# OUTSTANDING PEOPLE
# OF THE 20TH CENTURY

# OUTSTANDING PEOPLE
# OF THE 20TH CENTURY

**PUBLISHER**
Nicholas S Law

**EDITOR IN CHIEF**
Jon Gifford

**SENIOR EDITOR/PRODUCTION MANAGER**
Jocelyn Timothy

**EDITORIAL ASSISTANTS**
Barbara Cooper
Ann Dewison
Gillian George

All communications to: International Biographical Centre,
Cambridge CB2 3QP, England

# OUTSTANDING PEOPLE
# OF THE 20TH CENTURY

# 1999

International Biographical Centre
Cambridge, England

**ISBN: 0 948875 33 X**

Printed and bound in the UK by:
Biddles Limited, Woodbridge Park Estate,
Woodbridge Road, Guildford, Surrey GU1 1DA, England

# FOREWORD BY THE PUBLISHER

It is my great pleasure to publish *Outstanding People of the 20th Century* to celebrate the approach of the new Millennium. It is a work that has taken a considerable amount of time to research and produce and my thanks, along with those of my associates, are offered to the many learned societies and other organisations for recommending selected members for biographical inclusion. All such recommendations are carefully researched and questionnaires are sent to those who clear the final hurdle.

Once again, I must emphasise that there is no charge or fee for entry in *Outstanding People of the 20th Century* nor is there any obligation to purchase a copy. All entries have been checked most carefully by our own editors then submitted in proof form to the entrants for checking. However, in spite of this careful double checking, it is always possible that an occasional error may have occurred. If this has been the case, I offer my apologies in advance.

*Outstanding People of the 20th Century* is specially dedicated to a select few from all parts of the world. They are singled out for this honour by my senior editors and myself. A special feature on each one appears in the Dedication Section and in alphabetical order they are:

Professor Adetunji Ademuyiwa Adeyokunnu
Professor Louis Marie Pierre Allain,
    LFIBA
Efstathios Constantinos Arnis
Professor Alexander Balankin, FIBA
Dr James Daniel Barger, DDG, MOIF
The Honourable Dr Jack Gordon Beale, AO, JP,
    ME, Hon DSc,Hon LLD, DDG,
    LFIBA
Professor Alexander D Bruno, PhD
Clinton Ross Burnette, LFIBA, DDG,
    FWLA
Roberto Calderón-Sánchez, PE
Lurdes Camacho, FIBA
The Most Reverend Honourable Samuel
Emmanuel Carter, SJ, OJ, CD
Dr Ka Ching Chan, PhD
Fai Chut Cheng, DDG, LFIBA, MOIF
Dr Chiao-Liang Juliana Ching, MD, DDG,
IOM, LPIBA, MOIF
Dr Pesus Chou, DrPh
Dr Vsevolod Petrovich Chumenkov, PhD
Dorothy June Calvo Flores Cruz, FIBA
Professor Leon Ghiorghe Danaila, PhD
Dr Johanna Dobereiner
Dr Stephen E Draper, PhD, PE
Dr June B Ellis, PhD, DDG
Memduh Erdal
Dr Kjerstin Elisabeth Ericsson, PhD
Dr Myron Wyn Evans, PhD, DSc, FABI,
    LFIBA
Dr Dr Rong Remi Fang, PhD
Nancy Grace Augusta Forward

Dr Lawrence Jan Frateschi, PhD
Dr Alexander Gunther Friedrich
Dr Toru Funahashi, MD, DDG, LPIBA
Dr Angelo Graziolo, LFIBA
Dr Akihito Hagihara, DMSc, MPH
Professor He Xuntian
Dr Mahmoud Hijazy, PhD
Dr Ali Abbass Hussain Saleh, PhD, LFIBA
Professor Dr Mircea Gheorghe Ifrim, MD,
PhD, FIBA, DDG, IOM
Professor Dr Kazuyosi Ikeda, DSc, DLitt,
    DDG, IOM, LFWLA, LPIBA, MOIF
Professor Peter Uche Isichei, MD, DDG, FIBA,
    MOIF
Professor Shinji Itoh, MD, PhD, FIBA, IOM
Dr Thor Edward Jakobsson, PhD, FIBA
His Excellency Colonel Doctor Alhaji Yahya A J
    J Jammeh
Reverend Dr Andrew Jenkins
Dr Per Jespersen, PhD
Dr Christine Marie Kennefick, PhD, LFIBA, IOM
Reverend Young-Kyu Kim, ThD
Professor Eliezer Isaak Klainman, MD
Dr Edvard Kobal, DDG
Professor Dr Edgar Krau, PhD
Professor Dr Ryszard Jozef Kucha, LFIBA
Dr Vernette Trosper Landers, DDG, LFWLA,
    LPIBA, MOIF, IOM
Dr Dale Pierre Layman, PhD, DG, DDG, FABI,
    LPIBA, MOIF, IOM
Dr Miriam Lemanska, DSc, FIBA
Zhongying Li, DDG
Professor Valentin N Lukanin, LFIBA

Professor Michael H J Maes, PhD
Lee McCoy, DDG, MOIF
John Allen Mehaffey
Dr Yoshitsugu Miki, MD, DDG, LFIBA
Kenneth Andrew Mintz
Dr Eva Mae Nash-Isaac, PhD
Professor Alexander Ilyich Nesterov, FIBA
Dr Eunice Norton
Professor Masahiro Oka, DDG, FIBA
Antonia Camacho Okawa
Dr Henry Ostrowski-Meissner, PhD
Dr Clarence Henry Ott, PhD, CPA, CMA
Eugene Thomas Ouzts, LFIBA
Dr K N T Lakmal Peiris, MD, LFIBA
Dr Jose Ulysses Peixoto Neto
Dr Wladyslaw Radzikowski
Dr Muhammad Abdur Rahman, PhD
Mubarik Ahmed Rajpoot
HE The Honourable Professor Dr Hermann
      Rudolf Rauh, MA, CPhys, FInstP,
      FIM, OIA
Dr Zia Razzaq, DSc

Dr Justinas Rimas
Dr John Rosenknop, DrSci
Dr Holem Mansour Saliba, PhD
Professor Ya-Ching Shen, PhD
Dr Dong-Keun Shin
Professor Niki Stella Sideridou, MOIF
Albert L Simms
Dr Genovaite Sniraite Stulpiniene, FIBA
Professor Dr Der-Ruenn Su, PhD, DSc (Hon),
      DPhil (Hon), FIBA
Kerry Sutton, FIBA
Dr Masaki Tan, MD
Dr Ismail Hakki Olcay Unver, FIBA
Clive Thomas Walker, PhD
Richard LeRoy Welch, LFIBA
Professor Li Qing Yang
Dr Gili Yen, PhD
Dr Junichi Yoshida, MD, MS, FACS
Watson Toshinori Yoshimoto, IOM, LFIBA,
      MOIF
Professor Masataka Yoshimura, DEng
Zheqin Zhu

**Nicholas S Law**
Publisher

International Biographical Centre
Cambridge CB2 3QP
England

September 1999

# INTERNATIONAL BIOGRAPHICAL CENTRE RANGE OF REFERENCE TITLES

From one of the widest ranges of contemporary biographical reference works published under any one imprint, some IBC titles date back to the 1930's. Each edition is compiled from information supplied by those listed, who include leading personalities of particular countries or professions. Information offered usually includes date and place of birth; family details; qualifications; career histories; awards and honours received; books published or other creative work; other relevant information including postal address. Naturally there is no charge or fee for inclusion. New editions are freshly compiled and contain on average 80-90% new information. New titles are regularly added to the IBC reference library.

Titles include:

Dictionary of International Biography

Who's Who in Asia and the Pacific Nations

International Authors and Writers Who's Who

International Who's Who in Community Service

International Who's Who in Education

International Who's Who in Medicine

International Who's Who in Music and Musicians' Directory, Volume One, Classical and Light Classical

International Who's Who in Music, Volume Two, Popular Music

Men of Achievement

The World Who's Who of Women

International Who's Who in Poetry and Poets' Encyclopaedia

Outstanding People of the 20th Century

2000 Outstanding Scientists of the 20th Century

2000 Outstanding Artists and Designers of the 20th Century

2000 Outstanding Scholars of the 20th Century

2000 Outstanding Intellectuals of the 20th Century

Enquiries to:
**International Biographical Centre**
**Cambridge CB2 3QP**
**England**

# DEPUTY DIRECTORS GENERAL OF THE IBC

Prof Frank A Abban, LPIBA, DDG, *Ghana*
Prof S A Abbasi, DDG, *Hong Kong*
Mr Azmi Abdulazid, DDG, *Malaysia*
His Excellency S R Absy, FIBA, DDG, *Bahrain*
Dr Mustafa A Abu-Lisan, DDG, *England*
Chief Adewrele Adejumo, LFIBA, DDG, IOM, *Nigeria*
Dr Maurice Raphael Ades, DDG, *Israel*
Dr Jnan H Adhin, DDG, *Suriname*
Tulio S Aguilar Fajardo, FIBA, DDG, *Peru*
Mr Thomas Ernest Ainlay, FWLA, DDG, *Japan*
Ms Masako Akase, MOIF, LPIBA, DDG, *Japan*
Prof Mohammed Salim Akhter, DDG, *Pakistan*
Mr Abdullan Khaled Al-Ayoub, DDG, *Kuwait*
Dr Mohammed H K Al-Harbi, FIBA, DDG, *Saudi Arabia*
Dr Bader Eidan Al-Mahmeed, MOIF, DDG, *Kuwait*
Dr Khalil M H Al-Shamma', LFIBA, DDG, MOIF, *Iraq*
Dr M A Al-Thonayyan, LFIBA, DDG, *Saudi Arabia*
Prof Eila Marjatta Alahuhta, LFIBA, DDG, IOM, *Finland*
Dr Ayse A Alaylioglu, DDG, *South Africa*
Engineer Mr Yasser Ali Alhabibi, DDG, *Egypt*
Ms Zeba Ali, DDG, *Bangladesh*
Mr Jalal Alirza Aliev, DDG, *Azerbaijan*
Dr R J Alperin, LPIBA, DDG, IOM, *USA*
Dr Rowland Iwu Amadi, LFIBA, DDG, *West Africa*
Mr Jacob Oladele Amao, LFIBA, DDG, *Nigeria*
Rev Dr D L Amerasinghe, LFIBA, DDG, *Sri Lanka*
Prof An Zhixin, MOIF, DDG, *China*
Dr Spyros J Anapliotis, FIBA, DDG, MOIF, *Greece*
Mr Vikuotuolie Angami, FABI (USA), DDG, *India*
Prof B Angelopoulos, LPIBA, DDG, *Greece*
Prof Anatoly V Anisimov, DDG, *Ukraine*
Prof John Joseph Ansbro, DDG, IOM, *USA*
Ms Bella Aouad, LFIBA, DDG, *Lebanon*
Mr M A Aranda-Gomez, DDG, *Mexico*
Prof Sorab Jal Arceivala, DDG, *India*
Mr Arthur B Archer, DDG, *Barbados*
Ms Violet Archer, FIBA, DDG, IOM, *Canada*
Prof Aurel Ardelean, DDG, *Romania*
Dr A W M Ariff, LFIBA, LFWLA, DDG, *Malaysia*
Dr Eitoku Arima, FIBA, *Japan*
Mr Karl Erik Arons, DDG, *Latvia*
Mario Vernon Arroyo-Gomez, LPIBA, LFWLA, DDG, IOM, MOIF, *Gibraltar*
Dr Y Ashihara, LFIBA, DDG, IOM, *Japan*
Mr S-S Augustithis, DDG, MOIF, *Greece*
Professor Agnes Axmann, DDG, *Hungary*
Mr Roderick Honeyman Aya, DDG, IOM, *USA*
Prof Katsutoshi Ayano, LPIBA, DDG, IOM, MOIF, *Japan*
Prof Dr Ismail Hakki Aydin, DDG, *Turkey*
Dr K E Bader-Molnar, LFIBA, DDG, IOM, *Switzerland*

Dr Charles E Bagg, LFIBA, FWLA, DDG, *England*
Prof Bai Geng Yan, MOIF, DDG, *China*
Vjekoslav Bakašun, MD, PhD, DDG, LPIBA, MOIF, *Croatia*
Professor Bai Geng Yan, MOIF, DDG, *China*
Dr K Bala, DDG, IOM, *Malaysia*
Dr James D Barger, MOIF, DDG, *USA*
Ms Elisabeth Barker, FIBA, DDG, *USA*
Prof Andres Marcos Barrado, DDG, *Spain*
Ms Everlyn Bass, DDG, *USA*
Mr Elijah Sarwat Bassily, MOIF, DDG, *Egypt*
Dr Sarwat S Bassily, DDG, *Africa*
Mr Abdul R Batal, LPIBA, LFWLA, DDG, *Syria*
Prof Valentin D Batukhtin, DDG, *Russia*
Prof Yuriy Bazhora, DDG, *Russia*
Prof Charles P Beardsley, DDG, IOM, *USA*
Ms Georgia M Zeigler Beasley, DDG, *USA*
Mr James W Behrens, LFIBA, DDG, *USA*
Prof Sergei Belotserkovsky, DDG , *Russia*
Mr Roger Benebig, DDG, *New Caledonia*
Ms Charlene H Berry, LFIBA, DDG, IOM, *USA*
Mr Ismail Bhamjee, DDG, *Botswana*
Dr I M Bhatti, LPIBA, DDG, IOM, MOIF, *Pakistan*
Dr Chongthu Biakmawia, DDG, *India*
Mr Franco Bircher, LFIBA, DDG, *Switzerland*
Ms Irene M Bisiachi, LPIBA, DDG, MOIF, *Italy*
Mr Gerald Jude Boarman, DDG, *USA*
Dr Emmanuel Oti Boateng, DDG, *Ghana*
Mr Karic J Bogoljub, DDG, *Yugoslavia*
Dr Guy Boillat, LFIBA, DDG, MOIF, *France*
Professor Nikolay Lilov Bojkov, DDG, *Bulgaria*
Mr Makhaola D P Bolofo, DDG, *England*
Prof V Bondarenko, FIBA, DDG, *Russia*
Mr Nikolai A Borisevich, DDG, *Belarus*
Ms Shauna D Boulton, LFIBA, DDG, *USA*
Prof Romano Bozac, FIBA, DDG, *Croatia*
Mr Nikolai T Bozhilov, DDG, MOIF, *Bulgaria*
Col Ralph E Brandel, USMC Ret, DDG, MOIF, *USA*
Ms Patricia H Breen, LFIBA, DDG, *USA*
Lady of Soul Eleonora Bregu, MOIF, DDG, FIBA, *Albania*
Professor Hartmut D Breitkreuz, DDG, *Germany*
Dr Claudio Da Rocha Brito, DDG, LFIBA, *Brazil*
Mr Sabit Brokaj, DDG, *Albania*
Mrs Judith A Brooks, LPIBA, DDG, IOM, *USA*
Captain F W Brown, USN, LPIBA, DDG, IOM, *USA*
Sir George Noel Brown, DDG, *Belize*
Dr Josef Buchberger, DDG, *Switzerland*
Prof Aleksandra Bujakiewicz, DDG, *Africa*
Prof Amante Buontempo, DDG, *Malta*
Prof Giuseppe R Burgio, DDG, *Italy*
Mr Clinton Ross Burnette, DDG, LFIBA, *Australia*
Dr David Busumtwi-Sam, LFIBA, DDG, IOM, *Ghana*
Mr Valery S Buyanov, DDG, *Russia*
Mrs Merlene Hutton Byars, FIBA, DDG, *USA*

Mr Shaun Byrne DDG, *USA*
Prof E I Bystrov, LPIBA, DDG, IOM, MOIF, *Russia*
Dr Theodor Caba, LFIBA, DDG, *Romania*
Mr Heng-Wu Cai, DDG, *USA*
Ms Sondra L Campian, DDG, *USA*
Ms Margaret E Cannon-Wilson, FIBA, DDG, *USA*
Dr Guoping Cao, LFIBA, DDG, *China*
Dr Jinan Cao, LPIBA, DDG, MOIF, *Australia*
Dr Birger Carlqvist, LPIBA, DDG, *Sweden*
Ms Phillita T Carney, FIBA, DDG, *USA*
Mrs Gertrude E Carper, DDG, IOM, *USA*
Prof Alberto Carpinteri, LFIBA, DDG, MOIF, *Italy*
Dr Jorge M-G Carpizo, DDG, *France*
HRSH Leonard B Carr , MD, PhD, LPIBA, DDG, IOM, MOIF, *USA*
Prof Marion E Carter, LFIBA, DDG, MOIF, *USA*
Mr Manfredo Castro, LFIBA, DDG, *Philippines*
Mr Chen-Ting Ch'in, DDG, *China*
Prof Cha Jin Soon, LPIBA, DDG, IOM, *Korea*
Mr Chai Cheng Sheng, FIBA, DDG, IOM, *Singapore*
Ms Colleen Chanel, DDG, *USA*
Mr Scott Clay Chaney, FIBA, DDG, *USA*
Dr Chang Wan-Hsi (Mo jen), DDG, *Taiwan, China*
Dr Wen-Ying Chang, LFIBA, DDG, IOM, MOIF, *China*
Mr Xu Ping Chang, DDG, *China*
Dr Tapan Kumar Chatterjee, LFIBA, DDG, *Mexico*
Mr Moussallam Maher Chatty, DDG, *United Arab Emirates*
Mr John M Cheesman, LFIBA, DDG, IOM, *USA*
Dr Ricardo Chequer Chemas, LFIBA, DDG, MOIF, *Brazil*
Mr Chen Feng, DDG, *China*
Reverend Min-Yen George Chen, DDG, *Hong Kong*
Dr Pang-Chi Chen, LPIBA, DDG, IOM, MOIF, *Taiwan,*
Prof Chen Qi Qi, DDG, *China*
Prof Chen Weixian, DDG, *China*
Prof Yi-Feng Chen, DDG, *China*
Mr Fai Chut Cheng, MOIF, LFIBA, DDG, *Hong Kong*
Mr Charles Yang Chee Chew, DDG, *Australia*
Mrs Elsie T Childers, IOM, DDG, *USA*
Prof Tetsuro Chimura, DDG, *Japan*
Mr Michael Kuo-hsing Chin, DDG, IOM, *China*
Dr C Juliana Ching, LPIBA, DDG, IOM, *Hong Kong*
Dr Li Choy Chong, LPIBA, DDG, *Republic of Singapore*
Mr Shyam Kishore Chowdhary, DDG, FIBA, *India*
Mr Lowell Koon Wa Chun, DDG, *USA*
Professor Kyu-bok Chung, FWLA, DDG, *Korea*
Sir J R Ciancia Y Müller, LFIBA, DDG, IOM, *Spain*
Dr J Civasaqui, LPIBA, LFWLA, DDG, *Japan*
Lady Gloria F Clayton, LFIBA, DDG, *Australia*
Ms E Louise Clifford, LFIBA, DDG, IOM, *USA*
Prof Charles W Cline, LPIBA, LFWLA, DDG, IOM, *USA*

Mr J H Cockcroft, DDG, *England*
Mr Irwin Cohen, LFIBA, LFWLA, DDG, *USA*
Prof Vasko Solomon Čolančeski, DDG, *FYROM*
Dr Paolo Conti, DDG, *Italy*
Dr George Corder, LPIBA, LFWLA, DDG, *USA*
Mrs A Crafton-Masterson, FIBA, DDG, *USA*
Ms E A Crobaugh, DDG, *USA*
Prof Mario Fernando Crocco, DDG, *Argentina*
Dr S E Csordas, LFIBA, DDG, IOM, *Australia*
Dr Eva Anna Czajkowski, FIBA, DDG, *USA*
Dr Jean-Pierre L Daem, LPIBA, DDG, MOIF, *Canada*
Mr Alhaji M Danmadami, LFIBA, DDG, *Nigeria*
Mr Jaideep Das, LFIBA, DDG, MOIF, *India*
Dr Manfred A Dauses, LFIBA, DDG, *Luxembourg*
Dr Davey-Hayford, LPIBA, LFWLA, DDG, *Ghana*
Prof Blanche Davis, DDG, *USA*
Mrs L De Backer, LPIBA, LFWLA, DDG, *Belgium*
Mrs E Z de Brault, LPIBA, DDG, *Mexico*
Ms Helen G Deer, DDG, *USA*
Claude R DeLauter Jr, PhD, FIBA, DDG, IOM, *USA*
Dr Zlatko Dembic, DDG, *Norway*
Prof Ziji Deng, LFIBA, DDG, IOM, *China*
Prof Genrikh A Denisov, DDG, *Russia*
Prof Andrzej Denys, DDG, *Poland*
Mr Hasmukhroy Maganlal Desai, LFIBA. DDG, *India*
Dr Dharam Pal Dhall, LFIBA, DDG, MOIF, *Australia*
Mr Abdoulaye Diawara, DDG, *West Africa*
Dr C C Dickinson III, LFIBA, DDG, *USA*
Ms Doris Dillon, DDG, FIBA, *USA*
Prof Mile Dimitrovski, DDG, *Yugoslavia*
Dr Robert Ding Pooi Huat, FIBA, DDG, *Malaysia*
Mrs Jean C Dixon, DDG, MOIF, *Australia*
Dr Alfons F Doodoh, LFIBA, DDG, *Indonesia*
Mr Morton Downey, DDG, *USA*
Ms Mary Josephine Drayton, DDG, *New Zealand*
Miss Du Ying, DDG, IOM, *China*
Dr Bob  B Dugal, DDG, *Norway*
Professor Ioan-Florea Dumitru, DDG, *Romania*
Linda K Day Duntley, MA, LFIBA, DDG, MOIF, *USA*
Dr Pushparanee Durai, FIBA, DDG, *Malaysia*
Ms Patricia Dureska, LPIBA, DDG, MOIF, IOM, *USA*
Mr Karl Eickmann, LFIBA, DDG, *Japan*
Mr Arthur Eikenberry, LPIBA, DDG, *USA*
EUR ING Dr Adil Yassin Hag El Safi, DDG, *United Arab Emirates*
Professor Mohamed K El-Sorougi, FIBA, DDG, *Egypt*
Mr Elhamy Mostafa El Zayat, DDG, *Egypt*
June B Ellis, PhD, DDG, *USA*
Ms Jacquelyn Rose Ely, DDG, *USA*
Dr Ralph Stanton Emerson, DDG, *USA*
Ms Ester Erhomaa, LFIBA, DDG, IOM, *Finland*
Dr Alexei M Ermolaev, FIBA, DDG, *England*

Prof Zuey-Shin Hsu, LFIBA, DDG, IOM, MOIF, *Taiwan, China*
Dr Tien-tung Hsueh, LFIBA, DDG, *Hong Kong*
Mr Hua Lesun, DDG, FIBA, *China*
Ms Catherine Harding Hudgins, DDG, *USA*
Dr Norman N Huff, LPIBA, DDG, *USA*
Dr Frances W Hughes, LFIBA, DDG, *USA*
Prof William Derek Humpage, DDG, *Australia*
Mr Charles Orvis Hunter, DDG, *USA*
Mr Barney Hurwitz, DDG, MOIF, *Republic of South Africa*
Dr Kuei-Hsiang Hwang, LPIBA, LFWLA, DDG, IOM, MOIF, *China*
Rev Dr Prof Tzu-Yang Hwang, LPIBA, DDG, MOIF, IOM, *USA*
Dr Wen-Jyi Hwang, DDG, *Taiwan*
Alhaji Idris Ibrahim, LFIBA, DDG, *Nigeria*
Prof Mircea Gheorghe Ifrim, FIBA, DDG, IOM, *Romania*
Mr John Igo, DDG, *USA*
Prof Ljiljana Igric, DDG, *Yugoslavia*
Prof Dr Kazuyosi Ikeda, LPIBA, LFWLA, DDG, IOM, MOIF, *Japan*
Dr Dozie Ikedife, DDG, LPIBA, *Nigeria*
Prof Eiichi Ishibashi, DDG, MOIF, *Japan*
Mr Masamichi Ishihara, LFIBA, DDG, *Japan*
Prof Peter Uche Isichei, FIBA, DDG, MOIF, *Nigeria*
Prof S Issaragrisil, LPIBA, DDG, IOM, *Thailand*
Mr Masayuki Isshiki, Ph.D., DDG, *Japan*
Rev Anath E Jackson, LFIBA, DDG, *USA*
Mr Thirston H Jackson Jr, DDG, MOIF, *USA*
Prof Dr Drs H-J Jacobs, LPIBA, DDG, MOIF, *Germany*
Prof Dr George V Jandieri, DDG, *Georgia*
Dr Jørgen Jensen, LFIBA, DDG, *Denmark*
Prof Jon-Arild Johannessen, DDG, *Norway*
Dr Jane P Johnson, DDG, *USA*
Ms Margaret H Johnson, LFIBA, DDG, *USA*
Mr John B Jordanoglou, DDG, *Greece*
Chief Charles A Joshua, FIBA, DDG, IOM, MOIF, *USA*
Dr Gonzalez M Juana, FIBA, DDG, IOM, MOIF, *Sierra Leone*
Prof Natalia Juristo, DDG, *Spain*
Dr Kamaruzaman Jusoff, DDG, *Malaysia*
Dr Nella Kačergienė, DDG, FIBA, MOIF, *Lithuania*
Prof Simone Kadi, LPIBA, DDG, *France*
Dr Mirja A Kalliopuska, LFWLA, DDG, IOM, MOIF, *Finland*
Dr Bo Rolfsson Kallstrom, FIBA, DDG, *Sweden*
Prof Jawahar Kalra, DDG, MOIF, *Canada*
Dr Ghassan M Kansou, MOIF, LFIBA, DDG, *Lebanon*
Dr George Akaki Kanzaki, LPIBA, DDG, IOM, MOIF, *USA*
Dr Richard Willy R Kanzler, DDG, IOM, MOIF, *Republic of South Africa*
Assoc Prof Strashimir Karanov, DDG, *Bulgaria*
Dr Milan Karvas, DDG, *Slovakia*
Mr Kasumov Neimat Abbasuli Oglu, *Azerbaijan*

Ms Marlene M Katchur, LPIBA, DDG, MOIF, *USA*
Mr Michael G Katsonis, DDG, *USA*
Dr Shriniwas K Katti, DDG, *USA*
Ms Joyce E Kellberg, DDG, *USA*
Ms Sophy Kelly, DDG, *India*
Mr Richard Kemoli, DDG, *Kenya*
Mr James Sewell Kerr, DDG, FIBA, *West Indies*
Dr Rustom A Khatib, DDG, *Lebanon*
Profesor Vladimir Kh. Khavinson, DDG, *Russia*
Mr Ramaz Khetsuriani, DDG, IOM, *Georgia*
Mr Alexander F Khokhlov, DDG, *Russia*
Rev Dr Kim Kwang Tae, LFIBA, DDG, *Korea*
Prof Katsumi Kimura, DDG, *Japan*
Mr J Jerone King, DDG, *USA*
HSH Prince Dr George King de Santorini, Count de Florina, DDG, *USA*
Dr Samson B M Kisekka, LPIBA, DDG, IOM, *Uganda*
Dr Vihar Nikolov Kiskinov, DDG, *Bulgaria*
Prof Hirohisa Kitano, DDG, *Japan*
Dr Aggrey Kiyingi, DDG, *Australia*
Mr Tor G Kjoelberg, DDG, *Norway*
Prof Vladimir V Kliouev, DDG, *Russia*
Dr Edvard Kobal, DDG, *Slovenia*
Mr Toshiro Kobayshi, DDG, MOIF, *Japan*
Dr Spincer Sih-Ping Koh, FIBA, DDG, *China*
Prof Oleg A Kolobov, DDG, *Russia*
Prof Hisatoki Komaki, LFIBA, DDG, IOM, *Japan*
Lord Toshihiko Kono, DDG, *USA*
Dr Alfred V Kottek, LFIBA, DDG, IOM, *Austria*
Prof Ryszard Kozlowski, FIBA, DDG, *Poland*
Dr Alexei Krivolutsky, FIBA, DDG, *Russia*
Prof Dr Chang-Yang Kuo, DDG, *China*
Marvin Z Kurlan, MD, FACS, LFIBA, DDG, IOM, *USA*
Mr Kisho Kurokawa, LPIBA, DDG, IOM, *Japan*
Prof Volodimir G Kuz, DDG, *Ukraine*
Ms Tuulikki Kyllönen-Heikel, LFIBA, DDG, IOM, *Finland*
Prof Bernhard Kytzler, DDG, *Republic of South Africa*
Prof Aris Lacis, DDG, FIBA, *Russia*
Dr Armando Vicente Lago, IOM, DDG, *Argentina*
Dr Philip K H Lai, LPIBA, DDG, MOIF, *Hong Kong*
Dr Niki Laiopoulou, DDG, *Greece*
Mr Paul F Lalande, FIBA, DDG, MOIF, *France*
Mr Billy Lam, LFIBA, DDG, *Hong Kong*
Dr Luc Johan Lambrecht, LPIBA, DDG, MOIF, IOM, *Belgium*
Dr V Landers, LPIBA, LFWLA, DDG, IOM, MOIF, *USA*
Prof Dr M E Landsberg, FIBA, DDG, *Israel*
Dr Ted Lane, DDG, *USA*
Dr Dale Pierre Layman, Ph.D., MOIF, DDG, LPIBA, *USA*
Dr Harry C Layton, FIBA, DDG, IOM, *USA*
Dr William A Leavell, DDG, *USA*
Dr Charles L Leavitt, LPIBA, DDG, *USA*

Mr Andrew Siu-Woo Lee, LFIBA, DDG, MOIF, *Hong Kong*
Ms Angela W T Lee, DDG, *Hong Kong*
Dr Anne W M Lee, DDG, *Hong Kong*
Mr Don Yoon Lee, LFIBA, DDG, *USA*
Dr Irene Lee, DDG, *USA*
Dr Laurence A Lees, LFIBA, DDG, *Australia*
Miss Joy LeRoy, LFIBA, MOIF, DDG, *USA*
Prof Gorazd Lesnicar, DDG, *Slovenia*
Ms Zhongying Li, DDG, *China*
Prof Liang Dan-Fong, LPIBA, DDG, *Taiwan, China*
Eusebio G Lim, MD, LFIBA, DDG, *USA*
Ms Joan Pek Bee Lim, LFIBA, DDG, IOM, *Malaysia*
Dr Phillip K Lim, LPIBA, DDG, *USA*
Prof Chen-Chong Lin, LFIBA, DDG, *Taiwan, China*
Dr Chin-Ching Lin, LFIBA, DDG, *China*
Prof Chung-sheng Lin, DDG, *China*
Prof Jong-Teh Lin, LFWLA, DDG, *Taiwan, China*
Prof Ping-Wha Lin, DDG, MOIF, *USA*
Ms J C McKee Lindsay, LPIBA, DDG, IOM, *USA*
Prof Liu Chung Chu, DDG, *China*
Mr Liu Guohui, DDG, *China*
Prof Yanpei Liu, DDG, *China*
Dr Pek Liong Loa, LPIBA, DDG, IOM, MOIF, *Germany*
Mr Teimuraz D Lomtadze, DDG, *Russia*
Mrs Julia M LoTempio, DDG, *USA*
Dr Frederick Lundell, LFIBA, DDG, IOM, *Canada*
Prof Luo Yuanzheng, DDG, *China*
Prof Ren Liu Ma, DDG, *China*
Prof Teodor Maghiar, DDG, *Romania*
Ms Joan Mahaffey, LPIBA, DDG, IOM, *USA*
Dr Virendra B Mahesh, LPIBA, DDG, IOM, MOIF, *USA*
Mr Umaru-Sanda Maigida, LFIBA, DDG, IOM, *Nigeria*
Dr C O Majekodunmi, DDG, *Nigeria*
Mr Vladimir G Makhanov, DDG, *Russia*
Mr Faramaz Maksudov, DDG, *Azerbaijan*
Prof Lyubov T Malaya, DDG, *Russia*
Mr Hamid A Malik, DDG, *Saudia Arabia*
Dr Howard G(erald) Malin, LPIBA, LFWLA, DDG, IOM, MOIF, *USA*
Mr Gaudencio S Manalac, DDG, MOIF, *Philippines*
Ms Patricia J S Mapel, DDG, *USA*
Mrs Louise Martin, DDG, *USA*
The Hon John Ross Matheson, LFIBA, DDG, *Canada*
Mr Om Prakash Mathur, DDG, *India*
Mr Dmitry Mavlo, DDG, MOIF, *Russia*
Dr Patricia J Maybin, DDG, IOM, *USA*
Ms Mabel Mazzini, FIBA, DDG, IOM, *Argentina*
Dr Lucie Mba, DDG, *Gabon*
Dr Leland McClanahan, PhD, LFIBA, DDG, MOIF, *USA*
Mr Gary Albert McConnell, MOIF, DDG, *Norway*

Prof G McCormack, LFIBA, DDG, *USA*
Ms Lee McCoy, DDG, *USA*
Mr Paul McDonald-Smith, FIBA, DDG, MOIF, *Australia*
Mr Francis C Meddleton, LFIBA, DDG, *USA*
Prof Dr Mohamed A El-Fattah Mehaia, LFIBA, *Saudi Arabia*
Prof Dr Parakkat Ramakrishnan Menon, DDG, *India*
Mr Paul J Meyer, LFIBA, DDG, IOM, *USA*
Prof Dr Alexandru Mica, DDG, *Romania*
Mrs Pearl D Michaels, LPIBA, DDG, *USA*
Prof Dr H A Michalek, DDG, MOIF, *Austria*
Mr John Albert Middleton, LFIBA, *USA*
Mr Peter Mikhailenko, DDG, MOIF, *Ukraine*
Prof Alexander T Mikhailov, DDG, *Spain*
His Excellency Kari Juhani Mikkola, FIBA, DDG, *Sweden*
Prof James C Milln, DDG, *South Africa*
Dr Errol C Miller, DDG, *Jamaica*
Mr T E Miller, LFIBA, LFWLA, DDG, *USA*
Ms Carol Ann Mills, FIBA, DDG, *USA*
Mr James Milone, DDG, *USA*
Ms Hildegard M Minchenko, LFIBA, DDG, IOM, *USA*
Mr Mohamed A Mitkees, DDG, *United Arab Emirates*
Dr Elpis Mitropoulou, DDG, *Greece*
Dr Nver M Mkhitaryan, LFIBA, DDG, *Ukraine*
Mr Henry Stanley Rawle Moe, DDG, *Antigua*
Prof Sureswar Mohanty, DDG, *India*
Dr Victoria I Mojekwu, LFIBA, DDG, *Nigeria*
Dr Ntsu Mokhehle, MOIF, DDG, *South Africa*
Mr B Mollenhauer, LFIBA, DDG, *USA*
Mr Ralph E Montijo, LPIBA, DDG, IOM, *USA*
Mr Florian H Moore, MOIF, LFIBA, DDG, *USA*
Prof Omar K Moore, DDG, *USA*
Mr Michael Moraitis, LFIBA, DDG, *Greece*
Mr E A Mordi, DDG, *Nigeria*
Prof Hirotoshi Morii, DDG, *Japan*
Prof Mineo Moritani, DDG, *Japan*
Dr Minoru Mukai, MOIF, DDG, *Japan*
Dr Edwin Muniz Jr, DDG, *USA*
Mr Edahiko Murakami, LFIBA, DDG, IOM, MOIF, *Japan*
Dr Tadeusz Kordian Murawski, DDG, MOIF, *Poland*
Father Pius Murray, CSS, MOIF, DDG, *USA*
Mr George K Mwai, LPIBA, DDG, IOM, *Kenya*
Mr Jack Charles Myers, DDG, *USA*
Mrs Yong-Gyun Nah, LFIBA, DDG, *Korea*
Dr Shrinivas H Naidu, LFIBA, DDG, *USA*
Prof Esho Nakagawa, DDG, *Japan*
Sir Saburo Nakagawa, LPIBA, DDG, *Japan*
Dr Shigehisa Nakamura, LFIBA, DDG, IOM, *Japan*
Mr Kadaba V Narain, DDG, IOM, *Japan*
Mr Shiv Sahai Naraine, FIBA, DDG, *Guyana, South America*
Dr Eva Mae Nash-Isaac, DDG, *USA*

Mr Frederick L Neff, FIBA, DDG, *USA*
Prof Johan Theron Nel, LFIBA, DDG, IOM, MOIF,
   *Republic of South Africa*
Miss Elizabeth Nelson, LFIBA, DDG, *USA*
Prof Eviatar Nevo, LFIBA, DDG, MOIF, *Israel*
Dr Ngo Ba Thanh, DDG, *Vietnam*
Prof Dr Ngo Dat Tam, DDG, *Vietnam*
Prof Nguyen Canh Toan, DDG, MOIF, *Vietnam*
Prof Thu The Nguyen, DDG, *USA*
Dr Hiroshi Niimura, LFIBA, DDG, IOM, *Japan*
Mr Alexander G M Nijbakker, LFIBA, DDG,
   *Netherlands*
Dr Victor Alekseevich Nikerov, DDG, *Russia*
Dr Blazho Nikolov, DDG, *Bulgaria*
Dr Rev R N Nnamdi, DDG, *Germany*
Mrs Bessie Wherry Noe, DDG, *USA*
Prof Tasuku Noguchi, DDG, *Japan*
Dr Khalida I Noor, LPIBA, DDG,
   *Kingdom of Saudi Arabia*
Prof Henry Ian A Nowik, DDG, *USA*
Senator Cyrus N Nunieh, DDG, *Nigeria*
Ms Mary Devon O'Brien, LFIBA, DDG, *USA*
Ms Rosa Margot Ochoa, FWLA, DDG, *Mexico*
Dr Wilson R Ogg, LPIBA, LFWLA, DDG, MOIF,
   *USA*
Professor Katsuichiro Ohsaki, DDG, MOIF, *Japan*
Mr Masa Aki Oka, DDG, *Japan*
Prof Masahiro Oka, DDG, *Japan*
Prof U Okeke, DDG, *Nigeria*
Sir Josiah Onyebuchi Johnson Okezie, DDG,
   *Nigeria*
Dr Bartolomew E Okoduwa, DDG, *Nigeria*
Mr Akira Okuyama, LFIBA, DDG, *Japan*
Mr David V F Olateru-Olagbegi, DDG, *Nigeria*
Dr Tadanori Ondoh, DDG, *Japan*
Dr Vladimir I Onopriev, DDG, IOM, *Russia*
Dr Sazrar Opata, FIBA, DDG, *Ghana*
Ms C Jane Orlando, MOIF, DDG, *USA*
Mr Howard R Orms, DDG, *USA*
Prof Skender Osmani, DDG, *Albania*
Gladys S Ostrom, PhD, FIBA, MOIF, DDG, *USA*
Dr Pritam S Panesar, LFIBA, DDG, *Kenya*
Dr Lucy T Parker, LPIBA, DDG, IOM, *USA*
Dr Eugenia Pasternak, CM, PhD, LPIBA,
   DDG, IOM, *Canada*
Dr Howard John Peak, DDG, *Australia*
Ms Lou Peel, LFIBA, DDG, MOIF, *USA*
Dr Bozena Pejkovic, DDG, *Slovenia*
Lt Col Ralph M Persell, LFIBA, DDG, *USA*
Mr I R Perumal, DDG, *India*
Prof L A Petrov, DDG, MOIF, *Bulgaria*
Mr Gisli Petursson, FIBA, DDG, MOIF, *Iceland*
Mr Horst Willy Petzold, IOM, FIBA, DDG, *USA*
Prof Phan Huu Dat, DDG, *Vietnam*
Ms Danuta Piontek, DDG, MOIF, *Poland*
Mr Gavin Alexander Pitt, DDG, *USA*
Dr Ole Emil Plens, FIBA, DDG, *Sweden*
Professor Joze Pogacnik, DDG, *Slovenia*
Prof Vasile Popa, DDG, *Romania*
Mr Ion Popescu, DDG, *Romania*

Professor Katarina Popov-Pergal, DDG,
   *Yugoslavia*
Ms Dorothea Porter, LFIBA, DDG, *USA*
Dr Michael Leroy Porter, LPIBA, DDG, *USA*
Mr Malcolm Frederick Potter, DDG, *Australia*
Mr Krishna Prasad Pradhan, DDG, FIBA, *Nepal*
Ms Letricia E C Preston, DDG, *USA*
Ms Carol R Proctor, FIBA, DDG, *USA*
Dr Svein D Prydz II, LPIBA, DDG, IOM, MOIF,
   *Norway*
Dr Zbigniew Jerzy Przerembski, DDG, *Poland*
Dr Jerzy Z Przybojewski, FIBA, DDG,
   *Republic of South Africa*
Dr Raisa I Pshenichnikova, DDG, Russia
Mrs Lois Kathryn Pullig, DDG, *USA*
Dr Zvonimir Puretic, DDG, *Croatia*
Mr Robert Pwee Kong Joo, FIBA, DDG, IOM,
   *Republic of Singapore*
Prof Que Nguyen Anh, DDG, *Vietnam*
Dr Mariam Rajab, DDG, *Lebanon*
Dr Srinivasa S Rajan, LFIBA, DDG, *India*
Mr Anumolu Ramakrishna, DDG, *India*
Mr Harold Radj Ramdhani, DDG, *Suriname*
Dr Aspy Phiroze Rana, DDG, *India*
Dr A Satyanarayana Rao, DDG, *India*
Dr Usha Rao, DDG, *India*
Mr A Guinn Rasbury, LFIBA, DDG, *USA*
Dr Harun Ar Rashid, FIBA, DDG, *Bangladesh*
Mr Gerald Lee Ratliff, DDG, *USA*
Orlando M Recinos Argüello, DDG,
   *El Salvador*
Mr Harry Charles Reinl, DDG, *USA*
Dr Milan Remko, LPIBA, MOIF, *Czech Republic*
Dr Lonnie Royce Rex, DDG, *USA*
Jerome Reyda, QC, DDG, *Canada*
Mr Eugene E Rhemann, LPIBA, DDG, *USA*
Ms C L Richards, FWLA, DDG, *USA*
Ms Janet G Riebold, LFIBA, DDG, *USA*
Dr A Robertson-Pearce, FIBA, DDG, IOM,
   *England*
Ms Mary M Robben, LPIBA, MOIF, DDG, *USA*
Dr Ralph R Robinson, DDG, IOM, MOIF,
   *USA*
Ms Trudy Rodine-Wolfsehr, DDG, *USA*
Ms Irene B S Rodman, DDG, *USA*
Ms Elisabeth Anne Rooney-Ewing, DDG, MOIF,
   *USA*
Dr M H Rosen, LFIBA, LFWLA, DDG, *USA*
Ms Belle Sara Rosenbaum, IOM, DDG, *USA*
Dr Yuriy A Rossikhin, DDG, *Russia*
Ms Cecile I Rouchdy, LFIBA, DDG, MOIF,
   *Kingdom of Saudi Arabia*
Mr Abdul Razzak Rumane, DDG, *Kuwait*
Dr Blaž Rozman, LFIBA, DDG, MOIF, *Slovenia*
Dr P A Rubio, MD, PhD, LPIBA, DDG, *USA*
Professor Vladimir A Rusol, LPIBA, DDG, MOIF,
   *Russia*
Mrs Shikiko Saitoh, LFIBA, DDG, IOM, *Japan*
Prof Ahmad Salahuddin DDG, LFIBA, MOIF,
   *Africa*

Mr Mohammad Abdul Saleem, LFIBA, DDG, *United Arab Emirates*
Dr Ali Abbas Hussain Saleh, DDG, *Bahrain*
Dr Uday Salunkhe, DDG, *India*
Mr E F Sanguinetti, FWLA, DDG, *Argentina*
Mr Masakazu Sarai, DDG, *Japan*
Dr Kazuo Sato, FIBA, DDG, *Japan*
Dr Mitsuo Sato, DDG, *Japan*
Ms Geraldine Ogden Savari, DDG, *USA*
Prof Akiko Sawaguchi, DDG, *Japan*
Professor Adolf E Schindler, DDG, *Germany*
Mr Robert M Schmidt, DDG, LFIBA, *USA*
Prof Judith T Scholl, LFIBA, DDG, *USA*
Mr Werner N W Schramm, LPIBA, IOM, DDG, MOIF, LFWLA, *Germany*
Mr J-U Schroeder, MA, LFIBA, DDG, MOIF, *Germany*
Mrs Marjorie M Schuck, DDG, *USA*
Mr Leroy Bernard Schwan, DDG, *USA*
Mr Ainsworth D Scott, LPIBA, DDG, IOM, MOIF, *West Indies*
Mr Dennis Screpetis, LPIBA, DDG, *USA*
Mr Angelo A Sedacca, LFIBA, MOIF, DDG, *USA*
Prof Andrew Seim, DDG, *USA*
Jukka Tapani Seppinen, DDG, *Finland*
Dr Harry E Settanni, DDG, *USA*
Dr Shirish Shah, LFIBA, DDG, *USA*
Professor Dr Alexei N Shamin, DDG, *Russia*
Dr Isadore Shapiro, DDG, IOM, *USA*
Dr Harry Shanker Sharma, DDG, *India*
Mr Hamzeh Mohammed Shaweesh, FIBA, DDG, *Jordan*
Prof George V Shchokin, DDG, LFIBA, *Ukraine*
Mr Ralph Albert Sheetz, DDG, *USA*
Dr Muhammad M Mukram Sheikh, HLFIBA, DDG, IOM, *Botswana*
Dr Nimish Rameshchandra Shelat, LPIBA, DDG, *India*
Mr Roger Shen DDG, *USA*
Ms Bat-Sheva Sheriff, LFWLA, DDG, IOM, *Israel*
Ms Shi Bingxia, DDG, *China*
Professor Chun-Jen Shih, LFIBA, *Taiwan, China*
Prof Tso-Min Shih, DDG, *Taiwan, China*
Dr Sang-Tai Shim, DDG, *Korea*
Prof Koki Shimoji, DDG, LFIBA, *Japan*
Mr Sadao Shimoji, MOIF, DDG, *Japan*
Ms Marina V Shitikova, FIBA, DDG, *Russia*
Dr Leonid Vassilievich Shmakov, DDG, *Russia*
Dr M Murtuza Siddiqi, DDG, *Saudi Arabia*
Mr Islahuddin Siddiqui, DDG, *Pakistan*
Mr Robert D Siedle, LFIBA, DDG, *USA*
Mr Herbert Alfred Simmons, LFIBA, DDG, *USA*
Dr Teja Singh, LFIBA, DDG, IOM, *Canada*
Mr Aleksandre Sitnikov, DDG, *Russia*
Dr Valery K Smirnov, DDG, *Russia*
Mr Louis Smith, LFIBA, DDG, IOM, *USA*
Mrs Edwina Christine F Snow, DDG, *USA*
Ms Anne-Marie A Sondakh, DDG, *Indonesia*
Prof Song Zhongyue, DDG, *China*
Dr Igor Sourovtsev, DDG, *Russia*
Miss Callie J Spady, FIBA, DDG, *USA*

Mr Ion G Spanulescu, DDG, *Romania*
Dr David A Spencer, LFIBA, MOIF, DDG, LFWLA, *USA*
Mr Francis M J Spencer, LFIBA, DDG, *USA*
Ms Linda Bushell Spencer, DDG, *USA*
Mr Peter Stadler, LFIBA, DDG, *Denmark*
Ms Ursula Helena Stanescu, DDG, *Romania*
Mrs Joan E Starr, FWLA, DDG, *Australia*
Mr R St J Stephens, FIBA, DDG, *England*
Mrs E V Stewart, LFIBA, DDG, *USA*
Ms Annette Michelle Stokes, IOM, DDG, *USA*
Prof Dr Boyko S Stoyanov, LPIBA, DDG, IOM, MOIF, *Japan*
Ms M Strandell Thamm P E, DDG, *USA*
Professor Jovan Strikovic, FIBA, DDG, MOIF, *Yugoslavia*
Prof Roman G Strongin, LFIBA, DDG, *Russia*
Dr H Chien-Fan Su, FIBA, DDG, IOM, MOIF, *USA*
Dr T N Subba Rao, DDG, *India*
Mr Han Cheng Sun, DDG, *China*
Prof Qian Zhang Sun, DDG, MOIF, *China*
Mr Harta Susanto, DDG, *Indonesia*
Mrs B Sutton, LPIBA, FWLA, DDG, *England*
Prof Dr Shin'Ichi Suzuki, DDG, *Japan*
Dr Srikanta M N Swamy, LFIBA, DDG, IOM, *Canada*
Mr James E Sweeney, LFIBA, DDG, *USA*
Dr Nightingale C Syabbalo, DDG, *Kuwait*
Prof Emeric Szegho, LPIBA, DDG, *USA*
Dr Emmanuel H Tadross, LPIBA, DDG, IOM *Canada*
Mr Norio Takeoka, FIBA, DDG, *Japan*
Prof Ichiro Taki, DDG, *Japan*
Neva B Talley-Morris, FIBA, DDG, *USA*
Professor Yoshihiro Tanaka, DDG, *Japan*
Dr Zhichun Tang, DDG, *China*
Prof Giulio F Tarro, DDG, IOM, *Italy*
Prof Todor D Tashev, DDG, *Bulgaria*
Mr Percy C Tawodzera, MOIF, DDG, *Zimbabwe*
Mr Walter H Taylor, DDG, *Australia*
Mrs Nellie J Taze, LFIBA, DDG, *USA*
Mr Walter H Taylor, DDG, *Australia*
Mr Aik Chong Tek, DDG, *Indonesia*
Dr Aslan Kitovich Thakushinov, DDG, *Russia*
Mr Patrick C Thauberger, DDG, IOM, *Canada*
Mr Francis M C Thomas, LFIBA, DDG, *Sri Lanka*
Dr Walter Dill Thomas, LFIBA, DDG, *USA*
Ms Barbara M Thompson, DDG, MOIF, *USA*
Ms Mary J Thornton, LPIBA, DDG, IOM, *USA*
Mr Gary L Tipton, LFIBA, DDG, *USA*
Prof J H Tisch, LPIBA, LFWLA, DDG, *Australia*
Dr Ljerka Tiska-Rudman, FIBA, DDG, *Yugoslavia*
Dr Wolfgang Töglhofer, LFIBA, DDG, *Switzerland*
Mrs Florence W Toland, FIBA, DDG, *USA*
Mr Criton P Tomazos, DDG, *England*
Ms Lillian Del Toro, DDG, *USA*

Dr Tran Quang Hai, LFIBA, DDG, *France*
Dr Orville W Trosper, FIBA, DDG, *USA*
Mr Niklaus Troxler, DDG, IOM, *Switzerland*
Prof Tsai Chiu-Lai, LFIBA, DDG, MOIF, *China*
Ir Philip Kui Tse, DDG, LFIBA, *Canada*
Prof Pars Tuğlaci, FIBA, LFWLA, DDG, IOM,
    MOIF, *Turkey*
Mr Kenneth O Udeh, DDG, *Poland*
Prof Edward Ueno, LPIBA, DDG, IOM, MOIF,
    *Japan*
Dr David O Ukaegbu, DDG, *Africa*
Prof Arbo Valdma, LFIBA, DDG, *Germany*
Dr Carrie Temple Vance, DDG, IOM, *USA*
Professor Baidya Varma, DDG, *USA*
Dr Dorothy H Veon, MOIF, DDG, *USA*
Mr Juan Garbin Vereda, DDG, *Spain*
Constantin K Vereketis, LPIBA, DDG, *Greece*
Dr Ruslana Vernickaitè, FIBA, DDG, MOIF,
*Lithuania*
Ms Morwenna A Vincent, DDG, *Australia*
Dr Steven A Vladem, LFIBA, DDG, IOM, *USA*
Prof R F Vliegen, LFIBA, DDG, IOM, *Japan*
Mt Rev Dr Robert A Voice, DDG, *Canada*
Dr Mary L S Wainwright, LPIBA, DDG, IOM,
    *USA*
Dr Masami Wakisaka, DDG, MOIF, LPIBA, *Japan*
Ms Annette Walker, DDG, *USA*
Ms Annita C Walker, LFIBA, DDG, *USA*
W W Walley, MD, DDG, *USA*
Mr Wang Li Jun, DDG, *China*
Prof Wang Tao, LFIBA, DDG, *China*
Mr Rollin M Warner Jr, LFIBA, DDG, *USA*
Mr Norman Sidney Weiser, FIBA, DDG, *USA*
Ms Lois Campbell Wells, LPIBA, DDG, IOM,
    MOIF, *New Zealand*
Ms Nancy Weniger-Phelps, DDG, *USA*
Dr Don B Wethasinghe, LPIBA, DDG, *Sri Lanka*
Dr M R Wiemann Jr, LPIBA, LFWLA, DDG,
    IOM, MOIF, *USA*
Ms Eileen Vimy Wilhelm, DDG, *Australia*
George W Williams, JR, DDG, *USA*
Dr Joseph R Williams, DDG, *USA*
Mr Emmanuel A Winful, LPIBA, DDG, *Ghana*
Dr Abund Ottokar Wist, LFIBA, DDG, *USA*
Dr Azi Wolfenson, LPIBA, DDG, *USA*
Mr Wong Chin Wah, FIBA, DDG,
    *Republic of Singapore*
Mr Vincent W S Wong, LPIBA, DDG, IOM,
    *West Malaysia*
Mr Xie Guozhang, DDG, *China*
Prof Xu Benli, DDG, *China*
Dr Virendra Kumar Yadava, DDG, *India*
Dr Etsuo Yamamura, MOIF, DDG, *Japan*
Prof Masami Yamanaka, LPIBA, DDG, MOIF,
    *Japan*
Prof Ichiro Yamashita, LFIBA, DDG, IOM, MOIF,
    *Japan*
Mr Yan Yi, LFIBA, LFWLA, DDG, IOM, *China*
Prof Chen-Chung Yang, LFIBA, DDG, *China*
Mr Yang Shiliang, DDG, *China*
Dr George C Yeh, DDG, *USA*

Dr Chi-Tung Yeh, LPIBA, DDG, IOM, *China*
Mr Yew Mui Leong, LPIBA, DDG, *Hong Kong*
Prof Yulong Yin, DDG, *China*
Dr Vak Yeong Yoo, MOIF, DDG, LPIBA, *Korea*
Prof Dr Ken-ichi Yoshihara, LPIBA, DDG, IOM,
    MOIF, *Japan*
Mrs Florence S Young, LFIBA, DDG, *USA*
Dr Yu Bao Ming, MOIF, DDG, *China*
Dr Yu Xiaohui, LFIBA, DDG, *Japan*
Mr Chang Hee Yun, DDG, *Korea*
Dr Branimir Zamola, DDG, *Croatia*
Mr Raymond Eric Zbacnik, FIBA, DDG, *USA*
Dr Wendell E Zehel, DDG, MOIF, *USA*
Dr Zhang Fushan, LFIBA, MOIF, DDG, *USA*
Dr Zhang Wan Xin, DDG, *China*

# RESEARCH FELLOWS OF THE IBC

Professor Antoine Abondo, *Cameroon*
Dr Anna J Allen, *USA*
Dr Rowland Iwu Amadi, *West Africa*
Mr Mario V Arroyo-Gomez, *Gibraltar*
Professor Ba En-Xu, *China*
Mrs Katarina E Bader-Molnar, *Switzerland*
Margaret Baender, *USA*
Dr Isabel R Baumann, *Switzerland*
Ms Sheila Bellamy, *Australia*
Dr Guy Boillat, *France*
Dr Georges Antoine Borel, *Switzerland*
Ms Judith Anne Brooks, *USA*
Captain F W Brown, *USA*
Mrs Gertrude Esther Carper, *USA*
Professor Chung-Yi Chen, *Taiwan, China*
Mr James Dzu-Biao Chen, *Hong Kong*
Mr Michael Kuo-Hsing Ch'in, *Taiwan, China*
Dr C Juliana Ching, *Hong Kong*
Dr Frederick Foo Chien, *China*
Professor Kyu-bok Chung, *South Korea*
Mr Leonc Jusz Ciuciura, *Poland*
Ms Nancy Patricia Coe, *USA*
Ms Iris Colvin, *USA*
Dr Francesco De Napoli, *Italy*
Ms Panayote Elias Dimitras, *Greece*
Mr Eric Dixon-Cave Hiscock, *Canada*
Mr Luis Dolcet-Buxeres, *Spain*
Mr Robert Charles Dorion, *Central America*
Prof Hermann W Eichstaedt, *Germany*
Mr Ole Kristian Ersgaard, *Denmark*
Professor Litian Feng, *China*
Dr Marianne B Fleck, *USA*
Mr Wilhelm Flöttmann, *Germany*
Mrs Vivian E S Fox, *USA*
Professor Gao Hongxun, *China*
Dr Erwin E Girod, *USA*
Goh Han Teng, PhD, *Singapore*
Dr M Goldston-Morris, *Australia*
Mr Isaac Thoman Goodine, *Philippines*
Dr Francis Walter Graham, *Australia*
Dr Rhoda Grant, *USA*
Mrs Padmin Gunaratnam, *Singapore*
Ms Nancy L Thompson Gunnoe, *USA*
Ms Darlene Midori Hayashi, *USA*
Joy Alice Holm, PhD, *USA*
Mr Virapong Hongyok, *South Thailand*
Professor Dr Sadao Hoshino, *Japan*
Professor Zuey-Shin Hsu, *Taiwan, China*
Mr Louis Lim Kim Huat, *Tanzania*
Ms Mildred F Hutchins, *USA*
Professor Dr Kazuyosi Ikeda, *Japan*

Mr Ramnath Jeetah, *Mauritius*
Dr Mirja A Kalliopuska, *Finland*
Mrs Puriko Kase, *Japan*
Ms Marlene H Katchur, *USA*
Dr Jerry Alvin Kirk, *USA*
Dr Samson B H Kisekka, *Uganda*
Professor Gerrit K L'Abbé, *Belgium*
Dr Philip Lai, *Hong Kong*
Professor Li Ji-Ren, *China*
Professor Li Yiyi, *China*
Professor Li Yonming, *China*
Dr Joanne L Linn, *USA*
Mr Grigori Loutchansky, *Austria*
Mr Edward James MacGilfrey, *USA*
Ms Joan Mahaffey, *USA*
Mr Umaru-Sanda Maigida, *Nigeria*
Dr Francisca Martin-Molero, *Spain*
Professor Masaie Matsumura, *Japan*
Mr Joseph M Mayo, *USA*
Professor Ebden Lizo Mazwai, *South Africa*
Mr Paul J Meyer, *USA*
Dr Isutomu Mimura, *Japan*
Ms Hildegard-Kauth Minchenko, *USA*
Professor Iwao Miyachi, *Japan*
Ms Martha A Moore, *USA*
Ms Karen Wigley-Morrison, *USA*
Professor Dr Emil Mosonyi, *Germany*
Dr John Edward Mulvihill, *USA*
Professor Henry Ian A Nowik, *USA*
Ms Helen Mary Odamtten, *Ghana*
Professor Hidemichi Ota, *Japan*
Dr Danny Shiu-Lam Paau, *Hong Kong*
Dr Eugenia Pasternak, *Canada*
Dame Gwendolyn Brown Shepley Peacher,
    *USA*
Professor Tadeusz Popiela, *Poland*
Mr Nader E Rastegar, *USA*
Mr Robert John Richardson, *Canada*
Dr Ralph R Robinson, *USA*
Ms Donna Jo Rolland, *USA*
Dr Jim R Ropchan, *USA*
Dr Violet D Schaefer, *USA*
Mr Werner N W Schramm, *Germany*
Mr Clayton Winfield Scott, *USA*
Dr Isadore Shapiro, *USA*
Professor Shen Xiuzhi, *China*
Ms Anna Pearl Sherrick, *USA*
Dr V Maxine Shipley Stock, *USA*
Mr Ah-Tee Sim, *Singapore*
Mr Henri Martokoesoemo Soekrisno,
    *Indonesia*
Mr Haji Soemario, *Indonesia*

Mr Peter Stadler, *Denmark*
Ms Carlene Stinnette, *USA*
Dr Helen Chien-fan Su, *USA*
Dr Masuichi Takino, *Japan*
Professor Giulio Filippo Tarro, *Italy*
Mr Goh Han Teng, *Singapore*
Mr Walter D Thomas, *USA*
Professor R F Vliegen, *Japan*
Dr Sophie M Wolanin, *USA*
Mr Vincent W S Wong, *West Malaysia*
Dr Margaret S Woods, *USA*
Mrs Linda Wu Liu, *China*

Dr William L S Wu, *USA*
Professor Xia Zhen-Ao (Hsia Chen-Au), *China*
Ms Patricia Anne Yallop, *Australia*
Professor Ichiro Yamashita, *Japan*
Professor Fuqing Yang, *China*
Mr Yew Mui Leong, *Hong Kong*
Professor Dr K Yoshihara, *Japan*
Professor Zhang Shi-ding, *China*
Mr Zheng Dun Xun, *China*
Mr Yu Zhixue, *China*
Ms Situ Zhiwen, *China*

# CONTENTS

Deputy Directors General of the IBC      VIII - XV

Research Fellows of the IBC      XVI - XVII

Dedications Section      XXI - CCXI

Biographies      1 - 652

Honours List Section      654 - 711

# Dedications

## PROFESSOR ADETUNJI ADEMUYIWA ADEYOKUNNU

*For your Outstanding Contribution to Medicine, Paediatric Practice and Education*

# PROFESSOR ADETUNJI ADEMUYIWA ADEYOKUNNU

Professor Adetunji Ademuyiwa Adeyokunnu is devoted to his career in the field of medicine. In addition to the degrees of MB and DCH, earned respectively from the University of London in 1965 and the University of Glasgow in 1969, he obtained the professional qualifications of MRCP (UK) in 1972, FWACP (West Africa) in 1976, and FRCP, both London and Glasgow.

Since 1973 Professor Adeyokunnu has been a Consultant Paediatrician in his own country, Nigeria, as well as recently in Saudi Arabia, where he has served as Chairman of Paediatrics at the Royal Community Hospital at Jubail Industrial City since 1997. Moreover, in the former country he was appointed Professor of Paediatrics at the University of Ibadan in 1983.

Included among Professor Adeyokunnu's activities connected with his profession is his authorship of some 75 publications in journals. Furthermore, he enjoys membership of several national and overseas organisations, namely, the Nigerian Paediatrics Association, the Sickle Cell Club of Nigeria, the Genetic Society of Nigeria, the British Medical Association, the American Association of Advanced Science, the New York Academy of Sciences and the Saudi Paediatrics Association.

Professor Adeyokunnu was born on 26 May 1938 in Ilesha, Nigeria. He and his wife, Julianah, have a large family, consisting of three sons and three daughters.

*A biography of Professor Adetunji Ademuyiwa Adeyokunnu appears in the main section of this Edition.*

# PROFESSOR LOUIS MARIE PIERRE ALLAIN, LFIBA

*For your Outstanding Contribution
to Liberal Studies*

# PROFESSOR LOUIS MARIE PIERRE ALLAIN, LFIBA

Louis Marie Pierre Allain was born on 28 June 1933 in Brest, France, into a family of Breton descent. In 1936 the family moved to Southern France, where he was brought up. After obtaining his Baccalauréat at high school in Marseilles in 1950, he had three years of classes in Paris preparing for entrance to the Ecole Normale Supérieure and passed the required examination in 1953.

Louis Allain's studies at the Ecole Normale Supérieure, included two one-year stays at the University of Moscow, lasted until 1958. During the first two years, from 1953-55, he began learning Russian at the School for Eastern Languages, Paris. He then decided to change from Classics (Latin and Greek) to concentrate on Russian, so he had the first of his stays in Moscow from 1955-56. After returning to Paris he gained his "Agrégation de russe" in 1957. During his second stay in Moscow, from 1957-58, he had the opportunity to make a trip to China, visiting Beijing and Shanghai.

The strongest impression of Professor Allain's years of studies at the Ecole Normale Supérieure was the teaching of the Russian émigré poet Nikolaj Otsup (born in 1893), the former personal secretary to the St Petersburg Acmeist poet Nikolaj Gumilev, who was executed by the Bolsheviks in 1921. Otsup gave his student the keys he needed to understand the strange world of Soviet Russia, but above all introduced the young man to Russian literature and free Russian thought. At that time Professor Allain never imagined he would become the editor of Otsup's works in post-Soviet Russia and thus fulfill the latter's dearest and most passionate wish: to return to Russia with his poetry.

His studies at the Ecole Normale Supérieure completed, Louis Allain became a high school teacher for a short time, appointed to the Lycée Lakanal, Paris. However, he still had to do his compulsory military service, which lasted for 31 months because of the ongoing war in Algeria. Back to civilian life in January 1961, he became a high school teacher at the Lycée Saint-Charles, Marseilles. At the beginning of the next academic year he was appointed Assistant Lecturer in Russian at the Sorbonne, Paris, then two years later rose to Senior Lecturer. During that time he married Annie Luc, daughter of the French radio and TV pioneer Jean Luc. She, too, became a well-known specialist in Russian, and currently chairs the Department of Russian Studies at the University of Lille.

The year 1969 was a turning point in Professor Allain's life and career. He decided to leave Paris to be his own boss in a vacant chair of Slavistic Languages at the University of Lille, where he stayed for the rest of his career, at first as Managing Lecturer from 1969-81, then becoming Professor and Chairperson of the Slavic Languages Department from 1981-98, having completed his doctorate in Russian at the Sorbonne in 1979. He is now Professor Emeritus.

Professor Allain's time at Lille can be divided into two parts, before and after the fall of Communism. In the years from 1969-88 he had a few opportunities to visit Russia on grants from the French Ministry of Foreign Affairs. Although in this way he kept in touch with the Russian language, he was unable to publish papers in the Soviet Union, except once on the occasion of a French-Russian Symposium held in 1978 at the University of Lille. However, during that period he published about 30 papers elsewhere, as well as three books consisting of his doctoral thesis "La personnalité de Dostoïevski", "Dostoïevski et Dieu" and "Dostoïevski et l'Autre". Dostoyevski became one of his areas of specialisation, along with Pushkin, Chekhov, Gumilev - Otsup's favourite poet - and the Russian poetry of the Silver Age. Some lectures and papers were given in Russian in Eastern Europe, especially Hungary, while others were delivered in Western Europe (France, Belgium, the UK, West Germany) and the USA.

The fall of Communism was a crucial turning-point in Professor Allain's academic career. He was given the opportunity to publish in Russia many of the papers and studies he had been working on. As early as 1989 the first book on Russian literature written by a Western critic, "Studies of Russian Literature", was published by a St Petersburg firm. However, the main event was in 1992, when he became Russian editor for two Russian collections, "Literature of Russian Diaspora" and "Destinies. Evaluations. Memoirs", again published in St Petersburg. During the 1993-98 period about 27 books, among which he authored five, appeared in the two collections. He brought many unknown treasures to Russia, including at least three world "scoops", namely, Otsup's works, Poplavsky's novels and the last, hitherto unpublished book of Remizov.

Professor Allain has four children, born in 1965, 1966, 1969 and 1975 respectively. The eldest, his daughter Andree-Lise (born in 1965), is now a specialist in financial mathematics at the French bank Crédit Lyonnais. His second daughter, Juliette, is head of the Marketing Division of Fortant de France, a wine company located in Sète, while the third daughter, Laurence, is an economist at the International Monetary Fund in Washington DC. His youngest child, his son Alexandre, has just earned his diploma in archivistics and palaeography, and intends to become a library curator.

*A biography of Professor Louis Marie Pierre Allain, LFIBA, appears in the main section of this Edition.*

## EFSTATHIOS CONSTANTINOS ARNIS

*For your Outstanding Contribution to the
Foundation of Centrifugal Space Navigation*

# EFSTATHIOS CONSTANTINOS ARNIS

The son of an army officer, Efstathios Constantinos Arnis was born on 14 April 1931 in the village of Thermon, the ancient capital of the Aetolean confederacy. In 1939 the family moved to Athens, only to return to Thermon the following year, when Greece was drawn into World War II, but then settled in Athens once again in 1942.

The wartime years and the postwar unrest in neighbouring countries, combined with his experience in military service were critical in shaping the personality of Mr Arnis, who recognised the need for counteraction against conditions imposing hostile relationships among human beings. From 1950-51 he studied at the University of Athens Law School, but the lectures did not satisfy him, as he could find no indication in them as to the achievement of a peaceful society. Leaving his studies, in 1952 he participated in the international group which the Universal Council of Churches in Greece organised to help local farmers by constructing irrigation systems in the agricultural area of Pesta, near the town of Ioannina. Later on he focused his concern on environmental issues and conservation of wildlife, and in recent years has been a member of Greenpeace.

More and more, anything that carried Mr Arnis away from the habitual way of life gave him a reason for his existence. Seeking to escape from a world of unhappiness and living at the beginning of the space age, he turned his attention to the stars. Application of his decision to live in a peaceful world now moved forward. Systematically and continuously reading books on physics one after the other, he gradually engaged in increasingly complex analyses and sophisticated experiments in his laboratory at home. At the same time, to increase his knowledge still further, he frequently attended lectures at the School of Physics, University of Athens, during the period from 1961-70.

Through his independent approach, Mr Arnis was not only able to study at his own rhythm, without rules and limitations imposed from outside, but he also had more opportunity for a personal choice of pursuits. Having an aptitude for invention, he worked at home to produce mechanical designs for others, which brought him financial benefits. The years from 1967-70 were milestones in his life, as it was then that his theoretical analyses in the field of physics acquired official recognition in the form of four patents. In particular, his 1970 anti-gravity paper aroused interest. It received very positive comments from the Director of the Technological Applications Section at Democritos, the Hellenic Nuclear Research Centre, who implied that the work might in future be worthy of a Nobel Prize.

After following lessons at the Benos-Palmer Technological Schools in Athens, in 1972 Mr Arnis was awarded a Certificate as a Qualified Designer in Mechanical Engineering. To his surprise, the Professor of Mechanical Engineering Design asked him to re-design all the designs required for the lessons, collecting them in a volume for the School archives.

As happens all too often concerning new scientific ideas, Mr Arnis found his concepts for spaceships and space travel under gentle conditions of flight were met with scepticism, especially by physicists, who considered them unrealistic, a view taken in scientific circles both at home and abroad. However, the horizon has grown lighter since 1989, when he was invited to become a member of the Planetary Society. Admitted to the Hellenic Astronomical Society two years later on the recommendation of Dr Yannis Liritzis, a researcher of the Academy of Sciences in Athens, since 1992 he has served the society as Expert Secretary and by giving lectures. Also in 1992 he was selected for active membership of the New York Academy of Sciences. In addition, he is an associate member of the American Institute of Aeronautics and Astronautics and the American Association for the Advancement of Science, joining both by invitation in 1994, the year that he retired from his design activities.

Mr Arnis was twice asked to present his work at the Intersociety Energy Conversion Engineering Conference, held in 1996 and 1997 respectively, but on each occasion was unable to do so. However, the New York Academy of Sciences, DEMOCRITOS and other groups of scientists have had their attention drawn to his recent papers on "Determination of absolute motion" and "Distinction between gravity-acceleration applied to material bodies". Note has been taken of his sugggestions for new correct analyses of relativistic theories, the combination of superconductivity and free energy, and other matters.

Seeing the increasing turmoil in the world, Mr Arnis dreams of a spaceship to take him deeply into the infinite universe of God, where gentler secrets might offer his fellowmen a chance for a more spiritual and peaceful life in the new millennium. His plan for the immediate present is to establish his own observatory on a mountain near a monastery, where he can admire the stars and think of their creator.

*A biography of Efstathios Constantinos Arnis appears in the main section of this Edition.*

## PROFESSOR ALEXANDER BALANKIN, FIBA

*For your Outstanding Contribution to
Fractal and Fracture Mechanics*

# PROFESSOR ALEXANDER BALANKIN, FIBA

Professor Alexander Balankin is a research scientist and university educator, whose special interests lie in areas of solid and fracture mechanics. In particular, he has had notable success in his work on the theory of high velocity impact and armour piercing, the quantum-statistical approach to synergetics of a deformed solid, development fractal solid mechanics, contributions to statistical fracture mechanics, and the concept and theory of multifracta elasticity.

Although Professor Balankin has now been living in Mexico for several years, he was born in Moscow, Russia, on 3 March 1958. He studied at Moscow Engineering Physics Institute, earning a Master of Science degree in Solid State Physics in 1981, and PhD in Physics and Mathematics in 1986. He also holds a DrSc degree in Physics and Mathematics, obtained from Dzerzhinsky Military Academy, Moscow, in 1991.

Prior to embarking on his PhD studies in 1983 Alexander Balankin spent two years as a Junior Scientist at the Moscow Engineering Physics Institute, starting in 1981. In 1986 he was appointed a Senior Scientist at Dzerzhinsky Military Academy, where he became Head of the Research Laboratory in 1990 until leaving for Mexico in 1992. Joining Monterey Technological University in Mexico City, he held a professorial position there for the next five years, but in 1997 transferred to his current post of Professor of Mechanics at the National Polytechnic Institute, Mexico City. Furthermore, he has served the Mexican Government as Counsellor to the National Council for Science and Technology since 1995, while in 1999 he took on responsibility as Head of the Area of Material Engineering of the National Commission on Nuclear Safety and Safeguards, as well as acting as Consultant to the Mexican National Oil Company PEMEX.

In the course of his career so far, Professor Balankin has directed fourteen doctoral candidates in the preparation of their theses. He himself is the author or co-author of more than 140 articles in refereed journals, on solid state physics, solid and fracture mechanics, synergetics, and fractals, as well as author of two books and co-author of four others. In 1996 the firm Pleiades Publishing Inc selected one of his works for its Prize for Best Publication of 1995.

Professor Balankin has been the recipient of several other awards and honours. They include a State Prize of the USSR Ministry of Defence and a Prize from the USSR Academy of Sciences, awarded during his final years in Russia. He is classed as a National Researcher of Mexico at Level III, the highest level, a distinction he received some four years ago, while in 1997 he won the Romulo Garza Prize for Research and Technology Development of Mexico. As member of the Fracture Mechanics Section of the Mexican Academy of Material Sciences, he was recently elected Section President. Even more recently he accepted an invitation to become a Fellow of the International Biographical Association.

Professor Alexander Balankin and his wife Fatima have made their home on the outskirts of Mexico City. They have a teenage daughter, Asia, who was born on 27 September 1984.

*A biography of Professor Alexander Balankin, FIBA, appears in the main section of this Edition.*

## DR JAMES DANIEL BARGER
## DDG, MOIF

*For your Outstanding Contribution to*
*Pathology and Quality Improvement*

# DR JAMES DANIEL BARGER, DDG, MOIF

A specialist in the field of pathology, Dr James Daniel Barger has dedicated many years to his career. In addition to holding AB and BS degrees, both earned at the University of Dakota in 1939, MD from the University of Pennsylvania in 1941 and MS in Pathology from the University of Minnesota, he is a Diplomate of the American Board of Pathology.

For a number of years Dr Barger worked at hospitals in Arizona, but in 1964 he moved to Las Vegas, Nevada, to join the professional staff at the Sunrise Hospital and in 1981 was appointed to his present position of Senior Pathologist. Apart from his hospital commitments, he served as Medical Director of the South-West Blood Bank and Blood Services of Arizona and Nevada, an activity he has now discontinued, while at one time he was a Registered Quality Engineer in the State of California.

A member of the College of American Pathologists, Dr Barger distinguished himself by holding office as its President and was honoured by selection as Man of the Year for 1997. Included among the various organisations to which he gained admission are the American Association, the American Association of Pathologists and the American Cancer Society. He is also a Commander of the Knights of Lazarus, as well as a Deputy Director General of the International Biographical Centre and a Member of the Order of International Fellowship.

Dr Barger was born on 17 May 1917 in Bismarck, North Carolina, USA. He has two sons and two daughters.

*A biography of Dr James Daniel Barger, DDG, MOIF, appears in the main section of this Edition.*

# THE HONOURABLE DR JACK GORDON BEALE, AO, JP, ME, Hon DSc, Hon LLD, DDG, LFIBA

*For your Outstanding Contribution to Mankind Living in Harmony with the Environment*

# THE HONOURABLE DR JACK GORDON BEALE, AO, JP, ME, Hon DSc, Hon LLD, DDG, LFIBA

The Honourable Dr Jack Gordon Beale has enjoyed a long and successful career that spans 57 years as a Consulting Chartered Professional Engineer in Australia and includes 47 years as an international consultant in 60 countries in environmental policy, law and management, as well as in conservation, resource development, hydroelectric generation and engineering. Over the same 57 years he has held directorships in private and public companies, with interests including finance, investment, manufacturing, export and import. He is Chairman of Green Australia Ltd, an organisation that promotes landscape rejuvenation through ecological sustainable water, soil and vegetation programmes. In addition, he chairs the internationally respected Water Foundation of Australia and the Zenith Investment Group, which is involved in investment, property, energy and consulting. He represents Zenith in a hydroelectricity generating station network. Furthermore, he sits on the Advisory Committee of the Centre for Resource and Environmental Studies at the Australian National University.

Prior to establishing his private consultancy practice in 1942, Dr Beale had two years' experience as Manager and Engineer at a munitions works, as well as six years of mechanical, electrical, civil engineering and industrial training and experience. Between 1938 and 1942 he was also a part-time Lecturer in mathematics, physics, engineering design and trade courses at Sydney and Wollongong Technical Colleges. Moreover, 1942 was the year that he made his entry into politics, elected to the Legislative Assembly of New South Wales as Member of the South Coast Constituency. An outstanding parliamentarian, he was regularly re-elected until 1973. From 1965-71 he served as Minister for Conservation, his tasks including representing the New South Wales Government on the Australian Water Resources Council, the Australian Forestry Council and the Australian Agricultural Council. Similarly, during his term as Minister for Environment Control from 1971-73, he represented New South Wales on the Australian Environment Council. He wa a ranking Australian delegate to the 1972 United Nations Conference on the Human Environment. After retiring from politics, he spent the next three years as a part-time Senior Advisor for the United Nations Environment and Development Programmes, besides serving on the Science and Technology Council of New South Wales in 1975.

Dr Beale's achievements are many and varied. From the 1950 onwards he was engaged in formulatiung and initiating numerous environmental projects, often related to water conservation and irrigation and later including measures regarding pollution, environmental planning, development and legislation. Besides establishing the first comprehensive environmental reference library in Australia, he initiated the first survey of pollution and the environment of New South Wales, the first survey of environmental research in Australia, the first environmental impact assessment guidelines, the first river valley research on the sustainable development of natural resources and the first six major environmental investigations to be carried out with emphasis on human relations. He also successfully devised an economically drought-proof network of climatically distributed hydroelectricity generating stations, for which he was granted a patent in 1987.

A prolific writer, Dr Beale has published extensively on a wide range of subjects. Notable are his works on matters relating to the environment, including "Cyclical Environmental Management System" and "Protection and Management of the Environment", both of which appeared in 1975. "The Manager and the Environment: Theory and Practice of Environmental Management", written at the request of UNEP and published in 1980, was followed in 1981 by "Brown Australia", dealing with the degradation of the Australian landscape, and "Green Australia", which presented a comprehensive water, soil and vegetation programme for rejuvenation of the countryside. His numerous articles on various topics have appeared in professional, technical and general publications, while outspoken as always, he has frequently expressed his views at meetings and in the media.

In 1939 Jack Beale earned a Diploma in Mechanical Engineering with honours from Sydney Technical College. Four years later, at the age of 25, he became the youngest ever to be elected a Chartered Professional Engineer by the Institution of Engineers, Australia. He also holds a Master of Engineering degree from the University of New South Wales, awarded in 1976. In addition, despite his heavy load of professional commitments, he made time for study and research, both in Australia and at foreign educational institutions, such as the University of California, Massachusetts Institute of Technology and Harvard School of Design.

During his career, Dr Beale has been the recipient of numerous distinctions. They include appointment as Justice of the Peace for New South Wales in 1952. In 1973 he had the title of "The Honourable" conferred upon him by HM Queen Elizabeth II. The Australian National University established the Jack Beale Chair of Water Resources in 1989 and the Annual Jack Beale Water Resources Lecture series in 1990. In 1997 he was granted the highest honour of the University of New South Wales, namely, the degree of DSc (honoris causa), the same year that it established the Annual Jack Beale Global Environment Lecture Series. Her Majesty the Queen approved his admission to the Order of Australia for outstanding contributions to science, technology and environmental engineering, and the development of public policy. Most recently, the Australian National University bestowed on him its highest honour, the degree of LLD (honoris causa).

*A biography of The Honourable Dr Jack Gordon Beale, AO, JP, ME, Hon DSc, Hon LLD, DDG, LFIBA, appears in the main section of this Edition.*

# PROFESSOR ALEXANDER D BRUNO, PhD

*For your Outstanding Contribution
as a Mathematician*

# PROFESSOR ALEXANDER D BRUNO, PhD

Professor Alexander D Bruno is Head of the Mathematics Department at the Institute of Applied Mathematics of RAS in Moscow, Russia. A long-term member of Moscow Mathematical Society, during the present decade he has been admitted to the American Mathematical Society, as well as to the Academy of Nonlinear Sciences. In addition to publishing widely, he has participated in numerous international conferences held in Russia and elsewhere. Now his achievements in pure and applied mathematics are widely known.

Born in Moscow on 26 June 1940, Alexander Bruno was still very young when he began to show an interest in figures, which he was able to recognise before he knew any letters. He vividly remembers the day in 1945 when he sat turning over the pages of a book, fascinated by the changing page numbers. By the time he was approaching page 300, he understood how numbers were formed, that the rule could be applied to any number and that the range of numbers was infinite. That was the day he became a mathematician!

After completing his secondary education, Alexander Bruno commenced the study of Mathematics at Moscow State University, where he earned a Master of Science degree in 1962. He then embarked on postgraduate studies at the Institute of Applied Mathematics. There he prepared for a PhD, awarded by the USSR Academy of Sciences in 1966, the year after the Institute had appointed him as a Junior Researcher. In 1970 he qualified as Professor, but owing to somewhat unexpected circumstances was not promoted to the senior position until 1971. At the end of the 1980s he had his first taste of administration, as Head of a research group at the Institute, a position he held until 1995, when he took over responsibility as Departmental Head. Between 1992 and 1993 he also served as Head of the Department of Pure Mathematics at the Russian Open University.

Professor Bruno's duties have included giving courses in Nonlinear Analysis and Theory of Bifurcations. Moreover, since 1973 he has guided research students in Pure and Applied Mathematics. He has travelled abroad on numerous occasions, visiting institutes and universities in Poland, France, Germany and Italy. Starting with the International Congress of Mathematicians held in Moscow in 1966, he has so far taken part in a total of 42 international conferences, held in Russia, Ukraine and Uzbekistan, as well as in the former Czechoslovakia, Bulgaria, Germany, the Netherlands, Finland, France, Spain, Poland, Switzerland, Greece, Hungary, Japan and the USA.

Besides being the author of four monographs, Professor Bruno has published more than 170 papers, most of them subsequently translated into English. They are on Nonlinear Analysis, Number Theory and Applications in Mechanics, Celestial Mechanics and Hydrodynamics. In his book "Power Geometry in Algebraic and Differential Equations", published in 1998, he describes a new calculus, called power geometry, which is a development of differential calculus, oriented especially for solving nonlinear problems. It provides a very simple way of resolving singularities to find special solutions and discover asymptotics of solutions for equations and systems of equations of any kind - algebraic, ordinary differential or partial differential. It offers an alternative to algebraic geometry, differential algebra, nonstandard analysis and Lie group analysis, solving problems through simpler calculations.

In recognition of his accomplishments Professor Bruno has had his biographical details incorporated into many reference dictionaries.

*A biography of Professor Alexander D Bruno, PhD, appears in the main section of this Edition.*

## CLINTON ROSS BURNETTE, LFIBA, DDG, FWLA

*For your Outstanding Contribution to Film Script Writing*

# CLINTON ROSS BURNETTE, LFIBA, DDG, FWLA

A film producer and scriptwriter who began his career as a technological photographer, Clinton Ross Burnette is presently the Co-Director of Firebird Productions, a film production company he founded in New South Wales, Australia, as a subsidiary of Aurora Entertainment Corporation USA.

Mr Burnette's ties with the USA go back to his infancy, as he was born in the state of Mississippi on 30 July 1945. At the age of ten he arrived in Australia, where he attended elementary school. Four years later he was awarded the Elementary Certificate, the Resuscitation Certificate, the Proficiency Certificate and a Bronze Medallion by the Royal Life Saving Society of Australia. Possessed of exceptionally high intelligence, he achieved scholastic success at high school, obtaining A grades in English, Mathematics, Physics and Chemistry in his diploma in 1964. He was offered a place at college to study Physics with interest in Cosmology, but having a lifelong passion for photography opted to become a professional photographer instead. He also joined The Mustangs, an Anglo-American rock and roll group in which he played lead guitar between 1964 and 1967.

During the late 1960s Mr Burnette returned to the USA to study photography in Westpost, Connecticut, as well as following a course in creative writing. After qualifying with honours in Technological Photography and Cinematography in 1972, he spent three years as a forensic photographer with special expertise in infra-red, ultra-violet, fluorescence, macrophotography and microphotography, but in 1975 turned to commercial photography and also began writing articles on the artistic use of technological photography. Parallel with those activities he pursued studies which culminated in a qualification in Principles of Management and Industrial Psychology.

In Australia once more, Mr Burnette continued with his career in photography, establishing his own studio. In 1981 he undertook part-time study of computer technology and gained a certificate in programming. He then commenced working in the computer field, with an emphasis on graphic design that eventually led to his developing an interest in filmmaking.

While working in the States, Mr Burnette joined the Photographic Society of America and Associated Photographers International California chapter in 1972 and 1975 respectively; the former organisation was to publish his "How To" articles in its journal. After having music recorded by Columbine Records in Hollywood, he was admitted to membership of the American Society of Composers and Publishers. He is currently a bona fide member of the Royal Photographic Society of Great Britain.

*A biography of Clinton Ross Burnette, LFIBA, DDG, FWLA, appears in the main section of this Edition.*

## ROBERTO CALDERÓN-SÁNCHEZ, PE

*For your Outstanding Contribution
to Dredging*

# ROBERTO CALDERÓN-SÁNCHEZ, PE

Mr Roberto Calderón-Sánchez, PE, is the President of the Scientific Dredging Institute Incorporated, an organisation which he founded in July 1995 in San Juan, Puerto Rico. It has two main aims, one being to conduct research into the theory and practice of dredging, the other consisting of providing courses, seminars and workshops on dredging and related matters. In his capacity as President, he holds responsibility for Company organisation. Besides planning surveys to determine the type and content of the courses to offer, he engages in contacting prospective instructors. It is also essential for him to keep up-to-date with the latest developments in dredging, for which purpose he attends conventions and congresses in the United States and abroad. Among these, the 15th World Dredging Congress in Las Vegas, Nevada, in 1998, and the 14th World Dredging Congress in Amsterdam, The Netherlands, in 1995.

Born on 28 July 1930 in Carolina, Puerto Rico, Mr Calderón-Sánchez studied both in Puerto Rico and on the US mainland. In 1951 he was awarded a scholarship by the US Navy on obtaining the third highest grade in the qualifying examination held in Puerto Rico by the 10th Naval District. This enabled him to study at the Speed Scientific School, University of Louisville, in Louisville, Kentucky, from October 1951 until December 1952. Later on he had the opportunity for further study, attending courses of Louisiana State University Evening Division from 1955-59.

Furthermore, he holds a Bachelor of Science degree in Civil Engineering, obtained in 1969 from the University of Puerto Rico, Mayaguez Campus, called then the College of Agriculture and Mechanical Arts, where he pursued courses at its College of Engineering. It is remarkable that although he did not take the professional examination for his licence as engineer until sixteen years after graduation, after taking some review courses, he obtained the fifth highest grade of the 600 engineers that took the professional engineering examination with him in April 1987. This examination is the same given in the US for this purpose.

His Navy service as midshipman in 1952 in USS New Jersey BB-62 and Navy studies behind him, as a Civil Engineering graduate Mr Calderón-Sánchez worked for the Puerto Rico Highway Authority from 1969-1981. In May 1981 he was recruited in Puerto Rico for a position as Patent Examiner for the Civil Engineering Division of the US Patent Office in Washington DC. In April 1982 he resigned to accept a position as Construction Manager in Saudi Arabia with a private firm, but upon arrival there the conditions of work were not acceptable to him and he returned to Puerto Rico. He spent three years in private practice in surveying, but in 1985 was appointed Supervisor of Surveying with the Ports Authority of Puerto Rico, a post he now holds concurrently with his position as President of the Scientific Dredging Institute. The time he devotes to the Scientific Dredging Institute is after his office hours as Supervisor of Surveying, and on Saturdays, Sundays and vacations.

Among Mr Calderón-Sánchez's significant achievements is the 122-page report he wrote in 1989 on the damages caused by Hurricane Hugo to the ports facilities of the Ports Authority in Porto Nuevo. Containing some excellent recommendations for damage reduction on a future occasion, it has now been prepared for inclusion in the Archives of Puerto Rico.

A member of the College of Engineers and Surveyors of Puerto Rico, in the early 1970s Mr Calderón-Sánchez was twice elected to its Governing Board, serving for a year on each occasion. He enjoys the distinction of membership of the Society of Engineers of Puerto Rico, to which admission is by invitation only. In addition, he belongs to the American Society of Civil Engineers and the Association of Mechanical Engineers of Puerto Rico; having studied Mechanical Engineering for a time in the past, he was invited by his former classmates to join the latter organisation in 1997.

As a means of fulfilling his civic concerns he accepted the invitation to join Rotary International through the Río Pedras Club near his home. He also accepted the invitation extended to the citizens by the Athaeneum of Porto Rico in 1997 to express their points of view on the United States-Puerto Rico Political Status Act, HR 856, under consideration by the Committee on Resources of the House of Representatives. The Athaeneum undertook the translation of the testimonies and their submission to the White House and Congress of the United States.

For recreation Mr Calderón-Sánchez enjoys reading poetry, especially that of Ruben Dario. Married to Celeste O'Neill since 1988, he has two stepsons, Dr Luis F Pumarada-O'Neill and Mr Manuel E Pumarada-O'Neill.

*A biography of Roberto Calderón-Sánchez, PE, appears in the main section of this Edition.*

## LURDES CAMACHO, FIBA

*For your Outstanding Contribution to
Virtual Reality and Education*

# LURDES CAMACHO, FIBA

Lurdes Camacho is a very well known devoted Educational Technologist and Scientific Advisor. Her articles have been published locally and internationally, and she was a main contributor to "Teaching, Learning Information-Towards an Open Socratic School" published by the European Commission. She also has articles published in the journal "Educational Media International". Her book, which is regarded as an essential in the education world is entitled: "Memories of a Futuretime - Virtual Reality and Education".

Lurdes Camacho was born in the little town of Olhao, in Portugal, on the 16th April 1959. Her higher education includes a History Degree, which she acquired in 1982, an MSc cum laude Degree, in Multimedia Educational Communication, in 1995 and she is preparing her PhD Degree in Educational Communication. She began her long and dedicated professional career as a Teacher in a secondary school, between 1983-92 and then took up the important appointment of Educational Technologist at Universidade Aberta, from 1992-97. She was a Scientific Adviser for the Ministry of Culture in 1996-97, before taking up her present position of Coordinator of the Education and Training Department at the Institute of Cinema, Audiovisual and Multimedia in 1997. She has also been an Expert of Media, Information and Communication Technolgies and Youth at the Council of Europe since 1998.

Lurdes Camacho is an outstanding person of her community. She sits on several committees locally, and is a member of New York Academy of Sciences, the Portuguese Association of Computer Science and Education, and the Portuguese Association of Computer Science. She is also a Fellow of the International Biographical Association and has been nominated as Deputy Governor on the Board of Governors of the American Biographical Institute's Research Association. Her achievements have earned her biographical listings in several works, including Five Hundred Leaders of Influence, Who's Who in the World, Who's Who in Science and Engineering, and Who's Who of Professionals.

*A biography of Lurdes Camacho, FIBA, appears in the main section of this Edition.*

## THE MOST REVEREND THE HONOURABLE
## SAMUEL EMMANUEL CARTER, SJ, OJ, CD

*For your Outstanding Contribution to the
Development of the Local Church*

# THE MOST REVEREND THE HONOURABLE SAMUEL EMMANUEL CARTER, SJ, OJ, CD

The Most Reverend Samuel Emmanuel Carter has devoted the greater part of his life to the service of the Lord, including two dozen years as Archbishop of Kingston, Jamaica, retiring as Emeritus in November 1994. He took his first vows in the Society of Jesus on 24 August 1946, was ordained Priest on 19 June 1954, and in 1966 had the distinction of becoming the first Jamaican ever to be made a Roman Catholic Bishop, his consecration taking place on 25 April that year.

Born on 31 July 1919 in St Andrew, Jamaica, Samuel Carter was brought up in a family of five girls and another boy. Educated at St Aloysius Boys School and St Simon's College, he passed his High School Certificate at the latter institution, then remained there for a couple of years as a Latin Instructor. In 1941 he joined the Civil Service and was assigned to the Treasury Department, but left in 1944 for religious training and classical studies, entering the Jesuit Novitiate at Shadowbrook, Lenox, Massachusetts, USA. Once his vows were taken, he enrolled at Weston College, a Department of Boston College, where he obtained his MA in Philosophy in 1950. A year as an Instructor in Sociology at Holy Cross College, Worcester, Massachusetts, followed, prior to his return to Weston for theological studies leading to a Licentiate in Sacred Theology - STL - in 1955. A period devoted to Ascetical Theology studies in the UK followed.

Back in the USA in 1956 he attended Boston College School of Social Work, from which he received a Master's degree in Social Work. At the same time, he gained experience as a Caseworker and Marriage Counsellor for Boston Children's Service and the Family Service of Greater Boston. He also obtained a Certificate in Counselling and Family Life from the Catholic University of America.

His studies completed, Reverend Carter returned to Jamaica to serve as Assistant Parish Priest and Master of Ceremonies at Holy Trinity Cathedral Parish from 1958-59. Involved in founding Campion College, he became its Headmaster from its opening in 1960 until mid-1964, when he was appointed Rector of St George's College, the first Jamaican to hold that office. One of his tasks the following year was to attend the 4th and final session of the 2nd Vatican Council in Rome, as Adviser to Bishop McEleney. In February 1966 he was made Auxiliary Bishop of Kingston, with the Titular See of Cenculiana. From that year until appointed Archbishop of Kingston on 24 September 1970, he served as Vicar General of the Archdiocese of Kingston and Pastor of the Holy Cross Church.

Between 1966 and his retirement, Reverend Carter was elected to a total of seven terms as President of the Antilles Episcopal Conference. Besides representing the Conference at the 2nd, 3rd and 4th Synod of Bishops, held in Rome, from time to time he chaired one or other of the Conference's Commissions. In 1973 he was appointed by Pope Paul VI to the Roman Sacred Congregation for the Evangelization of Peoples, was elected to a four-year term as Chairman of the Caribbean Conference of Churches, became Director of the Christian Action for Development Fund, and joined the Commission of Enquiry set up to investigate the administration of justice, alleged police brutality and other related matters in the State of Grenada. Two years later he was elected Moderator of CIDSE (International Cooperation for Socio-Economic Development), while in 1976 he joined the Council of the University of the West Indies. President of Jamaica Council of Churches for two years running, namely, 1979 and 1980, he was later re-elected for the period 1991-93. The Pontifical Council for Promoting Christian Unity appointed him Co-Chairman of the Roman Catholic/Disciples of Christ Dialogue for 1983-95. In August 1987 he led the Caribbean Conference of Churches on a fact-finding mission to Haiti regarding the political situation and elections there, while in 1993 he was an Observer at the elections in Guyana. As a Papal appointee he attended the African Synod held in Rome in 1994, and was subsequently elected by AEC to attend the Synod of Americas held there in 1997. Chairman of the Board of LOVE FM Radio Station from 1993-95, since then he has held office as its Treasurer. Furthermore, he has provided his services to numerous other religious and secular bodies, including his current commitments as Vice-Chairman of the Board of Directors of the Jamaica Foundation for Children, and Chairman of the Association for Settlements and Commercial Enterprise for National Development.

Reverend Carter has been the recipient of a number of honours. In 1970 he was decorated Commander of the Order of Distinction by the Jamaican Government, which also bestowed the Order of Jamaica upon him in 1992. In 1976 he received the Rale Medallion, the Bicentennial Award of Boston College School of Social Work. In addition to an Honorary Doctorate in Divinity, awarded in 1966, he holds four Honorary Doctorates in Law, from the College of Holy Cross, Le Moyne College in Syracuse, Loyola University of Chicago and the University of the West Indies, besides a Doctorate in Sacred Theology - STD - from Boston College. As recently as 1996 he received a Doctorate in Divinity from Bethany College, in Bethany, USA.

*A biography of The Most Reverend The Honourable Samuel Emmanuel Carter, SJ, OJ, CD, appears in the main section of this Edition.*

# DR KA CHING CHAN, PhD

*For your Outstanding Contribution as
a Senior Lecturer in Science and Technology*

# DR KA CHING CHAN, PhD

A mechanical engineer engaged in research and lecturing at the University of New South Wales, Sydney, Australia, Dr Ka Ching Chan is well-established in a promising career, which he embarked on some eight years ago. He has already become known internationally, with numerous publications of his appearing in international journals and conference proceedings.

Although Ka Ching Chan originates from Hong Kong, born in Kowloon on 27 January 1965, he holds BASc and MASc degrees from Canada, awarded by the University of Toronto in 1987 and 1989 respectively. During his university studies he received a McAllister Summer Research Fellowship in 1986, as well as University Open Master's Fellowships in 1988 and 1989.

Leaving Canada for Australia, Dr Chan joined the University of New South Wales in Sydney in 1991, appointed to the position of Lecturer. There he also commenced preparations for a PhD, which the University awarded him in 1995. He was promoted to his present position of Senior Lecturer in 1997, after a short period earlier that year as a Visiting Assistant Professor at the Hong Kong University of Science and Technology.

In addition to his university degrees, Dr Chan is qualified as a Chartered Professional Engineer, as well as a Member of the Institution of Engineering, Australia. Furthermore, he has gained admission to the American Society of Mechanical Engineering, the Society of Mechanical Engineers and the Institute of Industrial Engineers.

Married to Miranda Wong since June 1990, Dr Chan has two sons, David Bertrand and James Michael. His recreational interests consist of music and photography.

*A biography of Dr Ka Ching Chan, PhD, appears in the main section of this Edition.*

## FAI CHUT CHENG, DDG, LFIBA, MOIF

*For your Outstanding Contribution to
Electrical Engineering Research*

# FAI CHUT CHENG, DDG, LFIBA, MOIF

Mr Fai Chut Cheng is a devoted researcher in the field of electrical engineering. For many years from 1957 onwards he worked in Harbin, China, in the High Voltage Section at the Central Laboratory of the Northeast Power Administration. However, since 1973 he has resided in Hong Kong, where his various posts have been mainly of a part-time or temporary nature. For most of the 1980s he worked at the University of Hong Kong, but in 1989 he transferred to Hong Kong Polytechnic University as a research assistant. In 1998 he reached retirement age, but he now hopes to continue as a non-salaried Honorary Research Fellow.

Born on 15 July 1933 in Shanghai, Fai Chut Cheng was the eldest boy in a traditional Chinese family. Brought up to believe that spiritual life was more important than material comfort, he developed a scholarly attitude, respecting cultural origins and classical works of all kinds, including those from abroad. At middle school he came to realise that good thinking was more important than learning new facts and that gaining good marks was secondary to attaining true ability. He started reading outside the school curriculum, his choice of books including Einstein's "The Evolution of Physics: The Growth of Ideas from Early Concepts to Relativity and Quanta". This helped him to develop the insight and imagination that later proved so useful to him in finding solutions to puzzles.

While at Tsinghua University, from which he graduated in Electrical Engineering in 1957, Mr Cheng found he had a need to explore matters to their origin, a need that his courses unfortunately did not satisfy. However, his work at Harbin, consisting mainly of research and development of overvoltages in electrical power systems, gave him valuable experience that provided a reliable background to his later theoretical investigations of engineering problems. Taking the opportunity to spend some of his free time on reading works by Hegel, he was strongly influenced by the philosopher's ideology of dialectics and view of the unity of opposites. Apart from that, during the latter part of the Harbin years, he developed an interest in Traditional Chinese Medicine. Through serving as a voluntary amateur between 1970 and 1972, he came to understand its underlying basis, in which the wholistic concept played such an important role, embodying the critical features of Chinese philosophy.

Since settling in Hong Kong Mr Cheng has benefitted greatly from his extensive background. Working part-time he was left with plenty of opportunity to pursue his personal project on analysis of electrical fields in power cables, which he began in the late 1980s and in which he put emphasis on the influence exerted by different electrical fields on the deterioration of cable insulation. His research provided the basis for his MPhil degree, awarded by the University of Hong Kong in 1990.

As a continuation of his project Mr Cheng began investigating the question of cable insulation design. It was in the early stages of that work that he had his greatest achievement ever, when he developed a formula for determining the insulation thicknesses of polymeric power insulation cables. The problem, a classic one that had puzzled investigators for nearly a century, had been without even a theoretical solution, so it was not surprising that his breakthrough attracted international attention. Interestingly, he used only a simple mathematical tool in his study. No complicated physical knowledge was required, the critical factor being to find the right idea, for which he drew on ways of thinking of both East and West. He presented the formula, an analytical expression of closed form and of sufficient accuracy for engineering purposes, in a paper that appeared in 1994 in the IEEE Transactions on Dielectrics and Electrical Insulation.

Continuing with the further stages of his project, Mr Cheng estimates that it will take at least five more years to complete, which he hopes that he will have the opportunity to do, despite being officially retired. He would then like to pursue deeper investigations or even use his engineering experience to aid him in seeking comparison and fusion of Eastern and Western philosophies.

*A biography of Fai Chut Cheng, DDG, LFIBA, MOIF, appears in the main section of this Edition.*

## DR CHIAO-LIANG JULIANA CHING, MD, DDG, IOM, LPIBA, MOIF

*For your Outstanding Contribution to Medicine and Business*

# DR CHIAO-LIANG JULIANA CHING, MD, DDG, IOM, LPIBA, MOIF

The daughter of Mr and Mrs Ching Tan, Chiao-Liang Juliana Ching was born in Hong Kong on 23 February 1955. A dedicated physician and businesswoman, she is known for her valuable contributions to the promotion of international understanding and cooperation, as well as to the advancement of humanity.

Dr Ching's preparation for her career in the field of medicine took place in the USA. As a student at Yale University she earned a Bachelor of Science degree summa cum laude in Biology, prior to commencing medical studies at the University of California at Davis, where she obtained her MD in May 1981. An internship and a year's residency at the University of California at Los Angeles Hospitals and Clinics were followed by a further residency at Harvard University Hospitals from 1983-85.

While in the United States, Dr Ching became a member both of the California Medical Association and the American Medical Association. After distinguishing herself through her medical services in Los Angeles, as well as at the Beth Israel Hospital and Brigham and Women's Hospital, she returned to Hong Kong, where she carries on her current activities. As a businesswoman she is the Director of two companies, namely, the Ideal Choice Development Ltd and Chi King Development Ltd. She has joined the Hong Kong Securities Professionals Alumni Association, while her range of leisure interests are represented by her membership of the Planetary Society, the Pacific Club and Friends of the Cultural Centre of Hong Kong. She is also an Elihu Yale Associate.

Dr Ching has been included in several biographical volumes, among them The First Five Hundred, International Directory of Distinguished Leadership, the Marquis Who's Who in the World, and, most recently, in the main and dedication sections of 2000 Outstanding People of the 20th Century. A Deputy Governor of the American Biographical Institute and Deputy Director General of the International Biographical Centre, she was selected as Woman of the Year 1991 and International Woman of the Year 1992. The latter organisation has honoured her with the International Order of Merit and as a Member of the Order of International Fellowship. Moreover, she has accepted an invitation to become a Life Patron of the International Biographical Association.

*A biography of Dr Chiao-Liang Juliana Ching, MD, DDG, IOM, LPIBA, MOIF, appears in the main section of this Edition.*

# DR PESUS CHOU, DrPh

*For your Outstanding Contribution
to Public Health*

# DR PESUS CHOU, DrPh

Dr Pesus Chou, who currently holds professorial and administrative positions at the National Yang-Ming University in Taipei, Taiwan, is dedicated to her career in university education and research. With interests lying within the field of public health, she has been responsible for numerous publications ranging from epidemiological studies to investigations into the use of Traditional Chinese Medicine.

Dr Chou was born on 9 November 1948 in Tainan, Taiwan. In 1967 she commenced her studies at the National Taiwan University in Taipei, earning her Bachelor of Science degree from its School of Pharmacy in 1971 and Master of Public Health from its Institute of Public Health in 1973. The following year she began twelve years of service with the Cancer Society of the Republic of China, at first as Secretary and then as Secretary-General. Added to that, in 1977 she became an Instructor in the Department of Social Medicine at the National Yang-Ming Medical College.

In August 1983 the Medical College promoted Ms Chou to Associate Professor, transferring her to its Institute of Public Health. She was almost immediately granted leave of absence for postgraduate study in the USA. There she spent two years at the Tulane University School of Public Health, obtaining a Master of Public Health degree in 1984, and majoring in Epidemiology for a Doctorate in Public Health, awarded in 1985, when she was also elected a member of the Delta Omega Honorary Public Health Society and received a Tulane Medical Alumni Association Student Recognition Award in 1985.

Apart from her main programme of study, in September 1983 Dr Chou had the opportunity to attend a six-day international seminar on Hansen's disease. Moreover, during the 1984 summer vacation she took part in a graduate summer session in epidemiology at the University of Minnesota and a programme in epidemiology run by the University of Massachusetts at Amherst, each three weeks in length.

On her return to Taiwan Dr Chou resumed her position at the National Ying-Ming Medical College, where she remained until February 1992. During the first few years of that period she paid two short visits to the USA, attending the Johns Hopkins School of Hygiene and Public Health summer programme in epidemiology in 1986 and the University of Michigan School of Public Health international graduate summer session in epidemiology in 1988, each lasting for nearly three weeks.

Dr Chou assumed her first duties with the National Yang-Ming University in August 1991, serving as Director of the Institute of Public Health until 1994 and as Dean of Student Affairs until 1997. In March 1992, August 1994 and March 1996 respectively, the university appointed her to her present positions of Full Professor at the Institute of Public Health, Director of the Preparatory Office of the School of Public Health and Director of the Community Medicine Research Centre. Her university appointments aside, she has been President of the Society of Preventive Medicine in China from 1993-99 and since May 1996 she has been Executive Director of the Human Rights Education Foundation, Taipei, as well.

Dr Chou is the author or co-author of more than 100 refereed papers written in Chinese or English and published in journals. Among the most notable are: "Review on Natural History and Screening of Cervical Cancer in Taiwan", published in 1990; "A Community-Based Screening for Liver, Cervical and Colorectal Cancer in Taiwan", as corresponding author in 1990; "Review on Risk Factors of Cervical Cancer" in 1991; "Community-Based Epidemiological Study on Isolated Systolic Hypertension in Pu-Li, Taiwan" and "Community-Based Survey on Blood Pressure, Blood Biochemistry, and Dietary Habits in Pu-Li, Tiawan", both as first author in 1992; "Analysis of Factors Related to Treatment and Prognosis of Leprosy Patients in Southern Taiwan", as first author in 1993; "Associated Risk Factors of Diabetes in Kin-Hu, Kinmen", as first author in 1994; "A Population-based Epidemiological Study on Cardiovascular Risk Factors in Kin-Chen", with others in 1995; "Factors Related to the Choice between Traditional Chinese Medicine and Modern Western Medicine among Patients with Multi-Method Treatment", "Prevalence of Coronary Heart Disease in Kin-Chen, Kinmen" and "A Door-to-Door Survey of Parkinson's Disease in a Chinese Population in Kinmen", all three with others in 1996; "An analysis of Unnatural Mortalities between 1990-1994 in A-Lein, Taiwan", as corresponding author in 1997; "Acupuncture Utilization in Taiwan" and "Progression to Type 2 Diabetes among High Risk Groups in Kin-Chen, Kinmen - Exploring the Natural History of Type 2 Diabetes", both as first author in 1998.

In recognition of her accomplishments Dr Chou was named One of the Top Ten Outstanding Young Women in the Republic of China in 1984. She was made an Honorary Citizen of Kinmen in 1992, while the following year she received a Cancer Prevention Special Contribution Award. Common Wealth, Taiwan's leading magazine, referred to her in its January 1998 issue as "One of the Most Influential Two Hundred People in Taiwan in the Past 400 Years". Furthermore, she is listed in three very recent editions of the Marquis Who's Who in the World and also in Five Hundred Leaders of Influence, and received a Twentieth Century Achievement Award from the American Biographical Institute.

*A biography of Dr Pesus Chou, DrPh, appears in the main section of this Edition.*

# DR VSEVOLOD PETROVICH CHUMENKOV, PhD

*For your Outstanding Contribution
to the Field of Science*

# DR VSEVOLOD PETROVICH CHUMENKOV, PhD

A Russian physicist who works in the section dealing with scientific-technical problems of cosmonautics at the Central Research Institute of Machine Building TSNIIMASH, Dr Vsevolod Petrovich Chumenkov has held the position of Leading Researcher there since 1986, when he was appointed on a competitive basis. He conducts research on exploration of the complex behaviour of non-linear systems, focusing on problems of self-organisation and chaotic dynamics, or deterministic chaos. In addition to holding six certificates as an inventor, he has filed successfully for two patents.

Dr Chumenkov was born on 18 September 1927 in Znamenskoye, Znamenski District, in the Omsk Region of Russia. His parents, both now deceased, saw to it that he had a fine upbringing and education. An excellent pupil at school, he completed his secondary education in 1945, receiving a Gold Medal and School-Leaving Certificate at the graduation ceremony on 4 July that year. After completing six years of service in the Soviet Army in 1951, he commenced studies in the Physics Faculty at Moscow State University, from which he graduated in December 1956. Awarded a postgraduate studentship he continued at the university and obtained the degree of Candidate of Technical Sciences in 1969. In 1980 he was granted the academic rank of Senior Researcher, while in 1986 he received a PhD, as well as being admitted as an Academician to the K E Tsiolkovski Russian Academy of Cosmonautics.

During his career Dr Chumenkov has been the author of three dozen scientific publications. They include three articles in the journal Zhurnal Technicheskoi Phiziki, one in Phizika Plazmy, one in Kosmicheskiye Issledovaniya, one in the bulletin Teplophizika Vysokikh Temperatur and two in the magazine Izmeritelnaya Technika. Participating in two All-Union Conferences held in the USSR in 1975, he presented a report at each. He was responsible for two reports delivered at the International Scientific Conference on Stability and Control of Transforming Nonlinear Systems, held at the Moscow State Aviation Institute from 27-29 June 1995, while the following year he presented as many as five reports at the International Conference on Scientific and Technical Problems of Cosmonautics and Rocket Engineering, held in Kaliningrad, Moscow Region from 23-25 April.

Dr Chumenkov serves as Scientific Secretary of a department of the Russian Academy of Cosmonautics. Admitted to the Central House of Scientists of the Russian Academy of Sciences in 1976, he also gained membership of Moscow Physical Society and the Russian Union of Scientists in 1989 and 1990 respectively. His honorary awards include the Jubilee Medal conferred upon him on 13 May 1996, in honour of the 50th Anninversary of TSNIIMASH.

Outside his professional life, Vsevolod Chumenkov's interests embrace chess, music, classical literature and philosophy. Married since 1960, he has a son and two daughters.

*A biography of Dr Vsevolod Petrovich Chumenkov, PhD, appears in the main section of this Edition.*

## DOROTHY JUNE CALVO FLORES CRUZ, FIBA

*For your Outstanding Contribution
to Education*

# DOROTHY JUNE CALVO FLORES CRUZ, FIBA

Ms Dorothy J C Flores Cruz has devoted her professional career to educating others in computer science. Herself an excellent student who won awards for academic achievement both at high school and university, she has always been ready to pass on her knowledge to others, to help them understand and learn. On several occasions during the present decade she has received recognition for her outstanding teaching.

Married to Samuel Tudela Cruz, Ms Cruz has two daughters, Felicity Marie and Mary Therese. She resides on the island of Guam, where she was born in Tamuning on 27 June 1948. Educated at John F Kennedy High School, Tumon, and the University of Guam, she graduated from the former in 1966 and achieved summa cum laude in her Bachelor of Arts degree in Mathematics and Secondary Education at the latter in 1970. She then embarked on postgraduate studies at the University of Hawaii, obtaining a Master of Science degree in Information and Computer Sciences in 1972.

After her return to Guam from Hawaii, Ms Cruz spent five years teaching at the University of Guam. Starting as an Instructor in Mathematics and Computer Science, she also coordinated the Computer Center, but after three years there she was appointed an Assistant Professor of Computer Science and became Department Chairman until leaving the university in 1977. In 1979 she joined the staff at Guam Community College as an Assistant Professor, rising to Associate Professor in 1981 and finally becoming full Professor of Computer Science from 1993 until retiring in 1997. In addition, she served a four-year term as Chairperson of the Computer Science Department in the 1980s and again in the 1990s. Furthering her own education, from time to time she gained credit hours, mostly at the Community College, but also over a longer period at the Central Texas College extension site at Subic Bay, Philippines, for which she took a year's sabbatical leave from 1990-91.

Her various achievement and teaching awards aside, Ms Cruz won 3rd place in an oratorical contest in 1964, and 1st place in a contest run by Guam Teen Magazine the following year, with a short story entitled "The Man on the Beach". As well as being included on the President's and Dean's Lists from 1967-70 and in three editions of Who's Who Among Students in American Universities and Colleges, she was the recipient of a four-year Salutatorian Scholarship and a two-year Graduate Scholarship, which supported her during her six years at university. Her recent awards and honours include a Commendation for Outstanding Service to Vocational Education in 1994, Professional Certification from the Institute of Academic Leadership Development in 1995 and three Outstanding Teacher Awards. In 1996, 1997 and 1999 respectively, she was listed in Who's Who Among America's Teachers, the International Who's Who of Professionals and the International Who's Who of Intellectuals. She will also appear on the Director General's Honours List and is one of the International Women of the Millennium.

Ms Cruz formerly held office in various organisations, besides serving on numerous committees at the University of Guam and Guam Community College. She was a member of Guam Federation of Teachers and Guam Community College Employees Association until 1997, and acted as Advisor to groups such as Guam Community College Student Body Association. Nowadays she is Treasurer and sits on the Board of Directors of Interfaith Volunteer Caregivers, Historian and Alternate Delegate for Phi Delta Kappa, and a Voting Member of the Association of Computing Machinery, in addition to her ordinary membership of the University of Guam Alumni Association, Chi Omicron Gamma, the National Community College Chair Academy, the Computer Society of the Institute of Electrical and Electronics Engineers and the International Biographical Association. A practising Catholic, she serves Our Lady of Lourdes Church, Yigo, as Eucharistic Minister and Lector of its Catholic Ministry, as Catechist for the Confraternity of Christian Doctrine, Chairman of the Liturgical Planning Committee and member of the Pastoral Planning Committee.

*A biography of Dorothy June Calvo Flores Cruz, FIBA, appears in the main section of this Edition.*

## PROFESSOR LEON GHIORGHE DANAILA, PhD

*For your Outstanding Contribution to
Neurosurgery and Psychology*

# PROFESSOR LEON GHIORGHE DANAILA, PhD

Born in Darabani, in Botosani County, Romania, on 1 July 1933, Professor Leon Danaila is a graduate of the Faculty of General Medicine of Jassy and of the Faculty of Psychology and Philosophy of Bucharest. After his graduation from the former in 1958, he worked for three years as a general practitioner with the Sanitary District of Comanesti and Darmanesti, Bacau County. Appointed resident neurosurgeon at the Neurosurgery Clinic of Bucharest by competitive examination in 1961, he has remained there up to the present. He completed his specialty residency in 1966 and became a Doctor of Medicine (PhD) in 1973, then was named a Senior Physician 2nd degree and Head of the Vascular Neurosurgery Department VII in 1981.

In 1991, by contest, Dr Danaila achieved the rank of Professor of Neurosurgery at Bucharest Faculty of Medicine and Professor of Psychoneurology at the Bucharest Titu Maiorescu University. A member of the Teaching Board of the former Faculty since 1992, he has served as Head of the Neurosurgery  Department of that institution since 1996 and became President of Romania Neurosurgery in 1996.

A year's Fulbright Scholarship granted in 1980 enabled Professor Danaila to work at the Neurosurgery Clinic at the University Hospital of New York. In July 1981 he travelled to the Netherlands for specialised studies in vascular neurosurgery and attended the Burdenke Neurosurgery Institute in Moscow. He has also attended lectures and seminars in Budapest, Dusseldorf, Brussels, Glasgow and Edinburgh, as well as taking a course in Paris.

Following his travels, Professor Danaila was able to perform the most complex of neurosurgical operations, including occlusion of an aneurysm of the arterial vertebro-basilar system, ablation of third ventrical tumours, carotidian and middle cerebral endarterectomy, and extra and intracranial anastomosis. Moreover, he succeeded in reducing operation mortality to percentages comparable to those reported by the world's most reputable neurosurgery clinics. Through his efforts, surgical mortality in Bucharest was reduced from 50% to 2-6% for acoustic nerve neuroma and from 37% to 3% for cases of intracerebral aneurysm. Such reductions were aided by the endowment of his operating theatre with a surgical microscope and laser. The department that he leads is unique for Romania.

Throughout his career Professor Danaila has communicated and published 241 scientific works, 41 of which appeared in foreign specialty journals. Several of these works are known as world novelties. They include "Logorrhea syndrome with hyperkinesia", "Ultrastructural changes of the cerebral substance and of the small vessels in the cerebral cortex determined by atherosclerosis", "The interaction of the two cerebral hemispheres in the integration of the language system" and "Histological studies of normal and pathological human cerebral tissue irradiated by CO2 laser". He has authored nine books and co-authored another eight, among them "Spinal Neurinoma", published in 1972, "Psychoneurology" in 1983, volumes 2 and 3 of "Vascular Diseases of the Brain and Spinal Cord" in 1985, "Romanian Neurosurgery", volumes I and II, appearing in 1986 and 1987 respectively, "Cardiovascular Thromboembolism" in 1987, "Psychiatric Surgery" in 1988, "The Treatment of Brain Tumours" in 1993, and "Alzheimer Disease" in 1996. Moreover, he sits on the editorial committees of the following journals: Romanian Journal of Reconstructive Microsurgery; Romanian Microsurgery; Romanian Journal of Neurology and Psychiatry; National Medical Review.

Besides being a corresponding member of the Romanian Academy, Professor Danaila is a member of the Romanian Medical Academy, the New York Academy of Sciences, the Union Médicale Balkanique, the Balkan Society of Angiology and Vascular Surgery, the International Society for Optical Engineering, the Société Française de Pharmacologie Clinique et de Térapeutique, the International Society of Psychoneuroendocrinology, the International Psychogeriatric Association and the European Association of Neurosurgical Sciences. He has been recognised on twelve occasions with an Inventor's Certificate and on ten additional occasions with an Innovator's Certificate, for his work on neurological and prosthetic appliances for cranial and meningeal usage. In addition to an award from the Romanian Academy in 1995 for his paper on "Treatment of the Cerebral Tumours", in 1996 he received the R E del Vivo International Award.

Leon Danaila is the son of Ghiorghe and Maria Danaila. He lives in Bucharest and is married to Alexandrina Ionescu.

*A biography of Professor Leon Ghiorghe Danaila, PhD, appears in the main section of this Edition.*

## DR JOHANNA DÖBEREINER

*For your Outstanding Contribution to
Biological N2 Fixation*

# DR JOHANNA DÖBEREINER

Dr Johanna Döbereiner has dedicated her career to conducting research in the field of soil biology, in which her main focus has been on nitrogen fixation. Combined with that, she has been responsible for the supervision and orientation of numerous Brazilian and foreign undergraduate and postgraduate students. A prolific writer, by 1995 she had more than 300 publications to her name. Moreover, during a period of nearly thirty years she participated in more than fifty international meetings with invited lectures.

Although Johanna Döbereiner has held Brazilian citizenship since 1956, she originates from Czechoslovakia, where she was born in Aussig on 28 November 1924. She attended university in the Federal Republic of Germany, earning a Bachelor of Science degree in Agromomy at the University of Munich in 1950, whereupon she emigrated to Brazil. The following year she started employment with the Brazilian Ministry of Agriculture, as a researcher in soil microbiology. A research grant from the Brazilian Research Council - CNPq - in 1957 was followed three years later by a research fellowship from the same source.

To further her education Dr Döbereiner travelled to the USA, where studies at the University of Wisconsin from 1961-63 culminated in a Master of Science degree in Agriculture. Her thesis for the degree was entitled "Manganese Toxicity in the Bean (Phaseolus vulgaris L.) Rhizobium symbiosis". Returning to Brazil, it was not long before she had the opportunity to attend a Soil Biology course that UNESCO organised specially for Latin Americans and which was held in Santiago, Chile. The next year - 1966 - a fellowship from the French Government and CNPq enabled her to follow a course on Soil Microbiology at the Institut Pasteur, in Paris, France. In the early 1970s she travelled to England twice. On the first occasion she spent a year in the Microbiology Department at Rothamsted Experimental Station, on an Overseas Development Authority Fellowship, while the second time a Royal Society Fellowship gave her the chance to work in the Nitrogen Fixation Unit at the University of Sussex.

In 1974 Dr Döbereiner left her position at the Ministry of Agriculture to join EMBRAPA (Empresa Brasileira de Pesquisa Agropecuária), where she has been carrying out research ever since, besides serving as Director of its National Centre for Research on Soil Biology until 1989. Receiving a fellowship from CNPq and a grant from the NAS, she appeared at the University of Wisconsin in 1975, for research in its Biochemistry Department. During the 1980s she received a research grant from FINEP, as well as two from NAS-BOSTID for work on nitrogen fixation in grasses and cereals in 1983 and on nitrogen fixation in sugar cane and cereals in 1986. In addition to a fellowship from CNPq, she had two grants from the European Economic Community, the first of which being for her cooperation with the Universities of Leuven, Belgium, and Dundee, Scotland, over nitrogen fixation in beans, while the second was for cooperation with Dr John Day of the University of Bristol, England.

In the course of her career, Dr Döbereiner has had numerous awards and honours bestowed upon her. She received the Frederico Menezes Veiga Prize from EMBRAPA for her outstanding research, the Agriculture prize from Bloch Editors Ltd, the Bernardo Houssay Science Prize for Agriculture from the OAS, the 1989 UNESCO Science Prize, the Premio Mexico de Ciencia y Tecnologia from the President of Mexico, and the TWAS Medal. She was decorated with the Order of the Rio Branco, which is presented to leading citizens by the Brazilian Government, the Order of National Merit of the Federal Republic of Germany, the Order of Merit of the Brasilia Superior Tribunal of Labour, and the Grand Cross, Brazilian Order of Scientific Merit. A member of the Brazilian Academy of Sciences, she was honoured to be elected its First Secretary in 1991 and Vice-President in 1995. Elected to the Pontificial Academy of Science, Vatican, Rome, she is also a Founding Member of the Third World Academy of Sciences and a Corresponding Member of the Argentinian Academy of Sciences. Two further distinctions consist of Honorary Citizenship of the City of Rio de Janeiro and the 1986 "A Lavoura" Distinction from the National Society of Agriculture. Moreover, she holds an honorary DSc from the University of Florida, Gainesville, USA, and a Dr honoris causa from the Federal Rural University of Rio de Janeiro, awarded in 1975 and 1980 respectively.

*A biography of Dr Johanna Döbereiner appears in the main section of this Edition.*

## DR STEPHEN E DRAPER, PhD, PE

*For your Outstanding Contribution to*
*Water Resources Engineering, Law and Policy*

# DR STEPHEN E DRAPER, PhD, PE

Dr Stephen Draper's career embraces water policy analysis, water resources and environmental engineering, engineering management and scientific-technical analysis. He holds a BS degree in General Science from the US Military Academy at West Point, Master of Science in Civil Engineering from Georgia Institute of Technology, for which he specialised in Construction and Photogrammetry, MBA in Management from C W Post, Long Island University, and JD in Environmental and International Law from Georgia State University, from which he also received an Award in American Jurisprudence in 1992. For his PhD, awarded by Georgia Institute of Technology in 1981, he submitted a dissertation entitled "Urban Rainfall-Runoff Modeling Using Remote Sensing Imagery". In addition to his degrees is his registration as a Professional Engineer - PE- in the States of Florida and Georgia.

Stephen Draper had an outstanding career in the army, during which he received numerous decorations, among them three Purple Hearts, two Bronze Stars, the Legion of Merit and the Gallantry Cross with Silver Star. He earned his Parachute Wings early on, and was awarded the Combat Infantryman's Badge. As a commissioned officer in the Corps of Engineers, he was posted to Europe, where he managed the allocation of US Army and Allied engineer resources and provided advice to the NATO Reserve Force.

Back in the USA, while Assistant Chief in the Planning Division of the South Atlantic Division his duties included supervision of navigation, flood control and beach erosion studies and preparation of environmetal assessments and environmental impact studies. Later, assigned to St Paul Engineer District, he directed Federal wetland regulation in five North Central states, coordinated environmental assessments and environmental impacts studies with official, conservation and local interests, and was the principal negotiator in the water rights dispute between the Federal Government and the Chippewa Nation of Leech Lake. As Commander of the 43rd Engineer Battalion, a 1200-man Army unit, he had responsibility for administration, finance, operations and logistics. Besides controlling operations and resource allocation in Southeastern and mid-Atlantic states, Central America and Europe, he coordinated certain operations in southeastern USA and Central America. He also supervised environmental assessments and environmental impact studies for engineering projects.

At one stage in his army career, Dr Draper served as Associate Professor of Physics at the US Military Academy, giving classroom instruction in mechanics and electromagnetism. He was also the principal investigator and lecturer on military applications of the electromagnetic spectrum. After leaving the army he became a Resident Expert at the Southeastern Office of the American Standards Testing Bureau. In that capacity he managed accident reconstruction and analysis in five southeastern states for a New York forensic engineering firm, as well as supervising and coordinating technical analysis by a multi-disciplined team. Nowadays a water resources consultant he provides water resources systems analysis and water-related accident reconstruction, analyses the causes of technical failure and makes environmental damage assessments. His expert services as a hydrology expert and technical director have been in demand in supervising and conducting research into environmental projects concerning water. In addition, he has been appointed to the Water Laws Technical Committee set up by the American Society of Civil Engineers to consider legal problems that civil engineers encounter in the water resources system. Within the Committee he chairs its Task Committee for Shared Use of Transboundary Water Resources, and is a member of the Task Committee on Model State Water Rights Code.

Dr Draper is the author or co-author of articles and papers in his field, published in journals and proceedings of meetings held locally, nationally and internationally. They include a paper on "Integrating Transboundary Water Sharing", presented at the 1st International Conference on Water Resources Engineering, held in San Antonio, Texas, by the American Society of Civil Engineers in August 1995. He was co-author of "ASCE Standards for Water-Related Policies, Laws, and Regulation", delivered at EOENV '97 International Symposium on Geology and Environment, held in Istanbul, Turkey in September. Both papers were subsequently published in the relevant proceedings.

Dr Draper is listed in Who's Who in the World, Who's Who in Law and Who's Who in Science and Engineering. In his professional capacity he is a member of the American Bar Association, the American Board of Forensic Examiners, the American Water Resources Association, the American Society of Civil Engineers, the National Academy of Forensic Engineers and the National Society of Professional Engineers.

*A biography of Dr Stephen E Draper, PhD, PE, appears in the main section of this Edition.*

## DR JUNE B ELLIS, PhD, DDG

*For your Outstanding Contribution to
Human Resource Consultation*

# DR JUNE B ELLIS, PhD, DDG

A human resource consultant who was born in Portland, Indiana, USA, and has recently retired to Dallas, Texas, June B Ellis has devoted many years to her career. In addition to her BA degree earned in 1942 at Mary Washington College, University of Virginia, and MS received in 1953 from Tulane University, New Orleans, she holds a PhD awarded by the International University in 1997. In recognition of her accomplishments she was named an Outstanding Tulanian in 1984.

In 1960 Dr Ellis was appointed to her first position, as Assistant Training Director of Social Services at East Louisiana State Hospital in Jackson. However, she moved to New Orleans in 1962 to spend a year as an Instructor at Tulane University School of Social Work, prior to becoming an Assistant Professor in the Department of Psychiatry at Tulane School of Medicine from 1963-68. During her last academic year at Tulane, she also became Executive Director of the Family-Service-Travelers Aid, an organisation in Fort Smith, Arkansas, continuing in that position for four years. Still in Fort Smith, from 1971 until retiring in 1998 she was President of the firm Child and Family Consultants and Director of the Human Resource Development Center, both of which she continues to own.

During those Fort Smith years, Dr Ellis was involved in various other activities. She sat on the Advisory Board of Suspected Child Abuse and Neglect, as well as on two commissions set up by the Governor of Arkansas, the first being on the status of women, the other on drug abuse prevention. She was also appointed to the Scholarship Selection Committee of the Whirlpool Corporation and has now been on the Advisory Board of Tulane University Center for Life Long Learning since 1996 and in 1998 was appointed Consultant in Gerontology at Tulane. Over the period from 1974-92 she acted as Consultant to two Swedish clients, Volvo Health Care in Gothenburg and Kontura Personal in Stockholm, also giving workshops at the Christian Counselling Center at Vellore, India, in 1974. Moreover, she was the author of three publications, namely, "TA Tally" in 1974, "TA Talk, terms and references in transactional analysis" in 1976, and "BEING" in 1982. Of the numerous papers she has presented "Love to Share: A Community Project Tailored by Oldstens for Latchkey Children" was selected as one of the ten most innovative ideas to emerge from 1972 American Ortho-Psychiatric Conference. In 1984 she was People to People's Delegate to the Republic of China.

A member of the American Association of Retired Persons, Dr Ellis was the Coordinator for its Western Arkansas Health Advocacy Service from 1995-97. Other organisations to which she gained admission as a member consist of the American Society for Training and Development, the American Academy of Psychotherapists, the American Group Psychotherapy Association, the American Orthopsychiatric Association, the Academy of Certified Social Workers, Western Arkansas Mental Health Association, including service on its Advisory Board, the Conference for Advancement of Private Practice in Social Work, the American Association of University Women, the American Association of Individual Investors and the National Association for Female Executives. She is also a former member of the Advisory Board of the Junior League of America.

*A biography of Dr June B Ellis, PhD, DDG, appears in the main section of this Edition.*

## MEMDUH ERDAL

*For your Outstanding Contribution
to Education*

# MEMDUH ERDAL

Memduh Erdal is a Businessman who was born on 20 March 1935 in Ortakoy, Northern Cyprus. He attended Ortakoy Elementary School in until 1947, and achieved a Certificate as a Certified Professional Manager from the Society of Business Pracitioners, based in the UK.

Mr Erdal established his own company, Memduh Erdal Co Ltd in 1952. He is also Director and Secretary of the Board of Directors of the Cyprus Credit Bank Limited, a post which he has held since 1978, and has been Founder and Chairman of the Board of Directors of Girne American University since 1987, and also founder of North Cyprus University College of Business Management Ltd, a private university established in 1985; he is among the Board of Trustee.

Mr Erdal was awarded the Silver Medal for Service from Queen Elizabeth in 1958 and the Gold Medal of the Association of Ski Instructors in Turkey in 1995. He was also given an Honorary PhD from South Eastern University, Washington, DC, in 1992. He has received an invitation from the President of Turkey to the Presidential Palace and also Letters of Achievement. He has been a Councillor for 16 years, and has been Acting Mayor for three months, for the Turkish Municipality of Nicosia in Cyprus and is a Member of the Girne Rotary Club. He is on the Board of Directors of Cyprus Credit Development and Investment Company Ltd and Chairman of the General Directorate of the Future American College, Primary School and Nursery School. Memduh Erdal is married to Sermin Ali Riza and they have a son, Tayfun, and a daughter, Tomur, as well as five grandchildren. Hunting, swimming, skiing, surfing and trap shooting are among his hobbies.

*A biography of Memduh Erdal appears in the main section of this Edition.*

## DR KJERSTIN ELISABETH ERICSSON, PhD

*For your Outstanding Contribution to*
*Cognitive Care Research*

# DR KJERSTIN ELISABETH ERICSSON, PhD

Dr Kjerstin Elisabeth Ericsson is a neuroscience educator whose background embraces nursing, administration and research. She presently serves as Senior Lecturer at the Karolinska Institute in Stockholm, Sweden, as well as Assistant Professor of Geriatric Nursing, appointed to the positions in 1992 and 1997 respectively. In addition, she is the author of various contributions to professional journals.

The daughter of Bertil Eurenius and Anna Maria Ericsson, Kjerstin Ericsson was born in Stockholm on 5 January 1938. After completing her secondary schooling she was employed as a laboratory assistant by Halland County Council from 1957-58. She then embarked on studies at St Eric Nursing College in Stockholm, becoming a Registered Nurse and qualifying as a Midwife in 1962. For the next two years she was a nurse working for Dalecarlia County Council, prior to accepting an appointment as district nurse with Gavle County Council from 1964-72. In that capacity she often had to deal with elderly people, a side of her work in which she developed a growing interest.

Returning to the Stockholm area, between 1976 and 1988 Dr Ericsson served as Chief Administrator of Geriatric Nursing for Stockholm County Council. From time to time during that period of her career she also took the opportunity for further education. Taking leave of absence to study at the University of Lyon, France, she earned a Certificate in Social Gerontology from the University of Lyon in 1979, as well as the degree of Maîtrise in Psychology in 1981. She obtained a Master's degree in Social Science in 1984 and PhD in 1985, both from the University of Uppsala, Sweden, while later still she returned to Lyon for the degree of Maîtrise in Sociology and Ethnology, awarded in 1988.

For the four years leading up to her appointment at the Karolinska Institute, Dr Ericsson was engaged in conducting research at Huddinge University Hospital. Among her activities while there was a study visit to Basel, Switzerland, for which she was subsidised by a second grant from the European Council in 1991 - back in 1974 an earlier grant from the same source had enabled her to travel to Lyon. Once at the Karolinska Institute, apart from her lecturing and research, her duties included sitting on its Examination Board for Doctoral Dissertations in 1992 and again in 1994. In 1993 she was on a similar examination board at the University of Umeå.

Dr Ericsson is a member of the American Association for the Advancement of Science and the New York Academy of Sciences. She has also been admitted to the International Psychogeriatric Association, the International Graphonomics Society and the International Association for Scientific Study of Intellectual Disability.

*A biography of Dr Kjerstin Elisabeth Ericsson, PhD, appears in the main section of this Edition.*

# DR MYRON WYN EVANS, PhD, DSc, FABI, LFIBA

*For your Outstanding Contribution
to Science*

# DR MYRON WYN EVANS, PhD, DSc, FABI, LFIBA

The son of Edward Ivor and Mary Evans, Myron Wyn Evans was born on 26 May 1950 in Craigcefnparc, in the coal-mining region of Wales, but now has his home and works in the USA, where he arrived in 1986, and works in Hungary. His father was a coalminer who held three medals, Bronze, Silver and Gold, awarded by the Mines Rescue Service. The boy's maternal grandfather, T Elim Jones, a self-educated Welsh-speaking miner who was also head deacon of Elim Baptist Chapel, as well as a composer and conductor, came from a Nonconformist Puritan background of miners and hill farmers of the coalmining valleys of South Wales. His origins go back further still to the Silures, ancient British Celts who inhabited South East Wales in Roman times.

Destined to break away from his family's mining tradition, Myron Evans developed an interest in science while at school. Subsequently entering Aberystwyth University, he gained a Bachelor of Science degree in 1971, then went on to obtain both his PhD and DSc, conferred by the university in 1974 and 1977 respectively. The year after obtaining the former doctorate he became a Junior Research Fellow at Wolfson College, Oxford. His research the previous year had been supported by a Science Research Council, Imperial Chemical Industries and National Research Council of Canada Fellowships. In 1976 he received the British Ramsay Memorial Fellowship, and later in his career the University of Wales Fellowship in 1984; the University of Wales Pilcher Senior Fellowship, Humboldt and IBM Fellowships in 1985.

While an Advanced Fellow of the Science and Engineering at Aberystwyth from 1978-83, Dr Evans distinguished himself during the first two years of that period by winning the Harrison Memorial Prize of the Royal Society of Chemistry and the Meldola Medal. In 1980 he journeyed to Italy, as a Visiting Scientist to the University of Pisa and the Scuola Normale Superiore. After a period in Ireland in 1985, as a visiting professor at Trinity College Dublin, he set off in 1986 for the USA for a visiting professorship at IBM in Kingston, New York. A visiting scientist at the University of Zurich, Switzerland, from 1989-90, and at Cornell University from 1989-92, he was also a Senior Associate and Research Associate at Pennsylvania State University in 1990 and 1992 respectively, as well as acting as science and technology advisor for the Welsh National Party of Plaid Cymru in 1991. In 1992 he became a Full Professor in the University of North Carolina and in 1995 he was not only a visiting professor both at York University, Toronto, and at the Indian Statistics Institute in Calcutta, but also assumed his present professional position with the Alpha Foundation in Budapest, Hungary. Additionally, since 1998 he has served as Director of the Alpha Foundation Institute for Advanced Study.

In the course of more than twenty-five years of research in physics and chemistry at international level, Dr Evans has contributed articles to professional journals and has published and edited some 500 communications and monographs, besides a book entitled "Modern Nonlinear Optics", published in 1997. In his research he pioneered the use of far infra-red rays for analysis of molecular dynamics, combining the technique with computer simulation and other spectral methods. This led to the formation of the European Molecular Liquids Group, of which he was the first scientific coordinator in 1980. Other pioneering achievements concerned the use of computer simulation for non-linear optical effects in molecular liquids, the technique of radiation-induced fermion resonance and the application of the Gauge Theory to electrodynamics.

Dr Evans is a member of the Optical Society of America, the American Institute of Physics, New York Academy of Sciences and Sigma Pi Sigma. His leisure interests consist of poetry, landscape photography and athletics.

*A biography of Dr Myron Wyn Evans, PhD, DSc, FABI, LFIBA, appears in the main section of this Edition.*

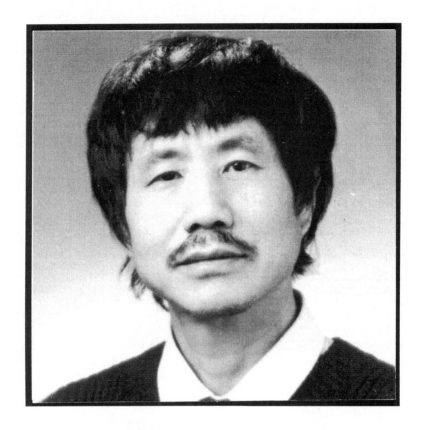

## DR RONG RÉMI FANG, PhD

*For your Outstanding Contribution to
Great Achievements in Physics Research*

# DR RONG RÉMI FANG, PhD´

The son of Kui Fang, a professor of physics now deceased, and Ruizhi Xiong, housewife, Rong Rémi Fang was born on 10 August 1958 in Ping-Jiang, Hunan, China. At school he was an unexceptional pupil until his last year at the First Middle School of Hunan, when he suddenly became outstanding in mathematics and physics. Convinced by his new-found ability and the influence of his father that his future career lay in the field of physics, in 1977, a year after his graduation from school, he entered Tsing-hua University, in Peking. After five years of study there, he graduated in experimental nuclear physics. Further studies at the Institute of High Energy Physics, Peking, culminated in 1985 with a postgraduate diploma in nuclear spectroscopy of gamma and beta-rays and in fast nuclear electronics.

From 1986-88 Dr Fang worked in the Department of Modern Physics at the University of Science and Technology of China in Hefei. In addition to lecturing in classical mechanics, special relativity and thermodynamics, he conducted research on nuclear electronics. He also installed, adjusted and operated HPD, a sophisticated piece of equipment presented by the French National Centre for Scientific Research, CNRS, for use in high energy physics experiments. As a result of his success, in January 1989 he was invited to France by LPNHE, Universities of Paris VI and VII, and the Centre for Nuclear Research in Strasbourg. At those institutions he participated in research involving international collaborations, at first focusing on the H1 Calorimeter-DESY and then on data acquisition and analysis at NA36-CERN, Geneva. As co-author he published the former research in Nuclear Instruments and Methods in Physics Research, Section A, and the latter in Nuclear Physics A. When his visit ended in 1993, he decided to remain in France, having found the laboratory research facilities there to be better than those in China, and in April 1995 was granted French citizenship.

An Engineer at the AERIAL Nuclear Irradiation Centre in Strasbourg since 1993, in that capacity Dr Fang has focused his attention on computer software for Dosimetry, as well as for simulation of particle detectors, the latter providing material for a doctoral thesis. He has also been engaged in working in nuclear electronics for beam shape control on electron accelerators, in respect of which he is the co-author of an article in Nuclear Instruments and Methods in Physics Research, Section B. In 1997 he successfully defended his thesis and was awarded a PhD by the Louis Pasteur University.

Although Dr Fang specialises in nuclear and high energy physics, in order to develop new particle detectors he has had to study classical physics, a field which most physicists regard as entirely mature, the forefront of research nowadays being applied and modern physics. However, he has added some new contents to classical physics, namely, the Rule of Change Accumulation, the Differential Equation of Electron(ion) Dispersion in inhomogeneous electrical fields, and two stability conditions for a system of multi-dielectrics with finite resistivities. These are proposed in four articles published between 1996 and 1998 in the journal Nuclear Instruments and Methods in Physics Research, Section A.

Dr Fang, who has recently been invited to become a member of the American Association for the Advancement of Science, as well as the New York Academy of Sciences, attributes his success to a good background in mathematics, rich experience of laboratory research, the amount of time he has devoted to his work, and good health. He keeps himself fit by taking exercise for thirty minutes each day, while for recreation he prefers music and dance.

*A biography of Dr Rong Rémi Fang, PhD, appears in the main section of this Edition.*

## DR NANCY GRACE AUGUSTA FORWARD

*For your Outstanding Contribution
as an Officier de la Légion d'Honneur*

# DR NANCY GRACE AUGUSTA FORWARD

Nancy Grace Augusta Forward, who now resides in Port Macquarie, New South Wales, Australia, was born on 30 August 1912, in Wellington, New Zealand, the daughter of C A Wake. She was educated in Australia and England, attending North Sydney Girls High School in New South Wales prior to travelling overseas to London to complete her studies at the Queen's College for Ladies, London. Married twice, she lost her first husband, Henri, during World War II. Her second marriage, to John Forward, took place in 1957, and he died on 19 August forty years later.

The greater part of Dr Forward's working life was based in England and Europe. Between 1936 and 1939 she was engaged in pursuing a career as a freelance journalist in Europe. After the occupation of France in 1940 she became actively involved with the Allied Escape Route Organisation for the next three years. From 1943-44 she served with the First Aid Nursing Yeomanry, FANY, and as a member of the Special Operations Executive was parachuted into France, where she worked with the Resistance Movement. An Executive Officer with the Foreign Office during the postwar period from 1946-48, she was attached to the British Embassies in Paris and Prague. From 1952-58 she served as an officer in the Women's Royal Air Force, assigned to the Air Ministry's Intelligence Section in London. Much later in her career, she authored "The White Mouse", a book published in 1985. She subsequently became the co-producer of the documentary based on the book "Nancy Wake" written by Russell Braddon.

Apart from an Honorary Doctorate conferred upon her by Griffith University in 1995, Dr Forward has been accorded several distinctions in recognition of her work in the Allied cause during the war. Thus she was decorated with the George Medal at a ceremony held at the British Embassy in Paris. Other decorations consisted of the Croix de Guerre with Palm and Bar, the Croix de Guerre with Star and the Médaille de la Résistance, all from France, and the US Medal of Freedom with Bronze Palm. France also honoured her as Chevalier de la Légion d'Honneur in 1970, and as Officier in 1988.

Besides being Patron of the Council of Ex-Servicewomen's Association (Victoria) Incorporated, Dr Forward is Vice-Patron of the Airborne and Special Forces Veterans Association of New South Wales. She has been a member of two London clubs, namely, the Royal Air Force and the Special Forces Club, as well as the Combined Services Returned Services League of Sydney.

*A biography of Dr Nancy Grace Augusta Forward appears in the main section of this Edition.*

# DR LAWRENCE JAN FRATESCHI, PhD

*For your Outstanding Contribution
to Health Economics Research*

# DR LAWRENCE JAN FRATESCHI, PhD

An educator and researcher, Dr Lawrence Frateschi is presently Professor of Economics and Statistics at the College of DuPage in Glen Ellyn, Illinois, USA, as well as Research Professor of Epidemiology and Biostatistics at the University of Illinois School of Public Health, Chicago. Moreover, in the course of his career he has been the author of numerous articles appearing in professional publications.

The son of Lawrence and Olga Frateschi, Lawrence Frateschi was born on 7 October 1952 in Chicago, where he was brought up and educated. As a student at the University of Illinois, Chicago, he earned a Bachelor of Science degree in Mathematics and Psychology in 1975, then went on to obtain a Master of Arts degree in Economics in 1979. From the same university in 1990 and 1992 respectively, he received a Master of Science degree in Public Health, specialising in Biostatistics and Epidemiology, and a PhD in Economics.

A Teaching Assistant in the Department of Mathematics and Lecturer in the Department of Information and Decision Sciences at the University of Illinois at Chicago from 1978-80, Dr Frateschi then spent a year employed as a Statistician at the Argonne National Laboratories. In 1981 he was appointed Assistant Professor of Economics and Statistics at the College of DuPage, rising to Associate Professor in 1986 and assuming his present position of Professor in 1990. In addition, while preparing for his Master's degree in Public Health he worked from 1989-90 as a Research Associate at the University of Illinois School of Public Health, Chicago, to which he returned in 1993 as Research Professor, a position he continues to hold.

Dr Frateschi has been admitted to the honorary societies of Phi Eta Sigma, Phi Kappa Phi and Delta Omega. He is also a member of the American Economics Association, the American Statistics Association, the American Public Health Association, the Society for Epidemiologic Research, the Midwest Economics Association, Illinois Economics Association and Illinois Public Health Association.

*A biography of Dr Lawrence Jan Frateschi, PhD, appears in the main section of this Edition.*

## DR ALEXANDER GUNTHER FRIEDRICH

*For your Outstanding Contribution to International Cooperation and Development Diplomacy*

# DR ALEXANDER GUNTHER FRIEDRICH

A native of Alt-Lietzegöricke, near Berlin, Germany, Alexander Gunther Friedrich was born on 6 November 1923, into a family background of several generations establishing and developing the forest products industry. He served in the 3rd PanzerGren Division, between 1942-45, and was wounded several times. His last assignment was as First Lieutenant at General Staff North.

Alexander Gunther Friedrich holds the degree of DSc (Dr.rer.nat), from Hamburg University, where he, after World War II studied both Economics and Natural Sciences. Between 1950-1966, Alexander Gunther Friedrich took up the positions of Researcher, Lecturer and Professor, which involved establishing guidelines for infrastructural planning, land use policies and industrialization, at the Universities of Hamburg, Oxford and Monrovia. Subsequently, he supported new research and training facilities overseas as FAO Section Chief at Headquarters in Rome, Italy.

Between 1966-79 he took up the appointment of Executive Secretary of the United Nations Industry Cooperative Programme, in Rome, Geneva and New York. He started the industrial globalization process within the United Nations system, introducing the term "Joint Venture" for enterprises with governments of developing countries in Latin America, Asia and Africa. He thus advised multilateral agencies, local entrepreneurs and transnational corporations, encouraging them to transfer managerial skills, technology and marketing systems, together with foreign direct investment and emphasizing their partnership in strengthening the international market economy with ecological, social, cultural and political objectives so that it created jobs and provided an income.

After this outstanding contribution to international cooperation and in development diplomacy, Dr Friedrich was invited home from 1978-89 as Chairman of the German Foundation for the International Development Forum at the Villa Borsig in Berlin, and in 1989-94 as Advisor to the Commission of the European Union at CARICOM and at ASEAN, where he concentrated on inter- and intra-regional cooperation.

Alexander Gunther Friedrich has been the recipient of several awards and honours during his long professional career. He was honoured with an Order of Merit, 1st class, the Iron Cross, 1st class and decorations and awards from Germany and the USA. His biographical detailes have appeared in "Five Hundred Leaders of Influence" and "Outstanding People of the 20th Century". He is a member of several associations i.e. on World Economic Affairs (DWG, Berlin); Foreign Policy (DGAP, Berlin); United Nations (DGVN, Bonn); International Development, (SID Rome).

In his leisure time, A G Friedrich enjoys history, modern painting, oldtimer motoring and rallies, hunting, skiing and golf. He was married with one son and two grandsons.

*A biography of Dr Alexander Gunther Friedrich appears in the main section of this Edition.*

## DR TORU FUNAHASHI, MD, DDG, LPIBA

*For your Outstanding Contribution as Chairman
of a Scholarship Fund in the Philippines*

# DR TORU FUNAHASHI, MD, DDG, LPIBA

Dr Toru Funahashi has had a long and distinguished career in the field of medicine. Apart from his responsibilities as a physician, he served the local medical association as arbitrator during the 1960s and as trustee in the early 1970s. The author of numerous medical reports in his particular field, he also spent two years as editor of the local medical newspaper.

The son of Takanobu Funahashi, a doctor and dermatologist with an interest in history and foreign languages, and Fusa Funahashi, who loved music, Toru Funahashi was born on 20 June 1926 in Kyoto, Japan. Expected to follow his father into the field of medicine, he began a medical course at a National High School in 1943, during World War II. Later that year the medical and technical students were sent to various factories, to cover the labour shortage. In Spring 1945, he entered the Medical Department of Osaka Imperial University, but was again sent to cover labour shortage until the war ended a few months later. Resuming his studies in the Medical Department, by then the Medical Faculty of Osaka University, he graduated in 1949. After a year's internship, he passed the state examination in 1950, thereby receiving a licence to practise medicine. His professional career as a Physician began in 1960, on completion of further studies consisting of three years of haematology at the Institute of Internal Medicine and seven years of human pathology at the Institute of Human Pathology. He graduated in pathologico-haematological studies in 1957 and received his licence as a Human Pathologist in 1958.

When Toru Funahashi visited his high school in 1946, he was saddened to see only the ruins of the laboratories. Among the weeds he found a number of badly burnt instruments. Picking them up one by one, he finally selected three badly discoloured microscope object lens, which he still keeps carefully in his room. They may well have been an inducement that led him to study microscopy as a tool of haematology and pathology! He later began collecting old microscopes.

Nowadays Dr Funahashi greatly appreciates having to overcome various difficulties in his student days in wartime. The experience taught him endurance and patience, besides encouraging him to be creative. For example, just after the war, he made a wooden centrifuger for himself, applying an electric motor from a used electric fan.

In the 1950s he became very interested in sound recording in the pre-electric era, from Edison's invention of the phonograph in 1877 to the introduction of electric recording techniques in 1924. Besides reading old documents on the subject, he began investigating and collecting old phonographs, which he restored whenever possible. The co-author of several reports on early sound recording machines, he has appeared on television and radio, as well as publishing in books and magazines. Moreover, he has lectured on the preservation of talking machines in the acoustic era.

In 1970, with friends he established the Osaka Audio Society. That same year he organised the first exhibition of Talking Machines in the Acoustic Era to be held in Japan. In 1973 he was instrumental in founding the first Talking Machine Museum in Japan, while five years later he set up a private research laboratory for the works of Thomas Alva Edison. Journeying to America to follow in the footsteps of that great inventor, Thomas Alva Edison, he was warmly welcomed wherever he went. He has friends with the same interest in several countries and corresponds with many of them.

In 1982 Dr Funahashi went with a group of Rotarians to the Island of Negros in the Philippines, where they were astonished to find the people in that permanently poor region so friendly and cheerful. Delighted with the visit, the visitors held a Brotherhood Signing Ceremony with a local Rotary Club. They also planned to return to the island annually, to provide free medical consultation. However, some five years later they decided to establish a scholarship fund for the young islanders, 48 of whom have benefitted from it up to now. Dr Funahashi, who has had great pleasure in serving as Chairman of the fund since 1989, believes it important to understand the scholars' situation and ambitions, and encourage them in their hopes. At first the young people seemed to stand on ceremony in contacting him, but now they talk or write to him frankly and call him "Second Father".

Having great sympathy for the young, Dr Funahashi has at present four Filipino foster-children. For some years he had no letter from his fourth foster-child, a West African girl, but recently the International Red Cross Association transmitted a letter from her, saying she was among the refugees there. He wonders how he can contact her.

Toru Funahashi lives in Osaka, in a house that was on the periphery of the 1995 Kobe-Osaka earthquake. Unfortunately the main part of the house, which included his collections, was badly damaged, so he lost most of his treasures. He and his wife now live in the undamaged section, which consists only of small rooms and his clinic. However, he is philosophical about the misfortune and tells his wife that some world they have never known before was coming, free of worldly-mindedness and love of gain.

*A biography of Dr Toru Funahashi, MD, DDG, LPIBA, appears in the main section of this Edition.*

## DR ANGELO GRAZIOLI, LFIBA

*For your Outstanding Contribution to
Medicine (Sexology) and Theology (Ethics)*

# DR ANGELO GRAZIOLI, LFIBA

Dr Angelo Grazioli is devoted to his career in the field of medicine, with his main concern being focused on the physical and psychological aspects of sexuality. A religious man, outside his professional life he is active in the Church of England in South Africa and holds a Bachelor of Theology honours degree, awarded in 1990. Although he originates from Sondrio, Italy, where he was born on 10 August 1955, he has spent the greater part of his life in South Africa, where he is married to Janneke and has two sons, Giancarlo and Riccardo.

As a medical student at the University of Cape Town Angelo Grazioli had an outstanding record, winning the Crichton Prize for Undergraduate Research in 1978, as well as the J T Louw Prize for Obstetrics and Gynaecology in 1979, the year he received his MB ChB. Having qualified, he began giving professional sexological counselling, to which he currently devotes 25-30 hours a week. After pursuing internships from 1980-81, he travelled to the USA, to conduct a residency in the Sexual Dysfunction Unit of the Loyola Strict School of Medicine in Chicago. He then returned to South Africa, where he has remained ever since.

In 1983 Dr Grazioli became a family practitioner, continuing in that capacity until 1988, when he assumed his present position as Director of the Sex Education and Dysfunction Unit of South Africa. He has also served as the Italian Government's Consular and Maritime Medical Practitioner for Cape Town and the Western Cape region since 1983. Between 1992 and 1993 he acted as Consultant to the Centre for Education Technology, Cape Town, in connection with its audiovisual programme for South African schools, entitled "Puberty: Time for Facts". He lectured in human sexuality in the Master's programme at the University of Stellenbosch from 1992-94 and sat on the AIDS Coordinating Committee of the Department of National Health and Population Development from 1992-95. In addition to serving the UK-based international journal Carer and Counsellor as South African Consulting Editor since 1993, since 1997 he has been Consulting Editor for the South African-based medical publication African Sexology Journal.

A public speaker who now fulfils between 60 and 80 engagements a year, Dr Grazioli has been addressing local and overseas audiences since 1979, with appearances at various professional, paraprofessional and public institutions and organisations, as well as on radio and television. He is the author of "The Management of Common Medical Disorders - A Formulary for Students", published in 1978, and "A Question of Love - Answers to Questions on Homosexuality", a book that appeared in 1998 in conjunction with his video "A Question of Love - Homosexuality, A Biblical Perspective". In addition, he has been responsible for sixteen articles in professional journals, eight papers presented at international congresses, and three radio and television productions.

Dr Grazioli is a member of the South African Medical and Dental Council, the South African Academy of Family Practice and Primary Care, the British Medical Association, the American Association of Sex Educators, Counsellors and Therapists, the Society for the Scientific Study of Sex, USA, and the Association of Christian Counsellors in South Africa. A former Trustee of the multiracial youth leadership development Outdoor Adventures, he was also on the committee of the George Whitefield College of Theology from its inception in 1989 until as recently as 1998. Within the Church of England in South Africa, CESA, he has a number of current commitments. Thus he is Kenilworth Rector's Warden and a member of the Kenilworth Council of St James Church. Besides serving on the CESA Ordination Selection Committee and the National Executive Committee, he has chaired the Social and Morals Committee since its inception in 1990. He is a Arbitrator for the Cape Area Council and a CESA Registrar as well.

*A biography of Dr Angelo Grazioli, LFIBA, appears in the main section of this Edition.*

# DR AKIHITO HAGIHARA, DMSc, MPH

*For your Outstanding Contribution
to Medicine*

# DR AKIHITO HAGIHARA, DMSc, MPH

A Japanese epidemiologist who holds degrees in two separate disciplines, namely, law and medicine, Dr Akihito Hagihara is presently an Associate Professor at Kyushu University School of Medicine, Fukuoka, appointed in 1995 after two years as a Research Fellow at Osaka University. Moreover, apart from being the author of a work entitled "Communication in Health", he is the contributor of various articles to professional journals.

Akihito Hagihara graduated from high school in the mid-1970s, whereupon he entered Tohoku University, from which he obtained a Bachelor in Laws degree in 1979. After three years on the legal staff at Kansai Electric Power Company, Osaka, he spent the period from 1982-84 on research at the Japan Energy Law Research Institute, then returned to the Electric Power Company. However, he resigned from there in 1987, to pursue medical studies at Osaka University, where he earned a Master's degree in Medical Science in 1989 His PhD Degree in Medical Science was awarded by the same university in 1993, the year he also received a Master's degree in Public Health from the University of Michigan, USA.

Since joining Kyushu University, Dr Hagihara has been a grantee of the Japan Ministry of Education. He has served as a Director of the Health Science Association of Fukuoka since 1991, while he also belongs to the Japan Society of Hygiene and Japan Society of Public Health.

Dr Akihito Hagihara was born on 21 February 1954 in Ichijima, Hyogo Prefecture, Japan. He and his wife, Naoko, have two sons, Seita and Kou-hey.

*A biography of Dr Akihito Hagihara, DMSc, MPH, appears in the main section of this Edition.*

## PROFESSOR XUNTIAN HE

*For your Outstanding Contribution to the
Development of Contemporary Music*

# PROFESSOR XUNTIAN HE

Professor He Xuntian, a well-known Chinese composer, is Professor and Chairman of the Musical Composition and Direction Department at Shanghai Conservatory of Music. As one of the most important musicians on the Chinese music stage, he has often been invited to attend international music festivals and international composers' conferences.

Born in 1953 in Suining, a small city in the province of Sichuan, He Xuntian studied music theory by himself at the early age of eight, and began to write music. He graduated from the Musical Composition Department at the Sichuan Conservatory of Music in 1982, but before that had written musical pieces for various art organisations. In pursuit of a complete evolution in music, he created the RD method of musical composition and became the first composer to base his works on his own theory.

He Xuntian's music has been published, broadcast and performed in over 65 countries and territories such as Austria, France, Germany, Britain, Netherlands, the United States, New Zealand, Japan, Singapore, Hong Kong and Taiwan. His major works include symphonies like "Tonal Patterns", 1985, "Four Dreams", 1986, and "Telepathy", 1987; chamber music such as "Two of the Earthly Branches", 1983, "Sounds of Nature", 1986, "Phonism", 1989, "Imagine the Sound", 1990, and "The Pattern of Sound Suite", 1997; folk orchestra music like "Caprice of Dabo River", 1982; and three new song albums, "Yellow Children", 1992, "Sister Drum", 1994, and "Voice from the Sky", 1996. Premieres of his works were launched by many world-famous orchestras, among them the Dresden String Orchestra of Germany, the BBC Philharmonic Orchestra of England, the Nieuw Ensemble of the Netherlands, the New York New Music Consort, USA, the Hong Kong Orchestra, Toronto Philharmonic Orchestra of Canada, and Tokyo Philharmonic Orchestra, Japan. In 1988, the He Xuntian Symphony Concert was held in Beijing Concert Hall by the China Musicians Association and the Central Orchestra.

Professor He's music has attracted worldwide attention. His "Sister Drum" is the first Chinese language album in the international music industry and has been distributed to over 65 countries worldwide. Both his musical composition and his musical theory have been written about and reviewed in over four hundred publications, among others in Time, Washington Post, Reuters, New York Times and Newsweek. Through his works, which are believed to have epoch-marking significance, he has made a great contribution to the search, rediscovery and remoulding of the soul of the Chinese nation. With a thorough revolution, he has broken through the monopoly of the dominant Western culture. As a Chinese composer with a very individualistic style, he is generally regarded as an important composer who is leading Chinese music out of the cultural desert. The emergence of his music marks the emergence of China's own school of music.

Professor He has won many awards at both national and international musical composition competitions, the major awards including the first prize at the Third National Musical Piece Competition in 1984, first prize at the First China Phonograph Awards in 1984, the Gold Tripod Award in 1995 in Taiwan, and third prize at the International Car-Marla-Von-Wettbewerbes fur Kammermusik in Germany in 1987. The International New Music Composers Competition presented him with the Outstanding Musical Achievement Award for 1989-90 in the USA; it is an award that goes to those who make remarkable achievements in the development of contemporary music.

*A biography of Professor Xuntian He appears in the main section of this Edition.*

## DR MAHMOUD HIJAZY, PhD

*For your Outstanding Contribution
as a Consultant Dermatologist*

# DR MAHMOUD HIJAZY, PhD,

Dr Mahmoud Hijazy has devoted many years to the medical profession. A Consultant in Skin and Genito-Urinary Diseases, he is currently the Owner and Director of the Dr Hijazy Medical Centre, based in Riyadh, Saudi Arabia. He is also the author of two books, one on each of his two specialties, while a textbook on paediatric dermatology in the process of publication.

The son of Hijazy Ali Hijazy and Amena Yousef Hijazy, Mahmoud Hijazy Hijazy was born on 17 August 1939 in Dair Senaid, Palestine. However, circumstances obliged him to study in Egypt, where he earned his MBBCh at Einshamas Medical School in Cairo in 1964. He also holds Diplomas in Venereology and Dermatology, DVD, and in Internal Medicine, DM, received in 1969 and 1971 respectively. His PhD in Dermatology and Venereology was awarded him in 1973.

Apart from an internship at the Demerdash University Hospital, Cairo, residencies in Cairo and training in the American University in Beirut, Lebanon, and Laser Surgery at Harvard Medical School in Boston. Dr Hijazy's early experience included general practice in medicine at the Saudi Military and Police Colleges in Riyadh, during the mid-1960s. In 1974 he set up as a Consultant Dermatologist and Venereologist in Riyadh, where he subsequently established his medical centre.

Dr Hijazy was honoured in 1970, named Man of the Year at the Arab American Congress held in Chicago. He has been admitted to the European Academy of Allergy and Clinical Immunology, the European Academy of Aesthetic and Restorative Surgery, the American Academy of Dermatology and the European Academy of Dermatology and Venereology. In addition, he was President of the Palestine Red Crescent Society. He has been honoured with inclusion in International Who's Who of Professionals.

Dr Mahmoud Hijazy is married to Raedah Halawa; they have two sons, Hany and Ramy, and two daughters, Reema and Sereen.

*A biography of Dr Mahmoud Hijazy, PhD, appears in the main section of this Edition.*

## DR ALI ABBASS HUSSAIN SALEH, PhD, LFIBA

*For your Outstanding Contribution
to Accountancy*

# DR ALI ABBASS HUSSAIN SALEH, PhD, LFIBA

Accountancy and administration combine to form the main professional interests of Dr Ali Abbass Hussain Saleh. Since 1995 he has made use of his experience and expertise in serving as a Consultant for the company of Cabouchon, based in Bahrain, United Arab Emirates.

The son of Abbass Hussain Saleh and Ameena Ali Hassan Saleh, Dr Hussain Saleh was born in Bahrain on 3 December 1956. After completing his secondary education in his homeland, he pursued further studies abroad, earning a Diploma in Business Training from London, England, in 1981, followed by a Bachelor's degree in Accounting and Auditing obtained from Pune University, Pune, India, in 1982.

On returning to Bahrain from India, Dr Hussain Saleh was appointed Head Accountant with the firm of Yusuf Bib Ahmad Kanoo, but in 1987 became a development trainee with the Bahrain Petroleum Company Limited. In 1988 he was awarded the degree of Master of Business Administration by Trinity College, USA, from which he also received his Doctorate in Business Administration in 1996.

In addition to being a freelance writer for Agora International, USA, Dr Hussain Saleh serves as editor for International Living. Admitted to membership of the National Geographic Society and the Institute of Professional Financial Managers in 1995 and 1996 respectively, he belongs to the High Lender Club and the Oxford Club, as well as the International Airline Passenger Association. Furthermore, he is a Life Fellow of the International Biographical Association and Deputy Governor of the American Biographical Institute. In recognition of his achievements during the last quarter of the 20th century, the latter organisation selected him for inclusion in its Five Hundred Leaders of Influence.

Dr Hussain Saleh's recreational pursuits consist of reading, swimming, collecting stamps, riding and driving. He married Elhaam Mohdi Ali in July 1986; they now have three sons, Hussain, Abbas and Hassan, and a daughter, Mariam.

*A biography of Dr Ali Abbass Hussain Saleh, PhD, LFIBA, appears in the main section of this edition.*

**PROFESSOR DR MIRCEA GHEORGHE**
**IFRIM, MD, PhD, FIBA, DDG, IOM**

*For your Outstanding Contribution to Science,*
*Education and UNESCO Achievements*

# PROFESSOR DR MIRCEA GHEORGHE IFRIM, MD, PhD, FIBA, DDG, IOM

Professor Mircea Ifrim describes himself as an Anatomist, Anthropologist, General Physician, Scientist and Educator. He was born in Calata, Cluj, Romania, on 4 May 1943. A distinguished education began in primary school and culminated in his Doctorate, progressing through the academic echelons to achieve the ranks of Chief Physician at the age of 35 and Full Professor at only 39 years of age.

Mircea Ifrim attained his MD in 1963 at the University of Bucharest, Romania, and his PhD at the Medical University of Cluj. He went on to pursue Postgraduate studies in Education Management at the University of Oradea in 1998. Concurrently, he embarked upon his university teaching career, beginning with the post of Assistant Professor at the Medicine University of Cluj, Romania, 1967-70. He then lectured in Medicine at this University until 1978 when he was appointed Visiting Professor at the Medicine University of Bucharest until 1990. He was, in 1991, appointed Dean and Founder of the Medicine Faculty in Oradea and also Director of the Medicine Research Institute, again in Oradea. He became Chairman of the Branch Academy of Science in 1996 and Vice Rector of Vasile Goldis University in Arad in 1997.

Professor Ifrim has made some important contributions to his chosen fields of research including the study of neuro-endocrine factors influencing connective tissue and the endocrine determinism in the appearance of some neural systems and heart malformations. He has published many distinguished works including Malformative Risk in Human Reproduction, 1983, and Connective Tissue Morphology and Pathology, published in 1988. His Human Anatomy Atlas, in three volumes in Romanian and English, is a unique monograph with not only illustrations like an atlas, but also essentialized texts involving the functional and clinical anatomy concept as well as medico-surgery applications and anatomy studies.

Professor Ifrim has been the recipient of numerous awards in honour of his achievements. These include the Scientist Merit Award from the Romanian Government, given in 1989, the Award from the Romanian Academy of Science in Bucharest, the Diploma with Honours for sporting anthropology research from the International Organization of Sports Medicine, a Gold Medal of the World Academy of Medicine "Albert Schweitzer" and numerous honorary doctorates. His biographical details have been listed in a number of international reference works. He has also been awarded the International Cultural Diploma of Honour in 1997, Man of the Year in 1998 and the Distinguished Leadership Award, also in 1998, and his name appears in numerous biographical directories. Professor Ifrim holds many distinguished professional memberships including the International Federation of Anthropology and Genetics in Sports, Warsaw, the National Union of Scientists, Bucharest, the Academy of Science and Culture, Brazil, from which he holds a Commander Degree, The Medical Science Academy of Poland and many others. He received the Honour Diploma for Human Rights Defence Award by the European Council ECOFOR for his social activities in promoting understanding, respect and even active tolerance among people, good international relationships and world peace when he, after 1989, became dignitary in the Government structures and General Secretary of CNR-UNESCO.

*A biography of Professor Dr Mircea Gheorghe Ifrim, MD, PhD, FIBA, DDG, IOM, appears in the main section of this Edition.*

## PROFESSOR DR KAZUYOSI IKEDA, DSc, DLitt, DDG, IOM, LFWLA, LPIBA, MOIF

*For your Outstanding Contribution to
Theoretical Physics and Poetry*

# PROFESSOR DR KAZUYOSI IKEDA, DSc, DLitt, DDG, IOM, LFWLA, LPIBA, MOIF

Currently Professor of Theoretical Physics at Osaka University and Poet, Dr Kazuyosi Ikeda was born on 15 July 1928 as the eldest son of the late Yosikatu Ikeda, company director, and Misao Ikeda, now residing in Fukuoka. His birthplace, on the coast some distance from Fukuoka City, was within ten minutes' walk of Kyushu University. Thus, spending his childhood in natural surroundings and an academic atmosphere, he was inspired to become a research scientist in the future, and a poet singing of the beauties of nature. At school he enjoyed both scientific and literary subjects. Even after entering the Department of Physics, Faculty of Science at Kyushu University in 1948, his interest in literature persisted and he wrote poems while researching in science.

After graduating in 1951, Kazuyosi Ikeda continued in the same department, pursuing a postgraduate course until 1956. His first scientific paper, "On the Theory of Condensation", presented at the International Conference on Theoretical Physics, Kyoto, 1953, was highly praised by famous scholars there, earned an award from the Yukawa Scholarship in 1954, and formed the dissertation for his DSc, received in 1957.

Appointed an Assistant in his department at Kyushu University in 1956, he became Associate Professor in 1960, then moved to Osaka University as Associate Professor in the Department of Applied Physics, Faculty of Engineering, in 1965, and rose to full Professor in 1968. In 1989 he joined the newly-established Department of Mathematical Sciences, Faculty of Engineering, as Professor of Theoretical and Mathematical Physics. Becoming Professor Emeritus at Osaka University in 1992, at the same time he served as Professor of Theoretical Physics at the International Earth Environment University, where he was installed as University President in 1995.

Dr Ikeda has contributed greatly to theoretical, mathematical and chemical physics, particularly to statistical mechanics of properties of matter and phase transitions by using mathematical-analytical methods to investigate an assembly of interacting molecules. His papers on the statistical-mechanical theory of condensation phenomena of gases and phase transitions in substances have been widely noticed and very highly evaluated in the international academic world. Interested in celestial mechanics, he theoretically investigated the orbit and motion of a comet recorded in the Japanese history "Nihon Syoki" as appearing in 634 and 635 AD.

Dr Ikeda has produced over 100 papers and monographs on the theory of properties of matter as applications of the principles of classical and quantum mechanics, the quantum statistical mechanics of gases and liquids, the statistical-mechanical theory of condensation of gases, the theory of thermodynamic properties of gases using cluster expansion, theoretical research on phase transitions by applying the theory of functions of a complex variable, the statistical-mechanical theory of gaseous and liquid helium, lattice gases, one-dimensional substances, solutions and so on, and theoretical-mechanical research on comets in ancient times. His numerous books on theoretical physics include "Statististical Thermodynamics", 1975; "Mechanics without the Use of Mathematical Formulae - from a moving stone to Halley's comet", 1980; "Invitations to Mechanics - from the fundamentals of calculus to the motion of a comet", with Appendix on a comet in ancient times, 1985; "Basic Mechanics", 1987; "Basis Thermodynamics - from entropy to osmotic pressure", 1991; "Graphical Theory of Relativity", 1998.

As a poet, Kazuyosi Ikeda emphasises that the true poem should have beauty of rhythm and sentiment. His poetry collection, "Bansyô Hyakusi", and his book, "The World of God, Creation and Poetry", appeared in 1986 and 1991 respectively. Besides serialising poems in the monthly magazine "Chishiki" since 1989, and Osaka University Newspaper since 1979, he has written essays on poetry. His poems in the fixed 7-and-5-syllable traditional Japanese metre sing of the hearts and minds of many things in nature. Full of lyrical emotion and scientific clarity, they have many enthusiastic admirers and appear in "kazuyosi's poetry on the Animate and the Inanimate", 1998, "Poems on Love and Peace", 1998 and in many world-famous anthologies, including "The First 100" (Barcelona-92, Olympoetry), "World Poetry" and "Parnassus of World Poets", and in many international journals, including "Poet", "Modern Poetry" and "Metverse Muse". Collections of his poems in English were published as "Poems on the Hearts of Creation", 1993, "Mountains", 1993, "North, South, East and West", 1996, and others. He has also serialised translations of Shakespeare's Sonnets into 7-and-5-syllable metre Japanese poems.

Below are two of his poems, one depicting the loneliness of a spiny lobster, gravely armoured, who has stately moustaches and knows no smile, the other portraying a slug's sad lazy life, particularly its pitiful death caused by salt. The English translations, by the author himself, are in the 7-and-5-syllable metre, like the original poems (expressed here in Romanised Japanese); thus in each poem a line has a 7-syllable first part and a 5-syllable second part.

## Ise-ebi

Ito ikamesiki nagaki Hige,
Se ni zo yoroeru kataki Kara,
Emi wo sirazaru Mi wa sabisi.
Hitori ayumu yo Umi no Soko.

## A Spiny Lobster

Ah, how dignified and long my moustachios are!
With a hard crust on my back, I am in armour.
I have no laugh and no smile, so nmy heart is lone.
On the bottom of the sea do I Walk alone.

## Namekuzi

Na-no-ha wo hamite nuranura to
Memesiku ikite Yo so sunete
Kutiosiki Mi no naru Hate wa
Sio wo kakerare tokete kiyu.

## A Slug

I eat greens indolently; my body's slimy
I live very sulkily and unmanlily.
On the day of the ending of my worthless life,
Ruthless salt, shaken on me, will melt down my life.

Professor Ikeda's sphere of pursuits is extensive. Science and poetry apart, his wide variety of hobbies and interests includes uncommon and rather unique ones such as watching Kabuki and Noh plays and performing Noh farces. In all fields he has the same goals. Through his science and poetry he wholeheartedly pursues beauty, whether in nature or the human world. This is his lifelong aspiration, supported by his strong religious belief that the Creator originally gave the world such beauty, which it is mankind's mission to discover, substantiate and polish.

Professor Ikeda is active and has various responsibilities in numerous organisations, including New York Academy of Sciences; Modern Poets Society, Board Member; World Parnassians Guild International, Honorary Director; American Biographical Institute Research Association, Deputy Governor, Continental Governor; Confederation of Chivalry, Grand Council; Accademia Ferdinandea di Scienze, Lettere ed Arti, Academician of Honour; Maison Internationale des Intellectuals, Senator; Accademia Internazionale "Trinacria" Lettere-Arte-Scienze, Academician of Merit; National and Professors-Students Coalitions for Unification of North South East West, Chairman of Osaka Branches; Olypoetry Movement, Honorary Founder, Representative of Japan; Council of the States for Protection of Life, Senator.

For his outstanding contributions to theoretical physics and poetry, he is listed in more than 38 international biographical volumes, including 17 dedication sections. His numerous distinctions include Chevalier Grand Cross, Golden Academy Award for Lifetime Achievement, 20th Century Achievement Award, Catania Prize, Pandit Prize, 2000 Millenium Medal of Honour, DLitt (hon), Dr of Environmental Science (hon), and titles of Grand Ambassador of Achievement and Knight of the Templar Order, Knight of the Lofsensic Ursinius Order, Knight of the Holy Grail Order, Knight of the University Knights Order, Knight of the San Ciriaco Order, and Knight of the Years 1995 of the International Writers and Artists Association. He is also included in the World Who's Who Hall of Fame, the IBC Director General's Honours List, the Millenium Hall of Fame and many more.

*A biography of Professor Dr Kazuyosi Ikeda, DSc, DLitt, DDG, IOM, LFWLA, LPIBA, MOIF, appears in the main section of this Edition.*

# STEPHANIE IKHUMEN

Stephanie Ikhumen served as a Secretary on Rehabilitaiton Programmes for the State of Illinois between 1970 and 1977. She then joined the staff of the University of Illinois in Chicago, working as a Lead Word Processor Operator in the Survey Research Laboratory from 1977 to 1979. After gaining an AA Degree in Business Administration from Central YMCA in 1979, she served as Secretary Transcriber in the Office of Business Affairs of the University of Illinois during 1979-80 and from 1980-86 as Administrative Secretary in the Department of Biological Chemistry. Between 1979 and 1983, Ms Ikhumen undertook coursework in Business Education and during 1984-85 studied Industrial/Organizational Psychology at Mundelein College. Since 1986, Ms Ikhumen has served as Administrative Secretary at the School of Public Health/Environmental and Occupational Health Sciences at the University of Illinois, Chicago. She also works as a professional residential real estate appraiser, having gained a Diploma in Real Estate Law from the School of Paralegal Studies in 1990. She has also completed a BA Degree in Management. Ms Ikhumen was born in Chicago on 17 June 1950.

## PROFESSOR PETER UCHE ISICHEI, MD, DDG, FIBA, MOIF

*For your Outstanding Contribution to Medicine and Medical Research*

# PROFESSOR PETER UCHE ISICHEI, MD, DDG, FIBA, MOIF

Professor Peter Uche Isichei is devoted to his career in the field of medicine. As physician, teacher, administrator and researcher, he played a pioneering role with success in four new medical schools in two different countries in the developing world. He was able to train doctors at basic and specialist levels, often under very difficult conditions. Moreover, he has been able to make some contribution to knowledge through medical research and has authored or co-authored many scientific publications in reputable international medical journals. During the present decade he has acted as an adviser and consultant to the World Health Organisation, as well as being a resource person for UNICEF Nigeria and the Federal Ministry of Health in Abuja, Nigeria.

Although Nigeria is Professor Isichei's homeland, his birth taking place in that country on 27 November 1932 in Asaba, he chose the University of Munich, Germany, to prepare for his career. After his pre-clinical study had been completed, the university, as was customary, encouraged him to do part of his studies abroad. Thus aided by a grant from the Warwick Educational Foundation, he attended the University of Oxford Clinical School from 1962-63.

Returning to Munich for his final year, Professor Isichei passed his "Staatsexamen" (MBBS equivalent) in 1964. Postgraduate work at the Max Planck Institute for Biochemistry, Munich, then led to his MD magna cum laude in 1966. His thesis, "Vergleichende Untersuchungen über die Leistungsfähigkeit moderner elektrophoretischer Analysen-metoden für die klinische Diagnostik", earned a distinction for its pioneering work on polyacrylamide gel electrophoresis. He continued at the Institute as a Postdoctoral Research Fellow, then in 1967 obtained a Diploma in Tropical Medicine and Hygiene, obtained through London School of Tropical Medicine and the Royal College of Physicians and Surgeons. At a later stage in his career he qualified as a Fellow of the Medical College of Pathology, Nigeria. Furthermore, as a Nuffield Foundation Fellow at the Postgraduate Medical College in Hammersmith, London, he prepared for an Advanced Certificate in Clinical Endocrinology, awarded in 1982. That year he also became a Bye Fellow at Robinson College, Cambridge.

Professor Isichei's university responsibilities began in Tanzania in 1969, as a Lecturer at the University of Dar-es-Salaam, but in 1971 he returned to Nigeria, to consecutive lecturing posts at the Ahmadu Bello University, Zaria, and the University of Nigeria, Enugu Campus. In 1977 he was appointed an Associate Professor at the University of Jos, where he is currently Professor of Clinical Biochemistry and Head of the Department of Clinical Pathology, holding both positions since the early 1980s. His administrative experience includes two recent two-year terms as Dean of the Faculty of Medicine at Jos. As a physician he has served as Consultant for the relevant university teaching hospitals during the whole period since 1969, while he was also Director and Head of the Clinical Biochemistry Diagnostic Laboratory at Jos University Teaching Hospital from 1977-95.

Some of the results of Professor Isichei's work in clinical biochemistry at the Max Planck Institute are included in a book dealing with polyacrylamide electrophoresis, published in Berlin in 1988. Although he contributed an article entitled "Genetic Markers in Nigeria" to "A History of Nigeria", a book written by his wife Elizabeth and which appeared in 1983, he is in general the author or co-author of numerous articles on medical subjects in national and international journals ranging from the Nigerian Medical Journal to Clinica Chimica Acta and Acta Endocrinologica. During the last few years he has been the principal investigator for an extensive thyroid disease project, from which several publications have emerged. As a result of the contributions made by him and his team to knowledge concerning iodine deficiency disorders, his department was selected by UNICEF as the reference laboratory for the fight against this scourge plaguing his country.

A life member of Oxford University Medical Society since 1963, at various stages of his career Professor Isichei became a member of the Nigerian Medical Association, the Association of Imunologists of Nigeria, the Association of Clinical Pathologists of Britain, the Association of Clinical Biochemists of Britain, the International Council for the Prevention of Iodine Deficiency Disorders and the University of Cambridge Society. He has recently received a number of awards and other distinctions from both the American Biographical Institute and the International Biographical Centre.

*A biography of Professor Peter Uche Isichei, MD, DDG, FIBA, MOIF, appears in the main section of this Edition.*

# PROFESSOR SHINJI ITOH, MD, PhD, FIBA, IOM

*For your Outstanding Contribution to Neuro-Psycho-Endocrinology*

# PROFESSOR SHINJI ITOH, MD, PhD, FIBA, IOM

Emeritus Professor Shinji Itoh, who was born on 16 February 1912 in Ise City, Mie-ken, Japan, has devoted many years to scientific research. Of particular note is his work in the field of neuroendocrinology, in which he is regarded as a pioneer.

Immediately after graduating from Nagoya University School of Medicine in 1935, Shinji Itoh started on his neuroendocrinological experiments. Working entirely on his own for four years, and without financial support, he discovered the existence of endocrinologically active peptide in the hypothalamus of various vertebrates. Following intravenous injection the peptide produced hyperglycemia, but this effect was not observed in adrenalectomized animals. Between 1939 and 1941 he published four papers on his observation. It was assumed that the peptide was secreted from hypothalamic neurons and subsequently affected the adrenal gland to cause hyperglycemia. At that time nobody knew that the central neurons could secrete such peptide, so his work was neglected.

Thereafter, in 1947 Professor B A Houssay received the Nobel Prize for his finding that the pituitary gland may secrete the hyperglycemic principle, since hypophysectomy reduced the symptoms of diabetes mellitus. Around 1950 many anatomists noticed that the anterior pituitary is connected to the hypothalamus by blood vessels. The feature was apparently shown by Professor G Harris as hypothalamo-hypophyseal portal vessels. To confirm hypothalamic control on adenohypophysis by the humoral factor, the active principle needed isolating from the hypothalamic tissue. The chemical structures of posterior pituitary hormones, oxytocin and vasopressin, were first shown by Professor V du Vigneaud, for which he received the Nobel Prize in 1955.

It was more than fifteen years before other peptide hormones regulating secretion of anterior pituitary hormones were classified. Nowadays chemical findings of such peptides have led to a new age of brain research, with modern techniques and instruments leading to the discovery of more than fifty peptide hormones. However, it will take many years to elucidate the physiological significance and important role of neuropeptides in cerebral functions such as memory, behaviour, emotions, imagination and introspection.

Professor Itoh studied in the USA at Columbia University Physicians and Surgeons from 1954-55 and the Rockefeller University from 1955-56. Returning to Japan, in 1957 he was appointed Professor of Physiology at Hokkaido University School of Medicine, where he remained until retiring in 1975. He also served as Professor at the Low Temperature Science Institute, Hokkaido University from 1965-75. On the occasion of the 1965 International Congress of Physiological Scienc In hes his fine work was referred to several times by Professor Houssay and Professor Harris, with whom he repeatedly co-chaired the meeting. In his department one of his assistants used neurohypophysectomized rats without harming the adenohypophysis, and found that stress produced its symptoms without neurohypophysis, indicating that corticotropin-releasing hormone (CRH) may exist in the brain and that vasopressin is not an essential stimulator of ACTH secretion. Another assistant of his developed a new assay for CRH and other hypothalamic hormones, microinjecting test material directly into the adenohypophysis. Professor Itoh wanted to use radioimmuno-assay (RIA) to prove the release of anterior pituitary hormone following the microinjection of hypothalamic extract, but at that time RIA was not developed sufficiently for common experiments.

After retiring from Hokkaido University as Emeritus Professor, Professor Itoh had the use of a small room at a pharmaceutical laboratory, where he conducted a large number of experiments with very little financial support and very poor equipment. Under those conditions and with only one assistant he carried out his experiments to observe the effects of neuropeptides on mental processes. Greatly interested in cholesystokinin octapeptide (CCK-8), which exists particularly abundantly in the frontal cortex, he found its analogues enhance memory processes and are effective for the treatment of some mental disorders. He noticed that the cholinergic system, NMDA receptor, proteinkinase C and protein synthesis are indispensable for memory processes, since inhibitors of these activities caused marked amnesia, but CCK-8 analogues effectively prevented this. He also reported that vasoactive intestinal polypeptide (VIP) disturbed memory processes. Moreover, CCK-4, the tetrapeptide of CCK-8, caused mental panic and serious depression. Although the CCK-4 content is normally very small in the brain, under some circumstances a relative increase causes pronounced mental disorders. Thus an adequate balance of these neuropeptides are important to preserve the normal mental condition. Further studies should be performed to elucidate mental physiology, together with interactions of various neuropeptides such as CRH, beta-endorphin, somatostatin, substance P, neurotensin, thyrotropin-releasing hormone (TRH) and others.

In addition to his work on peptides Dr Itoh has studied human adaptability to cold climates, particularly with regard to the Ainu, a group from Hokkaido, the northern island of Japan. He found their physiological and biochemical characteristics to differ from those seen in control Japanese subjects born on the main island and has published several books on the differences.

Professor Itoh emphasises the importance of man's brain in the changing world. The philosophical age of long ago, as seen in ancient Greece, China and India, was followed by the dark age of religion, but since then human knowledge has shown a marked development in the scientific field. It is not easy to imagine life in the future life, although technological advancement will surely bring great changes. The global effect of meteorological changes cannot be predicted precisely, but one fact is certain: ways to survive will be devised through brainwork.

*A biography of Professor Shinji Itoh, MD, PhD, FIBA, IOM, appears in the main section of this Edition.*

# DR THOR EDWARD JAKOBSSON, PhD, FIBA

*For your Outstanding Contribution
to the Natural Sciences*

# DR THOR EDWARD JAKOBSSON, PhD, FIBA

The son of Reverend Dr Jakob Jonsson and Mrs Thora Einarsdottir, Thor Edward Jakobsson was born on 5 October 1936 in Wynyard, Saskatchewan, Canada, where his Icelandic parents lived for six years. His ancestors had been workers, seamen, farmers and pastoral ministers. With his parents, two sisters and two brothers, he moved to Iceland in 1940, crossing the Atlantic on a passenger liner in a wartime convoy. He now recalls a happy upbringing in the Icelandic capital, Reykjavik, where he attended elementary and secondary school.

At Menntaskolinn high school, Reykjavik, Thor Jakobsson's main interests emerged as astronomy, philosophy and parapsychology. On finishing there in 1956 he enrolled in natural sciences at the University of Oslo, Norway. During the following years his studies were interspersed with prolonged stays in Iceland to earn his living. With his time divided between formal study, work, interests and family life, he earned a cand mag degree (BSc) in Geophysics in 1964. In 1966 he obtained a cand real degree (MSc) in Meteorology from the University of Bergen, where he remained for two more years, working on statistical meteorology and electronic computer operations.

Later in 1968 Mr Jakobsson returned to the country of his birth, Canada, accompanied by his wife, Johanna Johannesdottir, and two children, Thora and Vesteinn Atli. There he pursued research and studies at McGill University, Montreal, until 1973, when he obtained a PhD in Atmospheric Science, with a thesis entitled "Spectral Analysis of Marine Atmosphere Time Series". In January and February 1972, he participated as a meteorologist in a wintertime expedition on Canada's largest icebreaker, sailing north into the heavily ice-covered Baffin Bay between Canada and Greenland.

From 1973-79 Dr Jakobsson was a Research Scientist with the Atmospheric Environment Service, Toronto, Ontario, working mostly in the area of upper air data analysis for the purposes of studying short-term climate variations in the northern hemisphere, as well as building up support and knowledge of processes for climate modelling at AES. In his last year he was also involved in Arctic research. In connection with family and community life, his activities included membership of church committees, coaching children in soccer, minor participation in a political party (NDP), and contributing to the union of government officials.

Moving back to Iceland with his family in 1979, Dr Jakobsson has lived there ever since. He has worked as Research Scientist and Project Manager at the Icelandic Meteorological Service. In particular, in charge of sea ice research and sea ice service in Icelandic ocean waters, he has included sea ice modelling and remote sensing by weather satellites among his approaches. Since 1980 he has also been Adjunct Professor in Atmospheric Science in the Physics and Geophysics Department, University of Iceland. With his students he has been involved in European and international projects in the research areas of sea ice and atmosphere/ocean interaction in the North Atlantic. Besides the research and development connected with those projects and duties, he has participated at home and abroad in diverse committees and conferences on the atmosphere and the environment. Furthermore, he has proposed and encouraged Icelandic participation in developing the Northern Sea Route across the Arctic Ocean, connecting the North Atlantic with the Northern Pacific. He is a weekly presenter of weather forecasts on Icelandic State Television as well.

Since settling in Iceland Dr Jakobsson has been involved in the community, furthering public sport, such as jogging, long distance running and cycling, some events being combined with fund raising for charity. As a board or steering committee member he has served various societies and organisations, including the Vilhjalmur Stefansson Arctic Institute in Iceland; the National History Society of Iceland; the Society of Friends of the Arts in Hallgrimskirkja, Iceland's largest church, as Chairman; the Society of Greece-Iceland Friendship; working committees of the political party Framsoknarflokkur, now a government party; a health and vegetarian association; the Icelandic society of Friends of the Whales, as Vice-Chairman; the genealogical society Descendants of Richard Long (born in England in 1783), as Vice-Chairman. Moreover, he has been an editorial board member or editor of a few Icelandic journals dealing with various topics of nature and culture.

Dr Jakobsson is also the founder of an annual celebration of life and culture during the June and December solstices, the first one held in Iceland on 21 June 1985. Since then, links to solstice celebrations abroad have gradually been established and new ones encouraged, for the purpose of creating a global network of such festivals. In 1990 he founded the Odda Society, a cultural society of history and nature aiming to restore Oddi, in South Iceland, as a centre of cultural and environmental studies. Oddi, the site of the first school in Iceland, was established in the 11th century and during mediaeval times, the golden age of Icelandic literature, was the home of the learned and powerful family of Oddaverjar. He also founded Mork a Landi, an educational environment centre in the vicinity of the volcano Hekla. In 1996 he established an educational fund for informing the Icelandic public, particularly young people, about modern astrobiology research and the debate about the likelihood of extraterrestrial life. He is presently encouraging and assembling scientists and other interested people to hold conferences in Iceland and elsewhere in the year 2000, in celebration of the life and work of Giordano Bruno, the Italian Renaissance philosopher of infinity who was burned at the stake in Rome in 1600.

A member of several professional societies at home and abroad, Dr Jakobsson has supported the idea of world government since his twenties and at intervals has belonged to the World Federalist Movement. His favourite persons in history are Aristotle, Johannes Kepler and Mohandas K Gandhi. Finally, his wish for the next thousand years is that man may fare well, establish global and planetary peace, enjoy personal life despite difficulties, admire the infinite universe, and trust in God.

*A biography of Dr Thor Edward Jakobsson, PhD, FIBA, appears in the main section of this Edition.*

## HIS EXCELLENCY COLONEL DR ALHAJI YAHYA A J J JAMMEH

*For your Outstanding Contribution to Peace*

# HIS EXCELLENCY COLONEL DOCTOR ALHAJI YAHYA A J J JAMMEH

Colonel (retired) Doctor Alhaji Yahya A J J Jammeh is President of the Republic of The Gambia, elected in September 1996, with the inauguration taking place on 18 October 1996. The following September he was also elected Chairman of CILSS during its 12th Conference of Heads of State and Government, which was held in The Gambia.

His Excellency was born on 25 May 1965 in the village of Kanilai, Foni Kansala District, in The Gambia's Western Division. A bright child, intelligent and eager to learn, he began his primary education in 1972. Six years later he passed the Common Entrance Examination and was awarded a Government Scholarship. This enabled him to become a pupil at Gambia High School, from which he passed the General Certificate of Education 'O' Level in 1983, gaining credits in Geography, English, French, Biology and Physics, as well as passes in Chemistry and Oral English.

Colonel Jammeh's military career began on 1 April 1984, when he joined the former Gambia National Gendarmerie. In August he was assigned to the Special Intervention Unit of The Gambia National Army, but in April 1986 was transferred to the Special Guards Unit of the Mobile Gendarmerie and at the same time was promoted from Private to Sergeant. In December 1987 he was posted to the Gendarmerie Training School as an Escort Training Instructor, with further promotion to Cadet Officer. From August 1989 until the new year he served with the Presidential Guards, in charge of the Presidential Escort and commissioned Second Lieutenant in September. 1990 was spent on special assignments at the Kairaba Beach Hotel, as Security Officer for Visiting Heads of State at the ECOWAS Summit and as Officer-in-charge of the ECOWAS Peace Conference for Liberia.

His Excellency served as Officer Commanding of the Mobile Gendarmerie for the first five months of 1991, followed by two months as Officer Commanding of The Gambia National Gendarmerie's Military Police Unit. Five months into his next assignment, as Officer Commanding the Gambia National Army Military Police at Yundum Barracks from August 1991-November 1992, he received promotion to First Lieutenant. On the occasion of the visit of Pope John Paul II that February, he was specially assigned as Officer-in-charge both of His Holiness and entourage, and of VIP security at State functions including visiting Heads of State. In 1993 he was made Special Officer in charge of the close protection of the visiting ECOMOG Field Commander. In September 1993 he was sent to the USA, on a four-month Military Police Officers basic course at Fort McClellon, Alabama, from which he obtained a Diploma in Military Science. Later in 1994 he was appointed Chairman of the Armed Forces Provisional Ruling Council and Head of State. After promotion to Captain in November that year, he finally attained the rank of Colonel in August 1996, but retired from the Army early the following month, prior to the election.

In the last few years His Excellency has been the recipient of a number of honours. While in the USA, he was appointed Honorary Citizen of the State of Georgia and Honorary Lieutenant-Colonel ADC of Alabama State Militia in November 1993 and January 1994 respectively. He was decorated with the highest Libyan Insignia, Grand Commander of the Order of Al-Fatah, in 1995 and with the highest Chinese Insignia, the Order of Brilliant Jade with Grand Cordon of the Republic of China, in 1996. Besides receiving the 1997 Pan-African Humanitarian Award presented jointly by the Pan-African Foundation and the World Council of Culture, he was nominated Man of the Year 1997 by the American Biographical Institute, which also awarded him its Gold Record of Achievement in 1998. Yet another distinction was conferred upon him in September 1998, when he was appointed Honorary Admiral in the Alabama State Navy by the Governor of Alabama. He was awarded the Grand Order of Bravery by Colonel Gadaffi of Libya in November 1998, following this in December with the Islamic Worldwide Grand Prix from the Cheikhna Cheikh Saad Bouh Foundation of Dakar, Senegal. 1999 saw him receive an Honorary Doctorate of Civil Law from St Mary's University, Halifax, Canada, and he was appointed Deputy Governor of the American Biographical Institute Research Association in this year also, along with the 2000 Millennium Medal of Honour from the same Institute.

In his free time Colonel Jammeh enjoys a wide range of pursuits, embracing tennis, soccer, hunting, reading, correspondence, driving and riding motor-cycles, music and movies. He is interested in world events and is a keen animal lover. He is married, his wife being the former Zineb Souma.

*A biography of His Excellency Colonel Doctor Alhaji Yahya A J J Jammeh appears in the main section of this Edition.*

## REVEREND DR ANDREW JENKINS

*For your Outstanding Contribution to Youth and Community Organization*

# REVEREND DR ANDREW JENKINS

An outstanding person in his community, Andrew Jenkins has devoted most of his entire life to working with gangs, which have terrorised townships throughout America. He has met over two hundred gangs in the country and in the city of Philadelphia and became an East Coast Vice President and Representative for President Kennedy's nationwide Youth Organization United, that helped to work with gang activities throughout the United States.

Born and raised in South Philadelphia, USA, Andrew Jenkins was one of eleven children. He attended the John Bartram High School and then served three and a half years of duty with the United States Air Force, in Germany and Aviano, Italy. While in Italy, he attended the University of Maryland off campus courses, and then, with an honorable discharge, finished off his education at Temple University. He obtained a BA Degree in Human Services at Antioch University and is currently attending the True Holiness School of Ministeral Concepts for his Master's Degree. He also received an Honorary Degree from the Christian International University for Humane Letters.

Andrew Jenkins is a Founder and Vice President of The Young Great Society. He formed this society in a hope it would curtail gang shootings. He realised that to help with gang involvement, he would have to organize comprehensive, social, economic and educational planning for low-income residents, which he did through the society and with being President of Mantua Community Planners. During his seventeen years of President of Mantua Community Planners, he has organized employment, on the job training front, police community projects, recreation centers, youth clubs, trips, senior citizens, prison programs, credit union, community mini school, and architect workshops, which has helped the community expand and grow into a more secure place to live.

Andrew Jenkins served on the board of twenty four civic organizations in the Mantua Community. He is an Executive Board Member of the Citizen Crime Commission of Delaware Valley, a Board Member of Gaudenzia Inc (Drug Program), Mount Vernon Manor President and Owner, wich comprises of one hundred and twenty five apartment units, Advisory Board of Broad on South Streets at Philadelphia Senior Center, Associate Minister and Male Chorus Baritone-Bass Singer of Bible Way Baptist Church, Bass Singer at God's Community Choir, on the Advisory Board of Mantua Scatter Sites Tenant Association, a Board Member of West Philiadelphia Partnership, on the Advisory Committee of West Philadelphia Empowerment Zone, Financial Advisor and Supporter of Mantua Haverford Center, on the Advisory Committee of James Schuller's Memorial Boxing Gym and the President/CEO of Jenkins Consultants Inc. He was previously also employed in the following important positions: Community Representative of Philadelphia Anti-Poverty, Director of Relocation and Property Management, Director of Affirmative Action and Equal Opportunity Officer, and Executive Director, of Philadelphia Redevelopment Authority. He was the Chairman of the Center City Gallery 1 and 11 Shopping Mall and is presently serving as Deputy Mayor of Housing.

During his long and dedicated career, Andrew Jenkins has been the recipient of numerous awards and honours, including: Outstanding Man of the Year, from the City of Philadelphia in 1971; West Philadelphia Chamber of Commerce Award of Merit; Young Great Society Man of the Year Award, 1965; James Schuller Memorial Boxing Gym, Community Support Award, 1997; Maria Scott Ensemble Service in God's Work Award - African-American Community, 1996; Whitney Young Conference Service Award for Community Service Award, 1994; Governor Dick Thornburgh of Pennsylvania Community Service Award, 1984; Professional Service Award from the Crisis Prevention Network Inc, 1982; Gaudenzia Inc West Chester Campus Support and Dedication Award, 1995; The City of Philadelphia Redevelopment Authority Employee's Award, 1990; Mantua Community Planners Award as "Mayor of Mantua", 1971; National Black Association Appreciation Award, 1990; Role Model Award by Dr. Inez Thompson and Gospel Singer Thomasina James Johnson, 1995; Citation of the Commonwealth of Pennsylvania by the House of Representatives (Dave Richardson), 1995; Martin Luther King's Village Community Inc Cooperative Participation Award, 1982; City of Philadelphia Retirement Award (Redevelopment Authority), 1992; First United Baptist Church Loyal and Dedicated Services Award, 1984; University City High School Recognition of Services Award, 1975-76; Young Great Society Medical Center Community Devotion Award, 1969; Congressman Chaka Fattha Make a Difference Award, 1993; The Cub Scout Pack 422 Institutional Representative Award, 1961; The Young Great Society Outstanding and Devoted Service Award in 1976; and Mantua Community Leadership Award in 1982.

Andrew Jenkins is married to Patricia and they have four children, Eric, Denise, Andrea and Andrew Jr. In his leisure time, he enjoys writing poetry - and indeed has written more than two hundred and sixty poems - computer designing, graphics and restoration of old pictures, drawing and creating cartoon characters, singing, and writing his autobiography.

*A biography of Reverend Dr Andrew Jenkins appears in the main section of this Edition.*

## DR PER JESPERSEN, PhD

*For your Outstanding Contribution to
Philosophy as a Mirror of Life*

# DR PER JESPERSEN, PhD

Dr Per Jespersen, whose original choice of career was in the field of forestry, has been devoted to education and publishing from the 1970s onwards. Enjoying a reputation both at home and abroad, he is best known for his philosophical books designed specifically for children. Moreover, he has translated into Danish ten books from English, Swedish, Norwegian and German; they consist of philosophical or theological works, or fiction.

Born in Denmark on 14 January 1938, Per Jespersen graduated from Sanct Jorgens Gymnasium in Copenhagen in 1957, whereupon he commenced a four-year course of studies, which culminated in qualification as a forestguard in 1961. He then entered the Danish Civil Defence for his military service, which he completed in 1963. Several years in forestry followed, in which he started as Leading Forester on the Botogaard Estate in 1965. In 1966 he transferred to a similar position at the Schackenborg Estate, but left in 1970 to begin studies in preparation for a career in education. He graduated from Tonder Teachers College in 1973, while the following year he obtained a PhD in Theology.

Between 1973 and 1991 Dr Jespersen was engaged in teaching Danish, English and Philosophy at different schools in various places, including Bristol, England, in 1990. Furthermore, in 1976 he established the firm of SK Publishers for the purpose of publishing books on philosophy for children, or p4c. Since then 99 books have appeared, among them philosophical novels and short stories for children. In particular, the series about the children Kim and Marianne have proved very popular in Denmark. Books and teacher's manuals on p4c include "Filosofi med born" and "Born og filosofi", published in Sweden in 1999. Over the years hundreds of essays on p4c have been published in Denmark, Germany and Austria. They continue to appear in Sweden and the USA, the latter country's publications including "Analytic Teaching" from Viterbo College, Wisconsin. The main work for adults is the huge novel, "Når svanen dor", which deals with the apocalyptic year of 1986.

In addition to his publishing enterprise, Dr Jespersen has been involved in film production. Three films on p4c, namely, "Og så elsker jeg gyllelugt", with Marianne Albeck as producer, and "Du og jeg", directed by Lennart Pasborg, were produced by Magic Hour Film, of Lyngby, near Copenhagen and were also made available with English sub-titles. The only films in the world to deal with the theme of p4c at the time, they were shown many times on Danish Television. However, in 1998 he set up Peripas Film, a company that is now producing a new film on p4c. In English, with the title of "You And I, II", it is intended for worldwide distribution. The shootings have already been made and editorial work is underway.

Dr Jespersen's other current activities include serving as Project Leader in the Big Brother/Big Sister movement in the southern part of Jutland since 1994. In 1998 he established a private consultation - LÆSELINIEN - for children with reading difficulties. Children come there from a widespread area to receive practice in reading and to undergo philosophical therapy. The only place in the world where reading and spelling are taught through philosophy on a private basis, it helps the children to rediscover their human dignity and develop a new perspective on life. Moreover, the first to start the p4c movement in Denmark, he still lectures on it worldwide, Tarrant Wesleyan University and at Tarrant County Junior College at Arlington being among the many venues.

Per Jespersen is listed in the International Who's Who for 1999. He and his wife Anne have a son, Kim, and a daughter, Marianne.

*A biography of Dr Per Jespersen, PhD, appears in the main section of this Edition.*

**DR CHRISTINE MARIE KENNEFICK,
PhD, LFIBA, IOM**

*For your Outstanding Contribution
to the Sciences*

# DR CHRISTINE MARIE KENNEFICK, PhD, LFIBA, IOM

A materials scientist whose background includes engineering, Dr Christine M Kennefick has spent her adult life on studies and research. Presently a National Research Council Senior Associate at one of the US Air Force bases, she holds membership of the New York Academy of Sciences, the Materials Research Society, the American Ceramic Society and the American Physical Society. Her intellectual interests embrace applied mathematics, materials modelling and computer modelling.

Christine Kennefick was born on 4 July 1962 in Washington, District of Columbia, USA. After successfully completing her high school education she enrolled at Stanford University. An outstanding student, she obtained her Bachelor of Science degree in 1984, with distinction in the departmental honours programme. Continuing at the same university, she went on to prepare for a Master of Science degree, awarded her in 1986. Further work then led to a PhD from Cornell University in 1991.

After receiving her doctorate, Ms Kennefick became a National Research Council Association at the NASA Lewis Research Center in Dayton, Ohio, from 1991-93. In 1994 she travelled to Germany, where she spent two years as a Guest Scientist at the Max Planck Institute in Stuttgart. On her return to the USA she was offered a year's Postdoctoral Fellowship by the American Society for Engineering Education, which allowed her to work at the Army Research Laboratory in Aberdeen, Maryland, from 1997-98. She then transferred to the Wright Patterson Air Force Base in Dayton on her present Senior Associateship from the National Research Council.

*A biography of Dr Christine Marie Kennefick, PhD, LFIBA, IOM, appears in the main section of this Edition.*

## REVEREND YOUNG-KYU KIM, ThD

*For your Outstanding Contribution
to Theology*

# REVEREND YOUNG-KYU KIM, ThD

Reverend Young-Kyu Kim, who was born on 14 December 1954 in Hampyung, Jeonnam, Korea, has dedicated himself to his career as a theologian, contributing both to education and research. As a child Dr Kim devoted himself to Christian life under the influence of his pious mother. After school he pursued studies in diverse directions including medicine and technology, but eventually returned to the study of theology. He holds a Bachelor of Arts degree in Theology from Chong-Shin University, Seoul, a Master in Divinity from Hapdong Theological Seminary, Suwon, and a Doctorate in Theology from Göttingen University, in Germany, awarded in 1978, 1983 and legitimated in 1994.

After his return to Korea from Germany, Dr Kim settled in Seoul, where he became Director of the Research Institute for the Bible and Reformed Theology in 1995 and a Lecturer at Amyang University Theological Seminary in 1996. He has continued in both positions up to the present.

A member of the American Association for the Advancement of Science, Dr Kim has also been admitted to the New York Academy of Sciences. He is the author of various publications, notably "Biblica" in 1988, as well as the works "A Dialogical Document and the Metaplasmic Phase of the Pre-Mosaic Hebrew Behind Genesis 23" and "Calvin and the Old Testament", both of which appeared in 1993. His other recent publications reflect his confidence in a holistic emergence of all universal things, and his belief in a time when ethnic groups of the ancient Korean, old Sumerian, old Dravid, old Indo-European and Semitic lived historically together.

Reverend Kim is married; he and his wife, Bok-Im Kim, have two daughters, Sun-Shil and Sun-Yang.

*A biography of Reverend Young-Kyu Kim, ThD, appears in the main section of this Edition.*

**PROFESSOR ELIEZER ISAAK
KLAINMAN, MD**
*For your Outstanding Contribution to
Cardiology in the Community*

# PROFESSOR ELIEZER ISAAK KLAINMAN, MD

Eliezer Isaak Klainman was born on 12 April 1951 in Israel, and his expertise lies in the field of Cardiology.

He obtained his MD from Tel Aviv University in 1978, followed by a Certificate in Cardiology. His specialism is in Cardiology and Basic Science in Nuclear Cardiology. He is Professor and Lecturer in Medical Science and Cardiology at Ben-Gurion and Tel Aviv Universities, and also holds the post of Head Investigator of Clinical Trials. In addition, he is Cardiologist Expert in Physiology and Cardiac Rehabilitation at Beilison MC and Givatayin Cardiac and Rehabilitation Institute. In 1987 he founded the Macabi Cardiac Institute and was its Head until 1994. He then founded the Institute if Gigatayim and is still its Head.

Professor Klainman has contributed numerous articles to journals specialising in Cardiology, Cardiac Rehabilitation and Exercise Physiology including the International Journal of Cardiology, Clinical Journal of Cardiology and the European Heart Journal. In honour of his exceptional work in his field he has been the recipient of the Award of Excellence in Professional Medicine, granted in 1997, and an Honorary Certificate from the Rotary Club in 1996, as Founder of Mishmar-Hayarden Cardiac and Rebalition Institute at Gicatayin. His name is listed in the current edition of Who's Who in the World.

Professor Klainman is a member of the Israeli Cardiac Society, the Israeli Society of Hypertension and the New York Academy of Sciences as well as the European Heart Society and the American Association for the Advancement of Sciences. He is married to Yaffa and has three daughters, Hanna, Efrat and Michal.

*A biography of Professor Eliezer Isaak Klainman, MD, appears in the main section of this Edition.*

# DR EDVARD KOBAL, DDG

*For your Outstanding Contribution to the maxim: The Thing That Gives People Courage is an Idea (Georges Clemenceau)*

# DR EDVARD KOBAL, DDG

Dr Edvard Kobal holds responsibility as Director of the Slovenian Science Foundation, which is based in his country's capital, Ljubljana. He holds a Bachelor's degree in Chemical Technology, a Master's degree in the same discipline, and a Doctorate in Chemical Sciences, awarded by the University of Ljubljana in 1982, 1984 and 1991 respectively.

Dr Kobal assumed his present position with the Slovenian Science Foundation in 1994. Prior to that he spent five years working independently as an editor for the Educational Editorial Board of the National Publishing House, starting in 1989. For the latter part of that period, from 1992 onwards, he also acted as an advisor to the Ministry of Science and Technology. He has several publications to his credit, notably "The Movement "Science to Youth" and the Slovenes 1965-85", which appeared in 1987 and in its 2nd revised edition in 1993, "Chemical Information for Secondary Schools Students", which came out in 1991, "Chemistry for the Curious" which followed in 1994.

A member of the Slovenian Chemical Society since 1981, Dr Kobal is also in the affiliate membership programme of the International Union for Pure and Applied Chemistry. Moreover, after gaining admission to the Royal Institution of Great Britain in 1994 and the British Association for the Advancement of Science in 1996, he has continued with those memberships up to the present.

Born on 19 January 1957 in Logatec, Slovenia, Edvard Kobal married Doris Fajdiga in July 1989 and now has a son and a daughter. In his free time, apart from spending time with his wife and family, he finds recreation in painting.

*A biography of Dr Edvard Kobal, DDG, appears in the main section of this Edition.*

## PROFESSOR DR EDGAR KRAU, PhD

*For your Outstanding Contribution to
Psychology and Social Sciences*

# PROFESSOR DR EDGAR KRAU, PhD

Edgar Krau is a Professor at Tel Aviv University, a position he has held since 1981. He is the founder of an elaborate new theory of self-realization, in which he perceives that the search for self-realization is not a task which only appears before an élite, who has succeeded in satisfying all their needs, but constitutes the basic quest for life meaning in every human individual. Self-realization leads to the gratification of the person's main life aspirations, but entails compromises in other aspects of life. The vocational career is a main instrument for achieving self-realization, the embodiment of life meaning. The course of the career depends on a guiding end-stage image of self-realization elaborated early in adolescence and which is subsequently matched with society's and the invididual's occupational images. Career decisions are matches of images which have intentionally or unintentionally concealed characteristics. The latter account for career failures, especially when the guiding images are misconceived.

Professor Krau has also discovered the existence of socially and culturally bound models of socioeconomic management. It is proving, that enterprise management is not a purely economic activity, but is embedded in society's social and cultural profile which prescribes conditions and modes for the use of power. The neglect of the social consequences of management becomes destructive in the long run even to individual organizations, let alone to society as a whole. Professor Krau's opinion is that long-term proficiency in management leans on a collectivist value profile, which through the awareness of common goals achieves staff loyalty and uses power in the interest of the entire working collectivity.

Born on 9 April 1929 in Stanislau, Edgar Krau attended a high school in Cluj, Romania. He found himself being deported by the Nazis to Auschwitz and Kaufering, during World War II, in 1944-45. He began his university studies in Psychology and Education at Cluj University, between 1947-51, which lead to a university appointment, but was revoked the moment he applied for emigration to Israel, where his mother lived. His emigration was unfortunately denied and he was sent to the township of Gherla, where he took up the position of a high school teacher from 1952-61. His education being very important to him, he was admitted as a candidate for PhD, without a staff position, in 1955, presenting his doctoral thesis in 1960, entitled "Contributions to the Problem of Orientation in Action". This thesis caused problems as it contained a critique against the theory of "ustanovka" in Soviet psychology, but eventually got accepted from the University of Cluj in 1963. Edgar Krau's PhD title was finally recognized by the Romanian Superior Commission of Diplomas in 1964.

In 1961, Edgar Krau took up the position of Chief Research Fellow at the Institute of Pedagogical Sciences in Cluj, where he stayed until he emigrated to Israel in 1977. He was a Professor at the University of Haifa, between 1977-81, before taking up his present position at Tel-Aviv University.

During his professional career, Professor Krau has been recognized through his brilliant books and articles. His books have been acknowledged world wide and his papers presented at international meetings. His books are titled: "The Realization of Life Aspirations Through Vocational Careers", 1997, and "Social and Economic Management in the Competitive Society", and some of his articles are: "New Perspectives on Self-Realization", 1993, presented at the 101st Convention of the American Psychological Association, in Toronto, and "Life Career Planning and Prediction", 1994, at the XXIII International Congress of Applied Psychology, Madrid, Spain.

Professor Krau has been the recipient of several awards and honours. He was an invited guest of the Academy of Sciences, Moscow in 1968 and at the Institute for Experimental Psychology, Slovak Academy of Sciences, Bratislava, in 1970. He represented Romania on the International Test Commission at Liege, Belgium in 1971 and was a member of the International Test Commisssion, between 1971-73. In 1972 he recieved the Vasile Conta Prize of the Romanian Academy for contribution to the treatise "Psychology of Industrial Work", and also, in the same year, a Diploma of the High Center for Logic and Comparative Sciences, Bologna, Italy. He was on the Executive Committee of the Division of Psychology and National Development of the International Association of Applied Psychology, between 1982-86, the Chairman of the International Colloquium Human Resources Development in a Changing Society, in 1984, a member of the Executive Committee of the Association for Vocational and Career Counseling in Israel, since 1981 and the Editor-in-Chief of the bilingual AVCI Journal "Adam Veavoda" (Man and Work), since 1987.

Professor Krau's accomplishments in his life are so astounding that he is known world wide for his scientific activity concerns in psychology and social science.

*A biography of Professor Dr Edgar Krau, PhD, appears in the main section of this Edition.*

**PROFESSOR DR RYSZARD JOZEF KUCHA,
LFIBA**
*For your Outstanding Contribution
to Education*

# PROFESSOR DR RYSZARD JOZEF KUCHA, LFIBA

Born in the village of Husow, the district of Rzeszow, Poland on 4 May 1942, Ryszard Jozef Kucha received the degrees of MA in Education at the Human Science Faculty of Maria Curie-Sklodowska University in Lublin, in 1967, PhD in Education from the Faculty of Pedagogics and Psychology at the same University, in 1975, and the titles Senior Lecturer, in 1983, Assistant University Professor in 1991, and Professor, in 1997.

He has held several very important positions at the Maria Curie-Sklodowska University over the years, including: Vice Dean of Education and International Exchange Programmes, in 1984-90 and 1993-99; Head of the History of Education Department, at the Faculty of Pedagogics and Psychology, since 1984; and Editor of the academic magazine "Lublin Pedagogical Yearbook", edited by the Faculty of Pedagogics and Psychology, since 1993. He is also, concurrently, the Head of the Faculty of Pedagogics and Psychology Branch at Deblin Higher Military Aviation School, an appointment he has held since 1993. Other appointments include: Chair of Pedagogics of the State Lvov University, Ukraine, Institute of Pedagogics and Psychology of Professional Education, Ukrainian Academy of Pedagogical Sciences, Kiev and Lvov, Teacher's Training College of Nizhyn, Ukraine, the UNESCO Chair of the State Pedagogical Hercen University in St Petersburg, Russia, Department of Continuing Education, Bristol University, England, Department of Education at Umea University, Sweden, Department of Educational Foundations, College of Education, Saskatchewan University, Saskatoon, Canada, and the Hogeschool Gelderland Arnhem en Nijmegen, Arnhem, The Netherlands.

He has been a Visiting Professor at the Pedagogiska Institutionen, Umeå University, in 1993 and 1995, the Institute of Education at London University in 1994, Glasgow University in 1995, Hermann Gmeiner Akademie in Innsbruck, Austria, 1996, Vilna State University, Lithuania, 1993, Academy of Pedagogical Sciences, Kiev, Ukraine in 1997, The Chair of Pedagogics, State Lvov University, Ukraine in 1997 and 1998, Cattolica Universita di Milano, Italy, 1995, Catania Universita, Italy in 1996, The Chair of UNESCO at the State Pedagogical Hercen University, St Petersburg, Russia in 1998.

Professor Kucha's fields of investigation are in the history of elementary, secondary education in Europe, teacher training in the Kingdom of Poland for the years 1864-1915, education of national minorities, Polish-American education in the XIX and XX centuries, and European educational integration before the XXIst century. With regard to his investigations, Professor Kucha has published several articles and books, including: "Elementary Education in the Kingdom of Poland in the Years 1864-1944"; "Schools in Lublin in the Years 1864-1915"; "School of the Fourth Centuries. Secondary General School of Stanislaus Staszic in Lublin 1586-1986"; "Polish and Swedish Schools in the Nineteenth and Twentieth Centuries. A Historical Study"; "Education of Young Generations of Poles and Ukrainians in the Context of European Integration".

During his long and dedicated career, Professor Kucha has been the recipient of several grants from the Kosciuszko Foundation in New York, USA and Umeå University, Sweden. He is a member of the European Association for International Education, the International Standing Conference for the History of Education, the European Universities Continuing Education Network, the Polish Pedagogical Association, Lublin Scholar Association and on the Editorial Board of "Ars Educandi" a Gdansk academic magazine and "Pedagogics and Psychology of Professional Education" which is published in the Ukrainian language.

Professor Kucha is married to Ewa Anna Wawrzycka, who is an Elementary Class Teacher in the Primary School No 35, in Lublin. They have one daughter, Ewa Magdalena and she attained her secondary school certificate in 1999 and passed successfully her entrance examinations to the Marie-Curie-Sklodowska University.

*A biography of Professor Dr Ryszard Jozef Kucha, LFIBA, appears in the main section of this Edition.*

## DR VERNETTE TROSPER LANDERS, DDG, LFWLA, LPIBA, MOIF, IOM

*For your Outstanding Contribution to Education, Research and Community*

# DR VERNETTE TROSPER LANDERS, DDG, LFWLA, LPIBA, MOIF, IOM

Dr Vernette Trosper Landers has enjoyed a long and dedicated career in education in the public system, during which she not only taught at several levels in California, but was also involved in administration, counselling and project direction. Now retired, she resides in the Hi-Desert community of Landers, which she helped her late husband develop and where in 1992 she survived an earthquake that reached 7.6 on the Richter scale.

The daughter of LaVerne Stevens and Fred Trosper, Vernette Landers was born on 3 May 1912 in Lawton, Oklahoma, USA. However, in 1918 the family moved to California, where she attended school and subsequently entered the University of California at Los Angeles. From there she received her AB Honours degree in Spanish and French in 1933, MA in 1935 and EdD in 1953, with a total of nine honours altogether. Postgraduate study followed at the University of California at Berkeley and at Riverside, as well as at the University of Southern California at Los Angeles. She holds four teaching credentials from the State of California, two of them being for life.

Between 1935 and 1959 Dr Landers taught at secondary schools in the Montebello Unified School District, with a break from 1946-47 to serve as Professor of Spanish at Long Beach City College, and a second break in 1950, which she spent as an Assistant Professor at Los Angeles State College. Transferring to the Morongo Unified School District, 29 Palms, she taught the 8th grade at Yucca Valley Elementary School in 1959, but the following year became Dean of Girls at the 29 Palms High School. In 1965 she was appointed District Counsellor, a position she held until retiring in 1972. During the first two years of that final period of her professional career she was also responsible for coordinating adult education, while in 1967 she served as Director of the Title V Guidance Project.

In addition to her educational commitments, from 1962-82 Dr Landers was Clerk-in-charge of Landers Post Office. Moreover, as a writer she contributed articles to educational magazines and government publications for many years. After retiring she began publishing books in verse designed for children to read, totalling nine in all. The first of those, "Impy", appeared in 1974, and was followed by "Impy's Children" and "Talkie", both in 1975, "Nineteen O Four" and "Little Brown Bat" in 1976, "Slo-Go" in 1977, "Owls Who and Who Who" and "Sandy, the Coydog" in 1978, and finally "The Kit Fox and the Walking Stick" in 1980. Her verse was also included in the 1974 and 1975 editions of "New Voices in American Poetry", as well as in "An Anthology of World Peace and Brotherhood" in 1981.

During her career Dr Landers has been the recipient of numerous honours and awards. At university she was inducted into the honorary societies of Phi Beta Kappa, Pi Lambda Theta, Sigma Delta Pi, Pi Delta Phi and the Mortar Board. In 1967 she was named Soroptimist of the Year, while later distinctions included a Creativity Reognition Award from the International Personnel Research Association in 1972, selection as Poet Laureate for February 1981 by the Centre for International Studies and Exchanges, Rome, and a Diploma of Honour for Poetry by the Leonardo da Vinci Academy, Italy, in 1984. She holds a Certificate of Merit and two Certificates of Appreciation from Morongo Unified School District and in 1985 she had an Honorary Cultural DLitt conferred upon her by the World University. During the present decade she has received several honours from the American Biographical Institute and the International Biographical Centre, such as the Golden Academy Award for Lifetime Achievement, the International Honors Cup, the One in a Million Award, the International Woman of the Year Award, and the Platinum Record for Exceptional Performance.

A member of the American Association of Counseling and Guidance for 25 years, Dr Landers is a Life Member of the California Retired Teachers Association and a Life Fellow of the International Academy of Poets. The many other organisations which she joined include the Association of Women Deans and Administrators, the National League of American Penwomen, and Landers Women of the Moose. A lover of animals, she has been involved in crossbreeding bobcats with Siamese and Calico cats. She was married twice, but is now a widow. Her first husband, Major Paul A Lum, passed away in 1955, leaving her with a son, William Tappan. She has two more children, Lawrence and Marlin, from her marriage to Newlin J Landers, which lasted until his death in 1990.

*A biography of Dr Vernette Trosper Landers, DDG, LFWLA, LPIBA, MOIF, IOM, appears in the main section of this Edition.*

# DR DALE PIERRE LAYMAN, PhD, DG, DDG, FABI, LPIBA, MOIF, IOM

*For your Outstanding Contribution to Medical and Scientific Education, Writing and Research*

# DR DALE PIERRE LAYMAN, PhD, DG, DDG, FABI, LPIBA, MOIF, IOM

A medical and scientific educator, writer and researcher who is never afraid to speak his mind on issues on which he feels strongly, Dr Dale Pierre Layman regards himself as an eternal student, always ready to learn and extend his knowledge. As a professor in medical terminology, human anatomy and physiology at Joliet Junior College, he is much appreciated by his students, for whom he makes the lessons both interesting and fun. He likes to write his own classroom texts, some of which are incorporated in his textbooks "The Terminology of Anatomy and Physiology" and "The Medical Language: A Programmed Body-Systems Approach", published in 1983 and 1995 respectively.

Dale Layman was born on 3 July 1948 in Niles, Michigan, USA, as the son of Delphine Layman and the late Pierre Layman. An outstanding student at Niles High School, he graduated from there with honours in 1966. Two years at Lake Michigan College ended with an Associate in Science degree in 1968, after which he entered the University of Michigan at Ann Arbor, as a Michigan Public Junior Scholar. There he obtained a Bachelor of Science degree with distinction in Anthropology and Zoology in 1971, followed by a Master of Science degree in Physiology in 1974. He then became an instructor in human anatomy, physiology and histology at Lake Superior State College, now Lake Superior State University, but left in 1975 to join the staff at Joliet Junior College, Joliet, Illinois, where he still remains. Moreover, his enthusiasm for study and professional development spurred him on to obtain an Educational Specialist (EdS) qualification in Physiology and Health Science from Ball State University in 1979. For his PhD in Health and Safety Studies, awarded by the University of Illinois in 1986, he presented a dissertation entitled "The Runner: A Profile of Injury and Addiction". It had a very favourable reception and was cited in various publications.

His day-to-day teaching and his writing aside, Dr Layman concerns himself with matters directly or indirectly related to fields such as education, modern technological developments, social justice and the environment. At the beginning of the 1990s he participated in a protest against a proposed road development that threatened a unique wetland area. In 1994 he began campaigning for the status of teachers at Joliet Junior College, and indeed in the whole community college system of Illinois, to be upgraded from instructor to professor. This would increase the credibility of faculty members when applying for research grants or seeking publication. In 1995 he pressed for his college to have its name changed to the more historically accurate name of Joliet Pioneer College. With regard to molecular biology, his feelings are mixed. He recognises the advantages that genetic engineering can bring by providing improved vegetable crops, but then he asks what the potential long-term risks are for the consumer and for the environment. Furthermore, although information obtained from mapping of human genes can facilitate early diagnosis or prevention of a genetically-linked disease, it can also cause discrimination, for example, against persons applying for employment.

With regard to computers, Dr Layman knows well that used judicially they have many advantages. He is equally aware of the widening gap generated between the computer-literate and the computer-illiterate, a gap largely running along age, gender, racial and socio-economic lines. His fears for the future are that computers will dominate over human beings, directing their thoughts and actions, making them slaves to artificial intelligence. To counteract such situations he believes that people should be helped to develop computer-like modes of thinking, several elements of which already exist, such as programmed learning, iconic reasoning, and natural human reasoning upon the Common Ground Plane, or rectangular grid.

In his teaching, Dr Layman seeks to help his students understand the implications of molecular biology and the computer, and to develop alternative ways of reasoning. One such way is by using a grid, as in the example he presents in his paper entitled "1998 Influential Leadership in Medical and Scientific Education", prepared for a workshop on "Intuitive Geometry and the A&P (Human Anatomy & Physiology) Text" at the 12th Annual Conference of the Human Anatomy and Physiology Society at Fort Worth, Texas. The paper deals with the concept of geometric bodyspace, a wall or grid formed by modelling the human body as a collection of bricks or rectangles with cracks through which the light of knowledge shines. The idea is that while reading a textbook about the human body, the student can summarise and collect facts as rectangles having definite locations on a numbered grid, and so is guided to think geometrically and visually, not merely verbally. Thus verbal learning is strongly reinforced by the intuitive sense of Geometric Order in Space and the student can develop a chess-like thinking process, leading to greater critical understanding of the material read. Other advantages include narrowing of the gap between the computer-literate and computer-illiterate, reduction in the number of computers required by educational institutions and thus reduction in expenditure, and an insight into the Deep Structure of Universal Order, as symbolised by the Yin and the Yang, representing order and disorder.

Besides being admitted to the honorary societies of Kappa Delta Pi and Phi Kappa Phi, Dr Layman belongs to the American Association for the Advancement of Science, the Human Anatomy and Physiology Society and Illinois Community College Faculty Association. A Notable Author and Council Member on the Governing Board of the Text and Academic Authors Association, he has two linked biographical articles on its Internet site, in which he is referred to as a "Health writer who lives to write". Listed in various biographical volumes, he has also been the recipient of a number of distinctions from the American Biographical Institute and the International Biographical Centre.

*A biography of Dr Dale Pierre Layman, PhD, DG, DDG, FABI, LPIBA, MOIF, IOM, appears in the main section of this Edition.*

# DR MIRIAM LEMANSKA, DSc, FIBA

*For your Outstanding Contribution
as a Mathematician*

# DR MIRIAM LEMANSKA, DSc, FIBA

Miriam Lemanska was born on 11 May 1920 in the town of Lodz in Poland. She obtained her Master's Degree from the University of Lodz in 1952, following this with a Doctor of Science Degree at the Technion in Haifa, Israel, in 1967.

She began her working life as a Teacher at the Lyceum in Lodz while she was still studying, working from 1946 to 1952. She then proceeded to the Teacher's Academy at Lodz until 1954, and was Senior Assistant at Lodz University from 1953 until 1957. Dr Lemanska was then appointed a Research Worker for the Nuclear Research Institute in Warsaw, where she remained until 1958. She emigrated to Israel in August 1959 and began working as a Researcher for NRC Yarne, Israel, in 1960. She held this position until 1985 when she retired and then was promoted to a Researcher Consultant.

Dr Lemanska has contributed numerous articles to international refereed journals including the Journal of Nuclear Energy, the Journal of Applied Mathematical Physics and the International Journal of Impact Engineering. She has been honoured with an award from the Atomic Commission in Warsaw in 1958, and is a member of the Israel Nuclear Society.

Miriam Lemanska is a survivor of the holocaust, in which her parents and two sisters were unfortunately victims. She lives in Israel, and has a son, Alexander, a daughter-in-law, Margalit and two grandsons, Shachar and Daron.

*A biography of Dr Miriam Lemanska, DSc, FIBA, appears in the main section of this Edition.*

## ZHONGYING LI, DDG

*For your Outstanding Contribution to the
Research Field of Ionizing Radiation*

# ZHONGYING LI, DDG

Destined to become a nuclear physicist and professor, Ms Zhongying Li was born on 5 October 1943 in a village near Wuxi, in the province of Jiangsu, China. Her father Peihua Li (1918-47), an accountant in a Shanghai firm, died when she was only four years old, not long after the birth of her younger brother, who now teaches in high school. Undaunted by adversity, her mother Xiuqin Li (1918-87), a farmer, made a frugal living to support the four-member family and the bright and resolute children's schooling.

As a child Ms Li worked hard, aspiring to become a scientist and strive for the prosperity of her impoverished homeland, a wish that was to be fulfilled. After graduating from the Physics Department at Nanjing University in 1966, she became a researcher at the Institute of Nuclear Physics and Chemistry, China Academy of Engineering Physics, where she has now held the positions of Professor, since 1989, and Director of the Ionizing Radiation Measurement Laboratory since 1989 and 1993 respectively. Her first husband, Jingying Zhang (1941-83), was also a researcher and nuclear physicist at the same institute. Like her, he had obtained a BS degree from Nanjing University in 1966. When he later developed a chronic disease, she stoically bore pressures from all sides. Besides looking after him, she continued with her work at the Institute, while then and after his death on 22 October 1983, she had the household chores to do, as well as taking care of her two children, to whom she set an example through her never-failing motivation towards her career objective.

Ms Li has more than thirty years experience in the research field of ionizing radiation measurement and radiation protection. This has enabled her to acquire profound views in areas of radiation dosimetry, measurement technology in pulsed radiation field, value dissemination of a quantity in ionizing radiation, radiation protection, and application of nuclear technology. She achieved breakthrough results in dosimetry for photon and electron beams, corrections to account for lack of saturation on charge collection in an ionization chamber, and dosimetry for neutrons produced by a pulse reactor. In more than twenty papers published in scientific journals at home and overseas, she presented unique insights and a number of important research findings that were well received and highly regarded by Chinese and foreign experts. Early in 1999 the International Economic Centre, Hong Kong, selected two of those papers as Excellent Important Academic Achievements of the World's Ethnic Chinese.

Recently admitted to the American Biographical Institute's Research Board of Advisors, the New York Academy of Sciences, the International Radiation Physics Society and the American Association for the Advancement of Science, Ms Li continues to hold membership of the first three organisations. In addition, she is a Deputy Director General of the International Biographical Centre. Her achievements brought her a National Defence Great Achievement Award for Science and Technology in 1983, two Science and Technology Advancements Awards from the China National Nuclear Corporation in 1986, a Science Foundation Award from the China Academy of Engineering Physics in 1994, and Science and Technology Awards from the Scientific and Industrial Commission of National Defence in 1992 and 1995. Besides having her details included in prestigious international biographical publications, she has received nominations for various international awards.

Ms Li recently married Ke Qing Shi, a Beijing University graduate who was a senior engineer at Beijing Institute of Metrology before his retirement. She has two children from her first marriage, a son, Lu Zhang, and a daughter, Jue Li. The former, who now works for AT7T Inc, earned a BS degree at the China University of Science and Technology in 1993 and a Master's degree in Physics and Computer Science at the University of Oregon, USA, in 1998, while the latter received a BS degree from Sichuan University in 1994 and is employed by Exxon China Inc.

*A biography of Zhongying Li, DDG, appears in the main section of this Edition.*

**PROFESSOR VALENTIN N LUKANIN, LFIBA**

*For your Outstanding Contribution to
Road Engineering Education and Transport*

# PROFESSOR VALENTIN N LUKANIN, LFIBA

Born in March 1931 in the town of Orekhovo-Zuevo, Russia, Valentin N Lukanin graduated from the Automotive Engineering Department of the Moscow State Automobile and Road Technical University, MADI-TU. He was later to defend his PhD and DSc theses. In addition, he has had two Honorary Doctorates conferred upon him, one by the Higher Polytechnic Institute of Havana, the other by the Engineering University of Peru.

Following his graduation Professor Lukanin began working for a road transport company in the town of Lipetzk before returning to MADI-TU, where he has been teaching ever since. He currently holds the positions of Professor, Rector of the University, Head of its Motor Vehicle Engine Department and Director of its Energy-Ecological Problems Research Institute. A member of the Russian Academy of Transport, he serves as its Vice-President and is President of the International Association for Automotive and Road Engineering Education as well. He also holds membership of the International Engineering Academy and the International Higher Academy of Sciences.

In recent years Professor Lukanin has published various research papers, books and monographs, besides preparing a computerised textbook in the field. These publications include "Theoretical Foundations of Internal Combustion Engines", "Designing and Calculation of the Parts and Systems of Automotive IC Engines", "Acoustic Problems of Engines" and "Environmental Problems of Road Transport".

Professor Valentin N Lukanin remains devoted to the teaching and scientific research of the theory of internal combustion engines and the related ecological problems, as well as the environmental preservation problems connected with transport development.

*A biography of Professor Valentin N Lukanin, LFIBA, appears in the main section of this Edition.*

## PROFESSOR MICHAEL H J MAES, PhD

*For your Outstanding Contribution to
Psychiatric Research*

# PROFESSOR MICHAEL H J MAES, PhD

Professor Michael Maes has earned himself an international reputation for his work in the field of psychiatry. Not only has he contributed his services as a consultant, but has also conducted extensive research into psychiatric disorders, their diagnosis and treatment, the effects of various therapeutic drugs and the role played by factors such as pregnancy, stress and climatic variations. Throughout the 1990s he has been the recipient of several awards, starting with one from the European College of Neuropsychopharmacology in 1991. Apart from being the co-winner of five VVZ (Belgium) Prizes, two for clinical psychiatry, the others for biological psychiatry, he earned two Investigator Awards from NARSAD, USA, the same organisation from which he received the Klerman Award for Outstanding Research in 1998.

A prolific writer, since the mid-1980s Professor Maes is the author or co-author of over 300 papers, articles and book chapters, published or accepted for publication, many appearing in journals such as "Acta Psychiatrica Scandinavica", "Journal of Affective Disorders", "Journal of Psychiatry Research" and "Psychoneuroendocrinology". A number of other writings have been submitted or are in preparation. The co-editor of "Neurobiology and clinical views on aggression and impulsivity", which appeared in 1998, he is also the editor of "Current Opinion in Psychiatry. Clinical Psychiatry and Behavioral Medicine", 1997, and a further volume of the same book, published in 1999. Moreover, his editorial involvements have extended to include special supplements, year books, collections of abstracts and so on.

Born on 10 March 1954 in Ghent, Belgium, Michael Maes attended school in his home town and then went on to the University of Chent. where he qualified as a Physician in 1979. In 1986 he completed his specialisation as a Neuropsychiatrist, while in 1991 the University of Antwerp awarded him the degree of Docent, which qualified him to teach university students. He also received his PhD, after defending a thesis on "Clinical and Biological Diagnosis of Unipolar Depression".

For several years from the mid-1980s onwards Dr Maes was an Assistant Professor of Psychiatry at the University Hospital of Antwerp and Director of its Psychiatric Ward. During the same period he served as a Consultant Psychiatrist at a Psychiatric Center and engaged in private practice, dealing with cognitive and biological therapy for depression and anxiety disorders. However, towards the end of 1991 he left for the USA to spend four years as an Assistant Professor of Psychiatry at Case Western Reserve University, in Cleveland, Ohio. While still in America, where he received immigrant status in 1994, he also accepted responsibilities in Belgium, carrying out the duties of Ward Director and Departmental Scientific Director in the Department of Psychiatry, University of Antwerp, until 1999. His current commitments, assumed in 1995, 1996, 1997 and 1999 respectively, are as Director of the Clinical Research Centre for Mental Health, Antwerp, as Consultant Psychiatrist for IRCCS, Fatebenefratelli, Brescia and Milan, Italy, as Adjoint Professor of Psychiatry at Vanderbilt University, Nashville, Tennessee, USA, with appointment as Professor of Psychiatry pending, and as Professor of Psychiatry and Chairman of the Department of Psychiatry and Neuropsychology at the University of Maastricht, Netherlands.

Professor Maes has gained admission to the European College of Neuropsychopharmacology, the Belgian College of Neuropsychopharmacology, the New York Academy of Sciences and the American Association for the Advancement of Science. Other organisations to which he belongs include the European Association of Psychiatrists, the International Society of Psychoneuroendocrinology, the International Association of Suicide Prevention and the International Brain Research Organization. He is an active member of the Society of Biological Psychiatry, sits on the Steering Committee of the International Society for Research into Affective Disorders and officiates as Secretary of the World Psychiatric Association. In spring 1993 he was one of the founders of the Flemish Organization for Psychiatric Research, which he then served as Vice-Chairman.

Michael Maes is married to the former Carine Steyaert. Their daughters, Annabel and Eveline, both hold US citizenship, having been born there in 1992 and 1994 respectively.

*A biography of Professor Michael H J Maes, PhD, appears in the main section of this Edition.*

## LEE MCCOY, DDG, MOIF

*For your Outstanding Contribution
to Public Service*

# LEE MCCOY, DDG, MOIF

Lee McCoy resides in the beautiful city of Mobile, Alabama, USA. She is known there as a pillar of society as she is always available to anyone who needs help and advice.

Born on 27 July 1925, Lee McCoy is the mother of four children, Bernadette, Raymond, Richard, and Joan. She was a Consultant to the Citizens Advisory Committee of the Mobile Transit Authority, the Advisory Board of the National Organization on Disability, the World Committee for the International Decade of Disabled Persons, the Cultural Enrichment Task Force, Chamber of Commerce and Culture Mobile. Lee McCoy has also been a member of numerous committies and boards, including President of Mobile Chapter of Quota International in 1980-81, President of the Civic Round Table in 1981-82, on the Board of Friends of the Museum, between 1978-84, the National Organization on Disability, between 1982-89, Miss Wheelchair Alabama in 1980-84, the Joe Jefferson Players in 1986 and since 1981 the English-Speaking Union, of which she was President from 1995 until earlier this year. She is a member of the Mobile Historic Society, the Executive Women's Forum, the Mobile United Recreation and Culture Committee, the Mobile Opera Guild and Charter Member of the National Womens Museum of Arts.

Lee McCoy has presented over one hundred and fifty programs on International Decade in Alabama, USA, and Lisbon, Portugal. She is the only known woman in the country who buys and markets allied products to paint and has published an eighty four colour catalogue of sundry products. She has travelled and studied in fifty four countries, including a trip on Arts Color and Design in China. Having recorded her activities on twenty seven, one hundred and fifty page journal and 163 scrapbooks. Lee McCoy toured over four hundred and fifty homes in the United States speaking to people. In Mobile alone, she has initiated and co-chaired the British Faire in 1983, a one hundred and twenty event fair including the Magna Carta, which appeared on British television and also, on the same event, wrote a five page story for the British Heritage Magazine. She also initiated and produced the Banner Program on Mobile Streets, had a full scale replica of the CSS Hunley, the first submarine to sink a ship in wartime, built for display in the city museum, initiated a British park in Mobile and was the author of the book "Mobile, The Story of a Beautiful City". This book covers four hundred years of history, in fifty six pages, for visitors to Mobile.

During her long and extensive career, Ms McCoy has been the recipient of several awards and honours. She was awarded the Highest International Award for serving Quota Objectives from Australia, in 1980, the Lotus Award, from Spain, Birmingham, in 1981, the GPWC State Award in 1981-82, winner of the Gayfer Outstanding Career Woman Award for 1988, and the J C Penny Golden Rule Award in 1991. Lee McCoy was the Honoree at the reception of Senators and Representatives, and Honoured Guest at a luncheon by Honorable Jeanne Kirkpatrick, United Nations Mission, New York. She was also filmed for the Outstanding Mobile Women Series for TV WKRG.

Having worked full time for Mobile Paint Company, since the 1960's, Lee McCoy plans to retire in the near future from the company and spend her time lecturing on what she calls "Little Knowns". These are people such as Clara Barton, not only the President and Founder of the American Red Cross, but the person who changed the organization from a wartime relief agency to a disaster relief organization worldwide. She also presents "Spark Your Life" seminars through her company Lee McCoy Communications which was founded in 1998. On these people, Lee McCoy is currently writing a book, titled "Distinguished Southern Women", which is guaranteed to become a world wide best seller.

*A biography of Lee McCoy, DDG, MOIF, appears in the main section of this Edition.*

## JOHN ALLEN MEHAFFEY

*For your Outstanding Contribution
to Communications*

# JOHN ALLEN MEHAFFEY

John Allen Mehaffey, generally known as Jack, has been involved with the print media during his entire career, his various responsibilities including those of owner, editor and publisher of daily and weekly newspapers. At the same time, he has drawn on his extensive experience for the provision of consultancy services in sales, marketing and management. He is currently President of the company Mehaffey International, which has its base in Naples, Florida.

Jack Mehaffey was born on 18 October 1936 in Brainerd, Minnesota, USA. Already at school he showed interest in a business career and in 1954 he graduated from Minnesota School of Business. He is married to Mary Jean, with whom he has three sons, Mark A, Scott D and Chris D, all now adults.

Over the years Mr Mehaffey has been the recipient of a number of national awards for his achievements in the areas of news, editorial work and advertising. Besides being listed in the Marquis Who's Who in America, Who's Who in the Midwest, Who's Who in the World, Who's Who in Advertising, Who's Who in Finance and Industry and Who's Who in the Media and Communications, during the American Bicentennial in 1976 he was selected by The American Heritage Research for inclusion in the Library of Human Resources with the following citation: "In recognition of professional and civic attainments within the community of America, recognised by the citizenry of the Nation accorded to outstanding contributors to the growth and development of the American Republic". Moreover, he enjoyed the distinction of being a participant in the Re-Declaration of Independence at the Bicentennial Ceremonies held at the Liberty Bell in Philadelphia during Freedom Week.

In connection with his career Mr Mehaffey has been involved with numerous individual and company memberships. Apart from the Society of Professional Journalists Sigma Delta Chi, they include associations such as the Direct Marketing Association, the Marketing Association, the American Telemarketing Association and Florida's Southwest Direct Marketing Association. Among those directly connected with the press are the Association of Free Community Papers, the Central States Circulation Managers Association, Florida Press Association, Florida Advertising Publishers Association, Illinois Press Association, the International Press Club, Chicago, Deadline Club, Naples Press Club, Independent Free Press Papers of America, the National Press Club, the Newspaper Association of America, the National Newspaper Association, the Southeastern Advertising Publishers Association and the Suburban Newspaper Association. He has also gained admission to the American Entrepreneurs Association, the International Platform Association and Naples Area Chamber of Commerce.

John Mehaffey has for a long time been involved in numerous projects to help the disadvantaged. He and his family are benefactors of Right Friends who work to help vulnerable mentally handicapped adults and he attends many fundraising events. He is a member of numerous community and charity organizations.

*A biography of John Allen Mehaffey appears in the main section of this Edition.*

## DR YOSHITSUGU MIKI, MD, DDG, LFIBA

*For your Outstanding Contribution
to Cancer Research*

# DR YOSHITSUGU MIKI, MD, DDG, LFIBA

Yoshitsugu Miki was born on New Year's Day in 1954, in Neyagawa, Osaka, Japan. He is an Oncologist and achieved his Doctor of Medicine Degree at Osaka University in 1984. Whilst studying, he became aware that intravenously injecting cancer patients with the mumps virus could sometimes cause immediate regression of the cancer lesions. He was subsequently awarded the Kusumoto Prize and graduated in 1978. In 1980 Dr Miki became a graduate student in the Third Department of Internal Medicine, again at Osaka University, where he had the opportunity to work with Dr Tadamitsu Kishimoto. Since 1985 He has been President of his own clinic, the Miki Clinic, based in Neyagawa, and has continued his research on the effects of the mumps virus. He made the discovery that the mumps virus might reduce apoptosis in renal cancer cells.

Dr Miki has several publications which reflect his important findings, including an examination of scavenger receptors in renal cell cancer and an investigation into the effect of a high fat diet in the induction of various cancers. Further analysis of this has demonstrated that apoptosis was induced in the cancer cells at the early stage of carcinogenesis and Dr Miki subsequently published his findings in Cancer Research Volume 57, being the first to describe the ways in which tumour buds actively develop and resolve during the early phase of carcinogenesis.

Dr Miki is a member of the Japanese Cancer Association and is one of the Charles Darwin Associates of the New York Academy of Sciences. He lists his accomplishments of which he is most proud as discoveries in the fields of Carcinogenesis and apoptosis of cancer cells.

Dr Miki has been listed in editions of Who's Who in the World and other biographical dictionaries. He is a Life Fellow of the International Biographical Association. Yoshitsugu Miki is married to Machiko Tsuchiya.

*A biography of Dr Yoshitsugu Miki, MD, DDG, LFIBA, appears in the main section of this edition.*

## KENNETH ANDREW MINTZ

*For your Outstanding Contribution to
Librarianship and Literature*

# KENNETH ANDREW MINTZ

A Professional Librarian who is currently Head of Technical Services and Newsletter Editor at Hoboken Public Library, Hoboken, New Jersey, USA, Kenneth Andrew Mintz also enjoys an ever-growing reputation as a creative writer. His output includes poetry, essays and plays, but his greatest love is for writing fiction.

Kenneth Mintz was born on 15 March 1951 in Plattsburgh, New York. Already as a young child he loved to listen to stories and by the time he reached the age of ten he had begun to read classical authors such as Dickens and Hermann Melville. As a student at the University of Redlands, Redlands, California, he obtained a Bachelor of Arts degree in Creative Writing in 1973. Later, he pursued studies in Library Science at Southern Connecticut State University, New Haven, gaining a Master's degree in 1978.

In 1979 Mr Mintz served as assistant editor of the newsletter of the First Unitarian-Universalist Society of New Haven. At the same time, one of his early publications appeared, in the form of a booklet entitled "How the Library Can Help You". In 1980, after a short period as a temporary cataloguer at the public library in Medford, Massachusetts, he moved to Bayonne, New Jersey, to become a librarian at the public library there. That year saw the publication of his first novel, "The Holy Ghost". It was also around that time that he began in earnest to write poetry, which appeared in such publications as Connecticut River Review and Jersey City News. Similarly, his short stories were included in Entertain, Nightly Sounds, and New Voices. In the course of the decade, he saw three of his plays staged at the Greenhouse Theater in New York City, the Bayonne Playhouse and the Community Church of New York, while a fourth was produced by The Attic Ensemble of Jersey City, New Jersey.

Kenneth Mintz remained at Bayonne Public Library for eight years, during which he also edited the newsletter for the Unitarian Society of Rutherford, New Jersey, from 1984-85. After leaving Bayonne, he became a cataloguer at Hoboken Public Library from 1991 until taking on his present responsibilities there in 1999. Other activities from the late 1980s onwards included reviewing books for the Library Journal, New York City from 1988-93. Moreover, he started work on a trilogy of novels, as well as a collection of short stories. Ever versatile, having already been an actor in local theatre, since 1993 he has directed a drama group at the Community Church of New York.

During the last ten years numerous awards and honours have been bestowed upon Mr Mintz. Twice selected for the Editors' Choice Award of the National Library of Poetry, in 1989 and 1996, he received the Quill Poetry Award from Quill Books in 1991. At Hudson County Writing Festival he won the Essay Prize in 1994 and the Christmas Story Prize in 1997. From Bayonne Writers he received the Legion of Honor Award in 1989, the Special Legion Award in 1996 and the Group Founder's Competition Award in 1997, besides winning the Group Short Story Reading Competition in 1998. The same organisation named him Poet of the Year 1994 and Writer of the Year 1995. From the New Jersey Superbowl of Writing he received five awards, two for essay and one each for story, playwriting and short story. Other very recent awards include two from the New Jersey Olympics of Writing, for essay and playwriting respectively, as well as two Garden State Writing Challenge Awards, one for essay and one for poetry.

A member of the Bayonne Writers' Group, Mr Mintz held office as its Vice-President in 1986. He has been admitted to several other organisations including the American Library Association, New Jersey Library Association, Friends of the New York Public Library, the Poetry Society of America, the Academy of American Poets, The Modern Poetry Association and New York Academy of Sciences.

*A biography of Kenneth Andrew Mintz appears in the main section of this Edition.*

## EVA MAE NASH-ISAAC, PhD

*For your Outstanding Contribution
to Education*

# EVA MAE NASH-ISAAC, PhD

On 24 July 1936, in the parish of Natchitoches, Louisiana, USA, Eva M Nash-Isaac was born. The daughter of Earfus W Nash (deceased) and Dollie Mae Edward, she had an idyllic childhood, growing up in the beautiful countryside surrounding Louisiana.

Eva attended the John Adams Adult High School, in San Francisco, California. She graduated from there and went on to gain the degrees of BA, in Social Science, MS in Counselling, and MS in Education, from San Francisco State University in 1974 and 1985 respectively. She gained her PhD from Walden University, Minneapolis in 1995. Besides her degrees, she holds the credentials of Standard Teaching, Preschool, for grades kindergarten to twelve and adult classes, College Student Personnel Work, College Instructor in Psychology, and College Counsellor.

Dr Nash-Isaac began her professional career as a Nurse and Nurse's Aid in hospitals and nursing homes in San Francisco and Monterey, California. She then gained her degrees in education and took up the appointment of Regular Elementary School Teacher at Oakland Public Schools in California, USA, where she still teaches today. She taught kindergarten to sixth graders and also counselled the educationally disadvantaged and at-risk students. She also served on the Faculty Advisory Committee and on the School Advisory Committee. Concurrently, Dr Nash-Isaac has also held the appointments of Pupil Personnel Service Counsellor, for grades K-6, at the Garfield School, Oakland, California, between 1976-77 and at the Roosevelt Junior High School, Oakland, California, for grades seven to nine, for the year 1977-78. Besides being a teacher, Dr Nash-Isaac is an author, a lecturer at churches and schools on AIDS prevention and education and vocational skills and training, instructor, public speaker, practical nurse and a workshop presenter at the California Association for Counseling and Development, Los Angeles, her topic being Maximizing the Self Potential: A K-6 Academic Awareness Procedure. She is known in the education world as a pillar of society, who is willing to help anyone who needs it.

During her long and professional career, Dr Nash-Isaac had been the recipient of the Superteacher Award, from Oakland Unified School District in 1985-86, the Community Service Award, from California Association for Counselling and Development, in 1988, Phi Delta Kappa Five-Year Award in 1989 and 1990, a Honorary Diploma from St Labre Indian School, Ashland, Montana in 1991, a Certificate of Recognition for Beyond the Call of Duty, from the Board of Education, Oakland, California in 1990, and is listed in the biography of Who's Who in the World, published in 1991-92, Who's Who in America, Who's Who of American Women and Who's Who in American Education.

Eva Nash-Isaac is the Editorial Consultant of "Speech-Writer's Newsletter" at Ragan Communications, Inc. She is also a member of the California Association for Counselling and Development, Black Caucus, Phi Delta Kappa, the National Association for Female Executives, the National Alliance of Black Educators, the National Education Association, the International Platform Association, the Leadership Circle of the National Committee to Preserve Social Security and Medicare, the Commonwealth Club in California, and the World Affairs Council. She is commited to educating students to attain their maximum potential and maintaining the trust, enthusiasm and cooperation of all her students, families and associates, of which she is greatly effective and thanked.

*A biography of Eva Mae Nash-Isaac, PhD, appears in the main section of this Edition.*

## PROFESSOR ALEXANDER ILYICH NESTEROV, FIBA

*For your Outstanding Contribution to Science*

# PROFESSOR ALEXANDER ILYICH NESTEROV, FIBA

Professor Alexander I Nesterov, who was born on 22 June 1950 in Krasnogorsk, Russia, is devoted to research in the field of physics. He is currently carrying out his scientific work at Guadalajara University, Mexico, where he assumed the position of Professor and Researcher in 1994. Besides obtaining the degrees of PhD and Doctor of Science in Russia in 1976 and 1989 respectively, he qualified as a full Professor in 1991. He holds membership of the Mexican Academy of Science, the Russian Gravitational Society, the American Physical Society, the American Mathematical Society and the Mexican Physical Society.

Prior to taking up his post in Mexico, Dr Nesterov had spent many years at Krasnoyarsk University, where he became an Assistant Professor in 1977, rose to Senior Lecturer in 1980 and served as Associate Professor from 1984-86. A two-year break followed, after which he resumed his associate professorship in 1988, as well as being appointed as Senior Researcher. He held both positions until receiving promotion to full Professor in 1990. A Visiting Professor at Guadalajara University from 1993-94, he then assumed his current position there, although he still continued with his professorship at Krasnoyarsk University until resigning in 1997.

The co-author of "Dynamics of fields in general relativity", which appeared in 1985, Professor Nesterov has also had some sixty papers published in scientific journals. Besides receiving Honourable Mentions from the Gravity Research Foundation on three separate occasions, in 1993 he was the recipient of a grant from the International Science Foundation. He is listed in the 16th and 17th editions of Marquis Who's Who in the World and the 5th edition of Who's Who in Science and Engineering.

Professor Alexander Nesterov is married to the former Elena Dmitrievna. They have two sons, Sergey and Ilya.

*A biography of Professor Alexander Ilyich Nesterov, FIBA, appears in the main section of this Edition.*

# DR EUNICE NORTON

*For your Outstanding Contribution to*
*Uncompromising High Quality Classical Music*

# DR EUNICE NORTON

Dr Eunice Norton, who was born on 30 June 1908 in Minneapolis, Minnesota, USA, has dedicated many years of her life to classical music. A pianist of exceptionally high quality, she has performed widely in the USA and Europe, but has also contributed her expertise as a university professor and lecturer. In recognition of her accomplishments, she was recently honoured by receiving an Honorary Doctorate in Music, conferred by Wooster College in 1997.

A music student at the University of Minnesota from 1922-24, Eunice Norton then travelled to England, to study at the Tobias Matthay Pianoforte School in London for seven years. By that time she had already embarked on her professional career as a concert pianist, starting in 1927, the same year that she won the Bach Prize in a competition. The following year she distinguished herself by receiving the Chappell Gold Medal from the Chappell Piano Company. After leaving London in 1931, she had the opportunity to develop her technique further, through master classes with Artur Schnabel, at first in Germany and latterly in Italy.

Dr Norton has appeared as a soloist with leading orchestras, among them the London Symphony Orchestra, Queens Hall Orchestra, the BBC Orchestra, Berlin Symphony Orchestra, New York Philharmonic, Boston Symphony and Philadelphia Symphony, in addition to orchestras in Birmingham, Manchester, Leipzig, Vienna and many other US symphonies. She has held recitals at the Wigmore Hall and Queens Hall, London, and at numerous European and US venues. As a chamber musician, she has played in Budapest, as well as with the Juilliard and Griller String Quartets and the American Chamber Orchestra. Highlights of her career include a performance at the White House in Washington DC. She celebrated Beethoven Year with performances of the composer's 32 Piano Sonatas, while for the J S Bach Tricentennial she performed the 48 Preludes and Fugues.

Apart from her concert activity, Dr Norton has contributed to the world of music by giving master classes at various American universities. A Lecturer at the Carnegie Mellon University and the University of Pittsburgh, she has also been a Visiting Professor of Piano at the former institution. Drawing on her music studies in England during the 1920s and Germany in the early 1930s, she recorded a series of four lectures on the teaching of Tobias Matthey, and a similar series on the teaching of Arthur Schnabel. Besides being known as the Founder and Music Director of Pittsburgh New Fields of Music, Pittsburgh Concert Artists and Peacham (Vermont) Piano Festivals, she has served as President of Norvald Records Inc, a company engaged in producing classic CDs.

*A biography of Dr Eunice Norton appears in the main section of this Edition.*

## **PROFESSOR MASAHIRO OKA, DDG, FIBA**

*For your Outstanding Contribution
to Philosophy and Ethics*

# PROFESSOR MASAHIRO OKA, DDG, FIBA

Professor Masahiro Oka has dedicated his career to teaching college and university students, while also finding time to publish numerous books and articles. He holds a Master of Arts degree in Philosophy, obtained in 1948 after successfully completing a postgraduate course at Kyoto Imperial University, Japan.

For much of the 1950s Professor Oka was a member of the academic staff at Shudo Junior College, where he started as an Assistant in 1953. He soon rose to Lecturer and subsequently became an Assistant Professor, but in 1960 he transferred to Hiroshima Commercial College, at first with a similar status as at the Junior College, then later attaining full professorship. In 1973 he moved again, appointed full Professor at Hiroshima Shudo University. That year he also took sabbatical leave to travel to England for a year of study and training at the University of London, under Professor Coplestone, whose work he greatly admired. Since returning to Hiroshima Shudo University, he has continued with his duties there, adding responsibility for a postgraduate course from 1978 onwards.

Two of Professor Oka's earlier publications consist of a translation into Japanese of Copleston's "Contemporary Phi", as well as a book in German entitled "Einladung zum Denken". Other notable volumes of his include "Contemporary Philosophy", published in 1975, "Moral Education" and "German Ethical Theory", both of which appeared in 1976, and "Business Ethics", its first edition coming out in 1985 followed by the second edition in 1993. However, the most successful of his works is "The Idea of Education"; published in 1994, its quality was such that it was rewarded with the 3rd Cosmos Publishing Prize. A still more recent publication is his "Social Philosophy", which appeared in 1996.

A member of the Japan Society for Whiteheads Philosophy, Professor Oka has served in it as Director since 1988. In addition, he belongs to the Japanese Society for Ethics, the Kansai Ethical Society, the Philosophical Society of Western Japan and the Aristotelian Society.

For recreation Professor Oka enjoys reading and painting. He was born in Hiroshima on 15 February 1924, is married to Kazuko Miyake, and has a son, Takeharu, as well as two daughters, Atsumi and Shizuyo.

*A biography of Professor Masahiro Oka, DDG, FIBA, appears in the main section of this Edition.*

## ANTONIA CAMACHO OKAWA

*For your Outstanding Contribution
to Elementary Education*

# ANTONIA CAMACHO OKAWA

The daughter of Rafael Diaz Camacho and Tomasa Aguon Camacho, Antonia Camacho Okawa was born on 13 March 1949. She is now married to Ryo Okawa from Aomori, Japan, has three children, Chamie, Lanelle and Ray, teaches at an elementary school, and owns a business, namely, Okawa's Electrical Services.

On 7 June 1968 Mrs Okawa graduated from Hopwood Junior-Senior High School with the usual High School Diploma. The following day she started work in the public school system, teaching the 4th grade at Chalan Kanoa Elementary School. A year later she transferred her efforts to special education, continuing at Chalan Kanoa as a teacher of the deaf until 1975. After an eight-year break for family reasons, in July 1983 she became a Speech Language Clinician at the Commonwealth Health Center, providing her services as such for some eighteen months. Returning to the classroom in September 1985, she taught 1st grade at the William S Reyes School for five years, but in August 1990 moved to the William S Reyes Elementary School where she has been a kindergarten teacher ever since. Her work includes dealing with multilingual groups.

Parallel with her employment, Mrs Okawa has continued with her own education and professional development. In 1986 she earned an Associate of Arts degree in Elementary Education, awarded by the Northern Marianas College, while in 1991 she received a Bachelor of Arts degree in Elementary Education from the University of Guam. Moreover, she has attended numerous workshops on various educational themes such as classroom management, use of teaching aids, second language teaching, mathematics and science teaching, and parent-teacher relations. Most of the workshops were held on Saipan, but for a few she travelled to mainland USA, Hawaii and, recently, to Guam.

In recognition of her professional excellence and dedication, Mrs Okawa has been the recipient of several distinctions. Not only was she the 1991-92 Presidential Awardee for Excellence in Science and Mathematics Teaching, but also became a member of the William S Reyes Mathematics Task Force for the same period, and was selected as William S Reyes School Teacher of the Year. She had the honour of serving on the Accreditation Steering Committee and the Chamorro Bilingual Task Force from 1996-98, besides chairing the Parent Community Self Study Report Accreditation from 1997-98, and officiating as Treasurer of the William S Reyes Parent-Teacher Association from 1997-98. In addition to being named 1998 Teacher of the Year at the William S Reyes School, she was chosen to serve for the 1998-99 period both on the Planning Committee and on the Language Arts Task Force for standards and Benchmark. She is listed in the most recent issue of Who's Who in America.

*A biography of Antonia Camacho Okawa appears in the main section of this Edition.*

## DR HENRY OSTROWSKI-MEISSNER, PhD

*For your Outstanding Contribution to Nutritional Science and Herbal Therapeutic Extracts*

# DR HENRY OSTROWSKI-MEISSNER, PhD

A scientist whose research interests lie in the fields of biochemistry, nutrition, herbal and natural therapeutics and the environment, Dr Henry Ostrowski-Meissner has spent the greater part of his working life in Australasia, although he originates from Poland, where he was born in Grochowce on 18 April 1940. Now settled in New South Wales, Australia, he is presently the Executive Director of Research and Development at the Sydney-based firm of TTD International Pty Ltd, and is the author of 279 research and technical publications.

Dr Ostrowski-Meissner began his career in 1963, joining the Nutritional Biochemistry Laboratory, Department of Nutrition, IZ, in Balice, Cracow, where he remained for several years. Dr Ostrowski-Meissner holds three degrees from the College of Agriculture at the University of Cracow, Poland, obtaining a Bachelor of Science Degree in Agricultural Sciences in 1991, a Master of Science in Environmental Sciences in 1993 and a PhD in Nutritional Biochemistry in 1998. In 1967 he has completed a Diploma in Chemistry of Radioisotopes. In 1970 he moved to Lublin, to an appointment as Department Head for the Central Laboratory of the Feed Industry. In 1972 he completed a Diploma in Computer Techniques, specialising in commercial applications of linear programming techniques. On accepting an invitation from New Zealand's Research Advisory Council in 1973 and set off for the other side of the world, where for the next few years he led an extraction project at the Ruakura Research Centre in Hamilton. After the project was completed in 1976, he spent one year on researching herbal extraction techniques in Poland and the UK and in 1977 he made his way to Australia, becoming a Lecturer in Nutrition Biochemistry and Environmental Physics at the University of Sydney from 1978-79. He then spent three years in Indonesia, as Programme Leader at the Centre for Research and Development, returning to Australia at the beginning of 1983 to become as Director of AFIC-CSIRO. In 1993 he took up an appointment to his present position with TTD International Pty Ltd.

In 1996 the Chinese Academy of Sciences awarded him the title of Honorary Professor and Researcher. A Life Member of the SGVR, he was elected its President from 1991-96, while as an Executive Committee Member of the INFIC he has served as its Coordinator for Asia and the Pacific Region since 1984. In 1999 he was instrumental in establishing a Therapeutics Research Fund in Australia as an extension of the Charles Stuart Foundation with location at the Faculty of Health Studies and has accepted a position of the Chairman of the Fund, along with the title Honorary Researcher.

Dr Ostrowski-Meissner and his wife Teresa have a son, Witold, and three daughters, Misia, Henia and Rysia.

*A biography of Dr Henry Ostrowski-Meissner, PhD, appears in the main section of this Edition.*

## DR CLARENCE HENRY OTT, PhD, CPA, CMA

*For your Outstanding Contribution to
World Peace as a Citizen Ambassador*

# DR CLARENCE HENRY OTT, PhD, CPA, CMA

A Certified Public Accountant and a Certified Management Accountant (CEO) who originally contributed his expertise to various companies and the US Government, namely, Chief Accountant for G E X-Ray Corporation, Chicago, 1940-41; Public Auditor for Arthur Andersen & Co, Chicago, from 1941-43, Renegotiator of the US Army Air Corps with contracts in Chicago, 1943-45, Internal Auditor for David Bradley Manufacturing, (Sears), Bradley, Illinois, 1945-48, Controller-Treasurer for Manco Manufacturing Co, Bradley, 1948-59, and Owner and Operator of the Yellow Checker Cab Co, Kankakee, Illinois, from 1959-70. In 1970 he began a career in teaching, which has lasted up to the present. For most of that time he has held a professorial position at Southwestern Michigan College, appointed to the full-time faculty in 1973, and has now been an Adjunct Professor there since 1988. He also provides his services as a Curriculum Advisor. In 1994 he made a most generous donation to the College's endowment fund, allowing the establishment of The C H Ott Accounting Scholarship. In addition to his college commitments, since 1992 he has been deeply involved as a Citizen Ambassador with People to People International, in which capacity he has visited the UK, Australia and New Zealand, as well as countries in Europe, Africa and the Middle and Far East. His most recent mission was to Iran and Bahrain in May 1999.

Of European descent, Clarence Henry Ott was born on 20 January 1918 in Richmond, Michigan, USA, as the son of Ferdinand Quiram Ott, a cattle dealer and farmer, and Wilhelmina Radtke Ott, who was a first generation US citizen, Clarence Henry Ott was born on 20 January 1918 in Richmond, Michigan, USA, where he grew up with three brothers and two sisters. His paternal grandfather was a French General who had settled in Prussia, where he passed away. In 1885 the family, which had Court status in Prussia, emigrated to America. There the mother subsequently remarried and her son, Dr Ott's father, took her new husband's surname.

Dr Ott has an outstanding academic background, winning scholastic scholarships throughout his college career. As a student at Richmond High School he was selected as Salutatorian for the graduation ceremony. While at Valparaiso University, from which he obtained a BA degree in 1940, he was named Sophomore Scholar and was elected to Pi Gamma Mu, the National Social Science Honor Society. Returning to his studies later on, he received his MBA degree from the Northwestern University in 1970 and a PhD from the Southeastern University in 1980, the same year that he was awarded a Certificate in Management Accounting, thus joining an elite group of some 1,400 persons only. For that achievement he was honoured by the Board of Trustees of the Southwestern Michigan College. When he retired from full-time teaching at the College in 1988, a special banquet was held in his honour at the local Elks Lodge.

During the present decade, Dr Ott has travelled widely on behalf of People to People International. Furthermore, with his experience in financial management and investment, he was selected by the University of Pennsylvania Wharton School of Finance to lead an 18-man delegation to Russia and Estonia in 1992, to assist in education and organisation for adaptation to a capitalist system. While in the former USSR, besides attending professional meetings and discussions, visiting facilities and participating in informal gatherings with foreign colleagues, he gave a presentation on corporate securities at St Petersburg University of Economics. In the early autumn of the following year he accompanied 53 other American professionals on a two-week visit to China for the purpose of investigating opportunities for American investment. He found that capitalistic ideas in business and ownership existed, although the country was officially under a communist regime. Moreover, there appeared to be a wide range of diverse opportunities for investors.

Dr Ott has frequently engaged in public speaking. Besides being a member of the Speakers' Bureau at Rochester Institute of Technology while teaching there from 1970-73, he was also on the Speakers' Bureau at the Southwestern Michigan College between 1974 and 1988. A notable appearance for the latter was as a featured faculty speaker at the retirement dinner held for Dr Russell "M" Owen, President of the College. He broadcast on the local radio station, his talks on federal and local taxes being followed by question and answer sessions via telephone. Nowadays, he confines himself to speaking about his many and varied travel experiences.

Dr Ott has four children, who have all embarked on successful careers, James Richard Ott being a Doctor of Dental Surgery, Dennis McKay Ott an investment banker, Richard Darrel Ott a stockbroker, and Delene Michelle Illum a computer specialist. Sadly his wife, the former Helen Louis McKay, passed away in 1993, in the 51st year of their marriage.

*A biography of Dr Clarence Henry Ott, PhD, CPA, CMA, appears in the main section of this Edition.*

## EUGENE THOMAS OUZTS, LFIBA

*For your Outstanding Contribution
to Education*

# EUGENE THOMAS OUZTS, LFIBA

Teaching, preaching and flying have been all-important features in the career of Eugene Thomas Ouzts, who was born on 7 June 1930 at Thomasville, Georgia, USA, to parents Captain John Travis Ouzts and Livie Mae (Strickland) Ouzts. Now retired, he resides in Arizona, in an isolated area some seventeen miles north of Duncan.

From 1948-53 Eugene Ouzts served with the US Navy, but after his discharge he attended Harding University, in Searcy, Arkansas, as a ministerial student, majoring in Bible, Greek and Hebrew. In 1956 he was not only ordained a minister of the Church of Christ, but also graduated from Harding with a Bachelor of Arts degree on 31 May, the same day that he married Mary Olive Vineyard. While she taught in Augusta, he continued at Harding for a Master of Arts degree in Bible, awarded in May 1957.

Moving to Texas in August 1957, Mr Ouzts preached at Twitty and his wife taught at Shamrock. The next year he preached at Ropesville, Texas, but in 1959 he decided to join his wife in teaching, so he took education courses at the University of Arkansas. They both taught in DeValls Bluff, Arkansas, that year, and for the next five years in Caruthersville, Missouri. Eugene Ouzts also pursued postgraduate study at Murray State University, Kentucky, the University of Arkansas, the University of Arizona, Arizona State University and Northern Arizona University.

In August 1965 the Ouzts moved to Greenlee County, Arizona, where they still live. With his major emphasis on Secondary Science, Eugene Ouzts taught in Clifton from 1965 until retiring in 1992. He also gave night classes in Biology and World Religions for Eastern Arizona College. Concurrently with teaching, he preached at Morenci Church for most of the years from 1965-85, and has continued periodically since then for Morenci, Clifton and Safford. In the meantime, Mary Ouzts taught in Duncan, Morenci and Clifton, but gave it up the same year as her husband.

After training as private pilots in 1967, both Ouzts obtained their licences that year, then in 1969 bought their own Cessna 172. Later, they trained for instrument flying ratings and commercial certificates. They joined the Civil Air Patrol/United States Air Force Auxiliary in 1972 to fly. From 1st Lieutenant in 1980 Eugene Ouzts advanced through the ranks to Lieutenant-Colonel in 1989. By 1982 the unit commander had persuaded him to become the unit chaplain, while besides serving in this way as local chaplain, since 1985 he has served as Assistant Wing, or State, Chaplain as well. In addition to receiving the Meritorious Service Award in 1994, the Exceptional Service Award in 1997, he was named Arizona Wing Chaplain of the Year in 1984, the Thomas C Casaday Unit Chaplain of the Year 1985, Arizona Wing Safety Officer of the Year 1989, Arizona Wing Senior Member of the Year 1994, and Southwest Region Senior Member of the Year 1995.

For most of his years of teaching at Clifton High School from 1965-92, Mr Ouzts served as student activities adviser. He is a life member of the Military Chaplains Association, the Disabled American Veterans, the American Legion and the Air Force Association, as well as a member of Elks. Moreover, he has sat on the Board of Directors of Arizona Church of Christ Bible Camp, Tucson, since 1966, and is a member of the Airport Advisory Board, Clifton, Arizona. His avocations consist of flying, building and flying model aircraft, reading and gardening.

*A biography of Eugene Thomas Ouzts, LFIBA, appears in the main section of this Edition.*

## DR K N T LAKMAL PEIRIS, MD, LFIBA

*For your Outstanding Contribution
to Humanity*

# DR K N T LAKMAL PEIRIS, MD, LFIBA

Dr K N T Lakmal Peiris enjoys a dual career, divided between the fields of medicine and music. Not only does he serve as medical director of a clinic and member of a team of cardiac surgeons, but he is also an accomplished guitarist who has given concerts as a soloist in several countries. Although he now resides in Marbella, Málaga, Spain, he was born in Colombo, Sri Lanka, on 17 December 1959. When his father died in 1969, the nine-year-old boy, as the eldest child, was left to look after the family.

Dr Lakmal Peiris originally began earning his living by teaching Botany at his old school in Sri Lanka, but his dream was to become a surgeon. However, in 1976 he won a prize for a working model that he had designed of the Sun, Earth and Moon. Part of the prize was a selection for a scholarship enabling him to study at the Superior Institute of Medical Sciences, in Villa Clara, Cuba. There, in addition to studies finally leading to his MD in which he achieved 1st Class in 1987, from 1982-85 he took courses in Biostatistics and Scientific Research Methodology.

Arriving in Malaga in 1988, Dr Peiris spent a year as a Medical Officer at the European Medical Centre, but in 1989 was appointed to his present post of Medical Director at the Guadalmina Clinic in San Pedro. Since 1994 he has also been a member of the cardiac surgery team led by Dr A Iriarte. To date he is the author of some eighteen scientific papers, among which are "Surgical Treatment in Miastenia Gravis" in 1987, "Study of Reduced Glutation in Adults, New Borns and Diabetic Patients", for which he won the 1983 Provincial Prize in Biochemistry and Immunology, and "Emergency Surgical Treatment in Upper Digestive Bleeding", rewarded with the 1986 Provincial Prize in General Surgery. However, most notable is "The Value of the Isoenzymatic Pattern of the Lactic Dehydrogenase in the Diagnosis of Acute Myocardial Infarction", which won both the Provincial and the National Prizes for Cardiology in 1986.

It was while he was in his third year of medical studies that Dr Peiris began studying composition, orchestration and classical guitar, to which he was introduced by another medical student, Luis Meneses Columbié. Since then he has worked with masters such as Leo Brouwer, José Luis Martínez, David Russell, Luis Quiñones, Flores Chaviano and Hugo Geller. He performed as a guitar soloist at several music festivals in Cuba, formed a duo with Dr Meneses, and led a guitar group at the Institute of Medical Sciences. His first solo concert took place at the Provincial Museum in Villa Clara on 10 June 1987.

Since leaving Cuba, Dr Peiris has held concerts in Spain, England, Sweden, Germany, Portugal and Sri Lanka. He was both soloist and producer for "Vivencias", a CD recording made in 1995, the same year that he distinguished himself by becoming the first practising physician to record Agustín Barrios Mangoré's highly technical "Concerto Tremolo". Moreover, in 1998 he was responsible as producer for Nancy Casanova Dacosta's recording of Chopin. On 29 January 1999 he gave a classical guitar recital at the Illustrious Official Medical Council of the Province of Málaga, the first practising doctor ever to do so. Included in the programme was the world première of the solo guitar version of "Master, Sir", by the Sri Lankan composer Nimal Mendis and arranged by José Luis Martínez.

A nature lover, Dr Peiris keeps up his botanical interest through his fine collection of tropical orchids. His other main recreational interests consist of woodwork and foreign languages.

*A biography of Dr K N T Lakmal Peiris, MD, LFIBA, appears in the main section of this Edition.*

# DR JOSÉ ULYSSES PEIXOTO NETO, MD

*For your Outstanding Contribution*
*to Medicine*

# DR JOSÉ ULYSSES PEIXOTO NETO, MD

A medical practitioner deeply committed to his profession, Dr José Ulysses Peixoto Neto is well-known for his valuable contributions to the community. Apart from carrying out the regular demands of his career, in the late 1950s he was instrumental in founding the social security system of Crato, a city in the Brazilian province of Ceara. Some nine years later he became the founder of a local hospital, then in 1978 turned his efforts to establishing the Crato School of Law. In recognition of his achievements, he received an Award for Good Services from the Lions Club of Crato in 1993.

Born on 29 August 1930 in Crato, Dr Peixoto Neto has lived there for nearly all his life. However, as a young man he left to study at the Medical School of Pernambuco, where he earned his MD degree in 1955, after which he returned to his birthplace to set up in practice. He married the former Maria Isolda Cartaxo, with whom he had two sons and a daughter.

Over the years Dr Peixoto Neto has been the author of various writings, most notably a publication that appeared in 1976 under the title of "Himathantus Articulata in Medicine". Admitted to the American College of Physicians, the New York Academy of Sciences and the American Association for the Advancement of Science, he also belongs to the Brazilian Medical Association and the Brazilian Medical Clinic Society.

*A biography of Dr José Ulysses Peixoto Neto, MD, appears in the main section of this Edition.*

## DR WLADYSLAW RADZIKOWSKI

*For your Outstanding Contribution
to Education*

# DR WLADYSLAW RADZIKOWSKI

Dr Wladyslaw Radzikowski, a Polish econometrist and professor, began his working life some 56 years ago and plans to continue for many more. For most of that time he has been engaged in research on mathematical methods as applied to industry, especially with regard to management. He holds a Bachelor of Economics degree from the University of Lodz in 1953, as well as a Master of Industrial Economics degree and PhD in Mathematical Programming, from the Main School of Planning and Statistics in Warsaw in 1955 and 1964 respectively, while his Habilitation in Econometrics was awarded by the Economic Academy in Wroclaw in 1969.

In 1943, when only fourteen years old, Wladyslaw Radzikowski was obliged to become a metalworker. Employed as such by various firms during the war, after hostilities ceased he was able to return to his education. He also worked in enterprises and organisations in Lodz and then in Warsaw, becoming a clerk in 1947 and Head of Planning in 1949.

Remaining in Warsaw, in 1955 Dr Radzikowski was appointed Head of the Research and Development Department for Mathematical Methods at the Institute of Organisation in the Machine-Building Industry, but in 1964 transferred to a similar position at the Institute of Electrical Engineering. Two years later he joined the Institute of Industrial Economics and Organisation, where, as Deputy Director of Research, he was in charge of developing and implementing mathematical methods in machine building, metallurgy, fibre and other industries. Returning to the Institute of Organisation in the Machine-Building Industry in 1968, he was appointed Head Director. As such, his duties included designing and implementing of industrial corporations. His next post, at the Research and Development Centre of Informatics from 1971-74, was as Deputy Director of Research in charge of developing and implementing modular simulation models in management information systems. He is now Head of the Chair of Quantitative Management Techniques at the University of Warsaw School of Management and Professor at Nicolai-Copernicus University, Torun, appointed the former in 1974 and the latter in 1990.

Dr Radzikowski has travelled abroad on several occasions. During the mid-1960s he spent an academic year in Switzerland, pursuing postdoctoral studies at the Institute of Operations Research and Electronic Data Processing, University of Zurich. As a visiting professor he appeared three times at Fordham University Graduate School of Business Administration, New York City, during the second half of the 1970s. During the first half of the following decade he visited the Fachhochschule für Wirtschaft in West Berlin, as well as the University of Detroit, USA, while in the early 1990s he appeared at the Universities of Milan and Amsterdam.

Dr Radzikowski is currently project leader for two governmental research tasks, one on methods and models bases for management, the other on methods bases for controlling. A prolific author whose writing constitutes an integral part of his career, he has already published more than twenty books, in addition to some 280 other publications. Representative titles include "Mathematical and statistical methods in an enterprise", "Linear and nonlinear programming", "Project management", "Informatics in the national economy", "Informatics systems in organization and management", "Operations research in organization and management", "Optimization methods for logistics", and his latest work, "Controlling". In the last few years he has presented the following papers at international conferences: "Input-Out Methods in Transitional Economics", at PRIISM '96, Maui-Hawaii, 1996; "Mathematical Methods and Models Bases for Executives", at NSDI, St Croix, US Virgin Islands, 1996; "Quantitative Methods Bases (QMBs) for Management in the Perspective", at ICOQM, Jaipur, India, 1997; "A Time Series Approach to Generalization of Some Investment Evaluation Methods", at IDSI, Sydney, Australia, 1997; "Market Orientation of the Polish Car Producers", delivered at the High Technology Conference in Hebei, China, 1998.

Recognition and distinctions have come Dr Radzikowski's way. Apart from receiving five awards from the Ministry of Higher Education between 1968 and 1998, he was decorated with the Silver Cross of Merit in 1964, the Gold Cross of Merit in 1969. The Polonia Restituta Cross V Class was bestowed upon him in 1977; the Cross IV Class followed in 1985. He sits on the Presidium of the Committee for Organization and Management of the Polish Academy of Sciences, is President and former Vice-President of the Polish Economic Society, Warsaw Branch, and Vice-President of the Polish Branch of the Institute for Operations Research and Management Science, USA. He belongs to the Scientific Society for Organization and Management, which he formerly served as Vice-President and Chairman of its Main Scientific Board. Moreover, since early this decade he has held membership of the Verband der Hochschullehrer für Betriebswirtschaft, the International Input-Output Association and German Operations Research.

Wladyslaw Radzikowski has one main hobby, stamp-collecting. Born on 5 February 1929 in Lodz, Poland, he married Danuta Eleonora Kielkiewicz in 1947. His elder son, Pawel, earned a PhD in Econometrics and has now been working in New York City for some eighteen years, while the other son, Maciej, is an electronics engineer in Warsaw.

*A biography of Dr Wladyslaw Radzikowski appears in the main section of this Edition.*

# DR MUHAMMAD ABDUR RAHMAN, PhD

*For your Outstanding Contribution
as a Scientist in Aerospace Sciences*

# DR MUHAMMAD ABDUR RAHMAN, PhD

The son of Haji Sajjad Ali Khan and Momotaj Khanom, Muhammad Abdur Rahman was born on 1 March 1930 in Sylhet, Assam, India. At the age of twenty he left India for the USA, where he pursued studies at university and subsequently held positions in mechanical design engineering, as well as in aerospace engineering and in safety engineering. He is now engaged in scientific research for the purpose of invention. In addition to earning Bachelor and Master of Science degrees in Mechanical Engineering, both from the University of Toledo in 1953 and 1968 respectively, he holds a PhD in Engineering awarded by the California Coast University in 1985. He also qualified as a Registered Professional Engineer in the State of California.

After obtaining his first degree Dr Rahman worked in mechanical design for various consulting firms during the period from 1955-61. However, in 1962 he turned his attention to aerospace engineering, joining the Douglas Aircraft Company in Santa Monica, California. Continuing in that field, the following year he moved to North American Aviation Inc, in Los Angeles, but it was in 1964 that he had his greatest opportunity, when he became an aerospace engineer at the NASA Manned Spacecraft Center at the Gemini and Apollo Program Offices in Houston, Texas, remaining there until 1970. It was a source of extreme pride to him to be part of such a team, contributing to the work that culminated on 20 July 1969 in the first-ever landing on the Moon. As a foreign-born scientist, he owes his deepest gratitude to God Almighty for allowing him to play a role in such an event.

A safety engineer from 1975-86 with the US Department of Labor in Washington, Dr Rahman then embarked on his scientific research in 1987. His present interest is primarily focussed on the theory of superconductivity, the hypothesis on energy-gravity waves in the universe, and biomedical instrumentations to cover a heart pump, a device to improve blood circulation and equipment for special surgery. He has successfully filed for two patents, namely, a solar energy collector and a supersonic MHD generator system. Moreover, he is the author of various articles published in professional journals.

During the last few years Dr Rahman has been listed in two editions each of the Marquis publications Who's Who in the World, Who's Who in America, and Who's Who in Science and Engineering. A modest man, he is honoured to be included among so many prestigious personages.

A biography of Dr Muhammad Abdur Rahman, PhD, appears in the main section of this Edition.

## MUBARIK AHMED RAJPOOT

*For your Outstanding Contribution to
Education, Peace and the Urdu Language*

# MUBARIK AHMED RAJPOOT

The son of the late Abdul Majeed Rajpoot and Hajrah Begum Rajpoot, Mubarik Ahmed Rajpoot was born on 11 November 1937, in Lahore, Pakistan. He began his educational studies in Pakistan, but in 1968 emigrated to Oslo in Norway and became a Norwegian citizen. He received his BSc from various schools in Oslo in 1975. While studying in Pakistan, he took up the appointment of Office Clerk in a literary English monthly magazine, "Vision in Karachi", between 1962-63. But since settling in Oslo, he has held several important positions in various employment, some of which are: Working in a steel factory, for several years; Teaching Urdu to Norwegians in an evening school, from 1973-93; and since 1973, a bilingual teacher at Skolesjefen secondary school. He is also the Editor of the Akhbar-e-Pakistan, a first Urdu weekly newspaper in Scandinavia, and a freelance journalist and photographer.

Mubarik Ahmed Rajpoot is the author of several professional publications, the one book that has been recognised internationally being titled "Learn Urdu", which was published in 1988. It is the first of its kind in the Scandinavian language, financed by the Ministry of Education, Research and Church Affairs.

Being the first elected President of the Pakistan Workers Union, 1972, in Norway, Mubarik Ahmed Rajpoot has represented his community in the foreign Workers Union in Norway. He has also been a broadcaster on Radio/TV Islam Amadiyyah in 1981, and travelled extensively through Eastern Europe and walked through Bulgaria, Yugoslavia and Austria studying the culture, social structure and languages there. He took part in the 1981 peace march, where he walked from Copenhagen to Paris and has travelled throughout USA and Canada. He has been a member of the Oslo Journalists Club since 1975

Mubarik Ahmed Rajpoot is married to Robina S Latif. They have three children, a son, Khozemah M A Rajpoot, and daughters, Sidrah M A Rajpoot and Zoyah M A Rajpoot. He also has two sons from his second marriage, Osamah M A Rajpoot and Hamzah M A Rajpoot, and a daughter from his first marriage, Regina Nargis Rajpoot.

*A biography of Mubarik Ahmed Rajpoot appears in the main section of this Edition.*

## HE THE HONOURABLE
## PROFESSOR DR HERMANN RUDOLF RAUH,
## MA, CPhys, FInstP, FIM, OIA

*For your Outstanding Contribution to*
*Physics and Materials Science*

# HE THE HONOURABLE PROFESSOR DR HERMANN RUDOLF RAUH, MA, CPhys, FInstP, FIM, OIA

Hermann Rauh was born in Metzingen on 8 March 1946. He grew up in Rottenburg-upon-Neckar, however, where he attended primary and grammar school. It is the Swabian culture of this historic little town, so splendidly characterized in the works of the poeta laureatus, Sebastian Blau, to which, without doubt, he owes part of his mentality. Hermann's father Max handed down to him a disposition to rational analysis and early on encouraged a distinct interest in the natural sciences and their applications that was to determine his future course. His mother Katharina gave him the faculty for intuitive grasp and a marked linguistic bent, discernible in his oral and written accounts, which excel through clarity and intelligibility. Inherited from both parents, and even more prominent perhaps, are his artistic inclinations; these received particular support from the professional band musician, Walter Schöpe, who was at the heart of regular concert events in the Rauh family home. Hermann's violin and piano playing at that time, witnessed also in public appearances, was described as manifestation of an extraordinary musical talent, with perfect pitch and stupendous technique. After his father's premature death in 1962, Alfred Teufel, an honorary senator and distant relative, stood by his mother and took care of him, reinforcing his academic aspirations, while Richard Norz, a fatherly friend, acquainted him with life and ethos of the great scientists of the past. Already developed then were his open mind and tremendous thirst for knowledge, his enthusiasm and ingenuity, his dedication to a subject and its mastery, his seriousness and thoroughness, but also his sense of humour and his ability to marvel and to praise.

In 1965 Rauh entered the University of Tübingen to read physics, maths and chemistry. He felt particularly attracted to the lectures of Friedrich Lenz, which revealed to him the capacity of mathematical methods for providing quantitative solutions of physical real-world tasks. A theorist, impressed too by his friend Heinz Raidt's experimental activities, he eventually resolved to devote himself to applied research. In his thesis on point cathode electron guns, he introduced a powerful numerical approach, which made it possible to compute adequately, for the first time, the extremely complex electric field associated with devices of this kind. Proven a key tool for electron optical investigations and widely employed meanwhile, it opened up entirely new vistas of science and technology.

Rauh's fascination with solid state physics had already grown considerably when, after his graduation in 1971, he was offered work as an Associate in Alfred Seeger's department at the Max Planck Institute for Metals Research. This enabled him to gain insight into topics and techniques of a profound and lasting influence on his scientific aims. In a pioneering dissertation, for which he received his doctorate from the University of Stuttgart in 1975, he addressed the intricate problem of estimating theoretically the contribution of dislocations to the electrical resistivity of copper, and thereby laid the ground for numerous forthcoming studies on crystal defects and transport phenomena.

The decision in 1976 to accept an Assistant Professorship at the newly-founded University of Osnabrück meant a chance for continuing his own research and a direct responsibility for lecturing, but also an intense participation in development work. It was there that Rauh met Sigrid Löbker, a fine and thoughtful music pedagogue. They married in 1980. Sigrid is now a caring mother of their fabulous daughters, Anne-Kathrin and Christine, who show great promise on the violin and cello respectively, both as chamber players and as soloists: Anne-Kathrin, in a much-acclaimed recital given at 16, featured a sparkling performance of Bériot's scène de ballet; Christine won a spellbound audience's hearts with a mature rendition of Saint-Saëns' first cello concerto at her solo debut, aged 14.

The year 1980 also saw the beginning of a prolific collaboration with Ron Bullough, FRS, and later with Marshall Stoneham, FRS, during several visits and attachments to the renowned Harwell Lab. Resuming interests already pursued in Osnabrück, Rauh set about modelling microstructural evolution in nuclear reactor materials subject to high-energy particle irradiation, using the chemical rate theory approach. Here all sink types that together make up the spatially varying microstructure of the real material are assigned consistent sink strengths in an equivalent homogeneous continuum. He rigorously and originally derived sink strengths for voids, dislocations and free surfaces, appropriate to continuous and pulsed modes of irradiation respectively, enhancing comprehension of phenomena like void swelling and loop growth significantly. Analysing recombination processes of vacancies and self-interstitials, as occurring in irradiated solids, and of electrons and holes, as prevailing in semiconductor devices, was the objective of further thorough investigations. Seminal realisations were achieved when Rauh explored the kinetics of solute atom migration in the stress field of loaded cracks. His applications to modelling high-temperature brittle intergranular fracture of ferritic steels - a phenomenon strongly depending on sulphur segregation near crack tips - provided an understanding that enables corrective action to be taken against structural failure of service components involving welds.

Having obtained his habilitation in 1985, Rauh gladly accepted an offer from Sir Peter Hirsch, FRS, to join the Materials Department at the University of Oxford as a Visiting Fellow in 1986. Rauh's ties with this university and its cultural life, to which he contributed actively, were strengthened from 1988 when, simultaneously with affiliations to the Harwell Lab, he held a Research Fellowship at Wolfson College, Oxford, awarded by the President, Sir Raymond Hoffenberg, KBE.

In 1994 Rauh became Professor of Theoretical Foundations of Materials Development at Darmstadt University of Technology. His current attention focusses on a whole range of themes, including performance aspects of target materials for spallation neutron sources and magnetic properties of superconducting materials in electronic device applications. An International Ambassador by all means, committed to the sciences and arts he enjoys serving mankind by inspiring and educating the brightest students, by cultivating and disseminating the highest quality of scholarship, and by advancing innovative research of fundamental interest as well as of potential use to industry.

Rauh is a member of various learned societies, and holds Fellowships of the Institutes of Physics and Materials. Apart from meriting a dedication here, he was honoured with inclusion in a number of biographical reference works such as Dictionary of International Biography, 500 Leaders of Influence, and Who's Who in the World.

*A biography of HE The Honourable Professor Dr Hermann Rudolf Rauh, MA, CPhys, FInstP, FIM, OIA, appears in the main section of this Edition.*

# RAZOHARINORO

Mrs Razoharinoro has spent many years as a Certified Archivist, her work including administration and research. Appointed to the National Archives of the Republic of Madagascar in 1964, she has been the Chief Archivist there since 1969. In addition, since 1973 she has served as an Instructor in History at the University of Antananarivo. She edited the journal Tantara from 1973-95, and is also the author of various articles and reviews.

Born on 19 November 1936 in Antsirabe, Madagascar, Mrs Razoharinoro is the daughter of Rakotonjanahary and Razanamanana, both now deceased, the wife of Eugene Randriamboavonjy, and the mother of three children.. She holds a degree in Archives, obtained in 1964 from the Ecole Nationale des Chartres, Paris, France, and is a member of the Malagasy Academy. In recognition of her services to the country's heritage she was decorated Grand Officier de l'Ordre National de Malagasy.

## DR ZIA RAZZAQ, DSc

*For your Outstanding Contribution to
Education and Research*

# DR ZIA RAZZAQ, DSc

The son of Abdur and Surreyya B Razzaq, Dr Zia Razzaq was born on 16 March 1945 in Rawalpindi, Pakistan. He studied civil engineering, receiving a Bachelor of Engineering degree with Honours from the University of Peshawar in Pakistan in 1966, a Master of Applied Science degree from the University of Windsor in Canada in 1968, and a Doctor of Science degree from Washington University in St Louis, Missouri, USA, in 1974. His master's and doctoral research advisors were Dr William W McVinnie and Dr Theodore V Galambos respectively. He received the Morgan Award for excellence in teaching and research, the Lincoln Award, NASA fellowships and a Newport News Shipbuilding fellowship. In addition, he is listed in Who's Who Among America's Teachers, the International Who's Who of Professionals and Five Hundred Leaders of Influence.

Dr Razzaq is the author of over seventy-five publications in the areas of stability of metal structures, composite materials and structures, passive damping devices for vibration control of outer space structures, and other areas of structural mechanics. He has developed new structural theories and solution procedures, lateral-torsional buckling formulae, a natural frequency formula for a typical slender member of NASA's proposed space station, and a new column buckling formula for partially restrained columns which also unifies the famous column buckling load formulae for pinned or fixed end conditions developed by Leonhard Euler in the 1970s. Furthermore, he has conducted research on civil engineering structures, submarines, ship structures, stress analysis and fatigue of aircraft structural components, composite materials for guided missiles, side impact of automobile structures, parallel computing procedures for elasto-plastic stability problems, and in biomedical engineering. Together with Bruce G Johnston, he represented the entire North America for the stability of built-up structural members in a "World View" meeting held in France, in which representatives from several other continents also participated. He has made numerous presentations of his works at conferences and symposia held in USA, Canada, the United Kingdom, France, China, Turkey, Romania and Yugoslavia.

Now a professor at the Old Dominion University in Norfolk, Virginia, Dr Razzaq was previously on the faculty at Arizona State University in Tempe, Southern Illinois University at Carbondale and the University of Notre Dame in Indiana. In addition to having taught over forty undergraduate and graduate courses, he has guided a large number of Master's degree research projects and theses, as well as PhD degree dissertations. His earlier experience included working at the Tarbela Dam in Pakistan - the largest earthfill dam in the world; as a research and development engineer at the Chrysler Corporation in Michigan; as a research assistant at the University of Windsor and Washington University; as a teaching assistant at Windsor and as an instructor at Washington. He has also given national-level seminars on new LRFD procedures for timber structures in Chicago, Illinois, and Seattle, Washington, through the American Society of Civil Engineers.

He is the founder and President of Nepture Institute of Technology and Neptune Engineering Corporation. Besides being a member of the American Institute of Steel Construction, and a member of the committee on stability under the Council on Tall Buildings and Urban Habitat, which is a Member of UNESCO, he has served on several task groups of the Structural Stability Research Council. He is a member of the National Civil Engineering Honor Society of Chi Epsilon, as well as a Fellow of the American Society of Civil Engineers, and holds a Professional Engineer's licence. From 1985-91 he served as the chairperson of the task group on stability of beam-columns under SSRC. In addition, he is a specialist in earthquake, flood, wind and fire hazards mitigation. Serving as chair of the Architectural Committee of the ODF Associates, he is also a member of Friends of the Ferry Farm House in Virginia Beach, an organisation for historical preservation. In 1993, he became the founder and editor of a newspaper entitled "The Old Dominion Free Press".

With his wife, Shahida Yasmin Razzaq, Dr Razzaq now lives in Virginia Beach, Virginia, where he enjoys music, writing, travel, business and engineering. His children include two sons, Noor Z Razzaq and Faridoon Z Razzaq, born on 1 December 1980 and 1 January 1986 respectively.

*A biography of Dr Zia Razzaq, DSc, appears in the main section of this Edition.*

# DR JUSTINAS RIMAS

*For your Outstanding Contribution
to Management*

# DR JUSTINAS RIMAS

Justinas Rimas was born in the Kaunas Region of Lithuania on 17 December 1955, into the farming family of Antanina and Juozas. He had a brother, Remigijus, who unfortunately died in 1970 while rescuing a drowning friend. His sister, Violeta, is now married, has two sons and works as a finance manager at the confectionery plant of Kraft Jacobs Suchard Lietuva.

Finishing at the eight-year school of Margininkai in 1970, Justinas Rimas commenced special secondary studies at Kaunas Polytechnic School, completing the course in 1974. He then spent two years doing his military service. When that was over in 1976 he entered Kaunas Polytechnic Institute, from which he graduated in 1982 with the qualification of Engineer. Parallel with his studies he was also working, at first as a lecturer at Kaunas Polytechnic School and later as the Chairman of the pupils' trade union. In 1980 he was appointed Manager in the Personnel Department at Kaunas Gasification Administration, where he remained for a period of three years.

From 1983-90 Dr Rimas served as Assistant Chairman of the Planning Commission of Kaunas Executive Committee, but after Lithuania obtained its independence he transferred to the Savings Bank as Assistant to the General Manager at the Central Department in Kaunas. Between 1992 and 1994 he was Director of the Kaunas Branch of Vilnius Bank. In the meantime, he continued with his education as well, and was awarded a Master's degree in Business Management by the Vytautas Magnus University of Kaunas in 1994. From 1995-97 the Chairman of Kaunas State Tax Inspection, in 1998 he moved to Kaunus University of Technology, where he has been conducting research at the Finance Chair of the Faculty of Management since. His Doctorate in Management Sciences was conferred upon him in 1999.

Apart from his professional and research commitments, Dr Rimas has been active in community life. He joined with a group of artists to establish the Kaunas Art Fund in 1993. Besides becoming a member of Kaunas Rotary Club in 1995, in 1996 he gained admission to Lithuanian Art Collectors. In 1997 he was not only elected President of Lithuanian Boxing Association, but also as a member of the Lithuanian National Olympic Committee and the Finance Commission of the Lithuanian Federation of Economists and Industrialists. During the 1998 European Amateur Boxing Association Congress he was elected to the Association's Finance Commission. That year he was made a member of the Expert Commission of the Lithuanian Cultural and Sports Fund as well.

With another author Dr Rimas has published four books, namely, "Origin of Taxes and Social-Economic Expression", "Business and Taxes", "Taxes and Duties of Municipalities" and "For Businessmen about Taxes". Moreover, he has spoken and participated in many national and international theoretical and practical conferences on matters of economics, finances and taxes. In 1996 he visited the USA and Denmark, for studies at Los Angeles Tax Administration Institute and Copenhagen Tax Instruction Centre respectively.

As recreational pursuits Justinas Rimas enjoys lawn tennis, mountain skiing and travel. His wife Virginija, who has a Master's degree in Management, is a lecturer at Kaunas Higher Technical School. The couple have four children, two boys and two girls, born in 1980, 1998, 1989 and 1994 respectively. The eldest, Haroldas, has recently completed his first year in the Faculty of Management at Kaunas University of Technology. The elder girl, Justina, is in the 5th class at Kaunas Jesuitical Gymnasium, while her brother Tautvydas goes to the 2nd class at Anima School. The youngest, Gabriele, attends a dancing-school for children.

*A biography of Dr Justinas Rimas appears in the main section of this Edition.*

## DR JOHN ROSENKNOP, DrSci

*For your Outstanding Contribution to
Research and Teaching in Mathematics*

# DR JOHN ROSENKNOP, DrSci

Dr John Rosenknop, who now resides in Berlin, Germany, spent the earlier period of his career in the former USSR. The son of Selman Rosenknop and Maria Eidis, he was born on 28 December 1929 in Moscow, where he attended school. In 1947 he entered Moscow University, from which he graduated in Mathematics in 1952.

During his school and university studies, he several times became a winner both in the Moscow school Olympiads and in university students' competitions. From 1944 onwards he was a participant in the famous Dynkin's seminar. His first scientific achievement, which he carried out as a second-year student in the Department of Mechanics and Mathematics, concerned a problem set up by A N Kolmogorov, who presented it to the Dynkin's seminar, finding that it would take more than a week to solve. John Rosenknop found the solution two months later, at the same time that it was solved in Leningrad by an older, postgraduate student.

A year after going down from university, he succeeded in finding a post as a lecturer for external students of Moscow Regional Pedagogical Institute, where he continued to work until emigrating to West Germany in 1977. Many of his lectures in mathematics had to be given in a prearranged shortened time. Thus he developed experience in the economical exposition of mathematics, particularly the application of symbolic logic to a greater extent than usual.

After being awarded a scientific degree by the Kazan University in 1962 (later recognised as DrSci in West Germany), he was appointed to the staff at the Pedagogical Institute, at the Chair of Higher Algebra, Elementary Mathematics and Methods of Teaching Mathematics. There he devoted a good deal of time to the social work of the department, especially during the period nearer his emigration. His scientific research was independent and isolated. Contacts with colleagues abroad were impossible, but the field seemed to be important. In the following decades it was widely developed in connection with the Buchberger's Gröbner bases that became the main tool in the programming of solution of systems of nonlinear algebraic equations and in solving various closely related problems in computer mathematics.

Another of Dr Rosenknop's results was the establishment, at the end of the sixties, of connections between the algebra of polynomials of several variables and such a well-known geometric theory as combinatorial topology. Here the statement of a seemingly pure algebraic problem was unexpectedly interpreted in terms of objects of the topology.

After leaving the USSR Dr Rosenknop was involved mainly in the work of the well-known journal Zentralblatt für Mathematik. He has actively participated in several international mathematical congresses, the first held in Moscow in 1966, the others taking place in Berkeley, USA, Kyoto, Japan, Zurich, Switzerland, and Berlin, Germany, in 1986, 1990, 1994 and 1998 respectively. At a conference in Linz, Austria, in 1998, he received a special Gröbner-bases Co-Inventor Award. The author of more than thirty scientific publications, he also became an independent editor that year.

A member of Moscow Mathematical Society until 1977, he now holds membership of the American Mathematical Society, to which he was admitted in 1993. He has been honoured with inclusion in the 1998 and 1999 editions of the Marquis Who's Who in the World.

John Rosenknop is divorced and has no children. In his rare periods of free time, he prefers to travel.

*A biography of Dr John Rosenknop, DrSci, appears in the main section of this Edition.*

# DR HOLEM MANSOUR SALIBA, PhD

*For your Outstanding Contribution to
Mathematics and its Applications*

# DR HOLEM MANSOUR SALIBA, PhD

Dr Holem Mansour Saliba is dedicated to conducting research in the field of pure mathematics. Presently focusing on the functions of divisors, as well as the interpretation of certain New Testament verse with the use of mathematical logic, he has already achieved some interesting results in those areas.

Born on 25 January 1967 in Bteghrine, Lebanon, Dr Saliba attended university both in his homeland and in Russia. Pursuing studies in Pure Mathematics at the Université Libanaise, he earned the degree of Maîtrise from there in 1992. In June 1997 he received a PhD in Mathematics from the Lomonosov State University of Moscow, where he specialised in Mathematical Logic, Algebra and Theory of Numbers. Not only did he gain distinction in the relevant examinations set by the Supreme Certifying Committee of the Russian Federation, but his doctoral dissertation was also classed as excellent. He is deeply grateful to Professors Chubarikov, Arkhipov and Kaganova, from whose guidance he benefitted.

In his work on the mean value of the ternary function of divisors on sparse sequences, Dr Saliba has evaluated a new asymptotic formula for such function of divisors on the sequence of integral parts of non-integral exponents of the series of natural numbers. This result can be extended to the multi-valued function of divisors, which currently engages his attention. His other project started with applying mathematical logic to two verses from the New Testament. After many hundreds of years two particular verses of the Gospel had become subject to various interpretations, some of which showed a contradiction between the verses, whilst others attempted to explain that there was no contradiction. Through mathematical logic he not only succeeded in proving the absence of contradiction, but also demonstrated that the two verses were actually equivalent to each other. Thus the door was opened to him to see that many verses interpreted differently by different Christian sects were, in fact, not different, but the same. He is working on this now.

Outside his professional life, Dr Saliba enjoys three main recreational interests: theatre-going, visiting art galleries and football.

*A biography of Dr Holem Mansour Saliba, PhD, appears in the main section of this Edition.*

## PROFESSOR YA-CHING SHEN, PhD

*For your Outstanding Contribution
as a Chemistry Educator*

# PROFESSOR YA-CHING SHEN, PhD

Professor Ya-Ching Shen enjoys a career as an educator and researcher in the field of chemistry. In the former capacity he offers students two main courses, one in instrumental analytical chemistry, the other in the chemistry of natural resources. The chief areas of his research include the investigation of antitumour agents obtained from natural resources, the chemical modifications of lead compounds, and chemotaxonomy. He is presently involved in projects concerning the bioactive constituents of Taxus, Oleaceae and marine creatures. As an author he has some fifty refereed papers to his name, besides articles published in professional journals.

The son of Tiou Shen and Ching-Yin Wu, Ya-Ching Shen was born on 30 May 1953 in Taipei, Taiwan. He attended school in Taipei, after which he entered Taipei Medical College, where he earned a Bachelor of Science degree in 1976. Compulsory military service followed, but after its completion he embarked on postgraduate studies at the National Taiwan University, which led to a Master of Science degree in 1980. His next step was to work towards a PhD, awarded him by the same university in 1987. He also holds a Diploma in Pharmacy.

Appointed an instructor at the National Taiwan University in 1987, Dr Shen was promoted to Associate Professor in 1989, but left shortly afterwards to spend three years in the USA, conducting postdoctoral research at the University of North Carolina at Chapel Hil and at the University of California at San Diego. On returning to Taiwan in 1992, he accepted an Associate Professorship at the National Sun Yat-Sen University in Kaohsiung, where he has now held a full Professorship since 1997.

Professor Shen's other activities include consulting for the National Research Institute of Chinese Medicine, Taipei, from 1993-99. He has received grants from the National Science Council and the National Health Research Institute, was a Pharmacist in the Pharmacists' Association of Taipei from 1976-97, and is presently a member of the American Society of Pharmacognosy, the Chinese Pharmacy Association and the Chinese Pharmacists' Association.

Married to Show-Ching Dai since 1986, Dr Shen has two children. His leisure interests embrace gardening, identification of plants, nature, reading books and travelling for pleasure.

*A biography of Professor Ya-Ching Shen, PhD, appears in the main section of this Edition.*

## DR DONG-KEUN SHIN

*For your Outstanding Contribution
to Computer Science*

# DR DONG-KEUN SHIN

Dr Dong-Keun Shin, who claimed world leadership in computer sciences, conducts independent research to complete his theories and practices. Born in 1959 in Incheon, South Korea, he grew up in Seoul, Korea's capital city. From the time he was very young, he had dreams about creating his own theoretical world. After graduating from Po Sung high school in Seoul, he emigrated to the USA with his family in 1978, for better education. To make his dream come true, he chose to study computer science since the relatively new field provided good opportunities in research and industrial applications. Dr Shin received degrees in computer science from the University of California at Berkeley and the George Washington University. He worked for the former university's EECS Department as academic computing coordinator in his undergraduate years, and lectured in computer hardware and software courses at the latter in his graduate years. As an engineer, analyst or programmer, he has worked at several companies, including BT-Dialcom, Xerox, CBSI, SRA and Samsung Electronics. His current research interests include computer science theory and database systems.

While surveying hash functions for his doctoral dissertation, Dong-Keun Shin was the first to verify that there is no distinguishable difference between the performance of one relatively good and data-independent hash function and that of another. Dr Shin coined the term "phenomenon of relatively good (RG) solutions" in reference to the verification. Based on the first verification, he developed the hypothesis that the phenomenon of RG solutions is present in each group of polynomial time solutions for complex problems that basically require exponential time algorithms as solutions. He is preparing to verify the hypothesis for other complex problems. He has also contributed significantly to computer science by discovering and proposing best algorithms in the areas of sorting, hash functions, massive cross-referencing or the join database operation, and polygon clipping. His papers show that his algorithm for massive cross-referencing or the join, with its several versions, is best of its kind to date and his (mapping) hash function is the best hash method.

In early 1997, Dr Shin offered a challenge to the world's academic communities and computer scientists to refute the legitimacy of his verification and discoveries, as well as his claim to having made the greatest contribution to computer science. At that time, he sent letters to each nation's one or two highest political leaders, ministers of education or equivalent, the chairman of UNESCO, and heads of major universities and colleges in about 170 countries. Armed with his accomplishments, he expressed his desire to gain leadership in computer science academia through fair competition. He believes that any computer scientist with only a theory or idea can participate in such competition to win, regardless of racial, educational or social background. He also believes that the competition will create the academic hierarchy's uppermost group which must be very small. Computer scientists, who are examined through the competition and included in the group, will influence present and future students in the world to strive for a greater understanding of computer science. He thought that as the highest achiever in computer science he needed to take the mailing action to verify that his ideas were truly under his ownership and to stop any plagiarism. The schools to which he sent his challenging letters numbered over 4,300, but he has encountered no serious challenge as yet.

Moreover, on 3 July 1998 Dr Shin discovered a new sorting algorithm, Shin sort, which is the best solution to the problem of sorting and searching. This new algorithm seems to secure his victory in the battle for world leadership in computer science. In April 1999 he sent letters to some 1,200 press-related organisations worldwide. In his letters to the press, he proclaimed that he would lead people in computer science from the beginning of the 21st century, if no challenge arose. His letters leave world's computer scientists two options: to compete with him or to follow him. However, Dr Shin thinks that his involvement in experiments and application practices rather that pure research on computer science theory may put him at a disadvantage. If he loses, he will send letters to the world to announce the winner of the competition and will support the winner in his new leadership for world's computer science academia.

After designing and implementing a prototype of his sorting and searching software, he will eventually develop it into a Shin sort and search database management system (S³DBMS). S³DBMS creates Shin's trees in main or local memory for fast text/image/sound data retrievals. His press release in April 1999 shows that his sorting and searching scheme that traverses Shin's tree will replace current sorting and searching algorithms, hashing schemes and hash tables, and most trees including B-trees, due to the Shin sort/search algorithm's theoretical superiority. He believes that Shin sort will be used in most database systems and computer-based systems in future. As discoverer of the best solution for the sorting and searching problem, he may enjoy certain privileges, such as the right to write about sorting and searching theory and the publication of computer science textbooks.

Further details of Dr Shin's achievements can be found in his research collection entitled "A Collection of Research Processes for Genealogy and Proofs", thirty volumes of which have currently been submitted to the chairperson of the EECS Department, University of California at Berkeley. In Seoul, Korea, he has once lectured on computer-based systems for an introductory course at the University of Maryland's Asian Division. He is also involved in managing his family-owned Hwa Shin Building in downtown Seoul.

Although Dr Shin has accomplished his long-held dream of owning a theoretical world, he wants to serve mankind further with his creative talent. He plans to continue conducting computer science research and industrial computer applications, and to publish his theories and ideas in the computer science/engineering field.

*A biography of Dr Dong-Keun Shin appears in the main section of this Edition.*

## PROFESSOR NIKI STELLA SIDERIDOU, MOIF

*For your Outstanding Contribution
as an Educator and Writer*

# PROFESSOR NIKI STELLA SIDERIDOU, MOIF

A Greek writer, poet and former educator, Professor Niki Stella Sideridou has many productive years behind her, with numerous honours and prizes bearing witness to her accomplishments. For 35 years she served in secondary education, retiring in 1981 with the rank of Inspector General, and now enjoys the status of Honorary General Inspectress of Secondary Schools. She is a member of the Greek Literary Association, Honorary Chairman of the Greek Literateurs International Society and the International Writers and Artists Academy "Goddess Athena", a Distinguished Member of the International Writers and Artists Association and a Permanent Representative and Collaborator of the Greek Cultural Agency of Johannesburg. She is also a Distinguished Member of the Olympoetry Movement Committee, which bestowed the Honorary Ribbon of Lady of Olympoetry at a ceremony at Columbia University, New York.

The daughter of Giannis and Anna Siderides, both educators, Niki Stella Sideridou was born on 10 May 1915 in Smyrna. She was brought up in Roumeli, where her mother held an appointment as a teacher. In 1941 she married Professor Giannis Thomopoulos, by whom she had two daughters, Hegemoni and Melita, born in 1948 and 1956 respectively. In 1961 the marriage ended in divorce.

Professor Sideridou studied Philosophy, Literature and Pedagogics at the Universities of Athens and Uppsala (Sweden). During her teaching years she worked not only in Greece, but also for secondary schools in Addis Ababa, Ethiopia. She was the recipient of a number of prizes, medals, certificates and honorary distinctions from academic institutions in Greece and abroad. Noteworthy is the Roidis Prize from Athens Academy, awarded in 1956 for her study on "Andreas Karkavitsas and his Era". In 1961 the Supreme Council of National Education characterised her as a "writer of serious scientific works", while in 1993 she won the Giovanni Gronchi Award at the international competition held in Pontadera, Italy. Other bodies from which she has received awards include the Accademia Ferdinandea, the International Writers and Artists Association, the International Biographical Centre and the American Biographical Institute. During her career in education she has had recognition from official quarters for her eminent spiritual, educational, pedagogical, social, cultural, artistic and humanitarian work, as well as for her efforts concerning the environment and the cause of peace. Moreover, her humanitarian and peace activities have not only been acknowledged by the Red Cross both in Greece and Ethiopia, but also by UNICEF.

Since 1933 Professor Sideridou has been continously engaged in publishing articles, reviews and literary works in magazines and newspapers. In addition, she is the author of 21 books, including studies, travelogues, pedagogical works, a fairy tale for peace, and collections of poetry and short stories. Ever since her first book appeared in 1940, her works have received favourable reviews. Poems and other works of hers have been translated into various foreign languages. In addition to being published in foreign magazines and newspapers, they have been included in courses at universities abroad. Furthermore, she has frequently received invitations to participate in international congresses on poetry, literature, arts and communications.

Professor Sideridou has her home in Athens, where she still continues with her writing. Her leisure interests consist of reading good literature and theatregoing.

*A biography of Professor Niki Stella Sideridou, MOIF, appears in the main section of this Edition.*

## ALBERT L SIMMS

*For your Outstanding Contribution to
Suffering Humanity and Christian Education*

# ALBERT L SIMMS

Born on 21 January 1931, the son of Mr R J and Mrs Carrie B Simms, in the very clean and beautiful small community of Claremont, West Virginia, USA, where the main source of employment was coal mining, Albert L Simms spent his childhood playing softball, horse shoes, pitching, football, marbles and high rope jumping. He became a member of the Boy Scouts and at the age of seven years was converted unto Christianity, and became a Christian. He attended the First Baptist Church of Claremont, the Sunday Church and served as Superintendent at the Sunday School there. He was later appointed and elected to serve as a Deacon to the Church Board, singing as a Song Leader in a Quintet, working in the church vacation Bible School.

Albert Simms entered into Dubois High School of Mount Hope, West Virginia in 1945, graduating in 1950. While there, he sang in the Glee Club Chorus and became a member of the New Farmers of America, taking part in oratory contests at West Virginia State College. After graduation, he went into the ministry to preach. After ten months, he was licensed and three years later was called to the pastorage to receive his ordation, having begun his ministry at the age of sixteen. For eight years, he was a Minister, Deacon and Instructor of a class.

Being a Pastor and Evangelist, Mr Simms decided to take up employment to meet some of the expenses this incurred. He sought work at the Greenbrier Hotel as a bellman. While there he also served as Chaplain, holding services every Sunday for two years, with occasional broadcasts on local radio. He realised, after two years that the pressing demands of his ministry work would have to come first, so he left his employment and went into full time ministry and pastoring. In 1952, he became a member of the New River Valley Baptist Association, the West Virginia Baptist State Convention and the West Virginia State Baptist Minister Conference. He was elected as a statistician for the New River Valley Baptist Missionary Association in 1955 and enrolled in a three years general Bible course at the Appalachian Bible College, Bradley, West Virginia. After graduating from the college, Albert Simms entered a Home Study Course at College level, from the Division of Extended Studies of Southern Baptist Seminaries through the Home Study Institute, giving him access to Seminary extension courses. This comprised sixteen courses, based on a four year college level. He was awarded a Certificate in Religious Education, with credits that could be transferred to any accredited college. He received a Diploma for them all. Through the Home Study Institute education, Mr Simms was able to spend time with God, in prayer and meditation. He could attend conferences, group discussions, youth retreats, seminars and enjoy the reading of good literature.

Albert L Simms, is the Moderator of New River Valley Missionary Baptist Association, former member of West Virginia State Baptist Board of the Congress of Christian Education, former treasurer of New River Baptist Association, former field worker of the Hill Top Baptist Extension Seminary, former instructor of the West Virginia State Baptist Congress of Christian Education, former assistant instructor of the Hill Top Baptist Seminary Extension School, former member of Senator Holliday State Senator, on the Advisory Board of West Virginia, former Pastor of United Baptist Church of Winona, West Virginia, Shilo Missionary Baptist Church, Alderson, West Virginia, and Alumni of Appalachian Bible College. He is the Chairman of Hill Top Baptist Seminary Advisory Board, Chairman of West Virginia State Baptist Convention Ordination Committee, former historian of New River Valley Baptist Association and former Vice President of the Civic Club or Harlem Heights, Oak Hill, West Virginia.

During his lifetime, Albert Simms has been working with the poor and feeding the needy. He has supported work at foreign missions and three of the six churches at which he is Pastor and Administrator have been involved with this.

*A biography of Albert L Simms appears in the main section of this Edition.*

## DR GENOVAITE SNIRAITE STULPINIENE, FIBA

*For your Outstanding Contribution as the*
*One Who Moves Ends the Travel*

# DR GENOVAITE SNIRAITE STULPINIENE, FIBA

Genovaite Stulpiniene, who was born in Lithuania in 1932, is the Founder, Owner and President of three educational institutions, namely, the Institute of Law and Management, based in Kaunas, Lithuania, the G Stulpiniene College of Business Management and Languages, also Kaunas, and the Kaliningrad International Academy of Ecotechnology and Management, in Kaliningrad, Russia. Moreover, she is a member of the Section for International Relations of the Dante Alighieri Committee, besides having been admitted to the Academy of Natural Sciences and the International Society of Scientific Organizations of Education. She holds a Doctorate in Humanities.

During her whole career Dr Stulpiniene has been devoted to the field of education, both as a teacher and an administrator. After completing her studies at Ukmerge Girls High School in 1951, she spent fifteen years teaching at Ukmerge and Siauliai District Schools. For much of that period she continued with her own education as well, studying at first at Siauliai District Schools from 1952-55, then at Vilnius-Keplsa College of Music from 1956-59. Furthermore, in 1964 she began courses at Siauliai Pedagogical Institute. On finishing there in 1966, she was appointed Director of Sakyna Eight-year School, Siauliai District, for a couple of years. While an Instructor at Kaunas Polytechnical Institute from 1969-86, she held a similar post at Kaunas Technical College during the period from 1975-80, besides pursuing postgraduate studies at Vilnius University between 1978 and 1982.

In addition to distinguishing herself as the founder of non-state educational institutions in post-Soviet Lithuania, Dr Stulpiniene was the initiator of the first private studies in her country, organising vocational and higher education in the private sector from 1987 onwards. Since 1989 she has served as Rector of the Kaunas Management and Languages College, from which some 800 management specialists have graduated so far. Moreover, she became President of the G Stulpiniene Management College and of Institute of Management and Law, assuming the positions in 1993 and 1995 respectively. From time to time during the present decade she has travelled abroad for professional training, for that purpose visiting Oslo, Norway, in 1991, Finland each year from 1992 to 1997, Denmark in 1994, and St Petersburg, Russia, in 1997.

Apart from her history dissertation entitled "Cultural contacts with other countries", Dr Stulpiniene is the author of a lengthy work, "A Way to Recognition", which appeared in ten parts. A poet and creative writer, she is best known for two books of short stories, "Letters to My Father" and "Waiting for Spring", both published in 1990, and her 1994 film novel, "Woman's Life on Loan".

As leisure interests Dr Genovaite Stulpiniene enjoys the arts, or more particularly, literature and music. She has been married for many years and has a son, Zilvinas, who was born in 1967.

*A biography of Dr Genovaite Sniraite Stulpiniene, FIBA, appears in the main section of this Edition.*

**PROFESSOR DR DER-RUENN SU, PhD, DSc (Hon), DPhil (Hon), FIBA**

*For your Outstanding Contribution to Peace, World and Modern Physics*

# PROFESSOR DR DER-RUENN SU, PhD, DSc (Hon), DPhil (Hon), FIBA

The son of Pu-Kao Su and Mei-Chun Hsieh-Su, Professor Su Der-Ruenn was born on 11 March 1937 in a small village located in the southeast of Chekiang, China. In actual fact, his natural parents are Professor Buchin Su and Mrs B H Ma-Su. Professor Su who is the younger brother of Pu-Kao Su and well-known as a leading mathematician in China. His biographies are popular in modern China. It is a Chinese tradition that a boy may automatically become the son of his father's brother if required.

At the age of nine, after four years of education, Der-Ruenn Su arrived on the island of Taiwan. He earned a BS in Physics at the National Taiwan University, Taipei, and completed his reserve officer service in the Chinese Air Force. In the summer of 1960 he left for the USA. There he obtained his MS at the University of Pennsylvania and PhD at the State University of New York, serving as an assistant instructor at the former university, and working in a research position at the latter. Returning to China, he was a visiting professor at Fu-Jen University, Taiwan, the National Central University and the National Taiwan Normal University, and simultaneously a professor at the National Taiwan University in Taipei.

In the summer of 1961 Professor Su conducted postgraduate studies at the University of Pennsylvania under the guidance of Professor Charles W Ufford, choosing to investigate the Wigner correlation energy in atomic and surface physics. Around that time the membership of Mongolia in the United Nations was sensitive. Professor Su had made some influential political comments which seemed to have results. He later made some discoveries about the "commutation relation" of fermions in the field theory. Regarding the physics measurement theory, he believes that a plane, or surface, or any two-dimensional space, is immeasurable in a body or a three-dimensional space. For instance, because it is two-dimensional, not three-dimensional, a desk's "top-surface" is invisible and intangible. Therefore a living being in a three-dimensional space cannot be measured by creatures in other dimensions of any kind, unless there is a breakthrough into the dimensionalities. He has been trying hard to build up a dimensionality theory, even in his current research. Noticed by many other physicists, he has made some interesting breakthroughs in modern physics. In an autumn afternoon in 1962, Professor Su felt some enlightenment in the right direction. Since then, more or less, he became very careful and had been mastering the political problems. He has evolved and conducted the world changes in these years.

In mid-August 1963 Dr Su had a memorable and remarkable journey the first time he flew back to Taiwan from the USA. Leaving Seattle on 15 August, he was due to arrive in Taipei on 16 August, travelling via Anchorage and Tokyo. The first leg of the journey was uneventful. However, after the plane had taken off from Anchorage, at about 11 o'clock that evening, and had reached the stratosphere, he felt some discomfort between his eyes. A storm of wind and rain soon began, so about twenty minutes later the plane turned back to Anchorage, arriving just after midnight. It took off again at daybreak. On looking out of the window less than an hour later, he saw they were grounded on an "airfield" that was completely dark except for two lines of lights alongside the plane. There appeared to be no communication between the aircraft and ground, either. Some minutes afterwards the plane took off for Tokyo, where the passengers stayed overnight at a hotel. On the next day, 17 August, they grounded at Okinawa air base, where an Air Force operation was taking place with the newest type airplanes; he believes the stop was not in the original plan. When he finally reached Taipei his family confirmed that the plane had arrived a whole 24 hours behind schedule.

For a long time Dr Su did not wonder much about the experience, although he had noticed that the passengers looked a trifle strange after leaving the "dark airfield". More than 25 years later he was told that the "dark air base" was, in fact, a Soviet airbase. Surprisingly, however, after five more years he was informed that the flight had been to a place beyond human knowledge. Outer space flight?! In 1963 he had had no idea that creatures from outer space existed.

A member of the Chinese Physical Society and the American Physical Society, Professor Su is also a former member of the American Association for the Advancement of Science. He has written many important academic papers in physics and other academic fields, besides presenting theories in physics. Publication is scheduled for two books of his, namely, "The Collected Papers of Su Der-Ruenn: Quantum Physics 1966-1997" and "Quantum Mechanics, an intermediate aspect". His research interests include physics, human rights and deviating tendencies in society and political affairs, as well as the related definition of "progress of human civilization". He provides a stimulus and influence in the establishment of world peace and a peaceful world. Apart from the daily routine of university teaching and research, he has often participated in academic symposia and university activities regarding decisive action, although he rarely takes part in public activities.

Professor Su has been awarded numerous prizes for his work. They include two from the Government in 1973 and 1978 respectively, and the Six Arts Medal from the Chinese Ministry of Education in 1983. In 1989, the Year of World Peace, he received an honorary DSc from the Marquis Giuseppe Scicluna International University. It was awarded in recognition of his informative displays designed to promote worldwide awareness and to stimulate influential contributions to world peace. Moreover, as a result of his tremendous breakthroughs in physics theories he received an honorary DPhil from the Albert Einstein International Academy. His name can be found on a brass plate on the wall of the Academy.

*A biography of Professor Dr Der-Ruenn Su, PhD, DSc (Hon), DPhil (Hon), FIBA, appears in the main section of this Edition.*

## KERRY SUTTON, FIBA

*For your Outstanding Contribution to
Divination and Design*

# KERRY SUTTON, FIBA

A graphic artist and designer who has been involved with numerous projects both at home and abroad, Kerry Sutton is currently based in Auckland, New Zealand. He has travelled widely during his career, visiting countries in Latin America, Europe and the Far East, as well as spending longer periods in the USA, Canada and Australia. Over the last several years he has been engaged in freelancing, pursuing various courses and conducting research.

Kerry Sutton was born in New Zealand in 1944. After completing his secondary education he enrolled at Wellington Polytechnic, where studies in Industrial Design from 1962-64 led to the award of a Diploma. His major project during his third year consisted of the design of a two-seater Commuter Car. From 1965-66 he worked for General Motors (Frigidaire) Wellington, employed as a product designer for stoves and refrigerators. Later in 1966 he left for the USA for two years at the Art Center of Design in Los Angeles, studying Industrial Design with Transportation Design as an elective. Since that time he has also pursued studies in other areas such as black-and-white and colour photography, computers (Word Processing and Desktop publishing) and building biology.

After studying for two years at the Art Center College of Design, Mr Sutton moved to Canada. There he spent a year working for the Canadian Exhibition Commission in Ottawa, designing exhibitions for Government departments including Canada Post and the Department of Regional Economic Expansion. A year followed at De Nova Associates in Montreal, engaged in designs for trade show exhibitions for Moto Ski (snowmobiles), Air Canada office displays and other exhibits, as well as doing some freelance work. Moving to Toronto, he was involved at the waterfront complex of Ontario Place, his main responsibilities concerning graphics, interactive playground equipment and services for dispensing fast food. Remaining in Toronto, his other principal employer was Stan Ash Theatrical, where he was responsible for the detailing and supervision of cyclorama, lighting and staging baton installations for commercial educational and cable TV studios.

Before leaving Canada in 1974, Mr Sutton took a 4-week holiday in Brazil and returned to New Zealand, where he spent the early part of 1976 on finishing art and layout for consumer and institutional clients of the Christchurch firm of Hill Skinner Advertising. However, August 1976 found him in Australia. As a graphic artist for Australia Post, based in Sydney, he designed leaflets and new issue stamp displays, as well as exhibitions. In spring 1979 he embarked on his travels again, taking a 3-month trip to Europe, followed by 9 months in Latin America, journeying from Mexico City to Santiago de Chile. He then returned to Sydney and continued to work in the exhibition design area. Among the more prominent positions was Bettridge Stannard and Rose where he designed trade show stands and graphics for State government and industry. He also spent several months as an exhibition planner for the Museum of Arts and Sciences, with responsibility for designing the Museum's amateur radio and producing graphics for other projects.

Starting in January 1985, Mr Sutton spent two years travelling in Asia, developing his photographic skills. He also learnt basic Japanese and taught English conversation. Back in New Zealand, for much of 1987 he was responsible for the design and installation of trade show exhibitions, on behalf of the Peek Display Corporation, Auckland. In July 1988 he set off for South America and for the next twelve months travelled around Bolivia and Chile, from Arica in the north to Puerto Montt in the south. He finally returned to New Zealand to commence his present ongoing activities. One of the products he has recently designed is an Incense Burner-cum-Windchime that can show the 64 Hexagrams of the I-Ching. To go with it he has produced a booklet that explains the numerology of 8 and how the product works.

A biography of Kerry Sutton appears in the main section of this Edition.

## DR MASAKI TAN, MD

*For your Outstanding Contribution
Medicine and Surgery*

# DR MASAKI TAN, MD

The son of Chiyoshi and Masae Tan, Masaki Tan was born on 13 February 1946 in Akita, Japan. Nowadays a skilled surgeon and vice-director of a hospital, he prepared for his career at Tohoku University, Sendai, from which he obtained his MB in 1971 and MD in 1978. Furthermore, he pursued a law degree later, earning his LLB at Kinki University, Osaka, in 1985.

An Assistant Professor in the Department of Surgery at Tohoku University from 1973-84, Dr Tan then became Head of the Department of Surgery at Ohfunato Prefectural Hospital. He remained there until 1988, when he transferred to Kitakami Prefectural Hospital, again as Head of the Department of Surgery. In 1994 he accepted a similar appointment at Kitakami Prefectural Hospital, but resigned in 1998 to assume his present position as Vice-Director of Wakayanagi National Insurance Hospital, in Kurihara.

Dr Tan has been admitted to membership of the American Association for the Advancement of Science, ISPO and the New York Academy of Sciences. He is also known as the author of two publications of particular note. The first of those appeared in 1985, under the title of "Recent Advances on Chemotherapy", and was followed in 1986 by "New Applications of OK-432".

For recreation, Masaki Tan enjoys reading, watching movies, listening to music and travelling. He married Keiko Takahashi in January 1975; the couple have a son, Hiroki, and a daughter, Chihiro.

A biography of Dr Masaki Tan, MD, appears in the main section of this Edition.

## DR ISMAIL HAKKI OLCAY UNVER, FIBA

*For your Outstanding Contribution to
Sustainable Human Development*

# DR ISMAIL HAKKI OLCAY UNVER, PhD, FIBA

A Turkish civil engineer whose specialty lies in water resources management, Dr I H Olcay Unver has made a significant contribution to sustainable human development in his country. He is currently President of the Republic of Turkey Prime Ministry's Southeastern Anatolia Project (GAP) Regional Development Administration. Moreover, he is a member of the World Water Council, the Global Water Partnership, the International Hydropower Association, the International Water Resources Association, the American Geophysical Union, the American Society of Civil Engineers, the American Water Resources Association, the Canadian Water Resources Association, the Soil and Water Conservation Society of America, the World Association of Soil and Water Conservation, the Center for Irrigation Technology, Fresno, California, the Turkish Chamber of Civil Engineers and the New York Academy of Sciences.

As a student at the Middle East Technical University in Ankara Dr Ünver earned a Bachelor of Science degree in Civil Engineering with honours in 1979. Postgraduate studies led to a Master of Science degree in Civil Engineering from the same university in 1981. For his thesis, on "Computer-Oriented Design of Urban Stormwater and Wastewater Collection Systems", he developed two mathematical models for the hydraulic design of such systems, based on Turkish and US Standards. The models were applied to systems for the urban basin of Batikent, a town near Ankara.

Parallel with his studies, Dr Unver worked for the Municipality of Ankara between 1979 and 1980, as a Project Engineer engaged with urban sewerage. During the latter year he also consulted privately on water supply and distribution. He then departed for the USA, where he entered the University of Texas at Austin to prepare for a PhD, awarded in 1987 after presentation of a dissertation on "Simulation and Optimization of Real-Time Operation of Multiple-Reservoir Systems Under Flooding Conditions". The optimal control model that he developed combined state-of-the-art methods for river/reservoir simulations and the generalised reduced gradient technique for optimization. It has been successfully applied to the Highland Lakes System on the Lower Colorado River in Central Texas. His second model, an interactive real-time simulation one combining dynamic flow routing, reservoir operation capability, interactive input-output and on-screen graphics, is operational on the Lower Colorado River Authority's computer system.

After two years as a Water Resources Engineer for the Lower Colorado River Authority, Dr Unver left Texas in 1988 to return home, where he joined the State Planning Organization's Southeastern Anatolia Project Management Unit in Sanliurfa, as a Water Resources Specialist and Deputy Director. Appointed Regional Director of the GAP Regional Development Administration from 1989-91, he then left Sanliurfa for Ankara to assume his current position.

Turkey's biggest development project and one of the world's largest, GAP is an integrated, multi-sectoral project based on water resources development for a wide area and involves 22 dams, 19 hydropower plants and numerous irrigation schemes. The Regional Administration is responsible for planning, coordinating and monitoring all activities in agriculture, energy, transport-telecom, industry, health, education and urban-rural infrastructure within the area in question. Dr Unver has been active in approaching international organisations, financial institutions and foreign governments, securing finance or negotiating agreements on joint projects. Besides drawing up and implementing a sustainable development definition for GAP, he has designed support and partnership programmes for local initiatives and enterprises, as well as initiating special programmes to improve the status of women and other less-advantaged groups. Much of the work has been described in papers published in international journals or presented at national and international conferences and symposia. He has also lectured or given media interviews on GAP, water resources planning and management, and regional development.

Dr Unver was born in Turkey in 1957. Married with two children, he resides in Cankaya, a suburb of Ankara where his office is also situated.

*A biography of Dr Ismail Hakki Olcay Unver, PhD, FIBA, appears in the main section of this Edition.*

## CLIVE THOMAS WALKER, PhD

*For your Outstanding Contribution to
Nuclear Fuel Technology*

# DR CLIVE THOMAS WALKER, PhD

A nuclear fuel technologist and microbeam analyst, Dr Clive Thomas Walker has worked for more than twenty years at the European Institute for Transuranium Elements, where his current research interests include the behaviour of light water reactor fuel at high burn-up and the development of mixed oxide fuel for the nuclear incineration of plutonium. As well as gaining a Diploma in Metallurgy and PhD in Electrochemistry from the University of Surrey, Guildford, in 1971 and 1974 respectively, he became a Chartered Engineer in 1978 and Chartered Physicist in 1993. He is also a Fellow of the Institute of Materials, London, a Fellow of the Institute of Physics, London, and a Fellow of the Royal Microscopical Society, Oxford.

The son of Wilfred Wallace Walker and Vera May Walker, Clive Walker was born on 22 November 1947 in Colville, Leicestershire, England. After leaving school in 1964, he joined the Caterpillar Tractor Company in Leicester, employed as a laboratory technician. Parallel with his work, he continued with his education, earning the Ordinary National Certificate in Chemistry, Physics and Mathematics at Loughborough College of Further Education in 1967. Further part-time studies at Derby and District College of Technology led to the award of a Higher National Diploma Metallurgy in 1970. That year he was appointed a Plant Quality Assurance Engineer by Caterpillar Tractors, but not long afterwards he resigned from the company to pursue studies at the University of Surrey. There he encountered R T Grant, former Director of the Clinical Research Unit at Guy's Hospital, London. The ensuing friendship was to have a lasting influence on Dr Walker's thinking.

After leaving university in 1974, Dr Walker joined the Institute for Transuranium Elements - the European Commission's Nuclear Research Establishment based in Karlsruhe, Germany. In 1978 he became Head of the Institute's Electronic Probe Microanalysis Laboratory, a position he continues to hold. In addition, he has served as Deputy Head of the Technical Physics Unit since 1998. Other activities related to his career include representing the European Commission at the International Rise Fission Gas Release Projects from 1981-91, while in 1992 he appeared as a Visiting Scientist at Riso National Laboratory, Roskilde, Denmark. He is currently an Advisor to the Technical Committee on Microbeam Analysis of the International Organisation for Standardisation, to the International Congress on X-ray Optics and Microanalysis and to the European Conference on Applied Surface and Interface Analysis. Moreover, since 1993 he has held a seat on the Executive Board of the European Microbeam Analysis Society.

Following the nuclear accident at Three Mile Island in 1979, Dr Walker pioneered the use of electron probe microanalysis in the study of fission gas release from nuclear fuel. He subsequently supplied basic data on fission gas release for the development and validation of the Transuranus Computer Code, the European Reference Code for Nuclear Fuel Performance. Moreover, he made a major contribution to the establishment of the OECD/IAEA data base for evaluation of nuclear fuel performance and safety codes. With his colleagues J Ränsch and Giacchetti, he invented a secondary electron detector for analysis of radioactive materials in the scanning electron microscope. The device was granted US and French patents in 1983, as well as a British patent in 1984. In collaboration with others worldwide, he has contributed articles to various professional journals including Nature, Nuclear Technology and the Journal of Nuclear Materials. Presently, he is the Editor of "Modern Developments and Applications in Microbeam Analysis", the proceedings of the 6th International Workshop held by the European Microbeam Analysis Society in Konstanz, Germany, in May 1999.

In 1998 Dr Walker was honoured to be made a Freeman of the City of London. His activities outside his professional life include membership of the 94th Company of the City of London (The Engineers). He is married to the former Janet Patricia Vernon, daughter of Major Hubert Sidney Vernon of the Royal Electrical and Mechanical Engineers, the wedding having taken place on 9 September 1970.

*A biography of Dr Clive Thomas Walker, PhD, appears in the main section of this Edition.*

## RICHARD LEROY WELCH, LFIBA

*For your Outstanding Contribution as the Father of "Mental Photography"*

# RICHARD LEROY WELCH, LFIBA

A personal improvement company executive who originally started out in life insurance, Richard LeRoy Welch was born on 15 October 1939 in Lincoln, Nebraska, USA, as the son of Raymond Nathanial and Helen Lila Welch. Aptly named the "Father of Mental Photography", he has a reputation as a scientist, speaker, author and educator. His book, "Dynamic Brain Management", which appeared in 1996, was written in connection with his professional interests.

After graduating from high school, Mr Welch spent two years studying at the University of Nebraska, leaving at the end of 1959. He then entered insurance, based in Lincoln as an Agent for Guarantee Mutual Life in 1960. A couple of years later he became an Agent for Mutual Life of Omaha, with subsequent promotion to Manager. After serving as General Agent for Loyal Protective Life from 1969-70, he left Omaha for two years as Manager for Mutual Benefit Life in Dallas, Texas, from 1971-73, prior to assuming his final position in insurance, as Branch Manager for Great West Life in San Jose, California.

Armed with business management experience, in 1975 Mr Welch embarked on his present career, at first serving as Chief Executive Officer of the International Speedreading Institute and American Speedreading Academy. He has now been President and Chief Executive Officer of Educom Inc/Subliminal Dynamics and Brain Management since its founding in 1980.

Mr Welch is listed in Who's Who in America, Who's Who in the World and Who's Who of Entrepreneurs. Outside his professional life, he is a Mason and Shriner, whilst his leisure interests embrace sports, music and travel. Married to the former Donna Lee Gysegem since November 1991, he has a stepson, Shannon Panzo. From a previous marriage he has two daughters, Terri L Flowerday and Julie A Kuhl, who are themselves now married.

*A biography of Richard LeRoy Welch, LFIBA, appears in the main section of this Edition.*

## PROFESSOR LIQING YANG

*For your Outstanding Contribution as a
Composer and Music Educationist*

# PROFESSOR LIQING YANG

A well-known Chinese composer, Yang Liqing is Professor and Vice-President of Shanghai Conservatory of Music, Vice-Chairman of the Musicians Association of Shanghai, Vice-Director of the Committee for Music Theory and Composition of Shanghai Musicians Association, a member of the Chinese Musicians Association, Founding Member and Vice-Chairman of the Modern Music Society of Shanghai, Director of the Cultural Committee of the Overseas Scholars Association, Shanghai, and Director of Hong Kong International Centre of Educational Exchange.

Born on 30 April 1942 in Sichuan, China, Yang Liqing began learning to play the piano at the age of five, taught by his father, Yang Tilie, Professor of Piano at Shanghai Conservatory of Music. Graduating from Shenyang Conservatory of Music in 1970, he subsequently studied for his MA in Composition at Shanghai Conservatory of Music from 1978-80. One of the first Chinese after the Cultural Revolution to gain permission to travel to the West for educational purposes, from 1980-83 he studied composition under Alfred Koerppen and piano under Kurt Bauer in the Federal Republic of Germany. His teachers praised him as "a musician on whose future we can place high hopes". He gained his diplomas with honours in the master class for composition and advanced class for piano at the Staatliche Hochschule für Musik und Theater Hannover in 1983.

Returning to Shanghai, Professor Yang brought piles of records and scores which he used at Shanghai Conservatory of Music to pass on his newly-gained knowledge about modern composition to the students. An influential exponent of New Music, he has written numerous books and articles on the subject. Notable is his treatise "On the Historic Evolution of Orchedstration", published in 1986. Moreover, his book "The Compositional Techniques of Olivier Messiaen", which appeared in 1989, was subsequently referred to in the Newsletter of the European Foundation for Chinese Music Research as "the first book written by a Chinese on a Western avant-garde composer".

Professor Yang has received numerous commissions for compositions from organisations such as the GRAME-Centre National de Création Musicale, France, the Executive Committee of the Echoes of the Silk Road Grand Concerts, Japan, Singapore Symphony Orchestra, Hong Kong Chinese Orchestra, China National Symphony Orchestra, and others. His main works include: "Four Poems from the Tang Dynasty", for mezzo-soprano, piano and percussion, 1982; "Grievances at Wujiang", symphonic ballade for pipa and orchestra, 1986; "Festive Overture" for orchestra, 1987; "The Monument without Inscription", dance-drama music, 1989; "Elegy", erhu concerto, 1991; "Si", quintet for traditional Chinese instruments, 1997. His works have been performed in China, Germany, France, USA, Japan, South Korea, Singapore, Hong-Kong, Taiwan and elsewhere, by leading Chinese orchestras including the China National Symphony, the Central Philharmonic, Shanghai Symphony, Hong-Kong Philharmonic, as well as by foreign orchestras such as the Nagoya Philharmonic of Japan, the SWR Symphony and Philharmonia Hungarica of Germany, Singapore Symphony, and Seoul Symphony, South Korea.

Since the mid-1980s, Professor Yang has been the recipient of numerous awards and honours. He won the Chinese Record Prize in a Composition Competition in China in 1986, 1st Prize for Competition at Shandong 2nd Art Festival in 1989, and the Corolla Award at Shanghai Art Festival in 1990, the same year that he received a Grant from the Austrian Ministry of Sciences and Arts, as well as the German DAAD Scholarship. A Literary and Art Prize from Shanghai City in 1991 was followed by the title of Outstanding Young and Middle-Aged Expert from the State Council of China in 1993, and a Distinguished Achievements Award from Baogang Classic Art Foundation, Shanghai, in 1994. In 1995 he received two US grants, one from the Asian Cultural Council, the other from the Committee on Scholarly Communication with China. Besides being nominated for the Golden Cock Award for Best Movie Music in 1996, that year he won the Silver Medal in the Symphonic Composition Competition in Memory of Sun Yat-sen.

As a Guest Professor Yang Liqing taught in the Mozarteum Music Academy in Salzburg, Austria, in 1990, and at Cornell University, USA, in 1995. During those visits he was invited to conduct seminars and speak on the New Music of China, appearing at a number of colleges in Germany, Austria and Switzerland in the former period, and at two or three American colleges while at Cornell. Other activities of his include serving on the International Jury at the 2nd Asian Music Festival, held in 1990, and as President of the International Jury at the 6th Shanghai International Radio Music Festival in 1997.

*A biography of Professor Liqing Yang appears in the main section of this Edition.*

## DR GILI YEN, PhD

*For your Outstanding Contribution
to Economics*

# DR GILI YEN, PhD

An economist whose career embraces university education, research and administration, Dr Gili Yen not only has an excellent reputation in his own country, Taiwan, but is also known internationally through his professional publications. He is presently Senior Research Fellow at the Taiwan Research Institute in Taipei and Dean of the School of Management at Chaoyang University of Technology in Taichung, appointed to the former post in 1994 and to the latter in 1998.

The fifth child and second son of Tzeng-song and Yueh-yun Yen, Gili Yen was born on 8 March 1953 in Taipei. He finished his primary and secondary education in Keelung. Later, he studied at the National Taiwan University in Taipei, receiving Bachelor of Arts and Master of Arts degrees in Economics in 1975 and 1978 respectively. He then left Taipei to travel to the USA to pursue further studies which culminated in a PhD in Economics from Washington University in St Louis, Missouri, in 1983.

During the ten years or so prior to the first of his present appointments, Dr Yen held several positions at academic institutions. In addition to becoming an Associate Research Fellow at the Chung-Hua Institute for Economic Research from 1983-86, in 1985 he joined the National Central University as an Associate Professor at its Graduate Institute of Industrial Research, where he subsequently became Professor and Director. Instrumental in establishing the University's Graduate Institute of Financial Management, he transferred there in 1989, to serve as Professor and Founding Director until 1992. He then became a Senior Research Fellow and Division Director at Taiwan Institute of Economic Research, prior to his appointment at the Taiwan Research Institute.

Parallel with his research activities, from 1994-97 Professor Yen shouldered responsibility as First Vice-President of the China Development Industrial Bank. Between 1990 and 1997 he sat on the Board of Directors and Board of Supervisors of the China Steel Corporation, an enterprise based in Kaohsiung. He acted as an Advisor to the Executive Yuan - the administrative branch of the central government - from 1983-84 and again from 1989-90, while from 1987-93 he was involved as an Adjunct Professor at his alma mater, the National Taiwan University in Taipei.

With regard to publications, Professor Yen has experience both in editorship and in authorship. On behalf of the Pacific Economic Cooperation Council he edited a book entitled "New Directions in Regional Trade Liberalization and Investment Cooperation", published in 1994. In addition to being the author of "Empirical Studies on Business Finance and Government Policy in Taiwan", a collection of academic papers published in 1996, he contributed an article to the book "International Library of Management", published in 1998, and has authored or co-authored more than thirty articles in international journals such the Journal of Health Economics, Journal of Economics and Business, American Journal of Economics and Sociology, Managerial and Decision Economics, Review of Quantitative Finance and Accounting, Atlantic Economic Journal, Review of Pacific Basin Financial Markets and Policies, Economics and Finance Advances in Pacific Basin Business, Journal of Developing Areas, and others. Moreover, he sits on the Editorial Committees of two journals, namely, Advances Pacific Basin Business, Economics and Finance, and the Review of Pacific Basin Financial Markets and Policies.

Besides receiving the Outstanding Professorship Award from the National Central University in 1989 and the Outstanding Research Award from Chaoyang University of Technology in 1999; at various times during his career Dr Yen was granted research awards by the National Science Council. Earlier this decade he enjoyed the distinction of serving as Governor of the Chinese Economic Association, and as Secretary-General and Executive Director of the Chinese Finance Association. He continues to hold membership in both associations, as well as in the International Society for New Institutional Economics, in which he had the honour of acting as his country's representative in 1997.

Professor Gili Yen's recreational pursuits consist of reading, listening to music, playing table tennis, travelling and playing majong. He and his wife, the former Eva Chung-chiung Lin, have a son, Bernard Chih-hsun Yen, who is now studying at the University of California at Berkeley.

*A biography of Dr Gili Yen, PhD, appears in the main section of this Edition.*

## DR JUNICHI YOSHIDA, MD, MS, FACS

*For your Outstanding Contribution
to Surgery*

# JUNICHI YOSHIDA, MD, MS, FACS

Dr Junichi Yoshida is the Chief of the Division of General Thoracic Surgery at Shimonoseki City Hospital in Japan. Simultaneously, he has been involved in the prevention of MRSA cross infection using molecular epidemiology method or DNA analysis.

Junichi Yoshida graduated from Kyushu University, Faculty of Medicine, Japan, in 1981, gaining a MD degree. He then spent the following four years in surgical residency training in Kyushu University Hospital and its affiliated hospitals in Japan. He wrote his first paper while still in training, about the impalement chest trauma with an iron bar traversing the sternum and one of the costovertebral junction, which really impressed the medical world. In 1985, Dr Yoshida decided to take up an appointment in Chicago, USA as a Research Associate in the Department of Surgery, University of Illinois at Chicago. He also enrolled in the Graduate College there to study for a MSc degree in Surgery. In 1986, he defended a thesis regarding the anatomic study on the vagal nerve pathway from the central nervous system through the chest to the abdominal viscera to delineate where vagotomy should be performed, preserving the motor function of the stomach while abolishing gastric acid secretion. Dr Yoshida returned to Japan in 1988 as a House Officer in the hospitals affiliated with Kyushu University, until, in 1988, he became board certified by the Japanese Surgical Society.

In the 1990's there was an outbreak of methicillin-resistant S aureus (MRSA), outbreak which had been sporadic across Japan. Dr Yoshida was involved in the epidemiology there, but in 1993, with the crisis over, he took up the appointment of Assistant Professor in the Department of Surgery I, at Kyushu University. He majored in the prevention of noscomial infection and attained in 1996, a record of no detection of MRSA for seventeen consecutive months in the service of his Department. Concurrently, Dr Yoshida was also engaged in less invasive surgery, being laparoscopic, thoracoscopic and choledochoscopic procedures. In 1995, for two months, Dr Yoshida was invited as an instructor of endoscopic surgery at Sino-Japan Friendship Hospital, Beijing, and also in the same year, he was nominated as a Fellow of the American College of Surgeons. In 1996, he was still involved in the prevention of MRSA cross infection, using a molecular epidemiology method or DNA analysis, but also was appointed Chief, at the Division of General Thoracic Surgery, Shimonoseki City Hospital. A position he took to strengthen thoracoscopic surgery there.

Junichi Yoshida is the author of numerous professional articles, book chapters and conference papers, and has been accepted worldwide as one of the experts in his field. He sees his patients as though they were members of his own family and operates as such. He tells this policy to the postgraduate surgeons he trains, hoping that they will go on to be excellent surgeons with compassion, as he instills this in all his work.

Dr Yoshida is a member of the Warren H Cole Society, University of Illinois at Chicago. He is married to Yukimi, and they have two sons, Masashi Christopher and Hiroki Yoshida.

*A biography of Junichi Yoshida, MD, MS, FACS, appears in the main section of this Edition.*

## WATSON TOSHINORI YOSHIMOTO, IOM, LFIBA, MOIF

*For your Outstanding Contribution to the Conservation of Wildlife and the Preservation of their Natural Habitat*

# WATSON TOSHINORI YOSHIMOTO, IOM, LFIBA, MOIF

Watson T Yoshimoto (affectionately known as Yoshi) - general contractor, world-renowned sportsman and wildlife conservationist - was born on 21 November 1909 in Punalulu, Oahu, Hawaii, USA. His father, Yoshinosuke Yoshimoto, and his mother, Kou Nagawa Yoshimoto, had both arrived in Honolulu from Japan on the Manchuria Maru in 1907, to work on the sugar plantations.

Mr Yoshimoto began work as a carpenter's apprentice at the age of fifteen. In 1940 he formed the Oahu Construction Company, which he incorporated in 1947. In 1988 it was named one of the 250 largest public and private companies in Hawaii, while in 1990, his fiftieth year as a general contractor, he turned the limited company over to its employees. Since 1963 and 1967 respectively, he has been President of the W T Yoshimoto Corporation and Mak Bowl Incorporated.

Mr Yoshimoto's professional pursuits included service as President and Director of the General Contractors Association of Hawaii in 1954. Furthermore, he once served on the Board of Directors of Honolulu Iron Works, Honolulu Trust Company Limited, the City Bank of Honolulu, Aloha Motors Limited, Hawaii Thrift and Loan Company, and the Crown Corporation. He owned and operated the Classic Bowling Center from 1965 until dissolving its operations in 1992, after 28 years in the business.

Mr Yoshimoto's civic contributions have centred around the Outdoor Circle of Honolulu, the Bishop Museum of Honolulu and the Hawaiian Humane Society. In 1977 - in conjunction with his wife, Katherine Katsuyo Yoshimoto - he served as Co-Chairman of "Be Kind to Animals Week" under the auspices of the Hawaiian Humane Society, pursuant to a proclamation by Governor George Ariyoshi of the State of Hawaii. He was also Chairman of the General Contractors Division of the Honolulu Community Chest Campaign (now the Aloha United Fund) for 1961, 1963 and 1969.

However, it was in the outback that Mr Yoshimoto attained world renown as a wildlife conservationist, big game hunter, field trial enthusiast and outspoken proponent of the concept of "trophy hunting". Maintaining intense interest and participating in outdoor projects since 1950, he made substantial contributions to the Associated Field Trial Club of Hawaii, which honoured him in 1964 for his services as President in 1958 and 1959 and as Secretary-Treasurer from 1960-94. Besides citing him for his good sportsmanship and great generosity to dogdom (field trials) in Hawaii, in 1974 the organisation also established the W T Yoshimoto Derby Classic, a one-hour heat stake which ran its twentieth annual and final trial in 1994. In recognition of 42 years of service to field trials nationally, he was inducted into the Field Trial Hall of Fame in September 1991.

To date, Mr Yoshimoto has conducted hunting trips to 43 countries on six continents, besides to New Zealand, Papua-New Guinea, Ceylon and a number of other smaller islands. He has collected nearly every major animal, with 254 of them in the record class in the Safari Club International Record Book of Trophy Animals by January 1994. To herald his skill, determination and good sportsmanship, he was awarded by the Shikar-Safari Club International for the best Indian game trophy in 1962, with additional honours for the best African game trophy in 1971. In 1975 he won 1st Place in the Safari Club International Award for best African game trophy.

As a member of the Safari Club International Conservation Fund, he sponsors the American Wilderness Leadership School, which introduces American youth and teachers to the value and methods of conservation and makes them aware of the responsibilities involved in conserving the world's wildlife management, hunting skills, ethics and safety, fishing, hiking and riding. For his support and contributions to the school, in 1977 the Safari Club International honoured him as 1976 Man of the Year, its highest award. A member of the Club's Selection Committee for the International Hunting Hall of Fame Award and International Major Trophy Award, he himself received the former award in 1982 and the latter in 1983. Moreover, he was appointed President Emeritus of the Club's Hawaii Chapter, after serving as its President in 1978, 1979, 1980 and 1981. He belongs to many other organisations, most of them involved in outdoor wildlife conservation. On 5 December 1980, he was awarded the 24th "Weatherby Big Game Trophy Award", often called the "Oscar" of the hunting world, for his outstanding accomplishments in wildlife conwervation.

In 1978 Mr Yoshimoto established the non-profit W T Yoshimoto Foundation, which is dedicated to protection and perpetuation of all wildlife resources through assistance in education and conservation efforts. The Foundation also promotes sport hunting as a valuable wildlife management tool. One of its acts was to establish the W T Yoshimoto Foundation Endowed Fellowship in Animal Wildlife Conservation at the University of Hawaii at Manoa, giving provision for two scholarships annually. In addition, it operated the Wildlife Museum in Honolulu. Housing 370 specimens of mounted wild animals, the museum had the aim of educating the public regarding the ethics of sport hunting in wildlife conservation and game management, so that future generations could enjoy all wildlife and preserve the natural habitats. The entire contents of the museum were recently donated by the Foundation to the National Science Museum in Tokyo, Japan, where the opening ceremony for the Yoshimoto Collection took place on 6 March 1998.

*A biography of Watson Toshinori Yoshimoto, IOM, LFIBA, MOIF, appears in the main section of this Edition.*

# PROFESSOR MASATAKA YOSHIMURA, DEng

*For your Outstanding Contribution
to Engineering Research*

# PROFESSOR MASATAKA YOSHIMURA, DEng

Dr Masataka Yoshimura was born in Hyogo Prefecture, Japan, as the son of the late Gentaro Yoshimura and Saeko Yoshimura, who is still living. Nowadays he is a Professor in the Department of Precision Engineering at the Graduate School of Engineering at Kyoto University, where he has been employed for the past twenty-three years. He earned a Bachelor of Engineering degree in Mechanical Engineering and Master of Engineering degree in Precision Engineering from Kyoto University, from which he also received his Doctorate in Engineering in 1976.

Professor Yoshimura's research interests include the integrated optimization of product design and manufacturing, information systems for design and manufacturing, design optimization, concurrent engineering, and the dynamics of machine tools and industrial robots. In particular, he has conducted primary research in the following areas: analyses of the dynamics of industrial machines, machine tools, industrial robots, and their optimization; construction of design optimization methods for machines manufacturing high-performance products at high efficiency; concurrent design and manufacturing, and multidisciplinary optimization; construction of new manufacturing systems generating optimum design solutions from a systematic viewpoint; collaborative design generation based on knowledge and information systems; construction of innovative design and manufacturing systems based on networked information frame-systems. Internationally active, he is well-known as a pioneer and world authority in those areas of research, and contributes technical guidance and support for Asian countries such as Singapore and Taiwan.

In 1976 Professor Yoshimura received the Best Paper Award from the Japan Society for Precision Engineering. The following decade he became the recipient of two further Best Paper Awards, from the Japan Society for the Promotion of Machine Tool Engineering in 1985 and 1986. He has published more than eighty papers in English in the journals and proceedings of the American Society of Mechanical Engineers, in the International Journal of Production Research, in Concurrent Engineering: Research and Applications, in Structural Optimization, in MTDR,in CIRP and in publications of the Japan Society of Mechanical Engineers and Japan Society for Precision Engineering, as well as in numerous others. Moreover, he is the co-author of numerous books and contributions to books, notably "CAD/CAM/CAP", 1986, "Most Advanced Technologies of Machine Tools", 1988, and "Principles of CIM", 1993, all three in Japanese, plus the English publications of "Multicriteria Design Optimization", 1990, "Control and Dynamics - Manufacturing and Automation Systems: Techniques and Technologies", 1991, "Concurrent Engineering - Contemporary Issues and Modern Design Tools", 1993, "Control and Dynamics Systems - Concurrent Engineering Techniques and Applications", 1994, and "Design for X: Concurrent Engineering Imperatives", 1996.

A member of the Japan Society of Mechanical Engineers since 1967, Professor Yoshimura currently chairs its Research Committee and sits on its Steering Committee, assuming both responsibilities in 1998. He is also active in the American Society of Mechanical Engineers, serving as co-organizer of the Design Automation Conference since 1994. Other organizations to which he belongs consist of the Japan Society of Precision Engineers, the North American Manufacturing Research Institute of SME, the American Institute of Aeronautics and Astronautics, the International Society for Structural and Multidisciplinary Optimization, the Japan Society for the Study of Office Automation, The Institute of Systems, Control and Information Engineers and the Japan Society of Computational Engineering and Science.

In his free time, Dr Yoshimura finds recreation through listening to music, while he also enjoys travel. He is married to Machiko.

*A biography of Professor Masataka Yoshimura, DEng, appears in the main section of this Edition.*

## ZHEQIN ZHU

*For your Outstanding Contribution to*
*20th Century Chinese and World Music*

# ZHEQIN ZHU

A Chinese singer, known professionally as Dadawa, Miss Zhu Zheqin has been recording for the Warner Music Company since 1994. She already has an international reputation and in 1998 was admitted to membership of the American Society of Artists, Authors and Publishers.

One of Miss Zhu's earliest recordings was a song "The Story of a Red Crowned Crane", which was issued in 1990, and was followed two years later by her first album, "Yellow Children". In 1995, with her second album, "Sister Drum", she became the first Chinese singer in the international industry to have an album distributed worldwide. Her third album, "Voices from the Sky" came out in 1997, the year after her recording of the song "Tear Lake" with The Chieftains had appeared. Moreover, her voice can be heard on the soundtrack of two films, "The King of Nanling" and "Chinese Box", made in 1996 and 1997 respectively.

In 1990 Miss Zhu distinguished herself by winning 2nd Prize in the 4th Grand Prize TV Contest for Young Singers. Further success came her way in 1995, when her new album was selected as One of the Top Five Albums of the Year in World Music by Q Magazine and won the 20th Taiwan Jinding Phonograph Award for Best Album. 1997 was another year of glory. Not only was she named the Best Female Artist in YMC (Hong Kong Cable TV Station), but the movie Chinese Box received the Best Sound Track Award at the Venice Film Festival.

Zhu Zheqin is listed in Five Hundred Leaders of Influence, International Who's Who of Intellectuals and the 4th edition of Who's Who in Asia and the Pacific Nations. Born on 15 June 1968 in Guangzhou, China, she entered university after completing her middle school education, and gained a Bachelor of Arts degree in Chinese Literature in 1990. Singing is not her only pleasure; in her free time she enjoys reading, swimming, travelling and listening to funny stories.

*A biography of Zheqin Zhu appears in the main section of this Edition.*

# Biographies

# A

**AAGAARD-MOGENSEN Lars,** b. 30 March 1944, Randers, Denmark. Philosopher. m. Else Larsen, 1 son. Education: MA, SUNY, 1971; Mag art, Aarhus University, 1972; PhD, Aarhus University, 1980. Appointments: Aarhus University, 1972-77; Copenhagen University, 1977-78; Philosophical Research Center, Athens, Greece, 1978-79; Gent State University, Belgium, 1979-80; Washington University, St Louis, 1980-82; St Cloud State University, 1982-83; RIT, 1983-87; Wassard Company, 1987-; School of Visual Arts, 1993-. Publications include: Text, Literature and Aesthetics, Amsterdam, 1986; Idea of the Museum, 1988; World Making's Ways, 1987; Real Art, 1994; Hegel's Logic, 1998. Memberships: Phi Kappa Phi; Academy of American Poets; APA; Nordic Society of Aesthetics. Address: 3757 Main Street, Burdett, NY 14818-9631, USA.

**AARFLOT Rolf,** b. 1919, Borg, Sweden. Principal; Captain. m. Ingrid Lyttkens, 1 son, 1 daughter. Education: Military Officer, 1941; MSc, 1950. Appointments: Officer, Royal Lifegrenadiers, 1941; Principal, Secondary School, 1964. Publication: Jubilee Book of Lundells School, 1992. Honour: Knight of the Northern Star Order, 1972. Membership: South Rotary Club of Uppsala. Address: Tiundag 41, 752 30 Uppsala, Sweden.

**AARLI Johan Arild,** b. 1 May 1936, Kvinesdal, Norway. Neurologist. m. Gullborg Gullestad, 2 sons, 3 daughters. Education: MD, 1961, PhD, 1972, University of Bergen. Appointments: Professor of Neurology and Chairman, Department of Neurology, University Hospital, Bergen, 1977-; Dean, Faculty of Medicine, University of Bergen, 1985-87. Publications: 250 scientific papers on neurology; 3 books. Honour: Knight of 1st Class of St Olaus Order, 1997. Memberships: Association British Neurologists, Honorary Foreign Member; American Academy of Neurology, Correspondence Member; American Neurologic Association, Correspondence Member. Address: Haukeland Sykehus, 5021 Bergen, Norway.

**ABARA Okechukwu Nnamdi,** b. 26 May 1971, Afikpo, Nigeria. Engineer. m. Vera, 1 daughter. Education: BSc, Computer Science, Donetsk State Technical University, 1990-95; MSc, Computer Engineering, 1990-95. Appointments: Manager, Information Systems Engineer, Crucedoz Inv Company, 1995-99; Commercial Director, Systems Analysis, Alen Private Company, 1999-. Publications: Numerous Short Essays, Stories and 1 Novel, 1989-92. Honours: Several Educational and Social Service Awards. Membership: Association for the Defence of Rights of Foreigners. Address: Alen Private Company, Suite 340, House No 80, Artyoma Street, Donetsk 340055, Ukraine.

**ABASOVA Adilya Z,** b. 1942, Zangilan, Azerbaijan. Physicist. m. Abasov Gurban, 1 son. Education: Candidate of Physico-Mathematical Science, 1970, Degree of Physico-Mathematical Sciences, 1987, Azerbaijan State University. Appointments: Chief of Department in Parliament of Azerbaijan Republic; Professor of Baku State University. Publications: 70. Address: Institute of Physics, Azerbaijan Academy of Sciences, G Javid Prospekt 33, Baku 370143, Azerbaijan.

**ABATE Tsedeke,** b. 25 July 1952, Bobbi, Ethiopia. Entomologist. m. Azeb, 1 son, 2 daughters. Education: BS High Honours, 1977, MS, 1979, University Florida; PhD, Simon Fraser University, Canada, 1990. Appointments: Senior Researcher, Ethiopian Institute of Agricultural Research, 1994-98; Strategic Planning Coordinator, 1990-93. Publications: Over 100 articles and presentations. Honours: First Prize, Crop Science Society of Ethiopia, 1993, 1994. Memberships: Entomological Society of America; Annual Review of Entomology, International Correspondent. Address: IAR Nazareth Research Centre, PO Box 436, Nazareth, Ethiopia.

**ABBOTT Mary Elaine,** b. 23 April 1922, LaGrange, Illinois. Photographer. m. Harry Abbott, 1 son, 1 daughter. Education: BA Psychology and English (Liberal Arts), 1944, University of Iowa; Wisdom Literature; Ancient, Modern History; Writers' Workshop, University of Iowa; Certified Teacher, University of Chicago, Great Books. Appointments: Claire Allen Architect, Book Comm State Department History, National Trust; Advisor, International Platform Association; Resident Photographer, Comm Sculpture in Michigan; Lecturer, Manuscript Lorado Taft/Blackhawk. Honours: IPA Juried Shows, 1993-97, Awards; National Trust Hist Preservation; Jackson Historic District Commission; Buildings of Michigan; Claire Allen, Architect. Memberships: National Trust Historic Pres; Jackson Historic District Commission; IPA; Episcopal Church; Jackson Chorale; Junior League; Kappa Alpha Theta. Address: 721 Oakridge Dr, Jackson, MI 49203 3914, USA.

**ABD EL-SALAAM Khalafalla Mohamed,** b. 12 June 1943, El-Minia, Egypt. Professor. m. Professor Ehsan Abu El-Fotookh, 2 sons. Education: BS, Special Chemistry, Faculty of Science, 1963, MSc, Surface Chemistry, 1967, PhD, Surface Chemistry and Heterogenous Catalysis, 1970, Assiut University, Egypt. Appointments: Demonstrator, 1963-70, Assistant Professor, 1970-75, Associate Professor, 1975-79, Professor, 1979-, Assiut University; Professor, Physical Chemistry, Umm Al-Qura University, Saudi Arabia. Publications: About 100 works; Research on Surface Chemistry and Heterogenous Catalysis, Solid State Chemistry, Thermal Analysis. Honours: UNESCO postdoctoral fellowship to Tokyo Institute of Technology, Japan, 1973-74; Alexander Von Humboldt Stiftung postdoctoral Fellowship to Gottingen University, West Germany, 1977-78; Fulbright postdoctoral fellowship to Delaware Catalytic Center, Delaware University, USA, 1983-84. Membership: New York Academy of Science; American Association for the Advancement of Science. Address: 3 Dr Ezz El-Din Taha Street, Mantika Oula, Nasr City, Cairo, Egypt.

**ABDEL AZIZ Nabil Muhammad,** b. 6 January 1939, Cairo. Professor of Medieval History. m. Neveen Nasr Eldin Abdallah, 1 son, 2 daughters. Education: License History, 1962; Diploma of Education & Psychology, 1964; Magister, 1968; PhD, 1972. Appointments: Agent, 1980; Dean, 1981; Chief of Dept of History, 1981, 1991, 1998. Publications: 6 Arabic Sources; 4 books: Horses and its Sport, during the Mamluks Period, 1976; The Delight and Its Musical Instruments, during the Ayyoubids and Mamluks Periods, 1980; The Sultan's Kitchen, during the Ayyoubids and Mamluks periods, 1989; The Sport of the Hunting, during the Mamluks period, 1998; 4 studies. Memberships: Egyptian Historical Society; Arab Historians Society. Address: 60 Abou Bakr El Sadeek Street, Flat No 17, Heliopolis, Cairo, Egypt.

**ABDEL-AZIZ Osama,** b. 8 July 1939, Menofia, Egypt. Professor of Cardiology. m. Mahassen Ali Hassan, 1 son, 2 daughters. Education: MB, B.Ch, Cairo University, 1961; Master of Cardiology, Charles University, 1968; MD, Cardiology, Charles and Oxford Universities, 1971. Appointments: Professor, Head, Cardiac Department, Tanta

University, Egypt. Publications: Books on Cardiology and Electrocardiography. Memberships: Egyptian Society of Cardiology; American College of Cardiology; Egyptian Medical Association. Address: Cardiology Department, Faculty of Medicine, Tanta University, Tanta, Egypt.

**ABDELAZIZ Samir Fauad,** b. 26 March 1957, Cairo, Egypt. Consultant, Assistant Professor. m. Iman, 1 son, 2 daugters. Education: MBBch, 1982; MSc, 1986; MD, 1992. Appointment: Assistant Professor, Al Azhar University. Memberships: International Gynaecologic Cancer Society; World Oncology Network. Address: 10 Shazly St El Naam, Helmiat El Zeiton, Cairo, Egypt.

**ABDERRAHINAN Walid Ahmad,** b. 25 October 1944, Jerusalem. Research Scientist. m. Messbah A, 1 son, 2 daughters. Education: MSs, 1975; Phd, 1977; BSc, Water and Soil Science, 1987. Appointments: Director, Water Research Department, 1978-81; Coordinator, Water Research Group, 1981-89; Manager, Water Section, Research Institute, 1994-. Publications: More than 80 Technical Papers. Honours: 6 National and International Awards. Memberships: International Water Research Association; American Water Resources Association; National Water Well Association; International Association of Hydrocologists. Address: King Faud Univ Petrol Minerals; The Research Institute, Dhahran 31261, Saudi Arabia.

**ABDULHAMED Jassim,** b. 10 July 1952, Haditha, Iraq. Doctor; Paediatric Cardiologist. m. Nadia Hussain, 3 sons, 1 daughter. Education: MBChB, 1974; DCH, 1982; MRCP (Paeds), UK, 1986; FRCP Edinburgh, 1996; FACC, 1996; FCCP, 1996; FRCP LONDON, 1998. Appointments: Resident Doctor, Yarmouk Teaching Hospital, Baghdad, 1974-75; National Service, Medical Army Service and Rural Health, Iraq, 1975-79; Senior House Officer, Paediatrics, Althawra Children's Hospital, Baghdad, 1979-80; Senior House Officer, Paediatrics, 1980-81, DCH Candidate, 1981-82, Registrar, Paediatrics, 1982-85, Medical City Teaching Hospital, Baghdad; Clinical Attachment, Paediatrics, Westminster Children's Hospital, UK, 1985-86; SHO, Paediatrics, Leicester Royal Infirmary, UK, 1986-87; Registrar/Fellow, Paediatric Cardiology, Royal Hospital for Sick Children, Edinburgh, UK, 1987-89; Registrar, Paediatrics, Ninewells University Hospital, Dundee, UK, 1989-90; Senior Registrar, Paediatric Cardiology, Armed Forces Cardiac Centre, Riyadh, 1990-93; Consultant, 1993-95, Consultant and Acting Head of Dept, 1995-96, Consultant Cardiologist, 1997-, Paediatric Cardiology, Prince Sultan Cardiac Centre, Riyadh. Publications: Author and co-Author, 28 articles and abstracts in professional journals. Memberships: British Cardiac Society; Saudi Heart Association; British Paediatric Cardiologist Association; Association of European Paediatric Cardiologists. Address: Prince Sultan Cardiac Centre, PO Box 7897 Dept Paediatric Cardiology, Riyadh 11159, Saudi Arabia.

**ABDULKASAN Hadja Meriam,** b. 11 November 1959. Poblacion Buluan. Bachelor of Science in social Work. m. Hadji Abusama Salendab, 3 sons, 1 daughter. Education: BSc, Centro Escolar University, 1976-80. Appointments: Social Worker, 1981-. Memberships: Philippines Association of Social Work; Autonomous Region in Muslim Mindanao Employees Association. Address: Department of Social Welfare and Development, DSWD ARMM Regional Office, Cotabato City, Philippines.

**ABDULLAH Jafri Malin,** b. 5 December 1962, Kuantan, Pahang, Malaysia. Neurosurgeon. m. Dr Siti Fatimah Hj Abd Rahman, 3 sons, 2 daughters. Education: MD, USM, 1986;

Diplomate, Neurosurgery, Belgium, 1994; PhD, Belgium, 1995. Appointments: Lecturer, 1995-98; Associate Professor in Neurosurgery, Department of Neurosurgery, School of Medical Sciences, University Sains Malaysia, Kelantan, Malaysia, 1998-. Publications: 108 presentations as 1st presenter or co-author including special lectures and conferences; 50 papers as author or co-author in professional journals. Memberships: Malaysian Medical Association; University Sains Malaysia Medical Graduates Alumni Society; Belgium Neurosurgical Society; European Stereotatic and Functional Neurosurgical Society; International Stereotactic Radiosurgery Society; International Association of Pain; Malaysian Neurosurgical Society; Belgium Oncology Society; Malaysian Neuroscience Society; Asian and Australasian Neurosurgical Society (Malaysian delegate); International Society for Paediatric Neurosurgery; Asean Neurosurgical Society; Asean Society for Stereotactic, Functional and Computer Assisted Neurosurgery; Academy of Medicine, Malaysia; Fellow, International College of Surgeons; Associate International Member, American Association of Neurological Surgery. Address: University Science Malaysia, Jalan Sultanah Zainab II, Kehantan Kubang Kerian 16150, Malaysia.

**ABEDIN M Zainul,** b. 23 April 1953, Lakshmipur, Bangladesh. Teacher. m. Ayesha Begum, 1 son, 3 daughters. Education: BA, honours, Economics, 1973, MA, Economics, 1974, Dhaka University; PhD, Economics, Institute of Bangladesh Studies, Rajshahi University, 1989. Appointments: Lecturer, Economics, New Model Degree College, Sukrabad, Dhaka; Associate Instructor, Bangladesh Academy for Rural Development, Kotbari; Senior Faculty Member, Bangladesh Institute of Bank Management, Mirpur; Professor, Economics, Institute of Bangladesh Studies, Rajshahi University. Publications: 2 Books; Numerous articles in professional journals. Honours: Bangla Academy Award, Composing Poems. Memberships: International Institute for Development Studies; Institute of Bangladesh Studies; Rajshahi University Alumni Association; Bangladesh Economics Teachers Association; Bangladesh Economic Association; Indian Economic Association; Bengal Economic Association; Dhaka University Economics Department Alumni Association. Address: Institute of Bangladesh Studies, Rajshahi University, Rajshahi 6205, Bangladesh.

**ABEL Robert B,** b. 21 July 1926, USA. Oceanographer. m. Nancy Klein Abel, 1 son, 1 daughter. Education: Brown University, 1943-47; Columbia University, 1945; Johns Hopkins University, 1950-54; George Washington University, 1955-61; PhD, American University, 1969-72. Appointments: Chemical Oceanographer, Woods Hole Oceanographic Institute, 1947-50; Director of Oceanographic Surveys and Assistant to Director, US Naval Hydrographic Office, 1950-1960; Assistant Research Coordinator, Office of Naval Research, 1960-67; Director, National Sea Grant Programme, National Science Foundation, 1967-70; Director, UD Department of Commerce, 1970-77; Assistant Vice President, Texas A&M University, 1977-78; President, New Jersey Marine Sciences Consortium, 1979-93; Manager, Cooperative Marine Technology Program for the Middle East, 1979-; Senior Scientist, Stevens Institute of Technology, 1993-; Research Professor, Texas A&M University, 1993-. Publications: 3 Books; Over 100 Articles. Honours: Include, Order of Jules Richard, 1952; US Navy Distinguished Service Award, 1967; Man of the Year, National Sea Grant Association, 1973; Man of Year, Distinguished Service-COMPASS Award, 1987; Egyptian Government Award for Distinguished Achievement, 1991. Memberships: Several, Including Marine Technology Society; Explorers Club, Cosmos Club, New York Academy of Sciences; New Jersey Marine Fisheries Council; Middle East Institute. Address: Stevens

Institute of Technology, Davidson Laboratory, 711 Hudson Street, Hoboken, New Jersey 07030.

**ABOU-ALLAM Ragaa Mahmoud,** b. 28 January 1927, Fowa, Egypt. Professor Emeritus. m. Nawal Mohamed Hagras, 2 daughters. Education: BA, Cairo University, 1950; MA, Columbia University, 1962; PhD, New York University, 1965. Appointments: Consultant, Ministry of Education, 1967-74; Associate Professor, Kuwait University, 1974-77; Professor, 1977-81; Chair, Department of Education, Psychology, 1981-86; Professor 1986-96; Professor Emeritus, Cairo University, 1996-. Publications: Measurement and Evaluation of Academic Achievement; Introduction to Educational Research; Methods of Research in Psychology and Education. Memberships: National Association of Gifted Children. Address: 2 Road 259, New Maadi, Cairo 11435, Egypt.

**ABOU-TAHA Kais,** b. 28 February 1939, Yafa, Palestine. Physician. m. Fatima, 2 sons, 1 daughter. Education: MB, BCh, 1967; MD, 1974; MCCEE, 1981; Post Graduate Course in Diabetes, 1975. Appointments: Senior Medical Registrar; Specialist of Internal Medicine and Diabetology; UN Medical Examiner; DMP Canada. Publications: Medical Bouquet, 1984; Text Book in Diabetes, 1987; Diabetes and Children, 2nd Edition, 1990; A Guide to Cure, 1994; Cholesterol and the Heart, 1997; Hypertension, 2nd Edition, 1998; Educational Video Film on Diabetes. Memberships: American Diabetes Association; British Diabetes Association; Canadian Diabetes Association; International Diabetes Federation; Fellow, Royal Society of Medicine (Lon). Talented Painter. Address: Kais Abu Taha Med Ctr, Hamden St P O Box 46467, Abu Dhabi, United Arab Emirates.

**ABOUL NAGA Mohsen,** b. 28 January 1956, Port-Said, Egypt. Associate Professor; Architect. 1 son. Education: BSc Architectural Engineering, 1979, MSc Architectural Engineering, 1985, Cairo University; PhD Building Environment, 1990, University of Leeds, England. Appointments: Instructor, Architecture design, Housing, Execution Documents, 1980-84, Assistant Lecturer, Architectural Design, Housing, Planning, WD, and Environment, 1984-85, Assistant Professor, Full-time Engineering Faculty Member, 1991-96, Associate Professor, Full-time Engineering Faculty Member, 1997-, Cairo University; Instructor, Architecture Design, Projection, Building Construction, 1985-87, Full-time PhD Research Associate, 1986-90, University of Leeds, England; Visiting Professor, Engineering Faculty Member, 1994-95, Assistant Professor, Full-time Engineering Faculty Member, 1995-, UAE University, Al-Ain, UAE; Principle and Partner, EAG Consultancy, The Egyptian Architects Group, Cairo, 1980-. Publications: 5 international journal papers; 17 international conference papers. Honours: Particpated in 5 major projects 1991-; Design Prizes for 5 projects, 1982, 1983, 1991, 1993, 1994; Faculty Best Performance Research Award, 1998-99. Memberships: International Solar Energy Society; American Solar Energy Society; World Renewable Energy Network; Research Network, Lund University Centre for Habitat Studies; International Association of Housing Science; Chartered Institute of British Service Engineers; Registered Architect; Egyptian Societies of : the British Universities Graduates; Engineers; Solar Energy; Architects. Address: United Arab Emirates University, Municipality St POB 17555, Al Ain, Abu Dhabi, United Arab Emirates.

**ABOUSENNA Mona,** b. 16 August 1945, Cairo. Professor. Widow. 1 daughter. Education: Abitur German Language, 1963, Cairo; BA English Language & Literature, 1976, Cairo; MA American Literature, 1976, Ain Shams University; PhD

Comparative Drama, 1980, Ain Shams. Appointments: Professor English and Comparative Literature, Faculty of Education, Ain Shams University, 1990-; Head, English Dept, 1990-; Director, Centre for Developing English Teaching, 1990-. Memberships: Secretary General: Afro-Asian Philosophy Association; Averroes & Enlightenment International Association. Address: Faculty of Education, Roxy, Heliopolis, Cairo, Egypt.

**ABRAHAM Rebecca,** b. 11 April 1962, Calcutta, India. Faculty Head. Widowed, 1 son. Education: Bachelor of Science, 1982; Master of Business Administration, 1984; Doctor of Business Administration, 1989. Appointments: Assistant Professor, Nova Southeastern University, 1989-94; Associate Professor, Nova Southeastern University, 1994-. Publications include: Acculturation: A Review and an Exploratory Seven-Nation Comparative Study, 1996; The I C: An Etic-Emic Analysis in an Organizational Context, 1996; The Relationship of Vertical and Horizontal Individualism and Collectivism to Intrepreneurship and Organizational Commitment, 1997; Thinking Styles as Moderators of Role-Stress Job Satisfaction Relationships, 1997; Emotional Dissonance in Organizations: Antecedents, Consequences and Moderators, 1998; The Relationship of Differential Inequity to Job Satisfaction, Intention to Turnover and Self-Esteem, in press; Determinants of Receptivity to Expatriate Assignment, 1997. Address: Nova SE University, 3301 College Avenue, Fort Lauderdale, FL 33314-7721, USA.

**ABRAM Zoltan,** b. 9 December 1963, Seini, Romania. Hygienist; Writer. m. Noemi, 2 sons. Education: Degree in Medicine, 1989, Targu Mures; Degree in Journalism, 1991, Budapest; PhD, 1997. Appointments: Reader, University of Medicine & Pharmacy, Targu Mures; President, Prevention Health Promotion Association. Publications: Hungarians Around the World, 1995; The Muddy Nyarad, 1996; Communitas, 1996; Environmental Protection, 1997; Szentegyhaza, 1998; Dietetics, 1998; and articles. Memberships: President, Preventio; Secretary, Transilvanian Medical Society; New York Academy of Sciences; Secretary, Romanian Hygiene & Public Health Society; Co-President, Hungarian Folk High School Society. Address: Borsos Tamas 25, 4300 Targu Mures, Romania.

**ABRAMOV Anatoli A,** b. 30 May 1960, Tetyukhe, Russia. Physicist. m. Elena E Kudryavtseva, 1 son. Education: Diploma in Physics, Moscow State University, 1983; PhD in Physics and Mathematics, Russian Academy of Sciences, General Physics Institute, 1988. Appointments: Senior Research Fellow, General Physics Institute, RAS, 1993-96; Research Fellow, Rutgers University, 1996-97; Member of Technical Staff, Bell Labs Lucent Technologies, 1997-. Publications: Contributor, 46 Technical Papers; 4 Patents. Honours: Bell Labs President's Gold Award. Memberships: Optical Society of America. Address: Bell Labs, Lucent Techs, 101 Crawford Corner Road, Room 3N-502, Holmdel, NJ 07733, USA.

**ABRAMOVIC Biljana,** b. 15 December 1952. Professor. m. Borislav Abramovic, 1 daughter. Education: BS, 1975, MSc, 1979, PhD, 1983, Faculty of Sciences, University of Novi Sad. Appointments: Assistant, 1976-84, Assistant Professor, 1984-90, Associate Professor, 1990-95, Professor, 1995-, Faculty of Sciences, University of Novi Sad. Publications: About 50 articles; Catalytic Methods for the Determination of Noble Metals, Computer in Catalytical Analysis; Expert System for Catalytic Titrations; Books: Selected Topics of Microanalysis; Practical Exercises in Microanalysis. Memberships: Serbian Chem Society; Chem Society of Vojvodina; Associate Editor,

Chem series Rev of Research. Address: Vojvodina, Fruskogorska 30, 21000 Novi Sad, Yugoslavia.

**ABRUKOV Victor Sergeyevich,** b. 11 January 1952, Kazan, Soviet Union. Physicist; Educator. m. Abrukova Galina Vasiljevna, 1 son, 1 daughter. Education: Physicist, Leningrad State University, Leningrad, 1973-74; Physicist, Chuvash State University, 1969-74; Candidate in Physics and Mathematics, Institute of Chemical Physics of Academy of Sciences of Soviet Union, 1985; Doctor in Physics and Mathematics, Semenov Institute of Chemical Physics, Russian Academy of Sciences, Moscow, Russia, 1995. Appointments: Research Worker, Chuvash State University, 1974-76; Senior Research Worker, Chuvash State University, 1976-86; Head, Cheboksary Study Centre, All-Soviet Union Polytechnical Institute, 1986-96; Chairperson, Physics of Heat, Chuvash State University, 1996-; Professor, Cheboksary Study Centre, All-Soviet Union Polytechnical Institute, 1994-96; Professor, Chuvash State University, 1996-. Publications include: Challenges in Combustion and Propellants, 1996; Interferometric Techniques in Combustion, Gas Dynamic and Heat Transfer Research, Cheboksary, Russia, 1997; Interferometric Technique in Combustion, Gas Dynamic and Heat Transfer Research, Yokohama, Japan, 1998. Honours: Grant, Russian Foundation for Basic Research, 1993-95; Travel Grant, International Science Foundation, 1993; Grant, Russian Foundation for Basic Research, 1998-99; Grant, Russian Foundation for Basic Research, Volga Region, 1999-2000. Memberships: International Combustion Institute, 1993-; Physics and Engineering Faculty, Chuvash State University, 1997-; Scientific Council, Natural Sciences Institute, Chuvash State University, 1997-. Address: Chuvash State University, Moskovsky Prosp 15, 428015 Chebokary Chuvash, Russia.

**ABU-MANSOUR Mahasen Hasan,** b. 3 January 1953, Makkah, Saudi Arabia. Associate Professor of Linguistics. Education: BA English, King Abdul Aziz University, 1975; MA Linguistics, 1982, PhD Linguistics, 1987, University of Florida. Appointments: Assistant Lecturer, 1975-87; Assistant Professor, 1988-95; Head of English Department, Women's Campus, 1988-93; Associate Professor, 1996-; Dean of Admissions and Registrations, Women's Campus, 1995-. Publications: Epenthesis, gemination and syllable structure, 1990; Epenthesis in Makkan Arabic: Unsyllabified consonants Vs degenerate syllables, 1991; Closed syllable shortening and morphological levels, 1992; Optimality and conspiracy in the syllable structure of Arabic, 1995; Voice as a Privative Feature: Assimilation in Arabic, 1996. Honours: First Place High School Award, 1971; Saudi Arabian Government Scholarship to USA, 1979-87; Visiting Scholar, University of Massachusetts, 1993-94. Memberships: Arabic Linguistic Society; Linguistic Society of America; Linguistic Association of Canada and the USA. Address: PO Box 1222, Makkah, Saudi Arabia.

**ABU-SALAH Khalid Mustafa,** b. 9 February 1952, Tulkarm. Professor of Biochemistry. m. Fatinah Saleh-Nabulsi, 3 sons, 2 daughters. Education: PhD, University of Leeds, 1978; BSc, American University of Beirut, 1974. Appointments: Professor, King Saud University; Technical Consultant, Diagnostic Industry; Instructor, University of Leeds, 1976-78; Fellow, Institute of Biomedical Science. Publications: Fundamentals of Experimental Biochemistry, 1996; Techniques of Biological Analysis, 1991; Translator, Introducing Biochemistry, 1989; Contributed 20 Articles to Professional Journals. Honours: Research Grantee, 1980; Annual Award Prize, 1984; Scholarship, British Council; Deans Honour List. Memberships: Biochemical Society; International Association of Medical Laboratory Technologists; Saudi Chemical Society. Address:

King Saud University, PO Box 2455, Riyadh 11451, Saudi Arabia.

**ABU-SEADAH Abdel Razak,** b. 14 August 1947, Egypt. University Professor. m. Professor Ikhlass M Abbass, 1 son, 2 daughters. Education: BSc Chemistry and Botany, Faculty of Science, University of Cairo, Egypt; MSc Microbiology, Faculty of Science, University of Al-Azhan, Egypt; PhD Botany, Westfield College, University of London, UK. Appointments: Professor, Faculty of Science, Al-Azhan University; Professor and Director, The Regional Centre for Mycology and Biotechnology; Consultant for higher education and International Relationships, Al-Azhan University, 1992-95. Publications: 76 scientific papers under the author name Razak, A.A. Memberships: New York Academy of Science; Bioinorganic Scientists; American Association for the Advancement of Science; President, Egyptian Mycological Association; Vice President, International Mycological Association; Vice President, African Mycological Association; Editor in Chief, African Journal of Mycology and Biotechnology. Address: PO Box 8104, 13 Gaber ibu Hayan, 11371 Nasr City, Cairo, Egypt.

**ABUELMA'ATTI Muhammad Taher,** b. 15 October 1942, Cairo, Egypt. Professor. m. Soher Rose Ahmad Fares, 4 sons, 2 daughters. Education: BSc, Electrical Engineering, University of Cairo, Egypt, 1963; PhD, Electrical Engineering, University of Bradford, England, 1979. Appointment: University Professor, King Fahd University of Petroleum and Minerals, Saudi Arabia. Publications: Over 367 journal articles and conference presentations. Address: King Fahd University, Petroleum and Minerals Box 203, Dhahran 31261, Saudi Arabia.

**ABUL-HAJ Suleiman Kahil,** b. 20 April 1925, Palestine. Naturalised US Citizen, 1955. Pathologist. m. Elizabeth Abood, 11 Feb 1948, 3 sons. Education: BS, University of California at Berkeley, 1949; MS, 1951, MD, 1955, University of California at San Francisco. Appointments: Resident, University of California Hospital, San Francisco, 1949; Intern, Cook County Hospital, Chicago, 1955-56; Served to Major, US Army Medical Corps, 1956-62; Resident, Brooke General Hospital, 1957-59; Chief, Clinical and Anatomical Pathology, Walter Reed Army Hospital, Washington, 1959-62; Consultant, Armed Forces Institute of Pathology, 1960-96, California Tumor Tissue Registry, 1962-96, Tripler General Hospital, Hawaii, 1963-67, Camarillo State Hospital, 1964-70; Senior Surgical Pathologist, Los Angeles County General Hospital, 1963; Associate Professor, University of Southern California School of Medicine, Los Angeles, 1963-96; Director, Department of Pathology, Community Memorial Hospital, Ventura, California, 1964-80, General Hospital, Ventura County, 1966-74; Director, Pathology Service Medical Group, 1970-. Publications: Articles in professional journals, on research in cardiovascular disease, endocrine, renal and skin diseases, also cancer. Honours: Borden Award, California Honor Society, 1949; Achievement Certificate, Surgeon General, US Army, 1962. Memberships: Fellow, American Society of Clinical Pathologists; Fellow, College of American Pathologists; International College of Surgeons; World Affairs Council; Board of Directors, Tri-Counties Blood Bank; Board of Directors, American Cancer Society. Address: 105 Encinal Way, Ventura, CA 93001-3317, USA.

**ACCARDO Joseph John,** Jr., b. 7 July 1936, Baltimore, MD, USA. Writer, Editor. Education: AB, University of Notre Dame, 1958. Appointments: Reporter, TV Correspondent, United Press International, UP-Fox, Movietone Newsreel, 1959-1961; News Editor, Catholic Standard, 1961; Editor, National Academy of Sciences, 1962-64; Assistant Editor,

Transport Topics, 1964-68; Washington Editor, Chilton Publications, 1968-70; Chief Writer, Young and Rubicam, Burson-Marsteller, 1970; Free Lance Writer, Editor, Washington, DC, 1970-. Publications: World Conference on Shell Structures, 1964; Teamsters All, 1976; Contributor, Journals, Magazines, 1959-. Address: P O B 9700, Arlington, VA 22219-1700, USA.

**ACEVEDO Roberto,** b. 30 November 1950, Santiago, Chile. Chemist. m. Lucia Cecilia, 3 sons, 2 daughters. Education: MSc, 1974, University of Chile; PhD, 1981, University of London, UK. Appointments: Assistant Lecturer, 1971-74; Assistant Professor, 1974-83; Associate Professor, 1984-91; Full Professor, 1991-. Publications: Book: Atoms and Molecules, 1996; 57 papers in national journals; 26 publications in international congresses, conferences and lectures delivered;50 papers in international publications. Honours: Visiting Fellowship, 1982, Visiting Scholar, Dept Chemistry, 1993, University of Virginia; Honorary Research Fellow, 1984, 1985, 1990, 1991, Bursary of the EC DG-XII, 1991, Birkbeck College, University of London; Invited Speaker, Advanced Study Institute, NATO-ASI, Vibronic Processes in Inorganic Chemistry, Riva del Sole, Italy, 1988; Visiting Professor, Dept Biology and Chemistry, City University of Hong Kong, 1996; Member Editorial Board, Asian Journal of Spectroscopy; Co-Editor, Section of Chemistry, Ciencia al Dia. Membership: AAAS. Address: Casa 2950, Froilan Roa 5833, Macul Santiago, Chile.

**ACHARYA Ashwini Kumar,** b. 2 April 1968, Kamela, India. Teacher. m. Kanchan Lata, 1 son, 1 daughter. Education: MA, Hindi; Acharya Basic Teacher Certificate; Research Scholar, Lucknow University. Appointment: Primary Teacher, 1995. Memberships: Avadh Bharti Samiti, Haidergarh District Barabanki; Primary Teachers Association. Address: V & PO Kamda, Barabanki UP, India.

**ACHARYA Bipul,** b. Dinhata. Author; Editor. Education: Master of Arts in Economics; B Ed; MA; B Ed. Appointments: Outstanding Editor of Sahitya, a Bengali Magazine 1989-. Publications: Dui Banglar Kabita (a collection of Bengali poems); Samayita ( a collection of Bengali micro-poems); Sahitya Akash; Sarani. Honours: Sahitya Award for 14th Century, 1994; Sahitya Jagat Award, 1996; Marichika Sahitya Award, 1996; Nagrul 95 Award for Editing. Memberships: Kabita Club, Bangladesh; BCDA; CBJSPS. Address: Jyotish Bhawan, Godhulibazar, Dinhata, Coochbehar 736135, WB India.

**ACHARYA Vagish Shastri,** b. 24 July 1934, Sagar, Madhya Pradesh, India. Kundalini and Sanskrit Educator; Researcher. m. Rekha Tripathi, 3 sons. Education: Acharya in Word Philosophy, 1959; PhD, Paninian Grammar, 1964; DLitt, Semantics, 1969. Appointments: Founder, Laleshwar Sanskrit School, 1954; Teacher, Bharatiya College, 1956-59; Lecturer, Teekamani Sanskrit College, 1959-64; Senior Research Fellow, UGC, 1965-67; Deputy Director, Indological Institute, 1968-70; Director, Indological Research Institute, 1970-96; Founder, Director, Vagyoga Consciousness Institute, 1996-. Publications: Many books on Yoga-Tantra, Indian philosophy and Vagyoga, Kundalini and Mnemonic Sanskrit teaching. Honours: Kalidasa Award, 1966; Mahamahopadhyaya, 1982; Banabhatta Award, 1993. Memberships: Vagyoga Chetana Pitham; Academic Executives Council, Sampurnanand Sanskrit University; Other Indian and foreign universities. Address: B 3-131A, Shivala, Varanasi 221-001, Uttar Pradesh, India.

**ACOSTA Mario,** b. 16 April 1963, Mexico City, Mexico. Consultant, Pharmaceutical Educator, Researcher. m. Mirian

Coterrillo, 1 sons, 2 daughters. Education: MD, Hons, University of Mexico, 1985; M Neuro Science, 1989; PhD, Pharmaceutical Science, Cambridge University, England, 1995. Appointments: General Director, Medical Services, University of Mexico, 1988-90; Senior Professor, Medical Major, 1990-97; Clinical Researcher, 1991-93; Clinical Researcher, Addenbrooks Hospital University, Cambridge, UK, 1993-95; Chairman, Clinical Research, Boehringer Mangeim Institute, Mexico, 1991-93; Founder, President, Pharmaceutical Science College of Mexico, 1996-99. Publications: Contributor, Articles for Professional Journals. Memberships: AAAS; International Pharmacology Society; New York Academy of Sciences. Address: Urdaneta No 56, Navegantes Satélite 53100, Mexico.

**ADACHI Agnes Magdalene,** b. 26 October 1918, Budapest, Hungary. Author; Lecturer. m. Dr Masazumi Adachi, 2 sons. Education: Diploma, Montessori Liceum, Roma. Appointments: Chairperson, Greater New York Wallenberg Comm, Inc; Raoul Wallenberg Associate in WWII in Hungary. Publications: Child of the Winds, My Mission with Raoul Wallenberg; Wise Raoul; Gellert, fiction; Short Storys; Poetry: Homecoming & Four Seasons. Honours: Brendeis University National Women's Committee, in the 80th Philadelphia Council of Jewish War Veterans of US Brotherhood Award, 1987; Eleanor Roosevelt Award Commission for Women's Equality of the American Jewish Congress, 1995; Hadassah Queens-Jewish Region's Award, 1995; Yorkville Christian-Jewish Council's 1995 Distinguished Service Award; Raoul Wallenberg Movement for Humanity Certificate of Honour, 1996; Soroptimist International of New York 1996 Women of Distinguished Service Award. Membership: Soroptimist International of New York. Address: 69-02 Dartmouth Street, Forest Hills, NY 11375, USA.

**ADAMCZAK Eugeniusz,** b. 30 August 1935, Leszno, Poland. Publisher; Cartographer. m. Miroslawa, 1 son, 3 daughters. Education: Wroclaw University, 1953-58. Appointments: CEO. Ossolineum Publishing House of the Polish Academy of Sciences, 1969-92; Director, Romer Polish Cartographical Publishing House, Wroclaw Branch, 1992-. Publications: 80 Papers and Contributions on History of Science; Books, Portrety Ossolinskie, 1992; Knights and Commanders Crosses of the Orden Polonia Restituta, 1977,85. Honour: Golden Cross of Merit, 1970. Memberships: Polish Association of Book Publishers, Vice-president, 1979-80; Basketball Association. Address: Agrestowa 41, 53-006 Wroclaw, Poland.

**ADAMIETZ Irenaeus A,** b. 17 March 1955, Murcki, Poland. Physician, Researcher. m. Elisabeth J, 1 son, 1 daughter. Education: Physician, Medical Academy, Warsaw, Poland, 1979. Appointments: Registered Physician, 1981; Specialist, Radiology, 1989; Specialist, Radiotherapy, 1989; Assistant Physician, Department Diagnostic Radiology Regional Hospital, Wetzlar, Germany, 1981-84; Assistant Physician, Department of Radiooncology, 1984-86; Senior Staff Lecturer, Department of Radiotherapy and Special Oncology, Hannover Medical School, Germany, 1986-91; Vice Chairman, Associate Professor, Department of Radiation Oncology Johann Wolfgang Goethe-University, Germany, 1991-97; Director, Chairman, Clinic of Radiotherapy and Radio Oncology Ruhr University, Bochum, 1998-; Visiting Professor, Department of Radiation Oncology and Nuclear Medicine, Hahnemann University, Philadelphia, 1994. Publications: Over 250 presentations; Over 200 scientific publications, radiation oncology. Memeberships: German Society of Radiation Oncology; German Cancer Society; Multinational Association of Supportive Care in Cancer. Address: University Clinic of Radiotherapy and Radio Oncology, Hoelkeskampring 40, D-44625, Herne, Germany.

**ADAMS Carolyn B,** b. 18 October 1955, Sandersville, Georgia, USA. Register Evangelist; Song Writer. Divorced, 2 daughters. Education: Diploma, 2 year of Paramedica, 1973, Baldwin Area Voc High School. Honours: Certificate, Devoted and Invaluable Service, 1986, Resseau Chapel Apostilice Church; Plaque from Usher Board; Appreciation Certificate for Participation in 28th Youth Convention, 1987; Notable contributions from Resseau Chapel Sunday School, 1988; Award for Most Cooperative in Nursing School, 1988; Hollywood Song Jubilee Achievement, Songwrite of the Year, 1991; Special Honour of Excellence, Christ Church Ministries, Evangelistic Department, 1991; and many others. Publication: Written song which received Song of Excellence from Dottie Frost. Memberships: Americo Tech Career Institutes; First Class Association Martial Arts. Address: Lighthouse Ministries Evang Assoc, PO Box 3974, Eatonton, GA 31024, USA.

**ADAMS Glen C,** b. 19 June 1912, Trent, Washington. Publisher. m. Jean Pirie Evers, 1946, 1 son. Education: BA, Eastern Washington College, 1938; PhD, Gonzaga University, 1990. Appointments: Teacher, Burbank School, 1938-39; Farmer, 1939-51; Postmaster, Fairfield, 1951-72. Honours: Washington State Award, 1989; Nancy Blankenship Pryor Award, 1998. Memberships: Triangle Grange, 1929-; Eastern Washington Historical Society, 1977-84; Washington State Historical Society; Book Club of California; Alcuin Club; Farfield Chamber of Commerce, 1951-. Address: P O Box 287, Fairfield, WA 99012, USA.

**ADAMS James E Sr,** b. 1 March 1950, Highland Park, Illinois, USA. Chief Executive Officer of Television Station. m. Janet Y Adams, 2 sons. Education: GED, 1969, US Army; BOS, 1991, Jeff State. Appointments: President, CEO, Adams Agency; District Sales Manager, Cable Advantage; Owner, J & J Adams Entr Inc. Honours: Salesman of the Year, 1990; Lions Club Man of the Year, 1989-90; Business of the Year Nominee, 1996. Memberships: Country Music Association; Southern Gospel Music Association; Gospel Music Association; Lions Club; 70P No 50; Myer Panel; Platform Speakers Association; UFW; American Legion 40/8. Address: Adams Agy/Channel 12, 1703 Cogswell Avenue, Pell City, AL 35125-1646, USA.

**ADAMS Roy J,** b. 28 June 1940. Emeritus Professor. m. 2 daughters. Education: BA, summa cum laude, College of Liberal Arts, Pennsylvania University, 1967; MA, Industrial Relations, 1970, PhD, Comparative Industrial Relations, 1973, Industrial Relations Research Institute, University of Wisconsin. Appointments: Industrial Relations Specialist, Chase Manhattan Bank, New York, 1967-68; Chairman, Human Resources and Labour Relations Area, 1976-78, Assistant Professor, 1973-78, Associate Professor, 1978-83, Professor, 1984-97, Emeritus Professor, 1997-, Industrial Relations, McMaster University; Director, Theme School on International Justice and Human Rights, 1996-97. Publications: Numerous articles in professional journals. Memberships include: International Industrial Relations Association; Canadian Industrial Relations Association; Industrial Relations Research Association; International Sociological Association; International Political Science Association; Academy of Management; American Federation of Teachers; McMaster University Retiree's Association; Society for Human Resource Management; Periodical Writers Association of Canada; Canadian Authors Association. Address: 50 Whitton Road, Hamilton, Ontario L8S 4C7, Canada.

**ADDINGTON David John,** b. 11 July 1947, London, England. Legal Administrator; Arbitrator. m. (1) Moira Louise Meiklejohn, 2 daughters, (2) Mary Ann Mitchelson, 1 son, 1 daughter. Education: Polytechnic, Central London, 1963-64.

Appointments: Managing Clerk, Field Fisher Waterhouse, London, 1963-71; Litigation Manager, D Miles Griffiths Piercy & Company, London, 1971-73, Rubinstein Callingham, London, 1973-75, S Rutter & Company, London, 1975-77, Appleby, Spurling & Kempe, Bermuda, 1977-94, Mello Hollis Jones & Martin, Bermuda, 1994-; Member, Law Reform Committee, Bermuda Supreme Court Rules, 1989-, Committee of Bermuda Mediation and Arbitration Center, 1994-. Publications: Several articles in professional journals. Memberships include: Secretary, Anglican Church Synod and Ordinand; Lions Club; Bermuda Zone, Chairman, 1992-93; Association; Mariners Club; Institute of Management; Chartered Institute of Arbitrators. Address: Mello Hollis Jones & Martin, Reid House, 31 Church Street, Hamilton HM 12, Bermuda.

**ADDISON Alonzo Church,** b. 11 December 1965, Berkeley, California, USA. Specialist in Computer Graphics and New Media in Design and Education. Education: BSE, cum laude, Princeton University, 1988; March, 1992, Postgraduate, 1994, University of California, Berkeley. Appointments: Market Analyst, Transamerica Corporation, 1984-85; Design Consultant, Olympia & York, 1986-87; Computer Programmer, ALK Associates, 1988-89; Strategic Technology Consultant, ACA Group, 1989-; Project Director, University of California, 1992-; Vice President, Cyra Technology, 1993-. Publications include: The Failure of CAD: The Role of Computers in Design, 1992; A History of CAD in Architecture. Honours: American Institute of Architects Medal, 1992; University of California Fellowship, 1994-95, Doctoral Prize, 1996. Memberships: Director, Museum of The Future Consortium, 1994-; ACM Siggrath; ACADIA; National Eagle Scout Association. Address: 7927 Terrace Drive, El Cerrito, CA 94530, USA.

**ADE Wolfgang Roland,** b. 15 January 1947, Stuttgart, Germany. Physician. m. Shizuko Okawa, 1 daughter. Education: Applied Managerial Econs, 1972-74; Medical School, 1975-81, Universities of Hohenheim, Heidelberg and Tübingen. Appointments: Research Fellow, Tokyo Women's Medical College, 1982-83; Research & Scientific Officer, Juro Wada Commemorative Heart and Lung Institute. Publications: Autoregulated Extra and Intracorporeal Pump System for Perfusion, International Surgery, 1992. Memberships: ISCTS - The World Society of Cardio, Thoracic Surgeons, 1988, Secretary General; World Artifical Organ Immunology and Transplantation Society, Secretary, 1993-. Address: 20-7 Aoto 3 Chome, Katsushika-ku, Tokyo 125, Japan.

**ADEBULE Gbolahan Taiwo,** b. 12 October 1952, Jos, Nigeria. Medical Orthopaedic Surgeon. m. Ibisola Olufunmilayo, 2 sons, 2 daughters. Education: MB BS, 1976, College of Medicine, University of Lagos; FWACS, 1986, West African College of Surgeons; FICS, 1991, International College of Surgeons. Appointments: Consultant, 1986; Chief Consultant, 1997. Honours: Ricardo-Galeazzi SIcOT Scholarship, 1984; Pfizer Travel Fellowship, 1994. Memberships: Nigerian Medical Association; Nigerian Orthopaedic Association; SICOT; WOC; Nigerian Institute of Management. Address: 34 Sr Staff Quarters, PMB 2009, Igbobi, Lagos, Nigeria.

**ADENEYE Japhet Adekayode,** b. 17 September 1940, Odonoko, Nigeria. Lecturer; Researcher. m. Adebisi Olusola Osilowo, 4 daughters. Education: BSc, honours, Agriculture, 1967, PhD, Animal Science, 1972, University of Ibadan. Appointments include: Office Boy, Royal Exchange Assurance, Lagos, 1955-56; Audit Clerk, Federal Audit Department, Lagos, 1961-62; Science Tutor, Ahmadiyya College, Agege, Lagos, 1963-64; Junior Research Fellow, 1970-71, Laboratory Demonstrator, 1970-72, Senior Research Fellow, 1980-82, Reader, 1990-94, Professor, Dairy Science, 1994-, University of Ibadan; Research Fellow II, 1973-76, Research Fellow I, 1976-79, Senior Research Fellow, 1979-80, University of Ife. Publications include: Energy and Protein Requirements of Imported Holstein Cows for Milk Production at Ibadan, 1972. Honours include: Western Regional Scholar, 1956-60; Rockefeller Foundation Award, 1970-71. Memberships: Nigerian Society for Animal Production; Animal Science Association of Nigeria; Nutrition Society of Nigeria; Agricultural Society of Nigeria; Scripture Union, Nigeria; Odonoko-Odoroga Development Council. Address: Department of Animal Science, University of Ibadan, Ibadan, Oyo State, Nigeria.

**ADEYOJU Samuel Kolade,** b. 17 September 1936, Ijan-Ekiti. University Emeritus Professor. m. Dr Adeola, 1 son, 2 daughters. Education: BA, Hons, Exeter, 1963; PhD, LSE, London University, 1966; DIP Forestry, Oxford, 1968. Appointments: University Teacher, University of Ibadan 1966-96; Professor of Forestry. Publications: Over 90 Publications. Honours: Federal Government Scholarship, 1960-63; Post Gtaduate Scholarship, 1963-64; Comonwealth Scolarship, 1964-68; FAO Training Fellowship. Memberships: Commonwealth Forestry Association; Nigerian Forestry Association; Association of Advancement Agriculture Sciences in Africa. Address: Department of Forestry Resources, Management, University of Ibadan, Ibadan, Nigeria.

**ADEYOKUNNU Adetunji Ademuyiwa,** b. 26 May 1938, Ilesha, Nigeria. Physician. m. Julianah, 3 sons, 3 daughters. Education: MB, London, 1965; DCH, Glasgow, 1969; MRCP, UK, 1972; FRCP, London and Glasgow, 1986; FWACP, 1976. Appointments: Consultant Paediatrician, 1973-; Professor of Paediatrics, University of Ibadan, 1983-; Consultant Paediatric Haemotology Oncology, Programme Director, Deputy Chairman Saudi Arabian National Guard Hospital, Riradh, 1986-1996; Chairman of Paediatrics, Royal Commission Hospital, Jubail Industrial City Saudi Arabia, 1997-. Publications: 75 listed in journals. Memberships: British Medical Association; American Association of Advanced Science; New York Academy of Sciences; Saudi Paediatrics Association; Nigerian Paediatrics Association; Sickle Cell Club of Nigeria; Genetic Sociaty of Nigeria. Address: Chief Paediatrics Al Fanteer Hospital, P O Box 11720, Jubail Industrial City 31961, Saudi Arabia.

**ADHAM Fuad Mustafa,** b. 6 March 1954, Makkah, Saudi Arabia. Advisor. m. Azizah Abdulwahab Saati, 2 sons. Education: Concordia University, 1981; SAS University, 1985; Columbia University, 1994. Appointments: Associated with Saudi Arabian Television as interviewer, announcer and freelance writer; Manager, International Affairs, TRIAD International Marketing Ltd; Supervisor, Senior Supervisor, Flight Information Coordinator, Foreign Airlines Coordinator, Management Assessor, Advisor to Assistant Vice President Marketing Central Region, Advisor, Manager, Special Projects to Customer Services Training, Saudi Arabian Airlines; Management Trainee, Manger, Sales and Services, Manger, Operations, Unit Controller, General Manager, Central and Eastern Regions, Saudia Catering; Advisor to various companies. Honours: Several certificates of honour. Memberships include: Les Toques Blances; Chaîne Des Rôtisseur; Assessors Association; DCS, Saudi Arabian Airlines; International Flight Catering Association; Inflight Food Services Association; Handicap Children Association, Saudi Arabia; Arab Society for Human Resources Management, USA; National Restaurant Association. Address: PO Box 3576, Riyadh 11481, Saudi Arabia.

**ADHAMI Josif E,b.** 5 September 1925, Hochisht, Albania. Physician. m. 1 son, 1 daughter. Education: General Physician,

Med Pharm Inst, Bucharest, 1953; Specialised in Bucharest, 1952-53; Specialised in Moscow, 1957-58, Paris, 1967, Copenhagen, 1972, Asssistant Professor, 1963; MD thesis, 1964; Professor, 1972. Appointments: Professor of Internal Medicine; Professor of Hepatology and Gastroenterology; Head of Department, Internal Medicine and Hepatology, Gastroenterology. Publications: More than 250 scientific studies; 35 monographs; Student's medical text books; Editor, 15 scientific volumes in general scientific work; Honours: 1st Degree Award of Republic; Award of Merited Scientific Worker. Memberships: Vice Chief of Editorial Board, Tirana, 1960-61; Member, Editorial Board, 1994; Un Med Belk, 1963-; Member, IASL, 1974-; EASL, from foundation; Member Editorial Board, Journal of Hepatology, 1991-94; Member Scientists com of Hepato Gart Enter des pays Freucaplion, 1991-97; Med Chir Digest, 1997-; Chief of Editorial Board. Address: QSUT Nene Tereza, Tirana, Albania.

**ADO Yurii Mikhailovich,** b. 12 June 1927, Yalta, Crimea, Ukraine. Physicist. m. Ado Margarita Alexevna, 2 daughters. Education: Engineer, Moscow Aviation Institute, 1950; Candidat of Physics and Maths Science, 1957; Doctor of Physics and Maths Sciences, 1967; Professor, 1977. Appointments: Engineer, 1950, Postgraduate, Physics, 1953, Senior Scientist, 1957, Physical Institute of Academy of Sciences in Moscow; Head of Accelerator Department, 1964, Principal Scientific Researcher, 1988, Institute for High Energy Physics, Protvino. Publications: More than 130 publications. Honours: Russian Decoration, Friendship of Nations, 1986; State Prize, 1970. Membership: Head of Chair, Moscow State University. Address: Institute of High Energy Physics, Protvino, Moscow Region, 142284, Russia.

**ADSULE Prabhakar,** b. 8 December 1921, Indore. Writer, Lawyer. m. Muktamala. Education: MA, 1952; Research Scholars of Bombay University, 1952; LLB, Agra University, 1954. Appointments: Temporary Lecturer, Christian College, Indore. Publications: Unito Mystica, Science of Consciousness, 1992; Ath To Mriytuy Jidnaysa, 1997; Science of Phychic Condensate Phase of Patanjali, 1998. Memberships: Ex Lion; Member, Animal Welfare Board; Blue Cross Society, Indore. Address: 24 Yashwant Nivas Rd, Indore MP, India.

**ADUKU Henry A Kofi,** b. 16 February 1938, Akim Achiase, Ghana. Teacher. m. Juliana B Aduku, 3 sons, 4 daughters. Education: BA, Art, 1970; Diploma, Art Education, 1984. Appointments: Housemaster, Senior Housemaster, Assistant Headmaster, Headmaster, Mankessim Secondary Technical School. Honours: Awards of Certificates of Participation, Trade Fairs and Training of Youth and Unemployed, Ghana. Memberships: CHASS; GNAT; GAVA. Address: Mankessim Secondary Technical School, Mankessim, Ghana.

**ADVANI Chanderban G,** b. 23 July 1924, Hyderabad. Chief Executive Officer. m. Devi Khanchand Jagtiani, 1 son, 1 daughter. Education: LCC, UK, 1943; BA, 1949. Appointments: Managing Director, Narain Advani and Co, Karachi; Manager, Indo French Traders; Chief Executive Officer, Nephews International Inc, Japan; Proprietor, Nephews Commercial Corporation; President, GA Chandru Shokai. Honours: Key, Mayors of Bombay; Citation from the Mayors; Correspondent, Bharat Ratna. Memberships: Masonic and Shriners Clubs; Propeller Club of US Indian Chamber of Commerce; Yokohama Chamber of Commerce and Industry. Address: 35 Yamashita-cho, P O Box 216, Yokohama 231-8691, Japan.

**AFINOGUENOV Gennady E,** b. 15 June 1941, Leningrad, Russia. Microbiologist. m. Vera G Afinoguenova, 1 son, 1 daughter. Education: MD, 1964; MD.Sc.D, 1980; Professor,

1989. Appointments: Head, Scientific Research Center, St Petersburg Chemical Pharmaceutical Institute, 1980-81; Head, Wound Infection Department, Vreden Research Institute of Traumatology & Orthopedics, 1985-; Director, Testing Center, RF Ministry of Health, 1997-. Publications: 315 in Russia, 55 Abroad, 2 Monographs: Antiseptics in Surgery, 1987; Antimicrobial Polymers, 1993. Memberships: Russian Association of Clinical Microbiologists & Chemotherapists; Hospital Hygiene Society, Germany. Address: 23 Kuybishev Str, Apt 39, St Petersburg 197046, Russia.

**AFULEZI Uju Nkwocha,** b. Umuohiagu, Nigeria. Librarian. m. Carol Afulezi, 2 sons, 3 daughters. Education: BS, 1973, MS, 1974, Oregon; PhD, 1977, Missouri; MLS, 1992, Pratt. Appointments: Senior Lecturer; Senior Planning Officer; Executive Director; Librarian. Publications: The Igbo Question; Technique Planning in Education. Memberships: American Library Association; World Future Society; Planetary Society; Knight of St Columbus. Address: #5L 98-25 Horace Harding Expressway, Corona, NY 11368, USA.

**AGAÇI Feçor,** b. 16 March 1945, Berat, Albania. Pedagogue; Physician. m. Teuta Kurti-Agaçi, 1 son, 1 daughter. Education: GP Diploma, 1968, Medical Faculty, Tirana University; Diploma for Endocrinology, 1974; Doctor diploma, 1993; Assistant Professor, 1994; Visiting Professor of Endocrinology, 1993, University of Massachusetts Medical Centre; English and Russian Language documents. Appointments: General Practitioner, Berat, Albania, 1968-72; Pedagogue, Physiologic Pathology and Endocrinology, Medicine Faculty, Tirana University, 1972-; Chief Endocrinology and Diabetes Service, University Hospital Centre Mother Teresa, Tirana; Collaborated in Diabetes Unit of University Hospital of Geneva and Diabetes Endocrinology and Disease of Nutrition Service of Centre Hospitalier of Nevers, France; Collaborated with WHO Regional Office for Europe and International Diabetes Federation European Region. Publications: 43 published articles; 2 textbooks for students; 16 scientific sessions and conferences; 18 scientific reviews and opponences; scientific leader for 2 dissertations. Memberships: European Association for the Study of Diabetes; British Diabetic Association. Address: University Hospital Centre 'Mother Teresa', Endocrinology and Diabetes Service, Dibra Street, No 372, Tirana, Albania.

**AGAH Arvin,** b. 1964, Tehran, Iran. Professor. m. Jila Niknejad. Education: BA Highest Honours Computer Science, 1986, University of Texas at Austin; MS Computer Science, 1988, Purdue University; MS Biomedical Engineering, 1993, PhD Computer Science, 1994, University Southern California at Los Angeles. Appointments: Research Assistant & Scientist to Xerox Corporationn and IBM Corporation to 1994; Computer Consultant, Ernst & Young, Los Angeles, Slovak & Baron, Palm Springs, DRS Management, Los Angeles, 1994-95; Systems Analyst & Software Engineer, Ziffren, Brittenham, Branca & Fischer, 1991-95; Post-doctoral Fellow, Biorobotics Div, Robotics Dept, Mechanical Engineering Lab, Ministry of International Trade & Industry, Tsukuba, Japan, 1995-97; Visiting Lecturer, Dept Engineering Systems, University Tsukuba, 1996-97; Tenure-Track Assistant Professor, Dept Electrical Engineering & Computer Science, University Kansas at Lawrence, 1997-. Publications: 17 refereed articles and book chapters; 27 refereed conferences & workshops. Memberships: American Society of Engineering Education; American Institute of Aeronautics and Astronautics; Institute of Electrical & Electronics Engineers; Association for Computing Machinery. Address: University of Kansas Dept Electrical Engineering & Computer Science, Lawrence, KS 66045, USA.

**AGARWAL Girish Saran,** b. 7 July 1946, Bareilly, UP, India. Physicist; Director. m. Sneh Lata Agarwal, 2 daughters. Education: MSc, 1966, Banaras Hindu University, India; PhD, 1969, University of Rochester, USA. Appointments: Professor, School of Physics, University of Hyderabad, 1977-95; Director, Physical Research Laboratory, Ahmedabad, 1995-. Publications: Over 400 original publications in top-most journals of Physics and Optics. Honours: SS Bhatnagar Award in Physical Sciences, 1982; Meghnad Saha Award in Theoretical Sciences, 1987; Max-Born Award of Optical Society of America, 1988; Third World Academy of Sciences Prize in Physics, 1994; Einstein Medal of Optical and Quantum Electronics Society, USA, 1994; Goyal Prize in Physics, 1994; G D Birla Award for Scientific Research, 1995; R D Birla Award, 1996; Humboldt Research Award, 1997. Memberships: Fellow: American Physical Society; Optical Society of America; Third World Academy of Sciences; Indian Academy of Sciences, Bangalore; Indian National Science Academy, New Delhi. Address: Director, Physical Research Laboratory, Navrangpura, Ahmedabad 380053, India.

**AGARWALA Sanjay,** b. 18 October 1954, Varanasi, India. Doctor. m. Nisheeta, 1 son, 1 daughter. Education: MBBS, GS Medical College, 1978; MCPS, College of Physicians and Surgeons, 1978; D Orth, College of Physicians and Surgeons, 1981; MS, University of Bombay, 1982; M Ch Orth, University of Liverpool, UK, 1985. Appointments: Resident Medical Officer, King Edward Memorial Hospital, 1978-79; Resident Medical Officer, General Surgery, 1979-80; Resident Medical Officer, Orthopaedics and Traumatology, 1980; Registrar, 1980-82; Professor, Fellow, Registrar, The Robert Jones and Agnes Hunt Orthopaedics Hospital, 1982-83; Han Fellow, Registrar, Derbyshire Royal Infirmary, 1983; Visitor, Johns Hopkins Group of Hospitals, 1983; Stanley Johnson Microsurgical Centre Fellowship, Orthopaedic Registrar, 1984; Associate Fellow, Liverpool University, 1985; Acting Senior Registrar, Hartshill Orthopaedic Hospital, 1986; Consultant, P D Hinduja National Hospital, 1986-92; Head, Orthopaedics and Traumatology, 1992-. Publications: 8 Dissertations, Papers. Honours: Graduate Fellowship Award; Hand and Microsurgical Fellowship; Stanley Johnson Microsurgical Fellowship Award; Norman Roberts Prize; Many other Awards. Memberships: Indian Association of Laser Surgery and Medicine; Indian Rheumatology Association; Indian Orthopaedic Association. Address: 61 D Rd Churchgate, Mumbai 400 020, India.

**AGBAKOBA Olisa Charis,** b. 29 May 1953, Jos, Nigeria. Lawyer; Notary Public. m. Lilian, 3 daughters. Education: LLB Hons, University of Nigeria, 1977; BL, Law School of Nigeria, 1978; LLM, University of London, 1980. Appointments: Research Fellow, Institute of International Affairs, 1981; Guest Lecturer, Military and Command School, 1981; Law Practice, 1983; Senior Partner, Olisa Agbakoba and Associates, 1987; Founding President, Civil Liberties Organisation, 1987-95; President, Inter African Network for Human Rights and Development, 1995; Senior Partner, Human Rights Law Service, 1996. Publications: 25 publications. Honours: Roger Baldwin Medal; Patron of Law Students Association; Fellow, Institute of Administrative Management of Nigeria; Quality Magazine Man of the Year; Many other honours. Memberships: Nigerian Bar Association; International Bar Association; British Council on Managing Human Rights; American Bar Association; Many other memberships. Address: 39B Rumens Road, Ikoyi Lagos, Nigeria.

**AGEYEV Valentin,** b. 1 April 1947, Russia. Educational Psychologist. m. Ekaterina Koturga, 1 son. Education: Graduate, Physical Engineering, Moscow Engineering and Physical Institute, 1973; PsD, Psychological Sciences,

Academy of Pedagogical Sciences, Moscow, 1987. Appointments: Senior Research Worker, Institute of General and Pedagogical Sciences, 1981-86; Department Head, Science, Institute of Teachers Training, Voronezh, Russia, 1988-89; Head of Research Centre, Kazakhstan, 1989-91; Head Science, Private Experimental Centre, Russia, 1992-95; Head of Research Department, Institute of Training Officials, Government of Republic of Kazakhstan, 1996; Department Dean Science, Department of Philosophy and Politics of National University of Republic of Kazakhstan, 1997; Associate Professor, Department of Philosophy and Politics, National University of Republic of Kazakhstan, 1996-. Publications: Psychology of Creation; Contributor, Articles to Professional Journals. Honours: Diploma, Ministry of Education of Kazakhstan, 1991; Grant Soros, Kazakhstan Foundation, 1996. Memberships: International Affiliate of America Psychological Association; International Affiliate of Canadian Psychological Association. Address: 124-24 Furmanov St Almaty, 480091 Kazakhstan, Russia.

**AGGOR Francis Komla,** b. 24 February 1959, Anfoega, Ghana. Professor. m. Dale M, 2 daughters. Education: BA Hons, University of Ghana, 1979-84; MA, University of Western Ontario, 1986-87; PhD, University of California, Los Angeles, 1987-92. Appointments: Assistant Professor, JCU, 1992-98; Associate Professor, Director, Spanish Studies, John Carroll University, 1998-. Publications: 1 book; Articles in: Hispanófila; Estreno; Revista Hispánica Moderna; Bulletin of Hispanic Studies; Revista Canadiense de Estudios Hispánicos; Miguel Hernández Cincuenta Años; Cuadernos Hispanoamericanos; Mester; Silbos. Honours: Del Amo Dissertation Fellowship; Del Amo Graduate Fellowship. Memberships: Bhobu North America; Modern Language Association; Asociación Internacional de Hispanistas; Asociación de Amigos de Miguel Hernández; Hispanic Association for the Humanities. Address: Department of Languages and Cultures, John Carroll University, Cleveland, OH 44118-4520, USA.

**AGGREY Stephen,** b. 9 November 1955, Accra. Chemical Engineer. m. Gifty Odoi, 1 son, 1 daughter. Education: Associate Degree, Chemical Engineering, 1993; HND-Lab Management and Administration, 1994; Certified, Quality Assurance Management, 1998. Appointments: Assistant Research Officer, Ghana Atomic Energy Commission, 1977-79; Quality Control Supervisor, Cocoa Processing Company, Ghana, 1979-90; Head, Quality Control, Irani Brothers, Ghana. Honour: Award, Institute of Industrial Engineers, 1986. Memberships: American Society of Quality; American Chemical Society; Institution of Industrial Engineers; New York Academy of Sciences; Institute of Science Technology, England; Ghana Chemical Society. Address: Irani Brothers & Others Ltd, PO Box 170, Tema, Ghana.

**AGGREY-FORSON Samuel,** b. 21 September 1939, Enyan Obontser, Ghana. Educator. m. Ama Gyanwah Yankson, 4 sons, 7 daughters. Education: BA, 1968; Postgraduate, Education, 1971. Appointments: Assistant Headmaster, 1976, Headmaster, 1979, District Director of Education, 1990; Director, Ghana Education Staff Development Institute, 1997. Publictions: A Glossary of English Language Registers, 1976; The Examination Essay, 1980; Polish Up Your English, 1984; The General Paper Comprehension, 1986; The Universal English Primer, 1994. Memberships: Peoples Educational Association of Ghana; International Reading Association. Address: Ghana Education Staff Development Institute, PO Box 12, Ajumako, Ghana.

**AGIOBENEBO Tamunopriye J,** b. 28 February 1953, Bakana, Rivers State, Nigeria. Economist. m. Ada, 2 sons, 3 daughters. Education: BSc Hons Economics, 1976, ABU; PhD Economics, 1986, Pittsburgh. Appointments: Lecturer II, 1982, Lecturer I, 1986; Senior Lecturer, 1989. Publications: Over 50 publications including Introductory Microeconomics, 1996; Introductory Math Methods, Vol 1, 1997; Public Sector Economics, Vol 1, 1997; 13 journal articles; and others. Memberships: Life member, Nigerian Economic Society; Life member, Interdisciplinary Studies Association; American Economic Association; and others. Address: Box 324 Uniport Post Office, University of Port Harcourt, Port Harcourt Rivers State, Nigeria.

**AGRANOVSKI Igor Eugenievich,** b. 27 February 1964, Moscow, Russia. Engineer. m. Victoria, 1 daughter. Education: B Eng, Moscow, 1986; MSc, Chemical Engineer, Moscow, 1992; PhD, Australia, 1996. Appointments: Research Fellow, 1986-89; Senior Research Fellow, 1990-92; Senior Engineer, 1993; Lecturer, 1994-98; Senior Lecturer, 1999-. Publications: More than 40 Publications in Refereed Journals. Honours: 1st Prize for Best Paper. Memberships: Institution of Engineers; International Association of Aerosol Research; Russian Chemical Society. Address: Griffith University, Faculty of Ens, 4111 Brisbane, Australia.

**AGRAWAL Bhagwan Das,** b. 23 August 1932, Varanasi, UP, India. University Professor. m. Kailash Agrawal, 2 sons. Education: MA Mathematics; BSc; PhD. Appointments: Professor in Mathematics, Banaras Hindu University, 1958-96; Attended about 20 annual conferences of Indian Mathematical Society. Publications: 50 research papers in foreign and Indian Journals; Referee, research papers. Memberships: American Mathematical Society; Life member, Indian Mathematical Society, Progress of Mathematics, Mathematical Society, BMU and Ganita; Certain other mathematical societies. Address: Ck 52/11 Raja Darwaza, Varanasi 221 001, India.

**AGRAWAL Jai Prakash,** b. 16 June 1944, Bisaula, India. Scientist. m. Sushma Rastogi, 1 son, 1 daughter. Education: BSc, Lucknow University, 1965; MSc, 1967, PhD, 1970-71, Gorakhpur University. Appointments: CSIR Research Fellow, Gorakhpur University, 1967-71; JSO, Directorate of Inspection, General Stores, 1971-74; SSO-I, 1974-80, Assistant Director, 1980-84, Deputy Director, 1984-90, E.R.D.L, R&D Organization; Joint Director, H.E.M.R.L, R&D Organization, 1990-; M.Sc. (by research) and Ph.D. Guide for Poona and Delhi Universities; Adviser, Union Public Service Commission (UPSC), New Delhi; Referee for CSIR, Defence and International Journals; Expert for CSIR and DRDO Selections; Ph.D. Examiner for Indian Universities. Publications: 60 research papers, 13 techincal reports, 2 patents, 12 designs, 13 popular articles, 1 monograph; Freelance writer ( English and Hindi) for popular magazines such as Science Reporter, Popular Plastics, Plastics India, Industrial Products Finder and Vigyan Pragati (Hindi). Honours: Fellow, Royal Society of Chemistry, London; Ex-Marie-Curie Research Fellow; Ex-Indo-French High Level Research Fellow; Cash Award, Commendation Certificate; Dr Gorakh Prasad Vigyan Puraskar; DRDD Technology Award, 1996. Memberships: High Energy Materials Society of India; Indian Science Congress Association; Joint Secretary, Indian Society for Composite Materials, 1985-92; Member, Editorial Board of Popular Plastics and Packaging, 1985-91. Address: Joint Director, High Energy Materials Research Laboratory, Sutarwadi, Pune 411021, India.

**AGRAWAL Poonam,** b. 3 January 1958, Lucknow, UP, India. Academician; Scientist. Education: BSc, 1977, University of Udaipur; MSc Foods and Nutrition, 1980, GB Pant University of Agriculture and Technology; Doctoral in Biochemistry, 1985, IARI, New Delhi; Post-Doctorate in Biotechnology, Institute of

Wool Research, Aachen and Institute for Microbiology, University of Dusseldorf, W Germany, 1985-87. Appointments: Assistant Professor, Rajasthan Agriculture University Udaipur, 1983-91; Science Officer, Institute for Microbiology, University of Dusseldorf, 1987; Senior Scientific Officer, Gr I, Dept Biotechnology, Ministry of Science and Technology, New Delhi, 1988-89; Associate Professor, CS Azad University of Agriculture and Technology, Kanpur, 1991-95; Professor, PSSCIVE, NCERT, Bhopal, 1995-. Publications: 25 research papers in international and national scientific journals in field of clinical nutrition, Keratins and Keratinase, and studies on molecular basis of regulation of FMDH from Hansenula polymorpha and various other aspects of Nutrition and public health. Honours: Smt Bhagwati Devi Rastogi Trust Award for pioneering work on diabetes; Merit scholarship and honours during studies; Various other Fellowships; Merit and Appreciation Certificates by National Society of India for research. Memberships: Life member: Indian Association of Educational Planning and Administration; Association of Food Scientists and Technologists; Nutrition Society of India; International College of Nutrition; Society for Plant Biochemists/Biotechnologists; Indian Society of Agricultural Biochemists. Address: Pandit Sunderlal Sharma Central Institute of Vocational Education, 131 Zone II, MP Nagar, Bhopal 462 011, India.

**AGRAWAL Surendra Prasad,** b. 23 May 1929, India. Education: BSc, Agra University, 1949; BA, Agra University, 1952; Certificate, Library Science, 1952, MA, 1954, Aligarh Muslim University; French Course, School of Foreign Language, Government of India, New Delhi, 1966. Appointments: Member, Hindi Advisory Committee, Ministry of Coal, Government of India, New Delhi; Member, Board of Studies, School of Archival Studies, National Archives of India, Government of India, New Delhi. Publications: Many books, monographs including: Development of Documentation in India; Social Science Information, Concept Publishing Company, New Delhi, 1989; Second Historical Survey of Educational Development in India: Select Documents 1985-89 (jointly with J C Aggarwal), 1991; Modern History of Jammu and Kashmir: A Look Back into Ancient Glorious Kashmir Focussing Confrontation and Failures Leading to Present Turbulent Kashmir and a Peep Ahead, Co-author, 1996; Directory of LIS Education in India: Compendium on Library and Information Science Study in India, 1996. Honours: Degree Dr of Philosophy, Education (Hon), International University Foundation, 1988; Association of Government Librarians, Information Science (AGLIS), D R Kalia Award for NASSDOC; Freedom Fighters Samman Pension. Memberships: Fellow, IBA, Cambridge, England; Fellow, Society of Ethnobotanists, India; Life Member, Academy of Information Science; Board of Studies, School of Archival Studies, New Delhi, India; President, Shiksha Sansthan, New Delhi. Address: B-5/73 Azad Apartment, Sri Aurobindo Marg, New Delhi 110016, India.

**AGUILERA Ana Maria,** b. 16 October 1967, Barcelona, Spain. Professor of Statistics. Education: Degree, Mathematics, 1990, PhD, Mathematics, 1994, University of Granada. Appontments: Assistant Professor, 1990-96, Professor, 1996-, Department of Statistics and Operations Research, University of Granada. Publications: Several professional articles. Membership: Spanish Society of Statistics & Operations Research. Address: Cira de la Zubia, No 45 Portal 1, 4 C, 18002 Granada, Spain.

**AHANIN Maziar,** b. 11 January 1974, Iran. Businessman. 1 son. Education: Graduate, Business Management & Administration. Appointments: Sole Proprietor of: Maziar Clothing Ltd, retail & wholesale; Ahanin World Trading Inc,

importer, exporter. Honours: Various awards pertaining to management, supervisory, sales. Memberships: Canadian Fashion Association; Canadian Small Business Association. Address: 95 Scollard Street, Toronto Ont, Canada M5R 1G4.

**AHARONI Herzl,** b. 20 February 1937, Haifa, Israel. Scientist; Engineer; Educator. m. Miriam, 2 sons, 2 daughters. Education: BSc, 1964; MSc, 1967; Dipl.ing, 1970; DSc, Technion (IIT) Haifa, Israel, 1972. Appointments: Professor, Department of Electrical and Computer Engineering, Ben-Gurion University of the Negev, Beer-Sheeva, Israel. Publications: Over 100 in scientific journals and conferences. Honours: 3 Teaching Awards; Applied Electronics Award; Distinguished Research Professor. Memberships: Israel Crystal Growth Association; Israel Physical Society. Address: Department of Electrical & Computer Engineering, Ben Gunion University, PO Box 653, Beer Sheeva, Israel.

**AHLES-STARKS Shirley,** b. 2 December 1939, Washington, DC, USA. Music Teacher. m. Homer, 2 sons, 5 daughters. Education: DC Teachers. Appoitntments: Teacher, Singing, Piano, Drums. Honours: Many Awards throughout century. Address: P O Box 90135, Washington, DC 20090-0135, USA.

**AHMAD Nisar,** b. 1 April 1941, Okara, Pakistan. Scientist. m. Shahnaz Ahmad, 1 son, 1 daughter. Education: MSc, Government College, Lahore; PhD, Queens University, Belfast. Appointment: Chief Scientist, Government of Pakistan. Publications: Several articles in professional journals. Honours: Roll of Honour, Government College, Lahore, 1963; Open Gold Medal, Pakistan Academy of Sciences, 1996; Sitara-I-Imtiaz, 1997. Memberships: Fellow, Nuclear Society of Pakistan; Pakistan Physical Society. Address: Head APD PINSTECH, PO Nilore, Islamabad, Pakistan.

**AHMED Ahmed A,** b. 16 February 1942, Kalubia, Egypt. Professor. m. M M Eltouchi, 2 sons. Education: BSc, Faculty of Science, Cairo University, 1963; MSc, 1968; PhD, 1973. Appointments: Scholarship Student, 1964-65; Research Assistant, 1965-68; Assistant Researcher, 1968-73; Researcher, 1973-78; Associate Research Professor, 1978-1983; Researcher Professor, 1983-; Department Head, 1998-. Publications: Over 70 Scientific Articles, Technical Journals. Honours: Scientific Distinction Award; State Prize in Chemistry; Order of Arts and Science. Memberships: Chemical Society of Egypt; Society of Glass Technology; American Ceramic Society; American Association of Advancement of Sciences; New York Academy of Sciences. Address: Glass Research Department, National Research Centre, Dokki Cairo 12622, Egypt.

**AHMED Saleem,** b. 16 March 1945, India. Management Consultant; Educator. m. Joumana Ahmed, 2 sons, 1 daughter. Education: AEPT Power Tech, 1965, Karachi Polytech Institute Pakistan; BA Math, University of Karachi, Pakistan, 1965; BSME, Detroit Institute Technology, USA, 1971; MBA in Systems Approach, Baldwin Wallace College, 1980; PhD Marketing and Management, 1985, California Coast University Santa Ana, California, USA. Appointments: Project Engineer Union Carbide Corporation, Westlake, Ohio, 1977-85; Management Consultant, Saleem & Associates, Detroit 1986-89; President, Michigan Centre for Excellence Inc Dearborn, MI, 1990-, Society for Professional Advancement Inc, Dearborn, MI, 1990-. Publications: Author, Project Management Systems Approach for Plastic Engineering, 1990 The Excellence in Sales for Executives, 1991; Multi Level Marketing, 1991; The Psychology of Winning, 1992; The Job Connection, 1992; How to Close Sales Every Time, 1992

Others. Honours: Certified Manufacturing Engineer; Certified Plant Engineer; Who's Who in the Midwest; Who's Who in the World. Membership: ASTD. Address: Society for Professional Advancement Inc, PO Box 1727, Dearborn, MI 48121 1727, USA.

**AHN Chung Si,** b. 7 May 1944, Korea. Professor. m. Bong-Sook Sohn, 2 daughters. Education: BA, Political Science, Seoul National University, 1967; MA, Political Science, Seoul National University, 1971; PhD, Political Science, University of Hawaii, 1977. Appointments: Assistant Professor, Institute of Foreign Affairs, 1977-79; Assistant, Associate, Full Professor, Seoul National University, 1977-; Visiting Professor, Politics Department, Princeton University, 1988-89; Chairman, Department of Political Science, Seoul National University, 1991-93; Director, Institute of Social Science, 1994-96; Visiting Professor, Department of Political Science, National University of Singapore, 1996-97. Publications: Numerous Publications in various languages. Honours: Visiting Fellow, Institute of Southeast Asian Studies; Senior Fellow, Fulbright Hays Award; Visiting Fellow, Center of International Studies, Princeton University. Memberships: Jacob International Society for Collaborative Studies; Korean Association of Southeast Asian Studies; International Political Science Association; American Political Association; Korean Association of Political Science; Korean Association of International Studies. Address: Department of Political Science, Seoul National University, Shinlim-dong, Kwanak-ku, Seoul 151-742, Republic of Korea.

**AHSAN Nazmul,** b. 29 October 1955, Khulna, Bangladesh. Researcher. m. Rana Ahsan, 1 daughter. Education: PhD, Dhaka University, 1993. Appointments: Lecturer, Social Worker, 1981-87; Social Organizer, 1988-91; Researcher, 1992-. Publications: 10 professional articles in journals. Honour: Outstanding Theatre Activist and Playwright. Memberships: International Shakespeare Society; ITI, Bangladesh; Bangladesh Group Theatre Federation; SEAD, England. Address: 2 Farazipara Road, Khulna, Bangladesh.

**AIHARA Jun-ichi,** b. 2 July 1941, Tokyo. Chemistry Professor. m. Akiko Yoshimura, 1 son. Education: BSc, University of Tokyo, 1965; MSc, University of Tokyo, 1967; DSc, University of Tokyo, 1970. Appointments: Assistant Professor, Hokkaido University, 1970-81; Associate Professor, Shizuoka University, 1981-89; Professor, Shizuoka University, 1989-; Councillor of Shizuoka University, 1999-. Publications: Many papers, professional journals. Honours: Science Prize, 3M Japan, Ltd, 1989; Grand Prize, Shizuoka Asahi TV, 1992. Memberships: Chemical Society of Japan; American Chemical Society. Address: Shizuoka U Dept Chemistry, Faculty of Science, Oya Shizuoka 422-8529, Japan.

**AJANI Mehrunnissa,** b. 11 August 1944, Nairobi, Kenya. Company Secretary. m. Amirali, 1 son. Education: Diploma, Business, Polytechnical College, 1963; Diploma, Pitman's Secretary College, 1964. Career: Secretary, Dunlop Tyers, 1964-72, Phillips Electronics, 1973-76; Administration, 1976-94, Assistant Co-Secretary, 1995-96, Company Secretary, 1997-, Leitch Technology. Memberships: Canadian Society of Corporate Secretaries. Address: Leitch Technology Corporation, 24 Dyas Road, North York, Ontario M3B 1V7, Canada.

**AJIP ROSIDI,** b. 31 January 1938, Indonesia. Writer; Visiting Professor. m. Patimah, 3 sons, 3 daughters. Career: Chairman, Jakarta Arts Council, 1972-81; Chairman, Indonesian Publishers Association, 1973-79; President, Chairman of the Board, Dunia Pustaka Jaya Publishers, 1971-81, 1981-; Visiting

Professor, Osaka University of Foreign Studies, Japan, 1981-. Publications: 83 books in Indonesian and in Sundanese, some translated into 5 foreign languages. Honours: National Indonesian Awards, 1955-56, (for poetry), and 1957-58, (for prose); Australian Cultural Award, 1975; Indonesian Cultural Award, 1993. Memberships: Sundanese Writers Association; Indonesian National Cultural Body; Royal Institute of Linguistics and Anthropology, The Netherlands. Address: 5-25-21-422 Onohara Higashi, Mino, Osaka 562-0031, Japan.

**AKAHOSHI Kazuya,** b. 15 August 1960, Kitakyushu City, Japan. Gastroenterologist. m. Akiko, 2 sons, 1 daughter. Education: MD, Kagoshima University, 1986; PhD, Kyushu University, 1993. Appointments: Researcher, Kyushu University, 1989-91; Assistant Professor, 1994-97; Head of Gastroenterology, Aso Iizuka Hospital, 1997-. Publications: Gut, Research Article to Medical Journal; Radiology, Research Article to Medical Journal. Honours: Gastroenterological Endoscopy Society Award. Memberships: Japanese Society of Gastroenterology; Japan Gastroenterological Endoscopy Society. Address: Aso Iizuka Hospital, 3-83 Yoshio Town, 820 Iizuka, Fukuoka, Japan.

**AKAN Osman,** b. 3 August 1949, Ankara, Turkey. Professor. m. Guzin, 1 son. Education: BS, Civil Engineering, Middle East Technical University, 1971; MS, Civil Engineering, University of Illinois, 1973; PhD, Civil Engineering, University of Illinois, 1976. Appointments: Assistant Professor, Civil Engineering, Middle East Technical University, 1976-82; Associate Professor, Professor, Chairman, Civil and Environmental Engineering Department, Old Dominion University, VA, USA, 1982-. Publications: Over 80 Publications; Urban Stormwater Hydrology, 1993. Honours: Outstanding Journal Paper Award, 1987. Memberships: American Society of Civil Engineers; American Geophysical Union; Chi-Epsilon Honour Society. Address: Dept of Civil & Enviro Eng, Old Dominion University, Norfolk, VA 23529, USA.

**AKASE Masako,** b. 25 November 1933, Tokyo, Japan. Educator in the Humanities. Education: BA, 1957, MA, 1959, Waseda University. Appointments: Lecturer, 1968-70, Associate Professor, 1970-74, Professor, 1974-, Professor, Graduate Course, 1993-, Professor, Doctor Course, 1999-, Momoyama Gakuin University, Osaka. Publications: Author, books: Kafu Nagai and French Literature, 1976; Development of Comparative Studies, 1983; Kafu Nagai - Comparative Study, 1986; Comparative Literature, Comparative Culture, 1995; Kafu Nagai and French Culture, 1998. Honour: Mozume Sakuin Prize, 1990. Memberships: Japanese Comparative Literature Association, Governor, 1975-; France-Japanese Historical Studies Association, Trustee, 1980-. Address: 50-1-307, Kamikatsura, Maedacho, Nishikyoku, Kyoto, Japan.

**AKCHURIN Rauf,** b. 10 February 1945, Aktubinsk, USSR. Professor. m. Zharova Svetlana Petrovna. Education: Polytechnical Institute, Alma-Ata, 1967; Post Graduate Studies, Moscow State Institute of Electronic Engineering, 1976; D.Sc. Moscow State Academy of Fine Chemical Technology, 1993; Professor, 1996. Appointments: Assistant, Lecturer, Professor, Moscow State Academy of Fine Chemical Technology, 1978-. Publications: Physics Chemical Bases of Liquid Phase Epitaxy; Physics and Materical Science of Semiconductors with Deep Levels. Honours: State Prize in Science and Engineering. Memberships: Scientific Council, Russian Academy of Science.

**AKHMETEV Peter,** b. 2 February 1963, Moscow, Russia. Mathematician. 1 son. Education: DMath, Hon, Mathematical Institute Steklova, RAS, Moscow. Appointments: Researcher, Izmiran, Troitsk, Moscow Region, Russia, 1989-. Publications:

Contributor, articles to professional journals. Memberships: Moscow Mathematical Society; American Mathematical Society. Address: Moscow Region Troitsk, Mikrorayon B 32 14, 142092 Moscow, Russia.

**AKHOUNDZADEH Mohamad,** b. 1955, Iran. Diplomat. m. Shahla, 1 son, 1 daughter. Education: Civil Engineer, Town Planning. Appointments: CDA Delhi, Ambass-Dhaka, CDA London D G M F Affairs; Director, European Research Group, Amb-Pakistan; Adviser to the Minister of Foreign Affairs. Publications: Division of Sub-Continent and Creation of Bangladesh; Contributing Columnist, Iranian English Journals. Membership: Institute for Political and International Studies, Tehran. Address: Embassy of Iran, 2220 238 St 2 G 5/1 Diplomatic, Enclave Islamabad, Pakistan.

**AKIMOV Mikhail Nikolaevich,** b. 6 May 1957, Kilia, Ukraine. Physicist; Educator. m. Tatiana Yurievna Bobyleva, 1 daughter. Education: Student, Leningrad State University, USSR, 1974-80; Certificate Physicist, postgraduate, Leningrad State University, 1980-83; PhD, 1984. Appointments: Senior Lecturer, Department of Physics, and Applied Mechanics of the Saint Petersburg University of the Ministry of Internal Affairs; Lt-Colonel, Ministry of Internal Affairs of Russia. Publications: Articles in professional journals on plastic crystals, NMR, Birefringence Measurements; Textbooks. Honour: Honorary Emblem of Minister of Internal Affairs of Russia, 1996. Membership: DI Mendeleev Chemical Society. Address: Koroleva 24 k 36, 197349 Saint Petersburg, Russia.

**AKINJIOLA Raphael Agunbiade,** b. 20 July 1950, Ondo, Nigeria. Educational Administrator. m. Glory Agunbiade-Akinjiola, 3 sons, 2 daughters. Appointments: Class Teacher, High School, 3 years; Journalist, 2 years; Educational Administrator, 1980-. Publications include: UNCTAD and GATT - A Study in International Economic Bargaining Process, 1980; Crisis Management in Higher Education, 1985; Formative Evaluation Report, 1994. Memberships include: Philosophy Association of Nigeria; Conference of University Administrators, England; Nigerian Institute of Management. Address: National Universities Commission, Aja Nojanchukwu House, PMB 237, Garki GPO, Abuja, Nigeria.

**AKINMUYIWA Elijah Olufemi,** b. 24 April 1958, Edunabon. Secretary. m. Florence Bosede, 3 sons, 2 daughters. Education: Basic Course Certificate in Secretarial Studies, 1984; Advanced Certificate in Secretarial Studies, 1986. Appointments: Typist, Ile-Ife, 1975-81; Confidential Secretary to the Sole Administrator: Iseyin Local Govt Council, 1984, Ede Local Govt Council, 1986, Chairman, Atakunmosa Local Govt Council, Osu, 1987; Confidential Secretary to Under Secretary (Expenditure), Ministry of Finance & Economic Planning, Secretariat, Ibadan, 1988; Confidential Secretary to Assistant Director (Cabinet), 1989, Deputy Director (Cabinet), 1990, Director-General (Cabinet), 1991, Office of the Military Governor, Secretariat, Ibadan; Confidential Secretary to the Branch Manager, Thodel Savings & Loans Ltd (Mortgage Bankers), Ibadan Branch, 1991-94; Confidential Secreatry to the Corporate Affairs Manager, Dunlop Nigeria plc, Ikeja, 1994-97; Confidential Secretary to the Chief Engineer, Dunlop Nigeria plc, Ikeja, 1997-. Honours: Certificate of Award for the Completion of Bible Doctrine with the West African Mission, 1980. Memberships: Institute of Certified Secretaries & Reporters; Chartered Institute of Administration. Address: POB 29368, Secretariat Post Office, Ibadan, Oyo State, Nigeria.

**AKINSO Ayodeji,** b. 14 August 1957, Ondo, Nigeria. Banker. m. Stella, 2 sons, 1 daughter. Education: Certificate in Business Studies, 1978; Associate Chartered Institute of

Bankers, 1995; Diploma in Biblical Studies, 1998; Master Degree, Business Administration, 1998. Appointments: Branch Manager, UBA Plc, 1990; Head of Credits, 1991-93; Regional Credit Analyst, West Admin, 1993-96; Relationship Manager, 1997-. Publications: Turnaround Management in UBA; Raising Finance for Your Business; The Book Leviticus. Memberships: Chartered Institute of Bankers; Institute of Management. Address: United Bank for Africa; Iwo Road, Ibadan, Nigeria.

**AKINTUNDE Ifedayo,** b. 2 November 1933, Ondo, Nigeria. Consulting Engineer. m. Chief (Mrs) F O Akintunde, 2 sons, 1 daughter. Education: Engineering Practice in Government, Construction and Consultancy Respectively; Founder and Chief Executive of Profen Consultants Inc, 1976-. Publication: Technological Development Through Self-Reliance, book, 1994. Honours: Merit Award, Nigerian Society of Engineers, 1983; Certificate of Merit, Federal Ministry of Works and Housing, 1992. Memberships: Fellow, Institution of Civil Engineers; Fellow, Nigerian Society of Engineers; Fellow, Nigerian Academy of Engineering; American Society of Civil Engineers. Address: PO Box 6331 Agodi Gate, Ibadan, Oyo State, Nigeria.

**AKIRA Masanori,** b. 22 June 1955, Konoike, Osaka, Japan. Chest Radiology. Education: MD, Yamaguchi University, 1982; PhD, Osaka University, 1990. Appointments: Medical Staff, Osaka University, 1982-86; Medical Staff, 1986-92, Chief, 1992-, Department of Radiology, Kinki Chuo Hospital. Memberships: Japanese Society of Radiology; Japanese Society of Chest Diseases. Address: 39-12 Minamigaoka, Osaka, Kawachinagano 586, Japan.

**AKIYAMA Hidenori,** b. 2 April 1951, Ehime, Japan. Professor. m. Naoko, 1 son, 1 daughter. Education: BS, Kyushu Institute of Technology, 1974; MS, 1976, PhD, 1979, Nagoya University. Appointments: Research Associate, Nagoya University, 1979-85; Associate Professor, 1985-94, Professor, 1994-, Kumamoto University. Publication: High Voltage Pulsed Power Technology, 1991. Memberships: IEEE; JIEE; Physical Society of Japan. Address: Electrical & Computer Engineering, Kumamoto University, 2-39-1 Kurokami, Kumamoto 860, Japan.

**AKOEV Inal,** b. 17 April 1922, Moscow, Russia. Biophysicist; Radiobiologist. m. Akoeva Xeniya, 12 October 1920, 1 son. Education: Candidate of Bioscience, Academy of Veterinary Medicine, 1951. Appointments: Senior Scientist, Scientific Medical and Biological Department of Atom Bomb Experimental Range in Semipalatinsk, 1955-68; Dr of Bioscience, 1967; Founder, Laboratory of Radiation Biophysics, Institute of Cell Biophysics, USSR Academy of Science, 1968; Deputy Director, 1971-87. Publications: Author, more than 250 scientific papers including 6 monographies in Russian and 1 monography in English: Biophysical Insights into Cancer, 1989. Honours: 12 state medals and orders; Mark of Honor. Memberships: Founder and President, Section of Electromagnitobiology of Science Councils, USSR Academy Science, 1979-93; Regular membership, USA Bioelectromagnitology Society, 1981-91. Address: Microraion AB 5 F 21, 142292 Puschino, Russia.

**AKRAM M Chaudhry,** b. 30 September 1942, Jullundar, Pakistan. m. Munawar Sultana, 1 son, 2 daughters. Education: PhD, Warwick University. Appointments: Lecturer, Government College, Lahore, 1967-71; Lecturer, University of Zambia, 1973-81; Associate Professor, University of Bahrain, 1984-. Publications: 15 on Dynamic Models for Time Series Forecast. Honours: MA statistics Degree with Distinction, 1967. Memberships: Royal Statistical Society; International Institute of Forecasting. Address: #1 PO Box 28588, East Riffa, Bahrain.

**AKULIU Vladimir,** b. 28 July 1953, Moscow, Russia. Professor. 1 daughter. Education: MS, Moscow Institute of Physics and Technology, 1976; PhD, Lebedev Institute Moscow, 1980. Appointments: Junior Scientist, Lebedev Institute, 1976; Senior Scientist, General Physics Institute, 1983; Associate Professor, Moscow Institute of Physics and technology, 1984; Professor, Laboratoire Aime Cotton, France, 1996. Publications: 1 book; 69 Papers. Honours: 3 National Prize of USSR, 1978. Address: Lab Aime Cotton, Bat 505 Campus d'Orsay, Orsay 91405, France.

**AL BESHIR Mohamed Yousuf Ahmed,** b. 1 January 1941, Al Managil, Sudan. Advocate; Legal Consultant. m. Inam Al Haj Ahmed, 3 sons, 3 daughters. Education: LLB, University of Khartoum, 1966; Legal Profession Bar Exam, 1966. Appointments: Judge in Sudan, Judiciary of Sudan, 1966-76; Judge in Aden, Aden High Court, National Industries & Development Company Ltd, 1971-74; Company Secretary and Legal Adviser, Sharjah, 1976-77; Partner, Jaafar Alwan Al Jaziri & Associates, general practice law firm, 1978-. Memberships: National Geographic Society, USA, life member; International Living, life member; Highlander Club. Address: Jaafar Alwan Al Jaziri & Associates, PO Box 4253, Dubai, United Arab Emirates.

**AL MULHIM Mohammed,** b. 18 November 1963, Al-Ahsa. Educational Supervisor. m. Nora Al Mudhaffer, 2 sons, 2 daughters. Education: BSc Physics, 1986; Diploma Educational Evaluation and Measurement, 1997. Appointments: Physics Teacher, High Schools, 1986-94; Educational Supervisor for Physics, 1994-. Publications: Many articles in newspapers and magazines. Honour: Superiority Award for advanced level in Diploma. Memberships: Eastern Province Literary Club; Saudi Computer Association; Educational and Psychological Sciences Association. Address: PO Box 1708, Hoffouf 31982, Saudi Arabia.

**AL SAUD HRH Prince Saif Al Islam Bin Saud Abdul Aziz,** b. 1951, Riyadh, Saudi Arabia. University Lecturer; Businessman. m. Princess Modi Al Nimer, 2 sons, 4 daughters. Education: BS Media, 1989; MS Media, 1994; PhD Sociology First Class Hons, 1997. Appointments: Head of Information Office in Ministry of Interior; University Lecturer, King Saud University. Publications: The effect of drugs on Youths; The effect of the television advertisement on the Saudi Society. Address: PO Box 1121, Riyadh 11431, Saudi Arabia.

**AL-AMOUDI Omar Saeed Baghabra,** b. 29 October 1956, Hadhramouth, Yemen. Education. m. Taibah Mohammed Saeed Al-Amoudi, 2 sons, 2 daughters. Education: BS, King Fahd University, 1982; MS, 1985; PhD, 1992. Appointments: Lecturer, 1985-92; Instructor, 1992-95; Assistant Professor, 1995-98; Associate Professor, 1998-. Publications: More than 90 publications. Honours: First Honour throughout his undergraduate and graduate Studies; Excellence in Research Award; Involved in research into the durability of reinforced concrete in aggressive media andcharactisation and stabilisation of indigenous soils. Memberships: ACI-SAC; ASCE-SAC; Saudi Al Umran Society. Address: KFUPM Box 5058, Dhahran 31261, Saudi Arabia.

**AL-ANSARI Husain,** b. 15 July 1957, Kuwait. Library and Information Scientist. m. Haya Al-Othman, 1 son, 2 daughters. Education: BA Library Science, 1979, Cairo University, Egypt; MLIS, 1983, University Wisconsin at Milwaukee; PhD Information Studies, 1992, Florida State University.

Appointments: Assistant Professor, Library and Information Science Programme, Kuwait University; Director, Kuwait University Libraries, Kuwait University, 1994-. Publications: 8 publications including Directory of Libraries and Information Centres in Kuwait, co-author, 1999. Honours: Scholarship, Ministry of Education, Kuwait, 1975-79; Scholarship, Kuwait University, 1981-83, 1989-92; Award of Service, Distinguished Librarian, Faculty of Science, Kuwait University, 1987; Scole and the American Library Association Award, Distinguished PhD student, USA, 1989. Memberships: American Library Association; American Society for Information Science; Special Library Association; Arabian Gulf Chapter of SLA, President Elect, 1996-; AFLI; ASIS. Address: PO Box 17303, Khalidia 725645, Kuwait.

**AL-ASMARI Awad,** b. 11 January 1959, Balasmar. Staff Member. m. Haya Mohammed, 2 sons, 2 daughters. Education: PhD Electrical Engineering, 1991. Appointments: Associate Professor, College of Eng EE Dept, King Saud University. Publications: Over 30 papers in well known journals and conferences. Memberships: Senior Member, IEEE; Communication Society. Address: KSU EE Dept, POB 800 College of Engg, Riyadh 11421, Saudi Arabia.

**AL-DAKHIL Badr,** b. 8 December 1961, Riyadh, Saudi Arabia. Programmer. m. Nasseba, 1 son, 3 daughters. Education: Associate Degree, MIS, CMSU, USA, 1986. Appointments: Programmer, Saudi Arabian Monetary Agency, 1980-. Honours: Certificate of Recognition, 1989, 1999; Financial Award, 1993. Address: P O Box 42607, Riyadh 11551, Saudi Arabia.

**AL-DAWOOD Kasim,** b. 1 July 1961, Jubail, Saudi Arabia. Consultant Physician. m. Sita Al-Otaish, 3 sons, 2 daughters. Education: MBBS, Medicine, 1985; Fellowship in Family and Community Medicine, 1991; Master in Epidemiology, 1999; Diploma in Tropical Medicine, 1999. Appointments: Demonstrator, College of Medicine, 1987-91; Assistant Professor, Consultant, 1991-98; Chairman, Department of Family Medicine, 1994-96; Associate Professor of Medicine, 1999. Publication: Contributor, many articles on family medicine in professional journals. Memberships: AAAS; ISDE; IEA. Address: P O Box 2290, Al-Khobar 31952, Saudi Arabia.

**AL-HUSSAINI Emad K,** b. 1 January 1944, Assiut, Egypt. Professor of Electrical Communications. m. Safia Maarouf, 1 daughter. Education: BSc, Ain-Shams University, 1964; MSc, 1974, PhD, 1977, Cairo University; Research Fellow, Imperial College, London, 1976-77; University of Pennsylvania, Philadelphia, 1981-82. Appointments: Research Engineer, Egyptian Aeroorganization, Cairo, 1964-70; Served from Laboratory Engineer to Professor of Electrical Communications, Faculty of Engineering, Cairo University, 1970-. Publications: Over 50 papers in international journals and conferences. Honour: National Encouragement Award for Outstanding Engineering Research, Egypt, 1989. Memberships: Senior Member, Institute of Electrical and Electronics Engineers; Egyptian Engineering Society. Address: 23 Hamadan Street, Apt 301, 12211 Giza, Egypt.

**AL-JARALLAH Ahmed,** b. 1958, Riyadh, Saudi Arabia. Consultant Paediatricneurologist. Education: MBBS, 1983, College of Medicine, King Saud University; DCH, 1985, Royal College of Physicians & Surgeons, Dublin, Ireland; JBCP, 1989, Jordanian Medical Council, Amman; ABCP, 1997, Arab Council for Medical Specialisation, Damascus, Syria; FRICPCH, 1997, Royal College of Paediatrics and Child Health, London, UK; Postdoctoral Fellowship, University of Texas, SouthWestern Medical Centre, Dallas, 1998.

Appointments: Demonstrator, 1984; Registrar, 1988; Senior Registrar, 1989; Consultant, 1990. Publications: Many scientific papers locally and internationally. Honours: Several grants and awards from universities and research centres. Memberships: American Academy of Neurology; Fellow, Royal College of Paediatrics and Child Health. Address: PO Box 55902, Riyadh 11544, Saudi Arabia.

**AL-MUTAIRY Mohammad,** b. 9 August 1959, Saudi Arabia. Chief Executive Officer. m. W Al-Mutairy, 2 sons, 1 daughter. Education: Diploma in Business, ICS, England, 1978; Higher Management Skills, Chamber of Commerce. Appointments: General Manager, Tahani Corporation, 1980-90; Managing Director, Saudi Support Services Group, 1990-94; Chief Executive Officer, President, Saudi Groups, 1994-. Memberships: National Geographic Society; Disabled Children Society; Prince Salman Social Center. Address: Saudi Groups, PO Box 61816, Riyadh 11575, Saudi Arabia.

**AL-NAJJAR Musaed,** b. 17 September 1955, Kuwait. Assistant General Secretary. m. Maha Al-Shehab, 1 son, 1 daughter. Education: PhD, Psychology, Nottingham University, 1992. Appointments: Assistant Manager, Department of Research and Studies, Kuwait Police; Assistant General Secretary, National Committee for Drug Control. Publications: Self Esteem and Trait Anxiety in Relation to Drug Misuse in Kuwait; Personality Characteristics of Drug Abuse in Kuwait; Why People Take Drugs, a Study Case; Drug Abuse, A Brochure for Research Education Center, Kuwait. Memberships: Addiction Forum; International Association of Chief of Police; International Police Association; International Council on Alcohol and Addiction; Society for the Study of Addiction to Alcohol and Other Drugs; British Psychological Society; Psychological Services Section, American Psychological Association; Kuwait Anti-Drug Committee. Address: PO Box 34396, 73254 Kuwait, Kuwait.

**AL-NASSER Ibrahim,** b. 3 September 1953, Dawadmi, Saudi Arabia. Associate Professor; Professor. 4 sons, 3 daughters. Education: PhD, University of London, 1987. Appointments: Chairman, Department of Biochemistry, King Saud University, 1991-92. Publications: Principles of Practical Biochemistry; Biochemistry for Health Control. Address: PO Box 75250, Riyadh 11578, Saudi Arabia.

**AL-OMAR Ahmad Faisal,** b. 1 July 1939, Kazo, Hama, Syria. Professor. m. Hiam Alwani, 2 sons, 2 daughters. Education: BSc, Mechanical Engineering, 1963; MSc, Mechanical Engineering, 1966; PhD, Mechanical Engineering, 1968. Appointments: Dean, Faculty of Engineering, 1975-78, Dean, Faculty of Mechanical Engineering, 1984-86, 1995-97, Aleppo University; Dean, Faculty of Engineering, Sana'a University, 1989-91. Publications: 5 books, 12 papers, several articles. Memberships: Engineering Syndicate, Syria; Teachers Union, Syria. Address: PO Box 370, 21 Acasia Street, New Shabba Aleppo, Syria.

**AL-OUFI Saleh Abdullah,** b. 1955, Liyyah, Saudi Arabia. Legal Advisor. m. Sarah Abdullah Al-Edaily. Education: LLB, King Abdulaziz University, Makkah, 1976; Diploma, Regulation Studies, Institute of Public Administration, Riyadh, 1978; LL, Common Law, 1983, LLM, Admiralty Law, 1984, Tulane University, USA; Diploma, French Language, 1988, LLD, International Economic Law, 1988, Ottawa University, Canada. Appointments: Senior Attorney, Saud M Shawwaf Law Office, Riyadh, Saudi Arabia; Senior Legal Advisor, Contractual Affairs, Legal Department, Saudi Marketing & Refinery Corporation; Legal Advisor, Bureau of Experts, Council of Ministers, Government of the Kingdom of Saudi Arabia; Legal

Advisor, The Governor of Makkah; Adjunct Professor, International Arbitration, Institute for Diplomatic Studies, Ministry of Foreign Affairs; Adjunct Professor, Contract Law, Institute of Public Administration, Riyadh. Memberships: International Bar Association; APPIMAF; AIPPI; International Trademark Association. Address: PO Box 65965, Riyadh, Saudi Arabia.

**AL-RAMLAWS Ihats N,** b. 4 May 1971, Amman, Jordan. Area Sales Manager. Education: BSc Eng, Jordan University of Science and Technology, 1993. Appointments: Design Engineer, Zamil Steel, 1993-94; Engineering Group Supervisors, 1994-95; Area Sales Manager, 1995-. Memberships: Jordanian Engineers Association, 1993. Address: Samil Steel Bldgs Co Ltd, Al-Sadd St P O Box 19255, Doha, Qatar.

**AL-RIFAIE Jamal Sayyed Hashim,** b. 9 February 1948, Kuwait. Education: BSc, Natural Gas Engineering, Texas University, USA, 1973; Diploma, Production, Transport and Process of Heavy Crude Oil; Diploma, Building Crude, Gas and Products Tankers. Career includes: Natural Gas Engineer, Controller of Transport and Storage, Controller of Petrochemical & Transport, Director of Refining and Petrochemicals, Assistant Under-Secretary for Technical Affairs, Ministry of Oil, Kuwait; Member, Technical Team for Building 4 LPG Tankers, 1976-81; Participation, Sea Trial Test for LPG Vessels; Participation, Supervision, Gas Test for 4 LPG Vessels at Mina Al-Ahmadi; Participation on a Study Conducted by Norwegian Consulting House for Operations and Managing the LPG Fleet; Member, Head Hunter Committee, 1982-83; Chairman, Khafji Offshore Unused Associated Gas Project, 1993; Member, Permanent Council and Executive Board, World Petroleum Congresses, 1994-. Memberships include: Bahrain: Board Member, 1979-86, Deputy Chairman, 1986, Director, Finance Committee, 1982-86, Board Deputy Finance Committee Chairman, Gulf Petrochemical Industries Company; Tunis: Deputy Chairman, Phosphate Mines Investment Study Company, Soura Al-Wartan, 1986-88; Turkey: Board Member, Mediterranean Fertilizers Industry Companu, 1986-90; Board Member, Turkish Arab Fertilizers Company, 1986-89; Kuwait General Standard Specification Committee, Ministry of Commerce and Industry; Joint Exploration Project Committee, KPC; Deputy Chairman, Board of Conservation of Petroleum Resources, 1995-; Committee, Arabian Oil Company Concessin Agreement, 1995; Deputy Chairman, 1995-, Kuwait Oil Tanker Company SAK; Society of Petroleum Engineers, USA; Member, Oil and Gas Emergency Committee, State of Kuwait. Address: Ministry of Oil Kuwait, PO Box 22795, Safat 13088, Kuwait.

**AL-RUWAIH Fawzia Mohammed Ahmed,** b. 31 March 1952, Kuwait. Professor in Hydrogeology; Head of Geology Department. m. Ghadanfari Taleb, 2 sons, 3 daughters. Education: BSc, Kuwait University, 1973; MSc, 1975, PhD, 1980, University College, London, England. Appointments: Demonstrator, 1973-74; Assistant Professor, 1980-87, Associate Professor, 1988-97, Professor, 1997-, Geology Department, Kuwait University. Publications: 44 in field of hydrogeology; Numerous conference papers. Honours: Distinguished Research Award for Year 1994-95, Faculty of Science; Distinguished Research Award for Year 1995-96, Kuwait Foundation for the Advancement of Sciences. Memberships: Geological Society, England, 1977-; Groundwater Well Association, USA, 1978-; Editorial Board, Arab Gulf Journal of Scientific Research, Saudi Arabia, 1986-; Society of Science and Technology of Water, Bahrain, 1988-; International Desalination Association, Canada, 1990-; Editorial Board, Journal of Environmental Hydrology, USA, 1994-; The

Environment, Kuwait, 1994-. Address: Geology Department, Kuwait University Science College, PO Box 5969, 13060 Safat, Kuwait.

**AL-RUWAIS Abdulaziz,** b. 1 March 1953, Alyamamah. Professor; Consultant in Electrical Engineering. m. Nawal M Muqrin, 1 son, 4 daughters. Education: BSc Electrical Engineering, 1975, College of Engineering, King Saud University, Riyadh; MSc, 1978, University of Colorado at Boulder, USA; PhD, 1982, Ohio State University, Columbus, USA. Appointments: Part-time Consultant, Saudi Alamoudi Group, 1983-85, Advanced Electronics Company, 1990-91; Part-time Advisor, Royal Saudi Airforce, 1983-89, Signal Corp, Ministry of Defence and Aviation, 1989-; Member, Engineering Consulting Committee, 1994-, Chamber of Commerce Consulting Committee, 1995-, Ministry of Commerce; Member of Committee, for Secure Information Systems, 1995-, Advisory Committee of KACST for Research Planning and Funding, 1996-, King Abdulaziz City for Science and Technology; Teaching Assistant, 1975-80, Assistant Professor, 1982-83, Electrical Engineering Dept, King Abdulaziz University; Assistant Professor, 1984-87, Associate Professor, 1987-, Electrical Engineering Dept, King Saud University. Publications: Author or co-Author, 23 publications. Memberships: IEEE; IEE Communication Society; IEEE Aerospace and Electronic System Society. Address: KSU, Dean of College of Engineering, POB 800 Riyadh 11421, Saudi Arabia.

**AL-SAMARRAI Hafidh Salman,** b. 1 July 1950, Baghdad, Iraq. Doctor Engineer. m. Sabeeha N Alobaidi, 2 sons, 2 daughters. Education: BAE, University of Baghdad; MEng, University of Sheffield, England, 1976; PhD, Loughborough University of Technology, 1979. Appointments: University of Technology, Baghdad, 1979-82; Computer Consultant, 1982-87; Executive Director, Amoudi Electronic Systems, Saudi Amoudi Group, 1987-97; Vice President, SKAB Group for Commerce and Industry and CEO for Sadoca Environment Group, 1995-97; Information System Network Coodinator, Islamic Development Bank, OICIS-NET, 1997-. Publications: 2 books on computers and environment; Several articles. Honour: IEEE Service Award. Memberships: FBCS; SMIEEE; MITE. Address: PO Box 5925, Jeddah 21432, Saudi Arabia.

**AL-SHAIKH Abdulrahman Hassan,** b. 15 January 1959, Makkah, Saudi Arabia. Associate Professor. m. Al-Joharah, 1 son, 3 daughters. Education: BSc, honours, Engineering, 1982; MSc, Engineering, 1983; PhD, 1987. Career: Assistant Professor, 1988, Associate Professor, 1993, Chairman, Civil Engineering Department, 1995, King Saud University. Publications: Many articles in international journals and conferences. Memberships: ACI; ASCE; ACI-SAC. Address: King Saud University College of Engineering, Department of Civil Engineering, PO Box 800, Riyadh 11421, Saudi Arabia.

**AL-THANI Emad A,** b. 9 December 1957, Baghdad, Iraq. Mechanical Engineer. m. Nahdha J Hussain, 2 daughters. Education: BSc, Mechanical Engineering, Iraq, 1979; MSc, Mechanical Engineering, Iraq, 1982; PhD, Mechanical Engineering, Japan, 1994. Appointments: Assistant Lecturer, 1982; Lecturer, 1994, Head of Mechanical Engineering Department, 1995, Assistant Professor, 1999-, 7th of April University, Azzawiya, Libya; Consultant Engineer, 1994. Publications: 6 papers in national and international journals; Book in mechanical engineering, in Arabic. Memberships: Iraqi Engineers Union, 1979; Japanese Society of Mechanical Engineering, 1991. Address: 7th of April University, PO Box 15865, Azzawiya, Libya.

**AL-THOUR Khalid,** b. 26 September 1959, Sana'a, Yemen. Sedimentologist. m. Al-Fusail, Amani, 3 sons, 2 daughters. Education: BSc, Geochemistry, 1982; DAG (Diploma Applied Geology), 1984; MSc, 1988; PhD, 1992. Appointments: Sedimentologist, 1992; Assistant to the President of Sana'a Universiy, 1995-; Advisor of the President of Environment Protection Council, 1997-; DD of Student Affairs, Sana'a University, 1993-95. Publications: Six, 1989-97. Memberships: YRSG, 1982; SEPM, 1989; IAS, 1989; SCC, 1990, AREN, 1997. Address: Sana'a PO Box 2027, Sana'a, Yemen.

**ALAM Qaiser Zoha,** b. 16 March 1941, Patna, India. Educator; University Teacher and Researcher. m. Naheed Alam, 1 son, 1 daughter. Education: MA, 1963; PhD, 1968; PGDTE, 1980. Appointments: Lecturer in English, 1964-80; Reader in English, 1980-85; Professor, 1985-. Publications: 6 books; 50 research papers; 20 popular articles. Honours: Bihar Urdu Award, 1983; Gold Medal, 1997. Memberships: International Advisory Committee for World Linguistic Humour Conference, 1987; International Society for Humour Studies; American Book Club of India; Linguistic Society of India; Indian Association for English Studies; Indian Association for Commonwealth Literature and Language Studies. Address: 313B Road 3 Ashok Nagar, Ranchi 834002 Bihar, India.

**ALAM Shah Sufi M N,** b. 28 February 1953, Chittagong, Bangladesh. Envoy. m. Syeda Rokeya Begum, 2 sons, 1 daughter. Education: Honorary PhD. Career: United Nations World Peace Envoy in Bangladesh; Founder, Director General, Dayemi Complex, Bangladesh. Honours: Diploma of Honour, American Biographical Institute. Memberships: President, World Spiritual Assembly, New York, USA; Secretary General, International Organization for World Peace, Disarmament, Development & Human Rights, New York, USA; Founder, National Chairman, Bangladesh Youth Hostel Association; Executive Member, International Association for Religious Freedom, South Asia; President IARF Bangladesh Chapter. Address: 42/2 Azimpur Chotto, Dayera Sharif, Dhaka 1205, Bangladesh.

**ALAVANOS Alexandros,** b. 22 May 1950, Athens. Economist. m. Katia Charalabaki, 2 daughters. Education: Economics, Athens University. Appointments: Member, European Parliament, 1981-; President, Joined Delegation European Parliament, 1997-; Member, Dumittre on Foreign Affairs, 1994-. Publications: Notes on European Left; Notes on European Environment Policy; Greek of Constantinople. Address: European Parliament, Rue Wiertz, 1040 Brussels, Belgium.

**ALBARRACIN Dolores,** b. 9 November 1965, La Plata, Argentina. Social Psychologist. m. Martin Repetto, 1 daughter. Education: Lic Psicología, 1988; Professor of Letters, 1990; Doctorado Psycología, 1992; MA. Social Psychology, 1994; PhD, Social Psychology, 1997. Appointments: Fellow, National Council for Research; Assistant Professor, University of Florida. Publications: 20 including contributions to Journal of Applied Social Psychology. Honours: Dissertation Research Award; National Institute for the Humanities Grant. Memberships: American Psychological Association; American Psychological Society. Address: 8432 SW 46th Road, Gainesville, FL 32608-7199, USA.

**ALBECK Plea Sara,** b. 28 October 1937, Jersualem, Israel. Lawyer. m. Professor Shalom Albeck, 2 sons, 3 daughters. Education: LLM, Hebrew University, 1961. Appointments: Lecturer on Land Law and Law in Samaria; Lawyer, Horrowitz and Company, 1961-62; Deputy State Attorney, 1963-69; Director of Civil Department, State Attorney's Office, 1969-93;

Owner, private bar firm, 1993-. Publications: Many research articles on: Status of Women; Land Law; Land for Jewish Settlements. Memberships: Israel Bar Association, 1961-; National Association for Child Welfare, 1981-; Land Use Research Council, 1980-; Council for the Advancement of Women, 1994-; Land Redemption Fund, 1993-. Address: 9 Batei Machaseh Street, Jerusalem, 97500 Israel.

**ALBERT Winfried Hans Walther,** b. 3 March 1945, Eger, Germany. Medical Biochemist. m. Janet, 3 sons, 3 daughters. Education: PhD, Biology and Medical Biochemistry, University of Graz, Austria, 1970. Appointments: Research Assistant, Institute of Medical Biochemistry, University of Graz, 1969-70; Research Investigator, Department of Immunology, G D Searle Research Laboratory, High Wycombe, England, 1970-73; Laboratory Manager, 1973-80, Director, 1980-87, Senior Director, 1987-, Boehringer Mannheim GmbH, Roche Diagnostics, Penzberg, Germany. Publications: Improvement and Compatability of Laboratory Results in Life Sciences, 1991; Methods of Immunological Analysis I-III, 1993. Memberships: German Society for Clinical Chemistry; American Association for Clinical Chemistry; British Society for Immunology; German Society for Immunology; International Society for Oncodevelopmental Biology and Medicine; International Society for Preventive Oncology. Address: Roche Diagnostics, Nonnenwald 2, D 82372 Penzberg Bavaria, Germany.

**ALBRECHT Heinz,** b. 29 September 1948, Germany. Forensic Scientist. m. Deborah, 2 daughters. Education: MD, University of Göttingen, 1976; DipMentH, University of Auckland, 1996; FRANZCP. Appointments: Intermittently Acting Director, Regional Forensic Psychiatry Services, New Zealand; Honorary Senior Lecturer, Department of Psychiatry, University of Auckland; Psychiatrist-in-Charge, Acute Care Services, Kauri Unit, Mason Clinic, Regional Forensic Psychiatry Services. Memberships include: American Academy of Psychiatry and Law; New York Academy of Sciences. Address: PO Box 854, Robina DC 4226, Gold Coast, Queensland, Australia.

**ALBU Ioan,** b. 4 October 1920, Castau, Romania. Professor. m. Silvia, 1 son. Education: Doctor of Medicine, Surgery, University of Cluj, Romania, 1945; BA, 1949. Appointments: Assistant Professor, Department of Anatomy, School of Medicine, Cluj Sibiu, 1945-49; Associate Professor, University of Medicine, Timisoara, 1949-63; Professor, Head of Department of Anatomy, University of Cluj, Romania, 1963-90. Publications: Papilian's Textbook of Anatomy; Surgical Anatomy Textbook; 19 Manuals of Anatomy for Medical Students. Honours: Distinguished Physician; Distinguished Professor. Memberships: Emeritus Member, Romanian Academy of Medical Sciences; Anatomische Gesellschaft; European Teratology Society; Research Board of Advisors, American Biographical Institute. Address: Calca Turzii nr 44, 3400 Cluj, Romania.

**ALBUQUERQUE Roy,** b. 21 June 1950, Bombay, India. Public Relations Specialist. m. Lisette Maria, 2 sons, 1 daughter. Education: BSc, 1973; LLB, 1976; DPR, 1979; MA, 1990. Appointments: Public Relations Officer, Indian Express Group of Publications, 1979-81; Manager, Publicity and PR, Hindustan Diamond Co Ltd, 1981-89; Chief of Public Relations, TATA International Ltd, 1989-. Publications: Anchor, Star TV; The Golden Book of Manners and Etiquette, author. Memberships: Life Member, British Council; Life Member, Association of Business Communicators; Life Member, Advertising Club, Bombay, India. Address: Usha Sadan A-5A Colaba, Bombay 400005, India.

**ALCARAZ Jose Luis,** b. 3 July 1963, Hellin, Albacete, Spain. Engineering, Educator. Education: Bachelor, Murcia, Spain, 1981; Graduate in Industrial Engineering, Valencia, Spain, 1988; Doctor, Industrial Engineering, San Sebastian, Spain, 1993. Appointments: Assistant Lecturer, Valencia, Spain, 1988-89; Assistant Lecturer, San Sebastian, Spain, 1989-93; Assistant Lecturer, Bilbao, Spain, 1993-94; Full Professor, Bilbao, Spain, 1994-. Publications: Elasticity and Strength of Materials; Theory of Plasticity and Applications; Contributor, papers in International journals. Honours: Graduate Special Award. Memberships: European Mechanics Society; Spanish Association for Mechanical Engineering; New York Academy of Sciences. Address: Escuela De Ingenieros, Alameda Urquijo S/N, 48013 Bilbao, Spain.

**ALCOTT TEMPLE Leslie Jane,** b. 11 July 1951, Oklahoma City, USA. Artist; Writer. m. George Arthur Carlson, div, 1 son, 1 daughter. Education: Colorado Woman's College, University Denver, 1969-70; BS, Art and Elementary Education, 1973, Oklahoma City University; Central State University, Edmond, Oklahoma, 1973-74; Studied with Bruno Lucchesi, sculptor, New York and Italy, Jon Zahourek, painter, sculptor and anatomist. Appointments: Professional Artist of People, many different mediums, 1965-; Professional Author, 1981-; Tribal Diplomat and Advocate on behalf of all minority groups, especially women and children, 1981-; President, SLA Concrete Construction Inc, 1990-96; President, SLA Arch/Couture Inc, Environmental Enrichment Design Co, 1990-; Founder, President, Chairman of Board, American Association for the Benefit of the Tarahumara Indian Tribe, 1997-; Audience Development Committee, Denver Art Museum, 1993-94; Advisory Committee, Colorado Dept of Transportation, 1993-94; Docent, Colorada History Museum, 1998-; Marketing Committee, Artists of America Exhibition, 1999; Part time Teacher; Numerous exhibitions; Work included in Corporate and Private Collections. Publications: Featured in several books, articles and films; Poetry included in competitions; Co-author, The Tarahumara, 1977; Author, A Body of Work, 1981. Honours: Many awards and honours for both artistic works and construction affairs; Nominated, Mayor's Award for Excellence in the Arts, for Integrity and Service, Denver, 1997; Nominated, Governor's Award for Service in the Arts, as a Model of Integrity for Young Women, 1998. Memberships: Denver Art Student's League; Denver Art Museum; Sisters Cities International, Denver; Museo de las Americas; Women Construction Owners and Executives, Founder, Colorado, USA Chapter. Address: 2088 S Pennsylvania Street, Denver, CO 80210-4034, USA.

**ALCOVER Jose Sanchis,** b. 16 March 1938, Carlet, Valencia, Spain. Director. m. Amparo Berti Berti, 1 son, 2 daughters. Education: Master en Direccion Y Administracion de Empresas, Instituto Superior de Technicas Empresariales; Diploma of Finance, Wharton School, University of Pennsylvania; Diplomado en Planificacion Estrategica Internacional, Institut Europeen D'Administration des Affaires; Licentiate in Accountancy & Taxation, The Association of International Accountants; Programa Gerencia de Empresa PGE, Universidad Politecnica-CED; MA Economics, MBA, University of Detroit; Doctor en Ciencias Economicas y Empresariales, Doctor en Ciencias Politicas, Pacific Western University. Appointments: Presidente de: Electronica Espacial SA, Parkings y Edificaciones Cinco, SA, Tragroval SA; Consejero de Imelsa; Presidente y Director General de la Firma Electro Industrial Mediterraneo SA; Consejero Delegado e Inmobiliaria Clamasan SA; Delegado Comercial para Espana del Estado de Tucuman, Republic Argentina; Presidente de Trading Group Valencia. Memberships: various offices in professional associations in field of Business Management and economia y direccion. Honours: Oscar de Oro en Economia por el European Awards, 1990; Academico de Honour, Letra G, La Muy Ilustre Academia de Ciencias y Tecnologia del Consejo Mundial; Premio de Economia Ano 1994 por el Excmo Ayuntamiento de Valencia. Address: EIMSA, Duque de Gaeta 7Y9, Avenida Del Puerto 93, Valencia 16022, Spain.

**ALDOVA Eva,** b. 21 November 1922, Prague, Czechoslovakia. Microbiologist. Education: Doctor Rerum Naturalium, Charles University; RNDr, Candiadate Scientiarum Biologiae; CSc, Microbiologist, National Institute of Public Helath. Appointments: Retired; Working in Laboratory for Vibrionaceae, Plesiomonas Shigelloides Antigenic Scheme. Memberships: Serotyping Working Group; Subcommittee, Taxonomy of Vibrionaceae. Honours: Description of two microbial genera: Budvicia aquatica and Pragia fontium. Yersinia aldovae - the name was proposed by Hervé Bercovier et al. for a water Yersinia. Address: Nat Inst of Public Health, Srobarova 48, 100 42 Praha 10, Czech Republic.

**ALEKSANDROV Leonid N,** b. 27 September 1923, Dnepropetrovsk. Physicist; Educator; Researcher. m. Melnik Julia M, 1 son, 1 daughter. Education: University Diploma, 1950; Candidate, Science Degree, 1954; DrSc, 1964; Professor Solid State Physics, 1965; Merited Science and Engineering Worker of Russia, 1983-; Laureat State Prize of USSR, 1983-. Appointments: Head of Chair, Mordovian University, to 1965; Head Thin Films Research Lab, to 1978; Chief Scientist, Institute of Semiconductor Physics, Academy of Science of Russia; Professor, Novosibirsk Technical University, 1968-. Publications: 12 monographs; Over 400 reviews, original scientific papers, patents and textbooks. Honours: Chernov Award, 1963; Academy of Science Award, 1978, 1980; Gold Medal, 1988; 12 Government State Medal of USSR; Exhibition Medals, 1968, 1989; President Foundation for Science Award, 1993-96. Memberships: New York Academy of Science; Editorial Board Member, 2 international scientific journals. Address: Vojevodskogo Str 5, Apr 2, Novosibirsk 90, 630090 Russia.

**ALEMANY Gaspar,** b. 14 November 1959, Palma de Mallorca. Pharmacologist. m. Amaia Ortiz, 1 son. Education: Licenced in Pharmacy, 1982; Graduate in Pharmacy, 1984; Doctorate in Pharmacy, 1991. Appointments: Resident doctor in Clinical Chemistry, Son Dureta NHS Hospital, 1987-90; Hospital doctor in Clinical Chemistry, Juan March Balearic Govt Hospital, 1991; Chemist, 1994; Head of Analytical Chemistry Lab, Andratx, Baleares, 1994; Collaborative Professor, University of Balearic Islands, 1996; Pharmacy Inspector of NHS, 1997. Publications: 5 on catecholamines and metabolites, cannabinoids and buprenorphine. Honours: Juan March Grantee, 1978; Postdoctoral Balearic Govt Grantee, 1992. Memberships: American Association of Clinical Chemistry; International Association of Forensic Toxicology; Association of Spanish Toxicology. Address: Plz Espana 6, 07150 Andratx, Spain.

**ALEXANDER Constance,** b. 13 October 1939, Hillsboro, Ohio, USA. Stone Sculptor. m. Anfred Agee Alexander, 6 June 1959, 1 son, 1 daughter. Education: Graduate, Cincinnati Art Academy, 1961; Postgraduate, 1962; Postgraduate, Atlanta College of Art, 1977; Represented by Miller Gallery Cincinnati, also various galleries in Georgia and Florida; Exhibited in group exhibitions at Southeastern Artists Georgia Jubilee Festival (1st in sculpture award 1974), Southeastern Arts and Crafts Festival; Macon, Georgia, Colisuem, 1977 (1st in sculpture), World's Fair, Knoxville, Tennessee, 1982; David Schaeffer Gallery, Alpharetta, Georgia, 1988-93; Marble Festival, Jasper, 1989 (1st Place Award), Ariel Gallery, Soho, New York, 1989

(award of excellence), 90, 45th ann Penn and Brush Sculpture Exhibition, Soho, New York, 1991 (Excalibur Bronze Sculpture Foundry Award); Ariel Gallery, Soho, 1989-91; Tim Verstegen's The Dutch Framer Gallery, Canton, Georgia, 1989-93; Artistic Frames and Gallery, Jasper, Georgia, 1991-93; Buckhead Trinity Gallery, Atlanta, Georgia, 1994-98; Gallery 300 Atlanta, 1994; Represented in permanent collections Cincinnati Public Library, Georgia Institute Technology, Atlanta, Hartsfield International Airport, North Dekalb College, Coca-Cola International Headquarters. Membership: Society of Friends. Hobbies: Cross Country Rock Collecting; Photography; Poetry; Home Restoration. Address: PO Box 67, Canton, GA, 30114-0067, USA.

**ALEXANDER John B,** b. 21 November 1937, New York, New York. Scientist. Education: BGS Sociology, 1971, University Nebraska at Omaha; MA Education, 1975, Pepperdine University; PhD Education, 1980, Walden University; Engineering Management Programme, 1990, University California at Los Angeles, School of Engineering and Applied Science; Executive Programme in Management of Complex Organisations, 1991, Massachusetts Institute of Technology, Sloan School of Management; Programme for Senior Executives in National and International Security, 1993, Harvard University, John F Kennedy School of Government. Appointments: President, The Apollinaire Group (Independent writing and consulting), 1994-; Consultant, Director of Defense Research and Engineering, Office of the Secretary of Defense, The Pentagon, Washington DC, 1996-; Director for Scientific Liaison, National Institute for Discovery Science, Las Vegas, 1995-. Publications: 50 publications and presentations. Honours: Various US and foreign military awards for valour and service; National Award for Volunteerism from President Reagan, 1987; Aerospace Laureate, 1993, Inducted into the Laureate Hall of Fame, located in the Smithsonian National Air and Space Museum, Washington DC, 1997, Aviation Week & Space Technology; US Dept of Energy Weapon's Programme Recognition of Excellence Award, 1994. Address: 9521 Grand Canal Drive, Las Vegas, NV 89117-0860, USA.

**ALEXANDER Theron,** b. 31 August 1913, Springfield, Tennessee, USA. Behavioural Scientist; Developmental and Clinical Psychologist. m. Marie Bailey, 1 son, 1 daughter. Education: Princeton and Harvard Universities, US Navy; PhD, University of Chicago, 1949. Appointments: Staff Officer, Commander of 7th Fleet, United States Navy, 1944-45; Professor, Florida State University, 1949-54; Director, Child Guidance Clinic, 1954-57; Professor, University of Iowa School of Medicine, 1957-65; Professor, University of Miami School of Medicine, 1965-66; Professor, Director of Child Development Research Center, Temple University, 1966-80; Visiting Scholar, Stanford University, 1987-95. Publications: Psychotherapy in Our Society, 1963; Children and Adolescents, 1969; Human Development in an Urban Age, 1973; Developmental Psychology, 1980. Honours: Certificado, Estado de Sao Paulo, Brazil, 1977; Legion of Honor, 1979; Certificate for Distinguished Contribution to Psychology, American Psychological Association, Clinical Division, 1986. Memberships: Distinguished Fellow, American Psychological Association; Charter Fellow, American Psychological Society. Address: 50 Gresham Lane, Atherton, CA 94027-3918, USA.

**ALEXANDER Vedhamonickom,** b. 23 October 1956, Chathencode, India. Professor. m. Margaret, 1 son, 1 daughter. Education: BSc, Christian College, Marthandom, 1976; MEd, St Xaviers College of Education, Palayamkottai, 1979; MSc, St Josephs College, Trichy, 1981; PhD, University of Madras, 1987. Appointments: Assistant Professor, American College, Madurai, 1985; Assistant Professor, Loyola College, Chennai,

1985-95; Professor, Loyola College, 1995-. Publications: Several articles in professional journals. Honours: DST Grant, 1989, 1997, DAE, 1990, 1997, CSIR, 1997; DRDO, 1998. Memberships: Fellow, Indian Chemical Society; American Chemical Society; Royal Society of Chemistry, London. Address: Flat No 8, Redbrick Leela, 36 Tank Bund Road, Nungambakkam, Chennai 600 034, India.

**ALEXANDERSSON Hans-Olof,** b. 29 July 1950, Halmstad, Sweden. Senior Meteorologist. m. Gunilla, 1 son, 2 daughters. Education: Student Examination, Halmstad, 1970; PhD, Meteorology, 1987. Appointments: Amanuensis, Meteorological Department, Uppsala University, 1978-87; Senior Meteorologist, Swedish Meteorological and Hydrological Institute, 1987-. Publications: A Homogeneity Test Applied to Precipitation Data, Journal of Climatology; Homogenization of Swedish Temperature Data; Hemogeneity Test for Linear Trends. Honour: Finn Malmgren Prize. Membership: Swedish Meteorological Society. Address: Tallberga, Kaslinge, Vanga, 61790 Skarblacka, Sweden.

**ALEXANDROV Andrei,** b. 3 June 1996, Moscow, Russia. Neurologist. m. Natalia Alexandrova, 1 son. Education: MD, 1st Moscow Medical Institute, Moscow, Russia, 1989; Neurologist, Russian Academy of Medical Sciences, Moscow, Russia, 1991; RVT, The American Registry of Diagnostic Medical Sonographers, USA, 1996. Appointments: Resident, Russian Academy of Medical Sciences, 1989-91; Postgraduate Research Fellow, Universities of Toronto and New York State, 1991-95; Research Associate, Department of Neurology, University of Toronto, 1995-96; Research Fellow, Heart and Stroke Foundation of Canada, 1996-98; Instructor, Department of Neurology, 1997-; Director, Center for Noninvasive Brain Perfusion Studies, 1996-. Publications include: Measuring Carotid Stenosis, 1993; Do-not-resuscitate Orders in Acute Stroke, 1995; Correlation of Peak Systolic Velocity and Carotid Stenosis, 1997. Honours: Annual Scientific Award, Institute of Neurology, 1991; Personnel Award, Sunnybrook Hospital, 1992; International Fellowship, AHA, 1993; Robert G Siekert Young Investigator Award in Stroke, 1994; Department of Medicine Postgraduate Fellowship Award, University of Toronto, 1994; Canadian Stroke Society/Syntex Annual Award, 1994; World Federation of Neurology, Glaxo Junior Travel Fellowship, 1994; Junior Travel Fellowship, ANA, 1994; William Oldendorf Award, 1995; International Union of Angiology Prize, 1995; Award of Excellence in Stroke Research, European Stroke Society, 1995; Research Fellowship Award, HSFO, 1996, 1997. Address: 6431 Fannin Street, Room 7044 Houston, TX 77030, USA.

**ALEXANDROV Yuri Andreevich,** b. 26 May 1929, Karsun, Russia. Physicist. m. Svetlana S Alexandrova, 1 daughter. Education: Engineering Physics Institute, 1946-52; Candidate to PhD in Physics and Maths, 1959; Senior Scientist in Physics and Maths, 1964; DSc Physics and Maths, 1987; Active Member, New York Academy of Science, 1995. Appointments: Scientist, Physics Engineering Institute in Obninsk, 1952-59; Senior Scientist in Obninsk, 1959-62, in Dubna, 1962-65; Sector Leader in Dubna, 1965-89; Group Leader in Dubna, 1989-98. Publications: 108 publications, 2 books in Russian, 1 book in English. Honours: 3 medals. Memberships: Joint Institute for Nuclear Research, Dubna; Neutron Scattering Society of America, USA, 1992; Referee, Physical Review and Physical Review Letters. Address: Laboratory of Neutron Physics, Joint Institute for Nuclear Research, 4 Vekslera Str JINR Dubna, Moscow 141980, Russia.

**ALEXEEV Boris,b.** 2 May 1938, Orechovo-Zuevo, Moscow. Physicist; Educator. m. 1 daughter. Education: Degree in

physics, engineering, Moscow Institute of Physics and Technology, 1961; PhD, Moscow Institute of Physics and Technology, 1964; Doctor of Sciences, Computer Center of USSR Academy of Sciences, 1973; Professor of physics, Higher Attestation Commission of USSR, 1974. Appointments: Senior Research Scientist, Computer Center USSR Academy of Sciences, 1964-73; Head of Physics department, Moscow Aviation Institute, 1973-83; Head of Physics Department, Moscow Fine Chemical Technology Institute, 1983-; Visiting Professor, University of Provence, France, 1992-95; Visiting Professor, University of Alabama, USA, 1995 and 1997. Publications: More than 250 scientific works including 17 books. Honours and Awards: Meritorious Science and Technics Worker of Russia, 1989-; Meritorious Worker of Higher Professional Education of Russia, 1998-;President Stipend for outstanding Russian Scientists, 1994-. Memberships: Expert of the Higher Attestation Commission, USSR; Member of the Russian National Committee on Theoretical and Applied Mechanics, 1987-; Member of Organising Committee of Russian Academy of Sciences and Head of the Moscow Regional Committee, 1991; Academian of International Higher Education Academy of Sciences, 1993-; Member of the New York Academy of Sciences, 1995-. Address: 3d Frunzenskaya H 9 ap 130, 119270 Moscow, Russia.

**ALEXIADIS Minas,** b. 29 March 1948, Menetes Karpathos, Greece. Professor. m. Evi Mela, 3 sons. Education: BA, University of Ioanniya, 1967-72; MA, University of Ioannina, 1967-72; PhD, University of Ioannina, 1982; Post Doctoral Certificate, University College of London, 1982-83. Appointments: Professor, High School of Karpathos, 1975-77; Assistant, Tutor, Lecturer, Assistant Professor, Associate Professor, University of Ioannina, 1977-94; Associate Professor, Professor, University of Athens, 1994-. Publications: 10 Books; 32 Publications to Journals. Honours: Pan-Dodecanese Prize of Moskovis Foundation, 1982; Golden Cross of Dodecanese Church of Ecumenical Patriarche, 1995; Honorary Research Associate, King's College, London, 1989-90. Memberships: Greek Folklore Society; English Folklore Society; American Folklore Society; Greek Humanistic Society; Greek Society of Philologists; Philological Society, Parnassos; Panhellenic Association of Philogists; Historical Folklore Society of Dodecanese; Society of Karpathiam Studies; Union of Dodecanese University Professors; Cultural Foundation of Dodecanese. Address: Grammatothyrida 80723, 18510 Piraeus, Greece.

**ALEXIEVA Marina,** b. 16 January 1968, Sofia, Bulgaria. Banking Expert. Education: MA, English, 1995; Financial Manager, Re-Qualification in Finance, 1995. Appointments: Operations Manager, 1993-96; Banking Expert, International Payments Letters of Credit, 1996-. Membership: International Association of Crime Writers, Bulgarian Section. Address: 33 Tsar Osvobodittel Str, 1504 Sofia, Bulgaria.

**ALGNER Thomas,** b. 24 November 1962, Erlangen. Medical Doctor. Education: Baccalaureate in Philosophy; First Diploma in Theology, University of Munich, 1985; MD, University of Erlangen, 1992; Medical Thesis, University of Erlangen, 1992. Appointments: Post Doctor, Max Planck Society Connective Tissue and Rheumatology Research Units Erlangen, 1992-94; Associate for Research, Clinical Pathology, Department of Pathology, 1994-. Publications: Many Publications, 1992-. Honours: EULAR Award, European League Against Rheumatism, 1991. Memberships: New York Academy of Sciences; American Orthopedic Society; Endocrinology Society; International Society of Matrix Biology; American Society for Bone and Mineral Research; German Society of Pathology; International Society for bone and mineral

Research. Address: University Erlangen/Pathology, Krankenhaustr 8-10, Erlangen, D-91054, Germany.

**ALHALABI Bassem Abdo,** b. 2 October 1960, Damascus, Syria. Professor. m. Maha A Albitar, 1 son, 2 daughters. Education: BS, Electrical Engineering, Ohio University, 1984; MS, Purdue University, 1986; MS, Computer Engineering, University of Southwestern Louisiana, 1993; PhD, 1995. Appointments: Teaching Assistant, Robotics Lab Coordinator, 1984-86; Electrical, Computer Engineer, Manager, Alhalabi Industries Inc, 1986-90; Research Assistant, VLSI Lab Manager, Center for Advanced Computer Studies, 1990-95; Visiting Assistant Professor, University of South Alabama, 1995-96; Assistant Professor, Florida Atlantic University, 1996-. Publications: Virtual Education, Reality or Virtuality; Touching Students' Minds in Cyberspace. Honours: Outstanding Academic Award; USA Deans List. Memberships: Tau Beta Pi; Upsilon Pi Epsilon; Phi Kappa Phi Honour Society; Institute of Electrical and Electronic Engineers; Association for Computing Machinery; American Creativity Association. Address: 777 Glades Road, FAU, CSE Dept, Boca Raton, FL 33431, USA.

**ALI Imran,** b. 1 January 1963, Nanhera Anantpur, India. Environmentalist; Researcher. m. Seema Sultana Imran. Education: BS, MS College, Saharanpur, India, 1983; MSc, 1986, PhD, 1990, Roorkee University, India. Appointments: Junior Research Fellow, 1986-87, Senior Research Fellow, 1988-90, Research Associate, 1991-92, Pool Officer, 1993-96, Roorkee University; Scientist in Environmental Chemistry, National Institute of Hydrology, Roorkee, 1997-. Publications: Several articles in professional journals. Honours: Khosla Research Award, University of Roorkee, 1987. Address: National Institute of Hydrology, Roorkee 247667, India.

**ALI Syed Ahmed,** b. 8 August 1959, Hyderabad, India. Chemical Engineer. m. Anjum, 3 sons, 1 daughter. Education: B Tech, Chemical Engineering, Osmania University, Hyderabad, 1981; MS, King Fahd University of Petroleum and Minerals, 1984; PhD, Hokkaido University, Sapporo, Japan, 1997. Appointments: Research Assistant, Chemical Engineering, KFUPM, 1981-84; Engineer II, The Research Institute, KFUPM, 1984-90; Engineer I, 1990-96; Research Engineer, 1996-. Publications: Influence of Heteroatom Removal on Aromatic Hydrogenation, Fuel Processing Technology; Deep Desulfurization, Dearomatization and Cetane Improvements of Diesel Feedstock in a Single-Staged Reactor, Reaction Kinetics and Catalytsis Letters; Olefins can Limit Desulfurization of Reformer Feedstock, Oil and Gas Journal; Many other Publications. Honours: Distinction in B Tech, 1981. Memberships: American Institute of Chemical Engineers. Address: King Fahd University of Petroleum and Minerals, P O Box 341, Dhahran 31261, Saudi Arabia.

**ALICIAS Eduardo Jr Rezonable,** b. 10 August 1945, Vigan, Ilocos Sur, The Philippines. Professor. m. Teresita S Raquepo, 1 son, 2 daughters. Education: BSE magna cum laude, 1967, Divine Word College of Vigan; MA Education, 1977, Mariano Marcos State University, Laoag City; Dr Ed, 1981, University of the Philippines, Quezon City; Diploma in Education, 1986, British Council Fellow, University of London. Appointments: Principal, Immaculate Conception Minor Seminary, Vigan, 1971-76; Instructor, College of Education, UP, Quezon City, 1979-81; Assistant Professor, 1981-88, Associate Professor, 1988-, College of Education, Quezon City. Publications: Books: Data Organisation and Analysis in a Computer Environment, 1995, 1997; Classroom Observation and Related Fallacies: Lessons for Educational Administration, 1996; Humour and Madness, 1997. Memberships: Society of Educational Administrators and Researchers for Change Inc; University of

the Philippines Research Organisation for Better Education Inc; National Research Council of the Philippines. Address: University of the Philippines Campus, AB4-201 Hardin Ng Rosas, Diliman, Quezon City, The Philippines.

**ALIDI Abdulaziz S,** b. 5 September 1952, Al-Jubial, Saudi Arabia. Full Professor. m. Nahid E Algosaibi, 3 sons. Education: BS, Chemical Engineering; MS, Management Engineering; PhD, Chemical and Management Engineering. Appointments: Full Professor and Industrial Consultant. Honours: Excellence in Research Awards, 1991, 1994; Fulbright Fellowship, 1995. Memberships: AICHE; INFORMS; AOTS. Address: King Fahd University of Petroleum and Minerals, Box 1645, Dhahran 31261, Saudi Arabia.

**ALIEV Geibor Alizza Ogly,** b. 10 May 1923, Azerbaijan Republic. Political Figure. 1 son, 1 daughter. Education: Baku State University; Azerbaijan Industrial Institute, 1939-41. Appointments: Chairman, Supreme Council of Azerbaijan Republic, 1993-; President, Azerbaijan Republic, 1993-99. Publications: Author of more than 100 Publications. Honours: Honourary Doctor of Turkey University, 1994; Tbiliski University, 1996; Tashkent University, 1997. Address: President Palace, 19 Lstiglaliyat Str, Baku 370066, Azerbajan Republic.

**ALIEV Ozbek,** b. 25 March 1941, Azerbaijan. Chemist. m. Alieva Reyxan, 2 sons, 1 daughter. Education: Azerbaijan Pedagogical Institute, 1964; Candidate of Chemical Sciences, 1973; Doctor of Chemical Sciences, 1986. Appointments: Head, Laboratory of Institute of Inorganic and Physical Chemistry, Azerbaijan Academy of Sciences, Baku. Publications: 270 in professional journals, 20 patents. Address: Institute of Inorganic & Physical Chemistry, G Javid Pr 29, Baku 370143, Azerbaijan.

**ALIGIA Armando Angel,** b. 7 July 1955, Buenos Aires, Argentina. Physicist. m. Ana Gladis Rojas, 4 sons. Education: Technician in Chemistry, Otto Krause Industrial School No 1, Buenos Aires, 1973; University of Buenos Aires, 1974-75; Instituto Balseiro, Bariloche, 1976-79; PhD, Physics, 1984. Appointments: Staff Member, 1983-, Director, Theoretical Division, 1994-96, Centro Atómico, Bariloche; Instituto Balseiro, Bariloche, 1989-. Publications: 113 research articles in international journals. Honours: Alexander von Humboldt Fellowships, 1985-86, 1987. Address: Centro Atómico, 8400 Bariloche, Argentina.

**ALLAHVERDI Ali,** b. 14 May 1965, Gevas van, Turkey. Associate Professor. m. Hatice, 2 daughters. Education: BS, Petroleum Engineering, 1986; MS, Industrial Engineering, 1990; PhD, Industrial Engineering, 1992. Appointments: Assistant Professor, Marmara University, Turkey, 1993-95; Assistant Professor, Kuwait University, Kuwait, 1995-98; Associate Professor, 1998-. Publications: Contributor to Articles in Professional Journals. Honours: Dissertation Prize. Memberships: Operational Research Society; Institue of Operations Research and Management Science. Address: Department of Mechanical and Industrial Engineering, Kuwait University, P O Box 5969, Safat, Kuwait.

**ALLAHVERDIEV Surhay,** b. 21 May 1941, Yerevan. Researcher. m. Suzan Rakhmani, 1 daughter. Education: Moscow Academy of Agricultural, 1964; Candidate of Biological Sciences, Biochemistry, 1973; Elder Research Assistant, Plant Physiology, 1988; Doctor of Biological Sciences, Plant Physiology, 1992; Academician, International Informatization Academy, United Nations, 1998. Appointments: Head Laboratory of Plant Resistance, Institute of Botany, Baku,

1985-88; Head, Department of Plant Physiology, Baku, 1988-95. Publications: Physiological and Biochemical Mechanisms of Tolerance in Plants; Better Research, Moscow, 1993; Scientific Practical Studies, Istanbul, 1994. Memberships: Russian Society of Plant Physiology; Turkish Society of Biochemistry; FESPP (Federation of European Societies of Plant Physiology. Address: 74100 Bartin Orman Fakultesi, Bartin, Turkey.

**ALLAIN Louis Marie Pierre,** b. 28 June 1933, Brest, France. Literature Educator. m. Annie, 1 son, 3 daughters. Education: B Degree, 1950; Ecole Normale Superieure, 1953-58; Licence de Lettres Classiques, 1954; Scholar, Moscow University, 1955-56, 1957-58; Agregation de russe, 1957; Doctorate, Sorbonne, Paris, 1979. Appointments: School Teacher, Lycee, 1961; Assistant Lecturer, Sorbonne, 1961-63; Senior Lecturer, 1963-69; Managing Lecturer, University of Lille, 1969-81; Professor, Head of Department, Slavic Languages, 1981-98; Professor Emeritus, 1998-. Publications: Author, 8 books; Editor of several publications. Honours: Commander of Academic Palms, French Ministry of Education; Medal, City of Lille; Melanges Offerts au Professeur Louis Allain, Lille, 1996. Memberships: Alumni Ecole Normale Superieure; Intra Marine France; International Dostoevsky Society; Institute of Slavic Studies. Address: Rue Jules Guesde 408, Villeneuve d Ascq 59650, France.

**ALLAIN Serge,** b. 9 March 1930, Paris, France. Banker. m. Chantal Rain, deceased, 1 son, 1 daughter. Education: Licence Literature, 1950; Licence Law, Diploma, Political Science, 1951; Public Administration School (ENA), 1952. Appointments: Civil Servant, Ministry of Finance, 1954; Financial Attache, French Embassy in Brazil, 1962; Vice President of Credit Chimique, 1973; Controlling Body of Financial and Banking Activities, 1985. Honours: Knight of Ordre National du Merit, 1968; Judge, Paris Commercial Court, 1984; Knight of Legion of Honor, 1992. Membership: Polo Club de Paris. Address: 7 Av de Segur, 75007 Paris, France.

**ALLAKHVERDIEV Ali Ragym,** b. 4 March 1949, Baku, Armenian Republic. Professor of Medicine. m. Elnara Allakhverdieva, 2 daughters. Education: BSc, MSc, 1973, Azerbaijan Medical Institute; PhD, Medicine, 1980; DSc, Medicine, 1989; Professor, Medicine, 1992. Appointments: Scientific Researcher, Senior Scientific Researcher, Head, Clinic of Neurophysiology, Institute of Physiology, Academy of Sciences, Azerbaijan. Publications: 220 articles, 1 book. Membership: Azerbaijan National Academy of Creation. Address: Laboratory of Clinic of Neurophysiology, Institute of Physiology, Azerbaijan Academy of Sciences, Str Sharif-zade 2, Baku 370100, Azerbaijan Republic.

**ALLAKHVERDIEV Kerim Ragim,** b. 1 April 1944, Erevan, Armenian Republic. Professor in Physics. m. Zehra Allakhverdiev, 2 sons, 1 daughter. Education: BSc, MSc, Moscow Power Engineering Institute, 1967; PhD, Physics, 1967; DSc, Physics, 1982; Professor in Physics, 1985; 2 Years English courses in Moscow, 1967; 1 month English courses in BBC, London, England, 1975. Appointments: Leader, Optoelectronics Laboratory, Institute of Physics, Azerbaijan Academy of Sciences; Project Manager, Institute of Electronics, The Turkish Scientific and Research Council. Publications: 220 articles, 1 book, 5 patents. Honours: Azerbaijan State Prize, 1988; Krupp Stipendium, Germany, 1981-82; Window on Science Award of EOARD of USAF, 1996. Memberships: Azerbaijan Academy of Creation; European High Pressure Research Group; New York Academy of Sciences. Address: Laboratory of Optoelectronics, Institute of Physics Azerbaijan Academy of Sciences, 33 Avenue H Javid Baku, 370143 Azerbaijan Republic.

**ALLAN George Graham,** b. Glasgow, Scotland. Professor of Fibre and Polymer Science; Chemical Engineer. m. Margaret Muir Allingham, 4 sons, 2 daughters. Education: BSc 1st Hons, 1952, University Glasgow; BSc 1st Hons, 1952, University Strathclyde; Dip, 1951, Royal Technical College, Glasgow; PhD, 1955, Glasgow; DSc, 1970, Strathclyde. Appointments: Research Fellow, University Strathclyde, 1955-56; Research Scientist, DuPont, Wilmington, 1956-62; Senior Research Fellow, Weyerhaeuser, Seattle, 1962-66; Professor, University Washington, 1966-. Publications: Over 300 publications and book chapters; 70 patents. Honour: Awarded First DSc of University Strathclyde. Memberships: Royal Institute of Chemistry; American Chemistry Society; American Institute Chemical Engineering; Technical Association Pulp and Paper Industry, Tappi; Controlled Release Society. Address: 18411 60th Place NE, Kenmore, WA 98028-8907, USA.

**ALLAVENA Jean W C,** b. 29 June 1963, Monaco. Chief Operating Officer. m. Marie Pic-Paris, 3 daughters. Education: Graduate, HEC, Paris, 1986. Appointments: Chief Operating Officer, Lyonnaise Des Eaux, 1989-92, Paribas, 1986-88; Chief Financial Officer, Techpack International, Pechiney, 1992-96. Honour: Challenge Le Figaro, CPA, 1993. Memberships: Member of Committee, HEC Alumnis, Chairman of Career Commission; Automobile Club de France; Maxim's Business Club. Address: 28 Boulevard Victor Hugo, 92200 Neuilly/Seine, France.

**ALLEN Donald Ian,** b. 15 May 1938, Foster, Australia. Educator. m. Heather Margaret, 4 daughters. Education: B Com, 1960, B Ed, 1964, University Melbourne; MA, 1969, EdD, 1970, University of California at Berkley. Appointments: Teacher, 1961-67; Lecturer, Monash University, 1966-67; Associate Professor, Director of Professional Programmes, Simon Fraser University, 1970-79; Principal, Coburg State College, 1979-82; Executive Director, Victorian Dept of Education, 1982-87; Deputy Chair, Post Secondary, Educational Commission, 1988-92; Director, Policy & Planning Dept of Education, 1992-95; Deputy Secretary, Director of Higher Education, 1995-. Publications: 50 books, articles, on teacher education, curriculum. Honour: Fellow, Australian College of Education. Address: 24 Lofts Avenue, Kew, Vic 3101, Australia.

**ALLEN George Howard,** b. 6 January 1914, Boston, Massachusetts, USA. Publisher. m. Virginia Allen, 1 son. Education: MS; MBA; LLD. Appointments: General Manager and Assistant Publisher, McCall's Magazine; first Publisher, Better Living Magazine; first Publisher, Better Homes and Gardens Magazine; Publisher, Successful Farming Magazine; Publisher, Meredith Publications Annuals; Publisher, Woman's Day; Publisher: True Magazine; Mechanix Illustrated; Rudder Magazine; Electronics Illustrated; 20 Woman's Day Annuals; Group Publisher, CBS Special Interest titles including: Audio, Road and Track; World Tennis; American Photographer; Cycle World. Honours: Adelphia Award, 1936; Scholarship, Harvard Business School, 1936; Young Advertising Man of the Year, 1956; Achievement Award, Washington, DC, USA, 1956; Silver Anvil Award, American Public Relations Association, 1957; Bell Ringer Award, Salt Lake City Ad Club, 1957; Public Relations News Award, 1957; LLD, Honorary, University of Massachusetts, 1967; Henry Johnson Fisher Publisher-of-the-Year Award, 1981; Elected to the Hall of Fame, 1985; Distinguished Professional Service Award, 1986. Memberships include: The Advertising Council; Harvard Club of New York City; Metropolitan Club of New York; Economic

Club of New York; Sky Club of New York; Chair, Media Executive Roundtable Forum. Address: Consultant to Pub Management, 281 Harbor House Drive, Osprey, FL 34229-9742, USA.

**ALLEN James,** b. 12 December 1955, Derby, Connecticut, USA. Chief Executive Officer, Telecommunications. m. Nancy Marie McKenna, 1 son. Education: BA, Castleton State College, Castleton, 1977. Appointments: Director, National Cable Television Association, 1987-97; President and CEO, Secure Signals Inc, 1997-. Memberships: Coalition Opposing Signal Theft; American Society for Industrial Security; National Cable Television Association; CTAM; International Television Symposium; United States Golf Society. Address: 3910 Clares Court, Fairfax, VA 22033-4640, USA.

**ALLEX P C,** b. 11 September 1958, Philadelphia, Pennsylvania, USA. Environmental Scientist; Manager. m. div. 2 daughters. Education: AA & AS, Science & Management, 1985, Victor Valley Community College; BA Environmental Studies, 1988, California State University, San Barnado. Appointments: Senior Air Quality Specialist, South Coast Air Quality Management District, Public Advisors Office; State Enforcement Coordinator, U S Environmental Protection Agency; Environmental Consultant, Air Quality, Earth Tech Inc; Environmental Programme Manager, US Postal Service Facilities Dept, Washington DC; Senior Environmental Coordinator, USPS Western Region. Honours: Tribute of Appreciation, EPA, 1990; Commendation, EPA, 1990; Special Achievement Award, USPS, 1992; Outstanding Evaluation, USPS, 1992; Plaque for Appreciation of Efforts Involved with Strategic Plan Development, USPS, 1993. Memberships: Air & Waste Management Association, Transportation and Land Use Sub Committee; Women's Transportation Seminar, Orange County Chapter. Address: 1040 So Mt Vernon Avenue, Suite 6, 254, Colton, CA 92324, USA.

**ALLIK Jaak,** b. 8 October 1946, Tallinn, Estonia. Historian; Politician. m. Lembe Leppmets, 1 son, 2 daughters. Education: Tartu University, 1972. Career: Member of Parliament, 1990-92, 1995-; Minister of Culture, Estonia, 1995-. Honour: Merited Artist of Estonia, 1986. Membership: Estonian Theatre Union. Address: Ministry of Culture, Tallinn, Estonia.

**ALLISON John Langsdale,** b. 10 August 1930, Sutton Coldfield, Warwickshire, England. Naval Architect; Mechanical Engineer. m. Eunice Q Allison, 2 sons, 1 daughter. Education: Grad, 1956, Royal Naval Engineering College; BSc Eng, 1954, University of Nottingham. Appointments: Commissioned in RNVR; Engineer Officer, Royal Navy, 1954-56; Lecturer, Bromsgrove College of FE, 1958-66; Senior Research Engineer, Bell Aerospace, 1966-71; Chief Engineer, Ship Technology Bell/TMS, 1971-87; Chief Engineer, BLA Inc, 1987-. Publications: Numerous papers in professional journals. Honours: Vice Admiral Cochrane Award for Best Paper to a Section, Society of Naval Architects and Naval Engineers, 1992; Several patents, latest 1997. Memberships: Fellow, Institution of Mechanical Engineers; Fellow, Royal Institution of Naval Architects; Society of Naval Architects & Marine Engineers; American Society Naval Engineers; Naval Institute; and others. Address: 792 Tremaine Way, Severna Park, MD 21146-4328, USA.

**ALMENDROS MARTIN Gonzalo,** b. 21 September 1955, Madrid, Spain. Scientific Researcher. Education: BS, honours, Biological Sciences, 1977; PhD, Biological Sciences, 1980; Postgraduate Researcher, Consejo Superior de Investigaciones Cientificas, Madrid, 1978-85. Appointments: Researcher, 1985-90, Senior Researcher, 1990-; Project

Leader, 7 National and International Programs; Professor, International Course of Soil Sciences, University Autonoma Nacional, Mexico, 1990-; Member, Official Commission of Organic Fertilizers, Ministry of Agriculture, Spain, 1992-. Publications: Over 150 articles in scientific journals. Honours: 3 Postgraduate Research Fellowships. Memberships: Center of Environmental Sciences, Madrid. Address: Joaquin maria opez 60, E 28015 Madrid, Spain.

**ALMOND Paul,** b. 26 April 1931, Montreal, Canada. Film Maker; Novelist. m. Joan Harwood. Education: McGill University; BA, 1952, MA, 1954, Balliol College, Oxford. Appointments: Producer Director, CBC, 1953-66 and several television companies in New York, London and Hollywood for over 125 television productions; Writer, Producer, Director, feature films. Creative Works: Films: Isabel, 1968; Act of the Heart, 1970; Journey, 1972; Ups & Downs, 1982; The Dance Goes On, 1991; Director, Captive Hearts, 1987; Subject of book by Janet Edsforth, The Flame Within. Honours: Canadian Film Award, Best Feature Director, 1970; Best Television Director, 1979. Memberships: Directors Guild of Canada; Royal Canadian Academy of Arts. Address: PO Box 954, Malibu, CA 90265, USA.

**ALNAJJAR Ahmed Abdulaziz,** b. 21 March 1963, Khorfakkan, Sharjah, United Arab Emirates. Psychologist; Researcher; Consultant. m. Jamila Mohamed Alnajjar, 3 sons. Education: BA, Psychology, United Arab Emirates University, 1985; PhD, Social Psychology, University of Durham, England, 1991. Appointments: Social Worker, Ministry of Education, United Arab Emirates, 1985-86; Teaching Assistant, 1986-91; Lecturer, 1991-96, Assistant Dean for Student Affairs, 1991-93, Assistant Dean for Research, 1994-96, Faculty of Education, United Arab Emirates University; Lecturer, Faculty of Humanities and Social Sciences, United Arab Emirates University, 1996-; Consultant to Ministry of Interior, 1992-97; Director, Centre of Security and Social Studies, Ministry of Interior, 1993-96. Publications: Stress and Work Pressures, 1994; Social Care in the United Arab Emirates, 1995; Contributor of articles to professional journals. Honour: Sheikh Rashid Prize, 1991. Memberships: Affiliate, American Psychological Association; Afro-Asian Psychological Association; Sociologists Society; Customer Protection Society; University Lecturers Association. Address: PO Box 10244, Khorffakan, Sharjah, United Arab Emirates.

**ALI Ali Farid,** b. 29 August 1950, Egypt. Professor. m. Je ham Allam, 1 son, 2 daughters. Education: MS, 1948; MBBCh, 1974; MD, 1982. Appointments: Professor of Obstetrics & Gynaecology. Honours: From: Roma, 1994; USA, 1996, 1987; Cyarns Monla, 1998; Amsterdam, 1998. Memberships: American Associations of Laparoscopy & Infertility. Address: Sednawei Building, 13 El Montazha Street, Cairo, Egypt.

**ALON Azaria,** b. 15 November 1918, Ukraina. In Israel since 1925. Naturalist. m. Ruth, 2 sons, 1 daughter. Education: Tel Aviv University, 1962-65. Appointments: Member of Kibbutz Bet Hashitta, 1938-; Agricultural worker, youth movement leader, educator, teacher of biology; Pensioner, Chairman of the Board, Society for Protection of Nature, Israel; Writing, lecturing, broadcasting on conservation of Nature and Environment, 1951-. Publications: 100s of articles in daily papers, periodicals etc on nature, environment and conservation; 30 books on nature and environmental issues; Numerous booklets and brochures; Editor, Encyclopedia of Plant and Animal Life of Israel, 12 vols; Nature and landscape photography. Honours: Kol Israel (Israel Radio) Prize, 1962; Zimerman Prize for Environmental Activity, 1977; Israel Prize, 1980; Knesset (Israeli Parliament) Prize for Environmental

Activity, 1984; 500 Global Role of Honour, UNEP, 1987; Dr Honoris Causa, Weizman Institute, 1991; Yigal Alon Prize for Life Activity, 1994. Address: Kibbutz Beit Hashitta, 18910 Israel.

**ALONEFTIS Andreas,** b. 24 August 1945, Nicosia, Cyprus. Insurance Company Chief Executive Officer; Former Minister of Defence, Republic of Cyprus. m. Nethie Georgiades, 1 son, 1 daughter. Education: MBA, Southern Methodist University; Currently, Doctoral Student, Henley Management College, UK. Appointments: Senior Manager-Investments, Cyprus Development Bank, 1978-83; General Manager and Chief Executive Officer of CISCO, 1983-88; Minster of Defence, Republic of Cyprus, 1988-93; General Manager and Chief Executive Officer, American Life Insurance Company in Cyprus, 1993-95; Managing Director and Chief Executive Officer, Cyprialife Insurance Company, Cyprus, 1995-99; General Manager, Group Insurance, The Cyprus Popular Bank Group, 1999-. Memberships: Fellow, Association of International Accountants; Council Member, Association of International Accountants; Rotary Club of Nicosia; Propeller Club of America; Fulbright Association; Apocalypse Historical Research Society. Address: Cyprialife Insurance, PO Box 2535, Nicosia 1522, Cyprus.

**ALPER Howard,** b. 17 October 1941, Montreal, Canada. Chemist. m. Anne Fairhurst, 2 daughters. Education: Sir George William University; McGill University. Appointments: NATO Postdoctoral Fellow, Princeton University, 1967-68; Assistant Professor, State University of New York, Binghamton, 1968-71; Associate Professor, 1971-74; Associate Professor, University of Ottawa, 1975-77; Professor, 1978-; Chair, Department of Chemistry, 1982-85, 1988-91, 1991-94; Assistant Vice President, Research, 1995-96; Vice President, Research, 1997-. Publications: More than 400 Papers; 25 Patents, Organometallic Chemistry, Catalysis. Honours: Chemical Institute of Canada Inorganic Chemistry Award, 1980; Catalysis Award, 1984; Alfred Bader Award in Organic Chemistry, 1990; Commemorative Medal , 1992; Steacie Award, 1993; Urgel Achambault Prize in Physical Sciences, Maths, Engineering, 1996; Chemical Institute of Canada Medal, 1997; Bell Canada Forum Award, 1998. Royal Society of Canada, 1984; Guggenheim Fellowship, 1985; Killam Research Fellow, 1986; European Academy of Arts, Sciences and Humanities, 1996; Officer, Order of Canada, 1999. Address: University Ottawa Department Chemistry, 10 Marie Curie, Ottawa Ontario, Canada, K1N 6N5.

**ALSANIE Saleh,** b. 1 November 1959, Buraidah. Professor. m. Shikha I, 2 sons, 1 daughter. Education: BA, King Saud University, 1982; MA, Indiana University, 1985; PhD, Imam University, 1989. Appointments: Elementary Teacher, 1977-79; Principal, National Guard, 1979-82; Assistant Instructor, 1982-85; Lecturer, 1985-89; Assistant Professor, Imam University, Saudi Arabia, 1990-94; Associate Professor, 1994-. Publications: Religiosity as Therapy for Crime; Studies on Islamization of Psychology; Religiosity and Psychological Health; Positive Effects of Embracing Islam on the Attitudes among Prisoners in New York; Scientific, Ethical and Behavioural Requirements for Student Counsellors; Strategies of Phychological Security during crisis; Islamization of University courses on Psychology; Psychological and non Psychological Obstacles in Research among Saudi Social Scientists; Some Problems on Writing, Translating and Standardizing of Psychological Testing. Memberships: American Psychological Association; World Federation for Mental Health; Saudi Psychological and Educational Association; International Association of Muslim Psychologists;

International Council of Psychologists. Address: P O Box 30078, 11477 Riyadh, Saudi Arabia.

**ALTADILL-FELIP David,** b. 23 September 1966, Tortosa, Spain. Geophysicist; Researcher. m. Catalina Cordero, 1 daughter. Education: Graduate in Physics, 1991, University Barcelona; PhD Physics, 1997, University Ramon Llull. Appointments: Professor of Secondary School, Department of Education, Government of Catalonia, Tortosa-Tarragona, Spain, 1990-91; Award Holder, Geophysical Institute of Bulgarian Academy of Sciences, Sofia, Bulgaria, 1992-93, 1993-94; Scientific Collaborator, Ionospheric Dept, Observatori de l'Ebre, Roquetes, Spain, 1994-97; Award Holder, France Telecom, CNET, Lannion, France, 1996; Professor Holder, 1997-, Research Commission, 1998-, University Ramon Llull, Roquetes; Head of Ionospheric Department, Observatori de L'ebre, 1999. Publications: 16 papers in professional journals. Honours: Award of Foreign Ministry of Spain, 1992-93, 1993-94; Young Scientist Award, European Geophysical Society, 1995, International Association of Geomagnetism and Aeronomy, Uppsala, Sweden, 1997; Commission for Universities and Research from Govt of Catalonia, 1996; Invited Paper, Committee on Space Research, COSPAR, Nagoya, Japan, 1998; Invited Talk, International Union of Geodesy & Geophysics, Birmingham, UK, 1999. Memberships: European Geophysical Society; COSPAR Commission C; New York Academy of Sciences. Address: Observatori de l'Ebre, Horta Alta No 38, E-43520 Roquetes, Spain.

**ALTUKHOV Pavel,b.** 20 May 1946, Khabarovsk, USSR. Physicist. 1 son. Education: University, 1971; Doctor of Philosophy, AF Ioffe Inst, 1979; Doctor of Science, AF Ioffe, 1988. Appointments: Engineer, 1973-76; Junior Scientific Researcher, 1976-86; Senior Scientific Researcher, 1986-89; Leading Scientific Researcher, AF Ioffe Inst, 1989-. Publications: Significant publications, 1982, 1983, 1984, 1988, 1992, 1993, 1996, 1997, 1998; State prize of the USSR, 1998. Address: AF Ioffe Institute, Politekhnicheskaya St 26, 190421 St Petersburg, Russia.

**ALVINO Gloria,** b. 27 June 1931, Massachusetts, USA. Lecturer; Writer; Scientist; Pharmacist. Education: BS, Pharmacy, 1955; MS, Health and Human Services, 1992. Appointments: Researcher, Pharmacist, Lecturer, Entrepreneur, Surgical Supplies; Home Health Care Organizer, Chief Executive Officer, President, Heart to Heart Associates; Producer, Television Shows on Health Issues. Publications: The Human Energy Field. Honours: Alumni Achievement Award, 1985; MCP/AHS College Medal, 1998. Memberships: Toastmasters International Century Club; Auduboh Society; ISSEEM. Address: 32 Clark Road, Brookline, MA 02146-6030, USA.

**AMACHER A Loren,** b. 22 October 1938, Saskatoon, Canada. Neurosurgeon. m. Jane Elizabeth Tomlinson, 2 sons. Education: MD Hons, University of Western Ontario, 1962; FRCS, Royal College of Surgeons of Canada, 1969. Appointments: Associate Professor, Clinical Neurological Surgery, Pediatrics, University of Western Ontario, 1970-83; Professor of Neurosurgery, University of Connecticut, 1983-87; Director of Neurosurgery, Geisinger Medical Center, Danville, 1987-99. Publications: Professional papers; Book chapters; Commentaries; Presentations; Visiting professorships; Essayist; Novelist; Poet; Vocal musician. Honours: Harriman Award, Bucknell University, Lewisburg, Pennsylvania, 1994. Memberships: Numerous Professional Societies; Green Room Board; Weis Center for the Performing Arts; President, Pennsylvania Neurosurgical Society, 1997. Address: Penn State Geisinger Health System, Danville, PA 17822-1405, USA.

**AMANN Charles A,** b. 21 April 1926, Minnesota, USA. Engineering. m. Marilynn Reis, 1 son, 3 daughters. Education: BS, University of Minnesota, 1946; MSME, University of Minnesota, 1948. Appointments: Instructor, University of Minnesota, 1946-49; General Motors, Research Laboratories, 1949-91; Research Engineer, Supervisory Research Engineer, Assistant Department Head, Department Head, Research Fellow, Director; Principal Engineer, KAB Engineering, 1991-. Publications: Over 50; 18 patents. Honours: Clayton Prize, Institute of Mechanical Engineering; Colwell Award, SAE; Woodbury Award, ASME; Outstanding Achievement Award, University of Minnesota. Memberships: Fellow, SAE; ASME; National Academy of Engineering. Address: 984 Satterlee Road, Bloomfield Hills, MI 48304, USA.

**AMBARTSOUMIAN Eugenia N,** b. 23 October 1940, Tambov, Russia. Physicist. m. R.V. Ambartsoumian, 1 son, 1 daughter. Education: Diploma, Physicist Experimentator, Moscow State University, 1958-64; PhD, Institute of High Temperatures, Russian Academy of Sciences, 1981. Appointments: Junior Science Researcher, High Temperatures Institute of the Russian Academy of Sciences, Moscow, 1966-78; Senior Researcher, Scientist, Institute for Problems in Mechanics, Moscow, 1978-; Head of Science Research Group, Institute for Problems in Mechanics, 1981-. Publications: Contributor to over 60 articles, Professional Journals. Honours: Grantee, Foundation of Fundamental Investigations of Russia, 1995-99. Memberships: Society, Zhanie, Russia; Mendeleev Science Society; New York Academy of Sciences. Address: Academic Vargi Str 24-52, 117133 Moscow, Russia.

**AMBIKA G,** b. 14 May 1954, Kerala, India. Teacher; Researcher. m. V M Nandakumaran, 2 sons. Education: BSc, Physics, 1974; MSc, Physics, 1976; M Phil, 1980; PhD, 1988. Appointments: Junior Lecturer, Physics, 1976-77; Junior Lecturer, Physics, 1978-79; Lecturer, Physics, 1980-87; Lecturer, Physics, 1987-89; Post Doctoral Research Associate, 1989-94; Lecturer, Department of Physics, Government College, 1994-95; Lecturer, Department of Physics, Maharajas College, 1995-. Publications: 25 research papers, Nonlinear Dynamics and Chaos; Computational Aspects in Chaos and nonlinear Dynamics; 3 review articles. Honours: VS Subramonia Iyer Gold Medal, 1976; V Sivarama Krishna Iyer Gold Medal, 1976; Ross Gold Medal, 1976; Selected National Speaker in Nonlinear Dynamics under the Theoretical Physics Seminar Circuit Program. Memberships: New York Academy of Sciences; Indian Physics Association; Indian Complex Systems Society. Address: Department of Physics, Maharajas College, Cochin 682 011, India.

**AMBIKE Krishna Nilkanth,** b. 11 October 1925, Dahiwadi, Satara. Retired. m. Leelawati, 2 sons, 1 daughter. Education: MSc, Agriculture, First Class First. Appointments include: Lecturer in Agronomy, 1946-49; District Agricultural Officer, 1960-64; Technical Officer, Irrigation, Maharashtra State, Pune, 1970-74; Divisional Seed Certification Officer, Aurangabad, 1974-76; Deputy Director of Agriculture (PLanning), Maharashtra State Pune, 1976-83; Deputy Director of Agriculture (Planning), Maharashtra State; Retired, 1983. Publications: Soyabean Milk, 1947; Cotton Development in Maharashtra, 1965; Hybrid Seed Production, 1969; Response of Sorghum CSH - 1 and M-35-1 to Different Levels of NP and K, 1970; Agricultural Investment Experience (World Bank Project), 1982; On Farm Development of Irrigation Projects, 1971. Honours: BSc, Agriculture, Honours, 1946; MSc, Agriculture, Agronomy, First Class First, 1970; Seed Improvement Technology, IARI New Delhi, 1967; Special Advance Increment by Government of Maharashtra, 1982;

Fellowship of United Writers' Association India, Chennai, 1997. Memberships: General Secretary, Agricultural College Club, 1944; Pensioners Association Pune; Senior Citizens Organisation Telegram, Pune; Founder Member, Kaumudi Mandal of Common Motive Agriculture; Consultant, B R Agarwal Charitable Trust, Pune; Founder/ Chairman Anand Agro Consultancy; Vithal Mandir Family Trust, Vaduj. Address: 6 Gangotri Society, Bibawewadi Road, Pune 411037, India.

**AMENY Michael Andrew,** b. 18 June 1954, Lira, Uganda. Food Scientist. m. Gloria Ameny, 1 son, 2 daughters. Education: BSc, Biochemistry, Botany, 1979; MSc, Nutrition, Biochemistry, 1984; PhD, Food Science, 1994. Appointments: Vice President, Food Science Club, Dept of Food Science, 1991-92, Student Representative, Faculty/Staff Committee, Department of Food Science, 1992-93, Louisiana State University; Vice President, PTA University Terrace Elementary School, Baton Rouge, 1991-92; Member, Undergraduate Board, 1995-96, Postgraduate Committee, 1995-96, FAF; Member, Library Committee, 1995-; Patron, Food Science Club, Department of Food Science, Makerere University, Kampala, Uganda, 1995-96; Member, Task Force, Food Science Research Institute, Kampala, Uganda, 1996-98; NARO Biotechnology Committee, 1996-; Associate Editor, Uganda Journal of Agricultural Sciences, 1996-97; Committee of Agricultural Sciences, Minister of Agriculture on Food Technology, 1997-. Publications: Several articles in professional journals. Honours include: Several grants. Memberships: International Member, IFT; Fruits & Vegetables Products, IFT; Food Chemistry, IFT; International Society of Tropical Root Crops; Guild of the University of Wales; Professional Member, Institute of Food Technologists; American Horticultural Society; New York Academy of Sciences; International Association of Food Colorants; Crop Science Society of Africa. Makerere University, Department of Food Science Technology, PO Box 7062, Kampala, Uganda.

**AMERY Colin Lloyd,** b. 17 December 1938, Hutton, Essex, England. Barrister; Author. m. Yvonne Jean Gatton, 1 son, 1 daughter. Education: London School of Economics, 1957-58; BA, LLB, Auckland University, 1987-97. Appointments: Lawyer, 1962-68; Barrister, 1989-98; Journalist. Publications: New Atlantis - The Secret of the Sphinx, 1976; Odyssey of a Troubadour, 1982; Ten Minutes to Midnight, 1989; Multiple contributions in professional journals, magazines and newspapers. Memberships include: Law Society; Society of Authors; Executive Director, Lawyers Against Torture and Oppression Anywhere. Address: 19 Bill Phillip Place, Auckland Manurewa 1702, New Zealand.

**AMINOV Rashid Zarifovich,** b. 21 March 1938, Russia. Heat Power Engineer. m. Fedoseeba Svetlana, 2 daughter. Education: Candidate of Technical Sciences, 1966; Doctor of Technical Sciences, 1980; Professor, 1981. Appointments: Manager of Department, Heat Power Station, Saratov Polytechnical Institute, 1974; Head of Branch, Institute of Energy Research, 1990, Head of Department of Energy, Volga's Regions, 1995, Russian Academy of Science. Publications: 160 scientific articles in professional journals, 7 books, 14 patents. Honour: Honoured Worker of Science and Technique, Russia, 1997. Memberships: Full Member of the International Academy of Energy. Address: Department of Energy, Volga's Regions, Russian Academy of Sciences, 77 Politeknicheskaya Street, Saratov 410016, Russia.

**AMIR Hassan,** b. 14 September 1950, Zanzibar. Surgeon. m. Waheeda Amirali, 2 sons. Education: MBBS, 1976; MS, Surgery, 1980; FUICC, 1991. Appointments: Internship, 1976-77; Resident in Surgery, 1977-80; Consultant Surgeon,

Dubai Medical Centre, Red Crescent Society of I R of Iran, Dubai, UAE, 1981-88; Lecturer, 1988-92, Consultant Surgeon, 1988- Senior Lecturer, 1992-97, Associate Professor, 1997-, Research Coordinator, 1997-, Department of Surgery, Muhimbili University College of Health Sciences, University of Dar es Salaam, Tanzania. Publications: 27 Publications; Honours: International Cancer Research Technology Transfer Award, International Union Against Cancer. Memberships: Life Member, Association of Fellows of International Union Against Cancer; Fellow, Association of Surgeons of East Africa; Member, Medical Association of Tanzania; Fellow, Tanzania Surgical Association; Member Advisory Board, Asian Journal of Cancer. Address: P O Box 2863, Dar es Salaam, Tanzania.

**AMIRI Shabnam,** b. 26 November 1972, Tehran, Iran. Speech and Language Pathologist. m. Shahriar M Mirzaie. Education: BSc Degree, Iran Medical University, 1996. Appointments: Clinical Case Study, Dyslexic and Poor Readers; Clinical Study, Delayed Speech and Language Disorders in Pre-schoolers; Treatment of Stuttering. Publications: BSc Thesis on Voice Disorders and their Management; Translation, A Book in term of Reading, Writing and Dyslexia. Memberships: Speech Therapy Association. Address: 2ns floor No 26 Ally 146, South Rashgid St, Tehranpars, Tehran, Iran.

**AMLIE Jan Peder,** b. 23 September 1940, V Toten, Norway. Physician. m. May, 1 son, 2 daughters. Education: Medical School, Oslo, 1965; Specialist in Cardiology and Internal Medicine, 1973; MD, 1980. Appointments: Assistant Professor, 1980-83, Associate Professor, 1984-90, Professor in Cardiology, 1990-, Medical Dept 13. Publications: 105 scientific papers; FESC no 120, 1988; 1 symposium; 1 book. Memberships: President, Norwegian Society Cardiology; European Society Cardiology, Speciality Committee in Cardiology, EU/EOS. Address: Rikshospitalet, Pilestredet, 0027 Oslo, Norway.

**AMMAR El Sayed,** b. Damietta, Egypt. Professor of Pharmacology. m. Ahdab El Morshedy, 4 sons. Education: BSc, Pharmacology, Cairo University, 1961; PhD, Moscow, Russia, 1969. Appointments: Vice Dean, 1981, Professor Chairman, 1978, Faculty Pharmacology, Mansoura University, Egypt; Visiting Professor, College of Medicine, Ohio State University, USA, 1979-81. Publications: Over 50 articles in pharmacology, toxicology in USA, Russia, England, Japan, Yugoslavia, Egypt journals. Honours: Teaching Awards; Assiut University Award; Pharmaceutical Association Award. Memberships: American Society Pharmacological Experimental Therapy; Egyptian Pharmacologists; Association American Society Toxicology. Address: Faculty of Pharmacy, Mansoura, Egypt.

**AMMAR Hamed Mostafa,** b. 25 February 1921, Silwa, Aswan, Egypt. University Professor. m. Laila Lababidy, 1 son, 2 daughters. Education: BA, 1941, MA History, 1945, Cairo University; Diploma, 1947, MA, 1949, PhD Education, 1952, London University. Appointments: School Teacher, Consec University, 1941-45; Teacher and Professor, Faculty Education, Ain Shams University, Cairo, 1952-70; United Nations Regional Adviser in Human Development, 1970-85, Professor Emeritus, 1986-. Publications: Growing up in an Egyptian Village, 1954; Human Development in the Arab World, 2 vols, 1992; Educational and Cultural Innovations, 1998; and others. Honours: State Award, Egypt, 1996; Kuwait Award, 1995. Memberships: Few NGOs in Education, Social Welfare & Culture. Address: Faculty of Education, Department of Foundations of Education, Heliopolis, Cairo, Egypt.

**AMZAR Dinu,** b. 11 March 1943, Berlin, Charlottenburg. Writer, Mathematician. m. Moiken Bossung, 1 son. Education: Bachelor of Science, University of Mayence, Germany, 1967; Diploma in Mathematics, 1972. Appointment: Scientist, Federal Office of Statistics, 1973-83. Publications: Sehübungen an Rebengerippen; Gebiete den Grillen zu schweigen, Langholzabfuhren; In Sätzen In Ketten. Memberships: Heidegger Society; Humboldt Society; American Math Society, American Association for Advancement in Science; New York Academy of Science. Address: Lenaustrasse 2, 72488 Sigmaringen, Germany.

**ANAGNOSTOPOULOS John,** b. 15 May 1951, Athens. Electrical Engineer. Education: MS EE, Polytechnic University of New York, 1977. Appointments: Hardware, Software Design, Fellows Corp, Springfield, USA; Project Engineer; Artificial Intelligence Pioneer. Memberships: TEE Professional Engineers Club, Athens, Greece. Address: 13 Anaxagora Str, 17778 Athens, Greece.

**ANATI Emmanuel,** b. 14 May 1930, Florence, Italy. Archaeologist. m. Ariela Fradkin, 1 son, 1 daughter. Education: BA, Hebrew University, Jerusalem, 1953; MA, 1955; AM, Harvard University, 1959; Doctor of Letters, Sorbonne, Paris, 1960. Appointments: Researcher, Many Countries; Founder, Head, Centro Camuno di Studi Preistorici. Publications: Over 70 volumes Published; NumerousMonographs; World Journal of Prehistoric and Tribal Art; The Footsteps of Man; Le Orme dell'Uomo. Honours: Honorary Citizen of Capo di Ponte; Man of the Year, American Biographical Institute. Memberships: Rotary Club; International Committee on Rock Art; ICOMOS; IDAPEE. Address: Centro Camuno di Studi Preistorici, 25044 ES Capo di Ponte, Italy.

**ANCHEV Panko,** b. 25 March 1946, Varna, Bulgaria. Literary Critic, Publisher, Journalist. m. Donka Hristova, 2 sons. Education: MA, University of Veliko Tirnovo, 1971. Appointments: Editor, Radio Varna, 1972-73; Editor, G Bakalor Publishers, 1975-78; Editor in Chief, 1978-86; Chief, 1986-90; Chief, Andina Publishers, 1990-. Publications: Authors and Words; The Man in Words; The Conscience of Words. Memberships: Bulgarian Writers Union; Bulgarian Journalists Union. Address: Str Vladislav bl 24 flat 2, 9009 Varna, Bulgaria.

**ANDELSON Robert Vernon,** b. 19 February 1931, Los Angeles, CA, USA. Social Philosopher; Educator. m. Bonny Orange Johnson, 7 June 1964. Education: AA, Los Angeles City College, 1950; AB equiv, University Chicago, 1952; AM, 1954, PhD, 1960, University Southern CA; Ordained Min, Congl Ch, 1959. Appointments: Executive Director, Henry George School Social Science, San Diego Extension, CA, 1959-62; Instructor, Philosophy, Religion, Northland College, WI, 1962-63; Assistant Professor, Government, Philosophy, Northwestern State University, LA, 1963-65; Member, Faculty, 1965-, Member, Graduate Faculty, 1969-92, Professor, Philosophy, 1973-92, Professor Emeritus, 1992, Auburn University, AL; Inaugural Lecturer, Philosophy Lecturer Ser, University of Alabama, Birmingham, 1975; Member, Academic Staff, Ludwig von Mises Institute, 1983-; VP, International Union Land Value Taxation and Free Trade, 1986-88, President 1997-; Member, Director, Robert Schalkenbach Foundation, 1986-; Reviewer, Institutional Grant Applications, National Endowment for Humanities, 1987; Faculty Associate, Lincoln Institute land Policy, 1993-. Publications: Author, Imputed Rights: An Essay in Christian Social Theory, 1971; Editor, Co-author, Critics of Henry George, 1979; Commons Without Tragedy, 1991; Joint Author, From Wasteland to Promised Land: Liberation Theology for a Post-Marxist World, 1992; Land-Value Taxation Around the World (2nd Edition),

1997; Articles in scholarly journals. Honours: Assistant Sergeant at Arms, Republican National Convention, 1952; Research Award, Foundation Social Research, 1959; Research Award, Relm Foundation, 1967; 2 George Washington Honorary Medals, Freedom Foundation, 1970, 1972; Distinguished Research Fellow, American Institute Economic Research, 1993-. Memberships: Alabama Philosophy Society, President, 1968-69, 1978-79; Lee Co Republican Executive Committee, 1967-79; Editorial Board, American Journal Economics and Sociology, 1969-; Trustee, Henry George Foundation, 1971-75; Advisory Commission, 1975-; Editorial Board, The Personalist, 1975-80; AAUP, President Auburn Chapter, 1975-76; Southern Society Philosophy and Psychology. Address: 534 Cary Drive, Auburn, AL 36830-2502, USA.

**ANDEM Maurice Nwanang,** b. 31 December 1940, Big Town, Ibeno, Nigeria. m. Leila Mirjam Andem, 2 sons, 3 daughters. Education: St Joseph's College, Sasse, Buea, Cameroons, 1954-56; People's Friendship University, Moscow, USSR, 1968-73; University of Helsinki, Helsinki, Finland, 1973-80. Appointments include: Acting Associate Professor of Private International Law and Comparative Law, 1990-91, 1991; Associate Professor of Private International Law and Comparative Law, 1991-; Acting Professor of Public International Law, 1998; Chairman and Managing Director, Anton (Nigeria) Ltd, Lagos, Nigeria. Memberships include: Coach and Arbitrator, Fifth Willem C Vis International Commercial Arbitration Moot, Vienna, 1998; The British Inter-Planetary Society; Chairman, Finnish Space Law Association, 1995-; The International Institute of Space Law; Vice Dean, Faculty of Law, University of Lapland, 1996-2001, Director, Institute of Air and Space Law, University of Lapland, 1997-; Association of Law Teachers; Deacon, Christ for All Mission, Lagos, Nigeria. Address: Mastopolku 23, SF-96910, Rovaniemi, Finland.

**ANDERSON Charles William,** b. 8 May 1956, Geneva, Nebraska, USA. Associate Professor Computer Science. m. Stacey Lynn Brown, 2 sons. Education: BS Computer Science, 1978, University of Nebraska; MS Computer & Information Science, 1982, PhD Computer & Information Science, 1986, University of Massachusetts. Appointments: Since 1986: Senior Member of Technical Staff, GTE Labs, Waltham, MA, 1986-90; Assistant Professor, 1991-97, Associate Professor, 1997-, Computer Science Dept, Colorado State University. Publications: 8 refereed papers in professional journals including: Effects of Variations in Neural Network Topology and Output Averaging on the Discrimination of Mental Tasks from Spontaneous Electroencephalogram, 1997; 37 refereed conference papers. Honours: Various teaching awards; Member of 4 honorary societies. Memberships: ACM; IEEE; INNS. Address: Dept of Computer Science, Colorado State University, Fort Collins, CO 80523, USA.

**ANDERSON Garry Michael,** b. 17 May 1955, Houston, Texas, USA. Physician; Diagnostic Radiologist. Education: BS, Biology, Tarleton State University, Stephenville, Texas, USA, 1977; BS, Medicine, Texas A&M University, 1979; MD, Texas A&M University, 1981; Internship in Pathology, Scott and White Hospital, Temple, Texas, 1981-82; Resident in Diagnostic Radiology, 1982-86; Fellow in Imaging UCLA Center of the Health Sciences, 1986-87; Assistant Attending Clinical Professor, 1987-88; UCLA Center of the Health Sciences. Appointments: Diagnostic Radiologist, Community Radiology Medical Group, 1987-. Honours: Diplomate National Board of Medical Examiners; Diplomate American Board of Radiology; Member, Second Decade Council American Film Institute LA; Outstanding Young Alumnus Tarleton State University; Chief,

Radiology Resident, Scott and White Hospital. Memberships: Los Angeles Medical Association; California Medical Association; American Medical Association; Los Angeles Radiological Society; California Radiology Society; American College of Radiology; Radiological Society of North America. Address: 1813 Termino Avenue Apt 8401, Long Beach, CA 90815-2672, USA.

**ANDERSON Parker Lynn,** b. 19 April 1964, Wickenburg, Arizona. Education: Diploma, American School, Chicago. Appointments: Employee, Catholic Social Service of Yavapai. Publications: Roasting Roderick, aself-published journal of cinema commentary; Plays: The Startled Cowboys; Voices from the Past; The Sleeping Toad; Virgil Earp. Honours: Dictionary of International Biography; Intenational Who's Who of Intellectuals; Who's Who in America; Who's Who in the World; Who's Who in the West. Memberships: Prescott Fine Arts Association; Blue Rose Theatre. Address: P O Box 1285, Prescott, AZ 86302, USA.

**ANDERSON Ralph R,** b. 1 November 1932, Fords, New Jersey, USA. Professor. m. LaVeta Ann Anderson, 1 son, 1 daughter. Education: BS, 1953, MS, 1958, Rutgers University; PhD, University of Missouri, 1961. Appointments: Research Assistant, Rutgers University, 1957-58; Research Assistant, 1958-61, Instructor, 1961-62, Department of Dairy Science, University of Missouri; Assistant Professor, Animal Science, Iowa State University, 1962-64; Postdoctoral Fellow, Endocrinology, University of Wisconsin, 1964-65; Assistant Professor, 1965-68, Associate Professor, 1968-76, Dairy Science, Endocrinology; Professor, Department of Animal Sciences, Endocrinology, University of Missouri, 1976-98; Emeritus Professor, 1998. Publications: Numerous articles in professional journals. Honours include: Outstanding Faculty Member Award, UMC Dairy Club, 1988; Gamma Sigma Delta Graduate Teaching Award, 1982 and Research Award of Merit, 1994. Memberships: American Physiological Society; Endocrine Society; Society for Experimental Biology & Medicine; American Dairy Science Association; American Society of Animal Science; Federation of American Societies for Experimental Biology; Society for the Study of Reproduction; Sigma Xi; American Registry of Certified Animal Scientists. Address: S139 Animal Sciences Center, University of Missouri-Columbia, Columbia, MO 65211, USA.

**ANDERSON Richard Todd,** b. 7 November 1934, WI, USA. College President. m. Beatrice Joan, 2 sons, 1 daughter. Education: Bachelor of Science, University of Wisconsin, Stout, 1953-57; Master of Education, Marquette University, 1958-63; Doctor of Education, Marquette University, 1967-75. Appointments: Guidance Counselor, Waukesha County Technical College, 1963-65; Curriculum Coordinator, Waukesha County Technical College, 1965-66; Supervisor of Instruction, Waukesha County Technical College, 1966-68; Assistant District Director, Waukesha County Area Vocational, Technical and Adult Education District, 1968-73; President, Waukesha County Area Technical College District, 1973-. Honours: Chief Executive Officer Regional Award; Educator Alumnus of the Year Award; Waukesha YMCA Outstanding Corporate Leadership Award; Speakers Award; Award of Appreciation; Distinguished Service to the Community; Dictionary of International Biography, International Biographical Centre; Fulbright Scholarship; Distinguished Service Award; President of the Year; Eagle Award; AAWCJC Presidential Award; Recognition Award. Memberships: Administrators Association; American Management Association; American Technical Education Association; American Vocational Association; Community Colleges for International Development; Council for Occupational Education. Address:

Waukesha County Technical College, Office of the President, 800 Main St, Pewaukee, WI 53072, USA.

**ANDERSSON Lars,** b. 13 November 1947, Stockholm, Sweden. Researcher, Gerontologist. 1 daughter. Education: MA, Sociology, Stockholm University, 1972; PhD, Faculty of Medicine, Karolinska Institute, 1984; Associate Professor, Docent, 1989. Appointments: Research Assistant, Division of Stress Research, Karolinska Institute, 1973-78; Senior Researcher, Division of Stress Research, Karolinska Institute, 1979-97; Senior Researcher, Division of Geriatric Medicine, Karolinska Institute, 1998-; Director, Social Gerontology Section, Stockholm Gerontology Research Center, 1988-. Publications: Many Refereed Articles; Numerous Books, Book Chapters, Monographs; Special Reports, Non-Refereed Articles; Appointed expert in many committees. Honours: 5000 Personalities of the World, American Biographical Institute; Man of the Year, 1995, ABI; International Book of Honours, ABI; Dictionary of International Biography, International Biographical Centre; Men of Achievement, IBC. Memberships: Gerontological Society of America (fellow); Swedish Medical Research Council; WHO Fellowship; New York Academy of Sciences; Swedish Gerontological Society (President); Many othermemberships. Address: Stockholm Gerontol Rsch Ctr, Box 11382 Stockholm, Sweden.

**ANDO Yukio,** b. 9 July 1953, Beppu, Japan. Medical Doctor. m. Keiko Asahara, 3 sons. Education: Graduate, Kumamoto University School of Medicine, 1983; PhD, 1990. Appointments: Post Doctor Fellow, 1990; Assistant Professor, First Department of Internal Medicine, 1993; Visiting Professor, Umea Univeristy, Sweden, 1996. Honours: Travel Award of American Autonomic Society, 1996; Award of Kumamoto Medical Association, 1998. Memberships: Japanese Neurological Association; Advisory Memeber, Jalanese Autonomic Nervous System Society. Address: Kyomachi 1-11-20-301, Kumamoto 862, Japan.

**ANDRADE Ruymar,** b. 12 May 1042, Uba, MG, Brazil. Lawyer. m. Regina, 1 son, 1 daughter. Education: Law degree, 1971, C Mendes University, Rio de Janeiro; International Business, 1974, IIB, Rio de Janeiro; Certified Foreign Legal Consultant, Florida Supreme Court, USA. Appointments: President, Unipat Inc, Florida, USA; Senior Partner, R Andrade Advogados, Rio de Janeiro; Past President, Brazilian-American Chamber of Commerce, Florida. Publications: Technology as a Factor of Development, 1978; Brazilian Patent Law, 1997. Memberships: CIPA; ABA; BBA; AIPPI; ABAPI; INTA; ABPI. Address: 575 Palmer Avenue, Winter Park, FL 32789-2630, USA.

**ANDREADIS Ioannis,** b. 1 June 1960, Greece. Educator. m. Evangelia, 1 son, 1 daughter. Education: Diploma, Electrical Engineering, 1983; MSc, Electrical Engineering & Electronics, 1985; PhD, Instrumentation & Analytical Science, 1989. Appointments: Professor, TEI Kavalas, 1991-92; Lecturer, DUTH, 1992-. Publications: Over 50 articles in referred journals and conferences. Memberships: Technical Chamber of Greece; IEEE. Address: 16 Roosevelt, Crysoupolis Kavala, 64200 Greece.

**ANDREANI Domenico,** b. 5 March 1925, Taranto, Italy. Professor. m. Buccisano Elena, 1 son, 4 daughters. Education: MD, University of Pisa, Italy, 1948; Professor of Therapeurics, Catholic University, 1967-72. Appointments: Professor, Endocrinology and Metabolism, 1972-; Dean, Post Doctoral School of Endocrinology, 1984-. Honours: Fellow, Royal Society, London; East Presidet, 1983-86; President Italian Soc Endocrinology, 1988-90; Member, Royal Academy of Belgium,

C Bernard Lecture Prize, 1993. Memberships: American Diabetes Association; American Thyroid Association; European Endocrinology Federation; European Association Study of Diabetes; American Endocrinology Society. Address: Viale di Villa Grazioli n 3, 00198 Rome, Italy.

**ANDREEV Alexander V,** b. 14 October 1949, Peterburg, Russia. Researcher. m. Semenova Lioudmila, 2 sons. Education: Ural State University, Ekaterinburg, Russia, 1973; PhD, 1979; Professor, 1990. Appointments: Junior, Senior, then Leading Researcher, Permanent Magnets Laboratory, Ural State University; Leading Researcher, Institute of Physics, Academy of Sciences, Prague, Czech Republic, 1995-. Publications: Over 200 papers on magnetism. Membership: Editorial Board, Journal of Alloys and Compounds. Address: Brdickova 1916, 15500 Prague, Czech Republic.

**ANDREEVSKI Petre,** b. 25 June 1934, Sloestica, Macedonia. 1 son, 2 daughters. Education: Faculty of Philology, Skopje, 1963. Appointments: Dramatist; Journalist. Honours: Miladinov Brothers Award Denicia, 1968; 11 October Award, Denicia, 1968; Stale Poppy Award, Pirej, 1981; Ratsin's Award, All Faces of Death, 1996. Memberships: Independent Members of Macedonia; PEN Club. Address: Gramos St 5a, 91000 Skopje, Macedonia.

**ANDREGG Michael Murphy,** b. 22 December 1951, Reno, Nevada, USA. Teacher. m. Jo Ann, 1 daughter. Education: BS, Genetics, Zoology, Physical Anthropology, 1973, PhD, Genetics, 1977, University of California, Davis. Appointments: Director, Ground Zero Minnesota, 1983-; Professor, Master of Liberal Studies Program, University of Minnesota, 1985-; Professor, Justice and Peace Studies Program, University of St Thomas, St Paul, 1992-. Publications: On the Causes of War, 1997; Numerous articles in professional journals. Memberships include: International Studies Association; International Society for the Comparative Study of Civilizations. Address: Ground Zero Minnesota, PO Box 13127, Minneapolis, MN 55414, USA.

**ANDREJEVS Georgs,** b. 30 October 1932, Tukums, Latvia. Ambassador; Professor. m. Anita Brante, 1 son, 1 daughter. Education: Graduate, cum laude, 1959, MD, 1964, PhD, 1972, Faculty of Medicine, Latvian Medical Academy. Career: Professor, Chairman, Latvian Medical Academy, 1972-95; Member of Parliament, Latvian Parliament, 1990-94; Minister of Foreign Affairs, Latvia, 1992-94; Ambassador of Latvia to Canada, 1995-98; Ambassador of Latvia to the Council of Europe. Publictions: 274 scientific, 29 political, 4 monographs. Honour: Fellow, Royal College of Anaesthetists, 1995. Memberships: Latvian Academy of Sciences; European Academy of Anaesthesiologists; German Society of Anaesthesiologists. Address: The Latvian Embassy, 112 ent Street, Suite 208, Place de Villew Tower B, Ottawa, Ontario K1P 5P2, Canada.

**ANDREYEV Alexander,** b. 2 June 1958, Leningrad. Mathematician. m. Tatyana Andreyeva, 1 daughter. Education: Physics Faculty, St Petersburg State University, 1981. Appointments: Assistant Professor, St Petersburg University of Aerospace Instrumentation, Applied Mathematics Department, 1984-94; President, Softjoys Corporation, 1994-. Memberships: IEEE; IEEE Computer Society; ACM. Address: Softjoys Corporation, 16 Gastello Street, 19635 Saint Petersburg, Russia.

**ANDRIES Andrei,** b. 24 October 1933, Chisinau, Moldova. Physicist. m. Klimanova Lidia, 1 son. Education: PhD, 1964; Dr, 1974; Sc Moldova, 1978; Academician, 1984; Professor, 1992. Appointments: President, Academy of Science, Moldova, 1989;

Head of Laboratory, Institute of Applied Physics, 1971; Director, Centre Optoelectronics, 1993. Publications: More than 350 Publications. Honours: State Prize of Moldova, 1983; Merited Science Resaerch, 1984; Man of the Year, 1994; 20th Century Award, 1995; Order of the Republic of Moldova, 1996' Doctor honoris causa, University of Moldova, University of Ecology, Romania, University of Banat, Romania, 1997. Memberships: Romanian Association Science; Engineering Academy Science; European Academy; International Academy of Culture and Political Sciences, 1998. Address: 1 Stefan cel Mare, MD 2001 Kishinev, Moldova.

**ANDRIEVSKI Rostislav A,** b. 8 January 1933, Gorlovka, Ukraine. Scientist. m. Valentina Polunina, 2 daughters. Education: Engineer in Materials Science and Powder Metallurgy, 1955; Candidate of Sciences, 1968, Kiev Polytechnical Institute; DrSc, 1971, Moscow; Professor in Powder Metallurgy, 1971. Appointments: Student of Kiev Polytechnical Institute, 1950-55; Scientist, Ukranian Academy of Science, 1955-62; Head, Dept of Podolsk Technical Institute, 1963-76; Professor, Moscow Institute of Fine Chemical Technology, 1977-84; Deputy Director, Institute Physics in Frunze, 1984-90; Chief Scientist, Institute for New Chemical Problems, Chernogolovka, 1990-. Publications: 360 publications including 9 books. Memberships: Corresponding member, Kirghizstan Academy Sciences; Institute for Science of Sintering. Address: Institute of Problems of ChemicalPhysics, Russian Academy of Sciences, Chernogolovka, Moscow Region, 142432 Russia.

**ANDRZEJEWSKI Pawel,** b. 14 January 1954, Poznan, Poland. Mathematician. Education: MSc Math, 1977; PhD, 1988. Membership: European Mathematical Society. Address: Szczecin University, Math Institute, ul Wielkoposka 15, Szczecin, Poland.

**ANG Dang Dinh,** b. 16 March 1926, Ha Dong, Vietnam. Professor. m. Bui Thi Minh Thi, 2 sons, 3 daughters. Education: BS, Kansas Universty, 1955; PhD, CalTech, USA, 1958. Appointments: Professor, Chairman, Department of Maths, Saigon University, 1960-75; Professor of Maths, Ho Chi Minh City University, 1976-. Director, Labo Analysis, HCM City Universitym 1976-94; Honorary President, Ho Chi Minh Math Society. Publications: Over 120 Research Articles, Analysis and Mechanics; 5 Books, Analysis and Mechanics. Memberships: Vietnam Maths Society; American Maths Society. Address: Mathematical Faculty, College of Natural Sciences, Hochi Minh National Univrsity, Hochi Minh City, Vietnam.

**ANG Hooi Hoon,** b. 1964 Ipoh Perak, Malaysia. Lecturer in Pharmaceuticals. Education: BPharm Hons, University of Science in Malaysia, 1988; MSc, 1990; PhD, 1993; Doctoral Fellow, PHP Institute of Asia, Japan, 1995. Appointments: Graduate Assistant, School of Pharmaceutical Science, University of Science in Malaysia, 1988-90; Assistant Quality Control Manager, private firm, Ipoh Perak, 1992-93; Lecturer, School of Pharmaceutical Sciences, University of Science Malaysia, 1994-; Vice Chairman, Malaysian Pharmaceutical Society of Penang, 1994-95, Hon Secretary, 1995-. Publications: Over 100 publications in international refereed journals, research reports, invited lectures, seminars, workshops, congresses, symposiums and conventions. Honours: Many honours and awards in recognition of medical achievements; Sole recipient, 1996 ASAIHL Fellowship; Visiting Professorship, Faculty of Medicine, National University of Singapore; Young Scientist Awardee, international congresses, 1996, 1997; Sole recipient, 1997 TWAS South-south Fellowship and CAS Visiting Professorship to Beijing Medical University, 1998. Memberships: Malaysian Society of Parasitology and Tropical Medicine; Malaysian Microbiology Society; Japanese Society of Parasitology; Korean Society of Parasitology; Third World Academy of Science in Italy; Malaysian Natural Product Society; Malaysian Technology Forum; Malaysian Invention and Design Society. Address: School of Pharmaceutical Sciences, University of Science in Malaysia, Minden, 11800 Penang, Malaysia.

**ANG Minni,** b. 1 January 1966, Malaysia. University Lecturer. m. Elok Robert Tee. Education: ATCL, 1984; BSC, 1989; LTCL, 1994; PhD, 1998. Appointments: Temporary Teacher, SMP Taman Petaling, 1986; Research Assistant, University Malaya, 1989; Newsreader, Radio Television Malaysia, 1989-92; Staffworker, Scripture Union Malaysia, 1989-92; Teacher, Malaysia Symphony Orchestra, 1993; Head of Music Department, University Lecturer, University Putra Malaysia, 1995-. Publications: Articles to Journals; Compositions: Book, A Handbook of Basic Rock Rhythms for Drum Set, 1999. Honours: Best of Asia Pacific Award, 1998; Outstanding Service Achievement; CARI Top 5 Malaysian Sites; Who's Who in the World, 1999. Memberships: Malaysian Mensa Society; Kuala Lumpur Symphony Orchestra Society; Percussive Arts Society; International Computer Music Association; Audio Engineering Society; Acoustical Society of America. Address: U Putra Malaysia, Department Music Faculty Hmn Ecol, 43409 Upm Serdang Selangor, Malaysia.

**ANGEL Marina.** Professor of Law. Education: JD, Magna Cum Laude, Columbia Law School, 1969; LLM, University of Pennsylvania Law School, 1977; BA, Government, Barnard College, 1965. Appointments: Lecturer in Law, Rutgers Law School, 1970; Associate Professor of Law, Hofstra University Law School, 1971-78; Visiting Professor of Law, Hebrew University, 1979-83; Professor of Law, University of Athens - Temple University Law School, 1978-83, 1985, 1987-89, 1991; Visiting Professor, Wollongong University, 1992; Visiting Professor, Queensland University of Technology, 1992; Professor of Law, Temple University Law School, 1979-. Publications: Many publications. Honours: Pennsylvania Bar Association Anne V Alpern Award; Philadelphia Bar Association Sandra Day O'Connor Award; George P Williams Memorial Award; Temple Law Review Faculty Honoree, 1989; Temple Women's Law Caucus Honoree. Memberships: American Bar Association; Association of American Law Schools; Pennsylvania Bar Association; Philadelphia Bar Association; Association of the Bar of the City of New York; Sociaty of American Law Teachers. Address: Temple Univ Law School, 1719 N Broad St, Philadelphia, PA 19122 2504, USA.

**ANGELOFF Luben G,** b. October 1925, Kosevci, Omortag, Bulgaria. Agriculturalist. Education: Graduate, Economics, University of Sophia, 1953; Enrolled, Zootechnical Faculty, Agricultural Academy; MSc, Experimental Surgery, McGill University, Montreal, Canada, 1972. Appointments: Lecturer; Founder, Owner, Angel's Biomedical Laboratories Ltd, Canada. Publications: Over 70 scientific publications in the medical field; Books include: World Angel's Poetry, 1987; I am not Prometheus, I am Luben Angeloff From a Small Village, Kosevci, Omortag, Bulgaria, 1998; The Mirror of the Creator, in progress for the year 2,000. Honours: Diploma & Certificate, IV Congresso Latino Americano de Citologia, 1973; Bronze Medal, 1st International Exhibition of Scientific Films on Cancer, Buenos Aires, Argentina, 1978. Memberships: International Union Against Cancer; International AIDS Society; Pan American Cancer Cytology Society; International Society for Preventive Oncology; International Cryobiology Society; Musicians Guild of Montreal; American Society of Composers, Authors and Publishers; Member of over 50 International

Scientific Congresses. Address: Angel's Biomedical Laboratories Ltd., 3945 Brahms Street, Brossard, Quebec, Canada, J4Z 2W9.

**ANGELOV George,** b. 18 November 1943, Sofia, Bulgaria. Cybernetics Engineer. m. Konstanza Angelova, 1 son, 1 daughter. Education: Engineer, 1969; Economist, 1978; PhD, 1987; Diploma, Robotics. Appointments: Research Engineer, Central Research and Development, Institute of Automatization, 1969; Senior Consultant, State Committee of Science and Technology Progress, 1975; Research Engineer, Technical Cybernetics and Robotics Institute, Bulgarian Academy of Sciences, 1978; IIC, 1992. Publications: 18 inventories, including 2 patents in technical field, 1973-82; Publications in technical journals. Honour: Diploma, Inventor of the Year 1979 Award. Membership: New York Academy of Sciences, 1996-. Address: 32 L Karavelov, Sofia 1000, Bulgaria.

**ANGHELACHE Romeo,** b. 16 February 1964, Vatra Dornei, Romania. Physicist. m. Beatrice. Education: License in Physics, 1989; PhD in Condensed Matter, 1998. Appointments: High School Professor of Physics, 1989-90; Physicist Researcher and Network Administrator, 1991-. Publications: 18 scientific papers in peer reviewed literature. Honour: 2nd Award, National Conference on Philosophy of Science, 1986. Address: Institute Technical Physics, Mangeron Avenue 47, 6600 Iasi, Romania.

**ANGULO Chappie,** b. 3 March 1928, Detroit, Michigan, USA. Artist (Painter). m. Georgina, 1 son. Education: Art Schools, USA, England, Mexico, 1949-59. Career: Numerous (person and collective exhibitions, Mexico, USA, 1958-98. Memberships: International Art Association (NESCO); Salon Plustica Mexicana. Address: AP Postal 21 60.9, Mexico DF 0400, Mexico.

**ANIFANTIS Nikolaos,** b. 12 February 1955, Samos, Greece. Assistant Professor. m. Velaora Vasso, 1 son. Education: Mechanical Engineering degree, 1978, PhD Mechanical Engineering, 1985, University of Patras, Greece. Appointments: Research Assistant, 1978-86, Lecturer in Mechanical Engineering 1986-90, Assistant Professor in Mechanical Engineering 1990-, University of Patras. Publications: Over 20 articles to scientific journals. Memberships: Technical Chamber of Greece; NY Academy of Sciences; ISBE; IEEE Computer Society; AAAS. Address: 43 Sarantaporou St, 26223 Patras, Greece.

**ANISIMOV Oleg Alexandrovitch,** b. 16 March 1957, Leningrad, USSR. Scientist; Physical Geographer. m. Natalia Vladimirovna, 1 daughter. Education: Leningrad State University, 1974-1980; State Hydrological Institute, 1983-85; PhD, 1986. Appointments: Research Scientist, 1985, Leading Research Scientist, 1993, Deputy Head, 1996, Hydrological Institute; Consultant, State University of New York, 1995-96. Publications: More Than 60 Papers; Reports. Honours: Grantee, Alexander von Humboldt Foundation; USA National Science Foundation, USA Civilian Research & Development Foundation, International Science Foundation. Memberships: International Permafrost Association; World Climate Research Programme; American Geophysical Union. Address: Ap 71, 1/5 Kujbysheva Street, 197046 St Petersburg, Russia.

**ANKARABOYINA Apparao,** b. 11 November 1936, Berhampur, Ganjam District, Orissa, India. Researcher and Consultant. m. Bangam Swarajya Lakshmi, 2 sons, 3 daughters. Education: BSc (MPC) Distinction, 1956, Khallikote College, Berhampur; BSc Hons Geology and Geophysics,

1959, MSc Exploration Geophysics, 1966, IIT, Kharagpur; PhD Science, 1973, Jadavpur. Appointments: Senior Scientific Assistant, 1960-63, Scientist A - G, 1963-96, Consultant, 1996-, National Geophysical Research Institute, Council of Scientific and Industrial Research. Publications: Developments in Geoelectric Methods, 1997; 45 articles in scientific journals in the field of geoelectrical methods. Honours: Kern Forschung Analage (KFA), Germany, Fellowship, 1976-77; Invited by Elsevier Applied Science Publishers to write an article on Geoelectric Profiling, which covered his entire 23 years of research work, 1991; National Mineral Award, Government of India, 1997. Memberships: Life Fellow, Indian Geophysical Union, Association of Exploration Geophysicists, India; Life member, Indian Geological Congress; Hon member, Balaghat Association of Geologists and Research Workers. Address: H No 12-13-249 St 15, Tarnaka, Hyderabad 500 017, India.

**ANNAN Kofi,** b. 8 April 1938, Kumasi, Ghana. United Nations Secretary General. m. Nane Annan, 3 children. Education: University of Science and Technology, Kumasi; Macalester College, St Paul, Minnesota; Institut Universitaire des Hautes Etudes Internationales in Geneva; MSc, Massachusetts Institute of Technology. Appointments: Administrative Officer, Budget Officer, World Health Organization, Geneva, 1962; Deputy Director of Administration, Head of Personnel, Office of the United Nations High Commissioner for Refugees, 1980-83; Director of Budget, Office of Financial Services, 1984-87; Assistant Secretary General, Office of Human Resources Management and Security Coordinator, United Nations, 1987-90; Assistant Secretary General, Programme Planning, Budget and Finance, Controller, 1990-92; Secretary General for United Nations. Honours: Trustee Distinguished Service Award. Address: United Nations, New York 10017, USA.

**ANONGBA Patrick Norbert B,** b. 3 February 1960, Abidjan. Physicist. m. Varela Maria Teresa, 2 sons, 1 daughter. Education: Physical Engineer, Department of Physics, 1985; Department of Physics, Ecole Polytechnique Federale de Lausanne; Doctor of Science, Physics of Condenced Matter, 1989. Appointments: Assistant, Ecole Polytechnique Federale de Lausanne, Switzerland, 1985-90; Postdoctoral Research Associate, Institute of Physique Experimentale, Universite de Lausanne, Switzerland, 1990-92; Research Associate, Max Planck Institut fur Metallforschung, Stuttgart, Germany, 1992-94; Assistant Professor, UFR Sciences de Structures de la Matiere et de Technolgie, Universite de Cocody, Cote d'Ivoire, 1995-97; Associate Professor, 1997-. Publications: Many publications. Memberships: Swiss Physical Society; New York Academy of Sciences; Japan Society for the Promotion of Sciences. Address: GBAGBA, BP 498, Bingerville, Cote D'Ivoire.

**ANSARI Rashida Anees,** b. 22 April 1952, Kamptee, Nagpur, India. Teacher. m. 1 son. Education: DEd, 1972-74; BA Hindi Sudhakar, 1995. Appointments: Teacher 1979-; Director, Nagpur Mahanagar Palika, Karmchari Corporation Bank, Nagpur. Honours: Mayor Award, 1994; Babasaheb Ambedkar Best Teacher Award, 1995. Memberships: President, Vaishali Nagpur, Bahuddeshy Mahila Mandal; Secretary, Ekta, Vidharbha; VP, Tulsi Education Society; VP, Anjuman Maleghnimat Committee; Director, Raza Convent & Raza Silai School; Member: Jaibal Vikas Mandal, Nagpur; Noushakti Mitra Mandal. Address: Director, Corporation Bank, Vaishalinagar Q No 7/1, Nagpur 440017 MS, India.

**ANTHONISEN George Rioch,** b. 31 July 1936, Boston, MA, USA. Sculptor. m. Ellen, 1 son, 1 daughter. Education: BA, University of Vermont, 1961; National Academy of Design,

1961-62; Art Students League, 1962-64; Dartmouth College Medical School, 1967. Appointments: Many Group, Solo and Public Exhibitions. Honours: Exemplary Achievement in the Arts Award; Sculptor in Residence. Address: Box 147, Solebury, PA 18963, USA.

**ANTIA H M**, b. 6 November 1955, Indore, India. Scientist. Education: BSc, Indore University, 1973; MSc, Indian Institute of Technology, Bombay, 1975; PhD, Bombay University, 1979. Appointments: Professor, Tata Institute of Fundamental Research, 1979-. Publications: About 50 Papers, Various Astrophysical Journals; Numerical Methods for Scientists and Engineers. Memberships: Fellow, Indian Academy of Sciences; Member, International Astronomical Union. Address: Tata Inst Fundamental Rsch, Homi Bhabba Rd, Mumbai 400005, India.

**ANTIPENKO Yevgeny**, b. 25 July 1923, Eupatoria, Ukraine. Scientist. m. Margarita Mikhailova, 1 son, 1 daughter. Education: MD, Military Medical Academy, St Petersburg, 1946; PhD, 1950; DSc, 1964; Research into problems of repair of chromosomes, cytogenetic effects of nonthermal intensity microwaves in mammalian and genetic consequences of environmental pollution by people. Appointments: Teacher, Military Medical Academy; Head, Department Nuclear Firing Ground, Semipalatinsk, Russia; Professor and Laboratory Head, Institute Radiology and Oncology, Scientific Research Centre Hygiene, National Institute of Health, Institute of Ecohygiene and Toxicology, Kiev. Publications: Monograph, Residual Phenomena of the Acute Radiation Disease, 1963; Articles in professional journals. Memberships: Society of Radiobiology; Genetical Association; Hygienic Association. Address: Institute of Ecohygiene & Toxicology, Heroiv Oborony St 6, 252022 Kiev, Ukraine.

**ANTONESCU Niculae Napoleon**, b. 20 October 1934, Ederile, Romania. University Professor. m. Antonescu Lucia, 1 son. Education: Petroleum Technical High School, 1948-52; Diplomat Engineer, Petroleum Equipment Faculty, Petroleum and Gas Institute, Bucharest, Romania, 1952-57; PhD, 1966-70; Illinois Institute of Technology, Chicago, USA, 1972-73. Appointments include: Mechanical Engineer, Oil Drilling Company, Craiova, Romania, 1957-59; Assistant Professor, Petroleum, Gas and Geology Institute, Bucharest, Romania, 1959-68; Assistant Professor, Petroleum and Gas Institute, Ploiesti, 1968-70; Associate Professor, PGI Ploiesti, 1970-76; University Professor, PGI, Ploiesti, 1976-. Publications: Author, Co-author, 9 books, 95 articles in the specialty review; 90 papers presented at different scientific meetings; 120 research works for various companies; 10 patents. Memberships: Founder Member, Vice President, Romanian Tribology Association; Romanian Maintenance Association; Romanian Engineers Association; Reviewer, Applied Mechanics Review; Vice President, Balkan Tribology Association; Romanian Association of Fracture Mechanics. Address: 39 Buouresti Boulevard, Plolesti 2000, Romania.

**ANTONOV Anton Nikolaev**, b. 19 September 1943, Shumen, Bulgaria. Physicist. m. Krasimira Antonova, 1 son, 1 daughter. Education: MSc, 1968; PhD, 1972; DSc, 1989. Appointments: Senior Researcher, 1984-91, Professor, 1991-, Head of Nuclear Theory Group, 1995-, Institute of Nuclear Research and Nuclear Energy, Sofia, Bulgaria. Publications: 2 books in Nuclear Physics, Oxford, OUP, 1988; Berlin Springer, 1993; 120 scientific papers in journals. Honour: Award for Physics and Maths, Bulgarian Academy of Sciences, 1982. Memberships: Union of Scientists of Bulgaria; Union of Bulgarian Physicists. Address: Institute of Nuclear Research and Nuclear Energy, Boulevard Tzarigradsco Shosse 72, 1784 Sofia, Bulgaria.

**ANTONOVA Tatyana S**, b. 27 October 1947, Schuya, Russia. Scientist, Biologist. m. Puhno Stepan, 1 son. Education: D, Moscow University, 1973; PhD, Leningrad University, 1979; Special Course, Timiryasev's Academy of Agricultural Sciences, 1984. Appointments: All Russian Research, Institute of Oil Crops; Assistant, Lab Sunfe, Immunity; Senior SO; Chief of Lab Biotechnology; Chief of Lab, Sunflower Immunity, 1998-. Memberships: All Russian Botanical Society. Address: All Russian Research Institute of Oil Crops, Filatov Str 17, 350038 Krasnodar, Russia.

**ANTOUN Mikhail**, b. 20 August 1946, Khartoum, Sudan. Professor. m. Slavomira, 1 son, 2 daughters. Education: BPharm, University of Khartoum, 1968; PhD, University of London, 1974. Appointments: Assistant Professor, Pharmacognosy, University of Khartoum, Sudan, 1974-78; Associate Professor, 1978-81, Senior Research Scientist, Purdue University, West Lafayette, USA, 1981-86; Associate Professor, Medicinal Chemistry, UPR School of Pharmacy, San Juan, 1986-92, Professor, Medicinal Chemistry and Pharmacognosy, Faculty Chair Professor, Department Head, 1993-; Visiting Professor, Research Associate, School of Pharmacy and Pharmacal Sciences, Purdue University, 1979-81. Publications: Several articles in professional journals. Honours: Senior Scholar, University of Khartoum, 1968-69; Teaching Fellow, University of London, 1969-73; Fellow, Linnean Society of London, 1974-; Sigma Xi, 1991-. Memberships: American Chemical Society; American Association of Colleges of Pharmacy; American Society of Pharmacognosy. Address: Calle A, 6 La Antillana Trujillo, Alto, PR 00976, USA.

**ANTSIFEROV Vladimir N**, b. 26 November 1933, Vladivosotok, Russia. Metallurgist. m. Ljubob Terentjevna, 1 daughter. Education: High education, 1957; Doctor of Technical Sciences, 1973; Professor, 1974. Appointments: Head of Department, Powder Metallurgy, Perm Polytechnical Institute, 1984-86; Director, Supervisor of Studies, Centre of Powder Metallurgy, 1986-. Publications: 350 publications; 12 monographs. Honour: Soros Professor, 1995-97. Memberships: Corresponding Member, Russian Academy of Sciences, 1991; New York Academy of Sciences, 1997. Address: Engineering Center of Power Metallurgy, Perm Polytechnical Institute, 6 Prospekt Politeknicheskii, Perm 614061, Russia.

**ANTEZELEVITCH Charles**, b. 25 March 1951, Israel. Director of Research. m. Brenda Reisner, 1 son, 1 daughter. Education: BA, Queens College, City University of New York, 1973; PhD, State University of New York Health Science Center, 1978. Appointments: Postdoctoral Fellow, Experimental Cardiology Department, Masonic Medical Research Lab, New York, 1977-80; Assistant Professor, SUNY Health Science Center, 1980-83; Research Scientist, Masonic Medical Research Laboratory, 1980-83; Associate Professor, SUNY Health Science Center, 1983-86; Senior Research Scientist, Masonic Meidcal Research Laboratory, 1984; Executive Director, 1984-; Research Professor, SUNY Health Science Center, 1987-95; Gordon K Moe Scholar, 1987-; Professor of Pharmacology, SUNY Health Science Center, 1995-. Publications: 107 Original Articles, Book Chapters; 143 Abstracts. Honours: Van Horne Award; Fellow, Cardiovascular Section, American Physiological Society; Gordon K Moe Scholar; Senior Investigator to First Place Winner of Young Investigator Award; Distinguished Service Award; Leonard Horowitz Lecturer; Charles Henry Johnson Medal; Fellow, American College of Cardiology; Prsident, International Cardiac Electrophysiology Society; Many More Honours. Memberships: AHA; Basic Science Council; FASEB; APS; ISHR; ISCH; Cardiac Electrophysiology Society; New York Academy of

Sciences; Many other Memberships. Address: Masonic Medical Research Lab, 2150 Bleecker Street, Utica, NY 13501, USA.

**AOKI Masaki,** b. 5 November 1934, Shizuoka-ken, Japan. Educator. m. Nao Okai, 2 daughters. Education: MA, Tokyo Metropolitan University, 1967. Appointments: Professor, Matsuyama University, 1968. Memberships: French and French Literary Society of Japan; Japan Alpine Club; Himalayan Adventure Trust of Japan. Address: 2-5-25 Shoenji, 790-0904 Matsuyama, Japan.

**APOLLONOV Victor V,** b. 8 July 1945, Moscow, Russia. Physicist. m. Zoy Dobronevskaya, 1 daughter. Education: Diploma of Doctor, 1982 Diploma of Professor, 1991. Appointment: Head of Department, High Power Lasers, over 15 years. Address: Vavilov St 38, 117942 Moscow, Russia.

**APOSTOLOS-CAPPADONA Diane,** b. 10 May 1948, Trenton, NJ. University Professor. Education: BA, Special Honours, Religion, The George Washington University, 1970; MA, Religion, 1973; MA, Religion and Culture, The Catholic University of America, 1979; PhD, American Civilization, The George Washington University, 1988. Appointments: Lecturer in Religion and Art, Bellarmine College, 1974; Visiting Lecturer in Religion and Art, University of St Thomas, 1979; Lecturer in Religion and Arts, Humanities Institute, 1979-80; Lecturer in Religion, Mount Vernon College, 1980-85; Lecturer in Religion, The George Washington University, 1981-86; Visiting Lecturer in Religion and the Arts, The Catholic University of America, 1985, 1986, 1989; Visiting Faculty, Coolen House, 1992; Teaching Fellow, Graduate Theological Foundation, 1989-93; Adjunct Faculty in Christianity and Art, Pacific School of Religion, 1985-86, 1988-; Professorial Lecturer in Religion and Art, Georgetown University, 1978-; Visiting Professor, Sophia University, 1999; Adjunct Professor, Liberal Studies Programme, Georgetown University, 1985-; Visiting Research Professor, Centre for Muslim Christian Understanding, Georgetown University, 1996-. Publications: Many publications, Field of Religion, Art and Gender Studies. Honours: Fellowship, Centre for the Study of World Religions; Fellowship, National Endowment for the Humanities; Biography International; Foremost Women of the Twentieth Century; The World Who's Who of Women; The International Authors and Writers Who's Who; Many other Honours. Memberships: College Art Association; American Academy of Religion; The Society for Art, Religion and Contemporary Culture; Edward F Albee Foundation; Alden B Dow Creative Centre. Address: Ctr Muslim-Christian Understanding, Georgetown University ICC #260, Washington, DC 20057, USA.

**APOSTOLOY Anton,** b. 30 May 1951, Sofia, Bulgaria. Physicist. 1 daughter. Education: MS, Sofia University, 1974; PhD, Polymer Chemistry, 1993. Appointments: Physicist, Institute of Physical Chemistry, 1976-83; Research Associate, Institute for Protection Metals from Corrosion, 1983-84; Research Associate, Institute for Computing Technique, 1984-85; Research Associate, Laboratory on Structure and Properties of Polymers, 1985-1998; Research Associate, 1998-. Publications: Co-Author, Approximately 30 Articles, International Polymer Journals. Memberships: International Union of Crystallography; Union of Physicists in Bulgaria. Address: 116 Geo Milev Str, Bl 57 Apt 42, 1574 Sofia, Bulgaria.

**APPA Anna Anikó Kovacs,** b. 25 October 1948, Budapest, Hungary. Poet. Writer. m. Anthony Michael. Education: Diploma, Writer's Digest School; Diploma, Christian Writing School; CPN, Certified Professional Nutritionist; MREd, Adult Education; Teachers Diploma Graduate Studies; MA, 1983; BS, 1974-76. Appointments: Biology, Botany Research Assistant,

1969-74; Histology Lab Technician, Assistant, 1973-75; Office Manager, Medical, Business Assistant, 1978-79; Faculty Assistant, Manuscript Editor, Coordinator, 1979-81; Instructor, Supervisor, Counselor, Residential Advisor, 1981-83; Medical Executive, Clinical Research Assistant, 1985-86; Program Assistant, 1986-89; Science Writer, Editor, Abstractor, Freelance Academic Editing, 1989-91; Project Manager, Assistant Librarian, Gordon Conwell Theology Seminary, 1991-92; Biology, Latin Instructor, Essex Christian Academy, 1992-95; Biology, Botany Instructor, Gordon College, 1994-96; Poet, Writer, 1996-. Editor of: The Great Ragweed Season of 1984, Fact or Fantasy; A Comparison of Soluble Seed Proteins of Certain Acer Species; Many other Publications. Honours: Who's Who of Intellectuals, International Biographical Centre; International Woman of the Year; International Poetry Hall of Fame; Poet of the Year; Many other Honours and Awards. Memberships: National Association of Female Executives; Christian Writers Institute; Biology Advisory Committee; Many other memberships. Address: P O Box 2055, South Hamilton, MA 01982, USA.

**APPENROTH Klaus J,** b. 19 November 1948, Eisenach, Thur, Germany. Chemist. m. Dorothea Ruda, 1 son, 1 daughter. Education: Diploma Chemistry, 1972; Dr rer nat, 1978; Dr habil rer nat, 1991. Appointments: Scientific Assistant, Privatdozent, permanent academic position. Publications: 65 papers in photophysiology of plants especially duckweeds. Memberships: European Society Photobiology; American Society Photobiology; German Botanical Society. Address: University of Jena Inst Gen Botany, Dornburger Strasse 159, D-07743, Jena, Germany.

**APPIAH James Peter King,** b. 16 February 1951, Baman, Kumasi, Ghana. Writer; Apostle. m. Angela Mabel Asare, 1 daughter. Education: Unesco Certificate in Writing and Publishing, 1972; Certificate of Completion, Morris Cerullo School of Ministry, San Diego, 1981; BA, Literary Studies, Pacific Western University, 1990; Diploma in Journalism, Story Writing, ICS Scranton, 1993. Appointments: Library Assistant, Ghana Library, 1973-76; Founder, President, Followers of Christ International Church, FOCIC, 1974; Director, Adonten Literary Works, Kumasi, 1976-95; Ordained Bishop, Universal Ministries, 1980. Publications: The Lord of Praise, 1988; Prayer, The Key to a Triumphant Christian Living, 1992; Overcomers in the Blood, 1995; The Meaning of Pentecost, 1995; Ode to the Dead, Dedicated to the Princess of the People, 1998; Many other publications. Honours: Mondello Poetry International Award, First Prize, 1987; Honoured, City of Palermo (Unione Quartieri), 1988. Memberships: Morris Cerullo World Evangelism, Italy 1995-; United Christians Association in Italy, 1996; United Christians Association, 1998-; Ghana Young Pioneers; Ghana Youth Club; Ghana Association of Writers; United Christian Association; Christian Writers Forum; Member of the Adonten Royal Family of Asante, Mansa Nana. Address: Via San Giovanni, Bosco 126, 41100 Modena, Italy.

**APPLEBAUM Eric Scott,** b. 19 May 1962, Pasadena, California, USA. Physician; Allergist. m. Sandra Applebaum, 3 daughters. Education: BA, Queens College, Flushing, New York, 1983; MD, Albert Einstein College of Medicine, Bronx, New York, 1987. Appointments: Faculty of Medicine and Paediatrics, Albert Einstein College of Medicine, 1993-94; Medical Director, Allergic and Asthmatic Comprehensive Care of New Jersey, 1994-. Honours: Phi Beta Kappa, 1982; Distinction, Research, 1987; Several Scholarships. Memberships: Diplomate, American Board of Internal Medicine, American Board of Allergy and Immunology. Address: Allergic and Asthmatic Comprehensive Care PC, 50 Cherry Hill Road, Suite 301, Parsippany, NJ 07054-1101, USA.

**APRIKYAN Vardan Sergey,** b. 23 April 1957, Orenburg, Russia. Scientist. Education: DVM, Zoo Veterinary Institute, 1980; PhD, Institute of Immunology, Moscow, 1988; DSc, Institute of Immunology, 1996. Appointments: Laboratory Assistant, 1974; Post Graduate, 1984-87; Junior Researcher, Senior Scientist, Head of Project Group, Institute of Biochemistry, Armenia, 1988-; Leading Scientist, Head of Interdepartmental Project Group, 1997-98. Publications: More than 100 Scientific Publications. Honours: Honorary Awards; Competition of Young Scientists. Memberships: Armenian Society for Immunologists; Russian Society for Immunologists; International Society for Neurochemistry; New York Academy of Sciences. Address: Tbilisian Road 10 Ap 12, 375052 Yerevan, Republic of Armenia.

**ARAI Norio,** b. 17 September 1944, Yokosuka, Japan. Professor. m. Naoko Ito, 2 sons, 1 daughter. Education: BS Che, Nagoya University, Japan, 1967; MS Che, Nagoya University, Japan, 1969; PhD Che, Nagoya University, Japan, 1973. Appointments: Assistant Professor, Nagoya University, Japan, 1972-79; Associate Professor, Nagoya University, Japan, 1979-92; Professor, Nagoya University, Japan, 1992-. Publications: Special Issue of Energy Conversion and Management, 1997; More than 150 original papers. Honours: SCEJ Best Paper Award, 1982; ASME Awards, 1997, 1998. Memberships: ASME; AICHE; AIAA; Institute of Energy; Combustion Institute. Address: Rsch Ctr Advanced Energy, Nagoya University, Nagoya 464 8603, Japan.

**ARAKI Kenji,** b. 12 October 1934, Yokohama, Japan. University Professor. m. Kaneko, 1 son, 2 daughters. Education: B Eng, 1958, Yokohama National University, Japan; Dr Eng, 1970, University of Tokyo. Appointments: Professor, 1984-, Head of Dr course of Production Sciences Majors, 1994-96, and Head of Information Processing Centre, 1995-97, Saitama University; Invited Professor, National Tsing Hua University, Taiwan, 1975. Publication: Editor, Proceedings of the 3rd JHPS International Symposium on Fluid Power, Japan, 1996. Honours: Prizes for Best Paper, Fluid Power Technology Promotion Foundation, 1984, Japan Hydraulics and Pneumatics Society; 1996, The Society of Instrument and Control Engineers, 1998. Memberships: Japan-China Science & Technology Exchange Association, 1995-; Japan-Italy Science & Technology Cooperative Project (Artificial Intelligence), 1992-; Director, Japan Hydraulics and Pneumatic Society, 1990, 1992-98. Address: Saitama University Faculty Engineering, 255 Shimo okubo, Satana Urawa 358, Japan.

**ARAKKAL Antony L,** b. 15 December 1937, Kattoor, Kerala, India. Vice President of Advanced Engineering. m. Bridget Arakkal, 1 son. Education: BSc Engineering, 1964, Mech University of Kerala, India; MSISE, 1972, Illinois Institute of Technology, Chicago, Illinois. Appointments: President, A.E. Inc, 1986-93; Vice President Engineering, Airtex Products, 1993-. Publications: Hydraulic Machinery, 1968; Unipole Motors, 1981. Memberships: President, Institute of Industrial Engineers, Tristate Chapter; Former President, Society of Manufacturers, NC State; Member, International Rotary Club; Researcher, Patent for Unipole Motor. Address: RR3 Box 611E, Fairfield, IL 629837 9565, USA.

**ARANO Julio,** b. 10 November 1952, La Pae, Bolivia. Biomedical Engineer. m. Ruth Mary Quiroza, 1 son, 1 daughter. Education: University Costa Rica, 1981; University of Mayor de San Andrais, La Paz, 1997. Appointments: Founder, Professor, Electronics Systems Department, 1977-; Assistant Professor, University of Mayor de San Andris, 1978. Address: Calle Aviador #5, Casilla, 312275 San Miguel La Paz, Bolivia.

**ARBAB Ali Syed,** b. 1 October 1963, Kushtia, Bangladesh. Physician. m. Mahbuba Begum, 1 son, 1 daughter. Education: Bachelor of Medicine and Surgery, 1988; Doctor of Philosophy, 1998. Appointments: Medical Officer, Nuclear Medical Centers, 1989-95; Senior Medical Officer, 1995-98; Instructor, Radiology, Yamanashi Medical University, 1998-. Publications: Over 25 publications in international journals. Memberships: Society of Nuclear Medicine; Japanese Society of Nuclear Medicine; Bangladesh Atomic Energy Scientist Association. Address: Radiology, Yamanashi Medical University, Yamanashi 409-3898, Japan.

**ARBURY Andrew Stephen,** b. 3 March 1953, Midland, Michigan, USA. Art Historian. Education: BA, Albion College, 1975; MA, 1978, PhD, 1992, Rutgers University. Career: Art Historian, Curator, Roanoke College, 1984-88; Associate Professor, 1988-, Curator, 1997-, Radford University. Publications: Contributor to Dictionary of American Art, The Dictionary of Art, The Encyclopedia of Comparative Iconography. Honours: Fulbright Scholarship, 1981-83; Phi Beta Kappa. Memberships: College Art Association; Southeastern College Art Conference; Visual Resources Association; 16th Century Studies; American Association of Museums; American Society for Hispanic Art Historical Studies. Address: Radford University, Powell Hall, Box 6965, Radford, VA 24142, USA.

**ARCHULETA Keith Anthony,** b. 13 March 1955, Denver, Colorado, USA. Educational and Organisational Consultant. m. Iris, 1 son. Education: BA, honours, African and African-American Studies, 1978, BA, distinction, Communications, 1978, Stanford University; MA, Nonprofit Administration, University of San Francisco, 1992. Appointments: Founder, President, Emerald Consulting, 1992-; Project Administrator, Arts Education Funders Collaborative, 1994-; Site Administrator, Young African-American Achievers Program, 1995-97; Project Facilitator, SFUSD Elementary Arts Program, 1997-. Honours: Dinkelspiel Award for Service to Undergraduate Education, Stanford University, 1978; California Assembly Commendation, 1979; Outstanding Young Man of America, 1983. Memberships: Association for Supervision and Curriculum Development; Business for Social Responsibility; Fellowship of Companies for Christ International. Address: Emerald Consulting, 665 Dartmoor Lane Ste 154, Hayward, CA 94544, USA.

**ARDELEAN Petru,** b. 24 November 1943, Mihalt, Romania. Physicist. Niculina Ene, 1 son. Education: MS, Physics, University of Bucharest, 1967; Doctorate, University Babes, Bolyai, Cluj, 1979. Appointments: Physicist, Institute of Isotope and Molecular Technology, 1967-75; Researcher, 1975-90; Senior Researcher III, 1990-94; Senior Researcher II, 1994-. Publications: Introduction in Mass Spectrom, 1978; 51 papers published in journals. Memberships: Romanian Society of Physics; Romanian Mass Spectrometry Society; New York Academy of Sciences. Address: P O Box 700, R O 3400 Cluj Napoca 5, Romania.

**ARDILA Ruben,** b. 7 July 1942, San Vicente, Colombia. Psychologist. Widower, 1 son. Education: PhD Experimental Psychology, 1970, University of Nebraska, USA. Appointments and Memberships: Past President, Interamerican Society of Psychology; International Society of Comparative Psychology; Former Chairperson, several research institutions; Member: American Psychological Association; International Association of Applied Psychology; and others. Publications: 24 scientific books. Address: Apartado 88754, Bogota, Colombia.

**ARDREY-CURRY Saundra Elvira,** b. 26 August 1953, Louisville, Georgia, USA. Professor. m. William, 1 son, 1 daughter. Education: BA, Winston-Salim State University, 1975; PhD, The Ohio State University, 1983; MA, The Ohio State University, 1985. Appointments: Visiting Lecturer, University of North Carolina, 1978; Assistant Professor, 1983-88; Associate Professor, Western Kentucky University, 1998-; Director, African American Studies Department, 1995-. Publications: The Maturation of Black Political Power, 1990; Cleveland and the Politics of Resurgence, 1992; The Political Behavior of Black Women, 1993; Kentucky and the State of Human Rights, 1996. Honours: Outstanding Young Women of America, 1984; Rodney Higgins Award, 1989; University Outstanding Service Award, 1990; Invited Speaker at National Black Studies Conference, 1993; Outstanding African Americans, 1995. Memberships: The National Council of Black Political Scientists; National Association for the Advancement of Colored People; Alpha Kappa Alpha Sorority; National Council of Negro Women; The Washington Center for Internships and Seminars Liason Advisory Board. Address: Dept of Government, Western Kentucky University, Grise Hall, Bowling Green, KY 42101, USA.

**ARGIROV Julian Panajotov,** b. 19 February 1960, Sofia, Bulgaria. Researcher. Education: MSc in Heat and Mass Transfer Engineering, Sofia Technical University, 1986; Postgraduate studies, Institute of Nuclear Research and Nuclear Energy, 1990-93; PhD, 1999. Appointments: Solar Energy and New Energy Sources Laboratory, 1986-90; Fire PSA Leader, Risk Engineering Ltd, 1993-95; Researcher, Institute of Nuclear Research and Nuclear Energy, Sofia, 1995-. Publications: Articles in scientific journals in field of PSA methods; Papers at international conferences. Membership: New York Academy of Sciences, 1997-. Address: Institute of Nuclear Research and Nuclear Energy, Tzarigradsko chausee 72, Sofia 1784, Bulgaria.

**ARGTRIS John,** b. 19 August 1916, Volos, Germany. Professor. m. Inga-Lisa, 1 son. Education: 3rd Gymnasium, Athens; Technical Universities, Athens, Munich and Zurich, 1937-39. Career includes: Professor, Aeronautical Structures, University of London, Imperial College of Science and Technology, 1955-75, Visiting Professor, 1975-78, now Emeritus Professor; Director, Institute for Computer Applications, Stuttgart, 1984-. Publications include: Handbook of Aeronautics, vol 1, 1952; Energy Theorems and Structural Analysis, 1960; Modern Fuselage Analysis and the Elastic Aircraft, 1963; Recent Advances in Matrix Methods of Structural Analysis, 1964; Introduction into the Finite Element Method, vols I, II and III, 1986-88; Dynamics of Structures, 1991; An Overview of Aerolasticity, 1992; An Exploration of Chaos, 1994. Honours include: Gold Medal, Land Baden-Württemberg, 1980; Grand Cross of Merit, Germany, 1985; Grand Cross of Merit with Star, Germany, 1989; Henri Coenda Medal in Gold, 1992; Grand Cross of the Phoenix, Greece, 1996; Gold Medal of Argonauts, 1996. Memberships include: New York Academy of Sciences; ASME; National Academy of Engineering; Aeronautical Society of India; Greek Association of Computational Mechanics. Address: Institute for Computer Applications, 27 Pfaffenwaldring, 70569 Stuttgart, Germany.

**ARHONDONIS Bartholomew,** b. 29 February 1940, Imvros, Turkey. Ecumenical Patriarch. Education: Graduate, High Honors, Theological School of Halki, 1961. Appointments: Assistant Dean, Theological School of Halki, 1968; Director, Private Patriarchal Office, 1972; Member, Holy and Sacred Synod, 1974-. Honours: Congressional Gold Medal. Memberships: Society of Canon Law of the Oriental Churches; Founding Member and Vice President, Faith and Order Committee of the World Council of Churches; Vice Preside Fellow of the Orthodox Academy of Crete, Greece; Honor Member, Pro-Oriente Foundation in Vienna. Address: R* Patrikhanesi Fener, TR 34220, Istanbul, Turkey.

**ARINZE Emmanuel Nnakenyi,** b. 25 December 19 Sapele, Nigeria. Museologist. m. Maria Ndidi, 1 son, daughter. Education: Teachers Grade III Certificate, 1961; B Sociology, University of Ibadan, 1971; MEd, Educati University of Lagos, 1982; MSc, Sociology, University of J 1987; Criterion Referenced Implementation Certificate, 19 Appointments: Teacher, 1960-71; Museum Education Offic 1972; Co-ordinator, Nigerian National Museums Society, 19 1980-82; Head of Education Services, 1972-89; Cura National Museum, Jos and Lagos, 1974-78; Princip UNESCO Training Centre, Jos, 1974-76; Co-ordinator, Lac Museum Study Group, 1977-82; Head of Administrati 1978-80; Lecturer, Adult Education, 1979-82; Principal, Cer for Museum Studies, Jos, 1983-89; Assistant Direc Museums and Monuments, 1986-89; Director, Museums a Monuments, 1989-91; Lecturer, 1990-95; Chief Execut Heritage Consultancy Bureau, 1991-; Chairman, West Afric Museums Programme, 1992-; President, Commonwea Association of Museums, 1995-; Director, National Institute Cultural Orientation, 1993-96. Publications: Many professio works accompliched. Honour: Fellow, Salzburg Semir Memberships: ICOM; CAM; Museums Association of Nige Nigerian Folklore Society; West African Museums Programr Royal African Society, London; Botswana Society; Friends the Museum Association of Liberia; Friends of the Hist Museum of Ouidah; Lions Club International; MAG 55 Cl Plateau Club. Address: National Orientation Agency, PMB Abuja, Nigeria.

**ARITA Tatsuo,** b. 25 March 1928, Tokyo, Japan. Univers Professor. m. Kumiko Shigeta, 1 daughter. Educati Graduate, Faculty Political Economy, 1950, Graduate Sch 1951, DComm, 1986, Waseda University. Appointmer Professor, Meijo University, 1975-; Dean, Faculty Commerce, Chairman Graduate School of Commer 1989-91; Director, Placement Office, 1993-97; Chief Profess Graduate School of Commerce, 1995-. Publications: Pu Policy of Small Businesses in Postwar Japan, award winni 1990; Study of Small Businesses - History, Theory & Pol 1997. Memberships: Japan Economical Policy Associati Trustee 1983-; Japan Association Small Business Studies, V Chairman 1992-95, Managing Trustee, 1995-. Address: ; Miyukiyama Tenpaku, 468-0075 Nagoya Aichi, Japan.

**ARLINGHAUS Sandra Judith Lach,** b. 18 April 19 Elmira, NY, USA. Adjunct Professor m. William C Arlingha 1 son. Education: AB Maths, Vassar College; MA Geograp Wayne State University; Graduate study in Mathemat University of Chicago, University of Toronto, Wayne St University; PhD Theoretical Geography, University Michig Appointments: Founder and Editor, Solstice: An Electro Journal of Mathematics and Geography, 1990-; Found Director, Institute of Mathematical Geography, 1983-; Adju (full) Professor of Mathematical Geography Population-Environment Dynamics, University Michigan, Sch of Natural Resources and Environment, 1994-; Member, Bo of Trustees, Community Systems Foundation, 1994-; Planr Commissioner, City of Ann Arbor, Mayoral appointment, 199 Founder, International Society of Spatial Sciences, div Community Systems Foundation, 1995-; Director, Spa Analysis Div, Director of Fellowship Training Division, C 1996-; Adjunct Professor, College of Architecture and Url Planning, University of Michigan, 1997; Review Mathematical Reviews, 1991-. Publications: 3 handbooks book length refereed monographs; 42 articles in refereed professional journals and books; Numerous published reviews, invited articles, abstracts and reports. Memberships: Fellow, American Geographical Society; Regional Science Association; Association of American Geographers; American Mathematical Society; Mathematical Association of America; Michigan Society of Planning Officials. Address: University of Michigan School of Natural Resources, Ann Arbor, MI 48109, USA.

**ARNEZ Maja,** b. 17 June 1958, Ljubljana, Slovenia. Medical Doctor. m. Zoran Marij Arnez, 1 son, 1 daughter. Education: MD, Faculty of Medicine, University of Ljubljana, 1984, Specialst Consultant, Pediatrics, 1991, MSc, 1998. Appointments: Chief, Out Patients, Pediatric Clinic, University Department of Infectious Disease, University Medical Centre; Assistant Professor, Infectious Disease and Epidemiology, 1995-. Publications: Several articles in professional medical journals. Memberships: Slovenian Medical Association; Slovenian Pediatric Association. Address: Ribniska 5, 1000 Ljubljana, Slovenia.

**ARNEZ Zoran Marij,** b. 7 April 1953, Ljubljana, Slovenia. Medical Doctor; Surgeon; Professor of Surgery. m. Maja Arnez, 1 son, 1 daughter. Education: Medical Faculty, Ljubljana, 1971-76; Postgraduate, University Medical Center, Ljubljana, 1977; Specialist Certificate, 1983; PhD, 1989. Appointments: Resident, General Surgery, 1977-83, Member, Microsurgical Team, 1981, Professional Director, Department of Surgery, 1997, University Medical Center, Ljubljana; Specialist, 1983, Consultant, 1989, Head, 1990, University Department of Plastic Surgery and Burns, Ljubljana. Publications: Several articles in professional journals. Honours: Preseren Award, Students Research, 1976; Fellowship, Boris Kidric Foundation, 1977; Innovator of the Year, Ljubljana Television, 1987; Marko Godina Fellowship, 1987. Memberships: Slovenian Medical Society; International Society for Burn Injuries; Mediterranean Burns Club; Slovenian Society of Plastic Surgery; European Burns Association; International Society for Plastic, Reconstructive and Aesthetic Surgery; European Association of Plastic Surgeons. Address: Ribniska 5, 1000 Ljubljana, Slovenia.

**ARNIS Efstathios Constantinos,** b. 14 April 1931, Thermon, Greece. Designer in Mechanical Engineering. Education: Associate Student, Athens University, 1950-51, 1961-70; Technological Schools Benos-Palmer Graduate, Designer in Mechanical Engineering, Athens, 1972-. Appointment: Private practice in designings of mechanical engineering, 1952-94; Retired, 1994. Publications: 4 publications referring to the scientific field of energization of isolated physical systems. Memberships: Expert Secretary, The Hellenic Astronautical Society; Active member, The New York Academy of Sciences; Associate member, American Institute of Aeronautics-Astronautics; American Association for the Advancement of Science; The Planetary Society. Address: 10 Gortynos Street, Athens 112 54 Greece.

**ARORA Jagdish,** b. 15 January 1956, Udaipur, India. Librarian. m. Anita Arora, 1 son. Education: BSc, Biological Sciences, 1975; BLibSc, 1976; MLISc, 1977; MA, Political Science, 1980; PhD, Library Science, 1992. Career: Assistant Documentation Officer, ICRISAT, Patanchru, India, 1980-83; Documentation Officer, National Institute of Immunology, India, 1983-91; Deputy Librarian, Indian Institute of Technology, Delhi, 1991-. Publications: Several research papers. Honours: Need-cum-Merit Scholarship, Government of Rajasthan, 1971-75; CSIR Travel Fellowship, 1992, 1995; DST Travel Fellowship, 1995; Fulbright Fellowship in Library and Information Science, 1997-98. Memberships: Indian Library

Association; Medical Library Association of India. Address: Indian Institute of Technology, New Delhi, India.

**AROTIBA Godwin Toyin,** b. 2 May 1960, Mopa, Kogi State, Niger. Oral and Maxillofacial Surgeon. m. Marion M Arotiba. Education: BDS, 1985, College of Medicine, University of Lagos; FWACS, 1992, FMCDS, 1995, Lagos University Teaching Hospital. Appointments: Registrar, Senior Registrar, Lagos University Teaching Hospital, 1987-92; Lecturer, Consultant, College of Medicine, University of Lagos, 1992-97; Senior Lecturer, Consultant, 1998-. Publications: 15 articles in learned journals; 2 dissertations, 1991, 1995. Honours: 9 undergraduate awards including: Vice Chancellor's Prize, 1985; College Faculty Prize, 1982, 1985; Provost's Prize, 1982, 1985; 3 Fellowships, 1995, 1996, 1996. Memberships: Fellow, International Association Oral and Maxillofacial Surgeons; Fellow, International College of Surgeons; Fellow, International Union Against Cancer. Address: Dept Oral and Maxillofacial, College Medicine, University of Lagos, 12003 Lagos, Nigeria.

**ARSENE Melania Liliana,** b. 11 December 1956, Bucharest, Romania. Biochemist, Researcher. Education: BSc, University of Bucharest, 1979; MSC, University of Bucharest, 1980; PhD, University of Bucharest, 1998. Appointments: Biochemist, Drugs Factory, Bucharest, 1980-83; Biosynthesis Factory, Calafat, 1983; Researcher, Chemistry and Biochemsitry Energetics Institute, 1983-90; Senior Researcher, Chemistry Research Institute, 1990-. Publications: Over 40 Articles; 80 Scientific Communications to Professional Journals. Memberships: Romanian Biological Society; Romanian Biotechnology Bioengineering Society; New York Academy of Sciences. Address: Cozla nr 8 Bl A7 Apt 49, 74636 Bucharest, Romania.

**ARTHUR Owen Seymour,** b. 17 October 1949, Barbados. Economist. m. Beverley J Batchelor. Education: BA, Economics and History; MSc, Economics. Appointments: Assistant Economic Planner, 1974, Chief Economic Planner, 1979, National Planning Agency, Jamaica; Member, Barbados Senate, 1983; Member of Parliament, 1984; Leader of the Opposition, 1993; Prime Minister, 1994. Publications: Several articles in professional journals. Memberships: Board of Directors, Barbados Industrial Development Corporation, Central Bank of Barbados; Chairman, Barbados Agricultural Development Corporation; Barbados Economic Society; Barbados External Communications (BET) Sports Club. Address: Prime Ministers Office, Government Headquarters, Bay Street, St Michael, Barbados.

**ARUNCHALAM A,** b. 8 May 1970, Sivakasi, India. Lecturer. m. Ms Kusum. Education: BSc (Hons), 1990, MSc, Botany, 1992, Madurai Kamaraj University, Botany, Madurai, India; PhD, Botany, North-Eastern Hill University, Shillong, India. Appointments: Research Assigments: North- Eastern Hill University, Shillong, India, 1992-94; Senior Research Fellow, North-Eastern Hill University, 1994-96; Lecturer in Forestry, North-Eastern Regional Institute of Science and Technology, Nirjuli, India, 1996-. Publications: In refereed journals (national and international) and other professional journals; 26 research papers in scientific journals (national and international), 2 in books and edited volumes; Abstacts at symposia, workshops, conferences; popular articles in education journals and a newspaper. Honours: Junior and Senior Research Fellowships, Council of Scientific and Industrial Research, 1992-94, 1994-96; Science and Engineering Research Council's Visiting Fellowship, Department of Science and Technology, Government of India, 1998-99. Memberships include: President, Botanic Club, Department of Botany, North Eastern Hill University, 1994-95; Life Member, Arunachal Pradesh

Society of Land & Water Resources Management; Life Member, Indian Association of Soil and Water Conservationists, Dehra Dun; Life Member, Indian Society of Soil Biology and Ecology, Bangalore; Life Member, Indian Association of Tree Sciences, Solan. Address: NE Regional Institute of Science, Department of Forestry, Nirjuli 791 109, India.

**ARUTYUNOV Suren G**, b. 12 March 1938, Grozny City. General Director. m. Aeutyunova Dina Petrovna, 2 daughters. Education: Graduate, Khavcov Aviation Institute, 1961. Appointments: Foreman, Chief Foreman, Bureau Chief, Deputy Shop Manager, Deputy Chief Inspector, Deputy Chief Engineere, Komsomolsk Na Amuze Aviation Plant, 1961-66; Duputy Director, USSR Ministry of Aviation Industry Headquarters, 1978-82; General Director, Tushinsky Medicine, Manufacturing Plant, Public Company, 1982-. Publications: Over 30 Scientific Research and Engineering Papers. Honours: Symbol of Honour Order; Red Flag of Labour Order; Honorary Manufacturer of Russia. Memberships: Society of Logistics Engineers; Associated Member of International Academy of Informatisation; Associated Member of Russian Federation Academy of Transport. Address: Sushinskiy Machine Bldg Plant Stock Co, Svobada Street 35, 123362 Moscow, Russia.

**ARYSTANBEKOVA Akmaral**, b. 12 May 1948, Alma-Ata, Kazakhstan. Diplomat; Ambassador Extraordinary and Plenipontentiary. Education: PhD, Chemistry, Kazakh State University, 1975. Appointments: Member of the Kazakh Parliament, 1985-90; Chairman, Society of Friendship with Foreign Countries, 1983-89; Minister for Foreign Affairs of Kazakhstan, 1989-91; First Permanent Representative of Kazakhstan to the UN, 1992-. Publications: 10 Publications; Several Articles on International Affairs. Honours: State Award in Recognition of Distinguished State Service, 1996. Memberships: International Association of Permanent Representatives to the UN. Address: Permanent Mission of Kazakhstan to UN, 866 U N Plz Rm 586, New York, NY 10017-1822, USA.

**ASAKAWA Takeo**, b. 17 August 1936, Osaka, Japan. Professor. m. Mizohata Junko, 2 sons. Education: MD, Osaka University Medical School, 1962; PhD, Osaka University Graduate School of Medicine, 1967. Appointments: Assistant Professor, Osaka University Medical School, 1967; Career Investigator (Professor Earl W Sutherland, Nobel Prize Laureate) Fellow, The American Heart Association, USA, 1973-1975; Lecturer, 1973, Visiting Assistant Professor, 1975, Miami University School of Medicine; Associate Professor, Kumamoto University School of Medicine, 1977; Professor, Saga Medical School, 1979-; Councilor, Saga Medical School; Director, University Library; Director, Radioisotope Research Center. Honour: The Prize of The Japanese Journal of Pharmacology, 1996. Memberships: Japanese Biochemical Society; Japanese Pharmacological Society; Japanese Society for Neurochemistry; Japanese Inflammation Society. Address: Department of Pharmacology, Saga Medical School, 5-1-1 Nabeshima, Saga 849-8501, Japan.

**ASCHWANDEN Felix**, b. 22 February 1942, Lugano, Switzerland. Electrical Engineer. 1 son, 1 daughter. Education: Diploma, Electrical Engineer, Swiss Federal Institute of Technology, Zurich. Appointments: Design Engineer, Laboratories RCA Lts, 1973-. Publications: IEEE Transactions on Consumer Electronics. Honours: Chester W Sall Memorial Paper Award; 25 US Patents Granted. Memberships: IEEE. Address: 29 Alpenstrasse, 8800 Thalwil, Switzerland.

**ASHBACHER Charles**, b. 24 September 1954, Fort Riley, Kansas, USA. Computer Scientist; Mathematician; Writer. 1 daughter. Education: BS, 1980, Mount Mercy College, Cedar Rapids. Appointments: Instructor, Dept Mathematical Sciences, Mount Mercy College, 1983-89; Programmer, Analyst, Dept Physics and Astronomy, University of Iowa, Iowa City, 1990-92; Research Scientist, Decisionmark Corporation, Cedar Rapids, 1993-97; President, Owner, Charles Ashbacher Technologies, Hiawatha, Iowa, 1997-. Publications: Over 30 papers in mathematics and computing; Book review editor, Journal of Recreational Mathematics; PC software reviews editor, Mathematics and Computer Education; Videotape reviews editor, Mathematics and Computer Education; Books: An Introduction to the Smarandache Function, 1995; Collection of Problems on Smarandache Notions, 1996; Pluckings From the Tree of Smarandache Notions and Sequences, 1998. Memberships: Mathematical Association of America; American Mathematical Society; Association for Computing Machinery; Institute of Electrical and Electronic Engineers; AMA 2 Year Colleges; American Association for Artificial Intelligence; American Association for the Advancement of Science; School Science and Mathematics; Fibonacci Association; Duodecimal Society. Address: 119 Northwood Drive, Hiawatha, IA 52233-1407, USA.

**ASHKENAZY Vladimir**, b. 6 July 1937, Gorky, USSR. Musician. m. Thorunn Sofia Johannsdottir, 2 sons, 3 daughters. Education: Moscow Central School of Music, 1945-55; Moscow Conservatory, 1955-63. Appointments: Chief Conductor, Royal Philharmonic Orchestra, 1987-95; Chief Conductor, Deutsches Symphony Orchestra, 1989-2000; Chief Conductor Czech Philharmonic Orchestra, 1998-. Address: Kappelistr 15, 6045 Meggen, Switzerland.

**ASHRAF Mohammad Ghulam Rasool**, b. 9 July 1948, Nagpur, India. Educator. m. Zaheda Bano, 2 sons, 1 daughter. Education: BSc, 1969, MA Urdu, 1980, Nagpur University; BEd, 1972, Marathwada University; Training course in: New Mathematics and Science, 1970, New Education Policy, 1987, Government of Maharashtra, Population Education, 1996, State Council of Educational Research and Training, Pune. Appointments: Mathematics and Science Teacher, Islamic Urdu High School, Nagpur, 1968-72; Mathematics and Science Teacher, Nagpur Municipal Corporation High Schools, 1972-94; Head Master, NMC MAK Azad Urdu High School, Nagpur, 1994-; Tutor and Guide, various mathematics, science and Urdu Free Classes, 1968-; Translator, Examiner, Casual Announcer, AIR Nagpur, Resource Person, Compere, countless literary and educational programmes on all levels. Custodian of SSC and HSSC Examinations. Publications: poetry in all leading urdu magazines and journals in India; Translation of article, Sports in Britain; Critical Papers were read from AIR Nagpur and literacy programme; Stories, drama and articles on education, sports and literature in various journals. Honours: Shakir Aurangabadi Merit Prize, 1964; Chief Editor, Nawa-E-Subhnia School Magazine, 1964, Kaawis, 1990; Merit Certificate for academic success, 1972; Best Scribe Writer Award, 1984; Nav Ratna Puraskar Award in Education Field by Vichar, 1984; Many other awards of Appreciation. Memberships: General Secretary, Urdu Sabha; General Secretary & Founder Member, Anjuman-E-Katibeen calligraphic society; Patron, Shaheen Students Council; President, Zinda Dilan-E-Nagpur; General Secretary, Mohabbat Manch Nagpur; and others. Address: M A K Azad High School, NMC Asinagar, Ashok Nagar, Nagpur 17, India.

**ASKEROV Bakhram Mekhrali**, b. 1934, Azerbaija. Physicist. m. Ismet Askerova, 1 son, 2 daughters. Education: Diploma of Excellence, Baku State University, 1957; Ph

971; Professor, 1972. Appointments: Chairman, Physica Status Solidi Chair, 1971-; Vice Rector, Baku State University, 994-. Publications: Over 100 publications in professional Journals. Honour: Azerbaijan State Prize Laureate, 1974. Membership: New York Academy of Sciences. Address: Baku State University, 23 Z Khalilov Street, Baku 370145, Azerbaijan.

**ASMAR Alice,** b. Flint, Michigan, USA. Artist; Muralist; Photographer; Consultant; Teacher. m. (widow), 2 step-sons. Education: BA magna cum laude, 1949, Lewis & Clark College; MFA, 1950, University of Washington; Ecole Nationale Superieure des Beaux Arts, Paris, 1958-59. Appointments: Engineering Draughtsman, Aerodynamics, Boeing Aircraft, 1952-53; Teaching, Lewis & Clark College, 1955-57, and McGroarty Art Centre, 1990-98; Original line Engraver, Nambe Mills, Santa Fe, New Mexico, 1967-78; Illustrator & Article Coordinator, LA Times, 1978-81; Illustrator of Collage in Guide o American Law, 1984; Art Exhibits, 1950-98; Mural of Los Angeles at Metro Medical Mall, 1996. Publications: 72 Solo and 77 group exhibits throughout United States and Europe; in several hundred private and public collections; Featured in articles, books and videos. Honours: Many awards for art 1943-93 including Certificate of Appreciation from Burbank Coordinating Council for Community Involvement. Memberships: Burbank Chamber of Commerce; Committee Member, Art in Public Places; Honorary member, National League of American Pen Women; International Museum Artist Registration, life member; CA Lawyers for the Arts, Santa Monica Branch; Visual Arts & Galleries Association, NYC; Portland Art Museum; LA County Art Museum; Lewis & Clark College Alumni Association. Address: Asmar Studios, PO Box 1963, Burbank, CA 915073-1963, USA.

**ASSIS Andre Koch Torres,** b. 11 August 1962, Juiz de Fora, Brazil. Physicist. m. Hsu Su Chiao, 1 son, 1 daughter. Education: Bachelor, Physics, State University of Campinas, Brazil, 1983; PhD, Physics, 1987. Appointments: Post Doctoral, Culham Laboratory, United Kingdom Atomic Energy Authority, UK, 1988-89; Visiting Scholar, Center for Electromagnetics Research, USA, 1991-92; Professor, Institute of Physics, State University of Campinas, Brazil, 1989-. Publications: Weber's Electrodynamics, 1994; Relational Mechanics, 1999. Memberships: Brazilian Society of Physics; Brazilian Society for the History of Sciences. Address: Institute of Physics, State University of Campinas, 13083-970 Campinas - SP, Brazil.

**ASSUMPCAO Francisco B,** b. 7 September 1951, Sao Paulo, Brazil. Psychiatrist. m. 2 daughters. Education: Master, Psychology, 1985; Doctor, Psychology, 1988; Professor, Child Psychiatry, 1993. Publications: Child and Adolescent Psychiatry; History of Child Psychiatry in Brazil; Autism; Peruasioe Developmental Disorders. Memberships: Brazilian Psychiatry Association; Latin America Psychiatry Association. Address: R Manoel de Nobrega 1240/81, 04001-002 Sao Paulo, Brazil.

**ASTMAN Barbara Anne,** b. 12 July 1950, Rochester, New York, USA. Artist; Educator. m. Joseph Anthony Baker, 2 daughters. Education: AA, 1970, Rochester Institute of Technology, School for American Craftsmen, Rochester, New York; Graduate, 1973, Ontario College of Art & Design, Toronto, Ontario. Appointments: Faculty, Ontario College of Art & Design, 1975-; Faculty, York University, North York, Ontario, 1978-80, 1986; Coordinator of Colour Xerox Artists' Programme, Visual Arts Ontario, 1977-83; Board of Directors, Art Gallery at Harbourfront, Toronto, 1983-85, Arts Foundation of Greater Toronto, 1989-92; Appointed member, City of Toronto Public Art Commission, 1986-89; Member, Curatorial

Team, WaterWorks Exhibition, Toronto, 1988. Creative Works: 41 solo exhibitions; 95 group exhibitions, 1975-; Represented in 28 public and corporate collections; Many commissions for murals, Public Art. Honours: Many Ontario, Toronto and Canada Arts Council Grants. Address: 23 Alcina Avenue, Toronto, Ont M6G 2E7, Canada.

**ASUDANI Ghanshyam Hardayaldas,** b. 16 April 1967, Nagpur, India. Professor of English. m. Vaishali Ghodmare. Education: MA, English, 1995; BEd, 1996; PhD, in progress. Career: Professor, English, PWS College, Nagpur, 1996-97; Professor, English, Central School of Government of India. Honours: 2 Gold Medals, English Literature. Memberships: General Secretary, National Organization for the Integration of the Blind; National Federation of the Blind; National Association for the Blind. Address: 45D Hemu Kalani Square, Nagpur 440014 MS, India.

**ASUDANI Rajesh Hardayaldas,** b. 13 March 1976, Nagpur, India. Student. Education: BA, English Literature, 1997; LLB, in progress. Honours: Hinduja Merit Scholarship, Hinduja Foundation, Mumbai; Certificate of Appreciation, Chief Minister of Maharashtra & Human Resources Minister of India. Memberships: Secretary, National Organization for the Integration of the Blind; National Federation of the Blind; National Association for the Blind. Address: 45D Hemu Kalani Square, Nagpur 440014 MS, India.

**ASUDANI Vinod Hardayaldas,** b. 1 January 1969, Nagpur, India. Professor of English. m. Arti Gurnaney, 1 daughter. Education: MA, English, 1995; BEd, 1996; MA, History, 1998; PhD, in progress. Career: Professor, Head, Department of English, Shree Ramdeobaba Kamla Nehru Engineering College, Nagpur. Honours: 5 Gold Medals. Memberships: Vice President, National Organization for the Integration of the Blind; National Federation of the Blind; National Association for the Blind. Address: 45D Hemu Kalani Square, Nagpur 440014 MS, India.

**ATANOV Gennadiy,** b. 1 September 1939, Donetsk, Ukraine. Researcher, Educator. m. Lyudmila Tkalenko, 2 daughters. Education: MA, Kharkov Aircraft Institute, Ukraine, 1963; Candidate of Technical Sciences, 1970; Doctor of Physical Mathematical Sciences, 1978. Appointments: Assistant Professor, 1966; Associated Professor, 1970; Full Professor, Hydrodynamics Department, 1979; Head of Physics, Didactics of Physics Department, Donetsk State University, 1980; Rector, Donetsk Institute of Social Education, 1997-. Publications: 160 Works, Hydrodynamics; 80, Didactics. Honours: Grant, International Sciences Foundations. Memberships: Society of Water Jet Technology; International Artificial Intelligence in Education Society; Academy of Sciences; Ukrainian National Committee for Applied Theoretical Mechanics. Address: Donetsk State University, Donetsk 340055, Ukraine.

**ATLAN Henri,** b. 27 December 1931, Algeria. Biologist; Philosopher. m. Bela Rachel Kohn, 1 son, 1 daughter. Education: MD, 1958, PhD, 1973, Paris. Appointments: Research Associate, NASA, Moffettfield, California, 1966-68; Visiting Professor, Weizmann Institute, Israel, 1970-73; Professor, Head, Department of Biophysics, 1975-96, Scholar in Residence, Philosophy and Ethics of Biology, 1992-, Director, Human Biology Research Center, 1992-, Hadassah University Hospital, Jerusalem; Head, Biophysics and Nuclear Medicine, Hotel Dieu Hospital, Paris, 1991-97; Director of Research, Ecole des Hautes Etudes en Sciences, Sociales (EHESS), Paris, 1995-. Publications include: Theory of Self-Organization and Complex Systems, 1972, 1979, 1982,

1992; Philosophy of Knowledge Based on Intercritique of Science and Myth, 1986, 1991; Questions of Life Between Science and Opinion, 1994. Memberships: French National Ethics Committee; New York Academy of Sciences. Address: Human Biology Research Center, Hedassah University Hospital, Ein Karem, Jerusalem, Israel.

**ATTAH Judith Sefi,** b. 14 July 1933, Okene, Jamaica. Educator, Diploma. m. Christopher Okigbo, 3 daughters. Education: BA, University College, Dublin, 1957; Dip in Education, University of Reading, 1958. Appointments: Teacher; Principal; Chief Woman Education Officer; Assistant Director Teacher Training; Director Higher Education; Perm Delegate to Unesco; Permanent Anent Secretar; Fed Min of Science and tech; Perm Sec External Affairs; Ambassador, Italy, Greece, Cyprus. Honours: Order of the Federal Republic, 1979. Memberships: Sun Commission on the Prevention of Discrimination and Protection of Minorities, 1988-97. Address: Federal Ministry of Womens Affairs & Social Development, PMB 229, Garki, Abuja, Nigeria.

**ATTAPATTU John Ashmore Florian,** b. 17 November 1934. Senior Lecturer. m., 2 daughters. Education: Bachelor of Medicine, Bachelor of Surgery, MBBS, Ceylon, 1960; Master of Obstetrics, Gynaecology, MOG, Ceylon, 1969. Appointments: Pre Registration House Officer, 1960-61; House Officer, 1961; Medical Officer, 1962-65; Tutor, Lecturer, 1965-67; Registrar, 1967-69; Resident Obstetrician, Gynaecologist, 1970-71; Resident Obstetrician, Gynaecologist, 1973-74; Consultant Obstetrician, Gynaecologist, 1974-76; Consultant, Obstetrician, Gynaecologist, 1976-78; Consultant Gynaecological Surgeon, 1979; Consultant Obstetrician, Gynaecologist, 1979-84; Senior Consultant Obstetrician, Gynaecologist, 1984-85; Director, Senior Consultant, Obstetrician, Gynaecologist, Castle Street Hospital for Women, 1985-89; Locum Consultant Obstetrician, Gynaecologist, 1990; Director, Senior Consultant Obstetrician, Gynaecologist, 1990; Lecturer, Obstetrician, Gynaecologist, 1991-94; Senior Lecturer, Obstetrician, Gynaecologist, 1994-. Publications: Many Scientific Papers. Honours: Three Gold Medals Awarded for the Three Orations; Two Certificates of Merit, Ministry of Health; Commendation, Ministry of Teaching Hospitals; Twentieth Century Bronze Medal of Achievement, International Biographical Centre, England. Memberships: Sri Lanka Medical Association; Sri Lanka Medical Library; International Biographical Association; Royal Society of Medicine; New York Academy of Sciences; Many other memberships, Internationally. Address: 12 South Bend Road, Pine Gardens, Saint Michaels, Barbados.

**AUGUNAS Romualdas,** b. 14 April 1938, Siauliai. Photographer. m. Jefrosinija, 2 sons. Education: Studied, Kaunas Polytechnic School, 1954-58. Appointments: Numerous mountaineering photographic expeditions; Municipal Economy Designing Institute; Own business, ARFA. Creative works: Numerous exhibitions including: Under the Egyptian Sun; Mountains and People; Friendship Moments in Congo; In the Countries of Southeast Asia; On Mountain Peaks; That Large Small World; Other solo and group exhibitions. Honours include: Diploma, Baltic Republics Photography Exhibition, 1971; Silver Medal, All-Union Photography Exhibition, 1985; 2nd Prize, 18th Exhibition of Lithuanian Photographers, Chicago, USA, 1989; 1st Prize, 20th Exhibition of Lithuanian Photographers, 1991; Diploma, International Photography Exhibition, Kaunas, 1998. Memberships: Municipal Economy Designing Institute, 1961-91; Lithuanian Photographers Union. 1969; International Photoartists Federation, 1997. Address: Kalinausko 10-5, 2000 Vilnius, Lithuania.

**AUREL Ardelean,** b. 4 July 1939, Romania. Professor. m Dorina, 1 daughter. Education: MSc, Biology, Babes-Bolya University, Cluj, 1964; PhD, Biology, 1981. Appointments Professor, Cellular Biology, Vasile Goldis University of Arad Romania; Vice Rector, 1992, Rector, 1993-. Publications Several in professional journals. Honours: E Teodorescu Academy Award, 1982; Romanian Society of Biology Award 1997; Hungarian Academy Award, 1998. Memberships Academy of Scientists, Romania; International Society o' Ecology; Balkan Association of Biosciences. Address: Westerr University "V Goldis", Boulevard Revoloutziei 81, R 2900 Arad Romania.

**AUSTERMANN Christopher Brent,** b. 5 November 1971 Rolla, Missouri, USA. Educator. Education: Foreign Exchange Nakajo, Japan, 1991; Webster University, St Louis German-American Exchange; BS,Management Informatior Systems, International Business, Maryville University, 1994 Appointments: Internship, Rottenburg, Germany, 1993 Instructor, English, International Studies Education, Shiunji Japan, 1994-; Interpreter, Nagano Olympics, 1998; Cultural Linguistics Liason, Establishment of a Sister City Relationship Shiunji Niigata Japan and St James, MO, USA. Honours Graduation, Summa cum laude. Memberships: Alpha Lambda Delta, Omicron Delta Kappa; Japan Association of Language Teachers. Address: 99 Yoneko, Shiunji Niigata 957-0225 Japan.

**AVAK Khachatrian,** Professor, Rector. Education: PhD Armenian Literature, 1962, Professor, Armenian Literature 1985, Armenian Pedagogical Institute, Yerevan. Appointments Head of School dept of Vayk region Administration of Armenia, 1950-51; Student, 1951-55, Head of Student Dept, 1954-62 Head of Aspirant Dept, 1963-64, Manager of Scientific Lab o' Literature History, 1964-67, Docent of Chair of Armenian Literature, 1967-72, Dean of Psychological & Childhood Educational Faculty, 1973-79, Professor of Chair of Armenian Literature, 1979-85, Dean of Armenian Linguistics & Literature Faculty, 1985-91, Armenian Pedagogical Institute, Yerevan; Rector, Yerevan Hrachia Acharian University, 1991- Publications: 20 articles and monographs including, The Armenian Literature for 7th form, textbook in 7 publications, 1976-89; 4 presentations at professional conferences. Honours: Higher Award for Academic Excellence, 1953-55. Memberships: Academician of Ararat International Academy of Sciences; Academic Council of API; Academic Council of Faculty Literature API; Head of Academic Council of Hrachia Acharian, Yerevan; member, New York Academy of Sciences. Address: 1 Moscovian, University Hrachia Acharian, Yerevan, Armenia 375001.

**AVDULOV Marian Vladimir,** b. 18 August 1931, Moscow Russia. Geophysicist. Education: Graduate, Geological Faculty, Moscow University, 1956. Career: Research Engineer Geological Faculty, Moscow University, 1956-60; Physical Faculty, Moscow University, 1960-. Publications include: Phase transitions and problem of magma formation; Dynamic interaction between rock crystals in phase transitions of the first kind; Phase Transformations and Rock Genesis; The problem of Whole-Mantel Convection and Plate Tectonics. Membership New York Academy of Science. Address: Physical Faculty, MV Lomonosov Moscow University, Leninskie Gory, Moscow 119899, Russia.

**AVIRAM Uri,** b. 19 March 1936, Haifa, Israel. Social Work Educator. m. Ariella Avivi, 1 son, 2 daughters. Education: BA History and Education, 1962, The Hebrew University Jerusalem; MSW, 1966, Wayne State University; PhD Socia Welfare, 1972, University California at Berkeley; Certificate

Social Worker. Appointments: Counsellor, High School Teacher, Social Worker, Israel, 1957-72, Michigan, 1964-66, California, 1968-72; From Lecturer to Associate Professor, 1972-87, Dean, 1983-87, Tel Aviv University, Israel; Professor, Institute of Health, Rutgers University, New Jersey, USA, 1987-93; Zena Harman Professor Social Work, The Hebrew University, 1993-; Director, Paul Baerwald School of Social Work, 1993-; Visiting Faculty, Case Western Reserve University, University California at Berkeley, Cornell University; Member Advisory Committee, Psychiatric Services, Israeli Ministry of Health; Israeli Ministry of Labour and Social Affairs Commission on status and tasks of social workers, consultant in field of social policy, community care for severely mentally ill persons and the interface between psychiatry and law; Israeli Public Commission on Equal Rights Laws for Persons with Disabilities. Publications: Co-author, The Mentally Ill in Community Based Sheltered Care: a Study of Community Care and Social Integration, 1978; Community Mental Health in Israel, 1981; Psychiatric Treatment and Civil Liberties: The Involuntary Hospitalisation of the Mentally Ill in Israel, 1981; Contributor over 50 articles to professional journals and books; Active in scientific congresses and syposiums, 1974-; Contributor chapters to books. Honour: Henrieta Szold Award, City of Tel Aviv, 1983, for book. Membership: Medical Corps, Israel Defense Forces, 1954-57, reserve 1973-86. Address: 1 Etzion Gaver St Apt 6, 97803 Jerusalem, Israel.

**AWAD Adel,** b. 28 March 1949, Lattakia, Syria. Professor Doctor. m. Eng I Hatem, 2 sons, 1 daughter. Education: BSc, Civil Engineering, Damascus University, Syria, 1973; DEng, Environmental Engineering, Stuttgart University, 1983; DEng, Urban Planning, Stuttgart University, Germany, 1983. Appointments: Head, Environmental Engineering Department, Tishreen University, Syria, 1987-92; Visiting Professor, Jordan University of Science and Technology, Jordan, 1992-95; Professor, Tishreen University, Lattakia, Syria, 1995-. Publications include: More than 150 scientific publications; Earthquakes.. A Tragedy Shaking the World - Effect of Earthquake on Urban Environment, 1992; Fundamentals of Environmental Engineering, 1989; Select Researches in Environmental Science, 1994; Submarine Outfalls of Waste Water, 1996; Industrial Water Pollution Management, 1996; Women and Environment Protection, 1995. Honours include: Global 500 Honour Award, UNEP, 1990; Twentieth Century Honour Award for Achievement in Engineering, 1995; International Award of Recogition, 1995; International Man of the Year, 1995-96; Award of Best Scientific Book, 1996. Memberships include: National Marine Environmental Protection; National Environmental Urbanism; National Scientific Research and Standards; Protection of Land Environment in Lattakia Govemorate; Specialist Group, Waste Stabilization Ponds, IAWQ; Federal Germany Committee of Sewage Water Technology; Experts Committee for Water Resources, Legislation and Regulation of Water Resources Management in the Arab Region, affiliated to Arab League Educational Cultural and Scientific Organization, Tunis; Earthquake Research Institute, California, USA; American Biographical Institute Research Board of Advisors, North Carolina, USA; Specialist group, Hypertext System, affiliated to German Informatic Society.

**AWAJI Mitsuhiro,** b. 31 March 1965, Mukudani 712, Hayashita, Himeji. Physicist. Education: PhD, Okayama University of Science, 1992; Visiting Fellow, Oxford University, 1993-95. Appointments: Centre of Excellence Fellow, National Research Institute for Metals, 1995-97; Lecturer, Research Centre for Ultra High Voltage Electron Microscopy, Osaka University, 1997-98; Researcher, Japan Synchrotron Radiation Research Institute, 1998-. Publications: Professional Journals.

Honours: Nishina Prize; Japan Society for Promotion of Science Fellow for Research Abroad. Memberships: The Royal Microscopical Society; Physical Soceity of Japan; Japanese Society for Synchrotron Radiation Research. Address: Mukudani 712, Hayashita, Himeji, Hyogo 679-4211, Japan.

**AXELROD Glen Scott,** b. 4 November 1953, Newark, New Jersey, USA. Corporate Executive; Published Author. m. Jennifer, 2 sons. Education: BA Biology, 1975, Rutgers University; MSc Zoology/Ichthyology, 1978, Rhodes University, South Africa. Appointments: Assistant to President, TFH Pubs Inc, Neptune City, New Jersey, 1979-81; Assistant to Principal, Six Star Cablevision Group, Englewood, 1981-82; Executive Vice President, Breckenridge Development Corporation, Wayne, NJ, 1985-92; President, CEO Design Services, Riverdale, 1992-95; President, GJA Production Corporation, Mahwah, NJ, 1982-; Exec Vice President, 1996-97, President, CEO, 1997-, Board Directors, TFH Publications Inc. Publications: Patentee in field; Discovered new species of fish; Contributor articles to professional journals. Memberships: Trustee, Treasurer, Deerhaven Association, Mahwah, 1990-97; Fellow, Zoological Society London, 1978-. Address: TFH Publications Inc, One TFH Plz 3d & Union, Neptune City, NJ 07753, USA.

**AYALA José Iñigo,** b. 1 June 1955, Bukidnon, Philippines. Composer; Singer; Recording Artist. m. Jessica Sorongon, 2 sons. Education: BA in Economics, 1979; MBA studies. Career: Ethnic rock concert tours in Japan, India, rest of Asia; Currently records own compositions under Genesis label, Canada, USA. Honour: Short Story Award, Palanca Literary Awards, 1990. Membership: Original Pilipino Music. Address: Panorama House, 13 Lapanday Road, Davao City 8000, Philippines.

**AYIM Emmanuel Nuwokpor,** b. 15 July 1933, Avenui, Ghana. Medical Practitioner; Educator. m. Elsie Seyena Ayim, 2 sons. Education: University of Hamburg, 1960; MD, 1963; DTM & H,1961; Resident, Anaesthesia, Hamburg, Zurich, 1963-68. Appointments: Senior Lecturer, Anaesthesia, University of Dares Salaam, 1969-71; Senior Lecturer, 1974, Associate Professor, 1979-84, Professor, Head, 1984, University of Nairobi; Private Practitioner, Consultant, Director, Intensive Care, Mater M Hospital; Director, Special Care Unit, Gertrudes G Childrens Hospital. Publications: Numerous articles in professional medical journals. Memberships include: Society of Anaesthesiologists of East Africa; Kenya Medical Association; World Federal Society of Anaesthesiologists. Address: PO Box 14530, Nairobi, Kenya.

**AYREFLOR Maria Francisca Moscardó Ramis de.** Address: Fortuny 3 lo B, 07001 Palma de Mallorca, Baleares, Spain.

**AZAHARI Azril,** b. 23 Sept 1946, Pontianak, Indonesia. Educator. m. Poppy Rostina, 3 sons. Education: Graduate studies, 1978-79, MA, 1979, Sam Houston State University, Texas, USA; Doctoral studies, 1985-88, PhD, 1988, University of the Philippines. Appointments: Director, Agriculture Manpower Development Centre, 1994-; Vice-Dean, Graduate School, Trisakti University, 1994-. Honours: Fellowship, Government of Indonesia, 1965-68; World Bank Fellowship, 1978-79, 1985-88. Memberships: Academy of Management, 1995-; American Society for Quality, 1996-. Address: Jl Palapa V, No 26, Pasar Minggu, Jakarta 12520, Indonesia.

**AZCARATE Ismael Norberto,** b. 27 March 1944, Argentina. m. Haydee Beatriz Badano. Education: Master in Physics, University La plata, 1968; PhD, 1988. Appointments: Assistant Researcher, IAFE, 1976-80; Associate Researcher, IAR,

1980-83; Associated Researcher, IAR, 1983-95; Independent Researcher, 1995-. Memberships: Argentine Astronomy Association; International Astronomical Union; New York Academy of Science. Address: Calle 2 # 1532 D to C, 1900 La Plata, Argentina.

# B

**BA Le Huy,** b. 13 March 1947, Vietnam. Professor of nvironment. m. Education: Diplomas, 1974; PhD, 1986; DSc, )89. Appointments: Teaching in University, 1975-; Attended ıd reported 22 International Conferences. Publications: 6 ıecial books in Vietnamese; 64 papers published. ıemberships: Environment and Resources. Address: Institute r Environment and Resources, Vietnam National University, ɔchi Minh City, Vietnam.

**BA'ATHALLAH Sherif,** b. 4 September 1964, Egypt. Clinical ytogenetisist. m. Manal Kamel Balinas. Education: MBBCh, ıiro University, 1987; MSc, Cairo University, 1992. ɔpointments: Clinical Cytogenetisist, Childrens Hospital, Cairo niversity. Publications: Indications and Prospects of ınniocentesis. Memberships: American Society of Human ɘnetics; European Society of Human Genetics. Address: Fisal t Apt 3, 14 Abdel bary Sharab St, Giza 12111, Egypt.

**BAALES Michael,** b. 3 November 1963, Gerolstein, ɘrmany. Archaeologist. m. Sabine Gayck. Education: ıagister Artium, Archaeology, 1989, Dr rer nat, 1992, niversity of Cologne. Appointments: Scientific Co-Worker, ıaleolithic Research Centre, Roman-Germanic Central ıuseum Mainz, Schloss Monrepos, Neuwied. Publications: ınting economy and ecology of the Ahrensburgian Reindeer ınters in the uplands, monograph, 1996; Several articles in ɘrman, English and French publications. Memberships: ɘrman Society of Pre- and Protohistory; Friends of Antiquity ɔciety, Bonn. Address: Roman-Germanic Central Museum ainz, Schloss Monrepos, 56567 Neuwied-Monrepos, ɘrmany.

**BAASSIRI Ramez,** b. 1 January 1972, Canada. Director. ducation: BSBA, Finance, Boston University, 1991; BSBA, ɔcounts, University of Arizona, 1992; MBA, University of Hull, )97. Appointments: York International, 1988-92; AHB evelopment, 1992-93; Gulf Sail General Trading Company, td, 1993-. Honours: Gulf Sail Awards, 1994, 1998. ɪemberships: Round Table Artag-1, Dubai; Young ıtrepreneur Organization. Address: Gulf Sail General Trading ɔmpany, Ltd, PO Box 6713, Dubai, United Arab Emirates.

**BABA Yoshinobu,** b. 21 September 1958, Hitoyoshi, Japan. ʳofessor. m. Mikiko, 2 sons. Education: BA, Kyushu niversity, 1981; PhD, Chemistry, 1986. Appointments: Post ɔctor, Kobe Pharm University, 1986; Assistant Professor, Oita niversity, 1986; Associate Professor, Kobe Pharm University, )90; Professor, The University of Tokushima, 1997. ublications: Capillary Electrophysics of DNA; Integrated ıcrochip in DNA Analysis. Honours: Award for Young ʰarmaceutical Scientist. Memberships: American Association  Advertisement of Science; New York Academy of Science; ɪerican Chemical Society. Address: Univ Tokushina Dept ɘd Che, Shomachi, Tokushima 770-8505, Japan.

**BABENKO Dmitry,** b. 20 July 1970, Krasnodar, Russia. ʳawing Teacher. m. Helen Tsintsiruk, 1 daughter. Education: ʳtistic Graphics Faculty, Kuban State University, 1996. Career: ʳtist. Publications: Several articles in professional journals. ɔdress: PO Box 1670, Krasnodar 80, Russia.

**BABST Dean V,** b. 14 October 1921, Montana, USA. esearch Scientist. m. G Wyone Whittaker, 4 May 1947, 1 son,  daughters. Education: BA, 1947, MA, 1950, University of Ɉashington, USA. Appointment: Coordinator, Nuclear Age

Peace Foundation's Accidental Nuclear War Studies Program. Publications: 3 books; over 200 science articles. Honours: Graduate, Assis. Society, 1948-50; Alpha Kappa Delta, 1950; Peace Ambassador, 1992; International Man of the Year, 1992-93; Honorary Member, International Biographical Centre Advisory Conference, 1995. Memberships: UNA-USA; Veteran for Peace; International Physicians for Prevention of Nuclear War; Center of Defense Information. Hobbies: Oil Painting; Trout Fishing. Address: 4489 Juneberry Court, Concord, CA 94521, USA.

**BACH Gabriel,** b. 13 March 1927, Halberstadt, Germany. Judge. m. Ruth Arazi, 2 sons, 1 daughter. Education: LLB Hons, 1950, University College, London; Barrister at Law, 1949, Lincoln's Inn, London. Appointments: Assistant, Deputy State Attorney of Israel, 1953-69; Chief State Attorney of Israel, 1969-82; Justice of the Supreme Court of Israel, 1982-97. Publications: Articles in legal periodicals. Honours: Buchanan Prize, 1949 as Best Candidate of the Year at Lincoln's Inn; Fellowship of University College, London, 1998; Cited as Distinguished Friend of the City of Jerusalem, 1997. Memberships: Bnai Brith Organisation; Member of Council, Bnai Brith World Centre in Jerusalem. Address: 30 Radak Street, Jerusalem, Israel.

**BADARY Osama Ahmed,** b. 8 March 1961, Cairo. Professor. m. Mona Kamal, 1 son. Education: B Pharm, Ciaro University, 1983; D Biochem, Al Azhar University, 1985; MSc Pharmacology; PhD, Pharmacology. Appointments: Professor, Pharmacology and Toxicology, College of Pharmacy, Al Azhar Univeristy, Cairo, Egypt. Publications: Pharmacology Research; Onocology Research; Drug Development Research; Ethnopharmacol, Cancer Research; Anticancer Drugs. Honours: Grant, UGA, USA, 1990. Memberships: IFCC; SPT; ECCR. Address: 26th July Street, Building 2, Lebnan Square, El-Mohandessen, Cairo, Egypt.

**BADESCU Mihail Viorel,** b. 24 September 1953, Bughea De Jos, Arges, Romania. Educator. m. Jenica, 1 son, 1 daughter. Education: Bachelor, Dr Petru Groza College, 1972; MsD, Polytechnical Institute, Bucharest, 1977; PhD, Polytechnic University, 1993; Diplomate, World English Inst, 1995. Appointments: Inspector Engineer, IFA Viscofil, Bucharest, 1978-82; Researcher, Polytechnic Institute, 1982-90; Assistant Professor, Polytechnic University, 1990-93; Visiting Fellow, University of Southampton, 1995; Visiting Academic, University of Southampton, 1992; Lecturer, Associate Professor, Polytechnic University, 1993-. Publications: 3 Books; 140 Scientific Papers. Honours: Romanian Academy Prize for Physics, 1979. Memberships: International Solar Energy Society; European Astronomical Society; International Radiation Physics Society. Address: Faculty of Mechanical Engineering, Polytechnic University of Budapest, Bucharest 75590, Romania.

**BADUR Diana Isabel (Soltera),** b. 26 September 1957, Mayagüez, Puerto Rico. Educator. m. Gültekin Badur, 2 sons. Education: BA in English, 1978; MA in English, 1979; PhD in Curriculum and Instruction, 1982. Appointments: Professor of English, 1982-; Teaching composition, technical writing and literature at university level. Honour: Advanced Opportunity Fellowship, 1978-82. Memberships: National Council of Teachers of English; Illinois Association of Teachers of English. Address: Black Hawk College, 6600 34th Avenue, Moline, IL 61265-5870, USA.

**BAE Sang-Min,** b. 16 December 1958, Korea. Electronics Researcher. m. Yong-Hee Song, 2 daughters. Education: Bachelor's degree in Electronics, Hanyang University, Seoul,

1986; Master's degree in Instrumentation and Control, 1996, PhD course completion in Instrumentation and Control, 1998, Chungnam University, Taejon. Appointments: Researcher, Integrated Circuit Design, Hankook Electronic Co, Kumi, 1986-87; Senior Researcher, Instrumentation and Control, Korea Atomic Energy Research Institute, Taejon, 1987-. Publications: Reliability Centred Adaptive and Predictive Maintenance for Diesel Generator in Nuclear Power Plant; Hardware Oriented Reliability Centred Maintenance for Diesel Generator in Nuclear Power Plant; A New Automatic Topping Up Device for Battery in RWTF; Capacity Recovery of Class IE Nickel-Cadmium Battery; Fault Detection for the Steam Generator of Nuclear Power Plant. Honour: President's Award, Korea Atomic Energy Institute, 1990. Memberships: Korea Nuclear Society; Korea Instrumentation and Control Association; Korea Automatic Control Society. Address: PO Box 105, Yusong-gu, Taejon 305-600, Korea.

**BAENA Guillermina,** b. 25 June 1947, Mexico, DF. Professor. m. Sergio Montero, 1 son, 2 daughters. Education: Lic in Information Science, 1971; Dr, Latin American Studies, 1981. Appointments: Social Science Professor, Journalism, Political Communication, Writing, Research. Publications: Research Instruments; Writing Skilfully; Informative Journalist Genders; Chronic; Total Quality in Higher Education; Scientific Discourse Method; Political Credibility and Marketing Mix; Journalist Discourse; Quality and Higher Education. Honours: 3rd Place Fimpes Prize. Memberships: New York Academy of Sciences; Mexican Association of Communication Researchers. Address: Colonia Portales, Rumania 509 Bis, 03300 Mexico City, Mexico.

**BAGCHI Amitava,** b. 24 August 1926, Nagpur, Calcutta, India. Honour: Sahitya Tilar, for research work. Memberships: Life Member, Mikhil Bharat Baya Sahitya; Jamula, Benjiye Sahitya Parisad; Birbhine Sahitya Parisad. Address: Shyambati, Shantinieketan, Birbhaum, West Bengal, India.

**BAGI Annasaheb,** b. 12 August 1934, Kolhapur, India. Veterinary and Animal Science Consultant. m. Aarti S Duge, 1 son, 2 daughters. Education: BVSc, 1959; MSc Anatomy, 1975; PhD Anatomy, 1989. Appointments: Veterinary Officer, 1959-67; Lecturer in Anatomy, 1967-73; Assistant Professor Anatomy, 1973-82; Associate Professor Anatomy, 1982-88; Professor and Head of Anatomy, Veterinary College, Anand, 1988-94. Publications: Articles in professional journals; Handbook of Veterinary Immunology. Honours: Best Teacher Award, 1989. Memberships: Life member, World Association Veterinary Anatomists, USA; Indian Association Veterinary Anatomists. Address: 168/10 Hill Side Apartments, Mahatma Nagar, Nasik 422007, India.

**BAGNI Marialucia,** b. 7 June 1939, Viadana. Journalist. m. Gianni. Education: Degree, Political Science, Statistics. Appointments: Journalist, Successo, monthly magazine, Il Mond, weekly magazine; Press Officer, Assistant, President, Milan Stock Exchange. Honours: Several. Memberships include: Italian and European Union of Scientific Journalists. Address: Via Orti 14, 20122 Milan, Italy.

**BAHRAMI Mohsen,** b. 22 June 1954, Khomain, Iran. University Professor. Education: MSc, 1979, PhD, 1982, Mechanical Engineering, Oregon State University; BSc, Mechanical Engineering, Tehran Polytechnic, 1997. Appointments: Engineer, Nutech Engineers, USA, 1982-83; Advanced Robotcraft Technology, USA, 1983-85; Head, Aerospace Educational Planning Committee; Head, New Technologies Committee, NRC. Publications: More than 40 papers; 5 books (translated). Memberships: World Future

Society; ASME; IEEE; AIEE; AIAA; International Institute Space Law. Address: Amir Kabir University of Technolo Mechanical Engineering Department, 424 Hafez Aven Tehran 15, Iran.

**BAI Yu Hai,** b. 25 April 1941, China. Scientific Research. Zhao Yu Zhen, 1 son, 1 daughter. Education: Gradu Department of Physics, Jilin University. Appointmen Associate Professor, Institute of Acoustics, Acaemia Sin China. Publications: Over 50 articles in professional journ Honours: Scholarship, Max-Planck Institute of Solid St Physics, Germany. Memberships: Fellow, Acoustic Soci Physical Society of China; New York Academy of Scienc Address: Academia Sinica, Institute of Acoustics, Zhongguncun Street, Beijing 100080, China.

**BAILES Anthony James,** b. 1947, Bristol, Engla Musician. m. Anne Van Royen. Education: Bulmershe Colle of Further Education, 1965-67; Studies with Michael Wats Diana Poulton, Eugen Dombois. Appointments: Solo Conce Recordings, Europe, Scandinavia, 1971-. Publications: Introduction to 17th Century Lute Music; 32 Easy Pieces Lute. Honours: Grants, Henry and Lily Davies Fund; Edis Prize, Piéces de Luth. Memberships: Lute Society; Svens Gitarr och Luta Sallskapet. Address: Hollenweg 3A, Ch 41 Arlesheim, Switzerland.

**BAILEY Emmanuel F,** b. 30 November 1954, Liberia, W Africa. Pastor. m. Taylorie Major Bailey, 2 sons, 1 daugh Education: AS, 1978, Highland Park College; BS, 1980, Way State University; MDiv, 1983, Methodist Theological Sch DMin, 1988, St Mary's University; MA, 1990, Eastern Michig University; Certificate, 1996, Oxford University; Provisio Teacher Certificate, 1980, State of Michigan. Appointmer Pastor, Lee Ave United Methodist Church, 1981-83; Instruct Mott Adult High School, 1983-93; Pastor, Flint Park Uni Methodist Church, 1983-88; Pastor, Charity United Methoc Church, 1988-93; Pastor, Second Grace United Metho Church, 1993-; Supervising Pastor, Detroit West District, 199 Publications: I Want to Help But How? How to Help Griev People. Honours: Awards: Flint Urban Youth, 1986; Uni Methodist Church for Work with Children and the Poor, 19. Proclamation, City of Flint, Office of the Major, 1993; Afric Association, 1993. Memberships: African Association Michigan; Liberian Association; National Association Christian Counselors; Concerned Pastor Association Michigan; NAACP; Masons (Eurica Lodge). Address: 168 Rosemont Avenue, Detroit, MI 48219 4117, USA.

**BAILEY George Paul,** b. 17 June 1961, Denver, Colora USA. Systems Analyst. Education: Bachelor's degree Environmental Design, 1983, Master's degree in Urban a Regional Planning, 1994, University of Colora Appointments: Tektronix Inc, 1984-91; Information Graph Systems Inc, 1991-94, 1997-98; MCR Technology, 1994- Environmental Systems Research Institute Inc, 199 Memberships: Phi Kappa Tau; United States Junior Cham of Commerce; Kiwanis International Sports Car Club America. Address: PO Box 3037, High Mar Station, Bould CO 80307-3037, USA.

**BAILEY Joy Hafner,** b. 15 August 1928, Weehawkin, N Jersey, USA. Educational Administrator; Assistant Profess Counselor Education. 6 daughters. Education: BA, 1974; N 1975; EdD, 1977. Appointments: Counselor, Instructor, Te A&M University, 1976-80; Director, Student Support Servic Georgia State University, 1980-. Publications: Poetry, 19 article, 1998. Memberships: American Psychologi Association; American Association of Marriage and Fam

Therapists; Society of Psychologists in Management. Address: 635 Ashford Cove Drive, Lilburn, GA 30047, USA.

**BAIRD Marianne Saunorus,** b. 15 December 1953, Chicago, Illinois, USA. Nursing Specialist. m. Thomas William Baird, 1 daughter. Education: BSc, Nursing, Loyola University, Chicago, 1975; MNus, Adult Health, Emory University, 1982. Appointments: Clinical Nurse Specialist, Critical Care Services, Nursing Manager, Director, Supervisor, Operating Room an Surdgical Nursing, Rush-Presbyterian St Lukes Medical Center, Chicago; Case Manager, Pulmonary and Nephrology Services, St Joseph's Hospital of Atlanta. Publications include: Mosby's Critical Care and Emergency Drug Reference; Manual of Critical Care Nursing; Manual of Medical-Surgical Nursing; Mosby's Critical Care Consultant; Several articles in professional journals. Memberships: American Association of Critical Care Nurses; Society of Critical Care Medicine; American Holistic Nurses Association. Address: 3788 Glengarry Way, Roswell, GA 30075-2615, USA.

**BAJO Isa,** b. 25 December 1937, Tirana. Geologic Engineer, Geologist. m. Manushage Erindi, 3 sons. Education: Diploma, Geological Engineer, University of Tirana 1961; Candidate of Geological Sciences, Tirana Geological Institute, 1985; Dr Geologo-Mineral Sciences, 1995; Scientific Research Project Leader, 1996. Appointments: Scientist, N E Albania 1961-67; Copper, Chromite and Ferro-Nickel Deposits Exploration; Collaborator, Tirana and Fieri Geological Institute, 1978-88; Collaborator, Albanian Science Academy, 1989-91. Publications: Over 80 studies. Honours: 4 Awards, President of Albania. Memberships: Albanian Geological Association; Tirana Geological Institute; Albanian Science Academy. Address: Nolermarrja Gjeologice, Girokaster, Albania.

**BAKER Arthur Barrington,** b. 24 June 1939, Brisbane, Australia. Physician. m. Jane Colliss, 2 sons, 1 daughter. Education: MBBS, University of Queensland, 1963; DPhil, Magdalen College, University of Oxford, 1971; FFARACS, 1968; FFARCS, 1968; FRCA, 1991; FANZCA, 1992; FFICANZCA, 1993; DHMSA, 1982. Appointments: Reader in Anaesthesia, University of Queensland, 1972-75; Foundation Professor of Anaesthesia and of Intensive Care, University of Otago, 1975-92; Nuffield Professor of Anaesthetics, University of Sydney, 1992-. Honours: Court of Honour, Royal Australasian College of Surgeons, 1992; Orton Medal, Australian and New Zealand College of Anaesthetists, 1993; Joseph Professorship, ANZCA, 1997-2000. Publications: Over 100 publications. Memberships: Numerous memberships. Address: PO Box 345, Concord West, NSW 2138, Australia.

**BAKER J A II,** b. 12 December 1944, New York City, USA. Monetary Architect; Financial Engineer; Executive Coordination Consultant. Education: Postgraduate in Financial Services Management, The American College, 1994-; ChFC, CLU, Financial Planning Advisor; Associate Registered Investment Advisor. Appointments: Property/casualty/liability field underwriter, commercial and personal lines; Consultant Manager, Life Insurance, New York City, 1964-79; Supervisor, Physician's Planning Group, Attorney' Planning Service, Professional Service Corporation, New York City, 1979-81; CEO, JALB Enterpises, East Garden City, New York, 1980-; Board Directors, Medic Alert, Nassau County, 1985-87; Representative The Living Bank; Monitor, New York State Continuing Education Program, 1996-; Instructor, Continuing Professional Education Program, 1996-; Licencing courses, 1996-. Memberships: Citizen Ambassador International (nominated); American Automobile Assc; Fellow, Life Underwriters Council, Bethseda, Maryland; Emeritus National Association Life Underwriters DC, Chairman, 1972-74,

President Cortland Chapter, 1974-75; American Council Independent Life Undewriters; American Society of Financial Service Professionals; New York City Life Underwriters Association; Professional Insurance Agents; Fraternal Order of Police; New York Civil Service Retired Employee Association; General Agents Managers Association International, Chartered Member. Honour: Order of Malta, American Association, Pilgrim 99. Address: 149 E 23rd St Ste, 1200 New York, NY 10159-1200, USA.

**BAKER Richard Lee,** b. July 27th 1935, Grand Rapids, Michigan, USA. Book Publishing Company Executive. m. Frances Leona Gesink, 3 sons, 1 daughter. Education: Calvin College, Grand Rapids, 1954-56. Appointments: President, Baker Book House, Grand Rapids, 1957-97; Board Directors, 1981-86, Chairman, 1997-, President Board Directors, 1988-98, Christian Schools International Foundation. Memberships: Christian Booksellers Association; Evangelical Christian Publishers Association; Christian Reformed Church; Board of Directors, Evangelical Publishers Association, VP; Board of Directors, Lemstone Books, a division of Lemstone Inc. Address: 2240 Shawnee Dr SE, Grand Rapids, MI 48506-5335, USA.

**BAKHCHADJYAN Robert,** b. 27 February 1957, Gumry, Armenia. Physical Chemist. m. Tchakirian Isabelle, 1 son, 1 daughter. Education: Chemist, 1979, Yerevan State University; DSc Physical Chemistry, 1986, Institute of Chemical Physics, Armenian National Academy of Sciences, Moscow; French equivalence of diplomas, 1996, Paris. Appointments: Scientific Researcher, 1980, Senior Scientific Researcher, 1989, Institute of Chemical Physics, NAS of Armenia. Publications: Over 40 scientific articles and inventions in field of heterogeneous-homogenious chemical reactions; Heterogeneous Propagation of Chains, Chemical Kinetics, 1994. Honours: Grants of International Sciences Foundation, USA, 1994. Membership: New York Academy of Sciences, 1995. Address: ENSSPICAM, Ave Escadrille Normandie-Niemen, 13397 Marseille, France.

**BAKHTIYAROV Ikhtiyar Bakhram,** b. 17 June 1949, Agdam, Azerbaijan. Chemical Science Manager. m. B G Bakhtiyarova, 1 son, 2 daughters. Education: Doctor Diploma, 1980; Senior Research Attestat, 1988; Professor, 1996. Publications: 80 Publications; 3 Patents. Address: H Javid Pros 29, Inst Inorg and Phys Chem, Acad Sci, 370143 Baku, Azerbaijan.

**BAKIROV Alexander Grigiryevich,** b. 7 February 1915, Borskoye, Samara, Russia. Geologist. m. (1) Regitta Morgaleva, deceased 18 June 1977, (2), Valeria Tikhonova, 13 April 1990, 1 son. Education: Graduate, Geological Faculty of Tomsk Industrial Institute, 1939; Diploma with Honours, Postgraduate Course, Chair of Mineralogy and Crystallography under supervision of Professor A M Kuzmin; Defended Candidate Dissertation, 1948; Defended Doctorate Dissertation, 1970; Diploma of Doctor of Science, 1971; Elected for post of Professor of the chair of mineralogy and crystallography of Tomsk Polytechnic University, 1973. Appointments: Tomsk Polytechnic University, Chair of Mineralogy and Crystallography, 1939-; Served in the Soviet Army during the Second World War; Assistant, 1948-51, Associate Professor, 1951-72, Professor, 1972-; Head of combined chair of mineralogy and petrography, 1974-86. Publications: 102 publications on nickel ores of crust weathering, ultrabasic rocks, mineralogy, crystallography, geochemistry, petrology, ore deposits, tectonic, geomorphology, dowsing, parapsychology. Honours: 3 orders; 11 medals for participation in the Second World War.

Membership: International Academy of Energy-Information Sciences, 1992-. Hobbies: Parapsychology, Dowsing. Address: App 26, 5, Timakov Street, 634028 Tomsk, Russia.

**BAKOS John**, b. 10 March 1940, Greece. Private Club Consultant. m. Liliane, 1 daughter. Education: Business Administration, 1967, University Sacramento at California; Food & Beverage, 1995, Cal-Poly University, Pomona, California; Michigan State University School of Hospitality, 1997. Appointments: Director of Food & Beverage, Ambassador Hotel, Los Angeles, 1965; President, Standish Restaurant Corporation, 1974; COO & General Manager, Doublegate Country Club, 1983; COO & General Manager, The Piedmont Club, Lynchburg, 1995. Publications: various publications for the hotel & private club industry. Memberships: Club Managers Associations of America; International Club Network; Hotel & Restaurant Association of America. Address: The Piedmont Club, PO Box 1537, Lynchburg, VA 24505, USA.

**BAKSHI Mandeep Singh**, b. 29 June 1963, Bathinda, India. Lecturer. m. Gurinder Kaur, 1 son. Education: BA, 1982; MA, 1984; Doctorate, 1990. Appointments: Post Doctoral Fellow, Italian External Affair Ministry Fellowship, 1992-94; Visiting Scientist, University of Technology, Japan,1995-96; Lecturer, GND University, Amristar, 1996-. Publications: 40 in International Journals. Address: 1174 Ahata Niaz Mohd, 151001 Bathinda Punjab, India.

**BAKTHAVATSALAM Venkatrama**, b. 8 July 1943, Karasangal, Tamil Nadu, India. Chief Executive Officer. m. Nalini, 1 son, 1 daughter. Education: BE, Mechanical Engineering, MBA, Marketing & Finance, Madras University; DSc, Renewable Energy, Sri Venkateswara University, Tirupati, Andhra Pradesh. Career: Manager, Consultant, Industrial Engineer, Private Sector, Quasi Government, 1968-78; First Chief Executive, Agro Pumpsets & Implements Ltd, Hyderabad, 1978-84; First Managing Director, Non-Conventional Energy Development Corporation of Andhra Pradesh Ltd, 1984-89; First Managing Director, Indian Renewable Energy Development Agency Ltd, 1989-. Publications: Several publications in professional journals. Honours include: 16th All India Industrial Promotion Gold Award, 1994-95; Bharat Nirman Award; Award for Eminent Mechanical Engineer, Institution of Engineers, India, 1997. Memberships include: Energy & Environment Steering Committee, World Bank; President, International Association of Small Hydro; Vice President, Honorary Secretary, Solar Energy Society of India; Chairman, Board of Governors, Bharathidasan School of Energy, Trichy. Address: Managing Director, IREDA, Core 4A East Court, India Habitat Center, New Delhi 110003, India.

**BALAISIS Pranciskus**, b. 30 May 1942, Rokiskis, Lithuania. Radio Engineer. m. Ramona Jakubauskaite, 1 son, 1 daughter. Education: Engineer, 1965; PhDr, 1976; Habil Dr, 1987; Professor, 1994. Appointments: Engineer, 1965-70, Senior Engineer, 1970-71, Scientific Researcher, 1971-73, Senior Scientific Researcher, Head of Department, 1973-88, Professor, 1988-98, Kaunas University of Technology. Honour: Winner, Lithuanian National Science Award, 1995. Address: Birzelio 23-iosios 15-23, 3009 Kaunas, Lithuania.

**BALAKIN Alexander**, b. 8 August 1957, Kazan, Russia. Physicist. m. Marina Yablokova, 1979, 1 son. Education: Graduate, Kazan State University, Physics Faculty, 1974-79; Postgraduate, 1979-82; PhD, 1982. Appointments: Associated Professor, Department of Relativity Theory and Gravitation, Kazan University; Vice Director, Kazan Scientific Center of Gravitational Wave Research. Publications: 75 articles in Russian and international journals. Membership: Russian

Gravitational Society. Address: Department of Relativity Theory and Gravitation, Kazan State University, 18 Lenina Str Kazan, 420008, Russia.

**BALAKIRSKY Vladimir Boris**, b. 2 October 1957, Leningrad, USSR. Engineer. Education: MS, 1980; PhD, 1987. Appointments: LOMO, St Petersburg, 1980-90; Pargolovsky Zavod, St Petersburg, 1992-93; University Lund, Sweden, 1993-94; University Bielefeld, Germany, 1995-98; University Eindhoven, The Netherlands, 1999-. Publications: Papers in Problems of Information Transmission, IEEE Transactions on Information Theory. Memberships: Data Security Association, Confident, 1993-; IEEE, 1996-. Address: Grazhdansk Prosp 104-4-21, 195267 Saint Petersburg, Russia.

**BALAKRISHNAN B C**, b. 5 August 1928, India. Lexicographer. m. G Rajamma, 3 sons. Education: MA, 1953 Postgraduate Diploma, Linguistics, 1960; PhD, 1978 Appointments: Lecturer, Head, Department of Malayalam, S T Hindu College, 1953-59; Lecturer, Linguistics, Annamala University, 1960-61; Assistant Editor, Malayalam Lexicon University of Kerala, 1961-78, Chief Editor, 1978-88; Chie Editor, C V Exegetic Dictionary, 1988-98. Publications Numerous books and articles in professional journals. Honours Several. Memberships: Founder Secretary, Lexico Graphica Society of India, 1970-90, President, 1990-93; Academy o South Indian Literatures; Senate, Academic Council, Kerala University; Academic Council, Telugei University. Address Cultural & Lexicographical Research Institute, D-8, Jawaha Nagar, Thiruvananthapuram 41, India.

**BALALAYEV Vladimir Alekseyevich**, b. 3 December 1939 Leningrad, Russia. Physicist. m. Kolesova Margarita, 1 son Education: Diploma, Leningrad State University, 1962 Candidate of Physical, Mathematical Sciences, 1972; Senic Scientific Worker, 1977; Correspondence, Member of Russi Metrological Academy, 1992. Appointments: Junior Researc Worker, Senior Research Worker, Leading Research Worke Chief of Laboratory, Chief of Department, Vice Director of th Institute, Mendeleyev's Institute for Metrology, St Petersburc 1965-. Publications: 88 publications. Honours: Silver Medal fc secondary school, 1956; Decoration For Merits i Standardization, 1983; Medal, Veteran of Labour, 199( Decoration, Survivor of Blockaded Leningrad, 1993; Jubile Medal, Fifty Years of the Great Patriotic War 1941-1945, 199! Memberships: Editorial, Publishing Council, Mendeleyev' Institute for Metrology, 1979-; Scientific Council, Mendeleyev Institute for Metrology, 1980-; Candidate Dissertation Counc Mendeleyev's Institute for Metrology, 1982-. Address: 11 Varshavskaya str, Apt 70 196240 St Petersburg, Russia.

**BALANKIN Alexander**, b. 3 March 1958, Moscow Physicist; Professor. m. Fatima Balankina, 1 daughte Education: MSc Solid State Physics, 1981, PhD Physics Mathematics, 1986, Moscow Engineering Physics Institut DSc Physics & Mathematics, 1991, Dzerzhinsky Milita Academy. Appointments: Junior Scientist, Moscow Engineerir Physics Institute, 1981-83; Sr Scientist, 1986-90, Head Research Laboratory, 1990-92, Dzerzhinsky Military Academ Moscow; Professor of Monterey Technological Universi Mexico City, 1992-97; Professor of Mechanics of Nation Polytechnic Institute, Mexico City, 1997-. Publications: Auth and co-Author, 140 refereed journal articles on solid sta physics, solid and fracture mechanics, synergetic and fractal Author 2 books and co-author 4 books. Honours: State Prize Ministry of Defence of USSR, 1990; Prize of Academy Science of USSR, 1991; Prize of Pleiades Publishing Inc best publication in 1995, 1996; Romulo Garza Prize Research & Technology Development in Mexico, 199

National Researcher of Mexico, 1995. Memberships: National Consul of Strength of Materials, Russia; Counselor of National Consul for Science & Technology of Mexican Government; Russian Academy of Natural Sciences; National (Mexican) Academy of Sciences; Mexican Physical Society; President, Fracture Mechanics Section, Mexican Academy of Material Sciences. Address: SEPI-ESIME Ed 5 3er Piso, U P Adolfo Lopez Mateos, 07738 Zacatenco DF, Mexico.

**BALAYAN Mesrop,** b. 25 July 1925. Doctor of Psychology. m. 2 sons, 1 daughter. Education: Doctorate, Child Psychology, Sorbonne, Paris, 1962. Appointment: Dean, Faculty of Education, Isfaham State University. Publications include: Psychology of Puberty, 4th edition, 1992; Child Psychology, 2nd edition, 1998. Membership: International Association of Psychology. Address: c/o St Nerses Ehnohzlay Library, The Aem Cathedrale, Julfa Isfahan, PB 81735/115, Iran.

**BALDWIN Allen Adail,** b. 15 July 1939, St Augustine, FL, USA. Attorney at Law. Education: BA, Brigham Young University, 1969; JD, Southern University, 1975. Appointments: Teacher, High School; Attorney, 1975-. Publications: Tricks to Make the Angels Weep; Call in Not Heave; Redeem us From Virtue. Memberships: Various Bar Associations; American Trial Lawyers Association. Address: 308 Saint Johns Ave, Palatka, FL 32177-4723, USA.

**BALLER William Warren,** b. 12 June 1943, Lincoln, Nebraska, USA. School Psychologist; Neuropsychologist. m. Janet Elizabeth Thomsen, 1 son, 1 daughter. Education: BS Education and Liberal Arts Math and English, 1965, University of Nebraska; MA Education, 1967, PhD Psychology and Education, 1969, University Missouri; Postdoctoral Internship in Neuropsychiatry, 1974-75, Blackfoot State Hospital South. Appointments: Lecturer, 1965-67, Instructor, 1967-69, Special Education Teacher, University of Missouri; Assistant to Associate Professor of Education and Psychology, 1969-79, Professor of Education and Psychology, 1980-86, Idaho State University; Distinguished Professor of Human Behaviour, USInternational University, San Diego, 1979; Director, Bureau of Educational Research and Services, Idaho State University, 1979-83; Psychologist, Utica City School District, and Neuropsychologist consulting to local hospitals, 1986-. Publications: 47 refereed research and commentary. Honours: Phi Beta Kappa; Phi Delta Kappa; NDEA Teaching Fellow, University MO, 1965-68; Mu Epsilon Nu; Ford Foundation Career Scholar, 1963-65. Memberships: Elder, Musician, First Presbyterian Church of Utica; American Academy of Political and Social Scientists; American Legion; US Taekwondo Union Inc. Address: Utica City School District, 1115 Mohawk Street, Utica, NY 13501-3700, USA.

**BALOGUN Joseph Abiodun,** b. 1 January 1955, Jofin-Isanlu, Kogi, Nigeria. Physical therapy. m. Adetutu Olotu, son, 2 daughters. Education: BSc Physiotherapy, University of Ibadan, 1977; MS Orthopedic and Sports Physical Therapy, University of Pittsburgh, 1981; PhD Exercise Physiology, University of Pittsburgh, 1985. Appointments: Assistant Professor, Russell Sage College, Troy, New York, 1984-86; Senior Lecturer, Consultant Physiotherapist, Obafemi Awolowo University of Ile-Ife, Nigeria. Visiting Professor, University of Florida, 1988; Vice-Dean, Faculty of Health Sciences, Obafemi Awolowo University, 1990-91; Associate Professor, Texas Woman's University, 1991-93; Professor, Chairman, Physical Therapy , Associate Dean, Student Academic Affairs, College of Health Related Professions, 1993-. Publications: Over 70 articles published; Several chapters in textbooks; More than 12 published abstracts. Honours: SUNY 1993-94 Faculty Award, 1994, 98; American Physical Therapy Association Minority

Initiatives Award, 1996; Fellow, American College of Sports Medicine, 1996; Honorary Fellow, Institute of Public Health of Obafemi Awolowo University, 1997. Memberships: American Physical Therapy Association; American College of Sports Medicine; American Academy of Physical Therapy; United Kingdom Council for Professions Supplementary to Medicine; Nigerian Society of Physiotherapy; Nigerian Public Health Association. Address: 8708 Glenwood Road, Brooklyn, NY 11236, USA.

**BALTKAJS Janis,** b. 12 July 1935, Riga, Latvia. Pharmacologist. m. Sarmite Baltkaje, 1 son, 1 daughter. Education: Diploma, 1960, Riga Medical Institute; MD, 1965; MD habilitation, 1993, Latvia Academy of Medicine. Appointments: Senior Lecturer, 1967-72, Vice-Dean, 1969-88, Assistant Professor, 1972-94, Riga Medical Institute; Professor of Pharmacology, Latvia Academy of Medicine, 1994-. Publications: Co-author or author, 9 monographs; Over 100 publications; 3 author's certificates; 2 patents. Memberships: Latvian Society of Pharmacology; Latvian Physician's Journal; Institute of Pharmacology. Address: Salaspils iela 12-5-90, LV 1057, Riga, Latvia.

**BALZER Leslie Alfred,** b. 17 October 1944, Sydney, Australia. Investment Manager. m. Jannette Elaine Balzer, 1 son, 1 daughter. Education: BSc, Mathematics and Physics, BE (Hons 1), Mechanical Engineering, University of New South Wales; PhD, Control and Management Systems, University of Cambridge, England; Graduate Diploma, Applied Finance and Investment, Securities Institute of Australia. Appointments: Senior Development Officer in Engineering, Sugar Division, Assistant to Chief Mill Engineer, Project Engineer, Design Engineer, Assistant Engineer, CSR Ltd, 1962-76; Chairman, Manufacturing and Management Group, Senior Lecturer, Mechanical Engineering, University of Technology, Sydney, 1976-83; Manager, Advanced Technology Centre, NSW Department of Industrial Development, 1983-85; Dean, Faculty of Engineering, Royal Melbourne Institute of Technology, 1985-86; Chairman, Management Committee, Company Director, Centre for Innovation Development, Technisearch Ltd, 1985-86; Senior Executive, Pring Dean Ltd, 1986-89; Associate Principal, 1989, Principal, 1990, William M Mercer Inc; Director, John Ford and Associates Pty Ltd, 1990-91; Investment Manager Lend Lease Investment Management, 1991-. Publications: Over 30 papers in international research journals and for international and local conferences. Honours: Fellow, Australian Institute of Company Directors, Institution of Engineers, Australia, Institute of Mathematics and Its Applications, UK, Securities Institute of Australia; Associate Fellow, Australian Institute of Management; Colonial Sugar Refining Prize, AE Goodwin Memorial Scholarship, University of New South Wales; David Garrick Halmstad Memorial Prize, American Actuarial Education and Research Foundation, 1982; Outstanding Paper of the Year, Journal of Investing, 1994. Memberships include: National Committee of Futures Trading, Securities Institute of Australia; International Federation of Automatic Control; Australian Secretary, Asian-Oceanic Computing Industry Organization, 1984-85; Vice President, 1990-95, President, 1995-, Q-Group, Australia. Address: PO Box 785, Pymble, NSW 2073, Australia.

**BAMATRAF Abdulrahman M,** b. 6 October 1952, Mukalla, Yemen. Agriculturist, Environment Scientist. m. Samira Abdu Ali, 1 son, 4 daughters. Education: BSc, Soil Science, Baghdad University, 1974; MSc, Soil Science, Biometcorology, Utah State University, 1979; PhD, Soil and Water Science, University of Arizona, 1986. Appointments: Soil Officer, 1974-76; Farm Manager, 1979-82; Research Scientist, 1986-88; Assistant Director General, 1988-90; Professor, Soil and Water Science,

Faculty of Agriculture, Sana'a University, 1990-; Associate Dean for Scienitific Research, Sana's University, 1994; Director General, Agricultural Research and Extension Authority, 1994-97; Vice Minister, Ministry of Agriculture and Irrigation, 1997-. Publications: Papers published in scientific journals; Technical Reports; Constancy Reports Commissioned by several International Organisations. Honours: Certificate of Merit of Outstanding Achievement. Memberships: Honour Society of Agriculture; Yemen Society for Environmental Protection; Water Protection Society; COSPAR Associate; Hadramout Welfare and Social Society. Address: P O Box 13753, Sana's, Republic of Yemen.

**BAMEUL Franck,** b. 9 December 1965, Cherbourg, France. Entomologist; General Practice Physician. m. Gaetane Gaute. Education: MSc, University Bordeaux, 1993; MD, 1995; Intern, Bordeaux, 1994-95. Appointments: Consultant Specialist, Water beetle Specialist Group, UICN; Former Assistant, University Bordeaux. Honours: Special Prize Paul Pesson, 1994. Memberships: Society of Systematic Biologists; The Balfour Browne Club; Willy Hennig Society; Entomological Society of France.

**BANASZAK Grzegorz,** b. 10 February 1958, Gostyn, Poland. Mathematician. m. Beata Banaszak. Education: MS Math, 1982, Poznan, Poland; PhD Math, 1990, OSU, Columbus, USA; Hab in Math, 1996, Im Pan, Warsaw, Poland. Appointments: Szczecin University, 1982-86; GTA, Ohio State University, Columbus, 1986-90; Visiting Lecturer, Ohio State University, 1990-91; Postdoctorate, McMaster University, 1991-93; Szczecin University, 1993-94; Professor, Poznan, 1994-. Publications: articles in math journals; Editor, Proceedings of Alg K Theory Conference, Cont Math. Honour: Annual Award of Polish Mathematical Society, 1995. Membership: AMS. Address: Adam Mickiewicz University, Ul Matejki 48/49, 60769 Poznan, Poland.

**BANCIU Axente Constantin,** b. 13 October 1938, Bucharest, Romania. Chemist. m. Elsa Christa Witschel, dec, 1 son. Education: MSc, 1963, Technical University Dresden, Germany; PhD, 1974, Polytechnical Institute Bucharest, Romania. Appointments: Chemist, Chem Pharm Research Institute Bucharest, 1963-67; Chemist, Institute Physical Chemistry, Romanian Academy Bucharest, 1967-70; Scientific Researcher, 1970-78; Principal Senior Researcher, 1978-. Publications: 28 original papers on chemistry of complex compounds; Co-author 16 original papers and 6 patents. Memberships: Reviewer, Rev Roumaine Chim, 1975-; Fellow, Romanian Chemistry Society, 1992-; New York Academy Science, 1998-. Address: Inst Physical Chemistry of Romanian Academy, Spl Independentei 202, RO-77208 Bucharest, Romania.

**BANETH Gad,** b. 20 August 1959, Jerusalem. Veterinarian Researcher. m. Anat, 1 son, 2 daughters. Education: BSc, 1987, DVM, 1990, Hebrew University. Appointments: Lecturer, 1995, Department Head, 1997, Small Animal Medicine, School of Veterinary Medicine, Hebrew University. Publications: Hepatozoon Canis Infection in Two Dogs, 1995. Memberships: Israel Society for Parasitology; American Society of Tropical Medicine and Hygiene. Address: Kibbutz Tzora, 99803 Shimshon, Israel.

**BANIK Sambhu Nath,** b. 7 November 1935, Joypara, India. Clinical Psychology. m. Promila Banik, 2 daughters. Education: BSc, 1956; MSc, 1958; PhD, 1964; Postdoctoral Fellowship, 1965. Career: President, Family Diagnostics & Therapeutic Center; Executive Director, Presidents Committee on Mental Retardation; Director, Mental Health Administration. Honours:

Gold Medals, National & International Awards for Communit & Professional Services. Address: Family Diagnostic Therapeutic Center, 4400 MacArthur Boulevard North Wes Suite 305, Washington, DC 20007, USA.

**BAO Fucheng,** b. 20 November 1932, Yijing, Zhenyanç Anhui, China. Wood Science Researcher. m. Hu Rong, daughters. Education: Study, Department of Forestry, Anhu University, China, 1950-54; Advanced Study, Researc Institute of Forestry, Academy of Science, USSR, 1957-6C Advanced Study, College of Environmental and Forestr Science, SUNY, USA, 1983-84. Appointments: Professor c Wood Science, Chinese Academy of Forestry; Concurren Professor of Wood Science, Beijing Forestry University Nanjing Forestry University, North-East Forestry University Honour Professor, Anhui Agriculture University; Fellow International Academy of Wood Science. Honours: First Aware of Science and Technology Progress from: National Forestr Administration, 1998, State Forestry Ministry, China, 1995; Firs Award of Distinguished Science Book from the State Ministr of News and Publishing, China, 1987. Memberships: Vic President, China Wood Science Society; Chairman: Academi Committee of Wood Science and Technology Laboratory Technical Committee for Wood Basic Standarisation, of th State Ministry of Forestry, China. Address: Chinese Academ of Forestry, Beijing 100091, China.

**BAO Jishan,** b. March 1930, Fu County, Laoning Province China. Professor. m. Jingchun Na, 2 sons, 1 daughter Education: Graduate, 1955, Graduate Study degree, 1957 Speciality of Applied Geophysics, Beijing Institute of Geology Appointments: Teacher, Chengdu Institute of Geology, 1957- Director, Geophysical Prospecting Research Section an Director of Research Section of Geophysical Prospecting fo Petroleum, 1957-; Associate Professor, 1978-; Professor 1987-; Vice Director and Director of Applied Geophysics Dept and Vice Director of Research Institute for Applied Geophysics 1974-92. Publications: Digital Techniques of Seismi Prospecting, vol 1-4, 1973, 1974, 1977, 1987; Seismi Prospecting Principle and Methods, Vol 1, 1980; Digita Processing of Seismic Prospecting, 1990; 20 research papers 7 research achievement reports presented. Honours: 1 Honou Certificate, 5 second class Prizes and Honour Certificate c Chinese Expert by Patent Office of China, 1998; Governmen Subsidy granted by State Council of China, 1993- Memberships: Committeeman, Committee on Geophysica Prospecting for Petroleum of Chinese Petroleum Society Council member, Sichuan Petroleum Society; Director Chengdu Sifa Research Institute for New Technology; Director Chengdu Chengke Research Institute for New Technology c Geophysics; Vice Chairman, Committee on Geophysica Prospecting of Sichuan Petroleum Society; Council membe Chinese Association of Educationalist. Address: Dept c Information Engineering and Geophysics, Chengdu Universit of Technology, Shilidian, Chengdu, Sichuan Province 610059 China.

**BAOLIN Duan,** b. 6 January 1934, Jiangsu, China Professor. m. Chen Su Mei, 2 daughters. Education: Graduate Peking University, 1958. Appointments: Teacher, Professor Researcher on Folk Literature and Folklore, Vice Director Anthropology and Folklore Research Centre, Peking University 1958-98. Publications: The Study of Chinese Folk Literature 1981, 1985, 1998; Jokes - Human's Comic Art, 1991; an others; Chief Editor, Chinese and Foreign Folk Prosody, 1987 1991; The Study of Laughter - Comments on the Stories c Nasirdin Afant, 1988; Chief Compiler, A Dictionary of Foll Literature, 1988; A Study of World Folk Customs, 1989 Contemporary Satirical Folksongs, 1993. Honours: Include

Award, Premio Pitre, of Italy, 1996. Memberships: Vice President, Chinese Folklore Association; Chinese Popular Literature Society; Chairman, Beijing Folk Writers and Artists Association; International Society for Folk Narrative Research. Address: Department of Chinese, Peking University, 100871 Beijing, China.

**BAR-AM Benjamin,** b. 20 July 1923, Wiesbaden, Germany. Composer; Musicologist; Music Critic. Education: Studied with Paul Ben-Haim, Tel-Aviv; Ecole Normale, Paris, France; Music Teachers College Tel-Aviv; BA, University of Tel-Aviv. Appointments: Music Critic, Jerusalem Post, 1959-96; Secretary General, Israeli Composer's League, 1958-76; Chairman, 1976-78; Lecturer, Department of Musicology, Tel-Aviv University, 1973. Publications: Author, numerous articles on music; Compositions until 1975; Songs and songcycles for voice and piano, liturgical compositions for conservative synagogues in the US; Cantata, My Heart is Steadfast, psalms; Since 1988: Stimmen, for alto and instruments with text by Paul Celan; Symphony No 1; My Little Sister, for alto and piano trio, Abba Kovner; Lamentations, motet for alto, baritone and mixed choir, biblical. Address: Cremieux 22, Tel-Aviv, Israel.

**BAR-TAL Daniel,** b. 31 January 1946, USSR. Professor of Political Psychology. 1 son, 1 daughter. Education: BA Psychology and Sociology, Tel Aviv University, Israel, 1970; MS, Social Psychology, 1973, PhD, Social Psychology, 1974, University Pittsburgh, USA. Appointments: Lecturer, 1975-79, Senior Lecturer, 1979-83, Professor of Psychology, 1989-, School of Education, Tel Aviv University; Visiting Associate Professor, Department Psychology, Vanderbilt University, Nashville, Tennessee, 1981-82; Fellow Professor, 1983-89; Visiting Professor, Department of Psychology, Brandeis University, 1987-88. Publications: Author 3 books; Co-Editor, 10 books. Honours: Otto Klineberg Intercultural and International Relations Prize of SPSSI, 1991; President, International Society of Political Psychology, 1999-2000. Memberships: American Educational Research Association; American Psychological Association; European Association of Experimental Social Psychology; International Society of Political Psychology; Society for the Advancement of Social Psychology; Society for the Psychological Study of Social Issues; Society for Experimental Social Psychology; International Association of Applied Psychology. Address: School of Education, Tel Aviv University, Tel Aviv, Israel.

**BARABINO William A,** b. 11 February 1932, Bay Shore, New York, USA. Company Founder; Chief Executive Officer. 1 son, 2 daughters. Education: Fordham University, 1950; AS, SUNY College of Technology, Farmingdale, 1952; Diploma, Guided Missiles, USAF Air University; Studied, St Louis University, 1957; Diploma, Alexander Hamilton Institute, New York City, 1963. Appointments: District Manager, Piper Aircraft Corporation, Central America, 1960-62; Application Engineer, Laboratory for Electronics, Boston, Massachusetts, 1962-63; Marketing Manager, Special Equipment Division, Itek Corporation, Waltham, Massachusetts, 1963-65; Business Consultant, near Reading, Massachusetts, 1965-68; Director, Andover Institute of Business, 1968-70; Science and Technology Researcher, near Reading, 1970-; Consultant, CTS Corporation, Proctor and Gamble, Scovill Corporation, Goodyear Aerospace, American Environmental Products Inc, Plessey Co Ltd, General Motors, Ford Motor Co; Founder, Chief Executive Officer, Brief Necessities Agoura Hills, California, 1990. Publications: Low Tire Pressure Monitoring; Society of Automotive Engineers, 1970; Nations Business, 1979; Design News, 1979; Automotive Industries, 1980; Articles in professional journals; Several patents. Honours:

Rated pilot, Rated Navigator, USAF, Captain, 1952-59; Extraordinary Flying Skills, USAF, 1958, Chief of Staff, Guatemalan Air Force, 1962. Memberships: Republican Party; Presidential Task Force; American Legion; Veterans of Foreign Wars. Address: 5662 Walnut Ridge, Agoura Hills, CA 91301, USA.

**BARAKAT Nahla Salah,** b. 13 February 1963, Saudi Arabia. Lecturer. m. Eng Mourad El Newahi, 1 son. Education: BSc, 1985; MSc, 1990; PhD, 1996. Appointment: Lecturer, Research Associate, Department of Pharmaceutics Faculty of Pharmacy. Publications: 1991, 1995, 1998; Ideal Pharmacist, 1999. Membership: Egyptian Pharmaceutical Association. Address: Faculty Pharmacy, Khartom Square, Alexandria, Egypt.

**BARAN Neculai,** b. 2 August 1909, Tomesti Commune, Iasi County, Romania. Teacher, University Lecturer. m. Jeana Popovici, 1 son. Education: CUM LAUDE, 1929-32. Appointments: Substitute Teacher, National Highschool, 1934-35; Teacher, National Highschool, 1935; University Lecturer, Al I Cuza University, 1964-72. Publications: Archaeological Contributions to the Medieval History of Tomesti Commune, 1964; The Medical Conceptions of Doctor Dimitrie Caracas in Poemata Medica, 1965; An Outline of the Philosophical Language at Lucretius, 1965; Heraclitus in Dacoromania, 1966; Aspects of the Formation of Philosophical Terminology in the Thinking of the Roman People, 1967; Sextus Empiricus' Sceptic Doctorine, 1967; Chromatic Elements at Lucretius, 1968, 1969; Using Latin for the Harmony Among Peoples, 1969; The Post Ovidius in Romanian Literature, 1971; Teaching Latin to Young People, 1971; How Did Horatius Concirved the Pleasures of Life, 1975; Petrarca in Romanian Literature, 1975; The Stylistic Coordinates of the Chromatic Terminology at Lucretius, 1975; The Concept of Time and Duration in Latin, 1976; The Essential Features of the Latin Chromatic Vocabulary, 1983; Latin Adages and Reflections in Mihai Eminescu's Literary Works, 1997; Hippocrate's Oath, 1998. Honours: Doctorate, Classical Philology, 1971. Memberships: Studii Clasice, 1963; Societas Eirene, 1969; Association Vox Latina, 1970. Address: 18 Vascauteanu Street, 6600 Iasi, Romania.

**BARASAN Aabir,** b. 4 February 1963, Mymensingh, Bangladesh. Editor; Writer; Cultural Worker. m. Shanchita Sarma. Education: SSC, Science, 1978; HSC, Science, 1980; BA, 1987; Diploma, Recitation, Acting and Study in other subjects. Career: Founder, Sruti Cultural Academy and Dhabaman Literature Movement, 1993; Teacher of Recitation, Shilpakala Academy, 1997-. Publications: Poems in books, magazines and newspapers, 1986-97. Honours: congratulation Greetings, Avyatrik and Prochestra, 1995, 1997. Memberships: Pragatik; Bangladesh Shilpakala Academy; Abritti Samannaya Parishad. Address: Santana Market, Chasara, Narayanganj, Bangladesh.

**BARATTA Giovanni Battista,** b. 8 December 1942, Priverno, Italy. Astronomer. 2 daughters. Education: Degree, Physics, University La Sapienza, Rome, 1967. Appointments: Researcher, Consiglio Nazionale delle Ricerche, 1968-70; Astronomer, Osservatorio Astronomico, Rome, 1970-; Coordinator, Astronomical Observatory of Campo Imperatore, 1978-93. Publications: Numerous articles in professional journals. Honours: Grants, Accademia Nazionale Lincei, Edinburgh, 1972-74. Memberships include: International Astronomical Union. Address: Osservatorio Astronomico, Via Parco Mellini 84, I-00136 Rome, Italy.

**BARBER William,** b. 4 January 1942, Morristown, NJ, USA. Physical Educator, Teacher. m. Anita, 1 son. Education: BE,

University of Nebraska, 1967. Appointments: Recreational Director, Town of Morristown; Employment, Communication Director, M & M Mars; 1st Black Wrestling Coach, Track Coach, No Jersey Morris Catholic High School, 1967-73; Social Communications Worker, Urban 4H, 1967-73; Social record Director, Morristown Neighborhood House, 1967-; Sales Trainee, School Communication Worker, Social Case, GUidence Conselor, International Harvester, 1967-73; President, Barber Maintenance Cleaning Contractor; Manager of Building Opperations, Manager of Public Relations, Building Service Supervisor, AT and T, -1990; Intervention Instructor, Physical Health Educator Instructor, Passaic Technical Vocational Education; Mental HealthCounselor, St Clare Riverside Medical Centre. Honours: Jaycees Distinguished Service Award; Outstanding Citizen 4-H Club Award; Morris County Human Resource Award; NAACP Communications Award; Communication Service Award. Memberships: Charlest Menninger Society; Zeke HArris Science Club; Hands Across Morristown; New Jersey School Social Workers Council; Market Street Mission Christian Counselling Training; Many other memberships. Address: Passaic County Technical Institute, 45 Reiwhardt Road, Wayne, NJ 07470, USA.

**BARBOUR Blair Allen,** b. 12 August 1962, Huntington, West Virginia, USA. Electro-Optical Engineer. m. Susan L Barbour, 2 sons, 2 daughters. Education: BS Engineering Physics, 1984; MSEE Electro-Optical Engineering, 1986. Appointments: Member, University of Alabama Governing Board for Masters of Optics Programme; Chairman, Asbury CDC Governing Board; Member Alabama Optical Alliance Organisation. Publications: Over 30 national and international publications; 5 patents and patent pendings US and international. Honours: 2 best paper awards from AIAA; 1997 National Defense Industrial Association Award for innovative sensor technology development; Roy Nichols Performance Excellence Award. Memberships: Optical Society of America; SPIE; Sigma Xi Honour Society; Boys Youth Leader; Royal Ambassadors; Youth Soccer & Baseball Coach; Leader in Team Kid's International. Address: Nichols Research Corp MS, 913 4040 S Memorial Parkway Ste A, Huntsville, AL 35802-1399, USA.

**BARGER James D,** b. 17 May 1917, Bismarck, North Carolina, USA. Senior Pathologist. 2 s, 2 d. Education: AB, BS, University of Dakota, 1939; MD, University of Pennsylvania, 1941; MS, Pathology, University of Minnesota. Diplomate, American Board of Pathology; Registered Quality Engineer in California; Medical Director, South West Blood Bank, Blood Services, Arizona, Nevada; President, College of American Pathologists; Senior Pathologists, Sunrise Hospital, Las Vegas, Nevada, 1964-. Honours: Pathologist of the Year, 1977. Memberships: Various Societies; American Medical Association; American Association of Pathologists; American Cancer Society. Address: 1307 Canosa Avenue, Las Vegas, NV 89104, USA.

**BARKHAN Ronald Cecil,** b. 25 October 1916, Johannesburg, South Africa. Hypnotherapist; Psychotherapist; Relaxologist. m. widower. Education: PhD Psychology in Hypnotherapy, 1061, National University, Toronto, Canada. Honours: International Order of Merit 1991, International Roll of Honour for Distinguished Service to his profession, Hypnotherapy, 1983. Address: 102 Roslin Street, Sydenham, Johannesburg 2192, South Africa.

**BARMAN Bhaskar Roy,** b. 19 February 1950, Badurtala, Camilla, Bangladesh. Teacher. m. Mrs Shyamali Roy Barman, 1 son. Education: BA Hons English, 1970, Maharaja Bir Bikram College, Agartala; MA English, 1976, Calcutta University; BEd,

1993, Tripura University. Appointments: Teacher, Government Higher Secondary School under the Directorate of Education, Government of Tripura, India. Publications: Modern Stories: The Trap & Other Stories; Folktales of Tripura; Melange: An Anthology of Short Stories Translated into English from Bengali; The Rhymester, a novel translated into English from Bengali; Bouquet: An Anthology of Short Stories Translated into English from Bengali. Honours: The UWA Life-Time Achievement Award from United Writers Association, Chennai, India. Memberships: Writers Forum, Ranchi, India; Fellow, United Writers Association, Chennai. Address: South Bank of Girls Bedhjung Dighi, Itakhola Rd, Banamalipur, Agartala 799 001, West Tripura, India.

**BARMAN Dangshi,** b. 1 May 1943, Assam, India. Government Servant. m. Malaya Barman, 1 son, 2 daughters. Education: MA, Political Science; LLB; PhD, Land Reform Administration and Agrarian Reforms in Assam. Appointment: Additional Deputy Commissioner in Darrang District, Assam Civil Service. Publications: Good number of articles on Land Revenue Administration of Assam. Address: PO Mangaldoi, Darrang District, Assam, India.

**BARNA Susan M,** b. 3 September 1949, OH, USA. Entrepreneur. m. 11 September 1970, 2 daughters. Education: Nazareth Academy; Garland Junior College: Retailing, Fashion Modelling, Executive Management, MBO, Professional Assessment Centres, Graphic Arts Course, Computer, Word Processing, Public Relations Communications School, Career Related Training, Writing Seminars, Bar Association; Legal, Political, Drug, Violence, Crime Task Force Seminars; Accounting, Bookkeeping, Administrative Training, Personnel, Education, Fundraising, Medical and Health Services. Career: The May Department Stores, Management, Fashion, Advertising, Marketing, Administration; The Sherwin Williams Co, Manager, Field Progs, National Decorating Services Manager, National Decorating Consultant, Public Relations Mngr; Consumer, Industrial Chemical, Automotive Publications: Articles and appearances: Major Newspapers Magazines, Radio, TV; Public Relations Handbook; Heritage Decorating; Newsletters, Training Courses and other copyrigh material. Honours: International Fine Arts College of Fashion 1966; Merit Achievement Award, Cleveland YWCA, 1978 Outstanding Young Women of America, 1978; Greate Cleveland's Enterprising Young Women, 1987; Nationa Science Olympiad, 1992; 2000 Notable American Women 1994; Order of International Fellowship, 1995; IBC Advisor Board, 1995; Women's Inner Circle of Achievement, 1995 1996, 1997; International Woman of the Year, 1995; Twentiet Century Award of Achievement; World Who's Who of Womer 1994, 1995, 1996, 1997; International Who's Who o Contemporary Achievement, 1997; Presidential Seal of Honou 1996. Memberships: Treasurer, JA; Color Marketing Grour Speakers Bureau; Friends of the Library; Smithsonia Associates; First VP, Towne Center; Junior Auxiliaries, Medin County Hospital; Laurel School Parents, Board; NAFE Address: PO Box 41036, Brecksville, OH 44141-0036, USA.

**BARNES Junor Albert,** b. 10 May 1940, St Ann's Bay Jamaica. Research Biochemist, Lecturer. m. Florelda Efet Willis, 1 son. Education: BSc, Chemistry and Zoology, Londo 1973; MSc, Analytical Chemistry and Instrumentatio Loughborough, 1976; PhD, Chemistry, Birmingham, 198 Appointments: Post Doctoral Fellow, Alberta Heritag Foundation for Medical Research, 1983-86; Researd Associate, University of Alberta and University of Calgar 1987-90; Senior Lecturer, Biochemistry University of the We Indies, 1991-. Publications: Over 60 Publications. Honou Alberta Heritage for Medical Research Post Doctoral Fello

1983-86. Memberships: New York and Caribean Academy of Sciences; Canadian Institute of Chemistry; Institute of Biology. Address: University of West Indies, Department Preclin Sci Med Scis, Saint Augustine, Trinidad and Tobago.

**BARNES Mary Elizabeth,** b. 24 September 1938, Bladenboro, North Carolina, USA. Professor of Theology and Ethics. m. (1) 1 son, 2 daughters, div, (2) John W Eddins Jr. Education: BA, English, Meredith College, Raleigh, North Carolina, 1960; MDiv, Southeastern Baptist Seminary, Wake Forest, North Carolina; PhD, Theology and Ethics, Duke University, Durham. Appointments: Assistant Professor of Theology, Southeastern Baptist Seminary, 1984-91; Professor of Theology and Ethics, Baptist Seminary at Richmond, Virginia, 1991-. Publications: Books: An Affront to the Gospel? The Radical Barth and The Southern Baptist Convention, 1987; The Story of Discipleship: Christ, Humanity, and Church in Narrative Perspective, 1995. Memberships: American Academy of Religion; National Association of Baptist Professors of Religion. Address: Baptist Theological Seminary at Richmond, 3400 Brook Road, Richmond, VA 23227, USA.

**BARNES Melver Raymond,** b. 15 November 1917, Salisbury, North Carolina, USA. Science Chemist. Education: BA, Chemistry, Chapel Hill, North Carolina, USA, 1947; Math and Chemical courses at McCoy College, Baltimore; MD, University of Utah and University of California, Los Angeles. Appointments: Pittsburgh Testing Laboratories, Greensboro, North Carolina, USA, 1948-49; North Carolina State Highway and Public Works Commission, Raleigh, NC, 1949-51; Edgewood Arsenal, Edgewood, Maryland; 1951-61; Dugway Proving Ground, Dugway, Utah, USA, 1961-70. Publications: Several government science reports in closed literature and papers on natural sciences. Memberships: American Association for the Advancement of Science; American Chemical Society; American Physical Society; International Platform Association; Life Patron, International Biographical Association; American Biographical Institute Research Association; UN Association of the USA. Address: 1486 Swicegood Road, Linwood, NC 27299, USA.

**BARNES Patience Plummer,** b. 28 September 1932, Mt Vernon, New York, USA. Writer; Editor. m. James J Barnes, 1 son, 1 daughter. Education: BA Government, 1954, Smith College. Appointments: J Walter Thompson Company, New York City, 1950-55; Free Lance Writer & Editor, 1955-; Research Associate, Wabash College, 1988-. Publications: Editor: Free Trade in Books: A study of the London Book Trade since 1800, 1964; Authors, Publishers and Politicians: The Quest for an Anglo-American Copyright Agreement, 1815-54, 1974; Co-author: Hitler's Mein Kampf in Britain and America, 1930-39, 1980; James Vincent Murphy, Translator & Interpreter of Fascist Europe, 1880-1946, 1987; Private and Confidential: Letters from British Ministers in Washington to their Foreign Secretaries in London 1845-67, 1992; Co-author, 9 articles; Oral presentation 19 papers; Other work in progress. Memberships: The Athenian; League of Women Voters; Alumnae Association of Smith College; Friends of the Crawfordsville Public Library; Montgomery County Historical Society; The London Goodenough Trust for Overseas Graduates, UK; Metropolitan Opera Guild. Address: 7 Locust Hill, Crawfordsville, Indiana 47933, USA.

**BARNHART Stephen R.** Security Advisor. Education: AA, 1981, KCK Community College; BS Criminal Justice, 1990, PhD Higher Education Admin, 1994, TIU; MS Security Technology, 1992, CSTM; Various other professional and trade schools; Various seminars and programmes 1976-96. Appointments: Director of World Programmes, World Security

Organisation (WSO); Kentucky Colonel, Commissioned by the Governor of Kentucky; International Educational Adviser, The International Association of Personal Protection Agents; Presidential Commission on the American Agenda; other past positions. Honours: Special Merit Award, National Association of Chiefs of Police; Honorary Fellow, National Law Enforcement Academy; Silver Leader, Disabled American Veterans, Commanders Club; Citizens Committee for the Right to Keep and Bear Arms, Citizen of the Year, 1988-95. Memberships: American Society for Industrial Security, Kansas City Chapter, various posts; American Society of Law Enforcement Trainers; Academy of Security Educators & Trainers; Better Business Bureau; Security Associates Inc; International Freelance Photographers Association; Humane Society; Charter Member, Republican Presidential Task Force; Law Enforcement Alliance of America; AFL CIO International Union of Operating Engineers; Honorary Member, International Police Association; Grandview Chamber of Commerce; Missouri Burglar & Fire Alarm Association. Address: World Security Organisation Centre, 2 Sq Corpus 1 Fl 5, 5000 Veliko Tarnovo, Bulgaria.

**BARONE Michele,** b. 12 March 1948, Bitonto, Italy. Physicist. m. Crigno Canellopulos, 2 sons. Education: Dottore in Fisica, University of Bari, 1976. Appointments: Researcher, Centre Européenne pour la Recherche Nucléaire, Geneva, Switzerland; Project and Marketing Manager, Nucletec SA, Geneva; Project and Sales Manager, Cryophysics SA, Geneva; Senior Researcher, INFN-LNF, Frascati, Italy; Project Coordinator, Demokritos National Scientific Research Centre, Athens, Greece. Publications: Author or co-author, 80 papers in scientific journals; Editor, books: Ecologia ed economia dell'ambiente nell'antica Grecia, 1994; Frontiers of Fundamental Physics, 1995. Memberships: Italian Physics Society; Italian Vacuum Association; Greek High Energy Association. Address: Aretaiou 21, 11522 Athens, Greece.

**BARRICK Joan Lizbeth,** b. 19 January 1955, Levittown, Pennsylvania, USA. Education: BS, Waynesburg College. Appointments: Wistar Institute, 1976-81; Hahnemann University, 1981-82; Temple University, 1983-86; NIH National Institute of Health, 1988-98. Publications: 4 papers and 3 poster presentations in the field of human genetics. Address: NIH, 9000 Rockville Pike, Bethesda, MD 20814-1436, USA.

**BARRY Dana M,** b. 26 May 1949, Utica, New York, USA. University Technical Writer; Administrator. m. James F Barry, 4 sons. Education: BA, 1971; MS, Education, 1972; MS, Chemistry, 1974; PhD, 1985; Certified Professional Chemist, 1989-. Appointments: Clarkson University's Space Grant Program Administrator, 1993-99; Chemist, Chemical Consultant, Author and Administrator; Organiser, first Moonlink and NEARLink missions, Clarkson University, 1998. Publications: Author, 5 science books & journal features; Host, TV series, Sensational Science. Honour: International Women of the Year, 1992-93; APEX Awards for Publication Excellence, 1996, 1997, 1998, 1999. Membership: American Chemical Society; American Institute of Chemists; National Science Teacher Association. Address: 46 Farmer Street, Canton, NY 13617, USA.

**BARSOUM Marie Kamel Dawood,** b. 17 August 1932, Cairo, Egypt. University Professor. m. Alfons Barsoum, 1 son, 1 daughter. Education: BA, honours, Department of English Language & Literature, Faculty of Arts, Ain-Shams University, Cairo, Egypt, 1957; PhD, Trinity College, Dublin University, Ireland, 1965. Appointments: Assistant, 1959, Lecturer, 1966, Associate Professor, 1972, Professor, 1988, Department of English Language & Literature, Faculty of Arts, Ain-Shams University. Publications include: From Wyatt to Milton, 1972;

John Whiting and Some Major Trends in Twentieth Century Drama, 1985. Honour: Best Book of the Year Award, 1985. Address: 99-60 64th Avenue #2N, Rego Park, NY 11374, USA.

**BARTELS Eva,b.** 8 February 1950, Bratislava. Medical Doctor; Neurologist; Psychiatrist. m. 1 son, 1 daughter. Education: MD, Comenius University. Appointments: Assistant, Department of Neurology, Municiple Hospital, Altona, Hamburg, 1974-77; Assistant, Department of Psychiatry, Mepl Hospital, Ochsenzoll, 1977-78; Senior Assistant, Consultant, Dept of Neurology, University Hospital, Eppendorf, Hamburg, 1978-79; Mepl Hospital Bogenhausen, Munich, 1984-. Awards: Recipient of Young Investigators Award of American college of Angiology, 1992; Author: Color-coded duplex ultrasonography of the cerebral vessels, 1998; Co-editor, New trends in cerebral hemodynamics, 1997; Numerous articles to internal medical journals and numerous contributions/chapters to books; Reviewer for numerous American and European scientific journals. Honours: Recipient of the Young Investigators Award from the American College of Amgiology, 1992. Memberships: American Society of Neuriomaging, Neurosonology Research Group of the World Federation of Neurology; European Society of Neurosonology and Cerebral Hemodynamics; Treasurer American Institute of Ultrasound in Medicine. Address: Auweg 33, 85375 Neufahrn, Germany.

**BARTHOLOMEW Michael A,** b. 10 January 1951, London, England. Film Industry Executive; Entrepreneur. m. 1 child. Education: BSc Journalism, 1972, MSc cum laude, 1973, Medill School of Journalism, Northwestern University, Evanston, USA. Appointments: Reporter, The Associated Press, 1973-75; Brussels Bureau Chief, Radio Free Europe/Radio Liberty, Covering EU and NATO issues, 1975-85; Founder and President, BART IMS, media and government relations consultancy, European Affairs, 1985-94; Director European Union Affairs, Motion Picture Association, 1994-; Consensus builder bridging US industry and European policymakers. Publications: Contributor, Essays on Managing, 1990; Columnist, European issues, Wall Street Journal, International Herald Tribune. Memberships: Cercle Royal Gaulois Artistique and Litteraire; America-European Community Association; American Chamber of Commerce in Belgium; American Club Advisory Council; Centre for European Policy Studies; International Press Association. Address: 8 Chemin du Bonnier, 1380 Ohain, Belgium.

**BARTON John Joseph,** b. 19 March 1933, Rockford, Illinois, USA. Medical Doctor; Teacher; Researcher. m. div. 2 daughters. Education: BA, BS, MD, University Illinois; Rotating Internship, Cook County Hospital, 1961; Residency and Fellowship, Cook County/Northwestern Programme, 1965. Appointments: Faculty, Northwestern University Medical School; Director Obstetrics and Gynaecological Education, Cook County Hospital, 1965-69; Principal Investigator, Hektoen Institute; Participator, Northwestern University Gynaecology Pathology Laboratory; Currently: Chairman, Illinois Masonic Medical Centre, Chicago; Professor Obstetrics and Gynaecology, Rush Medical College; Lecturer, University Illinois College of Medicine. Various positions, American College Obstetrics and Gynaecology; Chairman and Member, Chicago Maternal and Child Advisory Committee, Chicago Dept Health, Perinatal Committee to Illinois Dept of Public Health, Governor's Aids Commission. Publications: 30 scientific articles. Honours: include: Co-recipient of the Central Association Scientific Prize Award for 1988. Memberships: Fellow, Chicago Institute Medicine, Board of Trustees; Fellow and Past President, Chicago Gynaecological Society, Advisory Council. Address: Bar T Ranch, 20516 Bunker Hill Road, Marengo, IL 60152 8003, USA.

**BARTZATT Ronald Lee,** b. 18 December 1953, Lincoln, Nebraska, USA. Chemist. Education: Lab Technician, 1973; BSc, 1976; MSc Chemistry, 1980; PhD Chemistry, 1982. Appointments: Lab Technician, 1973-76; Assistant Instructor, 1980-82; Research Biochemist, 1982-96; College Instructor & Chemist, 1996-. Honour: Phi Lambda Upsilon. Memberships: American Society of Clinical Pathologists; Planetary Society. Address: 4316 North 15 Street, Lincoln, NE 68521, USA.

**BARUZDIN Sergey Anatolievich,** b. 3 December 1950, Saint Petersburg, Russia. Radioelectronics Educator; Researcher. m. Baruzdina Ludmila Ivanovna, 1 son, 1 daughter. Education: Institute of Electrical Engineering, Sain Petersburg, 1968-74; PhD, 1984; Certificate of Senior Scientific Worker, 1989; Certificate of Docent, 1995. Appointments: Engineer, Main Geophysical Observatory, 1974-75; Engineer, 1975,77, Junior Scientist, 1978-85, Senior Scientist, 1985-89, Docent, 1989-, State Electrical Engineering University, Sain Petersburg. Publications: Functional Devices for Signal Processing; More Than 50 in the Field of Radio Engineering, Electronics and Physics. Honours: Bronze medal, Exhibition of Economics Achievement, 1986. Address: State Electrical Engineering University, 197376 Saint Petersburg, Russia.

**BARYKIN Nikolai Petrovich,** b. 11 August 1938, Stalingrad, Russia. Metallurgical Engineer. m. Taisiya Vasilievna Bulygina, 2 daughters. Education: Graduate, Kuibyshev Aviation Institute, 1962; Postgraduate, Moscow Institute of Steel and Alloys, 1964-67; Candidate of Technical Sciences, 1968; Assistant Professor Certificate, 1972; DSc, 1992; Professor Certificate, 1996. Appointments: Thermal Shop, Kuibyshev Bearing Plant, 1956-57; Foreman, Forge Shop, Ufa Motor-Building Plant, 1962-64; Teacher, Assistant Professor, Department Head, Ufa Aviation Institute; Head of Laboratory, Institute for Metals Superplasticity Problems, Russian Academy of Sciences, Professor, Ufa State Aviation University, 1988-. Publications: 120 articles in professional journals; 60 patents. Honours: Medal, Excellent Results, USSR Higher School Activity, 1984; Medal, Honoured Inventor of the Republic of Bashkortostan, 1988. Memberships: Scientific Council, Institute for Metals Superplasticity Problems; Specialized Council, IMSP. Address: Institute for Metals Superplasticity Problems, Khalturina 39, Ufa 450001, Russia.

**BASAK Jayanta,** b. 25 September 1965, Calcutta, India. Researcher; Educator. m. Raktima Basak. Education: BETelE (Hons) Electronics and Telecommunicarion Engineering, 1987, Jadavpur University; ME Computer Science and Engineering, 1989, Indian Institute Science, Bangalore; PhD, 1995, Indian Statistical Institute, Calcutta. Appointments: Programmer, 1993-95, Associate Professor, Machine Intelligence Unit, ISI, Calcutta, 1996-; Frontier Researcher, Brain Science Institute. Institute of Physical and Chemical Research, Japan, 1997-98, Computer Engineer, 1989-92, Programmer in Electronics and Communication Sciences unit, ISA, 1992-93; Visiting Scientist, Robotics Institute, Carnegie Mellon University, USA, 1991-92. Publications: 15 journal papers; 15 conference papers. Honours: 2 fellowships and 1 scholarship; Gold Medal Jadavpur University, 1987; Indian Science Congress Association Young Scientist Award, 1994; Indian National Science Academy Medal for Young Scientist, 1996. Memberships: IEEE; Indian Unit for Pattern recognition and Artificial Intelligence. Address: Indian Statis, Institute Machine Intelligence Unit, 203 BT Rd Bengal, Calcutta 700 035, India.

**BASARAN Erin,** b. 7 May 1941, Limassol, Cyprus. Electronics Engineer. m. Ocen, 1 daughter. Education: Master of Science, Light Current Electrical Engineering, Istanbul Technical University, 1968; Certificate in Education, Higher

Technical Institute, 1974. Appointments: Electronics Teacher, 13 Years; Curriculum Developer, 12 Years. Address: Interlingua Computers, P O Box 421, Lefkosa, TRN Cyprus, Via Mersin 10, Turkey.

**BASFORD Kaye Enid,** b. 10 August 1952, Ipswich, Queensland, Australia. Professor. m. Geoffrey Alan Basford, 1 son, 1 daughter. Education: AMusA Piano, 1972, Australian Music Examinations Board; BSc Hons I Mathematics, 1974, MLitSt Mathematical Statistics, 1977, PhD Mathematical Statistics, 1985, University of Queensland; FIS, 1983; FAIAST, 1998; CPAg, 1995; AStat, 1998. Appointments: Technologist B, 1974-80, Technologist A, 1981-84, (Statistical Consultant), Senior Professional Officer (Biometrician), 1985-87, Senior Lecturer in Biometry, 1988-93, Agriculture Dept, Reader in Biometry, School of Land and Food, 1998-, Deputy Dean, Faculty of Agricultural Science, 1993-95, School of Land and Food Systems, 1996, Deputy Director of Studies (St Lucia), Faculty of Natural Resources, Agriculture and Veterinary Science, 1997-, University of Queensland, Brisbane. Publications: Co-author, 2 books; 10 book chapters. Honours: 2 scholarships, 1970-73, 1974; Golden Lectern Award for Outstanding Lecturing, 1988; Australian Medal for Agriculture, Australian Institute of Agricultural Science & Technology, 1998; 4 Research Fellowships and Awards. Memberships: Institute of Statistics; Statistical Society of Australia; International Biometric Society; Classification Society of North America; International Association for Statistical Education; Institute of Mathematical Statisticians; Australian Institute of Agricultural Science & Technology; Australian Fulbright Association. Address: 3 McMahon Street, Bundamba, Qld 4304, Australia.

**BASHIRI Iraj,** b. 31 July 1940, Iran. University Professor. m. Carol L Sayers, 18 Apr 1968, 2 sons, 1 daughter. Education: BA, Pahlavi University, Shiraz, Iran, 1960-63; Non-Deg MA, Liverpool University, 1964-65; MA, 1966-68, PhD, 1968-72, Univ of Michigan, USA. Appointments: Assistant Professor, 1972-77, Associate Professor, 1977-87, Iranian Studies; Associate Professor, Iranian Studies, University of Texas, Austin, 1982; Associate Professor, Central Asian Studies, 1987-96; Professor, Central Asian Studies, 1996-. Publications: Persian for Beginners, 1972, 1975, 1981, 1991; Persian Syntax, 1975; The Fiction of Sadeq Hedayat, 1984; The Black Tulip, (novella in English and Persian), 1984; The Pearl Cannon, editor, 1986; Firdowsi's Shahname: 1000 Years After, 1994; From the Hymns of Zarathustra to the Songs of Borbad, 1995; Kamal Khujandi: Epoch and Its Importance in the History of Central Asian Civilization, 1996; History of a National Catastrophe, translation, 1996; many articles and essays in professional publications. Honours: Iran's Top Student in English Language, 1958; Top BA, Pahlavi University, Shiraz Iran, 1963; College of Liberal Arts, University of Minnesota, Distinguished Teacher, 1980; IREX Res Scholar, Tajikistan, 1993-94; Honorary Doctorate in History and Culture, Tajikistan State University, 1996; Honorary International Academician, Academy of Sciences of Tajikistan, 1997. Memberships: Founding Member, International Science Production Society, Kazakhtanon, 1992-; Board of Directors, the Borbad Foundation, Dushanbe, Tajikistan; Board of Directors, The Somonion Conference, Academy of Sciences, Tajikistan; American Association of Teachers of Slavic and East European Languages; American Association for Advancement of Slavic Studies; American Association for Central Asian Research; American Association for Central Asian Studies. Address: 518 8th St SE, Minneapolis, MN 55414-1208, USA.

**BASKAR Joseph Paul,** b. 9 June 1959, Dindigul, India. Development Social Worker. m. Mercy, 1 son, 1 daughter. Education: M Phil; MEd; MA. Appointments: Journalist;

Teacher. Memberships: Friends of United Nations; Food Information Action Network; Indian Institute of Public Administration; Global March Against Child Labour. Address: H2/22 Rani Mangammal Colony, Dindigul, Tamil Nadu 624008, India.

**BASSALO Jose Maria Filardo,** b. 10 September 1935, Belem, Para, Brazil. Physics Educator, Researcher. m. Celia Coelho, 2 sons, 1 daughter. Education: Civil Engineering, UFPA, 1958; Bachelor in Physics, University Brasilia, 1965; Master in Physics, IFUSP, 1973; Doctor in Physics, IFUSP, 1975. Appointments: Roads Municipal Department of Belem, 1958-85; Professor, Titular da UFPA, 1989-. Publications: Crônicas da Física Tomo 1; Tomo 2; Tomo 3; Tomo 4; Tomo 5; Nascimentos da Física. Memberships: Brazilian Physics Society; Brazilian Society of Science; Brazilian Society of History; New York Academy of Science. Address: Serzedelo Correa 347-1601, 66025240 Belem Para, Brazil.

**BASSETT Heather Marjorie,** b. 22 February 1930, Artarmon, NSW, Australia. Pathologist. Duncan James Bassett, 1 son, 2 daughters. Education: ASTC Nutrition, 1951; Postgrad Teachers' Certificate, 1954; MB BS, 1960; Postgrad Diploma Clinical Pathology, 1964; Compl Coppleson Course in Rehabilitation Medicine, 1982; FASEM, 1988. Appointments: RMD, Intern, R Prince Alfred Hospital, Sydney, 1960-61; Foundation Lecturer in Pathology, Papuan Medical College, 1962-67; Private clinic work when family were young; Foundation Assistant Medical Superintendent, Gosford District Hospital, 1972-73; Founding Area Health Physician in Geriatrics and Rehabilitation, 1974-77; Founder, Life member, Central Coast Community Chest, United Way; Founder, Life member, Central Coast Disabilities Council; Founder, Tri-Une Life Extension and Pain Management Clinics, Sydney and Gosford, 1985-; Preceptor, Milwaukee Pain Clinic, 1992. Publications: Official TPNC Govt Studies in Population Decline (Loloipa People); Also developed rapid diagnostic tests for Clostridium Welchii in Pig Bellies; Shared Studies in Burkitt Tumours, Mylob Ulcerans Epidemiology. Memberships: MAMA; MACAM; BSREM; FRSM; International Rehabilitation Medical Association. Address: 91 Donnsion Street, Gosford, New South Wales, Australia 2250.

**BASSILY Sarwat S,** b. Minia, Egypt. Business Executive. 2 sons, 2 daughters. Education: Graduated, Faculty of Pharmacy, Cairo University, 1961. Appointments: Several positions, Cairo University Hospitals and private pharmacies; Pharmacy Owner, Aswan, 1966; Established Advanced Biochemical Industries, now Glaxo-Wellcome-Egypt, 1978; Currently Chairman, Chief Executive Officer, Amoun Pharmaceutical Industries Co, Heliopolis. Memberships: Head, Association of Pharmaceutical Manufacturers in Egypt; Health Committee, National Democratic Party; Board Member, Federation of Egyptian Industries; Deputy, Coptic Denominational Assembly of Egypt. Address: Amoun Pharmaceutical Industries Co, 125 El Hegaz Street, Heliopolis, Egypt.

**BASSOE Carl Fredrik,** b. 5 August 1947, Sauda, Norway. Medical Doctor. m. Anne Margrethe, 1 son, 2 daughters. Education: MD, 1973; PhD, 1984; MA, 1993; Specialist, Internal Medicine, 1996. Career: Resident, Pathology, 1976-79; Research Fellow, 1980-82; Family Physician, Bergen, Norway, 1979-88; Officer, Occupational Medicine, Bergen, 1988-90; Resident, Internal Medicine, Voss-Vergen, 1990-94; Consultant, Haematology, 1994-. Publications: Phagocytosis, 1979; Leukemia, 1979; Measurement of Phagosyte Functions by Flow Cytometry, 1979; The Skinache Syndrome, 1995; Neural Networks, 1993; Natural Language Analysis, 1992 Memberships: Den Norske Laegeforening; Den Norske

Dataforening; Amnesty International. Address: Lyngvegen 14b, N 5082 Bergen, Norway.

**BASUC Donel,** b. 11 August 1963, Namoloasa, Romania. Professor; Lecturer. m. Florina Basuc, 1 daughter. Education: Master of Science Metalurgical Processing, 1983-88, Polytechnic Institute of Bucharest; PhD in forming of metals and heat treatment, 1992-97, University Polytechnic of Bucharest; Scholarships, 1995, 1997, Polytechnic of Turin, Visiting Professor, Polytechnic of Turin, 1998. Appointments: Process Engineer, Special Steels Holding, Romania, 1988-91; Assistant, 1991-98, Lecturer, 1998-, University Polytechnic of Bucharest. Publications: Colaboration in: Deformability of metallic materials, 1994; Considerations about numerical simulation of forming processes, 1996; Forming of metals, 1996; Forming of metals - rolling and close-die forging, 1998. Membership: Technical Forging Association of Romania. Address: Univ Politechnica of Bucharest, Fac SIM Splaiul Independentei 313, 77206 Bucharest 6, Romania.

**BATALOV Yuri Vasilyevich,** b. 25 June 1939, Semipalatinsk, Kazakhstan. Civil Engineer. m. Zoya Rodionovna Batalova, 2 sons. Education: Civil Engineering Technician, Semipalatinsk Agricultural Technical College, 1960; Civil Engineer, Ust-Kamenogorsk Civil & Highway Engineering Institute, 1965; Candidate of Economic Sciences Degree, Ordzhonikidze Moscow Institute of Management, 1977; Assistant Professor, 1982; Professor, 1992. Appointments: Assistant, Senior Teacher, Head of Department, Vice Rector, 1966-, Rector, 1986-, Ust-Kamenogorsk Civil & Highway Engineering Institute; Rector, East Kazakhstan Technical University, 1996-. Publications include: The Formation of the Administrative Personnel; Businessman's Dictionary. Honours: 8 Government Diplomas and Awards. Memberships include: Academy of Higher School Sciences, Kazakhstan; Academy of Natural Sciences, Kazakhstan; International Association for Automotive & Road Engineering Education; Association of Architectural Schools & Universities; International Association for the Exchange of Students for Technical Experience. Address: EKTU, Ul Lugovaya 19, Ust Kaneogorsk 492010, Kazakhstan.

**BATCHELOR Andrew William,** b. 16 February 1957, London, England. Lecturer. m. Valli, 2 daughters. Education: BSc, Eng, 1978; PhD, London, 1983. Appointments: Postdoctoral Research Fellow, Tokyo Institute of Technology, 1982-84; Research Engineer, Sugar Research Institute Mackay, Australia, 1984; Lecturer, South Australian Institute of Technology, 1986-88; Lecturer, University of Western Australia, 1989-92; Senior Lecturer, Nanyang Technological University, Singapore, 1992-. Honour: George Julius Award, Institution of Engineers, Australia. Memberships: Institution of Engineers, Australia; Japan Society of Tribologists; Society of Tribologists and Lubrication Engineers; American Society of Mechanical Engineers. Address: Nanyang Technical University, School Mechanical Production Engineering, Nanyang Avenue, Singapore 639798, Singapore.

**BATEMAN Philip Christiaan,** b. 5 January 1945. Writer; Creative Director; Researcher; Company Director; First World Creative Thinking Champion. m. Caroline Anne Bateman, 2 daughters. Education: Cert Com Art, 1970, Cape Technical College; Dip Adv (ICS), 1971; APR, 1979, Cape College for Advanced Technical Education; MCB (Dip), UK, 1987; F Inst C, UK, 1998; MCIJ, UK, 1998. Appointments: Creative Director, The Heritage Collection (Pty) Ltd and associated companies, 1979-, as well as author, researcher, part-time lecturer/tutor, director of companies (14), trustee; Consultant, 1974-79; Creative Manager and one of three founder editors of SA edition of Readers Digest (SARD), 1968-74; Commercial Artist, Writer, The Cape Argus, 1967-68; Authority on direct marketing psychology and copywriting. Publications: Financial Columnist, Woman's Value, 1993-97, Offshoots, and medical columnist, Wine, 1997-; Produced brochures for UN and EEC; Author thousands articles, brochures, booklets and mailings as well as books including: Generals of the Anglo Boer War, 1977; Pioneers of Southern Africa, 1978; Talk to Syfrets, (ms), 1983; plus numerous volumes in preparation; Designed Queen Mother's 80th Birthday Medallion, 1980; Contributor, MENSA In-News, Telicom, USA and numerous others; Major contributor Reader's Digest; Collaborated with Pulitzer author James Michener on world best-seller The Covenant, 1978-79. Honours include: Place Winner, BBC Poetry Competition, 1989 (anthologised); One of three winners in Wine Writers of the Year Competition, 1996; First WORLD CHAMPION Creative Thinking (Mind Sport, Olympiad, London 1997; Fourth in world in Creative Thinking, Hammersmith, 1998; Distinguished Leadership Award, ABI, USA, 1998; Outstanding Achievement Diploma for WORLD RECORD in Test of Poetic Ingenuity, 1999; published in anthology, St. Joseph's Literary Competition, 1999; awarded Senior Fellowship of ISPE (Society of extreme gifted), one of only 30 in world; Appointed to Board of Advisors, ABI, 1999; Included in: THE PEACE AUTOGRAPH display, International Museum of Peace and Solidarity, Uzbekistan, 1999; Featured in Who's Whos including 500 Leaders of Influence; Key speaker, MensAfrica (international MENSA gathering), 1999. Memberships: DMA, Chairman of Direct Mail Specialist Interest Group, 1997-; Life Member, ISPE; Life Member, Classical Association, UK; Council member, Free Market Foundation, 1998-; Cape Executive of SAAIE; Member of Chartered Institute of Journalists; Public Relations Society of Southern Africa; Fellow Institute of Copywriting; MENSA (Permanent Member); Life Member, British Society of Communicators; Poetic Genius Society, English Association (Guest of Honour, 1999). Address: Box 15410, Vlaeberg 8018, South Africa.

**BATES Susan Viola,** b. 23 May 1951, Columbus, Wisconsin, USA. Registered Nurse. m. Billie Dale Bates, 1 son, 1 daughter. Education: BSN, Olivet Nazarene College, Illinois, 1973; MSN, Governors State University, Park Forest South, Illinois, 1977. Career: Instructor, St Joseph Hospital School of Nursing, Joliet, Illinois, 1973-74; Project Coordinator, 1976-78, Assistant Director of Nursing, 1978-80, Our Lady of Mercy Hospital, Dyer, Indiana; Director of Nursing, 1981-84, Assistant Administrator, 1984-86, Culver Union Hospital; Director of Nursing, 1986-90, Director of Quality Risk Management, 1990-95, Visalia Community Hospital; Renal Case Manager, Kaweah Delta Hospital, 1996-. Membership: Sigma Theta Tau. Address: Kaweah Delta Hospital, 400 West Mineral King, Visalia, CA 93291, USA.

**BATRA Iqbal Singh,** b. 1 January 1949, Kanpur. Metallurgist. m. Brijender, 2 sons. Education: B Tech, Metallurgical Engineering, IIT Kanpur, 1970; MSc, Metellurgical Engineering, University of Mumbai, 1978. Appointments: Scientific Officer, Bhabha Atomic Research Centre, 1974-. Publications: 40 Publications, national and international journals. Address: Materials Science Div, BARC, Mumbai 400 085, India.

**BATU Suhe,** b. 1 July 1956, Huria Banner, Inner Mongolia, China. Teacher, Editor. m. Hasungowa, 1 daughter. Education: Bachelor of Literature, 1982. Appointments: Director, Journal of Inner Mongolia Teacher's College for the Nationalities, 1993; Vice Director, Department of Scientific Research, Inner Mongolia Teacher's College for the Nationalities, 1997. Publications: Outline of Khorchin Literature, 1993; Development f Mongolian Literature, 1995; On Typical Characters in Mongolian Literature, 1995; Outline of Mongolian Literature, 996. Honours: Young Qualified Personnel of Inner Mongolia, 996; Outstanding Young Intellectual of Inner Mongolia, 1996; Outstanding Achievements in Science and Technology for the outh of Inner Mongolia, 1996; Outstanding Achievements in ocial Science, 1997; Outstanding Achievements in Humane tudies and Social Science, Ministry of Education of China, 998. Memberships: Association of Mongolian Literature of hina, 1993; Association of Mongolian Periodicals of China, 994; Association of Journals of Social Science fo Colleges nd Universities of China, 1996; Association of Journals of olleges and Universities of Inner Mongolia, 1997. Address: ournals of Inner Mongolia Teachers College for the ationalities, Tong Liao, Inner Mongolia, China.

**BAUDET Fancis Andre,** b. 11 October 1946, France. eacher. m. Danielle Maillot, 1 son. Education: MPhilos, 1967; hD, Sociology, 1971. Appointments: Teacher, 1971-83; Qualified Teacher, University of Paris VIII, France, 1987-. ublications: Several contributions to professional journals. Membership: Jules Verne Society. Address: 46 Ave Lemonnier, 78160 Marly Le Roi, France.

**BAUMANN Ernst F,** b. 10 April 1943, New York City, New ork, USA. Geologist; Law Enforcer; College President and hairman. m. Kathleen Brennan, 5 daughters. Education: BA eological Sciences, 1967, Harvard University. Appointments: resident & Chairman, College of the Canons; Major, Civil Air atrol, USAF Aux. Publications: Toward a New World: Proof of e Existence of God; The Crucifixion: Proof of the Mock Trial f Jesus. Memberships: Space Defense Initiative; Planetary ociety; Concord Coalition; Knight of Columbus, Scribe (4th), ecorder (3rd). Address: 1101 Play Avenue, Canon City, CO 1212, USA.

**BAUMANN Herbert Karl Wilhelm,** b. 31 July 1925, Berlin, iermany. Composer; Conductor. m. Marianne Brose, 2 sons. ducation: High School; International Institut of Music; omposing with Paul Höffer and Boris Blacher; Conducting vith Sergiu Celibidache. Appointments: Conductor, chaikovsky Symphony Orchestra, 1947; Composer and onductor, Deutsches Theater Berlin, 1947-53; State Theater, chiller-Theater Berlin, 1953-70; Bavarian State Theater, 1unic, 1970-79; Freelance Composition and Conducting, 979-. Publications: Two ballets, Alice in Wonderland; Rumpelstilzgen; Music for orchestra, Chambermusic; Many ublications of his music on CD. Memberships: Verband 1ünchener Tonkünstler; Deutscher Componisten-Interessenverband, GEMA. Address: Apt 1419 ranziskanerstrasse 16, D-81669 Munich, Germany.

**BAUMANN-ANTCZAK Aleksandra,** b. 31 October 1962, Jstrow Wlkp, Poland. Doctor. m. Joseph Antczak. Education: 1D, 1987, University School of Medicine, Poznan; 1st degree nternal Medicine, 1991; PhD, 1994; 2nd degree Intern, 1995; Degree in Endocrinology, 1997. Appointments: Junior ssistant, Oncology Centre, Poznan, 1987-88; Assistant, 988-, Senior Assistant, 1995-, Dept Endocrinology, University chool of Medicine, Poznan. Publications: Papers on 21-OH as major autoantigen in autoimmune Addison's disease, 992-94. Honour: Award of Polish Ministry of Health, 1994. Membership: Polish Endocrine Society. Address: University chool of Medicine, Dept of Endocrinology, Przyhyazewskiego 9, 60-355 Poznan, Poland.

**BAVISOTTO Vincent S,** b. 21 January 1925, Buffalo, New ork, USA. Retired. m. Judy A Bavisotto, 1 son, 2 stepsons, 3 aughters. Education: BA, Biology, University of Buffalo, 1948;

MS, Biochemistry, Organic Chemistry, 1950, PhD, Biochemistry, Organic Chemistry, 1952, Pennsylvania State University. Appointments: Director of Research, Food and Beverage Division, Pfizer Inc, 1962-67; Technical Director, Theo Hamm Brewing Co, 1967-72; Associate Director of Research, Heublein Inc, 1972-74; Vice-President, Brewing and Research, Miller Brewing Co, 1974-90. Publications: Publications and patents in brewing, dairy science, meat industry, pharmaceuticals. Honour: Award Winner, American Chemical Society, Milwaukee Section. Memberships: Institute of Food Technologists, Wisconsin Section; President, ASBC, 1972; President, MBAA, 1988-89. Address: 5780 Mary Lane, Oconomowoc, WI 53066, USA.

**BAYBAYAN Estiller Elizabeth Gambala,** b. 19 December 1963, Veniegas, Llanera, Nueva Ecija. Education: BSSW, Wesleyan University, 1980-84; Eligibility Social Work Licensure, 1994. Appointments: DSWD National, 1989, 1989-90, 1989-92; LGU, Floridablanca, Pampanga, 1994, 1995-. Honours: Certificate & Plaque, Pusong Magiting Award, 1993; Plaque & Medal, Presidential Lingkod Bayan Award, 1993; Certificate of Appreciation, 1996; Certificate of Recognition, 1996, 1997, 1998; Resolution of Commendation, 1998. Memberships: PASWI, Philippine Association, 1985-; Rotary Club International, 1997-; PAJAPA Philippine Association, 1993-; Honor Awardees Association, 1997-. Address: MSWDO, Floridablanca, Pampanga.

**BAYKEEV Rustem Frunzevich,** b. 16 April 1957, Zelenodolsk City, Tatarstan, Russia. Biochemist; Educator. m. Romanova Albina Alexandrovna, 2 daughters. Education: Diploma, Kazan State Medical University, 1980; Diploma, Kazan State University, 1986. Appointments: Candidate of Biological Sciences, 1984; Doctor of Medical Sciences, 1993; Professor, Biochemistry, 1994; Assistant Professor, Kazan State Medical University, 1983-93; Associate Professor, 1993-94; Professor, Department of Biochemistry, 1994-. Publication: Tissue Destruction and Blood Coagulation, 1996. Honours: Grantee, Soros Foundation; Grantee, Russian Academy of Science. Address: Dekabristov St D8 KV 132, 420066 Kazan, Tatarstan, Russia.

**BAZHANOV Valentin A,** b. 10 January 1953, Kazan, Russia. Philosopher; Logician. m. Kopytova Luda, 2 daughters. Education: MA, Kazan University, 1975; PhD, Leningrad University, 1978; DSc, Institute of Philosophy, Academy of Sciences, USSR, 1988. Appointments: Assistant Professor, 1978-83, Dozent, 1983-86, Professor, 1989-93, Kazan University, Department of Philosophy; Dean, 1993-95, Chairperson, 1995-, Ulyanovsk Branch, Moscow State University. Publications: The Completeness of Quantum Theory, 1983; N A Vasiliev (1880-1940), 1988; Science as a Reflexive System, 1991; The Interrupted Flight, History of University Philosophy and Logic in Russia, 1995. Membership: Academy of Social Sciences of Russia. Address: Department of Philosophy, Ulyanovsk Branch, Moscow State University, Ulyanovsk 432063 POB 1602, Russia.

**BEALE Jack Gordon (The Honourable),** b. 17 July 1917, Sydney, New South Wales, Australia. Professional Engineer; International Engineering and Environment Consultant. m., 2 sons. Education: Honours Diploma, Mechanical Engineering, Associate, Sydney Technical College, 1939; Chartered Professional Engineer, 1943; Agricultural Engineering Research, University of California, 1952; MEng, University of New South Wales, 1965. Appointments include: Works Manager, Engineer, munitions, 1940-42; Manager, munitions ship hull construction, 1942-46; Member for South Coast, New South Wales Parliament, 1942-73; Minister forConservation,

1965-71, for Environment Control, 1971-73; Member, Australian Ministerial Councils: Water Resources, 1965-71, Environment, 1971-73, Agricultural, 1968; Director, private and public companies, 1942-; Consulting Chartered Professional Engineer, own practice, Australia, 1942-, overseas missions to 60 countries, 1952-; Chair, Water Research Foundation of Australia, 1955-; Senior Advisor, UNEP, UNDP,1974-77; Member, Advisory Committee, Centre for Resource and Environmental Studies, Australian National University, 1989-. Publications: Wholistic River Valley Planning, 1965; Management of Pollution, 1971; Guidelines for Assessment of Environmental Impact, 1971; UrbanEnvironmental Development, 1972; Sustainable Development of Natural Resources, 1972; Droughtproof Hydropower Network, 1985; Protection and Management of the Environinment, 1975; Cyclical Environmental Management System, 1975; The Manager and the Environment: Theory and Practice of Environmental Management, 1980; Brown Australia, 1981; Green Australia, 1981; Many professional, technical and general articles. Honours: Justice of Peace, New South Wales, 1952; Life Governor, Lifesaving Association of Australia, 1953; The Honourable, title conferred by Queen Elizabeth II, 1973; Life Governor, Water Research Foundation of Australia, 1976;Recognised for Contribution to Engineering Education, Institution of Engineers, Australia, 1988; Jack Beale Chair of Water Resources set up, Australian National University, 1989; Jack Beale Water Resources Annual Lecture Series, Australian National University, 1990-; Doctor of Science, honoris causa, confered by University of New South Wales, 1997; Jack Beale Lecture on the Global Environment, Annual Series, University of New South Wales, 1998-; Doctor of Laws, honoris causa, awarded by Australian National University, 1999; Order of Australia conferred with the approval of Queen Elizabeth II, 1999. Memberships include: Royal Agricultural Society of New South Wales; Commonwealth Parliamentary Association; Irrigation Association of Australia; Australian Museum Society; Art Gallery Society of New South Wales; Library of New South Wales Foundation. Address: 131 Toft Monks, 95 Elizabeth Bay Road, Elizabeth Bay, NSW 2011, Australia.

**BEATRICE Pier Franco**, b. 29 June 1948, Padua, Italy. Professor. m. Paola Isaia, 2 sons. Education: Graduate, Classics, Padua, 1970; PhD, Early Christian Studies, Catholic University of Milan, 1978. Appointments: Professor, Early Christian Literature, University of Padua, 1979-; Visiting Professor, University of Liege, 1996; Joseph Chair Professor, Patristic Theology, Boston College, 1998-99. Publications: Tradux Peccati; La Lavanda Dei Piedi. Memberships: International Association of Patristic Studies; North American Patristics Society. Address: Via Metastasio 16, I-35125, Padua, Italy.

**BECHTEL Sherrell**, b. 23 September 1961, Birmingham, USA. Psychotherapist. m. T M. Gray. Education: BSSW, 1989, MSSW, 1990, University of Alabama; LCSW, Georgia; LCSW, Tennessee; Certified Addiction Specialist; Certified Group Psychotherapist. Career: Private Practice, Employee Assistance Personnel, 1990-. Address: 109A Jordan Drive, Chattanooga, TN 37421-2662, USA.

**BECHTER Karl**, b. 2 August 1950, Germany.Neuropsychiatrist; Psychotherapist. m. Helga, 3 s. Education: MD, 1977; Research Assistant, Neurology, Psychiatry, 1977-78; Application as Neuropsychiatrist, 1983; Psychotherapist, 1998; PD Thesis, Psychiatry, 1996; Associate Professor, 1987-98. Appointments: Head of Department of Psychosomatic Psychotherapy, BKH Gunzburg. Honours: Kurt Schneider Prize; Theodore and Vada Stanley Foundation Award; Memberships: AEP; ISNIP; ISNV; WFBP. Address:

University of Ulm, Department of Psychiatry II, Ludwig Heilmeyer Str 2, 89312 Gunzburg, Bayern, Germany.

**BECHTEREVA Natalia Petrovna**, b. 7 July 1924, Leningrad Russia. Widowed, 1 son. Education: MD, 1st State Medical High School, 1947; PhD, Pavlov Institute of Physiology, 1951; DSc, Medicine, Institute of Experimental Medicine, 1959. Appointments: Scientific Worker, Institute Experimental Medicine, 1950-54; Senior Scientific Worker, Head of a Physiology Laboratory, Deputy Director, Leningrad Polenov's Neurosurgical Institute, 1954-62; Head, Department of Human Neurophysiology, 1962-90, Deputy Director; Director, Institute Experimental Medicine, Academy of Medical Science, 1970-90. Scientific Director, Head, Laboratory of Neurophysiology of Thinking and Consciousness, Institute of the Human Brain Russian Academy of Science, at present. Publications: More than 340 papers among them 120 in English; 11 monographs, 4 of them translated into English, German, Spanish. Honours USSR State Prize Winner in Science, 1985; McCulloch Medal USA Cibern Society, 1972; Hans Berger Medal, Germany 1970; Medal of Bulgarian Union Research Workers, 1984. Bechterevs Gold Medal of Russian Academy Science, 1997. Memberships: Full Member, Russian Academy of Science 1981; Russian Academy of Medical Science, 1975; Foreign Member, Austrian Academy Science, 1974; Finnish Academy Science, 1990; American Academy Medicine and Psychiatry 1994; International Academy Ecology, Human and Nature Protect Science, 1997; Honorary Member, Hungarian Electrophysical Society, 1968; J Purkinje Czech Neurophysiological and Neurosurgical Society, 1989; Vice President, International Union of Physiological Science 1974-80; Vice President, International Organization of Psychophysiology, 1982-94. Address: Kronverkskaya Street 29/37-33, St Petersburg 197101, Russia.

**BECKWITH David (Dave)**, b. 13 January 1955, Henderson North Carolina, USA. Internet Entrepreneur. Education Bachelor of Liberal Arts cum laude, Harvard University, 1986. Appointments: President, Charlotte Internet Society; Chief Executive Officer, IBMW; Founder, Idea Consultants. Memberships: Webmaster Guild; Internet Writers Network; New Civilization Network. Address: 1407 Iris Drive, Apartment 4, Charlotte, NC 28205-5291, USA.

**BEDOIRE Fredric Kurt**, b. 1 September 1945, Stockholm Sweden. Professor in History of Architecture. 1 son. Education BA, Stockholm University, 1969; Diploma, Royal Academy of Fine Arts (arch), 1972; PhD, Stockholm University, 1974. Docent, 1975. Appointments: Curator, Royal Armoury, Stockholm, 1969; Curator, Stockholm City Museum, 1970-73 Antiquarian National Board of Antiquities, 1974-78; Associate Professor, History of Architecture, Royal Institute of Technology, Stockholm, 1978-92; Professor, History of Architecture, Royal University College of Fine Arts (KKH) Arch Stockholm, 1992-; Vice Principal, Royal University College of Fine Arts, 1999-. Publications: (co-author) Stockholm - Architecture and Townscape, 1973, 1977, 1988; Large scale Work Places: Working Conditions in Factories and Offices 1981; Swedish Architecture - Drawings 1670-1970, 1986 Stockholm University: A History, 1987; Modern Architecture and Jewish Patronage, 1998. Address: Peter Myndes Backe 20, S-11846 Stockholm, Sweden.

**BEGJA Hamit**, b. 1 January 1929, Shkodra, Albania. Pedagogue. m. Liri, 2 sons. Education: Diploma in Psychology 1953. Appointments: Professor of Psychologyand Pedagogy Tirana University, 1953-93. Publications: 7 School Books; 32 Books; Hundreds of Articles. Honours: Professor, Academic Teacher of People. Memberships: Academy of Sciences

Association of Psychologists. Address: Academy of Sciences, Sheshi Fan Noli, Tirana, Albania.

**BEGUM Sharifa,** b. 16 January 1950, Comilla, Bangladesh. National Consultant. m. Mujibur Rahman, 1 son. Education: BA Hons Sociology, 1970, MA Sociology, 1971, Dhaka University. Appointments: Assistant Director, CWFP, 1975-85; Programme Officer, Asia Foundation, Dhaka, 1986-91; Curriculum Development Associates, 1994-95, Team Leader, FGD Team, 1993-94, Johns Hopkins University, Communication Programme, Dhaka, Training Officer, Care International, Dhaka, 1995-97; National Consultant (Sociologist), CPP, Tangail, 1997-; Programme Officer, USCCB (Canada in Bangladesh); Regional Field Coordinator, VAD Survey, Hellen Keller International. Address: CPP Project, Akar Takur, Tangail, Bangladesh.

**BEHARI Jitendra,** b. 16 January 1947, Agra, UP, India. Professor. m. Dr Rashmi, 2 daughters. Education: MSc Electronics, 1966, University Jodhpur; DIITD, 1968, PhD Solid State Physics, 1971, Indian Institute Technology, Delhi. Appointments: Assistant Professor, 1976-85, Associate Professor, 1985-95, Professor, 1995-, Jawaharfal Nehru University. Publications: 4 patents; 32 invited lectures and chaired sessions; Author or co-author, 78 articles in professional journals; Contributor 20 papers to conference proceedings; 22 papers to international conferences and symposia; 23 papers presented to national conferences & seminars; 7 technical reports. Honours: Fulbright Fellow, 1986; Career Award, 1984-86, Research Scientist 'B' award, 1986, University Grants Commission; Invited member, Electromagnetic Academy, USA. Memberships: Commission K, URSI; Senior member, IEEE; Indian Science Congress Association; Association of Physiologist & Pharmacologist Society of India; Life member, Biomedical Engineering Society of India; Indian Vacuum Society of India; Indian Physics Association; Active member, New York Academy of Sciences. Address: Jawaharlal Nehru University, School of Environmental Sciences, New Delhi 110067, India.

**BELCHANSKY Gennady,** b. 10 November 1936, Kiev, Ukraine. Scientist; Remote Sensing Ecologist. m. Tatiana Belchanskaia, 3 daughters. Education: BS Electrical and Computer Engineering, 1959; PhD Space Navigation and Control, 1962; PhD Space Control and Data Processing, 1972; Professor, Computer Science and Engineering, 1984. Appointments: Scientist, Institute Applied Mathematics, 1965-72, Scientific Fellow, Institute of USA Studies, 1965-74, Head of Department, Institute of Nature, 1974-78, Director, Institute of Cybernetics, 1978-89, Head of Dept, Aviation Institute, 1984-88, Head of Laboratory, Institute of Ecology, 1988-, Russian Academy of Sciences. Publications: 150 papers; 5 books. Honours: Henry Ford European Cons Awards, 1998. Memberships: IEE; New York Academy of Sciences; US National Geographic Society; Editorial Board, Earth Observatory and Remore Sensing. Address: Russian Academy of Sciences, Severtsov Institute, Moscow, Russia.

**BELDIE Camelia,** b. 15 September 1930, Urechesti, Vrancea. Chemist. m. Poinescu Ignat, 2 daughters. Education: PhD, Chemistry Faculty, University of Jassy, Romania. Appointments: Professor of Physical Chemistry; Vice-Recteur, 1979-84; Recteur, 1984-90. Publications: 65 published papers in Chemical Thermodynamics field. Memberships: Romanian Chemistry Society; Scientific People Association of Romania. Address: Al I Cuza University, Physical Chemistry Department, Splai Bahlui Stg 189, Iasi, Romania.

**BELINSKI Vladimir Alexeevich,** b. 26 Mar 1941, Soroki, USSR. Physicist; Researcher. m. Elena Serafimovna Vladimirova Belinskaia, 12 July 1968, 1 son. Education: Degree in Physics, Moscow Institute of Engineering and Physics, 1965; Postgraduate studies, Moscow Physics and Technology Institute and Landau Institute of Theoretical Physics, 1965-68; Degree in Physico-Mathematical Sciences, Institute of Theoretical Physics, Moscow, 1969; Doctorate in Physico-Mathematical Sciences, 1981. Appointments: Engineer, Research Institute of Optical Physics Measurements, Moscow, 1968-69; Researcher, 1969-81, Leading Researcher, 1981-90, Landau Institute of Theoretical Physics; Supervisor of Research, National Institute of Nuclear Physics, Rome, Italy, 1990-. Publications: Articles in professional journals. Honour: Landau Academic Prize, USSR Academy of Sciences, 1974. Membership: American Physical Society. Address: Via Nazionale Adriatica 225, 66023 Francavilla al Mare (CH), Italy.

**BELL Leon,** b. 14 July 1930, Liberty, MS, USA. Minister, Entrepreneur. Education: Dean, Central Centre of Mission, Baptist Seminary, 1957-59; Chaplain, Jackson State University, 1966-67; Director, Student Activities and Campus, 1967-69; Campus Religious Adviser, Instructor, 1969-75; Pastor, New Mount Zion Baptist Church, 1969-; Founder, Bells Robes and Worship, 1978-. Publications: Topnotch Introductory Essays for all Occasions; Program Outlines for Special Occasions in the Church. Memberships: Southern Christian Leadership; Mayors Task Force; General Missionary Baptist State Convention. Address: 4322 Beacon Place, Jackson, MS, 39213, USA.

**BELLANGER Gilbert,** b. 12 January 1944, Le Mans, France. Nuclear Engineer. m. Marie-Claude, 2 sons. Education: Diploma of Engineering, 1983; PhD, University of Dijon, 1989. Appointments: Head, Nuclear Materials Analysis Laboratory, 1965-85; Director, Materials and Corrosion Laboratory, 1985-99. Publications: Contributor, Articles, International Journals; 25 Papers. Memberships: International Society of Electrochemistry; Electrochemical Society; Institute of Corrosion; Nace International Corrosion Society. Address: 10 Ave de la Paix, F 21260, Selongey, France.

**BELLEROCHE Diesbach,** b. 10 April 1956, Paris. Genealogist; Editor; Bookseller. Education: Diploma, Ctr Internal de Glion, 1984. Appointments: Lecturer in field; Member, Twinning Commission, Fribourg CH/Rueil-Malmaison F, 1990-; Founder, Editor Bull de l'Institit Fribourgeois d'Heraldique et de Genealogiem 1989-93. Publications: Author: Notice genealogique sur la famille Liebert de Nitray, 1979; Descendance de Romain de Diesbach de 1716 a nos jours, Schweizer Lexikon, 1995; Les gardes-Suisses et leurs families, 1989; La Genealogie, sous la direction de Joseph Valynseele, 1991; Editor, web-site for geneaology. Awards: Recipient bronze medal of order Promerito Melitensi, 1993; Knight of Sovereign Order of Malte, 1991. Memberships: Society of Writers of Friebourg; Swiss Society; Heraldic and Genealogy Institute, SAR; Union des Francais de l'Entranger, 1985-95; Genealogy Society of Pas de Calais. Address: Chateau d'Alt Box 12, CH-1722, Bourgullion/Friebourg, Switzerland.

**BELLM Joan,** b. 20 June 1934, Alton, Illinois, USA. Drug Prevention Strategist. m. Earl D Bellm, 2 sons, 1 daughter. Appointments: Founder, Past President, CMEC; Founder, Past President, Illinois Drug Education Alliance; Executive Board, National Networker, National Federation of Parents for Drug Free Youth; Founder, Drug Watch International; Founder, International Drug Strategy Institute; Co-Founder, National Red Ribbon Campaign; Volunteer, numerous local, state and national government agencies. Publications include: Medical Marijuana; Drug User Accountability; Drug Advocates Push

Medical Marijuana; Let's Think About Harm Reduction; Heroin Distribution Proposal Real Danger. Honours: President Ronald Reagan Letter of Endorsement, 1981; American Legion, Department of Illinois Citation of Recognition, 1981, and Meritorious Service Award, 1982; Southern Illinois Law Enforcement Commission Award, 1983; Illinois Drug Education Alliance Award, 1984; Carlinville School Board Award, 1985; National Federation of Parents Outstanding Service Award, 1986; Illinois Alcoholism and Drug Dependence Association Award, 1986; Optimist International Award, 1987; Illinois Drug Education Alliance Award, 1988; Blackburn University Outstanding Citizen Award, 1989; Carlinville 1990 Citizen of the Year Award. Address: PO Box 227, Carlinville, IL 62626 0227, USA.

**BELOUSOV Vitalie**, b. 2 May 1930, Bälti, Moldova. Professor. m. Elena Belousov. Education: PhD, Mechanical Technology; Mechanical Engineer; University Professor. Career: Professor, Metal Cutting Tools & Creative Engineering. Publications: 300 scientific publictions including 15 books, 155 articles and 130 patents. Honours: 40 Gold Medals. Memberships: Romanian Scientists Academy; European Arts Academy. Address: Technical University of Iasi, 22 Copou Boulevard, Iasi 6600, Romania.

**BELOVA Eugenia**, b. 4 February 1960, Sverdlovsk, Russia. Scientist. m. Timophey Sergienko, 1 son. Education: Diploma, Radiophysics, Leningrad State University, 1977-83; PhD, Geophysics, 1998. Appointments: Assistant, Physics Department, Mine State Institute, 1985-90; Scientist, Polar Geophysical Institute, 1990-. Publications: 22 in professional leading journals. Address: Polar Geophysical Institute, 184200 Apatity, Murmansk Region, Russia.

**BELYAVSKAYA Ninel**, b. 6 October 1946, Korosten, Ukraine. Cytologist. m. Okulov Sergei M, 1 son, 1 daughter. Education: BSc, Kiev State University, Ukraine, 1969; PhD, Moscow State University, 1984; Certificate in Cytology. Appointments: Assistant, Institute of Botany, Kiev, 1969-72; Junior Scientist, Institute of Oncology Problems, Kiev, 1972-77; Junior Scientist, Institute Botany, Kiev, 1977-86; Scientist, 1986-93, Senior Scientist, 1993-. Publication: Modern Problems in Space Phytobiology, 1994. Honours: Honour Medal 1500 Anniversary of Kiev, 1982; Bronze Medal of Exhibition for achievements in public economy, Moscow, 1983. Memberships: Associate Member, Committee on Space Research; Active Member, New York Academy of Sciences; Ukrainian Botanical Society. Address: Ukrainian Academy of Sciences, Institute of Botany, Tereschenkovskaya St 2, 252004 Kiev 4, Ukraine.

**BELYAVSKIY Evgeniy Danilovich**, b. 26 August 1940, Taganrog, USSR. Radio-Physicist. m. Lyudmila Nikolaevna Volkova, 2 sons. Education: Engineering degree, Kiev Polytechnical Institute 1964; PhD in Radiophysics, Saratov University, USSR, 1970; Doctor of Physico-Mathematical Science, USSR, 1987. Appointments: Worker, Mechanical Plant, USSR, 1957-59; Engineer, 1965-70, Researcher, 1970-71, Senior Researcher, 1971-89, Head of Laboratory, 1989-96, Orion Research Institute, Kiev, Ukraine; Professor of Physics, Kiev Polytechnical Institute, 1996-. Address: Prospekt Majokovskogo 79, kv 212, 253232 Kiev, Ukraine.

**BENCZE Lóránt**, b. 6 December 1939, Sellye. Linguist. m. Zsuzsanna Örsi, 1 son, 2 daughters. Education: College Certificate, Theology, 1964; Teacher of English and Hungarian Literature and Linguistics, University Degree, 1969; PhD, History of Linguistics and Stylistics, 1972; CSc Linguistics, Hungarian Academy of Sciences, 1984; PhD, habil, Loránd Eötvös University, Budapest, 1996. Appointments: Form Master, Benedictine Secondary School of the Archabbey o Pannonhalma, Hungary, 1969-75; Senior Librarian, Library o the Hungarian Academy of Sciences, 1975-81; Assistan Professor, Depart of Modern Hungarian, Loránd Eötvö University, Budapest, 1981-89; Associate Professor, Head Section of Hermeneutics, Rhetoric and Discourse Analysis Loránd Eötvös University, 1989-92; Principal, Catholic Teache Training College Zsámbék, 1992-; University Professor, 1997- Publications: An Analysis of Romans XII 8-10, 1974; Conscious Tradition, Unconscious Construction of Subconscious Metaphors?, 1985; Uncertainty Principle and Symmetry i Metaphors, 1989; Reference and Socially Determined Knowledge, 1995; Function Oriented Iconography in Cultura Context, 1996. Honour: Count Kunó Klebersberg Medal, 1996 Memberships: President, Association of Church Colleges and Universities in Hungary, 1994-96, 1996-98. Address: 282 Szomor, Petofi Sandor u 32, Hungary.

**BENDL Jiri**, b. 26 October 1931, Hradec Kralove, Czech Republic. Scientist. m. Yvonna Bendlova-Mrazkova, 1 son, 1 daughter. Education: PhD, 1959; Dr Sc, 1977; Dipl Ing, 1956 Appointments: Engineer, Academy of Sciences, Prague 1956-59; Scientist, 1959-66; Senior Scientist, 1966-77; Head of Department, 1977-; Visiting Professor, Hannover, 1990 Publications: More than 100 Papers, Electrical Machines Memberships: Institute of Electrical Engineering; Academy o Sciences; OPTIM; EPNC; AMTEE; EDPE. Address: Institute o Electrical Engineering, Academy of Sciences, Dolejskova 18202 Prague 8, Czech Republic.

**BENES Solomon**, b. 28 March 1925, Iasi, Romania Physician. m. Liudmila. Education: MD, School of Medicine Bucharest, 1954; Appointments: Intern, Microbiolog Laboratory, Military Hospital, Bucharest, 1949-50; Fellow Microbiology Laboratory, 1950-51; Director, Clinic Laboratory Outpatients Department, 1951-52; Director, Research Laboratory Centre, Radiobiology Research, 1953-57, 1959-66 Chief Physician, Microbiology Laboratory, Mil Hospital 1967-73; Chief Physician, Clinic Laboratory Centre o Haematology, 1973-76; Associate, Medicine, Harvard Medica School, Boston, 1978-81; Assistant Research Scientist Assistant Professor, SUNY Health Science Centre, Brooklyn 1982-95; Senior Research Scientist, Assistant Professor SUNY Reasearch Foundation, Brooklyn, 1995-98; Retired 1998. Publications: Seminars in Infectious Diseases, 1983 Articles, Sexually Transmitted Diseases, Antimicrobial Agent and Chemotherapy, Journal; Clinical Microbiology, Proceedings of the 6th International Symposium on Human Chlamydia Infections. Address: 2828 Bragg St #3, Brooklyn, N 11235-1102, USA.

**BENITEZ Rene B**, b. 18 January 1962, Manila. Investmen Banker. m. Bettina Lorenzo, 1 son. Education: BA, Economics Claremont Colleges, Pitzer College, 1983; MA, Economics Yale University, 1985. Appointments: Senior Researcher NEDA, 1983-84; Policy Research Assistant, World Bank, 1985 Investments, Pru Bache Securities, 1985-88; Assistant Vic President, Sheaison Lehman Brothers, 1988-90; Vic President, Head of Syndications, Insular Investment and Trus Corporation, 1990-93; Director, Asian Oceanic Holdings 1992-93; Chief Executive Officer, Country Manager, DBS Securities, Inc, 1993-95; President, CEO, Amalgarne InvestmentBancorp, 1994-. Publiations: Articles, Nationa Security Review.Memberships: Phil Stock Exchange; Ph Economics Society; Rotary Club Makati. Address: 6805 Ayal Avenue, Makati, Philippines.

**BENNETT Alexander,** b. 27 July 1929, Edinburgh, Scotland. Ballet Director; Choreographer. Education: Trinity Academy, Edinburgh, 1934-47, Senior Leaving Certificate, 1946, 1947; Scottish Ballet School, 1946-48, Diploma Royal Academy of Dancing, London, 1948. Appointments: CPL British Intelligence, Germany, 1948-50; Principal, 1951-55, Guest, 1964, Ballet Rambert; Principal, 1956, Sadler's Wells Theatre Ballet; Principal, Royal Ballet, Covent Garden, London, 1957; Ballet Master, 1965-67, PACT Ballet Johannesburg; Ballet Master, Western Theatre Ballet, London, 1966-68; Ballet Master, Royal Opera, Covent Garden, 1969-70; Head of Vocational Studies, Arts Educational Schools, London, 1970-72; Ballet Master, Ballet Brasileiro da Bahia, Rio de Janeiro, Brazil, 1972-74; Ballet Master, National Ballet of Illinois, 1975-77; Director, Columbus Civic Ballet, Ohio, 1977-79; Founder/Director Scottish-American Ballet, 1980; Chattanooga Ballet, Tennessee, USA, 1980-86; Artistic Director, Twin Cities Ballet, Bloomington, Illinois, USA, 1986-. Honours: Howard D Rothschild Fellowship in Dance, Harvard University, Cambridge, Massachusetts, USA, 1995; Biographee in "Great Ballet Stars in Historic Photographs", 1985; Included in several biographical dictionaries. Address: 101 1st Street, North Meadow Village Normal, IL 61761, USA.

**BENNETT Isobel Ida,** b. 9 July 1909, Brisbane, Australia. Marine Biologist. Education: Somerville House, Brisbane. Career includes: Secretary, Librarian, Research Assistant, 1935-59; Only woman Scientist in Australian waters, HMDS Galathea, 1951; One offirst women to join ANARE Ship to Macquarie Island, 1959, 1960, 1965, 1968; Temporary Associate Professor, Stanford University, 1963; Professional Officer, University of Sydney, 1959-71; Invited as Specialist Lecturer on several P&O cruises; Co-opted to New South Wales Fisheries Department, 1974-79; Currently Consultant with Pittwater Council's Project AWARE. Publications: Australian Seashores, 1952-87; The Fringe of the Sea, 1966; On the Seashore, 1969; shores of Macquarie Island, 1971; The Great Barrier Reef, 1971-88; Discovering Lord Howe Island, 1979; Discovering Norfolk Island, 1983; Australia's Great Barrier Reef, 1987; Australian Seashores, 1992; A Coral Reef Handbook (co-editor), 1993; CD ROM of her collection of over 400 images of marine life donated to the people of Pittwater; Donated 3,000 slides of marine life to Australian National Library and Queenland Museum. Honours include: 5 species of marine animals named in her honour; MSc (Honoris Causa), Univ of Sydney, 1962; ANZAAS Mueller Medal, 1982; Whitley Memorial Award, Best Photography, 1982; AO, 1984; DSc (Honoris Causa), University of New South Wales, 1995. Memberships: ANARE Club; Life Member, Australian Coral Reef Society; Australian Federation of University Women; Australian Marine Science Association; Linnean Society of New South Wales; Royal Zoological Society of New South Wales Address: 30 Myola Road, Newport Beach, NSW 2106, Australia.

**BENNETT Rodney D,** b. 3 July 1958, Wichita Falls, Texas, USA. Music Educator. m. Marilyn K Spencer, 1 son. Education: BMusEd, 1982, BMus, Performance, 1982, Midwestern State University; MMus, Eastern New Mexico University, 1998. Appointment: Director of Bands, Munday Independent School District, Texas, 1983-. Honours: National Band Association Citation of Excellence, 1994; Texas Music Educators Association Leadership & Achievement Award, 1994. Memberships: Texas Music Educators Association; Phi Beta Mu; Texas Music Adjudicators Association; Texas Bandmasters Association; National Band Association; Kappa Kappa Psi; American School Band Directors Association; Association of Texas Small School Bands. Address: PO Box 776, Munday, TX 76371-0776, USA.

**BENNETT (Hammerberg) Janie Marie,** b. 25 October 1945, West Virginia, USA. Volunteer. m. Richard A Hammerberg, 1 son, 1 daughter. Appointments: First Grade Room Representative, Valley View Community Unit School, 1976-77; Volunteer, Cystic Fibrosis Foundation, 1977; Volunteer, Band Parent's Association, 1977-82; Volunteer, Operation Christmas, 1983; Honorary Heart and Sole Volunteer, Muscular Sclerosis Foundation, 1983-95; Volunteer, Uniersity of Illinois Office Friendly Program, 1982-1990; Volunteer, University of Illinois Kidney and Dialysis Transplant Hospital, 1982-1990; Volunteer Support Walk-A-Thoner, Many Charities, 1983-. Publications: Author of over 49 poetry-Anthology, 1990-1993. Honours: Customer Satisfaction Award, Babson Brothers Chemical Division, 1988; Inverted Pyramid President Award, Babson Brothers Chemical Division, 1990; Recognition Award, University of Illinois Hospital, 1990; Golden Poets Award, World of Poetry, 1991; Editors' Preference Award for Excellence, Creative Arts and Sciences, 1992; International Poet of Merit Award, National Library of Poetry, 1993; Editors Choice Award, The National Library of Poetry, 1993, 1994, 1995, 1996, 1997; Listed in many biographical publications including: Who's Who in the Midwest. Memberships: National Organisation for Women; Joliet Region Chamber of Commerce; Council for Working Women; International Platform Association; International Poetry Hall of Fame, 1997; American Business Women's Association Continuing Education Program, 1994-; The American Poetry Society, 1992-; International Society of Poets, 1992-; National Library of Poetry, 1992-; National Authors Registry, 1992-; National Multiple Scelrosis Society, 1983-. Address: 21307 Silktree Ctr, Plainfield, IL 60544, USA.

**BENTHEM Roelof Jan,** b. 2 August 1911, Hoogeveen. Expert in Nature Conservation and Landscape Development. 4 sons. Education: Trained in Landsurveying Problems. Appointments: Chief Landscape Planning, Netherlands State Forest Service; Emeritus Chairman, Initiator, Commission Environmental Planning of the World Conservation Union. Publications: Over 100 on Environmental Planning. Honour: European Prize for Nature Conservation and Landscape Development, 1969. Memberships: Past Chairman, Netherlands Society of Landscape Architects. Address: Hoge Duin en Dealse Weg 13, 2061 AD Bloemendaal, The Netherlands.

**BEQARAJ Xhevat,** b. 15 May 1936, Kute, Mallakaster. Journalist. m. Fatmira Veisllari, 2 sons. Education: Diploma, 1960, University of Tirana, Faculty of History & Philology. Appointments: Member of Commission of Literature for children in management of magazines Fatosi, Pionieri, Zeri i Rinise. Publications: Poetry: I have an accordion, 1965; My Path, 1966; Our Train, 1968; The House of Puppy, 1972; The Elephant and the Ants, 1974; The Wind Draws, 1984; Letters of the Autumn, 1988. Membership: League of Albanian Writers, Children's Commission. Address: Re Lidhja e Prizrenit, Oalatie shk 2 Apt 11, Tirane, Albania.

**BERDNIKOV Leonid,** b. 13 May 1947, Tambov, Russia. Astronomer. m. Tatiana Bednikova, 2 sons. Education: Department of Physics, Saratov University, 1973; MSc, Saratov University, 1973; PhD, Moscow University, 1986; PhD, Moscow University, 1994. Appointments: Junior Researcher, 1973-87, Researcher, 1987-92, Institute of Mechanics and Physics, Saratov University; Senior Researcher, 1992-94, Leading Researcher, 1995-, Sterberg Astronomy Institute, Moscow University. Publications: 140 papers in scientific journals. Memberships: Euro-Asian Astronomical Society; European Astronomical Society; International Astronomical Union. Address: Sternberg Institute of Astronomy, M V Lomomosov

Moscow State University, Leninskie Gory, Moscow 119899, Russia.

**BERDOWSKA Ewa Danuta,** b. 17 March 1949, Sosnowiec, Poland. Scientist; Physicist. m. Janusz Berdowski, 2 daughters. Education: MSc Physics, 1972, Silesian University, Katowice, Poland; PhD Physics, 1982, Technical University Mining & Metallurgy, Cracow. Appointments: Assistant, 1972-82, Tutor, 1982-91, Silesian Technical University; Tutor, Czestochowa University, 1991-; Head of Gas Sensors Research & Design Group, Central Mining Institute, Katowice, 1975-82; Head of Sensors Investigation Group, Experimental Mine of Coal, Mikolow, Poland, 1982-90. Publications: Author 2 books: Problems in Physics, 1990; Experiments in Physics, 1992; Author 32 articles in scientific journals. Honours: Government of Pland Grant, Warsaw, 1985, 1987; Polish Committee for Scientific Research Grant, 1994. Memberships: New York Academy of Sciences; European Acoustics Association, Paris; Polish Acoustical Society; Polish Physical Society. Address: Institute of Physics, Czestochowa University, Al Armii Krajowej 13, 42 200 Czestochowa, Poland.

**BERDOWSKI Janusz Marek,** b. 3 August 1945, Czestochowa, Poland. Scientist; Physicist. m. Ewa Koziol, 2 daughters. Education: MSc Physics, 1969, Silesian University, Katowice; PhD Physics, 1977, Gdansk University; DSc Physics, 1988, Poznan University. Appointments: Assistant, 1969-77, Tutor, 1977-89, Assistant Professor, 1989-91, Silesian Technical University, Gliwice; Research Scientist, Milltronics, Peterborough, Canada, 1989-90; Associate Professor, Czestochowa University, Poland, 1991-; Assistant Professor, Polish Academy of Sciences, Gliwice, 1994-; Head of Ultrasonic Transd Research and Design Group, Milltronics, Peterborough, 1989-90; Head of Ultrasonic Investigations of Coal Materials Dept, Polish Academy of Sciences, 1996-; Prorector for Science, Research and Foreign Cooperation, 1996-, Head of Solid State Physics Dept, 1997-, Czestochowa University. Publications: Book, Influence of Isotope Effects and Phase Transitions on the Interactions of Light and Surface Acoustic Waves in Antiferroelectric Crystals, 1987; 85 papers in scientific journals. Honours: Minister of Science, Higher School and Technics Award, Warsaw, 1978; President of Polish Academy of Sciences Award, 1979; Minister of National Education Award, Warsaw, 1989; Government of Poland Grant, 1986, 1988; Polish Committee for Scientific Research Grant, 1994. Memberships: Sci Couns, Institute of Coal Chemistry, Polish Academy of Sciences; IEEE; Lasers Electro-Optics Society of IEEE; European Acoustics Association, Paris; Polish Acoustical Society, Secretary Silesian Division, 1976-82; Polish Physical Society. Address: Czestochowa University Institute, Physics al Armii Krajowej 13, 42 200 Czestochowa, Poland.

**BERESNEVICH Vitaly,** b. 14 August 1952, Belarus, Minsk region. Mechanical Engineer. m. Bresnevich Galina, 2 daughters. Education: Mechanical Engineer, Riga Polytechnic Institute, 1975; Candidate of Technical Science, Riga Polytechnical Institute, 1984; DrScEng, Council of Riga Technical University, 1992. Appointments: Assistant, Doctoral student, Riga Polytechnical Institute, 1975-80; Researcher, Riga Technical University, 1980-85; Senior Researcher, Riga Technical University, Scientific Laboratory, 1985-. Publications: 130 in science (books, papers and patents), 1977-98. Honour: Honorary Diploma at the International Exhibition, Bulgaria, Plovdiv, 1985. Membership: New York Academy of Sciences, USA, 1996-. Address: 67, Sesku Street, Ap 82, Riga, LV 1082, latvia.

**BEREZIN Valentin,** b. 27 December 1937, Saratov, Russia. Physicist. m. Regina Berezina, 1 son. Education: Diploma,

Saratov University, 1960; BSc, 1964; Doctorate, 1984; Professorship, 1985. Career: Docent, Chair of Optics, 1967, Head, Chair of Chemical Physics, 1983, Dean, Physical Faculty, 1985-, Saratov University. Publications: 180 scientific publications. Honour: Honoured Worker, Higher School of Rossia. Memberships: International Higher School Academy of Sciences; Russian Academy of Quality; New York Academy of Sciences. Address: Department of Chemical Physics, Physical Faculty, Saratov University, 83 Astrakhanskaya Street, Saratov 410071, Russia.

**BERGER Daniel,** b. 26 May 1950, Lausanne, Switzerland. Engineer. m. Ayari Radhia, 3 sons, 1 daughter. Education: Physicist, Swiss Federal Institute of Technology, 1973; Mathematics University of Lausanne, 1973; PhD Physics, Swiss Federal Institute of Technology, 1977. Appointments: President, Oerlikon Contraves Dynatec, 1980-93; Vice President, Sales Oerlikon Contraves Defence, 1993-; Program Executive, Development IMD, Lausanne, 1996; President, AVIA, Swiss Air Force Officers Association, 1997-. Memberships: Alumni IMD; American Management Association; Swiss-USA Association. Address: Muhledaldenstrasse 3, CH 8956, Killwangen Aargan, Switzerland.

**BERGER Wolfgang H,** b. 5 October 1937, Erlangen, Germany. Oceanographer. m. Karen Thomas, 1 son, 1 daughter. Education: MSc, Geology, Boulder, Colorado, 1963; PhD, Oceanography, University of California, San Diego, 1968. Appointments: Assistant Professor, 1971, Associate Professor, 1974, Professor, Oceanographer, 1980-, University of California, San Diego; Director, Geosciences Division, Scripps Institution of Oceanography, 1994-96; Director, California Space Institute, 1998-. Publications include: Abrupt Climatic Change, 1987; Reidel Dordrecht Productivity of the Ocean, 1989. Honours: Prince Albert I Medal, 1991; Balzan Prize, 1993; Steinmann Medal, 1998. Memberships: Fellow, American Association for the Advancement of Science, American Geophysics Union; Senator, Helmholtz Association. Address: University of California, Scripps Institution of Oceanography, SIO UCSD 0215 La Jolla, CA 92093, USA.

**BERGHS Hubert Theodoor,** b. 20 February 1945, Bocholt. Reumatologist. m. Engelen Irene, 2 daughters. Education: MD, 1968, K U Leuven; Reumatologist, 1973. Publications: Articles in professional journals. Memberships: Belgian Association of Reumatology; Acknowledgement Commission of Reumatology. Address: Mosselerlaan 97, 3600 Genk Limburg, Belgium.

**BERGSTROM Anna M,** b. 25 March 1961, Sweden. Educator; University Professor. Education: BA French and Spanish, 1983, MA French and Education, 1986, University of Wisconsin; PhD French, 1995, Pennsylvania State University. Appointments: Teacher, French and Spanish, Glenbrook North High School, 1986-88; Visiting Lecturer in French, Indiana University, 1993-95; Assistant Professor of French, University of Delaware, 1995-99; Chair, Department of Teaching Processes, Communications and Learning, Institute of Education, Sweden, 1999-. Publications: in professional publications. Honour: General University Research Grant, 1999. Memberships: European Second Language Acquisition; American Associations of Applied Linguistics; American Association of Teachers of French; Delaware Council on the Teaching of Foreign Languages. Address: Stockholm Institute of Education, Box 34 103, 100 26, Stockholm, Sweden.

**BERGSTROM Yngve,** b. 29 December 1940, Forsa, Sweden. Professor. m. Birgit, 2 daughters. Education: PhD 1971; Docent 1971; Professor, Uppsala, 1983-89; Professor

Stockholm, 1989-. Appointments: Chairman several organisations and companies; Vice President, University of Palarna. Publications: Over 100 scientific publications. Address: Solvarbo 253, 783 95 Gustafs, Sweden.

**BERHAN Trebe Yemane,** b. 1 November 1948, Harar. Consultant; Specialist. m. Yalem Ambaye, 2 d. Education: MD, Medical Institute of LVOV, 1967-74; DDV Diploma, 1974-76; Dr med Diploma, 1976-78; PhD, Ministry of Public Health of Societ Union Central Research Institute, 1978; Post Doctoral Diploma, Medical Institute of LVOV, 1978-80; Certificate, Doctors Course in Leprosy, 1981; Certificate, Post Graduate Medical Education Course, 1986; Certificate, Health Education Work Shop, 1990; Certificate, Discovery Course in Medical Education, 1991. Appointments: Associate Professor, Lecturer, Specialists in Dermato-venereology, 1978-80; Registered in Ministry of Health, 1979; Medical Specialist, 1979; Senior Medical Specialist, 1982; Head, Outpatient Department, 1983-85; Chief Consultant Medical Specialist, 1985-88; Chairman, National Board of Dermatology, 1985-; Consultant, 1986; External Examiner, Addis Ababa University, 1986; Assistant Secretary General Scientific, 1986-91; Member of the Editorial Board, 1986-; Member, National Advisory Committee, 1986-90; Chairman, Ethiopia Red Cross, 1986-93; Short Term Consultant, 1988; Member, Research Committee, 1989-93; Member, Advisory Council International Society, 1989-; President, Ethiopia Dermatologists Association, 1993-; Director, Africa Consulting, 1993-; Consultant, 1993-; Cheif Executive Officer, 1994-; Region Chairman Lions Club International, 1995-; Secretary General, 1996-; Executive Committee Member, 1997-; Secretary General, African Association for Dermatology, 1997-. Publications: Many publications. Honours: Many Honours. Memberships: Numerouse Memberships. Address: P O Box 40193, Addis Ababa, Ethiopia.

**BERKA Petr,** b. 27 April 1959, Caslav. Computer Science Researcher and Educator. Education: Dipl Ing in Technical Cybernetics, 1983; PhD Bionics, 1991; Associate Professor in Computer Science, 1995. Appointments: Czechoslovak Academy of Science, 1983-87; Faculty of Informatics and Statistics, University of Economics, Prague, 1988-. Publications: Expert Systems for Environmental Data Management, 1995; Recognising Reliability of Discovered Knowledge, 1997; Knowledge Discovery is Financial Data, 1997. Memberships: Czech Society for Cybernetics and Informatics; European Coordinating Committee for Artificial Intelligence; New York Academy of Sciences. Address: VSE, Ekonomicka 957, 148 00 Prague 4, Czech Republic.

**BERKY Albin,** b. 1913, Czechoslovakia. Musician. m. Education: Graduate, Hons, Conservatory of Music; Graduate, University of Musical Art, Prague. Appointments: Soloist, Chamber Player, Prague International Spring Festival; Minister of Culture, Adjudicator for International Cello Competition, Prague Spring Festival; Principal Cellist, Prage, Bratislava, Brno, Ostrava, RTE Dublin, Ireland, Berlin Radio, Old Sach Czech Philharmonic, Slovak Philharmonic Orchestras, 1961-63; Soloist, World wide with major orchestras; Slovak String Quartet; Slovak State Piano Trio; Member, Princeton String Quartet, New York; Professor, Conservatory, and University of Musical Art, Bratislava; Professor, Royal Irish Academy of Music, Dublin, Royal Conservatory of Music, University of Toronto; Lakehead University, Thunder Bay; Harbord College Institute, Toronto; North York Board, Education in Toronto. Honours: State Soloist of Czechoslovakia, Minister of Culture, 1953, 1975. Address: The Heritage, 170 Vodden Street, Brampton L6V 2Z9, Canada.

**BERKY Albin Louis Jr,** b. 31 March 1953, Bratislava, Slovakia. Teacher; Music Educator; Musician; Performer. m. Julia, 1 son, 1 daughter. Education: Private Violin Lessons, University of Bratislava, 1964-69; Royal Academy of Music, Dublin, Ireland, 1964-70; Diploma in Music Education and Performance, State Conservatorium of Music, 1970-77; Decree, Qualified Saxophonist and Professional Musician, 1977. Appointments: Television and Radio Bratislava Recording Studios; Conservatorium Choir; Conservatorium Woodwind Quintet and Baroque Quartet; Professor, Woodwind Instruments, Theoretical Subjects, History of Music, Form, Harmony, National Conservatorium of Music, Bratislava, 1975; Professor, Conductor, Woodwind and Theoretical Subjects, School of Music Bratislava, 1975-77; Freelance Musician, Slovconcert Agency Saxophonist, 1977-80; Leader, Saxophonist Show Orchestra; Part Time Oboist, Chamber Groups and Orchestras; Oboist, Australian Chamber Orchestras, 1981; Woodwind Player, Oboist and Leader, Riverina Trio, 1981-86; Woodwind Lecturer, University of Sydney, 1986-; Director, Berky Music Academy, 1987; Woodwind Lecturer, Australian International Conservatorium, 1993-95; Teacher, Clarinet, Saxaphone, Oboe, Recorder, Chamber Music, 1978-96. Honours: 1st Prize, Oboe Competition, State Conservatorium of Music. Memberships: International Double Reed and Clarinet, Saxaphone Society; Management Board Charles Sturt University; NSW Music Teachers Association; President, Slovak Art Association. Address: 23 Merinda Avenue, Epping, NSW 2121, Australia.

**BERMAN Lev,** b. 18 September 1926, Elensky, Orlovsky Region. Education: Leningrad Polytechnical Institute, 1949; CandSc, Institute of Electric Communications, 1959; DSc, A F Ioffe Physicotechnical Institute, 1983. Appointments: Engineer, Electrosyla, Leningrad, 1949-55; Junior Researcher, Semiconductor Institute Academy of Science, 1955-59; Senior Researcher, Head of Research Group, A F Ioffe Physicotechnical Institute, 1959-. Publications: Nonlinear Semiconductor Capacitance, 1963; Introduction to the Physics of Varactors, 1968; Capacitive Methods of Semiconductor Research, 1972; Capacitive Spectoscopy of Deep Level Centers in Semiconductors, 1981; Purity Control of Semiconductors by the Method of Capacitance Transient Spectroscopy, 1995; More Than 100 Articles; 7 Inventions. Honours: Inventor of the Soviet Union, 1983; Prize Winner of the Award of Council of Ministers of Soviet Union, 1990. Membership: New York Academy of Sciences, 1995. Address: A F Ioffe Physicotechnical Institute, Polytechnicheskaya Str 26, 194021 St Petersburg, Russia.

**BERNHARD Michael Ian,** b. 29 April 1944, New York City, USA. Pharmaceutical Executive. m. Deborah, 1 son, 1 daughter. Education: BS, 1966, Tufts University; MS Transplantation/Immunology, 1969, NYU; PhD Tumour Immunology, Immunochemistry, Immunovirology, 1976, Cornell University School of Medical Sciences. Appointments: VP, Pharmaceutical Product Development, FEI Technologies, 1998-; Acting Section Chief, Monoclasal Antibody Section, Biological Response Modifiers. Publications: 3 patents issued, 3 pending, 1 provisional, 3 in preparation; 13 publications in professional journals; 18 abstracts. Honours: Richard Molin Memorial Foundation for Cancer Research Scientist of Year Award, 1977-78; Pratt Foundation Award for Outstanding Research, 1979; Becton Dickinson Exceptional Performance Stock Award, 1998; and many other fellowships, awards and invitations to speak. Memberships: American Association of Pharmaceutical Scientists; American Chemical Society; Food and Drug Law Institute; Drug Information Association; Regulatory Affairs Professionals Society; Association of Food and Drug Officials; NJ Pharmaceutical Quality Control

Association; Controlled Release Society. Address: 11 Harvey Drive, Summit, NJ 07901-1204, USA.

**BERNIK France,** b. 13 May 1927, Ljubljana, Slovenia. President of the Slovenian Academy of Sciences and Arts (SASA), Ljubljana; Literary Historian; Slavist; Educator. m. Marija Kanc, 14 July 1956, 1 daughter. Education: Graduated in Slavic Philology, University of Ljubljana, 1951; PhD, Literary Sciences, University of Ljubljana, 1960; Teaching Assistant, Slovene Literature, University of Ljubljana, 1951-57; Editor and Secretary, Slovenska Matica, Ljubljana, 1961-72; Titular Professor of Slovene Literature, University of Ljubljana, 1971-. Affiliated with the Slovenian Academy of Sciences and Arts' Research Centre; Scientific Adviser, Institute for Slovene Literature and Literary Sciences, SASA's Research Centre, 1977-; Elected Associate Member, 1983; Full Member, 1987, President, 1992-, Slovenian Academy of Sciences and Arts; Lecturer and Visiting Professor at various universities abroad; Editor-in-Chief, scholarly series: Collected Works of Slovene Poets and Writers, Ljubljana, 1981-; Author of a number of books and collection of essays: The Lyrics of Simon Jenko, 1962; Cankar's Early Prose, 1976, Simon Jenko, 1979; Problems of Slovene Literature, 1980; Typology of Cankar's Prose, 1983; Ivan Cankar: A Monograph, 1987; Slovene War Prose, 1941-80, 1988; Studies on Slovene Poetry, 1993; Slowenische Literatur im Europäischen Kontext, 1993; Ivan Cankar: Ein Slowenischer Schriftsteller des Europäischen Symoblismus, 1997. Memberships: Society for Slovene Studies, Bloomington, USA, 1991; Academia Scientiarum et Artium Europaea, Salzburg, Austria, 1993; Croatian Academy of Sciences and Arts, Zagreb, Croatia, 1994. Honours: Ambassador of Republic of Slovenia in Science, Ljubljana, 1994; Commandeur de l'Ordre de Saint Fortunat, Mainz Germany, 1996; International Cultural Diploma of Honor, Raleigh, USA, 1996; Eques commendator Ordinis sancti Gregorii Magni, Vatican, Rome, 1997; Golden Honorary Decoration of Freedom of the Republic of Slovenia, Ljubljana, 1997. Address: Zidovska 1, 1000 Ljubljana, Slovenia.

**BERSUKER Isaac B,** b. 12 February 1928, Kishinev, Moldova. Professor; Researcher. m. Liliya Bersuker, 1 son. Education: MS, 1952; PhD, 1957, D Sc, 1964, Leningrad. Appointments: Head of Lab of Quantum Chemistry, Academy of Sciences, Moldova, 1964-93; Senior Research Scientist, University of Texas at Austin, 1993-. Publications: 12 books; Over 300 research works. Honour: State Prize Laureate, 1979. Membership: Corresponding member 1972, Full member 1989, Academy of Science. Address: Dept of Chemistry, University of Texas, Austin, TX 78712, USA.

**BERTLES John Francis,** b. 8 June 1925, Spokane, Washington, USA. Physician; Educator. m. (1) Jeannette Winans, 1948, div 1978, 2 sons, 1 daughter, (2) Lila Rodriguez, 1981. Education: BS, Yale University, 1945; MD, Harvard University, 1952; Diplomate, American Board of Internal Medicine. Appointments include: Director, Haematology-Oncology Division, 1962-95, Assistant Attending Physician, 1962-64, Associate Attending Physician, 1964-71, Attending Physician, 1971-95, St Luke's Hospital Center, New York City; Assistant Clinical Professor of Medicine, 1962-67, Associate Clinical Professor, 1967-71, Senior Research Associate, Department of Biological Sciences, 1970-71, Associate Professor, 1971-74, Professor, 1974-95, Professor Emeritus of Medicine, 1995-, Columbia University; Visiting Professor of Medicine, Nuffield Department of Clinical Medicine, Radcliffe Infirmary, University of Oxford, England, 1977-78; Director, Transfusion Services, St Luke's Roosevelt Hospital Center, 1981-95; Attending Physician, Montefiore Medical Center, New York City, 1995-97; Clinical Professor of

Medicine, Albert Einstein College of Medicine, New York City, 1995-97; Consultant to government agencies. Publications: Articles in professional publications. Honours: Alpha Omega Alpha; American Society for Clinical Investigation; Career Scientist, Health Research Council, City of New York, 1962-75; Pioneer Award, National Sickle Cell Disease Programme, National Institutes of Health, 1997. Memberships: Fellow, American College of Physicians; American Society for Clinical Investigation; American Physiological Society; American Society of Hematology; American Federation for Clinical Research; American Chemical Society, Biochemical Division; New York Academy of Sciences; American Association of Blood Banks. Address: 67 Jared Drive, White Plains, NY 10605, USA.

**BERTOLAMI Orfeu,** b. 3 January 1959, São Paulo, Brazil. Physicist. m. Maria da Conceição Bento, 1 daughter. Education: Graduate, University of São Paulo, 1981; MSc, Institute of Theoretical Physics, São Paulo, 1983; Advanced Degree, Mathematics, Cambridge University, 1984; DPhil, Physics, University of Oxford, 1987. Appointments: Institut für Theoretische Physik, Heidelberg, Germany, 1987-89; Grupo Teórica Altas Energias, Lisbon, Portugal, 1989-91; Lecturer, Instituto Superior Técnico, Lisbon, 1991-; Scientific Associate at CERN (Theory Division), 1993-95; Instituto Nazionale Fisica Nucleare, Turim, 1994-95. Publications: Over 70, 45 of which in scientific international journals. Honours: Third Award, Essay Competition of Gravity Research Foundation, USA, 1999. Address: Institute Superior Tecn, Av Ronvisco Pais, P-1096, Lisboa Cedex, Portugal.

**BERTOTI Edgar Frigyes,** b. 13 August 1961, Miskolc, Hungary. Mechanical Engineer; Researcher. m. Réka Karczag, 1 son, 2 daughters. Education: MS in Mechanical Engineering, 1984; PhD in Mechanical Engineering, 1992. Appointments: Research Engineer, 1984-86, Assistant Researcher, 1986-89, Senior Researcher, 1989-, University of Miskolc; Humboldt Fellow, Germany, 1993-95; Fulbright Fellow, USA, 1995-96. Publications: Articles in: Computer Methods in Applied Mechanics and Engineering, 1993, 1995; Computational Mechanics, 1994; International Journal for Numerical Methods, 1996, 1998; International Journal of Solids and Structures, 1997. Honours: Humboldt and Fulbright Fellowships. Address: Department of Mechanics, University of Miskolc, Egyetemvaros, H-3515 Miskolc, Hungary.

**BERTRAND Jean Wilfrid,** b. 27 June 1945, Cayes-Jacmel, Haiti. Librarian. m. Ketly Sejour, 1 son, 1 daughter. Education: M Anthropology, State University of Haiti, 1972; M Library Science, ENSB, France, 1978. Appointments: Chief Librarian, Institut Francais d'Haiti, 1973-82; Chief Librarian, INAGHEI, 1977-82; State Archivist of Haiti, 1983-. Publications: Bibliotheques haitiennes aujourd'hui, 1975; Plea for a reorganisation of Haitian libraries, 1981; and others. Memberships: ACURIL; ICA; CARBICA. Address: Route Hopital Espoir, Rue Dubois #12, BP 12 99, Port-au-Prince, Haiti.

**BERVAR Marijan,** b. 10 July 1918, Vinkovci. Surgeon. m. Olga Jamnik, 1 son. Education: Graduate, 1941; Postgraduate in General, 1947, and Abdominal Surgery, 1950. Appointments: Professor, Military Medical Academy, 1976; Consulting Professor, I Pediatric Clinic, Belgrade, 1977; Head of Surgical Clinic, Military Medical Academy, 1980. Honour: Elected member, Scientific Society of Serbia, 1979. Memberships: Royal Society of Medicine, 1968; Societe Internationale de Chirurgie, 1973; Collegium Internationale Chirurgiae Digestivae, 1975. Address: Pristan 4, Maribor, Slovenia.

**BESSE Eryl,** b. 4 July 1958, Keele, Staffordshire, England. Solicitor; Avocat. m. Antonin Louis-Philippe Henri Besse, 1 son, 2 daughters. Education: Birmingham University and Limoges University, 1976-80, LLB, Law with French, First Class Honours; Qualified as Solicitor and Avocat Au Barreau de Paris. Career: Articled at and Assistant Solicitor, Freshfields, London; Assistant Solicitor and Avocat, Linklaters, London and Paris; Partner of Linklaters, May 1990. Memberships: Law Society; City of London Solicitors Guild. Address: Linklaters and Paines, 21 Boulevard de la Madeleine, 75001 Paris, France.

**BEST Melvyn Edward,** b. 8 March 1941, Victoria, Canada. Geophysicist. m. Virginia Marie Best, 1 son, 1 daughter. Education: BSc, honours, Mathematics and Physics, 1965, MSc, Physics, 1966, University of British Columbia; PhD, Theoretical Physics, Massachusetts Institute of Technology, 1970. Appointments: Geophysicist, 1972-77, Staff Geophysicist, 1977-78, Division Geophysicist, 1980-82, Manager Petroleum Engineering Research, 1982-85, Shell Canada Limited, Calgary, Canada; Leader, Research Group Royal Dutch Shell Exploration and Production Laboratory, The Hague, Netherlands, 1978-80; Subdivision Head, Atlantic Geoscience Centre, Halifax, Canada, 1986-90; Director Pacific Geoscience Centre, Member, Management Team, Geological Survey, Canada, 1990-94, Senior Research Scientist, 1994-97; Bemex Consulting International, Canada, 1997-. Honours: Meritorious Service Award, Canadian Society of Exploration Geophysicists, 1996. Memberships: Association of Professional Engineers, Geologists and Geophysicists of Alberta; Canadian Society of Exploration Geophysicists; Society of Exploration Geophysicists; Environmental and Engineering Society. Address: 5288 Cordvoa Bay Road, Victoria, British Columbia, V8Y 2L4, Canada.

**BESTER Frederik Christoffel Johannes,** b. 16 July 1961, Kokstad, South Africa. Specialist Physician. m. Jeanette Strydom, 1 son, 3 daughters. Education: MBChB, 1985, M Med (Int Med), 1993, University of Free State, Bloemfontein, South Africa; FCP, 1993, South Africa. Appointments: Intern, Universitas/Pelonomi hospitals, Bloemfontein, 1986; Medical Officer, Department Internal Medicine, UFS, 1987; Military Service, 3 military hospitals, Bloemfontein, 1988; Research Officer, Department Internal Medicine, UFS, 1989; Registrar, 1990; Registered as Physician, 1993; Consultant, Department Internal Medicine, UOFS, 1994; Went into private practice as specialist physician, 1994. Publications: co-author 11 articles in professional journals; 5 formal presentations outside South Africa. Honours: MER National merit bursary, 1984; Dux Student, UOFS, 1985; Second Prize, ICI Clinical research day, 1990; Special Award for articles, 1992. Memberships: South African Gerontological Society, founder member and secretary local branch and national executive committee member; South African Hypertension Society, 1989-; African Gerontological Society, founder member 1989; Mangaung Society for Care of the Aged; Voluntary Aid Bureau, Bloemfontein. Address: 1 Van Tonderstreet, Box 31058, 9317 Bloemfontein, South Africa.

**BETINIS Emanuel James,** b. 31 October 1927, Oak Park, Illinois, USA. Mathematician; Physicist. 2 sons, 1 daughter. Education: BS Chem/Math, 1950, Northwestern University; MS Applied Math, 1952, University of Illinois; MS Physics, 1979, University of Chicago. Appointments: Teaching, extensive college level teaching in mathematics and physics, in Illinois Institute of Technology, Chicago, Roosevelt University, Chicago, Elmhurst College, Illinois, College of Du Page, Glen Ellyn, Midwest College of Engineering, Lombard, North Park College, Chicago; Extensive knowledge and experience in solving engineering and physics problems leading to product development and computer simulation of product design and industrial processes, at Aerojet Engineering, Azusa, Northrop Aviation, Hawthorne, Atomics International, Canoga Park, IBM Corporation, Chicago, Batelle Memorial Institute, Wilbrook, CARA Corp, Oak Brook; Extensive experience in Fortran. Publications: author 12 publications in professional journals and essays including: Time Dilation Derived from the Electromagnetic Fields of a Moving Point Source, 1998; EM theory Schrödinger equation for faster-than-light quantum mechanics, 1998. Honours: Mathematics and Physics Honour Society; Fellow, British Interplanetary Society. Address: Elmhurst College, Department of Physics, Box 47 190 Prospect Avenue, Elmhurst, IL 60126-3271, USA.

**BETTELHEIM Karl Albert,** b. 23 April 1936, Vienna, Austria. Microbiologist. m. Shirley Mary Barton, 2 sons, 1 daughter. Education: BSc, honours, University of Leeds, 1959; Diploma, Imperial College, London, 1961; MSc, 1961, PhD, 1969, University of London; FRCPath, 1988; FASM, 1989. Appointments: Scientist, Senior Scientist, Center of Public Health, Colindale, London, 1961-68; Research Fellow, Imperial College, London, 1968-71; Lecturer, Medical Microbiology, Medical School of St Bartholomews Hospital, London; Scientist, NHI, Wellington, New Zealand; Senior Scientist, Fairfield Hospital (now VIDRL Melbourne), Australia. Publications: Over 160 papers in professional and medical journals. Memberships: Biochemical Society; Society of Applied Microbiology; Society of General Microbiology; Australian Society of Microbiology; New Zealand Society of Microbiology. Address: 2/40 Carwarp Street, Melbourne, Vic 3085, Australia.

**BEYREUTHER Roland,** b. 15 January 1938, Dresden, Germany. Professor Dr-Ing habil. m. Ute B Vogel, 1 son, 1 daughter. Education: Diploma in Engineering, 1962; Dr-Ing degree, 1968; Dr-Ing habil degree, 1971; Professor appointment, 1983; Deputy Director of Institute, 1985-90. Appointments: Scientific Assistant, Institute of Fibre Technology, Dresden, 1962-68; Scientific Collaborator, 1969-79; Departmental Head, Fibre Formation, 1981-; Departmental Head, Fibre Formation, Institute of Polymer Technology, Dresden, 1984-92, Institute of Polymer Research, 1992-. Publications: Author, book, Dynamik von Fadenbildungs-und Fadenverarbeitungsprozessen; Over 80 publications in professional journals. Honours: Recipient Science and Technology National Prize, 3rd Grade (in team), Government of GDR. Memberships: Scientific Head of Department of Fibre Formation in the Institute of Polymer Research, Dresden, Germany; Polymer Processing Society. Address: Institute of Polymer Research Dresden, Hohstrasse 6, D-01069 Dresden, Germany.

**BEZRUKOVA Alexandra Gennadievna,** b. 20 June 1944, Leningrad, USSR. Biophysicist. m. Bezrukov Sergei F, 1 son. Education: Diploma of Physics Faculty, Leningrad State University, 1969; Diploma of Candidate Biology Science, 1976; Diploma, Dr Physics, Math Science, 1997. Appointments: Junior Research Scientist, 1969-84, Senior Research Scientist, 1984-97; Professor, 1997-, St Petersburg State Technical University. Publications: 100 in Russian, 1971-; 10 publications in English. Honour: International Woman of the Year, 1997-98. Address: 195251 St Petersburg State Technical University, Department of Bioengineering, St Petersburg, Russia.

**BEZSMJERTNY Vitalyo Oleg,** b. 16 January 1964, Lvov, Ukraine. Education: Master of Philology, Lvov University, 1987-93. Appointments: Assistant Director, Middle School #52, 1993-95; President, Lvov Youth Trade Union, 1997, 1998; Chairman, Pensions Fund, Lvov Youth Trade Union, 1998; Chair, Lvov Youth Trade Union Association, 1998.

Membership: Lvov Youth Trade Union. Address: PO Box 6095, Lvov 290052, Ukraine.

**BEZVESILNAYA Elena,** b. 16 February 1948, Kiev, Ukraine. Chairman. Education: MS, National Technical University of Ukraine, 1972; PhD, Air Force Military Academy, Kiev, 1977; Doctor of Sciences, NTUU, KPI, 1991. Appointments: Engineer, NTUU, KPI, 1972-73; Doctor of Philosophy, 1972-76; Assistant Professor, 1976-80; Associate Professor, 1980-91; Professor, 1991; Chairman of Department, 1993-. Publications: 165 Scientific Works. Memberships: New York Academy of Sciences; Ukrainian Council of Conferment of DSc and PhD Degrees in the Speciality, Optics, Navigation and Mehanics; National Geographic Society. Address: Zankovetskaya 7 ap 25, 252001 Kiev, Ukraine.

**BHARADWAJ Prem Datta,** b. 20 May 1931, Gorakhpur, UP India. Professor of Physics. m. Vidya Wati Sharma, 3 sons, 1 daughter. Education: BS, 1950, NREC College, Khurja, UP India; MS, 1952, Agara College Agra, India; PhD, 1964, SUNY at Buffalo. Appointments: Assistant Professor of Physics, BR College Agra, UP India, 1952-54, 1959-60; Lecturer of Physics at Government Colleges, Director of Education, UP India, 1954-59; Assistant Professor of Physics, 1962-64, Associate Professor of Physics, 1964-66, Professor of Physics, 1966-, Chairman of Physics Dept, 1976-86, Niagara University, New York, USA; Visiting Professor, Department of Crystallography, Roswell Park Cancer Institute, Buffalo, 1970-71; Consultant, National Science Foundation, honorary, USA, 1966-71; Reviewer, Physics, New York State Regents Examination, honorary, 1976. Publications: Co-author, book, Intermediate Agriculture Physics and Climatology, 1954; Several publications in professional journals. Honours: Hind Rattan (Jewel of India) Award of 1994 for outstanding services, achievements and contributions among Non-Resident Indians, 1995, New Delhi; Rajiv Gandhi National Unity Award for excellence in outstanding services, achievements and contributions, 1995, New Delhi; Honoured by India Association of Buffalo for outstanding work in the field of education and community service, 1997; Named Man of the Year, 1999, American Biographical Institute, USA. Memberships: American Physical Society; Hindi Samaj of Greater Buffalo, New York, USA, co-founder, 1986; India Association of Greater Buffalo, New York, USA, co-founder, 1961. Address: 100 N Parrish Drive, Amherst, NY 14228-1477, USA.

**BHARGAVA Pushpa Mittra,** b. 22 February 1928, Ajmer, Rajasthan, India. Scientific Researcher; Consultant. m. Edith Manorawa Patrick, 1 son, 1 daughter. Education: BSc, MSc, PhD, Lucknow University, India, 1944, 1946, 1949. Appointments: Lecturer, Chemistry, Lucknow University, and Osmania University, Hyderabad, India, 1949-58; Scientist, 1958, Scientist E, 1964, Scientist F, 1972, Distinguished Scientist, 1975, Regional Research Laboratory, Hyderabad, India; Scientist-in-Charge, then Director, CCMB, Hyderabad, 1977-90; Visiting Fellow, Clare Hall, Cambridge, 1986; CSIR Distinguished Fellow, CCMB, Hyderabad, 1990-. Publications: About 120 major research publications in scientific journals and books; Learning Science, 1977; Proteins of Seminal Plasma, 1989; Life in 2099, in preparation. Honours include: National Citizens Award, India; Golden Jubilee Lecturer, The Institute of Engineers, India; Raghav Nath Bhargava Award; Prithvi Nath Memorial Award; CSIR Distinguished Fellowship; Wattumull Award, 1962; Ranbaxy Research Award for Medical Sciences, 1989; SICO Award for Biotechnology; VI A B Shah Memorial Lecturer; Fellow, World Academy of Art and Science; Cultural Festival of India Award; Goyal Prize for Biology, 1993; A.D. Rivla Award, 1994; Over fifty other awards and honours. Memberships include: Society for the Study of Reproduction;

American Fertility Society; New York Academy of Sciences; American Association for the Advancement of Science; Indian National Science Academy; Indian Academy of Sciences; National Academy of Sciences, India. Address: Indian Institute of Chemical Technology, Uppal Road, Hyderabad 50007, India.

**BHARGAVA Suresh Chandra,** b. 23 August 1938, Delhi, India. Engineer. m. Damyanti Bhargava, 2 sons, 1 daughter. Education: University Degree from Delhi, 1957; Engineering Degree, 1961. Appointments: Deputy Chief Engineer, Delhi Cloth and General Mills Ltd, 1961-65; Deputy General Manager, Modern Bakeries India Ltd, 1965-70; Assistant General Manager, Universal Tyres Ltd, 1970-74; Programme Officer, Area Development Services, UNICEF, New Delhi, 1974-80; Chief, Field Office, UNICEF, Lucknow, 1980-85; Zone Office, Representative, UNICEF, Lucknow, 1985-90; Chief, UNICEF, Hyderabad, 1991-. Membership: Institute of Engineers. Address: UNICEF, c/o UN Building Hyderabad Andhara, New Delhi, India.

**BHARUCHA Burjor Ardeshir,** b. 21 September 1955, Bombay, India. Medical Doctor (Paediatrics). Education: MBBS, 1977; Diploma in Child Health, DCH, 1981; MD Paediatrics, 1981. Appointments: Tutor, Lecturer in Paediatrics, 1981-86; Associate Professor of Paediatrics, 1986-94; Professor of Paediatrics, 1994-; Professor in Charge, Genetics Division & Paediatric Research Lab, 1992-. Publications: 80 in national and international medical journals & textbooks. Honours: Gold Medal in Pathology, Pharmacology, 1976; Rank of Merit at University Examinations, 1974, 1976, 1977, 1981. Memberships: Indian Academy of Paediatrics; Commonwealth Association for Mental Handicap & Developmental Disabilities; New York Academy of Sciences. Address: KEM Hospital, Seth GS Medical College Parel, Bombay, Maharashtra 400012, India.

**BHASKARAN Sambandam,** b. 11 July 1938, India. Professor. m. Banumathy, 2 daughters. Education: MA; MLitt; MA; PhD, Illinois. Appointment: Professor of Political Science. Membership: Indian Association of American Studies. Address: Department of Political Science, Annamalai University, Annamalai Nagar 608002, India.

**BHAT Gh Ahmed,** b. 20 April 1950, New Theed, Srinagar, Kashmir. Researcher; Teacher. m. Fatima Banu, 1 son, 1 daughter. Education: BSc, 1972; MSc, 1975; M Phil, 1987; PhD, 1996; Appointments: Lecturer, 1977-86; Senior Lecturer, 1987-91; Senior Lecturer, -1997; Reader, 1997-. Publications: 15 Publications. Memberships: J and K State Academy of Sciences; WWF; RMSI. Address: CORD Univ of Kashmir, Srinagar, Kashmir, India.

**BHAT Mohammad Yaseen,** b. 7 June 1976, Hanjigund, Kashmir, India. Actor. Career: Traditional Bhagat. Honours: Actor's Award. Memberships: National Bhond Theatgre; Wahthora Chadrose. Address: c/o Ahmad Bhat, R10 Hanjigund PO, Wahthora, Chadoora District, Budgam, Kashmir 191113, India.

**BHATT Balswaroop,** b. 24 September 1949, Hindaun, India. Teacher. m. Snehlata Bhatt, 1 son, 2 daughters. Education: BSc, 1969; MSc, 1971; PhD, 1976. Appointments: Lecturer, 1978-83, Senior Lecturer, 1983-93, Lecturer, 1996-98, Senior Lecturer, 1998-, University of West Indies, St Augustine, Trinidad; Associate Professor, Sultan Qaboas University, Oman, 1991-95; Professor, University Antioqula, Medellin, Colombia, 1995-96. Publications: 58 research papers in Fluid Dynamics; Author, Non-Newtonian Fluid Flows, 1982. Memberships: Life Member, Allahabad Mathematical Society;

Life Member, Indian Society of Theoretical Applied Mechanics; American Mathematical Society; Caribbean Academy of Sciences; New York Academy of Sciences; Caribbean Congress of Fluid Dynamics. Address: University of the West Indies, Dept of Mathematic and Computer Science, Saint Augustine, Trinidad, West Indies.

**BHATT Devendra Prakash,** b. 12 January 1958, Pithoragarh, India. Scientist. m. Neema Bhatt, 1 son, 1 daughter. Education: BSc, First Class Honours, Mathematics, 1976, MSc Chemistry, 1978, PhD, 1985, Kumaun University, Nainital. Appointments: Assistant Professor, Kumaun University Campus Almora, 1979-83; UGC Research Fellow, 1981-83; Scientific position at: Central Electrochemical Research Institute, India, 1983-94, National Physical Lab, India, 1994-; Publications: 47 research papers; Editor, Electroplating and Metal Finishing, 1997; Author 2 Hindi articles; 10 national and international conferences. Honour: Recipient, International Award, International Association of Educators for World Peace. Memberships: Fellow, Society for Advancement of Electrochemical Science and Technology; Electrochemical Society of India; The Vigyan Bharti, Jabalpur; Carbon Society of India; Convenor, Swadeshi Science Movement of India. Address: DRH-20, National Physical Lab Colony, New Delhi 110060, India.

**BHATT Sumer Chand,** b. 21 December 1933, India. Deputy Speaker. m. Kailash Bhatt, 2 sons, 1 daughter. Education: BA, honours, 1954; MA, Political Science, 1957; LLB, 1960. Appointments: Public Service, MLA, Haryana Vidhan Sabha, 1977-82, 1991-96; Chairman, Public Undertakings Committee, HVS, 1979-82, House Committee, Petition Committee, 1991-96; General Secretary, Haryana Pradesh Congress Committee, 1980-85; Deputy Chairman, 20 Point Programme High Powered Committee, Government of Haryana, 1982-86; Vice Chairman, Shivalik Development Board, Haryana, 1993-96; Deputy Speaker, Haryana Legislative Assembly, 1991-96. Publictions: Numerous articles in professional journals. Memberships include: Dwaraka Das Library; National Integration Center; Gandhi-In-Action, International Peace Committee. Address: Lajpat Bhawan, Sector 15B, Chandigarh, India.

**BHATTA Chandidas,** b. 30 March 1955, India. Medical Representative. m. Supriya, 1 son, 1 daughter. Appointments: Medical Representative, last 5 years. Publications: Jal Samukar Manso, The Flesh of Water Mollusc. Memberships: Cultural Organization. Address: Duttapukuk North 24, Pargana, India.

**BHATTACHARYA Bimalendu Bhusan,** b. 1 January 1942, Samastipur, Bihar, India. Educator; Researcher. m. Chitra Bhattacharya. Education: BSc Hons in Physics, 1959; MSc, 1961; PhD, 1974. Appointments: STA Geophysics, Geological Survey of India, 1962-65; Scientist, National Geophysical Research Institute (NGRI), 1965-77; Professor, Indian School of Mines, Dharbad, India, 1977-; Leader, Fourth Indian Scientific Antarctica Expedition, 1984-85; Visitor, Fulbright, Wisconsin University, Madison, USA, 1991-92. Publications: 65 in national and international journals. Honours: Coggin Brown Gold Medal in Earth Sciences, MGMI, Calcutta, India; National Mineral Award, Government of India. Memberships: Fellow, National Academy of Engineers, India; Fellow, Association of Exploration Geophysicists; Society Exploration Geophysicists, USA; American Geophysical Union; European Association Geophysicists & Engineers, the Netherlands; Computer Society of India. Address: Dept of Geophysics, Indian School of Mines, Dhanbao 826004, India.

**BHATTACHARYA Purusottam,** b. 30 December 1950, Howrah, India. University Teacher. m. Anindita Sanyal, 1 son, 1 daughter. Education: BA History (Hons), Calcutta University, 1970; BSc Economics, London School of Economics, 1974; MPhil, 1980, PhD, 1989, J L Nehru University. Appointments: Lecturer in History, Nabagram College, Calcutta University, 1981-82; Lecturer in International Relations, 1982-88, Reader in International Relations, 1990-, Joint Director, School of International Relations and Strategic Studies, 1993-, Jadavpur University, Calcutta; Reader in International Studies, Pondicherry University, 1988-90. Publications: Britain in the European Community, book, 1994; Papers in edited books and journals. Honours: Junior Research Fellow, JLNU, 1980; Research Grantee, UGC, 1986-87; International Visitor, USIA, Washington, USA, 1993; Fellow, Salzburg Seminar, Session 323, 1995. Memberships: Indian Council of World Affairs, New Delhi; London School of Economics Society; Calcutta Historical Society; West Bengal Political Science Association. Address: B-3/1 Parijat, 24 Mandeville Gardens, Calcutta 700 019, India.

**BHATTAR Venkata Rama,** b. 21 May 1966, Mysore. Sanskrit Pandit. m. Lakshmi Bhattar, 1 son, 2 daughters. Education: BA, 1987; MA, 1989; B Ed, 1990; M Ed, 1992; VEDA, 1990; AGAMA, 1982. Appointments: Sanskrit Pandit (Sanskrit & Religion Scholar), National High School, Bangalore, 1991-. Publications: 5 Sanskrit books; 3 Agama books. Honour: Outstanding Personality, 1998. Membership: KTK State Archak & Agamik Association, Bangalore. Address: Archak Asakta Poshaka Sabha Quarters, APS Road VV Puram, Bangalore 560004, India.

**BHATTI Illahi Bux M,** b. 11 August 1938, Khairpur, Sindh, Pakistan. Agricultural Researcher; Educator. m. Sakina Bhatti, 2 sons, 3 daughters. Education: MSc Agriculture, 1962, Sindh, Pakistan; PhD Plant Breeding, 1972, Wales, UK. Appointments: Director General, Agricultural Research, Sindh Province, Pakistan; Vice Chancellor, Sindh Agricultural University, Tandojam, Sindh. Publications: 204 including 5 books. Honours: 35 national and international awards. Memberships: Address: 139 Defence Society, Alam Rd, Hyderabad, Sindh, Pakistan.

**BHATTI Jawed Iqbal,** b. 1 November 1957, Gujranwala, Pakistan. Telecommunication Engineer. m. Irum. Education: BE, Electronics; MSEE. Appointments: Captain, Pakistan Army, 1980-87; Executive Engineer, WAPDA, 1997-; Publications: Flood Forecasting Telemetry of Pakistan. Memberships: Pakistan Engineering Council; Institute of Electrical and Electronic Engineers; American Radio Relay League. Address: Pakistan Water Power Devel, 144 - G Model Town, Lahore 54700, Pakistan.

**BHATTI Liaqat Ali,** b. 9 November 1951, Bikaner, India. Photographer. m. Kaneez Bhatti, 1 son, 2 daughters. Education: Postgraduate Diploma, Tourism and Hotel Management; Postgraduate Diploma, Journalism; Degree Course, Journalism. Honours: Appreciation Certificate and Trophy, Rajasthan Divas Samaroh Samiti; Certificate of Merit, Animal Welfare Board, India; 1st and 2nd Prize, Department of Environment, Government of Rajasthan; Japan Airlines Prize, 15th Photo Contest, Asian Cultural Centre for UNESCO, Japan, 1990; Consolation Prizes, 1st and 2nd National Photo Contest, Ministry J & B Photo Division, New Delhi, India; Certificate of Excellence, Indian Asthma Care Society; Sh. Hukum Singh Kchchhwa Smriti Puraskar, Thar Gair Nritya Foundation, Barmer. Address: Flat No 11, Government Hostel, M I Road, Jaipur, Rajasthan 302001, India.

**BHIKANE Anil Udhavrao**, b. 10 June 1965, Mankhed, India. Educator. m. Aruna Raghuveer Reddy, 2 sons. Education: Bachelor of Veterinary Science and Animal Husbandry, 1st Division, 1987, Master of Veterinary Science, Medicine, 1st with distinction, 1989, Veterinary College, Parbhani. Appointments: Veterinary Officer, Veterinary College, Parbhani, 1989-91; Assistant Professor of Veterinary Science, Agricultural College, Latur, 1991-93; Assistant Professor of Medicine, Veterinary College, Udgir, 1993-. Publications: Textbook of Animal Science, Part I, 1996, Part II, 1997; Textbook of Veterinary Science, 1997; Author of some 4 dozen research papers in field of veterinary medicine; 3 dozen popular articles. Honours: Merit Scholarships for Bachelor's and Master's studies; Certificate of Merit for securing highest marks in MVSc exam, 1988-89. Memberships: Life Member, Indian Veterinary Association; Life Member, Indian Society for Veterinary Medicine; President, Veterinarians Club, Udgir. Address: Department of Medicine, Veterinary College, Udgir 413-517, Dist Latur, India.

**BHIKKHUHI Kusuma**, b. 9 October 1929, Colombu, Sri Lanka. Lecturer. 3 sons, 1 daughter. Education: Science Teacher Professional Training, 1955; MSc, Theravada, 1969; BA, Theravada Buddhism, 1974; MA, Theravada; Phd, Buddhist, Pali University, 1998. Appointments: Science Teacher, Government School; English Teacher, University Scholarship, USA, 1969. Publications: MA, Thesis, Sati in Buddhist Meditation. Honours: Acting in Charge, Mahabodhi Society of India, 1998. Memberships: Sakyadhita International; First Bhikkhuni in Sri Lanka. Address: 50 Alwis Perera Mawatha, Katubedda, Moratuwa, Sri Lanka.

**BHUIYAN Md Shoaib**, b. 13 April 1964, Chandpur, Bangladesh. Computer Engineer. m. Runa Lisa Munni, 1 daughter. Education: MSc, University of Dhaka, Bangladesh, 1989; PhD, Nagoya Institute of Technology, 1996. Appointments: Scientific Officer, Bangladesh Atomic Energy Commission, Dhaka, 1990; Lecturer, University Grants Commission, Bangladesh, 1992; Research Associate, Nagoya Institute of Technology, 1996-; Lecturer, Nagoya College, Toyoake, 1996-, Faculty of Engineering, Department of Electrical and Computer Engineering, 1996-; Associate Advisor, Graduate School of Engineering, NIT, Nagoya, Japan, 1997-; Honours: Talent Pool Merit Scholarship, University of Dhaka, Bangladesh, 1985; Postgrad Research Scholarship, Government of Japan, 1992-96; Research Grantee, Principal Investigation Award, The Hori Information Science Promotion Foundation, Japan, 1998. Memberships: IEEE; IEICE of Japan; International Neural Network Society; IEEE Computer Society (Member - TC-PAMI). Address: Metjo Jutaku 2-508 Meijo 3-1, Nagoya, Kita 462-0846, Japan.

**BHUYAN Bijoy**, b. 28 August 1973, Guwahati, India. Artist. Education: Bachelor of Fine Arts, Maharaja Sayajira University of Baroda, 1996. Appointments: Organiser of many exhibitions, University of Baroda. Memberships: Friend Society. Address: Faculty of Fine Arts M S Universityof Baroda, Department of Sculpture, Baroda 390002, India.

**BI Ru-Chang**, b. 4 August 1940, Hebei, China. Professor. m. Bi-Cheng Chen, 1 son, 1 daughter. Education: Bachelor, Master, Leningrad University, USSR, 1960-65. Appointments: Research Assistant/Associate, Institute of Biophysics, Academica Sinica, 1966-80; Visiting Scholar, University of York, England, 1980-82; Associate Professor, Director of Department, Institute of Biophysics, Academia Sinica, 1983-. Publications: Many papers concerning various aspects of protein crystallography. Honours: National Award, 1982, 1986, 1988, 1995; Academy Awards. Memberships: Chinese Associations of Biophysics, Crystallography, Space Research

and Application; American Association for the Advancement of Science. Address: Academia Sinica, Institute of Biophysics, No 15 Datun Road, Chaoyang District, Beijing 100101, China.

**BIANCHI Robert Steven**, b. 30 November 1898, New York, New York, USA. Director of Academic and Curatorial Affairs. m. Anna M Haney, 1 daughter. Education: BA, 1965, Rutgers College, New Brunswick, New Jersey; MA, 1969, Phd, 1976, NY University's Institute of Fine Arts. Appointments: Curator, Department of Egyptian, Classical and Ancient Middle Eastern Art, Brooklyn Museum, 1976-90; Adjunct Professor, Columbia University and NYU, during 1980s; Global Art Historian; Director of Academic and Curatorial Affairs, Broughton International Inc, current. Publications: Book Review Editor, Journal of American Research Centre in Egypt; Contributing Editor, Minerva; Presenter on screen over 60 commercial and cable television broadcasts; Over 250 journal articles and book reviews; Author, 19 books, co-author 24 more; Curator or organiser or both, 7 international art exhibitions, 1995-, including Splendours of Ancient Egypt, Broughton International Inc, 1995. Honours: Bert H Hill Scholar, American School of Classical Studies, Athens, 1969; Fulbright-Hayes Fellow, Aegyptisches Museum, Berlin, 1977, 1978; Bourse Jacques Vandier, Musee du Louvre, Paris, 1981, 1982; J Clawson Mills Fellowship, Egyptian Dept, The Metropolitan Museum of Art, 1992-93. Address: 522 Valley Vista Blvd, Lewiston, Idaho 83501, USA.

**BIAO Zuo**, b. 12 February 1942, Changshu, Jiangsu, China. Professor. m. Qin Yi, 1 daughter. Education: Diploma, Majoring in English, Suzhou University, 1963-68; Diploma, Majoring in Comparative Study of Chinese and Western Cultures, China Academy of Cultures, 1987-89. Appointments: Dean, Foreign Languages Department, Nantong Normal College, 1977-87; Vice Dean, Dean, Foreign Languages Department, Chairman of the Centre of Language and Culture, Shanghai Martime University, 1987-. Publications: Concepts Concerning Comparative Literature, 1990; The Theory of Information Gap and Its Application, 1991; Variables in Reading Comprehension, 1992; Characteristics of Black English, 1993; Witty Translation, 1994; The Naming of Characters in Literary Works, 1995; Clarifying the Concept of Control, 1996; On the Rise of Estuary English, 1997; Translatability of Cultures, 1998. Honours: First Prize, Teaching Excellence, 1993; Shanghai Municipal Model Worker, 1994; National Excellent Teacher, 1995; National may 1st Labour Medal, 1996. Memberships: English Academic Committee of Shanghai Translators Association; Cultural Studies Committee of China Association for Comparative Study of English and Chinese. Address: Shanghai Maritime University, 1550 Pudong Avenue, Shanghai 200135, China.

**BICHEVIN Victor Vasily**, b. 25 March 1935, Krasnojarsk, Russia. Research Scientist. m. Aleksandra Andrei Popov, div, 1 son, 1 daughter. Education: BS, 1959, Tartu University, Estonia; PhD, 1972. Appointments: Junior Research Associate, Institute Physics, Tartu, 1960-63, 1963-72, Senior Research Associate, 1973-. Publications: Over 50 articles to professional journals. Memberships: European Physics Society. Address: Aardia 144/49, EE 2400, Tartu, Estonia.

**BIDLACK James Enderby**, b. 1 February 1961, Minneapolis, USA. Plant Physiologist; Plant Anatomist. Education: BS, Purdue University, 1984; MS, University of Arkansas, 1986; PhD, Iowa University, 1990. Career: Research Assistant, University of Arkansas, 1984-86; Research Assistant, Iowa University, 1986-90; Associate Professor, University of Central Oklahoma, 1990-. Publications: Numerous articles in professional journals. Honours: President's Partners

Excellence in Teaching Award, 1995; Biology and Pre-Med Teaching Awards, 1995; AAUP Distinguished Scholar Award, 1995. Memberships: Alpha Chi Sigma; American Society of Agronomy; American Association of University Professors; Council for Agricultural Sciences and Technology; Gamma Sigma Delta; Sigma Xi. Address: University of Central Oklahoma, Department of Biology, Edmond, OK 73034, USA.

**BIELENIN Kazimierz,** b. 29 January 1923, Brzesczcze. Archaeologist. m. Janina Czubryt. Education: MA, History of Art, Archaeology, Jagiellonian University in Cracow, 1952; PhD, Nicolas Copernicus University in Torun, 1963; Habilitated Dr, 1972; Professor, 1988. Appointments: Assistant, 1950, Curator, 1955, Assistant Professor, 1977, Vice Director, 1967-95, Museum of Archaeology in Cracow. Publications: Numerous works, including: Starozytne górnictwo i hutnictwo swietokrzyskie, 1974; The Holy Cross Mountains, Centre of the Largest Iron Producing Region on the Territory of non-Roman Europe, 2nd Edition, 1992; Eingetiefte Rennöfen der frühgeschichtlichen Eisenverhüttung in Europa in Festschrift Ur Richard Pittioni, 1967; Der Rennofen mit eingetieften Herd in seine formen in Polen in OFFA, 1983; Der Rennofen vom Typ Burgenland in der frühgeschichtlichen Eisenverhüttung Mitteleuropa in La siderrugie ancienne de l'Est de la France dans son contexte Europeen, 1994. Honours: Award of Merits, Region of Kielce, 1966; Award for Social Work for the City of Cracow, 1968; Award of Merits for Region of Cracow, 1973; Award for Preservation of Monuments, 1980; Gold Cross of Merits, 1977; Knight's Cross of Polonia Restituta, 1986; Officer's Cross of Polonia Restituta, 1995. Memberships: Comite pour la Siderurgie Ancienne de l'Union Internationales des Sciences Prehistoriques et Protohistoriques; Member of the Management, 1965; The Historical Metallurgy Society, Coleford, 1969-; Malopolska Branch, Associations of Lovers of Dabrowski Mazurka Traditions, President of the Board, 1994. Address: Muzeum Archaeological Cracow, ul Senacka 3, 31 002 Krakow, Poland.

**BIELINSKA-WAZ Dorota Joanna,** b. 9 June 1968, Poland. Physicist. m. Piotr Waz. Education: MSc, 1992; Doctor of Physics, 1998. Appointments: Research Assistant, Institute of Physics, 1991-98; Research Associate Adjunct, 1998-. Publications: Numerous Articles in Journals. Address: Krasinskiego 21/23/51, 47-100 Torun, Poland.

**BIERSCHENK Bernhard Friedrich,** b. 5 May 1941, Kassel, Germany. Senior Researcher, Psychology. Education: Fil lic, 1969; Fil Dr, 1972; Reader, 1972. Appointments: Deputy Professor, 1973-81; Senior Researcher, 1981-; Professor, University of Erlangen, 1976; Resident, Theoretical Psychology Edmonton, Canada, 1979-80; Visiting Fellow, National Science Eng, Research Council of Canada, 1981-82; Founding Member, Psychol Lab, Copenhagen Competence Research Center, 1994. Publications: 120 Books, Articles. Memberships: DGFP; American Psychology Association; New York Academy of Sciences. Address: Ljungsaetersvagen 10, 23641 Hollviken, Sweden.

**BIKTIMIROV Tofik Zijatdinovich,** b. 9 July 1952. Neurologist. m. Nailja Biktimirova, 1 son, 1 daughter. Appointments: Assistant, Department of Neurosurgery, Dean, Organizer, Department of Medicine, 1990, 1995, First Vice President, 1995-, Ulyanovsk State University. Honour: Honoured Doctor of Russia. Memberships: European Association for Palliative Care; Association of Palliative Care, Ulyanovsk. Address: 42 Leo Tolstoy Street, Ulayanovsk 422600, Russia.

**BILLINGS Richard Whitten,** b. 5 January 1924, Bar Harbor, USA. Association Manager. m. Norma Taraldsen, 1 son, 3 daughters. Education: AB, English, Colby College, 1948; MEd, Springfield College, 1951; ChFC, 1984, 1986, American College; PhD, Business Administration, LaSalle University, 1995. Appointments: Director of Membership and Adult Programming, Watertown YMCA, New York, 1948-50; Director of Extension, Schenectady YMCA, Director of Youth Work, Programming for Adults and Membership, 1951-56; Executive Director, Hudson Valley District YMCA, 1956-60; Executive Director, Association Island, Conference and Training Center of YMCA, New York, 1960-67; Executive Director, Eastern Region of US for the Fellowship of Christian Athletes, 1967-70; Executive Director, Association Island Recreational Corp, 1970-74; Director, Land Use Regulation Commission, State of Maine, Department of Conservation, 1974-76; Agent, John Hancock Mutual Life Insurance Company, 1976-86; Executive Director, Maine Association of Life Underwriters, Kennebec Valley Life Underwriters, Androscoggin Valley Life Underwriters, Independent Producer, The Chapman & Drake Insurance Agency, Owner, Maine Association Management Services, 1986-93; Owner, Maine Association Management Services, Executive Director, Kennebec Valley Life Underwriters, Androscoggin Valley Life Underwriters, Informed Notaries of Maine, 1993-94; Owner, Maine Association Management Services, Day Mountain Publications, Executive Director, Informed Notaries of Maine, Adjunct Professor, LaSalle University, 1994-. Publications: The Village and the Hill. Memberships include: Treasurer, Maine Insurance Agents Council, 1991-93; Trustee, Old Fort Western; Chairman of Trustees, South Parish Congregational Church, Augusta, Maine. Address: RR7, Box 1940, Augusta, ME 04330-9114, USA.

**BINKAUSEIENE Elena,** b. Lithuania. Chemist; Researcher. m. Boleslovas Juozapas Binkauskas, 1 daughter. Education: Degree in Chemistry, Vilnius University, 1971; D Physics Science, 1980. Appointments: Laboratory Assistant, Institute of Chemistry, 1971-72; Research Associate, 1972-86; Senior Researcher, Scientist, 1986-; Department Mamber Auditing Committee Institute of Chemistry, 1998-. Publications: Articles to Professional Journals; Patentee. Memberships: Lithuanian Association of Chemistry; Lithuanian Academy of Scientists; Tourist Club. Address: Rinktines 49-5, 2051 Vilnius, Lithuania.

**BINNS Patrick George,** b. 8 October 1948. Premier. m. Carol MacMillan, 3 sons, 1 daughter. Education: MA, Community Development, University of Alberta, 1971. Appointments: Development Officer, Government of Alberta; Rural Development Council, Prince Edward Island, 1972; Provincial Government of PEI, 1974-78, coordinating the establishment and administration of the regional services centres in eastern PEI; Elected to PEI Legislative Assembly, 1978; Provincial Legislature, and held several cabinet portfolios, 1979-84; MP, House of Commons, representing the riding of Cardigan, 1984-88; Parliamentary Secretary to Minister of Fisheries & Oceans; President, Island Bean Ltd and Pat Binns & Associates, 1988-96; Premier, President of the Executive Council and Minister responsible for Intergovernmental Affairs, 1996-; Planned and Constructed the Northumberland Arena; Founder and Active Organiser, Northumberland Fisheries Festival. Honours: Queen's Silver Jubilee Medal for Outstanding Public Service, 1978. Address: Office of the Premier, 95 Rochford Street, Box 2000, Charlottetown, PE, Canada C1A 7N8.

**BIONDIC Bozidar,** b. 16 November 1940, Zagreb, Croatia. Hydrogeologist. m. Zlatica Biondic, 2 sons. Education: Eng of Geology, Faculty of Mine, Geology and Petrol, University of

Zagreb, 1964; MA, 1974, PhD, 1982, University of Zagreb. Appointments: Hydrogeologist, 1964-78, Head, Division for Hydrogeology and Engineering Geology, 1988-92, Professor, 1990-, Vice Director, 1992-97, Director, 1997-, Institute of Geology, Zagreb; Proposer, Chairman, European Union COST 65 action, Hydrogeological Aspects of Groundwater Protection in Karstic Areas, 1990-95; Professor, Geotechnical Faculty, Varazdin University of Zagreb, 1998-. Publications: 65 scientific papers and over 220 professional reports. Memberships: International Association of Hydrogeologists; International Association of Engineering Geology; IAH Karst Commission; Croatian Geological Association; Croatian Association for Water Protection. Address: Travanjska 16, 10000 Zagreb, Croatia.

**BIRABUZA Andre,** b. 25 July 1952, Jenda. Physician. m. Angele Mugozi, 4 sons. Education: Doctor in Medicine, 1981; Nutrition Certificate, 1983; Pediatrician Preventive and Social, 1984; Special Training in General Pediatrics, 1984-88. Appointments: Director, National Reproductive Health Programme of Burundi; Publisher. Publications: 2 essays; Poetry; Fiction; Third essay in preparation. Memberships: National Economic and Social Council. Address: 19 Matana Ave, BP 2524, Bujumbura, Burundi.

**BIRCHAM Deric Neale,** b. 16 December 1934, Wellington, New Zealand. University Chancellor. m. Patricia, 1 son, 2 daughters. Education: BA, California University, USA, 1985; Doctor of Philosophy, Marquis Guiseppe Scicluna International University, 1985; Master of Business Administration, California University, 1987; Doctor of Literature, Marquis Guiseppe Scicluna International University, 1987; Doctor of Business Management, World University, USA, 1988; Doctor of Letters, University of Aetema Lucina, 1988; Doctor of Philosophy, PhD, The InternationalUniversity, 1994; Doctor of Science, International Open University, 1996; Doctor of Philosophy, Oxford International University, 1998; Doctor of Law, Bombay University, 1999. Appointments: Publicity, Public Relations, New Zealand Government, 1952-78; Head, Medical Photography, MedicalIllustrations Department, University of Otago, All Hospitals in theProvince of Otago; Director General, International Institute of Natural Medicine Inc; CEO President, Chair, Board of Directors, AstralInternational Incorporated Ltd; University President, Oxford International University; World President, Head of Council, Commonwealth Schools Council; Founder, World President, The Golden Circle. Publications: Author of Many Publications. Honours: Recipient of Many Honors, Awards and Titles. Memberships: Royal Photographic Society of Great Britain; Royal Society of Arts; New Zealand Professional Photographers Association; British Institute of Professional Photography. Address: 131 Tirohanga Road, Lower Hutt, Wellington, New Zealand.

**BIRCHER Andrea,** b. 6 March 1928, Bern, Switzerland. Nursing Professor. Education: RN Diploma, 1957; BS, 1961; MS, 1962; PhD, 1966; Clinical Nurse Specialist in Psychiatric Nursing and Certified Diplomate, American Psychotherapy Association. Appointments: Staff and Head Nurse, Assistant Professor, 1966-72; Professor, 1972-93; Professor Emeritus, 1993-. Publications: Numerous. Honours: Numerous. Memberships: Numerous. Address: 1161 Cypress Point Ln Apt 201, Ventura, CA 93003-6074, USA.

**BIRD Rebecca Yates,** b. 17 December 1963, San Antonio, USA. Drama Teacher. m. Steven Bird, 1 stepson, 1 daughter. Education: BFA, Acting, University of Texas, 1985; MA, Theatre, Hunter College, New York, 1998. Appointments: Adjunct Faculty, University of Tennessee, Chattanooga; 10m years professional theatre. Honours: Arts Recognition Award,

National Foundation for the Advancement of the Arts in Theatre, 1981. Memberships: Alpha Phi; Chattanooga Symphony Youth Orchestra Band; Board of Directors, Actors Equity Association. Address: 3227 Westonia Drive Chattanooga, TN 37412, USA.

**BIRKETVEDT Grethe,** b. 17 September 1942, Sarpsborg Norway. Medical Scientist; Writer; Musician. m. Per Birketvedt 1 daughter. Education: MEd, Teachers Training College, Stord Norway, 1964; MMus, Oslo University, Antioch College, 1969 MPhysEd, Oslo Medical School, 1983; MD, PhD, University o Tromso, Norway, 1995; Certificate of Teacher, Physics and Education; Music Diplomate; Medical Diplomate. Appointments Teacher, Norwegian Teaching Association, Sarpsborg 1964-67; Fulbright Scholar, USA, 1968-69; Musician Composer, Norwegian Composers Association, Oslo, 1969-83 General Practitioner, Medical Association, Oslo, 1982-92 Medical Scientist, General Practice Organization, Oslo 1992-93; Assistant Professor, Tromso Hospital, 1993-95 Visiting Scientist, University of Pennsylvania, 1995- Publications include: On a Distance, 1976; There Are Days 1978; Hildelin, A Symphonic Poem, 1980; In the Light of the Planet, 1994; Treatment of Overweight and Obesity in Genera Practice, 1998; Composer of Music. Honours: Writers Award University Altertumskunde, Germany, 1980; Norwegian County Medical Research Grantee, 1996. Memberships include: AAAS Fulbright Alumni Association; Norwegian Writers Association TONO Association; Norwegian Associationof Gastroenterology Norwegian Association of Music Composition; New York Academy of Sciences. Address: University of Pennsylvania Department of Medicine, Philadelphia, PA 19104, USA.

**BIRMAN Alexander,** b. 23 May 1946, Moscow. Physicist. m. Emily, 2 sons. Education: MSc, Moscow Physics Technical Institute, 1970; PhD, Institute of Applied Physics, Moscow 1975. Appointments: Senior Researcher, Institute of Applied Physics, Moscow, 1970-85; Leading Research Scientist Astrophysics Corporation, Moscow, 1985-93; Senior Optical Scientist, Dicon Fiberoptics Inc, Berkeley, CA, 1995- Publications: Contributor to Articles in Professional Journals. Memberships: IEEE, Optical Society of America; International Society for Optical Engineering. Address: 535 Pierce St Apt 2105, Albany, CA 94706-1055, USA.

**BIRNEY Leroy,** b. 13 January 1942, Dodge City, KS, USA. Missionary. 1 son, 2 daughters. Education: Student, Sterling College, KS, USA, 1960-62; BA, University of Kansas, 1964; Certificate, Emmaus Bible School, 1965; MA, 1968, MDiv, 1968; Trinity Evangelical Divinity School; ThD, International Seminary, Plymouth, FL, USA, 1986. Appointments: Ordained, 1969, 1984; Missionary in Colombia, South America, 1970-84; President, Founder, Missionary Action Inc, 1982-; International Ministry Teaching and Speaking in US, Latin, America, Africa, 1985-. Publications: Contributor to religious journals. Honours: Phi Beta Kappa, 1964; Faculty Scholar, Trinity Evangelical Divinity School, 1968, 1969. Memberships: Founder, Missionary Action Inc, 1982; Founder, Bethel Bible Institute in Honduras, 1987. Address: Missionary Action Inc, PO Box 1027, Bradenton, FL 34206-1027, USA.

**BIRSHTEIN Tatiana,** b. 20 December 1928, Leningrad, Russia. m. Mirlin David, 1 son, 1 daughter. Education: Leningrad University, 1951; Pedagogical Institute, Leningrad, 1954-58; PhD, Institute Macromol Comp, 1960; DSc, 1974. Appointments: Industrial Engineer, Leningrad, 1951-54; Junior Researcher, Senior Researcher, Principal Researcher, Institute Macromol Comp, 1958-; Professor, St Petersburg University, 1970-. Publications: Over 200 Articles. Membership: Advisory

Boards of Science Journals. Address: Institute Macromol Comp RAS, Bolshoi pr 31, 199004 Saint Petersburg, Russia.

**BISHOP Eliza H,** b. Crockett, Texas, USA. Writer; Researcher; Public Relations Executive. Education: BA, 1941, University of Mary Hardin-Baylor; Advanced Studies, University Indiana, 1950; Ohio State University, 1955; Texas A&M University, 1960. Appointments: Editor, Crockett Democrat, 1941-47; Newswriter, Houston Post, 1942-72; East Texas Editor, Houston Chronicle, 1947-81; Opened EB Promotions for Everybody, PR firm, 1978-; Volunteer, County Historical Commission Chairman, 1961-90; President, Texas Press Women, 1977-80. Publications: Author, Editor, Houston County History, 1980; Mini Histories, 1972-86; Historical Markers Map, 1974; Editor, Houston County , 1977, 1978, 1987, 1998. Honours: Communicator of Achievement, 1977; Best Texas County Historical Commission Chairman, 1972, 1974, 1976, 1978; Distinguished Service Award, City of Crockett, 1983-84; DAR Medal of Honour, 1990; Girl Scout Award, 1991. Memberships: National Federation of Press Women Inc; Texas Professional Communicators; Women in Communication Inc; Texas St Association of History; Texas Historical Foundation; Texas Museum Association; East Texas Historical Association. Address: 629 N 4th Street, Crockett, TX 75835-4035, USA.

**BISHOP Kim Irene,** b. 12 November 1960, Williamsport, Pennsylvania, USA. Pharmaceutical Executive. Education: BA, 1982, Franklin & Marshall College; MS, 1986, Villanova University; PhD, 1995, University of London. Appointments: Clinical Research Trainee, Devereux Foundation, Institute of Clinical Research and Training, Paoli, USA, 1982; Stock Broker Assistant, Prudential Bache Securities, Bala Cynwyd, USA, 1983-84; Freelance Data Analyst, Merck, Sharp & Dohme Research Labs, Presbyterian Hospital, Dept Cardiology, and Inter-American Pharmaceuticals Ltd, 1986-87; Clinical Research Coordinator and Data Analysis Specialist, Scheie Eve Institute, University of Pennsylvania Medical School, Dept of Ophthalmology, 1984-88; Senior Clinical Research Scientist, Allergan Pharmaceuticals, 1988-90; Contract Clinical Research Professional, ClinTrials Research International, Maidenhead, Berkshire, UK, 1994; Global Projects Liaison Manager, International Clinical Research Operations, Novartis Pharmaceuticals AG (world-wide HQ), Basel, Switzerland, 1996-. Publications: Co-author 11 research articles in respected scientific journals. Honours: British Association for Psychopharmacology Award, 1993, 1994; European Behavioural Pharmacology Society Award, 1994; Overseas Research Scholarship, 1991-94; Ciba Pharmaceuticals Medical and Clinical Development's Pride in Team Achievement Award, 1996; Regional Alumni Ambassador of Switzerland, Villanova University, 1996-. Address: Novartis Bld 5210.3.23, Dept Medical and Clinical Development, 4002 Basel, Switzerland.

**BISHOP Rosalinda,** b. 18 October 1950, Naga City, Philippines. Information Manage and Dance Choreographer. m. (div) Roy Bishop, 1 son. Education: BSc Education, 1969, MA Education, 1974, University Nueva Caceres, Philippines; MBA, 1979, Ortanez University, Philippines; AssociateDiploma Library Practice, 1990, Sydney Technical College, Australia; Master Library & Information Management, 1998, Charles Sturt University,Australia. Appointments: Teacher, Dept Education, Philippines, 1969-74;Research/Analyst, Armed Forces of Philippines, 1974-75; Foreign ExchangeOfficer, Central Bank of Philippines, 1975-80; Library Officer, ParliamentHouse, Canberra, Australia, 1981-82; Administrative Service Officer,Australian Bureau of Statistics, Canberra, 1982-86; Circulation Officer,University of Western Sydney, Sydney, 1986-88; Acquisitions Officer,Australian Catholic University, Sydney, 1988-94; Senior Library Supervisor, State Library of

New South Wales, Sydney, 1995-. Honours: Outstanding Migrant Award, 1984; Best Cultural Performance Award, 1991;1993 winner, Mrs Philippines Australia Beauty Pageant. Memberships: Girl Scouts of the Philippines, Trainer/Leader, 1969-74; Camarines Sur Teachers Musical Ensemble, Choreographer, 1969-74; Armed Forces of the Philippines Dance Troupe, Choreographer, 1975; Philippine Dance Ensemble,Director/Choreographer, 1985-; Philippine Australian Country Club, Secretary 1986-89; Filipino Women's Association, PRO 1987-91; Philippine Australian Entertainment Network, Treasurer 1997-; American Library Association, 1997-; Australian Library and Information Association 1997-; Association for Library Collections & Technical Services, 1998; Pilipino Magazine, Contributing Editor, 1998; Mrs Philippines Australia Beauty Quest, Protocol Manager & Choreographer, 1994-; Sydney Morning Herald Literary Club 1996-. Address: 7A Eulo Pde, 2112 Ryde, New South Wales, Australia.

**BISNAR Alowina Ruby,** b. 11 March 1943, Philippines. CPA. m. Orlando Y Bisnar. Education: BSC Commerce, Accounting; Money Market Management Certificate, Merrill Lynch, Wall Street, 1986; Money Market Management Certificate, Government Finance Officers Association, 1985. Appointments: Manager of Bonds and Investments, 1984-89, Manager of Financial Planning, 1989-94, Manager of General Accounting, 1994-97, Manager of Projects Accounting and Accounting Liaison for Customer Services, 1997-, Los Angeles Department of Water and Power. Honours: Member, Alpha Gamma Sigma, California State Honor Society, 1998. Membership: Secretary Treasurer, East Palmer Homeowners Association, 1996-97. Address: Los Angeles Department Water and Power, PO Box 51111 Room 405, Los Angeles, CA 90051-0100, USA.

**BISTRICEANU Marian,** b. 22 September 1941, Negoi, Dolj, Romania. Professor of Endocrinology. m. Pestrea Ioana, 1 daughter. Education: Faculty of Veterinary Medicine, Timisoara, 1965; Faculty of Medicine, Craiova, 1976. Appointments: Assistant, 1966-90, Lecturer, 1990-92, Assistant Professor, 1992-95, Professor, 1995-. Publications include: Immune Pathology of the Endocrine System Gynaecologic Endocrinology; Progresses in Medicine. Honours: Romanian Academy Award, 1983; Romanian Academy of Sciences Award, 1996. Memberships: Romanian Scientists Academy; Romanian Medical Sciences Academy; International Society of Endocrinology; Balcanic Medical Union; International Brain Research Organization. Address: 1100 Strada Madona Dudu, Bloc 4, Apartament 3, Craiova, Romania.

**BISWAS Dipak R,** b. 3 February 1949, India. Engineer. m. Bharati, 2 daughters. Education: MS, 1974, PhD, 1976, Materials Science and Engineering, University of California, Berkeley. Appointments: Manager, ITT/ALCATEL, 1981-88; Director, R&D Spectran, 1988-91; Director, R&D Fiberguide, 1991-94; Senior Scientist, Bellcore, 1994-96; Director, Production Development, Boston Optical Fiber, 1996-. Publications: Over 90, 10 US patents. Honours: Fox Awards, ITT, 1985; Team Award, Bellcore, 1995. Membership: American Ceramic Society. Address: 4 Saddle Hill Drive, Northborough, MA 01532, USA.

**BITTENCOURT Jose Augusto,** b. 8 June 1947, Araguari, MG, Brazil. Space Physicist, Educator. m. Rosangela Maria Gomes, 2 sons. Education: BSc, Chemical Engineering, Federal University of Minas Gerais, Brazil, 1970; MSc, Space Science, National Institute for Space Research, Brazil, 1972; PhD, Space Physics, Univeristy of Texas, Dallas, Texas, USA, 1975. Appointments: Research Assistant, University of Texas, 1973-75; Visiting Scientist, 1976; Research Scientist, INPE,

1975-; Professor, Space Science, Graduate School, 1982-87; Head of Aeronomy Department, Substitute Director, Space Sciences, 1989-92. Publications: Fundamentals of Plasma Physics; Advances in Space Research; Brazilian Journal of Geophysics; About 100 Published Papers, Well Known Scientific Journals, Space Science. Honours: NASA International University Fellowship; Golden Medal and Certificate Award for Outstanding Service. Memberships: URSI; American Geophysical Union. Address: Rua Taquaritinga 27, 12243180 San Jose dos Campos SP, Brazil.

**BITTERLICH Walter, b.** 19 February 1908, Reutte, Tyrol, Austria. Emeritus University Professor. m. Ilse Hauptmann, 2 sons, 2 daughters. Education: Dipl Ing, 1930; Dr nat techn, 1949. Appointments: Forester, Austrian Federal Forests, 1935-41; German soldier in Russia and Normandy, 1942; Discovery of the Angle Count Sampling, 1947; Forester, OBF, 1949-66; University Professor, University BOKU-Wien, 1967-78; Scientific work with FOB-Company in Salzburg, 1978-. Publication: The Relascope Idea, 1984. Honours: Honorary Member, Society of American Foresters, 1971; Osterreichisches Ehrenkreuz 1 Klasse fur Wissenschaft und Kunst, 1983; Preis Fachgebiet Forstliche Biometrie, University of Freiburg, Germany, 1983. Memberships: Epistolarium Societas Forestalis Fenniae; University-BOKU-Wien. Address: Dipling University, Rennbahnstrasse 4 A, Salzburg 5020, Austria.

**BJERKAAS Carlton Lee, b.** 17 April 1948, Fergus Falls, Minnesota, USA. Meteorologist. 3 sons. Education: BS, 1970, University of North Dakota; SM, 1977, Massachusetts Institute of Technology; MPA, 1983, Auburn University at Montgomery. Appointments: Weather Forecaster, 1971-73, Weather Recon, 1973-75, Radar Research Meteorologist, 1977-82, Operational Requirements and Test, Military Airlift Command, 1983-85, Chief Aerospace Environment Requirements, 1985-87, Assistant Chief of Staff, 1989-91, Director Comm Systems, Plans and Programmes, 1991-95, USAF; Senior Scientist, Science Applications, Intl Corp, 1995-. Publications: Numerous articles and technical reports, 1977-83; McGraw Hill Encyclopedia of Science and Technology, 1979. Memberships: Fellow, American Meteorological Society; American Association for Advancement of Science; American Society for Public Administration; NY Academy of Sciences; Academy of Political Science; Phi Beta Kappa; Sigma Xi; Phi Eta Sigma; Pi Alpha Alpha; Air Weather Association. Address: Science Applications Inl Corp, 619 W Highway 50, O'Fallon, IL 62269-1942, USA.

**BJURULF Per, b.** 29 March 1932, Jonkoping, Sweden. MD; Specialist in Internal Medicine. m. Carin Lindstrom, 2 sons, 2 daughters. Education: MD, 1957; Specialist in Internal Medicine, 1965; PhD, 1960. Appointments: Assistant Professor of Anatomy, 1960-63, and Preventive & Social Medicine, 1963-66, University Lund; University Professor and Head Dept of Preventive and Social Medicine, University Umea, 1966-69, Linkoping University, 1969-97; Head Physician in Preventive & Social Medicine, 1969-97, Deputy Chief Physician, 1971-81, Dean of Medical Education, 1971-73, 1981-84, Dean of Medical Faculty, 1987-92, Head of Centre for Community Medicine, 1992-95, Linkoping University. Publications: in anatomy, internal medicine and preventive medicine. Memberships: Swedish Medical Society; Swedish Medical Association; International Epidemiology Association; Bombay Natural History Society; Piraten Society; and others. Address: Gumhem, S 590 41 Rimforsa, Sweden.

**BLACKWELL Vickie, b.** 8 July 1951, Rockford, Illinois, USA. Nursing Administrator. m. (1) Jim Wright, 2 sons, 1 daughter, (2) Glen Blackwell. Education: ADN, 1972, BSN, 1983, MSN,

in progress. Appointments: Critical Care Team Leader and Head Nurse, 1972-83; Administrator, Director of Nursing S.N.F., 1984-97, Home Health, 1991-97; Owner, Wright Enterprises, 1992-. Publications: Several articles. Honours: Valedictorian, 1983; National Deans List, 1983; Hall of Fame; Woman of the Year. Address: 4150 San Ramon Drive, Corcnia, CA 91720, USA.

**BLADA Ioan, b.** 18 December 1932, Cioara, Romania. Quantitative Forest Geneticist. m. Elvira, 2 sons. Education: Forestry Faculty, Diplomas, Forest Engineering, Doctor in Forest Genetics. Appointments: Scientific Researcher, Forest Genetics; Head, Forest Genetics and Tree Breeding Laboratory ,Forest Research Institute, Bucarest, Romania. Publications: 53 Scientific Papers, Congresses and Symposia. Memberships: New York Academy of Sciences. Address: Forest Research Institute, Sos Stefanesti 128, RO 72904 Bucarest, Romania.

**BLAHA Vaclav, b.** 17 March 1931, Velesin, Czech Republic. Physician; University Professor. m. Alena Napravnikova, 2 daughters. Education: MD, 1955; Internal Medicine Qualification, I a II degree, 1960, 1964; Nuclear Medicine Qualification, 1968; University Professor of Nuclear Medicine, 1991. Appointments: Head, Dept Nuclear Medicine, 3rd Faculty of Medicine, Charles University, Prague, to 1996; Teacher, part-time, Institute of Biophysics, 3rd Faculty of Medicine, Charles University, 1996-. Publications: Many in periodical journals and monographs mainly concerning the radionucleide investigations of lungs, kidneys, hepatobiliary system and adverse reaction to radioactive drugs. Memberships: European Association of Nuclear Medicine; International Association of Radiopharmacology. Address: Hrusicka 2520/16, 141 00 Prague 4, Czech Republic.

**BLAHO Andras, b.** 18 September 1946, Kecskemet, Hungary. University Professor. m. 2 sons, 1 daughter. Education: MA, International Relations, 1970; MBA, International business, 1972; PhD, Economics, 1980; Dr Habil Oec, 1996. Appointments: Junior Assistant Professor, 1970-74; Assistant Professor, 1974-80; Associate Professor, 1980-96; Professor, 1996-; Chair of Department of World Economy, 1998-; Economic Affairs Officer, NY, 1982-97. Publications: Transnational Corporations on Global Development, 1980; Going Global, 1997. Address: U Econs, Kinisti la Utca 1-7, 1828 BP5 Budapest, Hungary.

**BLAJCHMAN Morris Aaron, b.** 3 January 1940, Montreal, Canada. Physician; Scientist. m. Janet Selick, 1 son, 1 daughter. Education: BSc, 1960, MD, 1964, McGill University; FRCP(C). Appointments: Professor, McMaster University, 1970-; Medical Director, Hamilton Centre, Canadian Red Cross, 1975-; Editor-in-Chief, Transfusion Medicine Reviews, 1987-. Publications: 275 scientific publications, 3 books. Honours: Gold Medal, RCPSC, 1979; Investigator Recognition Award, International Society for Thrombosis and Hemostasis, 1993; Governor General of Canada Commemerative Medal, 1994. Memberships: American Association of Blood Banks; American Society of Hematology; ASAS; International Society for Hematology; International Society for Thrombosis and Hemostasis; Canadian Society for Transfusion Medicine, president, 1990-92. Address: 118 Cline Avenue South, Hamilton, Ontario L8N 1X1, Canada.

**BLAND Janeese, b.** 20 February 1960, Evanston, Illinois, USA. Educator. Education: PB, University of Arkansas, Pine Bluff, 1980. Appointments: Educator; Author; Founder and President, The June Maria Bland Scholarship Foundation, 1992; Executive Producer and Writer, Janeese Bland Show, Century Cable TV, Santa Monica, show with million+ viewers,

1993-. Publications: The Soft Parade Anthology '98, 1998; The Sounds of Poetry '98, 1998. Honours: 3rd Runner Up Miss Illinois, 1982; Public Service Award, Fred Hampton Scholarship Foundation, 1983; NAACP Appreciation Award for Outstanding Public Service, 1984; State Bar of California's Wiley W Manual Award for outstanding contributions, pro bono services for the elderly and poor at Bet Tzedek Legal Services, 1996; State Community Leader of the Year, California, Quaker Oats Co andNW, 1995; State Community Leader of the Year Award, Illinois, 1998. Memberships: Chancellor's Community Task Force Rep, appointed by Chancellor of University of Arkansas, 1977; Elected Class Representative, Miss Freshman, University of Arkansas, 1977; Elected President, Student Bar Association, UWLA School of Law, California, 1995. Address: Sta Century Cable TV, JMB Show, PO Box 1387, Beverly Hills, CA 90213, USA.

**BLANKERT Beppie,** b. 13 April 1949, Medan, Indonisia. Choreographer. m. Kees Spanjers. Education: ML, 1974. Career: Teacher of Modern Dance & Workshops; Co-Founder, 2 Companies in Groningen: de Noord Nederlandse Dansgroep, Mezzing; Co-Founder, Dance School, Groningen; Founder, Artistic Director, Dansers Studio. Honours: Digital Award for Letters, Remember Me, 1987; Prize, Choreography & Production, Union of Theater & Concerthall Directors for Ives, 1992. Address: Entrepotdok 4, 1018 AD Amsterdam, The Netherlands.

**BLASIUS Nikolaus Heribert Arnold,** b. 6 December 1952, Daun, Germany. Orthopaedic Surgeon; Medical Educator; Researcher. m. Gerlinde Bohm Blasius, 2 sons, 1 daughter. Education: MD, 1978, University RWTH Aachen, Germany; Privatdozent Dr med Dr med habil, 1989, University Heidelberg; Assistant Surgeon, University of Bonn, 1979-80; Assistant Orthopaedic Surgeon, University Freiburg i Br, 1980-84; Consulting Orthopaedic Surgeon, University Heidelberg, 1985-92. Appointments: Professor, University RWTH Aachen; Director Orthopaedic Dept, Bethlehem Krankenhaus, Stolberg near Aachen; Medical Director, School for Physiotherapists. Publications: 5 publications including: Nachbehandlungsfibel Orthopadie, 1991; Ortopadie und Sport, 1999. Memberships: Stolberger Ortopadietag, Founder and President; German Society of Orthopaedic Surgeons; New York Academy of Sciences; European Society of Foot and Ankle Surgeons; CLS-HIP-Multicentre Study, Germany. Address: Bethlehem-Krankenhaus, Steinfeldstr 5, D-52222 Stolberg, Germany.

**BLAU Herbert,** b. 3 May 1926, Brooklyn, New York. Professor. m. Kathleen Woodward, 2 sons, 2 daughters, (3 from previous marriage). Education: BChE Chemical Engineering, 1947, NYU; MA Speach and Drama, 1949, PhD English and American Literature, 1954, Stanford University. Appointments: Assistant, Associate and Full Professor of English and World Literature, San Francisco State University, 1950-65; Professor of English, City College of CUNY, 1967-68; Provost, and Dean of the School of Theatre and Dance, California Institute of the Arts, 1968-71; Professor of the Arts (College and Conservatory), and Director of Inter-Arts Programme, Oberlin College, 1972-74; Dean, Div of Arts and Humanities, 1974-76, Professor of English, 1976-78, University of Maryland-Baltimore Co; Professor of English, 1978-84, Distinguished Professor of English and Comparative Literature, 1984-, University Wisconsin-Milwaukee; Co-Founder and Co-Director, The Actor's Workshop of San Francisco, 1952-65; Co-Director, Repertory Theatre of Lincoln Centre, NY, 1965-67; Founder and Artistic Director, KRAKEN, 1971-81. Publications: 6 books; Co-editor, Performance Issue(s); 98 articles; 7 plays; Very many workshops. Honours: 5 Fellowships; The Kenyon

Review prize for literary excellence, 1993; National Endowment for the Humanities grant, 1981, 1983, 1987, 1990, and Senior Fellowship, 1984; George Jean Nathan Award for Dramatic Criticism, 1984; President's (First) Distinguished Service Award, California State System, 1965. Address: Centre for 20th Century Studies, University of Wisconsin-Milwaukee, Milwaukee, WI 53201, USA.

**BLAZEJ Anton,** b. 10 March 1927, Nemsova. Professor. m. Krajcova Stepanka, 1 son, 1 daughter. Education: Chemical Technology, Ing.dr, DSc, Dr.h.c, Salford; Dr.h.c, Moscow. Appointments: Professor, President of the University, 20 years. Publications: 27 books, 352 scientific papers. Address:Nabelkova 4, SK 84105 Bratislava, Slovakia.

**BLECIC Milorad,** b. 8 May 1941, Piva, Montenegro. Writer. m. Nikolic Milina, 1 son, 1 daughter. Education: Belgrade University. Appointments: Literary Critic, Essayist, Monographer, Antologist, Literary Historian, 1963-. Publications include: Plants and Their Symbolics; Ivo Andric Beyond the Immense River of Life; Forests, Golden Forests and Other Plants; Stories From Pogledina; The Miraculous Apple and Other Stories; Father's Non Consecrated Pipes. Honours: Literary Award, Isidora Sekulic, 1974; Golden Badge of Culture & Education, Community of Serbia, 1991; Golden Bilberry for Literature, Eco-Fest, 1993. Memberships: Presidency, Writers Association of Serbia; Chairman, Commission for the Admission of New Authors, Wirters Association. Address: Udruzenje Knjizevnika Srbije, 11000 Beograd Francuska 7, Yugoslavia.

**BLESSINGER Timothy Louis,** b. 7 February 1953, Jasper, IN, USA. Educator; Publisher. Education: BS, Education, 1975; MS, Education, 1980; Post Graduate, Indiana University, 1985. Appointments: Teacher, English, Journalism, 24 Years; Owner, Blessinger International Publishing House Inc; Coach, Basketball, Tennis Track and Field for 20 years. Publications: A Lincoln, An American Hero, The Kentuckiana Years; Illinois Prairie Years; The Washington DC Years; The Seven Homes of Lincoln; Nancy Hanks; and many articles in School Corporation Newsletter and State Newspapers. Honours: Principal's Award for Outstanding Journalism, Nine; Dept of Ed Test Standards Cadre; Outstanding American, 1999; Many Teaching Awards. Memberships: Indiana State Teachers Association; Indiana High School Press Association; National Education Association; National Council of Teachers of English; International Reading Association. Address: Rr 2 Box 303A, Dale, IN 47523-9545, USA.

**BLICHERT-TOFT Mogens,** b. 9 September 1936, Spottrup Castle. Professor of Surgery. m. Birthe Blichert-Toft, 1 daughter. Education: Qualified Surgeon, 1975; Qualified Endocrine Surgeon, 1979; Surgical Oncology, 1979. Appointments: Chief Surgeon in Endocrine Surgery and Breast Cancer Surgery, Odense University Hospital, 1979-91, Rigshospitalet, Copenhagen University, 1991-; Professor of Surgery, 1983-. Honours: DMSc 1975; FRCS (Ed)(Hon), 1993; Corr Member, Society of Surgical Oncology, 1993; Honorary Silver Medal, Danish Surgical Society, 1992. Memberships: Royal College of Surgeons Ed; EORTC; SSO; Danish Surgical Society; President, Scandinavian Endocrine Surgery Section, 1981-85; Council Member, International Association of Endocrine Surgery, 1985-91; President, Danish Surgical Society, 1990-92; Council Member, European Society of Surgical Oncology, 1990-96, Treasurer, 1993-98; President, Danish Board Breast Cancer Cooperative Group, 1989-; Address: Rigshospitalet CE3104, Dept Endocrine Surgery, 2100 Copenhagen, Denmark.

**BLIKSRUD Liv**, b. 12 March 1945, Oslo. Professor. m. Petter Th. Bliksrud, 2 sons, 2 daughters. Education: MA, 1973, PhD, 1987, University of Oslo. Appointments: Lecturer, 1978-91, Postdoctoral Scholar, 1991-94, Professor, 1995-, in Scandinavian Literature, University of Oslo. Publications: Natur og normer hos Sigrid Undset, 1988, 1995; Sigrid Undset, 1997; Den smilende makten. Norske Selskap i Kфbenhaun, 1999 (under publication). Memberships: Life member, Clare Hall, Cambridge; Norwegian Academy of Science & Letters, Oslo; Royal Norwegian Society of Sciences and Letters. Address: Lyder Sagensgt 14, 0358 Oslo, Norway.

**BLINOVA Lidia D**, b. 4 April 1954, Tadjikistan. Research Scientist. m. Vladimir, 1 son, 1 daughter. Education: Diploma of Higher Education, Leningrad Electrotechnical Institute, Biomedial Electronics and Environmetal Safety; PhD, 1998; Physics and Mathematics, NPO Typhoon, Dbninsk, Russia. Appointments: Head of Regional Environmental Monitorine Laboratory, Khlopin Radium Institute. Publications: 1986; 1990; 1991; 1992; 1993; 1994; 1995; 1996; 1997; 1998. Memberships: Kalopin Radium Inst, St Petersburg, Russia; Emergency Responce Center, Radium Institue; Nuclear Society, Moscow. Address: Khlopin Radium Inst, 2nd Murinsky Prospect 28, 188537 St Petersburg, Russia.

**BLOK Suzanne Henriette Renie**, b. 1 January 1963, Bogota, Colombia. Dancer; Choreographer. Education: Diploma, Scapino Dansakademie Theater School, Amsterdam, 1985; Atheneum B, 1981. Career: Dancer, Various Companies; Creator of 25 Modern Dance Pieces of Which 12 are Full Length Evening; Founder, Satori. Honours: Choice of the Year, Rotterdam, 1993; European Commission Award for Young Artists, 1994; Dance Screen Award, 1994; Nomination, Phillip Moris, 1994. Address: Blok & Steel, Satori Foundation, 1 Jan v d Heydenstraat 87B, Amsterdam 1072 TM, The Netherlands.

**BLOKH Mark Yakovlevich**, b. 16 August 1924, Kiev, Ukraine. Linguist; Phylologist; Writer; Translator. m. Irina S Yenskaya, 1 daughter. Education: Moscow State Institute of Foreign Languages (now Moscow State Linguistic University), 1951; PhD Phylology, 1962, ScDr Phylology, 1978, Professor, 1981, Moscow State Pedagogical University. Appointments: Senior Teacher, Associate Professor, Professor, Head, Dept of Grammar and History of English, Moscow State Pedagogical University. Publications: 120 works in linguistics, phylology, linguistic methodology; Collections of fiction works (pen name Mark Lensky). Memberships: Central House of Scientists, Russian Academy of Sciences; Vice President, Moscow Association of Applied Linguistics; Doctorate dissertation Board of: Institute of Linguistics, Russia Academy of Sciences and Moscow State University. Address: Stroitelei ul dom 4 korp 1 kv 36, Moscow 117311, Russia.

**BOBIC Milos**, b. 30 June 1946, Belgrade, Yugoslavia. Architect. m. Mirjania Milanovie, 3 sons. Education: BA, University of Belgrade, 1972; PhD, 1988. Appointments: CEP, Belgrade, 1978-88; Professor, University of Belgrade, 1989-98; Docent, Academie Van Bouwkunst, Amsterdam, 1992-; Kuiper Compagnons, Rotterdam, 1996-. Publications: The Roof Above The Head, 1986; The Time Function of the City Spatial Structure, 1990; A Pattern Image, 1994; Strategie Voor Stedelijkheid, 1996. Memberships: Corporation of Graphic Designers; International Open Society Institute. Address: Kuiper Compagnons, Weena 723, Postbus 29059 3001, GB Rotterdam, The Netherlands.

**BOBIER Claude A**, b. 18 March 1934, Saint Etienne, France. Maitre of Conferences. m. Manissier H, 3 daughters. Education: DSc, University of Paris VI, 1974. Appointments:

Maitre Assistant, University of Paris VI, 1960-75; Professor University of Tunis, 1975-86; Maitre of Conferences, University of Bordeaux I, 1986. Publications: 80 scientific articles. Honour Order of International Ambassadors, 1998. Memberships: AGU AAPG; New York Academy of Sciences. Address: 6 Square D Gue, F33170 Gradignan, France.

**BOBYREV Valery Grigoryevisch**, b. 10 July 1938, Kursk Russia. Senior Lecturer. m. Julia Valentin Bobyreva, 1 son, daughter. Education: Diploma, Leningrad State Technological Institute; DSc, Volgograd Polytechnical Institute. Career: Senio Lecturer, Volgograd High School, Milicia; Senior Lecturer Volgograd State University, Faculty of Law, 1990-. Publictions Over 30 articles in professional journals. Address: Volgograd State University, Faculty of Law, 400062 Volgograd, Russia.

**BOCK Thomas Alexander**, b. 5 February 1964, Germany Physician, Scientist. m. E Irina, 1 son, 2 daughters. Education MD, 1989; Dissertation, 1990. Appointments: Intern, Aachen University Medical School, 1989-90; Visiting Scientist, NIH Bethesda, 1991-92; Fellow, National Center for Human Genome Research, 1992-93; Fellow, Head, Laboratory o Experimental Hematology, University Tubingen, 1995-Publications: Transgenic Scid Mice as Model for Human Hematopoiesis, 1995; Hematopoletic Stem Cells (editor), 1997 Biology of Hematology, 1999. Honours: Wilhelm Borchers Award; Friedrich Wilhelm Award; Visiting Fellow Award Address: University Tubingen, Department of Hematology and Oncology, Otfried Miller St 10, 72076 Tubingen, Germany.

**BOCKERIA Leo**, b. 22 December 1939, Russia. Cardiac Surgeon. m. Olga Alexandrovna, 2 daughters. Education: IM Sechenov First Moscow Medical Institute, 1959; MD, 1965 Postgraduate, 1965-68; Candidate of Medical Sciences, 1968 Doctor of Medical Science, 1973; Professor of Surgery, 1978 Appointments: Senior Scientific Worker, Bakoulev Center fo Cardiovascular Surgery; Russian Academy of Medica Sciences, 1968-74; Head of Labcratory, 1974-77; Deputy Director, 1997-94; Head of Department, Surgical Arrythmology 1979-; Head, Chairman, 1994-; Chief Cardiac Surgeon of the Ministry of Public Health, 1996-. Address: Leninsky pr 11 app 64, 117049 Moscow, Russia.

**BODART-BAILEY Beatrice M**, b. Schwerin, Germany Professor of Japanese History. m. John S Bailey, 1 daughter Education: BA Hons, 1972, MA, 1974, Asian Studies, PhD 1980, Australian National University. Appointments: Research Fellow, Research School of Pacific and Asian Studies Australian National University; Professor, Japanese Economi History, Kobe University, Japan; Professor, Faculty o Comparative Culture, Otsuma University, Japan. Publications 4 books; Over 20 major academic articles. Memberships European Japanese Studies Association; American Asian Studies Association; Australian Japanese Studies Association Asian Studies Conference, Japan. Address: Faculty o Comparative Culture, Otsuma University, Karagida 2-7-1 Tama-shi, Tokyo 206-8540, Japan.

**BODE Jurgen**, b. 27 March 1944, Yelzen. Professor. m Verena. Education: Diploma, 1969; PhD, 1971; Dr RER NAT HABIL, 1981; Professor, 1987. Appointments: GBF Gene Regulation and Differentiation Department. Memberships GDCH; GBCH; International Society of Gene Therapy and Molecular Biology. Address: Biotechnologie Forsch GmbH Mascheroder Weg, D-38124 Braunschweig, Germany.

**BODEY Gerald Paul**, b. 22 May 1934, Hazleton Pennsylvania, USA. Physician. m. Nancy Louise Wiegner, 1 son, 2 daughters. Education: Lafayette College, Easton

Pennsylvania, 1952-56; AB, magna cum laude, 1956; MD, Johns Hopkins University School of Medicine, Baltimore, Maryland, 1956-60. Appointments: Emeritus Professor of Medicine, University of Texas MD Anderson Cancer Center; Clinical Professor, University of Texas Health Science Center, Dental Branch, Houston, Texas, 1977-95; Professor of Internal Medicine and Pharmacology, University of Texas Health Science Center at Houston, Medical School, Houston, Texas, 1976-; Adjunct Professor of Microbiology and Immunology and Medicine, Baylor College of Medicine, Houston, Texas, 1975-;Chairman, Department of Medical Secialities, 1987-95 and Chief, Section of Infectious Diseases, 1975-95: The University of Texas M.D. Anderson Cancer Centre. Publications: over 950 papers in scientific journals, 60 book chapters and 420 abstractsHonours include: Honorary Member, Sociedade Brasileira de Cancerologia, 1978; Scholar of the Leukemia Society of America, 1984; Honorary Member, Mediterranean Medical Society; First Faculty Achievement Award in Clinical Research; Best Doctors in America, 1992-; Editorial Academy, The International Journal of Oncology, 1992-; First Professor Eugene Yourassowsky Award, Universite Libre de Bruxelles, 1995; The University of Texas M.D. Anderson Cancer Center Faculty Achievement Award in Clinical Research; Honorary Member, Academia Peruana de Cirugia, Peru; La Asociation Costarricense de Oncologia; Listed in 1983 by Institute for Scientific Information as one of the 300 most cited authors in all scientific literature. Memberships include: American Medical Association; Texas Medical Association; American Society of Hematology; Infectious Diseases Society of America; Sigma XI; European Society of Clinical Microbiology and Infectious Diseases; American Society of Microbiology; American Society of Clinical Oncology; American Society of Pharmacology and Clinical Therapeutics; Fellow, American College of Physicians; Fellow, American College of Chest Physicians; Fellow, Royal College of Medicine; Fellow, the Royal Society for Promotion of Health; Member, Lunar Quarantine Operations Team, Apollo 11, 12, 13 and 14, National Aeronautics and Space Administration; Member, Collaborative Cancer Treatment Research Program, Pan American Health Organisation 1976-84. Address: University Texas MDACC, 1515 Holcome, Houston, TX 77030, USA.

**BODIS Stephan,** b. 16 February 1958, Basel, Switzerland. Physician; Assistant Professor. m. Mirjam Christeler, 3 sons, 1 daughter. Education: Medical School, University Fribourg, Switzerland, 1978-80; Medical School, University Basel, Switzerland, 1980-84; Medical School Diploma, 1984; Graduate Record Examination, 1985; ECFMG Part 1 and 2, Bern, Switzerland, 1989-90; FLEX part 1 and 2, Boston, USA, 1994; American Board of Radiology, 1995. Appointments: Instructor, Medical School, University of Zurich, 1996-98; Privatdozent, Assistant Professor, Medical Faculty, University Zurich, 1998-. Publications: 16 Original Papers; Many Reviews, Meeting Reports, Published Lecturers. Memberships: ACR; ASTRO; ESMO; ESTRO; SASRO; VSAO. Address: Radiation Oncology, Ramistrasse 100, 8091 Zurich, Switzerland.

**BOERNER Sheila Fahey,** b. 10 December 1946, Minneapolis, Minnesota, USA. English Teacher. m. Ronald R Boerner, 3 sons, 3 daughters. Education: BS with distinction English, 1968, University Minnesota at Minneapolis; MA English, 1973, University Nebraska at Lincoln. Appointments: English Teacher, North Platte Senior High, North Platte, Nebraska, 1968-74; English Teacher, St Patrick's Junior Senior High, North Platte, Nebraska, 1994-. Membership: National Council of Teachers of English. Address: 1802 Birchwood Road, North Platte, NE 69101-5910, USA.

**BOGDANOFF Stewart R,** b. 16 August 1940, London, England. Educator; School Administrator. m. Eileen Dolan, 1 son, 2 daughters. Education: BS, King's College, Briarcliff Manor, New York, 1963; MA and Professional degree, NYU, 1965; Graduate work NYU, SUNY New Paltz, LIU, Harvard University, 1972-; Certificate in Administration & Supervision, 1988. Appointments: Coach, intramural director, curriculum writer, fundraiser Thomas Jefferson Elementary School, Lakeland School District, 1964-96; Physical Education Teacher, Lakeland School District, 1965-96; Head Teacher, 1984-96, Acting Principal, 1985-86, Thomas Jefferson Elementary School. Honours: Accolades and awards received throughout his life and career in education including Empire State Medal for Service to Youth, 1975; Outstanding Achievement in Education Award, Yorktown Jaycees; Named New York State Teacher of the Year, State Education Dept, 1983; Numerous distinguished community service awards; Point of Light Award from President Bush, 1992; Inducted into National Teachers' Hall of Fame, 1993; Honoured at the White House by Presidents, Ronald Reagan, George Bush and William Clinton; and many others. Memberships: American Alliance for Health, Physical Education, Recreation & Dance; Association for Supervision & Curriculum Development; Harvard Principals' Centre; International Platform Association; Kappa Delta Pi; NYS PTA; National Association of Sports for Cerebral Palsy, Les Autres; National Association for Sport & Physical Education; Phi Delta Kappa; and others. Address: 588A Heritage Hills, Somers, NY 10589, USA.

**BOGOLIUBOV Nikolay,** b. 30 November 1950, Moscow. Professor of Theoretical Physics. m. Tatiana Bogoliubova, 1 daughter. Education: Graduate, Physics Dept, St Petersburg University, 1968-74; PhD Theoretical Physics, 1980; DrSc, 1989. Appointments: Steklov Institute of Mathematics, St Petersburg, Russian Academy of Sciences. Publications: 2 books; 100 papers. Honour: Academician Krylov Prize of National Ukrainian Academy of Sciences, 1997. Address: Transportny 8 fl 16, 191040 St Petersburg, Russia.

**BOHUTOVA Josefa,** b. 16 January 1931, Zilina, Czech Republic. Physician. m. Vasil Bohut, 1 son, 1 daughter. Education: Charles University, Prague. Appointments: Professor, Radiology and Neuroradiology, Head, Clinic of Diagnostic Radiology, Postgraduate Medical School, Prague. Publications: Several in Radiology and Neuroradiology. Memberships: Czech Society of Radiology; President of the Czech Society of Neuroradiology; Slovak Society of Radiology. Address: Nemocnice Na Bulovce, Budinova 2, CZ 180 81 Praha 8, Czech Republic.

**BOICHENKO Alexander,** b. 17 October 1963, Moscow Region, Russia. Physicist. m. Yankovskaya, 1 son, 1 daughter. Education: Graduated with Honours, Moscow Engineering Physics Institute, 1986; PhD, Institute of General Physics, Moscow, 1992. Appointments: Junior Researcher, Institute of General Physics, Moscow, 1991-92; Researcher, 1992-94; Senior Researcher, 1994-. Address: Bolshoi Predtechenskii per 27/29 39, 123022 Moscow, Russia.

**BOIKOV Ilya,** b. 19 March 1941, Krementchug, Poltava Region, USSR. Mathematician. m. Svetlana Brusilovskay, 1 daughter. Education: Degree in Computer Engineering, 1963, Polytechnical Institute, Penza; Degree in Mathematics, 1968, Candidate of Science, 1973, Kazan State University; DSc, 1991, Siberian Branch of Academy of Science of USSR, Novosibirsk. Appointments: Engineer on Computer Plant, Penza, 1963-65; Engineer on Research Institute, Penza, 1965-68; Assistant, Dept Higher Mathematics, 1971-72, Associate Professor, 1972-74, Head, Dept Higher Mathematics,

1974-, Polytechnical Institute, Penza; Professor, State Technical University, Penza, 1991-; Professor, Teaching University, Penza, 1991-. Publications: 6 monographs; 35 main papers; 2 patents: Equipment to restore output signals, 1989; Device for Computation of Unit Impulse response, 1996; Editor, Optimal Methods of Calculations and Its Applications to Processing of Informations, collections of papers. Honours: 6 grants including State Science Grant, 1997-2000. Memberships: American Mathematical Society, 1994-; New York Academy of Sciences, 1995-; European Mathematical Society, 1997-; International Science Foundation; Novosibirsk University; Russian Foundation of Fundamental Investigation; Fundamental Investigation in Automation and Telemechanics, Computers, Cybernetics, Metrology, Communication. Address: Kirov Street 71-58, 440600 Penza, Russia.

**BOJADŽIEV Živko,** b. 14 April 1936, Sofia, Bulgaria. Linguist. m. Radka, 1 son. Education: MA, 1958, PhD, 1974, University of Sofia. Appointments: Assistant Professor, 1962-77, Associate Professor 1977-89; Professor, 1989-, Head, Department of General and Indo-European Linguistics, University of Sofia. Publications: Numerous on general linguistics, constrastive linguistics, history of linguistics. Membership: Societas Linguistica Europaea. Address: Zagore 1, 1124 Sofia, Bulgaria.

**BOJARIU Roxana,** b. 8 January 1962, Bucharest. Climatologist. m. Gelu Bojariu, 1 son, 1 daughter. Education: Diploma in Physics, 1984, Doctor in Geophysics, 1999, University of Bucharest, Faculty of Physics. Appointments: Teacher of Physics at Fundulea High School, 1984-87; Physicist at National Institute of Meteorology and Hydrology, Bucharest, 1987-90; Scientific Researcher, Dynamic Climatology Group, National Institute of Meteorology & Hydrology, 1990-. Publications: Climate Variability Modes due to Ocean-Atmosphere Interaction in the Central Atlantic, 1997. Membership: Romanian Meteorological Society. Address: Jean Steriadi no 8, BL I20, ap 10, sect 3, Bucharest, Romania.

**BOJIC Milorad,** b. 4 January 1951, Zemun, Yugoslavia. University Professor. m. Slavica Bojic, 1 son. Education: BSc, Mechanical Engineering, University of Belgrade, 1974; MS, Syracuse University, USA, 1977; PhD, Kragujevac University, 1984. Appointments: Associate Professor, 1990-95, Professor, 1995-97, Mechanical Engineering, Kragujevac University, Guest Professor, Center for Integrated Research in Science and Engineering, Nagoya University, Japan, 1997. Publications: Articles in professional journals. Memberships: Yugoslav Heat Engineering Society, Consulting Board, 1993-; Consulting Body on Rational Energy Consumption, Serbian Government, Belgrade, 1995-. Address: Kragulevacki Oktobar 141, 34000 Krguljevac, Yugoslavia.

**BOKOVOS Panayiotis,** b. 11 September 1935, Edessa, Greece. Writer; Politician; Economist. m. Sophia Nicopoulou, 2 daughters. Education: Degree in Law, University of Thessaloniki, Greece, 1959; Postgraduate Studies, Nancy, France, 1962; PhD, Economics, 1969. Appointments: Economics Consultant, Assistant Governor, National Mortgage Bank, Greece, 1976-77; Deputy, Thessaloniki Greek Parliament, 1977-81, 1981-85; Deputy Minister, Finance, 1977-81. Publications: Several Economic, Political and Literacy Books. Memberships: Greek Association of Economical Sciences; Association of Macedonian Studies; Lions Club; Association of Public Relations of Northern Greece. Address: 26 Filellinon St, Perea 57019, Greece.

**BOLKHOVITINOV Nikolai,** b. 26 October 1930, Moscow, Russia. Historian. m. Povelnenko Ludmila A. Education:

Candidate of Historical Sciences, 1959, Moscow City Pedagogical Institute; Dr Historical Sciences, 1966, Institute of History, USSR Academy of Sciences. Appointments: Junior, 1958, then Senior, 1962, Staff Member, Institute of History, USSR Academy of Sciences; Institute of World History, Russian Academy of Sciences, 1968-, Chairman Dept of History of the USA and Canada, 1988-92, Director, Centre for North American Studies, 1992-, Corresponding Member, 1987-, Academician, 1992-, USSR Academy of Sciences. Publications: Over 300 scholarly publications including 15 books. Honours: State Prize of Russian Federation, 1997, for a series of monographs on Russian-American Relations 1732-1867. Memberships: Full Member, Russian Academy of Sciences; Several foreign academies and societies. Address: Institute of World History, Leninski Prospect 32a, 117334 Moscow, Russia.

**BOLOGA Octavian Constantin,** b. 15 December 1948, Sibiu, Romania. Engineer; Professor. Education: Engineer, 1971-76, Technical University of Cluj-Napoca; ScD, 1986, Polytechnical University of Timisoara, Romania. Appointments: Engineer, Metal Manufacturing Companies, 1971; Teaching Assistant, 1976-79; Lecturer, 1979-90; Assistant Professor, 1990-93; Full Professor, 1993-; Head of Dept, Lucian Blaga University of Sibiu, Romania, 1994-. Publications: Plastics Forming Technology, 1994; Typified Processing Technologies, 1995; Editor in Chief, Journal Plastic Deformation, 1994-. Memberships: Scientists Association, Bucuresti; Engineering Association, Bucuresti, President of Sibiu Branch. Address: 10 Dobrun, 2400 Sibiu, Romania.

**BOLSHAKOV Vladimir,** b. 13 May 1946, Dnepropetrovsk. Professor. m. Irina Rossichina. Education: Graduate, Technological Faculty of Dnepropetrovsk Metallurgical Institute, 1969; Post Graduate Studies, Moscow Civil Engineering Institute, 1972; Doctor of Technical Science, 1986; Professor, 1987. Appointments: Junior Researcher, 1973; Assistant Professor, 1975; Head, Metal Technology Department, 1986-; Rector, President, 1987-. Publications: 16 Books; 546 Articles; 50 Patents. Memberships: Academy of Higher Education; European Society of Mathematics and Mechanics; Institute of Materialov; Iron and Steel Society. Address: 5-11 Acad Lazarian St, 320010 Dnepropetrovsk, Ukraine.

**BOLT Kevin Anthony,** b. 5 August 1961, England. Director, General Manager. m. Nobuko Matsuno, 1 son, 1 daughter. Education: BH, Hons, London University, 1984; RSA, UCLES, Certificate in Teaching English. Appointments: Director General, Industrial Products Ltd, 1993-; Director, General Manager, Polartech Asia Pacific Ltd, 1997-. Publications: What? Who? When? Why? Where?, 1995. Memberships: Institute of Directors. Address: Polartech Asia Pacific Ltd Unit 11, 12/F 10 Lee Hing St, Harbour Ind Ctr, Ap Lei Chan, Hong Kong.

**BONAIUTO Marino Marco,** b. 19 July 1963, Bologna, Italy. University Professor. m. Paola Perucchini, 1 daughter. Education: Degree in Psychology, 1987; PhD Social and Developmental Psychology, 1993. Appointments: Research Fellow, 1989-92, Postdoctoral Research Fellow, 1994-96, Researcher, 1996-98, Associate Professor, 1998-, University of Rome, La Sapienza; Research Fellow, European Community, University of Surrey, England, 1993-94. Publications: Articles to professional journals. Honour: Human Capital and Mobility Programme Fellow, EC, 1993. Memberships: Associazione Italiana Di Psicologia; European Association of Experimental Social Psychology; International Association People-Environment Studies. Address: Via Ghisalba 168, 00188 Rome, Italy.

**BONAPARTE Norton N Jr,** b. 10 April 1953, New York, USA. City Manager. m. Santa Zita, 1 son, 1 daughter. Education: BSc, Urban Studies, Worcester Polytechnic Institute, Massachusetts, 1975; Master Public Administration, Cornell University, Graduate School of Management, Ithaca, New York, 1977; Doctoral course in Public Administration, George Mason University, Fairfax, Virginia, 1983-86. Appointments include: Assistant to the Director, Minority Executive Placement Center, International City Management Association, Washington DC, 1976; Staff Assistant, Cornell University, Ithaca, New York, 1976-77; Director of Program Development, American Society for Public Administration (ASPA), Washington DC, 1981-83; Consultant (self-employed), Washington DC, 1983-84; Goverment Consultant, Institute Governmental Service, University of Maryland, 1984-87; Assistant Director for Program Operations, East Coast Migrant Head Start Project, Arlington, Virginia, 1987-88; General Manager, Owner, Auto Cleaning Service, Alexandria, Virginia, 1988; City Manager, Glenarden, Maryland, 1988-94; Senior Adjunct Instructor, National-Louis University, McLean, Virginia, 1989-; Instuctor, Potomac College, Rockville, Maryland, 1993; Instructor, Prince George's Community College, Largo, Maryland, 1994; Township Manager, Willingboro, New Jersey, 1995-. Memberships include: Chairman, Professional Municipal Management Joint Insurance Fund; Board of Directors, New Jersey Municipal Management Association. Address: Township of Willingboro, Municipal Complex, 1 Salem Road, Willingboro, NJ 08046, USA.

**BONAZZI Elaine,** b. Endicott, New York, USA. Opera Singer; Voice Teacher. m. Jerome Carrington, 1 son. Education: BM, Eastman School of Music. Career: Leading Roles with New York City Opera, Opera at the Forum, Metropolitan Opera, Netherlands Opera, Dallas Opera, Santa Fe Opera, Glimmenglass Opera, San Fransico Opera, Theatre of St Louis, Spoleto Festival, Berlin Opera, Washington Opera, Houston Opera, Mostly Mozart Festival, New York; Soloist with New York Philharmonic Orchestra, Philadelphia Orchestra, Glimmenglass Opera, San Francisco Opera, Cleveland Orchestra, National Symphony, Cincinnati Orchestra, Detroit Symphony, Minneapolis Symphony, Boston Symphony; Operas on NBC-TV, CBS-TV, ABC-TV; Judge at International Singing Competitions; Artist-in-Residence, State University of New York, Stony Brook; More operatic premieres than any other living American singer. Recordings: For various labels. Address: 650 West End Avenue, New York, NY 10025-7355, USA.

**BONCIOCAT Nicolae Ulpiu,** b. 26 June 1931, Arad, Romania. Chemical Engineer; Mathematics and Physics Diplomate. m. Ileana Cornelia Bonciocat, 1 son, 2 daughters. Education: Chemical Engineer, Politechnica University Timisoara, Romania, 1954; Mathematics and Physics Diplomate, West University Timisoara, Romania, 1958; PhD, Electrochemistry, Politechnica University Timisoara, Romania, 1971; Postdoctoral Training, University of Pennsylvania, USA, 1971-72; PhD, Guidance in Physical Chemistry, Romania, 990. Career: Assistant Professor, Politechnica University Timisoara, 1954-58; Chemical Engineer, "Solventul" Timisoara, 1958-60; Middle School Professor, Timisoara, 1960-62; Researcher, Pharmaceutical Research Institute, Bucharest, 1962-70; Chief, Corrosion Department, Centre of Physical Chemistry, Bucharest, 1970-80; Chief, Electrochemistry Department, Institute of Chemical and Biochemical Energetics, Bucharest, 1980-96; Director of Research, National Institute of Electrochemistry, Bucharest, 1996-; Associate Professor, Electrochemistry, Military Technical Academy, Bucharest, 992-. Publications: Numerous articles in professional journals. Honour: Medal, West University, Timisoara, 1997.

Memberships include: Institute of Microtechnology, Bucharest; National Institute of Electrochemistry; International Society of Electrochemistry; New York Academy of Sciences; Romanian Society of Electrochemistry. Address: Str Apusului 60 70 Bl 71 Sc 2, Apt 37, Bucharest 77561, Romania.

**BOND Alma Halbert,** b. 6 February 1923, Philadelphia, PA, USA. Author; Psychoanalyst. m. Rudy Bond, deceased, 2 sons, 1 daughter. Education: Postdoctoral Study of Psychoanalysis, National Psychological Association of Psychoanalysis, 1955; BA, Distinction in Psychology, Temple University, 1944; MA, New York University, 1951; PhD, Columbia University, 1962. Appointments: Psychoanalysis in private practice, 1953-91; Published Author, 1989-. Publications: Who Killed Virginia Woolf? A Psychobiography, 1989; Dream Portrait, 1992; America's First Woman Warri or: The Courage of Deborah Sampson, 1992; Is There Life After Analysis?, 1993; The Autobiography of Maria Callas, 1998; Numerous articles published in journals. Memberships: Dramatists Guild; American Society of Journalists and Authors; Florida Freelance Writers Association; Writers Guild; Psychoanalyst; American Psychological Association; Institute for Psychoanalytic Training and Research. Address: #1, 606 Truman Avenue, Key West, FL 33040, USA.

**BONDAR Vyacheslav,** b. 5 January 1948, Ukraine. Physicist. m. Spasska Larysa, 1 daughter. Education: MS Physics, 1970, PhD, Postgraduate Education in Solid State Physics, 1980, Lviv State University; Certificate, 1996, University Science Centre, Pennsylvania, Lviv Institute Menagm Technology Transfer. Appointments: Senior Lieutenant of Soviet Army, 1970-72; Engineer-Researcher, 1972, Senior Researcher, 1982-88, Head of Research Laboratory, 1988-, Department of Physics, Lviv State University. Publications: 126 articles; co-Editor, 1 book; 12 inventions. Honours: Grantee, Soros Foundation, 1993; Collaborative Research Grant, NATO, 1996, 1998; USA Government Conts, 1997, USA Government Programme, 1998. Memberships: Society of Inventors; Association Radioelectronic Materials, Higher School Academy Materials; Ukrainian Physical Society; International Society Optical Engineering; International Electrochemical Society. Address: 4 Pulyui St Apt 52, 290071 Lviv, Ukraine.

**BONDS Georgia Anna,** b. 30 December 1917, New York, New York, USA. Writer; Lecturer. m. Alfred Bryan Bonds, 2 sons, 2 daughters. Education: BA, University of North Carolina, Greensboro, 1938; MA, Louisiana State University, 1941; Postgraduate Study, University of North Carolina, 1941; Baldwin-Wallace College, 1960s. Appointments: Editor, Abstracts of Theses, Louisiana State University, 1940; Freelance Writer, Lecturer, 1943-; Editor, District Newspaper, United Methodist, Cleveland, 1979-91. Publications: Editor, English Translation of Wheat Growing in Egypt, 1954; Numerous magazine articles, 1941-. Honours: Girl Scout Awards: Thanks Badge, 1979; Thanks Badge II, 1997; International Friendship, 1984. Memberships: United Methodist Church; Girl Scouts of The USA; Phi Beta Kappa; Order of Eastern Star; American Association University Women; YWCA. Address: PO Box 768, Berea, OH 44017-0768, USA.

**BONNER Mary Winstead,** b. 20 April 1924, Nash County, North Carolina, USA. Retired Educator. m. Thomas Bonner. Education: BA, cum laude, Elementary Education, St Paul's College, 1946; MA, Virginia State University, 1952; Doctorate in Education, Oklahoma State University, 1968. Appointments: Professor, Department of Administration, Curriculum and Instruction, Emporia State University, 1964-86; ESU Faculty Senate, three years. Publications: 9 educational publications including: Pre- and Beginning Readers - Preparation of Future Teachers, 1974. Honours: Honorary Doctorate for contributions to education and humanitarian efforts, 1979, ESU; Ruth Schillinger Award for outstanding work in education, 1998. Memberships: Kansas Standarisation Committee; President, Emporia's NAACP chapter; Established first chartered sorority to welcome black women at ESU. Address: 2314 Sunset Lake Drive, Emporia, KS 66801-5369, USA.

**BOODHRAM Pardhomun,** b. 15 September 1950, Surinam, Mauritius. Police Officer. m. Satiavtee Nathoo, 4 daughters. Education: CSC, 1969, 1978; Diploma Modern Management, UK, 1978; Fellow, Institute of Administrative Management, India, 1993. Appointments: Police Officer. Publication: Police is a Religion. Honours: Commendation in Bravery, 1978; Long Service Award and Good Conduct Medal (Police), 1989. Memberships: Mauritius Billiard and Snooker Association; Institute of Administrative Management, India. Address: N40 SMF Married Quarters, Vacoas Mauritius.

**BOONPRAGOB Kansri,** b. 27 April 1947, Bangkok, Thailand. University Lecturer. Education: PhD, Botany, Ecology, 1987. Appointments: Lecturer, Ramkhamhaeng University, 1972-. Publications: Ecology Ramkhamhaeng University Press, 1996; Thailands National Greenhouse Gas Inventory, 1996. Memberships: Tropical Ecology; Lichenology; SIAM. Address: 59-23 Home Pl Sukapibarn 3, Bangkok 10240, Thailand.

**BOONYOROS Roongraung,** b. 16 June 1937, Chiang Mai. Educator. m. Vajira, 3 sons. Education: BA, 1957; MA, 1959; Diploma in Teaching (Secondary School), 1963. Appointments: Lecturer in Philosophy, 1965; Assistant Dean for Student Affairs, 1971; Head, Department of Human Relations, 1974; Dean, Faculty Humanities, 1976-80; Head Department Philosophy, 1983-94. Publications: Over 200 articles; 2 volume set on Buddhist Scriptures. Honours: Honour Award for Academic Service, 1996; Established Mahachulalongkorn University Chiangmai Campus, 1984, College of Social Science, 1992, Village Child Care Centre, 1979. Memberships: Buddhist Association, Chiang Mai; Philosophical Association of Thailand; Founder-member, Siddhattha Club. Address: Chiang Mai University Faculty Humanities, Huay Kaew Road, 50202 Chiang Mai, Thailand.

**BORCHERTS Vickie Wright Blackwell,** b. 7 July 1951, Rockford, Illinois. Nursing Educator; Management. m. (1)James Wright, (2)Glen Blackwell, 2 sons, 1 daughter. Education: ADN, 1972; BSN, 1983; PHN, 1991; MSN in progress. Appointments: Head Nurse, Acute Care, Critical Care, 1972-83; Home Health, Nursing Homes, 1984-98; Consulting, Blackwell Enterprises, 1992-. Honours: National Dean's List, 1983; Woman of the Year, 1998. Address: 4150 San Ramon Drive, Corcnia, CA 91720, USA.

**BORDELON Carolyn Grace Thew,** b. 28 December 1942, Shelby, Ohio, USA. Reading Specialist. m. Al Ramon. Education: BA, History, Political Science, Otterbien College, 1966; MA, Education, Bowling Green State University, 1972; Postgraduate, Ohio State University, 1986-. Appointments: Elementary Teacher, Allen East Schools, Ohio, 1966-68; Elementary Teacher, Marion Ohio City Schools, 1968-78; Chapter I REading Teacher, 1978-86; Reading Recovery Teacher, 1986-88; Reading Recovery Teacher, Dublin, City Schools, 1988-; Adj Instructor, Reading Department, Graduate Studies, Ashland University, 1996. Publications: The Parent Workshop; Octopus Goes to School. Honours: Excellence in Education Award; Chamber of Commerce; Teacher Award Grantee, Ohio Department of Education. Memberships:

Archaeological Institute of America; Ohio Education Association; National Education Association; Reading Recovery Council of North America; Phi Alpha Theta; Phi Delta Kappa. Address: 3958 Farlington Dr, Columbus, OH 43220-4531, USA.

**BORDEN William Vickers,** b. 27 January 1938 Indianapolis, USA. Writer. m. Nancy Lee Johnson, 1 son, 2 daughters. Education: AB, Columbia College, Columbia University, 1960; MA, University of California, Berkeley, 1962 Appointments: Chester Fritz Distinguished Professor of English Emeritus, University of North Dakota, USA. Publications Superstoe, novel, 1968, 1996; Slow Step and Dance, poems 1996; The Last Prostitute, play, film; Turtle Island Blues, play Memberships: Dramatists Guild; ASCAP; PEN. Address: RR 6 Box 284, Bemidji, MN 56601-8635, USA.

**BORDIN Ninel,** b. 27 December 1930, Moscow. Physicist m. Ratner Grigory, 1 son. Education: MS, Moscow Pedagogic Institute, 1952; PhD, All Union Scientific Research Institute o Current Source, 1966. Appointments: Teacher, Moscow 1952-58; Engineer, Senior Engineer, Senior, Scientist, All Union Scientific Research Institute of Current Source, 1958-92 Researcher, Jerusalem College of Technology, Israel, 1993- Publications: Modelling of Solar Cells and Solar Arrays, 1986 80 Articles to Professional Journals; 15 Inventions. Honours Bronze Medal, 1980; Medal of USR Astronaut Yuri Gagarin 1986. Memberships: Scientific Council, All Union Scientific Research Institute of Current Source. Address: Jerusalem College of Technology, 21 Havaad Haleumi St #16031, 91160 Jerusalem, Israel.

**BORIN Boris Michaylovitch,** b. 25 June 1935, Ukraine Teacher. m. Galing Borin, 2 sons. Education: Historian Diploma, Department of Oriental Studies, Leningrad University 1962-67. Career: Journalist, Moscow Radio, 1966-67; Teacher College & School, 1968-80; Language Instructor, US Air Force 1981-87. Publications: Aesop - Humor Fables, 1997. Address 7545 Hampton Avenue #314, Los Angeles, CA 90046, USA.

**BORN Ethel Wolfe,** b. 6 January 1924, Kasson, West Virginia, USA. Church Worker; Author. m. Harry Edward Born 2 daughters. Education: Student, Ecumenical Institute, Geneva 1983; BA, Mary Baldwin College, 1991. Publications: A Tangled Web - A Search for Answers to the Questions of Palestine 1989; By My Spirit, Methodist Protestant Women in Mission 1989-1939, 1990. Honour: Stanley S Kresge Award, United Methodist Foundation for Christian Higher Education, 1995 Memberships: President, United Methodist Women, 1972-76 Board Director, United Methodist General Board of Global Ministries, New York City, 1976-84; United Methodist General Committee on Christian Unity and Interreligious Concerns, New York City, 1988-96; American Association of University Women; National Association of Parliamentarians; National League of American Pen Women; Archivist, World Federation of Methodist Women; Pan-Methodist Commission on Cooperation; Governor on Board of Governors, Wesley Theological Seminary, Washington, DC; Trustee, Ferrun College Board of Trustees. Address: 3789 Knollridge Road Salem, VA 24153-1938, USA.

**BORNE Pierre Emile,** b. 3 June 1944, France. Professor. m M Plane, 2 sons, 2 daughters. Education: PhD, Automatic Control, 1970; DSc, Physics, 1976. Appointments: Assistant Professor, University of Lille, 1969-81; Professor, Head Automatic Control Department, 1981-, Director of Research 1982-, Ecole Centrale de Lille. Publications: 10 books, 1 encyclopaedia, 1 dictionary, over 230 articles in professional journals. Honours include: Chevalier dans l'ordre des palmes academiques, France, 1989; National Order of Merit in Education, Tunisia, 1997. Memberships: Fellow, IEEE; Fellow, Russian Academy of Nonlinear Sciences; Board of Directors, IMACS. Address: Ecole Centrale de Lille, Bd Paul Langevin, Villeneuve d'Ascq F 59651, France.

**BORODIN Natalia,** b. 26 Dec 1946, Bratislava, Slovak Republic. Writer. m. Jan Vadlejch, 1969. Education: PhD, Sorbonne University, Paris, France, 1987. Appointments: Professor; Screenplay Writer. Publications: Screenplays for cinema. Address: 220 Rue Saint Jacques, 75005 Paris, France.

**BOROVIKOV Valeriy Vasiljevich,** b. 16 November 1958, Bogdanovka, Ukraine. Researcher. div. Education: Engineer-Mechanic, A F Mozhayskiy Military Engineering Institute, St Petersburg, Russia, 1983; Candidate of Technical Sciences, 1991; Doctor of Technical Sciences, 1997. Appointments:Teacher, Doctorant, Docent of Sub-Faculty, A F Mozhayskiy Military Engineering Aerospace Academy, 1988-98; Commander, Guard Company, Cosmodrome, 1987-88; Holder Chair of Cosmodromes, 1998-. Publications: More than 110 articles, 1988-98; Monographs; Patentee in field of technology, transporting of dry materials, one scientific discovery. Memberships: Scientific Council on Conferment of Bachelor and DSc Degrees; Active Member, New York Academy of Sciences, 1996-. Address: Bogatyrskiy prospekt 53-3, kv 115, 197372 St Petersburg, Russia.

**BORRESON Glenn Leland,** b. 29 April 1944, LaCrosse, Wisconsin, USA. Lutheran Pastor. m. Mary E Jorgenson, 3 sons. Education: BA, 1966, Luther College; MDiv, 1970, MTh, 1978, Luther Seminary. Address: Pastor, Our Saviour's & Jordan Lutheran Churches, South Wayne, Wisconsin, 1971-74; Pastor, Grace Lutheran Church, Elroy, Wisconsin, 1974-78; Associate Pastor, First Lutheran Church, Decorah, 1978-88; Senior Pastor, Bethany Lutheran Church, 1988-. Publications: Author of sermon book, A Taste of God's Tomorrow, 1989; Editor & Co-Author, A Case for Excellence, 1998. Honour: Fellow in Academy of Parish Clergy, 1982-. Memberships: Academy of Parish Clergy; International Bonhoeffer Society. Address: 628 Tremont Street, Mauston, WI 53945-1230, USA.

**BORSARU Mihai,** b. 19 March 1941, Bucharest, Romania. Scientist. m. Ruxandra, 2 sons. Education: BSc, University of Bucharest, 1963; PhD, Nuclear Physics, Australian National University, 1974; Diploma, Education, University of Melbourne, 1978. Appointments: Research Physicist, Institute for Aut* omic Physics, Bucharest; Research Physicist, Niels Bohr Institute of Physics, University of Copenhagen; Senior Principal Research Scientist, Commonwealth Scientific and Industrial Research Organization. Honour: Excellence in Research, Australian Coal Association, 1995. Address: Queensland Centre for Advanced Technology, CSIRO PO Box 883, Kenmore, Qld 4069, Australia.

**BORZESZKOWSKI Hort-Heino von,** b. 30 May 1940, Liebenwalde. Physicist. Education: Diploma in Physics, 1963, Humboldt University, Berlin; Dr rer nat, 1967, Dr sc nat, 1973, Berlin Academy of Sciences. Appointments: Researcher at the Berlin Academy of Sciences, 1963-91; Department Head at Institute of Astrophysics, Academy of Sciences, 1976-82; Member, Scientific Staff, Einstein Laboratory for Theoretical Physics, Director, 1991. Publications: Author and co-author of 160 articles in journals and conference volumes; Co-author, 5 books including: The Meaning of Quantum Gravity, 1988. Memberships: International Commission on General Relativity and Gravitation; German Physics Society; International Astronomical Union; Italian Physics Society. Address: Institute

for Theoretical Physics, Technical University of Berlin, Hardenbergstr 36 PN 7-1, D 10623 Berlin, Germany.

**BOSE Subhasis,** b. 8 July 1957, Calcutta, India. Physicist; Researcher. 1 daughter. Education: BSc, University of Calcutta, 1977; MSc, Indian Institute of Technology, 1981; MPhil, 1982; PhD, 1990, Indian Institute of Technology. Appointments: Research Associate, Indian Association for the Cultivation of Science, 1991-93; Scientist, Department of Solar Energy, Government of India, 1995-; Senior Scientist, Ankur Scientific, Baroda, 1994. Publications: Articles to Professional Journals. Memberships: Materials Research Society of India; Solar Energy Society of India. Address: Energy Research Centre, Indian Association for the Cultivation of Sciences, 2A & B, S C Mullick Road, Jadavpur, Calcutta 700032, India.

**BOSE Sujit Kumar,** b. 10 October 1938, Udaipur, India. Educator. m. Kamala, 1 son, 1 daughter. Education: BSc, 1957, MSc Applied Mathematics, 1959, DSc Applied Mathematics, 1971, Calcutta University; Postdoctoral Research Engineer in Mechanics and Structures Department, 1972-74, Visiting Scholar, Mechanical, Aeronautical and Nuclear Engineering Dept, 1989, UC Los Angeles; Visiting Scholar, Computational Mechanics Centre, Civil Engineering Department, Georgia Institute of Technology, Atlanta, 1989; Visiting Scholar, Applied Mathematics Department, University of Twente, The Netherlands, 1989; Visiting Professor, S N Bose National Centre for Basic Sciences, Calcutta, 1990. Appointments: Lecturer in West Bengal Junior Educational Service, 1960-65; Assistant Professor, West Bengal Educational Service, 1965-75; Professor and Head of Department of Maths, Regional Engineering College, Durgapur, West Bengal, 1975-93; Professor in Mathematics at S N Bose National Centre for Basic Sciences, Calcutta, 1993-. Publications: 11 on Seismology; 5 on Elastodynamics; 4 on Response of Structures; 9 on Materials; 2 on Elastic Stability; 1 on Three Dimensional Stress Systems; 7 on Foundations; 2 on Fracture Mechanics; 2 on Fluid Mechanics; 5 on Control Theory; 1 on Nonlinear Dynamics. Memberships: Fellow, Indian Academy of Sciences; Society for Industrial and Applied Mathematics, USA; Insian Society for Theoretical & Applied Mechanics; American Mathematical Society; Calcutta Mathematical Society; Indian Statistical Institute. Address: BE 188 Salt Lake City, 700 064 Calcutta, India.

**BOSKOV Gordana,** b. 14 December 1936, Melenci, Yugoslavia. Film Director. Education: Degree, Film Institute, 1967. Honour: 1st Prize, Film Festival Palermo, Italy. Membership: Union of Drama Artists, Yugoslavia. Address: Dunavskikej 20/11, 11000 Beograd, Yugoslavia.

**BOSSERT James,** b. 11 March 1951, Rochester, New York, USA. Vice President, Quality. m. Nancy Bossert, 2 daughters. Education: BA, Psychology, St John Fisher College, 1973; MS, Applied Mathematics and Statistics, Rochester Institute of Technology, 1981. Appointments: Statistician, Xerox Corporation, 1981-84; Quality Consultant, Eastman Kodak, 1984-96; Vice President, Quality, Nokia Mobile Phones, 1996-. Publications: Procurement Quality Handbook, 1988; QFD, A Practitioner's Approach, 1989; Supplier Management Handbook, 1995. Membership: ASQ. Address: Quality Assurance, 1316 Wedglea Drive, Bedford, TX 76021, USA.

**BOTH Ioana,** b. 3 May 1964, Cluj-Napoca, Romania. Associate Lecturer in Romanian Literature. Education: MB Romanian Language and Literature and French Literature, 1986, PhD Literary Theory, 1997, Babes-Bolyam University, Cluj-Napoca. Appointments: Teacher Romanian Language and Literature, several secondary schools, 1986-90; Assistant,

1990-92, Lecturer, 1993-, Dept Romanian Literature, Babes-Bolyai University. Publications: 3 books; Over 300 studies, essays and articles in the fields of poetics, critical theory, Romanian and French Literature, published in volumes and literary reviews in Romania and abroad; French and Finnish literature translated into Romanian and published in Romanian reviews. Honours: The Best Editorial Debut, Prize of the Romanian Writers' Union, 1990; Best Young Writer, Prize of Moldavian Writers' Union, 1992. Membership: Romanian Writers' Union, 1990-. Address: New Europe College, Str Matei Voievod 18, 83222 Bucharest, Romania.

**BOUDJELKHA Mohamed Tidjani,** b. 5 December 1941, Guemar, Algeria. Professor. m. K Asma. Education: BS, 1965; MS, 1966; PhD, 1970. Appointments: Postdoctoral Research Associate, 1970; Maitre de Conferences, ecole Polytechnique, Algiers, 1970-73; Professor, University of Science and Technology, Algiers, 1974-94; Faculty, King Fahd University of Petroleum and Minerology, Dhahran, 1994-. Publications: Contributor of articles in professional journals. Memberships: American Mathematics Society; SIAM. Address: King Fahd University of Petroleum and Minerology, Box 170, Dhahran 31261, Saudi Arabia.

**BOUDREAU Beverly Ann Hayes,** b. 1 March 1940, Chicago, Illinois, USA. Health Care Professional. m. Frederick Boudreau, 1 son, 2 daughters. Education: Southwest College, Chicago, Illinois, 1968-70; Morainne Valley Community College, 1971-76; Seminars, workshops, US Army Reserve Family Programme, 1991-97. Appointments: Secretary-Technician, Northwestern Memorial Hospital, Chicago, 1984-86; Medical Assistant, Administrator, H Schachter, MD, Chicago, 1986-95; Administrative Assistant, Rehabilitation Medicine Clinic, Wheaton, Illinois, 1996-. Honours: Certificate of Achievement, US Army Reserve, Operation Beach Camp, 1996; Certificates of Appreciation, US Army Reserve, Instructor, Family Programmes, 1991-97; Participant, DuPage/Ulster Project, 1996-99. Memberships: Charter member, Family Program Advisory Council, US Army Reserve, 1991-96; Deacon, 1st Presbyterian Church, Glen Ellyn, Illinois, 1997-. Address: Rehabilitation Medicine Clinic, 26w171 Roosevelt Rd, Wheaton, IL 60187-6078, USA.

**BOUIC J H J Patrick,** b. 16 June 1967, Mauritius. Insurance Consultant. m. Nadia, 1 son. Education: BComm, 1989; ACII, 1992; Chartered Insurance Practitioner. Appointments: Managing Director, Valuers & Assessors Ltd, & City Brokers Ltd. Membership: Chartered Insurance Institute. Address: City Brokers Ltd, Labourdomman Street, Port Louis, Mauritius.

**BOURADJIEV Kostadin,** b. 17 July 1958, Plovdiv, Bulgaria. Musician. m. Jenny N Bouradjieva, 2 sons. Education: Diploma, Orchestra Conducting, Academy of Musical and Dance Arts, Plovdiv, Bulgaria, 1979-83. Appointment: Chief Artistic Director, Folk Ensemble Dobrudja, Dobrich, Bulgaria. Honours: Silver Lyre, Union of Bulgarian Musicians; Musical Award '97, Overall Contribution to Cultural Life in Dobrich. Membership: SABAM, Belgium. Address: Folk Ensemble Dobrudja, Ek Starija Dobrich, Dobrich 9300, Bulgaria.

**BOURCIER Richard Joseph,** b. 25 December 1930, New Bedford, USA. College Professor. m. Florence Michaud, 2 sons, 3 daughters. Education: AB, 1958, Assumption College, Worcester; MA French, 1959, Laval University, Quebec, Canada; PhD Comp Lit, 1983, SUNY Binghamton, NY. Appointments: Teacher, New Bedford Public School System, Massachusetts, 1958-59; Instructor of French, College of the Holy Cross, Worcester, 1961-68; Professor of French, Department Foreign Languages and Literatures, University of Scranton, 1968-. Publications: Editor, Proceedings of the 1988 International Colloquium on Georges Duhamel, 1884-1966; History and the Novel: Flaubert and the Legacy of Historical Fiction, 1984; 7 articles in professional publications; Reviewer, Critic of Civilisation: Georges Duhamel and His Writings, 1969; Psychologie de Salavin de Georges Duhamel, 1971; La Chronique des Pasquier et Cécile parmi nous de Georges Duhamel: Chronique et roman cyclique, 1986; Georges Duhamel et l'ideé de Civilization, 1994; Entretiens d'humanistes: Correspondance de Charles Nicolle et Georges Duhamel 1922-1936; 12 presentations. Honours: Chevalier dans l'Ordre des Palmes Académiques, French Government, 1995; Alpha Sigma Nu, National Jesuit Honour Society, Honorary member, 1995. Memberships: Modern Language Association; American Association of Teachers of French; American Association of University Professors; Association Internationale des Amis de Georges Duhamel et de l'Abbaye de Créteil; Institut Français; United States Amateur Ballroom Dancers Association. Address: 103 Belmont Avenue, Clarks Green, PA 18411-1101, USA.

**BOVA Davide,** b. 16 November 1961, Naples, Italy. Radiologist. m. Elizabeth Kendall, 3 daughters. Education: University of Florence Medical School, 1980-86; Internships in IV Clinica Medica, II Clinica Chirurgica, I Clinica Ostetrico-Ginecologica, 1986; Appointments: Residencies in Diagnostic Radiology, University of Florence, 1987, and University of Modena, 1988-90; MRI, Michigan State University, 1990-91; Nuclear Medicine, 1995-97, Diagnostic Radiology, 1997-, Loyola University Medical Centre; Assistant Radiologist, Ospedale Militare di Medicina Legale, Piacenza, 1988-90; Radiologist, Italian Field Hospital in Mozambique, 1993; Chief, Radiology Dept, Ospedale Militare di Medicina Legale, Piacenza, 1990-95. Publications: 21 articles or book chapters; 15 abstracts. Memberships: Chicago Radiological Society; Radiological Society of North America; American Roentgen Ray Society; Societa Italiana di Radiologia Medica. Address: Loyola University Medical Centre Nuclear Medicine, Dept 2160 S 1st Avenue, Maywood, IL 66153-5304, USA.

**BOWEN Gwendolyn Lorrayne,** b. 9 May, Denver, Colorado, USA. Dance Educator; Choreographer. Education: BA, University of Denver, 1951. Appointments: DP School, 1951-53; Founded Gwen Bowen School of Dance Arts, 1953-; Artistic Director, Premiere Dance Arts Company, 1960-. Memberships: DMA; DEA; AAPHERD; PDTA; KD. Address: 714 S Pearl Street, Denver, CO 80209 4213, USA.

**BOWEN Richard Antony,** b. 18 August 1935, Oxford. Mathematician. m. Patricia Rose Mason, 2 sons. Education: BSc, Mathematics, Birmingham, 1958; Diploma, Mathematical Physics, 1959. Appointments: Scientist, UKAEA Windscale and Dounreay; Scientist, British Railways Research; GERN, Geneva; ESOC, Germany. Publications: 12 Published Papers. Memberships: C Eng; MBCS. Address: Industriestrase 1, 64319 Pfungstadt-Eschollbruecken, Germany.

**BOWMAN Scotty,** b. 18 September 1933, Montreal, Canada. Head Coach. m. Suella Chitty, 3 sons, 2 daughters. Education: Graduate, Sir George Williams College. Honours: Winningest Coach in National Hockey League History. Address: Detroit Red Wings, Joe Louis Arena, 600 Civic Center Dr, Detroit, MI 48226-4408, USA.

**BOXILL Edith Hillman,** b. 8 November 1916, Providence, Rhode Island, USA. Professor of Music Therapy. 1 son, 1 daughter. Education: Bachelor of Music; Dalcroze Music Certificate; Master of Arts, 1974. Appointments: Founder, Director, Music Therapists for Peace Inc, 1988; Director of lusic Therapy, Manhattan Developmental Services, 1974-87; rofessor of Music Therapy, New York University, 1975-. ublications; Music Theraoy with the Developmentally andicapped, album and pamphlet, 1976; Music Therapy for ıe Developmentally Disabled, 1985; Music Therapy for Living, 989; The Miracle of Music Therapy, 1997. Honours: Lifetime chievement Award, American Association for Music Therapy, 995; Honorary Life Member, American Music Therapy ssociation, 1998; UN Non-Governmental Peace and :ooperation Award, 1999. Memberships: American Music ıerapy Association; American Society of Composers, Authors nd Publishers. Address: 375 Riverside Drive, Suite 11BB, ıew York, NY 10025, USA.

**BOYD-KJELLEN Gia,** b. 3 January 1943, Vasteras, .weden. Senior Administrator. m. Bo, 3 sons, 1 daughter. ducation: BSc, Stockholm University, 1984. Appointments: .dministrator, Ministry of Foreign Affairs, 1964-77; Social Jorker, Geriatric Medicine, London, 1978-80; Sweden, 984-86; Administrator, OECD, Paris, 1986-91; Advisor, lppsala University, Sweden, 1992; Secretary, Government teport on EU, 1993; Advisor, Minister of Spatial Planning on ¡ender, 1994; Senior Administrator, Nordic Council of linisters, Sweden, 1994-97; Initiator, Project Leader, Area Sea ;onference, 1998; Senior Administrator, Baltic Sea 2008, 998-. Publications: Disabled Youth, From School to Work; EU Jomen and Welfare; Transition of Disabled Youth, The Genua xperience. Memberships: Swedish Unifem Committee; :ooperative Organisation of Swedish Women. Address: .torgatan 22A, 75331 Uppsala, Sweden.

**BOYER Stephanie,** b. 22 January 1974, Williamsport, PA, ISA. Educator. Education: BS, Music Education, 1997. .ppointments: Music Teacher, Chorus Teacher, Waldorf, MD, JSA, 1997-. Memberships: National Residence Hall Honarary; Jational Teachers Association. Address: 2059 Red Spruce Ct, ıryans Road, MD 20616, USA.

**BOZANICH Richard Anton,** b. 27 July 1957, Long Beach, :alifornia. Journalist. Education: AB Journalism, 1979, Jniversity Southern California; MA Journalism/Public Affairs, 984. Appointments: Editor-in-Chief, Daily Trojan, University ;outhern California, 1979; Editor, Div of Research, Harvard 3usiness School, 1979-81; Writer/Editor, Los Angeles, 981-83, Editorial Intern, Washington DC Bureau, 1984, Los ıngeles Times; Copy Editor, The Dallas Morning News, 985-86; News Editor, Hollywood Reporter, 1986-87; Managing :ditor, Daily Variety, 1987-. Membership: NLGJA. Address: ı6-190 Avenida de las Montanas, Cathedral City, CA ı2234-1532, USA.

**BOZE Betsy,** b. 18 September 1953, Shreveport, USA. :ducation. 2 sons, 1 daughter Education: BS, Psychology, I974, MBA, 1975, Southern Methodist University; PhD, Jniversity of Arkansas, 1984. Appointments: Dean, University ıf Texas; Professor, Marketing, University of Alaska. Jemberships: American Council on Education; American ıssociation of State Colleges and Universities; American Jarketing Association; Academy of International Business. ıddress: 1409 Avenida Santa Ana, Rancho Viejo, TX 78575, JSA.

**BOZGA Ioan Victor,** b. 22 December 1941, Bucharest, ıomania. Electronics Engineer. m. Adriana Bozga, 1 son. :ducation: Transmissions, The Army Academy, 1975; nvention and Forecast, 1983, Science and Leadership, 1990, ³ost Academy Courses. Appointments: Head, Repairs Jepartment, Electronic Services, 1964-70; Teacher,

Improvement Courses, 1975-77; Designing and Implementation Systems, 1977-96; Designing and Research, Electromagnetica Company, 1996-98; Manager, Interactive S.A. Communication System Integrator, 1998. Publications: The Protection of Leadership by Technical and Organizational Means, 1990; Announcement and Alarm Systems of Population in Case of Accident, (Radio Activity, Chemicals, Natural Disasters). Address: Str Covasna, Nr 33, BL E-27, Et 1, Ap 6, Bucharest, Romania.

**BOZHILOV Nikolai Tzvetanov,** b. 4 September 1951, Sofia, Bulgaria. Entrepreneur. m. (1) 1 child, (2) Kate Shtereva Karapeneva, 1 child. Education: MSc, Economics, University of Varna, 1984. Career: Ships Officer, Navibulgar, Varna, 1974-79; Marketing Manager, Navibulgar, Varna, 1979-81; General Manager, Bulcon Container Service, 1982-85; Chief Officer, Captain, 1985-90; Founder, Owner, President, CEO Unimasters Logistics Ltd, Varna, 1990-; Chief Executive, Unimasters Ferry Ltd, Varna, 1993-, Intermodal Ltd, Varna, 1993-, Unimasters Logistics Group Ltd, Varna, 1993-, Varna Stock Exchange, Varna, 1994-; President, CEO, Unidata Ltd, Varna, 1994-, Universal Surveys Ltd, Varna, 1994-, Trademasters Ltd, Varna, 1994-, Unico Investment Ltd, Varna, 1994, Unimasters Air Ltd, 1995. Memberships include: Rotary Club; Bulgarian Shooting Association; Institute of Freight Forwarders, London. Address: Unimasters Logistics Group Ltd, PO Box 229, 40 Graf Ignatieu Street, BG-9000 Varna, Bulgaria.

**BOZHKOV Yuri Dimitrov,** b. 22 February 1962, Sofia, Bulgaria. Mathematician. Education: MSc, Sofia University, 1985; PhD in Mathematics, University of Warwick, 1993. Appointments: Research Team Member, ICTP, Trieste, Italy; Visiting Professor, University of Warwick, England, University of Trieste, Italy, State University of Campinas, Brazil; Currently Professor, Institute of Mathematics, Statistics and Computing Science, State University of Campinas. Membership: Union of Physicists, Bulgaria. Address: IMECC-UNICAMP, PO Box 6065, 13083970 Campinas, SP, Brazil.

**BOZIC Darijan,** b. 29 April 1933, Slavonski Brod, Croatia. Composer; Conductor. m. Marija Erceg, 2 sons, 1 daughter. Education: Diploma in Composition, 1958, Diploma in Conducting, 1961, University of Ljubljana, Academy of Music. Appointments: Orchestra member, National Opera, 1954-68; Conductor and Artistic Director, Slovene Philharmonic, 1968-70; Professor, University Ljubljana, 1980-88, University of Maribor, 1988-95; Artistic Director and Manager, National Opera, 1995-98. Publications: Scores, Books, Records, worldwide; Live Concert Performances, worldwide. Memberships: Military Officer, Slovene Army; Jazz and Electroacoustic Centre, University of Maribor. Address: Strossmayerjeva 8, Ljubljana SI-1000, Slovenia.

**BOZIC Vojislav,** b. 19 August 1931, Bajina Basta, Serbia, Yugoslavia. Professor. m. Milica, 1 daughter. Education: PhD, 1968; MA, 1964; Faculty of Economics; Doctor of Economics, 1968. Appointments: Manager, Account Electric Firm. 1953-57 Manager, Department of Planning, City of New Belgrade, 1959-63; Chief Advisor, Productivity and Standard of living in Federal Secretary of Labor, 1961-71; Professor, University of Belgrade, 1971-98. Publications: System of Control in Organization, 1980; Management Economics, 1991; Application Software, BOZOC, Co-Author, 1995; How to Run a Small Business, 1996; Economics of Business, 1996. Honours: Life Fellow, International Advisor, American Biographical Association, 1988; International Award and Charter, American Biographical Institute, 1998. Memberships: Scientific Society of Yugoslavia Economists; American Biographical Institute. Address: Srpskih Udanih Brigada 17,

11090 Belgarde Serbia, Yugoslavia.

**BOZKOWA Krystyna,** b. 12 July 1924, Poznan. Physician. m. Jozef Bozek, 1 son. Education: University Poznan, 1945-49; MD, 1950; PhD, 1951; Dr hab, 1960; Professor extraordinary, 1965; Professor ordin, 1975; Diploma of specialisation in Paediatrics, 1954. Appointments: Assistant, 1949-54, Adjunct, 1954-60, Medical Academy in Szczecin; Head of Dept Paediatrics, Deputy Director, 1960-70, General Director, 1970-91, National Research Institute of Mother and Child in Warsaw; Consultant, 1992-; Editor in Chief, Developmental Period Medicine, 1996-. Publications: Over 250; 10 textbooks. Honours: Honour Member: Swedish, 1976, Finnish, 1978, Hungarian, 1980, German, 1985, British, 1989, Paediatric Associations and Royal College of Paediatrics and Child Health, 1996; Expert of WHO, 1970-90; Commander of Polonia Restituta with Star, 1998; Chevalier of the French Legion d'Honneur, 1982; Commander of Finnish Great Lion, 1983. Memberships: Paediatric Research Society; International Association of CF; International Paediatric Association; Scientific Council of International Centre de L'Enfance in Paris, 1992-94. Address: M Kartowicza 16 m 2, 02-552 Warzawa, Poland.

**BRADY Donna Elizabeth Margaret,** b. 17 November 1955, Rockville Centre, NY, USA. Arts Administrator. Education: BA, Knox College, 1974; Regents Diploma, Northport High School, New York, 1973. Appointments: President, Performing Arts Resources, 1987-; Director, Technical Assistance Program American Dance Guild, 1985-87; Coordinator, TAP, American Dance Festival, 1981-85. Publications: Careers in the Performing Arts; various articles. Memberships: American Dance Guild, 1982-87; NYTAP, Treasurer, 1995-96, Co Chair, 1997, 1998; Artists Community Federal Credit Union, Secretary. Address: 88 E 3rd Street Apt 19, New York, NY 10003, USA.

**BRANDOW Stephen J,** b. 25 December 1960, Olean, New York, USA. Roman Catholic Priest. Education: AD, 1982, BA, 1985, Northwestern State University of Louisiana; Clinical Pastoral Education, Emory University Hospital, 1994; MDiv, Notre Dame Seminary, 1996. Appointments: Social work, Woodview Regional Hospital, Pineville, Louisiana, USA, 1985; Medical Administration, Service Vet Administration Hospital, Pineville, 1986-91; Par work, St Francis Cabrini Par, Alexandria, Louisiana, 1992; Our Lady of Lourdes Par, Marksville, Louisiana, 1993; Pastoral Intern, Our Lady of Prompt Succor Par, Alexandria, Louisiana, 1995; Associate Pastor, St Rita C Church, Alexandria, Louisiana, 1996-97; Chaplain, Central Louisiana St Hospital, Pineville, Associate, Pastor, Immaculate Heart of Mary Par, Tioga, Louisiana, 1997-; Chaplain, St Francis Cabrini Hospital, Alexandria, 1998-. Honours: Eagle Scout Class, 1974; National Eagle Scout Associate Life Member, 1977; Blue Key National Honor Fraternity, 1982; United Associate Christian Counselors Life Member, 1983; Phi Alpha Theta, 1984; Archbishop's Commission on Disabilities Archdiocese New Orleans, 1995-96; Treasurer, Central LA Ministerial Association, 1997-98. Memberships: National Eagle Scout Association; Louisiana Chaplain's Association United Association of Christian Counselors International. Address: 17 Azelea Road, Pineville, LA 71360, USA.

**BRANDT Andreas,** b. 29 December 1935, Halle. Painter. m. Kristina, 1 son. Education: Hochschule for Bildende Kunste, Berlin, 1955-61. Appointments: Freelance Artist, 1961-82; Professor, 1982-. Publications: Monographie Andreas Brandt, 1994. Honours: Camille Graeser Award; Fred Thieler Award. Address: Gotteskoogstrasse 22, D-25899 Niebuell, Germany.

**BRANOVER Herman,** b. 12 December 1931, Riga, Lat Professor of Magnetohydrodynamics. m. Fanya Naiberg, 1 s Education: MSc Engineering, 1953, DSc Physics, 19 Leningrad Polytechnic Institute; PhD Physics, 1962, Mos Aviation Institute; Full Professor, 1968, Soviet Ministry Higher Learning. Appointments: Engineer, Riga Design Bure 1953-54; Lecturer, Riga Technical College, 1954-59; Se Researcher, Latvian Academy of Science, 1959-70; Profes Riga Technology Institute, 1968-70; Professor, Tel-/ University, 1973-75; Professor, New York University, 1987 Professor, Ben-Gurion University, Israel, 1973-. Publicatic Over 250 scholarly papers and 20 books Magnetohydrodynamics, energy engineering and turbuler About 100 papers and books in Religion and Science Jewish Philosophy. Honours: A D Bergman Prize for r technology, Israel; Speaker of the Parliament Prize improving quality of life, Israel. Memberships: Latvian Acade of Science; Russian Academy for Natural Sciences; Mos International Energy Club; Editor in Chief, Encyclopedia Russian Jewry. Address: Omer Industrial Park, PO Box 3C Omer 84965, Israel.

**BRASHIER Edward Martin,** b. 30 September 1954, U Environmental Professional. m. Debra A Dillard-Brashie sons, 2 daughters. Education: AA; Bachelor; JD, Occupatic and Environmental Law. Appointments: Environme Remediation, Documentation, 1980-94; Board Chairm National Association of Environmental Professionals, 19 Publications: Several articles in professional journ Memberships: ASSE; AIC; ACS; ABCEP; OSHA. Address: Spring Street, Waynesboro, MS 39367, USA.

**BRASSEAUX Carl,** b. 19 August 1951, Lousiana, U History Professor; Writer. m. 2 sons, 1 daughter. Educat BA, Political Science, University of Southwestern Louisia 1974; MA, History, University of Southwestern Louisiana, 19 Law School, Louisiana State University, 1972; His Department, Louisiana State University, Baton Rou 1976-78; Doctorat, 3e cycle, North American Stud Universite de Paris, 1982. Appointments: Managing Ed Lousiana History, 1993-; Assistant Director, Center Louisiana Studies, University of Southwest Louisiana, 19 Curator, Colonial Records Collection, Center for Louisi Studies, 1980-; Professor, History Department, University Southwest Louisiana, 1998-; Associate Professor, His Department, USL, 1994-98; Assistant Professor, USL, 1991 Adjunct Assistant Professor, History Department, U 1987-90; Member, Graduate Faculty, USL, 1987-2C Member, USL Board of Editors, 1975-; Manager, Informa Systems, Center for Louisiana Studies. Publications: 13 boc 18 Magazine's and outstanding publications 1997-98 reference works, book length; 5 books in preparation pamphlets; 3 maps; 88 articles and chapters in books. Awa Kemper William Prize, 1979; honourable mention, 1975; Rol L Brown Prize, 1980; Presidents' Memorial Award, 1986; B prize, French Colonial Historical Society, 1987; Special Lifet Achievement Award from the Church of Jesus Christ of La Day Saints, 1987; Outstanding publications list 1997 Served on the Southeast Columbus Quincenten Commission, 1987-92; Golden Achievement Award, Bre Bridge Historial Society, 1989; Chevalier, l'Ordre des Paln Academiques, 1991; Featured selection of the History b club, 1994; National Daughters of the American Revolu Award, 1995; University Distinguished Professor of Histc University of Southwestern Louisiana, 1995. Address: Ce for Louisiana Studies, PO Box 40831, USL, Lafayette, LA 70504, USA.

**BRATHWAITE Alfred F,** b. 22 April 1941, Grenada. Pathologist. m. Vivian Isaacs, 1 son, 2 daughters. Education: MBBS, 1967, University of London. Appointments: Manager, Paho Lab Project, 1982-85; Consultant Pathologist, Freeport, Bahamas, 1985-. Publication: Thesis, Pathology of the Thyroid. Membership: Fellow, College of American Pathologists. Address: Hawaii Avenue, PO Box F41575, Freeport, Bahamas.

**BRATUKHIN Anatoliy,** b. 1937, Nizhniy Novgorod. Professor. m. Marina A, 1 son. Education: Graduate, Nizhniy Novgorod Polytechnic Institute, 1959; Defended Thesis, Degree of Candidate in Technics, 1992; Defended Thesis, Degree of Doctor in Technics, 1994. Appointments: Engineer, Deputy Engineer, Sokol Aviation Planit , Nizhniy Novgorod, 1959-81; Chief of Scientific Technological Headquarters, Deputy Minister, USSR Ministry of Aviation Industry, 1981-91; General Director, Aviation Industry, Department in Russian Ministry of Industry, 1992; Vice Chair, Russian Defence Industry State Committee, 1992-96. Publications: Over 300 Scientific Publications in Russia, China, Europe, USA, Aviation Issues. Honours: USSR State Award; USSR Council of Ministers Awars; Labour Red Flag Awards; Friendship Between Nations Award; Russian and Foreign Medals. Memberships: Russian and International Engineering Academies; Russian Academy of Transport; Russian Academy of Quality Problems; Active Members of American Society of Logistics Engineers; SAE (USA); New York Academy of Science; Chair of Russian Aviation Industry Council on CALS. Address: Moscow Aviation Technologies Institute, Skakovaya Street 5 Apt 18, 125040 Moscow, Russia.

**BRAUDO Evgeny,** b. 7 June 1934, Moscow. Food Chemist. m. Braudo Kostetskaya Irina S, 1 son, 1 daughter. Education: Engineer, I M Gubkin Moscow Petroleum Institute, 1957; PhD, Institute of Organoelement Compounds, USSR Academy of Sciences, 1971; DSc, A N Nesmeyanov Institute of Organoelement Compounds, USSR Academy of Sciences, 1990. Appointments: Researcher, Institute of Petroleum Refining, 1957-63; Researcher, Institute of Organoelement Compounds USSR Academy of Sciences, 1963-91; Head of Laboratory, Institute of Food Substances, Russian Academy of Sciences, 1991-96; Head of Laboratory, E N Emanuel Institute of Biochemical Physics, Russian Academy of Sciences, 1996-. Publications: More than 200 papers. Membership: Society Knowledge of Russia. Address: Profsojuznaja Str 136 4 272, 117321 Moscow, Russia.

**BRAUN Bennett G,** b. 7 August 1940, Chicago, Illinois, USA. Psychiatrist. 2 sons, 3 daughters. Education: BS, 1958-63, MS, 1962-64, Psychology, Tulane University; MD, University of Illinois, Chicago, 1964-68. Appointments: Medical Director, Associates in Behavioral Medicine Ltd, Skokie, Illinois; Chief, Section of Psychiatric Trauma, Rush-Presbyterian St Lukes Medical Center, Chicago; Clinical Associate, University of Illinois, Chicago; Assistant Professor, Rush Medical College; Attending Staff, Rush-Presbyterian St Lukes Medical Center, Chicago, Rush North Shore Medical Center, Skokie, Illinois. Publications: Numerous articles in professional medical journals, books and chapters in edited books. Honours include: Presidents Award, 1989, Morton Prince Award, 1991, Distinguished Service Award, 1993, Founding President and Fellow, International Society for the Study of Multiple Personality and Dissociation. Memberships: American Psychiatric Association; Illinois Psychiatric Society; Fellow, American Society of Clinical Hypnosis; Fellow, Society for Clinical and Experimental Hypnosis; Fellow, International Society of Hypnosis; American Orthopsychiatric Association; American Family Therapy Association; Academy of Psychosomatic Medicine; International Society for the study of

Dissociation; International Society for Traumatic Stress Studies; American Professional Society on the Abuse of Children; National Alliance for the Mentally Ill; American College of Forensic Examiners. Address: Associates in Behavioral Medicine, 9701 North Knox Avenue, Ste 103, Skokie, IL 60076, USA.

**BRAVINA Svetlana,** b. 16 April 1952, Ukraine, Physicist. m. Morozovsky Nicholas, 1 daughter. Education: MSc, 1976; PhD, 1988. Appointments: Senior Engineer, Institute of Physics 1983-86; Junior Research Scientist, 1986-89; Research Scientist, 1989-94; Senior Research Scientist, 1994-. Publications: More Than 80 Articles; 4 Patents. Membership: International Society for Optical Engineering. Address: Fl 122 Borshchagovskaya Str 2, 252055 Kiev, Ukraine.

**BRAY Eric Hans,** b. 23 October 1954, Stockton, California. English Educator. m. Mikjko Hirata, 1 son. Education: BA, University of California, 1984; MEd, Temple University, 1993; Teaching Certificate. Appointments: Teacher, Institute Bi Cultural, Tuxtla Gutierrez, Mexico, 1985-88; Instructor, Academy Director, Kyoto YMCA English School, Japan, 1989-94; Instructor, Doshisha University, 1994-96; Kansai University, Japan, 1996-97; Associate Professor, Yokkajchi University, Japan, 1997-. Memberships: Teachers of English to Speakers; Japanese Association of Lanuage Teachers; Japanese Archery Association. Address: Yokkaichi University, 1200 Kayo-cho, 512 Yokkaichi Mie-ken, Japan.

**BRAZHNIKOV Andrey V,** b. 28 October 1959, Kostroma, Russia. Researcher. m. Elena Karpenko, 1 daughter. Education: BS, Electrical Engineering, 1982; PhD, Electromechanics, 1985. Appointments: Chief of Laboratory, Research Institute, Krasnoyarsk, Russia, 1987-88; Chief, Two International Projects, 1991-92, 1993-; Director, Higher Educational Center, Krasnoyarsk, Russia, 1997-; Presentation of Scientific work at conferences in Bulgaria, 1990, 1993; Poland, 1994; USA, 1995, 1996; Australia, 1997. Publications: Over 50 scientific works including: Multiphase Inverter Electrical Drive with Different Versions of Induction Motor Rotor, PhD dissertation, 1985; Harmonic and Cyclical Modelling of Filters Having Variable Parameters, 1988; Multiphase Frequency Controlled Inverter Electric Drive with Induction Motor, 1990; Co-author, Electrical Drive Theory, 1991; Method of Compensating Filtering of Periodic Signals Components, 1991; Additional Resources of Control of Multiphase Inverter Drives, 1993; Prospects for Use of Multiphase Electric Drives in Field of Mining Machines, 1995; Improvement of Technical and Economic Characteristics of Drilling Rigs Owing to the Use of Multiphase Electric Drives, 1996; Hydrodynamic Modelling of Force Fields, 1997. Honours: Annual Prizes for Scientific Work, Russian Research and Higher Educational Institutes. Memberships: Institute of Electrical and Electronic Engineers; ABI Research Board. Address: Institute of Non Ferrous Metals, 95 Kr Rabochy Av, 660025 Krasnoyarsk, Russia.

**BREDEKAMP Caroline Margaret Ann,** b. 12 July 1966, Maquoketa, Iowa, USA. Teacher. Education: Associate of Arts, Early Childhood Education, Mount Saint Clare College, 1986; Bachelor of Arts, Elementary Education, 1988; Master of Arts, Elementary Education, Talented and Gifted Education, 1993. Appointments: Student Teacher, Horace Mann Elementary School, Iowa, 1988; Student Teacher, Harding, Elementary School, Iowa, 1988; Substitute Teacher, Maquoketa Community School, Preston Community School; Andrew Community School, East Central Community School, Iowa, 1988-91; Teacher, AEA 7 Agency, Iowa, 1991-92; Teacher, Central Community Schools, Iowa, 1993-. Honours: Dean's List; National Dean's List; Transfer Merit Scolarship; Smith Arey

Scholarship; Presidential Scholarship; Certificate of Superior Academic Scholarship Award; Academic All American; Who's Who Among American Junior Colleges; Iowa Talented and Gifted Association Research Award. Memberships: National Education Association; Iowa State Education Association; National Association of Gifted Children; National Parent, Alumni Association; Kappa Delta Pi; Omicron Delta Kappa; Mensa; American Association of University Women. Address: 115 1/2 S 2nd St Apt 3, Macquoketa, IA 52060-2948, USA.

**BREE Peter,** b. 23 September 1949, Driebergen-Rijsenburg, the Netherlands. Radio Producer; Presenter. Education: MO-A, 1972-73, English Language and Literature, University Groningen; Oboe with Han de Vries, 1973-79, Solo degree, 1979, Cor Anglais and Chamber Music degrees, 1981, Amsterdam Muzieklyceum; Scholarship with Neil Black, London, 1980-81. Appointments: Master of English, various grammar schools, Amsterdam, 1973-77; Principal Oboist, NOS Radio, Hilversum, 1977-79; Free-lance Oboist, mainly solo and chamber music, 1979-94; Producer AVRO Radio, Hilversum, 1980-83; Producer and Announcer Veronica Radio, Hilversum, 1982-92; Master classes at Royal Academy of Music, London, 1990; Reviewer CD-magazine DISK, Netherlands, 1991-92; Producer and Announcer, Concert Radio, Amsterdam, 1994-98; Producer and Announcer AVRO Radio, Hilversum, 1998-. Publications: Writer of various articles in Escape Magazine, 1969-72; Recordings for Dutch radio, 1977-94; 9 gramophone recordings; edition of François Devienne: the Six Sonatas for oboe and basso continuo, 1989-90. Honours: Dutch government scholarship for further studies with Neil Black in London, 1980; Awards from Dutch Cultural Ministry to commission compositions from Ruud Bos, 1979 and Leo Samama, 1981; Award from Arts Council of GB to commission composition from Dr Edmund Rubbra, 1980; Silver Vriendenkrans Award of the Society of Friends of the Concertgebouw and the Royal Concertgebouw Orchestra, Amsterdam, 1981; Dedicatee of 7 compositions; Honorary Doctor of Music, Marquis Guiseppe Scicluna International University Foundation, Delaware, USA, 1988. Memberships: Founder and Vice-Chairman, Live Music Now the Netherlands, 1980-85; Comite d'Honneur of Association Internationale de Musique, France; Chairman, The Academy of the Begynhof, Amsterdam, 1987-; and others. Address: Middenweg 166, 1097 TZ Amsterdam, The Netherlands.

**BREGU Eleonore,** b. 8 April 1953, Erseke, Albania. Head of the Holy Mission Eleonore. 1 son, 3 daughters. Education: Jurisprudence, Faculty of Law, Tirana, Albania. Appointments: Lady of Soul, Divine Connection, 1987-98. Publications: Rowing in no Returning; The Man in Front of the Human Being; Sacred Message from the Spiritual Connection with Saint Marie; Sacred message from Vanga. Honours: Saintless; Lady of Soul; Nomination, Holy Mission with the Name, Eleonore; Extension of the Mission in 13 Nations; Diploma, American Biographical Institute; Deputy Governor in the Board of Governors, ABI; Deputy Director General, International Biographical Centre. Memberships: Order of International Fellowship; International Biographical Assocaition; Research Board of Advisors, ABI. Address: Holy Mission Eleonora, St Muhamet Gjollesha, Tirana, Albania.

**BRENDER-SHEINBAUM Chava,** b. 29 November 1951, Tel-Aviv, Israel. Scientist. m. Moshe Brender, 2 sons, 1 daughter. Education: BSc, Chemistry, 1971; MSc, Physical Chemistry, 1975; PhD, Physical Chemistry, Bar-Ilan University, Ramat-Gan, Israel, 1982. Appointments: Research Assistant, 1971-82, Research Associate, 1982-, Bar-Ilan University, Ramat-Gan, Israel. Publications: Articles in professional journals. Honours: Michael Landau Prize; Mifal Hapais Prize.

Memberships: Israel Physical Society; Israel Chemical Society Israel Polymer and Plastics Society. Address: Department o' Physics, Bar-Ilan University, 52900 Ramat-Gan, Israel.

**BRENNAN Ngairetta Joy,** b. 23 September 1929, Australia Environmentalist. m. John Brennan, 1 son, 2 daughters Education: BSc, Hons, 1977. Appointments: President, Men ot the Trees, 1982-; Vice President, Greening Australia Queensland, 1982-. Honours: Member, Order of Australia. 1995; Advance Australia Award, 1995. Address: 5/26 Rees Avenue, Clayfield, Qld 4011, Australia.

**BRERETON Vera Ann,** b. 3 February 1949, St Vincent West Indies. Tourism Consultant. m. Richard Oliver Rayside. Education: BA, Honours, University of the West Indies. 1969-72; Postgraduate Diploma, Tourism Studies, University ot Surrey, England, 1977-78. Appointments: Director, Tourism, St Vincent, 1978-85; UNDP/WTO Tourism Development Advisor, British Virgin Islands, 1985-88; OAS Regional Tourism Education and Training Consultant, 1988-95; Tourism and Services Manager, Catman 15 Department of Tourism, 1995-. Honours: Regional Award, Caribbean Tourism Organization, 1995. Membership: American Society for Training and Development. Address: Caribbean Tourism Organisation, Sir Frank Walcott Building, 2nd Floor, Culloden Farm, St Michael, Barbados, West Indies.

**BRETON Philip J,** b. 29 March 1916, Mutrie Sask, Canada Musician; Composer. Career includes: First played piano, Montmartre Saskachewan, Canada, age 5; First public performance, 1927; First dance band performance, 1929; First composition, 1929; First professional broadcast job, Regina Saskatchewan, Canada, 1936; First continuos professional engagement, Larry's Swing band and Vaudivillo Show, 1938. First Classical Opus, Regina, 1940; First composition performed coast to coast on network cbc, April 1942; Breton Orchestra, Montmartre, Saskatchewan, 1929-38; Larry's Swing Band and Vaudeville 9 Travelling, 1938-39; Walter Dalke's Orchestra, Regina, 1939-40; Freelancing combo work, Regina, 1940-41; Walter Budd Orchestre, Regina, 1941-42; wrote songs, 1942-45; Combo work, Regina, 1945-46; Pat Perry's Jazz Band, Regina, 1946-48; Hank Winder Orchestra, Omaha, Nebraska, USA, 1948-53; Tony Bradley's Orchestre, Omaha, Nebraska, 1953-64; Dick Wickman's Orchestra Omaha, 1964-65; Don Hamsa Orchestra, Omaha, 1970-72; Dick Wickman Orchestra, Omaha, 1972-74; Greg Spevak Orchestra, Omaha, 1974-87. Creative Works: 800 popular songs, 1929-98; 75 Classical Opus, 1940-55; World Without War - 1964, 1965; Manuscriptotechicomomusicology; 83 songs published, 1968. Address: 2509 Farnam Street, Omaha, NE 68131-3613, USA.

**BRETTSCHNEIDER Marla Ann,** b. 16 May 1965, New York, USA. Professor. Education: BA, Political Science, State University of New York, Binghamton; MA, Politics, PhD, Politics, New York University. Appointments: Assistant Professor, Political Philosophy, Political Science and Womens Studies, Bloomsburg University, 1993-96; Assistant Professor, Political Philosophy, Political Science and Womens Studies, University of New Hampshire, 1996-. Publications: Cornerstones of Peace: Jewish Identity Politics and Democratic Theory, 1996; The Narrow Bridge: Jewish Views or Multiculturalism, 1996. Honour: Gustavos Meyers Human Rights Award, 1997. Address: Department of Political Science, University of New Hampshire, HSSC UNH, Durham, NH 03824-3586, USA.

**BREW-GRAVES Samuel Henry,** b. 11 October 1934, Cape Coast, Ghana. Paediatrician; International Health Developmen'

Consultant. m. Charlotte, 1 son, 2 daughters. Education: St Thomas's Hospital Medical School, 1956-61; Diploma, Sick Children's Hospital, Toronto, Canada, 1966; Paediatric Fellow, Johns Hopkins Medical Institute and MPHJHU School of Public Health, 1967; FMC; FWACP; FRSH. Appointments: Head, Pediatrics, Military Hospital, 1968-71; Director, Army Health Military Hospital, 1971-74; United Nations WHO Staff Member, Chief of Mission in Uganda and Nigeria, 1974-79; Managing Director, Radmed Consultancy; Chairman, Cliffpoint Holdings. Publications: Over sixty articles, abstracts and papers in professional medical journals. Honours: Chairman, Ghana Football Association, 1972-74; National Sports Administration Award, 1973. Memberships: St Thomas's Hospital Alumni; Johns Hopkins Medical and Surgical Association; Johns Hopkins School of Hygiene and Public Health; Paediatric Association of Nigeria; Association of Olympic Medical Officers; Academy of International Military Sports. Address: Radmed Consultancy Services Ltd, PO Box 9492, Airport Accra, Ghana.

**BREWSTER Robert Gene,** b. 7 July 1936, Birmingham, AL, USA. Singer; Educator. 1 son. Education: Diploma, Howard High School, Chattanooga, TN, USA, 1954; BMus, Piano, Honors, Wheaton College, Wheaton, IL, USA, 1954-58; MMus, Voice, Distinction, Indiana University, Bloomington, IN, USA, 1958-59; DPhil, Performance Practices and Musicology, Washington University, St Louis, MO, USA, 1963-66. Appointments include: Teacher, Music and French, Director, Concert Choir, Westfield High School, Westfield, AL, USA, 1959-60; Chairman, Department of Music, Director, Concert Choir, Miles College, Birmingham, AL, USA, 1960-62; Chairman, Division of Fine Arts and Music, Director, Concert Choir, Jackson State College, Jackson, Mississippi, 1962-63; Chairman, Department of Music, Dillard Univrsity, New Orleans, LA, USA, 1974; Coordinator, Voice Area, University of Miami, Coral Cables, FL, USA, 1974-82; President, Administrator, Fashion Suite, Showroom Inc, New York, NY, USA, 1983-. Honours include: Metropolitan Opera District Auditions Winner, 1965; Fulbright Scholar for Vocal Study in Germany, 1966-68; Graduate Fellow, Stipend in Addition; Deutsche Akademische Austauscht Dienst Award, 1968-70; Distinguished Professor, Dillard University, 1974. Memberships: National Association of Schools of Music; National Association of Teachers of Singing; American Musicological Society; College Music Society; American Association of University Professors; Phi Mu Alpha Music Fraternity; Florida Vocal Teachers Association; The National Arts Club, New York, London, Los Angeles. Address: 475 W 57th St Apt 18A, New York, NY 10019-1778, USA.

**BREZEANU Gheorghe,** b. 29 October 1948, Ditesti, Prahova. Professor. m. Doinita, 1 son. Education: Engineering, University Politehnica, Bucharest, 1972; PhD, Microelectronics, 1981. Appointments: Assistant Professor, Electronics Faculty, University Polytechnica, Bucharest, 1972-86; Lecturer, Electronics Faculty, 1989-90; Associate Professor, 1990-92; Professor, 1992-. Publications: 1 Monograph; 3 Books; 5 University Handbooks; 4 Patents; Over 100 Papers. Honours: Award, Romanian Academy. Memberships: IEEE; Electronics Devices Society; International Semiconductor Conference. Address: Drumul Taberei 64, 77387 Bucharest, Romania.

**BRIDGE Dorothy,** b. 10 February 1938, Sydney, Australia. Teacher. m. Robert Bridge (dec), 2 sons, 1 daughter. Education: Creative Writing Advanced Course, 1973-75; Journalism Course, 1988. Appointments: Writer, Journalist, Song Writer, 1976-; Secretarial Positions; Creative Writing Teacher, Cairns College of TAFE, 1994-; Various voluntary activities. Publications: 10 books; Cassette Tape of 4 songs, Songs from Cairns, 1987; Film Script, Gold, 1984; Children's

Play, 1983; Stories, articles, poems, songs in numerous publications. Honours: Cultural Award, Mulgrave Shire Council, 1994; Prize Winner, Bush Ballad Competition, 1994; Literature Representative, Cairns City Council, RADF Committee; Winner, The Examiner/Pacific International Competition, 1990; Nominee, Cairns Businesswoman of the Year, 1989; Certificate & Gold Bicentennial Medallion, Australian Consolidated Press, 1988; Recited Poem, Bicentenary Year in the Mulgrave Shire, Opening Ceremony of Australia Day, 1988; 3rd Prize, Ian Mudie Award for Short Story, 1987; Winner, New Idea Compt, 1987; First Prizes, Pre Teen Story & Factual Story, Arts Festival, 1985; Queensland Day Poetry Award, 1983. Address: 21 Blue Hills Crescent, Freshwater, Cairns, Qld 4870, Australia.

**BRINCHUK Mikhail,** b. 4 February 1945, Belorussia. Lawyer. m. Lidiya, 1 son, 1 daughter. Education: Diploma, International Law, Patrice Lumumba Peoples Friendship University, Moscow, 1973; Postgraduate, Institute of State and Law, USSR Academy of Sciences; Diploma of Candidate of Legal Sciences, 1978; Diploma of Doctor of Legal Sciences, 1991. Appointments: Director, Center for Environmental Legal Studies, Institute of State and Law, 1992-; Head of Chair, Academic School of Law, 1996-98; Professor, Environmental Law, Moscow State Juridical Academy, 1994-98; Correspondent, Journal, Environmental Liability, 1996-97. Publications: Legal Protection of the Atmospheric Air, 1985; Legal Protection of the Environment from Pollution by Toxic Substances, 1990; Ecological Law (Environmental Law), 1998; Over 150 articles in professional journals. Memberships: Commission on the Environmental Law, International Union of Nature Protection and Natural Resources; European Council for Agricultural Law; High Environmental Council Under the RF State Duma. Address: Russian Academy of Sciences, Institute of State & Law, Center for Environmental Legal Studies, Znamenka Str 10, 119841 Moscow, Russia.

**BRINCK Ulrich,** b. 25 September 1958, Hannover, Germany. Physician. Education: Medical Study, University of Gottingen; MD, 1988, University Wurzburg; PhD, 1998, University Gottingen. Publications: Over 50 original articles in professional journals. Membership: German Society Pathologists. Address: Dept of Pathology, Robert Koch Str 40, 37085 Gottingen, Germany.

**BRINTON Byron Charles,** b. 25 January 1912, Fessenden, North Dakota, USA. Editor; Publisher. m. Roberta Lee Wright, 3 sons, 2 daughters. Education: Junior Certificate with Honours, Journalism, University of Oregon, 1934. Honours: Northwest Bonneville Advisory Board, Its' Full Life; Twice Honored by State for Service to Agriculture, 1990's. Memberships: Both US Forest and Bureau of Land Management Boards; Oregon Geographic Names Board; Twice represented public before Congress, once before the Federal Power Commission; Founding President, Anthony Lake Ski Area Association, 1930s. Address: PO Box 70, 2517 Valley Avenue, Baker City, OR 97814, USA.

**BRITT-DORRAH Maisha,** b. 22 October 1944, Laurens, South Carolina, USA. Organizational Development Consultant. 2 daughters. Education: Associate in Science, Law Enforcement, 1981, BSc, Criminal Justice, 1984, Philadelphia College of Textiles and Science; MA, Administration, Antioch University, 1986. Appointments: Police Officer, Philadelphia Police Department, 1973-79; Sergeant County Detective, Philadelphia District Attorneys Office, 1979-90; Consultant, M Dorrah-Britt & Associates, 1990-. Honours: Murrell Dobbins High School Hall of Fame, 1988; National Library of Poetry Editors Choice Award, 1997. Memberships: International Society of Poets; International Association of Women Police;

National Association of Chiefs of Police; Fraternal Order of Police; International Platform Association; American Association of University Women. Address: PO Box 1381, Dover, DE 19903-1381, USA.

**BRITTAN Leon,** b. 25 September 1939, London. Vice President. m. Diana, 2 Step daughters. Education: MA, Trinity College, Cambridge; Henry Fellow, Yale University. Appointments: Called to Bar, Temple, 1962; Conservative Candidate, North Kensington General Elections, 1966, 1970; MP, Cleveland and Whitby, 1974-83; MA, Richmond, North Yorkshire, 1983-88; Vice Chairman, Employment Committee of Parliamentary Conservative Party, 1974-76; Opposition Spokesman, Devolution and House of Commons Affairs, 1976-78; Opposition Spokesman on Devolution and Employment, 1978-79; Minister of State, Home Office, 1979-81; Chief Secretary to the Treasury, 1981-83; Home Secretary, 1983-85; Secretary of State, Trade and Industry, 1985-86; Member, Vice President, European Commission, 1989-; Publications: The Conservative Opportunity; Milestones for the Sixties; Rough Justice; Infancy and the Law; Many other publications. Memberships: Chairman, Cambridge Unversity Conservative Association; President, Cambridge Union; Chairman, Bow Group; Vice Chairman, National Association of School Governors and Managers; Many other memberships. Address: 200 rue de la Loi, 1049 Brussels, Belgium.

**BROAD Robin,** b. 26 January 1954, Manchester, USA. Academic. m. John H Cavanagh, 1 son. Education: BA summa cum laude, Economics, Williams College, 1977; MPA, 1980, PhD, 1983, Woodrow Wilson School of Public and International Affairs, Princeton University. Appointments: University Professor, Research Associate, Xavier University, Mindanao, Philippines, 1977-78; Economic Researcher, Chulalonghorn University, Bangkok, Thailand, 1979; Visiting Research Associate, UP, Manila, Philippines, 1980-81; International Economist, 1983-84, InterAmerican Development Bank Desk Officer, 1984-85, US Treasury Dept, Office of Multilateral Development Banks; Senior Staff Economist, US Congressman Charles E Schumer, 1985-87; International Affairs Fellow, Council on Foreign Relations, Resident Associate, Carnegie Endowment for International Peace, 1987-88; Grantee, John D and Catherine T MacArthur Foundation, International Peace and Security Programme, 1988-90; Assistant Professor, 1990-96, Associate Professor, 1996-, The International Development Programme, School of International Service, The American University. Publications: 2 books; 2 monographs; 4 book chapters; 7 refereed, 6 non-refereed journal articles; Over 19 newspaper and miscellaneous publications; other non-refereed Philippine publications. Honours: 10 grants and fellowships.

**BROCK Randall,** b. 24 November 1943, USA. Poet. Education: BA, History, 1962-70; MFA, Creative Writing, 1972-73. Appointments: Poet. Publications: 18 Chapbooks, Poetry , 4 Cassette Tapes, Poetry to Music. Honours: Centrum Scholar, 1977; Honourable Mention Poetry Exhibition, 1998. Memberships: SOPA; PEN, USA, West; P and W. Address: P O Box 1673, Spokane, WA 99210, USA.

**BRONSHTEN Vitaly Aleksandrovich,** b. 9 October 1918, Moscow, Russia. Astronomer. m. Klionskaya Ittas, 1 daughter. Education: Mechanic, Mathematics Faculty, Moscow University, 1947. Appointments: Assistant Professor, Moscow State Pedagogic Institute, 1945-52; Scientific Consultant, Moscow Planetarium, 1952-64; Scientific Secretary, All Union Astronomical Geod Society, 1964-83. Publications: 15 books; 250 scientific papers. Memberships: Honorary Member of American Society of Amateur Astronomers; Astronomical

Society of Russia, 1990-. Address: Varshavskoe Road 16 Ap 130, Moscow 113105, Russia.

**BRONSTEIN Mihail,** b. 23 January 1923, Leningrad, Russia. Economist. m. Barskaya Bella, 1 son, 1 daughter. Education: Political Economy, Leningrad University, 1949; Candidate of Economic Sciences, Leningrad University, 1954; Doctor of Economic Sciences, 1965. Appointments: Leningrad University; Estonian Academy of Sciences. Publications: Over 300 scientific works, including: Land and economic relations, 1978; Economic extimation of natural resources, 1981. Memberships. Academy of Sciences, Estonia; International Association of Agricultural Economics; International Union of Economists. Address: Sole 47-78, EE 0003 Tallinn, Estonia.

**BROOKEY Robert S,** b. 14 September 1928, Los Angeles, CA, USA. Chemical Engineer. m. Carolyn Patch, 1 s. Education: BS, Chemistry, University of California, Berkeley, 1950; MS, Chemical Engineering, 1950; PhD, Chemical Engineering, University of Wisconsin, 1952. Appointments. Chemical Engineer, E I Du Pont de Nemours and Co, 1950; Research Chemical Engineer, Esso Research and Engineering Co, 1956; Research Chemical Engineer, Esso Standard Oil Co, 1957; Assistant Professor, The Ohio State University, 1960, Associate Professor, 1964; Professor, 1992; Emeritus Professor, 1992-. Publications: 5 Books and Reviews; Over 125 Papers. Honours: North American Mixing Forum Outstanding Research Award; Fellow, American Physical Society; Senior Research Award; Fellow, American Institute of Chemists; Senior Fellowship in Science; Sigma Xi, Honourary Research; Alpha Gamma Sigma; Phi Beta Delta, Many others. Memberships: Memberships in 8 Technical Societies. Address: Department of Chemical Engineering, 121 Koffolt Laboratories, 140 West 19th Avenue, Columbus, OH 43210-1180, USA.

**BROOKS Delora DeShields,** b. 18 May 1930, New Jersey, USA. Medical Writer; Medical Technologist. m. Eugene L Brooks, 2 daughters. Education: Columbia University, 1951; Washington Square College, 1952, 1953, 1958-59; AA, 1961, Westchester Community College; Vassar College, 1968; BS, 1981, SUNY at New Paltz. Appointments: Medical Technician and Technologist at various Hospitals and Laboratories including: The Private Medical Group of New Rochelle, 1958; Greenwich Hospital, 1962; Ossining Medical Laboratory, New York, 1960-61; Research Assistant, Columbia Presbyterian, New York, 1962-63; Demir Laboratory, Mt Vernon, 1960-61; DeShields Medical Laboratory, New Rochelle, as Owner and Director, 1961-63; Harlem Valley State Hospital, Wingdale, 1967; Research Technologist, Wassaic Developmental Centre, 1982. Publications: 10 publications including: Incidence of Eosinophils in Psychopathic and Mentally Normal Patients, 1953. Honours: American Medical Technologist of the Year Award, 1967; Commendation from County of Dutchess, State of New York, 1991; Honoured throughout the United States at a Breakfast of Champions yearly in various states. Memberships: VP of New York State Chapter of American Medical Technologist, 1960; Association in the American College of Medical Technologist, 1961; Secretary, New York State Society and New York Association of Clinical Laboratories, 1962; Registry of Medical Technologists International, 1962; Teacher of Medical Self Help - Office of Civil Defense, New Rochelle, 1954; American Medical Writers Association; American Medical Technologists Registry; American College of Medical Technology, Associate. Address: Dutchess Avenue, Box 67, Millerton, NY 12546, USA.

**BROOKS-KORN Lynne,** b. 6 July 1951, Detroit, Michigan, USA. Artist. m. Howard Brooks-Korn. Education: MFA and BFA, University of Michigan, Ann Arbor, Michigan, USA, 1976;

1973. Career: Solo Exhibitions include: 51 solo exhibitions since 1990 including: Academy of Performing Arts, Prague, Czech Republic; California State University, Chico, California; Musee de Art Contemporain, Chamalieres, France; Musee de Syndicat d'Initiative de Corlay, Corlay, France; Maclaurin Art Gallery, Ayr, England; Caveau-Musee Les Vignerons, de Roueire, Paris, France; Carlsbad Museum, Carlsbad, New Mexico; Minot State University, Minot, Northern Dakota; Grants Pass Museum of Art, Grants Pass, Oregon; Las Vegas Library Galleries, Las Vegas, Nevada; Aberdeen Arts Centre, Aberdeen, Scotland; Red River Valley Museum, Vernon, Texas; College of Eastern Utah, Price, Utah; Carson-Newman College, Jefferson, Tennesee; The Lurie Company, San Francisco Art Festival Museum, Edmonds, Washington; Margaret Harwell Art Museum, Poplar Bluff, Missouri; Nicolaysen Art Museum, Casper, Wyoming, USA; North County Museum of Arts; Park Raoids, Minnesota; Merced College Art Gallery, Merced, California; Napa Valley College, Napa, California; The Merrick Art Gallery Associates, Brighton, Pennsylvania; Group Exhbitions: 227 group exhibitions since 1990 including: US Embassy, Africa; l'Office du Tourisme, Luneville, France; Franc-Waret Castle, Brussels, Belgium, Galerie Am Ritterhof, Salzgitter, Germany; Galerie Am Markt Hofgeismar, Germany, Bryn Mawr College, Bryn Mawr, Pennsylvania; San Bernardino County Museum, Redlands, California; Ohio State University, Mansfield, Ohio; San Francisco State University, San Francisco, California, USA; Emporia State University, Emporia, Kansas; Eastern New Mexico University, Portales, New Mexico, USA; World Trade Center, New Orleans, Louisiana; Brenau University, Gainesville, Georgia, Austin Peay State University, Clarksville, Tennesee; Painted Bride Art Center, Philadelphia, Pennsylvania; East Tennessee State University, Baltimore, Maryland; Orange County Center for Contemporary Art, Santa Ana, California; Freeport Art Museum, Freeport, Illinois; Johns Hopkins School of Medicine, Baltimore, Maryland; Photogroup Center, Smithsonian Institution's National Museum of American Art, Artspace, Richmond, Virginia, USA. Honours: 17 awards for art since 1990. Address: 700 Loma Vista Ter, Pacifica, CA 94044-2425, USA.

**BROWN Barry S,** b. 26 September 1937, Brooklyn, New York, USA. Psychologist. m. Ann F Brown, 1 son, 2 daughters. Education: AB, Brooklyn College, 1958; MS, 1959, PhD, 1963, Western Reserve University. Career: Research Administrator, National Institute on Drug Abuse, 1975-92; Adjunct Professor, University of North Carolina, Wilmington, 1992-; Senior Investigator, Friends Research Institute, Baltimore, Maryland, 1995-. Publications: Over 100 journal articles, chapters and books. Honours: Award, Outstanding Service to the Field of Drug Abuse, National Association of State Alcohol and Drug Abuse Directors, 1986; Grant Awards, National Institute on Drug Abuse, 1994, 1996, 1998. Memberships: Editorial Board, Substance Use and Misuse, Journal of Drug Issues, Journal of Substance Abuse Treatment; Journal of Behavioral Health Services and Research. Address: PO Box 1695, Carolina Beach, NC 28428-1695, USA.

**BROWN Bradford C,** b. 17 February 1958, Waterbury, CT, USA. Executive. m. Alicia A Billings. Education: Bachelor of Arts, Political Science, Providence College; Master of Arts, Harvard University; Juris Doctor, Catholic University of America. Appointments: President, Western Stratagies, Nelson Communication Group; Executive Vice President, Shandwick Public Affairs. Publications: Pepperdine Law Review; The Washington Post; The Washington Business Journal; Austin American Statesman; San Antonio Business Journal; Virginian Pilot; San Diego Business Journal; Attourney Desk Library,

Co-Author. Address: Shandwick Pub Affairs, 655 15th St NW Ste 475, Washington, DC 20005, USA.

**BROWN Calvin A Jr,** b. 13 September 1931, Athens, Georgia, USA. Retired Physician. m. Joy San Walker, 2 daughters. Education: BS Biology, Morehouse College, Atlanta, Georgia; MD, Meharry Medical College, Nashville, Tennessee. Appointments: Assistant Professor, Department of Preventive Medicine, Emory University Medical School (first African American to be granted a Faculty Appointment), 1968-81; Developer, Co-Director, Director, Atlanta Southside Comprehensive Health Center, Atlanta, Georgia, 1966-69; Medical Director, Pineview Convalescent Center, Atlanta, Georgia, 1968-76; Member, Committee on Curriculum Revision, Emory Medical School, 1969; Member, Advisory Group, Georgia Regional Medical Program, 1969-74; Physician, Atlanta (Thikol) Job Corp Center, 1970-73; Chief of Staff, Martin Luther King Sr Nursing Home, 1971-74; Developer, Co-Director, Henry County Health Access Station, 1971-73; Chief Physician, Fulton County Jails, 1971-83; Developer, Medical Director of Health Care, Atlanta City Jail, 1980-84; Regional Medical Consultant, Peace Corp, 1982; Consultant, St Paul Insurance Company, 1984; Developer, Initial Director, Emergency Room, Hughes Spalding Medical Center, 1986-87; Founder, 1989, President, 1989-, Brown Medical Associates; Many civic positions. Honours: Honorary DSc, Morehouse College, 1987, Morehouse Medical School, 1998. Memberships: Life member, Alpha Phi Alpha Fraternity; Atlanta Medical Associiation; Georgia State Medical Association; National Medical Association; National Association for the Advancement of Colored People, life member; Sigma Pi Phi Fraternity (Kappa Boule); National Alumni Association of Morehouse College, life member. Address: 2947 Oldknow Drive NW, Atlanta, GA 30318, USA.

**BROWN Lester R.** Environmentalist; Researcher. Education: BS Agricultural Science, 1955, Rutgers University; MS Agricultural Economics, 1959, University of Maryland; MPA Public Administration, 1962, Harvard University. Appointments: President and Senior Researcher, Worldwatch Institute, non-profit research institute devoted to analysis of global environmental issues; Advisory Committee, Institute for International Economics; Advisory Council, Committee for the National Institutes for the Environment; Board of Directors, Environmental and Energy Study Institute; Board member, Institute for Sustainable Development, Poland; Advisor, Clean up the World Project, Australia; Advisory Council, International Fund for Agricultural Research; International Council, Earth Day 2000; Advisory Committee, Eco-Policy Centre, Rutgers University; Board of Advisors, International Fund for China's Environment; Advisory Committee, UN's Foundation; Advisory Board, Centre for a New American Dream. Publications: 18 books including: Tough Choices: Facing the Challenge of Food Scarcity, 1996; The World Watch Reader, 1998; 3 book series; Publisher of World Watch; Beyond Malthus: Nineteen Dimensions of the Popular Challenge, 1999; Author numerous articles. Honours: Too numerous to list including: 19 honorary degrees; UN Environment Prize, 1987; Gold Medal, Worldwide Fund for Nature, 1989; Selected as one of 100 Who Have Made a Difference, by the Earth Times, 1995; Selected as one of Audubon Society's 100 Champions of Conservation, 1998; 3 literary awards. Address: Worldwatch Institute, 1776 Massachusetts Avenue NW, Washington DC 20036-1904, USA.

**BROWN Opal Diann,** b. 8 August 1958, USA. Medical Technologist; Nurse. m. T David Brown. Education: BS, Medical Technology, 1981; BS, Nursing, 1993. Appointments: Biomedical Reference Laboratories, Fairmont, 1981-82;

Fairmont General Hospital, 1982; BG Thimmappa, Maryland Inc, Bridgeport, 1982-83; Pocuhontas Memorial Hospital, 1984-87; Alexandria Hospital, 1987-88; Richland Memorial Hospital, 1988-; RN, Midland Regional Center, South Carolina Department of Special Needs, Columbia, 1994-. Memberships: American Society of Clinical Pathologists; Sigma Theta Tau; ANA; Student Nurses Association. Address: 232 Laurel Meadows Drive, West Columbia, SC 29169-2361, USA.

**BROWN Reginald R, Jr.,** b. 18 March 1946, Baton Rouge, LA, USA. Law Enforcement Officer. m. Charlotte, 2 sons, 2 daughters. Education: Southern University, 1964-65. Appointments: Attorneys Disciplinary Board; Major and Sheriff's Administrative Assistant, East Baton Rouge Sheriff's Office, 1975-. Honours: Presidents U.S.A. Award, Law Enforcement; Golden Deeds Award, City of Baton Rouge, 1997; S.U. Trail Blazers Award 1998. Memberships: S.U. Alumni; NAACP. Address: P O Box 881, Baton Rouge, LA 70821-0881, USA.

**BROWNSTEIN Erica M,** b. 18th January 1960, Newark, Ohio, USA. Educator. m. David Brownstein, 1 son, 1 daughter. Education: Teaching Certificates in Chemistry, Mathematics and Physics; BS Chemistry, cum laude, 1987, Ohio Dominican College; PhD, 1997, from Mathematics, Science & Technology Programme, Ohio State University. Appointments: Physics and Chemistry Teacher, Sheridan High School, 1988-90; Taught Physics and Elementary Science Methods and Science in Elementary Classrooms, OSU, 1993-94; Assistant Programme Coordinator, National Centre for Science Teaching and Learning, 1990-94; Research Associate for Department of Theory and Practice, Mike Beeth, 1996; Co-taught an integrated science, mathematics and technology workshop for high school science and mathematics teachers, 1996; Supervised mathematics, science and technology interns in technology designated sites, 1996-97; Taught Physiology, Ohio Dominican College, 1998; Taught Physics, AP Physics and Computer Science, Eastmoor High School Columbus Public Schools, 1998-. Publications: Co-author 1 refereed article and 6 papers in professional journals; 6 presentations with and 5 without papers. Memberships: American Association of Physics Teachers; National Science Teachers Association; Science Educators of Central Ohio; National Association for Research in Science Teaching; American Educational Research Association; American Educational Teachers of Science. Address: Ohio Dominican College, 755 Denison Avenue, Columbus, OH 43215, USA.

**BROZOVSKY John A,** b. 30 April 1951, Spokane, Washington, USA. Accounting Professor. m. Sue Ewen King, 1 son. Education: BBA International Business, 1975, MPA Accounting, 1978, University of Texas; PhD Accounting, 1990, University of Colorado. Appointments: Teaching Assistant, 1977, Computer Programmer, 1974-77, University of Texas; Lecturer, California State University-Fresno, 1983-86; Research/Teaching Assistant, University of Colorado, 1986-89; Assistant Professor, 1989-96, Associate Professor, 1996-, Virginia Tech. Computer Programmer, Texas State Health Dept, 1978-80; EDP Auditor, City of Austin, 1980-81; Senior Internal Auditor, Enserch Corp, 1981-83. Publications: Co-author, 22 refereed journal articles; 2 invited articles and 2 electronic articles; 3 books and parts of books; 5 refereed proceedings and 12 presentations. Honours: IICCP Award of Excellence, 1981; ANBAR Electronic Intelligence Citation for Excellence, 1997; Lybrand Cerificate of Merit, Institute of Management Accountants, 1997, 1998; Several fellowships and research grants. Memberships: American Accounting Association; American Economic Association; American Tax Association; Institute of Management Accountants; National

Tax Association. Address: 9000 Newport Road, Catawba, VA 24070, USA.

**BRÜCK Miroslav,** b. 9 July 1964, Skalica, Slovakia. Polygrapher. m. div. 1 daughter. Publications: 3 Poetry books, Media - Polish, Slovakia, Bulgaria. Membership: Klub Nezavislych Spisovatelov (Club Independent Writers), 1995-. Address: Pod Hajkom 15, 909 01 Skalica, Slovakia.

**BRUESKE Berneta Dallas Thompson,** b. 3 September 1908, Quincy, Minnesota, USA. Poet. m. L. F. Brueske, 3 sons, 2 daughters. Education: Country School of Quincy Township, Minnesota. Career: Poet; Mother. Publications: Thank You Lord, 1989. Address: 260 Streamwood, Irvine, CA 92620, USA.

**BRUESKE Charlotte,** b. 1 January 1934, Plainview, MN, USA. Poet. Education: AA Degree, Pasadena City College, 1976; BA, California State University, 1984; Continuing Studies, Fuller Theological Seminary, Orange County, CA. Poet; Composer. Publications: Once in a Coon's Age; The Ancestors of Gottlob August Bruss and Bertha Pauline Goede; A Search for the Records of the Orphans of Dannan; Composer, Lyrical Numerous Works; Evergreen; Every New Day; Because of Love; I Heard a Robin Sing Today; Where Love Abides; Anthology, To Every Life; Poems of the Season; The Bells on the Steeple; Consider the Lilies; Life Friend; Lift Up One Another; To Touch the World by Love. Honours: Certificate of Merit, Virginia Baldwing Talent Agency. Address: 260 Streamwood, Irvine, CA 92620, USA.

**BRUESKE Jhana,** b. 24 October 1943, Minnesota, USA. Artist; Poet. Career: Artist; Animal Behavior Consultant; Poet. Publication: I Heard A Robin Sing Today. Address: c/o 260 Streamwood, Irvine, CA 92620, USA.

**BRUNER Violet,** b. 1 November 1922, Depauw, Indiana, USA. Artist. m. Lester Windell, 1 son, 2 daughters. Education: AB, 1943, AM, 1958, University of Louisville, Kentucky; MS, Education, Indiana University, Southeast, 1995. Appointments: Commercial Art, Advertising, 1944-; Art Teacher, 1966-71; Art Gallery Director, 1973-87. Publication: Human Symbiosis, 1967, 1997. Honour: International Poetry Hall of Fame. Memberships: Society of Friends; Daughters of the American Revolution; American Humanists; National Museum of Women in Art. Address: 4675 Davis Mill Road, NW Ramsey, IN 47166, USA.

**BRUNO Alexander Dmitrievich,** b. 26 June 1940, Moscow, USSR. Mathematician. 2 sons. Education: MS, Mathematics, Moscow State Univ, 1962; PhD, Physics, Mathematics, Institute of Applied Mathematics, 1966; Professor, Physics, Mathematics, Inst of Appl Math, 1970. Appointments: Junior-, 1965; Senior-, 1971; Leading Researcher, 1987; Head of Mathematical Department, 1995. Publications: Transac Mos Math Soc 25-26; Local Methods in Nonlinear Diff Eq; The Restricted 3-Body Problem; Power Geometry in Algebraic and Diff Eq. Memberships: Moscow Mathematical Soceity; American Mathematical Society; Institute of Applied Mathematics; Academy of Non-Linear Sciences. Address: Inst of Applied Mathematics, Miusskaja Sq 4, Moscow 125 047, Russia.

**BRYDEN Michael MacLaren,** b. 24 April 1938, Melbourne, Australia. Professor. m. R Elizabeth, 2 daughters. Education: Bachelor of Veterinary Science, 1962; Doctor of Philosophy, 1968; Doctor of Science in Veterinary Medicine, 1970; Doctor of Science, 1984. Appointments: Biologist, Australian National Antarctic Research Expeditions, 1964-67; Instructor in Anatomy, Cornell University, 1967-70; Senior Lecturer in eterinary Anatomy, University of Sydney, 1970-72; Reader in natomy, University of Queensland, 1973-87; Professor, Head f Department, Veterinary Anatomy, University of Sydney, 988-. Publications: 6 Books; 100 Scientific Papers; 18 Major Government Reports; 19 Popular Articles. Memberships: ustralian Institute of Biology; Australian Mammal Society; Soceity for Marine Mammalogy; Royal Zoological Society of Jew South Wales; Society of the Sigma Xi. Address: Department of Veterinary Anatomy and Pathology, University f Sydney, NSW 2006, Australia.

**BUCHANAN Bruce,** b. 10 September 1947, Washington DC, USA. Advertising Photographer; Metal Artist. Education: University of New Orleans, Louisiana; Long Beach City College, California; Ocean Corp, Houston, Texas; Industrial Welding School, Belle Chasse, Louisiana. Appointments: ormer Chair, Social Action Committee, Unitarian Universalist Church; Former Deep-Sea Diver and Pipe Welder; Expert on Workers Compensation Issues; Literacy Volunteer; Founder, ree Meal Kitchen; Founder, Injured Workers Group. Publications: Photographs published widely; Metal art featured n several local, national and international publications; Articles n literary journals and newspapers. Memberships: Art Directors Club of Portland, Maine; Artists and Blacksmiths Association of Jorth America. Address: PO Box 556, Bar Mills, ME 4004-0556, USA.

**BUCHNER Daniel Richard,** b. 29 July 1963, Chicago, Ilinois, USA. Military Defence Engineer. Education: Bachelor's Degree, Electrical Engineering, Christian Brothers University, Memphis, Tennessee, 1985; Master's Degree, Electrical Engineering, University of Missouri at Rolla, 1994. Appointments: Engineering Assistant, Owens Engineering Company, Jackson, Tennessee, 1985; Associate Engineer, 1985-86, Engineer, Electronics, 1986-91, Boeing, St Louis, Missouri; Journeyman Engineer, Science Applications International Corporation, St. Ann, Missouri, 1991-92; BDM International Inc, Fairview Heights, Illinois; Assistant Staff Member, 1992-93; CAS, Inc,St Ann, Missouri; Journeyman Engineer, 1993-94; Senior Analyst, 1994-97; CAS, Inc, Senior Analyst, 1997- present, Huntsville, Alabama. Honours include: Certificate of Appreciation, Hazelwood School District, Florissant, Missouri,1988; Five Year Service Award, Boeing, St Louis, Missouri, 1990; Letter of Appreciation, President of CAS nc, 1995; Note of Appreciation, Army Aviation Electronic Combat Project Manager, 1996; Fellow, International Biographical Centre, Cambridge, England, 1998; The Twentieth Century Award for Achievement, International Biographical Centre, Cambridge, England, 1998; Listed in numerous biographical dictionaries. Memberships: Army Aviation Association of America; Armed Forces Communications and Electronics Association; Association of Old Crows; Institute of Electrical and Electronic Engineers; IEEE Aerospace and Electronic Systems Society; Association of the United States Army; Madison Church of Christ; Tau Kappa Epsilon Alumni Association. Address: 17 Allen Street, Madison, AL 35738-1505, USA.

**BUDAEV Vladimir Michailovich,** b. 25 October 1955, Moscow, Russia. Architect. m. Budaeva Olga, 5 May 1979, 1 d. Education: Diploma, Architecture, Moscow Architectural Institute, 1984. Appointments: Head, Architectural Artistic Planning Institute, Academician A T Polyansky; Headed design and construction, Chief Architect, Memorial, Pobedy Park; Head, Construction, Central Museum of Great Patriotic War; Chief Architect, Constructor, Central Obelisk, Pobedy Park; Chief Architect, Cathedral of Georgiy Pobedonosetz and Synagogue Memorial, Poklonnaya Gora; Architect, Constructor, Monument of Peter the Great, Moskva River; Design and Construction, Moscow Zoo; Architect, multi-storey municipal buildings. Publications: Several papers in professional journals. Honours: Honoured Architect, Russia; Medal, Holy Sergiy Radonezsky, Russian Orthodox Church. Membership: Union of Architects of Russia. Address: Petrovka 26-28, 103051, Moscow, Russia.

**BUDAGUAN Boris,** b. 22 May 1957, Baku, Russia. Head of Department. m. Olga Budaguan, 1 son, 1 daughter. Education: MSc, 1980; PhD, 1985; DSc, 1993; Professor, 1995. Career: Postgraduate, 1982-85, Senior Researcher, 1989-92, Professor, 1993-96, Head of Department, 1996-, Moscow Institute of Electronic Technology; Senior Researcher, Russian Academy of Sciences, 1986-89. Publications: Numerous papers in international journals; 5 books. Honours: Grant, International Science Foundation, 1993; Grant, President of the Russian Federation, 1998. Membership: New York Academy of Sciences. Address: Moscow Institute of Electronic Technology, Moscow 103489, Russia.

**BUDNIK Patricia M,** b. 2 July 1936, Riverside, New Jersey, USA. Teacher; Professor. 2 sons. Education: BEd, 1967, MEd, 1972, University of Miami, Coral Gables; DEd, Nova University, Fort Lauderdale, 1991. Appointments: Teacher, Dade County Public Schools, Miami, 1967-; Visiting Professor, Hunan Educational College, Changsha, China, 1994, 1995, 1996, 1997; Adjunct Professor, Nova Southeastern University, Fort Lauderdale, 1996-. Publications: 2 Practicums, 1989, 991. Honours: Grantee, Foundation of Excellence in Public Education, 1986, 1987; Grantee, Broward Community Foundation, 1990. Memberships: United Teachers of Dade-Steward; National Association for the Education of Young Children; International Reading Association; Florida Reading Association; St Andrews Presbyterian Church Choir; Sunday School Superintendent and Teacher, Evangelism Explosion Team. Address: 1820 North 45th Avenue, Hollywood, FL 33021-4104, USA.

**BUDRIUNAS Ramunis Aloyzas,** b. 29 January 1938, Kaunas, Lithuania. Scientist. m. Danute, 1 son, 1 daughter. Education: Engineer of Forestry, Lithuanian Agricultural Academy, 1959; Doctor of Natural Science, 1971; Senior Researcher of Ecology and Biogeocenology, 1977. Appointments: Forestry Officer, 1959-61; Researcher, Institute of Botany, Lithunaian Academy of Sciences, 1961-74; Director, Kaunas Botanical Garden, 1975-; Assistant Professor, Vytautas Magnus University, 1997-. Publications: Co-Author, The Reservation of Zuvintas, 1968; Landscape Ecology and Aesthetics, 1975; Trees and Shrubs Grown in Lithuania, 1987. Memberships: Kaunas Nature Protection Society; Lithuanian Table Tennis Association; European Table Tennis Union, Veterans Committee; Kaunas Healthy City Project. Address: Z E Zilibero 6, LT-3018 Kaunas, Lithuania.

**BUGIS Ahmed A,** b. 12 February 1956, Makkah, Saudi Arabia. Accountant. m. Nawal, 1 son, 3 daughters. Education: Technical Translation Diploma, Carnegi Mellon University, 1977; Bachelor of Science, Accounting, Clarion, 1980. Appointments: Auditor, Treasurer, Budget Specialist, Head of Budget and Finance, Royal Saudi Armed Forces, 1981-90; Director of Finance, International Islamic Relief Organisation, 1990-91; Senior Accountant, Group Leader, Saudi Aramco, 1991-. Memberships: Saudi Accounting Association; Saudi Computer Society; American Accounting Association; American Management Association; Institute of International Auditors; Institute of Management Accountants. Address: P O Box 2660, Dhahran 31311, Saudi Arabia.

**BUI Khanh The,** b. 18 June 1936, Binh Thuan. Professor of Linguistics. m. Nguyen Thi Mao, 1 son, 1 daughter. Education: First Degree, Graduate of Foreign Languages, Hanoi University of Teachers; Graduate of Linguistics, National University of Hanoi; Doctor, National University of Hanoi, 1981. Appointments: Dean, Faculty of Oriental Studies; Director, Centre for V-mese and SEA Studies; Vice Rector, University of HCM City. Publications: Co-Author, Cham Language; Co-Author, Ksingmul Languages; Introduction to Linguistics; A Cham Grammar. Memberships: Executive Committee, Linguistics Society of Vietnam. Address: Dept of Oriental Studies, University of Social Science and Humanities, 12 Dinh Tien Hoang St, Ho Chi Minh City, Vietnam.

**BUINOVA Lyudmila Nikolaevna,** b. 7 January 1941, Sverdlovsk, Russia. Senior Scientific Researcher. m. Igor Martemianov, 1 daughter. Education: Graduate, Ural State University, 1964, PhD, 1975. Appointments: General Scientific Field of Proposed Activity, Investigation of Structure and Mechanical Properties of Ordered and Aged Metallic Alloys. Publications: 90. Address: Laboratory of Phase Transformations, Institute of Metal Physics, Urals Division of Russian Academy of Sciences, 18 S Kovalevskaya Str GSP-170, Ekaterinburg 620219, Russia.

**BULANOV Nikolai,** b. 19 May 1945, Tyumen, Russia. Scientific Worker. m. Bulanova Margarita N, 1 son, 1 daughter. Education: Diploma of Physical-Engineer, 1969; Diploma of Physical and Mathematical Sciences Kandidat, 1975; Certificate of Senior Scientific Worker, 1982. Appointment: Senior Scientific Worker researching properties of liquids. Publications: Thermophysical Properties of Liquids in Metastable (Superheated) State, book, 1988; About 50 articles. Membership: Institute of Thermal Physics, Urals Branch of Russian Academy of Sciences. Address: Lab of Energetics & Cryogenics, Institute of Thermophysics, Urals Branch of Russian Academy of Science, 91 Pervomaiskaya Str GSP-828, Ekaterinburg 620219, Russia.

**BULAVIN Leonid Anatolievich,** b. 18 August 1945, Poltava, Ukraine. Physicist. m. Svitlana Bulavina, 1 son. Education: MS, 1967; PhD, 1973; DSc, 1990. Appointments: Scientific Researcher, 1970-79; Assistant Professor, 1979-83; Associate Professor, 1983-90; Professor, 1990-; Dean, Department of Physics, 1990-. Publications: Over 200 scientific papers including: Neutron Study of Liquid; Physics - Problems and Tests; Critical Phenomena in Liquid. Memberships: Academician, High School Academy; Correspondent Member, Ukrainian National Academy of Sciences; European Association of Deans; Ukrainian and American Physical Society. Address: Department of Physics, TG Shevchenko Kiev University, 6 Prospekt Academika Glushkova, Kiev 252127, Ukraine.

**BULIGESCU Lucian,** b. 17 October 1929, Ploeshti, Romania. Doctor. m. Lia, 1 son. Education: School of Medicine Cluj, magna cum laude, 1953; Doctor es Sciences, 1957; Doctor Docent, 1974. Appointments: Professor, Chief of Department Internal Medicine and Hepatology, Fundeni Hospital, Chaussee Fundeni, Bucharest; Chief of Chair of University. Publications: 14 books; 500 works. Memberships: President, Romanian Association for Study of Liver; Belgium Society of Gastroenterology; French Society for Gastroenterology; French Association Study of Liver; New York Academy of Sciences. Address: str Precupetii Vechi 23, Sector 2, Bucharest, Romania.

**BULLARO Grace R,** b. 11 July 1949, Salerno, Italy. Educator; Public Speaker; Book Reviewer. m. Frank, 2 sons.

Education: PhD, SUNY Stony Brook, 1993; MA, SUNY Stony Brook, 1989; BA, CUNY City College, 1971. Appointment: Graduate Teaching Assistant, Comparative Literature State University of New York at Stony Brook, 1988-92; Adjunct Assistant Professor, Foreign Language Department Nassau Community College, 1990-; Sub Assistant Professor, English Department, City University of New York, Lehman College, 1991-. Publications: Il Piacere, Gradiva, 1990-91; Bla Runner, Riverside Quarterly, 1993; Dissertation, 1994; Swept Away, Italian Culture, 1995; Seduction of Mimi, Italian Cultu 1996; Chapter in Flowers and Revolution, 1997; Sev Beauties, Italian Culture, 1997; Ciao Professore in Fore Italicum, 1999. Honours: Phi Beta Kappa, CUNY City College 1972; President's Award for Excellence in Teaching, SUN Stony Brook, 1991; CUNY University Senate, 199 Senate-Lehman College 1997-99. Membership: Univers Faculty Executive Committee, Lehman College, Bronx, N York, 1999-. Address: CUNY Lehman Coll, English De Bedford Park Blvd W, Bronx, NY 10468, USA.

**BULYCHEV-OKSER Michael,** b. 17 February 198 Moscow, Russia. Pianist; Composer. Education: Piano Studi with Dr A Bakulov, Central Music School for Gifted Childre Moscow Conservatoire, 1988; Attended Professor Voskrensky masterclasses, Moscow State Conservatoi 1994-96; Study of Composition with famous Russian compos Professor Khrennikov, Moscow State Conservatoire, 1990-9 Scholarship study, Pre-college Division, Manhattan School Music, Piano and Composition, New York, USA, 1996-9 Entered College Division, Piano Department, Manhattan Scho of Music, Scholarship Student, since 1998; Scholars Student, Composition Programme, La Schola Cantorum, Pai France, 1998; Scholarship Student Piano Music Festiv Puigcerda, Spain, 1999. Career includes: Moved to USA, 199 Piano Recital, Del Terzo Studio, Weill Hall, Carnegie Ha 1996; Solo Piano Recital, Hubbard Hall, 1996; Chamber Mus Concert, Myers Recital Hall, 1996; Author's Solo Compositi Concert, Hubbard Hall, Manhattan School of Music, Pr Division, 1997; Elva Van Gelder Memorial Award Concert,199 Grand Founders Day Concert, Performed as Soloist w Manhattan Philamonic Orchestra, 1998; Solo Piano Recital Senior Citizens, Brooklyn, 1998; Recital de Piano in La Soc Cantorum, Paris, France, 1998; Debut Performance, Rac WQXR with the Manhattan Philharmonic Orchestra, 199 Young Musicians Concert, Carnegie Hall, New York 1999; S Piano Recital in Italian Culture Center of Long Island, N York, 1999; Spring Music Program Concert, Oyster Bay, N York, 1999; First Prize Winner Piano Recital, Puigcerda, Spa 1999. Honours: Eva Van Gelder Memorial Award, Manhatt School of Music, 1996; Richard Kimball Award in Compositi 1996, 1997; First Prize Award, 1996-97, Young Artis Concerto Competition for Young Instrumentalists, Sar Lawrence College, 1997; Carl Owen Memorial Scholarsh 1997; Parents' Association Award for Achievement in Musi and Theory Studies, 1997; La Schola Cantorum Summ Composition Programme Scholarship, Paris, 1998; Manhatt School of Music Scholarship, 1998; First Prizewinner, Pia Concerto Competition, Manhattan School of Music, 1998; Fi Prize Winner International Piano Competition, Puigcerc Spain, 1999. Address: 499 East 8th Street, Apt 2C, Brookly NY 11218, USA.

**BUMPUS Jamie Edward,** b. 27 November 1969, Union C Tennessee, USA. Journalist. Education: BA, Communicatio History, University of Tennessee at Martin, USA, 199 Appointments: Executive Editor, Copy Editor, Staff Writer, T Pacer, University of Tennessee at Martin, 1988-93; Journalis Staff Member, Governors School for the Humanities, Univers of Tennessee at Martin, Summer 1993; Sports Editor, T

Fulton (Kentucky), Leader, 1993-95; Sports Color Commentator, WOBT-TV, Union City, Tennessee, 1996; County Reporter, The Jackson, (Tennessee) Sun, 1996; News Director, WCMT-AM-FM/WCDZ-FM, Martin, Tennessee, 1996; Copy Editor, State Gazette, Dyersburg, Tennessee, 1996-. Honours: Society of Professional Journalists Outstanding Member, 1992-93; Wilson Hall Newswriting Award, 1992-93; Society of Professional Journalists Region 12 Best Sports Story Second Place, 1993; Kentucky Press Association Weekly Class I Best Sports Feature Second Place, Fall 1994; Kentucky Press Association Weekly Class I; Best Sports Story, First Place, 1994. Address: 737 Campground Road, Troy, TN 38260, USA.

**BUNCH Richard Alan,** b. 1 June 1945, Honolulu, Hawaii, USA. Educator; Writer. m. Rita Anne Glazar, 1 son, 1 daughter. Education: AA, Napa Valley College, 1965; Harlaxton Manor, Grantham, Lincolnshire, England, 1966; BA, Stanford University, 1967; MA, University of Arizona, 1969; MDiv, 1970, DD, 1971, Graduate Work, Philosophy, 1972-75, Vanderbilt University; Graduate Studies, Asian Philosophy, Temple University, 1975-76; JD, University of Memphis, 1980; Teaching Credential, Sonoma State University, 1988. Appointments: Teaching Assistant, Philosophy, Vanderbilt University, 1973-74; Instructor, Philosophy, Belmont University, 1973-74; Attorney, Horne & Peppel, Memphis, 1981-83; Assistant Professor, Law, Memphis State University, 1982-83; Associate News Editor, Napa Valley Times, 1985-86; Instructor, Philosophy, Chapman University, 1986-87; Instuctor, Philosophy Sonoma State University, 1990-91; Adjunct Humanities Faculty, Napa Valley College, 1985-. Publications: Summer Hawk, 1991; Night Blooms, 1992; Wading the Russian River, 1993; A Foggy Morning, 1996; Santa Rosa Plums, 1996; South By Southwest, 1997; Rivers of the Sea, 1998; Sacred Space, 1998. Honours: Pushcart Poetry Prize Nominations, 1988, 1997; Grand Prize, Ina Coolbrith National Poetry Day Contest, 1989; Winner, Jessamyn West Poetry Prize, 1990. Memberships: Academy of American Poets; Russian River Writers Guild. Address: 248 Sandpiper Drive, Davis, CA 95616, USA.

**BUNTS Frank E,** b. 2 March 1932, Cleveland, Ohio, USA. Artist. m. Jean Grassle Bunts. Education: BA, MA, 1964, Yale University, Cleveland Institute of Art, Case Western Reserve University. Creative Works: Represented in 6 public collections in USA and China; Over 130 solo and group exhibitions including Intercommunication Centre Artists Database, Tokyo Opera City, Tokyo, 1998; VIA Art Foundation, New York, continuing to 2001; 35 reviews and reproductions. Address: 15 W 24th Street, New York, NY 10010-3214, USA.

**BUNYON Ronald S,** b. 13 March 1935, Philadelphia, PA, USA. Educator; Poet. m. Josephine L Winbush, 1 son. Education: AS General Engineering, 1965, Mitchell College, Connecticut; BSc cum laude (1st in Class), Administration and Industrial Engineering, 1969, University of New Haven; MSc Urban Studies and Education, 1971, Southern Connecticut State College; MSc Urban and Environmental Administration and Management, 1992, continuing as a PhD Candidate, Rensselaer Polytechnic Institute; Various other courses in universities 1976-. Appointments: Educator 13 years, OIC International, Ghana, 1973-75, NJ Dept Education - COED, 1985-87, Passaic County Tech-Voc High School, 1987-89, Bergen County Technical School, 1989-; Management 18 years, Project Administrator, Community Progress Inc, New Haven, Entrepreneurial Management Training Specialist, Opportunities Industrialisation Centre, Philadelphia, Assistant Vice President, Drexel University, Philadelphia, Manager, Business Ventures International Inc; Technical 7 years, Designer, Lo-Ti-Tek Manufacturing Engineering, Philadelphia,

Designer, Draftsman radar system, H L Yoh Engineering Consultant Inc, Philadelphia, Senior Mechanical Designer, General Dynamics Inc. Publications: NASA, Commercial Applications of Space Programme Components; Poetry: Black Life Poetic Thinking, Life Poetic Thinking II; 3 vols, African American Original Family Stories; Philosophic Thinking. Memberships: Founder and Director, Bugain School, 1998, in Lashibi Tema, Ghana; Master Mason; PhD International, Berne University. Address: Business Ventures Intl Inc, PO Box 1324, Philadelphia, PA 19105, USA.

**BUREAU Jean Paul,** b. 6 June 1940, Nevers. Professor. m. 1 son, 1 daughter. Education: MD, 1970; MS, Tropical Ecology, 1972; Professor, 1974; Professor, 1st class, 1992. Appointments: Assistant, Montpellier Medical School, 1968; Assistant, Faculty of Medicine, 1970; Professor, 1974; Montpellier Faculty of Medicine, 1978. Publications: Numerous articles in professional medical journals. Memberships: Several. Address: Lab Histology and Cyrogenetics, Faculty of Medicine, 2 rue Ecole de Medecine, 34000 Montpellier, France.

**BURGER Henry G,** b. 27 June 1923, New York, USA. Vocabulary Scientist. m. Barbara Grace Burger. Education: BA, Columbia College, 1947; MA, 1965; PhD, 1967. Appointments: US Army, 1943-46; Social Science Consultant, 1956-67; Anthropologist, Southwestern Cooperative Educational Laboratory, 1967-69; Professor of Anthropology, University of Missouri, 1969-93; Founding Editor, Publisher, The Wordtree, 1984-. Publications: 97 Including 11 Books, Manuals or Monographs; 37 Articles or Book Chapters; 31 Communications; 15 Journal Columns; 3 miscellaneous. Honours: Phi Beta Kappa, 1947; Faculty Research Grant, National Science Foundation, 1970. Memberships: American Translators Association; National Association for the Practice of Anthropology; American Association of Applied Linguistics; American Society for Information Science; American Translators Association; Modern Language Association. Address: The Wordtree, 10876 Bradshaw Street, Overland Park, KS 66210 1148, USA.

**BURGIN Mark S,** b. Kiev, Ukraine. Mathematician; Philosopher; Computer Scientist. m. Lyubov Burgina, 1 son. Education: BS, MS, 1965-68, PhD, 1971, Moscow University, School of Mechanics and Mathematics; DSc, Institute of Philosophy, National Academy of Sciences, Ukraine, 1989. Appointments: Junior Scientific Researcher, Institute of Computer Systems, Moscow, 1971-78; Senior Scientific Researcher, Department of Automated Systems, Research Institute of Fishery and Oceanography, Moscow, 1978-80; Vice Chief, Computer Department, Institute of Design of Machinery Factories, Kiev, 1981-82; Lecturer, Kiev State University, 1982-85; Senior Scientist, Institute of Pedagogy, Kiev, 1985-90; Consultant, Institute of Economics, Kiev, 1987-90, Research Center "Ecology", Kiev, 1990-93; Leading Scientist, Department of Artificial Intelligence, Institute of System Technology, 1990-92; Leading Scientist, Research Center of Science, National Academy of Sciences of Ukraine, Kiev, 1992-94; Professor, Institute of Content and Methodology of Education Kiev, 1996-97, International Solomon University, Kiev, 1993-98; Head, Assessment Laboratory, Research Center of Science, National Academy of Sciences of Ukraine, Kiev, 1994-98; Chief Scientist, Institute of Psychology, Kiev, 1995-98; Leading Scientist, Institute of Statistics, Kiev, 1996-98; Professor, Kiev State University, 1997-98; Visiting Scholar, University of California, Los Angeles, USA, 1998-; Honorary Professor, Aerospace Academy of Ukraine. Publications: Over 700 scientific works including several books. Memberships include: American Mathematical Society; Association for Computing Machinery; New York Academy of

Sciences; Ukrainian Academy of Information Sciences; IEEE; Computer Society; Academy of Original Ideas; International Association of Fuzzy-Set Management and Economics; European Association for Logic, Language and Information; International Association for Foundations of Sciences, Language and Cognition; Society for Computer Simulation International; American Philosophical Association; Psychological Society of Ukraine; Pedagogical Society of Ukraine; International Association of Artificial Intelligence. Address: 1620 South Bentley Avenue #200, Los Angeles, CA 90025, USA.

**BURLACU Constantin**, b. 20 January 1949, Botosani, Romania. Journalist, Educator. m. Elisabeta Busaga, 1 son, 1 daughter. Education: BS, University Nicolas Doubrowa, Santiago, Chile, 1994; MA, Pacific Wstern University, 1996; D Hon, University Nicolas Doubrowa, 1994. Appointments: Chairman, League of National Defense, Nwe York City, 1985-; Publisher, NEW Right Mag, New York City, 1985; Dep, Mem, Assembly of International Parliament for Safety and Peace, Sicily, Italy, 1993-; Professor, University Nicolas Doubrowa, 1996-. Publications: The History of Nationalism in Eastern Europe, A Study of its Origin and Background in Romania, 1996; History of Moldova and its connection with Political and Social Circumstance from the Earliest Time to the Present Day, 1998. Honours: Republican Presidential Task Force, Washington, 1989; Order of Merit, National Senatorial Commission, 1991; Legion of Merit, Washington, 1993; Appointed, Knight Sovereign Nobel Religious Order of St Tatjana, Belgium, 1994; Citizen of Year, Principality of Hutt River Province, Australia, 1995. Memberships: Republican National Commission, Washington, 1985; American Federation of Police, Miami, 1990; National Representative, Senatorial Commission; National Representative, Congressional Commission; Fredom Army; Conservative Caucus; Amnesty International; American Defense Commission; American Security Council; Liberty Lobby. Address: 464 Woodward Ave, Ridgewood, NY 11385, USA.

**BURLAKA Dmytro Petrovych**, b. 4 January 1952, v Dmytroushky. Biologist. m. Halyna M Burlaka, 1 son, 1 daughter. Education: Graduate in Biology, Physiology, 1978, Shevtsnenko State University, Kyiv; Diploma Medical Radioelctronics, 1980; Candidate in Biological Sciences, 1992, Institute Experimental Pathology, Oncology, Radiobiology, Kyiv. Appointments: Senior Lab Worker, IEPOR, 1978-84, Junior Researcher, 1984-92, Researcher, 1992-95, Senior Researcher, 1995-. Publications: Articles to professional journals 1979-99. Membership: Euroscience. Address: Institute Experimental Pathology, Oncology, Radiobiology, Vasylkivs'ka 45, 252022 Kyiv, Ukraine.

**BURLAKOV Victor**, b. 10 November 1952, Ryasan, Russia. Physicist. m. Strizhova Nataliya, 2 sons. Education: Diploma of Physic-Ingeneer, Moscow Physical Technical Institute, 1970-76; PhD, 1982; Dr of Physical Mathematical Sciences, 1993. Appointments: Engineer, 1976, Junior Scientific Researcher, 1979, Scientific Researcher, 1986, Senior SR, 1988, Leading SR, 1994, Russian Academy of Sciences. Publications: More than 70 publications in scientific journals. Honour: Medal of 850th Anniversary of Moscow. Membership: Association of Spectroscopists. Address: Laboratory of Spectroscopy of Semiconductor Structures, Institute for Spectroscopy, Russian Academy of Sciences, Troitsk, Moscow 142092, Russia.

**BURNETT Arthur Louis**, b. 15 March 1935, Spotsylvania County, Virginia, USA. Judge; Adjunct Law Professor. m. Frisbieann Lloyd. Education: BA, Howard University, 1957; JD,

New York University School of Law, 1958. Appointments: Attourney, U S Department of Justice, 1958-65; Assistant, US Attourney, 1965-68; Legal Advisor, General Counsel, Metropolitan Police Department, 1968-69; US Magistrate Judge, Assistant General Counsel, Civil Service Commission, OPM, 1975-80; US Magistrate Judge, 1980-87; Superior Court, DC, 1987-; Adjunct Law Professor, Catholic University, 1997-; Howard University, 1998-. Publications: Author of substantial number of law review and law journal articles. Honours: Phi Beta Kappa; Summa Cum Laude; Attorney General's Sustained Superior Performance Award; US Civil Service Commission's Distinguished Service Award; Director's Award; ABA Judge Edward R Finch Award; FBA Presidents Award; NBA Presidents Award; Ollie Mae Cooper Award; ABA Flashner Award, as Oustanding Special Court Judge, 1985; ABA Judicial Award of Excellence, General Jurisdiction Judge, 1999. Memberships: American Bar Association; Criminal Rules Advisory Committee; Superior Court Library Committee; Many others. Address: Superior Court of District of Columbia, 500 Indiana Avenue NW Room 1020, Washington, DC 20001, USA.

**BURNETTE Clinton Ross**, b. 30 July 1945, Mississippi, USA. Film Producer. Education: High School Diploma, 1964; Studied Photograhy, Westport, Connecticut, USA, qualified with honours in technological photography and cinematography, 1972. Appointments: Forensic Photographer; Established own photographic studio. Publication: How To, articles published in Photographic Society of America journal. Membership: Photographic Society of America, 1972; Associated Photographers International, California, 1975; American Society of Composers and Publishers. Address: Firebird Film and Television Productions, POB 1643 Crows Nest, New South Wales 2065, Australia.

**BURZYNSKI Stanislaw Rajmund**, b. 23 January 1943, Lublin, Poland. Medical Doctor. m. Barbara Burzynski, 1 son 2 daughters. Education: MD, distinction, 1967, PhD, 1968, Medical Academy, Lublin, Poland; ECFMG Certificate, Baylo College of Medicine, Houston, Texas, 1971; Licence, Medicine Texas State Board of Medical Examiners, 1973. Career Research Worker, 1961-62, Teaching Assistant, 1962-67 Intern, Resident, 1967-70, Medical Academy, Lublin, Poland Research Associate, 1970-72, Assistant Professor, 1972-77 Baylor College of Medicine, Houston, Texas; President Burzynski Research Institute Inc. Publications: Numerou articles in professional journals. Honours include: Lady Libert Award, 1997; Gold Medal, American Institute of Polish Culture 1997; Medal, Heart for Hearts, Lublin, Poland, 1997; Memoria Medal of Zamoyski's Lyceum, Lublin, Poland, 1997 Memberships: American Academy of Medical Ethics; America Association for the Advancement of Science; America Association for Cancer Research; American Chemical Societ American Medical Association; Harris County Medical Societ Inter-American Society for Chemotherapy; International Unio of Pure & Applied Chemistry; New York Academy of Science Parenteral Drug Association; Society for Neuroscience; Texa Medical Association; Sigma Xi; World Medical Associatio Address: 20 West Rivercrest Drive, Houston, TX 77042-212 USA.

**BUSTAMANTE Pilar**, b. 22 July 1950, Cadiz, Spai Professor. m. Joaquin Bosque. Education: BS, Pharmac University of Granada, Spain, 1974; PhD, University Granada, Spain, 1979. Appointments: Instructor, University Granada, Spain, 1976-78; Assistant Professor, University Alcala, Spain, 1981-82; Associate Professor, University Alcala, Spain, 1982-84; Professor, Pharmaceutics, Univers of Alcala, Spain, 1984-. Publications: Problem Solving: Physic Pharmacy, co-author with A Martin, 1993; Physical Pharmac contributing editor, 1993; Numerous research papers. Memberships: UNICEF; New York Academy of Sciences; ADFG, Spain. Address: Gotri 30 5D, 28039 Madrid, Spain.

**BUTANI Partab Hassasing,** b. 23 December 1928, Karachi, Pakistan. Animal Activist. m. Kala. Education: BA, History and Economics; MA, History and Economics; BCom; Diploma, Dramatic Arts; Certificate of First Aid. Appointments include: Senior Consumers' Assistant, Bombay Electric Supply and Transport Undertaking (BEST), Bombay, 1949-83; Honorary Animal Welfare Officer, Animal Welfare Board of India; Director, Stray Dog Lovers' Association, Vashi, New Bombay. Publications: Several articles in professional journals. Honours: Several national and international prizes during academic and service career. Memberships include: Blue Cross of Hyderabad; Beauty Without Cruelty; Bombay Natural History Society; American Centre Library, Bombay; Bombay Society for Prevention of Cruelty to Animals; Indian Council of World Affairs, Bombay. Address: 91-1 Mulund Colony, Mulund (West), Bombay 400082, India.

**BUTKIN Vladimir D,** b. 27 June 1928, Obyachevo, Russia. Scientist, Teacher. m. Galina D Chekanova, 1 daughter. Education: BS, Mining Electomechanics, 1950; PhD, Mining Electromechanics, 1980. Appointments: Head of Open Pit, 1950-55; Deputy Director, Director, Scientific Research Institutes, 1955-89; Head of Department, Professor, Higher Educational Institution, 1989-. Publications: 286 Published Scientific Works. Honours: Miner's Glory Medal. Memberships: Russian Technological Academy. Address: c/o Andrey V Brazhnikov, Academy of Non Ferrous Metals, 52 Tolstoy St, Apt 21 Krasnoyarsk 660028, Russia.

**BUTLER Kathleen,** b. 22 September 1963, Berkeley, California, USA. Museum Administrator. m. Michael Steven Shackley. Education: BA, Mills College, 1985; MA, 1987, PhD, 1994, UC, Berkeley. Appointments: Lecturer, UC, Berkeley, 1992; Assistant Registrar, 1993-96, Administrative Coordinator, 1996-98, Assistant Director, 1998-, Phoebe Hearst Museum of Anthropology. Publications: Article, Annals of Tourism Research, 1995. Honours: Dissertation Completion Grant, 1992-93; Humanities Graduate Research Grant, 1990, 1992. Memberships: American Association of Museums; College Art Association; American Studies Association; Association of College and University Museums and Galleries. Address: Phoebe Hearst Museum of Anthropology, 103 Kroeber Hall, University of California, Berkeley, CA 94720-3712, USA.

**BUTNARIU Dan,** b. 1 February 1951, Romania. Mathematician. m. Hadasah, 1 daughter. Education: BA Mathematics, 1974; MA Mathematics, 1975; PhD Mathematics, 1980. Appointments: Assistant, 1975-79; Lecturer, 1979-80; Senior Lecturer, Polytechnic Institute Iasi, Romania, 1980-84; Postdoct, Weitzmann Institute, Rehovat, 1984-86; Senior Lecturer, 1986-89; Associate Professor of Maths, 1990-96; Professor of Maths, University Haifa, Israel, 1997-. Publications: 50 papers; 1 book. Honours: Prize for Young Scientists of Romanian Math Society, 1974; Prize of Balcanic Mathematical Union, 1980. Memberships: Israel Mathematical Union; American Mathematical Society; Society of Industrial & Applied Maths. Address: University of Haifa, Dept of Mathematics, 31905 Haifa, Israel.

**BUTSKHRIKIDZE Garbert,** b. 15 December 1938, Kutaisi, Georgia. Mining Electromechanical and Automation Engineer; Educator. m. Nargiza J Alibegashrili, 2 daughters. Education: BSc, Mining Engineering, Georgian Polytechnic Institute, Tbilisi, 1962; PhD, 1969; DSc, Moscow Mining Institute, 1988. Appointments: Assistant Professor, 1968-79, Dean, 1979-84,

Associate Professor, 1984-89, Georgian Politechnic Institute; Professor, 1989-, Dean, 1989-92, Head of Department, 1992-, Georgian Technical University. Publictions include: Research of Processes Dependendences on the Basic of the Correlation Analysis, 1994; Control Methods of Separation Processes of Manganese Ozes by Density, 1994. Memberships: Georgian Mining Society; Georgian National Peoples Academy. Address: 15 Vaja Pshavela Street, 380060 Tbilisi, Georgia.

**BUTTERFIELD Eric Gaynor,** b. 1 May 1941, Argentina. Senior Partner, International Consulting. m. Ana Vaccaro, 1 son. Education: PhD, Business Administration, Michigan University, USA; MBA, Business Administration, University of Buenos Aries. Career: Senior Partner, International Consulting; President, Organization Development Institute, Buenos Aries; Visiting Professor, Tufts University, USA; Research Fellow, The Fuller American Foundation. Memberships: ODI; ASQC; AQP; AMA; New York Academy of Sciences; ODN. Address: Florida 141 Piso 2, (1005) Buenos Aires, Argentina.

**BUZO Zihni,** b. 25 February 1912, Berat, Albania. Consulting Engineer. m. Elaine Johnson, 2 sons. Education: BSc CE, University of California, Berkeley, 1934; MSc E, Harvard University, Cambridge, 1935. Appointments: Sanitary Engineer, Department of Health, Albania, 1935-39; Design and Construction Engineer, Australia, 1940-46; Environmental Engineering Consultant, Staff Member, WHO, Genevam 1959-74; Engaged in many water development projects. Honours: Order of Australia; Fellow, Honorary Institution of Engineers, Australia. Membership: American Society of Civil Engineers. Address: 30 Dangar Street, Armidale, NSW 2350, Australia.

**BYARS Donna,** b. Rock Island, Illinois, USA. Artist. m. John w Freeman, 1 son. Education: Parsons School of Design, New York City, 2 years. Appointments: Artist-in-Residence, Palisades Interstate Park, New York, 1976; Collage Instructor, New School for Social Research, New York City, 1980; Drawing Instructor, 1980-, Gallery Director, 1984-88, Parsons School of Design; Presenter, National Sculpture Conference, Cincinnati, 1987; Panellist, New York Foundation for the Arts Inc, 1990; Solo shows: 55 Mercer Street, New York City, 1975; AIR Gallery, New York City, 1977, 1979, 1984, 1987; Hudson River Museum, Yonkers, New York, 1989; University of Southern Maine, Portland, 1992; Group shows, 1971-, include: Hudson River Museum; AIR Gallery; Sculpture Center, New York City; Stephens College, Columbia, Missouri; Hillwood Art Gallery, Long Island University, C W Post; New York Feminists Art Institute; Virginia Museum of Fine Arts, Richmond; Max Hutchinson's Sculpture Fields, Kenoza Lake, New York; Fine Arts Museum of Long Island; Parsons School of Design, New York City; Franklin Furnace, New York City; Katonah Museum, New York; Gallery of Contemporary Art, University of Colorado Springs; Scales Fine Art Center, Wake Forest University, Winston-Salem, North Carolina; Spencer Museum of Art, University of Kansas, Laurence; Center for Curatorial Studies, Bard College, Annondale-on-Hudson, New York; Archer M Huntington Art Gallery, College of Fine Arts, University of Texas, Austin; Women Sculptors of the 90s, Snug Harbor; In permanent collections: Museum of Fine Arts, Santa Fe, New Mexico; Chicago Art Institute; VA Museum; Commissions: Wave Hill, Bronx, New York; Long Island University, C W Post; Bard College; Max Hutchinson's Sculpture Fields. Memberships: AIR Gallery, 1979-89; College Art Association. Address: 453 Cooper, Accord, NY 12404, USA.

**BYARS Merlene Hutto,** b. 8 November 1931, West Columbia, South Carolina, USA. Artist; Accountant; Writer. Widow, 4 sons. Education: Student, Palmer College, Midlands

Tech, University South Carolina, 1988-; Diploma in Journalism, International Corr School, 1995; Longridge Writers Group, 1995. Appointments: Accountant, State of South Carolina, 1964-93; Retired, 1993; President, Merlene Hutto Byars Enterprises, Cayce, 1993-; Designer, Collegiate Licensing Company, US Trademark, 1989-; Pub Lintheads, 1986; Olympia-Pacific: The Way It Was 1895-1970, 1981; Did Jesus Drive a Pickup Truck, 1993; The Plantation Era in South Carolina; Producer, Lintheads and Hart Times, play, 1986; Creator, Quilt which hung in South Carolina State Capital for bicentennial celebration, 1988; Designer, Saxe Gotha Twp Flag, 1993; Author: The State of South Carolina Scrap Book, Orangeburg District, 1990; A Scrap Book of South Carolina, Dutch Fork, Saxe Gotha, Lexington County, 1994; The Plantation Era of South Carolina, 1996; Interviewed and exhibited art work at Oxford University, England, 24th International Congress on Arts and Communications, 1997. Honours: Recipient, numerous awards for quilting South Carolina State Fair, 1976-; Certificate for rose research test panel Jackson and Perkins, 1982; Formost Women in Community Award, 1969-70; Cayce Amb Award, City of Cayce, 1994; Fellow, International Biographical Association; Cayce Museum History. Memberships: Life Member, Women's Missionary Society, United Lutheran Church, 1954-; Member, Education Foundation University South Carolina, 1969-98; Member, Thomas Cooper Library Society, University of South Carolina, 1997; Member, The University of South Caroliniana Society, 1997-; Member, Education Think-tank for Retired Faculty and Staff, University of South Carolina, 1998-; Treasurer, Airport HS Booster Club, 1969-76; Secretary, Saxe Gotha Historical Society; Lexington County, 1994-96; National Museum Women in the Arts, 1997-. Address: 1842 Evelyn Street, Cayce, SC, USA.

**BYRON Julie Anne,** b. Sydney, Australia. Author; Photographer. Career: Author. Publications: Amazing Psychic Experiences of the Famous, 1993, Japanese translation, 1995; Many articles published. Address: 6 Lazar Place, Chapman, Canberra, ACT 2611, Australia.

# C

**CABRIJAN Tomislav,** b. 22 October 1934. Educator, Internist, Endocrinologist. m. Ivanka Tusek, 1 son, 1 daughter. Education: MD, University of Zagreb, 1959; Internal Medicine Specialist, University of Zagreb Medical Clinic, 1968; PhD, University of Zagreb, 1975; Full Professor, Internal Medicine, 1987. Appointments: Ward Internist; Endocrinologist, Sisters of Mercy University Hospital, 1968-70; Head of Centre, Diabetes Department, Endocrinology, 1970-90; Head of Department, Endocrinology, Diabetes and Metabolic Diseases, 1990-; Consulting Endocrinologist and Diabetes Expert, Ministry of Science and Technology, 1987-; Acting Director, Sisters of Mercy University Hospital, 1990-. Publications: Obesity ans Apnea Syndrome, 1992; Taking Care of Your Diabetes, 1995; Urgent States in Endocrinology, 1996; Contributor, Articles to Professional Journals. Honours: Fellowship of Alexander Von Humboldt Foundation. Memberships: Croatian Academy of Medical Sciences; German Diabetes Association; European Association for the Study of Diabetes; American Endocrine Society; Croatian Endocrine Society; Roman Catholic. Address: Petrova 110, HR 10 000 Zagreb, Croatia.

**CAI Guang Yu,** b. 27 November 1936, Jiangxi, China. Research Professor. m. Li Lian Zhi, 3 daughters. Education: BTech, Department of Petroleum Refining, China University of Petroleum, Beijing, 1954-58. Appointments: Research Assistant, 1958-78, Research Associate, 1978-84, Associate Professor, 1985-88, Professor, 1989-, Dalian Institute of Chemical Physics, Chinese Academy of Sciences. Publications: Over 90 professional articles in journals and magazines. Honours: 7 times Prize of Academia Sinica, 1983, 1984, 1987, 1988, 1991, 1992, 1996; 2 times Prize of Chinese National Invention, 1964, 1997. Memberships: Committee member, Chinese Active Carbon Association. Address: Dalian Institute of Chemical Physics, Chinese Academy of Sciences, PO Box 110, Dalian 116 023, China.

**CAI Yumin,** b. 16 December 1960, Huiyang, Guangdong, China. Enterprise Administrator,. m. Xiaohong Ye, 1 son. Education: Master of Management Engineering, China Textile University, 1996, Doctor of Textile Engineering, 1998. Appointments: General Manager, Huizhou Trade Development General Corporation, 1989; Director General, Huizhou Textile Enterprise Group Corporation, 1991. Publication: The Strategy of Huizhou Textile Industry Development, 1991. Honours: Prominent Youth of China, 1993; Honorary Citizen, City of Albany, New York, USA, 1998. Memberships: United Associations of Chinese Youth; Association of Chinese Young Enterprisers. Address: Director General, Textile Industry General Corporation, Huizhou, Guangdong 516001, China.

**CAIN Lyle J,** b. 19 November 1957, Halstead, Kansas, USA. Electrical Engineer. m. Karen Sue, 2 sons. Education: BSEE, Kansas State University, 1980; MBA, Manufacturing Operations, University of Missouri, 1988. Appointments: Design Engineer, 1980-81; Equipment Design Engineer, 1981-82; Engineer, 1982-1986; Senior Engineer, 1986-90; Staff Engineer, Allied Signal, 1990-. Address: Allied Signal Inc D/ET2 FC39, 2000 E 95th Street, Kansas City, MO 64131-3095, USA.

**CAIVANO Jose Luis,** b. 26 March 1958, Junin, Buenos Aires, Argentina. Professor; Researcher. m. (1) Marcela Fiorillo, div, 1 daughter, (2) Mabel López. Education: Bachelor, 1977, National College, Junin; National Professor of Music, 1979, National Conservatory, Buenos Aires; Architect, 1984, Buenos Aires University, Argentina. Appointments: Research Fellow, 1986-89, Adjunct Professor, 1988-1993, 1997-, Full Professor, 1993-96, Director, Research Programme, 1997-, Buenos Aires University; Research Associate, Indiana University, 1989, 1994; Research Fellow, 1990-94, Postdoctoral Research Fellow, 1995-97, Adjunct Researcher, 1997-, National Council of Research. Publications: 2 books; 13 articles in journals; 24 articles in proceedings of Congresses; Editor, AREA, research in architecture and design, 1994-, Monograph series, Serie Difusion, 1994-, 4 Congress Proceedings, and anthologies of research by fellow members FADU, UBA, 1994, 1997; Translator 1 book and 1 article. Honours: 5 university grants; Award to the scientific and technological production, Buenos Aires University, 1992, 1993, 1994. Memberships: President, Argentine Colour Group, 1994-2000; Chairman, Study Group of the International Colour Association; Advisory Board, International Society for the Interdisciplinary Study of Symmetry; Member several editorial boards and advisory boards; International Scientific Board, Journal Visio; New York Academy Sciences; International Association for Semiotic Studies; Study Group on Photography of the International Association for Semiotic Studies; International Association for Semiotics of Space; International Association for Visual Semiotics; International Society for Computational Modelling of Creative Processes; and others. Address: Sanabria 2783, 1417 Buenos Aires, Argentina.

**CALAMAR Gloria,** b. 7 September 1921, NYC. Painter; Artist. 3 sons. Education: 3 year certificate, Otis Art Institute, Los Angeles; 2 year studio, Art Student's League of New York; BA Art History, SUNY at New Paltz; Graduate work in Art History and Art Education, SUNY; Tulas W Batik Workshop, Yogyakarta, Java, Indonesia. Appointments: Artist in Residence, Orange County Community College, SUNY, Mount Saint Mary College, Santa Barbara City College; Lecturer 13 art groups; Judge 3 art contests; Over 50 one-artist shows in the USA and other countries, 4 juried shows and 3 invitational shows. Publications: Featured in several biographical books and magazines. Honours: Heritage Club Award for Paintings of Victorian Houses, Santa Barbara Art Association, 1979; National Endowment for the Arts Grant to Individual Artists, 1980-81; Artist Residency Grant, Dorland Mountain Colony, Temecular, 1983; Otis/Parsons' North gallery, Los Angeles, 1989. Memberships: Woodstock Art Association, New York; Charter member, Artists' Equity Association, NY; Life member, Art Students League of New York. Address: PO Box 844, Summerland, CA 93067, USA.

**CALDERÓN-SÁNCHEZ Roberto,** b. 28 July 1930, Carolina, Puerto Rico, USA. Civil Engineer. m. Celeste O'Neill, 2 stepsons. Education: University of Louisville, Speed Scientific School, 1951-52; Louisiana State University, Evening Division, 1955-59; BS, Civil Engineering, University of Puerto Rico at Mayagüez, 1969. Appointments: Civil Engineering, Puerto Rico Highway Authority, 1969-81; Patent Examiner, US Patent Office, Civil Engineering Division, 1981-82; Private Practice, Surveying, Puerto Rico, 1982-85; Supervisor of Surveying, Ports Authority of Puerto Rico, 1985-; President, Scientific Dredging Institute Inc, 1995-. Publication: Report on the damages caused by Hurricane Hugo in 1989 including damage-reduction recommendations, which has been prepared for inclusion in the Historical Archives of Puerto Rico. Memberships: College of Engineers and Surveyors of Puerto Rico; Society of Engineers of Puerto Rico; American Society of Civil Engineers; Elected to Governing Board, College of Engineers, Architects and Surveyors of Puerto Rico, 1970-71, 1972-73; Association of Mechanical Enginees, Puerto Rico. Address: Scientific Dredging Institute Inc, 6 Azucena Street, Santa Maria, San Juan, PR 00927, USA.

**CALHAMER Allan Brian,** b. 7 December 1931, Hinsdale, Illinois, USA. Inventor. m. Hilda Morales, 2 daughters. Education: AB, Harvard, 1953. Appointments: Inventor, Diplomacy Board Game, 1959; Systems Analyst, 1958-65; US Postal Service, 1969-1992. Publications: Significant Factors in the Thirty Six Year Cycles of Presidential Elections, 1996; Arsenal, 1998; On Balance. Honours: Game of the Year, 1976, 1977; Product Hall of Fame, 1993; Hall of Fame, Games. Address: 501 N Stone Ave, La Grange Park, IL 60526 5523, USA.

**CALHOUN Craig,** b. 16 June 1952, Illinois, USA. President, SSRC and Professor of Sociology. m. Pamela F DeLargy, 2 children. Education: BA, University of Southern California, 1972; MA, Columbia University, 1974; MA, Manchester University, 1975; DPhil, Oxford University, 1979. Appointments: Research Associate, Columbia University, 1973-74; Director, Interim Dean, Adjunct Professor, Associate Professor, Professor of Sociology, University of North Carolina, 1977-96; Visiting Research Associate, University of Khartoum, 1983; Visitng Professor, Beijing Foreign Studies University, 1989; Director, Chair, Professor, New York University, 1996-; President, Social Science Research Council, 1999-. Publications: The Question of Class Struggle; Sociology; Neither Gods Nor Emerors: Students and the Struggle for Democracy in China; Critical Social Theory: Culture, History and the Challenge of Difference; Nationalism; Articles and Chapters. Honours: National Merit Scholar; USC Resident Honours Program; USC and Haynes Foundation Scholarships; Manchester University Faculty Scholarship. Address: Department of Sociology, New York University, 269 Mercer Street, New York 10003-6687, USA.

**CALLEJA GUIJARRO Tomas,** b. 31 December 1922, Navares de Ayuso SG, Spain. Writer; Teacher. m. Gregoria Martin, 4 daughters. Education: Arts Diploma; Sociology Diploma. Appointments: Educational Teacher, Ministerial Commission, Planning Pedagogy of General Basic Education. Publications include: La Arqueologia la Historia y la Leyenda en torno a Las Vegas de Pedraza; Era el Arcipreste de Hita Segoviano?; Las Mojadas de Caballar; Aventuras en cuevas, Leyendas de las Pirámides. Honours: National Prize, Childrens Literature; Prize of Poetry; Diploma UNICEF Spain. Memberships: Association of Writers & Artists, Spain; Spanish Friends of Archaeology; Society of Spanish & Medieval Studies. Address: Melilla 12 60 B, 28005 Madrid, Spain.

**CALVER Richard John,** b. 16 December 1955, Australia. International Civil Servant; Author. Education: BSc, University of Western Australia, 1973-76. Appointments: Australian Social Security Department, 1977-80; Australian Foreign Service, 1980-93; United Nations Peacekeeping, former Yugoslavia, 1993-98. Publication: A History of Jensen, 1991. Memberships: Association of Jensen Owners, USA; Jensen Car Club, Australia; Jensen Owners Club, England. Address: UN Headquarters, Box 870, 10001 Zagreb, Croatia.

**CAMACHO Lurdes,** b. 16 April 1959, Olhao. Educational Technologist; Scientific Adviser. m. Joao M Camacho. Education: History Degree, 1982; MSc, Multimedia Educational Communication, 1995; PhD, Educational Communication. Appointments: Teacher, Secondary School, 1983-92; Educational Technologist, Universidade Aberta, 1992-97; Scientific Adviser, Ministry of Culture, 1996-97; Institute of Cinema, Audiovisual, Multimedia; Co-ordinator of Education and Training Department, 1997-; Expert, Media, Information and Communication Technologies and Youth CoE, 1998-. Publications: Memories of a Future Time Virtual Reality and Education; Contributor, Teaching, Learning Information Towards an Open Socratic School Ec; Educational Media International; Several articles in professional journals. Memberships: New York Academy of Sciences; Portuguese Association of Computer Science and Education; Portuguese Association of Computer Science. Address: R 4 de Infantaria #7 2 Frt, 1350-266 Lisbon, Portugal.

**CAMBEL Bohuslav,** b. 29 October 1919, Slovenska Lupča, Slovak Republic. Retired Professor. m. Olga Hrivnakova, 2 sons, 2 daughters. Education: RNDr, 1948; DSc, 1963; DrHC, 1968. Appointments: include: Assistant, 1945-53, Head, Dept of Mineral Resources & Geochemistry, 1952-63, Subdean, 1952-53, Associate Professor, 1953-57, Professor, 1957, Director, Geological Institute, 1958-63, Dean, 1959-61, Faculty of Natural Sciences, Comenius University; Vice Rector, Comenius University, 1953-57; Director, Geological Institute, Slovak Academy of Sciences, 1963-89; Rector, 1966-69, Head, Dept of Geochemistry, 1969-80, Comenius University. Publications include: Geochemistry and Petrology of argillaceous-quartz metamorphic rocks of the Malé Karpaty Mts crystalline complex; Thermodynamics of metamorphic conditions of the West Carpathian crystalline complex; Geochemistry of pyrrhotites and pyrits of various genetic types, 1969; Geochemistry of chaclopyrite, in Acta Geologica, 1974. Honours include: Golden Medal, Slovak Academy of Sciences, 1989; Golden Medal, Czech Academy of Sciences, 1989; State Award. Memberships: Mineralogical Association of Russia; Committee, International Association of Geochemistry & Cosmochemistry, 1968-73; Czech Association on Geology & Mineralogy; Chairman, Mineralogical-Geochemical Section, Carpathian-Balkan Geological Association; Slovak Geological Society. Address: Hummelova 17, 811 03 Bratislava, Slovak Republic.

**CAMERY John William,** b. 5 February 1951, Cincinnati, Ohio, USA. Computer Software Engineer. Education: BA Hons Mathematics, 1972, University of Cincinnati; MS Mathematics, 1974, Carnegie-Mellon University. Appointments: Mathematician, US Army Communications Electronics-Engineering Agency, Washington DC, 1975-83; Computer Specialist, US Army Management Systems Analysis Agency, Washington DC, 1983; Mathematician, Defense Communications Agency, Washington DC, 1983-86; Programmer Analyst, General Sciences Corp, Laurel, Maryland, 1986-87; Software Engineer, Sygnetron Protection Systems, Timonium, Maryland, 1987-88; Consultant, Martin Marietta Ocean Systems Operations, Glen Burnie, Maryland, Automation Consultants Inc, Baltimore, 1988-89; Computer Software Engineer, RDA Logicon, Leavenworth, 1989-. Publications: Co-author, Simulation Techniques for a Multiple CPU Military Communication System, 1976; Pentagon Consolidated Telecommunications Centres System (PCTCS) Video Subsystem Reference Manual, 1982. Honours: University Honour Scholarship, Dean's List, 1968-69; Carnegie-Mellon University Teaching Fellowship, 1972-73; Spot Award for support of the 25ID Ramp-up Exercise, 1995. Memberships: American Mathematical Society, 1974-; Christian Church; Greater Cincinnati Amateur Radio Association; International Platform Association; Republican Party; Societe Mathematique de France. Address: 655 Sheridan Ct, Leavenworth, KS 66048-4449, USA.

**CAMPBELL Alistair Te Ariki,** b. 25 June 1925, Rarotonga. Poet; Novelist. m. (1) Fleur Adcock, (2) Meg Andersen, 3 sons, 2 daughters. Education: BA, 1954, Victoria University of Wellington; Diploma of Teaching, 1954, Wellington Teachers College. Appointments: Editor, New Zealand Dept of Education, 1955-72; Senior Editor, New Zealand Council for Educational Research, 1972-87. Publications: 12 books of verse; Trilogy of novels, 1989-93; Novel, 1998. Honours: New Zealand Book Award for Collected Poems, 1982; Island to Island, memoir, 1984; Pacific Islands Artist Award, 1998; Hon DLitt, Victoria University, 1999. Memberships: President, PEN International, New Zealand Centre, 1977-79. Address: 4B Rawhiti Rd, Pukerua Bay, Wellington, New Zealand.

**CAMPBELL Barbara Ann,** b. 31 July 1959, Seattle, Washington, USA. Podiatrist. m. Allan Dyer, 23 April 1988, divorced 23 December 1997. Education: BS, Pre Med, KSU, 1977-81; Masters Degree Candidate, Nutrition, KSU, 1981-82; DPM, CCPM, 1982-86; Podiatric Surgical Resident, CHMC Phoenix, Arizona, USA, 1986-87. Appointments: Associate Podiatrist, Quinlan Foot and Ankle Center, Scottsdale, Arizona, 1987-95; Private solo practice, Paradise Valley, Arizona, 1995-. Honour: Board Certified in Primary Podiatric Medicine, ABPOPPM, 1994. Memberships: JDF; AF; ACFAOM; ACFAS, 1987-97; APMA; AZPMA; ADA; Rainbow Home Health Advisory Board; Examination Committee, ABPOPPM. Address: Barbara A Campbell DPM Ste C-123, 10575 N Tatum Boulevard, Paradise Valley, AZ 85253, USA.

**CAMPBELL Patricia Barbara,** b. Worcester, MA, USA. Education Researcher. m. Tom R Kibler, 1 daughter. Education: BS, LeMoyne College, 1969; MS, Syracuse University, 1971; PhD, Syracuse University, 1973. Appointments: President, Campbell-Kibler AssociatesDirector of Grants; Director of the Project on Sex and Stereotyping in Education; Tenured Associate Professor of Research. HOnours: Willystine Goodsell Award, 1990; Betty Vetter Award, 1998. Memberships: American Educational Research Association; National Science Foundation; United States Department of Education. Address: Campbell Kibler Associates, Groton Ridge Heights, Groton, MA 01450, USA.

**CAMPOS-CHRISTO Marcelo,** b. 6 June 1929, Belo Horizonte, Brazil. Medical Doctor. m. Magda Lucia Figueiredo, 4 sons, 3 daughters. Education: MD, Federal University Minas-Gerais, 1952; Postgraduate, University Sao Paulo. Appointments: Doctorate, 1956, Assistant Professor, 1958, Associate Professor, 1961, Professor, 1978, Federal University Minas Gerais. Publications: Several articles in professional journals. Memberships: American College of Surgeons; Brazilian College of Surgeons; Brazilian Society of Cardiovascular Surgery; New York Academy of Sciences. Address: Rua Dias Toledo 76, 30380670 Belo Horizonne, Brazil.

**CAMRASS Joan,** b. 27 April 1926, Harrogate, England. Archivist. m. Dr Rex Camrass. Education: MA (Oxon), University of Oxford. Appointments: Head of Geography Dept, Roundhay High School, Leeds, England, 1948-60; Burnie High School, Tasmania, 1960; Ulverstone High School, Tasmania, 1961; National Bahá'í Archives Officer, New Zealand, 1978-. Publications: Australia: Five Geographic Studies, Curriculum Resource Book Series, University BC, 1972; Arohanui - Letters from Shoghi Effendi to New Zealand, 1981. Memberships: FRGS, Fellow of the Royal Geographic Society; Association for Bahá'í Studies, New Zealand. Address: PO Box 51422, Pakuranga, Auckland, New Zealand.

**CAMUNAS Caroline.** Health Volunteer; Associate Professor. Education: Diploma, Kingston Hospital School of Nursing, New York, 1965; BS, Long Island University, Brooklyn, 1975; EdM, 1981, EdD, 1991, Teachers College, Columbia University, New York. Appointments: Staff Nurse, Clinical Research Center, Albany Medical Center, 1965-66; Staff Nurse, Eye Institute, 1966-68; Staff Nurse, 1968-71; Head Nurse, 1971-76, Surgical Metabolism Unit, Senior Supervisor,

General Clinical Research Center, 1976-81, Administrative Nurse, Clinician, Eye, Medicine and Surgery, 1981-83, The Presbyterian Hospital, New York; Visiting Fellow, Joseph and Rose Kennedy Institute of Ethics, Georgetown University, Washington, DC, 1994-95; Adjunct Faculty, Adelphi University, Garden City, New York, 1996, 1997; Associate, Nurses Executives Associates Inc, Washington, DC, 1990-; Adjunct Associate Professor, 1994-97, Associate Professor, Program Coordinator, Nursing Education, 1997-98, Teachers College, Columbia University; Volunteer, Heath Volunteers Overseas, Washington, DC, 1997-. Publications: Numerous papers in professional journals. Honours include: Amanda Silver Distinguished Service Award, New York Counties Registered Nurses Association, 1988; American Journal of Nursing Book of the Year Award, 1991. Memberships include: American Association of Bioethics; American Nurses Association; American Nurses Foundation; American Society for Bioethics and Humanities; American Society of Law, Medicine and Ethics. Address: 309 West 105th Street, New York, NY 10025, USA.

**CANDAN Ercan,** b. 6 March 1967, Turkey. Researcher. m. Sennur, 2 sons. Education: BSc, Gazi University, Turkey, 1988; M Met, Sheffield University, UK, 1994; PhD, 1998. Appointments: Assistant Professor, Zonguldak Karaelmas University, Turkey. Publications: Various Papers, Journals of Materials Science, Scripta Materialia; Key Engineering Materials; 2nd International Advanced Technologies Symposium. Memberships: Institute of Materials. Address: Beyas Apt #16-4, Yenisehir Ergenekon Mah, Karabuk, Turkey.

**CANNON-WILSON Margaret Erickson,** b. 26 May 1923, Marquette, Michigan, USA. Adjunct Professor. m. Dr John Penshing Cannon dec'd, 1 son, 2 daughters. Education: BA, Art Education, University of Americas, Mexico; MA, Art, California University, Fullerton. Appointments: Art History and Art Appreciation, University of the Americas, Mexico, Cypress and Cerritos Colleges, California University, Fullerton; Drawing and Painting, Cerritos, Cypress and Fullerton Colleges, Escula de Artes Activo, Ensenada, Mexico; Life Drawing, Whitier Evening College and California University, Fullerton. Art History, Chapman University; Founding Member, Chicano Art Association. Creative Works: Exhibitions at Laguna Museum of Art; Cerritos College Gallery; California University, Fullerton; University of the Americas, Mexico; La Mirada Festival of Arts, Orange County Art Association; Los Angeles Art Association; University of California, Irvine; San Diego Art Institute. Memberships: C Jung Institute, San Diego; San Diego Art Institute. Address: 1640-65 Maple Drive, Chula Vista, CA 91911, USA.

**CANOVA-DAVIS Eleanor,** b. 18 January 1938, San Francisco, CA, USA. Protein Biochemist, Biotechnology. m. Kenneth Roy Davis, 10 Feb 1957, 2 sons. Education: BS, 1968, MS, 1971, San Francisco State University; PhD, University of California Medical Center, San Francisco, 1977. Appointments include: NIH Postdoctoral Fellow, University of California, Berkeley, 1977-80; Assistant Research Biochemist, University of California Medical Center, SF, 1980-84; Senior Scientist, Liposome Technology, Menlo Park, CA, 1984-85; Senior Scientist, Genentech, 1985-. Publications include: Strategies for an Analytical Examination of Biological Pharmaceuticals, 1990; Isolation of a Cyclic Imide Variant of Human Growth Hormone, 1991; Chemical Heterogeneity as a Result of Hydroxylamine Cleavage of a Recombinant Fusion Protein, 1992. Honours include: Earl C Anthony Trust Award, 1975; Chancellor's Patent Fund Awards, 1976; Travel Allowance Award, 1979. Memberships: American Chemical Society; The Protein Society; American Peptide Society; California

Scholarship Federation, President, 1954-55. Address: 1203 Edgewood Road, Redwood City, CA 94062, USA.

**CANTLIFFE Daniel J,** b. 31 October 1943, New York, New York. Educator. m. Elizabeth Lapetina, 4 daughters. Education: BS, 1965, Delaware Valley College; MS Horticulture, 1967, PhD Plant Physiology, 1969, Purdue University. Appointments: Assistant Professor, Assistant Horticulturist, 1974-76, Associate Professor, Associate Horticulturist, 1976-81, Professor, 1981-, Assistant Chairman, 1983-84, Acting Chairman, 1984-85, Chairman, 1985-, Coordinator of Horticultural Sciences Graduate Programme, 1985-88, 1991-, University Florida, Vegetable Crops Dept, Acting Chairman, Fruit Crop Dept, 1991-92, Professor, Chairman, Horticultural Sciences Dept, 1992-. Publications: Editor, Symposium of the Timing of field production of vegetables, 1987; 1 monograph; 1 bulletin; 12 book chapters; 121 refereed publications; 156 non refereed publications; 192 miscellaneous publications. Honours: Many Awards of Appreciation and Merit; Awards for Best Papers and Research Awards; Citation of Appreciation, in Gratitude for Distinguished Services Rendered to the American Society for Horticultural Science as President 1994-95; Hon membership in the Florida Seed Association, 1996, in recognition for the effort and special assistance provided to the Florida seed, plant, and garden supply industries; United States Dept of Agriculture Group Honour Award for Excellence, 1997; Outstanding Researcher Award, 1997, Career Award from the American Society for Horticultural Science in recognition of distinguished research on horticultural crops or plants; 1997 Seed Science Award from the Crop Science Society of America in recognition of distinctive service to the development and use of quality seeds in agriculture; and many others. Memberships: 12 societies and associations. Address: Horticultural Sciences Dept, PO Box 110690, University of Florida, Gainesville, FL 32611-0690, USA.

**CAO Houde,** b. 5 October 1930, Ningbo, Zhejiang, China. Craftsman and Sculptor. m. Qiu Meirong, 3 sons, 3 daughters. Education: All accomplishments achieved through self study. Appointments: Director of Arts and Crafts, Institute of Ningbo, 1960; Director of Arts and Crafts, Institute for Buddhist Figures of Ningbo, 1982; Vice Director of Arts and Crafts School of Ningbo, 1964; Part work and part study Polytechnological School. Publications: publications up to several hundred pieces works have been display and awarded prizes at major exhibitions at home and abroad. Memberships: Invited Researcher, China Buddhist Culture Institute, 1993; Advanced Member, Arts and Crafts of Society of China, 1991; Council Member, Zhejiang Folk Art Academy, 1988; Vice General Secretary, Poem and Ci Society of Ningbo, 1992. Address: No 401 2 Houying Lane, Ningbo, Zhejiang, China.

**CAO Xiaowen,** b. 21 May 1936, Mengcheng, China. Physics Professor. m. Liu Zhirong, 1 son, 1 daughter. Education: BS, Hefei University of Technology, 1957-61. Appointments: Head Group, Institute of Physics, Academy Sinica, Beijing, 1961-71; Head, Branch of Applied Superconductivity, Xibei Institute of Cryogenic Electronics, 1971-78; Associate Professor, Institute Plasma Physics, Academy Sinica, 1978-1999. Publications: 150 Papers. Memberships: Chinese Institute Physics; Chinese Cryogenic Institute. Address: 10 Science Road, 230031 Hefei, P R China.

**CAO Zheng Kang,** b. 19 February 1940, Hangzhou, China. Engineering Designer. m. Shi Cong, 1 son, 1 daughter. Education: Bachelor Engineering, 1963, HoHai University. Appointments: Worker, 1963, Senior Engineer, 1986, Vice Chief Engineer, 1991, Shanghai Municipal Engineering Design Institute. Honour: China National Golden Award for Excellent

Design, 1994. Memberships: Academic Committee, Shanghai Civil Engineering Association; Director, China Rock & Soil Anchorage Engineering Association. Address: Shanghai Municipal Engineering Design Institute, 3 Guo Kang Road, Shanghai 200092, China.

**CAPLINGER Gregory Earl,** b. 25 March 1953, England. Physician; Scientist; Educator. Education: BA/BS Biology, 1974; MD, Metropolitan Collegiate Institute, 1982; MD, 1982; Postgraduate studies in Internal Medicine, Harvard Medical School, 1986; DSc in Immunology, Sussex College of Technology, 1987. Appointments: Director of Clinical Medicine, International Institute of Medical Science, Santo Domingo, Dominican Republic, 1988-; Director of Immuno-Oncology, International Institutes of Health, 1996-99. Honours: Ambassador General, British West Indies Health Confederation; Current nomination from SGH for Nobel Prize in Medicine, 1999-2000. Memberships: British College of Physicians and Surgeons; International Association of Christian Physicians. Address: International Institute of Medical Science, Centro Ottorino, Avenida 27 de Febrero, Santo Domingo, Dominican Republic.

**CAPPELØRN Niels Jørgen,** b. 11 February 1945, Denmark. Director. Education: Dr hc, St Olaf College, 1996; Master of Divinity, University of Copenhagen, 1977. Appointments: Assistant Lecturer, University of Copenhagen, 1977; Assistant Priest, Holy Ghost Church, 1978-; General Secretary, Danish Bible Society, 1980-93; Director, Royal Orphanage Publishing Company, 1984-93; Director, Søren Kierkegaard Research Centre, 1994-; Examiner, University of Copenhagen and University of Aarhus, 1988-. Publications: Søren Kierkegaards Papirer, Indeks; Bibelsyn; Fra Tekst til Praediken; Word Pictures, Søren Kierkegaards Journals, Notebooks, Booklets, Sheets, Scraps and Slips of Paper; Kierkegaards Dagboger i Udvalg; Søren Kierkegaards Skrifter; Kierkegaard Studies, Yearbook; Kierkegaard Studies, Monograph Series. Memberships: Søren Kierkegaard Society; Union of Danish Publishers; Editorial Committee for the New Translation of the Bible; Danish Bible Society. Address: Store Kannikestraede 15, DK-1169, Copenhagen K, Denmark.

**CARBOGNANI Lante,** b. 16 May 1951, Caracas, Venezuela. Chemist. m. Miren Arambarri, 1 son, 3 daughters. Education: Chemist, 1977, Simon Bolivar University (Caracas). Appointments: Teacher, Simon Bolivar University, 1977-78; Research Chemist, Flavours and Fragrances, Nectaroma, SCS, 1978-80; Research and Management positions, PDVSA-Intevep, 1980-. Publications: 52 in Petroleum Chemistry, 22 in peer reviewed journals 1981-. Honour: Team Member, UNESCO Meritory Achievement Award, Intevep, 1991. Memberships: AAAS; Simon Bolivar University Graduate Association; Venezuela Scientific Association. Address: PDVSA-Intevep, PO Box 76343, 1070A Caracas DF, Venezuela.

**CAREVIC Olga,** b. 9 April 1925, Novi Sad. Professor. m. Kolja. Education: DPH, 1951; DSc, 1961; Docent, 1964; Professor, Scientific Adviser, 1979. Appointments: Professor Emeritus, University of Zagreb; Honours: European Movement, Croatia Award for Humanity; Medal for Scientific Research; Award from Town Zagreb for Democracy. Memberships: JSSX; YUTOX. Address: Palmoticeva 7, Zagreb 10000, Croatia, Russia.

**CAREY Keith,** b. 13 January 1958. Editor. m. Lois Lynn Schuricht, 1 son. Education: BA, honours, History, 1980. Appointment: Managing Editor, Global Prayer Digest. Publication: Global Prayer Digest. Address: USCWM Global

Prayer Digest, 1605 East Elizabeth Street, Pasadena, CA 91104-2721, USA.

**CARLSON Lars A,** b. 14 November 1928, Stockholm, Sweden. Professor of Medicine. m. Anette Asplund, 1 son, 1 daughter. Education: MD, 1956, PhD, 1960, Karolinska Institute, Stockholm. Appointments: Assistant Professor Medicine, 1960-68, Professor Internal Medicine, 1973-93, Karolinska Institute; Professor Geriatrics, Uppsala University, 1968-72; Head, King Gustaf V Research Institute, 1973-93. Publications: 500 scientific international publications. Memberships: President, European Society of Clinical Inv; President, European Athsclerosis Society, 1970-78; FRCP Edin, 1970-. Address: King Gustaf V Research Institute, Karolinska Hospital, S-171 76 Stockholm, Sweden.

**CARLUGEA Zenovie,** b. 28 October 1950, Crusetu-Maiag, Gorj, Romania. Teacher; Writer. m. Zoia Nastasescu, 1 son, 1 daughter. Education: University of Bucharest Faculty of Romanian Literature and Language, Romanian-Latin Section. Appointments: First Degree Professor; Methodic Professor of the Inspectorate Gorj County. Publications: Editor, 7 Romanian publications; Poetry: Happinesses, 1994; Crystal Clouds, 1995; Icy Banks, 1997; Attick in Heliopolis, 1997; Critical Essays: Lucian Blaga's Poetry, 1995; Alexandru Macedonsky: Luring Castle, Essay on the Macedonskian Baroque, 1997; Bpancusi today, 1999; Contributor to professional journals. Honur: Grand Prize for Poetry, Tudor Arhgezi, National Literature, 1994. Memberships: Scientific Secretary, Academic Society Zalmoxis; President, Philologic Science Society Gorj; Ecaterina Teodoroiu High School Principal, Targu-Jiu. Address: Str 11 Iunie, Bl 3, Sc B, Ap 18, 1400 Targu-Jiu, Gorj, Romania.

**CARPINTERI Alberto,** b. 23 December 1952, Bologna, Italy. Professor. Education: PhD, cum laude, Nuclear Engineering, 1976, PhD, cum laude, Mathematics, 1981, University of Bologna, Italy. Appointments: Researcher, Consiglio Nazionale delle Ricerche, Bologna, Italy, 1978-80; Assistant Professor, University of Bologna, 1980-86; Visting Professor, Lehigh University, Bethlehem, USA, 1982-83, Tsinghua University, Beijing, China, 1996, Tongji University, Shanghai, China, 1996, Malaysia Institute of Technology, Johor Bahru, 1997; Professor, Structural Mechanics, 1986-, Director, Department of Structural Engineering, 1989-95, Founding Member, Director, Graduate School in Structural Engineering, 1990-, Politecnico di Torino, Italy. Publications include: Mechanical Damage and Crack Growth in Concrete: Plastic Collapse to Brittle Fracture, 1986; Structural Mechanics: A Unified Approach, 1997. Honours: Robert l'Hermite International Prize, Paris, 1982; JSME Medal, Japan Society of Mechanical Engineers, Tokyo, 1993; Doctor of Physics Honoris Causa, The Constantinian University, USA, 1994; International Cultural Diploma of Honor, American Biographical Institute, 1995; Honorary Professor, Nanjing Architectural and Civil Engineering Institute, China, 1996. Memberships: Réunion Internationale des Laboratoires d'Essais et de Recherches sur les Matériaux et les Constructions; American Society of Civil Engineers; European Structural Integrity Society; European Mechanics Society; New York Academy of Sciences. Address: Chair of Structural Mechanics, Politecnico di Torino, 10129 Torino, Italy.

**CARROLL Howard,** b. 28 July 1942. Attorney. m. Eda Stagman, 2 daughters. Education: Juris Doctor, DePaul University; Bachelor of Science Business Administration, Roosevelt University; Graduate Studies, Urban Studies, Loyola University. Appointments: Attorney, Carroll and Sain, Illinois; Committeeman, 50th Ward Democratic; Treasurer, Democratic Party of Chicago and Cook County; Professor, Complementary Faculty, College of Health Sciences. Publications: Honours:

Recipient of Many Honours and Awards, 1971-. Memberships: Zionist Organization of Chicago; Budlong Woods B'nai B'rith; West Rogers Park B'nai B'rith; Ner Tamid Congregation of Northtown; Northtown Community Council; B'nai B'rith Council of Greater Chicago; Young Adults Division of State of Israel Bonds; Governmental Agencies Division of jewish United Fund. Address: 2929 W Allison Ave, Chicago, IL 60645-4203, USA.

**CARTER George Edward,** b. 16 September 1934, Leominster, MA, USA. Teacher, Professor. m. Betty K Tonsing, 4 sons, 2 daughters. Education: BA, California State University, 1961; MA, 1962; PhD, University of Oregon, 1970. Appointments: Adjunct Professor, Wartburg College, 1996-97; Senior Consultant, Educational Advisory Services International, 1997-; Adjunct Professor, Indiana Purdue University, Fort Wayne, 1997-. Publications: A Review of Slavery. Honours: Fulbright Scholar; National University of Lesotho, Lesotho. Memberships: Midwest African Studies Association; American Association of University Professors; Association for Documentary Editing; American Studies Association; Anti Slavery Society for Protection of Human Rights. Address: 1809 Florida Dr, Fort Wayne, IN 46805, USA.

**CARTER Rosalynn,** b. 18 August 1927, Georgia, USA. Author; Lecturer. m. James Earl Carter Jr, 3 sons, 1 daughter. Education: Graduate, Georgia Southwestern College, 1946. Appointments: Board of Directors, The Friendship Force, 1981-; Board of Advisors, Habitat for Humanity, 1984-; Vice Chair, Board of Trustees, The Carter Center Inc, 1986-; President, Board of Directors, Rosalynn Carter Institute of Georgia Southwestern State University, 1988-; Distinguished Fellow, Emory University Institute for Womens Studies, 1990-; Chair, Carter Center Mental Health Task Force, 1991-; Policy Advisory Board, The Atlanta Project, 1991-; Co-Founder, Every Child By Two Campaign for Early Immunization, 1991-. Publications: First Lady From Plains, 1984; Everything to Gain: Making the Most of the Rest of Your Life, 1987; Helping Yourself Help Others: A Book for Caregivers, 1994; Helping Someone with Mental Illness: A Compassionate Guide for Family, Friends and Caregivers, 1998. Honours include: Numerous honorary degrees; Georgia Woman of the Year Award, 1996; Jefferson Award, American Institute for Public Service, 1996; Lifetime Achievement Award, National Mental Health Association, 1997. Address: 1 Woodland Drive, Plains, GA 31780, USA.

**CARTER Samuel Emmanuel,** b. 31 July 1919, St Andrew, Jamaica, West Indies. Roman Catholic Archbishop. Education: BA, Philosophy, Weston College, Massachusetts, 1950; MA, Philosophy, 1950; STL, 1955; MSW, Social Work, Boston College, 1958; DD, Honorary Doctor of Divinity, 1966. Appointments: Latin Instructor, St Simons College, 1939-41; Civil Servant, Treasury Department, 1941-44; Jesuit Novitiate, Shadowbrook, Lenox, Massachusetts, 1944-; First Vows in Society of Jesus, 1946; Assistant Parish Priest, Master of Ceremonies, Holy Trinity Cathedral Parish, 1958-59; Founder, First Headmaster, Campion College, 1960-64; Rector, St Georges College, 1964; Auxiliary Bishop of Kingston, first native born Roman Catholic Bishop in the English-speaking Caribbean, 1966-70; Archbishop of Kingston, 1970-94. Honours: LLD, Honorary Degree, Doctor of Law, 1970; CD, Commander of the Order of Distinction, 1970; LLD, Honorary Degree, Doctor of Law, 1976; Rale Medalion, 1976; LLD, Honorary Degree, Doctor of Law, 1979; STD, Doctor of Sacred Theology, 1988; LLD, 1988; OJ, Order of Jamaica, 1992; DD, Doctor of Divinity, 1996. Memberships: Education Advisory Council; Ministry of Education; Jamaica Teachers' Association; Jamaica Catholic Educational Association; Jamaica Save the Children Fund; Jamaica Mental Health Association; St

George's College Old Boys' Association; Many other memberships. Address: P O Box 36, 77 Halfway Tree Rd, Kingston 10, Jamaica.

**CASAS Alberto,** b. 31 October 1958, Zaragoza, Spain. Honorary Professor. m. Resurreccion del Pozo. Education: Grad Physics, 1980, University Zaragoza, Spain; PhD Physics, 1985, Universite Autonoma de Madrid, Spain. Appointments: Teaching Assistant, temporal staff, Universite Autonoma Madrid, 1981-86; Flemming Fellow, University of Oxford, UK, 1986-88; Staff Professor, University Santiago, Spain, 1988-90; Fellow CERN, Geneva, Switzerland, 1991-93; Permanent Staff member, Consejo Superior de Investigaciones Cientificas, Madrid, 1990-; Temporary Staff member, University California at Santa Cruz, 1995-96; Scientific Associate, CERN, Geneva, 1998-99; Honorary Professor, Universite Autonoma, Madrid, 1996-97. Publications: Contributor articles to international scientific journals that have collected over 1500 citations; Referee: Zeitschrift Physics, Germany, Physics Letters, The Netherlands, Phys Rev Letters, New York. Membership: Royal Spanish Society of Physics. Address: Av Artesanos 165, 24760 Tres Cantos, Madrid, Spain.

**CASASENT David,** b. 8 December 1942, Washington, DC, USA. Professor. m. Paula, 2 sons, 3 daughters. Education: BS, Electrical Engineering, University of Illinois, 1964; MS, Electrical Engineering, University of Illinois, 1965; PhD, Electrical Engineering, University of Illinois, 1969. Appointments: Technician, Antenna Laboratory, University of Illinois, 1962; Technician, Charged Particles Research Laboratory, 1962; Engineer, Circuit Design, Digital Equipment Corporation, 1963; Teaching Aid, Department of Computer Science, University of Illinois, 1963; Research Assistant, 1964-69; Assistant Professor, Carnegie Mellon University, 1969-74; Associate Professor, 1974-75; Full Professor, 1975-. Publications: 33 Published Books; 48 Editorships; 661 Published Papers. Honours: SPIE President's Award; Many Other Honours. Memberships: Eta Kappa Nu; Fellow, Institute Electrical and Electronic Engineers; Fellow, Optical Society of America; American Institute of Physics; Fellow, past-president, Society of Photo Optical Instrumentation Engineers; New York Academy of Science; President, International Neural Network Society, 1999-. Address: Carnegie Mellon University, Electrical and Computer Engineering Department, Pittsburgh, PA 15213, USA.

**CASTEL Viviane Sabine Etiennette du,** b. 21 March 1965, Luxembourg (Grand Duché). Political Analyst. m. Jean Marc Suel. Education: Lic, Germanic Studies, German Institute, Strasburg, 1989; Graduate, Defence and Strategy, Higher School International Studies, Paris, 1990; Graduate, Diplomacy and International Organisation Administration, University of Paris, 1992; Department of Political Science, University of Nice, France, 1995. Appointments: Stage in analyst EEC, CEE DGIII EG, Brussels, Belgium, 1990-91; SGDN, Paris, 1991-92; Political Analyst, Paris, 1992-; Teacher, Economics Courses Descartes, Paris, 1992-98. Publications: From Königsburg to Kalingrad: Europe in Front of a New Russian Overlands, 1996; Articles to professional journals. Memberships: Institut Français des Relations Internales, Les Fontaines, Group Rencontre. Address: Rue de Mezieres 15, 75006 Paris, France.

**CASTELLANO Carlos Eduardo,** b. 18 October 1947, Tucuman, Argentina. Doctor in Chemistry. m. Nora Gutierrez, 3 sons. Education: Bach, 1965; Licenciado in Chemistry, 1970; Doctor in Chemistry, 1974. Appointments: Researcher, National Institute of Physical Chemistry, Theoretical and Applied, 1970-75; Researcher, ALAR, Aluminio Argentino, 1975-80; Process Engineer, ALAR, 1980-85; Production Superintendent,

1985-90; Maintenance Manager, 1990-92; Production Manager; Operations Manager, 1995-99. Publications: Many different publications in the electrochemical field in different international magazines. Membership: The Minerals, Metals and Materials Society. Address: Aluar Alumino Argentino SAIC, Ruta Provincial, No 4 Parque Industrial, Puerto Madryn 9120, Argentina.

**CASTELNUOVO Daniele Augusto,** b. 29 October 1947, Siena, Italy. Bank Executive. m. Elisabetta Ajo. Education: LLD, Siena, 1971; German, Brussels, 1986. Appointments: Economist, Banca Commerciale Italiana, 1976-80; Senior Associate, Conference Board, Europe, 1981-82; Director General, European Industry Steelworks Association, 1982-83; Bank Executive, Euromobilare, 1986-96, Credito Emiliano, 1996-97, Banca Akros, 1997-; Lecturer, Finance, University of Siena. Publications: Several articles in professional journals. Membership: Royal Society of Arts, London. Address: 24/1 via Tolstoi, 20146 Milan, Italy.

**CASTILLO Diana M,** b. 22 July 1945, Pontiac, Michigan, USA. Religious Organisation Administrator. Education: AA Humanities magna cum laude, 1992, BA English magna cum laude, 1994, University of Cincinnati, Ohio; BA, Rescue College Administration, Denver Rescue Mission, Colorado, 1999. Appointments: Delayed Birth Certificate Clerk, WV State Health Dept, Charleston, 1979-86; Proofreader, Fiecke Web, Cincinnati, 1987, Anderson Publishing Company, Cincinnati, 1987-88, Press Community Papers, Cincinnati, 1987-88, Dixie News, Erlanger, Kentucky, 1989; Word Processing Specialist, University of Cincinnati, 1990-94; Desk Clerk, Grand Canyon National Park Lodges, Arizona, 1996; Supervisor, Sunshine Rescue Mission's Hope Cottages, Flagstaff, Arizona, 1996-98. Publications: Involved in Writing, DTP, Layout and Design for several publications; Newsletter Reporting in Mountain Friends, Flagstaff Christian Fellowship, 1998; Editor and proofreader several newsletters and books; Created Women's Centre Lines, a newsletter for the Women's Centre; Wrote and designed a Christian tract for homeless people; Composed 7 Christian songs. Honours: Presidential Scholarship, WV State College, Institute, WV, 1985; Alpha Sigma Kappa Honour Society, 1992, Golden key National Honour Society, 1993, University Cincinnati. Memberships: Bible Study Fellowship, Port Angeles, Washington; International Platform Association; International Union of Gospel Missions; Aglow Fellowship; Women in Communications Inc; Freelance Editorial Association. Address: 4 S San Francisco Street=330, Flagstaff, AZ 86001, USA.

**CASTRO Francisco Ferreira de,** b. 28 June 1923, Floriano-Piaui, Brazil. Lawyer; Educator. m. Iracema da Costas Silva Castro, 1 son, 2 daughters. Education: BS Economics, 1941, Acad Com, Pe Champagnat, Brazil; LLB, 1948, Minas Gerais Federal University, Belo-Horizonte, Brazil; LLD, 1967, Brasilia University. Appointments: State Rep Legislative Assembly, 1950-54; Vice Governor, Substitute Governor, State Government Piaui, 1954-58; State Lawyer, Teresina, 1960-62; Fed Dep Nat, Congress, Brasilia, Brazil, 1958-62; Adviser Juridical Affairs of Presidency, Federal Government of Brasilia, 1962-64; Professor of Constitutional Law, University of Brasilia, 1962-70; Professor of Political Science, 1963-89; Lawyer, Supreme Tribunal and Superior Federal Appeals Tribunal, Brasilia, 1964-. Publications: The State's Aim: Main Doctrines, 1956; Modernization and Democracy, 1967; Contributor articles to professional journals; Active Historic and Geographic Inst Fed District, Brasilia. Honours: Juridical Medal, Medal of Centenary Clovis Bevilaqua Brazilian Government, 1959; Grand Cross Medal Piaui State Renascenca Merit Order, 1997. Memberships: Former President, Fed Dist Sect, Labour Party,

Brasilia; Brazil Lawyers Order; Planetary Society, Pasadena, USA; Congress Club. Address: SML MI 09, Conj 05 Casa 16, 71540095 Brasilia Distrito Federal, Brazil.

**CEGLEDY Janos,** b. 4 May 1937, Budapest. Musician. m. Chiyoko, 1 son. Education: BA, Victoria University, New Zealand, 1960; LRAM, 1964; LGSM, 1964. Appointments: Guest Professor, Piano Toho Music University, Tokyo, 1968-81; Professor of Piano, 1981-; Guest Lecturer, Musashino Academia Musicae, Tokyo, 1982-; Adjudicator, various national competitions in Japan. Creative works: Composer various piano compositions, 1981, 1986, 1992, 5 Jewish Songs, 1987, Vibrations, 1996, Pieces for double bass, 1997; Concert pianist tours include Australia, New Zealand, Japan, Middle East, Liszt Festival, Washington, 1993, others. Publications: Editor, Beethoven Piano Sonatas, duet Anthologies, 2 vols, Strauss Duets, 2 vols, Debussy Duet, Beethoven Pieces. Honours: DAAD Stipendium West German Government, 1961-63. Memberships: Japan Federation of Musicians; Leschetizky Society of Japan, President 1991-; Grand Lodge Mass.

**CEILLEY Roger,** b. 18 May 1945, Cedar Falls, Iowa, USA. Dermatologist. 2 sons, 1 daughter. Education: BA, 1967, University Northern Iowa; MD, 1971, University of Iowa; Dermatology, 1977, University of Iowa. Appointments: Instructor, 1976-77, Assistant Professor, 1977-79, Assistant Clinical Professor, 1979-, Department of Dermatology, University of Iowa, Iowa City; Fellowship Director, Mohs Micrographic Surgery and Cutaneous Oncology, 1990-; Private Practice, West Des Moines, 1979-. Publications: Author or co-Author, 84 published papers; 17 books or book chapters; 312 exhibits, films, tapes, special presentations, interviews, lectures. Honours: President, American Academy of Dermatology, 1997; President, American Society of Dermatologic Surgery, 1988-89; Chairman, National Coalition for Sun Safety, 1996-; Honorary member, Pacific Dermatological Association, 1991; and others. Memberships: 50 professional affiliations, 30 collegiate, university, university hospitals and national committees. Address: 804 38th Street, West Des Moines, IA 50265-3178, USA.

**CEKOVIC Zivorad,** b. 11 September 1934, Gornji Milanovac, Serbia. Professor. m. Radmile, 2 sons. Education: BS, Chemistry, University of Belgrade, 1960; PhD, Department of Chemistry, University of Belgrade, 1964. Appointments: Instructor, 1967; Assistant Professor, 1970; Associated Professor, 1976; Professor, 1983. Publications: Principals of Organic Synthesis; Experimental Organic Chemistry. Honours: Medal for Science Achievement. Memberships: Serbian Chemistry Society; Serbian Scientific Society; New York Academt of Science. Address: P O Box 158, 11001 Beograd, Yugoslavia.

**CELA Bashkim,** b. 7 April 1952, Tirana, Albania. Engineer. m. Ilira, 2 sons. Education: Petroleum Engineer, 1975, Faculty of Geology & Mines; Diploma, 1983, School of Specialisation into Hydrocarbons, Torino; PhD, 1987. Appointments: Engineer, 1976-80; Lecturer, 1980-84; Vice Dean, Faculty of Geology & Mines, 1985-89; Chief of Drilling Chair, 1988-94; Responsible of Wells Drilling Section, 1994-. Honour: Diploma of Specialisation of Turin Polytechnic, Italy. Membership: Society of Pteroleum Engineers, 1992-. Address: Section of Petroleum Engineering Dept, Faculty of Geology & Mining, Tirana, Albania.

**CELICHOWSKI Jan,** b. 3 August 1960, Poznań, Poland. Neurophysiologist. m. Hanna Celichowska, 2 sons, 1 daughter. Education: MS, University School of Agriculture, 1983; PhD, 1989, Habilitation, 1996, Nencki Institute of Experimental Biology. Appointments: Assistant, 1983-89, Adjunct, 1989-97, Professor, 1997-, University School of Physical Education, Poznán; Director, Poznán-Ille-et-Vilaine Foundation, 1993-. Honours: Awards, Ministry of Physical Culture and Tourism, 1992, 1998. Memberships: Polish Neuroscience Society; Polish Physiological Society; International Brain Research Organization. Address: 9/9 Chełmońskiego Street, 60-754 Poznań, Poland.

**CELLINI William Quirino Jr,** b. 12 March 1951, Ardmore, PA, USA. Electrical Engineer; Systems Engineer. Education: BS, Electrical Engineering, Drexel University, Philadelphia, PA, USA, 1974; MBA, Operations Research, University of Pittsburgh, PA, 1975. Appointments: MSEE Courses/Credits: 11/33 George Washington University, Washington, DC; Professor Registration: PE, Electrical Engineering, VA, USA, 1987. Publications: Contributor, IEEE Standards Board, New York, NY, USA; NFPA, Quincy, MA, USA; AEE, Atlanta, GA and AESAL, Paris, France. Memberships: IEEE; NFPA; SAME; ASEE; WCA; LOCA; USNI; NLUS; AFA; AUSA; AMNH; NGS; NAS; NIAF; PS, SSI; NASS; NTHP; SICS; AFP, OAS. Address: 1303 Delaware Avenue #811, Wilmington, DE 19806, USA.

**CENTURION Oscar,** b. 13 March 1955, Paraguay. Architect. m. Lorraine. Education: Diploma in Architecture, 1980; Diploma in Planning, Edinburgh University, 1983; Certificate, 1996. Appointments: General Director, Cultural Heritage; President, Paraguay National Committee. Honours: COPAPH 95. Memberships: International Council of Museums; CCPC; World Heritage Center of Conservation. Address: A Velazquez 332, Asuncion, Paraguay.

**CEREPNALKOVSKI Ilija,** b. 2 August 1932, Galicnik. Mechanical Engineer. m. Veselinka, 2 daughters. Education: Mechanical Faculty, Belgrade, 1959; PhD, Mechanical Engineering Sciences, Skopje, 1979. Appointments: Heat Plants and Air Conditioning Systems, Textile Industry, 1959-61; Locomotive Maintenance, Railway, 1961-64; Design, Building and Operation of Heat and Power Systems, Steel Plant, 1965-69; University Professor, Refrigeration and Compressors, 1970-. Publications: Over 150 scientific and engineering articles in professional journals. Memberships: International Institute of Refrigeration; Engineering Energy Association of Macedonia; Heat Engineering Association of Macedonia; Heat and Power Institute, University Sv Kiril i Metodij, Mechanical Faculty. Address: Faculty of Mechanical Engineering, Naselba Karpos 2, 91000 Skopje, Macedonia.

**CERIC Emir,** b. 19 April 1944, Bosanska Dubica, Bosnia Hercegovina. Biochemistry. m. Nada Meic, 1 son, Igor. Education: BSc, Chemistry, 1968; MSc, 1976; DSc, 1979. Appointments: Engineer, 1968-71, Assistant Product Manager, 1971-74, Product Manager, 1974-79, Chief Engineer, R&D, 1979-84, Manager, R&D, 1984-94, Project Manager, 1994-, Ina Refinery, Rijeka; Science Assistant, 1978-, Lecturer, 1981-82, University of Technology, Zagreb; Lecturer, Business School, Zagreb, 1992-93; Consultant, Engineering Co, BJ, Zagreb, 1992-96. Publications include: Petroleum Technology, 1984; Technology of Base Oils, 1994. Memberships: Croatian Commission for Fuel & Lubricants; Committee for Petroleum, Croatian Academy of Sciences. Address: F-Candeka 23A, Rijeka 51000, Croatia.

**CEROVSKY Nevenka,** b. 16 November 1958, Zagreb. BScE. m. Davor Cerovsky, 1 daughter. Education: BSc Economics, 1982, Zagreb University. Appointments: Director of Finance Development of Pliva, 1992-93; Finance Director of Pliva, 1993-96; Director of Cosmetics Division of Pliva, 1996-98; President of Neva d.o.o. Pliva Group, 1998-. Honour:

Decorated by President of Croatia for the Achievements in Economy. Membership: Croatian Association of Economists. Address: Neva d.0.0. Pliva Group, Tuskanova 41, 1000 Zagreb, Croatia.

**CERRI Robert,** b. 25 December 1947, Boston, USA. Photographer. Education: BA, Psychology, University of Kentucky, 1976. Appointments: School Teacher, Bocaraton, Palm Beach County School System; Head Psychologist, Open Door, Bocaraton, Florida; President, Robert Cerri Photography & Design; Vice President, Sales and Marketing, ADC Entertainment Inc. Publications: Several photographs in Newsweek, Time Life, Vogue, National Geographic as well as various professional journals and magazines. Memberships: Meeting Professional International; National Trust for Historic Preservation. Address: Robert Cerri Photography, PO Box 801536, Aventura, FL 33280, USA.

**CHAE Chi-Bom,** b. 25 September 1940, Seoul, Korea. Professor. m. Hyo-Sun Bang. Education: BS in Chemistry, Seoul National University, 1963; PhD in Biochemistry, University of North Carolina at Chapel Hill, 1967. Appointments: Professor, University of North Carolina at Chapel Hill, USA, 1970-93; Professor, Pohang University of Science and Technology, Pohang, Korea, 1993-. Memberships: American Society of Biochemistry and Molecular Biology; Korean Society of Biochemistry. Address: Department of Life Sciences, Pohang University of Science and Technology, 790-784 Pohang, Korea.

**CHAIBEDDERA El'Mehdi,** b. 4 February 1953, Mostaganem. Teacher. m. Belajouzi, 7 s. Education: Degree in French. Appointments: Teacher, 25 Years. Honours: Medaille D'Argent Institute Academique; Grand Prix International. Memberships: Academie International. Address: Cite le s160 Logts Bt D3 No 21, 27000 Mostganem, Algeria.

**CHAIBI Mohamed,** b. 28 April 1956, Tazouguart, Errachidia. Naval Military Officer. m. Assif Malika, 2 daughters. Education: BMath, 1976; Deck Officer, 1979; Telecom Engineer, 1988; Diploma Electrons and Heperfrequencies, 1990; DElectrons, 1993. Appointments: Deck Officer; Chief Telecom Officer; Chief Electron Department; Director, Telecom School; Chief, Studies and Planning Officer. Publications: Several articles in professional journals. Honour: Citation a l'ordre de la Nation, 1984. Address: BP 6321, Rabat Institus, Rabat, Morocco.

**CHAKLADER Snehamoy,** b. 22 March 1935, Dacca, Bangladesh. Teacher. m. Mita Chaklader, 1 daughter. Education: BA, 1956, MA, 1958, PhD, 1974, Calcutta University. Appointment: Reader, Political Science, Burdwan University. Publications include: Government & Politics of the People's Republic of China, 1978, 1980, 1984, 1996; Language Problem & Politics in India, 1981; Linguistic Minorities in Indian Federal Process, 1981, 1989; Caste Problem & Politics in India, 1987, 1997; Sociolinguistics - A Guide to Language Problem in India, 1990; Evolution of Socialist Thought, 1991. Memberships: International Sociological Association; Indo-Canadian Association; Indian Political Science Association; West Bengal College & University Association. Address: 10A Old Calcutta Road, P O Rahara 743186, West Bengal, India.

**CHAKRABORTY Tithi,** b. 23 September 1971, Calcutta. Research Scholar. Education: MA Ancient Indian History & Culture, 1995, Calcutta University; Research work on the Terracotta Temples at Bengal and Bangladesh. Appointments: Student Musicologist, Calcutta Museum, Town Hall, Calcutta. Publications: Freelance journalism in Bengali newspapers on Drama, Art, features and others, 1994, 1996, 1997; Article, on Terracotta Rasamanchos of Howrah district. Honour: Financial Grant, CAST, Govt of West Bengal, 1997-98. Membership: Rasehimbanga Itahas Samsad, West Bengal. Address: P 9 Niva Park Extension, Brahmapur, Calcutta 70009, India.

**CHAM Wai Kuen,** b. 20 July 1957, Hong Kong. Professor. Education: BSc, 1979; MSc, 1980; PhD, 1983. Appointments: Professor 1998-. Publications: 24 refereed journal papers; 54 conference papers; 2 patents. Memberships: CEng; MIEE; MHKIE; StMIEEE. Address: Chinese University of Hong Kong, Dept Electronic Engineering, Shatin, Hong Kong, China.

**CHAMBERS Johnnie L Tucker,** b. 28 September 1929, Crocket County, Texas, USA. Teacher. m. Boyd Chambers, 3 sons, 1 daughter. Education: BEd, Sul Ross State University, Alpine, Texas, 1971. Appointments: Teacher, 1st and 2nd Grades, Candelaria Elementary School, Texas, 1971-73; Head Teacher, K-8, Ruidosa Elementary School, Texas, 1973-77; Head Teacher, K-8, Presidio Ind School District, at Candelaria Elementary School, 1977-91, Teacher, 2nd and 3rd Grades, 1991-93, Teacher, Pre-Kindergarten, Kindergarten and 1st Grade, 1993-; Acting Principal, Candelaria Elementary and Junior High, 1995-, Head Teacher, Pre-K to 8th Grades, 1996-97, Teacher, Pre-K, Kindergarten, 1st and 2nd Grades, 1996-97. Honours: Awards, Boy Scouts of America, 1969, 1983; Winner, Litter Glitter Award, 1994-95. Memberships: Texas Teachers Association; Phi Alpha Theta. Address: Number 1 Education Avenue, Candelaria, TX 79843, USA.

**CHAMBERS Raymond John,** b. 16 November 1917, Newcastle, New South Wales, Australia. Professor Emeritus. m. Margaret S Brown, 1 son, 2 daughters. Education: BEc, 1939, DScEcon, 1973, University of Sydney. Appointments: Lecturer, School of Management, Sydney Technical College, 1945-53; Senior Lecturer, Professor of Accounting, University of Sydney, 1953-82; Professor Emeritus, 1983-; Visiting Professor, 1962-85. Publications: Eight books; Five volumes of articles in professional journals. Honours include: AO, (Officer of the Order of Australia), 1978; Gold Medal American Institute of CPA's 1967; Three honourary doctorates; Leverhulme Foundation Fellowship, Waseda University Tokyo, 1971; Alpha Kappa Psi Foundation Award, 1976; Gordon Fellowship, Deakin University, 1989; Inaugural AAANZ Award, Outstanding Contribution to the Accounting Research Literature, 1996. Memberships include: Australian Society of Certified Public Accountants, National President, 1978; American Accounting Association; Accounting Association of Australia and New Zealand; Societa Italiana di Storia della Ragioneria. Address: 18 Amy Street, Blakehurst, NSW 2221, Australia.

**CHAN Chok Wan,** b. 19 August 1945, China. Consultant Paediatrician. m. Catherine, 4 daughters. Education: MB, BS (HK), 1971, University of Hong Kong; M Med (Paediatrics) 1976, University of Singapore; MRCP (UK), 1976, Royal College of Physicians of UK; FRCP (Ireland), 1986, FRCP (London), 1992, Royal College of Physicians of Ireland and London; FHKAM (Paed), 1993, Hong Kong Academy of Medicine; FRCPCH (UK), 1997, Royal College of Paediatrics and Child Health. Appointments: Honorary Lecturer, 1978-97 Honorary Associate Professor, 1997-, University of Hong Kong; Consultant Paediatrician, Hong Kong Sanatorium and Hospital Hennessy Child Health Clinic, both 1981-. Publications: 3 books: Screening All Preschool Children in Hong Kong, 1981 Growth and Development in Hong Kong: State of Asia Children, 1986; 5 articles. Memberships: President, Association of the Paediatric Societies of Southeast Asian Region President, the Federation of Medical Societies of Hong Kong President, Hong Kong Society of Child Neurology and Developmental Paediatrics; Elected Council Member, Hon

Kong Academy of Medicine; Standing Committee Member, International Paediatric Association. Address: Room M10 Floor, Hennessy Centre, 500 Hennessy Road, Causeway, Hong Kong.

**CHAN Fo Kwong,** b. 6 September 1929, Hong Kong. Managing Director. m. Miss Cheng Kwai Ching, 4 sons, 2 daughters. Education: BA, Wellington English College. Appointments: Chan Kwong Kee Emporium, 1947; Managing Director, Chan Kwong Kee Emporium Co Ltd; Founder and Curator, Chan Fo Kwong Museum, 1990-; Director: Pok Oi Hospital, Yuen Long Public Secondary School Board, Yuen Long Merchants Association Kindergarten; Chairman, Hong Kong International Kite Association. Honours: Certificate of Recognition of Services, 1996. Memberships: Honorary Life President, Yuen Long Town Hall; Hong Kong Chan Clan General Association, Yuen Long Br; Hong Kong NT Chung San; Fellow, Countrymen Association: Hong Kong Chinese Martial Arts Association; Hon President, Yuen Long Shap Pat Heung Scouts Association; Secretary, Yuen Long Merchants Association. Address: Hong Kong International Kite Association, No 89 Letter Box Block B, 3F 32-34 Tai Tong Rd, Yuen Long NT, Hong Kong.

**CHAN Ka Ching,** b. 27 January 1965, Hong Kong. Senior Lecturer. m. Miranda Wong, 2 sons. Education: BASc, 1987, MASc, 1989, University Toronto; PhD, 1995, University NSW. Appointments: Lecturer, 1991-97, Senior Lecturer, 1997-, University NSW. Publications: Numerous publications in international journals and conference proceedings. Memberships: CPEng; IEAust; ASME; IIE; SME. Address: 49 Jervis Drive, Illawong, NSW 2234, Australia.

**CHAN Monnie Yuet Hung,** b. 14 July 1966, Hong Kong. Educator; Philanthropist. m. Alan Fai-lun Lam, son. Education: LTCL Pianoforte, 1994; Trinity College of Music, London; MA Education, 1997, London University; PhD Candidate Education, Hull University. Appointments: Author. Publications: Piano Examination - Technique and Further Education, 1993, 1994; 400 Specimen Aural Tests, 1993, 1994; Music Theory, 1994. Memberships: Incorporated Society of Musicians, UK; Founder and Chairperson of Hong Kong Music Educational Members Association; Founder and Chairperson, Schooling Foundation for China; President, Hong Kong Outstanding Teachers Association. Address: Room 612 New Town Tower, No 10-18 Pak Hok Ting Street, Shatin NT, Hong Kong.

**CHAN Paul Kay Sheung,** b. 1 July 1964, Hong Kong. Doctor. Education: MBBS, 1988; MSc, 1994; Dip.LSHTM, 1995; MRCPath, 1997; FHKCPath, 1997; FHKAM, 1998. Appointments: Medical and Health Officer, Government Virus Unit, 1991-96; Assistant Professor, Department of Microbiology, Chinese University of Hong Kong, 1996-. Publications: Several articles in professional medical journals. Memberships: Royal College of Pathologists; Hong Kong College of Pathologists; Hong Kong Academy of Medicine. Address: Chinese University of Hong Kong, Department of Microbiology, Shatin, Hong Kong.

**CHAN Wing Yee,** b. 7 May 1960, Hong Kong. Pathologist. 1 son, 1 daughter. Education: MB BCh, Wales, 1983; Dip Occ Med, Cuhk, 1988; MRC Path, UK, 1995; MIAC, 1996. Appointments: Senior House Office, Geriatric Medicine, Royal Gwent Hospital, 1984; SHO, Geriatric and Chest Medicine, St John's Hospital, London, 1985; Medical Officer, Community Health, Christian Medical Service, 1986-; General Practice, 1987-89; Pathology, Kwong Wah Hospital, Hong Kong, 1990; MO, Prince of Wales Hospital, 1992; SMO, 1996; Associate Professor, A and C Pathology, Chinese University of Hong

Kong, 1997-. Publications: American Journal of Pathology; Human Pathology. Memberships: Royal College of Pathologists, UK; International Academy of Cytologists. Address: Chinese University of Hong Kong, Dept of Anatomy and Cell Pathology, Shatin, Hong Kong, China.

**CHANDA Surajit,** b. 7 April 1970, Calcutta. Painter. Education: Bachelor Visual Arts, 1996; Pursuing Master of Visual Arts. Appointments: Professional Artist. Honour: National Scholarship, Govt of India, 1997-99. Address: F 5 School Rd, PO Sodepur, West Bengal, India.

**CHANDLER Danny Ricardo,** b. 4 April 1962, Columbus, Mississippi, USA. Business Systems Analyst. m. Reta C Boone, 1 son. Education: BA, Mathematics, 1984; AA, Business Administration, 1989; Emergency Medical Technician, 1990. Appointments: South Central Conference Executive Committee; Madison Parks and Recreation Committee; Madison Chamber of Commerce; Founder, Mississippi FOCUS. Publication: Contribution to Message Magazine. Honour: C E Mosely Pioneer Service Award. Membership: Mississippi Academy of Sciences. Address: 505 McLaurin Street, Madison, MS 39110-8613, USA.

**CHANDRA Prakash,** b. 16 October 1936, Calcutta, India, arrived in Germany, 1960. m. Angelika Chandra, 3 children. Education: BS, University of Delhi, 1956; MSc, University of Nagpur, 1958; Drphilnat, University of Frankfurt, 1965; Dr med habil, 1971. Appointments: Research Assistant, University of California, Berkeley, 1958-60; Research Associate, University of Hamburg, Germany, 1960-63; Research Associate, Lecturer, Professor, University of Frankfurt, Germany, 1971-73; Professor, Head of Department, University of Frankfurt, 1973-; Director, NATO-ASI, Corfu, Greece, 1978, 1981; Maratea, Italy, 1985. Publications: Methods of Molecular Biology, 1973; Over 200 articles to professional journals. Honours: Leukemia Prize, German Society of Pediatrics Oncology, 1978; Semmelweis Medal, University of Budapest, 1980; University Medal of Tel Aviv University, 1986; Memberships: Fellow, Royal Society Chemistry, London; New York Academy of Sciences. Address: Breitlacher St 45A, D 60489, Frankfurt, Germany.

**CHANDRAN Sathish,** b. 28 March 1962, Kuala Lumpur, Malaysia. Network Technology Manager. m. Priya Sarada, 1 son, 1 daughter. Education: BTech Electronics and Communications Engineering, 1984, University of Kerala, India; MSc, Radio Frequency Communications Engineering, 1989, University of Bradford, England; PhD, Antennas and Microwave Engineering, 1993, Loughborough University, England. Appointments: Lecturer, Communications Engineering, Federal College of Technology, Malaysia, 1985-86, 1988; Testing, Planning and Commissioning Engineer, Standard Elektrik Lorenz AG, Malaysia, 1987-88; Science and Engineering Research Council, UK, Sponsored Research Assistant, Dept Electronics and Electrical Engineering, Loughborough University of Technology, 1989-91, 1991-93; Engineering and Physical Research Council, UK, Sponsored Senior Research Associate, Dept Electrical and Electronic Engineering, University of Nottingham, 1994-96; Senior Radio Networking and Designing Engineer, Perwira Ericsson, Malaysia, 1996-; Network Technology Manager, Radio Network Planning and Transmission Network Planning, American Standards Division, Ericsson, Malaysia, 1998-; President, Founder, International Union of Radio Science, Malaysia; Chairman, Founder, Institute of Electrical and Electronics Engineering, Antennae and Propagatus Chapter, Malaysia. Publications: 13 journal papers; 15 conference papers. Honour: Ivar Ahlgren Research Award, Ericsson Radio Systems, Sweden. Memberships: Fellow, Royal Society of Arts, Commerce & Manufacture, UK; Fellow, Remote

Sensing Society, UK; Senior Member, IEEE, USA; IEE, UK; Royal Society of New Zealand; Sigma Xi, Scientific Research Society; MENSA; Institution of Engineers, Malaysia; Chartered Engineer, Engineering Council, UK. Address: No 32 Jalan S G 6/8, Sri Gombak, 68100 Batu Caves, Selangor, Malaysia.

**CHANDY Kumblankal Thomas,** b. 8 February 1946, Kerala, India. Agronomist. Education: Philosophy, Sacred Heart College, Kodaikanal; BSc, GB Pant University of Agriculture and Technology, 1973-76; Theology, D'Nobili College, Pune, 1976-80; MSc, Agronomy, GB Pant University of Agriculture and Technology, 1980-82. Appointments: Farm Manager, D'Nobili College, Pune, 1976-80; Research Officer, Research Department, Indian Social Institute, 1982-84; Director, Vocational Courses in Agriculture & Animal Husbandry, St Josephs College, Jakhama, 1984-87; Teacher, St Josephs College, 1984-87; Preparer, Department of Agricultural Education, Indian Social Institute, New Delhi, 1987-88; Director, Department of Agricultural Education, Indian Social Institute, 1988-98; Agriculture trainer recognised by GUT of India; Evolved 45 rural and agricultural technologies; Senior Fellow, Department of Agricultural Education, 1998-. Publications include: Paddy Production, 1987; Rabbit Rearing, 1987; Matching Poverty Alleviation with Sustainable Land Use, 1993; Evaluation Report, 1995; Written and edited 600 booklets in English on Agriculture, Animal Husbandry, Environment, Natural Resource Management; Edited 300 booklets in Hindi. Memberships: Indian Society of Agronomy; Indian Society of Tuber Crops. Address: Indian Social Institute, 10 Institutional Area, Lodhi Road, New Delhi 110 003, India.

**CHANG Anne Bernadette,** b. 24 August 1963, Malaysia. Medical Consultant. Education: MBBS, 1988; FRACP, 1995; PhD, 1998. Appointments: Intern, 1990; Registrar, 1991-94; Fellow, 1995-97; Consultant, Respiratory Paediatrics, 1997. Publications; Many publications in Thorax, Archives Disease, International journals. Honours: St Vincents Hospital Award; NHMRC Scholarship; Queen's College Exhibitionist. Memberships: RACP; TSANZ. Address: Department of Respiratory Medicine, Mater Misericordiae Children's Hospital, South Brisbane, Queensland 4101, Australia.

**CHANG Fakuan,** b. 27 October 1924, Ying Shang County, Anhui Province, China. Professor of Classical Literature. m. Wnag Xiu Chun, 2 sons, 1 daughter. Education: Professor, Beijing Education College, 1978; Professor, East Japanese Finance University, 1987; Director, China Rhizome Art Society, 1993. Memberships: Beijing Poems Socity; Xiang Shan Poems Society. Address: 24-1-501 Zhi Chun Li, Shuang Yu Shu Street, Beijing 100086, China.

**CHANG Fook-Hoe,** b. 5 October 1945, Johore, Malaysia. Research Scientist. m. Kee Chang, 2 sons. Education: BSc, 1972; PhD, 1978. Appointments: Tutor, Victoria University of Wellington, 1974-79; Scientist, New Zealand Oceanographic Institute, 1979-92; Scientist, National Institute of Water and Atmospheric Research Limited, 1992-. Publications: Contributions to Professional Journals and Books. Honours: DSIR Study Award, 1984-85; DSIR Travel Award, 1984. Memberships: New Zealand Marina Sciences Society; Royal Society of New Zealand. Address: National Institute of Water and Atmospheric Research Limited, 301 Evans Bay Parade 14-901, Kilbirne, Wellington, New Zealand.

**CHANG H K,** b. 9 July 1940, Shenyang, China. President; University Professor. Min-min Chou, 1 son, 1 daughter. Education: BS, Civil Engineering, National Taiwan University, 1962; MS, Structural Engineering, Stanford University, 1964; PhD, Fluid Mechanics, Biomedical Engineering, Northwestern

University, 1969. Appointments include: Assistant Professor, Associate Professor, 1969-76, State University of New York, Buffalo; Associate Professor, 1976-80, Professor, Biomedical Engineering, Physiology, and Adjunct Professor, Chemical Engineering, 1980-84, McGill University, Montreal; Visiting Professor, Université Paris-Val de Marne, 1981-82; Professor, Biomedical Engineering, Physiology, Biophysics, 1984-90, Department Chair, 1985-90, University of Southern California, Los Angeles; Founding Dean, School of Engineering, Professor, Chemical Engineering, Hong Kong University of Science and Technology, 1990-94; Dean, School of Engineering, Director, Pittsburgh Bioengineering Institute, Professor, Chemical Engineering, Medicine, University of Pittsburgh, 1994-96; President, University Professor, City University of Hong Kong, 1996-. Publications: Over 100 scientific articles; Author, 2 books; 1 Canadian patent. Honours: Honorary Professor, Peking Union Medical College, Chinese Academy of Medical Sciences, 1987-, Northeastern University, 1998-. Memberships: American Institute of Chemical Engineers; American Physiological Society; Founding Fellow, American Institute of Medical and Biological Engineering; Fellow: Hong Kong Academy of Engineering Sciences; Hong Kong Institution of Engineers; Senior Member: American Society of Civil Engineers; Biomedical Engineering Society. Address: Office of the President, City University of Hong Kong, 83 Tat Chee Avenue, Kowloon Tong, Hong Kong.

**CHANG Huo-Shan,** b. 18 December 1928, Taiwan, China. Chairman Telecommunications Company. Education: BS, National Cheng Kong University, 1951. Appointments: Chairman, TECOM Co Ltd; Chairman, BayCom Opto Co Ltd. Publication: Successful Business Management, 1995. Honour: National Award of Excellence Winners. Membership: Rotary Club of Taipei Southeast. Address: No 23, R&D Road 2, Science-Based Industrial Park, Hsin-Chu, Taiwan, China.

**CHANG Kun-Hsiung,** b. 14 October 1936, Taiwan. Professor; Researcher; Director. m. Hwang Su-Zen, 2 daughters. Education: BS, 1960, National Taiwan University; MS, 1962-64, PhD, 1964-68, University of Tokyo, Japan. Appointments: Dean, College of Science, 1985-86, College of Marine Science, 1986-89, National Sun-Yat-Sen University; Associate Professor and Professor, National Taiwan University, 1968-93; Researcher and Director, Institute Zoology, Academia Sinica, 1968-96; Director, Science Division, Science Attache, Taipei Economic and Cultural Representative Office in Japan, 1993-. Publications: Over 100 fishery-zoological and ecological research reports in refereed papers, conference papers and other publications. Honours: Award of Golden Hand, the 10 Most Excellent Outstanding Youth of Country, 1973; Film Academy Award for film of oceanographic science, 1978; Award of Golden Horse (Documentary film), Taiwan, 1981; Outstanding Scientist Award of the Country, Taiwan, 1983; Distinction in Research of Biological Science, Taiwan, 1984. Memberships: Chinese Biological Society, Society of Streams, Taiwan; Ichthyological Society of Japan. Address: Science Division TECROJ, 5-20-2 Sirokanedai Minato-ku, Tokyo 108-0071, Japan.

**CHANG Naikwang Luke,** b. 28 November 1928, Zhejiang, China. Professor; Acupuncturist. 1 son, 2 daughters. Education: MD, National Jiangsu Medical School, 1956. Appointments: Chairman, Surgical Department, Yangzhou No 1 Municipal Peoples Hospital; Professor of Anatomical Department, San Francisco California University; Professor, Medical University of South Carolina, Charleston, USA. Honours: President, New York Chinese Medical Centre. Memberships: American Association of Clinical Anatomists and American Society of Acupucturists. Address: New York Chinese Medical Centre,

58-05 Hollis Court Blvd, Fresh Meadows, NY 11365-1731, USA.

**CHANG Ni-Bin,** b. 21 April 1960, Taipei, Taiwan. Professor. m. Wen-Ling Huang. Education: BS, Civil Engineering, National Chiao-Tung University, China, 1983; MS, Environmental Systems Engineering, Cornell University, 1989; PhD, Environmental Systems Engineering, 1991. Appointments: Environmental Technician, Bureau of Environmental Protection, 1985-86; Environmental Engineer, Department of Environmental Engineering, Housing and Urban Development Bureau, 1986-87; Deputy Manager, Ecology and Environment Inc, 1991-92; Deputy Manager, Division of Environmental Engineering, Fichtner Pacific Engineers Inc, 1992; Associate Professor, Department of Environmental Engineering, National Cheng Kung University, 1992-97; Professor, 1997-. Publications: Many Publications. Honours: Rank 1 Advanced National Exam of Environmental Engineering; Rank 1 National Exam of Professional Engineering; Rank 3 General National Exam of Environmental Engineering; Rank 2; Russell Ackoff Award; Class A Research Award, 1994, 1995, 1996; Outstanding Research Award; Best Research Award. Memberships: New York Academy of Science; American Society of Mechanical Engineers; International Air and Waste Management Association; International Solid Waste Association; American Water Resource Association; American Society of Civil Engineers; American Association for Advancement of Science; Chinese Society of Civil and Hydraulic Engineering; Many other memberships. Address: National Cheng Kung University, Department of Envioronmental Engineering, Tainan, Taiwan.

**CHANG Shi Chuan,** b. 16 October 1954, Ping Tung. Chest Physician. m. Jung Shu Lin, 2 sons. Education: MD, China Medical College, 1980; PhD, National Yang Ming Medical College, 1990. Appointments: Attending Physician, Chest Department, Veterans General Hospital, Taipei; Professor, Department of Medicine, School of Medicine, National Yang Ming University. Publications: Many Publications. Honours: Research Award, Taiwan Medical Foundation; The Best Researcher, Veterans General Hospital; The Best Teacher, Veterans General Hospital; Research Award, National Science Council. Memberships: American College of Chest Physicians; American Thoracic Society; Journal of Internal Medicine; Chinese Medical Jounral; Thoracic Medicine. Address: Vets Gen Hosp Chest Dept, No 201 Sect 2 Shih Pai Rd, Taipei, Taiwan 11217, Republic of China.

**CHANG Wan-hsi,** b. 6 June 1920, Kiukiang, Kiangsi Province, China. Professor. m. Tsung Li-chung, 2 sons, 3 daughters. Education: Graduate, 1939, Dept Politics, Military Academy. Appointments: General Editor, General Manager, Kung Li Pao, 1943-44; Staff, Secretary of the Commander in Chief, Office of Navy General Headquarters, 1949-53; Deputy Station Chief of Military Broadcasting Networks, Tsoying, 1953-56; Chief of Morgue of Military Newsagency of Ministry of National Defense, 1959-60; Senior Officer of Secretariat of National Assembly, 1967-74; Selected Rank Compiler of Secretariat of National Assembly, 1974-81; Director of Library of National Assembly, 1981-; Associated Professor of Soochow University, 1961-90; Visiting Professor of Chinese Literature Institute, Canton College, Hong Kong, 1991-98. Publications: Over 50 books of poems, novels, novelettes, short stories, prose, theory and collections of works. Honours: Hon D Litt, MGSIUF, USA, 1988, WU, USA, 1989; Hon D H, AEIAF, USA, 1990; Wide range of honours at home and abroad including: Golden Tripod Prize, Government Information Office of China and Chia Hsin Literature Foundation, 1991; Mo Jen's (pen name) Special Room was opened in Wuhan, China, 1993 to

display all his publications; Honorary doctorates in literature and humanities from International University Foundation, Albert Einstein International Academy Foundation and World University Roundtable. Address: 14 Alley 7, Lane 502, Chung Ho Street, Peitou, Taipei, Taiwan.

**CHANG Yih,** b. 12 July 1958, Tainan, Taiwan. Engineering Consultant. m. Kui-Hsiang Lij, 1 son, daughter. Education: BS, Chung Cheng Institute of Technology, 1976-80; MS, Chiao Tung University, 1982-84; PhD, Stanford University, 1988-91. Appointments: Consultant, Chung Sheng Institute of Science and Engineering, 1992; Supervisor, Department of Health, The Executive Yuan, 1993; Supervisor, Automotive Research and Testing Center, 1994; Professor, Chung Cheng Institute of Technology, 1996-98; Consultant, President Officer, RiTEK Co, 1998; Director, Flat Panel Display Division, 1999. Publications: IEEE Photonics Technology; J Material Processing Technology; Applied Physics Letters; Zeitschrift fur Metallkunde; Journal of Polymer Science; Mettallurgical and Materials Transaction; Crystal Resaerch Technology; Many other publications. Honours: 2nd Class Graduate Award; 1st Class Graduate Award; Research Award; Best Teaching Award. Memberships: IEEE; TMS; ASM International; American Association for the Advancement of Science; Abrasive Machining Society; Chinese Society of Defence Science and Technology; Chinese Crystal Growth Society; Chinese Society of Mechanical Engineers; Many other memberships. Address: 14F, No1, Jung Jeng Road, Chung Ho City 135, Taiwan.

**CHAO Tzu-Chieh,** b. 3 September 1953, Taichung, Taiwan. Surgeon, Researcher. m. I-Shiu Chen, 2 sons. Education: MD, China Medical College, 1979; MS, University of Illinois at Chicago, 1989; PhD, University of Illinois at Chicago, 1993. Appointments: Resident in Surgery, Chang Gung Memorial Hospital, 1981-85; Fellow, General Surgery, Chang Gung Memorial Hospital, 1985-86; Attending Surgeon in General Surgery, 1986-; Research Associate, University of Illinois College of Medicine, 1989-92; Lecturer, Chang Gung University, College of Medicine, 1993; Associate Professor, Surgery, Chang Gung University, College of Medicine, 1993-. Honours: Biomedical Research Scholarship, Chang Gung Memorial Hospital, 1987-92; Eleanor B Pillsbury Scholarship, University of Illinois Hospital, 1990-92. Memberships: Collegium Internationale Chirurgiae Digestivae; The Society for Leukocyte Biology; The Society for Experimental Biology and Medicine. Address: 12th Fl 406 Chang Gung Med Village, Taoyuan 33333, Taiwan.

**CHARTERIS Richard,** b. 24 June 1948, Chatham Islands, New Zealand. Musicologist; Writer; Editor. Education: BA, Victoria University, Wellington, New Zealand, 1970; MA with 1st Class hons, University of Canterbury, 1972; PhD, 1976, Universities of Canterbury and London. Career: Rothmans Research Fellowship, University of Sydney, 1976-78; Research Fellowship, University of Queensland, 1979-80; Australian Research Council Chief Investigator, Music Department, University of Sydney, 1981-90; Australian Research Council Senior Research Fellow (Reader), Music Department, University of Sydney, 1991-94; Professor in Historical Musicology and Australian Research Council Senior Research Fellow, Music Department, University of Sydney, 1995-. Publications include: Author of over 100 books and editions devoted to the music of Johann Christian Bach, John Coprario, Alfonso Ferrabosco the Elder, Domenico Maria Ferrabosco, Giovanni Gabrieli, Adam Gumpelzhaimer, Hans Leo Hassler, Thomas Lupo, Claudio Monteverdi and others, and mostly in the series Corpus Mensurabilis Musicae, Musica Britannica, Recent Researches in the Music of the Baroque Era, Boethius Editions, Fretwork Editions, King's Music Editions, Baroque

Music Series; and books on composers, music and early sources in the series Boethius Editions, Thematic Catalogues Series, Musicological Studies and Documents and Altro Polo. Contributions to: Numerous journals and magazines; Music Letters; Early Music; Royal Musical Association Research Chronicle; Musica Disciplina; Chelys; The Galpin Society Journal; MLA Notes; The Huntington Library Quarterly; Studies in Music.. Honours: Fellow, Australian Academy of the Humanities, 1990. Address: Music Department, University of Sydney, NSW 2006, Australia.

**CHASE Steven Reginald,** b. 16 November 1956, Montreal, Canada. Film Director. m. Kim Chase, 1 daughter. Education: School of Graphic Design, Dawson College. Honours: Over 400 International Film Awards. Membership: Directors Guild of America. Address: Reactor Films, 1330 4th Street, Santa Monica, CA 90401, USA.

**CHATTERJEE Tapas Kumar,** b. 9 June 1956, Calcutta, India. Physiotherapist. m. Joyce. Education: MCom, Calcutta University, 1980; Yoga Therapy and Yoga for Health, University Jadavpur, 1981. Career: Private Practice, 1982-. Publications: Rog Sarata Yoga; Yoga-Deep; Bayam O Yoga-Asana; Ashud Theke Pathya Boro; Barama Bayam; Basta Loker Sustha Sarir. Address: 130/1A Bidhan Sarani, Calcutta 700004, West Bengal, India.

**CHATTERJI Susanta,** b. 1 February 1931, Rajdia, India. Chemist. 1 daughter. Education: BSc Chemistry Hons, 1950, MSc Applied Chemistry, 1952, D Phil, Applied Chemistry, 1958, Calcutta University. Appointments: National Research Fellow, Government of India, 1958; Research Fellow, Swedish Institute, 1959-61; Research Fellow, 1962-67, Lecturer, 1967-71, Birkbeck College, University of London; H & H Industri A/S, Denmark, 1972-79; Teknologisk Institut, Denmark, 1980-82, 1983-90. 1991-92; TOCTEN invitee 1982 to India (UNDP); Director, Tech Service, MAC spa Modern Advanced Concrete, Treviso, Italy, 1982; Professor of Civil Engineering, Kanazawa University, Japan, 1990-91; Freelance Consultant, 1994-. Publications: Over 200 papers in different journals. Honours: National Research Fellow, India, 1958; Fellowship of the Swedish Institute, 1959-61; Research Fellow, DSIR, UK, 1962-67; Grantee, DSIR, Denmark, 1973-89. Membership: New Yord Academy of Science, USA. Address: Carl Bernhardsvej 13B St 4, 1817 Frederiksberg C, Denmark.

**CHATTOPADHYAY Ajit Kumar,** b. 29 February 1936, West Bengal, India. Electrical Engineering Teacher; Researcher. m. Sumitra, 1 son, 1 daughter. Education: BE, Calcutta University, 1958; M Tech, IIT, 1963; PhD, UMIST, 1971. Appointments: Lecturer, KG Engg Institute, Bankura, 1959-60; Associate Lecturer, 1960-62, Lecturer, 1962-68, Assistant Professor, 1968-86, Indian Institute of Technology, Kharagpur; Professor, 1976-96, Head, 1992-95, Indian Institute of Technology; AICTE Emeritus Fellow, BE College, Howrah, 1996-. Publications: More than 100 in the Field of Power Electronics and Drives in International Journals and Conference Records. Honours: Bimal Bose Award, 1986; Bharatia Cutler Hammer Prize, 1986; Tata Rao Prize, 1993; IEEE Fellow Award, 1991; Man of the Year, 1998. Memberships: National Academy of Engineering; The Institute of Electrical and Electronics Engineers, USA; Institution of Engineers; Institution of Electronics and Telecommunications; Indian Society of Technical Education. Address: Flat 3B, 48/1 Laxmi Narayan Tala Road, Howrah 711 103, India.

**CHATTOPADHYAYA Rajagopal,** b. 20 November 1957, Calcutta, India. Biochemist; Religious Historian. m. Moushumi, 2 sons. Education: MS Chemistry, 1980, I.I.T. Kanpur; PhD,

1987, UCLA; Postdoctoral positions, 1988-90, University of California at Berkeley, 1990-93, Baylor College of Medicine. Appointments: Lecturer in Biochemistry, 1993-96, Senior Lecturer in Biochemistry, 1996-, Bose Institute, Calcutta. Publications: Swami Vivekananda in the West, 1994; World's Parliament of Religions, 1893, 1995; Swami Vivekananda in India, 1998. Honours: Scientific work from Bose Institute cited among the four most significant advances in Physics in the Britannica Book of the Year, 1996. Address: Bose Institute, P 1/12 Cit Scheme VII M, Calcutta 700054, India.

**CHATTY Mousallam Maher,** b. 17 April 1955, Damascus. Information Technology Director. m. Lina Chorbaji. Education: BSc, Mathematics, Physics, 1981. Appointments: Software Design Manager, 1984-87, Project Manager, 1987-90, Sakhr/Al-Alamiah Kuwait; Information Technology Director, Al-Yousuf Dubai, 1991-. Publications: Contributor of several articles in professional journals. Memberships: IEEE; Europe and Middle East Oracle User Group. Address: Yousuf Habib Al-Yousuf, PO Box 25, Creek Road, Binyas Street, Dubai, United Arab Emirates.

**CHATURVEDI Mahashweta,** b. 2 February 1950, Etawah UP, India. Reader. m. U K Chaturvedi, 2 sons, 1 daughter. Education: MA English, 1966, Sanskrit, 1969, Hindi, 1978; Dip Jourl Sm, 1980; Sangeet Prabhaker, 1983; Sahityacharya, 1984; PhD, 1984; D Litt, 1991; LLB, 1993. Appointments: From Lecturer to Reader, 1984-, RPPG College, Meerganj, Bareilly, India. Publications: 20 books in Hindi, including stories, yajureda Rahasya, 1982; Jyoti Kalash, 1982; Apamanu Pariksha, 1992; Epic poetry, Viveka Vijay, 1997; 8 English poetry collections including: Voice of Agony, 1985; Throbbing Lyre, 1995; Way of Melody, 1997; Back to the Vedas, forthcoming. Honours: Viveka Award, 1990; Ambedker Fellowship, 1994; Sahitya Bharti, 1994; Michael Madhusudan Award, 1995; Subhadra K C Gold Medal, 1995; Gold Medal USA, 1996; Rotaract Ratna, 1996; Shashi Mani Award, 1997; Writer Award, 1998. Address: Professor Colony, Bareilly College Campus, Shyamganj Bareilly 243 005, India.

**CHATZIGIANNI Emmy B,** b. 1 January 1960, Athens, Greece. Histiopathologist. m. Fotis Chimonas. Education: Graduate, Medical School of Athens, 1986; Specialized in Pathology, 1990. Appointments: Head of Research Medical Immune Center, 1st Surgical Department of Athens; Head of Resaerch Programs, Department of Anestesiology, University of Athens; Teacher, 4th and 6th Year, Medical School in Immunohistochemistry; Pathology Department, 3rd Hospital of IKA of Athens. Publications: 18 Medical Papers, International Congress; 48 Papers, Greece; 15 Papers, International Medical Journals; 26 Papers, Greek Medical Journals. Memberships: Cell Stress and Chaperones. Address: 17 Sp Dariotou str, GR 145 61 Kifissia, Athens, Greece.

**CHAUDHRY Abduljabbar Iqbal,** b. 2 February 1951, Toba Tek Singh, Pakistan. Histotechnologist. Education: BS, MT, 1978. Appointments: Senior Medical Technologist, Main Trust Hospital, Faisalabad, Pakistan, 1982-85; Senior Medical Technologist, Central Hospital Al-Kufra, Lybia, 1986-87; Senior Histotechnologist, King Abdulaziz University Hospital, Jeddah, Saudi Arabia, 1987-99; Senior Histotechnologist, Umm-Al-Qura University, Makkah, Saudi Arabia, 1999-. Publication: Manual of Histotechnology. Memberships: National Society for Histotechnology, USA; Institute of Biomedical Sciences, London, England. Address: Chak No 308 GB, Viachak No 333 GB, District Toba Tek Singh, 36330 Pakistan.

**CHAUDHRY Altaf Hussain,** b. 1 June 1935, Gujrat. Agriculturist. m. Shamim Akhtar, 4 sons, 4 daughters.

Education: BSc, Agricultural, 1956, MSc, Agricultural, 1962, Plant Breeding from Sindh. Appointments: Research Assistant, 1956-64; Assistant Botanist, 1964-68; Oilseeds Botanist, 1968-86, 1987-88; Director, ARI, Tando Jam, 1987-92; Director General, Agricultural Research, Sindh, 1988-89; Project Director, National Oilseeds Development Project, 1992-97. Publications include: Scope of Safflower in Pakistan, 1985; Improvement Research on Groundnut, 1986; Oilseeds Testing in 'dobari' lands of Sindh Province, 1988; Research and Production of Safflower in Southern Pakistan, 1989; Organizational Set-up and Activities - ARI, 1989. Address: House No 229 Street 19, G 10/2 Islamabad, Pakistan.

**CHAUDHURI Kripasindhu,** b. 29 March 1943, Nityananadapur, India. Teacher; Researcher. m. Minati Chaudhuri, 2 sons, 2 daughters. Education: BSc, honours, 1964, MSc, 1966, PhD, Fluid Mechanics, Visva-Bharati, 1970. Appointments: Lecturer, Mathematics, Visva-Bharati, 1967-68; Lecturer, Mathematics, 1969-75, Reader, Mathematics, 1975-83, Professor, Mathematics, 1983-, Jadavpur University. Publications: Several articles in professional journals. Memberships: Indian Mathematical Society; Calcutta Mathematical Society; Indian Science Congress Association; National Academy of Sciences, India; National Council of Education, Bengal; Indian Academy of Comparative Religion; Association for Improvement of Mathematics Teaching; Mathematical Association, Jadavpur; Fellow, National Academy of Sciences, India. Address: 39A Ajanta Road, New Santoshpur, Calcutta 700 075, India.

**CHAUHAN Girwer Singh,** b. 13 December 1946, Raipur, UP India. Professor; Educator. m. Mrs Urmila Chauhan, 1 son, 2 daughters. Education: BSc Hons Ag and AH, 1968; MSc Food Technology, 1970; PhD Food Technology, 1982. Appointments: Senior Research Assistant, 1971-74; Assistant Professor, 1974-83; Associate Professor, 1983-93; Professor, 1993-. Honours: University Merit Award, 1967-68; FAO Scholarship, 1968-70; ICAR's Senior Fellowship, 1980-82; Canadian Award, 1989-90. Memberships: Association Food Scientists and Technologists, India; Vice President, AFST (1), 1994-95, President, 1998-99. Address: 1/304 Phoolbagh, Pantnagar 263145, India.

**CHAUHAN Suneet P,** b. 28 March 1958, Rewa, India. Maternal-Fetal Medicine Specialist. m. Laura Anne, 2 daughters. Education: BA, 1979; MD, 1983; Board Certified Obstetrician and Gynaecologist, 1995; Board Certified, Maternal-Fetal Medicine, 1997. Career: Assistant Professor, 1994-98; Private Practice, 1998-. Honours: 16 Awards for Clinical Research in Obstetrics; 4 Teaching Awards. Memberships: Society of Maternal-Fetal Medicine; Phi Kappa Ki. Address: 853 North Church Street, Suite 403, Spartanburg, SC 29303, USA.

**CHAZANOFF Daniel,** b. 1 March 1923, New York City, USA. Musician; Music Educator. m. Nina Trachtenberg, 1 son, 1 daughter. Education: BSc Education, Instrumental Music, 1949, Ohio State University; MA, 1951, EdD, 1964, Music and Music Education, Columbia University. Appointments: Director of Music, retired, Rochester, NY Public Schools; String Instructor, Columbia University; Music Appreciation Instructor, Bx Community College, CUNY; Guest Lecturer, Eastman School of Music, Brookport SUC and Roberts Wesleyan College. Publications: Over 250 publications. Honours: 2 research grants; Delegate, 8th National Conference, US National Commission for UNESCO; and others. Memberships: Music Educators National Conference; Life member, National Honorary Music Society; and others. Address: 114 Penarrow Rd, Rochester, NY 14618-1724, USA.

**CHEAL MaryLou,** b. 5 November 1926, St Clair Co, MI, USA. Research Psychologist. m. James Cheal, 2 sons, 1 daughter. Education: BA, 1969, Oakland University, Rochester; PhD Psychology, 1973, University of Michigan. Appointments: Various teaching and research posts, 1968-76; Charles A King Postdoctoral Fellow, Neuropsychology Lab, McLean Hospital and Research Fellow, Dept Psychiatry, Harvard Medical School, 1976-77; Assistant-Associate Psychologist, Neuropsychology Lab, Ralph Lowell Labs, Mailman Research Centre, McLean Hospital, and Lecturer on Psychology, Dept Psychiatry, Harvard Medical School, 1977-83; Faculty Research Associate, Dept Psychology, 1983-87, Faculty, Women's Studies, 1986, Adjunct Associate Professor, 1987-91, Adjunct Professor, 1993-, Dept Psychology, Arizona State University; Visiting Professor, Air Force Systems Command University Resident Research Programme Appt, AFHRL/OTE, 1986-88, Research Psychologist, University of Dayton Research Institute, 1986-94, Williams Air Force Base, Arizona; Senior Research Psychologist, University of Dayton Research Institute, Air Force Armstrong Lab, Mesa, Arizona, 1994-95. Publications: Author or Co-author, 67 papers in professional journals; Invited referee to 30 scientific journals. Honours: Tempe All-American Woman for Women Who Create, 1985; Society of Sigma Xi; Various university honours and research awards. Memberships: American Association for Advancement of Science, Fellow; American Psychological Association, Fellow; American Psychological Society, Charter Fellow; International Brain Research Organisation; Psychonomic Society; Arizonia Supreme Court of Foster Care, Review Board Chair; and others. Address: 127 E Loma Vista Drive, Tempe, AZ 85282-3574, USA.

**CHEHABEDDINE Jamil Abdullkarim,** b. 25 Sept 1962, Beirut, Lebanon. Telecommunications and Electronics Engineer. m. Saginaz Jamil, 1 son, 1 daughter. Education: BSc, Excellent with Honours, Telecommunications and Electronics, Beirut Arab University, 1986; Short training courses in installation and use of various marine and landbase telecommunications systems. Appointments: Manager, Microwave, Satellite Communications and Earth Stations Departments, Inteltec, 1986-93; Managing Director, Globlink, 1993-95; Projects Consultant, Technical Team Leader, Technical Manager, Telesat, 1994-98; Head, Electronics Department, Middle East Airports Services, 1998-. Publication: Author, telecommunication design application under Lotus, in progress. Honours: Mentioned in Financial Times, 1989; Award, Sierra Digital Channel Banks Series, Sierra Systems, California, 1991. Membership: AMSAT, 1993. Address: PO Box 136339, Beirut, Lebanon.

**CHELIKU Mehmet,** b. 15 January 1936, Elbasan, Albania. Pedagogue; Linguistics Researcher. m. Fatbardha Luniku, 1 son, 1 daughter. Education: Diploma in Linguistics, 1958, Tirana University; Candidate of Science, 1981; Docent, 1984; Doctor of Science, 1990; Professor, 1994. Appointments: Scientific Researcher, Albanian Academy of Science, Tirane, 1958-73; Head of Department of Albanian and Foreign Languages and Literature, Elbasan, 1973-92; Rector, A Xhuvani University of Elbasan, 1992-96; Pedagogue and Researcher, 1997-. Publications: 4 books on linguistics and university textbooks; 5 books to be published; Over 200 different titles. Honours: Mesues i Popullit, 1993; Punonjës i Shquar i shkences dhe i Teknikes, 1987; MP, 1992-96. Memberships: Vice Chairman and member, Parliamentary Commission of Education and Science; Proposed to be a member of Albanian Academy of Science. Address: Faculty of Philology, University of Elbasan A Xhuvani, Elbasan, Albania.

**CHELLIAH Muthuvel,** b. 14 November 1954, Tiruchi, Tamilnadu, India. Scientist. m Nalini. 1 son, 1 daughter. Education: MS, Meteorology, University of Hawaii, 1980; PhD Meteorology, University, MD, College Park, 1985. Appointments: Resident Phys Scientist, NWS, 1992-; Resident Associate, University of MD, College Park, 1985-88. Honours: US Department of Commerce, Gold medal, 1997. Memberships: Former President, Tamil Sangam of Metropolitan Washington and Baltimore; Former Assistant Editor, Thendral Magazine; Founder Editor of Mullai, Newsletter published by Tamil Sangam of Metro Washington. Address: 7165, Morninglight Trail, Columbia, MD 21044, USA.

**CHEN Bingqing,** b. 9 January 1940, Wuxim Jiangsu, China. Senior Engineer. m Wang Wenxui, 1 son, 1 daughter. Education: Ferrous Metallurgy Department, Beijing University of Science and Technology, 1959-64; Studied in Thermal Engineering Department, Qinghua University, 1983-84. Appointments: Anshan Iron and Steel Corp, 1964-85; Senior Engineere, Iron and Steel Research Institute, 1985-. Publications: Smelting Reduction and Direct Reduction, co-auth, 1996; over 20 papers on iron and steel in journals. Honours: A Patent 'A Coal Gasification Based DRI Production Process Based on Shaft Furnace', Awarded the Gold Prize in the Sixth New Technology and New Production Conference, China. Memberships: China Metallic Society; Baosteel Automatic Society. Address: Room 601 No 10 Baolin 9th Village, Baosan, Shanghai 201900, China.

**CHEN Charng-Ven,** b. 25 October 1944, Yunan, China. Attorney-at-Law. m. Suzy K W Chen, 1 son, 1 daughter. Education: LLB, National Taiwan University, 1967; LLM, University of British Columbia, 1969; LLM, Harvard, 1970; SJD, Harvard, 1972. Appointments: Adjunct Professor of Law, National Chengchi University and Soochow University Graduate School of Law, 1972-; Advisor to Central Bank of China, Ministry of Foreign Affairs, 1988-; Advisor to the Cabinet, 1988-; Senior Partner, Lee and Li Attorneys-at-Law, Taipei, Taiwan. Publications: Numerous articles on transnational legal problems. Honours: Honorary President, Harvard Club of China on Taiwan, 1989-; Recipient, Order of Resplendent Banner with Special Cravat from the President of the Republic of China, 1989; Recipient, other medals and awards, government of Republic of China on Taiwan. Memberships: Chairman, Taipei European Schools Foundation, Taiwan, 1994-; Director, 1993-, Vice Chairman, 1992-93, Vice Chairman and Secretary General, 1990-92, Straits Exchange Foundation; Taipei-Moscow Economic and Cultural Coordination Commission, 1992; Vice President, 1992-, Secretary-General, 1988-92, The Red Cross Society of Republic of China; Director, China Airlines, 1992-; Director, Novartis (Taiwan) Co Ltd, 1993-; International Issues Planning Committee, Faculty of Arts and Sciences, Harvard University, 1990-; Taipei Bar Association, Hsinchu Bar Association and Kaohsiung Bar Association; The Commercial Arbitration Association of Republic of China. Address: Lee and Li, 201 Tun Hua N Road 7th Floor, Taipei, Taiwan.

**CHEN Chi-Yao,** b. 19 November 1930, Taiwan, China. Insurance Director. m. Chen-Chou Hsu-Hwei, 1 son, 2 daughters. Education: BA, 1953; Doctorate Program, Wharton School, University of Pennsylvania; Associate Professor of Insurance. Appointments: Honorable Chairman, Non-Life Underwriter's Society of ROC, 1996-; Chairman, Risk Management Society of Taiwan, 1998-; Director of the Board, Guarantee Fund of Compulsory Automobile Insurance, 1998-; Member, Insurance Committee, Consumers' Foundation of ROC, 1993-; Chairman, Chiyung Insurance Foundation, 1998-; Director of the Board, Insurance Society of ROC; President,

Taipei South-East Rotary, 1993-94; Managing Director, Institute of Internal Auditors, Taipei Chapter. Publications: Reinsurance 1976; Reinsurance - Studies on Current Problems and Trend 1987; Reinsurance - Principle and Practice, 1996; Risk Management and Insurance, 1993. Honours: Outstanding Book, Society of Insurance, 1971; National Council of Science 1994, Japan Risk Management Society, 1994; Outstanding Insurance Employee of the Year, Ministry of Finance, 1975 Outstanding Employee, Taipei Chamber of Commerce, 1978 Outstanding Contributions to the Insurance Profession, Hall of Fame, International Book of Honor, American Biographical Institute, 1986; Honorary Professor, Hunan College of Insurance and Economics, China, 1991; Honorary Professor Institute of Insurance Education China, 1991. Memberships Risk Management Society of Taiwan; Insurance Society of ROC; Japan Risk Management Soicety; Rotarian, Taipe Southeast Rotary Club. Address: 2d Fl No 5 Ally 5 Ln 5 Sec 3 Jen Ai Road, Taipei, Taiwan.

**CHEN Chih-Hsin (Zhi-Xin),** b. 8 February 1931, Shao-Xing Zhejiang, China. Retired Professor; Private Researcher Consultant. m. He Xiu-Hua, 1 son, 1 daughter. Education: BS Mechanical Engineering, 1952, Qing-Hua University, Beijing. Appointments: Engineer, Chang-chun First Auto Manufactory 1952-55; Lecturer, Harbin Military Engineering Institute, 1955-60; Associate Professor, Xian Armor Engineering Institute, 1961-70; Senior Researcher, Beijing Armor Technology Research Institute, 1970-80; Professor, Shanghai University of Technology, 1980-93; Retired Professor, Private Researcher and Consultant, 1994-. Publications: 3 books Theory of Conjugate Surfaces, vol I, 1974, vol II, 1977; Fundamentals of the Theory of Conjugate Surfaces, 1985; Over 50 articles to professional journals. Honours: First Class Merit Award, 1978; National Natural Science Award, 1987; Science and Technology Advance Award, 1986. Memberships: Delegate, China National people's Congress, Beijing, 1978-83; Delegate, Shanghai People's Congress, 1983-88; Major Captain, Chinese People's Liberation Army, 1956-80; Member, ASME, 1980-; IEEE Computer Society, 1998-; Association for Computing Machinery, 1998; National Geographic Society, USA, 1996-; Founding member, Shanghai Society for Modern Design Theory and Methodology Research, Vice Chairman 1987-. Address: Lane 200 House 23 Room 401, Wu-Ning Lu, Shanghai 200063, China.

**CHEN Chong-Maw,** b. Taiwan. Professor. m. JoAnn Gong-rong, 1 son, 2 daughters. Education: BS, 1958, National Taiwan Normal University; PhD, 1967, Kansas University, USA; Postdoctorate, McMaster University, Canada, 1967-69, Roche Institute of Molecular Biology, NJ, USA, 1969-71. Appointments: Assistant, Associate and Full Professor, University of Wisconsin at Parkside, 1971-; Wisconsin Distinguished Professor, 1988-. Publications: 59 refereed papers; 46 abstracts; 7 book chapters; 6 scientific review articles; 12 international symposium papers. Honours: NSF, USDA and NIH grants; 2 Excellence in Teaching Awards; Wisconsin Distinguished Professor. Memberships: 6 scientific associations. Address: University of Wisconsin at Parkside, Wood Rd, Kenosha, WI 53141, USA.

**CHEN Chunhua,** b. 14 March 1964, Zhejiang Province China. Senior Engineer. m. Chunhua Qing, 1 son. Education Doctorate, Qindao Ocean University, 1998. Appointments: Research on Marine Chemistry, Marine Exploitation Plan Design and Research Institute, Hainan Province, 1990-; Director, Marine Environment Department. Publications: More than ten research papers in Chinese scientific journals; 2 Prizes for Science and Technology progress, Hainan Province Ocean

Department. Address: Hainan Marine Administration Bureau, Yiyuan Building 10, Haifu Road 69, Haikou 570203, China.

**CHEN Eric Yu-Hai,** b. 31 May 1960, Hong Kong. Psychiatrist. m. Linda C W Lam, 1 daughter. Education: MBChB, 1985; MA, Oxon, 1985; MRCPsych, 1990. Appointment: Associate Professor, University of Hong Kong. Publictions: Over 30 articles in international journals. Memberships: Royal College of Psychiatrists, England; International Neuropsychiatric Association. Address: University of Hong Kong, Department of Psychiatry, Pokfulam Road, Queen Mary Hospital, Hong Kong.

**CHEN Gong,** b. Haicheng, Liaoning, China. Professor of Physical Education and Sport Science. m. Yuan Li, 1 son, 1 daughter. Education: BPhysEd, 1976, Shenyang Physical Education Institute, China; MPhysEd, 1981, Beijing Physical Education University, China; DPhysEd, 1990, University Arkansas, Fayetteville, USA. Appointments: Tenured Associate Professor, San Jose State University, California; Vice Director, Centre for International Sport and Human Performance, SJSU; Director, SJSU Self-defense Research Institute. Publications: 2 books on creativity; 2 books on self-defence; 1 book on racquetball; 1 book on weight training; 1 book on Tai Chi; 1 book on badminton; 4 book chapters. Honours: Arthur Broten Young Scholar Award, 1994; SJSU College Teaching Research Award, 1997; SJSU Teacher Scholar Award, 1998; Hon Professor of Shenyang Physical Education University. Address: Dept of Human Performance, San Jose State University, One Washington Square, SPX Building #56 San Jose, CA 95192-0054, USA.

**CHEN Gui-Qiang,** b. 25 May 1963, Zhejiang Province, China. Professor. m. Anna Chen, 1 son. Education: BS Mathematics, 1982, Fudan University, Shanghai; PhD Mathematics, 1987, Academia Sinica, Beijing. Appointments: Assistant Professor, Academia Sinica, Beijing, 1987-89; Associate Scientist, Courant Institute of Mathematical Sciences, New York University, 1987-89; Assistant Professor, University of Chicago, 1989-94; Associate Professor, 1994-96, Professor, 1996-, Northwestern University, Evanston, USA. Publications: Over 70 scientific research papers in various international journals; Editor, 2 research monographs. Honours: Alfred P Sloan Fellow, 1991-97; Argonne, University of Chicago Fellow, 1989-91; Chinese National Prize of Sciences, 1990; and others. Memberships: American Mathematical Society; Society for Industrial and Applied Mathematics; Institute for Advanced Study; Berkeley Mathematical Science Research Institute. Address: Northwestern University, Dept of Mathematics, Evanston, IL 60208-2739, USA.

**CHEN Han-Jung,** b. 17 October 1951, Taiwan. Neurosurgeon. m. Yu-Chu Hou, 1 son, 1 daughter. Education: MB, 1977; PhD, 1992. Appointments: Director, Department of Neurosurgery, Chang Gung Memorial Hospital, Kaohsiung. Publication: Essential Neurosurgery. Honours: President, 5th Annual Meeting of Taiwan Neurosurgical Society; Scholarship, Takeda Foundation, Japan. Memberships: American Association of Neurological Surgeons; Executive Committee, Asian Society of Stereotactic, Functional and Computed Assistant Neurosurgery; Executive Committee, Taiwan Neurosurgical Society. Address: Chang Gung Memorial Hospital, Niao-sung Hsian, 83305 Kaohsiung Hsien, Taiwan.

**CHEN Huiyuan,** b. 27 May 1956, China. Professor. Education: BA, English Language and Literature, Yunnan University, China, 1982; MSc, Foreign Language Education, University of Rochester, USA, 1994; PhD candidate in Linguistics, Guangdong University of Foreign Studies, China,

1996-99. Appointments: Translator, Interpreter, China-Australian Joint Agricultural Development Project, 1982-84; University Professor in English and Linguistics, 1984-98. Study area and interest: Second Language Acquisition and Psycholinguistics. Publications: Papers published both inside and outside China. Honour: AAUW International Fellowship, 1992-93. Address: Department of Foreign Languages, Yunnan University, Kunming, Yunnan, China.

**CHEN Jaw-Wen,** b. 10 April 1959, Taipei, Taiwan, China. Professor. Education: Doctor of Medicine, Kaohsiung Medical College, China, 1977-84; Post Doctoral Research Fellowship, Stanford Unviersity School of Medicine, 1997-98. Appointments: Rotating Internship, 1983-84; Residency, 1986-89; Subspecial Fellowship, 1989-91; Chief Residency, 1990-91; Clinical Lecturer, 1991-98; Clinical Research Fellowship, 1991-93; Attending Physician, Division of Cardiology, Veterans General Hospital of Taipei, 1993-; Assistant Professor, Medical School, National Yang-Ming University, 1998-. Publications: When you can not hide, Poetry, 1984; 28 Published Medical Papers; 8 Conference Papers and Abstracts. Honours: Clinical Teaching Award, Veterans General Hospital. Memberships: The Society of Internal Medicine; Republic of China Society of Cardiology; Society of Emergency and Intensive Care Medicine; Formosan Medical Association; American Heart Association; International Society of Lipids and Atherosclerosis. Address: Vet Gen Hosp, 201 Shih Pai Rd Sect 2, Taipei, Taiwan.

**CHEN Jiaming,** b. 6 March 1952, Xiamen, Fujian, China. Professor. m. Lufeng Huang, 1 son. Education: MA, Wuhan University, 1985; PhD, The Graduate School, Chinese Academy of Social Sciences, 1989. Appointments: Assistant Professor, 1985, Lecturer, 1986, Associate Professor, 1991, Professor, 1994-, Department of Philosophy, Xiamen University. Publications: Books: Contemporary Methodology of Western Philosophy and Social Sciences, 1991; Constitutive and Regulative Principles: Kant's Methodology of Philosophy, 1992; Trends of Modern Social Thoughts (editor), 1992; Translations of books: L Stevenson's Seven Theories of Human Nature, 1988; The Age of Reason, 1989. Honour: K C Wong Fellow, British Academy, 1995. Memberships: President, Society for Foreign Philosophy Research, Fujian Province, 1996-; Council Member, Chinese Society for Modern Foreign Philosophy Research, 1996-; Chief Editor, Journal of Xiamen University, 1998-. Address: Department of Philosophy, Xiamen University, Xiamen, Fujian, China.

**CHEN Juh Wah,** b. 10 November 1928, Shanghai, China. Engineering Educator. m. Han Lin Chen, 2 sons, 1 daughter. Education: BS, Chemical Engineering, Taiwan College of Engineering, 1953; MS, 1957, PhD, 1959, Chemical Engineering, University of Illinois. Appointments: Chairman, Department of Thermal & Environmental Engineering, 1970-85; Distinguished Visiting Professor, National Cheng Kung University, 1991-92; Dean of Engineering, Southern Illinois University, Carbondale, 1989-. Honours: Outstanding Alumnus Achievement Award, National Cheng Kung University; Gold Medal, Ostrava Technical University, Czech Republic; Outstanding Leadership Award, Cheng Kung University Alumni Association. Memberships: ASEE; AIChE; ASME; ACS; Sigma Xi; Tau Beta Pi. Address: College of Engineering, Southern Illinois University, Engineering Building Complex, Room A108, Carbondale, IL 62901, USA.

**CHEN Kao,** b. 21 March 1919, China. Electrical Engineer. m. May Y Yoh, 2 sons, 1 daughter. Education: BSEE, Jiaotong University, China, 1942; MSEE, Harvard University, USA, 1948;

DSEE, Polytechnic University, USA, 1952; Registered Professional Engineer, New York, New Jersey, 1954-. Appointments: British Industries Scholar, 1945-47; Ebasco International Power Systems Engineer, 1953-56; Fellow Engineer, Westinghouse Electric Corporation, 1956-83; Engineering Consultant, N.A Philips Lighting Corporation, 1983-86; Owner, President, Carlsons Consulting Engineers, 1987-. Publications: 3 books, over 95 papers and articles in professional journals. Honours: IEEE Centennial Medal, 1984; IAS-IUSD Award of Merit, 1985; IEEE Richard Harold Kaufmann Award, 1992; IEEE Distinguished Lecturer, 1996, 1997. Memberships: Life Member, National Society of Professional Engineers; Illuminating Engineering Society; Life Fellow, IEEE; Power Engineering Society. Address: 11816 Caminito Corriente, San Diego, CA 92128-4550, USA.

**CHEN Kuoxian,** b. 29 December 1933, Shanghai, China. Aeronautical Manufacturing Technology Researcher. m. Wang Lisheng, 3 daughters. Education: BSc, 1957, China Aeronautical University. Appointments: Researcher, Prof Senior Engineer, Aeronautical Industrial Ministry, 1987-. Publications: Power Spinning and its Application, 1966; Power Spinning Technology, 1986. Honours: Specialist with Eminent Contribution, 1991; Government Special Subsidy, 1991; National Science & Technology General Meeting Award, 1979; Minister Science & Technical Progress Award, 1983, 1987, 1989, 1991. Memberships: Board Director, China Forging and Stamping Institution; Vice Chairman, China Metal Spinning Committee of Forging and Stamping Institution. Address: 201# Keging Building No 6, 15# Fuxing Road, Beijing 100038, China.

**CHEN Lai-Juh,** b. 19 June 1963, Taipei, Taiwan. Semiconductor and TFT-LCD Technologist. m. Lee Chung-Mann, 1 son, 1 daughter. Education: BS, Tatung Institute of Technology, Taipei, Taiwan, 1986; PhD, Chemical Engineering Department, Tsing-Hua University, Hsinchu, Taiwwan, 1992. Appointments: Process Engineer, 1992-95, Project Manager, 1995-96, Section Manager, 1995-97, Department Manager, 1997-99, Electronics Research and Service Organization (ERSO); Director of LCD Fab, Acer Display Technology Inc, 1999-. Publications: Over 40 in journal and conference papers; 20 patents. Honours: Research Achievement Award, Industrial Technology Research Institute, Hsinchu, Taiwan, 1995; One of Taiwan Hundred Outstanding Young People, China Times, Taipei, 1995; Award of Research Publication, Industrial Technology Research Institute, Hsinchu, 1999; Award of Young People, China Youth Corps, Taipei, Taiwan, 1999.

**CHEN Long,** b. January 1943, Fuzhou, Fujian. Professor. Education: Graduate, 1960, History Department, Xiemen University. Appointments: Researcher in fields of archaeology, relics, ethnodogy, geographical name, local chronicle, culture for tea and technological history; Professor, Vice Director, Fujian Museum; Chief Editor, Fujian Relics and Museum. Memberships: Council member, Chinese Museum Association; Standing committee, Fujian Natural Science Museum; Vice President, China's Exchange Centre for Research of Tea Culture; National Association of Fujian; Evaluation Commission of Professional Titles; Special Professor, History Institute of Fujian Provincial Academy of Society Science. Publications: One million word research papers, books and monographs. Honours: Scientific Achievements Prizes, including Province level and state level, many times; Gained high reputation. Address: Fujian Provincial Museum, West Lake Park, Fuzhou, China.

**CHEN Mei-Lien,** b. 15 November 1958, Chuang-Hwai, Taiwan. Environmental Educator. m. Pei Jung Kuo, 1 daughter. Education: Bachelor of Public Health, National Taiwan University, 1981; Master of Public Health, 1983; Doctor of Philosophy, 1992. Appointments: Lecturer, National Yang Ming University, 1985-92; Associate Professor, National Yang Ming University, 1992-. Publications: The Science of the Total Environment, many Journals. Memberships: Standing Member of Board, National Public Health Association of the Republic of China; Member, New York Academy of Sciences. Address: Nat Yang Ming Univ, 155 Li-Long St Shih Pai, Taipei, Taiwan.

**CHEN Min-Yen George,** b. 2 February 1934, China. Minister; Social Welfare Activist. m. Wen-Yu Shem Chen, 1 son, 1 daughter. Education: Civil Engineering; Economics; Biblical Hermeneutics. Appointments: Minister at Large, 1952-; Executive Director, Bonisa Foundation, Holland, 1985-; Senior Adviser, International Aid Inc, USA, 1986-; Associate Partner, Asia Evangelical Mission, USA, 1986-; Consultant, Action Love, Hong Kong. Publication: Translator, Thompson Chain Reference Bible to Chinese. Honours: Honorary Citizen, Anqing City, China, 1995, Daye City, China, 1998, Weixi County, China, 1998; Honorary Hospital Director in China, Daye Christian Hospital, Anqing Municipal Hospital, Huancheng Hospital, Qian Wu Hospital; Honorary President, Zhongshau Huan Cheng Social Welfare Foundation. Address: Flat C 17/F Tower 21, Riviera Gardens Tsuen, Hong Kong.

**CHEN Ming-Der,** b. 4 November 1961, Taipei, Taiwan. Academic Researcher. m. Yu Hui Ling, 1 son. Education: BSc, Biology, Tunghai University, 1984; MSc, Biology, Tunghai University, 1986; PhD, Tunghai University, 1996. Appointments: Assistant, Tunghai University, Veterans General Hospital, 1984-86; Assistant Researcher, Taichung Veterans General Hospital, 1988-89; Associate Research Specialist, Taichung Vet Gen Hospital 1989-. Publications: Many Articles to Professional Journals. Honours: Eli Lilly-Roc Award; Academic Awards. Memberships: International Association of Bioinorganic Scientists; American Diabetes Association; New York Academy of Sciences; Endocrinology Society of ROC; AAAS. Address: Taichung Vets General Hospital, Division End/Met, No 160 Sect 3 Chang-Kang Rd, 40705 Taichung, Taiwan.

**CHEN Ming-Fong,** b. 13 October 1949, I-Lan, Taiwan. Doctor; Medical Professor. m. Mei-Yuh Tsai, 1 son, 1 daughter. Education: MD, 1975, National Taiwan University, Medical College; PhD, 1990, Graduate Institute of Clinical Medicine. Appointments: Visiting Staff of Internal Medicine, (Cardiology), 1981-; Chief of Critical Care Medicine, National Taiwan University Hospital, 1993-; Professor of Internal Medicine, 1995-. Honours: National Science Council Outstanding Researcher Award, 1990-93, 1995-97; Best Post Presentation Award, 1996, Society of Internal Medicine of Taiwan; Award of Colleague Foundation of Medicine, 1996; Best Teacher Award, 1998, National Taiwan University Hospital. Memberships: Fellow, American College of Cardiology; Fellow, European Society of Cardiology; Critical Care Medicine, USA; Taiwan Society of Cardiology; Secretary-General, Society of Internal Medicine of Taiwan. Address: No 7 Chung shan S Rd, Taipei, Taiwan.

**CHEN Nian,** b. 31 October 1948, Shanghai, China. Government Executive Officer. m. Nai Li Wang, 1 son, 1 daughter. Education: MB, Shanghai Medical University, 1982 M in Medicine, 1984; PharmM, University of Queensland Australia, 1984, PhD, Medicine, University of Queensland Australia, 1992. Appointments: Mechanical Engineer, Shanghai Numbering Machine Co., 1968-73; Electrical Engineer 1973-78; Research Officer, Queensland University, 1989-92 Pharmacologist, Princess Alexandra Hospital, Brisbane,

Australia, 1993-94; Senior Science Officer, Chemical Assessment Division, National Occupational Health and Safety Commission, Australia, 1994-; Director, Nellian Australia, 1996-; Member of the National Gene Technology Task Force, 1998-. Memberships: ASCEPT, ASBMB. Address: P O Box 346, Marrylands 2160, Australia.

**CHEN Rong-Chi,** b. 10 November 1938, Hsinchu, Taiwan. Professor of Neurology. m. Chaw-Fang Chou, 1 son, 2 daughters. Education: MD, National Taiwan University Medical College, 1964; Neurology Residency, University of Wisconsin, Madison, 1973. Career: Resident, Staff Physician, Lecturer, Associate Professor, Professor, Chief, Department of Neurology, Vice Superintendent, National Taiwan University Hospital; Superintendent, En Chu Kong Hospital. Publications: 150 articles in professional medical journals. Honours: Paper Excellence Award, Wisconsin Neurological Society, USA, 1973; Research Article Excellence Award, Chinese Medical Association, Taiwan, 1986; Excellent Textbook Award, Ministry of Education, Taiwan, 1990. Memberships: Formosan Medical Association; Chinese Medical Society; China Medical Association; Taiwan Neurological Society; Chinese Society of Medical Rehabilitation; Society of Psychiatry, China; Chinese Society of Medical Ultrasonics; Taiwan Epilepsy Society; Taiwan Stroke Society; Neuroscience Society, China; American Academy of Neurology; American Neurological Association; World federation of Neurology. Address:En Chu Kong Hospital, 399 Fuhsing Road, Sanhsia Town, Taipei Hsien 237, Taiwan.

**CHEN Shan-Ben,** b. 15 December 1956, Lianyun Port City, China. Educator. m. Shao, 1 son. Education: BS, 1982; MS, 1987; PhD, 1991. Appointments: Assistant Professor, 1982; Lecturer, 1987; Associate Professor, 1995; Professor, 1995. Publications: IEEE Translation Autom Contributions; Int J of Sys Sci; IEEE Translationm Systems Management and Cyb. Memberships: IEEE; New York Academy of Sciences; Chinese Welding Society; Committee of Chinese Welding Society. Address: P O Box 436, No 92, West Dazhi St, Harbin 150001, China.

**CHEN Shawn Hsiao-Yun,** b. 25 September 1963, Taiwan, China. Managing Director. m. Serina Sun Chai-Wu. Education: BPharm, National Defense Medical Center, Taipei, Taiwan, 1982-86; MBA, Asian Institute of Management, Makat, Philippines, 1993-94. Appointments: Product Manager, Pfizer Pharmaceutical Company, 1988-92; Director, Business Development Asia Pacific, IMED Corporation, 1995-96; Managing Director, Asia Pacific, Alaris Medical Systems Incorporated, 1997-. Membership: American Chamber of Commerce, Singapore. Address: Alaris Medical Systems, 65 Chulla Street No 40-04, OCBC Center, Singapore 049513, Singapore.

**CHEN Shenglin,** b. 2 January 1937, Meixian, Guangdong, China. Historian. m. Zhu Jufang, 2 sons. Education: Bachelor, History Department, Zhongshan University, 1954-58. Appointments: Lecturer, 1978-80; Associate Professor, 1980-85; Professor, Design in History, Zhongshan Unviersity, 1984-96; PhD Supervisor, 1986. Address: History Department, Zhongshan University, Guangzhou, China.

**CHEN Shu Xuan,** b. 30 March 1936, Fuzhou, Fujian, China. Professor. m. Shuxia Chen, 1 son, 1 daughter. Education: BA, Xiamen University, 1959. Appointments: Technical Term, Hunan Rodio Research Institute, 1959-62; Lecturer, Huaqiao University, 1962-74; Associate Professor, Xiamen University, 1974-. Publications: Theory Substance - Base of Crossing Theory at Natural Subjects, 1994; Thinking Engineering - Man's Brain Intelligent Activity and Thinking Model, 1994. Honours:

3rd Class Prize, National Mechanical and Electronic Department, 1989; Fujian Natural Science Excellent Thesis Prize, about Microcompute system of MM-1000 Friction Tester, Fujian Science and Technology Association, 1991. Membership: China Thinking Science Institute, Fujian; Director, Fujian Instrument and Appearance Association. Address: 19-502 Baicheng, Xiamen University, Xiamen, Fujian, China.

**CHEN Shyi-Ming,** b. 16 January 1960, Taipei, Taiwan, China. University Professor. Education: BS, 1982, Dept Electronic Enginerring, National Taiwan University of Science and Technology; MS, 1986, PhD, 1991, Dept Electrical Engineering, National Taiwan University. Appointments: Associate Professor, 1991-96, Professor, 1996-98, Dept Computer and Information Science, National Chiao Tung University, Hsinchu; Professor, Department of Electronic Engineering, National Taiwan University of Science and Technology, Taipei, 1998-. Publications: Over 100 papers in refereed journals and conference proceedings. Honours: Winner of 1994 Outstanding Paper Award, Journal of Information and Education; Winner of 1995 Outstanding Paper Award of Computer Society of Republic of China; Winner of 1997 Outstanding Youth Electrical Engineer Award of Chinese Institute of Electrical Engineering; Editor, Journal of Chinese Grey Systems Association. Memberships: Senior Member, IEEE; ACM; IFSA; Executive Committee Member: Taiwanese Association for Artificial Intelligence, and Chinese Fuzzy Systems Association. Address: National Taiwan University of Science & Technology, 43 Sect 4 Keelung Rd, Taipei 106, Taiwan.

**CHEN Sinn Wen,** b. 24 September 1961, Tainan, Taiwan, China. Professor. m. Wenyuj Shieh, 1 son, 2 daughters. Education: BS, Chemical Engineering, National Taiwan University, 1979-83; MS, Materials Science, University of Wisconsin, 1985-87; PhD, Materials Science, University of Wisconsin, 1987-90. Appointments: Research Associate, University of Wisconsin, 1990-91; Senior Scientist, Alcoa Technical Center, 1991-92; Associate Professor, National Tsing Hua University, 1992-97; Professor, National Tsing Hua University, 1997-. Publications: 26 Published Papers. Honours: Young Investigators Achievement Award; NSC Research Award; Invited Speech. Memberships: TMS; AICLE; CMRS. Address: National Tsing-Hua University, Departmen of Chemical Engineering, Hsinchu 30043, Taiwan.

**CHEN Wei-Yin,** b. 5 April 1950, Taipei, Taiwan. Education: Researcher. m. Tsuei-Ju Kao. Education: BS, Chemical Engineering, Tunghai University, 1973; MS, Chemical Engineering, Polytechnic Institute, New York, 1975; MS, Applied Mathematics, University of New York, Stony Brook, 1975; PhD, Chemical Engineering, City University of New York, 1982. Appointments: Senior Research Engineer, 1981-85, Fuel Research Manager, 1985-87, Gulf South Research Institute; Research Assistant Professor, Louisiana University, 1987-90; Assistant Professor, 1990-93, Associate Professor, 1993-98, University of Mississippi. Publictions: Over 100 in professional journals. Honours: Numerous Research grants on Fossil Fuel Ultilization. Memberships: American Institute of Chemical Engineers; American Chemical Society; Combustion Institute; Sigma Xi; Chinese Institute of Engineers. Address: Department of Chemical Engineering, University of Mississippi, Anderson Hall University, MS 38677, USA.

**CHEN Wu-Tong,** b. 20 November 1935, Anxi, Fujian, China. Historian. m. Gui-fang Feng, 1 son, 1 daughter. Eduction: BA, Department of History, Xiamen University, 1958. Appointments: Editor, Higher Education, Peoples Education Publishing House, 1958-72; Teacher, Department of Chinese Language and

Literature, Guangxi University, 1972-75; Teacher, Department of History, Central University for Nationalities 1975-. Publications: Over 80 papers in professional journals; over 10 books. Honours: 2nd Class Prize, Guangming Daily, 1984; 2nd Class Prize, Government of Henan, 1994; 2nd Class Prize, Bejing Municipality, 1994. Memberships: Executive Council, Chinese Institute of Ming Dynasty; Chinese Society of Minority Histories; Chinese Society of Peasant War; Beijing History Society. Address: Central University for Nationalities, Beijing, China.

**CHEN Xiao Hong**, b. 6 February 1967, Tianjin, China. Researcher. Education: Mechanics and Engineering Science, Peking University, China. Appointments: Technical Reviewer, ICCM-11, ICFSS-3, 1997; Consultative Editor, Chinese Figures Dictionary, 1997; Postdoctoral Research Fellow, University of Sydney, 1996-. Publications: Over 20 refered journal and conference papers; Book chapter for ACS Volume. Honours: Certificate of Honour, Chinese Figures Dictionary, 1997; Premier Paper Award, ACCM-1, Japan, 1998. Memberships: American Association for the Advancement of Science, 1997-; Australian Composite Structures Society, 1997-; Chinese Australian Academics Society, 1998-. Address: Dept of Mechanical and Mechatronic Eng, Univ of Sydney, Sydney, NSW 2006, Australia.

**CHEN Xiaojun**, b. 7 November 1956, Henan, China. Associate Professor. m. An Li, 1 daughter. Education: PhD, Xian Jiaotung University; PhD, Okayama Science University. Appointments: Lecturer, Xi'an Jiaotong University; Postdoctor, University Delaware; Research Fellow, University New South Wales; Associate Professor, Shimane University. Publications: 50 Research Papers, International Journals. Memberships: GAMM; Japan Math Society; Japan Applied Maths Society; Japan OR. Address: Shimane University, Dept Math and Computer Sci, Matsue 690, Japan.

**CHEN Yansheng**, b. 6 October 1926, Beijing, China. Teacher. m. Ying Yao, 1 son, 1 daughter. Education: Graduated, Department of Aeronautics, Shanghai Jiaotong University, 1949. Appointments: Lecturer, 1955, Associate Professor, 1978, Professor, 1986, Beijing University of Aeronautics and Astronautics; Tutor to doctoral students in Mechanics, appointed by Ministry of Education, Chinese State Council, 1986. Publications: Theory and Application of Hydrostatic Bearings, textbook in Chinese, 1980; Stability of Multirecess Hybrid-Operating Oil Journal Bearings, 1985; Foundation of Tribology, textbook in Chinese, 1991. Memberships: Standing Committee, Chinese Association of Tribology; Chinese Association of Mechanical Engineering. Address: 23988 Greening Drive, Novi, MI 48375, USA.

**CHEN Yu**, b. 10 September 1942, Beijing, China. Acupuncturist (MD). m. Paul L Munson, 1 son. Education: MD, 1965, Capitol Medical College; OMD, 1977, Chinese Traditional Medical School, Beijing; MS, 1981, Union Hospital and Chinese Academy of Medical Sciences, Beijing; Training in English Language, Cambridge, England. Appointments: Physician, Guan Su Province, China, 1968-73; Resident Physician, Yen Shan Oil Factory, Worker's Hospital, Beijing, 1974-78; Attending Physician, National Research Institute for Family Planning, Beijing, 1982-83; WHO Research Fellow, Karolinska Inst, Stockholm, 1983-85; Fellow, University of Texas at Houston, 1985-87; Research Fellow Pharmacology, University North Carolina, 1987-90; Acupuncturist, N Carolina, 1989-93; Licensed Acupuncturist in Maryland, 1993-. Publications: Papers on endocrinology, molecular genetics, and acupuncture; many inventions. Honours: Best Essay, First International Conference on Chinese Micro Acupuncture

Therapy, San Francisco, 1995; Large illustrated feature on Dr Yu Chen and her work in Baltimore Sun on Dec 2, 1997. Memberships: Diplomate in Acupuncture of the National Commission for the Certification of Acupuncturists, 1989; Licensed Acupuncturist, Maryland, 1982-. Address: 1520 Taylor Avenue, Baltimore, MD 21234, USA.

**CHEN Zu-Fen**, b. 1926, Shanghai, China. Appointments: Research Fellow, Shanghai Municipal Arts & History Research Institute, 1992; Councelor, Shanghai Municipal Political Consultative Council, 1993; Professor, Calligraphy & Painting Research Institute, 1994; Creative Councelor, China National Arts Institute, 1995; Senior Fellow, China National School of Famous Artists, 1996; Consulting Editor, China Internation Cultural Exchange Press, 1996; Deputy Chairman, Worldwode Buddhist Culture Society, 1997; Artistic Director, World Famous Artists Association, 1998; Senior Fellow, Xin Shenzhou Gallery 1998. Publications: Calligraphy Artists of the Modern Era; Self Practice Manual of Calligraphy; Auto Biography, Survival Against All Odds. Honours: 1st Class Award, Special Award, International Literature & Arts Expo; Gold Award, Red Latern Expo of Arts; Special Award, Lion Cup. Memberships: Society of Famous Calligraphy & Painting Artists; International Salon c Modern Artists. Address: Hall of the Humanities Research c Shanghai, 41 Sinan Road, Shanghai 2000020, China.

**CHEN Zueng-Sang**, b. 6 November 1952, Tainan, Taiwan Professor. m. Hsien-Tsu Lee, 2 daughters. Education: PhD National Taiwan University, 1984. Appointments: Professo Department of Agricultural Chemistry, National Taiwa University, 1989; Chairman, Soil Remediation COmmittee c EPA, Taiwan, 1997. Honours: Science Achievement Awarc Agricultural Association of China; Science Achievement Awarc Chinese Agricultural Chemical Society. Memberships International Union of Soil Science; International Society fc Ecology; Soil Science Society of America; Internation Association on Water Quality; Chinese Agricultural Chemic Society; Agricultural Association of China; Chinese Society c Soil and Fertilizer Sciences. Address: Dept Agr Chem N Taiwan U, No 1 4th Sect Roosevelt Rd, 10617 Taipei, Taiwan

**CHENG Benny Ngo**, b. 16 February 1963, Calooca Philippines. Research Engineer. m. Xiaojing F Chen Education: PhD, Mathematics, Massachussetts Institute Technology, 1987; PhD, Statistics, University of Californi Santa Barbara, 1994. Appointments: Visiting Assista Professor, Mathematics, University of Arkansas, Fayettevill 1987-88; Member, Information and Computing Staff, NAS JPL, 1994-. Honour: Top Ten Outstanding Young Scientists the Philippines, 1988. Membership: American Geophysic Union. Address: Jet Propulsion Laboratory, 4800 Oak Gro' Drive, MS 300-323, Pasadena, CA 91109, USA.

**CHENG Fai Chut**, b. 15 July 1933, Shanghai, Chin Electrical Engineering Researcher. Education: BS, Electric Engineering, Tsing Hua University, Beijing, China, 1957; MP Electrical Engineering, University of Hong Kong, Hong Kor 1990. Appointments: Engineer, Northeast Pow Administration, Central Laboratory, Harbin, China, 1957-7 Technician, Tomoe Electrics Co, Hong Kong, 1973-7 Lecturer, School of Science and Technology, Hong Kor 1976-80; Part time Demonstrator, University of Hong Kor 1980-88; Temporary Teacher, Haking Wong Technical Institu Hong Kong, 1987-88; Evening Visiting Lecturer, Hong Kc Polytechnic, 1988-89, 1990-93; Research Assistant, 1989-9 Teaching Assistant, 1992-93, Hong Kong Polytechnic; Part ti Research Assistant, Hong Kong Polytechnic, 1994-9 Honorary Research Fellow, Hong Kong Polytechnic Universi 1998. Publications: Insulation Thickness Determination

Polymeric Power Cables, 1994; Discussion on Insulation Thickness Determination of Polymeric Power Cables, 1995. Honours: Outstanding Achievement Medal, 1997; Gold Star Award, 1997; Silver Medal, 1997; Distinguished Leadership Award, 1997; Twentieth Century Achievement Award, 1997; Most Admired Man of the Decade, 1997; Millenniuum Hall of Fame Statue, 1998; 1997 Man of the Year, Commemorative Medal, 1997. Memberships: Associate Member, 1988-, Hong Kong Institution of Engineers; Associate Member, 1992-, Institution of Electrical Engineers (UK); Senior Member, 1995-, Institute of Electrical and Electronics Engineers (US); Member, 1995-, New York Academy of Sciences; Life Fellow, International Biographical Association, 1997-; Life Patron, American Biographical Institute Research Association, 1997-. Address: Hong Kong Polytechnic University, Department of Electrical Engineering, Hung Hom, Kowloon, Hong Kong.

**CHENG Haw Zen,** b. 11 September 1954, Taipei, Taiwan. Computer Specialist. m. Chung-neng Cheng. Education: B EE, 1978, National Cheng-Kung University; MSc Computer, 1983, Utah State University. Appointments: Specialist, Computer Graphics, Taiwan Television Ent Ltd; Consultant, Asia Television Ent Ltd, Hong Kong. Memberships: IEEE Networking the World; Association for Computing. Address: 164-6 Chien-Kuo Road 2nd Fl, Hsin-Tien, China.

**CHENG Winston T K,** b. 2 June 1950, Taiwan, China. Educator; Researcher. m. Feng-Ying Chen, 2 sons. Education: BSc, 1975; MSc, 1979; PhD (CNAA), 1985. Appointment: Professor, Department of Animal Science, National Taiwan University, Taiwan, China. Publications: Outstanding Scientific Research Award, China, 1986, 1997 and 1998. Honours: Award of the Ten Outstanding Youths in Republic of China, 1986; Academic Research Award, Chinese Society of Animal Science, 1986. Memberships: Chinese Society of Animal Science, China, 1975-; Society for Study of Fertility, 1983-; American Society of Animal Science, USA, 1985-. Address: Chairman, Department of Animal Husbandry, National Taiwan University, Taipei, Taiwan.

**CHEONG Keng-Liang Kenneth,** b. 22 April 1958, Singapore. University Administrator. Education: BSc (Hons), Teesside Polytechnic, 1983; MSc, The Victoria University of Manchester, 1985; Certified Data Processor, Institute for Certification of Computer Professionals, 1986; LTCL, Trinity College of Music, London, 1987; Chartered Engineer, The Engineering Council, 1991; Diploma in Business Administration, National University of Singapore, 1993. Appointments: Information Systems Officer, National Computer Board, 1985-94; Senior Consultant, International Corporate Management Pte Ltd, 1987-94; Assistant Registrar, 1994-98, Assistant Director, 1998-, National University of Singapore. Honour: Singapore Armed Forces Good Service Medal, 1994. Memberships: Institute of Electrical and Electronics Engineers; British Computer Society; Singapore Computer Society; MENSA Singapore.

**CHERIAN Mathew Punnachalil,** b. 5 September 1949, Thiruvamkulam, Saudi Arabia. Pediatrics Consultant. m. Aleena, 2 sons, 1 daughter. Education: MB, BS, Calicut Medical College, India, 1972; DCH, Christian Medical College, 1976; MD, 1977; MRCP, Royal College of Physicians of Ireland, 1989. Appointments: Junior Resident, Safdarjang Hospital, India, 1974; CMC Hospital, India, 1975-76; Registrar in Pediatrics, CMC Hospital, 1977-78; Consultant, Medical Trust Hospital, 1978-80; Consultant, Aramco Medical Organization, 1980-. Publications: Several in Various Pediatric Journals of World. Memberships: International College of Tropical Medicine; Royal College of Physicians of Ireland;

American College of Tropical Medicine. Address: Saudi Aramco, PO Box 1356, 31311 Rastanura, Saudi Arabia.

**CHERKAOUI Mohamed,** b. 22 April 1945, Boujad. Research Director. m. Khadija, 2 sons, 1 daughter. Education: MA, Philosophy, 1967; MA, Sociology, 1972; Bsc, Statistics, 1972; PhD, Sociology, 1975; Doctorate es Lettres, 1981. Appointments: Assistant Professor, 1972-73; Research Officer, National Center for Scientific Research, 1976-85; Director, CNRS, 1986-. Publications: Les Paradoxes de la reussite Scolaire, 1979; Les Changements du Systeme Educatif en France, 1982; Sociologie de l'education, 1986; Classical Tradition in Sociology, 1997; Naissance d'une Sciene Sociale, 1998; Central Currents in Sociological Theory, 1999; Dictionnaire de Sociologie, 1999. Memberships: French and International Sociological Assocaition; Editorial Board of French Review of Sociology. Address: 54 Blvd Raspail, Maison des Scis de L'Homme, 75006 Paris, France.

**CHERKASOVA Maria Valentinovna,** b. 13 March 1938, Moscow, Russia. Ecologist; Journalist. m. Alexander Dulov, 1 son, 1 daughter. Education: Student, 1956-62, Postgraduate, 1965-68, Moscow University; PhD, Biology, 1984. Career: Staff, Zoological Museum, Moscow University, 1962-65; Head, Biology & Nature Protection Department, Znaniye-Sila Magazine, 1968-73; Department of Rare & Endangered Species, Research Institute for the Protection of the Environment, 1973-88; Coordinator, Socio-Ecological Union, 1988-90; Director, NGO Center for Independent Ecological Programs (CIEP) of the Socio-Ecological Union, 1990-. Publications: Over 150 articles and books including: They Must Survive; the Greatest Threat to the Sustainable Development; Russian Fords, Where Are You?. Honours: Global 500 Roll of Honour, UNEP, 1992; 1 of 25 Women Ecologists, UNEP's 25th Anniversary, 1997. Memberships: Socio-Ecological Union; Childwatch International Research Network; Ecology & Children Health Association. Address: 103104 Russian Federation, Malaya Bronnaya 51 12-12, Moscow, Russia.

**CHERNESKEY Russell,** b. 2 May 1929, Fenwood, Saskatchewan, Canada. Accountant; Consultant. m. Juliette Reta Majeau. Education: Technical Studies, Radar Electronics, Royal Canadian Air Force; Arts and Science, St Patricks College affiliated with University of Ottawa, St Pauls College affiliated with University of Manitoba, Simon Fraser University, Burnaby British Columbia; Business Administration, University of British Columbia; Commerce, University of Alberta; Institute of Chartered Accountants, British Columbia and Alberta; Postgraduate, Computers and Systems, Investments, Law amd Taxation. Appointments: Articled Student, Chartered Accountant, British Columbia and Alberta; Controller, Central Fabricators Ltd, Alberta, Frankel Engineering Ltd, Alberta; Business Manager, Bryan Anderkson & Associates, Law Firm, Alberta; Principal and President, Keywest Consulting Corporation. Memberships: Past Member, Admissions Requirement Committee, University of Alberta; Past Membership Chairman, Sara International, Edmonton Chapter; Past Director and Chairman of Finance, Alberta Bosco Homes (A Society for Children and Adolescents); Past Director and Safety Committee, St Anne's Natural Gas Cooperative; Board of Governors Newman Theological College and St Joseph's Seminary; Internatioanl Who's Who of Professionals; Several University Alumni's. Address: Keywest Consulting Corporation, Westgate Business Park, 10271-178 Street, Edmonton AB T5S 1M3, Canada.

**CHERNOV Ivan Petrovich,** b. 14 January 1935, Altai, Russia. Physicist. m. Nadejda Bezzubtzeva, 1 son, 1 daughter. Education: PhD, 1966, Polytechnic University of Tomsk;

Professor, 1981. Appointments: Head of Laboratory, Research Institute of Nuclear Physics, Tomsk, 1966-71, 1973-81; Researcher, Nils Bohr Institute, Copenhagen, 1971-73; Professor, Head Physics Department, Polytechnic University of Tomsk, 1981-. Publications: Hydrogen & Helium Analysis, 1988; Contributor of articles to professional journals. Memberships: Russian Physics Society; International Ecological Academy of Science. Address: 15/15 Studentcheskaya Str, 634004 Tomsk, Russia.

**CHERNYAKOV Sergei Mikhailovich,** b. 29 January 1950, Murmansk, Russia. Physicist. 1 son, 1 daughter. Education: Diploma of the Petrozavodsk's University, 1972. Appointments: Military Service, 1972-74; Scientist, 1974-96; Head of Observatory, 1996-. Publications: More than 40 scientific publications. Memberships: The Natural Philosophy Alliance; The Interstellar Propulsion Society; The National Geographic Society. Address: Geophysical Observatory Loparskaya, Polar Geophysical Institute, Kola Scientific Center of the Russian Academy of Sciences, 15 Khalturina Str, Murmansk 183010, Russia.

**CHERNYSHOV Eugenij Eizhenievich,** b. 30 January 1958, Leningrad. Radioelectronics Engineer. m. Elena Cheznyshova, 1 daughter. Education: Leningrad Mechanical Institute, 1981; Doctor of Technical Science, Academician of International Informatization Academy, Academician of Transport Academy, 1995. Appointments: Teacher, Higher schools of St Petersburg, 1981-; Professor, Baltic State Technical University, 1993-; Rector, Instrument Engineering Academy, 1994-; General Director, Principal Designer of Radioavionica Corp, 1991-. Publications: Monographs: Airborne Expert Systems of Aviation Complexes; Airborne Computing Systems; Signal Processors of Aerospace Systems; Space Signal Processing in Adaptive Phased-Array Radars; Radioengineering Devices and Systems; Also over 100 scientific works published worldwide. Honours: Order of International Fellowship; International Order of Merit; Presidential Seal of Honour, 1996. Memberships: St Petersburg regional management of NTO RES; St Petersburg Society of Scientists; Editorial Board, Radioelectronics and Communication; Intergovernmental Russian-Italian Commission for defence complex conversion. Address: MOIF IOM, PO Box 111, St Petersburg 198103, Russia.

**CHETTY Ravindra,** b. 18 October 1962, Tanzania. Barrister at Law. m. Shalmila, 3 sons. Education: BA, Jurisprudence, 1986, Balliol College, Oxford University; Council of Legal Education, London, 1986-87; Called to Bar, Middle Temple, 1987; Called to the Bar, Mauritius, 1987. Appointments: Barrister at Law, Private Practice, 1987-; Lecturer at Council of Legal Education, Mauritius, 1991-; Past Member of Law Reform Commission; Member, Sports Research Unit. Memberships: Past President, Rotary Club of Port Louis Citadelle; President, Mauritius Football Association; Vice Chairman, Mauritius Child Care Society. Address: 6th Floor, PCL Building, 43 Sir William Newton Street, Port Louis, Mauritius.

**CHIANG Kao-Fei,** b. 23 March 1947, Kiang-Si Province, China. Professor of Education. m. Han-Shiow Liu, 2 daughters. Education: BSEE, Chung Cheng Institute of Technology, 1968; MSEE, 1972; Engineer Degree, University of Southern California, 1978; PhD, Research Institute of Electronics and Electrical Engineering, National Chen Kung University, 1988. Appointments: Electronics Department, Chung Shan Institute of Science and Technology, 1972; Visiting Scholar, Information Systems Laboratory, Stanford University, 1985-86; Program Director, 1988; Associate Professor, Nan-Tai Institute of Technology, 1993. Publications: International Journals of System Science; International Journals of Electronics.

Memberships: IEEE. Address: 5F #28 Alley 14 Lane 283, Sec 3 Roosevelt Road, Taipei, Taiwan.

**CHIANG Kin Seng,** b. 18 August 1957, Zhongshan, China. Professor. m. Yuan Li, 1 son, 1 daughter. Education: BE honours, Electrical Engineering, 1982, PhD, 1986, University of New South Wales, Australia. Appointments: Research Officer, Department of Mathematics, Australian Defence Force Academy, Canberra, 1986; Research Scientist, Senior Research Scientist, Division of Applied Physics, Commonwealth Scientific and Industrial Research Organization, Sydney, 1986-93; Visiting Scientist, Electrotechnical Laboratory, Tsukuba City, Japan, 1987-88; Project Leader, Optical Fibre Technology Center, University of Sydney, 1992-93; Associate Professor, Professor, Department of Electronic Engineering, City University of Hong Kong, 1993-. Publications: Over 100 papers in international journals and conference proceedings, 1982-. Memberships: Optical Society of America; International Society for Optical Engineering; Australian Optical Society; Institute of Electrical and Electronic Engineers. Address: City University of Hong Kong, Department of Electronic Engineering, Kowloon, Hong Kong.

**CHICHENEUVE Alex N,** b. 1 July 1966, Moscow. Business Man, Education: Master of Science, Moscow Institute of International Relations. Appointments: Vice General Director, Federal Contract Corporation Roscontractive. Memberships: Liverpool Cotton Association; London Sugar Association. Address: Capital Leasing, 5 Orlikov Ln, 107801 Moscow, Russia.

**CHICHILNISKY Graciela,** b. 27 March 1946, Buenos Aires. Mathematician; Economist. 1 son, 1 daughter. Education: PhD Programme in Mathematics, Massachusetts Institute of Technology, 1967-68; MA, 1970, PhD Mathematics, 1971, PhD Economics, 1976, University of California at Berkeley. Appointments: Professor of Economics, 1980-, UNESCO Professor of Mathematics and Economics and Professor of Statistics, 1995-, Director, Programme on Information and Resources, 1994-, Columbia University; Associate Editor of Editorial Board, 15 professional journals; Advisor and Contributing Author, Intergovernmental Panel on Climate Change, IPCC, Working Group II, 1993-96; Member of the Second National Forum on Biodiversity of the NRC, the Smithsonian Institution, the Library Congress, and the American Association for the Advancement of Science, 1996-97; Member of the Technical and Scientific Advisory Committee for the International Programme on R&D, Ministry of Environment, Water Resources and Legal Amazon, Brazil, 1997-. Publications: 171 articles; 11 books; 7 book reviews; 14 working papers. Honours: Leif Johansen Award, 1995. Memberships: American Mathematical Society; American Economic Association; American Statistical Association. Address: 405 Low Library, Columbia University, 116th & Broadway, NY 10027, USA.

**CHIEN Chin-hsiang,** b. 13 February 1948, Taipei, Taiwan. Professor; Researcher. m. Song-nan Chow, 2 sons, 1 daughter. Education: BS, College of Agriculture, National Taiwan University, 1970; MS, College of Science, New Jersey State University, 1972; PhD, Institute of Agricultural Chemistry, National Taiwan University, 1983. Appointments: Professor, Institute of Biochemistry, National Yang-Ming University. Publications: 30 journal articles, 60 conference papers. Membership: Editor, Journal of Genetics and Molecular Biology, 1990-. Address: Institute of Biochemistry, College of Life Sciences, National Yang Ming University, Shipai, Taipei, Taiwan.

**CHIGBOH Nnaemezie,** b. 4 November 1947, Eke. Civil Engineer. m. 2 sons, 3 daughters. Education: WASC, 1971; FH, Mainz, Germany, Diploma in Engineering, 1976; The Salford University, Msc, Transport Engineering, 1980. Appointments: Civil Engineer, Boer Engineering Consultants, 1976-77; Geri Consulting Co, Frankfurt, 1977-79; Fed Cap Dev Authority, Head, Transportation Unit, 1981-. Publications: Impact of Railways to Nigeria. Economy, 1980; Transfer of Technology, 1985; Contract Consultancy in the Development of Abuja, Railway Network for Abuja; Alternative Water Scheme to Karu; Ogbuanu the 4th of Eke, 1997. Memberships: Institute of Highway Transport; Institute of Transport Engineering; Washington International Road Federation; Council of Reg Engr Nigeria. Address: Federal Capital Development Authority, PO Box 1772, Abuja FCT, Nigeria.

**CHIHARA Goro,** b. 20 July 1927, Tokyo, Japan. Scientist. m. Suzuko Yasuda, 1 son, 1 daughter. Education: BPharm Sci, 1952; PhD, 1957; DPharm Sci, Tokyo University, 1962. Appointments: Head Biochemistry, Tokyo University Hospital, 1956; Head Chemotherapy, National Cancer Centre Research Institute Tokyo, 1962; Professor, Kyoto University, 1985; Professor, Kyoto Pharmaceutical University, 1988; Professor, Teikyo University, 1988; Special Scientific Advisor, 1990. Publications: Immunopotentiation, 1973; Immune Modulation Agents, 1984; Immunomodalatory Agent from Plants, 1999. Memberships: International Association Immunopharmacology; International Society Preventive Oncology. Address: Tanacho 49-15 Aoba-ku, Yokohama 227-0064, Japan.

**CHILADZE Tamaz,** b. 5 March 1931, Signakhi. Writer. Education: Graduated, Tbilisi State University, 1954. Appointments: Chief Editor, Khelovneba, magazine, 1973-81; Chief Editor, Mnatobi, literary magazine, 1997-. Publications: Author of novels, poems, plays and essays, 1951-. Honours: Shota Rustave National Award, 1992; State Prize of Georgia, 1997. Memberships: Georgian Writers Union; Writers Association, Otaridi. Address: 380072 Georgia Tblisi, Simon Chikrovani St 22, ap 7, Georgia.

**CHILDERS-EPLEY Thelma,** b. 28 December 1918. Education: BS, Indiana University, Bloomington, Indiana, USA, 1941; MA, California State College, Los Angeles, CA, USA, 1958; Postgraduate Work, University of Southern California, Los Angeles, CA, USA, 1964-65. Appointments include: Instructor, Occidental College, Eagle Rock, CA, 1952-61; Reserve Teacher, Los Angeles Unified School District, Los Angeles, CA, 1955-57; Instructor, California State College, Northridge, CA, 1958; Teacher, Adult Education, Los Angeles USD, Los Angeles, CA, 1964-69; Specialist, Gifted Programs, Los Angeles Unified School District, 1958-65; Educational Consultant, Schools, State Boards of Education, USA, 1975-86; Advisory Boad, Gifted Groups, Los Angeles, CA, 1958-75. Publications: Annotated Bibliography on Gifted, book, 1958; Professional articles to numerous journals, 1958-78. Honours: Achievement Awards, The Association for Gifted, California, 1958-75; Achievement Awards, Delta Kappa Gamma Society, 1989-90; Woman of the Year, Delta Kappa Gamma Society, 1990. Memberships: World Future Society, 1979-92; National Association for Gifted, 1958-92; World Council on Gifted, 1980-98; Delta Kappa Gamma Society, , 1955-; Associated Administrators of Los Angeles University School District, 1975-98; California Retired Teachers Association, 1975-; California Coordinators of Newspapers in Education, 1982-92. Address: Leisure World, Laguna Hills, CA, USA.

**CHILDERS-WILSON Julia M,** b. 6 February 1950, Fort Wayne, Indiana, USA. Project Manager. m. Robert Kenneth Wilson. Education: Associate in Customer Service Certificate,

1992, Life Office Management Association; Certificate of Excellence in Project Management, 1992, American Management Association; Certification of Project Management Professional, 1992, Project Management Institute; Bachelors in Information Management, 1995, University of Phoenix. Appointments: Senior Consultant, AT&T Global Solutions, 1995; Director and Senior Programme Manager, Vanstar Corporation, 1996; Project Executive, 1997, Practice Leader and Principal, 1997, Practice Manager and Principal, 1998, Practice Executive and Principal, 1998-, IBM Corporation. Publications: 3 books including: The Implementation Coordinator: How to Coordinate Information Systems Implementations, 1994; 5 papers presented at conferences; 4 presentations at conferences. Honours: Various grants and scholarships, 1967-; Focus on the Producer Award, Pacific Mutual Life Insurance Company, 1989; President's Citation, PMI, 1991, 1996; VIP Award, PMI, 1993; Volunteer of the Year Award, PMI Employees' Federal Credit Union, 1994; Women in Project Management, 1994; IBM Stock Options Award, 1998. Memberships: Life Office Management Association; American Management Association; Project Management Institute; PMI-Orange County Chapter; Pacific Mutual Employee's Federal Credit Union, Board of Directors; National Association Female Executives; FLMI Society of Southern California; World Future Society. Address: PO Box 8054, Newport Beach, CA 92658, USA.

**CHING Chiao-Liang Juliana,** b. 23 February 1955, Hong Kong. Education: BSc, summa cum laude, Biology, Yale University, USA; MD, University of California at Davis, USA, 1981; Residency, UCLA Hospitals and Clinics, 1981-83, Harvard University Hospitals, 1983-85. Appointments: Medical work, Beth Israel Hospital and Brigham Women's Hospital, and UCLA Hospitals and Clinica; Director, Ideal Choice Development Ltd, and Chi King Development. Honours: Woman of the Year; International Woman of the Year. Memberships: California Medical Association; American Medical Association; Hong Kong Securities Professionals Alumni Association; Planetary Society; Pacific Club; Elihu Yale Associate; Friends of the Cultural Centre of Hong Kong; Deputy Governor, American Biographical Institute; Deputy Governor General, International Biographical Institute. Address: 4 Mount Butler Drive, Jardine's Lookout, Hong Kong.

**CHIPEUR Gerald David,** b. 28 June 1960, Walla Walla, Washington, USA. Lawyer. m. Dr Barbara E Chipeur, 2 daughters. Education: Louise McKinney Scholarship, Concordia College, 1979-81; LLB, 1984, LLM, 1990, Faculty of Law, University of Alberta. Appointments: Lecturer, 1989-92, Adjunct Professor, 1993-97, Canadian University College; Partner, Fraser Milner, Barristers & Solicitors; Fellow, International Academy for Freedom of Religion and Belief; Contributing Editor, Charter and Human Rights Litigation Quarterly. Publications: Columnist, Family Practice, the Canadian Newspaper of Primary Care; 70 legal publications; 11 legislative bills drafted; testimony before 8 legislative committees; over 60 speeches and presentations. Memberships: National Council of the Canadian Bar Association, various other posts with the Canadian Bar Association; International Commission of Jurists, Canadian Section; National Association Health Lawyers; Associate Member, Centre for Constitutional Studies; Canadian Journal of Clinical Medicine; Co-Chair, Canada for Tomorrow Committee; Member of the board of Canadian University College, Gimbell Eye Foundation, Sherwood Park Care Centre, North America Medical Inc.. Address: Fraser Milner, 30th Floor 5th Avenue Place, Calgary, Alberta, Canada T2P 4X7.

**CHIRCEV Elena,** b. 10 June 1955, Deva, jud Hunedoara, Romania. Professor of Music. m. Andrei Chircev, div 1989, 1 son, 1 daughter. Education: Graduated, Academy of Music, Cluj-Napoca, 1978; Doctorate in Musicology, 1998. Appointments: Lector, GH Dima Academy of Music, Cluj-Napoca, 1986; Professor, School of Music, 1978-86. Publications: Studies in reviews. Address: Str Scortarilor Nr 3, Block D6, Sc 2, Apt 21, Cluj-Napoca, Romania.

**CHIRCULESCU Andy Remus Marius,** b. 30 June 1948, Drobeta, Romania. Physician. m. Mihaela, 1 son. Education: MD, 1972; PhD, 1977. Appointments: Hospital Intern, 1972-74; Resident Physician, 1974-77; Pathologist Chief, 1977-78; University Assistant, 1978-; Senior Lecturer Tenure, 1991; Senior Fellowship in Pathology, 1992. Publications: Author of 234 Original Papers, 187 Published, 47 Communicated. Honours: Certificate of Honour, 1998; Man of the Year, American Biographical Institute, 1998. Memberships: Secretary of the Section of Anatomy; National Committee of the Romanian Society of Normal and Pathologic Morphology, 1987; Union Medicale Balkanique, 1982; Romanian Society of Acupuncture; Romanian Scientists Association; Romanian Society of Biophysics in Acupuncture; Romanian Society of Psychoneuroendocrinology; Associations of Medical Sciences, 1991; Romanian Assocaition of Anatomists; Physicians Order of Romania; European Biomedical Research Assocaition; National Congress of Normal and Pathological Morphology. Address: 14-Dr Severeanu, Bucharest 76228, Romania.

**CHITESCU Ion,** b. 19 July 1947, Bucharest, Romania. University Professor. m. Rodica Chitescu, 2 daughters. Education: Master Mathematics, 1970, Mathematics PhD, 1975, Faculty Mathematics, University Bucharest. Appointments: Assistant Professor, 1970-80; Lecturer, 1980-91; Associate Professor, 1991-, Faculty Mathematics, University Bucharest. Publications: 37 papers in field of Measure and Integration Theory, Function Spaces, Hausdorff Measure and Dimension-Fractals, Random Sequences, Probability & Statistics, Optimization. Honour: National Romanian Academy Prize 1985 for monograph, Function Spaces. Memberships: AMS; Mathematical Reviews referee; Board, Mathematical Journal, Mathematical Studies and Researches, Romania. Address: Str Henri Coanda 44, sector 1, cod 71119, Bucharest, Romania.

**CHITTISTER Joan D,** b. 26 April 1936, DuBois, Pennsylvania, USA. Author; Lecturer; Benedictine Sisters of Erie. Education: St Benedict Academy, Erie, 1954; BA, Mercyhurst College, Erie, 1962; MA, University of Notre Dame, Indiana, 1968; PhD, Pennsylvania State University, 1971. Appointments: Elementary Teacher, 1954-59; Secondary Teacher, 1959-74; College Instructor, 1969-; President, Federation of St Scholastica, 1971-78; President, Conference of American Benedictine Prioresses, 1974-90; President, Leadership Conference of Women Religious, 1976-77; Prioress, Benedictine Sisters of Erie, 1978-90; Executive Director, BENETVISION, A Research and Resource Centre for Contemporary Spirituality, 1990-. Publications: 20 books including: Wisdom Distilled from the Daily, 1990; Heart of Flesh: A Feminist Spirituality for Women and Men, 1998; In Search of Belief, 1999; Columnist for National Catholic Reporter; Numerous articles and lectures on religious life, peace-making and women's issues. Honours: 6 Honorary LLD, 1 Honorary Doctorate of Sacred Theology, 2 Honorary Doctorates of Humanities; 2 book Awards; Distinguished Alumna of the Year, Mercyhurst College, 1986; Woman of the Year Award, The Women's Roundtable, Erie, 1990; Pope Paul VI Teacher of Peace Award, Pax Christi National Assembly, 1990; US Catholic Award for Furthering the Cause of Women

in the Church, US Catholic Magazine, 1992; Catherine of Alexandria Award, 1994; Ruth Bayley Peace Award, Peacelinks, 1994; Pennsylvania Honour Roll of Women, 1996; National Ethics Award, Summit on Christian Ethics, Washington DC, 1996; Notre Dame Alumni Association Women's Award of Achievement, 1997; Service to Society Award, Penn State University Alumni Society, 1999; and many others. Memberships: Benedictine Sisters of Erie; American Benedictine Academy; Speech Communications Association; Board of Directors: National Catholic Reporter, Erie Community Foundation; Council Member, International Committee for the Peace Council. Address: St Scholastica Priory, 355 East 9th Street, Erie, Pennsylvania 16503, USA.

**CHIU Pi-Ru,** b. 27 January 1950, Taipei, Taiwan. Associate Professor of Nursing. Education: DSc, Nursing, 1994. Appointments: Associate Professor and Director, Department of Nursing, College of Medicine, Fu Jen Catholic University, 1998-. Publications: The Structural Design of Patient Classification Systems, 1996. Honour: National Science Institute Research Award, 1997. Memberships: Secretary, Nursing Research Committee, Nurses Association of China; Academic Committee, Lambda Beta; Sigma Theta Tau. Address: Department of Nursing, Fu Jen Catholic University, 510 Chung Chen Road, Hsing Chung, Taiwan.

**CHIU Ying-Chech,** b. 25 May 1937, Canton, China. Professor of Chemistry. Education: BSc, Chemical Engineering, Cheng Kung University, Tainan, Taiwan, 1959; PhD in Chemistry, Baylor University, Waco, Texas, 1965. Appointments: Senior Research Chemist, Shell Development Company, Houston, Texas, USA, 1969-81; Professor of Chemistry, Chung Yuan Christian University, Chungli, Taiwan, 1981-. Publications: Patentee: Steam Foam Well Cleaning, 1972; Tall Oil Pitch Soap, 1974; Process of Displacing Oil, 1976; Aqueous Anionic Surfactant, 1976. Honour: Distinguished Research Professor Award, 1988-93. Memberships: American Chemical Society; New York Academy of Sciences. Address: Department of Chemistry, Chung Yuan Christian University, Chungli, Taiwan, China.

**CHMELA Pavel,** b. 2 July 1936, Pozdechov, Moravia, Czech Republic. Professor of Physics. m. Marie Snajdrova, 1 son, 1 daughter. Education: Mgr, 1959, Rer.Nat.D, 1967, PhD, 1968, Palacky University, Olomouc; D Habil, A Mickiewicz University, Poznan, 1986; Principal Research Fellow, Presidium of Czech Academy of Sciences, Prague, 1990; Professor of Physics, Czech Republic, 1995. Appointments: Assistant Professor, 1960-66, Research Fellow, 1966-74, 1976-88, Palacky University, Olomouc; Associate Professor, Head, Physics Department, Military Technical College, Cairo, Egypt, 1974-76; Principal Research Fellow, 1988-95, Professor of Physics, 1995-, Technical University, Brno. Publications: 66 original research papers, 55 reports and communications, 17 reviews. Honours: Award, Union of Czech Mathematicians and Physicists, 1981; Award, Palacky University, Olomouc, 1981, 1986, 1987; Award, Physical Section, Union of Czech Mathematicians and Physicists, 1990. Memberships: Union of Czech Mathematicians and Physicists; International Commission for Optics. Address: Uvoz 6, 602 00 Brno Moravia, Czech Republic.

**CHO Hyung Suck,** b. 8 October 1944, Seoul, Korea. Professor. m. Eun Sue Kim, 1 son, 1 daughter. Education: BS, Seoul National University, 1971; MS, Northwestern University, USA, 1973; PhD, University of California, Berkeley, USA, 1977. Appointment: Professor, Department of Mechanical Engineering, Korean Advanced Institute of Science and Technology. Publications: 240 articles in international journals nd conference proceedings; Editorial Board Member several ternational journals including: Robotica; LFICA Control ngineering Practice; Advanced Robotics. Honours: Humboldt ellow, 1984-85; Tatcher Bros Award, Institute of Mechanical ngineering, England, 1998. Memberships: ASME; IEEE; PIE; KAST. Address: Korea Advanced Institute of Science & echnology, 373-1 Kusong-dong, Yusong-ku, Taejon 305-701, orea.

**CHO Jun-Dong**, b. 21 July 1957, Seoul. Professor. m. Keum J Choi, 2 sons. Education: BS, 1980, Sungkyunkwan niversity; MS, 1989, Polytechnic University; PhD, 1993, orthwestern University. Appointments: Samsung Electronics, 980-95; Sung Kyun Kwan University School of Electrical and omputer Engineering, 1995-. Honours: High Performance esign Automation for MCM and Package, World Scientific, 996; Design Automation Conference, Best Paper Award, 993. Membership: IEEE, senior member. Address: epartment ofElectrical and Computer Engineering, Sung Kyun wan University, 300 Chunchun dong, Suwon, Korea 440-746.

**CHO Myong Won**, b. 2 September 1932, Kwangjn, Republic Korea. Professor. m. Young Jwa Suh, 2 sons. Education: A, Chonnam National University, 1959; MA, University of awaii, 1967; PhD, Chonnam National University, 1974; Post octoral Fellow, University of Edinburgh, 1979-80. ppointments: Instructor, Chonnam National University, 959-68; Assistant Professor, Chonnam National University, 968-73; Associate Professor, 1974-79; Professor, 1978-98; meritas, 1998-. Publications: Modern Foreign Langauge ducation, 1981; Travels, Landscape, Peoplescape and elf-Scape, 1983; Dictionary of English Teaching, 1991; anguage Learnability, 1998; Out There, 1998. Honours: ecipient from British Council and Hornby Foundation for ostdoct Fellowship, 1979-80; Professional Research Award om the East West Centre 1973-74; Schlarship from the East 'est Centre, 1965-67. Memberships: Korea Association of eachers and English, President, 1986-90; International ssociation of teachers of English as a Foreign Language; eachers of English and Other Languages. Address: Yang 2 ong Suh Ku, Keumho Apt 3-201, 502-222 Kwangju Chonnan, epublic of Korea.

**CHO Zang-Hee**, b. 15 July 1936, Seoul, Korea. Researcher. ducation. m. Jung-Suk Cho, 3 daughters. Education: BS, 960, MS, 1962, Electronics, Seoul National University, Korea; hD, Applied Physics, Uppsala University, Sweden, 1966; i.D, Physics, Stockholm University, Sweden, 1972. Career: esearch Staff, Swedish Atomic Research Council, 1966-71, esearch Supervisor, 1971-72, Associate Professor, Physics, 972-76, Institute of Physics, University of Stockholm; Visiting cientist, Wallenberg Fellow, Brookhaven National Laboratory, pton Long Island, New York, 1970-71; Adjunct Associate rofessor, Associate Research Physicist I-III, Applied Science nd Engineering, University of California, Los Angeles, 972-77; Associate Research Radiation Physicist IV, University f California, San Diego, 1977-78; Professor, Electrical cience, 1978-95, Visiting Chair Professor, 1995-97, Korea dvanced Institute of Science & Technology, Seoul; Visiting rofessor, 1984-, Radiology Department, Professor, Radiology, o-Director, Imaging Research Center, 1979-84, Columbia niversity, New York; Professor, Radiological Sciences, irector, NMR Imaging Research, University of California, vine, 1984-. Publictions: Over 180 scientific and technical apers in professional journals. Honours include: National cience Prize, Korea, 1995; Science Prize, National Academy Sciences, Korea, 1997. Memberships; Elected Member, US ational Academy of Sciences-Institute of Medicine, 1997; ational Academy of Sciences, Republic of Korea, 1998

Address: Department of Radiological Sciences, University of California, Irvine, CA 92697, USA.

**CHODAK Stanislaw**, b. 1 January 1931, Szpikolosy, Hrubieszow, Poland. Lawyer; Public Prosecutor. m. Zofia Nowosielska, 1 daughter. Education: Faculty of History, Catholic University of Lublin, 1950-54; LLM, 1955, Maria Curie-Sklodowska University, Lublin. Appointments: Assistant Public Prosecutor, City of Lublin, 1955-66; Associate Public Prosecutor and later Regional Public Prosecutor, Province of Lublin, 1966-; Lecturer and Professor of Criminalistics of Faculty of Laws for postgraduate students of laws, public prosecutor's trainees and judge's trainees, 1966-. Publications: Numerous books and articles dealing with the problems of Criminatistics and Formal and Substantive Legality; Issues of collection and examination of material evidences and traces of crime in penal proceedings concerning offences against life and health. Honours: Gold Medal of National Education, 1960; Order of Polonia Restituta, Class III, 1968, Class II, 1978, Class I, 1997. Memberships: Catholic Schools Association; Association of Polish Lawyers. Address: Wallenroda Street 11/10, 20 607 Lublin, Poland.

**CHOH Sung Ho**, b. 7 November 1935, Chungjin, Korea. Professor of Physics. m. Sul Ja Kim, 1 son, 1 daughter. Education: BS Physics, 1958, Seoul National University; MS Experimental Physics, 1960, Graduate School, Seoul National University; PhD Physics, 1968, Graduate School, Brown University, USA. Appointments: Full Time Instructor, Yonsei University, 1961-63; Post-doctoral Fellow, McMaster University, Canada, 1968-71; Associate Professor, Professor, Dept Physics, Korea University, 1971-. Publications: Over 200 scientific papers. Honours: Recipient National Order Mokreon, 1987; Academic Award of Samil Moonwha Foundation, 1990. Memberships: American Physical Society; Canadian Association of Physicists; International EPR Society; Fellow, Korean Physical Society; Korean Academy of Science & Technology; Institute of Physics, UK. Address: Joogong Apt 1001-402, Choongang-dong 67, Gwacheon Kyunggi-do 427-010, Korea.

**CHOI Dong Ryong**, b. 15 February 1945, Tokyo, Japan. Geologist. m. Chong-Ih Choi, 1 son, 1 daughter. Education: BSc, 1967, DSc, 1972, Hokkaido University, Sapporo, Japan. Appointments: Chief Engineer, Kokusai Kogyo Co Ltd, Tokyo, 1973-77; Postdoctoral Fellow, Assistant Professor, University Miami, USA, 1977-84; Senior Research Scientist, Australian Geological Survey Organisation, Canberra, 1985-88; Consulting Geologist, Canberra, 1988-. Publications: Belize Reef Foundation, Seismic Study, 1981, Drilling Study, 1984, US National Science Foundation. Memberships: Geological Society of Australia, of America, of Japan; American Association of Petroleum Geologists; New Concepts in Global Tectonics Group. Address: 6 Mann Place, Higgins, ACT 2615, Australia.

**CHOI Moo Young**, b. 2 June 1957, Seoul, Korea. Professor. m. Keumsook Lee, 1 son, 1 daughter. Education: BS, Seoul National University, 1979; MS, Seoul National University, 1981; PhD, Stanford University, 1984. Appointments: Assistant Professor, 1987-91, Associate Professor, 1991-97, Professor, 1997-, Seoul National University. Publications: About 70 publications (research papers) in professional journals. Memberships: Fellow, Korean Physical Society; Member, American Physical Society. Address: Department of Physics, Seoul National University, Seoul 151742, Korea.

**CHOI Yong-Eui**, b. 29 June 1960, Kimje-kun, South Korea. Plant Biologist. m. Joung-Yeon Han, 2 sons. Education:

Graduate Biology, 1984, MSc Biology, 1986, PhD, 1994, Chonbuk National University, South Korea. Appointments: Researcher, Genetic and Physiology Division, National Institute of Agricultural Science and Technology, RDA, Korea, 1985-86; Research Assistant, Department of Botany, Chonbuk National University, Korea, 1994-96; Researcher, Korean Ginseng and Tobacco Research Institute, Korea, 1996-98; Chief Researcher, PanaxBio Co Jinankun, Chonlabukdo, Korea, 1998-; Researcher, Nara Institute of Science and Technology, Japan, 1998-. Publications: Author or co-Author, 24 papers in professional journals; 7 patents in Korea, 1996-99. Memberships: Korean Society of Botany; Korean Society of Plant Tissue Culture; Korean Society of Plant Resources; International Society of Plant Morphologists. Address: 1314-94 Douckjin-Dong, 561-190 Chonju, South Korea.

**CHOI Young Deuk,** b. 12 May 1961, Seoul, Korea. Doctor, Professor. m. Kwang Hee Baek, 2 daughters. Education: MD, PhD, 1998; Appointments: Assistant Professor, Yonsei University College of Medicine. Publications: Around 50 Articles for Urological Genital System. Memberships:Corresponding Member, American Urological Associations; Active Member, Korean Urological Asociation. Address: Dept Urology, Yongdong Severance Hospital, Youngdong P O Box 1217, Seoul, Korea.

**CHOLAYYA Pramila,** b. 20 January 1939, Sholapur, India. Artist. m. U Cholayya, 1 son, 1 daughter. Education: Government Diploma, Fine Art, 1980. Appointment: Director, Chitrakalamandira School of Art, Udupi. Creative Works: Exhibitions of paintings in Kyushu, Japan, 1996. Membership: Karnataka Lalitkala Academy. Address: Chitrakalamandira School of Art, Udupi 576 101, Karnataka, India.

**CHON Kyum Koo,** b. 17 March 1952, Cheju, Korea. Professor. m. Lee Eun Joo, 2 sons. Education: BS, SungKyunKwan University, 1979; MA, 1982; PhD, University of Massachusetts, 1989. Appointments: Research Intern, East West Center, Hawaii, 1982-83; Teaching Assistant, University of Massachusetts, 1983-88; Researcher, SungKyunKwan University, 1989-92; Assistant Professor, Associate Professor, Taegu University, 1992-; Director, Korean Institute of Stress, 1996-. Publications: Durkeim and the Social Construction of Emotions; Rules of Hope; Disentangling the Stress Labyrinth. Honours: Academic Achievement Award, Taegu University; 1st Class, Licence, Korean Mental Health Clinical Psychologist. Memberships: Health Psychology Division; IAAP; American Institute of Stress; Korean Association of Health Psychology. Address: 110-101 Nokwon Mansion, 761 Jisan-dong, Taegu, Korea.

**CHOPRA Perveen Ji,** b. 12 August 1934. Musician. m. Sh Som Ji, 2 sons, 1 daughter. Education: SSLC. Career: Agent. Honours: Several music awards. Memberships: Punjab Association; Regional & Religious Associations. Address: 3/71 Parag Roopnagar, New Mig Colony, Bandra E, Mumbai 40005, India.

**CHOPYK Dan B,** b. 2 January 1925, Beneva, Ukraine. Educator. m. Alexandra Koudryasheva, 3 sons, 1 daughter. Education: Philosophy, Ukrainian Theological Seminary, 1945-47; BCom, University of Birmingham, England, 1953; MA, 1962, ABD, 1968, University of Colorado, USA; PhD, Ukrainian Free University, 1970; Academician, International Informatization Academy, 1997. Appointments: Teacher, Public Schools, Denver-Jeffco, Colorado, USA, 1958-65; Instructor, Regis College, Colorado, 1965; Teaching Fellow, University of Colorado, Boulder, 1966-67; Assistant Professor, Associate Professor, Professor, 1969-96, Professor Emeritus, 1996-,

University of Utah, Salt Lake City; President, World Cossack Academy, affiliated with World Distributed University, Brussels, Belgium, 1998. Publications: 3 collections of poetry; Numerous publications in field of Slavic linguistics, Slavic folklore and civilisation, including: Systemy Fonem SULM, 1976; Navchannya Movy, 1976; G S Skovoroda: Fables and Aphorisms, 1990; Movoznarchi praci, 1994; G S Skovoroda: His Life and Times, 1994; Metodologia izuchenia inostrann iazyka, 1994; Skovoroda's Fables: Analysis, 1995. Memberships: Ukrainian Free Academy of Sciences; Shevchenko Scientific Society; AATSEEL; American Association for Advancement of Slavic Studies; Ukrainian Historical Society; Rocky Mountain Modern Language Association; International Association of Ukrainists; International Informatization Academy; World Cossack Association; RMASS, President, Executive Board; Canadian Association of Slavists. Address: 106 Guadeloupe Drive, Toms River, NJ 08757, USA.

**CHOU Loke Ming,** b. 4 November 1946, Singapore. Academic. m. Renee Lim, 1 daughter. Education: BSc Hons, 1969; PhD, 1975. Appointments: Science and Education Department Head, Singapore Science Centre; Lecturer, 1977-82; Senior Lecturer, 1982-88; Associate Professor, 1988-98; Professor, National University of Singapore, 1998-. Publications: Over 200 Scientific Publications. Honours: Outstanding Science Lecturer Award; Teaching Excellence Award. Address: Department of Biological Science, National University of Singapore, 10 Kent Ridge Crescent, Singapore 119260, Singapore.

**CHOU Pesus,** b. 9 November 1948, Tainan, Taiwan. Public Health Director. m. Gin-Kai Lin, deceased. Education: BS, School of Pharmacy, 1967-71, MPH, Institute of Public Health, 1971-73, National Taiwan University; MPH, 1983-84, DrPH, 1984-85, School of Public Health and Tropical Medicine, Tulane University, USA. Appointments: Secretary, Secretary General, Cancer Society of China, 1974-86; Instructor, Department of Social Medicine, 1977-83, Associate Professor, 1983-92, Director, 1991-94, Professor, 1992-, Institute of Public Health, Dean of Student Affairs, 1991-97, Director, Preparatory Office of School of Public Health, 1994-, Director, Community Medicine Research Center, 1996-, National Yang-Ming University; President, Society of Preventive Medicine, China, 1993-98; Executive Director, Human Rights Education Foundation, Taipei, 1996-. Publications: Numerous articles in professional journals. Honours: One of Top Ten Outstanding Young Women in China, 1984; Delta Omega, 1985; Honorary Citizen of Kinmen, 1992; Cancer Prevention Special Contribution Award, 1993. Address: National Yang-Ming University, Shih-Pai, 11221 Taipei, Taiwan.

**CHOU Tise-Sheng,** b. 27 September 1937, Honan, China. Senior Scientist; Professor. m. Kan Yan-Shi, 2 sons, 1 daughter. Education: BS, Chung-Cheng Institute of Technology, 1962; DEng, Catholic University of Leuven, Belgium, 1976. Appointments: Instructor, Military Academy 1965-68; Chemical Engineer, 1968-76, Scientist, 1976-80 Division Deputy Director, 1980-83, Senior Scientist, 1982- Division Director, 1983-86, Program Manager, 1986-89 Institute of Nuclear Energy Research; Technical Superintendent, 1982-90, Commissioner, 1985-87, Chun Shan Institute of Science and Technology; Professor Feng-Chia University, 1985-88; Advisor, Taiwan Power Company, 1989-91; Chief Advisor, Yu Sheng Technology Ltd 1991-97. Publications: Over 60 research reports on radioactiv waste management. Honours: Representative of China, Pacif Nuclear Council, 1990-93; Academician, International Informatization Academy, 1994-. Memberships: Chinese

Institute of Engineers; Chinese Chemical Society; Pollution Protection Society of Radiation, Biology and Chemistry; Chinese Nuclear Society. Address: Institute of Nuclear Energy Research, PO Box 3-27, Lungtan 325, Taiwan.

**CHOUDHARI Ramesh Madhav,** b. 25 March 1950, India. Assistant Professor. m. Shobha, 2 daughters. Education: BSc Physics and Maths, 1970; MSc Theoretical Nuclear Physics, 1972; BE Electrical Engineering, 1976; MS Computer Science, 1983; PhD Computer Science, 1994. Appointments: Programmer/Analyst, MG Consultantcy Services Ltd, Bombay, 1977-80; Assistant Professor, Clafflin University, 1983-84; Assistant Professor, South Carolina State University, 1985-. Publications: 23 publications in Computer Science, 1982-98. Honours: Government Open Merit Scholar, 1968-72; Research Scholar, University of Bombay, 1972-73. Memberships: Life Member of South Carolina Academy of Sciences; National Geographic Society; Institute of Electrical and Electronics Eng-Computer Society; Riverbanks Society. Address: South Carolina State University, P O Box 7725, Orangeburg, SC 29117, USA.

**CHOUDHARY Suresh,** b. 25 January 1950, Parli Vaisnath. Physician. m. Saros, 2 sons, 2 daughters. Education: MB, BS, Degree, 1976. Appointments: Private Clinic. Honours: Mr Medico, Health, Body Building Competition. Address: Vaidynath Clinic, Ganeshpar Parli, Vaijnath, Dist Beed, India.

**CHOUDHURY Dilip Kumar,** b. 1 September 1946, Pakowa, India. Physicist. m. Nilima Niogi, 2 daughters. Education: BSc, Gauhati University, 1965; MSc, 1967, PhD, 1970, Delhi University; Postdoctoral Research, Delhi, 1970-71, Oxford University, England, 1971-74. Appointments: Senior Research Associate, Daresbury Laboratory, England, 1974-76; Visiting Fellow, Tata Institute, Bombay, 1976-78; Lecturer, 1978-83, Reader, 1983-88, Professor, 1988-, Gauhati University. Publications: 75 research papers, 3 books. Honours: Honorary Mention Citation, Erice, Italy, 1973; Thawani Fellowship, 1988; Kamal Kumari national Award, Science & Technology, 1994. Memberships: ICTP, Trieste, Italy; Assam Science Society; Indian Physics Association; New York Academy of Sciences; American Biographical Institute. Address: Department of Physics, Gauhati University, Guwahati 781014, India.

**CHOUDHURY Rezaul Karim,** b. 1952, Shakharunja, Joypurhat, Bangladesh. Landlord. m. Laila Choudhury, 2 sons. Education: MA, Political Science, Rajshahi University, Bangladesh. Publications: 6 books of poetry. Honours: Obtained many awards and honours. Address: Maurika, Badurtala, Bagura 5800, Bangladesh.

**CHOW Chun Lam James,** b. 25 November 1966, Hong Kong. Physicist. Education: BSc First Class Hons Applied Physics, 1992, City University, Hong Kong; PhD Physics, 1995, University of Hong Kong, Hong Kong. Appointments: Demonstrator, University of Hong Kong, 1995; Croucher Research Fellow, University of Cambridge, UK, 1995-97; Research Associate, 1997-98, Part-time Research Associate, 1998-, University of Toronto, Canada; Research Fellow, McMaster University, Canada, 1998-. Publications: Over 15 presentations and seminars at international conferences and universities in North America, Europe and Asia; Over 45 publications in cited journals, reports and conference proceedings; Science manuscript writer of Chinese newspaper. Honours: Chartered Physicist and European Physicist in the UK and Europe respectively; Sir Edward Youde Memorial Scholarship, 1990-91, Fellowship, 1993-94, 1994-95; CMA Donor Scholarship 1990-91; 11 other Fellowships, travel grants and Scholarships 1993-98. Memberships: IEEE, USA; IEE, UK;

Canadian Association of Physicists; American Physical Society; Institute of Physics, UK; New York Academy of Sciences; IEEE Computer Society; Electrochemical Society. Address: Department of Physics and Astronomy, McMaster University, Hamilton, Ontario, Canada L8S 4M1.

**CHOW Song-Nan,** b. 20 November 1942, Taiwan. Physician; Researcher; Educator. m. Chin-Hsiang Chien, 2 sons, 1 daughter. Education: MD, College of Medicine, National Taiwan University, 1968; PhD, Institute of Clinical Medicine, National Taiwan University, 1983. Appointments: Professor, Department of Obstetrics and Gynaecology, National Taiwan University, 1988-; Chairman, Division of Gynaecology, National Taiwan University Hospital, 1994-; Chairman, Research Institute of Laser Medicine, National Taiwan University, 1993-. Publications: 110 referee journal papers; more than 95 conference papers. Memberships: President, The Taiwan Association of Gynaecology, 1995-; President, Global Vista Medical Foundation, 1997-; Editor-in-Chief, Journal of Genetics and Molecular Biology, 1990-. Address: National Taiwan University Hospital, 7 Chung-Shan South Road, Taipei, Taiwan.

**CHOWDHARY Brahma Ram,** b. 12 December 1941, Surpaliya, Nagaur Raj, India. Teaching University Professor. m. Bhanwari Devi, 1 son, 4 daughters. Education: BVSc, AH, 1963, PhD, 1980, Rajasthan Agricultural University, Bikaner; MSc, University of Canterbury, Lincoln College, Christchurch, New Zealand, 1967. Appointments: Demonstrator, Extension, College of Veterinary and Animal Science, Bikaner, Rajasthan, India, 1963; Assistant Professor LPM, 1967; Associate Professor, LPM, 1975; Professor and HCD-LPM, 1994. Publications: Books on Animal Production and Allied Field in English: Sheep Production, 1975; Wool Science, 1980; Camel Production, 1994; Eco-Culture, Nutrition and Livestock Production, 1998; 75 research papers. Memberships: Society of Animal Production; WUS. Address: Hirakunj-Alok Sadan, Sharma Colony Rani Bazar, Bikaner 334001, India.

**CHOWDHURY Nirmalendu,** b. 1 February 1942, Karimganj, Assam, India. Veterinary Scientist. m. Amita (Dutta) Chowdhury, 1 daughter. Education: BVSc, Assam Agricultural University, 1964; MVSc, UP College Veterinary Science, 1968; DSc, State University Gent, Belgium, 1975; Postdoctorate, Kumamoto University Medical School, 1980-81. Appointments: Associate Professor, Assam Agricultural University, 1975-80; Associate Professor, Punjab Agricultural University, 1982-87; Professor, 1988-. Publication: Helminthology, editor, 1994. Honours: Research Fellow, CSIR, ICAR, 1969; Belgian Ministry Education, 1970; Japan Society Promotion Science, 1980. Memberships: Fellow, Belgian Society Parasitology; Indian Society Parasitology; World Association Advancement of Veterinary Parasitology. Address: Department of Parasitology, College of Veterinary Science, P A U Ludhiana 141004, India.

**CHOWDRI Nisar Ahmad,** b. 15 April 1959, Srinagar. Doctor. m. Neelofar, 1 son, 1 daughter. Education: MBBS, 1984; MS, 1988. Appointments: Senior Resident, 1988-91; Lecturer, 1991-98; Assistant Professor, 1998-. Publications: 22 Publications. Honours: Bronze Medal for 2nd Position, MBBS; 3rd Position Certificate of Merit, MBBS; Fellowship, Association of Ind Surgeons. Memberships: Association of Surgeons of India; Association of Plastic Surgeons of India; National Academy of Burns. Address: Hassi Bhat, Rainawari, 190003 Srinagar, India.

**CHOWNING Orr-Lyda,** b. 30 November 1920, Oregon, USA. Dietitian. m. Eldon Wayne Chowning. Education: BSc, Foods & Nutrition, Oregon State College, 1943; MA, Columbia University, 1950; Diet Intern, Scripps Metabolic Clinic, LaJolla,

1944. Career: Senior Assistant Dietitian, Providence Hospital, Portland, Oregon, 1945-49; Dietitian, St Lukes Hospital, New York City, 1949; Cafeteria Food Service Supervisor, Met Life Insurance Company, New York City, 1950-52; Opened Diet Department and Dietitian, McKenzie Willamette Hospital, Springfield, 1955-59; Foods Director, Erb Memorial Student Union, University of Oregon, Eugene, 1960-63; Set Up Food Service and Dietitian, Cascade Manor Retirement Home, Eugene, 1967-68; Owner, Operator, Secretary, Treasurer, Veranda Kafe Inc, Albany, 1971-80, Chownings Adult Foster Home Inc, Albany, 1984-. Publication: A Phenylalanine Deficient Diet. Honours: College Scholarship, 1939; Mu Beta Beta, 1942; Kappa Delta Pi, 1950. Memberships: American Dietetic Association; Oregon Dietetic Association. Address: Chownings Adult Foster Home, 4440 Woods Road North East, Albany, OR 97321-7353, USA.

**CHOYCE Lesley,** b. 21 March 1951, Riverside, New Jersey. Author. m. Education: BA, 1972, Rutgers University; MA American Literature, 1974, Montclair State College; MA English Literature, 1983, CUNY. Publications: 56 books including: The Republic of Nothing, novel, 1994; The Coastline of Forgetting, poetry, 1995; Nova Scotia: Shaped by the Sea, history, 1996; 2 CDs: Long Lost Planet, music & poetry, 1996; Sea Level, music & poetry, 1998; 3 film & video credits; 3 music videos: Traction, Long Lost Planet, Beautiful Sadness. Honours: Finalist for Canadian Science Fiction and Fantasy Award, 1981; First Place in short fiction and the novel, Writers' Federation of Nova Scotia Literary Competition; The Order of St John Award of Merit; Short listed for the Stephen Leacock Medal, 1987; Dartmouth Book Award, 1990, 1995, short-listed, 1991-93; Pierian Spring Editor's Award for poetry; Event Magazine's Creative Nonfiction Competition, winner, 1990; Ann Connor Brimer Award for Children's Literature, 1994, shortlisted 1992-93; Manitoba's Young Reader's Choice Award, finalist, 1994; Authors Award, Foundation for the Advancement of Canadian Letters, co-winner, 1995; First Place, Canadian Surfing Championships, 1995. Address: 83 Leslie Road, East Lawrencetown, NS Canada B2Z 1P8.

**CHRISTENSEN Halvor Niels,** b. 24 October 1915, Cozad, NE, USA. Biochemist. m. Mayme Matthews, 2 sons, 1 daughter. Education: Bachelors Degree, University of Nebraska at Kearney, 1935; MA, Chemistry, 1937; PhD, Biochemistry, 1940. Appointments: Associate in Biochemistry, Harvard Medical School, 1940-42; Director, Department of Chemical Research, Childrens Hospital, Boston, 1942-44; Professor, Chairman, Biochemistry Department, 1947-49; Chairman, Biochemistry, Tufts University; Nobel Guest Professor, University of Uppsala, Sweden; Carlsburg Laboratory, Copenhagen, 1968-70. Publications: Author of some 270 Publications. Memberships: Adjunct Professor of Pediatrics, University of California, San Diego, 1989-99. Address: 7450 Olivetas Ave Apt 204, La Jolla, CA 92037, USA.

**CHRISTIAN Cora L,** b. 11 September 1947, St Thomas, Virgin Islands. MD; MPH. m. Simon B Jones-Hendrickson, 1 son, 1 daughter. Education: BS Biology, 1967, Marquette University, Milwaukee; MD, 1971, Jefferson Medical College; MPH, 1975, Johns Hopkins University School of Public Health and Hygiene; Residency, Freedmen's Hospital, Howard University Medical Centre, 1971-74; Diplomate: American Academy of Family Practice, 1974-, Board of Quality Assurance & Utilisation Review, 1988-, American College of Forensic Examiners, 1995-. Appointments: Lecturer, Thomas Jefferson University, 1991-; Medical Director, Hess Oil Virgin Islands Corporation's Medical Unit, 1991-; Consultant, NY-Virgin Islands AIDS Education and Training Centre, Training Centre for Health Professionals, Cicatelli Associates,

1992-; Family Practice, self-employed, 1971-; Federal Aviation Medical Examiner, 1976-. Publications: 15 articles in professional publications; 84 presentations and speeches. Honours: Wilmot Blyden Scholarship, US Virgin Islands, 1963; John Hay Whitney Fellowship, 1969; National Urban Coalition Fellowship, 1974; Seikyo Culture Award, Tokyo, 1987; SGI Peace & Friendship Award, 1989; 1990 Individual Member Recognition Award, American Medical Review Research Centre, 1990; 1st Recipient of VI Public Health Award, 1996; Paul Harris Fellow, 1997; Physician Award for Community Service, VI Medical Society, 1997. Memberships: President, VI Medical Society; President Elect, US Virgin Islands Medical Society; Associate member, Society of VI Historians; American Academy Family Physicians; American College of Occupational and Environmental Medicine; American Cancer Society; International Association for Medical Assistance to Travellers; and others. Address: Hess Oil Virgin Island Corp, 40 E G La Grange, Frederiksted, VI 00841, USA.

**CHRISTODOULIDES Andreas Demosthenes,** b. 24 October 1918, Oekos, Cyprus. Educationalist. m. Loulla, 1 son, 1 daughter. Education: Teacher's Diploma, 1939, University of London; Associate, 1946, BA, 1953, Acad Diploma, 1955, University of London; Diploma of Educational Organisation and Supervision, 1961, University Northwestern, USA. Appointments: Elementary School Teacher, 1939-46; Lecturer at Teachers' Training College, 1946-49; Headmaster, Morphou Model School, 1949-51; Assistant Inspector of Schools, 1951-59; Chief Inspector of Schools, 1959-70; Founder and President, Cyprus Educational Research Association, 1961-84; Founder and Alternate President, Pancyprian School for Parents, 1968-96; Director, Department of Primary Education, Ministry of Education, Cyprus, 1970-77; Head of Service for Cypriots Living Overseas, Cyprus Presidency, 1977-82; Dean of Administration and Coordinator of Education Programme, Intercollege, Nicosia, 1983-; Various positions (educational and expatriate associations). Publications: Reading Primer, 1949; The Story of Communications, 1950; For Parents, 1967; We and Our Children, 1981; Editor and Contributor: Cyprus Educational Res Bulletin, 1961-84; Family and School magazine, 1970-97; Avgerinos newpaper children, 1982-83, subsequently periodical for children, 1983-96; Wrote numerous articles for local newspapers and gave numerous lectures and seminars for teachers and parents. Honours: Honorary Plaque, Cyprus Federation of Parent Associations, 1971; Honorary Presid, Cyprus Expatriates Association, 1986; Honorary Presid, Pancypria School for Parents, 1996; Honorary Dean, Intercollege, 1998. Memberships: American Educational Research Association; Cyprus Educational Research Association; Cyprus Family Planning Association; Cyprus Branch of IBBBY; Cyprus Association for Mental Health; Cyprus Anti-Cancer Society; President, Kalopanayiotis Cultural Centre; President, Kalopanayiotis Expatriates Association; Kalopanayiotis Community Welfare Council. Address: Flat 53, 24 Michalakopoulos Str, 1075 Nicosia, Cyprus.

**CHRISTOPHORY Jul,** b. 22 April 1939, Luxembourg. Director. m. Marielle Ruppert, 1 son, 1 daughter. Education: Doctor of Philosophy, Kings College, London, 1964. Appointments: Director, National Library, 1984-96; Director, European Commission Representation, 1996-. Publications: Luxembourgeois, Qui Etes-Vous?; A Short History of Literature in Luxembourgish; Luxembourg, World Bibliographical Series. Memberships: Institut Grande-Ducal, 1982; Rotary Luxembourg, 1998. Address: Ferme de Grevels, 8059 Bertrange, Luxembourg.

**CHU Ching-Cheng,** b. 13 October 1957, Taiwan, China. Publisher; Communicator. m. Yun-Chiu Yang, 1 son, 1

daughter. Eduction: BA, Soochow University, Taiwan; MBA, Bloomsburg University, USA. Appointments: President, Successmart International Marketing Group; Publisher, Success, magazine, Chinese edition. Address: 3F-1 No 79 Hsin Tai Wu Road, Section 1 Hsichih, Taipei County, Taiwan, China.

**CHU Paul Kim-Ho,** b. 19 October 1956, Hong Kong. Professor. m. Wileen, 1 son, 1 daughter. Education: BS, Ohio State University, 1977; MS, Cornell University, 1979; PhD, 1982. Appointments: Professor, City University of Hong Kong, 1996-; Professor, Peking University, 1997-; Advisory Professor, Fudan University, 1994-; Advisory Professor, Southwest Jiaotong University, 1998-; Professor, Southwestern Institute of Physics, 1998-. Publications: 120 Publications; 120 International Conference Papers. Memberships: American Chemical Society; Asia Pacific Microanalysis Association; Bohmishe Physical Society; Fellow, Hong Kong Institution of Engineers; Institute of Electrical and Electronic Engineers; Materials Research Society. Address: City University of Hong Kong, 83 Tat Chee Ave, Kowloon, Hong Kong, China.

**CHU Shih-Fan (George),** b. 6 December 1933, Hupei, China. Profesor; Chair. m. Li-Ming Kuo Chu, 1 son, 1 daughter. Education: MS, 1965, PhD, 1968, University of Illinois; BA, Taiwan University. Appointments: Assistant Professor, 1967-70, Associate Professor, 1970-80, Professor, 1980-, Chair, Economics Department, 1992-; Visiting Professor, Wuhan University, Huazhoung University of Science and Technology, National Taiwan University. Publications: Several articles in professional journals. Honours: Fulbright Grant; IIE Scholarship; Ford Foundation Fellowship. Memberships: AEA; SEA; ES; WSSA. Address: 4490 Gibraltar Drive, Reno, NV 89509, USA.

**CHUA Hai Joo James,** b. 19 June 1951, USA. Nuclear Scientist. Education: BS Nuclear Engineering, 1975, Manchester University, UK; M Nuclear Science, 1977, PhD Nuclear Science, Columbia University. Appointments: President, The Big Apple International Group of Companies, Aerospace & Scientific Research Inc, Advance Tech (China) Ltd, The Big Apple Design team, Missile Fabrication Composites Inc, Space Science Inc, Wailic Investments (HK) Ltd, Mamina (Tokyo) Group of Companies; VP, American Aerospace Corporation, China (PRC) Procurement Group, JC Star Consortium (Europe); Director, Starlight Manufacturing Group of Companies. Memberships: AIAA; AAAS. Address: The Big Apple International Group of Companies, Macpherson Rd, PO Box 103, Singapore 913404, Singapore.

**CHUA Tuan-Meng,** b. 20 January 1944, Muar, Johor, Malaysia. Housing Developer. m. Siow-Gek Seah, 3 sons. Education: Advanced Diploma in Commercial Management, Jersey, UK, 1980; BA, Management, Australia, 1984. Appointments: Chairman, Chamber of Commerce, Muar, 1990-; Vice-Chairman, Chamber of Commerce and Industry, State of Johor. Honours: Distinguished Member Award, Lions International, 1991; Honorary Doctor of the University in Community Leadership, St Clements University, Prospect, South Australia, 1999. Memberships: Fellow, International Commercial Management Institute, Jersey; Fellow, President's Council, American Institute of Management, USA. Address: PO Box 45, 501 Jalan Mohamadiah, Muar 84000, Johor, Malaysia.

**CHUBB Scott Robinson,** b. 30 January 1953, New York, USA. Research Physicist. m. Anne Lauren, 2 daughters. Education: BA, Princeton University, 1975; MA, State University of New York, 1978; PhD, State University of New York, 1982. Appointments: Research Associate, Northwestern University, 1982-85; National Research Council Fellow, 1985-88;

Physicist, Sachs Freeman Associates, 1988-89; Research Physicist, Naval Research Laboratory, 1989-. Publications: More than 50 publications. Honours: Member, Sigma Xi; National Research Council Award. Memberships: American Physical Society; Sigma Xi; American Geophysical Union. Address: 9822 Pebblewiegh Court, Burke, VA 22015, USA.

**CHUMENKOV Vsevolod Petrovich,** b. 18 September 1927, Znamenskoye, Omsk Region, Russia. Physics Researcher. m. R S Domnina, 1 son, 2 daughters. Education: Physics Faculty, Moscow State University, 1956; Postgraduate Studentship, 1969. Appointment: Leading Researcher, TSNIIMASH, 1986-. Publications include: Numerous articles; Two reports at international conferences; "Stability and Control of Transforming Nonlinear Systems", 1995; Five reports at the International Conference "Scientific and Technical Problems of Cosmonautics and Rocket Engineering", 1996; Six inventors certificates and two patents; Altogether 36 scientific works. Honours: Gold Medal, second. sch. grad. 1945; Jubilee Medal, in honour of the 50th Anniversary of TSNIIMASH, 1996. Memberships: Central House of Scientists of the Russian Academy of Sciences, 1976; Moscow Physical Society, 1989; Russian Union of Scientists, 1990. Hobbies: Chess; Music; Classic Literature; Philosophy. Address: 28 Korolev Prospect, Flat 215, City Korolev, Moscow 141070, Russia.

**CHUNG Chia Mou (Charles),** b. 21 February 1918, Guangdong, China. m. Betty Lee, 1 son, 3 daughters. Education: BS, 1947, MS, 1948, State University of Washington, USA; Graduate Study, 1948-51, NYU, USA. Appointments: Editor, Central Police College, China; Professional Officer, Executive Yuan, China; Revisor, Secretariat of the United Nations, New York City. Publications: Road for the Republic of China to be Readmitted to the United Nations, 1994; China Anthology, 1996, co-editor; Chung's Selected Essays, 1998. Memberships: Adviser, Kwangtung Community Association, Taipei; Chairman, Central Police University Alumni Association of Eastern US; Adviser, Eastern US Chapter, World Federation of Hakka; Eastern US Hon VP, National Cheng-Chi University Alumni Association. Address: 165 Park Row Apt 20F, New York, NY 10038-1138, USA.

**CHUNG Hung-Yuan,** b. 10 August 1952, Ping Tung, Taiwan. Electrical Engineer. m. Mei Ying Liu, 2 sons, 1 daughter. Education: PhD, Electrical Engineering, National Cheng Kung University. Appointments: Professor, National Central University. Publications: Over 46 Papers, Journals. Memberships: IEEE, Life Member, Institute of Chinese Engineers. Address: National Cevtral University, Dept of Electrical Engineering, Chung Li 32054, Taiwan.

**CHUNG Sang-Koo,** b. 6 January 1938, Kimhae, Korea. University Professor. m Kyung-In Lee, 1 son, 1 daughter. Education: BSEE, Seoul National University, 1962; Student, Technical University, Berlin, 1964-66; MSEE, 1972, DSc, 1974, Washington University, St Louis. Career: Postdoctoral Fellow, Washington University, 1974-75; Research Fellow, Regensburg University, Germany, 1975-78; Professor, 1978-, Dean, School of Engineering, 1981-83, Dean, Graduate School, 1990-94, Ajou University, Korea; Visiting Scholar, University of California, Los Angeles, USA, 1983-84; Guest Researcher, ABB Semiconductor AG, Switzerland, 1996. Memberships: Fellow, Korea Institute of Telematics & Electronics; IEEE; Korean Institute of Electrical Engineers; New York Academy of Sciences. Address: Ajou University, 5 Wonchun-dong, Paldal-ku, Kyung-gi, Suwon 442-749, Korea.

**CIANCAGLINI Humberto Rafael,** b. 6 September 1918, Salta, Argentina. Civil and Electronic Engineer. m. Cora M

Gutierrez, 2 sons. Education: Dipl Civil Engineer, 1943; Postgrad Course, Engineer Specialist in Radio Communications, 1946. Appointments: Professor, University Buenos Aires; Member of the Director Boards of: Argentine Scientific Council, Atomic Energy Argentine Committee, Space Research Argentine; Council, State Secretary of Communications. Honours: Eminent Engineer, 1985, IEEE; Diploma De Merito (Electronica), Konex Foundation, 1983; Prize for Professional Activities, Argentine Academy of Engineering. Memberships: IEEE, Life Senior Member; American Association for Advancement of Science; New York Academy of Science; and others. Address: Lafinur 3383 Dep 12A, 1425 Buenos Aires, Argentina.

**CIESLIKOWSKA Teresa Maria,** b. 1 October 1926, Lwow, Poland. Researcher. m. Sawomir Cieslikowski, 1 son, 1 daughter. Education: MA, 1952; Doctor, 1964; Habil, 1967. Appointments: Teacher Assistant, 1958-63; Assistant Professor, 1964-68; Habil Professor, 1968-75; Associated Professor, 1975-91; Professor, 1991-. Publications: Author 3 books, 1965, 1966, 1995; Co-Author 1 book, 1996. Membership: Societas Scientiarum Lodziensis. Address: W Wroblewskiego 59 B 29, 94-035 Lodz, Poland.

**CIGNA Arrigo,** b. 18 December 1932, Milano, Italy. Scientist. m. Luciana Rossi, 2 daughters. Education: Physics degree, University of Milan, 1958; Libera docenza, Health Physics, 1967, Speleology, 1969, University of Rome. Appointments: Scientist, Health Physics Laboratory, Ispra Centre, CNRN (National Committee for Nuclear Energy), 1958-59; Army service, at Radiation Protection Laboratory of CAMEN (Centre for Military Appliances of Nuclear Energy), 1959-60; Requested to set up the Environmental Radioactivity Laboratory, Casaccia Nuclear Centre, CNEN (National Committee for Nuclear Energy), Rome, 1961-74; Faculty of Mathematical, Physical and Natural Sciences, University of Rome, 1968-74; Director, Environmental Protection Division, Department Radiations and Health & Safety Protection (RAD), 1974-81; Director ad interim, Laboratory for the Study of the Marine Environment, Fiascherino (La Spezia), 1980-81; Director, Energy and Environment Research Centre "Forte di S Teresa" ENEA (former CNEN); Invited Professor, University of Padua, 1983; Consultant for environmental questions, Department of Nuclear Fuel, Department of Nuclear Fuel, Energy Research Centre of Saluggia (Vercelli), 1984-90; Scientific Advisor to Director of the Environment Sector, 1991-94; Health Physicist, IFEC plant, Energy Research Centre of Saluggia (Vercelli), 1992-94; Invited Professor, University of Milan, 1994-95; Retired, 1994. Memberships include: Board, Società Speleologica Italiana, 1964-, Chairman, 1970-79; Union Internazionale de Radioécologie, 1986-, President, 1973-81, Board Honoary Member, 1981-. Address: Fraz Tuffo, 1-14023 Cocconato, Italy.

**CILI Petro Ilia,** b. 12 January 1931, Albania. Geologist. m. Violeta, 2 sons. Education: Diploma, Ing Geologist, 1957. Appointments: Manager, Memberships, Different Geological Explorative Groups; Chief of Cabinet, Geology of Albania; Chief of Geological Sector of Institute of Geological Mining Research; Chief of Cabinet, Geological Mapping; Scientific Worker, 1988-. Publications: Author, Co-Author, 9 Geological Cartographics, Exploratives, Regional Works; Co-Author, Geological, 1969; Tectonic, 1970; Ore Deposits, 1976; Metelogenic, 1986; Co-Author, Maps of Albania of Carpato-Balkanic, Tectonic Map; Geology of Albania, of Tectonics of Karpeto-Balkans; Structured Geology; 15 Articles Published in Scientific Magazines. Honours: Medal of Work; Medal for Distinguished Work in Mines and Geology; Order of Distinguished Work in Mines and Geology; Prize of Republic of II Grade Memberships: Association of Geologists of Albania.

**CIRRITO Joseph James,** b. 21 June 1926, Caltavuturo Italy. Geographer. m. Daphne Faith Lemmer, 1 daughter Education: BA, 1954, University of Americas; Certificate, 1958 Aeronautical Chart and Information Centre; Certificate, 1959 Air University; Certificate, 1963, Industrial College of the Armed Forces; Certificate, 1967, Alexander Hamilton Institute Certificate, 1968, Newspaper Institute of America; Certificate 1974, American Management Association. Appointments Designer, Contract Assignments, Buffalo, USA, 1954-57 Research Analyst, Aeronautical Chart and Information Centre St Louis, USA, 1957-59; Associate, The Editorial Group Ltd Buffalo, USA and Johannesburg, SA, 1959-; Consultant, J Cirrito Associates, Johannesburg, 1978-. Publications Research papers and reports in professional journals Technical Articles, Wings Over Africa, World Airnews, and Mining Survey. Honours: Certificate, Originated Data System Improvement, US Dept of Air Force, 1958; Alumni Honour Roll University of the Americas, 1963; Commendations Successfully Completing Difficult Assignments, Clients & Corporations, 1960-96; Klein Memorial Writing Award, 1967 Memberships: Life member, National Defense Industrial Association; Member: Loyal Order of Moose; Transvaal Aviation Club; South African Voluntary Euthanasia Society Address: PO Box 4171, Witbeeck 1729, South Africa.

**CIRSTOIU Ada,** b. 27 October 1972, Balcesti, Romania Professor. Education: Faculty of Philology (Romanian-Russian). Appointments: 3 years of teaching Romanian, Russian and Latin. Publications: Articles in professional journals. Honours: Diploma of Association for the Paradoxical Movement; 3rd Award at the 3rd National Literature Contest, ASU. Address: Op 1, CP 71, Craiova, Dolj 1100, Romania.

**CISMASIU Cristina Sanda,** b. 11 December 1949, Brasov Romania. Mathematician. m. Nicolae, 1 son. Education Graduate in Mathematics, 1972; Doctor in Mathematics, Babes Bolyai University, Romania, 1987; Appointments: Computer Analyst, Electronic Computation Center, 1972-76; Assistant Senior Lecturer, Reader, Transilvania University, 1976-99 Publications: 5 International Journals; 17 Articles in Romanian Journals; 6 Courses and Books. Address: Transilvania University, Bd Eroilor 29, 2200 Brasov, Romania.

**CIUPA Radu V,** b. 20 June 1949, Oradea, Romania University Professor. m. Alexandra, 1 daughter. Education MSc, Faculty of Electrical Engineering, Technical University of Cluj, Napoca, 1972; MA, Faculty of Economics, University Babes Bolyai Cluj, 1978; PhD, Medical Electronics Equipment 1990. Appointments: Researcher, 1976-78; Assistant Professor, Technical University of Cluj, Napoca, 1978-90 Professor, 1990-; Vice Dean, 1992-. Publications: 7 Published Books; 66 Published Scientific Papers. Memberships European Society of Biomechanics; Biomedical Engineering Society. Address: Str Vlahuta NO 21, Bl. Cl Sc 3, Ap 37. RC 3400 Cluj Napoca, Romania.

**CIVIDJIAN Grigore Alexandru,** b. 12 January 1936 Kishinev, Moldavia. Electrical Engineering Educator. m. Xenia Andrei Kishinsky, 1 son, 1 daughter. Education: Diploma Engineering, Polytechnic Institute, Bucharest, 1958; PhD Polytechnic Institute, Issay, 1970; Degree, Mathematics University of Craiova, 1971. Appointments: Worker, Local Industry, Craiova, 1958-60; Designer, Project Institution Craiova, 1960-67; Assistant Professor, 1967-69, Lecturer 1969-77, Associate Professor, Engineering, 1977-89

Professor, Head, Department of Electrical Apparatus, 1989-, University of Craiova; Consultant, Electroputer Research Institute, Craiova, 1970-95, Electrical Engineering Research Institute, Bucharest, 1981-95. Publications include: Electrical Apparatus, 1972; Several articles in professional journals. Honours: Grants, St Petersburg Technical University, 1973, University of Central Lancashire, England, 1994, University Paul Sabatier, 1995. Memberships: Electrical Fuses Club; Electrostatica Society. Address: Dezrobirii F 1-1-1, RO 1100 Craiova, Romania.

**CLARK Patricia Dianne,** b. 17 March 1956, Toronto, Canada. Executive Director. m. Daniel M Clark, 21 August 1980, 2 sons. Education: BPHE, 1981, University Toronto; Business Certificate, 1986. Appointments: National Sales Representative, Owl Instruments, 1982-83; Employee Fitness Coordinator, Texaco Canada, 1983-84; Executive Director, Ontario Group Fitness Office, 1984-91; Programme Director, Ontario Fitness Council, 1984-89; Executive Director, Ontario Association of Sport and Exercise Sciences, 1984-. Honours: Fitness Leadership Award, Ontario Fitness Council, 1992; Prov Fitness Citation, Prov Government, 1994. Memberships: Ontario Association of Sport and Exercise Sciences; CSEP/FACA; Leaside HS Alumni Association; Humber College Fitness Leadership Advisory Committee; Seneca College Fitness Instruction Advisory Committee. Address: Ontario Association of Sport & Exercise Sciences, 75 Broadway, Orangeville, Ontario L9W 1K1, Canada.

**CLARKE Arthur Charles (Sir),** b. 16 December 1917, Minehead, England. Author. Education: Physics, 1st class honours, Mathematics, Kings College, London. Career: RAF, 1936; Assistant Editor, Physics Abstracts, Institution of Electrical Engineers, 1948-50; Chairman, British Interplanetary Society, 1950; Director, Underwater Safaris, Colombo. Publications include: Across the Sea of Stars; From the Oceans, From the Stars; More Than One Universe; A Meeting With Medusa; The Nine Billion Names of God; Prelude to Mars; The Sentinel; Tales From Planet Earth; An Arthur C Clarke Omnibus; The Best of Arthur C Clarke; Four Great S.F. Novels; Of Time and Stars; 2001 Deep Range, Moondust (anthologies). Honours include: Oscar Nomination for 2001 Screenplay, 1969; Commander of the British Empire, 1989; Freeman of Minehead; Nobel Peace Prize Nomination, 1994; NASA Distinguished Public Service Medal, 1995; Asteroid 4923 named Clarke, IAU, 1996. Memberships include: Society of Authors; H G Wells Society; Science Fiction Writers of America; Astronomical Society of the Pacific;Fellow, Royal Astronomical Society. Address: 25, Barnes Place, Colombo, Sri Lanka.

**CLAUDEL Bernard Michel,** b. 20 May 1932, Strasbourg, France. Retired Professor. m. Martine Gouilleux, 3 sons. Education: Ecole Normale Superieuse, Paris, France, 1952-56; Agregation des Sciences Physiques, 1956; Doctorat es Sciences, 1962. Appointments: Professor of Chemical Physics and Chemical Engineering, National Institute of Applied Sciences at Lyon, France. Publications: 3 books: La Catalyse au Laboratoire et Dans L'Industrie, 1967; Elements of Chemical Kinetics, 1969; Bases du Genie Chimique, 1977; Numerous publications in various scientific journals. Address: 154 rue Anatole France, 69100 Villeurbanne, France.

**CLAUSEN Claus Andreas,** b. 1 August 1922, Fredrikstad, Norway. Emeritus. m. Astrid, 2 daughters. Education: Mag Art, 1955. Appointments: University Lecturer, University of Bergen, Norway; Associate Professor. Publications: Diverse Publications on Marine Zoology in International Biological Journals. Membership: International Association of Meiobenthologists. Address: Ekornvegen 19, 5046 Radal, Norway.

**CLAUSEN Sten-Erik,** b. 13 September 1943, Oslo, Norway. Senior Researcher. m. Liv Arnet Clausen, 2 daughters. Education: Degree in Psychology, University of Oslo, 1974. Appointments: Senior Researcher, Norwegian Institute of Urban and Regional Research, 1987-; Lecturer, University of Oslo, 1990-. Publications: Applied Correspondence Analysis, 1998; Articles in professional journals. Memberships: Foreign Affiliate, American Psychological Association; Norwegian Psychological Association. Address: Elgveien 12, 0852 Oslo, Norway.

**CLAYTON Nicola Susan,** b. 22 November 1962, Newcastle Upon Tyne, UK. Professor. Education: BA Hons, Zoology, 1984; University of St Andrews, 1984-87; PhD, 1987; University of Bielefeld, West Germany, 1987-90; EGI and Linacre College, Oxford. 1990-92; Departmental Demonstrator in Animal Behaviour, 1992; BA Hons, Department of Zoology, Oxford, 1992-95; Assistant Professor, University of California Davis,1995-98; Associate Professor, 1998-. Honours: 1st Year Class Prize; 2nd Year Class Prize; 3rd Year Class Prize; O Level Prizes; A Level Prizes; Pembroke College Book Prize; Domus Scholarship; ICI Scholarship; Alexander von Humboldt Stiftung; NATO Post Doctoral Fellowship; Junior Research Fellowship, Linacre College; Departmental Leadership in Animal Behaviour; Ten Year AFRC University Research Fellowship; Nominated for an Alan T Waterman NSF Award. Memberships: ABS; ASAB; American Association for the Advancement of Science; American Ornithological Union; American Psychological Association; Audubon British Ornithological Union; European Neuroscience Association; Experimental Psychology Society; International Behavioral and Neural Genetics Society; International Society of Neuroethology; National Geographic Society; New York Academy of Sciences; Royal Society for the Protection of Birds; Society for Neurosciences. Address: Universty of California, Neuro Physiol Behavioural Dept, Briggs Hall, Davis, CA 95616, USA.

**CLEATON-JONES Peter Eiddon,** b. 5 March 1941, Johannesburg, South Africa. Medical Practitioner; Dental Surgeon. m. Marguerite Ginette France Thorpe, 1 son. Education: BDS, 1963; MBBCh, 1967; PhD, 1975; DSc (Dent), 1991; DTM&H, 1980; DPH, 1982; DA, 1975. Appointments: Dental Officer, Soweto, 1963; Surgical/Medical Intern, Soweto, 1968; Dental Researcher, Medical Research Council, University of Witwatersrand, Director of Research Council, 1968-. Publications: 280 full publications. Honours: Medical Research Council Silver Medal, 1990; Trendley Dean Memorial Award, International Association for Dental Research, 1998; many others as well. Memberships: SA Medical Association; British Medical Association; International Association for Dental Research. Address: MRC University Witwatersrand, Dental Research Institute Pvt Bag 3, Wits 2050, South Africa.

**CLEMENTS Christopher John,** b. 21 January 1946, Ledsham, England; New Zealand nationality. Public Health Physician. m. Vivien Driscoll, 2 sons. Education: MB BS, 1969, The London Hospital, University of London; LRCP, MRCS, 1969; D Obst, 1972, University Auckland; DCH, 1973, Royal College of Physicians, London; MSc, 1980, Faculty of Community Medicine, University of Manchester; MCCM, 1980, New Zealand; MFPHM, 1980, Royal College of Physicians, London; Fellow, Australasian Faculty of Public Health Medicine, 1994, Royal Australian College of Phsyicians. Appointments: University Teacher, Canada, UK, NZ; Clinical Obstetrics, Registrar, Waikato Hospital, NZ, 1971; Immunization Programme Reviews, Inner Mongolia, China, Afghanistan,

Swaziland, Kazakstan, 1986-96; Primary Health Care, Medical Director, Hospital del Valle Apurimac, Peru, 1973-74, Chief Medical Officer, Save the Children Fund, Bangladesh Project, 1977, Afghanistan Project, 1977-78; Resident Clinical Paediatrics, University Western Ontario, Alder Hey Children's Hospital, UK, Lancaster Royal Infirmary, UK, Westminster Children's Hospital, London; Specialist in Community Medicine, Dept Health, New Zealand, 1980-85; Assistant Director, National Head of Disease Control, Dept Health, Head Office, Wellington, NZ, 1983-85; Medical Officer, Expanded Programme on Immunization, World Health Organisation, Geneva, 1985-. Publications: Editor: WHO/EPI quarterly news sheet; New Zealand Health Review; Consultant Editor, Annals of Tropical Paediatrics; Reviewer various professional bulletins and journals; Author over 100 published articles and book chapters. Address: WHO Expanded Programme on Immunization, 1121 Geneva 27, Switzerland.

**CLERVOY Jean Francois,** b. 19 November 1958, Longeville Les Metz. Astronaut. m. Laurence Boulanger, 1 son, 1 daughter. Education: Ecole Polytechnique, Diploma, 1981; Ecole Nationale Superieure De L'Aeronautique et de L'Espace, 1983; Ecole Du Personnel Navigant D'Essais et de Reception, 1987. Appointments: Space System Engineer, 1983-; Astronaut, 1985-; Flight Test Engineer, 1986-; Mission Specialist, NASA, 1992. Honours: NASA Space Flight Medal; NASA Exceptional Service Medal; Chevalier Ordre National Du Merite; Chevalier Ordre National De La Legion D'Honneur. Memberships: Association of Space Explorers; French Aeronautics and Astronautics Association. Address: NASA JSC/Code CB, Houston, TX 77058, USA.

**CLODE William Henry,** b. 20 July 1927, Funchal. Medical Doctor. m. Maria Helena Migueis, 3 sons, 2 daughters. Education: Graduated in Medicine, 1952; Internship, 1954-60; Medical Research Associate, Brookhaven National Laboratory, New York, USA, 1961-62; Chief, Service Institute Port Oncologia, 1963. Appointments: More than 70 publicationss on nuclear medicine and cancer. Honours: 7 awards. Memberships: International Society for Preventive Oncology; Sociedade Port Medic Nuclear; Society Cien Med, Lisboa. Address: Av Roma 85-5 Dt, 1700 Lisboa, Portugal.

**CLOUSE R Wilburn.** Education: BA Chemistry, 1959, David Lipscomb University, Nashville; Economics, Management, part-time, 1960-63, University Tennessee, Nashville; MA Economics, 1968, Middle Tennessee State University; PhD Educational Administration, 1977, George Peabody College, Vanderbilt University; Postdoctoral experience, UNC, Chapel Hill, North Carolina, 1981. Appointments: include: Founder and Director, Centre for Entrepreneurship Education, Vanderbilt University, 1997-; Associate Director, Corporate Learning Institute, 1984-87, Research Associate, Learning Technology Centre, 1984-88, Director, Programme of Library & Information Science, 1988-89, Associate Professor, Dept of Educational Leadership, Peabody College of Education and Human Development, 1977-, Vanderbilt University. Publications: 19 books and monographs; 37 articles; Early Career Publications in Chemistry: Heterogeneity of the Carbohydrate Moeity of Crystalline Ovalbumin, 1963; An Automatic Determination of Protein-Bound Hexose, 1962; 47 presentations and invited addresses; 15 book and research article reviews. Honours: Sam Walton Free Enterprise Fellow, 1997; Peabody Round Table Honoree, 1988, 1992; Peabody Outstanding Faculty Award, 1983. Memberships: National Council for Science & Premedical Education, Harding University, 1980-90; Editor, Executive Entepreneur, 1998; Editorial Review Board or Editorial Advisor, Psychology - a Journal of Human Behaviour, The Institute for Memetric Research, Operational Research

Quarterly; Policy Reviewer, National Centre for Research in Vocational Education; Grant Reviewer, Research Grants, Social Sciences & Humanities Research Council of Canada; and others. Address: Vanderbilt University, Peabody College, PO Box 514, Nashville, TN 37202-0075, USA.

**CLURMAN Judith,** b. 3 November 1953, Brooklyn, New York, USA. Conductor. m. Bruce Ruben, 1 son. Education: BMus, 1977; MMus, 1978. Appointments: Music Director, Conductor, The New York Concert Singers, The Judith Clurman Chorale, Project Youth Chorus; Conducted Premieres by Leonard Bernstein, William Bolcom, Philip Glass, Stephen Paulus, Ned Rorem, Christopher Rouse, Ellen Taaffe Zwilich; Conducted World and US Premiere, Mozart's Newly Discovered Canons in Conjunction with the Mozart Bicentennial; Artistic Director, Music of the Jewish Spirit Series at the 92nd Street, New York City; Teacher, Juilliard School, 1989-. Publications: Editor, Choral publictions for European American Music, Lawson Gould and Transcontinental Music. Membership: American Choral Directors Association. Address: 75 East End Avenue, Apt 9L, New York, NY 10028-7915, USA.

**CLYNE Michael George,** b. 12 October 1939, Melbourne, Australia. University Professor. m. Irene Donohoue Clyne, 1 daughter. Education: BA Hons, 1960, MA, 1962, University of Melbourne; Postgraduate Studies, Bonn, Utrecht, 1961-62; PhD, Monash University, 1965. Appointments: Tutor, Lecturer, Senior Lecturer in German, 1962-72, Associate Professor of German, 1972-88, Professor of Linguistics, 1988-, Monash University; Visiting Professor, Universities of Stuttgart, 1972-73, Heidelberg, 1997. Publications: 24 books and about 240 articles in field of linguistics Books include: Pluricentric Languages, 1992; Inter-Cultural Communication at Work, 1994; The German language in a changing Europe, 1995; Undoing and redoing corpus planning, 1997. Honours: Fellow, Academy of the Social Sciences in Australia, 1982; Fellow, Australian Academy of Humanities, 1983; Honorary Life member, Applied Linguistics Association of Australia, 1988; Member, Order of Australia, 1993; Austrian Cross of Honour for Science and the Arts, 1st Class, 1996; Honorary PhD, University of Munich, 1997; Jacob and Wilhelm Grimm Prize, 1999. Address: Department of Linguistics, Monash University, Clayton, Victoria 3168, Australia.

**COBANI Hysen H,** b. 5 November 1932, Libehove. Agronomist. m. Vnjesa, 1 son, 1 daughter. Education: Professor, 1995; Agricultural University of Tirana, 1951-55; Doctor of Science, 1985. Appointments: Scientific Researcher, Agricultural Researched Institute of Lushnje, 1955-60; Agronomist in Chief, Agricultural Enterprise, 1960-77; Researcher, Director, Research Institute for Vegetables, 1977-94; President, TARADIA Co Ltd, 1995-. Publications: Over 120 Programmed Articles; Over 30 Scientific Articles; Over 12 Technical and Scientific Books; Brochures. Honours: First Class Work Order, Chairman of Parliament. Memberships: Chairman, Association, Rain and Rural Familty; Member, Board of Directors, Seeds and Saplings Association of Albania. Address: Rruga A Kasemi, Pallati 69/1, Shk1, Apt 3, Tirane, Albania.

**COBAS M Margarita,** b. 1 March 1949, Santiago de Cuba. Professor; Director. m. R Pomes, 1 daughter. Education: BSc, Physics, University of Oriente, Santiago de Cuba, 1970; PhD, Technical Sciences, University of St Petersburg, 1976; Dr Degree, Technical Sciences, National Commission of Academic Degrees, Cuba, 1978. Appointments: Professor, Director, Center for Scientific Equipment, Ministerium of Science, Technology and Environment, Cuba. Publications: Over 40 in professional journals and conference proceedings.

Memberships: Cuban Physics Society; Academic, Cuban Academy of Sciences; Scientific Council, Center for Scientific Equipment, Cuba. Address: Ave Camaguey No 11238, Cerro, Havana City, Cuba.

**COCKRILLE Stephen,** b. 19 January 1945, Washington DC, USA. Art Director. m. Eva Vagreti, 2 sons. Education: BA, West Virginia State College, 1968; MA, University North Dakota, 1972. Appointments: Graduate Teaching Assistant, University North Dakota, Grand Forks, 1971; Design Assistant, Thomas Clayton Printing, New York, 1974-75; Art Director, West Side Printing and Graphics, NYC, 1975-76; Studio Manager, Graphic Concern Inc, New York, 1976-78; Independant Art Director, New York, 1978-84; President, Textart Inc, New York, 1984-97; Retired 1997; Judge, New England Book Show, Boston, 1987. Publications: Producer numerous basal educational programmes for national distribution, 1984-97. Honours: Selected for presentation to the Jordanian Minister of Education and staff on the US textbook industry, New York, 1995; Recipient Honorable Mention, New England Book Show, Boston, 1992; Pupil's Editor and Theme Posters, Boston, 1992; Bronze Award Dimensional Illustrators Awards Show, New York, 1992; 1st place Award, Educational School Division, New York Book Show, 1994. Address: 1150 Kings Crown Rd, Woodland Park, CO 80863, USA.

**COHEN Ellis Avrum,** b. 15 September 1945, Baltimore, Maryland, USA. Film Producer; Author; Investigative Journalist. Education: Associate in Arts, Communications Department, Community College of Baltimore, 1965; Certificate of Law, School of Law, University of West Los Angeles, 1992. Appointments: Vice President, 1970-72; Editor in Chief, New York Magazine, 1972-76; Producer, 1972-77; Director, 1974-77; Producer, Director, 1976; Senior Press Agent, 1978-79; Movie Producer, Aunt Mary, 1979; Vice President, 1979-80; TV Movie Producer, 1982-90; President, Chief Executive Officer, Hennessey Entertainment, 1983-; Movie Producer, First Steps, 1984; Movie Producer, Love Mary, 1985; Author, Danger Evidence, 1995; Television Spokesperson, 1997-98; Movie Producer, Dangerous Evidence: The Lori Jackson Story, 1999. Publications: Avenue of the Stars, 1990. Honours include: Mayor's Award; Award of Excellence; Best TV Movie; Golden Halo Award; Luminas Award of Excellence. Memberships: Producers Guild of America; Writers Guild of America; Academy of Television Arts and Sciences; National Writers Union; Investigative Reporters and Editors; HTML Writers Guild; Society of Professional Journalists; International Federation of Journalists; Amnesty International, USA. Address: Hennessey Entertainment Ltd, P O Box 481164, Los Angeles, CA 90048-9319, USA.

**COHEN Marvin Lou,** b. 3 March 1935, Montreal, Quebec, Canada. Professor. 1 son, 1 daughter. Education: AB, University of California, Berkeley, 1957; MS, University of Chicago, 1958; PhD, 1963. Appointments: Member, Techincal Staff, Bell Telephone Laboratories, Murray Hill, 1963-64; Senior Scientist, Lawrence Berkeley Laboratory, 1965-; Assistant Professor of Physics, University of California, 1964-66; Associate Professor of Physics, 1966-69; Professor of Physics, 1969-95; University Professor, 1995-. Honours: Alfred P Sloan Fellow; Elected Fellow, American Physical Society; Guggenheim Fellow; Oliver E Buckley Prize for Solid State Physics; Elected National Academy of Sciences; Lawrence Berkeley Laboratory Certificate of Merit; Julius Edgar Lilienfeld Prize of the American Physical Society; Outstanding Performance Award. Memberships: Committee of the National Academy of Sciences; Lawrence Berkeley Laboratory Staff Committee; Frank Isakson Prize Committee; American Physical Society Isakson Prize Committee; American Physical Society

Lilenfeld Prize Committee; National Academy of Sciences Nominating Committee for Selection of the NAS President; American Academy of Arts and Sciences. Many other memberships. Address: 201 Estates Dr, Piedmont CA 94611-3315, USA.

**COHEN Renee Snell,** b. 2 July 1945, Paris, Texas, USA. Educator. 1 son. Education: AAS, 1965, Paris Junior College; British and American Literature, French and German, University of Houston, 1966-67; BC TESL Teaching Qualification, University of British Columbia, Vancouver, 1974; BA Oriental Art History & Japanese, 1977; MEd TESL, 1983. Appointments: Teaching English to Immigrants, Vancouver Community College, 1974-77; Teacher of English, UBC, 1978-79; Teacher of Music and English, University of Oriental Studies, Los Angeles, 1979-81; Teacher of English, Fo Kwan Shan, Buddhist College & Monastery, California Extension, 1981-82; Freshman English, Paris Junior College, Texas, 1987-88; First & Second Grade, Abundant Life Christian Academy, Paris, Texas, 1985-88; SUNY, Sullivan County Community College, Toyama Campus, Japan, 1989-91; Ogaki Women's College, Dept International Studies, Japan, 1991-. Publications: English Consultant, Evergreen Haiku Society, 1992-; 5 poetry presentations; 5 research articles; 3 poetry translations; Book, The Story of Chiune Sugihara, textbook, 1992; 4 books of translations; Ogaki Grass, monograph, 1992; 13 journal publications; 4 anthologies; Several Award winning poems in collections. Honours: 3 scholarships. Memberships: Japan Association for Language Teaching; JALT Bilingualism National Interest Group; Evergreen Haiku Society; Licensed Teacher of Japanese 13-stringed Zither; Japan Todo Musical Association; New York Academy of Sciences. Address: c/o Susan Guest, 690 ES 31 Street, Paris, TX 75460, USA.

**COHEN-ALMAGOR Raphael,** b. 24 October 1961, Petach Tiqva, Israel. Lecturer. m. Zehavit, 1 son, 1 daughter. Education: BA, Political Science, Sociology, Anthropology, Tel Aviv University, 1983-85; MA, Political Science, 1985-87; D Phil, Politics, St Catherine's College, Oxford, 1987-91. Appointments: Lecturer, Faculty of Law, Hebrew University, 1992-95; Senior Lecturer, Department of Communication, University of Haifa, 1995-. Publications: The Boundaries of Liberty and Tolerance, 1994; Middle Eastern Shores, 1994; (ed.), Basic Issues in Israeli Democracy, 1999; (ed.), Liberal Democracy and the Limits of Tolerance, 1999. Memberships: Israel Press Council; 21st Century Trust. Address: Department of Communication, University of Haifa, Mt Carmel, Haifa 31905, Israel.

**COHEN-SABBAN Nessim,** b. 4 August 1930, Cairo. Director. m. 2 sons, 1 daughter. Education: Audit College, Cairo University, 1956; Audit College, Tel Aviv University, 1961. Appointment: Internal Auditor, Playknits, New York. Publications: Who's Who, 1997 and 1998. Address: 1013 Avenue Y, Brooklyn, NY 11235-5013, USA.

**COLBY Frank G,** b. 10 April 1915, Muhlhausen, Thur, Germany. Independant Scientific Consultant. m. Renee R Hiller (dec), 1 son, 1 daughter. Education: Chemical Engineering degree, 1939, DSc General Sciences and Chemistry, 1941, University Geneva, Switzerland. Appointments: Chemical Consultant, various companies, Havana, Cuba, 1941-46; Research Chemist, Industrial Tape, New Brunswick, NJ, 1946-47; Chemical Literature Specialist, Commercial Solvents, Terre Haute, IN, 1947-51; Director of Research and Information, R J Reynolds Tobacco, Winston-Salem, 1951-83; Independant Scientific Consultant, Research Analysis, New York, NY, 1983-. Publications: Book chapter, Smoking and Health, 1984. Memberships: President, International Students

Union, Geneva, 1935-41; President Founder, Film Friends Society, Winston-Salem, 1952-75; Chairman, WS Chamber Music Society. Address: 186 Riverside Dr Apt 6A, New York, NY 10024-1007, USA.

**COLE Louis Biddle,** b. Amarillo, Texas, USA. Retired Air Force Colonel; Air Force Junior ROTC Instructor. m. Leona Lewis Cole, 4 daughters. Education: BBA, West Texas State, 1940; Air Force Professional Schools, 1946-71; MEd, University of New Orleans, 1976. Appointments: Flight and Ground Instructor, Civilian Pilot Training; Pilot, Educator, Logistics in the USAF; Instructor, Air Command and Staff School; Aerospace Science Instructor, Air Force Junior ROTC. Honours: Air Medal, 1945; Air Force Commendation Medal, 1960, 1967; Phi Delta Kappa, 1967; kappa Delta Pi, 1967; Pi Kappa Pi, 1967; Legion of Merit, 1971; Outstanding Instructor, 1976, 1986, 1989; 17 consecutive yearly awards for excellence in AFJROTC program. Memberships include: Past President and Director, University of New Orleans Chapter of Phi Delta Kappa; Service Key President, World Aerospace Education Organization and World Aerospace Education Organization of America; Weather Reconnaissance Associations; Civil Air Patrol. Address: 4500 Leo Street, Marrero, LA 70072-3842, USA.

**COLEMAN Bernell Roche,** b. 26 April 1929, USA. m. Annie Richardson, 1 son, 1 daughter. Education: BS Biology, 1952, Alcorn A&M College; University of Illinois Professional College, 1959-60; PhD Physiology, 1964, Loyola University Stritch School of Medicine. Appointments: Research Assistant, Assistant and Associate Professor Physiology and Biophysics, Lecturer in Physiology various Schools of Medicine, 1952-76; Visiting Lecturer in Physiology, University Illinois College of Medicine, Chicago, 1972-76; Visiting Associate Professor of Physiology, Rush Medical College, Chicago, 1973-76; Professor of Physiology and Biophysics, 1976-, Chairman, Department of Physiology and Biophysics, 1996-, Howard University College of Medicine, Washington DC; Graduate Professor of Physiology and Biophysics, Howard University Graduate School of Arts and Sciences, Washington DC, 1977-. Publications: Co-author 85 papers in professional journals. Honours: 5 fellowships; Award for Meritorious Research, University of Health Sciences, Chicago Medical School Board of Trustees, 1975. Memberships: American Heart Association, Nation's Capital Affiliate; Sigma Xi; American Association for the Advancement of Science; American Physiological Society; AAUP; Phi Rho Sigma Medical Society; International Congress of Physiological Sciences; Council of Basic Science of the American Heart Association; Federation of American Societies of Experimental Biology; New York Academy of Sciences; Charter Member, American Society of Hypertension; Association of Black Cardiologists; International Society of Hypertension in Blacks. Address: 14200 Myer Ter, Rockville, MD 20853-2350, USA.

**COLEMAN Marilyn Adams,** b. 27 March 1946, Lancaster, DC, USA. Research Scientist. m. George E Coleman III, 1 son, 1 daughter. Education: BSc, 1968, SC; PhD Developmental Physiology, Auburn. Appointments: Assistant Professor, Ohio State University, 1976-81; President, Mac Associates, 1971-; President, Quimmune, 1993-. Publications: Over 200. Honours: Top Young Executive, 1985, Esquire Magazine; Numerous other awards. Memberships: Address: Mac Associates, 2532 Zollinger Rd, Columbus, OH 43221, USA.

**COLLINS Daniel,** b. 19 November 1963, Florida, USA. Vice President of Sales. 2 sons, 1 daughter. Education: Business Management, Fortune 500 University, 1985; Business Management, National Education Institute, 1988; Sales

Marketing, National Association of Sales Professionals Education, 1996. Career: Regional Field Trainer, Transworld Systems Inc, 1986-90; Vice President, Business Development, Armot Associates, 1990-94; Vice President, Sales, Sarah Louis Inc, 1994-. Publications: Several articles in professional journals. Honours include: Proclamation, Governor of North Carolina; Master Salesman Award, 1996. Memberships: American Management Association International; Association Records Managers & Administrators; Association Information & Image Managers. Address: 128 Sarasota Center Boulevard, International Trade Center, Sarasota, FL 34240, USA.

**COLLINS James Duffield,** b. 20 December 1919, Logansport, Indiana, USA. Research and Development Engineer. m. Barbara Cook Collins, 1 son, 1 daughter. Education: BS, United States Merchant Marine Academy, 1946. Appointments: Process Engineer, Marine Engineer, Design Project Engineer, Senior Project Engineer, Editor-at-Large. Publications: The Effects of Residual Magnetism on the Corrosion Fatigue Properties of Type H10 Stainless Steel Compressor Blades, 1976; The Effects of Low Temperature Magnetic Cycling on the Properties of Ferromagnetic Materials, 1980. Membership: Society of Naval Architects and Marine Engineers. Address: 5228 Bevedere Drive, Indianapolis, IN 46228-2137, USA.

**COLLINS Joely Meri,** b. 8 August 1972, Vancouver, BC, Canada. Actress; Producer. Education: Langara College, Arts Programme, Vancouver, 1990; RADA, Summer Shakespeare Intensive, 1996. Appointments: Rachael, in TV series Madison, 1994-97; Completed first documentary, Summer Love, with mum, 1997-98. Honour: Canadian Gemini Award for Best Lead Actress in a TV Series, 1996, for Madison. Memberships: Academy of Canadian Cinema and Television; ACTRA; UBCP; SPCA; Greenpeace; Western Canadian Wilderness Committee.

**COLOMBO Armando Walter,** b. 7 August 1960, Mendoza, Argentina. Professor, Dr of Engineering. m. Fabiola Espinoza, 1 son. Education: BSc, Electronics, 1979; Diploma of Engineering Electronics, 1990; MSc, Control Systems Technician, 1994; PhD, Dr, Engineering, 1998. Appointments: Certified in Engineering, Project Engineer, 1982-86; Assistant Professor, 1986-90; Visiting Researcher, Slovenia, 1988; Assistant Researcher, 1991-94; Visiting Researcher, Spain, 1992; Assistant Researcher, 1995-98; Professor, Researcher, Portugal, 1999-. Publications: Contributor of more than 40 articles to Professional Journals; Books; Book Chapters. Honours: 3 International Grantees. Memberships: IEEE; Gesellschaft Fur Informatiks. Address: Rua a Ver o Mar, Lote 35, 2815 Boteguin, Charneca de Caparica, Portugal.

**COLOMBO Arrigo,** b. 11 September 1921, Busto Arsizio, Italy. Philosopher, University Professor. m. Marie-Josephe Beauchard. Education: Licence in Scholastic Philosophy, 1948; Licence in Theology, 1952; Doctor in Philosophy, State University, Milan, 1956; Research Scholarship, Humboldt Foundation, Germany, 1963-66; Habilitation, Theoretical Philosophy, 1966. Appointments: Professor of Philosophy, Faculty of Education, University of Lecce, 1966; Associate Professor, 1981; Founder, Director, Centro Interdipartimentale di Ricercasul l'Utopia, 1982; Founder, Director, Laboratorio di Poesia, 1986; Founder, Movimento per la Società di Giustizia e per la Speranza, 1998. Publications: Il Destino del Filosofo Le Società del Futuro: Saggio Utopico Sulle Società Postindustriali; Utopia e Distopia; La Russia e la Democrazia Il Riemergere Della Democrazia Diretta; l'Utopia Rifondazione di un'Idea e di una Storia; Materiali per l'Utopia, Il Diavolo Genesi Storia Orrori di un mito Cristiano che avversa la Società di Giustizia. Memberships: Society for Utopian Studies; Associazione Internazionale per lo Studio delle Utopie; Moreanum Angers Correspondent; Cristiani per il Socialismo; Democrazia Proletaria. Address: Via Monte S Michele 49, 73100 Lecce, Italy.

**COLVIN Greta W,** b. 24 March 1962, Odessa, Texas, USA. Entrepreneur. 1 son. Education: AA, Radio, Television, Film, 1982; BA, University of Texas, 1987; MA, English, 1998. Career: Owner, Paradigms Inc; Owner, W C Advertising; Owner, Imase Inc. Honour: Dale Carnegie Graduate, 1993. Memberships: Licensed Broadcaster; Licensed Private Investigator; Licensed Paralegal; Licensed Insurance Board of Texas. Address: 11623 Whisper Valley Street, San Antonio, TX 78230-3737, USA.

**CONAND Chantal,** b. 10 April 1943, Poland. University Professor. m. François Conand, 3 daughters. Education: Doctorate, Biological Oceanography, Marseilles, 1974; Doctor es National Sciences, Brest, 1988. Appointments: Assistant Professor, University of Marseilles, 1964-68, University of Dakar, Senegal; Researcher, ORSTOM. New Caledonia; Professor, University of La Reunion, France. Publications: 92 in Marine Science. Honour: Best Thesis in the Pacific. Memberships: International Society Reef Studies; French Habeufic Association; French Coral Reef Association; Western Indian Ocean Marine Science Association. Address: Rte du Piton Bois de Nefles, 97490 Sainte Clotilde, France.

**CONDREA Lydia,** b. Chisinau. Linguist; Educator. m. Arcady Condrea, 1 son, 1 daughter. Education: Masters' Degree in French Philology and Teaching Methodology, State University of Chisinau, Moldova, 1977; Master's Degree in Romance Linguistics, University of Washington, USA, 1990; PhC in Romance Linguistics, University of Washington, USA, 1994. Appointments: French Instructor, Head of French Section, Washington Academy of Languages Adjunct Faculty, Seattle Pacific University; French and Spanish Teacher, West Seattle High School, Seattle, Washington. Publication: Le rythme Comme Un Des Parametres du System Linguistique, 1995. Honour: Recognition of Outstanding Teaching, Institute of Arts, Chisinau, Moldova, 1980. Memberships: International Society for Functional Linguistics; Modern Language Association; National Geographic Society; Washington and National Education Association; Greenpeace; Women in the Arts; American Orff-Shulwerk Association. Address: 12563 N Densmore Avenue N, Seattle, WA 98133, USA.

**CONIAVITIS Thomas,** b. 3 March 1939, Agrinion, Greece. Professor of Sociology. m. Lotta Gellerstedt, 1 son, 1 daughter. Education: BA, 1965, Panteion University, Athens; PhD, 1977, Docent, 1985, Uppsala University, Sweden. Appointments: Various teaching positions at Departments of Sociology, Uppsala and Orebro Universities, 1975-; Director, Foundation for Mediterranean Studies, Athens, 1985-88; Professor Sociology, Department Political Science and International Relations, Panteion University, Athens, 1986-; Head of Department, 1990-92; Various positions as Adviser or Boardmember in educational institutions. Publications include: Irrationality - Rationality; Max Weber - Georg Lukacs: a settlement, 1977; Methodological Pluralism; To the criticism of existing sociology, 1984; Pluralism in Sociology: A methodological approach, 1993. Address: Prometheus 5, GR 151 26 Maroussi, Greece.

**CONRAD John W.** Professor of Fine Arts; Entrepreneur. m. Barbara Jean Daugherty, 1 son, 1 daughter. Education: BS, Art Education, Indiana University of Pennsylvania, 1958; 6 month programme in Photography, US Army, 1958-59; MFA,

Ceramics, 1963, Carnegie-Mellon University; EdD Ceramic Research, University of Pittsburgh, 1970. Appointments: Art Instructor, Penn Hills High School, 1959-64; Adjunct Instructor, Carnegie-Mellon University,1961-64; Professor of Fine Arts, 1966-, Art Dept, Head of Ceramic Programme, Chairman of Department, 1980-82, 1985-88, Academic Senator, 4 terms, Mesa College; Exhibited ceramics and sculpture in 24 exhibitions; Ceramics Consultant; Developer and Owner, Falcon Company, 1982-. Publications: Author 8 books; several magazine articles. Honours: Distinguished Alumnus 1993 Award for accomplishments as artist, educator and entrepreneur in area of ceramic arts; NISOD Teaching Excellence Award, 1993; Organiser, 51 ceramic exhibits in San Diego. Memberships: Allied Artists and Three Rivers Art Association, Pittsburgh; Ceramic Artists of San Diego; National Council of Education Ceramic Arts; Allied Craftsmen of San Diego. Address: 770 Cole Ranch Road, Encinitas, CA 92024, USA.

**COOK Colin Burford,** b. 20 January 1927, London, UK. Doctor of Medicine. m. Elizabeth Stacey. Education: MD, 1951, London University, UK. Appointments: Diplomate of the American Board of Psychiatry & Neurology, 1979. Publication: Jazz Improvisation & Harmony, 1998, pen name Alan Phillips. Memberships: AMA; American Society of Psychoanalytic Physicians; American Guild/League of Authors. Address: 373 Strawberry Hill Avenue, Stamford, CT 06902, USA.

**COOK Mary Elizabeth,** b. 5 January 1943, Muscogee County, USA. Teacher. m. Robert James Cook, 1 son. Education: BS, Alabama State University, 1965; Georgia State University, 1973; Elementary Education, Supervision, Administration, Troy State University. Appointments: Teacher, Wacoochee High School, Salem, 1960-69; Teacher, Stewart County Board of Enducation; Teacher, Richland Junior High School, Georgia; Teacher, Fox Elementary School, 1973-94; Teacher, Gentian Elementary, 1994-96; 3rd Grade Teacher, Forrest Road Elementary, 1996-97; Teacher, Cusseta Road Elementary School, 1997-. Memberships: Sigma Rho Sigma; Kappa Delta Pi; Muscogee Association of Educators; Georgia Association of Educators; National Teachers Association; International Reading Association; National Association of Female Executives; American University of Women; National Council of Teachers of Mathematics. Address: 4655 Illini Drive, Columbus, GA 31907-6613, USA.

**COOKE Philip,** b. 31 August 1954, Charlotte, North Carolina, USA. Television Director. m. Katheen Cooke, 2 daughters. Education: BA, Oral Roberts University, 1976; MA, University of Oklahoma, 1986; PhD Candidate, Trinity College. Appointment: President, Phil Cooke Pictures Inc. Honours: Numerous awards in television. Membership: Academy of Television Arts and Sciences. Address: Phil Cooke Pictures Inc, 1612 N Pass Avenue, Burbank, CA 91505-1729, USA.

**COOPER Barbie Perkins,** b. 22 August 1950, Columbus, Georgia, USA. Writer. m. Phil Cooper, 1 son. Education: English & Communications study at College. Appointments: Business Writer for a communications firm; Correspondent for Construction Equipment Guide; Screenwriter; Award winning poet; Editor, College & Family related military publications; Continuity/Script Supervisor for commercial; Voice-overs for commercial projects. Publications: 6 editorials in the Post & Courier; 2 articles. Honours: Many awards and honorable mentions for literary works. Memberships: The Dramatists Guild; SC Writers Workshop; NC Writers Network; Scriptwriters of SC; National Association of Female Executives; Writers Workshop, Los Angeles; Writers Connection, Script Consultant/Reading Analyst, the Writers Workshop, Los

Angeles; The Scriptwriters Network. Address: 641 Palmetto Street, Mount Pleasant, SC 29464-4440, USA.

**COOPER Peter John,** b. 2 August 1960, Barford St Martin. Journalist. Education: MA Politics, Philosophy & Economics, 1982, Oxford University. Appointments: Editor, Gulf Business Magazine, Dubai. Honours: IBP Financial Journalist of the Year, 1991, 1993. Membership: Friend of the Royal Academy. Address: Motivate Pub, PO Box 2331, Dubai, United Arab Emirates.

**COPELAND John Howard,** b. 13 October 1950, San Diego, California, USA. Film Maker; Producer. m. Shannon Gloria Casey. Education: BA Communications/Theatre, 1973, Chapman College, Orange, California. Appointments: Executive Vice President, Netter Digital Entertainment Inc, Board of Directors (Secretary); Co-Producer, TV pilot, Babylon 5 - The Gathering, 1993; Supervising Producer, TV series, Hypernauts, 1995-96; Producer, The Wild West, TV documentary, 1993; Producer: TV movie, Siringo, 1994; Babylon 5 Series and 5 movies, 1993-98, Crusade, 1998. Honours: Emmy Nomination, Best Information Series, 1993, The Wild West; Emmy Award, Babylon 5, 1993, Babylon 5, 1994; Best Vision of the Future Award, Space Frontier Foundation, Babylon 5, 1994, 1996; E Pluribus Unum Award, Best Television Series, Drama, Babylon 5, 1997; Hugo Award, Best Dramatic Presentation, Babylon 5, 1996, 1997. Memberships: Academy of Television Arts and Sciences; Directors' Guild of America. Address: Netter Digital Ent Inc, 5125 Lankershim Boulevard, North Hollywood, CA 91601, USA.

**CORBIER Philippe André,** b. 2 March 1947, Amiens. Physiologist Educator. m. Colette Fuzillier, 2 sons. Education: Diploma of the Faculty of Pharmacy, 1971; Doctor ès Sciences, University of Paris II. Appointments: Research Scientist, Developmental Endocrinology, Laboratory of Endocrinology, CNRS, Orsay, France, 1972-94; Instructor, Physiology, University of Paris II, 1972-99. Publications: Contributor of Articles to Scientific Journals. Memberships: New York Academy of Science. Address: 18 rue Charles de Gaulle, 91400 Orsay, France.

**CORCHON Luis C,** b. 28 March 1949, Madrid, Spain. Economist. m. Maria Del Mar. Education: PhD, Economics, London School of Economics, 1986. Appointments: Professor, University of Alicante, 1988-97; Professor, University Pompeu Fabra, 1997-98; University of Carlos III, Madrid, 1998-. Publications: Quarterly Journal of Economics; JET; 16 Other Papers in International Journals; 2 Books. Memberships: Associate Editor: Revista Espanola de Economia, Journal of Public Economic Theory. Address: University of Carlos III, C/Madrid 126, 28903 Getafe, Madrid, Spain.

**CORCOS Thierry,** b. 8 October 1954, Tunisia. Medical Doctor. m. Laure Dehen, 2 daughters. Education: Internat des Hopitaux de Paris, 1978; Educational Commission for Foreign Medical Graduates, Philadelphia, 1980; MD, Paris, 1982; Certified Specialist, Cardiology, Paris, 1983. Appointments: Resident, Medicine and Cardiology, Paris Hospitals, 1978-82; Resident, Cardiology, 1982-83, Clinical and Research Fellow, 1983-84, Montreal Heart Institute, Canada; Chef de Clinique, Assistant des Hopitaux, Paris, 1984-87; Co-Director, Department of International Cardiology, Director, Heart Research Center, Parly II Medical Surgical Center, Le Chesnay, France, 1987-; President, Francophone Meeting on International Cardiology, 1997-. Publications: Over 200 in professional medical journals. Honours: Golden Word, Best Francophone Meeting, 1997. Memberships: Fellow, French Society of Cardiology; European Society of Cardiology; American College of Cardiology; Society for Cardiac Angiography & Interventions; International Fellow, American Heart Association. Address: 20 Rue des Ecoles, 75005 Paris, France.

**CORDELL Beulah Faye,** b. 3 May 1939, Clifty, Arkansas, USA. Special Educator. m. Jack Cordell, 2 sons. Education: BSE, English, Social Studies, 1987, ME, Special Education, 1994, University of Arkansas. Career: Director, One-Room School; Outreach Teacher of GED and ESL, Northwest Technical Institute; Teacher, Youth at Risk, Bentonv County Alternative School. Honours: Beta Phi Teaching Excellence Award, 1993. Memberships: Council for Exceptional Children; Ozark Literacy; Beaver Lake Literacy Council. Address: 1100 Monitor Road, Springdale, AR 74764, USA.

**CORNELL Bengt Henrik Jonas,** b. 8 November 1938, Stockholm, Sweden. Writer; Director. m. Agreta Ekmannen, 1 son, 2 daughters. Education: University study in literature and philosophy, Swedish Film Institute Film School, 1994-95. Career: Novelist, Critic, Director and Writer of feature films, including Hugs and Kisses, 1967-; Films for TV in Stockholm and Copenhagen, 1975-; Theatre Director, City Theatre in Stockholm, 1970-. Honours: Several awards for the Swedish Film Institute; Prix Europa 1991 for Best TV Feature Film, Guldbaggen, for Best Script 1993 in the Film Institute's Competition. Memberships: SNS; FERA. Address: Kanalallen 13, 115 25 Stockholm, Sweden.

**CORTES John Emmanuel,** b. 11 September 1956, Gibraltar. Biologist. m. Valerie Diane Pearce, 1 son, 1 daughter. Education: Bachelor of Science, University of London, Royal Holloway College, 1979; Doctor of Philosophy, Magdalen College, Oxford, 1984. Appointments: Manager,Gibraltar Health Authority, 1988; General Manager, Gibraltar Health Authority, 1990; Director, Gibraltar Botanic Gardens, 1991; Managing Director, Wildlife Ltd, Gibraltar; Justice of the Peace, 1994. Publications: co-author, The Birds of Gibraltar; co-author, The Flowers of Gibraltar; Numerous Publications on Gibraltar and Region on Ecology and Conservation. Honours: Gibraltar Heritage Award. Memberships: Chartered Biologist; Member, Institute of Biology; Fellow, Linnean Society; Member, Institute of Ecology and Environmental Management; General Secretary, Gibraltar Ornithological and Natural History Society. Address: 8/8 Buena Vista Road, Gibraltar.

**COSTA George (formerly Adel George Costandy),** b. 27 January 1951, Cairo, Egypt. Internist. Education: MD Hons, 1975, Cairo University, Egypt; ECFMG, USA. Appointments: Rotating Intern, Cairo Univ Hospital, 1975-76, Army Hospital, 1976-77; Lab Technician, phlebotomist, NY Labs, 1977-79; Ear, Nose and Throat resident, Cairo, 1978-79, 1982-83, 1984-86; Respiratory Therapist trainee, Mt Vernon Hospital, NY, 1989; Pediatric clerk, Interfaith Medical Centre, NY, 1990; Resident in Internal Medicine, Woodhull Hospital, NY, 1991. Membership: New York Academy of Science. Address: 5929 Reno Avenue, Temple City, CA 91780-1529, USA.

**COSTAMAGNA Sixto Raul,** b. 29 August 1951, Oliva Province, Argentina. 1 son, 1 daughter. Education: Degree in Biochemistry; Master in Parasitology. Appointments: Management Laboratory Hospital Evac, 1978; National University of Sud, 1979. Publications: Atlas of Parasitology; Papers, microscopy journals. Memberships: Argentine Protozoologica Association; Spanish Parasitology; American Association for the Advancement of Science. Address: Undiano 373, 8000 Bahia Blanca, Argentina.

**COWASJEE Saros**, b. 12 July 1931, Secundrabad, India. Author; Educator. Education: BA, 1951, St John's College, Agra, India; MA, 1955, Agra College; PhD, 1960, University of Leeds. Appointments: Professor of English, 1971-95, Professor Emeritus of English, 1995-, University of Regina; Assistant Editor, Times of India Press, Bombay, 1961-63; Instructor in English, University of Regina, 1963; Research Associate, University of California, Berkeley, 1970-71; Visiting Commonwealth Professor, University of Aarhus, 1975; Guest Lecturer, numerous universities in Europe, Australia, N America, India, Fuji and Singapore. Publications: 11 books of criticism, fiction and plays; Editor, 24 novels and anthologies including: The Oxford Anthology of Raj Stories, 1998; Contributor to various publications and numerous articles; General Editor, Arnold Publishers' Literature of the Raj series, 1984-. Honours: J N Tata Scholarship for postgraduate studies at Leeds University; Recipient 4 Canada Council Leave Fellowships. Memberships: Association Canadian University Teachers Eng; Canadian Association Commonwealth Literature & Language Studies; Author's Guild of India; Writers Union of Canada; Zorastrian. Address: Dept of English, Regina University, Regina Sask, Canada S4S 0A2.

**COX Frances Plake**, b. 15 October 1919, Goodyear, Arizona, USA. Educator. m. N James Cox, 2 sons. Education: BA, Education, Elementary Certificate, Arizona State University, 1941; California Life Elementary Certificate, 1955; Special Learning Handicapped Credential, 1972; Additional university credits to doctorate level plus, San Francisco State College, Santa Clara University, Notre Dame College, University of California at Berkeley, University of California at Santa Cruz, San Jose State University, Fresno State College. Appointments: Classroom Teacher, Phoenix, Arizona, 1941-49, Fresno City Schools, California, 1949-50, Fresno County Schools, 1953-56, Portland Public Schools, Oregon, 1960-64; Master Teacher, Fresno State College, 1953, Oregon State University, 1962; Resource Specialist, Palo Alto Unified Schools, California, 1964-87. Honours: Arizona State University Award, Most Popular Girl, 1941; Outstanding Senior Alumnus Award, 1941; Mortar Board, 1941; WHO Award for Outstanding Service, Palo Alto Schools and California Teachers Association, 1986. Memberships: Certified Pilot, Member, Civil Air Patrol, 1941-42; Sigma Phi Gamma, 1941-47, Treasurer; Parent-Teacher Association, Phoenix, Fresno, Portland and Palo Alto Schools, 1941-86; Remedial Reading Teachers Organisation, 1961-73; National Education Association/California Teachers Association, 1976-86, Leader, Political Action Representative; Resource Specialists Organisation, 1984-86; International Platform Association, 1986-96; Commonwealth Club of California, 1986-99; California Retired Teachers Association, 1987-99; Sierra Club, 1996-98. Address: 911 La Mesa Drive, Portola Valley, CA 94028, USA.

**COX Frank D (Buddy)**, b. 20 December 1932, Shreveport, Louisiana, USA. Oil Company Executive; Exploration Consultant. m. Betty Jean Hand, 1 son, 2 daughters. Education: BS, Business Administration, Louisiana Tech University, 1956; Postgraduate, Centenary College, 1958-59; Certified Professional Landman. Appointments: Various Positions, Exxon Corporation, Houston, 1955-86; Chief Landman, V P Coal Resources, 1980-86; Private Practice, Houston, 1986-89; Senior V P, Energy Exploration Management Company, Houston, 1989-94; Vice President, Manager, T Bar X Limited Company, Houston, 1994-; Vice President, Director, Power Exploration International, Houston, 1994-; Partner, East Texas Reef Fund Limited, 1994-; Land Manager, Thomson-Barrow Corporation, 1994-; Tecolotita Inc, 1994-. Honour: Named, Distinguished Military Graduate, Louisiana Tech University, Ruston, 1955. Memberships:

American Association of Professional Landmen; Houston Association of Professional Landmen; West Houston Association of Professional Landmen; West Houston Exxon Annuitant Club; 100 Club of Greater Houston, Louisiana Tech University Foundation; Crimestoppers Inc; Pi Kappa Alpha Educational Foundation; Omicron Delta Kappa Foundation; Delta Sigma Pi. Address: 14830 Carolcrest St, Houston, TX 77079-6312, USA.

**COX Paul H B**, b. 16 April 1940, Venlo, Holland. Film Director. 2 sons, 1 daughter. Appointments: Film Director, The Journey, 1972; Illuminations, 1976; Inside Looking Out, 1977; Kostas, 1978; Lonely Hearts, 1981; Man of Flowers, 1983; My First Wife, 1984; Cactus, 1986; Vincent, 1987; Island, 1989; Golden Braid, 1990; A Woman's Tale, 1991; The Nun and the Bandit, 1992; Exile, 1994; Lust and Revenge, 1996; The Hidden Dimension (Imax-3D), 1997; Molokai, 1998; Innocence, 1999; Many other Films Directed. Publications: Home of Man, The People of New Guinea, 1972; Human Still Lives from Nepal, 1978; Mirka, 1982; I Am, 1997; Reflections, 1998. Honours: Exile, Australian Film Institute Award; A Woman's Tale, Grand Prix, International Flanders Film Festival, Ghent; Australian Human Rights Award; Australian Film Institute Award; Vincent, Jury Prize, Istanbul International Filmdays; Cactus, Selected for Director's Fortnight, Cannes Film Festival; My First Wife, Flanders International Film Festival; Houston Film Festival; Rio De Janeiro Film Festival; Australian Writers Guild Award; Australian Film Institute Award; Man of Flowers, Warsaw Film Festival, Cannes Film Festival; Figueira Da Foz Film Festival; Valladolid Film Festival; Chicago Film Festival; Australian Film Awards; Lonely Hearts, Uppsala Film Festival; Australian Film Institute Award; Many tributes from all over the world.

**CRACIUN Constantin**, b. 10 July 1943, Marasesti, Romania. Geologist. m. Lidia Ecaterina Craciun. Education: PhD, University of Bucharest, 1984. Appointments: Senior Researcher, Research Institute for Soil Science and Agrochemistry. Publications: 108 papers, 3 books, 1 patent. Memberships: Romanian National Society of Soil Science; Romanian Society of Geology; European Nuclear Society; Romanian Association of Nuclear Energy. Address: ScD apt #51, Drumul Taberii 105 Bl A9, 77461 Bucharest, Romania.

**CRAIN Christina Melton**, b. 18 March 1966, Dallas, TX, USA. Attorney. m. Nathan E Crain. Education: BA, Government Dean's List, The University of Texas at Austin, 1988; JD, Oklahoma City University School of Law, 1991. Appointments: Associate, Nichols, Jackson, Dillard, Hager & Smith, LLP, 1991-93; Name Partner, Kirk, Griffin and Melton, 1994-96; Senior Vice President and General Counsel, Shoponline, at present; Estate Planning, Elder Law, General Corporate, Ad Litem, Attorney and Counselor at Law, President, Christina Melton Crain PC, at present. Honours: Silver US Congressional Medal of Honor for Volunteerism, 1987; Certificate of Achievement, 1996; Junior League of Dallas Peas and Carrots Award for Outstanding Volunteerism, 1997; Distinguished Service Award, 1997; Outstanding Volunteer Award, 1994; Outstanding Young Republican Woman of the Year, 1994 and 1995; DAYL Outstanding Committee Chair of the Year Award, 1997; YRNF Outstanding Young Republican Woman of the Year, 1995; Dallas Outstanding Young Lawyer, 1997-98. Memberships: American Bar Association; Texas Young Lawyers Association, Prevention of Domestic Violence, 1992-93, Needs of Senior Citizen, 1992-; Dallas Bar Association; Dallas Association of Young Lawers; Federal Bar Association; Texas Women Lawyers Association; Dallas Estate Planning Council; Estate Planning Council of North Texas; Senior Network Alliance; National Academy of Elder Law

Attorneys; Friends of the Dallas Public Library, , VP of Special Events; National Association of Women Executives; Pi Beta Phi, Dallas; Dallas Heart Ball; Nursing Home Ombudsman; Dallas Museum of Art; Dallas Historical Society. Address: Christina Melton Crain PC #104-944, 5521 Greenville Avenue, Dallas, TX 75206, USA.

**CRAPON DE CAPRONA Noël François Marie, (Comte),** b. 23 May 1928, Chambéry, Savoie, France. Lawyer; UN Senior Official. m. Barbro Sigrid Wenne, 2 sons. Education: Diploma, Institute of Comparative Law, 1951; LLB, University of Paris, 1952; Postgraduate Studies, School of Political Science, 1952-54. Appointments: Assistant Manager, St Catalina Estancias, Argentina, 1947-48; Editor, Food and Agriculture Organization of the United Nations, 1954-57; Liaison Officer, UN and Other Organisations, 1957-65; Chief, Reports and Records, 1966-72; Chief, Conference Operations, 1972-74; Secretary General, 1974-78; Director, FAO Conference, Council and Protocole Affairs, 1974-85. Publication: The Longobards, a tentative explanation. Honours: FAO Silver Medal, 25 Years of Service; Medal of Honour, City of Salon de Provence. Memberships: Society in France of the Sons of the American Revolution; Alumni Association COllege St Martin de France and Ecole des Sciences Politiques. Address: Lojovägen 73, S-18147 Lidingö, Sweden.

**CRAWFORD Kevan Charles,** b. 26 January 1956, Salt Lake City, USA. Nuclear Physicist. Education: BS, Chemical Engineering, 1978, MS, Nuclear Engineering, 1983, PhD, Mechanical Engineering, 1986, University of Utah. Career: Manager, Reactor Operations, 1981-83, Professor, Engineering, 1984-95, A&M University of Utah. Honour: Fulbright Professor, Minsk, belarus, 1994-95. Memberships: American Nuclear Society; Fulbright Association; Phi Kappa Phi. Address: Precision Engineering Corporation, 3781 South 3145 East, Salt Lake City, Utah 84109-3744, USA.

**CREASIA Joan C,** b. 14 August 1941, Burlington, Vermont, USA. Educator; Nurse. m. Donald Creasia, 2 daughters. Education: BSN, University of Vermont, 1964; MS, Nursing, University of Tennessee, 1978; PhD, University of Maryland, 1987. Appointments: Staff Nurse, Psychiatry Unit, Massachusetts Mental Health Center, Boston, 1964-65; Instructor, D'Youville School of Nursing, Cambridge, Massachusetts, 1965-66; Staff Nurse, Boston Lying-In Hospital, Boston, Massachusetts, 1966-67; Staff Nurse, Medical Surgical Units, Norwood Hospital, Norwood, Massachusetts, 1967-70; Staff Nurse, Nursing Supervisor, Oak Ridge Hospital, Oak Ridge, Tennessee, 1971-74; Staff Nurse, Supervisor, Frederick Memorial Hospital, Frederick, Maryland, 1977-78, 1986-92; Research Assistant, Nursing, University of Maryland, Baltimore, 1980-83; Instructor, Coordinator, Assistant Professor, Medical Surgical, Nursing, Frederick C.C, Frederick, Maryland, 1978-80, 1981-83; Assistant Professor, Coordinator, RN-BSM Program, University of Maryland School of Nursing, Baltimore, 1983-90, Associate Professor, Chair, RN-BSN/MS Programs, 1990-94; Director, Statewide Programs, University of Maryland School of Nursing, 1991-94; Instructor, Nursing, University of Tennessee, Knoxville, 1994-97; Associate Dean, Academic Programs and Interim Dean, Medical University of South Carolina College of Nursing, Charleston, 1994-95; Dean, College of Nursing, University of Tennessee, Knoxville, 1995-. Publications: Conceptual Foundations of Professional Nursing Practice. Honours: Outstanding Achievement in Indirect Nursing Research Award, 1987; National Research Service Award; Professional Nurse Traineeship Award; Outstanding Leadership Award, Maryland Nurses Association. Memberships: ANA; NLN; Sigma Theta Tau; Phi Kappa Phi. Address: 605 Scotswood Circle, Knoxville, TN 37919, USA.

**CRINEL Cicos C,** b. 24 March 1952, Craiova, Dolj, Romania. Professor. m. Lucia Dima Cicos, 1 son. Education: Chem Fac, University Craiova, 1976. Appointments: Professor, 1976-78; Pr Res, 1978-94; Pr Chem, 1994-. Publication: Catplisis Rev Roum Chimie-Bucarest, Annales University Craiova. Memberships: ACS; SRC; SRMM. Address: BD MAI BI, 16A AP3, 1100 Craiova DJ, Romania.

**CRISTEA Minerva,** b. 24 April 1943, Lunca-Bihor, Romania. Professor. m. Cristea Viorel Valentin, 1 daughter. Education: Engineering Diploma, 1965; PhD Physics, 1984. Appointments: Instructor, 1965, Assistant, 1968, Lecturer, 1978, Deputy Professor, 1990, Full Professor, 1994, Politechnica University Timisoara, Romania. Publications: 13 textbooks for students; 3 patents; 75 papers in scientific journals or international conferences volumes. Honour: Excellent Lecturer, 1980. Memberships: Romanian Society of Physics; Society for Multidisciplinary Research from West Region of Romania. Address: Technical University of Timisoara, P ta Horatiu 1, 1900 Timisoara, Romania.

**CRIVOI Aurelia,** b. 5 November 1946, Ghinkautsi, Moldova. m. Jon Crivoi, 2 sons. Education: PhD, University of Chisinau. Appointment: Lector, Professor, of the University. Publications: 13 manuals, 140 articles. Membership: University Senate, special thesis member. Address: 2009 Chisinau, A Mateevici Str No 60, State University, Moldova.

**CROITORU Victor Miron,** b. 17 August 1943, Bucharest, Romania. Professor. m. Amelia, 1 daughter. Education: Diploma, Engineer, 1966; Doctor, Engineer, 1976. Career: Instructor, 1967; Assistant Professor, 1970; Lecturer, 1976; Associate Professor, 1990; Professor, 1992-. Publications: 75 papers, 62 oral presentations, 15 books, 28 patents. Honour: Prize, Romanian Academy. Memberships: ILM; EALE. Address: Polytechnical University of Bucharest, Faculty of Electrics & Telecommunications, Splaiul Independentei 313, R 77206 Bucharest, Romania.

**CROUT Charles John,** b. 6 May 1947, Chambersburg, Pennsylvania, USA. Vice President Technology. m. Brenda S Crout, 2 sons, 1 daughter. Education: Associate in ME, 1967, BSME, 1971, Penn State University; Postgrad Studies, George Washington University, 1978, University Wisconsin, 1980, Penn State (including Executive Management Programme), 1983, 1991. Appointments: Engineering Manager, Chief Engineer, Chambersburg Engineering Co, 1971-94; CEO, Charles J Crout, PE, Engineering Services, Chambersburg, 1987-94; President, Contemporary Forming Technology, Cleveland, 1994-95; VP Product Operations, Forging Developments International Inc, Cleveland, 1995-98; VP Technology, Ajax Manufacturing Company, Euclid, Ohio, 1998-. Publications: Co-Author, Impact Die Design Mnaual, 1985, 1989; Forge Engineering and Die Design Manual, 1995; Concepts of Forging, 1995, 1998; Various papers presented to technical conferences between 1976-98; 7 US patents. Memberships: American Society of Mechanical Engineers; American Society for Materials; Forging Industry Education and Research Foundation; Society of Manufacturing Engineers. Address: 39371 Stonefield Pl, Avon, OH 44011-1779, USA.

**CRUZ Dorothy June Calvo Flores,** b. 27 June 1948, Tamuning, Guam. Educator. m. Samuel Tudela Cruz, 2 daughters. Education: BA, Mathematics, University of Guam, 1970; MSc, Information and Computer Sciences, University of Hawaii, 1972. Appointments: Project Headstart Helper, Department of Education, 1966; Precinct Official (Clerk) for Special Election, Government of Guam, 1969; Computer Science and Math Instructor, Computer Center Coordinator,

University of Guam, 1972-75; Computer Science Assistant Professor, 1979-81, Computer Science Associate Professor, 1981-93, Computer Science Department Chairperson, 1985-89, 1992-96, Computer Science Professor, 1993-97, Guam Community College; Retired, 1997-. Honours include: Graduate Scholarship Award, 1970-72; Outstanding Teacher Awards, 1993-94, 1996-97; Commendation for Outstanding Service to Vocational Education, 1994; Professional Certification Award, 1995; Outstanding Teacher/Advisor Award, 1997; Listed in numerous biographical dictionaries. Memberships include: National Honor Society, 1964-66; Guam Federation of Teachers, 1985-97; Business Professionals of America; Advisor, Computer Science Organization, 1991-97; Advisor, Guam Community College Yearbook Staff, 1991-92; Advisor,Guam Community College Student Body Association, 1992-97; Faculty Council, National Honour Society, 1993-97; Advisor, National Association of Secondary School Principals, 1996-97; Computer Science Advisory Committee, 1983-89, 1991-97; Eucharistic Minister, Lector, Catholic Ministry of Our Lady of Lourdes Church, Yigo, Guam, 1986; Board of Directors, Treasurer, Interfaith Volunteers Caregivers Inc. 1991-; University of Guam Alumni Association, 1993-; National Community College Chair Academy, 1995-; Institute of Electrical and Electronics Engineers Computer Society, 1996-. Address: PO Box 11142, Yigo, Guam 96929 0142, Guam.

**CSABA László,** b. 27 March 1954, Budapest, Hungary. Economist. m. Gabriella Onody, 1 son, 1 daughter. Education: BA, 1976; MA, 1978; Bp Uni Econ, 1984; PhD, 1996; Postdoc/Professor, Hungarian Academy Science, 1997; Dr habil oec Bp Uni Econ. Appointments: Fellow, Institute of World Economics, Bp, 1976-87; Senior Economist, Kopint-Datorg, 1988; Honorary Professor, College of Foreign Trade, 1991; Full Professor, Bp Un Econ, 1997; Visiting Professor, Milan, 1991, Helsinki, 1993, Frankfurt, 1997, Berlin, 1998. Publications: Author, 5 monographs; Editor, 2 coll columes; Author, 130 publications in journals and chapters in 18 countries. Memberships: Vice President, European Association for Comparative Economics, 1990-94, 1996-98; Co Chairman, Committee on Economics, Hungarian Academy Science, 1996-. Address: Kopint Datorg, Csokonai 3, 1081 Budapest, Hungary.

**CSETENYI Arthur Istvan,** b. 13 September 1954, Szeged, Hungary. Computer Scientist. m. Maria Istvan. Education: PhD, 1980, Budapest University of Sciences, 1980; C Sc, 1989, Hungarian Academy of Sciences. Appointments: Budapest University of Economic Sciences, 1978-; Visiting Professor, Oulu University, 1984-85, Wageningen University, 1986, Ruhr University of Bochum, Germany, 1987-89, Pennsylvania State University, 1997-98. Publications: Papers on mathematical ecology, I-II, 1986-88. Memberships: ACM; IEEE; American Mathematics Society; New York Academy of Sciences. Address: 21/A Utas, 1025 Budapest, Hungary.

**CUBERO Jose I,** b. 1 August 1939, Seville, Spain. Professor of Genetics. m. Maria-Teresa. Education: PhD, 1970; PhD, Biology, 1973. Appointments: Director, Faculty of Agricultural Sciences, Spain, 1986-91; Chairman, ICARDA Board of Trustees, 1986-89. Publications: 5 books, over 200 articles in professional journals. Memberships: European Plant Breeding Association; AEP; Sociedad Espagñola de Genética. Address: ETSIAM, Dept de Genetica, Av Menendez Pidal s/n, 14080 Cordoba, Spain.

**CUCNIK Valerija,** b. 26 November 1963, Jesenice, Slovenia. Designer. Divorced. Education: Architecture, University in Ljubljana; Organisation and Computer Information, University in Maribor; Music School Jesenice, Piano and Cello.

Appointments: Exhibitions of drawings and paintings, 1994-98; Several Radio and TV appearances. Publications: You'll Know It's For You, poetry, 1991; For Thirsty Birds, poetry, 1996. Memberships: Cultural Society Dr France Preseren Zirovnica; Vasovalci, Music Group. Address: Breznica 28A, 4274 Zirovnica, Slovenia.

**CURRIE Larry,** b. 30 December 1946, Rome, Georgia, USA. Insurance Executive. m. Linda, 2 sons, 1 daughter. Education: University North Dakota, 1967-68; Gadsden State, 1972-74; CLU Designation, 1984, MS Management, 1995, American College. Appointments: USAF, 1966-72; Appointed Agent, State Farm Insurance, 1974; Agency Manager, 1981; Agency Director, 1988; Field Executive, 1995-; Board of Directors, Kid One Transport, 1998-. Publications: Editor, Multiple Risk Management Newsletter, 1996-98; Articles published in newsletter, 1997, 1998. Memberships: NALU; Society of Financial Service Professionals, National Chair, Leadership & Management Section 1998-; Shelby Co Republican Party, Executive & Committee 1998-. Address: 5513 Afton Drive, Birmingham, AL 35242-4202, USA.

**CURTIS Carol Lynne,** b. 17 December 1946, Salt Lake City, Utah, USA. Educator. m. Enel Laik, 1 son, 1 daughter. Education: BS Sociology, 1969, University of Utah; Language Training, 1969, TESL Training, 1969, Peace Corp; Post-Graduate Education Certificate, 1994-, University of South Pacific, Fiji; Training for museum work, 1985-86. Appointments: Researcher for Anthropologist, Lae Atoll, Marshall Islands, 1975-76; Researcher-Writer, Hand-crafts of the Marshall Islands, 1977; Community Organiser for Utahans Against Hunger, Utah, 1979; Teacher, Rock Point Community School, Arizona, 1979-82; Part-time Teacher, Alaska then Marshall Islands, 1982-87; Grants Manager, Alele Inc, Majuro, MI, 1985-90; Accountant, Grants Manager, 1991-92, Curator, 1992-94, Grants and Fund Raising Programme Manager, 1994, Alele Inc; Teacher, MI High School, Bilingual-Bicultural, 1994-. Publications: 1 book; 2 articles; 1 book chapter. Address: PO Box 714, Majuro, Republic of the Marshall Islands, MH 96960.

**CUTRUBUS Christina Nina,** Publisher; Owner. Education: University of Utah, Salt Lake City, 1954-56. Career: Publicist,Metro-Goldwyn-Mayer, MGM, Paramount Pictures, Walt Disney Productions, United Artists, Cinerama Productions; Owner, Phonic Arts Agency; Owner, University Services Corporation, 1971; Editor, Publisher, Utah Ballet West Magazine; Originator, Owner, Publisher, Editor, Utah Preservation/Restoration Magazine; Personal Representative, Press Agent, His Eminence Archbishop Iakovos. Publications: The Salt Lake Temple: A Monument to a People; D. Alt: Impressions of an Impressionist. Memberships: Zeta Phi Eta; Salt Lake Advertising Club; Salt Lake Chamber of Commerce. Address: PO Box 58247, Salt Lake City, UT 84158-0247, USA.

**CYTRYCKI Slawomir,** b. 17 December 1951, Lodz, Poland. Economist. m. Elzbieta, 2 sons. Education: University of Lodz, 1970-71; Leningrad Institute of Economics and Finance, Diploma Cum Laude, Master of Economics, 1971-74. Appointments: Assistant Lecturer, University of Lodz, 1974; Head of International Department, National Committee of the Polish Students' Association, 1974-77; Deputy Director, Ministry of Science, Higher Education and Technology, 1977-82; Special Assistant to the Under Secretary General, United Nations Secretariat, New York, 1982-87; Advisor to the Prime Minister, Deputy Chef de Cabinet of the Prime Minister, 1987-89; Deputy Chief of Cabinet of the President, 1989-91; Managing Director, Bank Handlowy w Warszawie SA, 1991-. Honours: Encomienda de la Orden del Aguila Azteca, 1979; Cross of Merit, Bronze, 1986, Gold, 1989; Knight's Cross,

Polonia Restituta, 1999. Address: Bank Handlowy w Warszawie SA, ul Chalubinskiego 8, 00-950 Warsaw, Poland.

**CYWINSKI Zbigniew,** b. 12 February 1929, Torun, Poland. Structural Engineering Educator. m. Helena Wilczynska. Education: BSCE, Technical University of Gdansk, 1953; MSCE, 1955; PhD, Engineering, 1964; DSc, Engineering, 1968. Appointments: Instructor, Assistant Professor, 1953-65; Consulting Engineer, University of Baghdad, 1965-66; Assistant Professor, 1966-70; Assistant Professor, University of Mosul, 1970-73; Associate Professor, 1973-79; UNESCO Expert, Somalia, 1979-80; Professor, Structural Engineering, 1980-87; Professor, University of Tokyo, 1987-88; Technical University of Gdansk, 1988-. Publications: Structural Mechanics I, 5 editions, 1973, II, 2 editions, 1976; Numerous articles in professional journals. Honours: Ministry Award, 1976; Rector Award, 1994. Memberships: ASCE; Polish Society of Theoretical and Applied Mechanics; International Association of Bridge and Structural Engineering; Polish Society of Bridge Engineers. Address: ul Msciwoja 50/32, 80-357 Gdansk, Poland.

**CZAPLINSKI Kazimierz,** b. 16 April 1926, Pulawy. Civil Engineer. m. Wanda, 3 sons, 1 daughter. Education: MS, English, Gdansk University of Technology, 1952; PhD, Wroclaw University of Technology, 1967; Professor, 1990. Appointments: Site Manager, 1949-52; Main Engineer, Mostostal, Wroclaw Place, 1952-62; Assistant Professor, Wroclaw University Technology, 1963-72; Associate Professor, 1972-89; Professor, 1990-. Publications: Realization of Construction Objects, Erections of Structures; Co-Author, Construction Design Methodology; Over 150 Articles. Memberships: National Council of Lay Catholics; Polish Society of Civil Engineers. Address: Szolc-Rogozinskiego 3, 53-209 Wroclaw, Poland.

# D

**D'AMICO Ann,** b. 24 August 1957, Pittsburgh, Pennsylvania, USA. Writer; Public Relations Professional. m. John T Rago, 2 daughters. Education: BA, Duquesne University, 1979; MA, 1987. Appointments: Communications Associate, Public Relations, Duquesne University, 1979-89; Coordinator, University Relations, 1989-93; Executive Director of Public Affairs, 1993-. Memberships: Public Relations Society of America; International Association of Business Communications; Council for Advancement and Support of Education. Address: Duquesne University, 600 Forbes Ave Pub Affairs Off, Pittsburgh, PA 15282, USA.

**D'HONDT John Patrick,** b. 18 November 1953, Pittsfield, Massachusetts, USA. Author; Performer. Education: BSc, Education, North Adams State College, North Adams, Massachusetts, USA. Publications: The Bunny Book, novel, 1991. Honours: Fellowship at Mount Angel Abbey Library, Oregon, 1996; Requiem for The Singing Nun, performed by the author, San Francisco, California, 1997. Membership: PEN Center, USA West. Address: PO Box 14251, San Francisco, CA 94114, USA.

**D'SOUZA Alan S,** b. 11 January 1954, Calcutta, India. Real Estate Agent; Tax Consultant; Pianist; Author. m. Mary Ann C Diaz, 2 daughters. Education: BS, Physics, Northeast Missouri University, 1974; Postgraduate, University of New Orleans, 1984-85. Appointments: Business & Estate Consultant, Hinsdale-Oakbrook (III) Associates, 1979-82; Pianist, Marriott Hotels, Lake of the Ozarks & Canal Street, New Orleans, 1982-84; Revenue Officer, IRS, Baton Rouge, 1985-89; Tax Consultant, Pianist, Writer, Baton Rouge, 1989-. Publications: Latin Jazz, series, 1995-96; Customer Service Manual, Beckley Cardy Company; DSK Favorites: Our Best Home Cooking co-author); Several articles in professional journals. Memberships: Society of Professional Journalists; Academy of Political Science; Jazz Society, Baton Rouge; Smithsonian Institute. Address: 15728 Council Avenue, Baton Rouge, LA 70817, USA.

**D'SOUZA Mary Augusta,(Sister of the Cross)** b. 26 March 1938, Pune, India. Educationalist. Education: Secondary Teacher Training, 1959; MLit, 1979. Appointments: Teacher, 1962-90, 1993-; Principal, 1990-93; Coordinator, Goa YCS/YSM, 1993-; Animator, Young Students Movement, 1970-. Honours: Best Teachers National Award, B Lyons Club, Aurangabad, 1990; Rotary Club, Kholapur, 1991. Membership: Sisters of the Cross, Chavanod, France, 1993-. Address: Holy Cross Convent, Bastora, Bardez Goa 403507, India.

**DA COSTA German,** b. 14 September 1942, Montevideo, Uruguay. Physicist. m. Ana Maria Isern, 2 sons, 2 daughters. Education: Docteur en Physique, 1974, France; Doctorat d'Etat es Sciences Physiques, 1982, France. Appointments: Full Professor, Physics Department, University Simon Bolivar, Caracas, Venezuela; Head of Laboratory of Optics and Fluids. Publications: 60 in refereed scientific journals and proceedings of international congresses. Honour: National Prize for the best work of the year, National Research Council, Conicit, Venezuela, 1995. Address: Residencia Puerta del Este, Torre Oeste Apt 231, California Norte Caracas, Venezuela.

**DAALDER Joost,** b. 28 September 1939, Bergen, Netherlands. Professor of English. m. Geertruida, 3 sons, 2 daughters. Education: Cand Litt, University of Amsterdam, 1960; Drs Litt, 1965. Appointments: Lecturer, Senior Lecturer,

University of Otago, New Zealand, 1966-76; Lecturer, Senior Lecturer, Flinders University of South Australia, 1976-82; Reader, 1983-98; Professor, 1998-. Publications: Scholarly Editions of Renaisance Texts; Over 70 Scholarly Articles. Address: Sch of Humanities, Flinders University, GPO Box 2100, Adelaide, SA 5001, Australia.

**DACI Hinajet,** b. 11 August 1936, Diber. Lecturer. m. Mirvjen, 2 daughers. Education: Electrical Engineer, 1960; MSc, 1987; PhD, 1993; Professor, 1994. Appointments: Lecturer, 1960-73, 1982-91, 1998-; Electrical Engineer, Paper Mill, 1973-81; Dean, Electrical Engineering Faculty, 1992-97. Publications include: Computerize Measurement Systems; Transducers; Electrical Measurements. Memberships: New York Academy of Sciences; National Council of Energy; Scientific Council, MDMK. Address: Fakulteti i Inxhinieas Elektruke, Universiteti Politeknik, Bul Deshmoret e Kombit, Tirane, Albania.

**DACKOW Sandra Katherine,** b. 19 May 1951, Paterson, New Jersey, USA. Symphony Conductor; Educator; Musical Arranger. Education: Bachelor of Music, Master of Music; PhD, Eastman School of Music, Rochester, New York. Appointments: Music Director, Hershey, Pennsylvania, Symphony Orchestra; Music Director, Ridgewood, New Jersey, Symphony Orchestra; many Guest conducting appearances in US and other countries. Publications: Over 50 arrangements published for young orchestras; Pride of Ridgewood Award; ASCAP Awards annuals. Memberships: ASCAP; Music Educators National Conference; Conductors Guild; American String Teachers Association. Address: 27-33 Corsa Terrace, Ridgewood, NJ 07450-3145, USA.

**DADAWA Zhu Zheqin,** b. 15 June 1968, Guangzhou, China. Artist. Education: BA, Department of Chinese Literature, 1990. Appointments: Artist, Recording contract, 1994-. Creative Work: Recordings: Yellow Children, 1992; Sister Drum, 1995; Voice from the Sky, 1997; Soundtrack: The King of Wanling, 1996; Chinese Box, 1997; Songs: The Story of a Red-Crowned Crane, 1990; The Tear Lake with the Chieftains, 1996. Honours: 2nd Prize, National 4th Grand Prize Young Singers, TV Contest, 1990; One of Five Albums of the Year, Q Magazine; Best of the Top Ten in the World, Shanghai Xinmin Evening Newspaper, 1995; Best Album of the Year, the 20th Taiwan Jinding Phonograph Award, 1995; The Best Sound Track of Venice Film Festival Prize, 1997; The Best Female Artist in YMC, 1997. Membership: ASCAP, 1998.

**DAEHNHARDT Rainer,** b. 7 December 1941, Wien, Austria. Historian. m. Paula, 1 son, 4 daughters. Education: Bachalerat, Deutsche Schule Lissabon, Goethe Realgymnasium Frankfurt. Appointments: Academic Member, Naval Academy, Lisbon. Publications: 54 Books; 350 Articles. Honours: Medal of Honour, Vasco Da Gama. Memberships: Post, Academy of Antique Arms; American Society of Arms Collectors; Gesellschaft fur Waffenkunde, Arms and Armour Society. Address: Portuguese Acad Antique Arms, Rua Visconde Da Luz 9, P-2750 Cascais, Portugal.

**DAESCU Constantin,** b. 21 May 1943, Bucharest. Chemist. Teacher. m. Ana-Elena, 1 son, 1 daughter. Education: Engineer, Politechnical University, 1966; PhD, 1977. Appointments: Assistant, Politechnical University , 1966-77; Professor, 1977-. Publications: Drug Chemistry and Technology; Drugs Industry. Memberships: Romanian Chemical Society; New York Academy of Science. Address: 11-13 Take Ionescu, 1900 Timisoara, Romania.

**DAFALLAH Abdullah Ahmad,** b. 25 October 1940, Khartoum. Medical Biochemist. m. Fathia, 2 sons, 2 daughters. Education: MBBS, 1965; Academic Diploma in Biochemistry, 1969; PhD, 1973; MSc, 1974. Appointments: Medical Officer, Ministry of Health, Sudan, 1967-68; Assistant Professor, College of Medicine, 1973-79; Associate Professor, 1980-88; Chairman, Department of Biochemsitry, 1980-82; Associate Professor, Consultant, College of Medicine, King Faisal University, Saudi Arabia, 1989-99. Publications: 20 Articles, top professional journals. Honours: Senior Scholar British Council; Senior Scholar Michigan State University; Senior Scholar W.H.O.. Memberhips: Life member, Sudan Medical Association; Fellow, Royal Society of Tropical Medicine and Hygiene; Member, British Biochemical Society; Member, Sudanese Doctors Union. Address: College Medicine, P O Box 2114, 31451 Dammam, Saudi Arabia.

**DAGA Satya Narayan,** b. 16 December 1948, Dewas, India. Engineer. m. Padma Daga, 1 son. Education: BSc, honours, Vikram University, 1966; BESc, honours, Jabalpur University, 1969. Career: Deputy General Manager, 1991-94, Senior Deputy General Manager, 1994-95, Additional General Manager, 1995-, BHEL, Bhopal (India). Publications: 40 technical papers in national and international conferences. Honours: Gold Medal, Vikram University, 1966; Gold Medal, Jabalpur University, 1969; Title, Man of the Year, American Biographical Institute, USA, 1997. Memberships: Fellow, Institution of Engineers, India; Member, American Society of Mechanical Engineers, New York, USA; Member, Indian Institute of Industrial Engineering. Address: Barkhera 13-N5 A Sector, Bhopal 462021, India.

**DAGAN Gedeon,** b. 24 December 1932, Rumania. Professor of Hydrology. m. Ora, 3 daughters. Education: Hydraulic Engineering and Applied Mathematics, Bucharest University, 1956; DSc, Technion, Haifa, Israel, 1965. Appointments: Professor of Hydrology and Fluid Mechanics, Technion, Haifa, Israel, 1962-76; Faculty of Engineering, Tel Aviv University, 1976-. Publications: 5 books; numerous articles. Honours: Fellow, AGU, 1989; Doctor Honoris Causa, University Paris V, 1996; Stockholm Water Prize, 1998. Membership: American Geophysical Union. Address: Department Fluid Mechanics and Heat Transfer, Tel Aviv University, Ramat Aviv, Israel.

**DAGNINO-PASTORE Jose,** b. 19 November 1933, Buenos Aires, Argentina. Economist. m. 2 daughters. Education: MA Econ, University of California; Am Econ; PhD Econ, Harvard University, 1963. Appointment: Staff, Professor, Director and trustee of Universities and research institutes; Minister of the Economy, BA Province; Secretary to the National Development Council; ME of Argentina; Ambassador at large for financial affairs in Europe; Governor for the Interaction Development Bank; The World Bank; International Monetary Fund; Partner Econometrica; Syndic, Director, Chairman of banks, enterprises and foundations; Consultant to a few Latin American National and over a dozen international institutions. Publications: 60 papers published in 4 languages and 20 countries; Chair member, Academy of Economic Sciences; Academy of Strategic; Trustee, Argentine Council for International Relations; Member, Executive committee of the Interamerican Dialogue; Vice-chairman, National Endowment for the Arts and Other Foundations. Address: Reconquista 379 4th Fl, 1003 Buenos Aires, Argentina.

**DAGUM Estela-Bee,** b. 30 November 1935, Cordoba, Argentina. Economist; Statistician. m. Camilo Dagum, 3 sons. Education: PhD Economics, 1960. Appointments: Senior Researcher, Mathematica, Princeton, NJ, 1966-68; Professor, National University of Mexico, 1968-70; Chief, 1972-80, Director, 1981-93, Time Series Staff, Statistics Canada, Ottawa, Canada; Professor, Fac Statistical Sciences, University Bologna, 1994-. Publications: Author of the XIIARIMA method adopted by majority of statistical bureaus; Over 100 articles in scientific journals. Honours: Julius Shiskin Award, 1980; Crystal Globe Award, 1996. Memberships: Fellow, American Statistical Association, 1980; Elected member, International Statistical Institute, 1985; Honorary Fellow, International Institute of Forecasters, 1996; Vice President, InterAmerican Statistical Institue, 1998-2000. Address: University Bologna Faculty Statistical Sciences, Via Delle Belle Arti 41, 40126 Bologna, Italy.

**DAHL Marilyn Olive,** b. 12 February 1931, Broderick, Saskatchewan, Canada. Association Executive; Nurse. m. Lloyd Theodore, 2 sons, 1 daughter. Education: Diploma, 1953, Victoria Hospital School of Nursing; BSc N, 1979, PhD, 1995, University UBC; MA Communications, 1988, Simon Fraser University. Appointments: Nursing Supervisor, Victoria Hospital, Prince Albert, Saskatchewan, 1953-54; Swift Current Union Hospital, 1954-55; Saskatoon University Hospital, 1955-56; Dr Rygiels Children's Hospital, Hamilton, Ontario, 1969-71; Riverview Psychiatric Hospital, Coquitlam, BC, 1971-77; Instructor, Douglas College Faculty of Nursing, 1980-88; Research and Consultant, Hearing Health Care, 1979-95; President and CEO, MD Enterprises, 1993-95; President, Canadian Hard of Hearing Association, 1985-92; President, International Federation of Hard of Hearing, 1992-94; President, Canadian Deaf and Hard of Hearing Forum, 1992-94; Core Committee, Institute for Hearing Accessibility Research, UBC, 1994-; Executive Director, Western Institute for the Deaf and Hard of Hearing, 1995-. Publications: Editor, IFHOH Journal, 1990-92; Editor, Jerusalem Congress Report, 1993; To Hear Again: A Training Manual; a Self-Help Guide to Better Hearing; numerous publications in professional and consumer journals; numerous national and international presentations and briefs consumer advocacy. Honours: Order of British Columbia, 1993 - named Canada's Foremost Advocate for the Hard of Hearing; Commemorative Medal for 125th anniversary of Canadian confederation for volunteer service, 1993; Marilyn Dahl Award of Merit established by Canadian Hard of Hearing Association, 1994. Memberships: International Federation of Hard of Hearing; Canadian Hard of Hearing Association; Western Institute for Deaf & Hard of Hearing; Institute for Hearing Accessibility Research; Alumni, UBC & SFU. Address: Western Inst for Deaf & Hard of Hearing, 2125 W 7th Avenue, Vancouver BC, Canada V6K 1X9.

**DAI Zhiliang,** b. 24 November 1939, Shanghai, China. Professor; Senior Engineer. m. Hua Nanzhen, 2 daughters. Education: Graduate, Shanghai East China Science and Engineering University, 1964. Appointments: Engineer, Beijing Class Design and Research Institute, 1964-; President, Professorship, Senior Engineer, Vice President, Bengbu Design and Research Institute for Glass Industry, 1982-; Engineer, Beijing Centre, 1993-; Visiting Professor, Wuhan Industry University. Publications: Several articles in professional journals. Memberships: Steering Committee, International Commission on Glass; Chinese Ceramic Society; Vice Director, China Architectural and Industry Glass Association. Address: Bengbu Glass Design Research Institute, Tushan Road, Anhui Bengbu 233018, China.

**DALAI Ajay Kumar,** b. 13 April 1959, Puri, India. Professor of Engineering. m. Debasmita Dalai, 1 son, 1 daughter. Education: BSc, honours, Chemistry, 1979; BScTech, Petro-Chem Tech, 1982; MTech, Chemical Engineering, 1989; PhD, Chemical Engineering, 1990; PEng, 1993. Appointments:

Production Engineer, 1984-85; Research Assistant, 1989-96; Research Associate, Lecturer, 1990-96; Assistant Professor, 1996-98; Associate Professor, 1998-. Publications: Over 15 papers in professional journals. Honours: NSERC Fellowship; Sask Power Fellowship; Indian National Scholarship Award; Best Volunteer in 1994-95, Hindu Society. Memberships: AIChE; CIC; CSChE; APEGGA; ACS. Address: Department of Chemical Engineering, University of Saskatoon, 110 Science Place, Saskatoon S7N 5C9, Canada.

**DALE Virginia House,** b. 9 September 1951, Rochester, New York, USA. Ecologist. m. Leonard Charles Hensley, 5 February 1987, 1 son, 1 daughter. Education: BA, 1974, MS, 1975, Mathematics, University of Tennessee, Knoxville; PhD, Mathematical Ecology, University of Washington, Seattle, 1980. Career: Research Associate, Forest Research Laboratory, Oregon State University, 1981; Assistant Professor, Department of Biology, Pacific Lutheran University, 1981-82; Instructor, Department of Biology, University of Puget Sound, 1982-83; Research Scientist, 1984-94, Associate Director, 1994-96, Senior Scientist, 1996-, Environmental Sciences Division, Oak Ridge National Laboratory; Adjunct Faculty, Ecology and Evolutionary Biology, University of Tennessee, Knoxville, 1993-. Publications: Books: Effects of Land Use Change on Atmospheric CO2 Concentrations: Southeast Asia as a Case Study, 1994; Tools for Environmental Decision-Making Research, 1999; Numerous articles in professional journals. Honours include: Martin Marietta Performance Improvement Process Award, 1989; Technical Publication Award, East Tennessee Chapter of the Society of Technical Communication, 1991, 1992; International Techinical Communications Competition Award of Excellence, 1991; Martin Marietta Technical Achievement Award, 1991; Hammer Award, Vice President Al Gore, 1997. Memberships include: USDA Forest Service Committee of Scientists; Associate Editor, Ecosystems; National Science Foundation; Environmental Protection Agency Scientific Advisory Board; Sigma Xi; National Research Council. Address: Environmental Sciences Division, Oak Ridge National Laboratory, PO Box 2008, Oak Ridge, TN 327831, USA.

**DALENS Bernard Jacques,** b. 6 June 1949, Petite Rosselle. Anaesthesiologist Paediatrician. m. Assali, Helene, 2 sons, 2 daughters. Education: Medical Thesis, 1979; Certification, Anaesthesiology, 1979; Certification, Paediatrics, 1980; PhD, 1986. Appointments: Assistant Professor, Anaesthesiology, 1980-83; Consultant, 1983-. Publications: Over 200 Publications; Pediatric Regional Anesthesia; Regional Anesthesia in Infant and Children; Principals and Practice of Pediatric Anesthesia. Memberships: SFAR; ADARPEF; APA; ASA; IARS; ESRA. Address: 10 Rue Massillon, F-63000 Clermont-Ferrand, France.

**DALWADI Thakor,** b. 30 October 1959, Anand, Guj, India. Engineer. m. Daxaben, 2 sons. Education: SSC, 1976; Diploma, Electrical Engineering, 1979; Post Diploma, Refrigeration, Air Conditioning, 1980. Appointments: Trainee Engineer, L D College of Engineering, 1979-80; Trainee Engineer, MIS Air Conditioning Co Ltd, 1980-81; Junior Engineer, Jyoti Ltd Mogar, 1981-82; Technical Executive, MIS Power Build Ltd, 1983-. Honours: Sharpshooter, IIIrd in India; NCC Ist and IInd Passed. Memberships: Technical Executive, MIS Power Build Ltd; Lion Club Anund. Address: OPP D N High School, Prajapati Bhooran, Station Road, Anand, 388001 Guj, India.

**DALY Donald Francis,** b. 6 August 1928, Bridgeport, Connecticut, USA. Investor. m. Sandra Godfrey, 2 sons, 4 daughters. Education: AB, 1950, Yale College. Appointments:

US Army, 1950-57; Hemphill Noyes, 1957-63; Vice President, Scudder Stevens and Clark, 1963-78; Partner, Brundage Story & Rose, 1978-95; Senior Vice President, Mellon Bank, 1995-. Honours: Distinguished Service Cross, 1953; Bronze Star & Purple Heart. Memberships: Investment Counsel Association of America, former governor; Fellow, NY Society Security Analysts; Union Club; Commander, Order of St John; Yale Club, NY; Pilgrims; Philadelphia Estate Planning Council. Address: 321 South Roberts Rd, Bryn Mawr, PA 19010, USA.

**DAMODARAN Sivakumar,** b. 4 November 1944. Muttappalam. Social Psychiatrist. m. M Girija, 1 son. Education: BA, 1965; MSW, 1967; JD, 1971; PhD, 1996. Appointments: Research Investigator, Research Guide in Social Work. Publications: 72 Research Articles. Memberships: Several Including IAMCR; IASSW; WAPR; ISSRF; ISSA; BSPS; ISTD; IEA; ISLE; IAEA. Address: Population Research Center, University of Kerala, Kariavattom, Thiruvananthapuram 695581, Kerala, India.

**DANA Uriel,** b. 12 November 1954, Chicago, Illinois, USA. Fine Artist. Education: Sculpture and Museum Management, College of Marin, Kentfield, California, 1981-83; Painting Apprentice of Gage Taylor, San Rafael, California, 1983-85. Appointments: Fine Artist, Illuminarium Gallery, Corte Madera, California, 1984-87, Isis Rising Gallery, Santa Monica, 1984-87, 1987-88, Center Art Galleries, Honolulu, and Maui, Hawaii, 1987-88, Dyansen Galleries, Maui, Hawaii, 1989; Hanson Galleries, Sausalito, LaJolla and Carmel, 1989-90; Sierra Galleries, Tiburon, 1990, Eaton Galleries, Sausalito, 1990; Conacher Gallery, San Francisco, 1991-95, Fine Art Collections, Kona, Hawaii, 1992-95, Addi Galleries, Maui, Hawaii, 1992-95. Publications: Columnist, Living on the Edge and Angel in A G-String. Honours include: Award of Honour, San Francisco Arts Commission, 1985; Editors Choice Award, Outstanding Poets of 1998, National Library of Poetry; Who's Who of American Women, 21st Edition. Address: PO Box 2163, Sausalito, CA 94966, USA.

**DANAILA Leon Ghiorghe,** b. 1 July 1933, Darabani. Neurosurgeon. m. Alexandrina Ionescu. Education: Graduate, Faculty of General Medicine, Jassy; Graduate, Faculty of Psychology and Philosophy, Bucharest. Appointments: General Practitioner, Sanitary District of Comanesti and Darmanesti, Bacau County, 3 years; Resident Neurosurgeon, Neurosurgery Clinic of Bucharest, 1961; Senior Physician, Head, Vascular Neurosurgery Department VII, 1981; Professor of Neurosurgery, Bucharest Faculty of Medicine, Professor of Psychoneurology, Bucharest University, 1991 Publications: Numerous articles in professional journals and magazines. Memberships: President, Romanian Neurosurgery, Corresponding Member of Romanian Academy, 1997; Romanian Medical Academy; New York Academy of Sciences; L'Union Medical Balkanique; Balkan Society of Angiology and Vascular Surgery; Biomedical Optics Society; International Society for Optical Engineering; Societe Francaise de Pharmacologie Clinique et de Terapeutique; International Society of Psychoneuroendocrinology; International Psychogeriatric Association; European Association of Neurosurgical Sciences; Membre de la Société de Neurochirurgie de Langue Française; World Federation of Neurosurgical Societies. Address: Institute of Cerebro Vascular Disorders, Bucharest, Romania.

**DANILOV Vladimir Ivanovich,** b. 25 October 1947, Gur'evsk, Kemerovo, Soviet Union. Physicist. m. Sabantseva Elena Victorovna, 9 August 1968, 2 sons. Education: Engineer of Metallurgy, Siberian Steel and Iron Institute (SSII), 1970; Candidate of Physical and Mathematical Sciences, SSII, 1979;

Senior Research Assistant, Institute of Strength Physics and Material Sciences (ISPMS), 1990; Doctor of Physical and Mathematical Sciences, ISPMS, 1995. Appointments: Leading Research Assistant of Strength Physics Laboratory, Institute of Strength Physics and Material Sciences. Publications: Approximately 100 to science journals and proceedings; Monographs: Structure Levels of Plastic Deformation and Fracture, 1990; Physical Mesomechanics and Computer-Aided Design of Materials, 1995. Honours: 2 Diploma of 2nd Degree, Contest of Fundamental Science Works by Siberian Branch, USSR, 1987, 1990. Address: Institute for Physics of Strength and Materials Science, Siberian Division of Russian Academy of Science, 2/1 Prospekt Akademicheskii, Tomsk 21, 635021, Russia.

**DARMANOVIC Srdjan,** b. 18 July 1961, Cetinje, Montenegro, Yugoslavia. Politicologist; Assistant Professor. Education: Graduate, Faculty of Political Sciences, Belgrade, 1984; MA, Political Sciences, Belgrade, 1994; PhD, in progress. Appointments: Assistant Professor, Law Faculty, Podgorica, Montenegro University; Member, Federal Parliament of Yugoslavia; Director, Center for Democracy and Human Rights, Podgorica. Publications: Books: Malformed Democracy - The Drama of Yugoslav Postcommunism, 1993; The Real-Socialism: Anatomy of Collapse, 1996; Several articles in professional journals. Membership: Montenegro Academy of Sciences and Arts. Address: Vukice Mitrovic 016, YU 8100 Podgorica, Yugoslavia.

**DARMON Rene-Yves,** b. 10 September 1938, Algeria. Professor. m. Nicole, 1 son, 1 daughter. Education: ESSEC, 1961; MBA, Columbia University, 1963; PhD, Wharton School, University of Pennsylvania, 1973. Appointments: Product Manager, 1964-65;Sales Administration Manager, 1966-68; Consultant, 1973-; Assistant Professor, Universite Laval, 1968-73; Associate Professor, 1973-79; Visiting Associate Professor, McGill University, 1976-78; Associate Professor, 1979-83; Professor, 1983-90; Professor of Marketing, ESSEC, 1990-; Head of Marketing Department, 1991-92, 1998-; Dean of Research, 1992-. Publications: 48 Articles in Professional Journals; 17 Books; 4 Book Chapters. Honours: Outstanding Paper Award; Excellence in Reviewing Award; Award for Best Applied Paper in Marketing; Best Paper Award; Mu Kappa Tau Top Paper Award; Best Stidsen Award of Excellence; Honorable Mention Award; Mu Kappa Tau Award for the Best Article. Memberships: Association Francaise de Marketing; European Marketing Academy; Academy of Marketing Science; Administrative Sciences Association of Canada; INFORMS; American Marketing Assocaition. Address: Ecole Sup Scis Econ Commls, Av Bernard Hirsch BP 105, 95021 Cergy-Pontoise, France.

**DAROOWALA A Razzaque,** b. 11 January 1953, Karachi, Pakistan. Engineer; Investment Banker; Project Consultant. m. Farzana, 1 son, 3 daughters. Education: B Eng (Mech); MBA; MA Economics; Postgrad Diploma Computer Science; Diplomaed Associate, Institute of Bankers in Pakistan; Technical Diploma, Japan International Co-op Agency. Appointments: Deputy Superintendent Engineer, Karachi Shipyard & Engineering Works Ltd; Vice President, MIS, Creditline and Computer Division, NDFC, current. Honours: 1st Position in Matriculation, (10th grade), in whole Karachi, 1968; 2nd Position in Intermediate, (12th grade), in whole Karachi, 1970; All Scholastic Academic Career. Memberships: Adjunct Faculty Member, Institute of Business Administration, University of Karachi; Rotary International; Association of Overseas Technical Scholarships; MENSA International; JCs; Japan Culture Centre; Computer Society of Pakistan; Pakistan Engineering Council; Institute of Engineers, Pakistan. Address:

KDA 7 Chandni Chowk, 2 New Era Apts SC 10, Karachi Sindh 74800, Pakistan.

**DARRABY Jessica L,** b. 17 June, Canada. Lawyer; Author. Education: BA, 1974, University of California at Los Angeles; MA, 1976, University California at Berkeley; JD, 1979, BoaltHall School of Law, University California at Berkeley. Appointments: Attorney, private practice; Law Professor, adjunct, 1988-; Gallery Director & Owner. Publications: Art Artifact & Architecture Law, legal treatise updated annually, 1995-98. Honour: Canada Council Fellowship. Address: Pepperdine School of Law, Malibu, CA 90263, USA.

**DARWISH Ahmed Yehia,** b. 6 May 1951, Cairo, Egypt. Medical Doctor. m. Sherine Fawzy, 1 son, 1 daughter. Education: MB BCH, 1974, Ein Shams University, Cairo; MSc, Pediatrics, 1982, Cairo University. Appointments: Director of Human Genetics Lab, Cairo University; Director of Human Genetics Centre; Genetic Counsellor to: As salam International Hospital; Behman Hospital for Handicapped; Wady El Nile Hospital. Honours: Medal of Honour, Physician Syndicate, Egypt, 1980; Diploma of Outstanding Achievement, Physician Syndicate, Egypt, 1982. Memberships: American Society of Human Genetics; Egyptian Society of Human Genetics; Egyptian Red Crescent; European Society of Human Genetics; Egyptian Society of Pediatric Neurology. Address: Str No 78 No 8 3rd Flr, El Maadi, Cairo, Egypt.

**DAS Asrukana,** b. 25 March 1945, Barisal, Bangladesh. General Secretary, YWCA. m. David Pronab Das, 1 son, 1 daughter. Education: Bachelor of Arts, Economics, 1967; Masters of Arts, Economics, 1970. Appointments: School Teacher, 1971-72; General Secretary, YWCA of Dhaka, Bangladesh, 1972-80; National General Secretary, YWCA of Bangladesh, 1980-. Honours: Service Award, 1995, 1997. Memberships: Young Women's Christian Association of Dhaka, Bangladesh. Address: YWCA of Bangladesh, 3/23 Oqbal Road, Mohammadpur, Dhaka 1207, Bangladesh.

**DAS Banarasi,** b. 16 October 1955, Akorhi, Mirzapur, Uttar Pradesh, India. Teacher. m. Vimala Devi, 1 son. Education: Sahityacharya (equivalent to MA in Sanskrit), 1982; BTC, 1988; MA, Hindi Literature, 1993. Appointment: Assistant Teacher, Government Basic School, Mirzapur. Publications: Sri Hanumad Vandana, 1982; Sri Vindhyavasinicharitamrit, 1989; Sri Ashtabhujakatha Manjari, 1991; Paryavarankaumudi in Sanskrit, Hindi and English, 1993; Utsarg, 1995; Hymn to Lord Hanuman, 1995; Gandhari, 1996; Adyatan, 1997; Silver Poems, 1998. Honours: Sanskrit Literature Award, Uttar Pradesh Government Sanskrit Academy, 1995; Gram Ratna Award by Gram Panchayat Akorhi, Mirzapur, 1996; Winged Word Award, International Socio-Literary Foundation, 1997. Address: S/O sri Molai, Post Akorhi, Mirzapur 231307, UP, India.

**DAS Barij Baran,** b. 1 January 1934, Calcutta, India. Social Worker. m. Ratna, 3 daughters. Education: BCom, Calcutta University, India, 1954. Appointments: Executive, International Oil Co, 1968; Chairman, World Armwrestling Federation; General Secretary, World Armsport Federation, 1970-. Publications: WAF Book of Armwrestling; WAF Book of Armsport; WAF Book of How to Armwrestle. Honours: Citation by Museum of Mirik, India. Memberships: Chairman then General Secretary, World Armsport Federation; Founder Indian Armsport Federation; Indian Power Lifting Federation; Indian Strengthlifting Federation. Address: 63 Sarat Bose Rd, Calcutta 7000025, India.

**DAS Kamala,** b. 31 March 1934, Malabar, India. m. 1adhava Das, 3 sons. Education: Honoris Causa. ppointments: Chairman, Kerala Forestry Board; President, :hildrens Film Society, Kerala State; President, Sanghamitra ociety for Womens Welfare. Publictions: Several books of oems. Honours: Asian World Prize; PEN Prize, Poetry; ahitya Academy Award; Nominated, Nobel Prize. Address: loyal Stadium Apts, Kadavanthara, Kerala, India.

**DAS Swapan Kumar,** b. 15 October 1955, Calcutta, India. iraphic Artist. Education: Diploma in Fine Arts, Government ollege of Arts and Crafts, Calcutta, 1979; Post-Diploma in iraphic Arts, Kala Bhavan, Santiniketan, Visva, Bharati Jniversity, 1982; Research on Printmaking, Aichi Prefectural irt University, Nagkute, Japan, 1986-88. Career: Freelance irtist. Honours: West Bengal State Akademi, 1976-77, 979-80, 1983; Academy of Fine Arts, Calcutta, 1977-78, 979-80, 1981-82, 1985-86; Birla Academy of Art and Culture, 977, 1981; Mahakosal Kala Parishad, Madhya Pradesh, 977-78, 1980-81, 1985-86; National Scholarship in Graphic irt, 1980-82; The Xaverian Art Award, Calcutta, 1984, 1985; All idia Fine Arts and Crafts Society, New Delhi, 1986; Monbusho icholarship, Government of Japan, 1986-88; West Bengal itate Government Arts Exhibition, 1986, 1990; Norwegian iternational Print Triennial, Norway, 1989; Critics Circle of idia, New Delhi, 1989; Ramdhenu Award, Calcutta, 1989; rativa Award, Calcutta, 1989; Special Certificate, International iennial Print Exhibtion, Taipei Fine Arts Museum, Taipei; iraphic artwork reproduced as poster for Festival of India, JSA. Address: H B 16/1 Janapath, Ashininagar, Baguihati, :alcutta 700059, India.

**DAS GUPTA Manash,** b. 13 July 1956, Shillong, India. ecturer. m. Chandana Das Gupta. Education: Bachelor of icience; Master of Science; Doctor of Philosophy; Fellow, idian Chemical Society. Appointments: Lecturer, 1977-1988; ienior Lecturer, 1988-93; Lecturer, Selection Grade, 1993-. ublications: Contributor of 10 Research papers in International ournals. Honours: Certificate of Merit Scholarship; Debate :hampionship. Memberships: Indian Science Congress ssociation; Society of Kinetics of India; Meghalaya Science iociety. Address: St Anthonys College, Shillong 793001, ilaghalaya, India.

**DATUBO-BROWN Difini,** b. 28 April 1944, Nigeria. Medical ratitioner. m. Emily Datubo-Brown, 2 sons, 2 daughters. :ducation: MBBS, Ibadan, 1974; FRCS, England, 1980; FRCS, :dinburgh, 1980. Appointments: Consultant, Burns and Plastic iurgeon, 1982-; Professor, Department of Surgery, 1995-. ublications include: Alternative Techniques for Scrotal teconstruction; Inhibition of Human Fibroblast Growth in Vitro y a Snake Oil. Memberships: Nigerian Association of Plastic ind Reconstructive Surgeons; New York Academy of Sciences; :ommonwealth Fellow, Association of Commonwealth Jniversities. Address: College of Health Sciences, University if Port Harcourt, Port Harcourt, Nigeria.

**DAUGHDRILL James H Jr,** b. 25 April 1934, LaGrange, ieorgia, USA. College President. m. Elizabeth Gay Daughdrill, son, 2 daughters. Education: BA, Emory University, 1956; ilDiv, magna cum laude, Columbia Theological Seminary, 967; DDiv, Davidson College, 1974. Appointments: President, <ingston Mills Inc, Cartersville, Georgia, 1956-64; Minister, St indrews Presbyterian Church, Little Rock, Arkansas, 1967-70; iecretary of Stewardship, Presbyterian Church of the US, 970-73; President, Rhodes College, 1973-. Memberships: foung Presidents Organisation; World Business Council; Chief :xecutives Organization, 1984-86. Publications: Mak Talk, 971; New Directions for Higher Education (co-author).

Honours: Omicron Delta Kappa; McCallie School Alumnus of the Year, 1981; Memphis Educator of the Year, 1982; Spirit of Life Humanitarian Award, City of Hope, Los Angeles, 1984; Community Service Award, Rotary Club of Memphis, 1986; Planner of the Year Award, Society of Professional Planners, 1989; Distinguished National Eagle Scout Award, 1991; Named National Honorary Member, Kappa Delta Epsilon, 1997. Address: 91 Morningside Park, Memphis, TN 38104-3037, USA.

**DAUKANTAS Jurgis,** b. 20 December 1946, Stolzenau, Germany. National Board Certified Counselor. Education: Associate of Arts, Magna Cum Laude, Lesley College, 1971-73; Bachelor of Arts, Psychology, University of Massachusetts, Boston Dorchester, 1974-76; Certificate, Computer Programming, Operations, 1979-80; Master of Arts, Counseling and Guidance Psychology, University of Northern Colorado, 1980-82; CACREP approved Program, 1980-82; ME D Candidate, Counseling Psychology, Cambridge College, 1998-. Appointments: Medical Corpsman, Radio Operator, Computer Operator, United States Army, Berlin, Germany, 1964-67; Replacement Teacher, Substitute Teacher, Boston Public Schools, 1997-. Memberships: Amercan Counseling Association; Massachusetts Mental Health Counselor's Association; International Biographical Centre. Address: 86 Otis St Apt 43C, Cambridge, MA 02141-1700, USA.

**DAUS Arthur Steven,** b. 6 February 1957, Louisville, Kentucky, USA. Physician; Neurological Surgeon. m. Victoria Schilla, 1 son, 1 daughter. Education: BS Physics magna cum laude, 1977, Vanderbilt University; MD, 1981, St Louis University School of Medicine; Internship, 1981-82; Residency in Neurological Surgery, 1982-88, University of Kentucky; Neurological Surgeon, 1988. Appointments: Practising Neurological Surgeon, Joplin, Missouri, 1988-. Honours: Phi Beta Kappa, Alpha of Tennessee, Vanderbilt University, 1976; First Honorable Mention, Resident's Competition, Southern Neurological Society, 1984; Kentucky Colonel, 1985; Kentucky State Resident Award, 1985, Committee on Trauma, American College of Surgeons; Physicians Recognition Award, 1990-94, 1993-97, 1996-2000 with Special Commendation for Self Directed Learning, American Medical Association. Memberships: AMA; American Association Neurological Surgeons and Joint Sections of Pain, Tumours, Neurotrauma and Critical Care, and Disorders of the Spine and Peripheral Nerves; Congress of Neurological Surgeons; Southern Neurosurgical Society; Southern Medical Association; National Coalition of Physicians Against Family Violence; Missouri Medical Association; Jasper-Newton Co. Medical Society; and others. Address: 5 Teal Drive, Joplin, MO 64804, USA.

**DAVANKOV Vadim,** b. 20 November 1937, Moscow, Russia. Chemistry Professor. m. Etichia Farmaki, 2 sons. Education: Technical University of Dresden, Germany, 1962; PhD, 1966, DrSc, 1975, Professor, 1980, Russian Academy of Sciences, Institute of Organo-Element Compounds. Appointments: Junior Research Fellow, 1962-68, Senior Research Fellow, 1968-75, Head of Dept, 1975-, Deputy Director, 1988-94, Russian Academy of Sciences, Institute of Organo-Element Compounds. Publications: Ligand Exchange Chromatography, 1988; Over 400 scientific publications and patents. Honours: Tswett Medal for Chromatography, 1975; State Award of Russian Federation, 1996; Chirality Medal, 1999. Memberships: Academy of Natural Sciences of Russia; American Chemical Society; International Union of Pure and Applied Chemistry; Head of Scientific Council on Chromatography, Russian Academy of Sciences. Address: Russian Academy of Sciences, Institute of Organo-Element Compounds, Vavilov Str 28, 117813 Moscow, Russia.

**DAVENPORT Thomas R H,** b. 5 January 1926, Madras, India. Historian. m. Gwen Elizabeth Matthews, 1 son, 2 daughters. Education: BA, honours, Queens College, Oxford, 1949; MA, Rhodes University College, 1949; PhD, University of Cape Town, 1960; Hon D Litt, Rhodes University, 1994. Appointments: War Service, Sounth African Artillary, 1945; Lecturer, Senior Lecturer, University of Cape Town, 1953-65; Associate Professor, 1965-75, Professor, Head of Department, 1975-90, Rhodes University. Publications: The Afrikaner Bond. The History of a South African Political Party, 1966; South Africa: A Modern History, 4 editions, 1977, 1978, 1987, 1991, fifth edition forthcoming; Christianity in South Africa (with Richard Elphick), 1997; The Birth of a New South Africa, 1998; Several articles in professional journals. Memberships: Past President, South African Historical Society; Fellow, Royal Historical Society. Address: 78C Palymra Road, Newlands 7708, South Africa.

**DAVEY Eleanor E Britton,** b. 28 August 1910, Colorado Springs, USA. Science Educator. m. Herbert M Davey, 1 daughter. Education: AB, University of Northern Colorado, 1934; MS, Arizona State University, 1967. Appointments: Credit Advisor, Montgomery Ward, Denver, Colorado, 1936-38; Swimming Instructor, Colorado State University, Fort Collins, 1938; English Teacher and Swimming Instructor, East High School, Cheyene, Wyoming, 1939-40; Full time mother, 1940-57; Director of Physical Education and English Teacher, 1957-63, Science Department Chairperson and Biology Teacher, 1963-76, Xavier College Preparatory, Phoenix; Awards Director, Science Fair, Arizona State University, Tempe, 1974-88; Professor of Biology, University of Arizona, Tucson, 1980; Arizona Director, Presidential Awards Programme, National Science Foundation, Arlington, Virginia, 1983-98. Publications: Co-author, book, Strength Through Leadership, 1963; Author, Student Text, Air Pollution - Man and the Environment, 1971, Individualized Instruction, Can it Work?, 1980; Contributor, text, Units on Energy for Middle/Junior High Level, 1979; Author for Arizona Section, book, Mothers of Achievement in American History 1776-1976, 1976. Honours: 3 National Science Foundation Scholarships, 1961, 1962, 1967; Outstanding Science Teacher Award, 1965; Arizona Mother of the Year, 1969; Woman of the Year, Phoenix Business and Professional Women, 1972-73; Outstanding Biology Teacher of Arizona, 1973; American Society for Microbiology Award, 1973, 1974, 1976; Arizona Science Teachers Association set up a fund in the name of Eleanor E Davey to Promote Excellence in Science Education, 1983; Arizona Nevada Academy of Science, Distinguished Service Award for Contributions to Science, 1997; and many others. Memberships: 10 professional associations. Address: 242 E McLellan Boulevard, Phoenix, AZ 85012-1141, USA.

**DAVEY Kenneth Richard,** b. 21 February 1952, Seymour, Victoria, Australia. Engineering Educator; International Researcher. m. Madeleine Sophie Behan Davey, 3 daughters, 1 deceased. Education: BChEng, Royal Melbourne Institute of Technology, 1974; MEngSc 1976, PhD, 1980, University of Melbourne. Appointments: Resident Tutor, Engineering, Queens College, University of Melbourne, 1976-79; Postdoctoral Research Fellow, Research Scientist, CSIRO, Division of Food Processing, Brisbane, 1980-83; Consultant, Food Industry and Australian Government, 1980-; Senior Research Scientist, 1984-90, Leader, Engineering Studies Group, 1984-88, Senior Lecturer (Professor), 1991-, University of Adelaide; Director, Food Technology Research Group, University of Adelaide, 1994-; Senior Visiting Research Professor, Laboratoire de genie de l'hygiene et des procedes alimentaires, Institut National de la Recherche Agronomique, Paris, 1995; Senior Visiting Professor, Department of Food

Science, Cornell University, Ithaca, New York, 1998. Publications: Papers in professional journals, conference proceedings, contributions to books, patents. Honours include: Competitive academic scholarships; Fellow, Institution o Engineers, Australia; Fellow, Institution of Chemical Engineers, UK; Fellow, Australian Institute of Food Science and Technology. Memberships include: Institution of Engineers Australia; Institution of Chemical Engineers, UK; Australian Institute of Food Science and Technology; Society for Applied Bacteriology, England; Naval and Military Club, Melbourne Address: 27A Yeltana Avenue, Wattle Park 5066, Australia.

**DAVIES Gillian,** b. 5 April 1940, Abersoch, N Wales. Judge Education: Certificat d'etudes Francaises, Premier Degree Grenoble University, 1957-58; Barrister at Law, Inns of Cour School of Law, 1958-61; PhD, Law, University of Wales, 1997 Appointments: Chairman, Board of Appeal, European Paten Office, 1997-; Honorary Professor, University of Wales, 1994- Formerly, Visiting Lecturer, Centre for Commercial Law Studies; Visiting Lecturer, University of Kent. Publications Piracy of Phonograms; Private Copying of Sound and Audio Visual Recordings; Co-author: Challenges to Copyright and Related Rights in the European Community; Copyright and the Public Interest; Copinger & Skone James on Copyright Memberships: Association Littéraire et Artistique Internationale Address: European Patent Office, Erhardtstrasse 27, D-80298 Munich, Germany.

**DAVIS Adam Brooke,** b. St Louis, MO, USA. Professor. m Andrea Wiedermann, 3 sons, 1 daughter. Education: PhD University of Missouri, 1991; BA, English, University o' Michigan, 1983; MA, University of Michigan, 1984 Appointments: Guest Professor, Freiburg, 1991-92; Assistant Professor of English, Truman State University, 1991-97 Associate Editor, The Chariton Review, 1998-; Associate Professor, 1997-; Director of Graduate Teachers o' Composition, Truman State University, 1997-. Publications Kulturelle Perspektiven auf Schrift und Schreibprozesse, 1995 Rhetoric Review, 1998; The Sixteenth Century Journal, 1998 New Literary History, 1998; Bestia; Many other publications Memberships: Medieval Academy of America; Medieval Association of the Midwest; American Association of University Professors; Missouri Folklore Society; National Council o1 Teachers of English; Conference on College Composition and Communication; Alexander von Humboldt Association o' America; International Society of Anglo Saxonists; Phi Kappa Phi. Address: McClain Hall 314a, Truman State University, Kirksville, MO 63501, USA.

**DAVIS Concelor Dominquez,** b. 17 July 1957. Mental Health Therapist; Counsellor. m. Rasute Jankeviciute. Education: BBA, Accounting, Marketing, St Mary's University, San Antonio, 1991; MA, Counselling, MTI Institute, Los Angeles, 1996. Appointments: Owner, Davis Industries, San Antonio; Owner, Eva's Crystal Place, San Antonio; Councellor, Borgess Hospital, Kalamazoo; Fiscal Officer, Passages Alternative Living; Resident Coordinator, Hallmark, Chicago Mental Health Counsellor, Columbia Woodland Hospital Publications: The Enroy Method, An Approach to Cognitive Behavior Psychotherapy; Its Time to Wake Up; Live for Christ; First Love Then Marriage. Honours: Nominated, Businessman of the Year; Good Conduct Medal, Foreign Service Memberships: Illinois Counselling Association; Delta Sigma Ph Fraternity. Address: 5820 N Kenmore Ave Apt 802, Chicago, IL 60660-3763, USA.

**DAVIS Lennard J,** b. 16 September 1949, New York City Professor; Writer. 1 son, 1 daughter. Education: BA, 1970 Columbia College, New York; École Practique des Hautes

Etudes, Paris, 1972-73; PhD, 1976, English and Comparative Literature, Psychoanalytic Training Clinic, Faculty of Medicine, 1975-76, Columbia University; Psychoanalytic Training Clinic, Yale University, 1976-77. Appointments: Assistant Professor, 1977-85, Associate Professor, Film Division, 1985-86, Columbia University; Assistant Professor, Brandeis University, 1986-89; Visiting Associate Professor, Brown University, Graduate Programme, 1988, University Pennsylvania, 1989-90, Hobart & William Smith Colleges, 1991-92; Assistant Professor, 1992-95, Associate Professor, 1995-97, Professor, 1997-, Binghamton University, SUNY; Editorial Board, Corporalities, United University Professions, 1997-, Mediaevalia, 1996-, Advisory Board, Novel, 1998-, The Encyclopedia of the Novel, 1996-, The Eighteenth Century: Theory and Interpretations, 1985-, Arkansas Review, 1992-97. Publications: Author or co-Editor, 10 books. Memberships: Founding member, Committee on Disabilities in the Profession, the Modern Languages Association; Co-founder, Group for Early Modern Cultural Studies; and others. Address: SUNY Binghamton Dept English, Binghamton, NY 13902, USA.

**DAVIS Lowell Livingston,** b. Urbana, Virginia, USA. div. Education: BS Morehouse College; MS Atlanta University; MD Howard University. Appointments: Capt Mc USNR 1970; Clinical Associate Professor; Surgeon, USC Medical School, California, USA. Memberships: FACC; FACS; FACA; FICA; FCCP. Address: Ste 316 12111 Chandler Boulevard, Valley Village, CA 91607, USA.

**DAVIS Lowell Livingston,** b. 14 December 1922, Urbana, Virginia, USA. Cardiothoracic Surgeon. Divorced. Education: BS, Morehouse College, 1949; MSc, Atlanta University, 1950; MD, Howard University, 1955; Graduate School of Medicine, University of Pennsylvania, 1959-60. Appointment: Cardiothoracic Surgeon, 1967-. Memberships: FACS; FICS; FACA; FICA; FCCP; FACC; Society of Thoracic Surgeons; American Association of Thoracic Surgery; Western Thoracic Surgery Association. Address: 4518 186 St, F 202, Redondo Beach, CA 90278-4669, USA.

**DAVIS Patricia M,** b. 16 November 1932, Lloydminster, Canada. Literacy Educator. m. Harold M Davis, 1 son, 1 daughter. Education: BA, Dallas Baptist College, 1981; MA, University of Texas, 1988; PhD, 1994. Career: Teacher, Trainer, Summer Institute of Linguistics, Ministry of education, Peruvian Amazon Region, 1963-84; Literacy Trainer, Summer Institute of Linguistics, England, 1979, 1988, University of Oregon, 1985-88; International Literacy and Education Consultant, Summer Institute of Linguistics, Dallas, 1995-. Publications: Cognition and Learning, 1991; La ensenanza del Castellano como segunda lengua entre los grupos etnolinguisticos de la Amazonia, 1997. Honour: Outstanding Dissertation of the Year Award, International Reading Association, 1996. Memberships: International Reading Association; Comparative and International Education Society; Alpha Chi; Kappa Delta Pi; Phi Kappa Phi. Address: Summer Institute of Linguistics, 7500 West Camp Wisdom Road, Dallas, TX 75236, USA.

**DAYAL Promod K,** b. 3 November 1940, Bilsanda, India. m. Jyotsana Dayal, 1 son, 1 daughter. Education: BSc, 1959; BDS, 1964; MDS, 1975; Dip Jour, 1974; Dip Appl Psych, 1982; Dip Naturopath, 1984. Appointments: ABSM Institute Dental Science, Mangalore, 1993-96; Government Dental College, Ahmedabad, 1990-98; Professor and Chairman, Department Oral Medicine, and Associate Dean, KMC College Dental Surgery, Mangalore, 1996-. Honours: 150 awards, including: National (India) Award for Dental Research; Indo-German Award for Oral Cancer Research; Representative (India) in SE

Asia; Fellowships: International College of Dentists, Royal Society of Health, Pierre Fauchard Academy. Memberships: International Association Dental Research; International Association Dentomaxillofacial Radiology; Editor, Indian Journal of Dental Research. Address: Department of Oral Medicine and Radiology and Associate Dean, KMC College of Dental Surgery, Mangalore 575001, India.

**DE CRÉE Carl,** b. 19 June 1957, Brussels. Professor; Researcher. Education: MD, cum laude, 1981, MA, 1986, Certificate in Physical Education and Sports Medicine, cum laude, 1984, MPE, cum laude, 1985, MSc, 1992, University of Leuven. Appointments: Scientific Assistant, Clinical Research Unit, St Bartholomew's, Antwerp, 1981-83; Medical Adviser, Takeda Pharmaceuticals Inc, Oaska, 1987; Scientific Adviser, Europalia Project, Japan in Belgium 1989, Brussels, 1989; Project Leader, Department of Human Movement, University of Limburg, Maastricht, 1991-92; Seminars and Publications Manager, VLANAJO, Association of Independent Health Insurances, Lier and Association of Flemish Health Insurances, Malines, 1992-93; Visiting Professor, Universities of Copenhagen, 1986, Coimbra, 1992, Kyoto, 1993; Associate Professor, Institute for Gyneco-Endocrinological Research, 1992-99; Principal Lecturer, De Montfort University, Bedford, England, 1995-99; Research Professor, Institute for Gyneco-Endocrinological Research, Leuven, 1999-. Publications: Several articles in professional journals. Honours include: Minority Scientist Development Award, 1988-89; Achievement Award, IGER, 1998. Memberships include: American College of Sports Medicine; Belgian Society for Sports Medicine and Sports Science; British Association of Sports and Medicine; American Endocrine Society; Flemish Association of Sexology; New York Academy of Sciences; Friends of the London Philharmonic; Vereniging Vrienden van het Concertgebouworkest. Address: Institute of Gynecol-Endocrine Research, PO Box 134, B-3000 Leuven 3, Belgium.

**DE FLORA Antonio Cesare,** b. 2 July 1940, Genova, Italy. Biochemistry Educator. m. Patrizia Bonavera De Flora, 2 sons, 2 daughters. Education: Maturita classica "Liceo C. Colombo", Genova, Italy, 1958; MD, honours, University of Genova, 1964. Appointments: Assistant Professor, 1970-73, Associate Professor, 1970-73, Professor, Biochemistry, 1973-, Scientific Coordinator, Biology Area, 1995-, University Genova, Italy; Head, Biochemistry Department, Genova, 1981-90; Visiting Scientist, Medical Research Council, Mill Hill, England, 1970; Director, Target Project Biotechnology I, 1988-96, Biotechnology II, 1997-, National Research Council, Rome; Chairman, Scientific Committee, Siena Consortium, Siena, Italy, 1992-. Publications: 200 articles in professional journals; 2 patents. Honours: Research Grants, National Research Council, Rome, 1968-; European Union, Bruxelles, 1986-90; Citta di Genova Prize, Mayor of Genova, 1997. Memberships: International Council Scientific Union (COBIOTECH), Paris, France; Board, Biotechnology (EU) Bruxelles, Belgium; Federation of European Biochemistry Societies; Biochemical Society; Italian Biochemical Society. Address: University Degli Studi de Genova, 1st Policattedra Chim Biol, Viale Benedetto XVI, I-16132 Genova, Italy.

**DE FORD Douglas A,** b. 26 November 1945, San Jose, Costa Rica. Scientist Engineer. div, 3 sons, 1 daugher. Education: University of Costa Rica, 1963; Mechanical Engineering, Industrial Business Administration, ITESM Monterey Institute of Technology, 1964-70; MSc, Biotechnology, Teesside University, England, 1983-85; PhD, Biochemical Engineering (Scale-up/down Biotechnical Operations/Processes), 1985-88; Postgraduate Studies,

National University, Costa Rica, 1990. Career: Industrial Engineer, Dole Standard Fruit Company, 1970-75; Chief Engineer, CCSS National Health Service, Costa Rica, 1975-83; University Professor, Bio-Engineering and Industrial Engineering, 1975-83, 1990-94; Scientific Research Engineer, Northeast Biotech Centre and Beecham Pharmaceuticals, England, 1983-88; General Manager, Ancla Laboratories, Costa Rica, 1988-90; Director of Research and Development, CCSS National Health Service, Costa Rica, 1990-94; International Consultant, UN Industrial Development Organization, Vienna, Austria, 1994-96. Publications include: Tropical and Sub Tropical Bio Therapeuticals, Nutritionals of Value and Other Bio Chemicals; Biotechnological Unit Operations for Agrindustrialization. Honours: 2 Scholar Grants, England, 1983-88. Memberships: Institution of Chemical Engineers, England; Federal College of Engineers and Architects, San Jose; College of Electrical, Mechanical and Industrial Engineers, San Jose; National Commission of Biotechnology, San Jose. Address: 2600 Dodge Avenue, Helena, MT 59601-0510, USA.

**DE LA ISLA DE BAUER Maria de Lourdes**, b. 4 February 1934, Queretaro, Mexico. Plant Pathologist. m. Reinald Bauer, 2 daughters. Education: Ing. Agr, ITESM, Monterrey, Mexico, 1955; MSc, University of Minnesota, USA, 1957; Dr.sc.agr, Göttingen Universität, Germany, 1967. Appointments: Professor, Department of Plant Pathology, Chairman, Department of Plant Pathology, Coordinator, Agronomy Section, Mexican Academy of Sciences. Publications: 3 books and numerous scientific articles. Honours: Premio al Saber, 1954; A.V. Humboldt Fellowship, 1963-67. Memberships: Mexican Society for Plant Pathology; President Mexican Society for Sustainable Agriculture & Agronomy Section, Mexican Academy of Sciences. Address: Colegio de Postgraduados, CP 56230 Montecillo, Edo de Mexico, Mexico.

**DE LACERDA Davi Abrantes**, b. 11 February 1972, Fortaleza, Brazil. Physician; Scientist. Education: Graduate, 1989, Colegio Christus; Research Fellow, 1994, Harvard Medical School; Medical Doctor Diploma, 1998, University of Sao Paulo Medical School. Appointments: Research Fellow: Harvard Medical School, 1992-94, Institue Pasteur, 1994, University of Sao Paulo, 1995-97; Visiting Fellowship, Clinical: Hopital Cantonal, Geneve, 1995, L Maximilian University, Munich, 1996, T University, Dresden, 1998. Publications: A Point Mutation in Collager alpha 1 (XI) Causes Autosomic Condrodysplasia in Mice (CHO), 1995; Violence Against Women in Sao Paulo, 1996. Honours: Anatomy Award USP, 1991. Membership: American Association for the Advancement of Science. Address: Sitio Catole CX Postal 45, 63180 Juazeiro do Norte - CE, Brazil.

**DE LEO Diego**, b. 11 July 1951, Rovigo, Italy. Psychiatrist. m. Cristina, 2 sons. Education: Grad Medicine, 1977; Specialty in Psychiatry, 1981; PhD in Social and Behavioural Sciences, 1988, University Leiden, The Netherlands. Appointments: Director of Psychogeriatric Service, University Padova, Italy; Director, WHO Collaborating Centre for Suicide Prevention, Padova, Italy; Director, Australian Institute for Suicide Research and Prevention, Brisbane, Australia. Publications: Author and Co-Author, 22 books and 180 scientific publications. Honour: Stengel Award Winner, 1991. Memberships: President, International Academy for Suicide Research; Vice President, International Association for Suicide Prevention. Address: Psychogeriatric Service, Via Vendramini 7, 35137 Padua, Italy.

**DE LEON Pedro S**, b. 29 June 1954, Sta Barbara, Pangasinan, Philippines. Professional Mechanical Engineer. m. Rebecca R de Leon, 3 sons, 2 daughters. Education: BSc

Mechanical Engineering, 1977, St Louis University, Philippines; MSc Mechanical Engineering, 1995, Technological University of Philippines, Manila; MBA, 1996, PhD Science Education, 1998, Virgen Milagrosa University Foundation, San Carlos City, Philippines. Appointments: Various Instructor and Engineering posts, 1978-92; Professorial Chair Holder in field of Engineering, Pangasinan State University, 1997-98; Engineering Review Manager, Northern Philippines Review Centre, Sta Barbara, Pangasinan, 1993-; Consultant, Fire Extinguisher Manufacturing Division, RC Balingit Trading Dagupan City, 1994-; Associate Professor, part-time, VMUF College of Engineering, San Carlos City, 1995-; Assistant Professor, Pangasinan State University College of Engineering, Urdaneta City, 1992-. Publications: 4 articles; Co-author, Strength of Materials, 1998; Coauthor, Engineering Management, 1997; Solutions to Problems, in Power Plant Engineering, 1996. Honours: Professorial Chair Holder Award in the field of Engineering given by the Pangasinan State University, 1997; The Outstanding Mechanical Engineer Award in the field of Education bestowed by the Philippine Society of Mechanical Engineers, 1996. Memberships: American Society of Mechanical Engineers; PRO, Northern Luzon, Philippine Society of Mechanical Engineers, National; Past President, PSME, Pangasinan Chapter; Southeast Asian Mathematical Society; Asia-Pacific Physics Peachers & Educators Association; Association of Management & Industrial Engineers of the Philippines; Filipino Inventors Society; Philippine Association of Graduate Education, Region I. Address: Lucao District, Dagupan 2400, The Philippines.

**DE MARINO Donald Nicholson**, b. 28 September 1945, Greensburg, USA. International Business Affairs. m. Betsy Reiver De Marino, 4 sons. Education: BA, 1967. Career: Director, Mack & Nicholson, West Chester, 1972-76; Business Consultant, The Nicholson Group Incorporated, New York City, 1976-81; Senior Project Officer, US-Saudi Arabian Joint Commission on Economic Corporation, Riyadh, Saudi Arabia, 1981-84, Director, 1985-87; Manager, Litton Industries Offset Investment Programs, Riyadh, 1984-85; Senior Project Advisor, The Arab Investment Company, Riyadh, 1985; International Business Consultant, Principle, De Marino Associates, Coatesville, 1987-88; Deputy Assistant Secretary, Africa, Near East & South Asia US Department of Commerce, Washington, 1989-90; US Advisor, Tata Group of India, 1991-; Chairman, National US-Arab C of C, 1991-; President, De Marino Associates Incorporated, 1992-; Lecturer, Wharton School of Advanced Management Program, 1994-96. Honours include: Chevalier, Sovereign Military Order of Temple of Jerusalem; Distinguished Service Award, Government of Saudi Arabia, 1987. Address: 43 Longview Road, Coatesville, PA 19320-4311, USA.

**DE MARTINO Kenneth**, b. 11 July 1960, Malta. Managing Director. m. Madeleine Busuttil, 3 daughters. Education: Certificate, Modern Management, British Careers TRG College, 1981, Business Management, Alexander Hamilton Institute, 1984, Managing Assertively, Guardian Business Services England, 1988, Financial Services, Thomas Cook Group, 1990. Appointments: Assistant Sales Manager, 1984-86, Sales Manager, 1986-88, Area Manager, 1988-91, North Africa Thomas Cook Group London; Managing Director, Thomas Cook Malta Ltd, 1991-98; Chairman, Thomas Cook Financial Services Malta Ltd, 1999-; Managing Director, KDM Holdings Ltd, 1999-. Memberships: Secretary General, Scout Association of Malta; Institute of Commercial Management England; Malta Institute of Management; President, Association of Licensed Foreign Exchange Dealers; Vice President, Malta Association of Incoming Tourism Agents. Address: Thomas

Cook Malta Ltd, 11 Piaxxetta Tower Road, Sliema SLM16, Malta.

**DE MENDONCA Rui,** b. 18 November 1959, Azores. Medical Doctor, Obstetrician, Gynecologist. m. Teresa Taylor Kay. Education: MD, BChir, University of Lisbon, 1985; Postgraduate, Institute of Superior Clencias Sociais E Politicas, 1993. Appointments: Specialist, Obstetrician, Gynecologist, Portuguese Government, Portuguese Medical Association; General Teaching, Medicine and Surgery Hospital; 1985-87; Complementary Teaching, 1988-89; Maternal, Fetal, Reproductive Medicine, Staff Hospital University Santa Maria, 1990-91; Gynecologist, Oncology, Pathology Staff, Instituto Portugues de Oncologia, 1992; Hospital Assistant, Ob, Gyn Hospital, Ponta Delgada, 1994-; Specialist in Obstetrics and Gynecology, 1994-; Director for Development, Centre for Reproductive Medicine, 1995-. Publications: Contributor to Articles, Professional Journals. Memberships: Obstetrician and Gynecologists Junior Committee; Committee for the Study of Perinatal Mortality; Founder, Azores Br, The National Centre for Bioethic Studies; European Society of Human Reproduction and Embryology. Address: Rua Do Poco 2 Santa Cruz, 9560 Lagoa S Miguel Azores, Portugal.

**DE PAOLA Domingos Q,** b. 13 March 1954, Brazil. Doctor; Plastic Surgeon. m. Nelia, 1 son, 1 daughter. Education: Medical School, Rio de Janeiro, 1977; Plastic Surgeon Training, 1980; Coz Laser Training, 1996. Appointments: Head, Plastic Surgery Services, 1979-88; Head Director, IEDS State Hospital, 1988-95; Health Minister, Quality Program, 1995-96; Head Director, Specializing in Plastic and Laser Surgery, CCPR, Rio de Janeiro, 1995-. Memberships: Brasilian Plastic Surgery Society; International College of Surgeons; American Society for Aesthetic Plastic Surgery; Brasilian Society of Aesthetic Medicine; Brasilian Laser Society of Medicine and Aesthetic Medicine. Address: Rua siqueira Campos 93 gr, 605 & 801 Copacabana, Riode Janeiro, Brazil 22031-070

**DE SZY Gerard Charles,** b. 11 October 1939, Debreen. Economist. 2 sons, 1 daughter. Education: Licence is Sciences Commerciales, University Geneva, Switzerland, 1960; Laurea n Economics e Commercio, University Genoa, Italy, 1963; Laurea in Giurisprudeuza, 1986; Diploma in Psychology, Jniversity Lubina, Slovenia, 1996. Appointments: Financial Analyst, Royal Dutch Shell Company, 1964-65; International Official, European Union Commission, 1965-69; Research Economist, Battelle Memorial Institute, 1969-73; Senior Financial Analyst, SIFIDA, 1973-75; Senior International Offical, European Union Commission, 1981-85; University Professor, nternational Centre for University Studies, 1986-. Publications: Narcissism; Contemporary Economic Theories; Micro Economics; Development and Under Development; Many other publications. Honours: President, International Centre for University Studies; Rector, Centro Interuniversitaries Tichese; Vice President, International Centre for Applied Psychology. Memberships: Slovenian Psychologist Association; American Psychological Association; Association of Fiduciari del Canton Ticino; Lawyers Association; European Association for nternational Education. Address: Via Mofa 16, 6850 Mendrisio Ticino, Switzerland.

**DE VOS Leo Joseph,** b. 6 December 1946, Ostend, Belgium. Professor. m. Williane Schotsaert, 1 son, 1 daughter. Education: Lic Social and Military Sciences (high distinction), Royal Military Academy, Brussels, 1965-69; Studies, Royal Higher Institute for Defense, 1976, 1980-81; Lic, Modern History (highest distinction), Catholic University Leuven, 1976; Certificate Profound Knowledge French, Royal Military Academy, 1976; Certificate Superior Officer, Royal Higher Institute for Defense, 1981; PhD, History, 1984. Appointments: Officer, Belgian Armed Forces in Germany, 1969-75; Assistant, Chair of History, Royal Military Academy, 1975-80; Part-time Assistant, Catholic University Leuven, 198083; Intelligence and Operations Offiocer, Logistic Grouping Support, Armed Forces of the Interior, 1981-83; Major, active duty, -1985; Lt-Colonel, Armed Reserve Forces, 1985; Associate Professor, Professor, 1990-, Royal Military Academy; Lecturer, KUL Pennsylvania, 1991; Teacher, Royal Higher Institute for Defence, Royal Military Academy. Publications: Over 100 articles, 20 books include: Veldslagen in de Lage Landen, 1995; De Eerste Wereldoorlog, 1996, 2nd edition, 1996. Honours: Prijs van de repetitor, Royal Military Academy, 1981; Prijs Generaal Minister Baron de Greef, 1991; Prix J de Saint-Genois, Académie Royale des Sciences, des Lettres et des Beaux-Arts de Belgique, 1991, Marcel Minnaertprijs, Unie Nederland-Vlaaderen, 1996. Memberships include: Chairman, Belgische Sectie van Internationale Vereniging voor Militaire Geschiedenis; Chairman, Scientific Council, Royal Army Museum, 1993-. Address: Korbeek-Lostraat 80, 3360 Bierbeek, Belgium.

**DE VRIES Linda Elizabeth Rachel,** b. 6 July 1957, Beaufort West, Cape, South Africa. Researcher; Educator; Business Woman. m. Steven, 3 sons. Education: B Comm, 1978; Secondary Teacher Diploma, 1979; Psalmody International Diploma; Honours in Business Economics, 1981; Honours in Business Administration, 1990; MBA, 1991. Appointments: Chair, Director, Founder Member, Femvest, 1998; Chairperson, Christian Education; Director, Broadcape, 1998; Consultant to Peru Government, 1997 and Namibia; Senior Lecturer, University Western Cape; Teacher, Senior Schools, Guest Faculty. Publication: Econofun: Going and Growing, 1994. Honours: Various scholarships; Best papers & proceedings; Women of Worth Nomination, 1998. Memberships: Academy of Management; South African Academic Development Association; South African Association of Management Scientists; Western Cape Education Department. Address: 61 David Atkins Street, 7490 Charlesville, Cape, South Africa.

**DEAN Colin Leslie,** b. 3 September 1953, Australia. Poet; Philosopher. Education: BSc; BA; BLitt(Hon); MA; BLitt(Hon). Career: Resident Poet for ASP; Gamahucher Press; Working for a PhD. Publications: Evil Flowers, Poems by C Dean; Poisonous Flowers, Poems by C Dean; Wetflowers, Poems by C Dean; The Australian Aboriginal Dreamtime; Epistemiology; The Nature of Philosophy; A Moral Philosophy; A Consequence of the epistemiological Holism of Qume; The Religions of the Pre-Contact Victorian Aborigines. Membership: Australian Institute of Physics, 1984. Address: 72 Plume Street, Norlane, Geelong 3214, Australia.

**DEAN George Arthur,** b. 19 September 1931, Detroit, MI, USA. Medical Doctor, Art Historian. m. Vivian, 2 sons, 2 daughters. Education: BA, Wayne State University, 1953; MD, Wayne State University, 1956. Appointments: Professor, Wayne State University; Professor, University of Michigan. Honours: Alpha Omega Alpha Honourary Medical Fraternity, 1956; Familty Physician of the Year, 1985. Membership: Founder and President, Chess Collectors International. Address: 1135 Charrington Rd, Bloomfield, MI 48301-2114, USA.

**DEB Mrinal K,** b. 28 March 1949, Dibrugarh, India. Educator. m. K Deb, 1 son. Education: BSc, 1971; MSc, 1973; Bachelor of Education, 1990; PhD, 1991. Appointments: R K Mission, 1976; Presently Reader, Department of Zoology, St Anthony's College, Shillong. Publications: Vision Research, 1990; Current Science, 1993; Cytobios, 1994; Geobios, 1995.

Memberships: Meghalaya Science Society; Zoological Society, Calcutta; North East Education Society. Address: St Anthony's College, Bomphile Road, 793-001 Shillong, India.

**DEB Suash,** b. 26 October 1960, Karimganj, Assam, India. Researcher. Education: BE, Mechanical Engineering, Jadavpur University, Calcutta, 1984; MTech, Computer Science, University of Calcutta, 1987; Postgraduate, Computer Vision, Stanford University, USA, 1991. Appointments: Trainee Engineer, CESC (India) Ltd, 1984-85; Systems Executive, Webel Computers Ltd, Calcutta, 1987-88; Research Scientist, SI, Calcutta, 1988-. Honours: Asian Expert Consultant, ARPA, Department of Defense, Federal Government of USA, 1996; Guest of Honour, International Conference on Advanced Robotics, Intelligent Automation, Vienna, Austria, 1996. Memberships: Senior Member, Institute of Electrical and Electronics Engineers, USA; Regional Editor, IEEE Robotics and Automation, 1994-96; Editorial Board, Robotics and Computer Integrated Manufacturing, 1996-. Address: 162/170 Lake Gardens, 700045 Calcutta, India.

**DEBRECENI Laszlo,** b. 30 July 1936, Beremend. Physician. m. Judit Sztarcsevich, 2 sons. Education: Medical University, 1960; Certicate in Internal Medicine, 1965; Certificate in Clinical Laboratory, 1969; PhD, 1977; Certificate in Neuroendocrinology, 1987. Appointments: Head, Clinical Laboratory, Hospital Mohacs, 1969-97; Head, Internal Medicine, 1991-96; Director, Mohacs Hospital, 1990-95; Research Associate, Heart Disease Research Foundation, New York, 1988-. Publications: Acupuncture in Clinical Medicine, 1988; Clear Consciousness, 1994; Theory and Praxis of Modern Acupuncture, 1996; Healing and Faith, 1997. Memberships: New York Academy of Science; Member of the Corps, Hungarian Academy of Science; Fellow, International College of Acupuncture and Electro-Therapeutics. Address: Szabadsag stv 28, 7700 Mohacs, Hungary.

**DECK Richard Allen,** b. 6 May 1953, Concord, New Hampshire, USA. Political Scientist; Consultant; Writer; Director; Human Rights Activist. m. JoAnn Marie Passariello Deck. Education includes: BA, summa cum laude, 1972-77; MA, Economics, 1981-82; MCP (ABT), Planning, 1979-82; AM, Political Science, 1982-85; PhD (ABD), Political Science, 1986; MALS Liberal Studies (Film), 1994; Phd, Political Science, 1998. Appointments: Research Assistant, Chairperson, Department of Political Science, Macalester College, St Paul, Minnesota, 1975-76; Legislation Analyst, Education Committee, New York State Assembly, Albany, 1979; Co-Chair, Graduate Assembly, University of California, Berkeley, 1981-82; Head Teaching Assistant, Introductory International Relations Course, Stanford University California, 1984; SSRC-MacArthur Foundation Fellow in International Peace and Security Studies, Singapore, 1986-88; USC-UCLA Joint Fellow in National and International Security, Los Angeles, California, 1989; Research Fellow and Project Coordinator on Asian Regionalization, Asia/Pacific Research Centre, Stanford University, California, 1991-92; Vice President Catalyst Concepts, Berkeley, California, 1993-98; Founding Director, Asia-Pacific Regional Policy Research Institute, Emeryville, California, 1998. Publications include: Future Cross-Cultural Educational Opportunities in Southeast Asia and North America: Fiscal and Political Dilemmas; The Association of Southeast Asian Nations and the East Asia Economic Group/Caucus; Singapore's Strategic Culture, Peace, Conflict, and Strategic Culture in the Asia-Pacific Region; Singapore's Foreign Policy, The Singapore Puzzle. Memberships include: International Studies Association; American Political Science Association; Association for Asian Studies; Academy of Political Science,

New York City. Address: Catalyst Concepts, PO Box 8393, Berkeley, CA 94707, USA.

**DEERING Anne-Lise,** b. 20 June 1935, Oslo, Norway. Artist; Realtor; Ceramic Artist. m. div. 3 sons, 1 daughter. Education: BA Art, 1977, Postgraduate courses in medallic art, computer graphics design, 1990-91, Pennsylvania State University; Licensed Realtor, 1991; Graduate, 1993, Realtors Institute; Completed courses in residential real estate appraisal, 1995. Appointments: Research Assistant Biophysics, Yale University, 1955-57; Ceramic Artist, Potter, 1977-; Real Estate Sales, Coldwell Banker University Realty, 1992-93, Century 21 Corman Associates, 1993-98. Publications: Feature articles, Ceramics Monthly, 1987; Newsletter Editor, Central Pennsylvania Guild of Craftsmen, 1994. Honours: 1981 juried status, PA Guild of Craftsmen; 1978 Artist status, Art Alliance of Central PA; PSU Jurors Choice Award for Sculpture, 1977. Memberships: PA Guild of Craftsmen and Central PA Guild of Craftsmen, various offices; Chairman, Art Alliance of Central PA members juried exhibit, Board of Directors, various other offices; Charter member, American Museum of Women in the Arts; American Medallic Sculpture Association; Washington Potters; Seattle Metals Guild; Realtor member, National Association of Realtors; Central PA and Pennsylvania Association of Realtors. Address: 2731 NE 135th St, Seattle WA 98125, USA.

**DeFLEUR Melvin Lawrence,** b. 27 April 1923, Portland Oregon, USA. University Professor. m. Margaret Hanus DeFleur. Education: BS Psychology cum laude, St Louis University, Missouri; MS Psychology, PhD Sociology, University of Washington at Seattle. Appointments: Instructor and Assistant Professor, Dept Sociology, Indiana University 1954-63; Professor Sociology, Dept Sociology, University of Kentucky, 1963-67; Chairman, Dept Sociology, 1968-73, Associate Dean for Research, The Graduate School, and Director, Office of Grants and Research Development 1974-76, Washington State University; Professor of Speech Communication and Professor Sociology, University of New Mexico, 1976-80; Chairman, Department Sociology, 1981-85; Professor of Communication, School of Communication, and Professor Sociology, 1985-87, University of Miami; John Ben Snow Endowed Chair in Mass Communications, S I Newhouse School of Public Communications, Syracuse University 1987-94; Chairman, School of Mass Communication and Public Relations, 1994-97, Professor of Communication, Dept of Mass Communication, Advertising and Public Relations, 1997, Boston University. Publications: 11 books and monographs including: Understanding Mass Communication, 1981; Milestones in Mass Communication Research, 1983; Theories of Mass Communication, 1966; approx 50 journal articles. Honours: Fullbright Professor Sociology, Argentina, 1961-62; 1971; Distinguished Kentucky Educator, student body of University of Kentucky, 1966-67; Outstanding Educator of America for teaching at Washington State University, 1975; Alumni Merit Award for Distinguished Service, St Lou University, 1992. Membership: Association for Education Journalism and Mass Communication. Address: Boston University, 640 Commonwealth Avenue, Boston, MA 02215 USA.

**DEFORD Frank,** b. 16 December 1938, Baltimore Maryland, USA. Writer; Editor. m. Carol Penner, 28 August 1965, 1 son, 2 daughters. Education: BA, Princeton University. Appointments: Writer, Sports Illustrated, 1962-89; Commentator, Cable News Network, 1980-86, National Public Radio, 1980-89, 1991-, NBC, 1986-89, ESPN, 1992-97; HBO 1997-; Editor-in-Chief, The National, 1989-91; Writer, Newsweek Magazine, 1991-93, 1996-; Contributing Editor

Vanity Fair, 1993-96. Publications: Five Strides on the Banked Track, 1969; Cut'N'Run, 1971; There She Is, 1972; The Owner, 1974; Big Bill Tilden: The Triumphs and the Tragedy, 1977; Everybody's All-American, 1981; Alex: The Life of a Child, 1982; Spy in the Deuce Court, 1987; World's Tallest Midget, 1988; Casey on the Loose, 1989; Love and Infamy, 1993; Contributions to numerous magazines. Honours: Sportswriter of the Year, National Association of Sportswriters and Sportscasters, 1982-88; Emmy, 1988; Cable Ace, 1996. Address: Box 1109 Greens Farms, CT 06436, USA.

**DEGARMO Mark Borden,** b. 11 February 1955, Sharon, USA. Dancer; Choreographer. Education: Oberlin College, 1974-75; BA, Dance, The Juilliard School, 1979-82. Career: Artistic Director, Mark DeGarmo & Dances, Dynamic Forms Inc, 1982-; Teaching Artist, Lincoln Center Institute, 1986-. Memberships: Dance USA; World Dance Alliance American Center; United Federation of Teachers, Lincoln Center Institute Chapter. Address: Mark DeGarmo & Dancers, c/o Dynamic Forms Inc, 179 East 3rd Street, Suite 24, NY 10009-7754, USA.

**DEHEER Nicholas Andrew,** b. 15 September 1930, Cape Coast, Ghana. Consultant in Public Health Medicine. m. Babina Dorsina Sackey, 4 sons, 6 daughters. Education: MB, BS, LRCP, MRCS, London University, 1958; DPH, DTM&H, Liverpool University, 1961; MFPHM, England, 1985; MFCH, England, 1987. Appointments: Regional Medical Officer, Ghana, 1963-67, 1972-73; Chief Medical Nutritionist, Ghana, 1967-72; Regional Secretary, Commonwealth of West African Health Secretariat, Lagos, Nigeria, 1973-81; Consultant in Public Health Medicine, England, 1984-93. Publications include: History of the West African Health Secretariat; Handbook on Health Education for Basic Schools; First Aid User Mannual for Schools. Memberships: Ghana Medical Association; British Medical Association; Historic Churches Preservation Trust, England; Fellow, West African College of Physicians, 1976; Honorary Fellow, WA College of Nurses, 1979. Address: PO Box 12632, Accra, Ghana.

**DEIVASIGAMANI Thiruppaasoor Vajjiravel, (Desini),** b. 15 January 1936, Chennai. Poet Translator. m. K. Gowri Ammal, 2 daughters. Education: BCom, Hons; BGL; BL; BLitt; MA. Appointments: Assistant Editor, Grama Rajyam; Associate Editor, Porul; Sub Editor, Tamil, British Information Services, Madras; Member-Secretary, State Official Language (Legislative) Commission, Tamil Nadu; Director, Law Department, TN Secretariat. Publications: Kavithai-k-Kaavalar; More than 25 books; Chief-Editor of 34 volumes of Kavithai, the pioneer Tamil poetry journal, 1962-96. Memberships: Founder, Elango Youths League, 1947; President, Kamban Tamil Writers' Association; President, Kalaivani Dramatic Troupe; First Secretary, Madras Poets' Academy; President, National Tamil Poets' Congress. Address: 4/2 Malleeswarar Koil St, Mylapore, Chennai 600004, India.

**DEJONCKERE Philippe Henri,** b. 11 July 1949, Ronse. University Professor. m. Thiry Suzanne, 2 daughters. Education: MD, 1973, PhD, 1981, Lic Occup Medicine, 1975, ORL Specialist, 1976, Laureate Conservatory Music, 1971, Louvain; Lic Forensic Medicine, 1986, Liege; Dipl Statistics, 1978, Paris VI. Appointments: Lecturer, 1983, Associate Professor, 1986, University Louvain (B); Visiting Professor, University Lille, 1986; Guest Professor, University Kurume, Japan, 1996; Professor and Chairman, Institute of Phoniatrics, Utrecht University, Netherlands. Publications: 250 scientific articles; 6 books. Honours: Paul Guns Prize, 1975; Van Lawrence Prize, 1997; Knight Crown Order (B), Knight Order of King Leopold (B). Memberships: Several ORL and Phoniatric Societies; Collegium Medicorum Theatri; Voice Foundation; European Laryngological Society. Address: Institute of Phoniatrics, Utrecht University, PO Box 85500, 3508 GA Utrecht, The Netherlands.

**DEKHTYAR Yuri,** b. 19 June 1947, Riga, Latvia. Physicist. m. Galina Dekhtyar, 2 daughters. Education: Mechanical Engineer, 1971; PhD Physics/Mathematics, 1982; DSc Physics, 1992. Appointments: Professor, Head of Institute, Riga Technical University, 1973-. Publications: 196 publications. Honour: Latvian State Prize, 1989. Memberships: Material Research Society; Latvian Medical Engineering and Physics Society, President. Address: Riga Technical University, 1 Kalku Street, LV 1658 Riga, Latvia.

**DEL VOLGO Marie-José,** b. 28 January 1952, Tunis. Physician; Researcher; University Educator. m. Roland Gori, 1 daughter. Education: Doctorate Medicine, University of Aix Marseilles II, 1978; Doctorate Sciences, University of Aix Marseilles I, 1988; Doctorate Psychology, University Aix Marseilles I, 1995. Appointments: Physiology Monitor to Science Assistant Practitioner, University Aix Marseilles II, 1974-86; Maitre de Conférences and Hospital Practitioner, University Aix Marseilles II, 1986-. Publication: L'instant de dire le myth individuel du malade dans la medecine une moderne, 1997. Memberships: International Center Research in Clinical Psychopathology; Society Neurosciences; Society Physiology; Society History and Epistemology of Life Science. Address: 101 rue Sylvabelle, 13006 Marseille, France.

**DEL CASTILLO Roberto Antonio,** b. 15 July 1940, Colon, Panama. Medical Technologist. m. Mytle Uubu Gibbs, 1 son, 2 daughters. Education: BSc, 1971, Universidad de Panama; Medical Technologist, 1973, Universidad de Panama. Appointments: Medical Technologist, 1973-76; Chief Technologist, Seguro Social Blood Bank, 1976-. Publications: Incidence of Hepatitis B Surface Antigen in Donors at the Blood Bank of CSS Hospital, 1987; Incidence of HIV in Donors at the Blood Bank of CSS Hospital, 1991. Membership: AABB. Address: PO Box 11243, Estafeta Betania 6, Panama.

**DELLA-GIUSTINA Jo-Ann,** b. 6 September 1951, Springfield, USA. Lawyer. Education: BA, 1972, Clark University; MA Programme, 1973-75, San Diego State University; MA, 1983, Columbia College; JD, 1987, Chicago-Kent College of Law; PhD Programme, current, CUNY, John Jey College. Appointments: Assistant Corporation Counsel, City of Chicago, 1987-88; Assistant Public Defender, Cook County, 1988-90; Judicial Law Clerk, Illinois Appellate Court, Justice David Cerda, 1990-98. Publications: Civil Rights Law Report, 1986; Blossom of the Flower, poetry, 1990. Honour: Order of COIF, 1998. Memberships: Academy of Criminal Justice Sciences; American Society of Criminology; Justinian Society of Lawyers; National Italian-American Lawyers Association; National Association of Women Lawyers. Address: 322 W 57th Street Apt 33J, New York, NY 10019, USA.

**DELLAVECCHIA Michael Anthony,** Ophthalmologist. Education: BA, Physics, LaSalle College, Philadelphia, 1970; MS, Biomedical Science and Engineering, 1972, PhD, 1984, Drexel University; MD, Temple University, 1976. Appointments include: Resident, Anatomical and Clinical Pathology, 1977-80, Chief Resident, 1979-80, Fellow, Surgical Pathology, 1980-81; Resident, Ophthalmology, 1981-84, Temple University Hospital; Fellow, Ophthalmology Project, Orbis Inc, New York City, 1985; Vice President, Medical Director, Co-Founder, Mega Med Electronics, Hatfield, 1984-86; Associate, John Reichel MD Ltd, Bryn Mawr, 1984-95; Associate Staff, Clinical Instructor,

Temple University Hospital, 1986-; Instructor, Wills Eye Hospital, 1986-, Scheie Eye Institute, 1986-96; Professor, Department of Biomedical Engineering, Drexel University, 1991-; Attending Staff Ophthalmology, Graduate Health Systems, Philadelphia College of Osteo Medicine, 1995-. Publications: Several articles in professional medical journals. Honours: Numerous Federal Emergency Management Association Certificates and Fellowships. Memberships include: IEEE; AMA; American Society of Laser Medicine and Surgery; American Society of Clinical Pathology; International Society of Photoinstrumentation Engineers; American Academy of Ophthalmology; Intercounty Ophthalmology Society. Address: 6131 Grayes Avenue, Philadelphia, PA 19142-3207, USA.

**DELPACHITRA Sarath Bandula,** b. 18 February 1955, Sri Lanka. Academic. m. Nayana Devika, 2 sons, 1 daughter. Education: BSc Honours, Agriculture, University of Sri Lanka; Post-Graduate Diploma in Commerce, University of Canterbury, New Zealand; MCom, Economics, University of Lincoln, New Zealand; PhD, Economics, University of Southern Queensland. Appointments: Assistant Manager, Sri Lanka State Plantations Corporation; Deputy Director, General Treasury, Sri Lanka; Senior Academic, New Zealand. Publications: Articles in professional journals. Honours: United Nations Development Programme Fellow; Research Fellow, University of Southern Queensland. Memberships: International Energy Economics Association; Economics Society of Australia; New York Academy of Sciences. Address: Faculty of Business, University of Southern Queensland, Baker Street, 4350 Toowoomba, Queensland, Australia.

**DEMBER Jean Wilkins,** b. 29 January 1930, Brooklyn, New York, USA. Consultant; Trainer. m. Clarence, 1 son, 5 daughters. Education: Master of Human Services, Lincoln University, Pennsylvania, 1988. Appointments: Political Candidate, Legislative, 1975, 1977, 1979; Chairman, Headstart Corporation, 1985-89; Founder, Afrikans United for Sanity Now!; Consultant, Multicultural Services in Community Mental Health, 1980-. Publication: Sex Isn't Strawberry Jam. Honours include: NAACP Service Award, Greenhaven Prison, 1975; Service Award, Central Branch NAACP, 1978; Political Leadership Award, Gordon Hights Cultural and Social Club, New York, 1981; National Evangelization Award, National Office for Black Catholics, 1982; Poetess Public Service, Humanitarian Award, Chi Rho Chapter of Omega Psi Phi, 1982; Who's Who Among African Americans; Dr Martin Luther King Award, Lifer's Committee, Auburn Prison, 1982; King's Park Mental Health Hospital Commemoration Committee, 1982; Service Award, Political Leadership, 1997; Who's Who in American Women. Memberships: National Association for the Advancement of Coloured People; National Black United Front, Houston Chapter; Institute for Interracial Harmony. Address: 55 Court Street, North Babylon, NY 11704, USA.

**DEMIAN, Aurel Mihai** b. 9 November 1929, Arad, Romania. Chemical Engineer. m. Doina, 1 son. Education: Diplomat Chemistry Engineer, 1953; Doctor Engineer, 1964. Appointments: Engineer in Tobacco Industry, 1952-54; Researcher, Romanian Academy of Science, 1954-65; Professor, Chemical Technology, Military Technical Academy, 1965-. Publications: 52 published papers. Membership: University Solidarity, Romania. Address: Military Technical Academy, Bv Regina Maria 81-83 Sect 5, Bucharest, Romania.

**DEMIRAJ Shaban,** b. 1 January 1920, Valona, Albania. Linguist. m. Fatime Saraci-Demiraj, 1 son, 1 daughter. Education: High Pedagogical Institute, 1948; University of Tirana, 1954. Appointments: Second School Teacher, Albanian Language and Literature, Tirana, 1948-54; Lecturer, Historical

Grammar of the Albanian Language, 1954-90, Vice Dean, Faculty of History and Philology, 1962-66, Head, Chair, Albanian Language, Faculty of History and Philology, 1966-90, Professor, 1972-90, Professor Emeritus, 1990-, University of Tirana; President, Albanian Academy of Sciences, 1993-97. Publications: 11 books in Albanian Language, Over 50 articles, monographs and communications in Albanian, English, French, Italian, German. Memberships: Association Internationale d'Etudes Sud-Est Européen; Academy of Sciences and Arts of Kossovo; Central European Academy of Science and Art; Albanian Academy of Sciences. Address: Rruga Margarita Tutulani V/1, 1 ap 7, Tirana, Albania.

**DENG Bo,** b. 28 December 1934, Hunan, China. Analytical Chemist. m. Jianwei Chen, 2 daughters. Education: Graduated, Department of Chemistry, Peking University, 1957; Postgraduate Research Institute, Tsinghua University, China, 1964. Appointments: Assistant, 1957-64; Lecturer, 1965-79; Associate Professor, 1979-88; Professor, 1988-. Publications: Atomic Absorption Spectrophotometry, 1982; The Application Statistical Methods to Analysis, 1984; Instrumental Analysis, 1991; The Application of Computer in Statistical Processing of Analysis Data, 1989; Statistical Methods of Processing Analysis Data, 1995. Memberships: Council, Chinese Society of Analytical Instrumental; Chemistry Society of Beijing Municipal and Chinese Society of Spectrum Analysis; Board Member, Spectroscopy and Spetral Analysis; Analytical Instrumental. Address: Department of Chemistry, Tsinghua University, Beijing 100084, China.

**DENG Xiao Min,** b. 15 June 1953, Guangxi, China. Professor. m. Wei Quan He, 1 son, 1 daughter. Education: BA, Guangxi Normal University, 1972-76; Postgraduate Study, Guangzhou Foreign Languages Institute, 1978-79; Visiting Scholar, Lewis & Clark College, Portland, Oregon, 1988-89. Appointments: Professor, English, Guangxi Normal University; Visiting Professor, Chinese, Chinese History & Culture, Concordia University, Portland, Oregon; Director, American Office, Shanghai Institute of International Finance, Los Angeles, California. Honours: Outstanding Professor, Guangxi Normal University, 1987; Excellent Achievement Award, Scientific Research, Guangxi Normal University, 1992. Memberships: World Future Society, USA; International Study Association for Cross-Cultural Human Resource Development, China. Address: 15 North Valencia Street, Apt 14, Alhambra, CA 91801-2760, USA.

**DENHAM Frederick Ronald,** b. 21 October 1929, Middlesbrough, UK. Management Consultant. m. Enid Lynn, 2 sons, 1 daughter. Education: BScHons, University of Durham, 1951; PhD, Applied Science, University of Durham, 1953; MBA, University of Buffalo, 1960. Appointments: Union Carbide Canada, Supt of Engineering and Maintenance, 1956-61; Stevenson and Kellog, 1961-90; Professor, York University, 1969-72; Trustee, North York Board of Education, 1972-78; KPMG, Vice Chairman, 1990-92; Director, Proctor and Redfern, 1994-97; Director, A T Kearney Ltd, 1994-98. Publications: Co-Author, Distribution Management Handbook; Co-Author, Profitable Logistics Management. Memberships: Institute of Management onsultants; Engineering Institute of Canada; Rotary International. Address: 20 Queen Street West, Suite 2300, Toronto, Canada, M5H 3R3.

**DENISOV Nikolai Nikolaevich,** b. 11 November 1956, Kozelsk, Kaluga. Scientist; Physicist; Mathematician. m. Marina Nikolaevna Chernova, 20 March 1981, divorced 1992, 2 daughters. Education: Mathematician, Moscow State University, 1974-79; Postgraduate course, Physicist, 1981-85. Appointments: Student, 1974; Engineer, 1979; Senior

Research Worker, 1992. Address: Research Institute for Physico-Technical and Radioengineering Measurements, Mendeleevo Solnechnogorsk District, Moscow Region 141570, Russia.

**DENISOVA Nataliya Andreevna,** b. 21 April 1947, Russia. Mathematician. m. Alexander V Rezvov, 1 son, 1 daughter. Education: MD, Mathematics, 1971, PhD, Mathematical and Theoretical Physics, 1976, N I Lobachevskii N Novgorod State University. Appointments: Assistant Research Associate, 1971-72, Postgraduate, 1973-75, Associate Professor, 1976-, N Novgorod State University. Publications: 22 scientific publications, 12 lecture notes in the field of theoretical and mathematical physics. Address: Mechanic and Mathematic Faculty, N I Lobachevskii Nizhny Novgorod State University, 23 (Korpus 2) Prospekt Gagarina, GSP34 Nizhny Novogord 603600, Russia.

**DENISSE Jean Francois,** b. 16 May 1915, St Quentin, Aisne, France. Retired. m. Girondot Myriam, 2 daughters. Educations: Student, Ecole Normale Supérieure, 1936; Agrégation, Physical Science, 1949; Doctor, Physical Science, 1949. Appointments: Director of Station de Nancay, 1956; Director, Paris Observatory, 1963; Director, Institute National d'Astrophysique et Géophysique, Chairman, Centre d'Etudes Spatiales, 1967; Chairman, COSPAR and ESO, Centre for Space Studies, 1978. Publications: Publications on Astrophysics and Plasmas Physics - Commandeur de la Légion d'Honneur; Commander, Legion of Honour. Memberships: Corresponding Member for Correspondent Member, Royal Astronomical Society and Société Royale des Sciences, Liège, Belgium; Academia Europea, Academy of Sciences, 1967. Address: 48 rue Mr Le Prince, 75006 Paris, France.

**DENYS Sylvia,** b. Butler, Pennsylvania. Lawyer. Education: BA English and Philosophy, 1970, MA, 1977, Duquesne University; JD, Student Instructor in Legal Writing, 1979, Duquesne University School of Law. Appointments: Private Law Practice, 1982-91, 1993-; Attorney, Neighbourhood Legal Services Association, 1979-81; Judicial Law Clerk, Superior Court of Pennsylvania, 1981-82; Assistant Professor of Law, Duquesne University School of Business, 1982-89, 1990-91; Academy for Advancement of Science, Pecs, Hungary, 1992-93; Visiting Professor, School of Medicine, Pecs, 1991-92; Adjunct Professor, Janus Pannonius School of Law, Pecs, 1991-92; Practice in Civil Rights and Employment, Labour Law, 1994-; Associate Editor of Duquesne Law Review, 1978-1979. Honours: Fulbright-Hayes Fellow to Hungary, 1990; Grant from Hunkele Foundation, 1988; Selected member, Team 92 of the Delegation of European Communities. Memberships: Federal Bar Association; Association of Trial Lawyers of America; Allegheny County Bar Association; Pennsylvania Bar Association; American Inns of Court; and others. Address: 1710 Allegheny Building, 429 Forbes Avenue, Pittsburgh, PA 15219, USA.

**DESHPANDE Krishna Sriniwasrao,** b. 27 June 1946, Sunjoti, India. Veterinary Educator. m. Shailaja, 1 son, 1 daughter. Education: BVSc &AH, 1968; MVSc, 1970; PhD, 1981. Appointments: Veterinary Officer, 1970-75; Professor of Animal Genetics and Breeding, 1975-97; Associate Dean and Principal, Veterinary College, Parbhani, 1997-. Publications: 97 research papers; 10 popular articles; 3 textbooks. Honour: Certificate for Meritorious Service, 1996. Memberships: Indian Society of Animal Genetics and Breeding; Executive Veterinary Teachers' Association. Address: Veterinary College, Parbmani, India.

**DESWAL Renu,** b. 24 January 1964, Delhi, India. Research Scientist. m. Mr Sunil Chowdhary, 1 son. Education: BSc, 1985; MSc, 1987; PhD, 1994. Appointments: Research Associate, School of Life Sciences, 1994-95; Research Scientist, Centre for Plant Molecular Biology, 1995-98; Research Scientist, National Centre for Plant Genome Research, New Delhi, 1998-. Honours: Junior Research Fellowship, University Grant Commission, 1988-90; Senior Research Fellowship, 1990-93. Memberships: New York Academy of Sciences, 1995-; Third World Organisation for Women in Science, TWOWS; Signal Transduction Society, Germany; Life Member, Society of Biological Chemists, SBC, India; . Address: Jawharlal Nehru University, Centre for Plant Molecular Biology, New Delhi 110 067, India.

**DEV Gautam,** b. 8 July 1935, Lahore, India. Service Director. m. Mrs Sudesh, 2 sons. Education: BSc, Hons, Delhi University, 1957; Associate IARI, Indian Agricultural Research Institute, 1959; PhD, 1963. Appointments: Associate Professor, Soils, Punjab Agricultural University, 1965-75; Professor, Soils, 1975-89; Director of Research, HP Agricultural University, 1985-88; Director, India Programme, Potash and Phosphate Institute of Canada, 1989-. Publications: Scientific Reviews in Journals. Honours: Fellow, Indian Society of Agricultural Chemists; Honorary Assignment, Research Board of Advisors, American Biographical Institute; Man of the Year; FAI Prize, Fertiliser News Paper; Fellow, Indian Society of Soil Science; 12th International Congress of Soil Science Commemoration Award; FAI Silver Jubilee Award; FAI Prize for Fertiliser News Paper; Central Governement Prize for Agriculture. Memberships: Indian Society of Soil Science; International Society of Soil Science; Indian Society for Nuclear Techniques in Agriculture and Biology; Indian Society of Agricultural Chemists. Address: Potash and Phosphate Inst, Can India Program, Sector 19, Gurgaon 122016, India.

**DEVANARAYANAN Sankaranarayanan,** b. 11 November 1940, Thiruvananthapuram. University Professor. m. Chitra, 1 son, 1 daughter. Education: BSc, University College, 1961; MSc, 1963; PhD, Indian Institute of Science, Bangalore, 1969; Diploma, University of Uppsala, 1971; DSc, International University of California, USA, 1999. Appointments: Senior Research Assistant, Indian Institute of Science, 1969-70; SIDA Fellow, Institute of Physics, Uppsala, Sweden, 1970-71; Lecturer, University of Kerale, 1971-75; Reader, 1975-84; Professor, 1984-; Professor, University Puerto Rico, Riopiedras, USA, 1989-91; Professor and Head, University of Kerala, 1993-. Publications: Monograph in Physics; About 100 Research Articles in Professional Journals. Honours: Merit Scholar; SIDA Fellow, Institute of Physics; Visiting Professor, Puerto Rico. Memberships: Indian Cryogenic Council; American Physical Society; United Writers' Association; Indian Physics Association; Indian Science Congress Association; Chairman, Board of Studies in Physics; Member, Faculty of Science; Academic Council; Senate. Address: TC 16/173 G-9, PRS Enclave, E V Rd, 695014 Thiruvananthapuram, Kerala, India.

**DEVKOTA Surendra Raj,** b. 10 January 1962, Gorkha, Nepal. Environment Consultant. m. Kachan Devkota, 1 son. Education: MSc, Environmental Engineering, 1992. Appointments include: Assistant Lecturer of Ecology, Tribhuwan University, Central Department of Botany, Kirtipur, Kathmandu, Nepal, 1992-93; National Consultant/Environmental Engineer, Kathmandu Valley Vehicular Project Emission Project, Kathmandu, 1993; EIA Team Member, Environmental Engineer, IUCN, Nepal, 1994; Air Pollution Expert, Environmental Engineer, World Bank, MEIP, RAS, 1994-95; National Consultant, Industrial Waste

Management Expert, Industrial Pollution Control Management Project, Nepal, 1994-95; Environmental Consultant, Marium Leather Industry, Nepal, 1995-96; Environmental Consultant, Environmental Consultant, Nepal Environmental and Scientific Services Ltd, Kathmandu, 1996; Environmental Consultant, Development Resource Mobilisation Network, Kathmandu, 1996; Research Associate/Field Coordinator, 1996; Member of the Environment Protection Council of Nepal 1996-; Environmental Consultant, Ministry of Population and Environment, HMG/N, 1997. Publications: Around 12 scientific articles published in national and international journals. Membership: International Society for Ecological Economics; Asian Institute of Technology Alumni Association. Address: PO Box 5279, Kathmandu, Nepal.

**DEW John,** b 1944, Santiago de Cuba. Director. Appointments: Set and Costume Designer; Principal Stage Director, Bielefeld, 1982-95; Artistic Director, Municipal Theatres, Dortmund. Address: Stadt Theatre Dortmund, Kuhstr 12, 44137 Dortmund, Germany.

**DEWAN Kum Kum,** b. 4 July 1950, New Delhi, India. Professor. m. S M Dewan, 1 daughter. Education: BA Hons Mathematics, 1969, MA Mathematics, 1971, Delhi University; PhD, 1980, Postdoctoral Fellow, 1991-92, ITT, Delhi. Appointments: Lecturer in Mathematics, 1972-85, Reader in Mathematics, 1985-93, Professor in Mathematics, 1993-, Jamia Millia Islamia; Visiting Assistant Professor, Concordia University, Canada, 1987. Publications: Over 30 research papers in professional journals. Honours: Junior Research Fellow, UGC, 1971, IIT, 1971, CSIR, 1972; Teacher Fellow, 1977. Memberships: Forum for Inter-Disciplinary Mathematics, Treasurer 1995-; Academic Forum; Indian Mathematics Society; ISIAM. Address: Asian Games Village, B-812 Nakka Singh Block, New Delhi 110049, India.

**DEWITT Michelle,** b. 13 November 1962, Grand Haven, Michigan, USA.Sales Consultant. Education: AA, Business Major, Muskegon CommunityCollege, 1983; BBA, General Marketing, Western Michigan University, 1985;COMM 549, 1991. Appointments: Office Manager, Tony Betten Ford, 1985-89;Instructor, Muskegon Business College, 1987-88; Account Executive,Structural Concepts Corp, 1989-90; Public Relations Director, VertiMarkGroup Inc, 1990-96; Manager, Development & Promotions, Gnu Media, LLC,1997; Sales Consultant, MVP Specialist Saturn of Grand Rapids, 1997-.Publications: Competitive Intelligence, Competitive Advantage, RealInternet Tactics, 1997. Honours: Interchange Spotlight. Memberships:Business Marketing Association; Business Professional AdvertisingAssociation; Ameican Marketing Association. Address: 460 Hampton Lane NW Apt 2A, Grand Rapids, MI 49544-4577, USA.

**DEXTER Barrie Graham,** b. 15 July 1921, Kilsyth, Vic, Australia. Retired. m. Judith Craig, 1 son, 2 daughters. Education: MA Hons, Melbourne, 1947; DipEd, Melbourne, 1947. Appointments: Student Teacher, Housemaster, Brighton Grammar School, Melbourne, 1940; Corporal, 2/6 Australian Independent Company, AIF, New Guinea, 1941-43; Lieut, RAN, 1944-47; Teacher, Resident Master, Wesley College, Melbourne, 1947; Joined Department of External Affairs, 1948; University of London and Middle East Centre for Arab Studies, Lebanon, 1950-51; Australian Legation, Egypt, 1951-54; Australian High Commission, Pakistan, 1956-58; Australian Embassy, Washington, DC, USA, 1960-63; High Commissioner in Ghana, 1963-64; Ambassador to Laos, 1964-68; Member, Commonwealth Council for Aboriginal Affairs, 1967-76; Director, Commonwealth Office of Aboriginal Affairs, 1967-72, Secretary (Permanent Head) of Department, 1972-76;

Ambassador to Yugoslavia, Romania and Bulgaria, 1977-80 High Commissioner in Canada and Commissioner in Bermuda 1980-83; Retired, 1983. Honour: CBE, 1981. Memberships Institute of Aboriginal and Torres Strait Studies, Canberra Address: 11/79 Collings Street, Pearce, ACT 2067, Australia

**DEYANOVA Liliana Dimitrova,** b. 27 September 1951 Sofia, Bulgaria. Professor. m. Deyan, 2 sons. Education Graduate, Philosophy, Sociology, St Kliment Ohridski Sofi University; PhD, Sociology, 1988; Habilitation, General Sociology, 1990. Appointments: Research Fellow, Research Centre for Sociological Studies of Youth, 1974-75; Assistan Professor, Department of Sociology, St Kliment Ohridski Sofi University, 1975-89; Head of Laboratory, Sociology of Everyda Life, 1990-; Associate Professor, Sofia University, 1990 Publications: Many Publications. Memberships: Institute fo Critical Social Studies; Sociological Problems Academi Review; Critical Theory Series in the Critique and Humanis Publishing House. Address: Department of Sociology, S Kliment Ohridski Sofia University, 15 Tsar Osvoboditel Blvd 1000 Sofia, Bulgaria.

**DHAMODARAN Tathamangalath Kesavan,** b. 10 Apr 1959, Eyyal, Kerala, India. Scientist. m. M K Sreedevi, 1 son 1 daughter. Education: BSc Chemistry, 1979; MSc Chemistry 1981; PhD Wood Preservation, 1998; Training in Wood Science and Technology, UCNW, Bangor, UK, 1994 Appointment: Scientist, Wood Science, 1982-. Publications: 4 scientific papers; 7 technical research reports; 3 popula articles; 2 information bulletins. Honours: ODA-TCT Award fo Training in Wood Science and Technology, 1994, UK. Address Tathamangalath House, PO Thalore, Via. Ollur. Trichur Dt Kerala State, India.

**DHAR Dipok Kumar,** b. 1 January 1961, Lalmonirha Bangladesh. Physician. m. Mousumi Mojumdar, 1 daughter Education: MBBS, Mymensingh Medical College, 1985; PhD Shimane Medical University. Appointments: Assistant Surgeon Mymensingh Medical College; Consultant Surgeon, Kumudir Hospital, Mirzapur, Bangladesh; Lecturer, Shimane Medica University, Japan. Publications: Transplantation; Hepatology Oncology; American Journal of Surgery. Memberships International Society for Esophageal Disease; Japanes Surgical Society; New York Academy of Sciences. Address Tenjin Cho 233-2, 693 Izumo, Japan.

**DHAWAN Satish,** b. 25 September 1920, Srinagar Kashmir, India. Professor; Aeronautical Engineer. m. Nalini, son, 2 daughters. Education: BA Mathematics and Physics 1938, MA English Literature, 1941, BE Mechanica Engineering, 1944, Punjab University, Lahore; MS Aeronautica Engineering, 1947, University of Minnesota, USA; Aeronautica Engineer, 1949, PhD, Aeronautics and Mathematics, 1951 California Institute of Technology, USA. Appointments: Senic Scientific Officer, 1951-52, Assistant Professor of Aeronautica Engineering, 1952-55, Professor and Head of Department o Aeronautical Engineering, 1955-62, Director, 1963-81, India Institute of Science, Bangalore; Visiting Professor o Aeronautics, California Institute of Technology, 1971-72 Chairman, Space Commission and Secretary to Governmen of India, Department of Space, 1972-82; Chairman, India Space Research Organisation, 1972-82; Senior Advise Department of Space, 1984-85; Member, Space Commissior 1984-. Honours: Padma Shri, 1966, Padma Bhushan, 1971 Padma Vibushan, 1981, Government of India; 6 honorar doctorates; Aryabhata Medal, 1983, Indian National Scienc Academy; Madhya Pradesh Government Pandit Jawaharla Nehru Award in Engineering and Technological Sciences 1983; Karnataka State Award, 1984; Om Prakash Bhasi

Foundation Award, 1981, for Science and Technology in the discipline of Space Science and Technology; Parikh Memorial Award, 1986; Watumull Foundation Medal Award, 1987; G M Modi Science Award, 1988; Vikram Sarabhai Memorial Award, 1998. Memberships: Space Commission; Chairman Governing Council, Raman Research Institute, Bangalore, Board of Trustees; Electronics Commission; Defence Research and Development Council; Radar and Communications Development Board; Atomic Energy Commission; and others. Address: 7/11 Palace Cross Road, Bangalore 560 020, India.

**DHONDT Guido Dominique Constant,** b. 10 February 1961, Belgium. Fracture Mechanics Researcher. m. Barbara Elisabeth Euler, 1 son, 1 daughter. Education: Civil Engineer, Catholic University of Louvain, Belgium, 1983; Master of Arts, Princeton University, 1985; Doctor of Philosophy, 1987. Appointments: Partner, Theoretical Research Associates, Groebenzell, Germany, 1993-96; Fracture Mechanics Expert, Motoren und Turbinen Union, Daimler-Chrysler Aerospace Agency, Germany, 1987-. Publications: About 40 Publications in Professional Journals, 1983-. Honours: Young Engineering Prize, Flemisch Engineering Organisation, 1984. Memberships: ABAQUS German Fracture Mechanics Group; DVM Mixed Mode Fracture Mechanics Group; Society of Industrial and Applied Mathematics; German and International Association of Computational Mechanics. Address: Enzianstrasse 14, D-82194 Groebenzell, Germany.

**DHULIPALLA D Lakshmi Narayana,** b. 12 January 1925, Chintalapudi, India. m. D Jagatsarvam, 1 son, 2 daughters. Education: BA, honours, 1948, MA, honours, 1950, PhD, 1954, Andhra University. Appointments: Research Officer, Vizag Urban Survey, Department of Statistics, Andhra University, 1954-55; Sri Venkateswara University, Tirupati, 1955-. Publications include: Employment and Economic Development - A Study in Technical Aspects, 1958; Economics of Farm Management in Cuddapah District 1968-1969, 1974; Farm Mechanization - A Study of the Impact on Production and Employment, 1980; Population Growth and Economic Growth, 1985. Honours: Gold Medal, Best Doctorate, Andhra University, 1956. Memberships: AP Economic Association; Indian Society of Labour Economics; Indian Economic Association. Address: Sri Venkateswara University, 5/8 Vidyanagar, Tirupati, India.

**DI Hui Zhi,** b. 31 January 1926, Jiangsu, China. Doctor of Pulmonology. m. Yin Shouzheng, 1 son, 2 daughters. Education: MD, 3rd Military Medical College, 1951. Career: Director, Chief Doctor, Expert Department, Wuhan General Hospital. Publications include: Pratical Handbook of Medical Doctors, 1980. Honours: 3rd Prize, three times, Science, Preventive & Convalescent Medicine. Memberships: Vice President, Hubei Branch of China Antituberculosis Association. Address: Wuhan General Hospital, Guangzhou Division, PLA, Wuhan 430070, China.

**DI CASTRI Francesco,** b. 4 August 1930, Venice. Research Scientist. m. Valeria Vitali, 1 son, 1 daughter. Education: BA, 1947; VMD, 1958; PhD honoris causa, 1982. Appointments: Director Division, UNESCO, 1971-84; Assistant Director General, UNESCO, 1990-92. Publications: 35 books; 700 scientific articles. Honours: Global 500 Roll of Honour, United Nations; Commander of the Order of the Italian Republic, 1998; Award, High Scientific Merit, Canada, 1982; and many others. Memberships: Academy Agriculture France; Academies of Science, Italy and Russia; Academy Forestry, Italy. Address: 49 Allee du Pic Saint Loup, 34980 Saint Clement de Riviere, France.

**DI MELCHIORRE Silvio,** b. 23 May 1972, Buenos Aires, Argentina. Airline Consultant; Political Scientist. Education: Political Scientist with specialty in International Relations, University of Buenos Aires, 1997. Appointments: Managing Director, BII Worldwide, Buenos Aires, 1991-92; President, SDM Internacional, Buenos Aires, 1993-95; Consulting in Field, Buenos Aires, 1993-95; Banking Mediator, Buenos Aires, 1995-96; Founder Director, Biblioteca Silvio Di Melchiorre, Buenos Aires, 1996-97; Airline Consultant, Buenos Aires, 1996; Airways Policy Adviser, Buenos Aires, 1997-. Publications: Editor, Director, Tain Magazine, Buenos Aires, Boletín Informativo Internacional, Buenos Aires, 1989-90; Author: Information Service, IO Club, 1992; TV novel, Ramses II, 1995; Political Expression, Airways Policy, 1998; Banking publication, La Banque, 1998. Memberships: Donor Publications to Library of University Del Salvador, Buenos Aires, 1996-97; Instituto del Servicio Exterior de la Nación, Buenos Aires, 1997-98; Bolsa de Comercio de Buenos Aires, 1997-. Address: Bartolomé Mitre 1676, Piso 3, Dpto 11, Cuerpo 2, CP 1037 Buenos Aires, Argentina.

**DIAB Hassan,** b. 1 June 1959, Beirut, Lebanon. University Professor. m. Nuwar Mawlawi, 2 sons, 1 daughter. Education: BSc Hons Communications Engineering, Leeds Metropolitan University, Eng, 1981; MSc, Distinction, Systems Engineering, University of Surrey, 1982; PhD Computer Engineering, University of Bath, 1985. Appointments: Trainee Engineer, 1979-80, Systems Engineer, 1982, IBM UK Labs Ltd, Winchester and Portsmouth; Assistant Professor, 1985-91, Associate Professor, 1991-97, Professor, 1997-, Chairman, Department of Electrical and Computer Engineering, Faculty of Engineering and Architecture, 1998-2001, American University of Beirut, Lebanon; System Analyst Consultant, Hariri Foundation, Beirut, 1986-90; IEAust Coordinator in the Middle East, Institution of Engineers in Australia, 1991-. Publications: Book, Design and Implementation of a Flight Simulation System, 1992; 30 papers in refereed journals; 25 papers in conference proceedings; 8 abstracts in conference proceedings; 10 papers submitted for publication; 22 technical reports. Honours: 2 academic awards; Overseas Research Scholarship, 1983-85; Registered Chartered Engineer, 1988; Fulbright Research Award, 1988; Research Award in Engineering, 1989-90, AUB; 1992 Young Arab Scientists Shuman Prize in Engineering, Amman; Senior Member, IEEE, 1993; Fellow, Institution of Engineers, Australia, 1995. Memberships: IEEE, USA; IEE, UK; IEAust, Australia; Engineering Syndicate, Beirut; Lebanese Association for the Advancement of Science, Beirut. Address: American University of Beirut, Faculty of Engineering and Architecture, PO Box 11-0236, Beirut, Lebanon.

**DIACONESCU Paula,** b. 14 March 1929, Draganesti, Romania. Linguist; Professor. m. Solomon Marcus. Education: Licentiate Letters, Bucharest University, 1953; Doctor's degree Philology, 1968, Bucharest University. Appointments: Assistant Professor, 1953-69, Associate Professor 1969-86, Faculty of Letters, University of Bucharest. Publications: author, Elemente de Istorie a Limbii Romane Literare Moderne, 1974. Honours: Academic Prize, Timotei Cipariu, Romanian Academy for Structura si Evolutie in Morfologia Substantivului Romanesc, 1970; Title of Confereutiar Evidentiat, 1986. Address: Str, Sfintii, Voievozi 41-45, Apart 32, 78109 Bucharest, Romania.

**DIACONU Jean,** b. 10 February 1944, Bodesti, Jud Vilcea, Romania. Professor. m. Lucia, 1 son ,1 daughter. Education: Graduate, Carol Davila, University of Bucharest, 1968; Graduate , Philosophy University of Bucharest, 1977; Doctor in Medical Science, 1982; Graduate in Implantology, Romanian Society of Oral Implantology with European Academy of Oral

Impantology, 1991. Appointments: Chief Doctor of Stomatology, Lehliu Gara Hospital, 1968-72; Chief Doctor of Stomatology, Pipera Industrial Platform, 1972-73; Chief Doctor of Stomatology, I L Caragiale Medical Centre, 1973-76; Chief Doctor of Stomatology, Dr I Cantacuzino Hospital, 1976-92; Chief Doctor of Stomatology, N Gh Lupu Hospital, 1992-. Publications: The Side Effects of the Xilin and of the both, Xilin and Adrenalin Combinated in Local and Loco-Regionl Anesthesia, 1970; During Broque Dermatitis With Oral Lesions at a 4 Years Old Child, 1972; Bullous Lesions, 1977; Contributions at the Study of the Pathogenic and Saptophyte Flora with Oral Nose Pharynx Localization, 1978; 18 Articles and Reports, Scientific Symposiums. Honours: Order Sanitary Merit; Order of the Medical Doctors of Romania. Memberships: UNAS; Order of the Medical Doctors of Romania. Address: 31 major Coralvu Bl P 3A, Scara 1 Etj 1 Apt 5 Sector 2, 73291 Bucharest, Romania.

**DIACONU Mircea A,** b. 2 October 1963, Boroaia, Suceava. Teacher. m. Antonela Daniela, 2 sons. Education: Degree of Lecturer. Career: Doctor in Philology. Publications: Studies: Poezia de la Gândirea, 1997; Mircea Streinul Viata Si Opera, 1998; Instantanee Critice, 1998; Several articles in professional journals. Memberships: Writers Society; Research Board of Advisors, American Biological Institute. Address: 29 George Enesecu Avenue, Bl sc 6, Apt 30, Suceava 5800, Romania.

**DIANKOV Yavor,** b. 17 January 1961, Sofia, Bulgaria. Economist. m. Milena Diankova, 1 son, 1 daughter. Education: Diploma, University, Sofia, Bulgaria, 1985. Appointments: Private Specialisation, 1985-89; International Trade, 1989-93; Executive Director, Company Stromex, 1993-97; Executive Director, C Atex Commerce, 1998-. Publications: Books, features, scientific publications; Led Zeppelin (translation) 1990; Karate-Do Classik, 1991; Karate-Do The Way in My Life (translation), 1992; The Doors of the Life Philosophy (Poetry), 1993; Self-Defence for Everybody, 1994; Spirit Without Chains (translation), 1995; The Letters of the Zen-Monk to the Master of the Sword (translation), 1996; Nyu Mon Karate-Do (translation), 1997; The Martial Arts and Health, 1998. Memberships: Bulgarian Writers Union; President, World ju Jitsu, Bulgaria, 1998-; President, Japan Karate Association (JKA), Bulgaria. Address: 3 Haidushka Poliana Str, 1612 Sofia, Bulgaria.

**DICKENSON Timothy,** b. 14 November 1959, Dallas, TX, USA. Chemical Engineer. m. Cara Jeannette, 3 daughters. Education: AS, Pre Engineering, Murray State College, 1980; BS, Chemical Engineering, Oklahoma State University, 1983. Appointments: Assistant Superintendent, 1989-90; Technology Leader, Assistant Production Superintendent, 1990-95; Plant Manufacturing Leader, 1995-97; Plant Manufacturing Leader, Polymeric and Pure MDI, 1997-. Honours: 8 Polyurethane Technology Center Awards; Man of the Year; Two Thousand Notable American Men; Men of Achievement. Memberships: Christ Church Assembly of God; Shady Oaks Assembly of God. Address: 2906 Prairie Hill Ct, Houston, TX 77059-3570, USA.

**DICKSON Robert Bradley,** b. 31 May 1948, Vicksburg, MIS, USA. Minister, Educator, Business Owner, Administrator, Consultant. Education: Bachelor of Arts, Religion and Philosopy, 1971; Master of Religious Education, 1976; Graduate, Specialist in Religious Education, 1988; Doctor of Divinity, Anchor Theological Seminary, 1995. Appointments: Pastor, Staff, Churches in Texas, Arkansas, Indiana, Florida, 1968-93; Vice President, Institutional Development, Volunteer Position for Anchor Theological Seminary; Owner, Founder, Optima Graphics, 1986-; Founder, Director, Growth Equipping and Evangelism Ministries. Publications: Biblical Stewardship.

Memberships: Texarkana Chamber of Commerce; GW Baptist Religious Education Association; National Association of Church Business Administrators. Address: Optimus Publishing Company, 411 East Hoadley Road, Pine Bluff, Arkansas 71602-9547, USA.

**DIENSTAG Eleanor Foa.** Author; Journalist; Corporate Writer. Education: Graduate, History, Smith College. Appointments: Staff Speechwriter to the Chairman and Chief Executive Officer, American Express, James D Robinson, 1978-83; President, Eleanor Foa Associates, founded in 1983; Monthly Columnist, New Choices, magazine, currently; Articles, essays and reviews have appeared in The New York Times, Harper's, The New Republic, The New York Observer, Ms, McCall's and Working Woman. Publications: Whither Thou Goest: The Story of An Uprooted Wife, 1976; In Good Company: 125 Years at the Heinz Table, 1994; American Society of Corporate Secretaries: Fifty Years of Change and Growth, 1996. Honours: Awards, IABC; Awarded Literary Residencies at Yaddo and the Virginia Center for the Creative Arts. Membership: President 1996-8, American Society of Journalists and Authors. Address: Eleanor Foa Associates, 435 E 79th St, New York, NY 10021-1034, USA.

**DIETERLE Brian,** b. 4 April 1941, North Dakota, USA. Medical Practitioner. divorced, 3 daughters. Education: BS, 1963; MS, 1964; PhD, 1970; MD, 1987. Career: Interna Medical Practitioner. Publications: Several scientific professional publications, 1965-69. Memberships: Rho Ch Society; Medical Association of America. Address: 221 Staggs Road, Ste 201, Branson, MO 65616, USA.

**DIFALCO John P,** b. 24 November 1943. Attorney. m Carolyn DoFalco, 1 son, 2 daughters. Education: BA, 1965, JD 1968, Ohio State University, Columbus; MA, 1986, University Northern Colorado at Greeley; Postgraduate studies in Publi Administration. Appointments: Attorney, Hearing Office and Director, US Postal Service, 1970-77; Labour Relation Specialist, City and County of Denver, 1977-80; City Attorney Greeley, Colorado, 1980-87; Shareholder and Partner, attorney law firm, John P DiFalco & Associates PC, 1987-. teaching publications; 83 articles; 40 presentations. Honours President's Award, Metropolitan Denver City Attorney Association; Outstanding City Attorney, 1986, Colorad Municipal Attorneys Association; Paul Harris Fellow Rotar International; numerous awards and honours from Postal an Federal Associations; and others. Memberships: includ American Bar Association; Colorado Bar Association; Feder Bar Association; Colorado Trial Lawyers Association; Industri Relations Research Association; National Public Employ Labour Relations Association; American Arbitratic Association; National Institute of Municipal Law Office International Platform Association; Society for Professionals Dispute Resolution; American Association of Adult Continuing Education; various corporate directorship Address: 1136 E Stuart Street Ste 4102, Fort Collins, C 80525 1173, USA.

**DIGNADICE Francis,** b. 24 April 1966, Manila, Philippine Lawyer. Eduction: LLB, University of the Philippines, 199 Career: Legal Counsel, Anglo Asian Strategic Management In Puerto Awl lord, Inc, Grand International Airways, In Memberships: Christian Legal Society of the Philippin Aksyon Demokratiko. Address: 25th Floor, Antel Building, 1 Valero Street, Sakedo Village, Makati City, Philippines.

**DILLARD John Robert,** b. 14 March 1955, Sylva, No Carolina, USA. Corporate President. Education: BSBA, w honours, dual concentration in Economics and Finan

Western Carolina University, Cullowhee, North Carolina, USA, 1977; JD, The Cumberland School of Law of Samford University, Birmingham, AL, USA, 1980; PhD, Economics, with honours, Southwest University, 1989; Accepted for graduate study in Economics, Woollsy Hall, University of Oxford, Oxford, England, 1990. Appointments: Part time Faculty at Southern Institute, Birmingham, AL, 1979; Part time Faculty at Blanton's Junior College, Asheville, North Carolina, 1981; Solo Attorney, North Carolina, 1980-81; Partner, law firm of Alley, Killian, Kersten & Dillard, PA, Waynesville, North Carolina, 1981-85; Senior Vice President and Counsel for Commonwealth Land Title Company, Asheville, North Carolina, 1985-93; President, Stewart Title of North Carolina Inc, Asheville, North Carolina, and State Manager and Senior State Counsel for Stewart Title Guaranty Company for the state of North Carolina, 1993-; Adjunct Faculty, Asheville-Buncombe Technical Community College, Instructor of Economics, Marketing, Business Law and Insurance, 1990-93; Adjunct Faculty, Mars Hill College, Instructor of Management (Labor Relations), 1992. Honours include: Unsung Brother Award, 1974; North Carolina Banker's Scholarship, 1976; Alpha Phi Sigma National Honor Society, 1977; University Nominee for Truman Fellowship, 1977; Delegate to International Law Society, 1979; Human Relations Award Dale Carnegie Institute, 1987; Special Achievement Award, Dale Carnegie Institute, 1987. Memberships: North Carolina State Bar; North Carolina Bar Association; North Carolina Bar Foundation; North Carolina Real Property Section; North Carolina Land Title Association. Address: 4 Wagner Branch Drive, Asheville, NC 28804, USA.

**DILLING Kirkpatrick,** b. Evanson, Illinois. Lawyer. m. Elizabeth, 1 son, 3 daughters. Education: Administrative Mechanical Engineering, Cornell University; Pre-Law, Northwestern University; Law Training, Northwestern University; DePaul University; Special French Studies, Ecole Faubier, Switzerland; Sorbonne University. Appointments: Private, Aircraft Armament Officer, Special Courier, US Army Air Corps, 1943-46; Specialist, Food, Drug, Device and Cosmetic Law; Partner, Dilling and Dilling Law Firm, 1948-; Admitted, US Supreme Court, 1952. Publications: Various Publications of Public Health Law. Memberships: Illinois Bar; General Counsel, Cancer Control Society; Adelle Davis Foundation; Episcopal Church; Delta Upsilon, Phi Delta Phi Fraternities; American Bar Association; Chicago Bar Association; Association of American Trial Lawyers; Midwest Pharmaceutical Advertising Council; Tower Club; Cornell Society of Engineers; Rolls Royce Owners Club. Address: 1120 Lee Road, Northbrook, IL 60062-3816, USA.

**DILLINGHAM Marjorie Carter,** b. 20 August 1915, Dicknell, Indiana, USA. m. William Pyrle Dillingham Junior, deceased, 1 son, 1 daughter. Education: PhD, Spanish, Hispanic Minor History, Florida State University, 1970. Appointments: United States Representative, Hemispheric Conference on Taxation in Rosario, Argentina; Taught at Duke University, the University of Georgia, Florida State University, Panama Canal Zone College, St George's School of la Habana, Cuba, and secondary schools in Florida; Directed Traveling Spanish Conversation Classes from Florida State University. Honours: Winner, Delta Kappa Gamma International Fellowship for Graduate Research; Recipient of Delta Kappa Gamma; Presented a paper before the National Meeting of the American Association of Teachers of Spanish and Portuguese in New York; Named to the Putnam County Educational Archives Hall of Fame. Memberships: Phi Kappa Phi; Sigma Delta Pi; Beta Pi Theta; Kappa Delta Pi; Alpha Omicron Pi; Delta Kappa Gamma. Address: 2109 Trescott Drive, Tallahassee, FL 32312, USA.

**DILLON Jean Katherine,** b. 18 May 1925, Birmingham, Alabama, USA. Federal Employee Retired; Business Owner. m. Roy Lerone Morris, div 1969, 2 daughters. Education: BA, Business, Huntingdon College, Montgomery, 1950. Appointments: Secretary, Bookkeeper, H.T. Fitzpatrick, CPA/Attorney, Montgomery, 1948-50; Secretary, Budget Technician, Director of Buget, Deputy Chief of Staff, Comptroller, HQ Air University, Maxwell Air Force Base, Alabama, 1950-58; Executive Secretary, Administrative Assistant, Deputy Chief of Staff, Comptroller, HQ Air University, Maxwell Air Force Base, Alabama, 1958-86; Administrative Assistant, State Coalition of Domestic Abuse Shelters, Montgomery, 1987; Owner, Operation, The William Cook House, 1989-. Honours include: 1st Runnerup, Federal Secretary of the Year, 1986. Memberships include: Nauvoo Historical Society; Board Director, Alabama Highland Games; American Legion Auxiliary; American Association of University Women. Address: 929 Parkwood Drive, Montgomery, AL 36109, USA.

**DILMAC Sukran,** b. 27 July, Kütahya, Turkey. Associate Professor. Education: BSc, 1980, MSc, 1982, PhD, 1990, Istanbul Technical University. Appointments: Teaching and Research Assistant, Department of Materials, Civil Engineering Faculty, Istanbul Technical University, 1982-91; Project Manager, Energy Systems Department, Marmara Research Center, Tübitak, 1993-97; Associate Professor, Corlu Engineering Faculty, Trakya University, 1997-. Publications: Several articles in professional journals. Honours: Grant, UNESCO-ICTP, 1989; Grant, Deutscher Akademischer Austauschdienst, 1995. Memberships: New York Academy of Sciences; Clean Energy Foundation; International Solar Energy Society. Address: Gundogdu Sok #66/1, 34010 Istanbul, Turkey.

**DIMITROV Vasili,** b. 9 October 1937, Tiraspole, Moldova. Professor. m. Faina, 1 son. Education: BSc, 1958, MSc Organic Chemistry, 1960, Moscow Chemical-Technological Institute by Mendeleev name; PhD Physical Chemistry, 1968, Senior Scientific Researcher in Thermophysics, 1968-77, Doctor of Sci in Chemical Physics and Mathematics, 1968-82, Institute for Pure and Applied Mechanics, Siberian Department of USSR Academy of Sciences, Novosibirsk, Academycity; Professor in Hydrodynamics, 1983-1991, Kishinev Polytechnic Institute by S Lazo name; Academician, Academy of Cybernetic Sciences of Ukraine, 1993-. Junior Scientific Researcher, Institute of Chemical Kinetics and Combustion, 1960-63, Senior Scientific Researcher, Institute for Pure and Applied Mechanics, 1963-83, Siberian Dept of USSR Academy of Sciences; Professor, Head of Department, Department of Continuum Mechanics, Kishinev Polytechnic Institute by S Lazo name, 1983-91; Professor-Researcher, Institute for Industrial Mathematics, Beer-Sheva, Israel, 1991-96; Professor-Researcher, Department of Geophysics and Planetary Sciences, Tel Aviv University, 1993-. Honours: Special Award for the Contribution in the Environment Protection of the region of Yasnaya Polyana (Tolstoy's memorial), 1966, All-Union Research Institute of Oil-Chemistry Industry; Gold Medal, Siberian Branch of USSR Academy of Sciences, 1978; Plus several diplomas and other medals and Distinction Prizes. Memberships: USSR National Council on: Hydraulic Problems; Combustion Problems; Member of Board, Head Sub-Committee on Kinetics, USSR National Knowledge-Bank AVOGADRO; Consulting Professor with USSR National Centre of Cosmonauts; International Combustion Institute; European Geophysics Society. Address: 2/9 Mendeli St, Bat-Yam 59475, Israel.

**DIMITROVA Ditka**, b. 6 October 1937, Bourgas, Bulgaria. University Professor. m. Venelin Dimitrov, 2 daughters. Education: MSc Mechanical Engineering, 1963, Technical University in Sofia; DrSc, 1975, Institute for Physical and Chemical Researches Karpov-Moskov; Professor, 1985, High Testing Commission at States Committee of Science and Technical Progress, Sofia. Appointment: Professor, University of Chemical Technology, Faculty of Inorganic Chemistry, Department of Mechanics, Borgas, Bulgaria. Publications: Co-author, 12 papers in professional journals. Membership: Union of Bulgarian Scientists. Address: Higher Institute of Chemical Technology, Faculty of Inorganic Chemistry, Dept of Mechanics, Eng 8010 Bourgas, Bulgaria.

**DINDA Biswanath**, b. 4 August 1947, West Bengal, India. University Teacher. m. Chitralekha Das, 1 son, 1 daughter. Education: BSc Honours, 1967, MSc in Chemistry, 1969, PhD in Chemistry, 1974, Calcutta University. Appointments: Lecturer in Chemistry, B N Mahavidyalaya, 1973-81; Lecturer in Chemistry, Calcutta University Post-Graduate Centre, Agartala, 1981-86; Reader in Chemistry, 1987-93, Professor of Chemistry, 1993-, Tripura University, Agartala; Currently Head of Chemistry Department, Dean of Science Faculty, Member of Senate and Syndicate, Tripura University. Publications: 40 research papers in scientific journals of international repute; Recent Advances on Vegetable Tannins, book. Honour: Honorary Member, Sigma Xi, USA, 1978. Memberships: Life Member: Indian Chemical Society, 1982-; Indian Science Congress, 1990-; Institution of Chemists, India, 1990-; Indian Association for Cultivation of Science, 1990-. Address: 8/1 Middle Road, Calcutta 700075, India.

**DINEFF Peter**, b. 2 July 1947, Sofia, Bulgaria. Educator. m. Valia Velkowa, 2 daughters. Education: MS, Technical University of Sofia, 1971; PhD, Technical University of Sofia, 1978. Appointments: Design Engineer, Computer Institute, Sofia, 1971-74; Researcher, Technical University, Sofia, 1978-88; Senior Researcher, Technical University, Sofia, 1988-91; Associate Professor, Technical University, Sofia, 1991-. Publications: Electrophysical and Electromechanical Technology, author, 1991; Electrotechnology, 1998; Contributor, articles to professional journals. Honours: Recipient Medal Expo '85, Plovdiv, Bulgaria; Patent's Office of Bulgaria, 1985. Memberships: IFIA, 1995-96; New York Academy Sciences, 1995-96; FNTD, Bulgaria. Address: Technical University of Sofia, Kliment Ochridski 4, 1710 Sofia 100, Bulgaria.

**DING Dajun**, b. 28 April 1923, Anqin, Anhui Province, China. Professor. m. Ms Fanqin, 2 sons, 4 daughters. Education: B Eng, 1948. Appointments: Assistant, 1948-53, Lecturer, 1953-78, Professor, 1979-93, Nanjing Institute Technology. Publications: 37 Chinese text, reference and monograph books on concrete masonry and mechanics; Over 270 papers in Chinese and 140 in 10 foreign languages; Stiffness and Cracking of RC Flexural Members; Finite Fundamental Member Method; New Strength Theory of Transversely Reinforced Masonry. Honours: Personal Award, National Scientific Congress Prize, 1978; Prize of 4th Degree, National Prize of Natural Science, 1982; Prize of 1st Degree of Excellent Test, China State Construction Ministry, 1996; Provincial prizes. Memberships: IABSE; New York Academy of Science; CTBUH, India; IBHS; Honorary President, Jiangsu Province; Chairman, Limit State Design Committee of Concretet and Masonry Buildings Group of Council on Tall Buildings and Urban Habitat, USA; Honorary Director, International Federation Highrise Structures, India. Address: Civil Engineering College, Nanjing Institute of Technology, Nanjing 210096, Jiangsu, China.

**DING Fa Zhang**, b. 15 September 1940, Shanghai, Ch Editor in Chief. m. You Yu Hua, 2 daughters. Educat Graduate, Fudan University, Shanghai, 1966. Car Journalist, Jiangxi Daily, 1966-73; Lecturer, Fudan Univers 1973-83; Editor in Chief, Shanghai Youth Paper, 1983- Shanghai Evening News, 1988-. Publications: Several artic in professional journals and magazines. Memberships: Bo Chinese News Press Society; Board, Chinese Fore Friendship Society; Chief, Academy of China Evening N Association; Board, Shanghai Writers Society; Vice Chairm Shanghai News Workers Society. Address: Xinmin Even News Press, yan An Zhong Road 839, Shanghai 2000 China.

**DINGLI-ATTARD dei baroni Inguanez Marcel V**, b. 21 1951, Floriana, Malta. Cultural and Economic Affairs Exp Humanitarian; Peacemaker. m. Mary Ann, 2 daught Education: B Phil Philosophy, 1976, a pontifical univers Benedictine Order in Rome; D Pol Sc habilitatus, 1990, s recognised institution, Republic of El Salvador. Appointme Honorary Consul of Malta, State of Missouri, USA; He Malta's Consular Post, Missouri; President, Albert Eins (1879-1955) International Academy Foundation; Cultural Economic Affairs Expert, Nevis Island Administrat Government of St Kitts and Nevis, West Indies; Special En International Association of Educators for World Peace, N UN (ECOSOC) and UNESCO; Special Representat International Association of Educators for World Peace, N UN (ECOSOC) and UNESCO to the Albert Eins (1879-1955) International Academy Foundation; Notary Pu County of Jackson, State of Missouri, 1985. Honours: Dipl in Recognition of Scientific and Research Activity in fiel Biocenotics, 1985, Polish Biocenotics Society; Honorary Co for Peace, 1989, Malta; World Server, 1990, UN in New Y Knight of Grace of the Constantinian Order of St Georg Naples, 1978. Address: US Federal Building Rms 201-20 301 W Lexington Street, Independence, MO 64050, USA.

**DIRGELA Petras**, b. 21 February 1947, Zvaginiai villa Klaipeda, Lithuania. Writer. m. Dalia Eugenia Yodkaite, 2 s Education: University of Vilnius, 1965-72. Appointme Journalist, 1967-72; Literary career started 1971; Scena Script Writer, 1972-76; Vice Chairman, Lithuanian Wri Union, 1990-94; Vice President, Lithuanian PEN Cen 1990-98. Publications: Most important historical nov Kulgrinda, 1985; The Yoldia Sea, vol 1, 1987, vol 2, 19 Kingdom, the Books of Homeless, 1997. Honours: Grant of Foundation Pour une Entraide Intellectuelle Europeene, 19 Art Prize of Lithuanian Republic, 1997. Membersh Lithuanian Writers Union; International PEN Club. Addre Tuskulenu 60-6, Vilnius, Lithuania.

**DITCHEV Stefan Petrov**, b. 10 March 1940, Mana Bulgaria. Mechanical Engineer. m. Maria Stefanova Ditch 2 daughters. Education: MSc, 1963, DSc, 1984, Techr University, Sofia; PhD, Higher Institute of Food and Fla Industries, Plovdiv, 1973. Appointments: Vice Rector, R Higher Institute of Food and Flavour Industries, 1975 1984-89, 1995-, Head, Department of Food Enginee Equipment, 1975-93. Publications: 215 in total, 22 monogra 20 inventions, 70 papers in international conferences symposiums. Honours: Golden Badge of Honoured Inve Bulgaria; Golden Medal and Diploma, Intellectual Activit INPEX; Engineer of the Year, 1991. Memberships: Ukrai Academy of Technology and Cybernetics; International Inst of Refrigeration, Paris; Association of Frozen Fo Association of Energy Engineers; New York Academy Sciences; Australian Research Council. Address: Hig

Institute of Food Industry, 26 Maritza Boulevard, 4000 Plovdiv, Bulgaria.

**DIXIT Mithilesh,** b. 1 September 1946, Etawah, India. Teacher. m. G R Dixit, 2 daughters. Education: MA, Hindi, 1968; PhD, Hindi, 1989; MA, Sanskrit, 1992. Appointments: Lecturer, Hindi, YDPG College, Lakhimpur Kheri; Lecturer, GDHGPG College, Moradabad; Reader, Head, BDMM Girls Postgraduate College, Shikohabad. Publications: Collections of poems and essays, several research papers, articles and poems in professional journals and magazines; Editor, Ruta quarterly. Honours include: Dalit Gaurav Samman, Dehradun, 1994; Ati Vishisht Sahitya Samman, 1994; Sahitya Sadhana Rashtriya Samman, 1994; Rashtra Bhasha Ratna, 1996; Kailasho Devi Smriti Purashar, 1996; Anushanga Purashar, Hindi Sansthan, 1997; Sahitya Seva Samman, 1997. Memberships: International Goodwill Society of India; Red Cross Society; St Johns Ambulance Brigade; St Johns Ambulance Association; International Sai Seva Organization; Bhartiya Hindi Parishad; Sahitya kala Manch; Acharya Kul; Saraswati Sadhana parishad. Address: 536 A/2 Nai Basti, Shikohabad UP, India.

**DMITRIEV Alexander,** b. 19 January 1935, Leningrad, Russia. Conductor. m. Ludmila Dmitrieva, 1 son. Education: choir, school, 1944-53; choir and composition, conservatoire, 1953-58; orchestra and conducting, 1958-61; Vienna Hochschule für Musik, 1968-69. Appointments: Chief Conductor, Radio SO Petrosavodsk, 1961-77; Chief Conductor, Maly Opera, Leningrad, 1971-77; Chief Conductor, Academic SO, Philharmic, St Petersburg, 1977; Chief Conductor, Staranger SO Norway, 1990. Honour: People Artist of USSR, 1990. Membership: Professor, St Petersburg Conservatoire. Address: St Petersburg Philharmonic, Ul Brokskogo, Saint Petersburg 190011, Russia.

**DMITROV Valeri,** b. 17 July 1953, Irzhavets Village. General Director. m. Shaposhnikova Olga, 1 son. Education: Engineer, Mechanician Degree, Moscow High Technical School n.a. Bauman, 1977; Engineer-Mathematician Degree, Moscow Electronic Industry Institute, 1982; Candidate in Technics, MHTS n.a. Bauman, 1985. Appointments: Engineer, Scientific Research Institute of Machine Building Issues, 1977-81; Senior Research Engineer, Senior Scientific Specialist, Monolit Institute, 1981-85; Chief Designer, Tushinsky Machine Building Plant, 1985-; General Director, NTO Integro, 1989-. Publications: Co-Author, Common Concept of Engineering of Automated Machine Building Enterprises, 1988; Generalised Concept of Computer-Aided Integrated Manufacturing in the Machine Building Industry, 1993. Honours: USSR Cosmonautics Federation Medals, XXX Aniversary of Y.A. Gagarin's Flight, V.P. Makeev Medal; M.V. Keldysh Medal. Memberships: Society of Logistics Engineers, Russian SOLE Chapter; International Informatization Academy; International CALS Congress. Address: NTO Integro, Svoboda Str 35, 123362 Moscow, Russia.

**DÖBEREINER Johanna,** b. 28 November 1924, Aussig, Czechoslovakia. Scientist in Agricultural Microbiology. m. Jürgen Döbereiner, 2 sons, one deceased, 1 daughter. Education: University of Munich Agriculture, 1963; MSc, University Wisconsin, Dr Hon Causa, University Florida, 1975. Appointment: Researcher of EMBRAPA, 1951-. Publications: More than 500 papers; 18 international prizes. Memberships: Brazilian Academy Science; Third World Academy Science; Pontifical Academy of Sciences. Address: CNPAB/EMBRAPA, Seropédica 23851- 970, Rio de Janeiro, Brazil.

**DOBRESCU Emilian,** b. 22 May 1933, Bucharest, Romania. Economist. m. Eugenia Viorica Poenaru, 1 daughter. Education: Economics Faculty, Lomonosov University, Moscow, 1956; DEcons, Bucharest, 1963. Appointments: Assistant, 1956, Lecturer, 1958, Professor, 1967, Economics Faculty, Bucharest; Vice President, 1972-78, President, 1981-82, State Planning Committee; Vice President, National Council for Science & Technology, 1983-88; Senior Researcher, Member, Science Council, National Institute for Economic Research, Romanian Academy, 1990-98; Member, Advisory Group, Romanian Presidency, 1993-96; Member, Economics Council, Romanian Presidency, 1998. Publications: More than 100 papers and books, including: The Rate of Economic Growth, 1968; The Structure of Romanian Economy, 1968; The Correlation Between Accumulation and Consumption, 1971; The Optimum of the Socialist Economy, 1976; Economic Measurement, 1989; Macromodels of the Romanian transition Economy, 1996, 1998. Memberships: Romanian Academy; Association de Comptabilite Nationale, Paris; Science Council, Journal of Applied Microeconomics, Bucharest; International Great Master Chess Study Composition. Address: Str Uruguay Nr 2, Bl 8, Ap 2, 71266 Bucharest 1, Romania.

**DODSON John Richard,** b. 13 June 1948, Melbourne, Australia. Professor. m. Mary Power, 4 sons, 1 daughter. Education: BSc, honours, 1970, MSc, 1971, Monash University; PhD, ANU, 1976. Appointments: Lecturer, University of Canterbury, Christchurch, New Zealand; Lecturer, Senior Lecturer, Associate Professor, University of New South Wales; Chair in Geography, University of Western Australia. Publications: Over 100. Memberships: Chair, National Committee for Quaternary Research; National Committee for Geography; President of Holcene Commission. Address: Department of Geography, University of Western Australia, Nedlands, Perth, WA 6907, Australia.

**DOEBLER Bettie Anne,** b. 26 August 1931, Atlantic City, New Jersey, USA. Professor of English; Writer. m. John W Doebler, 1 son, 1 daughter. Education: BA magna cum laude, 1953, MA, 1955, Duke University; PhD, University Wisconsin at Madison. Appointments: Instructor - Associate Professor, Dickinson College, Carlisle, Pennsylvania, 1961-70; Associate Professor - Professor, Arizona State University, Tempe; Director, Interdisc, Humanities Programme, 1989-93. Publications: Death in the Sermons of John Donne, 1974; essays in ELH, Anglia Shakespeare Studies, and others; Rooted Sorrow; Dying in Early Modern England, 1994. Memberships: Phi Beta Kappa; Shakespeare Association of America; Modern Language Association. Address: Arizona State University, Department of English, Tempe, AZ 85287, USA.

**DOEHRING Ekkehard,** b. 30 October 1954, Braunschweig. Physician. m. Martina, 1 s, 1 d. Education: Dr med, 1982; Habilitation, 1988; Paediatrician, 1988; Professor, 1995. Appointments: Paediatric Training, 1981-90; Research Fellow, Parasitology, 1991-94; Medical Director, 1995-98. Memberships: Many. Address: Rosa Luxembourg Str. 3, 16816, Neuruppin, Germany.

**DOGGER Ada Ruth,** b. 4 November 1925. Retired Scientist, Educator. m. James, 3 sons. Education: BS, Microbiology, Nutrition, 1963; MS, Radiological Health Physics and Pharmacology, 1965. Appointments: Scholarship Committee Advisor; Faculty Advisor; Cancer Research; Information Coordinator; Science Writer, Investigator; Research Assistant; Assistant Professor; Researcher, Instructor; State Radiological Safety Officer; Instructor; Education Representative; Chairman.

Publications: Mutagenic Effects of Gamma Irradiation on Antibiotic Producing Actinomycetes; Listen Please; Rainbow of Hope; Out of Chaos (forthcoming); The Essence of Joan. Honours: Women in Science; Phi Kappa Phi; NIH Fellow. Memberships: GA Education for HI; Board of Directors, Childrens Theatre; International Platform Association; American Security Council; Antrhro Society of America; Science Section and Group of ASGB; Many other memberships. Address: P O Box 208, Gore, VA 22637-0208, USA.

**DOLL Gerhard Michael,** b. 28 January 1962, Landau, Germany. Orthodontist. Education: Studies, Dentistry and Medicine, Mainz, Vienna and Johannesburg University, 1981-89; Dental Examination, 1987; Medical Examination, 1989; Dr.Med.Dent, Mainz University, 1992. Appointments: Trainee, Radiology, Radiologic Clinics of Mainz University and Cologne, 1989-95; Surgical Training, England, 1992-93; Lecturer, Senior Lecturer, Orthodontics, Johannes Gutenberg University, 1995-. Publictions: Several articles; Books: Experimental Studies and Phantom Examinations on Computed Tomography of the Thorax, 1997; Skin Realations of Dental Personnel on Application of Latex Gloves, 1997. Memberships: International Association of Dento-Facial Radiologists; German Scientific Society of Dentists; German Orthodonic Society; European Orthodonic Society. Address: Department of Orthodontics, Augustusplatz 2, D 55131 Mainz, Germany.

**DOLLFUS Audouin,** Astronomer. Appointments: Aeronautics: Pilot Instructor, gas and hot-air balloons; Pioneer, Balloon Astronomy; First telescopic observations from upper atmosphere on board balloons, 1954-59; Astronomy: Solar Physics: Physics of the solar corona; Outer solar corona; Solar plasma activity survey; Solar magnetic fields; Physics of planetary bodies: Telescopic exploration of the Solar System; Polarimetric analysis of Solar System objects; Space Research: Soviet Craft MARS-5; NASA missions; Lunar samples. Honours: Harold Jeffries Lecture, RAS, London, 1974; Tissandier International Astronautical Federation Award, 1991; Galabert International Astronautics Award, 1973; Janssen Gold Medal, Societe Astronomique de France, 1988; Great Award, French Academy of Sciences, 1988. Memberships: International Academy of Astronautics, trustee; Royal Astronomical Society, London; Royal Astronomical Society of Canada; Astronomical and Geophysical Society, Soviet Union; New York Academy of Sciences; Explorers' Club, New York; Societe des Explorateurs Francais; Assoc Francaise pour l'Advancement des Sciences, Past President; Societe Astronomique de France, Past President; Aero Club de France, trustee. Address: Observatoire de Paris Meudon, Sec d'Astrophysics, 5 Pl Jules Janssen, 92195 Meudon Princ Cedex, France.

**DOLOCAN Voicu,** b. 18 September 1939, Romania. Professor. m. Elena, 2 sons. Education: Diploma in Physics, 1963; PhD, 1970. Appointments: Assistant Professor, University Bucharest, 1963-70; Lecturer, 1970-90; Professor, 1990-. Publications: Physics of Solid State Devices, 1978; Tunneling Phenomena, 1989; Superconductivity, 1997; Semiconductor Quantum Structures, 1997. Honour: Diploma Romanian Academy. Memberships: New York Academy of Science; Romanian Physics Society. Address: Bd Tineretului 1 Bl 5 Sc A, Bucharest, Romania.

**DOMANSKA Ewa Helena,** b. 20 December 1963, Poznan, Poland. Historian. Education: PhD, Poznan University, Poland, 1995. Appointments: Assistant Professor, Department of History, Poznan University, Poland, 1995. Publications: Encounters, Philosophy of History After Postmodernism;

Microhistories: Encounters in between Worlds, 1999. Address: Dept of History, Adam Mickiewicz University, Sw Marcin 78, 61-809 Poznan, Poland.

**DOMARKAS Vladislavas,** b. 17 August 1939, Kartena, Lithuania. Professor. m. Sakalausrkaite Stanislava, 1 son, 1 daughter. Education: Kaunas Polytechnic Institute, 1956-61; Diploma Electrical Engineer, 1961; Doctor Technical Sciences, 1967, KPI; Doctor Habilitation of Technical Sciences, 1977, KPI. Appointments: Engineer, Assistant Professor, Associate Professor, Professor, KPI, 1961-93; Prorector, KPI, 1980-83, Rector, 1983-92; Deputy Minister of Foreign Affairs of the Republic of Lithuania, 1993-94; Minister of Education and Science of the Republic of Lithuania, 1994-96; Professor, Department of Public Administration, Kaunas University of Technology, 1997-. Publications: Books: Piezo electric transducers for measuring devices, co-author, 1975; Ultrasonic Echoscopy, co-author, 1988; Over 100 papers in scientific periodicals. Honour: Rank of the Envoy Extraordinary and Minister Plenipotentiary of the Republic of Lithuania. Membership: Associate member, Lithuanian Academy of Sciences. Address: Perkuno al 74, 3000 Kaunas, Lithuania.

**DOMI Mahir,** b. 12 March 1914, Elbasan. Linguist. m. Vediha, 1 son, 1 daughter. Education: Diploma, University of Grenoble, Faculty of Classic, Philology and Literature. Appointments: Teacher and 1 Year Director, Normal Middle School of Elbasan, 1942-47; Chief, Department of text's School, Ministry of Education, 1947-50; Chief, Department of Linguistic, Literature and Folklore, Institute of Study, 1950-53; Professor, Institute of Pedagogy, 1953-55; Chief, Department of Albanian's Grammar and Dialectology, and Extern Professor, University of Tirana, 1955-89. Publications: About 300 articles and reports; Sintax of Albanian Language; Phonetics and Grammar of Present Albanian Language, Chief Editor, 1976; Orthography of Albanian Language, Collaborator, 1973; Vocabulary Orthographical of Albanian Language, Collaborator, 1976; Vocabulary of Albanian Language, 1954; A Xhuvani Works 1 + 2, 1980; Historical Morphology of Albanian Language, 1961; Terminological Dictionaires Multi-Languages, 15 volumes; Problems of Present Albanian's Phonetics and Grammar, 1972; Albanian Dialectology, Chief Editor in 5 volumes, 1971; Albanian Language's Alphabet and the Congress of Manastire, Chief Editor; Annual Bibliography of Turcology, Collaborator; Grammar of Albanian Language 1 + 2 volumes, Chief Editor, 1995-96. Honours: Professor, 1958; Member of Albanian's Academy of Sciences, 1972; People's Teacher, 1977; Price of Republic, First Class, 1974; Order of Red Flag of Work, First Class, 1985; Distinguished Workman of Science, 1995. Memberships: International Committee of Onomastic, 1981-; President, IFLA, Albania, 1972-95; French Linguistic's Association, 1980-; Albanian Academy of Science, 1972-; Albanian Association of Studies of East-South Europe, 1966-75; Commission of History of Ideas AIESSE; Vice Chairman, International Albanian Committee for Atlant of Europe's Languages. Address: Pr M Shyri P 54, Sh 2 Ap 16, Tirana, Albania.

**DOMPREH Victoria Primrose,** b. 1 February 1943, Akim Oda, Ghana. Teacher. m. Charles Dompreh, 2 sons.Education: BA, Education, University of Cape Coast, Ghana, 1972; Dip.TEFL, University of Sydney, Australia, 1975. Appointments: Teacher, Ghana, 1964-82; Headmistress, 1982-84, Principal, 1984-89, Nigeria; Proprietress, 1990-. Membership: Ghana National Association of Private Schools. Address: Victory Schools Ltd, PO Box 45, Akim Oda, Ghana.

**DONALD J Robert,** b. 24 April 1950, Bangalore, S India. Educationist. m. Nalina, 1 son, 1 daughter. Education: DLitt, umanistic Psychology; PhD, Humanistic Psychology; FAGE, cademy of Higher Education; MA, Philosophy and sychology; Bachelor of Liberal Arts, Spicer Memorial College. ppointments: Teacher, Spicer Memorial Higher Sec School; ecturer, Philosophy and Psychology; Registrar, Spicer lemorial College; Asst Professor, Philosophy and Psychology; ssociate Director of Education, South India Union of angalore; Principal, SDA Junior College; Director of Public ffairs and Religious Liberty, South India Union of SDA's; rincipal, Lowry Memorial Junior; Director of Education, South dia Union of SDA's. Honours: Cited as the Prominent Citizen f Karnataka, 1995; Citation of Merit Certificate; Outstanding eople of the 20th Century; The International Directory of istinguished Leadership, 9th Edition, 1998; Man of the Year, 999, ABI. Publications: 33 Papers Presented In Seminars, onferences; 11 Articles; 5 Books and Monographs. lemberships: South India Union of SDA; SDA International oard of Education; SDA Accrediting Association; Spicer lemorial College. Address: 4-7 Saunders Road, Frazer Town, angalore 560 005, India.

**DONG Xijiu,** b. 10 February 1925, Jinan, Shangdong, China. rofessor of Chinese Dance History. m. Chao Tong, 2 sons, 2 aughters. Education: BA, Chinese Literature, Beijing (Peking) niversity, China, 1949. Appointments: Chief, Dance Division, rt Research Institute, Cultural Ministry, China, 1947-79; eputy Director, Dance Research Institute, Cultural Ministry, hina, 1980-87. Publications: The History of Chinese Dance; he Skill Road; The Dance of Tang Dynasty; The Illustration of icture of Chinese Dance History. Memberships: National Art wards; Committee Member, China Dance Association. ddress: Academic Arts China, 17 Qian Hai W Street, Beijing, hina.

**DONG Yu-fen,** b. 11 May 1940, Kaiyuan, Liaoning, China. enior Engineer. m. Bi Shu-Mei, 1 son, 1 daughter. Education: achelor, Jilin University of Technology, 1960-68; Qinghua niversity, 1983-85. Appointments: Transportation Team of ipeline Company of China Oil Department, 1978-88; Senior ngineer, Professional Chief Engineer, 1988-. Publications: 32 esearch papers, 89 science articles. Honours: Chinese cience and Technology Delicate City Golden Award, 1993; hinese Patent International Fair Golden Award, 1994. lemberships: Chinese Scientific Association; Director, Chinese utomobile Journal. Address: POB 11 Tieling, Lianong 112001, hina.

**DONGRE Lahan Raj,** b. 12 November 1959, Out Suranga elly, India. Medical Practitioner. m. Jyothi, 1 daughter. ducation: BA; LLB; DHMS. Memberships: Indian hangeological Society; Chairman, Society for Participatory evelopment and Re-Education. Address:C/O Siddartha Clinic . No 1-2-277, M G Road, Sirpur Kaghaznagar, Adilabad AP, dia.

**DONOGHUE John Charles,** b. 19 September 1950, swego, New York, USA. Engineer; Manager. m. Ann Marie erry, 1 son, 1 daughter. Education: BS, Electronic echnology, Chapman College, 1981; Graduate Courses, oftware Engineering, University of California, Irvine, 1981-82; A, Management, University of Redlands, 1987; Law Student, Vestern State University, Fullerton, 1988-89; Graduate Course, omputer Science, Azusa Pacific University, 1991-93. ppointments: US Air Force, Air Force Systems Command entral Inertial Guidance Test Faculity, Holloman AFB, 969-79; Senior Systems Engineer, Grumman Data Systems, 978-79; Manager, Software and Digital Systems Independent esearch and Development, Lockheed Aircraft Services, ntario, Canada, 1979-85; Manager, Northrop Grumman

Military Aircraft Systems Division, 1985-. Honours: Air Force Commendation Medal, 1976. Memberships: Northrop Corporation Software Council, 1987-97; University of California Software Improvement Network, 1988-; Capability Maturity Model Correspondence Group, Software Engineering Institute, 1993-; Los Angeles Software Improvement Network, University of Southern California, 1994-; Charter Member, Software Inspection and Review Organization, Sunnyvale, California, 1981-; New York Academy of Sciences, 1995-; National Space Society, 1995-; IEEE; IEEE Computer Society; Northrop Management Club. Address: 13739 Lighthouse Court, Fontana, CA 92336-3443, USA.

**DOR Caplyn,** b. 13 November 1952, Buffalo, New York, USA. Visual Artist. m. Kenneth, 1 son. Appointments: Creative Artist, New York State Council, 1992-. Honours: International Gold, CAPI Award of Excellence; TINT Artistic Excellence Achievement Award; Best of Show. Memberships: Arts Council of Buffalo and Erie County; International Artist Group; WNY Artist Group. Address: 4246 Mistymeadow Ln, Hamburg, NY 14075-1336, USA.

**DORNELLES ALVES Juares,** b. 23 November 1954, Porto Alegre. Engineer. m. Maria Fillipi Dornelles, 1 son. Education: USP-SP, Engineering, 1989; Postgraduate in civil construction in 1981. Appointments: Engineer, Construction Dumez Ltd, 1986-87; Area Director, Lix Da Cunha Construction, 1988-91; President, Ventturini Engineering, 1991-. Honour: Top Imobiliário, San Paul, Brazil, 1996; O EMPREITEIRO' National Classification of the Best Construction of the Year, 1997. Address: Ventturini Eng. Const. E. Ger. Ltd, Avenue Sumare 991 Perdizes, San Paul, CEP-05016 091, Brazil.

**DOROSHENKO Ryurik Aleksandrovich,** b. 28 October 1948, Guriev City, Kazakhstan. Physicist. m. Tatyana Mitrofanova, 1 son. Education: Bashkirian State University, 1971; PhD Degree, 1982, Physical Institute of USSR Academy of Sciences. Appointments: Senior Researcher, 1983-90, Head of the Laboratory of Antiferromagnets and Ferrities, 1990, Institute of Molecular and Crystal's Physics, Ufa. Publications: The Photomagnetic Phenomena in Yttrium-Ferruterous Garnets, 1992; Influence of the Light on the Magneto-Ordered Crystals, 1996. Membership: Physical Society of Russia. Address: Laboratory of Antiferromagnets and Ferrities, Physics Department Bashkir Scientific Center of the Russian Academy of Sciences, 6 K Marxa Str Ufa 450025, Russia.

**DORSETT Mary Alice,** b. 4 February 1926, Dade City, Florida, USA. Businesswoman. 1 son, 1 daughter. Education: Paine College, Augusta, Georgia, 1945-46; The Trade and Professional School for Women and Girls, Washington, DC. Career: Founder, Faith Mission, 1962; Business Women, 47 years. Publication: Wings. Honours: TOBA's Unsung Hero Award; Dr M L King Drum Major Award; Plaques from Hillsborough Community College, Links, Sherriff's Department, Greeks Literature. Memberships: Grand Union Society; National Council of Negro Women; Tampa Urban League; NAACP. Address: PO Box 4896, Tampa, FL 33677, USA.

**DORSEY-MURPHREE Betty Jo,** b. 15 January 1932, Brownsville, PA, USA. Professor. m. Marshall W, 2 sons, 3 daughters. Education: BA, Asbury College, USA, 1950-53; Graduate, Northwestern University, IL, USA, 1954-55; Postgraduate Certificate in Education, University of London, 1963; Diploma in Education, University of London, 1967-68; PhD, Sociology, University of London, 1969-74. Appointments: Administrator, Teacher, 1955-1965; Teaching Assistant, University of Rhodesia, 1967-68; Lecturer, Education, University of Rhodesia; Research Fellow, University of

Rhodesia, 1969-70; Research Fellow, University of Rhodesia, 1970-74; Research Associate, St Anthony's College, Oxford University, 1975; Research Associate, St Antony's College, Oxford University, 1977-79; Senior Associate, 1982; Chairman of Department of Education, University of Zimbabwe, 1982-85; Visiting Professor, Stanford University, 1989-90; Senior Associate, Oxford University, 1993-; Consultant, World Bank, Ford Foundation, Canadian International Development Agency, UNESCO. Publications: 32 Publications, 2 forthcoming; 26 Conferences and Seminars; Honours: Honourary Professor of Graduate Studies, University of Belgrade, 1988; Outstanding Alumnus Award, Asbury College; Cited in: Who's Who in the World; 500 Notable Women; Who's Who in International Education. Memberships: Association of Sociologists of Southern Africa; Comparative and International Education Society; National Education Association of Zimbabwe; International Sociological Association; Sociology of Education Research Committee; History and Comparative Education Society of Southern Africa. Address: 46 Aberdeen Road, Avondale, Harare, Zimbabwe.

**DOTSENKO Alexander,** b. 19 August 1948, St Petersburg, Russia. Physicist. m. Elena Dotsenko, 2 sons. Education: MS, Physical Mechanics, 1971; PhD, Theoretical Physics, 1976. Appointments: Head, Optical Glass Department, Vavilov State Optical Institute, 1971-96; Deputy Director, Corning Scientific Center, St Petersburg, 1997-. Publications: 140 scientific articles, proceedings of conferences and patents, including 3 books. Memberships: Russian Physical Society; Russian Optical Society; American Ceramics Society; International Glass Commission, (TC10 "Optical properties of glasses"). Address: Corning Scientific Centre, 4 Birzhevaya line, St Petersburg 199034, Russia.

**DOU Hua Shu,** b. 24 August 1958, Shandong Province, China. Research Scientist. m. Ying Ying Chen, 1 son. Education: BSc, Northeast University, Shenyang, 1982; MSc, Northeast University, Shenyang, 1984; PhD, Beijing University of Aeronautics and Astronautics, 1991. Appointments: Teaching Assistant, 1984, Lecturer, 1987, Northeast University; Postdoctor, 1991, Associate Professor, 1993, Tsinghua University; Visiting Researcher, Tohoku University of Japan, 1994; Associate Professor, Hosei University of Japan, 1995; Research Scientist, Sydney University, Australia, 1996-. Publications: AIAA Journal; Transactions of ASME; Computational Mechanics; Computer Methods in Applied Mechanics and Engineering; Journal of Non Newtonian Fluid Mechanics; Journal of Engineering Thermophysics; Acta Mechanica Sinica; Acta Aerodynamica Sinica; Fluid Enginering. Honours: Outstanding Achievement for Teaching and Research, Tsinghua University, 1994; Second Prize of Science and Technology Progress, Ministry of Mechanical Industry of China, 1994; Second Prize of Science and Technology, Ministry of Aeronautical Industry of China, 1995. Memberships: A1AA, 1993; ASME, 1993. Address: Dept of Mechanical Engineering, University of Sydney, NSW 2006, Australia.

**DOUGLAS Vincent Fredric,** b. 31 March 1949, Johnstown, USA. Publisher. m. Patrice, 1 son, 1 daughter. Education: BS, MEd, Indiana University of Pennsylvania. Appointments: President, American Education Publishing, 1990-97; Senior Vice President, McGran Companies, 1997-. Address: 4944 Hampsted Square East, New Albany, OH 43054, USA.

**DOUGLASS John F,** b. 13 December 1951, Rochester, Minnesota. Teacher. Education: BA, Harvard University, 1974; MA, University of South Florida, 1976; MS, University of Michigan, 1979; Appointments: Assistant, Division of Mammals, Field Museum, 1967-68; Summer Research Assistant,

American Museum, 1969; Teaching Assistant, Universi[ty] Michigan, 1976-82; Lepidopterist, Allyn, Museum Entomology, Peru Expedition, 1980; Teacher, Duluth Ce[n] High School, 1983; Teacher, St John's High School, Tol[e] Ohio, USA, 1983-; Organizer, Lepidopterist, Allyn Muse[um] Congo Expedition, 1991. Publications: Bibliography of American land tortoises; Butterflies of Okapiland; Many oth[er] Honours: President, Class of 1970; Honorary Fresh[man] Scholarship; Interviewer, Harvard Radcliffe Commi[ttee] Memberships: Lepidopterists Society; many others. Addr[ess] 3347 Airport Hwy, Toledo, OH 43609, USA.

**DOURAKI Thomais,** b. Rentina, Greece. Legal Adv[iser] Academic. Education: Graduate in Law, Law Faculty, Ath[ens] 1972; Postgraduate in Public International European L[aw] University of Paris I & II; MA, Administrative Law, 1974; Law, European Community, 1975, 1976; PhD, cum la[ude] 1984. Appointments: Ministry of National Economy, Ath[ens] 1977-; Jean Monnet Fellow, European University Insti[tute] Florence, 1990-92; External Professor, National Schoo[l] Public Administration, Athens, Cyprus Academy. Publicati[ons] 41 books, articles on human rights, research studies. Hon[our] ECHR and the Right to liberty, Paris, 1986. Memberships: [I] Academy of International Law, The Hague, Netherlands; Ce[ntre] for Ethics, Law and Medicine, Freiburg University, Germa[ny] International Institute for Humanitarian Law, San Remo; Fre[nch] Association for International Law, International Institut[e] Human Rights (Strasbourg). Address: 28 Achaias St[reet] Ambelokipi, Athens, Greece.

**DOW Marguerite Ruth,** b. 13 June 1926, Ottawa, Ont[ario] Canada. Professor of English and Drama. Education: English Hons, 1949, B Ed, 1971, MA English, 1970, Unive[rsity] of Toronto, Ontario; Certificate in Drama, 1955, Que[en's] University; Senior Cert in Drama, 1956, Banff School of [Fine] Arts, University of Alberta. Appointments: Laboratory Assis[tant] Division of Applied Biology, 1944-46, Librarian, Aeronau[tical] Library, 1947-48, National Research Council; Librarian, J[oint] Intelligence Bureau, Defence Research Board, 1949 Teacher of English, Ontario High Schools, 1950-65, inclu[ding] Head of the English Department, Laurentian High Sch[ool] Ottawa, 1959-65; Associate Professor English & Dra[ma] 1965-72, Professor, 1972-85, Professor Emerita, 1985-, Fac[ulty] of Education, University of Western Ontario. Publicati[ons] Editor, Light from Other Windows, anthology, 1964; Author, Magic Mask, textbook of Theatre Arts, 1966; Co-aut[hor] Courses of Study in the Theatre Arts, grades 7-12, 1[9] Editor, We are Canada/Nous Sommes Canadiens, 1[9] Co-Editor, An Early Ontario Harvest, receipts from southeastern counties, 1983; Co-author, Loyalist Vignettes Sketches, 1984; Contributor, The Canadian Encyclopae[dia] Second Edition, 1988; Author, 54 articles in professi[onal] journals. Honours: Numerous awards and medals inclu[ding] Grant of Armorial Bearings, Kings of Arms, England, 1[9] Silver Badge of Service, Monarchist League of Canada, 1[9] Life Fellow, World Literary Academy, 1986; Universit[y of] Western Ontario renamed the Canadian Heritage Wr[iting] Award the Marguerite Ruth Dow Canadian Heritage Wr[iting] Award, 1995. Memberships: Member and held office in m[any] Clubs, Committees and associations. Address: 52 [Bay] Avenue, Apt 2, Ottawa, Ontario, Canada K1S 2G2.

**DOWRIDGE Donald L,** b. 28 November 1956, Baltim[ore] Maryland, USA. Motivational Consultant. 1 son. Education: Management Marketing. Appointments: Founder, [D] Enterprises, 1992; Distributor for TPN (The Peoples Netw[ork] 1998. Publications: 6 books. Honours: Letter Congratulations, President of USA, 1995; Distinguished Cit[izen] of the Year, Tampa, Florida, 1996. Memberships: Tampa

Metro Jaycees. Address: PO Box 22722, Tampa, FL 33622-2722, USA.

**DOYLE Gloria Thorpe,** b. 25 December 1951, St Louis, MO, USA. Teacher. m. Jerry Nelson, 2 sons. Education: BS Degree, Hampton University, 1973; MA Degree, Hampton University, 1975; Adv Certificate, NC Central University, 1984. Appointments: Mathematics Teacher, Syms Junior High, Hampton, USA, 1973-80; Visiting Professor, Hampton University, USA, 1973-79; Mathematics, Computer Programming Teacher, NC, USA, 1980-82; Computer Education Specialist, Durham City, USA, 1982-85; Math, Computer Programming Teacher, Computer Coordinator, Durham, USA, 1985-. Publications: Computer Programming Booklet, Editor, 1984. Honours: NC Hamtonian of the Year, 1992; Durham Teacher of the Year, 1984; Jiffy Lube Teacher of the Year, 1989; Hillside Parent Award, 1995. Memberships: National Education Association; NC Association of Educators; National Council of Teachers of Mathematics; NC Council of Teachers of Mathematics; International Society of Technology in Education; Delta Sigma Theta Sorority, Inc; National Hampton Alumni Association; Hillside PTSA; Parent Boosters Club; Hillside PIE Club; Advanced Placement Computer Science Teachers List Serv; APCS Institute; Mt Calvary United Church of Christ. Address: 1811 Primrose Place, Durham, NC 27707-4333, USA.

**DRAGAVTSEV Victor,** b. 18 October 1935, Sochi, Russia. Geneticist. m. Nataly, 1958, 2 daughters. Education: Graduate, Agricultural University, 1958; Dr of Biology, 1963; Professor of Genetics, 1985; Correspondence, Agricultural Academy, 1991. Appointments: Senior Scientist, Botany Institute in Alma-Ata, 1958-68; Head, Plant Genetical Laboratory, Novosibirsk, 1968-85; Deputy Director, Krasnodar Agricultural Institute, 1985-90; Elected by Director of VIR, 1990. Publications: 220 including 5 monographs. Honour: Honorary Promoter of science of Russia. Memberships: Eucarpia; London Linnean Society; N T Vavilov Society of Geneticists and Breeders; Botanical Society of Russia.

**DRAPALIK Betty R,** b. 7 April 1932, Cook County, Illinois, USA. Artist. m. Joseph J, 1 son, 1 daughter. Appointments: Secretary, Assistant Director, Arden Shore Boys Home, Lake Bluff, Illinois, USA; Secretary Clerk, Service School Command, Great Lakes Naval Base, USA; Retired. Publications: Articles, The Artists Magazine. Honours: 1st Place, LCAL Fine Arts Festival; 2nd Place, Watercolour, 1997, 1998; Best of Show; Recent Works, Purchase Award. Memberships: Midwest Watercolor Society; Red River Watercolor Society; Lake COunty Art League; International Platform Association; Lakes Region Watercolour Guild; National Association of Women in the Arts; Art Institute of Chicago; Kenosha Art Association; Community Gallery of Art; Deerpath Art League. Address: 2018 W Grove Ave, Waukegan, IL 60085-1607, USA.

**DRAPER Stephen,** b. 17 March 1942, Columbus, Georgia, USA. m. Lucy Hargrett, 1 daughter. Education: PhD, Water Resources and Physics, Georgia Institute of Technology; JD, Environmental and International Law, Georgia State University; MBA, Management, C W Post, Long Island University; MSCE, Construction and Photogrammetry, Georgia Institute of Technology; BS, General Science, US Military Academy, West Point; Professional Engineer, Registered in Georgia; Professional Engineer, Registered in Florida. Appointments: Water Policy Analyst; Water Resources Enginering; Engineering Management. Publications include: Coordinating Water Use Policy and Regulation and Water Quality Policy and Regulation, 1994; Shared Use of Transboundary Water Resources, 1995; Standardizing the Shared Use of Transboundary Water Resources, 1995; Integrating Transboundary Water Sharing, 1995; Sharing Transboundary Water Resources: A Review of Standards, 1995; Managing Transboundary Water Sharing, 1996; Sharing the Resource - Water Doesn't Recognize Boundaries, 1996; ASCE Standards the Water-Related Policies, Laws, and Regulation, 1997; International Duties and Obligations for Transboundary Water Sharing, 1997. Honours: Gallantry Cross with Silver Star; Legion of Merit; Bronze Star; Soldier's Medal; Purple Heart; Air Medal; Meritorious Service Medal; Commendation Medal; American Jurisprudence Award, Georgia State University, 1992; Special Actions Award, Womens Equity Action League, 1976. Memberships: American Bar Association; American Board of Forensic Examiners; American Water Resources Association; American Society of Civil Engineers; National Academy of Forensic Engineers; National Society of Professional Engineers. Address: The Draper Group, 1401 Peachtree St NE Ste 500, Atlanta, GA 30309, USA.

**DRAYTON Mary Josephine,** b. 13 January 1916, Dunedin, New Zealand. Retired Teacher; Local and Regional Councillor. m. Ronald Wilfred Drayton (dec). Education: MA Honours, History, 1937; Diploma in Education, 1940. Appointments: Head of Department, 1947-57, First Assistant, 1955-57, Acting Principal, 1957-59, Whangarei Girls High School; Principal, Tauranga Girls College, 1959-1980s; Elected to University of Waikato Council, 1979, Court of Convocation, 1987-94; Pro-Chancellor, 1986-87, Chancellor, 1988-91, Waikato University; Member, 1985-89, Deputy Mayor, 1986-89, Chairperson, Town Planning Committee, 1986-89, Tauranga City Council; Director, Trust Bank, Bay of Plenty, 1988-91; Member, Tauranga District Council, 1989-92; Regional Councillor, Bay of Plenty, 1989-92, re-elected, 1992-95, 1995-98, Deputy Chairperson, Resource Planning Committee, 1992-95, Chairman, Resource Planning Committee, 1995-98, Bay of Plenty Regional Council; Chairperson, Tauranga Sub-Region Landfill Working Party, 1991-92. Honours: Woolf Fisher Travelling Fellowship to Hawaii and California, 1971; MBE, 1980; Paul Harris Fellow, 1987; Commemoration Medal, 1990; Honorary Doctorate, University of Waikato, 1993. Address: 197 Ngatai Road, Tauranga, New Zealand.

**DREW Sharon Lee,** b. 8 November 1946, Los Angeles, CA, USA. Sociologist. 1 son, 1 daughter. Education: BA, Oganizational Sociology, California State University, Long Beach, 1983; Graduate Work in progress, California State University, Dominguez Hills, 1998. Honours: California Tomorrow, 1990; California Sociological Association, 1991; California State University Dominguez Hills' Older Adult Center, 1994. Hobbies: Gardening/Horticulture; Aquarium Hobbyist; Theatre; Music; Personal Development; Reading. Address: 927 N Chester Avenue, Compton, CA 90221, USA.

**DRIES Alice F,** b. 16 December 1926, USA. Ornamental Horticulture. m. Joseph Dries, 1 son. Education: MS, 1965; 90 credits towards Doctorate. Career: Educator, Danville Area College, 28 years. Publications: Several articles in professional journals and magazines. Honours: 4, 1975, 1989, 1990, 1997. Memberships: AAUW. Address: RR1, Box 22214, Old Fort, NC 28762-9801, USA.

**DRIESBACH Walter Clark Jr,** b. 3 July 1929, Cincinnati, Ohio, USA. Sculptor; Instructor. m. Susan Sanders Driesbach, 1 son, 2 daughters. Education: Diploma, 1952, School of the Dayton Art Institute under Robert Koepnick; Studio Assistant to Joseph Kiselewski, sculptor, New York, 1954-55; Graduate study under Charles Cutler, Art Academy of Cincinnati, 1955-56. Appointments: Taught Sculpture Workshop, 1956, Sculpture Instructor Summer 1958, Guest Instructor in

Sculpture, 1960, Instructor Sculpture 3D Design, 1970-83, Instructor, Foundation Dept, 1983-87, Art Academy of Cincinnati; Drawing Instructor, 1970-71, Instructor in Sculpture and 3D Design, 1978-93, Thomas More College; Instructor in Sculpture, Drawing & 3D Design, University of Dayton, 1966-72; Instructor in Sculpture and Drawing, Wilmington College, 1963-66; Instructor in Sculpture and Drawing, Memphis Academy of Arts, 1956-58. Creative Works: Sculptures in 110 private collections across the US, in Portsmouth, England, and Honduras; Sculptures in the collections of 11 Educational Institutions and Corporations; 15 solo exhibits; Participated in 32 Group Shows. Honours: Represented in 3 Sculpture Publications, 1970, 1980, 1989; Memphis Fellowship Show, 1st Award for Sculpture, 1956; Zoo Arts Festival Fleischmann Purchase Prize 1964; Ohio State Fair, Professional Sculpture Div, 1st Prize, 1966, 2nd Prize, 1968; Ohio State Fair, Cash Award, Fine Arts Exhibition, 1971; Fine Woodworking Exhibition, Emery Gallery, 2nd Prize, 1986. Membership: Cincinnati Carvers Guild. Address: 2541 Erie Avenue, Cincinnati, OH 45208, USA.

**DRUMMOND Richard Henry,** b. 14 December 1916, San Francisco, California, USA. Theological Professor. m. Pearl Estella Drummond, 2 sons, 1 daughter. Education: BA, 1938, MA, 1939, University of California at Los Angeles; PhD, University of Wisconsin, 1941; BD, Lutheran Theological Seminary, Gettysburg, Pennsylvania, 1944; Postdoctoral Studies, UCB, UCLA, Tokyo School of Japanese Language, San Francisco Theological Seminary. Appointments: Pastor, Japanese Church of Christ, (Presbyterian), San Francisco, 1947-49; Fraternal Worker, Japan, 1949-62 (PC USA); Professor, Christian Studies and Classical Languages, Meiji Gakuin University, Tokyo, 1958-62; Visiting Professor, 1968-69, 1976-78, 1986-87; Professor of Ecumenical Mission and History of Religions, University of Dubuque Theological Seminary, 1962-84; Florence Livergood Warren Professor of Comparative Religions, University of Dubuque Theological Seminary, 1984-87; Visiting Professor, Atlantic University, 1987-89, Old Dominion University, 1989; Professor of Ecumenical Mission & History of Religions, Emeritus, University of Dubuque Theological Seminary, 1987-. Publications: Several articles in professional journals, six books. Honours: Phi Beta Kappa, UCLA; Research Fellowship, University of Wisconsin, 1940-41; Teaching Fellowship, Gettysburg Theological Seminary, 1941-44; Faculty Fellowship, Sealantic Fund, 1968-69; Outstanding Educator of America, 1972, 1974; University Fellow, University of Dubuque, 1991. Address: 3662 Pennsylvania Avenue, Apt L-147, Duburque, Iowa 52002, USA.

**DRYSDALE James Wallace,** b. 11 May 1937, Edinburgh, Scotland. Biochemistry Professor. m. Ann Marie Drysdale, 2 sons. Education: BS, honours, 1960, MSc, 1963, Edinburgh University Medical School; PhD, University of Glasgow Medical School, 1965. Career: Assistant Lecturer, Biochemistry, University of Edinburgh; Assistant Lecturer, Biochemistry, Glasgow; Assistant Professor, Physiological Chemistry, MIT, 1966-68; Principal Research Associate, Harvard Medical School; Professor of Biochemistry, Tufts Medical School, 1984-. Publications: Numerous papers in professional journals. Address: Tufts University School of Medicine, Biochemistry & Pharmacology, 136 Harrison Avenue, Boston, MA 02111, USA.

**DU Zhen-Ping,** b. 2 June 1962, Nanjing, China. Senior Software Engineer, Research Fellow. m. Jian-Jian Zhao, 2 sons. Education: BE, Automatic Control, Southeast University, China, 1984; ME, Automatic Control, 1987; PhD, Automatic Control, 1990. ME with Distinction, Electrical and Electronic Engineering, University of Canterbury, New Zealand, 1994. Appointments: Post Doctoral Fellow, Transportation Systems

and Power Systems, University of Canterbury, New Zealand, 1991-93, 1995-96; Asia Area Manager, CHART Instruments Ltd, New Zealand, 1996-98; Senior Software Engineer, Forum 8 New zealand Ltd, 1998-. Publications: Over 20 papers published in Transportation Research IEE Proceedings, IFAC Proceedings etc. Memberships: Referee of IEE Proceedings-Generation, Transmission and Distribution; International Federation of Automatic Control. Address: 20 Woodbury Street, Avonhead, Christchurch, New Zealand

**DUAN Ruo-fei,** b. 20 February 1936, Wuhan, China. Professor. m. Zhang Ying, 1 son, 1 daughter. Education: Graduate, Philosophy Department, Peking University, 1961. Appointment: Director, Editor-in-Chief, Contemporary Trend of Thought, magazine. Publications: Collected Works of Duan Ruo-fei, 1992. Honours: Title, State Rank Expert, China, 1992; Several honours of outstanding contributions to social science from the government of China. Address: 87 Jiu'er Lane, Beijing 100009, China.

**DUAN Yun-Bo,** b. 27 September 1962, Shandong, China. Researcher; Professor Computational Science and Engineering. m. Cai-Xia Yu, 1 son. Education: BSc Physics, 1983, Department of Physics, Shandong Normal University, China; MSc Atomic and Molecular Physics, 1989, Department Physics, Liaoning University, China; MSc Molecular Spectroscopy and Laser Spectroscopy, 1996, Postdoctoral Fellow of Japan Society for Promotion of Science, 1997-98, Dept Physics, PhD Computer Science, 1997, Department Electronics and Computer Science, Toyama University, Japan; PhD Chemical Physics, 1996, Kanazawa University, Japan; Post-doctoral Researcher, Dept Chemistry, Ohio State University, 1999. Appointments: Assistant Professor, teaching General Physics and Atomic and Molecular Physics, 1983-86, Lecturer, teaching General Physics and Quantum Mechanics, 1989-93, Department of Physics, Yantai Normal University, China; Professor, Institute for Computational Science and Engineering, Ocean University of Qingdao, China, 1998-. Publications: Co-author 45 articles in professional journals. Memberships: Chinese doctoral association in Japan; American Association for the Advancement of Science. Address: 9-301 Arisawa 811, 930 Troyama, Japan.

**DUDEK Jaromir,** b. 4 June 1929, Sobesice. Pharmacist, Consultant. m. Ladislava, 1 daughter. Education: PhMr, Masaryk University, 1952; RNDr, Komensky University, 1968; Specialist in Pharmacology and Toxicology, 1984. Appointments: Pharmacist, 1952-54; Examiner, Social and Clinical Pharmacy, 1954-99; Management of Pharmacy, 1954-89; Spokesman of Clinical Pharmacy, 1981-91; Researcher in Clinical Pharmacy, 1989- 90; Hospital Pharmacist, Faculty Hospital, 1989-92; Health Institute, 1993-99. Publications: Free Open Drugs; Information for Rational and Secure Medical Treatment; Lexicon for Health. Memberships: Pharmaceutical Society; Department of Social and Clinical Pharmacy Hradec Kralove. Address: General Health Ins, Havlickova 3, 305 88 Plzen, Czech Republic.

**DUDEK Wieslaw Aleksander,** b. 6 September 1953, Glogow, Poland. Mathematician; Educator. m. Izabela Grozdzinski, 2 sons. Education: MSc, Mathematics, Algebra, Department of Mathematics, University of Wroclaw, Poland, 1978; Higher course of didactics, Pedagogical University of Czestochowa, Poland, 1985; Dr, mathematics, Department of Higher Algebra, State University of Khishiniev, Molodova, 1990. Appointments: Assistant, Lecturer, and Assistant Professor, Institute of Mathematics, Pedagogical University of Czestochowa, 1978-90; Adjunct, Institute of Mathematics, Technical University of Wroclaw, 1990-. Publications: About 50 cientific works in different professional journals; Problems in inear Algebra and Analitic Geometry, 1985; On Some Classes -groups and Generalizations, 1990; Editor of professional urnal : Quasigroup and Related Systems. Memberships: merican Mathematical Society; Polskie Towarzystwo Iatematyczne (Polish Mathematic Association); Polish ssociatio of Filately. Honours: Prize, J Marcinkiewicz Competition, 1977; Rector's Prize, Pedagogical University of zestochowa, 1980, 1981, 1983, 1985, 1987, 1989; Prize of he Director of Institute Mathematical Technical University of Vroclaw, 1997. Address: Institute of Mathematics, Technical Iniversity, Wybrzeze Wyspianskiego 27, 50-370 Wroclaw, oland.

**DUDZIK Carol**, b. 28 November 1950, Evergreen Park, linois, USA. Teacher; Attorney. m. Terrence Dudzik. ducation: BA, 1972, MA, 1975, Western Illinois University; MEd, 1981, University of Illinois at Urbana; JD, 1987, John Marshall Law School. Appointments: Attorney, Private Practice; nstructor, Moraine Valley Community College; Educator, Chief Megotiator, North Palus Education Association, Illinois ducation Association Legal Dept, 1988; Cook County rbitrator. Honours: 10 year Service Award, St Patricia Church, 988; North Palus School District Certificate for Service, 1989, 998. Memberships: Chicago Bar Association; National ducation Association. Address: Conrady Jr High School, 96th nd Roberts Rd, Hickory Hills, IL 60457, USA.

**DUDZINSKI Piotr Antoni**, b. 14 November 1949, Sroda laska, Poland. Mechanical Engineering Educator; Consultant. n. Jolanta Anna Wasiela, 1 child. Education: MSc, 1973, Tech.Sc, 1977, Wroclaw University of Technology; Doctor Iabilitatus, Technical University, Dresden, 1991. ppointments: Lecturer, 1977-85, 1987-88, 1991-95, Professor, 995-, Wroclaw Technical University; Alexander von Humboldt ellow Fridericana University of Karlsruhe, Germany, 1985-87, Iniversity of Berlin, 1993; Staff, Technical University, Dresden, 989-91; Consultant, Interactor, Gevelsberg, Germany, 1995-, Building Mechanization and Mineral Mining Research Institute, Varsaw, 1995-. Publications: Several articles in professional ournals. Honours: Polish Ministry of Education Award, Varsaw, 1978, 1979; Fellow, Polish Academy of Sciences, 994. Memberships: International Society for Terrain Vehicle Systems; International Association for Automation and Robotics Construction; Societas Humboldtiana Polonorum; New York cademy of Sciences. Address: Wroclaw University of echnology, 1-16 Wybrzeze Wyspianskiego 27, 50 370 Vroclaw, Poland.

**DUGAR Chand Ratan**, b. 11 April 1953, India. President, Director. m. Kamala. Education: B Com, Hons, Calcutta Iniversity, 1969-72; Chartered Accountants Examination .C.A., 1970-74. Appointments: Audit Article Clerkship, 971-75; Senior Assistant, 1975-76; Chief Accountant, Commercial Manager, Vice President Finance and Market, oint President Eastern Spinning Mills, 1976-91; Advisor, ndophil Textile Mills, Phillipines and Thailand, 1992; General Vlanager, 1992-97; President, Director, 1997-. Honours: Development Citra Award; Many other awards. Memberships: nstitute of Chartered Accounts of India. Address: PT Elegant extile Industry, Menara Batavia Level 16, JL K H MAS, Vlansyur Kav 126 Jakarta, 10220 Indonesia.

**DUKIC Dragutin**, b. 28 November 1952, Matesevo. Jniversity Professor. m. Stana, 1 daughter. Education: Graduate, Faculty of Natural Sciences, Department of Biology, 976; MS, Faculty of Agriculture, 1982; PhD, Faculty of /eterinary, 1987. Appointment: Dean, Faculty of Agronomy, Cacak University. Publications include: Microbiology of Grain,

Flour, Germ and Concentrates, 1993; Microbiology Handbook, 1994. Memberships: Serbian Society for Microbiology; Yugoslav Society for Microbiology; Yugoslav Society for Soil Study; Serbian Society for Biology. Address: Cara Dusana 34, Faculty of Agronomy, 32000 Cacak, Yugoslavia.

**DUKOV Ivan Ljubomirov**, b. 25 June 1942, Haskovo, Bulgaria. Chemical Engineer. 2 sons. Education: MSc, 1967, PhD, 1973, DSc, 1996, University of Chemical Technology and Metallurgy, Sofia. Appointments: Research Fellow, 1973-83, Lecturer, 1983-88, Reader, Associate Professor, 1988-. Publications: 60 papers in professional journals. Memberships: New York Academy of Sciences; Union of Scientists of Bulgaria. Address: Department of Inorganic Chemistry, University of Chemical Technology and Metallurgy, 1756 Sofia, Bulgaria.

**DUMA Didi**, b. 31 October 1936, Romania. Hydraulic Engineer. m. Maria, 1 daughter. Education: BSCE, Civil Engineering, 1965; PhD, Hydraulic Engineering, 1984. Appointments: Chief Researcher and Designer, Hydraulic Engineering Research Institute, Bucharest, Romania; Head, Computational Department, Institute for Research and Environmental Engineering, Bucharest, Romania; Senior Project Manager, Consoer Townsend Envirodyne Engineers, Chicago, USA, 1991-. Publications: Over 100 scientific papers in various professional magazines, 2 technical books on hydraulics. Honours: Romanian Academy Award, 1982. Memberships: American Society of Civil Engineers; American Water Resources Association. Address: Consoer Townsend Envirodyne, 303 East Wacker Drive, Ste 600, Chicago, IL 60601, USA.

**DUMAS Charles**, b. 9 July 1945, USA. Associate Professor; Writer; Actor; Director. m. Josephine, 2 sons, 2 daughters. Education: AA, 1974; BA, 1975; JD, Yale Law School, 1978. Appointments: Associate Professor, Pennsylvania State University; President, Hudson Legal Services; Researcher; President, Dumas Enterprises; Artistic Director, Loaves and Fish Company. Honours include: NAACP Best Actor; Earl Warren Fellow, Yale Law School; Emmy Award. Memberships: yale Club; AEA; SAG; AFTRA; Writers Club; Dramatist Guild. Address: Pennsylvania State University, School of Theatre Arts, State College, PA 16801, USA.

**DUMITRU Spiridon**, b. 28 September 1942, Brasov, Romania. Professor of Physics. m. Aurelia Dumitru, 1 son, 1 daughter. Education: Faculty of Physics, Babes-Bolyai University of Cluj, 1960-65; Licentiate, Theoretical Physics, 1965; PhD, University of Craiova, 1976. Appointments: Physicist, Solid State Physics Laboratory, Faculty of Physics, Babes-Bolyai University of Cluj, 1965-68; Assistant, 1968-78, Lecturer of Physics, 1978-92, Department of Physics, University of Brasov; Professor of Physics, Department of Physics, Transilvania University of Brasov, 1992-. Publications: Books: Microphysics - Solved Problems/Exercises and a Critical Examination of the Question of Uncertainty Relations Significance, 1984; Numerous articles in professional journals. Honours: Prize, Dragomir HURMUZESCU, Romanian Academy, 1995. Memberships: Romanian Physical Society; European Physical Society. Address: University Transilvania Din Brasov, Faculty of Mechanical Engineering Technology, B dul Eroilor 29, 2200 Brasov, Romania.

**DUNAEVSKY Oleg**, b. 18 February 1928, Belyi, Russia. m. Ludmila Ossadchaya, 2 daughters. Education: Graduate, Leningrad Medical Institute, 1955; Dissertation for Master Degree, 1963; Dissertation for Doctor Degree, 1969; Title of Professor, 1974. Appointments: Physician, Leningrad Hospital of Infectious Diseases, 1957-62; Assistant, Department of Infectious Diseases, Leningrad Institute of Advanced Studies for Doctors, 1962-68; Rector, Kalinin State Medical Institute, 1974-87; Head, Department of Infectious Diseases and Epidemiology, Tver Medical Academy, 1968-. Publications: Differential Diagnostics of Jaundice, 1977; Pecularities in the Course of Infectious Diseases in Elderly and Old Persons, Co-author, 1982; Differential Diagnostics of Liver Diseases, 1985; Viral Hepatitis and Differential Diagnostics of Liver Diseases, 1993; HIV-Infections, 1995; Guidance to Internal Diseases; Infectious Disesase, Co-author, 1996; Differential Diagnostics of Major Infectious Diseases Characterized with Retching, Diarrhoea and Stomachaches, Co-author, 1997. Honours: Order of Honour, Znak Pochiota, 1976; Golden Medal, German Democractic Republic Government, 1982; Order of Red Labour Banner, 1986; State Order of Friendship of Russian Federation, 1998; Distinguished Scientist of Russia, 1992. Memberships: Chairman, Oblast Region Association of Physicians Infectious Diseases, Editorial Body Epidemiology and Infectious Diseases Journal; Chairman, Tver Department of Russian Children Fund; Member, International Academy of Informatization; Corresponding Member, Russian Academy of Medicine; Member, Order of International Fellowship. Address: Ploschad Square Slavy, Dom 1, kv 148, 170000 Tver, Russia.

**DUNBAR Gary Leo,** b. 5 February 1949, Cadillac, Michigan, USA. University Professor. m. Deborah S Dunbar, 1 son, 1 daughter. Education: BA, 1971, BS, 1975, Eckerd College; MA, 1976, MS, 1977, Central Michigan University; PhD, 1988, Clark University. Appointments: Director, Brain Research Laboratory, 1988-; Professor, Department of Psychology, 1995-, Central Michigan University; Director, Graduate Programmes in Experimental Psychology, CMU, 1995-. Publications: Over 100 published articles, abstracts, book chapters; 1 book: Psychology & Human Behaviour. Honour: 1997 Michigan Professor of the Year, Carnegie Foundation for Advancement of Teaching and Council for the Advancement and Support of Education. Memberships: Society for Neuroscience, President elect for Michigan Chapter; Faculty for Undergraduate Neuroscience, President 1994-95. Address: 3314 Saratoga Springs Drive, Mount Pleasant, MI 48858-9696, USA.

**DUNGAN John Russell (Duggan),** b. 31 October 1927, Cambridge, Massachusetts, USA. Lawyer, Corporate Director, Chief Financial Officer. m. Nancy Beaton, 3 sons, 3 daughters. Education: AB, Harvard College, 1950; LLB, Suffolk University, 1954; MMP, Harvard Business School, 1957; LLM, Boston University, 1963; BS, Bentley College, 1964; JD, Suffolk Law School, 1968. Appointments: President, Boston Television and Appliance Co, 1950-54; Corporate Director, Secretary, Corporate Counsel, Treasurer, Acushnet Company, 1966-80; Director of Treasury Services, General Cinema Corporation, 1980-83; Vice President of Finance, Omni Resources Corp, 1983-; Retired. Honours: 11th Earl of Lymerick; 11th Viscount Dungan of Clane; 11th Baron Dungan of Castletown; 61st High King of Ara, Coonagh; HIgh Chief of the Name and Clan; Hereditary Lord of the Manor of Castletown; Knight of the Golden Chain. Memberships: Harvard Club of Boston, 1950; Harvard Varsity Club, 1950; Kittansett Club, 1966; President, New Bedford Chamber of Commerce, 1977-78; Director, 1967-1980; President, New Bedford Taxpayers Association, 1977-79; Chairman, United Way of Greater New Bedford; Library and Parish Trustee. Address: 923 North Elm Avenue, Hastings, NE 68901, USA.

**DUNGAN John Russell Jr, (Viscount Dungan of Clane, Prince of Ara),** b. 12 December 1953, Boston, Massachusetts, USA. Physician; Consultant Anaesthesiologist. m. Nancy Elizabeth Perkins-Dungan, div, 1 son, 2 daughters. Education:

AB magna cum laude, 1977, Harvard College; EdM, 19 Harvard University; DDS, 1984, Baylor University; MD ( laude, 1989, Creighton University. Appointments: Instruc Anaesthesiology, Boston University School of Medic 1986-89; Attending Anaesthesiologist, Boston City Hosp 1986-89; Chief of Anaesthesia, Tobey Hospital, Wareh Massachusetts, 1989-91; Chief Anaesthesia, 1991-, Chie Surgery, 1995, Mary Lanning Hospital, Hastings, Nebra; President, Hastings Anaesthesiology Associates, 19' Publications: 5 books and journal articles. Honours: John E Scholar, 1967; Cum Laude Society, Tabor chapter, 19 National Merit Scholar, 1971; International Fe English-speaking Union, 1971-72; John Harvard Scholar, 19 1977; Harvard College Scholar, 1976; Phi Beta Kappa Harvard College, 1976; 12th Viscount Dungan of Clane 62nd hereditary Ptince of Ara, High King of Ara and Chief of Name and Clan; Hereditary Head and Commander, Mili Order of the Knights of Leinster; Hereditary Knight of Golden Chain; Kentucky Colonel, Honorable Order of Kentu Colonels, 1985, 1990; Acting Chief and President, the ( Dungan, 1998-. Memberships: National Board Anaesthesiology; American Society of Anaesthesiolog Nebraska Society of Anaesthesiologists; and others. Addre Heartwell Park, 923 N Elm Avenue, Hastings, NE 68901-4( USA.

**DUNLAP John Daniel III,** b. 5 February 1959, Cass C Michigan, USA. Environmental Protection. m. Jane Marg; Austin, 1 son, 2 daughters. Education: BA, Political Scien University of Redlands, 1981; Masters of Public Policy Environmental Policy, Claremont Graduate School, 19 Appointments: Public Advisor, South Coast Air Qu Management District, 1989-93; Chief Deputy Direc Department of Toxic Substances Control, 1993-94; Chairn California Air Resources Board, 1994-. Publications: W Regulators Need Now to Go with Sound Science: The Skill the Anthropolotist, the Economist and the Diplomat - and Mind Set of the Entrepreneur, 1997. Honour: Alumni Ca Achievement Award, University of Redlands, 19 Memberships: Chairman, Troop Committee, Boy Scout America, Alta Loma & Auburn, California, 1994 Commonwealth Club. Address: PO Box 2815, Sacramento, 95812, USA.

**DUNMORE John,** b. 6 August 1923, Trouville, Fran University Professor. m. Joyce Megan Langley, 22 April 19 1 son, 1 daughter. Education: BA (Hons), London, 1950; P New Zealand, 1962; Publications: French Explorers in Pacific, 1966-69; The Fateful Voyage of the St Jean Bapti 1969; Norman Kirk: A Portrait, 1972; Pacific Explorer, 19 New Zealand and the French, 1990; The French and Maoris, 1992; Who's Who in Pacific Navigation, 1992; Journal of La Perouse, 1994-95. Publications: Numer learned journals and periodicals. Honours: New Zealand B of the Year, 1970; Legion of Honour, 1976; Academic Pai 1986; New Zealand Commemoration Medal, 1990; Mas Medal, 1993. Membership: Australasian Language Literature Association, President, 1980-82. Address: Pounamu Avenue, Greenhithe, Auckland, New Zealand.

**DUPAGNE Nestor,** b. 29 June 1922, Tillier, Belgi Gynaecologist. m. Lucy Chatelain, 2 sons. Education: Mec Doctor, 1948; Licence in Dental Sciences, 1949; C Resident, 1958, Woman's Hospital, New York. Appointme Attending Gynaecologist, Brussels ParcLeopold Cl Memberships: Fellow, American College of Surgeons; N York Academy of Sciences. Address: 15 rue du Village, 1 Chastre, Belgium.

**DURANI NACK Clair,** Artist; Writer; Business Woman. m. Prince Durani. Education: New York University. Appointments: President, Founder, Owner, The Claire Durani Nack Corporation & Subsiduaries, The Durani Company, The CDN Company, Princess Enterprises Company, The Book Companies of CDN. Publications: Various French, British and American publications. Membership: Library of Congress, Washington, DC. Address: 416 East Street, Rensselaer, NY 12144, USA.

**DURLABHJI Yogendra,** b. 7 April 1950, Jaipur, India. Managing Partner. m. Nirmala Durlabhji, 2 daughters. Education: BA Honours, History, MA, History, St Stephen's College, Delhi University, 1967-72; MA, International Relations, California State University Graduate School, San Jose, 1972-73; Advanced Diploma in Educational Studies, Churchill College, University of Cambridge, 1978-79; Associateship, Institute of Education, University of London, 1979-80. Appointments: Teacher, History, English, Mathematics, Master-in-charge of Tennis, The Doon School, Dehradun, Uttar Pradesh, 1974-75; Teacher, History, English, Master-in-charge of Basketball, Mayo College, Ajmer, Raj, 1977; Currently Managing Partner, M/s K S Durlabhji, gems and jewellery, Jaipur. Honours: Kishan Prashad Memorial Prize, 1970, Vice-President, Games and Sports, 1971-72, David Raja Ram Prize, Katy Man of the Year, Special Citation for Academic and Sports Achievements by College Principal, St Stephen's College, 1972; St Stephen's College Squash Colours, Delhi University Squash Colours, Blazer, Gold Medal for Outstanding Performance; Cambridge University Squash Colours; Sportsman of the Year, Churchill College, 1977-78. Memberships: CII National Sports Committee; CII National Committee on Education and Literacy; The Belvedere, Oberoi; Chambers, Taj; President, Wodehouse Society, St Stephen's College; Life Member: Ashok, Jai and Jaipur Clubs; Cricket Club of India; Rajasthan Polo Club; Oxford and Cambridge Society of India; Founder Member: The Almost Wimbledon Club, Jaipur; Stephanians in Rajasthan; President, Rajasthan Squash Rackets Association; Chairman: Confederation of Indian Industry, Rajasthan State Council; Durlabhji Environment Friendly Trust; Sanskar; Honorary Member: International Lawn Tennis Club of India; Trustee: Durlabhji Trust for Development; Santokba Durlabhji Memorial Trust. Address: Emerald House, D-31 Subhash Marg, C-Scheme, Jaipur 302 001, Rajasthan, India.

**DUTTA Nilima,** b. 28 February 1934, Calcutta, India. M. Mr Nirmal Dutta, 1 son. Education: Government College of Arts & Crafts, University of Calcutta, 1954; MA, University of Calcutta, 1957. Appointments: Art Teacher, Brahmo Girls Schoo, 1957-94. Honours: Outstanding Contribution to Indian Art. Memberships: Academy of Fine Arts, Calcutta; All India Fine Arts and Crafts Society; Birla Academy of Arts and Culture. Address: Plot 217, A Block, Bangur Avenue, Calcutta 700055, India.

**DUYCK Kathleen Marie,** b. 21 July 1933, Portland, Oregon, USA. Musician; Poet; Social Worker. m. Robert Duyck, 2 sons, 1 daughter. Education: Diploma, St Marys Academy, 1950; BS, Home Economics, Oregon State College, 1954; MSW, University of Washington, 1956. Career: Principal Cellist, Phoenix College Orchestra & Scottsdale Symphony; Adoption Worker; Poet. Publications: Poems in anthologies. Honours: Several Editors Choice Awards, NLP of USA. Memberships: Arizona Cello Society; International Society of Poets. Address: 4545 East Palomino Road, Phoenix, AZ 85018, USA.

**DVARECKAS Vytautas,** b. 20 September 1928, Lithuania. Professor of Geography. m. Daniele, 1 son, 1 daughter, dec'd.

Education: Vilnius University, 1953; Professor, 1991. Appointments: Teacher, 1947-48; Manager, Weather Forecasting Department, Vilnius Hydrometeorology Station, 1956-57. Honour: Lithuania State Award Laureate. Memberships: Chair, UNESCO; Chair, Council of Science Dissertations. Address: P Vileisio 13-21, Vilnius, Lithuania.

**DWIJEN Dwijendra Nath Banerjee,** b. 10 November 1950, Dinajpur, Bangladesh. Teacher. m. Minakshi Banerjee, 3 sons. Education: Kavyatirtha, 1972; MA, 1975; B Ed, 1978; LLB, 1983. Appointments: Assistant Teacher, Rajshani Collegiate School, Bangladesh. Publications: Sanchita Sanglap, 1993; Santan Dharma Shiksha, 1995; Sanchita Sanglap Volume II, 1998; Magazine, Unmes, Moni-Mukta. Honours: Best Teacher of the National Educational Week, 1995. Memberships: Founder, President, The Varendra Shishu Theatre, Rajshahi; Adviser, The Unmas Shilpi Gusthi, Rajshahi; Adviser, The Padma Kalir Mala, Rajshahi; Dramatist and director of the theatre. Address: Rajshahi Collegiate School, Dist Rajshahi, Bangladesh.

**DWIVEDI Dinesh Chandra,** b. 20 September 1951, Surat, India. Deputy General Manager. m. Shailja, 1 son, 1 daughter. Education: BE, Electrical Engineering, Birla Institute of Technology and Science, 1972. Appointments: Engineer Trainee, J K Synthetics, 1972-73; Management Trainee, 1973-74; Assistant Engineer, 1974-78; Engineer, Africa Synthetic Fibres, 1978-80; Senior Engineer, 1980-82; Superintendent Electrical Engineer, J K Synthetics, 1982-84; Assistant Manager, 1984-87; Deputy Manager, 1987-90; Project Manager, Jaykeytech, 1990; Senior Manager, 1990-95; Assistant General Manager, 1995-97; Deputy General Manager, 1997-. Address: c/o PT Indorama Synthetics Tbk, P O Box 2, Purwakarta 41110, West Java, Indonesia.

**DWIVEDI Suresh Chandra,** b. 1 January 1952, Ballia, India. Professor of English and American Literature. m. Smt Prabha Dwivedi, 1 son, 2 daughters. Education: BA, 1967, Gorakhpur University; MAEng, 1969, PhD, 1976, Vidyapith; DLitt, 1988, California, USA. Appointments: UGC Fellow, MG Kashi Vidyapith, 1969-72; Lecturer in English, A D College, 1972-84; Shri Aurobindo College, Delhi University, 1975-76; Reader, Allahabad University, 1985-98, Director, 1998-. Publications: The Poetry of Robert Frost, 1978; Twentieth Century American Poetry, 1985; Perspectives on Nissim Ezekiel, 1988. Honours: Rahul Award, 1986; Grierson Award, 1990; Bhogpuri Shirouani, 1998. Memberships: Director, National Service Scheme; Life member, ASRC, Hyderabad; Literary Criterion, Indian Association of American & English Literature; and others. Address: Dept of English, University of Allabahd, Ilahabad UP, India.

**DYMNIKOVA Irina,** b. 21 May 1943, Russia. Physicist. 1 son, 1 daughter. Education: MSc, Hons, Elementary Particle Theory, Leningrad University, 1966; PhD, Theoretical and Mathematical Physics, Estonia, 1978; Doctor Habilitatis, Theoretical Physics, Warsaw University, 1992. Appointments: Research Worker, A J Ioffe Physico Technical Institute, Leningrad, 1966-88; N Copernicus Astromical Center, Warsaw, 1990-96; Professor of Physics, Institute of Mathematics and Physics, University of Olsztyn, Poland. Publications: Nonsingular Cosmology with the Initial de Sitter Stage, 1975; Nonsingular Black Hole, 1990. Honours: Award, Gravity Research Foundation. Memberships: International Society on General Relativity and Gravitation; New York Academy of Sciences; National Geographic Society; The Planetary Society. Address: Inst of Maths and Physics, Zolnierska 14, 10-561 Olsztyn, Poland.

**DYR Wanda,** b. Sadoles, Poland. m. 2 sons. Education: Master Biology, 1980; PhD, 1989, Medical Academy, Warsaw. Appointments: Senior Lecturer, Medical Academy, Warsaw, 1980-89; Adjunct, Institute of Psychology and Neurology, Warsaw, 1989-91; Visiting Scientist, Institute of Psychological Research, Indianapolis, 1991-92. Honour: Postdoctoral Grant, Kosciuszko Foundation, New York, 1991. Memberships: European Society Biomedical Research Alcoholism; International Biomedical Research Alcoholism; European Behavioural Pharmacology Society. Address: Institute of Psychiatry and Neurology, Al Sobieskiego 1/9, 02-957 Warsaw, Poland.

**DZEMESHKEVICH Sergei,** b. 19 February 1950, Baku, Azerbaidjan. Cardiosurgeon. m. Valentina Dadichkina, 1 son, 1 daughter. Education: MD, Moscow Medical University, 1973; PhD in Medicine, 1976; DSc in Medicine, 1984; Qualifed as Professor of Surgery, 1993. Appointments: Research Fellow, 1876-85, Head, Division of Artificial Organs, 1985-88, Head, Department of Heart Surgery, Deputy Director, 1988-98, Research Centre of Surgery, Moscow; Professor, Department of Cardiovascular Surgery, Cardiology Research Centre, Moscow, 1998-. Publications: Author, 250 articles and 4 books in cardiosurgery and transplantology. Honours: Winner, USSR State Award, 1984; Award, International Society of Cardiothoracic Surgery, 1996; Award, International Society of Artificial Organs, 1997. Memberships: International College of Surgeons; International Society of Artificial Organs; International Society of Cardiothoracic Surgery; New York Academy of Sciences; Russian Society of Cardiovascular Surgery. Address: Leninsky Str 123-1-163, 117513 Moscow, Russia.

**DZHANAKHMEDOV Akhad,** b. 23 November 1946, Baku, Azerbaijan. Scientist. m. Sima, 2 sons. Education: Diploma in Mechanics, 1969; PhD, 1973; Research Fellow, Brunel University, UK, 1975-76; DSc, 1989; Professor, 1990; Academician, 1997. Appointments: Lecturer, 1973-79; Associate Professor, 1979-89; Head of Department, Professor, 1990. Publications: 150 papers including monographbook, textbook and patents; Author, Thermo-Mechanical Theory of Wear. Memberships: Editorial Board, Scientific Journal, Friction and Wear, 1994; Vice President, Engineering Charity Society. Address: Azer State Oil Academy, Azadlig Avenue 20, 370010 Baku, Azerbaijan Republic.

**DZHEPAROV Fridrikh,** b. 3 January 1947, Samarkand. Physicist. m. Ignatyuk Tatiana, 1 daughter. Education: Physics Department, Moscow State University, 1970; Postgraduate Course, 1975; PhD, 1976; DSc, 1991. Appointments: Junior Research Staff, 1975; Senior Research Staff, 1982; Leading Research Staff, 1991; Chief of Laboratory of Neutron Physics, 1997. Publications: More than 100 scientific articles on statistical physics spin dynamics, neutron physics, beta-NMR and NMR. Honours: 5 awards of annual ITEP scientific competitions; Medal on 850 years of Moscow. Memberships: Scientific Counsel of Institute of Theoretical and Experimental Physics; Scientific Counsel on Magnetism of Russian Academy of Science; Scientific Counsel Nuclear Methods for Investigations of Condensed Media of Russian Academy of Science. Address: Institute for Theoretical and Experimental Physics, B Cheremushkinskaya 25, Moscow 117259, Russia.

**DZIDONU Clement Kwaku,** b. 23 November 1955, Accra, Africa. Academic. 2 daughters. Education: Diploma, Distinction in Journalism, London School of Journalism, England, 1979-80; BSc, honours, Computer Science and Operations Research, University of Surrey, Guildford, England, 1980-83; PhD, Computer Science and Operations Research, Trinity College,

Dublin, Ireland, 1984-88. Appointments: Lecturer, Chief Examiner, School of Systems and Data Studies, University of Dublin, 1984-89, 1991-96, Senior Research Fellow, 1996-; Lecturer, Chief Examiner, Department of Industrial Engineering, National University of Ireland, 1989-91; Senior Lecturer, Department of Computer Science, National University of Science and Technology, Zimbabwe, 1996-98; Executive Director, International Center for Internet and Telecommunciation Technologies, Accra, Ghana, 1998-. Publications include: Simplified Illustrated Guide to Computer Hardware Jargon, 1994; Desktop Guide to Computer Software Processing and Applications Jargon, 1994; The Computer Jargon Book, 1994; Demystifying the Computer, 1994; Fundamentals of Computers and Computing, 1995; All You Need to Know About Computers, 1995; Emerging Electronic Messaging and Educational Technologies: A Technological Opportunity for Supporting EDE Among Geographically Spread Institutions, 1998. Memberships: Association of Professional Computer Consultants; Institution of Programmers & Analysts; British Computer Society; Irish Computer Society; Institute of Industrial Engineers; European Institute of Industrial Engineers; Operational Research Society; Institute of Statisticians; New York Academy of Sciences. Address: International Center for Internet and Telecommunication Technologies, PO Box AN 19782, Accra, Ghana.

**DZIOPAK Józef,** b. 24 August 1947, Hyżne, Poland. Educator. m. Elena Neverova-Dziopak, 4 daughters. Education: M in Tech, Civil Engineering, 1967, Rzeszów, Poland; MSc Engineering, 1972, PhD Engineering, 1983, Cracow University of Technology; DSc Engineering, 1993, Wroclaw University of Technology; Certificated Civil and Sanitary Engineering. Appointments: Vice Director, Institute Sanitary Engineering and Environmental Protection, Cracow, 1984-88; Head Division, Sanitary Engineering and Technical Infrastructure, Cracow, 1991-; Head Department, Water Supply and Sewage Systems, Czestochowa, Poland, 1994-98; Director, Institute Environmental Engineering, Czestochowa, 1997; Dean, Faculty Environmental Engineering and Protection, Czestochowa, 1997-99; Expert, Ministry Environmental Protection, Warsaw, 1993-. Publications: 2 monographs; Author 61, Co-author 65 publications; Author 6, co-author 11 patents; Author 30 and co-author 25 projects realised; Co-author 51 expert opinions. Honours: Testimonial Award, World Exhibition Achievements, Plovdiv, 1985; Special Award, Science Progress Centre, Katowice, 1985; Collective Award, Impex XIII, Pittsburgh, 1997; Special Merit Award, 2nd Messe Kansai, Osaka, 1997; Award of Excellence, Golden Key Award, London International Inventions Fair, London, 1997; Award for the 1st Category of International Water Supply Symposium, Tokyo, 1998. Memberships: International Academy of Ecology and Life Protection Sciences, St Petersburg, Russia; International Network of Engineers and Scientists for Global Responsibility, Germany; Section of Sanitary Engineering, Polish Academy of Sciences, Warsaw; Polish Geothermal Association, Cracow. Address: ul Juliusza Lea 244/8, 30-133 Krakow, Poland.

# E

**EBISIKE Eze,** b. 19 February 1937, Owerri Imo State. Management Consultant; Author. m. Mercy Obodotie, 3 sons. Education: Philosophy, 1963-66; Theology, 1967-70; Print, Electronic Journalism; BA Hons, 1966; Diplomas in Theology, 1970, in Mass Media, 1972; Management Consultancy and Achievement Mot Orientation; Diplomas in Management Consultancy, 1983, in n-Ach Orientation, 1981. Appointments: Catholic Priest Curate and Parish Priest, Imo State, 1970-71; Catholic Priest, Religious Broadcaster, Journalist, PR with CSN, Lagos, 1972-76; Resigned from Priesthood; Sub-Editor, Lagos Shopping News Magazine, 1978; Management Consultancy, 1980-98. Publications: 18 books; Editor, 7 books, 1970-98. Memberships: Okponkwume Progressive Union; Lagos Country Club, Ikeja, Lagos, Nigeria. Address: Upman Ltd, 360 Herbert Macaulay Street, Yaba PMB 1181, Yaba Lagos, Nigeria.

**EBO Antona,** b. 10 April 1924, Bloomington, Illinois, USA. Franciscan Sister of Mary. Education: BS, Medical Records Administration, St Louis University, 1962; MHA Hospital Executive Development, St Louis University, 1970; MTh, Aquinal Institute of Theology, 1978. Appointments: Franciscan Sister of Mary, St Louis, 1946-; Executive Director, St Clare Hospital, 1967-71; Assistant Executive Director, St Marys Hospital Medical Centre, 1970-74; Executive Director, Wisconsin Catholic Health Association, 1974-76; Chaplain, St Marys Hospital Medical Centre, 1978-81; Voulunteer Chaplain, University of Mississippi Medical Centre, 1981-87; Councilor General, St Louis, 1987-91; Pastoral Associate, St Nicholas Catholic Church, 1992-. Honours: Featured in Catfish and Crystal; Ebony Magazine; Liguori Magazine; Certificate of Commendation; Elected Delegate National Black Catholic Congress; Harriet Tubman Award; Honourary Doctorate; LHD, Loyola University Memberships: Human Rights Commission; National Black Sisters Conference; Madison Housing Authority Commissioner; Many other memberships. Address: St Nicholas Church, 701 N Eighteenth St, St Louis, MO 63103, USA.

**ECHAURREN Juan Carlos,** b. 21 July 1966, Santiago, Chile. Researcher. Education: Instrumentation and Automatization University Technician, 1988; Post-grade in Systems Civil Engineer, Mariscal Sucrie University, 1994-97. Appointments: Research, Electronic Technician,Specialized Equipment. Publications: Radio Transmission and its Application to the AutomaticControl; Polynomic Structure for MassDistribution in Horizontal and Vertical Environment Through of Physics Mathematical Model; Exact Solutions of Polynomial order for the equations of Schröedinger and Wheeler-DeWitt through the use of methods in Laplace's Transformables. Memberships: AAPT; APS; Planetary Society; National Geographic Society. Address: Rupanco 7-H, Poblacion, Los Lagos,Chuquicamata Segunda Region, Chile.

**ECHU Ibrahim,** b. 11 May 1964, Kogi State, Nigeria. Training and Research Officer. m. Education: BA (Hons) Theatre Arts, 1990, University of Jos; MSc Political Economy and Development Studies, 1997. Appointments: Public Relations Officer, 1994-97, Training and Research Officer, 1997-, Public Relations Department, Industrial Training Fund Headquarters. Publications: 77 articles in The Herald, New Horizon and others; 6 papers presented at postgraduate school, Unijos, 1993-94. Honours: 1st Prize, UNESCO National Essay Competition at Tertiary level, 1989; 2nd Prize, Voice of Nigeria (VON) National Essay Competition, 1993. Address: c/o PO Box 73, Ejule, Kogi State, Nigeria.

**EDDLEMAN George David,** b. 20 August 1936, Winston-Salem, North Carolina, USA. Composer; Arranger. m. Miriam Yanes Eddleman. Education: Appalachian State University, 1958; BSc, Virginia Commonwealth University, 1964; MMus, Boston University, 1971; Dr of Musical Arts. Appointments: Music Teacher, Groves High School, Savannah, Georgia, 1959-60; Director, Third Army Chorus, Ft McPherson, Georgia, USA, 1960-62; Music Teacher, La Fayette Junior School, 1982-98; Guest Lecturer, New York City Opera, 1985-89; Senior Editor, Silver Burdett Ginn, 1972-96; Adjunct Professor, College of St Elizabeth, Morristown, New Jersey, USA, 1977-; Lecturer, Chautaugul Institution, 1994-. More than 350 publications including Kolot Min Hashorah, 1995. Address: 12 James Court, Rockaway, NJ 07866-3048, USA.

**EDMOND Lauris Dorothy,** b. 2 April 1924, Dannevirke, New Zealand. Writer. m. Trevor, 1 son, 5 daughters. Education: Trained Teachers Certificate, 1943; Speech Therapy Diploma, 1944; BA, Waikato University, 1968; MA, Hons, Victoria University. Appointments: Teacher, English, French, Senior Classes, Huntly College, Heretaunga College, 1968-72; Regional Tutor, Massey University, 1980-94; Creative Writing Courses; Workshops; Continuing Education Classes, Polytechnics, Summer Schools; Literary Groups. Publications: Many Books, Poetry, Drama, Fiction. Honours: PEN NZ Best First Book, 1975; Commonwealth Poetry Prize, 1985; OBE, For Services to Poetry and Literature, 1986; Lilian Ida Smith Award for Poetry, 1987; Mobil Radio Award, For Best Dramatic Production, 1987; Honorary DLitt, Massey University, New Zealand, 1988; Scholarship in Letters, 1990; Short Listed for National Book Awards, 1992, 1996; Lifetime Achievement Award, 1999. Memberships: Katherine Mansfield Memorial Fellowship; 1981. Address: 22 Grass St, Oriental Bay, Wellington, New Zealand.

**EDSALL David,** b. 12 January 1954, Flint, Michigan, USA. Counsellor. Education: Fundamentals of Hebrew and Greek, Flint Bible Institute. Appointments: Administrative Assistant, Yeshua the Messiah Government; Coequal Member, Council of All Apostles. Publications: The Vision Document; The Vote Book; The Enigma, III Volumes. Memberships: The Christian Council. Address: The Christian Council, P O Box 372, Flint, MI 48501-0172, USA.

**EDWARDS Vanessa Adele,** b. 17 December 1965, Port Macquarie, Australia. Author. Education: BA, 1990; Master of Letters, 1993; MA Hons, 1997; JP, 1998. Publications: Narcissistic Neurotics, 1993; The Space Between, 1997; Various contributions to professional journals. Memberships: Association for the Study of Australia; Associate, Centre for Australian Literature and Language Studies; NSW Women Justices' Association. Address: PO Box 12, 2444 Port Macquarie, Australia.

**EDWARDS William J,** b. 18 May 1962, USA. Public Defender. Education: BA, Loyola College, 1985; JD, Western State University College of Law, San Diego, 1991. Appointments: Certified Law Clerk, Office of the Public Defender, San Diego, 1989-90; Certified Law Clerk, Sheela & Sheela, San Diego, 1990-91; Certified Law Clerk, Office of the Public Defender, San Bernardino, 1991; Attorney, Law Clerk, 1991-95, Deputy Public Defender, 1995-, Office of the Public Defender, Riverside County. Publications: Numerous articles in professional journals. Honours: Professional of the Year, Association of Retarded Citizens of California, 1996. Memberships: State Bar of California; American Bar Association; National Association of Criminal Defense Lawyers; California Public Defender Association; California Attorneys for Criminal Justice; American Association on Mental Retardation.

Address: Office of the Public Defender, 46209 Oasis Street, Suite 314, Indio, CA 92201-5963, USA.

**EFROS Alexei,** b. 11 August 1938, Saint Petersburg, Russia. Physicist. m. Irina, 2 sons. Education: PhD, Ioffe Institute of Russia, 1962; Doctor of Science Degree, 1972. Appointments: Chief Scientist, Ioffe Institute; Distinguished Professor of Physics, University of Utah. Publications: About 100 papers; 2 books. Honours: Landau Award; Humboldt Award. Memberships: American Physics Society. Address: Dept of Physics, University of Utah, Salt Lake City, UT 84112, USA.

**EFROS Victor,** b. 11 June 1942, Russia. Physicist. m. Ninel Pushkina, 1 son. Education: MSc, Moscow State University, 1966; PhD, Kurchatov Institute, Moscow, Russia, 1974; DSc, 1987. Appointments: Junior Scientist, Kurchatov Institute, Moscow, 1967-74; Senior Scientist, 1974-89; Head Scientist, 1989-. Publications: 90 Articles in Professional Journals. Honours: Kurchatov Prizes, 1973, 1990; Nomination, Man of the Year, American Biographical Institute, USA. Address: Russian Research Centre 'Kurchatov Institute', 123182 Moscow, Russia.

**EGENHOFER Max J,** b. 9 October, Friedrichshafen, Germany. Professor. m. Stefanie M Egenhofer, 1 son, 1 daughter. Education: Dipl Ing, Surveying Engineering, 1985, Stuttgart University, Germany; PhD Surveying Engineering, 1989, University of Maine. Appointments: Graduate Research Assistant, Institute of Geodesy and Photogrammetry, Swiss Federal Institute of Technology, 1982-83; Graduate Research Assistant, 1983-84, Research Assistant, 1985, Institute for the Applications of Geodesy in Constructions, University of Stuttgart; Graduate Research Assistant to Research Assistant Professor in Surveying Engineering, 1985-92, Cooperating Assistant Professor, 1991-94, Cooperating Associate Professor, 1994-, in Computer Science, Assistant Professor in Surveying Engineering, 1992-94, Associate Director, 1993-96, Director, 1997-, National Centre for Geographic Information and Analysis, Associate Professor in Spatial Information Science and Engineering, 1994-, Libra Professor of the College of Engineering, 1998-, all at the University of Maine. Publications: 21 invited conference talks; Member 7 Editorial Boards; Book and article reviewer; Organiser of 14 conferences and workshops. Address: University of Maine National Centre of Geographic Information, Dept Spatial Information Science & Engineering, Boardman Hall, Orono, ME 04469-5711, USA.

**EGGERTSSON Thorsteinn,** b. 25 February 1942, Keflavik, Iceland. Author; Songwriter; Journalist. partner. Johanna Fjola Olafsdottir, 2 daughters. Education: Illustrator, Akademiet for Fri & Merkantil Kunst, Copenhagen, 1965; Teachers University of Iceland, 1982. Appointments: Journalist, Graphic Designer, Rock Singer, Author, Writer and Director of various musicals and night club shows; Songwriter, over 400 lyrics recorded. Honour: International Poetry Hall of Fame, 1997. Memberships: Scandinavian Association for Composers and Lyricists; STEF, Iceland; Icelandic Writers Union. Address: Skipholt 18, 105 Reykjavik, Iceland.

**EICHLER Margrit,** b. 28 September 1942, Berlin, Germany. Sociologist. m. Donald Payne, 1 son. Education: Universitaet Goettingen, 1963-65; Freie Universitaet, Berlin, 1965-66; MA, 1968, PhD, 1972, Sociology, Duke University. Appointments: Lecturer, 1971, Assistant Professor, 1972-75, Adjunct Professor, 1975-77, Department of Sociology, University of Waterloo; Associate Professor, 1975-80, Professor, 1980-, Department of Sociology, Ontario Institute for Studies in Education; Appointed to Department of Educational Theory,

1975-, Cross-appointed to Department of Sociology, 1981-, Cross-appointed to University College, 1997-, University of Toronto; Director, Institute for Gender Studies and Women's Studies, University of Toronto, 1999-; Visiting Scholar, Canadian Research Institute on Law and the Family, University of Calgary, 1990-91; Nancy Rowell Jackman Chair in Women's Studies, Mount Saint Vincent University, 1992-93. Publications: 18 books and monographs; 62 book chapters and bibliographies; 47 articles in refereed journals and encyclopedias; 23 technical reports, conference proceedings; 22 book reviews, magazine/newspaper articles; Over 200 paper presentations. Honours: Elected FRCS, 1994; Distinguished Visiting Professor, University of Alberta, 1985; LLD h.c. Brock University, 1991; Outstanding Contribution Award of the Canadian Sociology and Anthropology Association, 1996; Various student awards. Memberships: in 20 editorial and other boards and in associational functions; Addiction Research Foundation; American Sociological Association; Association of Universities and Colleges in Canada; Canadian Research Institute for Advancement of Women; Canadian Sociology and Anthropology Association; Ontario Law Reform Commission; Royal Society of Canada SIRCH; Social Science Federation of Canada; Social Sciences and Humanities Research Council; and others. Address: Ontario Institute for Studies in Education at the University of Toronto, 252 Bloor Street W, Toronto, Ont M5S 1V6, Canada

**EICHOLZ Marti,** b. 10 December 1939, Indiana, USA. Administrator; Author. m. Robert Edgar, 2 sons. Education: BS Education, 1960; MS, Supervision and Administration, 1962; PhD, Educational Counselling, 1997. Appointments: Elementary School Teacher; Administrator; College Instructor; Radio Talk Show Host; Author; Founder, Executive Director Institute for Transformation LLC; President, CEO, MECA Profiles. Address: Institute of Transformation LLC, 550 Kirkland Way #405, Kirkland, WA 98033, USA.

**EIDUKAS Danielius,** b. 21 July 1932, Utena, Lithuania. Engineer. m. Laima. Education: Engineer, Kaunas University of Technology, 1957; PhD, 1963; Habil Doctor, 1970; Academician, 1976. Appointments: Senior Engineer, 1957-59; Head of Department, 1959-62; Scientific Secretary, 1964-88; KTU Professor, 1972; Professor, Chairman and Member of Habilitation and Study Committee, 1988-. Publications: 61 Scientific works, including 459 articles and theses, monographs, 27 manuals. Honours: National Science Award, 1973, 1995. Membership: Honorable member, Russian Academy of Metrology. Address: Avieciu 6-1, 3000 Kaunas, Lithuania.

**EISELIN Rolf,** b. 6 November 1925, Zurich, Switzerland. Architect; Artist. Education: Arch dipl, EPFZ; Reg Architect State of Illinois, USA and Switzerland. Appointments: Architect Skidmore, Owings & Merrill, Chicago; and other firms in New York, Boston, Paris, Zurich; Own practice at present; Individual exhibition, prints: San Francisco Museum of Modern Art; Group exhibitions, architecture: University Zurich; sculpture: Oakland Art Museum; painting: University of California; prints: US National Museum, Washington DC; Kunsthaus Zurich; photography: San Francisco Museum of Modern Art; Curator practice: Prints USA exhibition, world tour. Honours: Award for Outstanding Photography at national exhibition 'Photography USA', 1989; Medal of Honour, national exhibition of prints Jersey City Museum, USA; Represented in several collections. Memberships: Swiss Engineers and Architects Association; Swiss Painters, Sculptors and Architects Society; California Society of Printmakers, former president. Address: Rés La Côte 60, 1110 Morges, Switzerland.

**EISHINSKII Alexandr Moiseevich**, b. 1 October 1936, Dnepropetrovsk, Ukraine. Mathematician. Div. Education: Degrees, 1954, 1965. Appointments: Teacher of Mathematics; Science Research Worker. Membership: New York Academy of Sciences. Address: Serova 3, Apt 7, 32000 Dnepropetrovsk, Ukraine.

**EISSA Hany Mokhtar**, b. 10 June 1953, Damietta, Egypt. Professor. m. 2 sons. Education: BVSc, 1976, MVSc, 1980, Cairo University; Dr.Med.Vet, Germany, 1985. Career: Demonstrator, Theriogenology, 1977-80, Assistant Lecturer, 1980-85, Lecturer, 1985-90, Assistant Professor, 1990-95, Professor, 1995-, Cairo University. Publications: Over 35 original articles in professional journals. Honours: Prize, Academy of Technology and Sciences, Egypt, 1994, 1996; State Prize, 1996; OIE Meritorious Award, Paris, 1997. Memberships: Society for Theriogenology, USA; Egypt Veterinary Medicine Syndicate; Egypt Veterinary Medicine Association; Egypt Society of Animal Reproduction Fertility; Egypt Society of Experimental Surgery. Address: Department of Theriogenology, Faculty of Veterinary Medicine, Giza 12211, Egypt.

**EL BAZ Osama**, b. 2 January 1964, Cairo, Egypt. Manager. m. Fihaa Gamaledin Quarasham. Education: BS, Faculty of Science, Cairo, 1985; MS, Faculty of Science, Mansoura, Egypt, 1987; PhD, MBA, Marketing, 1999. Appointment: Chemist, Urology & Nephrology Center, Mansoura, 1986-89, Erfan Hospital, Jeddah, Saudi Arabia, 1989-92; Medical Representative, Saudi Health Service Co, Jeddah, Saudi Arabia, 1992-93; Laboratory Product Specialist, 1993-94, Product Manager, 1994-96, Managing Director, 1996-, Alash Trading Company. Address: Alash Trading Co, PO Box 116, Mansours 35511, Egypt.

**EL EBIARY Mustafa**, b. 15 August 1959, Alexandria. Physician. m. Isabel, 1 son. Education: BS, 1977; MD, 1982; PhD, 1993. Appointments: Internship, University of Alexandria Hospital, 1983-84; Residency, Pulmonary and Critical Care Medicine, 1984-88; Clinical and Research Fellow, University of Barcelona, 1988-90; Chief Researcher, 1990-, ICU Consultant, 1992-, Hospital Clinic, Barcelona; Associate Professor of Medicine, University of Barcelona, 1992-98; Pulmonary and Critical Care Consultant, Cl Remei, Barcelona, 1998-; Professor of Medicine, University of Barcelona, 1998-. Publications include: Legionella pneumonia requiring admission to ICU, 1997; Community-acquired pneumonia in the elderly: Clinical and nutritional aspects, 1997; Impact of invasive and non invasive quantitative culture sampling on outcome of ventilator-associated pneumonia: A pilot study, 1998. Honours: Several. Memberships: Sociedad Española de Neumologia y Cirugia Toracica; American Thoracic Society; Sociedad Española de Medicina Intensiva y Unidades Coronarias; New York Academy of Sciences; European Society of Intensive Care Medicine; American Association for the Advancement of Science; European Respiratory Society. Address: Av Barcelona 21, 2° 2a, 08750 Molins de Rei, Spain.

**EL ISSA Jiries Spiro**, b. 16 August 1948, Damascus, Syria. Banker. m. Hala El Deek, 1 son, 2 daughters. Education: AA, Bir Zeit University, Palestine, 1967; BA, Business Administration, 1969, MBA, 1978, American University of Beirut. Appointments: Finance Department, Royal Jordanian Airlines, Amman, 1969-; Investments Officer, Central Bank of Jordan, Amman, 1970-; Vice President, Credit, Citibank NA, Amman, 1975-; Senior Manager, Credit, Arab Bank PLC, Amman, 1983-. Membership: Rotary International. Address: Arab Bank, PO Box 950544, Amman 11195, Jordan.

**EL KHAMLICHI Abdeslam**, b. 16 March 1948, Al Hoceima. Neurosurgeon. m. El Fassi Jaouhara, 1 son, 2 daughters. Education: Medical School, Mohamed V University, Rabat, 1966-71; Internship and Training: Department of Internal Medicine, 1972, Department of Neuropsychiatry, 1972, Department of Neurosurgery, 1973-74, Department of General Surgery, 1975, University Hospital Centre of Rabat; Department of Neurosurgery, University Hospital of Rabat, 1975-76; Department of Neurosurgery, CHU Vaudois, Lausanne, 1976-77; Department of Neurosurgery, Hopital Neurologique, Lyon, France, 1977-78. Appointments: Assistant Professor, 1976-80, Associate Professor, 1980-84, Professor, 1984-, Neurosurgery, Medical School of Rabat; Head Department Neurosurgery, University Hospital Centre of Rabat, 1983-. Memberships: President, Hassan II Foundation for prevention and cure of Nervous System Diseases; President, Moroccan Society Neurosurgery; Moroccan Society Neurosciences/Neurological Sciences/Medical Sciences; President, Maghreban Federation of Neurosurgical Societies; PanAfrican Association Neurological Sciences; Congress of Neurological Surgeons; WHO Committee of Experts in Neurosurgery; New York Academy Sciences; Editor, Maroc Medical; Review Board, Acta Neurochirurgica; Review Board, Surgical Neurology; International Editorial Board, Neurosurgery; and others. Address: Hopital des Specialities, Dept Neurosurgery BP 6444, Rabat, Morocco.

**EL KHOLI Mohamed Bahgat**, b. 25 September 1942, Cairo, Egypt. National Research Center Professor. m. Moushira El Tabaa, 1 son, 1 daughter. Education: BSc, 1964, MSc, 1972, PhD, 1979. Appointment: General Manager, Arab Ceramic Company. Publications: Numerous scientific papers, international journals, 1980-. Membership: National Association of Advanced Technology of New Materials. Address: National Research Center, Department Ceramic, Cairo, El Doki, Egypt.

**EL MASRI Youssef M I**, b. 25 September 1944, Beirut, Lebanon. University Professor. m. Elsen Josine, 3 sons. Education: BS Physics, 1968; MS Physics, 1969; PhD Nuclear Physics, 1974, La plus distinction, University of Louvain, Belgium; Postgraduate, Nuclear Engineer, Radioprotection Pedagogy. Appointments: Research Fellow and University Assistant, 1969-74; Research Associate, 1975-78; Research Group Senior, 1979; Research Group Leader, 1988; Lecturer, University of Louvain, 1988-93; Professor in Nuclear Physics, University of Louvain, 1993; Invited Scientist or Professor at: Jülich, Germany; Lawrence Berkeley Laboratory, USA; IISNR Center, Grenoble, France; Cyclotron Institute of Texas A&M University, USA. Publications: 75 international publications in PRL, PR and other journals; 58 communications at international NP conferences. Honour: Honorary Rank of Commander de l'ordre de la Couronne, awarded by Albert II, King of Belgium, 1997. Memberships: Belgian Physical Society; European Physical Society. Address: Institute of Nuclear Physics, University of Louvain, Chem du Cyclotron 2, B-1348 Louvain-La-Neuve, Belgium.

**EL-MALLAWANY Raouf**, b. 28 May 1951, Pont Said, Egypt. Professor. m. Hoda Abo El-Ghait, 1 son, 1 daughter. Education: BSc, Physics, Alexandria University, 1973; MSc, Physics, 1978; PhD, Menofia University, 1986. Appointments: Professor of Physics, Faculty of Science, Menofia University, Egypt. Publications: Over 50 International Articles on the Physical Properties of the New Non-Crystalline Solids 'Tellusite Glasses'. Honours: Egyptian State Award. Memberships: Materials Research Society; Arab Materials Science Society. Address: University Accomadation Building No 9, Somoha 21615, Alexandria, Egypt.

**EL-MELEIGI Mohamed,** b. 13 May 1947, Egypt. Professor. m. Zakia M Hassan. Education: BSc, 1959, MSc, 1972, PhD, 1978, North Dakota State University. Appointments: Research Associate, 1978, Assistant Professor, 1982, Associate Professor, 1984, Head of Department, 1984-, Professor, 1988. Publications: Over 50 in professional journals and books. Honour: First Grade of Honour and Helaly Award, 1969. Membership: American Phytopathological Society. Address: College of Agricultural Plant Protection, PO Box 1482, Burydah, Saudi Arabia.

**EL-SHERIF Mahmoud A,** b. 7 July 1942, Cairo. Electrical Engineering Educator. m. Jeylan Talaat, 1 son, 2 daughter. Education: BSc in Comm Engineering, Cairo University, 1966; Diploma in Electronic Engineering, Alexandra University, Egypt, 1977; MSc in Elecetro Physics, 1980; MSEE, University Pennsylvania, 1983; PhD, Electrical Engineering, Drexel University, 1987. Appointments: Engineer, Egyptian Telecom Organisation, Cairo, 1966-67; Radar Instructor, Air Defence Institute, Alexandria, 1967-77; Chairman, Radar Department, 1977-81; Dean Engineering, Air Defence College, Alexandria, 1987-89; Research Professor, Drexel University, Philadelphia, 1989-94; Director, Founder, Fiber Optics and Photonics Lab, 1994-. Honours: 1st Class Medal of Distinguished Performance, President of Egypt, 1971; Medal, Certificate of Appreciation, Egyptian Engineering Association, 1987. Memberships: Fellow, Optical Society, America; IEEE, America; Ceramic Society; International Society of Optical Engineers; Society for Advancement of Material and Processing Engineers. Address: 1117 Hillcrest Rd, Narberth, PA 19072-1223, USA.

**ELAZAR Daniel Judah,** b. 25 August 1934. Political Science Educator. m. Harriet J Fienberg, 2 sons, 1 daughter. Education: MA, Political Science, University of Chicago, 1957; PhD, Political Science, 1959; Degree Hon, Jewish Institute, Religion Hebrew Union College; Degree Hon, Gratz College, Philadelphia. Appointments: Assistant Professor, Political Science, University of Illinois, 1959-63; Associate Professor, Political Science, Temple University, Philladelphia, 1964-67; Professor, Political Science, 1967-. Director, Centre for the Study of Federalism, 1967-. Publications: The American Partnership, 1962; American Federalism, A View from the States; Explorig Federalizm: Covenant and Polity in Biblical Israel; Covenant and Commonwealth; Convenent and Constitutionalism; Covenant and Civil Society. Memberships: Association of Jewish Studies; American Political Science Association; Award Section on Federalism and Intergovernmental; International Association Centres for Federal Studies; Phi Beta Kappa. Address: Department of Political Studies, Bar Ilan University, 52900 Ramat Gan, Israel.

**ELEZI Besim,** b. 20 March 1935, Saranda, Albania. Surgeon. m. Marika, 1 son, 1 daughter. Education: MA, 1957; Candidate of Medical Science, 1964; Docent, 1972; Doctor of Medical Sciences, 1988; Professor, 1989. Appointments: Chairman, Department of Surgery, University Hospital Centre of Tirana. Publications: 2 Monographs, Hydatidosis; 2 textbooks; Around 100 Papers and Reports. Honour: Distinguished Scientific Worker. Memberships: Albanian Surgical Society; Member, Permanent Committee, Eurosurgery. Address: Spitali No 1, Tirana, Albania.

**ELEZI Ismet,** b. 5 April 1920, Albania. Lawyer. m. Meliha Elezi, 2 sons. Education: Graduated as Lawyer, 1951, Postgraduate Training Course, 1957-60, Leningrad; Doctorate in Law, 1961, Professor, 1972, University of Tirana. Appointments: Scientific Secretary, Institute of Sciences, 1955-57; Scientific Secretary, Tirana University, 1957-66;

Chairman, Criminology Department, 1957-90, Member, Scientific Council, 1957-98, Faculty of Law, Tirana; Chairman, Legal Department of Government, 1966-85; Board Member, Reconciliation of Disputes Foundation, Albania, 1995-98. Publications: Penal Procedure of the Popular Republic of Albania, Tirana, 1953; Fundamental Rule of Law in the Popular Republic of Albania, 1959; Penal Law, special part, 1968, 6th editions, 1995; Penal Law, general part (co-author), 1973, 2nd edition, 1975; Constitutional Law (co-author), 1984; The History of the State and the Law in Albania (co-author), 1987, 2nd edition, 1994; Criminology, 1989, 2nd edition, 1994; Penal Code Commentary, general part (co-author), 1997; 15 monographs; More than 80 articles and conference papers. Honours: Order of Distinguished Merit in Social and State Services, Republic of Albania, 1985; Republic Prize, 1985. Address: Fakulteti i Drejtesise, Rr Dora D'Istria, Shqiperi, Tirana, Albania.

**ELFTMAN Susan Nancy,** b. 3 April 1951, Oakland, California, USA. Physician Assistant. Education: AA, Chabot College, 1971; BS, Medical Science, 1980; BA, Zoology, University California, Berkeley, 1973; MPH, UCLA, 1990. Appointments: Southern California Medical Center, San Diego, USA, 1981-82; Memorial Medical Center, Long Beach, California, USA, 1982-87; Harriman-Jones Medical Group, Long Beach, California, 1986-90; Pamela Kushner MD, Long Beach, California, 1990-. Honours: Magna Cum Laude, Silver Key (Honor) Society, Outstanding PA Student, Outstanding Woman in Health Sciences, 1980; Mothers and Babies, March of Dimes, Los Angeles County, 1990. Memberships: American Academy of Pennsylvania; American Society for Prophylaxis in Obstetrics; California Academy of Pennsylvania. Address: 275 Ximeno, Long Beach, CA 90803, USA.

**ELIAVA Avtandili,** b. 15 June 1944, vil Khobi, Georgia. Physicist. 1 daughter. Education: Tbilisi State University, 1967; Junior Scientist, 1967, Institute Applied Mathematics, TSU, 1967; Postgraduate, 1990; Candidate Physico-Mathematical Science, 1995. Appointments: Junior Scientist, Institute Applied Mathematics, TSU, 1967; Special Student, Researcher of Laboratory of Theoretical Physics, Joint Institute Nuclear Research, 1975-77; Junior Scientist, Institute Applied Mathematics, TSU, 1977-. Publications: 20. Membership: Bull Georgian Academy Science, 1968. Address: 17 Kekelidze Str, 380079 Tbilisi, Georgia.

**ELIAVA Lamzira,** b. 25 July 1938, Georgia. Philosopher. Education: Tbilisi State University, 1961; Postgraduate, Kiev, 1977; Candidate of Philosophical Science, 1978; Reader, Philosophy, Moscow, 1981. Appointments: Senior Laboratory Assistant, 1962, Head, 1971-74, Senior Teacher, 1979, Reader, 1979-, Study of Philosophy Department, Tbilisi State Pedagogical University. Publications: Several professional articles. Membership: Georgian Philosophical Society, 1963-. Address: 17 Fl 34 Kekelidze, 380079 Tbilisi, Georgia.

**ELIAVA Liana,** b. 31 August 1939, Georgia. Philologist. Producer. m. Robert Vinonen. Education: Tbilisi State University, 1962; All Soviet State Institute of Cinematography, Moscow, 1970. Appontments: Assistant Producer, Georgia Film Studio, 1961-66; Producer, Georgia Film, Tbilisi. Creative Works: 8 Films, 2 Scenarios, Collected Verses, 1977, Verses, 1996. Membership: Georgian Cinematographical Union. Address: 17 Fl 34 Kekelidze, 380079 Tbilisi, Georgia.

**ELINSON Jack,** b. 30 June 1917, New York City. Sociomedical Scientist. m. May Gomberg, 3 sons, 1 daughter. Education: BS, College of the City of New York, 1937; MA, 1946, PhD, 1954, George Washington University.

ppointments: Professor Emeritus, Sociomedical Sciences, Columbia University; Senior Research Scholar, Institute for Health, Rutgers University. Publication: Co-author, Sociomedical Health Indicators, 1979. Honours: Leo G Reeder Award, American Sociological Association, Washington DC, 985; Dennis J Sullivan Award, New Jersey Public Health Association, 1990; AAPOR Award for Exceptionally Distinguished Achievement, 1993; Award for Outstanding Contribution to Development of New Jersey Graduate Program in Public Health, 1994. Memberships: Institute of Medicine; Board of Directors, Public Health Association of New York City, 976-77; Chair, Medical Sociology, American Sociological Association, 1977-78; President, American Association for Public Opinion Research, 1979-80. Address: Columbia University, Sociomedical Sciences, 600 West 168 St, New York, NY 10032, USA.

**ELLIOT Elisa Louise,** b. 21 November 1956, Minneapolis, MN, USA. Microbiologist. 1 s, 1 d. Education: Texas A & M University, 1974-76; BS, Microbiology, Minor in Chemistry, Texas Tech University, Lubbock, 1977; PhD, Microbiology, University of MD, College PK, 1984. Appointments: Assistant Professor, Seafood Microbiology, University of Alaska Fishery Industrial Technology Center, AK, 1984-87; Microbiologist, US Department of Agriculture, 1987-89; Microbiologist, US Food and Drug Admin, 1989-. Publications: Many Publications. Memberships: National Shellfisheries Association; American Society for Microbiology; American Association of University Women; Sigma Xi. Address: FDA Ctr for Food Safety and Applied Nutrition, HFS-615, 200 C St SW, Washington, DC 20204-0001, USA.

**ELLIS June B,** b. 17 June, Portland, Indiana, USA. Human Resource Consultant. 1 son, 1 daughter. Education: BS, Mary Washington College, University of Virginia, 1942; MS, Tulane University, 1953; PhD, International University, 1977. Appointments: Training Director, East La State University, 960-64; Assistant Professor, Tulane School of Medicine, Department Psychiatry, 1963-68; Executive Director, Family Service-Travelers Aids, Ft Smith, Arkansas, 1967-71; President, Child and Family Consultant, Ft Smith, 1971-; Director, Human Resource Development Center, Ft Smith; Member, Advisory Board, Suspect Child Abuse and Neglect; Consultant, Volvo Health Care, Goteborg, Sweden, 1974-92; Kontura Personal, 1974-92; Tulane University Outstanding Alumni, 1984 Tulane Alumni Board, 1978-88. Publications: Author: TA Tally, 1974; TA Talk, Terms and References in Transaction, 1976; BEING, 1982. Memberships: Arkansas Government's Commission on Status of Women, 1970-73; Arkansas Government's Commission Drug Abuse Prevention; Advisory Board, Junior League America; Scholarship Selection Committee, Whirlpool Corporation; American Society Training and Development; American Academy Psychotherapists; American Group Psychotherapy Association; American Orthopsychiatric Association; Academy Certified Social Workers; West Arkansas Mental Health Association; Conference for Advancement of Private Practice in Social Work; Episcopalian; American Association of Retired Persons; Western Arkansas Health Advisory Service Coordinator, 1995-97; Advisory Board, Tulane University Life Long Learning, 1997; American Association of University Women; American Association of Individual Investors; National Association of Female Executives. Address: 3437 Westminster Avenue, Dallas, TX 75205, USA.

**ELLYETT Clifton Darfield,** b. 10 January 1915, Christchurch, New Zealand. Physicist. m. Ngaire Frances Warren, 2 sons, 2 daughters. Education: MSc Double Hons Chemistry and Physics, 1936, 1937, NZ; PhD, 1949,

Manchester University, UK; FRAS; FAIP; FAIE. Appointments: Senior Demonstrator in Chemistry, 1936, Assistant Lecturer to Reader in Physics, 1938-64, University of Canterbury, NZ; Foundation Professor of Physics, University of Newcastle, NSW, Australia, 1964-80. Publications: 68 articles, mainly geophysics, in refereed journals; 1 book. Honours: Sundry Scholarship Awards; ICI Senior Research Fellowship; Dr h.c., University of Newcastle; and others. Memberships: Patron, The National Herbalists Association of Australia; President, The Central Coast Community College, NSW, Australia. Address: PO Box 84, Ourimbah, NSW 2258, Australia.

**ELMER Michael Bendik,** b. 26 February 1949, Copenhagen. Judge. m. Lise Skovby. Education: Cand Jur, 1973, Copenhagen University; Advocate, 1982. Appointments: Civil Servant, Ministry of Justice, Copenhagen, 1973-77, 1978-82; Deputy Judge, Hilleroed, 1977-78; Head of Division, Ministry of Justice, Copenhagen, 1982-87, 1988-91; High Court Judge (ai), Copenhagen, 1987-88; Deputy Secretary, Ministry of Justice, Copenhagen, Head of Department on Human Rights and Community Law, 1991-94; Advocate General, EC Court of Justice, Luxembourg, 1994-97; Vice President, Maritime and Commercial Court, Copenhagen, 1998-. Publications: Books and articles on Danish and European Law. Memberships: Chairman or member of numerous government and international committees. Address: Maritime and Commercial Court, Bredgade 70, DK-1260 Copenhagen K, Denmark.

**EMELYANOV Alexander Alexandrovitch,** b. 2 July 1948, Lipetsk, USSR. Physicist. m. Nina Pavlovna Belova Emelyanova, 1 son, 1 daughter. Education: Physicist, State University, Tomsk, USSR, 1971; PhD, Polytechnical Institute, Tomsk, 1979; DSc, East-Kazakhstan Technical University, Ust-Kamenogorsk, Kazakhstan, 1998. Appointments: Senior Research Associate, High Voltage Research Institute, Tomsk, 1974-80; Dean, General Technical Faculty, Associate Professor, Power Engineering Institute, Alma-Ata, 1980-87; Head Dept, Kazakh National Technical University, Ust-Kamenogorsk, Kazakhstan, 1987-96; Senior Research Associate, 1996-98, Head Dept, 1998-, East-Kazakhstan Technical University. Publications: Articles to professional journals; Author of proceedings 1973-. Address: Ul Lugovaya 29 Apt 31, 492010 Ust-Kamenogorsk, Kazakhstan.

**EMELYANOV Emelyan,** b. 7 November 1934, Poland. Marine Geologist. m. Lydia Emelyanova, 1 son, 1 daughter. Education: Vilnius University, 1958; Candidate of Geological Mineralogical Sciences, Institute of Oceanology of AS USSR, 1963; Doctor of Sciences, Institute of Oceanology, AS USSR, 1981; Research Professor, Highest Council of the USSR, 1983. Appointments: Scientific Collaborator, Chief of Geological Group, Southern Department of Institute of Oceanology, 1958-63; Head, Atlantic Geology Department, PP Shirshov Institute of Oceanology, RAS, and Professor of Kaliningrad State University, 1993-98. Publications: 250 scientific publications; Sedimentogenesis in the Atlantic Ocean Basin, 1982; Types of Bottom Sediments of the Atlantic Ocean, 1975; Geochemistry and Sedimentology of the Mediterranean Sea, 1986. Honours: 3 medals from the government of Russia for the excellent job, 1970, 1986, 1996; Diploma of Russian Geographical Society, 1970; Award, German Geological Society, 1997. Memberships: Russian Academy of Natural Sciences, 1991; New York Academy of Sciences, 1995; Lithuanian Society of Natural Sciences, 1997. Address: 23600 Kaliningrad, Institute of Oceanology, Russia.

**EMERSON Ralph Stanton,** b. 1912, Foxcroft, Maine, USA. Medical Doctor. Education: BA, Cornell University, 1933; MD, Cornell University Medical College, 1936. Appointments: Army

Surgeon, European Theatre Hospital; Founder, Doctor, Surgical Practice, Roslyn Heights. Publications: 1 book, several articles in professional medical journals. Memberships: Fellow, American College of Surgeons; American Medical Association; Nassau County Medical Society; Medical Society of the State of New York; New York Schools High School Athletic Association; Roslyn Kiwanis Club. Honours: Theodore Roosvelt Award, nassau-Suffolk Hospital Council. Address: 115 Warner Avenue, Roslyn Heights, NY 11527-1025, USA.

**EMMERSON Bryan Thomas,** b. 5 September 1929, Townsville, Queensland, Australia. Professor of Medicine. m. Elva Brett, 2 sons. Education: MBBS, 1952, MD, 1962, PhD, 1973, University of Queensland; FRACP, 1957. Appointments: Professor of Medicine, Consulting Physician, Princess Alexandra Hospital, Brisbane, 1974-94. Publications: 160 scientific articles; 2 books on gout. Honours: Prizes for research; Officer of Order of Australia, 1997. Memberships: Hon Life Member, ANZ Society of Nephrology, 1988; Hon Fellow, Queensland Institute of Medical Research, 1994. Address: Princess Alexandra Hospital, Ipswich Rd, Brisbane, Qld 4102, Australia.

**ENDO Tamio,** b. 5 April 1949, Sakai, Japan. Associate Professor. m. Oda Harumi, 1 daughter. Education: BEng, 1976, MEng, 1978, Gifu University; DEng, 1987, Kyoto University. Appointments: Assistant Professor, 1978-87, Associate Professor, 1987-, Mie University, Japan; Visiting Researcher, University of California, 1995. Publications: in professional journals. Memberships: Japan Society of Applied Physics; Physical Society of Japan; Material Research Society, USA. Address: Tabata Ueno, Anoh, Mie 514-2325, Japan.

**ENG Charis,** b. 17 January 1962, Singapore. Physician; Scientist. Education: BA Hons, University of Chicago, 1982; Phd, 1986; MD, 1988; Residency, Internal Medicine, Beth Israel Hospital, Boston, 1988-91; Medical Oncology Fellowship, Dana Farber Cancer Inst, Boston, 1991-94; Human Cancer Genetics Fellowship, University of Cambridge, UK, 1992-95. Appointments: Instructor, 1994-95; Assistant Professor, Medicine, Dana Farber Cancer Institute, Harvard Medical School, Boston, 1995-98; Associate Professor, Medicine and Human Cancer Genetics; Director, Clinical Cancer Genetics Program, Ohio State University, 1999-. Publications: 110 Original Articles in Peer Reviewed Journals. Honours: Sigma Xi; Alpha Omega Alpha. Memberships: American Society of Human Genetics; American Association for Cancer Research. Address: Ohio State University, 420 W 12th Ave, #690C MRF, Columbus, OH 43210, USA.

**ENGAN Terje,** b. 22 September 1956, Alen, Roros, Norway. MD; Consultant in Oncology. m. Ann Elisabeth Hegle, 1 son, 1 daughter. Education: MD, 1982, University Tromsoe; MD, PhD, 1995, University Trondheim. Appointments: Consultant Oncologist, Department of Oncology, University Hospital of Trondheim; Fellow, Norwegian Cancer Society. Publications: Thesis, NMR Spectroscopy of Human Blood Plasma in Malignant Disease, 1995; Publications in international medical journals. Memberships: Norwegian Cancer Society; ESTRO; Norwegian Medical Association. Address: University Hospital Trondheim, Dept of Oncology, N-7006, Trondheim, Norway.

**ENGEL Margorie L,** b. 12 November 1943, Baltimore, Maryland, USA. Author; Speaker. m. Stephen Boyle, 5 daughters. Education: BA English and Sociology, Western Maryland College, 1965; MA Special Education Programme Development, 1975, Fairfield University; Executive MBA, 1987, University of New Haven; PhD Law, Policy and Society, 1998, Northeastern University. Appointments: Education Programme

Development, public and private schools in Virginia, Califor New York and Connecticut, 1965-76; Public Relations, Fairf University, 1976-78; Partner, New Business Developme Merger and Acquisitions, Siebert Associates, 1978- President, Hamilton-Forbes Associates, Practical Solutions Families Complicated by Divorce and Remarriage, 198 Publications: Books: The Divorce Decisions Workbook Planning and Action Guide; The Canadian Divorce Decisi Workbook; Weddings a Family Affair; Divorce H Sourcebook: a Resouce and Reference Guide; entry Divorce in Women's Studies Encyclopedia. Membershi Stepfamily Association of America, President; Children's Ri Council, Advisory Board; Massachusetts Governor's Advis Commission on Responsible Fatherhood and Family Sup Commissioner; Massachusetts Bar Association, Family L Section and MA Probate and Family Court Committ Massachusetts Council on Family Mediation Inc; Notary Pul Massachusetts; Authors Guild; International Platf Association; Newcomen Society of the United States. Addre 25 Walnut Street, Boston, MA 02108-3612, USA.

**ENGLISH Lyn Denise,** b. 5 May 1953, Brisbane. Associ Professor. Education: PhD, University of Queensland, 19 Med; BEd; Dip T. Appointments: Associate Profess Queensland University of Technology, 1992-. Publicatio Mathematical Reasoning: Analogies, Metaphors and Imag Mathematics Education: Models and Processes; Handbool International Research in Mathematics Education. Honou Outstanding Thesis Award; Outstanding Dissertation Aw Practical Implications Award. Address: Queensland Univer Tech, Victoria Park Rd, Kelvin Grove, Brisbane, QLD 40 Australia.

**ENNIS Sharon Lynn,** b. 27 October 1951, Washington [ Multicultural Music Teacher. m. W Frank Ennis, 1 son daughter. Education: BS Elementary Education cum lau 1973, Carson-Newman College; Masters equiv, mu endorsement, 1982, Central Washington University; Certific Elementary Teacher 1-6, mid school, Teacher of Music K Appointments: Kindergarten and Music Teacher, Green Ac Kindergarten, Louisville, 1974-75; Teacher, third grade, Gr County School District, Corinth, Kentucky, 1976-78; Longte sub/fourth grade, Bracken County School District, 1978- Longterm sub bilingual-Spanish, Moses Lake (Wash) Sch District, 1980-81, Longterm sub/fourth grade, 1981-84; Teacl third & fourth grade, Wicomico County School Distr Salisbury, MD, 1984-88, Teacher Music K-6, 1988-; Mu Director of Choirs and Congregations, Pianist, Kentuc Tennessee, Washington & Maryland, 1971-88; Teacher Priv piano lessons, various communities; Teacher, Vacation Bil School, various areas, 1971-88; Presenter 1st US/Russia Jc Conference on Education, Moscow. Publications: Vocabula and Science Activities, curriculum to accompany textbo 1982; Symbols of Holidays, elementary holiday musi programme, 1995; Music Curriculum, 1994, lessons multicultural music activities and traditions, 1988-95; a others; To Russia with Music, 1997. Memberships: Deln Elementary School PTA; Singer, Salisbury Choral Socie Adult Choir Director, First Baptist Church of Fruitland, Fruitla MD; NEA, Maryland State Teachers Association; Wicom County Education Association; People-to-People Internatio Delta Omicron, international music fraternity, 1998; and othe Address: Delmar Elementary School, 811 S. Second Stre Delmar, MD 21875, USA.

**EPERIN Anatoli,** b. 15 October 1930, Barnaul, A Region.Engineer, Physicist. m. Eperina Anfia Ivanovna, 2 so 1 daughter. Education: Diplomas of Engineer, Tor Polytechnical Institue, 1954; Doctor of Science, 19

Professor, 1995. Appointments: Engineer, Shift Engineer, Main Engineer, Siberian Chemical Plant, Tomsk, 1954-71. Main Engineer, Leningrad NPP, 1971-83; Director, LNPP, 1983-96; Director, Education Research Center, 1996-. Publications: 93 Scientific Works; 75 Inventions; 48 Patents, Russsia; 1 International Patent; 7 Monographs. Honours: Lenin Prize, 1965; State Prize of USSR, 1985; Government Prize of RF, 1996. Memberships: RF Nuclear Society, 1993; St Petersburg Engineer Academy, 1993; International Academies of Information Technologies, 1993; Ecology and Safe Activity, 1995; Energy, 1995. Address: ul 50 let October 8 kv 27, Sosnovy Bor Leningraskaya obl, 188537 Russia.

**ERBER Georg Arthur,** b. 20 June 1950, Berlin, Germany. Senior Research Officer in Economics. m. Barbara Hannelore Gabelmann, 1 son, 1 daughter. Education: Diploma, Economics, Free University, Berlin, 1975; Dr.rer.pol, 1980; Assistant Professor, Statistics, Econometrics, Free University, Berlin, 1975-81. Appointments: Researcher, Economics, German Institute for Economic Research, Berlin, 1981-; Visiting Professor, Zhejiang University, Hangzhou, China, 1987; Thammasat University, Bangkok, Thailand, 1987-88, 1992-93; Academician Counselor, National Planning Institute, Lima, Peru, 1989, 1990; Economics Educator, Ecole National D'Administration, Lao, 1994. Publications include: Future Perspectives of Germany in International Competition: Industry Policy Implications of the New Growth Theories, 1998. Memberships: American Economics Association; International Atlantic Economic Society; German-British Yacht Club. Address: German Institute of Economic Research, Konigin-Luise Street 5, Berlin D-14195, Germany.

**ERBOVA Karla,** b. 30 April 1933, Plzen. Assistant Manager. m. Ing Milos Halouska, 1 son, 1 daughter. Education: Studies for graduated assistant of manager, State Institute for Stenography, 1974-76. Publications: 10 books of poem collections; Various almanachs; Contributor of articles and poems to journals and newspapers; Poetry broadcast with Czechoslovak and Czech Broadcasting Corporation; Author at literary meetings. Honours: Prize of Czech Broadcasting Corporation for poetry James fights with Angel, 1987; Prize of Town of Plzen for lifetime work, 1995; Many regional literary prizes. Memberships: Community of Writers; Czech Centre on the International Pen Club; National Library Society, Chairwoman 1995-97. Address: Jasminova 49, 106 00 Praha 10, Czech Republic.

**ERDAL Memduh,** b. 20 March 1935, Ortaköy, North Cyprus. Businessman. m. Sermin Erdal, 1 son, 1 daughter. Education: Certified Professional Manager Certificate, Society of Business Practitioners, UK. Appointments: Established own company, Memduh Erdal Co Ltd, 1958; Director-Secretary, Board of Director, Cyprus Credit Bank Ltd, 1978; Founder, Chairman, Board of Directors, Girne American University, 1987. Honours: Silver Medal for Service, Queen Elizabeth II, UK, 1958; Honorary PhD, South-Eastern University, Washington DC, 1992; Gold Medal, Association of Ski Instructors, Turkey, 1995. Memberships: Founder Member, Turkish Chamber of Commerce, Cyprus; Councillor, 16 years, Acting Mayor, 3 months, Turkish Municipality of Nicosia, Cyprus; Girne Rotary Club. Address: Board of Directors, Girne American University, Via Mersin 10, Karaoglanoglu Girne, Trncyprus, Turkey.

**EREMIN Yuri,** b. 5 October 1947, Moscow, Russia. Mathematician. m. Natalya Grishina, 1 son, 1 daughter. Education: PhD, Mathematical Physics, 1976, DSc, Mathematical Modelling, 1989, Moscow State University. Appointments: Senior Scientist, 1982-93, Head, Research Group, 1993-, Applied Mathematics and Computer Science

Faculty, Moscow State University. Publications: More than 180 scientific papers; 1 book. Address: Applied Mathematics and Computer Science Faculty, Moscow State University, Vorobyov Hills, 119889 Moscow, Russia.

**ERGIN Mehmet,** b. 25 May 1936, Yozgat, Turkey. Chemical Engineer. m. Uysal Ergin, 1 son, 1 daughter. Education: Chemical Engineer Diploma, 1960; PhD, 1969, Glasgow University; Associate Professor, 1974, Full Professor, 1980, Hacettepe University. Appointments: VP, Islamic Academy of Sciences, 1986; President, Turkish Scientific and Technical Research Council, 1988-91; President, Turkish Atomic Energy Authority, 1996-97; Chairman, Chemistry Dept, Fatih University, present. Publications: Over 50 articles, technical reports and editor, 2 books. Memberships: Chamber of Chemical Engineers; IUPAC; Islamic Academy of Sciences. Address: Fatih University, Department of Chemistry, Buyukcekmece, Istanbul 34900, Turkey.

**ERICSSON Kjerstin Elisabeth,** b. 5 January 1938, Stockholm, Sweden. Neuroscience Educator. Education: RN/Midwife, St Eric Nursing College, Stockholm, 1962; Certificate, Fin, D'Etudes de Ière Annee, Ecole Inter Enseign Inf, Lyon, France, 1978; University Certificate, Social Gerontology, University Lyon, France, 1979; Maitrise Psychology, University Lyon, 1981; Master of Social Science, University Uppsala, 1984; Maitrise Sociology and Ethnology, University of Lyon, 1988; PhD, University Uppsala, 1985. Appointments: Laboratory Assistant, Halland County Council, Sweden, 1957-58; Nurse, Dalecarlia County Council, Swedem, 1962-64; District Nurse, Gavle County Council, 1964-72; Geriatric Nursing Chief Administrator, Stockholm County Council, 1976-88; Researcher, Huddinge University Hospital, 1988-92; Senior Lecturer, Karolinska Institute, 1992-; Assistant Professor, Geriatric Nursing Research, Karolinska Institute, 1997. Publications: Contributor of articles in professional journals. Honours: Grant, Swedish 3M, Stockholm, 1973; Grants, European Council, Lyon, France, Basel, Switzerland, 1974, 1991. Memberships: AAAS; International Psychogeriatric Association; International Graphonomics Society; New York Academy of Sciences; International Association for Science Study of Intellectual Disability. Address: Karolinska Institute, Department of Geriatric Medicine, Huddinge University Hospital M98, 14186 Huddinge, Sweden.

**ERMAKOV Voldemar Valentinovitch,** b. 9 November 1936, Russia. Physician; Healthcare Manager, Educator. m. Tatiana, 1 son, 1 daughter. Education: MD, Medical School, Moscow; Candidate of Medical Science, Gamaleia Institute of Epidemiology, 1969; Medical Diplomat, Diplomat in International Medicine. Appointments: Research Officer, Institute of Tropical Medicine, Moscow, 1960-62; Malariologist, WHO, Dacca, East Pakistan, 1963-65; Director, The WHO International Training Course on Epidemiology, Moscow, Prague, Geneva, Alexandria, 1969-81; Dean, Faculty of International Health Central Institute of Advanced Medical Studies, 1980-86; Director, The Who International Training Course for Public Health Administrators, Moscow, 1980-86; Associate Professor, Faculty of International Health, Russian Medical Academy of Postgraduate Studies, 1993-. Publications: Contributor of articles to professional journals; International Quarantine monograph, 1982, Moscow, pp319. Address: Apt 26, 31 Leningradskoe Shosse, 125 212 Moscow, Russia.

**ERMOLIEV Yuri Michailovich,** b. 3 November 1936, Briansk, Russia. Mathematician. m. Ljudmila, 1 daughter. Education: Candidate Degree, University of Kiev, Ukraine, 1959; Doctor Degree, Maths, 1972; Full Professor, 1974. Appointments: Research Institute of Cybernetics, Kiev, Ukraine,

1960-72; Researcher, Senior Researcher, Head of Resaerch Department, Institute of Cybernetics, 1972-79, 1984-91; Project Leader, International Institute of Applied Systems Analysis, Austria, 1979-84, 1991-. Publications: Nondifferentiable and Stochastic Optimization. Honours: Ukraine State Prize in Science; USSR State Prize in Science; Kjell Gunnarson's Risk Management Prize. Membrships: National Academy of Science; New York Academy of Sciences. Address: Inst Applied Systems Analysis, Schloss, A-2361 Luxembourg Law, Aust, Austria.

**ERNEST David J,** b. 16 May 1929, Chicago, Illinois, USA. Musician; Educator. m. Prudence, 4 sons. Education: BMEd, 1951, Chicago Musical College, Chicago, Illinois; MS, 1956, University of Illinois; Fulbright Scholar, Sorbonne, University of Paris, France, 1958-59; EdD, 1958, University of Colorado, Boulder. Appointments: Instrumental Music Teacher, Illinois Public Schools, 1955-56; Instructor, Oboe, double-reed specialist, woodwinds, music education, University of Colorado, 1956-58, 1959-61; Chairman, Div of Fine and Applied Arts, Glenville State College, 1961-63; Professor of Music and Music Education, Department of Music, St Cloud State University, Minnesota, 1963-, Departmental Chairman, 1969-79, Professor Emeritus, 1996-. Publications: Many articles in professional publications. Honours: Full Scholarship Chicago Musical College, 1949-51; Fulbright Scholar to France, 1958-59; Danforth Associate, 1962. Address: 1455 25th Street, South East St Cloud, Minnesota 56304, USA.

**EROFEYEV Vladimir,** b. 20 August 1959, Nizhny Novgorod, Russia. Professor. m. Tatyana Turina, 1 son, 1 daughter. Education: MS in Mechanics, Nizhny Novgorod State University, 1981; PhD Mechanics of Solids, St Peterburg Technical University, 1986; D Sci Mechanics of Solids, Moscow State University, 1994. Appointments: Research Fellow, Senioe Research Fellow, Head of Laboratory, Research Institute for Material Testing, Nizhny Novgorod, Russia 1981-86; Head of Laboratory, Vice Director, Mechanical Engineering Research Institute, Russian Academy of Sciences, 1986-; Professor, Nizhny Novgorod State University, 1997-. Publications: Nonlinear Waves in Elastic Media with Dispersion, 1986; Microstructured Solids, 1996. Membership: Russian Acoustical Society. Address: 85 Belinskogo str, Nizhny Novtorod 603024, Russia.

**ESLAMI Mohamad Reza,** b. 8 March 1945, Tehran, Iran. University Professor. m. Mrs Minoo Nezami, 1 son, 1 daughter. Education: BSc in ME, 1968, Tehran Polytechnic, Iran; MSc in Me, 1970, PhD in ME, 1973, Louisiana State University, USA. Appointments: LSU, NASA Soace Shuttle Team, 1970-73; Assistant Professor, 1973-77, Associate Professor, 1977-89, Professor, 1989-, Amirkabir University of Technology; Associate Professor, LSU, 1977. Publications: Over 110 technical papers, 7 books. Honours: 3 award plaques from American Society of ME. Memberships: Associate Fellow, American Institute of Aero and Astro; Honor member, Iranian Society of Mech Engineering; American Society of Mech Engineering. Address: Mechanical Engineering Department, Amirkabir University, Hafez Avenue, Tehran, Iran.

**ESAN Gabriel A,** b. 24 February 1956, Orin-Ekiti, Nigeria. Computer Analyst. m. Cecilia Yemisi, 2 sons, 1 daughter. Education: NCE, Maths, Chemistry; BSc, Mathematics; PGD, Computer Science. Appointment: System Manager. Publications: Computerisation of Accounting System; Mathematical Award. Memberships: Mathematical Association of Nigeria; Computer Association of Nigeria. Address: Fed Road Safety Commission, Ibadan Computer Section, Oyo State, Nigeria.

**ESKIN James Aaron,** b. 7 July 1953, Boston, Massachusetts, USA. Public Affairs Strategist. Education: BA, Urban Affairs, The George Washington University, Washington, DC, USA, 1975. Appointments: Director of Communications, Agriculture Council of America, 1974-81; Corporate Communications Director, Associated Milk Producers Inc, 1982-96; Principal, Jim Eskin, Public Affairs Strategist, 1996-. Publications: More than 50 guest column credits in daily newspapers and business journals; Publisher, monthly Stratagems newsletter, 1996-. Memberships: Business for Social Responsibility, 1995-; Public Relations Society of America, 1995-; Steering Committee, Greater San Antonio Chamber of Commerce Education, 1997-; Executive Director, San Antonians for a Major Sports Complex, 1983-89. Address: 11851 Belair #204, San Antonio, TX 78213-4858, USA.

**ESKOV Valery Mathew,** b. 13 October 1948, Poltava. Biophysicist. m. Filatova Olga Eugene, 2 sons. Education: DSc, Biophysics, Russian Academy of Sciences, 1979; MSc, 1994. Appointments: Assistant, Medical Institute, Samara, Russia, 1971-81; Senior Lecturer, Agricultural Institute, Samara, Russia, 1981-87, Polytechnic Institute, Donetsk, Ukraine, 1987-88; Senior Lecturer, Professor, Pedagogical Institute, Togliatty, Russia, 1988-96; Professor, State University, Surgut, Russia, Director, Science Education Center, 1996-. Publications include: Introduction to the Compartmental Theory of the Respiratory Neuron Networks, 1994. Honour: V Tatishev Prize. Memberships: International Academy of Information Communication Controll in Engineering Natural Science; Russian Academy of Natural Science; Association of Creative Pedagogy. Address: Surgut State University, Energetikov 14, 626400 Surgut, Russia.

**ESMAEL Haresad,** b. 5 September 1956, Kuala Lumpur, Malaysia. Managing Director. Education: MBA, Harvard, 1986. Address: 3 JLN Jaya Bandar Tun Razak Cheras, Kuala Lumpur 56000, Malaysia.

**ESSALI Mohamed Adib,** b. 30 March 1954, Yabroud, Syria. Psychiatrist. m. Emtithal Rezk, 2 sons, 1 daughter. Education: MD, 1979, Faculty of Human Medicine, Damascus University; PhD, 1990, London University, UK; MRCPsych, 1992, Royal College of Psychiatrists, UK; Advanced Studies in Substance Abuse, Johns Hopkins University, USA, 1996. Appointments: Resident, Damascus Hospitals, 1979-85; Psychiatrist and Neuroscientist, Academic Dept Psychiatry, Charing Cross and Westminster Medical School, University of London, 1986-90; Psychiatrist, Oxford Regional Training Schemes in Psychiatry, 1990-93; NIDA-Humphrey Fellow, Johns Hopkins University, USA, 1995-96; Head, Department of Psychiatry, Al-Tal Hospital, Al-Tal, Syria, 1993-; Professor of Psychiatry, Faculty of Human Medicine, Damascus University, 1997-. Publications: Author and coauthor 12 papers in professional publications. Honours: Young Scientist Award, 5th Winter Workshop on Schizophrenia Research, Austria, 1990; Young Investigator Award, International Congress on Schizophrenia Research, Tucson, Arizona, 1991. Memberships: 11 professional bodies including: The Royal College of Psychiatrists, UK; British Association for Psychopharmacology; Arab Federation of Psychiatrists; also: Referee to journals in field of psychiatry; Commentator, ACP Journal Club and Evidence-based Medicine. Address: 27 Al Zahrawi Street, Damascus, Syria.

**ESSANG Okon Ita,** b. Akwa Ibom, Nigeria. m. Akon Essang, 3 daughters. Education: Cambridge School Certificate, 1950-54; Diploma, Forestry. Appointments: Queens Commission, 2nd Lt, Nigerian Army, 1960; Adjutant General, PSO, 14th Division, Biafran Army, 1968-69; Commissioner for Education, Lands and Finance, 1978-79; Chairman, TPT

Corporation, 1979-82. Honours: PhD honoris causa, Albert Einstein International Academy Foundation of America; PhD honoris causa, Southland University; Albert Einstein Cross of Merit, 1991. Memberships: Institute of Management Consultants. Address: Plot 337, Eta Agbo Road, Layout by Unical, PO Box 856, Calabar Cross River State, Nigeria.

**ESTEVES Jorge M Sa,** b. 25 June 1963, Aveiro, Portugal. Professor; Researcher. m. I Valdoleiros (div), 2 daughters. Education: Licenciatura in Electronic and Telecommunications Engineering, 1986; Project work for Engineer Diploma, Teletrafic Engineer, 1987, Portugal Telecom; Master Computer Science, 1990; PhD Mathematics, 1996. Appointments: Senior Engineer, Network Design Centre, Portugal Telecom, 1987-; Officer Engineer, Portuguese Navy, 1987-89; Director, School for Technicians of Electronic and Informatic, 1989-; Professor, University Aveiro, Math Department, Senior Research Member, 1990-98. Publications: MSc and PhD theses; Book on numeric computation of INESC, 1997; Article in an American journal, ORSA, 1996; Article at Proceedings of the 15th Teletrafic Congress, USA, 1995; Several articles and conference abstracts. Memberships: Portuguese Math Society; Apdio, Portuguese Operations Research Society; Senior member, Ordem Dos Engenheiros; Research Member, Instituto De Eng de Sistemas e Computadores. Address: Department of Maths, University Aveiro, 3800 Aveiro, Portugal.

**ESTRIN Genrikh Yakovlewitsch,** b. 5 November 1933, Moscow, Russia. Engineer. m. N G Brezgunova, 1 son. Education: Degree, Civil Engineering with Honours, Moscow Institute of Civil Engineers, 1955; Postgraduate, All Union Science Research Institute, Moscow, 1976. Appointments: Construction Chief, MK38, Moscow, 1955-68; Head of Group, Central Science Research Institute, Moscow, 1972-73; Chief Specialist, 1973-76, Senior Science Worker, 1976-88, Head of Division of Structural Engineering, 1988-. Publications: Progressive Steel Constructions, 1971; Joints of Steel Building Constructions, 1992; Articles to professional journals. Honours: Recipient, Medals Exhibition of National Economy Achievements, Moscow, 1977-90; Grantee, International Science Foundation, 1992. Membership: New York Academy of Sciences, 1996. Address: TsNJJ Promzdaniy, Borovskoje Chaussee 58/1-306, 119634 Moscow, Russia.

**ESTRIN Herman A,** b. 2 June 1915, North Plainfield, New Jersey, USA. Educator. m. Pearl Simon, 1 son, 1 daughter. Education: AB Languages and Literature, 1937, Drew University, Madison; AM Curriculum and Teaching, 1942, Professional Diploma, Director of Guidance, Phi Delta Kappa, 1947-50, EdD, 1954, Post-doctoral study in field of speech, communication arts and curriculum development in higher education, 1956-61, Teachers College, Columbia University. Appointments: Instructor of English, 1946-48; Assistant Professor of English, 1949-53; Course Supervisor, Department of English, Division Technology, 1950-73; Associate Chairman, Department of English, 1950-63; Associate Professor of English, 1953-58; Professor of English, Graduate Division, 1958-70; Professor of English, 1958-81; Professor Emeritus, 1981-; 26 lectures, workshops and presentations given nationally and internationally including: University of Alaska, 1972; University of British Columbia, 1978; University of Paris, France, 1978, 1979. Publications: 13 books including: The Teaching of Technical Writing, co-editor, 1975, one of the 1977's 10 best sellers of NCTE's publications; 5 brochures; 400 articles in educational and scholarly journals; Editorial Advisory Board Member 5 journals and other professional publications. Honours include: Recipient, the Eugene Best Memorial Award for Distinguished Teaching of English, 1973; Exceptional Achievement Award, The Association of Teachers of Technical Writing, 1984; Distinguished Alumni Award, Teachers College, Columbia University, 1988; L'Officier in L'Ordre of Palmes Academiques, University of Paris, 1991; Sterling Olmstead Award, 1994; English Educator of the Year, 1995. Memberships include: American Society of Engineering Education; National Council of Teachers of English; National Council of College Media Advisors; New Jersey Council of Teachers of English; New Jersey Collegiate Press Association; College English Association; Phi Beta Kappa; Omicron Delta Kappa; Tau Delta Phi; Alpha Phi Omega; Phi Beta Sigma; Kappa delta Pi. Address: 315 Henry Street, Scotch Plains, NJ 07076-1408, USA.

**ETO Hajime,** b. 16 June 1935, Tokyo. Professor. Education: BA, 1959, MA, 1962, University of Tokyo; PhD, Systems Science, Tokyo Institute of Technology, 1979. Appointments: Hitachi Ltd, 1962-76; University of Tsukuba, 1976-99; Chiba Keizai University, 1999-. Publications: R and D Strategies in Japan, The National and Corporate Approach; R and D Management Systems in Japanese Industry. Memberships: New York Academy of Science; American Association for the Advancement of Sciences. Address: Nakano 3-43-17-305, Nakano-ku, Tokyo 164-0001, Japan.

**ETVERK Toomas,** b. 9 May 1944, Rakvere, Estonia. Information Professional. m. Katrin Etverk, 1 son, 2 daughters. Education: Electronics Engineer, Technical University Tallinn, Estonia, 1968. Appointments: Engineer, Institute for Cybernetics, Estonian Academy of Science, Tallinn, Estonia, 1968-75; Head of Department, 1975-83, Scientific Director, 1983-89, Estonian Institute for Information, Tallinn, Estonia; Director for Library Science, Estonian National Library, Tallinn, Estonia, 1989-1900; Director, Teek Ltd, Library Service Company, Tallinn, Estonia, 1990-; Lecturer, Pedagogical University Tallinn, Tallinn, Estonia, 1992-. Publications: Articles in journals; Scientific and Technical Information, in Russian; Informatics, Library, in Estonian. Address: PO Box 502, Tallinn, EE0010, Estonia.

**ETXEBA Carlos,** b. 10 March 1929, Bilbao, Spain. Poet; Playwright. Education: Qualified in Commerce, 1949; Studied English, French, German, Italian. Appointments: Technical Translator of English, German, French and Italian, to 1987; Retired 1987-. Publications: 10 theatrical productions including: El Amore a los Hijos, 1990; Musica de Piedra, 1998; 7 Poetry publications: Luna Azulada, 1976; El Mar esta Dentro de Ti, 1991; Voces Poeticas, 1997; and others. Honours: Premio, Catania e Il Suo Vulcano, 1994; Premio, U Liotru Di Catania, 1995; Premio, Catania Duomo, 1995; Attestato di Merito de la Accademia Ferdinandea, 1995; Premio, La Sicula Athenae, 1996; Premio Primavera Catanese, 1997. Memberships: Asociacion Colegial de Escritores, 1985; Asociacion de Autores de Obras de Teatro, 1990; Asociacion Artistica Vizcaina, 1950; Sociedad General de Autores, 1985. Address: Heros No 9-1C, 49009 Bilbao, Spain.

**EUBA Femi,** b. 2 April 1941, Lagos, Nigeria. Theatre Educator. m. Addie Jane Dawson. Education: Diploma, Acting and Speech and Drama, Rose Bruford College of Speech and Drama, Kent, England, 1965; MFA, Playwriting, Yale School of Drama, New Haven, 1973; MA, Afro-American Studies, Yale Graduate School, 1982; PhD, Literature, University of Ife, Nigeria. Appointments: Acting, 1965-; Director of Plays; Lecturer, Dramatic Arts, 1976-80, Senior Lecturer, Dramatic Arts, 1982-86, University of Ife; Teaching Assistant, Afro-American Studies, Yale University, 1980-82; Visiting Professor, Theatre and Speech, College of William and Mary, 1986-88; Assistant Professor, 1988-91, Associate Professor, 1991-95, Professor, 1995-, Theatre/English, Louisiana State

University. Publications: Plays include: The Yam Debt, 1964; Down by the Lagoon, 1965; The Game, 1968; Tortoise, 1969; The Devil, 1970; The Wig and the Honeybee; The Gulf, 1991; Crocodiles, 1995; Scholarly Book: Archetypes, Imprecators and Victims of Fate: Origins and Developments of Satire in Black Drama, 1989. Honours include: Association of Nigerian Authors Literary Award, 1988; Phi Kappa Phi, 1997; Louisianna State University Alumni Association Faculty Excellence Award, 1997. Memberships: Black Theatre Network; African Literature Association; Association of Theatre in Higher Education; South Western Theatre Convention; Theatre Communications Group; Library of Congress; The Drama League; British Equity. Address: Louisianna State University, PO Box 16352, Baton Rouge, LA 70893-6352, USA.

**EVALD Pierre,** b. 15 June 1944, Copenhagen. Researcher, Lecturer. 2 sons. Education: Cand Phil, 1965; Professional Librarian, 1971; Osho University, 1989. Appointments: Senior Lecturer, The Royal School of Library and Information Science. Publications: Several Books and Periodical Articles in English and Danish in the field of LIS and Social Anthropology. Memberships: Danish Library Assocaition; Institute of Library Management; Local Committee of Environmental Preservation. Address: Museumsatien 8, 9999 Skagen, Denmark.

**EVANS Charlie Anderson,** b. 29 Dec 1945, Columbus, Georgia, USA. Chemist. div., 3 sons. Education: BS, Chemistry, Georgia Institute of Technology; PhD, Chemistry, University of Georgia, 1974; Postdoctoral work with André Rassat, Centre d'Etudes Nucléaire, Grenoble, France, 1973-74, with James Bolton, University of Western Ontario, Canada, 1974-76. Appointments: Part-time faculty, Mathematics Department, Georgia Institute of Technology, Atlanta, 1967-68; ESR Applications Chemist, Varian Associates, Florham Park, New Jersey, 1976-80; Adjunct Professor, Chemistry Department, Drew University, Madison, New Jersey, 1978; NMR Applications Chemist, 1980-81, NMR Applications Laboratory Manager, 1981-84, JEOL (USA) Inc, Cranford, New Jersey; Scientist, Bertex Laboratories, Cedar Knolls, New Jersey, 1984-87; NMR Group Leader, Schering-Plough Research Institute, Bloomfield and Kenilworth, New Jersey, 1987-96; Adjunct Professor, Chemistry Department, Fairleigh-Dickinson University, Madison, 1988-; Senior Scientist, Small Molecule NMR Group, Schering-Plough Research Institute, Kenilworth, 1996-. Honours: Muscogee Foundation Scholarship, 1964-68; NDEA Title IV Fellowship, 1971-73; Fulbright Fellowship, 1973-74; President's Award, Schering-Plough, 1989; Best Paper, Eastern Analytical Symposium, 1995. Memberships: American Chemical Society; American Association for the Advancement of Science; New York Academy of Sciences. Address: Schering-Plough Research Institute, K-15-0450 2015 Galloping Hill Road, Kenilworth, NJ 07033, USA.

**EVANS Dewitt,** b. 5 August 1929, Bessemer, Alabama, USA. Foundation Administrator. m. Jacqueline Abel Evans, 1 son, 1 daughter. Education: University of Maryland, 1960-61; BA Degree, 1976, MAT Degree, 1979, University of District of Columbia, Washington DC; Postgraduate Studies, Howard University School of Divinity, Washington DC, 1980; University of Michigan, Dearborn, 1991-92; Auburn University, Montgomery, 1994; Christian Writer's Seminar, Samford University, Birmingham, Alabama, 1997. Appointments: Founder, President, Chairman, CEO, Institute for the Preservation of African American Literature Inc, 1987-; Founder, President, Chairman, CEO, National Consortium for African American Affairs Inc, 1994-; Founder, President, Chairman, CEO, Dewitt H Evans Scholarship Fund Foundation Inc, 1998-. Publications: Chapter Editor, Oracle Magazine,

1982-89; Contributing Writer, Afro-American Newspaper Washington, DC, 1982-89; Publisher/Executive Editor, Famil Focus Newsletter, 1993-; Works in Progress: A Concise Histor of the Institute for the Preservation of African American Literature Inc; My Cup Runneth Over: A Genealogical Historical and Psychoanalytical Memoir of the Journey of a American Family in the Global Context, vols 1-V; A Critique o the Ideological Character of Moral Judgement; Glossolalia Speaking in Tongues. Honours: 30 Years honorary nava service; Honorary Discharge Certificate, US Navy, 1946-76 Good Conduct Medals and Awards, US Navy, 1946-76; Recru Petty Officer Award, US Navy, 1947; Gregg Shorthand Certificate, 1974; National Dean's List, 1976; Marquis' Who'' Who in the South and Southwest Achievement Award, 1997 IBC International Man of the Year Achievement Award Cambridge, 1998; IBC Outstanding People of the 20th Centur Achievement Award. Memberships: Omega Psi Phi, 1982- Kiwanis International Inc, 1983-89; Grand United Order of Oddfellows in America and Jurisdiction, Washington, DC 1983-89; Panhellenic Council, 1985-89; Institute for the Preservation of African American Literature Inc, 1987-; Nation Consortium for African American Affairs Inc, 1994-; Dewitt I Evans Scholarship Endowment Fund Foundation Inc, 1998 National Association for the Advancement of Colored People 1987, 1998-. Hobbies: Bibliophile; History; Music; Philanthrop Address: Route 1, Box 25A, Fitzpatrick, AL 36029-9501, US/

**EVANS Hugh E,** b. New York, USA. Physician. m. Ruth, son, 1 daughter. Education: BA, Columbia College, New Yor 1954; MD, State University of New York, 1958. Appointment Professor of Pediatrics; Professor of Preventive Medicine an Community Health. Publications: Numerous Articles Professional Journals. Memberships: Society for Pediatr Research; American Academy of Pediatrics; American Medic Association; New York Academy of Science. Address: UMDN 150 Bergen Street, Newark, NJ 07103, USA.

**EVANS Myron Wyn,** b. 26 May 1950, Craigcefnparc, Wale Physicist. m. Laura Jean Evans. Education: BS, 1971, Ph 1974, DSc, 1977, Wales. Education: BS, 1971, PhD, 197 DSc, 1977, Aberystwyth University, Wales. Appointment Junior Research Fellow, Wolfson College, Oxford, 197 Advanced Fellow, Science and Engineering, Research Counc Aberystwyth, Oxford, 1978-83; Visiting Scientist, University Pisa, Scuala Normale Superiore, 1980, University of Zuric 1990, Cornell University, 1989, 1991; Visiting Professor: Trin College, Dublin, 1985, IBM, Kingston, NY, 1986; Yo University, Toronto, 1995, Indian Statistical Institute, Calcutt 1995; Visiting Scientist, Cornell University, 1989-92; Universi of Zurich, 1989-90; Research Associate, Pennsylvania Sta University, 1990; Professor, Alpha Foundation, Budapes Hungary, 1995-; Director, Alpha Foundation for Advance Study, 1998-; National Committee, British Science a Engineering Research Council. Publications: Editor, Mode Nonlinear Optics, 1997; 500 monographs; Articles professional journals. Honours: Leverhulme Fellow, Humbol Fellow, British Imperial Chemical Industries Fellow, 1974; NF Canada Fellow, 1974; Junior Research Fellow, Wolfs College, Oxford, 1975; British Ramsay Memorial Fellow, 197 IBM Fellow; Harrison Memorial Prize, Royal Society Chemistry, 1978; Meldola Medal, 1979; Sigma Pi Sigm Memberships: Optical Society of America; American Institute Physics; New York Academy of Sciences. Address: 82 L Lane, IThaca, NY 14850, USA.

**EVANS VANDERBILT Clara,** b. 28 October 1940, Oran County, North Carolina, USA. Physician Assistant. divorced son, 2 daughters. Education: Certificate, Physician Assista Duke University, 1971; BS, Philosophy, SUNY, 198

ertificate, Physician Assistant, Pennsylvania. Appointments: hysician Assistant, Surgery, Resident, Montefiore Medical enter, Albert Einstein College Medicine, Bronx, New York, SA, 1971-78; Director, Physician Assistant, Surgery, esidency, 1978-; Preceptor, Physician Assistant, Student urgery Clerkship Physician Assistant Program, Touro College, ix Hills, New York, 1985-95; Harlem Hospital, CUNY, New ork City, 1980-95. Honours: Distinguished Alumnus Award, uke University Physician Assistant Alumni, 1993. lemberships: Fellow, American Academy Physicians ssistants, Vice President, 1975-76, 10th Anniversary ppreciation Award, 1989; New York State Soicety Physician ssistants, Founding President, 1975, President, 1976; merican Academy Physician Assistants, Board Directors, 972, 1974; National Commission Certified Physician ssistants, Board Directors, 1977-84. Address: Montefiore ledical Center, 111 E 210th Street, Bronx, New York 10467, SA.

**EVMENOV Leonid Fyedorovich,** b. 22 July 1932, Cherikov, logilyov district. Philosopher. m. Zoya Zhigalkovich, 1 son, 1 aughter. Education: University, 1955; Candidate of hilosophy, 1961; Doctor of Philosophy, 1976; Professor, 1979; Member of National Academy of Sciences of Belarus, 1991. ppointments: Assistant Professor of Philosophy, 1961; dviser to Secretary of Communist Party of Belarus, Central Committee, 1970; UNESCO Secretariat Specialist of the rogramme P-4, 1971; Chair of Ethics, Aesthetics, Head, elarusian State University, 1975; National Academy of ciences of Belarus, Institute of Philosophy & Law, 1981; Head f Dept of Scientific Information in Social Sciences, National cademy of Sciences of Belarus, 1983; Advisor to the hairman of the Supreme Soviet of the Republic of Belarus, 994-95. Publications: Dialectics & Revolution; Philosophy of ntimarxism & Dialectics; Totalitalism and Human Rights; uclear Age: Humanism and Human Rights; Total Crisis and luman Rights; Problems of Human Rights International deology, Principles and Imperatives. Address: Masherov rospect 51, corp 1 aprt 213, 220035 Minsk, Rep of Belarus.

**EVREINOV Eduard,** b. 13 June 1928, Korma, Russia. nformation Scientist. m. Makaeva Sultanat, 1 son, 1 daughter. :ducation: MS, 1950; MS, 1952; PhD, 1959; Grand PhD, 1968; rof, 1972; Grand PhD, 1994; Prof EM, 1995. Appointments: )irector Computer Department, 1952; Vice Director IM cademy of Science, 1959; Director-General VGPTI, 1956; 4ead of Chair CS, 1993. Publications: 300 scientific works; 23 nonographs. Honours: Lenin Prize, N2, 1957; International nformation Prize, 1992; Medal UN, 1995; Diploma of Honour, 1981; Medal IIA, 1998. Memberships: Academician, numerous lepartments and academies; President, RIA; President, WDU. address: 11A Tverskaya 5-6, Moscow 103009, Russia.

**EZEKWE Michael Obi,** b. 16 November 1944, Nigeria. m. :dith I Ezekwe, 4 sons, 1 daughter. Education: BS, Animal Science, University of Nigeria, 1971; MS, Animal Nutrition, Pennsylvania State University; PhD, Animal Nutrition, Pennsylvania State, 1977. Appointments: Assistant Professor, Principal Investigator, Virginia State Univesity, 1978-97; USDA-CSREES; Associate Professor, Director of Swine Development Centre, Alcorn State University, 1997-. Publications include: Effect of Grain Supplementation on Reproductive Performance and Nutritional Status of Gestatin and Lactating Spanish Does, 1995; A Seasonal Reproductive Performance of Virginia Brush Goats Used for Meat Production, 1996; Environmental Effects on Yield and Agronomic Traits of Purslane, 1997; Characterization of Purslane as a Viable Vegetable Crop in the United States, 1994; The Effects of Gestational Fructose-Rich Diet on Serum Metabolities of

Pregnant Gilts and the Progeny, 1989; Lipid Composition of Purslane (Portulaca Oleracea) Harvested at Different Growth Stages, 1990; Evaluation of Purslane Seeds From Different Geographical Locations for Oil Contents and Fatty Acids Quality, 1993; Omega-Three Fatty Acids in Purslane (Portulaca Oleracea) Tissues, 1991; The effects of Maternal Fasting on Postnatal Performance of Pigs, 1990. Honours: President, VSU Chapter, 1990-93, Sigma Xi; Gamma Sigma Delta; First Place Outstanding Paper Award in Animal Science, ARD Biennial Research Symposium, New Orleans, Louisiana, 1994; Feed compositions comprising Purslane leaves and Methods of Using Thereof, US Patent. Memberships: American Society of Animal Science; American Society of Nutritional Science. Address: Alcorn State University, 1000 ASU Drive #1374, Lorman, MS 39096, USA.

# F

**FABRIKANT Craig,** b. 1 August 1952, Buffalo, New York, USA. Psychologist. m. Carol Golub, 1 son, 1 daughter. Education: BA General Psychology, 1974, MA Counselling and Guidance, 1977, MA Counselling Psychology, 1977, Fairleigh Dickinson University, Dept Psychology, Teaneck, New Jersey; PhD Clinical Psychology, 1983, Florida Institute Technology, School of Psychology, Melbourne, Florida. Appointments: Psychology Intern, 1977-78; Adjunct Instructor in Psychology, 1980-83; Consultant, Psychological Service Centre, Cedar Lane, 1983-84; Staff Therapist and Supervisor, 5th Avenue Centre for Counselling and Psychotherapy, NYC, 1984-85; Senior Clinical Psychologist, North Jersey Developmental Centre, Totowa, NJ, 1978-85; Adjunct Instructor, Department of Psychology, Fairleugh Dickinson University, 1983-85; Chief Psychologist and Director of Clinical Services, Cedar Grove Residential Centre, Division of Youth and Family Services, Department of Human Services, 1985; Chief, Section of Psychology, Institute for Child Development, Hackensack Medical Centre, NJ, 1985-96; Private Practice, NJ, 1984-; Executive Director, Co-Owner, Pascack Centre for Human Development, NJ, 1986-. Publications: Author or co-author 6 articles, 2 book reviews and 25 international and national presentations and communications; 4 medical grand rounds; 4 workshops and colloquium. Memberships: American Psychological Association, 4 divisions; Council for Exceptional Children; National Association of Gifted Children; Council on Learning Disabilities; World Federation for Mental Health; Association for the Advancement of Psychology; American College of Forensic Examiners; and others. Address: 750 Martin Avenue, Oradell, NJ 07649-2300, USA.

**FABRIZIO Tuula,** b. 13 May 1931, Helsinki, Finland. Physician; Medical Editor. m. John A Fabrizio, 2 sons. Education: Medical School, University of Helsinki, 1957; DMS, University Central Hospital, Helsinki. Appointments: Emergency Departments, Park City Hispital, Bridgeport, 1964, Norwalk Hospital, 1966-69, Milford Hospital, 1973-77, St Vincent's Medical Centre, Bridgeport; School and Well Baby Clinic Physician, Norwalk, 1969-73; Occupational Health Services, Lowered Fee Clinic for Uninsured People, 1979-. Honours include: Bronze Medal, Finnish Medical Association, 1980; Plaque, Finnish Medical Journal, 1982. Memberships: American Medical Association; Fairfield County Medical Association; Connecticut State Medical Society; American College of Emergency Physicians; American Public Health Association; American Association for Automobile Medicine; International College of Pediatrics; Academy of Political Science; American Medical Writers Association. Address: 42 Stevens Street. Norwalk, CT 06850-3525, USA.

**FADARISHAN Stephen,** b. 24 November 1953, Scranton, PA, USA. Electrical Engineer. m. Ines. Education: First Class FCC Licence, 1970; BS, Electrical Engineering, 1982. Appointments: Design Engineer, Locus Inc, 1982-84; Design Engineer, General Instrument, 1984-85; Lead Systems Engineer, Norden Systems, 1985-89; Software Engineer, Westinghouse, 1989-90; Software Engineer, Boehringer Mannheim, 1990-91; Technical Adviser, Cummins Engine Co, 1992-. Honours: Eta Kappa Nu; Electrical Engineering Honour Fraternity. Memberships: AIIM; ACM; STC. Address: Cummins Engine Engring Standards, Box 3005 M/C 50111, Columbus, IN 47202-3005, USA.

**FAHIM Fawzia A,** b. 9 December 1931, Fayoum, Egypt. Professor. m. Salah El Mahdy, 2 sons, 1 daughter. Education:

BSc, 1954; Diploma in Education, Psychology, 1985; MSc, 1962; PhD, 1965. Appointments: Demonstrator, 1957-62; Governmental Grant, 1962-65; Lecturer, 1967-74; Assistant Professor, 1975-80; Professor, 1980-; Head of Environmental Biology Department, 1983-87. Publications: 65 Publications. Memberships: Egyptian Society of Biochemistry; Mediteranian Society of Tumoz Mankin Onocology; Egyptian Society of Tumor Manken Onocology; New York Academy of Sciences; Patients Welfare; Environmental Protection; AAAs. Address: 19 Mohamed Hegab St, 11351 Cairo, Egypt.

**FALLON Stephen Michael,** b. 18 September 1954, Washington, DC, USA. Professor. m. Nancy Hungarland. Education: AB, English, Princeton University, 1976; MA, English, McGill University, 1978; PhD, English, University of Virginia, 1985. Appointments: Assistant Professor, Liberal Studies, University of Notre Dame, 1985-90; Chair, Professor of Liberal Studies, 1992-95; Associate Professor, Program of Liberal Studies, Department of English, University of Notre Dame, 1990-. Publications: Milton Among the Philosophers; National Endowment for the Humenitus Fellow. Honours: James Hally Hanford Distinguished Book Award; Milton Society of Service. Memberships: Modern Language Association; Milton Socity of America. Address: U Notre Dame, 368 Decio Hall, Notre Dame, IN 46556-5644, USA.

**FAN Zhen Zeng,** b. 18 September 1960, Shijiazhuang, Hebei, China. Doctor. m. Zhang Li Ping, 1 son. Education: Doctor, He Bei Medical University, 1996. Appointments: 1982-. Publications: Phychosis and Behaviourism of Neurosurgery, 1988; Medical Answer, 1996; Medical Introduction, 1997. Memberships: China College of Medicine. Address: 223 He Ping West Road, Xin Hua District, Affilliated Hospital Two, He Bei Medical University, Shijiazhuang, He Bei 050000, China.

**FANELLI Leslie,** b. 27 May 1957, Cincinnati, OH, USA. Artistic Director. m. Anthony Fanelli, divorced, 1 daughter. Education: BS, Theatre and Urban Affairs, CUNY Baccalaureate, 1986. Appointments: Artistic Director and Founder, Theatre in Motion. Honours: New York City Mayor's Very Special Arts Award, 1993; Clinton Administration Commendation, 1993. Memberships: New York City Arts-in-Education Roundtable; Arts Horizons; Artpride, New Jersey, USA. Address: 245 Livingston Avenue, New Providence, NJ 07974, USA.

**FANG Qi-Cheng,** b. 22 November 1929, Zhejiang, China. Professor of Medicinal Chemistry. m. Sun Liu-Nan, 1 son, 1 daughter. Education: BS Pharmaceutical Chemistry, 1952, Medical College, Peking University, China; PhD Pharmaceutical Sciences, 1958, Moscow Sechenov 1st Medical Institute, USSR. Appointments: Assistant, Department of Pharmaceutical Sciences, Beijing Medical College, 1952-54; Graduate Student, Moscow Sechenov 1st Medical Institute, 1955-58; Research Associate, 1959-79, Associate Professor, 1979-85, Professor, 1985-, Vice Chairman, Department of Chemistry of Natural Products, 1959-78, Chairman, 1979-94, Member, Specialist Group, 1995-, Institute of Materia Medica, CAMS and PUMC; Consultant and Visiting Scholar, Division of Chemistry and Life Sciences, Research Triangle Institute, North Carolina, USA, 1987-88. Publications: Co-worker over 100 scientific papers published in international and domestic journals, in the field of chemical studies on alkaloids, flavonoids, saponins, triterpenoids, taxoids. Honours: 5 Prizes awarded by National Science Meeting, 1978; Second Grade Prize of National Inventions, for Anisodamine, 1981; First Grade Prize of Science and Technology Progress, Ministry of Public Health, 1996; Third Grade Prize of National Sciences and Technology Progress, 1997; Special Government owance awarded for Outstanding Contribution in velopment of the Medical and Pharmaceutical Undertakings, 2-. Memberships: Committee of Drug Evaluation, Ministry Public Health, China, 1992-95; Commission of armacopoeia of China, 1975-96; Board of Editors of Chinese armaceutical Journal, 1978-98; Co-Editor in Chief, Book: dern Studies on the Traditional Chinese and Herb Medicine, ols, 1994-98; Board of Editors, Journal of Asian Natural oducts Research, 1997-. Address: Institute of Materia dica, Chinese Academy of Medical Sciences, Peking Union dical College, 1 Xian Nong Tan Street, Beijing 100050, na.

FANG Rong Rémi, b. 10 August 1958, Ping-Jiang, Hunan, ina. Physicist. Education: Diploma, Nuclear Physics, ing-Hua University, Beijing, 1982; Master Degree, High ergy Physics, Institute of High Energy Physics of China, 35; PhD, High Energy Physics, University Louis Pasteur, ance, 1997. Appointments: Lecturer, Modern Physics, iversity of Science and Technology, China, 1985-88; Visiting sociate Professor, High Energy Physics, University of Paris 1989-91; Engineer, Aerial Nuclear Irradiation Centre, 1993-. blications: Several articles in professional journals on Rule Charge Accumulation, Electron Dispersion and related ics. Memberships: American Association for the vancement of Science; New York Academy of Science; low, American Biographical Institute. Address: 14 Rue rivaux, 67200 Strasbourg, France.

FANG Rongli, b. 10 October 1940, Suining, Sichuan, China. acher. m. Zhang Juyin, 28 September 1969, 2 daughters. ucation: Undergraduated Student, Menchilieve Institute of emical Engineering, Moscow, 1959-63; Undergraduated dent, Modern Chemistry Department, China University of ience and Technology. Appointments: Researcher, Chinese tional Department of Nuclear Industry, 1988-; Professor of Department of Materials Sciences and Technology, uthwest Institute of Technology, Mianyang, Sichuan, China. blications: Over 60 papers published in international ademic symposium proceedings and academic journals; 4 onographs: Bases of Environment Pollution Analyse; Mixing aterials of Cement; Engineering of Sillicate Reaction; Industry esidue and Cement Mixing Materials. Honours: Significant hievement, National Department of Nuclear Industry and the tional Science and Technology Symposium, 1978; Second ize, Youth Science and Technology Achievement of Sichuan ovince, 1993; Third Prize, Sichuan Province Science and chnology Achievement, 1996; Gold Prizes, Chinese Patent hievements Fairs, 1993. Memberships: Council, Chinese ment Industry Association; Chinese National Higher ucation Guiding Committee of Inorganic Material Specialty; ouncil, Sichuan Province Building Materials Industry sociation; Specialist Group of Senior Professional dgement Committee of Building Engineering and Building aterials Specialty in Colleges and Universities in Sichuan ovince. Address: Department of Materials Science and chnology, Southwest Institute of Technology, Mianyang, chuan, China.

FANG Zhongda, b. 20 May 1916, Shanghai, China. Plant athology. m. Yu Hanying, 2 sons. Education: PhD, Wisconsin hiversity, USA, 1948; Professor, Nanjing Agricultural hiversity, 1952. Honour: Outstanding People Record of ambridge University. Membership: American hytopathological Society. Address: Department of Plant athology, Nanjing Agricultural University, Nanjing 210095, hina.

FARACHOV Adalat Nurulla, b. 1936, Masally Region, Azerbaidjan. Teacher. m. Sabirova Nasiba A, 1 son, 2 daughters. Education: Dr.biol, Professor, 1991, Moscow. Appointments: Scientific and Pedagogical Fields. Publications: Several articles in professional journals. Membership: Biological Faculty, Pedagogical University. Address: F1 Seyidbayli Street, Apt 28, Block 2, Baku 370001, Azerbaidjan.

FARAIDY Abdulaziz, b. 15 May 1945, Taif, Saudi Arabia. Public Administrator. m. Nora, 4 sons, 2 daughters. Education: BS, California State University, Los Angeles, 1970; MPA, South California, Los Angeles, 1982. Appointments: Commande of Shooting Range Public Security; Chief Instructor for Officers Institute, Hospital Administration Security Forces Hospital in Riyadh, General Director, Civil Defense for Riyadh Region (currently). Honours: King Abdulaziz Leadership, 1999; King Abdulaziz Medal; King Faisal Medal; Leadership Military Medal. Memberships: American Society for Public Administration; American Society Safety Engineers; American Society Fire Engineering. Address: PO Box 26894, Riyadh 11496, Saudi Arabia.

FARELL Edward, b. 20 January 1943, Toronto, Canada. Engineer. m. Susan, 1 son, 3 daughters. Education: MSc, distinction, Telecommunication Systems, University of Essex, England, 1971. Appointments: Senior Development Engineer, Program Manager, Satellite Systems, Raytheon & RCA; Telecom Consultant, ITU, World Bank, IDB & Administrations. Publications: Over 20 papers in professional journals. Memberships: Association of Professional Engineers, Ontario. Address: E. Farell Consulting Co. Ltd., 349 Brunswick Avenue, Toronto, Ontario M5R 2Z1, Canada.

FARID Reza, b. 11 February 1941, Iran. Professor of Medicine. m. Simin, 1 son, 1 daughter. Education: MD, Mashad University, Iran; DTCD, Wales University, UK; Diplomate, American Academy of Asthma Allergy Immunology. Appointments: Professor of Medicine, Head of Immunology, Ghaem Hospital, Mashad. Publications: 17 books; 60 articles; all in medicine. Memberships: FCCP; Fellow, AAAAI; Fellow, American College of Allergy. Address: Dept of Immunology, Ghaem Hospital, Mashhad, Iran.

FASHAKIN Joseph Bandele, b. 6 September 1937, Akure, Nigeria. Professor of Nutrition. m. Janet Morenike, 3 sons, 2 daughters. Education: BSc, McGill; MSc, Michigan State; MSc, MIT; DSc, Harvard. Appointments: University Professor. Publications: 28. Honours: 8 Awards. Memberships: 3 associations. Address: PO Box 1745, Akure, Nigeria.

FATTORINI Ivan, b. 28 February 1941, Belgrade. Pediatric Surgeon. m. Zeljka, 1 son, 1 daughter. Education: Graduate, Zagreb University Medical School, 1965; Residency in General Surgery, 1967-69; Postgraduate Studies, Sport Medicine, 1969-71; Residency in Pediatric Surgery, 1969-72; Board Exam in Pediatric Surgery, 1972. Appointments: Consultant Pediatric Surgeon, 1986; Chief of Outpatients, Childrens Hospital, Zagreb, 1989-91; Director of the Hospital and Chief of Division of Urology, 1991-; President, Croatian Society of Pediatric Surgeons, 1997-; Official Physician, National Olympic Team, 1984, 1988, 1992; Medical Committee, 1990-; President, Medical Committee, Basketball Club CIBONA Zagreb, 1976-; President, Medical Committee, Ministry of Education and Sports of Republic of Croatia, 1991-; Head, National Delegation of the T-DO, The Council of Europe, 1991-; Headquarters, Croatian Army Medical Corps, 1991-95; President KIWANIS Club Zagreb, 1993-94; Coordinator, Medical Committee, Football Club, Croatia Zagreb, 1996-; Editorial Boards: Paediatria Croatica, 1991-, European Journal of Pediatric

Surgery, 1999-. Honours: City of Zagreb Award for the Year of 1993; Order of the Croatian Star with the Effigy of Katarina Zrinska, 1996; Man of the Year, American Biographical Institute, 1997; Honorary Member of the Association of Pediatric Surgeons of Bosnia and Herzegovina, 1997. Memberships: Croatian Medical Association; Croatian Surgical Society; Croatian Urological Society; Croatian Society of Sport Medicine; FIMS; Medical Committee, FIBA; World Federation for Mental Health; World Association of Croatian Physicians; KIWANIS Club Zagreb; KIWANIS Club International; Many other Memberships. Address: Childrens Hospital Zagreb, Klaiceva 10000, Croatia.

**FEDELLE Estelle**, b. Chicago, Illinois, USA. Painter; Educator; Writer. Education: Art Institute of Chicago; Northwestern University; Institute of Design; American Academy of Fine Arts; Privately. Career: Owner, Teacher, Demonstrator, Fedelle Art Studio; Exhibited at 50 one-man shows and group shows, Chicago Visual Arts Center, Illinois State Fair, Chicago Public Library, Kenosha Public Library, Barron Galleries, Chicago and Las Vegas, Grand Central Gelleries, New York, American Artists Professional League, elsewhere; Weekly Columnist, Art and You, The Leader newspapers, Chicago, 1974-; Lectures and demonstrations, Eastern and Midwestern United States. Publications: How to Begin Painting for Fun, book, 1965; Contributions to other art books. Honours: 75 awards for paintings, including Honorary PhD, Colorado State Christian College, 1973, and Certificates of Merit. Memberships include: American Portrait Society; American Society of Artists; International Fine Arts; National League of American Penwomen; Municipal Art League; Regent Art League; Park Ridge Art League. Address: 1500 S Cumberland, Park Ridge, IL 60068, USA.

**FEDORCHENKO Alexandr I**, b. 4 June 1954, Amurskaya Oblast, Russia. Thermo and Molecular Physics Scientist. m. Fedorchenko Elena Andreevna, 1 son. Education: Graduate, Department of Applied Mathematics, Novosibirsk State Technical University, 1971-76; Postgraduate Student of Institute of Thermophysics, 1980-83; Candidate of Physics and Mathematical Science. Appointments: Senior Researcher Scientist of Laboratory of Disperse Systems, Institute of Thermophysics, 1989-91; Senior Researcher of Laboratory of Turbulent Flow, 1991-. Publications: Books: High Temper Dust-Laden Jets in Plasma Technology, 1990; Plasma Jet in the Development of New Technology, 1990; High Velocity Acceleration of Macrobody, Theory, Practice, Perspectives, 1994; Above 40 papers in science journals and proceedings of conferences. Honours: 1st Award of Young Science Conference, Institute of Thermophysics, 1987; 3rd Award Applied Research Competition of Siberian Division, RAS, 1990. Membership: Editorial Board Member, J of Magnetohydrodynamics and Plasma Research, New York, 1996. Address: Institute of Thermophysics SBRAS, Prosp Academician Lavrentyev 1, 630090, Novosibirsk, Russia.

**FEENEY Mary Katherine**, b. 7 October 1934, Niagara Falls, New York, USA. Registered Nurse. m. Gerald E Feeney, 4 daughters. Education: BS, Nursing, Niagara University, 1956; MS, Human Resource Management, SUNY, 1981. Appointments: Public Health Nurse, Herkimer County; Past Coordinator, Herkimer County Long Term Health Care. Memberships: Board Director, Executive Committee, Oneida/Herkimer Coalition for Tobacco Control. Address: 146 Stateroute 169, Little Falls, NY 13365-9556, USA.

**FEHER Tibor**, b. 9 January 1932, Ujvidek, Yugoslavia. Professor of Hormone Biochemistry. m. Katalin Grosser, 2 daughters. Education: Diploma Chemist, 1955, Natural Science Department, University of Szeged, Hungary. Appointmer Scientific Consultant, Medical University of Budape Publications: Author (Contributor) 5 books; 280 articles professional journals. Memberships: European Endocr Society; Professor, NY Academy of Science. Address: Oktol 6U 8, 1051 Budapest, Hungary.

**FEHR Manfred**, b. 25 March 1936, Jena. Engineer. Giomar Yemail, 1 son, 1 daughter. Education: PhD Chemi Engineering, 1978; Fluent 5 languages. Appointmer Professional activities in 18 countries; International consulta with 31 clients; Lecturer and Professor of 5 universiti Publications: 78 journal and newspaper articles, 1980-98 book, 1995. Honours: 27, 1963-98. Memberships: Past a present member of 26 professional associations in vario countries. Address: Caixa Postal 811, 38400 974 Uberlan MG, Brazil.

**FEIGHT Cheryl**, b. 21 March 1949, Rapid City, Sou Dakota, USA. Administrator; Computer Manager; Consultar Multimedia, Web Development, Creativity. m. Mark Feight daughter. Appointments include: Director, Fine Arts Compu Resources, 1974-; Director, Arts Outreach; College of Fi Arts; University of South Dakota; Vermillion, South Dako Honours: Scholarship, University of North Carolina, School Business Administration, 1984; Outstanding Young Women America, 1979; Friends of Education Award, SD Association Elementary School Principals, 1983; Vermillion Area A Council Board of Directors, 1978-81; Scholarship Recipie Foundation for the Arts in SD, 1984; Visiting Professor, IB Rochester, Minnesota, Summer 1991; IBM Roches Courseware Development Award, November 199 Memberships: American Film Institute; American Council the Arts. Address: University SD College Fine Arts, 414 E Cla Street, Vermillion, SD 570069-2307, USA.

**FEIN Paul Stockser**, b. Springfield, Massachusetts, US Journalist. Education: Cornell University. Appointmen Journalist, articles have appeared in general interest, spo and tennis magazines around the world. Publications: Articl have appeared in Le Monde du Tennis, France; Tenr Magazin Germany, Match Ball, Italy; Tennis, USA; Tenr Week, USA; International Tennis; Australian Tennis Magazin Tenis Solo Tenis, Mexico; Sport, USA; Women's Sports ar Fitness, USA; Players Magazine, USA; Tennis Tidnjnge Sweden; Tennis Report, Taiwan; Tennis USA. Honour Community Service Award of Springfield Tennis Opportuni Program, 1987; New England Lawn Tennis Association Med Award, 1988; Tennis Writer of the Year Tennis Week, 199 Tennis Writer of the Year Award, Tennis Week, 1996; Tenr Writer of the Year Award from Tennis Week, 199 Memberships: US Tennis Writers Association; Nation Sportswriter and Sportscasters Association; Associatic Internationale de la Presse Sportive; US Tennis Associatio US Professional Tennis Association; National Senior Wome Tennis Association; AARP; United States Professional Tenn Registry. Address: 39 Beekman Drive, Agawam, M 01001-2608, USA.

**FEKETE-BERKY Julia**, b. 20 July 1957, Slovakia. Musicia Teacher. m. Education: Majored in Piano Accordian, School Music, Bratislava, 1964-70; Flute, 1970-72; Majored in Flut State Conservatorium of Music, 1972-76; Mus Ed ar Performance, Hons, 1976-78; Flute, University of Bratislav 1978-81. Appointments: Junior Choir, Radio Bratislav 1963-64; Vocal Section, 1972-74; Flute Lecturer, Nation Conservatroium of Music, 1974-76; Principal Flautis Conservatorium Orchestra, 1976-78; Principal Flautist, Nation Orchestra, 1976-81; Woodwind Section, Bratislava Rad

Orchestra, 1976-81; Flautist, Singer, Professional Orchestras, Recording Studios, Music Festivals, Shows, Television and Radio, 1972-81; Teacher, Lecturer, Conservation Centre, 1981-86; Co-originator of Woodwind Teaching, Riverina Region of NSW, 1981-86; Member, Berky Trio, Flute, Principal Flautist of Opera Ensemble, Sydney, 1987-. Honours: 1st Prize, National Flute Competition, 1976; 2nd Prize, National Flute Competition, 1978; 1st Prize, University Competition for all Instruments, 1981; 1st Prize, Newcastle Mattara Festival, 1982. Memberships: Secretary, Management Committee National Orchestra; Flute Society; NSW Teachers Association; AMEB Examiner, NSW. Address: 23 Merinda Avenue, Epping 2121, NSW, Australia.

**FELBER Sonja Veronika,** b. 21 March 1965, St Pelten. Mechanical Engineer. Education: E Graduate, University Technology Vienna, 1992; DSc, 1994; Research Scientist, OMV, Vienna, Austria, 1991-92. Appointment: Assistant, University Technology, Vienna, 1993-. Memberships: Austrian Welding Foundation; Austrian Iron and Steel Institute; International Institute of Welding. Address: Department of Materials Science and Testing, Vienna University of Technology, Karlsplatz 13, A1040 Vienna, Austria.

**FELTUS James Jr,** b. 16 April 1921, Gloster, Mississippi, USA. Senior Bishop. m. Hazel Luter, 7 sons (1 dec), 3 daughters. Education: PhB, 1946, Xavier University, New Orleans; MEd, 1963, Southern University, New Orleans; BD, 1954, DD, 1955, Campbell College, Jackson; MRE, 1973, Baptist Theological Seminary, New Orleans; PhD, 1998, University of Biblical Studies, Oklahoma City. Appointments: Substitute Teacher, Orleans Parish School Board, 1954-74; District Superintendent #8, Louisiana, 1953-65, Overseer of British Honduras, 1955-73, Church of God in Christ Incorporated; Pastor, First Church of God in Christ United, New Orleans, 1945-; Presiding Senior Bishop & Founder, Church of God in Christ United, New Orleans, Jamaica, London, Africa and the Virgin Islands, 1974-. Honours: Member, District Attorney's Committee Against Drugs, 1988-89; Honorary Civil Sheriff, 1983-; Colonel of the Staff to Louisiana Governor Edwards, 1987; New Orleans Mayor's Certificate of Appreciation, 1987; President, Interdenominational Ministerial Alliance, 1987; NO City Council's Certificate of Recognition, 1986, Leadership Award, 1987; Declaration of Bishop James Feltus' Day by Mayor of NO, 1987; Phi Delta Kappa's Man of the Year Award, 1990; Citation of Honour, US Senate, 1990; Charter Member of the International Association of Chiefs of Police; Member of the American Association of Christian Counsellors. Address: Churches of God in Christ United, 2453 Josephine Street, New Orleans, LA 70112, USA.

**FENG Boyang,** b. 4 September 1952, Changchun, Jilin, China. Musicologist. m. Wei Wang, 1 son. Education: Jilin College of Arts, 1978-82. Appointment: Teacher, 1982-. Publictions: Manchu Shaman Music as Viewed From Cultural Anthropology; The Analysis of the Social Values of Manchu Shaman Music; Instructions to Musical Works Appreciation. Honours: Chang Bai Shan Literature and Art Award; Excellent Teaching Achievements Award. Memberships: Board, Chairman of Manchu Music, Research Institute in Chinese Musicians Association; Chinese Religion Institute; Music History in Chinese Musicians Association. Address: Jilin College of Arts, No 11 Zhou Road, Changchun 130021, China.

**FENG Jincheng,** b. 5 December 1939, Ninbo, Zhejiang Province, China. m. Ji Jinqiu, 1 son, Feng Zheng. Education: Graduate, Diploma of Physics, Nanjing University, China, 1962. Appointments: Technician, Physics Engineer, 1962-70; Physics Engineer, 1971-72; Agriculture Engineer, 1973-78; Lecturer of

Mathematics, Nanjing Forestry University, 1978-86; Associate Professor of Mathematics, Nanjing Population Administration College, 1986-88; Associate Professor of Physics, The Frontier Science Institute of the National Labour and Personnel Department, 1988-89; Professor of Physics, Qiongzhou University, China, 1990-. Publications: More than 20 Articles, International Conference or Journals; Fuzzy Pattern Recognition; Fuzzy Mathematics and Its Application in Forestry. Honours: Reward of Science and Technique Achievements for Root Irrigation at National Level; Reward of Scientific Congress; Specialist with Outstanding Achievements; Specialist with Science and Technique Achievements at National Level; World Science and Technique Consultative Specialist; Session Chairmen of ICNNSP; Outstanding People of the 20th Century, International Biographical Centre. Memberships: Vice Chairman of Hainan Branch of China's Electronics Society; Executive Council of China Engineering Probability and Statistics Society; Member of the Editorial Board of Journal of Data Acquisition and Processing. Address: Department of Physics, Qiongzhou University, 572200 Hainan, China.

**FERGUSON Dell, Dayle Wendell Jordan,** b. 6 May 1954, Washington, Georgia, USA. Education. m. Jerry L Ferguson, 3 sons. Education: Alpena Community College, Alpena, Michigan, Diploma, 1972; Auditing, Georgia State University, 1983-87. Appointments: Performer, I Lost It At the Movies, musical, 1982; Singer, Sweet Adelines Inc, Tulsa, 1981; Entertainer, Artist; Writer, numerous articles in profile magazines, journals. Publication: Times in Life, book. Honours: Irwin Berlin Award, 1982; Musical, Panama Canal, Times Clash, Siemmes and Allis Journal, 1983. Membership: YWCA of Greater Atlanta. Address: 2853 The Meadows Way, College Park, GA 30349, USA.

**FERNANDES Ernest (Reverend Father),** b. 25 March 1941, Anjuna, Goa, India. Pastor-Principal; Teacher; Sportsman. Education: MA, 1974; B Ed, 1975. Appointments: Teacher-Principal, 1975-98; Trustee of the School and Church; Vice-President of All India National Association of Catholic Schools, India; Executive Committee Member of Sports Authority of India. Publications: in school magazines. Honours: National Award for Sanchayika, children's bank; Giant International for Sports Promotions in Education. Address: Our Lady of Lourdes Parish, Kalyan, Mumbai, Maharashtra, India.

**FERNANDEZ Crispulo Jr,** b. 10 May 1941, Manila, Philippines. Businessman. m. Teresita Toribio, 3 sons, 3 daughters. Education: Liberal Arts, 1959, University of Sto Tomas; Chemical Engineering, 1962, Manoua Institute of Technology; Economics AB, 1971, University of the East. Appointments: Conference Supervisor, Manila Electrical Company, 1970-73; Man Liaison Officer, Philippines Petroleum Corporation, 1973-75; General Manager, Fernandez Trading, 1976-84; President, Fernandez Farms, Inc, 1977-90; Owner, Fernandez Tenements, 1985-98; President and CEO, Fernandez-Navarro Development Corporation, 1995-98. Honours: Senator No 26255, Jaycees International, 1978; Most Outstanding Jaycee, Cainta Jaycees, 1980; Most Outstanding Farmer, Philippines Jaycees, 1983; Rotarian of the Decade, Rotary Club of Cainta, 1998; Knight York Cross of Honour, York Rite Masonry, 1988; Knight Commander Cross of Honour, Scottish Rite Masonry, 1985. Memberships: As above plus: Friends of Ortigas Foundation; Philippines Chamber of Commerce and Industries, NCR. Address: 317 A Mabini Street, 1900 Cainta Rizal, The Philippines.

**FERNANDEZ Julio Angel,** b. 5 April 1946, Montevideo, Uruguay. Astronomer. Education: Degree of Licenciado in

Astronomy, University of the Republic, Montevideo, Uruguay, 1974. Appointments: Assistant, Astronomy Department, University of the Republic, Montevideo, Uruguay, 1970-76; Visiting Astronomer, National Observatory, Madrid, Spain, 1979; Researcher, Max-Planck Society, Max-Planck Institut für Aeronomie, Germany, 1980-82; Researcher, Max-Planck Society at the Max-Planck Institut für Kernphysik, Germany, 1983; Visiting Professor, Observatorio do Valongo, Rio de Janeiro, Brazil, 1984-86; Professor, Astronomy Department, Faculty of Sciences, University of the Republic, Montevideo, 1986-. Publications: Author, about 50 research papers, several books and popular articles for magazines and newspapers including: On the Existence of a Comet Belt Beyond Neptune, 1980; Origin and Nature of Comets, 1983; Some Dynamical Aspects of the Accretion of Uranus and Neptune: The Exchange of Orbital Angular Momentum with Planetesimals, 1984; Cometary Dynamics, 1998. Memberships: Editorial Advisory Board, Planetary and Space Science, journal; International Astronomical Union; Planetary Society; President, Astronomical Society of Uruguay; Small Bodies Names Committee of the International Astronomical Union for the term 1997-2000; Organizing Committee, International Astronomical Union Commission 14, 1994-2000. Address: Facultad de Ciencias, Departamento de Astronomia, Igua 4225, 11 400 Montevideo, Uruguay.

**FERNANDO Ellekuttige Malcolm,** b. 24 September 1951, Colombo, Sri Lanka. Naval Officer. m. Nilanthi, 1 daughter. Education: Chartered Engineer, 1973-77; MSc, Defence Studies, 1989-90. Appointments: Deputy Director, 1992-96; Commandant Defence Academy, 1997-98; Director, Electrical Engineering, 1998-. Honours: Dissertation for Masters Degree, 1990. Memberships: Institution of Engineers. Address: Sri Lanka Navy Headquarters, P O Box 593, Colombo 01, Sri Lanka.

**FERRARA José Vicente,** b. 19 November 1931, Chihuahua, Chihuahua, Mexico. Chemical Engineer. m. Consuelo Fernández, 4 sons, 2 daughters. Education: Bachelor in Chemical Engineering, University of Dayton, USA, 1952; MS, Chemical Engineering, Massachusetts Institute of Technology, 1954; Seminar in Work Simplification, Lake Placid, New York, 1975; AD-2 Course in Business Administration, IPADE, Monterrey, Mexico, 1977. Appointments: Production Manager, Fábrica de Papel Monterrey, 1954-55; Plant Manager, Química Industrial de Monterrey; Production Manager, 1958-60, President, Chief Executive Officer, 1960-, Productos Químicos Monterrey SA de CV; President, Bienes Ionmobiliarios de Monterrey, 1964-; President, Cajas de Cartón Sultana, 1977-; President, Reactivos y Equipos SLP, 1978-. Memberships: President, Movimiento Familiar Cristiano, 1960-65; Unión Social de Empresarios Mexicanos, President, 1970-72; Sierra Madre Tennis Club, Board of Directors, 1971-73; Casino de Monterrey; Casino del Valle; Club Internacional. Address: Privada Rio Tiber #100, Colonia del Valle, Nuevo Leon, Mexico 66250.

**FERRARA Richard Anthony Jr,** b. 13 November 1963, Providence, Rhode Island, USA. Management. Education: High School Diploma, La Salle Academy, 1981; BS, Management, Boston College, 1986; MBA, Marketing, Cornell University, 1991. Appointments: Director of Programs, Junior Achievement of Rhode Island; Assistant Manager, Customer Service, Comsearch Inc; Assistant Manager, Sales Administration, Canon, USA, Inc. Honour: Canon Spirit Award, Address: 849 Van Dyck Court Sunnyvale, CA 94087, USA.

**FERRAZZI Enrico,** b. 11 September 1953, Italy. Medical Doctor. Education: Graduate, cum laude, Milan University

School of Medicine, 1978; Graduate, cum laude, Milan State University First School of Obstetrics and Gynaecology, 1982; Perinatal Medicine, National Council of Research, 1985. Career: Research Fellow, 1987, Consultant, 1991, Associate Professor, 1998, Department of Obstetrics and Gynaecology, San Paolo Biomedical Sciences Institute, University of Milan. Publications: Several articles in the fields of perinatal medicine and diagnostic ultrasound in major scientific international journals. Memberships: Italian Society of Obstetrics & Gynaecology; Italian Society of Perinatal Medicine; Italian Society of Ultrasound in Obstetrics and Gynaecology; International Society of Ultrasound in Obstetrics and Gynaecology; Society of Maternal Fetal Medicine. Address: University of Milan, Department of Obstetrics and Gynaecology, ISBM San Paolo Via Rudini 8, 20142 Milan, Italy.

**FERREIRA DA SILVA Antonio,** b. 1 April 1947, Conceição do Jacuípe, Berimbau, Bahia, Brazil. Physicist; Researcher. m. Vera Conceicão da Silva. 1 son, 1 daughter. Education: BSc, Federal University of Bahia, 1970; MSc, University of Campinas, 1975; PhD, 1979, Docent in Physics, 1985, Linköping University, Sweden. Appointments: Visiting Researcher, University of Kyoto, Japan, 1979; Head, Division of Science and Technology, 1981-82, Senior Researcher, 1986-, Instituto Nacional Pesquisas Espaciais, São José dos Campos, Brazil; Visiting Researcher, Brown University, USA, 1982; Consultant, Brazilian National Resesarch Council, 1986-; Visiting Scientist, Linköping University, 1996; Consultant, Condensed Matter Physics. Publications: More than 120 international publications. Honour: One of Brazilian Scientists most cited internationally, Science Ranking (Brazilian), 1999. Memberships: American Physical Society; Brazilian Physical Society; New York Academy of Sciences. Address: INPE/LAS CP 515, 12201970 São José dos Campos, São Paulo, Brazil.

**FERRERO Marc,** b. 1 June 1955, Glendale, California, USA. Producer. m. Maureen, 1 son, 1 daughter. Education: BA, 1978, USC. Appointments: President, Magic Window Productions. Honours: Gold Award, Worldfest Houston; Silver Award, Worldfest Charleston; Silver, Houston International Film Festival; Silver, US International Film and Video Festival; Bronze, Columbus Film abd Video International. Memberships: Themed Entertainment Association; Academy of Television Arts and Sciences; IAAPA; ITVA. Address: Magic Window Productions Inc, Suite 390 20300 Ventura Boulevard, Woodland Hills, CA 91364-2448, USA.

**FERRY Joan Evans,** b. 20 August 1941, Summit, New Jersey, USA. School Counselor; Municipal Auditor; College Instructor. Education: BS, University of Pennsylvania, Philadelphia, 1961-64; Typing, Shorthand, Lansdale School of Business, Lansdale, Pennsylvania, 1962; EdM, Temple University, Bethlehem, Pennsylvania, 1967. Appointments: Adjunct Faculty, Bucks County Community College; American Red Cross Instructor, Swimming, Lifesaving and Water Safety; Assistant Manager, Holiday House Pool and Recreation Center; Elementary School Counselor, Pennridge Schools; Instructor, American Institute of Banking; Municipal Auditor; Notary Public; Private Counselor; Private Instructor, Swimming, Diving, Racing; Real Estate Partnership. Publications: Learning Styles of Elementary School Children; Angola: A Nation in Ferment; Social Science Ethnography of the Open Space Classroom; Relationships of Selected Variables in a Fifth Grade Classroom; Studies in the Care of the Chronically Ill and Disabled. Honours include: World Intellectual of 1993; Gold Record of Achievement, USA, 1994; Service Recognition Award, National Ski Patrol, USA, 1994; Spring Mountain MOM Award, 1995; World Outstanding Service and Dedication, Spring Mountain Ski Patrol, Pennsylvania, 1996. Memberships:

Sierra Club; The Nature Conservancy; National Wildlife Federation; Dublin Ambulance Squad. Address: 834 Rickert Road, Perkasie, PA 18944, USA.

**FERTIG-DYKES Susan Beatrice,** b. 9 January 1944, Panay, Philippines. Writer; Producer; Director; Talent Scout. m. George M Dykes III, 2 sons. Education: University of Oregon, 1963-64; Loyola University, Chicago, 1980-81; BA with distinction Communications, 1982, University of Missouri. Appointments: Veterans Administration, Director of Broadcast Services, 1983-86; The White House, Office of Special Placement, 1989; US Department of Veterans Affairs, Director of Policy and Special Projects, 1989; Director of Publishing and Visual Communication, US Dept of Agriculture, USDA, 1989-93; Founder/Director, Institute of Cultural Affairs, Croatia, Bosnia, 1993-97; Manager, Human Resource Development, and Civil Society Initiatives, World Vision International, 1997-. Publications: Contributing Author, Beyond Prince & Merchant: Citizen Participation and the Rise of Civil Society, 1997. Honours: The Brent School Award for Leadership Scholarship, Character, 1961; University of Missouri Award 1982 for Greatest Contribution to the Department of Communication. Memberships: National Academy of Television Arts and Sciences; International Association of Facilitators; Women in Film a Vidndeo; Top Trainers Network. Address: 205 S Yoakum Pky Apt 1021, Alexandria, VA 22304-3826, USA.

**FERZAN N,** b.19 January 1935, Oroomieh, Iran. University Lecturer. 2 daughters. Education: MSc, Tabriz University; Post Graduate Cert; Cranfield University; Silsoe, UK. Appointments: Lecturer; Author; Technical Adviser; Publisher. Publications: Automative Engines; Repair, Volume 1; Repair, Volume2. Honours: MEM; MECH, Eng, Iran; Corrosion Assn Iran. Address: PO Box 13145-119, Terhan, Iran.

**FIDELMAN Uri,** b. 19 May 1936, Haifa, Israel. Lecturer. 1 son, 1 daughter. Education: MSc, Mathematics, Hebrew University, Jerusalem, 1966; DSc, Technion, Israel Institute of Technology, Haifa, 1982. Appointment: Lecturer, Technion, Israel Institute of Technology; and Dept of Behavioural Sciences, Emek Israel College. Publications: 45 journal articles. Address: Technion Israel Institute Technology, Department General Studies, Haifa, 32000, Israel.

**FIERRO Alfredo E,** b. 22 August 1965, San Salvador, El Salvador. Commercial Officer. Education: Business Administration, Graduate with Honours, University of Catolicz Argentina, 1989. Appointments: Area Director, International marketing, SADE Ind Group, 1988-91; Senior Trader, Export Division, SA ALBA, 1992-94; Commercial Officer, British Embassy, Buenos Aires, 1994-. Honours: Sir Proby Cautley, D Group Award for Export Achievement. Memberships: American Marketinf Association; Association Argentina de Marketing. Address: Brit Embassy, Dr Luis Agote 2412, 1425 Buenos Aires, Argentina.

**FILIPOVIC Nada,** b. 16 June 1949, Backk Palanick. Assistant Professor. m. Slavico, 1 son, 1 daughter. Education: BC, Technology, 1973; MS, 1984; PhD, 1998. Appointments: Head of Scientific Laboratory, 1975-82; Assistant, Baking Technology, 1982-98; Assistant Professor, 1998-. Publications: 5 Research Papers; 2 Books; 2 Patents. Memberships: National Chemical Society. Address: Faculty of Technology Center for, Cereal Technology, 1 Cara Lasara Blvd, Novi Sad 1000, Yugoslavia.

**FILIPPOVA Irina,** b. 21 July 1965, Russia. Radiation Protection Officer. 1 son. Education: Saint Petersburg Institute f Hygiene and Sanitation, 1982-89. Appointments: Head of Radiation Protection Department, National Board for Health Protection, 1989-97; Head of Supervision Department, Estonian Radiation Protection Centre, 1997-98; Memberships: Estonian Association of Radiologists. Address: ERPC, Kopli 76, EE 007 Tallin, Estonia.

**FIMREITE Norvald,** b. 12 May 1935, Sogndal, Norway. Professor. m. Solveig Fimreite, 1 daughter. Education includes: PhD. Appointments: Professor, University of Tromso, 1972-80; Professor, Telemark College, 1981-99. Publications: About 80 scientific publications. Membership: Association of Norwegian Research Workers, Board Member, 1992-96. Address: Ovre Borgvin 33, 3800 Bo, Norway.

**FINE Marlene G,** Director. Education: BA, Speech, University of Massachusetts, 1970; MA, Speech Communication, University of Minnesota, 1972; PhD, Communication Studies, University of Massachusetts, 1980; MBA, University of Massachusetts, 1984. Appointments: Teaching Associate, 1970-72; Instructor, 1972-74; Lecturer, Teaching Associate, 1974-79; Acting Director of Writing, 1980; Senior Partner, 1978-83; Financial Analyst, 1983; Associate Dean, 1984-85; Director, Master in Business Administration Program, 1985-89; Assistant Professor, 1985-91; Associate Professor, 1991-95; Chair, Department of Marketing and Communication, 1993-95; Dean of Graduate Studies, Emerson College, Boston, Massachusetts, 1995-1999; Director, Graduate Programme in Communications Management, Simmons College, Boston, Massachusetts. Publications: 18 Publications; 4 Book Reviews; 41 Conference Presentations; 14 Professional Speeches. Honours; Dictionary of International Biography, International Biographical Centre; World Who's Who of Women, IBC; Professor of the Year Award, 1989; Award for Outstanding Service of the MBA Program; Beta Gamma Sigma; Shaeffer Eaton Award for Academic Excellence; Pi Kappa Delta; Delta Sigma Rho - Tau Kappa Alpha; Award Winning Inter-Collegiate Debater. Memberships: Council of Graduate Schools; National Communication Association; International Communication Association; Eastern Communication Association; Academy of Management; Association for Business Communication. Address: Communications Management, Simmons College, 300 The Fenway, Boston, MA 02115, USA.

**FINKBEINER Claudia Hilde,** b. 16 August 1957, Heilbronn-Sontheim, Germany. Professor. Education: Abitur, Elly-Heuss-Knapp-Gymnasium, Heilbronn,1976; Studies, 1976-80, 1980-82; Graduate Studies, Heidelberg, Karlsruhe, 1990-91; Dr.ed, summa cum laude, 1994; Postgraduate, Justus Liebig University, Giessen, Germany, 1994-96; Postgraduate, University of California, Berkeley, USA; Taipei Normal University, Taiwan, 1996-97. Appointments: Inservice Training, Heidelberg, 1980-82; Teacher, English as a Foreign Language and Physical Education, Baden-Wurttemberg, Germany, 1982-94; Lecturer, English, State Institute for Teacher Training, Ludwigsburg and Teachers Training College, Heidelberg, 1987-97; Professor, Foreign Language Research, Kassel University, 1997-. Publications include: Zur Förderung expliziter und impliziter Lernstrategien im Englischunterricht: ein notwendiges Desiderat?; Sind gute Leserinnen und Leser auch gute Strategen?; The promotion of explicit and implicit learning strategics in English instruction: a necessary aim?; Teaching English in the European Dimension. Honours include: Award, Outstanding Innovative Ideas for Foreign Language Teaching, Ernst Klett Textbook Publishers, 1992; Award, Outstanding Empirical Pedagogical and Methodological Dissertation, Goettingen University, and Arbeitskreis der Sprachenzentren, Sprachinstitute und Fremdspracheninstitute (AKS), 1997. Memberships: International Reading Association; Association of Language Awareness; Teachers of English to Speakers of Other Languages; Board, German Society of Foreign Language Research; Fachverband Moderne Fremdsprachen; German Society of Applied Linguistics; Arbeitskreis Sprachen; Empirical Pedagogical Research Group, German Society of Educational Sciences; German Society of American Studies. Address: Dep.08, Teaching English as a Foreign Language and Foreign Language Research, University of Kassel, Georg-Forster Str 3, 34 109 Kassel, Germany.

**FINKELSTEIN Honora Ellen,** b. 18 July 1941, Midwest, Wyoming. Writer, Minister. m. Jay L, 1 son, 3 daughters. Education: BA, Rice University, 1963; MA, University of Texas at El Paso, 1976; PhD, University of Houston, 1976. Appointments: Assistant Professor, Houston Baptist University, 1976-79; Lifestyle Editor, Arundel Newspapers, 1987-88; Producer, Kaleidoscope for Tomorrow, 1992-94; Founder, Sunweavers Inc. Publications: Beautiful Skin; Magicians; Pieces of Eight. Honours: Faculty Woman of the Year, HBU, 1979; 1st Place Award, Suburban Newspapers of America, 1987. Memberships: Phi Kappa Phi Honor Society. Address: Sunweavers Inc, 12202 Nutmeg Lane, Reston, VA 20191, USA.

**FIORENTINO Carmine,** b. 11 September 1932, Brooklyn, Kings County, New York, USA. Education: Blackstone School of Law, Chicago, Illinois, 1954; LLB, John Marshall Law School, Atlanta, Georgia, 1957; Studies at Hunter College, New York City, 1951, Columbia Broadcasting School, New York City, 1952, Famous Writers School, Westport, Connecticut, 1962. Appointments: New York State Workmen's Compensation Board, New York State Department of Labor, 1950-53; Court Reporter-Hearing Stenographer, Governor Thomas E Dewey's Committee of State Counsel and Attorneys, 1953; Public Relations Secretary, Industrial Home for the Blind, Brooklyn, 1953-55; Legal Stenographer, Researcher, Law Clerk, various law firms, Atlanta, 1955, 1957-59; Secretary, Import-Export Firm, Atlanta, 1956; Private law practice, Atlanta, 1959-63; Attorney-Advisor, Trial Attorney, US Department of Housing and Urban Development (HUD) and Office of HUD General Counsel, Washington DC; Legal Counsel, Peachtree Federal Credit Union, 1963-74; Acting Director, Elmira, New York Disaster Field Office, US Department of Housing and Urban Development, 1973; Candidate, US Administrative law Judge, Director, Vice President, General Counsel, The Hexagon Corporation, Atlanta; Currently in private law practice. Publications: Non-fiction and poetry; Composer: words and music, popular songs and hymns; Washington newspapers. Honours include: Government awards. Membership include: Bar Member, State of Georgia and District of Columbia; US Supreme Court; US District Court, District of Columbia; US Second Circuit Court of Appeals; US District Court, Northern District of Georgia. Address: Suite R-4, 4717 Roswell Road, NE, Atlanta, Georgia 30342, USA.

**FIRSOVA Nataly,** b. 1 April 1948, Leningrad, Russia. Professor. m. Vladimir Zagoradny, 2 sons. Education: Graduate, Leningrad University, 1971. Appointments: Junior Scientific Research Worker, 1971-74, Assistant to Chair of Mathematical Analysis, 1975-81, Institute of Textile Industry; Professor, Military School, 1981-88; Senior Scientific Researcher, 1988-. Publications: Several professional articles. Honours: Prize, City Competition, 1971. Memberships: Union of Scientists, St Petersburg. Address: ul Saltykova Schedrina dom 22 kv 1, St Petersburg 191028, Russia.

**FISCHER Peter,** b. 3 November 1963, Steyr, Austria. Engineer; Researcher; Project Manager. Education: Masters Degree, Technical University of Graz, Austria, 1990; Doctor in Technical Sciences, 1998. Appointments: Research Advisor University of Linz, Austria; Research Advisor, Technical University of Graz, Austria; Computation Specialist, Project Manager, Technology Center, Steyr, Austria. Publications Stochastic Dynamics of Finite Element Systems; Approximately 20 Scientific Papers. Honours: Engineering Award of Victor Kaplan Foundation, Research Award of Austrian Automotive Industry Association. Memberships: New York Academy of Sciences. Address: Brunnerstrasse 6, A-4400 Steyr, Austria.

**FISCHER Steven Thomas,** b. 10 June 1972, Baltimore, Maryland, USA. Independent Producer, Director. Education Visual and Performing Arts Degree, University of Maryland 1998. Appointments: Creator, Childrens Animated Television Series, 1991; Director, Promotional Documentary or AmeriCorps, 1996-97. Publications: There's a Blue Dog Under My Bed, 1991. Honours: International Television Association Festival, 1995, 1997. Memberships: Directors Guild of America International Television Association; Independent Feature Project; International Animated Film Association. Address Cinema and Radio Ventures, Inc, P O Box 3866, Crofton, MD 21114-3866, USA.

**FISHER Leonard Everett,** b. 24 June 1924, New York City USA. Artist, Author. m. Margery Meskin, 1 son, 2 daughters Education: BFA, Yale University, 1949; MFA, Yale University 1950. Appointments: US Army Topographer, Major European and Pacific Invasions; Dean Emeritus, Paier College of Art Artist/Author. Publications: Illustrator of over 260 books, author of over 80 of these; designer of 10 US Postage Stamps Collections of original art and manuscripts in: The Library of Congress; Butler Art Institute; Mt Holyoke College; The University of Connecticut, Oregon, Minnesota, Southern Mississippi; Brown University; The New York Public Library Westpoint Public Library; Housatonic Museum. Honours Pulitzer Prize Painting Scholarship; Medalion of the University of Southern Mississippi; Christopher Medal; National Jewish Book Award; Regina Medal of the Catholic Library Association Kerlan Award of the University of Minnesota; Prencio Grafico Fiera, Internazionale Di Bologna. Memberships: Authors Guild PEN; Society of Illustrators; Silvermile Guild of Artists; Society of Childrens Book Writers and Illustrators. Address: 7 Twin Bridge Acres Rd, Westport, CT 06880, USA.

**FISHER Mary Maurine,** b. 19 July 1929, Schenectady, New York, USA. Federal Government Official. m. Eugene T Fisher (dec), 2 sons. Education: Certificate, 1952, Strayer College Certificate, 1989, University of Virginia. Appointments: Credit Manager, General Electric Credit Corp, Washington DC, 1950-70; Business Specialist, US Small Business Administration, Washington DC, 1970-; Member of the President's Advisory Committee on: Small and Minority Business Ownership, 1979-85, Native American Affairs 1979-80, Reservation Development, 1978-79, Native American Economic Development, 1977-78. Honours: 4 Special Achievement Awards, Small Business Administration, 1974 1978, 1990, 1992; 3 Certificates of Special Achievement, SBA 1982, 1984, 1986; 3 Certificates of Appreciation, SBA, 1983 1987, 1989; Certificate of Special Appreciation, SBA, 1984; 2 Awards of Appreciation, SBA, 1984, 1985; Award of Excellence, 1985, Award of Superior Performance, 1986 President's Advisory Committee, SBA; 4 High Quality Performance Awards, SBA, 1991, 1993, 1994, 1994; Student of the Year, University of Virginia, 1980. Memberships: Faifax Little League; Fairfax Industrial Development Authority; Warren Woods-Joyce Heights Civic Association, VP 1958-; Friends of Fairfax; National Contract Management Association. Address 4203 Lamarre Drive, Fairfax, VA 22030-5133, USA.

**FITCHETT June Wiseman,** b. 29 May 1942, Marion, North Carolina, USA. Director, Resident Activity Therapy. 1 son, 1 daughter. Education: BA, Western Carolina University, 1968. Appointments: Director, Resident Activity Therapy and Volunteers, Victoria Health Care Center, Smoky Mountain Diagnostic Laboratories; Resident Services and Activity Coordinator, Givens Estate Methodist Retirement Center; Writer, Asheville Citizen-Times; Social Worker, County of Buncombe; Personnel Director, Rehabilitation Coordinator, Lions Industries for the Blind; Job Placement Coordinator, Handicapped and Organizational Development Coordinator, Thoms Rehabilitation Hospital; Coordinator, Title II Job Placement Program, County of Buncombe and City of Asheville; Teacher, Counsellor, High School Dropouts Neighborhood Youth Corps, Asheville, North Carolina; Teacher, Jackson County Public Schools. Honours: Outstanding Young Women of America, 1971; Outstanding Service Award, Asheville Area Mayors Committee for Employment of the Handicapped, 1980; Listed in numerous biographical dictionaries. Memberships: Board, Buncombe County Council on Aging; North Carolina Activity Professional Association. Address: 226 Forest Hill Drive, Asheville, NC 28803-2406, USA.

**FITTER Perin Savakshaw,** b. 24 August 1948, Eldoret, Kenya. Environment Conservationist. Education: BSc, honours, University of Pune, 1968. Career: Teacher, Patron, Wildlife Club, 12 years; Western Kenya Coordinator for Wildlife Clubs of Kenya, 7 years; Coordinator for Environment Conservation Project, 6 years. Honour: Global 500 Laureate of UNEP. Memberships: Global 500 Forum of UNEP; Project Director, Kenya Neem Foundation. Address: Kenya Neem Foundation, PO Box 1268, Kisumu, Kenya.

**FITZ-WILLIAMS McFauland Patrick,** b. 6 October 1940, Sekondi, Ghana. Cardio Vascular and Thoracic Surgical Consultant, Cardiologist. 4 sons, 4 daughters. Education: MD Hons, Lvov Medical College, 1969; Diploma in General Surgery, 1971; PhD, 1979; Proficiency Certificate in Thoracic Surgery, 1980. Appointments: Medical Officer, 1974; MO; Registrar, Surgical Department; Surgeon, I/C Bolga Hospital, Ghana; Lecturer, Thoracic Medicine, USSR; Lecturer, Thoracic Medicine, Ghana; Head of Cardio Thoracic Unit; Consultant of Narh Bita Hosp; Medical Director, The New Achimota Clinic. Publications: Over 20 publications; 4 Patents. Hoours: 4 Certificates of Achievement; Knight Commander. Memberships: Member and Fellow of over 25 associations. Address: The NewAchimota Clinic, P O Box AH 382, Achimota, Via Accra, Ghana.

**FITZPATRICK James D,** b. 21 October 1938, Syracuse, NY, USA. Lawyer. Education: Bachelor of Science, Holy Cross College, Worcester, 1960; Juris Doctor, Syracuse University College of Law, 1963. Appointments: Partner, Bond, Schoeneck and King Attourneys, 1988-; Member, New York, American and International Bar Association, 1999; Speaker, New York State Bar. Honours: Afghanistan Freedom Fighter Award, 1989; Honored Friend of El Salvadore Award, 1991; Republican Senatorial Medal of Freedom; Republican Presidential Legion of Merit; Torch of the Heart Award. Memberships: New York State Bar Association; International Platform Association; The Americas Guild; Syracuse Cerebal Palsy and Mental Retardation Inc; The Consortium for Childrens Services; World Future Society. Address: 201 Croyden Road, Syracuse, NY 13224-1917, USA.

**FJERDINGSTAD Erik,** b. 4 October 1940, Copenhagen, Denmark. Environmental Physical Chemist. Education: Magister Scientiarum in Physical Chemistry, 1966; BEd, 1967; DPH, 1972. Appointments: Instructor, 1967 to Associate Professor, University of Copenhagen, 1976-. Publications: Articles in professional journals. Honours: Scholarship to NHH, 1972. Memberships: American Association for the Advancement of Science; New York Academy of Science; Planetary Society; Danish Society of Materials Research. Address: Bredebovej 23 lmt, DK-2800 Kgs Lyngby, Denmark.

**FLECKER Peter,** b. 24 May 1953, Novy Bor, Czech Republic. Biochemist. Education: Dipl Chem, 1980; PhD, 1983. Appointments: Liebig Fellow, University Munich, 1984-86; Assistant Professor, University Karlsruhe, 1986-88; Head, Enzymology Department, Paul Ehrlich Institute, 1988-91; Head, Protein Engineering Laboratory, University Mainz, 1992-. Publications: In Eur J Biochem, FEBS Lett. Honour: Liebig Award, 1984-86. Memberships: Active member, New York Academy Science; German Chemical Society; German Society Biochemistry and Molecular Biology. Address: Kraftstr 11, 63065 Offenbach, Germany.

**FLEETWOOD Daniel Mark,** b. 3 August 1958, Seymour, Indiana, USA. Physicist. m. Betsy E Fox, 3 sons. Education: BS, 1980, MS, 1981, PhD, 1984, in Physics, Purdue University, W Lafayette. Appointments: Senior Member Technical Staff, 1984-89, and Distinguished Member Technical Staff, Sandia National Laboratories, Albuquerque, New Mexico. Honours: Co-inventor of protonic memory chip, Discover Magazine's 1998 Computer Hardware and Electronics Technology of the year; 6 time Winner of IEEE Nuclear and Space Radiation Effects Conference Best Paper Award. Memberships: Fellow, IEEE; International Correspondence Chess Master; Phi Beta Kappa. Address: Sandia National Labs, PO Box 5800 MS 1083, Albuquerque, NM 87185-1083, USA.

**FLEROV Vladimir,** b. 11 August 1938, Irkutsr, Russia. Physicist. m. Galina Demina, 1 son, 1 daughter. Education: Latvian University, 1955-60; DPhys, 1981. Appointments: Technologist, Semiconductor Plant, 1960-64; Researcher, Institute of Physics, 1964-90; Lecturer, Air Force Academy, 1980-92; Researcher, Nuclear Reactor, 1992-98. Publications: Over 50 articles in professional journals. Honours: Medal for Conquest of Virgin Islands, 1957; Medal for Labor, 1986. Memberships: Planetary Society. Address: 31 Dzirnavu Street #24, LV-1010 Riga, Latvia.

**FLORESCU Grigore-Vagil,** b. 22 May 1938, Oradea, Romania. Lawyer, Professor. m. Rodica, 2 daughter. Education: BL, Bucharest University, 1959; Doctor of Law, 1976; Master of European Law, 1971; Diploma Fed Study, 1971; Diploma of Centre of Research of Academy of International Law, the Hague, 1976. Appointments: Judge, 1959-65; Chief Legal Counsel, Ministry of Industry, 1965-91; General Counsel, Ministry of Justice, 1991-93; Lawyer, Professor of Commercial Law, Bucharest, 1994-.Publications: Over 50 study books, Law. Memberships: Member of the Bucharest and Paris Bar; American Abitration Association; International Artitral Centre of the Austrian Chamber of Commerce, Vienna; Austrian Chamber of Commerce, Vienna. Address: 8-10 Palntelor Bloc A Apt 31, Sector 2, 70308 Bucharest, Romania.

**FLORIAN Carmen,** b. 26 June 1947, Rupea, Romania. Musicologist. m. Calin Florian, 1 son. Education: Graduate, Ciprian Porumbescu Music Conservatorium, Bucharest, 1970. Appointments: Literary Secretary, Theatre; Romanian Union of Composers; General Manager, Controceni National Museum, 1994-97. Publications: Vocatie si destin - Dinu Lipatti, 1986; Pagini din jurnalul unei regasiri - Dinu Lipatti, 1987; Maturii despre Dinu Lipatti, 1994. Honour: Medal, Diploma, Madonna

Romena, Mons Dr Ioan Robu, Archbishop of Bucharest, 1997. Address: Str Pictor Luchian No 1, Sect 2, Cod 73, 358 Bucharest, Romania.

**FLOYD Nancy Lynn,** b. 6 February 1936, Wynona, Oklahoma, USA. Quill Pen Maker; Quilligrapher; Teacher. m. Ken Floyd (dec), 1 son, 3 daughters. Education: BS Ed Elementary and Physically Handicapped, 1962, MS Ed Learning Disabilities and Multiply Handicapped, 1970, Illinois State University; UVA Postgrad Visiting Scholar, Professional Certificate, Early Childhood Special Education, 1975. Appointments: Teacher, Physically and Multiply Handicapped, Elgin, Illinois, 1962-73; Teacher of Student Teachers, Master Teacher, Elgin, 1968-73; Head Start Handicapped Coordinator and Founder, Charlottesville, Virginia; Quill Pen Maker, 1979-; TV feature interviews with Peter Jennings, ABC, 1983, Jamie McIntyre, CBS - Capitol Ed, 1998, PBS, 1991, 1996, 1997. Publications: Mother, May I, an Honorary Memorial to Mother Teresa; Mother M Teresa, a Pencil in God's Hands; Let us Pray; O Lord Use Me As Well. Address: Lewis Glaser Quill Pens Inc, 1700 Sourwood Pl, Charlottesville, VA 22911, USA.

**FLUTURE Vladimir,** b. 16 December 1938, Galati-Romania. Professor of Surgery. m. Sandru Voichita, 1 son, 1 daughter. Education: Grad 1961, Medical University Timisoara; MD 1971. Appointments: Professor of Surgery; Permanent Member, Romanian Academy of Medical Science; Vice-President, National Committee for Hepatic Transplantation; Chief of Emergency Surgical Clinic, City Hospital Timisoara. Publications: 92 papers in field of vascular surgery, transplantation and liver surgery. Honours: Visiting Professorship, Dept Surgical, Basel University, Switzerland, 1995; President, Timisoara Surgical Society, 1993. Memberships: Permanent Member, Romanian Academy Medical Science; International Society Surgery, 1966; European Digestive Surgery, 1998. Address: Spitalul Municipal, Str GH Dima Nr 5, 1900 Timisoara, Romania.

**FOBES Jacqueline Theresa Mitchell,** b. 5 June 1946, Calgary, Alberta, Canada. Educational Psychologist; Consultant. m. Dr. James L Fobes. Education: AA, 1969; BA, 1975; MA, 1977; PhD, 1988. Appointments: Monterey Schools, California, 1981-89; Psychiatric Institute Washington DC, 1982-93; Pleasantville Board of Education, New Jersey, 1993-. Publications: 23 publications, research papers presented at conventions and civic groups, 1970-. Memberships: Atlantic County Psychologists Association; American Association of University Women. Address: 807 Blue Teal Drive, Absecom, NJ 08201-4235, USA.

**FOLEY Jack,** b. 8 September 1940, Neptune, NJ, USA. Poet; Writer. m. Adelle, 1 son. Education: BA, Cornell University, 1963; MA, University of California, Berkeley, 1965. Appointments: Author and Performer of Poetry; Executive Producer, Poetry, KPFA Radio, Cover to Cover, current show; Organizer, Poetry Serios Larry Blakes. Editor, Poetry Flash; Editor, Poetry USA, 1990-95. Publications: Poetry Books: Letters, Lights, Words for Adelle, 1987; Gershwin, 1991; Adritt, 1993; Exites, 1996; New Poetry from California - Dead, Requim, 1998; Her Blackness Sparkles!, 1995. Memberships: PEN, Oakland; Poets and Writers; MLA. Address: 2569 Maxwell Avenue, Oakland, CA 94601, USA.

**FOLGER William M,** b. 13 May 1916, Lockport, New York. Actor; Journalist. m. Frances Morlan, dec, 1 son, dec, 1 daughter. Education: BS General Business, 1938, University of Illinois; MA Political Science, 1975, Maxwell School, Syracuse University. Appointments: Religion and Transportation Writer, Buffalo Courier-Express; Newswriter, NBC, Washington;

Newscaster, Washington Post Radio; News Commentator, Wish Radio, Indianapolis; Journalism Professor, Syracuse University, University of Northern Colorado; Freelance Actor. Honours: Freedom Foundation Award; American Association of Religion and Psychiatry Award; 3 Page One Awards, Western New York Newspaper Guild, one for consistently fine reporting, 2 for interpretive reporting; Screen Actors Guild American Scenes Award; Denver Westword Award for Actor in Best Ensemble Play of 1989. Memberships: Society of Professional Journalism, President Colorado Chapter; President, Religious Newswriters Association of US and Canada. Address: 172 Newport Street, Denver, CO 80220-6018, USA.

**FOLKE Jens,** b. 16 August 1953, Gentofte, Denmark. Environmental Chemist. m. Karen, 2 sons. Education: Fil. Dr., Environmental Chemistry, 1985; MSc, Biochemistry, Org Chemistry, 1990; MEM, Master of Environmental Management, 1998. Appointments: Scientist, Analytical Chemistry, Assessment of Toxicity, 1980-81; Scientist, Analytical Chemistry, Mass Spectrometry, 1981-82; Senior Scientist, Environmental and Analytical Chemistry, 1982-86; Project Manager, Environmental Impact Assessment, Industrial Effluents, Cleaner Technology, Head of Environmental Chemistry Group, COWI Consult, Consulting Engineers and Planners, 1986-90; Director, Danish Branch, European Environmental Research Group, 1991-. Honours: Scholarship from University of Copenhagen; Hede-Nielsen Prize; Certificate, Best Technical Paper; many other honours. Memberships: Technical Association of the Pulp and Paper Industry; The Environmental Auditors Registration Association; Danish Society of Professional Engineers; Scientific and the Concertation Committees. Address: Ostergade 16, 3250 Gilleleje, Denmark.

**FOMENKO Vladimir Ivanovich,** b. 14 June 1937, Volgogzad, Russia. Metrologist. m. Galina Nikolayevna Fomenko, 1 son. Education: Diploma, Engineer, Leningrad Institute of Aircraft Instrument Making, 1961; Postgraduate, Org I Mendeleev Institute for Metrology, 1974. Appointments: Chief Science Secretary, DI Mendeleev Institute for Metrology, 1968-95. Publications: Two monographs. Memberships: Physics Society of Russia; Corresponding Member, Metrology Academy of Petrovskaya Academy of Russia. Address: DI Mendeleev All-Russia Research Institute for Metrology, 19 Moskovsky Prospekt, St Petersburg 198005, Russia.

**FOMETESCU VDumitru Doru,** b. 27 May 1949, Ciuperceni, Gorj, Romania. Physician. m. Nicolita Vlad, 2 daughters. Education: Faculty of Medicine, Bucharest, 1973; Residence, Internal Medicine, Bucharest, 1978; Diploma, 1980, University of Medicine, Bucharest. Appointments: Districtual Hospital, To-Jiu, Gorj, 1980-. Publications: 3 books of poetry and essays. Honour: The Great Award of Literature, 1992, Festival, Tudor Arghezi. Memberships: Geminative Fluid magazine, Founder member, President; Prosens magazine, President; DVF Cultural Foundation, President. Address: Spitalul T Vladimirescu, 1400 Targu Jin, Jud Gorj, Romania.

**FOMICHEV Vadim,** b. 24 October 1941, Russia. Physics. m. Galina Sakharova, 1 son, 2 daughters. Education: Physical Faculty, St Petersburg University, 1964; PhD, 1967; DSc, 1975; Professor, 1981. Appointments: Associate Professor, 1967-77, Director, Institute of Physics, 1978-94, Head of Laboratory, 1994-, St Petersburg University. Publications: Over 100 papers. Honour: State Prize in Science, 1989. Membership: Advisory Board, International Conferences on VUV Radiation Physics, 1987-95. Address: Physics Research Institute, St Petersburg

University, 1 Uliyanovskaya Street, St Petersburg 198904, Russia.

**FOMICHOV Vladimir A,** b. 1 September 1950, Moscow, Russia. Professor. m. Olga S Fomichova, 1 son. Education: MSc, honours, Applied Mathematics, Moscow Institute of Electronic Engineering, 1973; PhD, 1983. Appointments: Professor, Computer Science, KE Tsiolkovsky, Russian State Technological University, Moscow; Associate Professor, Moscow State Institute of Electronics and Mathematics. Publications: Numerous articles in professional journals; One monograph in Russian. Memberships: Editorial Board of the international journal Informatica, Ljubljana, Slovenia, 1992-; Associate Editor of the electronic international journal Educational Technology and Society, Germany, 1998--; Cybernetics Academy, Stefan Odobleja, (secretariats in Milan, Italy, Bucharest, Hungary, head office, Lugano, Switzerland); Moscow Mathematical Society; International Society for Artificial Intelligence in Education; International Association for Cybernetics. Address: Universitetsky Prosp 9, Flat 22, Moscow 117296, Russia.

**FOMICHOVA Olga S,** b. 12 January 1958, St Petersburg (Leningrad), Russia. Educator. m. Vladimir A Fomichov, 1 son. Education: MSc, English, German, Moscow State Pedagogic Institute, 1980; PhD, Philology, Moscow State Linguistic University, 1990. Appointments: Head of the Studio Culture Ecology and Foreign Languages, Moscow Children and Teenagers Palace for Creative Work, 1990-. Publications: Numerous articles in professional journals. Memberships: International Association for Cybernetics; Associate Editor of the electronic international journal, Educational Technology and Society, Germany, 1998-; International Society for Artificial Intelligence in Education, Leeds, UK. Address: Universitetsky Prospect 9, Flat 22, Moscow 117296, Russia.

**FOMIN N,** b. 21 October 1950, Novgorod, Russia. Professor of Physics. m. Valentina, 1 son. Education: St Peterburg Technical University 1973; PhD, Institute of Physics, Belarus, 1978; Doctor of Science, Moscow Institute for Problems in Mechanics, 1985; Full Professor, 1990. Appointments: Institute of Pure and Applied Machanics, Novosibirsk, Russia, 1973-76; Heat and Mass Tranfer Institute, Minsk, Belarus, 1973-76; Junior Scientist, 1976-85; Senior Scientist, 1985-; Head of Laboratory. Publication: Monograph, Speckle Photography for Fluid Mechanics Measurements, Springer, 1998. Membership: Board of Directors, Belarus Physical Society. Address: Heat and Mass Transfer Institute, Minsk 220072, Belarus.

**FONG Francis,** b. 21 June 1956, Hong Kong. Senior Lecturer. m. Betsy Ip, 2 sons. Education: BMusEd, honours, 1979; MMusEd, 1992. Appointments: Executive Officer, Ethnic Music Centre of Western Australia, 1984-90; Lecturer, 1990-92; Senior Lecturer, 1992-, Hong Kong Academy for Performing Arts. Honour: Selected as one of 75 most prominent graduates o have contributed to the community in 75 years of University of Western Australia, 1988. Memberships: Founder, Chairman, Musical Director, Hong Kong Christian Chinese Orchestra, 1997-. Address: c/o Hong Kong Academy for Performing Arts, Gloucester Road, Wan Chai, Hong Kong.

**FONG Hiram Leong,** b. 15 October 1906, Honolulu, Hawaii, USA. Attorney. m. Ellyn Lo, 3 sons, 1 daughter. Education: BA Degree, Univrsity of Hawaii, 1930; LLB Degree, Harvard Law School, 1935. Appointments: Clerk, 1924-27; Chief Clerk, 1930-32; Founder, Cosmopolitan Law Firm, Fong, Miho, Choy and Robinson; US State Senator; Founder, Chairman, Finance Enterprises, Finance Securities, Finance Investment, Finance Factors Building, Finance Insurance, Market City; Founder,

Chairman, Emeritus of Finance Factors and Grand Pacific Life Insurance Company; President, Finance Factors Foundation, Market City Foundation, Hiram Leong Fong and Ellyn Lo Fong Foundation, Ocean View Cemetary Ltd; Chairman, Highway Construction Company Ltd; Director of Several Companies. Honours: Hall of Fame; National Award for Outstanding Service to Brotherhood from the National Conference of Christians and Jews; Citation of Meritorious Service; Horatio Alger Award; Citation for Outstanding Public Service; Social and Rehabilitation Service Medallion; Golden Plate Award; Award for Outstanding Service to the Nation; Many Other Honours and Awards. Memberships: Post Office and Civil Service Committees; Address: 1102 Alewa Drive, Honolulu, HI 96817-1507, USA.

**FONG Lina,** b. 7 November 1948, Hong Kong. Social Worker. m. Timon Pak Yeung Wong, 2 daughters. Education: University of Hong Kong, 1970; Master in Social Work, University of Hawaii, 1974; PhD, Social Work, University of Southern California, 1990. Appointments: Assistant Professor, University of Louisville, 1990-94; Director, Social Work Program, Lewis-Clark State College, 1994-95; Director of Field Education, East Tennessee State Unviersity, 1995-96; Professor, Associate Graduate Director, Andrews University, Michigan, 1996-97; Associate Professor, University of Texas, 1997-. Honours: Crusade Scholar, 1985-88. Memberships: National Association of Social Workers; International Association of Schools of Social Work; International Council of Social Welfare; International Federation of Social Workers; Society of Spirituality; National American Association for Christian and Social Work. Address: 206 N Montevideo Ave, No5, Edinburgh, TX 78539-2819, USA.

**FONSECA Ivan Claret,** b. 11 July 1938, Santo Eslevao. Doctor. m. 1 son, 2 daughters. Education: MD, 1964. Appointment: General Surgeon, Nanuque, Brazil, 1965-; Lecturer, Environment, High Schools and Universities, 1973-. Publications: 72 books, numerous articles in professional journals. Honours: Lyons International Honour, Nanuque, Brazil, 1975; Global 500 Award, UNEP, Mexico, 1990; Rotary International Honour, Brazil, 1995; Grande Oriente do Brasil Honour, 1995. Memberships: Geographic and Historic Institute of Minas Gerais State; Brazilian Surgeons College; Doctors and Writers Brazilian Society. Address: Pocos de Caldas Street, 165 Nanuque, Minas Gerais, Brazil.

**FORD David Fairbanks,** b. 20 March 1958, Boston, Massachusetts, USA. Museum Director. m. Mrs Kenneth V Schott, deceased, 1 son. Education: BA, Brown University, 1980; MA, University of Virginia, 1983; Art Students League, New York City, 1984-90. Appointments: Liturgical Arts Consultant and Independent Arts Researcher, 1984-92; Director, Main Street Museum of Arts, Hartford, Vermont, USA, 1992-98. Publications: Big Fish and Good Lookin Women, author w Jack Rowell, 1995; Vermont Genealogy, 1996; OTM, 1998. Memberships: Hartford Historical Society; WEHGS. Address: 5 Mill Road, White River Junction, VT 05001-3308, USA.

**FORD Guillermo Patricio,** b. 2 September 1910, Buenos Aires, Argentina. Accountant (retired). m. Patricia M M Keegan, 1 son. Education: Faculty of Economic Sciences, Buenos Aires University, 1939-46. Appointments: Junior Clerk, Ussher's Grocery Store, 1924-27; Accountancy Clerk, Great Southern Railway, 1927-30; Senior Auditor, Deloitte Plender Griffiths & Co, 1930-50; Financial and Administrative Manager, RCA of America, 1953-64, Atma-Chloride SA, 1964-76, Buenos Aires. Honours: Honorary President, Federation of Irish-Argentine Societies; Hon Editor, Southern Cross; Permanent contributor to Human Rights cause. Memberships: Professional Council of Economic Sciences; Irish Catholic Society; Hurling Club; Argentine Automobile Club; Accion Católica. Address: Charcas 3965 3A, 1425 Buenos Aires, Argentina.

**FORD Lincoln Edmond,** b. 14 May 1938, Boston, USA. Physician; Scientist. 4 daughters. Education: AB, Harvard College, 1960; MD, University of Rochester, 1965. Appointments: Honorary Research Fellow, University College London, 1971-74; Assistant Professor, Associate Professor, Medicine, University of Chicago, 1974-96; Professor, Medicine, Krannert Institute, Indiana University, 1996-. Publictions: 70 in medical and scientific professional journals. Memberships: Biophysical Society; American Physiological Association; Society of General Physiologists. Address: University of Ind Merd Schkrannert Institute of Cardiology, 1111 West 10th Street, Indianapolis, IN 62024800, USA.

**FORTNER Rosanne White,** b. 13 November 1945, Logan, West Virginia, USA. Professor Environmental Science Education. m. Richard D Fortner, 2 sons. Education: BA Biology, 1967, West Virginia University; MA Earth Science Education, 1973, Oregon State University; EdD Science Education, 1978, Virginia Polytechnic Institution. Appointments: Middle School Science Teacher, Roanoke County, Virginia, 1967-69, 1971-76; Faculty, 1978-, Professor, 1992-, Ohio State University; Coordinator, Ohio Sea Grant Education Programme, 1983-. Publications: Over 50 in environmental science education. Honours: Fellow, American Association for the Advancement of Science, Ohio Academy of Science; NAAEE Research Award, 1992. Memberships: President, National Marine Educators Association, 1988-89; Board Directors, North American Association for Environmental Education, 1986-89; Sigma Xi; Phi Beta Kappa; National Science Teachers Association; American Geophysical Union. Address: OSU School of Natural Resources, 2021 Coffey Road, Columbus, OH 43210-1085, USA.

**FORTOV Vladimir Yevgenievich,** b. 23 January 1946, Noginsk, Moscow, Russia. Minister of Science and Technologies of the Russian Federation, Moscow, Russia. Education: MSc, Space Research and Plasma Thermodynamics, 1968; Candidate Science, 1971, Physics of Intense Shock Waves in Dense Plasma, 1971; DSc, Physics in Strong Coupled Plasmas, 1976, Moscow Institute of Physics and Engineering. Appointments: Postgraduate Student, Moscow Institute of Physics and Engineering, 1968-71; Researcher, Head of Laboratory, Institute of Chemical Physics, USSR Academy of Sciences, 1971-86; Division Director, Institute of Chemical Physics, USSR Academy of Sciences, 1986-92; Director, Scientific Research Center of Thermophysics and Pulse Influences, 1992-93; Professor, High Energy Density Physics, Moscow Institute of Physics and Engineering, 1991-. Publications: Thermophysical Properties of Gas Phase Nuclear Reactor Work Media, 1980; Physics of Nonideal Plasma, 1987, 1989; Thermophysical Properties of Hot Dense Plasma, 1991; Intense Shock Waves and Condensed Matters Under Extreme Conditions, 1994. Honours: USSR State Award in Physics and Mathematics, 1986; Red Banner Order for Investigations in Physics and Computational Mathematics, 1987; Russian Government Award, 1996; For Public Service to Motherland Order, 1996. Memberships: Corresponding Member, USSR Academy of Sciences, 1987; Academician, Russian Academy of Sciences, 1991, Vice President, 1996; American Physical Society; New York Academy of Sciences European Academy of Sciences and Arts; International Planetary Society; International Academy of Astronautics; US National Academy of Engineering. Address: Mechanical Engineering Research Institute. Address: Scientific

Board for Low Temp Plasma Physics, Russian Academy of Sciences, 13/19 Izhorskaya Str, Moscow 127412, Russia.

**FOSTER Frank Benjamin,** b. 23 September 1928, Cincinnati, Ohio, USA. Musician; Bandleader; Jazz Educator; Composer; Arranger. m. Cecilia A Foster, 3 sons, 1 daughter. Education: High School Diploma, Cincinnati, Ohio, 1946; Honorary PhD, Music, Central State University, Wilberforce, Ohio, 1983; Honorary PhD, Humane Letters, College of St Rose, Albany, New York, USA, 1988. Appointments: Assistant Professor, Music, SUNY at Buffalo, 1972-76; Adjunct Assistant Professor, Livingston College of Rutgers University, 1977-79. Publications: In Defense of Be-Bop, essay, 1979; Jazz and the Electronic Revolution, essay, 1984. Honours: Grammy Award, 1987; Grammy Award, 1990. Memberships: Local 802 American Federation of Musicians; ASCAP; NARAS. Address: 1235 Post Road, Scarsdale, NY 10583-2132, USA.

**FOSTER Richard Donithan,** b. 11 January 1971, Richmond, Virginia, USA. Author; Journalist. m. Lisa Kayne Bricker Foster. Education: BSc, Virginia Commonwealth University, 1994. Appointments: Staff Writer, Richmond Times Dispatch, 1992-94; Staff Writer, Roanoke Times, 1994-97; Assistant Editor, Style Weekly Magazine, 1997-. Publication: The Real Bettie Page, 1997. Membership: Society of Professional Journalists. Address: 11302 Bridgemont Road, Apt 202, Richmond, VA 23235, USA.

**FOULIS Iain P L,** b. 9 August 1937, Farnborough, Hants. Retired. Education: Diploma of Spanish, 1960-61. Appointments: Argyll and Sutherland Highlanders, 1957-59; Cyprus, Service Medal, 1958; Language Teacher, English, Madrid, 1960-61; Bank of London and South Africa, Bahamas, Guatemala, Nicaragua, 1962-65, 66; Sales, Toronto; Language Teacher, Madrid, Spain, 1966-83; Retired Landowner, 1983-. Memberships: Friends of the Spanish Castles, 1973; Friends of Saint James Way, 1971. Address: Edificio Cuzco Soledad 11, Postal 5-2-C, San Augustin De Guadalix, 28750 Madrid, Spain.

**FRADKIN Efim Samoilovich,** b. 30 November 1924, Shedrin, Belarussia. Professor. m. Frima M Fradkina, 2 daughters. Education: PhD, DSc, 1952, Lebedev Physical Institute, Moscow. Appointments: Senior Research Scientist, 1948-64; Full Professor, Head, Quantum Field Theory and Statistics Department, 1964-, Lebedev Physical Institute, Moscow; Visiting Professor: Institute for Advanced Studies, JCTP, California and Massachusetts, Institutes of Technology, CERN, University of New York, Stony Brook, Cambridge University, Saclay CE, University of Tokyo, Rome, Paris and others. Publications: 250 scientific publications in basic areas of Quantum Field Theory and Quantum Statistics. Honours: E Tamm Award, 1980; Laureate of Dirac, 1988, Sakharov 1996; Medals. Memberships: Academia Pontaniana, Italy 1983; Academician, Academy of Sciences, Russia, 1990-. Address: PN Lebedev Physical Institute, Russian Academy o Sciences, 53 Leninsky Prospekt, Moscow 117924, Russia.

**FRANCIS John Charles,** b. 8 February 1957, Sunderland England. Telecommunications Consultant. m. Gabriele, 1 son Education: BSc Hons, Mathematics, University of East Anglia England, 1982; MSc, Digital Techniques, Heriot Wat University, Scotland, 1984; PhD, Electrical and Electronic Engineering, 1986. Appointments: Post Doctoral Researche Heriot Watt University; Director, SLL; Consultant, Ascom Project Leader, Swisscom; Rapporteur ETSI; Project Leade Eurescom. Publications: Casual Reasoning a System Approach. Memberships: Swiss Group for Artificial Intelligenc and Cognitive Science; Gorilla Foundation; ETSI NA6 UMT.

Task Force; GSM MoU 3GIG. Address: Swisscom Corp Tech, Ostermundigenstr 99, CH-3000, Bern, Switzerland.

**FRANGOPOL Petre T,** b. 26 May 1933, Constantza, Romania. University Professor. m. Maria Iosefina. Education: Chemical Engineering, Polytechnical University, Iasi, 1956; Postgraduate, Nuclear and Applied Physics, Bucharest University, 1957; PhD, Polytechnical University, Timisoara, 1967; Postdoctoral Fellow, National Research Council, Ottawa, Canada, 1970-71, University of Washington, 1970-71, Dozentenstipendium Humboldt Marburg-Lahn, 1972. Appointments: Head of Laboratory, Institute of Atomic Physics, Bucharest; Professor, Biophysics and Medical Physics, "Al I Cuza" University, Iasi. Publications: Ocver 180 scientific publications, 50 articles in cultural magazines. Honour: Prize, C Miculescu, Romania Academy, 1991. Memberships: German Chemical Society; Romania Chemical Society, French Society of Medical Physics; Romania Biophysics Society. Address: "Al I Cuza" University, PO Box 1637, R 6600 Iasi 7, Romania.

**FRANK Judith Ann (Jann),** b. 10 February 1938, Fresno, California, USA. Retired Businesswoman, Financial and Community Worker. Education: BA, Liberal Studies, California University, Fullerton, 1989; Postgraduate studies, Counselling, Human Development and Community Service, CSUF, 1990-91; Postgraduate studies, Counselling and Psychology, Chapman University. 1991-93. Appointments: Physical and Occupational Intern, Rehabilitation Institute of Southern California, 1978-80, 1992-93; Founder, President, Distant Drums Native Arts, 1994-97; Founder, President, Jann Frank Enterprises, 1996-98. Honours include: Commendation for Volunteer Service, Orange County Council of Women in Chambers of Commerce, 1980; Woman of Distinction in Social Sciences, Fullerton College, 1984; Distinguished Service Award, Rehabilitation Institute of Southern California, 1993; Twentieth Century Achievement Award, 1997; International Woman of the Year, 1997-98; Millennium Hall of Fame, 1997-98. Memberships: Board, Native American Institute; National Museum of the American Indian; Library of Congress. Address: 601 West Santa Fe Avenue #85, Placentia, CA 92870, USA.

**FRANKE Jack Emil,** b. 8 July 1965, Pine Bluff, Arkansas, USA. Teacher. m. Lyudmila Vagun, 1 daughter. Education: BA, University of Texas, 1987; MA, Monterey Institute of International Studies, 1992; PhD, St Petersburg State University, 1995. Appointments: Russian Interpretor, Marine Resource Corp, 1988-90; Associate Professor of Russian, Defence Language Institute, 1990-94; Director, Computer Aided Study, George C Marshall Center, Garmisch-Pa, Germany, 1994-97. Honours: Army Achievement Medal; Commanders Medal, Civilian Service, 1998; International Who's Who for Professionals, 1998; US Army Europe Employee of the Year; International Distinguished Leadership, 1999; Research Board of Advisors, 1999. Memberships: Ganbaru Black Belt Association; United States Judo Federation; American Council of Teachers of Foreign Language; Computer Aided Language Instruction Consortium. Address: 370 Clay Street #13, Monterey, CA 93944, USA.

**FRANKENBERG Eliezer,** b. 7 July 1945, Lebanon. Biologist. m. Sabina Krol, 2 daughters. Education: BSc, 1970; MSc, 1972; PhD, Hebrew University, 1978; Postdoctoral, Ruhr University, Germany, 1980. Appointments: Chief Scientist, Nature Reserves Authority, Israel; Senior Research Associate, Lecturer, Hebrew University; Adjunct Senior Lecturer, Ben Gurion University. Honours: SSAR Prize, 1975; Science Faculty Prize, 1976; Heinrich Herz Stiftung, 1979; Smithsonian Institution, 1980. Memberships: Israel MAB Committee; IUCN/SSC-RSG; IUCN-CEM; Zoological Society of Israel;

Representing Israel in UNEP-CUS, UNEP-COBD conventions. Address: 12 Rachel Hameshoreret Street, 96348 Jerusalem, Israel.

**FRANTSUZOV Anatolii Alexeevich,** b. 1 April 1933, Leningrad, USSR. Physicist. m. L P Frantsuzova, 3 sons. Education: Diploma of Physicist, Leningrad University, 1956; PhD, Experimental Physics, 1965; DSc, Semiconductor Physics, 1987. Appointments: Leading Scientist, Institute of Semiconducting Physics, Siberian Division of Russian Academy of Science. Publications: 33 papers in scientific journals, 1957-95. Address: Laboratory of Low Temperature Electronics, Siberian Division of Russian Academy of Science, 13 Prospekt Lavrentieva, Novosibirsk 90, 630090, Russia.

**FRANTSUZOVA Stella Borisovna,** b. 17 April 1935, Vinnitsa, Ukraine. Scientist; Pharmacologist. m. Mr Mark Landsman, 1 daughter. Education: Graduated, 1959, Kiev Medical Institute, Curative Faculty; Candidate of Medical Science, 1968; Doctor of Medical Science, 1978; Professor, 1988; Kiev Public Patent Institute, 1980. Appointments: Physician, 1961-66; Junior Science Worker, 1966-68; Senior Science Worker, 1968-76; Head, Laboratory of Pathophysiology and Experimental Pharmacology, Scientific Research Laboratory Centre of National Medical University, Kiev, Ukraine, 1976-. Publications: 207 scientific publications, 4 books, 10 patents, 12 methodical documents. Honour: Title and Badge "Inventor of the USSR". Memberships: Pharmacological Committee, Ministry of Health, Ukraine; Special Science Council for Academic Degrees Conferment; Editorial Board for 2 medical science journals; Ukrainian Society of Pharmacologists. Address: Institutskaya str 24/7 apt 35, 252021 Kiev, Ukraine.

**FRANUS Edward Andrew,** b. 19 January 1916, Golonog, Poland. Psychologist; Ergonomist. m. Danuta, 2 daughters. Education: Diploma of Schoolmaster, 1935; Diploma of Gymnasialmaster, 1938; MSc, Jagellonian University, 1950; D Phil, 1958; Habil Doctor, Docent, 1968; Full Professor, 1978; Professor Emeritus. Appointments: Gymnasial Professor, 1938-39; Assistant, Jagellonian University, 1946-50; Elder Assistant, Lecturer, 1951-58; Adjunct, Lecturer, 1959-68; Assistant Professor, 1968-78; Full Professor, 1978-86; Director of the Chair, 1968-86; Vice Dean of Faculty, 1972-75; Vice Director of Institute of Psychology, 1979-80. Publications: Author of many publications. Honours: Golden Cross of Merit; Knight Cross of Renaissance of Poland; 4 Awards from Ministry of Education; 4 Awards, President of Jagellonian University; 2 Awards of Achievement, International Biographical Centre. Memberships: Union of Polish Teachers; Association of Universal Learning; Polish Psychological Association; Commission of Ergonomics PAN; Polish Ergonomics Association; Editorial Board of Semiyearbook Ergonomia. Address: ul Lea 77 m II, 30 058 Krakow, Poland.

**FRATESCHI Lawrence Jan,** b. 7 October 1952, Chicago, USA. Health Economist. Education: BS, University of Illinois, Chicago, 1975; MA, Economics, 1979; MS, Public Health in Biostatistics and Epidemiology, 1990; PhD, Economics, 1992. Appointments: Lecturer, 1978-80; Statisician, 1980-81; Professor, Economics and Statistics, 1981-. Publications: Numerous Articles Published. Honours: Phi Eta Sigma, 1972; Phi Kappa Phi, 1975; Delta Omega, 1990. Memberships: American Economics Association; American Public Health Association; Midwest Economics Association; American Statistics Association; Illinois Public Health Association; Illinois Economics Association. Address: Coll of DuPage, 422 22nd St, Glen Ellyn, IL 60137-6700, USA.

**FRAZER Robbin,** b. 1920, Elnora, Alta. Company President. Education: BA, Social Communication and Public Relations, Ottawa University, 1982. Appointments: Elementary School Teacher, Brazilian Traction Light and Power, 1947-53; Media Relations Officer, Public and Industrial Relations Ltd, 1956-67; Director of Public Relations, Banff School of Fine Arts and Management Centre, 1961, 1962; Various Support Positions, House of Commons, 1963-82; Supervisor of Public Information, Conference Board of Canada, 1973-75; President, Spectrum Three Consulting, 1976-; Alta Prov Information Officer, Canada Mortgage and Housing Corporation, 1978-79; Executive Assistant to Assistant Deputy Ministry of SPACE, 1982; Telecommunications Personnel and Policy Analyst Government Telecommunications Agency, 1986, 1987; President, World Bestravel Associates, 1988-; Faculty Member, Algonquin College of Applied Arts and Technology, 1988-91; Administration National Office, Canadian Public Personnel Management Association, 1990; Director, National Client Services, Government Leaders Training Institute, Custom Learning Systems, 1991-93; President, Life Long Learning Horizons and Associates, 1994-; Independent Associate, P.P.L-Legal Care of Canada Inc., 1999-. Publications: Welcome to Greater Vancouver; Various Government Publications and Reports; Many other Publications. Memberships: Canadian Public Relations Society; Business and Professional Women's Association of Ottawa; Canadian Association for Distance Education; Ottawa Distance Learning Group; Canadian Association of Home Based Business; Many other memberships. Address: Spectrum Three Consulting, Suite 201, 7080 Glacier Street, Powell River, BC, V8A 1R7, Canada.

**FREAS George Wilson II,** b. 27 October 1955, Franklin, KY, USA. Computer Consultant. m. Cynthia Anne, divorced 1990, 1 son. Education: BS, Computer Science, Western Kentucky University, Bowling Green, KY, USA, 1979; MS, Computer Science, University of Alabama in Huntsville, Huntsville, AL, USA, 1994. Appointments: President, Synergistic Consultants Inc, 1991; Software Consultant, Bell South Telecommunications, 1995; Adjunct Professor of Computer Science, American Institute of Computer Sciences, 1997. Publications: Canhy Canon, 1991; GEN7 Software, 1993; LALL - LL(1) Parser Generator, 1992. Membership: Educational Software Cooperative. Address: PO Box 2885, Huntsville, AL 35804-2885, USA.

**FREEDMAN Daniel,** b. 28 March 1958, Montreal, Canada. Internet Executive. Education: Vanier College, Montreal, Canada. Appointments: Writer, Producer, Director, Executive Producer, CFCF-12, Montreal, Quebec, Canada; News Director, CFCF-12, Montreal. Publications: Managing Editor, Paul Kogan's Baseline, New York; Director of New Business Development, Multimedia, Reed. Memberships: Elseuer, Boston, New York; Online Director, PBS The Business Channel, Washington DC. Address: 1640 19th Street, Washington DC 20009, USA.

**FREEMAN Arthur Merrimon III,** b. 10 October 1942, Birmingham, Alabama. Psychiatrist. m. Linda Poynter, 2 sons, 1 daughter. Education: AB Philosophy, 1963, Harvard University; MD, 1967, Vanderbilt University School of Medicine; Resident, Chief Resident, Johns Hopkins University, 1968-72. Appointments: Assistant Professor, Stanford University, 1974-77; Professor, Vice Ch Department of Psychiatry, University of Alabama, 1977-90; Director, Appalachian Hall Hospital, Asheville, North Carolina, 1993-96; Dean, 1993-96, Professor, Ch Department of Psychiatry, 1991-, LSUMC-S. Publications: Psychiatry for the Primary Care Physician, 1979; Binding and Treatment Response in Depressed Outpatients,

1993. Honour: Best Doctors in America, 1996-97. Memberships: American Psychiatry Association, Fellow 1978-; American College of Psychiatry, Fellow 1986-; Sou Psychiatry Association, Fellow 1991-; American Association Chmn of Depts of Psychiatry, 1991-. Address: 5929 E Ridge Dr, Shrevport, LA 71106 2423, USA.

**FREGA Ana-Lucia,** b. 25 November 1935, Buenos Aires, Argentina. m. Guillermo Coronel. Education: Higher Degree in Piano, National Conservatory of Music, 1954; DMus, National Rosario, Argentina, 1996. Appointments: Principal School of Performing Arts, Teatro Colon, Buenos Aires, 1980-90; Visiting Professor in Spain; Profesoor in Argentina. Publications: More than 50 books published. Membership: President, International Society Music Education, 1994-2000; Member, Executive Board International Music Council, UNESCO, 1998-2004. Address: Anchorena 1484 7 Piso Dpto 16, 1425 Buenos Aires, Argentina.

**FREIBERT Lucy M,** b. 19 October 1922, Louisville, Kentucky, USA. Emerita Professor of English. Education: AB, Spalding College, 1957; MA, University of St Louis, 1962; PhD, University of Wisconsin, Madison, 1970. Appointments: Elementary and secondary schools, Louisville, 1947-60; Associate Professor of English, Spalding College, 1960-71; Professor of English, University of Louisville, 1971-93. Publications: Hidden Hands: An Anthology of American Women Writers, 1790-1870, 1995; Numerous publications in Arizona Quarterly and Canadian Literature, and others. Honours: Distinguished Teaching Award, 1986; Trustees Award, 1991; Women of Distinction Award, 1993. Memberships: MLA; NOW; NWSA. Address: 1507 Hepburn #2, Louisville, KY 40204, USA.

**FREIRE Mario Marques,** b. 21 March 1969, Seia, Portugal. University Professor. m. Teresa M P Marques Freire. Education: Licentiate Degree in Electrical Engineering, University of Coimbra, Portugal, 1992; MSc, Systems and Automation, University of Coimbra, Portugal, 1994. Appointments: Research Engineer, Institute of Telecommunications at Coimbra, Portugal, 1992-; Student Assistant, University of Beira Interior, 1994-95; Research Assistant, University of Beira Interior, Portugal, 1995-. Publications include: Performance Implications of Partial Chirp Compensation in a Semiconductor Optical Booster Amplifier for Dispersion Supported Transmission at 10/Gbit/s, 1998; Multi-Quantum Well Laser Parameters for Simulation of Optical Transmission Systems up to 40 Gbit/s, 1998; Assessment of Blocking Performance in Wavelength Division Multiplexed Ring Networks with Bidirectional Links, 1999. Memberships: Member, Order of Engineers, Portugal; New York Academy of Sciences; Association for Computing Machinery; Institute of Electrical and Electronic Engineers. Address: Maiorais, Caixa Pessoal No 857, P-6200 Tortosendo Beira Baixa, Portugal.

**FREMLING Lennart,** b. 12 January 1946, Stockholm, Sweden. Member of Parliament. m. Margaretha Fremling, 1 son, 1 daughter. Education: MSc, 1968. Appointments: Head, Investigation Section, Vehicle Department, Swedish Road Safety Authority, 1975-91; Member of Parliament, 1991-. Address: Riksdag, 100 12 Stockholm, Sweden.

**FRIDLYANDER Yosif,** b. 28 September 1913, Andizhan, USSR. Academician; Professor. m. Satarova Tamara Ph, 2 daughters. Education: Moscow Higher Technical School, 1937. Appointments: Senior Technician, Engineer, Peading Engineer of All-Union Institute of Aviation Industry; Head of Laboratory of Research Institute of Aviation Materials; Corresponding Member, USSR (now Russian) Academy of Sciences, 1976, member, 1984. Publications: Over 400 including 40 patents.

onours: Lenin Prize; USSR State Prize. Memberships: Chair, cientific Council, Structural Materials for New Technologies. ddress: Research Institute of Aircraft Sciences, 17 Radio Str, loscow 117005, Russia.

**FRIEDLANDER Daniel,** b. 4 November 1933, Chicago, inois, USA. Journalist; Marketer. m. Shirley Tishcoff, 2 sons, daughter. Education: University of Colorado. Appointments: ewspaper and Wire Services Editor, Publisher, Company resident. Honours: State of Illinois Resolution for Outstanding ontributions to Journalism; Chicago Press Veterans ssociation. Memberships: International Vice President ssociation for Corporate Growth and many other irectorships. Address: Friedlander Comm Ltd, 2203 Lakeside rive, Bannockburn, IL 60014, USA.

**FRIEDMAN Hal Marc,** b. 29 December 1965, Trenton, ichigan, USA. College History Instructor. m. Lisa Sampsell riedman, 1 son. Education: BS Political Science and History, 987, Eastern Michigan University; MA History of International elations, 1991, PhD History of US International Relations, 995, Michigan State University. Appointments: Numerous aching posts, 1988-; Science and Technology Instructor, yman Briggs School, Michigan State University, 1995; Adjunct ecturer in History, Department of Social Sciences, University f Michigan-Dearborn, 1998; Full-Time, Early American History nstructor, Social Science Division, Henry Ford Community ollege, Dearborn, 1996-; Part-time, Associate Graduate aculty Member, Metropolitan Detroit Region, College of xtended Learning, Central Michigan University, 1997-. ublications: 211 articles abstracted; 10 articles; 5 book eviews; 2 theses microfilmed; 1 Monograph, forthcoming. onours: 1 scholarship, 1986, 4 fellowships, 1989, 1990, 1992, 995, 2 travel grants, 1993, 1994, 2 research grants, 1994, 995; Member 4 honour societies; Visiting Fellow, Humanities esearch Group, University of Windsor, 1995. Memberships: )mohundro Institute for Early American History and Culture; Vorld History Association; American Historical Association; )rganisation for American Historians. Address: Henry Ford CC ocial Science Division, 5101 Evergreen Road, Dearborn, MI 8128-2407, USA.

**FRIEDMANN Yohanan,** b. 28 March 1936, Zakamenné, `SR. Professor of Islamic Studies. m. Zafrira, 2 daughters. ducation: BA, 1959, MA, 1962, Hebrew University; PhD, 1966, IcGill University. Appointments: Professor of Islamic Studies, lebrew University, Jerusalem. Publications: Shaykh Ahmad irhindi, 1971; Prophecy Continuous, 1989. Address: 115 Uziel treet, Jerusalem 96431, Israel.

**FRIEDRICH Alexander Gunther,** b. 6 November 1923, Alt ietzegoericke, Germany. UN Diplomat (retired). m. div. 1 son. ducation: DSc, 1950, Hamburg University. Appointments: esearcher, Lecturer, Professor, Universities of Hamburg, )xford and Monrovia, IFAO Section Chief at H Q Rome, 950-66; UN Executive Secretary, Industry Cooperative rogramme, Rome, Geneva, New York, 1966-79; Forum hairman, German Foundation for International Development, erlin, 1979-89; Advisor, European Commission, 1989-94; ontributed to international cooperation and development by tarting in 1966 the globalization process in UN, encouraged oreign Direct Investment in developing countries of Latin merica, Asia and Africa, Joint Ventures. Memberships: ssociations: World Economic Affairs; Foreign Policy; United ations; International Development. Address: Kennedy Ufer 1, 50679 Cologne, Germany.

**FRIEDRICH Fabian,** b. 2 May 1965, Blumenau, Brazil. iochemist. Education: Graduate, Biochemistry, University

Federal of Santa Catarina, Brazil, 1988; Master Degree, Parasitology, 1993, Doctorate, Cell and Molecular Biology, 1996, Institute Oswaldo Cruz, Brazil. Appointment: Molecular Biologist, PCR Nucleotide Sequencing, Institute Oswaldo Cruz, Brazil. Publications: Numerous in scientific refereed journals. Membership: Brazilian Society of Virology. Address: Rua Içara 122, 89030-170 Blumenau, Brazil.

**FRIESS Donna Lewis,** b. Los Angeles, California, USA. m. Kenneth Friess, 2 sons, 1 daughter. Education: BA, University of Southern California; MA, California State University at Long Beach, California; PhD, United States International University, San Diego Campus. Appointments: Full time College Professor, Cypress College; Author; Professional Lecturer. Publications: Cry the Darkness: One Woman's Triumph; Circle of Love (published in 6 languages), 1993; Whispering Waters, 1998. Honours: Recognized by US Justice Department for work to protect children, 1995; Highest Honor, Nomination for American President's Service Award, 1996. Memberships: Founding Member, American Coalition Against Sexual Abuse; Board Member, Mothers Against Sexual Abuse; Honor Board Member, Child Abuse Listening and Mediation; Honor Board, One Voice (Against Sexual Abuse). Address: 31506 Paseo Christina, San Juan Capistrano, CA 92675, USA.

**FRIGGIERI Oliver,** b. 27 March 1947, Furjana, Malta. Professor of Maltese Literature; Author. m. Eileen Cassar, 1 daughter. Education: BA, cum laude, 1968; MA, 1975; PhD, 1978. Appointments: Full Professor, Head, Department of Maltese, University of Malta. Publications: Author of numerous articles published in international academic journals; Translator of various works from Latin, English and Italian into Maltese; His works include: Storia delle letteratura Maltese, 1986, Le vituel du crepuscule, 1991, Dizzjunarju ta' Termini Letterarji, 1996, La menzogna, 1997, Poeziji, 1998; Guest speaker in numerous international congresses held throughout Europe. Honours include: Premio Mediterraneo Internazionale, 1988. Membership: Association Internationale des Critiques Literaires, Paris. Address: University of Malta, Faculty of Arts, Department of Maltese, Msida, Malta.

**FRISCH Celia,** b. 27 December. Violinist; Chamber Music Coach; Educator. m. Al Frisch, deceased April 1976, 1 daughter. Education: Graduate, High School, Roxbury, Massachusetts. Appointments: Private Violin Teacher, Massachusetts; Chamber Music Coach, New York; Member, Crystal Strings Trio, Massachusetts, Marjorie Posselt Chamber Group, Boston, Ondricek Ensemble, Boston; Freelance Violinist under Arthur Fiedler, Milton Katmis, Dean Dixon and Lukas Foss, Boston and New York; Assistant Director, Strings Chamber Music, New York; 1st Violinist Brwyn Mawr String Quartet, Boston and New York; President, Myra Music Company, Tarrytown, New York, 1976-; Lecturer on music, travel, books and other topics. Publications: The Animals Nobody Knows, author, 1981. Memberships: ASCAP; Songwriters Guild; Wagner Society of New York; Ethical Culture Society of Westchester; Chamber Music America; Hudson Valley Music Guild; Rockland County Book and Discussion, New York; Bohemian, New York City. Hobbies: Writing; Walking; Swimming; Reading; Music; Traveling. Address: Myra Music Company, 177 White Plains Road, #33F New York, NY 10591, USA.

**FRISCHHOLZ Robert Walter,** b. 6 June 1964, Weiden, Germany. Computer Scientist. Education: Diploma, Computer Science, 1991; PhD, Engineering Science, 1998. Appointments: Computer Scientist, 1991-94, Group Leader, 1994-96, Fraunhofer Institute; Department Leader, Mikromak Gmbh, 1996-98; Head of Development, DCS AG, 1998-.

Publications: Several articles in professional journals. Memberships: IEEE. Address: Herdegenweg 9, 90427 Nürnberg, Germany.

**FRISTACKY Norbert,** b. 8 November 1931, Puchov, Slovakia. Scientist; Educator. m. Hilda Fristacka, 1 son. Education: Dipl Ing, Electrical Engineering, 1954, PhD, Technical Cybernetics, 1964, Slovak Technical University. Appointments: Assistant Professor, 1954, Docent, 1970, Professor, 1985, Head, Computer Science and Engineering Department, 1978-1990, Rector, 1990-91, Slovak Technical University; Lecturer, worldwide. Publications include: Programmable Logic Professors, 1981; Logic Circuits, 1986; Digital Computers, 1993. Honours: Czech Technical National Society Prize, 1981; Slovak Literary Fund Prizes, 1986, 1993; Computer Society IEEE (USA) Computer Pioneer Award, 1996; Slovak University of Technology Medal, 1997. Memberships include: American Czech Society of Arts & Sciences; IEEE, USA; IEE (UK); Slovak Society for Computer Science. Address: Slovak Technical University, Department of Computer Science & Engineering, Ilkovicova 3, 812 19 Bratislava, Slovakia.

**FROESCHLE Guenter,** b. 30 June 1954, Germany. Surgeon. m. Simone Krohn, 4 sons, 2 daughters. Education: MD, 1984; Engineer, 1988. Appointments: Surgeon, 1991; Orthopaedic Surgeon, 1993; Associate Professor, 1995. Publications: Several medical publications. Honour: Roggenbuck Grantee. Memberships: German Surgical Association; Degum Ver Nordwestdent; CHIR; DGM; DGC. Address: Kreiskrankenhaus Stormarn, Schutzenstr 55, 23843 Bad Oldesloe, Germany.

**FROLOV Vladimir Nicolaevich,** b. 20 August 1941, Bekovo, Russia. Nuclear Power Plant Operator. m. 30 Apr 1968, 2 sons. Education: Certificate in Engineering, Power Engineering Institute, Moscow, 1964; Certificate in Nuclear Engineering, Obninsk Physical Engineering Institute, Russia, 1985. Appointments: Operator, Engineer, 1964-73, Deputy Chief, Technology Department, 1977-82, 1983-86; Novovoronezh Nuclear Power Plant; Head, Equipment Department, Loviisa Nuclear Power Plant, Finland, 1973-76; Supervisor, Nuclear Scientific Centre, Tazhura, Tripoli, Libya, 1982-83; Deputy Director, Scientific Production Department, Pripyat, Chernobyl, Ukraine, 1986-91; State Inspector, Consultant, Scientific Production Department, Navigator, Information and Technology, Kiev, 1991-. Publications: Operation of the Reactor Installations of the Novovoronezh Nuclear Power Plant, 1972; Everything Comes in Bunches, 1996. Honours: Labour Veteran Medal, Kiev, 1990; Medal for Liquidation of Consequences of Chernobyl Catastrophe, 1990. Memberships: USSR Communist Party, 1977-90; Ukrainian Nuclear Society, 1996-. Address: Apt 308, Kashtanova Str 5, 253225 Kiev, Ukraine.

**FROST Juanita C,** b. 4 August 1926, Rockford, Illinois, USA. Middle Management. m. Thomas Tapenden Frost, deceased, 1 son, 1 daughter. Education: Little Rock University. Appointments: Executive Director, Camp Fire Girls, 1967-1973; Executive Assistant, Board of Trustees, Scott and White Memorial Hospital and Scott, Sherwood and Brindley Foundation, 1973-. Memberships: Daughters of the King; St Francis Church; Episcopal Diocese of Texas; Temple Civic Theatre Guild 1997-. Address: 3001 Las Moreas Drive, Temple, TX 76502 1643, USA.

**FROYLAND Gary Allan,** b. 3 December 1971, Mackay, Australia. Mathematician. Education: BSc, University of Queensland, 1992; PhD, University of Western Australia, 1997. Appointments: PhD Researcher, University of Western Australia, 1993-96; Research Officer, University of Western Australia, 1996-97; Research Fellow, University of Tokyo, 1997-. Honours: University Medal, University of Queensland; Ethel Raybould Prize in Mathematics; Postgraduate Research Award; Japan Society for Promotions of Science. Memberships: Australian Mathematical Society; Australia and New Zealand Industrial and Applied Mathematics. Address: S Georges College, Mounts Bay Road, Crawley, WA 6009, Australia.

**FRYBA Ladislav,** b. 30 May 1929, Studenec. Professor. m. Dagmar Frybova. Education: Department of Civil Engineering, Czech Technical University, Prague. Appointments: Head of Bridge Department, Railway Research Institute; Professor Institute Theoretical and Applied Mechanics, Academy of Sciences of Czech Republic. Publications: 160 papers; 6 books; Co-author 5 other books. Memberships: President Czech Society for Mechanics; Engineering Academy, Czech Republic; President, European Association for Structural Dynamics; Chairman of Committee of Experts, European Rail Research Institute, Utrecht. Address: Institute of Theoretical and Applied Mechanics, Academy of Sciences, Prosecka 76, CZ 190 00 Prague 9, Czech Republic.

**FRYDRYCH Iwona Krystyna,** b. 17 April 1956, Lodz, Poland. Textile Engineer. m. Waldemar, 1 daughter. Education: MSc, 1979, PhD, 1986, DSc, 1995, Textile Faculty, Technical University, Lodz. Appointments: Assistant, 1979-, Adjunct 1987-, Institute of Textile Metrology, Clothing and Nonwovens Textile University, Lodz; Deputy Director, Institute of Textile Architecture, 1987-. Publications: Over 70 papers in professional journals. Honours: Group Award, Ministry of National Education, 1991; Achievements in Technics Department of PAN, 1992. Memberships: President, Laboratory Commission of GCA; Polish Textile Engineers; Committee Cotton Testing Methods, ITMF; Association of Applied and Theoretical Mechanics. Address: Czernika 1B-13, 92 538 Lodz, Poland.

**FU Earl,** b. 6 June 1950, Taipei, Taiwan. Dentist; Educator m. Ching-Hwa Gau, 2 sons. Education: Bachelor of Dental Surgeon, 1974, National Defense Medical Centre, Taiwan; Certificate in Periodontics, 1981, Doctor of Science in Oral Biology, 1982, Boston University, USA. Appointments: Teaching Assistance and Residency, 1974-78, Associate Professor, 1983-95, Professor, 1995-, Chairman, 1997-, Periodontal Dept, National Defense Medical Centre, Taiwan; Visiting Associate Professor, Loma University, USA, 1993-94. Publications: Editor, Chinese Dental Dictionary, 3rd Edition 1984; Contributor articles to professional journals, 1974-. Honours: Army Commendation, 1990; Best Performance in Education, 1986, 1991, NDMC. Memberships: Dental Association of Republic of China, 1974-; Councillor 1989-91, 1997-; Academy of Periodontology, ROC, 1983-; President 1991-93; Fellow, International College of Dentistry. Address: 4F 92 Sect 2 An-Ho Rd, Taipei, Taiwan.

**FU Shiying,** b. 11 November 1919, De Hui City, China. Professor. m. Zhan Shunhua, 4 daughters. Education: MB ChB, 1943, Moukden Medical College. Appointments: Professor of Cardiology in Harbin Medical University; Tutor of Doctoral Degree Postgraduates and Postdoctoral Academic Exchange Station. Publications: Practical Electrocardiography, 1995; Advances in Cardiovascular Diseases, 1980. Honours: Awards from MOH, 1987, 1996, and Province, 1990, 1996. Memberships: Chief Member, Chinese Medical Association; Member of Associations of Chinese Internal Medicine and Chinese Cardiology. Address: The First Hospital and Research nstitute of Cardio Vascular Disease of Harbin Medical University, Harbin 150001, China.

**FU Shou-Cheng Joseph,** b. 19 March 1924, Beijing, China. Biochemist; Physical Organic Chemist. m. Susan B Guthrie, 3 sons. Education: BS and MS, 1944, Catholic University Beijing, China; PhD Chemistry, 1949, Johns Hopkins University. Appointments: Assistant Chemist, Catholic University Beijing, 1941-44; Junior Instructor, Johns Hopkins University, 1947-49; Scientist, National Cancer Institute, 1951-54; Chief Enzyme and Bio-Organic Chemistry Lab, Dana Faiber Cancer Institute, Boston, 1956-66; University Professor Chemistry and Chairman Chemistry Board, Chinese University Hong Kong, 1966-70; Concurrent, Research Fellow, National Cancer Institute, 1949-51; Bissing Fellow, from Johns Hopkins University to University College, University London, 1955; Research Associate, Children's Hospital Medical Centre and Harvard Medical School, 1956-66; University Dean, Science Faculty, Chinese University Hong Kong, 1967-69; Honorary Professor and Academic Consultant, Inner-Mongolia (AR) Medical College, Huthot, China, 1988-. Publications: in field of Organic Chemistry, proteins and enzymes, chemical kinetics and reaction mechanism, cancer chemotherapy and prevention, vision research, aging & nutrition. Memberships: Fellow, AAAS; American Association Cancer Research; American Society Biological Chemistry; NY Academy Sciences; Fellow, Royal Society Chemistry; Sigma Xi. Address: UMDNJ New Jersey Medical School, 185 S Orang Avenue, Newark, NJ 07103, USA.

**FUCHS Lorelei E,** b. 20 June 1950, New York City, New York, USA. Theologian; Educator; Religious Sister. Education: BA, Wheeling Jesuit University, 1972; MA, University of Notre Dame, 1991; MTh, STL, 1997, PhD Candidate, 1997-; Catholic University of Louvain, Belgium. Appointments: Associate Director, Graymoor Ecumenical & Interreligious Institute, New York City; Lecturer, Centro Pro Unione, Rome, Italy. Publications: A few articles in ecumenical journals, 1993-; Editor, Annual Journal for the Week of Prayer for Christian Unity; Co-editor, Encounters for Unity. Memberships: Faith and Order Commission; National Association of Diocesan Ecumenical Officers, USA; North American Academy of Ecumenists. Address: Graymoor Ecumenical & Interreligious Institute, 475 Riverside Drive, Room 1960, New York, NY 10115-1909, USA.

**FUCHS Michael,** b. 9 December 1964, Ulm, Germany. Instructor in Medicine; Gastroenterologist. Education: Abitur, 1984; MD, 1991, Internship, Departments of Medicine, Surgery and Radiology, 1991-92, PhD, Medicine, summa cum laude, 1993, Albert-Einstein University of Ulm; Residency, 1992-93, Instructor in Medicine, 1996-, Department of Medicine, Medical University Lubeck; Senior Research Fellow, Division of Gastroenterology, Brigham and Women's Hospital, Harvard Medical School and Harvard Digestive Diseases Centre, Boston, 1993-96; USMLE Step 1 and 2, 1997. Publications: Author or co-Author, 2 book chapters; 8 original articles; 11 oral presentations; 11 abstracts, 9 presented at national and international meetings. Honours: German Research Council Grant, 1993-95, 1997-99, 1999-2001; Young Investigator Award, European Association for the Study of Liver, 1995; Postdoctoral Fellow, Falk-Foundation, Germany, 1995-96; ADHF Postdoctoral Fellowship, 1995-96; Research Scholar, Alfred Jarchow Foundation, Germany, 1997. Memberships: German Gastroenterology Association; Gastroenterology Research Group; American Association for the Advancement of Science; American Association for Study of Liver Disease; New York Academy of Sciences; European Association for the Study of the Liver; American Society for Cell Biology; American

Physiological Society. Address: Medical University Luebeck Division Gastroenterology, Ratzeburger Allee 160, D-23538 Lubeck, Germany.

**FUENTES Martha Frances Ayers,** b. 21 December 1923, Ashland, Alabama, USA. m. Manuel Solomon Fuentes, 11 Apr 1943. Education: BA, University of South Florida, USA, 1969. Appointments: Playwright; Author. Publications: Pleasure Button, full length play, 1995-96; Jordan's End, 1998; Faith for Today. Memberships: Dramatist Guild; Florida Theatre Conference; North Carolina Writer's Network; Florida Studio Theatre. Hobbies: Theatre; Swimming; Travel; Animal Rights; Environmental Protection; Gardening. Address: 102 Third Street, Belleair Beach, Florida, 34786-3211, USA.

**FUIOREA Ion,** b. 1 June 1953, Muereasca, Romania. Professor. m. Luminita Cristian, 1 son, 1 daughter. Education: Engineer in Aircraft, MSc, 1977; Mathematics, 1985; PhD, Composite Materials Design, 1994. Appointments: Engineer on Bucharest Airport in Maintenance of Airplanes, 1977-81; Lecturer in Military Technical Academy (MTA), 1981-90; Senior Lecturer in MTA, 1990-96; Professor in Aircraft Design and Composite Structures in MTA, 1996-. Publications: Mechanics, 1988; Mechanics, 1990-91, 1992, 1993; Composite Materials The Mechanical Answer Design, 1995; Finite Element for Aircraft Structures, 1997. Memberships: Officer with the rank commender; International Society for the Advancement of Material and Process Engineering. Address: Str Marcu M Ruxandra Nr 4, BL B5 Sc B Ap 33, Bucuresti, Coo 77306, Romania.

**FUJINO Kazuo,** b. 22 September 1925, Tokyo, Japan. Emeritus Professor. m. Junko Suzuki, 1 son, 1 daughter. Education: Bachelor's degree, University of Tokyo, 1950; PhD, University of Tokyo, 1962. Appointments: Research Worker, The Whales Research Institute, Tokyo, 1950-64; Program Chief, US Department of Interior, Department of Commerce, Honolulu, 1964-71; Affiliate Faculty, University of Hawaii, Honolulu, 1965-71; Professor Kitasato University, Sanriku, Japan, 1972-91; Dean, Kitasato University, 1982-86. Publications: Population genetic studies on marine fish, 1999; Over 100 original and/or reviewing scientific papers, 1953-97. Honour: Superior Performance Award, US Department of Interior, 1969. Membership: Honorary member, President, Japanese Society of Fish Genetics and Breeding Science, 1980-90. Address: 2-28-22 Shakujiidai Nerima, 177-0045 Tokyo, Japan.

**FUJINO Masako,** b. 6 August 1958, Sapporo. Pharmacologist; Astrologer; Amateur Astronomer. Education: Phd; Medical School Graduate. Appointments: Pharmacology Member, 1989-; Astronomy Member, 1992-; Astrology Member, 1993-. Publications: Speech in E C Compiling in International Congress of Physiology; AFA Bulletin, Astrological Basis Issue, USA. Memberships: Japan Pharmacological Society; Astronomical Society of Japan; Research Member, American Federation of Astrology. Address: Uzumi-cho 1-1-6 Makomanai, Minami-ku Sapporo 005, Japan.

**FUJITA Sei,** b. 20 March 1928, Kyoto-City, Japan. Political Economist. m. Hiroko, 1 son. Education: Doctor in Sociology, Hitotsubashi University, 1965. Appointments: Professor, Economics, Osaka City University, 1975-91; Osaka University of Economics and Law, 1991-. Publications: Soviet Commodity Production - Its Semi Permanent Continuation (in Japanese); The Soviet Economy as a Social Experiment - Lessons from the 20th Century. Memberships: Association for Comparative Economic Studies; Amnesty International; Japan Braille Library.

Address: 4-5-11 Mukogaoka Uenoshiba, Sakai-shi 593-8303, Japan.

**FUKAC Jiri,** b. 15 January 1936, Znojmo, Czech Republic. Musicologist. m. Jitka, 2 d. Education: PhDr, Musicology, University in Brno, 1954-59; Dozent, 1990; Professor, 1994. Appointments: 8 Books about Musicology; 200 Articles. Memberships: International Musicology Society; Czech Musicology Society. Address: Milenova 4, Brno 63800, Czech Republic.

**FUNAHASHI Toru,** b. 20 June 1926, Kyoto City, Japan. Human Pathologist; Physician. m. Shizuko Tsuji, 2 daughters. Education: Graduate, Medical Faculty, Osaka University, 1949; Hematologist, 1950-53, Human Pathologist, 1953-60, Alma Mater. Appointments: Trustee, Local Medical Association, 1970-72; President, Rotary Club of Moriguchi, Osaka, Japan, 1993-94. Publications: Nineteen professional publications in journals and magazines. Memberships: Medical Volunteer, Island in the Philippines; Rotary Club of Moriguchi. Address: 7-18 Sanae-cho, Moriguchi-shi, Osaka 570-0072, Japan.

**FUNAYAMA Shinji,** b. 31 May 1951, Sendai, Japan. Scientist; Chemist; Educator. m. Noriko Saito, 1 daughter. Education: BPharm, 1975, MS, 1977, PhD, 1980, Tohoku University, Japan. Appointments: Research Associate, University of Illinois at Chicago, 1980-83; Research Fellow, Tohoku University, 1983-84; Resident Head, Kitasato University, 1984-90; Instructor to Assistant Professor, Tohoku University, 1990-96; Associate Professor, Aomori University, 1996-. Publications: The Alkaloids:Treasurehouse of Poisons and Medicines, 1998; Numerous articles inprofessional journals. Memberships: Consultant Editor, Journal of Research and Education in Indian Medicine; Editorial Reviewer, PharmaceuticalBiology; Japan Association of Herbs, Board of Directors, 1991-; American Society of Pharmacognosy; Japanese Society of Pharmacognosy; Pharmaceutical Society of Japan.

**FUNG Margaret C,** b. 4 February 1934, Nanking, China. Government Official. m. John Fung, 1 son, 2 daughters. Education: BA, 1955, National Taiwan University; MSLS, 1959, Marywood College, USA; PhD, 1983, Indiana University, USA. Appointments: Assistant Librarian, St John's University and Harvard-Yenching Library, Harvard University, 1959-65; Deputy Librarian, Chinese University of Hong Kong, 1966-67; Associate Professor, National Taiwan University, 1967-74; Professor and Director of Libraries, National Taiwan Normal University, 1977-81; Visiting Professor, University of Illinois, USA, 1984-87; Executive Director Chinese Studies, Wang Institute of Graduate Studies, USA, 1984-87; Professor, National Chengchi University and National Taiwan University, 1990-97; Ministerial Member of Examination Yuan China 1990-; President, Library Association of China, 1998-99. Publications: Reflections on Civil Service System and Library Information Science, 1996; The Evolving Social Mission of the National Central Library in China, 1928-1966, 1994; Primer of Library Automation, 1990; Library and Information Science, 1982; Library and Information, 1979. Honours: Distinguished Service Award of Examination Yuan, 1994; IU Louise Maxwell Award, 1994; The Chinese-American Librarians Association Distinguished Service Award, 1989; Outstanding Service Awards, Library Association of China, 1979, 1984; Member Phi Tan Phi; Beta Phi Mu; Honorary Citizen of Dallas, Texas. Memberships: American Library Association; American Society for Information Science; Asian Pacific American Library Association; CEAL; Association for Asian Studies; Chinese American Libraries Association; Library Association of China;

Welcome International Club; ZONTA International. Address PO Box 2-53, Mucha, Taipei, Taiwan.

**FUREN Shirley A,** b. 9 December 1936, Pomona, California USA. Art Dealer. m. Walter E Furen, 1 son, 2 daughters Education: Bachelor Degree, University Studies, University c New Mexico; Certified Medical Assistant. Career: Realtor Washington, DC; Model, California; Santa Fe Opera; A Dealer. Memberships: Episcopal Church; Capital Busines Womens Association; Council on International Relations Sacramento Capitol Club. Address: 644 Alto Street, Santa Fe NM 81501, USA.

**FUREY Susan M,** b. 13 May 1946, Philadelphia Pennsylvania, USA. Professional Educator. m. Francis J Furey 2 sons. Education: Masters Education, 1995, Director o Curriculum Certificate, 1994, Doctoral candidate, 1994- Widener University. Appointments: School Board Director 1991-95; Political Action Director for PSEA, 1993-; Professiona Educator, 30 years. Publications: Publisher's Plus (letter t Editor). Honour: Friend of Education Award, 1995 Memberships: Phi Kappa Phi Honour Society; Pennsylvania State Education Association; Kappa Delta Pi Honour Society National Education Association. Address: 507 Bryn Maw Avenue, Bala Cynwyd, PA 19004-2526, USA.

**FURUYAMA Renee,** b. 15 February 1957, Honolulu, Hawaii USA. Social Worker; Lobbyist; Community Organizer. m. Joe Fischer. Education: MSW, 1988; MURP, 1993. Appointments State Geriatric Case Manager, 1992-95; Public Policy Director Mental Health Association, Hawaii, 1995-98. Honour Scholarship, 1982-84. Memberships: National Assocition o Social Workers; American Friends, Service Committee; Hawai Committee for Africa. Address: 1371-4 Hunakai Street Honolulu, HI 96816, USA.

# G

**GABBASOVA Zukhra,** b. 11 October 1967, Novosibirsk, Russia. Physicist. m. Tagir Kh Gareyev, 1 son. Education: Master of Physics, 1989; PhD, Theoretical Physics, 1995. Appointments: Junior Scientist, Bashkir Science Centre, Russia, 1989; Participation in All-Union and European Conferences, Mocow, 1990, Novgorod, 1991; Junior Scientist, Calabria University, Italy, 1992; Scientist, Bashkir Science Centre, Russia, 1996. Publications: Numerous publications. Memberships: Junior Scientist, Physics Department, Bashkir Science Centre, Russia, 1989; J S Physics Department, Calabria University, Italy, 1992; General Physics Institute of AS, Moscow, Russia, 1992; Scientist, Physics Department, Bashkir Science Centre, Ufa, Russia, 1996. Address: Laboratory of Antiferromagnets & Ferrities Physics Department, Bashkir Centre of Russian Academy of Science, 6 K Marxa Str Ufa, 450025, Russia.

**GACESA Nikola,** b. 14 December 1924, Stikada-Gracac. University Professor of Economic History. m. Ivanka, 1 daughter. Education: BA, Faculty of Philosophy, Belgrade, 1954; PhD, Economic History, University of Belgrade. Appointments: Professor of Economic History, University of Novi Sad, 1977-97; Head, History Department, University of Novi Sad; Member of the Managing Board of Matica Srpska, Novi Sad; Head, Manuscript Department, Matica srpska, Novi Sad. Publications: Agricultural Reform and Resettlement in Yugoslavia, 1945-48; Studies in Agriculture, 1995. Membership: Historical Society of the Republic of Serbia. Address: Fruskogorska 33, 21000 Novi Sad, Yugoslavia.

**GADZIJEV Misa Eldar,** b. 17 August 1945, Ljubljana. Surgeon. m. Marijeta, 2 sons, 1 daughter. Education: MD, 1970; Surgeon, 1978; PhD, 1989; Professor, 1992; Hig degree Consultant, 1997. Appointments: President, Surgical courses, International Hepaatobiliary School Ljubljana; Member of the State Ethical Committee; President, Professional Medical Committee; Member Scientific Committee, IHPBA. Publications: Over 100 papers including: Atlas of Internal Liver Anatomy, 1996. Memberships: International Hepato-Pancreato-Biliary Association; International Gastro-Surgical Club; Slovenian Medical Association. Address: University Medical Centre Ljubljana, Division of Surgery, Surgical Courses, Dept of Gastroenterologic Surgery, Zaloska 1 SI 1000 Ljubljana, Slovenia.

**GAFFNEY Jeffrey Steven,** b. 28 July 1949, San Bernardino, CA. Research Chemist. m. Nancy A Marley, 1 s, 2 d. Education: BS, University of California, 1971; MS, 1973; PhD, 1975. Appointments: Graduate Research Assistant, University of California, 1971-75; Postdoctoral Research Associate, Brookhaven National Laboratory, 1975-77; Associate Chemist, 1977-80; Chemist, 1980-85; Staff Member, Los Alamos National Laboratory, 1985-88; Faculty Adjunct, Adjunct Research Chemist, New Mexico Institute of Technology and Mining, 1992-; Chemist, Argonne National Laboratory, 1989-; Grand Mentor, DOE/OBER Global Change Education Program, 1998-. Publications: 118 Publications. Honours: Gifted and Talented Teaching Award; Certificate of Recognition; Chemistry Awards; Many others. Memberships: American Chemical Society; American Association for Aerosol Research; American Geophysical Union; American Association for the Advancement of Sciences. Address: Argonne Natl Lab, 9700 Cass Ave Bld 203, Argonne, IL 60439-4843, USA.

**GAFITANU Mihai,** b. 16 September 1934, Iasi, Romania. Professor of Mechanical Engineering. m. Gafitanu Eliza, 2 sons. Education: ME, 1957; PhD, 1968. Appointments: Assistant, 1957-62, Lecturer, 1962-69, Assistant Professor, 1969-72, Professor, 1972-, Vice Dean, 1964-72, Vice Rector, 1972-76, Head of Department, 1985-96, Rector, 1976-84, 1996-, Technical University of Iasi. Publications: 9 books, 14 text and handbooks, 13 patents, 67 papers in scientific journals, 162 papers in proceedings. Honour: Romanian Academy Prize, 1985. Memberships: Vice President, Romanian Tribology Association, 1981-; National Council of Academic Evaluation and Accreditation; National Council of Academic Titles and Diploma Accreditations, 1991-; Various professional stages abroad. Address: Titu Maiorescu str nr 24A, bl H5 app 11, 6600 Iasi, Romania.

**GAGIU Constantin,** b. 24 August 1944, Valea Danului-Arges. Scientific Researcher. m. Florica, 1 son, 1 daughter. Education: Bucharest Politechnical University, 1969; Doctor in Science, 1975, V P Goriacikin Institute, Moscow; Scientific Researcher first degree, 1990, Agricultural and Silvical Science Academy, Bucharest. Appointments: Scientific Researcher, 1969-72, 1975-80, ICMA Buch; Doctorand Inst V P Goriacikin, Moscow, 1972-75; Ing first degree, Minist Agric, 1980-90; Manager, Minist Agr, 1990; General Manager, Institute Romatest, 1990-98. Publications: Reliability in operating conditions of tractors, 1995; 165 scientific works; 50 publications (other technical books and articles). Honour: Diploma for honorary manager, ATTR. Memberships: Vice President: ATTR; SIMAR. Address: Armenis str nr 8-10 bl j 5 ap 3 sector 3, Bucharest, Romania.

**GAGOVIC Milorad,** b. 2 August 1938, Bezuje. Physician. m. Ljubica Gagovic, 1 son, 1 daughter. Education: Diploma, 1963, Faculty of Medicine, Belgrade University; Postgraduate Studies Diploma, 1981, Novi Sad University; MD, 1986, Novi Sad University. Appointments: Gynaecologist, Obstetrician, 1964-, Medical Centre, Vrbas. Honours: Municipal October Award, 1984; Various citations and charters in recognition of scientific and occupational achievements. Memberships: Yugoslav Association of Gynaecologists-Obstetricians; Medical Societies in Yugoslavia. Address: Ul Sava Kovacevic 99, Vrbas 21460, Yugoslavia.

**GAGRAT Rustam Jehangir,** b. 5 November 1959, Bombay, India. Lawyer. m. Lia, 1 son. Education: BA, Elphinstone College, Bombay, 1979; BA Hons, Downing College, Cambridge University, 1981; MA, 1985; Solicitor, Bombay, 1984; Solicitor, UK, 1987; PIL, Harvard University Law School, 1993. Appointments: Advocate Supreme Court of India; Solicitor, Supreme Court of England; Partner, Gagrat and Co, Advocates and Solicitors, Bombay and, Partner, Gagrat and Co, Supreme Court Advocates, Delhi; Company Director, Trustee of the Public and Private Trusts. Honours: Tata Scholar, Cambridge University; Rustomji Mulla Prize of the Bombay Law Society; Presented Papers at International and Domestic Law Conferences. Memberships: Supreme Court of India Bar Association; Bombay Bar Association; Bombay Law Society; The Law Society of England; International Bar Association; International Law Association; Oxford and Cambridge Society. Address: 9 Om Ratan, New Worli, Bombay 400 025, India.

**GAI Moshe,** b. 18 August 1949, Baghdad, Iraq. Professor of Physics. m. Helen Hart-Gai. Education: BSc, Hebrew University, Jerusalem; MSc, 1976, PhD, 1980, SUNY at Stony Brook. Appointments: Research Associate and Lecturer, 1980-84, Assistant Professor, 1984-89, Associate Professor, 1989-94, Yale University; Professor, University Connecticut,

**1994-.** Membership: Fellow, American Physical Society, 1998-. Address: 17 Parker Place, Branford, CT 06405 4416, USA.

**GAIDAR Boris,** b. 19 January 1946, Zaporoj'e, Ukraine. Neurosurgeon. m. Lutchinsckaya Tatiana A, 1 son, 1 daughter. Education: Medical Institution, Alma-Ata, Kazakhstan, 1963-69; Postgraduate, Neurosurgery, Military Medical Academy, Leningrad, 1980-83. Career: Neurosurgeon, Alma-Ata City Hospital, 1969-72; Neurosurgeon, Regional Military Hospital, 1972-80; Senior Teacher, Neurosurgical Department, Military Medical Academy, Leningrad-St Petersburg, 1983-92; Chief, Neurosurgical Department, Military Medical Academy, Leningrad-St Petersburg, 1992-. Publications include: Sonography in Diagnosis of Aortic Arch Branches Diseases, 1994; Optimization of Cerebral Blood Flow in Neurosurgical Patients. Membership: Vice President, National Association of Neurosurgeons. Address: Vyborg Quay 3, St Petersburg 194175, Russia.

**GAIGALAS Algirdas Juozapas,** b. 27 February 1933, Pakruojis, Lithuania. Geologist. m. Birute Svetlauskaite, 1 son. Education: Doctor of Geology and Mineralogy, 1962; Professor, 1980. Appointments: Scientific Worker, 1957-63, Senior Research Worker, 1963-71, Head of Sector, 1971-79, Professor, 1979-, Institute of Geology and Geography, Academy of Sciences, Lithuania. Publications: Over 400 scientific publications, 350 popular ones, 11 books. Memberships: President, Lithuanian Natural Society; Leader, Working Group, Scandinavian Ice Cover of Southeastern Part of Inqua. Address: Vilnius State University, Faculty of Natural Sciences, Ciurlionio Street 23, Vilnius, Lithuania.

**GAILEY Frances,** b. 26 June 1932, Watertown, New York, USA. College Professor Emerita. Education: BS, Syracuse University, 1949-53; MS, Cornell University, 1958-59; PhD, Ohio State University, 1969-72. Appointments: Dietitian, Wheaton College, Wheaton, Illinois, USA, 1959-60; Teacher, Homer Central School, Homer, New York, USA, 1960-61; Assistant Professor, Associate Professor, Professor, Home Economics, SUNY College at Oneonta, 1961-93. Honours: Phi Upsilon Omicron; Kappa Omicron Phi; Omicron Delta Kappa, Leadership. Memberships: American Association of Family and Consumer Sciences; International Approval Services; American Standards Testing and Materials; SUNY College at Oneonta Foundation Board. Address: 46 Woodside, Oneonta, NY 13820, USA.

**GAKHOKIDZE Ramaz,** b. 17 May 1945, Tbilisi, Georgia. Chemist. m. Rusudan, 1 son, 2 daughters. Education: Chemist, Tbilisi State University, 1967; Candidate of Chemical Sciences, 1971; Postdoctoral Fellow of Purdue University, 1976-77; Doctor of Chemical Sciences, 1984. Appointments: Senior Research Worker, 1971; Docent of Tbilisi State University, 1974; Head of Laboratory, Bioorganic Chemistry, 1983; Professor, 1984; Head of Department of Bioorganic Chemistry, 1990-. Publications: Saccharinic Acids, Advances in Chemistry; On Mechanism of Acid Rearrangement of Carbohydrates; Reports of Academy of Science of USSR; Acid Transformation of Sulphonates of Aldoses; Journal of Organic Chemistry; Biological Active Compounds of Flora of Georgia; Investigation of Water Solublle Polysaccharides of Some Plants of Georgia, Chemistry of Natural Products; Total of 247 publications. Honours: Laureate of First Grade Prize of Georgian Council of Ministers; Laureate of P Melikishvili Prize; Laureate of Georgian Ministry of Education Prize; Laureate of Georgian State Prize. Memberships: American Society of Pharmacognosy; Italian Ecological Scientific Committee; European Ecological Committee. Address: 82 Barnov Str, 380028 Tbilisi, Georgia.

**GAL Gheorghe Sorin,** b. 23 August 1953, Abram, Bihor, Romania. Mathematician. m. Doina Rodica, 1 son, 1 daughter. Education: Graduate, Faculty of Mathematics, Babes-Bolyai University, Cluj-Napoca, 1976; Master Degree, 1977, Doctor in Mathematics, Faculty of Mathematics, Babes-Bolyai University, Cluj-Napoca, 1993. Appointments: Mathematician, Computer Center, Oradea, 1978-90, Reader, 1990-93, Lecturer, 1993-96, Professor, 1996-, Head, Department of Mathematics, University of Oradea. Publications: Publications in research journals; Reviewer mathematical reviews; Referee for various journals. Memberships: American Mathematical Society; New York Academy of Sciences; Planetary Society. Address: Cantacuzino 21 B1 AN 45 #8, 3700 Oradea, Bihor, Romania.

**GALDETSKII Anatoly,** b. 2 October 1956, Kiev, USSR. Physicist. m. Alena Kovalenkova, 1 son. Education: High Degree Diploma, 1978, Postgraduation in MPhil, PhD Diploma, 1982, Moscow Physical Technical Institute. Appointments: Junior Scientist, Moscow Institute of Radioengineering and Electronics of Academy of Science, 1981-87; Senior Scientist, State Research and Production Corporation "ISTOK", 1987-91; Head Scientist, "Istok", 1991-. Publications: Proceedings of International Vacuum Microelectronics Conferences, 1991-97; Mikroelektronika, 1997. Address: Vacuum Microelectronics Department, Research & Production Corp "ISTOK", Fryazino, Moscow 141120, Russia.

**GALERIU Constantin,** b. 21 November 1918, Bacau, Romania. Professor, Christian Orthodox Theological Academy; Priest. m. Argentina Cristina, 4 sons. Education: MTheol, Faculty of Christian Orthodox Theology, Bucuresti University, 1952; DTheol, 1973. Appointments: Consultant, University Professor of Practice and Fundamental Theology; Accredited PhD Supervisor; Spiritual Father Confessor; Professor of History and Philosophy of Religion; Missionary Priest; Ecumenical Evoy. Publications: Sacrifice and Redemption; The Structure of Sacrifice; Twilight Dialogues; Receive This Treasure; The Transfiguration of Christ-Transfiguration of Nature; Fidelity of Orthodox Church. Honours: Doctor Honoris Causa, Ecological University of Bucuresti; Award of the Senate of the Bucuresti University, 1992; Award of Honour, Titu Maaiorescu University, 1942. Address: Str Silvestru 36, Bucuresti, Romania.

**GALESANU Mihail Romeo,** b. 9 May 1932, Brasov, Romania. Physician. m. Corina, 1 son, 1 daughter. Education: Graduate, Medical Faculty, University of Medicine and Pharmacy, Carol Davila, Bucharest, 1957. Appointment: Professor, Head, Department of Radiology and Oncology, University Gr T. Popa of Iassy, 1982-. Publications: Numerous books and articles in professional medical journals. Honour: Diploma, Educational Minisdtry of Romania, 1989; 2nd Prize Teaching Program, 1986. Memberships: Academy of Medical Sciences of Romania; EACR, Nottingham; EUSOMA, Milano ESTRO, Brussels; ARRS, USA; President, Romanian Society for Radiation Oncology; Founding Member, BUON, Athens DEGRO, Tubingen. Address: PO Box 1-60, RO 6600 Iasi Romania.

**GALIAN Laurence,** b. 5 April 1954, Manhattan, New York USA. Author; Musician. m. Naila. Education: Music Education Hofstra University, 1972-74; Operatic Conducting, University of South Florida, 1975; Hofstra University (University Withou Walls at New College), 1995-97. Appointment: Senior Dance Accompanist, Hofstra University, 1981-. Publications: Balle Music (Compact Disc), 1993; Beyond Duality: The Art of Transcendance, 1995. Membership: International Guild of Musicians in Dance. Address: PO Box 297, Jericho, NY 11753-0297, USA.

**GALLAGHER Jack B,** b. 27 June 1947, Brooklyn, New York, USA. Composer; Music Educator. m. April Lorenz, 19 August 1977, 1 son, 1 daughter. Education: BA cum laude, Hofstra University, 1969; MFA, Cornell University, 1975; D of Mus Arts, Cornell University, 1982. Appointments: Trumpet, National Orchestral Association, New York City, 1968-70; Teacher, Bethpage Public Schools, New York, 1969-71; Graduate Teaching Assistant, Music, Cornell University, 1971-75; Instructor, Music, The College of Wooster, Ohio, 1977-81; Assistant Professor, 1981-83, Associate Professor, 1983-91, Professor, 1991-, Acting Chair, Department of Music, 1992-93. Publications: Compact disc recordings: Symphony in One Movement: Threnody, 1994; Berceuse, 1995; The Persistence of Memory, 1996; Proteus Rising From the Sea, 1995; Toccata for Brass Quintet, 1994; Capriccio, 1998. Honours: Recipient, 1st Prize, Virginia College Band Directors Association, 1987; Ohio Arts Council Individual Artist Fellowship, 1992, 1996; Ohio Music Teachers Association Composer of the Year, 1996; Fellow, The Yaddo Corporation, 1984. Memberships: Society of Composers Inc; American Music Center; Broadcast Music Inc; Cleveland Composer's Guild; International Trumpet Guild; Pi Kappa Lambda; Sigma Alpha Iota. Hobbies: Films; Reading; Sports. Address: The College of Wooster, Scheide Music Center, Wooster, OH 44691, USA.

**GALLOS Jordan Chris,** b. 26 August 1922, Cleveland, Ohio, USA. Food Facilities Consultant. 1 son, 1 daughter. Education: NC State University, 1940-41, 1945-46; University of Missouri, 1943. Appointments: Member, Office of Strategic Services, WWII; Food Service Dealer, Designer, Sales, Manager, Dreco Inc; Johns G Kolbe Inc; Ezekiel Weilman Co; Florence Equip Co; Joseph Equip Co; Butler Enteprises; Szabo Food Services, Director Food Facilities, Chicago. Publications: Food Service Magazines; If I had Only Known - That this too would pass, Autobiography. Memberships: ISFSC; FCSI; Optimist Club; Masonic Lodge Shriner; Orthodox Church. Address: 1527 Dewitt Road, Sparta, North Carolina 28675, USA.

**GALTUNG Johan,** b. 24 October 1930, Oslo. Professor of Peace Studies. m. Fumiko Nishimura, 3 sons, 1 daughter. Education: PhD equivalents in Mathematics, 1956, Sociology, 1957. Appointments: Professor of Sociology, Columbia University, 1957-60; Director and Founder, International Peace Research Institute, Oslo, 1959-70; Professor of Peace Studies, 1969-; Director, TRANSCEND, a peace network, 1993-. Publications: 80 Books in Social Sciences, Peace and Conflict Studies. Honours: Dr honoris causa at 6 and Honorary Professor at 4 universities around the world. Address: 51 Bois Chatton, F-01210 Versonnex, France.

**GAMBOTTO Antonella,** b. 19 September 1965, Sydney, Australia. Writer; Author. Education: Killara High School Sydney, 1982. Appointments: Contributing Writer, RAM Magazine, Sydney, 1983; Contributing Writer, New Musical Express, Sounds, Zig Zag Magazine, The Daily Star, 1984-86; Editorial Consultant, GQ Magazine, Freelance Translator, London; Winner of Cosmopolitan's New Journalist of the Year Award, 1987-88; Contributing Writer, Independent On Sunday Review, Sunday Telegraph, Penthouse, London, 1989-91; Senior Contributing Editor, Penthouse Magazine, Contributing Writer, Australian, Cosmopolitan, Cleo, Billy Blue, Sydney, 1989-91; Senior Contributing Editor, Mode Magazine, Playboy Magazine, Contributing Writer, Cleo Magazine, Literary Critic, Sydney Morning Herald, Guest Interviewer, Face The Press, Guest Commentator, TVTV, Sydney, 1992-93; Contributor to Love Cries, Senior Contributing Editor, ELLE Magazine, Contributing Writer, Mode Magazine, Literary Critic, Sydney Morning Herald, Sydney, 1994; Co-Judge, Sydney University Literary Competition, Senior Contributing Editor, ELLE Magazine, Contributing Writer, Harper's Bazaar, Literary Critic, Sydney Morning Herald, and The Australian, Sydney, 1995-. Publications: Lunch of Blood, An Instinct for the Kill, The Pure Weight of the Heart.

**GAN Woon-Song,** b. 6 March 1943, Singapore. Acoustician. m. Siu Hui Chong, 2 sons, 1 daughter. Education: BSc, Physics, Imperial College, London, 1965; PhD, Acoustics, 1969. Appointments: Postdoctoral Research Assistant, Imperial College and Chelsea College, London, 1968-70; Associate Professor, Physics, Nanyang University, Singapore, 1970-79; Founding Director, Acoustical Services Singapore Ltd, 1976-. Publications: Over 100 papers in professional journals. Honours: UNESCO Research Fellowship, 1970, 1973. Memberships: Senior Member, Institute of Electrical and Electronics Engineers, USA; Fellow, Southern African Acoustics Institute, Institution of Electrical Engineers, England, Institute of Acoustics, England. Address: c/o Acoustical Services Singapore Pte Ltd, 209-212 Innovation Centre, NTU, Nanyang Avenue, 39798 Singapore.

**GANACHARI Neelkantji,** b. 10 June 1916, Hosur, India. Social Worker. m. Irsavva, 4 sons, 2 daughters. Education: Studied Gandhian philosophy, Jamanalal khadi Institute, 1941. Appointments: Imparted the importance of khadi at several villages; Went to jail for beliefs, 1942-44; Entered Kalahal village of Ramdurg Taluk of Belgaum District, 1948; Taught social values, freeing society from bad habits, Kalahal village; Work extended to whole of Karnatak; Service in field of Education; Established schools in villages; Worked to establish social peace and communal harmony in villages; A true Gandhian. Address: Sureban, Ramdura Belgaum, Karnataka, India.

**GANDHI Madan Gopal,** b. 31 August 1940, Lahore, India. Professor. m. Smt Sushma Bhardwaj. Education: MA, English, 1964, MA, Political Science, 1966, PhD, Political Science, 1974, Punjab University, India; DLitt, Honorary, World Academy of Arts and Literature and World Congress of Poets, California, USA. Appointments: Dean of Social Sciences; Dean of Education; Head, Department of Political Science; Director, Directorate of Distance Education, 6 years; Director, Haryana Warehousing Corporation, 3 years; Dean, Faculty of Social Sciences, and Dean, Faculty of Education; Professor and Head, Department of Political Science Director, Centre for Third World Study and Research; Member, Indian Council of Social Science Research, Government of India; Member, Indian Council of Philosophical Research, Government of India; Visiting Fellow, St John's College, Cambridge, England, 1989-90. Publications: Gandhi and Marx, 1969; Gandhian Aesthetics, 1969; Modern Political Analysis, 1976; Modern Political Theory, 1981; Articles and research papers in various national and international journals; Creative writing: collections of poetry in English: Kundalini, 1982; Ashes and Embers, 1982; Haikus and Quatrains, 1983; Petals of Flame, 1985; Luteous Serpent, 1986; Meandering Maxe, 1987; Freak Stair, 1988. Honours: Selected among First Five Hundred, International Biographical Centre, Cambridge, England; International Man of the Year, 1991-92, 1996-97, International Biographical Centre, Cambridge and American Biographical Institute, North Carolina, USA; Elected Most Admired Man of Decade, American Biographical Institute, USA; Selected World Intellectual, International Biographical Centre, Cambridge, 1993; One-In-A-Million Honour, International Biographical Centre, Cambridge; Invited Life Fellow, American Biographical Institute's Research Association; Nominated for ABI's Lifetime Achievement Award; Invited Deputy Governor, ABI's current

Research Board of Advisors; Member, Board of Advisors, International Centre Democracy, Maryland, USA; Tagore Medal, 1961; Nominated for National Excellence Award; Nominated for Rajiv Gandhi Award; Chief Editor, MDU Journal of Arts and Social Sciences and Former Joint Editor, Indian China Review. Member, Haryana Granth Academy. Address: MD University, Rohtak 124001, India.

**GANDHI Ravinder Singh,** b. 4 April 1960, Tarin, India. Scientist. m. Varinder Gandhi, 1 son, 1 daughter. Education: BSc II, 1978, BSc, 1979, Guru Nank Dev University, Amritsar; MSc Dairying (Animal Genetics and Breeding), 1982, PhD Animal Genetics and Breeding, 1987, NDRI, Karnal. Appointments: Scientist, 1986-91; Scientist, Senior Scale, 1991-.Publications: 47 research articles; 2 review articles; 5 popular articles; 14 abstracts. Honours: Various scholarships and distinctioncertificates; Junior, Senior Research Fellowship, NDRI, 1980, 1983; Invited by Board of Governors, NYAS, USA, to become a Member, 1996; Outstanding Young Indian Award, Karnal Junior Chamber, for Scientific and TechnologicalDevelopments, 1997; Outstanding Young Person Award, Indian Junior Chamber, 1997; Invited by National Geographical Society of USA to become a member, 1998; Who's Who in the World, 15th Edition. Memberships: Life Member: Indian Dairy Association; Indian Society of Animal Production and Management; Agricultural Research Services Scientists Forum; Member: New York Academy of Sciences; Indian Society of Life Sciences; Indian Society of Animal Genetics & Breeding; Karnal Cultural Forum. Address: 28 Officers Colony, Behind DC's Residence, Karnal 132001, India.

**GANE Patrick Arthur Charles,** b. 28 December 1953, Saltash, Cornwall, England. Scientist. m. Sarah, 1 son. Education: BSc, Imperial College London, 1976; ARCS, Associate of the Royal College of Science, 1976; PhD, University of Plymouth, 1979. Appointments: Research Fellow, University of Exeter, 1979-81; Research Group Leader, English China Clays International, 1981-94; Director, Segan Ltd, 1994-; Research Director, Omya Pluss Staufer AG, 1995-. Publications: Over 50 publications and patents. Memberships: Technical Association of the Pulp and Paper Industries; Guild of Cornish Composers. Address: Omya, Pluss-Staufer AG, Baslerstrasse, CH-4665 Oftringen, Switzerland.

**GANESH Gani Kannusamy,** b. 12 March 1941, Srirangam, TN, India. Industrialist. m. Jane Janaki, 24 August 1961, 3 sons, 2 daughters. Education: B Comm, 1960; M Comm, 1961; DSc, 1963. Appointments: Proprietor, Ganesh Silk Factory and Kannusamy & Co; Sales Manager, Vickers Plc London, 1965-75; Director, Paperodex Shreepack Ganeshwari Group, Bangalore and Krishnagiri, India, 1975-85; Chairman and ChiefExecutive Officer, Ganeshwar Inficons, Bangalore India and Washington DC, USA, 1985-. Publication: Packaging Management, 1987; Quality Control and Waste Management; Crew Education and Training. Honours: Rotary Youth Leadership Award, Rotary Intl. Foundation Counsellor, 1953; Junior Chamber International Senatorship, 1965; Paul Harris Fellow, USA, 1983; Baden-Powell Fellow, World Scouts Foundation, Geneva, 1986; Fellow, Institute of Management; Fellow, Institute of Packaging Professionals. Memberships: Indo-American Chamber of Commerce, Chairman 1992; US-India Business Council, Washington DC, USA, Director 1994; All India Management Association; Bangalore Management Association; American Management Association; Institute of Quality Assurance UK; Institute of Directors London UK; Freemasons Society; Public Relations Society; World Wide Fund for Nature. Address: PO Box 12 Ganeshcenter, Multiplex Kailashagiri, Krishnagiri 635001, India.

**GANGOPADHYAY Mohini Mohan,** b. 1 January 1939 Sialdanga, Manihara, West Bengal, India. Teacher. m. Git; Gangopadhyay, 3 sons, 1 daughter. Education: SF Wes Bengal Board of Secondary Education, Calcutta, 1960; Kaby; Pran, 1974; Kalbya Bhaskar, 1975; Sahitya Sudhakar, 1978 Eai Samayer Charan Kabi, 1985. Appointments: Head Teache: 1960; Reporter and Regular Writer, various journals, 1955- Editor Ketaki, bi monthly magazine, 1967-. Publications: Aba: Prthibi, 1984; Buker Gopane Astraouli, 1985; Kanch Ghar; Agun, 1989; Sei Masus, 1990; Rakter Ujan Thele, 1993; Ma Bhater Larai, 1993; Shasyer Malat, 1993; Bispathar, 1994 Pratibadi Samayer Mukh; Chande Ek Katha Jami, 1997 Honours: Nazrul Award, 1980; Jasimuddin Award, 1981 Jibanananda Award Siliguri, 1990; Kanpur Kheya Kanpur 1991; Padma Ganga Award Calcutta, 1992; Silver Medal, 1992 Silver Medal, Nikhil Bharat Banga Sahity Sammelan, 1997 Bronch Medel, 1996; Asimananda Akademic Award, 1996 Mallik Akademi Award, 1996; Anil Chattopadhayay Award 1997; India International Friend Society Award Delhi, 1997 Mallabhum Sahitya Award, Calcutta, 1998. Memberships Demorcalic Writers and Artist Association, West Bengal; Al Bengal Primary Teachers Association West Bengal; Folklore Cultural Research Centre Purulia District; Journalis' Association Purulia; Little Magazine Editor Associatior Calcutta. Address: Sialdanga, PO Manihara 723168, Purulia West Bengal.

**GANGULY Sambhu Nath,** b. 23 December 1947, Calcutta West Bengal, India. Writer; Critic. Education: MA, English 1971; MA, Bengali, 1975; MA, History, 1979; MPhil, 1982; PhD 1988; DLitt, 1996; FGSI, 1997. Career: Eminent Writer anc Literary Critic; Authority on Mediaeval Bengali Literature Publications: 18 books; About 100 research articles Membership: Secretary, Bangya Sanskriti Charcha Kendra association of eminent professors. Address: 22 Krishna Das Paul Lane, Calcutta 700 006, West Bengal, India.

**GANIEV Fuat Ashrafovich,** b. 1 August 1930 Bashkortostan. Philologist. m. Yunaleeva Rumia Aynutdinovna, 2 sons. Education: Graduate, Kazan State University, 1954 Candidate of Philology, 1964; Doctor of Philology, 1978 Professor, 1985. Appointments: School Teacher, 1954-55 Director, 1955-56; Head, Editorial Office, 1957-59; Researcher 1962-88; Department Head, 1988-. Publications: 200 and 1C capital dictionaries. Honours: Honoured Scholar of Tatarstan 1989; Tatarstan State Prize Laureate, 1994; Honoured Scholar of the Russian Federation, 1996. Memberships: Corresponding Member, Academy of Sciences, Tatarstan, 1992; Society of Orientalists. Address: Zelenaya str 11, Flat 55, 420043 Qazan Tatarstan, Russia.

**GANTZAROU Alexandra,** b. 26 April 1972, Vienna, Austria Doctor. Education: Foreign Language Certificates, 1992, 1995; Degree of Medicine, Athens University, 1996. Appointments: House Officer, Health Centre of Alexandria, 1996-98; Participant in Research Project, Hypertension Centre, 1998; Resident in Internal Medicine, Agios Pavlos Hospital, 1998-. Honours: Scholarships of the State Institution, 1990-96; Rank 1 at Graduation amoung 174 graduates, 1996; Success Rank 1, National University, 1990. Memberships: British GMC. Address: 42 V Tzella Str, GR 43100 Karditsa, Greece.

**GAO Jie,** b. 16 November 1961, Beijing, China. Physicist. m. Zhang Yaling, 1 daughter. Education: Bachelor Degree, 1983, Master Degree, 1986, Tsinghua University, Beijing, China; PhD study, IHEP Academia Sinica, 1986-89; Doctor Degree, 1992, University of Paris; Habilitation, 1996, University of Paris - Sud XI. Appointments: Foreign Physicist, LAL of CNRS, 1990-92, Ingenieur de Recherche, CNRS (functionary of France), 1993-

Publications: 12 articles in Nucl Instr and Methods (NIMA), 1990-98; 4 Articles in other scientific journals. Membership: Overseas Chinese Physics Association. Address: Lab de L'accelerateur Lineaire, IN2P3/CNRS, 91405 Orsay, Cedex, France.

**GAO Qingdi,** b. 22 May 1942, Shandong, China. Physicist. m. Feng Ding, 2 daughters. Education: Graduate, Tsinghua University, 1966. Appointments: Professor, Director, Tokamak Physics Division, Southwestern Institute of Physics, 1990-. Honours: Special Government Subsidy for Outstanding Contribution to Developing Science and Technology in China, issued by the State Council, 1993. Memberships: Chinese Physics Society; Chinese Nuclear Society. Address: P O Box 432, Chengdu, Sichuan 610041, China.

**GAPONOV Sergei,** b. 3 December 1964, Voronezh, Russia. Biologist. Education: Diploma, honours, Department of Biology and Soil Sciences, Voronezh State University, 1986, Postgraduate, 1990; Decree of Merit, Medicine and Parasitology, Cambridge, 1996. Appointments: Lecturer, Zoological Division, Department of Biology, 1985-95, Doctor of Biology, 1990, Associate Professor, 1995-, Voronezh Sate University. Publications: 60 scientific and methodological articles in professional journals. Honours: Talented Researcher Award, Russian Academy of Sciences, 1994-96; Lauriate, Russian Academy of Natural Sciences, 1995; Lauriate, European Academy of Sciences, 1996. Memberships: New York Academy of Sciences; All-Russian Entomological Society; Russian Parasitological Society. Address: Revolution Avenue, House 26/28, Apt 98, 394000 Voronezh, Russia.

**GAPOSCHKIN Peter John Arthur,** b. 5 April 1940, Boston, Massachusetts. Computer Programmer. Education: BSc, 1961, MIT; MA, 1965, PhD Physics, 1971, University of California at Berkeley. Appointments: Senior Analyst, Informatics, Palo Alto, California, 1979-80; Programmer Analyst, S F Municipal Railway, 1983-. Honours: Upper Dean's List, MIT, 1961; Able Toastmaster Silver Award, 1987; Advanced Toastmaster Gold Award, 1998. Memberships: American Astronomical Society; American Mathematical Society; Toastmasters International. Address: 1823 1/2, Delaware St, Berkeley, CA 94703-1328, USA.

**GARATTINI Silvio,** b. 12 November 1928, Bergamo, Italy. Director. m. Anny Fagnoni, 3 sons, 2 daughters. Appointments: Director, Mario Negri Institute for Pharmacological Research, Milan, Italy. Publications: Author or co-Author Over 120 papers in professional journals. Honours: Marzotto Prize for Medicine for Study of Antitubercular Drugs, 1954; The City of Bergamo Prize, 1955; Prize from Vittorio Emanuele Foundation sponsored by Lombardy Institute of Sciences & Letters, 1956; Pope John XXIII Prize for Cancer Chemotherapy, 1970; Honorary Citizen of Texas, USA, 1974; Cavaliere Legion d'Onore Francese, 1984; Le Porte di Milano Pitagora Prize, Catanzaro, Italy, 1988; Premio Rhone Poulenc Pharma per la Chemioterapia Antitumorale, 1989; Premio Internazionale Castello di Pietrarossa, Italy, 1990; Several honorary doctorates. Memberships: European Society for the Study of Drug Toxicity; International Brain Research Organisation; International Society for Research on Aggression; Italian Society of: Biological Psychiatry; Cancerology; Chemotherapy; Pharmacology; Teratology; National Academy of Medicine; New York Academy of Sciences; Polish Pharmacological Society; Royal College of Biological Psychiatry; Society of Biological Psychiatry; International Society Study of Xenobiotics; Member of the Committee for Proprietary Medicinal Products (CPMP) of the European Agency for Evaluation of Medicinal Products (EMEA); Honorary Fellowship

of the Faculty of Pharmaceutical Medicine of the Royal Colleges of Physicians, London; Commentatore della Repubblica Italiana; and others. Address: Istituto di Ricerche Farmacologiche, Mario Negri, Via Eritrea 62, 20157 Milano, Italy.

**GARBAR Isaac Joseph,** b. 20 January 1939, Minsk, USSR. Researcher; Educator. m. Larisa Rakhlin, 1 daughter. Education: MSc, Physics, Minsk University; PhD, Engineering, Institute of Aircraft, Kiev, 1978; DSc. Engineering, Institute of Railway Transport, Moscow, 1988. Appointments: Researcher, Senior Engineer, Senior Researcher, Leading Researcher, Head of Research Group, Research Institute, Minsk, 1966-91; Senior Researcher, Invited Lecturer, Ben-Gurion University, Beer-Sheva, Israel, 1991-; Visiting Professor, Tohoky University, Japan, 1996. Publications: Articles to professional journals and conference proceedings. Memberships: International Coordination Committee, Tribology Division, American Society of Mechanical Engineering; Fellow, Israel Tribology Society. Address: Bialic 31/6, Beer-Sheva, 84340 Israel.

**GARBER Helen Kolikow,** b. 9 August 1954, Brooklyn, New York, USA. Photographer. m. Dr Stuart Garber. Education: BS, 1976, SUNY at New Paltz; Computer Graphics Programme, UCLA, 1988-92; Otis Parsons Photography Programme, 1992-94. Appointments: Owner, Helen K Garber Photography Studio, Venice, California, 1992-, clients include: Hilton Hotels, Doubleday Books, Random House, Penguin USA, Minolta, AGFA, The Getty Centre; One Woman Show: Paul Kopeikin Gallery, Los Angeles, 1998. Publications: Book, Parents at Last, 1998; Photographs in various newspapers & magazines. Honours: Photo of the Year, Publicity Club of LA, 1997, Appointed to Santa Monica Arts Commission, 1998. Memberships: Advertising Photographers of America; American Society of Picture Professionals; California Lawyers for Arts. Address: 324 Sunset Avenue Studio D, Venice, CA 90291, USA.

**GARCIA DE LEON PENICHE Rosa Raquel,** b. 8 January 1965, Mexico DF. Systems Engineer. m. Roberto, 2 sons. Education: College School UPIICSA, 1986; Marketing Masters, Technológico de Monterrey, 1995. Appointments: Benchmark Coordinator, IBM PoughKeepsie, New York, 1989-90; Honours: Marketing Excellence Award, IBM, Mexico, 1989; Marketing Excellence Award, IBM, Mexico, 1990. Memberships: ACM; Puanetary Society. Address: Paseo de los Jardines 298, Col Paseos Taxquena, 04250 Mexico City, Mexico.

**GARESTSKY Radim,** b. 7 December 1928, Minsk, Belarus. Geologist. m. Galina, 1 daughter. Education: BSc, Geology, Moscow Oil Institute, 1952; DPh, Geology, Geological Institute, Moscow, 1961; DSc, Geotectonics, Geological Institute, USSR, 1969. Appointments: Researcher, Geology Institute, USSR, 1952-71; Head, Department of Geotectonics, 1977-; Director, Institute of Geochemistry and Geophysics, Belarus, 1977-93; Professor, Belarus University, 1981-; Vice-President, Belarus Academy of Sciences, 1992-97. Publications: 17 scientific monographs; 500 articles. Memberships: Chief, Belarus Committee, Intern Geological Correlation Programme, 1989-; President, Belarus Geological Society, 1993-; President, Union of All-World Belarussians, 1993-; Belarus Academy of Science, 1972-; Russian Academy of Science, 1994-; American Geophysical Union, 1993-. Address: 15/49 Kulman Street, Minsk 220100, Belarus.

**GARFUNKEL Adi,** b. 15 August 1939, Romania. Dental Educator. m. Maya, 1 son, 1 daughter. Education: DMD, School of Dental Medicine, Jerusalem, 1963; Anaesthesiologist, 1969;

Oral Medicine Specialist, University of Pennsylvania, USA, Fellow, Immunology, 1972. Appointments: Chairman, Department of Oral Medicine, Hadassa, Jerusalem, 1975; Dean, Faculty of Dental Medicine, Jerusalem, Israel, 1986; Director, Middle East center of Dental Education, 1997; Professor of Oral Medicine, Hebrew University of Jerusalem; Medical College of University of Pennsylvania. Publications: Over 100 papers in medical textbooks. Honours: Honorary Member, ADA; Doctor honoris causa, Carol Davila University; Honorary Member, Burma Dental Association. Memberships: Alpha Omega; Israeli Dental Association; American Dental Association; Member of various editorial boards. Address: Department of Oral Medicine, Hadassah Medical Center, PO Box 12000, Jerusalem 91120, Israel.

**GARLEA Valentina,** b. 28 April 1949, Dobrovat, county Iasi, Romania. Living tomograph. m. Petru Garlea, 2 foster daughters. Education: Life. Appointments: Permanent MEDISAN Collaborator; Diachronic and Synchronic investigations into the human body; Psychometric Clairvoyant. Publications: The Phenomenon called Valentina (talks with Valentina recorded with a commentary by Florin Gheorghita), 1997; numerous interviews with, as well as articles about, her in various national newspapers, magazines and journals. Memberships: Founding member and permanent counsellor of ANATECOR, Romanian Association for Complementary Therapies. Address: Str Ciric 38A bl. V, Sc D et 11 ap 4, 6600 Iasi, Romania.

**GARMIRE Gordon Paul,** b. 10 March 1937, Portland, OR, USA. Astrophysicist. m. Audrey B Garmire, 3 sons, 3 daughters. Education: AB, Harvard, 1959; PhD, MIT, 1962. Appointments: Assistant-Associate Professor Physics, MIT, 1964-67; Associate Professor Physics, Caltech, 1967-72; Professor, 1972-81, Evan Pugh Professor, 1985-, Pennsylvania State University. Honours: Guggenheim Fellow, 1974; Senior Fulbright Fellow, 1973-74; Evan Pugh Professor, 1985-; NASA Exceptional Scientific Achievement Award, 1978. Membership: AAS Chair High Energy Astrophysics Division, 1985, 1998-2000. Address: Pennsylvania State University, 525 Davey Laboratory, University Park, PA 16802, USA.

**GARNER Bruce Le Grange,** b. 27 May 1962, Hastings, New Zealand. Genealogist. m. Vicki. Appointments: Principal Genealogist, New Zealand Family History Services, 1991-. Honours: New Zealand Video Industry Awards 1988, Runner Up, Best Retailer of the Year. Memberships: Australian Association of Genealogists and Record Agents; Association of Professional Genealogists. Address: P O Box 181, Seaford, VIC 3198, Australia.

**GARRETT Linda Oaks,** b. 9 April 1957, Oklahoma City, Oklahoma, USA. Teacher; Writer. m. John Charles Garrett. Education: BM, Oklahoma Baptist University, 1981; MDiv, 1986, PhD, 1993, Southwestern Baptist Theological Seminary. Appointments: Teaching Fellow, Southwestern Baptist Theological Seminary, 1987-88; Teaching Fellow, University of North Texas, 1993-94; Assistant Professor Theology, Judson College, 1995-96. Publications: Articles in Biblical Illustrator, 1993, 1995. Honour: W T Connor Award, Southwestern Baptist Theological Seminary, 1987. Memberships: AAR; SBL. Address: 3925 Cannock Drive, Birmingham, AL 35242, USA.

**GARRIGLE William Aloysius,** b. 6 August 1941, Camden, New Jersey, USA. Trial Lawyer. m. Rosalind Chadwick-Garrigle, 3 daughters. Education: BS, LaSalle University, 1963; LLB, Boston College Law School, 1966. Appointments: Trial Lawyer, 1966-. Honours: Admitted to the Bar of New Jersey, 1966, US District Court of New Jersey,

1966, US Court of Appeals of the 3rd Circuit, 1973, US Supreme Court, 1973; Certified Civil Trial Attorney, New Jersey Supreme Court, 1982-; Certified in Civil Trial Advocacy, National Board of Trial Advocates, 1989-; Diplomate, American Board of Trial Advocates, 1992-; American Board of Professional Liability Attorneys, 1994-. Memberships: American Bar Association; New Jersey State Bar Association; Burlington County Bar Asociation; Camden County Bar Association; International Association of Defense Counsel; Federation of Insurance and Corporate Counsel; Tavistock Country Club; Master, Camden Inn of Court. Address: 223 East Main Street, Moorestown, NJ 08057-2905, USA.

**GARTMAN Max Dillon,** b. 3 May 1938, Mobile, Alabama, USA. Professor. 2 sons, 1 daughter. Education: BA, 1960; MA, French; PhD, Romance Languages, 1974; Certificates, Universite de Nice. Appointments: Professor, French & Spanish, Samford University, 1965-82; Head of Department, 1976-82; Professor, Chair, Foreign Languages, University of North Alabama, 1982-; Director, Center for Critical Languages, 1995-. Publications: Several articles in professional journals. Honours: Outstanding Faculty Award, 1992-93. Memberships: Chair, Alabama Association of Foreign Language Teachers; Chair, Southern Conference on Language Teaching, 1976; President, Alabama Consortium for the Advancement of Foreign Language Education; President, Alabama Association of Teachers of French, 1994-96; Board, Alabama Humanities Foundation. Address: 122 Lambeth Street, Florence, AL 35633, USA.

**GASPARSKI Wojciech Wladyslaw,** b. 10 October 1936, Warsaw, Poland. Professor. m. Renata S Gasparska, 2 sons. Education: MSc Engineering, 1959, Silesian University of Technology, Gliwice; PhD, 1969, Polish Academy Sciences, Warsaw; DrS (Habilitation), 1978, Warsaw Technical University, Faculty of Architecture, Poland; Professor of Humanities, 1985, Poland. Appointments: Research Fellow, Institute of Praxiology, 1967-71, Chairman of Design Methodology Unit, 1969-86, Associate Professor, 1971-89, Vice Director, 1971-73, Director, 1973-75, Vice Chairman Department Praxiology and Science of Science at Institute of Philosophy and Sociology, 1976-86, Chairman, 1986-91, Professor, 1993-, Logic of Language and Action Department, Institute Philosophy and Sociology, Vice Chairman, 1987-96, Chairman, 1996-, Academic Board, Institute Philosophy and Sociology, Member Council Research Institutes, 1990-96, Chairman of Science Studies Committee, 1993-, all at Polish Academy of Sciences; Chief Consultant, 1998-, Principal, 1995-98, Collegium Invisible, Warsaw. Publications: Author, co-Author, Editor and co-Editor 21 books in English, Polish and Russian; Author and co-Author over 260 papers; Editor-in-Chief or member of Editorial board 9 journals. Honours: Fulbright Fellowship, USA, 1981; Knight Cross of Polonia Restituta in 25th Anniversary of Polish Society of Cybernetics, 1986; Honorary member, Austrian Society for Cybernetics; Honorary member, UK Systems Society; Honorary President, The Learned Society of Praxiology, 1994; Medal of the National Education Commission, Poland, 1998; Several grants and fellowships. Address: Tolwinskiego St 10 15, Warsaw, Poland.

**GATES Carolyn Helm,** b. 23 July 1935, Kempen County, Mississippi, USA. Stockbroker. m. James Pickens Gates, 2 sons, 1 daughter. Education: BA cum laude, Psychology, University of Memphis, 1976; Postgraduate studies, Shelby State University, 1979, Fogelman College of Business, University of Memphis, 1979-83, State Technology University. Appointments: General Contractor, C H Gates Construction, Memphis, Tennessee, 1975-76; Commissioner, 1977-94, Chair, 1989, Shelby County Commission, Memphis; Board Member,

Gates Mortgage and Equity Corporation, Memphis, 1979-84; Vice-President, Manager, Board, The Gates Companies, Memphis, 1984-96; Registered Representative and Agent, New York Life and Annuity Company, Memphis, 1996-97; Registered Investment Specialist, Union Planters Bank and Financial Services, Memphis, 1997-. Honours: Appointed to Defense Advisory Committee on Women in the Services, 1986-89; Outstanding Women of Memphis Award; Outstanding Service Award, Memphis City Schools; Outstanding Memphis State Graduate. Memberships: Memphis State University National Alumni Association, 1983-92, President, 1990-92; National Association of Counties, Steering Committee for Health and Education; Tennessee County Services Association; Tennessee County Commissioners Association; University of Tennessee Round Table; English Speaking Union; Honorary Lifetime Member, Shelby County Parent-Teacher Association; Task Force on Education; American Heart Association; Others. Address: 7430 Mimosa Road, Germantown, TN 38138, USA.

**GATEV Velichko,** b. 10 July 1929, Nicopol, Bulgaria. Doctor. m. Borjana Stefanova, 2 daughters. Education: MD, Sofia, 1953; PhD, 1964; DMSc, Moscow, 1972; Professor, Sofia, 1974. Appointments: Junior Research Associate, Research Institute of Pediatrics, Sofia, 1960-68; Senior Research Associate, 1968-74; Head of Laboratory of Physiology, 1968-92; Professor, 1974-92; Professor, National Centre of Hygiene, Sofia, 1992-; Science Secretary Medical Board, Conc of Ministers, 1992-. Publications: In Development Medicine and Child Neurology; Motor Control; Morphophysiology Child Character. Memberships: International Society of Development Neurosciences; International Brain Research Organisation; EEG and Clinic Neurophysiology; Society of Child Development and Care. Address: National Centre for Hygiene, Dim Nestorov Str 15, 1431 Sofia, Bulgaria.

**GATZA Louise,** b. 17 February 1939, St Charles, VA, USA. Cosmetologist, Medical Transcriptionist, Author. 2 daughters. Education: Associate Degree, Triton College, River Grove, Illinois, 1993; Certificate with Honours, Medical Transcription, College of Du Page, Glen Ellyn, Illinois, 1993. Appointments: Owner, Manager, Fashionette Beauty Salon, Chicago, Illinois, USA, Retired; Author, Medical Reference Text, 1995; Publications: Yes STD's Cause Cancer. Memberships: Past Illinois Registered Cosmetologist; Indiana Registered Cosmetologist; Past Member National Association of Medical Trans; IFCA Bible Church. Address: Noblesville, IN 46060-9027, USA.

**GAUR Yagya Dutta,** b. 1 January 1941, Jodhpur, India. Researcher and Teacher. m. Kusum Gaur, 1 son, 1 daughter. Education: BSc, 1960; MSc, 1962; PhD, Microbiology, 1976. Appointments: National Fellow, Microbiology; Project Coordinator, Biological Nitrogen Fixation, cum Principal Scientist, All India Coordinated Project, Indian Agricultural Research Institution, New Delhi, India. Publications: 100 publications. Honour: Best Teacher Award, Indian Agricultural Research Institute, New Delhi, 1996. Memberships: Life Member, Society of Plant Biochemistry and Biotechnology; Association of Microbiologists of India. Address: Department of Microbiology, IARI, New Delhi 110012, India.

**GAUS David Sheerin,** b. 4 August 1943, Indianapolis, IN, USA. Publisher. Education: BA, Zoology, University of Chicago, 1964; MA, Biology, Northwestern University, 1965. Appointments: Peace Corps Teacher, Nigeria, 1966-67; assorted jobs and projects, 1968-80; Publisher, Sci-Notes Newsletter, 1981-. Publications: Sci-Notes, largely self written, on virology, heterotoxicity. Memberships: Delta Upsilon;

Returned Peace Corps Volunteers. Address: 566 1/2 N Keystone Ave, Indianapolis, IN 46201-2040, USA.

**GAUSS Karl Frederik,** b. 19 July 1956, Elmira, NY, USA. Internist. m. Paula Ann Tuite, 2 sons, 1 daughter. Education: BS Biology, 1981, SUNY College of Arts and Sciences, Geneseo; MD, 1985, Residency in Internal Medicine, 1985-88, SUNY Upstate Medical Centre, Syracuse. Appointments: Assistant Clinical Instructor, Department of Internal Medicine, 1988-95, Clinical Assistant Professor, Department of Medicine, SUNY HSC at Syracuse, 1995-; President, Cortland County Medical Society, 1992-; Chairman, Department of Internal Medicine, Cortland Memorial Hospital, 1989-93, Executive Committee of Medical Staff, 1989-93, 1995-97, Director, Pacemaker Clinic, 1989-; President, CEO PHI Aeomedical Consultants, Inc, 1989-95; Aviation Medical Examiner, Cortland County, 1988-; Attending Physician, Member Medical Staff, Cortland Memorial Hospital, 1988-; Director and Staff Physician, Moravia Health Centre, 1992-93; Consulting Physician, Tully Hill Drug and Alcohol Rehabilitation Centre, 1990-92; Board Directors, Flying Physicians Association, 1994; Medical Director, Cortland Residential Facility, 1997-. Publications: 8 presentations and radio shows for public education; 12 slide shows and lectures. Memberships: American Geriatric Society; American College of Physicians; American Society Internal Medicine; NY State Society of Internal Medicine; NY State Medical Society, Cortland County Delegate; Cortland County Medical Society; Flying Physicians Association; Aerospace Medical Association; Robert Wood Johnson Foundation Counsellor, Substance Abuse; Aircraft Owners and Pilots Association. Address: 166 Madison Street, Cortland, NY 13045, USA.

**GAUTAM Prem Lal,** b. 12 December 1947, Kandayana, India. Director of Research. m. Kamla Gautam, 1 son, 2 daughters. Education: BSc, Agriculture, Punjab University, 1968; MSc, Genetics, 1970, PhD, Genetics, 1974, Indian Agricultural Research Plant Breeding Institute, New Delhi. Appointments: Assistant Professor, 1974-79, Associate Professor, 1979-85, Associate Director, 1979-81, Joint Director, 1985-91, Associate Dean, 1987-91, Plant University of Agriculture and Technology, Pantnagar; Dean, College of Forestry, 1991-97, Director of Research, University of Horticulture and Forestry, Nauni Solan, India. Publications: 146. Honours: Punjab University Medal, 1968; Lal Bahadur Shastri Gold Medal, 1968; ICAR Merit Scholarship, Junior Research Fellowship, Senior Research Fellowship; CIDA/NSERC Canadian Research Associateship Award, 1983, 1984; Gran Vikas Sansthan Honour, 1989. Memberships: Indian Society of Genetics and Plant Breeding; Indian Society of Crop Improvement; Indian Society of Plant Genetic Resources; Indian Society of Tree Scientists; Asian Network on Forestry Education; IUFRO Working Party on Medicinal Plants. Address: National Bureau of Plant Genetic Resources, Pusa Campus, New Delhi 110012, India.

**GAVIN Mary Jane,** b. 1 September 1941, Prairie Du Chien, Wisconsin, USA. Staff Nurse. m. Alfred William Gavin, 1 son, 1 daughter. Education: Pre-Nursing, magna cum laude in Chemistry, 1961, North Central College, Naperville, Illinois; BS RN, 1964, University of Wisconsin, Madison; Postgraduate Deep Muscle Therapy Training, 1980, Primer Method of Canada. Appointments: Staff Nurse, Eye, Ear, Nose, Throat Surgery, UW Hospitals, Madison, 1964-69; VA Home Response, 1969-. Honours: Gave up scholarship to UW at Madison 1959, so could attend Christian College at North Central College; Journalism Award, 1959. Memberships: President, Monona Grove American Legion Auxiliary Unit 429, 1990-; Task Force for the Handicapped; Wrote the materials that made Federal Law USC 351 null and void in 1990, rewritten as USC 1151; Eastside Evangelical (Wisconsin Synod) Lutheran Church, Madison. Address: 702 Fairmont Avenue, Madison, WI 53714-1424, USA.

**GAVISH Motti,** b. 5 December 1954, Bucharest, Romania. Electronic Systems Engineer. m. Vira, 1 son. Education: BSEE, Technion, Israel, 1978; MSEE, Tel Aviv University, 1984; PhD, Tel Aviv University, 1995. Appointments: Electronic Engineer, Israel Defense Forces, 1978-81; Development Engineer, Tadiran Ltd, Communication Division, 1981-82; Signal Processing Engineer, Elta Ltd, Radar Division, 1982-86; Lecturer, Center for Technological Education, Holon, 1985-86; Expert Engineer, Tadiran Ltd, Systems Division, 1986-90; Senior Scientist, Elta Ltd, Communications Systems Division, 1990-98; Chief Engineer, 1998-. Publications: Contributor to Numerous Articles to Professional Journals. Memberships: Institute of Electrical and Electronics Engineers (IEEE), Senior Member. Address: 1/13 Ben Yosef St, 69125 Tel-Aviv, Israel.

**GAVRILA Lucian,** b. 10 January 1941, Romania. Biologist. m. Gavrila Cecilia, 2 daughters. Education: Diploma, Biologist, Bucharest University, 1965; Research Fellow, Harvard University, USA, 1975. Appointment: Professor of Genetics, Bucharest University, 1965-. Publications: Several scientific original papers, 20 books. Honours: Romanian Academy of Sciences Prizes, 1975, 1977. Memberships: International Genetics Federation, 1988; European Genetics Federation, 1993. Address: Faculty of Biology, Allea Portocalelor 1-3, Bucharest, Romania.

**GAYLES-FELTON Anne R,** b. 4 June 1923, Marshallville, Georgia, USA. Educator. m. Ambrose M Felton, dec. Education: BS, Fort Valley State College; MA, 1949, Prof Diploma, 1955, Columbia University; Doctor of Education, 1961, Indiana University. Appointments: Professor of Education, Florida A&M University. Publications: 2 books; 3 monographs; 60 articles; 4 studies. Honour: Teacher of the Year, Florida A&M University. Memberships: 5 Honor Societies; Delta Sigma Theta; Association of Teacher Educators. Address: 609 Howard Avenue, Tallahassee, FL 32310, USA.

**GAYOOM Abdul Maumoon (H E),** b. 29 December 1937, Male, Maldives. Politician. m. Nasreena Ibrahim, 2 sons, 2 daughters. Education: Al-Azhar University, Cairo. Appointments: Research Assistant, Islamic History, American University, Cairo, 1967-69; Lecturer, Islamic Studies, Philosophy, Abdullahi Bayero College of Ahmadu Bello University, Nigeria, 1969-71; Teacher, Aminiya School, 1971-72; Imam at Friday Prayers, 1972-73, 1973-74; Manager, Government Shipping Department, 1972-73; Writer, Translator, Presidents Office, 1972-73, 1974; Imam at Friday Prayers, 1973-74 Undersecretary, Telecommunications Department, 1974; Director, Telephone Department, 1974; Special Undersecretary, Office of the Prime Minister, 1974-75; Deputy Ambassador to Sri Lanka, 1975-76; Undersecretary, Department of External Affairs, 1976; Deputy Minister of Transport, 1976; Perm Representative to UN, 1976-77; Minister of Transport, 1977-78; President, Republic of Maldives, Commander-in-Chief, Armed Forces, 1978-; Governor, Maldives Monetary Authority, 1981-; Minister of Defence and National Security, 1982-; Minister of Finance, 1989-93; Minister of Finance and Treasury, 1993-; Member, Constituent Council of Rabitat Al-Alam Al-Islami. Honours include: Hon D Letters, Aligarh Muslim University of India, 1983; Hon PhD in Political Science, Marquis Giuseppe Scicluna International University Foundation, USA, 1988; Global 500 Honour Roll (UN Environment Programme), 1988; Hon D Letters, Jamia Millia Islamia of India, 1990; Man of the Sea Award, Lega Navale

Italiana, 1990; Hon D Letters, Pondicherry University of India, 1994, Knight Grand Cross of St Michael and St George, 1997; World Health Organisation Health-for-All Gold Medal, 1998. Address: The Presidents Office, Boduthakurufaanu Magu, Male 20-05, Republic of the Maldives.

**GAZSO Lajos Gaspar,** b. 21 March 1946, Budapest. Biologist. m. Anna Gyarmati, 1 daughter. Education: MSc, 1971, PhD, 1974, Eotvos Lorand University, Faculty of Natural Sciences, Budapest; Postdoctoral Fellow, University of Manchester. Appointments: Scientific Director, National Research Institute for Radiobiology and Radiohygiene, Budapest. Publications: 2 books; 98 scientific publications. Memberships: International Union of Radioecology; European Society of Radiation Biology; and others. Address: National Research Institute for Radiobiology and Radiohygiene, Anna u 5, H 1221 Budapest, Hungary.

**GE Qin-Sheng,** b. 24 February 1917, Shanghai, China. Professor Reproductive Endocrinology and Infertility. m. Tseng Hsien Chiu, 1 son. Education: Graduate, BS, Shanghai Medical University, 1942; House Staff, Chung Ho Hospital, Beijing, 1943-48. Appointments: Assistant, Instructor, Assistant Professor, Dept Obstetrics and Gynaecology, PUMC Hospital, 1948-53; Professor, Division of Reproductive Endocrinology, Department of Obstetrics and Gynaecology, PUMC Hospital, 1979-. Publications: Published around 80 papers and chapters in 4 books. Honours: 2nd Prize, Ministry Public Health, 1986; First Prize, Ministry Public Health, 1996; 3rd National Scientific Prize, 1997. Memberships: International Menopause Society; North America Menopause Society; International Federation of Pediatric and Adolescent Gynecology; Executive Committee, International Society of Gyneclogic Endocrinology; Editor in Chief, Journal of Reproductive Medicine; Chairman WHO Collaborating Centre for Research in Human Reproduction. Address: No 26 Beijige Third Lane, Dongdan, Beijing 100005, China.

**GEBAUER Kurt,** b. 18 August 1941. Sculptor. m. Libuse Lukasova, 3 sons. Education: Sculpture, Academy of Fine Arts, Prague, 1969. Appointments: Professor, Academy of Arts, Design and Architecture, Prague; Studio of Sculpture. Publictions: Several articles in professional journals. Address: Delostrelekca 3, 160 00 Prague 6, Czech Republic.

**GEHLAWAT Jagdish Kumar,** b. 11 September 1937, Nizampur Majra, - Dist Sonepat, Haryana State. Educator. m. Vimal Gehlawat, 1 son, 2 daughters. Education: B Chem Eng, 1962, MSc Tech, 1965, PhD Tech, 1969, Bombay. Appointments: Works Manager, Laxmi Starch Ltd, 1969-71; R&D Manager, Gharda Chemicals Ltd, 1971-73; Technical Director, Universal Starch-Chem Allied Ltd, 1973-75; Assistant Professor, 1975-77, Professor, 1977-98, Indian Institute of Technology, Kanpur; Chairman, Gehlawat Agro Pvt Ltd, 1998-. Publications: Over 100 publications including 3 books. Honours: NOCIL Award 1983 by Indian Institute of Chemical Engineers for excellence in design and construction of a process plant; Chemical Engineering Award 1997 by Institution of Engineers India for excellence in innovative process development. Memberships: Expert Committee on Sugar Industry, Technology Information Forecasting and Assessment Council 1988-90; Advisory Board, National Sugar Institute, Kanpur, 1991-97; Fellow and Chartered Engineer, Institution of Engineers, India; Life member IICHE, IPPTA, STAI and IMS; Founder President, People Oriented Science and Technology Society. Address: 248 RK Vihar IP Extn, 110-092 New Delhi, India.

**GEIMAN Stephen R,** b. 8 October 1947, Waynesboro, USA. Educator. m. Lisa H Geiman, 2 sons, 1 daughter. Education: BSc, 1969. Career: Member, State Education State Tennis Sol Committee; High School Outstanding Track Coach; High School PE Teacher, 1969-98. Memberships: AAHPERD; ASCD; VAHPER; VHSCA. Address: Rr 2, Box 310, Waynesboro, VA 22980, USA.

**GELMAN Leonid Moiseevich,** b. 15 April 1949, Kiev, Ukraine. Scientist; Educator. Div, 1 daughter. Education: MS, Honours, National Technical University of the Ukraine, Kiev, 1972; PhD, 1987, Doctor of Sciences, 1993, Acoustical Institute, Russian Academy of Sciences. Appointments: Engineer, 1972-82; Junior Researcher, 1982-87; Professor, Department of Orientation and Navigation, 1984-, Professor, Department of Nondestructive Testing, 1984-, National Technical University of the Ukraine; Senior Researcher, 1987-93; Leading Researcher, 1993-94; Chief Researcher, 1994-95; Head, Laboratory of Vibroacoustic Diagnostics, 1995-98; Professor, Department of Mechanical Engineering, Zhitomar Institute of Engineering and Technology, 1998-. Publications: Over 120 scientific works; 17 patents. Honours: US International Science Foundation and Government of the Ukraine Award, 1995; Civilian Research and Development Foundation Award, USA, 1996; MacArthur Foundation Award, 1997; Acoustical Society of America Award, 1998; Lady Davis Trust Award, 1999. Memberships: Ukrainian Society of Nondestructive Testing; Acoustical Society of America; New York Academy of Sciences; Russian Acoustical Society; Acoustical Society of Japan; International Institute of Acoustics and Vibration; Narragansett Chapter, Acoustical Society of America; Chicago Chapter, Acoustical Society of America; London Institute of Electrical Engineering. Address: Vibroacoustic Diagnostics, International Technical University of the Ukraine, 103 Kiev 252103, Ukraine.

**GENIUSAS Algis Tomas,** b. 12 August 1932, Kaunas, Lithuania. University Professor. m. Isolde Gabriele Geniusiene, 1 son, 1 daughter. Education: Diploma with Honours, cum laude, 1961, Leningrad (St Petersburg) University; PhD, 1969, University of Latvia; Dr Habilis Diploma in Humanitarian Sciences, 1988, Moscow University. Appointments: Professor, Academy of Sciences of Lithuania, 1990-92; 1st Deputy Director General of Lithuanian Newsagency ELTA, 1992-93; Professor, Vilnius and Kaunas Universities, 1996-. Publications: Shakespeare Readings, Academy of Sciences of the USSR, Moscow, 1984-85, 1990; University publications, 1968-98. Memberships: United Nations Association of Lithuania, President 1993-; International Federation of Free Journalists, London, 1995-. Address: Kalvariju 172 81, 2042 Vilnius, Lithuania.

**GEOGHEGAN Michel Henry,** b. 11 January 1937, Bradford, Yorkshire. United Nations. m. Annemarie, 3 sons, 3 daughters. Education: Diploma, Chinese Studies, 1955-57; BSc, 1957-60; MA, 1972-73. Appointments: UK Foreign Service, London, 1960-62; Brussels, 1962-64; Manila, 1964-66. Memberships: Earth Society; Communications Coordination Committee. Address: 90 12 181st Street, Jamaica, NY 11423, USA.

**GEORGANTOPOULOS Georgios,** b. 10 March 1941, Derveni Corinthias. Professor. m. Despina Georgantopooulou, 1 son, 1 daughter. Education: BSc Mathematics, 1973; PhD Phisicomathematics, 1976. Appointments: Lecturer, University Patra, 1973-80; Professor, Hellenic Air Force Academy, 1980-. Publications: 50 publications in international journals; 14 academic books. Memberships: FDP AGARD/NATO; Hellenic Mathematical Society. Address: Air Force Academy, Dekeleia Attikis, Athens, Greece.

**GERALD William,** b. 15 December 1918, Irwin County, Georgia. Pastor Emeritus; Musician; Recording Artist. m. Myrtle Boyce, 4 sons. Education: Alumnus Howard University; Cortez Business College. Appointments: Founder of Five Churches; District Bishop, Maryland, USA; Radio Minister, WBGR; Consecrated to the Bishopric, 1988. Publications: Several books; Gospel Songs; Dramas; Hymns; Semi-classics; Poems. Honours: International Poetry Hall of Fame. Memberships: Bible Way Church World Wide; Lighthouse Apostolic Church; International Biographical Centre; american Federation of Televsion and Radio Artists. Address: 620 Severn Ave, Annapolis, MD 21403, USA.

**GERAMY Allahyar,** b. 20 July 1966, Kermanshah, Iran. m. Maryam Moghaddas Bayat, 1 daughter. Education: DDS, Tehran University of Medical Scis, 1984; MSc, Orthodontics, Tehran University of Medical Science, 1995. Appointment: Assistant Professor of Orthodontics, Shiraz Medical Science University, 1995-. Publications: Researches published in American and European journals of orthodontics. Address: Shiraz Medical Science University Dental School, Ghasrodasht Avenue, Shiraz Shiraz, Iran.

**GEREIGHTY Andrea Ann Saunders,** b. 20 July 1938, New Orleans, LA, USA. Writer; Poet. m. Dennis A Gereighty Jnr, deceased, 1 son, 2 daughters. Education: BA, LA State University in New Orleans, USA, 1974; English Certificate on Scholarship from English Speaking Union; MA, University of New Orleans, USA, 1978-. Appointments: Shell Oil Records Retrival, 1956-60; Owner, Founder, CEO, New Orleans Field Services, 1960-. Address: 257 Bonnabel Boulevard, Metairie, LA 70005 3738, USA.

**GERIMON Paul,** b. 14 October 1954, Dinant, Belgium. Singer. Education: Classic Humanities, Superior Diplomas, Violin and Voice, 1972; Opera Studio Brussels, 1975-78; Centre Musique Baroque, Paris, 1991-92. Appointments: Guest Soloist, Deep Bass, La Monnaie of Brussels, 1975-2000; Festival d'Aix, 1989-98; Berliner Philarmoniker, 1995; Barbican Centre, 1998; Brooklyn Academy, 1999; Théâtre des Champs Elysées, 1999. Publications: M Klobe; Du Mont; L'Orfeo; Euridice Orphee D'Or 1991 de L'Acadamie du Disque Lyrique. Memberships: Union des Artistes, Brussels. Address: 32 Rue Saxe-Cobourg, B-1210 Brussels, Belgium.

**GEROVA JANZOVA Maria,** b. 1 February 1926, Zilina. Physiologist. m. Jan Gero, 1 d. Education: MD, 1950; PhD, 1956; DSc, 1992. Appointments: Assistant Professor, Faculty of Medicine, Bratislava, 1951; Postgraduate Student, Institute of Cardiovascular Dis, Prague, 1952-56; Scientific Worker, Physiologist, Institute Norm Pathol Physiology, Bratislava, 1956-. Publications: Elasticity of Sinocarotoid Region; Chapter in The Coronary Artery; More than 400 articles in journals. Honours: Jessenius Silver Medal; J Golden Medal; Laufberger Medal. Memberships: CS Physiol Society, 1956; American Physiol Society, 1994; American Heart Association, 1996; International Union Physiol Sci, Council Member, 1986; Expert, Clinical Cardiology, Member, Editorial Board. Address: Belehradska 6, 83104 Bratislava, Slovakia.

**GHAFOOR Abdul,** b. 10 February 1928, Mansehra, Pakistan. m. Taheera Ghafoor, 1 son, 1 daughter, deceased. Education: BA, Honours, Urdu Language and Literature, 1955; PhD, Honours, Engineering, USA, 1995. Appointments: Lt Colonel and Acting Brigadier, Engineer Corps, Pakistan Army, 1952-77; Chief Engineer, Government of Punjab, Provincial Government of Pakistan, 1977-79; Director of Works and Chief Engineer, Private Limited Construction Company, 1979-81; General Manager and Chief Engineer, Saudi Development

Company, Jeddah, 1981-82; Chief Resident Engineer, private Consulting Engineers firm, Pakistan, 1982-85; Project Director, Riyadh, Saudi Arabia consultant engineers company, 1985-86; Chief Engineer, consulting engineers firm, Pakistan, 1987; Chief Engineer, construction company, Pakistan, 1988-90; Director of Works in Pakistan, private trading and finance company, 1990; Chairman, Chief Executive, Private Ltd Consulting Engineers, 1990-. Publications: Numerous articles in professional magazines and newspapers. Honours: Several medals and letters of appreciation. Memberships: American Society of Civil Engineers; Fellow, Institution of Engineers, Pakistan; Pakistan Engineering Council. Address: House no 36, Street 5, F-8/3, Islamabad, Pakistan.

**GHAHREMANI-GHAJAR Mohamed Ali,** b. 14 April 1945, Tehran, Iran. Central Bank Employee. m. Sohaila Mostafari-Kashani, 1 daughter. Education: BA, 1969, MA, 1971, University of Cincinnati, USA. Career: Employee, Central Bank of Iran, 1974-. Publications: Various articles in professional publications. Address: Bank Markazi Jl Iran, Ferdowsi, PO Box 11365-8551, Tehran, Iran.

**GHANASHEV Ivan Petrov,** b. 28 May 1960, Sofia, Bulgaria. Physicist. m. Vania Georgieva, 1 son, 1 daughter. Education: Sofia University, Bulgaria; Nagoya University, Japan; MSc, 1986, PhD, 1992, Microwave Permittivity Measurements. Appointment: University Professor, Department of Radio Physics and Electronics, Sofia University. Publications: Over 70 publications including: Method for computing wave attenuation coefficients of electromagnetic waves in anisotropic plasma columns, 1994; Dispersion of dipolar electromagnetic waves in a radially inhomogeneous axially magnetised plasma column, 1997; High-density flat plasma production based on surface waves, 1998. Honours: 1st Prize, International Physics Olympical, Moscow, 1979; 1st Prize, NCA Software Design Contest, Bulgarian Academy Sciences, 1982. Memberships: IEEE; American Vacuum Society; Japanese Society Applied Physics; American Institute of Physics. Address: Nagoya University, Department Electrical Engineering, Furo cho Chikusa Ku, Nagoya 464 01, Japan.

**GHARAATI Abdoul Ali,** b. 27 December 1942, Isfahan, Iran. Academic Member. m. Zahra, 2 sons, 1 daughter. Education: BA, Education and Philosophy; MA, Education; PhD, Education. Appointments: Teacher, Primary Schools; Teacher, High Schools; Instructor, Teachers Training Centre; Academic Member, Dean, Faculty of Education. Publications: Logic of Learning; 5 Papers on Education. Honours: Numerous Awards. Memberships: The Iranian Society of Education; The Society for Better World. Address: Isfaham University, Faculty of Education, Hezar Jerib St, Isfaham, Iran.

**GHARSE Sunil,** b. 12 April 1942, Belgaum, Maharashtra, India. Technical Director. m. Neeta, 1 son, 1 daughter. Education: B Engineering, 1963; Postgraduate in Industrial Engineering and Management, Bombay University, Gold Medallist; Postgraduate Alumnus of Indian Institute of Management, Ahmedabad; BE Hons; PG DIE, Bombay; FIE; FIETE; FIWWA; FI IIE; MIIWE. Appointments: Executive Director, Nathani Steel Ltd, Entel Ltd, SLM Ltd (Swiss Loco Manufacturers); Technical Director, Midtown Projects & Consultants. Honours: Several rewards and awards for Excellence in Performance in Siemens, Crompton Greaves and others. Memberships: Fellow: Institution of Engineers, India; Institute of Electrical and Electronic Engineers, USA; Institute of Electronic and Telecom Engineers; Institue of Industrial Engineers; Institute of Welding Engineers; Indian Water Works Association. Address: 4/6 Kamana Coop Housing Society, K Gadgil Road, Prabhadevi, Bombay 400028, India.

**GHAZALY Zeinab,** b. 14 December 1953, Eygpt. Vice Chairman for Commercial and Technical Affairs. m. 2 daughters. Education: BSC Faculty of Commerce, Ain Shams University, 1980; Masters in Business Administration, Ain Shams University; Diploma in Marketing, Aim Shams University, 1998. Honours: Honoured by Her Excellency First Lady Mrs Suzanne Mubarak for contributing Blood Donation Campaign. Memberships: Eygptian Business Women Association; 21st Century Business Women Association; Inner Wheel, West Club; Honoree Membership, Lions (El Salam) Club. Address: 106 El Nil Street, Agouza, Eygpt.

**GHNAIM Othman Ezzat,** b. 23 December 1957, Jordan. Civil Engineer. m. Abeer Khalafawi, 1 son, 1 daughter. Education: BSc Civil Engineering, Kuwait University, 1980; Master's Certificate in Construction Risk Management, George Washington University. Appointment: Managing Partner, Middle East Engineering Consultants (MEECON), 1985. Memberships: Kuwait Engineers Society; Jordan Engineers Society; UAE Engineers Society. Address: PO Box 8733, Dubai, United Arab Emirates.

**GHONEIM Ibrahim M,** b. 5 March 1958, Cairo, Egypt. Assistant Professor of Theriogenology. m. Sana A E Emara, 1 son, 1 daughter. Education: BVSc, Cairo University, 1981; Master Veterinary Medicine, 1985; Doctorate Veterinary Medicine, Zurich University, 1989. Appointment: Assistant Professor of Theriogenology, Faculty of Veterinary Medicine, Cairo University. Publication: Breeding Activity of the Camel Animal Reproductive Science, 1986. Memberships: Egyptian Veterinary Medicine Association; Egyptian Society for Animal Reproduction and Fertility. Address: Theriogenol Department, Faculty Veterinary Medicine, Giza 12211, Egypt.

**GHORASHI Mehrdaad,** b. 2 February 1964, Tehran, Iran. Mechanical Engineering Educator, Researcher and Consultant. m. Marjaaneh Nikpour, 1 son, 1 daughter. Education: BSc in Mechanical Engineering, 1987; MSc in Mechanical Engineering, 1989; PhD in Mechanical Engineering, 1994; MSc in Economic and Social Systems Engineering, 1998. Appointments: Consultant, RST Company, Tehran, 1987-89; Manager of Quality Control Department, Indamine Company, Tehran, 1988-90; Manager of Research and Development Department, Mazda Company, Tehran, 1990-95; Lecturer, 1990-94, Assistant Professor of Mechanical Engineering, 1994-, Chairman of the Naval Engineering Division, Mechanical Engineering Department, 1996-, Sharif University of Technology; Member, Higher Education Planning Council, Tehran, 1996-. Publications: 6 papers in professional journals; 5 papers in proceedings of conferences; 7 articles in Ettelaat newspaper; Ten articles in Kayhan newspaper. Honours: Awards from the Minister of Road and Transport, Minister of Education and Training, President of Sharif University of Technology, 1994; Award for Graduation as first PhD in Mechanical Engineering in Iran. Membership: American Society of Mechanical Engineers. Address: Sharif Univ Tech, Mech Eng Dept, Azadi St PO Box 11365-9567, Tehran, Iran.

**GHOSE Aurobindo,** b. 1 November 1935, Bangladesh. Lecturer; Assistant Professor. m. Chandrima Ghose, 1 son, 2 daughters. Education: IA, 1961; BA, 1963; MA, 1965. Appointments: Lecturer, 1968, Assistant Professor, 1980, in National Language and Literature. Honours: Provincial Drama Competition, Dhaka, 1969; 2nd Place, English Essay Competition, Nawabganj, 1960; Govt of the People's Republic of Bangladesh, Ministry of Information and Brode Caste, 1980, 1985. Address: Kaliganj Babupara, Post Raja Rampur, Dist Chapai Nawabganj, Bangladesh.

**GHOSH Ashok,** b. 15 February 1962, Burdqan, WB, India. Plastics Professional; General Manager. m. Manasi Ghosh. Education: MISE degree in Mechanical Engineering; Postgrad Diploma in Industrial Safety; Leadership Management Course; BA Public Administration; Specialisation course in Polymer Technology. Appointment: General Manager (Works) in M/S Creative Wares Ltd, Calcutta. Honours: Commendation of C-in-C in Indian Navy for Modification Work on Surface to Surface Missile; Outstanding Contribution in Indian Plastic Industry for 5 years. Memberships: Society of Engineers; Indian Value Engineering Society; National Institute of Quality and Reliability; Indian Plastic Institute. Address: Creative Wares Ltd, 27 Thakurpukur, Calcutta 700063, India.

**GHOSH Hrishikes,** b. 1 November 1933, Calcutta, India. Chemical Engineer. m. Roma Ghosh, 1 daughter. Education: BChE, Jadavpur University, 1955. Appointments: Engineering Trainee, Sindri Fertilisers and Chemicals, 1955-57; Project Engineer, 1958-61, Head, Chemical and Industrial Division, 1961-66, APV Engineering Company, Ltd, Calcutta; Project Manager, 1966-71, Senior Manager, 1972-75, Deputy General Manager, 1975-87, General Manager, Head, Heat and Mass Transfer Division, 1988-89, Chief Consultant, 1989-91, Engineers India Ltd; Advisor, Petro-Chemicals, Development Consultants Ltd, Calcutta, 1992-. Publications: Several technical articles on heat transfer and energy saving; A book of Verse and Stories. Honours: Government of India Scholarships and Prizes, 1951-55; Marquis, Who's Who in the World, 1997. Memberships: Technical Advisory Committee, Heat Transfer Research Inc, USA, 1978-91; Indian Institute of Chemical Engineers, 1976-91, 1998-; Chairman, Heat Transfer Committee, Member, Process Equipment Committee, Bureau of Indian Standard, New Delhi, 1985-91; President, Social (Puja) Festival, Delhi, 1983, 1988, 1990, Executive Member 1977-82. Address: 621 Anand Kunj Vikas Puri, 110 018 New Delhi, India.

**GHOSH Kanjaksha,** b. 3 December 1952, Bhagarpur, India. Doctor; Haematologist; Medical Scientist. m. Mrs Uma Sarkar, 2 sons. Education: MBBS, 1976; MD, 1980; Diploma National Board, 1983; MRCPath, 1992; MRCP (UK), 1993; MRCP, 1993. Appointments: Resident Medicine and Cardiology, 1977; Senior Research Fellow, ICMR, 1977; Research Officer, ICMR, 1980; Senior Research Officer, ICMR, 1983; Lecturer, Haematology, Postgraduate Institute Medical Education and Research, 1983; Assistant Professor, 1985; Senior Specialist, Kuwait, 1987; Overseas Researcher, UK, 1991; Assistant Director, Institute of Immunohaematology, 1994; Associate Professor and Director, BMT, Sullan Qabous University, Muscat, 1997. Honours: National Merit Scholarship, 1968; Talent Search Fellowship, ICMR, 1977; Gold Medals in Physiology and Pharmacology. Memberships: Indian Society Haematology and Blood Transfusion; Indian Society of Human Genetics; Association Physics India; National Academy Medical Science; New York Academy Science; SASAT. Address: 703/3A Nestle Apartments, Pandurang Budhkar Marg, Worli, Bombay 400013, India.

**GHOSH Narayan C,** b. 14 September 1949, Satirpara, Banglasesh. Reader in Mathematics. m. Sarmistha Biswas, 1 son 1 daughter. Education: SSC, Dhaka Board, 1964; BSc (Hons), Burdwan University, 1969; MSc, Applied Mathematics, Jadvpur University, 1972; ICA, Indian Statistical Institute, 1990; PhD, Jadavpur University, 1990. Appointments: Reader, S N Bose School for Mathmathics and Mathematical Sciences; Recorder in Mathematics Section, Indian Science Congress; Principal Investigator, NCERT project on Mathematics Education; Programme Coordinator, NR Sen Centre of Pedagogic and Professional Mathematics; Executive Editor,

Journal of Pure and Applied Physics; Editor, Journal of Air Land and Sea; Member, Editorial Board, Journal of BHV Mathematical Society; Guest Scientist, International Centre for Theoretical Physics, Italy, 1990; Assistant Secretary, All India Science Teacher's Association, (WB branch); Former Member, Council of Calcutta Mathematical Society; Executive Editor, International Journal of Enviroment Pollution Minimisation, Editing two monographs i) Some Aspects of Mathematics Teaching Methodology and ii) Energy Generation and Environment Pollution, Mathematical Views; Ex-Member, Text Book Writing Committee of West Bengal Board of Secondary Education. Publications: Many research papers including: Micro and Macro Form of Studies of Turbulence with espective Use of Differential and Integral Methods, 1998; ModernTheory of Turbulence and its Applications in Meteorology, 1998.Memberships: Indian Statistical Institute; Bangladesh Mathematical Society; Indian Science Congress Association; Institute of ScienceEducation and Culture; Indian Association for Cultivation of Science;Banaras Mathematical Society; All India Science Teachers; Association; Ramanujan Mathematical Scoiety; Association for Improvement of Mathematics Teaching; National Environment Science Academy; Institute of IndianEnviroment Engineering; SN Bose Centre for Research and Study of Minimising Environment Pollution. Address: Department of Mathematics, SN Bose School for Mathematics and Mathematical Sciences, Aghor Smritie, Roy Bahadur C Mukherjee Road, Hooghly, West Bengal, India.

**GHOSH Prabhat Kumar,** b. 1 March 1941, Calcutta, India. Analytical Laboratory Chemist. m. Sati Basu, 1 son. Education: BSc, Calcutta University, 1961; Post-Graduate Diploma in Management, Business Management, AIMS, New Delhi, 1987. Appointments: Apprentice Chemist, Metallurgical Laboratory, 1961-63, Chemist, 1963-68, M/s Electrosteel Castings Ltd; Chemist, 1969-76, JE, 1976-87, AE, 1987-93, DE, 1993-97, GRSE Ltd; Assistant Manager, M/s Garden Reach Shipbuilders and Engineers Ltd, Calcutta, 1997-. Publication: Work Instructions for Ferrous and Non-ferrous Chemical Analysis at GRSE Ltd, for accreditation of chemical laboratory, 1995. Address: FD-466, Flat 9, Sector III, Salt Lake, Calcutta 700091, West Bengal, India.

**GHOSH Stanley,** b. 21 October 1921, India (United States citizen). Educator. m. Olga Domonkos, 2 sons, 2 daughters. Education includes: PhD, Indiana University, USA, 1950. Appointments: United Nations, Food and Agriculture Organization; US Government Executive; Currently Professor of Management and Strategic Planning, Graduate Division of Professional Studies, Hawaii Pacific University, Honolulu. Publications: Numerous. Memberships: Several. Address: Hawaii Pacific University, 1166 Fort Street, Honolulu, HI 96813, USA.

**GHOSH Sujit,** b. 24 October 1964, India. Senior Manager. m. Debarati, 1 son. Education: BE, Civil, 1987; MSc, Canada, 1990; PhD, Canada, 1993. Appointments: Post Doctoral Fellow, National University of Singapore, 1994-95; Technical Manager, Pioneer International Ltd, 1996-97; Business Development Manager, Pioneer International Ltd, 1998-. Publications: Over 20 publications, International Journals and Conferences. Honours: ASTM's York Dale Memorial Award. Memberships: American Concrete Institute; Singapore Concrete Institute. Address: Pioneer Gt World Ctr Twr E, 1 Kim Seng Prom 10-01/02/03, Singapore 237994, Singapore.

**GHRIST John Russell,** b. 6 February 1949, Hammond, Indiana. Computer Technician. m. div. 4 sons, 1 daughter. Education: BSc, 1997, Indiana University. Appointments: 30 years of radio broadcasting: Religious Music Host, WYCA

Hammond, Indiana, 1967-71; News Reporter, WJOB Hammond, 1971-73; Music Show Host, WFLM Crown Point, Indiana, 1979-85; Disc Jockey, WTAS Beecher, Illinois, 1982-86; News/Copy Writer, WLCL Lowell, Indiana, 1981-83; Traffic Reporter, WLTH Gary, Indiana, 1985-88; Shadow Traffic Reporter, WLS/WMAQ Chicago, Illinois, 1985-87; Disc Jockey, WFXW Geneva, Illinois, 1985-89; Host of Elgin Hour, Jazz Casual, Producer for Plant Man radio shows, WEPS Elgin, Illinois; Communications Engineer, 1985-90, Land Acquisition Plat Specialist, 1990-94, Computer Technician, 1994-, Illinois Department of Transportation. Publications: Author, 5 books: Valley Voices, 1997; Jct 20, The Story of Udina, 1996; Radioville, The Town that Never Was, 1996; Billy Sunday The Dundee Prophet, 1995; Plato Centre Memories, 1998. Honours: Illinois Reaches Out State of Illinois, Springfield, 1994; Indiana Bell Pioneers Community Service Award, Crown Point, 1987; USDA Soil Conservation Award, Crown Point, 1997; Inducted into the Elgin Historical Society Hall of Fame, 1997; Elgin Schools Community Service Award, 1998; Mayor's Heritage Community Service Award, Elgin, 1998. Memberships: Valley Amateur Radio Association; Udina Historical Association. Address: Illinois Department of Transportation, 201 Centre Ct, Schaumburg, IL 60196-3169, USA.

**GIBBS Louise Elizabeth,** b. 14 November 1914, Puerto Rico, USA. Teacher; Guidance Counsellor. Education: New York University, 1944-53; MA, 1959-61. Appointments: Guidance Counselor, Elementary Secondary High School, College of New Rochelle, 1975-78, Kingsborough Community College, 1980-82. Honour: Award, New York Association for Counseling and Development, 1997. Memberships: Association of Concerned Counselors. Address: 775 Concourse Village East, Bronx, NY 10451, USA.

**GIBSON Susan,** b. 2 September 1945, Perrin Field, Texas. Social Worker, Social Services. Education: BA, Sociology, University of Texas. Appointments: Division of Development Disabilities, 1982-98; Service Provider, 1986-98; Division of Vocational Rehabilitation, Independent Living Counselor, 1995-98; Susan Gibson and Associates Agency, 1998-. Honours: Woman of the Year, 1995-96. Address: P O Box 1369, Kingston, WA 98346-1369, USA.

**GIBSON Susan Lee,** b. 9 February 1945, Perrin Field, Texas, USA. Social Services. Education: BA, Sociology, University of Texas. Appointments: Contractor, Division of Developmental Disabilities, 1982-99; Agency, 1995-99. Honours: International Woman of the Year, 1995-96; Key of Sucess; Certificates of Appreciation. Memberships: Division of Vocational Rehabilitation. Address: Susan Gibson and Associates, P O Box 1369, Kingston, WA 98346-1369, USA.

**GIELEN Uwe Peter,** b. 15 August 1940, Berlin, Germany. Professor of Psychology. Education: MA, Psychology, Wake Forest University, Winston Salem, North Carolina, 1968; PhD, Social Psychology, Harvard University, 1976. Appointments: Assistant Professor, 1977-80, City University of New York; Associate Professor, 1980-87, Professor, 1987-; Chairman, 1980-1990, Department of Psychology, St Francis College, Brooklyn, New York. Publications: Founding Editor, World Psychology (journal), 1995-; 7 co-edited books include: Psychology in the Arab Countries, 1998; The Family and Family Therapy in International Perspective, 1998; Psychology in International Perspective, 1992. Memberships: President, International Council of Psychologists, 1994-95; President, Society for Cross-Cultural Research, 1998-99; Director, Institute for International and Cross-Cultural Psychology, St Francis College, 1998-. Address: Department of Psychology, St

Francis College, 180 Remsen Street, Brooklyn, NY 11201, USA.

**GIL Michael Iosif,** b. Kharkov, Ukraine. Professor. m. Luba, 2 sons, 1 daughter. Education: MS 1967; PhD 1983; Doctor of Science 1991. Appointments: Professor, Ben Gurion University, Israel, 1991-. Publications: Norm Estimations for ...., 1995; On Stability of ...., 1998. Membership: American Mathematical Society. Address: Department of Mathematics, Ben Gurion University, PO Box 653, 84105 Beersheba, Israel.

**GILBERT Armida Jennings,** b. 10 July 1953, Sumter, South Carolina. Educator. Education: BS, University of South Carolina, 1976; MA, University of South Carolina, 1986; PhD, University of South Carolina, 1989. Appointments: University of South Carolina, 1989-90; Kent State University, 1990-98; Auburn University, 1998-. Publications: 18 Publications; 22 Professional Papers Presented. Honours: Research Appointment for Emerson and Woman, Kent State University Research Council; Nominee, 1993 National Endowment for the Humanitites Summer Stipend for Emerson Women; Teaching Development Award, Women Writers, A Course Proposal; Outstanding Essay Award. Memberships: Modern Languages Association; Philological Association of the Carolinas; Advisory Board and Founding Member, Ralph Waldo Emerson Society. Address: 1634 North Donahue Drive, Auburn, AL 36832, USA.

**GILES Howard,** b. 22 December 1946, Cardiff. Professor. m. Jane, 1 son. Education: BA Hons, University of Wales, Bangor, 1968; PhD, University of Bristol, 1971; DSc, 1996. Appointments: Professor, Social Psychology, University of Bristol, 1984-88; Professor of Communication, University of California, Santa Barbara, 1989-. Publications: Over 300 Publications. Honours: Many Honours and Awards. Memberships: Fellow, British Psychological Society; Gerontological Society of America; American Psychological Society; President, International Communication Association, 1998-99. Address: 998 Camino del Rio, Santa Barbara, CA 93110, USA.

**GILL Glenda Eloise,** b. 26 June 1939, Clarksville, Tennessee, USA. College Professor. Education: BS, 1960; MA, 1964; PhD, 1981. Appointments: College Professor, University of Texas, El Paso, 1970-75; Professor, Simpson College, 1981-82; Professor, Tuskegee University, 1982-83; Professor, Winston Salem State University, 1984-90; College Professor, Michigan Technological University, 1990-. Publication: White Grease Paint on Black Performers. Honours: NEH Grants to Iowa, 1974; Yale, 1985; UNC, Chapel Hill, 1989; Duke, 1991. Memberships: Modern Language Association; American Society for Theatre Research; Eugene O'Neill Society. Address: 1100 Agate, Apt 5, Houghton, MI 49931, USA.

**GILLESPIE Lyall Leslie,** b. 23 July 1919, Queanbeyan, NSW, Australia. Former Public Servant; Current Local Historian; Author. m. Norma Joan Bogg, 2 sons, 2 daughters. Education: Radio Course certificate, 1943, Melbourne Technical College; Accountant, ASA, 1952. Appointments: Various positions in Department of Interior, Immigration, Works and Territories and the Public Service Board, 1937-58; Assistant Director of Works, Canberra, 1958-60; Assistant Administrator, Northern Territory, 1960-63; Chairman, Town Management Boards, Alice Springs, Katherine and Tennant Creek, 1961-63; Chairman, Northern Territory Tourist Board, 1962-63; Assistant Secretary, Dept of the Interior, Canberra, 1964-72; Director, Commonwealth Brickworks (Canb) Ltd, 1968-72; Commissioner for Housing, Dept of the Capital Territory, Canberra, 1973-78; City Manager, Dept of the Capital Territory, Canberra, 1978-82; Local Historian and Author,

1982-. Publications: A Pictorial History of the Read/Reid Family in Australia 1849-1979; Aborigines of the Canberra Region; A Pictorial History of Telopea Park School 1923-83; The Southwell Family, Pioneers of the Canberra District 1838-1988; Canberra 1820-1913; Ginninderra Forerunner to Canberra; Early Verse of the Canberra Region; Early Education and Schools in the Canberra Region. Honour: Companion of the Imperial Service Order (ISO), 1983; Order of Australia Medal (OAM), 1999. Memberships: Associate, Australian Society of Certified Accountants; Fellow, Australian Institute of Management; Associate (Tech), Institution of Radio and Electronics Engineers (Aust); Life member, Horticultural Society of Canberra; Life member, Canberra and District Historical Society; Australian Rock Art Research Association; and others. Address: Lynora, 18 Ferdinand Street, Campbell, ACT 2612, Australia.

**GILLMAN Karen Lee Hein,** b. 16 September 1937, Wichita, Kansas, USA. Psychologist. m. (1) Louis Thomason, 2 daughters, (2) Richard Gillman. Education: BS, Oklahoma State University, Stillwater, 1959; MS, Virginia Polytechnic Institute and State University, Blacksburg, 1974; PhD, State University of New York at Albany, 1985. Appointments: Director, Outpatients Services, Greene County, Mental Health Clinic, Cairo, New York; Director, Student Assistant Programme, Rennselaer County, New York Unified Services; Director, Intensive Day Treatment, St Lawrence Psychiatric Center, Ogdensburg, New York, USA. Honours: National Science Foundation Fellow, 1961; Board of Examiners of Psychologists, Maine, 1998. Memberships: American Psychological Association; Central ME Psychological Society; American Association for Marriage/Family Therapy. Address: RR5 Box 5215, Winslow, ME 04901, USA.

**GILLMAR Jack Notley Scudder,** b. 18 October 1943, Honolulu, Hawaii, USA. Real Estate Executive; Educator; Author. m. Janet Thebaud, 1 son, 1 daughter. Education: BA, Penn, 1965; MA, Harvard, 1967; MA, PGI, 1994. Appointments: Volunteer Peace Corps, Micronesia, 1967-70; Trustee and President, Scudder Gillmar Estate, 1973-; Trustee, Parker School Trust, 1991-; Trustee and President, Friendship Garden Foundation, 1971-. Publications: Beauty as Experience and Transcendence, 1994; Specimens of Hawaiian Kapa, 1979; Impact of an In-country Peace Corps Training Program, 1970. Memberships: The Pacific Club; Fulbright Association. Address: Scudder Gillmar Estate, PO Box 2902, Honolulu, HI 96802-2902, USA.

**GILMORE Gordon Ray,** b. 7 September 1935, Mesa, Arizona, USA. Engineer; Manager. m. Donna K Gilmore, 3 sons. Education: BS, Petroleum Engineering, 1958; MS, Management, 1968. Appointments: Active Duty, Navy, 1958-83; President, John Brown, US Services Inc, 1995. Publications: Various articles in professional journals. Honours: Legion of Merit; Navy Marine Corps Medal for Heorism; Bronze Star Medal with Combat V. Memberships: Retired Officers Association; American Legion; National Rifle Association; Association of Civil Engineer Corps Officers. Address: 1405 Corte Canalette, Bakersfield, CA 93309-7129, USA.

**GILYOV Anatoliy V,** b. 12 July 1952, Vipolzovo, Russia. Scientist; Teacher. m. Nataliya N Lustchik, 1 son, 1 daughter. Education: BS, Mining Mechanics, 1979; PhD, Mining Mechanics, 1985. Appointments: President, Electromechanical Faculty of Krasnoyarsk State Academy of Non Ferrous Metals and Gold, 1986; Head of Department, Mining Machines and Complexes of KSANFM and G, 1987; Deputy Rector, KSANFM and G, 1996-. Publications: 124 Published Scientific Works. Honours: Annual Prizes by Educational and Scientific Research

Institutions of Krasnoyarsk. Memberships: Member, Several Higher Educational Associations of Russia. Address: c/o Audrey B Brazhnikov, Academy of Non Ferrous Metals, 52 Tolstoy St Apt 21, Krasnoyarsk 660028, Russia.

**GINOS James Zissis,** b. 1 February 1923, Hillsboro, Illinois, USA. m. Chrisilla, 2 sons. Education: BA, Columbia College, 1954; MSci Chemical Engineering, 1962, PhD, Organic Chemistry, 1964, Stevens Institute of Technology, 1964; Diploma, Athens College, Greece, 1943. Appointments: Assistant Scientist, Brookhaven National Laboratories, New York, USA, 1964-68; Research Associate Professor, Sinai School of Medicine, New York City, 1968-70; Associate Scientist, 1970-74, Scientist, 1974-75, Brookhaven National Laboratories, New York; Research Associate, 1975-89, Associate Research Professor, Neuroscience, 1989-93, Cornel University Medical College; Senior Research Associate, Neuro-oncology Laboratory, Mem Sloan Kettering Cancer Center, New York City, 1980-84; Associate, Lab Mem Nuclear Medicine, Cyclotron, 1984-93; Retired, 1993. Publications: Numerous scientific research articles and reviews. Memberships: American Chemical Society; American Association for the Advancement of Science; American Society for Clinical Pharmacology. Address: 200 Winston Drive, Apt 3016, Cliffside Park, NJ 07010, USA.

**GIRELLI Carlo Maria,** b. 18 September 1958, Milan, Italy. Doctor of Medicine. 2 daughters. Education: Degree, 1983; Gastroenterology Speciality, 1987. Appointments: Lieutenant Doctor, Italian Army, 1984; Assistant, S Giuseppe Hospital, Milan, 1985; Assistant, 1990, Medical Manager, 1997, Busto Arsizio Hospital. Publications: 25 mainly in the field of Gastroenterology, but also in internal medicine, oncology and infectious diseases. Memberships: New York Academy of Sciences; American Association for the Advancement of Science; European Association for Gastroenterology and Endoscopy; Gruppo Italiano Studio Malattie Inflammatorie Intestinali; Club del Tenue. Address: Azienda Ussl #3, Plazza Solaro 3, Busto Arsizio Varese, Italy.

**GIRIN Alexander,** b. 1 February 1951, Georgiyevich, Ukraine. Mechanical Engineering Educator. m. Larisa Pavlovna Girina, 1 daughter. Education: Graduate, Novosibirsk State University, 1973; Postgraduate, Odessa State University, 1979; DSc, 1985. Appointments: Laboratory Assistant, Institute of Hydrodynamics, Novosibirsk, 1972-73; Teacher, Odessa State University, 1979-88; Assistant Professor, 1988-. Publications: Several articles in professional journals. Membership: New York Academy of Sciences. Address: Malinovskogo Street 71, Apt 137, 270000 Odessa, Ukraine.

**GIRITLI Ismet,** b. 17 April 1924, Sebastopol, Turkey. Lawyer; Writer. m. Suna Agaoglu, 1 son, 1 daughter. Education: Graduate, Istanbul University School of Law; PhD, 1955; Full Professorship, 1964. Appointments: Chairman, Turkish Broadcasting Corporation, 1964-68; Dean, School of Journalism, Marmara University. Publications: Author of over 50 books and thousands of articles. Memberships: Academia Mexicana del Derecho Internacional, 1976; Palmes Académiques, France, 1985. Address: Nisantas, Ihlamur yolu 56/9, 80200 Istanbul, Turkey.

**GIRKA Volodymyr,** b. 8 September 1957, Kharkiv, Ukraine. Physicist. m. Viktoriya Bilous, 1 daughter. Education: MSc, Physics, 1980, PhD, Physics, 1984, Kharkiv State University. Appointments: Junior Scientific Researcher, 1980; Scientific Researcher, 1987; Assistant, 1989; Senior Teacher, 1993; Senior Scientific Researcher, 1994; Associate Professor, 1997-. Honour: International Science Foundation Fellowship,

1994. Membership: Ukrainian Physical Society. Address: Sumska Street 17, Apt 62, 310023 Kharkiv, Ukraine.

**GIRMAN Sergej**, b. 14 February 1939, Russia. Neurobiologist. m. Kalabuchova V, 2 sons. Education: Radio Engineer, Rjazan Radio Institute, 1961; PhD, Neurophysiology, Moscow State University, 1981. Appointments: Researcher, Moscow State University, 1967-84, Institute of General Genetics, 1984-90, Institute of Development Biology, 1990, Russian Academy of Sciences, Moscow. Publications: Contributor of articles in professional journals. Honours: Grants, 1993, 1994-95, 1995-97, 1997-2000. Membership: New York Academy of Sciences. Address: Solntsevsky Avenue 34-8, 119620 Moscow, Russia.

**GIUSTI Susan Marie**, b. 24 March 1970, Beaver, Pennsylvania, USA. Financier. Education: Associates degree in Mass Communications, Harrisburg Area Community College; BA Speech Communications, York College. Appointments: WITF-PBS Affiliate, Harrisburg, 1993-96; Dauphin Deposit Bank, Harrisburg, 1996-. Address: 790 N Highlands Drive Apt H, Harrisburg, PA 17111, USA.

**GIVEN David R**, b. 8 November 1943, Nelson, New Zealand. Consultant. m. Karina, 2 sons, 1 daughter. Education: BSc, honours, 1965; PhD, Botany, 1970; Certificate, Theology, Moore, 1975. Appointments: Scientist, DSIR, New Zealand, 1966-91; Postdoctoral Fellow, Canadian National Research Council, 1973-74; Consultant, Self Employed, 1991-97. Publications: 166 professional publications. Memberships: Riccarton Bush Trust Board; Past President, Friends of Christchurch Botanic Gardens; Christchurch Agenda 21; Chairman of the Board, Christchurch Branch, New Zealand Bible College. Address: David Given & Associates, 101 Jeffreys Road, Christchurch 5, New Zealand.

**GIZA David Alan**, b. 16 May 1958, Chicago, Illinois, USA. Attorney. m. Karen Van Maldegiam. Education: BSC, DePaul University, 1981; JD, John Marshall University, 1984; Illinois Bar, 1985. Appointments: US District Court, 1985; Attorney, Private Practice, Chicago, 1985-86; Associate, Larry Karchmar Ltd, Chicago, 1986-87; Kovitz, Shifrin & Waitzman, Chicago, 1987; Attorney, W W Grainger Inc, Skokie, 1987-91, Lincolnshire, 1991-93; Division Attorney, 1993-96, Senior Attorney, 1996-98, Assistant General Counsel, 1998-, W W Grainger Inc. Memberships: Trustee, Village of Libertyville; Chairman, Camp Lake Center Lake Rehabilitation District; American Trial Lawyers Association; American Corporate Counsel Association; Illinois State Bar Association; Chicago Bar Association; Lake County Bar Association. Address: W W Grainger Inc, USA.

**GIZEJOWSKI Marian Antoni**, b. 17 January 1951, Zielona, Gora, Poland. m. Zofia Patyna-Gizejowska, 1 daughter. Education: BSc, C Engg, 1972; MSc, C Engg, 1974; PhD, C Engg, 1981. Appointments: Junior Instructor to Assistant Professor, Warsaw University of Technology, 1975-; Postdoctoral Fellow, University of Sydney, 1983; Senior Lecturer University of Zimbabwe, 1988-94; Visiting Professor, University of British Columbia, 1991. Publications: Over 120 publications. Honours: 3 awards. Memberships: ASCE; IABSE; ESDEP of SCI. Address: Surowieckiego 4 m 92, 02 785 Warsaw, Poland.

**GJERDE Rosalie Prince**, b. 23 May 1941, Fort Bregg, California, USA. Music Educator. m. Marion Wilbur Gjerde, 2 sons, 1 daughter. Education: BA, Humboldt State University, 1963; California Lifetime Credentials (Teaching). Appointments: Teacher, Fort Bragg Schools, 1964-69; Consultant, Mendocino

Schools, 1978-79; Teacher, Music Department, College of the Redwoods, 1971-78; Owner, Principal Teacher, Gjerde Music Studio, 1979-. Publications: Various choral compositions and choral responses; Numerous articles in professional journals. Memberships: Nationally Certified Member, Music Teachers National Association; National Guild of Piano Teachers; California Association of Professional Music Teachers; Music Teachers Association of California. Address: 315 Park Street, Fort Bragg, CA 95437, USA.

**GJERMANI Linda**, b. 9 February 1962, Tirana, Albania. Educational Researcher; Consultant. m. Mishel Gjermani, 27 September 1984, 2 children. Education: University Diploma, University of Tirana, 1984; MS, University of Twente, Enschede, Netherlands, 1997. Appointments: High School Teacher, Kruja, Albania, 1984-85; Teacher, Middle School, Tirana, 1985-87; Editor-in-Chief, Institute of Pedagogical Research, Tirana, 1987-94; CAtholic Relief Services, Tirana, 1996-98; Researcher, 1994-; Project Director, UNICEF, Tirana, 1994-97; Soros Foundation, Tirana, 1996-98; Catholic Relief Services, Tirana, 1996-98; Consultant, Children's Aid Direct, 1998; World Bank, 1998-99. Publications: Pedagogical Review, 1996, 1997; Education in Albania: A National Dossier, 1997; The Parents and the School-Possible Friends, 1998; Editor-in-Chief, Vocational Education, 1987-93; Contributor of articles to magazines. Memberships: Representative, Property with Justice, Albania, 1993; Fellow, Albanian Physicists Association; Education Development Centre. Address: Pall 39 Shk 4 Ap 46, R R Kongresi I Lushnjes, Tirana, Albania.

**GJIKA Viktor**, b. 23 June 1937, Korga. Film Maker. m. Flora Gjika, 1 daughter. Education: Diploma, High Institute of Cinema, Moscow, 1960. Appointments: Director, Photography, 1960, Film Director, 1965, Director, Cinema, 1984-90; President, Treuikfilm; Artistic Director, Telehrberia. Honours: Republic Awards, 1964, 1979, 1984; Cup of National Film Festival, 1979, 1981; Honour Diploma, International Film Festival, Istanbul, 1979; Grand Prix, Festival of Lodz, Poland, 1960. Memberships: Inernational Jury, Inernational Film, Festivals; Vice President, European Film College, Danimarka; Vice Chairman, Association of Albanian Film Makers. Address: Rr Ded Gjon Luli P 5 Sh 3, Apt 33, Tirana, Albania.

**GJONI Klement**, b. 25 November 1951, Kucove, Albania. Geologist Engineer. m. Vjollca, 1 son. Education: Diploma, Geology Engineering, University of Tirana, Albania, 1973; Certificate, Technical University of Clausthal, Germany, 1997. Appointments: Production Engineer, 1974-84, Exploration Engineer, 1987-89, Chief of Editing and Training Department, 1987-92, Vice Director, Training Department, 1992-, ALBPETROL. Publication: Editor, Nafta Shqiptare, magazine, 1987-99. Memberships: Chairmanship, Democratic Party, Fier, 1997; Geologists and Geophysics Association. Address: ALBEPTROL, Quendra e Kualilikimit, Patos, Albania.

**GLADKOVSKY Victor Andreevich**, b. 29 May 1925, Yekaterinburg, Russia. Science Worker. m. Jnna Gubasheva, 1 son. Education: Graduate, Mechanical Department, Ural State Technical University, 1948; Doctor Technician, Leningrad State Technical University, 1970. Appointments: Science Worker, Institute of Physics and Metals, Yekaterinburg and Institute of Metallurgy, Teeljabinsk, 1948-; Head, Chair of Strength of Materials, Perm State Technical University 1962-93, Professor, 1993-. Publications: Over 200 research papers, 15 inventions. Memberships: Several. Address: 29a Komsomol Pr, Perm State Technical University, Perm 614600, Russia.

**GLAZEBROOK Susan Gwynfa Mary,** b. 8 February 1956, Bowden, Cheshire, England. Tax and Banking Lawyer. m. Greg Kane, 2 sons. Education: BA, History, 1975, MA, 1st class honours, History, 1978, LLB, honours, 1980, Dip.Bus, Finance, 1994, Auckland University; DPhil, French Legal History, Oxford University, 1988. Career: Junior Lecturer, History, University of Auckland, 1976-79; Worked in Rouen, France, 1981-83; Research Assistant, Auckland University, 1984; Part-time Tutor, Accountancy and English, Oxford, 1985; Part-time Lecturer, Department of Commercial Law, University of Auckland, 1991-94; Partner, Simpson Grierson Butler White, 1986-. Publications: Several articles in professional journals. Memberships: New Zealand Committee of the Pacific Economic Co-operation Council; International Bar Association; Inter-Pacific Bar Association; International Fiscal Association; New Zealand Law Society; Board of Trustees, National Provident Fund; Director of Counties Manukau Health Ltd. Address: Simpson Grierson, 92-96 Albert Street, Auckland, New Zealand.

**GLEASON David Michael,** b. 15 March 1950, Cleveland, Ohio, USA. Physical Scientist. m. Boonrueng Paancahreon. 2 daughters. Education: BS, Mathematics, 1973, MSc, Mathematics, 1974, MSc, Geodetic Science, 1984, Ohio State University. Appointments: Geodetic Scientist, Mathematician, Defense Mapping Agency, 1975-86; Physical Scientit, Air Force Research Laboratory, 1986-; Develops gravity models to make airborne and spaceborne navigation more autonomous. Publications: Over 35 single-authored refereed R&D papers. Honours: Ohio State University, Heisakanen Award for Geodetic Science R&D, 1986; Institute of Navigation Thurlow Award for Navigation R&D, 1991; Selected as one of 2000 Outstanding Scientists of 20th Century, 1999. Memberships: Institute of Navigation; American Geophysical Union. Address: Air Force Research Lab VSBI, 29 Randolph Road, Hanscom AFB, MA 01731 3010, USA.

**GLOUSCHENKOV Vladimir,** b. 16 December 1941, Kuibyshev, Russia. Researcher; University Educator. m. Kaleria Shishkanova, 1 son, 1 daughter. Education: Diploma Engineer (MEng equivalent), Metallurgical Engineering, 1964, Candidate of Science (PhD equivalent), Mechanical Engineering, 1972, Samara State Aerospace University; International academic sabbatical and consulting activity, Harbin Institute of Technology, China, 1993, European Institute for Joining of Materials, Denmark, 1994, Capital Space Machinery Corporation, China, 1995, 1996, Shanghai Academy of Spaceflight Technology, China, 1997. Appointments: Research Engineer, 1964-68, Project Manager, Research Laboratory for Impulse Processing of Metals, 1970-74, Director, Research Laboratory for Impulse Processing of Metals, 1974-84, Founder, Director, Research Laboratory for Advanced Materials Processing, 1986-, Samara State Aerospace University; Teaching: Assistant Professor, 1970-76, Associate Dean, 1972-78, Associate Professor, 1976-, Department of Metallurgy and Mechanical Processing, Samara State Aerospace University. Publications: Co-author, over 115 professional publications and 88 Russian patents. Honours: USSR National State Prize; Title of USSR National Inventor; Regional Prize in Science and Technology; Gold and Bronze Medals, USSR National Exhibition of Technological Achievements; Outstanding Achievements Award, Ministry of Education. Memberships: President, International Association for Magnetic Metal Forming; Minerals, Metals and Materials Society; New York Academy of Sciences; European Section, American Welding Society; International Association for Continuing Engineering Education. Address: App 59, 153 Molodogvardeyskaya St, 443001 Samara, Russia.

**GLOWINSKI Roland,** b. 9 March 1937, Paris, France. Professor. m. Angela Rimok, 2 daughters. Education: BSc, Ecole Polytechnique, Paris, 1958; PhD, Mathematics, University of Paris, 1970. Appointments: Scientific Director, INRIA (France), 1971-85; Professor, Mathematics, University of Houston, 1985-. Publications: Several articles in professional journals. Honours: Seymore Cray Prize, 1988; Grand Prix Marcel Dassault, French Academy of Sciences, 1996. Memberships: French Academy of Sciences; AMS; SIAM; Academia Europaea. Address: Department of Mathematics, University of Houston, Houston, TX 77204-3476, USA.

**GLOWNIA Jan,** b. 14 January 1940, Kwaczala, Poland, Academic Teacher. m. Janina Gorka, 1 son, 1 daughter. Education: MSc, University of Mining and Metallurgy, 1962; Master, Metallurgical Plant, 1962-66; PhD, 1971. Appointment: Professor, University of Mining and Metallurgy, 1992. Publications include: Microsegregation in dendritic single crystals of nickel-rich alloys, 1987. Memberships: Metals, Minerals and Materials Society. Address: ul Milkowskiego 8/51, 30-349 Cracow, Poland.

**GLOZMAN Janna M,** b. 28 December 1940, Moscow, Russia. Neuropsychologist. m. Naum Glozman, 1 son. Education: MSc, Linguistics, Moscow Linguistic University, 1963; MSc, Psychology, Moscow University, 1970; PhD, Medical Psychology, Moscow University, 1974; Senior Research Diplomate in Medical Psychology, 1982. Appointments: Translator, Institute of Medical Information, 1963-70; Researcher, 1970-77, Senior Researcher, 1977-93, Leading Researcher, 1993-, Moscow University; Visiting Scholar, New Medico Rehabilitation Centre, Troy, New York, 1991; Assistant Professor, Moscow Academy of Postgraduate Training, 1992-96; Visiting Professor, University of North Carolina at Wilmington, 1996. Publications: 6 books, over 170 articles in Russia and abroad, 1970-; Editorial Board, Neuropsychology Review. Honours: Achievement Medal, Academy of Physical Education and Reducation, Krakov, Poland; Medal, 850 years of Moscow; Medal, Veteran of Labour. Memberships: Russian Neurological Association; New York Academy of Sciences. Address: Apt 118, 25 Narodnogo Opolchemia, Moscow 123154, Russia.

**GNIADECKA Monika,** b. 29 March 1967, Warsaw, Poland. m. Robert Gniadecki. Education: Medical School, Warsaw, 1991; PhD, Copenhagen University, Denmark, 1994. Appointments: Registrar in Dermatology, Warsaw Medical School, Poland, 1992-94; Research Fellow, Department of Dermatology, National University Hospital and Bispebjerg Hospital, Copenhagen, Denmark, 1994-. Publications: Non-Invasive Methods and The Skin, Co-author, Handbook; Articles in various journals. Membership: International Society of Skin Imaging. Address: University of Copenhagen, Department of Dermatology, Bispebjerg Bakke 23, 2400 Copenhagen, Denmark.

**GO,** Tian Kang, b. 18 November 1932, Amoy, China. Professor. m. Mitsuko Omata, 2 sons. Education: BA, Far Eastern University, 1953; BA, Columbia University, 1985; PhD, University of Tokyo, 1966. Appointments: Lecturer, Associate Professor, Professor, Rissho University, Tokyo, 1962-73; Professor, Chuo University, Tokyo, 1973-; Part time Lecturer, University of Tokyo, 1972-77; University of Kyoto, 1974; Hitotsubashi University, 1982; Visiting Professor, Beijing University, 1997-98. Publication: The Evolution of Finance Capitalism in the United States 1873-1914, 1972. Address: 65 Shu Ming Dong Du, Amoy City, Fujian, China.

**GODA Yoshimi,** b. 24 February 1935, Sapporo, Japan. Civil Engineering Researcher; Educator. m. Toshiko Fukuda, 2 sons, 3 daughters. Education: Beng, 1957, DEng, 1976, University of Tokyo; MSc, Massachusetts Institute of Technology, 1963. Appointments: Researcher, Port and Harbour Research Institute, Ministry of Transport, Japan, 1957-64, Chief, Hydraulic Model Test Section, 1964-67, Chief, Wave Research Group, 1967-78, Director, Hydraulic Engineering Division, 1978-80, Director, Maritime Hydrodynamics Division, 1980-84, Deputy Director, 1984-86, Director General, 1986-88; Professor, Civil Engineering, Yokohama National University, 1988-. Publictions include: Random Seas and Design of Maritime Structures, 1985. Honours: JSCE's Paper Encouragement Prize, 1968; JSCE's Paper Prize, 1976; JSCE's Publication Awards, 1987, 1997; ASCE's International Costal Engineering Award, 1989. Memberships: Japan Society of Civil Engineers; American Society of Civil Engineers; International Association of Hydraulic Research. Address: Yokohama National University, Department of Civil Engineering, 79-5 Tokiwadai, Hodogaya-ku, Yokohama 240-8501, Japan.

**GODBOLE Shrikant,** b. 18 June 1950, Khamgaon. Banker. m. Mrs Kavita, 2 sons. Education: SSC. Appointments: Lecturer, Various Venues, 1987-. Telling Programmes, Various Venues, 1986-. Publications: Natak Zalech Pahije; Problem - Problem; Molkarin Yeta Ghara; The Spirit; Dey Re Hari Khatlyavari; Asave Prem Shejari; Western Style Haldi Kumkum; Bhadyane Dene Aahe; Rangeet Swayamwar; Yugdrashta; Nan Ting Too Aani Pari Rani; Prism; Ek Hota Lakoodtodya; Many Articles in Magazines, Newspapers. Honours: Gunwant Kamgar Kalyan Puraskar; Best Story Award; Best Citizen Award; Best Play Write, 1981-1985; Best Acting, 1981, 1985; Best Producer Award; Best Director Award, 1981, 1985; Outstanding Services Award; Best Performance Award; UWA Life Time Achievement Award; Man of the Year, American Biographical Institute; MSPI, Outstanding Personalities. Memberships: Akhil Bhartiya Marathi Natya Parished; Vidarbha Sahitya Sangha Nagpur; Vidarbha Lekak Sangha Nagpur; Kala Manch; Swarvihar; Labour Welfare Board, May other Memberships. Address: The United Western Bank Ltd, Hospital Road, Gondia 441614, India.

**GODETTE Franklin Delano Roosevelt,** b. 3 November 1932, North Harlowe, NC, USA. Attorney at Law. m. Eunice Godette, 2 sons, 1 daughter. Education: BA, 1955, JD, 1958, Howard University. Appointments: Attorney at Law. Honours: Certificate of Appreciation as Associate Editor, Howard Law Journal, Howard University School of Law, 1958; Certificate of Award for Outstanding Accomplishments in Criminal Justice from Ebenezer Presbyterian Church, USA, 1984. Membership: North Carolina State Bar, 1958-. Address: 1140 Adams Creek Road, Havelock, NC 28532, USA.

**GODOLI Giovanni,** b. 10 March 1927, Firenze, Italy. Astronomer. m. Maria, 1 son. Education: PhD, Physics, 1949; Libera Docenza, Astrophysics, 1956. Appointments: Astronomer, Arcetri Astrophysical Obervatory, 1951-67; Director of Catania, Astrophysics Observatory; Full Professor of Astronomy, Catania University, 1967-76; Full Professor, Solar Physics, Florence University, 1976-. Publications: About 200 publications, Solar and Stellar Physics. Honours: Borgia Prize of the Academia Nazionale dei Lincei. Memberships: International Astronomical Union; European Physical Society; European Astronomical Society. Address: Corso Dei Tin, Firenze 50122, Italy.

**GOELLNER Claud Ivan,** b. 4 October 1957, Passo Fundo, RS. Professor. 2 daughters. Education: Agronomist,

Universidade de Passo Fundo, 1980; MSc, 1983, University Federal Rio Grande do Sul; PhD, University of Leon, Spain. Appointments: Professor of Toxicology and Ecotoxicology; Advanced Professor of Toxicology and Ecotoxicology of Agronomy and Veterinary School, University Passo Fundo; Professor of Toxicology of Foods, Food Engineering School, University of Passo Fundo and Universidade Regional Integrada-Erechim; Professor of Toxicology, Biochemistry and Pharmacy Course, Universidade Regional Integrada-Erechim, RS. Publications: 100 papers in scientific journals in Brazil and abroad; 2 books published about Toxicology of Pesticides, 1993. Memberships: ISSX; Centre for Toxicology Studies of Rio Grande do Sul. Address: University Passo Fundo, Campus 99001970 Passo Fundo, Brazil.

**GOESCHEN Karl Klaus Günter,** b. 18 April 1948, Kiel, Germany. Medical Doctor; Gynaecologist. 4 sons, 1 daughter. Education: Christian Albrechts University, Kiel, 1966-69; Medical University, Lübeck, 1969-72; Medical Assistant, 1972, Medical Doctor, 1973, Doctor's degree, 1973, PhD, 1984, Free University, Berlin; Qualified as Professor, Medical School, Hannover, 1989. Appointments: Medical Assistant, Stadt Krankenhaus, Rendsburg, 1972-73; Medical Officer, German Army, 1973-74; Assistant Doctor, Martin Luther Hospital, Berlin, 1974-79; Assistant Professor, Senior Consultant, Institut Perinatale Medizin, Berlin; Chief Consultant, Medical School, Hannover, 1985-95; Chief of Department, Frauen Klinik Klinikum, Osnabrück, 1995-; Chief, Midwifery School, Osnabrück. Publications: Cardiotokography Practice, 1979; Hypotension in Pregnancy, 1988; Treatment with Prostaglandins, 1989; More than 300 scientific publications. Memberships: Secretary, Gesellschaft für Pränatal und Geburtsmedizin; Editorial Board, Zeitschrift Perinatalmedizin; Dtsch Ges Gyn Gebh; Norddeutsche Ges Gyn Gebh; Deutsch Gessellschaft für Perinatale Medizin. Address: Frauenklinik Klinikum, Am Finkelhügel 1, 48076 Osnabruck, Germany.

**GOETZ Raymond,** b. 14 May 1922, Rockford, Illinois, USA. Law Professor; Labor Arbitrator. m. Elizabeth Morey Goetz, 4 sons, 2 daughters. Education: JD, 1950, MBA honours, 1963, University of Chicago. Appointments: Professor of Law, University of Kansas, 1965-87; Permanent Arbitrator, 1979-83, Panel of Salary Arbitrators, 1979-83, Major League Baseball Clubs and Players Association; Permanent Umpire, Ford Motor Company and UAW, 1984-89; AT&T and CWA Panel of Arbitrators, 1986-94. Publications include: Employee Benefit Trusts Under Section 302 of Labor Management Relations Act, 59; Regulation of Uninsured Employee Welfare Plans Under State Insurance Law; Secondary Boycotts and the LMRA: A Path Through the Swamp; Arbitration After Termination of a Collective Bargaining Agreement; Collective Bargaining Agreements as Contracts; labor Law Decisions of the Supreme Court During the 1977 Term; The Kansas Public Employer-Employee Relations Law. Memberships: National Academy of Arbitrators; American Bar Association. Address: University of Kansas Law School, Lawrence, KS 66045, USA.

**GOFFIGAN Christopher,** b. 10 June 1960, USA. Research Associate. Education: AAS, Management, AAS, Merchandising, Tidewater Community College, 1982; Professional Communication Certificate, Christopher Newport College, 1989; Certified Professional Consultant, International Guild of Professional Consultants, 1997. Appointments: Library Aide, Tidewater Community College, 1980-82; Inventory, Miller Rhodes, Virginia Beach, 1984, 1988; Telephone Sales Representative, Energy Savings Exterior Inc, Virginia Beach, 1985, Sears Service Center, 1985-86; Credit Clerical, Sears Credit Central, Virginia Beach, 1986-87; Telephone Interviewer, Issues Answers, Norfolk, 1988; Research Associate, Leading ational Advertisers/Competitive Media Reporting, 1990-. onours: Certificate of Appreciation, Military Mail Call, 1984; amed Knight Chevalier, Venerable Order of the Knights of ichael the Archangel, 1992; Honorary Sargent at Arms, ational Association of Chiefs of Police, 1993; Gold Seal ward, National Association of Chief of Police, 1995; Honorary hief, National Association of Chiefs of Police, 1995; ternational Poet of Merit Award, International Society of oets, 1996; Editors Choice Award, National Library of Poetry, 996, 1997; International Poetry Hall of Fame, 1997. emberships: International Society of Poets; International uild of Professional Consultants; US Marshals and Peace fficers Association of America; American Federation of Police nd Concerned Citizens; National Geographic Society; merican Biographical Institute Research Association; ember, American Police Hall of Fame and Museum. Address: 40 Cason Lane, Virginia Beach, VA 23462, USA.

**GOGELIA Artshil,** b. 10 December 1941, Tbilisi, Georgia. ournalist. m. 1973, 2 sons, 1 daughter. Education: Institute of port, 1961; Georgian University Philologist, 1967. ppointment: Chairman, Georgian TV and Radio Corporation. ublications: Honorable Diploma of Georgian Government; onorable Journalist of Georgia. Membership: International ederation of Journalists. Address: 209 Nutsubidze Str, 380086 blisi, Georgia.

**GOGOVI Geoffrey Kwao A,** b. 1938, Ghana. m. Comfort riscilla, 3 sons, 3 daughters. Education: BA, honours, niversity of Ghana, 1966; Diploma, TEO, University of Leeds, 973; MA, University of Lancaster, 1974. Appointments: School laster, 1966-72; Inspector of Schools, 1974-77; Lecturer, CC, 1977-79, 1985-, University of Ilorin, 1979-85; Head, epartment of English, UCC, 1989-91, 1997-98, Dean, Arts, 990-93. Publication: Colonial Language Policies and Their ffects on Modern WA States, 1990. Honour: Commonwealth ellowship, 1972-74. Memberships: Ghana English Studies ssociation; Linguistics Association of Ghana. Address: B114 ff Carl-Reindorf Road, Cape Coast, Ghana.

**GOH Ronald,** b. 18 November 1944, Singapore. Company irector; Audio Engineer. m. Dora Lee, 2 sons, 1 daughter. ducation: Singapore Polytechnic. Appointments: Sales lanager, 1965, Sales Director, 1968, Managing Director, 992-, Electronics and Engineering Pte Ltd. Honours: umerous Commercial Outstanding Awards from Trade rinciples. Memberships: Audio Engineering Society; The lighlander Club; The Oxford Club. Address: Electronics and ngineering Pte Ltd, 285 Outram Road, Singapore 169069, ingapore.

**GOH Ronald,** b. 18 November 1944, Singapore. Company irector; Audio Engineer. m. Dora Lee, 2 sons, 1 daughter. ducation: Singapore Polytechnic. Appointments: Sales lanager, 1965, Sales Director, 1968, Managing Director, 992-, Electronics & Engineering Pte Ltd. Honours: Numerous ommercial outstanding awards from trade principals. lemberships: Audio Engineering Society; The Highlander lub; The Oxford Club. Address: Electronics and Engineering te Ltd, 285 Outram Road, Singapore 169069.

**GOLBERG Dmitri Victorovich,** b. 21 March 1961, Moscow, Russia. Materials Science. m. Galina, 2 daughters. Education: 3S, Moscow Institute of Steels and Alloys, Moscow, Russia, 978-83; MS, 1978-83; PhD, I P Bardin Central Research nstitute for Ferrous Metallurgy, 1986-90. Appointments: Junior Researcher, Researcher, I P Bardin Central Research Institute or Ferrous Metallurgy, 1983-93; Visiting Scientist, University of Tsukuba, Japan, 1993-94; Visiting Scientist, Max Planck

Institute für Eisenforschung, Germany, 1994-95; Visiting Scientist, National Institute for Research in Inorganic Materials, Japan, 1995-96; Visiting Scientist, National Research Institute for Metals, 1996-97; Researcher, National Institute for Research in Inorganic Materials, Japan, 1997-. Publications: 32 Papers in Refereed International Journals; 3 patents. Honours: Honourable Diploma, Moscow Institute of Steels and Alloys; Student with the Highest Performance in the Degree MS; Best Paper Award, Japan Society of Electron Microscopy, 1997-98. Memberships: Japan Society for Metals; Japan Society of Electron Microscopy, Materials Research Society. Address: National Institute Research Inorg Mater, Namiki 1-1, Ibaraki Tsukuba 305-0044, Japan.

**GOLD Gretchen,** b. 10 January 1967, Minnesota, USA. Artist. m. Neal Goldberg. Education: BS, University Wisconsin. Appointments: Art Director, Med-O-Lark Summer Camp; Teacher, K-12, several schools. Honour: Recognised for work as art teacher for children. Membership: Woman's Caucus for Art, national. Address: 334 Beacon Street, Boston, MA 02116-1004, USA.

**GOLDEN Harvey E. Rheumatologist. m. Inge Hirsch Golden,** 2 sons, 1 daughter. Education: BA, 1953, Grinnell College, Iowa; Northwestern University Medical School, Chicago, 1962; Internship Straight Medicine, Los Angeles General Hospital, 1962-63; Residency in Internal Medicine, 1963-65, Fellowship in Rheumatology, 1965-66, Mayo Clinic, Rochester, Minnesota; Fellowship in Rheumatology, Northwestern University Medical School, 1966-67. Appointments: Associate in Medicine, Northwestern University Medical School, Chicago, 1967-69; Assistant Professor of Medicine, Chicago Medical School, 1969-72; Assistant Professor of Medicine, 1972-78, Associate Professor of Medicine, 1978-98, Professor of Medicine, 1998-, Rush Medical College, Chicago; Senior Attending, Presbyterian-St Luke's Hospital, Chicago, 1980-. Publications: Author or Co-author, 13 articles, 16 abstracts and letters. Honour: Philip Hench Scholarship Award (Mayo Foundation) for achievement in Rheumatology, 1967. Memberships: Fellow, American College of Physicians; American College of Rheumatology; Chicago Rheumatism Societyl Arthritis Foundation, Illinois Chapter; American Society Clinical Rheumatology; American Medical Association; Chicago Medical Society; Illinois State Medical Society. Address: Rheumatology Assocs SC, 1725 W Harrison St Ste 1039, Chicago, IL 60612-3862, USA.

**GOLDIN Ian Andrew,** b. 3 March 1955, South Africa. Chief Executive. m. Theresa, 1 son, 1 daughter. Education: BSc, Mathematics, 1974-76, BA, Honours, Economics, 1975-77, University of Cape Town; MSc, Economics, London School of Economics, 1978-79; Doctorate, Oxford University, 1979-83. Appointments: Economist, South Africa Labour and Development Research Unit, 1976-78; Visiting Professor, Acting Head of Economics Department, University of Cape Town, 1980-81; Lecturer, Economics, Oxford University, St Peters College, Oxford, 1981-83; Director, Trade and Commodity Markets, Landell Mills Commodities Ltd, London and New York, 1984-88; Director of Programmes, Organization for Economic Co-operation and Development, Paris, 1988-92; Principle Economist, World Bank, Washington, DC, USA, 1992-95; Principle Economist, European Bank for Reconstruction and Development, London, 1995-96; Chief Executive, Managing Director, Development Bank of Southern Africa, Johannesburg, 1996-. Publications include: The Economics of Sustainable Development; Economic Reform, Trade and Agricultural Development; Modelling Economywide Reforms; Trade Liberalization: Global Economic Implications.

Address: No 5 Lawley Road, Westcliffe, Johannesburg 2193, South Africa.

**GOLDING Raymund Marshall,** b. 17 June 1935, Westport, New Zealand. Retired Vice Chancellor. m. Ingeborg Anna Maria Carl, 2 daughters. Education: BSc, 1957, MSc, 1958, University of Auckland; PhD, 1963, University of Cambridge; Fellow: New Zealand Institute of Chemistry 1966; Institute of Physics 1969; Royal Australian Chemical Institute 1974; Royal Society of Arts 1977; Australian Academy of Technological Sciences and Engineering 1995. Appointments: Professor, Theoretical and Physical Chemistry, University of New South Wales, 1968-86; Pro-Vice Chancellor, 1978-86; Vice-Chancellor, James Cook University of North Queensland, 1986-96; Director, St Georges Hospital, 1982-86; Council member, Papua New Guinea University of Technology, 1986-93; Director various enterprises, 1990-97; Trustee, World Wide Fund for Nature, 1988-94; Currently: Chairman, Australasian Marine Science Consortium; New South Wales Chiropractic Registration Board Education Committee; Chiropractors and Osteopaths Board of Queensland; Honorary Chairman, Australian Chapter PACON International; Director, PACON International; Chairman, Management Committee, National Unit for Multidisciplinary Studies of Spinal Pain, Townsville General Hospital; Member many other committees. Publications: Wave Mechanics, 1969; Chemistry, Multistrand Senior Science for High School Students, 1975; The Goldings of Oakington, 1992; Over 100 research papers since 1957. Honours: Easterfield Award, 1967; Honorary Fellow, Korean Chemical Society, 1985; DSc, University NSW, 1986; Awarded Officer of the Order of Australia General Division, 1994; The Pacon International Award, in Honolulu, 1996. Memberships: Fellow, 5 Institutes and Societies. Address: Lot 2 Tolson Road, Mooloolah, QLD 4553, Australia.

**GOLDMAN Stanford Milton,** b. 28 November 1940, Salt Lake City, USA. MD; Medical Educator. m. Harriet Kaplow, 1 son, 1 daughter. Education: BA cum laude, BRE, 1961, Yeshiva University, New York; MD, 1965, Residency, Bronx Municipal Hospital Centre, 1966-69, Chief Resident, 1968-69, Albert Einstein College of Medicine, Bronx, New York; Internship, Jefferson University Medical Hospital, Philadelphia, 1965-66. Appointments: include: Professor and Chairman of Diagnostic Radiology, 1993-, Profesor of Urology, 1995-, University of Texas Medical School at Houston; Adjunct Professor of Radiology, 1994-, Adjunct Professor of Urology, 1994-, Baylor College of Medicine, Houston; Medical Director of Radiology Technology, Houston Community College, School of Technology, Houston, 1994-; Professor of Radiology, 1995-, Adjunct Radiologist, 1995-, M D Anderson Cancer Centre, Houston; Chief, Dept of Radiology, Hermann Hospital, Houston, 1993-; Physician-in-Chief, Dept Radiology, Lyndon Baines Johnson Hospital, Houston, 1993-. Publications: Author or co-Author: 15 abstracts; 21 invited articles in journals; 128 refereed original articles in journals; 27 book chapters; 4 books; 157 oral presentations; 52 exhibits; 40 other publications. Honours: Certificate of Appreciation for over 20 years of teaching and research, Armed Forces Institute of Pathology, Div of Radiological Pathology, 1993; Radiology Classroom and Library named in honour for 20 years of devotion and service, Francis Scott Key Medical Centre, 1993; Albert Einstein Distinguished Alumnus Award, 1996; Many more Certificates of Appreciation and Merit and other awards and fellowships for excellence in research, teaching and scientific exhibits. Memberships: Member of 27 professional associations and societies. Address: University of Texas Medical School, Dept of Radiology, 6431 Fannin MSB 2.132, Houston, TX 77030 1501, USA.

**GOLDSTEIN Stanley Irving,** b. 1 October 1925, Bronx, New York, USA. Pharmacist; Podiatrist. m. Hortense, 3 sons. Education: BSc Pharmacy, 1949; DPM, 1957; Podiatric Surgeon; Attended College of Medicine and Surgery, Bologna Italy. Appointments: Assistant Chief Pharmacist, Dr Berner Pharmacy, Rivington, New York; Extern, Beth-Israel Hospital and various clinics, NYC; Director, Podiatric Medicine and Surgery, AFL, New York; Chief Podiatric Surgeon, Helen Hayes Hospital, Stormy Point, New York; Lecturer, Seaton Hall College of Medicine. Publications: Medical articles in professional journals. Memberships: Fellow, International College of Foot Surgeons; Past VP, Jewish War Vets. Address 561 S Main St #Route 304, New City, NY 10956-2926, USA.

**GOLEMI Bardhyl,** b. 11 May 1933, Saranda. Professor. m. Golemi Lavdi, 1 son, 1 daughter. Education: BSc Engineering 1955, PhD, 1978, Professor, 1980, Tirana University, Albania. Specialisation, 1972, Bupelec Paris, France. Appointments. Head of Dept, 1968-75, Head of Education Sector, 1960-75, Tirana University; Scientific Secretary, Scientific Academy 1976-80; Deputy Minister of Education Albania, 1981-91; General Secretary, National Commission for Qualification, Albania, 1982-90; President, UNESCO Albanian Commission 1982-90. Publications: Theoretical Foundations of Electric Technic, 1975, 1998; Synthesis of Electrical Circuits, 1980 Oscillations in Nonlinear Circuits, 1980; Editorial Board Albanian Dictionary Encyclopaedia, 1984. Honour: Republic Prize First Grade for Oscillations in Nonlinear Circuits, 1980 Memberships: Member of Senate, Tirana University, 1978-90; Electrical Engineering Association; Editorial Board, Journal of Applied Electromagnetism, Athens, Greece. Address Akademie Shkencare, Tirane, Albania.

**GOLOVASHKIN Aleksander Ivanovich,** b. 16 January 1935, Murom, Russia. Physicist. m. Emma Georgievna, 2 daughters. Education: Moscow State University, 1958 Candidate of Sciences, 1965; Associate Professor, 1982 Senior Scientific Worker, 1975; Soros Associate Professor 1995. Appointments: Head of Sector, 1974, Laboratory, 1986 Vice-Director of Division, 1995, of P N Lebedev Physical Institute. Publications: Over 200 articles to professional journals, 1960-. Honours: Order of Red Banner, 1981; Medals Labour Veteran, 1995, and 850 Years of Moscow, 1997 Memberships: P N Lebedev Physical Institute, 1958-; Physical Society of Moscow; Moscow Engineering-Physics Institute Address: Oktober Str 91-2-24, 127521 Moscow, Russia.

**GOLOVCHINER Gregory,** b. 11 July 1963, Moscow, Russia Physician. m. Kristina, 2 sons. Education: MD, 1986, Moscow School of Medicine; Resident, Cardiology, 1986-88, Institute for Transplantology, Moscow. Appointments: Invasive Cardiology Institute for Transplantology, Moscow, 1988-92; Resident Internal Medicine, Soroka Medical Centre, Beer Sheva, Israel 1994-99. Publications: 11 in medical journals. Membership Israel Medical Association. Address: 103/64 Irushalaim Boulevard, 84801 Beer Sheva, Israel.

**GOLTSOV Victor Alexeevich,** b. 13 March 1936, Omsk Siberia, Russia. Scientist; Professor. m. Lyudmila F Kollegova 1 son, 1 daughter. Education: Graduate, 1958, Ural Polytechnic Institute, USSR; DSc first degree, 1964; Associate Professor 1967; DSc second degree, 1977; Full Professor, 1974 Appointments: Engineer in Industry, 1958-60; Postgraduate Assistant Professor, Senior Scientific Worker, Ural Polytechnic Institute, 1960-73; Chairman of Physics Dept, Donetsk State Technical University, 1973-; Head of Scientific Research Laboratory of Interaction of Hydrogen with Metals and Hydrogen Technologies. Publications: 400 papers in professional journals. Memberships: Member several advisory ommittees; Ukrainian Physical Society; Academician: Engineering Academy of Ukraine; International Engineering Academy, Moscow; International Academy of Informatization, Moscow; Chairperson of Permanent Working International Scientific Committee on Hydrogen Treatment of Materials, Coral Gables, USA, Donetsk, Ukraine. Address: Donetsk State Technical University, 58 Artyom Street, 340000 Donetsk, Ukraine.

**GOLU Mihai,** b. 4 March 1934, Poienari-Gorj. Psychologist; University Professor. m. Elena Filip, 2 sons. Education: College or Primary School Teachers; Master's, 1958, Faculty of Psychology, Moscow; PhD, 1962, University Bucharest; Postdoctoral Advanced Studies, Carnegie-Mellon University, Pittsburg, 1973-74. Appointments: Assistant Professor, 958-62; Lecturer, 1962-82; Full Professor, 1982-, University of Bucharest, Dept of Psychology; Ministry of Education, 991-92; Ministry of Culture, 1992-93. Publications: 15 books; 50 papers in fields of psychology and neuropsychology. Honours: Medal Pablo Picaso, UNESCO, 1992; Medal Jan Amos Comenius, Cheh Academy of Science, 1992. Memberships: President, Association of Psychologists of Romania; President, National Society for Education; Member of Boards: Institut of Psychology an Idnstitut for the Study of the Totalitarism; Active member of the Academy of Scientists. Address: 22 Libertati Bloc 102, Scara 5 Apt 89, 72200 Bucharest, Romania.

**GOLUB Vladyslav,** b. 5 December 1940, Znamenka, Ukraine. Mechanical Engineer. m. Maria Barskaya. Education: Engineer, 1977; MSc, 1977; DSc, 1985; Prof, 1991. Appointments: Leading Designer, Machine Plant, Berdychev, Ukraine, 1965-68; Chief Designer, Design Institute, Kyiv, Ukraine, 1968-71; Senior Engineer, 1971-77, Senior Research Worker, 1977-84, Head of Lab, 1984-86, Head of Dept, 1986-, Institute of Mechanics, National Academy of Science, Kyiv, Ukraine. Publications: 3 books, 1983, 1989, 1994; 160 articles and patents, 1973-98. Honours: Jubilee Medal for Valiant Labour, 1970; Recipient, Academy Prize, 1989; State Prize of Ukraine in Field of Science and Technology, 1991. Memberships: Fellow, EUROMECH European Mechanics Society; German Society on Applied Math and Mechanics; National Ukrainian Committee on Theoretical and Applied Mechanics; Ukrainian Physics Society; New York Academy of Sciences. Address: Institute of Mechanics, 3 Nesterov Str, 252057 Kyiv, Ukraine.

**GOMES Celeste Regina,** b. 16 May 1960, Sao Paulo, Brazil. Writer; Editor. Education: BA, English Literature, Montclair State College, 1982. Appointments: Associate Editor, 16 Magazine, 1982-87, then Freelance Writer, until 1991; Executive Editor, Country Song Roundup, 1991-95; Managing Editor, Travel Weekly Supplements, 1995-. Memberships: Country Music Association, 1988-; Academy of Country Music, 1991-. Address: Travel Weekly Supplements, 500 Plaza Drive, Secaucus, NJ 07094-3626, USA.

**GOMEZ DE MIER Vicente,** b. 11 September 1933, Santa Maria de Redondo, Spain. Professor. Education: Diplomado, Gestion Financiera, Madrid, 1980; Master, Direccion de Empresas, Barcelona, 1986; Licenciado, Ciencias Fisicas, Madrid, 1964; Doctor, Teologia Moral, Madrid, 1994. Career: Professor, Researcher, Manager, Education Centres at El Escorial. Publications include: Cien años de reformismo (1875-1975), 1976; De la tolerancia a la libertad religiosa, 1997; Numerous articles in professional journals. Memberships: Real Sociedad Espanola de Fisica; European Society for Catholic Theology; Colegio de Doctores y Licenciados; Asociacion para el Progreso de la Educacion. Address: Real

Monasterio, 28200 S L El Escorial, Spain.

**GONG Fangzhen,** b. 2 December 1923, Shanghai, China. Social Scientist. m. Miss Yang, 1 son. Education: BA, 1946. Appointments: Consultant, 1991, Research Fellow, Shanghai Academy of Social Sciences, 1992. Publications: Wisdom of Chinese Culture, 1992; Wisdom of Byzantine, 1994. Honour: Award of Shanghai, History of the Zoroastrianism. Memberships: Chinese Society of Sino-Foreign Relations; Shanghai Society of Religions. Address: Institute of Religion Course, Shanghai Academy of Social Science, 622-7 Huaihai Road M, Shanghai 200041, China.

**GONG Pixiang,** b. 13 January 1955, Huaiying, Jiangsu, China. Jurist. m. Liu Fenling, 1 daughter. Education: LLB, Nanjing Normal University, 1982; SJD, School of Law, Renmin University of China, 1997. Career: Professor of Law, 1992; President, Nanjing Normal University, 1996. Publications include: The Course of the Modernization of Legal System in China, 1991; Karl Marx's Thought on Philosophical Jurisprudence, 1992; The Philosophy of Law and the Modernisation of Legal System, 1998. Honours: 2nd Prize, Research of Social Science, Jiangsu University; Winner, National Special Allowance, State Council, China, 1992; Chinese Outstanding Young Jurist, China Law Society, 1995; Outstanding Middle-Aged amd Young Expert, State Council, China, 1997. Memberships: Director, China Law Society; Vice President, Jurisprudence Association of China; Vice President, Jurispurdence and Constitutional Science Research Association, Jiangsu; Executive President, Chinese Society of Law History. Address: Nanjing Normal University, 122 Ninghai Road, 210097 Nanjing, China.

**GONZALEZ-BOGEN Americo,** b. 3 July 1927, Porlamar, Margarita Island, Venezuela. University Professor; Researcher. Education: MD, 1953, Central University of Venezuela; Specialist in Surgery, 1956; Doctor of Medical Sciences, 1958, UCV; Postgraduate studies, several universities in Europe and Japan; Studied Philosophy. Appointments: Professor, 1958, Professor Titular, 1958-83, Central University of Venezuela; Surgeon, Hospital Vargas, Caracas, 1956-78; Professor in Clinical and Therapeutic Surgery, UCV, 1958-78; President and Researcher, International Seminar the Respiratory Pulse, 1978-, private research, scientific interpretation of the respiratory function, with the lung as an active viscera, the visceral effector of the vagus-sympathetic nerve. Publications: Author 3 books; Editor, International Seminar, The Respiratory Pulse, scientific review, 1992, 1993. Memberships: International Seminar The Respiratory Pulse, President; New York Academy of Sciences; Medical Federation of Venezuela. Address: International Seminar, The Respiratory Pulse, Av Universitaria Edif Caribana At 43, Valle Abajo, Caracas 1040, Venezuela.

**GOOCH Nancy Jane,** b. 19 December 1941, Ann Arbor, Michigan, USA. Mortgage Originator. Education: BA, 1963, Western Michigan University; MA, 1968, Eastern Michigan University. Appointments: Real Estate Administrator, Chinelly Real Estate, Florida, 1980-86; Mortgage Originator, Emac Mortgage, Ann Arbor, Michigan, 1987-98. Publications: Past Editor, ASHAM magazine; Representative, Saddle & Bridle Magazine. Membership: American Saddlebred Association of Michigan, past Board of Directors. Address: BMAC, 325 E Eisenhower Parkway, Ann Arbor, MI 48108-3355, USA

**GOODENOUGH Belinda Jane,** b. 13 May 1964, Kidderminster, England. Psychologist. m. Mitchell Landrigan, 1 daughter. Education: BA Honours, Class I, Psychology, 1988; PhD, Psychology, 1992; Registered Psychologist, New South

Wales. Appointments: Associate Lecturer, 1988-92, Senior Research Assistant, 1992-94, Lecturer, 1995-, University of New South Wales, Australia; Research Officer, 1994-98, Hospital Scientist, 1999-, Sydney Children's Hospital; Consultant Research Psychologist, University of Technology, Sydney, 1998-. Publications include: Book chapters and articles in professional journals. Honours: Australian Postgraduate Research Award, 1988-92; Overseas Trust Award, 1996; National Health and Medical Research Council Grant, 1997-98; Clinical Initiatives Award, 1999. Memberships: International Association for Study of Pain; Australian Pain Society; Australian Psychological Society; International Association for Study of Humour. Address: 485 Gardeners Road, Rosebery, NSW 2018, Australia.

**GOODMAN Steven Roy,** b. 12 August 1963, New York, USA. Educational Consultant, Attorney. Education: AB, Cum Laude, Duke University, 1985; MS, Education, University of Pennsylvania, 1989; JD, University of Southern California, 1989; Certificate, Hague Academy of International Law, 1994. Appointments: Faculty Member, The Wharton School; Executive Director, College Admissions Institute of America; Independent Admissions Consultant, 1986-. Honours: US Speaker, United States Information Service, Liberia; Chairman, Philadelphia Bar Association, International Law Committee; Election Observer, South Africa. Memberships: District of Columbia Bar; Philadelphia Committee on Foreign Relations. Address: Tilden Gardens 502, 3020 Tilden Street NW, Washington, DC 20008-3081, USA.

**GOONERATNE Malini Yasmine,** b. 22 December 1935, Colombo, Sri Lanka. University Professor of English Literature. m. Brendon Gooneratne, 1 son, 1 daughter. Education: D Litt, Macquarie; PhD, Cambridge; BA Hons, Ceylon. Appointments: Visiting Professor, Edith Cowan University, WA, 1991; Research Fellow, Literary Criterion Centre, Dhvanyaloka Mysore, India, 1990; Foundation Director, Post-Colonial Literatures and Languages Research Centre, Macquarie University, 1988-93; Associate Professor English, 1976, Senior Lecturer, 1972, University Ceylon, 1965; External Adviser, Department of English, University of the South Pacific, 1993; Editorial Consultant, Westerly, University of West Australia, 1993; National Coordinator, Commonwealth Visiting Fellow, 1989; Vice Chair, Commonwealth Section, International Association of University Professors of English Triennial Conference, 1989; Convener, New and Post-Colonial Literature Section, Australasian Universities Language and Literature Association; Personal Chair in English Literature. Publications: Poetry; 9 books of non-fiction; 2 novels. Honours: Rockefeller Foundation Fellow, 1995; External Adviser to Department of English, University of South Pacific, 1995; National Committee for Review of Australian Honours and Awards, 1994; Edith Cowan University Visiting Professorial Fellow, 1991, University Michigan, 1991; Eleanor Dark Foundation Writing Fellow, 1991; Order of Australia for distinguished service to literature and education 1990; and others. Memberships: Patron, Jane Austen Society of Australia; VP, Federation Internationale des Langues et Litteratures Modernes; Order of Australia Association; Australian Society of Authors; Asia Society; and others. Address: Macquarie University Department of English Linguistics, Humanities Division, N Ryde, NSW 2109, Australia.

**GOPAL Lallanji,** b. 15 June 1934, Allahabad. Professor. m. Krishna Kanti Gopal, 5 sons. Education: BA, 1951; MA, 1953; DPhil, Allahabad, 1958; PhD, London, 1962; Visharad, 1948; Dipl in French, 1958. Appointments: Lecturer, Allahabad Varsity; Reader, Banaras Hindu University; Sayajirao Gaekwad Professor of Indian Culture and Civilisation, BHU; Head, Department of Indian Philosophy and Religion, BHU; Director,

Centre of Advanced Study in Philosophy; Professor and Head Department of AIHC and Archaeology, BHU; Convenor, Purana Research Committee, BHU; Coordinator SAP in AIHC and Archaeology, BHU; Dean, Faculty of Arts, BHU; Rector and Acting Vice Chancellor, BHU; Editorial Fellow, PHISPC. Publications: 25 books; Editor 25 books; 250 articles. Honours: British Council Scholarship, 1960-61; ICHR Senior Fellowship, 1994-96; Govt of India Humanities Research Scholarship, 1954-56; UGC National Lecturer, 1977, 1987; Chakravikrama Gold Medal, 1986; Honorary Vidyachakravarti, 1981; Honorary Vidyavachaspati, 1996. Memberships: Nominated member: EC Jamia Milia Islamia; EC BHU; Academic Council Hyderabad University; Academic Council Aligarh Muslim University; FRASc, London; FNSI; Chairman, UGC History Panel; Chairman, Secretary, Treasurer and President NSI; President (Ancient History), Indian History Congress; General President, Panjab History Congress; President Indian History and Culture Society; Secretary (Historical Archaeology) Archaeology Society of India; Secretary Indian History and Culture Society; Nominated member: ICHR; IHRC; Rastrabhasha Parishad; Member EC of ESI. Address: Guurdham Colony, Varanasi UP, India.

**GOPYCH Petro Mykhaylovych,** b. 17 February 1947, Komarivtsi, Ukraine. Educator; Scientist. m. Tabanova Raisa, 2 sons. Education: MSc Physics, 1971; PhD Physics and Mathematicss, 1974; DrSc Physics and Mathematics, 1992, Kharkiv State University. Appointments: Postgraduate, KhSU and Joint Institute for Nuclear Research, Dubna, Russia, 1971-74; Senior Researcher, 1974-79; Senior Lecturer, 1979-80; Associate Professor, 1980-90, KhSU; Spinal Trauma, 1990; Leading Researcher, KhSU, 1992-. Publications: 130 publications including textbook, Nuclear Spectroscopy, Kharkov, 1980. Honour: First Class Kharkiv State University Prize for the Best Lecturer, 1989. Memberships: Ukrainian Nuclear Society, 1996; New York Academy Sciences, 1995. Address: 27 Pushkin Street, PO Pokotilovka, Kharkiv 312140, Ukraine.

**GORANOVA Svetla,** b. 20 July 1946, Bulgaria. Physician. m. Parven, 1 son, 1 daughter. Education: Medical Academy, 1971; PhD, 1977. Appointments: Chief Assistant, Pediatrition, University of Hospital of Pediatrics; Head of Department for Diabetic Children. Publications: 35 Publications. Memberships: JSPAD; EASD. Address: Bankja Faculty Pediatric Hospital, Department for Diabetes Children, Sheinovo Strasse 8, Bankja, 1720 Bulgaria.

**GORBAN Alexander,** b. 19 April 1952, Omsk, USSR. Full Professor in Modelling and Simulation. m. 4 children. Education: Novosibirsk Special School for Physics and Mathematics, 1965-67; Novosibirsk State University, 1967-70; Omsk Pedagogical Institute, 1971-73; Candidate of Physics and Math, Kuibyshev State University and Pedagogical Institute, 1980; Doctor of Physics and Math, Krasnoyarsk Institute of Biophysics, 1990. Appointments: Engineer, Omsk Railway Engineering Institute, Research Division, 1973-76; Junior Researcher, Omsk State University, Laboratory of Kinetics, 1976; Junior Researcher, Tomsk Polytechnic Institute, Laboratory of Kinetics, 1977; Engineer, Institute of Theoretical and Applied Mechanics, USSR Academy of Sciences, Siberian Branch, Novosibirsk, 1978; Engineer, Institute of Catalysis, USSR Academy of Sciences, Siberian Branch, Novosibirsk, 1977-78; Junior Researcher, 1978-1983, Senior Researcher, 1983-89, Head of the Nonequilibrium Systems Laboratory,1989-95, Deputy Director and Head of the Computer Sciences Department, 1995-, Computing Center, USSR (Russian) Academy of Sciences, Siberian Branch. Publications include: Scattering Rates Versus Moments:

ternative Grad Equations, 1996; Short-Wave Limit of ydrodynamics: A Soluble Example, 1996; Relaxational ajectories: Global Approximations, 1996; On Completeness the Class of Functions Computable by Neural Networks, 996; High Order Orthogonal Tensor Networks: Information apacity and Reliability, 1997; Back-Propagation of Accuracy, 97; Information Content of Nucleotid Sequences and Their agments, 1997. Memberships: Full Member, Russian sychological Association, 1989; Active Member, International formatization Academy, 1994; American Society of echanical Engineers, 1997. Address: Academgorodok, omputing Center, Krasnoyarsk 660036, Russia.

**GORBATENKO Igor,** b. 14 August 1953, Kherson, Ukraine. otechnologist. div, 1 son, 2 daughters. Education: Kherson ate Agricultural Institute, 1970-75; Postgraduate, Institute of olecular Biology and Genetics, 1975-78; PhD, 1979; DSc, 92. Appointments: Junior Researcher, Institute of Molecular ology and Genetics, Kyiv, 1975-81; Senior Researcher, stitute of Irrigated Farms, Kherson, 1981-85; Head, Kherson epartment, Institute of Agricultural Biotechnology, 1985-98. ublications include: Handbook of Genetics of Agricultural nimals, 1997. Memberships: New York Academy of Sciences. ddress: Starostina St 1 Ap 30, 325024 Kherson, Ukraine.

**GORDIETS Boris,** b. 3 September 1941, Chelabinsk, ussia. Scientist; Physicist. m. Valentina Gordiets, 1 son. ducation: Graduated, Moscow Physical-Technical Institute, 65, Candidate of Sciences, PhD equivalent, 1968; Doctor of ciences, Research Professor equivalent, 1982. Appointments: ading Scientist, Lebedev Institute of Physics, Russian cademy of Sciences, 1986-; Invited Professor, Instituto uperior Technico, Lisbon, Portugal, 1993-. Publications: 2 ientific books; 146 scientific publications in various scientific urnals and books. Address: Instituto Superior Technico, Ave ovisco Pais, 1096 Lisbon, Portugal.

**GORDON Irwin Glenn (Yashad),** b. 7 December 1965, ooklyn, New York, USA. Genealogist; Archivist; Stand-up omedian. Education: BA, Judaic Studies, Brooklyn College, 89; MLS, Information and Library Science, Pratt Institute, 93. Appointments: Secretary, SEEK Study Organization, ooklyn College, 1987; Candidate, Vice President, Abe Stark llel House, Brooklyn College, 1987; Candidate, Board of rectors, Amalgamated Warbasse Houses, Brooklyn, 1993-96; chival Consultant, US Trust Co, New York, 1994-95; bstitute Teacher, Public School 90, Brooklyn, 1996; Project enealogist, Bureau of Missing Heirs, Ceres, California, 1996; oject Archivist, Equitable Life Assurance Society, New York, 96-97; Stand-up Comedian, New York Comedy Club, 1997-; ecording Secretary, Chmielniker Sick and Benevolent Society Poland, Workmen's Circle, New York, 1999-. Publications: ticles: Observations/Tatzpiyos, editorial column, Hatikvh wspaper, 1988-89; Review Contributor, National enealogical Society Quarterly, Arlington, Virginia, 1997-98; twork: Tevas No'ach, 1982; Member, 1988; Chai, 1988; chor, 1989; Har Sinai, 1989; BiVrachas Chanukah!, 1991, ef-Tidom, 1992; Tikvah, 1993. Honour: Beta Phi Mu, Theta apter, 1994. Memberships: Co-Founder, Editor-in-Chief and itor Emeritus, Hatikvah newspaper, 1987-89; President, hool of Information and Library Science Study Association, 92-93. Address: 445 Neptune Avenue, Apt 17-B, Brooklyn, Y 11224-4516, USA.

**GORDON Marjorie,** b. 28 July, New York, New York, USA. usician. m. Nathan Gordon, 1 son, 1 daughter. Education: A, cum laude, Hunter College. Career: Professor, Voice, uquesne University, 1957-59, Wayne State University, 61-91, National Music Camp, Interlochen, 1963-65,

Meadowbrook School of Music, 1966-71, University of Michigan, 1970, Michigan State University, 1971; Soloist, Teacher, American University Wolf Trap Program, Washington, 1973; Special Education Consultant, Detroit Grand Opera Association; Adjunct Professor, Oakland Community College. Leading Roles: New York Philharmonic Symphony Soloist, 1950; New York City Opera debut 1955. Principal Roles: Chautauqua Opera Company, 12 years; Soloist with major orchestras. Concerts Abroad: Europe, Israel; Summer stock opera engagements, USA. Creative Works: Radio; Television; Recitals in USA, Greece, Europe, Canada, Israel. Memberships: AFTRA; Florida Music Teachers Association; Michigan Music Teachers Association; American Guild of Music Artists; Music Teachers National Association; National Opera Association; National Association of Teachers of Singing; International Platform Association; Metropolitan Opera Guild; Boca Raton Music Study Club; Broward County Music Club; Central Opera Service. Address: 24 Del Rio Boulevard, Boca Raton, FL33432-4734, USA.

**GORDON Nathan L,** b. 8 February 1915, New York, New York, USA. Violist (Musician). m. Marjorie Gordon (Soprano), 1 son, 1 daughter. Education: Violin Scholarship, Cleveland Institute of Music, 1927; Violin Scholarship, Cleveland Settlement School, 1930; State and National High School Violin Championship, 1931; Double Fellowship, Violin and Viola, Juilliard School, 1932-36. Appointments: Principal and Solo Viola, Chautauqua Symphony, 1936-60; Metropolitan Opera Orchestra, 1936-37; Principal and Solo Violist, Pittsburgh Symphony, 1937-39; First Desk Viola, NBC Symphony with Toscanini, 1939-54; Solo Debut, Town Hall, New York City, 1944; First Viola, Symphony of the Air, 1954-55; Principal and Solo Viola, Pittsburgh Symphony, 1955-57; Principal and Solo Violist, Detroit Symphony, 1957-85; Soloist: Greece, Israel, U.S.A., Canada, etc. Conducting: Founder and Conductor, Dearborn Symphony, 1960-85; Conductor, Detroit Women's Symphony, 1963-73; Guest Conductor, Toledo Symphony and others; Chamber Music in Schools: Founder and Violist, Gateway to Music, Pittsburgh, 1955-58; Excursions in Music, Detroit, 1960-80; Regional Director, Upward Bound, Michigan, 1974-77; Co-Director, Kaleidoscope Series, Michigan, 5 years; Guest Artist, Budapest String Quartet; Gordon-Cole String Trio, 1995-. Teacher: Dalcroze School, New York, New York; Interlochen, Michigan; Academy of the Arts, Michigan; Duquesne University, Pittsburgh, Pennsylvania; Carnegie Institute, Pittsburgh, Pennsylvania; University of Michigan, Ann Arbor, Michigan; Oakland University at Meadowbrook, Michigan; Wayne State University, Detroit, Michigan; Indiana University, Bloomington, Indiana; University of Bowling Green, Ohio. Honours: Dearborn City Citation, 1987; Artist-Teacher of the Year, American String Teachers Association, 1993. Memberships: American Federation of Musicians; The Bohemians, New York City; American Viola Society; New York Viola Society; Detroit Musicians League; Chamber Music America; Mu Phi Epsilon (Honorary); Music Teachers National Association (Certified); Broward County Music Teachers Association; Boca Raton Music Teachers Association; Michigan Council for the Arts; Palm Beach County Arts Council; American String Teachers Association. Address: 24 Del Rio Boulevard, Baco Raton, Florida, USA.

**GOREV Nikolai Borisovich,** b. 24 March 1957, Dnepropetrovsk, Ukraine. Physicist. m. Inna F Kodzhespirova, 1 son. Education: MSc, Dnepropetrovsk State University, Dnepropetrovsk, Ukraine, 1980; PhD, Kharkov State University, Kharkov, Ukraine, 1989. Appointments: Engineer, 1980-86, Junior Researcher, 1986-89, Researcher, 1989-91, Senior Researcher, 1991-, Institute of Technical Mechanics, Dnepropetrovsk, Ukraine. Publications: 45 publications.

Honour: Badge, Inventor of the USSR, 1990. Membership: Ukrainian Physical Society, 1992-. Address: 10-2 Pravda Ave Apt 63, Dnepropetrovsk, 320081 Ukraine.

**GOROKHOV Igor M,** b. 6 April 1932, Leningrad, USSR. Isotope Geochemist. m. Irina A Ostrovskaya, 1 daughter. Education: Certificate as Research Chemist, with honours, Leningrad State University, 1954; PhD, Chemical Sciences, Leningrad Technological Institute, 1965; DrSc, Geological and Mineralogical Sciences, Institute of Geochemistry, Kiev, Ukraine, 1981. Appointments: Junior Research Fellow, V G Khlopin Radium Institute, Leningrad, 1954-61; From Junior Research Fellow to Principal Research Fellow, Institute of Precambrian Geology and Geochronology, Russian Academy of Sciences, St Petersburg, 1961-. Publications: Graphical Methods of Isotope Geology, co-author, 1974; Rubidium-Strontium Method of Isotope Geochronology, author, 1985; Contributor, over 100 articles to scientific publications. Honours: Medals for Scientific Service, Czech Geological Survey, Prague, 1986, Slovakia Geological Survey, Bratislava, 1986; Grantee, Presidium, Russian Academy of Sciences, Moscow, 1994, 1997. Memberships: Board, Council on Isotope Geology and Geochronology, Moscow, 1973-91; Commission on the Upper Precambrian, Moscow, 1988-; Editorial Board, Chemical Geology, Amsterdam, Netherlands, 1987-; Elected, New York Academy of Sciences, 1995. Address: Institute of Precambrian Geology and Geochronology, Russian Academy of Sciences, nab Makarova 2, St Petersburg 199034, Russia.

**GORPINTCHENKO Tatjana,** b. 11 July 1946, Saransk City. Centre Director. m. Victor Gorpintchenko, 1 son. Education: Plant Biochemistry, 1969, Mordovinian State University; PhD, 1972, DSc, 1996, Moscow State Technological Institute of Food Industry. Appointments: Institute of Biochemistry, Academy of Science of USSR, 1972-77; Director, Russian Centre for Quality Control of Plant Varieties, 1977-. Publications: Over 70 scientific papers. Honours: Order of People Friendship, State Award, 1988; Title of Honoured Agricultural Worker of Russian Federation, 1996; Medal, 850 anniversary of Moscow, State Award, 1997. Memberships: National Delegate of Russia, International Association for Cereal Science and Technology; ICC Executive Committee member. Address: Russian Centre for Quality Control of Plant Varieties, 6 Listvenichnaja allee, Moscow 127550, Russia.

**GORSKY Michael,** b. 16 May 1950, Daugavpils, Latvia. Teacher. m. Nina Gorska, 1 son, 1 daughter. Education: Riga Technical University, 1967-69; Daugavpils Pedagogical University, 1969-73. Appointments: Chemistry Teacher, Iecava Secondary School, 1972-; Head, Bauska Regional Chemistry Teachers Methodological Council, 1976-; Chief, Program of Advanced Chemistry Teaching, Iecava Secondary School, 1978-; Member, Chemistry Teaching Methodological Council, Ministry of Education, Latvia, 1979-89; Lecturer, Manager, Programs of Raising the Level of Teachers Skills, Latvia, Russia, Estonia, 1982-; Member, Editorial Board, Teachers' Newspaper, 1987-89; Member, Scientific Methodological Council of Chemistry Teaching, Ministry of Education, USSR, 1987-91; Member of Council, Ministry of Education, Latvia, 1988-90; Head, Chemistry Teaching Methodological Council, Ministry of Education, Latvia, 1989-90; Member, Chemistry Council Center for Curriculum Development and Examinations, Latvia, 1991-; Member, Scientific Council, Institute of Education Development, Latvia, 1993-94; Methodologist, Riga Natural School, 1997. Publications: 45 research and methodological works; 10 books. Honours: Luda Berzina Prize Laureate, 1996; Valerija Seiles' Prize Laureate, 1997. Memberships: Vice President, Latvian Chemistry Teachers Association; Latvian

Association of History of Science. Address: Ozolu Street 9-9 Iecava, LV 3913, Latvia.

**GOSBEE Rebecca Ann,** b. 22 February 1951 Charlottetown. Nurse. Education: BN, Nursing, Dal housi University, 1980; RN, prince Edward Island School of Nursing 1973 ; MSc N, Nursing, University of Toronto, 1984 Appointments: Clincal Nurse Specialist, Charlottetown PE 1986-90; Instructor, University of New Brunswick Distan Education, 1987-; Executive Director, Association of Nurses 1990-. Publications: Numerous Publications for ANPE Memberships: Canadian Nurses Association; Canadian Nurse Protective Society; Canadian Nurse Specaialist Interest Group Canadian Nurses Respiratory Group; Salvation Army, Re Sheild Appeal Campaign. Address: Assoc of Nurses od PI Island, 17 Pownal St, Charlottetown PE, Canada, C1A 3V7.

**GOSLIN Gerald Hugh,** b. 7 January 1947, Detroit, Michigar USA. Concert Pianist. Education: Music, Cass Technical Hig School; Wayne State University. Appointments: Judge Leontyne Price Vocal Arts Competition, 12 Years; Judge, Vere Opera Association Vocal Competition, 2 Years; Host, Pian Hour, WHND; Numerour Concerts. Honours: Dictionary c International Biography, International Biographical Centre Order of International Fellowship; 2000 Outstanding People c the 20th Century; International Book of Honour; Man of th Yeaf, American Biographical Institute; Annual Associate, AB 2000 Millennium Medal of Honours. Memberships: America Choral Directors Association; American GUild of Organists Presbyterian Association of Musicians; Detroit Federation c Musicians. Address: 19782 Olympia, Redford, MI 84240-1334 USA.

**GOSWAMI Atanu Bihari,** b. 14 May 1931, Calcutta, India Consulting Hydrogeologist; Adviser, Water Resources Education: BSc, Honours, Geology, 1951, MSc, Geology, 1953 Certifice and Diploma, French, 1970-71, Calcutta University PhD, Jadavpur University, 1995. Career: Geological Assistan 1954-55; Assistant Geologist, 1955-60; Geologist (Junior 1960-66; Geologist (Senior), 1966-80; Director, Geologica Survey of India, 1980-89; Technical Consultant, "Project Life' Rotary International, 1989-90; Hydrogeologist Consultan KFW-GKW, Germany, 1991-93; Senior Research Scientis School of Water Resources Engineering, Jadavpur University 1990-92, 1998-; Consulting Hydrogeologist, Water Resource Management Adviser, Various Water Assessments an Management Projects, India, 1990-. Publications: 3 books o the water resources of different parts of India; Over 60 pape in national and international professional journals. Honou Award, Original Contributions in Coastal Hydrology, MMC 1968. Memberships: Indian Science Congress Associatio Alumni Association, Presidency College, Calcutta; Minin Geological and Metallurgical Institute of India; Mohan Baga Athletic Club, Calcutta; Founder Member, Association of India Geohydrologists and Indian Society of Earth Science International Study Group Member on Rapid Geomorphologic Hazards, IGU, 1989-; Several International Working Group UNESCO, 1982-89. Address: 89/2 Maharani Indria Devi Roa Pallisree, Calcutta 700060, India.

**GOSWAMI Dinesh Chandra,** b. 2 January 1940, Bikane India. Musician, Teacher. m. Urmila, 1 son, 2 daughter Education: Master of Music, 1967; Diploma, Instrument Music, 1969; LLB, 1974; MA, Hindi, 1976. Appointment Government Service, 1959-97; Legal Draftsman, 1985-9 Retired, 1997. Publications: Articles on Music in leadir magazines. Honours: Sangeet Rasajna. Memberships: Al Jury. Address: 2-688 Malaviya Nagar, Jaipur, India.

**GOSWAMI Vagishkumar V,** b. 4 June 1965, Baroda. Religious Head. m. Alka, 2 sons. Education: Master of Arts; Doctorate in Naturopaty. Appointments: Vice President, Eye Camps, Nairobi, 1995; President, Vishwakathakar Samelan, 996; Chairman, Medical Doctors Seminar, 1997; Vice Chancellor, Vallabh Vidyapith, Baroda, 1998. Publications: Sanskrit; Gujarati; Gokul Tahukya Mor; Shri Dwarkadhish Prabhu Pragatya Varta; Bhartiya Sankriti Braj-Bhasha; Rashtriya Aikya and Maha Prabhu Vallabh. Honours: Shikhar Sanman and Gold Medal, 1988; Prashasti Patra By Uttar Bharat Sanakritik Sangh, 1988; Vrajsahitya Ratnakar, 1990; Manav Samajratna, 1990; Sahitya Varidhi, 1990-91; Harit Rishi Puraskar, 1992; Abhinandan, 1996; Prashasti Patra, 1996; Vidhya Vachaspati, 1997. Memberships: Gujarat Hindi Academy; Vakpati Foundation; Vallabh Vidyapith; Encyclopedia of Pushtimarg; Chief Editor Shree Vallabhelite Forum; Quaterly Hindi Magazine Pushti Path. Address: Bethak Mandir, Kevda Baug, Madan Zampa Road, Baroda - 390 001, Gujarat, India.

**GOTO Shohachiro,** b. 5 January 1933, Nobeoka, Miyazaki, Japan. Professor of Economics. m. Takako, 3 daughters, Kaeko, Chizuko, Mikiko. Education: Bachelors Degree of Economics, Japan, 1961; Master of Economics, Graduate School, 1963; Degree of Economics, Meiji University, 1976. Appointments: Assistant, Meiji University, Japan, 1963-67; Lecturer, 1967-90; Assistant Professor, 1970-75; Professor, 1975-. Visiting Scholar, UCLA, USA, 1979-80. Publications: Fundamental Theory of Economic Policy, 1974; Analysis of Productivity and Economic Policy, 1993; <I-S> Analysis and Economic Policy, 1993; A Study in the Principles of Economic Policy, 1999. Memberships: Japan Economic Policy Association. Address: 2-6-29 Nishi Lashiwadai, Kashiwa 277-0886, Chiba, Japan.

**GOTTSCHALL Carlos Antonio Mascia,** b. 18 April 1939, Santa Maria, Rio Grande do Sul, Brazil. Medical Doctor; Researcher. m. Elisabete Maria Santos Gottschall, 2 sons, 1 daughter. Education: MD, 1963, Master's degree in Pneumology, 1975, PhD in Cardiology, 1977, Federal University of Rio Grande do Sul, Brazil. Appointments: Head of Research University, 1970-74, Director, Laboratory of Haemodynamics and Interventional Cardiology, 19820, Professor of Cardiology, Postgraduate Medical School, 1988-, Director, Institute of Cardiology, 1993-, Porto Alegre, Rio Grande do Sul; Consultant, Federal Agency for Postgraduate Education, National Council of Science and Technology Development, Brasilia, 1993-. Publications: Cardiac Function: From Normality to Failure, 1995; 103 articles in professional and general journals including Journal of Invasive Cardiology and more than 400 medical congress papers, 1964-99. Honours: Merit Award, Brazilian Society of Cardiology, 1985; Award for for 30 years Coronariography in Brazil, 1996. Memberships: Fellow, Brazilian Society of Cardiology, 1964-; Brazilian Society of Hemodynamics and Interventional Cardiology, Founder, President, 1981-82; Society for Cardiac Angiography and Interventions, USA, 1991-; International Andreas Gruntzig Society, USA, 1993-; Latin American Society for Interventional Cardiology, Founder, 1995. Address: Rua Prof Ulisses Cabral 1100, CEP 91330-520, Porto Alegre, RS, Brazil.

**GOULD Richard Martin,** b. 19 August 1971, Auburn, Cayuaga County, New York State. Sales Marketing Consultant. Education: JD, 1966; AB, 1963, Ohio Northern University; University of Arizona, 1966; University of Buffalo, 1968. Appointments: Gould & Associates, Sales Marketing Consultant. Memberships: International Platform Association; Alpha Epsilon Pi; Phi Alpha Delta; Phi Beta Lambda. Address:

Gould & Associates, PO 6701, 128 La Perdiz Ct, San Rafael, CA 94903 3541, USA.

**GRABOVAC Ivo,** b. 28 August 1934, Split, Croatia. Law Educator. m. Milojka, 1 son, 1 daughter. Education: Faculty of Law, Zagreb, 1960; LLM, 1965; LLD, 1967. Appointments: Clerk, Harbourmasters Office, Split, 1955-61; Assistant, Faculty of Law, Split, Assistant Professor, 1965-71, Associate Professor, 1971-76, Professor, 1971-, Dean, 1978-80, 1994-96. Publications: 21 books; 650 scientific articles in professional journals. Honours: State Award of Croatia for Scientific Achievements, 1988; Award, City of Split, 1991; Award, County of Split and Dalmatia, 1996. Memberships: Croatia Maritime Law Association; International Maritime Committee; Croatian Academy of Science & Art. Address: Odeska 14, 21000 Split, Dalmatia, Croatia.

**GRAFF Darrell Jay,** b. 8 September 1936, Cedar City, Utah, USA. Professor. m. Joyce Richens, 1 son, 3 daughters. Education: AA, DixieCollege, 1956; BS, 1958, MS, 1960, Utah State University; PhD, University of California, Los Angeles, 1963. Appointments: NIH Postdoctoral Fellow, Rice University, 1964; NSF Postdoctoral Fellow, Rice University, 1965; Professor, Physiology, Weber State University, 1965-. Publications include: Intestinal Absorption of Metal Ions and Clelates, 1985; Human Physiology Laboratory Manual, 1998. Memberships: AAAS; AARP; ASP. Address: Weber State University, 3750 Harrison Boulevard, Ogden, UT 84408, USA.

**GRAHAM Christopher,** b. 28 January 1946, Dayton, Ohio, USA. Attorney; Lawyer. m. Marsha Carol Gum, 3 daughters. Education: Lawrenceville School, 1964; BS, Business Administration, 1968, JD, 1971, University of Missouri, Columbia; LLM, Taxation, Georgetown University, 1973. Appointments: Law Clerk, Missouri Supreme Court, 1971-72; Administrative Law Judge, State of Missouri, 1997-. Elected Offices: City Attorney, City of Jefferson, Missouri, 1977-81; Missouri House of Representatives, 1983-91. Memberships: Missouri, Florida and American Bar Association; Lions Club; Phi Gamma Delta; Colonel, US Army Reserves, 1972-. Address: 1204 Major Drive, Jefferson City, MO 65101-3660, USA.

**GRAHAM Lanier,** b. 6 March 1940, Oklahoma, USA. Art Historian; Curator; Educator. m. Gloria K Smith, 1 daughter. Education: BA, 1963; MA, 1966; PhD, 1968. Appointments: Curator, Museum of Modern Art, New York City, 1965-70, Fine Arts Museum of San Francisco, 1970-76, IAD, 1976-82, National Gallery of Australia, 1984-87, Norton Simon Museum, 1987-91; Lecturer, Art History, California State University, 1992-. Publications include: Leonardo Studies, 1961; Georgione Studies, 1964; Three Centuries of American Painting, 1971, 1977; French Art, 1973, 1975;Claude Monet, 1974; The Rainbow Book, 1975, 1979; The Spontaneous Gesture: Prints and Books of the Abstract Expressionism, 1987; Vincent Van Gogh, 1990; Marcel Duchamp and the Surrealist Tradition, 1991; Sacred Visions: World Art and Architecture, 1991 and 1992; Goddesses in Art, 1997. Memberships: Institute for Aesthetic Development; CAA; ICOM; World Print Council; Society of Architectural Historians; Society for Literature and Art.

**GRAHAM Lois C,** b. 20 March 1917, Denver, Colorado, USA. Eductor. m. Milton C Graham, 2 sons, 2 daughters. Education: BA, Ouachita Baptist University, Arkansas, 1939. Honour: Governor's Distinguished Service Award, 1989. Memberships: AAUW; Delta Kappa Gamma; Retired Public Employees of Nevada; Emergency Planning Committee. Address: PO Box 1543, Hawthorne, NV 89415, USA.

**GRAINGER Gareth,** b. 5 October 1950, Blue Mountains, NSW. Deputy Chairman; Author. m. 1 son. Education: BA, LLB, LLM, University of Sydney, 1974-86; LLM, first class honours, University of Technology, Sydney. Appointments: Solicitor, Private Practice, 1976-82; NSW Public Service, 1982-86; Assistant Secretary, Commonwealth Department of Primary Industry and Energy, 1986-89; General Manager, State Rail Authority, 1989-92; Head, Resources and Marketing, Special Broadcasting Service Company, 1992-93; Visiting Associate Professor, Bond School of Law, 1993. Publications: Australian Fisheries and the Administrative Appeals Tribunal, 1988; Gatt Disputes, 1989; Last Polynesian War Lord, 1992; Transport Volume Halsbury's Laws of Australia, 1996; Australian Constitutional Monarchy, 1994. Honours: British Foreign and Commonwealth Office Scholarship, 1988; International Order of Merit, 1994. Memberships: Chairman, National Plain English Speaking; President, Australia-Britain Society (NSW); President, English Speaking Union (NSW); Founding Counsellor, Australia for Constitutional Monarchy; Fellow, International Biographical Association. Address: 74 Elizabeth Bay Road, Elizabeth Bay, New South Wales 2011, australia.

**GRAMS Betty Jane,** b. 13 March 1926, Lead, South Dakota, USA. Minister; Educator; Writer. m. Monroe D Grams, 1 son, 2 daughters. Education: BA, North Central Bible College, 1948, 1963; Machails Music School; Latin America Advanced Theological Training, 1982. Appointments: Minister to Latin America, Bolivia, Argentina; Teacher, Director of choirs and music, Bolivia; Director, Women's Ministry, 5 countries, SA. Publications: Ministrando con Musica; Mujeres Llenas de Gracia; Women of Grace; Families Can Be Happy; many articles. Memberships: Instituto de Superacion Ministerial; Missionary and Ordained Minister, Assemblies of God. Address: 6161 Manchester Ln, Davie, FL 33331-2970, USA.

**GRANT Linda Kay,** b. 24 May 1940, Peona, Illinois, USA. Journalist. div. 1 son. Education: BS, Northwestern University; Postgrad Studies, New School for Social Research and Tufts University. Appointments: Reporter, Researcher, Associate Editor, Senior Writer, Fortune Magazine, 1971-78, 1995-98; Staff Writer to Senior Writer, LA Times, 1978-84; Senior Business Correspondent, LA Times in NYC, 1991-93; Contributing Editor, LA Times Magazine, 1991-93; Senior Writer, US News and World Report, 1993-95. Publication: Author, Face of Hong Kong. Honours: Overseas Press Club Award for best reporting from abroad, 1967; Gerald Loeb Award for Distinguished Business and Financial Journalism, 1981, 1982. Membership: Women's Leadership Forum. Address: 271 Midland Avenue, Rye, NY 10580 3849, USA.

**GRANZOTTI Joao Antonio,** b. 14 May 1942, Franca, Brazil. Professsor. m. Clelia Agostini, 2 sons. Education: Medical Degree, 1968; Master, 1973; Doctor of Medicine, 1975. Appointments: Assistant Professor of Pediatrics, 1973; Associate Researcher, University of Ilinois, Chicago. Publications: Publications in Pediatric Cardiology. Honours: Diploma and Medal, Brazilian Academy of Art, Culture and History, 1992-93, 1997-98. Memberships: Brazilian Cardiology Society; Pediatrics Society. Address: Rua Guaranta, 356 Ribeirao Preto, E S Paulo, Zip 14040 190, Brazil.

**GRASZ Lynne Anne Morian,** b. 22 September 1943, Los Angeles, California, USA. Education: BS, University of Nebraska, 1966; Simmons College, Boston, Women's Management Program, 1982. Appointments include: CBS School of Management, 1980; President, CEO, Grasz Communications, New York City, 1990-93, 1997-; Ex Director, Broadcast Designers' Association, 1994-97; Ex Director, Promax International, Los Angeles, USA, 1989-90; Ex Director,

Television Information Office, New York City, 1985-89; Director, Communications, CBS, Broadcast Group, New York City, 1981-85. Publication: Aliteracy, BPME Promotion College Textbook. Honours: 2 Emmy's; National Headliner Award; Religion in Media Award; Golden Mike Award; BPME President's Award. Memberships: Promax; BDA International; National Broadcasting Society; AWRT. Address: Grasz Communications, 130 West 67th St Ste 25C, New York, NY 10023-5914, USA.

**GRAZIOLI Angelo,** b. 10 August 1955, Sondrio, Italy. Medical Doctor. m. Janneke, 2 sons. Education: MBChB, 1979; BTh Hons, 1990. Appointments: Internships, 1980-81; Residency, Loyola School of Medicine, Sexual Dysfunction Unit, Chicago, 1982; Family Practitioner, 1983-88; Trustee, Outdoor Adventures, 1988-93; Committee Member, George Whitefield College of Theology, 1989-98; AIDS Coordinating Committee, Dept National Health and Population Development, 1992-95; Consultant to Centre for Education Technology, Cape Town, 1992-93; Lecturer in Human Sexuality, Masters Psychology Programme, University Stellenbosch, 1992-94; Director, Sex Education and Dysfunction Unit of South Africa, 1988-; Italian Governments Consular and Maritime Medical Practitioner for Cape Town and Western Cape Region, 1983-; Consulting Editor various professional journals; Various offices within the Church of England in South Africa; Professional Sexological Counsellor, 1979-; Public speaker, 1979-. Publications: Book: A question of love - Answers to Questions on Homosexuality, 1998; Video: A Question of Love - Homosexuality, a Biblical Perspective, 1998; The Management of Common Medical Disorders - a Formulary for Students, 1978; 16 professional journal articles; 8 international congress papers; 3 radio and television productions. Honours: University of Cape Town: Crichton Prize for Undergraduate Research, 1978, J T Louw Prize for Obstetrics and Gynaecology, 1979. Memberships: SA Medical and Dental Council; SA Academy of Family Practice/Primary Care; BMA; American Association Sex Educators Counsellors and Therapists; Society for Scientific Study of Sex, USA; Association of Christian Counsellors in SA. Address: 9 Montrose Avenue, Claremont 7708, South Africa.

**GREBENNIKOV Andrey V,** b. 3 May 1956, Uzhgorod, USSR. Scientist. m. Galina V Grebennikova. Education: Engineer Degree, Moscow Institute of Technology, 1980; Doctor of Philosophy, Moscow Technical University of Communications and Informatics, 1991. Appointments: Engineer, 1980-83; Junior Research Assistant, 1983-88; Senior Research Assistant, Associate Professor, 1988-98. Publications: 45 articles in scientific journals. Membership: IEEE Microwave Theory and Techniques Society. Address: VLSI, Institute of Microelectronics, 11 Science Park Road, Singapore Science Park II, 117 685 Singapore.

**GREGOR Marlene Pierce,** b. 22 April 1932, Oak Park, Illinois, USA. Teacher, Science Consultant. m. Harold L, 2 sons, 1 daughter. Education: MS, Illinois State University, USA; BS, University of Illinois, USA. Appointments: Teacher, Wethersfield Comm Unit, 1953-54; Teacher, Prairie Central Schools, 1966-91; Retired; Consultant, Chair, School Outreach of Fell Arboretum, 1995-. Publications: Blue Ribbon Season, 1992. Honours: Honors Science Teacher, 1985-87; Teacher Excellence Award, 1989; Finalist, Presidential Award for Excellence in Science Teaching, 1991; Illinois Creative Nutrition Education Award, 1989. Memberships: Secretary, Science Teachers Association, 1989-91, 1991-93; Advisory Board Member, Center for Scientific Literacy, 1991-92. Address: 107 Market Street, Bloomington, IL 61701, USA.

**GREKOV Dimitar,** b. 22 January 1958, Belitza, Bulgaria. Associate Professor Dr. m. Stanka Grekova, 2 daughters. Education: MSc, 1984, PhD Sericulture, 1988, Agricultural University, Plovdiv, Bulgaria. Appointments: Assistant Professor, 1988-96, Associate Professor, 1996-, Agricultural University, Plovdiv. Publications: 65 scientific papers; 1 textbook and 1 manual, university teaching materials. Honour: Honorary Professor, Ukraine Academy of Science. Membership: Union of Bulgarian Researchers. Address: Higher Agricultural University, 12 Mendeleev Street, Plovdiv 4000, Bulgaria.

**GRENFELL Raymond F,** b. 23 November 1917, West Bridgwater, PA, USA. Physician. m. Maude Byrnes Chisholm, 4 sons. Education: BS. University of Pittsbugh, 1939; MD, 1941. Address: 190 Ridge Drive, Jackson, MS 39216, USA.

**GRIECO-TISO Pina,** b. 27 March 1954. Secondary School Teacher; Author. m. Alfredo Tiso, 17 January 1981, 3 sons. Education: English, French, Spanish, Psychology, 1973-75, DipEd, 1976, Monash University; Italian Language, Literature and Culture, Melbourne University, 1978-79. Appointments: Teacher: Springvale High, Paisley High, Werribee High, Karingal Secondary, Carwatha Secondary, Brighton Secondary, Dandenong High, Dandenong School of Foreign Languages, Princes Hill School of Foreign Languages, Bon Beach Secondary, Mordialloc-Chelsea Secondary College; Currently Teacher, English, French, Parkdale Secondary College; Runs street children's projects, East Bentleigh Clinic; Organiser, aerosol art competitions state and nation wide. Publications: Multi-lingual textbook for travellers, 1980; Young adult fiction: Blitz - a Bomber's Nightmare, 1991; Time Out, 1993; Sticks and Stones, 1998; Poetry and short stories in anthologies and magazines. Honours: FAW 1st and 2nd Regional Prizes for Short Stories and Poetry, 1987, 1988, 1989, 1990; Coolum Short Story and Poetry Prizes, 1989, 1990; Rockhampton Poetry Award, 1989. Memberships: ASA, 1991-; NBC, 1991-; FAW, 1991-; ALITRA, 1993. Address: 18 Daley Street, Bentleigh 3204, Victoria, Australia.

**GRIESSER Gerhard (Gerd),** b. 31 July 1918, Stuttgart. Professor Emeritus of Medical Informatics. m. Gisela Breuer. Education: Medical State Board Examination, 1942, Berlin; Promotion Dr med, 1942, University Tuebingen; Habilitation for General Surgery and Venia legendi in Surgery (Senior Lecturer), 1959, 1960; Additional study in Statistics and Mathematical Statistics, 1960, 1963, Faculty of Economy, University of Tuebingen; Extension of Venia legendi to Medical Statistics and Documentation, 1963. Appointments: include: Full Professor for Medical Statistics and Documentation, Head of Institute of Medical Statistics and Documentation, Christian Albrecht University of Kiel, 1964-79; Chairman, State Health Council of Schleswig-Holstein, 1968-92; Chairman, Schleswig-Holstein Cancer Society, 1968-87; Member of Faculty of Medical Academy of Luebeck, 1965-72; Lecturer in Health Care Systems Analysis and Hospital Organisation and Operations for Students of Informatics, 1977-94; President, Christian Albrecht University at Kiel, 1979-85; Professor Emeritus, 1986; Co-Founder of ITK Information Technology Kiel Ltd as Enterprise for Technology Transfer and Innovation in Computer Applications and for Designing and Planning Hospital Information and Communications Systems, 1986; Executive Manager ITK, 1986-91; Founding member, FIT Research Institute for Information Technology Kiel R.A, as a Non-Profit-Making Organisation, 1990; Free Lance Consultant for Hospitals on Information Systems, 1992. Publications: 7 books; Contributor to 11 books; 125 publications about surgical and cardio-surgical topics, and medical informatics. Honours: MIA Award for best publication in Medical Informatics of the

Year 1979; Cross of Merit, 1st degree, of the Order of Merit of Germany, 1981; Knights Cross, 1985; and others. Memberships: 13 scientific associations and 5 editorial boards. Address: Barstenkamp 51, D-24113 Molfsee, Germany.

**GRIGAS Jonas,** b. 10 April 1938, Lithuania. Physicist. m. Rita Morkunaite, 2 daughters. Education: MS, Physics, 1961, PhD, 1968, DSc, 1980, Vilnius University. Appointments: Engineer, Institute of Radiomeasurements, Vilnius, 1961-63; Assistant Professor, 1963-70, Head, Laboratory of Microwave Spectroscopy of Ferroelectrics, 1965-, Associate Professor, 1970-82, Professor, 1982-, Vilnius University. Publications: Microwave Dielectric Spectroscopy of Ferroelectrics and Related Materials, 1996; Over 150 papers in professional journals. Honours: Award, National Science and Technology, 1986; Meritorious Science Worker Award, 1996. Memberships include: Lithuanian Academy of Sciences. Address; B Sruogos 36-24, 2040 Vilnius, Lithuania.

**GRIJALVA-CHON Jose Manuel,** b. 13 November 1959, Hermosillo, Sonora, Mexico. Oceanologist. m. Reina Castro, 2 daughters. Education: BSc Oceanography, 1985, University Baja California, Mexico; MSc Marine Ecology, 1986, Dr Sc Marine Ecology, 1995, CICESE, Ensenada, BC, Mexico. Appointments: Professor, University of Sonora, 1986-. Memberships: Sea of Cortes Researchers Association, Mexico, Secretary 1997-99; Oceanologists Association, Mexico; Mexican Society Planktology. Address: Universidad de Sonora-Dictus, Rosales y Niños Héroes s/n, 83000 Hermosillo, Mexico.

**GRINALDI Polly,** b. 24 July 1932, Philadelphia, Pennsylvania, USA. Health Carer. m. John Grimaldi, 3 sons, 3 daughters. Education: Registered Nurse, Bryn Mawr College, 1950; BS, Biology, Washington College, 1953; Dietetics, University of Delaware, 1978. Appointments: Creator, The Right Way by Polly, first US Wellness franchise; Presenter, The Right Way by Polly weekly television show on Health, Diet and Exercise; Large patient practice. Publications: Author of 9 books and manuals on natural healing (complementary medicine). Honour: Outstanding Achievement in conquering Arthritis, nominated by her patients. Address: 416 New London Road, Newark, DE 19711-7010, USA.

**GRIMHOLT Unni,** b. 20 October 1960, Oslo, Norway. Researcher. 1 son. Education: MSc, 1988; PhD Immunogenetics, 1994. Publications: ongoing since 1993. Address: Norwegian College of Vet Medicine, PO Box 8146, Dept of Morphology, Oslo 0033, Norway.

**GRINDLEY Bruce Alan. b. 1 March 1948,** Woking, England. Estate Agent. 1 son, 1 daughter. Appointments: Brokerage Clerk, Lloyds Brokers, 1965-67; Clerk to Branch Manager, Abbey Life, London, 1967-86; Director, Sunway Properties, Tenerife, 1986-94; Director, Tenerife Property Shop, 1994-. Honours: Best International Estate Agent, 1996, 1997; Gold Award, Best Spanish Estate Agent, 1998. Memberships: International Real Estate Institute; National Association of Estate Agents

**GRINSPUN Doris,** b. 29 October 1952, Santiago, Chile. Executive. m. Ricardo, 2 sons. Education: MSN, University of Michigan, 1991; PhD Studies, University of Toronto, 1993-94; PhD Studies, New York University. Appointments: Staff Nurse, Haematology Department, Hadassah Medical Center,1974-75; Sergical Department, Meir Gen Hospital, 1975-78; Intensive Care Unit, Loewenstein Rehab Hosp, Israel, 1978-79; Staff Nurse, Assistant Head, University of Michigan Hospital, 1979-84; Assistant Head Nurse, Queen Elizabeth Hospital,

Toronto, 1984-90; Director of Nursing, Mount Sinai Hospital, Toronto, 1990-96; Executive Director, Registered Nurses, 1996-. Publications: Author of numerous articles and book chapters. Honours: Mount Sinai Hospital Management Leadership Award, 1993; The Ella May Howard Award, 1992; Physical Medical and Rehab, Clinical Service Award, 1989; University of Michigan Hospital Award for Professional Contribution, 1988; Helen Carpenter Award for Doctoral Study in Nursing, 1993; R Faye McCain Award, 1989. Address: Reg Nurses Assoc of Ontario, 438 University Ave Ste 1600, Toronto, ON M5G 2K8, Canada.

**GRITZNER Jeffrey Allman**, b. 10 January 1997, Newaygo County, MI, USA. Geographer. m. Yvonne Gastineau, 2 sons, 1 daughter. Education: AB, University of California at Berkeley, 1966; AM, 1974, PhD, 1986, University of Chicago. Appointments: Director, Public Policy Research Institute, University of Montana; Professor of Geography, UM; Senior Associate and Director, Africa Program, World Resources Institute; Senior Program Officer, National Academy of Sciences. Publications: 11 books, 8 published reports, 17 chapters in books, 31 articles, 53 professional papers. Honours: Fulbright NDEA Title IV, Ford Foundation, National Science Foundation; fellowships. Memberships: American Association for the Advancement of Science; American Geographical Society; Association of American Geographers; Gamma Theta Upsilon; The Hakluyt Society. Address: 378 One Horse Creek Road, Florence, Montana 59833, USA.

**GROMOV Boris Fyodorovitch**, b. 11 May 1927, Vil Strykabkovo, Bolsheselsky district, Yaroslavl Region, Russia. Scientist; Engineer. m. Zoya Ivanovna Gromova, 1 daughter. Education: Engineer of Physics, Moscow Power Institute, 1951; Doctor of Physics and Mathematicss, 1961, 1966; Professor, 1969; Real Member, New York Academy of Science, 1996. Appointments: Junior Researcher, 1951; Researcher, 1953; Senior Researcher, 1956; Head of Research Laboratory, 1958; Head of Research Department, 1962; Head of Research Section, 1964; Deputy Director for Scientific Works, 1974; Director Adviser, 1997. Publications: Main publications are of closed character. Honours: Lenin Prize Laureate, 1961; State Prize Laureate, 1981; Honoured Scientist and Engineer of Russia, 1996; Orders and Medals of the Soviet Union and Russia, 1966-98. Address: Gorky St 60 Apt 38, 249020 Obninsk Kaluga, Russia.

**GROMOV Valery**, b. 2 June 1940, Leningrad, Russia. Scientist. m. Svetlana Gromova, 2 daughters. Education: State Technical University, St Petersburg, 1963; Candidate of Science, 1976; Senior Research Assistant, 1983. Appointments: Engineer, 1963, Chief of Testing Bureau, 1966, Senior Research Assistant, 1972, Chief of Laboratory, 1977-. Honours: Gagarin's Medal and Diploma, 1978, 1981; State Prize of Russia, 1983; Diploma, World Exhibition of Invention, 1995, 1997. Memberships: International Society for Terrain Vehicle Systems; Committee of Space Research; Board of Trustees, Lunar Geotechnical Institute. Address: VN11 Transmash, Zarechnaya St 2, St Petersburg 198323, Russia.

**GRÖNEMEYER Dietrich H W**, b. 12 November 1952, Clausthal-Zellerfeld, Germany. Radiologist. m. Christa Grönemeyer, 21 October 1977, 1 son, 2 daughters. Education: MD, University of Kiel, 1981; PhD, University of Witten-Herdecke, 1990; Qualified as Professor, 1996. Appointments: Assistant Professor, Biomedical Technology, 1978-82, Assistant Professor, Radiology, 1982-84, University of Kiel; Assistant Professor, Radiology, 1984-88, Director, Institute of Diagnostic and Interventional Radiology, 1988-90, Chairman, Institute of Diagnostic and Interventional Radiology,

1990-, Chairman, Medical Computer Science, 1990-, Professo Chairman, Department of Radiology and Microtherapy, 1997 University of Witten-Herdecke. Publications: Numerou including: Interventionelle Computertomographie, 198 Interventional Computed Tomography, 1990; Open Fie Magnetic Resonance Imaging, 1999. Memberships: Society Minimally Invasive Therapy; Deutsche Röntgengesellscha Schmertztherapeutisches Kolloqium; Research ar Development Centre for Minimally Invasive Therapy, Berli Research and Development Centre for Microtherapy, German European Congress of Radiology; Editorial Board, Minimal Invasive Therapy. Address: Institute for Microtherap Universitätsstrasse 142, 44799 Bochum, Germany.

**GRONOSTAJSKI Jerzy**, b. 28 October 1933, Chełn Professor. m. 1 son, 1 daughter. Education: MSc, Wrocła University of Technology, 1956; PhD, 1963; Habilitation, 196 Appointments: Head, Metal Forming Department, 1965 Associate Professor, 1967, Professor, 1976, WU Publications: Over 230 including 6 books and 30 patent Honours: Bachelor's Cross of Poland Renaissance Orde 1976; Medal of National Education Committee, 1986; Medal Country Defs, 1987; Medal of WUT, 1970; Medal of SIMI 1974. Memberships: Committee of Metallurgy, Polish Academ of Science, 1967-; President, Committee Civil and Mechanic: Engineering, 1987-; PAs Wroclaw Branch, 1990-; Preside Scientific Council of the Military Institute of Engineerin Address: Podwale 54/7, 50-039 Wroclaw, Poland.

**GROSSMANN Jan**, b. 4 January 1949, Havirov. Seni Lecturer. m. Danuta Grossmannova-Szarowska, 1 daughte Education: Conservatoire, Ostrava, 1972; MA, Janace Academy of Music Arts, Brno, 1979; Senior Lecturer, Academ of Music Arts, Bratislava, 1993. Appointments: Clerk, Janacek Philharmonic Orchestra, 1979-82; Music Theory Teache Conservatoire, Ostrava, 1982-83; Music Theory an Composition Teacher, Music Schools, Ostrava, 1983-89; Mus Theory Teacher, University Ostrava, 1989-; Composition ar Music Theory Teacher, Conservatoire, Ostrava, 1991-9 Creative Works include: Peter - Rock, organ, string quarte 1987; About the Horrors, alto, harp, 1988; Precatio bon; soprano, alto, bass, organ, 1993; Lava me, cantata sacr; soprano, string quartet, 1993. Memberships: Centre of Creativ Activities, Ostrava; Association of Musicians and Scientist Society of Czech Composers; The Contrast '90-the Art Clu Address: Myslbekova 13, 702 00 Ostrava 1, Czech Republic

**GROUIOS George**, b. 10 April 1968, Florina, Greec Assistant Professor of Motor Behaviour. m. Irine Koidot Education: BEd, Thessaloniki, Greece, 1984; MEd, 1985, Phl 1988, Manchester, England. Appointment: Assistant Professc of Motor Behaviour, Aristotelian Universty of Thessalonik Greece. Publications: Over 40 international publications highly refereed scientific journals. Memberships: New Yo Academy of Sciences; American Association for th Advancement of Science; British Association of Sport Science Greek Psychological Association; Greek Neuroscienc Association. Address: 37 Peston Street, 54453 Thessalonik Greece.

**GROVER Gautam**, b. 26 March 1976, New Delhi, Indi Businessman, Animal Rights Activist. Education: SSC, Columbus School, New Delhi, 1994. Appointments: Preside of People for Animals, Indias Largest Animal Welfa Organization. Publications: First Aid for Animals. Membership People for Animals. Address: BA/1A, Ashok Vihar 1, Del 110052, India.

**GROZA Petru Mircea,** b. 14 February 1921, Deva, Romania. Physiology Physician. m. Groza Simona Ileana, 2 sons, 1 daughter. Education: Professor, Medicine University of Bucharest, Physician Doctor Docent, 2nd Degree Researcher Academician. Appointment: University Professor Dr Doc Academician. Publications: Human Physiology, 1974; Human Physiology, 1980; Physiology, 1991; Abdominal Secretion and Motility; Physiology Manuals. Memberships: GOSPAR; Intercosmos Society; Medical Science Academy Bucharest; Medical Science Academy, New York; Davis University; Honour Member, Malta Academy; Medical Science Academy Paris; Medical Science Academy, Moscow. Address: Aleee Alexandru 28, 63 Bucharest, Romania.

**GRUBAR Jean-Claude,** b. 5 May 1944, France. Professor. Education: Docent in Psychology, 1974. Appointment: Professor, University of Charles de Gaulle, Lille III. Publications: Several professional articles in scientific journals. Honours: Awards, 1993, 1996. Memberships: Several. Address: University Charles de Gaulle, Lille III, Department of Education, 35 Rue Ste Barbe, 59208 Tourcoing, France.

**GRUBER Andreas Walter,** b. 24 August 1968, Vienna, Austria. Neurosurgeon. m. Renate. Education: MD, University of Vienna Medical School, 1992. Appointments: Neurological Surgeon, Department of Neurosurgery, University of Vienna, 1992-. Publications: Contributor of articles in books and journals, 1992-. Memberships: Österreichische Gesellschaft fur Neurochirurgie; Österreichische Gesellschaft für Chirurgie; Österreichische Gesellschaft für Neurologie, Neurochirurgie Intensivmedizin; World Federation of Interventional and Therapeutic Neuroradiology; Osterreichische Gesellschaft für Neuroradiologie. Address: University of Vienna Medical School, Department of Neurosurgery, Waehringer Guertel 18-20, 1090 Vienna, Austria.

**GRUBNIK Vladimir V,** b. 22 March 1950, Odessa, Ukraine. Surgeon. m. Tatyana A Zolotaryova, 1 daughter. Education: MD, 1973; PhD, 1975; DrMedSci, 1988; Professor of Surgery. Appointments: Surgeon, District Hospital, 1973-75; Surgeon, Odessa Oblast Hospital, 1975-77; Associate Professor, 1977-85, Chief, Surgical Department, 1985-99, Odessa Medical University. Publications: 195 scientific publications, 1968-99; 6 books. Honour: Recipient, Government Prize in Science, 1990. Memberships: New York Academy of Sciences, 1994; European Association of Endoscopic Surgery, 1996; Russian Association of Endoscopic Surgery, 1997. Address: 148/2 Schors str no 12, 270036 Odessa, Ukraine.

**GRUSKA Jozef Damas,** b. 11 December 1933, Rabčice, Slovakia. Computer Scientist. m. Viera Grusková, 1 son, 1 daughter. Education: Graduate, high school, Prievidza, 1953; Graduate, Mathematics, Commenius University, Bratislava, 1958; PhD, Computer Science, Slovak Academy of Sciences, 1965. Appointments: Scientist, Slovak Academy of Sciences, Bratislava, Slovakia (Mathematical Institut, Institut of Technical Cybernetics, Computer Center, 1958-68, 1970-74, 1985-90, 1993-97; United Nations Computer Research Center, Bratislava, 1975-85; Professor, University of Minnesota, USA, 1968-70; University of Hamburg, 1990-93; Masaryk University, Brno, Czech Republic, 1997-. Publications: More than 100 publications; Book Foundations of Computing. Honours: Medal, Slovak Academy of Sciences, 1993; IFIP Silver Core Award, 1996; IEEE Computer Pioneer Award, 1996; Gold Medal of Masaryk University, Brno, Czech Republic, 1997. Memberships: Slovak Union of Mathematics and Physicists, 1958-; Slovak Cybernetics Society, 1960-90; European Association in Theoretical Computer Science, 1985-, Council Member, 1985-91; IFIP Specialist Group on Foundations of Computer Science, Chair, 1989-96. Address: Subežná 13, 81104 Bratislava, Slovakia.

**GRYAZNOV George M,** b. 26 December 1926, Kovzov, Russia. m. Zoya Roumyantseva, 1 son. Education: Graduate, Gorkii University, 1952; Doctor Sci Theses, 1969; Professor, Moscow Engineering Physics Institute, 1977-98. Appointments: Computing Engineer, 1952-56; Jet Designer, 1957-61; Co-Chief Designer, Space Nuclear Reactors, 1962-72; President, State, Krasnaya Zwezda, 1972-97; Founder, Space Nuclear Energetics: Thermoionic Reactor Topaz. Publications: 183 publications, 79 patents, 1 monograph; Peace Nuclear Power, 1971; Simp Space Nuclear Power, 1989, 1990, 1991, 1992, 1993, 1994. Memberships: Electrotechnical Academy of Russia, Moscow, 1993; Technology Academy of Russia, Moscow, 1994. Address: ul Kolomenskii pr 1 1 15, Moscow 115446, Russia.

**GRYGUTIS Barbara,** b. 7 November 1946, Hartford, CT, USA. Artist. 1 son. Education: BFA, University of Arizona; MFA, University of Arizona. Appointments: Numerous Major Public Art Projects; Many Exhibitions. Publications: Architecturama; Data Book; Work Ethic was Inspiration for New St Paul; Chevy Art Cruises Into Town; Tucson's Tiled '54 Chevy Sparks Albuquerque Art Flap; Albuquerque Art Project; A Temple Tempe; Amphitheater to Grace Garden; A Talk with Barbara Grygutis and Peter Warshall; Il Concorso La Ceramica Nell Arredo Urbano; La Ceramica Nell' Arredo Urbano; Barbara Grygutis, The Alene Dunlop Smith Garden; Tucson, Art, Sand, Mules and Taillights; Women in Clay, The Ongoing Tradition; On the Ceramist as Sculptor; Impressions of Arizona. Honours: Arizona Artist Award; Albuquerque Conservations Association Award of Merit; National Endowment for the Arts. Address: 135 S 6th Avenue, Suite C, Tucson, AZ 85701, USA.

**GU Jin,** b. 19 December 1923, Guangdong, China. Editor, Photographer. m. Peng Shu-Qin, 2 sons, 1 daughter. Education: Majoring in Sociology, Tsinghua University, Beijing, 1946-48. Appointments: Senior Editor, Director of Editing, Reporting Department, China Pictorial. Publications: Editor to several albums including, As The Dragon Stirs, 1989. Memberships: National Journalists Association of China; Chinese Photographers Association; China Senior Professors Association. Address: China Pictorial Magazine, 33 Chegonzhuang Xilu Haidian District, Beijing 100044, China.

**GU Zhimin,** b. 1 July 1927, Beijing, China. Doctor of Medicine. m. Wong Wenjing, 1 son, 1 daughter. Education: Graduate, 1952, Dept Medical Science, Anhui Medical University; Graduate, 1957, First 2-year Chinese Medical Course, Shanghai, China; ICCI Hon Doctor of Medicine, 1987. Appointments: Advisor, first Shanghai Hospital attached to PLA Air Force, 1987; Medical Director, International Old Folk Association (HK) of UN, 1987; Advisor of Daqing (China) Fourth Hospital, 1994. Honours: Prize at 15th Zagrebu Yugoslavie (1987) International Exhibition of Inventions for Equilibrium Detector and Equilibrator for Channels and Network; The article The Theory on the Equilibration of Bioelectricity and its Medical Effects, was issued at the World Medical Physics and Biological Engineering Conference in 1988; Invention won prize at Beijing China 1992 International Exhibition of Inventions. Memberships: Advisor, Association de Acupuncture China en Argentina, 1993; Official member, Chinese Society of Somatic Science Beijing, 1993. Address: Room 301, 65 Huanghe Road, Shanghai, China 200003.

**GUAN Fengnian,** b. 28 October 1938, Changtu, Liaoning, China. Water Resources and Hydrolic Engineering. m. S Q Zhang, 3 daughters. Education: BS, Hydraulic Engineering

Department, Dalian Engineering College, 1964. Appointments: Technician, Engineer, Senior Engineer, Professor, Heilonjiang Provincial Investigation, Design and Research Institute for Water Resources and Hydropower Engineering, 1964-. Publications include: Manual of Culvert and Sluice Design, 1975; Situ Experimental Research of Normal Frost Heaving Forces Acting on Slab Foundation Bottom, 1982; Horizontal Frost Heaving Forces Acting on Structures, 1981; Culvert, 1985; Frost Heaving in Soil and Its Prevention of Damage to Hydraulic Structures, 1985; Aqueduct, 1986; Retaining Wall design in Hydraulic Structures, 1998 and others. Honours: 4th Prize, Science and Technology Advance, Heilongjiang, 1987; 3rd Prize, Science and Technology Advance, China Academy of Sciences, 1988; 2nd Prize, Outstanding Design, Heilongjiang, 1993. Memberships: Association of Glacial and Frozen Soil, 1980-85; Vice Director of Hydraulic Structure Speciality, Heilongjiang Provincial Society of Water Resources & Hydropower Engineering, 1980-95; Committee, Harbin City Experts Consultants Committee, 1994-. Address: No 52 Qingbin Road, Nangang District, Harbin 150080, Heilongjiang, China.

**GUCKLEROVA Marie Jehlicková,** b. 18 July 1941, Opava, Silesia, Czech Republic. Writer; Engineer of Economy; Publishing Executive. m. 31 October 1963, 2 sons. Education: Diplomas, 1964, 1967, University of Economist Graduates, Prague. Appointments: Engineer of Economy, State Musical Publishing House, Prague, 1964-78; Consultant, cultural firm Capon, New York City, USA, 1968-71; Editor, Czech Foreign Broadcasting, 1968-71; Chief Editor, Publishing House Work, 1978-90; Publishing Executive, 1990-. Publications: Author: Cultural-economic publications, engaged by Czech Ministry of Culture, 1966; Fairy-Tales, 1975, 1976, 1977, 1979, Phonograph records, The Water Castle, 1980; Fairy Tales, 1980, 1994, 1995; Audiotapes, Fairy-Tales from Castles, Seas and Woods, 1992- Book, The Celtic Crown, The Celts - The Ancestors of the European American. Address: Klobouenicka 7, 140 00 Prague, Czech Republic.

**GUENTHER Charles John,** b. 29 April 1920, St Louis, Missouri, USA. Author; Teacher. m. Esther Laura Klund, 1 son, 2 daughters. Education: AA, 1940, Harris Teachers College; BA, 1973, MA, 1974, Webster University; LHD (Hon), 1979, Southern Illinois University; Fellow in PhD, St Louis University, 1976-79. Appointments: US Army Engineers and US Air Force, 1942-75; Adjunct instructor or professor, various college in US, 1976-90; Reviewer, St Louis Post-Despatch and other journals, 1953-. Publications: 10 books of poems and translations including: Phrase/Paraphrase, 1970; Modern Italian Poets, 1961; Voices in the Dark, 1974; The Hippopotamus, 1986; Moving the Seasons, 1994. Honours: Order of Merit, Italian Republic, 1973; many other awards. Memberships: Poetry Society of America, past Midwest VP; Past President, Missouri and St Louis Writers Guilds; St Louis Poetry Centre. Address: 9877 Allendale Drive, St Louis, MO 63123, USA.

**GUENTHER Herbert,** b. 17 March 1917, Bremen, Germany. Professor Emeritus. m. Ilse Guenther, 2 daughters. Education: PhD, Indian Philosophy and Linguistics, Munich University, Germany, 1939; PhD, Indian Philosophy, Vienna University, Austria, 1943. Appointments: Docent, Vienna University, 1943; Assistant Professor, Lucknow University, India, 1950; Assistant Professor, Chairman, Tibetan Studies, Varanaseya Sanskrit Vishvavidyala, India, 1956; Professor, Head, Department of Far Eastern Studies, University of Saskatchewan, Canada, 1964; Visiting Professor, Yale University, New Haven, USA, 1967; Visiting Professor, Toronto University, Canada, 1971; Professor Emeritus, Far Eastern Studies, University of Saskatchewan, Canada, 1984. Publications: Over 30 books and 90 articles in

professional journals. Honours: DLitt, University of Saskatchewan, 1983; Citation and Presentation, Ceremonial Scarf and Silver Plaque, Outstanding Contributions to Indian Culture, Anantajyoti-Vidyapith, Lucknow, India, 1987. Address: 1320 13th Street East, Saskatchewan SK, S7H 0C6, Canada.

**GUESS Jeffrey,** b. 1948, Adelaide, Australia. Poet; Educator. Appointments: Taught in both country and metropolitan high schools, TAFE colleges and universities; Runs numerous writing workshops; Invited Judge for major poetry competitions, including the John Bray Award. Publications: Poetry published widely and has appeared in most Australian newspapers and magazines; Appears regularly in leading literary magazines and major newspapers; He is also published in America, Canada, New Zealand, England and Wales; His work is frequently anthologised; 6 collections of poetry; Co-edited three anthologies of poetry and edited a book of community writing; Co-written textbook on teaching poetry in primary schools and a textbook entitled Writing Poetry for tertiary students. Honours: Winner numerous first prizes for his writing; Awardee free writing grants; His papers, manuscripts and letters are held by the Defence Force Academy Library, Canberra in the Australian Special Research Collection. Address: PO Box 1039, Gawler, SA 5118, Australia.

**GUETZLOE Douglas Michael,** b. 15 June 1954, Tampa, FL, USA. Governmental and Public Relations Officer. m. 2 sons, 1 daughter. Education: BSc, Florida State University, 1977. Appointments: Chairman, Ax the Tax Committee; Outstanding Republican for Orange County. Honour: Republican Party Executive Committee. Address: Advantage Consultants, 3660 Maguire Boulevard Ste 103, Orlando, FL 32803, USA.

**GUGLIELMI Angelo,** b. 2 April 1929, Arona, Italy. President, Managing Director. m. Alberta Montanari, 1 son, 1 daughter. Education: Degree, Italian Literature. Appointments: RAI, National Broadcaster, 1955; Managing Director, RAI3, 1987-95; President, Managing Director, Istituto Luce SpA, 1995-. Publications: Avanguardia e Sperimentalismo; Vent'anni d'impazienza; Vero e Falso; Il Piacere della Letteratura; La letteratura del Risparmio; Carta Stampata; Autarchia Impossibile; Corsari e Gentiluomini; La Brutta Addormentata; Senza Rete. Address: Istituto Luce SpA, Via Tuscolana 1055, 00173 Roma, Italy.

**GUHA R P,** b. 23 June 1929, Calcutta. Teacher. m. A Guha, 1 son, 1 daughter. Education: PhD; D Litt; MHM. Appointments: Principal; Chairman. Honours: FUWA; M M Academy Award; Man of the Year, American Biographical Institute, USA. Memberships: ASISC; World Poetry Society; Poets International Writers Forum. Address: Patratu School of Economics, PO PT Ps 829119, PB 13 Hazaribagii, India.

**GUIBERT Vincent,** b. 3 April 1966, Paris, France. Consultant (Management). Education: Ecole Normale Superieure, 1992; MEcons; PhD, Econs; Master in Maths; Master in Computer Science. Appointment: Senior Consultant (Boss and Consultant) in Strategic Issues. Honours: Medal of the French National Defense; Medal of the Order of Malta. Memberships: former Vice President, Conference Olivaint; Order of Malta. Address: 1 Rue Erlanger, 75016 Paris, France.

**GUIDO Gianluigi,** b. 26 September 1963, Cutrofiano, Lecce, Italy. Consumer Researcher; Consultant. Education: DSc, 1987, LUISS University, Rome; MIBA, 1990, US International University, San Diego, CA; PhD, 1996, University of Cambridge, England; Commercialist Dr, University Bari, Italy; Official Auditor, 1992. Appointments: Researcher, Institute San Paulo, Turin, Italy, 1987-88; Researcher, US International niversity, San Diego, 1989-90; Professor Management, niversity Lecce, Italy, 1990-93; Research Scientist, University a Sapienza, Rome, 1994-; Professor of Market Analysis, niversity of Padua, 1998-; President, Guido Marketing esearch, Lecce, Italy, 1995-; Board Directors, Society Trans ub, Lecce; Researcher, ISTAO-Olivetti, Ancona, 1987; nancial Consultant, EFIM, Rome, 1988. Publications: Author, he Financial Innovations of Interest Rate Swaps, 1988; larketing & Distribution: Strategies for a Changing Europe, 991; The Economy of the Titles Market, 1994. Memberships: otary Scholar, Rotary Foundation, 1989; Scholar, British ouncil, 1993; Grantee, INSEAD International Scholarship, 992; American Marketing Association; Association Consumer esearch; Italian Association Marketing Research. Address: 13 ia Trento e Trieste, 73024 Maglie Lecce, Italy.

**GUIDRY Anne Mooney,** b. 6 March 1948, Houston, Texas, SA. Teacher; Composer; Recording Artist; Producer. m. litchell Guidry. Education: Studied music at University of exas at El Paso, 1967-69, University of Houston, 1972-74; BA, 1986, Sam Houston State University, Huntsville, Texas. ppointments: Performer, 5 years, Sam Houston Folk Festival; roducer, Composer, Recording Artist, In Flight, 1980, 'averick, 1986, United Way Telethon, 1983; Danced in movie, Irban Cowboy, 1980; President of In Flight Music United, 979-97, Blue Heron Music & Art, 1998-. Publications: All Jngs on the Maverick release, 1986, 2 collections, 1979, Back ) the Country, Depth Perceptions, Western Opera; The El aso Desperado Rides Tonight, 1997; Notable Women of exas, 1984. Honours: Farrish Foundation Scholarship, 1966; ominee for W C Handy Blues Award, 1987; Permanent music ollections: Archive of Contemporary Music, NYC, Blues oundation, Memphis, Barker Texas History Centre, University f Texas at Austin. Memberships: Austin Songwriters Group; rofessional Finance Club; Professional Marketing lanagement Club. Address: PO Box 632311, Nacogdoches, X 75963-2311, USA.

**GUIK Lev Aronovitch,** b. 26 November 1939, Bobrujsk, elarussia. Mechanical Engineer; Educator; Researcher. m. udmila Vladimirovna, 3 sons. Education: Degree, Mechanical ngineering, 1962; Candidate of Science, 1970; DSc, 1992. ppointments: Assistant Professor, 1969-98, Head of epartment, 1995-, Kaliningrad State Technical University; eputy Chairman, Regional Technical Center, Kaliningrad, 994-; Expert, UN Industrial Development Organization, ienna, 1995-. Publications include: Some Mechanics and imulations of Rotary Cutting, 1997. Honours: Honoured wentor of the Russian Federation; State Scientific Prize /inner, President of Russia. Membership: Russian Academy f Natural Sciences. Address: Kaliningrad State Technical niversity, Sovjetsky Prospect 1, 236000 Kaliningrad, Russia.

**GUJRAL Shiela,** b. 24 January 1924, Lahore. Poet, Writer, ocial Worker. m. Inder Kumar Gujral, 2 sons. Education: lasters Degree, Economics; Diploma in Journalism, Panjab niversity; Diploma in Montessori Training. Appointments: ducator; Social Worker; Part Time Writer. Publication: 26 ublications, Poetry. Honours: World of Poetry, Golden Poet ward, 1989, 1990; Nirala Award, 1989; Best Hindi Poetry ward of the Year; Mahila Shiromani Award, 1990; D Litt, Vorld Academy of Art and Culture, 1992; Editor's Choice ward for Outstanding Achievements in Poetry; Huh lansolhoen Poetry Highest Award, Korea; Soka Gokkai niversity Award of Highest Honour for Making Outstanding ontribution in the World of Poetry; Shiromani Sahitkar Award; elhi Ratan Award. Memberships: Delhi Parent Teachers ssociation; Bhartiya Grameen Mahila Sangh; National PTA;

Zakir Hussain Society; Balkanji Bari, Childrens Association. Address: 5 Janpath, New Delhi 110011, India.

**GULIK van der Elisabeth Thecla Maria,** b. 19 December 1947, Amsterdam, The Netherlands. Education: Analytical Chemist, 1969, Westeinde Hospital, The Hague; Physician, 1980, Catholic University, Nÿmegen. Appointments: Analytical Chemist, Westeinde Hospital, The Hague, 1967-69, St Radboud Hospital, Nijkegen, 1972-73; Physician, Boerhaave Hospice, Haarlem, 1980; Assistant Pathologist, Wilhelmina Gasthuis, Amsterdam, 1980-81, Slotervaart Hospital, Amsterdam, 1981-82, Free University Hospital, Amsterdam, 1982-83, Erasme Hospital, Brussels, 1985; Researcher Pathology, several University Hospitals, Paris, France, 1983-88; Physician, Bureau of Driving Licenses, Rijswijk, Netherlands, 1990-92; Physician of Insurance, General Administration Office, Amsterdam, 1990-96; Joint Executive Organization, Zoetermeer, 1996-98; Physician of needs assessment, Needs Assessments Netherlands Advice NV, Amsterdam, 1998-. Publications: Reports; Lectures in field. Honour: Grantee, 1985, Association Naturalia et Biologia, College de France, Paris. Memberships: Dutch Royal Academy of Medicine; Dutch Organisation of Pathologists; Dutch Association of Insurance Medicine; Syndicat des Médecins Anatomo-, Cyto-Pathologistes Français, Marseille, France; Société Française de Pathologie, Toulouse, France. Address: Smedemanstraat 2, NL 1182 HT Amstelveen, The Netherlands.

**GULLESTAD Marianne,** b. 28 March 1946, Kristianand, Norway. Research Professor. m. Jan Terje Faarlund, 2 daughters. Education: PhD, 1984. Appointments: Lecturer, Department of Social Anthropology, Bergen, Norway, 1976; Researcher, funded by Ministry of Family and Consumer Affairs (FAD) and Norwegian Research Council for Science and Humanities (NAVF), 1976-77; Research Fellow, NAVF, 1977-82; Research Fellow, Urban Research Program, NAVF, 1982-84; Visiting Scholar, Department of Anthropology, University of Chicago, 1983-85; Research Fellow, NAVF, 1984-86; Research Fellow (Forsker NAVF), NAVF, 1986-; Visiting Scholar, Department of Anthropology, University of Chicago, 1988-89, 1994; Senior Research Fellow, Norwegian Research Council (NFR), 1992-96; Research Professor, Norwegian Centre for Child Research, 1989-. Publications: 13 books include: Family and Kinship in Europe, French edition, 1995, English edition, 1997; Chapters; Articles. Honours: Eilert Sundt's Award for excellent research; Allforsk's award, for Excellence in Research and Publication. Membership: Royal Norwegian Academy. Address: Oscars Gate 73, N 0256, Norway.

**GULO Lev,** b. 17 July 1930, Ukraine. Doctor of Medical Science; Professor. m. Margarita Revyakina, 1 son. Education: Leningrad Military Medical Academy, 1954; Biological Faculty, State University, Leningrad, 1960; Candidate of Medical Science, 1965; DSc, 1990; Professor, 1991. Career: Military Service, 1954-56; Manager, Medical Rescue Station, St Petersburg, 1956-59; Clinical Theraputist, Lecturer, Assistant Professor, Head of Faculty, Professor, Institute for Advanced Medical Studies. Publications: 150 medical articles, 5 monographs. Memberships: Russias Scientific Society of Gerontologists and Geriatricians; Russian Society of Gastroenterologists; Council of Therapists of St Petersburg Municipal Health Committee. Address: Institute for Advanced Medical Studies, Saltykov Schedrin Str 41, 193015 St Petersburg, Russia.

**GUNDERSON Joanna,** b. 14 May 1932, New York, New York, USA. Writer; Publisher; Playwright. m. Warren Gunderson, 1 son, 1 daughter. Education: BS, School of

General Studies, Columbia University, 1954; Study at Santiniketan, West Bengal, Sanskrit. Appointments: Writer, 1957-; Publisher (Red Dust), 1963-; Playwright, 1985-; Reviewer for Beckett Circle, 1995, 1996. Publications: Published in Rampike, 1985, 1986, 1990; Frank and However, 1987; Midland Review, 1988; Plays produced, 1990, 1992, 1994-98; NEA grants, 1979-85. Address: 1148 5th Avenue, New York, NY 10128, USA.

**GUNTER Gordon Pennington,** b. 18 August 1909, Goldonna, Louisiana, USA. Zoologist. m. (1) Lottie LaCour, 6 June 1932, (2) Frances Monette Hudgins, 6 September 1957, 4 sons, 1 daughter. Education: BA, Louisiana State Normal College, 1929; MA, University of Texas, 1931; PhD, 1945. Appointments: Biologist, US Bureau Fisheries, intermittently, 1931-38; Marine Biologist, Texas Game, Fish and Oyster Commission, 1939-45; Research Scientist, Institute of Marine Science, University Texas, 1945-49, Director, 1949-55; Professor, Zoology Marine Laboratory, University Miami, Florida, USA, 1946-47; Senior Marine Biologist, Scripps Institution Oceanography, University California, La Jolla, 1948-49; Director, Gulf Coast Research Laboratory, Ocean Springs, Mississippi, 1955-71; Director Emeritus, 1971-; President, 1974, World Mariculture Society; President, Mississippi Academy Sciences, 1964-65; Founder Editor, Gulf Research Reports, 1961-74; Publications: Gunter's Archievs No 1-12; Contributed over 435 articles on marine biology to professional and popular publications. Honours: The "Gunter Library", the Gulf Coast Research Laboratory was named for him; A research vessel to be named the "Gordon Gunter". Memberships: Sigma Xi; Phi Kappa Phi; Advisory Panel Commercial Seafoods Division La Commission of Wildlife and Fisheries, 1953-54; Vice Chairman, Biology, Committee Treatise on Marine Ecology, 1942-57; Principal Investigator, Plankton Studies, OTEC Program, Gulf of Mexico, 1978-82. Address: 127 Halstead Road, Ocean Springs, MS 39564-5316, USA.

**GUO Hanmin,** b. 4 April 1945, Ping Dingshan, HeNan, China. Teacher. Yu You Qin, 1 son, 1 daughter. Education: BA, Zhengshan University, 1963-68; MA, HuNan Normal University, 1980-83. Appointments: Professor, HuNan Normal University; Director, Institute of Researches in Chinese Modern History. Publications: Social Ideological Trends in the Late Period of the Qing Dynasty; Guang Ming-Cup Champion for High Quality Academic of Science, 1992. Memberships: Vice President, HuNan Historical Association; Vice President, Tansitong Research Institute. Address: Department of History, Hunan Normal University, Hunan, China.

**GUO Hongji,** b. 3 May 1948, Baoding, Hebei, China. Historian; Professor; Senior Editor. m. Wang Meijuan, 1 son. Education: Graduate, Baotou Iron & Steel College, 1970, Qinghai Normal University, 1981. Appointments: Technician, Chinese No 4 Metallurgical Construction Company, 1970-78; Historian Professor, 1981-, Editor-in-Chief, Journal, Qinghai Normal University. Publications: Confucian Ethics and Chinese Cultural Changes, 1996; Neo-Nationalism, 1996; Cultural Nationalism, 1997; The Overturned Civilization, 1998; Middle Kingdom Complex in the Late 20th Century, 1999. Memberships: Director, Chinese Periodicals Association; Managing Director, Chinese Universities Journal Institute. Address: #541 Building 14 36 W Wusi Road, 810008 Xining Qinghai, China.

**GUO Jingyi,** b. 26 January 1927, Shanghai, China. Teacher. 2 sons, 2 daughters. Education: Diploma, Department of Economics, Gt China University, Fudan University, 1948-52. Appointments: Senior Research, Professor, Director of Post Graduate School, Fudan University, 1952-98. Publications: The West German Economy, The Development of Federal Germany. Honours: First Class Prize for Graduate Teaching Fudan University, 1992-93. Memberships: Shanghai Economic Association; World Research Group. Address: Room 403 No 4 Fourth Dormitory, World Economic Institute, Fudan University Shanghai 200433, China.

**GUO Qixin,** b. 28 January 1964, Shanghai. Scientist Educator. Education: Bachelor, 1990; Master of Engineering 1992; Doctor of Engineering, 1996. Appointments: Assistant Professor, 1992-97; Associate Professor, Saga University 1997-. Publications: Contributor to Professional Journals Membrships: IEEE; The Institute of Electrical Engineers of Japan; Japan Society of Applied Physics. Address: Saga University, Honjo 1, Saga 840, Japan.

**GUO Ying-lan,** b. 22 February 1942, Henan Province China. Research Professor. m. Wang Xian-ye, 1 son, daughter. Education: Henan Agricultural University, 1965 Appointments: China Association for Science and Technology 1965-72; Institute of Microbiology, Academia Sinica, 1973- Publications: 3 books; 54 papers, including 64 new species, 9 new combinations, 122 new records for China and 1 new name. Membership: Secretary General, Mycological Society of China; Deputy editors-in-chief of Mycosystema. Address Mycology Dept, Institute of Microbiology, Academia Sinica Beijing 100080, China.

**GUO Yu Huai,** b. 4 October 1934, Shanxi, China. Official. m Zhang Qing Shu, 1 son, 1 daughter. Education: Graduate Biology Department, Shanxi Normal Institute, 1956 Appointments: Deputy Governor, Shanxi Province, 8 years First Deputy, 5 years; chairman, Provincial Politica Consultative Committee; General Director, Shanxi Yellow River Diversion Project; President, Historiography Researching Institute, Shanxi. Publications: Several books, numerous articles in professional journals. Address: 3 Dong Ji Hu Yen Street, Tai Yian, Shanxi 030009, China.

**GUO Yude,** b. 9 March 1931, Shenyang, China. Researcher Education: Medicotherapeutic Faculty, Dalian Medical University, 1948-54. Appointments: Researcher, Hubei Medical University, 1954-. Publications include: Urgency of ENT Diseases; Otitis Media in Children; Concise Atlas of ENT Operations; Symposia of Clinical Audiology. Honours: 2nd Degree, Academic Scientific Progress, Hubei, 1987. Address Jie Fang Road No 238, Department of Otolaryngology, 1st Hospital of Hubei Medical University, Wuhan 430060, China.

**GUO Zuyu,** b. 6 DEcember 1962, China. Biochemist. m. Qi Li, 1 son, 1 daughter. Education: PhD Biochemistry, 1992 Appointments: Senior Research Scientist, Rhone Poulenc Publications: Over 30 publications and 1 patent. Memberships AAAS; AAPS; ISSX. Address: Rhone Poulenc Rorer, 500 Arcola Road No W12, Collegeville, PA 19426 3930, USA.

**GUPTA Manash Ranjan,** b. 10 November 1956, Calcutta India. Professor of Economics. m. Pampa Dasgupta, 1 son Education: BA, 1976, MA, 1979, PhD, 1987, University of Calcutta. Appointments: Lecturer, Indian School of Mines Dhanbad, Bihar, India, 1980-84; Lecturer, 1984-85, Reader 1985-89, University of Burdwan, West Bengal; Professor Jadavpur University, Calcutta, 1989-. Publications: 45 papers in professional journals include: Wage determination of a child worker: A theoretical analysis; Imperfect competition, Foreign Enclave and Export Subsidy. Honour: Panchan an Chakrabort Memorial Award, 1998-99. Address: Arabinda Sarani Basunagar, PO Madhyamgram 743 275, Dist North 2

Parganas, West Bengal, India.

**GUPTA Nippun,** b. 3 November 1964, New Delhi. Advertising Executive. Education: 3 tier programme, Indian Institute of Management, Ahmedabad; Postgrad Diploma Advertising, Institute of Marketing Management, New Delhi; BA, University of Allahabad. Appointments: Account Group Manager, Ammirati Puris Lintas Advertising, Bombay, 1986-90; VP, Trikaya Grey Advertising, New Delhi, 1990-. Memberships: Visiting Faculty, Indian Institute of Mass Communications; Times School of Marketing, New Delhi; India Habitat Centre; Delhi Advertising Club; Noida Golf Club. Address: L-169 Sector-25, Jalvayu Vihar-II, 201301 Noida, India.

**GUPTA Prem Prakash,** b. 18 December 1946, India. Professor. m. Sarita, 1 son. Education: MBBS, 1968; MD, Paediatric Medicine, 1973. Appointments: Assistant Professor, Paediatrics at Medical College, Jaipur, India, 1973-79; Associate Professor, Jaipur, 1979-84; Associate Professor, Tripoli, Libya, 1984-85; Associate Professor, Jodhpur, Ajmer, Jaipur, 1986-93; Professor, Paediatrics, Medical College, Kota, 1993-; Superintendent, JK Lon Mother and Child Hospital, Kota, 1995-. Publications: About 45 publiations in medical journals, mostly on Neonatology. Memberships: Indian Medical Association; Indian Academy of Paediatrics; Respiratory, Neonatology, Tuberculosis Chapter of IAP; Thalassaemia Society. Address: Medical Superintendent, J K Lon Mother and Child Hospital, Kota 324001, India.

**GUPTA Ramesh Chandra,** b. 28 September 1950, Ratangarh, India. Educator in Medical College. m. Usha Gupta, 3 daughters. Education: MBBS, 1974; MD, Biochemistry, 1979. Appointments: Senior Demonstrator in Biochemistry, 1974-79; Assistant Professor in Biochemistry, 1979-94; Associate Professor in Biochemistry, 1994-98; Professor of Biochemistry, 1998-. Publications: Over 50 research papers on clinical biochemistry; 1 book on Practical Biochemistry. Memberships: Association of Clinical Biochemists of India; Nutrition Society of India. Address: Dept Biochemistry, Government Medical College, Kota Rajasthan, India.

**GUPTA Ravi N,** b. 25 May 1975, Bargarh, Orissa, India. Student. m. Ashalata. Education: Bachelor of Fine Arts. Honours: All India Art Contest 1995; Orissa State Art Exihibition 1998. Address: c/o Satyanarayan Medical Hall, Godbhaga District, Bargarh, Orissa, India.

**GUPTA Rohit B,** b. 3 July 1969, Bombay, India. Engineer. m. Priti Gupta. Education: BE, University of Massachusetts, Amherst, USA, 1989; MSc, Glasgow Caledonian University, 1991. Appointments: Director, Ducon, 1992-97; Managing Director, Peenar Technology, 1998-. Memberships: CEMA; ASHRA; PIMMA. Address: 6 Alpana, 2d Fl Pedder Road, Bombay 400 026, India.

**GUPTA Roshan Lall,** b. 9 January 1928, Solan, India. Surgeon. m. Indira Gupta, 2 daughters. Education: MBBS (Lucknow), 1951; FRCS Edinburgh, 1954; FRCS England, 1957; Master of Surgery (Lucknow), 1960. Appointments: Professor and Head of Department of Surgery, Medical College Meerut, retired 1988. Publications: Textbook of Surgery, 1996; Year Book of Surgery, 1994-98; Recent Advances in Surgery, Nos 1-7, 1987-97; Colour Atlas of Surgery, in press; The Medico-Legal Aspects of Surgery, 1998. Honours: Professor Emeritus Surgery, 1988-; Professor S P Srivastava Oration Award of Indian Medical Association, 1982; Godrej Karai Memorial Oration Award of Association of Thoracic and Cardiovascular Surgeons of India, 1984; B C Roy National Award of Medical Council of India for Eminent Teacher in

Surgery, 1984; Dr S N Mathur Oration Award; and others. Address: 215 East Saket, Meerut 250 001 UP, India.

**GUPTA Shreesh Kumar,** b. 13 November 1936. Cardiologist. m. Smt Mala Devi, 2 sons, 1 daughter. Education: Merit Medical Student, Government Medical College, Nagpur, 1954-62; MD, Nagpur University. Publications: Shree Mala, (Epic in Hindi); Mini Shree Mala, (Epic in English); Shir Symbols The Satya Sagare (English); God's Original Book (English); Science of God (English); Ishwar Krat Prakratic Ishwareeya Kitab (God's Book in Nature by God Himself) (Hindi); Coronary Exercise, 1972. Honours: Man of the Year 1997, with Commemorative Gold Medal Award, ABI, USA; 2000 Millenium Medal of Honor, American Biographical Institute, USA; Twentieth Century Achievement Award, ABI, USA; Outstanding Achievement Diploma in Honor of Contribution to make God's knowledge in all religions as one exact "Science of God" by their natural proof. Address: Goshala Ward, Gondia, Maharashtra, 441601, India.

**GUPTA Uma,** b. 15 February 1957, Meerut City, India. Researcher; Consultant. Education: MA, 1978, MPhil, 1979, PhD, 1983, Psychology, Meerut University, India. Appointments: Research Fellow, 1983-84; General Fellow, 1986-88; UGC Research Scientist "A", 1988-93; UGC Research Scientist "B", 1993-. Appointments: Assistant Editor, 1988-93, Editor, 1994-, Pharmacopsychoecologia; Honorary Member, Research Board of Advisors and Professional Women's Advisory Board, ABI, Raleigh, North Carolina, USA. Publications: 3 books; Over 60 research papers; Research work extensively cited. Memberships: Life Member, Indian Academy of Applied Psychology; Cashier, 1988-93, Secretary, 1994-, Pharmacopsychoecological Association. Address: UGC Research Scientist, Department of Basic Principles, Institute of Medical Sciences, Banaras Hindu University, Varanasi 221005, India.

**GUPTHA Soneil,** b. 24 August 1953, Jaipur, India. Doctor. m. Leena S Guptha, 2 sons. Education: MBBS 1976, Distinction in Physiology, Biochemistry Medicine and Therapeutics, Gynaecology and Obstetrics, MD (Med and Ther), 1980, University of Rajasthan, India; FICA, 1983, American College of Angiology, USA; FCCP, 1983, American College of Chest Physicians; MRCP (1), 1985, Royal College of Physicians, UK; Dip Pharm Med, 1994, Royal Colleges of Physicians and Surgeons, UK; AFPM, 1995, Faculty of Pharmaceutical Medicine, UK. Appointments: 1976-90, various positions as senior house officer, registrar, and associate professor in hospitals and academic institutions in India and UK; Medical Officer, Senior Medical Officer, Medicines Control Agency, Department of Health, London, UK, 1990-91; Pharmaceutical Physician, Clinical Research and Medical Affairs, Merck Sharp & Dohme Ltd, UK, 1991-95; Honorary Consultant, MRC Lipoprotein Team, Hammersmith Hospital and Charing Cross Hospital, London, UK, 1994-96; Associate Director Research Administration, 1995-96, Senior Associate Medical Director, Clinical Research, 1997-, Pfizer Inc, Groton, USA. Publications: Thesis: Clinical Study of Natural History of COPD; 35 papers and abstracts; 5 book reviews; 11 invited lectures. Memberships: American College of Chest Physicians; American College of Cardiology; American Heart Association; Association of Physicians of India; Cardiological Society of India; European Atherosclerosis Society; European Society of Cardiology; European Society of Hypertension; International Atherosclerosis Society; International College of Angiology. Address: 127 Five Fields, Madison, CT 06443, USA.

**GURAYA Sardul Singh,** b. 12 October 1930, Kotmajlis, Gurdaspur, Punjab, India. Professor. m. Surinder Kaur, 2 sons,

1 daughter. Education: BSc, Hons, 1954, MSc, Hons, 1956, PhD, 1959, DSc, 1971, Punjab University; Postdoctoral Fellowship, University of Kansas Medical Centre, Kansas City, USA, 1962-64. Appointments: Demonstrator, Punjab University, 1954-59; Assistant Professor, Gorakhpur University, 1960-62; Pool Officer, Council of Scientific and Industrial Research, 1965-66; Reader, Udaipur University, 1966-71; Professor and Head, Punjab Agricultural University, 1971-86; Professor and Dean, 1986-90, Professor, 1990-93, Punjab Agricultural University, Ludhiana; Emeritus Scientist, Council of Scientific and Industrial Research, 1993-95; Emeritus Professor, Punjab Agricultural University, Ludhiana, 1996-. Publications: 9 books, 27 chapters in books, 373 original research papers, 6 reviews. Honours: Fellow, Indian National Science Academy; Fellow, National Academy of Sciences, India; Fellow, National Academy of Agricultural Sciences; Fellow, Punjab Academy of Sciences; SS Bhatnagar Prize, 1973; Basanti-Devi Amir Chand Prize, 1990; National Lecturer, UGC, 1976-77; PhD, Honoris Causa, International University Foundation, USA; MS Randhawa Best Book Award, 1985; International Man of the Year, IBC, 1997; Man of the Year, ABI, 1997. Memberships: Executive Council, Indian Society for General and Comparative Endocrinology; Executive Council of the Indian Society for Invertebrate Reproduction; Indian Society for the Study of Reproduction and Fertility; International Cell Research Organization, UNESCO; National Committee, International Union of Biological Sciences; Executive Council, Indian National Science Academy; Vice President, Association of Progressive Zoologists; Executive Council, National Academy of Agricultural Sciences; National Committee for Research on Human Reproduction; Editorial Boards of several journals; Advisory committees, groups and scientific panels of various scientific and educational organizations of India, UNESCO and WHO. Address: 32-G, Saraba Nagar, Ludhiana, 141004, India.

**GURD Alan Robert**, b. 4 October 1940, Northern Ireland. Surgeon. m. Ruth Imrie, 4 sons, 1 daughter. Education: MB BCh, 1964, MCh, 1969, Queens, Belfast; FRCS, Edinburgh, 1967. Appointments: Staff, Royal Victoria Hospital, 1974-76; Staff, Cleveland Clinic, 1976-. Publications: Articles in professional journals. Honour: Board of Governors, Cleveland Clinic. Memberships: British Orthopaedic Association; American Academy of Orthopaedic Surgeons. Address: 17754 Lost Trail, Chagrin Falls, OH 44023, USA.

**GURVICH-LISHCHINER Sophia D**, b. 19 September 1929, Moscow. History and Criticism of Literature. m. Gurvich Joseph, 1 son. Education: Graduate 1951, Moscow University; PhD Literature, 1964, Institute World Literature, Moscow Academy of Science. Appointments: Scientific Worker, Leader of Group in Institute of World Literature, Moscow, 1955-90; Scientific Adviser, University Tel-Aviv, Israel, 1991-. Publications: Over 130 books, papers and book chapters on Russian Literature. Address: University of Tel Aviv, PO Box 15245, 75051 Rishon Le Zion, Israel.

**GURVICH Victor A**, b. 24 December 1951, Moscow, Russia. Physicist; Engineer. m. Irina, 1 son, 1 daughter. Education: MS, Mechanical Engineering, Moscow Institute of Electronics, 1974; PhD, Medical Engineering, Institute of Medical Devices, Moscow, 1986. Appointments: Engineer, Russian Research Institute for Light Engineering, Moscow, 1974-77; Chief of Laboratory, X-Ray Image Intensifiers Mosroentgen INc, Moscow, 1977-92; General Manager, ALVIM Research and Development Ltd, Jerusalem, Toronto, 1993-; Project Leader, Ministry of Industry and Trade, Jerusalem, 1995-98; Scientific Secretary, Mosroentgen Inc 1982-92. Publications: Patentee in field; Contributor of scientific articles to professional journals. Honours: Silver Medal, Exhibition of Economic Achievement,

USSR, 1985; Medal, Inventor of the USSR, 1986; Recipient of Diploma, International Technical Exhibitions, Plovdiv, Bulgaria, 1985, Leipzig, Germany, 1987. Memberships: American Association of Physicists in Medicine; Russian Association of Physicists in Medicine; Israeli Association of New Entrepreneurs. Address: 39 Slender Fernway, Toronto, Ont M2J 4P4, Canada.

**GUSEV Anatoli**, b. 15 March 1949, Moscow, Russia. Scientist, Space Science. m. G Pugacheva. Education: Graduate, Moscow Engineering Physical Institute, 1972; MS, Institute of Cosmic Research, Academy of Science, Russia, 1972; PhD, Physics of Plasma, Institute of Nuclear Physics, Moscow University, 1985. Career: Engineer, Institute of Electromechanics, 1972-75; Senior Scientist, Institute of Nuclear Physics, Moscow University, 1975-92; Visiting Professor, State University of Campinas, Brazil, 1993-. Publications: Numerous articles in professional journals. Honour: Medal, USSR Industrial Progress Exhibition, 1978. Memberships: European Geophysical Union; Sociedade Brasileira de Fisica. Address: University of Campinas, IFGW-DRCC, CP 6165, 13083-970 Campinas-SP, Brazil.

**GUTH Deborah L A**, b. 14 February 1950, Cardiff, South Wales. University Lecturer. m. Michael Cohen, 1 daughter. Education: BA, honours, 1972, MA, 1973, University of Sussex; Doctorat de IIIème cycle, Université de Paris-Sorbonne, 1980. Appointments: Postdoctoral Fellow, 1980-83, Lecturer, English Literature, 1983-, Tel Aviv University, Israel. Publications: Several articles in professional journals. Memberships: MLA; George Eliot Society; Toni Morrison Society. Address: Department of English, Tel Aviv University, Ramat Aviv, Israel.

**GUTHRIE Phillip Patrick**, b. 19 August 1962, Baltimore, Maryland, USA. Television Program Production Manager. Education: Diploma, Joppatowne Senior High, Maryland, 1980; BA, University of Maryland, College Park, 1984; Diploma, Dale Carnegie Management Seminar, 1990. Career: Executive Producer, WBFFTV-FOX-45, Baltimore, 1985-92; Senior Producer, Program Manager, Cable 17, Baltimore, 1992-95; Public Affairs Producer, WMARTV-NewsChannel 2, Baltimore, 1995; Program Production Manager, TCI Communications, Baltimore, 1995-. Honours: Grand Prize, Audio Entertainment, Alpha Epsilon Rho, 1984; 3rd Place, 1992, 2nd Place, 1994, Organizational News, ITVA; Silver Award, Public Service Announcements, International Television Association, 1997; Emmy Award Nomination, National Academy of Television Arts & Sciences, 1997; Cable Ace Award Nomination, National Cable Television Association, 1998; Received 5 Telly Awards, 1998. Memberships: National Academy of Television Arts and Sciences; International Television Association; American Film Institute; Advertising Association of Baltimore. Address: 2231 Redthorn Road, Baltimore, MD 21220, USA.

**GUTMAN Aron**, b. 4 June 1936, Zhitomir, Ukraine. Physicist. m. Nijole Gutmaniene, 2 sons, 1 stepson. Education: Department of Physics and Mathematics, Vilnius University, 1958; PhD, Theory and Mathematical Physics, Leningrad University, 1962; DSc, Biophysics, Kaunas Medical Institute, 1975; Professor, Biophysics, Kaunas Medical Academy, 1990. Appointments: Chair, Physics and Biophysics, Kaunas Medical Institute, 1965-73; Senior Research Fellow, Laboratory Neurophysiology, Kaunas Medical Institute, 1973-89; Chief Researcher, Kaunas Medical Academy Laboratory Neurophysiology, 1989-. Publications: 2 monographs (Russian); 50 papers (Russian and English). Memberships: International Academy of Social and Natural Science, Moscow; Society of Neuroscience, USA. Address: Medical Academy 9, Mickeviciaus St, Kaunas 3000, Lithuania.

**GUTU Ion,** b. 2 November 1939, Hincauti, Edinet, Moldova. Professor of Psychology and Physiology. m. Elena Capatina, son, 1 daughter. Education: Undergraduate, Moscow University, 1962-67; Doctorate, 1970. Appointments: Researcher, Academy of Science, Moldova, 1970-74; Lecturer, State University of Moldova and Pedagogical University of Moldova, 1974-81; Vice Rector, 1981-85, First Vice Rector, 1985-92, Rector, 1992-, Pedagogical University of Moldova. Publications: Physiology of the Nervous System; Dictionary of Psychology and Physiology of the Nervous Activity; Human Physiology; Concept of Undergraduate Pedagogical Education in Moldova; The Basics of Anatomy, Physiology and Hygiene of Students; Functional Organization of Birds' Visual System. Honours: Eminent Worker in the Field of Public Education; Worker Emeritus in the Field of Public Education; Order of the Working Glory. Memberships: Psychologists Association; Teachers Association. Address: Str A Doga 28/1, Apt 37, Chisinau 2024, Moldova.

**GUTU Modest,** b. 14 March 1937, Lipcani, Bessarabia. Marine Zoologist. m. Olimpia Serban, 1 son. Education: Theoretical Licence, 1954; Faculty of Biology, 1967. Appointments: Researcher, Gr. Antipa National Museum of Natural History, Bucharest, 1967-, Institute of Oceanology, Havana, 1973, Oceanography Museum, Monaco, 1980, 1987; Member, Several science expeditions. Publications: Over 110 articles in professional journals. Honours: First Prize and Trophy for two books, 1976, 1982; Richard Prize, French Science Academy, 1986; Jubilee Medal, Gr. Antipa Museum, 1993; International Man of the Year, 1998. Memberships: Romanian Society of Biological Sciences; International Commission for Science Exploration of the Med Sea; Crustacean Society, USA. Address: Muzeul "Grigore Antipa", Siseaua Kisselef 1, 79744 Bucharest 2, Romania.

**GUU Yeong-Yan,** b. 9 December 1967, Taiwan (Kaohsing). Engineer. 1 daughter. Education: PhD 1997, National Cheng-Kung University. Appointments: Assistant Professor of Mechanical Engineering Dept, National Cheng-Kung University, 1995-97. Publications: Articles to professional journals in the field of coating technology. Address: 279 Chung Cheng 2nd Rd, Mei-Nung Town, Kaohsiung 843, Taiwan.

**GVELESIANI Anzori,** b. 12 August 1937, Tbilisi, Georgia. Geophysicist; Physicist. Education: Honours, Tbilisi State University, 1960; Postgraduate, 1969; Candidate Physical-Mathematical Science, 1970; Dr Physical-Mathematical Science, 1980; Senior Scientist, 1982; Professor, 1997. Appointments: Junior Scientist, 1961; Senior Scientist, 1972; Leading Scientist, 1980; Head of Department, 1991. Publications: More than 100 articles, 1963-97; Monographs, 1979, 1998; Conferences, 1970, 1973, 1980. Memberships: Georgian Geophysical Society; Georgian Physical Society; Georgian Byron's Society; Georgian Opera and Ballet Society. Address: Institute of Geophysics, 1 Alexidze Street, 380093 Tbilisi, Georgia.

**GYANGA Thimma Reddy,** b. 1 July 1939, Obulumpalle (AP), India. Teacher. m. Savithri Gyanga, 1 daughter. Education: BE (Hons) Mechanical Engineering, 1962, Government College of Engineering, Anantapur; Advanced Diploma Production Engineering, 1969, Borough Polytechnic, London, UK; MSc Machine Tools, 1970, UMIST Manchester University; PhD Machine Tools, 1980, Regional Engineering College, Warangal. Appointments: Associate Lecturer, 1962-65, Lecturer, 1965-73, Assistant Professor, 1973-80, Regional Engineering College, Warangal, AP; Professor, NBKR Institute of Science and Technology, Vidyanagar, 1980-87; Director, Kavikulguru Institute of Technology and Science,

Ramtek, MS, 1987-. Publications: 12 papers published. Honours: Gem of India, 1996, All India Achievers Conference; One of Rising Personalities of India; 5000 Personalities of the World, 7th Edition, ABI; Selected for the National Award of 1998 as best Engineering College Principal by the Indian Society for Technical Education; 500 Leaders of Influence, 8th Edition, ABI. Memberships: Associate, Machine Tool Technology, Manchester; ISTE, MISTE; Fellow, Institution of Engineers; Senate member, Nagpur University; Former Senate member, SV University, Tirupati. Address: Kavikulguru Institute of Technology & Science, Ramtek 441106 MS, India.

# H

**HA Chang-Sik,** b. 30 January 1956, Pusan, Korea. Professor. m. Sheon-Ja Han, 1 son, 2 daughters. Education: PhD Polymer Science, 1987, Korea Advanced Institute of Science and Technology (KAIST). Appointments: Professor, Dept Polymer Science and Engineering, Pusan National University, Korea, 1982-; Visiting Scholar: University of Cincinnati, 1988-89, Stanford University, USA, 1997-98. Publications: 200 scientific papers in refereed journals; 10 books, author or co-author. Honours: Best Paper of the Year, Korea Institute Rubber Ind, 1990; Polymer Science Award, Polymer Science of Korea, 1995. Memberships: American Chemical Society; Society of Polymer Science, Japan; Polymer Society of Korea; Korean Chemical Society; Polymer Processing Society; Korean Institute of Rubber Industries. Address: Pusan National University, Department of Polymer Science & Engineering, Pusan 609-735, Korea.

**HA Quang Phuc,** b. 1 January 1958, Vietnam. Lecturer. m. Hoa Nguyen, 2 daughters. Education: BE, Electric Engineering, 1980; PhD, Engineering Science, 1992; PhD, Electrical Engineering, 1997. Appontments: Lecturer, Ho Chi Minh City Pedagogical University of Technology; Senior Research Associate, University of Sydney. Publications: Over 50 Papers; Contributions to books. Memberships: MIEEE; MIEAust; CPEng. Address: University of Sydney, Department of Mechanical Engineering, J 07, Sydney, NSW 2006, Australia.

**HABUKA Hitoshi,** b. 25 March 1957, Akita, Japan. Researcher. m. Satoko, 1 son, 1 daughter. Education: Bachelor, Niigata University, 1979; Master, Kyoto University, 1981; Dr, Hiroshima University, 1996. Appointments: Researcher, Semiconductor Crystal Growth Technology; Chief Researcher. Publications: Research Papers, Electrochemistry; Crystal Growth; Applied Physics. Memberships: American Association for the Advancement of Science; American Chemical Society; Electrochemical Society; Japan Society of Applied Physics; Society for Chemical Engineers: Chemical Society of Japan; Japanese Association for Crystal Growth. Address: R and D Centre, Shin Etsu Handotai, 2-13-1, Isobe, Annaka Gunma 379-0196, Japan.

**HADDAD Emile K,** b. 14 June 1958, Lebanon. Engineer. m. Dina, 1 son, 1 daughter. Education: BE, Civil Engineering, 1982. Career: Senior Vice President, Marlborough Development Corporation, 1988-93, Bramalea, 1993-96; President, Lennar Communities, 1996-. Memberships: Building Industry Association; Urban Land Institute. Address: Lennar Corporation, 24800 Chrisanta Drive, #200, Mission Viejo, CA 92691, USA.

**HADLEY Eleanor Martha,** b. 17 July 1916, Seattle, Washington, USA. Economist. Education: BA Politics, Economics and Philosophy, 1938, Mills College; Studied Japanese language in Tokyo, 1938-40; PhD Economics, 1949, Radcliffe College; PhD, Harvard. Appointments: Office of Strategic Services, Far East Branch; Staff, President Truman's Commission on Migratory Labour, 1950-51; Staff, arranged Senate hearings on Migratory Labour for Senator Hubert Humphrey, 1951-52; Washington Representative, National Consumers League, 1952-53; Washington Representative, American (later National) Association of Social Workers, 1953-56; Associate Professor of Economics, Smith College, Dean, class of 1962, 1956-65; Economist, US Tariff Commission, later, International Trading Commission, 1967-74; Group Director, International Division, General Accounting Office, 1974-82; Professional Lecturer, Economics Dept, George Washington University, 1972-84; Visiting Lecturer, Jackson School of International Studies, University of Washington, 1987-94. Publications: Antitrust in Japan, 1970 and numerous journal articles. Honours: Fulbright Research Scholar, Japan, 1962; 3rd Order of the Sacred Treasure, Government of Japan, 1986; Honorary member, Mortar Board/Tolo Alumni Association, University of Washington, 1986; Mortar Board endowed Hadley Scholarship, Jackson School, University of Washington, 1995; Distinguished Contribution to Asian Studies, Association for Asian Studies, 1997; Hon LLD, Mills College, 1998. Address: 807 SW 207th Place, Seattle, WA 98166, USA.

**HAFFNER Agnes Cristina,** b. 22 May 1948, Ahuachapan, El Salvador. Master of Public Administration. 1 son, 2 daughters. Education: Library Sciences and Documentation Certificate, 1974, Inter-American Institute of Agricultural Sciences, Turrialba, Costa Rica; Administration of Agricultural Science Libraries Certificate, 1978, Tropical Agriculture International Centre, Cali, Colombia; AA Criminal Justice (Hons), Union County College, Cranford, New Jersey; BA Public Administration Summa Cum Laude, 1996, MPA (Hons) 1997, Kean University, Union, New Jersey; Notary Public of the State of New Jersey, 1998-. Appointments: Chief Librarian School of Agricultural Science, National University of El Salvador, and Coordinator, National Centre of Agricultural Information and Documentation, 1970-80; Production Manager, Inland Casket Manufacturing, Riverside, California, 1984-86; Office Manager, Purchasing Dept, Harvard-Industries-ESNA Division, Union, New Jersey, 1986-89; Legal Secretary (bilingual), Almeida & Livingston, Counsellors at Law, Newark, New Jersey, 1989-90; Legal Secretary, State of New Jersey Division of the Ratepayer Advocate, Newark, New Jersey, 1990-; Secretary of the Board of Directors, Acting Property Manager (voluntary position), The Private Terrace Condominium Association, Elizabeth, New Jersey, 1998-. Publications: Editorial Assistant, First Guide to Graduate Programmes in Public Affairs and Administration, 1997, Assessment for Fanwood Township, NJ, 1996; Editor, Thesis in Agricultural Sciences, National Univesity of El Salvador, 1979. Honours: New Jersey Association Legal Secretaries, Union County Chapter, Scholarship, 1993; Mountainside Professional Women's Club Scholarship, 1993-94; Business and Professional Women's Club of Westfield NJ, 1994, o Clark, NJ, 1994, Scholarships. Memberships: Various alumni associations; American Association for Public Administration. Address: 675 Garden Street, Private Terrace, Unit No 16, Elizabeth, NJ 07202, USA.

**HAFIDI Moulay El Hehdi,** b. 28 October 1956, Morocco. Engineer. m. Benlafqih Hafida, 1 son, 1 daughter. Education: Diploma, Forestry Engineering, 1982; MSc, Environmental and Renewable Resources, 1996. Appointments: Head Desertification Control Section, 1983-90, Head, 1990-94, Provincial Office of Forestry, Errachidia; Head, Environmental and Protected Areas Section, Provincial Office of Forestry, Nador, 1996-. Publication: Food Habits and Preferences of Barbary Sheep in the High Atlas National Park, Morocco. Honour: Global 500 Honour Award, UNEP, 1993. Memberships: Global 500 Forum; Tafilalet Association, Morocco. Address: Service Provincial des Eaux et Forets, Nador, Morocco.

**HAGAR Susan Anne Mack,** b. 5 April 1948, Philadelphia, Pennsylvania, USA. School Psychologist. m. James N Hagar, 1 son, 1 daughter. Education: BA, 1970, MEd, 1975, Temple University, Philadelphia; MS with honours, School Psychology, Eastern College, Saint Davids, Pennsylvania, 1997; Certified

School Psychologist, School Counsellor, Teacher. Appointments: Teacher, Philadelphia, Pennsylvania, and Plattsburgh, New York; Reading Teacher, Gladwyne, Pennsylvania, Montessori School; School Psychologist, Bethlehem Area School District, Bethlehem, Pennsylvania. Honour: Recipient, Congratulatory Letter from First Lady Barbara Bush, 1990. Memberships: American Psychological Association; National Association of School Psychologists; National Education Association; Pennsylvania Psychological Association; Pennsylvania School Counselors Association. Address: 3414 West Union Street, Allentown, PA 18104-5947, USA.

**HAGIHARA Akihito**, b. 21 February 1954, Ichijima, Hyogo, Japan. Epidemiologist. m. Naoko, 2 sons. Education: LLB, Tohoku University, 1979; M in Med Science, Osaka University, 1989; DMSc, 1993; MPH, 1993. Appointments: Legal Staff, Kansai Electric Power Co, 1979-82, 1984-87; Researcher, Japan Energy Law Research Institute, 1982-84; Research Fellow, Osaka University, 1993-95; Assistant Professor, Kyushu University, 1995-. Publications: Communication in Health; Contributor, Articles in journals. Honours: Grantee, Japan Ministry of Education. Memberships: Director, Health Science Association; Japan Society of Hygiene; Japan Society of Public Health. Address: Kyushu University School of Medicine, 3-1-1, Maidashi, Fukuoka 812-8582, Japan.

**HAGNI Richard Davis**, b. 29 April 1931, Howell, Michigan, USA. Professor. m. Rachael S, 2 sons, 2 daughters. Education: BA Geology, Michigan State University, 1953; MS Geology, 1954; PhD, Geology, 1962. Appointments: Instructor, Department of Geology and Geophysics, University of Missouri-Rolla, 1956-60; Assistant Professor, Department of Geology and Geophysics, 1960-66; Associate Professor, Department of Geology and Geophysics, 1966-77; Gulf Oil Foundation Professor, 1984-90; Chairman, Department of Geology and Geophysics, 1985-; Curator's Professor of Geology, 1991-. Publications: 18 Publications. Honours: Best Paper Award; Named, Gulf Oil Professor of Geology; Missouri Academt of Science membership Award; Honorary Keramos Member; Named, University of Missouri Curators' Professor; Named, Fellow, Missouri Academy of Science; Named, Most Distinguished Scientist, Missouri Academy of Science. Memberships: International Association on the Genesis of Ore Deposits; Paragenesis Commission; International Council of Applied Mineralogy; Steering Board for the International Congress on Applied Mineralogy; International Mineralogical Association; Commission on Applied Mineralogy; International Geological Congress; American Association of Professional Geologists; Geological Association of America; Society of Economic Geologists; Mineralogical Society of America; Many other memberships. Address: 27 Johnson Street, Rolla, MJO 65409-0410, USA.

**HAHM Sung Deuk**, b. 4 March 1963, Yeocheon, Kyungsang, Korea. Professor. m. Jungmi Oh, 2 daughters. Education: BA, 1985, Yonsei University, Seoul; MPA, 1989, University of Texas at Austin; PhD Public Policy, 1993, Carnegie-Mellon University. Appointments: Assistant Professor, Georgetown University, Washington DC, 1994-97; Professor, Korea University, Seoul, 1996-. Publication: After Development, 1997. Address: Korea University Department of Public Administration, 5-1 Anam-dong, Sungbuk-ku, Seoul 136-701, Korea.

**HAIDER Daud**, b. 21 February 1952, Doharpara, Pabna, Bangladesh. Writer. Education: SSC, Dhaka, 1970; BA, honours, Comparative Literature, Calcutta, India, 1977. Appointments: Literary Editor, Daily Sambad, Dhaka, 1974;

Freelance Journalist, Calcutta, 1978-86. Publications: Over 10 books, poetry, essays and novels. Honours: Berlin Akademie der Künste, 1987; Berlin Senate, 1988. Address: Eisenacher Street 24, 10781 Berlin, Germany.

**HAIMOWITZ Natalie**, b. 27 May 1923, New York City, NY, USA. Clinical Psychologist. m. Morris L Haimowitz, 3 daughters. Education: BA, Psychology, Brooklyn College, 1944; MA, Clinical Psychology, Ohio State University, 1945; PhD, Human Development, University of Chicago, 1948. Appointments: Ohio State University Psychological Clinic, 1944-45; Externe Counseling Center, University of Chicago, 1946-47; Postdoctoral Trainee, Mental Hygiene Clinic, US Veterans Administration, 1949-51; Clinical Trainee, International Transactional Analysis Institute, 1967-69; Teaching Trainee, International Transactional Analysis Institute, 1969-71; Trainee, Cancer Counseling and Research Center O. Carl Simonton, MD Fort Worth, Texas Phase I and Phase II, 1978; One week training with Milton Erikson MD, Phoenix, Arizona, 1975. Appointments: Research Assistant, Committee on Human Development, University of Chicago, 1945-46; Faculty, Department of Psychology, Brooklyn College, 1947-48; Instructor, University of Chicago, 1953-58; Clinical Private Practice, 1955-; Chief Psychologist, Women's and Children's Hospital, 1955-59; Psychologist, Milwaukee Psychiatric Services, 1960-64; Co-Director, Haimowoods Institute, 1972-; Faculty, University of Wisconsin, Parkside, Department of Psychology, Behavioral Science Division, 1978-79. Publications: Human Development, 1960, 1966, 1973; Suffering is Optional, 1976; Success in Psychotherapy, 1952, 1987. Address: 1101 Forest Avenue, Evanston, IL 60201, USA.

**HAIRALD Mary Payne**, b. 25 February 1936, Tupelo, Mississippi, USA. Teacher; Coordinator, Secondary Education. m. Leroy U Hairald, 1 son. Education: Associate of Arts, Itawamba Community College, 1955; Bachelor of Commerce, Business Education, Master of Business Education, University of Mississippi, 1957, 1963; Additional graduate work, University of Southern Mississippi, Mississippi State University, University of California, University of Mississippi. Appointments: Cooperation Education Teacher, Coordinator, Nettleton High School, 1970-; Local Coordinator for Academic Year in America, 1988-; Social Science Teacher, Nettleton High School, 1959-70; Business Education Teacher, John Rundle High School, Grenada, 1957-59. Honours: Regional IV Vocational Teacher of the Year, 1996; National Vocational Teacher of the Year, 1997; Public Education Forum Award for Excellence, 1997; Wal-Mart Teacher of the Year, 1997. Memberships: American Vocational Association; Cooperative Work Education Experience Association; Marketing Education Association; Mississippi Association of Vocational Educators; MACVET; MAME; DECA; AAUW; Ladies' Civitans; Phi Delta Kappa. Address: PO Box 166, Nettleton, MS 38858 0166, USA.

**HAIRE Ian James Mitchell**, b. 2 July 1946, Belfast, Northern Ireland. Professor; Church Leader. m. Mary Christine Haire, 2 daughters. Education: Classics, Theology, Worcester College, Oxford University, 1965-69; BA, honours, Theology, 1969, MA, Theology, 1973, University of Oxford; Diploma, Theology, Hendrik Kraemer Instituut, Leiden, 1972; PhD, Theology, University of Birmingham, 1981. Appointments include: Missionary, Indonesia, 1972-84; Minister, Uniting Church, Darwin, Australia, 1985-86; Professor, New Testament, Trinity College, Brisbane, 1987-; Principal, 1992-; Professor, Head, School of Theology, Griffith University, 1994-; National President-Elect, The Uniting Church in Australia, 1997-. Publications include: The Character and Theological Struggle of the Church in Halmahera, Indonesia, 1941-1979, 1981. Memberships: Australian and New Zealand Society for

Theological Studies. Address: Griffith University, Trinity College, GPO Box 674, Brisbane, Qld 4001, Australia.

**HAIRSTON Walter Albert,** b. 14 September 1928, Winston, Salem, NC, USA. Military, Education. m. JeaneHe O Hairston, 2 sons, 5 daughters. Education: BS, Morgan State University, 1959; Loyola College Med, 1970; Command and General Staff College, 1974; National Defense University, 1979. Appointments: Teacher to Dean Department, Commandant USA Reserve School, 1978-. Honours: Commendation Ribbon with medal Pendant; Outstanding Instructor Command Gen Staff; Graduated, cum laude, Morgan State University; Rank of Colonel. Memberships: Kappa Alpha Psi; Kappa Delta Pi; Reserve Officers Association; American Legion. Address: 14300 Robcaste Rd, Phoenix, MD 21131, USA.

**HAISCH Bernhard Michael,** b. 23 August 1949, Stuttgart, Germany. Astrophysicist. m. 3 children. Education: BS High Distinction Astrophysics, 1971, Indiana University, Bloomington; PhD Astronomy, 1975, University Wisconsin, Madison. Appointments: Research Associate, JILA, University Colorado, 1975-77, 1978-79; Visiting Scientist, Astronomical Institute, Utrecht, The Netherlands, 1977-78; Research Scientist, Lockheed Palo Alto Research Laboratory, 1979-83; Visiting Fellow, Max-Planck-Institut fur Extraterr Physik, Garching, Germany, 1991-94; Deputy Director, Centre for EUV Astrophysics, University California at Berkeley, 1992-94; Editor-in-Chief, Journal of Scientific Exploration, 1988-; Associate Editor, Scientific Editor, The Astrophysical Journal, 1993-; Staff Scientist, Staff Physicist, Lockheed Martin, Palo Alto, 1983-. Publications: Over 100 papers in scientific journals and various conference proceedings; Article, Flares on the Sun and Other Stars, 1991; Books: Solar and Stellar Flares, 1989; The Many Faces of the Sun, 1998; 1 patent. Memberships: Editorial Board, Solar Physics, 1992-95, Speculations in Science and Technology, 1995-; International Astronomical Union; American Astronomical Society; Fellow, Royal Astronomical Society; Associate Fellow, American Institute Aeronautics and Astronautics; European Astronomical Society; Society for Scientific Exploration; Phi Beta Kappa; Sigma Xi; Phi Kappa Phi. Address: Solar and Astrophysics Laboratory, Lockheed Martin, Division H1-12, Building 252, 3251 Hanover St, Palo Alto, CA 94304, USA.

**HAJEK Jan.** Address: Adamiho 4, Bratislava, SL 84105, Slovakia.

**HAJNAL Györgi,** b. 25 March 1936, Budapest, Hungary. Vicarius Foraneus. Education: Completed studies at Academy of Theology, Esztergom, 1959; Completed studies at Technical Academy, Budapest, 1964; Librarian's degree, 1973; Pastoral Psychology, 1985. Honours: Golden Pen Award for Outstanding Educators; Honorary Citizen of the 14th District; Honorary Citizen of Budapest; Golden Teachers Desk. Memberships: Committee of Cathecesis; Liturgical Committee; Hungarian Society of Psychiatry. Address: Zoborhegy tér 4/a, H-1141 Budapest, Hungary.

**HALL David Spencer,** b. 23 November 1936, Nashville, Tennessee, USA. Choral Director; Vocal Instructor. Education: BA Music Education, 1958, Austin Peay University, Clarksville; MA Music Education, 1959, Eastern New Mexico University, Portales, New Mexico; M Mus Choral Conducting, Temple University, Philadelphia. Appointments: Music Instructor: USAF in Tripoli, Libya, France and West Berlin; Mastbaum High School, Philadelphia, 1970-72; Upper Darby High School, Pennsylvania, 1973-84; Director of Music, Haverford High School, 1984-86; Director of Choral Activities, Nazareth Academy High School, Philadelphia, 1992-. Memberships:

Music Educators National Conference; American Choral Directors Association. Address: 729 South 3rd Street, Philadelphia, PA 19147-3310, USA.

**HALL Jerry F,** b. 3 December 1934, Childress, Texas, USA. Writer. m. Dorothy Sue, 1 son, 1 daughter. Education: Reporter, Editor, Texas newspapers; Information Assistant to Vice President, Southwestern Bell Telephone Company. Publications: I Love a Farmers Market, 1987; Hello, Texas, 1990. Memberships: Sigma Delta Chi; Public Relations Society of America; Life Member, University of Texas Alumni Association; TLC Birding Society. Address: 707 Cypress Creek Road, Wimberley, TX 78876, USA.

**HALLET Charles,** b. 4 September 1933, Sougné-Remouchamps, Belgium. Jesuit Priest. Education: BA, Université Catholique, Louvain, 1959; BPhil, Ecole des Hautes Etudes Philosophiques et Scientifiques, France, 1961; DD, P Universidad Católica de Chile, 1979. Appointments: Vice Grand Chancellor, 1991-, Director, Department of Theology, 1993-, Universidad Católica del Norte, Antofagasta, Chile; Episcopal Vicar of Education, Archdiocese of Antofagasta, 1991-. Publications: 13 books; 50 articles. Honour: Knight, Order of Leopold II, Belgium, 1996. Membership: New York Academy of Sciences, 1995. Address: Eduardo Orchard 1637, Casilla 1147, Antofagasta, Chile.

**HALSTEAD Diane Claire,** b. 21 March 1940, Chicago, Illinois, USA. Microbiologist. Education: MS, Loyola University Stritch School of Medicine, 1970; PhD, Medical College of Pennsylvania, 1977; Diplomate, American Board of Medical Microbiology, 1985-. Appointments: Director, Microbiology, Immunology, Allentown Hospital, Pennsylvania, 1976-85; Visiting Assistant Professor, 1981-85, Adjunct Associate Professor, 1985-91, Adjunct Professor, 1991-, Medical College of Pennsylvania; Embryologist, Reprotech, Allentown, Pennsylvania, 1985-87; Laboratory Director, Mauch Chunk Medical Center, Jim Thorpe, Pennsylvania, and Director, Microbiology, Virology, Immunology and Flow Cytometry, Health Network Laboratories, Clinical Laboratory, Lehigh Valley Hospital, Allentown, 1985-93; Director, Microbiology, Virology, Immunology, Mol Dx, Baptist-St Vincent's Health System, Faculty, Baptist-St Vincent's School of Medical Technology, Jacksonville, Florida, 1993-; Clinical Professor, Department of Paediatrics, University of Florida College of Medicine, Jacksonville, 1994-. Publications: Rapid Virus Diagnosis, 1981; Medically Important Infections Caused by Normal Oral Flora: Selected Case Studies, 1985; Non-cultural Methods for Diagnosis of RSV Infections, 1987; Others. Honours: Beta Beta Beta, 1962; Medical College of Pennsylvania Alumnae Citation, 1995. Memberships: Current: American Society of Microbiology; American Society of Clinical Pathologists; Pan-American Group for Rapid Viral Dx; American Academy of Microbiologists; Fellow, American College of Microbiology; Fellow, College of Physicians of Philadelphia; Florida Association for Clinical Microbiology, Co-Chair; Jacksonville Area Microbiology Society; Organiser, Jacksonville Microbiology Users Group; First Coast Infectious Disease-Clinical Microbiology Symposium Inc, President, Co-Chair. Address: 17 Ponte Vedra Colony Circle, Ponte Vedra Beach, FL 32082, USA.

**HAMAOKA Takafumi,** b. 24 December 1962, Ehime, Prefecture. Physician. m. Shitomi, 1 son, 1 daughter. Education: MD, School of Medicine, Ehime University, Japan, 1989; PhD, Tokyo Medical University of Tokyo, 1993. Appointments: Research Associate, Department of Biochemistry, Biophysics, University of Penn, USA, 1990-91; Researcher, WHO Collaborating Center for Health Promotion in Sports Medicine, Tokyo, 1993-; Assistant Professor, Department of Preventative Medicine, Tokyo Medical University. Honours: Research Award, Tokyo Metropolitan Government; Young Investigators Award, 1st European College of Sports Science. Memberships: New York Academy of Sciences; American Association for the Advancement of Science. Address: 3-1-2 Minami Kasai, Edogawa Ku, Tokyo 134, Japan.

**HAMED Mohamed,** b. 31 January 1946, Suez, Egypt. Professor. m. Mona Thabet, 1 son, 1 daughter. Appointments: Engineer, Egypt Electric Authority, Cairo, 1969-79; Lecturer, 1978-83, Assistant Professor, 1983-89, Faculty of Engineering, Head, Department of Electrical Engineering, 1985-92, Professor, 1989-, Vice Dean for Research Development, 1992-93, Dean in Duty, 1993, Faculty of Engineering, Port Said; Board Director, Electric Distribution Company, Ismailia, 1986-93; Consultant, General Authority for Educational Buildings, Cairo, 1993-; Scientific Committee for Universities Staff Promotion, Highest Congress of Universities, Cairo, 1995-. Publications: Numerous articles in professional journals. Memberships: New York Academy of Sciences; American Association for Development of Science. Address: Port Fouad City, 25 El Ebour Zone, Port Said 42523, Egypt.

**HAMER David John,** b. 5 September 1923, Melbourne, Victoria, Australia. Naval Officer; Politician. m. Barbara McPherson, 2 sons, 1 daughter. Education: MA, Monash University, 1976. Appointments: Served, Royal Australian Navy, 1937-68; Director of Naval Intelligence, 1962-63; Captain (D), Destroyer Squadron, 1963-65; Federal Politics as Member of Parliament for Isaacs, 1969-74, 1975-77; Senator for Victoria, 1978-80; Deputy President of the Senate, 1983-90. Publication: Can Responsible Government Survive in Australia?, 1994; Bombers versus Battleships, 1998. Honour: Distinguished Service Cross, 1945. Address: 2/77 Caroline Street, South Yarra, Victoria 3141, Australia.

**HAMLIN Lisa Kathleen,** b. 8 March 1962, Nashville, TN, USA. Librarian, Metaphysician. Education: BMs, MMs, MsD, University of Metaphysics. Advanced Studies Degree, Pastoral Psychology, University of Metaphysics; MLS, Vanderbilt University; BS, Elemetary Education, Belmont University; Honorary Degrees, Progressive Universal Life Church; PhD, Metaphysical Science; PhD, Parapsychology, Doctorate in Divinity. Appointments: Student Library Assistant, Belmont University, 1979-83; Library Technical Assistant, 1984; Graduate Assistant to the Director, Vanderbilt University, 1984-85; Librarian, Cataloging Librarian, 1985-86; Library Meida Specialist, Mt Juliet Elementary, 1987-89; Head of Technical Services, Brentwood Library, 1990-; New Thought Pastor, Spiritual Counselor, 1996-. Publications: Many Poems Published. Honours: Scholarship in Library Science; National Poet of the Year; Editors Choice Award; International Woman of the Year, International Biographical Centre. Memberships: Tennessee Library Association; Association of Research and Enlightenment; Institute of Noetic Sciences; International Metophysical Ministry; Chronic Fatigue and Immune Dysfunction Syndrome Society; Interstitial Cystitis Association; Nature Conservancy; Surfriders Foundation; Environmental Defense Fund; Center for Marine Conservation; World Jewish Congress; B'nai B'rith Foundation of the US. Address: 4853 Cimarron Way, Antioch, TN 37013, USA.

**HAMMAD Ihab,** b. 6 April 1958, Alexandria, Egypt. Dentist. m. Khalil Amani, 1 son, 2 daughters. Education: BDS, Alexandria University, 1980; MS and Certificate in Prosthodontics, University of Minnesota, USA, 1985; DSc, Boston University, USA, 1988. Appointments: Assistant

Professor, University of Minnesota, 1985-86; Assistant Professor, 1988-90, Associate Professor, 1997-, Alexandria University; Associate Professor, King Saud University, Saudi Arabia, 1991-97. Publications: Several in international specialised journals including Journal of Prosthetic Dentistry and Journal of Prosthodontics. Honour: S D Tylman Award, American Academy of Fixed Prosthodontics, 1986. Memberships: Egyptian Dental Association; Saudi Dental Society; New York Academy of Sciences; American Academy of Fixed Prosthodontics. Address: Alexandria University School of Dentistry, Champollion Street, Azarita, Alexandria, Egypt.

**HAMMOND Elizabeth Hall Atwater,** b. 22 September 1921, New Haven, Connecticut, USA. Marriage and Family Therapist. m. Alden Wellington Hammond, 3 sons, 1 daughter. Education: BA, Vassar College, 1943; MA, Assumption College, 1979. Career: Licensed Marriage and Family Therapist, Massachusetts; Licensed Certified Social Worker, Massachusetts; Owner, Private Practice, Family Focus. Publications: My Mommy......She Has Long Feet: A case study from a family systems perspective, Pediatric Social Work, The Official Journal of the International Association for Pediatric Social Services, 1982; Several articles in professional newsletters. Honours: Certificate of Recognition, Worcester (Massachusetts) Area Community Mental Health Center, 1985; Talk Show Panelist, Greater Worcester Cablevision, 1986. Memberships: Clinical Member of the American Association for Marriage and Family Therapy; American Association of University Women; Founder, Central Massachusetts Alliance for Mental Health, 1982; Confirmed Communicant and Licensed Pastoral Lay Eucharistic Minister, Holy Trinity Episcopal Church, Diocese of Western Massachusetts. Address: 34 Finlay Road, Fiskdale, MA 01518-1237, USA.

**HAMMOND Karen,** b. 20 December 1954, Baton Rouge, USA. Salesperson; Former Journalist. m. Ralph E Hammond. Education: BS, Journalism,. University of Colorado, 1978. Appointments: Telemarketer, First Meridian Mortgage; Salesperson, LinkCell Corporation, Toyota of Dallas, Telecable of Richardson, Plano, Plano Cellular, Brewer Communications, Publishing Concepts, Dallas; US Attorney, Northern District of Texas; Reporter, Lakewood Sentinel Newspaper. Memberships: National Organization for Women; Women in Communication. Address: 3500 Hillridge Drive, Apt 118, Plano, TX 75074-4367, USA.

**HAN Jingxing,** b. 8 November 1924, Luannan County, Hebei. Geological Surveyor; Petroleum Exploration Engineer. m. Yang, 1 son, 1 daughter. Education: North East University, Beijing University, 1945-52. Appointments: Chief Engineer, Song Liao Basin Petroleum Prospecting No 2 Petroleum Prospecting Party of MGMR, 1955-64; Chief Engineer, Si Chuan Petroleum Prospecting No 2 Petroleum Prospecting Party, 1964-76; Chief Engineer, North China Petroleum Prospecting, North China Bureau of Petroleum Geology of MGMR, 1976-80, 1985-95; Responsible Person, Institute of Petroleum Geology of MGMR, 1980-85; Retired, 1995-. Publications: Co-author, The generation and evolution of the Hehuai Basin, book chapter, 1989; Vice Chief Editor, Prospecting and Discovery of Oil and Gas in China, 1992. Honour: National Certificate of Merit and Medal for being one of the discoverers of Da Qing oil field. Membership: Geology Institute of China. Address: Petroleum Geological Bureau, Funiu Road, Zhengzhou 450006, China.

**HAN Pao Teh,** b. 19 August 1934, Shantung, China. Architect; Professor. m. Sharon Hsiao, 1 son, 1 daughter. Education: BS, National Chengkung University, 1958; MArch, Harvard University, 1965; MFA, Princeton, 1967. Appointments:

Professor and Chairman, Department of Architecture, Tunghai University, Director, National Museum of Natural Science; President, Tainan National College of the Arts. Publications: Spiritual Dimension of Architecture, 1972; Architecture, Culture and Society; Essays on Ming and Ching Architecture, 1976; The Story of Chinese Landscape Design, 1992. Memberships: Chinese Institute of Architect; Chinese Institute of Urban Planning; Chinese Association of Museums. Address: #61 Jen Ai Road, Section 2, Apt 5C-1, Taipei, Taiwan.

**HAN Rusheng,** b. 1 September 1936, Beijing. Professor. m. Li Weijin, 1 son. Education: Graduated, Department of Physics, Peking University. Appointments: Department of Physics, Peking University, 1959-; Associate Professor, 1985; Professor, 1991-; Director, Theoretical Condensed Matter Physics Group, Institute of Theoretical Physics Academic Sinica, 1990-; Director, Center for Computational Physics of Peking University, 1994-. Publications; Physics in High Temperature Superconductivity; A New Family of Fullerenes; Physics in Life Science; Many Papers. Honours: First Class Prize of Development of Science and Technology; Special Class Prize of Peking University; Second Class Prize of Development of Science and Technology. Memberships: National Academic Committee of Statistical Physics and Theoretical Condensed Matter; Academic Committee of Institute of Theoretical Physics; CCAST, Committee of Senier Advisers and Coordinators. Address: Department of Physics, Peking University, 100871 Beijing, China.

**HAN Xue-Zhang,** b. 5 January 1912, Beijing, China. Barrister. m. Wei-Xion Gu, 1 daughter. Education: Bachelor of Law, Shanghai Institute of Law and Politics. Appointments include: Adviser of All-China Bar Association. Publication: The Problem of Criticising and Inheriting Law, 1956. Honour: Xuezhang Han Lawyer Foundation established, 1997. Memberships: Vice-President, All-China Bar Association; President, Honorary President, Shanghai Bar Association. Address: Room 901, Building 3, 246 Wu-xing Road, Shanghai 200030, China.

**HAN Youngyearl,** b. 10 June 1938, Seoul, Korea. Educator. m. Eunb-Mo Kim, 2 sons, 1 daughter. Education: BSc, Electronic Engineering, Seoul National University, 1956-60; MSc, Electrical Engineering, 1974-76, PhD, Electrical Engineering, 1976-79, University of Missouri-Rolla. Appointments: Researcher, Siemens & Halske Company, Germany, 1961-64; Professor, Hanyang University, 1980-; Policy Consultant, Ministry of Interior, Korea, 1981-92; Research Steering Committee, Ministry of Communications, Korea, 1985-93; Visiting Professor, University of Colorado, 1987-88, University of Oregon, 1994-95; Steering Committee, Asia-Pacific Conference on Communication, 1992, International Telecommunication Union, SG7 Seoul Conference, 1994, Korea Section, ITU-CCITT and ITU-CCIR, 1985-89; Judging Consultant, Bureau of Patent, Korea, 1993-95; Director, Research Institute of Telecommunication and Information Sciences, Hanyang University, 1998-. Publications include: Information Theory, Information Systems (book). Honours: Achievement Award, Korea Institute of Communication Science, 1989; Order of Merit Award, Government of Korea, 1993; Presidential Citation Award, Government of Korea, 1993. Memberships: Institute of Electrical and Electronics Engineers; Korea Institute of Communication Sciences; Korea Institute of Telematrics and Electronics. Address: Department of Electronic Communcation Engineering, Hanyang University, Hangdang-Dong Sungdong-ku, Seoul 133-791, Korea.

**HANCKEL Norman Paul,** b. 5 December 1929, Adelaide, South Australia. Wine Consultant. divorced, 1 son (deceased),

2 daughters. Education: High Distinction, Horticulture, Roseworthy College; SA Institute of Technology; Top Distinction in Business Administrative. Appointments: Production Manager, S Smith and Sons, Yalumba Wines; Director and Chief Executive, Hungerford Hill Ltd; Full time Commissioner, Industries Assistance Commission, Australian Government; Director, Head, New South Wales Government Department of Industrial Development; Presiding Member, Chairman, South Australian Government Onkaparinga Catchment Water Management Board. Hobbies: Golf; Tennis; Landscape Painting; Camping. Address: 43 Alexandra Avenue, Rose Park, SA 5067, Australia.

**HANDA S M,** b. 8 May 1942, Lahore, Pakistan. Professor and Researcher. m. Aruna Handa, 1 son, 1 daughter. Education: BSc, Hons, Zoology, 1963; MSc, Hons, Zoology, 1964; PhD, Zoology, 1970. Appointments: Lecturer in Zoology, 1970, Reader in Zoology, 1981, PU, Chandigarh; Director, Pb Dst, Chandigarh, 1991; Professor of Zoology, 1994. Publications: 80 papers. Honours: Government of India Scholarship for doing PhD; Attended and chaired numerous conferences, seminars. Memberships: Life Member, ISCA, Calcutta; Life Member, AICCG, Kalyani; Life Member, NISA, Chandigarh. Address: Department of Zoology, Panjab University, Chandigarh 160014, India.

**HANEKE Dianne Louise,** b. 23 February 1941, San Francisco, California, USA. Professor of Education. m. John P Haneke, 1 son, 2 daughters. Education: BS, Southern California College, Costa Mesa, 1964; MSEd, 1971, CAS, 1990, PhD (in progress), University of New York, Albany. Appointments: Classroom Teacher, Grades 5-6, Los Angeles City Schools, California, 1964-66; Reading Specialist, Grades K-12, Greenville, Cairo, Durham, New York, 1971-89; Professor of Education, Mount Saint Mary College, Newburgh, New York, 1990-92, Concordia University, Austin, Texas, 1992-. Publications: A Woman After God's Own Heart, 1983; A View From The Inside: An Action Plan for Gender Equity in New York State Administration (co-author), 1990. Honours: Alumnus of the Year Award, Southern California College, 1979; Distinguished Service Award, Southern California College Education Department, 1988, Southern California College Alumni Association, 1994; Distinguished Contributor Award, Southern California College Alumni Association, 1988. Memberships: Association for Supervision and Curriculum Development; Association of Teacher Educators; American Educational Research Association; Capital Area Reading Council, Austin; Christian Educators Association International; College Reading Association; Delta Kappa Gamma; International Reading Association; National Council of Teachers of English; National Reading Conference; Phi Delta Kappa; Texas Directors of Field Experience; Texas State Reading Association. Address: 2927 Flower Hill Drive, Round Rock, TX 78664-6300, USA.

**HANKIN Joseph N,** b. 6 April 1940, New York, USA. College President. m. Carole G, 2 sons, 1 daughter. Education: Bachelor of Arts, Social Sciences, City College of New York, 1961; Master of Arts, History, Columbia University, 1992; Doctor of Education, Administration of Higher Education; Doctor of Letters, Honoris Causa, Mercy College, 1979; Doctor of Humane Letters, Honoris Causa, College of New Rochelle, 1996. Appointments: Fellow, Department of History, City College of New York, 1962-63; Lecturer, 1963-65; Lecturer, Brooklyn College of the City University of New York, 1963; Lecturer, Queens College of the City University of New York, 1964; Course Assistant, Department of Higher and Adult Education, Columbia University, 1965; Director, Evening Division, Summer Session, Harford Junior College, 1966-67;

Occasional Lecturer, 1965-; President, Harford Junior College, 1967-71; Adjunct Professor, Visiting Professor, Columbia University, 1976-; President, Westchester Community College, 1971-. Publications: Many publications. Honours: American Association of Community Colleges, 25 Year Service Award; Child Care Council of Westchester, Joey Award; Westchester 2000 Meritorious Service Award; Boys Town of Italy, Educator of the Year Award; Many other awards. Memberships: American Arbitration Association; American Association of Junior Colleges; American Association of Higher Education; American Association of Retired Persons. Address: 4 Merion Dr, Purchase, NY 10577, USA.

**HANSEN Anne Katherine,** b. 29 October 1928, Coulter, Iowa, USA. Poet; Writer; Educator. Education: BA, Education, Chapman University, 1958; MA, University of Redlands, 1971; Lifetime Teaching Credential, Orange, California. Appointments: World of Poetry, 1988-92; International Council, City Hall, San Bernardino, California, 1993-95; International Society of Poets, 1993-. Publications: Poetry Book: Listen To My Heart, 1998. Honours: Golden Poet Awards, 1988, 1989, 1990, 1991, 1992; Poet of Merit, 1993-94, 1996. Memberships: American Association of University Women (Secretary); Danish Brotherhood in America (Treasurer); Church of the Nazarene (Board Member). Address: 1632 North Sepulveda Avenue, San Bernardino, CA 92404, USA.

**HANSEN Magnus Bang,** b. 24 May 1936, Denmark. Headteacher. m. Asta, 1 son, 2 daughters. Education: Teacher Certificate, 1958. Appointments: Lieutenant, Artillery, 1960; Headteacher, 1965; President, Headteachers of Danish State Special Schools, 1970-85; City Council, 1974-81. Publications: The Rise of Subculture Bridges; Children With Psychotic Behavior. Honour: Medal of Merit. Memberships: Lions Club of Denmark. Address: Sydskraenten 4, 4400 Kalundborg, Denmark.

**HANSON Murray,** b. 26 May 1948, Albert Lea, Minnesota. Pastor. m. Mary Ann, 1 son, 1 daughter. Education: Bachelor of Arts, Minnesota State University, 1970; Master of Divinity, University of Dubuque Theological, 1973; Doctor of Ministry, 1980. Appointments: Intern, SunnysidePresbyterian Church, 1972; Associate Pastor, Lakeside Presbyterian Church, 1973-77; Pastor, Third Presbyterian Church, Rockford, IL, 1977-. Publications: Tour Organizer and Host. Honours: University of Dubuque Theological Seminary Alumni Award. Memberships: Greater Rockford Clergy Association; Many more. Address: 3d Presbyn Church, 1221 Custer Ave, Rockford, IL 61103-4667, USA.

**HANSTEEN Johannes Mathias,** b. 7 March 1927, Arendal, Norway. Theoretical Physicist. m. Ellen Karlsrud, div 1989, 2 sons, 1 daughter. Education: Cand Real, University of Oslo, 1955; Dr Philos, University of Bergen, 1976. Appointments: Research Assistant, University of Oslo, 1953-56; Fellow, Nordic Institute of Theoretical Physics, Copenhagen, 1957-59; Research Associate, University of Oslo, 1959-66; Professor, Theoretical Atomic Physics, University of Bergen, 1967-. Publications: Numerous articles on atomic collision physics and nuclear physics; Contributions to international conference proceedings, 1956-99. Memberships: Norwegian Physical Society; European Physical Society; American Physical Society; European Academy of Science, Arts and Letters; New York Academy of Sciences. Address: Department of Physics, University of Bergen, Allegaten 55, N-5007 Bergen, Norway.

**HAO Deqian,** b. 8 March 1927, Qian Yuan, Shenxi, China. Economy. m. Wang Ning Zhen, 2 sons, 1 daughter. Education: Graduate, Philosophy Department, Beijing University, 1952; Graduate, Economic Research Department, People's University of China. Appointments: Lecturer, Beijing Railway College, 1955; Associate Professor, 1981, Professor, 1989, Lanzhou Railway College. Publications: On Production and Consumers; On the Development of Railway Must Pay More Attention to the West Region. Memberships: Director, Lanzhou Railway College Social Science Department, 1983-87; Gansu Provincial Economic Council, 1983-95. Address: Department of Social Science, Lanzhou Railway College, Lanzhou, Gansu, China.

**HAPSMITH Linda T,** b. 7 February 1963, Salt Lake City, UT, USA. Academic Advisor. m. Michael C Hapsmith, 1 daughter. Education: BS, Child and Family Development, University of Utah, 1984; MS, Educational Psychology, University of Utah, 1989. Appointments: Advising Programs Coordinator, Pennsylvania State University, Hazleton Campus, 1995-97; Academic Adviser, Pennsylvania State University, 1997-. Publication: Attachment to Pets Among Eighth Graders, 1990. Honour: Woman of Achievement Award, Utah Federation of Business and Professional Women, 1991. Membership: National Academic Advising Association. Address: Pennsylvania University - Hazleton, Highacres, Hazleton, PA 18201, USA.

**HARARY Keith,** b. 1953, New York, New York. Research Scientist, Science Journalist; Author. m. Darlene Moore. Education: BA Distinction Psychology, magna cum laude, 1975, Duke University; PhD Psychology, 1986, Graduate School of The Union Institute; Specialised training in crisis and suicide intervention, individual and family counseling, Mental Health Centre, Durham, North Carolina, 1972-76. Appointments: Crisis Counsellor, Durham Mental Health Centre, 1972-76; Research Associate, Psychical Research Foundation, 1973-76; Research Associate, Department of Psychiatry, Maimonides Medical Centre, 1976-79; Director of Counseling, Human Freedom Centre, 1979; Research Consultant, SRI International, 1980-82; Design Consultant, Atari Corporation, 1983-85; Freelance Science Journalist, 1988-98; Editor at Large, Omni Magazine, 1995-98; President and Research Director, Institute for Advanced Psychology, 1986-. Publications: Co-author, Who Do You Think You Are? Explore Your Many-Sided Self with Berkeley Personality Profile, 1994; Co-author, 6 30-day altered state of consciousness series; Co-author, The Mind Race; 43 articles in professional publications; Over 50 feature articles; 24 articles in Omni; Very many television and radio appearances. Memberships: American Psychological Society; American Psychological Association; Association for Media Psychology; Member Board Directors, American Society for Psychical Research, 1993-. Address: 98 Main Street, Suite 637, Tiburon, CA 94920, USA.

**HARDAS Kshama,** b. 25 June 1978, Belgaum. Kathak Dancer; Computer Science Graduate. Education: Alankar in Kathak Dance, with special distinction, 1998; BSc, Computer Science, Nagpur University, 1999. Career: Kathak Densuas; Participant, various dance dramas including Shrikrishna Sangetika, 1992, Geet-Geeta, 1993, Durga Zali Gouri, 1994, Nagpur; Special performances, Deshmukh Memorial Festival, Wardha, 1992, Vividh Kala Mahotsav, Ramtek, 1993, and Nagpur, 1994, Neeri Auditorium, Nagpur, 1994, Balirampanth Pande Memorial Festival, Nagpur, 1996, Indian Food in International Market, Seminar, Nagpur, 1996, 12th Adivasi Yuvak Mahotsav, Gadchiroli, 1996; 12th All India Road Congress Convention, Nagpur, 1997, India-Israel Cultural Association 2nd Annual Function, 1997, Kal-Ke-Kalakar Sammelan, Sur Singar Samsad, Bombay, 1998. Honours: 1st Award, Inter-School Classical Solo Dance Competition, 1992, 1993, 1994; 2nd Place, Inter-State Classical Dance

Competition, 1995; 1st Place, SCZCC 10th Yuva Sangeet Nritya Mahotsav, Ujjain, 1996; Represented Maharashtra State, SCZCC 10th Yuva Sangeet Nritya Mahotsav, Khajjuraho, 1996; Represented Nagpur University, winning 2nd Award in Classical Dance, 12th West Zone Inter-University Youth Festival, Anand (Gujrat), 1996; Represented West Zone, All-India Inter-University Youth Festival Bombay, Kshitij, 1997; Nrityashree Award, Kiran Mahotsav All-India Level Kathak Contest, 1998; Singarmani Award, 1998. Address: Kathak Sadhana Kendra, 52 Madhav Nagar, Nagpur 440-010, Maharastra State, India.

**HARDIN Hal,** b. 29 June 1941, Nashville, USA. Attorney. Education: BS, Middle Tennessee University, 1966; JD, Vanderbilt University, 1968. Appointments: Fingerprint Technician, FBI, 1961; Director, St Louis Job Corps Centre, 1968; Assistant District Attorney, Nashville, 1969-71; Private Practice, 1971-75; Presiding Judge, Nashville Trial Courts, 1976-77; US Attorney, Middle District, Tennessee, 1977-81; Practice of Law, Nashville, 1981-; Instructor, Government Aquinas College, Tennessee State College; Adjunct Professor, Federal Sentencing, Nashville Law School. Memberships: ABA; National Association of Criminal Defense Attorneys; Nashville Bar Association; Tennessee Bar Association. Address: 219 2nd Avenue North Ste 300, Nashville, TN 37201-1618, USA.

**HARDIN L Ann,** b. 2 August 1947, Findlay, Ohio, USA. Social Worker; Individual, Marriage and Family Therapist. m. John W Hardin, 2 sons, 1 daughter. Education: Bachelors in Social Work, Masters in Social Work, University Missouri, Columbia; Certified Clinical Social Worker. Appointments: Director, Option Program, Project Concern International, 1975-78; Student Internship, University of Missouri Medical Centre, Neonatal Intensive Care Unit, 1983; Graduate Student Assistant, Missouri Association for Social Welfare, 1984-85; Adjunct faculty, University of Guam, School of Social Work, 1990, 1991, 1998; Individual, Marriage and Family Therapist, Navy Family Service Centre, Guam, 1985-92; Senior Individual, Marriage and Family Therapist, Superior Court of Guam, Client Services and Family Counseling Division, 1992-. Publications: 2 Chapters in book, Family Violence in Guam, 1997; 25 presentations, including Hong Kong, 1996 and Sydney, Australia, 1998. Honours: Outstanding Graduate Student, 1985; Social Worker of the Year, 1991; Awarded The Ancient Order of the Chamori, Governor of Guam and the Guam Legislature, 1991. Memberships: National Association of Social Workers; Academy of Certified Social Workers; Guam Association of Social Workers, various positions; Guam Association of Individual, Marriage and Family Therapists; American Counseling Association; American Association of University Women; American Association of Christian Counselors. Address: Superior Court of Guam, PO Box 4324, Agana, GU 96932, USA.

**HARDING Christopher Philip,** b. 4 August 1944, Keynsham, Somerset, England. Retired Consultant. Education: SFPE, 1977; DPhE, 1978; FIBA, 1985; AAABI, 1986; MCC, 1988; PhD, 1988; Kt.MSS, 1989; SRFP, 1990. Appointments: CIAE, 1969-83; Good News, 1983-86; Eltran, 1985-87; Computer Consultants, 1987-88; Point One Advisory Group Inc, 1988-90. Publications: Numerous in professional journals. Honours include: Biography of the Year Award, Historical Preservations of America, 1987; Certificate of Recognition, General Achievements, International Who Who's of Contemporary Achievement, 1997; Certificate for Special Projects Participation, ISPE Special Projects Co-Ordinator, 1998; Outstanding Achievement Diploma, Outstanding Contribution to ISPE, 1998. Memberships: MENSA; International Legion of Intelligence; International Society for

Philosophical Enquiry; The Mega Society; Rockhampton Leagues Club; Frenchville Sports Club Limited; Brothers Leagues Club Capricornia. Address: Box 5271 Mail Centre, North Rockhampton, Qld 4702, Australia.

**HARDISH Patrick Michael,** b. 6 April 1944, Perth Amboy, New Jersey, USA. Composer; Librarian. Education: Juilliard School, 1969-72; BA, 1976, Queens College, CUNY, 1973-76; MS, 1980, Pratt Institute, 1976-80; Graduate Work, Columbia University, 1978-80. Appointments: Library Assistant, Columbia University Music Library, 1978-84; Co-Director and Co-Founder, Composers Concordance, 1983-; Senior Librarian, New York Public Library, 1984-. Honours: Meet the Composer Awards, 1978, 1982, 1983, 1992, 1997; Virginia Center for the Creative Arts, Fellowships, 1981, 1982, 1985, 1986, 1988; Sonorous for Sax Quartet. Memberships: American Music Center; BMI; New Jersey Guild of Composers, Program Committee; Music Library Association. Address: 713 Lincoln Drive, Perth Amboy, New Jersey 08861-2313, USA.

**HARE Sandra Florence,** b. 23 October 1952, Philadelphia, PA. Medicine. 1 daughter. Education: BA Biological Sciences, 1974, Clark University; Pharmacology, Loyola University Stritch School of Medicine, Illinois, 1974-75; MPH, 1978, University Illinois School of Public Health; MD, 1983, University Health Sciences, Chicago Medical School, North Chicago, Illinois. Appointments: Residency in Internal Medicine, Mercy Hospital and Medical Centre, 1984-87, Clinical Assistant in Medicine, University Illinois Medical Centre, 1985-87; Cook County Hospital, Dept Internal Medicine, 1987-; Attending Staff Physician, Cermak Health Services, Illinois, 1987-92; Internal Medicine Physician, North Suburban Clinic, Ltd, Illinois, 1992-98; President, CEO, Renaissance Medicine Ltd, Wilmette, Illinois, 1998-. Publications: National Technical Information Services environmental health criteria documents on Lead and Hydrogen Cyanide, co-author. Honours: Jonas Clark Scholarship 1970-74; American Association of University of Women Gloucester County Scholarship, 1970; Bamberger Award for Leadership, 1971. Memberships: American College of Physicians; American Medical Association; Illinois State Medical Society; Cook County Medical Society; American Society Internal Medicine. Address: 3612 Lake, Wilmette, IL 60091, USA.

**HARIBHAKTI Vishnubhai Bhagwandas,** b. 8 October 1929, Baroda, India. Chartered Accountant. m. Usha Haribhakti, 2 sons, 1 daughter. Education: BCom, Bombay University; Chartered Accountant, 1st Rank in final examination. Appointments: Founder, Senior Partner, Haribhakti and Co, Chartered Accountants; Formerly: Director, Board of Directors, Central Bank of India; Director, National Rayon Corporation Ltd; Special Executive Magistrate; Member, All India Board of Technical Studies in Management; Member, Faculty of Commerce, University of Bombay; Member, Faculty of Commerce, M S University, Baroda; Visiting Professor, Sydenham College of Commerce and Economics, Bombay; Currently: Director, The Prudential IC and CI Trust Co Ltd; Director, several public limited companies. Publications: Taxation of Non-Residents in India, book; Accountant's Role in Evaluation of Capital Investments, conference paper; Several articles on taxation policy, public finance and management accounting, other topics. Honour: G P Kapadia First President Gold Medal, Final Chartered Accountants Examination. Memberships: Institute of Chartered Accountants of India, President, 1967-68; Indian Merchants' Chamber, Bombay, President, 1978, Member, Managing Committee; Founder Director, Rotary Club of Bombay Mid-Town, President, 1987-88; Past District Treasurer, Rotary District 3140; Managing Committee, Associated Chambers of Commerce and dustry of India. Address: 42 Free Press House, 213 Nariman oint, Mumbai 600021, India.

**HARKARE Manohar,** b. 22 December 1914, Nagpur, India. an of Literature, Spirituality and Yoga Authority in Whole orld. m. Smt Shalinibai, 2 sons, 3 daughters. Education: BSc, Sc, MA, BT, MA (Music); BFA. Career: Opened many spiritual eep secrets in Ved, Upnishad, Bhagvadgita, Ramayan, ahabharat, Bible and Kuran; Worked to create a better ociety to engender world peace; Known world-wide for arkaya Pravesh; Teacher of Prime Minister of India, Atal hari Vajpayee, 1941; Close associate of Mahatma Gandhi nd Guruji Golwalkar; Freedom Fighter. Publications: Writer of 6 books including: Enigma of Death and Birth; Book on the cientific side of Indian Music. Memberships: Founder Member, ishwa Hindu Parishad and Jansangh; President, Vaidik Viswa. ddress: 85 Ramana Marutinagar, Nagpur 440 009 aharashtra, India.

**HARRIS Bruce,** b. 19 November 1953, San Antonio, Texas, SA. Mining Consultant. m. Sharon L Huddleston. Education: ED, 1970. Appointments: Director, 1984, Owner, Vacation ranson Magazine, 1994-96; Owner, Heavy Metal Mining ompany, 1995-; Owner, EPI Services, 1997-. Publications: old Miner's Handbook, author; Modern Gold Dredging, author. lemberships: Apple Squires of the Ozarks, 1993-; Reference ibrary Chairman, 1994-97; Lending Librarian, 1998-. Address: leavy Metal Mining Company, PO Box 9256, Springfield, MO 5801-8256, USA.

**HARRIS Godfrey,** b. 11 June 1937, London, England. Public olicy Consultant. m. Barbara DeKovner-Mayer, 3 sons. ducation: AB, Stanford University, 1958; MA, University of alifornia, Los Angeles, 1960. Career: Task Force, University f California, Los Angeles, 1958-60; Intelligence Officer, US rmy, Fort Hancock, New Jersey, 1960-62; Lecturer, epartment of History and Political Science, Rutgers niversity, 1961-62; Foreign Service Officer, Department of tate, 1962-65; Management Analyst, Bureau of Budget, xecutive Office of the President, 1965-67; Special Assistant the President of IOS Development Company Ltd, 1967-68; resident, Chief Executive Officer, Harris/Ragan Management iroup, 1968-. Publications include: Books: Promoting nternational Tourism, 1986; The Ultimate Black Book, 1988; oncentration, 1997; Don't Take Our Word For It!, 1998; lumerous articles. Honours include: National Defense Medal; rmy Commendation Medal. Memberships include: Phi Beta appa; International Ivory Society; Association of Management onsultants; American Academy of Consultants; Ephebian ociety, Los Angeles; California Seal Bearer Society; American oreign Service Association. Address: Harris/Ragan lanagement Group, 9200 Sunset Boulevard, Suite 404, Los ngeles, CA 90069, USA.

**HARRIS Jeffrey Saul,** b. 13 March 1949, Pittsburgh, ennsylvania, USA. Physician. 1 son, 2 daughters. Education: 3S, Molecular Biophysics, Yale University, 1971; MD, niversity of New Mexico, 1975; MPH, Managed Care rganisation, University of Michigan, 1982; MBA, Executive lanagement, Vanderbilt University, 1988. Appointments: resident, J Harris Associates Inc, 1979-; Director of Health lanagement, Northern Telecom Inc, 1983-88; Medical irector, Aetna Health Plans, 1990-91; National Practice eader, Alexander and Alexander Consultant General ractitioners, 1991-94; Senior Vice-President, Health, Safety nd Claims Industrial Indemnity, 1994-97. Publications: Various n themes including occupational medical practice, strategic ealth management, integrated health management. Honours: residential Award, Aetna, 1996. Memberships: American

Medical Association; ACOEM; ACPM; ACMQ. Address: 386 Richardson Way, Mill Valley, CA 94941, USA.

**HARRIS Robert Dalton,** b. 24 December 1921, Jamieson, Oregon, USA. History Educator. m. Ethel Imus. Education: BA, Whitman College, 1951; MA, 1953, PhD, 1959, University of California, Berkeley. Appointments: Teaching Assistant, University of California, Berkeley, 1956-59; Instructor in History, 1959, Professor, 1961-86, Emeritus Professor, 1986-, University of Idaho. Publications: Necker, Reform Statesman of Ancient Regime, book, 1979; Necker and Rev of 1789, 1986. Memberships: American Historical Association; American Association of University Professors. Address: 928 East 8th STreet, Moscow, ID 83843-3851, USA.

**HART John Arthur Lewis,** b. 4 September 1937, Melbourne, Australia. Orthopaedic Surgeon. m. Jan, 1 son, 1 daughter. Education: University of Melbourne. Appointments: Senior Lecturer, 1973-96, Clinical Associate Professor, 1996-, Department of Surgery, Monash University; Assessor, National Health and Medical Research Council, 1982-; Examiner, Orthopaedic Surgery, 1992-; Board, Orthopaedic Surgery, 1994-, Royal Australasian College of Surgeons; President Australian Orthopaedic Association 1998-99. Publications: Several articles in professional journals. Honours: ALESA Major Bursary Victorian Science Talent Quest, 1955; International Cultural Diploma of Honour, 1990; Life Member, Sports Medicine Australia, 1991; Honorary Fellow, Australian College of Sports Physicians, 1993; LO Betts Memorial Gold Medal, Australian Orthopaedic Association, 1997. Memberships include: Australian Orthopaedic Association; AO Alumni Association; Society of International Chirurgy and Traumatoloy (SICOT); International Society for Arthroscopy and Knee Surgery. Address: 16 Riversdale Court, East Hawthorn, Vic 3122, Australia.

**HARTAL Paul,** b. 1936, Hungary. Artist, Writer, Teacher. m. Penny Fromme, 2 sons, 1 daughter. Education: MA, Concordia University, Montreal, 1977; PhD, Columbia Pacific University, USA, 1986. Appointments: Founder, Centre for Art, Science and Technology; University Instructor; Project Director. Publications: Brush and Compass; The Kidnapping of the Painter Miro; several articles. Memberships: New York Academy of Sciences. Address: Box 1012, St Laurenmt, Quebec, Canada, H4L 4W3.

**HARTLEY Elise Moore,** b. 3 March 1953, SLC, Utah. Freelance Designer; Pastor. m. Edward A. Education: BFA, Costume Design for Theatre, University of Utah, 1976. Appointments: Fashion Designer Assistant, 1978; Costumiere, Milliner, 1986; Milliner, Utah Opera, 1986-90; Coordinator of Childrens Ministries, 1996-. Honours: Best Costume Design Award; Lagoon Opera House Award; Childrens Ministry Award. Memberships: First Presbyterian Church, Ordained Deacon; Pastor Nominating Committee. Address: 446 Wall Street, Salt Lake City, UT 84103 1751, USA.

**HASEEBUDDIN Syed,** b. 9 August 1970, Hyderabad, India. Development Manager. Education: BS Industrial Chemistry, 1991, MS Polymer Sciences, 1993, Kakatiya University, Warangal, India; PhD, 1997, Osmania University, Hyderabad. Appointments: Manager in Application Research and Development, OEM Coatings, ICI India Ltd, Calcutta, 1997-. Publications: 12 papers in professional journals and conferences. Honours: Young Scientist Award, 1994, for best presentation of research paper; Indian Paint Association Award, 1997; Complimentary Membership from Surface Coatings International (JOCCA) England; Senior Research Fellowship, Council of Scientific and Industrial Research,

1995-97. Memberships: New York Academy of Sciences, active; Oil and Colour Chemists Association, England; Associate member, Oil Technologists Association of India. Address: D No 13-7-89 Yellam Bazaar, Warangal 506 002, India.

**HASHMI Ziauddin Syed,** b. 24 February 1960, Pakistan. Pharmaceutical Scientist. m. Shameem, 1 son, 1 daughter. Education: BScHons, 1982; MSc, 1983; PhD, 1993. Appointments: Research Assistant, 1983; Microbiologist, 1983; Lecturer, 1984-88; Demonstrator, 1989-92; University of Sydney, Post Doctoral Fellow,1993-1994; Course Consultant Lecturer, 1994-. Publications: Lomefloxacin Sensitivities; Lomefloxacin disc susceptibility criteria - a reappraisal; Late quinolone resistance in Pseudomonas aeruginosa; Outer membraine changes in quinolone resistant Pseudomonas aeruginosa; Quinolone resistance in Pseudomonas aeruginosa; Bactericidal Activity of Lomefloxacin. Honours: Glaxo Prize; New Zealand University Grants; Merit Scholarship; Summer Studentship; Research Studentship. Address: 31 Watson Pl, Papatoetoe, Manukau City, Auckland, New Zealand.

**HASSEL Sven,** b. 19 April 1917, Denmark. Author. m. Dorthe, 1 son. Education: Military Education. Appointments: Shipboy; Soldier; Production Chief; Professional Writer. Publications: Legion of the Damned; Wheels of Terror; Comrades of War; Marchbattalion; Assignment Gestapo; Monte Cassino; Liquidate Paris; SS General; Reign of Hell; Blitzfreeze; Bloody Road to Death; Court Martial; OGPU Prison; The Commissar. Memberships: Danish Authors Union; German Authors Union. Address: Francese Perez Cabrero 2, 08021 Barcelona, Spain.

**HASTY Linda Lorraine,** b. 16 November 1946, Shelbyville, Tennessee, USA. Professor; Educator. m. Doyle E Hasty, 2 sons. Education: BSc, Business Education, 1968, MBEd, 1979, Middle Tennessee State University, Murfreesboro, Tennessee, USA; Doctorate, Higher Education, Nova Southeastern University, Ft Lauderdale, Florida, USA, 1994-. Appointments: Instructor, English Grades 7-9, West Middle School, Tullahoma, Tennessee, 1968-71; Instructor, English, Reading, West Middle School, Tullahoma, Tennessee, 1976-77; Instructor, Assistant Professor, Associate Professor, Professor, Motlow State Community College, 1978-. Publication: Journal of Business Education, Teaching Word Processing Without Sophisticated Equipment, 1980. Honours: Certified Professional Secretary, 1980; Teaching Excellence Award, Motlow State Community College, Tullahoma, Tennessee, 1981; 1st Place Keyboarding Award, Staffing Solutions, Tullhoma, Tennessee, 1995; Certified Manager, 1995; Certified Professional Résumé Writer, 1998. Memberships: American Association of University Professors; Tennessee Business Education Association. Address: 412 Riverbend Country Club, Shelbyville, TN 37160-7221, USA.

**HASUNUMA Kohji,** b. 12 November 1943, Tokyo. Biologist. m. Miyako, 1 son, 1 daughter. Education: Bachelor of Science, Tokyo University, 1966; Master of Science, Tokyo University, 1968; Doctor of Science, Tokyo University, 1971. Appointments: Research Associate, Tokyo University, 1971; Associated Professor, National Institute for Basic Biology, 1979; Professor, Kihara Institute, 1990-. Publications: Signal Transduction in Plants, 1996; Light Signal Transduction, 1999; 3 reviews; 8 Original Papers on light signal transduction. Honours: 20th Century Achievement Award, American Biographical Institute, 1998; Distinguished Leadership Award, ABI, 1998; Magnificient and Distinguished Deeds, ABI, 1998; Deputy Director General, International Biographical Center, 1998; Hall of Fame, ABI, 1998; 2000 Milennium Medal of

Honour, ABI, 1998; International Man of the Year, IBC 1997-98; Citation of Meritorious Achievement, IBC, 1998 Decree of Merit, IBC, 1998; 20th Century Award fo Achievement, IBC, 1999; Memberships: New York Academy o Sciences; International Biographical Centre; America Biographical Institute for Academic Degree; Internationa Journal of Cell Biology, Cytologia; Natural Science in Nationa Institution; Board of Advisors, ABI. Address: Yokohama City University, Kihara Institute for Biological Research an Graduate School of Integrated Sciences, 641 12 Maioka ch Totsuka ku, Yokohama 244 0813, Japan.

**HASZPRA Otto,** b. 11 September 1928, Budapest, Hungary Civil (Hydraulic) Engineer. m. div. 2 sons, 1 daughter Education: Dipl Engineer, 1951, Dr Techn, 1967, Technica University Budapest; Candidate of Sc, 1966, Doctor of Techr Sc, 1973, Hungarian Academy of Science; Europa Engineer o FEANI, 1994. Appointments: Assistant Professor, Associate Professor, Technical University of Transport, Szolnok, 1951-56 Research Engineer, Head of Section, Head of Dept, Scientifi Deputy Director, Research Centre of Water Resources Development, VITUKI, Budapest, 1956-79; Adviser, Lecturer o 5 continents, 1968-; Visiting Research Engineer, Iowa Institute of Hydraulic Research, 1968-69; UN Expert, 1979-; Professo of Hydraulics, Head of Dept of Hydraulic Engineering Research Professor, Technical University of Budapest, 1979- Publications: Over 300 including: Modelling Hydroelastic Vibrations, 1978, 1979, 1979, 1980; Concise Hungarian-Esperanto Dictionary (co-editor, author), 1996 Honours: Roland Eotvos, 1978; Pro Esperanto, 1987; Alber Szent-Gyorgyi, 1993; and others. Memberships: Internationa Academy of Science, San Marino-Paderborn; New York Academy of Science; Hungarian Academy of Science; Nationa Committees of IAHR, ICOLD; Universal Esperanto Association Hungarian Hydrologic Society. Address: Technical University of Budapest, Department of Hydraulic Engineering, HU-1521 Budapest, Hungary.

**HATCH Ann M,** b. 3 March 1956, Tachikowa, Japan. Public Relations Specialist. m. Jim Hatch, 1 s. Education: BA, Appliec Communications; MA, Political Science. Appointments Reporter, Editor, Auburn University at Montgomery, 1983-86 News Services Coordinator, Auburn University, 1986-88 Interim Director, University Relations, Auburn University, 1987 Assistant Director of Public Information, Media Relations Texas Womans University, 1988-94; Interim Director, Public Information, Texas Woman's University, 1994-95; Director o News and Information, Texas Woman's University, 1995- Honours: Grand Awards; Awards of Excellence in Achievement in Writing; Business Communicator of the Year; Finalist Katie Awards; More than 30 others. Memberships: Council for Advancement and Support of Education; Association of Texas Colleges and Universities; American Association of State Colleges and Universities; Alliance for Higher Education; Leadership Denton. Address: Texas Woman's University, P O Box 425619, Denton, TX 76204, USA.

**HAW Boon Hong,** b. 14 February 1969, Penang, Malaysia. Business Development Partner. m. 2 s. Education: MBA, Trinity University, USA. Appointments: Managing Director, BN Billionaire Network; Co-founder of Ansted University; Business Development partner for Clayton University. Memberships: Million Dollar Round Table; Malaysian Insurance Institute; Highlander Club; Chartered Institute of Business Administration. Address: 3 Lebuh Rambai 4, 11060 Penang, Paya Terubong, Malaysia.

**HAWES Nancy Elizabeth,** b. 28 October 1944, Philadelphia Pennsylvania, USA. Mathematics Educator; Associate Pastor

Education: BS Mathematics Education, 1966, Millersville University; MAT, 1970, Purdue University; M Div, 1979, Eastern Baptist Theological Seminary. Appointments: Penncrest High School, Rose Tree-Media School District, 1966-68; Upper Merion Area High School, Upper Merion Area School District, 1968-; Assistant Pastor, 1975-82, Associate Pastor, 1990-, Wesley A M E Zion Church; Pastor, St John A M E Zion Church, 1982-88; Pastor, Mt Tabor A M E Zion Church, 1988-90. Memberships: Upper Merion Area Education Association; Pennsylvania State Education Association; National Education Association; Association of Teachers of Mathematics of Philadelphia and Vicinity; Pennsylvania Council of Teachers of Mathematics; National Council of Teachers of Mathematics; Mathematical Association of America; Philadelphia Zoological Society; Philadelphia Orchestra Association; Philadelphia-Baltimore Conference of A M E Zion Church. Address: 2230 Dermond Avenue, Upper Darby, PA 19082, USA.

**HAYASHI Mitsuhiko,** b. 3 September 1930, Okazaki, Japan. Retired Physicist. m. Etsuko Ito, 2 daughters. Education: BSc, 1958, MSc, 1960, Nagoya University; PhD, Tokyo Institute of Technology, 1971. Appointments: Research Associate, 1960-70, Assistant Professor, 1970-75, Associate Professor, 1975-76, Nagoya University; Professor, 1976-96, Professor Emeritus, 1996-, Toyama Medical and Pharmaceutical University. Publications include: Introductory Physics, 1966; Ultrafine Particles, 1984. Memberships: Physical Society of Japan; American Physical Society. Address: 831-2758 Kitayama Obata, Moriyama-ku, Nagoya 463-0011, Japan.

**HAYASHI Takemi,** b. 8 October 1938, Nagoya, Aichi, Japan. Physics Teacher. m. Mariko Tsurumi, 1 son, 1 daughter. Education: BS, Nagoya University, 1961; MS, 1963; DSc, 1966. Appointments: Research Fellow, Hiroshima University, 1966-83; Lecturer, 1983; Associate Professor, Kure Japan National College of Technology, 1983-85; Professor, 1985-91; Professor, Kogakkan University, 1991-. Publications: Articles to Professional Journals. Memberships: Physical Society of Japan; American Physical Society. Address: Kogakkan University, 1704 Kodakujimoto Cho, Ise Mie 516-8555, Japan.

**HAZARIKA Nurara,** b. 28 February 1942, North Lakhimpur, Assam, India. m. Ansar Hussain Hazarika, 1 son, 1 daughter. Education: BA Hons in History, 1978; MA, History, 1980; MPhil, 1983. Appointments: Lecturer in History, Women's College, Shillong; Self employed in small scale industry, Aesthetics, presently. Address: Lower Lachaumeire, Shillong 793001, Meghalaya, India.

**HAZELTINE Joyce,** b. Pierre, SD. Secretary of State. m. Dave, 2 s, 1 d. Education: Huron University; Northern State University; Black Hills State University. Appointments: Elected Secretary of State, 1986; Inaugurated, 1987; Re-elected, 1990; Inaugurated, 1991; Re-elected, 1994; Inaugurated, 1995; Re-elected, 1998; Inaugurated, 1999. Honours: Outstanding Alumni Award; Outstanding Young Woman of America. Memberships: Pierre Area Chamber of Commerce; Mother of the Year Committee; SD Literary Council Charter; General Foundation of Women's Clubs; South Dakota Breast and Cervical Cancer Control Outreach Program. Address: 500 E Capitol Avenue, Ste 204, Pierre, SD 57501-5070, USA.

**HE Ji-Fan,** b. 30 June 1937, Shanghai, China. Solid Mechanics Educator; Researcher. m. Bang-An Ma. Education: MSc, Tsinghua University, Beijing, 1959. Appointments: Assistant, 1959-79, Lecturer, 1979-86, Associate Professor, 1986-96, Professor, 1996-, Tsinghua University, Beijing. Publications: Articles to professional journals. Memberships:

Chinese Society of Theoretical and Applied Mechanics; Chinese Society of Composite Materials; Chinese Society of Vibration Engineering. Address: Department of Engineering Mechanics, Tsinghua University, Beijing 100084, China.

**HE Qiansan,** b. 26 November 1932, Chengdu, Sichuan, China. Musicologist. m. Zhong Zilin, 1 son. Education: Study, Department of Musicology, Central Conservatory of Music, Beijing, 1957-62; Advanced study, Chinese Academy of Social Sciences, 1978-80. Appointments: Associate Professor, 1986; Vice Chairman, Department of Musicology, 1984-88; Professor, 1992. Honours: First Prize for Chinese National Achievement in Teaching and Research, 1993; Grant, Asian Cultural Council, 1993. Memberships: Chinese Musicians Association; Director, Society for Musical Aesthetics, China. Address: Central Music Institute, Baojia Street, Beijing 100031, China.

**HE Qing,** b. 26 September 1959, Hunan, China. Senior Engineer. m. Yan Cheng, 1 son. Education: BS, North East University of Technology, Shenyang, China, 1982; MS, General Research Institute for Non-Ferrous Metals, Beijing, China, 1989; PhD, University of Tennessee, USA, 1998. Appointments: Research Engineer, General Research Institute for Non-Ferrous Metals, Beijing, 1982-86, 1989-92; Research Assistant, Oak Ridge National Laboratory, 1992-97; Post Doctoral Research Associate, Oak Ridge National Laboratory, 1998; Senior Engineer, Seagate Technology Inc, 1998-. Publications: 50 Articles to Professional Journals; 40 Presentations on Conference; 4 US Patents. Honours: Outstanding Research Award, 1986; Outstanding Research Award, 1991. Memberships: American Physics Society; Materials Research Society; Sigma Xi Scientific Research Associate. Address: 10650 Brunswick Road, Apt 102, Bloomington, MN 55438, USA.

**HE Shao-Xun,** b. 21 July 1920, Beijing, China. Professor. m. Xiao Qing-Cheng, 2 sons, 1 daughter. Education: BS, 1942, Southwestern Associate University. Appointments: Professor of Geology, Central South University of Technology, Changsha, China. Publications: Stereographic Projection used in Structural Geology, 1979; Ductile Shear Zone and Metallogeny, 1996. Honour: Progressive Award of Science and Technology, 1991, National Education Committee of China. Memberships: Geological Society of China; International Association of Structural/Tectonic Geologists. Address: Central South University of Technology, Department of Geology, Changsha 410083, China.

**HE Wei,** b. 25 November 1942, Linxiang City, Hunan, China. Philosophy Research Fellow. m. Tao Xian Ping, 2 sons. Education: BA, Philosophy Department, 1962-67, Diploma, 1967, Wuhan University. Appointments: Teacher, Hunan Education College, 1968-80; Research Fellow, Hunan Academy of Social Sciences, 1994-. Publications include: Make a Start of Course of Keen Perception, 1990. Membership: Vice Board Chairman, Hunan Society of Philosophy, 1978-. Address: Hunan Academy of Social Sciences, Institute of Philosophy, Changsha, Hunan, China.

**HE Xuntian,** b. 15 May 1953, Sichuan, China. Composer. 1 son. Education: BA, Department of Composition, Sichuan Conservatory of Music, 1982. Appointments: Lecturer, Composition, 1982-86, Associate Profesor, Vice Chairman, Composition Department, 1987-91, Sichuan Conservatory of Music; Vice Chairman, Composition and Conducting Department, 1991-97, Professor, Composition, 1996-, Chairman, Composition and Conducting Department, 1998-, Shanghai Conservatory of Music. Publications include: Tonal Patterns, 1985; Four Dreams, 1986; Sounds of Nature, 1986;

Telepathy, 1987; Phonism, 1989; Imagine the Sound, 1990; Sister Drum, 1994; Voice from the Sky, 1996; The Pattern of Sound Suite, 1997. Honours: 1st Prize, 3rd National Musical Piece Competition, China, 1984; 1st Prize, 1st China Phonograph Awards, Shanghai, 1986; Jinding Phonograph Award, Taiwan, 1995; 3rd Prize, International Carl-Marla-Von-Wettbewerbes fur Kammermusik, Germany, 1987; Outstanding Musical Achievement Awards, USA, 1989-90. Memberships: Chinese Musicians Association; ASCAP. Address: 20 Fen Yang Road, Shanghai Conservatory, Shanghai 200031, China.

**HEAD Willis Stanford,** b. 21 June 1953, Memphis, Tennessee, USA. Musician. m. Lynn. Education: BMus Education, 1975, MMus, Education, 1980, Arkansas University. Appointments: Percussion Instructor, Dixie Music Camp, Jonesboro, Arkansas, 1972-81; Timpanist Tupelo (Miss) Symphony Orchestra, 1973-74; Northeast Arkansas Symphony, Jonesboro, 1974-81; Band Director, Mammoth Spring (Arkansas) High School, 1975-77; Founder/ Director, Lindenwood Percussion Studio, Memphis, 1980-; Percussionist, Memphis Symphony & Little Symphony, 1981-; Lecturer, Mid-South Bible College, Memphis, 1982-; Percussion Instructor, Shelby State Community College, Memphis, 1984-; Percussion Consultant, Harding Academy, Memphis, 1985-;, Osceloa (Arkansas) High School, 1986-, Millington (Tennessee) High School, 1987-; Timpanist, Jackson (Tennessee) Symphony Orchestra. Memberships: Percussion Arts Society; Phi Mu Alpha; Kappa Delta Pi; National Association of Recording Arts & Sciences. Address: 652 South Prescott Street, Memphis, TN 38111-4325, USA.

**HEAP Denise Elaine,** b. 30 November 1954, Houston, Texas, USA. Accountant; Writer. Education: BA Mathematics, BA, German, 1977, Texas Christian University; Fulbright Fellowship, University of Augsburg, 1977-78. Appointments: Hänssler-Verlag, Stuttgart, Germany, 1979-80; Accountant, Lingen Oil and Gas, 1981-84; Controller and Treasurer, ITAG Exploration Inc, 1984-89; President/Owner, Translations Verbation, Houston, Texas, USA, 1989-95; Controller, Corrocean USA Inc, Houston, Texas, USA, 1994-97; Office Manager and Controller, ICM America LLC, Malvern, Pennsylvania, USA, 1997-. Publications: Published letters in Immigrant Genealogy Society, 1994. Honours: Fulbright Fellowship, 1977-78; National Science Foundation Honorary Member, 1977; Notable Women of Texas, 1984; Texas German Society, 1989-95. Memberships: Fulbright Association, Lifetime Member; Houston Association for Film and Television; Volunteer for Consular Corps and Institute for International Education, 1981-95; Chairman, TCU Links/Houston, 1981-95. Address: 7824 Waldeck Cemetery Road, Round Top, TX 78954, USA.

**HEARD Michal (Mickie) Louise,** b. 30 January 1950, Jamestown, New York. Children's Pastor; Educator. m. (div), 2 sons, 2 daughters. Education: Postgraduate Diploma Philosophy, 1985, University of Aberdeen, Scotland; Masters Religious Education, 1991, Trinity Divinity School, Deerfield, Illinois. Appointments: Minister of Education, Westhill Christian Fellowship, Aberdeen, Scotland, 1983-85; Minister of Christian Education, Village Presbyterian Church, Northbrook, Illinois, 1985-96; Director of Children's Ministry, Christ Church, Oakbrook, Illinois, 1996-. Publication: Contributor, Healing the Children of War, 1994. Memberships: Founder, Association of Christian Entrepreneurs for Educational Paradigms, 1998; AFTRA; ASCD; Founding member, Opening the Door Network, 1996. Address: 2284 Scott Road, Northbrook, IL 60062-6041, USA.

**HECHT Isaac,** b. 28 December 1913, Baltimore, Maryland, USA. Education: BS, Economics, Johns Hopkins University, 1936; LLB, University of Maryland, 1938. Appointments: Court of Appeal of Maryland; Supreme Court of United States; United States Court of Appeals for the Fourth Circuit; United States District Court, District of Maryland; Tax Court of United States. Memberships: Bar Association of Baltimore City; Maryland State Bar Association Inc; Maryland Bar Foundation Inc; American Bar Association; American College of Trust and Estate Counsel; Association of Life Insurance Counsel; Baltimore Estate Planning Council; Clients' Security Trust Fund of the Bar of Maryland; National Client Protection Organization Inc; Judicial Conference of the Fourth Circuit; Baltimore Association of Tax Counsel. Address: 315 N Charles St, Baltimore, MD 21201, USA.

**HEDRICK Wyatt,** b. 28 September 1951, Roswell, New Mexico, USA. Pharmacist. m. Marcia. Education: BS Pharmacy, 1974, University New Mexico; MSc Hospital Pharmacy, 1978, University of Houston. Appointments: Resident, Pharmacy, University of Texas, Medical Branch Hospitals, Galveston; Pharmacist, Memorial General Hospital, Las Cruces, New Mexico, 1978; Pharmacist, Columbia Medical Centre West, El Paso, Texas, 1978-. Memberships: American Society of Health-System Pharmacists; Texas Society of Health-System Pharmacists; El Paso Area Society of Health-System Pharmacists. Address: 1028 Quinault Drive, El Paso, TX 79912-1223, USA.

**HEFFER Janet Cassandra Smith,** b. 24 January 1947, Ogden, Utah, USA. Professional Figure Skater; Advertising Executive. m. James Edward Heffer, 8 June 1968, 1 son, 1 daughter. Education: University of Colorado; University of Wisconsin; Majored in English and Italian; Master's credits in English Literature. Appointments: Figure Skating Professional and Choreographer, Sun Valley; Legal Secretary; Skating Professional, Denver, Denver Country Club, Creative Concepts in Advertising; Advertising, US Department of Agriculture, Patton, currently. Publications: Sermons Donne By A Genius, thesis; Papers on the metaphysical poetry of John Donne vs Ben Johnson; Thesis on Romeo and Juliet. Honours: Gold Medallist, US Figure Skating; Kappa Kappa Gamma; Colorado Musicians Guild; US Midwestern Figure Skating Champion. Memberships: Denver Civic Ballet; Symphony Guild; Central City Opera Association; United States Golf Association; United States Tennis Association; Republican Committee woman, 1971-75; United States Figure Skating Association. Address: 4505 South Yosemite #117, Denver, CO 80237, USA.

**HEICK Alex,** b. 25 January 1949, Copenhagen, Denmark. Physician; Neurologist. m. Annelise Dal, 1 son, 2 daughters. Education: MPsych, Copenhagen University, 1978; MD, University of Copenhagen, 1979; Certified Specialist of Neurology, 1995. Appointments: Royal Danish Army Medical Corps, 1979-80; Intern, Department of Orthopedic Surgery, Kommine Hospital, 1981-82; Department of Medicine, Bispeberg Hospital, 1982-83; Resident, Department of Neurosurgery, Rigshospitalet, Copenhagen, 1983-85; Resident, Department of Neurology, Roskilde Sygehus, 1985-91; Consultant, Department of Neurology, Glostrup University Hospital, 1994-. Publications: Books and scientific articles in professional journals. Memberships: Danish Neurological Society; AAAS; Masons. Address: Department of Neurology, Glostrup University Hospital, Glostrup 2600, Denmark.

**HEINTZE Michael,** b. 8 March 1958, Goslar, Wissenschaftlicher Angestellter. Education: Erstes Staatsexamen für das Lehramt an Gymnasien, 1983; Promotion, 1987; Habilitation, 1998. Appointments:

Vissenschaftlicher Angestellter, University Göttingen, Institut ür Lateinische und Romanische Philologie des Mittelalters, 984-88; Wissenschaftlicher Assistent, University Giessen, stitute für Romanische Philologie, 1988-94; Lehrbeauftragter, Iniversity Giessen, Institut für Rom. Phil., 1994-96; Vissenschaftlicher Angestellter, University Frankfurt/Main, stitut für Romanische Sprachen und Literaturen, si nce 1997. ublications: König, Held und Sippe. Untersuchungen zur hanson de geste des 13. und 14. Jahrhunderts und ihrer yklenbildung, 1991; Other books and articles on French and rovençal Lit of the Middle Ages and Spanish Lit of the Golden ge. Honours: Scholarship, Conseil Général de la Vienne, niversity of Poitiers, France, 1980-81. Memberships: Société encesvals; Société Internationale Arthurienne; Association Iternationale d'Etudes Occitanes; International Courtly iterature Society. Address: Gartenstrasse 28, D-35390 iessen, Germany.

**HEISS Frederick William,** b. 3 March 1932, Kansas City, SA. Political Science Educator; Public Administrator; Policy Iesearcher. Education: BSBA, University of Denver, 1958. ppointments: Denver Urban Ohbs University Colorado, 970-82; Director, MPA Graduate Program, 1982-85; hairman, Department of Public Administration, Virginia Commonwealth University, Richmond, 1985-91, Professor, 991-; Director, Met Study, National Academy of Public dministration, Washington, 1974-76; Director, Science echnology, NSF, Denver, 1976-78; National Chairman, cience and Technology Transfer, 1977-78; Consultant, US ivil Service, Utah, 1975; Director, Capital Area Study and rogram, Richmond, 1987-93; Visiting Professor, Huanghe niversity, Henan, China, 1989. Publications include: Urban Iesearch and Urban Policy, 1975. Memberships: Beta Theta 'i; ASPA. Address: 321 Bighorn Drive E-5, Estes Park, CO 0517, USA.

**HEITMAN Susan Marie,** b. 16 August 1954, Detroit, Michigan, USA. Artist. m. Roger Melvin, 1 d. Education: BFA, astern Michigan University, 1988; MA, 1995. Appointments: eacher, Crafts, 1995-96; Coordinator, Crafts, Northville Christian Assembly, 1997; Co Chair Person, Exhibitions, Ann rbor Women Painters, 1997-98; Chair Person, 1998-. ublications: Articles to magazines and newspapers. Honours: Masters Fellowship; Exceptional Merit Award; Symposium Arts nd Science. Memberships: Ann Arbor Women Painters; Ann Irbor Art Center; Paintcreek Center for The Arts; Detroit Artists Market; East Michigan University Alumni Association; Northville Assembly of God. Address: 5303 Napier Road, Plymouth, MI 8170-5033, USA.

**HELD Gerhard,** b. 5 March 1944, Vienna, Austria. Meteorologist. m. div. 2 sons, 1 daughter. Education: PhD Meteorology, 1968, University of Vienna, Austria; Registered Natural Scientist. Appointments: Research Officer - Specialist Iesearcher, Radar Meteorologist, Atmospheric Physics Div, National Physical Research Laboratory, CSIR, Pretoria, 970-84, Research Area Leader, 1990; Senior Environmental Consultant, Technology Research and Investigations, Eskom, Iohannesburg, 1992; Invitee to various international onferences and working groups; Assistant Editor, Austrian Meteorological Journal, Wetter und Leben, 1965-67; Referee o 6 professional journals; Examiner and Supervisor for doctoral nd MA/MSc theses; Organiser, international and national meteorological conferences in Austria and South Africa, art xhibitions and invited Lecturer at Advanced Winterschool on Atmospheric Sciences, 1996. Publications: 29 papers in efereed journals; 100 research or contract reports; 2 extended ook reviews; 1 book chapter in Cloud Dynamics; 2 book chapters in Air Pollution and its Impacts on the South African

Highveld, and Principal Editor; 48 papers in proceedings of international and national conferences. Memberships: South African Council for Natural Scientific Professions; South African Institute for Physics; National Association for Clean Air; South African Society for Atmospheric Sciences, Founder Member, Council Member, President, 1998-; Environmental Scientific Association, founder member, Chairman, 1997-; Board of Trustees, International Life Sciences Institute, South Africa. Address: Queenswood, 1171 Dormer Avenue, 0186 Pretoria, South Africa.

**HELLWIG Birgitta Öman,** b. 11 June 1932, Borås, Sweden. Mathematician. m. Günter Hellwig, 1 son, 3 daughters. Education: Filosofie kandidat, 1954, Uppsala University, Sweden. Appointments: Technical Officer, Imperial Chemical Industries Ltd, Birmingham, England, 1957; Assistant, Mathematics Department, Uppsala University, Sweden, 1958; Teaching Fellow, Harvard University, Cambridge, Massachusetts, 1959; Senior Mathematician, Republic Aviation, Farmingdale, New York, 1960; Member Research Staff, Systems Research Centre, Lockheed Electronics Co, Bedminster, New Jersey, 1960-61; Translator Mathematics Textbooks, Addison-Wesley Pub Co, Reading, Massachusetts, 1964; Reviewer, Mathematics Reviews, Ann Arbor, Michigan, 1968-; Assistant to Applicants' Lawyers by Procs, European Court of Human Rights, Strasbourg, France, 1989-. Publications: Articles on Differential Operators in scientific journals, 1967-. Membership: Nordisk Kommitte for Mänskliga Rättigketer. Address: Pommerotter Weg 27, D-52076, Aachen, Germany.

**HELMERICKS Harmon Robert,** b. 18 January 1917, Gibson City, IL, USA. Explorer. m. Martha Magdalen Morlang, 3 sons, 2 daughters. Education: Student, University Arizona, 1940-41. Appointments: Sheet Metal Worker, Army Engineers, Seaward Alaska, 1941-44; Associate with Constance Helmericks in Study of Arctic, 1944-46; Writer, Lecturer on Arctic America, 1946-; Organizer expedition by air north of Arctic Circle Alaska and Canada, 1947; Co-Founder, with Martha M Helmericks Arctic Tern Fish-Freight Company, 1952; Chairman Board, Colville Inc; Co-Discoverer, with Martha M Helmericks and Atlantic Richfield, of Prudhoe Bay Oil Field, 1968; Assistant Curator, Kansas City Museum; Consultant Arctic Oil Operation Gulf Oil Company, Sohio Oil Company, Union Oil Company; Founder, with Martha M Helmericks, Arctic Schools for Boys, 1974; Arctic Consultant to Eastman Kodak Company; Chairman Board, Colville Environment Services; Director, Alaska Interior Resources; Master Guide Alaskan Game Commission; Active in Conservation in Africa, India, Europe Arctic Institute North America; Airplane Owners and Pilots Association. Publications; Oolak's Brother, 1952; Arctic Hunters, 1955, with Constance Helmericks; We Live in the Arctic, 1947; Our Summer With the Eskimos, 1948; Our Alaskan Winter, 1949; Flight of the Arctic Tern, 1952; Arctic Bush Pilot, 1968; The Last of the Bush Pilots, 1968, 1990; Magazine articles; Films for American Motors Corp, TV shows on Arctic research. Memberships: Daedalians; Circumnavigators. Address: 930 9th Avenue Fairbanks, AK 99701-4303, USA.

**HENDERSON James,** b. 7 August 1940, Sudbury, Canada. Legislator, Physician, Psychoanalyst. m. Karen Santolini, 3 sons. Education: MD, University of Western Ontario, 1964; MPH, Johns Hopkins University, 1966; CRCP, FRCP, Royal College, 1969; DABPN, 1973; Diploma Phychoanalysis, 1980. Appointments: Associate Professor, Faculty of Medicine, University of Toronto, 1969-; Member, Legislative Assembly of Ontario, 1985-95. Honours: Gold Medalist, University of Toronto, 1970; American Phychiatric Association, Fellow, 1980;

Special Award of Distinction, 1987. Memberships: OPA; CPA; CMI; AOA; AKK; APA. Address: 455 Spadina Avenue Suite 205, Toronto Ont, Canada, M5S 2G8.

**HENDRICKS Edward David,** b. 29 July 1946, Bridgeport, CT, USA. Consultant. m. Elizabeth, 1 son, 1 daughter. Education: BA, BS, Summa Cum Laude, University of North Carolina at Charlotte, 1975; MA, State University of New York, Albany, 1976. Appointments: President, CEO, ACME, The International Association of Management Consulting Firms, 1979-95; President, Edward D Hendricks and Associates Inc, 1996-. Publications: The Insiders Guide to Consulting Success, 1997; Successful Business Networking 1998; Get on the Right Track, 1999. Honours: Certified Association Executive, 1991; Certified Management Consultant, 1998. Memberships: Institute of Management Consultants; American Society of Association Executives; National Speakers Association; New York Society of Association Executives; MENSA. Address: 354 Anton St, Bridgeport, CT 06606-2119, USA.

**HENEMAN Robert Lloyd,** b. 17 January 1955. Professor. m. Renée Brausch Heneman, 1 son, 1 daughter. Education: BA, Economics and Psychology, Lake Forest College, 1977; MA, Labour and Industrial Relations, University of Illinois, Urbana-Champaign, 1979; PhD, Labour and Industrial Relations, Michigan University, 1984. Appointments: Human Resource Specialist, Pacific Gas & Electric Company, San Francisco, 1979-80; Graduate Research Assistant, Michigan University, East Lansing, 1980-83; Assistant Professor, 1984-89, Associate Professor, 1989-92, Management and Human Resources, Ohio University, Columbus; Associate Professor, Director, Graduate Programs in Labour and Human Resources, Fisher College of Business, Ohio University, Columbus, 1992-. Publications: Staffing Organizations; Merit Pay: Linking Pay Increases to Performance Ratings. Honours: Scholar Athlete Awards, Lake Forest College, 1972, 1973; Psi Chi, 1977; Phi Kappa Phi, 1979; Sigma Iota Epsilon, 1983; Outstanding Teacher Awards, Ohio State University, 1992, 1994, 1995, 1996, 1997. Memberships: Academy of Management; Industrial Relations Research Association; Society for Industrial and Organizational Psychology; American Compensation Association; Society for Human Resource Management. Address: 4815 Lytfield Drive, Dublin, OH 43017-2174, USA.

**HENNEBERG Alexandra E,** b. 28 October 1956, Braunschweig, Germany. Medical Director. m. Hans-Joachim Henneberg, 2 sons, 1 daughter. Education: Final Medical Examination, University of Bonn, 1982; Promotion (Dr med), University of Tübingen, 1982; Habilitation (Priv Doz), University of Ulm, 1993. Appointments: Medical Director, Hospital for Parkinson's Disease, Bad Nauheim; Guest Lecturer, University of Ulm and University of Giessen. Publications: Books: Parkinson - zu neuem Gleichgewicht finden, author, 1997; Immunological Alterations in Psychiatric Diseases, co-author, 1997; Parkinson - na und?!, co-editor, 1998; Author or co-author, 8 book chapters; Articles and abstracts in journals; Numerous papers. Honours: Scholarship, Deutsche Studienstiftung, 1975-82; Hertie Foundation Award, 1985; Stanley Foundation Award. Memberships: New York Academy of Sciences; German Society for Neurology; German Society for Neuropathology and Neuroanatomy; German Society for Neurochemistry; German Society for Neurogenetics; International Society for Pathophysiology; International Society of Neuroimmunomodulation; Liga gegen Epilepsie; Society for Immunology; German Neuroscience Society; Deutsche Gesellschaft für Psychiatrie, Psychotherapie und Nervenheilkunde. Address: Hospital for Parkinsons Disease, Franz Groedel Strasse 6, D-61231 Bad Nauheim, Germany.

**HENNING Daniel H,** b. 1 August 1931, Cleveland, Ohio USA. Professor Emeritus. Divorced, 1 son, 1 daughter. Education: BS, Biology and Social Sciences, Bowling State University, 1957; MS, Conservation and Public Administration University of Michigan, 1959; PhD, Public Administration and Forestry, Syracuse University, 1965; MSU, Billings Appointments: Professor Emeritus, Public Administration Environmental Affairs; Environmental Training Consultant Southeast Asia; Senior Fulbright Research Scholar, Southeast Asia, 1988-89; Visiting Lecturer, Chinese University of Hong Kong, 1973-75; Visiting Associate Professor, Public Administration, University of New Mexico, 1990-91 Publications: Managing the Environmental Crisis, 1989, 1998 Environmental Policy and Administration, 1997. Memberships International Society for Tropical Foresters; IUCN Commission on Education and Training; IUCN Council for Environmental Law; American Society for Public Administration. Address 17008 East Lake Shore, Bigfork, Montana 59911, USA.

**HENRY Carolyn S,** b. 31 January 1955, Newton, KS, USA Professor, Family Relations. Education: BSE, Oklahoma Christian College, 1976; MS, University of Tennessee Knoxville, 1981; PhD, The University of Tenessee, Knoxville 1984. Appointments: Director, Career Planning and Placement Pepperdine University, 1977-80; Assistant Professor, South Dakota State University, 1985-88; Assistant Professor 1988-93 Associate Professor and Interim Head, 1995-97, Professor 1997-, FRCD Department, Oklahoma State University Publications include: Family System Characteristics, Parenta Behaviors, and Adolescent Family Life Satisfaction, 1994 Validation of the Adolescent Family Life Satisfaction, 1995 Grandchildrens' Perceptions of Grandparental Support in Divorced and Intact Families, 1995; Family Structure and Interpersonal Relationship Quality of Young Adults, 1995 Adolescent Social Competence, Parental Qualities, and Parental Satisfaction, 1995; Family Resources and Adolescent Family Life Satisfaction in Remarried Family Households, 1995 Adolescents' Perceptions of Family System Characteristics Parent-Adolescent Dyadic Behaviors, Adolescent Qualities, and Adolescent Empathy, 1996; Predictors of Life Satisfaction Among Low-Income Rural Youth, 1997; Adolescent Social Competence and Parental Satisfaction, 1997; Family Stressor Events, Family Coping Strategies, and Adolescent Adaptation in Farm and Ranch Families, in press. Memberships: Clinical Member, AAMFT; National Council on Family Relations American Association of Family and Consumer Sciences Address: Oklahoma State University, FRCD Department Stillwater, OK 74078, USA.

**HENRY Roy Monroe,** b. 27 October 1939, Chicago, Illinois USA. Financial Planner. m. Meredith, 1 son, 1 daughter Education: 1st Class Airman, USAF, Turkey, 1957-61; BBA Kennedy, Western, 1990. Appointments: Estimator, Con P Curran Printing Co, St Louis, 1961-64; Sales Man, Prudential Insurance Company, 1964-72; President, Roy M Henry and Associates, Chesterfield, MD, 1972-76; St Louis Financial Planners, 1976-83; First Financial Planners Inc, 1983- Honours: Guest Speaker, Purdue University, Yale University Stanford University; Financial Planner of the Year, 1987. Memberships: Missouri Athletic Club; International Association of Registered Financial Cons; Non Profit Investwatch Fellow Life Underwriting Teaching Council; International Association Financial Planners. Address: 2031 Kehrsboro Dr, Chesterfield MO 63005-6512, USA.

**HENSLEIGH Howard Edgar,** b. 29 October 1920 Blanchard, Iowa, USA. Lawyer. m. Janice Lee Pedersen, 1 son 2 daughters. Education: BA, 1943, JD, 1947, State University of Iowa; International Law, Columbia Law School, 1954-55

Appointments: Intelligence Officer, ETO, Parachute Infantry, WWII; Deputy Assistant General Counsel, International Affairs, Office of Secretary of Defense; Deputy Assistant to the Secretary of the Treasury, National Security. Publications: Comments Editor, Iowa Law Review, 1946-47. Memberships: American Bar Association; International Law Society. Address: 50 School Street, Carlisle, MA 01741-1709, USA.

**HERDLEIN Richard J,** b. 12 August 1944, Valdosta, GA, USA. College Administrator, Professor. 1 son. Education: BA, St John Fisher College, 1966; MA, Niagara University, 1970; Certificate of Specialization, Niagara University, 1970; MS, Niagara University, 1976; PhD, University of Pittsburgh, 1985. Appointments: Dean of Student Affairs, University of Pittsburgh; Vice President for Student Affairs, Thomas Moore College; Vice President for Student Affairs, Associate Professor, Medaille College. Honours: Outstanding Young Men of America; Person of the Year; Administrator of the Year; Most Respected Doctor; Who's Who in the East. Memberships: National Association of Student Personnel Administrators; Buffalo Council on World Affairs; American Association of Higher Education; Leadership Buffalo; Centre for Entrepreneurial Leadership. Address: 47 Fairchild Dr, Amherst, NY 14226-3328, USA.

**HERMAN Leszek,** b. 25 May 1950, Cieszyn, Poland. Medical Electronics Engineer. m. Ewa Szpikowska, 1 son, 1 daughter. Education: Automatics Engineer, 1975, MSc, Electronics, 1980, Technical University of Silesia. Appointments: Engineer, ZNSM, Szczecin, 1977-79; Manager, Polish Television, Szczecin, 1979-80; Engineer, Meratronik, Szczecin, 1980-83; Engineer, 109 Military Hospital, Szczecin, 1983-85; Designer, Meramont, Szczecin, 1985-87; Engineer, (Warski) Szczecin Shipyard, 1987-90; Co-Owner, Baltic Electric S.C, Neurocomputing Division, 1992-. Publications: Several professional articles. Memberships: Honorary Member, Association for Logic Programming, Imperial College, London; New York Academy of Sciences. Address: ul Okulickiego 75 B, PL-71-035 Szczecin, Poland.

**HERMAN Mary Margaret,** b. 26 July 1935, Plymouth, Wisconsin, USA. Research Physician. m. Dr Lucien Jules Rubinstein, deceased, 2 stepsons, 1 stepdaughter. Education: BS, 1957, MD, 1960, University of Wisconsin at Madison, USA. Appointments include: Senior Staff Scientist, Section of Neuropathology, Clinical Brain Disorders Branch, MIMH, NIH; Consultant Neuropathologist, District of Columbia Medical Examiner's Office; Teaching Associate and Consultant, Neuropathology, District of Columbia General Hospital. Publications include: Over 150 full-length scientific articles. Honours include: Weil Award, American Association of Neuropathologists, 1974; Phi Kappa Phi; Sophomore Honorary Society; Alpha Chi Omega; Received a Regent's and Johnson Foundation Scholarship; Merck Faculty Development Award, 1969; Research Career Development Award, 1967-72. Memberships include: American Association for the Advancement of Science; The American Medical Association; American Society for Investigative Pathology; American Society for Cell Biology; International Academy of Pathology; International Society of Neuropathology; Society for Developmental Biology; Society for Neuroscience; Society of Biological Psychiatry; Society for in vitro Biology. Hobbies: Tennis; Music; Gardening. Address: 125 S Reynolds Street, Alexandria, VA 22304-1152, USA.

**HERMANS Johannes J Rob,** b. 10 August 1966, Amby, Netherlands. Researcher in Pharmacology. Education: DSc, 1988, PhD, 1992, University of Maastricht; Postdoctoral Fellow, Philipps University, Marburg, Germany, 1994-95. Appointments: Postdoctoral Research, 1996-99,

Pharmacokinetics, Department of Pharmacology and Toxicology, 1999-, University of Maastricht. Publications: Contributor of various articles to professional journals. Honours: Postdoctoral Fellowship, Alexander von Humboldt Stiftung, 1994-95; Research Grant, Dutch Kidney Foundation, 1996-99. Address: Department of Pharmacology and Toxicology, University of Maastricht, PO Box 616, 6200 MD Maastricht, Netherlands.

**HERNADI Ferenc,** b. 23 November 1929, Balmazujvaros. University Professor. m. Dr Eva Gonczol, 1 daughter. Education: MD, 1954; CSc, 1966; DSc, 1972. Appointments: Professor, Institute of Pharmacology, University Medical School of Debrecen, Hungary. Publications: 208. Honours: Issekutz Award, 1994; Paracelsus Award, 1996. Memberships: Hungarian Society of Chemotherapy; International Society of Chemotherapy. Address: University Medical School of Debrecen, Dept Pharmacology, POB 12, H 4012 Debrecen, Hungary.

**HERON Thomas Anthony Edmond,** b. 10 July 1945, Brisbane, Australia. Mechanical Engineer. div. 1 son, 1 daughter. Education: BE, Mechanical, First Class Hons, 1980; ME, Mechanical, 1983; MPA, 1991; Graduate Diploma in Executive Leadership, 1993. Appointments: Principal Adviser, Engineering, 1989-94, Senior Principal Adviser, Technology, 1994-, Division of Workplace Health and Safety. Honours: NACO Australia Prize for Design Analysis, 1979; Australian Institute of Refigeration, Air Conditiong and Heating Award, 1979; W W Marriner Award for best technical paper, Australia and NZ, 1985. Memberships: Registered Professional Engineer with Board of Professional Engineers, Queensland, Australia. Address: Division of Workplace Health and Safety, 30 Makerston Street, Brisbane, Queensland 4000, Australia.

**HERRMANN Lorena Joyce,** b. 2 February 1925, Atchison, Kansas, USA. Music Teacher; Organist; Writer. m. William Ernest Herrmann, 2 sons, 1 daughter. Education: BMusEd, cum laude, College of Emporia, Kansas, 1947; MMusEd, University of Oklahoma, 1950. Career: Private Piano and Organ Students, Kansas and Oklahoma, 1947-; Vocal Music Educator, Jefferson Elementary School, Ponca City, Oklahoma, 1947-49; Senior High School and Fogarty Junior High School, Guthrie, Oklahoma, 1950-53; Assistant Professor, Instructor, 1968-83, Associate Professor, 1983-92, Chairman, Department of Music, 1990-92, St Mary of the Plains College, Dodge City, Kansas. Publications: Concert Reviews for SMPC Advance, The Diapason; Book: Zion Lutheran Church (editor). Memberships: Mu Phi Epsilon; Phi Delta Kappa; MENC; KMEA; MTNA; KMTA; American Guild of Organists; National Guild of Piano Teachers; Dodge City Area Piano Teachers League; Kansas Authors Club; Zion Lutheran Church. Address: 10508 135 Road, Offerle, KS 67563-9204, USA.

**HESS George Franklin II,** b. 13 May 1939, Oak Park, Illinois, USA. Lawyer. m. Diane R Hess, 1 son. Education: BS, Colorado State University, 1962; JD, Suffolk University Law School, 1970; LLM, Boston University Law School, 1973. Career: Private Law Practice. Memberships: American Bar Association; Florida Bar Association; Broward County Bar Association. 2524 Castilla Is, Fort Lauderdale, FL 33301-1505, USA.

**HESSE Axel Ernst,** b. 16 July 1935, Berlin-Koepenick. Ethnomusicologist. m. Flora Perez Diaz, 1 son, 1 daughter. Education: Diploma of Musicology, Berlin, 1961; Postgraduate, Ethnomusicology, Havana, 1963-65; PhD, 1970. Appointments: Institute of Musicology, University of Leipzig, 1965-70; Institute of Musicology, Humboldt University, Berlin, 1970; Academy of

Sciences, Berlin, 1987-89; Ciplice Folksound Archives, 1989; Professor, University of Salamanca's 1254 Music Chair, Francisco Salinas, 1990-93; Street Musician "Arcos en Compania" (with Flora), 1994; Retired, 1998; Scientific Come Back, 1999. Publications: Music Life of Latin America 1492-1969, 1994; Articles on Latin American and German Folk Music; Transculturation Theory. Honours: IOM; DDG; Order of International Ambassadors, 1995; Golden Needle of the League of Peoples Friendship; Mens Inner Circle of Achievement, ABI. Memberships: International Folk Music Council; Committee, GDR-Portugal; Folklore Initiativ Komitee, Chairman; International Council of Traditional Music. Address: The Multidisciplinary Salinas Colloquium on Rhythm, Calle Compania 36-BJ, E-37002 Salamanca, Spain.

**HESTHAMMER Jonny,** b. 7 March 1965, Bergen, Norway. Geologist. m. Hilde Anita Larsen. Education: Candidatus Magisterii, University of Bergen, 1988; MSc, University of British Columbia, 1991; PhD, University of Bergen, 1995-. Appointments: Field Geologist, Geological Survey of Canada, Vancouver, 1988-90; Geologist, Husky Oil, Calgary, Canada, 1991; Senior Geologist, Statoil, Bergen, 1991-. Publications: Several articles in professional journals. Honour: Eage Distinguished Lecturer Award, Geneva, 1997. Memberships: Norsk Geologisk Forening; European Association of Geoscientists and Engineers. Address: Veslefrikkveien 26, 5142 Fyllingsdalen, Norway.

**HETHCOTE Herbert Wayne,** b. 8 November 1941, Villisca, Iowa, USA. Professor. m. Leslie Marshall, 2 sons. Education: BA, Applied Mathematics, University of Colorado, 1964; PhD, Mathematics, University of Michigan, 1968. Appointments: Professor of Mathematics, University of Iowa, 1979-. Publications: Gonorrhea Transmission Dynamics and Control, 1984; HIV Transmission and AIDS in the United States, 1994. Memberships: Society for Mathematical Biology; Society for Industrial and Applied Mathematics. Address: U Iowa Math Dept, Iowa City, IA 52242, USA.

**HETHERINGTON Bonita Elizabeth,** b. 27 May 1946, Marion County, IA, USA. Teacher. m. Thomas O, 1 son, 1 daughter. Education: BA, Cental College, IA; Masters, Indiana University; Postgraduate, Texas Tech. Appointments: Teacher, Schley County Schools, 1968-71; Teacher, Montezuma Ind Schools, Buena Vista, 1971; Teacher, Bryan Ind Schools, 1979-82; Teacher, Lubbock Ind Schools, 1982-1988; Teacher, Lewisburg Area Schools, 1989-; Language Arts Specialist, 1992-. Honours: Consultant for Muleshoe Ind School District, Texas for Gifted, 1986-88; Instructor for Institute for Teachers of Disadvantaged Gifted, 1987-88; Selected to be a member of a federal grant program Goals 2000-Educate America Consortium, 1996-; Named, One of 17 showcased teachers from the state at the PA Association of Childhood Education International. Memberships: NEA; PSEA; LAEA; IRA; Keystone RA; Susquehanna RA; National Council of Teachers of English; Union County Historical Society; Education Committee; Alpha Delta Gamma; Epsilon Sigma Alpha; Christ's Evangelical Lutheran Church. Address: 1615 Market St, Lewisburg, PA 17837-1231, USA.

**HETZEL Basil Stuart,** b. 13 June 1922, London, UK. Medical Scientist. m. Anne Gilmour Fisher, 3 sons, 2 daughters. Education: MD, 1949; Fulbright Research School, Cornell, NY, 1951-54; Research Fellow, Chemical Pathology, St Thomas's Hospital, London, 1954-55; FRACP, 1958; FRCP, 1972; FFPHM, 1980; FTS, 1981. Appointments: Michell Professor of Medicine, Adelaide University, 1964-68; Professor, Social and Preventive Medicine, Monash University, 1968-75; Chief, CSIRO Human Nutrition, 1975-85; Executive Director,

International Council for Control of Iodine Deficiency Disorders, 1985-95; Chairman, International Council for Control of Iodine Deficiency Disorders, 1995-. Publications: The LS Factor; The Story of Iodine Deficiency; SOS for a Billion. Honours: Lt Governor, South Australia, 1992; Chancellor, University of South Australia, 1992-98; Honorary Doctorate, University of South Australia, 1999. Memberships: President, Endocrine Society of Australia; President, Australian Society for Epidemiology and Research in Community Health; Deputy Chairman, International Epidemiological Association; Life Member, Australian Nutrition Foundation; Life Member, Public Health Association of Australia; Life Member, Australian Epidemiol Association; Companion of the Order of Australia; Anzac Peace Prize RSL. Address: Health Development Foundation, 8th Flr Samuel Way Bldg, Womens and Childrens Hospital 72 King William Road, North Adelaide, SA 5006, Australia.

**HEYDEN Van der Ulrich,** b. 7 September 1954, Ueckermunde. Historian; Political Scientist. m. Barbara, 2 daughters. Education: History Diploma, 1981, PhD History, 1984, Humboldt University, Berlin; PhD Political Sciences, 1997, Free University Berlin. Appointments: Assistant, International Affairs, Humboldt University, Berlin, 1984; Research Fellow, Institute for Economic History, Academy of Sciences in Berlin, 1984-86; Research Fellow, Institute for World History, Academy of Sciences in Berlin, 1986-91; Research Fellow, Centre for Modern Oriental Studies in Berlin, 1992-95; Current research: the relationships between Germany and South Africa in the late 19th century. Publications: 9 books including short monographs; 13 edited books; General editor from 3 book series; About 70 articles and chapters in books plus various popular articles; About 300 book reviews. Memberships: Berlin Association of Mission History; Association Brandenburg-Princes Town-One World; Brandenburg Institute for Development Policy. Address: Humboldt University Berlin Institute African Studies, Prenzlauer Promenade 149 152, 13189 Berlin, Germany.

**HICKCOX Leslie Kay,** b. 12 May 1951, Berkeley, California, USA. College Professor. Education: BA, Physical Education, University of Redlands, California, 1973; MA, Physical Education, University of the Pacific, 1975; MEd, Physical Education, Teachers College, Columbia University, 1979; MEd, Health Education, 1987, MEd, Guidance, Counselling, 1988, EdD, Education, Curriculum, Instruction, 1991, Oregon State University, Corvallis. Appointments: Coordinator, Women's Athletics, Instructor, Physical Education, College of Marin, 1976-77; Coordinator, Recreation, Instructor, Physical Education, State University of New York, Stony Brook, 1981-83; Instructor, Health, Physical Education, Linn Benton Community College, Oregon, 1985-94; Instructor, Communication, Human and Interdisciplinary Studies, Marylhurst University, Oregon, 1986-95; Education Supervisor, Health Educator, Oregon State University, 1988-90; Instructor, Health, Physical Education, Portland Community College, 1994-95; Coordinator, Health, Physical Education, Recreation, Instructor, Health, Physical Education, Rogue Community College, 1995-97; Coordinator and Associate Professor, Health, Physical Education, Western Montana College, 1997-99; Assistant Professor, Health Education, Northeastern Illinois, 1999-. Publications: Learning Styles: A Survey of Adult Learning Style Inventory Models, book chapter, 1995; Articles on experiential learning and gender studies. Honours: Kappa Delta Phi; Phi Delta Kappa. Memberships include: American College of Sports Medicine; Association for Advancement of Health Education; Association of Supervision and Curriculum Development; Council for Adult and Experiential Learning. Address: 2635 N Baldwin Street, Portland, OR 97217, USA.

**HICKEL Walter Joseph,** b. 18 August 1919, Claflin, Kansas, 3A. Business Executive. m. Ermalee Strutz, 6 sons. pointments: Civilian Aircraft Inspector, Army Air Corps, 42-46; Property Owner, Developer and Manager, 1946-66, 70-90; Governor of Alaska, 1966-69, 1990-94; US Secretary, partment of the Interior, 1969-70; Chairman of the Board, kel Investment Company, property ownership and velopment, 1970-90, 1995-; Chairman, Founder, Yukon cific Corporation, 1982-90; Founder, Secretary-General, The rthern Forum; Founder, Institute of the North, Alaska Pacific iversity. Publications: The Potential and the Promise of the ctic, special report, 1970; Who Owns America?, 1971; eothermal Energy, special report, 1972; Planning acroprojects, article, 1987; Going Up in Flames: The omises and Pledges of Alaska Statehood Under Attack, -author, 1990; The Wit and Wisdom of Wally Hickel, 1994; ticles in newspapers and periodicals. Honours include: Boss Year, National Secretaries Association, Juneau, 1968, chorage, 1974; Alaskan of Year, 1969; Man of Year, Ripon ciety, 1970; Best Non-Fiction Book Award, Alaska Press ub, 1972; William A Egan Outstanding Alaskan Award, aska State Chamber of Commerce, 1987; Grand Cordon, der of the Sacred Treasure, Japan, 1988; 11 honorary ctorates. Memberships include: Board of Trustees, Alaska cific University, 1959-91; Alaska-Nippon Kai, 1968-; uestrian Order of the Holy Sepulchre, 1968-; Knights of alta, 1970-; Life Trustee, National Recreation and Park sociation, 1975-; Board of Trustees, Alaska Council on onomic Education, 1977-; Pioneers of Alaska, 1979-; -Chairman, Board of Directors, Commonwealth North, 1979-; aska SeaLife Center Board of Governors, 1995-. Address: ) Box 101700, Anchorage, AK 99510-1700, USA.

**HICKEY Phyllis A,** b. 25 February 1957, Malden, assachusetts, USA. School Principal. Education: BA, havioral Sciences, Certification in Elementary Education 1-8, nhurst College, 1979; MA, Computer Education, Eastern onnecticut State University, 1987; Norwich Diocesan incipals' Leadership Academy, 1998. Appointments: 8th rade Teacher, 1979-92, Principal pro-tem, 1984-92, omputer Coordinator, 1987-92, Principal, 1992-, St Mary hool, Putnam, Connecticut. Honours: Nominee, Presidential ward for Excellence in Mathematics, 1992; Nominee, IBM echnology and Learning Teacher of the Year Award, 1992; olunteer Service Award, Holy Family Home and Shelter, illimantic, Connecticut, 1994; Appreciation Award, ortheastern Communities Against Substance Abuse, 1994; ominee, National Catholic Education Association stinguished Teacher Award, 1995. Memberships: National atholic Education Association; Delta Kappa Society Society ternational; New England Association of Catholic evelopment Officers; National Association of Students Activity dvisor. Address: St Mary School, 23 Marshall Street, Putnam, T 06260-1403, USA.

**HICKS Peter Alastair,** b. 20 August 1945, Kampala, ganda. Food Engineer. m. Constance Lilian, 1 son, 1 aughter. Education: BSc Hons, Reading, 1968; M Eng Sc, ydney, 1983. Appointments: H J Heinz Co Ltd, London, 964-68; Unilever Australia P/L, 1969-70; Food Engineer, asetsart University, 1977-78; Visiting Fellow, University of S acific, Samoa, 1981; Lecturer, University of W Sydney, 970-83; Senior Regional Agroindustries Officer, FAO of UN, 984-. Publications: Over 150 Technical papers in field; eynote Speaker at 22 International Conferences and 10 ational Conferences. Memberships: Chairman, Food ngineering Group, Australian Institute of Food Science and echnology, 1972-74, Fellow; Council for Education in World itizenship, 1964; Asian Association of Agricultural Engineers;

Thai Association of Food Technology. Address: Food and Agr Orgn UN, Maliwan Mansion, Phra Atit Rd, Bangkok, Thailand.

**HIDEN Robert Battaile Jr,** b. 8 May 1933, Boston, Massachusetts, USA. Lawyer. m. Ann Eliza McCracken, 2 sons, 1 daughter. Education: BA, Princeton University, 1955; LLB, University of Virginia School of Law, 1960. Appointments: Officer, US Navy, 1955-57; Partner, 1968-98, Of Counsel, 1999-, Sullivan and Cromwell, New York City; Vestry, Junior Warden, 1970-76, 1982-86, 1999-, St John's Church, Larchmont, New York; Trustee, 1979-85, Secretary and Trustee, 1990, Larchment Yacht Club, New York; Trustee, Hampton University, 1984-; Member, University of Virginia Law School, Dillard Scholarship Selection Committee, 1984-98. Publications: Articles in various legal periodicals, 1958-96. Honours: China Service Medal, 1956; Order of the Coif, 1959; Raven Society, 1959; Omicron Delta Kappa, 1959. Memberships: Association of Bar of City of New York; American Bar Foundation; New York State Bar Association; Dean's Council, University of Virginia Law School. Address: 2 Walnut Avenue, Larchmont, NY 10538-4232, USA.

**HIGGINSON William J.** Consultant; Editor; Publisher. Education: Certificate with Honours in Japanese language and Area Studies, Institute of Far Eastern Languages, Yale University; BA, Southern Connecticut State College, New Haven. Appointments: Teaching writing privately since 1972; Director of Project Culture, Leesburg State Prison, New Jersey, 1977-78; Instructor of English, Nutrition, Creative Writing and Communications at the Union County College, Cranford, New Jersey, 1979-90; Administrator, Office of Cultural and Heritage Affairs, County of Union, Elizabeth, New Jersey, 1983-91; Chair, Department of English, New Mexico Academy for Sciences and Mathematics, 1998-. Publications: Author of several professional publications including: Haiku World: An International Poetry Almanac, 1996; The Seasons in Haikai, 1996; The Haiku Seasons: Poetry of the Natural World, 1996; Haiku Compass: Directions in the Poetical Map of the United States of America, 1994; Met on the Road: A Transcontinental Haiku Journal, 1993; Ten Years' Collected Haiku, vol I, 1987; The Healing and Other Poems, 1986; The Haiku Handbook: How to Write, Share and Teach Haiku, 1985; Paterson Pieces: Poems, 1969-1979, 1981; Death is and Approaches to the Edge, 1981. Memberships: PEN, New Mexico; Haiku International Association; Haiku Society of America. Address: PO Box 2740, Santa Fe, NM 87504, USA.

**HIGHMAN Barbara,** b. 14 August 1942, Washington, DC, USA. Physician; Dermatologist. 1 son, 1 daughter. Education: MD, University of Michigan Medical School, 1967; Straight Medicine Internship, Baylor University Affiliated Hospitals, 1967-68. Appointments: Dermatology Residency, Henry Ford Hospital, 1968-71; Fellow in Dermatology, John Hopkins University, 1971-72; Diplomate, American Board of Dermatology, 1973-. Honours: Physicians Recognition Award; Continuing Medical Education Award. Memberships: American Academy of Dermatology; Society for Investigative Dermatology; National Foundation for Dermatology; Anne Arundel County Medical Society and Medical Chirurgical Society; Prince George's Medical Society. Address: 3335 Old Line Avenue, Laurel, MD 20707, USA.

**HIHARA Katsuji,** b. 16 February 1949, Okuarata, Taka-gun, Hyogo, Japan. University Professor. m. Masami Yoshida, 1 son. Education: Bachelor of Commercial Science, Kwansei-gakuin University, 1971; Master of Business Administration, Kobe University, 1973; Doctor of Business Administration, Kobe University, 1996. Appointments: Assistant, 1975-76, Assistant Professor, 1976-79, Associate

Professor, 1979-88, Professor, 1988-89, Toyama University, Toyama, Japan; Professor, Kobe University of Commerce, Kobe, Japan, 1989-; Head, Graduate School of Business Administration, 1992-93, Head, Department of Business Administration, 1992-93, Kobe University of Commerce. Publications: Inflation Accounting, in Japanese, 1984; Income Concepts of Inflation Accounting, in Japanese, 1995. Memberships: American Accounting Association, USA; Japan Accounting Association, Japan. Address: 2-30-22 Yokoo, Suma-ku Kobe Hyogo 654-0131, Japan.

**HIJAZY Mahmoud,** b. 1939, Palestine. Consultant Dermatologist; Venerologist. m. Raedah Halawa, 2 sons, 2 daughters. Education: MBBch, 1964; DVD, 1969; DM, 1971-; MD(PhD) DVD, 1973. Appointments: Skin and Genitourinary Dis Consultant - Owner and Director of Dr M Hijazy Medical Center; President of the Red Crescent, 1969-72. Publications: Book on skin diseases; Book in Genitourinary Diseases; Textbook, Pediatric Dermatology. Memberships: Academy Allergy and Clinical Immunology; Aesthetic and Restorative Surgery; American Academy of Dermatology; European Academy of Dermatology and Venereology. Address: Prince Mamdouh Bin Abdul Aziz St, Sulimania, Riyadh 11422, Saudi Arabia.

**HILL Debora Elizabeth,** b. 10 July 1961, San Francisco. Writer. Education: H BA, 1983, Sonoma State University. Appointments: Talk show host Rock Jour Viacom, San Francisco, 1980-81; Interviewer; Biographer, Harrap Ltd, London, 1986-87; Editor, North Bay Magazine, Cotati, California, 1988; Guest feature writer, Argus Courier, Petaluma, California, 1993-95; Concept developer, BiblioBytes, Hoboken, New Jersey, 1994-95, White Tiger Films, San Francisco, 1995-, Star Trek/Voyager, 1997-98, Star Trek/Deep Space Nine, 1998; Feature Writer, The Econs Press, 1996-; Associate Producer, White Tiger Films, 1995-97. Publications: Author, The San Francisco Rock Experience, 1979; CUTS from a San Francisco Rock Journal, 1982; Punk Retro, 1986; Gale Research-Resourceful Woman, 1994; St James Guide to Fantasy Writers, 1996; A Ghost Among Us, 1996; St James Guide to Famous Gays and Lesbians, 1997; Jeromes Quest, 1997; Rumour Has a Memory, 1999; Super Girls: The Co-ed Murders, 1999; Co-writer, Cons Producer, The Danger Club, Danger Club II; Contributor stories & articles to professional journals. Memberships: The Online Wordbiz Directory; The Hollywood Direct Access Directory; Writers for Hire. Address: 110 Grant Avenue, Petaluma, CA 94952-4809, USA.

**HILL Marianne Theresa,** b. 29 August 1945, Richmond, VA, USA. Economist. 1 daughter. Education: BS, Mathematics, University of Maryland, 1969; MSc, Economics, London School of Economics, 1970; PhD, Economics, Yale University, 1983. Appointments: Senior Economist, Governors Economic Council, 1980-85; Assistant Professor, Public Finance, University of Akron, 1986-90; Senior Economist; Center for Policy Research and Editor, 1990-. Publications: Various articles in professional journals and newspapers; Elgar Companion to Feminist Economics, 1999. Memberships: International Association for Feminist Economics; Unitarium Universalist Church, Jackson, USA; Childrens Defense Fund. Address: Center for Policy Research, 3825 Ridgewood Rd, Jackson, MS 39211, USA.

**HILL-WARREN Ernestine,** b. 17 December 1927, Rosebud, Texas, USA. Mayor. m. Floyd, 2 daughters. Education: BS, Texas College of Medicine, Prairie View A and M University. Appointments: 1st Black Mayor, Rosebud, Texas; 47 Years of Learning Public School. Address: 805 N 8th St, Rosebud, TX 76570, USA.

**HILT Mary Louise,** b. 17 May 1947, Muskegon, Michigan, USA. Artist. Education Layton School of Art, Milwaukee, Wisconsin, USA, 1966-68. Career: One Woman Show, Harvar Law School, 1987; 15 Exhibits, Various Venues, 1987-97; Tw Person Show, Fruenthal Center for Performing Arts, 1989 Group Shows, Bravos Gallery, 1987, 1990-92, 1994, 1996 Designed and Ran Art programme, The Kelliher Cente 1994-96; One Woman Show, Armenian Genocide Collection 1995-96; Massachusetts State House Portrait Exhibit, 199! Group Show, Allied Artists, 1997; Group Show, New Englan Watercolour Society 6th North American Open Show, 1998 Honours: Cambridge City Council Award; 2nd Annual Nev England Artists Competition Publicity Award, 1994 Memberships: Allied Artists of America; Chamber o Commerce, Cambridge, MA, USA. Address: Hilt Studio, 3 Richdale Ave, Cambridge, MA 02140, USA.

**HINOSHITA Fumihiko,** b. 21 November 1955, Kyoto, Japan Nephrologist. Education: MD, 1981, PhD, 1986, Tokyo Medic and Dental University. Appointments: Expert Clinician, Torid Kyodo Hospital, 1987-91; Research Associate, Department of Pathology, Harvard Medical School, Boston, 1991-9: Nephrologist, Toranomon Hospital, Tokyo, 1992-97; Chie Nephrologist, Hiratsuka Kyosai Hospital, 1997-98; Associat Professor, International University of Health and Welfare Tochigi, Japan, 1998-. Honours: 1st Prize, Seven Universitie English Oratorial Contest, Tokyo, 1978; Delegate, 32nd Japa and America Student Conference, 1980; Numerous grants Ministry of Education, Japan. Memberships: Internationa Society of Nephrology; Japanese Society of Internal Medicine American Society of Nephrology; Japanese Society o Nephrology. Address: International University of Health an Welfare Hospital, 537-3 Iguchi, Nishi-Nasuno-machi, Nasu-gur Tochigi 329-2763, Japan.

**HIRAKATA Hideo,** b. 12 March 1958, Nishinomiya, Japan Anesthesiologist. m. Chikako, 1 son. Education: MD, 1987 PhD, 1997, Kyoto University. Appointments: Kyoto Universit Hospital, 1987-88, 1997-; Tazuke Kofukai Medical Researc Institute, Kitano Hospital, 1988-97. Publications: in professiona journals of Anesthesiology. Membership: American Societ Anesthesiologists. Address: Kyoto University Hospita Department of Anesthesia, 54 Shogoin Kawahara Cho 606-8507 Sakyo-ku, Kyoto, Japan.

**HIRAMATSU Morihiko,** b. 12 March 1924, Oita, Japan Local Official. m. Teruko Mihara, 2 daughters. Education BLaw, Law School, Tokyo University, 1949. Appointments Employee, Ministry of International Trade and Industry 1949-64; Director, Industrial Environmental Protection Division Enterprises Bureau, 1964-65; Director, Petroleum Planning Division Mining Bureau, 1965-67; Director, Export Insurance Division Trade Promotion Bureau, 1967-69; Director Electronics Policy Division Heavy Industries Bureau, 1969-73 Director, General Affairs Division, Basic Industries Bureau 1973-74; Deputy Director General, Minister's Secretary National Land Agency, 1974-75; Vice Governor, Oita Pret 1975-79; Governor, 1979-83, 1983-87, 1987-91, 1991-95 1995-. Publications: Exhortations to the One Village, On Product Campaign; Think Globally, Act Locally; Ideas From Regional Perspective; The Road to the United States of Japan Honours: National Order of Cruzeiro Do Sul, 1988; Ramo Magsaysay Award, Philippines, 1995. Membership: Chairman Kyushu Governors' Association, 1991-. Address Chancellor/Governors Official Resid, 8-20 Niagemachi, Oit City, Oita Pref 870, Japan.

**HIRASAWA Eiji,** b. 22 August 1950, Toyama, Japan Biochemist. m. 1 son, 2 daughters. Education: BSc, Toyam niversity, 1973; MAgric, Kyoto University, 1977; DAgric, Kyoto niversity, 1981; DSc, Osaka City University, 1985. ppointments: Research Associate, Osaka City University, )79-88; Instructor, ibid, 1988-94; Associate Professor, ibid, ¥94-96; Professor, ibid, 1996-. Publications: Basic ochemistry, author, book, 1998. Honour: Alex von Humboldt ellow, 1984-86. Memberships: Botanical Society of Japan; apan Society of Plant Physiologists; American Society of Plant hysiologists. Address: Yamasaka 3 3 14, 546 0035 Osaka, apan.

**HIREMATH Satish, b.** 23 March 1969, Solapur, India. Artist. . Education: DMC, BFA, Painting, Dharawad University; MA, ainting, Gulburga University, 1998. Career: Freelance Artist, japur, Karnataka. Honours: Merit Award, All India Exhibition Shahabad, 1996; Merit Award, All India Exhibition at Mysore asara, 1996; Scholarship, All India Fine Arts & Crafts Society, 997; District Level Exhibition Award, Best Painting, 1997. ddress: c/o Chinchali House, Shirdhar Newas, Near Alankar uilding, Bijapur 586101, Karnataka, India.

**HIROMOTO Toshiro, b.** 2 January 1952, Kyoto, Japan. rofessor. m. Setsuko Kanda, 3 sons. Education: Doctor of ommerce. Appointment: Professor of Accounting, itotsubashi University, 1993-. Honours: Outstanding lanuscript Award, 1983, Literature Award, 1994, Japan ccounting Association; Literature Award, Japan Cost ccounting Association, 1998. Memberships: Japan Accounting ssociation; Japan Cost Accounting Association. Address: 15-6 aruyama-cho, Hachioji, Tokyo 192-0021, Japan.

**HIRSCH Martin Alan, b.** 26 March 1947, New York City, ew York. Dentist. m. Noreen Ellen, 2 daughters. Education: S, 1968, CUNY; DMD, 1972, University of Pennsylvania; peciality Prosthodontics, 1975, University of Iowa; Speciality laxillofacial Prosthetics, 1976, University of Chicago. ppointments: Dental Extern, The Coatsville (PA) Hospital, 971-72; Dental Intern, Mt Sinai Hospital, NYC, 1972-73; esident, Veterans Hospital, Iowa City, 1973-75, University hicago Hospital and Clinics, 1975-76; Assistant Professor )tolaryngology, Abraham Lincoln School of Medicine, niversity of Illinois Medical Centre, Chicago, 1976-77; irector, Maxillofacial Prosthetics Clinic Centre for Craniofacial namolies, University Illinois Medical Centre, Chicago, 976-77; Assistant Professor, University Illinois College of entistry, 1977-93; Staff, Department of Dentistry, University linois Hospital Medical Centre, 1979-83; Staff, Department of urgery, Dental Section, Cuneo Hospital, Chicago, 1979-87; abrini Hospital, Chicago, 1979-92; Staff, Department entistry, Illinois Masonic Medical Centre, Chicago, 1979-; lember, Head and Neck Treatment Centre, 1981-; Senior taff, Columbus Hospital Department of Surgery, Dental ection, Chicago, 1979-; Private Practice, General Cosmetic nd Prosthetic Dentistry, Chicago, 1979-; Attending Catholic lealth Partners, Chicago, 1998-; Adjunct Instructor, University f Chicago Hospitals and Clinics, 1975-76. Publications: peaker, Dental conferences, symposiums, seminars; Made resentations to lay audiences on radio and TV. Memberships: peaker, American Cancer Society, Chicago Division; hairman, Professional Education Committee, 1981-85; Oral ancer Committee, 1982-86; ADA; Illinois Dental Society; hicago Dental Society. Address: 1578 Hazel Ln, Winnetka, IL 0093-1313, USA.

**HIRSCHBERG Jenö, b.** 11 May 1928, Miskolc, Hungary. hysician. m. Clara Hirschberg, 2 sons. Education: MD, 1952, ledical University, Budapest; PhD, 1976; DSc, 1985, lungarian Academy of Sciences; Specialisation: )to-rhino-laryngology, 1957, Phoniatrics, 1979, Paediatric

ORL, 1980, Audiology, 1996. Appointments: Air Physician, Hungarian Army, Air Force, 1952-56; Oto-rhino-laryngo-bronchological Department, Heim Pál and Madarász Children's Hospital, Budapest, 1956-, Chairman, 1967-93, Scientific Consultant, Department of ORL, Phoniatrics and Pedaudiology and Cleft Palate Centre, 1993-. Publications: 253 in 11 languages; 3 patents; Editorial Board, 5 international journals; 9 books; Co-author 11 books. Honours: Hon member, 6 associations in field; 5 Medals: Kempelen, 1968, 1998; Gutzmann, 1980; For children, 1992; Cseresnyés, 1996. Memberships: Hungarian Society of ORL; Hungarian Association of Phonetics, Phoniatrics and Logopedics; International Association of Logopedics and Phoniatrics; Union of European Phoniatricians; International Association of Phonosurgeons; European Society of Pediatric Otorhinolaryngology; International Federation of Otorhinolaryngological Societies; Hungarian Association of Plastic Surgery, Hungarian Society of Bronchology, Hungarian Section of Pediatric ORL. Address: Children's Hospital ENT Cleft Pl, Madarász u 22/24, 1131 Budapest, Hungary.

**HIRST Scott Bill, b.** 30 June 1953, Westerly, Rhode Island, USA. Education: AA, Liberal Arts, 1978, Rhode Island Junior College, now Community College of Rhode Island; BA, Political Science, University of Rhode Island, 1980. Appointments: Thames River Tube Co Inc, Ashaway, Rhode Island; Electric Boat Corporation, Groton, Connecticut, 1981-96; Moderator Voting District No.1, Town of Hopkinton, Rhode Island, 1988-90; Alternate Delegate, 1992 Republican National Convention, Houston, Texas and Alternate Delegate, 1996 Republican National Convention, San Diego, California; Elected Hopkinton Town Council, Rhode Island, 1996; Board of Fire Commissioners, Ashaway Fire District, Rhode Island, 1994-97; Memberships: President, Hopkinton Historical Association, 1984-85; President, 1997-, Mowry Family Association; Master one term, North Stonington Grange No 138; New London County (Connecticut) Pomona Grange No. 6, 1968-; Freemason; Odd Fellows; Goodenow Family Association; Avery Memorial Association; American Political Items Collectors; Life Member, The Denison Society, Mystic, Connecticut; The Thomas Minor Society; Westerly, Rhode Island, Lodge No. 678, Benevolent Protective Order of Elks; The Nye Family of America Association Inc., East Sandwich, Massachusetts. Address: 20 Maple Court, Ashaway, RI 02804-9630, USA.

**HJALTASON Jon, b.** 24 January 1959, Akureyri, Iceland. Historian. m. Lovisa Bjork Kristjansdottir, 3 daughters. Education: BA, 1986, MA, 1990, History, University of Iceland. Appointments: Freelance Writer, 1987-; Part-time Teacher, 1987-97; Founder, Holar, book publishing company, 1991-. Publications: Author 7 books including Nonni and the House of Nonni, 1993; The Forger and his Judge, 1995; Co-author, The History of the Icelandic Freezing Plants 1942-1996, 1997; Articles in newspapers and magazines including Culprits in the History of Iceland, 1995. Memberships: Historical Society (Iceland); Chairman, Historical Society of Eyjafjorour. Address: c/o Amtsbokasafnid a Akureyri, V Brekkugoetu, 600 Akureyri, Iceland.

**HO Betty Juenyu (Yulin), b.** 20 November 1930, Nanking, China. Researcher; Writer. m. div, 2 sons (1 dec), 2 daughters. Education: BS Biology, 1952, Columbia University. Appointments: Laboratory Technician, Rat Laboratory, Columbia Presbyterian Medical Centre, 1953-54; Pianist, Accompanist, Ecole de Ballet Mara Dousse, Lausanne, Switzerland, 1959-60; Piano Teacher, Le Manoir, English Teacher, Institut Montcalm, Lausanne 1960-61; Research Director, Juvenescent Research Corporation, 1963-; Presently reorganizing The Living Body Bible: Secrets for Youthful Living. Publications: 10 including: 101 Ways to live 150 years Young and Healthy, 1992; A Unique Health Guide for Young People, 1994. Honours: Royal Patronage for Life, awarded by Prince Kevin, Principality of Hutt River Province, Queensland, Australia, 1994. Membership: Order of International Fellowship. Address: 807 Riverside Drive Apt 1F, New York, NY 10032, USA.

**HO Tsan Fai,** b. 28 August 1972, Hong Kong. IT Management. Education: BEng, 1994; MPhil, 1996; M.Arts, 1997; MBA. Appointments: Project Manager, Information Networking Laboratories, 1996-98. Memberships: IEEE; IEE; ACM; HKEA. Address: 33 Braemar Hill Road, Block 10, Flat 1B, Braemar Hill Mansion, North Point, Hong Kong.

**HO Zhi Chien,** b. 3 March 1924, Guangdong, China. Professor of Medicine. m. Dr Guo Wen Hua, 2 daughters. Education: BA, 1947; MD, 1952; Honorable PhD, 1992. Appointments: Lecturer to Professor, Professor, and Dean of Faculty of Clinical Nutrition, 1984-97, Sun Yat-sen University of Medical Sciences, Guangzhou, China. Publications: 97 original articles; 13 books as editor and writer. Honours: 13 provincial and national awards; Highest Award, Ryerson University, Canada. Membership: Chair, Chinese Infant & Maternal Association. Address: Department of Clinical Nutrition, Sun Yat-sen University of Medical Science, Guangzhou, China 510089.

**HOANG Van Son,** b. 16 June 1938, Hanoi, Vietnam. Medical Doctor. m. Duong Thi Nguyet Minh, 1 son, 1 daughter. Education: MD, 1962; Specialist Doctor Grade 2, 1982; PhD, 1985. Appointments: Head of Department, Hospital Nghe An, 1962-68; Hospital Viet Xo, Hanoi, 1968-71; Hospital Viet Duc, Hanoi, 1971-77; Institute of Paediatrics, 1977-; Associate Professor, University Blida, Algeria, 1989-94, University Hanoi, 1994-. Publications: 124 articles in medical journals. Honours: Medal, 1962, Vietnam Youth Union; Order of Resistance Grade 3, 1987; Medal, 1996, Health Care Services, Ministry of Health, Vietnam. Memberships: Vietnam Association Clinical Biochemists; International Federation Clinical Chemistry; International Society Enzymology; American Association Clinical Chemistry; International Association Therapeutic Drug Monitoring and Clinical Toxicology; New York Academy of Sciences; National Geographic Society, Washington; Australian Association of Clinical Biochemists. Address: 14 Duong Thanh, Hanoi, Vietnam.

**HOBBS Lottie Beth,** b. 7 July 1921, Rowden, Texas, USA. Author; Publisher. Education: BS, Abilene Christian University, 1943. Appointments: Editor, The Family Educator, 1976-94; President, National Pro-Family Forum Inc, 1977-94. Publications: Author of books: You Can Be Beautiful, 1959; Daughters of Eve, 1963; If You Would See Good Days, 1965; Victory Over Trials, 1968; Your Best Friend, 1969; Choosing Life's Best, 1988. Address: Harvest Publications, 6501 E Lancaster, Fort Worth, TX 76112, USA.

**HOCHMAN Larry Berman,** b. 21 November 1953, Paterson, New Jersey, USA. Composer; Orchestrator. m. Diane Hochman, 1 stepson, 1 daughter, 1 stepdaughter. Education: Eastman School of Music, 1971-72; Bachelor of Music, Manhattan School of Music, 1972-75. Appointments: Co-Founder, with Larry Gates, Newfound Music Productions. Compositions include: Symphonic Poem: In Memoriam, 1993; Phantom of the Opera, Regal Entertainment, (national tour); Dona Nobis Pacem, Choir at the Abbey of the Abbey of Regina Laudis, Children's Choir of Luxembourg; American Portraits, suite for orchestra; Music for films: The Watchman, 1983; Not

for Publication, 1983; Amazing Stories, (TV Show), 1986; Views of a Vanishing Frontier, (documentary), 1988; Yad Vashem (documentary); Lester Horton Warm Up (modern dance video); TV themes: CNN World News Tonight; NHL All Star Game; America's Toughest Assignment (CBS); 15 themes AMC (Cable TV); Co-Composer, HBO animated spl, Alexander and the .... Very Bad Day; Arranger: The Mailman and the Pirhana; Orchestrator: (films) On the Wing, 1986; Dead of Winter, 1986; The Ascent; TV films: The Guardian; Grand Larceny; Ransom of Red Chief; Composer, with Marc Elliot (Off-Broadway play) One Man Band; Orchestrator, (Broadway musical) Late Nite Comic, 1987; Orchestrator, (regional production), "1492", 1992; Funny, You Don't Look Like a Grandmother, 1993; Jane Eyre (Toronto), 1998; King David (Broadway, Alan Menken, composer); Cinderella (TV Musical Disney); Director, vocal arranger (Broadway production), Do Black Patent Leather Shoes Really Reflect Up?, 1982; Arranger, Orchestrator, Copacabana (live musical, written and directed by Barry Manilow, 1990-91); Orchestrations include Albums for Mandy Patinkin, Audra McDonald, Dawn Upshaw; Phantom of the Opera (Joyce Agency); Fascinatin' Rhythm pre-Broadway, 1997. Honours: New Jersey Theatre Group Applause Award, 1998; various CLIO awards and other advertising awards for Newfound Music; ASCAP Award, 1985. Membership: American Federation of Musicians; Board of Directors, Pushcart Players; BMI. Address: 10 Kershner Place, Fair Lawn, NJ 07410-5307, USA.

**HODGE Mary Therese,** b. 19 September 1951, Northern Billerica, USA. m. William B Hodge, div, 1 son, 1 daughter. Career: Ironworker, Regency Architectural Metals Group; Own Construction Company, Terris Associates, New Haven. Honour: 1st Female in USA on Launch Crew of 688 Class Nuclear Submarine, 1980; Scheduled to work on the sea trials of the submarine with Admiral Hyman Richover (Father of Nuclear Navy). Address: My Mothers' Kitchen, 56 State Street, Suite 8, New London, CT 06320, USA.

**HODGES Raymond John,** b. 9 May 1943, Australia. Chartered Chemist. m. Delma Mackey, 1 son, 1 daughter. Education: BSc, honours, Newcastle, New South Wales, 1965; PhD, Kensington, New South Wales, 1969; Commercial Pilots Licence, Civil Aviation Authority, Melbourne, 1980. Appointments: BHP Shortland, 1959-65; Postdoctoral Fellow, Hull University, England, 1969-72; Research Officer, BHP Shortland, 1972-75; Associate Professor, Monash University. Publications: MOGAS for Aeroplanes, co-author, 1984; Instrumental Analysis, an Introduction, 1997; Numerous other articles in professional journals. Honours: Commonwealth Scholar, 1960-69; Postdoctoral Fellow, 1969-72; Air Safety Award, 1980; Royal Aeronautical Society Medal, 1984; 10 research grants, 1977-97. Memberships: Fellow, RACI, 1983-; Fellow, AIPet, 1980-; AIE, 1978-. Address: RMB 4333, Rickard Drive, Morwell, Victoria 3840, Australia.

**HOEVELMANN Gerd Heinrich,** b. 20 February 1956, Siegen, Germany. Self Employed. m. Jutta Hoevelmann, 2 daughters. Education: MA, Philosophy, Linguistics, University of Marburg, 1984. Appointments: Assistant, Department of Philosophy, University of Marburg, 1984-92; Self Employed, 1992-. Publications: 150 publications on philosophy and history of science, linguistics, psychology, biology, semiotics, cultural history, parapsychology, space science. Memberships: Society for Scientific Exploration; Committee on Space Research; International Astronautical Federation; Language Origins Society; Parapsychology Association. Address: Hoevelmann Communication, Carl-Strehl-Str 16, 35039 Marburg, Germany.

**HOFEREK Mary J,** b. 1 November 1943, East Orange, New rsey, USA. Database Administrator. Education: BA, Health d Physical Education, Trenton State College, 1965; MA, Jucation, University of Michigan, 1969; PhD, Physical Jucation, University of Wisconsin, 1978. Appointments: atabase Administrator; Adjunct Professor. Memberships: EE; ASM. Address: 87 Oak Shade Road, Gaithersburg, MD 878, USA.

**HOFFHEIMER Daniel Joseph,** b. 28 December 1950, ncinnati, Ohio, USA. Lawyer. 3 daughters. Education: ploma, Phillips Exeter Academy, 1969; AB, cum laude, arvard College, 1973; JD, University of Virginia Law School, 76. Appointments: Associate, 1976-84, Partner, 1984-, Taft, ettinius & Hollister. Publications include: Wandering Between vo Worlds: Employment Discrimination Against Aliens, 1976; nployment Discrimination Against Aliens, 1976; Law and odernization in China: The Juridicial Behavior of the Chinese ommunists, 1977; China and the International Legal Order: n Historical Introduction, 1979; Practitioner's Handbook, -author, 1991; Practitioners' Handbook, co-author, 1991; xth Circuit Federal Practice Manual, Co-author, Editor, 1993. emberships include: President, Federal Bar Association, 87-88; President, Cincinnati Bar Association, 1992-93; ellow, American Bar Foundation; Fellow, Ohio Bar oundation; National Conference of Bar Presidents; Ohio upreme Court Commission on Racial Fairness, 1993-; nerican, Federal, Ohio State and Cincinnati Bar Associations; oard of Governors, Estate Planning, Probate and Trust Law ection; Advisory Board, Ohio Federal District Court Review; ustee, Judges Hogan and Porter Memorial Trust of the ederal Bar Association; Numerous community activities. ddress: 3672 Willowlea Court, Cincinnati, OH 45208-1816, SA.

**HOFFMAN Russell David,** b. 14 August 1956, Connecticut, SA. Computer Programmer. m. Sharon Leah Hoffman. Jucation: Pennsylvania State University, 1974 (DNF); omputer Processing Institute, Bridgeport, Connecticut, 1980. opointments: Owner, Chief Programmer, The Animated oftware Co. Publications: All About Pumps; The Heart: The ngine of Life; Editor, Stop Cassini Newsletter; Webmaster, ww.animated software.com. Address: Animated Software, PO ox 1936, Carlsbad, CA 92018-1936, USA.

**HOGAN Edward Patrick,** b. 12 November 1939, St Louis, issouri, USA. Educator. m. Joan M Ford, 2 sons, 3 daughters. Jucation: BS, General Studies, 1961, AM Geography, 1962, nD Sociology and Anthropology, 1969, St Louis University. opointments: Professor and Head Department of Geography, 967-91, Professor of Geography and South Dakota State eographer, 1991-, Assistant Vice President Academic Affairs, 991-, South Dakota State University. Publication: Co-author, eography of South Dakota, 1998. Honours: SDSU Educator the Year, 1997; NCGS Distinguished Teaching Award, 1989. emberships: Association of American Geographers; SD eographical Society; National Council for Geographic ducation. Address: Office for Academic Affairs, SDSU ookings, SD, USA.

**HOLDEN Helge,** b. 28 September 1956, Oslo, Norway. rofessor of Mathematics. m. Ingvill M Stedoy, 4 sons. ducation: Dr philos, University of Oslo, 1985. Appointments: ssociate Professor, Norwegian Institute of Technology, 986-91; Professor, Norwegian University of Science and echnology, 1991-. Publications: Solvable Models in Quantum echanics, co-author, 1988; Stochastic Partial Differential quations, co-author, 1996; More than 90 research papers.

Membership: Norwegian Academy of Technological Sciences. Address: Karisvingen 14C, 7040 Trondheim, Norway.

**HOLDEN Mary Gayle,** b. 21 October 1948, Charlottesville, Virginia, USA. Attorney. m. Peter R Holden, 4 sons. Education: BA, Roanoke College, 1970; JD, University of Virginia Law School, 1980. Appointments: Miller, Canfield, Paddock and Stone, 1979; McGuire, Woods, Battle and Booth, 1980-83; Sole Practitioner, 1983-84; Frank, Bernstein, Conway and Goldman, 1985; In House Counsel, 1985-88; Calligaro and Mutryn, 1988-89; Leonard, Ralston and Stanton, 1990-97; Hopkins and Sutter, 1997-. Memberships: Virginia State Bar, 1980-; American Bar Association, 1980-88; District of Columbia Bar Association, 1998-; Board of Directors, American Cancer Society, 1997-; Loudoun County Affirmative Action Committee, 1995-; Board of Directors, Committee for Dulles, 1985-; Jackson Field Home for Girls, 1988-89; Fairfax Choral Society, 1983-; County Leadership Extension Council, 1995-; Loudoun Chamber of Commerce, 1996-; Zonta International, 1997-. Address: Hopkins and Sutter, 888 16th St NW, Washington, DC 20006-4103, USA.

**HOLECEK Milan,** b. 10 February 1956, Hradec Kralove, Czech Republic. Physiologist. m. Katerina, 2 daughters. Education: MD, 1981; PhD, 1985. Appointments: Assistant Professor, 1981-91; Associate Professor, 1992-. Publications: 50 Original Papers. Memberships: ESPEN; ISAAR; Physiol Soc; Hepatol Soc. Address: Dept of Physiology, Medical Faculty Charles Univ, Simkove 870, 500 01 Hradec Kralove, Czech Republic.

**HOLEN Norman Dean,** b. 16 September 1937, Cavalier, North Dakota, USA. College Professor. m. Ilene G Holen, 1 son, 1 daughter. Education: BA, 1959, Concordia College; MFA, 1962, State University of Iowa; Postgrad Study, 1972, University Minnesota. Appointments: Instructor, Chairman, Northwestern College, Orange City, 1962-63; Instructor, Concordia College, 1963-64; Professor, 1964-, Department Chair, 1967-68, 1979, 1987-88, Augsburg College, Minneapolis. Publications: 13 articles in professional journals and reviews; 13 commissioned sculptures, in public collections; 20 one-person exhibitions; 92 group shows; 116 competitive exhibitions with 16 national and 2 international awards. Honours: 18 educational grants and awards; 15 awards of excellence and travel grants including: In Memoriam Award, national, Allied Artists of America, 1983; National Sculpture Society Travel Grant, 1984; Mabel Pew Myrin Trust Grant, 1987; NSS Fellow. Memberships: National Sculpture Society; Allied Artists of America; Society of Minnesota Sculptors. Address: 7332 12th Avenue S, Minneapolis, MN 55423, USA.

**HOLLA Malathi K,** b. 6 July 1958, Bangalore, India. Bank Officer. Education: MA Psychology. Appointments: Assistant Manager, Syndicate Bank, Bangalore. Honours: Total Medals won so far: 153 gold, 28 silver, 8 bronze; Women Championship with Trophy 7 times; Retained National Championship 1981-; Outstanding Youth in Sports, 1988; Dasara State Award for outstanding performance in sports from Government of Karnataka, 1988; Rajyothsava Award from Government of Karnataka for Outstanding Sports Woman of the Year, 1989; Outstanding Disabled Sports Person Award in Public Sector Banks, 1989; His Excellency the Governor of Karnataka conferred the Karnataka State Award for outstanding sports person in Athletics in 1990-91; His Excellency, the President of India conferred the Arjuna Award for outstanding sports woman of the year 1995-96; K K Birla Foundation Award for Excellence in Sports for year 1995-96; Prathiba Shree award, 1996; Prathibha Rathna Award, 1997; Best Citizen of

India Award 1998-99; and others. Address: Syndicate Bank, 28 Residency Road, Bangalore 560025, India.

**HOLLMEN Arno Ilmari,** b. 19 November 1930, Helsinki, Finland. Professor; Phycisian. m. Ulla Margareta Kiuru, 1 son, 2 daughters. Education: MD, 1956, Turku University; PhD, 1967, Helsinki University; Assistant Professor, 1971, Professor, 1974, Oulu University. Appointments: Anaesthesia Registrar, Copenhagen University Hospital, 1959, Helsinki University Hospital, 1960-62; Consultant Anaesthetist, Kuopio Central Hospital, 1963-65, Oulu County Hospital, 1965-72; Professor and Chairman, Dept of Anaesthesia, Oulu University Hospital, 1972-92; Senior Lecturer, 1992-; Visiting Professor, University of Stanford, 1970-71, University of California, 1976-77, University of Columbia, New York, 1983, 1985, University of Texas, San Antonio, 1985-86; Clinical Professor, University of Texas, San Antonio, 1986-94. Publications: 200 in international medical journals and textbooks. Honours: Honorary Member, Finnish Society of Anaesthesiologists, 1990, Australian Society of Anaesthetists, 1979; Elected Fellow of Royal Society of Anaesthetists, England, 1995; First Class Knight of Finnish White Rose Order, 1977. Memberships: Scandinavian Society of Anaesthesiologists; European Academy of Anaesthesiologists; New York Academy of Sciences; Scientific Committee of National Defence; Society of Parliament members and researchers in Finland; Society of Research of the Future. Address: Yrjonk 25C17, 00100 Helsinki, Finland.

**HOLLOS Mate,** b. 18 July 1954, Budapest, Hungary. Composer. Education: F Liszt Academy of Music, Budapest. Appointments: Managing Director, Hungarian Records Limited; President, Hungarian Composers Union. Publications: Articles in music periodicals. Honours: Award, The Audience at the Rostrum of New Recordings of the Hungarian Radio, 1992; Erkel Prize, 1997; Béla Bartók - Ditta Pásztory Prize, 1998. Memberships: Hungarian Composers Union; Jeunesses Musicales; Union of Hungarian Creative Artists. Address: Bimbo ut 5, H-1022 Budapest, Hungary.

**HOLLOSI Miklos,** b. 24 October 1941, Budapest. Chemist. m. Ilona Laczko, 2 daughters. Education: MSc, 1965; PhD, 1967; DSc, 1990. Appointments: Assistant Professor, 1967, Associate Professor, 1982, Full Professor, 1991, Chair, 1993, Department of Organic Chemistry, Eotvos University, Budapest. Publications: Over 130 papers in international journals. Honours: Natural Sciences Award of Eotvos University, 1990; Academy Award, 1996. Memberships: European and American peptide Society; Hungarian Academy of Sciences. Address: H 1518 Budapest, PO Box 32, Hungary.

**HOLMES David Jeffrey,** b. 24 February 1945, Somerville, New Jersey, USA. Autograph Dealer. m. Barbara Ware Holmes, 1 daughter. Education: BA, Springfield College; MA, Northeastern University. Appointment: Dealer in rare books and manuscripts, 1972-. Memberships: Antiquarian Booksellers Association of America; Professional Autograph Dealers Association. Address: David J Holmes Autographs, 230 So Broad St 3rd Fl, Philadelphia, PA 19102, USA.

**HOLSTI Ole Rudolf,** b. 7 August 1933, Geneva, Switzerland. Professor, Researcher. m. Ann Wood, 1 son, 1 daughter. Education: BA, Stanford University, 1954; MAT, Wesleyan University, 1956; PhD, Stanford University, 1962. Appointments: Instructor, Assistant Professor, Stanford University, 1962-67; Research Coordinator, Associate Director, Stanford University, 1962-67; Associate Professor, Professor, University of British Columbia, 1967-74; Professor, University of California, 1978-79; George V Allen Professor, Director of Undergraduate Studies, Chairman, 1974-98, Emeritus, 1998-.

Publications: Content Analysis: A Handbook with Application fc the Study of International Crisis; Enemies in Politics; E enemigo en Politica; Content Analysis for the Social Scienc and Humanities; The Analysis of Communication Conten Developments in Scientific Theories and Compute Techniques; Crisis Escalation War; Unity and Disintegration i International Alliances, Comparative Studies; Change in th International System; American Leadership in World Affairs Vietnam and the Breakdown of Consensus; Public Opinion an American Foreign Policy; Encyclopedia of US Forieg Relations; Many Articles and Chapters. Honours: Bes Published Paper Award, International Studies Quartely; Nevi Stanford Award; Howard Johnson Distinguished Teachin Award; Alumni Distinguished Undergraduate Teaching Awarc Memberships: International Studies Association; Internationa Soceity for Political Psychology;Western Political Scienc Association; Peace Science Society; American Politica Science Association; International Studies Association President 1978-79; Many Other Memberships. Address: Dep Pol Sci, Duke University, Durham, NC 27708, USA.

**HOLTZ Aliza,** b. 10 January 1952, New York, NY, USA Biomedical Consultant. Education: BA Biology, Psychology Education, 1973, Brandeis University; PhD Biology, 198C Boston University. Appointments: Research Scientist, NY Stat Psychiatric Institute, 1980-82; Manager Special Projects, MEE Communications, 1983-84; President, Holtz Communications 1985-. Publications: Author or co-Author, numerous articles i professional journals. Memberships: New York Academy c Sciences; American Medical Centres Association; America Association of the Advancement of Science. Address: 275 F Washington Avenue, New York, NY 10032 1203, USA.

**HOLYER Erna Maria,** b. 15 March 1925, Germany. Autho Artist; Educator. m. G W Holyer. Education: AA, San Jos Evening College, 1964; DLitt, World University, 1984; Diploma Writers Digest School, 1987. Career: Freelance Artist, 1958- Freelance Writer, 1960-; Instructor, MAEP, Adult School, 1968- Publications: 13 books, 1965-97. Honours: Congress Challeng Trophy, 1991; DFA, 1992. Memberships: CWC; NLAPW; Worl University Doctoral Round Table. Address: 1314 Rimroc Drive, San Jose, CA 95120, USA.

**HOLZ Dietmar Alexander,** b. 2 November 1962, Hamburg Germany. Engineer. m. Annette Holz, 4 sons. Education Masters Degree, Material Engineering, 1990, PhD, Cerami Processing, 1994, Technical University of Hamburg Appointments: Research Assistant, Technical University o Hamburg, 1990-95; Material Development, Magnetic Products Philips Components, 1995-98; Advanced Ceramics an Modules, Process Development, Philips Components, 1998- Publications: 15 papers in professional journals including Fabrication of Low-to-Zero Shrinkage Reaction-Bonded Mullit Composites, 1995; Reaction Bonding of Aluminium Oxide (RBAO) Science and Technology, 1995. Address: Schulstrass 11a, 24640 Schmalfeld, Germany.

**HOMMA Toshiaki,** b. 2 October 1954, Tokyo, Japan Respiratory Physician. m. Fumiko Tange, 1 son, 2 daughters Education: BS, 1980, MD, PhD, 1984, University Tsukuba Appointments: Chief Instructor, Seiranso Hospital, 1985-86 Assistant Professor, Tsukuba University, 1986-88, 1997- Research Associate, National Jewish Hospital, Denver, USA 1989-93. Publications: Sports Medicine Guide, 1994 Laboratory Medicine, 1996; Practice in Internal Medicine, 1997 Memberships: Japanese Society of Respiratory Care Medicine Japan Internal Medicine; Japanese Thoracic Society. Address 14-25 Onogawa, Tsukuba Ibaraki 305-0053, Japan.

**HON Giora,** b. 20 December 1950, Afula, Israel. Philosopher. 1 son, 1 daughter. Education: BSc Physics, 1975; MSc History Phil Science, 1977; PhD History Phil Science, 1984. Appointments: Lecturer, University Haifa. Address: University Haifa, Department Philosophy, Mt Carmel, 31905 Haifa, Israel.

**HONG Chu-Wan,** b. 20 September 1959, Kang-Shan, Taiwan. Materials Scientist; Process Engineer; Manager; Educator. Education: BS, 1987, Dipl-Ing (MS), 1991, Dr-Ing (PhD), 1995, Technical University Hamburg-Harburg, Germany. Appointments: Research Scientist, Mercedes-Benz, Stuttgart, Germany, 1991; Visiting Researcher, Nippon Steel Corp, Kawasaki, Japan, 1992; Research Scientist, Technical University, Hamburg-Harburg, 1992-94; Head of Laboratory, University of Erlangen-Nürnburg, 1994-98; Project Manager, Siemens Matsushita Components, Austria, 1998-; Guest Lecturer, University of Erlangen-Nürnberg, Germany, 1999-. Publications: 4 patents; 1 book; Papers published in refereed journals. Honour: Award of the Max Planck Society, 1993. Memberships: American Ceramic Society; German Society of Materials Science. Address: Am Muehlgarten 47, D-91080 Spardorf, Germany.

**HÖNIG Johannes Franz,** b. 15 July 1956, Dülmen, Germany. Plastic Surgeon. Education: MD, 1986, DMD, 1988, University of Ulm, Germany; PhD, University of Göttingen, Germany, 1995; Diplomate, German Board, Plastic and Reconstructive Surgery. Appointments: Resident, University of Ulm, 1985-86, University of Würzburg, 1986-88; Senior Resident, University of Göttingen, 1989-93; Instructor, Plastic and Reconstructive Surgery, 1992, Consultant, 1993, Professor, 1995; Lecturer, Craniofacial and Plastic Surgery, University Medical School, Göttingen, 1993-94; General Manager, Medline Publishers, 1992. Publications: Author, numerous books and articles; Editor, Author, Plastic Surgery Patient Adviser, 1994; Inventor, multipoint contact osteosynthesis plate; Patentee in field. Memberships: Art Collection, Göttingen, 1991; Founder, Bernhardt Rosevelt Gelschefarth Society, Germany, 1996; German Society of Plastic and Reconstructive Surgery; American Society of Plastic and Reconstructive Surgery; New York Academy of Science; German Society of Craniofacial Osteology, Chairman, 1994-97; European Association of Aesthetic Plastic Facial Surgeons, President, 1997-98. Address: Homann-Föge-Weg 3, D-37073 Göttingen, Germany.

**HOOKHAM Eleanor King,** b. 5 April 1909, Oklahoma, USA. Artist; Painter (lithographic art, etchings); Writer. m. (1) George Lawrence Salley, 9 July 1934, divorced 28 March 1940, (2) Robert Ernest Hookham, 5 November 1943, 1 daughter. Appointments: Artist Exhibitor, Leonard Clayton Gallery, New York City, New York, USA, 1938; One Woman Show, Montross Gallery, New York City, 1939-41; Painted Portrait of President of Senate, Phillip Beall Hangs in Florida Senate, 1943; Painted Portrait of D N Nathanial M Salley, Salley Building, Florida State University, Tallahassee; Painted Portrait of Dr Timothy Lehmann, Hangs in Lehmann Building, Elmhurst College; Taught art in own home, Elmhurst, Illinois, USA, 1946-83; Group Show, Johnson Gallery, South Michigan Avenue, Chicago, Illinois, 1959-60, 1961; Group Show, Chicago Midwest Artists, Illinois State Art Museum, 1964; One Woman Show, Galerie Internationale, New York City, New York, 1962-63; 1964, 1965; Group Show, International Federation Culturelle Feminine, 1968; Musée D'Art Moderne, also Athens, Greece and in Plais, 1969; One Woman Show, Pensacola Art Museum, Florida, One Woman Show, 1969; Galerie Marcel Bernheim, 1965-1984; Galerie Bernheim-Jeune, 1985-92. Publications: Creative Art and the Subconscious, author, 1979;

Compilation Of My Color Theory, author; Biography, El King, 1997; Eleanor King Hookham, biography. Honours include: Medaille D'or L'Academie De Lutece, 1979; Gold Medal, Group Show, Museum in Sony Building, Osaka, Japan, 1980; Gold Grand Prix Humanitaire De France, Paris, France, 1984; Palme D'Or, Paris Critiques, Paris, 1981; Medaille Vermeil, Arts Science Et Lettres, Paris, France, 1989; Medaille Lifetime Achievement for Promoting Art, Illinois Arts, 1995; Alliance, Sidney R Yates Award, Chicago, Illinois, 1995; Honorary Doctorates of Arts: Honoris Causa Di Maestro, Seminario Internationale D'Arte Moderna, Salsumaggiore Terme, Italy, 1982; Doctor Honoris Causa, Cultural Academie De France, Paris, France, 1980; Doctor of Art, Elmhurst College, Elmhurst, Illinois, USA, 1987. Memberships: Founding Member, Elmhurst Artists' Guild, President, 1951-53, 1971-73; Founder, 1974, Elmhurst Art Museum; Founder, 1974, Elmhurst Fine Arts and Civic Centre Foundation; President, 1981-91; Daughters of the American Revolution, Regent, 1961, 1962; Colonial Dames of America, Chapter XIV, Chicago, 1981; National Arts and Letters, Chicago. Hobbies: Golf; Swimming. Address: 289 Adelia Street, Elmhurst, IL 60126, USA.

**HOPPE Ulf-Peter,** b. 10 January 1955, Schlüchtern, Hessen, Germany. Scientist. m. Ulrike Hoppe, 2 daughters. Education: Dr rer nat, 1985; Postdoctoral qualification, 1995. Appointments: Principal Scientist, Norwegian Defence Research Establishment. Publications: 30 articles in scientific journals. Honours: Silver Cross of Honour, German Federal Armed Forces. Memberships: EGS; COSPAR; Norwegian Geophysical Association. Address: Norwegian Defence Research Establishment, Division for Electronics, PO Box 25, 2007 Kjeller, Norway.

**HOPPENSTEIN Abraham Solomon,** b. 9 October 1931, Benoni, South Africa. Barrister; Merchant Banker. m. Judith Taubene, 2 sons, 2 daughters. Education: Degrees in Commerce and Law, 1949-54, University of Witwatersrand, Johannesburg; International Fellowship, Aspen Institute for Humanistic Studies, Aspen, Colorado, 1988. Appointments: Various significant positions in South Africa, 1949-75; South Africa's first Trade Commissioner to Israel, South African Embassy, Tel Aviv, 1975; Counsellor, Political Affairs, South African Embassy, Washington DC, 1976-77; Member, National Executive Councils of the South African Jewish Board of Deputies and of the South African Zionist Federation, 1978; Consul General for South Africa, Washington DC, 1979-80, New York, 1980-86; Member, Board of Trustees, Temple Israel Centre, White Plains, New York; Member, Board of Directors, Ben Gurion University Associates, New York, 1989-92; Member Board of Trustees, Helen Keller International, 1997-; Member Board of Directors, The Alliance Foundation, and Israel Medical Development Inc (Schneider Children's Hospital, Tel Aviv), 1992-; Member, Board of Governors, Polo Club of Boca Raton, Florida, 1998-; Investment and Merchant Banker, Vice President International Business Affairs, Allen & Company Inc, New York, 1986-92; Chairman, President and Chief Executive Officer, Chartrex International Ltd LLC, Chairman and Director, other corporations, 1956-; Advocate, Supreme Court of South Africa, 1971-; Attorney, Notary Public and Conveyancer of the Supreme Court of South Africa, 1958-71. Honours: Honorary member, NY Chamber of Commerce, 1980; Honorary member, Lions International, 1979; Israel-South Africa Chamber of Commerce, Tel Aviv, 1976. Memberships: Economic Club of New York; Foreign Policy Association, New York; Global Economic Action Institute. Address: PO Box 812373, Boca Raton, FL 33481-2373, USA.

**HORGAN Susan Bedsow,** b. 24 November 1947, Chicago, IL, USA. Television Producer; Writer. m. Patrick Horgan, 1 son.

Education: Bachelor of Arts, University of California, Irvine. Appointments: Producer, As The World Turns; Head Writer, As The World Turns; Producer, One Life To Live; Associate Head Writer, One Life To Live; Executive Producer, One Life To Live. Honour: Daytime Emmy, Best Series Writing Team. Membership: NATAS; WGA. Address: The Haunted Ink Bottle, 91 Cedar Road, Wilton, CT 06897-3628, USA.

**HORIGOME Hitoshi,** b. 28 July 1956, Ina, Nagano, Japan. Paediatric Cardiologist. m. Yumi Sakamoto, 1 son, 1 daughter. Education: MB, 1982, MD, 1991, University of Tsukuba. Appointments: Clinical Trainee, Tsukuba University Hospital, 1982-83; Medical Staff, Kanagawa Children's Medical Centre, Yokohama, 1984-85, Ibaraki Children's Hospital, Mito, 1985-92; Instructor, University of Tsukuba, 1992-. Publications: Magnetocardiography, book, 1997; Contributor of articles to professional journals. Membership: Foster Parent, Plan International, Tokyo, 1995-. Address: 2-5-20 Umezono, 305-0045 Tsukuba, Ibaraki, Japan.

**HORVATH Werner,** b. 13 November 1949, Linz, Austria. Radiologist; Artist. m. Ilse Beham, 1 son, 1 daughter. Education: MD, University of Vienna, 1975; Assistant in Radiology, Hospital Barmh Bruder Linz, 1978-82, Oberarzt, 1983-88, Primarius, 1988. Appointments: Chief Radiologist, X-Ray Department, Hospital Barmh Bruder, 1988-; Authorized Representative, Radiation Protection, 1988-; Continued Education, 1988-. Publications: Numerous articles in professional journals; Numerous art exhibitions. Honour: Senator Putter Prize, German Society of Phlebology, 1982. Memberships: Austrian Society of Radiology; Austrian Society of Ultrasound; German Society of Phlebology; Austrian Society of Angiology; Medical Society of Upper Austria. Address: Krankenhaus der Barmherzigen Bruder, Seilerstatte 2, A-4020 Linz Upper-Austria, Austria.

**HOSRI Fernand,** b. 20 January 1942, Beirut, Lebanon. Corporate Executive. m. Eugenie Saad, 1 son, 2 daughters. Education: Proficiency in Italian, Dante Alighieri Institute, Rome, 1959; French Baccalaureate, College des Freres, Beirut, 1961; Proficiency in English, Michigan University, 1963; BA, Political Science, American University of Beirut, 1967. Appointments: Founder, Managing Director, Ets F.A Hosri, Beirut, 1966, Mobilier Confort, Beirut, 1971, Jorica Traders (Overseas) Ltd, Limassol, Cyprus, 1990, Jorica Hoteliere France Sarl, Agen, France, 1990, Makas Est. For Safety Equipment, Jeddah, Saudi Arabia, 1992, IMFAH Real Estate Co, Beirut, 1997; Executive Director, SACOTEL Sarl, Beirut, 1978. Publications: Lebanese Pound Crisis in Lebanon, 1986; Several articles in professional journals. Honours: Medal, Diploma of Honour, Terra Santa Mission, Jerusalem, 1959; Apostolic Benediction, Pope Paul VI, 1969; Honour Roll Certificate, Lions Club International Foundation, 1983; Lions President Plaque of Appreciation, 1984; Lions Medal of Merit, 1986; Lions Highest Plaque of Appreciation for Life Membership, 1993; Apostolic Benediction, Pope John Paul II, 1996; International Grand Prix to the Commerical Prestige Europe, Monaco, 1997; Golden Athena International Economic Performance Award, Athens, 1998. Memberships: Founder, President, Phoenicia Sporting and Cultural Club, Ghebaleh, Lebanon, 1964, Hosri Family Association, Beirut, 1993; Co-Founder, Member, Lebanese Insurance Brokers Association, Beirut, 1982; Chairman, The Saint Nohra Charitable Trust, Ghebaleh, 1994; Life Member, The Internatonal Association of Lions Clubs; Life Fellow, The Oxford Club, USA; Honorary Member, The Girl's Education Association, Beirut; Beirut, Jeddah and Agen (France), Chambers of Commerce and Industry; Beirut Businessmen Association; Comfort Inn Primevere Hotel Owners Association,

Paris; Lebanese Office Stationary and Engineering Equipment Importers Association; The Lebanese Political Association; National Fire Protection Association, USA; The Institute of Professional Managers, UK; Alumni Association of the American University of Beirut. Address: Pasteur St F Hosri Building, PO Box 11-565, Beirut, Lebanon.

**HOSSAIN Zaker,** b. 30 April 1940, Murshidabad. Advocate. m. Hosne Ara Begum, 3 sons, 1 daughter. Education: BA Hons, Calcutta; MA LLB, Dhaka; SPL Law Training, University of California, USA; Fellow, Centre for International Legal Study, Salzburg, Austria; EX EPCS (Admn) Counsel. Appointments: Counsel, Cadre, Visiting Lawyer, California University, USA; Apellate Division, Supreme Court. Publications: Judicial Management in Bangladesh; Law articles. Memberships: California Bar Association; International Bar Association, UK; Honourable Society of Inner Temple, England; Red Cross Society; Life Member, Bangladesh Children's Hospital; Law Asia; Supreme Court Bar Association; Intellectual Property Law Section, California, USA; Anjuman-E-Mafidul Islam. Address: President, Environmental Defense Association of Bangladesh, 27 Gandaria Keshab Banerjee Rd, Dhaka, Bangladesh.

**HOSTON Germaine Annette,** b. 27 July, Trenton, New Jersey, USA. Professor. Education: AB, Politics and East Asian Studies, Princeton University, 1975; MA, 1978, PhD, 1981, Government, Harvard University. Appointments: Assistant Professor, Associate Professor, Professor, Johns Hopkins University, 1992-; Professor of Chinese and Japan Politics, Director, Institute for Transpacific Studies in Values, Culture and Politics. Publications: Marxism and the Crisis of Development in Prewar Japan, 1986; The State, Identity and the National Question in China and Japan, 1994; Numerous articles in professional journals. Memberships include: Vice President American Political Science Association; Association for Asian Studies. Address: Department of Political Science, 0521 University of La Jolla, California, San Diego, 9500 Gilman Drive, CA 92093-0521, USA.

**HOU Tianzhen,** b. 5 February 1940, Hejin, Shanxi Province, China. Biologist. m. Mao GuoYing, 2 sons. Education: BSc, 1964, Forestry and Soil College, Shen Yang; Foreign Language Institute, Xian, 1984-85; University of Minnesota, Mineapolis, USA, 1986-87, 1991-93. Appointments: Director, Forest Physiology and Biochemistry Department, Xinjiang Academy of Forestry Science, 1964-98. Publications: Author, Experimental evidence of a plant meridian system I, II, III, IV, V, 1994, 1997; Inventor, Plant Treatment Process Patent, USA, 1997. Honour: Great Achievement Award of Science and Technology, Xinjiang Government, 1981. Memberships: Fellow, Xinjiang Committee of Biological Science and Technology, 1985-88; Fellow, China Committee of Forest Physiology and Biochemistry, 1988-98. Address: Xinjiang Academy of Forestry Science, Urumqi 830002, China.

**HOUSTON Brian Christopher Michael,** b. 27 December 1938, Calcutta, India. Military Engineer. m. Heather S D Houston, 1 daughter. Education: BSME, Air Force College, 1957; Hamilton County Police Academy, 1973; MDiv, Virginia Theological Seminary, 1984; Lasalle University BS/MS Security Management. Appointments: Retired Lt Col, military, 23 1/2 years; Royal Canadian Airforce Pilot, 1957-65; Royal Marines/ZZ Reg SAS, 1965-79. Honours: 3 Purple Hearts; Bronze Star; Silver Star; Croix de Guerre and CIB with 2 Stars. Memberships: Fraternal Order of Masons; National Association for Counter Terrorism; Life Member, NRA and Founder Second Ammendment Task Force. Address: 1207 Sunrise Court, Herndon, VA 22070, USA.

**HOWAT Peter Aran**, b. 23 February 1949, Hokitika, New ±aland. Professor. m. Jeanette, 1 son, 1 daughter. Education: p Ed, 1970, Otago; BSc, 1971, Canterbury; Dip Tchng, 1971, nristchurch; MSc, 1978, PhD, 1979, Illinois. Appointments: ±acher, Greymouth HS, New Zealand, 1972-75; Head, ±partment of Health Promotion, Curtin University, Australia, ±80-; Co-Director, Curtin University Centre for Health omotion Research; Australian Editor, American Journal of ±alth Behaviour, 1991-. Publications: 150 refereed journal ±icles, book chapters, reports and conference proceedings. ±nours: Avery Brundage Scholarship, University of Illinois, ±78, 1979; Graduate, University Illinois MSc and PhD ±ogrammes; National Honour Society, Phi Kappa Phi. ±emberships: Australian Health Promotion Association, ±ational Secretary 1992-95; Public Health Association of ±stralia, WA State President, 1993-95; Injury Control Council WA, President 1992-94. Address: Head, Department of ±alth Promotion, School of Public Health, Curtin University, ±O Box U1987, Perth, WA 6845, Australia.

**HOWE Drayton Ford Jr**, b. 17 November 1931, Seattle, ±ashington, USA. Lawyer. m. Joyce A Howe, 1 son. ±ucation: AB, University of California, Berkeley, 1953; LLB, ±stings College of Law, 1957; Admitted to California Bar, ±58. Appointments: Lawyer, Internal Revenue Service, ±58-61; Tax Department Supervisor, Ernst & Ernst, San ±ancisco, 1962-67; Lecturer, Tax Matters, University of ±lifornia Extension, 1966-76; Principal, Bishop, Barry, Howe, ±ney & Ryder, San Francisco, 1968-. Memberships: California ±r Association; California Society of CPA's. Address: Bishop ±rry Howe Et Al, 275 Battery Street, 12th Floor, San ±ancisco, CA 94111-3305, USA.

**HOWES Lawrence Guy**, b. 23 October 1951, Melbourne, ±stralia. Physician; Medical Researcher and Educator. m. Jan ±inton, 1 son, 2 daughters. Education: MBBS, 1975, PhD, ±84, University Melbourne; Fellow, Royal Australasian College ± Physicians, 1982. Appointments: NH asnd MRC Travelling ±esearch Fellow, 1983-85; Senior Lecturer, University ±elbourne, 1986; Senior Staff Clinical Pharmacologist, Austin ±ospital, Melbourne, 1992-; Professor of Clinical Pharmacology ±d Medicine, UNSW, St Georges Hospital, Sydney. ±blications: Over 110 publications or book chapters in ±rdiovascular medicine. Memberships: Royal Australasian ±ollege of Physicians; High Blood Pressure Council of ±stralia; Australasian Society of Clinical and Experimental ±armacologists and Toxicologists; Cardiac Society of ±stralia and New Zealand. Address: 93A Woodlands Avenue, ±garno 2210, New South Wales, Australia.

**HRIB Jiří**, b. 16 September 1942, Frýdek-Místek. Plant ±ysiologist. m. Marie Malá, 1 daughter. Education: Engineer, ±66, PhD, 1973, University Agric Brno; Mendel University of ±griculture and Forestry, Brno, now. Appointments: Scientist, ±ience Film Laborarory, 1967-73; Institute Vert Zoollology, ±73-74; Institute Botany, 1974-83; Institute Experimental ±hytotechnics, 1984-87; Institute Syst and Ecol Biology, ±87-91, Czechoslovak Academy Sciences, Brno; Senior ±ientist, Institute of Plant Genetics and Biotechnology, Slovak ±cademy of Sciences, Nitra, 1991-. Publications: Over 90 ±ticles in professional scientific journals; The Co-Cultivation of ±ood-Rotting Fungi with Tissue Cultures of Forest Tree ±ecies, 1990; Research films: Auth, Ontogeny of the Alga ±enedesmus quadricauda, 1973; Co-author, Regeneration of ±e Cap in the Alga Acetabularia mediterranea, 1980. ±emberships: Czech Botanical Society, Prague; Czech ±ience Film Association, Brno; International Association for ±ant Tissue Culture, Rehovot; International Association of

Sexual Plant Reproduction Research, Wageningen. Address: Ukrajinska 17, 625 00 Brno, Czech Republic.

**HRISTOV Marin**, b. 15 November 1949, Pleven, Bulgaria. Professor. m. Zveta Hristova, 1 daughter. Education: MSc Engineering, 1972, PhD Electronics, 1979, Technical University, Sofia. Appointments: Research Officer, Technical University, Sofia, 1972-75; Assistant Professor, 1975-86; Professor, Dean of Faculty, Head of ECAD Laboratory, 1986-. Publications: Electronic Devices, 1985, 1992, 1995; CAD in Electronics, 1988. Memberships: IEEE; IEE, London, UK; New York Academy of Sciences; Eurochip; Europractice. Address: Mladost IV bl 470 entr 2 41, 1715 Sofia, Bulgaria.

**HRYNIEWICZ Zdzislaw**, b. 24 October 1946, Kwakowo, Poland. Researcher; Educator. m. Elzbieta Szymanska, 1 son, 1 daughter. Education: MSc (mgr), Mathematics, 1969, University of Gdansk; Postgraduate study, 1975-78, PhD Elastodynamics, 1981, Institute of Hydroengineering, PAS, Gdansk; DSc, Wave propagation, Structural dynamics, 1993, Technical University of Gdansk. Appointments: Graduate Research Assistant, Technical University of Gdansk, Department of Mathematics; Graduate Research Assistant, 1971-81, Assistant Professor, 1981-94, Associate Professor of Applied Mathematics, 1994-, Technical University, Dept of Civil Engineering, Koszalin. Publications: 33 publications in professional journals in the field of Elastodynamics, wave propogation and vibration of solids. Honours: 7 research grants and fellowships; 7 awards granted following the visits connected with these grants and fellowships including the Minister of National Education Award, Warsaw, granted for research achievement, 1984, 1990. Membership: European Association for Structural Dynamics. Address: Zdzislaw Hryniewicz Technical University, Raclawicka 15, 75620 Koszalin, Poland.

**HSU Chung-Ping**, b. 21 January 1955, Keelung, Taiwan. Surgeon. m. Kuan Yoa-Hua, 2 sons, 1 daughter. Education: MD, 1980, National Defence Medical Centre. Appointments: Chief of Surgical Emergency, Coordinator of Nutritional Support Service and Attending Surgeon of Thoracic Surgery of Taichung Veterans General Hospital. Publications: Author or co-author 50 articles in professional journals. Honours: Formosa Medicine Foundation Award, 1994; National Science Association Council Award for Study of Medicine (group B), 1995, 1998. Memberships: New York Academy of Science; International Society for Diseases of the Oesophagus; International Society of Surgery; American College of Chest Physicians; Asian Pacific Society of Respirology; Surgical Association of ROC; Chest and Critical Care Medicine, ROC; Association of Thoracic and Cardiovascular Surgery; Digestive Endoscopy Society, ROC; Chinese Association for Endoscopic Surgery. Address: 8F #19-2 Ln 52 Sect 3, Reh-Her Rd, Taichung Taiwan, Taiwan.

**HSU Hsiu-Sheng**, b. 26 October 1931, China. Professor. m. Barbara Chew, 1 son, 3 daughters. Education: BSc, 1955, McGill University, Canada; MS, 1956, PhD, 1959, University of Pennsylvania, USA. Appointments: Postdoctoral, University of Pennsylvania, 1959-62, Johns Hopkins Medical School, 1963-64, Oxford University, 1973; Professor of Microbiology and Immunology, Medical College of Virginia, VCU, Richmond, VA, USA. Publications: Pathogenesis and immunity in murine palmonellolosisis, 1989; Is Salmonella an intracellular pathogen, 1993. Honours: Research grants from American Thoracic Society and US National Institute of Allergy and Infectious Diseases. Membership: American Society for Microbiology. Address: Department of Microbiology and

Immunology, Medical College of Virginia, VCU, Richmond, VA 23298-0678, USA.

**HU Can,** b. 31 October 1949, Taipei, Taiwan. Scientist. m. Li-Wen Yu Hu, 1 son, 1 daughter. Education: BS, National Taiwan University, Taipei, 1968-72; MS, University of Kentucky, Lexington, 1975-76; PhD, Massachusetts Institute of Technology, Cambridge, 1976-80. Appointments: Senior Scientist, Becton Dickinson Polymer Research, Dayton, Ohio, 1984-88; Project Scientist, Baxter Healthcare Corporation, Irvine, California, 1988-. Publictions: 34 in scientific journals, 12 US patents and many other European and Japanese patents. Memberships: American Chemical Society; Society for Biomaterials. Address: Bentley Division, Baxter Healthcare Corporation, 17511 Armstrong Avenue MS/3M, Irvine, CA 92614, USA.

**HU Dongsheng,** b. 6 December 1925, Beijing, China. Historian of Peking Opera. m. Nieh, Jeanchu, 2 daughters. Education: BA, Yengchin University in Beijing, 1950. Appointments: Historian of Peking Opera; Head, Editorial Board, History of Peking Opera in China. Publications: History of Peking Opera in China, vol I, 1989, vol II, 1990. Honour: 1st Prize for Social Science, Beijing, 1991. Membership: Association of Chinese Dramatists. Address: Beijing Normal University, Lize 3D Building 4-301, Beijing 100875, China.

**HU Jane Hwa,** b. 6 March 1940, China. Health Scientist, Administrator. m. Wen-Jin Woan, 1 son, 1 daughter. Education: BA, Biology, New York University, Washington Square College, 1963; PhD, Medical Physiology, College of Physicians and Surgeons, Columbia University, 1968. Appointments: Health Scientist Administrator, National Institutes of Health, Bethesda, Maryland, 1978-97; Member, Defense Advisory Committee on Women in the Services, The Pentagon, Washington, DC, 1991-93; Chairman, China Foundation, Washington, DC, 1997-. Publications: A Sojourner, 1994; To Love, 1995; A Philosopher on the Ivy Roof, 1995; A Life of Learning to Love, 1996. Memberships: Phi Beta Kappa; Sigma Xi. Address: 9216 Falls Chapel Way, Potomac, MD 20854, USA.

**HU Jinlian,** b. 26 August 1961, Hubei, China. Educator. m. Ping-Biao Chen, 1 son. Education: BEng, Wuhan Institute of Textile Science and Technology, China, 1982; MEng, China Textile University, 1986; PhD, Textile Department, University of Manchester Institute of Science and Technology, 1994. Appointments: Lecturer, Chengdu Textile School, Sichuan, China, 1982-83; Assistant Lecturer, 1986-87, Lecturer, 1987-90, Wuhan Institute of Textile Science and Technology; Assistant Professor, ITC, Hong Kong Polytechnic University, 1994-. Publications: Over 100 publications in textile science. Honours: 4th Prize for paper, Clothing Research and Design Centre of China and Journal of Chinese Garments, 1987; 3rd Prize for Paper, Science and Technology Association, 1988; Scholarship of Technical Cooperation, British Council and Chinese Government, 1990-94; Honorary Professor, Wuhan Institute of Textile and Science and Technology, 1997-. Memberships: Chinese Textile Engineers Society, 1987-; Fellow, Textile Machinery Society, Japan, 1995; Hong Kong Institution of Textiles and Clothing, 1996; Fellow, Textile Institute, 1998. Address: Hong Kong Polytechnic University, Hung Hom, Kowloon, Hong Kong.

**HU Yaozhong,** b. 5 December 1961, Jiangxi, China. Professor. m. Jun Fu, 1 son. Education: BA, Department of Mathematics, University of Jiangxi, Nanchang, China, 1978-82; MA, Institute of Mathematical Sciences, Academia Sinica, Wuhan, China, 1982-84; PhD, Department of Mathematics and Computer Science, Louis Pasteur University, France, 1991-92.

Appointments: Assistant Lecturer, 1984-88, Lecturer, 1988-9 Institute of Mathematical Sciences, Academia Sinica, Wuha China; Maitre de Conferences Invité, Department c Mathematics and Computer Science, Louis Pasteur Universit France, 1992-93; NAVF Postdoctoral Researcher, Departme of Mathematics, University of Oslo, Norway, 1993, 1994-9! Postdoctoral Research Associate, Center for Stochast Processes, Department of Statistics, University of Nor Carolina, Chapel Hill, 1993-94; Alexander von Humbol Research Fellow, Ruhr University-Bochum, Germany, 1994 Visiting Assistant Professor, Department of Mathematic University of California, Irvine, 1996-97; Assistant Professo Department of Mathematics, University of Kansas, 1997 Publications: Numerous articles in professional journal Memberships: New York Academy of Sciences; America Mathematical Society; Chinese Mathematical Society; Chines System Engineering Society. Address: Department c Mathematics, University of Kansas, 405 Snow Hall, Lawrence KS 66045-2142, USA.

**HUA Kien A,** b. 17 March 1958, Danang, Vietnam University Professor. m. Chau M Hua, 1 son, 2 daughters Education: BS, 1982; MS, 1984; PhD, 1987. Appointments Associate Professor of Computer Science and Director c Database Systems Laboratory, University of Central Florida Publications: Over 60 in journals and conference proceedings Honours: Best paper and Best presenter awards from the 199 International Conference on Computer Design; Associate Cha and Program Vice-Chair for a number of internationa conferences. Memberships: ACM; IEEE. Address: University c Central Florida, School of Computer Science, Orlando, Fl 32816, USA.

**HUA Lesun,**b. 3 April 1935, Suzhow, PRC. Scientist c Electronics and Geophysics. Education: Graduate, Tzinghu University. Appointments: Research Professor, Shangha Acoustics Laboratory, Academia Sinica; Technical Presiden Shihang Laboratory; Deputy Governor, Continental Governo Abira; Deputy Director General, IBC. Publications: Time-varyin filtering for elimiating multiple echos in profiling sonar, signa processing in geosonal, PA-1 parametric transmitter and it' applications. Honours: Gold medal, Shanghai Talent Circle c Science and Technology; Outstanding Achievement Scientis Title, Ministry of Communications; World Lifetime Achievemer Award, ABI DDG of IBC; Honorable Title, AB Accomplishments: Development for first generation militar sosar, China; Development of Geosonar used in extra shall water; Development of green techniques with STS. Referenc Works: International leaders in Achievement, 1997; 500 leader of influence, 5 edition; The biographies of the famous person i the contemporary world, volume of China. Address: 45 Xiao-Mu-Qiao Road, Shanghai 200032, PR China.

**HUANCHENG Ma,** b. 28 December 1962, Hunan, China Teacher. m.Wu Jianrong, 1 son. Education: PhD, Forestry 1997. Appointment: Associate Professor, 1997. Publication Proceedings of Salt Resistance and Physiology of Populu Euphratica, 1998; Membership: China Association of Forestry Address: Soil Science and Natural Resources, Southeas Forestry College, White Dragon Temple, Kunming 650223 China.

**HUANG Annian,** b. 28 October 1936, Wujin County, Jiangsu Province, China. Professor. m. Lyu Qi Xiang, 1 daughter Education: Graduate, Dept History, Beijing Normal University Appointments: Assistant, Lecturer, Associate Professor Professor, Beijing Normal University, 1958-98. Publications: US History in 20th Century, 1988; The Rise of America 1492-1898 1992; On the Social Economic History of US, 1993 ontemporary World History 1945-95, 1997; The Social Welfre olicy in US since 1945, 19998; and others. Memberships: merican History Research Association of China, VP; China ssociation for American Studies, standing member of council; he Journal of American (USA) International Contributing ditors in China. Address: 100875 Dept of History, Beijing ormal University, Waidajie No 19, Xinjieke, Beijing, China.

**HUANG Barney Kuoyen**, b. 27 January 1931, China. rofessor; Company President. m. Lindy W, 2 sons, 1 aughter. Education: BS in Agricultural Engineering, National aiwan University, 1954; MS, Agricultural Engineering, niversity of Illinois, 1960; PhD, Agricultural Engineering, urdue University, 1963; System Analysis and Control, Stevens istitute of Technology, 1964; Experimental Stree Analysis, Jayne State University, 1966; Computer and Processing ystems, Princeton University, 1967; System Synthesis and omputation, Princeton University, 1968; Research istrumentation, Polytechnic Institute of Brooklyn, 1969; dvanced Hybrid Computation, Pennsylvania State University, 969; Physics of Differential Equations, University of Visconsin, 1970; Nonlinear Systems, University of Santa Clara, 970; Mechanics and Aerodynamics, Syracuse University, 971; Noise Control in Engineering Design, Syracuse niversity, 1973; Engineering Design of Machine Mechanisms, )klahoma State University, 1973. Appointments: Assistant, lational Taiwan University, 1954-58; Graduate Assistant, niversity of Illinois, 1958-60; Graduate Assistant, Purdue Jniversity, 1960-62; Assistant Professor, 1963-67; Associate 'rofessor, 1967-73; Full Professor, North Carolina State Jniversity, 1973-93; President, International Innovative echnology Inc, 1993-; President, Air Pruning Technologies, 998-; Distinguished Professor, Branden University, 1998-. 'ublications: Author and Co Author of over 150 Technical and tesearch Articles and Books; Patentee, over 30 patents. lonours: Sigma Xi; Tau Beta Pi; Gamma Sigma Delta; Alpha :psilon; Lins Fellowship, 1965, 1971, 1974, 1976; ASAE Paper ward; ASAE AE50 Award, 1999; Many other awards. lemberships include: American Society of Agricultural :ngineers. Address: 3332 Manor Ridge Drive, Raleigh, NC '7603-4845, USA.

**HUANG Chih-Yao**, b. 31 May 1963, Hsinchu, Taiwan. :lectronics Engineer. m. Chien-Ting Hsu. Education: BS, lational Tsinghua University, 1985; MS, 1987, PhD, 1994, lational Chiaotung University. Appointments: Part-time ecturer, National Chiaotung University, 1992-93; Postdoctoral ellow, National Nano Device Laboratory, 1994-95; R&D lenior Engineer, Mosel/Vitelic Inc, 1995-98; Part-time ssociate Professor, Chunghua University, 1997-98; Technical ssistant Manager, Winbond Corporation, 1998-. Publications: leveral articles in professional journals and patents. lembership: IEEE Electron Device Society. Address: No 32, ane 248, Sect 2, Ching-kuo Road 300, Hsinchu, Taiwan.

**HUANG Cun-Bing**, b. 11 June 1944, Guiyang, China. 'rofessor. m. Wei-Fang Xia, 2 sons. Education: Guiyang lealth School, 1962; Guiyang Medical College, 1972; MSc, 1D, Nanjing Medical University and Nantong Medical College, 983. Appointments: Pathologist, Medical Laboratory echnician, Sinan Hospital, 1962-78; Pathologist, Lecturer, )irector, Zunyi Medical College, 1982-88; Research Fellow, Jmea University, 1989-91; Professor, Nantong Medical College, 1993-95; Research Pathologist, Karolinska Inst, 991-92, 1995, 1997-98; Professor, Nanjing Medical University, 997-; Editor, Publisher, Anticancer Digestion and Discussion, 996-; Research Professor, Director, Stockholm Anticancer nst, 1993-. Publications: J Nantong Med College, 1983; Chin J Oncol, 1984; Acta Acad Med Zunyi, 1985, 1986, 1987, 1988;

Chin J Digest, 1986; Cancer, 1986; Anticancer Res, 1988; Histopathology, 1988; Stress Med, 1991; In Vivo, 1992; Scand J Gastroenterol, 1993; Anticancer Digestion and Discussion, 1996, 1997, 1998; Chin Med J, 1998. Honours: 2 Excellent Science and Technology Progress Awards in Cancer Histogenesis and Early Diagnosis; 2 Excellent Papers in Cancer. Memberships: AAAS; New York Academy of Science; Swedish Cancer Society; Chinese Medical Association. Address: Stockholm Anticancer Inst HB, S-12246 Enskede, Stockholm, Sweden.

**HUANG Jingheng**, b. 28 November 1935, Min-Qing County, Fujian Province, China. Teacher. m. Ran Hainan, 2 sons. Education: BD, 1957, Shanghai First Medical College; Visiting Scholar, American Health Foundation, 1987, Centre for Health Promotion Research and Development, Texas University, 1987, UCLA, 1988, Victorian Health Promotion Foundation, Aut, 1995. Appointments: Department of Epidemiology, Shanghai First Medical College, 1957-86; Department Health Education, Shanghai Medical University, 1986-. Publications: Over 40 science articles and 7 books. Honours: Eradicated Schistosomiasis Medal, gold finished; Excellent Teacher; Special Subsidy by the State Council; Exemplary Health Educator by NPHCC and MOH. Membership: VP, China Health Education Association; Deputy President of Shanghai Health Education Association; Member of Expert Advisory Committee on STDs, AIDS and MOH. Address: Department of Health Education, Shanghai Medical University, 138 Yi Xue Yuan Road, Shanghai 200032, China.

**HUANG Lie-De**, b. 26 January 1922, Quan Zhou City, China. Professor. m. Zeng Shu Ying, 3 sons. Education: Graduate, Fudan University, 1951; Professor, Tong Ji University; CSIAM, Tsinghau University. Appointments: Professor, Tongji University, China. Honours: Chinese Excellent Scientist; Distinguished Leadership; Outstanding Scientists of the 20th Century; Centures World Celebrity; Chinese Science and Inventor; World Mathematician; Chinese Scientific Celebrity; Personal Citation; Outstanding Service to the Teaching Profession and Researcher on Astronautical Mathematics. Memberships: CSIAM. Address: Department of Applied Mathematics, Tongji University, Shanghai 200092, China.

**HUANG Shiping**, b. 18 September 1946, Min qing, Fuzhou, China. m. 1974, 1 son, 1 daughter. Education: Fujian TV College, 1980. Membership: Huaxia Poetry Friend Society. Address: No 167 Min qing Xi Men Road, 350800 Fuzhou, China.

**HUANG Wann-Chu**, b. 6 February 1944, Kaushiung, Taiwan. Professor of Physiology. m. Ying-Sheue Hsieh, 1 son, 1 daughter. Education: BS, National Normal University, Taipei, 1967; MS, National Defence Medical Centre, Taipei, 1973; PhD, University of Alabama at Birmingham, 1981. Appointments: Instructor, 1973-78, Associate Professor, 1981-86, Chairman, 1986-91, Professor, 1986-93, National Defence Medical Centre, Taipei; Research Associate, University of Alabama at Birmingham, USA, 1978-81; Director of Medical Affairs, 1993-95, Professor, 1995-, Tzu Chi College of Medicine, Hualien, Taiwan. Publications: Author or co-author, research articles in professional journals; Editor, Renal Physiology, 1985; Editorial Board, Journal of Nephrology, Republic of China, 1985-95, Chinese Journal of Physiology, 1987-96; Deputy Editor-in-Chief, Acta Nephrologica, Republic of China, 1996-. Honours: Excellent Research Awards, National Science Council, Taiwan, 1987-94, 1998; Excellent Teaching Service Award, Ministry of Education, Taiwan, 1996. Memberships: Chinese Physiological Society;

The Pharmacological Society in Taiwan; Biophysical Society, Republic of China; International Society of Nephrology; International Society of Hypertension; High Blood Pressure Council, American Heart Association; Society of Chinese Bioscientists in America. Address: Tzu Chi College of Medicine and Humanities, Graduate Institute of Medical Science, 701, Section 3, Chung-Yan Road, Hualien 970, Taiwan, China.

**HUANG Yuan Qing,** b. 5 August 1963, Shanghai, China. Artist; Teacher. m. Tu Huiqi, 1 daughter. Education: Graduate, Shanghai University of Science and Technology, 1985; Fine Arts Department of Shanghai Normal University, 1987-89. Appointment: Lecturer, Film and Television College of Shanghai University. Creative works: Exhibitions include: Contemporary One - Hundred Calligraphists Stone-etching Exhibition, Lou Yang Museum, 1991; China-Shanghai Modern Calligraphy, Shanghai Art Museum, 1991; Three Person Art, Shanghai, 1993; Shanghai Modern Art, Yokohama, 1993; Painting Exhibition for Asia Art Seminar, Shanghai Hilton, 1994; International Biennial of Modern Calligraphy, China Art University, 1995; 20+1 Chinese Contemporary Art, Shanghai Art Museum, 1996; Shanghai Modern Art Treasure, Image and Abstract, Shanghai Orient Museum, 1997; Movement, Germany, 1997; Handover-Contemporary Artist Invitational, Hong Kong Exhibition Center, 1997; 20+1 Chinese Contemporary Exhibition, International Forum, Tokyo, 1998; Tian Yu Centre, Shanghai, 1999; Liu Haishu Art Museum, Shanghai, 1999; Biz Art, Shanghai, 1999. Honour: Prize of Excellence at International Ink-Water Works, Toronto, 1992. Address: NU 118 LN 24, Cheng Shan Road, Rm 402, Shanghai 200126, China.

**HUBER Thomas Wayne,** b. 2 September 1942, Eddy, Texas. Microbiologist. m. Doris Marie Huber, 1 son, 2 daughters. Education: BA Microbiology, 1964, PhD Microbiology, 1968, University of Texas at Austin. Appointments: Postdoctoral Fellow, Centre for Disease Control, Atlanta, Georgia, 1968-70; Assistant Professor, University of Texas Medical School, San Antonio, 1970-74; Associate Professor, University of Texas School of Public Health, 1974-81; Chief, Bureau of Labs, Houston Health Dept, 1974-81; Associate Professor, Texas A&M College of Medicine, Temple, 1981-; Microbiologist, Central Texas Veterans Health Care System, VA Hospital, Temple, Texas, 1981-. Publications: Author or co-Author 26 articles or book chapters. Honours: Diplomate, American Board of Medical Microbiology, 1973; Burroughs Welcome Visiting Professor, 1990-91; President, Southwestern Association Clinical Microbiology, 1996-97; Sigma Xi. Memberships: American Society for Microbiology; American Academy of Microbiology; Southwestern Association for Clinical Microbiology. Address: 4809 Arrowhead Drive, Temple, TX 76502-1451, USA.

**HUCHRA John Peter,** b. 23 December 1948, Jersey City, New Jersey, USA. Astronomer. m. Rebecca Henderson, 1 son. Education: BS, Massachusetts Institute of Technology, 1970; PhD, California Institute of Technology, 1976. Appointments: Center Fellow, Harvard-Smithsonian Center for Astrophysics, 1976-78; Astronomer, 1978-89, Senior Astronomer, 1989-, Smithsonian Astrophysical Observatory; Lecturer, 1979-84, Professor of Astronomy, 1984-, Harvard University; Visiting Scientist, Space Telescope Science Institute, 1986, 1990; Centennial Lecturer, Utah State University, 1987; Visiting Lecturer, University of Minnesota, 1988; Associate Director, SAO-OIR Division, 1989-98, Harvard College Observatory, 1990-98; Vaughan Visiting Professor, University of Texas, 1991, Caltech, 1991, University College of Santa Cruz, 1993; Director, F L Whipple Observatory, 1994-98; Scientific Editor, Astrophysical Journal, 1998-2000. Publications: Author, over

250 scientific papers in peer-reviewed journals. Honours: Various Research Grants, NASA, 1979-, Smithsonian Institution, 1980-, National Science Foundation, 1984-89; Newcomb-Cleveland Award, 1989, Fellow, 1994-, American Association for the Advancement of Science, 1989; Aaronson Prize, University of Arizona, 1991; Fellow, American Academy of Arts and Sciences, 1991-; Fellow, American Physical Society, 1992-; Member, National Academy of Science, 1993 Lyman Spitzer Lecturer, Princeton University. Memberships include: Sigma Xi; American Astronomical Society; International Astronomical Union; Royal Astronomical Society; Astronomical Society of the Pacific. Address: Harvard-Smithsonian Center for Astrophysics, 60 Garden Street, Cambridge, MA 02138, USA.

**HUDSON Walter Tiree,** b. 10 April 1943, Lynchburg Virginia, USA. Artist. 2 Sons. Education: GED, 1968. Career Exhibitions: Lynchburg Public Library; Lynchburg Recreation Department; Community Market. 1999; Holiday Inn Select 1999. Publications: The Glass Eye, 1960. Memberships Blueridge Chapter 82nd Airbourne Division Club; Lynchburg Stamp Club; Church of Jesus Christ. Address: 3475 Fort Ave Apt 326, Lynchburg, VA 24501-3834, USA.

**HUGHES Lenore Harris,** b. 30 March 1914, Aspenwall, Nebraska, USA. Teacher; Writer; Artist. m. Delbert Littrell Hughes, 2 step-sons. Education: Teaching Certificate, Peru Nebraska State Teacher's College, 1934; BA, University of Omaha, 1939; AB Religious Education, Kentucky Christian College, 1943; MA Art and English, Phillips University, Enid, Oklahoma, 1947. Appointments: Teacher, rural schools, 1933-35; Teacher, High Schools and Colleges, 1939-78, Journalism, 1958-78; Religious Education Director, various churches, 1946-50; Department of the Army, Fort Bliss, 1951-54; Free Lance Writer; Artist. Publications: Articles for numerous newspapers and magazines; Weekly column, El Paso Inc; Showings of paintings and photographs; Self-published books: How to Write and Publish a Book, 1977; 6 other books and 4 books of poetry. Honours: Ordained as a Religious Education Director, 1947; Outstanding Journalism Teacher, Interscholastic Press Conference, Austin; Order of the Golden Quill, Texas, 1977; Golden Key winner in the field of journalism, Columbia Scholastic Press Association, NYC, 1973. Memberships: El Paso Art Association; Women's Dept of the Greater Chamber of Commerce, El Paso; The Woman's Club of El Paso; First Christian Church, El Paso; United Amateur Press Association, publishing own bulletins, Interrobang, ?Mark, and The Fossils. Address: 1831 Murchison Street, Suite #348, El Paso, TX 79902, USA.

**HUI John Jun,** b. 27 September 1953, Shanghai, China. Television Producer. m. Susan Guangsu Zhang, 1 son, 1 daughter. Education: BA, People's University, China, January 1983. Appointment: President, Globe Net Advertising Ltd; Television Producer. Publications: Many books and papers. Honour: Media Award in China. Memberships: Director, China National Editorial Media Association; Director, Canadian-Chinese Film & TV Association. Address: Globe Net Advertising Ltd, Grace Court Apartment, No 2-6 Pi Ku Lane, Xidan, Xi Cheng District, Beijing 100032, China.

**HUI Keung,** b. 31 January 1962, China. Engineer. Education: BSc, Engineering, 1st Class Honours, 1987; PhD, 1995. Appointments: HVAC Engineer, 1987-89; Consultant Engineer, 1994-95; Visiting Lecturer, 1995-96; Research Fellow, 1996-98; Visiting Assistant Professor, 1998-, Hong Kong University. Publications: Articles in International Journal of Control, 1994, 1997, 1999, IEE Proceedings and IMechE Proceedings, 1995, 1997, Automatica, 1999. Honour: Croucher Foundation Scholarship, 1989-91. Memberships: Chartered

Institute of Building Services Engineers; Institution of Mechanical Engineers; Hong Kong Institution of Engineers. Address: 40 Hing Fat Street, B7-17/F, Hong Kong.

**HUIDOVICI Elia,** b. 30 December 1967, Romania. Professors Assistant. m. Dumitru Tiberiu. Education: MD, University of Medicine and Pharmacy, 1993; Junior Assistant, Department of Physiology, University of Medicine, 1994; Resident Doctor, Infectious Diseases, 1994; Professors Assistant, Physiology, 1998; PhD, Student in Physiology, 1998. Appointments: Professors Assistant, Department of Physiology, University of Medicine, Bucharest; Resident Doctor, Infectious Diseases, Colentina Hospital, Bucharest. Publications: 6 Publications, Articles in journals. Memberships: Romanian Society of Physiology Sciences; Federation of European Physiological Societies. Address: Str Calea Vitan 108 Bl V 35 Sc 1, Ap 24 Sector 3, Bucharest, Romania.

**HULL Andrea Douglas,** b. 13 March 1949, Sydney, Australia. Director; Professor. Education: University Sydney. Appointments: Executive Director, Department for the Arts, Western Australia, 1988-94; Director, Strategic Development Division, Australia Council, 1987-88; Director, Policy and Planning Australia Council, 1982-87, Director, Community Arts Board Australia Council, 1979-82; Senior Project Officer, 1973-79; Secondary School Teacher, Borough Haringey UK, 1972-73, National Travel Director, National Union Australia University Students, 1970-71; Premier's CI for the Arts, 1996-; Board Member, Melbourne Theatre Company, 1996-; Chair, Arts and Tourism Industrial CI, 1995-98; Member, Bundanon Trust Residency Committee, 1996-; Trustee, Victoria Arts Centre Trust, 1995-, Board Member, National Academy of Music, 1995-; Board Australia-Korea Foundation, 1992-; Director, Australian Institute Arts Administration, 1992-96; Director, Australian-Japanese Foundation, 1992-95; CI and Executive, Australia Abroad Council, 1991-94; Western Australia Art Gallery Board, 1988-95; Perth Theatre Trust, 1988-95; Western Australia Museum Board, 1988-95; Library and Information Service Western Australia Board, 1988-95; Western Australia Symphony Orchestra Board, 1988-95; Western Australia Health Promotion Foundation Board, 1988-95; UNESCO Advisory Committee Cultural and Heritage Conventions and Recommendations, 1986-88; Sidney Myer Performing Arts Award Committee, 1984-94, Joint Liaison Australia CI Commonwealth Tertiary Education Committee, 1985-88; Curriculum Development Centre Education and Arts Advisory Committee, 1985-86; Commissioner Commonwealth Tertiary Education Commission, 1983-86; National Student Travel Guide to Australia, 1971; A Directory of Festivals Held Throughout Australia, 1975, 1976, 1978; Review of Tertiary Arts Education and Training, 1987; Chapters in various publications on cultural policy and cultural tourism. Hobbies: Yoga; Tennis; Swimming; Theatre. Address: Victorian College of the Arts, 234 St Kilda Road, Southbank, Vic 3006, Australia.

**HUM Peng Jong Alex,** b. 21 October 1967, Singapore. Scientific Researcher; Entrepreneur. m. Priscilla Yang Meiling. Education: BEng, Honours, 1992; PhD, Microwave Engineering, 1997. Appointments: Lecturer, Nanyang Polytechnic, 1995-96; Technical Staff, Centre for Wireless Communications, 1996-. Publications: Numerous in international refereed journals and at conferences, 1992-. Membership: IEEE.

**HUNG Tzu-chen,** b. 20 October 1957, Peng-Hu, Taiwan. Engineering Educator. m. Jeanne Gei-Mei Shih, 1 son, 1 daughter. Education: BS, 1980, MS, 1982, Nuclear Engineering, Tsing-Hua University, Taiwan; MS, 1987, PhD, 1989, Mechanical Engineering, UCLA. Appointments: Scientist,

Physical Research Inc, California, 1988-89; Engineer, Argonne National Laboratory, USA, 1990-92; Director, Global Energy Tech Inc, Illinois, 1993; Associate Professor, I-Shou University, Taiwan, 1993-. Publications: Over 70 publications in journals, conferences & reports. Honours: Reviewer, 2 international journals, 1995-; Associate Editor, journal of cogeneration report, Taiwan, 1997-; National Science Council Awards, 1994, 1997; 1996 paper honour, Chinese Nuclear Society. Memberships: Chinese Society of Solar Energy; Chinese Society of Cogeneration; Kaohsiung Metropolitan Development Foundation. Address: 452 Jeou-Ru 2nd Rd, Kaohsiung, Taiwan.

**HUNGNESS Lisa Sue,** b. 12 May 1971, Chicago, Illinois, USA. English Teacher. Education: BA English, 1994, MA Cultural Education, in progress, Indiana University at Bloomington. Appointments: Graduate Student Teacher of English, Matravers School, Westbury, England, 1994; English Teacher, Lebanon High School, Ohio, 1995-; Freelance Technical Consultant/Software Evaluator, South-Western Educational Publishing, Cincinnati, Ohio, 1996-. Publications: American Literature for Life and Work: Teachers' Test Bank, 1997; C2000 Assessment Portfolio & Test Bank, 1999; Forever Young. Honours: National Council of Teachers of English Teacher Researcher Grant Award, 1998; Ashland/OEA Teacher Achievement Award, 1998; Area Progress Council of Warren County Inc Excellence in Teaching Award, 1997; Jiffy Lube Excellence in Teaching Award, 1997; and others. Memberships: National Education Association; Ohio/National Council of Teachers of English; Greater Cincinnati Council on World Affairs; League of Women Voters; Phi Delta Kappa. Address: 8904 B Harperpint Drive, Cincinnati, OH 45249, USA.

**HURRIBUNCE Ashwin Chitason,** b. 25 November 1960, Sydenham, Durban, South Africa. Radiologist; Educator. m. Sharon Louise Miller, 1 son, 1 daughter. Education: MB, ChB, University of Natal, Durban, 1983; Fellow, Faculty of Diagnostic Radiology, College of Medicine of South Africa, 1991; MMed, Diagnostic Radiology, University of Witwatersrand, Johannesburg; Various military courses including Senior Medical Command and Staff Course, 1996, Joint Staff Course, 1997. Appointments: Various hospital positions, 1984-92, mainly at Chris Hani Baragwanath Hospital, Soweto, including Senior Specialist in Radiology, 1991-92; Teaching positions include Lecturer, Department of Radiology, University of Witwatersrand, 1988-90, 1991-92; Assistant Director, Lieutenant Colonel, National Peacekeeping Force, 1993-94; Director Training, Brigadier, Profession of Arms, South African Military Health Service, South African National Defence Force, 1994-98; Brigadier General, 1998-99, Deputy Chief, 1998, Acting Chief, 1998-99, Chief, Major General, 1999-, Joint Training, Profession of Arms, Department of Defence; Curricular Lecturer, Profession of Arms, South African Defence College, currently; Member, Chairperson, National Standards Body 08, South African Qualifications Authority, 1998-. Honours: Unitas Medal, South African National Defence Force; Long Service Medals, Mkhonto we Sizwe; Military Merit Medal. Memberships: African National Congress, 1975-, Executive Member, Southern Natal Health Desk, 1990-94, Committee Member, National Sub-Commission on Academia, Research and Technology, 1992-93, Chairman, Health Department Commission on Organisational Structure, 1992-93, Member, Health Department Women's Health Commission, Deputy Director, Personnel Directorate, Military Health Service; Committee Member, Medical Graduates Association, University of Natal, 1991-92, 1992-93. Address: PO Box 10194, Centurion 0046, South Africa.

**HUSAR Alexandru,** b. 26 April 1926, Ilva Mare, Nasaud, Romania. Professor. m. Margareta Husar. Education: BA, Philosophy and Letters, University of Bucharest, 1945; PhD, Philosophy, University of Bucharest. Appointments: V Babes, Cluj-Napoca; Professor of Aesthetics and Theory of Literature; University Alexandru Ioan Cuza, Iasi, Romania. Publications: The Return to Literature, 1970; Ars Longa, Fundamentals of Arts, 1980; Metapoetica, Philosophy of Arts, 1983; Sources of Arts, 1988; The European Idea, 1993; The Lessons of History, 1995; Anti-Gog, In Dialogue with Papini's Gog, 1997; Searchings through Memory, 1998. Membership: President, Society of History and Philology, Iasi. Address: 6600 Iasi, 9 Rozelor Str, Romania.

**HUSSAIN Ahmed Gouda,** b. 21 May 1942, Sharkia, Egypt. Professor of Geophysics. m. Sanaa Abdul Latif, 1 s, 3 d. Education: BSc, Cairo University, 1963; High Diploma of Geophysics, 1967; MSc, Cairo University, 1970; PhD, 1974. Appointments: Researcher, 1974; Associate Professor, 1979; Professor of Geophysics, 1985; Head Department of Geophysics, King Abdulaziz University, Saudi Arabia, 1987-90. Honours: National Prize of Geosciences, 1978; Republic Medal, Grade 1 for Science and Arts, 1979. Memberships: Faculty South Sciences; National Research Institute of Astronomy and Geophysics. Address: 9 Officers Buildings, Nasr Eddin, Haram Street, Giza, Eygpt.

**HUSSAIN Rizwan,** b. 19 March 1959, Dacca, East Pakistan. Scientist. m. Suad Saeed, 2 sons, 1 daughter. Education: BSc, 1979; MSc, Analytical/Inorganic Chemistry, 1982; PhD, Polymer Chemistry, 1993. Appointments: Scientific Officer, 1986-91, Senior Scientific Officer, 1991-, Pakistan Institute of Nuclear Science and Technology. Publications include as co-author: X-ray crystallinity studies of palladium polyacrylate; Differential thermal analysis of some rare earth nitrates; Indoor air pollution - its effects and remedies; A study of gamma radiation induced molecular weight changes in poly (phenyl methacrylate), poly (methyl methacrylate) and their copolymers. Honours: Listed in various biographical dictionaries; International Man of the Year 1997-98, IBC. Memberships: Member International Radiation Physics Society, USA; Member Pakistan Institute of Chemists; Member Pakistan Society for Advancement of Science and Technology; Life Member Pakistan Nuclear Society; Life Member Chemical Society of Pakistan; Life Member Pakistan Society for Semiconductor Science and Technology. Address: H#23A Street 3 Valley Road, Westridge 1, Rawalpindi, Pakistan.

**HUSSAIN SALEH Ali Abbass,** b. 31 December 1956,. Bahrain. Accountant. m. Elham Mahdi Ali, 3 sons, 1 daughter. Education: BCom, Pune University, India, 1982; Diploma, Business Training, London, 1984; MBA, USA, 1988; Doctorate, Business Administration, USA, 1996. Career: Development Trainee, Bahrain Petroleum Company Limited. Memberships: Institute of Professional Financial Managers. Address: Area 406, House 1160, Road 627, Sanabis, Bahrain.

**HUSZAR Arlene Celia,** b. 1 May 1952, New York, NY, USA. Attorney. m. Victor M Yellen, 1 daughter. Education: BA, Florida Atlantic University, 1973; JD, University of Florida, 1976. Appointments: Sole practice, 1979-80; Managing Attorney, Florida Institutional Legal Services, 1980-; Publications: Adoption, 1992; Termination of Parental Rights, 1997. Memberships: Eighth Judicial Circuit Bar Association, Board of Directors, 1994-; Florida Academy of Professional Mediators; North Central Florida Mediation Council, Florida Bar, 1977-; District of Columbia Bar, 1979-; US Supreme Court Bar, 1982-; Certified Federal and Circuit Court Mediator. Address:

Florida Institutional Legal Services, 1110 NW 8th Ave Ste C, Gainesville, FL 27320, USA.

**HUTCHEON Wilda Vilene Burchell,** b. 9 September 1919, Fort Fairfield, Maine, USA. Artist; Fine Arts. m. Philip S Hutcheon. Education: Graduate, 1944, Art Federal Design School; Hon DFA, 1990, London, England. Appointments: Superintendent, Art Dept, Maine Exhibition, 1952-58; Curator of Fine Arts, Nylander Museum, 1959-62; Teacher, Art, Loring Air Force Wives. Creative Works: One woman shows include Woodfords Congregational Church, Portland, Maine, 1967, Talent Tree Gallery, 1974, Maine State, Poland Springs, Restigouche Museum, New Brunswick, Canada, 1978, Madison Avenue, NYC, 1978, Orunquit Art Centre, 1978, Woods Edge Gallery, Perham, Maine, 1994; Group shows include Talent Tree Gallery, Augusta, 1974, Laguna Beach, California, 1986-87; Exhibited in permanent collections and private collections. Honours: International Art Gold Medal Best in Show, IPA, Washington; International Creative Achievement Award, New Orleans; International Best of Show, New England; International Distinguished Award for Outstanding Achievement and Service in creative art with induction into Distinguished Leadership Hall of Fame; Commander, Kentucky Colonels; National Award for Service, Professional Photographers of America, 1962; Hastings Cup for Continued Excellence, PPANE, 1964; President's Club for Outstanding Merit, MPPA, 1969; Numerous awards at art shows; Woman of the Year, Caribou Business and Professional Women, 1997; Achievement Award, AAUW, 1997. Memberships: Maine Association of Women in Fine and Performing Arts; Business and Professional Women's Club; International Platform Association; and others. Address: 26 Home Farm Rd, Caribou, ME 04736-2473, USA.

**HUYNH Dang Huy,** b. 25 October 1934, Quang Nam. Professor. m. 1 son, 1 daughter. Education: Dr C, 1985, Academia of Science, Moscow; Ecology of Animals, Biodiversity. Appointments: Researcher, 1961-. Publications: 102 scientific works including 12 monographic books. Memberships: Vietnam Association for Conservation of Nature and Environment; Chairman, Zoological Society of Vietnam. Address: Council of IEBR, National Centre for Natural Sciences and Technology, Ngia Oo Caulnag Hanoi, Vietnam.

**HWANG Kao-Pin,** b. 27 June 1952, Taiwan. Medical Diplomate. m. Ying Lu, 1 son, 2 daughters. Education: BMed, 1977; Master Tropical Medicine, 1982; PhD, Infectious Diseases, 1988. Appointments: Chief, Research Center for Tropical Medicine, Kaohsiung Medical College; Chief, General Pediatrics, Kaohsiung Medical College Hospital; Chairman, Hospital Infection Control Committee, Kaohsiung Medical College Hospital. Honours: Mead Johnson Pediatric Research Award, Pediatric Association of the Republic of China; Annual Nestlé Award for Pediatric Research, 1986, 1988. Memberships: President, Nosocomial Infection Control Society of the Republic of China; Director, The Infectious Diseases Society of the Republic of China. Address: No 243 Chien-Hsin Road, 807 Kaohsiung, Taiwan.

**HWANG Seong Sik,** b. 15 June 1963, Korea. Research Engineer. m. Min Soon Kee, 3 sons. Education: PhD, 1997. Appointment: Research Engineer, Korea Atomic Energy Research Institute, 1989-. Publications: Several articles in professional journals. Membership: Corrosion Science Society of Korea. Address: Korea Atomic Energy Research Institute PO Box Yusong 105, Taejon 305-600, Korea.

**HWANG Wen-Jyi,** b. 12 December 1966, Taipei, Taiwan. Educator; Researcher. m. Wan-Shin Cheng. Education

Diploma, Electronic Engineering, National Taipei Institute of Technology, 1987; MS, 1990, PhD, 1993, University of Massachusetts. Appointment: Associate Professor, Department of Electrical Engineering, Chung Yuan Christian University, Taiwan. Publications: Over 20 papers in professional journals. Membership: IEEE. Address: Chung Yuan Christian University, Department of Electrical Engineering, Chungli 32023, Taiwan.

# I

**IAKOVLEV Anatoly Ivanovych,** b. 1 November 1937, Kharkiv, Ukraine. Economist; Academic. m. Nina Khitushchenko. Education: MEng, 1961; DSc, 1969; DSc, 1982; Professor, 1986. Appointments: Engineer, 1961-64; Assistant Professor, 1967-70, Associate Professor, 1970-84, Head, Professor, Chair, Department of Economics and Marketing, Economic Faculty, 1984-, Kharkiv State Politechnical University. Publications include: Economics of Machine-Building Industry, 1980; Economic Estimation of Automation Instruments, 1982; Improvement of the Economic Estimation of High Quality Technique, 1993; Social-Economic Effectiveness of Innovations Under Market Conditions, 1994; Effect Calculation of International Projects, 1997. Honours: Winner, Ukrainian Professors Competition, 1990; Academician, Academy of Engineering Sciences, Ukraine, 1991; Honoured Professor of Ukraine, 1991. Memberships: International Project Management Association; Journalists Association of Ukraine. Hobbies: Journalism; Sports; Theatre; Fine Literature. Address: 22 Krasnoshkolnaya Naberezhnaya Street, Apt 53, Kharkiv 310125, Ukraine.

**IANKOV Ianko Nikolov,** b. 13 August 1944, Klissuritza, Montana district. Lawyer. m. Elka Petkova, 1 son, 1 daughter. Education: LLB, 1973; LLM, 1974; Assistant Professor, 1974; Associate Professor, 1995. Appointments: Senior Research Fellow, Institute for Legal Sciences, 1992-; Member Bulgarian Parliament, 1990-91; Political Prisoner, 1982-89; Research Fellow, Institute for Legal Studies, Bulgarian Academy of Sciences, 1974-82. Publications: Prognostics/Theoretical and Methodological Problems, 1993; Document for Identity/Political Documentary, Vol 1, 1994, Vol 2, 1995, Vol 3, 1998; Introduction to the Psychology of Law, 1998; Numerous articles. Memberships: Liberal Congress Party, President, 1990-; Union of Lawyers Democrats, President, 1991-; Basic Institute for Research and Defence of Human Rights; BIRD of Human Rights, President, 1995-. Address: 7 Pirotska Street, Sofia 1000, Bulgaria.

**IANKOV Ivan Iankov,** b. 15 August 1949, Koinare, Bulgaria. Economist. m. Roumiana Iankova, 1 son. Education: Degree, Industrial and Civil Building Engineer, High Institute of Civil Engineers, 1975; Degree in International Economic Relations, Foreign Trade Academy, Moscow, 1982. Appointments: Building Institute of Investigation Research, 1975-79; Trade Representative, Technoexport, Tripoli, Libya, 1983-86; Bioinvest, Benghazi, Libya, 1986-89; Economist, Agroengineering Ltd, Sofia, Bulgaria, 1990-91; Crude Oil Trader, JV Quorum, Moscow, Russia, 1991-94; Director, Petroquorum Ltd, Moscow, 1994-. Publication: Building Light Steel Structure, co-author. Address: Petroquorum Ltd, 17/2 Bolshaija Nikitskaija Str, 103009 Moscow, Russia.

**IANNELLO Silvia,** b. 9 May 1948, Catania, Sicily, Italy. Medical Educator; Clinical Investigator in Internal Medicine. m. Francesco Belfiore, 2 daughters. Education: MD, University Medical School of Catania, 1973; Specialist, Haematology, 1978, Diabetology, 1982, University of Catania; Visiting Research Associate, University of Southern California, Los Angeles, 1982. Appointments: Resident, Internal Medicine, 1973-77, Ministry of Education Fellow, 1977-80, Clinical Investigator in Internal Medicine, 1982-, University of Catania. Publications: Advances in World Diabetes Research, 1984; Numerous articles in international Professional Journals. Memberships: ADA; IDF; EASD; EASO. Address: Via XX Settembre N19, I-95027 San Gregorio, Catania, Italy.

**IBADINOV Khursand,** b. 22 March 1944, Tajikistan. Astrophysicist. m. V M Korovina, 1 son. Education: Pedagogical University, 1959-64; Diploma, Physics, St Petersburg, Russia DSc, 1967-69. Appointments: Senior Assistant, 1964, Junior Research Worker, 1972, Senior Research Worker, Head Laboratory of Experimental Astrophysics, 1992, Vice Director Institute of Astrophysics, Tadjik Academy of Sciences Publications: Over 80 in professional journals. Memberships International Astrophysics Union; COSPAR; European Astrophysics Society; European-Asian Astrophysics Society Tajik Astronomical Society, President, 1992. Address: Tadjik Academy of Sciences, Institute of Astrophysics, Bukhoro Street 22, 734042 Dushenbe, Tajikistan.

**IBADOV Subhon,** b. 25 January 1944, Isfara, Tajikistan. Astrophysicist. m. Shahrubonu Saidmahmud, 1 son, 2 daughters. Education: Graduate, Moscow University, 1966 PhD, 1970; DSc, 1996. Appointments: Senior Scientist 1970-89, Head, Comets/Asteroids Department, 1989-, Institute of Astrophysics, Tajikistan Academy of Sciences. Publications Over 120 papers in professional journals. Honour: Gold Medal, 1960. Memberships: European Astrophysical Society; International Meteor Organization; COSPAR; International Astrophysical Union. Address: Tadjikistan Academy of Sciences, Institute of Astrophysics, 734042 Dushanbe, Tadjikistan.

**IBOK Udo John,** b. 1 August 1945, Ikot Ekpene, Nigeria. Lecturer. m. Affiong Udo Ibok. Education: BSc Chemistry, 1972, Ahmadu Bello University, Zaria; PhD Chemical Metallurgy, 1975, Cardiff, Wales. Appointments: Lecturer II, Admadu Bello University, 1976-79; Lecturer I, Senior Lecturer, Reader, Professor, University of Calabar, 1979-. Publications: Author and Co-Author, 43 papers in scientific publications; 3 chapters in books; Editor, Laboratory Techniques and Analytical Manual, 1989; 2 books in preparation; 7 monographs and reports; 20 conference, workshop and seminar papers; Book reviewer. Honours: 2 academic awards; 3 scholarships including: Ford Foundation Scholarship for Postgrad Studies in the UK, 1972-75. Memberships: Newport and District Metallurgical Society; South Wales Metallurgical Society; Institute of Metallurgists, London; Associate Member, Institution of Mining and Metallurgy, London; Nigerian Mining and Geosciences Society; Chemical Society of Nigeria; Science Association of Nigeria; Nigerian Society for Biological Conservation. Address: Dept of Chemistry, University of Calabar, Nigeria.

**IBRAHIM Ahmed,** b. 15 September 1945, Dongola, Sudan. Urological Surgeon. m. Zeinab Hassan Satti, 5 sons, 1 daughter. Education: MB, BCh, 2nd Class Honours, Cairo University, 1966; Fellow, Royal College of Surgeons of Edinburgh; 1973; Fellow, International College of Surgeons, 1998. Appointments: Lecturer in Urology, 1975-78, Associate Professor of Urology, 1978-86, University of Khartoum; Associate Professor of Urology, 1986-93, Professor of Urology, 1993-, College of Medicine, King Saud University, Saudi Arabia. Publications: More than 68 publications in international, regional and local medical journals in the field of urology and surgery. Membership: British Association of Urological Surgeons. Address: PO Box 1544, Abha, Saudi Arabia.

**IBRAHIM Fayez Joseph,** b. 1947, Mashghara, Lebanon. Vice President, Group Administration and Personnel. m. Souraya Dimachkieh, 1 son. Education: Lebanese Baccalaureate (Part I), Good Shepherd Secondary College, 1966; Lebanese Baccalaureate (Part II), Good Shepherd Secondary College, 1967; Masters Degree in Law, Faculty of Law, 1971. Appointments: Lawyer, Bureau of mr Fouad Rizk,

971-72; Lawyer, Bureau of Mr Edmond Dallal, 1973-75; Legal Advisor, Banque du Liban et D'outre-Mer, 1975-76; Employee Relations Manager, Mannai Trading Co, 1976-; Personnel Manager, Mannai Trading Co, 1978-; Group Personnel Manager, Mannai Corporation, 1983-; Senior Executive-Group Administration and Personnel, Mannai Corporation, 1987-; General Manager-Group Administrator and Personnel, Mannai Corpn, 1992-; Vice President-Group Administration and Personnel, Mannai Corpn, 1994-. Publications: Personnel Policy Guide, 1993; Manual of Administration, Personnel Policies and Procedures, 1997. Memberships: Alexander Hamilton Institute, New York; Fellow, Institute of Management (IM); Fellow, Institute of Management Services (IMS). Address: Mannai Corp Ltd, Rayyan Rd P O Box 76, Doha, Qatar.

**IDOGAWA Tohru,** b. 17 February 1929, Hitachi-ohta, Ibaraki, Japan. Professor Emeritus. m. Reiko Fujioka, 1 son, 1 daughter. Education: B Eng, 1952, D Eng, 1967, University of Tokyo. Appointments: Professor of Hokkaido University, 968-77; Professor, University of Tsukuba, 1977-92, Professor Emeritus, 1992-. Honours: Awardee of Distinguished Paper Prize, Society of Instrument and Control Engineers, 1969; Awardee of Sato Prize for Distinguished Papers of the Acoustical Society of Japan, 1996. Memberships: Society of Instrument and Control Engineers; Acoustical Society of Japan; Acoustical Society of America; Catgut Acoustical Society; French Society of Acoustics. Address: 1-14-39 Gakuencho, Higashi-kurume, Tokyo 2030021, Japan.

**IFRIM Mircea G,** b. 4 May 1943, Calata, Cluj, Romania. Anatomist; General Physician; Scientist; Educator. m. Feng Shen. Education: MB, Medical University, Bucharest, 1963; MD, Medical University, Cluj, 1971; Postgraduate, Educational Management, University Oradea, 1989; D Honoris Causa, 998. Appointments: Assistant Professor, Medical University, Cluj, 1967-70; Lecturer, Medical University, Bucharest, 1970-78; Visiting Professor, Medical University, Bucharest, 1978-90; Professor, Medical University, Bucharest, 1991-; Dean, Founder, Faculty of Medicine, Oradea, 1991-; Director, Medical Research Institute, Oradea, 1991-; Chairman, Academy of Sciences, Oradea, 1996-; Vice Rector, V Goldis University, Arad, 1997-. Publications: Numerous papers in professional journals. Honours include: Award, Romanian Academy of Sciences, Bucharest, 1988. Memberships: International Society of German Language Speaking Anatomists; International Federation of Anthropology and Genetics in Sports; National Society for Normal and Pathological Morphology; National Union of Scientists, Bucharest; Academy of Sciences and Culture, Sao Paulo, Brazil. Address: University of Oradea, Medical Faculty, 1 Decembrie Street, 3400 Oradea Bihor, Romania.

**IHAN Alojz.** Address: Spodnji Rudnik 1/37, 1000 Ljubljana, Slovenia.

**IJALA Ezekiel Patrick Olupot,** b. 11 March 1947, Mbale, Uganda. Supply Chain Manager. m. Esther Wanza, 2 sons, 2 daughters. Education: Diploma, Chartered Institute of Transport, UK; Diploma, Chartered Institute of Purchasing and Supply, UK. Appointments: Chief Supplies Officer, The East African Community, 1976-77; Materials Manager, The Associated Vehicle Assembles, Mombasa, Kenya, 1977-85; Principal Purchasing and Supplies Officer, The Uganda Cooperative Bank, Kampala, 1985-90; Director of Operations, Government Central Purchasing Corporation, Republic of Uganda, 1990-92; Procurement Specialist, The Northern Uganda Reconstruction Programme, Office of the Prime Minister, Republic of Uganda, 1992-95; National Consultant on Import Operations and Techniques, Training Advisor on Import

Training, ITC/UNCTAD, Kampala, 1995-96; Head of Procurement, The National Medical Stores Corporation, Republic of Uganda Entebbe, 1996-. Memberships: Fellow, Chartered Institute of Transport, UK; Fellow, Chartered Institute of Purchasing and Supplies, UK; Fellow, British Institute of Management; Institute of Logistics, UK. Address: PO Box 9179, Kampala, Uganda.

**IKANI Samuel Sule,** b. 4 January 1964, Idah, Kogi State, Nigeria. Architect. m. Ojunuyo Valentina Ikani, 1 daughter. Education: BSc Hons Architecture, 1989; MSc Architecture, 1991; National Diploma, Civil Engineering, 1985. Appointments: Academic Planning Officer in Charge of Environmental Science Discipline, Nigerian Universities, 1993-. Publications: The Menace of Soil Erosion on Residential Buildings; Cultural Centre, Idah: Towards Cultural Rival in Igala Land. Address: National Universities Commission, Academic Planning Dept, PMB 237 Garki GPO, Abuja, Nigeria.

**IKEDA Kazuyosi,** b. 15 July 1928, Fukuoka, Japan. Professor, Theoretical Physics; Poet. m. Mieko Ikeda, 1 son, 1 daughter. Education: Graduate Degree, Rigakusi, 1951. Postgraduate, 1951-56, Department of Physics, Faculty of Science, Kyushu University; DSc, 1957; Degree, Honorary Doctor of Environmental Science, 1993; Degree, Honorary Doctor of Literature, 1995. Appointments: Assistant, 1956-60, Associate Professor, 1960-65, Department of Physics, Faculty of Science, Kyushu University; Associate Professor, Department of Applied Physics, 1965-68, Professor, 1968-92, Professor, Department of Mathematical Sciences, 1989-92, Professor Emeritus, 1992-, Faculty of Engineering, Osaka University; Professor, 1992-, President, 1995-, International Earth Environment University, Japan. Publications include: Statistical Thermodynamics, 1975; Mechanics without Use of Mathematical Formulae, 1980; Invitation to Mechanics, 1985; Basic Thermodynamics, 1991; Graphical Theory of Relativity, 1998; Bansyoo Hyakusi (collection of poems), 1986; The World of God, Creation and Poetry, 1991; Poems on the Hearts of Creation,1993; Mountains, 1995; North South East West, 1996.Honours include: Yukawa Commemorative Scholarship Award, 1954; International Order of Merit, 1990; Chevalier Grand Cross, 1991; 20th Century Award for Achievement, 1993; Prize Catania, 1994; Knight of Templar Order, 1995; Gold Star Awards, 1996. Memberships include: New York Academy of Sciences; Physical Society of Japan; Modern Poets Society; World Parnassians Guild International; World Literary Academy; International Academy of Poets; Confederation of Chivalry; Maison Internationale des Intellectuels; Accademia Ferdinandea di Scienze Lettere ed Arti; Accademia Internazionale Trinacria Lettere-Arte-Scienze; Order of International Fellowship; American Biographical Institute Research Association; International Biographical Centre; International Biographical Association; United Writer's Association. Address: Nisi 7-7-11 Aomadani, Minoo-si, Osaka 562-0023, Japan.

**IKEDA Kiyohiro,** b. 19 February 1956, Kamamoto, Japan. Professor. 1 son, 1 daughter. Education: BEng, Tokyo University, 1978; MEng, Tokyo University, 1980; PhD, University California at Berkeley, 1984. Appointments: Research Associate, Nagaoka University of Technology, 1984-87; Associate Professor, Nagaoka University of Technology, 1987-93; Associate Professor, Engineering, Tohoku University, Sendai, Japan, 1993-96, Professor, 1996-. Publications: Echelon Modes in Uniform Materials, 1994; Mode Switching and Recursive Bifurcation in Granular Materials, 1997. Memberships: American Society of Civil Engineers; Japan Society of Civil Engineers; Japan Society for Industrial and Applied Mathematics; Japan Society for Computational

Engineering and Science. Address: Tohoku University, Department Civil Engineering, Aoba, 06 Sendai 980-8579, Japan.

**IKEDA Tadasu,** b. 15 March 1947, Yonago, Japan. Professor. m. Mitsuko Nadao, 4 daughters. Education: DrMedSc, Tottori University, 1980. Appointment: Professor, Tottori University Faculty of Medicine. Honour: Shimoda Mitsuzo Award, 1986. Memberships: Fellow, Japan Diabetic Society; American Diabetes Society. Address: Munakata 451-13, Yonago 683-0017, Japan.

**ILANGO Balakrishna,** b. 13 July 1938, Mayiladuthurai, India. Teacher. m. Ganga Devi, 1 son, 1 daughter. Education: BE, Electrical Engineering, 1960; MSc, Electrical Machine Design, 1963; PhD, Power Electronics, 1971. Appointments: Professor, Power Systems, 1976-85; Head, Electrical Engineering Department, 1985-89; Member, Secretary, Tamil Nadu State Council for Science and Technology, 1989-90; Principal, Regional Engineering College, 1990-95; Vice Chancellor, Bharathiar University, 1997-. Publications: Several articles in professional journals. Honours: 3 1st Prizes for Projects; Probono Publico Award, 1994. Membership: Indian Society for Technical Education. Address: Bharathiar University, Coimbatore 641046, India.

**ILIA Stefanllari,** b. 5 June 1943, Erseke. Professor. m. Rozeta, 2 sons. Education: Graduate in Philology, 1967, Peking University; Postgrad in France and Sweden; D Philological Sciences, 1983; Professor, 1995. Appointments: Chief of Sector of Theoretical Subjects; Chief of English Dept, 1974-90. Publications: English-Albanian Dictionary; Albanian-English English-Albanian Dictionary; English-Albanian Dictionary of English Idioms. Memberships: Member of Scientific Council of Faculty of Modern Languages; Member of Senate of Tirana University. Address: Fakulteti i Gjutiëve të Huaja, Tirana, Albania.

**ILIE Virgil Pascal,** b. 3 May 1964, Bucharest, Romania. Film Director. m. Ioana Ilie, 1 son. Education: International Academy for Studies of World Religion and Culture. Appointments: Assistant Decorator, 1985-89; Journalist, 1990-; Television News Director, 1995-96; Film Director, Producer, 1996-; Founder, Kogaion Film. Creative Works: Film Director of Pilgrimage to the Holy Land, Older Days' Little Paris, Today's Metropole of Contrasts, Awakening, Tismana and Prislop, Monasteries in Moldova, Bucharest, Kogaion - The Sacred Mountain, Pontus Euxinus - Romanian Black Sea Shore. Membership: International Organization of Journalists. Address: Constantin Sandu Aldea Str. 13, App 6, Bucharest 1, Romania.

**ILIEVA Emilia V,** b. 21 August 1955, Bulgaria. Education: MA English Language and Literature, University of Sofia, Bulgaria; PhD African Literature, Russian Academy of Sciences. Appointments: Lecturer, University of Sofia, 1980-82; Senior Research Fellow, Institute of World Literature, Russian Academy of Sciences, 1989-93; Senior Lecturer, Department of Literature, Egerton University, 1994-. Publications: in Research in African Literatures; Articles in professional publications including: Enchanted Reality, The World of the African Village, Encyclopedia of Post-Colonial Literature in English. Memberships: Russian-South African Friendship Association; Writers Association of Kenya. Address: Dept of Literature, Egerton University, PO Box 536, Njoro, Kenya.

**ILIEVSKA-ARSOVA Milena,** b. 27 June 1947, Sofia, Bulgaria. Medical Doctor. m. Goce Arsov, 2 daughters. Education: School of Medicine, 1970; Specialization, Internal Medicine, 1976; PhD, 1995. Career: Department of

Gastroenteropathology, Internal Clinic, Medical Faculty, Skop 1971-73; Skopje Health Centre, 1973-74; Clinic Gastroenteropathology, Medical Faculty, Skopje, 197. Publications: Several papers in professional journa Memberships: Macedonian Association of Gastroenterolog International Hepato Pancreato Biliary Association. Address: 5 Perisa Savelic, 9100 Skopje, Macedonia.

**ILYUSHIN Michael A,** b. 8 June 1945, Kuibyshev Regio Russia. Chemistry Professor; Researcher. m. Shugalei Iri Vladimirovna, 1 October 1983, 1 daughter. Education: Engine Chemist Technologist Diploma, Leningrad Lensovet Institute Technology, 1969; PhD, Leningrad, 1975; Doctor of Chemic Sciences, St Petersburg State Institute of Technology, 199 Appointments: Engineer, LTI, 1969-72; Aspirant, Po Graduate, LTI, 1972-75; Researcher, LTI, 1975-78; Assista Professor, LTI, 1978-93; Associate Professor, SPSIT, 1993-9 Professor, SPSIT, 1995-. Publications: Nitronium Salts Organic Chemistry, 1983; Estimation of Dentistry ar Detonation Velocity of Tetrazole, 1994; Initiating Explosive Status and Prospects, 1997; Photosensitive Explosi Compounds and Compositions and their Initiation by Sing Laser Pulse, 1997. Honours: Honourary Medal, The Inventor the USSR, 1981; Honourific Title, Soros Associate Professc 1997; Dictionary of International Biography, Twenty Six Edition, International Man of the Year, 1997-98, Internation Biographical Centre, 1998; 2000 Outstanding People of th 20th Century, 1998. Memberships: All Russian Chemic Society, 1972. Address: State Institute of Technolog Moscovsky Prospect 26, 198013 Saint Petersburg, Russia.

**IMAMALIJEV Tofik Eijub Oglu,** b. 24 May 1948, Bak Azerbaijan. Inventor; Patent Engineer; Mechanics Enginee Medical Staff. m. 6 February 1971, 1 daughter. Educatio Graduate, Leningrad Institute of Precise Mechanics, Optics ar Computer Facilities, 1972; Azerbaijan Society Institu Inventions Creativity, 1973; International Scientific ar Educational Association, Znanie, 1996. Appointments: Vic Rector, Azerbaijan Society Institute Inventions Creative 1974-79; Chief, Patent Department of Scientific Cente Geophysics, 1977-84; Director, Centre of Inventior Methodology, 1979-; President, Azerbaijan Inventors Unior 1989-. Publications: The Structural Analysis, 1976; Role Differentiation in Creative Collective, 1978; Methods c Psychological Activization of Creativity, 1979; Discovery c Primary Life Forms, 1997. Honours: Number of patents computer programs; awards; Prize, Young League c Azerbaijan for Science and Techniques Achievements, 198 Membership: Azerbaijan Republic Advice of Young Scientis and Specialists, 1981-84. Address: Director of Invention Centre, CMI Post Box 211, 370000 Baku Centre, Azerbaijan

**IMAMURA Nobutaka,** b. 13 April 1943, Hiroshima, Japar Researcher; Educator; Physician and humanitarian support. m Hiroko Harada, 3 sons, Yoshitaka, Sohkichi, Shigehirc Education: MD, Medical School, 1968, Postgraduate, PhD 1973, Hiroshima University. Appointments: Assistant Professo Research Institute, Nuclear Medicine and Biology, 1984-; Gues Professor, R E Kavetsky Institute of Experimental Oncology 1996-; Kiev Postgraduate Medical School, 1998-. Publication 20 books, over 200 articles in professional journals includin Blood, Brit. J. Haemat, Europ. J. Hematol. Honours: Hiroshim Medical Association Award for achievement of aggressive natural killer cell leukemia/lymphoma, 1988; Japan Society In Award, 1992; Minister of Health Ukraine Award, 199€ Hiroshima Peace Grant Award, 1997, 1998, 1999 Memberships: Guest Editor, Experimental Oncology, 1996- Counselor, Japan Society of Hematology, Japan Society c Clinical Hematology; International Advisory Committee

Modeling of Developing Systems. Address: 14-24 ishi-Asahimachi, Minamiku Hiroshima 734-0002, Japan.

**IMANAKA Makoto,** b. 21 June 1951, Amagasaki City, apan. Professor, Mechanical Engineering. m. Yukiyo Uemura, daughters. Education: BEng, Himeji Institute of Technology, apan, 1973; MEng, 1975, DEng, 1986, Nagoya University, apan. Appointments: Researcher, Koei Chemistry Company td, Osaka, 1976-79; Senior Researcher, Industrial Research nstitute, Hyogo, 1979-90; Associate Professor, 1990-97, rofessor, 1997-, Osaka University of Education. Publications nclude: Effect of adhesive layer thickness on fatigue strength f adhesively bonded butt, scarf and butterfly type butt joints, 996; Estimation of fatigue strength for adhesively-bonded lap ints based on fatigue failure criterion under multiaxial stress onditions, 1998; Fatigue failure criterion of CFRP/Matal joints nder multiaxial stress conditions, 1998. Memberships: Japan ociety of Mechanical Engineering; Japan Society of Materials cience; ASTM; Chemical Engineering Society of Japan; dhesion Society of Japan. Address: Osaka University of ducation, Asahi Gaoka, Kashiwara City, Osaka, 582-8582, apan.

**IMRE László Károly,** b. 4 August 1929, Apatfalva, Hungary. niversity Professor. m. Emöke Nádas, 2 daughters. ducation: Diploma, Mechanical Engineering, Technical niversity, Budapest; PhD, 1965; DSc, 1985. Appointments: ecturer, Technical University, Budapest, 1951-57; Assistant rofessor, 1957-65; Associate Professor, 1965-87; Professor, 987-; Deputy Director, 1987-92, Institute of Thermal Energy nd Systems Engineering. Publications include: Handbook of rying, 1974; Solar Drying, 1996. Honours: Gold Medal of nventors, 1971; Academic Prize, 1984. Memberships: IEEE; hairman of Hungarian Solar Energy Society; Board Member f International Solar Energy Society, 1992-98 Address: echnical University of Budapest, Department of Energy, Iuegyetem rkp 3, H-1111 Budapest, Hungary.

**INDRUCH Igor Peter,** b. 12 May 1936, Ostrava. Educator of nformation Technology. m. Dagmar, 1 son, 1 daughter. ducation: Agricultural University, 1963; Postgraduate, Dip, esearcher Work, 1965; Diploma, CSC, Czech Academy of cience, 1972; Postgraduate, Researcher Work, Charles niversity, 1982. Appointments: Researcher, Czech Academy f Sciences, 1964-84; Head of Computer and Information entre, 1984-90; Head of Science Team, Academy of griculture, 1990-92; Educator, Information Technology, usiness Academy, High School, 1992-. Publications: esearch on Peaceful Use of Nuclear Energy; Dynamic ystems of Selectional Procedures; Innovations from griculture; Information Services in Rural Areas. Memberships: cademy of Science; New York Academy of Science; NESCO; Association of the Teachers of English. Address: alackeho 308, 757 01 Valasake Mezirici Moravia, Czech epublic.

**INGRAM David Eric,** b. 9 January 1939, Miles, Queensland, ustralia. Applied Linguist; University Professor. m. Nelly ohokau Ingram, 2 sons, 3 daughters. Education: Teaching ertificate, 1957, Queensland Teachers' College; A Ed, 1962, A, 1965, University of Queensland; MA Applied Linguistics, 971, PhD, 1978, University of Essex, England. Appointments: rimary School Teacher, Wynnum North, 1958-60, High School eacher, Caboolture, 1961-63, Camp Hill, 1963-66, French ubject Master, Bremer SHS, Ipswich, 1967, Brisbane SHS, 969-71, Queensland Education Department; Colombo Plan xpert, ESL, Australian Dept External Affairs, Phnom Penh, ambodia, 1968; Lecturer and Senior Lecturer, Mt Gravatt ollege of Advanced Education, Brisbane, 1972-83; Lecturer,

Principal Lecturer and Head, Department of Education Studies, Darwin Institute of Technology, 1983-86; Director, Institute of Applied Linguistics, Brisbane College of Advanced Education, 1986-89; Professor of Applied Linguistics and Director, Centre for Applied Linguistics and Languages, Griffith University, Brisbane, 1990-. Publications: Numerous articles in books, journals and other forms published around the world including: International Second Language Proficiency Ratings. Honours: Numerous research grants from various bodies for research in aspects of applied linguistics, especially language policy and language assessment; AFMLTA Medal for Outstanding Service to Language Teaching in Australia, 1994; Fellow, Australian College of Education, 1987-92; Mellon Foundation, Fellow and Adjunct Fellow, National Foreign Language Centre, Washington DC, 1993-94, 1995-99; Mellon Foundation Fellow and Adjunct Fellow, National Foreign Language Center, Washington DC, 1993-94, 1995-99; and others. Memberships: Life Member, Modern Language Teachers Association of Queensland; Life Member, Queensland Association for the Teaching of English to Speakers of Other Languages; Applied Linguistics Association of Australia; Association for Language Learning, Britain; Uniting Church of Australia. Address: 30 Coburg St E, Cleveland 4163, Australia.

**INNIS Michael Derrick,** b. 8 July 1919, Bakkar, India. Physician. m. Elizabeth Osborne, 2 sons, 1 daughter. Education: MBBS, Madres, 1942; DTMandH, Liverpool, 1956; FRCPA, 1961; FRCPath, 1971. Appointment: Consultant Haematologist, Princess Alexandra Hospital, 1960-79. Publications: Articles in Nature, the Lancet, Oncology, British Medical Journal. Memberships: Australian Medical Association; British Medical Assocation; American Association for the Advancement of Science. Address: 1 White Dove Court, Wurtulla, Qld 4575, Australia.

**IOANOVICIU Damaschin,** b. 28 January 1935, Oradea, Romania. Physicist. m. Marina Sabau, 1 daughter. Education: Physics, Faculty of Mathematics and Physics, 1959; Doctorate in Physics, 1973. Appointments: Principal, Physicist, Senior Researcher of IIIrd Degree, 1961-86; Senior Researcher of IIIrd Degree, 1991-92; Principal Researcher first Degree, Institute of Isotopic and Molecular Technology, 1992-. Publications: 72 Papers in reviews, Scientific; Book Chapters. Honours: Representative of Romania, Committee Organizing Mass Spectrometry Conferences, 1984-87. Memberships: Romanian Society for Physics; Romanian Society for Mass Spectrometry; New York Academy of Science. Address: Inst of Isotope and Molec Tech, Donath 65-103, POB 700, R-3400 Cluj Napoca, Romania.

**ION Crudu,** b. 29 August 1927, Mihoveni, Romania. University Professor. m. Aspasia, 1 son. Education: Mechanical Engineer, "Gh Asachi" Technical University, Iasi, 1951. Appointments: Chief of Department Staff, 1963-74, Assistant Dean, 1972-74, Rector, 1974-81, Chief of Department, 1981-90, "Dunarea de Jos" University of Galatzi. Publications: Several articles in professional journals. Memberships: Vice President, Romanian Tribology Association; Tribology Society, Germany. Address: Eroilor Str Nr 22, Galati 6200, Romania.

**IONESCU Mircea N,** b. 23 September 1935, Sinaia, Romania. Geological and Geophysical Prospecting Engineer. m. Marcela, 1 son, 1 daughter. Education: Graduate, 1960, Oil, Gas and Geology Institute, Bucharest; Specialisation, 1967, Mining Institute I M Plehanov, Sankt Petersburg; PhD Geology, 1976, University of Bucharest. Appointments: Associate Professor, Lecturer and University Conferencier, Mining Institute of Petrosani, Romania, 1960-83; University Conferencier and Professor, Oil and Gas University of Ploiesti,

Romania, 1981-. Publications: Ore Deposits Course, 1969; Mining Engineer's Manual, 1984; Economical Geology, 1984; Petrology, 1992; More than 60 articles in Professional Journals. Memberships: President, Geology Society of Romania, Ploiesti Branch; President, Mineral Resources Division, Prahova Scientists Foundation. Address: Str Sandulesti No 11, B1 Zl5 Sc 1 Ap 34 Sect 6, Bucharest, Romania.

**IP Horace Ho-Shing,** b. 9 January 1957, Hong Kong. Computer Science Educator. m. Annie Wai-Lan Ng, 1 daughter. Education: BSc Applied Physics with Hons, 1980, University of London; PhD Image Processing, 1983; Postdoctoral Research Associate, University College London, Imaging Processing Group, 1983-84. Appointments: Research Fellow, Research Computing Unit, Imperial Cancer Research Funds Laboratory, London, 1984-87; Project manager, Senior Engineer, Cambridge (Eng) Consultants, 1987-89; Senior Lecturer, City University Hong Kong, Department of Computer Science, 1989-91, Principal Lecturer to University Senior Lecturer, 1991-96, Professor, Head of Department of Computer Sciences, 1996-. Publications: Co-Editor, Lecture Notes in Computer Science 1024: Image Analysis Applications and Computer Graphics, 1995; Contributor Chapters to books; Associate editor, editorial board, Pattern Recognition, 1995-; Editor, Journal Computer-Aided Design and Computer Graphics; Special Issue Editor, Real-Time Imaging Journal; Chair Editorial Advisory Board, The IT Magazine, 1994-; Editor-in-Chief, Hong Kong Computer Journal, 1993-94; Contributor articles to professional journals; Reviewer various journals; Conference proceedings; Research grants. Memberships: IEEE; Engineering Council, Institute Physics, UK; Institute Electrical and Electronics Engineers; Hong Kong Institution Engineers; Hong Kong Computer Society; Hong Kong Society Multimedia & Image Computing; International Association Pattern Recognition. Address: City University Hong Kong, Tat Chee Avenue, Kowloon, Hong Kong.

**IPATOV Sergei Ivanovich,** b. 10 November 1952, Moscow, Russia. Applied Mathematician in Astronomy. m. Artjuhova Valentina. Education: Moscow State University, Department of Mechanics and Mathematics, 1970-75, PhD (Kandidat of Physical and Mathematical Sciences), 1982, Doctor of Physical and Mathematical Sciences, 1997. Appointments: Keldysh Institute of Applied Mathematics of Russian Academy of Sciences, Moscow, 1975-, now as Leading Scientist; Lecturer, Moscow State University, 1998. Publications: Published more than 100 scientific articles in journals: Earth, Moon and Planets, 1987; Icarus, 1992; Solar System Research, 1992. Memberships: European Astronomical Society; Euro-Asian Astronomical Society, 1995-; New York Academy of Sciences, 1995-96; Corresponding Member, Russian Academy of Natural Sciences, 1998; Associate, Committee on Space Research, 1996-. Address: Keldysh Institute of Applied Mathematics, Miusskaya Sq 4, Moscow 125047, Russia.

**IQBAL Hasan Mahmood,** b. 10 June 1955. m. 2 children. Education: Higher School Certificate, 1st Division, 1972; MBBS, Dhaka University, 1979; Diploma in Tuberculosis and Chest Diseases, Dhaka University, 1982. Appointments: Assistant Surgeon, SSMC Mitford Hospital, Dhaka, 1979-81; Medical Officer, Madergaij Thana Health Complex, Jamalpur, 1981; Resident Medical Officer, IDCH, Dhaka, 1982-85; Junior Consultant, Institute of Diseases of the Chest and Hospital Dhaka, 1985-86; Senior Physician, TB Control and Training Institute, Dhaka, 1992-96; Superintendent TB Control and Training Institute, Dhaka, 1992-96; Consultant, Gopalgang TB Clinic, 1996. Publications: Multidrug Resistant Tuberculosis and Its Management; Publications in various journals. Memberships: British Thoracic Society, England; Executive

Member, National TV Relief and Rehabilitation Society Bangladesh; Executive Member, Bangladesh Chest and Hea Association; Bangladesh Medical Association; National and T Association of Bangladesh. Address: Iqbal Chest Centre, 43 Bara Magh Bazar, Dhaka, Bangladesh.

**IRANDOUST Said,** b. 23 September 1960, Tabri: Azerbaijan, Iran. Professor. m. Airi Aulikki Hirvonen, daughters. Education: MSc Chemical Engineering 1984; Ph Chemical Reaction Engineering, 1989. Appointments: Assista Professor, 1990-94; Associate Professor, 1994-1998 Professor, 1998-, Dept of Chemical Reaction Engineering Chalmers University of Technology; Visiting Scientis University of Waterloo, Canada, 1990. Publications: 26 paper in professional journals in the field of Chemical Reactio Engineering and Engineering Education; 4 scientific reports Honours: Pedagogical Prize at the School of Chemica Engineering awarded by the student federation, 1987, 1996 Pedagogical scholarship awarded by Chalmers, 1994. Address Chalmers University of Technology, SE-412 96, Göteborg Sweden.

**IRELAND Kevin Mark,** b. 18 July 1933, Auckland, Nev Zealand. Writer. m. Caroline Gaunt, 2 sons. Publications Poetry: Face to Face, 1963; Educating the Body, 1967; A Lette From Amsterdam, 1972; Orchids, Hummingbirds and Othe Poems, 1974; A Grammar of Dreams, 1975; Literary Cartoons 1978; The Dangers of Art: Poems, 1975-80, 1980; Practice Night in the Drill hall, 1984; The Year of the Comet, 1986 Selected Poems (Oxford Poets Series), 1987; Tiberius at the Beehive, 1990; Skinning a Fish, 1994; Anzai Day: Selectec Poems, 1997; Fiction: Sleeping with the Angels, 1995; Blowing My Top, 1996; The Man Who Never Lived, 1997; Non-fiction The New Zealand Collection, 1989; Under the Bridge and Ove the Moon: A Memoir, 1998. Honours: New Zealand Nationa Book Award for Poetry, 1979; Order of the British Empire fo Services to Literature, 1992. Membership: Former President PEN, New Zealand. Address: 8 Domain Street, Devonport Auckland 1309, New Zealand.

**IRITANI Toshio,** b. 30 July 1932, Tokyo, Japan. Professor m. Yukie Umeda. Education: BE, 1955, MA, 1957, Tokyo University of Education; PhD, Clark University, Massachusetts USA, 1962. Appointments: Research Associate, MIT, 1960-61 Visiting Researcher, University of Geneva, 1961-62; Instructor 1963-64, Professor, 1964-98, Tokai University; Professor Chofu Women's College, 1998-. Publications: The Value of Children, 1979; Group Psychology of the Japanese in Wartime 1986; Power: A Study of Social and Psychological Analysis 1993. Honours: Distinguishing Award, Mainichi Newspapers Wundt Medal, German Psychological Society; Plack Distinguishing Award, 1980. Memberships: Psychological Association, Japan; International Mozart Society, 1997-; International Council of Psychologists, 1997. Address: 3-21 4 Chôme Daita, Setagaya, Tokyo 155-0033, Japan.

**ISHAN M,** b. 6 August 1982, Multan, Pakistan. Student. Education: Degree, 1994. Honour: Award, 1996. Address: M Iqbal Engg Complex, 3779 Railway Road, Multan, Pakistan.

**ISHIDATE Motoi,** b. 25 December 1930, Tokyo, Japan. Cytogenetics. m. Etsuko, 1 daughter. Education: Graduate, 1956, Department of Biology, Tohoku University; Degree of Medical Sciences, 1966, Tohoku University. Appointments: Cytogenetic screening for environmental mutagens and/or carcinogens; Consultation and evaluation of mutagenic activities of chemicals. Publication: In Vitro Chromosomal Aberration: Data Book, 1988. Honour: Japanese Environmental Mutagen Society, 1997. Memberships: Japanese Cancer

Research Association; Japanese and USA Environmental Mutagen Societies. Address: 5-23-11 Koenji-Minami, Suginami-ku, Tokyo, Japan.

**ISHIGOHKA Takeshi,** b. 10 March 1944, Tokyo. Professor. m. Terue, 1 son, 1 daughter. Education: Bachelor of Engineering, Seikei University, 1962; Master of Engineering, 1964; Dr of Engineering, 1970. Appointments: Assistant, Department of Electrical Engineering, Seikei University, 1970-77; Lecturer, 1977-78; Associate Professor, 1978-89; Professor, 1989-. Publication: Superconducting Generator with Excitation Transformer, 1973. Honour: Matsunga Prize, 1974. Memberships: Institute of Electrical Engineers of Japan; IEEE; Cryogenic Association of Japan. Address: 2-4-13 Akatsuki-cho, Hachioj-shi, Tokyo 192-0043, Japan.

**ISHIGURO Toyosuke,** b. 7 August 1929, Nagoya, Japan. International Business Consultant; Educator. m. Aiko Kuroki, 1984. Education: BA, honours, Kwansai Gakuin University, Japan, 1957; BA, Political Science, Pasadena University, 1962; MA, Political Science, University of Southern California, 1964; JD, Loyola University, 1976. Appointments: Instructor, Department of Asian Studies, University of Southern Carolina, 1962-64; Legal Assistant, Fredrick W Hill Law Office, Los Angeles, 1973-77; Associate, Iwasaki, Thomas & Sheffield, 1977-87; Adjunct Professor, Law, Loyola University, 1979-; President, Ishiguro & Associates, Beverly Hills, 1988-; Lecturer, Japan External Trade Organization to Japanese Business Organizations; Speaker to various groups including the Californian Bar Association. Publications: 4 books on American Law in Japanese, several articles. Memberships: Phi Delta Phi; Phi Sigma Sipha. Address: 2042 Ajax Circle, West Covina, CA 91792-1501, USA.

**ISICHEI Peter Uche,** b. 27 November 1932, Asaba, Nigeria. Physician, Professor. m. Elizabeth, 3 sons, 2 daughters. Education: 2M BBS, University of Munich, 1958-61; BM Bch, University of Oxford, 1962-63; MBBS, University of Munich, 1964; MD, University of Munich, 1966; DTM, H, London School of Tropical Medicine, 1967; FMC Path, Postgraduate Medical College, 1975. Appointments: Lecturer, University of Dar-es Salaam,Tanzania, 1969-70; Lecturer, Ahmadu Bello University, 1971-72; Senior Lecturer, University of Nigeria, 1973-76; Associate Professor, University of Jos, 1977-83; Clinical Subdean, University of Jos, 1980-81; Professor, University of Jos, 1981-. Publications: Numerous publications, National and International. Honours: Wawick Foundation Grant, Oxford University Clinical School, 1962-63; Postdoctoral Research Fellow, Max Planck Institute for Biochemistry; Nuffield Foundation Fellowship; Bye Fellow, Robinson College, Cambridge; Decree of Merit, International Biographical Centre; 20th Century Acheivement Award, IBC; 20th Century Achievement Award, American Biographical Institute; Man of the Year Award, ABI; The Professional Performance Award; Medical Excellence Award; Acheivement in Research Award. Memberships: Oxford University Medical Society; Nigerian Medical Association; Association of Immunologists of Nigeria; Association of Clinical Pathologists of Britain; Association of Clinical Biochemists of Britain; International Council for the Prevention of Iodine Deficiency Disorders; University of Cambridge Society; Order of International Fellowship; International Biographical Association. Address: Faculty of Medicine, University of Jos, PO Box 6594 (Private), Jos, Nigeria.

**ISKANDEROV Ibragimjan,** b. 8 May 1932, Kazakstan. Economist. m. Sanobar A Salimova, 2 sons, 3 daughters. Education: Post Graduate, Moscow State Economic Institute, 1961; Graduate, Tashkent Financial and Economic Institute,

1953. Appointments: Director, 1971-75; Rector, 1975-1976; Senior Scientific Secretary, 1976-1984; Deputy Chairman, Council of Ministers of Uzbekistan, 1987-89; Vice President, Academy of Sciences of Uzbekistan, 1990-96. Publications: Over 300 Publications. Honours: State Award of Uzbekistan; Award of Red Labour Flag; Award of Peoples Friendship; Three Awards of Communist Party, Supreme Council, Council of Ministers; Award of Kyrgyzstan Republic. Memberships: Ecosan International Organization; Knowledge Society of Soviet Union; Society of Friendship of Turkey and Uzbekistan. Address: 70 Gogol Str, Uzbekistan Academy of Sciences, Tashkent 700047, Uzbekistan.

**ISLAS YÉPEZ Oscar Alberto,** b. 2 December 1966, Mexico City. CPA. Education: Bachelor, Accounting, CPA, 1988, Tax Specialist, 1993, Master in Finance, 1998, Universidad Panamericana. Appointments: Financial Analyst, Mexico, Smithkline & French, 1989-91; Financial Planning Manager, Pharma Mexico, 1991-92, Comptroller, Pharmaceuticals Mexico, 1992-95, Acting Finance Director, Brasil, 1996-97, Special Projects Director, Mexico, 1997-99, Smithkline Beecham; Comptroller, Mexico, axo Wellcome, 1999-. Honours: Scholarship, high school studies, 1981, Ad Honorem Scholarship, 1984, Universidad Panamericana; Mexico's Best Student, El Diario de Mexico journal, 1988. Memberships: Alumni Council, 1989-, Academic Board, 1991-, Universidad Panamericana Accounting School; Part-time Faculty, Universidad Panamericana Business and Accounting Schools, 1989-. Address: Cerro San Andres #240, 04200 Mexico City, Mexico.

**ISMAIL Taymour,** b. 13 December 1967, Iran, Tehran. Hospital Administrator. Education: BA International Relations and Law, 1991, American University Washington DC; MSc Health Care Administration, 1999. Appointments: PA Assistant for CEO, Saudi Amoudi Group; Director of 1st Home Health Care Programme in Saudi Arabia. Publications: in Caring Magazine, 1997. Membership: American Hospital Association. Address: United Doctors Hospital, PO Box 50602, Jeddah, Saudi Arabia.

**ISSA Yousry Moustafa,** b. 7 January 1945, Cairo, Egypt. Professor of Chemistry. m. A L El-Ansary, 2 sons, 1 daughter. Education: BScAgr, Soil Science, Faculty of Agriculture, Alexandria University, 1965; BSc, Applied Chemistry, 1968, MSc, Analytical Chemistry, 1971, PhD, Analytical Chemistry, 1974, Faculty of Science, Cairo University, Giza. Appointments: Instructor, 1968-72, Lecturer Assistant, 1972-74, Lecturer, 1974-79, Assistant Professor, 1979-84, Professor of Analytical Chemistry, 1984-, Faculty of Science, Cairo University, Giza; On loan as Assistant Professor, Faculty of Education, King Abdel Aziz University, Mecca, Saudi Arabia, 1977-79, Associate Professor, Faculty of Education, Um El-Kora University, Mecca, 1979-81. Publications: More than 280 in international periodical journals. Honour: State Prize in Chemistry, Egyptian Academy of Science, 1989. Memberships: Egyptian Chemical Society, 1968-; Life Member, Indian Chemical Society, 1979-; Egyptian Analytical Chemical Society, 1989-; Editorial Boards: Egyptian Journal of Analytical Chemistry; Asian Journal of Chemistry; International Journal of the Spanish Society of Analytical Chemistry. Address: Chemistry Department, Faculty of Science, Cairo University, Giza, Egypt.

**ITAKETO Umana Thompson,** b. 30 October 1969, Edem Aya, Ikot Abasi, Nigeria. Engineer. m. Ima Andrew Eshiet, 2 daughters. Education: BEng, Honours, Upper Class, 1985; MEng, Systems and Control, 1989; PhD student, University of Owerri, Nigeria. Appointments: Assistant Lecturer, University of

Nigeria, Nsukka, 1987-88; Instrumentation and Control Engineer, Mobil Producing Nigeria, Eket Ak, Ibom State, Nigeria. Publications: The Design and Implementation of Interface Level Controller, 1985; Investigations into Appropriate Controller Types and Tuning Methods for Improved Systems Response; The Development of Optimal Control Strategy for Non-Linear Control Systems under Dynamic States, 1998; The Development of Performance Criteria for Optimal Control Studies of Non-Linear Systems, 1998. Memberships: Nigerian Society of Engineers; Council of Registered Engineers of Nigeria; International Federation of Automatic Control; Institute of Electrical and Electronic Engineers; ISA, Address: Engineering Department, Mobil Producing Nigeria, QIT, c/o Mobil Court, 3 Clement's Inn, London, England.

**ITANTIS Evangelos,** b. 31 October 1934, Palama, Greece. Professor. m. Helen, 2 daughters. Education: PhD, Mathematics, University of Athens, 1969. Appointments: Research Fellow, Research Center Democritos, 1967-74; Professor, Mathematics, University of Patras, Greece, 1974-. Publications: Over 50 Scientific Research Papers in various profesional journals; several textbooks. Address: University Patras, Department of Mathematics, Patras, Greece.

**ITKIS Sinovij I,** b. 20 August 1935, Russia. Engineer; Metallurgist. m. Ludmila Itkis, 1 son, 1 daughter. Education: Graduate, Diploma, Metallurgical Faculty, Chelyabinsk Polytechnical Institute, 1963; Postgraduate, 1965-68. Appointments: Engineer, Technician, Head of the Shift, Head of the Foundry Section, Chelyabinsk Tube Plant, 1963-65; Head, Industrial Laboratory Foundry of Technology, 1970-73; Lecturer, Instructor, General Chemistry Department, 1973-86; Professor, General Chemistry Department, 1986-91, Head, General Chemistry Department, 1991-97, Chelyabinsk Technical University. Publications include: Oxidizing mixtures in conveyer production of steel castings, 1973; Prognosis of Construction Strength of Moulds Collection of Papers, 1991; Phenomenological description of chemical and structural transformations of moulding mixtures, 1994; Synthetic approach to structure formation, 1995; Development of organic-silicate binding composition for making moulds and cores, 1997. Address: 145 Svobodu Street, Apt 1, 454090 Chelyalinsk, Russia.

**ITO Kenichi,** b. 7 March 1938, Tokyo, Japan. President. m. Yasuko, 1 son, 1 daughter. Education: Graduate, Law School, Hitotsubashi University, 1960. Appointments: President, The Japan Forum on International Relations Inc; Trustee, Executive Director, The Global Forum; Professor, International Politics, Aoyama-Gakuin University, Tokyo; Board Member, Institute of International Studies, Kajima Institute of International Peace, Japan International Rescue Action Committee, Japan Association of International Relations; Advisory Commission, Official Development Assistance, Japanese Ministry of Foreign Affairs. Publications include: Kokka to Senryaku; Taikoku to Senryaku; Futatsu no Shogeki to Nihon; Chiheisen wo Koete; Chokindai no Shogeki. Address: 17-12-1301 Akasaka 2-chome, Minato-ku, Tokyo 107, Japan.

**ITOH Shinji,** b. 16 February 1912, Ise City, Mie Prefecture, Japan. Professor Emeritus; Medical Researcher. m. Eiko Itoh, 2 sons, 2 daughters. Education: Graduated 1935, Nagoya Medical College; PhD, 1941, Nagoya University School of Medicine. Appointments: Lecturer, 1941, Associate Professor, 1947, Nagoya University School of Medicine; Professor, Hokkaido University School of Medicine, 1957. Publications: 44 Monographs; 34 books (edited by others); 224 original papers; 157 scientific reviews. Honours: Hokkaido Prize of Science and Technology, 1968; Hokkaido Medical Association Prize, 1971;

The Sun Rising Prize (Government), 1985. Memberships: American Association for the Advancement of Science; European Neuroscience Society; International Biometeorological Society; Japan Biometeorological Association; Japan Endocrinological Society; Japan Neuroendocrinology Society; Japan Physiology Society; Japan Neuroscience Society. Address: 2-6-31 Nishikoori, Otsu 520 0027, Japan.

**ITTU Gheorghe,** b. 8 March 1944, Dobromir, Ct Romania. Agronomist. Education: Agronomist, Faculty of Agronomy, 1967; PhD, Plant Breeding and Genetics, 1983. Appointments: Agronomist, 1967-71; Researcher, 1971-85; Senior Scientist, 1985-. Publications: 90. Honour: Ion Ionescu Dela Brad Award, Romanian Academy of Sciences, 1990. Memberships: International Triticale Association; Romanian Society of Agronomists. Address: Research Institute for Cereals and Industrial Crops, Fundulea 8264, Jud Calarasi, Romania.

**IVANISHKO Yuri Alexandrovich,** b. 13 February 1954, Russia. Physiologist; Research Ophthalmologist. m. Natacia Nikhailovna, 2 daughters. Education: MB Surgery, Rostov State Medical University, 1976; MD Ophthalmology, 1978; PhD, Scientific Research Institute, Moscow, 1983. Appointments: Chief Director, Rostov State Medical University, 1982. Publications: New Principles; More Than 50 Scientific Works; 2 Dissertations. Address: Ophthalmology Centre Inter YUNA, B Sadovaja Str 115, 344021 Rostov-on-Don, Russia.

**IVANJICKI Olga O,** b. 10 May 1931, Belgrade, Yugoslavia. Painter; Sculptor; Writer. Education: Academy of Arts, Belgrade, 1955; MA, 1957; Ford Foundation Grant, 1962; Fulbright Artist in Residence, Rhode Island School of Design, 1978. Career: Exhibits, 1955-; Numerous One-man shows; Paintings in Museum of Modern Art, Belgrade, Museum of Modern Art, Skopje, Metropolitan Museum of Arts, New York, USA, Museum of Modern Art, New York, USA. Publications: Olja, Cosic, 1982; The Mirror of Love, 1995; Brain Storm, novel, 1995; Olja, 1996. Honours: July 7th Award, 1988; International Woman of the Year, 1995; Best Painter of the 20th Century, Yugoslavia, 1996. Memberships: ULUS; MEDIALA. Address: 19 Kosancicev Venac, 11000 Belgrade, Yugoslavia.

**IVANKOVIC Radmilo,** b. 31 December 1933, Batina, Yugoslavia. Deputy Director. m. Ljiljana, 1 son, 1 daughter. Education: Dipl.Eng, Department of Electrical Engineering, Belgrade, 1958; MS, Department of Electrical Engineering, Belgrade, 1977. Appointments: Supervisory Engineer, 1959-64, Technical Director, 1965-68, Thermal Power Plant "Kolubara", V Crljeni; Chief of Power Analysis Division, Electric Power Industry of Serbia, 1968-76; Chief, Supervision Division, Thermal Power Plant "N Tesla", Obrenovac, 1976-80; Chief, Research and Development Division, Electric Power Industry of Serbia, 1980-84; Deputy Director, Electric Power System Control, Electric Power Industry of Serbia, 1984-. Publications: Several books and papers. Honours: Gold Medal, Power Association of Serbia, Belgrad, Yugoslavia, 1985; Honorary for Contribution to Quality of Life, Clean Air Association of Serbia, Belgrad, 1992; Honorary for Contribution to Nikola Tesla Museum, Nikola Tesla Museum, Belgrade, 1993. Memberships: President, Power Association of Serbia, Belgrade, Yugoslavia; President, Board of Directors, Thermal Power Plant "Nikola Tesla", Obrenovac; Representative, Yugoslavia UCPTE. Address: Sumadijski trg 6/VII-24, 11030 Belgrade, Serbia.

**IVANOV Ivan Petrov,** b. 28 January 1944, Valtchitran, Pleven, Bulgaria. Associate Professor, Chemistry. m. Guinka Troanska-Ivanova, 2 sons. Education: MSc, 1968, PhD, 1976, University of Chemical Technology, Sofia; Assistant Professor,

1976, Associate Professor, 1997, Department Chemistry Biochemistry, Medical University, Sofia, Bulgaria. Appointments: Assistant Professor, 1976, Associate Professor, 1997, Department of Chemistry and Biochemistry, Medical University, Sofia. Publications: More than 30 papers published in Bulgaria and international journals. Membership: Union of the Scientists in Bulgaria. Address: Medical University of Sofia, Department Chemistry and Biochemistry, 2 Zdrave Street, 1431 Sofia, Bulgaria.

**IVANOV Ivan Tanev,** b. 9 October 1951, Samuilovo, Bulgaria. Physicist; Educator. m. Tanka Ganeva Marcheva, 1 son. Education: University degree, 1974, Sofia (Bulgaria) State University; PhD, 1995, Stara Zagora Medical Institute. Appointments: Controlling Physicist, Nuclear Electrostation, Kozloduy, Bulgaria, 1974-76; Physicist Chemical Plant, 1976-84, Assistant Professor Medical Institute, 1984-98, Associate Professor, Head of Department of Physics and Biophysics, Thracian University, 1998-, Stara Zagora. Publications: 18 papers in international journals; 2 patents. Honour: Award of the Ministry of Chemical Industry, Sofia, 1981. Membership: Union of Bulgarian Scientists. Address: Flat 26, Armejska Str 16, E 6000, Stara Zagora, Bulgaria.

**IVANOV Leonid,** b. 13 April 1938, Kiev, Ukraine. Physician. div, 1 daughter. Education: Graduate, Kiev Medical University, 1961; Candidate of Medical Sciences, 1970; Habilitation, Doctor of Medical Sciences, 1987, Professor, 1992. Appointments: Physician, Rural Hospitals, Ukraine; Junior, Senior Research Worker, Kiev Institute of Gerontology, 1965; Professor, Saratov Medical University, 1990; Physician, Germany, 1995. Publications: Numerous publications in professional medical journals. Memberships: Russian, Ukrainian, German & Austrian Societies of Gerontology. Address: Eigenheimgasse 5, 92334 Berching, Germany.

**IVANOV Valeri A,** b. 29 May 1935, Bryansk, Russia. Scientist. m. div. 1 daughter. Education: Dipl Engineer, 1957; Dr techn Sc, 1970; Academician of Russian Engineering Academy, 1993; Professor, 1973. Appointments: Engineer of Research of Experimental Laboratory of Bryansk Machine Building Works, 1957; Assistant, Docent, Leningrad's Polytechnical Institute, 1962; Professor, Head, Institute of Nuclear and Thermal Power Plants of St Petersburg State Technical University, 1972. Publications: 27 books; 300 papers; 80 inventions. Honours: Award of USSR government, 1983; Honoured Worker of Science and Technology, Russian Federation, 1995; Honoured Worker of Russian United Energy System, 1996. Memberships: International Energetics Academy; Internationale Engineering Academy. Address: Favorskogo d 18 k 58, 195220 St Petersburg, Russia.

**IVANOV Vladimir,** b. 29 May 1945, Perm, Russia. University Professor; Researcher Applied Physics, Mathematics and Mechanics. m. Elena P Orlova, 1 son, 1 daughter. Education: MSc Physics and Mathematics, 1968, Perm State University; PhD, 1978, Institute Hydrodynamics of Academy of Sciences of USSR, Siberian Branch; DSc Physics and Mathematics, 1990, Supreme Attestation Commission of USSR Council of Ministers, Moscow; Cambridge First Certificate in English, 1993, University of Cambridge, UK. Appointments: Assistant Lecturer, 1972-76, Lecturer, 1976-78, Full Professor, 1990-93, Perm State Technical University; Research Engineer, Perm Aircraft Engine Building Works, Calculation and Theoretical Division, 1968-72; Researcher, 1978-87, Senior Researcher, 1987-90, Chief Researcher, 1990-93, Institute of the Mechanics of Continua, Ural Branch of Russian Academy of Sciences, Perm; Scientific Advisor, Soviet All-Union Abstract Journal, Mechanics, 1978-90; President, University of Information

Technologies and Computer Modelling, 1993-; Director of Marketing, Official Representative in Russia, AMPER Company, San Francisco, 1993-; Director, International Account, Official Representative in Russia, Mutual Data Incorporated, New York, 1993-. Publications: 107 in professional scientific journals, scientific and public newspapers; 2 monographs. Honours: Academician, Academy of Electrotechnical Sciences of Russia, 1993; Corresponding member, International Academy of Informatization, 1993; Active member, New York Academy of Sciences, 1997. Memberships: Scientific Council, PSTU; Advisory Council on Support of Small and Medium-Size Business, Perm Region Administration; Society of Industrial and Applied Mathematics; Minerals, Metals and Materials Society; International Association for Maths and Computers in Simulation; AMS; and others. Address: University of Information Technology & Computer Modelling, PO Box 1847, 614051 Perm, Russia.

**IVANOV Vladislav,**b. 18 February 1936, Staraya, Russa, Russia. Educator. m. 1 son. Education: Engineering, Mozhaisky Academy, 1959; Dok Tech Sci, Mendeleev Instititute of Metrology, 1982; Professor, Institute Fine Mechanics and Optics. Appointments: Lt, 2nd Lt, 1956-61; Head of Laboratory Institute Electroavtomatika, 1965-69; Mendeleev Institute of Metrology, 1969-84; Professor, Chairman of Department, Institute of Fine Mechanics and Optics, 1985-. Publications: Invention of magnetic resonance imaging, 1960; Creation of Two National Standards, 1978; Creation of New Science, Groupponics; Author, Metrological Assurance of Gyroscopes, 1983; Orbital Gyrocompassing, 1993; Three Ways, poetry, 1991; Gleams of Our Time, poetry, 1998. Memberships: American Mathematics Society: American Instr Society; Peter the Great Academy. Address: Stoikosty 27-303, 198261 Saint Petersburg, Russia.

**IVANOVA Shoileva,** b. 16 February 1951, Sofia, Bulgaria. Physician. m. Peter Shoilev, 1 son. Education: MD, Medical Academy, Sofia, 1976; Associate Professor, 1992; PhD, 1997. Appointments: Postgraduate Student, 1975-79; Research Worker, Bulgarian Academy of Sciences, 1979-91; Chief, Laboratory of Autoimmunity, Military Medical Academy, Sofia, 1991-. Publications: Over 120 in experimental and clinical immunology. Memberships: Association of Scientists in Bulgaria; National Society of Immunology; European Society of Esthetical Medicine. Address: Military Medical Academy, 1731 Sofia, Bulgaria.

**IVANOVA Tania,** b. 9 September 1946, Sofia, Bulgaria. Engineer. m. Mintcho, 2 daughters. Education: Radiotechnics, Technical University, Sofia, 1969; PhD, Physics, Central Laboratory for Space Research, Sofia, 1981. Appointments: Engineer, Scientific Group on Space Physics, 1969-73; Research Fellow, Central Laboratory for Space Research, 1973-84; Associate Professor, Space Research Institute, 1984-; Head of Space Biotechnology, 1987-. Honours: Golden Medal for Science. Memberships: New York Acadmey of Science, 1995-97; International Science Council on Biological Life Support Systems, 1995-. Address: Space Rsch Inst, 6 Moskovska Str PO Box 799, 1000 Sofia, Bulgaria.

**IVANYI Attila S,** b. 13 November 1942, Budapest, Hungary. University Professor. m. 3 daughters. Education: Mechanical Engineer, 1966; MBA, 1972; DMS, 1978. Appointments: Rand Leader, Lang Machine Factory, 1970; Assistant Professor, 1974, Associate Professor, 1980, Professor, 1987-, Budapest University of Economic Sciences. Publications: Several articles in professional journals. Honour: Award, Ministry of Education, 1983. Membership: Value Analysis Society of Hungary. Address: Mandula u 31, Budapest 1025, Hungary.

**IVLEV Boris Ivanovich,** b. 1 April 1947, Elets, Russia. Physicist. m. Irina Pavlova, 1 daughter. Education: MSc, Physics, Moscow Physical Technical Institute, 1970; PhD, Theoretical Physics, Landau Institute for Theoretical Physics, Moscow, 1973; DSc, Physics and Mathematics, Landau Institute for Theoretical Physics, 1980; Diploma, Senior Scientific Researcher, Moscow, 1983. Appointments: Junior Researcher, 1973-80, Senior Researcher, 1980-83, Leading Researcher, 1983-89, Head of Superconductivity Department, 1989-90, Landau Institute, Moscow; 2 semesters as Visiting Profesor, University of Southern California, 1991; Consultant, Los Alamos National Laboratory, 1991-97; Research position, Swiss Federal Institute of Technology, Zurich, 1992-94; Professor, University of San Luis Potosi, Mexico, 1994; Consultant, Oak Ridge National Laboratory, 1995-99. Publications: 111, 1970-. Memberships; American Physical Society, 1993; Mexican Academy of Sciences, 1996; American Association for the Advancement of Science, 1996. Address: 2616 Mission Road #106, Tallahassee, FL 32304, USA.

**IWAMA Hiroshi,** b. 28 November 1960, Kamaishi, Iwate, Japan. Anaesthesiologist. m. Naomi Suzuki, 2 daughters. Education: Bachelor in Medicine, 1986, Oita Medical University, Oita, Japan; Doctor of Medicine, 1994, Fukushima Medical College, Japan. Appointments: Researcher in Forensic Medicine, Oita Medical University, 1986-87; Resident in Emergency Medicine, Nippon Medical School, Tokyo, 1987-89; Staff Anaesthesiologist, Central Aizu General Hospital, Aizunakamatsu, Japan, 1989-92; Staff Anaesthesiologist, Fukushima Medical College, 1992-94; Director of Anaesthesiology and Emergency Medicine, Central Aizu General Hospital, 1994-. Publications: Many articles in professional journals. Memberships: Japan Surgical Society; Japanese Association of Acute Medicine; Japan Society of Anaesthesiology; Japan Society of Pain Clinicians; Japanese Society of Intensive Care Medicine; Japanese Dental Society of Anaesthesiology. Address: Department of Anaesthesiology, Central Aizu General Hospital, 1-1 Tsuruga-machi, Aizuwakamatsu City 965-0011, Japan.

**IWASAWA Yasuhiro,** b. 13 March 1946, Saitama, Japan. University Professor. m. Yumiko Iwasawa, 2 sons. Education: BS, 1968, MS, 1970, Dr, 1973, University of Tokyo. Appointments: Research Associate, Lecturer, Associate Professor, Yokohama National University, 1972-84; Associate Professor, 1984, Professor, 1986-, University of Tokyo. Honours: Progress Award for Young Chemists, Chemistry Society of Japan, 1979; Japan IBM Science Award, 1990; Inoue Science Award, 1996; Catalysis Society of Japan Award, 1999. Memberships: Chemistry Society of Japan; Catalyst Society of Japan; Surf Science Society of Japan; Applied Physics Society of Japan; American Chemical Society. Address: Dept of Chemistry, Graduate School of Science, The University of Tokyo, 7-3-1 Hongo Bunkyo ku, Tokyo 113-0033, Japan.

**IWATA Yoshikazu,** b. 20 May 1936, Osaka, Japan. Neurosurgeon. m. Hisako Shizukuishi, 1 son, 2 daughters. Education: MD, Osaka University Medical School; PhD, Osaka University Postgraduate Medical Course. Appointments: Rotating Internship and Resident at St Luke's and Children's Medical Centre at Philadelphia, 1971-72; Vice President of Minoh City Hospital, Osaka, 1992-. Publications: Articles in professional journals. Memberships: Japan Neurosurgical Society; New York Academy of Sciences. Address: Department of Neurosurgery, Minoh City Hospital, 5-7-1 Kayano, Monoh Osaka, 562 0014 Japan.

**IYENGAR Bhanu,** b. 23 May 1938, India. Doctor; Pathologist. m. N V Parthasarathy, 2 daughters. Education: MBBS, 1961, LH Medical College; MD, 1967, PhD, 1984, MA Medical College; FAMS, 1994, Institute of Pathology. Appointments: Demonstrator, 1963-69, Lecturer, 1969-80, Assistant Professor, 1980-83, Associate Professor, 1983-85, MA Medical College; Deputy Director, 1983-91, Director, 1992-98, Institute of Pathology; Director, Professor, Department of Pathology, Dr RPGMC, Kangra, 1998-. Honours: Doctor Bagabati Acharya Oration Award, IAPM, 1994; Fellow, National Academy Medical Sciences, 1994; TB Patel Oration Award, Gujarat Cancer Society, 1997. Memberships: International Society Environmental Toxicology & Cancer; New York Academy of Sciences; Pan American Society Pigment Cell; International Academy Pathology. Address: Institute of Pathology (ICMR), PB No 4909, New Delhi 110029, India.

**IYER Sarang Nath,** b. 21 June 1926, Pune, India. Pharmaceutical Quality & Good Manufacturing Practices Consultant. m. Lalitha, 2 sons. Education: BSc, 1944, MSc, Chemistry, 1947, Lucknow University; PhD, Microbiology, University of Iowa, USA, 1957. Appointments: Analyst, Laboratory of Public Analyst, MP Government, Lucknow, 1945-46; Senior Research Assistant, Mango Necrosis Scheme, ICAR, Lucknow University, 1947-51; Senior Scientific Assistant, Biochemistry Division, Central Drug Research Institute, Lucknow, 1951-54; Analytical & Quality Assurance Manager, Parke Davis India Ltd, Mumbai, 1957-69; Laboratory Manager, 1969-80, General Technical Manager, 1980-83, General Manager, Corporate Services, 1983-86, Johnson & Johnson Ltd, Mumbai. Publications: 15 Research Papers, 1948-57. Memberships: Indian Pharmaceutical Association; Association of Microbiologists of India; Society of Biological Chemists of India; Sigma Xi; New York Academy of Sciences. Address: 63 Bharat Tirtha, 409 V N Purav Road, Mumbai 400071, India.

**IYYANGAR Madabhushi Padmanabha,** b. 18 August 1939, India. Professor. m. M Srinivasamma, 2 sons, 2 daughters. Education: Bachelors Degree, Sri Venkateshwara University, 1959; Masters Degree, Madras University, 1966; Doctorate, PhD, APAU, 1986. Appointments: Professor, University Head, Veterinary Anatomy, Veterinary Science College. Publications: Histological Studies on the test of Indian Buffalo; Gross Anatomical Studies on the Pudendal Nerve in the Male Buffaloes; Teratoma of Testes in a Cock; Gross, Histological and Histochemical Observations on the Structure of Buccal Glands of the Buffaloe; Histochemistry of the Ureter of Goat; Histological Structure of the Pelvis and the Pattern of its Distribution in Goat; Histology and Histochemistry of the Urinary Bladder of Goat; Histological and Histochemical Studies on the Structure of Cortex of Kidney and the Goat; Age Changes in the Bursa of Fabricius in the desi Birds; Histological Observations on the Balano Prepucial Adhesions in Buffalo Calves; A Study on the Histological Intimacy Between Cotyledons and Caruncles of Ovarian Placenta; Morphological Studies on Gravid Uteri of Deccani Ewe; Histological and Histochemical Structure of the Female Urethra of Indian Buffalo. Memberships: All India Association of Vety Anatomists. Address: Department of Veterinary Anatomy, Veterinary Science College, Rajendrangar Hyderbad, 500070, India.

**IZAKOVICOVA Zita,** b. 15 July 1959, Trnava, Slovak Republic. Landscape Ecologist. Education: Faculty of Natural Sciences, Comenius University, 1979-84; RNDr, MSc, 1986. Appointments: Chairperson, Scientific Board, Institute of Landscape Ecology, Slovak Academy of Sciences; Coordinator of Scientific Projects. Publications: Over 50 Scientific and Professional Articles; 4 Text Books; 6 Scientific Books. Honours: Award Plaquette, Perfectly projects. Memberships:

Slovak Scientific Committee on Problems of the Environment; Slovak Ecological Society, Section of the Applied Ecology; Slovak Geographical Society; International Association of Landscape Ecology. Address: Institute of Landscape Ecology of SAS, Stefanikova 3, 814 99 Bratislava, Slovakia.

**IZMIROVA-MOSHEVA N A,** b. 23 May 1934, Sofia, Bulgaria. Chemist. m. Ivan Al Izmirov, 1 daughter. Education: BA, Chemistry, Sofia State University, 1958; PhD, Toxycology and Ecology, Medical Academy, 1978; ScD, Sofia Medical Academy, 1981. Appointments: Research Worker, Institute of Hygiene and Occupational Health Medical Academy, Sofia, 1959-92; PhD Dissertation, 1977; Habilitation, 1980; Senior Research Worker, Intoxicological Department. Publications: 60 Research Publications, 1968-99; Noninvasive screening methods for prophylaxis, diagnostics and treatment of man, 1999. Honour: Certificate of Authorship for Inventions. Memberships: Union of Scientists; Scientific Consultant, Sofia University, Nathional Oncology Centre. Address: Hygitest Association, 15 Dimitar Nestorov St, Sofia 1431, Bulgaria.

**IZOSIMOV Igor,** b. 24 February 1954, Russia. Physicist. m. 1 daughters. Education: Graduate, St Petersburg University, 1977; PhD, 1984; DSc, 1997. Appointments: Senior Scientist, 1991, Leading Scientist, 1992. Publications: Over 100 in professional journals and conference proceedings. Memberships: VG Khlopin Radium Institute; Chernobil Association; Russian Nuclear Society. Address: VG Khlopin Radium Institute, 1 Roentgen Street, St Petersburg 197022, Russia.

**IZRAEL Yuri Antonievich,** b. 15 May 1930, Tashkent, Russia. Scientist. m. Elena Sidorova, 1 son, 1 daughter. Education: Degree, Physics, Tashkent State University, 1953. Appointments: Engineer, Researcher, Geophysics Institute, Academy of Sciences, Russia, 1953-56; Senior Scientist, Head of Laboratory, Deputy Director, Director, Institute of Applied Geophysics, State Committee for Atomic Energy, 1963-70; 1st Deputy Head, 1970-74, Head, 1974-78, Main Department of Hydrometeorological Service, USSR Council of Ministers; Coordinator, Chairman, Soviet Side, Joint USSR-US Commission on Cooperation in Environment Protection, 1972-88; 2nd and 1st Vice President, World Meteorological Organization, 1975-87; Chairman, USSR State Committee on Hydrometeorology and Control of Natural Environment, 1978-88; Chairman, Governmental Commission, Aral Sea and Comission on Lake Baikal, 1987-89; Director, Laboratory on Monitoring Environment and Climate, Academy of Sciences, Russia, 1978-90; Chairman, USSR State Hydrometeorology Committee, 1988-91; Director, Institute of Global Climate and Ecology, Academy of Sciences, 1991-. Publications: Over 200 scientific articles in professional journals. Honours include: State Prize, 1981; The Sukachev Gold Medal of Ac. Sc. of the USSR, 1983; Gold Medal of the Ettore Majorana Int. Sci. Centre in Italy, 1990; UN-UNEP Sasakawa Prize, 1992; Gold Medal, Prize, International Meteorological Organization, 1992. Memberships: Russian Academy of Sciences; Russian Academy of Ecology; International Academy of Astronautics; Deputy, Supreme Soviet of the USSR; Honorary Member, Hungarian Meteorological Society. Address: Institute of Global Climate and Ecology, Glebovskaya 20B, Moscow 107258, Russia.

**IZZAT Mohammad Bashar,** b. 1 October 1964, Syria. Cardiothoracic Surgeon. Education: MD, 1987; MS, 1996; FRCSI, 1991; FRCSEd, 1997; FRCSEng, 1998; FRCS(CTh), 1996; FCS, 1996; FICS, 1995; FACC, 1998; FCCP, 1998. Appointments: Associate Professor and Head, Section of Cardiac Surgery, The Chinese University of Hong Kong;

Consultant Cardiothoracic Surgeon, Damascus University, Syria. Publications: Several books and research papers on cardiac surgery. Memberships: EACTS; STS; ICS. Address: PO Box 33831, Syria.

# J

**JÁ'RAI Antal**, b. 25 August 1950, Biharkeresztes, Hungary. Mathematician. m. Ilona Matisz, 2 sons, 1 daughter. Education: Master's, 1974, PhD, 1976, Kossuth Lajos University, Debrecen, Hungary; Candidate of Maths, 1990, Habil, 1994, Kossuth Lajos University. Appointments: Research Assistant, 1974-76, Research Fellow, 1976-90, Associate Professor, 1990-, research topics: Functional Equations and Measure Theory; 15 years experience in computer programming; 21 system programmes, 20-30 other programmes, 7 world records in computational number theory. Publications: Over 40 research papers in mathematics; 3 lecture notes; 1 book; Over 20 technical reports. Honours: Pro Universitate, Debrecen, 1974; Grünwald Géza Award, 1979; Ministry Award, 1990, for Outstanding Contributions to the Conference, IFSE. Memberships: Bolyai János Mathematical Society; Neumann János Computer Science Society, Hungary. Address: Keleti Ká'roly u 8 IV 1, Budapest II, H-1024 Hungary.

**JAAKKOLA Maritta S**, b. 9 March 1959, Helsinki, Finland. Consultant in Pulmonary Medicine; Visiting Associate Professor. m. Dr Jouni J K Jaakkola. Education: MD, 1984, DSc Respiratory Epidemiology, 1994, Specialist in Pulmonary Medicine, 1995, University of Helsinki; Diploma in Epidemiology and Biostatistics, 1990, McGill University, Canada. Appointments: Resident, 3 Finnish hospitals, 1984-85, 1986-87, 1987-91; Laboratory Physician, Transplantation Laboratory, University of Helsinki, 1985-86; Research Fellow, Respiratory Epidemiology Unit, Department of Epidemiology and Biostatistics, McGill, 1987-89; Researcher, Academy of Finland, 1992-93; Senior Registrar, Department of Pulmonary Medicine, University of Helsinki, 1992-94; Resident, Department of Pulmonary Medicine, Rikshospitalet, Oslo, Norway, 1995; Consultant in Pulmonary Medicine, Finnish Institute of Occupational Health, Helsinki, 1996-; Visiting Associate Professor, Department of Epidemiology, School of Hygiene and Public Health, Johns Hopkins University, Baltimore, USA, 1997-. Publications: Co-author, 15 journal articles; Author or co-author, 5 books and chapters in books. Honours: Young Investigator Award, Finnish Pulmonary Association, 1993; Reviewer, American Journal of Epidemiology, European Respiratory Journal, and Indoor Air; Author, First Finnish University textbook in Pulmonary Medicine. Memberships: European Respiratory Society; American Thoracic Society. Address: Kimmeltie 11 C 31, 02110 Espoo, Finland.

**JACHYMSKI Jacek Robert**, b. 28 June 1959, Lodz, Poland. Mathematician. m. Zofia Bukowczyk, 2 sons, 1 daughter. Education: MSc, 1981, PhD in Mathematics, 1987. Appointments: Assistant, 1981-87, Adjunct, 1987-, Institute of Mathematics, Technical University of Lodz. Publications: Articles in Bulletin of the Australian Mathematical Society, 1993, 1996, Aequationes Mathematicae, 1994, 1997, Journal of Mathematical Analysis and Applications, 1995, 1996, 1999, Proceedings of the American Mathematical Society, 1996, 1997, Nonlinear Analysis, 1998; Journal of Combinatorial Theory, 2000. Memberships: Polish Mathematical Society; American Mathematical Society; Japanese Association of Mathematical Sciences; New York Academy of Sciences; Academic Mountain Club, Lodz. Address: Institute of Mathematics, Technical University of Lodz, Zwirki 36, 90-924 Lodz, Poland.

**JACINTO Juan C**, b. 4 June 1954, Havana City, Cuba. Physician. m. G de la Madrid. Education: MD, University of Havana, 1979. Career: Endocrinologist, Ameijeiras Bros Hospital, 1985. Honour: Premium, Annual Scientific Journey National Hospital, 1996. Membership: Diabetology Group Havana City, 1998. Address: National Hospital, PO Box 8066 Boyeros, Habana 10800, Cuba.

**JACKOBOICE Sandra Kay**, b. 22 July 1936, Michigan USA. Artist. m. Edward James Jackoboice, 2 sons. Education Weekly Workshops, Helen Aves, Lost Wax Process Jewellery Design, 1968-78; Michigan State University, East Lansing 1955-56; Continuing Education Classes, Kendall School o Design, Grand Rapids, 1978-80; BA, Aquinas College, Grand Rapids, 1989. Appointments: Art Programme Development and Direction, Franciscan Life Process Centre, 1991-; Colour Plus Studio, 1991-; Board of Trustees, Arts Council of Greate Grand Rapids, 1997-99. Creative Works: Solo and Group Exhibitions 1993-, throughout USA and Poland; Corporate Collections at Butterworth Hospital, Downtown Managemen Board, Grand Rapids, and Monarch Hydraulics, Corporate Offices; Numerous individual collections; Represented ir several galleries and art museums. Memberships: CIVA American Society of Botanical Artists; Great Lakes Paste Society, co-Founder, President, 1997-; Ada Council for the Arts; Artists Alliance; Grand Rapids Art Museum, Women's Committee; Grand Valley Artists' Association; Midwest Paste Society; Rivertown Artists' Guild. Address: PO Box 6775, Lake Drive SE, Grand Rapids, MI 49516, USA.

**JACKSON Darcy Wilma Demille**, b. Chicago, Illinois, USA Writer, Columnist. m. Gordon C, 4 daughters. Education Bachelor's Degree, University of Michigan; Michigan State University Clinical Certificates. Appointments: Columnist, Flin Journal, 1982-; Treasurer, Alumni Board of Governors University of Michigan; Michigan Human Resources Board Delegate. Honours: Pionees, Journalism Award; Choice Award Forum Magazine. Memberships: Eta Phi Beta Sorority Inc Alumni Association. Address: 615 Lippincott Blvd, Flint, M 48503, USA.

**JACKSON Geraldine**, b. 30 October 1934, Barnesville Georgia, USA. Credit Clerk. m. Alphonso Smith dec'd, 1 son Appointment: Credit Clerk, Sterling Jewelers, 24 years Honours: Superior Accomplishment Award, US Postal Service Illinois, 1970. Memberships: NAACP: Georgia Sherif Association; National Association of Police Chiefs; Nationa Law Enforcement Officers Memorial Fund. Address: 1890 Myrtle Drive South West 422, Atlanta, GA 30311, USA.

**JACKSON John Charles**, b. 12 March 1939, Columbus Ohio, USA. Retired Teacher. m. Carol. Education: Bachelor o Science, Education, Ohio State University; Double Major Social Studies, Ohio State University, 1961. Appointments Teacher, Grades 7-12, Bokescreek Local, 1961-62; Teacher Grades 7-8, Grandview Heights, 1962-91. Honours: Ohio State University College of Education Alumni Society; Caree Teacher Award; Martha Holden Jennings Foundation Scholarship. Memberships: Franklin County Retired Teachers Association; Ohio Retired Teachers Association; Ohio State University Alumni Association. Address: 5741 Aspendale Drive Columbus, OH 43235-7506, USA.

**JACOB Karen Hite**, b. 14 February 1947, Wilkinsburg Pennsylvania, USA. m. John B Jacob, 1 son. Education: BM University of North Carolina, Greensboro, 1969; MAT University of North Carolina, Chapel Hill, 1970. Appointments Artistic Director, Creator, Carolina Pro Musica, professiona early music ensemble specializing in medieval to baroque music, 1977; Ensemble tours SE USA and own series Earl Music at St Mary's; Solo and duo recitals; Teacher; Music

Director for St John's Episcopal Church, Charlotte, North Carolina, 1981-91; Appearances on public radio and commercial television; Early keyboard specialist, New Orleans Institute of Performing Arts Workshop, 1983; Music Director, Caldwell Memorial Presbyterian, Charlotte, North Carolina, 1992-. Recordings: The Angel So Did Sound It, compact disk. Publications: Editor: Newsletter for Southeastern Historical Keyboard Society, 1981. Contributor to: The American Organist. Honours: Mu Phi Epsilon, 1967; Honorary Citizen of New Orleans, Louisiana; 1993 Performance in Europe; 1995 USIA Grant to Teach Music in Russia. Memberships: Founding Member, Board of Directors: Southeastern Historical Keyboard Society; Past Treasurer, Editor; American Guild of Organists. Hobbies: 13th-18th Century Recipe Cooking; Gardening; Sailing. Address: PO Box 32022, Charlotte, NC 28232, USA.

**JACOBSEN Arland Dean,** b. 25 September 1941, Mitchell, South Dakota, USA. Education Administrator. m. Wilhelmine T, 1 son, 1 daughter. Education: BA, Augustana College (Sioux Falls), 1963; Study, University of Chicago, 1964-65; BD, Luther Seminary, St Paul, Minnesota, 1967; PhD, Claremont Graduate University, Claremont, 1978. Appointments: Director, CHARIS Ecumenical Center and Fargo/Moorhead Communiversity, 1983-; Assistant Professor of Religion, Concordia College, Moorhead, Minnesota, 1979-83; Visiting Assistant Professor, Loyola Marymount University, 1978-79. Publications: The First Gospel: An Introduction to Q, 1992; Ecumenical Shared Minstry and the United Methodist Church, 1995; Numerous articles and reviews. Memberships: Society for Biblical Literature; Society for Advancement of Continuing Education for Ministry. Address: 1915 12th Ave S, Moorhead, MN 56560-3114, USA.

**JACOBSEN Joyce Penelope,** b. 27 May 1961, Berkeley, CA, USA. Professor. m. William S Boyd, 1 son, 1 daughter. Education: AB, Economics, Harvard College, 1982; MSc, Economics, London School of Economics, 1983; PhD, Economics, Stanford University, 1991. Appointments: Visiting Assistant Professor, Northwestern University, 1991; Visiting Assistant Professor, Harvard University, 1989, 1992, 1994; Assistant Professor of Economics, Rhodes College, 1988-93; Assistant Professor of Economics, Wesleyan University, 1993-; Associate Professor of Economics, Wesleyan University. Publications: Do Men Whose Wives Work Really Earn Less?, 1996; Marriage and Migration, Comparing Gains and Losses from Migration for Couples and Singles, 1997; Workforce Sex Segregation in Developing Countries, General Patterns and Statistical Relationsships for Developing Countries in the Western Hemisphere, 1997; What Data do Economists Use?, 1997; Many other publcations. Honours: Presidential Scholar, 1978; Detur Prize for first year grades, Harvard College, 1979; Phi Beta Kappa, Radcliffe College, 1982; Abba P Lerner Studentship, London School of Economics, 1982-83; First Year Fellowship, Stanford University, 1983-84; Omicron Delta Epsilon, Rhodes College, 1989. Memberships: Society of Labour Economics, 1996-; International Association for Feminist Economics, 1991-; American Economic Association, 1988-. Address: Department of Economics, Wesleyan University, Middletown, CT 06459, USA.

**JACOBSEN Klaus,** b. 23 March 1939, Copenhagen. Surgeon. m. Kirsten Klinge Jacobsen, 3 sons. Education: MD, 1965, Postgrad Diploma as General Practitioner, 1967, Postgrad Diploma as Orthopaedic Surgeon, 1981, PhD Bio Mechanics, 1981, University of Copenhagen. Appointments: Senior Registrar, Gentofte and Glostrup Hospitals, 1975-79; Senior Registrar, Orthopaedic Hospital, Rigshosp, 1979-84; Consultant, Orthopaedic Surgical Dept, Gentofte Hospital, 1984-85; Senior Consultant, Head Orthopaedic Dept, Frederiksberg Hospital, 1985-97; Chief District Surgeon, Thule

Inuit Population, the northernmost people in the world, Greenland, 1997-. Publications: Biomechanics of the human knee joint (ligaments), thesis, 1981; Over 40 papers in international scientific journals. Honours: Danish Council for Sports Injuries, 1974; Foundation for the Handicapped, 1974; Guildahl Foundation, 1981. Memberships: Danish Orthopaedic Society, member executive committee, 1986-90, Chairman, 1988-90; European Society of Knee Surgery and Arthroscopy; Scandinavian Orthopaedic Society; Danish Surgical Society. Address: Chefdistrikts Laegen B121, DK 3971 Qaanaaq Hospital, Greenland, Denmark

**JACOBSEN Shirley Marie,** b. 1 August 1944, Sioux City, Iowa, USA. Business Administration. m. Gerald L, 4 sons. Education: Bachelor of Career Arts, Business Administration, 1993; Pilgrimage Diploma, State of Israel, City of Jerusalem, 1994. Appointments: Business Administration, 1973-; Songwriter, Writer, 1995-; Editor, 1997-98. Publications: Feelings of the Heart; A Cancer Review; Successful Telemarketing Business; A Second Start in Life; Songs: Perfect Peace; He'll Take You Back; Some Water to Drink; From Thorns to Gems; You Put my Life Together Again; a composition, son et lumiere; I Just Stood There, a poem. Honours: The Millennium Plaque and Medal; Certificate of Merit; Citation of Meritorious Achievement; Decree of Merit; Pictorial Testimonial; Certificate of Dedication; Certificate of Inclusion; Twentieth Century Achievement Award; International Cultural Diploma of Honour; Notable Author Award; Notable Christian Service Award; Excellence in the Arts Award; National Dean's Award; National Sales Award; Editor's Choice Award.Memberships: International Biographical Association; American Biographical Institute; Delta Epsilon Chi. American Association of Bible Colleges. Address: Songwriter, A Forager, P O Box 1699, Chandler, TX 75758, USA.

**JAGADEESH Anumakonda,** b. 13 August 1947, Nellore, India. Renewable Energy Expert. m. Vaiderbhi Devi, 1 son, 2 daughters. Education: PUC, 1962, BSc, 1965, V R College, Nellore; MSc, 1976, Sri Venkateswara University, Tirupati; PhD, 1985, University of Roorkee. Appointments: Teacher of Physics, V R College, Nellore, 1968-89; Researcher, Danish Folkcentre for Renewable Energy, Denmark, 1989-90; Researcher in Wind Energy, ENEA CRE CASACCIA, Rome, 1990-92; Director, Murugappa Chettiar Research Centre, Chennai, India, 1993-95; VP, Advanced Radio Masts Ltd, Hyderabad, 1995-96; Director, Infrastructure Consulting and Engineers Pvt Ltd, Bangalore, 1996-97; Freelance Wind Energy Consultant, 1997-. Publications: Over 100 research papers in international and national journals; Presented papers at several international conferences and seminars; Over 150 popular articles and letters to the Editor on energy, environment, science and technology and appropriate technology; 2 monographs. Honours: Margaret Noble Foundation Award in Energy Technology, 1994; Golden Jubilee of Independence of India Award, 1997; United Writers Association, Chennai, Lifetime Achievement Award, 1998; CBR Award in Science and Technology, Hyderabad, 1998. Memberships: Associate member, Sigma Xi Scientific Society, USA; Fellow, Royal Meteorological Society, UK; CEU, Rome; Solar Energy Society of India; IPV Prima Viri, Rome; Energy Environment Group, New Delhi. Address: 2.210 (Upstairs) Nawabpet, 524 002 Nellore, India.

**JAGADGURU RAMANANDACHARYA Rambhadracharya Swami,** b. 14th January 1950, Jaunpur, India. Monk; Educator. Education: MA; DLitt in Sanskrit Grammar; Studied subjects related to Sanskrit grammar, philosophy and vedic literature; Studied works of Hindu saint-poet Tulsidas; Listen and dictate Sanskrit, Hindi, Gujarati and English (blind since 2 months old).

Career: Followed monastic path since 1983, devoting himself to prayer, teaching and promoting the Indian culture at home and overseas; Established a monastery in Chitrakoot, India for himself and his disciples; Working towards establishing a university for those with special needs like physically and mentally handicapped to help them maintain their independence and carve their way in the world. Publications: 50 books in Sanskrit and Hindi related to Hindu scriptures in prose and verse, including Critical and Analytical Study of Prasthantrai, consisting of three scriptire texts of holy origin. Honours: Gold Medal for his work; Merits and certificates in national debates; Outstanding scholar and exponent of Vishistadvait philosophy. Address: Tulsipeethadhiswar, Tulsipeeth, Amodvan, Chitrakoot, Satna 210 404, Madhya Pradesh, India.

**JAGGERNAUTH Deonarine Dulip Joseph,** b. 21 July 1953, Princes Town, Trinidad, West Indies. Senior Petroleum Engineer. m. Allison Garcia, 1 daughter. Education: BSc, 1978, MSc, 1979, Petroleum Engineering. Appointments: Reservoir Engineer, Production Engineer, Special Projects Engineer, Senior Reservoir Engineer, Technical Superintendent. Publications: Several articles in professional journals. Honours: Section Service Award, Trinidad and Tobago; Long Service Award; Kermit Waldron Award. Memberships: Society of Petroleum Engineers; Kansas Alumni Association; Kansas Engineering Society. Address: 638 Ocean Avenue, West Coast Drive, Gulf View La Romain, Trinidad.

**JAIN Alok,** b. 9 December 1966, Vidisha, India. Engineering Educator. m. Ritu Jain, 2 sons. Education: BE, Electronics and Instrumentation, 1988; MTech, Computer Science and Technology, 1992. Appointments: Lecturer, 1989-96, Reader, 1996-, SA Technological Institute, Vidisha, India. Publications: 12 research papers in professional journals. Memberships: IEE, England; IEI, India; ISTE, New Delhi, India. Address: 79 Bans Kuli, Vidisha 464001, India.

**JAIN Lakhmi,** b. 1 October 1946, India. Educator. m. Sandhya Jain, 2 daughters. Education: PhD, ME, BE, honours. Appointment: Director, Knowledge-Based Intelligent Engineering Systems Centre, University of South Australia. Publications: 150 research papers, books, edited books, conference proceedings. Membership: Fellow, Institution of Engineers, Australia. Address: KES University of South Australia, The Levels, Adelaide, SA 5095, Australia.

**JAIN Mahavir Saran,** b. 17 January 1941, Buland Sahar. Professor. m. Ela, 1 son, 1 daughter. Education: MA, 1960; D Phil, 1962; D Litt, 1967. Appointments: Lecturer, Reader, Professor, Jabalpur University, 1964-84; Visiting Professor of Hindi Language and Literature, University of Bucharest, 1984-88; Professor, Head of Department, 1988-92; Director, Central Institute of Hindi, 1992-. Publications: 26 Book Length Publications; 89 Research Papers; 40 Articles; Anya Bhasha Shikshan; Parinisthit Hindi ka Dhwanigramik Adhyayan; Parinisthit Hindi Ka Rupgramik Adhyayan; Bhasha Avam Bhasha Vigyan; Vishwa Chetna Avam Sarvadharma Samabhav. Honours: Literary Award of the Government; Honoured by, Andhra Pradesh Hindi Prachar Sabha; Honoured by Indian Cultural Institute; Doctorate of Literature; International Cultural Diploma of Honour, American Biographical Institute. Memberships: Linguistic Society of India; Advisory Committee, National Council for Promotion of Urdu Language; Advisory Committee, Central Institute of Indian Languages. Address: Central Institute, Sansthan, Agra 282005, India.

**JAKOBSSON Thor Edward,** b. 5 October 1936, Wynyard, Sask, Canada. Research Scientist. m. Johanna Johannesdottir,

1 son, 1 daughter. Education: Geophysics, 1964; Meteorology, 1966; PhD, Atmospheric Science, 1973. Appointments: Researcher, Bergen University, Norway; Research Scientist, Atmospheric Environment Service, Canada; Researcher, Project Manager, University Teacher, Icelandic Meteorological Institute, University of Iceland. Publications: Scientific and popular books, papers and articles. Memberships: American Meteorological Society; Canadian Meteorological and Oceanographic Society; International Society of Biometeorology; The Planetary Society. Address: Espigerdoi 2, 108 Reykjavik, Iceland.

**JALALY Hossein,** b. 11 September 1943, Tehran. Civil Engineer. m. Farzane Masoumi, 1 son, 1 daughter. Education: MSc Civil Engineering, 1966, University Tehran; PhD, 1972, DSc, 1976, Structural Engineering, University Paris. Appointments: Site Engineer, Armeh Construction Co, 1966; Research Engineer, Technical Centre of Steel Structures, Paris, 1968-76; Research Fellow, Concrete, Imperial College of Science & Technology, Tehran; Associate Professor, Civil Engineering, Sharif University of Technology, 1978-83; Technical Director, Bandab and Lar Consulting Engineers, 1981-87; Professor, University Tehran, 1983-90; Managing Director, Ab-Niru Consulting Engineers, Tehran, 1987-. Publications: 52 published papers; Reports written for professional conventions worldwide. Memberships: International Commission on Large Dams, 1987-94; High Council Dam Engineering, Iran, 1996-; European Convention for Construction of Steelwork, 1971-78; American Concrete Institute, 1978-85. Address: 18 Sinak Alley, North Sohravardi Avenue, Abbas Abad, Tehran 15779, Iran

**JAMES Martin Jonathan,** b. 22 September 1961. Dancer. m. Adrienne Jane, 1 son, 1 daughter. Education: New Zealand School of Dance. Appointments: Ballet Dancer, Royal New Zealand Ballet, 1981; Principal Dancer, English National Ballet, 1987-90; Deutsch Open Berlin, 1990-94; Royal Danish Ballet 1994-. Honours: Five Hundred Leaders of Influence, American Biographical Institute, 1996; Men of Achievement, International Biographical Centre, 1997; International Directory of Distinguished Leadership, ABI, 1997; Dictionary of International Biography, IBC, 1999. Address: 71A Store Kengensgade, DK 1264, Kopenhagen, Denmark.

**JAMES Randy,** b. 19 April 1969, Shreveport, Louisiana, USA. College Teacher. Education: BA, Louisiana University, 1991; MA, Eastern Kentucky University, 1992; PhD, University of Southwestern Louisiana, 1998. Career: English Composition Instructor. Honour: Delta Beta Rho Scholarship, 1989. Memberships: Sigma Tau Delta; Research Association of Minority Professors; National Black Graduate Student Association. Address: USL Box 44707, Lafayette, LA 70504, USA.

**JAMIALAHMADI Mohammad,** b. 6 June 1953, Iran. Professor. m. P Shoghi, 1 daughter. Education: Bachelor of Industrial Chemistry, 1977; Post Graduate Diploma, Chemical Engineering, 1978; MSc, Chemical Engineering, 1980; PhD, Chemical Process Engineering, 1982. Appointments: Lecturer, Chemical and Petroleum Engineering, Abadan Inst of Technology, National Iranian Oil Company, 1982-87; Visiting Professor, Senior Research Fellow, Department of Chemical and Materials Engineering, University of Auckland, New Zealand, 1987-92; Professor, Department of Chemical and Petroleum Engineering, 1992-. Publications: 190 Papers in International Journals and Conferences. Honours: TMS Award, 1992; Iranian Society of Chemical Engineering and Chemistry Award, 1993; TMS Award, 1994; TMS Award, 1995; Mike Ackrill Award, 1997; Iranian Award from his Excellency Mr

Khatami the President of Iran, 1998. Memberships: Royal Society of New Zealand; Iranian Chemical Engineering Society; Iranian Petroleum Engineering Society; Iranian Oil Co, Research Centre Council; Iranian SOciety of Chemistry and Chemical Engineering; Editorial Board of Chemical Engineering and Processing Journal. Address: School of Petroleum Eng, University of Petroleum Industry, Ahwaz, Iran.

**JAMMEH Yahya Alhaji J J,** b. 25 May 1965, Kanilai Village, Foni Kansala District, Western Division. Head of State; President of Gambia. m. Tuti Faal-Jammeh. Appointments: Military career, Gambia National Gendarmerie, then Gambia National Army, 1984-96; Elected First President of Second Republic Gambia, 1996; President of Republic of The Gambia, 1996; Chairman, CILSS during its 12th Conference of Heads of State and Government held in The Gambia, 1997. Honours: Honorary Citizen of State of Georgia, USA, 1993; Honorary Lt Col ADC, Alabama State Military, USA, 1994; Decorated with highest Libyan Insignia, Grand Commander of the Order of Al-Fatah, 1995; Decorated with highest Chinese Insignia, The Order of the Brilliant Jade with Grand Cordon of China, 1996; 1997 Pan-African Humanitarian Award; Appointed Honorary Admiral, Alabama State Navy, 1998. Address: Office of the President, State House, Banjul, The Gambia.

**JAN Bilal Ahmad,** b. 22 October 1972, Srinagar, Kashmir, India. Film Director. Education: BSc, 1996; Computer Course, 1994; Film Appreciation Course, 1998; PG Diploma in Kashmiri, Kashmir University, 1998-99. Appointments: Freelance Film Director, short and documentary films; Production Film Bilal; Stage Actor, 4 years; Radio, 4 years; TV documentary, 3 years. Honours: Cultural Merit Certificate, 1988; Invitation for 5th International Film Festival, Mumbai, India. Membership: World Wide Fund for Nature. Address: Bagi Sunder Balla Chattabal, Srinagar 190010, Jammu Kashmir, India.

**JANA Atanu,** b. 10 April 1962, Manipal, India. Teacher; Researcher. m. Madhumita SenGupta, 1 d. Education: BSc (D Tech), Gujarat Agricultural University, 1984; MSc (Dairying), 1989; PhD (Dairy Tech), 1999. Appointments: Research Assistant, Department of Dairy Technology, SMC College of Dairy Science, Gujarat Agricultural University, 1984-89; Assistant Professor, 1989-. Publications: The Effects of Homogenization Conditions on the Textural and Baking Characteristics of Buffalo Milk Mozzarella Cheese; Process Standardization for Manufacture of Mozzarella Cheese from Homogenized Buffalo Milk; Many others. Honours: ICAR, Junior Fellowship; Dictionary of International Biography, International Biographical Centre; Twentieth Century Award for Achievement, IBC. Memberships: Indian Dairy Association; Soho Club; Dairy Science College Staff Club; Ahmedabad Bengal Cultural Association; Anand Durga Puja Celebration Committee; External Examiner Rajasthan Agricultural University, Bikaner; Rajendra Agricultural University, Pusar, Bihar; Dairy Science College, Rainpur, Madhya Pradesh. Address: Department of Dairy Technology, SMC College of Dairy Science, Anand Campus, Anand 388 110, Gujarat State, India.

**JANABI Hatif,** b. 1952, Kadisia. Poet; Writer; Translator. m. hatha. 1 son. Education: BA, Arabic Literature, University of Bagdad, 1972; MA, Polish Literature, Warsaw University, 1979; PhD, Drama, Warsaw University, 1983. Career: High School Teacher, Arabic, Kirkuk, Iraq, 1973-76; Lecturer, Arabic, Warsaw University, 1979-85; Lecturer, Arabic Literature and Drama, University of Tizi-Ouzu, Algeria, 1985-88; Visiting Scholar, Department of Near Eastern Languages and Cultures, Indiana University, Bloomington, 1993-94; Lecturer, Arabic Language, Literature and Culture, Warsaw University, 1988-. Publications: Numerous books and articles in professional journals in Arabic, English and Polish. Honours: First Public Prize, 12th, 13th & 14th Miedzynarodowy Listopad Poetycki, 1989, 1990, 1991; 1st Prize, Best Collection of Poems, 14th Miedzynarodowy Listopad Poetycki, Poznan, 1991; 1st Prize, University of Arkansas Press Annual Award for Arabic Literature, 1995; Fellowship, Polish Ministry of Culture, 1997-98; Award, The Metafora Review in Literature, Poland, 1997. Memberships: Polish Pen; Polish Oriental Association; Middle East Studies Association; Union of Polish Writers. Address: ul Smyczkowa 11/82, 02 678 Warsaw, Poland.

**JANACEK Bedrich,** b. 18 May 1920, Prague, Czechoslovakia. m. Elisabet Wentz, 1 January 1951, 1 son. Education: Soloist examination in organ idem, State Conservatory of Music, Prague, 1942; Master class for organ, 1945-46; Diploma Ex, 1946; Choir Master Degree, Royal High Music School, Stockholm, 1961; Organist various concerts, Europe, USA, 1942-, including Royal Festival Hall, London, other concert halls in England, Belgium, the Czech Republic, Germany, Hungary, Italy and Sweden; also Soloist with orchestras; Teacher organ, State Conservatory of Music, Prague, 1946-48; Parish Musician, Cathedral Parish, Lund, Sweden, 1965-85. Honours: Recipient, City of Lund Cultural Prize, 1980, 1988; Royal Distinction Litteris et Artibus, Stockholm, 1993; Composer, organ compositions and choral works including 2 cantatas with orchestra, compositions for brass and organ. Address: Kyrkogatan 17, S 222 22 Lund, Sweden.

**JANAN Firdous Ara J,** b. 28 December 1945, Satkhira, Bangladesh. Physician. m. Anm Atai Rabbi, 1 son, 2 daughters. Education: MBBS, Dhaka, 1968; MD, USA, 1975; FCPS Medicine, 1975; FRCP, Edinburgh, 1997. Appointments: House Surgeon, Gynaecology and Obstetrics, 1968; House Physician, Medicine, 1968-69; Medical Officer, Paediatric Unit, 1971; Resident Medical Officer, IPGMR, Dhaka, 1971-72; Deputed to FCPS course in Medicine, 1972-74; Resident Medical Officer, IPGMR, Dhaka, 1974-77; Assistant Professor of Medicine, IPGMR, 1977-81; Associate Professor of Medicine, Sir Salimullah Medical College, Dhaka, 1981-87; Associate Professor of Medicine, Mymensingh Medical College, Mymensingh, 1987; Associate Professor, Centre for Medical Education, 1987; Associate Professor of Medicine, IDCH, 1987-89; Associate Professor, Centre for Medical Education, 1989-90; Professor of Medicine, Sir Salimullah Medical College and Mitford Hospital, 1990-93; Professor of Medicine, Dhaka Medical College, 1993; Professor and Head, Department of Medicine, Dhaka Medical College, 1996-. Publications: Study of a Family of Cleido-Cranial dysostass with Agenesis of Gall Bladder in the Father, 1977; Tackling Tuberculosis in Industry; Hypertension in Secretariat Population of Bangladesh, 1979; On Some Liver Diseases in Bangladesh, 1979; Studies of Chronic Idiopathic Jaundice, 1990; A Case of True Hermaphrodite, 1990; Rheumatic Fever: Its Prevention and Control, 1977; Abdominal Tuberculosis, 1991; Kartagener's Syndrome in An Old Man of 60 Years, 1993; Prevalence of Pheumatic Fever in a Urban Population of Bangladesh, 1996; Tuberculosis of Gall Bladder; Drug Induced Diseases; Prevalence Type and Aetiology of Anaemia in School Children of Urban Rural Children of Bangladesh. Memberships: Bangladesh Medical Assocation; Association of Physicians of Bangladesh; Bangladesh Renal Assocation; Bangladesh Cardiac Society; Bangladesh Gastro-enterology Society; Society of Surgeons of Bangladesh; Bangladesh Endocrine Society; Bangladesh National Association for Medical Education. Address: Department of Medicine, Dhaka Medical College, Dhaka 1000, Bangladesh.

**JANARDAN Yadav,** b. 5 January 1963, Narpatganj, India. Educator; Freelance Writer. m. Asha Prabha, 1 son, 1 daughter. Education: BA, Hons, Hindi, FBG College, 1986; MA, Hindi, PG Dept Hindi, LNMU Darbhanga, 1990; BEd, Hindi, Govt Teacher Training College, Saharsa, 1994; LLB, CKM Law College, Araria, 1995. Appointments: Primary School Teacher, 1994-; Voluntary Lecturer, JDSSM College, Forbesganj, 1991-94. Publications: 43 publications in magazines and journals; Collaborated in 8 books of poetry and short stories; 10 broadcasts; Other literary works unpublished or part published; Sub Editor, Kala Patrika Purnia and Sarokar Patrika Raniganj. Honours: Awarded Purnia Shree by Kala Sahitik Manch, Purnia, 1994, for Hindi Literary Work; Awarded Surbhi Shree by Surbhi, 1995, for contribution to Hindi Literature; Certificate and Cup for Hindi Literary Work by Kshetriya Rachnatmak Vikash Manch, 1997; Certificate of Acharya by Jamini Academy, 1998, for Outstanding Hindi Literary Works in prose and poems. Memberships: VP, Fanishwar Nath Renu Smriti Punj, Forbesganj, Araria; Founder member, Renu Sahitya Parishad Araria; General Secretary, Akhil Bhartiay Sahitya Parishad. Address: AT + PO Narpat Ganj - 854335, Dish-Araria, Bihar, India.

**JANARSHANA SWAMY Gajaraj,** b. 16 February 1936, Mandya. Government Services, Retired. m. Narayanamma, 1 son, 2 daughters. Education: SSLC, 1955-56. Appointments: Junior Assistant; Senior Assistant; General Superintendent; Assistant Administrative Officer. Honours: Honoured by the Social Activities. Memberships: Social Services Organisation. Address: No 68 University of Agricultural Sciences Layout, 7th B Cross Raj Mahal Vilas Ext 2nd Stage, Sanjaynagar, Bangalore 5600094, India

**JANAS Frantisek,** b. 15 September 1946, Nova Lhota, Czech Republic. Publisher. m. Jana Janas, 1 son, 1 daughter. Education: Academy of Business, Brno, 1982. Appointment: Editor, Publisher, Edice 33, Brno. Publications: About 40 classic books edited and published, 1979-, including works of Baudelaire, Edgar Allan Poe and Franz Kafka. Memberships: Association of Czech Bibliophiles; Club of Friends of Fine Art. Address: Hercikova 4, 612 00 Brno, Czech Republic.

**JANI Sushma,** b. 26 September 1959, India. Physician; Pediatrician. m. Nitanjan Jani, 1 son, 2 daughters. Education: MBBS, University of Gujrat, India, 1982; General Psychiatry, Indiana University, 1987; Clinical Psychiatry, Johns Hopkins University, 1989; Diplomate, University of Maryland, 1994. Career: Director, Assistant Professor, University of Maryland, 1990-. Honours: First Class Honour, B J Medical School, 1980; Teacher of the Year, University of Maryland, 1998. Membership: American Academy of Child & Adolescent Psychiatry. Address: 10485 Owen Brown Road, Columbia, MD 21044 3835, USA.

**JANKOVIC Draga,** b. 21 September 1925, Knjazevac, Serbia. Ichthyologist. m. Belus, div, 1 son. Education: BSc, 1950; PhD, 1958. Appointments: Head of Limnology Department. Honours: Order of the Golden Wreath. Memberships: Academy of Environmental Biology, India; Europe Ichtyolog Society, Frankfurt. Address: Karadjordjeva St 13/11, Zemun 11080, Yugoslavia.

**JANOVIČ Sakrat,** b. 4 September 1936, Krynki, Poland. Writer. m. 2 sons. Education: Electrical engineering, technical school, Bialystok; Teacher's extramural studies, Bialystok; Magisterium, Polish Phililogy, 1973, University of Warsaw. Appointments: Journalist, 1956-70; Instructor Educational, 1971-81; Member, Belarusian Independent Publishers, 1980-; Writer, 1982-; Leader, Belarusian Democratic Union, 1990-.

Publications: Over 20 prose books - lyrical miniatures, sho stories, novelettes, novels, essays, plays, studies; Joine organisation of Belarusian Independent Publishers, 1980 Memberships: International Eurasian Academy of Sciences Belarusian Associations of Writers, Belaviesha, Poland Address: 16-120 Krynki, ul Sokolska 9, Poland.

**JANSARI Jagdishchandra,** b. 28 August 1939, Karachi Pakistan. Industrial Engineer. m. Nirmala, 1 son. Education BE, Mechanical Engineering, MS University of Baroda, India 1962; MS, Industrial Engineering, North Carolina Stat University, USA, 1965. Appointments: Supervising Enginee 1975-79, Manager, 1979-84, Senior Manager, 1984, Chie Manager (MS), 1984-86, Chief Manager (IE), 1986-91, Genera Manager, 1991-97. Publications: Several papers in professiona journals. Memberships: President, Indian Institute of Industria Engineering, Baroda; Senior Member, Institute of Industria Engineers, USA; Executive Member, Baroda Productivit Council. Address: 8B Nivruti Society, Karelibaug, Barod (Gujarat) 390018, India.

**JANSEN Lambertus,** b. 27 October 1934, Salt Lake City Utah, USA. Judge. m. Lanita, 1 son, 1 daughter. Education: BS Westminster College, 1958; JD, University of Utah, 1968 Appointments: Director, Utah Housing Development Agency 1969-71; Private Law Practice, 1968-83; Hyatt Legal Services 1983-87; Shanley Law Offices, 1987-92; City Court Judge Oswego, 1992-. Memberships: American Judges Associatior New York Bar Association; Utah Bar Association; New York Association of City Court Judges; Oswego County Ba Association. Address: 30 Talisman Terrace, Oswego, N 13126-6142, USA.

**JANUSKEVICIUS Laimis,** b. 8 November 1951, Lithuania Dendrologist. m. Rita Januskeviciene, 1 son, 1 daughter Education: Forestry Engineer's Diploma, Lithuanian Agricultura Academy, 1975; Doctor of Natural Sciences, 1988 Appointment: Head, Department of Dendrology, Kauna Botanic Garden, Vytautas Magnus University, 1980 Publications: Author and co-author, 7 books on dendrology Memberships: Corresponding Member, The Nordic Arboretur Committee; Centre of Development of Hardy Landscap Plants; Chairman, Dendrologist Society of Lithuania. Address Zilibero 6, Kaunas 3019, Lithuania.

**JARALLAH Jamal,** b. 5 April 1958, Al-Ula, Saudi Arabia Physician. m. Nabiha, 4 sons, 2 daughters. Education: MBBS King Saud University, 1983; MSc, 1986; MRCGP, Roya College of General Practitioners, 1987; Appointments Resident; Demonstrator, Department of Family and Communit Medicine; Lecturer, Department of Family and Communit Medicine; Assistant Professor, Department of Family an Community Medicine; Consultant in PHC; Associate Professo Department of Family and Community Medicine; Professo Department of Family and Community Medicine. Publication 28 Papers Published; Community Diagnosis Health Actior Referral Sysytem in, Quality Assurance in Primary Health Car Memberships: Royal College of General Practitioners; Worl Organization of National Colleges; Saudi Society for Family an Community Medicine. Address: College of Medicine, Universit Hospital, King Saud University, Riyadh 11472, POB 7805 Saudi Arabia.

**JASENTULIYANA Nandasiri,** b. 23 November 1938 Ambalangoda, Sri Lanka. Lawyer. m. Shanthi Jasentuliyana, sons. Education: LLB, University of Ceylon, Sri Lanka; LLE University of London, England; LLM, McGill University, Canada Attorney-at-Law, Ceylon Law College, Sri Lanka; Diploma Academy of American and Comparative Laws, Dallas, Texas

JSA; Attendance Certificate, The Hague Academy of International Law, The Netherlands. Appointments: Intern, F J and G De Sarams, 1960-61; Attorney at Julius and Creasy, 1962; Programme Officer, Asia Foundation, 1962-63; United Nations Official, 1965-; Executive Secretary, United Nations Conference on the Peaceful Uses of Outer Space (UNISPACE), 1981-82; Executive Secretary, United Nations Conference on Nuclear Energy (UNPICPUNE), 1986-87; Member, Board of Trustees of International Space University, 1989-; President, International Institute of Space Law, 1993-; Director, United Nations Office for Outer Space Affairs (OOSA), 1988-; Deputy to the Director-General, United Nations Office at Vienna, 1994-. Publications include: Books: Manual of Space, 4 volumes, 1979; Perspectives on International Law, 1995; Foreign Policy of Sri Lanka and the United Nations, 1998; Chapters: The International Regulatory Regime for Satellite Communications: The Meaning for Developing Countries, 1994; Future Perspectives of Space Law, 1995; The Development of Space Law From a Third World Perspective, 1997. Honours: All Round Student of the Year, Richmond College, 1958; Ceylon Law College Scholarship for Standing First of the Order of Merit, 1959; Editor, Ceylon Law College Review, 1961; Commonwealth Scholar, 1963-64; Testimonial Award of International Astronautical Federation, 1982; Book Award, International Academy of Astronautics, 1989; Elected as Academician of International Academy of Astronautics, 1990; Elected Academician of Russian Academy of Cosmonautics, 1996. Address: UN - Office for Outer Space Affairs, Vienna International Centre, Room F-832, PO Box 500, 1400 Vienna, Austria.

**JAVAKHISHVILI Nodar,** b. 7 October 1954, Georgia. Banker. m. Marina Chaduneli, 1 son, 1 daughter. Education: Tbilisi State University, 1972-77; Diploma, honours, Banking, 1977. Appointments: Senior Economist, Deputy Governor, Republican Bank, 1977-91; Governor of Rustavi, Branch of the Republican Bank, 1991-92; Governor, Isani Branch of The Social Bank, 1992; President, National Bank of Georgia, 1993; Governor, National Bank of Georgia, 1995-98. Address: 39 Chavchavadze Avenue, Tbilisi 380062, Georgia.

**JAYARAM Chandraprabha,** b. 29 June 1979, Bangalore, India. Bharatha Natyam Classical Dancer. Education: Studied b.u.c, Bangalore University; Passed senior exam in Bharatha Natyam Classical Dance in merit. Honour: Recognised by the Indian Institute of Talent Search, Mysore, India. Membership: Affiliated to above institute. Address: No 31 8th Cross Agrahara Dasarahalli, Magadi Road, Bangalore 560079, Karnataka State, India.

**JAYAWARDANA Pushpa Lalanie,** b. 7 August 1951, Colombo, Sri Lanka. Medical Officer; Senior Lecturer. m. M A J Jayawardana, 1 son, 1 daughter. Education: MBBS, Ceylon, 1975; MSc, Community Medicine, 1990; MD, Community Medicine, 1994. Appointments: Department of Health, Sri Lanka, 1975-82; NHS, UK, 1983-85; Medical Faculty, University of Peradeniya, Sri Lanka, 1986-97; Medical Faculty, University of Kelaniya, Sri Lanka, 1998-. Publications include: Ventilatory function of factory workers exposed to tea dust; Ventilatory function in brass workers of Gadaladeniya, Sri Lanka. Memberships: Kandy Society of Medicine; Peradeniya Medical School Alumni Association; Society of Occupational Medicine, London; Sri Lanka Medical Association; College of Community Physicians, Sri Lanka; Nutrition Society. Address: Department of Community and Family Medicine, Faculty of Medicine, Thalagolla Road, Ragama, Kelaniya, Sri Lanka.

**JAYRAJ Susai Manickam Joseph Arul,** b. 6 September 1961, Royapuram. Professor. m. Angeline Mary, 2 daughters.

Education: BA, 1983; MA, 1985; M Phil, 1987. Appointments: Teacher, St Joseph's College, Tiruchirapalli, 1986; Coordinator of the National Service Scheme, Alma Mater, 1990-94; Commissioned Officer, 2 TN Armoured Squadron, National Cadet Corps; Troop Commander, NCC Unit of St Joseph's College. Publications: Josephite; Jivan; The Cadet; Focus; Poems 97; Wanderlust; Sybiline Leaves; The Quest; Day Spring. Honours: Man of the Year. Memberships: Writers' Forum. Address: Dept of English, St Joseph's College, Tiruchirapalli 620002, India.

**JEDLICKA Miroslav Frantisek,** b. 30 September 1929, Simonovice, Czech Republic. Scientist in Photonics. m. Olga Marie Souckova, 2 sons. Education: MSc Electrotechnical Engineering, 1952, Faculty of Electr Engineering, PhD, 1961, Czech Technical University, Prague. Appointments: Scientist, Research Institute for Vacuum Electronics and TESLA Vacuum Engineering, Prague, 1952-92; President, Czech and Slovak Society for Photonics, 1992-. Publications: Photoelectricity, book; Co-author 6 books on Photoelectronic Image Devices and Camera Tubes; Author and co-Author over 250 papers in scientific and professional journals about photoelectronic materials and related problems. Memberships: Czech and Slovak Society for Photonics; European Optical Society; International Measurement Confederation. Address: Jemenska 581, 16000 Prague, Czech Republic.

**JEEVAN RAO Ande,** b. 5 October 1956, Nizamabad, India. Lecturer. m. Vijaya Kumari, 1 son, 2 daughters. Education: MSc, Botany, 1979; M Ed, 1998; M Phil, Botany, 1992; M Com, 1998; MA Lit Eng, 1988; PG Dip, Higher Education 1995; Master in Science, Arts, Commerce, Education, Faculties. Appointments: Lecturer in Botany, Government College, Mortad, India, 1980. Honours: State Award for University and College Teachers, Government of Andhra Pradesh, India, 1993. Memberships: SCST and BC Welfare Association; New AP HB Colony Welfare Association. Address: Government Jr College, Mortad, Nizambad AP, India.

**JEHN Lawrence A,** b. 7 August 1921, Dayton, Ohio, USA. Professor Emeritus Computer Science. m. Betty L James, 5 sons, 4 daughters. Education: BME, 1943, University Dayton; MS, 1949, University Michigan. Appointments: Professor Mathematics, 1950-68; Professor Computer Science, 1968-88. Honours: Cofounder of the Annual Computer Science Conference of ACM, Major Contribution to Computer Science Education. Memberships: Association for Computing Machinery; Sigma Xi Scientific Research Society. Address: 12285 N Spring Creek Rd, Parker, CO 80138, USA.

**JELIC Svetislav,** b. 1 January 1944, Belgrade. Head of Department. Education: Primarius, 1982; PhD, Medicine, University of Belgrade, 1988. Appointments: Department for Hematoncology and Allergy with Clinical Immunology, Clinical Hospital, Belgrade, 1969-80; Head, Department for Chemotherapy, Institute of Oncology and Radiology, Belgrade, 1981-94; Head, Department of Chemotherapy, Head, Hematological Laboratory, Institute of Oncology and Radiology, Belgrade. Publications: 20 articles in books and monographs, 165 articles in national or international journals, 158 articles as abstracts. Memberships: Serbian Medical Association; European Society for Medical Oncology; Central and Eastern European Oncology Study Group; Hellenic Society Against Lung Cancer; Multinational Association of Supportive Care in Cancer; European Association of Haematology; Balkan Union of Oncology. Address: Institut za onkologiju i radiolgiju, 11000 Beograd, Pasterova Street 14, Yugoslavia.

**JENG Woei-Lih,** b. 3 April 1945, Fu-kien, China. Educator. Education: BS, 1967; MS, 1971; PhD, 1976. Appointments: Instructor, 1976-77; Associate Professor, 1977-82; Professor, 1982-. Publications: Articles in professional journals. Address: National Taiwan University Institute of Oceanography, PO Box 23-13, Taipei 106, Taiwan.

**JENKINS Shirley Mae Lymons,** b. 9 August 1936, Wilcox County, Alabama, USA. Retired Teacher. Education: Bachelor of Science Degree, Knoxville College; Advance Academic Degree, AA, University of Alabama; Masters of Arts, Atlanta University. Appointments: Teacher, Boykin High School, 1959-62; Teacher, Camden Academy, 1962-68; Teacher, Leeds Elementary School, 1968-89; Retired, 1989. Honours: Soror of the Year, 1988-89; Service Award Delta Sigma Theta Sorority; Outstanding Service Certificates; Distinguished Alumni Award; National Association of Equal Opportunity in Higher Education; Outstanding young Woman of America; Knoxville College Alumni Award; Knoxville College Football Team Award; Knoxville College Student Body Award; Outstanding Young Women in America, 1981; Service Award, Delta Sigma Theta, 1985-88; Knoxville College Alumni Award, 1991, Student Body Award, 1993; Honorary Doctorate in Humanities, Knoxville College, 1994; Miles College Plaque, 1998. Memberships: Sixth Avenue Baptist Church; Life Member, Phi Delta Kappa Sorority; Delta Sigma Theta Sorority; Knoxville College Alumni Association; National Council of Negro Women; Treasurer, Birmingham Knoxville College Alumni Chapter; Alabama Retired Teachers Association. Address: 2692 20th St W, Birmingham, AL 35208, USA.

**JENKINS Andrew,** b. 20 July 1936, Philadelphia, Pennsylvania, USA. Deputy Mayor of Housing; Executive Director. m. Patricia Jenkins, 2 sons, 2 daughters. Education: University of Maryland, 1957; Temple University, 1961; BA Human Services, 1984, Antioch University; PhD, International Christian University; Hon degree, 1996, Humane Letters; Presently pursuing a Master's degree at True Holiness Temple Inc, School of Ministerial Concepts; Ordained Minister, Jamerson's School of Ministry. Appointments: City Official, City of Philadelphia; Deputy Mayor of Housing. Publications: Currently writing autobiography. Honours Numerous including: Outstanding Young Man of the Year, City of Philadelphia, 1971; West Philadelphia Chamber of Commerce Award of Merit, Young Great Society Man of Year Award, 1985; Maria Scott Ensemble Service in God Work Award, 1996; US House of Representative Congratulation Award by Bill Gray Congressman, 1984; Community Service Award by Governor Dick Thornburgh of Pennsylvania, 1984; Mantua Community Planners' Awarded as Mayor of Mantua, 1971; National Black Association Appreciation Award, 1990; Citation, Philadelphia City Council, 1982; Citation, Commonwealth of Pennsylvania by the House of Representatives, 1995; Martin Luther King's Village Community Inc Cooperative Participation Award, 1982; City of Philadelphia Retirement Award (Redevelopment Authority), 1992. Memberships: Citizen Crime Commission of Delaware County Executive Board Member; Gaudenzia Inc Board Member; Associate Minister, Bible Way Baptist Church; and many others. Address: Executive Director, Redevelopment Authority of the City of Philadelphia, 1234 Market Street 8th Floor, Philadelphia, PA 19107, USA.

**JENKINS Catherine Ann,** b. 5 May 1949, Cincinnati, OH. 2 sons, 1 daughter. Education: Bachelor of Sciences, Speech Pathology, 1976; Master of Education, Special Education, 1988. Appointments: Educator, Cincinnati Public Schools, 1976-98; Co-Founder, President, Regional Director, National Suttering Project, Cincinnati, 1984-87; Director, Disabilities 50Chs, 1996-. Publications: Different Friends, 1994; Co-Author,

Training Manual for Disability Coordinates, 1998-99. Memberships: National Writers Assocation. Address: P O Box 40208, Cincinnati, OH 45240-0208, USA.

**JENSEN Poul Erik Hyldgaard,** b. 13 April 1959, Skorping, Denmark. Associate Professor. Education: Biology, Part 1, 1982, Biology, Part 2, 1984, Natural Sciences Embedseksamen, Biology, specialisation in Protein Chemistry, 1986, PhD, Natural Sciences, Institution of Molecular Biology and Plant Physiology, 1991, Aarhus University; PhD studies, Natural Sciences, Duke University Medical Center, Durham, North Carolina, USA, 1987-89; PhD studies, Natural Sciences, 1989-91, PhD, Medicine, 1993, Postdoctoral Fellow, 1994, Institution for Medical Biochemistry and Biophysics, Umeå University, Sweden. Appointments: Research, 1994-95, Assistant Professor of Immunochemistry, 1995, Institution for Medical Biochemistry and Biophysics, Umeå University; Assistant Professor of Immunochemistry, 1995-99, Senior Lecturer in Immunochemistry, 1999, Department for Immunology and Immunochemistry, Umeå University; Head of Neuroimmunological Laboratory, Neurocentret, Rigshospitalet, Copenhagen University Hospital, Denmark, 1999-. Publications: Mechanisms of Proteinase Inhibition by Human α2-Macroglobulin and Pregnancy Zone Proetein, dissertation, 1993; Use of PEG with Covalently Coupled Hydrophonic Groups in Aqueous Two-Phase Systems - Methods and Protocols, 1998; Co-author, about 2 dozen others, mostly on research concerning human α2-macroglobulin. Address: Fredrik V's vej 21, nb 90, 2100 Copenhagen E, Denmark.

**JEON Rak-Keun,** b. 9 April 1938, Umsong, Korea. Engineer. m. Choon-Ja Choi, 1 son, 2 daughters. Education: BEng, Haw Yang University, Seoul, 1961. Appointments: Lieutenant, Air Force; Engineer, Hyun Dai Construction Company; Project Manager, Sam Whan Corporation; Executive Managing Director, Dae Woo Corporation; President, Kyungnam Metal Company; President, Dong Hyun Inc, Architects and Engineers. Address: Song Pa Ku, 21-6 Seok Chon Dong, Seoul 138-190, Korea.

**JESBERG Robert O,** b. 17 November 1947, Springfield, IL, USA. Science Educator. m. Ruth Marie Andreas, 2 daughters. Education: Bachelor of Arts, Susquehanna University, 1965-69; Masters, Education, Temple University, 1969-71; Principals Certificate, Temple University, 1971-74. Appointments: Science Educator, Centennial School District, 1969-; Science Consultant, K'Nex Ind Inc, 1994-; Science Coordinator, Centennial School, 1996-98; Adult Evening School Director, Centennial School, 1984-97; Consultant to Science Program, Singapore American Schools, 1993. Publications: Microchip Measuring, The Science Teacher Magazine, 1986; K'Nex Educator Guide, 1995; K'Nex Racer Energy Educator Guide, 1996; K'Nex Bridges Educator Guide, 1996. Honours: Outstanding Science Supervisor, Pennsylvania, 1989; Outstanding Educator, Pennsylvania, 1987; Outstanding Contribution and Service, Pennsylvania, 1987. Memberships: National Science Foundation, Earth and Computer Sciences, 1984, Astronomy and Space Science, 1989, 1991, 1992, Commonwealth Excellence in Science Teaching Alliance, 1995, 1996, 1998; PA Science Teachers Association, 1986; National Science Teachers Association, 1987; Bucks County Science Teachers Association, 1992; PA State Team of the Mid Atlantic Eisenhower Math Science Consortium, 1995-. Address: 116 Blue Jay Rd, Chalfont, PA 18914-3104, USA.

**JESPERSEN Per,** b. 14 January 1938, Copenhagen. m. Anne, 1 son, 1 daughter. Education: PhD, Theology, Teacher, Education. Publications: 100 Books on P4C. Memberships:

ternational Who's Who. Address: Randerup 40, 6261 edebo, Denmark.

**JEUNG Eui-Bae,** b. 26 October 1961, In-Jae, Korea. ofessor. m. Hyun-Hi Jeung, 1 son, 1 daughter. Education: √M, 1984, MS, 1986, Seoul National University; PhD, iiversity of British Columbia, Vancouver, 1993. Appointments: esearch Associate, Washington University, St Louis, 1993-95; ill Lecturer, 1995-97, Assistant Professor, 1997-, Chungbuk ational University, Korea. Publications: 12 scientific blications, 1993-. Memberships: Korean Association for boratory Animal Science; Endocrine Society, 1993; Korean ciety for Veterinary Science. Address: College of Veterinary edicine, Chungbuk National University, Cheongju 361-763, rea.

**JEVRIC Olga,** b. 29 September 1922, Belgrade, Serbia. :ulptor. Education: Graduate, Music Academy, Belgrade, 46; MA, Academy of Visual Arts, 1948. Appointments: Editor Chief, Dictionary of Visual Arts, Serbian Academy of iences and Arts. Honours: Award, International OUN :hibition, Sloven-Gradec, 1966; Award, Republic of Serbia, 79. Membership: Serbian Academy of Sciences & Arts. ldress: 35 Knez Mihajlova, 1100 Belgrade, Serbia.

**JEWELL Judy Ann,** b. 15 July 1946, Seattle, Washington, ;A. Pastor; Educator. m. Dr Crowell E Jewell Senior, 1 :pson, 1 stepdaughter. Education: Glacier High School oloma, Seattle, Washington, USA, 1964; AA, Highline mmunity College, 1968; BA, Central Washington University, 70. Appointments: Teacher: Ethel Boyce Elementary School, 71-72; Rollings Elementary School, 1973-74; Bremerton iristian School, 1975-76; Christian Life School, 1976-78; irist The King Academy, 1979-83; St Anthony Junior/Senior gh School, 1983-85; Young Adult and Singles Ministry ordinator, Church of the Good Shepherd, 1987-88; Minister Christian Education and Chaplain, First Congregational urch and Pilgrim School, 1988-90; Pastor, University Temple ited Methodist Church, 1990-95; Director of Pastoral Care d Counseling, Bayview Manor Retirement Residence, 1995-; :e President, Serene Alternatives II, 1996-. Memberships: sociation of Professional Chaplains; United Methodist sociation of Health and Welfare Ministries; Chaplain's ecutive Committee; American Association of Pastoral unselors; Washington Pastoral Counseling Association; iiversity of Washington Environmental Health and Safety combinant DNA Committee; Board of Discipleship of the ited Methodist Church - Education Section Co Chair; Task rce on Aging, Church Council of Greater Seattle; Washington sociation of Homes for the Aging - Chaplains Forum -Chair. Address: Serene Alternatives II, 16727 80th Avenue √, Stanwood, WA 98292, USA.

**JEYASEELAN Sithamparapillai,** b. 26 September 1953, Sri nka. Senior Engineer. m. Chandragowry, 2 sons. Education: :c Hons Instrumentation and Control Engineer, 1980, iiversity of Westminster, London, England. Appointments: :ld Inst Engineer, GeoSystems Pty Ltd, Perth, WA, 1981-85; sistant Field Seismologist, Seismograph Services Ltd, 'elaide, SA, 1985-86; Research and Development Engineer, acker Communications Ltd, Adelaide, 1986-87; Electrical gineer, Tulsa Pty Ltd, Adelaide, 1987-88; Senior Engineer, IP Steel, Whyalla, SA, 1988-96; Senior Engineer, Water irporation, Perth, WA, 1996-. Memberships: Chartered gineer, Engineering Council, UK; Corporate Member, stitution of Electrical Engineers, UK; Corporate Member, stitute of Measurement and Control, UK; Corporate Member, stitute of Engineers, Australia. Address: 34 Central Avenue, dross 6153, Australia.

**JHA Udayanatha, (Ashok),** b. 6 April 1959, Bittho, Distt. Madhubani, India. Teacher. m. SMT Nanda Jha, 3 sons. Education: Shastri, 1975; Vyakaranacharya, 1978; Sahityacharya, 1980; MA in Sanskrit, 1983; PhD, 1989; DLitt, 1997. Appointments: Lecturer, Vyakarana, 1978-82; Lecturer, Sahitya, 1982-. Publications: 5 books, over 200 research articles. Honours: Gold Medal & Sahitya Ratna Award, 1989. Memberships: Convenor Bishwa Sanskrit Pratishthanam, Madhubani District, 1980-84; Secretary, Sanskrit Department of State Bishwa Hindu Praishad, Bihar, 1987-90; Joint Secretary, State Union of Sanskrit Teachers, Bihar, 1989-92. Address: Sadashiv Kendriya Sanskrit Vidyapith, Puri, Orissa, India.

**JI Yong-Xing,** b. 25 February 1936, Xing'an, China. Linguist. m. Wang Jin-Xiu, 2 sons, 1 daughter. Education: Guangxi Teachers' University, 1957-61, 1961-63; Peking University, 1979-81. Appointments: Assistant, GTU, 1963-68; Editor, 1969-78; Lecturer, 1981-85; Associate Professor, 1985-89; Visiting Professor, QUT, Australia, 1990-91; Professor, GTU, 1992-. Publications: 3 books: Analysis of Grammatical Construction, 1983, 1987, 1990; Co-author, Introduction to Linguistics, 1987, 1989; Syntactic Theory of Ancient Chinese, 1998; 17 articles and conference papers. Honours: Outstanding Award of Scientific Research, 1986, 1991; Outstanding Award of Teaching, 1987; Excellent Award for Book, 1991. Memberships: Linguistic Society of China; All China Association for Teaching Chinese as a Foreign Language; and others. Address: Dept of Chinese Language and Literature, Guangxi Teachers University, Guilin, Guangxi 5411004, China.

**JIANG Ding Xian,** b. 10 November 1912, Wuhan, China. Professor. m. Xiao Shufang, 1 son, 2 daughters. Education: Diplomas, 1934. Appointments: Vice President, Central Conservatory of Music, Beijing, 1961-84; Director, Compositional Department, 1950-84; Professor, 1942-. Honours: Lifelong Professor, 1993-; Enjon Subsidy for Outstanding Expert from the Government. Memberships: Association for Chinese Musicians; CPPCC. Address: Dept of Compose, Central College of Music; 43 Bao Jia Jie Xi Cheng District, Beijing 100031, China.

**JIANG Guorui,** b. 8 July 1954, China. Mathematician; Computer Scientist. m. 1 daughter. Education: Doctoral student, Institute of Systems Science, Academia Sinica, 1992-94; Visitor, Department of Computer, Tsinghua University, 1997-98. Appointments: Lecturer, 1987; Assistant Professor, 1992; Professor, 1996; Deputy Director of Department of Mathematics, 1994, Department of Computer, 1998. Honours: Second Class Award of Science and Technology Progress, Hebei, 1991; Outstanding Contributor Expert, Hebei Province, 1992; Person with Ability of Striding Over Century, 1997. Membership: Mathematics Institute. Address: Department of Mathematics, He Bei Normal University, Shi Jia Zhuang 050091, China.

**JIANG Shaoyu,** b. 25 January 1940, Shanghai, China. Professor. m. Xu Fulian, 1 son. Education: Graduate, Department of Chinese Language and Literature, Peking University, 1962. Appointments: Professor, Department of Chinese Language and Literature, Peking University. Publications include: An Outline of Classical Chinese Vocabulary, 1989; A Study of the Language of Tang Poetry, 1990; Introduction to the Study of Early Modern Chinese (Ancient Mandarin), 1994. Honour: State Expert with Outstanding Contributions, 1992. Memberships: Former Vice Secretary General, All China Society of Linguistics. Address: Department of Chinese, Peking University, Beijing, China.

**JIANG Xin,** b. 16 March 1917, Ho-Peh Province, China. Professor. m. Su-Zhen Wang, 2 Sons. Education: United Universities, 1943; MA of the Educational Researches Institute, Northwest Normal University, 1947; Sorbornist, France, 1949-54. Appointments: Assistant in Pedagogy, Lecturer, Educational Researches Institute of the Northwest Normal University 1947-48; Professor and Teacher of French, Foreign Affairs College, 1955-90. Publications: Cheif Editor, French - Chinese Practical Dictionary of International Life, 1962. The I Ching has been writen only through usurpation and distortion of Fu Hgi's Original Hexograms System, 1987; It is Right Time Now to Catching a Counterfeit, 1989; New Exploration on Confucius' Relations with Hi Ching, 1990; Leibnig Binary Number System is Quite Different from Fu Hsi's, 1990. Memberships: Vice Chairman, Beijing Resaerch Society of Choui, 1982-; Chinese Learned Society of Confucius, 1990-. Address: 242 Grey Building, Foreign Affairs College, Beijing 100037, China.

**JIANG Xuefeng,** b. 22 November 1946, Zhenjiang, China. Teacher. m. Guang Xia Zhang, 1 daughter. Education: Graduate, Shanghai Jiao Tong University, 1970. Appointments: Teacher, Software Teaching Group, Computer Science, Society of Guizhou, China. Publications: Software Engineering; Information Retrieval; English for Computer Technology and Application. Memberships: Chinese Computer Association; Physical Science Association. Address: Dept of Computer Science, Guizhou University, Guiyang Guizhou Prov, 550025, China.

**JIANG Yeon Fuh,** b. 10 April 1954, Taoyuan, Taiwan. Researcher; Engineer. m. Jian Ming Her, 2 daughters. Education: BS 1976; MS 1978; PhD 1991. Appointments: Associate Chief Director; Associate Scientist; Senior Specialist. Journal articles and conference proceedings, 1991-. Memberships: IEEE; CAC. Address: 3F No 30-1 Hernyang St, Chungli 320, Taiwan.

**JIANG Zhen-Ying,** b. 13 November 1949, China. Educator. m. Chaohua Fang, 1 daughter. Education: Diploma, Shanghai Normal University, 1974; Certificate, Shanghai Traditional Chinese Medical College, 1979; Diploma, English Department, Shanghai Foreign Language Institute, 1983; Master of Science, College of Health, University of Utah, 1987; Doctor of Philosophy, College of Health, 1991. Appointments: Chief Director, Correction Office, Shanghai Farm, 1968-72; Faculty, Division Head and Coach, Shanghai Traditional Chinese Medical College, 1974-83; Adjunct Faculty, College of Health, University of Utah, 1983-91; Vice President of Academic Senate, Member of President Advisory Council, Chair, Department of Science, Mathematics, Health and Physical Education, Barstow College, 1991-; Guest Professor in Shanghai Medical University and East China Normal University, 1999-. Publications: How to Teach Deaf Swim; The History of Breathing Meditation and Its Relationship to the Health of Human Body; The Study of Technique Principal and Characteristics of One Arm Giant Swing Backward; The Effects of Breathing Medication of Postworkout Recovery; A Study of the Nutrition Analysis of Barstow College Students. Honours: Career in Education Award; Humanitarian Award; AGS Award; Golden Apple Pin; Leadership Exemplified Award; Service Award, Barstow College, 1999. Memberships: American Alliance for Health, Physical Education, Recreation and Dance; American Association for Health Education; National Association for Sports and Physical Education; National Education Association; California Teachers Association; American Heart Association; American Red Cross; American Coaching Effectiveness Program. Address: Barstow College, 2700 Barstow Road, Barstow, CA 92311, USA.

**JIAO Zhao-Ping,** b. 7 October 1951, Wuhu, Anhui, China. Academic Administrator and Educator. m. Li-Ping Xie, daughter. Education: Bachelor, Construction Engineering, Hefe University Tech, China, 1974; Master of Solid Mechanics, Hefe University Tech, 1979. Appointments: Assistant Lecture Lecturer, Assistant Professor, Professor, Dean, Department c Construction Engineering, Hefei University Tech, 1981-94 Professor, Dean of Department of Civil Engineering, Vic President of University, South China Construction University 1994-. Honours: Honours of Excellent Youth in Science an Technology, Ministry of Machine Building and Electroni Industry, 1992; National Specialist Allowance, China, 199: Memberships: Vice Chairman, Computer Mechanic Community, Guangdong Province; Director, Mech Society Guangdong Province, 1995-; Chinese Society of Theoretica and Applied Mechanics. Address: South China Constructio University, No 248 Guangyuan Zhong Road, 51040 Guangzhou, China.

**JINDAL Manu Parkash,** b. 27 May 1974, Patiala. Advocate Education: BA Hons Political Science, 1995, LLB, 1998, Gur Nanak Dev University. Appointments: Worked in the courts wit Sh V K Sareen, advocate, over 2 years. Publications: Hundred of articles about his Unique Collection of newspapers, which i made into a house of newspapers. Honours: Entry as 'Record' in Manorama year Book, 1996, 1997, 1998, under titl India in Records; Inclusion in Limca Book of Records, 1997 1998, as a National Record. Memberships: Life member, Re Cross Society, Jalandhar; Life member, Youth Hostel Association of India; Life member, PAHAL, a socia organisation; American Centre Library. Address: 42/77 Gree Model Town, Jalandhar 144003, Punjab, India.

**JINDAL Tarsem,** b. 8 July 1951, Jaitu, Punjab, India Specialist. m. Sushil Jindal, 1 son, 1 daughter. Educatior MBBS, 1973; MD, Pediatrics, 1977. Appointments: Consultar Pediatrician, Bhatinda, 1979-86; Senior Pediatrician, Jaipu Golden Hospital, Delhi. Publications: Several articles i professional journals. Honours: Distinguished Science Awarc Memberships: Indian Medical Association; Indian Academy c Pediatrics; National Neonatology Forum; Breast-Feedin Promotion Network of India (BPNI). Address: 13 1st Floor, Kap Vihar, Pitampura, Delhi 110034, India.

**JISHIASHVILI David,** b. 28 January 1950, Tbilisi, Georgia Physicist. m. Manana Kvachantiradze, 1 son, 1 daughte Education: Graduated, Tbilisi State University, 1971; Candidat of Science, 1981; Doctor of Science, 1995. Appointments Head of the laboratory, Laboratory of Composite Films, Institut of Cybernetics Georgian Academy of Sciences; Professo Materials Science Department, Georgian Technical University Publications: 55 publications in refereed journals. Honours First Prize, Mendeleev Scientific Society, 1981; Internationa Man of the Year for 1997/98. Membership: Georgia Optoelectronic Society. Address: 5 Euli Street, 380086 Tbilis Georgia.

**JOB Raymond Franklin Soames,** b. 13 July 1954, Dubb Australia. Academic. 2 sons, 1 daughter. Education: BA Hons University of Sydney, 1977; PhD, University of Sydney, 198E Appointments: Part Time Tutor, 1977-1980; Behaviora Scientist, 1979-82; Senior Behavioural Scientist, 1980-8: Psychologist, 1983-85; Lecturer, 1985-89; Senior Lecture 1990-; Elected, Vice-President, Australian College of Roa Safety, 1998-99; Elected, Secretary, International Commissio for the Biological Effects of Noise, 1998-2000. Publication: Many Published works, Books, Monographs, Book Chapter Journal Articles, Conference Proceedings, Published Abstract Reports, 1981-98. Honours: Rostrum Cup, Public Speakin

972; Tasman-Lovell Memorial Medallion; Visiting Fellowship, wedish Instute, 1994; 500 Leaders of Influence, 1997; 2000 )utstanding People, International Biographical Centre, 1997. .ddress: Dept of Psychology, University of Sydney, NSW 2006, .ustralia.

**JOGLEKAR Satish Dinkar,** b. 25 February 1949, Junnar, ndia. Educator; Researcher. Education: Pre-degree, 1966, re-professional, 1967, BSc, 1969, S P College, University oona; MSc, 1971, IIT, Bombay; PhD, 1975, SUNY at Stony rook. Appointments: Research Associate, Fermilab, Batavia, 975, Institute for Advanced Study, Princeton, 1975-77, niversity of California at Berkeley, 1977-79; Research ssociate, 1980-81 IIT Bombay; Lecturer, 1981-83, Assistant rofessor, 1983-91, Professor, 1991-, IIT Kanpur. Honours: ellow, Maharashtra Academy of Sciences, 1993, National cademy Sciences, India, 1996. Memberships: Institute for .dvanced Study, Princeton; American Physical Society; New ork Academy Sciences. Address: Indian Institute Technology Kanpur, Dept of Physics, Kanpur 208016, India.

**JOHANNESSEN Jon-Arild,** b. 8 December 1949, Mehamn. rofessor. m. Siri Hopland. Education: PhD, Stockholm niversity. Appointments: Professor, 1994-. Publications: 8 ooks; 35 double blind reviewed scientific papers. Honours: 1CB Awards, 1997; Norbert Wiener Award, 1997; MCB wards for Excellence, 1998. Membership: International ybernetic Society. Address: Evenvollen 46, 2623 Gausdal, lorway.

**JOHANSEN Roberto,** b. 19 September 1944, Chihuahua, lexico. Entomologist. Education: National Autonomous niversity of Mexico, 1964; Faculty of Medicine; Faculty of ciences, 1965-69; Postgraduate Studies, Entomology, lational School of Agriculture's Postgraduate College; MSc, iology, National Council of Science Scholarship, UNAM aculty of Sciences, 1974; DSc, Biology, 1977. Appointments: ssociate Researcher, Institute of Biology, 1975-88; Professor, nsect Morphology, Division of Higher Studies, 1982-84; Head f Department, 1985-87; Coordinator, 1987-91. Publications: .uthor of some 80 publications; Articles; Reports; Monographs; ook Chapters about Insecta Thysanoptera. Honours: Medals, iplomas, UNAM, 1986, 1990, 1995; Title, National lesearcher; Board Certified Entomologist, 1996-; ntomological Society of America. Memberships: Sociedad lexicana de Historia Natural; Sociedad Mexicana de ntomologia; Sociedade Entomologica do Brasil; Academia lexicana de Ciencias; Asociación Etnobiológica Mexicana; ntomological Society of America. Address: Instituto De iologica UNAM, Departmento De Zoologia; AP 70-153 Mexico 4510, DF, Mexico.

**JOHARJI Ghazi,** b. 1 February 1957, Beirut. Doctor. m. amar M Al Shible, 2 sons, 1 daughter. Education: MBBS, 984; Certificate, Clinical Training, Otolaryngology, 1989; iploma, Otorhinolaryngology, 1992; Fellowship, Laryngology nd Voice, 1993. Appointments: Senior Registrar, torhinolaryngologist, Riyadh Medical Complex, Saudi Arabia, 993-; Consultant Otorhinolaryngologist, Al-Osrah International lospital, Riyadh, 1997-; Member, Quality Management lepartment, Riyadh Medical Complex, 1997. Publictions: everal professional articles in medical journals. Memberships: audi Otorhinolaryngology Society; Fellow, International college of Surgeons. Address: PO Box 2055, Riyadh 11196, audi Arabia.

**JOHNSON Arnold,** b. 15 September 1955, Baton Rouge, A, USA. Public Relations Marketing. Education: BSc, 1977.

Membership: International Drug Programme, 1997. Address: 2480 78th Avenue, Baton Rouge, LA 70807, USA.

**JOHNSON J Chester,** b. 28 September 1944, Chattanooga. Financial Executive, Poet. m. Freda Stern, 1 son, 1 daughter. Education: Harvard University, 1962-65; BSE, University Arkansas, 1967. Appointments: Senior Analyst, Moodys Investors Services, 1968-71; Head Publisher, Financial Research, Advertising, Group the Morgan Bank, 1972-77; Department Assistant Secretary, US Treasury Department, Washington, 1977-78; Chairman, Princiapal, Government Financial Associations Inc, 1979-; Board of Directors, Chairman, Financial Company, New York State Environmental Facilitites Corporation, 1991-95; Chairman, Federal Task Force to Create National Development Bank; Chairman, Federal, Inter Agency, Task Force for Improvement Governmental Financial Reporting; Chairman, Fund to Assure Public Infrastructure; National Infrastructure Bond Coalition, 1988-91. Publications: OH America, 1967; Family Ties, Internecine Interregnum, 1981; For Conduct and Innocents, 1982; Shorts, For Fun, Not for Instruction; It's a Long Way Home, An American Sequence; Shorts, On Reaching Forty; Exile, Martin; The Professional Curiosity of a Martyr; Freda's Appetite; Lazarus Come Forth; Plain Bob; Psalms in The Book of Common Prayer of the Episcopal Church. Honours: Young South Poets Award; International Poets Award. Memberships: National Association Industrial Public Fiancial Advisors; National Society Mcpl Analysts. Address: 315 E 86th St Apt 16 Ge, New York, NY 10028-4780, USA.

**JOHNSON Jane Penelope,** b. 1 July 1940, Danville, Kentucky, USA. Writer; Poet. m. William Evan Johnson, 15 July 1958, 2 sons. Education: Graduate, Famous Writers School, 1967; Graduate, Newspaper Institute of America, New York. Appointments: Freelance Writer; Advisor, International Society of Poets. Publications: Contributor to World Soccer Magazine; Poetry in many national and international anthologies including American Poetry Anthology, Best Poems of 1997, Best Poems of 1998; Perceptions in Harmony. Honours: 30 Editors' Choice Awards; Semi-Finalist, North American Poetry Open; Honorary Doctor of Letters, London, England, 1993. Memberships: Kentucky Society for Gifted Education; Menninger Sponsor (Mental Health); Charter Member, Peale Center for Christian Living, Pawling, New York. Address: PO Box 8013, Gradenside Branch, Lexington, KY 40504, USA.

**JOHNSON Martha Brown,** b 10 October, Mississippi. Educator. 1 daughter. Education: Master, Public Administration, University of San Francisco; Master of Arts, Secondary Education; Bachelor of Social Science, Jackson State University, Jackson; San Mateo School of Law; College of Notre Dame; Roosevelt University; Chicago State University; Georgia State University. Appointments: Volunteer, Open Door Homeless Shelter, Red Cross of America; Volunteer, Atlanta's Ministry of International Students, ARMIS; Volunteer, Docent Programme, High Museum of Art; Organization Industrial Center Est, Menlo Park, CA, 1978; Executive Director, Neighborhood Housing Services, Menlo Park, 1980-82; Instructor, Humanities, Social Science, English, San Mateo High School, 1978-86; Instructor, Atlanta Public School System, 1987-. Publications: Newspaper and Magazine Articles, Religion, Education and Philosophy; Original Poetry. Honours: National Endowment for the Humanities; Oak Tree Award Winner, Teacher of the Year, 1988. Memberships: Ebenezer Church; Organization of American History Teachers; Georgia Council for the Humanities; National Council for Excellence in Critical Thinking; High Museum of Art; Toni Morrison Society. Address: 1445 Monroe Drive, Appartment F-16, Atlanta, Georgia 30324, USA.

**JOHNSON Martin C,** b. 16 November 1933, Santa Fe, New Mexico, USA. Pediatric Neurosurgery. m. Priscilla B, 1 son, 2 daughters. Education: AB, Stanford University, 1955; MD, Stanford University School of Medicine, 1959. Appointments: Surgical Internship, Stanford University, 1959-60; Assistant Surgical Resident, Presbyterian Medical Center, 1963-64; Mayo Foundation Fellowship Neurosurgery, 1960-61; US Navy Reserve (UC), 1961-63, Active Duty, Reserve, rank of Lt Commander, 1968; Assistant -Chief Neurosurgery president, University of Cincinnati, 1964-68; In private practice neurosurgery, Portland, Oregon, 1968-; Staff, Emanuel Hospital, Neurosurgical Consultant, Shriners Hospital for Crippled Children; Colonel, MC, USAR. Memberships: Fellow, American College of Surgeons; Fellow, American Academy of Pediatrics; Multnomah County Oregon medical societies; American Medical Association; Congress of Neurological Surgeons; American Association of Neurological Surgeons; Pan Pacific Surgery Association; Society for Critical Care Medicine; American Academy of Pediatrics; Northwest Pediatric Neurological Surgery; Portland Academy of Pediatricians; International Society for Pediatric Neurosurgery; American Society of Pediatric Neurosurgery; Multnomah Athletic Club; Columbia Aviation Club. Address: 31870 SW Country View Ln, Wilsonville, OR 97070-7476, USA.

**JOHNSON Robert Leland,** b. 1 May 1933, Denver, Colorado, USA. Attorney at Law. m. Pamela Gay, 1 son, 1 daughter. Education: Yale University, 1955; Juris Doctor, University of Denver, 1958; BA, English, 1962; Human Development Certificate, 1978. Appointments: Assistant Regional Councel, United States General Services Administration; Law Clerk, Justice O Otto Moore of the Colorado Supreme Court; Lecturer, Child Development, University of Colorado, 1978-83; Private Practice, Sole Practitioner, 1962-. Publications: 10 Publications. Honours: Certificate of Merit, University of Denver, 1958; Community Leader of America, 1969, 1972; Denver Opportunity Certificate of Merit, 1967; Colorado Society of the Sons of the American Revolution Patriot Medal, 1976. Memberships: American Bar Association; American Judicature Society; Colorado Trial Lawyers Association; Denver Bar Association; Legal Aid and Public Defender Committee; Familty Law Committee; Interprofessional Committee; Economics of Law Practice Committee; Lawyer Referal Committee; Law Day, USA, Committee; Adams County Bar Association; Colorado Bar Association; Colorado Assocaition for the Gifted and Talented. Address: 534 Pearl St #306, Denver, CO 80203, USA.

**JOHNSON Wylie Pierson,** b. 28 March 1919, Montgomery, Alabama, USA. m. Lurene Hall, 9 November 1946, dec June 1997, 1 son, 2 daughters. Education: BS, Mechanical Engineering, Auburn University, 1942; Utility Management, Georgia Tech; Business Management, La Salle University Correspondence School; Economics night classes, sponsored by Alabama Power; Real Estate Law night classes, University of Alabama at Birmingham. Appointments: Ensign in Navy; Chief Engineer, Executive Officer, rank of Lieutenant, USS Grainger, 1946; Junior Engineer, Senior Engineer, 1947, Supervisor, Transmission Lines, 1952-58, Superintendent of Transmission, 1958-66, Superintendent of Special Services, 1966-74, Manager, General Services, 1974-76, Alabama Power; Retired, 1976. Publications: Numerous articles to professional journals. Honour: AUM School of Business Outstanding Leadership Award, 1999. Memberships include: Chairman, Transmission and Large Substation Committee, Southeastern Electric Exchange, Atlanta; Senior Member, IEEE, chairman, Alabama Section; Birmingham Engineers Club; Shades Valley Exchange Club; President, Vestavia Hill Exchange Club; Montgomery Chapter, Sons of the American Revolution; Advisor, High School Junior Achievement Program Chairman, United Appeal for Alabama Power; Vice President Montgomery Genealogical Society; President, Board o Directors, Pike Road, Alabama Volunteer Fire Department Clerk, Chief Inspector, Mt Meigs. Address: 621 Royal Towe Drive, Birmingham, AL 35209, USA.

**JOINER Elizabeth Garner,** b. 15 February 1939, Atlanta Georgia, USA. Professor. m. Buford Norman. Education: AB La Grange College, Georgia, 1959; MA, University of Georgia 1964; PhD, Ohio State University, 1974. Appointments Teacher, French and English, Franklin County High School Georgia, USA, 1959-60, Winder-Barrow High School, Georgia 1960-62; Graduate Teaching Assistant, University of Georgia 1962-64; Instructor, 1964-65; Instructor of French Winthrop College, South Carolina, 1965-68; Assistant Professor 1968-74; Assistant Professor, French, University of South Carolina, Columbia, USA, 1974-77; Associate Professor 1977-84; Professor, French, 1984-. Publications: Textbooks First Year French, 1974; Départs, 1978; Horizons, 1984; Vidéo Vérité, 1994; Monograph: The Older Foreign Language Learner, 1981; Editor of Developing Communication Skills 1978; Contributor, articles to scholarly books and journals, book chapters, etc including Teaching Listening: How Technology Can Help, 1997; Chevalier dans l'Ordre des Palmes Académiques, 1991. Honours: Phi Beta Kappa; Phi Kappa Phi Memberships: American Association of Teachers of French American Council on the Teaching of Foreign Languages Modern Language Association. Address: 9 Cassia Court Columbia, SC 29209-4226, USA.

**JOKL Miloslav Vladimir,** b. 9 February 1933, Prague Czech Republic. University Professor. m. Jana Spetova, 2 sons. Education: MSc, 1956; PhD, 1963; DSc, 1975. Appointments: Laboratory Head, Institute of Hygiene and Epidemiology, Prague, 1956-77; University Professor, 1977-. Publications include: Microenvironment, 1989. Honours: Medal Czech Medical Society, 1983; Medal, Technical University of Kosice, 1993; Gold Medal, Technical University of Prague, 1998. Memberships: Society of Environmental Technology Society of Built Environment. Address: 60 Na Orechovce, CZ 162 00, Prague 6, Czech Republic.

**JOLOS Rostislav,** b. 11 January 1942, Vladivostak, Russia. Physicist. m. L V Jolos, 1 son, 1 daughter. Education: St Petersburg State University, St Petersburg, 1964; PhD, 1968; DSc, 1977; Professor, 1994. Appointments: Chief, Scientific Group (Sector) in Bogoliubov Laboratory of Theoretical Physics, Joint Institute for Nuclear Research, Dubna. Address: Joint Institute for Nuclear Resarch, 4 Vekslera Str, JINR Dubna, Moscow 141980, Russia.

**JONCZYK Leon,** b. 25 July 1934, Katowice, Poland. Painter: Graphic Artist; Art Historian; Art Theoretician; Art Critic. Education: Art studies, Poland and Netherlands; Dr Prof, Art History and Theory, University (PUL), London. Appointments: University Professor, PUNO; Head of Graphic Art Dept, PUNO/APA; President, Association of Graphic Artists, Munich. Publications: Illustrated monographs about his art; Publications by the artist about experimental printing; Articles in Leonardo; Articles and books about other artists. Memberships: Petite Confrontation Europeenne; ISAST, San Francisco; National and international academies for Art, Sciences and Humanities in Paris, Bordeaux, Naples, Rome. Address: Franz Joseph Str 30/IV, 80801 Munchen, Germany.

**JONES Harold M,** b. 25 March 1934, Chicago, IL, USA Musician. m. Wanda Jeannette, 3 sons. Education: Sherwood Music School, 1951-53; Julliard School of Music, 1955-59.

Appointments: Soloist, Bach Aria Orchestra; New York Sinfonieta; American Symphony Orchestra; Brooklyn Phylharmonic; National Orchestral Association; Municipal Concerts Orchestra; Symphony of the New World; Yachats Music Festival; Audubon String Quartet; Fresk Quartet; Faculty, Manhattan School of Music, Manhattanville College; Westchester Conservatory. Honours: Outstanding Woodwind Player; Arion Award; Key to the City, Jackson, Tennessee. Memberships: National Flute Association. Address: 100 W 94 St, New York, NY 10025, USA.

**JONES Hazel Emma,** b. 6 April 1919, Footscray, Victoria, Australia. Retired Librarian. m. Clifford Henry Jones dec'd, 2 sons, 3 daughters. Education: BA, University of Melbourne, 1943; Associate, Australian Library and Information Association, 1974; Certificate, Sheffield School of Interior Design, 1995. Appointments: Librarian, University of Melbourne, 1935-45; Cataloguer, Church of England Grammar School, 1969-70; Commonwealth Department of Works, 1970-71; Librarian, Greenslopes Repatriation Hospital, 1971-72; Librarian, Acting Librarian, State Department of Health, 1973-94. Publications: Several annual reports. Memberships: Foundation Member, Australian Institute of Librarians and Community Activities; Secretary, Treasurer, President, ALIA. Address: 35 Greer Street, Bardon, Queensland 4065, Australia.

**JONES Jack W,** b. 17 September 1940, Daytona Beach, Florida, USA. Professional Musician. Education: BMus, Stetson University, DeLand, Florida, 1962; Master of Sacred Music, Union Theological Seminary, New York City, 1964; Doctor of Musical Arts, The Juilliard School, New York City, 1973. Appointments: Instructor in Music, Mercer University, Macon, Georgia, 1964-68; Organist, Director, First Baptist Church, Columbus, Georgia, 1967-70; Associate Organist, Choirmaster, Cathedral Church of St John the Divine, New York City, 1970-73; Director of Music Activities, USMA, West Point, New York, 1973-75; Associate Professor of Music, Ouachita University, Arkadelphia, Arkansas, 1975-76, Palm Beach Atlantic College, West Palm Beach, Florida, 1976-78; Organist, First Baptist Church, West Palm Beach, 1976-78, Van Nuys, California, 1978-79; Concert Artist, Palm Beach, 1979-; Organist, Director of Music, Royal Poinciana Chapel, Palm Beach; Director, Founder, Masterworks Chorus, Palm Beaches, 1979-; Music Director, Stage Co of Palm Beaches, 1978-80, Florida Repertory Theatre, 1981-85; Pianist, Burt Reynolds Dinner Theatre, 1980-81; Artistic Director, Gilbert and Sullivan Light Opera, Palm Beach, 1985-, Teen Music Theatre, Palm Beach, 1985-92; Artistic Director, Co-Founder, International Children's Chorus, Palm Beach, 1988-90; Music Director, Culture Theatre Inc, 1993-97, Burt Reynolds Institute of Theatre Training, 1995-96. Memberships: American Choral Directors Association; American Guild of Organists, Palm Beach Chapter; Palm Beach Chamber of Commerce; Governor's Club; Federation Music Club; Civic organisations. Address: 125 Harvard Drive, Lake Worth, FL 33460-6332, USA.

**JONES Martha L,** b. 12 June 1945, Brooklyn, New York, USA. Social Worker. m. Steve R Jones, 1 daughter. Education: B, Juniata College, 1967; MSW, University of Maryland, 1972; PhD, The Fielding Institute, 1990. Appointments: President, Executive Director, Founder, Common Sense Adoption Services and Common Sense Associates; Supervisor, United Methodist Childrens Home, County Child Welfare. Publications include: The Pennsylvania Model: A Guide for Responding to Child Sexual Abuse, 1987; Working with the Unmotivated Client, 1990; Managing Anarchy and Role Conflict, 1990; Role Conflict: Case of Burnout or Energizer?, 1993. Honour:

Pennsylvania Social Worker of the Year, 1997. Memberships: National Association of Social Workers; International Transactional Analysis Association; Executive Women International; Association of Women Therapists; Academy of Certified Social Workers. Address: Common Sense Adoption Services, 5021 East Trindle Road Mechanicsburg PA 17055-3622, USA.

**JONES Thomas Evan,** b. 3 April 1937, Kenosha, Wisconsin, USA. University Professor; Author; Speaker; Consultant (Policy Analyst). Education: BA, Wheaton College, Illinois, USA, 1958; MA, Harvard University, USA, 1963; PhD, Johns Hopkins University, 1964; DSSc, New School for Social Research, 1975. Appointments: Junior Instructor, Johns Hopkins University, Baltimore, 1963-64; Assistant Professor, University Connecticut, Storrs, 1964-67; Member, Faculty, New School for Social Research, New York City, USA, 1972-74; Adjunct Associate Professor, Polytechnic Institute, New York, 1976-78; Consultant, Hudson Institute, New York, 1978-81; Research Coordinator, Goals for Global Society Project, 1975-76; Research Fellow, UNITAR, 1975-76; Seminar Leader, IBM, White Plains, New York, 1973-76, Consultant, Jomar Labs, 1993-. Publications: Author, Options for the Future, 1980; Contributor, articles to professional journals, chapters to books. Aspen Institute Fellow, 1975; International Institute Applied Systems Analysis Fellow, 1975; NSF Fellow, 1972-75; World Future Society, Vice President, New York City Chapter, 1972; International Platform Association. Address: 1648 Cottle Avenue, San Jose, CA 95125-3809, USA.

**JOSAS Tomas,** b. 7 March 1940, Klabai, Silale, Lithuania. Civil Engineer. m. Stase, 2 sons. Education: Diploma Civil Engineer, Kaunas University of Technology, 1965. Appointments: Chairman of Panevezys Council; Mayor, Panevezys City; Panevezys County Governor. Publications: Publications in local newspapers. Address: Vasario Igsios g 27, LT 5319 Panevezys, Lithuania.

**JOSEPH Joseph S,** b. 16 November 1952, Tsada, Cyprus. Professor. m. Eleni Joseph, 2 daughters. Education: BA, Panteion University, Greece; MA, University of Stockholm, Sweden; PhD, Miami University, USA. Appointments: University of Cyprus; University of Alabama, USA; Gustavus Adolphus College; Harvard University, USA; Minister Plenipotentiary, Cyprus. Publication: Cyprus: Ethnic Conflict and International Politics, from Independence to the Threshold of the European Union, book, 1997. Memberships: International Studies Association; British International Studies Association; American Political Science Association. Address: 13 Alfios Street, 2313 Latakamia, Cyprus.

**JOSEPHS Stephanie,** b. 29 September 1965, Willmar, Minnesota, USA. Communications Consultant. m. Nate Josephs, 1 daughter. Education: BA Journalism, 1989, University of Minnesota; Life Operations Management Association course, level 1, 1997. Appointments: Intern, Mona, Meyer & McGrath Public Relations, Bloomington, Minnesota, 1988; PR Manager, The Kit Company, Minneapolis, 1988; Communications Assistant, 1989-90, Communications Administrator, 1990-93, Marketing Services Manager, 1993-94, AAA Minneapolis; Corporate Communications Specialist, MSI Insurance Companies, Arden Hills, Minnesota, 1994-; Independent Marketing Communications Consultant, 1998-. Honours: Recipient 8 Life Communication Associations Awards of Excellence, 1994-97. Memberships: Public Relations Society of America; Toastmasters International. Address: 720 108th Avenue Northwest, Coon Rapids, MN 55448, USA.

**JOSHI Jagmohan,** b. 20 March 1933, Dhanoa, India. Agronomist, Consultant. m. Santosh Sharma, 3 sons. Education: MS, Panjab University, 1960; PhD, Ohio State University, 1972. Appointments: Lecturer, 1956-61; Assistant Agricultural Officer, 1961-66; Research Associate, 1966-73; Researcher Associate, 1973-77; Resarch Assistant Professor, 1977-85; Resaerch Associate Professor, 1985-96; Professor, 1997-. Publications: 10 Publication: Co Author, Soybeans for the Tropics, 1987; Contributing Editor, Technologies for Sustainable Agriculture in the Tropics, 1993; Contributor, Articles to Professional Journals, 1974-. Memberships: American Society of Agronomy Corporation; Crop Science Society of America; Soil Science Society of America; Agricultural Scientists of Indian Origin; American Soybean Association. Address: Univ Md Eas Shore Trigg Hall, Princess Anne, MD 21853, USA.

**JOSHI N M,** b. 11 January 1936, Pune, India. Professor of Education. Education: MA; MEd; PhD. Publications: 28 books in Marathi published. Honour: Honour by Maharashtra Government for best literature. Memberships: 20 institutions. Address: Gandhali Apartments, 1013 Sadashivi Peth, Pune 411030, India.

**JOSHI Rangnath Nathrao,** b. 29 July 1940, Aite, Tq. Bhoom Osmanabad District, India. Law, Prominent Poet, Writer, Actor, Singer. m. Pilubai, 1 son, 1 daughter. Education: HMDs; BTMD; D Lit, Colombo; D Lit, Nanded. Appointments: Composer of 7000 Poems, Lyrics, Marathi, Hinid, English, Sanskrit; Singer; Performer, 1005 Performances; Approved Poet, All India Radio; Artist of Radio; TV Chief Guest; President; Chairman. Publications: Sangram Tutari; Dhaktya Tuljapurchi Tuljabhavani; Bhavdara, Dundhubi, Gitbhavani, Tuljabhavani Mahina; Sachitra Gitashree; Lokmata Ahilyadevi Holkar; Dharmatma; Shri Manik Prabhu Gitayan; Bhaktikaustubha; Ahilyadevi Holkar Gitayan, Shrikashi Jagadguru Charitra Gitganga. Honours: Four First Prized, 1953, 1974, 1976, 1980; 1997, 1999 Special Merit Certificates; Many Medals, Awards, Cups, Honours, Certificates. Memberships: All India Rajendra Samajik Kalyan Parishad Patna; Cultural Kala Pathak Ahmednager; Teachers Seminar of Songs; President, Marathawada University day, Pesident Sahitya Sammelen; Many other memberships. Address: 335 Kaviraj, Near Papnash, Tirtha, At PO Tq Tuljapur, Osmanabad, Maharashtra State, India 413601.

**JOU Jong-Jhy,** b. 15 April 1952, Chia Yi, Taiwan. Professor. m. Li-Ping Chung, 1 son, 2 daughters. Education: BS, 1973, National Central University, Taiwan; MS, 1978, PhD, 1982, Florida State University, USA. Appointments: Teacher, Suway High School, Hualien, Taiwan, 1975-76; Associate Professor, 1982-86, Professor, 1986-, Feng Chia University, Taichung, Taiwan. Publications: Articles in professional journals 1996-. Memberships: Chinese Society Mechanical Engineering; Chinese Society Mathematics; University Reform Union; University Professor Union. Address: Feng Chia University Department of Applied Maths, 100 Wenhwa Road, Taichung 40724, Taiwan.

**JOUVE Daniel Gabriel,** b. 12 October 1938, Paris, France. Consultant. m. Alice Higgins, 2 sons, 1 daughter. Education: Licence en Droit, University of Paris, 1959; Diplome d'Etudes Superieures d'Economie, 1960; Diplome de l'Institut d'Etudes Politiques de Paris, 1960; MBA, Harvard University, USA, 1963. Appointments: Lending Officer, Assistant Manager of Paris Branch, The Chase Manhattan Bank, 1965-68; Development Manager, General Manager, President, Technic Union, Groupe Expansion, 1968-74; Publisher, Founder, Le Nouvel Economiste, 1974-78; General Manager, Russell

Reynolds Associates Inc, 1978-86; President, Founder, Jouv & Associäs, 1986-. Publications include: Men Money ar Motivation; Dix Conseils pour räussir dans votre premier jo Dix Conseils pour vos relations publiques personelles; Vot Carrier, Conseils pour le piloter; Paris: Birthplace of the US. Le Recrutement. Memberships: Board Member, The Friends Franklin, Philadelphia, USA; International Board, World Pape Boston, USA; Harvard Business School Alumni Council; Boa Member, Les Amis du Musée de Blerancourt; Conseiller Tl French Library and Cultural Center (Boston); Honorary Citiz of Vergennes (Vermont). Address: 9 Pl Vauban, 75007, Par France.

**JU Dehua,** b. 9 October 1938, Jiangsu, China. Professor. Guanghua Chen, 1 son. Education: Graduate, Qingh University, 1961; Post-Graduate, 1966. Appointments: Fuzh University, 1966; East China University if Science a Technology, 1974-; Visiting Scholar, University of Marylan 1981-84; ASTI, 1990-. Honours: Talent Nominee Awar Shanghai; State Science and Technology Achievemer Award; State Distinguished Expert Award. Memberships: IEE ACM. Address: Dept of Computer Science, East Chir University of Science and Technology, 130 Meilong R Shanghai 2000237, China.

**JU Ding De,** b. December 1937, Chuxiong, Yun Na Researcher; Teacher. m. Lu Gui mei, 1 son. Education: BS 1958, Department of Chemistry, Yunnan Universi Appointment: Professor, Solar Energy Cell Material Stud 1995-. Publication: New Views on Gai-x AlxAs/GaAs Solar C Structure, 1996. Honour: Second Prize, China Airpla Company, 1996. Membership: Solar Energy Research Institu of Yun Nan Normal University. Address: Solar Energ Research Institute, Yun Nan Normal University, Kun Ming, Y Nan 6500092, China.

**JUENEMANN Rick,** b. 19 October 1921, Washington, US Poet; Writer; Artist. m. Launa J Bullen, 1 son, 2 daughter Career: Background in singing, 1936-40; Freelan professional artist, 1952-95; Stage production, Vagabond Kin 1962; Sold over 3,000 original oil paintings to buye worldwide; Played Thaddeus, Living Last Supper, li dramatization, 1985; Featured extra, Chattahoochie, movi 1988; Television and video commercials, 1988; Sang in cho The Witness, religious play, 1991-95; Several featured par The Living Witness, religious play, 1996; Featured in stage ar video production, The Majesty of Christmas, religious pla 1997. Publication: God Created It All To Him Be the Glor 1992. Honours: Golden Poet Award, 1989, 1990, 1991, 199 Address: 641 Holland Avenue, PO Box 6751, Cayce, S 29171-6751, USA.

**JUG Karl,** b. 12 September 1939, Essen, German University Professor. m. Ulrike Sünderhauf, 1 son, 2 daughte Education: Dipl-Phys, Universität Frankfurt, 1964; Dr phil na Universität Frankfurt. Appointments: Research Associa University of Frankfurt, 1965-67, Illinois Institute of Technolog 1967-69; Assistant Professor, 1969-71, Associate Professc 1971-74, St Louis University; Professor, Universität Hannove 1975-; Visiting Professor, Florida State University, 1970, Joh Hopkins University, 1971, University of Stuttgart, 1972-7 Indian Institute of Technology, Madras, 1987, Jagiellonia University, Krakow, 1989, Academy of Science, Prague, 199 Moscow State University, 1996, 1997, University of Paris, 199 Publications: Mathematik in der Chemie, 1981, 1993; 1 original articles in international journals of chemistry a physics. Honours: Corresponding Member, European Academ of Arts, Sciences and Humanities, 1984-; Membe Humboldt-Gesellschaft, 1993-. Memberships: America hemical Society; American Physical Society; unsen-Gesellschaft; Ges Deutscher Chemiker; International ociety of Mathematical Chemists; World Association of heoretically Oriented Chemists; New York Academy of ciences. Address: Raarangerweg 2, 31832 Springe, iermany.

**JUKNA Ceslovas, b.** 14 September 1932, Lithuania. Head, pecial Zootechnics Department. m. Stefanija Jukniene, 1 son. :ducation: Graduate, Lithuanian Veterinary Academy, 1962; ssociate Professor, 1970; Habil.Dr, 1975; Professor, 1977. :areer: Teacher, 1967-, Dean, 1968-90, Head, Special ootechnics Department, 1972-, Lithuanian Veterinary cademy. Publications: Several articles in professional urnals. Honours: Bonus, Council of Ministers, Russia, 1986; istinguished Scientist in Lithuania, 1986; Order of Gediminas, th degree, 1996. Memberships include: Council, Lithuanian gricultural Sciences. Address: Baltijos 51-24, 3008 Kaunas, ithuania.

**JUNANKAR Pramod Nagorao, b.** 21 May 1943, India. rofessor. m. 2 children. Education: BSc, 1961-64, MSc, 964-66, University of London; PhD, University of Essex, 1984. ppointments: Include, Visiting Fellow, Australian National niversity, 1984-87; Guest Lecturer, University of Warwick, 984-85; Principal Research Fellow, University of Warwick, 984-85; Lecturer, University of Essex, 1969-88; Senior ecturer, Australian National University, 1988-92; Visiting ellow, University of London, 1989; Reader in Economics, ustralian National University, 1993-97; Visiting Fellow, ustralian National University, 1994; Professor, University of Vestern Sydney. Publications: Editorial Boards; Journal lefereeing; Book Reviews; Conference Papers; Seminars; Aonographs; Books, Economics of Unemployment: Causes, onsequences and Policies; From School to Unemployment? he Labour Market for Young People; Marx's Economics; nvestment: Theories and Evidence. Honours: Graduate ursary; Leverhulme Research Studentship. Memberships: merican Economics Association; Economic Society of ustralia; Royal Economics Society. Address: Department of conomics and Finance, University of Western Sydney, Aacarthur, Campbelltown, PO Box 555, New South Wales 560, Australia

**JURENAS Kajetonas, b.** 29 July 1955, Kupiskis, Lithuania. rchitect. m. Grazina Jureniene, 1 son. Education: Honour Diploma, 1977, Vilnius Engineering-Construction Institute, rchitecture Faculty. Appointments: Architect, Institute of Urban Projection and Construction, 1977-90; Architect, K Jurenas Studio of Architecture and Design, 1991-. Career: Projected nd realised over 50 public and living buildings. Membership: icencing Committee of Lithuanian Architects. Address: Stalupenu 4-11, LT 5400 Siauliai, Lithuania.

**JURGAITIENE Kornelija, b.** 19 March 1958, Kaunas, ithuania. Scholar; Diplomat. 1 son. Education: Grad, 1981, /ilnius University; Postgrad Studies, Institute of World iterature, Moscow; PhD Modern American Literature, 1990; IATO Democratic Insts Fellowship, 1993-94. Appointments: lead of Foreign Relations Dept, Lithuanian Academy of Sciences, 1988-92; Head of Int Programmes Dept, Lithuanian State Agency for Research and Development, 1992-93; Senior Programme Officer, UNDP/Lithuania, 1993-94; Charge 'Affaires, Embassy of the Republic of Lithuania, Norway, 994-96; Ambassador Extraordinary and Plenipotentiary, imbassy of the Republic of Lithuania, Norway, 1996-. ublications: Romantic Nationalism and the Challenge of :uropeanisation: a Case of Lithuania, 1993; Democracy in heory and Practice, co-ed, 1993; European Integration and

National Adaptations, 1996; The Baltic States: Re-Nationalisation of Political Space, Neo-Nationalism and Regionality, 1997. Honour: Grand Cross of the Norwegian Order of Merit, 1998. Address: LR Ambasada Norvegijos Karalysteje, Gimle terasse 6, Oslo 0244, Norway.

**JURSENAS Ceslovas, b.** 18 May 1938, Ignaline Region, Lithuania. Journalist. m. Jadvyga, 1 son. Education: Graduate, Vilnius University, 1960. Appointments: Chairman, 1993-96; Member Seimas, 1996-; Chairman, Lithuanian Democratic Labour Party, 1996-. Honours: 1000 World Personalities, 1982. Memberships: Lithuanian Democratic Labour Party, 1996-. Address: Seimyniskiy 30-16, Vilnius, Lithuania.

**JUSEVICIUS Antanas, b.** 6 April 1953, Kaunas City. Wood Sculptor. m. Raimonda, 2 sons. Appointments: Restoration, Various Churches of Lithunaia, 1981-88; Creative Work, Wood Sculptures, 1998-93; Various Exhibitions. Honours: Winner Comp Lithuanian Sculptors, Šepka, 1996; Scholarship of Ministry of Culture, Lithuania, 1998; Diploma, Ministry of Internal Affairs. Exhibitions: 1994-Vilnius, 1995-Rokiškis, Vilnius, 1995-Rokiškis, Kaunas, 1996-Rokiškis, 1997-Kėdainai, Raseiniai, Alytus, Kaunas, 1998- Kaunas, Rumsiškės, Germany (Münsteinach); Wood Sculptors Symposium Germany, 1998. Memberships: Lithuanian Folk Art Society. Address: Baranausko 22-25, 3000 Kaunas, Lithuania.

**JUSKEVICIUS Sarunas, b.** 6 October 1956, Klaipeda, Lithuania. Soloist. m. Virginija, 1 son, 1 daughter. Education: Theoretical Department, Klaipeda St Simkus Music College, 1971-75; Faculty of Music Teaching, Klaipeda Faculty, Lithuanian Conservatory, 1975-79. Appointments: Teacher, Kartena Secondary School, Kretinga District, 1979-83; Soloist, 1983-86; Director, Klaipeda Republic's Opera Theatre, Klaipeda Culture Centre, 1986-87; Soloist, 1987-; Director, Klaipeda Music Theatre, 1987-89. Membership: Lithuanian Theatre Union. Address: Laukininku 7-61, LT 5800 Klaipeda, Lithuania.

**JUSOFF Kamaruzaman, b.** 28 March 1958, Kelantan. Associate Professor. m. Rohaita A Fathel, 4 daughters. Education: PhD, 1992. Appointment: Associate Professor, 1994. Honours: Common Forestry Book Prize, 1979-80; OrSS Award, 1989-92; Travel Grant Award, 1992-, Excellence Service Awards, 1992, 1993; British Chevening Research Award, 1995-96; 20th Century Award, 1997. Memberships: Malaysian Remote Sensing Society. Address: Faculty of Forestry, University Putra Malaysia, Serdang, 43400 Selangor, Malaysia.

**JUSSAWALLA Meheroo, b.** 15 July 1923, India (US Citizen). Telecommunications Economist. m. F Jussawalla (dec), 1 son, 1 daughter. Education: MA, 1945, Madras University; PhD Economics, 1963, Osmania University. Appointments: Dean Social Science, Osmania University; Visiting Professor, Hood College MD, St Mary's College MD; Senior Research Fellow, East West Centre, Honolulu. Publications: 14 books; 150 journal articles. Honours: Awards from Pacific Telecommunications Council, Hawaii, 1996, Atwater Institute Canada, 1990, Fest Schrift, 1998. Memberships: Institute for International Communications, London; International Telecom Society, Pacific Telecom Council. Address: 1601 East West Centre, Honolulu, HI 96848, USA.

**JUTRAS Cindy M, b.** 23 August 1953, Massachusetts, USA. VP, Software Business Applications for Manufacturers. m. B Glenn Jutras. Education: BA Mathematics with Physics, 1975, Merrimack College; MAS Computer Science, 1978, Boston

University. Appointments: Data Processing Manager, Barry Controls, 1975-1977; Project Analyst, ADL Systems, 1977-78; Manager, Product Management Interactive Management and Systems, 1978-83; Manager, Manufacturing Consulting, The Ask Group, 1984-94; VP, Product Strategy, MK Group Computer Associates, 1994-. Publications: Virtually Vertical Manufacturing, 1998; VVM, Transforming the Supply Chain, 1998. Membership: Supply Chain Council. Address: Computer Associates, 1 Tech Drive, Andover, MA 01810 2452, USA.

**JYOTHI Narayana,** b. 2 November 1955, Bangalore. Businessman. m. Ms Gowramma, 1 son, 1 daughter. Education: SSLC. Honours: City Police Night Watch Committee Award. Memberships: President, Karnataka for Kannada Cawallikendra, Bangalore; Vice President, Gokula Welfare Association; Special Police Officer; Secretary, State Kannada Journalim Association. Address: No 16 Vivekanda Road, Gokula Extn, Devasandra K R Puram, Bangalore 36, India.

# K

**KABASAWA Uki,** b. 21 January 1965, Namerikawa, Japan. ᵼysicist. Education: Bachelor Degree, 1988, Master Degree, 90, Osaka University. Appointments: Researcher, Central ᵼsearch Laboratory, 1990-96, Engineer, Electronic Device ᵼnufacturing Equipment and Engineering Division, 1996-99, ᵼgineer, Instruments, Beam Technology Center, 1999-, ᵼachi Ltd. Publications include: Studies of High-Temperature ᵼperconductors, vol 1, 1989, vol 6, 1990; Advances in ᵼperconductivity VI, vol 2, 1994. Memberships: American ᵼsociation for the Advancement of Science; New York ᵼademy of Sciences; The Physical Society of Japan; The ᵼan Society of Applied Physics. Address: Hitachi Ltd, ᵼstruments, Beam Technology Center, 882 Ichige, ᵼachinaka-shi, Ibaraki-ken 312-8504, Japan.

**KABASHI Mirush,** b. 17 April 1948, Shkoder. Actor. m. ᵼeodhora, 2 daughters. Education: High Academy of Arts, ᵼ64-70. Appointments: Actor, 87 roles in theatre, 22 roles in ᵼematography, Participator in over 100 Concerts, Television ᵼcles, 1971-. Publications: Hundreds of articles, Magazines ᵼd press of Albania. Honours: Award of International Festival Experimental Theatre, Cairo, 1997. Memberships: Vice ᵼesident, National Association of Creators and Actors of ᵼanian Satire and Humour. Address: Albania RTV, Tirana, ᵼania.

**KABBANI Sami,** b. 3 Jan 1937, Damascus, Syria. Professor Cardiovascular Surgery. m. Sally, 2 sons, 1 daughter. ᵼucation: BSc, American University of Beirut, Lebanon, 1958; ᵼ), American University of Beirut, 1962; Intern, American ᵼiversity of Beirut, 1962-63. Appointments include: Professor ᵼ Surgery, Damascus University Medical School, 1979-; ᵼrdiovascular Surgeon, Western Heart Institute, San ᵼancisco, California, USA, 1982-83; Chairman, Department of ᵼrdiovascular Surgery, Damascus University Medical School, 97-. Publications include: Diseases of the Heart and Vessels, 92; Experience with Assisted Circulation, 1994; Arterial ᵼronary Revascularization, 1997; Initial Experience with Mitral ᵼmograft Replacement, 1997. Honour: First Degree ᵼesidential Appreciation Award, 1972. Memberships: Arab ᵼyrian) Medical Society, 1969-; American College of ᵼrgeons, 1970-; Denton College of Surgeons, 1970-; Denton Cooley Cardiovascular Society, 1973-; Association of ᵼoracic and Cardiovascular Surgeons of Asia, 1978-; ᵼlifornia Medical Society, 1982-; Arab-American Medical ᵼsociation, 1982-; American College of Cardiology, 1983-; ᵼrian Cardiovascular Association, 1994-; Mediterranean ᵼsociation of Cardiology and Cardiac Surgery, 1998. Address: ᵼmascus Medical School Department Surgery, PO Box 2837, ᵼ) Box 2837, Damascus, Syria.

**KABDEBO Thomas George,** b. 5 February 1934, Budapest. ᵼiversity Librarian; Doctor of History. m. Agnes Wohl, 2 ᵼughters. Education: PhD, University of Budapest, Cardiff, ᵼndon, Manchester. Appointments: Assistant Librarian, ᵼiversity of Cardiff, London; Sub Librarian, University of ᵼnchester; Librarian, University of Guyana, Westminster City ᵼiversity, London, Maynooth Ireland; Librarian, St Patricks ᵼllege, Maynooth and NUI Maynooth. Publications: Hundred ᵼngarian Poems; Diplomat in Exile; Hungary; Evelo; Irorszag ᵼt arca; Blackwell's Missions; The Hungarian Irish Parallel; ᵼnden Idok; Az istenek; Amonnan; The Poetry of Attila Jozsef; ᵼnube Trilogy. Honours: Prix de Poesie; Prix de Historie; Pro ᵼtria, Hungarian State Award for Cultural Achievements; ᵼngarian Order of Merit; Fust Translation Prize of the

Hungarian Academy. Memberships: PEN Club. Address: The Library, St Patricks College, Maynooth, Co Kildare, Ireland.

**KAČERGIENĖ Nella,** b. 19 October 1935, Minsk, Belarus. Physician; Pediatrician. Education: Kaunas Paramedical and Obstetrical School, 1950-54; Kaunas Medical Institute, 1956-62; Hematology Department, Institute of Pediatrics, USSR Academy of Medical Sciences, 1968-70, Postgraduate, 1970-73; Candidate of Science Degree, 1973, Doctor of Science, 1986, USSR Academy of Medical Sciences; Doctor Sci habilitas, Vilnius, 1993. Career: Pediatrician, Prienai District Central Hospital, 1962-67, Republican Vilnius Childrens Hospital, 1967-68, Department of Pediatrics, Lithuanian Scientific Research Institute of Experimental and Clinical Medicine, 1973-85; Senior Research Worker, Lithuanian Scientific Research Institute of Mother and Child Health Care, 1985-91; Leading ChiefScientific Researcher, Centre of Pediatrics, Vilnius University Childrens Hospital, 1991-97; Chief Scientific Worker, Centre of Pediatrics, Vilnius University, 1998-. Publications: Over 190 scientific works. Honours include: Several diplomas of honour; Platinum Record, Superior Talent and Success in Business and the Arts, American Biographical Institute, 1996. Memberships include: Lithuanian Pediatric Academic Council; Russian Academy of Medicine Science Committee of Biorhythmology, Moscow; National Geographic Society, USA; International Society of Bromeorology, USA; International Committee for Research and Study of Environmental Factors, CIFA, Belgium; Lithuanian National Committee of the United Nations Children's Fund. Address: Viršuliškių 89-22, 2056 Vilnius, Lithuania.

**KADA Morihiro,** b. 5 May 1947, Osaka, Japan. Semiconductor Packaging Manager. m. Takako Hayama, 1 son, 1 daughter. Education: Bachelor of Applied Physics, 1970. Appointments: Department General Manager, VLSI Development Laboratories, 1994-98; Departmental General Manager, System LSI Development Center, Sharp Corporation, 1998. Publications: Several articles in professional journals. Memberships: Electronic Industries Association of Japan; Semiconductor Equipment and Materials International; Institute for Advanced Micro-system Integration. Address: 25-9 Higashikatazoe, Kawachinagano, Osaka 586-0045, Japan.

**KADHUM Abdul-Ameer Sahib,** b. 1956, Babylon, Iraq. University Professor. m. Ashwaq M Ali, 1 son, 3 daughters. Education: BSc, 1977, MSc, 1979, PhD, 1995, all in Chemical Engineering. Appointments: Assistant Lecturer, Institute of Technology, Baghdad, 1979; Lecturer, 1981; Assistant Professor, 1995; Consulting Chemical Engineer for Oil Companies, 1995. Publications: Translation, Fluid Flow for Chemical Engineers, 1992; Many papers published in journals. Memberships: Institution of Chemical Engineers, UK; Engineers Union, Iraq. Address: PO Box 15865, Azzawiya, Libya.

**KADIJEVIC Djordje,** b. 6 January 1933, Shibenik, Croatia. Film Director; Art Historian. m. Danica, 1 son, 1 daughter, deceased 1997. Education: Graduated Art History, 1960. Appointments: Art Critic, 1959-; Film Director, 1967-. Appointments: Film festival in Pula for debut directory, 1967; Chianzano, Italy. Honour: Award for Best TV-Serial, 1988. Memberships: AICA; Association of Serbian Film Workers. Address: Praska 35, 1100 Belgrade, Serbia.

**KAGEYAMA Taro,** b. 13 February 1949, Kobe, Japan. Theoretical Linguist; Educator. m. Reiko Jinnaka, 2 daughters. Education: BA, 1971, MA, 1973, Osaka University of Foreign Studies, Japan; PhD, University of Southern California, USA, 1977. Appointments: Instructor, Kobe Gakuin University, Japan, 1973-74; Assistant Professor, 1978-80, Associate Professor,

1980-87, Osaka University; Professor, Kwansei Gakuin University, 1987-. Publications: In Japanese: Lexical Structures, 1980; Grammar and Word Formation, 1993; Verb Semantics, 1996; Word Formation and Conceptual Structure, 1997. Honours: Ichikawa Award, 1980; Kindaichi Award, 1994. Memberships: Linguistic Society of America; Linguistic Society of Japan; English Linguistic Society of Japan. Address: Kwansei Gakuin University, Uegehara 1-1-155, Nishinomiya 662-8501, Japan.

**KAHOA Linda Lou**, b. 7 March 1943, Springfield, Greene Co, Missouri, USA. Public Relations Consultant. m. G M "Mike" Kahoa, 2 sons, 1 daughter. Education: SW Missouri State University. Appointments: Editor, Milking Shorthorn Journal, 1974-78; Owner Sales Management, Public Relations Home Based, 1980-. Publication: Editor, 100 Year History of Roger Mills County, UK, 1994. Memberships: Washita Battlefield Historical Society, Secretary, Editor; Platonic GWFC Club. Address: Kahoa Productions RR 1 Box 106, Cheyenne, OK 73628 9759, USA.

**KAIRUKI Hubert Mwombeki C**, b. 24 June 1940, Bukoba, Tanzania. Medical Doctor. m. Kokushubila Kairuki, 3 sons, 2 daughters. Education: MB, ChB, 1968; MRCOG, Royal College of Obstetricians and Gynaceologists, 1974; M Med, 1974. Appointments: Director General, Mission Mikocheni Hospital; Chairman, Mission Mikocheni Health and Education Network; Vice-Chancellor, Mikocheni International University. Honours: Pope Paul II's Award for Distinguished Service, 1990; Fellow, Royal College of Obstetricians and Gynaecologists, 1992; Hunterian Professorship, 1993. Memberships: Medical Association of Tanzania; Association of Private Hospitals in Tanzania; Association of Gynaecologists of Tanzania; International Federation of Gynaeology and Obstetrics; SOFIGO; Tanzania Association of Private Universities; New York Academy of Sciences. Address: Mission Mikocheni Hospital, PO Box 65300, Dar-es-Salaam, Tanzania.

**KAJINO Akihide**, b. 29 January 1955, Sapporo, Japan. Orthopaedist; Rheumatologist. Education: MD, 1989, Honorary Lecturer, 1993, Nippon Medical School, Tokyo. Appointment: Chief Surgeon, Department of Orthopedics, Shitaya Hospital. Publications: Several articles in professional journals. Memberships: Japanese Orthopaedic Association; Japan Rheumatism Association; Japanese Association of Rehabilitation Medicine. Address: Shitaya Hospital, Department of Orthopaedics, 3-12-40 Negishi Taito-ku, 110-0003 Tokyo, Japan.

**KAJITANI Motohisa**, b. 8 May 1937, Gifu, Japan. University Professor. m. Yoko Shimizu, 1 daughter. Education: BA, 1961, University of Tokyo; MA, 1964, Kyoto University, Japan. Appointments: Non-resident member, Queen Elizabeth House, Oxford, 1972-74; Visiting Professor, Dept Sociology, UCLA, 1990; Chairman, Meijo University Library. Publications: Press and Empire, 1981; Sociologie Globale, 1987; Essays in International Sociology, 1999. Honour: Awarded life membership from International Sociological Association, 1997. Membership: International Sociological Association. Address: Meijo University, 501 Shiogamaguchi, Nagoya 468, Japan.

**KAJIWARA Kagemasa**, b. 5 October 1958, Tokyo, Japan. Neuroscientist. m. Shiori, 1 daughter. Education: Bachelor of Dentistry, 1984; PhD, 1988. Appointments: Research Asistant, Kanegawa Dental College, 1988-90; Research Worker, 1988-90, Lecturer, 1996-; Tokai University. Lecturer, 1990-95; Lecturer, Keio University, 1993-96. Memberships: AAAS; Physiological Society of Japan; Molecular Biology Society of

Japan. Address: Institute of Medical Science, Tokai Universit Bohseidai, Isehara 259-1193, Japan.

**KALAFATI Dmitriy D**, b. 11 March 1914, Moscow, Russi Professor. m. Natali Kalafati, 1 son, 1 daughter. Educatio Odessky Politechnical Institute, 1940; PhD, 1948; DSc, 196 Appointment: Professor, Moscow Power Institute. Publicatior Six books, 98 publications in scientific journals. Addres Energeticheskay a 16, Kor 1, K 140, 111116 Moscow, Russi

**KALAPESI Roshan Minocher**, b. 21 May 1925, Bomba Designer. Education: BSc Hons, University of Bombay, 194 J J School's Art Diploma, Institute of Paris; Design and Colo Psychiatry, Eric Dust. Appointments: Joined Family Busines Shannon Chemical Works, 1948-60; Managing Directc Shannon Chemical Works, 1965-; Publications: Tŀ Splendoured One; Cyrus the Great; Pinnochio, Calcutta Scho of Music; Oliver, Calcutta School of Music; Several Magazine and Newspaper, World Wide. Honours: Dictionary International Biography, International Biographical Centr World Who's Who of Women, IBC; International Directory Distinguished Leadership, USA. Address: 2 Burhani Mahal, ![ L Jagmohandas Marg; Mumbai 400 006; India.

**KALE G B**, b. 1 December 1947, Nagpur, India. Scienti Officer. m. Mrs Sharayu, 1 son, 1 daughter. Education: BS 1967; BE, 1971; MSc (Tech), 1979; PhD (Tech), 198 Appointments: Group Leader, Diffusion and EPMA Laborator Publications: About 70 publications in scientific journa Address: Materials Science Division, BARC, Mumbai 40008 India.

**KALE Govind**, b. 2 June 1950, Bembale, Taluka Madŀ District, Solapur, Maharashtra State. Storekeeper. m. Suma V Lakade, 2 s, 1 d. Education: SSC, March, 1970; B com, Pa II, March, 1972. Appointments: Muster Karkoon, 197 Assistant Store Keeper, 1974; Store Keeper, 1993. Publicatio Dastaiwaj, poetry, 1994. Honours: Balakawi Thombare Awar Sudhakar Nerelekar Award; Granthottejak Awar Memberships: Storekeeper Union; Organiser, Rashtra-prer Sanghatana. Address: Solapur PatBandhare, Vasaha Gurunanak, Solapur 413003, India.

**KALEDIENE Birute**, b. 27 December 1934, Baltrusiai, Sak area, Lithuania. Trainer. m. Vytautas Kaleda, 2 daughter Education: Higher Education Diploma, 1957, Agricultur Academy, Faculty of Agronomy; Trainer's Profession Certificate, 1973, Sports College of Lithuania. Appointment Athlete, track and field, 1955-64; Member of National Tear world record in javelin, 1958, in Tbilisi, 1949, 1957; Bronz Medal, 1960, Olympic Games in Rome; 4th Place, 1964, Toky Olympics; Triner, 1964-. Honours: European Vice-Champioı 1958; 12 times Champion of Lithuania; 3 times Champion the USSR; Master of Sports of the Highest Class of the USS and Lithuania; Highest Category Trainer of Lithuania; Fair Pla Award, 1996. Memberships: Lithuanian Athletics Associatioı President of Athletics Veterans Association. Address: Zeim 28a 47, LT 3000 Kaunas, Lithuania.

**KALEMBASA Stanislaw Jon**, b. 6 May 1941, Polan Professor. m. Dorothe, 1 son, 1 daughter. Education: Phľ 1971, Assistant Professor, 1978; Associate Professor, 198 Professor, 1992. Appointments: Professor, Head, Soil Scienc and Plant Nutrition, Department of Agriculture and Pedagogic University, Siedlce. Publications: 272 in professional journal Honour: Knight of the Order of the Cross of the Polis Reneissance. Memberships: International Soil Science Societ Address: ul 3 Maja 54, 08 110 Siedlce, Poland.

**KALGIN Yuri,** b. 10 November 1948, Kostroma, Russia. Physicist. m. Orlova Galina, 1972, 2 sons. Education: Graduate, Physics Faculty, Moscow State University, 1973; PhD, Physics and Mathematics, 1992; Senior Scientist, 1993. Appointments: Head, Ionaspheric Laboratory, 1997-; Senior Scientist, 1993-. Publications: 21 publications in scientific journals in the area of dynamics in lower thermosphere, 1978-97. Membership: COSPAR Associate Member, 1994-. Address: Institute of Applid Geophysics, Rostokinskeya 9, 129128 Moscow, Russia.

**KALISNIK Miroslav,** b. 8 April 1927, Videm Ob Savi. Physician; Educator. m. Nevenka Orazem, 1 son, 1 daughter. Education: MD, 1952, Medical Faculty in Ljubljana; PhD, 1960, University in Ljubljana. Appointments: Demonstrator, University Medical Faculty in Ljubljana, 1947; Assistant, 1953; Assistant Professor, 1961; Associate Professor, 1967; Full Professor, 1972; Emeritus Professor, 1996. Publications: Over 200 research articles; 4 books. Honours: Vice Rector, 1991-93; Scientific Co-worker, Slovenian Academy Sciences and Arts, 1963. Memberships: Slovenian Medical Journal, Editor, 1967-80, Chief and Responsible Editor, 1980-88; Acta Stereologica, Chief Editor, 1982-; Slovenian Medical Orthography, Chief Editor, 1979-. Address: Prijateljeva 9, 1000 Ljubljana, Slovenia.

**KALLIONTZIS Constantine,** b. 1 December 1954, Athens, Greece. Civil Engineer. Education: BSc Honours, Class I, 1977, PhD, 1981, Leeds University, England. Appointment: Computational Hydraulics, privately owned office specialising in Applied Computational Engineering, Nea Smyrni, Athens, 1982-. Publications: Contributor to journals Computers and Structures, 1996, 1997, Earthquake Engineering and Structural Dynamics, 1998, Communications in Numerical Methods in Engineering, 1998, International Journal of Offshore and Polar Engineering, 1998. Membership: Greek Technical Chamber. Address: Computational Hydraulics Office, 70 Omirou Street, Nea Smyrni 17 121, Athens, Greece.

**KALMBACH Gudrun,** b. 27 May 1937, Grosserlach, Germany. Professor. Education includes: PhD, Mathematics, University of Göttingen, 1966. Appointments: Lecturer, University of Illinois, Urbana, USA, 1967-69; Assistant Professor, University of Massachusetts, Amherst, 1970-71, Pennsylvania State University, University Park, 1969-75; Professor of Mathematics, University of Ulm, Germany, 1975-. Honours: 3 medals; 2 books dedicated to her 60th birthday. Memberships: American Mathematical Society; AWM; DGHK; Emmy Noether Verein; FDP; GFPI; NY Acady of Scis; OIA. Address: PF 2744, D-89017 Ulm, Germany.

**KALTENBACH Anneliese,** b. Karlsruhe Durlach. Senior Civil Servant. Education: Maturity Certificate; Diploma, Commercial French; Diploma, Commercial English; Russian Language, Literature Studies; PhD, Paris University, 1962. Appointments: English, French Interpreter and Translator; Senior Civil Servant, German Embassy, Paris; Press and Information Office of the Federal Government, Bonn. Publications: Ludwig Haeusser, Historian et Patroite 1818-1867, 1965. Honours: Gold Medal, Robert Schuman, 1966; Chevalier dans l'Ordre des Palmes Académiques, 1968; Officier dans l'Ordre des Palmes Académiques, 1995; Officier de l'Ordre de Leopold, 1971; Commander, Oranje Nassau Orden, 1971; Commandeur, Ordre du Mérite du Grand Duché de Luxembourg, 1974; Officier dans l'Ordre National du Mérite de la République Française, 1975; Commandeur dans l'Ordre National du Mérite de la République Française; Federal Merit Cross First Class of the Silver Medal, German, French Youth Office. Memberships: AIDLUPA, 1961; Association des

Membres de l'Ordre des Palmes Académiques, 1968; International Biographical Center; American Biographical Association. Address: Duerenstrasse 29, D 53173 Bonn, Federal Republic of Germany.

**KAMABE Hiroshi,** b. 24 February 1960, Ayabe, Kyoto, Japan. Assistant Professor. Education: BS, 1982, MSc, 1984, Toyohashi University of Technology; PhD, Nagoya University, 1994. Appointments: Research Assistant, Mie University, Japan, 1984-94; Assistant Professor, 1994-98, Visiting Researcher, Technical University of Eindvoven, 1996; Assistant Professor, Gifu University, Japan, 1998-. Publications: Stochastic Process (co-auth); Technical papers to IEEE journals, 1989, 1991, 1993. Memberships: IEEE; IEICE. Address: 6-34 Daifuku, Gifu 502-0934, Japan.

**KAMAMI Yves-Victor,** b. 9 April 1958, Paris, France. Medical Doctor. m. Corinne Dilouya, 2 sons, 1 daughter. Education: Prizewinner, Paris Medical University, 1986; Graduate, Oto-Rhino-Laryngology, 1987. Appointments: Resident, Paris Area Hospitals, 1982-87; Assistant, Foch Hospital, 1988-92; ENT Consultant, Paris Hospital, 1989-92; Consultant, Saint Cloud Hospital and London Diagnostic Centre, London, currently; Private Practice, Astor Medical Centre, currently. Publications: Snoring: How to cure it with laser, book, 1991; Laser in Medical Practice, book, 1997; 11 medical articles. Memberships: French Society of Oto-Rhino-Laryngology; French Society for Laser Medicine and Surgery; Corresponding member, American Academy of Otolaryngology-Head and Neck Surgery; Honorary member, South African Society of Oto-Rhino-Laryngology; European Sleep Research Society; American Society for Laser Medicine and Surgery; International Association for the Study of Pain. Address: 43BD Malesherbes, 755008 Paris, France.

**KAMAN Jiri,** b. 31 March 1926, Dolni Loucky, Czech Republic. Veterinary Anatomy Professor. m. Anna, 1 daughter. Education: DVM, 1954; Candidatus Sci, 1962; Docent, 1964; DSc, 1990; Professor, 1993. Appointments: Assistant Lecturer, 1954-63; Doc, 1964; Reader, Veterinary Anatomy, Head, Anatomical Institute, 1965-70; Head Researcher Team, Institute of Pathology, 1971-89; Professor of Anatomy, 1990-93; Professor, Postgraduate Study, 1972-92; Cons State Breed Pigs F, 1975-89; Cons Transplant Centre, Medical Faculty, 1969-89. Publications: Co-Author, 35 Textbooks; 3 Science Books; Over 350 Articles in Scientific and Professional Journals. Honours: State Agricultural Publishing House Award; Czech Founder Technician Award; Ministry of Education Award. Memberships: Czech Anatomy Society; Czech Zoological Society; Czech Biological Society; International Com Avian Anatomical Nomenclature; World Association of Veterinary Anatomy; European Association of Veterinary Anatomy. Address: Sumavska 25, 602 00 Brno, Czech Republic.

**KAMBHAMPATI Venkata Sambasiva Rao,** b. 16 July 1965, Marlapalem Village, India. College Educator; Researcher. m. Venkata Suvarna Kambhampati, 1 son, 1 daughter. Education: BE, Industrial Production, 1st Division, University of Mysore, 1987; ME, Systems and Information, 1st Division, BITS, Pilani, 1990; PhD, Decision Support Systems, 1st Division, Indian Institute of Technology, Delhi, 1996. Appointments: Lecturer, G N D Engineering College, Bidar, 1987-88; Lecturer, College of Engineering, Osmanabad, 1988-89; Engineer, G E (I) Ltd, Bahadurgarh, 1990; Research Scholar, Indian Institute of Technology, Delhi, 1991-95; Reader, S R K P G Centre, Nandyal, 1995-96; Assistant Professor, V R Siddhartha Engineering College, Vijayawada, 1996-; Consultant to Madanapally Institute of Technology and Science. Publications:

Co-author of 5 research papers in international journals, 2 in national journal and 2 in conference proceedings. Memberships: Life Member, Indian Society for Technical Education; Life Member, Indian Society for Mechanical Engineers; Life Member, System Society of India; Life Member, Computers and Information Science Society. Address: Computer Science and Engineering Department, V R Siddhartha Engineering College, Vijayawada 520007, Andhra Pradesh, India.

**KAMBLE Jagannath Sitaram,** b. 5 October 1961, India. m. Sunandabai, 2 sons, 1 daughter. Education: DNM; NN CAL; MN. Publications: Uddhwasta; Jwalamukhi. Membership: Muktangan Sahitya Mandal, Beed. Address: Raj Kaml Tadpatri Center, Ahamad Nagar Road, Beed Maharastra 431122, India.

**KAMEI Tsutomu,** b. 29 May 1960, Shimabara, Japan. Researcher. Education: Diploma in Medicine, 1985, MD, 1985, PhD, 1989. Appointments: Physician, Saitama Childrens Medical Center, 1989; Researcher, Shimane Medical University, 1990; Director, Administrative Director, Shimane Institute of Health Sciences, 1994; Part-time Lecturer, Kanazawa Medical University, 1998, Ochanomizu University, 1999. Publications: Several articles in professional journals. Memberships: WFMH; IUHPE; Japanese Society for Alternative Medicine and Treatment. Address: Shimane Institute of Health Sciences, 223-7 Enya-cho, 693-0021 Izumo Shimane, Japan.

**KAMENOV Borislav,** b. 18 April 1936, Sofia, Bulgaria. Geologist. m. Nadejda Angelova, 1 son, 1 daughter. Education: MSi, 1959, Higher Mining and Geological University, Sofia; PhD, 1972, Bulgarian Academy of Sciences, Geological Institute. Appointments: Prospector, 1959; Assistant Professor, Sofia University, 1966; Lecturer, 1971; Associate Professor, 1981; Professor, 1997; Adviser for the Ministry of Mineral and Water Resources, Somalia, 1974-77. Publications: Over 50 scientific papers in magazines; 3 monographic books. Memberships: Bulgarian Geological Society; Bulgarian Antarctic National Committee, President. Address: Sofia University, 15 Bd Tzar Osvoboditel, Sofia 1000, Bulgaria.

**KAMENOVA Gjulemetova,** b. 7 November 1939, Sofia, Bulgaria. Associate Professor; Historian of Fine Arts (Visual). m. Kiril Gjulemetov, 3 daughters. Education: School of Art, Sofia, 1958; Academy of Fine Arts in Sofia, 1958-63; Studied, graduated, History and Theory of Art, Sankt Peterburg, Academy of Arts, Russia, 1963-67. Appointments: Historian of Art, National Institute of Monuments, Sofia, 1966-70; Editorial Staff, Magasin of Art, 1970-72; Assistant, Academy of Fine Arts, Sofia, 1972; Doctor, 1986; Associate Professor, 1987-. Publications: Books on medieval mural paintings in the Bulgarian churches; Articles in books for education in visual art. Memberships: AICA; ICOMOS. Address: 15 Elemag St Bl 307 ap 60, 1113 Sofia, Bulgaria.

**KAMEYAMA Michitaka,** b. 12 May 1950, Utsunomiya, Japan. Professor. m. Kimiko Owashi, 1 son, 2 daughters. Education: B Engineering, 1973, Master of Engineering, 1975, Doctor of Engineering, 1978, Tohoku University, Sendai, Japan. Appointments: Research Associate, 1978-81, Associate Professor, 1981-91, Professor, 1991-, Tohoku University. Honour: Fellow, IEEE, 1997. Memberships: Institute of Electrical and Electronics Engineers. Address: 6-10-8 Minami Yoshinari, Sendai Miyagi 989-3204, Japan.

**KAMIENSKA-CARTER Eva Hanna,** b. 19 February 1960, Warsaw, Poland. Designer; Artist. m. Bernard Owen, 2 daughters. Education: Masters Degree, Architecture, Warsaw Technical University, Warsaw, Poland, 1983; Graduate with

Honours, Art Institute of Pittsburgh, 1991; Certificate to Practice Art, Ministry of Culture, 1983. Appointments: Free Lance Artist, Design Consultant, Warsaw, Poland, 1983-87; New York City, Detroit, Boston, 1987, 1991, 1991; Partner, Designer, Carter-Kamienska Design, Pittsburgh; Art Teacher, Carnegie Museum of Art, 1991-92; Pittsburgh Centre for the Arts, 1991-92; Set Designer, Motion Pictures, 1994-. Memberships: Pittsburgh Center for the Arts; Associated Artists of Pittsburgh. Address: 853 Phineas St, Pittsburgh, PA 15212-8026, USA.

**KAMILI Azra Nahaid,** b. 28 August 1958, Srinagar. University Teacher. m. Zaffar Abbas Khatib, 2 sons. Education: MSc; M Phil; PhD. Appointments: Assistant Research Officer, 1984-85; Lecturer, Degree College, 1985-86; Lecturer, University of Kashmir, 1986-97; Reader, 1997-. Publications: 15 Publications in scientific journals. Memberships: Life Member, Oriental Science, Kashmir University; Executive Council Member of KUTA. Address: CORD, University of Kashmir, Srinagar, Kashmir, India.

**. KAMRAVA Mehran,** b. 1 February 1964, Karaj, Iran. Professor. m. Melisa Canli. Education: PhD, Social, Political Science, University of Cambridge, 1989. Appointments: Assistant Professor, Political Science, California State University. Publications: Revolutionary Politics, 1992; The Political History Of Modern Iran: From Tribalsim to Theocracy, 1992; Politics and Society in the Third World, 1993; Democracy in the Balace, Culture and Society in the Middle East, 1998; Cultural Politics in the Third World, 1999. Memberships: American Political Science Association; Middle East Studies Association. Address: 9007 Ehwanda Avenue, Northridge, CA 91325, USA.

**KAN Chu-Cheng,** b. 19 October 1924, Hsiu Jen County, China. Electronics Company Executive. m. Man Chih, 2 sons, 1 daughter. Education: MPA, Century University, 1978. Appointments: Research Associate Fellow, Institute of International Relations, Taiwan, 1967-77; Chief Director, Research, Development and Evaluation Commission, Taiwan, 1977-82; Counsellor, Ministry of Finance, Taiwan, 1982-84; Ministry of Economic Affaris, Taiwan, 1984-85; Embassy China, South Africa, 1985-89; Chairman, Mustek Ltd, Johannesburg, South Africa, 1990-; Chairman, CEO, Continental Weapons (Pty) Ltd, Johannesburg, South Africa, 1994-. Memberships: Association of Chinese Industrialists, South Africa; Confederation Employers South Africa. Address: PO Box 6692, Halfway House 1685, South Africa.

**KAN Min,** b. March 1934, Hefei, China. Research Professor. m. Wang Dao Hong, 3 daughters. Education: BS Degree in Solid State Physics, Fudan University, 1956. Appointments: Vice President, Southwest China Institute of Applied Magnetics, 1980-86; Vice President, Shanghai University of Science and Technology, 1987-95. Honours: The First Award of Electronics, Industry Ministry of PR China, 1980; Diploma of Outstanding Achievement of China State, 1993. Memberships: Shanghai Committee of CPPCC, 1987-. Address: Shanghai University, Jiading District, Shanghai 201300, China.

**KANAGY Steven Albert,** b. 26 September 1956, Chicago, USA. Foundation Administrator. Education: Kendall College, Illinois, 1974-76; W Carey College, Hatiesburg, 1980. Appointments: Staff Worker, Longbeach Public Library, 1978; Manager, Kanagy Art Foundation Inc, Longbeach, 1982-; Lead Director, 1997-; Distributor, Amway Corporation, Michigan, 1984-; Manager, Partner, Southeastern Restorations and Industrial Trading, 1992-; Lead Director, Kanagy Art Foundation Inc, 1998. Publications: Articles. Memberships: American Management Association; National Trust for Historica eservation; National Geographic Society; International atform Association. Address: PO Box 1014, Long Beach, MS ₦560-1014, USA.

**KANAILAL Das,** b. 1 January 1939, Manuchak. Teacher; urnalist. m. Arati, 2 sons, 2 daughters. Education: BA, 1962; ₦ Hons, 1964; BT, 1966; MA, 1969. Appointments: ₦achership, 1963; Editor, Journalist, 1982. Publication: ₦ngrami Nandigram. Memberships: West Bengal Union of ₦urnalist; Midnapur District News Papers Association. ₦dress: Sarat Rashmoni Bhaban, P O Manuchak, Midnapur, ₦est Bengal, India.

**KANAKA Jiri,** b. 28 June 1925, Prague, Czech Republic. ₦ysician; Gynecologist. m. Dajo, 1 son, 1 daughter. ₦ucation: MD, Charles University, 1950; PhD, 1965; DSc, ₦69; Professor, 1987. Appointments: Founder, Member, ₦ernational Study Group of Detection and Prevention of ₦ncer, 1968-83; President, Czech Society, 1976-88. ₦blications: 279 publications; 10 monographs. Honours: ₦vard of Minister of Health; JE Parkynje Medal; Medal, 650th ₦niversary of Charles University. Memberships: 3rd Medical ₦culty; IFCPE. Address: Dept Gyne Obs Third Med Fac, ₦arles University, Srobarova 50, 100 00 Prague 10, Czech ₦public.

**KANDA Selichi,** b. 22 May 1927, Kobe. Professor in ₦emistry. m. Atsuko, 1 son. Education: Bachelor, Osaka ₦iversity, 1953; DSc, Osaka University, 1962. Appointments: ₦tructor, Osaka City University, 1953; Inst, Osaka University, ₦62; Professor, Tokushima University, 1964. Publications: 40 ₦emical research papers in scientific journals; Organic ₦miconducting Polymers, 1968. Membership: Chemical ₦ciety Japan. Address: Kami Hachman Nishi Yama 498, ₦kushima 770-8041, Japan.

**KANDEEL Elsayed Ezzat,** b. 26 September 1938. ₦ofessor; UN Expert. m. Fikrya, 2 daughters. Education: BSc ₦ri Sc, 1960, MSc, 1963, PhD, Forest and Wood Science, ₦wa State, USA, 1968; FIWSc, UK, 1974. Appointments: ₦rector, Forestry Dept, Alexandria University. Publications: ₦2 international publications in USA, Egypt, Middle East and ₦urope. Memberships: Fellow, Institute of Wood Science, UK; ₦ppi, USA; For Pr So, USA. Address: Meteorolgy and Envir. ₦r. College, PO Box 9034. King Abdul Aziz University, Jeddah ₦4413, Saudi Arabia.

**KANDIAH Silva,** b. 15 October 1950, Singapore. Airline ₦anager. m. Chrystaleen, 1 d. Education: BA Hons, English, ₦iversity of Singapore, 1973. Appointments: Airline Executive, ₦76-84; Airline Manager, 1984-92; General Manager, SATS ₦curity Services, 1992-. Honours: Colombo Plan Award, 1970. ₦emberships: International Association of Chiefs of Police; ₦orldwide Church of God; Airline Club of Singapore. Address: ₦ate Security Services Pte Ltd, P O Box 3, Singapore, Changi ₦rport, Singapore 9181.

**KANDRAC John Jr,** b. 22 February 1953, Cleveland, Ohio, ₦SA. Education: BSc, Bowling Green State University, Ohio, ₦SA, 1984. Appointments: US Department of Defense, ₦entagon, Washington, DC, USA; US Department of Defence, ₦hina Lake NAWC, China Lake, CA, USA; US Department, ₦ISA Headquaters, Arlington, VA, USA. Honours: Outstanding ₦oung Man of America, 1984; Second place, Pentagon recipe ₦ontest, Washington, DC, 1990; Who's Who in Media and ₦ommunications, ist Edition, 1998. Memberships: BCA, ₦ioCommunications Association, Inc.; AFCEA, Armed Forces ₦ommunications and Electronics Association; NPS, Nikon

Professional Services; NRA, National Rifle Association. Address: PO Box 762, Newington, VA 22122, USA.

**KANEKI Tadashi,** b. 18 April 1944, Tokyo, Japan. Division General Manager. m. Sumiko Kaneki, 2 daughters. Education: BS, Mechanical Engineering, 1967, MS, Mechanical Engineering, 1969, Tokyo University, Japan. Appointments: Department Manager, Compressor Design, Tsuchiura Works, Hitachi Ltd, 1986-93; Department Manager, Industrial Machinery Department, 1994-96, Division General Manager, Environmental System and Plant Engineering Division, 1996-, Hitachi Ltd. Honour: Speaker Presenter, Design Automation of Centrifugal Compressors, Turbo-Machinery Symposium, 1978. Memberships: ASME; JSME. Address: Ibaraski Prefecture, 1-11-18 Tsuwa, Tsuchiura T300, Japan.

**KANG Sa-Ouk,** b. 10 Feb 1952, Seoul, Korea. Professor of Biophysics. m. Jung-Hwa Lee Kang, 1 son, 1 daughter. Education: BS, Microbiology, College of Liberal Arts and Sciences, 1974, MS, Microbiology, Graduate School, 1976, Seoul National University, 1974; PhD, Biophysics, Institut für Biophysik, Justus Liebig Universität, Giessen, 1983. Appointments: Lecturer of Biology, Korea Military Academy, 1976-79; Part-time Lecturer, 1978-79, Assistant Professor of Biophysics, 1984-88, Associate Professor of Biophysics, 1988-93, Department Chairman, 1991-93, Professor of Biophysics, 1993-, Department of Microbiology, College of Natural Sciences, Seoul National University; Research Assistant, Institut für Biophysik, Justus Liebig Universität, Giessen, Germany, 1979-83; Research Associate, Department of Biophysics and Theoretical Biology, University of Chicago, USA, 1983-84; Vice-Dean, Student Affairs, College of Natural Sciences, 1993-95, Director, Research Centre for Molecular Microbiology, 1999-, Director, Institute of Microbiology, 1999-, Seoul National University. Publications: NMR-spektroskopische Untersuchungen zur Aktivität von L(+)-Ascorbinsäure und ihren Folgeprodukten in chemischen und biologischen Systemen, dissertation, 1983; A possible enzymatic catabolism of L-ascorbic acid via α-ketoaldehyde, 1985; Co-author, about 80 contributions to journals and books. Memberships: Microbiological Society of Korea, 1984-; Korean Biophysical Society, 1995-; Korean Society for Free Radical Research, 1995-; Korean Society for Molecular Biology, 1995-; Korean Magnetic Resonance Society, 1995-; American Society of Biochemistry and Molecular Biology, 1997-; American Chemical Society, 1999-; International EPR Society, 1999-; European Calcium Society, 1999-. Address: Seoul National University, Shinlim-dong, Kwanak-ku, 151-742 Seoul, Korea.

**KANINSKI Pavel Sergeyevich,** b. 29 October 1954, Yaroslavl. Research Scientist. m. Galina, 1 s. Education: Graduate, Polytech Institute of Yaroslavl, 1972-77; Postgraduate, Electro Chemistry, Engineering Technologist Diplomat, 1981-84; Doctor of Chemical Sciences, 1987. Appointments: Engineer, Polytech Institute of Yaroslavl, 1977-82; Senior Engineer, 1982-85; Science Colaborator, 1985- 87; Senior Science Collaborator, 1987-89; Head of Department, 1989-91; Chief of Research, Centre Spektrum Yaroslavl, 1991-. Publications: Method of Preperation Fatty Acids Butyl Esters; Method of Preperation mono and diphtalonitrils; Method of Regeneration Exhausted Lubricant Coolant Liquids. Honours: Medal of the USSR Economic Achievement Exhibition; Premium of Leninsky Komsomol of Region. Memberships: New York Academy of Sciences; Academy Natural Sciences of Russian Federation; Directorate Music Likers Organisation. Address: Yaroslavl 62, Post Office Box #108, 150062 Yaroslavl, Russia.

**KANKA Jiri,** b. 28 June 1925, Prague, Czech Republic. Physician; Gynaecologist. m. Dagmar, 1 son, 1 daughter. Education: MD, Charles University, Prague, 1950; PhD, Charles University, 1965; DSc, 1969; Professor, Obstetrics and Gynaecology, 1987. Appointments: Founder Member, International Study Group of Detection and Prevention of Cancer, 1968-83; President, Czech Society CPC, 1976-88; Registrar, Obstetrics and Gynaecology, 1964-. Publications: 279 Publications; 10 Monographs. Honours: Award of Minister of Health; Award of Czech Medical Association; J E Purkynje Medal; Medal Awarded 650th Anniversary of Charles University. Memberships: International Federation of Cervical Pathology and Coloscopy. Address: Department Obstetrics and Gynaecology, Third Medical Faculty, Charles University, Srobarova 50, 100 00 Prague 10, Czech Republic.

**KANNIS Theodore John,** b. 5 February 1931, Perth, Western Australia, Australia. Optometrist. 1 son, 3 daughters. Education: Diploma of Optometry, 1954, University of Western Australia. Appointments: Honorary Liaison Consultant, Australian Pensioners League, (44 years - a record). Honours: BEM, 1970; OBE, 1979; AM, 1992; Order of Australia; CIT WA; Citizen of the Year for Western Australia, 1998. Address: 122 Murray Street, WA 6000, Australia.

**KANNO Akira,** b. 1 December 1932, Tokyo, Japan. Banker. m. Yasuko Matsumoto, 1 son, 1 daughter. Education: BLL, Tokyo University, 1955; MA, Economics, Yale University, 1963. Appointments: Executive Director, Bank of Japan, 1986-92; Deputy Governor, Export, Import Bank of Japan, 1992-94; Vice Chairman, Senior Executive Director, Japanese Bankers Association. Address: Kouyama 4-12-14, Narima-ku 176-0022, Japan.

**KANO-SUEOKA Tamiko,** b. 26 June 1932, Kyoto, Japan. Professor. m. Noboru Sueoka, 1 daughter. Education: BS, Kyoto University, 1956; MA, Radcliffe College, 1960; PhD, University of Illinois, 1963. Appointments: Research Assistant, California Institute of Technology, Pasadena, 1956-58; Research Associate, Princeton University, New Jersey, 1963-67; Research Staff, Princeton University, 1968-72; Assistant Professor, Molecular, Cellular and Developmental Biology, 1973-79, Associate Professor, 1979-85, Professor, 1985-, University of Colorado. Publications: Biochemical Action of Hormones, 1983; Progress in Nucleic Acid Research and Molecular Biology; Contributor of articles to professional journals. Memberships: American Association of Cancer Research; American Society for Biochemical and Molecular Biology. Address: University of Colorado, Campus Box 0347, Boulder, CO 80309, USA.

**KANSAL Mitthan Lal,** b. 5 February 1962, Renukot, Uttar Pradesh, India. Assistant Professor of Civil Engineering. m. Goldy Kansal, 2 sons. Education: BSc with distinction, Civil Engineering, 1985, MTech Honours, Civil Engineering, 1988, Kurukshetra University; Postgraduate Diploma in Operations Management, IGNOU, 1996; PhD, Civil Engineering, Delhi University, 1996-97. Appointments: Research Fellow, Water Resources Management Centre, REC Kurukshetra, 1986-89; Research Scholar, Indian Institute of Technology, Delhi, 1989-90; Scientist B, NIH, Roorkee, 1990-91; Lecturer in Civil Engineering, 1991-96, Assistant Professor of Civil Engineering, 1996-, Delhi College of Engineering. Publications include: Co-author: Role of Engineers in Combating the Effect of Drought Menace, 1988; Role of Computers in Water Resources Education and Training in India, 1989; Rapid Determination of Optimum Moisture Content of Engineering Soils for Embankment Construction, 1990; Author: Institute-Industry Link in Engineering Education for Upgradation - An Indian

Perspective, 1994; Co-author: Reliability Analysis of Wate Distribution Systems Under Uncertainty, 1995; Stochast Hydraulic Reliability of a Water Distribution Network, 199€ Identification of Monitoring Stations in Water Distributio System, 1997; A Study on Financial and Contractual Issues i BOT Projects, 1998. Memberships: Life Member, Institution Engineers, India; Life Member, Indian Society of Technic Education; New York Academy of Sciences. Address: 15, Typ V, New Campus of Delhi College of Engineering, Bawar Road, Delhi 110-042, India.

**KANTOR Vladimir,** b. 30 March 1945, Moscow. Philosoph Literature. m. Marina Kisseleva, 1 son, 1 daughter. Educatio Moscow State University, 1963-69; Postgrad work, 1970-7 PhD Philosophy, 1974; DSc Philosophy, 1988. Appointment Head of Dept, Member of Editorial Board, Journal Questions Philosophy, 1974-. Publications: 8 books, 1978-. Honour Heinrich Böll Prize, 1992, Germany; Soros Prize, 199 Moscow. Membership: Union of Russian Writers, 1988 Address: ul Borisa Galushkina 15-81, RU 129301 Moscov Russia.

**KAPLAN Ben-Zion,** b. 13 February 1936, Tel-Aviv, Israe Professor of Electrical Engineering. Education: BSc, 197 MSc, 1964, Electrical Engineering, Technion, Haifa; DPh Applied Science, Sussex University, England, 197 Appointment: Professor, Department of Electrical ar Computer Engineering, Ben-Gurion University, Beer-Shev; Israel; Established the Frederick and Alice Kotek Laboratory f Magnetic and Electronic Systems. Publications: 118 referee journal publications. Honours: Prize in Applied Electronic Polish-Jewish-Ex-Servicemen's Association, London, 199; Incumbent of the Konrad and Chinita Abrahams-Curiel Chair Electronic Instrumentation. Memberships: Senior Membe IEEE; Israeli Committee, URSI, Metrology Subcommitte (Commission A). Address: Department of Electrical ar Computer Engineering, Ben Gurion University, PO Box 65; Beer Sheva, Israel.

**KARAGODOVA Tamara Yakovlevna,** b. 25 April 194! Saratov, Russia. Physics Educator; Researcher. m. Alexande 2 d. Education: Diploma of Physicist, 1967; Diploma Candidate of Sciences, 1973; Diploma of Doctor of physica Mathematical Sciences, 1997. Appointments: Assistant, Sta Technical University, Saratov, Russia, 1972-75; Associa Professor, SSTU, 1976-97; Professor, 1997-. Publication Optics and Spectroscopy; JETP; Izvestiya of Russian Academ of Science; Proceedings SPIE; Canad J Physics. Honour Individual Grant of International Science Foundadtion; Grant International Soros Science Education Program. Membership SPIE; Association of Spectroscopists. Address: SST Polytechniceskaya 77, 410054 Saratov, Russia.

**KARAPANDZIC Miodrag R,** b. 25 April 193€ Rgaje-Prokuplje. Professor of Plastic and Reconstructiv Surgery. m. Mirjana, 1 daughter. Education: School Stomatology, 1957; School of Medicine, 1966; Specialist Maxillo-Facial Surgery, 1966; Specialist of Plastic Reconstructive Surgery, 1976; DrSci, 1976. Appointment Professor of Maxillo Facial Surgery, 1976; Professor of Plast and Reconstructive Surgery, 1989; Director of Plastic ar Reconstructive Surgery Clinic, 1989; President of Exam Boa for Plast and Recon Surgery, 1989. Publications: Origin method in Plast and Rec Surgery of Lips, 1974; Grabb Encyclopaedia of FL V 1, 1990; 193 articles, presentations ar publications in domestic, European and international medic journals; 4 text books; 2 surgical films of rare disease Honours: First Class Golden Decoration, President of th Republic. Memberships: Serbian Medical Associatio

Yugoslavian Plastic and Reconstructive Surgical Association; European Association of Plastic and Recononstructive Surgery. Address: Jove Ilica 87/III, 11000 Belgrade, Yugoslavia.

**KARAZIJA Stasys,** b. 14 December 1930, Kupiskis reg, Lithuania. Forester. m. Aldona Gabrilaviciute, 2 daughters. Education: Forestry Engineer, 1954, Lithuanian Academy Agriculture; Candidate of Science, 1965; DSc Biology, 1980; Professor, 1993. Appointments: Employed in forest enterprises, 954-60; Researcher, Lithuanian Forest Research Institute, 960-, Head of Dept, 1973, Deputy Director, 1989, Director, 994, Chairman Senate, 1997; Lecturer, University of Agriculture, 1990-. Publications: Over 100 scientific publications; Books: Forest Typology in the Southern Baltic Region, Co-author, 1977; Plants of Lithuanian Forest, co-author, 1977; Silviculture, manual, co-author, 1979; Types of Lithuanian Forests, 1988; Forests and Protected Areas, 994; Lithuanian Oak Forests, co-author, 1997. Honours: Awarded Bronze Medals at Exhibition of Achievements of National Economy of USSR, 1968, 1973. Memberships: Corresponding member, Lithuanian Academy of Sciences; IUFRO (International Union of Forestry Research Organisations). Address: Pramones pr 83-106, LT 3041 Kaunas, Lithuania.

**KARCHEV Todor,** b. 28 May 1945, Ljubimetz, Bulgaria. Associate Professor. m. Violeta Doncheva, 2 daughters. Education: MD, Medical University of Sofia, 1969; PhD, 1983; DSc, 1997. Appointments: Assistant Professor, Associate Professor, Medical University, Sofia. Publications include: Lymphoid Throat Ring in Normal and Pathological State, 1978; Textbook of Pediatric Otorhinolaryngology, 1981; Textbook of ENT Diseases, 1994. Memberships: European Society of Pediatric ORL; European Society of Rhinology; New York Academy of Sciences. Address: ENT Department, Medical University, 8 Belo More Street, 1527 Sofia, Bulgaria.

**KARDO-SYSSOEV Alexei,** b. 7 June 1941, Leningrad, Russia. Physicist. m. Helen Kardo-Syssoeva, 2 sons, 2 daughters. Education: Master's degree in Physics, 1964; PhD, Physics, 1973; Qualification as Professor, 1987. Appointments: Senior Scientist, Laboratory Head, Ioffe Physical Technical Institute, Russian Academy of Sciences; General Manager, Pulse Systems Group, Russia. Publications: Contributor, more than 150 publications in field of semi-conductor physics, devices and electronics. Honour: Soviet State Prize, USSR State Prize Committee, 1987. Address: Bldg 75/2, Flat 3 M, Toresa, 194214 St Petersburg, Russia.

**KAREVSKI Ljupco,** b. 24 June 1947, Skopje, Macedonia. Professor. m. Violeta, 1 son, 1 daughter. Education: Faculty of Medicine, 1972; Specialist in Orthopaedics, 1979; Postgraduate Studies, 1984; Doctoral Dissertation; Professor. Publications: More than 100 Publications. Honours: Golden Plaque of Yuot; Plaque of MDC, 1990; IAEA Cert, 1997; Cert of Appreciation, 998. Memberships: Macedonian Doctors Chamber; Macedonian Assocaition of Orthopaedics. Address: Faculty of Medicine, Ul Bojmija 4/27, 91000 Skopje, Rep of Macedonia.

**KARGER Delmar William,** b. 9 May 1913, Cape Girardeau, Missouri, USA. Industrial and Management Expert. m. (1) Paula E Miller, 5 July 1935, deceased, (2) Edith Kennedy Loring, 11 Jan 1962, deceased, (3) Ruth Lounsberry Rivard, 31 Oct 1970, 3 daughters. Education: BS, Electrical Engineering, Valparaiso University, 1935; MS, General Engineering, University of Pittsburgh, 1947. Appointments include: Registered Professional Engineer; Surveyor, US Army, 1935; Assistant Plant Engineer, International Harvester Co, 1941-42; Assistant Chief Manufacturing Engineer, Manufacturing and Repair Division, Westinghouse Electric Corporation, 1942-45; Management Consultant, Booz, Allen & Hamilton, New York City, 1951; Manager, new products, Government and Industrial Products Division, 1958-59; Professor, Head of Department Management Engineering, Rensselaer Poly Institute, Troy, New York, 1959-63; Founding Dean, School Management, 1963-70; Ford Foundation Professor Management, 1970-78; IE and Management Consultant, US, Canada, Brazil, European, Scandinavian Middle East Countries, 1978-; President or Director, of several companies; Industrial Management Consultant. Publications include: Author: (with F Bayha), Engineered Work Measurement, 1957; The New Product, 1960; (with R G Murdick), Managing Engineering and Research, 1969; (with A B Jack) Problems of Small Business in Developing and Exploiting New Products, 1963; (with R G Murdick) New Product Venture Management, 1972; How to Choose a Career, 1978; Strategic Planning and Management: The Key to Corporate Success, 1991. Honours: Recipient, McKinsey Prize, 1967; Wiley Prize, 1978; Fellow, American Association for the Advancement of Science; Fellow, American Institute Industrial Engineers, past National Vice President, Director, Inter-Soc Affairs. Memberships include: Methods-Time Measurement Association Standards and Research, President, 1958-60; New Product Management and Development Association, Vice President, Director. Address: 404 Circle Drive, DeFuniak Springs, FL 32433-2564, USA.

**KARIMOV Anvar Saidovich,** b. 21 May 1935, Tashkent, Uzbekistan. Professor. m. Karimova Svetlana, 1 son, 2 daughters. Education: Engineer Electromechanics, 1957, Tashkent Polytechnical Institute. Appointments: Engineer of Manufacture, 1958; Assistant, Docent, Professor, Chief of Theoretical and General Electro-Engineering Dept, 1958-. Publications: Over 100 publications; 20 patents of USSR. Honour: Excellent of Higher Education of USSR. Membership: International Academy of Electro-Engineering Science. Address: Electromechanical and Electron Devices Dept, Tashkent State Polytechnical Institute, Str Aksaj 13, Tashkent 700042, Uzbekistan.

**KARIMOV Farshed,** b. 16 October 1949, Tajikistan. Physicist. m. 1 son, 1 daughter. Education: Physics Department, Tajik State University, 1966-68; Diploma, Physicist, Moscow State University, 1968-72. Appointments: Explorational Expedition, Academy of Sciences, Tajikistan Institute of Seismoresistant Constructions and Seismology, 1980-90; Professor, Tajik State University, 1990-96; Vice President, Engineering Academy, Tajikistan, 1997-. Publications: 60 professional papers. Memberships: Correspondent, Engineering Academy, Tajikistan; American Geophysical Union. Address: Akademicheskaya str 10, 734013 Dushanbe, Tajikistan.

**KARIMOV Kamal,** b. 14 February 1948, Tashkent. Professor. m. Shokhista Karimova, 2 sons, 1 daughter. Education: Student, Tashkent State University, 1966-72; Postgraduate, Institute of Mechanics, Uzbekistan Academy of Sciences, 1975-78; Bachelor of Technical Sciences, 1980; Doctorate of Technical Sciences, 1991; Professor, 1992; Special Course, Kaunas Technical University, Lithuania, 1985-88. Appointments: Engineer, Junior, Senior, Leading and Chief Research Worker, Institute of Mechanics, Academy of Sciences, Uzbekistan, 1972-91; Head, 1991-94, Vice Rector, 1994-95, Tashkent State Technical University; Diplomat, Ministry of Foreign Affiars, Uzbekistan, 1995; Diplomat, Embassy of Uzbekistan, Iativa, 1995-97; Diplomat, Embassy, Uzbekistan, Russian Federation, 1997-. Publications: 2 monographs, 15 inventions, over 100 scientific researches. Honour: Uzbekistan Youths Prize Laureate, 1977. Membership:

Corresponding Member, Academy of Engineering, Uzbekistan. Address: Massiv Besh Agach 4/78, 700027 Tashkent, Uzbekistan Technical University, Uzbekistan.

**KARP Maria Ludwika,** b. 11 August 1939, Gorlice, Poland. Librarian. m. Master of Polish Philology, 1963. Appointments: Manager, Library of Faculty of Mining, University of Mining and Metallurgy in Krakow. Honour: Krakow Silver Award. Membership: Stowarzyszenie Bibliotekarzy Polskich. Address: al Mickiewicza 30, Block A4 30 059 Cracow, Faculty of Mining, University of Mining and Metallurgy, Poland.

**KARPISEK Ladislav Stephan,** b. 20 June 1924, Sabinov, Czechoslovakia. Researcher. m. Helena Erna Kutena, 1 son. Education: Mechanical Engineering degree, 1949, Charles University, Prague. Appointments: Development Engineer, CHEP, Sydney Australia; Managing Director, LSK Industries Pty Ltd and LSK International Research Pty Ltd, Sydney, Australia. Publications: Over 1000 patents and patent applications in materials handling, packaging, locks and security, horticulture, medical and scientific, combustion and rotary piston machines, and many other fields. Address: PO Box 2352, Taren Point, NSW 2229, Australia.

**KARRAY Fakhreddine,** b. 20 January 1960, Sfax, Tunisia. University Professor. m. Neila, 1 son. Education: Ing Dip, 1964, University of Tunis; PhD, 1989, University Illinois Urbana-Champaign. Appointments: Faculty of University of British Columbia and Lakehead University; Professor, University of Waterloo, currently. Publications: 65 in textbooks, journals, encyclopedias, proceedings. Honour: Best Paper Award of the World Automation Congress, 1998. Memberships: IEEE; Professional Engineer of Ontario. Address: Dept of System Design Engineering, University of Waterloo, Waterloo, Ont N2L 3GI, Canada.

**KARSHENBOIM Savely,** b. 6 January 1960, Leningrad, Russia. Physicist. Education: Leningrad State University, 1983; PhD, 1992, St Petersburg State University. Appointments: Engineer, 1983, Junior Researcher, 1989, Researcher, 1995, Senior Researcher, 1995-, D I Mendeleev Institute for Metrology, Leningrad. Publications: Author or co-author, 63 papers in professional journals. Memberships: St Petersburg Physics Society; Association of Spectroscopists. Address: D I Mendeleev Institute for Metrology, 19 Moskovsky Prospect, St Petersburg 198005, Russia.

**KARTASHEVICH Anatoly,** b. 19 February 1949, Slutsk, Minsk, Belarus. Engineer. m. Tatiana, 1 son, 1 daughter. Education: Diploma, Belarussian Agricultural Academy, 1971; Candidate of Science in Engineering, 1980; PhD, Engineering, 1993. Appointments: Dean, International Relations, 1993-96, First Vice Rector, 1996-, Belarussian Agricultural Academy. Publictions: 260, including 70 patents and 4 books. Honour: Outstanding Teacher of Belarus. Memberships: Academician, Belarussian Academy of Engineering, Belarussian Academy of Engineering and Technology, Russian Academy of Agricultural Engineering. Address: 4 Michurin 3, Gorki 213410, Belarus.

**KARUNAIRAJAN Richards D,** b. 24 May 1936, Manipay, Sri Lanka. Journalist. Div. 2 daughters. Education: Trained in printing and publishing, 1956-59, India; Diploma in Rural Social Leadership, Xavier University, Philippines, 1978. Appointments: Executive Officer, Church Information Office, London; Journalist, Sun and Weekend, Colombo, Sri Lanka; Consultant, South East Asia Rural Social Leadership Institute, Philippines; Information Officer and Editor, Radio Television Seychelles; Production Editor, South London Newspapers; Freelance, Canada. Publications: Biogas Technology, 1975; Education for

Development, 1978; a number of features on children and rural development. Memberships: International Federation of Organic Agricultural Movements; Serendeebam. Address: 6 Lyngrove Crescent, Richmond Hill, Ontario L4B 2B7, Canada.

**KARVAS Milan,** b. 5 June 1932, Bratislava, Slovakia. Company Executive; Doctor. m. Viera, 1 son, 1 daughter. Education: Diploma, 1957, Faculty of Chemistry, Technical University Bratislava; Doctor Diploma, 1968, Academy of Sciences, Bratislava; Postdoctoral Study, Eth Zurich, 1971-72; Habilitation as Docent, 1996, Komenius University, Bratislava. Appointments: Partner of Private Company, Synkola (Synthetic Contracts Laboratory), Bratislava; Associate Professor, Faculty of Natural Sciences, Komenius University, Bratislava. Publications: Author or co-author, 63 original papers in international journals; 104 patents; Over 45 lectures on domestic and international symposiums. Honours: Prize of Slovak Academy of Sciences, 1960; Award of Czechoslovak Ministry of Economics, 1982; Gold Medal of Slovak Chemical Society, 1994. Memberships: Board of Accreditation, Committee of Slovak Government; Slovak Chemical Society; Swiss Chemical Society; Rotary Club Bratislava; National Committee of UIPAC. Address: Gajova 15, 81109 Bratislava, Slovakia.

**KARYDIS Michael,** b. 28 August 1950, Athens, Greece. Professor. m. Mainwen Jones. Education: BSc Natural Sciences, 1973, University of Athens, Greece; PhD, 1978, University of Wales. Appointments: Researcher, Greek Atomic Energy Commission, Athens, 1979-81, National Centre of Marine Research, Director of the Hydrob Station and Public Aquarium of Rhodes, 1982-86; Professor, Department of Environmental Studies, University of the Aegean, 1987-97, Chairman of the Marine Science Dept, 1998-. Publications: 31 articles to professional journals. Memberships: American Society Limnology and Oceanography; American Ecological Society; American Phycol Society; British Phycol Society. Address: Department of Environmental Studies, University of the Aegean, 81100 Mytilini, Greece.

**KARYONO Tri Harso,** b. 15 December 1956, Yogyakarta, Indonesia. University Lecturer; Thermal Comfort Researcher; Architect. Education: BArch, Bandung Institute of Technology, 1984; MA, Architecture, University of York, England, 1989; PhD, Architecture, Sheffield University, England. Appointments: Lecturer, Schools of Architecture at University of Indonesia, University of Tarumanagara, University of Mercu-Buana, University of Bina Nusantara. Publications: Thermal Comfort for the Indonesian Workers in Jakarta, 1995; Discrepancy between actual and predicted thermal votes, 1996; Thermal Comfort in the Tropical South East Asia Region, 1996. Address: New York Academy of Sciences, 1996. Address: Pondok Benda Indah N1/35, Pamulang, Tangerang 15416, Indonesia.

**KASAMATSU Tadashi,** b. 29 September 1967, Osaka, Japan. Optoelectronic Researcher. m. Yuki Utada, 1 son. Education: BE Electrical Engineering, 1990, ME Electrical Engineering, 1992, Kyoto University, Kyoto, Japan. Appointments: Researcher and Developer, injection-locked ArFexcimer laser and diode-pumped solid-state lasers, NEC Corporation, 1992-, currently Assistant Manager Opto-elctronics and High Frequency device Research Laboratories. Publications: Applied Physics Letters, 1995; Applied Optics, 1997. Memberships: Japan Society of Applied Physics; Laser Society of Japan; Optical Society of Japan. Address: NEC Corp, 4-1-1 Miyamae-ku, Miyazaki, Kawasak 216, Japan.

**KASATKIN Alexandr Petrovich,** b. 29 July 1944, Rodniki, anovo Region, Russia. Physicist. m. Nina Loginova. ducation: Graduated, Nizhny Novgorod University, 1966; ploma of Candidate of Physico-Mathematical Science, 1973; ertificate of Senior Research Worker, 1976. Appointments: ostgraduate Student, 1966-69; Junior Research Worker, )69-70; Senior Research Worker, 1970-. Publications: Near ) scientific and methodics publications. Address: Laboratory Dielectric Covers, Physico-Technical Research Institute, zhny Novgorod State University, 23 (Korpus 3) Prospekt agarina, Nizhny Novgorod 603600, Russia.

**KASPERCZAK Henry,** b. 10 July 1946, Zabrze, Poland. ootball Coach. m. Marguerite Nowak, 3 sons, 2 daughters. ducation: Diploma in Physical Education, University of arsaw, 1978; Diploma in Training, Professional Coach, 1992-. opointments: Footballer, Stal Mielec, 1965-66, Legia arsovie, 1966-68, FC Metz, 1978-79, 73 selections for the ational team from 1968-78; Trainer, FC Metz, 1979-84, 'inner, French Cup, 1984, AS St Etienne, 1984-87, Racing lub of Strasbourg, 1987-89, Racing Paris, 1989-90, Finalist, 'ench Cup, 1990, Montpellier HSC, 1990-92, Quarter Finals European Cupwinners Cup, Lille OSC, 1992-93, National eam, Ivory Coast, 1993-94, 3rd place in African All-Nations up, Tunisia, 1994, National Technical Director and Trainer, unisian National Team, 1994-98, Finalist, African All-Nations up, 1996, Olympic Games, Atlanta, 1996, Quarter Finalists, frican All-Nations Cup, 1998, World Cup, France, 1998, SC astia, 1998. Honours: 3rd Place in World Cup, Germany, )74; 5th Place World Cup, Argentina, 1978; Silver Medal, lympic Games, Montréal, 1976; Elected Best Trainer in 'ance, 1991. Membership: UNECATEF. Address: 19 rue des octeurs, Charcot, 42100 St Etienne, France.

**KATILIUS Ramunas,** b. 15 October 1935, Kaunas, thuania. Physicist. m. Elmira Katiliene, 2 sons. Education: iploma, 1959, Vilnius University, Faculty of Physics and aths; Postgrad, Institute of Physics and Maths, Lithuanian cademy of Science, 1959-62; Candidate of Physics and lathematical Science, 1969, Institute of Semiconductors, ∍ningrad; Dr Phys and Math Sci, 1986; Hab Dr Nat Sci, 1993; hief Research Fellow, 1989. Appointments: Junior Research ellow, Institute of Physics and Maths, Lithuanian Academy of cience, Vilnius, 1962-66; Junior Research Fellow, Institute of emiconductors, Leningrad, 1966-72; Junior and Senior esearch Fellow, A F Ioffe, Physical-Technical Institute, ∍ningrad, 1972-88; Senior and Chief Research Fellow, emiconductor Physics Institute, Vilnius, 1988-; Professor of hysics, 1991-, Extraordinary Professor, 1991-93, Vytautas lagnus University, Faculty of Environment Research, Kaunas, 'thuania. Publications: Research in the field of Theoretical hysics and Solid State Physics; 110 publications including ∍view articles and chapters of books in English; Books: 'uctuation Phenomena, in Russian, 1989; Statistical Physics nd Physical Kinetics, in Lithuanian, 1998. Honours: Lithuanian ational Science Award, 1995; Citation index, over 400. lemberships: Lithuanian Physical Society; Board member, pen Society Fund-Lithuania. Address: Antakalnio 90 25, LT 040 Vilnius, Lithuania.

**KATKEVICIUS Vlades,** b. 18 March 1937. Engineer. m. rute, 2 daughters. Education: Kaunas University of echnology, Faculty of Electrical Engineering, Diploma, 956-61. Appointments: Senior Lecturer, Kaunas University of echnology, 1962-69; Associate Professor, Kaunas University f Technology, 1969-89; Professor, Kaunas University of echnology, 1989-95; Mayor, Kaunas City Municipality, 995-97; Vice Minister, Minstry of Public Administration eforms and Municipals of the Republic of Lithuania, 1997-.

Publication: Over 100 Scientific Articles, published locally and Internationally; Scientific Training Film on Asynchronical Induction Electrical Engines; 7 Inventions. Honour: Habilitate Doctor, 1993. Memberships: Lithuanian Conservative Party, Kaunas Branch, Chairman, 1993-95; Lithuanian Conservative Party, Board Member, 1993-96; Kaunas University of Technology Senate; Lithuanian Union of Engineers. Address: Sjeinio 33-5, LT 3000 Kaunas, Lithuania.

**KATKEVICIUS Vygantas,** b. 12 July 1962, Ukmerge, Lithuania. Economist. Education: PhD (Doctor of Economics), 1984, Vilnius University. Appointments: Director of Economic and Finance Dept, Ministry of Agriculture, Lithuania.

**KATOH Yoshimitsu Yuki,** b. 3 October 1953, Aich, Japan. Neuroanatomist. m. Keiko Katoh (Suzuki), 1 son, Taihei, 1 daughter, Yasuyo. Education: Medical Technologist, Fujita Health University, 1976; PhD, School of Medicine, Fujita Health University, 1986. Appointments: Associate Professor, Department of Anatomy, School of Health Sciences, Fujita Health University, 1998. Honour: Grant-in-Aid for Scientific Research (C), Ministry of Education, Science, Sports and Culture of Japan, 1996-98. Memberships: Japan Neuroscience Society; Japanese Association of Anatomists; Bulletin of the Fujita Medical Society. Address: Department of Anatomy, School of Health Sciences, Fujita Health University, Toyoake, Aichi 470-1192, Japan.

**KATPATAL Yashwant Bhaskar,** b. 9 January 1966, Jabalpur (MP), India. Educator; Researcher. m. Meenal Pimplikar, 1 son. Education: M Tech, 1988, PhD, 1992, Dr H S Gaur University, Sagar, India. Appointments: Assistant Professor (Ad hoc), Dr H S Gaur University, Sagar, 1988-89; Senior Project Fellow, National Env Engineering Research Institute, Nagpur, India, 1992-93; Senior Lecturer, Civil Engineering, Visvesvaraya Regional College of Engineering, Nagpur, 1993-. Publications: Journal articles: Tectonic strain ratio computed..., 1992; Departures from true Ellipticity...., 1993; Finite strain from oriental.., 1994; Contribution to books: Computers in urban planning and urban management, 1998; The Indian Precambrian, 1998; 3 papers presented in international conferences and 8 in the area of Remote Sensing and GIS at national conferences, seminars and symposiums. Honours: Young Scientist Award, MPCOST, 1993; Best Lecture Award, IWWA, 1998; Merit Scholarship, MPCOST and UGC during M Tech 1985-88. Memberships: Life Member, Journal of Indian Remote Sensing Society; Fellow, Journal of Geological Society of India; Journai on GIS "GIS@Development". Address: QR No 31, URCE Campus, Nagpur 440 011, India.

**KATUKOORI Rajireddy,** b. 19 July 1968, Nagaram, India. Researcher. m. Vasantha, 1 daughter. Education: MA; DCCP; PGDCA (PhD). Appointment: Research Project Fellow, 1997. Publiction: Dimensions of Daklit Literature and the Dynamics of Change. Membership: Indian Changeological Association. Address: H No 1-26 Post Nagaram, Mndl Hasanparthy, District Warangal 371, India.

**KAUFFMAN Teresa Jo,** b. 24 August 1951, San Francisco, California, USA. Creative Artist; Professor. Education: BA, University of California, Berkeley; MA, University of Texas, Austin; PhD, The Union Institute. Appointments include: TV News Anchor and Reporter, ABC Affiliate in Texas; Worked in TV, video, film and radio in public, network affiiate, cable, radio and corporate video environments, over 25 years; Canada, California, Texas, North Carolina; Senior Writer-Producer-Director, created first frame by frame animated computer art cartoon, Ampex Corporation, Redwood City, California, 1980; Professional Artist; Expressive arts/communication therapist, Holly Hill Psychiatric Hospital 1994-6; Founder/director of Finding a Voice at Creative Spaces, (art, writing, media, music). Publications: The Script as Blueprint: Content and Form Working Together - Writing for Radio, Television, Video and Film; Secret Place; Publications and invited lectures in interdisciplinary studies, psychology, communication and creative expression. Music compositions include: Little Miss Puppet Talks to the Angels; The Seasons Change. Creative Works include: Art (painting) - solo shows, 1st place, impressionistic painting, acrylic - Fine Arts competitition, North Carolina State University; Illustrator, stationary and cards, magazines, newsletters, books, music books. Honours include: Professional Member of the Year, 1993, The National Broadcasting Honour Society; Outstanding Lecturer of the Year, College of Social Sciences and Humanities, North Carolina State University, Raleigh, 1996; 2 EMMY nominations and over 15 first place national awards. Award winning shows include: Otters From Oiled Waters; The Seasons of Change; Habitat for Humanity; Little Miss Puppet Talks to the Angels; Front Porch; Secret Place; Wake Visual Arts; Raleigh Conservatory of Music I and II; I'm One Person or Another; Raleigh Conservatory; The Rainbow. Memberships: Elected Full Member of theAmerican Psychological Association; American Association for Humanistic Psychology; The Berkeley Honor Society; California Scholastic Federation; Phi Kappa Phi Academic Honor Society; Invited Member, National Association of Television and Broadcasting; Public Relations Consultant, Raleigh Conservatory of Music; former Vice President and Board Member, Wake Visual Arts Association; former Board Member, The Texas Consumer Association. Address: 407 Furches Street, Raleigh, NC 27606-4017, USA.

**KAUFMAN Asher Selig,** b. 7 July 1925, Edinburgh, Scotland. Physicist. m. Josephine Hilda Corman, 1 son, 1 daughter, deceased. Education: BCs, University of Edinburgh, 1945; BSc, Hons, Physics, 1948; PhD, 1954. Appointments: National Service, 1945-47; National Secretary, Bnei Akiva Youth Movement, 1948-49; Research, Associated Electrical Industries Research Laboratory, 1954-59; Research and Teaching, Hebrew University of Jerusalem, 1959-87; Professor Emeritus, 1987-, Honorary Research Fellow, 1998-, College of Judea and Samaria, 1998-. Publications: The Temple of Jerusalem: Tractate Middot, part 1, 1991, part 2, 1997; Papers on the Temples of Jerusalem and Shiloh, ancient metrology, location of Mount Sinai, ionized gases, spectroscopy, high-temperature measurement. Honours: Newton Scholarship in Natural Philosophy, 1943; Crum Brown Silver Medal in Chemistry, 1943. Memberships: Institute of Physics, UK; European Physical Society; Israel Physicial Society; Societies for archaeological exploration and Judaic studies. Address: 54 Helahuz Street, Jerusalem 96269, Israel.

**KAUNECKAS Jonas,** b. 6 June 1938, Pasvalys. Priest. Education: Panevezys Land reclamation Technical School, 1958; Vilnius State University, 1972; Kaunas Priest Seminary, 1977. Appointments: Engineer, Alytus District Land Reclamation Institutions, 1958-72; Assistant Pastor in Telsiai Cathedral, 1977-83; Pastor of Skaudvile, 1984-90; Professor & Director spiritual in Priest Seminary, 1990-. Publications: Homilies in the magazine The Church News. Honours: The Title of monsignor, 1993; Vytis Cross Order of Lithuania for Bravery, 1998. Memberships: Member and Secretary, Catholic Committee for Defense of Believers' Rights, 1978-88; Publisher of underground magazines, The Chronicle of the Catholic Church of Lithuania, and The Future of Lithuania, 1975-88; Presbyterian Council and of the college of Consultors of Telsiai Diocese; Editorial Board, The Church News. Address: Telsiu kunigu seminarija, Katedros 6, LT 5610 Telsiai, Lithuania.

**KAUR Jasjeet,** b. 19 November 1964, Meerut, India. Lecturer; Research Associate. m. Dr G S Sodhi, 1 son, daughter. Education: BSc, Meerut University, 1984; MSc Organic Chemistry, Meerut University, 1986; PhD Biotechnology, Punjabi University, Patiala, 1992; Training i Instrumentation, Ranbaxy Laboratories Ltd, Gurgaon, India 1997; Centre for Electronics Design and Technology, Mohal India, 1997. Appointments: Project Assistant, Defenc Research and Development Organisation, New Delhi, 1988-91 Senior Research Fellow, Council of Scientific and Industria Research, New Delhi, 1991-94; Research Associate, Delh University, 1995-; Lecturer, College for Applied Sciences fc Women, Delhi, 1997-. Publications: 20 research papers; presentations in seminars; 2 articles; 2 patents. Honour: Youn; Scientist Awardee, 1997. Memberships: Indian Scienc Congress Association; Indian Academy of Forensic Science Address: 38 Jagriti Enclave, I P Extension II, Delhi 110092 India.

**KAVALIAUSKAS Paulius,** b. 6 February 1945, Anykscia Lithuania. Geographer. 2 sons, 2 daughters. Education: MSc Geography, 1967; Dr Sc, Landscape Science, 1974; Habil Dr Land Management, 1993. Appointments: Professor Department of General Geography, Vilnius University. Honours V V Adamkus Award on Environment Protection, 1995 Memberships: Association of Lithuanian Geographers Independent Center of Strategic Research. Address: Rygo 17-42, LT 2017 Vilnius, Lithuania.

**KAVDIA Indra Singh,** b. 22 June 1941, Udaipur, Rajasthan India. Government Servant. m. Chandra Kumari, 1 son, daughter. Education: MA, University of Rajasthan, Jaipur, 1961 Diploma, Developmental Administration, University c Manchester, 1982. Appointments: Collector and Distric Magistrate, Banswara, 1970; Chief Executive Office Ganganagar Sugar Mills Ltd, Sriganganagar, 1970-75; Deput Secretary to Govt (Mines), Jaipur, 1974-75; Collector an District Magistrate, Kota, 1975-76; General Manager, State Road Transport Corporation, Jaipur, 1976; Resident Directc (Rajasthan), National Textile Corporation Ltd, New Delh 1976-80; Managing Director, State Warehousing Corporatior Jaipur, 1980; Directorand Special Secretary to Governmen Jaipur, 1980-81; Commissioner,Departmental Enquiries, Jaipu 1981; Area Development Commissioner, Kota, 1982-83 Chairman and Managing Director, Jaipur Metals and Electrica Ltd, 1983-90; Chairman, State Road Transport Corporatior Jaipur, 1990-91; Chairman and Managing Director, State Agr Industries Ltd, Jaipur, 1991; Secretary to Govt, 1991-93; Jaipu Development Commissioner, 1993; Principal Secretary t Government and Director, State Institute of Publi Administration, 1995-. Honours: Man of the Year, 1998 American Biographical Institute; Distinguished Leadershir 1997, ABI; Research Board of Advisors, Honorary Membe ABI; Five Thousand Personalities of the World, ABI; Fiv Hundred Leaders of Influence, 1999, ABI; Outstanding Peopl of the 20th Century, International Biographical Centre; Birl Award of Excellence, Rajasthan Chamber of Commerce an Industries; Rajasthan State Award, Jaipur Metals an Electricals. Memberships: Indian Institute of Publi Administration; Indian Economic Association; Institute c Economic Growth; Institute in Industrial Engineering. Address D-17-B Shanti Path, Tilak Naar, Jaipur 302004, India.

**KAVERIN Alexei Mihailovich,** b. 7 August 1949, Moscow Russia. Physicist. m. Vera Chirkova, 3 daughters. Educatior Graduate with honours, Urals Polytechnical Institute, 1972 Appointments: Institute of Thermal Physics, Ural Branch c Russian Academy of Sciences, 1972-, Senior Scientific Worke Defended a candidate dissertation, 1982. Publications: Mor than 20 articles in scientific journals. Address: Laboratory of Energetics and Cryogenics, Institute of Thermophysics, Urals Division of Russian Academy of Sciences, 91 Pervomaiskaya Str GSP-828, Ekaterinburg 620219, Russia.

**KAVVAS M Levent,** b. 24 May 1948, Ankara, Turkey. Professor. m. Jale, 1 son, 1 daughter. Education: BS, Civil Engineering, Middle East Technical University, Ankara, Turkey, 1970; MS, Civil Engineering, Colorado State University, Ft Collins, 1972; PhD, Civil Engineering, Purdue University, Indiana, 1975. Appointments: Visiting Associate Professor, School of Civil Engineering, Purdue University, 1980-82; Associate Professor, University of Kentuckt, 1982-85; Associate Professor, University of California, 1985-90; Co-Director, Center for the Study of Hydroclimatology in the Pacific Rim, 1996-; Professor, University of California, 1990-. Publications: 87 technical papers in professional journals; Book: New Directions for Surface Water Modeling; Co-Author: Earth System Science Encyclopedia and Hydrology of Disasters. Honours: Fulbright Scholar, 1970-75; Phi Kappa Phi, 1973; Research Award, Foreign Specialists, Ministry of Construction, Japan, 1989. Memberships: American Geophysical Union; American Society of Civil Engineers; IAHS; EGS. Address: Department of Civil and Environmental Engineering, University of California, Davis, CA 95616, USA.

**KAWAHARA Fred Katsumi,** b. 26 February 1921, Penngrove, California, USA. Chemist. m. (1) Sumiko Hayami, (2) Andrea L Eary, 2 sons, 2 daughters. Education: BS Hons, 1944, University of Texas; PhD Chemistry, 1948, University of Wisconsin; Post PhD Fellow, 1951-53, University of Chicago. Publications: 60 peer reviewed papers; 20 US patents; 1 British patent; 6 textbook chapters; 2 books. Honours: Fellow, American Institute of Chemistry; Superior Service Award, 1952. Membership: Fellow, American Institute of Chemistry. Address: 1632 Cumberland Street, Covington, KY 41011-3716, USA.

**KAWAHATA Masahiro,** b. 8 September 1936, Tokyo, Japan. Professor. m. Keiko Kohra, 1 son. Education: BE, Mechanical Engineering, 1960, ME, Control Engineering, 1963, PhD, Systems Engineering, 1966, University of Tokyo. Appointments: Managing Director, New Media Development Association, Ministry of International Trade and Industry; Special Advisor, Fujitsu Ltd; Board Director, Fujitsu Research Institute; Visiting Professor, Stanford University. Honours: Award, Minister of International Trade and Industry, 1986; Pioneer Award, University of Washington, 1995; Honour, Public Understanding of High Technologies, Ministry of International Trade and Industry, 1996; Provost's Distinguished Visiting Professor, University of Southern California, 1997. Memberships: Board of Trustees, Seijo University; Board Member of Virtual World Consortium; Secetary of IEEE; Advisory Panel of PEMM. Address: 3-18-2 Denenchofu Ota-ku, Tokyo 145, Japan.

**KAWAI Iroku,** b. 13 March 1928, Oita City, Japan. Emeritus Professor. m. Yoshiko Kobayashi, 1 son. Education: PhD, 1976, Hiroshima University. Appointments: Emeritus Professor, Hiroshima University, 1991; Professor Clinical Psychology, Dept Human Science, Yasuda Women's University, Hiroshima, 1998-. Publications: School Refusal, in Japanese, 1989; Co-editor, Three Psychologies, 1995. Memberships: Japanese Psychological Association; Japanese Association for Behaviour Analysis. Address: 11 8 1001 Uchikoshi cho, Nishiku, Hiroshima 733-0004, Japan.

**KAWANO Kenji,** b. 16 June 1967, Japan. Researcher. Education: BS, 1992; MSc, Physics, 1994; PhD Engineering, 1998. Appointments: Researcher, Railway Technical Research

Institute, Tokyo, 1994-96, Toyohashi University Tech, 1996-. Address: Toyohashi University Tech, Toyohashi Aichi, Toyohashi 441-8580, Japan.

**KAYANDE Shyam Radhakrishna,** b. 5 September 1942, Nagpur, India. Reader in History. m. Kunda Jog, 1 son, 1 daughter. Education: BA, 1962, MA, 1964, Nagpur University; PhD, Poona University, 1984. Appointments: Botard Member, Studies in History, University of Poona; Chairman, Board of Studies in History, Convenor, Refresher Course, North Maharashtra University; Chairman, Board of Studies in History, Academic Council, Maharashtra State Board of Secondary and Higher Secondary Education, Pune; Head, Department of History, Pratap College; Vice President, Khandesh Itihas Parishad; Contingent Officer, Maharashtra State, NCC Republic Day Camp, New Delhi; Associate, Maharashtra Public Service Commission, Mumbai; Section President, Maharashtra Itihas Parishad. Publications: Books: Mwghal Bharat, 1979; Jivandhara Rajdharachi, 1987; Numerous articles in professional journals. Memberhsips: Khandesh Itihas Parishad, Dhule; Maharashtra Itihas Parishad, Pune; Rajwade Sanshodhan Mandal, Dhule; Mahareshtra Itihas Shishak, Pune; Sane Guruji Vachanalaya Amalnes. Address: Teachers Quarters, Pratap College, Amalner 425401, Jalgaon, India.

**KAYE Keith Woodhill,** b. 8 February 1942, Capetown, South Africa. Professor. m. Valda Noreen, 3 daughters. Education: Medical School, University of Witwatersrand, Johannesburg, South Africa, 1960-62; Bachelor of Science, Anatomy and Physiology, 1963; Bachelor of Sciences, Anatomy and Paleoanthropology, 1964; Student Demonstrator, Department of Anatomy, 1965-66; Clinical Years, Medical School, Doctor of Medicine, 1964-67. Appointments: Instructor, Department of Urologic Surgery, 1979-83, Clinical Assistant Professor, 1983-88, Clinical Associate Professor, 1988-92, Clinical Professor of Urology, 1992-93, University of Minnesota; Professor of Urology, University of Western Australia; Director, Urological Research Centre. Publications: 59 Publications. Memberships: Minnesota University Society; Society for Minimally Invasive Surgery; American Fertility Society; American Urological Association; Endourology Society; Australian Medical Association; The Urological Society of Australasia; Royal Australasian College of Surgeons; Australian Prostate Health Council. Address: 9 The Coombe, Mossman Park 6012, Australia.

**KAZILIUNAS Adolfas,** b. 4 January 1942, Lithuania. University Professor. m. Terese Stankunaite, 1 son, 1 daughter. Education: Engineer, 1967, Doctor, 1976, Kaunas; Habilitus Doctor, 1989, Leningrad. Appointments: Head of Central Laboratory of Textile Factory, 1975-90; Head of Lithuanian State Quality Inspectorate, 1991-95; Professor, Vilnius University, 1995-. Publications: 108 publications; 38 patents (inventions). Honours: Awarded 2 silver medals at exhibitions of inventions in Moscow, 1979, 1985. Memberships: Vice President, Lithuanian Society of Commodity Science; Lithuanian Society of Quality. Address: Didlaukio 58-64, LT 2000 Vilnius, Lithuania.

**KAZIMIANEC Jelena,** b. 4 October 1954, Vilnius, Lithuania. Philologist. 1 son. Education: Master of Linguistics, Moscow State University, Russia, 1972-78; Postgraduate Study in Philology and Linguistics, Russian Academy of Pedagogical Science, Moscow, 1984-87; PhD, Russian Academy of Pedagogical Science, 1987; Dr, Humanitarian Science, Scientific Board of Lithuania. Appointments: Lecturer, Pedagogical University, Vilnius, Lithuania, 1978-84; Associate Professor, Pedagogical University, Vilnius, Lithuania, 1987-90; Associate Professor, Jilin University, Changchung, China,

1990-95; Associate Professor, Pedagogical University, Vilnius, Lithuania, 1995-. Publications include: Teaching Russian for Foreigners, 1996; Semantics and Pragmatics of the Russian Language, 1996; New Items in Theory and Practice of Description and Teaching the Russian Language, 1997. Honour: Coach, Winners of International Student Olympiad in China, 1994. Memberships: International Program Director, Pedagogical University, Slavonic Faculty, Vilnius, Lithuania; American Association of Advanced Slavonic Studies. Address: Liudo Giros 74-61, Vilnius 2035, Lithuania.

**KAZIMIANEC Valentin,** b. 13 March 1948, Lithuania. Physicist. 1 son. Education: MSc Physics, Hons, 1971, Vilnius University; Post-grad study in Radioelectronics, Kaunas Scientific Research Institute of Radiomeasurements, Lithuania, 1972-75; Doctor (earlier Candidate) of Cybernetics, 1975, Kaunas University of Technology; Doctor Informatics and Measurements, 1991, St Petersburg Electrotechnical University, Russia; Doctor habilitus Engineering Science, 1993, Scientific Board of Lithuania. Appointments: Senior Researcher, Projects Manager, Vilnius Scientific Research Institute of Electronics, 1971-92; Expert, Relations with scientific and educational organisations, St Petersburg (Russia), Council of Science and Education Major's Dept, 1992-93; Expert, WAN planning, Lithuanian Telecom, 1993-94; Councillor of Chairman of Management Board, Computer Technologies Implementation, Lithuanian Savings Bank, 1994-95; Leading Engineer, WAN Implementation, Lithuanian Railroads, 1995-96; Chief Inspector Intranet Creations, Customs Dept of Ministry of Finance of Lithuania, 1996-. Publications: Coauthor, monograph on intellectual measurement systems based on broadband wave registrators; About 70 scientific articles on process modelling, wave theoretical analysis, data registration and processing, special software creation; 2 patents; Coauthor 18 scientific research reports. Honour: Highest Certifying Commission, Moscow, Russia, Senior Research Fellow, 1982. Membership: St Petersburg Association of Scientists, Russia. Address: Liudo Giros St 74-61, 2035 Vilnius, Lithuania.

**KEENER Craig,** b. 4 July 1960, Massillon, Ohio, USA. Professor; Writer. Education: BA, Central Bible College; MA, 1985, MDiv, 1987, Assemblies of God Seminary, 1985, 1987; BA, Central Bible College. Appointments: Visiting Professor, Eastern Seminary, 1996-98; Assistant Professor and Professor, Head Seminary, 1992-96. Publications: 8 books including: The IVP Bible Background Commentary: New Testament, 1993; Over 80,000 in print; Paul, Women and Wives; And Marries Another; The Spirit in the Gospels and Acts; Matthew Commentary; Defending Black Faith; plus many articles. Address: Eastern Seminary, 6E Lancaster Avenue, Wynnewood, PA 19096-3430, USA.

**KEEY Roger Brian,** b. 11 March 1934, Birmingham, England. Professor. m. Daphne, 1 son, 3 daughters. Education: BSc, Birmingham University, 1954; PhD, 1957. Appointments: Chemical Engineer, DCL Ltd, 1957-62; Lecturer, Reader, 1962-78; Professor, 1978-97; Director, Wood Technology Research Centre, 1997-. Publications: Kiln Drying of Lumber; Drying of Loose and Particulate Materials. Honours: Procter and Gamble Award, Drying Research. Memberships: FRSNZ; FIChemE; FIPENZ; FNZIC; CEng. Address: 25 Montclare Ave, Christchurch 8004, New Zealand.

**KEH Huan Jang,** b. 3 November 1955, Taiwan. Chemical Engineer; Educator; Researcher. m. Sue-Jean Chen, 1 son, 1 daughter. Education: BS, 1978, National Taiwan University; MS, 1980, University Florida; PhD, 1984, Carnegie Mellon University. Appointments: Professor, Dept Chemical

Engineering; Director, Research Centre for Petrochemical Industry; Associate Dean, College of Engineering, National Taiwan University. Honours: Outstanding Research Awards, National Science Council, Taiwan, 1992, 1994, 1997; Excellence in Teaching Award, Ministry of Education, Taiwan, 1993. Memberships: Chinese Institute of Chemical Engineers; International Association of Colloid and Interface Scientists. Address: Dept Chemical Engineering, National Taiwan University, Taipei 106-17 Taiwan, China.

**KEIRANS Leonids,** b. 11 May 1925. Professor. Education: Qualified Teacher of Biology and Geography in basic school, 1948, Daugavpils Teachers College; Qualified Teacher of Geography in secondary school, 1952, Pedagogical College of Latvia; Scientific degree Candidate of Pedagogical Sciences, biology teaching methodology, 1963, Dr paed, branch of biology teaching methodology, 1988, Sankt-Petersburg Pedagogical College; Certified by Latvian Scientific Board, 1991. Appointments: Teacher, Raudas Basic School, 1952-56; Lab Assistant, Lecturer, Senior Lecturer, 1956-, Head of Botany Department, 1972-93, Professor Emeritus, 1995-, Daugavpils Pedagogical College (later University); Member of Promotion and Habilitation Council, Pedagogical Science, same university, also University of Latvia, 1992-. Publications: 125 works; 20 books including, Development of Teaching Methodologies in the Field of Biology, 1997. Address: Saulesiela 66-3, Daugavpils, LV-5403 Latvia.

**KELEKIAN Hilda,** b. 8 June 1961, Beirut, Lebanon. Artist, Industrialist. m. George Darido. Education: AA, Interior Design, Lebanese American University, 1983; BS, Interior Architecture and Fine Arts, University of New York, 1985; DSM, Textiles, Institute of Taraky, 1991; Honorary Diploma in Fine Arts, Societe des Beaux Arts, France, 1994; Honorary Diploma, International Exhibition of Miniature Art, Stockholm, 1996. Appointments: Artist; Parchmentor; Miniaturist; General Manager, Co-Owner, Kokosport Uniforms Factory, Company for Professional Clothing. Creative Works: Displays of Parchments in seven museums, USA and Europe; Art Exhibitions worldwide. Honours: La Toile d'Or France, 1995; Gold Medal, Biennal of Artists, Stockholm, 1995; Gold Medal, Arts de Prestige, France, 1996; Laureate of Merit and Development, France, 1996; Honoured Artist of the European Community, 1996. Memberships: Chairman of several exhibitions; UNESCO; Federation National de la Culture, France. Address: Portemilio 3504 C, Kaslik, Lebanon.

**KELEKIAN Lena,** b. 18 May 1959, Beirut. Artist; Icon Painter; Geologist; Designer. Education: BSc, Geology, American University of Beirut, 1981; DTh, Institute Superieur, Pour La Formation Religieuse, 1992; Certificates in Restoration, Conservation of Icons, Murals, University of London, 1992, 1993, 1995; Honorary Diploma in Fine Arts, 1994; Degree of Professor, 1996. Career: Artist, Iconographer, Restorer, Geologist; Co-Owner, Kokosport Uniforms Factory Co; Art Exhibitions, Worldwide; Permanent Display of Icons in 7 Museums, USA and Europe. Honours include: Medal, Star of Macedonia, 1994; Gold Medal, Biennal of Artists, Stockholm, 1995; 1st Prize, Joudraniyat, City of Beirut, 1997. Memberships include: AUB Alumni Association; UNESCO; American Geological Association; European Geological Association. Address: Portemilio 350C, Kaslik, Lebanon.

**KELLEHER Catherine,** b. 3 May 1947, Jersey City, New Jersey, USA. Nursing; Public Health; Health Services Research. Education: BSN, Georgetown University School of Nursing, 1969; MS, University of California, San Francisco Medical Center, School of Nursing, 1970; MPH, Harvard University, 1979; DSc, Johns Hopkins University, 1985;

Appointments include: Recreational Therapist Assistant, 1966, Rehabilitation Therapist Assistant, 1967, Willowbrook State School, Staten Island; Practical Nurse, New York Hospital, Cornell Medical Center, 1968; Graduate Nurse, University of California, San Francisco, 1969; Staff Nurse, McAuley Neuropsychiatric Institute, St Mary's Hospital, San Francisco, 1970-71, 1974; Postgraduate Research Nurse, 1971-74, Faculty, 1973-74, University of California, San Francisco Medical Center; Director, Video Telemedicine Project, Nepal, The Thomas A Dooley Foundation, New York, 1975-76; Audiovisual Supervisor, Brookdale Hospital Medical Center, Brooklyn, 1976; Consultant, Staff, Home Care Research Initiative Program Office, Robert Wood Johnson Foundation, 1995-97; Co-Principal Investigator, Implementation and Evaluation of Health Outcomes and Evaluation Plans for Home Health Patients with Diabetes, Department of Health, New York, 1997. Publications: Numerous articles in professional journals. Honours include: Woman of the Year, American Biographical Institute, 1996, 1997. Address: 100 Riverside Drive, Apt 14E, New York, NY 10024-4822, USA.

**KELLEMS Jann,** b. 5 October 1951, Jacksonville, USA. Healthcare Systems Consultant. Education: Flagler College, 1970-73; Certificate, Managing Quality Healthcare Systems, Florida International University, 1994; AGPAM Certified Patient Accounting Technician, 1995. Appointments: Clerk, 1977-85; Patient Accounts Representative, Assistant Patient Accounting Director, 1985-88; Insurance Manager, 1988-96; SMS Senior Healthcare Consultant, National Implementations, 1996-. Address: Shared Medical Systems, 100 West Cypress Creek Road, Suite 1050, Fort Lauderdale, FL 33309, USA.

**KELLEY Lee,** b. Boston, Massachusetts, USA. Acting Coach. Education: BA, Liberal Arts, University of Massachusetts; Leland Powers School of Radio, TV and Theater, Boston, Mass. Career: Broadway tutor and coach, Annie, Peter Pan, Evita, Oliver, Broadway Babies, Sunday in the Park, 1978-83; Audition and Acting Coach, Soaps, Guiding Light, All My Children, TV Series, Commercials, Industrial films, 1984-. Honours: Phi Beta Kappa; Phi Kappa Phi; Pi Sigma Alpha; Who's Who In Entertainment; Who's Who of Emerging Leaders in America. Memberships: Actors Equity; Screen Actors Guild; American Federation of Television and Radio Artists; The Dramatists Guild; International Platform Association. Address: 400 W 43rd St Apt 7J, New York, NY 10036 6304, USA.

**KEMOLI Richard,** b. 3 December 1935, Maragoli, Kenya. Institutional Finance Manager. m. Annette, 1 son, 3 daughters. Education: Alliance High School, Kikuyu, Kenya, 1955; Cambridge Overseas Certificate, Makerere University College, Kamapala, Uganda; BSc, Econ, London, 1962. Appointments: Senior Executive, Commonwealth Development Corporation, 1962-95; Director, Kenya Revenue Authority, Kenya Breweries, Johnson Wax; Chairman, UNGA Group, Bamburi Cement Ltd and Kenya Capital Partners. Honour: MBE, 1995. Memberships: Several professional and charitable institutions. Address: Kenya Capital Partners Ltd., Norfolk Towers, Kijabe Street, PO Box 43233, Nairobi, Kenya.

**KEMURDJIAN Alexander,** b. 4 October 1921, Ordzhonikidze. Mechanical Engineer. m. Valda Kemurdjian, 1 son. Education: Diploma, Mechanical Engineer, 1951; MSc, 1957; DSc, 1971; Professor, 1977. Appointments: Senior Lieutenant, World War II; Engineer, 1951; Senior Research Worker, 1956; Head of R&D Department, 1959; Chief Designer, Research Institute, 1969; Chief Research Worker, 1991-. Publications: 150 with 5 monographs. Honours: Order of the Red Star, 1944; Order of the Great Patriotic War, 1945, Grade II, 1995; Order of Lenin, 1971; Sign of Honour, 1983; Lenin Prize Winner, 1973; Higher School Prize Winner, 1986; Academician, Academy of Cosmonautics, 1993; Silver Medal and Diploma, 44th World Exhibition of Invention, Research and Industrial Innovation, Brussels Eurica, 1995; Order of Courage, 1997; Several medals; Minor planet named after him by the International Astronomical Union, 1997. Memberships: European Geophysical Society; Planetary Society, Pasadena, USA; Committee on Space Research. Address: VN11 Transmash, Zarechneya Str 2, St Petersburg 198323, Russia.

**KENNEFICK Christine Marie,** b. 4 July 1962, Washington, District of Columbia, USA. Materials Scientist. Education: BSc with distinction, 1984, MSc, 1986, Stanford University; PhD, 1991, Cornell University. Appointments: National Research Council Associate, NASA, Cleveland Ohio, 1991-93; Guest Scientist, Max Planck Institute, Stuttgart, Germany, 1994-96; Fellow, American Society for Engineering Education, Materials Scientist, US Army Research Lab, Maryland, 1997-98; National Research Council Associate, Air Force Research Lab, Dayton, Ohio, 1998-. Memberships: New York Academy of Sciences; Materials Research Society; American Ceramic Society; American Physical Society. Address: Air Force Laboratory, AFRL/MLBC, 2941 P Street Ste 1 Building 654, Wright Patterson AFB, Ohio 45433-7750, USA.

**KENVIN Roger Lee,** b. 1926, New York, USA. Writer; Publisher. m. Verna Rudd Trimble, 2 daughters. Education: BA, Bowdoin College, 1949; MA, Harvard University, 1956; MFA, 1959, DFA, 1961, Yale University. Appointments: Professor, Chair, Theatre and Dance, California Polytechnic, San Luis Obispo, 1983-88; Publisher, July Blue Press, Alexandria, New Hampshire, 1997-. Publications: Krishalight, 1976; Harpo's Garden, 1997; The Cantabrigian Rowing Society's Saturday Night Bash, 1998. Memberships: Maine Writers & Publishers Alliance; New Hampshire Writers Project. Address: 575 Fairview Avenue, Arcadia, CA 91007, USA.

**KEPEZINSKAS Kazimieras,** b. 10 January 1937, Trakai, Lithuania. Geologist. m. Valentina Kepezinskas, 1 son. Education: MSc, 1960, Dept Geology, Moscow University; PhD, 1965, Novosibirsk University; Habilitated Doctor of Physical Science, 1974, Novosibirsk Institute Geology and Geophysics. Appointments: Junior Research Scientist, Moscow University, 1960-62; Junior, Senior Research Scientist, Head of Department, Institute of Geology and Geophysics, Novosibirsk, 1962-92; Senior Research Scientist, Institute of Geology, Lithuania, 1992-. Publications: Author and Co-author, 180 scientific articles, 6 books and 5 geological maps. Memberships: Lithuanian Geological Union; Russian Mineralogical Society. Address: Gabijos 65-38, LT 2000 Vilnius, Lithuania.

**KERIMOVA Elmira,** b. 31 December 1942, Gezamboy, Azerbaijan. Physicist. m. Guseinov Nadir, 1 daughter. Education: Azerbaijan State University, 1963; Scientific degree of candidate of physico-mathematical science, 1970; Degree of doctor of physico-Mathematical sciences, 1992. Appointments: Head of Laboratory, Institute of Physics, Baku, Azerbaijan. Publications: 170 publications, 8 patents. Address: Institute of Physics, Azerbaijanian Academy of Sciences, G Javid Prospect 33, Baku 370143, Azerbaijan.

**KERIS Valdis,** b. 26 January 1961, Riga, Latvia. Neurosurgeon; Neurologist. m. Sandra Mihalenoka, 1 son, 1 daughter. Education: MD, 1985, Medical Academy of Latvia; PhD, 1991; DSc, 1996. Appointments: Research Fellow, 1985-87, Cons Researcher, 1997-98, Medical Academy of Latvia, Riga; Cons, 7th Clin Hospital, Riga, 1987-; Assistant

Professor Neurosurgery and Neurology, Riga Stradina University, 1998-. Publication: Transluminal Angioplasty of Precerebral and Cerebral Arteries: Experimental and Clinical Aspects, 1996. Memberships: European Association Neurosurgery Societies; European Federation Neurology Societies; World Federation Neurosurgery Societies. Address: Riga 7th Clin Hospital, 2 Hipokrata St, LV-1038, Riga, Latvia.

**KERR James Sewell,** b. 17 Janauary 1922, Jamaica. Queens Cousel; Attorney at Law. m. Hyacinth Clarke, 2 sons, 4 daughters. Education: Senior School Certificate, Lincolns Inn, 1954-57; Called to the Bar, 1957. Appointments: Crown Council, 1962-64; Acting Legal Attache, Jamaica High Commission, London, 1964; Resident Magistrate, 1964-67; Director of Public Prosecutions, 1967-77; Judge of Appeal, Jamaica, 1977-88; Judge, Cayman Islands Court of Appeal, 1984-; Ombudsman, Parliamentary Matters, 1991-; Judge, Turks and Caicos Islands Court of Appeal, 1995-; Ombudsman, Political Matters, 1998-. Honour: Order of Jamaica, 1987. Memberships: Constitutional Commission, 1992-92; Judicial Service Commission, 1988-94; Committee on Political Tribalism, 1996-97. Address: Court of Appeal, P O Box 695, Kingston, Jamaica.

**KESSLER Alan F,** b. 13 September 1947, Ways City, Kansas, USA. Engineer. m. Karen Maxwell, 1 son, 1 daughter. Education: BS Agricultural Engineering, cum laude, Machine Design Option, 1969, Kansas State University; MS Engineering, Mechanical Engineering, Machine Design, 1970, Purdue University; Pre MBA Programme, 1982, MBA Programme partially completed, University Wisconsin, University Texas; Raytheon Advanced Management Programme, 1994, Harbridge House Inc. Appointments: Project Development Engineer, 1970-74, Senior Development Engineer, 1974-78, Development Engineering Supervisor, 1978-79, Development Engineering Manager, 1979-83, Senior Principal Engineer, 1983, Manager, Production Support Engineering, 1983-84, Manager, Product Development Engineering, 1984-86, Manager, Unitary Design Engineering, 1986-87, The Trane Company; Vice President, Engineering and Topton Operations, Caloric Corporation, Raytheon Appliance Group, 1991-92; Chief Engineer, 1992, Vice President Engineering, 1992-93, Vice President Engineering and Quality, 1997-, Amana Refrigeration Inc; Vice President, Engineering and Quality, Raytheon Appliances, 1993-97. Publications: 15 papers; 3 patents. Honour: Kansas State University College of Engineering, Distinguished Member Hall of Fame, 1997. Memberships: American National Standards Institute; Air Conditioning and Refrigeration Institute; Association of Home Appliance Manufacturers; Air Conditioning and Refrigeration Centre; and others. Address: Amana Appliances, 2800 220th Trail, Amana, IA 52204, USA.

**KEUM Yong Yeon,** b. 12 December 1958, Taebaek City, Korea. Researcher. m. Dong Ryung Han, 2 sons. Education: BSc, 1978-82, MSc, 1982-84, Seoul National University, Korea; PhD, Universite Pierre et Marie Curie, 1996. Appointments: Lecturer, Department of Physics, Kangreung National University, Korea, 1985-88, Department of Physics, Sang-Ji University, Wonju, Korea, 1986-88; Assistant Professor, Department of Physics, Sang-Ji University, 1988-91; Researcher, Laboratoir Physique Theorique et Hautes Energie Paris, France, 1992-96; Lecturer, Department of Physics Education, Seoul National University, 1997-98; Research Fellow, Asia Pacific Center for Theoretical Physics, Seoul, 1996-98; Monbushou Research Fellow, Theory Division, KEK, Tsukuba, Japan, 1998-. Publications: Several articles in professional journals. Honours: Prize, Seoul National University, 1982; Prize, 3rd Military Academy School, 1985;

CEA Fellowship, France, 1994-96; Honorable Mention, Gravity Research Foundation, 1997; Monbushou Fellowship, Japan Government, 1998-99. Address: KEK Theory Group, 1-1 Oho Tsukuba, Ibaraki 305-0801, Japan.

**KHALEEFA Omar Haroon,** b. 1 January 1962, Al-Rahad, Sudan. Psychologist; Researcher. m. Ikhlas Ashria, 2 daughters. Education: BA, honours, 1985, MS, 1987, University of Khartoum; PhD, University of Newcastle-upon-Tyne, 1995. Appointments: Teaching Assistant, University of Khartoum, 1986-91; Assistant Professor, Psychology, University of Bahrain, 1996-. Publications: Over 30 articles in professional journals. Honours: International Prize, International Sociological Association, 1994; Prize, International Institute of Islamic Thought, USA, 1994; Best Researcher in Psychology in the Arab World, Shoman Foundation, 1997. Memberships: IACCP; APA; ICP; ECHA; WCGT; ISA. Address: College of Education, University of Bahrain, Department of Psychology, PO Box 32038, Bahrain.

**KHALIKOV Abdukarim,** b. 30 December 1947, Dushambe Sity. Professor; Engineer. m. 3 sons, 1 daughter. Education: Dipl Eng, Electronical Technology; Diploma Candidate, Technical Science; Dr, Technical Science. Appointments: Teacher; President, Algorithm, SPF. Publications: 155 scientific works; 4 monographs. Honours: Many diplomas. Address: Technological University, Kuibyshev Street 10, Dushanbe, 734025 Tajikistan.

**KHALIKOVICH Khalikov Abdukarim,** b. 30 December 1947, Kanibadam, Tagikistan. Professor. 3 sons, 1 daughter. Graduate, Elements and Devises Computers Technical, 1974; Doctor of Technical Science, Institute of Cybernetic, Uzbekistan, 1991. Appointments: Vice Director, VNIIPOU VNIIPVTI VNIIPAS GKVTII, Academy of Sciences, USSR. Publications: 155 Scientific Works. Honours: Honorary Member, Academy of Information of Education Ministry of Russian Federation. Memberships: Coordination Centre of Information Community of Independent States; Expert Council on Science and Technical of Federation of Engineering Institutes of Central Asian Countries. Address: 754055 Republic of Tajikistan, Dushanbe-city, Dehoti Street 23,20-43, Tajikistan.

**KHAN H A,** b. 22 June 1935, Dharwar, Karnataka, India. Professor. m. Razia, 1 son, 1 daughter. Education: BA, Hons, 1956; LLB, 1961; MA, 1962; MLS, 1969; PhD, 1986. Appointments: Assistant Librarian, Karnatak University, 1962-67; Deputy Librarian, Mysore University, 1967-71; Reader, Library Science, 1971-86; Mysore University Librarian, 1980-82; Professor, 1986-95. Publications: 2 research documents; Assessment of Public Libraries in Karnataka, 1979; Public Libraries and Their Services in Karnataka, 1982; Over 60 research articles. Memberships: Life Member: Indian Library Association; Indian Association of Special Libraries and Information Centres; Society for Information Science. Address: 62 HIG HUDCO Colony, Bannimantap, Mysore 570 015, India.

**KHAN Abbas-Haider,** b. 14 January 1998, Quetta-Haider. Professor. m. 1 son, 1 daughter. Education: PhD, 1978, UK; Postdoctorate, 1995-96, USA. Appointments: Lecturer, 1972; Professor, 1993-. Honours: Overseas Fellowship, 1974; Fulbright Award, 1995, USA; DAAD Fellowship, Germany, 1998. Memberships: American Chemical Society; Chemical Society of Pakistan; Pakistan Society of Biochemistry. Address: Institute of Biochemistry, University of Balochistan, Quetta, Pakistan.

**KHAN Ahmed Qasim,** b. 18 January 1950, Lahore, Pakistan. Computer Software Executive. m. Mahnaz Faridi, 1 son. Education: Graduate Engineer, Electrical Communication Engineering; Chartered Engineer, Advanced Computer Engineering. Appointments: Junior Engineer, Telephone Industries of Pakistan, 1967-74; Development Engineer, MAREIK Earth Station Project, Elektrisk Bureau, Oslo, Norway, 1979-81; Chief Consultant, Haukeland Hospital, Bergen, 1981-82; Head of Department, Industrial Projects Department, University of Bergen, 1982-84; Managing Director, SCS Scandinavian Computer Systems, Norway, 1984-87, SCS Scandinavian Computer Systems (Pvt) Ltd, Pakistan, 1987-. Memberships: Institute of Electrical and Electronics Engineers, USA; Computer Society, USA; Norwegian Society of Chartered Engineers; New York Academy of Sciences. Address: 233, G9/4, Islamabad, Pakistan.

**KHAN Lurey,** b. 11 November 1927, Camden, New Jersey, USA. Writer. m. John Lewis Thomas, 1947, deceased August 1978, 1 daughter. Education: Student, Boston College, 1945-46, 1963-65, Harvard University, 1966. Appointments: Medical Technician, New England Hospital, Boston, 1954-58, Children's Hospital, Boston, 1958-61; Research Assistant, Harvard Medical School, Boston, 1961-66; Bacteriologist, HP Hood and Company Inc, Charlestown, Massachusetts, USA, 1966-68; Brewing Chemist, Carling Brewing Company, Natick, Massachusetts, USA, 1968-72; Research Assistant, Harvard Medical School, Boston, 1972-77; Administrator, Sears Roebuck and Company, Boston, 1978-80; Medical Technologist, Smithkline Beecham Company, Waltham, Massachusetts, 1981-93. Publications: Author: One Day, Levin....He Be Free, William Still and the Underground Railroad, 1972; Contributor, short stories and articles to journals and magazines. Honours: Creative Writing Grantee, Mary Roberts Rinehart Foundation, 1978; Mary Lizzie Saunders Clapp Scholar Schlesinger Library, Radcliffe College, 1985. Memberships: Authors Guild; Authors League America; Roman Catholic. Hobbies: Swimming; Cooking; Hiking; Reading. Address: #E206 791 Tremont Street, Boston, MA 02118, USA.

**KHAN Mohammad Islam,** b. 20 June 1968, Lucknow, India. Sculptor. m. Education: BFA, 1992, MFA, 1996, Lucknow University. Appointments: Freelance Artist; 1 and 2 year research on scholarship and fellowship, 1995, 1992-94; Training of blind student in Sur Smarak Mandal, Sur Kuti Runakata Agra, 1993; Art Teacher, Eram Intermediate College, Indira Nagar, Lucknow; Training of many college students in Naini Tal Raj Bhavan, 1994. Creative works: Represented in collections of work in India; Private collection in Italy and India; 2 one man shows in UP State Lalit Kala Academy, Lucknow, 1994-95; Many group shows; Attended 3 artist camps in Lucknow, 1992, 1996, 1997. Honours: Governor of UP, 1995; Dept of Culture UP, 1993; College of Arts and Crafts, Lucknow, 1987. Membership: Joint Secretary, UP Artists Association, Lucknow. Address: 727 Sheikh Pura Colony, Aliganj, Lucknow 0, UP India.

**KHAN Muhammad Mansoor,** b. 10 April 1939, Wadhona. Teacher. m. Tahira, 2 sons. Education: BA, 1959; MA, English, 1961; PhD, English, 1975. Appointments: Assistant Lecturer; Lecturer, Assistant Professor; Assistant Professor, Professor, 1985-. Publications: Emily Dickinson's Poetry; The Butterfly Throb; Several Poems and Articles published in journals. Memberships: American Book Club; Indian Association of American Studies. Address: Mehta Colony Parasia Road, Chhindwara 480001, India.

**KHAN Sohail A,** b. 10 February 1955, Nagpur, India. Physician. m. Arshia, 2 sons, 1 daughter. Education: BSc, 1974; MSc, 1976; MBBS, 1982; MD, 1986. Appointments: Physician, Government Medical College Hospital, Nagpur, India; Physician, Ministry of Health, Riyadh, Saudi Arabia; Resident, Barc Hospital, Bombay; Resident, MGM Hospital, Bombay; Resident, Prince Aly Khan Hospital, Bombay; Resident, Holy Spirit Hospital, Bombay. Memberships: Royal Society of Health, London; Indian Medical Association; Planetary Society; New York Academy of Sciences; American Assocaition for the Advancement of Sciences. Address: Artawiah Med Ctr, Artawiah, Riyadh 11952, Saudi Arabia.

**KHAN Taimur,** b. 28 January 1967, Panisail, Birbhum, India. Lecturer. Education: MP, 1983; HS, 1985; BA Beng Hons, 1988; MA Beng, 1992; Running with research on Bengali poems. Appointments: Part time Lecturer on Bengali, Hiralal Bhakat College, Nalhati, Birbhum, 1998-. Publication: Kothay Pa Rakhi, 1994. Membership: DANA. Address: Dadpur, Panisail, Birbhum 731224, West Bengal, India.

**KHANAM Jasmina,** b. 23 February 1959, West Bengal. Teacher. m. Nasimul Gani, 1 daughter. Education: B Pharm, 1981; M Pharm, 1983; PhD, 1993. Appointments: Lecturer, V L College of Pharmacy, India, 1983-86; Lecturer, Jadavpur University, India, 1992-. Publications: in the Journal of the Institution of Engineers, 1990, 1996. Memberships: Life Member: Indian Pharmaceutical Association; Indian Association for the Cultivation of Science; ISTE. Address: Dept Pharmaceutical Technology, Jadavpur University, Calcutta 700 032, India.

**KHANAPURE Subhash,** b. 10 November 1954, Parli Vaijnath, India. Research Scientist. m. Anita V Choudhary, 1 son. Education: BSc, Chemistry, Marathwada University, 1975; MSc, Organic Chemistry, 1977; PhD, Organic Chemistry, National Chemical Laboratory, Poona University, 1983. Appointments: Research Officer, National Chemical Laboratory, 1983; Post Doctoral Fellow, Cancer Drug Research Laboratory, Institute for Chemical Research, Kyoto University, Kyoto, Japan, 1983-85; Research Associate, Southern Methodist University, 1985-88; Senior Research Scientist, 1988-91; Senior Research Scientist, Florida Institute of Technology, 1991-98. Publications: 64 Publications. Honours: Junior, Senior, Research Fellowships, Council of Scientific and Industrial Research; Monbusho Scholarship, Ministry of Education, Japan. Memberships: American Chemical Society. Address: NitroMed Inc, 12 Oak Park Drive, Bedford, MA 01730, USA.

**KHANDELWAL Ashok Kumar,** b. 1 June 1960, Jamshedpur, India. Advocate. m. Ranjna Khandelwal, 2 sons. Education: BA; BSc, LLB. Publication: Poetry book. Honours: Namrin Kalyan Samitee Award; Roy Award. Memberships: Lions Club of Jamshedpur; Yawanar Samitee, Jamshedpur. Address: 178/D Line No 1, Kashidih Sakehi, Jamshedpur 1, India.

**KHANDELWAL Ishwari Prasad,** b. 16 January 1937, Chindwara, India. Engineer. m. Urmila, 1 son, 2 daughters. Education: BEng, honours, Mechanical Engineering, University of Jabalpur, 1960. Appointments: Plant Engineer, Head of Department, Rashtriya Chemicals and Fertilizers, 1961-73; Chief Engineer, Production Manager, Works Manager, Managing Director, Albright and Wilson Chemicals India Ltd, 1973-. Memberships: American Society of Mechanical Engineers; Fellow, Institute of Mamagement, Institution of Industrial Managers, India. Address: "Urmish", Sai Section, Ambarnath 421 501, Thane, Maharashtra, India.

**KHANNA Pardeep K,** b. 4 February 1956, Ferozepur, Punjab, India. Scientist. m. Veena, 1 son, 1 daughter. Education: BSc,1975; MSc, 1977; PhD, 1980; Postdoctorate, 1983. Appointments: Assistant Professor, 1983-86, Associate Professor, Mycologist, 1986-94, Professor, Senior Mycologist, 1994-, PAU Ludhiana, India. Publications: Over 75. Honours: University Merit Certificate and Fellowship in BSc, University Merit Certificate and Fellowship in MSc, 1975-77; CSIR, JRF/SRF Fellowship in PhD, 1977-80; French Government Fellowship, 1981-83; Plant Science Colloquium Award of DBT, Government of India, 1986-87. Memberships: Life member, Association of Microbiologists of India; Life member, Mushroom Society of India; Indian Phytopathological Society; BioEnergy Society of India. Address: Dept of Microbiology, PAU, Ludhiana PB, India.

**KHARCHENKO Vera Konstantinovna,** b. 4 August 1949, Tver, Russia. Teacher. 1 son. Education: MA, Novosibirsk Pedagogical University, 1970; PhD, St Petersburg Pedagogical University, 1970-73; DSc, Moscow Pedagogical University, 1990. Appointments: Assistant, Department of Russian Language, 1973-78, Lecturer, 1978-81, Assistant Professor, 1981-91, Head, Department of General Philology, 1991-, Belgorod State University; Director, Belgorod Philological Research Institute, 1997-. Publications include: How to Do Research; Functions of the Metaphor; Types of Linguistic Analysis with Commentaries and Patterns; Indirect Meanings of the Word; The Dictionary of Childrens Speech; The Paradoxes of Childrens Speech. Memberships: University Board; Two Dissertation University Boards. Address: Chernyshevskogo 6 kv 19, 308612 Belgorod, Russia.

**KHARLAMOV Alexander,** b. 13 June 1953, Moscow. Physicist. m. Vera Barteneva, 1 s, 1 d. Education: MS, Physics, 1976; PhD, 1982; Doctor of Physics, 1998. Appointments: Researcher, 1976-83; Senior Researcher, 1983-93; Professor of Physics, 1994-. Publications: 34 Publications in Science Area. Memberships: ACP; AAAS. Address: Rua da Saudade 106, Gafanha da Encarnagao, 3830 Ilhavo, Portugal.

**KHATIBI Abdol Ali,** b. 27 April 1958, Iran. Lecturer in Marketing Management. Education: BEngg, Hiet, India, 1983; BScEngg, Newport, USA, 1987; MBA, 1991, PhD, Developing Mechanical Design, 1993-94, Osmania, India, MBA, 1989, PhD, Production and Planning, 1999, Newport, USA. Appointments include: Engineering Trainee, Engineer, Madras Airport, 1984-88; Lecturer, Aircraft Engineering, 1987-88, 1991, HIET; General Manager, Production Programmer and Product Designing, 1988-91, Progress Manager, 1992, PLtdCo; Vice President and Lecturer, Institute of Tech Engineering, Malaysia, 1995; Business Development and Consultant, Pasma Group, from Taiwan in Malaysia, 1995-97; Planner and Lecturer, KA College, Malaysia, 1995-97; Consultant, International College, Malaysia, 1996-97; Head of Department and Lecturer, KOP Educators and Consultants, Malaysia, 1996-97; Marketing Coordinator, Research Coordinator, 1997, MBA Coordinator, May, Dec, 1998, Deputy Director, February 1998, D Director, March 1998, University Telkom Melaka, Malaysia. Publications: Research papers, contributions to national and international publications. Memberships: Institute of Engineers and Technicians, London; India Aeronautical Society of India; India Society for Technical Education. Address: University Telekom Faculty Management, Jalan Ayer Keroh Lama, Malaka 75450, Malaysia.

**KHATRI M H,** b. 4 September 1942, Pakistan. Senior Scientific Officer. m. 4 sons, 2 daughters. Education: MSc, Applied Physics, Karachi University, 1973; PhD, Ionic Physics, University of London, 1980. Publications: 26 articles in professional journals. Memberships: Pakistan Association of Scientists & Scientific Progression. Address: SUPARCO, Ionospheric Research Division, Sector 28, Gulzar-e-Hijri, Off University Road, PO Box 8402, Karachi 75270, Pakistan.

**KHAVARI-NEJAD Ramazan-Ali,** b. 21 January 1943, Babol, Mazandaran, Iran. Botanist. m. Behnaz Eshragh, 2 daughters. Education: DIC in Botany, Imperial College of Science and Technology, London, 1969; MSc in Plant Physiology, 1969, PhD in Botany, 1972, Imperial College of Science and Technology, University of London. Appointments: Assistant Professor, Department of Biology, University of Isfahan, Isfahan, 1972-77, 1978-79; Adjunct Professor, Department of Biochemistry, Michigan State University, East Lansing, USA, 1977-78; Associate Professor, 1980-94, Professor, 1995-, Department of Biology, University of Teachers Education, Tehran. Publications: Articles in journals such as Photosynthetica, and Acta Horticultura; Effects of CO2 enrichment preconditioning on chlorophylls contents and photosynthetic CO2 exchange in tomato plants, in book Progress in Photosynthetic Research, 1987; Books in Farsi: Photosynthesis, 1991; An Introduction to BASIC Programming, 1993; Biostatistics, 1996; An Introduction to Plant Growth and Development, 1997; Plant Respiration, 1997; Photosynthesis in Higher Plants, 1997; Principles of Biostatistics, microcomputer edition, 1997; Plant Physiology (cells, respiration, photosynthesis), 1998. Honours: Royal College of Science Scholarship in Botany, Imperial College of Science and Technology, London, 1970; British Council Fee Remission Scholarship, 1970-72; Fulbright Grant, 1977-78; Distinguished Professor, University of Teachers Education, Tehran, 1994. Address: Department of Biology, University of Teachers Education, 49 Mobarezan, Tehran 15, Iran.

**KHAZAN Victor,** b. 18 March 1947, Dniepropetrovsk, Ukraine. Scientist. m. Alla Deynega, 1 son, 1 daughter. Education: Dniepropetrovsk State University, 1970; Candidate of Science, 1980; Senior Scientist, 1988; DPhil, 1993. Appointments: Engineer, Higher Engineer, Junior Scientist, Senior Scientist, Institute of Geotechnical Mechanics, Ukraine Academy of Science, 1978-88; Senior Scientist, Head of Laboratory, Institute of Technical Mechanics, 1988-91; Head of Laboratory, Head of Department, Institute of Nature Management and Ecology, 1991-. Publications: Over 100 scientific works and inventions, several books. Address: 48 Kosior Street, Apt 24, Dniepropetrovsk 320085, Ukraine.

**KHETSURIANI Ramaz.** Address: 51 Iosefidze Str, apt 95, 380060 Tbilisi, Republic of Georgia.

**KHIN-NWE-OO,** b. 30 August 1950, Yangon, Myanmar. Microbiologist; Researcher. Education: MB, BS, Institute of Medicine, Yangon, 1974; Diploma in Bacteriology, 1982; MMedSc, Microbiology, 1994. Appointments: Assistant Surgeon, Ag San Tb Hospital, Yangon, 1978-81; Medical Officer, National Health Laboratory, Yangon, 1981-83; Research Officer, Department of Medical Research, 1983-91, Senior Research Officer, 1991-94, Research Scientist, 1994-97, Deputy Director, 1997-, Yangon. Publications: Articles in international journals, 1989, 1991, 1993, 1995, 1996, 1997, local journals, 1989, 1990, 1991, 1992, 1993, 1994, 1995, 1996, 1997. Honours: Fellowship, Japan, 1991-92; Best Poster Award, Myanmar, 1993. Memberships: Lifelong Member, Myanmar Medical Association, 1978-; Lifelong Member, Microbiology Association, 1992-. Address: 90 Sabaichan 2nd Lane, Hlaing, Yangon, Myanmar.

**KHONIK Vitaly Alexandrovich,** b. 17 December 1955, Kemerovo. Physicist. m. E Paschenko, 1 daughter. Education:

Graduate, Voronezh Politechnic Institute, 1978; Candidate of Sciences, Physics and Math, 1983; DSc, Physics and Math, 1992; Professor, 1994. Appointments: Engineer - Physicist, 1978-81; Postgraduate Student, 1981-83; Junior Researcher, 1984-85; Senior Researcher, 1985-91; Assistant Professor, 1991-92; Professor, 1992-. Publications: 170 publications in solid state physics. Honour: Soros Professor, Open Society Institute, Soros Foundation, 1997. Address: General Lizyukov Str 44 Apt 86, Voronezh 394053, Russia.

**KHOROSHILOVA Eugenia**, b. 9 August 1947, Stavropol, Russia. Chemist. m. Oleg Semyonov PhD, 1 son, 1 daughter. Education: Diploma, High School, 1955-56; Diploma, Lomonosov Moscow State University, 1966-71; PhD, Institute of Spectroscopy of Academy of Sciences, 1985. Appointments: Research Chemist, Institute of Elementorganic Compunds, 1971-76; Research Scientist, Zelinski Institute of Organic Chemistry, 1976-81; Senior Scientist, Institute of Spectroscopy of Academy of Science, 1981-. Publications: 40 scientific publications; 5 patents. Honours: High School Gold Medal, 1966; Medal, 850 Years of Moscow, 1988. Memberships: Mendeleev Chemical Society; Society of Inventors and Innovators, Russia; Invited to New York Academy of Sciences. Address: Institute of Spectroscopy RAS, 1420092 Troitsk, Russia.

**KHOSRAVI Amir**, b. 8 August 1948, Birjand, Iran. Lecturer. m. Soraya, 3 sons. Education: BSc, 1970, MSc, 1972, PhD, 1980, Cambridge University, Trinity College. Publications: 1 paper in Proceedings of American Mathematical Society, 1982; Several papers in Iranian journals and proceedings. Membership: Iranian Mathematical Society. Address: Department of Mathematics, University for Teacher Education, Dr Mofateh Avenue, Tehran 15614, Iran.

**KHOZEIMEH Issa**, b. 25 December 1939, Tehran, Iran. Engineer Educator. m. Nahid Khozeimeh, 2 daughters. Education: Associate in Arts, 1962; Bachelor of Science, George Washington University, 1966; Master of Science, George Washington University, 1973; D Eng, George Washington University, 1984; DSc, George Washington University, 1994. Appointments: Junior Engineer, Potomac Electric Power Company, 1967-68; Engineer Substation Design, Potomac Electric Power Company, 1968-71; Substation Design Engineer, Potomac Electric Power Company, 1971-73; Designs Standards Engineer, Potomac Electric Power Company, 1973-79; Senior Engineer, Potomac Electric Power Company, 1979-80; Chief Electrical Engineer, David Volkert and Associates Inc, 1980-88; Manager, Utilities Division, Metropolitan Washington Airports Authority, 1988-. Publications: 21 research papers, publications, recognitions, 1977-1993. Honours: School of Engineering Service Award, George Washington University, 1976; General Alumni Association Service Award, George Washington University, 1977; Engineer Alumni Association Service Award, George Washington University, 1978; Certificate of Appreciation, Engineer Council, 1984, 1985; Distinguished Service Award, Engineer Council, 1986; Distinguished Senior Engineer Award, Maryland Society of Professional Engineers, 1997; Distinguished Alumni Service Award, George Washington University Alumni Association, 1997,1999. Memberships: SIGMA XI, 1985; ETA KAPPA NU, 1979; NSPE, 1975; IEEE, 1962-; ISA, 1978; ASEM; NICE; NIEMS; SES; WSE; ASQC; IES; CES; BES; AFEA; EC and M-EIEP, 1978; GWU-EAA, 1967-. Address: P O Box 557, Glen Echo, MD 20812-0557, USA.

**KHURSHID Zahiruddin**, b. 8 February 1947, Kamptee, India. Information Professional. m. Foukia Khurshid, 1 son, 2 daughters. Education: BA (Honours), 1969, MLS, 1972, University of Karachi, Karachi, Pakistan, MSLIS, 1978, Pratt Institute, Brooklyn, New York, USA. Appointments: Head of Cataloging Department, King Fahd University of Petroleum and Minerals, 1983-87; Manager, King Fahd University of Petroleum and Minerals, 1987-93, Senior Manager, King Fahd University of Petroleum and Minerals, 1993-. Publications: 25 articles to professional refereed journals. Honour: Scholarship, Pratt Institute, New York, USA. Memberships: Life Member, Beta Phi Mu, International Library Science Honor Society; Arabian Gulf Chapter, Special Libraries Association; Life Member, Pakistan Library Association. Address: King Fahd University of Petroleum & Minerals, Box 450, Dhahran 31261, Saudi Arabia.

**KIANGI Daud Abdala**, b. 7 October 1955, Kilimanjard, Africa. Engineer, Manager. m. Margreth Msuya, 3 daughters. Education: BSc Hons Engineering 1983; MSc Project Management 1987. Appointments: Technical Advisor and Consultant to Coffee Industry, Tanzania. Honours: Best Worker, By Local Labour Organisation, Tanzania, 1991. Memberships: National Geographic Society. Address: P O Box 732, Moshi, Africa.

**KIEHNE Anna**, b. Preston, Minnesota, USA. Consultant. m. Lyman F Loveland. Education: BA, Business Administration, 1969; Certificate, Systems Analysis, 1984; Masters, International Business, 1992. Appointments: Consultant, 1990-; Vice President, Bowest Corp. Memberships: Institute of Management Accountants; American Management Association. Address: 15085 SW Chardonnay Ave, Tigard, OR 97224, USA.

**KIHANA Toshimasa**, b. 17 September 1955, Iyomishima, Japan. Gynecological Oncologist. m. Mieko Daigen, 1 s, 1 d. Education: MD, Ehime University School of Medicine, 1982; PhD, 1993. Appointments: Chief, Obstetrics and Gynecological Section, Ehime Prefectural Central Hospital. Honours: Grants in Aid, Ministry of Education, Science Sports and Culture of Japan, 1993, 1995, 1998. Memberships: Japan Society of Obstetrics and Gynecology; Japanese Cancer Association; Japan Society of Clinical Oncology. Address: 617-21 Higashi-ishi, Matsuyama 790-0932, Japan.

**KIKAWA Kazuhiko**, b. 7 July 1943, Yamaguchi, Japan. Physician. m. Naoka Higa, 1 son, 1 daughter. Education: BM, 1970, Kumamoto University, Japan; MD, 1976, Pennsylvania, USA; Dilpomate, 1977, American Board of Internal Medicine; Fellow, American College of Physicians, 1985. Appointments: From Physician-in-Chief to Assistant Director, 1980-91; Director, 1991-, Fukuoka Tokushukai Hospital; Chairman, Tokuwakai Social Welfare Corporation, 1995-; Board of Directors, Tokushukai Medical Corp; Council member, Japan-N American Medical Exchange Foundation, 1997-. Publications: Nephron, 1983, 1989; Journal of Cardiography, 1978; Japanese Journal of Medicine, 1990; Consultant, USA, 1995. Memberships: Council member, Japanese Society Internal Medicine; Japan Hospital Association; Japan Hospital Quality Assurance Society. Address: 2-54 Suku-Kita, Kasuga Fukuoka, 816-0864, Japan.

**KIKUCHI Soka Kazuhiro**, b. 3 April 1934, Yokohama, Japan. Marine Consultant. m. Yukiko Gotoh, 1 son, 1 daughter. Education: Master degree of Political Science and Economy, Waseda University. Appointments: Chief European Representative of Yokohama Marine Products, 1972-97; Stayed in London, UK, as Chief European Representative; President, MBC International, Marine Consultant; Life Member, International Association of Ports and Harbours. Honour: Tea

Master of Tea Ceremony. Address: 12 20 3 Chome Nagata Kita, Minami ku Yokohama 232-0071, Japan.

**KILGORE Janice,** b. 6 July 1955, Dallas, Texas, USA. Music Education. Education: Graduated with Honours, Justin F Kimball High School, Dallas, TX, USA, 1973; Music and Christian Education, Oral Roberts University, Tulsa, OK, USA, 1973-76; AA, graduated with honors, Mountain View College, Dallas, TX, USA, 1979; Recording Technician, Cedar Valley College, Dallas, TX, 1981; BMus, Music Education, North Texas State University, Denton, TX, 1983; Doctoral Candidate in Music Education, Vocal Pedagogy, University of North Texas, 1990; State Certified Teacher, All Level Music, Choral, 1991; Yamaha Educational Systems, Buena Park, CA (Certified Yamaha Music Instructor, Keyboard), 1987. Appointments include: Coordinator, Chairperson, District Vocal Music Program; Choir Director/Class Keyboard Instructor, Music History Instructor, Junior High and High School levels; Class Keyboard Instructor, Baldwin Family Music, 1987-89; Private Piano Instructor and Class Music Theory, Oak Cliff Music Co, 1978-80; Director: St Luke United Methodist Church of Dallas, 1989-90; First United Methodist Church of Waxahachie, 1990-93; Trinity United Methodist Church of Duncanville, 1993-94. Publications: 10 1 creative training ideas, contributing author, 1998. Honours: Outstanding Choir Member, 1969, 1972; Student Member, Dallas Symphony Orchestra, viola, 1973; Missionary Service Award, United Methodist Women, 1986; Nominated for Woman of the Year, International Biographical Centre, 1996-97; Sigma Alpha Iota, Marion Flagg Scholarship Recipient, 1997. Memberships: Texas Music Educators Association; Texas Choral Directors Association; Texas Orchestra Directors Association; Music Educators National Conference; Dallas Music Educators Association; Choristers Guild; International Association of Jazz Educators; American Guild of English Handbell Ringers. Address: 317 Oak Meadow Lane, Cedar Hill, TX 75104-3283, USA.

**KILJUNEN Kimmo Roobert,** b. 13 June 1951, Finland. Member of Parliament. m. Marja Liisa, 2 sons, 2 daughters. Education: MA, Social Sciences, Helsinki University, 1973; M Phil, Development Studies, Sussex University, 1977; D Phil, 1985; Docent, Helsinki University, Joensuu University, 1986. Appointments: Study Programme Assistant, University of Helsinki, 1972-73; Liaison Officer, Finnish UN Association, 1974-75; British Council, Fellowship, University of Sussex, Institute of Development Studies, 1975-78; Researcher, Labour Institute for Economic Research, Helsinki, 1979-81; Member Finnish UN Delegation, 1979; Secretary General, Kampuchea Inquiry Commission, 1980-82; Research Fellow, Academy of Finland 1981-85; Secretary General International Peace Bureau, Geneva, 1984-85; City Councillor, Vantaa, 1985-; Director, Institute of Development Studies, Helsinki University, 1986-95; Consultant, UNICEF, Kenya Country Office, Nairobi, 1989-91; Transition Policy Coordinator, UNDP, New York, 1993-94; Member of Parliament, Finland, 1995-; Serves on many parliamentary committees including: Foreign Affairs, 1996-; Grand Committee, Member, 1995, Vice-Chair, 1999-; Defence, 1999-; Vice-Chairman, Finnish Delegation to OSCE Parliamentary Assembly, 1995-. Publications: Namibia, The Last Colony, 1981; Kampuchea, Decade of the Genocide, 1984; Region to Region Cooperation Between Developed and Developing Countries; Finland and the New International Division of Labour, 1992. Honours: President Urho Kekkonen Foundation, Literature Award. Memberships: Vice-Chairman Finnish Red Cross International Committee, 1992-93; UNU/WIDER'S Academic Advisory Council, 1993-96; Chairman, Finland South Africa Association, 1995-97; Chairman Finnish Committee for European Security, 1995 Address: Linnoittanpolku 3 G 15, FIN 01280 Bantaa, Finland.

**KIM Byung Kyu,** b. 25 May 1950, Ulsam, Korea. Professor. m. Kyung Hee Hong, 2 sons. Education: BS, Pusan National University, 1973; MS, Ohio University, 1981; PhD, Virginia Polytechnic Institute and State University, 1984. Appointments: Professor, Pusan National University; Editorial Board, Journal of Applied Polymer Science and Journal of Polymer Engineering. Publications: Over 180 papers in professional journals. Memberships: New York Academy of Sciences; Society of Plastic Engineers. Address: Pusan National University, Pusan 609-735, Korea.

**KIM Dong Ik,** b. 12 December 1959, Jeju, Korea. Professor; Director. m. Sung-Hee Park, 2 sons. Education: MD, 1980-84, MS, 1986-88, PhD, 1996. Appointments: Staff, Division of Vascular Surgery, Samsung Medical Center, 1994-; Professor, Department of Surgery, College of Medicine, Sungkyunkwan University, 1997-; Director, Division of Vascular Surgery, Samsung Medical Center, 1999-. Publications include: Venous dynamics in leg lymphedema, 1999; Changes in lymphatic function after complex physical therapy for lymphedema, 1999; Factors affecting intraoperative electroencephalographic changes during carotid endarterectomy, 1999. Honour: Investigators Award, Samsung Medical Center, 1997. Memberships: Board, Korean Society for Vascular Surgery; Fellow, International College of Angiology; European Society for Vascular Surgery; International Union of Angiology; International Society of Lymphology; Asian Vascular Society; Korean Surgical Society; Korean Society of Transplantation; Japanese College of Angiology; Japanese Society for Vascular Surgery. Address: Division of Vascular Surgery, Samsung Medical Center, 50 Ilwon-Dong, Kangnam-Ku, Seoul 135-710, Korea.

**KIM Dong-Won,** b. 16 February 1969, Suwon, Korea. Researcher. m. Mi-Sook Song. Education: PhD, Korea Advanced Institute of Science and Technology, 1996. Appointments: Member of Research Staff, Samsung Advanced Institute of Technology, 1996-. Honours: J Electrochemical Society, 145, 1958, 1998. Memberships: Electrochemical Society. Address: 102-12 Moonji-Dong, Yusung-Gu, 305-380 Taejon, Korea.

**KIM Hak Yang,** b. 6 June 1956, Seoul, Korea. m. You Jeon Lee, 2 sons. Education: MD, College of Medicine, 1982, MS, Graduate School of Medicine, 1985, PhD, 1996, Kyung Hee University. Appointments: Associate Professor, Hallym University, 1997-. Publications: Articles in Journal of Gastroenterology and Hepatology, 1997; Helicobacter, 1997. Memberships: Korean Association of Internal Medicine; Korean Society of Gastroenterology; Korean Society of Gastrointestinal Endoscopy. Address: 445 Kildong, Kangdongku, Department of Internal Medicine, Kangdong Sacred Heart Hospital, Seoul 134-010, South Korea.

**KIM Hyung-Il,** b. 11 April 1953, Pusan, Korea. Professor. m. Hyung-Sook Jee, 1 son, 1 daughter. Education: Bachelor of Dentistry, Seoul University, 1978; Master of Dentistry, 1985, PhD, 1989, Chosun University. Appointments: Captain, Korean Army, 1978-81; Instructor, 1986-89, Assistant Professor, 1989-93, Associate Professor, 1993-98, Professor, 1998-, Pusan University; Visiting Researcher, Kyushu University, 1991-92. Publications include: Dental Materials, 1995. Memberships: Korea Research Society for Dental Materials; Japanese Society for Dental Materials and Devices; International Association for Dental Research. Address: Department of Dental Materials, College of Dentistry, Pusan University, 1-10 Ami-Dong, Seo-Gu, Pusan 602-739, Korea.

**KIM Ki Hoon,** b. 23 January 1933, Taegu, South Korea. Professor. m Soo Wha Chai, 1 son, 1 daughter. Education: BA, Seoul National University, 1956; MRE, New York Theological Seminary, 1960; MA, Clark University, 1962; PhD, University of Connecticut, 1968. Appointments: Professor, Economics, Central Connecticut University, 1967-; Water Commissioner, City of New Britain, Connecticut, 1984-; Director, Connecticut Institute for Asian and American Studies, 1990-95; Director, Center for Korean and Japanese Studies, 1995-. Publications: Over 20 articles in professional journals. Honours: Citations and Awards; Included in Who's Who in the World and Who's Who in America. Memberships: AAUP; American Economic Association. Address: Central Connecticut University, 1615 Stanley Street, Rm 115A, Marcus White Hall, New Britain, CT 06050, USA.

**KIM Phyo,** b. 23 March 1956, Tokyo, Japan. Neurosurgeon; Professor. Education: MD, University of Tokyo, 1980; PhD, Mayo Graduate School of Medicine, 1996-. Assistant Professor, University of Tokyo, 1990-96; Professor, Dokkyo University School of Medicine, 1996-. Honours: Galbraith Award, Congress of Neuro Surgeons; Galenus Award, Japan Neurosurgical Society. Memberships: AANS; JNS. Address: Dept of Neurosurgery, Dokkyo University School of Medicine; 880 Kitakobayashi Mibu Machi, Tochigi 321 0293, Japan.

**KIM Pyung-Soo,** b. 4 December 1939, Seoul, Korea. Martial Arts Educator, 10th Dan. m. Sonnya Kim, 1 son, 1 daughter. Education: BA, Hankuk University of Foreign Studies, 1963. Appointments: Founder, Cha Yon-Ryu International Martial Arts Association, 1968-; Faculty of Rice University and University of Houston, 1969-. Publications: Palgue 1,2,3; Palgue 4,5,6; Palgue 7 and 8. Honours: Grandmaster of the Year, International Martial Arts Hall of Fame; World Karate Union Hall of Fame; Texas Martial Arts Hall of Fame; Cha Yon-Ryu chosen Best School of 1997, Texas Martial Arts Hall of Fame. Address: Cha Yon-Ryu International Martial Arts Association, 1740 Jacquelyn, Houston, TX 77055, USA.

**KIM Sang Wook,** b. 24 March 1952, Seoul, Korea. Professor. m. Mee Sook Ahn, 2 sons. Education: PhD, Han Yang University, 1979. Appointments: Professor, Department of Chemical Engineering, University of Seoul, 1979-; Director, The Environmental Engineering Center, University of Seoul, 1998-; Vice President, Korean Society of Industrial Engineering Chemistry; Guest Director, The Japanese Society of Plastic Recycling; Chairman, Recycling Committee, Korean Society of Automotive Engineers. Publications: 118 papers in international journals and conferences; 326 papers in domestic journals and conferences; 6 books. Honours: 1st Science Prize, Materials Research Society Of Korea, 1993; 45th Cultural Prize, Science, Seoul Metropolitan Government, 1996; 6th Excellent Paper Prize of Science and Technology, Korean Federation of Science and Technology Society, 1996; 20th Century Achievement Award, 1999. Memberships: NAE: JSPR: SPE; IEEE; KIEE: KIEEME; KSCT; KIChE; PSK; KSIEC; KSAE. Address: A-401 Hyundai Riverville, 135-1 Kwangjang-Dong, Kwangjin-ku, Seoul 143-210, Korea.

**KIM Tae-chang,** b. 1 August 1934, Cheong-Ju, Korea. Intercultural Relations Specialist, and Public Philosopher. m. Hyo-Ae Oh, 1 daughter. Education: BA, Political Science, Yonsei University, Korea, 1957; MA, International Studies, University of South Carolina, USA, 1970; PhD, International Relations, Yonsei University, 1980. Appointments: Teacher, English, French and German, High Schools, Korea; Program Asistant, United States Operation Mission, Korea; University Professor, 1969, Chair, Department of Public Administration,

1977-80, Chair, Department of Political Science and International Relations, Director, Social Science Research, -1986, Dean, College of Social Sciences, Director of the Institute of National Unification Studies, Director, Institute for the Study of International Relations and Ideologies, Dean, Graduate School of Public Administration, Chungbuk National University, Korea; Visiting Professor, Faculty of Law, University of Tokyo, and Kita-Kyushu University, Japan; Dean Faculty of Humanities, Kyushu Women's University, Fukuoka, Japan; Visiting Professor, Chinese Academy of Social Science, People's University of China, Beijing, Academy of Social Science and Open University, Ho Chi Minh City, Vietnam, ASEAN Institute for Health Development, Mahidol University, Bangkok, Centre for Urban Planning and Environmental Management, University of Hong Kong; Academic Advisor, Hanbeck Research Foundation, Seoul, Japanese Research Centre, Taiwan National University, Taipei. Publications: Author, editor and translator of numerous books and articles from English, Japanese, French and German including: Man, God and Reality, 1989; The Philosophy of Happiness Together, 1992; the 21st Century and Intellectual Challenge, 1993; Creating a New History of Future Generations, 1994; Why Future Generations Now?, 1994; Self and Future Generations, 1999. Honours: Cheong-ju City Award of Distinguished Achievement, 1982; Republic of Korea National Medal of Distinguished Service, 1987; Chungbuk Province Award of Distinguished Achievement, 1989. Address: 303 St Paulia Kita Osaka, Shimoshinjo 5-26-10, Higashiyodogawaku, Osaka 533-0021, Japan.

**KIM Theresa Ki-ja,** b. 12 February 1933, Seoul, Korea. Professor. m. Yang-su Lee, 1 son, 2 daughters. Education: BA, English Language and Literature, 1959, MA, English Literature, 1964, Sookmyung Womens University, Seoul, Korea; MA, English Literature, Fairleigh Dickinson University, 1969; PhD, Performance Studies, New York University, 1988. Appointments: Adjunct Instructor, 1974-76, Adjunct Assistant Professor, 1978-88, Adjunct Associate Professor, 1988-89, Department of Theatre, Brooklyn College, City University of New York; Instructor, Department of Fine Arts, Fairleigh Dickinson University, 1976-77; Visiting Associate Professor, Department of Theatre Arts, University of Iowa, 1989-90, Department of Theatre and Dance, Trinity College, Hartford, 1990, Department of Drama, New York University, 1992; Assistant Professor, Department of Theatre Arts, State University of New York, Stony Brook, 1991-. Creative Works: Numerous theatrical experience as director, actor and make-up artist. Honours: Korean Society Travel Grant, 1992; SUNY Travel Grant, 1992, 1995; Korea Foundation Fellowship, 1996; Fulbright Senior Scholar Research Grant, 1997. Memberships: International Society for Shamanic Research; Association for Theatre in Higher Education; Association for Asian Studies; Association for Asian Performance. Address: SUNY at Stony Brook, Department of Theatre Arts, Stony Brook, NY 11794, USA.

**KIM Won Andrea,** b. 10 March 1943, Seoul, Korea. Architect. m. Park Chung-Ai Kim, 1 son, 1 daughter. Education: BS Architecture, 1965, Seoul National University; Diploma, 1973, Bowcentrum Postgrad International, Rotterdam, The Netherlands. Appointments: Architect, Kim Swoo-geun Atelier, Seoul, 1965-70; Principle Partner, Wondoshi Architects, Seoul, 1973-75; Principle, Architects' Group Forum, Seoul, 1976-; President, Feng-shui/Geomancy Research Centre, Seoul, 1981-91; Head Community Planning, Architectural Institute of Korea, Seoul, 1984-96. Principal Works include: National Theatre for Traditional Performing Arts, 1984 (Korean Institute of Architects Special Award, 1991); National Reunification Education Centre, 1987 (KIA Award, 1992); Catholic Martyrs'

Monument and Memorial Chapel (KIA Award 1986); Kwang-ju Catholic University (KIA Award, 1998); Author, essays on architecture, Light and Shadow, 1982. Memberships: Secretary General, Kim Swoo-geun Cultural Foundation, Seoul; Korean Catholic Bishop's Council for Arts, Seoul; Society National Modern Art Museum; Korean Institute Architects; Korean Society Interior Designers; Korean Institute Interior Designers. Address: Architects Group Forum 1-94, Dong Soong-dong Jongro-gu, Seoul 110-510, Republic of Korea.

**KIM Yong Pal,** b. 6 May 1914, Jeong-Eup, Korea. Educator. m. Bok Soon Kim, 1 son, 5 daughters. Education: MA, Korean Literature, 1964-65, Doctorate Course, 1966-67, Kon-Kuk University, Seoul, Korea. Appointments: Head, Instruction Department, High Schools, Kyong-Ki, Su-Do, Suk-Myng, 1945-65; Lecturer, Poetics, College of Literary Arts, Kon-Kuk University, 1964-70; Clerk, translating Japanese into English, Bank of Tokyo, New York Agency, 1970-79. Publications include: Poetry: Ruins, 1952; A Toad's Talk, 1970; Pulses of Time, 1990; Mr Melange's Camela, 1995; Prose: Stroll in the Wood of Lebanon Cedar, 1995. Honours: Golden Poet Award, World of Poetry, 1985-88; Poetry Award, Korean Literary Society of America, 1990; Outstanding Achievement in Poetry, National Library of Poetry, USA, 1993-95. Memberships: Korean Literary Association, 1953-; Korean Branch, Pen International, 1953-; Advisor, Korean Literary Society of America, 1993-. Address: 31-41 23rd Street #4M, Astoria, NY 11106-4057, USA.

**KIM Young-Kyu,** b. 14 December 1954, Hampyung, Jeonnam, Korea. Theologian. m. Bok-Im Kim, 2 daughters. Education: BA, Theology, Chong-Shin University, Seoul, 1978; MDiv, Hapdong Theological Seminary, Suwon, 1984; ThD, Göttingen University, Germany, 1994. Appointments: Director, Research Institute for the Bible and Reformed Theology, 1995-; Lecturer, Anyang University Theological Seminary, 1996-. Publications: Biblica, 1988; A Dialogical Document and the Metaplasmic Phase of the Pre-Mosaic Hebrew Behind Genesis 23, 1993; Calvin and the Old Testament, 1993. Memberships: American Association for the Advancement of Science; New York Academy of Sciences. Address: Dong-Yoo-Joo-Tack B102, 17-12 Seok-Chong-Dong, 138-190 Seoul, Korea.

**KIM Young-Wook,** b. 25 September 1958, Seoul, Korea. Professor. m. Ki-Young Lee, 2 sons. Education: BS, Yonsei University, 1981; MS, 1983, PhD, 1990, Korea Advanced Institute of Science and Technology. Appointments: Research Scientist, Korea Institute of Science and Technology, 1990-96; Professor, Seoul City University, 1996-98; Professor, University of Seoul, 1998-. Publications: 70 papers; 8 patents. Honour: Best Paper Award, Korea Institute of Science and Technology, 1990. Memberships: American Ceramic Society; Korea Ceramic Society. Address: Department of Materials Science, University of Seoul, 90 Jeonnong-Dong, Dongdaemoon-Gu, Seoul 130-743, Korea.

**KIMBELL Michael Alexander,** b. 15 March 1946, Glen Cove, New York, USA. Composer; Piano Technician. m. Edith Maria Guenther, 1 son. Education: BA, Music, Haverford College, 1967; DMA, Composition, Cornell University, 1973. Appointments: Assistant Professor, Johnson State College, Vermont, 1971-75; Assistant Professor, University of the Pacific, California, 1975-78; Freelance Composer and Piano Technician, 1978-. Honours: National Endowment for the Humanities Summer Stipend, 1975; Music Teachers Association of California Composers Today First Prize, 1979; Britten-On-The-Bay Competition Fifth Prize, Woodwind Quintet, 1997; Southern Arizona Symphony Orchestra First Prize, Arcadian Symphony, 1998. Memberships: National Association

of Composers, USA; Piano Technicians Guild; American Musicological Society. Address: 209 Hillcrest Drive, Daly City, CA 94014-1028, USA.

**KING Joy Rainey,** b. 5 August 1939, Memphis, Tennessee, USA. Poet. m. Guy King, 1 son, 1 daughter. Education: Graduate, Whitehaven High School, 1957. Career: Retired Medical Secretary. Honours: International Poetry Hall of Fame; Millennium Hall of Fame; Woman of the Year, 1997; International Woman of the Year, 1998; Marquis Who's Who of American Women, 21st edition. Memberships: Poets Guild; Writers Guild; International Society of Poets. Address: 3029 Willow Branch, Herrin, IL 62948, USA.

**KING Valeria G,** b. 16 June 1958, Durham, North Carolina, USA. Associate Professor of Music. Education: BA, MA, Music Education North Carolina Central University; MM, Music Theory, Florida State University. Appointments: Associate Professor of Music, Southern University, New Orleans; Director, Louisiana Institute for Music Technology, Southern University, New Orleans. Creative Works: Chavalier J Boulougne de Saint Georgies Symphonie Concertante Opus 11 No 2 in D Major A New Edition with Commentary. Memberships: College Music Society; Association for Technology in Music Instruction; Louisiana Institute for Music Technology. Address: 7231 Suffolk Drive, New Orleans, LA 70126-1529, USA.

**KINOSHITA Akitoshi,** b. 5 August 1959, Nagasaki City, Japan. Doctor. m. Yukiko Fukikawa, 1 son, 2 daughters. Education: MD, 1984, PhD, 1993, Nagasaki University. Appointments: Staff, 2nd Department of Internal Medicine, Nagasaki University School of Medicine, 1984-86, 1988-92; Chief, Pulmonary Division, Hokusho Central Hospital, 1986-88; Nagasaki Municipal Citizens' Hospital, 1992-96; Nagasaki-Chuo National Hospital, 1996-. Memberships: Japanese Respiratory Society; Japan Society of Clinical Oncology; Japanese Society of Internal Medicine; Japan Society for Bronchology. Address: 2-241-14 Kushima, Omura 856-0835, Japan.

**KINZIG WOLFRAM U,** b. 7 March 1960, Mannheim, Germany. Professor of Church History. m. Maria del Carmen Rascon Chavez, 1 son, 1 daughter. Education: University of Heidelberg, 1978-1988; Unversity of Lausanne, 1985-1986; Christ Church, Oxford, 1986-1987; Trinity College, Cambridge, 1987-88; Doctor of Theology, Heidelberg, 1988; Habilitation, Historical Theology, Heidelberg, 1991; Appointments: Fellow, Peterhouse, Cambridge, 1988-1992; Fellow, King's College, Cambridge, 1992-1995; Privatdocent, University of Heidelberg, 1992-1996; Professor of Church History, University of Bonn, 1996. Publications: In Search of Asterius, 1990; Erbin Kirche, 1990; Novitas Christiana, 1994; Memberships: Fellow, 21st Century Trust, London. Address: Pestalozzil Strasse 7 H, 53757 Sankt Augustin, Germany.

**KIPRIJANOVA Radmila,** b. 30 May 1940, Skopje, Macedonia. Professor. m. Branko Radovanovic, 2 daughters. Education: Inorganic Technology, Faculty of Technology, Skopje, 1964; Master Studies: Scuola Enrico Mattei di studi sugli idrocarburi, Milan, Italy, 1968; Doctoral Studies, Faculty of Technology, Zagreb, 1974. Appointments: Vice-Dean 1980-82, Dean, 1982-84; Dean, 1984-86, Faculty of Technology; Minister of Science, Technological Development and Informatics of the Republic of Macedonia; Member of the Executive Council, 1986-90; President of the Assembly of the Republic Community of Science, 1983-84; Member, Scientific Board of the Research Project, Strategy of the Technological Development of Yugoslavia in the Beginning of the 21st Century, 1987; Federal

Vice-Minister for Development, 1990-92; Rector of Ss. Kiril and Metodji University in Skopje, 1994-96; Reelected 1996-98. Publications: 73 articles in professional journals; 9 projects; 5 books; 1 monograph. Honours: Goce Delcev Prize for significant achievements in the field of science; Many rewards and recognitions for teaching and research at the University. Memberships: Chemical and Technological Association of Macedonia; Many chemical and technical associations of former Republics of the Yugoslav Federation. Hobbies: Music; Literature; Painting. Address: Bul, Krste Misirkov, bb 91000 Skopje, Macedonia.

**KIRALY Laszlo,** b. 19 January 1954, Zalaegerszeg, Hungary. Composer. m. Katalin Weber, 1992, 1 son. Education: Diploma of Academy of Music Ferenc Liszt, Budapest, 1983. Appointments: Scolarship for Electronic Music Studio of Ghent University, 1980, Music Producer, 1981-, Hungarian Radio, First Publications of Score and Record, 1980, 1983; Radio recordings, 1978-, Creation of Hungarian Requiem, in the Great Hall of Academy of Music Ferenc Liszt; Contemporary Music to the Hungarian National Philharmonica, 1984-93. Memberships: Jewish-Christian Association; Hungarian-Flemish Friends' Circle, Member of Honour. Address: Danko u 20, H 1086 Budapest, Hungary.

**KIRCHHOF Lutz,** b. 15 May 1953, Frankfurt, Germany. Lutenist. Education: Studied lute 14 years under Lothar Fuchs; Read Musicology, Frankfurt, specialising in Historical Lute Literature, 1972; Passed final exam summa cum laude, 1979, Frankfurt Musikhochschule. Appointments: Frankfurt Studio fur Alte Musik, 1973-80; Founded own lute consort, 1976, giving numerous concerts on radio and television; First gramaphone recording, 1980, other recordings following; Guest Tutor, Lecturer on Lute, Frankfurt University's Musikwissenschaftliches Institut, 1981, 1983; Tutor, private pupils; Recitals, Vienna Musiksommer 1988, Festspiele in Schwetzingen, Berlin Horizonte-Festival, repeatedly invited to international Berlin Gitarren-Festival; Established Frankfurter Lautentage, 1988, now renamed Internationale Lautentage which is yearly; Formed circle of lute researchers, 1990; Toured Australia performing and giving music classes, 1994; Founded ensemble, Liuto Concertato, 1995; Initiated founding of German Association for Lute, 1996, combined with Festival of European Lute Music in Lindenmuseum in Stuttgart. Publications: Book: Tutor for the Renaissance and Baroque Lute, 1983; CD: World Festival of the Lute, 1993; CD, celebrating the 400th birthday of the Princess Elisabeth of Hessen, 1997; 2 LPs, 15 CDs, 1980-97. Honours: First Prize in Jugend musiziert, 1972; Award of the German Record Critic, 1993. Address: Hauptstrasse 26, 35781 Weilburg 6, Germany.

**KIREMIRE Enos Masheija Rwantale,** b. 15 February 1945, Kigezi, Uganda. Inorganic Chemist. m. Merab Kambamu Kiremire, 2 sons, 1 daughter. Education: BSc, Honours, Makerere University, Uganda, 1970; PhD, University of New Brunswick, Canada, 1977. Appointments: Lecturer I and II, 1977-83; Senior Lecturer, 1984-88; Associate Professor, 1989-. Publications: 8 in refereed journals; 18 conference papers; 1 contribution to a book; 2 text books. Honours: Commonwealth Visiting Scholarship, University of New Brunswick, 1971-76; Nuffield Foundation Fellowship, University of Sussex, England, 1981-82; Visiting Lectureship, University of Michigan at Ann Arbor, USA, 1991-92; Visiting Professorship, University of Witwatersrand, South Africa, 1997-98. Memberships: Royal Society of Chemistry; American Chemical Society; New York Academy of Sciences; Zambian Chemical Society. Address: Department of Chemistry, University of Zambia, PO Box 32379, Lusaka, Zambia.

**KIRTY Dave,** b. 13 March 1935, Gujdrat, India. Techno-Legal Consultant; Engineering Manager. m. Purnima Bhatt, 1 son, 2 daughters. Education: BE, Civil Engineering, Gujarat University; LLB, MA, Economics, Bombay University; PhD, Diploma in Law, USA; Diploma in Journalism and Communications, Calcutta. Appointments: Senior Engineer, India's First Atomic Power Station, Tarapur, India's First Satellite Communication Centre, Ahmedabad, US Government works in India, Parsons Engineering Science Inc, USA; Techno-Legal Consultant, Municipal Corporation of Greater Bombay; Irrigation Consultant, Government of Iran; Engineering Consultant, UCC Oman; Techno-Legal Consultant, Midwest Consulting Engineers; Design Engineer, Chambal Hydel and Irrigation Scheme. Publications include: Public Undertakings and Law, 1995; Proposed Arbitration and Concilliation Bill, 1995; Foundations and Law, 1996; Unconscionable Contract Terms, 1996. Memberships: American Arbitration Association, New York; Fellow, Institution of Engineers, Indian Council of Arbitration, Institute of Valuers, Indian Institute of Bridge Engineers; Construction Management Association of America. Address: Ghar, Sagrika Society, Juhu Tara Juhu, Mumbai 400049, India.

**KISELEVA Galina,** b. 17 February 1962, Tavda Region, Sverdlovsk. Teacher of Painting. m. Kiselev Andrey, 2 daughters. Education: Diploma, Pedagogical Institute, 1995. Appointments: Teacher, Kindergarten, 1981-94; Teacher, Private School, 1994-96; Teacher, School State. Publications: Publications on International Conference, Interaction of Arts, Theory Methodology, Humane Education. Honours: Diploma, Third Degree, Regional Competition, Teacher of the Year. Memberships: Post Graduate, State Pedagogical University. Address: 70 let Oktybrya St 55, Apt 185, Togliatti, Region of Samara, Russia.

**KISHITA Kazutaka,** b. 25 December 1946, Ibusuki, Japan. Business Professional; Chemist. m. Keiko J Kishita, 2 sons. Education: AA, Chemistry, 1968; BA, Chemistry and Natural Science, 1971. Appointments: General Manager, 1983-87; Director, 1987-91, Research and Development; Executive Vice President, Three Bond of America, 1991-97; President, Three Bond Manufacturing, 1997-. Honours: Torrance Education School District Award, 1991-94; Palos Verdes Education School District Award, 1991-94. Memberships: California Chamber of Commerce; Torrance Area Chamber of Commerce. Address: Three Bond, 20815 Higgins Court, Torrance, CA 90501, USA.

**KISLIAKOV Dimitar Savov,** b. 23 December 1960, Sofia, Bulgaria. Civil Engineer. m. Teodora Kisliakova, 1 son. Education: MSc, Civil Engineering, 1986; PhD, 1990. Appointments: Design Engineer, Energoproekt, Sofia, 1986-87; Lecturer, 1990-94, Senior Lecturer, 1994-, Department of Hydrotechnics, University of Architecture, Civil Engineering and Geodesy, Sofia. Publications: More than 20 publications in professional journals and conference proceedings. Memberships: GAMM, Germany; Euromech; Bulgarian Society on Large Dams. Address: University of Architecture, Civil Engineering and Geodesy, 1 Chr Smirnenski Blvd, 1421 Sofia, Bulgaria.

**KISSANE Sharon Florence Mrotek,** b. Chicago, Illinois, USA. Writer; Teacher. 2 daughters. Education: BA, English and Speech, De Paul University, Chicago, 1961; MA, Communications, Northwestern University, 1963; PhD, Education, Loyola University, Chicago. Appointments: Technical Writer, Editor, 1962-63; Instructor, 1963-68; Financial and Business Writer, 1969-71; Director, 1972-73; Free Lance Writer, 1973-89; President, Kissane Communications, 1979-.

Publications: Linguistics Theory Applied to the Teaching of Reading and the Languages Arts, 1970; Contributing Editor of Sharpening the Mother Tongue, 1970; Co-Author, Polish Biographical Dictionary, 1992; What is Child Abuse, 1993; Gang Awareness, 1995; Career Sucess for People with Physical Disabilities, 1997; Mousie Garner's Autobiography, 1999. Honours: Dale Carnegie Scholarship, 1958; Honorable Citizen of Korea, 1966; Prix de New York for Painting, 1971; Cite de Locre; 3rd Place for American Artist Award, 1998. Memberships: Phi Kappa Delta Education Fraternity; Chapter Kappa Gamma Pi Social Sciences Fraternity; Barrington Area Proffesional Women's Organization; Society of Midwest Consultants; Writers Guild of America; Board Member, Barrington Area, United Way. Address: Kissane Comms Ltd, 15 Turning Shire Dr, South Barrington, IL 60010 9597, USA.

**KITAMURA Hironori,** b. 18 December 1920, Fukuyama, Hiroshima-Ken. Anatomist; Educator. m. Mitsuko Yasuda, 1 son, 1 daughter. Education: DDS, 1942, Tokyo Medical Dental University; D in Medical Science, 1960; BA Psychology, 1972, Nippon Management University; PhD, 1984, Union University. Appointments: Assistant Professor, Tokyo Medical and Dental University, 1956-61; Research Associate, Dental School, University Washington -at Seattle, 1961-63; Research Associate, Cleft Palate Research Centre, University Pittsburg, 1963-65; Professor Anatomy, Kanagawa Dental College, Yokosuka, Japan, 1965-88; Professor Emeritus, 1988-; Oralanatomy Educator, School Dental Hygienists, 1987-97. Publications: Atlas of Developmental Anatomy of Face, 1966; Embryology of Mouth and Related Structures, 1989; Colour Atlas of Human Oral Histology, 1992; Oral Embryology and Pathohistology, 1998; Dental Malformations and Pathohistology, 1998. Memberships: Japanese Association Anatomists, Councillor 1956-; Japanese Association Oral Biologists, Councillor 1965-. Address: Minami-ku, Nagata Higashi, 3-8-5-406, Yokohama 240, Japan.

**KITKAUSKAS Kazys Napoleonas,** b. 5 January 1931, Utena, Lithuania. Architect; Engineer. m. Sulniute Laimute, 1 son, 1 daughter. Education: Building Engineer, 1960, Kaunas Politechnical Institute; Doctor of Humanities/History of Architecture, 1980. Appointments: Institute of Preservation and Restoration of Monuments, 1960-82; Head of Architectural Dept, The Castle Research Centre, Lithuanian Castles, 1993-98. Publications: Books: Vilnius Cathedral, 1977; Vilnius Castles, 1989; and others. Honours: Laureate of the National Prize, 1990; Gediminas Order of the 4th degree, 1995, of the 3rd degree, 1999. Memberships: Architects' Union; Lithuanian National Committee of ICOMOS; State Commission for Monument Protection; Academy of Sciences of Lithuanian Catholics; Conservative Party (Homeland Union) of Lithuania. Address: Ligonines 4-3, Vilnius, Lithuania.

**KIZAWA Makoto,** b. 18 April 1925, Kiryu, Japan. Professor Emeritus. m. Yukiko, 2 sons. Education: BEng, 1948, DEng, 1969, Dept Electrical Engineering, University of Tokyo. Appointments: Electrotechnical Lab, Tokyo, 1948-70; Professor, Osaka University, Toyonaka, 1970-80; Professor, 1980-83, VP, 1983-87, University of Library and Information Science. Publication: Digital Magnetic Recording, in Japanese, 1979. Memberships: IEE of Japan; Information Processing Society of Japan. Address: 3-13-6 Hachimanyama, Setagaya-ku, 156-0056 Tokyo, Japan.

**KJOSSEV Kirien Tzvetanov,** b. 9 November 1963, Sofia, Bulgaria. Surgeon. m. Elena K Kjosseva, 2 sons. Education: Medical Doctor, Certified by Medical Academy, Higher Medical Institute, Sofia, 1987; Surgeon, Certified by Higher Medical Institute, Sofia, 1995. Appointments: Staff Surgeon, Surgical

Unit, County Hospital, Kjustendil, Bulgaria, 1990-92; Staff Surgeon, Department of General Surgery, Military Medica Academy, Sofia, Bulgaria, 1992-. Publications: More than 60 scientific articles in English language in journals. Memberships Bulgarian Surgical Society, 1995; New York Academy of Sciences, 1995; International Society of Surgery, 1996. Address: PO Box 159, 1606 Sofia, Bulgaria.

**KLACZAK Adam,** b. 16 February 1928, Cracow, Poland Technical Manager. m. Maria Chrzanowska, 27 June 1954, deceased July 1987, 1 son, deceased April, 1992. Education: Diploma in Engineering, University Tech, Cracow, 1951; DTech Scis, 1970; Certificate Engineering. Designer Desinging Department, Cracow, 1951-67, Chief Checking Staff, 1970-78. Consultant, 1981-89; Academic Teacher University Tech, Cracow, 1967-70; Member, supervision staff, Polservice, Libya, 1978-81; Technical Manager, Office, Cracow, 1989-. Publications: Articles in professional journals. Honours: Gold Award, City of Cracow, 1987. Address: Odrzanska 10/12, 30-408 Cracow, Poland.

**KLAINMAN Eliezer Isaak,** b. 12 Apr 1951, Israel. Cardiologist. m. Yaffa Klainman, 3 daughters. Education: MD, Tel-Aviv University, 1978; Certificate in Cardiology; Specialist in Cardiology and Basic Science in Nuclear Cardiology, Beilinson Medical Centre, Petach-Tigua, 1979-86. Appointments: Head and Founder, Mishmar Hayarden Cardiology and Rehabilitation Institute, Givat; Professor, Lecturer in Medical Science and Cardiology, Ben-Gurion and Tel-Aviv Universities; Head Investigator, clinical trials; Cardiologist Expert in Exercise Physiology and Cardiac Rehabilitation, Beilinson Medical Centre and Givatayim Cardiology and Rehabilitation Institute. Publications: Articles in journals of cardiology, cardiac rehabilitation and exercise physiology including International Journal of Cardiology, Clinical Cardiology, Journal of Electrophysiology, European Heart Journal, JACC, others. Honours: Honorary Certificate, Rotary Club, 1996; Excellence in Professional Medicine Award, Cardiology Institute, 1997. Memberships: Israeli Cardiology Society; Israel Society of Hypertension; New York Academy of Sciences; European Heart Association; American Association for the Advancement of Science. Address: 13 Opsterland Street, 43350 Raanana, Israel.

**KLAUER K J,** Emeritus University Professor. m. Rosemarie Klauer-Bohme, 1 son, 2 daughters. Education: Dr.phil, 1958; Postdoctoral, 1967. Appointments: Teacher, Disabled Children, 1959-63; Professor, Special Education, 1963; Professor, Education, 1968-. Publications: Numerous books and articles on educational psychology and special education. Memberships: American Educational Research Association; European Association for Research in Learning & Instruction. Address: Robert Stolz Weg 15, D 42781 Haan, Germany.

**KLAUSS Kenneth Karl,** b. 8 April 1923, Parkston, South Dakota, USA. Education: BMus, Composition, University of Southern California, 1946. Career: Composer, Horton Theatre, Los Angeles, 1948-50; Private Instructor, San Francisco, 1950-61; Composer/Pianist, Hollywood, 1961-85; Lecturer/Instructor, University of Southern California, Southern California Institute of Architecture, 1967-77. Creative Works: Story of the World (drawings, poems, music in 8 volumes), 1952-88. Honour: Honorable Mention, University of Ohio Opera, 1952. Membership: Founder and Patron, Klauss/James Archive and Art Museum, Parkston, South Dakota. Address: 440 Wren Drive, Los Angeles, CA 90065, USA.

**KLAWUN Christoph,** b. 1 December 1961, Stuttgart, Germany. Chemist. m. Elizabeth Kate, 1 daughter. Education:

Diploma, Chemistry, Univesität des Saarlandes, Germany, 1990; PhD, Analytical Chemistry, University of California, 1995. Appointments: Chemist, Software Engineer, Applied Automation, Bartlesville, Oklahoma, 1995-. Publications: Many publications. Honours: Graduate Student of the Year, 1995; Nominated, 1996 Elsevier Chemometrics Award. Memberships: American Chemical Society; Instrument Society of America. Address: Applied Automation Inc, P O Box 9999, Bartlesville, OK 74005, USA.

**KLEIHAUER-WARD Elke Magreta**, b. 5 January 1962, Stratford, Canada. Tool and Dye Maker; Teacher. m. Thomas Charles, 2 sons, 2 daughters. Education: Certificate of Qualification, Tool and Die Maker; Certificate of Apprenticship, Tool and Die Maker; Bachelor of Education, University of Western Ontario. Appointments: First Female Tool and Dyemaker, Canada; First Female Machine Shop Teacher, Canada. Address: North Lambton Secondary School, P O Box 40, Forest ON, Canada, N0N 1J0.

**KLEIN George**, b. 28 July 1925, Budapest, Hungary. Professor; Research Group Leader. Education: MD, Karolinska Institute, 1951; DSc, University of Chicago, 1966; MD, University of Debrecen, 1988; PhD, Hebrew University, 1989; DSc, University of Nebraska, 1991; PhD, 1994. Appointments: Instructor, History, 1945; Instructor, Pathology, 1946; Research Fellow, 1947-49; Assistant Professor, Cell Research, 1951-57; Professor, Tumor Biology, Head of Department, 1957-93; Research Group Leader, Microbiology and Tumor Biology Center, 1993-. Publications: More than 1000 Papers, Fields of Experimental Cell Research, Cancer Research; Many Books. Honours: Robert Koch Gold Medal; Orden Nacional al Merito de la Republica de Colombia; Kaposi Award; Thomas P Infusino Prize; Many Other Awards, Honours. Memberships: Royal Swedish Academy of Scienes; Foreign Member, Finnish Scientific Society; National Academy of Sciences of the United States; Hungarian Academy of Sciences; American Association of Immunologists; American Philosophical Society; French Society of Immunology; Many other Memberships. Address: P O Box 280, 2-171 77 Stockholm, Sweden.

**KLIMCHOUK Alexander**, b. 29 August 1956, Odessa, Ukraine. Hydrogeologist; Speleologist. m. Yablokova Natalia, 2 sons. Education: MS, Geomorphology, Kiev State University, 1983; PhD, Hydrogeology, National Academy of Sciences, 1999. Appointments: Technician, Engineer, Senior Engineer, Head of Karst and Speleological Division, Scientist, Institute of Geological Sciences, National Academy of Sciences, Ukraine, 1973-. Publications: Over 130 scientific papers in professional journals. Memberships: Vice President, National Association of Soviet Speleologists, 1992-; Bureau Member, Union International of Speleology; President, Ukrainian Speleological Association, 1992-97; President, UIS Commission on Karst Hydrogeology and Speleogenesis, 1994-; National Speleology Society, USA; Ukrainian Speleology Association. Address: Kibalchicha Str 7A kv 59, 253183 Kiev, Ukraine.

**KLIMEK Marek**, b. 8 October 1964, Cracow, Poland. Obstetrician and Gynaecologist. m. Malgorzata Patrzyk, 15 March 1986, 1 daughter. Education: MD, 1989, PhD, 1992, qualified as Associate Professor, 1998, Jagiellonian University. Publications: More than 60 in professional medical journals. Memberships: Polish Gynaecological Society; European Association of Gynaecologists and Obstetricians; New York Academy of Sciences; European Society for Gynaecological Endoscopy. Address: Szlak 3/5, 31-161 Cracow, Poland.

**KLISCH Egbert**, b. 6 May 1965, Cologne, Germany. Physicist. Education: Diploma in Physics, 1993; PhD, 1998.

Appointments: Assistant Professor, University Extension, 1990-; Scientist, University of Cologne, 1993-99. Publications: 1 Book; Contributor to papers for professional journals. Address: Drachenfelsstr 36, 50939 Cologne, Germany.

**KLUBOVICH Vladimir Vladimirovich**, b. 26 March 1933, Voronichi, Grodno, Belarus. Director of Institute of Technical Acoustics. m. Galina Klubovich, 1 son. Education: Engineer, Byelorussian State University, 1956; PhD, 1963, DSc, 1973, Physical Technical Institute, Byelorussian Academy of Sciences, Minsk; Professor, Institute of Solid State and Semiconductors Physics, Byelorussian Academy of Sciences, Minsk, 1979. Appointments: Teacher, Yuradishevskaya Secondary School, 1957-58; Senior Scientists, Physical-Technical Institute, Minsk, 1958-75; Head, Laboratory on Ultrasonics, Physical Technical Institute, Minsk, 1975; Leader, Vitebsk Branch of Institute of Solid State and Semiconductors Physics, Vitebsk, 1975-94; Director, Institute of Technical Acoustics, Vitebsk, 1994. Publications: 350 including: Ultrasonic Rolling and Drawing of Metals, in English, 1972; The Ultrasound Working of Materials, Minsk, Nauka I Technika, in Russian, 1981; Excitation and Stabilization of Autoresonance Impacting Oscillators in Ultrasonic Technological Systems, in English, 1990; The Topological Classification of Grain Interfaces in Polycrystalls, in Russian, 1992. Honours: Winner, State Prize of BSSR, 1984; Awards of the order, Sign of Honor, 2 medals. Memberships: Scientific Technical Society of Belarus; Scientific Council on problem, Solid State and Semiconductors Physics; Scientific Council on problem, Strength and Plasticity; Corresponding Member, Belarus Academy of Sciences. Address: Institute of Technical Acoustics, Belarus Academy of Sciences, 13 Ludnikov Prospect, 210717 Vitebsk, Belarus.

**KLUTZOW Friedrich W**, b. 6 August 1923, Bandoeng, Java, Dutch East Indies. Neuro-Pathologist. 1 son, 1 daughter. Education: MD, 1951, University of Utrecht, Netherlands; Internships, University Hospital, Utrecht, 1951-53; Newton Wellesley Hospital, Massachusetts, USA; Residency, OBS/GYN, Lawrence and Memorial Associated Hospital, New London, Connecticut, 1954-56; Pathology and Neuropathology, University of Wisconsin, 1968-71; AFIP, 1971-72. Appointments: Chief of Staff, Community Memorial Hospital, Oconto Falls, Wisconsin, 1965-68; Neuropathologist, Minneapolis, Minnesota, 1972-75; Chief Pathology and Laboratory Medicine, Brockton, Massachusetts, 1975-83; Wichita, Kansas, 1983-87; Chief of Staff, DVA Medical Centre, Bath, New York, 1987-90; Clinical Associate Professor Pathology, Rochester, 1988-92; University South Florida, 1994-. Publications: Several publications in professional journals; Principal author, Neuropathology Manual: Practical Approach, 1996. Honours: Outstanding Career Award, Washington DC, 1990; Plaque honouring 22 years of Clinical Leadership. Memberships: NY Academy of Sciences; American Association Neuropathologists; Fellow, College American Pathologists; International Society Neuropathology. Address: PO Box 7846, Sarasota, FL 34278-7846, USA.

**KMIELIAUSKAS Antanas**, b. 3 August 1932, Lithuania. Artist. m. Rita Vasiliauskaite, 1 daughter. Education: Vilnius Art Institute, 1951-57. Appointments: Teacher of Art, Children Art School, 1963-78; Teacher, Anatomy and Drawing, Vilnius Art Academy, 1979-. Address: Sigro 28-2, LT 2014 Vilnius, Lithuania.

**KNEPPER Ronald**, b. 9 May 1955, Fort Wayne, Indiana, USA. Sculptor. m. Carol Brentegani Ferreira Dos Santos, 3 daughters. Education: BFA, Indiana University, 1982; MA, New Mexico State University, 1985; MFA, Mills College, 1987.

Appointments: Visiting Artist, Biola University, La Mirada, California, 1986; Kent Institute of Art and Design, Canterbury, England, 1989; 1990; Guest lecturer, Bilkent University, Turkey, 1989-90; Professor, Purdue University, Fort Wayne, USA, 1992; Director, Kouros Gallery, NYC, USA, 1994-95; Instructor, Parsons School of Design, NYC, USA, 1995-. Memberships: Gallery Advisory Board, Mills College, 1985-87; Co-Chair, Names Project AIDS Quilt, Fort Wayne, 1994. Address: 186 Pinehurst Avenue Apt 5A, New York, NY 10033-1730, USA.

**KNOLL Gregg A,** b. 10 May 1949, Milwaukee, Wisconsin, USA. Artist; Printmaker; Educator. Education: BFA with honors, Layton School of Art and Design, Milwaukee, WI, USA, 1973; MA, University of Iowa, Iowa City, IA, USA, 1977; MFA, University of Iowa, 1979. Appointments: Founder, Master Printer, Green River Press, 1976-; Founder Hand-Papermaking Facility, University Iowa, Iowa City, 1979-84; Visiting Artist, Faculty, University Iowa, 1979-84; Juror Graham Scholarship Com University Iowa, 1980-83. Honours: Grumbacher Gold Medallion Merchandise Award, Wustum Museum Fine Arts, 1989; Mary Ann Naczinski Memorial Purchase Award, 1989; SC Johnson Wax Purchase Award, 1990; 1st Place Award, 7th Annual Regional Art Exhibition Gallery Ten, Rockford, IL, 1993; Rotary Club Award, Northern National Art Competition, Nicolet College, Rhinelander WI, 1993; 2nd Place Award, Wustum Museum of Fine Arts, Racine, WI, 1998. Memberships: University Iowa Alumni Association; College Art Association of America; Milwaukee Art Museum. Address: Green River Press, PO Box 356, South Milwaukee, WI 53172-0356, USA.

**KNUDSEN Dagfinn Andreas,** b. 11 April 1942, Drevja, Norway. Metallurgist. m. Karin Nilssen, 1 daughter. Education: Engineers Degree, Metallurgical Techniques, Trondheim Tekniske Skole, 1967. Appointments: Assistant Engineer, Ardal Verk ASV, 1967-72; Project Engineer, Sunndal Verk ASV, 1972-86; Process Engineer, Franzefoss Bruk AS, 1986; Service Engineer, Ostlandsmeieriet AL, 1989; Service Engineer, Autodisplay AS, 1991. Publications include: Teknisk Ukeblad, 1991, 1992; Helgeland Arbeiderblad, 1992. Membership: National Geographic Society. Address: Bergheim i Drevja, N-8650 Mosjoen, Norway.

**KO Hyeongseok,** b. 14 August 1962, Chonju. Professor. m. Eunjoo Lee, 1 son. Education: BS, 1985, MS, 1987, Seoul National University; PhD, 1994, University of Pennsylvania. Appointments: Assistant Professor, University Iowa Computer Science Dept, 1994-95; Assistant Professor, Seoul National University, School of Electrical Engineering, 1995-. Publications: Co-author 4 papers in international journals. Honour: Creative Researcher Grant Award, The Creative Research Initiatives of the Korean Ministry of Science and Technology. Memberships: ACM; IEEE. Address: Seoul National University, School of Electrical Engineering, Seoul 151-742, Korea.

**KOBAYASHI Herbert S,** b. 6 February 1929, Webster, Texas, USA. Design Engineer; Real Estate Developer; Farmer. m. Haruko Orita, 1 son, 2 daughters. Education: BSEE, University of Houston, 1951; MSEE, University of Michigan, 1958; MS, Industrial Engineering, 1969. Appointments: US Army, 1954-56; Design Engineer, SIE, Houston, 1960-61; Design Engineer, Boeing Aerospace, Huntsville, Alabama, 1961-62; New Orleans, Louisiana, 1962; Aerospace Technologist, NASA, Houston, 1963-89; President, Kobayashi Inc. Publications: 2 patents in bit synchronizer, 1972; 3 patents in doppler radar, 1984-89. Memberships: IEEE; AIAA; Institute of Nagivation. Address: 1428 FM 528W, Webster, TX 77598, USA.

**KOBAYASHI Nagao,** b. 21 January 1950, Nagano, Japan. Professor of Chemistry. m. Yayoi Enomoto, 2 daughters. Education: DSc, 1978; Doctor of Pharmacy, 1986. Appointments: Assistant Professor, Chemical Research Institute of Non-aqueous Solution, 1983-85; Assistant Professor, 1986-95, Associate Professor, 1995, Pharmaceutical Institute; Full Professor, Dept of Chemistry, Graduate School of Science, 1995-, Tohoku University. Publication: Phthalocyanines, Chemistry and Functions, 1997. Memberships: Japan Chemistry Society; Polymer Society of Japan. Address: Department of Chemistry, Graduate School of Science, Tohoku University, Sendai 980-8578, Japan.

**KOBAYASHI Toshiro,** b. 20 May 1939, Sapporo, Japan. University Professor. m. Fumiko Fukuda, 1 son, 1 daughter. Education: Bachelor of Engineering, 1962, Doctor of Engineering, 1972, Hokkaido University. Appointments: Fuji Electric Corporation, Research and Development Department Ltd, 1962; Associate Professor, Nagoya University, 1973; Professor, Toyohashi University of Technology, 1982-. Honours: Mishima Prize, Iron and Steel Institute of Japan, 1997; Fellow, ASM, ASM International, 1998. Memberships: DDG; MOIF, IBC. Address: 21-16 Kodare, Ogasaki-cho, Toyohashi 441, Japan.

**KOBLANSKA Zdzislawa Bogumila,** b. 27 September 1935, Lwow, Poland. Fine Artist. Education: Graduated in Scenography, 1963, Academy of Fine Arts, Cracow, Poland, 1955-61. Appointments: Artistic works at the private atelier; Advertising graphics, 1963-74; painting, specimen tapestry, scenography, travelling, 1974-; writing of book, 1995-. Publications: Exhibitions of paintings, tapestry and scenography with catalogues; book in preparation. Memberships: Union of the Polish Plastic Artists; Circle of All Arts Lovers of Zwierzyniec, Cracow Quarter. Address: ul Tarnowskiego 10, 30 528 Cracow, Poland.

**KOCIAN Ludovít,** b. 24 December 1947, Trstená, Slovakia. Biologist; Zoologist. m. Elena Okrucká, 2 daughters. Education: MSc, Faculty of Science, Comenius University, Bratislava, 1970; RNDr, 1974; PhD, 1982; Docent, 1997. Appointment: Senior Lecturer, Faculty of Natural Sciences, Comenius University, Bratislava. Publications: 45 including: On the nesting biology of the rock pipit, Anthus spinoletta (L, 1758) in Slovakia (co-author), 1982; Project of a State Nature Reserve in the Tatra National Park from the Zoological point of View (co-author), 1989; Effect of the Downhill Ski Track in the West Tatra (Roháce) on the Occurrence of Land Vertebrates, 1992; Occurrence of a melanistic Common vole, Microtus arvalis (Pallas, 1779) in Slovakia (co-author), 1992; Structure and Dynamics of Breeding Bird Communities in Three Parks of Bratislava (co-author), 1995; Spread of the bluethroat Luscinia svecica svecica in Slovakia (co-author), 1996; Bird communities of the Western Tatras-Roháce Mountains between 1870-1996, 1998. Memberships: Slovak Ornithological Society; Czech Ornithological Society; Slovak Zoological Society. Address: Faculty of Natural Sciences, Comenius University, Mlyn dolina B1, SK-84215 Bratislava, Slovakia.

**KOCIJAN Jus,** b. 16 June 1964, Ljubljana. Control Engineer; Educator; Researcher. m. Mateja Skrbec, 1 son. Education: BSc, 1988, MSc, 1990, PhD, 1993, all in Electrical Engineering, University Ljubljana. Appointments: Junior Researcher, 1988-93, Teaching Assistant, 1990-95, Assistant Professor, 1995-, University Ljubljana. Publications: Papers in professional journals; Books: Robust Multivariable Control: a View of Theory and Practice, 1995; Dynamic Control Systems Design, 1996; Practicum of Dynamic System Identification, 1998; Editor, Proceedings of IFAC/IMACS Workshop, Artificial

Intelligence in Real-Time Control, 1995. Honour: University Award for Student Research Work, 1989. Memberships: IEEE, Control Systems Society; New York Academy of Sciences; Automatic Control Society of Slovenia; Slovenian Society for Modelling and Simulation; Slovenian Artificial Intelligence Society. Address: University of Ljubljana, Faculty of Electrical Engineering, Trzaska 25, 1000 Ljubljana, Slovenia.

**KOEPSEL Wellington Wesley,** b. 5 December 1921, McQueeney, Texas, USA. Electrical Engineer. m. Dorothy Adams, 1 son, 2 daughters. Education: BSc, 1944, MSc, 1951, Electrical Engineering, University of Texas; PhD, Electrical Engineering, Oklahoma State University, 1960. Appointments: Assistant Professor, Southern Methodist University, 1951-59; Associate Professor, University of New Mexico, 1960-63; Associate Professor, Duke University, 1963-64; Professor and Head, Department of Electrical Engineering, Kansas State University, 1964-76; Professor Emeritus, 1984-, Adjunct Professor, 1996-98, University of Texas. Publications: Contributor to articles in professional journals. Memberships: Eta Kappa Nu; Sigma Xi; Senior Member, IEEE. Address: PO Box 26806, Austin, TX 78755-0806, USA.

**KOESTENBLATT Marlene Charney,** b. 10 August 1945, Brooklyn, New York, USA. m. Nicholas Kushner, 1 son. Education: BA, Huntern College, NY, 1967; MA, Fairleigh Dickinson University, 1980; EdD, Indiana University of Pennsylvania, 1998. Appointments: Counselor, 1977-78; Practicum Student, 1978-79; Consultant, Counselor, 1979-80; Advisory Board Member, 1982-84; Consultant, Counselor, 1982-84; Graduate Assistant, 1984-85; School Psychologist Extern, 1985; Consultant, Instructor, 1985-86; Advisory Board Member, 1985-87; Associate, 1986-89; Learning Specialist, 1989; Learning Specialist, Counselor, 1989-91; Advisory Board Member, 1991-92; Coordinator of Enrichment and Individualized Instruction, 1991-92; Consultant, 1992-93; Delaware Valley Network Member, Delaware Valley, PA, 1993-; Education Committee Member, Mayor's Commission on People with Disabilities, 1995-; Coordinator of Services for Students With Learning Disabilities, Community College of Philadelphia, 1993-; Advisor to the Chair, American Psychological Association Committtee on Disability Issues in Psychology, 1997-. Publications: Characteristics of Cognitively, Perceptually Impaired Students and Associated Accommodations; Application of Neuropsychological Paradigms to the Processes and Products of Technical Writing; Many others. Honours: Business and Professional Women's Hawkin's Scholarship; Association for Children and Adults with Learning Disabilities Certificate of Recognition; BA Conferred with Honour. Memberships: Association on Higher Education and Disability; National Academy of Neuropsychology; American Psychological Association; National Association of School Psychologists. Address: Ctr on Disabilities CC of Phila, 1700 Spring Garden St, Philadelphia, PA 19130-3936, USA.

**KOGANTI Varaprasad R,** b. 1 January 1952, Macharam, AP, India. Teacher and Researcher in Organic Chemistry and Chemical Education. m. Kanakatara K, 1 son, 1 daughter. Education: BSc, 1974; MSc, 1976; MPhil, 1st rank, 1981; PhD, 1988. Appointments: Lecturer, Chemistry, 1979-86, Senior Lecturer, 1986-92, Associate Professor, 1992-, New Science College; Research in Chemical Education, Diagnostic Test in Organic Chemistry, 1996, 1997, 1999. Publications: Ten research papers of national and international reputation. Honours: Teacher Fellow, UGC, New Delhi, 1983-86; Guest Lecturer, University of Kentucky, USA, 1992; Resource Person for Teacher Training (UG and PG Levels), 1997-; Distinguished Teacher Awardee, 1997. Memberships: Board of Studies, Osmania University, Hyderabad; Andhra Pradesh College

Teachers Association; Indian Science Congress. Address: New Science College, Ameerpet, Hyderabad 500 073, AP, India.

**KOGURE Shinichi,** b. 11 November 1950, Kiryu, Gunma, Japan. Associate Professor; Neurophysiologist. m. Kogure Atsuko, 3 sons, 1 daughter. Education: Master of Engineering, 1975, MD, 1979, Gunma University. Appointments: Assistant Professor, Nippon Medical School, 1979-89; Associate Professor, Soka University, 1989-; Visiting Scientist, University of British Columbia, Canada, 1994-95; Research Fellow, Institute of Oriental Philosophy, 1989-. Publications: Brain Mechanisms of Sensation, 1981; Neural Mechanisms of Epilepsy through Kindling Research, 1993. Honour: Investigator's Award of Japan Epilepsy Research Foundation, 1997. Memberships: Japan Epilepsy Society; American Epilepsy Society; New York Academy of Sciences. Address: 405-11 Tonogaya Mizuho, Nishitama, Tokyo 190-1212, Japan.

**KOH Seok-Keun,** b. 3 May 1958, Seoul, Korea. Researcher. m. Mi-wha Choo, 1 son, 1 daughter. Education: BS, Yon-Sei University, 1981; PhD, Rutgers University, USA, 1989. Appointments: Associate Professor, Kyoto University, Japan, 1989; Senior Researcher, Principal Researcher, KIST, Thin Film Technology and Research Centre, Korea, 1991-. Publications: 100 articles; 40 patents including US Patent, 1998. Memberships: American Physics Society; Material Research Society. Address: PO Box 131, KIST, Thin Film Technology and Research Centre, Cheongryang, 130-650 Seoul, Korea.

**KOHLER William Curtis,** b. 22 May 1942, Wharton, New Jersey, USA. Physician; Sleep Specialist. m. Barbara Bauman Kohler, 1 son, 2 daughters. Education: BA, 1964, Oberlin College, Ohio; MD, University of Florida, 1968, Intern in Paediatrics, 1968-69, Resident in Paediatrics, 1969-70, Resident in Neurology (Adult), 1970-73, Fellow in Paediatric Neurology, 1970-73, University Florida College of Medicine, Gainesville, Florida. Appointments: Major, US Air Force, 1973-75; Faculty Associate, Centre for Neurobiological Sciences, 1970-76, Assistant Professor of Paediatrics, 1973-76, Electroencephalographer (Child Neurology), 1973-76, Assistant Professor of Neurology, 1975-76, Assistant Professor of Neuroscience, 1975-76, Clinical Assistant Professor of Paediatrics, 1976-91, Clinical Assistant Professor of Neurology, 1976-90, University of Florida College of Medicine; Consultant, Child Neurology and Paediatrics, 1973-94, Assistant Medical Director, Region 11B, 1976-77, Division of Children's Medical Services, State of Florida; Clinical Assistant Professor, 1974-75, Clinical Associate Professor, 1975-76, Dept Paediatrics, University Texas Health Science Centre, San Antonio, Texas; Medical Director, Lancaster Youth Development Centre, 1975-76; Electroencephalographer, Telediagnostic Systems, 1976-79, Tallahassee Neurological Clinic and Tallahassee Memorial Regional Medical Centre, 1976-94; Private Practice, Tallahassee Neurological Clinic, Tallahassee, Florida, 1976-94; Medical Co-Director, The Sleep Disorders Centre, Deaconess Medical Centre, Billings, Montana, 1994-96; Private Practice, The Sleep Centre of Montana, Billings, 1996-; Medical Director, The Sleep Centre at Saint Vincent Hospital and Health Centre, Billings, 1996-. Publications: 8 papers in professional journals; 1 abstract; numerous presentations. Address: The Sleep Centre of Montana, 1233 30th St North, Billings, MT 59101, USA.

**KOHLI Rajesh,** b. 23 February 1957, Madras, India. Marketing Medical Consultant. m. Rachana, 2 daughters. Education: MCom; DEM; AMIBM, India. Appointments: Marketing Endoscopic line of business and specialising in them in last 8 years. Honours: Bharath Vikas Award; Rashtreeya

Ekta Award. Membership: Indo German Chamber of Commerce. Address: Near Koramangala Club, No 86 17th D Main 6th Blk, Koramangala, Bangalore 560 095, India.

**KOHOUT Jaroslav,** b. 19 May 1927, Klatovy, Czechoslovakia. Professor. m. Nada Vybiralova, 1 son, 1 daughter. Education: PhD, 1953; Doctor of Sciences, 1968. Appointments: Head, Department of Sociology and Psychology, 1963-72; Dean, Faculty of Management, 1972-85; Deputy Scientific Secretary, Czechoslovak Academy of Sciences, 1985-92; Professor, Czech Management Institute and Technical University, Prague. Publications: 12 monographs; 1 novel; More than 100 papers and articles published in Czech Republic and abroad. Honour: Gold Medal, Presidium, Czechoslovak Academy of Sciences. Membership: Corresponding Member, Czechoslovak Academy of Sciences. Address: Department of Psychology, School of Economics, Nam W Churchilla 4, 130-00 Prague 3, Czech Republic.

**KOHRING Victor Heinz,** b. 2 August 1958, Waukegan, Illinois, USA. State Legislator. Education: AA, 1985, Matanuska-Susitna Community College; BA, 1987, MBA, 1989, Alaska Pacific University. Appointments: Wasilla Planning and Utilities Commission, 1991-94; Matanuska-Susitna Borough Economic Development Commission, 1993-94; Alaska Housing Finance Corporation Board, 1991-94; State Representative, District 26, 1995-. Membership: Wasilla Chamber of Commerce, Chugiak-Eagle River Chamber of Commerce. Address: PO Box 870515, Wasilla, AK 99687, USA.

**KOJIMA Seiji,** b. 22 April 1951, Tokyo, Japan. Associate Professor. m. Toshiko Iiyama, 1 son. Education: BS, 1974, DSc, 1979, University of Tokyo. Appointments: Research Associate, 1980, Assistant Professor, 1981, Associate Professor, 1994-, University of Tokyo; Editor, Journal of the Physics Society of Japan, 1998-. Publications: 152 papers for scientific journals in the field of condensed matter physics. Memberships: Physics Society of Japan; Chemistry Society of Japan; Japan Society of Applied Physics. Address: Institute of Materials Science, University of Tsukuba, Tsukuba, Ibaraki 305-8573, Japan.

**KOKOT Franciszek,** b. 24 November 1929, Olesno Sl. Physician. m. Malgorzata Skrzypczyk, 4 sons. Education: Medical studies, 1948-53; Defense of doctor thesis, 1957; Defense of habilitation thesis, 1962; Extraordinary professor, 1969; Ordinary professor, 1982. Appointments: Technician, Dept Chemistry, Silesian University Medical School, 1949-50; Assistant and Senior Assistant, Dept Pharmacology, 1950-57; Assistant Professor, 1957-62, Associate Professor, 1962-69, Extraordinary Professor, 1969-74, Dept Internal Medicine; Extraordinary Professor, Dept Nephrology, 1974-82; Ordinary Professor, 1982-, Head of Dept. Publications: Author over 600 scientific publications and several chapters in 30 textbooks. Honours: Dr h.c. Medical School of Wroclaw, 1990, Katowice, 1993, Szczecin, 1995, Kosice, 1997, and Lublin, 1997; Honorary member, 7 foreign societies of nephrology; L Pasteur Medal, Strasbourg, 1985; F Volhard Golden Medal, 1991; International Distinguished Medal, USA, 1991. Memberships: International Society Nephrology; European Society Nephrology; President, Polish Society Nephrology, 1989-98; FRCP, Edinburgh, 1994. Address: Ul Francuska 20, 40-027 Katowice, Poland.

**KOLAR Jaromir Jan,** b. 30 July 1926, Ostrava, Czech Republic. Radiologist. m. Olga. Education: MD, summa cum laude, 1950, Professor of Radiology, 1980, Medical Faculty, Charles University, Prague. Appointments: Lecturer, Clinic for Diagnostic Imaging, Postgraduate Medical School, Prague.

Publications: 17 monographs, 474 papers in profession: medical journals. Honour: Rajewski Medal, Europea Association of Radiology, 1993. Memberships: Czech Medic: Association; Czech Radiological Association; Internation: Skeletal Society. Address: Preslickova 5, Praha 10, CZ 106 0( Czech Republic.

**KOLESOV Sergey,** b. 11 December, Kiev, Ukraine Merchant Marine Officer. m. Elena Kaliazina. Education Petrozavodsk River School, Russia, 1986-9( Technician/Navigator, Voice of Prophecy Bible Schoc 1993-94; World English Institute, USA, 1996-98. Appointment: 3rd, then 2nd Officer, White Sea, Omega Shipping Compan: Russia, 1990-94; 2nd Officer, N Square Ltd, Greece, 1994-9! 2nd, then Chief Officer, Aquarian Shell Marine, Greece 1995-98; Receiving/Filing Agent, International Registries, US/ 1994-; Chargé d'Affaires, Hutt River Principality, Australi: 1995-. Honours: Radio Prague DX Diploma; HAC-DX Diplom: Berlin, Germany; Numerous Diplomas, East and West Radi Club, Germany; Honorary Listener, Radio Sofia, Bulgaria Memberships: Radio Prague Monitor Klub; Radio Mosco' Friendship Club Member; International Listeners' Club, Belgiu: Club DX de Radio Havana, Cuba; Radio Bucharest Short Wav Listeners Club; World Wide Country Club, Tennessee, US/ Radio Slovakia International Club. Address: PO Box 174 Kie' 252150 Ukraine.

**KOLEV Spas Dimitrov,** b. 19 October 1958, Sofia, Bulgari: Chemistry Educator. m. Snezhana Bakalova, div, 1 sor Education: Diploma in Higher Education (Chemistry), 198: University of Sofia; PhD Chemistry, 1988, Technical Universit of Budapest, Hungary. Appointments: Assistant Professo University Sofia, 1982-83, 1988-90, 1992; PhD, student an: Researcher, Technical University Budapest, 1983-8t Research Fellow, University Twente, The Netherlands 1990-92; Researcher, La Trobe University, Australia, 1996 Publications: Over 60 scientific articles in professional journa and conference proceedings. Honours: Recipient, Ronal Belcher Memorial Award, 1988; Adjunct Senior Researc Fellow, University South Australia, 1998. Membership: Unic of Scientists, Bulgaria. Address: La Trobe University Department of Chemistry, Bundoora, Victoria 3083, Australi:

**KOLHE Sadashiv,** b. 4 May 1969, Palasi, India. Singe: Musician. m. Sulochanabai, 3 sons. Education: Publi Education. Appointments: Director, Gramin Vikas Natya Kal: Pathak, Palashi; Singer, All India Radio. Publications: Sever: articles in leading newspapers. Honours: Awards from loc: bodies. Address: At Palasi Post Shevadi, Ta Loha Distric: Nanded, India.

**KOLPAKOV Andrei,** b. 24 September 1941, Moscow Russia. Physicist. m. Olga Kolpakova, 1 son. Education Graduate, Physicist, Moscow State University, 1965; Degree c Doctor of Physico-Mathematical Science, 1994. Appointment: Senior Assistant Professor, 1979-; Professor, 1994 Publications: X-Ray Dynamical Difraction, 1988; X-Ra' Difraction in Crystals With One-D Variation of the Lattic Parameter, 1989; X-Ray Difraction in Super-Lattices, 1992; 10( publications in scientific journals and 1 patent. Membershiɟ International Union of Crystallography. Address: Physica Faculty, M V Lomonosov Moscow State University, Leninski Gory, Moscow 119899, Russia.

**KOMAROV Fadei Fadeevich,** b. 20 August 1945, Mogile\ Belarus. m. Valja, 1 son, 1 daughter. Education: MSc, Physics Belorussian University, 1969; Candidate of Physics an Mathematics, 1974; PhD, 1982. Appointments: Postgraduate Solid State Physics Department, 1969-75, Chief, Institute c

Applied Physical Problems, 1975-; Vice Director, Institute of Applied Physical Problems, 1981-92; Head, Solid State Electronics Chair, 1988-, Belorussian University. Publications: 8 monographs, 6 reviews and articles, 37 patents, 228 publications in journals, 261 abstracts and reports. Honours: Soros HonoraryProfessor, 1995-. Memberships: Corresponding Member, National Academy of Science, Belarus, 1996; Belorussian Vacuum Science and Technology Society; Several editorial boards. Address: Institute of Applied Physics Problems, 7 Kurchatov Street, Minsk 220064, Belarus.

**KOMAROVSKIKH Konstantin F,** b. 4 September 1934, Kolivan, Novosibirsk, Russia. Physicist. m. Mochova Nina I, 2 sons. Education: Physicist, Leningrad, St Petersburg University, 1958; Candidat Degree, Moscow Physics Technical Institute, 1968; Dr, Leningrad Polytechnic Institute, 1982. Appointments: Engineer, Senior Research Assistant, Head of Laboratory, Research Institute of Physics Problems, 1964-73; Head of Laboratory, Institute Biological Instrument Making, 1973-78; Head of Department Laboratory, Science Production Association, Avangard, 1978-83; Head, Physics Chair, Northwest Polytechnic Institute, 1983-92; Professor, Physics, Northwest Polytechnic Institute, 1993-. Publications: Published more than 110 works including 1 monograph; 9 inventions. Honours: Medal, 1970, 1991. Memberships: Corresponding Member, Russian Academian of Natural Science; International Professor Association, accredited by UNIDO (UN). Address: North West Polytechnic Institute, 5 Khalturina Street, St Petersburg 191186, Russia.

**KOMATINA Dejan,** b. 14 December 1964, Belgrade, Yugoslavia. Education: BSc, 1989, MSc, 1993, PhD, finishing, Faculty Civil Engineering, University Belgrade. Publications: River Renaturalisation, 1992; Solid-Liquid Open Channel Flow, 1997. Memberships: International Association of Hydraulic Research; Yugoslav Society of Mechanics; Yugoslav Committee on Large Dams. Address: Jovana Bijelica 29, 11000 Belgrade, Yugoslavia.

**KOMLEVA Gabriela Maria,** b. 27 December 1938, Leningrad. Ballerina; Teacher. m. A Sokolov-Kaminsky. Education: As ballet dancer, The Vaganova Ballet School, Leningrad, 1948-57; As rehearsal master, The State Conservatory after Rimsky-Korsakov, Leningrad, 1979-84. Appointments: Prima Ballerina, 1957-88, Guest Star, 1989-90, Maryinsky (Kirov) Theatre, St Petersburg; Ballet Teacher and Coach, 1978-88; Ballet Mistress, 1989-; TV Hostess of Ballet Programmes, St Petersburg, 1985-90; Professor of Choreography Dept, The State Conservatory after Rimsky-Korsakov, 1987-; Member of Editorial Board, Newsletter of Belarussian Ballet, 1993-; Artistic Director, St Petersburg Ballet Master Classes, 1993-; President, English Society of Russian Style Ballet, 1994-. Creative Works: As ballerina, all main roles in classic and modern Maryinsky repertoir; Main roles in about 30 ballet films including Bayarderks; TV hostess of 17 ballet programmes; Restager 11 important ballets; Guest Teacher and Choreographer of master classes and Summer courses in USA, Canada, England, Switzerland, Taiwan, Norway and Japan. Honours: State Prize Russian Federation, 1970; Prize Varna Competition, 1966; Prize Choreography Competition, Moscow, 1967; Named Honoured Artist Daghestan, 1968; Honoured Artist Russia, 1970; National Artist of Russia, 1975; National Artist of USSR, 1983; Best Actor of Year, Leningrad, 1968; Best Actor of Year in TV films, Leningrad, 1982; Best Rehearsal Master, 7th Moscow Competition, 1993. Memberships: Union of Theatre Figures of Russia. Address: 198005 St Petersburg, Fontanka Reka 116 kv 34, Russian Federation.

**KOMORI Teruhisa,** b. 3 July 1954, Suzuka, Mie, Japan. Lecturer. m. Eri Oda, 2 s. Education: MD, Mie University School of Medicine, 1989. Appointments: Lecturer, Mie University School of Medicine, 1993. Publications: Many Articles, 1983-. Memberships: Japanese Society of Psychiatry and Neurology, World Federation of Biological Psychiatry; International Society of Neuroimmunomodulation. Address: Dept of Pyschiatry Mie University, 2-174 Edobashi, Tsu 514-8507, Japan.

**KONAGAYA Masaaki,** b. 3 January 1949, Choshi, Chiba, Japan. Physician; Neurologist. m. Yoko Uchiyama, 1 son, 1 daughter. Education: Graduate, 1975, Nagoya University School of Medicine; Graduate, 1979, Postgraduation School of Nagoya University; Doctor of Philosophy, Medical Science, Board of Clinical Neurology. Appointments: Assistant Professor, Nara Medical University, 1981; Director of Neurology, Suzuka National Hospital, 1990-; Assistant Professor, Nagoya University School of Medicine, 1995-. Publications: Shinkeinaika, 1995; No to Shinkeinaika, 1996; Over 300 scientific papers in Clinical Neurology. Memberships: Counsillor, Japanese Association of Neurology; Japan Society of Neurovegetative Research; Japanese Association of Neurological Therapeutics. Address: Dept Neurology, Suzuka National Hospital, 3-2-1 Kasado cho, Suzuka Mie 513, Japan.

**KONDILI Anesti,** b. 30 January 1943, Korce. Cardiologist. m. Aleksandra, 2 daughters. Education: Grad, 1965, Faculty of Medicine, Tirana University. Appointments: Petagogue, Faculty of Medicine, Dept Semiology, Dept Cardiology, 1965-; Specialisation in field of cardiology and haemodynamics, 1970-71; Specialist in Cardiology, 1972-; Specialisation for cardiovascular reanimation in Paris, 1973-74; Organiser and Chief of Coronary Intensive Care Unit, Clinic of Cardiology, 1976-; Obtained title, Doctor, 1981 Assistant Professor, 1988, Professor in Faculty of Medicine, 1991; Dean of Faculty of Medicine, 1997; Member of High Commission of medical expertise, 1984-, and its chief, 1989-; Member of the board of Bulletin of Medical Science, 1980-. Publications: 3 textbooks for university students: Electrocardiography and phonocardiography, 1972; Diagnosis of the internal diseases, 1975; Cardiology, 1991; 3 monographs; 23 articles in Bulletin of Medical Sciences; 45 articles in scientific magazines; 5 articles in foreign magazines; 18 others on various subjects; Participated and read his papers in 15 international conferences & seminars and 27 national conferences and seminars. Honours: Naim Frasheri Order Class II, 1979; Order of Labour Class I, 1989. Address: Rr Elbasanit, P4, Sh4, Ap 7, Tirane, Albania.

**KONDO Yutaka,** b. 24 November 1949, Shizuoka City, Japan. Professor. m. Noriko Mochizuki, 1 son, 2 daughters. Education: BS, Geophysics, University of Tokyo, 1972; MS, Geophysics, University of Tokyo, 1974; DS Geophysics, University of Tokyo, 1997. Appointments: Research Associate, 1976-89, Assistant Professor, 1989-92, Professor, 1992-, STEL, Nagoya University. Honours: Alexander von Humboldt Fellowship, 1978-79; Tanakadate Award, 1986; Horiuchi Award, 1990. Memberships: Society of Geomagnetism and Earth, Planetary and Space Sciences; Meteorological Society of Japan; American Geophysical Union. Address: Nagoya University, STE Laboratory, 3-13 Honohara, Toyokawa, Aichi 442, Japan.

**KONEVETSKY Alexander,** b. 18 January 1926, Russia. Russian Philologist. m. Irina Konevetsky, 1 son. Education: M Philology, 1952, Vilnius Pedagogical University, Lithuania; Doctor (Candidate) Philology, 1960, Vilnius University; Doctor Habilius Philology, 1979, Saratov University, Russia. Appointments: Assistant Lecturer, 1952-54, Senior Lecturer,

1954-63, Assistant Professor, 1963-80, Professor, 1980-, Vilnius Pedagogical University, Slavonic Faculty. Publications: Participated in 10 scientific conferences and seminars in Vilnius, St Petersburg, Riga; Books: Word-formation of adverbs, 1976; Historical grammar of Russian language, 1989; 26 scientific articles in Proceedings of Vilnius, St Petersburg, Riga, Saratov Universities. Honours: Higher Certifying Commission, Moscow, Russia Professor of Philology, 1981; Honoured Man of Science of Lithuania, 1986. Address: Erfurto 46-23, 2043 Vilnius, Lithuania.

**KONO Takeshi,** b. 30 August 1954, Osaka, Japan. Dermatologist. Education: MD, Osaka City University Medical School, 1980; PhD, 1984. Appointments: Medical Staff, Department of Dermatology, Osaka City University, 1984-89; Assistant Professor, Department of Dermatology, Osaka City University, 1989-. Honours: Osaka Mayor Award, 1991. Memberships: Councilor, Japanese Society of Investigative Dermatology. Address: Dept of Dermatology, Osaka City University Medical School, 1-4-3 Asahi machi Abeno Ku, Osaka 545 8585, Japan.

**KONSTANTINOV Igor Eduardovich,** b. 24 March 1969, Georievka, Russia. Thoracic and Cardiovascular Surgeon. 2 sons. Education: K.MD. St. Petersburg, Russia, 1992. Appointments: Resident Cardiovascular Surgeon, Pokrov Hospital, St Petersburg, 1992-94; Clinical Fellow, Lunkoping Heart Centre, 1994-97; Carolinas heart Institute, Charlotte, 1997-98; Heart Institute for Children, Oak Lawn, 1989-. Publications: Articles to professional journals. Memberships: Scandinavian Society Thoracic Surgery; New York Academy of Sciences.

**KONSTANTINOV Mihail M,** b. 5 March 1948, Sofia, Bulgaria. Mathematician. m. Ema Vankova, 1 son. Education: MS, Mathematics, Plovdiv University; PhD, Mathematics, Bulgarian Academy of Sciences. Appointments: Dean, Faculty of Transport Engineering, Professor, Mathematics, University of Architecture and Civil Engineering. Publications: 500, including 12 books. Memberships: American Mathematical Society; Union of Bulgarian Mathematicians. Address: UACEG, 1 Chr Smirnenski Bould, 1421 Sofia, Bulgaria.

**KONSTANTINOV Vladimir,** b. 29 August 1958, Siauliai, Lithuania. Conductor. m. Svetlana, 1 son, 1 daughter. Education: Klhipeda BT of Lithuanian Music Academy, 1975-79. Appointments: Choirmaster, Klaipeda Peoples Opera Theatre, 1976-87; Chief Choirmaster, Conductor, 1987-; Aukurhs Choir Founder, Opera Based on HC Andersen, 1993-. Honours: Winner of Several Choir Competitions; The Simkus Prize. Memberships: Lithuanian Theatres Union; Lithuanian Choirs Society. Address: Debreceno 72-13, LT 5810 Klaipeda, Lithuania.

**KOOMSON Jane Comfort,** b. 31 March 1948, Kromantse, Ghana. Typist. m. J K A Bessah, deceased, 2 sons, 2 daughters. Education: Government Secretariat, 1976. Appointment: Secretary to Headmistress, Mfantsiman Girls Secondary School, Saltpond, 1976-. Honour: Choir Certificate, 1997. Address: Mfantsiman Girls Secondary School, Saltpond, Ghana.

**KOPEIKA N S,** b. 12 November 1944, Baltimore, Maryland, USA. Electrical Engineer. m. Miriam Sirota, 2 sons, 1 daughter. Education: PA, Electrical Engineering; BSc, 1966; MSc, 1968; PhD, 1972. Appointments: Department of Electrical and Computer Engineering, Ben Gunion University of the Negev; Lecturer, 1973; Senior Lecturer, 1976; Associate Professor, 1981; Professor, 1987; Department Chairman, 1989-93.

Publications: Over 130 journal papers, international journals; Over 95 conference papers; Textbook: A System Engineering Approach to Imaging, 1998. Memberships: OSA; SPIE; IEEE. Address: Ben Gurion University of the Negev, P O Box 653, Beer Sheva, Israel.

**KOPP Maria S,** b. 14 January 1942, Budapest, Hungary. Medical Doctor; Psychologist. m. A Skrabski, 2 daughters. Education: MD, 1968; Psychologist Diploma, 1977. Appointments: Head, Organizer, Department of Clinical Epidemiology, National Institute of Occupational Health, 1968-73, Head, Department of Clinical Epidemiology, 1973-82, Department of Psychiatry, 1982-93, Director, Institute of Behavioral Sciences, 1993-, Semmelweis University of Medicine. Publications: 101 scientific articles in professional journals. Memberships: International Society of Behavioral Medicine; European Society of Health Psychology; Hungarian Psychophysics Society; Hungarian Health Psychology Society; Hungarian Psychiatry Society. Address: Bela Kiraly Ut 19, H 1125 Budapest, Hungary.

**KOPPE William,** b. 7 May 1949, Chicago, USA. Defender of Christ. m. Cathy Urbaniak, 1 son, 1 daughter. Education: Diploma, Maine Township East Park Ridge, 1967; Degree, University of San Francisco, 1971. Appointments: Knight of thy blessed Virgin Mary, Rome, Italy; Founder and Actual Blood of Defenders of Christ, Jerusalem. Publications: Poetry, True Blue; Bo Bo not Bozo, John Paulaskas. Memberships: Alumni, University of San Francisco; Dank; UHVA; Christian Coalition. Address: 8970 N Parkside Ave Apt 401, Des Plaines, IL 60016-5514, USA.

**KORABIOWSKA Monika,** b. 13 November 1966, Cracow, Poland. Physician. Education: Medical Study, Jagiellonian University, Cracow; Doctor degree, 1992, Cracow. Honour: Humboldt Scholarship, 1995-98. Membership: New York Academy of Science. Address: Department Pathology, University of Gottingen, Robert Koch St, 37075 Gottingen, Germany.

**KORB Jan,** b. 30 July 1937, Trutnov, Czech Republic. Scientist. m. Lubica Korb, 1 son. Education: MSc, University of Chemical Engineering, Prague, 1961; PhD, Institute of Organic Chemistry and Biochemistry, Prague, 1966; DSc, Institute of Molecular Genetics, Prague, 1990. Appointments: Senior Scientist, Head, Department of Biopolymer Micromorphology, Institute of Molecular Genetics, Academy of Sciences, Czech Republic. Publications: Over 50 scientific publications. Honours: Biochemistry Awards, Academy of Sciences, Czech Republic, 1967, 1975. Memberships: European Association for Cancer Research; Czech Society for Electron Microscopy; Czech Society for Biochemistry and Molecular Biology. Address: Institute of Molecular Genetics AS CR, Flemingovo n 2, 16637 Prague 6, Czech Republic.

**KORJAGIN Yuri D,** b. 20 April 1942, Arti, Sverdlovsk. Engineer; Metullurgist, 1 d. Education: Graduate, Metallurgical Faculty, Urals Polytechnical Institute, 1964; Engineer Technician, Heat of the Laboratory Metalloceramics, Kamensk-Uralsk Foundry Plant, 1964-67; Postgraduate Studies, 1967-70; Candidate Thesis Defense, 1972. Appointments: Lecturer Instructor, Metallurgist Department, 1971-98; Deputy Dean, Metallurgical Faculty, South Urals State University, 1994-99. Publications: 108 research papers; 24 author's certificates on inventions of methods Heat treatment steels aluminium and magnesium alloys; Influence of Modes of Deformation and Thermal Processing on Structure and Properties of Alloys for Modern Engineering, 1992; Influence of Modes Thermomechanical of Processing on Formation of ucture and Properties Supereasy Magnesium Alloys, 1995; ructure and Properties of Alloys of System Al-Mg-Li, rengthening by Thermal Processing and Deformation, 1991. ddress: 454080 Cheljabinsk, 86 Kommuna Street, Apt 36, ussia.

**KORLINSKI Wladyslaw,** b. 26 April 1933, Orlow, Poland. ofessor. m. Anna Szczerska, 2 sons, 1 daughter. Education: Sc, 1957, PhD, 1968, DSc, 1978, Technical University of dz, Poland. Appointments: Professor, Technical University of dz, and of Bielsko-Biata Branch of Lodz Technical University, 88-; Professor, Knitting Technology Research Institute, 94-. Publications: 3 books; 80 scientific articles, 1965-98. nours: Gold Cross of Merit, 1987; Medal of National mmittee of Education, 1991; 20 awards from the Rector, 70-98; 3 awards from Minister of Education, 1977, 1989, 90. Address: Bracka 41-11, 91 709 Lodz, Poland.

**KORNIYCHUK May,** b. 2 May 1937, Vladivostok, Russia. athematician. Education: Mathematics. Appointments: Junior d Senior Scientific Collaborator, Senior Teacher, Manager, epartment of High Military School. Publications include: athematics Models of Optimization and Estimation of eliability of Function Compound Systems. Honours: Medal, ood Work, High Education Ministry, Russia, 1979. emberships: Kiev Mathematical Association; Academy of esearch Air and Space. Address: Oles Gonchar str 37a, Apt , Kiev 252034, Ukraine.

**KOROVINA Vera Mikhaylovna,** b. 8 June 1937, Kamenets, dolsk, Ukraine. Physicist. m. Ibadinov Kh, 1 son. Education: aduate, Tajik State University, 1959; Postgraduate, 1963-66; ploma of Doctors Degree, 1968. Appointments: Senior ssistant, 1959, Senior Lecturer, 1966, Professor, Department Optics and Spectroscopy, 1968, Tajik State University. blications: Over 40 articles in Soviet scientific journals. nour: Honourable Worker in Education, Tajikistan, 1997. embership: Tajik Physical Society. Address: Kovalja 5/4 ap , Dushanbe 734063, Tajikistan.

**KORSAKAITE Ingrida,** b. 31 October 1938, Birzai, huania. Art Historian. m. Rimvydas Racenas, 2 daughters. ducation: Diploma Art History and Theory, 1961, Repins stitute of Painting, Sculpture and Architecture, St Petersburg; octor of Humanitarian Sciences, 1970, Lithuanian Academy Sciences. Appointments: Senior Researcher, Lithuanian ademy of Sciences, 1961-89, Institute of Culture and Arts of thuania, 1990-; Stipendiate, International Youth Library, unich, 1988; Visiting Scholar, Chicago, 1991. Publications: clude 8 Monographs. Honour: Order of Grand Duke ediminas. Memberships: Lithuanian Artists' Association; thuanian Section of AICA; Lithuanian Section of IBBY; sociation of Lithuanian Art Historians; Society of History and lture of Reformation in Lithuania; Martynas Muzvyoles Club Bibliophiles, Vilnius. Address: V Grybo 41-23, LT 2055 nius, Lithuania.

**KORSHUNOV Fedor Pavlovich,** b. 15 May 1934, Belarus. ysicist. m. Korshunova Evgenia Alfonovna, 1 daghter. ucation: MS, Physics and Electronics, Academy of zhaiskiy, Leningrad, 1957; PhD, Solid State Physics, stitute of Physics, Academy of Sciences, Belarus, 1966; DSc, stitute of Steel and Alloys, Moscow, 1973. Career: Senior esearch Engineer, 1962-68, Senior Researcher, Laboratory Radiation Effects, Institute of Solid State and Semiconductor ysics, National Academy of Sciences, Belarus, 1968-85; ad, Laboratory of Radiation Effects, Institute of Solid State d Semiconductor Physics, National Academy of Sciences, larus, 1985-94; Deputy Director, Head, Laboratory of

Radiation Effects, 1994-. Publications: Over 350 professional publications. Honours: Belarussian State Award in Science, 1980; 3 medals, Order, Sign of Honour, 1986. Membership: Corresponding Member, National Academy of Sciences, Belarus, 1984. Address: Institute of Solid State and Semiconductor Physics, National Academy of Sciences, P Brovki Str 17, Minsk 220072, Belarus.

**KORTOV Vsevolod,** b. 3 January 1939, West Siberia, Russia. Physicist. m. 1960, 1 son. Education: Engineer Physicist, 1962; Doctor, 1966; Doctor of Sciences, 1976. Appointments: Assistant, 1962; Assistant Professor, 1965; Full Professor, 1976; First Vice Rector, Urals State Technical University, 1988. Publications: More 450 publications in scientific journals; 65 patents. Honour: Academician, Russian Academy of Natural Sciences, 1994. Membership: Russian Physical Society. Address: Urals State Technical University, 19 Mira Str, Ekaterinburg 620002, Russia.

**KORZENIOWSKI Krzysztof (Kris),** b. 3 December 1935, Lodz, Poland. Electrical Engineer; Educator. m. Miroslawa Halina Rajf, 2 sons. Education: MSc, Electrical Engineering, 1960, PhD, Electrical Engineering, 1975, Lodz University of Technology; Certified Electrical Engineer, Poland; Registered Engineer, Papua New Guinea. Appointments: Electrical Engineer, Project Engineer, Instruction Laboratory Manager, Electrical Industry Export Manager, 1959-60; Senior Research Fellow, Lodz University of Technology, 1970-81; Principal Lecturer, UNESCO Project, Kwara State College of Technology, Nigeria, 1981-84; Associate Professor and Electrical Engineering Consultant, Papua New Guinea University of Technology, Lae, 1985-. Honour: Silver Jubilee Award, Papua University of Technology, 1992. Memberships: Fellow, Institute of Engineers, Papua New Guinea; Senior Member, Institute of Electrical and Electronics Engineers, USA; Society of Instrument and Control Engineers, Japan. Address: Papua New Guinea University of Technology, Private Mail Bag, Lae, Morobe Province 411, Papua New Guinea.

**KOSAKOVSKYY Anatoliy Lukianovich,** b. 8 October 1952, Netreba Rovensky, Ukraine. Otolaryngologist. m. Nadia Kosakovska, 1 daughter. Education: Degree, 1973, MD, 1975, Chernivetsky Medical Institute, Ukraine; Candidate of Science, Kyiv State Institute of Advanced Medical Training of Physicians, Ukraine, 1985; DSc, Kyiv State Institute, 1994. Appointments: Intern Otolaryngologist, Rovensky Region Hospital, Rovno, 1975-76; Otolaryngologist, Volodymyretsky (Ukraine) District Hospital, 1976-80; Head, Otolaryngology Department, Volodymyretsky District Hospital, 1976-80; Clinical Resident, Kyiv (Ukraine) State Institute of Advanced Medicial Training Physicians, 1980-82; Head, Board of Young Scientists, Kyiv State Institute, 1984-85; Assistant Professor, Kyiv State Institute, 1985-96; Head, Department of Overseas Development and International Economic Relations, Kyiv Medical Academy of Postgraduate Education, 1994-98; Professor of Otolaryngology Pediatric Department, Kyiv Medical Academy of Postgraduate Education, 1997-; Prorector, International Relations, Kyiv Medical Academy of Postgraduate Education, 1998-. Publications: 2 Monographs; Over 140 articles in professional journals. Honours: Best Young Rationalizer of the City of Kyiv, 1984; Named Honoured Inventor of Ukraine Supreme Soviet of Ukraine, 1990; Honoured Inventor and Rationalizer, Board of Invention and Rationalization Organization of Ukraine, 1991. Memberships include: New York Academy of Sciences; Kyiv Science Society of Otolaryngology; Rectorate, 1995-, Science Council, 1997-, Tzaole Union Com., 1995-, Kyiv Medical Academy of Postgraduate Education. Address: PO Box 70, Kyiv 252179, Ukraine.

**KOSHIBE Heihachiro**, b. 4 June 1926, Tokyo, Japan. Agrotechnologist. m. Masako Nakayama, 2 sons. Education: MA, Plant Genetics, Tokyo Agricultural University. Appointments: Chief Executive Officer, Mikado Seed Growers Co Ltd; Chairman, Chiba Overseas Trade Cooperative; Executive Committee, ASSINSEL, Nyon, Switzerland. Publication: Horticulture and Agricultural Seeds. Honour: Recipient, Yellow Medal and National Order No 5A, Emperor of Japan, 1997. Memberships: District Governor, Rotary International, 1993-94; Honorary Life Member, FIS; Executive Vice President, Japan Seed Trade Association; Chairman, Election Control Commission; Policemen's Friendship Association, Chiba. Address: 7-6-28 Makuhari-Hongo, Hanamigawa, Chiba City 262-0033, Japan.

**KOSTIAL Pavol**, b. 5 July 1949, Zilina, Slovak Republic. Professor. m. Maria Kostialova, 2 daughters. Education: Comenius University, Bratislava, 1972; PhD, 1981; Associate Professor, 1987; Full Professor, 1998. Appointments: Vice Rector, University of Zilina, 1993-1996; Dean of the Faculty, Industrial Technologies, 1996. Publications: The Utilization of the Ultrasonic Waves in the Study of Surfaces and Interfaces. Memberships: New York Academy; Scientific Boards of Several Universities. Address: Trenéin University, Faculty of Industrial Technologies, T. Vansovej 1054-45, SK 020 32 Puchov, Slovak Republic.

**KOSTIAL-SIMONOVIC Krista**, b. 19 December 1923, Osijek, Croatia. Physiology Researcher; Educator. m. Ivan Simonovic, 15 July 1953, 1 son. Education: MD, Medical Faculty, Zagreb, Croatia, 1949; DSc, 1955. Appointments: Research Assistant, Institute of Medical Research and Occupational Health, Zagreb, 1950-55, 1955-62, Research Advisor, 1962-; Honorary Research Assistant, University College, London, 1953; Head Department, Biophysics Institute Medical Research and Occupational Health, 1958-62, Head, Department of Mineral Metabolism, 1962-89, Deputy Director, 1964-89, Consultant, 1989-; Postgraduate Teacher, Medical Faculty, Faculty of Pharmacy, Faculty of Natural sciences, 1963-; Consultant, WHO, Copenhagen, IAEA, Vienna, EPA, Washington, 1979-. Publications: Articles in professional journals; Member, editorial board, professional journals. Honours: Gold Medal, President of Republic, 1965; Ruder Boskovic Award, Republican Research Council, Zagreb, 1969; Life Achievement Award, Ministry of Science and Technology, Zagreb, 1992; Danica Hrvatska Medal, 1996. Membership: Croatian Academy of Sciences and Arts. Address: 19 Amruseva, 10000 Zagreb, Croatia.

**KOSTOV George**, b. 18 October 1943, Srem, Bulgaria. Chemical Engineer. m. Velichka Kostova, 1 son, 1 daughter. Education: Diploma, Chemical Engineering, Higher Institute of Chemical Technology, 1968; MSc, 1968; PhD, 1980; DChemSci, Bourgas University, 1996. Appearances: Vice Rector, Higher Institute of Chemical Technology, Bourgas, 1983-89; Head, Fluoropolymere Laboratory, Bourgas, 1984-92; Director, Center for Electronic Beam Technology, 1993-, Dean of Faculty, 1997-. Publications include: Thermally Stimulated Depolarization Analysis of Radiation Grafted Ion-Exchange Copolymers of LDPE and PTFE, 1992; Radiation Initiated Graft Copolymerization of 4-Vinylpyrioine onto Lope and PTFE Films and Aion-exchange Membranes Therefrom, 1996; Novel Fluorinated Monomers Bearing Reactive SideGroups, Part 1. Preparation and Use of CICF²CFCII as the Telogen, 1995; Syntesis and Polymerization of Fluorinated Monomers Bearing a Reactive Lateral Group. Part 2. Synthesis of Nonconjugated Dienes, 1997. Honours: Cyril and Methodi Medal, 1st Degree, Bulgarian Ministry of Education and Science, 1987; Monbucho Scholarship, Japanese Ministry of Education, Osaka & Tokyo

Universities. Memberships: New York Academy of Science Bulgarian Polymer society; Bulgarian Polymer Scienti Council; Bourgas University Academy Council. Addres University "Prof. A.S. Zlatarov", 1 Prof Yakimov Str. Center Electron Beam Technology, 8010 Bourgas, Bulgaria.

**KOSTRAUSKAS Pavelas**, b. 25 October 1927, Lithuan. Electrical Engineer. m. Zinaida, 1 son, 1 daughter. Educatic Candidate of Science, 1959; DSc, 1978. Appointmen Assistant Professor, MDC, 1962; Professorship, PR, 197 Head of Department of Electrical Machines, 1982-8 Publications: 248 articles, books and patents. Honou Honoured Inventor, 1968. Memberships: Academic Council Protocol, 1995; Corresponding Member, International Acader of Engineering, 1996. Address: Ukmerges 9-24, LT 30 Kaunas, Lithuania.

**KOSTRUBALA Mark Anthony**, b. 13 August 196 Chicago, Illinois, USA. Fiction Writer. Education: BA, 199 University of Iowa. Career: Fiction Writer. Publication: Fi novel, Dark Legacy, 1996. Address: 10227 S Kostner Avenu Oak Lawn, IL 60453-4210, USA.

**KOTLER Philip**, b. 27 May 1931, Chicago, Illinois, US. Professor. m. Nancy Kotler, 3 daughters. Educatio Economics, DePaul University, 1948-50; MA Economics, 195 University of Chicago; PhD Economics, 1956, MI Postdoctoral studies, Sociology, University Chicago, 195 Mathematics, Harvard University, 1960. Appointments: Teach on marketing management, new products marketing, marketi strategy and other marketing fields; Researcher in same are Editorial adviser for marketing journals; Consultant to companies. Publications: 17 books on marketing; Author co-author 114 articles; Invited lectures at 24 universitie Honours: 20 scholastic honours, awards and fellowshiµ including: First recipient of Award for Excellence in Health Ca Marketing, 1985. Memberships: Marketing Science Institut Management Analysis Centre; EST; College on Marketin Institute of Management and Science; American Marketi Association; Member of Board, Peter F Drucker Foundation fi Nonprofit Management. Address: 301 Keystone Cou Glencoe, IL 60022-1957, USA.

**KOUDRYASHEVA Alexandra A**, b. 1 Jan 1934, Tul Russia. Scientist; Educator. m. Dan B Chopyk. Education: B Biology, 1965; Doctor of Technical and Biological Science All-Union Institute of Food Industries, USSR; PhD, Technic and Biological Sciences, Higher Attestation Committee Soviet Ministers of USSR, 1983; Assistant Professor's Diplom 1975, Professor's Diploma, 1985, USSR Higher Certificatic Committee. Appointments: Head, Radiation Microbiolog Laboratory, All-Union Food Industry Research Institute, USSI 1961-71; Professor, Chairman, Dean, Department Commodities and Microbiology, Russian Economic Academ Moscow, 1971-93; President, ICONAHR, 1993-. Publicatior Microbiological Basis of Preserving Fruit and Vegetables, 198 BAS "Alexandrina": Its Applications in the Food Industr Cosmetics and Medicine, 2nd edition, 1997; Microbiolog Sanitation and Hygiene, 1997; XXth Century Violations Again Human Health. Honour: Laureate, International Prize, 199 Memberships: Academician, International Informatic Academy; New York Academy of Sciences; All-Unic Microbiological Association. Address: 106 Guadeloupe Driv Toms River, NJ 08757, USA.

**KOUSHKI Parviz Amir**, b. 28 April 1943, Sabzevar, Ira Academician. m. Alison M Larkin, 1 son, 1 daughter. Educatio BSCE/MSCE, 1965, Department of Civil Engineerin University of Azarbijon; Diploma English Proficiency, 196

lew York University; MSCE Traffic, 1970, Department of Civil ngineering, University of Massachusetts, Amherst; PhD ransport, Department of Civil and Environmental Engineering, Iniversity of Wisconsin, Madison. Appointments: Assistant Professor, Advisor to Mayor, Municipality of Tehran, Co-Director, Centre for Urban Studies, Tehran Polytechnic Iniversity, 1975-79; Assistant Professor, Clarkson University, ISA, 1979-82; Associate Professor, King Saud University, Saudi Arabia, 1982-90; Associate Professor, University of Alaska, USA, 1990-92; Professor, Department of Civil ngineering, Kuwait University, 1992-. Publications: Over 120 ournals, proceedings and research report publications. lonours: Certificate and Monetary Awards, Outstanding Project Management, Kamkar Construction Company, 1964; Certificate of Outstanding Project Supervision, Secretary of Housing and Jrban Development, 1966; Honorary Mention, National Essay Contest, American Society of Civil Engineers, 1981; Distinguished Faculty Award, 1994, Outstanding Research Award, 1996, Kuwait University. Memberships: Persian, and American Society of Civil Engineers; Transportation Research Board, USA; International Association of Travel Behaviour; World Safety Organisation; Volunteers in Technical Assistance; Human Factors Society; World Bank, Rooster of Consultants; New York Academy of Sciences; Editorial Board of Journals in USA, UK and Iran. Address: Kuwait University, Civil Engineering Department, PO Box 5969, Kuwait 13060.

**KOUTKOVA Alice S,** b. 7 April 1931, Taganrog, Russia. Educator. Widow, 1 son, dec 1978. Education: Designer, Taganrog Aviation College, 1951; English Educator, Rostov Pedagogical Institute, 1959; Degree in Methodology in English, 1975; Qualified as Assistant Professor, 1979, Professor, 1989; Laureat Diploma, 1990. Appointments: Designer, Taganrog Aviation Plant; English Educator, Taganrog Radio Institute and Novocherkassk State Technical University, 1959-84; Head, English and French Languages Department, Novocherkassk Polytechnic Institute, South Russia State Technical University, 984-.(F4)Publications: More than 210 scientific works including: Computers and Programming, 1969; Man - Computer Future, 1987, 1995; CAD Systems, 1988; World of PCs, 1997; Business English, 1998; USA: Land and People, 1999; Internet and Virtual Reality, 1999. Memberships: MALP, 1992; Teachers of English to Speakers of Other Languages, 1993; Science and Methodology Council for State Education Committee for Foreign Languages, 1994; National Association of Teachers of English, 1996; Active Worldwide Member, New York Academy of Sciences, 1996. Address: B Khmelnitsky 51-16, 346428 Novocherkassk, Russia.

**KOVAC Stefan,** b. 19 April 1928, Slovakia. Professor. m. Klara, 1 son, 1 daughter. Education: Engineer of Chemistry, 951; Dr, 1952; PhD, 1959; DSc, 1987. Appointments: Associate Professor, 1962; Professor, 1989; Head of Organic Chemistry Department, Slovak Technical University, 1990-93; Head of Department of Chemistry, Trnava University, 1994-; Vice President for Developmental Affairs, Trnava University, 996-. Publications: 130 Scientific Papers; 15 Patents; 2 Books on Organic Chemistry; 2 Books on Spectral Methods in Organic Chemistry; 13 Text Books on Organic Chemistry for Faculty Students. Honours: Silver and Gold Medals, Slovak Technical University and Trnava University. Memberships: Slovak Chemical Society; British Chemical Society; American Biographical Institute Research Board of Advisers. Address: University of Trnava, Department of Chemistry, Hornopotocna 23, 91843 Trnava, Slovakia.

**KOVACH George Daniel,** b. 29 December 1951, Fairfield, California, USA. Theatre; Literature. m. Anne Marie Pleskovic deceased, 2 daughters. Publications include: Passion of a

Peasant; Blessed Be...Thine; Three Dreams of Obsession; Poetry and Tales for the Little Ones; Candleberry Tale; Love and the Wind; Adventure of Thicket Hallow; George and the Jester; Enchanted Melody; Other Side of Darkness; Tales and Legends of Immortality. Honours include: Fellowship, International Biographical Association, 1996; Member, International Fellowship, 1996; Research Board of Advisors, 1996; Twentieth Century Achievement Award, 1997. Memberships: American Society of Composers, Authors & Publishers, 1978; International Platform Association, 1995; International Biographical Centre, FIBA, MOIF, 1996. Address: 328 William Street A, Downingtown, PA 19335, USA.

**KOVACHEV Ljubomir,** b. 26 November 1942, Dimitrovgrad, Bulgaria. Surgeon. m. Amelia Panteleeva, 1 son. Education: MD, Medicine, 1972, MD, Surgery, 1978, PhD, 1985, Sofia University. Appointments: Registrar in Surgery, 1972-75; Assistant Professor in Surgery, 1976-85; Associate Professor and Head, Department of General Surgery, 1987-; Dean of Foreign Students, 1987-93. Publications: Contributions to: International Surgery, 1991; Surgery, Radiology and Anatomy, 1993; Japanese Journal of Surgery, 1995; The Lancet, 1996; Other journals. Memberships: International Gastro-Surgical Club; International College of Surgery; Eurosurgery; National Geographic Society. Address: George Kochev St 39, Entr D, Apt 2, 5800 Pleven Lovec, Bulgaria.

**KOVALCHENKO Mikhaylo Savich,** b. 2 March 1934, Vinnitsa, Ukraine. Materials Science. m. Vira Sinelnikova, 1 son. Education: Degree of Engineer, Kyiv Polytechnic Institute, Ukraine, 1956; PhD, Ukraine Academy of Sciences, Kyiv, 1962; DSc, 1974; Professor, 1976. Appointments: Engineer, 1956-58, Junior Research Fellow, 1958-59, Senior Engineer, 1958-62, Senior Research Fellow, 1962-67, Head of Department, 1968-, Institute for Problems of Materials Science, Ukraine National Academy of Sciences; Educator, 1958-68, Professor, 1988-96, Kyiv Polytechnic Institute; Expert, Higher Certification Committee, Moscow, 1982-91, Ukraine, 1993-96. Publications include: Hot Pressing, 1962; Radiation Damage of Refractory Compounds, 1979; Theoretical Principles of Hot Treatment of Porous Materials by Pressure, 1980. Honours: State Prize, Science and Technology, Ukraine, 1994; Title, Merited Worker in Science and Engineering of the Ukraine, Ukraine President, 1998. Address: Institute for Problems of Materials Science, Ukraine NAS 3, Krzhizhanovsky Str, Kyiv-142, 252142, Ukraine.

**KOVALEV Evgueni Evguenievich,** b. 7 July 1929, Tikhvin, Leningrad, Russia. Radiation Physicist; Researcher; Administrator. m. Nora Kolesnikova. Education: Engineer, Moscow Institute of Engineering Physics, 1952; PhD, 1956; DSc, Institute of Biophysics, Moscow, 1969. Appointments: Senior Scientist, 1956-59, Head of Laboratory, 1959-64, Institute of Biophysics, Moscow; Head of Division, 1964-75, Head of Department, 1975-90, Institute of Biomedical Problems, Moscow; Director, Research Center of Spacecraft Radiation Safety, Moscow, 1990-97. Honours: Decorated, USSR Government, 1961, 1963, 1986; Named, Honoured Scientist of Russia, Russian Government, Moscow, 1976; USSR State Prize, Moscow, 1978. Memberships: New York Academy of Sciences; National Science Committee on Radiation Protection. Address: Research Center of Spacecraft Radiation Safety, 40 Schukinskaya, Moscow 123182, Russia.

**KOVALEVICH Oleg,** b. 30 Dec 1937, Moscow, Russia. Scientist. m. Kovalevich Irina, 2 daughters. Education: Moscow Engineering, Physics Institute, Doctor, 1969; Professor, 1996. Appointments: Head of Laboratory, Kurchatov Institute, Chief of Department, USR Nuclear Regulatory Body; Deputy Director,

Scientific and Engineering Centre of Nuclear and Radiation Safety. Publications: About 100 publications. Honour: Goverment awards. Memberships: Russian Nuclear Society; ASME; New York Academy of Science. Address: Nal M Gorkogo 32/34-98, 113035 Moscow, Russia.

**KOVARSKI Victor,** b. 31 December 1929, Kharkov, Ukraine. Professor. m. Kovarskaya Brigitta, 1 son. Education: MSc, Physics, Kishinev University, 1952; Candidate of Science, Ukraine Academy of Sciences, Institute of Physics, 1959; Doctor of Sciences, Kiev Institute of Theoretical Physics. Appointments: Assistant Lecturer, 1952-60; Senior Researcher, 1961-63; Senior Researcher, Theoretical Physics, Institute of Applied Physics, 1963-69; Head of Laboratory, Physical Kinetics, 1969-; Full Professor, Theoretical, Mathematical Physics, 1971-; Corresponding Member, Academy of Sciences, 1972-92; Full Member, Academy of Sciences, 1992. Publications: About 200 Scientific Publications; 5 Books. Honours: State Prize Laureate, Science and Technology; Professor Emeritus. Memberships: Scientific Councils of the Former USSR Academy of Sciences; Head, Scientific Councils of the Moldavian Academy Sciences. Address: Academy Str, MD 2028 Kishinev, Moldova.

**KOVERDA Vladimir,** b. 16 September 1946, Polevskoi. Scientist. m. Margaret, 1 daughter. Education: DSc, Phys and Maths, 1973. Appointments: Senior Research Worker, 1976-88; Deputy Director, 1988-97; Director, 1998-. Publications: Spontaneous Crystallization of Supercooled Liquid, Co-author, VP Skripov, in Russian, Nauka, Moscow, 1984. Memberships: Corresponding Member, Russian Academy of Sciences. Address: Laboratory of Phase Transformations, Institute of Thermophysics, Urals Division of Russian Academy of Sciences, 91 Pervomaiskaya Str GSP 169, Ekaterinburg 620219, Russia.

**KOYASSAMBIA Jean-Baptiste.** Address: S/C Godeca BP, 1838 Bangui, Republic of Centrafricaine, Africa.

**KOZAI Toyoki,** b. 25 September 1943, Tokyo, Japan. Professor. m. Michiko, 2 sons, 1 daughter. Education: BS, 1967, Department of Horticulture, Chiba University; MS, 1969, PhD, 1972, Department of Agricultural Engineering, University of Tokyo. Appointments: Research Assistant, Department of Agricultural Engineering, Faculty Agriculture, University of Osaka Prefecture, 1973-77; Post-doctoral Fellow, Centre for Agro-Biological Research, Wageningen, The Netherlands, 1974-75; Associate Professor, Department Horticulture, 1977-90, Professor, Department Bioproduction Science, 1990-, Faculty of Horticulture, Chiba University; Visiting Researcher, Department Biological and Agricultural Engineering, Cook College, Rutgers University, New Jersey, USA, 1989. Honours: Prize for Academic Achievement in Growth Regulation and Mass-propagation of in vitro plantlets by Physical Environment Control, awarded by Japanese Academy of Agricultural Sciences and Yomiuri Newspaper Co, 1997; 3 Prizes for Academic Achievements, 1982, 1991, 1992. Memberships: Various offices in numerous academic societies, symposia, conferences, congresses and workshop organisation including: Editorial Advisory Board Member, Scientia Horticulturae, an international journal sponsored by the International Society for Horticultural Science; Editorial Board Member, Plant Cell, Tissue and Organ Culture; Society of Agricultural Meteorology of Japan; Japanese Society of Environment Control in Biology, Chief Director; Japanese Society of High Technology in Agriculture, Vice-Pesident. Address: Department of Bioproduction Science, Faculty of Horticulture, Chiba University, 648 Matsudo, Matsudo Chiba 271, Japan.

**KOZELJ Mirta,** b. 4 November 1956, Ljubljana, Slovenia Medical Doctor. Education: MD, 1981; PhD, 1993 Appointments: Specialist, Internal Medicine, Cardiology Publications include: Lipomatous hypertrophy of the interatria septum: Diagnosed by echocardiography and magnetic resonance imaging, 1995; Percutaneous translumina angioplasty in a transplanted kidney with fibromuscula dysplasia, 1996; A case of Candida parapsilosis prosthetic valve endocarditis cured by medical treatment, 1997 Tachycardia induced cardiomyopathy in dogs: Relatior between chronic supraventricular and ventricular tachycardia 1997. Memberships: World Medical Association; Slovenian Medical Association; Slovenian Society for Emergency Medicine. Address: University Medical Centre, Department of Cardiovascular Disease, Zaloska 7, 1000 Ljubljana, Slovenia

**KOZHOUHAROV Ivan Hristov,** b. 14 September 1950 Triavna, Bulgaria. Conductor. 1 son. Education: Music School Rousse, Bulgaria; Music Academy, Sofia; N A Rimsky-Korsakov Conservatory, St Petersburg, Russia Appointments: Chief Conductor, Opera House, Bourgas; Music Director, Bourgas State Philharmonic Orchestra, Bulgaria Conductor, New Chamber Ensemble and Camerata Classica Sofia, Bulgaria. Honour: Grand Prize, International Competition Hungarian Television, Budapest, 1980. Address: Bourgas State Philharmonic Orchestra, 1 Vola Street, 8000 Bourgas, Bulgaria

**KOZLOV Anatole A,** b. 16 May 1947, Perm, Russia Sociologist. m. Shereshevskaja Elena, 2 sons. Education Historical Faculty degree, 1971, Urals University; PhD ir Sociology, 1979; Professor, 1988. Appointments: Head o Sociology, Department, North West Academy of State Service St Petersburg; Head of Youth Problems Laboratory, Socia Research Institute, St Petersburg; Vice President, Academy o Humanities, State University. Publications: 14 books; Over 15( papers. Memberships: N34 Committee, Youth Sociology International Sociology Association; Russian Sociologists Society; Vice President, Academy of Humanities. Address: 9 ya Liniya V O 61, NW State Service Academy, 199004 S Petersburg, Russia.

**KOZLOV Leonid,** b. 13 December 1935, Russia. Professo of Foundry. m. Vinogradova Nina, 1 daughter. Education Diploma in Engineering, 1958; PhD, 1965; DSc, 1983 Appointments: Technical Director, Foundry Shop, 1958-60 Postgraduate, Moscow State Institute for Steel and Alloys 1960-63, Assistant, Associate Professor, Professor, 1964- Guest Professor, IIT, India, 1970-72. Publications: Over 200, 3 textbooks. Honours: Labour Red Banner Order, 1980 Honoured Scientist of Russia, 1996. Membership: Internationa Committee of Foundry Technicians Association; President o CIATF, 1996. Address: Leninsky Prosp 18-9, Moscow 117071 Russia.

**KPAKIWA Steven James (HRH Prince),** b. 12 Septembei 1947, Kainkordu. International Scientist; Research Professor m. Ramona Kpakiwa, 1 daughter. Education: BA, PhD International Relations, Bradford Colleges, USA, 1971-76; BSc Political Studies, University of California, USA; MA, Sociology PhD, Political Science, SJD, Constitutional Law, Doctorate Common and Civil Law, London University; LLM, Internationa Human Rights, Somerset University, School of Law, 1986; JD Bernadean University, College of Law, 1985; JD, DCS International Business Law and International Management 1988; SJD, PhD, International Government Studies, 1987; PhD Political Economy and Government, 1988. Career: Internationa Scientist, Research Professor, International Educatior Consultant. Publications: Numerous professional articles ii journals and magazines. Honours include: Diploma ecognition of Excellent Religious Moral and Humanitarian ualities; Medal of the Holyland; Honorary titles include: Free ninker, Elder, Fair and Universal Philosophy. Memberships clude: American Society of International Law; American olitical Science Association; International Association of ducators for World Peace; International Bar Association, ngland; Common Law Bar Association; International Cultural orrespondence Institute, Madras, India. Address: International ducational Services, Postfach 102163, 34021 Kassel, ermany.

**KRAJEWSKI Joyce,** b. 17 November 1952, Cuyahoga. ducator. m. Divorced. Education: Business and Marketing, uyahoga Community College, 1970s, 1990s; Certified, egistered and Qualifies Health and Fitness Specialist, ational Academy for Health and Fitness, 1997; American Red oss, different subjects: Child abuse, Disaster, Church nurse; any different workshops and adult education programmes. ppointments: Television Workshop Inc, voiceover, 1985; rofessional Sales Training, Kirlins, 1993; Animal Disaster eam, 1995; Greater Cleveland Chapter of Sweet Adelines, 96. Honours: Cleveland Advertising Club, Runner Up, 1986; ertificate of Thanks, Outstanding Volunteer Service, 1996; ominated Olympic Games Torch Relay, 1996; Finalist, anhattan Model Search, 1996; Table Topics Toastmaster, 97. Membership: Toastmaster International. Address: 19603 oby Rd, Cleveland, OH 44137, USA.

**KRALJ Metka,** b. 30 April 1956, Ljubljana, Slovenia. ologist; Science Educator. Education: BSc Biology, 1979, aculty of Biotechnics, University Ljubljana; MSc, 1985, stitute Hydraulics and Environmental Engineering, Delft, The etherlands; MSc Cell Biology, 1991, PhD Cell Biology, 1998, edical Faculty, University Ljubljana. Appointments: esearcher in Freshwater Ecology, Institute of Biology, ibljana, 1982-86; Assistant Professor for Cell Biology, edical Faculty, Ljubljana, 1986-95; Assistant Professor for cience -Biology, Faculty of Education, Ljubljana, 1995-. iblications: Articles in scientific journals. Address: Ob zici 7, 17 Ljubljana, Slovenia.

**KRAMER Christer Jonas,** b. 2 May 1947, Sundsvall. neumatologist. m. Ulla, 2 daughters. Eduction: Physician, 77; Rheumatologist, 1985. Career: Rhuumatologist, elleftea Hospital; Organizer, Annual Spring Meeting, wedish Association of Rheumatology, 1991 and Update of ondartropaty, Human Brain Institute, St Petersburg, Russia. iblications: Several articles in professional medical journals. emberships: Swedish Rheumatology Association; Hjukens amfällighets Forn; Swedish Association of Physicians; entern. Address: Hjuken 88 92291 Vindeln, Sweden.

**KRANJC Andrej Aleksej,** b. 5 November 1943, Ljubljana, ovenia. Geographer; Archaeologist. m. Maja Ravbar, 1 son. ducation: Diploma, Geography and Archaeology, 1971; agister, 1977; Doctor of Sciences, 1986. Appointments: ead, 1988-95, Scientific Adviser, 1995, Lecturer in Physical eography, 1996, Karst Research Institute; Head, dministative Board, Scientific Research Centre, Ljubljana, 95-. Publications: Books: Cave Sediments, 1989; Dolenjski aski Svet, 1990; Editor, Acta Carsologica. Honours: Palmes ademique, 1997; National Award for Research, Slovenia, 98. Memberships: Karst Research Institute; International eographical Union; Association Française de Karstologie. ddress: Rozna C6, SI-6230 Postojna, Slovenia.

**KRANJNIK Eduard,** b. 19 November 1942, Prague, zechoslovakia. Mathematician. m. Ludmila Dudova, 2 aughters. Education: Charles University, Prague, 1962-67;

Doctor in Natural Sciences, 1988; PhD, Czech Technical University, 1988. Appointments: Assistant Professor, Czech Technical University, 1970-92; Associate Professor, 1992-. Publications: Signal Processing III Theory and Applications, 1986; Signal Processing VI Theory and Applications. Memberships: Society of Czech Mathematicians and Physicists; IEEE. Address: Preslickova 11, 106 00 Prague 10, Czech Republic.

**KRASIKOV Nikolai Nikolayevich,** b. 13 September 1938, Kovrov, Vladimir region, Russia. Education: Geophysicist, Leningrad Mining Institute, 1962; Doctor Technical Science, Leningrad Technological Institute, 1983; Professor of Physics, 1990-. Appointments: Researcher; Associate Professor; Chief Researcher; Head of Department. Publications: Over 200 scientific works in different journals. Honours: Grantee of Education Ministry; Soros Professor. Memberships: Academy of Electrical Engineering (Russia); New York Academy of Sciences; Euroscience. Address: Nogina per 5-46, 601901 Kovrov, Russia.

**KRASNOV Igor Borisovich,** b. 26 November 1931, Tula, Russia. Neurohistologist. m. Ptushkina Svetlana, 2 daughters. Education: Sechenov Moscow Medical Institute, 1949-56; Institute of Brain Research, Moscow, Postgraduate Course, 1956-59, PhD, 1962; Washington University Medical School, St Louis, USA, Postdoctoral Fellow, 1967. Appointments: Junior Research Scientist, Institute of Brain Research, 1959-64; Senior Research Scientist, Institute of Biomedical Problems, Moscow, 1964-91, Leading Research Scientist, 1991-98. Publications: 145 articles, chapters in books and theses. Honours: The Gagarin Diploma of USSR Federation of Cosmonautics, 1988. Membership: Scientific Commission F of Committee on Space Research. Address: Institute of Biomedical Problems, Khoroshevskoye Shosse 76A, 123007 Moscow, Russia.

**KRASNY Sergey Anatolyevich,** b. 23 September 1966, Minsk, Belarus. Surgeon. m. Larisa Mikhailovna Beregovtzova, 1 son, 1 daughter. Education: Diploma with honours, 1989, Intern, 1989-90, Minsk State Medical Institute. Appointments: Urologist, Minsk Children's Diagnostic Centre, 1990-92; Junior Researcher, 1992-96, Senior Researcher, 1996-97, Leading Researcher, 1997-, Research Institute of Oncology and Medical Radiology, Minsk. Publication: Treatment of Renal Cancer Patients with Local and Regional Spread of the Process, 1995. Memberships: Corresponding member, International Academy for Techs, 1997-; Belorussian Urologists Organisation. Address: Research Institute for Oncology and Medical Radiology, Lesnoy-2, 223052 Minsk, Belarus.

**KRAU Edgar,** b. 9 April 1929, Stanislau, Poland. Professor of Organisational Psychology. m. Mary Epure, 1 daughter. Education: MA, 1951, PhD, 1964, Psychology, University of Cluj, Romania. Appointments: University of Cluj, Romania, 1963-77; Head, Psychology Department, Academy of Romanian Republic, Cluj, 1968-77; Professor, University of Haifa, Israel, 1977-81; Professor, Tel-Aviv University, Israel, 1981-97. Publications: Treatise of Industrial Psychology (co-auth), 1967; Self-realization, Success and Adjustment, 1989; The Contradictory Immigrant Problem, 1991; Organizations and Management: Towards the Future (co-auth), 1993; The Realization of Life Aspirations through Vocational Careers, 1997; Social and Economic Management in the Competitive Society, 1998; Over 60 papers in leading scientific journals. Honours: Vasile Conta Prize, Romanian Academy, 1972; Award of High Centre for Logic and Comparative Sciences, Bologna, Italy, 1972; Honorary Mention, Journal of Vocational Behaviour, 1986; Honorary Biography/Bibliography,

Revue Européenne de Psychologie Appliquée, 1993. Memberships: Israel Psychological Association; International Association of Applied Psychology; Affiliate Member, American Psychological Association; Active Member, New York Academy of Sciences. Address: 2 Hess Str, 33398 Haifa, Israel.

**KRAUSE Stephen W,** b. 27 November 1956, Kingston, New York, USA. Principal Consultant. m. Susan J Steinbach, 2 s, 1 d. Education: BS, Business, University of Minnesota, 1974-78. Appointments: Programmer, Analyst, Pennzoil, 1978-79; Programmer, Analyst, International Business Machines, 1979-81; Senior Associate Programmer, Analyst, 1981-86; Application Development Specialist, 1986-90; Advisory Systems Engineer, 1990-92; Consulting Account Manager, Bachman Information Systems, 1992-94; Project Integration Team Leader, Thrifty Payless Inc, 1994-95; Staff Sales Consultant, Oracle Government, Oracle Corporation, 1995-98; Principal Consultant, IMPAC Services, 1998-. Honours: Oracle Club Excellence, 1998; IBM Systems Engineer Symposiums Award; IBM Division Award. Address: 6583 Artemis Ln, West Linn, OR 97068, USA.

**KRAVCHUK Leonid Makarovych,** b. 10 January 1934, Velykyy Zhytyn Village, Rivne Region, Ukraine. Economist; Creator of independent state of Ukraine. m. Antonina M Kravchuk, 1 son. Education: Graduate in Economics, Taras Shevchenko Kyiv State University, 1958; PhD Economics, 1970; Honoured professor of numerous national and foreign universities. Appointments: Lecturer of Political Economy, Chernovtsy Financial College, 1958-60; Political Activist, 1960-90; President of Ukraine, 1991-94; Parliamentary Deputy of Ukraine, 1980-. Publications: Book, There is such a State-Ukraine; Many articles, interviews and other publications in magazines and newspapers. Honours: Order of the Great Prince Yaroslav Mudryy of 5th Degree, 1996, 4th Degree, 1999; Order of International Personnel Academy for the Development of Science and Education, 1998. Memberships: Supreme Council Committee of Ukraine on International Affairs with Commonwealth of Independent States; Chairman of State Commission in carrying out of administration reforms in Ukraine; Chairman of Ukrainian Council of Peace and Ukrainian Society, The Intellect of Nation. Address: 2 Frometovskaya Str, 252039 Kyiv, Ukraine.

**KREININ Mordechai E,** b. 20 January 1930, Tel Aviv, Israel. Professor of Economics. m. Marlene, 3 daughters. Education: MA, 1952, PhD, 1955, University of Michigan; BA, Tel Aviv University, 1951; Visiting Professor, 15 institutions in US, Europe and Australia. Publications: 10 books; 200 articles in professional journals. Honours: Distinguished Faculty Award, 1967; Michigan Boards of Trustees Distinguished Awards, 1984. Memberships: Past President, current Board Member, International Trade and Finance Association; American Economic Association. Address: 1411 Sherwood Avenue, East Lansing, MI 48823-1851, USA.

**KRIEGER David,** b. 27 March 1942, Los Angeles, USA. Peace Foundation President. m. Carolee Krieger, 2 sons, 1 daughter. Education: Graduate, Occidental College, Los Angeles; MA, PhD, Political Science, University Hawaii at Manoa; JD, Santa Barbara College of Law. Appointments: Associate, Centre for the Study of Democratic Institutions; Coordinator, of the Disarmament and Development Project, Foundation for Reshaping the International Order; Faculty Member, University of Hawaii and San Francisco State University; Adjunct Faculty Member, University of California at Santa Barbara and Santa Barbara City College; Lecturer, throughout the world on issues of peace, security, international law, and the abolition of nuclear weapons; Judge protem and

arbitrator for Santa Barbara Superior Court; Advisory Counc Global Resource Action Centre for the Environment, New Yor International Council of the Institute on the Holocaust ar Genocide, Israel, the International Institute for Peace, Vienn Peace Resources Cooperative, Japan, Transnation Foundation for Peace and Future Research, Sweden, War ar Peace Foundation, New York, Whistler Foundation, Canad Deputy Chair, International Network of Engineers ar Scientists for Global Responsibility, Germany; Board membe Lawyers Committee on Nuclear Policy, New York; Committe of 100 for Tibet; Scholar, World Association of Internation Studies; International Steering Committee of Middle Powe Initiative; Founder, Nuclear Age Peace Foundation, Preside 1982-. Publications: 10 and many studies of internation issues; Editor of 3. Honours: Bronze Medal of Hungaria Engineers for Peace, 1995; Peace Award of the War ar Peace Foundation, 1996; Soka Gakkai International Peace Culture Award, 1997; Soka University Award of Highe Honour, 1997; and others. Address: 1187 Coast Village Rd S 121, Santa Barbara, CA 93108-2794, USA.

**KRIEMELMAN Sheila,** b. 15 September 1941, Honolul Hawaiia, USA. Artist; Teacher. m. Arthur L Kriemelman, 1 so 1 daughter. Education: BS Art Education, 1963; MS Studio A 1983. Appointments: Adjunct Associate Professor Fine Ar Iona College, 1982-98. Creative Works: 23 Solo Exhibitio throughout United States; Many Group Exhibitions 198 including: Three Artists, 3 days, NYC, 1992; Hudson Riv Contemporary Artists Association, NYC, 1993; Art of th Northeast, USA, 1994; Honolulu Academy of Arts, 1995; Ea Hampton Visual Arts Festival, NY, 1996; Maui Arts and Cultur Centre, Wailuku, Maui, 1997; B'nai B'rith Klutznick Nation Jewish Museum, Washington DC; Works in private a corporate collections in the US, England and Australi Represented in 4 current galleries and 12 collections; W murals in 3 public installations, 1977, 1979, 1987. Publication 4 catalogues; Article, Craighead, the Litany of the Great Rive 1992. Honours: 11 awards including: Jules L Bauer Memori Award for a watercolour, 1983; Best in Show, Mamaronec Artists Guild's Members Juried Show, 1983; Molly M Canad Award for oils and acrylics, 1993; First Prize: Grace Huntle Pugh Award for oils and acrylics, 1994. Memberships: Nation Association of Women Artists; New York Society of Wome Artists; New York Artists Equity; College Arts Associatio Mamaroneck Artists Guild Inc. Address: 148 Greene Stree New York, NY 10012, USA.

**KRIER Fernande Germaine,** b. 31 May 1940, Chauffaille France. Professor and Researcher in Linguistics. Educatio Graduated, German, French, Italian, University of the Saarlan Saarbrücken, Germany, 1969; DEA, General Linguistics, 197 Doctor of General Linguistics, 1975, Doctor of Humane Letter 1983, University of Paris V, Sorbonne. Appointments: Lectur in General Linguistics, University of Paris, Sorbonne, 1973-7 Assistant Professor of Romance Languages, University of Kie Germany, 1976-85; Visiting Professor of Romance Language University of Trier, 1985-86; Professor of Germanic Language University of Rennes II, France, 1986-. Publications: Maltese Contact with Italian. A Phonological, Grammatical ar Semantic Study, 1976; The Border Area of Franco-Provenç and Swiss-German in Valais (Switzerland), 1985; Numerou articles in various international journals of linguistics, 1975 Memberships: Association of Former Trainees of the Europea Union, Brussels, 1970-; Société Internationale de Linguistiqu Fonctionnelle, Paris, 1974-; Societas Linguistica Europae Vienna, 1977-; Société de Linguistique de Paris, 198 Address: Université Rennes II Haute Bretagne, 6 Avenu Gaston Berger, F-35043 Rennes, France.

**KRIPA Bujar Skender,** b. 23 June 1956, Tirana, Albania. Electronic Engineer. m. Iris Kongoli, 2 daughters. Education: Electronic Engineer, Polytechnic University of Tirana, 1981; Informatic Specialist, Society "Bull", Paris, France, 1984, 1988; Doctor, Electronic Engineering, University of Rome, Italy, 1996. Career: Electronic Engineer, Albanian Radio Television, 1981-84; Researcher, Institute of Information and Applied Mathematics, Science Academy of Albania, 1981, 1991; Informatic Educator, Polytechnic University of Tirana, 1985-90; Electronic Engineer, Groupe Schneider Vanoni Sud S.P.A, Italy, 1992-; Automation Educator, Professional States Institute, Vanoni, Italy, 1988. Publications: Several articles in professional journals. Address: Viale Maraini No 15, Interno 7, 2100 Rieti, Italy.

**KRISHEN Kumar,** b. 22 June 1939, Srinagar, Kashmir, India. Scientist; Technologist. m. Vijay L Raina Krishen, 3 daughters. Education: BA, Jammu and Kashmir University, 1959; BTech, 1962, MTech, 1963, Calcutta University; MS, 1966, PhD, 1969, Kansas State University. Appointments: Junior Research Fellow, Research Fellow, Institute of Radio Physics and Electronics, Calcutta University, 1963-64; Research Assistant, 1964-66, Instructor, 1966-68, Assistant Professor, 1968-69, Kansas State University; Staff Scientist, Staff Engineer, Lockheed Electronics Company Incorporated, 1969-76; Microwave Program Manager, 1976-77, Microwave Program Scientist, 1977-78, Manager, 1978-82, Manager for Research and Development Programs, 1982-86, Manager for Advanced Programs, 1986-88, Assistant to Director for Technology and Advanced Projects, 1988-90, NASA/Johnson Space Center; Chief Technologist, New Initiatives Office, Johnson Space Center, 1990-94; Chief Technologist, Technology Transfer and Commercialization Office, NASA Johnson Space Center, 1994-. Publications: Numerous articles in professional journals. Honours include: Houston Leadership Award, 1993; Performance Award, NASA Johnson Space Center, 1994, 1995; Fellow, Society for Design and Process Science, 1996; Outstanding Technological Achievement Award, Texas Association of Minority Business Enterprises, 1997. Memberships include: IEEE; National Management Association; American Association for the Advancement of Science; Sigma Xi; Eta Kappa Nu; Phi Kappa Phi. Address: 127 Long Grove Drive, Seabrook, TX 77586, USA.

**KRISHNA Simile Srinivasan,** b. 14 September 1932, Thanjavur, Tamil Nadu, India. Researcher; Educator. m. Shyamala, 2 daughters. Education: BSc, 1952; MSc, 1955; PhD, 1960. Appointments: Lecturer, 1963-81; Reader, 1981-91; Professor, 1991-93; Emeritus Professor and Scientist, 1993-; all in field of Entomology in Zoology. Publications: Over 125 research papers in journals published in Brazil, Canada, China, Germany, India, Java, Kenya, Malaysia, the Netherlands, Nigeria, Philippines, Switzerland, UK, USA and West Indies. Honours: National Research Fellow, Government of India, 1961-63; Emeritus Scientist Fellowship, Council of Scientific and Industrial Research, New Delhi, 1993-96. Memberships: Association for the Advancement of Entomology, India, Life Member; Association for the Advancement of Zoology, India; Indian Academy of Entomology; Japanese Society of Applied Entomology and Zoology; Zoological Society of Japan; Entomological Society of Canada; Entomological Society of America. Address: 22/46 Sai Darshan Apt IV Fl, II Main Rd Kasturbanagar, Aydar Chennai 600 020, India.

**KRISHNA MURTHY Bangalore Laxminarayan Sastry,** b. February 1919, Bangalore, India. Retired Assistant Commissioner of Police. m. Mrs Radhamma, 2 sons, 3 daughters. Appointments: Police Constable; Police Head Constable; Police Sub Inspector; Circle Inspector; Assistant Commissioner of Police; Police Service 1942-74, when retired. Publications: 28 true cases investigated during his career. Honours: Indian Independence Medal, 1947; President's Police Medal, 1960; Best Investigation Award for 1973, by the Home Minister, Government of India, 1975; Hundreds of commendation certificates and praise. Address: No 45 Mico Layout, Mahalaxmipura, Bangalore 560086, India.

**KRISTOPAITIS Adolis-Jonas,** b. 11 June 1925, Balaneliai, Pakruojis District, Lithuania. Painter. m. Genovaite Kristopaitiene, 1 son. Education: Institute of Applied and Decorative Arts, Kaunas, 1948-50; Learning painting-restoring in Vilnius Restoration Centre, 1980. Appointments: Participated in exhibitions in Lithuania, USSR, Poland, Czechoslovakia, Finland, 1954-; Has arranged 8 personal exhibitions; Has created palcards, illustrations for Lithuanian magazines, 1970-85; Has worked in National M K Ciurlionis Museums in Kaunas as Painter-Restorer 1980-. Publications: Reproductions in all albums of Lithuanian Painting; In a number of Lithuanian newspapers and magazines, 1970-90. Honours: Recipient Medal at International Plener of Belowesze in Poland, 1969; Honorary Diploma, 1985, Supreme Soviet of LSSR. Membership: Lithuanian Artists' Association, 1961-. Address: Varniu 26-46, LT 3026 Kaunas, Lithuania.

**KRIVONOSOV Alexej,** b. 1 September 1925, Moskva, Russia. Linguist; Philosopher. m. Maina Troitskaja, 1 son, 1 daughter. Education: DrSc, 1976; Professor, 1976; PhD, Humboldt University, Berlin. Appointments: Head, Scientific and Technical Dept, Professor, General Linguistic Dept, Moskow Linguistic University. Publications: 176 papers; 4 books: Sistema Neizmenjaemych Klassov Slov v Nemetskom Jazyre, 1974; Die Modalen Partikeln in der Deutschen Jegenwartsprache, 1977; Estestvenny jazyk i Logika, 1993; Jazyk Logika Myshlenije, 1996. Memberships: Scientific Board, Moscow Linguistic University; Scientific Board, MoskowLomonosov-University; Scientific Board, Ivanovo University. Address: 129090 Moskva, ul Giljarovskogo 19 Apt 12, Russia.

**KRIVORUTSKI Leonid,** b. 10 April 1939, Lipovets Village, Russia. Professor of Energy. m. Vinnitskaia Alla Romanovna, 1 daughter. Education: Engineer of Power Engineering, Industry of Ural Polytechnical Institute, 1975; PhD, 1975; Doctor of Technical Sciences, 1989. Appointments: Electrician, 1966; Chief Engineer, Scientific Institute, 1966; Chief of Laboratory, Sigerian Energy Institute, 1976; Chief of Department, SEI, 1990; Scientific Researcher, SEI, 1992. Publications: 115 Including 5 Monographics. Memberships: Association of Consumets of Energy and Fuel; Centre of Energy Policy. Address: Kola Scientific Centre RAS, Fersman Str 14, Appatiti Murmansk 184200, Russia.

**KRONAST Wolfgang,** b. 28 February 1952, Konstanz, Germany Physicist. m. Ingrid Wolz-Kronast, 3 daughters. Education: Degree in Physics, University of Freiburg, 1978; PhD, University of Freiburg, 1985. Appointments: Scientific Research, GSI, Darmstadt, 1978-79; Research, University of Freiburg, Germany, 1979-86; Process Engineer, 1986-87; Scientific Lecturer, University of Applied Science, Furtwanden, 1988-. Publiations: Study of Transfer Ionisation Systems, X; International Conference on the Physics of Electronic and Atomic Collisions; Abstracts of Papers, 1977; Alignement of Cd after Photoionisation with Synchrotron Radiation, 1984; A Miniaturized Single Chip Silicon Membrane Microphone with Integrated Field Effect Transistor, 1994; A Single Chip Condenser Microphone using Porous Silicon as Sacrificial Layer for the Air Gap, 1998. Address: University of Applied

Sciences, Mechatronic and Microsystems, Gerwigstr 11, Furtwangen, D 78120, Germany.

**KRONENBERG Julia,** b. 29 August 1947, Hungary. Psychiatrist. m. Jona Kronenberg, 2 daughters. Education: MD, 1974; Child, Adolescent and Adult Psychiatry, 1982, 1984. Publications: Co-author 12 original articles; 3 papers; 2 review articles; 3 invited papers; 44 papers presented at scientific meetings; 2 papers published as abstracts; 2 other publications. Address: Rehov Hasbor 12, Hod Hasharon, Israel.

**KRTOLICA Jelica,** b. 4 February 1953, Skopje. Dentist. m. Gragan, 1 son, 1 daughter. Education: Dental Technician, Secondary Medical School, 1967-71; Faculty of Dentistry, Skopje, 1971-76; Specialization in Prosthetic Dentistry, Skopje, 1983-86. Appointments: KRKA, Novo Mesto, 1977-78; Replek, Macedonia, 1978-81; Jugotrgovija, Macedonia, 1981-83; Faculty of Dentistry, 1983-91; Private Dental Practice, Skopje, 1991-. Honours: Award of Appreciation, World Dental Congress, 1997. Memberships: Chamber of Private Dentists, 1991; Macedonian Chamber of Dentistry, 1995; FDI, 1996. Address: Bul AVNOJ br 28./25, 91000 Skopje, Republic of Macedonia.

**KRUEGER Caryl Waller,** b. 1 April 1929, Chicago, Illinois, USA. Author; Lecturer. m. Cliff Krueger, 2 sons, 1 daughter. Education: BS,Speech, Graduate Studies, Northwestern University, 1950 Graduate Studies, University of Chicago, University of California at San Diego. Publications: Books: Family Traditions; 1001 More Things to Do with Your Kid; 1001 Things to do with Your Kids; 222 Terrific Tips for Two; Working Parent-Happy Child; Six Weeks to Better Parenting; The Ten Commandments for Grandparents; 101 Ideas for the Best Ever Christmas; Single with Children; 365 Ways to Love Your Child; The Family Party Book; The Little Book of Poems; Prayers and Pearls; Articles to Parade, Sunset, Parents, L A Times, Christian Science Monitor and others. Honours: Centennial Woman of Achievement; Alpha Omicron Pi; Named Writer of the Year, Chicago Advertising Club, 1959; Woman of the Year, Panhellenic Hawaii, 1968; Recipient Service Award, Camp Fire Girl Council, Honolulu. Memberships: Pen Women; Women in Communications; AAUW; Phi Beta; Hidden Meadows Newcomers Club, Founder; President, Oahu League Republican Women, Honolulu; Community Concert Association; Rancho Santa Fe, California; MENSA. Address: 28455 Meadow Mesa Ln, Escondido, CA 92026 6507, USA.

**KRUPINSKA Jolanta,** b. 5 July 1928, Zytomierz, Ukraine. Full Professor; Pharmacologist. m. Thaddeus, 1 daughter. Education: Diploma, Faculty of Medicine, Jagiellonian University Cracow, 1949; Department of Pharmacology, 1950-72. Appointments: MD, 1950; Full Professor, 1987; Head, Faculty of Pharmacy, Department of Pharmacodynamics, Cracow, 1972-88; President, Cracovian Branch, Polish Pharmacological Society, 1968-91; President, Commission of Chronopharmacology PAN, and of Monitoring of Drugs, PAN. Publications: 125. Honours: Awards: Ministry of Health; Rectors, MA; Cross of Merit, Medal of National Education. Membership: Polish Pharmacological Society. Address: Kielecka Str 9/16, Cracow 31526, Poland.

**KRUPKOVA Olga,** b. 3 April 1960, Brno, Czech Republic. Mathematician. m. Demeter Krupka, 2 daughters. Education: MSc, 1984, PhD, 1992, Charles University, Prague; Doc (Habilitation), 1996, Masaryk University, Brno. Appointments: Researcher, Masaryk University, Brno, 1984-90; Assistant Professor - Associate Professor, Silesian University, Opava, 1990-. Publications: The Geometry of Ordinary Variational Equations, 1997; Articles in professional journals.

Memberships: American Mathematical Society; Union of Czech Mathematicians and Physicists. Address: Silesian University, Department of Maths, Bezrucovo nam 13, 74601 Opava, Czech Republic.

**KRUSOS Denis Angelo,** b. 27 Oct 1927, New York, New York, USA. Chairman of the Board; Chief Executive Officer. m. Catherine Bezas, 1 son, 1 daughter. Education: BEE, City College of New York, 1949; MSEE, Newark College of Engineering, 1951; JD, St John's University, 1969. Appointments: Development Engineer, Republic Aviation and Fairchild Engineering Corporation, Farmingdale, New York 1952-56; Senior Engineer, American Boach Arma Corporation Westbury, New York, 1956-60; Founder, Officer, Director Automation Labs Inc, Mineola, New York, 1955-65; Founder Chairman of the Board, Director, Integrated Electronics Huntington, New York, 1966-83; Founder, Chairman of the Board, Director, Visual Sciences Inc, Huntington, 1969-83 Chairman of the Board, Color Q Inc, Dayton, Ohio, 1969-92 Founder, President, Director, Panafax Corporation, Woodbury New York, 1977-82; Founder, Chairman of the Board, Chie Executive Officer, Director, CopyTele Inc, Huntington, 1982- Vice-Chairman, Shanghai CopyTele Electronics Co Ltd Shanghai, China, 1995-. Publications: Over 170 patents in fla panel display technology. Memberships: Institute of Electrica and Electronics Engineers; New York State Bar Association American Bar Association; Suffolk County Bar Association Address: 1 Lloyd Harbor Road, Lloyd Harbor, NY 11743-9701 USA.

**KRYSA Oleh,** b. 1 June 1942, Poland. Violinist. m. Tatiana Tchekina, 3 sons. Education: DMA, Moscow Conservatory Teacher, David Oistrakh. Career: Solo Recitals and Soloist with leading orchestras in major halls; Leader, Beethoven String Quartet, 1977-87; Professor of Violin, Kiev Conservatory Moscow Conservatory, Manhattan School of Music, New York Eastman School of Music, Rochester, New York. Honours Prizewinner of Wieniawski, Paganini, Tchaikovsky and Montreal International Competitions. Address: 265 Westminster Rd, Rochester, NY 14607, USA.

**KRZAK Zygmunt,** b. 12 July 1933, Hamlet Grójec Prehistorian. Education: MA, 1955; PhD, 1967; Assistant Professor, 1988; Professor, 1995. Appointments: Assistant 1955; Adjunkt, 1968; Assistant Professor, 1988; Professor 1995. Publications: Main books: The Zlota Culture, 1976 Megality Europy, 1994. Honour: Golden Cross of Merit Address: ul Kasprzaka 5 m 3, 01 211 Warsaw, Poland.

**KRZESINSKA Marta,** b. 15 July 1949, Kielce, Poland Physicist; Researcher; Educator. m. Andrzej Krzesinski, 2 sons Education: MSc, Physics, 1972, PhD, Physics, 1983, Silesiar University, Katowice. Appointments: Assistant, 1972-73, Senio Assistant, 1976-84, Silesian Technical University, Gliwice Assistant Professor, Institute of Coal Chemistry, Polish Academy of Sciences, Gliwice, 1984-. Publications: Single author of articles in Phys Stat Sol, 1984, 1986, Ultrasonics 1986, Acoust Lett, 1995, Fuel, 1996, 1998, Energy Fuels, 1997 Int J Rock Mech Min Sci, 1997, Appl Acoust, 1998, othe journals. Memberships: American Chemical Society; Europear Acoustics Association; Polish Acoustical Society. Address Tarnogorska 114 D, 44-100 Gliwice, Poland.

**KRZYSZKOWSKA Maria,** b. 11 November 1927, Warsaw Poland. Dancer - Prima Ballerina. m. Zbigniew Nowicki Education: Student, Leon Woizykowski's Ballet School Warsaw, 1940-44. Appointments: Prima Ballerina, New Theatre-Warsaw, 1947-50; Opera Poznán, 1950-53 Opera-Warsaw, 1953-65; Great Theatre, Warsaw, 1965-77 irector of ballet: Great Theatre Warsaw, 1970-80, 1985-96; usical Theatre, Warsaw, 1996. Honours: Recipient of Highest olish State Decorations, 1979, 1986; Ministry Culture and Arts rizes, 1967, 1985; Town of Warsaw Prize, 1987. Membership: olish Scene Artists Union, Vice Chairman, 1968-72, hairman, 1983. Address: ul Rynek Starego Miasta 26 m 8, 0-272 Warsaw, Poland.

**KSANFOMALITY Leonid V,** b. 28 January 1932, Kerch, ussia. Astronomy; Space Research. m. Irina Shoulgina, 1 aughter. Education: Diploma, Engineer, Mechanics, 1956; andidate, Physics and Mathematics, 1963; Doctor, Physics nd Mathematics, 1978. Career: Chief of Laboratory, lastumany Observatory, Academy of Sciences, 1957-67; hief of Laboratory, Space Research Institute, Moscow, cademy of Sciences, 1968-. Publications: Over 260 in rofessional journals, including 4 books. Honours: State wards, 1964, 1966, 1976, 1985; Scientific Awards, 1970, 997. Memberships: International Astronomical Union; New ork Academy of Sciences; COSRAR. Address: Space esearch Institute, Profsojuznaja 84/32, 117810 Moscow, ussia.

**KSENOFONTOV Vyacheslav Alexeevich,** b. 24 August 946, Donskoy, Moscow. Physicist. m. Lyudmila V senofontova, 2 daughters. Education: Kharkov State niversity, 1970; PhD, 1988; Senior Scientist, 1996. ppointment: Senior Scientist, Laboratory Physics of Solids, harkov Physico-Technical Institute. Publications: Branch remium, 1988; More than 40 papers. Address: Department of ondensed Matter Physics, Kharkov Physico-Technical stitute, Ukrainian National Academy of Sciences, 1 cademicheskaya Str, Kharkov 310108, Ukraine.

**KŠICOVÁ Danuse,** b. 26 April 1932, Brno, Czech Republic. rofessor. m. Evzen Petrov, 1 daughter. Education: Faculty of rts, Brno University, 1951-56; PhDr, 1969; CSc, 1970; DrSc, 991. Appointments: Lecturer, Masaryk University, Brno, 1956; enior Lecturer, 1961; Associate Professor, 1990; Professor, 995. Publications: Russian Poetry in F Táborský terpretation; The Romantic and Neoromantic Long Poems; ussian Literature of the 19th and Early 20th Century in Czech ranslation; Russian Poetry at the Turn of the Century; Art ouveau - Word and Image; Co-Author of two books; Many ther publications. Honours: Silver Plaque of Brno University; lemorial Plaque of Brno Skauting. Memberships: Literary ssociation; Academy of Russian Studies; Czech Committee Slavists; IAWIS; Visual Literacy Association. Address: Arne ovaska 1, 66088 Brno, Czech Republic.

**KUANG Zong-lian,** b. 26 February 1920, Beijing, China. harmaceutical Researcher. m. Lin Zunyun, 1 daughter. ducation: BSc, 1945, Shanghai St John's University. ppointments: Researcher of High Pressure Hydrogenation, ortheast Pharmaceutical Factory, Shenyang; Shenyang ational Pharmaceutical Research Institute, 1955; Tianjing, 959; Beijing, 1960; Shandong Xinhua Pharmaceutical Factory, 961. Publication: Synthesis of Caffeine with dimethylurea as w material, 1965. Honours: National Invention Prize, Beijing, 964; National Science and Technology Mass Meeting Award, eijing, 1978. Memberships: Chinese Pharmaceutical ssociation. Address: Admin Office, Retired Personnel of handong Pharmaceutical Factory, Zhangdian District, Zibo ity, Shandong Province 255005, China.

**KUBECEK Vladimir,** b. 17 April 1949, Jablonec, Czech epublic. Scientist, Radar Electronics. m. Stanislava, 1 son, 1 aughter. Education: MSc, cum laude, Physical Engineering, zech Technical University, Prague, 1973; PhD, Electronics,

Military Academy, Brno, 1981. Appointments: Senior Scientist, Chief Scientist, Radar and Passive Sensors, Research and Development Department, Tesla Pardubice, 1973-93; Technical Director, ERA a.s, 1993-98. Publications: 38 research reports, 19 papers in scientific and technical journals, 9 patents. Memberships: IEEE; AFCEA; Association of Czech Electrical Engineers; PhD Committee, Military Academy, Brno. Address: Brozikova 435, 530 00 Pardubice, Czech Republic.

**KUCHA Ryszard,** b. 4 May 1942, Husow Village, Poland. Educator. m. Ewa Anna Wawrzycka, 1 daughter. Education: MA Education, 1967; PhD Education, 1975; Habilitation, 1983; Assistant Professor, 1983-90; Associate Professor, 1991-96; Full Professor, 1997. Appointments: Head History of Education Dept, 1984-, Vice-Dean Faculty Pedagogics and Psychology, 1984-90, 1993-99, Maria Curie-Sklodowska University, Lublin; Professor, Higher Pedagogical University, Kielce, 1991-96; Visiting Professor, Saskatchewan University, Canada, 1991, Umea University, Sweden; Editor-in-Chief, Lublin Pedagogical Yearbook, 1993-. Publications: History of Elementary Education in the Kingdom of Poland (1864-1914), 1982; History of Education in Lublin (1864-1915), 1995; Polish and Swedish Schools in the 19th and 20th Centuries, 1995; 13 books; 105 articles. Honours: 7 Rector's Awards. Memberships: European Association for International Education; European Universities Continuing Education Network; International Standing Conference for the History of Education; Polish Pedagogical Association; ASO. Address: Boleslawa Chrobrego 24/58, 20-611 Lublin, Poland.

**KUCHINSKI Vladimir Georgievich,** b. 26 March 1948, Leningrad, Russia. Electrophysicist. m. Zinaida Molchadskaya, 9 November 1968, 1 son, 1 daughter. Education: Engineer-Electrophysicist, Leningrad Politechnical Institute, 1972; PhD Degree, 1978; Dr of Science Degree, 1994. Appointments: Head, High Power Supply Systems Department, Efremov Institute, Responsible Person in Russia on Power Supply Systems of International Thermonuclear Experimental Reactor. Publications: More than 70 papers. Memberships: Scientific Secretary, Scientific Board for Pulse Power Energy Systems, Russian Academy of Sciences. Address: Scientific Board for Pulse Power Engineering, Russian Academy of Sciences, D V Efremov Research Institute for Electrophysical Apparatus, St Petersburg 188631, Russia.

**KUCINGIS Algimantas,** b. 3 June 1927, Kaunas, Lithuania. Researcher. m. Irena, 2 daughters. Education: Textile Engineer, Stockinet Factory, 1959-61; Senior Research Fellow, 1961-64; Chair, Materials Research Lab, 1964-87; Chief Research Fellow, Lithuanian Textile Institute, 1987-92. Publications: Author or co-author 7 inventions, over 120 publications, 2 monographs on Textile Research. Memberships: Kaunas City Council Deputy, 1990-95; Participant Sajudis-Lith National Movement for Independance; Union of Lithuania's Political Prisoners and Exiles; Kaunas Deputies Club; Council member, Reviewer of Scientific Studies, Kaunas University of Technology. Address: Kulvos 6-7, LT 3026 Kaunas, Lithuania.

**KUDIRKA Juozas,** b. 19 March 1939, Lithuania. Ethnologist. m. Lilija Kudirkiene, 1 daughter. Education: Graduate, Faculty of History and Philology, Vilnius University, 1960-65; Doctor of History, Lithuanian Academy of Science, 1969; Habilitated Doctor of Arts, 1995. Appointments: Junior Research Fellow, Lithuanian Institute of History, Lithianian Academy of Science, 1969-74; Junior Research Fellow, Lithuanian Institute of Philosophy, Sociology and Law, 1974-80; Senior Research Fellow, 1980-; Chairman, Folklore Department, 1986-90.

Publications: 24 publications. Address: Architektu 25-73, LT 2043 Vilnius, Lithuania.

**KUDRAVIEC Anatol,** b. 1 January 1936, Belarus. Journalist. m. Leus Lubov, 1 son, 1 daughter. Education: Diploma, Belarussian State University, Philological Faculty, 1963. Appointments: Belarusian Radio, 1963-65; Publish House, Literature and Arts, 1965-66; Newman Magazine, 1975-. Publications: On the Green Party; Late Apples. Honour: Order of Fellowship. Memberships: General Assembly of OUN; Administration of Writers Union. Address: 39 Slavinski St Apt 22, Minsk 220086, Belarus.

**KUHLER Renaldo Gillet,** b. 21 November 1931, Teaneck, New Jersey, USA. Scientific Illustrator. 1 daughter (adopted). Education: BA History and Fine Arts, University of Colorado; Independent study Museumology and Museum Technical Training; Self taught in the field of Scientific Illustration. Appointments: Curator of History, Eastern Washington State Historical Society Museum, 1962-67, North Carolina State Museum of Natural Sciences, 1969-. Publications: Illustrations for, Reptiles of North Carolina, 1995, American Firearms and the Changing Frontier, 1962. Membership: National Trust for Historic Preservation. Address: North Carolina State Museum of Natural Sciences, 210 N Salisbury St, Raleigh, NC 27611-1740, USA.

**KUISMANEN Kimmo Kauki Kalevi,** b. 4 March 1950, Lahti, Finland. Architect. m. Marita Näsi, 1 son, 3 daughters. Education: Architect MSc, Oulu University, Finland, 1976. Appointments: Private Architect, 1974-; Managing Director, Case Consult Ltd, 1992-. Publications: Exhibitions in many countries. Honours: 6 First Prizes at Architectural Competitions. Memberships: SAFA; ATL; President, Oulu Wine Club. Address: Nokelantie 5, 90140 Oulu, Finland.

**KUK Michael Louis,** b. 11 January 1949, Clinton, Iowa, USA. Fire Chief. Education: MSc, Columbia Pacific University, 1988. Appointments: Fire Chief, Ward, 1 Fire District, 1975-85; Fire and Safety Technician, OLIN Chemicals, 1976-79; Fire Chief, PPG Industries, 1979-81; Fire Chief, Savanna Army Depot, 1989-. Publications: Numerous fire related articles. Honours: Numerous commendations for rescues and firefighting. Memberships: International Association of Fire Chiefs; Iowa Firemens Association; Illinois Firefighters Association; Tri-City Music Society, Local 67; VFW Post 8486; AMVETS Post 28; Vietnam Veterans Association; Brigade International. Address: 652-8th Avenue South, Clinton, Iowa 57232-5608, USA.

**KUKAGOWSKA Ewa,** b. 20 April 1962, Sosnowiec. Physiologist. m. Andrzey Kukagowski, 1 son. Education: Silesian University, Katowice, 1986; Doctor's degree, 1996, Silesian Medical Academy; Post-grad studies in Occupational & Environmental Hygiene, Silesian Technical University. Appointments: Dept of Computer Service and Organisational Counselling Metekon, 1986-87; Institute of Occupational Medicine and Environmental Health in Sosnowiec, 1988-. Publications: in professional journals. Address: ul Dzieciotow 45/1, 40 532 Katowice, Poland.

**KUKETAEV Temirgali,** b. 6 November 1939, Karaganda, Zhetkimshet. Physician. m. Rakhima Kuketaeva, 2 sons, 1 daughter. Publications: 244 publications in science journals, 2 monographs in physics; 5 patents. Address: Chair of Physical Department, Karaganda State University, 28 Universitetskaya Str, Karaganda 470074, Kazakhstan.

**KUKLA Lubomir,** b. 21 August 1955, Brno, Czech Republi Paediatrician. 1 daughter. Education: MD, 1980; Degree Paediatrics, 1985; PhD Paediatrics, 1987; MPH cum laud 1996. Appointments: Paediatrician, Research Worker, 198 Social Paediatrician, Research Worker, 1987; Head Department of Preventive and Social Paediatrics, Researc Institute of Child Health, Director of National Centre for proje ELSPAC, Temporary Adviser of WHO for Czech Republi 1989; Member of International Coordinating Executiv Committee of ELSPAC, 1997-. Publications: Head author of book in English and 1 in Czech; 2 book chapters in Englis Several book chapters in Czech; Over 20 articles in journal Over 40 lectures especially in International Congresses ar Conferences; Over 20 posters. Memberships: Europea Society for Social Paediatrics; European Science Foundatio International Society for Prevention of Child Abuse ar Neglect; Secretary General, Czech Society for Soci Paediatrics; of Czech Medical Association J E Purkyne; Czec Paediatric Society of Czech Medical Association J E Purkyn Scientific Council of Ministry of Health of CR; Scientif Commission for Paediatrics and Genetics of Internal Gra Agency of Ministry of Health CR; Executive Board, Czec Committee for UNICEF; Editorial Board of Journal of Czec Physicians; and others. Address: Research Institute of Chi Health, CEJL 91, 602 00 Brno, Czech Republic.

**KUKUSHKIN Alexander,** b. 9 March 1939, Moscow, Russi Physicist. m. G P Zlobina, 1 son, 1 daughter. Educatio Graduated, Moscow State University, 1962; PhD, 1966; DS 1981; Professor, 1987. Appointments: Scientific Researche 1965-68, Assistant Professor, 1968-73, Associate Professo 1974-87, Full Professor, 1987-, Moscow State Universit Publications: 3 books; 150 papers in scientific journal Professor of Biophysics, 1987; Stalin's scholarship, 1959-6 Honour: Medal in Honour of 850's Moscow. Membershi Photobiology Society. Address: Physical Faculty, M Lomonosov Moscow State University, Leninskie Gory, Mosco 119899, Russia.

**KULANDAISWAMY Vangalampalayam C,** b. 14 July 192 Thennilai, India. Former Vice Chancellor. m. Dr Soundraval 1 son, 1 daughter. Education: BE, Andhra University, 195 DSS, University of Madras, 1955; MTech, Hydraulics, I Kharagpur, 1956; PhD, Hydraulics, Hydrology and Wat Resources, University of Illinois, 1964; DLitt, honoris causa University of Jaffna, Sri Lanka, 1980; DSc, honoris caus Alagappa University, Tamil Nadu, 1997; DLitt, honoris caus Pondicherry University, 1997. Appointments: Professor Hydraulics, 1965-71, Dean, Postgraduate Studies ar Research, 1971-74, College of Engineering, Director Technical Education, 1974-78, Department of Educatio Government of Tamilnadu; Vice Chancellor, Madurai Kamara University, 1978-79; UN Expert and Adviser, UNESC 1979-81; Vice Chancellor, Anna University, Madras, 1981-9 Vice Chancellor, Indira Gandhi National Open University, Ne Delhi, 1990-94. Publications: Over 90 professional article Honours: Ministry of Irrigation Gold Medal, 1973; Leverhulm Fellowship, 1975; Akademi Award for Tamil Literature, 198 Indira Gandhi National Integration Award, 1989; Central Boar of Irrigation and Power Diamond Jubilee Gold Medal, 199 Scroll of Honour, 1991; Padma Shri, 1992; Swan Pranavananda Saraswati Award, 1994. Memberships: Fello National Academy of Sciences, India, Institution of Engineer India, Indian National Academy of Engineering, Comput Society of India, Tamil Nadu Academy of Sciences. Addres 23 MGR Road, Besant Nagar, Madras 60090, India.

**KULIKAUSKIENE Regina Volkaite,** b. 10 September 191 Kedainiai, Lithuania. Archaeologist. m. Pranas Kulikauskas, daughter. Education: Vytautas Magnus University, Kaunas, 1936-39; Diploma, Historian-Archaeologist, Vilnius University, 1940. Appointments: Senior Lecturer, 1941-62, Head, Archaeological Ethnographic Chair, 1952-62, Vilnius University; Scientific Worker, Institute of Lithuanian History, 1962-92. Publications include: Lithuanians in the 9th-11th c.c, 1970; The Material Culture of Lithuanians in the 9th-13th c.c, 1978, 1981; Lithuanian Ethnogenesis, 1987; Ancient Lithuanian Clothes and Their Decorations/1st-16th centuries, 1997. Honour: Title, Deserved Worker in Science, 1976. Memberships: Lithuanian Academy of Science; Council, Institute of Lithuanian History, Honorary Member, Council, Lithuanian Society of Archaeologists. Address: Kuosu 6, 2055 Vilnius, Lithuania.

**KULIKOVSKAYA Svetlana,** b. 12 January 1950, Russia. Visual Artist. 1 son. Education: Bachelor of Arts, Westminster College Salt Lake City, Utah, USA. Honours: Manhattan Art International Award of Merit, 1995; Musee Des Arts d'unet Artiste. Memberships: Amnesty International; National Museum Women in the Arts. Address: 185 Elm St #1, Cambridge, MA 02139-1426, USA.

**KULKARNI Kumar B,** b. 1 November 1943, India. Physician. m. Kamal. 2 sons. Education: MBBS, Bombay University, 1968; DCH, College of Physicians and Surgeons, 1970; Diploma in Russian Language Studies, 1988. Appointments: House Physician, Surgeon, 1968-70; General Practice, 1970-72; General Duty Medical Officer, Air India, 1971-72; Private Practice, 1972-; Lecturer, Physiology, 1996-97. Publications: 68 papers on diverse topics in Clinical Paedatrics have been published in National and International journals. Honours: Sir Dinshaw Petitt Memorial Award; Soviet Land Prize; Environment and Development Essay Award; Outstanding Person Award. Memberships: Gwalior Branch, Indian Medical Association; Indian Academy of Pediatrics. Address: Swami Vivekanand Marg, 3 Bank Colony, Gwailor 474001, India.

**KULKARNI Meghaasham Dattatraya,** b. 1 June 1952, Chopada, India. Veterinarian. m. Asha Kulkarne, 1 son, 1 daughter. Education: BSc, Biology; BVSc & AH, 1st Class with Distinction, Nagpur Veterinary College, Nagpur, 1977; MVSc, Medicine, 1st Class with Distinction, Postgraduate Institute, Punjabrao Krishi Vidyapeeth, Akola, 1979. Appointments: Animal Health Specialist, All-India Coordinated Research Project on Cattle, 1980-86, Scientist S-2, Principal Investigator, Physiological Adaptation of Crossbred Cattle, 1986-89, Principal Veterinary Officer, Veterinary Polyclinic and A I Centre, 1989-97, Mahatma Phule Krishi Vidyapeeth, Rahuri; Associate Professor of Veterinary Science, College of Agriculture, Pune, 1997-98; Associate Professor, Head, Department of Veterinary Medicine, KNP College of Veterinary Medicine, KNP, Shirval, 1998-. Publications include: Effect of birth weight growth rate on calf mortality, 1994; A note on optimum birth weight for survival in crossbred calves, 1994; Studies on blood glucose profile in Trypanosomiasis infection in buffaloes, 1994; Epidemiological investigation of Enterotoxaemia in cattle, 1995; To evaluate sire effect on mortality and its heritability estimates in three breed crosses of Holstein Friesian, Jersey, Gir, 1996; Evaluation of sire on the basis of mortality in offsprings and its heritability estimates in triple crosses (BFG), 1997; Haemodynamic studies in trypanosomiasis in buffaloes (Bubolus bubal), 1998; Climatological effect on incidence of dermatitis in crossbred cattle, 1998. Honours: Books Award, Jawaharlal Nehru Memorial Fund; Active Member, New York Academy of Sciences, 1996; Bishnu Sudhama Memorial Award, Indian Veterinary Association, 1998. Address: Department of Veterinary Medicine, K N P College of Veterinary Science,

Shirval, Dist Satara (MS) 412 801, India.

**KULLANDER Sven Gunnar,** b. 9 March 1936, Karlstad, Sweden. Physicist. m. Eva Elisabeth, 2 sons, 2 daughters. Education: MSc, Royal Institute of Technology, Stockholm, 1961; PhD, Physics, Uppsala University, 1964; Swedish Doctor's Degree of Philosophy, Uppsala University, 1971; Docent, Uppsala University, 1971. Appointments: Research Assistant, The Enrico Fermi Institute, University of Chicago, 1961-63; Research Engineer, The Gustaf Werner Institute, (GWI), Uppsala University, 1964-65; Staff Member, CERN, Geneva, 1966-72; Associate Professor, Uppsala University, 1973-78; Professor, Uppsala University, 1979-; Director of GWI, Uppsala University, 1979-86; Head, Department of Radiation Sciences, 1986-89; Dean, Faculty of Mathematics and Natural Sciences, 1989-93. Publications: About 170 papers in fields of accelerators, nuclear physics and elementary particle physics; Books: Mikrokosmos, Studieförlaget, 1984; Out of Sight, 1994. Memberships: Swedish Physical Society; European Physical Society; Finnish Society of Sciences and Letters; Royal Swedish Academy of Sciences; Royal Academy of Arts; Royal Society of Sciences. Address: Uppsala University, Department of Radiation Science, PO Box 535, 751 21 Uppsala, Sweden.

**KUMAKHOV Muhaddin Abubekirovich,** b. 29 July 1928, Anzorovo, Kabardino-Balkarskaya, Russia. Linguist. m. Zara Yusufovna, 1 son, 1 daughter. Education: Graduate, 1952, Tbilisi University, Georgia; BSc, 1955; Doctor Philology, 1966. Appointments: Scientist, 1954, Professor, 1978, Chief Scientist in Caucasian Languages and Comparative Linguistics, 1990, Institute Linguistics, Russian Academy of Sciences. Publications: Author of 150 publications including 10 monographs. Honours: Member of Russian Academy of Natural Sciences, 1991; Honoured Doctor of Lund University, Sweden, 1997. Address: 117333 Moscow, Leninskiy avenue 57 136, Russia.

**KUMAR Santosh,** b. 15 June 1961, Ghazipur, India. Reader. m. Subhra Roy, 1 daughter. Education: BSc, 1979; MSc, Geography, 1981; MSc, Geology, 1983; PG Diploma, Spectroscopy, 1987; PGC, 1991; PhD, Geology, 1991; PhD, Geology, 1993. Appointments: Junior Research Fellow, 1985-86; Project Officer, Scientific Officer, 1987-88; Senior Research Fellow, 1989-91; Research Associate, 1992-93; Research Scientist, 1993-96; Pool Officer, 1996-97; Reader, Geology, Nagaland University, 1997-. Publications: 21 research papers in professional journals. Honours: External Scholarship, Government of India. Memberships: Fellow, Geological Society of India; Member of several working groups. Address: Department of Geology, Nagaland University, Nagaland, India.

**KUMAR Udaya,** b. 14 November 1951, Bangalore, India. Professor. m. Gayathri Dharshinee, 1 son, 1 daughter. Education: BSc, 1970; MSc, 1972; M Tech, 1974; PhD, 1983. Appointments: Deputy Engineer, Bharat Electronics, 1974; Lecturer, 1977, Assistant Professor, 1984, Professor, 1990-, Principal, 1997-, Dr Ambedkar Institute of Technology, Bangalore. Publication: Advanced Microprocessors and IBM-PC Assembly Language Programming, 1996. Honour: Vikas Ratna Award, 1996. Memberships: IEEE, USA; ACM, USA; MISTE, India; CSI, India. Address: Dr Ambedkar Institute of Technology, Near JB Campus, Bangalore 560056, India.

**KUMARASINGHE Gamini,** b. 23 June 1944, Sri Lanka. Medical Doctor. m. Sepalika, 2 sons. Education: MBBS, 1968; D Path, 1979; FRCPath, 1993; FRCPA, 1994. Appointments: Registrar and Senior Registrar, The Hospital for Sick Children, Gt Ormond Street, London, 1977-83; Head, Dept of Laboratory

Services, King Khaled Hospital, Saudi Arabia, 1984-88; Head, Division of Microbiology, National University Hospital, Singapore, 1989-. Publications: mainly on epidemiology and mechanisms of antibiotic resistance, evaluation of new antimicrobial agents and hospital acquired infections. Memberships: Hospital Infection Society, UK; American Society of Microbiology; International Society for Human and Animal Mycology; Singapore Society of Pathology; and others. Address: National University Hospital, Division of Microbiology, Lower Kent Ridge Road, 119074 Singapore.

**KUME Kristaq,** b. 9 July 1949, Vlora, Albania. Mathematician. m. Violeta Kanxheri, 2 sons, 1 daughter. Education: Diploma Mathematician, 1972, State University of Tirana; Candidate of science, 1983; Doctor of science, 1991. Appointments: Scientific Researcher, 1973-75, 1981-94, Director, 1994-, National Institute of Zootechnical Research; Mathematician, Agriculture Enterprise Thumana, 1975-81. Publications: Books: Mathematical statistical methods in animal husbandry, 1974; Mathematical Programming Models in Agriculture, series 4 editions, 1980-87; Mathematical methods in Selection and Animal Breeding, 1992; 2 thesis; 14 original articles in the field of mathematical programming and its application in agriculture, 1975-85; Series of 12 original articles in the field of genetics and selection, 1986-90, 4 during 1988-91; Series of 10 original articles and presentations in international symposiums in the field of the study of Authocthone genetic resources, 1992-98; Series of 8 original articles and presentations in the field of anthropology of Albanian populations, 1990-98. Honours: Medal of Work, 1982; Order of 3rd Class Work, 1990; Reader, 1987; Professor, 1995. Memberships: FAO-CIHEAM International Network for Small Ruminants; Albanian Anthropology Association; New York Academy of Science; Association for the Protection of Authochthonous Breeds. Address: National Institute of Zootechnical Research, Tirana, Albania.

**KUNARATNAM Kanthia,** b. 30 April 1934, Erlalai, Sri Lanka. Senior Professor of Physics. m. Pushpawathy, 1 son, 2 daughters. Education: BSc (Cey) First Class Hon in Physics, 1958, University of Ceylon, Colombo; PhD (Lond), 1963, DIC (Lond), 1963, Imperial College, London. Appointments: Assistant Lecturer, 1958-63, Lecturer Gr II, 1963-68, Lecturer Gr I, 1969-75, University of Ceylon, Colombo & Peradeniya; Professor, 1975-85, Senior Professor, 1985-, Dean Faculty of Science, 1977-78, 1984-88, Vice-Chancellor, 1994-96, University of Jaffna, Sri Lanka. Publications: PhD thesis, 1963; Articles in international journals on interpretation of magnetic anomalies and spatial and time variation of geomagnetic fields. Honours: Dr Hewavitharne Memorial Prize for Phys University of Ceylon, Colombo, 1958; Commonwealth University Academic Staff Fellowship, UK, 1971; ICTP, Italy, Associateship, 1986-93; Royal Society London, Developing Country Fellowship, 1988-89; Number of travel awards by prestigious international institutions. Memberships: Sri Lanka Association of Adv Sci, 1958-93; Associate member, ICTP, Italy, 1986-93; Jaffna Science Association, 1993-. Address: Dept of Physics, University Jaffna, Thirunelvely, PO Box 57, Jaffna, Sri Lanka.

**KUNDU Mridula,** b. 1 March 1968, Bhara, Bankura, India. Lecturer. Education: BA, 1989; MA, 1992; MPhil, 1995; Research work continuing since 1995. Appointment: Lecturer, Tamralipta Mahavidyalaya, 1997-. Publications include: Rhetorical Aspects of T S Eliot and Suddhindranath Dutta's Poetry; Impersonality Theory: Eliot and Suddhindranath; Poetic Theory of Suddindranath; Word's Marriage in Poetry of Nirendranath Chacroborty; Literary Universalization. Memberships: Jadavpur University, India; National Library,

India; Ramkrishna Mission Institute of Culture, India. Address: Tamralipta Maharadyalaya, Tamluk Midnapore WB, India.

**KUNDU Subhas C,** b. 2 November 1947, Midnapur, India. Teacher; Researcher. m. Shikha, 2 sons. Education: MSc Genetics, 1970; PhD, Genetics, 1975. Appointments: Assistant Professor, Professor, Manipur University, 1976-93; Professor Head, Biotechnology Centre, Indian Institute of Technology 1994-. Publications: Papers in Chromosoma, Experimental Cell Research, Methods in Enzymology, Can J Biochemistry, JBC, Cytogenetics and Cell Genetics, Genetical Research, Eur J Cell Biology. Honours: Post Doc, Moscow, Germany, England, Canada. Memberships: Chairman, Eastern Zone; All Inda Biotech Association. Address: Biotechnology Centre, Indian Institute of Technology, Kharagpur 721302, India.

**KUNEVA Mariana,** b. 7 August 1955, Sofia, Bulgaria. Scientist. Divorced, 1 son. Education: MSc, University of Sofia 1978; PhD, Institute of Solid State Physics, Bulgarian Academy of Sciences, 1997. Appointments: Design Engineer, Institute of Special Optics, Sofia, 1978-88; Physicist, 1988-90, Research Associate, 1990-, Institute of Solid State Physics, Bulgarian Academy of Sciences, Sofia. Publications: Several articles in professional journals. Honours: Bronze Medal, Painting Ministry of Culture, 1979. Memberships: Bulgarian Physica Union, 1979-; Bulgarian Section of SPIE, 1998-. Address Institute of Solid State Physics, 72 Tzarigradsko Chaussee Boulevard, 1784 Sofia, Bulgaria.

**KUPKA Valerij,** b. 23 December 1962, Khomut, Zeleny Hai Ukraine. Teacher. m. Ivana, 1 son, 1 daughter. Education: PhD 1998; Diploma in Russia Language and Literature and History Philosophical Faculty, Safarik University in Presov Appointments: Postgrad, 1990-94, Research Assistant, 1994- Russian Dept, Philosophical Faculty, Presov University Presov. Publications: Inconstancy, 1994; Skomoroshina, 1995 A Fly in the Ear, 1998. Memberships: Obec Slovenskych Spisovatelov (Slovak Writers Community). Address: Vazecka 12, 08005, Presov, Slovakia.

**KURAMITSU Rie,** b. 27 November 1950, Fukuoka, Japan College Professor. Education: Master of Engineering, Osaka University, 1978; Doctor of Agriculture, Hiroshima University 1998. Appointments: Technical Official, Osaka University 1978-83; Part-time Instructor, 1987-91; Instructor, 1991-95 Associate Professor, 1995-99; Professor, Akashi Nationa College of Technology, 1999-. Publications: Organic Chemistry 1993; Synthesis of Salty Peptides and its Application to Food Systems. Memberships: Japan Society for Bioscience Biotechnology and Agrochemistry; Brewing Society of Japan Address: Akasha Nat Coll Tech, Uozumi, Akashi, Hyogo 674-8501, Japan.

**KURANE Ryuichiro,** b. 18 April 1945, Nagano, Japan Director Applied Microbiology Dept. m. Hiromi, 1 son, 2 daughters. Education: BS, 1969, MS, 1971, PhD, 1974 University Tokyo. Appointments: Researcher, Senior Researcher, 1974-88, Head Lab, 1988-93, FRI, Japan Professor, Tokyo University Agriculrural Technology, 1990-93 Director, Planning, NIBH, 1993-95; Director, Applied Microbiology Dept, 1995-; Co-Chair, Environmental Bio Sp Comm, OECD, 1994; Co-Chair, BCIPP, OECD, 1995-98 Co-Chair, BSID, OECD, 1998-. Publications: Bioconversion 1993; Bioremediation, 1998; and others; Editor, J Clean Product Processes, 1998-. Honours: Award Ministry State fo Science and Technology, 1984; Ministry Science and Technology Award, 1995, 1994; Ichimura Academy Prize Prince Mikasanomiya, 1995. Memberships: Biochemistry Biotechnology and Agriculture; Bioengineering and Ferment and others. Address: National Institute Bioscience Human Technology, 1-1 Higashi, 305-8566 Tsukuba Ibaraki, Japan.

**KURDIANI Michael E,** b. 1 January 1954, Tbilisi, Georgia. Linguist; Theoretician of Literature and Art; Poet. m. Nino Vadachkoria, 2 sons, 2 daughters. Education: Tbilisi State University, 1976; Doctor of Philological Sciences, 1998; Professor of Kutaisi, 1994, Tbilisi, 1999, State Universities. Appointments: Academician of the Gelati Academy of Sciences, Academician, Secretary, 1995-; Editor-in-Chief, bilingual scientific journals Bulletin of Kutaisi State University, 1994, Memoirs of Gelati Academy of Sciences, 1996; Head of Chair, General Linguistics, 1994; Chief Scientific Worker in Arn Chikobava Institute of Linguistics, 1998. Publications: Genesis of Versification of Kartvelian Languages; Futurism; Navanena, co-author; Common-Kartvelian Versification System and General Linguistic Theory of Versification; Dadaists in Circassian Dress; Chronicle (Verses and Poems), Volume 1, 1982, Volume 2, 1987; The 30th February, theatrical novel, co-author, 1989. Memberships: Demographic Society of Georgia, President, 1990-94; Georgian Writers Union, 1992. Address: L Asatiani Str 64, 380007 Tbilisi, Georgia.

**KURDIEH Ishaq M,** b. 15 November 1939, Palestine. Engineer. m. Rosemary Guidry, 3 sons, 2 daughters. Education: BSEE, 1964; MSEE, 1969. Appointments: Design Engineer, 1964-68; Project Engineer, 1969-73; Senior Engineering Consultant, 1974-78; Project Director, 1979-84; Engineering Manager, 1985-92; Engineering Advisor, 1993-95; Project Director, 1996-99. Honours: High School medal, 1958; American Friends of MID EAST Scholarship, 1959; Fulbright Award, 1959; Fluor Daniel/King Aziz University Award, 1994. Membership: Muslim Student Association - IEEE (USA); Who is Who in the World 1999. Address: 105 Old Stone Road, Norwich, NY 13815, USA.

**KURODA Yasuo,** b. 31 March 1947, Saga, Japan. Professor. m. Setsuko. Education: MD 1971, PhD 1981, Kyashu University, School of Medicine, Japan. Appointments: Assistant Professor, Kyushu University School of Medicine, 1976; Associate Professor, 1988, Professor, 1996, Saga Medical School, Japan. Address: Department of Internal Medicine, Saga Medical School, Saga 849, Japan.

**KURODA Yukiaki,** b. 22 May 1926, Nara, Japan. Emeritus Professor. m. Sachi Harada, 2 sons. Education: Associate Professor, Osaka University, 1963; Head of Laboratory, National Institute Genetics, 1966; Professor of National Institute Genetics, 1984; Emeritus Professor, 1990; Professor, Azabu University, 1990. Publications: Invertebrate and Fish Tissue Culture, 1988; Antimutagenesis and Anticarcinogenesis Mechanisms, 1990. Memberships: Japanese Tissue Culture Association; Genetic Society of Japan; Environmental Mutagen Society of Japan; Japan Society of Cell Biology; Japan Society of Develop Biologists. Address: 24-8 Hatsunedai Mishima, Shizuoka 411-0018, Japan.

**KUROPATENKO Valentin Fyodorovich,** b. 18 December 933, Rechitsa, Byelorussia. Mathematician; Mechanic. m. velina Kuznetsova, 2 daughters. Education: St Petersburg University, 1956; First Higher Degree, 1965; Second Higher Degree, 1978; Assistant Professor, 1969; Professor, 1983. Appointments: Engineer; Senior Research; Head of Division; Head of Department. Publications: Investigation of Material strength under Dynamic Loading, monographs; 80 articles in journals. Honours: State Prize Winner US, 1968; Order, 1984; Medals. Memberships: International Information Academy, 993; Petrovskaya Academy of Sciences and Arts, 1995.

Address: Federal Nuclear Center of Russia, PO Box 245, Snezhinsk 454070, Russia.

**KURYGIN Anatoly,** b. 17 September 1932, Zaborie, Ryazan Region, Russia. Surgeon. m. L Lushnikova, 1 son, 1 daughter. Education: Military Medical Department, Kuibyshev Institute, 1956; PhD, 1979; Professor of Surgery, 1981. Appointments: Regimental Surgeon, 1956; Senior Surgeon, Tank Division, 1960; Postgraduate, 1961; Senior Teacher, 1971; Vice Chief of Surgery Clinic, 1977; Senior Surgeon, Russian Force Contingent in Germany, 1982; Chief of Department and Clinic of Emergency Surgery, Military Medical Academy, 1985; Major-General, Medical Services, 1989. Publications: 10 monographs, 190 scientific articles. Honours: State Prize of USSR, 1987; Meritorious Science Worker of Russia, 1992; Badge of Honour, 1984; The Excellent Teaching Prize of USSR, 1989; State Scientific Prize, 1994. Memberships: Pirogov Surgical Society; State Committee of Experts of Russia; St Petersburg Academy of Sciences & Arts; Fellow, Russian Community of Surgeons and its Administration. Address: Military Medical Academy, 194175 Lebedeva 6, St Petersburg, Russia.

**KUTAS Saulius Aloyzas Bernardas,** b. 21 June 1935, Kupiskis. Engineer. m. Marija, 2 daughters. Education: Dipl Ing, Kaunas University of Technology, 1958. Appointments: Head of Lithuanian Nuclear Safety Inspectorate; Minister of Energy; Deputy Minister of Energy; Deputy Chief Engineer, Lithuanian Energy System. Publications: 8 Booklets; 30 Articles. Memberships: Lithuanian Member Committee WEC; International Energy Economist Association. Address: Tverecius 24-9, LT 2040 Vilnius, Lithuania.

**KUTI Abdul Fatayi Demola,** b. 16 April 1937, Lagos State. Judge. m. Shade, 9 sons, 1 daughter. Education: O Level, Latin Language, English Language, History, Yoruba Language, 1956; A Level, British Constitution, University of London, 1957; A Level, History, 1957; A Level, Economic and Public Affairs, University of London, 1958; LLB Hons, University of Hull, 1958; Call Certificate, Barrister and Solicitor of the Supreme Court, 1964; Post Graduate Course, University of Makerere, Uganda, 1964; Diploma Institue of Advanced Legal Studies, 1988; Carnegie Endowment Scholar in Diplomacy, International Law and Development Economy, Institute of Public Administration and Political Science. Appointments: Chairman, Newly Constituted Miscellaneous Offences Tribunal, 1990-92; Two Term Chairman, Armed Robbery Tribunal, 1985-87, 1987-91; Honourable High Court Judge, Federal Capital Territory Abuja, 1985-. Publications: Many Publications. Honours: Paul Harris Fellowship; Lawson Special Award of Honour; Presidential Recognition; Certificate of Honour; Many other honours. Memberships: Rostrum Club; International Society for Reform of Criminal Law, Parole and Early Release Based in Ottawa; Royal Society of Literature; Society of the Middle Temple; Nigerian Bar Association; Criminal Forum Faculty of Administration of Rutgers; Many other memberships. Address: High Court of Justice, Abuja, Nigeria.

**KUTKA Nicholas,** b. 17 December 1926, Czechoslovakia. Physician. Widower, 2 sons. Education: MD, 1951; PhD, 1962. Career: Associate Professor, Baylor College of Medicine; Chief, Nuclear Medicine, Veterans Affairs Medical Center; Consulting Physician, several hospitals. Publications: Numerous in nuclear medicine. Memberships: Society of Nuclear Medicine; American College of Nuclear Physicians; American Society of Nuclear Cardiology; Texas Medical Association. Address: P.O. Box 20183, Houston, Texas 77225-0183, USA.

**KUTRA Raimondas,** b. 3 June 1954, Lithuania. Banker. m. Liudmila Kutriene, 2 daughters. Education: Vilnius University, 1978. Appointments: AB Vilniaus Bankas, Deputy Chairman of Managing Board, 1991-; Director, VISA CEMEA Board, 1995-98. Address: AB Vilniaus bankas, Gedimino pr 12, LT 2600 Vilnius, Lithuania.

**KUTTNER Bernard A,** b. 13 January 1934, Berlin, Germany. Lawyer; Former Judge. m. Maria Marta Kuttner, 1 son, 2 daughters. Education: AB cum laude, Dartmouth College, 1955. Appointments: Former Editor, Trial Techniques Newsletter; Certified Trial Attorney, Specialist, by Supreme Court of New Jersey; Judge, State Division of Tax Appeals. Publication: A Code of Ethics for Governmental Officials. Honour: Nominee, Pro Bono Publico Award, American Bar Association. Memberships: Past Chairman, Trial Techniques Committe of American Bar Association; Former President, Essex County Bar Association; Past Chairman, Community Health Law Project; Past Chairman, Essex County Park Commission; Irvington Jaycees and Lions; President, Institute for Ethical Behaviour. Address: Kuttner Law Offices, 24 Lackawanna Place, Millburn, NJ 07041, USA.

**KUZMICH Nicolai,** b. 28 November 1950, Kobrin, Republic of Belarus. Artist; Jeweller; Enameller. m. Tatyana, 1 son, 1 daughter. Education: Diploma, 1982, Minsk Artistical Specialised School. Publication: Research of Byzantinesque Enamels, 1998. Honours: Medal of Saint Vladimir, State Prize for Moral Renaissance, 1987. Membership: Artists Union of Republic of Belarus. Address: Gavrilova str 35-45, Brest, Belarus.

**KUZMIN Vadim,** b. 9 December 1948, Sverdlovsk, Russia. Historian. m. Lubov Zlobina, 1 son. Education: Diploma, 1971, Ural State University; PhD History, 1981; Doctor of Historical Science, 1994. Appointments: Assistant, 1975, Senior Lecturer, 1978, Assistant Professor, 1984, Professor, 1997-, Ural State University, Faculty of History, Department of International Relations, Chair of Eastern Studies. Publications: Over 70 including: The Preparing and the Signing of the Saadabad Pact, 1937, in Russian, 1992. Memberships: Association of European Studies; Russian Society of Orientalists; Sverdlovsk Regional Branch of Russia-Japan Society. Address: Zavodskaya 14, Apt 74 Ekaterinburg 620028, Russia.

**KUZMIN Yuriy,** b. 28 September 1931, St Petersburg. Researcher. m. L Iljina, 1 son. Graduate, Military Medical Academy, 1967; Dr of Medicine, 1993; Professor, 1994. Appointments: Researcher, Institute of Physiology, 1960-71; Head of Lab, Speech Pathology, St Petersburg Research Institute of ETN and Speech Pathology, 1971-85; Head of Department, 1985-. Publications: 120 Publications; Co-Author of 2 Monographs; 9 Presentations at International Congress. Memberships: Society of Otolaryngology of Russia; Committee of Speech Pathology. Address: P O Box 198 013, 9 Bronnitskaya Street, St Petersburg, Russia.

**KUZNETSOVA Tamara Vasilievna,** b. 11 April 1948, Kurilsk, Sahalinskaya, Russia. Physicist. m. Yurl Oslapovich Pukas, 2 daughters. Education: Graduate, secondary school with honour silver medal, 1973; Graduate, Leningrad State University, Department of Physics with Honour Diploma, 1973; Postgraduate Student, Academy of Sciences of the USSR. Appointments: Junior Research Worker, 1974; Research, 1986; Senior Research Workers, Institute of Terrestrial Magnetism, Ionosphere and Radio Wave Propagation of Russian Academy of Sciences, 1990; Doctor of Philosophy, 1981; Senior Scientist, 1998. Publications: About 70 publications. Memberships: Associate, COSPAR scientific commission D on Space Plasmas in the Solar System; European Geophysic Society, 1995. Address: Russian Academy of Science IZMIRAN, Moscow Region, 142092 Troitsk, Russia.

**KVINT Vladimir L,** b. 21 February 1949, Russia. Economi 2 daughters. Education: MSc, Mining Electrical Engineerir PhD, Economics, 1972; DSc, Economics, 1988. Caree Director, Emerging Markets, Arthur Andersen; Professc Management Systems and International Business, Fordha University Graduate School of Business, New York; Adjur Professor, International Business, New York University Ste Graduate School of Business; Member, Bretton Woo Committee, Washington, DC; Deputy Chairman of the Boar ELBIM Bank, Moscow; Board Member, PLD Telekom Inc, Ne York. Publications: 250 articles, 17 books, including: TI Barefoot Shoemaker: Capitalizing on the New Russ International Joint Ventures. Honour: Honourary Doctc University of Bridgeport. Membership: Russian Academy Natural Sciences. Address: Fordham University, Lincoln Cent Campus, 113 West 60th Street, NY 10023, USA.

**KWAN Vincent Po Chuen,** b. 24 July 1959, Hong Kong S₹ Solicitor. m. Nikki L K Tan, 1 daughter. Education: BSoc S 1983; LLB, 1987; LLM, 1992; MSc, 1999. Appointments: Ci Servant, 1983-87; Solicitor, Deacons Graham and Jame 1988-93; Executive Director, Chuang's Group, 1993-9 General Manager, Legal, Sino Group, 1997-. Membership Solicitor, HKSAR, England and Wales; ACT Australia; FCC Address: Flat 1E Phase 1, Blessings Gd 95 Robinson Roa Hong Kong.

**KWON Joon Taek,** b. 10 March 1935, Kimpo, Kore Retired Chemist. m. Moon Ja Kwon, 1 son, 1 daughte Education: BS, 1957, University Illinois, USA; MS, 1959, Ph 1962, Cornell University; Sophomore standing, Seoul Natior University, Korea. Appointments: Postdoctoral Research a Teaching Fellows, 1962-64, Instructor, 1964-65, Univers British Columbia, Canada; (Associate) Research Chemi Chemcell Ltd, Edmonton, Alberta, 1965-67; Senior Researe Chemist, Celanses Research Company, New Jersey, US. 1967-70; Senior Research Chemist, 1970-78, Princip Research Chemist, 1978-, ABB Lummus Global In Bloomfield, New Jersey, -1999. Publications: Holder of 14 L Patents and UK, German and Japanese patents; Contributor 13 professional articles on inorganic and industrial chemis and 3 thesis for advanced degrees. Honours: Grant in a University British Columbia, Canada, 1964-65; Industrial gra in aid, NRC, Canada, 1965-67; Scouters Key, District Award Merit, Vigil Honour in the Order of the Arrow, Silver Beav Award, Boy Scouts of America. Memberships: America Chemical Society; Royal Society of Chemistry, UK, MRS CChem; Korean Chemical Society, recording secretary in No America, life member; Catalysis Society of Metropolitan Ne York; American Section, Thermal Analysis Society, New Yo Society of Chemical Industry; Past New Jersey Chapt President, Korean Scientists and Engineers in Americ Address: 142 Derby Drive, Freehold, NJ 07728-2767, USA.

**KWON Joong-Ho,** b. 5 May 1954, Korea. Professor. m. B Park, 2 sons, 1 daughter. Education: BS, Kyungpook Nation University, 1979; MS, 1981; PhD, 1984. Appointmen Principal Investigating Officer, Korea Atomic Energy Ins 1981-92; Professor, Dept of Food Science and Technolog Kyungpook National University, 1993-. Publications: 1! Research Papers; 15 Patents. Memberships: IFT; KSFS Address: Department of Food Science and Technolog College of Agriculture, Kyungpook National University, Tae 702 701, Korea.

**KWONG Donald,** b. 10 February 1968, Sacramento, California, USA. Contracts Administrator. Education: BA, Economics, University of California, Santa Cruz, 1991. Appointments: Student Trainee, Management and Purchasing, 1987-91, Purchasing Agent, 1991-93, US Department of Energy; Procurement Specialist, PRC Environmental Management Inc, 1993-95; Procurement Consultant, San Jose Minority Business Development Center, 1995-96; Contracts and Subcontracts Administrator, Aerotherm Corporation, DynCorp Aerospace Technology, 1996-. Honours: Performing an Exceptional Endeavor Recognition Award, 1991, Suggestion Award, 1992, US Department of Energy; Safety Award, Aerotherm Corporation, 1997; Performance Excellence Award, DynCorp Aerospace Technology, 1997. Memberships include: Business and Subcontract Management Special Topic Committies, 1996-; Department of Defense Western Regional Council for Small Business Education & Advocacy, 1997-. Address: Aerotherm Corporation, 580 Clyde Avenue, Mountain View, CA 94043, USA.

**KYLE George William,** b. 9 August 1945, Westerley, Rhode Island, USA. Computer Engineer. m. Miriam. Education: AA Personal Management, AS Data Processing, 1976; BGS Computer Engineering, 1982. Appointments: US Navy, Retired, 1963-83; Clinton Power Station, 1983-97; Pioneer Services and Engineering, 1997-. Address: P O Box 325, Clinton, IL 61727, USA.

# L

**LA SCALA Massimo**, b. 15 October 1959, Bari, Italy. Electrical Engineer. m. Attolico Antonia, 2 sons. Education: Laurea in Ingegnezia, 1984; PhD, Politecnico Bozi, Politecnico Bari, 1989. Appointments: Assistant Professor, Universita di Bazi, 1990-92; Associate Professor, Universita di Napoli, 1992-96; Associate Professor, Politenico Bari. Publications: Over 70 publications on international journals in electrical engineering. Memberships: IEEE; Associazione Elettrotecnica Italiana. Address: Via Pisacane 19, 70126 Bari, Italy.

**LACIS Aris**, b. 1 August 1936, Latvia. Cardiac Surgeon. m. Aija, 2 sons. Education: Profesor, Cardiac Surgery. Career: Chief, Latvian State Childrens Center for Cardiology. Publications: 32 scientific papers in professional medical journals. Memberships: Inernational Society for Cardiovascular Surgery; Association of European Paediatric Cardiologists. Address: Raunas 45/3-108, Riga, LV 1084, Latvia.

**LACKMAN Conway L**, b. 21 April 1938, Cincinnati, USA. Consultant. 2 daughters. Education: BA, 1960, Ohio Wesleyan University; MBA, 1964, Arizona State University; PhD, 1973, Cincinnati University. Appointments: Director of Marketing Research, ATT, RJR, 1974-91; Principal, International Consulting Group, 1991-. Publications: 150 articles in journals. Honour: Omicron Delta Epsilon National Economics Honorary Society. Memberships: American Marketing Association; Eastern Economic Association. Address: 112 Washington PL=9J, Pittsburgh, PA 15219 3504, USA.

**LACOVA Margita**, b. 8 November 1932, Vysna Sebastova, Presov, Slovakia. Chemist; University Teacher; Professor; Doctor. m. Dr Jan Lac, 2 June 1932, 1 son, 2 daughters. Education: Faculty of Sciences, Comenius University, Bratislava, studied chemistry, 1952-57, MSc, 1957, PhD 1967, Professor, 1975. Appointments: Research worker and University Teacher. Publications: Author of more than 100 scientific publications and more than 30 inventions from research work. Honours: Awarded medals of Comenius University and of Faculty of Natural Science, 1982; Medal of City Office, Bratislava, 1985; Medal of Slovak Chemical Society, 1982. Memberships: Slovak Chemical Society; National Geographic Society; New York Academy of Sciences. Address: Department of Organic Chemistry, Comenius University, Mlynska Dolina Ch-2, 84215 Bratislava, Slovakia.

**LACY Norris J**, b. 8 March 1940, Kentucky, USA. Professor. m. Susan Houston Lacy. Education: AB, Murray University, 1962; MA, 1963, PhD, 1967, Indiana University. Appointments: Assistant Professor, Professor, French, University of Kansas, 1966-88; Visiting Associate Professor, University of California, Los Angeles, 1975-76; Professor, French and Comparative Literature, Washington University, 1988-98; Edwin Erle Sparks Professor of French, Pennsylvania State University, 1998-. Publications: The Craft of Chrétien de Troyes: An Essay on Narrative Art, 1980; Reading Fabliaux, 1993; A Camelot Triptych, 1997; Co-author: The Arthurian Handbook, 1988, 1998. Honours: President, Mid-America Medieval Association, 1980-81; International President, 1984-87, Honorary International President, 1987-, International Arthurian Society; Knight of the Order of Academic Palms, 1988; President, Midwest Modern Language Association, 1994-95. Memberships: Modern Language Association; Medieval Academy of America; International Arthurian Society; American Literary Translators Association; American Association of Teachers of French; Société Rencesvals; International Courtly Literature Society; Medieval Romance Society; America Society of French Academic Palms. Address: Department of French, Pennsylvania State University, University Park, P/ 16802, USA.

**LADYGHINA Margaret F**, b. 26 May 1944, b Sonkovo, Tve reg, Russia. Candidate of Medical Sciences. m. div. Educatior Diploma, 1968, Leningrad Medical University; Postgrad Diplomate, St Petersburg Medical Academy; Candidate Medica Sciences, 1997. Appointments: Competitor District Dispensar of Dermatology, Leningrad, 1969; Dermatologist, Centra District Hospital, Volkhov, Russia, 1970-82; Dispensary c Dermatology, St Petersburg, 1982-96; Municipal Dermatolog Dispensary, St Petersburg, 1997-. Publications: 1 article in fiel of dermatology, 1994; 1 Patent. Membership: Science Societ Tarnovsky. Address: J Hagek 8 Apt 27, 192281 St Petersburg Russia.

**LÅG Jul**, b. 13 November 1915, Flesberg, Norway Professor. m. Ingrid Brenner, deceased 1979, 1 son, daughter. Education: Cand agric, 1942, Dr agric, 1949, Th Agricultural University of Norway. Appointments: Professor i Soil Science, AUN, 1949-85; Rector, AUN, 1968-71 Publications: More than 200 scientific papers; 5 books i Norwegian; Editor of 13 books in English; President, Th Norwegian Academy of Science and Letters, 1976-85 Chairman, The Working Group Soils and Geomedicine, 1986- Memberships: Scientific academies in Norway, Denmark Finland, Poland and Sweden; Honorary Member, Soviet So Science Society; Correspondent Member of German So Science Society. Address: Langbakken 2, 1432 Ås, Norway.

**LAGERBERG Dagmar Anna-Greta**, b. 25 July 1941 Stockholm. Child Health Researcher. Education: BA, 1963 PhD Sociology, 1975, University of Uppsala. Appointments Research Assistant, Department of Social Medicine, 1964-73 Associate Professor, 1983, University Uppsala; Researche Central Unit of Child Health, University Hospital, Department c Pediatrics, 1976-. Publication: Child Abuse and Neglect - / Dilemma to the Child Health Services?, 1998. Honou Decorated Kt Chevalier of Palmes Academiques, President c France, 1992. Memberships: Scientific Council of Nationa Board of Health and Welfare, Stockholm, 1984-; Swedisl Writers' Union, 1981-. Address: Vaksalagatan 42 B, S-753 3 Uppsala, Sweden.

**LAI Chuk Ling Julian**, b. 5 March 1961, Hong Kong Educator; Researcher. m. Liu Yee Ping Winnie. Educatior BSc, University of Toronto, 1985; PhD, University of Hong Kong, 1995. Appointments: Demonstrator, Department c Psychology, University of Hong Kong, 1989-93; Lecture 1993-96, Assistant Professor, 1996-, Department of Applie Social Studies, City University of Hong Kong. Publication Author and co-author of 8 journal articles including: Differentia predictive power of the positively versus the negatively worde items of the Life Orientation Test, 1994; Unemployment an psychological health among Hong Kong Chinese women, 1997 Memberships: Graduate Member, Registered Psychologis Hong Kong Psychological Society; International Association c Applied Psychology; International Affiliate, America Psychological Association. Address: Applied Social Studies City U, Tat Chee Ave, Kowloon, Hong Kong.

**LAI Ruay-Sheng**, b. 10 November 1957, Taiwan. Physiciar m. Pei-Ching Lee, 1 s, 2 d. Education: MB, Teipei Medica College, Taiwan, 1984. Appointments: Staff Physiciar Veterans General Hospital, Kaosiung, Taiwan; Assistar Professor, Foo-Ying Institute of Technology. Publications: The Lancet, 1996, 1998. Memberships: American College of Ches

Physicians. Address: Vet Gen Hosp-Kaohsiung, 386 Ta-Chung 1st Road, Kaohsiung 813, Taiwan.

**LAI Shih-Kung,** b. 15 November 1957, Taiwan. Professor; Centre Director. m. Chiung-Ku Lee. Education: BSE, National Cheng Kung University, 1979; MCRP, Ohio State University, 1985; PhD, University of Illinois at Urbana-Champaign, 1990. Appointments: Visiting Associate Professor, National Chung Hsing University Graduate Institute of Urban Planning; Associate Professor, currently Professor, Department of Land Economics and Administration, Director of Centre for Land Management and Technology, National Chung Hsing University, Taipei. Memberships: American Planning Associatin; Chinese Planning Association. Address: National Chung Hsing University, 67 Section 3 Min Sheng East Road, Taipei, Taiwan, R.O.C.

**LAI Yongjin,** b. 27 December 1935, Xiaoxi, Pinhe, China. Teacher. m. Yang Juanjuan, 1 son, 1 daughter. Education: Certificate of Graduation, Fujian Teacher's College, 1958. Appointments: Fujiang Teachers' Training College, 1956-58; Qingzhou Paper Mill of Fujian, 1959-63; Teaching, Gaokeng Primary School and Guoqiang Middle School of Pinhe, 1964-84; Teaching in Pinhe Senior Vocational School, 1985-. Publications: The Environment for Mandarin Ducks Life Through the Winter; Acoyus Found in China (in Pinhe County). Honour: The Method of Raising Mandarine Ducks, article, won Third Prize, 1991. Memberships: Chinese Zoology Institute, 1982; Fujian Plant Institute, 1980. Address: 62 Zhongdong Street, Xiaoni, Pinghe, Fujian 363700, China.

**LAI Yukman,** b. 25 February 1949, Canton, China. Artist. m. Ming-Yau Ng, 3 daughters. Education: Diploma, 1974, Hong Kong Sir Robert Black College of Education; BA, 1986, University of East Asia, Macau. Appointments: Curator of C C Arts Gallery, Vancouver; President, Chinese Canadian Artists Federation in Vancouver; Lecturer of Art, Simon Fraser University, Vancouver; Board Director, Richmond Art Gallery Association, Vancouver; 7 solo exhibitions, 25 collective exhibitions; Represented in 10 public collections and 4 corporate collections. Publications: Painting, Calligraphy & Seals of Yukman Lai, 1990; My Rockies: Landscape Paintings by Yukman Lai, 1993; Yangtze River: A Sentimental Journey, Landscape Paintings of Yukman Lai, 1997; and others; 10 articles on art. Honour: 1st Class Prize, The Whole China Taibai Cup Compt of Chinese Painting, 1989. Memberships: Life member, Chinese Canadian Artist Federation, Vancouver; Fellow, Huang Pu Art Academy, Shanghai. Address: 20 East Pender Street, Vancouver BC, Canada V6A 1T1.

**LAI Zongsheng,** b. 9 March 1943, Fuzhou, China. Professor. m. Meilin Xu, 1 daughter. Education: Graduate, Department of Physics, East China Normal University, 1961. Career: Associate Professor, 1986-92, Professor, 1992-, Department of Electrical Engineering, Chairman, Supervisor, PhD Students, 1993-, East China Normal University; Visiting Scholar, University of Alberta, Canada, 1991, 1992. Publications: Over 80 professional papers in journals. Memberships: IEEE; New York Academy of Sciences; American Association for the Advancement of Science. Address: Department of Elecrical Engineering, East China Normal University, 3663 Zhong Shan Road (N), Shanghai 200062, China.

**LAIRD John E,** b. 19 July 1943, Philadelphia, Penn, USA. Freelance Photographer. 1 son, 1 daughter. Education: Photography, Commercial Art Courses, Sinclair College, 1982-83. Appointments: Contributing Photographer, Sinclair College Newspaper, 1982-83; Exhibitions, Photographs,

Paintings, Dayton Visual Arts Centre, 1992-93. Publication: As I see It. Honours: Honourable Mention, National Photo COntest, 1988, Finalist, 1998; Photographers Forum Magazine Award of Excellence. Memberships: Dayton Visual Arts Centre. Address: P O Box 9445, Dayton, OH 45409-9445, USA.

**LAKIS Juozas,** b. 12 March 1943, Tausiunai, Shalchininku District, Lithuania. Sociologist. m. Genovaite Navaslauskaite, 1 son, 1 daughter. Education: Master Humanitarian Sciences, 1967, Vilnius University; PhD Sociology, 1972, Moscow Lomonosoff University; Habilitated Dr Etnosociology, 1993, Vilnius Pedagogical University; Fellowship, 1997, Columbia University, New York. Appointments: Head of Laboratory of Educational Sociological Research, Vilnius Pedagogical University; Director, Lithuanian Conflict Prevention Centre; Researcher, Central European University Research Support Scheme. Publications: 50 articles and books of scientific reflection; 70 articles reflecting social and political issues. Memberships: Lithuanian Sociologist Association, member Research Board; National Business Confederation, member of Board, Head of Commission for Education and Ethics. Address: Zirmunu 133-25, LT 2012 Vilnius, Lithuania.

**LAL Avtar,** b. 27 September 1960, Amritsar, Punjab. Pharmacologist; Researcher; Medical Educator; Clinical Pharmacologist. m. Jyoti, 1 son, 1 daughter. Education: MBBS, 1984; MD Pharmacology, 1988; DM Clinical Pharmacology, 1991. Appointments: Junior Resident/MD Pharmacology, Department of Pharmacology, Medical College, Amritsar, Punjab, 1987; Senior Resident, 1989, Senior Resident/DM Clinical Pharmacology, 1989, Department of Clinical Pharmacology, Postgraduate Institute of Medical Education and Research, Chandigarh; Lecturer, Department of Pharmacology, Mahatma Gandhi Institute of Medical Sciences, Savagram, District Wardha, Maharashtra, 1991; Lecturer, Department of Pharmacology, Jawahar Lal Nehru Medical College, Aligarh Muslim University, Aligarh, Uttar Pradesh, 1992; Lecturer, 1993, Senior Lecturer, 1995, Department of Pharmacology, University College of Medical Sciences and Guru Teg Bahadur Hospital, Delhi. Publications: Contributor over 45 articles in professional journals and chapters in books; Referee to journals. Memberships: Indian Pharmacological Society; Association of Physiologists and Pharmacologists of India; Indian Society of Clinical Pharmacology and Therapeutics; Indian Academy of Neurosciences; Indian Medical Association; Delhi Society for Promotion of Rational Drug Use; Indian Medical Association Academy of Medical Specialists. Address: 80 Gagan Vihar, Delhi 110 051, India.

**LAL Harbans,** b. 20 July 1947, Talwandi Bhai, Punjab, India. Teacher. m. Veena Agrawal, 1 son, 1 daughter. Education: MSc, 1969; PhD, 1975. Appointments: Demonstrator, 1970-72; Lecturer, 1976-81; Reader, 1981-88; Associate Professor, 1988-. Publications: 101. Honours: WHO Fellowship Award, 1983; Nutrition Society of India, Young Scientist Award, 1983; Fellow, International Academy of Ophthalmology, Brussels, 1989; Fellow, Association of Clinical Biochemists of India, 1997. Memberships: Life Member, Nutrition Society of India, 1982; Life Member, Association of Clinical Biochemists of India, 1986, Vice President, 1995. Address: Department of Biochemistry, Pt B D S PGIMS, Rohtak 124001, Haryana, India.

**LAL Kishori,** b. 14 September 1947, Palampur, India. Teacher. m. Raj Kumari, 1 son, 1 daughter. Education: BSc, MA, English Literature; PhD, Journalism. Appointments: Lecturer, 1978; Reader, 1993-. Publications include: Quest and Reminiscences, 1975; Lingerings of Love, 1983; Epics of Despair, 1993; Passions Progress, 1995. Honours include:

Excellence Award in Freelance Journalism, 1996; United Writers Excellence Award in Literature, 1997; Commendation Card for Devotion to Duty, General Officer Commanding-in-Chief, Southern Command, 1997. Memberships include: United Writers Association of Madras. Address: Department of English, National Defence Academy, Khadakwasla, Pune 411 023, India.

**LALCHANDANI V D,** b. 15 July 1942, Mehar, Sindh. Teacher. m. Meera, 2 sons, 3 daughters. Education: BSc, 1967; MSc, 1969. Appointments: Lecturer, 1969; Professor, 1986. Publiations: 19 Papers Published. Honours: Dr K R Raminathan Physics Teaching Aid Award, 1987; Best Teaching Aid Award, 1997. Memberships: Indian Association of Physics Teachers; Indian Physics Association; Instrument Society of India; Hindi Vigyan Sahitya Parishad. Address: Dept of Physics, CMD College, Bilaspur 495 001, India.

**LALL Ajai Livingstone,** b. 1 December 1958, AP, India. Mission Director. m. Indu, 1 son, 2 daughters. Education: BA, India; BS, USA; MA, India; PhD; DD; D Lit , India. Appointments: Director, Central India Christian Mission; National Youth Council of India; India Bible Publishers. Memberships: Evangelical Fellowship of India; Fellowship of Evangelical Churches of India. Address: Central India Christian Mission, P O Box 11, Damoh Madhya Pradesh, 470 661 India.

**LAMAUSKAS Jonas,** b. 25 February 1941, Kaunas, Lithuania. Principal. m. Aldona, 2 sons. Education: Kaunas J Gruodis School of Music, 1955-59; Lithuanian Conservatory, 1959-64. Appointments: Laboratory Assistant, 1961-62, Senior Laboratory Assistant, 1962-64, Lithuanian Conservatory; Instructor, Music Department, Siauliai Pedagogical Institute, and Siauliai College of Music, 1964-66; Principal, Siauliai Conservatory, 1966-. Honours: Honoured Culture and Education Worker, 1975, Honoured Art Worker, 1989, of the Lithuanian Republic. Memberships: International Lions Clubs Association; Lithuanian College Principals Association; Lithuanian Musical Association. Address: S Neries 8-2, LT 5400 Siauliai, Lithuania.

**LAMBERT Kathy Kristensen,** b. 24 February, California, USA. Legislator; Educator. m. Daryl Lambert, 2 sons, 2 daughters. Education: AA, College of Marin, 1975; BA, University of Washington, 1984. Appointments: Vice Chair, Children and Family Services Committee, 1995-96; Member, Appropriations and Law and Justice, 1995-; Assistant Majority Floor Leader, Washington State House of Representatives, 1996-98. Publications: Childrens History Novel on Martin Luther King Jr, 1991. Honours: Outstanding Legislator of the Year, Family Law Section of Bar, 1996. Memberships: Republican Party; Washington Education Association; PTA. Address: PO Box 1138, Woodinville, WA 98072, USA.

**LAMBRECH Régine,** b. 21 November 1950, White Plains, NY, USA. Teacher. Education:Bachelor of Arts, French and Secondary Education, 1972; Master of Arts, French, 1975; Doctor of Philosophy, French, 1985. Appointments: Associate Professor, French, English, 1983-84; Chargée des Relations Internationales, 1984-88; Director of International Relations, 1989; Professor, Program Administrator, Ecole Centrale De Lyon, 1983-. Publications: 19 Publications; Numerous Reviews. Honours: Phi Sigma Iota; Phi Kappa Phi; Deans List; Alpha Mu Gamma; Distinguished Alumna, Penn State University, 1996. Memberships: NAFSA; Association of International Educators; European Association for International Education; Modern Languages Association; Union des Professeurs de Langues Etrangères dans les Grandes Ecoles; SIETAR; IAIE. Address:

Le Brévent, 47 Ave Valioud, F-69110 Ste Foy-Lès-Lyon, France.

**LANDAU Iddo,** b. 2 August 1958, Jerusalem, Israel. University Senior Lecturer. m. Yael. Education: BA, Philosophy and History, 1984, MA, Philosophy, 1986, Hebrew University of Jerusalem; PhD, Philosophy, McGill University, Canada, 1991. Appointments: Lecturer, 1993-97, Senior Lecturer, 1997-, Philosophy Department, Haifa University, Israel. Publications: Several articles in professional journals. Honours: Haezrachi Prize, 1985; McGill Major Fellowship, 1986-88, 1989-90; Alon Fellowship, 1992-95. Membership: American Philosophical Association, 1992-. Address: 7 Menachem Beilis Street, 34814 Haifa, Israel.

**LANDERS Vernette,** b. 3 May 1912, Lawton, Oklahoma, USA. Educator; Counsellor; Community Development Worker. m. (1) Paul A Lum, dec, 1 stepson, (2) Newlin Landers, 2 stepsons. Education: AB, honours, University of California, Los Angeles, 1933; MA, 1935; EdD, 1953; Teaching Life Diploma; General Pupil Personnel Services Life Diploma. Appointments: Teacher, Montebello, California Schools, 1935-45, 1948-50, 1951-59; Freelance Writer, 1944-; Professor, Long Beach City College, 1946-47, Los Angeles State College, 1950; Dean of Girls, 29 Palms High School, 1960-65; District Counselor, Morongo Unified School District, 1965-72; Coordinator, Adult Education, 1965-67; Director, Guidance Project, 1967; Clerk, Volunteer, Landers Post Office, 1962-83; Secretary, Landers Volunteer Fire Department, 1972; Vice President, Landers Association Inc, 1969-71; Director, Secretary, Desert Ears, Emergency Radio Service, 1970-73. Publications include: Impy, 1974; Talkie, 1975; Impy's Children, 1975; Who and Who Who, 1978; Sandy The Coydog, 1979; The Kit Fox and the Walking Stick, 1980. Honours include: Platinum Record for Exceptional Performance, American Biographical Institute, 1996. Memberships include: International Academy of Poets, London. Address: 632 North Landers Lane, PO Box 3839, Landers, CA 92285, USA.

**LANDES William Alan,** b. 23 April 1945, New York, USA. Publisher. m. Sharon Gorrell, 1 son, 2 daughters. Education: AA, RADA; AS, Orange County Community College; BA, BS, Hunter Lehman College; MA, California State University; PhD, UCLA. Appointments: Manager, USAF, 1967-69; Associate Producer, New World Productions, 1971-72; Entertainment Editor, Showcase Magazine, 1972-75; Director of Theatre, Artistic Director, Players, USA, 1975-78; Artistic Director, Merrick Studios, 1978-79; Vice President, Publisher, Players Press, 1980-. Publications: Musicals; Plays; Texts; Films. Memberships: SAG; AFTRA; DGA; PGA; Dramtist Guild. Address: The Empire, PO Box 1344, Studio City, CA 91614-0344, USA.

**LANDSBERGIENE Grazina,** b. 1930, Anyksciai, Lithuania. Pianist. m. Vytautas Landsbergis, 1 son, 1 daughter. Education: Vilnius Academy of Music, 1959. Appointments: Accompanist, National Theatre of Opera and Ballet, 1958-85; Associate Professor, Vilnius Academy of Music, 1990-; Concerts with various singers. Honour: Vilnius Glory Award, 1998. Membership: Chairperson, Vytautas Landsbergis Foundation. Address: Traidenio 34-15, LT 2000 Vilnius, Lithuania.

**LANDYMORE Roderick William,** b. July 1946, Ottawa, Ontario, Canada. Professor. m. 3 children. Education: BSc Hons, 1967, MD, 1972, Residency in General Surgery, 1975-79, Dalhousie University, Halifax, Nova Scotia; Internship, Rotating, Graduated with distinction, 1971-72; Residency, Thoracic and Cardiovascular Surgery, New York University Medical Centre, New York, 1979-81; McLaughlin Travelling

Fellowship, Duke University, University of Pennsylvania, 1981-82. Appointments: General Practice, Woodlawn Medical Clinic, Nova Scotia, 1972-75; Associate Staff, General Teaching Unit, Halifax Infirmary Hospital, 1972-75; Clinical Instructor in Surgery, NYU Medical Centre, 1979-81; Assistant Professor, 1982-86, Associate Professor, 1986-94, Professor, 1994, Department Surgery, Head Cardiovascular Surgery, Victoria General Hospital, 1989-94, Dalhousie University, Halifax; Medical Officer - 33rd Battalion, Instructor, Lecturer, Royal Canadian Army, 1990-94; Chairman Dept Cardiac Sciences, King Fahad National Guard Hospital, Riyadh, Saudi Arabia, 1994-98. Publications: Author and Co-author 83 peer reviewed and invited abstracts; 96 manuscripts; 4 book chapters. Honours: 15 research grants; Reviewer or advisory board 8 professional journals; 2 patents. Memberships: Medical Society Nova Scotia; Canadian Cardiovascular Society; Canadian Society of Cardiovascular and Thoracic Surgeons; American Association for Academic Surgery; Society Thoracic Surgeons; New York Academy of Sciences; American Association for Thoracic Surgery, limited membership; European Association for Cardio-Thoracic Surgery; Association of Military Surgeons of United States; The Saudi Heart Association. Address: 526 West Lawrencetown Road, Lawrencetown, Nova Scotia, B2Z 1S5, Canada.

**LANE Vivian**, b. 26 May 1938, Girardville, PA, USA. Educator. Education: BS, Major Education, 1960; MSW, Major Social Work, 1981. Appointments: Educational Counselor, 1960-70; Social Work, Inner City Youth, 1975-79; Educational Counselor, Community Outreach, 1982-. Honour: HS Valedictorian, 1956. Memberships: Kappa Delta Pi, Honorary; National Association Social Workers. Address: PO Box 186, Clifton Heights, PA 19018-0186, USA.

**LANGBACKA Ralf Runar**, b. 20 November 1932, Narpes, Finland. Theater Director, Manager, Professor. m. Birgitta Danielsson, 2 sons, 1 daughter. Education: MA, ABO Akademi, Finland, 1956. Appointments: Artistical Director, 1960-63; Director, 1963-65; Artistical Director, 1965-67; Director, 1967-71; Artistical Director, 1971-77; Professor of Arts, 1979-83; Managing and Artistical Director, 1983-87; Professor of Arts, 1989-93; Visiting Professor, 1994-97; Freelance Director, Denmark, Norway, Germany and Sweden, 1960-97. Publications: Teatterikirja, 1977; Bland annat om Brecht, 1982; Moten med Tjechov, 1986; Denna Langa dag, Detta Korta Liv, Dikter, 1988; Olga, Irina Och Jag (Play), 1991; Brecht og Det Realistiske Teater, 1998; Krocketspelaren, 1998; About 500 Articles on Literature, Film, Theatre, Politics. Honours: The Critics Spurs Award, 1963; Pro Finlandia Medal, 1973; Award of Svenska Litteratursallskapet i Finland, 1982; Award of the MiddleNordic Countries, 1984; Award of the Swedish Culture Foundation in Finland, 1989; Honorary Prize of the Culture Foundation, Finland-Sweden, 1994; The Henrik Steffens Award, Germany, 1994; Honorary Member of Finnish Theatre Directors Association, 1995. Memberships: Nordic Theatre Union, 1983-96; Chairman, Finnish Centre of The International Theatre Institute, 1983-95. Address: Hopeasalmenranta 1B, 00570 Helsinki, Finland.

**LANGER Jerzy Jozef**, b. 25 February 1946, Bad Harzburg, Germany. Professor of Chemistry. m. Anna, 2 sons. Education: MSc Chemistry, 1969; MSc Physics, 1972; PhD Organic Phys Chemistry, 1974; DSc Physics and Theoretical Chemistry, 1989. Appointments: Adjunct Chemist, 1976-89,Assistant Professor of Chemistry, 1989-96, Associate Professor ofChemistry, 1996-, A Mickiewicz University, Faculty of Chemistry. Publications: About 50 publications in scientific journals; 45 conference communications; 5 patents. Honours: Award for Scientific Achievements, 1988, Ministry of National Education, Warsaw; Award for Scientific Achievement, 1991, QMW University of London. Memberships: Fellow, Royal Society of Chemistry; C Chem; Sigma Xi, USA; EMRS; AAAS; WATOC; International Society for Molecular Electriconics and Biocomputing. Address: A Mickiewicz University, Faculty of Chemistry, Grunwaldzka 6, PL-60780 Poznan, Poland.

**LANGFORD Carol Ann**, b. 20 July 1940, Chicago, USA. Pediatrician. m. (1) Arthur G Robins, (2) George B Wolfenden, 2 sons. Education: University of Chicago Laboratory School; BA, Stanford University, 1962; MD, University of Chicago, 1969. Appointments: Peace Corps, 1963-64; Misson Hospital, Kwa Zulu, 1972-74; Training Fellowships, Childrens Hospital, Boston; Consultant, Langford Resort Hotel; Assistant in Pediatrics, Massachusetts General Hospital; Instructor of Pediatrics Harvard Medical School. Publication: Aloe Queen of Medicinal Plants. Memberships: Duxbury Art Association; American Academy of Pediatrics; Museum of Fine Arts; Sierra Club; Duxbury Historical Society. Address: Boston Evening Medical Center, 388 Commonwealth Avenue, Boston, MA 02215, USA.

**LAPIN Slava (Izyaslav) P**, b. 26 June 1930, Leningrad, Russia. Psychopharmacology. m. Natalia Annalova, 1 son, 1 daughter. Education: MD, Internal Medicine, 1953; DMed, Pharmacology, 1971; Professor, 1972. Appointments: Assistant Professor, Pediatric Medicine, 1956-60; Chief, Laboratory of Psychopharmacology, Bekhterev Psychoneurology Research Institute, 1960-. Honour: Kravkov Medal of Honour for Merits in Soviet Pharmacology, 1974. Membership: Honorary Member, British Association for Psychopharmacology, 1984. Address: 88-136 Nevsky Prospect, St Petersburg 191025, Russia.

**LARA-ROSANO Felipe**, b. 22 March 1938, Puebla, Mexico. Systems Engineer. m. Guadalupe Elisa Velazquez, 1 son, 1 daughter. Education: Engineer, 1962, University Puebla; MSc, 197o, National University, Mexico (UNAM); PhD, 1973, UNAM. Appointments: General Director, Barros Sierra Foundation, 1975-77; Senior Researcher, UNAM, 1978-; Head Graduate Department for Engineering, 1991-93; Head Academic Senate for Mathematics, Physics and Engineering, 1993-97; Director Centre for Instrumentation Research, 1997. Publications: 35 international scientific publications. Honour: Doctor Honoris Causa, International Institute for Advanced Systems Research and Cybernetics. Memberships: New York Academy of Sciences; Mexican Academy of Sciences; IEEE; Mexican Academy of Engineering. Address: UNAM, Apartado 70-418, Coyoacan, Mexico City 04510, Mexico.

**LARBI Madonna Owusuah**, b. 18 February 1953, Accra, Ghana, West Africa. Programme Administrator, Executive Director. 1 son. Education: Diploma in Journalism, 1974; Human Rights Diploma, 1989. Appointments: Administrative and Liaison Consultant, United Nations Fund for Population Activities, Ghana; Public Affairs Consultant, World Bank Office, Ghana, 1980-81; Communications Team Assistant, Amnesty International, Ghana, 1988-90; Executive Director, National Organization of Immigrant and Visible Minority Women of Canada, 1990-91; Programme Officer, English Speaking Africa and Asian MATCH International Centre, 1991-92; Executive Director, MATCH International Centre, 1992-. Memberships: Board Member, SOS Children's Villages, Canada, 1993-; North South Institute, Ottawa, Canada, 1996-98; YWCA, Canada, 1994-96; UNESCO, Ottawa, Canada, 1993-; Media Watch, Canada, 1992-94; Gender Group of WETV International Development; Member of Research Centre, Ottawa, Canada. Address: MATCH International Centre, 200 Elgin St, Ste 1102, Ottawa, ON K2P 1L5, Canada.

**LARDREAU Guy,** b. 28 March 1947, Paris, France. Professor. m. Esther Lardreau-Cotelle, 1 son. Education: Philosophy, 1972. Appointments: Professor de Chaire Supérieure, Khagne. Publications include: Discours philosophique et discours spirituel, 1985; Fictions philosophiques et science-fiction, 1988; La Véracité, 1993; Présentation criminelle de quelques concepts majeurs de la philosophie, 1997. Honour: Grand Prix de la science-fiction française, 1988; Honoured by the French Academy, 1989. Memberships: College International of Philosophy. Address: 17 rue Piron, 21000 Dijon, France.

**LARKIN Anatoly,** b. 14 October 1932, Moscow, Russia. Physicist. m. Larkina Tatiana, 2 sons. Education: MS, Moscow Physics Engineering Institute, 1956; PhD, Kurchatov Institute of Atomic Energy, 1960; DSc, Kurchatov Institute of Atomic Energy, 1965. Appointments: Researcher, Kurchatov Institute of Atomic Energy, 1957-66; Professor, Moscow State University, 1970-91; Head, Department of London Institute for Theoretical Physics, 1966-95; Professor, Theoretical Physics Institute, University Minnesota, 1995. Honours: London Prize in Low Temperature Physics, 1990; Hewlett-Packard Prize, 1993; World Congress on Superconductivity Award of Excellence, 1994. Memberships: Corresponding Member, Soviety Academy of Science, 1979; Full Member, Russian Academy of Science, 1991. Address: Russian Academy of Sciences, Chernogolovka, Noginsk District, Moscow 142432, Russia.

**LARSKY Nikolai,** b. 3 January 1937, Moscow, Russia. Painter. Education: Graduate, Art Faculty, Moscow Polygraphic Institute, 1965. Career: First Personal Exhibitions of Paintings, Moscow 1962; Yearly Exhibitions of Non-Conformist Art, Moscow, 1965-88; Placard Exhibitions, Moscow, 1965, 1967, 1972, 1975; Exhibitions of Soviet Placard in Poland, England, Cuba, Austria, 1967-68; Placard Exhibitions in Latvia, Lithuania, 1972-74; Exhibitions of Moscow Painters, 1976, 1977; Joint Exhibitions of Paintings in Moscow, 1988, 1990; Personal Exhibitions of Paintings "Corrosions", Moscow, The Arbat Gallery, 1988, 1989, 1990; Placard Exhibition "Ecology", Moscow, 1990; Joint Exhibitions of Paintings in Italy, 1991, France, 1991; Personal Exhibitions of Paintings in Severodvinsk and Kandalaksha, Russia, 1991; Exhibition of Paintings "Ecology", Moscow, 1992; Personal Exhibition of Water Colours, Moscow, 1996; Personal Exhibition of Oil Paintings & Water Colours, Moscow, the "Yamanouchi" Office, 1996; Joint Exhibition of Paintings, Moscow, 1997. Publications: Several articles in professional journals; Catalogues of works. Honours: Diploma, Best Placard of the Year, Moscow, 1966; 2nd Prize, Circus Placard, Moscow, 1967. Memberships: Russian Union of Painters; International Federation of Painters. Address: Shipilovsky proezd 41-3-285, 115551 Moscow, Russia.

**LARSON Janice,** b. 29 September 1948, Houston, Texas, USA. Computer Science Educator. m. Harold Vernon Larson, 2 sons. Education: AA, Computer Science, San Jacinto College, 1981; BA, Computer Information Systems, University Houston, Clear Lake, 1984; MA, Computer Information Systems, University Houston, Clear Lake, 1988; Postgraduate in Instructional Technology, 1994-. Appointments: Programmer Control Applications, Houston, 1985-86; Texas Eastern Pipeline, Houston, 1988-90; Instructor, Computer Science, San Jac into College, Houston, 1990-94; Adjunct Computer Science, San Jac International College, Houston, 1995; Adjunct Computer Science, UH-CLC, 1996; Reader, ETS, 1996-97. Publications: Associate Editor, Technology and Teacher Education Annual, 1995; Editor of Phi Deta Kappa Newsletter, 1995; Nonlinear Pattern Recognition, 1984. Memberships:

IEEE; UH Alumni Association; Kappa Delta Pi International Honor Society; Phi Delta Kappa Professional Fraternity. Address: 11309 Forbes Road, Houston, TX 77075, USA.

**LARSON Roger Keith,** b. 27 April 1924, Cadillac, MI, USA. Medical Director. m. Frances Appel, 2 sons, 2 daughters. Education: Northwestern University, 1942; Wheaton College, 1943-44; MD, University of Illinois, Chicago, 1947; Internship, Cook County Hospital, Chicago, 1947-49. Appointments: Director, UCLA Medicine Clerkships Harbor General Hospital, 1954-57; Private Practice, Internal Medicine, Fresno, 1957-61; Chief of Medicine, Valley Medical Center of Fresno, 1961-90; Medical Director, AIDS Professional Education and Training Centre, 1990-94. Publications: 38 Medical Publications; 9 Nonmedical Publications. Honours: Distinguished Service Award, American Heart Association, 1969; Henry E Randel Award, Central Valley Lung Association, 1980; Kaiser Award for Excellence in Teaching, UCSF, 1981; Establishment of the Roger K Larson, Distinguished Visiting Professorship, UCSF, 1989; Fresno Madera Medical Society Award for Outstanding Services, 1991; Laureate of California Chapter of American College of Physicians Award, 1992. Memberships: American College of Physicians; CMA; AAAS; American Thoracic Society. Address: Valley Medical Center of Fresno, 445 South Cedar Avenue, Fresno, CA 93702-2907, USA.

**LARY Banning K.** Education: Fork Union Military Academy; University of Miami; University of Texas, Austin; Arthur Wise Real Estate School; University of California, Los Angeles, Playwriting Seminar; Renaissance Art School; Allstate Contractors College; ACTV Video Producers Workshop. Appointments: Website Positioning Specialist; Freelance Writer & Editor; Book Designer, Publisher, American Multimedia Publishers; Video Producer, Publisher, Promedion; Executive Director, Legal Development Resources; Creative Director, Hankins Laboratories; Editor, Art Director, The White Paper; Advisory Board, American Academy of Poetry Therapy; Editor-in-Chief; Writer, Ghost Writer, Graphic Designer, Painter Contractor, Estimator, Manager, Designer, Tradesman. Publications include: Taxes, Trading and the IRS, 1997; Foreign Currency Fluctuations Make Trade an Attractive Industry, 1998; Strategic Keywords in Web Page Design, 1998; Meta Tags in Web Page Submissions, 1998. Address: American Visionary Artists, PO Box 3551, Austin, TX 78764-3551, USA.

**LATFOULLIN Ildous,** b. 23 October 1938, Kazan, Russia. m. Foedorova Svetlana, 2 daughters. Education: Kazan Medical Institute, 1963; MD, 1985; Professor, 1988. Publications: More than 160 articles and 2 monographs. Membership: Petrovsky's Academy. Address: Kazan Medical University, Butlerou Str, 420000 Kazan, Russia.

**LATHAM William P,** b. 4 January 1917, Shreveport, USA. Composer; Educator. m. Joan M Seyler, 1 son, 2 daughters. Education: Degrees in Composition and Theory, Cincinnati College of Music, Ohio; PhD Composition, 1951, Eastman School of Music, University of Rochester, New York. Appointments: Theory and Composition Teacher, University of Northern Iowa, 1946-65, Professor, 1959; Professor of Music and Coordinator of Composition, 1965-84, Director of Graduate Studies in Music, 1969, Distinguished Professor of Music, 1978, Professor Emeritus, 1984-, Faculty, School of Music, North Texas State University. Creative works: Composer of over 100 works, about 65 have been published, many performed throughout the USA, Canada, Europe and Japan. Honours: Numerous Awards and Commissions, 1962-. Memberships: ASCAP. Address: PO Box 50373, Denton, TX 76206-0373, USA.

**LAURE Carlos Julio,** b. 11 June 1933, Teofilo Otoni, MG, Brazil. University Professor. m. Maria de Lourdes Rodrigues, 3 sons, 1 daughter. Education: Bachelor of Chemistry, 1956-61; DSc, Biochemistry, 1962-69; Assistant Professor, 1969-75. Appointments: Private Docent, 1975-81; Associate Professor, 1981-. Publications: Author, Co-Author, 17 articles in professional journals in German and English. Memberships: Brazilian Biochemical Society; Society of Toxinology; Sao Paulo Academy of Science. Address: Department of Biochemistry, Faculty of Medicine, Ribeirao Preto, 14.049 Ribeirao Preto SP, Brazil.

**LAURINAVICIUS Laimis,** b. 5 June 1949, Lithuania. Chief Currency Examiner; Associate Professor. 2 daughters. Education: Faculty of Radioelectronics, Kaunas Polytech Institute, 1967-72; Post Grad, Institute of Semiconductor Physics, Academy of Science; Candidate of Technological Science; Habil Dr of Technological Science. Appointments: Senior Engineer, Group Manager, Vilnius Institute, 1974-75; Designing Engineer, Research Fellow, Institute of Semiconductor Physics, Academy of Science, 1975-88; Senior Lecturer, Vilnius Civil Engineer, 1988-90; Associate Professor, Vilnius Technical University, 1990-; Manager, Currency Examination Division, Bank of Lithuania, 1997-. Publications: About 100 Studies; 30 Inventions. Address: Pamenkalnio 3/5-16, LT 2001 Vilnius, Lithuania.

**LAURINAVIČIUS Romualdas,** b. 2 July 1935, Laplegiai vil, Lithuania. Scientist; Biologist. m. Danute Švegždaite, 1 son. Education: Graduate, Lithuanian Academy of Agriculture, 1959; Postgraduate, 1961-64; Candidate of Biology, 1965; Moscow State University, 1966; Senior Research Worker, 1973; PhD, 1994. Appointments: Scientific Research Worker, 1964-71, Chief, Research Group of Space Biology, 1971-86, Chief, Department of Gravitational Physiology, 1986-, Institute of Botany Lithuanian Academy of Sciences. Publications: 85 scientific publictions in the field of gravitational and space plant physiology; 8 inventions. Memberships: Lithuanian Society of Plant Physiologists; Associate Member, Committee on Space Research (COSPAR). Address: Antakalnio 92-14, 2040 Vilnius, Lithuania.

**LAUTNER Peter,** b. 11 February 1959, Györ, Hungary. Historian of Ancient Philosophy. m. Judit Anka, 2 sons. Education: Ma, Classics and Philosophy, Eötvös University, Budapest, 1986; PhD, Hungarian Academy of Sciences, 1992. Appointments: Reader, Ancient Philosophy, Eötvös University, Budapest, 1989-94; Fellow, Senior Fellow, Research Group for Classical Studies, Hungarian Academy of Sciences, 1994-; Short-time Fellow, Warburg Institute, London, 1993; A W Mellon Research Fellow, American School for Classical Studies, Athens, 1994; Fellow, Netherlands Institute for Advanced Studies, 1995-96; Fellow, Centre for Hellenic Studies, Washington DC, 1996-97. Publications: Co-auth: Simplicius on the Void, 1992; Simplicius on Aristotle's De Anima 1.1-2.4, 1995; Simlicius on Aristotle's Physics 5, 1997; Simplicius on Aristotle's De Anima 2.5-12, 1997.Memberships: American Philological Association; Institute of Classical Studies, London. Address: Váci Mihály utca 22, H-2083 Solymár, Hungary.

**LAVE Judith Lister Rice,** b. 18 May 1939, Campbellton, NB, Canada. Professor of Health Economics. m. Lester B Lave, 1 son, 1 daughter. Education: BA first class hons, 1961, Queen's University, Kingston, Ontario; MA Economics, 1964, PhD Economics, 1967, Harvard. Appointments: Lecturer-Assistant Professor, Graduate School of Industrial Administration, 1966-71, Associate Professor of Economics and Urban Affairs, 1973-78, Carnegie Mellon University; Professor of Health Economics, Graduate School of Public Health, 1982-, Professor of Economics, Department of Economics, 1985-, Professor of Business Administration, Joseph M Katz Graduate School of Business, 1987-, Professor of Psychiatry, Department of Psychiatry School of Medicine, 1989-, Co-Director, Centre for Research on Health Care, 1993-, Vice Chair, Department of Health Services Administration, Graduate School of Public Health, 1994-, University of Pittsburgh; Interim Director, Health Administration Programme, 1997-; Commissioner, Prospective Payment Assessment Commission, 1993-97, Melecavic Payment Advisory Commission, 1997-. Publications: Board of Editors, 8 Journals and Publications; Author or co-Author, 77 peer reviewed articles; 40 invited papers; 4 books; 6 book reviews; 5 reports written under contract. Honours: Woodrow Wilson Fellow, 1961-62; Administrators Citation, HCFA, 1982; Elected member of Institute of Medicine, 1990; Honorary degree, Queen's University, 1994; Fellow, Association for Health Services Research, 1995; Distinguished Fellow, Association for Health Services Research, 1997; and others. Memberships: American Economic Association; American Public Health Association; Association for Health Services Research and Foundation for Health Services Research; National Academy of Social Insurance; Institute of Medicine; International Health Economics Association; Fellow, Employee Benefits Research Institute. Address: Graduate School of Public Health, University of Pittsburgh, Pittsburgh, PA 15261, USA.

**LAVIN Duchesne,** b. 24 May 1933, Sydney, Australia. Teacher of Religion and Music. Education: ATCL (T) Violin, 1954; LTCL, 1970; LMusA, FTCL, 1971; FLCM, Piano, 1972; MMusEd, 1972; Diploma, Teaching English as a Second Language, 1979; LAGM, Piano, 1982; FTCL, Harpsichord, 1986. Appointments include: Teacher, Private Instrumental Music, High School Australia and Papua New Guinea, 1953-69; Lecturer, Music, Port Moresby Teachers College, 1970-71; Teacher, Private and Classrooms, High Schools, Australia, 1977-. Publications include: With Music and Song; Songs of Papua New Guinea, books I and II; Make and Play Bamboo Flutes; Pacific Rhythm and Song; Kada Kakaili; Songs for a Happy Christmas; Pentatonic Miniatures; Sing Sing; Two Masses in English; Misa to Rot. Honours: Gold Medal, Trinity College, London, 1970; Certificate of Appreciation, City of Sydney Cultural Council, 1987. Memberships: APRA; Australian Institute of Music Teachers; MIMT. Address: OLSH Convent, Kensington, Sydney, NSW 2033, Australia.

**LAVOIPIERRE Alain Maurice,** b. 12 May 1951, Mauritius. m. Gail Webb, 2 daughters. Education: MBBS, Melb, 1974; FRACR, 1980. Appointments: Intern RMO, St Vincent's Hospital, Melbourne, 1975; Junior RMO, Royal Children's Hospital, Melbourne, 1976; Radiology Registrar, 1977-80, Radiologist, 1980-83, St Vincent's Hospital; Director of Radiology, Fairfield Hospital, 1985-93; Partner, Radclin Medical Imaging, Melbourne, 1983-, Chairman 1995-98. Publications: Several papers, book chapters and books. Honours: Philips Prize, RA. CR, 1996; Cabrini Clinical Education and Research Foundation Prize, 1997. Memberships: Royal Australasian College of Radiologists; Australian Medical Association; Radiological Society of North America. Address: Radclin Med Imaging, 183 Wattletree Rd, Malvern, VIC 3144, Australia.

**LAVRENCHENKO Georgy Konstantinovich,** b. 22 December 1939, Ahtanisovskaya, Krasnodarsky Region, Ukraine. Professor of Low Temperature Physics and Engineering. m. Yekateryna Ivanovna, 1 son. Education: Honours Diploma, Engineering-Mechanics of Refrigerating and Compression Machines and Plants, Odessa Technology Institute of Refrigerating Industry, Ukraine, 1964; Technical

Science Candidate Degree, 1971; Doctor of Technical Science, Highest Certificate Commission of USSR, 1986. Appointments: Engineer, Problem Laboratory of Odessa Technology Institute, 1964-66; Head Instructor,1966-74, Assistant Professor, 1974-86, Odessa Technology Institute of Refrigeration Industry; Professor, Head of Department of Cryogenics Plants, 1986-97, Professor, Department of Engineering Thermophysics, 1997-, Odessa State Academy of Refrigating. Publications: Dissertation, Energy characteristics on thermo-electrical batteries of refrigerating systems, 1971; Dissertation, Forming of the effective multi-component working fluids and creation on its base the compression throttle refrigerating systems, 1986; Over 200 scientific articles and books on low temperature physics problems, refrigerating and cryogenic techniques, technic thermodynamics, thermophysics and energetics; Over 50 patents in low temperature engineering. Honours: Certificate, Honoured Scientist and Technician of Ukraine, 1991; Certificates of Academician, Academy of Refrigeration, Moscow, 1995, and Ukraine, 1996. Memberships: International Institute of Refrigerating, Paris, 1986; Active Member, New York Academy of Sciences, 1994. Address: State Academy of Refrigerating, Sofiyevskaya Str 23, flat 12, 270026 Odessa, Ukraine.

**LAWN Connie Ellen,** b. 14 May 1944, USA. Reporter; Writer. 2 sons. Education: BA, Simmons College; Harvard University Courses; L'Institut d'Etudes Politiques Courses. Appointment: Reporter, The White House, 1968-. Publictions: 3 books. Memberships: White House & State Department Correspondence Association; Radio-Television Gallery; Washington Independent Writers. Address: 3622 Stanford Circle, Falls Church, VA 22041-1317, USA.

**LAWRENCE Kathy,** b. 12 September 1949, Arkansas, USA. RN Educator. 2 sons. Education: CC Special Education, 1975; ADN, 1977; BSN, 1992; MSN, 1994. Appointments: Head Nurse, Acting Supervisor, Medical Center Hospital, Odessa, 1978-80; Assistant Head Nurse, Memorial General Hospital, Elkins, West Virginia, 1980-81; Staff Nurse, United Hospital Center, Clarksburg, West Virginia, 1981-83; Primary Nurse, Physicians Office, Naidu Clinic, Odessa, 1985-88; Nursing Supervisor, University of Texas Medical Branch, Galveston, 1988-95; Case Manager, Outcomes Evaluation and Nursing Research, 1995-. Memberships: ANA; Texas Nurses Association; American Association of Diabetes Educators; American Association of Medical Assistants; American Association of Intravenous Theapists; American Radiological Nurses Association; American Association of Neuroscience Nurses; American Medical-Surgical Nurses; Case Management Society; American Intravenous Nurses Society; Alpha Nu Chi; Sigma Theta Tau. Address: 5405 Abvenue Q Rear, Galveston, TX 77551, USA.

**LAWRENCE William Henry Jnr (Fr. Neal),** b. 22 January 1908, Clarksville, TN, USA. Education: AB, Harvard English Literature and Pre-Medicine, Harvard College, 1929; Naval Military Government School Columbia University, 1944-45; MA, Public Law and Government, Columbia University, 1947; St John's Seminary, Minnesota, USA, 1955-60, ordained Catholic Priest; Diploma, Franciscan Language School, Japan, 1960-62; Oxford University, Merton College Summer Session, 1965. Appointments include: Business Executive, 1929-43; U.S. Navy, Lieutenant Commander USNR, 1943-53; U.S. Foreign Service, General MacArthur's Headquarters, Diplomatic Service, 1947-49; USIS Singapore, Malaya, Taiwan 1949-51; Catholic Priest (Monk), St Anselm's Benedictine Priory and Church, Tokyo, 1960-; Sophia University, International College, Ethics and Philosophy, 1963-80; Shirayuri Women's College, Professor English Literature Department 1966-84; Seikei University, 1968-81; Keio University, Oral English, 1968-81; Advisor, Keio International Center, 1981-83.Publication include: Saburo Kurusu, Man and Diplomat, 1970; Soul's Inne Sparkle - Moments of Waka Sensations, 1978; Rushing Ami Tears, 1983; Sparkling Moments - Tanka Poems in English 1993. Honours: Honorary Doctor, Doctor of Literature, World Congress of Poets in Cairo, 1990; Michael Madhusuda Academy, Calcutta, India, Award for Creative Works, 1992 Order of the Rising Sun, Gold Rays with Rosette, award from the Emperor and Government of Japan, 1993; Golden Dov Award in Peace Medallion, Waka/Tanka, Excellence in Ancien Poetic Form, 1995. Memberships include: Asiatic Society c Japan, Honorary Member, Senior Vice President; Association of Foreign Teachers in Japan; International House of Japan Board of Directors, Harvard Club of Japan and Music for Youth Columbia University Alumni Association; American Poetr Association, USA; Japan Pen Club. Address: St Anselm' Benedictine Priory, 4-6-22 Kamiosaki, Shinagawa-ku, Tokyo Japan.

**LAWSON Jennifer,** b. 8 June 1946, Birmingham, AL, USA Television Production, Programming. m. Anthony Gittens, 2 sons. Education: Master of Fine Arts, Columbia University 1974; Honorary Doctor of Letters, 1991. Appointments Director, CPB Program Fund, 1989; Executive Vice President PBS, 1989-95; Consultant, 1995; Executive Producer, A Woman's Place, 1998; Executive Producer, Africa, 1998 Memberships: National Academy of TV Arts and Sciences Address: 1838 Ontario Pl NW, Washington, DA 20009 2109 USA.

**LAWSON Melanie Kay,** b. 2 August 1955, Fort Valley Georgia, USA. Reading Specialist. m. Robert Scott Lawso Senior, 1 son, 1 daughter. Education: MEd degree in Schoo Administration, Abilene Christian University, 1992; Masters Candidate in Higher Education, Texas Technical University Lubbock, Texas, USA, 1995. Appointments: Associate Teacher, Head Start AISD, 1984-88; Head Start/Prekindergarten Teacher, AISD Woodson Head Start Abilene, Texas, USA, 1988-90; Early Childhood Teacher Hardin-Simmons University, 1990 and 1991; English as a Second Language, AISD Pilot Program, Abilene, Texas 1990-92; Kindergarten Teacher, AISD, Jane Long Elementary School, Abilene, Texas, 1992-93; Training Manager, 7th Services Squadron, United States Air Force, Dyess AFB, Texas, 1994-97; Reading Support Teacher, NKC School District, Oakwood Manor Elementary School, Missouri, USA, 1997-. Honours: Scholarship, Big Country AEYC, Local Affiliate of National AEYC, 1985; Scholarship, Key City Reading Conference, 1989; President's Trust Fund Scholarship, Texas Association for Education of Young Children, 1996. Memberships: Higher Education Student Association; Golden Key Honor Society; Phi Delta Kappa (Professional Educational Honor Society); Big Country Association for the Education of Young Children, President, 1994-92, Current Past President former President-elect, membership, Chairperson and Workshop Presenter; Served on Abilene's Children Today; National and Southern Association for the Education of Young Children; Texas Association for Gifted and Talented; Kappa Delta Pi; Teachers of English to Speakers of Other Languages; International Reading Association; Missouri Educator's Association. Address: 1702 Yorktown Drive, Abilene, TX 79603-4216, USA.

**LAX Emeric Imre,** b. 28 March 1925, Tg, Mures, Romania. Professor of Radiology. m. Agneta Blau, 2 daughters. Education: MD, 1950; Doctor in Science, 1972; Primarius and Dozent, 1973; Full Professorship, 1984; Emeritus Professor, 1994. Appointments: Emeritus Professor of Radiology, Hebrew

University of Jerusalem. Publications: More than 50 publications in speciality journals; Co-Authorship in 3 books. Honours: Best Teacher Award, 1991, The Szent-Gyorgyi Albert Medal, 1997. Memberships: The Isralli Assocaition of Radiologists; The Romanian Society of Radiologists; American Society of Radiologists. Address: Hadassah University Hospital, Radiology Dept, Jerusalem 91120, Israel.

**LAZAR Imre,** b. 4 May 1957, Budapest. Internist; Medical Anthropologist. m. Edit Balogh, 2 sons, 1 daughter. Education: MD, 1981, Semmelweis Medical University; Internist, 1986; Psychotherapist, 1990; PhD in Medical Anthropology and Behavioural Medicine, 1998. Appointments: Internist, 1981; Lecturer in Medical Anthropology and Behavioural Medicine, 1990; Head, Psychosomatic Department, St Imre Hospital, 1991; Deputy Head, Department of Medical Anthropology, Institute of Behavioural Medicine, Semmelweis Medical University, 1993-. Publications: Books: Psychoneuroimmunology, 1991; Human Ecology I-II, 1998; 5 chapters in book, Behavioural Sciences, 1998; 4 lecture notes. Memberships: Founding member, Commission of Ethical Relationships of IUAES, 1995; Council member: Hungarian Crohn Association, 1995-; Association of Hungarian Socialpsychiatry, 1995; Association of Psychooncology, 1993-95. Address: H 1089 Budapest, Noyvarad 74, Hungary.

**LAZAREV Sergei,** b. 12 March 1957, Tayga, Russia. Radiophysicist. m. Tatiana, 1 daughter. Education: Diploma, Tomsk University, 1979; PhD, Optics, 1988. Appointments: Researcher, Tomsk Medical Institute, 1980; Researcher, Institute of Atmospheric Optics, Russian Academy of Sciences, Tomsk, 1981, Senior Researcher, 1990-. Publications: 44, 6 patents. Address: Siberian Division, Russian Academy of Sciences, 1 Prospekt Akademicheskii, Tomsk 55 634055, Russia.

**LAZAREV Vladimir,** b. 10 October 1925, Moscow, Russia. Researcher. m. Karlasheva M, 1 son. Education: Dip.Ing, 1951; DSc, 1965; Professor, 1968. Appointment: Chief Researcher, Institute of Information Transmission Problems, Russian Academy of Sciences. Publications: 355 books and papers, 1953-98. Honour: Meritorious Science and Technics Worker of Russia, 1990. Memberships: New York Academy of Sciences; Humboldt Gesellschaft; Academy of Technology Society of Russia. Address: Ostrovitjanova St 33-36, 117279 Moscow, Russia.

**LAZARIS Andreas,** b. 21 May 1965. MD; Pathologist. Education: BM, Athens University Medical Faculty, 1989; Specialisation in Pathology, 1994; Doctoral thesis, Grade A, Athens University Medical Faculty, 1995. Appointments: Resident in Pathology, Hippokration Hospital, Athens, 1990-94; Research Coordinator, Research Laboratory, First Propadeutic Surgical Department, Athens University Medical School, 1992-93; Compulsary Service as Specialist Pathologist, Department Pathology, Volos General Hospital, 1996-97; Lecturer in Pathology, Athens University Medical School, 1998-. Publications: 34 in international medical journals and congress proceedings. Honours: 1st Monograph Award, 24th Annual Hellenic Medical Congress, Scientific Committee, 1998; 2nd Award, Union of Medical Armed Forces Scientists, 1994; Award, Greek Union of Tumour Markers, 1996. Memberships: Hellenic Society of Anatomic Pathology, 1994-; New York Academy of Sciences, 1997. Address: Department of Anatomic Pathology, 75 Mikras Asias Street, Goudi, GR-115 27, Athens, Greece.

**LAZAROIU Dumitru-Felician,** b. 19 Jan 1926, Ploiesti, Romania. Professor; Scientific Consultant. m. Céline Varenne,

2 daughters. Education: Diploma in Electrical Engineering, 1949, PhD in Technical Sciences, 1968, Polytechnic University, Bucharest; Complementary specialisation, Romania, Russia, Hungary, France, Japan. Appointments: University Assistant, 1949-57, Assistant Professor, 1957-72, Professor, 1972-82, reintegrated, 1990, Polytechnic University, Romania; Research Engineer, Electrical Equipment Industry, Bucharest, 1949-58; Technical Director, Electronica Works, Bucharest, 1958-64; Scientific Director, Electrotechnical Research Institute, Bucharest, 1964-69; General Director, Electronic and Electrotechnical Department, Ministry of Industry, 1969-72; General Director for Higher Education and Research, 1972-75, Ministry of Education; International activity, UNESCO, International Labour Organisation, International Electrotechnical Commission and Underwriters Laboratories Inc; Quality Manager, Elscint, France, 1984-96; Independent International Quality Consultant, Paris, 1996-. Publications: Author, co-author, 26 books on electrotechnical and electronic equipment, automatic systems and systems reliability; More than 100 articles and research papers; 7 patents, USA, Japan, France, Germany, elsewhere. Honours: Gold Medal for Patents, Caen, 1972; Romanian Academy Award, 1973. Memberships: Scientists Association of Romania, 1993; French Association of Scientists and Engineers, 1995; EURINGs, 1995; New York Academy of Sciences, 1996. Address: 19 Rue de Penthièvre, F-75008 Paris, France.

**LAZAROVICI Philip,** b. 1 October 1949, Roman, Romania. Scientist. m. Janina, 1 s, 1 d. Education: BSc, Biology, 1975; MSc, Zoology, 1976; PhD, Toxicology, 1981. Appointments: Teaching Assistant, Hebrew University of Jerusalem, 1974-80; Scientist, Agricultural Research Organization Bet-Dagan, Israel, 1980-82; CNRS Research Fellow, France, 1982; Post Doctoral Fellowship, Weizmann Institute of Science, Israel, 1982-84; Visiting Scientist, New York University Medical Center, 1984; Visiting Associate, National Institute of Child Health and Human Development, NIH, USA, 1985-88; Golda Meir Fellow, The Hebrew University, Jerusalem, 1988-89; Lecturer, School of Pharmacy, 1989; Guest Scientist, National Institute of Child Health Human Development, NIH, USA, 1990; Senior Lecturer, School of Pharmacy, 1994; Guest Researcher, Frederick Cancer Research and Development Center, NIH, USA, 1993-94; Adjunct Visiting Scientist, National Institue of Child Health and Human Development, NIH, USA, 1995-96. Publications: Numerous Publications. Honours: Award of Distinction, Faculty of Science, 1978; CNRS, Research Award. Memberships: Israel Physiology, Pharmacology and Biochemical, Molecular Biology Societies; International Society of Toxicology; European Societies of Toxinology and Toxicology; American Society of Toxinology; International Society of Tetanus; American Society for Neuroscience; New York Academy of Sciences; American Chemical Society. Address: Moshe Zvi Segal 30/6, Ramot Ghimel, Jerusalem, Israel.

**LAZARUS Harold,** b. 16 January 1927, New York City, USA. Distinguished Professor of Management. 2 sons. Education: BA, cum laude, New York University, 1949; MS, Columbia University School of Business, 1952; PhD, Columbia University, 1963. Appointments: Dean, School of Business, Hofstra University; Professor, New York University Graduate School of Business; Teacher, Columbia, Harvard, Cornell Universities; President, North American Management Council; Research Director, AT&T Manpower Laboratory; Director, 26 Corporation Boards. Publications: Over 100 articles and books. Honours: Teacher of the Year, New York University, Hofstra University; Citibank Award, Management Publications; Ford Foundation Fellow. Memberships: President, Eastern Academy of Management; Phi Beta Kappa; President, Mid-Atlantic

Association of Colleges of Business Administration; Board, World Management Council; Academy of Management; New York School of Psychiatry. Address: 20191 East Country Club Drive, TH8, Aventura, FL 33180-3016, USA.

**LEAVELL Debbie Susann,** b. 24 May 1952, Detroit, Michigan, USA. Instructor Language Arts. m. Rev Joseph G Leavell Sr, 1 son. Education: AA, Highland Park Community College; Bachelors & Masters in Secondary Education, Wayne State University. Appointments: Educator, 1974-; Evangelist, 1986-. Publications: Freelance Writer of articles & poetry. Honour: Spirit of Detroit Award, 1990, for youth ministry. Membership: Association for Supervision and Curriculum Development. Address: Levey Medical School, 25300 W 9 Mile Rd, Southfield, MI 48034-3906, USA.

**LEBED Andrei,** b. 29 January 1959, Dnepropetrovsk, Ukraine, USSR. Physicist. m. Natalia Lebed. Education: Master, Moscow Institute of Physics and Technology, 1982; PhD, Landau Institute, Moscow, Russia, 1985. Appointments: Associate Professor of Physics, Okayama University, Japan; Associated Member, Landau Institute, Moscow, Russia. Honour: Soviet Youth League Prize in Physics, 1990. Memberships: American Physical Society; Associated member, Landau Institute, Moscow. Address: Department of Physics, Faculty of Science, Okayama University, Okayama 700-8530, Japan.

**LECHEVALIER Hubert A,** b. 12 May 1926, Tours, France. Professor Emeritus. m. Mary Jean Pfeil, 2 sons. Education: Licence of Natural Science, Laval University, Quebec City, Canada, 1947; MS, 1948; PhD, Rutgers University, 1951. Appointments: Assistant Professor, Microbiology, College of Agriculture, Rutgers University, 1951-56; Associate Professor, Microbiology, 1956-66; Professor, Microbiology, Waksman Institute of Microbiology, 1966-91; Professor Emeritus, The State University of New Jersey, 1991-. Publications: Author, Co-Author of over 100 Scientific Papers; Co-author, co-editor of 10 Books. Honours: Sigma Xi; Honorary Member, Société Française de Microbiologie; Lindback Award for Distinguished Research; Charles Thom Award; Bergey Trust Award; New Jersey Inventors Hall of Fame. Address: 131 Goddard Nisbet Road, Morrisville, VT 05661-8041, USA.

**LECHNER Helmut,** b. 19 May 1927, Graz, Autria. Nerologist. m. Maria Bauer, 2 daughters. Education: MD, Karl Franzens University of Graz, 1951. Appointments: University of Zurich Hospital; Extraordinary Professor, 1968; Ordinary Professor, 1972. Publications: 510 Scientific Papers; Co-Author 45 Scientific Books. Honours: Honorary Member, Stoke Council of the American Heart Disease; Honorary Member, Peruvian Society of Clinical Neurophysiology; Honorary Member, Polish Epileptic Society; Honorary Member, Greek Society of Neurology and Psychiatry; Man of the Year, American Biographical Institute; Golden Award of Styria with the Star of the Province of Styria; Honorary Citizenship, City of Pula; Honorary Doctorship, Aristotelian University of Thessaloniki. Memberships: Institute for Clinical Neurophysiology and Neurorehabilitation. Address: Institute of Clinical Neurophysiology and Rehabilitation, Humboldstrasse 47, A-8010 Graz, Austria.

**LECONA Horacio,** b. 24 August 1959, Mexico. Engineer. m. Carmen Correa, 1 son. Education: Bachelor Degree in Communications, Masters Degree in Art Administration and in Organisational Systems. Appointment: Coordinator, Nacional de Danza Del Instituto Nacional De Bellas Artes, Mexico. Membership: International Society for the Performing Arts;

Association of Performing Arts Presenters. Address: Atlixco 147-4, Col Condesa, DF 06140, Mexico.

**LECROY Hoyt Franklin,** b. 8 October 1941, Cherokee Co, Alabama, USA. Music Educator. m. Karen Adams LeCroy, 2 sons, 1 daughter. Education: BA, Jacksonville State University, 1963; MMus, E Carolina University, 1966; PhD, University of Southern Missouri, 1978. Appointments: Public School Music Educator, Music Supervisor, College Professor, 1963-; Music Education, Faculty of Heinhardt College, 1998-. Publications: More than 50 publications in state, national and international journals; National Editorial Board, Music Education Journal. Memberships: Music Educators National Conference; Georgia Music Educators Association; College Music Association. Address: Lake Arrowhead, Box 3031, Waleska, GA 30183, USA.

**LEE An-Chen,** b. 13 August 1956, Chiayi, Taiwan. Educator; Professor. m. Chiu-Chen Ding, 2 sons. Education: BS, Mechanical Engineering, 1978, MS, Mechanical Engineering, 1980, National Tsing Hua University, Taiwan; PhD, Mechanical Engineering, 1986, University of Wisconsin-Madison, USA. Appointments: Associate Professor in Mechanical Engineering Department, 1986-90, Director, Production Automation Centre, 1993-95, Professor, Mechanical Engineering Department, 1990-, National Chiao Tung University. Publications: Over 50 research papers in well-known international journals. Honours: Distinguished Research Award, National Science Council, Taiwan, 1993-94, 1995-96, 1997-98; Distinguished Engineering Professor Award, Chinese Society of Mechanical Engineering, Taiwan, 1995. Memberships: Member, 1988, Editorial Board, 1992-, Journal of Chinese Society of Mechanical Engineering; Editorial Board, International Journal of Applied Mechanics and Engineering, 1996-; Chinese Society of Automation, 1988. Address: National Chiao Tung University, 1001 Ta Hsueh Road, Hsinchu 300-10, Taiwan.

**LEE Andrew,** b. 2 October 1961, Taipei, Taiwan. Conductor. Education: University Studies, Music, Musicology, History, Art History, Conducting; Private Studies, Violin, Piano, Theory, Composition, Conducting. Appointments: Chief Conductor, Lemberger Philharmonic, 1993-. Address: 1963 Ludgate Crescent, Gloucester, Ontario, K1J 8L3, Canada.

**LEE Anne W M,** b. 21 February 1952, Hong Kong. Oncologist. Education: MB BS, 1976, Medical Faculty, University of Hong Kong; DMRT, 1982, FRCR, 1983, Royal Marsden Hospital, UK; FHKCR, 1992, FHKAM, 1993, Institute of Radiology and Oncology, Hong Kong; Stanford University, USA, 1988; Princess Margaret Hospital, Canada, 1988. Appointments: Medical and Health Officer, 1977-85, Senior Medical and Health Officer, 1985-91, Consultant (D2), 1991-93, Institute of Radiology and Oncology, Queen Elizabeth Hospital, Hong Kong; Consultant (D2), 1993-94, Chief of Service (D2), 1994-95, Chief of Service (D3), 1995-, Administration of Dept of Clinical Oncology, Clinical management of cancer patients, Training of doctors in oncology and radiation therapy, Clinical researches (especially on nasopharyngeal carcinoma), Department of Clinical Oncology, Pamela Youde Nethersole Eastern Hospital, Hong Kong. Publications: 17 invited oral presentations; 5 free submission and oral presentations; 5 poster presentations; 25 papers; 5 invited articles in professional journals; 2 book chapters on Complications of radiation therapy; Editor, International Journal of Radiation Oncology, Biology and Physics; Hong Kong Radiographers Journal; American Journal of Clinical Oncology; Journal of the Hong Kong College of Radiologists. Memberships: 2 Hospital Governance & Consultation Bodies; 3 Expert/Grant Awarding Panels; 5 Professional Education and Examinations Bodies;

various offices, Hong Kong Head and Neck Society; Hong Kong College of Radiologists; Hong Kong Society of Radiation Therapy and Oncology; Hong Kong Chemotherapy Society, 991-; Asia Oceanian Clinical Oncology Association, 1992-; Hong Kong Paediatric Haematology and Oncology Study Group, 1994-; American Association for the Advancement of Science, 1997-. Address: Dept of Clinical Oncology, Pamela Youde Nethersole Eastern Hospital, 3 Lok Man Rd, Chai Wan, Hong Kong.

**LEE Benjamin L,** b. 16 November 1954, Taiwan. Professor. m. Jine-Shew Lee, 1 daughter. Education: BS, 1980; MS, 1981; Doctor of Industrial Technology, 1992. Appointments: Manager, China Glory Printing, 1984-89; Assistant Professor, Central Michigan University and Eastern Michigan University, 1992-97; Associate Professor, California State University, Los Angeles, 1997-. Publications include: The Successful Editor; Modern Printing Technology and Management; Printing Paper; Binding; Printing Ink; To Turn Paper Into Gold by Printing; International Trade of Printing. Honours: Outstanding Alumni Award, 1984; Honorable Educator Award, 1985; Faculty Fellow, Academic Service-Learning, 1996. Memberships: National Association of Industrial Technology; Graphic Arts Technical Foundation; International Graphic Arts Education Association. Address: Department of Technology, California State University, 5151 State University Drive, Los Angeles, CA 90032, USA.

**LEE Carla Ann Bouska,** b. 26 November 1943, Ellsworth, Kansas, USA. Nursing Health Care Educator. m. Gordon Larry Lee. Education: RN, Marymount College, Salina, Kansas, 1964; BSN, University of Kansas, 1967; MA, 1972, EdS, 1975, Master n Nursing, 1984, Wichita University; PhD, Kansas University, 1988. Appointments: Staff Charge Nurse, Ellsworth County Veterans Memorial Hospital, 1964-65; Critical, Coronary and Surgical Nurse, Medical Center, University of Kansas, 1966-67, Watkins Memorial Hospital and Student Health Center, 1965-66; Assistant Director, Chief Instructor, School of Nursing, Wesley School of Nursing, Wichita, 1967-74; Assistant Professor, Chairperson Nurse Clinician, Practitioner, Wichita University, 1974-84; Assistant Professor, Graduate Health Administration Program, Wichita University, 1984-92; Associate Professor, Director, Nurse Practitioner Program, Fort Hays University, 1992-95; Associate Professor, Coordinator, Postgraduate Nursing Studies, Clark College, Ohaha, 1995-. Memberships include: Kansas Nurses Association. Address: 1367 North Westlink Avenue, Wichita, KS 67212, USA.

**LEE Dominic Tak Shing,** b. 12 October 1967, Hong Kong. Academic Psychiatrist. m. Kathy Chan. Education: MBChB, Hons, 1991; MRCPsych, 1996. Appointment: Assistant Professor, Psychiatry, 1995-. Publications: Detecting Postnatal Depression in Chinese, British Journal of Psychiatry, 1998. Memberships: Marcé Society; American Psychosomatic Society; Royal College of Psychiatrists. Address: The Chinese University of Hong Kong, Department of Psychiatry Rm 134041, 11 F Prince of Wales Hospital, Shatin New Territories, Hong Kong.

**LEE Edmund,** b. 2 March 1968, San Francisco, California. Photojournalist. Education: Associates of Science in Photography, 1992, City College of San Francisco; BA Journalism with Photojournalism emphasis, 1997, San Francisco State University. Appointments: Sports and News Stringer Photographer, various newspapers, 1992-94; Staff Photographer, Metro Newspaper Group, 1994-95; Stringer Photographer, Pacifica Tribune, 1995-96; Photography Intern, 1997-98; Part-time Staff Photographer, Contra Costa Sun, 1998-. Honours: Winner and various awards for photography. Memberships: Asian American Journalists Association, Bay Area Chapter; National Press Photographers Association; San Francisco Area Press Photographers Association. Address: 7 Crestview Avenue, Daly City, CA 94015-4502, USA.

**LEE Elhang,** b. 19 December 1947, Seoul, Korea. Professor of Physical Science. m. Namsoo Chang, 1 son, 1 daughter. Education: BSEE, Seoul National University, 1970; MS, 1972, MPhil, 1975, PhD, 1977, Yale University, USA. Appointments: Research Fellow, Yale University, 1977-78, Princeton University, 1979-80; Research Specialist, Monsanto Company, 1980-84; Senior Scientist, Team Leader, AT&T Bell Laboratories, 1984-90; Vice-President, Electronics and Telecommunications Research Institute, Korea, 1990-98. Publications: 1 book; Over 250 papers and articles in scholarly journals worldwide; Over 100 talks and speeches worldwide. Honours: Distinguished Academic Award, Korean Physical Society, 1995; National Medal of Honour, Korea, 1996; Fellow, Royal Chartered Institution of Electrical Engineers, UK, 1997; President, Institute of Electrical and Electronics Engineers/LEOS Korea. Memberships: Korean Academy of Science and Technology; New York Academy of Sciences; Fellow, Korean Physical Society; Fellow, Optical Society of Korea; Fellow, MRS, Korea; Sigma Xi; American Association for the Advancement of Science; Future Studies. Address: Inha University School of Electrical and Computer Engineering, Inchon 402-751, Korea.

**LEE James J,** b. 27 August 1939, Taiwan. Environmental Scientist. m. Margie Lee, 1 daughter. Education: PhD, Environmental Science; MS, Geography. Appointments: President, International Environmental Protection Association; President, World Federation of Taiwanese Associations. Publications: Articles in Taiwan Ecological Series; Over 100 papers. Memberships: American Solar Society; American Geographers Society. Address: 14306 Parkvale Road, Rockville, MD 20853, USA.

**LEE Ming-Kwei,** b. 15 November 1951, Taiwan. Electrical Engineer. m. I-Chen Chou, 2 sons, 1 daughter. Education: BS, 1975, Chung Yuan College of Science and Engineering, Taiwan; MS, 1979, Nat Cheng-Kung University, Taiwan; PhD, 1983. Appointments: Associate Professor, Electrical Engineering, 1983-88, Professor, 1988-, National Sun Yat-Sen University, Kaohsiung, Taiwan; Visiting Scholar, Bell Lab, AT&T, Holmdel, New Jersey, 1987-88. Publications: 60 papers; 10 patents. Honour: Outstanding Teaching Award, Ministry of Education, Taipei, 1988. Memberships: IEEE; Chinese Institute Engineering; Chinese Institute Electrical Engineering. Address: National Sun Yat-Sen University, Department of Electrical Engineering, Kaohsiung 80424, Taiwan.

**LEE Ming-Yih,** b. 11 September 1954, Taiwan. Professor. m. Shu Chuan Chou Lee, 2 daughters. Education: PhD, Mechanical Engineering, University of Minnesota, USA, 1981. Appointments: Professor and Chairman, Department of Mechanical Engineering and Graduate Institute of Mechanical Engineering, Chang Gung University, Taiwan. Publications: Over 120 journal articles in the area of Mechanical Engineering and Robotics. Honours: Gold Medal, International Exhibition of Ideas and Inventions; Golden Brain Prize, National Invention Contest, Taiwan; Best Paper Awards, 1st National Conference on Applied Mechanism and Robotics, USA; 1st Place, Best Paper Award, SME 4th World Conference on Robotic Research, USA; etc. Memberships: IEEE; ASME. Address: 401 Chang Gung Med Vill 10th Fl, Taoyuan, Taiwan.

**LEE Roland Robert,** b. 18 July 1954, Cleveland, Ohio, USA. Neuroradiologist. Education: BA Physics, 1975, California Institute of Technology; MA, Physics, University of California at

Berkeley, 1977; MD University of California at Los Angeles, 1985; Residency in Diagnostic Radiology, Brigham and Women's Hospital, Harvard Medical School, Boston, 1986-90. Appointments: Fellowship, MRI, Long Beach Memorial Medical Centre, California, 1990-91; Fellowship, Neuroradiology, University of California at San Francisco, 1991-92; Assistant Professor, Radiology, Johns Hopkins Hospital, 1992-97; Associate Professor of Radiology, University of New Mexico, and Director of Neuroimaging/Magnetic Source Imaging, VA Medical Centre, Albuquerque, 1997-. Publications: Articles in professional journals; Book Editor, Spinal Imaging, 1995. Honours: J Froehlich Award, California Institute of Technology, 1974; Outstanding Teacher Award, UC Berkeley, 1976, Johns Hopkins, 1994; Regent's Scholar, UCLA, 1981-85; Outstanding Reviewer for Radiology, 1994-97; Outstanding Teacher Award, University of New Mexico, 1998. Memberships: AMA; ACR; ASNR; RSNA; ASSR. Address: 815 Piedra Larga Place, NE Albuquerque, NM 87123, USA.

**LEE Soon-Bok,** b. 17 December 1951, Korea. Professor. m. Jin-Sun Lee, 1 son, 1 daughter. Education: BS, Seoul National University, 1974; MS, Korea Advanced Institute of Science and Technology (KAIST), 1976; PhD, Stanford University, USA, 1980. Appointments: Consultant, NucTech San Jose, CA, 1980; Principal Researcher, KIMM, 1981-87; Professor, KAIST, 1988-. Publications: 27 journal papers; 2 patents. Honours: Excellent Researcher Award, 1983; National Honour of Korea, 1984. Memberships: ASME; IEEE; SEM; KSME Director Editor. Address: KAIST Mechanical Engineer Department, Science Town, Taejon 305-701, Korea.

**LEE Sungho H,** b. 3 November 1946, Kyonggi-do, Republic of Korea. m. Hwadong Kim, 17 February 1973, 2 children. Education: BA, Yonsei University, Seoul, Korea, 1970; MA, 1975; Student, Ruhr University, Bochum, Germany, 1976-77; EdD, George Washington University, 1980; Instructor, 1975-76, Assistant Professor, 1981-85, Associate Professor, 1986-90, Professor, 1991-, Dean, College of Education, 1998-, Yonsei University; Director, University Evaluation Korean Council for University Education, Seoul, 1983-90; Member, Presidential Commission for Electoral Reform, 1986-87; Member, Presidential Commission, 21st Century, 1989-93; Assistant Minister, Ministry of Education, Korea, 1993; Member, Presidential Commission for Rebuilding Nation, 1998-. Publications: Author: Shaking Parents and Straying Children, 1997 (award Chosun Daily Newspaper Co, 1997); Co-auth: Scientific Development and Higher Education, 1989 (award NSF, 1986); Academic Profession in the World, Award Carnegie Foundation, 1995; 20 books and numerous articles. Memberships: Board Trustees, Korean Higher Education Association, 1994-; Consultant, New Community Development Movement Association, Seoul, 1996-98; National Advisory Committee for Education Policy, Seoul, 1996-98; Board of Trustees, National Institute of Curriculum Development, 1998-99. Hobby: Golf. Address: Yonsei University Department of Education, Shinchonding 134, 120-749 Sodaemoon-ku Seoul, Korea.

**LEE Tony J F,** b. 10 November 1942, Taiwan. Professor. 1 son, 1 daughter. Education: BS, Pharmacy, Taipei Medical College, 1963-67; PhD, Pharmacology, West Virginia University School of Medicine, 1969-73; Postdoctoral Fellow, University of California, Los Angeles, 1973-75. Appointments: Assistant Professor, 1975-80, Associate Professor, 1980-87, Professor, 1987-, Department of Pharmacology, Southern Illinois University School of Medicine, Springfield; Visiting Professor, Sun Yat-sen University of Medical Sciences, Guangzhou, 1987-; Science University of Tokyo, Japan, 1990; Adjunct Professor, Taipei Medical College, Taiwan, 1996-. Publications:

Several articles in professional journals. Honours: NIH and American Heart Association Grantee. Memberships: American Society for Pharmacology and Experimental Therapeutics, American Association for the Advancement of Science; Society for Neuroscience; American Heart Association Stroke Council; American Heart Association High Blood Pressure Research Council. Address: Southern Illinois University School of Medicine, PO Box 19230, Springfield, IL 62794-9230, USA.

**LEE William Johnson,** b. 13 January 1924, Oneida, Tennessee, USA. Attorney. m. Marjorie Anne Young, 2 sons. Education: Akron University, 1941-43; Denison University, 1943-44; Harvard University, 1944-45; JD, Ohio State University, 1948. Appointments: Served with USAAF, 1943-46; Research Assistant, Ohio State University Law School, 1948-49; Ohio Assistant State Liquor Control Director, Chief of Liquor Purchases, Permit Chief, Assistant Permit Chief and Attorney Examiner, Department of Liquor Control, 1951-57; Assistant Counsel, Hupp Corporation, 1957-58; Part-time Instructor, College of Business Administration, Kent State University, 1961-62; Lawyer, General Practice, 1959-62; Attorney, Papy & Carruthers, 1962-63; Special Counsel, City Attorney's Office, Fort Lauderdale, Florida, 1963-66; Private Law Practice, Fort Lauderdale, Florida, 1965-66; Assistant Attorney General, Office of the Attorney General, State of Ohio 1966-70; Administrator, State Medical Board of Ohio, 1970-85; Practice of Law, 1985-. Memberships: Editorial Board, Ohio State Law Journal, 1947-48; Broward County Bar Association; Akron Bar Association; Columbus Bar Association; Franklin County Trial Lawyers Association; Association of Trial Lawyers of America; American Legion; Phi Kappa Tau; Pi Kappa Delta; Delta Theta Phi; Experimental Aviation Association of Southwest Florida. Address: Apple Valley, 704 Country Club Drive, Howard, OH 43028-9530, USA.

**LEE Yiu-Bun,** b. 18 November 1970, China. Assistant Professor. m. Man-Chu Leung. Education: BEng, 1993, PhD, 1997, Chinese University of Hong Kong. Appointments: Visiting Assistant Professor, Chinese University of Hong Kong, 1987-98; Assistant Professor, Computer Science Department, Hong Kong University of Science and Technology, 1998-. Publications: Numerous publications in leading journals and conferences. Memberships: Institute of Electrical and Electronics Engineers; Association of Computing Machinery. Address: Flat 7, 6/F, Block d, Lok Nga Court, Ngau Tau Kk, KLN, Hong Kong.

**LEE Yuan-Pern,** b. 25 January 1952, Hsinchu, Taiwan. Professor. m. Su-Yuen Fu, 1 son, 1 daughter. Education: BS Chemistry, 1973, National Taiwan University; PhD Chemistry, 1979, University California at Berkeley, USA. Appointments: Research Associate, National Oceanic and Atmospheric Administration, Environmental Research Laboratory, USA, 1979-81; Associate Professor, 1981-85, Professor, 1985-, National Tsing Hua University; Adjunct Research Associate, Institute of Atomic and Molecular Sciences, Academia Sinica, 1988-; Director, Regional Instrument Centre at Hsinchu, 1991-. Publications: Over 75 in professional journals. Honours: National Chair Professor, Ministry of Education, 1997-2000; Scholar Medal, Chinese Chemistry Society, 1996; Outstanding Scholarship, Foundation for promotion of outstanding scholars, 1995-2000; Endowed Chair on Advanced Energy Engineering, University Tokyo, 1997; Outstanding Research Award, National Science Council, Taiwan, 1989-95; 16th Wu Shan-Liang Award, 1993; Scholar Award in Basic Science, Ministry of Education, Taiwan, 1990; Chung-Shian Academic Research Award, 1988; Best Article Award, J of Chinese Chemistry Society, 1986; Outstanding Teaching Award, National Tsing Hua University, 1986. Memberships: Sigma Xi; Chinese

Chemical Society, Taiwan; American Physical Society. Address: 9th Fl 57 Lin-Sheng Rd, Hsin-Chu 300, Taiwan.

**LEGRICE Hylton,** b. Auckland, New Zealand. Ophthalmologist; Businessman. 2 sons, 1 daughter. Education: MB, CHB (New Zealand), University of Otago, 1958; FRCS (England), 1956; Diploma in Ophthalmology, University of London-Institute of Ophthalmology, 1964; FRACS, 1968; FRACO, Royal Australian College of Ophthalmologists, 1974; FRCOphth (England), 1978; Diploma in Obstetrics, University of Auckland. Appointments: Senior Surgical Registrar, Croydon Eye Unit, London, England; Senior Registrar, Senior Resident Surgical Officer, Moorfields Eye Hospital, London; Part-time Visiting Surgeon, Honorary Surgeon, Auckland Group Hospitals, 1970-; Visiting Surgeon, Mercy Hospital, Auckland, 1970-; Consultant Ophthalmic Surgical Practice, Auckland, 1970; Foundation Clinical Reader in charge of Undergraduate Teaching in Ophthalmology, Auckland University Medical School, 1972-83; Director, Deputy Chairman, Chairman, Southern Cross Healthcare Group, 1984-, Southern Cross Hospital's Trust, 1984-, Southern Cross Benefits Ltd, 1984-; Director, Allied Properties Ltd, 1986-89, Montana Wines Ltd, 1987-, Metlifecare Group Ltd, 1994-, several Private Company interests; Director, Chairman, Fund of New Zealand, 1985-86; Ministerial Appointee, Foundation Member, Board of Directors, Deputy Chairman, Chairman, New Zealand Symphony Orchestra (COE) Ltd, 1989-96. Honour: Officer, Order of the British Empire, 1995. Memberships: Honorary Surgeon, Auckland Cricket Association, 1972-; Ophthamological Society of New Zealand, Council, 1974-86, President, 1986-87; Ministerial Medical Appointee, Optician's Board, Wellington, 1979-87; Auckland Medico-Legal Society, Council, 1981-89, President, 1988. Address: Apartment 4, 123 St Stephens Avenue, Parnell, Auckland 1, New Zealand.

**LEI Xian,** b. July 1942, Pingyao County, Shanxi Province. Professor; Procurator. m. Wang Guifang, 2 sons, 1 daughter. Education: LLB, 1968, Beijing Institute of Political Science and Law. Appointments: Director of General Office of Security Bureau of Yuci City, Shanxi Province, 1972-78; Chief-Prosecutor of Jingzhong Procuratorate, Shanxi Province, 1978-84; Associate Professor, Vice Chief-Prosecutor of Shanxi Province, 1984-1990; Director of Bureau of Personnel Education and Training of the Supreme People's Procuratorate (SPP), 1990-96; President and Professor of National Prosecutors College of China, Commissioner of the Procuratorial Commission affiliated to SPP, Secretary-General of the Chinese Foundation for the Education of Senior Prosecutors, 1990-. Publications: 8 books including: A Textbook of Investigation of Procuratorial Organs, 1995; The Education of Procurators and the Development of Procuratorial Cause, 1996; More than 20 compositions also. Memberships: Standing Committee of Chinese Procuratorial Society; Standing Committee of China Political Science Society; China Law Society; Senior Advisor, China Success Research Organisation. Address: National Prosecutors College, Xixiazhuang, Shijing District, Beijing 100041, China.

**LEINWAND Freda,** b. 25 January 1932, Toronto, Ontario, Canada. Photographer. Education: Columbia University, New York City, 1965-67. Appointments: Solo Shows: Radcliffe College, Cambridge, MA, USA, 1981; Group Shows: University Toronto, Canada, 1972; Soho Photo Gallery, New York City, 1972; American Institute Graphic Arts, New York City, 1976; Lowe Art Gallery, Syracuse University, 1982; Galamaqundi Club, New York City, 1988; Westbeth Gallery, 1972-98; Audart Gallery, New York City, 1998. Publications: Contributor to publications including New York Times, Popular Photography, MS Forbes, Family Health, Woman's World, Medical

Economics; many books. Membership: American Society of Picture Professionals. Address: 463 West Street, New York, NY 10014, USA.

**LEITAITE Judita,** b. 27 December 1959, Kaunas, Lithuania. Singer; Mezzo-soprano. m. Dauksys Algimantas, 1 son, 1 daughter. Education: Lithuanian Music Academia, 1984; Studied under Elisabeth Schwarzkopf. Appointments: Laureate of the M Glinka Vocal Contest and Laureate at a vocal contest in Finland. Address: Papilenu 11-44, LT 2000 Vilnius, Lithuania.

**LEKA Elmas,** b. 18 February 1930, Vlore, Albania. Engineer. m. Drita Leka, 2 daughters. Education: Ing dryling diplomate, 1954, High Institute of Petrol and Gas; Candidate of Science, 1982; Docent, 1986; DSc, 1994; Professor, 1998. Appointments: Production Engineer, 1954-57; Chief of Technical Department, Ministry of Industry and Mines, 1957-66; Chief Engineer, Geological Enterprise, Tirana, 1967-71; Chief, Dryling Department, Science Institute of Geology and Mines, 1971-81; Chief, Science Department, Ministry of Industry and Mines, 1981-90. Publications: 4 books; 7 learned texts and scientific technical instruction, Tirana University; 3 scientific studies; 30 other studies and projects of important theoretical and practical values; Nearly 20 scientific articles refereed in different scientific reviews. Memberships: Scientific Council, Ministry of Industry and Mines; Institute of the Studies and Projects of Geology and Mines; Institute of Mineral Technology and Metallurgical Institute. Address: Geological Research Institute, Blloku Vasil Shanto, Tirana, Albania.

**LEMANSKA Miriam,** b. 11 May 1920, Lodz, Poland. Mathematician. 1 son. Education: Master's Degree, Lodz University, Poland, 1952; Dr of Science, Technion, Haifa, Israel. Appointments: Teacher, Lyceum, Lodz, 1946-52; Prelector Teacher, Academy of Lodz, 1951-54; Senior Assistant, Lodz University, 1953-57; Research Worker, IBJ Nuclear Research Institute, Warsaw, 1956-58; Researcher, Soreq, NRC, Yavne, Israel, 1960-85; Retired. Publications: Several in professional journals. Honour: Award, Atomic Commission of Warsaw, 1958. Membership: Israel Nuclear Society.

**LEMBERGS Aivars,** b. 26 September 1953, Latvia. Economist. m. Inara, 1 son, 1 daughter. Education: Faculty of Education, Latvian State University, 1977. Appointments: Laboratory Assistant, 1974-75; Engineer, Economist, Ventspils Port Plant, 1977-78; Politician, 1978-88; Chairman, Executive Committee of Ventspils City, 1988-91; Chairman, Ventspils City Council, 1994-. Publications: 13 Publications; 9 articles in the Independent Morning newspaper. Honour: Honorary Member, Latvian University. Membership: President, Latvian Transit Business Association. Address: 36 Juras, Ventspils, LV 3600, Latvia.

**LENNERSTAD Håkan Elof,** b. 3 April 1952, Sweden. Mathematics Researcher. m. Doris Marie Nielsen, 2 sons, 2 daughters. Education: MS, Chalmers University of Technology, Goteborg, 1977; PhD, 1990. Appointments: Mechanic, Volvo, Goteborg, 1978-82; Researcher, Mittag-Leffler Institute, Stockholm, 1989; University SC Columbia, 1990; Assistant Professor, Chalmers, 1991; University Kariskrona/Ronneby, 1992-. Publications: Patentee; Research Papers, Education Papers. Memberships: Swedish Mathematical Society; American Mathematical Society; Swedish Society of Inventors. Address: University Karlskrona/Ronneby, Dept of Mathematics, 371 79 Karlskrona, Sweden,

**LENNON Joanna Leslie,** b. 5 May 1948, Los Angeles, California, USA. Executive Director. m. Gene Knauer.

Education: BA Social and Political Philosophy, 1970; Teaching Credential, 1979; MS Wildland Resource Science, 1981; PhD Candidate Wildland Resource Science, University of California at Berkely. Appointments: Various teaching and research posts, 1970-80; Deputy Director, Ecological Analysts Inc, Concord, California, 1981; Teaching Associate, University of California at Berkeley, 1981; Project Director, Cynefin Education Conference, Wales, UK, 1982; Project Director, Nature Conservancy Council, London, UK, 1982-83; Executive Director, National Resources Institute, San Francisco, 1983; Founder/Executive Director, East Bay Conservation Corps, Oakland, California, 1983-. Publications: 12 papers and plans in the field of forest guides and urban conservation. Honours: US Forest Service Certificate of Merit, 1978; Graduate Fellowship, Dept of Forestry, UC Berkeley, 1980-82; University Honour Society; National Forestry Honour Society; NASCC Special Award, 1986-87. Memberships: Prtanean, National Women's Society; National Association of Service and Conservation Corps, President. Address: East Bay Conservation Corps, 1021 Third Street, Oakland, CA 94607, USA.

**LEONE Aurelio,** b. 21 July 1942, Rome, Italy. Physician; Researcher. m. Elena Archilli, 3 children. Education: Degree, Medicine, University of Rome, 1966; Certificate, Cardiology, 1969; Certificate, Internal Medicine, University of Pise, 1972; Certificate, Hygiene & Preventive Medicine, University of Genoa, 1977. Career: Assistant Chair, Pathology, Anatomy, University of Rome, 1966-69; Researcher, Clinical Physiology, Medical School, University of Pise, 1969-73; Assistant Professor, Cardiology, City Hospital, La Spezia, 1973-87; Chief, Division of Medicine, City Hospital, Pontremoli, 1987-. Publications: Several articles in professional journals and books. Memberships: Royal Society of Health, England; New York Academy of Sciences; Eques Sancti Gregorii Magni; Lions Club. Address: Division of Medicine, City Hospital, Via Provinciale 27, 19030 Castelnueovo, Magra, Italy.

**LEPS Ants Arvo,** b. 26 January 1936, Pärnu, Estonia. Professor. m. Virve Pold. Education: BA, 1961, University Illinois; MA, 1965; PhD, 1979, UCLA. Appointments: Assistant Physicist, Nuclear Chicago Corporation, Des Plaines, Illinois, 1959-60; Engineering Writer, General Dynamics Corp, Pomona, California, 1962-65; Technical Publications Analyst, System Development Corp, Santa Monica, California, 1965-70; Instructor, Santa Monica College, 1968-70; Research Associate, Institute for Educational Development, El Segundo, California, 1970-71; Consultant Instructional Design, Northridge, California, 1972-; Professor, Dept Radio-TV-Film, California State University, Northridge, 1979-; Coordinator, MA Programme in Mass Communication, 1981-90, Professor, 1988-; Consultant to various TV, film and educational agencies, Estonia, 1990-91. Publications: Author, co-editor, Art of Multi-Image, 1978; Co-Author, Mass Media and the Individual, 1983; Contributor, Chapter on educational and instructional TV to The Encyclopedia of Educational Media Communications and Technology, 1988; Presenter, various media conferences, 1980-; Contributor articles to professional journals. Honour: Teaching of Year Award of Excellence, 1991. Memberships: Board Directors, Build Rehabilitation Industries, North Hollywood; Advisory Committee, Glendale Community College; CFA; Academy TV Arts & Sciences; Society Motion Picture and TV Engineers; International TV Association; Association for Multi-Image, various offices; American Psychological Association; International Interactive Communications Society; Broadcast Education Association; Life member, AECT; and others. Address: California State University, Northridge, Dept Radio-TV-Film, Northridge, CA 91330, USA.

**LESKI Jacek Marek,** b. 1 July 1963, Gliwice, Poland. Biomedical Educator; Researcher. m. Iwona Wanda Fortunka, 2 daughters. Education: MSc, 1987, PhD, 1989, DSc, 1995, Silesian Technical University. Appointments: Assistant, 1988-89, Assistant Professor, 1989-95, Associate Professor, 1995-97, Professor, 1998-, Silesian University. Publications: Author, A new possibility of non-invasive elctrocardiological diagnosis, 1994; Over 100 publications in professional journals. Memberships: IEEE; EMBS. Address: Zwyciestwa 57/20, 44-100 Gliwice, Poland.

**LESLIE Mae Sue,** b. Forrester, Arkansas, USA. Writer. m. Gerald Leslie, 1 son, 1 daughter. Education: BA, Journalism, Sam Houston University, 1966; Diploma, Nursing Home Social Worker, 1968. Appointments: Freelance Writer; Nursing Home Social Worker; Several Secretarial Positions. Publications: Several short stories in professional magazines. Honours: Honorable Mention Certificate, Fantasy Contest, 1989, for Cartoon, 1990; Award, Short Story, 1994; Award, Short Nonfiction, 1994; Award, Short Essay, 1994; Semi-Finalist, Screenplay, 1996. Membership: National Writers Union. Address: 802 Carol Street, Bellaire, TX 77401-4713, USA.

**LEUNG Hung-Fat Frank,** b. 3 October 1964, Hong Kong. Assistant Professor. m. Winnie W Chan. Education: BEng, 1988, PhD, 1992, Electronic and Information Engineering, Hong Kong Polytechnic University; MIEEE, IEEE, 1992; AMIEE, IEE, 1995. Appointments: Engineer Trainee, Development of PABX and Telephone Systems, Lambda Industrial Ltd, 1986-87; Research Assistant, R&D, 1988-89, 1992, Visiting Lecturer (part-time) Teaching, 1988-90, 1991-92, Lecturer, Research and Teaching, 1992-93, University Lecturer, Teaching and Research, 1993-94, Hong Kong Polytechnic; Assistant Professor, Teaching and Research, Hong Kong Polytechnic University, 1995-. Publications: 13 international journal papers; 45 international conference papers; 5 other publications. Honours: Sir Edward Youde Memorial Fund Council Fellowship, 1989, 1990. Address: Department of Electronic and Information Engineering, The Hong Kong Polytechnic University, Hung Hom, Kowloon, Hong Kong.

**LEVASSEUR Lee,** b. 8 April 1950, Hartford, Connecticut, USA. Fine Artist. m. div. 1 son. Education: BS Art Education, 1973, Southern Connecticut State University, New Haven. Appointments: 5 major exhibitions in France, Buenos Aires, America, Portugal and Israel, 1991-. Publications: Featured in International Art Magazine, 1991 and Cable TV Documentary, 1992. Honours: Artitudes International Art Competition, Gallery 54 NYC, 1989; SOHO International Art Competition, Winter 92, Ariel Gallery, NYC. Address: Organic Surrealism, 525 E Main St #40, Branford, CT 06405, USA.

**LEVEE John Harrison,** b. 10 April 1924, Los Angeles, USA. Artist; Designer. m. Suzanne. Education: BA, University of California, Los Angeles, 1948; Postgraduate, New School of Social Research, New York City, 1949. Appointments: Visiting Professor, Art, University of Illinois, 1965, New York University, 1967-68, University of Southern California, 1971. Creative Works: One-man shows include Andre Emmerich Gallery, New York City, 1957-59, 1962, 1966, Gimpel Fils, London, 1958, 1960, 1966, Galerie de France, 1961, 1962, 1964, 1969, Nora Gallery, Jerusalem, Haira, Israel, Museum of Art, Moose Gallery, Toronto, 1963, Phoenix Museum of Art, 1964, University of Illinois, Krannert Art Museum, 1965, Tel Aviv (Israel) Museum, 1969, Margo Leavin Gallery, 1970, Konig Galerie, Geneva, 1971, Galerie la Toabis, Paris, 1975, Palm Springs (California) Museum, 1978, Museum, Nice, France, 1980, Galerie La Closerie des Lilacs, Paris, 1983, 1986,

Galerie 1900-2000, Paris, Galerie de Poche, Paris, 1990; Many architectural projects, France, USA. Honours: Prizes, Watercolor Association, 1955, 1956, Commonwealth of Virginia, Biann, Purchase Award, 1966, Grand Prix Woolmark Foundation, 1974-75, Grand Prix Biennal de Paris, 1969, Ford Grantee, 1969, Tamarind Fellow, Los Angeles, 1969. Address: 19 rue Notre Dame des Champs, Paris 6, France.

LEVIN Victor J, b. 20 October 1934, Gorky, Vitebsk, USSR. Geologist. m. Iraida Ar Charlampova, 2 daughters. Education: ngineer-geologist, Mining Institute, Sverdlovsk, USSR, 1957; PhD, Academy of Sciences, Sverdlovsk, USSR, 1969. Appointments: Main Geologist, parties of Geology Expedition, Cheljabinsk, USSR, 1957-69; Head, Petrologies Laboratory of men Reserve Academy of Sciences, Miass, USSR, 1969-75; Main Geologist, Central Party of AO Ural Geol Mapping Expedition, Ekaterinburg, Russia, 1975-; Curator on rare Metals, 1995-. Publications: 140 scientific articles; Author, Co-author, 4 monographs, 1974, 1990, 1994, 1997. Honours: Honorary prospecting of Depths, 1995; Honoured Geologist of Russia, 1999. Memberships: New York Academy of Sciences; International Academy of Mineral Resources; International Association on Genesis Ore Deposits; Ural Petrography Council. Address: AO Ural Geol Mapping Expedition, 55 Fainera str, 620014 Ekaterinburg, Russia.

LEVINE Michael S, b. West Hollywood, CA, USA. Professor of Genetics. m. Lily Mirels, 2 sons. Education: BA, Genetics, University California at Berkeley, 1976; PhD, Molecular Biophysics and Biochemistry, Yale University, 1981. Appointments: Assistant, Associate, Professor, 1984-90, Department Biological Sciences, Columbia University; Professor, Biology, 1991-96, UCSD; Professor, Genetics, University California, Berkeley, USA, 1996-. Publications: Over 100 articles in professional journals. Honour: Award in Molecular Biology, National Academy of Sciences, 1996. Memberships: Fellow, American Academy of Arts and Sciences; National Academy of Sciences. Address: University California, Department MCB Division Genetics, 401 Barker Hall, Berkeley, CA 94720, USA.

LEVITSKY Yuri, b. 10 March 1931, Perm, Russia. Linguist. m. Rimma Korneevskaya, 1 son. Education: Candidate Diploma, 1970; Docent Certificate, 1978; Doctor Diploma, 1987; Professor Certificate, 1989. Career: Teacher, English, Secondary School, Perm, 1953-57; Engineer, Permskiye Motory, 1957-63; Teacher, English, Chair of Romantic and Germanic Languages, Perm University, 1963-66, Senior Teacher, 1969-74, Head of the Chair of Foreign Languages, 1975-85, Professor, 1988. Publications: 144 publications in Russian, English and German. Address: PO Box 7115, Perm Centre, Russia.

LEVY John-Claude Serge, b. 17 May 1942, Cannes, France. Professor. m. Rouy Helen, 2 sons, 1 daughter. Education: ENS Fellow, 1962; 3rd Cycle Doctorate, 1969; Doctorate of State, 1972. Appointments: Lecturer, University of Paris, 1966; Professor, University of Paris, 1985. Publications: Systems a Memoire; Other publications. Memberships: Fellow of ENS. Address: 5 Place de Rungis, 75013 Paris, France.

LEWANDOWSKI George, b. 14 December 1949, Ostroda, Poland. Priest. Education: Doctor of Evangelic Theology, 980-83; Professor, Catholic University of Lubon, 1990. Appointments: Chief, Pastoral and Theology Studies, Academy of Catholic Theology, Warsaw; Judge, Metropolitan Court. Publications: 8 books, over 100 articles in periodicals. Memberships: Society of Polish Theologists. Address: Niemcewicz 7/9, Apt 182, 02-022 Warsaw, Poland.

LEWANDOWSKi Jerzy Boleslaw, b. 14 August 1948, Lodz, Poland. m. Halina, 1 daughter. Education: MSc, 1974, DSc, 1980, Associate Professor, 1990, Professor, 1992, Technical University of Lodz; Professor, Warsaw University of Technology, 1994. Appointments: Head of Department Production Management, 1990-; Vice-Dean, Faculty of Management, 1990-92, 1997-99; Chief Editor, Scientific Bulletin of Technical University of Lodz - Management, 1992-; Rector, College of Economics, 1994-95. Publications: 10 books include: Ergonomics, 1995; Maintenance Management, 1997; Total Quality Management, 1998; 150 journals. Memberships: The Polish Ergonomic Society; Polish Academy of Sciences; Ergonomics and Occupational Safety Committee of the National Economic Chamber. Address: Skalna 63, 92-007 Lodz, Poland.

LEWIN Pearl G, b. 25 April 1923, Brooklyn, New York, USA. Psychologist. m. S Z Lewin, 2 sons. Education: BA, Hunter College, New York, USA, 1943; MS, University of Michigan, 1947; PhD, New York University, USA, 1980. Appointments: Inspector Chemist, Quartermaster Corps, US Army, 1943-45; Chemist, Chemical Warfare, US Army, 1945; Assistant Psychologist, Bureau of Psychological Services, University of Michigan, 1947-48; Research Assistant, Chemistry, Freelance, New York City, 1955-71; Adjunct Lecturer, 1973-74, Instructor, 1974-79, Assistant Professor, 1979-80, City University of New York; Senior Psychologist, Manhattan Family Court, New York City, 1982-87; Consultant, Freelance, 1987-; Ancillary Appointments: Coordinator, Student Services, 1974-76, Administrator, Academic Regulations, 1974-76, New School Library Arts, Brooklyn College, City University of New York. Publication: Sexist Humor, 1979. Memberships: American Psychological Association; Pi Lambda Theta; Phi Kappa Phi. Address: 4231 N Walnut Avenue, Arlington Heights, IL 60004-1302, USA.

LEWIS Elaine Marie, b. 4 April 1969, Miami, Florida, USA. Special Educator. m. Jim F Lewis. Education: BS, Special Education, 1991; MS, Special Education, 1995; Completing a EDD, Special Education. Appointments: Special Education Teacher, 1991-; ESE Chairperson, 1996-. Publications: Use of Music to Increase Language, Social, Skills with Children with Autism, 1996. Memberships: Autistic Society of America; Council for Exceptional Education. Address: 1680G Windorah Way, West Palm Beach, FL 33911, USA.

LEWIS Horacio Delano, b. 17 January 1944, Panama. Educator. m. Susan, 1 son, 2 daughters. Education: BS, Morningside College, 1967; MA, Northeastern Illinois University, 1972; Certificate, Harvard University, 1989; PhD, Columbia Pacific University, 1996. Appointments: Senior Specialist, Lecturer, Brown University; Assistant Dean, Director, Indiana University; Education Associate, Delaware Department of Education and Adjunct Professorships. Publications: Several Publications. Honours: Jefferson Public Service Award; Republic of Panama President Gold Medal of Achievement. Address: 12 Bristlecone Ct, Newark, DE 19702-3508, USA.

LEWIS Janet, b. 13 August 1950, Yankton, South Dakota, USA. Higher Education Administrator. m. James J Lewis, 2 sons. Education: BA, Sioux Falls College, 1972; MA, University of South Dakota, 1977; PhD, University of Nebraska, Lincoln, 1986; Institute for Educational Management, 1991. Appointments: Tenured Associate Professor, USD, 1982-95; Special Assistant to the President, 1990-91; Program Director, Master of Science in Administration, Chair, Speech Communication Department, USD, 1992-95; Dean, Continuing Education and Director, State-Wide Educational Services, 1995-. Publications: The Multidisciplinary Team in the Public

Schools; Speech and Language Pathology in the Public Schools. Memberships: Advisory Committee, Global Summit on District Education, Washington DC, 1996; 1998 Annual Conference Planning Committee UCEA; 1997 Annual Conference Planning Committee, WCET; Chair, University Advisory Committee, LERN, 1997-. Address: University of South Dakota, 414 E Clark Street, Vermillion, SD 57069, USA.

**LEWIS John,** b. 1 September 1949, Canton, Illinois, USA. Education: Associate Degree Horticulture, Danville Junior College, 1969; BS, Horticulture University of Illinois, 1971; Boomer School of Design, Hawaii, 1976; AFS Commentating School, 1986. Appointments: Vice President, Nouvette Trading Ltd, importer of silk flowers from Europe and China; Lecturer on National Circuit for Trends and Design Concepts; Supervises factory productions in China. Publications: Frequent contributor to PFD Magazine, 1992-. Memberships: AIFD; PFCI; Tennessee State Florists Association; Washington State Florist Association. Address: 5810 Ashridge Road, Memphis, TN 38141, USA.

**LEWIS Ludella,** b. 5 December 1946, Greenville, USA. CPA. 2 sons, 4 daughters. Education: BSBA, Roosevelt University, 1980; PhD, 1994; MBA, 1995. Appointments: Supervising Senior Auditor, 1984-91; Ludella Lewis & Company, 1987-; Village Treasurer, Budget Director, 1990-91. Memberships: Illinois CPA Society; American Society of Notaries; National Notary Association; National Association of Female Executives; American Association of University Women. Address: PO Box A3512, Chicago, IL 60690, USA.

**LEWIS Mark Richard,** b. 4 February 1962, Spokane, Washington, USA. Aerospace Engineer. Education: AA, Highline Comm College, 1982; BSA&A, 1986, MSA&A, 1991, University of Washington. Appointments: Senior Propulsion Engineer, Boeing; Adjunct Professor, Bellevue Comm College; Performance Engineer, Boeing. Publication: AIAA paper, Aerodynamic testing for HSCT: A shock tube design study. Memberships: Tau Beta Pi, Golden Key; American Institute of Aeronautics and Astronautics. Address: 15405m Des Moines Mem Dr, Apt 3202, Burien, WA 98148, USA.

**LEWIS Mary Jane,** b. 22 July 1950, Kansas City, MO, USA. Educator; Communication; Writer; Video Producer. Education: Der, Stephens College, 1971; MA, 1984, PhD, 1996, New York University. Appointments: Adjunct Professor, New York University, 1988-92; Lecturer, Video Producer, University of Hawaii, 1992-. Publications: Godey's Ladys Book, Contributions to the Promotion and Development of the Fashion Magazine in Nineteenth Century. Memberships: America, UMI, 1996; AAUW; Film and Video Association of Hawaii; Hawaii Com TV Producers; KAQ Alumni; National Association of Historical Preservation; NEA; New York University Alumni; The Fashion Group Inc. Address: 91-513 B Hapalua Street, Ewa Beach, HI 96706, USA.

**LEWIS Milton James,** b. 15 October 1941, Newcastle, New South Wales, Australia. Academic. m. Elizabeth Anne Beadman, 1 daughter. Education: BA, (Honours), University of New South Wales, 1962; MA, 1973, PhD, 1977, Australian National University. Appointments: Teacher, Researcher, Tertiary Institutions, Australia, England, New Guinea, 1965-81; Research Fellow, Social Medicine, 1982-84, Research Fellow, History, 1984-85, Senior Lecturer, School of Public Health, 1986, Research Fellow, Public Health, 1988, Senior Research Fellow, 1989-91, Australian Research Council Senior Research Fellow, 1991-95, Senior Research Fellow, 1996, NHMRC Senior Research Fellow, 1997-, University of Sydney. Publications include: Managing Madness: Psychiatry and

Society in Australia 1788-1980, 1988; Disease, Medicine and Empire (with R Macleod), 1988; New Perspectives on the History of Medicine (with H Attwood and R Gillespie), 1990; A Rum State: Alcohol and State Policy in Australia, 1992; Sex Disease and Society (with S Bamber and M Waugh), 1997 Thorns on the Rose: The History of Sexually Transmitted Diseases in Australia, 1998; Histories of Sexually Transmitted Diseases and HIV/AIDS (with P Setel and M Lyons), 1999 Memberships: Australian Society of History of Medicine; New South Wales Society of History of Medicine; Australian Public Health Association; Australian Association for History Philosophy & Social Studies of Science. Address: Department of Public Health & Community Medicine, University of Sydney, Sydney, NSW 2006, Australia.

**LEWIS Sylvia,** b. 28 April 1927, Akron, Ohio, USA. Writer Editor; Associate Executive. m. Allen Lewis, 2 sons, 2 daughters. Education: University Michigan, 1945-47; University Akron, 1961-62. Appointments: Editor, Akron Jewish News, 1948-50; Columnist, Na'Amat Woman, 1993-98; National President, Na'Amat USA, 1993-97; President, Planned Parenthood, Summit, Portage and Meding Counties, 1999-. Honours: Inducted into Ohio Women's Hall of Fame, 1995; J C Penney Golden Rule Award, 1994; Named one of No Ohio's Top Women Professionals by No Ohio Live Magazine. Address: 277 Keith Avenue, Akron, OH 44313-5301, USA.

**LEWTER Helen Clark,** b. 14 January 1936, Millis, Massachusetts, USA. Teacher. m. Alvin Council Lewter, 2 sons, 1 daughter. Education: BA, University of Massachusetts, 1958; MS, Old Dominion University, 1979. Appointments: Teacher, Framingham, Massachusetts, 1960-63, Virginia Beach, Virginia, 1963-65, Chesapeake, Virginia, 1965-67, 1979-. Honours: City of Chesapeake, Virginia, Public Schools Elementary Teacher of the Year, 1984; Kappa Delta Pi, 1985; Phi Kappa Phi, 1985; Who's Who in American Education, 1996-, Who's Who in American Women, 1997- Who's Who in America, 1997-, Who's Who in the World, 1997-, Who's Who in the South and Southeast, 1997, Who's Who Among America's Teachers, 1998, Dictionary of International Biography, 1997-. Memberships: International Reading Association; Virginia Reading Association; Chesapeake Reading Association; National Education Association; Virginia Education Association; Chesapeake Education Association; Delta Kappa Gamma Teachers' Sorority; International Platform Association; Deep Creek Baptist Church. Address: 428 Plummer Drive, Chesapeake, VA 23323, USA.

**Li Bi Wan,** b. February 1940, Xiangtan, Hunan, China. Professor. m. Xu Xuelu, 1 son, 2 daughters. Education: BA, Peoples University of China, 1961. Appointments: Tutor of Graduate Students, Beijing Institute of Business. Publications: Marketing Information Analysis and Management, 1989; Commercial Enterprise Management, 1996. Honour: 2nd Prize, Beijing Technology Study Competition. Memberships: Vice President, Committee of Commercial Enterprise Culture Study, National Commercial Culture Study. Address: Graduate Department, Beijing Institute of Business, 33 Fucheng Road Beijing, China.

**LI Chunbao,** b. 12 November 1928, Jinzhou, China. Professor. m. Dingfang Ji, 1 son, 2 daughters. Education: B Degree, 1952, Beijing University, China; PhD, 1985, State Education Commission, China. Appointments: Lecturer and Associate Professor, 1952-80, Professor and Chief of Department of Electronic Engineering, 1980-84, Teacher of PhD, 1985-95, Dalian Maritime University, China; Chief of Organising Committee, International Conference on The Construction and Life of the Information Society, Beijing, 1989 ublications: Since 1980: To construct a vector field with given url function and divergence function, 1981; The correlative otential function and a new method for solving Maxwell quation, 1984; The correlative potential function and its pplication in electromagnetic wave theory, 1985; The nathematical theory and physical concept of a new method for olving Maxwell's equation, 1989; Editor, The Way Leads to the nformation Society (book of conference), Tokyo, 1990, Beijing, 992; The mathematical modelling of cyclones in the tmosphere using a new computational equation, 1996. lonours: Outstanding Scientific Paper Prize, Chinese lectronic Institute, 1986; Top Grade of Scientific Technology rize, State Education Commission, China, 1987; Outstanding cientist Prize, State Science Commission, China, 1991; Man f the Year, ABI, 1998; Cited among Five Hundred Leaders of nfluence, ABI, 1999. Memberships: Fellow, Chinese Electronic nstitute; Senior Member, IEEE.

**LI Desheng,** b. 17 October 1922, Shanghai, China. etroleum Geologist. m. Zhu Qichang, 1 son, 3 daughters. ducation: BS Geology, 1945, National Central University. ppointments: Chief Geologist, China Research Institute of etroleum, 1963-; Academician, Chinese Academy of ciences, 1991-. Honours: National Science Prize, 1st Class, 982; 2 National Science & Technology Progress Awards, pecial Class, 1985; AAPG Distinguished Achievement Award, 994. Memberships: Geological Society of China; Chinese eophysical Society; Life member, American Association of etroleum Geologists, 1988-. Address: PO Box 910 of Beijing, eijing 100083, China.

**LI Dongfan,** b. 21 September 1937, Tangyin, Henan, China. cientific Researcher. m. Shiyao Li, 2 daughters. Education: raduate, Department of Chemistry, Northwestern University, hina, 1962. Appointments: Assistant Professor, 1978, ssociate Professor, 1986-, Director of Research Subjects, alian Institute of Chemical Physics. Publications: Thirty rticles in professional journals. Honour: Significant chievement of Science and Technology, Chinese Academy of ciences, 1978. Memberships: Fellow, Chinese Science and echnology Society, Chinese Chemical Society, Chinese etroleum Society. Address: Dalian Institute of Chemical hysics, Chinese Academy of Sciences, PO Box 110, Dalian 16023, China.

**LI Feng,** b. 30 June 1949, Shanghai, China. Medical ducator. m. Meng Zhi Hong, 1 son. Education: MD, Shanghai irst Medical College, 1973-79; MPH, School of Public Health, 979-83; PhD, Shanghai Medical University, 1987-90. ppointments: Assistant Teacher, Shanghai Medical University, 979-85; Lecturer, Shanghai Medical University, 1986-92; ssociate Professor, Shanghai Medical University, 1992-97-; irector, Shanghai Medical University, 1997-. Publications: 6 ooks; 40 Theses. Honours: Elitist Young Scholar of ationwide Universities, 1990; Excellent Teaching Fellowship, 997. Memberships: Chinese Rural Health Association; hinese Health Education and Health Promotion Association; hinese Preventative Medical Association; Chinese Medical ssociation. Address: Dept of Health Education, Shanghai ledical University, Shanghai 200032, China.

**LI Heng Rang.** Address: Southwest Bureau of Petroleum, eology No 116 Yihuanlu, Chengdu Sichuan 610081, China.

**LI Hsien-Wen,** b. 3 October 1946, Taiwan. Professor. m. ung-Meh Chen Li, 1 son, 2 daughters. Education: BS leteorology, 1969, MS Oceanography, 1972, National Taiwan niversity; Dr rer nat, 1977, Kiel University, Germany. ppointments: Professor, Department Oceanography, 1980-,

Dean, College of Science and Technology, 1995-, National Taiwan Ocean University. Publications: A Numerical Predictive Model of Tidal Current Northeast of Taiwan, 1996; Preliminary Study of 'Mad-dog' Wave, 1998. Honour: Award for Excellent Teachers in Universities and Colleges, Ministry of Education, 1991. Memberships: IUGG, Chinese Taipei, 1993-; SCOR, Chinese Taipei, 1995-; AGU, 1998-. Address: Department of Oceanography, National Taiwan Ocean University, Keelung 20224, Taiwan.

**LI Jiangang,** b. 3 November 1961, Lujiang, China. Scientist. m. Xiangbo Chen, 1 son. Education: BS, Engineering, 1982; MS, Physics, 1985, PhD, Physics, 1990, Institute of Plasma Physics. Appointments: Manager, HT-6M Department, Division of Physics, Associate Professor, 1992-94, Division Head of Tokamak, Professor, 1994-99, Assistant Director, 1999-, Institute of Plasma Physics, Hefei. Honours: 3rd Class Award for Science and Technology Development, 1996, 100 Talent Project, 1996, 2nd Class Award for Science and Technology Development, 1997, 3rd Class Award for Natural Science, 1997, Chinese Academy of Sciences. Address: Institute of Plasma Physics, 10 Science Road, Hefei 230031, China.

**LI Jing Rong,** b. 11 September 1929, China. Physician. m. Chen Xuan Mei, 3 sons, 1 daughter. Education: Bachelor degree, 1956, Beijing Medical University; Advanced Study, Chinese Traditional Medicine course, 1959-60. Appointments: Resident Physician 1956-70, Neurologist before 1960, Assistant 1956-60, Neurosurgeon 1960-, Lecturer 1978-83, First Affiliated Hospital of Hunan Medical University, Changsha; Attending Physician 1970-78, Neurosurgeon 1970-74, Head Trauma Rescue Party and Dept Hsiang-Qian Railway Compaign Headquarter Hospital, Zhi Jiang; Vice Professor and Vice Charge Physician, Hunan Medical University, Changsha, 1983-88, Guangzhou Medical College Research Institute of Neurosciences, and 2nd Affiliated Hospital of GMC, 1986-; Professor, Guangdon Provincial Colleges and University Senior Degree Judgement Bureau, Guangzhou, 1988-; Vice Director, Neurosurgical Dept, Research Institute of Neurosciences of Guangzhou Med College and 2nd Affiliated Hospital of GMC, 1988-94; Editor, J Neurology and Neurosurgery, Fascicle of Foreign Medical Sciences, 1978-83. Publications: 26 papers in professional journals. Honours: 2nd and 3rd Prize Outstanding Thesis Award, 1993, 1994, 1996, 1998. Memberships: Fellow, Guangzhou Municipal Neurosurgeon Association; New York Academy of Sciences; Guangzhou Overseas Exchange Association; 7th and 8th CPCCC Guangzhou Municipal Committee; International Neurotrauma Society; Malaysia Ipoh Yok Choy Boys and Girls' High School and Perak Girls' Middle School Alumni Association in Guangzhou; Guangzhou Medical College overseas Chinese Association; Editorial Board Member, J Neurology and Neurosurgery Foreign Medical Sciences, Chinese J of Otorhinolaryngology-Skull base Surgery, Guangzhou Medical College J, J of US Chinese Medicine. Address: 250 Chang Gang Don Rd, Guangzhou 510260, Guangdon, China.

**LI Jinlu,** b. 6 December 1939, Shandong, China. Professor of Physical Chemistry. m. Shuting Wang, 2 sons, 1 daughter. Education: Graduated, Department of Applied Chemistry, Tsinghua University, 1963; DEng, Department of Hydrocarbon Chemistry, Kyoto University, Japan, 1998. Appointments: Assistant, Department of Chemical Engineering, 1963-78, Lecturer, Department of Chemistry and Chemical Engineering, 1978-87, Associate Professor, Department of Chemistry, 1987-96, Professor, 1996-, Tsinghua University, Beijing. Publications: 70 papers in international journals including Applied Catalysis, Catalysis Today, and domestic journals, international and domestic conferences. Honours: State Award,

1978; Award from Education Minister, 1986. Memberships: Catalysis Committee, Chemical Society, China; Academic Committee, State Key Laboratory of China; Chemical Technology. Address: Department of Chemistry, Tsinghua University, Beijing, China.

**LI Junbai,** b. 1 December 1964, Neimonggol. Professor. m. Yuxin Huang, 1 daughter. Education: PhD, 1992; Post Doc, 1993-96. Appointments: Vice Chairman, Scientific Committee of Institute; Chairman, Colloid and Interfaces Laboratory; Head of International Joint Laboratory. Publications: Co-Author of over 40 publications in international journals. Address: Inst Photorg Chem, Chinese Academy of Science, Beijing 100101, China.

**LI Ke,** b. 14 November 1931, China. Professor. m. Guilian Zhang, 2 sons, 1 daughter. Education: BSc, Central Party School of China, 1956. Appointment: Professor, Philosophy and Social Science. Publications include: Knowledge of Making You Wise. Honours: 2nd National Prize, 1983; 1st Class Expert of China Special Subsidiary, 1992. Memberships: Committee, Philosophy Task Group for Chinese 8th and 9th Five Year Plans. Address: President of the Party School of Hainan, Hai Kou City, Hainan 570001, China.

**LI Li,** b. 28 November 1942, Jincheng, China. Professor. m. Ning Kang, 1 daughter. Education: BS, Peking University, 1966. Appointments: Associate Research Scientist, 1986, Research Scientist, 1993, Professor of Physics, 1994. Publications: Over 60 scientific papers in international journals on chemical physics and spectroscopy research fields. Address: Department of Physics, Tsinghua University, Beijing 100084, China.

**LI Lite,** b. 3 May 1948, Xi'an, Shanxi Province, China. Professor. m. Ma, 1 son. Education: Bachelor Degree, Northwest Agricultural University, 1981; Masters Degree, Food Processing Engineering, Hokkaido University, 1985; Doctoral Degree, Food Processing Engineering, Hokkaido University, 1988. Appointments: Associate Professor, Department of Food Science, 1988-93; Post Doctoral Research, Japan, 1993-94; Vice President, Professor, Beijing Agricultural Engineering University, 1994-95; Vice President, Professor, China Agricultural University, 1995-. Publications: Many Publications on Food Science. Honours: First Class Award of Excellent Achievements in Education of Universities at Beijing; Great Award of UNUWA; Award of Beijing Excellent Invention; Award of Excellent thesis of CSAE. Memberships: Chinese Academic Society of Agriculture; Chinese Society of Agricultural Engineering; Society of Engineering; Chinese Institute of Animal Products Processing. Address: Center for International Exchange, China Agricultural University, Beijing 100083, China.

**LI Paul Mang Wah,** b. 5 April 1940, Hong Kong. Legal Executive. m. Jeanny Kwok Ching, 1 son, 1 daughter. Education: BA Hons, 1963, University of Hong Kong; College of Law, England, 1969-70; Chinese Law Diploma, 1987, University of East Asia, Macau. Appointments: Assistant Solicitor, M/S Rowdget Young & Co, 1971-74; Assistant Solicitor, M/S Ho & Wong, 1974-75; Partner, M/S K M Lai & Li, 1975-; Hong Kong Law Society's Criminal Law & Procedure Committee, 1991-; Council Member, Hong Kong Society of Notaries, 1993-; China Appointed Attesting Officer, 1991-. Honours: Various community services awards, 1975-. Memberships: Chinese General Chamber of Commerce; Hong Kong Jockey Club; Hong Kong Golf Club; Kowloon Club; Hong Kong Rifles Association; Hong Kong Automobile Association; South China Athletic Association. Address: M/S K M Lai & Li,

10 and 11th Fls Luk Hoi, Tong Bldg, 31 Queen's Road Central Hong Kong.

**LI Pei Yuan,** b. 9 January 1923, Lasting County, Hebei Province, China. Professor of Modern Chinese. m. Xinda Shu, 2 sons. Education: BS 1946, Beijing University. Appointments: Professor, University of Languages of China; Lecturer, Beijing University. Publications: Over 10 textbooks on teaching foreigners Chinese. Address: University of Language of China, Hai Dian District, 15 Xue Yuan Lu, Beijing 1000083, China.

**LI Qing Chang,** b. 5 July 1936, Hebei. Medical Doctor. m. 1 son, 1 daughter. Education: Zhang jia kou medical institutes, 1960. Appointments: Doctor, 1960-82; Head, Department of Medical Hospital, 1982-90; Head, Hospital of Develop area of Qing Huang dao, 1990-94. Publications: Over 500 articles; 10 major scientific research, items and many honorary titles; Lead of Medical Institutes and Lead of Hospital of Medical University Hebei, China, 1994-99. Memberships: Member of International Stereotactic Radiology Institutes. Address: No 19 Shi Fu Rd, Hebei Province Gao Cheng 052600, PR China.

**LI Shiyao,** b. 21 March 1940, Chengdu, Sichuan, China. Scientific Researcher. m. Dongfan Li, 2 daughters. Education: Graduate, Department of Chemistry, Northwestern University China, 1958-62. Appointments: Assistant Professor, 1978-86; Associate Professor, Director of Research Subjects, 1987-95; Professor, Leader of Research Group, 1996-, Dalian Institute of Chemical Physics. Publications: Numerous articles in professional journals. Honours: National Significant Award of Science and Technology, Chinese National Congress of Sciences, 1978; Progressive Award of Science and Technology, Chinese Academy of Sciences, 1996. Memberships: Chinese Science and Technology Society; Chinese Chemical Society; Chinese Petroleum Society. Address: Dalian Institute of Chemical Physics, Chinese Academy of Sciences, PO Box 110, Dalian 116023, China.

**LI Stan Z,** b. 18 August 1958, China. Researcher. Education: BEng, 1982, Hunan University, Changsha, China; MEng, 1985, National University of Defense Technology, Changsha; PhD, 1991, University of Surrey, Guildford, England. Appointments: Research Fellow, School of Electronic and Electrical Engineering, University of Surrey, England, 1990-91; Research Fellow, 1991-94, Lecturer, 1994-97, Senior Lecturer, 1997-, School of EEE, Nanyang Technological University, Singapore. Publications: 5 books and book chapters including: Markov Random Field Modeling in Computer Vision, 1995; 19 journal papers including: 6 papers in IEEE Transactions and International Journal of Computer Vision. Honours: Excellent Paper Award, National Conference on Radar Signal Processing, 1985; 3 year Full Scholarship from British Council 1988-91; Paper nominated for Marr's Prize at International Conference on Computer Vision, 1990; Excellent Paper Award, Asian Conference on Computer Vision, 1993. Memberships: Senior Member, IEEE; IEEE Computers Society. Address: School of Electrical and Electronic Engineering, Nanyang Technological University, Nanyang Avenue, Singapore 639798.

**LI Weilin,** b. 24 August 1963, Hebei, China. Senior Geologist. m. Li Ping, 1 son. Education: BSc, 1985, Dept Petroleum Geology, China University of Geoscience. Appointments: Senior Geologist, 1995, Director, Database Division, 1996, Institute of Petroleum Geology, MGMR, China; Vice Director, Data and Information Centre, China National Star Petroleum Corporation, China, 1998. Honours: Third Grade Science & Technical Progress Award, Ministry of Geology and Mineral Resources for project: Lognormal Analysis System for Petroleum Resource Assessment, 1990; Strategy Data File ystem of Natural Gas Resource Exploration, 1996. Membership: China Geology Association. Address: Institute of etroleum Geology, CNSPC 31 Xueyuan Road, Haidian istrict, Beijing 100083, China.

**LI Weixuan,** b. 11 November 1939, Shanghai, China. rofessor. m. Pingping Xu, 2 daughters. Education: Full rofessor, Certified by Chinese Authority; PhD Equivalent, epartment of Computer Science, University of Ottawa. ppointments: Professor, CHangsha Railway University, 978-79; Visiting Professor, University of Waterloo, 1982-83; isiting Professor, Simon Fraser University, 1989-90; Visiting rofessor, University of Ottawa, 1990-91; Part Time Professor, arious Departments, University of Ottawa. Publications: Graph heory, 1980; Applied Mathematics, 1981; Optimal Sequential earch, 1984; 26 Papers. Honours: Distinguished Research ward; Distinguished Contribution Award; Best Research aper Award; Excellent Teaching Award; Part Time Professor the Year Award. Address: Changsha Railway Inst, Changsha 10075, China.

**LI Wen-ren,** b. 30 May 1914, Fuzhou, China. Cardiothoracic urgeon. m. Pan Pei-zhen, 4 daughters. Education: BSc, eking Yen-Ching University, 1937; MD, University of New ork. Appointments: Associate Professor, Medical College, handong University, 1947-49; Director, Chief Surgeon, uzhou Union Hospital. 1950-70; Vice President, Professor, ujian Medical College, 1959-70; Director, Fujian Provincial ospital, 1971-86; Founder, Director, Fujian Provincial esearch Institute, 1978-88. Publications: 60 papers, 4 books. onours: 12 Awards. Memberships: Life Member, International ongress on Hyperbaric Medicine; Chinese Medical ssociation; Chinese Society of Hyperbaric Medicine; Fujian ssociation of Cardiothoracic Surgery. Address: Fujian rovincial Hospital, Fuzhou 350001, China.

**LI Xiangting,** b. 6 April 1940, Ji Ling, China. m. Zang Hong, son, 1 daughter. Education: Graduated, Central Conservatory f Music, 1963; Studied in Department of National Music. ppointments: Teacher, 1963; Associate Professor, 1986, rofessor, 1996, Central Conservatory of Music; Visiting cholar, University Music School, Cambridge, England, 989-90; Research Associate, Centre of Music Studies, niversity of London, 1990-94. Publications: On the Aesthetics nd Musical Thought of the Performance with Gu Qin, Tang ynasty (monograph); Recordings: Chine: L'Art du Qin Li iangting (CD); Soul of China Gu Qin Recital (CD). lemberships: Vice President, Beijing Gu Qin Research ociety; National Committee, Musicians' Association of China; ouncil Member, International Culture Exchange Centre; astern Artists' Association, UK. Address: Central onservatory of Music, 43 Bao Jia Street, Beijing 100031, hina.

**LI Xiao-Ping,** b. 15 June 1960, Shaanxi, China. eophysicist. m. Cui-Rong Liu, 3 daughters. Education: BS, hina University of Mining and Technology, 1981; PhD, ergakdemie Freiberg, 1989. Appointments: Research eophysicist, Xian Branch, China Central Mining Research stitute, 1982-86; Visiting Scientist, Bergakdemie Freiberg, 986-89; Research Geophysicist, Deutsche Montan echnologie, 1989-92; Research Scientist, University of arlsruhe, 1992-97; Research Scientist, German Geological urvey, 1997; Senior Geophysicist, Petroleum Geo-Services, 997-; Adjunct Professor, China University of Mining and echnology, 1996-. Publications: Several articles in rofessional journals. Honours: Marquis' Who's Who in the orld, 1999/2000; Outstanding People of 20th Century, IBC ambridge; Five Hundred Leaders of Influence, 1999, ABI;

Memberships: Society of Exploration Geophysicists; European Association of Geoscientists & Engineers. Address: Donskiveien 74E, N-1346 Gjenttum, Norway.

**LI Xuerong,** b. Taizhou, Jiangsu, China. Professor of Mechanical Automation and Mechanical Engineering. m. Ren Zhijin, 2 sons, 1 daughters. Education: Bachelor of Engineering, National Tung-Chi University, 1948. Appointments: Professor of Mechanical Automation, Changsha Communications University. Publications: A New Method for CAD of Dimension Synthesis; International Conference of Mechanical Transmission and Mechanism Tianjing University, 1997. Address: Balizhung Beili, No 313 1 303 Shilibao Dajie, Beijing 100025, China.

**LI Yan Fang,** b. 26 December 1937, Shenyang, Liaoning, China. College Teacher. 1 son, 1 daughter. Education: Graduated, Biology Department, Northeast Normal University of China, 1962. Appointments: Cytogenetics Professor, Director of Master Degree. Publication: Botany, 1995. Honours: Excellent Teacher, 1995; The Government Special Award, 1997. Memberships: Vice President, Jilin Botany Institute; Associate Editor, Chinese Botany Bulletin; Vice President, Jinlin Genetics Institute. Address: PLA Agric/Livestock Husbandry University, Biology Teaching/Research Unit, 175 Xian Avenue, Changchun, Jilin 130062, China.

**LI Yao-Juan,** b. 8 June 1933, Fengnan, Hebei, China. Professor. m. Liang Ke-jun, 1 son, 2 daughters. Education: BSc, 1953, Northeastern University; MSc, 1956, Mining University of China. Appointments: A career Professor. Publication: Practive of Application of Systems Engineering Method for Guiding the Treatment of Patients Suffering from Varied Chronic Diseases. Memberships: Executive Director, Chinese Computer Simulation Society; World Consuls Specialist of Science & Technology; and others. Address: Hebei Institute of Science & Technology, 45 Xinhua West Road, Thangshan, Hebei, China 063009.

**LI Yi,** b. 23 August 1965, Shanghai, China. Associate Professor. m. Cheng Chun. Education: BA, Chemistry, 1987; MBA, 1999. Appointments: Vice-Director, Research and Development Centre and Electronic Ceramics Division, Shanghai Institute of Ceramics, Chinese Academy of Sciences, 1995-. Membership: Chinese Ceramic Association. Address: 1295 Ding-Xi Road, 200050 Shanghai, China.

**LI Yin-an,** b. 17 May 1937, Jiangyin, Jiangsu, China. Physicist, Plasma Physics. m. Ru-wen Zhao, 1 son, 1 daughter. Education: Diploma, Zhengzhou University, Henan, China. Appointment: Professor, Institute of Physics, Chinese Academy of Sciences, 1990-. Publications: Physics Dictionary: On Plasma Physics, 1985; Controlled Thermonuclear Fusion, 1992; Numerous papers in professional journals. Honour: Meritorious Certificate of Excellent Book, 1995. Memberships: Vice President, Asian-African Association for Plasma Training; Associate Director, Asian-African Association for Plasma Training Research and Training Centre; Associate Director, Association for Plasma Studies of China. Address: Institute of Physics, Chinese Academy of Sciences, PO Box 603-4, Beijing 100080, China.

**LI Zaiting,** b. Shanghai, China. Professor. m. Wu Weiping, 1 son, 1 daughter. Education: Chemical Engineering, Tsinghua University; Graduate, Petroleum Processing, Petroleum University, 1956. Appointments: Project Head, 1960-79; Director of Research Dept, 1980-88; Technical Director of Petroleum Processing Research Division, 1989-93; Editor in Chief, Petroleum Processing and Petrochemicals, 1994-98.

Publications: Over 50 academic papers; 7 patents. Honours: Outstanding Contribution Certification, State Council of China, 1992; 1st Invention Prize, National Science and Technology Committee of China, 1995. Address: Research Institute of Petroleum Processing, PO Box 914, Peking 100083, China.

**LI Zhishen**, b. 21 November 1935, Weiyuan, Sichuan Province, China. Teacher. m. Jinglin Zhang, 2 daughters. Education: BS. Mathematics Department, Lanzhou University, China, 1957. Appointments: Lecturer, 1978-84, Associate Professor, 1990-, Professor, Mathematics Department, Lanzhou University. Publications: Articles in Equations of Mathematical Physics, Vols I and II. Honours: 2nd Awards om Achievements in Science and Technology, Gansu Province, 1986, 1987; 2nd Award on Achievements in Science and Technology, Chinese Supervisory Bureau on Technology, 1989. Membership: Chairman, Branch Committee, China's Technical Committee for Standardization of Quantities and Units. Address: Mathematics Department, Lanzhou University, Lanzhou 730000, China.

**LI Zhongying**, b. 5 October 1943, Wuxi, Jiangsu Province, China. Nuclear Physicist; Professor. m. (1)Jingying Zhang, (2)Keqin Shi, 1 son, 1 daughter. Education: BS, 1966, Nanjing University. Appointments: Researcher, 1968-88, Professor, 1989-, Director, 1993-, Ionizing Radiation Measurement Laboratory, Institute of Nuclear Physics and Chemistry, China Academy of Engineering Physics. Honours: Great Achievement Award of Science & Technology conferred by Ministry of Nuclear Industry, 1983; Sciences and Technology Advancement Award conferred (twice)by China National Nuclear Corporation, 1986; Sciences and Technology Advancement Award conferred by Industrial Commission of the National Defense, 1992, 1995; Science Foundation Award conferred by China Academy of Engineering Physics, 1994. Memberships: New York Academy of Sciences; International Radiation Physics Society. Address: China Academy of Engineering Physics, PO Box 525-89, Chengdu Sichuan 610003, China.

**LIANG Bin-Shiang**, b. 10 December 1965, Kaohsiung, Taiwan. Computer Scientist; Information Engineer. m. Shu-Er Huang, 1 daughter. Education: BS, 1991, Master's degree, 1991, Doctoral Candidate, 1993-, Department of Computer Engineering, National Chiao-Tung University. Appointments: Adjunct Lecturer, Department of Information Engineering, Chung-Hua Polytechnic Institute, 1993-94; Training Course Lecturer, Chung-Sun Institute of Science and Technology, 1996; Adjunct Lecturer, Department of Material Science and Engineering, National Chiao-Tung University, 1997-, Professional Information Course, Training Division, Taiwan Provincial Government, 1998-; Lecturer, National Computer Course, Tze-Chiang Foundation of Science and Technology, National Tsing-Hwa University, 1998-99; Reviewer, IEEE Inter-Net Computing, 1998-, IEEE Software, 1999-; General Manager, FlowRing Technology Corporation, 1999-. Publications: Co-author, 3 articles in journals and 11 papers published in conference and workshop proceedings. Honour: Winner, National Programming Contest, University Group, Ministry of Education, 1991. Memberships: Student Member, Computer Society, Institute of Electrical and Electronics Engineers, 1993-; Engineering Management Group, 1994-, Engineering Computer-Based System Group, 1994-. Student Member, Association of Computing Machinery, 1993-; Student Member, Computer Society of the Republic of China, 1996-; Chinese Association of Software Quality, 1997-. Address: 3rd Floor, 59, 87 Lane, Naan-chung Street, Hsinchu, Taiwan.

**LIANG Suzhen**, b. 26 August 1944, Jiangsu, China Researcher. m. Guixiang Gu, 1 daughter. Education: MLIS Canada, 1985. Appointment: Information analysing and research, 1973-. Publications: Application of Micro-Computers in Libraries, 1990; Development and Using of Information Resources in Agriculture. Membership: Chinese Society o Agricultural Scientech Information. Address: Information Center, China Academy Agricultural Science, 30 Baishi Qiac Road, Beijing 100081, China.

**LIANG Xian-Yuan**, b. 18 July 1930, Guangdong, China Retired Professor. m. Yan-zhi Ye, 1 son, 2 daughters Education: BSc, Department of Biology, Zhongshan University 1953. Appointments: Assistant Researcher, Preventive Schistosomiasis, 1953-56; Assistant Scientist, Institute o Oceanology, Chinese Academy of Sciences, 1956-80 Assistant Professor, 1985, Instructive Professor for MSc Students, 1986, Department of Biology, Zhongshan University Publications: 40 papers and monographs, 1957-96 Memberships: Chinese Society of Zoology; Chinese Society o Oceanology and Limnology; Chinese Society of Scientific Fisheries; Chinese Society of Crustaceans; Councillor, Chinese Society of Malacology; International Society of Medical and Applied Malacology. Address: 25-204 Suzhou-yuan, Jinar University, Guangzhou, China.

**LIAO Chihong**, b. 16 April 1957, Fuzhou, Fujian, China. m Wang Bin, 1 son. Education: Bachelor of Engineering, Nationa Xian Highway University, Xian, China, 1982; Master o Engineering, 1989, Doctor of Engineering, 1992, Yokohama National University, Yokohama, Japan. Appointments Assistant, National Xian Highway University, China, 1982-86 Doctor Fellow, Japan Science and Technology Agency, Tokyo 1992-95; Director, Sun-Rainbow Co Ltd, Tokyo, 1996-97 Fellow, Japan Science and Technology Corporation, Tokyo 1998-. Publications: How to Keep Fit by Chinese Qigong, 1992 Advanced Combustion Science, 1993; Halon Replacements Technology and Science, 1995; Qigong: The Ideas and the Practice, 1998. Membership: Japan Association for Fire Science and Engineering. Address: National Research Institute of Fire and Disaster, 3-14-1-Nakahara, 181-0005 Mitaka Tokyo, Japan.

**LIAO Quan Wen**, b. 18 December 1946, Quanzhou University Professor. m. Yang Youting, 2 sons. Education: BSc 1968; MSc, 1982. Appointments: Director of Editoria Department, Xiamen University Publishing House, 1987-90 Associate Dean, Dean of Business Management Dept 1990-96, Head of Social Science Academy, Associate Chie Complier of Xiamen University Journal, 1996-, Xiamer University. Publications: Introduction of Management Systen Project, 1988; High Education System Project, 1990. Honours Human Resource Management, won the First Prize of Secon Fujian Province Humanities and Social Science Exceller Achievements in 1994; National Expert with Special Dedicatio enjoying State Council Subsidy, 1993; Prize Chiyu Internationa Excellent Academic Achievement in Japan for Huma Resource Development, 1994; Second Prize of Third Fujia Province Humanities and Social Science Exceller Achievement in 1998 for Personnel Administration Work; Socia Remuneration System and Social Compensation Systen Human Resource Development in East Asia, Second Prize Xiamen Humanities and Social Science Excellent Achievemen Human Resource Development in China, First Prize of Chin National Economic Management Association, 1997; Huma Resource Development and Management, Business Recruitin System, 1998. Memberships: Director, China Busines Management Association; Director, China Social Econom System Project Association; Managing Director, China Nationa

Economic Management Association; Vice Board Chairman of Fujian Province Technological Economy & Management Modernisation Association. Address: Xiamen University, Block 12-101 Seaside, Fujian 361005, China.

**LIAQATH D M,** b. 6 January 1950, Chikballapur. Social Worker. m. Farhat Begum, 3 sons. Education: Diploma in Rural Development Management. Appointments: Consultant; Several Organisations. Memberships: Life Member, Indian Institute of Public Administration, new Delhi; Chairman, Farmers Development Agency. Address: Railway Station Road Cross, Chikballapur 562 101, India.

**LIAW Der-Cherng,** b. 28 October 1958, Taiwan, China. Teacher. m. Yau-Yuh Tsay, 1 daughter. Education: BS, Control Engineering, National Chiao Tung University, 1982; MS, Electrical Engineering, National Taiwan University, 1985; PhD, Electrical Engineering, University of Maryland, 1990. Appointments: Postdoctoral Research Associate, Systems Research Center, University of Maryland, 1990-91; Director, Institute of Control Engineering, National Chiao Tung University, 1994-95; Visiting Professor, Institute for Systems Research University of Maryland, 1996-97; Associate Professor, Department of Control Engineering, National Chiao Tung University, 1991-. Publictions: Global stabilization of axial compressors using nonlinear cancellation and backstepping design; Contact friction compensation for robots using genetic earing algorithms; Reliable control of nonlinear systems; Quadratic polynomial solutions of the Hamilton-Jacobi nequality in reliable control design. Memberships: IEEE; IEEE Control Systems Society; IEEE Circuit and Systems Society. Address: Department of Electrical and Control Engineering, National Chiao Tung University, Hsinchu 300, Taiwan, China.

**LIBBY Ronald T,** b. 20 November 1941, Los Angeles, California. University Professor. 2 daughters. Education: BA, 1965, Washington State University; MA, 1966, PhD, 1975, University of Washington. Appointments: Senior Lecturer, Victoria University, New Zealand, 1987-89; Professor and Chair, Southwest State University, Minnesota, 1989-96; Professor and Chair, Political Science Dept, St Joseph's University, 1996-. Publications: 5 books including: Eco-Wars: Political Campaigns and Social Movements, 1999; 12 articles and contributions to collections; Associate Editor, Journal of Policy Studies; Editor 8 other publications. Honours: Nominated for the Gladys M Kammerer Award of the American Political Science Association, 1992; Nominated for Robert H Ferrell book prize for Distinguished Scholar for American Diplomacy award, and other book prizes and awards; Treasurer-elect, New Zealand Political Science Association, 1988; J Allen Smith Dissertation Fellowship, University of Washington, 1971; Linden Mander Award for best paper in International Relations at University of Washington, 1970; and others. Address: 37 Revere Rd Apt #7, Drexel Hill, PA 19026, USA.

**LIBUS Zofia,** b. 27 March 1930, Wilno, Poland. Chemist. m. 1 daughter. Education: MS, 1952; PhD, 1957; DSc, 1981; Professor, 1997. Appointments: Postdoctoral Fellow, Polish Academy of Sciences, Warsaw, 1957-62; Head, Physical Chemistry Department, Technical University of Gdansk, 1963-. Publications: 35 in professional chemical journals, 40 oral contributions or posters presented at conferences. Honours: 3 Awards, Minister of National Education, 1971, 1976, 1982; Cross of Merit, 1980, 1990; Medal, National Education Committee, 1997. Membership: Polish Chemical Society. Address: ul M. Gomolki 35, 80-279 Gdansk, Poland.

**LIGHTBOURNE Alesa M,** b. 29 July 1952, Carmel, California, USA. Writer. 3 sons. Education: BA, Anthropology,

1974; MA, English, Writing, 1986; PhD, Communications, 1996. Appointments: Principal, Lightworks, 1989-; formerly Corporate Writer, College Instructor, High School Teacher. Publications: Fiction and non-fiction works appear in over 100 publications. Honours: Awards from Washington Press Association, 1990, American Forest Products Association, 1997; Hemlock Awards, 1996; Motorola Quality Award. Memberships: Zones of Peace International, Eastside Peace Coalition; Mothers Against Violence in America; UC Santa Cruz Alumni. Address: 16013 SE 31st St, Bellevue, WA 98008-5701, USA.

**LILEY Elizabeth E,** b. 14 November 1964, Lafayette, Indiana, USA. Journalist; Publicist. m. Roman Goz. Education: Bachelor, Purdue University, 1986. Appointments: Reporter, Acting Bureau Cheif, Journal and Courier; Reporter, Editor, Burlineton Free Press; Associate Director Public. Honours: Mavis Doyle Outstanding Vermont Journalist. Memberships: Champlain Association of Retarded Citizens; Ledgewood South Condominium Association; Hospice of the Champlain Valley and Spectrum Youth Services. Address: 4145 Maquam Shore Road, Swanton, VT 05488, USA.

**LILLIE Betty Jane,** b. 11 April 1926, Cincinnati, Ohio, USA. Professor. Education: BS Ed, College of Mt St Joseph, 1955; BA, College of Mt St Joseph, 1961; MA, Providence College (Theology), 1967; MA, Providence College (Biblical Studies), 1975; PhD, Hebrew Union COllege, 1982. Appointments: Teacher, Athenaeum of Ohio, Cincinnati, 1982-99; Professor, Evening College, University of Cincinnati, 1984-99. Publications: Various Books, Articles, Reviews. Honours: Graduate Student Scholarship; Honorary Memberships; Research Board of Advisors; Honorary Member, Advisory Council, International Biographical Centre; Woman of the Year, American Biographical Institute, 1993, 1994, 1995, 1996, 1997; International Woman of the Year, International Biographical Centre,1992-93, 1996-97; Lifetime Achievement Award, ABI, 1995; Millenium Hall of Fame, ABI, 1998; Presidential Seal of Honor, IBC; Order of International Fellowship, IBC. Memberships: Catholic Biblical Association; Society for Biblical Literature; Biblical Archaeology Society; Eastern Great Lakes Biblical Society; Council on the Study of Religion; Woman's Center for Theological Studies; Ohio Humanities Council. Address: 2704 Cypress Way, # 3, Cincinnati, OH 45212-1773, USA.

**LIN Amy,** b. 22 January 1948, Taiwan. Engineer; Real Estate Investor. m. Edward Y Lin, 1 son, 1 daughter. Education: Bachelor Degree, Business Administration, 1967-71; MEng, 1973-75. Appointments: Senior Industrial Engineer, AL Engineering & Consulting Group; Real Estate Investor. Memberships: Apartment Owners Association; International Institute of Industrial Engineers. Address: PO Box 14404, Irvine, CA 92623-8404, USA.

**LIN Bingyi,** b. 8 January 1937, Fuzhou, China. Professor. m. Zhang Meizhen, 2 sons. Education: BA, 1962, Fudan University. Appointments: Teacher, 1962; Lecturer, 1980; Associate Professor, 1986; Director of History Department, 1987; Professor, 1995. Publications: Chinese History, 1996; History Textbooks for Schools, 1991. Honour: National Exemplary Teacher Prize, 1991. Membership: Shanghai History Research Association. Address: Department of History, Shanghai Education College, 1045 Huihai Rd M, Shanghai 200031, China.

**LIN Bor Luh,** b. 4 March 1935, Xiaman, Fujian, China. Professor. m. Hsin Lee, 3 sons. Education: BS, National Taiwan University, 1956; MS, University of Notre Dame, 1960; PhD, Northwestern University, 1963. Appointments: Professor,

Mathematics, University of Iowa, 1972-; Chair, Department of Mathematics, University of Iowa, 1993-. Publications: More than 80 Papers. Honours: Honorary Professor of Mathematics, Harbin University of Sciences and Technology, 1996. Memberships: American Mathematical Society. Address: Dept of Math, Univ of Iowa, Iowa City, IA 52242 0001, USA.

**LIN Chao-Tien**, b. 23 November 1939, Taiwan. Teacher. m. Mei-Huei. Education: MA, NTU, Taiwan, 1966; PhD, UBC, Canada, 1988. Appointments: Professor of Philosophy, Department of Philosophy, National Taiwan University. Honours: From Classical Logic to Confirmation Logic. Address: Department of Philosophy, National Taiwan University, College of Liberal Arts, 1 Roosevelt Rd, Section 4, Taipei 106, China.

**LIN Chih-Min**, b. 2 March 1959, Taiwan. Professor. m. Hsiu-Hui Wang, 1 son, 1 daughter. Education: BS, 1981; MS, 1983; PhD, 1986. Appointments: Deputy Section Head of System Engineering of a missile system, Chung Shan Institute of Science and Technology, 1986-92; Professor, Department Electrical Engineering, Yuan Ze University, Taiwan, 1993-. Publications: 26 journal papers; 46 conference papers. Honours: Recipient Invention Award, Ministry of Education, Taiwan, 1986; National Medal, Ministry of National Defense, Taiwan, 1990; Research Award, National Science Council, Taiwan, 1994, 1996, 1997, 1998. Memberships: IEEE Control System Society, Executive Secretary, Taipei Section, 1996. Address: Yuan-Ze University Elec Engineering, 135 Far East Rd, Chung-Li Tao-Yuan 32026, Taiwan.

**LIN Fen**, b. 1 July 1951, Zhejiang, China. Doctor. m. Jin Gui-Fen, 1 son. Education: Graduate, 1973, Dept of Medicine, Zhejiang Medical University. Appointments: Attended Zhejiang Medical University for advanced studies, 1975, 1983; Director, First Hospital of WenLing City, 1993-. Publications: 4 works; 118 research papers in medicine in internal and external journals; 4 have been international academic exchanges. Honours: Conferred the title for Special Technical Top-Notch Personnel, 1990; Gained prizes in science and technology 8 times. Memberships: Society of Traditional Chinese Medicine and Western Medicine; Editorial Department, Journal of Applied Clinical Paediatrics. Address: WenLing First Hospital, Zhejiang Province 317500, China.

**LIN Hai-Jui Henry**, b. 22 December 1937, Taiwan. Utility. m. Hsing-Mei Pan, 2 daughters. Education: MB, 1967, Taipei Institute Technology; HRM, 1997, Academy of San Yet Xian University. Appointments: Chief of BLR Auxi, 1976-81; Department Chief of Turbine, 1981-94; Deputy Manager, 1994-. Honours: Heat Exchanger Committee Recognition, 1992; Asia Power-Gen, 1997; Pennwell Conferences & Exhibitions. Membership: ASME. Address: 73-8F Hsin Ten Road, 810 Kaohsung, Taiwan.

**LIN Maw-Wen**, b. 24 November 1946, Taipei, Taiwan. Oil Company Executive. m. Kai-chi Ho, 1 son. Education: BA, Tamkang University, Taipei, 1970; MS, Tennessee Technological University, USA, 1974; PhD, National Chiao Tung University, Taipei, 1995. Appointments: Research Assistant, Ministry of Interior, Taipei, 1971-72; Senior Planner, Research and Development Division, 1974-79, Section Chief, Planning Division, 1980-88, Senior Specialist, 1989-90, Deputy Director, Information Systems Division, 1990-91, Director, Information Systems Division, 1991-, Chinese Petroleum Corporation, Taipei; Associate Professor, Tamkang University, 1977-92; Associate Professor, Fu-Jen Catholic University, Taipei, 1992-. Publications: Time Series Analysis and Forecasting, 2nd edition, 1991; Research and Development Reports. Honours: Excellent Talents Award, Ministry of

Economic Affairs, 1980; Award for Research and Development Report held by Ministry of Economic Affairs, 1982-87; 2nd Prize, 1983-84, 1st Prize, 1985, Award for Research and Development Report held by Executive Yuan; Outstanding Information Systems Award, Republic of China, 1991; Outstanding Information Talents Award, Republic of China, 1993; Honoured as Successful Enterprise Manager of Republic of China, 1995. Memberships: Permanent Member, Chinese Statistical Association, 1976-; Permanent Member, Chinese Management Association, 1980-; Founder Member, Chinese Energy Economics Association, 1984-; International Association for Energy Economics, 1986-; Chinese Open Systems Association, 1993-, Supervisor, 1997. Address: 83 Chung-Hwa Road, Sec 1, Taipei 10031, Taiwan, China.

**LIN Mo-Yen**, b. 1917, Shanghai, China. Attorney-at-Law. Education: BA, Tai Yen Chinese Literature Academy, Shanhai, 1939; BLL, National Fuh Tan University, Shanghai, 1943. Appointments: Judge Advocate, 1944-55; Attorney-at-Law, 1955-; Manager, Central Motion Picture Corporation, Taiwan, 1955-57; Chairman, Tian Hsiang Tourism Development Company Ltd, 1970-; Chairman, Victory Development Corporation, 1971-. Publications: On National Recovery - The Certainty of Chinese Communists Surrender. Honours: Armed Forces Citation, Government of the Republic of China, by President Chiang Kai-Shek, 1960. Memberships: Lawyers Association of Taipei; World Association of Lawyers of the World Peace Through Law Centre; Society for Strategic Studies of China; Doctoral Member, Philosophy of Law, World University Round Table, USA. Address: 10F-6 Rainbow International Building, 106 Hsin Yi Road, Section 3, Taipei, Taiwan, China.

**LIN Shu-Kun**, b. 24 March 1957, Hanchuan, Hubei, China. Chemist. 1 son, 1 daughter. Education: BSc, Wuhan University, 1982; MSc, Academia Sinca, 1985; PhD, Eth-Zurich, 1992. Appointments: President, Molecular Diversity Preservation International, 1995-. Publications: Over 40 Publications, Refereed Scientific Journals. Memberships: American Chemical Society; New Swiss Chemical Society. Address: Molecular Diversity Preservation, Saengergasse 25, Basel CH-4054, Switzerland.

**LIN Yue-Shan**, b. 10 October 1952, Taipei, Taiwan. Obstetrician and Gynaecologist; Laporoscopist; Gynaecologic Oncologist; Pharmacist. m. Yen-Fen Chou, 2 sons, 1 daughter. Education: Bachelor of Pharmacy, Taipei Medical College, 1975; Bachelor of Medicine, National Cheng Kung University, 1989. Appointments: Propagandist, Taiwan Cyanamid Co Ltd, 1977-80; Manager, Lin Teh Yuang Co Ltd, 1981-84; Resident, Ob/Gyn, National Cheng Kung University Hopsital, 1989-93; Visiting Staff: Ob/Gyn, NCKUH, 1993-95, Chi Mei Foundation Hospital, 1995-. Publications: 22 papers in national and international journals. Memberships: Association of Ob/Gyn, ROC, Taiwan; Chinese Association of Gynecologic Endoscopist; American Association of Gynecologic Laparoscopist; International Gynecologic Society; Accreditation Council for Gynecological Endoscopy. Address: Chi-Mei Foundation Hospital, 901 Chung Hwa Road, Yung-Kany Tainan, Taiwan.

**LINČIUVIENĖ Donata**, b. 3 December 1938, Kaunas Lithuania. Philologist; Editor; Translator. m. Augustinas Linčius, 1 daughter. Education: Graduate, 1961, Philological Faculty Vilnius University. Appointments: Editor, Mintis (Idea), 1962-69 Editor, Belles-Lettres, Vaga, 1969-94; Editor, Edition Centre Institute of the Lithuanian Literature and Folklore, 1994-. Publications: Translations from French: Théodore-Valensi Berlioz, 1973, G Perec, Les Choses, 1992, H Bazin, Cri de

Chouette, 1994; A Mourois, Le Cercle de Famille, 1998. Membership: Lithuanian-French Association. Address: P Vileisio 9-11, LT 2055 Vilnius, Lithuania.

**LINDGREN Kaj Brynolf**, b. 4 December 1922, Varkaus, Finland. Professor Emeritus. m. Riitta Haahti, 2 sons, 3 daughters. Education: MA, 1948; DPhil, 1953. Career: Lecturer, German, 1954-62, Associate Professor, German Philogy, 1962-, Professor, 1964-89, University of Helsinki. Honours: Goethe Medal, Gold, 1968; Knight Commander of Finish Lion, 1975; Jacob and Wilhelm Grimm Award, 1981. Memberships: Wissenschaftlicher Rat des Instituts fur Deutsche Sprache, Mannheim; Finnish Academy of Science and Letters. Address: Aamutie 8 B, SF-02210 Espoo, Finland.

**LINDO J Trevor**, b. 12 February 1925, Boston, MA, USA. Psychiatrist. Education:AB, Boston latin School, Boston College, New York University, 1946; Columbia University; Certificate, University of Freibourg, Switzerland, 1953; MD, University of Lausanne, 1957; University of Paris; State University of New York; Kings COunty Hospital; 1957-61; Neuropathology Seminars, Yale University. Appointments: Associate Attending Psychiatrist, St Johns Episcopal Hospital; Clinical Instructor of Psychiatry, Columbia University; Psychiatric Consultant, Brooklyn Bureau of Community Services; Superior Psychiatrist, Ct Valley Hospital, 1961-64; Assistant Visiting Psychiatrists, 1964-66; Senior Psychiatrist, 1966-; Psychiatrist, Bedford Stuyvestant Community Mental Helath Centre, 1976-; Assistant Clinical Professor of Psychiatry, Columbia University, 1981-; Associate Clinical Professor of Psychiatry, 1983-85; Psychiatric Consultant, Marcus Garvey Manor, 1983; Medical Director, Community Mental Health Centre, 1986-. Honours: Fellow, American College of International Physicians, 1983; Distinguished Physician of America, 1990; Life Member, American Psychiatric Association. Memberships: Memorial National Medical Assocaition; Lyndon B Johnson Health Centre; American Psychiatric Association; World Federation for Mental Health; Dr Thomas Matthew Crown Heights Civic Association; Black Psychiatrist of America; Caribbean Federation for Mental Health Professionals; Many other memberships. Address: 1265 President ST, Brooklyn, NY 11213, USA.

**LING Beibei**, b. 6 January 1936, Shanghai, China. Professor of Biophysics. m. Yufang Zhao, 2 sons. Education: BSc, Physics, Peking University, 1957. Appointments: Institute of Atomic Energy, Chinese Academy of Sciences, 1957-58; Assistant Professor, Associate Professor, Full Professor, Director, Harbin Engineering University, 1958-89; Visiting Scientist, University of Michigan, Visiting Professor, State University of New York, USA, 1981-83; Professor, Vice-President, Dean of Graduate School, Zhejiang University t HuaJiaChi, Zhejiang Agricultural University, 1989-. Publications: Over 5 books and chapters including: The Principles of Nuclear Reactor Engineering, 1982, 1989; Basic Principles of Quantum Mechanics, 1988; Basic Radiobiology, 1997; Applications of Radiotracer Technique to Molecular Biology, 1997; Over 70 papers including: A laser Raman spectroscopic study of irradiated TMP in aqueous aerated solutions, 1991; The theory of time-dependent stochastic dynamics of radiation damage and repair of biological systems, Parts I and II, 1992; x-ray irradiation effects on DNA's unscheduled synthesis and replication of barley embryos during their imbihition, 1995; Protection of EGCG on DNA from radiation damage, 1995. Honours include: 2nd Science and Technology Prize, Committee of National Education of China, 1986. Memberships: Director, Biophysical Society of China; Director, Agricultural and Forest Committee, Degree and Graduate Student Education Society, China; Vice-Chairman,

Academic Committee, Nuclear Agronomy Key Laboratory, Agricultural Ministry; Vice-Chairman, Graduate Student Education Society, Zhejiang Province; Standing Committee of Zhejiang Province, CPPCC; Vice-President, Zhejiang Province Committee, China Democratic League. Address: Institute of Nuclear Agricultural Science, Zhejiang University, Hua Jia Chi Campus, 268 Kai Xuan Rd, Hangzhou 310029, P R China.

**LING Chung Mei**, b. 5 May 1931, China. Biochemist. m. Amy Hsieh, 2 daughters. Education: BS, National Taiwan University, 1958; MS, Illinois Institute of Technology, 1962; PhD, Illinois Institute Technology, 1965. Appointments: Head, Virology Laboratory, Abbott Laboratory, North Chicago, Illinois; Research Fellow, Abbott Laboratory, North Chicago, Illinois; Chairman, General Biology Corporation. Honours: Fellow, American Academy of Microbiology, 1982; Life Time Deputy Governor of Board of Governors, 1989; First Five Hundred, International Biographical Centre, 1991. Memberships: American Society Biochemists; American Chemistry Society; American Society Clinical Chemistry; Society of Sigma Xi. Address: KangLing Biotech Corp, 59 Kwang Fu S Rd, Hsinchu Hsien 30316, Taiwan.

**LING Yong Yong**, b. 3 February 1935, Shanghai, China. Professor of Mathematics. m. Neng Di Zhang, 3 daughters. Education: BSci Mathematics, 1957, Peking University, Department of Mathematics and Mechanics. Appointments: Research Assistant, Institute of Mathematics, Chinese Academy of Sciences, Peking; Department of Applied Mathematics, Chinese Sciences and Technology University, Peking, 1957-63; Assistant, Lecturer, Department of Mathematics, Hebei University, Tianjing, 1963-70; Lecturer, Associate Professor, Professor, Department of Applied Mathematics, Tongji University, Shanghai, 1971-. Publications: Author or co-Author 11 papers in professional publications including: The Theory of Time-Dependent Stochastic Kinetics of Radiobiology Effects and the Repair of DNA Systems after Stopping Irradiation, 1995. Honours: Science and Technology Progressive Prize, 2nd class, Committee of National Education of China, 1991; National Achievement in Science and Technology Fulfilled Diploma, Committee of National Science and Technology of China, 1992. Memberships: International Society of Offshore and Polar Engineers, USA; Sciences and Technology Society of China; Society of Relativistic Astrophysics and Gravitation of China; Mathematics Association, Shanghai; Mathematics Society of China. Address: Dept of Applied Mathematics, Tong Ji University, Shanghai 200092, China.

**LINTON John LeRoy**, b. 9 July 1945, Salt Lake City, UT, USA. Photographer; Writer for educational improvement video tapes. m. Blanch Ann Yardley Linton, 15 December 1967, 5 children. Education: BA, Brigham Young University, Provo, USA, 1969. Appointments: Film Producer, KBYU-TV, Provo, UT, 1967-72; Film Producer, BYU Motion Picture Studio, Provo, UT, 1973-76; Producer, Director, Linton Productions, Salt Lake City, UT, 1976-79; Producer, Director, Seven Star Pictures, Salt Lake City, 1979-83; Instructor, Chemistry, Physics, Geology, Biology, Altz High School, Sandy, UT, 1984-86; Media Production Specialist, Jordan School District, Sandy, UT, 1986-89; Producer, Writer, Director, Linton Productions, Sandy, UT, 1989-; Board of Directors, Video Journal of Education, Salt Lake City, UT, 1992-. Publications: The Video Journal of Education, vols I-VIII, photographer, writer, 1991-98. Honours: Silver Award, Utah Advertising Federation, 1977; 1st Place Small Business, Days of '47 Committee, Salt Lake City, 1985; Award of Merit, Salt Lake Tribune, Salt Lake City, 1985; Centennial Certificate, Brigham Young University, Provo, UT, 1975; Learning Award, Learning Magazine, Chicago, Illinois,

1976; Cine Award, Council on International Non Theatrical Events, Washington, DC, USA, 1976; Golden Spike Award of Merit, PRSA/IABC, 1988. Memberships: Sandy City Chamber of Commerce; American Society of Curriculum Development. Address: 10 Northridge Lane, Sandy, UT 84092-4902, USA.

**LIOU Tsung Dao**, b. 15 August 1943, Taiwan, Republic of China. Government Officer. m. Lai Chen Yin, 1 son, 2 daughters. Education: Doctor, De Landbouwwetenschappen, Landbow Universiteit Wageningen, Netherlands, 1987. Appointments: Senior Scientist, Director, Fengshan Tropical Horticultural Experiment Station, 1993. Address: Fengshan Tropical Horticultural Experiment Station, TARI Fengshan, Kaoshsung 83017, Taiwan, Republic of China.

**LIOUBIMOVA Zarema**, b. 2 June 1937, Moscow. Physiologist, Professor. m. L Lioubimova, 2 sons. Education: Biology and Chemistry, 1959; Post Graduate Student, 1959-61; Doctor, Biology Sciences, 1972. Appointments: Head of Department, St Petersburg University, 1988-. Memberships: Council of Applied Physics; Council for Exceptional Children. Address: Leningradskoe Shosse, D 94 K 1 KW 63, Moscow, 125565, Russia.

**LIRKOV Alexander Lubomirov**, b. 16 Dec 1942, Sofia, Bulgaria. m. Petkova Romy, 9 July 1967, 1 son. Education: MSc, Chemical Engineering, 1967, PhD, 1987, University of Chemical Technology and Metallurgy, Sofia. Appointments: Research Fellow, Institute of Radioelectronics, Sofia, 1967-69; Assistant Professor, Technical University of Sofia, 1969-92; Associate Professor, TU, 1992-. Publications: 40 papers published in numerous journals. Memberships: Union of Scientists of Bulgaria, 1975; American Electopl & Surf Fin Soc., 1995; American Electrochemical Society, 1993. Address: Department of Chemistry, Technical University, Sofia 1797, Bulgaria.

**LITVIN Vladimir**, b. 10 February 1932, Dnepropetrovsk, Ukraine. Geographer. m. 30 January 1960, 2 daughters, Elena, Tatiana. Education: Diploma, Moscow University, 1955; Candidate of Geographic Science, 1964; Doctor of Geographic Science, 1980; Professor, 1988. Appointments: Science Worker in Polar Institute of Fishery and Oceanography, 1955-66; Scientific Worker in Atlantic Branch of Institute of Oceanology, 1966-86; Head, Ocean Geography Department, Kaliningrad University, 1987-. Publications: 300 publications including books, Morphostructure of Oceans, 1987; Dissection and Ocean Bottom Morphometry, 1990; World of Submarine Landscapes, 1994; Morphostructure of Earth, 1995. Honour: Honoured Scientist of Russian Federation, 1966; F P Litke Gold Medal of Russian Geographic Society, 1966. Memberships: Russian Geographicical Society, 1970; European Union of Coastal Conservation, 1994; Academician of Russian Ecological Academy, 1995; European Union of Coastal Conservation, 1993. Address: Kaliningrad University, A. Nevsky Street 14, 236041 Kaliningrad, Russia.

**LITVINOV Vladimir**, b. 20 January 1946, Ukraine. Scientist. m. Valeria Litvinov, 1 daughter. Education: MSc, 1969; PhD, 1975; DSc, 1987. Appointments: Research Associate; Professor; Laboratory Manager. Publications: 150 articles in scientific journals. Memberships: American Physical Society; New York Academy of Science and Arts. Address: 6150 North Kenmore Avenue, Apartment 13B, Chicago, IL 60660-2720, USA.

**LIU Ben-Chieh**, b. 17 November 1938, Chungking, China. Teacher. m. Jill Jyh-Huey, 2 sons, 1 daughter. Education: BA, Economics, National Taiwan University, 1961; MA, Memorial

University, 1965; MA, Washington University, 1968; Ph Washington University, 1971. Appointments: Fulbrig Professor of Management, Chicago State University, 1982 Fulbright Professor, Dr, International Business Institut 1996-98. Publications: 5 books; More than 180 article Leading professional journals. Memberships: America Economic Association; American Statistical Associatio Society for Advancement of Management; Southern Economi Association; Society for Information Management Science Address: Chicago State University, 9th at Kings Drive, Chicag IL 60628, USA.

**LIU Hanli**, b. 6 March 1960, Beijing, China. Biomedic Engineering. m. Anqi Wu, 2 sons. Education: MS, Physic Wake Forest University, 1990; PhD, Physics, Wake Fore University, 1994. Appointments: Research Associat University of Pennsylvania, 1992-96; Assistant Professc Biomedical Engineering, University of Texas at Arlingto 1996-. Honours: Outstanding Young Scientist Awar Outstanding Young Faculty Award. Memberships: SPIE; OS. Address: University of Texas at Arlington, Arlington, TX 7601 USA.

**LIU Jin**, b. 12 March 1955, Shanghai, China. Businessma m. Div. 1 son. Education: Graduate, 1987, History Departmer Shanghai East China Normal University. Appointmen General Manager, 1997-, Chairman of Board of Director Shanghai Hengtong Group Co Ltd. Honour: Chaine d Rotisseurs Membership, 1996. Memberships: Directc Shanghai Public Relations Association. Address: Shangt Hengtong Group Co Ltd, Hengtong Intl Mansion, 23 Floor 8! Chang Ning Lu, Chang Ning District, Shanghai, China.

**LIU Keh Fei**, b. 11 January 1947, Beijing, China. Physi Professor. m. Yao Chin Liu, 1 son, 1 daughter. Education: B Tunghai University, 1968; MS, SUNY, Stony Brook, 1972; Ph SUNY, 1975. Career: Research Scientist, CEN Saclay, 197 Research Associate, Adjunct Assistant Professor, UCL 1976-80; Associate Professor, 1980-86, Professor, 198€ University of Kentucky. Publications: Over 100 articles professional journals. Honours: 1st Prize, Theoretical Physic Academia Sinica, 1987; Grand Challenge Award, Departme of Energy, 1988, 1989; Alexander von Humboldt Award f Senior Scientist, Germany, 1990; University Resear Professor, 1992-93; Fellow, American Physical Society, 199 Memberships: American Physical Society; Overseas Chines Physics Association; Bluegrass Chapter, National Conferenc of Community & Justice. Address: University of Kentuck Department of Physics & Astronomy, Lexington, KY 4050 USA.

**LIU Mengjun**, b. 25 April 1965, Wangdu, Hebei, Chin Researcher. m. Qi Jinbo, 1 daughter. Education: Bachelor Agriculture, Hebei Agricultural University, China, 1984; Mast of Agriculture, 1987; Doctor of Science, Beijing Medic University, China, 1993; Post Doctor, National Horticultu Research Institute, South Korea, 1997. Appointmen Assistant Professor, 1987; Lecturer, 1991; Associate Professc 1993; Professor of Pathology, Research Center of Chines Jujube, Hebei Agricultural University, China, 199 Publications: A Taxonomic Study on the Genus Ziziplus; Flo of Wild Fruit Tree in China. Honours: 1 of 100 National Go Examples for Young Researchers; 1 od 10 Most Outstandi Young People of Hebei Province. Membershij Vice-Chairman, Fruit Committee, Chinese Association 1 Agricultural Technique Popularization; Vice-Chairman, Het Youth Association for Science and Technology. Addres Research Center of Chinese Jujube, Hebei Agricultu University, Baoding, Hebei 071001, China.

**LIU Qing,** b. 25 October 1938, Hubei Province, China. Professor. m. Madam Pin Ni, 1 daughter. Education: Bachelor Degree, Chemical Engineering of Polymers, Dalian University of Technology, 1963. Appointments: Department Director, Polymer Sunthesis and Application, Beijing Chemical Engineering Research Institute of Chinese Chemical Engineering Ministry, 1963-72; Department Director, Polymer Synthesis Materials, Research Institute, Beijing Yanshan Petrochemical Corporation, 1972-83; General Engineer, Deputy Director, Research Institute of Beijing, Yanshan Petrochemical Corporation, 1983-96; Deputy Director, National Science Research Center for Synthesis of Nevel Rubber and Technology, 1996-. Publications: Styrene Butadiene Thermoplastic Block Copolymer, 1985; Modification of Tire Tread, 1996; Computer Simulation of Polymeric Process of SBS, 1997. Honours: Award of National Science Conference for N2O4 Sealing Material, 1978; Award of Nawarded, National Science Conference for Cis Polybutadiene Rubber Industrial Technology, 1978; First Class of National Technology Scientific and Technological Advance Price for SBS Integral Industrial Technology with the Capacity of 10000ta, 1996. Memberships: Standing Council, China Synthetic Rubber Industry. Address: No 15 Fenghuangting Road, Fangshan Dist Beijing 102550, China.

**LIU Rang-Su,** b. 18 February 1935, Henyang, Hunan, China. Professor of Physics; Physicist in Solid State. m. Li Ji-Yong, 1 son, 1 daughter. Education: Student, Yuoyong Middle School, Henshan, 1953-59; Graduate, Hunan University, Changsha, 1959-64; Visiting Professor, University of Waterloo, Waterloo, Canada, 1990-92; University of New South Wales, Sydney, Australia, 1998 Professional Certification: Technician; Lecturer; Associate Professor; Professor. Appointments: Technician, Shanghai Electrical Apparatus Research Institute, The Ministry of Machinery Industry, Shanghai, 1964-71; Technician, Xiangxiang Chemical Factory, Hunan, 1971-79; Lecturer, Department of Basic Courses, Hunan University, 1979-86; Associate Professor, Department of Physics, Hunan University, 1986-92; Professor, Department of Physics, Hunan University, 1992-; Director, Institute of Physics for Functional Materials, Hunan University, Changsha, 1994-. Publications: 2 books in Chinese; 70 papers in Chinese; 20 papers in English, in professional journals including: A Model of Double-Layer Structural Units of Amorphous Alloys, 1986; Microscopic Mechanism of the High Strength of Amorphous Alloys, 1989; Structure Factors of Rapidly Quenched Metals, 1992; Simulation Study on the Microstructure Transitions of Liquid Metals During Rapid Cooling Processes, 1995; Resistivities and Temperature Coefficients of Resistivity of Amorphous Alloys with High Content of Metalloid, 1996; Heredity and Stability of Microstructures of Liquid Metals During Solidification Processes, 1997. Honours: Prize of Progress of Science and Technology, Education Committee of Hunan Province, 1987; Prize of Progress of Science and Technology, Ministry of Machinery Industry, China; Grants for Natural Science, National Natural Science Foundation of China, 1993, 1996. Memberships: The Chinese Physical Society, 1985; The Chinese Materials Research Society, 1993; The Program Committee of IPMM'99. Hobbies: Sport; Climbing; Writing. Address: Department of Physics, Hunan University, Changsha, Hunan, China.

**LIU Shih-Chao,** b. 9 July 1921, Peking. m. May-Tsan Liu, 4 daughters. Education: PhD, Mathematics Department, University of Wisconsin, USA, 1965. Address: 10 Range 4 Lane 51 Sec 2, Yenchiuyuan Road, Nankang, Taipei, Taiwan.

**LIU Siang-Chun,** b. 16 September 1937, Changhua, Taiwan. Materials Science Educator; Researcher. m. Joyce

Chen, 2 daughters. Education: Diploma, Taipei Institute of Technology, 1959; MS, Department of Metallurgical Engineering, University of Missouri at Rolla, USA, 1983. Appointments: Served with Taiwanese Reserve Officers Training Corps, 1959-61; Teaching Assistant, 1963-69, Instructor, 1969-75, Associate Professor, 1975-97, Professor, 1997-, Taipei Institute of Technology. Publications: Case Studies in Ceramic Product Development Manufacturing and Commercialization, 1997; Phase Stability of the Al-N System, 1997; Thermodynamics of the Al-C-N-O system for the Production of Aluminium Nitride, 1997; Theoretical Oxygen Pressures for the Active-to-Passive Transition in the Oxidation of Alpha-Silicon Carbide, 1997; Thermodynamic Evaluation for the Co-existence of Al2O3-MgO-MgAl2O4 with Al-Mg Alloy, 1998; Thermodynamic Modeling of Iron Bath Smelting-Energy Balance of SRF, 1998; Thermochemistry of the Al-Mg-O System, 1998; Thermodynamics of the Mg-C-N-O System for Evaluation of MgO-C Bricks, 1998; Other publications in professional journals. Memberships: Metallurgical Society; American Ceramic Society. Address: Department of Materials and Mineral Resources Engineering, National Taipei University of Technology, 1 Chung-Hsiao East Road, Section 3, Taipei 10643, Taiwan, China.

**LIU Xiangsheng,** b. 31 January 1939, Hunan, China. Cultural Worker. m. Xiuying Huang, 1 May 1967, 2 sons. Education: Department of Library and Information Science, Wuhan University, 1960-64. Appointments: Department of Library Science Research, National Library of China, 1964-69; "5.7" Cadre School, 1970-71; Section of Book Selection, 1971, Office of Library Operation, 1972-74, Deputy Director, Section of Classification Systems and Thesaurus, 1974-83, Deputy Director, Department of Acquisition and Cataloguing Chinese Books, 1984-85, Deputy Director, Director, Department of Library Science Research, 1985-95, National Library of China; Secretary General, China Society for Library Science, 1995-. Publications: Theory and Use of Chinese Thesaurus, 1980; Theory of Subject Indexing Language and Subject Indexing, 1985; General Chinese Author Numbering Tables, 1992; Training Textbook for Book Classifying, 1993; Textbook for Classified Chinese Thesaurus, 1994. Memberships: Standing Council, China Society for Library Science; Deputy Director, Academic Committee, China Society for Library Science. Address: National Library of China, 39 Baishi Qiao Road, Beijing 100081, China.

**LIU Xuanhuang,** b. 13 August 1935, Nanchang. Mathematics Educator. m. Changying Shi, 3 sons. Education: BSc, 1956, MSc, 1959, Central China Normal University. Publications: About 50 papers. Membership: Democratic Alliance of China. Address: Jiangxi Elec University, Dept Math, Nanchang 330032, China.

**LIU Yanpei,** b. 1 February 1939, Tianjin, China. Mathematician. m. Fengxiu Li, 1 son, 1 daughter. Education: Graduate, National University of Science and Technology of China. Appointments: Visiting Research Scientist, Rutgers University, USA, 1987, 1990; Visiting Professor, University of Rome, La Sapienza, 1989, 1992; Visiting Distinguished Professor, University Cincinnati, USA, 1997; Professor, Academia Sinica, 1986-, Northern Jiaotong University, 1994-; PhD Advisor, 1989-. Publications: Monographs: Embeddability in Graphs, 1995; Enumerative Theory of Maps, 1998; Theory of Rectilinear Layouts, 1996; Rectilinear Embeddings: Theory & Methods, 1994; Embeddability Theory of Graphs, 1995; Transportation Networks: Theory & Methods, 1998. Memberships: AMS; New York Academy of Sciences. Address: North Jiaotong University, 801 Tower 2, 100044 Beijing, China

**LIU Yong-Li,** b. 5 May 1959, Heilongjiang Province, China. Teacher. m. Yan-Li Zhang, 1 son. Education: Bachelor's degree, 1982, Master's degree, 1985, Northeast Agricultural University of China; Doctorate in Agriculture, Hokkaido University, Japan, 1996. Appointments: Assistant, 1985-88, Lecturer, 1988-96, Associate Professor, 1996-99, Northeast Agricultural University of China; Visiting Scholar, Hokkado University, Japan, 1996-99. Publications: Organ Formation and Plant Regeneration of Tara Vine (Actinidia arguta Planch) Cultured in Vitro, 1995; Organ Formation and Plant Regeneration from Internodal Segments of Actinidia kolomikta Maxim in in-Vitro Culture, 1997; Efficient Propagation Method of Tara Vine (Actinidia arguta Planch) by Etiolation Culture, 1997; Effects of Cold Acclimation and Freezing Solution Treatment on the Survival of Frozen Lateral Buds Excised from in Vitro-Cultured Shoots of Tara Vine (Actinidia arguta), 1998; Plantlet Regenration, Organ Formation and Somatic Embryogenesis from in Vitro-Cultured Root Tissue of Actinidia kolomikta, 1998. Memberships: Japanese Society for Horticultural Science; New York Academy of Sciences. Address: Faculty of Agriculture of Agriculture, Hokkaido University, North 9 West 9, Sapporo 060, Japan.

**LIU Yu,** b. 23 May 1964, Junzhou City, China. Professor; Educator. m. Ya Juan Liu. Education: Master Phil, 1990, PhD, 1994, INSA, France; Post-doctoral degree, 1996, Hong Kong University of Science and Technology. Appointments: Professor of Environmental Engineering, Beijing Institute of Light Industry, 1997-. Publications: 14 technical papers in professional journals; Book in Chinese, Biofilm Reactor Engineering. Honours: Lee Kuan Yew Award, Singapore, 1998; Outstanding Researcher, Beijing Government, 1998. Memberships: American Association for Advancement of Sciences; New York Academy of Sciences. Address: Beijing Institute of Light Industry, Department of Chemical Engineering, 11 Fucheng Road, Beijing 100037, China.

**LIU Yuecui,** b. 26 January 1949, Chenxi, Hunan, China. Teacher, Researcher. Education: Graduate, Southmiddle Forest College; Bachelor of Agriculture. Appointments: Tutor, Postgraduate of Forestry; Management Major, Northwest Forest College; Vice Professor, 1993-. Publications: Forest Inventory Plan, Teach Yourself Books; Forest Mensuration and Forest Management; Forest Calculation and Measuring Managment. Honours: 2nd Grade Award, Province Science and Technology; International Outstanding Artistic Work Award; International Outstanding Accounting Treatise Award; 20th Century Special Studing Field Contribution Award; National Outstanding Treatise Works Award. Memberships: Forestry Management Branch of China Forest Association; Forest System Engineering SOciety of China; China Educationalist Association; World Literature and Artisitic Studying Centre. Address: Department of Forestry, Northwest Forest College, #93 Yanling Shaanxi, China.

**LIU Yung-Hsien,** b. 2 January 1962, Kaohsiung, Taiwan. Obstetrician; Gynaecologist. m. Li Chin Chang, 2 sons, 1 daughter. Education: MD, 1988, Kaohsiung Medical College. Appointments: Embryologist, Infertility Clinic, Yuan's General Hospital; Visiting Staff, Department of Obstetrics and Gynaecology, Kaohsiung Medical College. Memberships: European Society Human Reproduction and Embryology; American Society for Reproductive Medicine; AAAS; New York Academy of Science. Address: 169 Howjinn West Rd, Nan Tze Kaohsiung 811, Taiwan.

**LIVENGOOD Charlotte Louise,** b. 18 June 1944, Los Angeles, California, USA. Education: BS, Secondary Education, Texas A&I University, 1968; MEd, Personal

Guidance and Counseling, North Texas University, 1971; Certificate of Secondary Teaching, Texas; Certificate of Counselor, Texas. Appointments: Counselor, Gus Grissom High School, Huntsville, 1971-72; Teacher, West Springfield High School, 1972-73; Education Specialist, US Department of Defense, El Paso, Texas, 1975-78; Instructor, El Paso (Texas) C.C, 1977-78; Employee Development Specialist, US Office of Personal Management, Dallas, 1978-79; Personal Management Specialist, Department of Veterans Affairs, Houston, 1979-87; Labour Relations Specialist, Department of Veterans Affairs, Department of Veterans Affairs Medical Centre, Houston, 1987-89; Personal Staffing Specialist, Department of Veterans Affairs, Houston, 1989-90; Employee Development Specialist, Academy Training Officer, HUD, Fort Worth, 1990-95; Associate Professor, Arizona State University, 1995-; Training Officer, Department of the Treasury, Bureau of Engraving and Printing, Fort Worth, 1995-. Memberships include: ASTD; AAUW; American Personal and Guidance Association; Texas State Teachers Association; Department of Veterans Affairs Employee Association. Address: US Department of the Treasury, Bureau of Engraving and Printing, Western Currency Faculty, 9000 Blue Mound Road, Fort Worth, TX 76131-3304, USA.

**LIVINGSTON Lee Franklin,** b. 20 February 1942, Boston, Massachusetts, USA. Investor. m. Elaine, 2 sons. Education: School of Visual Arts, New York University, Georgetown University, NY Institute of Finance. Appointments: President, Imperial Consultants Inc. Honour: NJ Man of the Year, 1992. Memberships: Treasurer, AEMT Community Development Corp; Board of Trustees, American Red Cross; President, Amshe Emeth Memorial Temple, 1995-97; Board of Directors, Women Aware Shelter for Victims of Domestic Violence; Treasurer, Jewish Social Service Committee. Address: 12 Derby Lane #4 N, Brunswick, NJ 08902-4729, USA.

**LIVINGSTON Margery Elsie,** b. 29 October 1940, Petoskey, Michigan, USA. Education: BS, honours, Taylor University, 1962; MA, high honours, Wheaton College, 1983; Studies, Columbia Theological Seminary, 1964-65, 1979, University of Paris, Sorbonne, 1970, Daystar International University, 1980, West Chester University, 1989. Appointments: Teacher, Waterford (MI) School System, 1962-64; Educational Missionary, County Division, BCM International, Union County, New Jersey, 1965-69; Educational Missionary, BCM International & AIM International, Albertville, France, 1969-70; Educational Missionary, BCM & AIM Watsa, Zaire, 1970-81; Counselor, Therapist, BCM & AIM Amani Counselling Center, Nairobi, Kenya, 1983-84; Counselor, Therapist, BCM International, Upper Darby, Pennsylvania, 1985-97; Organizer, Director, Member Care Ministries for BCM, 1988-. Publications: Commit Thy Way (editor); Living in Community. Honours: Billy Graham Evangelistic Association Scholar, 1981-83; Graduate magna cum laude, 1983. Memberships: Association of Christian Counselors; Association of North American Missions; American Psychological Association; Alpha Chi; Conservative Baptists of America; BCM International Licensed Psychologist, Commonwealth of Pennsylvania. Address: 74 Ida Red Avenue, Apt 202, Sparta, MI 49345-1279, USA.

**LO Chiu-Yuen Benson,** b. 4 April 1934, Hong Kong. Electronic Engineer. m. Tang Shit-fong, 2 sons, 1 daughter. Education: Certificate in Telecommunications, 1964, Hong Kong Technical College; Diplomas in Telecommunication Engineering, 1964, 1968, British Institute of Engineering Technology (Correspondence), Sydney, Australia; Full Technological Certificate, 1984, City & Guilds of London Institute, UK. Appointments: Radio Technician, Fairco Radio Corporation, 1950-61; Technician, Cable & Wireless, HK, Ltd

961-85; Production Engineer, Golden Eagle Electronics Manufactory Ltd (HK), 1985-98. Memberships: Licentiateship Diploma, City & Guilds of London Institute; Institution of Incorporated Engineers in electronic, electrical and mechanical Engineers; Engineering Council; Alumni Association of Electronic Engineering, Hong Kong Polytechnic University; American Society of Certified Engineering Technicians. Address: 11/FL Flat B6, 1044 King's Rd, Quarry Bay, Hong Kong, China.

**LO Samuel E,** b. 23 November 1929, Tainan, Taiwan. Minister; Professor. m. Charlotte Lo, 2 sons. Education: ThB, Tainan Theological College, 1953; BA, Pasadena College, 1956; MA, MDiv, Boston University, 1962; Certificate, Humanities, Harvard University, 1963; PhD, Philosophical Theology, New York University, 1968; MA, Educational Administration, Point Loma College, San Diego, 1988; PhilD, Religion, Somerset University, England, 1989. Appointments: Pastor, Two Presbyterian Parishes, New York, 1960-69; Assistant Professor, Research Professor, Seton Hall University, 1968-73; Personnel Administrator, Support Agency, Presbyterian Church, USA General Assembly, New York City, 1973-74; Business Sectors Management and Teaching, Essex College, New Jersey, 1975-80; Professor, Theology, Tainan and Taiwan Theological Seminaries, 1981-84; Parish Associate, Northminster Presbyterian Church, San Diego, 1985-87; Minister of Youth, Taiwan Lutheran Church, San Diego, 1986, Olympic Presbyterian Church, Los Angeles, 1987-88; Managing Director, Flamingo Garden Incorporated & Taiwanese-American Committee on Aging in Southern California, 1987-89; Minister, English Congregation, Canaan Taiwanees Christian Church, Mountain View, California, 1989-91, Chatham Presbyterian Church, New Jersey, 1991-96; Retired, 1996. Publications: 2 books. Honours: Scholar, New York University, 1968; 2 American Historical Association Grants. Memberships: Council on Scientific Study of Religion; American Academy of Religion; Philosophical Association of America; American Association of University Professors; Association for Asian Studies; Presbytery of Newton; Presbyterian Church, USA; American Association of Retired Persons; Retired Clergypersons. Address: 560 Carriage Drive, Plain City, OH 43064, USA.

**LO Virginia Wong Yee-Ching,** b. 13 May 1934, Hong Kong. Social Worker. m. John Lo, 2 daughters. Education: BA Social Welfare, 1958, University of California at Berkeley; Masters in Social Work, 1962, NY University. Appointments: Deputy Superintendent of Social Service of Society for the Aid and Rehabilitation of Drug Abusers, Hong Kong, 1969-92; Temporary Advisor, UN WHO, Regional Office for Western Pacific Working Group on Early Intervention Programmes in Drug Abuse. Publications: Treatment of Drug Dependence in Therapeutic Community, and Aftercare, 1981; The Female Addict in Hong Kong, 1983; Rehabilitation of Young Addicts, 1987. Memberships: Drug Awareness Committee of Lions Club International, Hong Kong and Macau, 1987-92; Chairperson of Programme Sub-Committee of Drug Awareness Committee, 1987-88, 1988-89. Address: Dept of Social Work, Hong Kong Shue Yan College, Wai Tsui Crescent Braemar Hill Road, North Point, Hong Kong.

**LOBODA-CACKOVIC Jasna,** b. 29 March 1930, Homec, Slovenia. Researcher; Physicist; Artist; Sculptor; Painter. m. Zlinko Cackovic. Education: Diploma in Physics, 1960, MSc Solid State Physics, 1964, University Zagreb; Promotion work and PhD, 1970, Fritz-Haber Institut der Max-Planck Gesellschaft, Berlin, and University of Zagreb; Learned art from Father Peter Loboda and self taught. Appointments: Scientist, Atom Institute Ruder Boskovic, Zagreb, 1960-71; Honorary

Assistant, University Zagreb, Croatia, 1961-65; Post doctoral, 1970-72, Scientist, 1972-97, Fritz-Haber Institut der Max-Planck Gesellschaft, Berlin. Career: Over 150 sculptures and relief; 1000 paintings presented at various exhibitions, in professional journals and books, 1968-; Permanent representation, Bildhauergalerie Plinthe, Berlin, 1987-95. Publications: Over 65 scientific articles to professional journals and books. Honours: Euro medal in gold, Art and Culture, Exhibition Zurich, 1989; Euro art plaquette, Exhibition Paris, 1989; 3 European Art Honorary Prizes, Germany, 1994-95; 2nd and 3rd places for sculpture and photography at international exhibitions, Germany, on the Internet, 1995, 1998. Memberships: New York Academy of Science, 1996; Deutsche Physikalische Gesellschaft, 1972-95. Address: Im Dol 60, 14195 Berlin, Germany.

**LOEBER Dietrich André,** b. 4 January 1923, Riga, Latvia. University Law Professor. m. Anita Hasselblatt, 1955, 4 children. Education: Dr iur, University of Marburg; Diploma, Hague Academy of International Law; MA, Columbia University New York. Appointments: Attorney at Law, 1954-66; Editor of law journal, Osteuropa-Recht, 1955-60; Research Associate, Max Planck-Institute of Foreign and International Private Law, Hamburg, 1958-70; Exchange Scholar, Lomonosov University, Moscow, 1961; Research Associate, Harvard Law School, 1963-64; Professor, University of Kiel, 1966-; Visiting Professor, 1970, 1974, University of California, Los Angeles; Stanford University, 1971, 1973; University of Adelaide, 1977; Columbia University, 1980-81, 1983; University of California, Berkeley, 1985, 1986; University of Latvia, Riga, Spring 1991; Tartu University, Fall 1991; Dean Faculty of Law, University of Kiel, 1985-87. Publications: About 5 books and 130 articles including: Urheberrecht der Sowjetunion, 1966, 1981; Der hoheitlich gestaltete Vertrag, 1969; Diktierte Option, 1972, 1974; East-West Trade, 4 vols, 1976-77; Ruling Communist Parties and Their Status Under Law, 1986; Regional Identity Under Soviet Rule, 1990. Honours: Dr iur honoris causa, University of Latvia, 1991; Three Stars Order (Latvia), 1995; Great Medal, Academy of Sciences of Latvia, Riga, 1995. Memberships: Scientific Board, 1984-90, Federal Institute of Communist and International Studies, Cologne; Vice President, 1986-92, Director for European Affairs, 1992-94, Association for the Advancement of Baltic Studies, USA; Foreign Member, Academy of Sciences, Latvia, Riga, 1990-; Emeritus Professor, 1989. Address: Gehlenkamp 14, Hamburg D22559, Germany.

**LOEFFLER Elke Susanne,** b. 11 April 1967, Tuebingen. Economist. Education: MEc, 1990, Washington University, St Louis; Diploma in Economics, 1993, Master Political Science, 1995, University of Tuebingen; Doctor of Administrative Sciences, 1998, Speyer. Appointments: Research Institute for Public Administration, 1993-97; Public Management Service, OECD, 1997-. Memberships: Verein Fuer Social Politik; CAPAM; Freiherr-Vom-Stein-Gesellschaft. Address: OECD PUMA, 2 Rue Andre Pascal, F 75775 Paris Cedex 16, France.

**LOENNING Per,** b. 24 February 1928, Bergen, Norway. Bishop; Professor. m. Ingunn Bartz-Johannessen, 3 sons, 1 daughter. Education: Cand theol, 1949; Dr theol, 1955; Dr philos, 1959, University Oslo; Dr litt (h.c.), 1986, St Olaf College, Northfield, Minnesota. Appointments: Bishop of Borg, 1969-75; of Bergen, 1987-94; Professor, University Oslo, 1976-81, Centre d'Etudes Decumeniques, Strasbourg, 1981-87; Member of Parliament, 1957-65. Publications: 43 books on philosophy, theology, devotion, essays including: Studies on Pascal 1958, 1980 Kierkegaard, 1954; Creation - an Ecumenical Challenge. Honour: Pax Christi Award, St John's University, Collegeville, Minnesota, 1975. Memberships: Royal Norwegian Society of Sciences; Norwegian Academy of

Sciences and Humanities. Address: Lovenskiolds Gate 19a, N-0260 Oslo 2, Norway.

**LOGUNOV Anatoly A,** b. 30 December 1926, Obsharovka, Samara, Russia. Theoretical Physicist. m. Eshliman Anna N, deceased, 1 son, deceased, 1 daughter. Education: Graduate, Lomonosov Moscow State University, 1951; Doctor of Physics and Mathematics, 1959; Professor, 1961; Corresponding Member, USSR Academy of Sciences, 1968; Full Member, USSR Academy of Sciences, now Russian, 1972. Appointments: Vice Director, Laboratory Theoretical Physics Joint Institute of Nuclear Research, Dubna, 1956-63; Director, Institute for High Energy Physics, Protvino, 1963-74; Vice President, Academy of Sciences, 1974-91; Rector, Moscow State University, 1977-92; Director, State Research Center, Institute for High Energy Physics, 1993-. Publications: More than 400: Lectures on Relativity and Gravitation Theory; The Updated Analysis of the Problem; On the Dynamics of Electron; Relativistic Theory of Gravitation; The Third Irisated Bridge; General Principles of the Quantum Field Theory; Introduction to Axiomatic Quantum Field Theory. Honours: Lenin Prize, 1970; The State Prize, 1973, 1984; Hero of Socialist Labour, 1980; Order of Honour, 1962; Four Order of Lenin, 1971, 1975, 1980, 1986; Order of Merit Native Country, 1995; Order of Pole Star (Mongolia); Order of Yugoslavian Banner, Yugoslavia; Golden Medal Merit for Science and Humankind, Czechoslovakia; Lyapunov Medal; Gibbs Medal. Memberships: Doctor Honorary, Universities of Helsinki, Finland; Prague, Czech; Havana, Cuba; Belgrade, Yugoslavia; Berlin, Germany; Sofia, Bulgaria; Bratislava, Slovakia; Vasada, Soka, Tokai, Japan; Full Professor Honorary, Institute of Fundamental Research, Molise, Italy. Address: SRC Institute for High Energy Physics, 1 Pobeda Str, 142284, Protvino, Moscow, Russia.

**LOJDA Ladislav,** b. 18 January 1926, Litohor. Research Worker, Veterinary Medicine. m. Jirina Simova, 2 sons. Education: Diploma Medicus Veterinarius, 1950; Doctor of Veterinary Medicine, 1950; Candidate of Science, 1968. Appointments: Veterinary General Practitioner, 1950-56; Specialist, Reproduction of Domestic Animals, 1956-58; Region Veterinary Specialist, 1958-62; Senior Research Worker, 1962-92. Publications include: Heredopathology of Reproduction in Domestic Animals, 1971; Cytogenetics of Animals, 1989; History and Perspectives of Genetic Prevention in Veterinary Medicine, 1996. Honour: Medal, Merits of Development in Veterinary Sciences, 1977. Memberships: Genetic Society, Academy of Sciences, Brno; Cytogenetic Society, Academy of Sciences, Praha; Czech Biology Society, Academy of Sciences, Brno. Address: Listi 7, 614 00 Brno, Czech Republic.

**LOKHOV Rudolf Yermolaevich,** b. 14 December 1939, Tskhinval, Russia. Bio-Organic Researcher. m. Svetlana S Lokhova, 1 son. Education: Diploma, Politechnical Institute, Kiev, 1963; PhD, Chemistry, Research Institute of Organic Products, Moscow, 1971. Appointments: Engineer, Technologist, Vitamins Factory, Umanski, Russia, 1963-71; Consultant in Oncology, Krupp-Stal, Dusseldorf, Germany, 1991; Consultant in Oncology, Sandoz, Switzerland, 1992; Director, Republican Centre of Medico-Biological Problems, Vladikavkaz, Russia, 1992-96; Director, Research Institute of Biochemical Engineering of Cells, International Academy of Technological Sciences, Vladikavkaz, 1993-; Professor, North Ossetian State University, Vladikavkaz, 1993-. Publications include: Nutrition and Cancer: Nonorthodox Approaches, 1993; Introduction to Nanobiology, 1999. Memberships: Russian Federation of the Academy of Technological Sciences; New York Academy of Sciences. Address: 51 Mamsurova Street, Vladikavkaz 362008, Russia.

**LOLJA Saimir A,** b. 16 March 1963, Elbasan, Albania. Industrial Chemist. m. Iliriana, 1 son. Education: BSc Industrial Chemistry, 1987; Military Chemical Certificate, 1987; PhD Industrial Chemistry, 1994; Oil Industry Operations and Economics Certificate, 1995; Wharton Executive Development Progress Certificate, 1995. Appointments: Assistant-Researcher, 1987-91, Researcher & Lecturer c Chemical Processing Plant Design & Economics, 1991- University Tirana Faculty of Natural Sciences; Teaching Schedule Executive, 1993-96. Publications: Book Fundamentals of Design & Economics, 1998; Papers in professional journals. Memberships: Affiliate Member, ICHemE Active Member, NYAS; Association for the Protection & Preservation of the Natural Environment of Albania. Address University of Tirana Faculty of Natural Sciences, Bu Deshmoret e Kombit, Tirana, Albania.

**LONG Yaoting,** b. 27 February 1941, Wuhan, China Chemist. m. Lu Miaoqin. Education: Graduate, Huazhong University of Science and Technology. Appointments Environmental Chemistry. Publications: Environmental Analysis; Environmental Monitoring and Analysis; Ion Mobility Spectra of Selected Amines and their Applications in Field Testing with the Use of a Portable IMS Device; Selective Determination of Dimethoate Using Ion Mobility Spectrometry with Single and Mixed Alternate Reagent Ions. Address Research Center for Eco-Envioronmental Sciences, Chinese Academy of Sciences, Beijing 100085, China.

**LOOMER Gerald Earl,** b. 5 May 1947, Hot Springs, South Dakota, USA. Teacher. 1 son, 1 daughter. Education: BS Physics, St John's University, 1969; MS Physics, South Dakota School of Mines and Technology, 1972. Appointments: South Dakota School of Mines and Technology, 1969-71; Philip High School, South Dakota, 1972-74; Lakefield High School Minnesota, 1974-78; Central High School, Rapid City, 1978-89 TI-IN Network, San Antonio, Texas, 1987-88; Stevens High School, Rapid City, 1988-. Honours: South Dakota Teacher o the Year, 1983; National Presidential Award for Excellence in Science Teaching, 1984; NASA Teacher in Space Finalist 1985; Finalist Phi Delta Kappa 75 Young Leaders in Education St John's Outstanding Alumni Award; SDSM&T Centennial 100 Alumni Award; SDSM&T Mines Award, 1994. Memberships American Association of Physics Teachers; National Science Teachers Assocaition; National Education Associations; PH Delta Kappa International; Knights of Columbus; National State Teachers of the Year; South Dakota Science Teacher Association; Beginning Experience of Western South Dakota South Dakota Academy of Science; Minnesota Academy of Science; The Challenger Center; Roman Catholic Church Address: 435 Viking Dr #WwOP, Rapid City, SD 57701-9558 USA.

**LOOMIS Janice Kaszczuk,** b. 26 June 1952, New Britain Connecticut, USA. Artist; Figurative Sculptor. m. Richard, sons. Education: Summa cum laude, BFA Sculpture, Hartford Art School, University of Hartford, 1987. Appointments Founding President, Society of Connecticut Sculptors Secretary, American Medallic Sculptors Association; Board Member, Connecticut Womens Artists; Instruction Chairman West Hartford Art League. Honours: Numerous Awards Memberships: American Medallic Sculpture Association Society of Connecticut Sculptors; Connecticut Women Artists Canton Artists Guild; National Sculpture Society. Address: Hudson St, Enfield, CT 06082-5950, USA.

**LÓPEZ HUIDOBRO Fernando Arturo Pedro Jesús,** b. 3 July 1958, Barcelona, Spain. Chartered Accountanc Education: 1st Biology, 1979, University of Barcelona

Certificate in Banking, STUCOM, 1982, Barcelona; Certificate in COBOL machine code, STUCOM, 1982, Barcelona; Certificates in machine codes, BIT, 1983, Barcelona; English Language, University Barcelona, 1982-85, British Council Institute, 1986-87; Chartered Analytic Accountancy, INEM, 1990, Barcelona; 1st Librarian, 1990, University Barcelona; Diploma Databases, European Social Fund, 1991, Barcelona; Chartered Marketing, Fomento del Trabajo Nacional, 1992, Barcelona; 1st Economy, 1993, University Barcelona; Certification Mediterranean Politicals, 1998, International Course, Institut Català de la Mediterrània d'Estudis i Cooperació. Appointments: Participant various seminars, conferences, meetings, symposia, in field of economics and politics, 1990-. Memberships: Club Natació Montjuïc, Barcelona; Reader CataloniaLibrary, Barcelona; UNICEF, Spain; National Geographic Society, Washington DC, USA; The Folio Society, London, England. Address: Mata 28 Principal 4, Barcelona 08004, Spain.

**LOPUSZANSKI Jan Tadeusz,** b. 21 October 1923, Lwow. Theoretical Physicist. m. Barbara Zaslonka, 1 son. Education: MA, 1950, University Wroclaw; PhD, 1955, Jagellonian University, Cracow; Pls Professor, University Utrecht, 1958, NYU, 1960-61, IAS Princeton, 1964-65, SUNY at Stony Brook, 1970-71, University Gottingen, 1984, 1991-92. Appointments: From Assistant to Associate Professor, 1947-68, Full Professor, 1968-95, retired, 1995, Vice Dean Mathematics, Physics, Chemistry, 1957-58, Wroclaw University; Dean, 1962-64, Director, 1970-84, ITPN UN. Publications: Original over 100; 5 Books; Editorial Board, Progress in Physics, Reports on Mathematics Physics. Honour: Officer Cross of Polonia Restituta, 1981. Memberships: Polish Academy of Sciences; Polska Akademia Umiejetnosci, Cracow; Polish Physics Society; IAS Princeton; International Association Math. Phys; IUPAP. Address: Wroclaw University Institute of Theoretical Physics, Pl Max Born 9, 50204 Wroclaw, Poland.

**LORD Thomas R,** b. 14 March 1943, Washington DC, USA. University Professor. m. Jane T Lord, 1 son, 2 daughters. Education: BS, 1965, PhD, 1983, Rutgers University; MS, College of New Jersey, 1969. Appointments: Postdoctorate Training, Birmingham University, England; Professor, Indiana University of Pennsylvania; Professor, Burlington College, Pemberton, New Jersey. Publications: Over 50 papers in Science and Science Education Journals. Memberships: National Association for Research in Science Teaching; National Science Teachers Association; National Association of Biology Teachers; Society for College Science Teachers. Address: Indiana University of Pennsylvania, Weyandt Hall, Room 114, Indiana, PA 15705, USA.

**LORENTE,** Hererra Juan B, b. 10 October, 1960, Jeses del Marquesado, Granada. Publisher. Education: Batchlor's INUP, Barcelona, Spain, 1994; MbH Pacific Westen University, 1990. Appointments: Partner and Co-founder of the Publishing House Idea Books, 1993-; Dir Telemarketing Ediociones Atrium, Barcelona, 1980-92; Product Manager, Editorial Marin, Barcelona, 1992-93. Publications: Libr. Agri. Idea Wood, other titles Idea Books, 1998-. Memberships: Mem collaborator Ayuda en Acción, Barcelona, 1992; Spanish Army, 1980-82. Address: Idea Books SA, Rosellon 186 10 4a, 08008 Barcelona, Spain.

**LORENTZ George,** b. 25 February 1910, St Petersburg, Russia. Mathematician. m. Tanny nee Belikov, 1 son, 4 daughters. Education: Canidate, University of Leningrad, 1936; Dr rer nat, University of Tuebingen, 1944. Appointments: University of Leningrad, 1932-42; Universities of Frankfurt and Tuebingen, 1946-49; Toronto, 1949-53; Wayne State, 1953-58;

Syracuse, 1958-68; Texas at Austin, 1968-80. Publications: 135 papers, 8 books. Honours: Students, Honorary Dr degrees, Tuebingen, 1977, Wuerzburg, 1996. Memberships: American Mathematical Society; Mathematical Association of America; Deutsche Mathematische Vereinigung. Address: 2750 Sierra Sunrise Terrace 404, Chico, CA 95928, USA.

**LORSCHEIDER Fritz,** b. 27 August 1939, Rochester, New York, USA. Professor, Medical Science. m. Juliet Brand, 1 son, 3 daughters. Education: BSc, University of Wisconsin, 1963; MSc, 1967, PhD, 1970, Michigan State University. Appointments: Assistant Professor, 1970-73, Associate Professor, 1973-80, Professor, 1980-, Department of Physiology & Biophysics, Faculty of Medicine, University of Calgary. Publications: 170 papers and scientific communications in physiological research. Memberships: American Physiological Society; American Society for Biochemistry & Molecular Biology; Canadian Physiological Society. Address: Faculty of Medicine, University of Calgary, 3330 Hospital Drive NW, Calgary, Alberta T2N 4N1, Canada.

**LOSY Jacek Jerzy,** b. 16 June 1955, Poznan, Poland. Neurologist. m. Jadwiga Polcyn, 2 sons. Education: MD, 1980, PhD, 1986, University School of Medicine, Poznan, Poland. Appointments: Assistant Professor, Department Neurology, 1994, Head Department Neuroimmunology, 1997-, University School of Medicine, Poznan; Chief Medical Advisory Board, Polish Multiple Sclerosis Society, 1991-. Honours: Jacqueline du Pre Fellowship, International Federation Multiple Sclerosis Societies, 1988; Ministry Health Award, Polish Ministry Health, 1995. Memberships: International Neuroimmunology Society; World Federation Neurology; Polish Neurology Association. Address: Department Neurology, Przybyszewskiego 49, 60-355 Poznan, Poland.

**LOTHROP Monica Ward,** b. 5 September 1958, Norristown, Pennsylania, USA. Financier. m. Howard J Lothrop, divorced. Education: Management Trainee, York Bank and Trust Co, York, Pennsylvania, USA, 1980-81; Accountant, Volvo White Truck Corp, Greensboro, North Carolina, 1981-84; Financial Analyst, Dairymen Inc, Greensboro, North Carolina, USA, 1984-86; Accounting Manager, Kraft Dairy Group, Memphis, Tennessee, USA, 1986-88; Controller, Green Duck Corporation, Hernando, Mississippi, 1988-89; Assistant Controller, American Signature, Olive Branch, Mississippi, 1992-93; Plant Controller, Smurfit Recycling Company, Memphis, Tennessee, USA, 1991-92, 1993-94; Consultant, Women's Collateral Funding, Philadelphia, Pennsylvania, 1995-96; Instructor, Data Processing Trainers, Philadelphia, Pennsylvania, 1995-; Finance Director, Borough of Norristown, Norristown, Pennsylvania, 1995-. Memberships: Institute of Management Accountants; Association of Certified Fraud Examiners; American Association of University Women, Editor; Government Finance Officers Association; Pennsylvania State Tax Collectors Association; Superkids of Montogery County, Board Member; Pennsylvania Public Risk Management Association; Montgomery County Children and Youth, Director. Address: 915 Cooke Lane, Norristown, PA 19401, USA.

**LOTT Davis Newton,** b. 8 May 1913, San Antonio, USA. Advertising Agency Executive, Publisher. m. Arlene Marion Peterson, 3 daughters. Education: BS, Northwestern University, 1935; Post Graduate, UCLA. Appointments: Better Homes and Gardens and Successful Farming, Des Moines, Iowa, 1935-36; Abbott Labs, North Chicago, Illinois, 1936-37; Copywriter, J Walter Thompson, Chicago, 1938-39; Owner, President, Lott Advertising Agency, LA, 1939-41, 46-; President, USA Corporation, Marina Del Rey, California; President, Lott Publishers, Santa Monica, California. Publications: Rules of the

Road; Handbook of the Nautical Road; Emergency Shiphandling Manual; Collision Prevention; Treasure Trail; Star Spangled Broadcast; Mystery of Midnight Springs; Dodge City Justice; The Inaugural Addresses of the American Presidents; The Presidents Speak; See How they Ran; The Presidents Illustrated; Jimmy Carter and How We Won. Honours: George Washington Medal for Literature; Excellence Freedoms Found. Address: 13222 Admiral Ave Unit B, Marina Del Rey, CA 90292, USA.

**LOTTERMOSER Werner Ernst Alfred,** b. 27 April 1955, Braunschweig, Germany. Physicist. m. Claudia Hoffmann, 1 son, 1 daughter. Education: Diploma in Physics, 1981, PhD, 1986, University of Frankfurt; Habilitation, University of Salzburg, Austria, 1996. Appointments: Research Assistant, University of Frankfurt, University of Salzburg, 1982-92; Assistant Professor, 1992-96, Professor of Mineralogy, Crystallography and Solid State Physics, 1997-, University of Salzburg. Publication: The Single Crystal Mössbauer Spectroscopy (MBS) compared with Powder-MBS, Magnetometry and Neutron Diffraction, 1996. Membership: German Society of Crystallography. Address: Auenstrasse 10, D-83435 Bad Reichenhall, Germany.

**LOUCHEV Oleg Anatolievich,** b. 12 June 1960, Moscow, USSR. Researcher. m. Irina Baum, 1 son, 1 daughter. Education: MS, Chemical Engineering, Moscow Institute of Chemical Engineering, Moscow, 1982; PhD, Applied Physics, Turkmenistan Academy of Sciences, Ashkhabad, 1986. Appointments: Research Centre for Technological Lasers, Russian Academy of Sciences, Troitsk, 1987-89, 1992-94; Energy Institute, Russian Academy of Sciences, Moscow, 1990-91; National Institute for Inorganic Materials, Tsukuba, Japan, 1995-. Publications: Around 50 publications in refereed journals and conference proceedings. Honour: Recipient, Leninski Komsomol Award for Achievements in Science and Technology, 1986. Membership: Active Member, New York Academy of Sciences, 1994. Address: NIRIM, 1-1-Namiki, Tsukuba, Ibaraki 305-0044, Japan.

**LOUGHEED Alan Leslie,** b. 13 April 1927, Nanrango, Queensland, Australia. Educator. m. Jill Blackmore, 2 sons, 1 daughter. Education: BA, 1955, BCom, 1960, BEcon, 1st Class Honours, 1964, PhD, 1974, Queensland. Appointments: School Teacher, 1945-62; Tutor, 1963-64, Lecturer, 1964-68, Senior Lecturer, 1968-83, Associate Professor, 1984-92, Honorary Research Consultant, 1993-, Department of Economics, University of Queensland; Visiting Scholar, University of Kent, England, 1971, 1976-77, 1988; Visiting Lecturer, University of New England; Visiting Research Scholar, Centre for Business History in Scotland, University of Glasgow, 1996. Publications: Author, co-author, 12 books including: The growth of the international economy 1820-1960, 1971, 4th edition, 1999; Technological diffusion and industrialisation before 1914, 1982; The Brisbane Stock Exchange, 1994-1984, 1984; 28 articles and papers including: International economic relations - past and future, 1972; The cyanide process and gold extraction in Australia and New Zealand, 1987; The Discovery, Development, and Diffusion of New Technology: the cyanide process of gold extraction, 1887-1914, 1989; Industry and technical change, 1994; The London stock exchange boom in Kalgoorlie shares, 1895-1901, 1995; Want of novelty and patent litigation: the case of the cyanide process of gold extraction 1892-1902, 1995; Technological advance in the manufacture of chemicals: the case of cyanide, 1888-1930, 1986. Honour: Outstanding Achievement Medal, University of Queensland, 1964. Memberships: Economic Society, Queensland Branch, Treasurer, 1967-70, Vice-President, 1973, 1974, 1976, President, 1975; Australia and New Zealand

Economic Society; Australian Economic History Association; Australian Mining History Association; Centre for Business History in Scotland. Address: 2 Titan Lane, Buderim, 4556, Sunshine Coast, Queensland, Australia.

**LOUISY Calliopa Pearlette,** b. 8 June 1946, St Lucia, West Indies. Governor-General of St Lucia. Education: BA, 1969, University of West Indies; MA, 1975, Laval University, Canada; PhD, 1994, Bristol University, England. Appointments: Pupil Teacher, Laborie Girls Primary School, 1958-60; Graduate Teacher, St Joseph's Convent Secondary School, 1969-76, St Lucia A Level College, 1976-81; Tutor of French, OCOD Teacher Training Summer Workshops, Dominica, 1980-86; Principal, St Lucia A Level College, 1981-86; Dean, Division of Arts, Science and General Studies, Sir Arthur Lewis Community College, 1986-94; Vice Principal, 1994-95, Principal, 1996-97, Sir Arthur Lewis Community College; Governor General of St Lucia, 1997-. Publications include: Dilemmas of Inside Research in a Small-Country Setting: Tertiary Education in St Lucia, 1997; Harmonisation and Diversification of Tertiary Education in the Caribbean, 1998. Honours: Grand Cross of the Order of St Lucia, 1997; International Woman of the Year, 1998. Address: Government House, Castries, St Lucia, West Indies.

**LOVALLO William R,** b. 16 November 1946, Newark, New Jersey. Behavioural Scientist. Education: BA Psychology, 1968, University California at Los Angeles; MA Experimental Psychology, 1970, University Colorado; PhD Biological Psychology, 1978, University Oklahoma. Appointments: Research Associate, 1979-81, Research Assistant, 1973-74, Research Psychologist, 1974-79, Research Associate in Psychology, 1979-81, Research Health Science Specialist, 1982-87, Assistant Director to Acting Director, 1979-86, Associate Research Career Specialist, 1987-, Director, 1986-, Behavioural Sciences Lab, Vice Chairman, 1987-88, Chairman, 1988-90 Research and Development Committee, Oklahoma City Veterans Affairs Medical Centre; Associate Chief of Staff for Research (interim), Oklahoma City Veterans Affairs Medical Centre, 1991-92; Adjunct Assistant to Associate Professor, 1979-91, Professor of Psychiatry and Behavioural Sciences, 1991-, University of Oklahoma Health Sciences Centre; Associate Director, Research Network on Mind-Body Interactions, John D and Catherine T MacArthur Foundation, Chicago, 1994-; Professor of Psychiatry and Psychology, 1994-, Professor of Psychology and Social Sciences, 1994-, Rush-Presbyterian-St Luke's Medical Centre. Publications: Author or co-author 85 scientific papers, 7 review articles, 1 book: Stress & health: Biological and psychological interactions, 1997; Editor, Handbook of research methods in cardiovascular behavioural medicine, 1989; 6 Book chapters; 94 presentations at scientific meetings and published abstracts. Honours: Fellow, 3 international societies; Elected member, Academy of Behavioural Medicine Research; Various stipends, awards and letters of commendation for excellence in teaching and outstanding contributions to Research Development. Address: VA Medical Centre (151A), 921 NE 13th Street, Oklahoma City, OK 73104, USA.

**LOVELL-SMITH Hugh David,** b. 19 November 1951, Christchurch, New Zealand. Medical Practitioner. m. Sally Ann Henders, 2 sons, 1 daughter. Education: BA, 1972; MBChB, 1978. Appointments: General Practitioner, 1982-; Fellow, Master of General Practice Programme, Dunedin School of Medicine, 1996-; Clinical Senior Lecturer, Department of General Practice, Christchurch School of Medicine, 1997-; Spokesman on Health, Natural Law Party. Publications: Numerous publications on Maharishi Vedic approach to health in professional journals. Memberships: Fellow, Royal New ealand College of General Practitioners; President, Maharishi ledical Association of New Zealand. Address: Hillmorton ledical Centre, 21 Coppell Place, Christchurch 8002, New ealand.

**LOW Victor Nelson,** b. 25 August 1931, NYC, USA. Senior istory Lecturer. m. Helga Low, 2 sons. Education: BA, 1951, niversity Chicago, Illinois; MA Comparative Education, 1962, olumbia University Teachers College, New York; PhD African istory, 1967, University of California, Los Angeles. ppointments: Education Officer, Nigeria, 1960-61; Lecturer lamic History and Law, Addis Ababa University Ethiopia, 967-69, President pro tem Inter-Faculty Association, 1968-69; isiting Assistant Professor, 1969-72, Acting Director, 1970-71, isiting Lecturer, 1976-77, Michigan State University, East ansing; Visiting Senior Lecturer, 1972-73, Senior Research ellow, 1978-80, Senior Lecturer, 1979-82, Hebrew University Jerusalem, Israel; Senior Lecturer, Tel Aviv University, 978-80; Senior Lecturer, Head, History Division, 1973-75, hmadu Bello University, Nigeria; First Chief Examiner in istory, Nigerian Universities Joint Matriculation Board, 974-75; Senior Lecturer, Head, Department of History, 975-76, University of Ibadan Jos Campus, Nigeria; Senior ecturer, Tel Aviv University, Israel, 1978-80; Visiting Associate rofessor, Dartmouth College, Hanover, NH, 1990, 1991. ublications: Editor, Hebrew University (Magnes) Press, acmillan Company, New York, The Grolier Society, New ork; Books: Three Nigerian Emirates: A Study in Oral History, 972; African History and Societies to 1914: a Critical Survey f Relevant Books (with special reference to West Africa), 2 ols, in press; In Progress: The Rebbe and the Yekke: A Family omance; Lyme Road Letters; A Lucky Life; Editor, Bailey ridge (FM 5-277), 1986; Co-editor, History of Modern Israel, t 1: Zionism, 1979, Pt 2: Israel, 1982; Several articles and views in professional publications. Fellowships: Ford oundation Foreign Area Research Fellow, 1963-65; Foreign anguage Fellow in Classical Arabic (INDEA), 1966-67 ddress: 171 Lyme Road, Hanover, NH 03755-6608, USA.

**LOWDIN Per-Olov,** b. 28 October 1916, Uppsala, Sweden. esearch Scientist, Educator. m. Karin, 1 son, 1 daughter. ducation: Swedish Degree, Filosofie Licentiat, Uppsala niversity, 1935; DSc, 1948.Appointments: Lecturer, echanics and Mathematical Physics,Uppsala University, 942-48; Assistant Professor, Theoretical Physics, 1948-55; ssociate Professor, Swedish Natural Science Research ouncil, 1955-60; Research Associate, Consultant, Visiting rofessor, USA; Founder, Leader, Uppsala Quantum hemistry Group, 1955-82; Professor, Quantum Chemistry, ead of Department, 1960-82; Professor Emeritus, 1983-; raduate Research Professor of Chemistry, Physics, University f FLorida, 1960-92; Founder, Leader, Florida Quantum Theory roject, 1960-82; Founding Director, 1983-. Honours: Honorary resident, International Academy of Quantum Molecular cience; Honorary President, European Academy of Arts, cience, Humanities; Honorary President, World Association of heoretical Organic Chemists; Niels Bohr Medal; Heyrovsky edal; Many other honourary positions and awards. emberships: Swedish, Norwigian, Danish and Finnish ational Academies of Science; Royal Academy of Arts and ciences; American Philosophical Society; Fellow of the merican Physical Society; The Explorers Club; American hemical Society; British Physical Society; Many other emberships. Address: Department of Quantum Chemistry, ppsala University, Box 518, S-75120, Uppsala, Sweden.

**LU Bin,** b. 27 October 1932, Suzhou City, Jiangsu Province, hina. Professor. m. Xiucen Yang, 1 son, 2 daughters. ducation: Graduate, Department of Pharmacy, Shandong

Medical College, 1952. Appointments: Teaching Assistant, Sandong Medical College, 1952; Lecturer, Sichuan Medical College, 1960; Associate Professor, West China University of Medical Sciences, 1983; Professor, West China University of Medical Sciences, 1987. Publications: Co-Author, Drug Microencapsulation, 1992; Editor in Chief, New Techniques and New Dosage Forms of Drugs, 1998; Over 50 Scientific Papers. Memberships: National Pharmacopoeia of China; Pharmacy Association of China. Address: West China University of Medical Sciences, 17 Renminnanlu 3 Duan, Chengdu 610044, China.

**LU Chan-Nan,** b. 23 August 1958, Chiayi, Taiwan. Educator; Consultant. m. Jau-Rong Lai, 1 daughter. Education: BSc, 1981, National Taiwan University; PhD, 1987, Purdue University; Master in Engineering, 1993, Rensselaer Polytechnic Institute. Appointments: Development Engineer, G E Co, 1983-84; Lead Engineer, Harris Corp, 1987-89; Associate Professor, 1989-93, Professor, 1993-, Chairman of EE Dept, 1997-, National Sun Yat-Sen University. Publications: Co-author, 25 journal papers; Author and co-author, 4 other journal publications including: discussion on Treatment of inequality constraints in power system state estimation, 1995. Honours: Young Engineer Award, Chinese Institute of Electrical Engineering, 1997; Research Awards, National Science Council, 1991-98. Memberships: Senior member, IEEE; Chinese Institute of Electrical Engineering. Address: Department of Electrical Engineering, Nat Sun Yat-Sen University, Koahsiung 804, Taiwan.

**LU Daofa,** b. 5 January 1940, Shandong, China. Senior Vice President. m. Gao Meihua, 1 daughter. Education: Beijing University, 1960-66. Appointments: Aircraft Assembler, 1966-70; Aircraft Designer, 1970-75; Assistant to Chief Engineer, 1975-77; Technical Director of Aircraft Structural Shop, 1979-82; Manager of Aircraft Manufacturing Engineering, 1982-84; Deputy Director of Technical Updates, 1984; Director, NC Machining Centre, 1984-85; Director of Technology Office, 1985; Senior Vice President, General Manager of Production Support, 1986-96; Senior Vice President, General Manager of Aeronautic Production, Shenyang Aircraft Corporation, 1997-. Publications: 7 compositions and thesis. Honours: Worker of the Year, National Planning Committee, National Economy and Trade Committee, National Science Committee, Ministry of Aviation, provincial government, municipal government and corporate; First Prize of Science and Technology Advance, Ministry and Provincial government for Aircraft Accessories Supply System Engineering; Many Second level Acievements and Second Prize granted by the Ministry and provincial government; Many other safety and environment protection awards. Memberships: 10th, 11th, 12th and 13th People's Congress of Huanggu District; Vice President, China Aviation Industry Technical Equipment Engineering Association; Executive General Director, China Aviation Industry Northeast Region Economy and Technology Society; China Successful People Study Association. Address: No 1, Lingbei Street, Huanggu District, Shenyang City 110034, Liaoning Province, China.

**LU Huisheng,** b. 19 November 1935, Shanghai, China. m. Wu Xiujing, 2 daughters. Education: Department of Naval Architecture, Shanghai Jiao Tong University, 1954-59. Appointments: Ship Model Towing Tank, in charge, 1959-60; Flying Mechanics Section in charge, 1960-61; Ship Hydrodynamics Section, Deputy Chief, 1961-85, and Ocean Engineering, Vice Editor-in-Chief, 1982-85, Ship Hydrodynamics Section, Associate Professor, 1985-92, Ship Hydrodynamics Section, Professor, 1992-. Publications: Experimental Study on Open Rudder, 1982; Experimental

Study of Hydrodynamic Performance of Ship Rudder, 1985; A Laser Track-Attitude-Meter and Its Application, 1988; Computer Simulation of Ship Manoeuvring Motion in Restricted Water, 1990; A Study of Efficiency of MHDS Propulsion, 1991; Ship Manoeuvrability Criteria and Their Application in Primary Design, 1992. Honour: Ex Thesis Prize, 1989. Memberships: Chinese Naval Architecture Engineering Association, 1979; Ship Manoeuvrability Speciality Group, 1979-88; Chinese Ocean Association, 1982; Ocean Engineering, Vice Editor-in-Chief, 1982-85; Chinese Navigation Association, 1982; Steering Specialty Committee, 1986-; Vice Director, Ship Model Navigation Subspecialty Committee, 1988-. Address: Department No 1, Shanghai Jiaotong University, Shanghai 20030, China.

**LU Kau U,** b. 10 July 1939, Canton, China. Professor, 1 daughter. Education: BS, Electrical Engineering, Taiwan University, 1961; PhD, Mathematics, California Institute of Technology, 1968. Appointments: Assistant Professor, 1968-75, Associate Professor, 1975-79, Professor, 1979-, California State University, Long Beach. Publications include: Mathematical Investigation of Bode's Law and Quantilization of Gravity: Astrophysics and Space Science, 1995. Memberships: American Mathematical Society; American Physical Society; General Relativity Society. Address: Department of Mathematics, California State University, Long Beach, CA 90840, USA.

**LU Qing Bin,** b. 26 September 1965, Pinghe, Fujian, China. Scientist. m. Ning Ou, 1 daughter. Education: MS, Fuzhon University, China, 1989; PhD, University of Newcastle, Australia, 1997. Appointments: Lecturer; Post Doctoral Fellow; Research Associate. Publications: Papers in Physical Review Letters; Physical Review; Surface Science. Honours:Postgraduate Excellence by Australian Institute of Physics, 1995; Science and Technology Agency Fellowship of Japan, 1996. Memberships: American Physical Society; American Chemical Society; American Vacuum Society. Address: Rutgers U Dept Physics and Astron, Piscataway, NJ 08855, USA.

**LU Songwei,** b. 26 September 1965, Zhejiang, China. Researcher. m. Jian Yang. Education: BSc, Materials Science and Engineering, 1986, Zhejiang University; MSc, Materials Science and Engineering, 1989, Shanghai Institute of Optics and Fine Mechanics, Chinese Academy of Science; PhD, Materials Science and Engineering, 1998, Institut fuer Neue Materialien, Germany. Appointments: Research Engineer, Research and Development Division, Shanghai CITIC - Jiading Industrial Co Ltd, Shanghai, 1989-93; Research Engineer and Manager, Research and Development Division, Shanghai Guowei Industrial Co Ltd, Shanghai, 1994; Research Associate, Department of Ceramic and Materials Engineering, Clemson University, USA, 1998-. Publications: Co-author 14 journal articles. Honours: Exemplary Student Award, Zhejiang University, 1983, 1984, 1985, 1986, Scholarship, 1984, 1985. Memberships: American Association for the Advancement of Science; American Ceramic Society; Materials Research Society. Address: Department of Ceramic and Materials Engineering, Olin Hall, PO Box 340907, Clemson University, Clemson, SC 29634-0907, USA.

**LU Steven Zhiyun,** b. 25 November 1941, Shanghai, China. Professor. m. Shiru Zhao, 2 sons. Education: BS, Qinghua University, Beijing, 1965; MS, 1984, PhD, 1986, Department of Mechanical & Aerospace Engineering, Cornell University. Career: Chairman, Department of Mechanical Engineering, New York Institute of Technology, Old Westbury. Publications: Several articles in professional journals. Honour: NSF SBIR

Award, 1988. Memberships: AIAA; ASME. Address: New Yo Institute of Technology, 268 Wheatley Road, Henry Schu Hall, Old Westbury, NY 11568, USA.

**LU Xiaohu,** b. 30 November 1962, Jintan, China. Chemis Researcher. m. Haiyan Tang, 2 sons. Education: BS, 198 MSc, 1989, University of Science and Technology of Chir (USTC); Tech Licentiate, 1996, PhD, 1997, Royal Institute Technology, Sweden. Appointments: University Lecture University of Science and Technology, 1989-92; Researc Engineer, 1997-98, Assistant Professor, 1998-, Royal Institu of Technology, Sweden. Publications: About 80 scienti papers; Book, Introduction to Molecular Spectroscop Honours: Yilida Experimental Science Scholarship USTC 1986; Outstanding Research Paper Award, Anhui Associatic of Science and Technology, 1988; Chairman Prize, Chines Academy of Science, 1989; USTC Award, Development Science and Technology, 1991; The USTC Yilida Awar Outstanding Young Teacher, 1992; USTC Outstanding Awar for book, Introduction to Molecular Spectroscopy, 199 Memberships: Chinese Chemical Society; America Association for the Advancement of Science. Address: Roy Institute of Technology, Highway Engineering, Brinellvagen 3 100 44 Stockholm, Sweden.

**LU Yuxin,** b. 23 October 1953, Shanghai, China. Historia Linguist. Education: BA, 1982, Haerbin Normal University; M/ 1992, Doctor of Arts, 1998, St John's University. Appointment Instructor, Shanghai Medical College, 1982-85; Researche National Language Institute, 1986-90; Instructor, 1988-9 Researcher, 1997-98, Ibaraki University, Japan; Teachir Assistant, St John's University, 1990-96; Assistant Professc Dowlling College, 1999-. Publications: 1 book and 1 journ article in Chinese; 2 articles in English; 4 books and Variou articles in Japanese; Various presentations in New Yor Tokyo, Prague, Denver and Haerbin. Honours: Sever fellowships and travel and research grants; 4 research award Memberships: American Historical Association; Association fe Asian Studies; Senninkai; Kindaigo Kenkyukai; America Sino-Japanese Study Group; Community College Gener Education Association. Address: 112-29 15th Avenue, Colleg Point, NY 11356, USA.

**LU Zhong Yi,** b. 7 January 1946, Chongqing, Chin Paediatrician. m. Tian Xi, 2 sons, 1 daughter. Education: BS 1969, Chongqing Medical University. Appointment Paediatrician, 1969-86, Chief Doctor in PICU, 1987-9 Associate Professor, Vice Director, 1991-96, Professor, Vic Director, 1996-, Children's Hospital, Chongqing Medic University. Publications: 11 journal articles in field paediatrics; One of editors of 4 books on paediatric medicin Honours: 3rd Prize of Progress in Science & Technology Sichuan Province: Pathogen study on Autumn diarrhea infants and children in Chongqing area, 1987, The length stay time for endotracheal intubation through nasal route, 199 2nd Prize of Progress in Science & Technology of Chongqin The changes of disorder of glucose metabolism ar insulin-receptor in critical ill children, 1997. Memberships: Vic Chairman, Dept of Paediatrics, Chongqing Medical Universi Vice Director, Children's Hospital, Chongqing Medic University; Head, Division of Paediatric Emergency. Addres Children's Hospital, Chongqing Medical University, 136 Zho Er Road, Chongqing 400014, China.

**LUARASI Aleks,** b. 22 March 1941, Luaras, Alban Lawyer. m. Yllka, 1 son, 1 daughter. Education: Lawye University of Tirana, 1963; Doctor, 1981; Professor, 199 Appointments: Lawyer, 1963-71; Editor, Professor, Chief Department, Public Law, Faculty of Law, University of Tiran

1972-99; Minister, General Secretary, Council of Ministers of Albania, 1991; Cp, European Commission for Democracy through Law, Venice Commission, 1992-98. Publications: Co Author, Many Textbooks for Law Schools; Monographs; Papers; The State Law in Albania in the Times of Scanderbeg. Address: Akedemia e Shkencave, Tirana, Albania.

**LUGOMER Stjepan,** b. 16 April 1944, Podgajec, Croatia. Research Scientist. m. Branka Turk, 1 son. Education: BSc, 1967, MSc, 1970, PhD, 1974, all in Physics, Zagreb, Ljublana. Appointments: Coordinator Tech Project, 1984-90; Senior Research Scientist, 1990-98, Scientific Advisor, 1998-, Ruder Boskovic. Memberships: Croatian Physical Society; Croatian Vacuum Society; New York Academy of Sciences. Address: Bozidara Magovca 52, Zagreb 10020, Croatia.

**LUIK Hans,** b. 7 November 1954, Tallinn, Estonia. Chemist. m. Lea Maripuu. Education: Diploma Engineer, Tallinn Technical University, 1978; PhD, Chemistry, Institute of Chemistry, Tallinn, 1987. Appointments: Engineer, 1978-81, Junior Researcher, 1981-87, Researcher, 1987-90, Senior Researcher, 1990-94, Head, Department of Oil Shales and Shale Oil, 1994-, Institute of Chemistry. Publications: More than 50 scientific and popular publications, 1980-98. Memberships: New York Academy of Sciences; National Geographic Association. Address: Vana-Parnu maantee 10-1, EE-0016 Tallinn, Estonia.

**LUKOSEVICIUS Viktoras,** b. 9 August 1939, Kaunas, Lithuania. University Teacher. m. Emilija Lukoseviciene, 2 sons. Education: Diploma Engineer of Geodesy, 1962, Kaunas Polytechnical Institute, Lithuania; PhD Engineering, 1966, Institute of Surveying, Aerial Photography and Cartography, Moscow; Associate Professor, 1970, Kaunas Polytechnical Institute. Appointments: Head of Basic Science Department, Kaunas Polytechnical Institute, 1967-70; Head of Civil Engineering Department, KPI, 1970-81; Vice Dean and Associate Professor, Panevezys Faculty of Kaunas University of Technology, 1981-87; Head of Civil Engineering Department, Associate Professor and Faculty Council Chair of Panevezys Faculty, KTU, 1988-. Publications: Over 50 scientific articles; Participant conferences in USA, Brasil, Sweden, Norway, Russia and elsewhere. Honours: Fellowship winner, NATO and Italy National Science Council Competition, 1996. Memberships: Senate member, Kaunas University of Technology; International Association for Continuing Engineering Education; Association for the Advancement of Baltic Studies; Council member, Lithuanian Liberal Society; Board member, Panevezys Department, Lithuanian Scientists' Union; President, Panevezys Lithuanian & Swedes' Society; Lithuanian K Dineika Health Society; N Rerich Society; Lithuanian Geographers' Society. Address: Statybininku 56-66, LT 5309 Panevezys, Lithuania.

**LUKSENIENE Janina,** b. 29 January 1944, Ukmerge, Lithuania. Restoration Scientist. m. Luksenas Antanas, 1 son. Education: Diploma, Vilnius University, 1967. Appointments: Chemist, Restoration Centre of Lithuanian Art Museum, 1969-83; Head of Restoration, Centre of Lithuanian Art Museum, 1983-94; Head of Department of Scientific Reesarch, Restoration Centre of Lithuanian Art Museum, 1994-. Publications: Catalogue of Exhibitions; Conservation and Restoration in Estonia; A GUid to the Museums of Lithuania. Memberships: Member, International Council of Museums. Address: A Gostauto 5/12-88, LT 2001 Vilnius, Lithuania.

**LUMBROSO Henri Raphael,** b. 7 April 1921, Alexandria, Egypt. Research Physical Chemist; Professor. m. (1)Nicole Bader (div), (2)Ruth Urbainczyk, 2 sons, 2 daughters.

Education: BS, 1939, University Paris; BS Physical and Natural Science, 1946, Engr Ecole Nationale; DS Physical Science, University Paris. Appointments: With ENSCP, 1940-42; CNRS, 1946-85; Physical Chemist, Research Director, Paris, 1957-85; Professor, 1960-70. Publications: Articles in professional journals. Honour: Recipient Marguerite di la Charlonie Award, French Academy of Sciences, 1967. Address: Lab Chimie Generale, University Paris VI, 4 Place Jussieu, F-75252 Paris, France.

**LUMSDEN Ian Gordon,** b. 8 June 1945, Montreal, Quebec. Art Gallery Director. m. Katherine Elizabeth, 1 son. Education: BA, 1968, McGill University; Museum Management Institute, University California at Berkeley, 1991. Appointments: Curator Art Dept, The New Brunswick Museum Saint John, 1969; Curator, 1969-83, Director, 1983-, Beaverbrook Art Gallery; Director, Artsatlantic, 1994-; Advisor, Carol Hoorn Fraser Trust, 1992-; Programming Committee, 49th Parallel Centre for Contemporary Canadian Art, 1990-92. Publications: Sargent to Freud: Modern British Paintings and Drawings in the Beaverbrook Collection; Early Views of British North America, 1994; Gainsborough in Canada, 1991; Drawings by Carol Fraser 1948-86, 1987; 20th Century British Drawings in the Beaverbrook Art Gallery, 1986; New Brunswick Juried Exhibition, 1984; Recent Acquisitions 1978-83, 1983; The Murray and Marguerite Vaughan Inuit Print Collection, 1981; Mexican Works from the Vaughan Collection, 1979; Fredericton Collects, 1979; 8 others. Memberships: Canadian Cultural Property Export Review Board, 1982-85; Artsatlantic Advisory Committee, 1977-94; CAMDO, 1971-, Treasurer 1998-; Advisory Committee, Atlantic Conservation Centre, Canadian Conservation Institute; Canadian Museums Association; Atlantic Provinces Art Gallery Association; American Association of Museums. Address: 725 George Street, Fredericton NB, Canada E3B 1K6.

**LUN Xiao,** b. 3 January 1912, Pi Xian, Sichuan, China. Radiochemist; Researcher. m. Louisa, 2 s. Education: BS, Tsing Hua University, 1939; MS, University of Illinois, 1948; PhD, 1951. Appointments: Director, Great China Alcohol Plant, Jintang, 1941-47; Research Associate, University of Illinois, 1951-52; Physical Chemist, Petroleum Experimental Station, Bureau of Mines, Bartlesville, 1952-55; Professor, Institute of Physics, Beijing, 1956-58; Associate Director, No 5 Laboratory, Institute of Physics, Beijing, 1956-58; Director, No 16 Lab, Institute of Atomic Energy, Beijing, 1959-79, Department of Isotopes, 1979-83, Research Division of Isotopes, 1981-83; Professor, China Institute of Atomic Energy, Beijing, 1984-; ; Editor in Chief, Journal of Isotopes, 1988-. Publications: Contributor of Articles to Professional Journals. Honours: Congressman 5th National Peoples Congress, Beijing, 1978-83; Honorary Certificate of National Defence Society of Science and Technology; Honay Chairman, Isotope Society of China; Certificate of Appreciation American Nuclear Society; Ho Leung Ho Lee Foundation Award; Grantee national Natural Science Foundation. Memberships: AAAS; Chinese Academy of Sciences; New York Academy of Sciences; Chinese Nuclear and Radiochemical Society; Phi Lambda Upsilon; Sigma Xi. Address: 12 Yuetan Beijie, Ste 206, Beijing 100045, China.

**LUNDSTEN Ralph,** b. 6 October 1936, Ersnäs, Sweden. Composer; Filmmaker; Artist; Author. Appointments: Owner, Andromeda, 1959-. Recordings: More than 550 opus and 68 records, 12 short films, art exhibitions; Lustbarheter, book with CD. Compositions: Nordic Nature Symphony No 1, The Water Sprite; Johannes and the Lady of the Woods; A Midwinter Saga; A Summer Saga; Bewitched; Landscape of Dreams; The Seasons; Erik XIV and Gustav III, 2 ballets about Swedish Kings; Cosmic Love; Ourfather, Nightmare; Horrorscope;

Shangri-La; Universe; Discophrenia; Alpha Ralpha Boulevard; Paradise Symphony; The New Age; Pop Age; Music for Relaxation and Meditation; Cosmic Phantazy; The Dream Master; The Gate of Time; The Ages of Man; Sea Symphony; Mindscape Music; Nordic Light; The Symphony of Joy; The Symphony of Light; The Symphony of Love; In Time and Space; Inspiration, 1996. Honours: Grand Prix Biennale, Paris, France, 1967; The Swedish Film Institute Prize, 1964-67; 40 other awards for music and film making; Schwingungen Preis, Oscar of Electronic Music, 1997. Address: Frankenburgs väg 1, SE-132 42 Saltsjö-Boo, Sweden.

**LUNDY-SLADE Bettie B,** b. 16 February 1924, Marinette, Wisconsin, USA. Retired. m. Jim Slade, 2 sons, 1 daughter. Education: Licences, Nurse, Physiatric Technician, Electronics Technician. Appointments: US Navy Waves, 1944-50; Den Mother, Cub Scouts; S S Teacher, Lutheran Church; General Dynamics; Teledyn Ryan, Cubic. Publications: Do You Have a Minute; Growing Up During Depression. Honours: Letters of Appreciation, Mother Teresa, General Norman Schwarzkopf, Queen Elizabeth II; Senator Cashman Award, 1937. Memberships: International Society of Poets; National Park and Conservation; Smithsonian Association; National Museum of Women in Arts; Auduban Society. Address: 6315 Thorn Street, San Diego, CA 92115-6908, USA.

**LUNKIM Tongkhojang,** b. 1 January 1937, Kamu village, Manipur, India. Doctor of Theology; Minister. m. Chongnu, 2 sons, 4 daughters. Education: D Div, M Div, Serampore College (University); M Theol, Fuller Theological Seminary, USA. Appointments: Administrative Secretary, Kuki Christian Church, 1979-; Kuki Bible Translator, 1964-72; President, Kuki Baptist Convention, 1958-59, General Secretary, 1959-68; Chairman, Kuki Movement for Human Rights, 1996-; Co-worker, Disaster Emergency Service Incorporation, and Senior Minister of Imphal Christian Church, 1982-. Address: K C C Office, PO Imphal 795001, Manipur, India.

**LUO Ching-Hsing,** b. 10 January 1958, Taiwan. Professor, Biomedical Instrumentation and Modelling. m. Shio-Shiin Lee, 4 sons. Education: BS Electrophysics, 1980, National Chao Tung University, Taiwan; MS Electrical Engineering, 1982, National Taiwan University; MS Biomedical Engineering, 1988, Johns Hopkins University, USA; PhD Biomedical Engineering, 1991, Case Western Reserve University, USA. Appointments: Professor in Electrical Engineering Department, National Cheng Kung University. Publications: Engineering Mathematics, I, II, 1997; Solutions of Engineering Mathematics, I, II, 1998; Patents: Speed Training System for Athletic Experts, 1998; The Application of Solar Cells to Infrared Controllers, 1998. Honours: Numerous scholarships; Supreme Award in the Microcomputer Application System Competition, by Ministry of Education, 1997; The Li Foundation Biomedical Engineering Fellowship, 1997-98. Membership: Biomedical Engineering Society of China. Address: Department of Electrical Engineering, National Cheng Kung University, Tainan 701, Taiwan.

**LUO Peng fei,** b. 20 May 1949, Guangdong, China. Doctor. 2 sons. Education: BSc, 1970, Zhongsan Medical University; MSc, 1982, Kunming Medical College. Appointments: Chief Professor of Interventional Radiology Dept, Guangdong Provincial Hospital. Publication: Chief Editor, Clinical Interventional Radiology, 1997. Honour: Outstanding Medical Scientist of China, 1992. Membership: China Medical Association. Address: Guangdong Provincial Peoples Hospital, Guangzhou, China.

**LURIE Ranan Raymond,** b. 26 May 1932, Port Said, Egypt. Naturalised US Citizen, 1974. Political Cartoonist. m. Tamar Fletcher, 2 sons, 2 daughters. Education: Herzelia College, Tel-Aviv, Israel; Jerusalem Art College. Appointments: Served as Major, Israeli Army Reserve, 1950-67; Correspondent, Maariv Daily, 1950-52; Features Editor, Hador Daily, 1953-64; Editor-in-Chief, Tavel magazine, 1954-55; Staff Political Cartoonist, Yedioth Aharonot Daily, 1955-66; Political Cartoonist, Life Magazine, New York City, 1968-73; Contributor, New York Times, 1970-; Syndicated, United Features, 1971-73, Los Angeles Times, New York Times, 1973-75, King Features and Editors Press, 1975-, Universal Press, 1982-; Contributing Editor, Political Cartoonist, Newsweek International 1974-76; Editor, Political Cartoonist, Vision Magazine of South America, 1974-76; Staff Political Cartoonist, Honolulu Advertiser, 1979; Political Cartoonist, The Times, London, 1981-83; Political Analyst, Cartoonist, The Asahi Shimbun, Tokyo, 1983-84; Senior Analyst, Political Cartoonist, US News and World Report, Washington, 1984-85; Chief Editorial Director, Editors Press Service, 1985; Political Cartoonist, Time Magazine, 1994-97; Editor-in-Chief, Cartoon News, 1997-: Senior Adjunct Fellow, Center for Strategic and International Studies, Washington; Lecturer; TV Political Cartoonist and Analyst, MacNeil/Lehrer News Hour; Exhibited, Israel, Canada, USA. Publications: Some dozen books of cartoons published in Israel, USA. Germany, UK, Japan, China. Honours include: Highest Israeli Journalism Award, 1954; John Fischetti Political Cartoon Award, 1982; UN Society of Writers Award for Excellence, 1995; Hubert H Humphrey First Amendment Freedoms Prize, 1997. Memberships: Association of Editorial Cartoonists; National Cartoonists Society of America; Honorary Associate Member, Asahi Shimbun; MENSA. Address: 9 Mountain Laurel Drive, Creenwich, CT 06831, USA.

**LUTHER Amanda Lisa,** b. 27 April 1959, La Mesa, California, USA. TV Producer. m. Jeffrey Henry Luther, 2 daughters. Education: UCLA, 1977-79; BA, Fine Arts, Columbia College, 1979-81. Appointments: Producer, Saban Entertainment; Coordinating Producer, Telepictures. Membership: ECO. Address: 37402 Harrow Court, Palmdale, CA 93550, USA.

**LUTZE Ruth Louise,** b. 19 April 1917, Boston, USA. Textbook Editor. Education: AB Hons 1938, Radcliffe College; Graduate work, Boston University. Appointments: 40 years textbook editor, Leading English course series; Book Reviewer. Address: 110 Circuit Road, Winthrop, MA 02152-2819, USA.

**LUYO Jaime,** b. 23 July 1944. Electrical Engineer; Professor. 2 sons. Education: BSc, honour, Universidad Nacional de Ingenieria, Peru, 1967, Diploma, Electrical Engineer, 1970; Certificate, Electrical Engineer, Duke University, University of Texas, 1971; MSc, Rensselaer Polytechnic Institute, 1973; Economics Graduate School Certificate, Universidad Nacional Mayor de San Marcos, 1979. Appointments: Assistant Professor, 1968-69, Associate Professor, 1971-76, Director, Control Systems Laboratory, 1973-77, University Planning Director, 1985-87, Head, EE Graduate School, 1987-88, Chairman, School of Electrical Engineering, 1989, UNI Engineering Faculty Organization; Head, Control System and Electronics Engineering Department, 1981-84, Dean, Electronics Engineering Faculty, 1990-92, 1993-95, 1995-98, President, Committee of Admissions, 1994, Vice President, Committee on Admissions, 1996, University Nacional Mayor de San Marcos. Publications: Numerous articles in professional journals. Honours include: Conimera First Award, 1981, 1991; 2nd Engineer of the Year Award, The Peruvian Engineers Society, 1996. Memberships

Peruvian College of Engineers; New York Academy of Sciences; Peruvian Electrotechnical Association; American Association for the Advancement of Science; Institute of Electrical and Electronics Engineers; National Geographical Society. Address: Los Eucaliptos 408, (R San Felipe), Lima 11, Peru.

**LUZAJ Isuf,** b. 21 February 1913, Kanina, Albania. m. Drita Mezin, 3 sons, 2 daughters. Education: PhD, 1930-34; D-Litt, 1934-36. Appointments: University Argentina, 1944-60; Lice Albania, 1937-39; University Cregoriana, Rome, Ialy, 1945-48; University of Hampshire, Hasrvard, Indiana, Illinois, 1960-92. Publications: books: Refimet Albania, 1938; Utopia Marksiste-Italy, 1947; Diaspora Italy, 1948; Los Rio Bajan Rojos Argentina, 1954; Egzistenca Dhe Boshesia Italy, 1996; over 92 unpublished books of poetry, philosophy, paleontology, history, sociology, dialogues, monologues and politics; Numerous articles in professional journals. Honours include: Gold Medal of Peace, USA, 1950; Academic Award, Outstanding Educator, Argentina, 1952; Gold Medal of Peace, Lima, 1965; Award, Outstanding Accomplishment, USA, 1984. Address: 1724 North Oak Park Avenue, Chicago, IL 606707 4426, USA.

# M

**MA Jian-Guo,** b. 27 March 1961, Shanxi, China. Assistant Professor. m. Lanping Li, 1 daughter. Education: BSc, 1982, MSc, 1988, Lanzhou University of China; PhD, 1996, Gerhard-Mercator University, Germany. Appointments: Research Fellow, Gerhard-Mercator University, Germany, 1991-96; Research Fellow, Technical University of Nova Scotia, Canada, 1996-97; Assistant Professor, School of EEE, NTU, Singapore, 1997-. Publications: Over 60 journal papers; Engineering of Electromagnetic Fields in hgh-Tc Superconductors, 1996. Memberships: Senior Member, IEEE. Address: School of EEE, NTU, Singapore 639798, Singapore.

**MA Ren Liu,** b. 17 April 1934, Zhejiang, China. Professor. m. Wang Rui Qi, 3 daughters. Education: Student, Shanghai Fudan University Biology Department, China, 1952-53; Student, Excellent Diploma, Harkov Animal Husbandry College, Soviet Union, 1954-59. Appointments: Assistant and Lecturer, 1959-79, 1979-86, Associate Professor, Shanxi Agricultural University, China, 1986-92; Full Professor, Shanxi Agricultural University, China, 1992-94, Retired 1994. Publications: Over 10 books and more than 90 articles, 1960-98. Honours: Gold Cock Prize, XX World's Poultry Congress, New Delhi, India, 1996. Memberships: Directing Member, Poultry Branch Society of the AHVS of China, 1984; WPSA, 1989; Edificatory Committee Member, Agricultural Engineering Society of China, 1991. Address: Building No 4, Room 702, Xiaohongmiao Nanli, Guangwai, Xuanwu District, Beijing 100055, China.

**MA Wenhai,** b. 17 August 1954, China. Assistant Professor; Illustrator. m. Shuqing Zhai, 1 daughter. Education: BFA, Scene Design, Central Academy of Drama, Beijing, 1982; MFA, Scene and Costume Design, Carnegie Mellon University, 1984. Appointments: Lecturer, Central Academy of Drama, Beijing, 1984-87; Artist-in-Residence, 1987-93, Assistant Professor, 1993-98, Duke University, Durham, North Carolina, USA. Publications: Illustrator, children's books: Red Means Good Fortune; Old Brother, Younger Brother; The Painted Fan; The Making of the Monkey; The Swan's Gift; The Pavilion Garden Liberated. Membership: Society of Children's Book Writers and Illustrators. Address: Drama Program, Duke University, 206 Bivins Building, Durham, NC 27704, USA.

**MA Xiaohui,** b. 11 March 1965, Tangshan, China. Musician; Erhu Soloist. Education: BA, 1987, Shanghai Conservatory of Music. Appointments: Soloist, Traditional Chinese Music Orchestra of Shanghai, 1987-; Concertmaster of Traditional Chinese Music Orchestra of Shanghai, 1993-; Adviser, Hongkong Youth Music Society. Honours: First Prize, National Competition of Cantonese Music, 1987; Nomination of 10 Best Young Artists of Shanghai Award, 1993; Award of 1995 Baogang Cup for Outstanding Performance of Classical Art. Membership: Shanghai Musicians' Association. Address: Shanghai National Orchestra, 336 Xinhua Road, Shanghai 200052, China.

**MA Xiaoqian,** b. 12 March 1964, Wuhan, China. Teacher. m. Zhang Ling. Education: Bachelor of Engineering, 1987, Master of Engineering, 1990, PhD, Engineering, 1995, Huanzhong University of Science and Technology. Appointments: Associate Engineer, Wuhan Iron and Steel Design and Research Institute, 1990-92; Associate Professor, School of Electric Power, South China University of Technology, 1995-. Publications: As co-author, 6 papers in professional journals including: The cold and fired test and application of a slit bluff-body burner, 1997; Comparison of methods for metallurgical furnace cooling and heat recovery 1997; Analysis of pulverized coal current flow flame stabilit conditions, 1998; Intensified heat transfer under low Re numbe and the method of evaluation of energy, 1998. Address: Schoc of Electric Power, South China University of Technology Guangzhou 510641, China.

**MABUTO Nobulali Prospina,** b. 3 December 1936 Johannesburg, South Africa. Lecturer and Tutor in Nursing Services. m. Mxolisi Mabuto, 1 son, 1 daughter. Education Diploma in General Nursing, 1963; Diploma in Midwifery, 1965 Certificate in Clinical Care, Instruction and Administration 1972; Diploma in Nursing Education, University of the North Pietersburg, 1977; BA, Nursing Administration and Community Health Science, University of South Africa, Pretoria, 1987 Appointments: Professional Nurse, Cardiology Unit, 1973-74 Intensive Care Unit, Cardiology Section, 1974-75, Baragwanath Hospital, Bertsham, Johannesburg; Nursing Tutor, Senio Professional Nurse rank, 1978-80, Chief Professional Nurse rank, 1980, allocated to Audio-Visual Centre, 1981-86 Classroom Based Nurse Educator, Student Clinical Follow-up Evaluator, 1987-94, Head of Department, Member of College Senate, Member of Students Representative Council, 1995- Baragwanath College of Nursing; Health talks on radio Ikwekwezi Radio Station, SABC, 1999; Health talks anc research, Phelang-Philani Projects, 1999. Memberships Transvaal Nurse Educators, Vice-Chairman, 1980-82 Coordinator, 1982-85; South African Regional Healtr Committee, South African Health Social Services Organisation 1992-94; South African Nursing Council; Democratic Nursing Organisation of South Africa; Nursing Educators Profession Society. Address: 968 Mofolo Central, PO Dube, 1852 Soweto South Africa.

**MACDONALD Hugh Ian,** b. 27 June 1929, Toronto, Ontario Canada. Professor, University Administrator. m. Dorothy Marion, 2 sons, 3 daughters. Education: B Com, University of Toronto, 1952; MA, Oxford University, 1954; B Phil, Oxforc University, 1955; LL D, University of Toronto, 1974; D Univ The Open University, 1998. Appointments: Lecturer Economics, University of Toronto, 1955; Dean of Men, 1956; Assistant Professor, Economics, 1962; Chief Economist, Government of Ontario, 1965; Deputy Provincial Treasurer 1967; Deputy Treasurer and Deputy Minister of Economics, 1968; Deputy Treasurer, Deputy Minister of Economics and Intergovernmental Affairs, 1972; President, York University, 1974-84; Director, York International, 1984-94; President Emeritus, Professor of Economics and Public Policy, 1994-. Publications: Various Publications. Honours: Governor General's Medal; Cody Trophy; Candian Centennial Medal; Queens Silver Jubilee Medal; Officer of the Order of Canada Knight of Grace of the Order of St Lazarus of Jerusalem; Citation of Merit, The Court of Canadian Citizenship; Medal of the Dominican Republic; Commemorative Medal for the 125th Anniversary of Confederation of Canada; Award of Merit, Canadian Bureau for International Education. Memberships: Director Canadian Rhodes Scholars Foundation; Chairman, Hockey Canada; The Commonwealth of Learning; Ballio Annual Fund Appeal in Canada; Advisory Board, Internationa Master of Business Administration Program; Many other Memberships. Address: York University, Rm 226R, Schulich School of Business, 4700 Keele Street, Toronto, Ontario, M3J 1P3, Canada.

**MACIJAUSKAS Aleksandras,** b. 18 May 1938, Kaunas Photo Artist, Complier of Books. m. Burdaite Nijole, 1 son, 1 daughter. Appointments: Photocorrespondent, Vakarines Naujienos Newspaper, 1967-73; Executive Secretary, Lithuanian Photo Artists Union, 1973-1974; Chairman,

Lithuanian Photoartists Union Art Council, 1979-89; Chairman of Kaunas Department, 1978-94; Many Exhibitions. Honours: International Golden Rose, Photoforum, 1969; Grand Prix, Land of Amber 2, 1971; Gold Medal, International Exhibition, Golden Eye, 1972; Grand Prix Exhibition of Humour, 1973; Grand Prix, Salon International, 1975; Gold Medal, Exhibition of Humour, 1976; Grand Prix, Vitkovice 78, 1978; Prize, Gold Medal, Best Photo, 1984; Lithuanian National Prize, 1995; Gediminas Order, 1998. Memberships: Lithuanian Journalists Union; International Federation of Artistic Photography. Address: Taikos pr 63-56, LT 3036 Kaunas, Lithuania

**MACIOLKA Michael Eugene,** b. 18 September 1936, Lasek. Priest. Education: Graduate, 1960, Archdioce Theological Seminary, Poznan; D Theol, 1967, Catholic University of Lublin. Appointments: Parish Vicar, Lwowek Poznanski, 1960-61, Leszno Wielkopolskie, 1967-68; Academic Youth Chaplain of Poznan, 1969-75; Editor Catholic weekly, Przewodnik Katolicki, 1975-80; Managing Director, Ksiegarnia SW Wojciecha, publishing house, 1980-90; Polish Primates Procurator for the Printing Matters of Catholic Church, 1984-90; Member of Publishing Matters of the Government and Episcopate, 1980-89; Member Press Council, 1984-89; Parish Priest of Mary Church in Oborniki, 1990-; Lecturer of Theological Faculty of Poznan, 1974-. Publications: Editor-in-Chief, Chrzescijanska Wizja Cztowieka, Christian Vision of Man, John Paul II in Poland; Encyclopedic and Catholic magazine publications. Honours: Award granted by Ministry of Culture for Entirety of Work, 1985; Award granted by City Council of Poznan for the Contribution to the Cultural Development of the City of Poznan, 1985; Award for the Popularisation of Social Science of Church, 1987, granted by Odiss Publishing House in Warsaw. Memberships: Scientific Society; Polish Theologians Society. Address: ul Koscielna 2, 64-600 Oborniki, woj Poznan, Poland.

**MACKAY William Morton,** b. 26 March 1934, Dundee, Scotland. Educator. m. Catherine Kirk, 2 sons, 1 daughter. Education: MA, Honours, 1956, Diploma Education, 1957, University of St Andrews; Diploma of Theological Studies, Free Church of Scotland College, Edinburgh, 1959. Appointments: Teacher, Buckhaven High School, Scotland, 1959-61; St Andrew's College, Lima, Peru, 1961-78; Teacher, 1961-64, Supervisor of Studies 1965, Headmaster, 1966-78; Teacher, Lothian Region, 1978-85; Principal, Presbyterian Ladies' College, Melbourne, Australia, 1986-97. Publication: Thomas Chalmers: A Short Appreciation, 1980. Honours: Diploma of Honour for services to Education in Peru, 1981; Moderator of Synod Presbyterian Church of Eastern Australia, 1993. Memberships: Australian College of Education; Association of Heads of Independent Schools of Australia; Associate Fellow, Australian Principals Centre; Associate, Royal Scottish Geographical Society. Address: 53 Lauderdale Street, Edinburgh, EH9 1DE, Scotland.

**MACKERRAS Colin Patrick,** b. 26 August 1939, Sydney, Australia. Academic. m. Alyce Barbara Mackerras, 2 sons, 3 daughters. Education: BA, 1961, University Melbourne; BA Hons, 1962, PhD, 1970, Australian National University; Master Letters, 1964, University Cambridge, England. Appointments: Foreign Expert, Beijing Foreign Studies University, 1964-66, 1986, 1995; Research Scholar, 1966-69, Research Fellow, 1969-73, Department of Far Eastern History, Australian National University; Foundation Professor in School of Modern Asian Studies, 1974-, Chairman, 1979-85, Co-Director of Key Centre for Asian Languages and Studies, 1988-96, Head of School, Modern Asian Studies, 1996-, Griffith University. Publications: Author or co-Author 35 Books; Numerous articles in journals and chapters in books; Also book reviews. Honours:

International Visitor to USA, 1977; Gold Citation for the Media Peace Prize, UN Association for Australia, 1981, shared; Albert Einstein (1879-1955) International Academy Foundation Cross of Merit (ECOM) Award, 1993. Memberships: Different positions: Asian Studies Association of Australia; Chinese Studies Association of Australia; Queensland History Teachers' Association. Address: 19 Allambee Crescent, Capalaba, Queensland 4157, Australia.

**MACKEY Niloufer,** b. Bombay, India. Mathematician. m. D Steven Mackey. Education: BSc, St Xavier's College, Bombay; PhD, State University of New York, Buffalo, 1995. Appointment: Assistant Professor, Western Michigan University, Kalamazoo, 1995-. Honours: American Fellow, American Association of University Women, 1996; National Science Foundation Grantee, 1997-. Memberships: American Mathematical Society; Mathematical Association of America; Society for Industrial and Applied Mathematics; International Linear Algebra Society; Association for Women in Science; Association for Women in Mathematics; American Association of University Women. Address: Western Michigan University, Department of Mathematics & Statistics, Kalamazoo, MI 49008, USA.

**MADAN MOHAN RAO Gutti,** b. 27 November 1926, Jandrapet, India. Professor. m. Vimala Devi, 2 sons, 3 daughters. Education: BSc, Andhra University, 1948; BSc Hons, University of Madras, 1950; MA, University of Madras, 1953; PhD, University of Toronto, Canada, 1968. Appointments: Lecturer, Andhra, 1950-51; Head of Biology Department, 1950-57; Lecturer, Head of Department, Sir Theagaraya College, 1951-57; Chairman, Postgraduate Department of Zoology, 1957-83; Professor, Chairman, Sir Theagaraya College, 1957-77; Vice Principal, Sir Theagaraya College, 1967-72; Research Professor, Diabetes Research Center, New York Medical College, 1977-78; Principal, Sir Theagaraya College, 1972-83; Senior Researcher, Center for Health and Drug Research Tripoli, 1978-86; Professor of Psysiology, The Great Al-Fateh University; Director, Vimala Institute, 1992-. Publications: 61 Publications. Honours: Bourne's Prize of Presidency College; Caithness Prize of the University of Madras. Memberships: Linnean Society of London; Society for Experimental Biology and Medicine; New York Academy of Sciences. Address: 21 Second Main Road, Ramakrishna Nagar, Madras 600 057, India.

**MADE GOWDA Natkal M,** b. 10 April 1947, Netkal, India. Chemistry Professor. m. Bharathi, 3 daughters. Education: BSc, Chemistry and Physics, University of Mysore, India, 1969; MSc, Chemistry, University of Mysore, India, 1971; PhD, Chemistry, University of Mysore, India, 1978. Appointments: Assistant Professor, 1989-92; Associate Professor, 1992-96; Chairman, Professor, Chemistry, Western Illinois University, 1996-. Publications: 110 Papers, Conference Presentations; 68 Papers. Honours: 5 Faculty Excellence Awards; 1 Outstanding Research Award; 5 Other Honours. Memberships: American Chemical Society; IUPAC; American Institute of Chemists; Illinois Science Academy; Phi Kappa Phi US National Honours Society; Sigma Xi. Address: Department of Chemistry, Western Illinois University, Currens Hall 214B, Maconb, IL 61455, USA.

**MADHAVAN Kutty Shirley,** b. 20 July 1942, Kerala, India. Teacher. m. V K Madhavan Kutty, 2 daughters. Education: BA Hons English, 1962; AMI Montessovi Diploma, Pre-School Education, 1974. Appointments: Principal, The Magic Years, Montessovi Pre School, India. Memberships: Association Montesovi International, Amsterdam; Managing Committee, Madras; Working Committee Andhna Pradesh Montessori Association, Hyderabad. Address: 25 Rahindra Nagar, Nr Lodi Gardens, New Delhi, India.

**MADIAN Mohammed,** b. 3 January 1947, Cairo, Egypt. Professor of Philosophy. m. Hikmat Zahra, 1 son, 2 daughters. Education: BA, 1969, AM, 1976, PhD, 1983, Cairo University. Appointments: Demonstrator, 1969, Lecturer, 1983, Professor, 1998, Cairo University; Assistant Professor, Sultan Qaboos University, Oman, 1987-91. Publications include: The Method in "Principia Ethica", 1988; Philosophical Analysis, 1988; Ethical Intuitionism, 1988; Inquiry into the Problem of Meanings, 1989; Inquiry into the Logic of Ethical Criticism, 1990. Honours: Andre Laland Prize of Philosophy, 1969; Mostafa Abdel Razek Prize of Philosophy, 1983; Zaki Nagib Mahmoud Prize of Philosophy, 1984. Membership: Egyptian Philosophical Society. Address: Department of Philosophy, Cairo University College of Arts, Orman Giza, Cairo, Egypt.

**MADJIROVA Nadejda Petrova,** b. 7 November 1945, Plovdiv. Phsycian; Psychiatrist. m. Petko Valkov, 1 daughter. Education: Medical Education, 1971, Higher Medical Institute, Plovdiv; Specialist in Psychiatry, 1975, Medical Academy, Sofia; PhD Psychiatry, 1985. Appointments: Doctor, Bulgarian Psychiatric Hospital, Radnevo, 1971; Assistant Professor, Department of Psychiatry and Medical Psychology, Plovdiv, 1976; Consultant, Children with psychic problems, 1978-; Chief Assistant-Professor, 1985; Associate Professor, Department of Psychiatry and Medical Psychology, 1989, Lecturer Child Psychiatry, 1989-, Higher Medical Institute, Plovdiv; Lecturer Psychiatry, Medical Faculty, Pazardjik, 1989-91. Publications: Monographs: Chronobiological Aspects in Psychiatry, 1995; Child Complexes, 1996. Contributor articles to professional journals. Memberships: International Society for Chronobiology; President, Bulgarian Chronobiology and Biometeorology Society; Society for Child Psychiatry; Psychiatric Society in Bulgaria; New York Academy of Sciences. Address: Peter Stoev 123, 4004 Plovdiv, Bulgaria.

**MAEDA Yutaka,** b. 7 January 1956, Osaka, Japan. Scientist. m. Keiko, 2 daughters. Education: Bachelor of Engineering, 1979; Master of Engineering, 1981; Dr of Engineering, 1990. Appointments: Teacher, 1979-88; Research Associate, 1988-92; Lecturer, 1992-95; Associate Professor, Kansai University, 1995-. Publiations: IEEE Trans on Neural Networks; IEICE Trans Inf and Syst; Electronics Letters; Neutral Networks. Memberships: IEEE; INNS; IEE of Japan; IEICE; SICE of Japan. Address: Kansas U Dept Elec Engrng, 3-3-15 Yamate-cho, 564 Suita, Japan.

**MAEGAARD Jan Carl Christian,** b. 14 April 1926, Copenhagen. Composer; Professor of Musicology. m. Kirsten Offer Andersen (div), 2 daughters. Education: Music theory, composition, music history, piano, double bass, 1945-50, conducting, 1952, The Royal Danish Conservatory of Music; State certificate as music teacher in music theory and music history, 1953; Musicology, 1951-57, University of Copenhagen; Mag art, 1957; Studies in Los Angeles, 1958-59, 1964; Dr Phil, 1972. Appointments: Freelance musician, 1949-56; Music critic at various newspapers, 1952-60; Teacher, Royal Danish Conservatory of Music, 1953-58; Teaching Assistant, University Copenhagen, 1959-61; Associate Professor, 1961-71; Full Professor, 1971-96; Guest Professor, SUNY at Stony Brook, 1974; Professor of Music, University California at Los Angeles, 1978-81. Publications: Author or co-author 7 books; 50 important articles; Contributor to 7 reference works; Composer much printed music and recorded music; Mentioned in 17 biographical works. Memberships: Danish section, ISCM; Society for Publishing Danish Music; Member of directorium, International Musicological Society, 1989-96; Royal Danish Academy of Sciences and Letters; Norwegian Academy Science and Letters; Danish Composers' Association, with

offices attached. Address: Duevej 14 6, 2000 Frederiksberg, Denmark.

**MAES Michael,** b. 10 March 1954, Ghent, Belgium. Psychiatrist; Director; Professor. m. Carine Steyaert, 2 daughters. Education: MD, University of Ghent, Belgium, 1979; Psychiatrist, 1986; PhD, University of Antwerp, Belgium, 1986. Appointments: Director, Clinical Research Center for Mental Health, Antwerp, Belgium; Professor of Psychiatry and Chairman, Department of Psychiatry, University of Maastricht, the Netherlands; Adjoint Professor, Psychiatry, Vanderbilt University, Nashville, Tennesse, USA; Consultant Psychiatrist, IRCCS, Brescia, Italy. Publications: 300 in international journals on psychoneuroimmunology of psychiatric disorders (depression, schizophrenia). Memberships: Society of Biological Psychiatry; World Psychiatric Association (WPA), section of Affective Disorders; International Society of Psychoneuro (ISANE). Address: Department of Psychiatry and Neuropsychology, University Hospital of Maastricht, Postbus 5800, 6202 AZ Maastricht, The Netherlands.

**MAHABIR Errol,b.** 25 February 1931. Education: BA Adminst. & Mgmt. Appointments: Chairman & MD, Eminent Services International Ltd; Eminent Holdings Ltd; Chairman, Business Forms & MiCr Services; Chairman, Carib Containers Ltd; Chairman, Damus Ltd; Chairman, Damus Roofing, Systems Ltd; Chairman, General Packaging Ltd; Director, Associated Brands Ltd; Director, Consolidated Biscuits Ltd; Director, Sunshine Snacks Co Ltd; Served as member of San Fernando Council, 1959-66; Deputy Mayor of San Fernando, 1960-63; Mayor of San Fernando, 1963-66; Member of Parliament, 1966-86; Served in Governments of Trinidad & Tobago. Memberships: Trade & Economic Missions to South America, USA, Canada, Europe, The Far East. Participant in Commonwealth Heads of Government Meetings; Served as Deputy Political Leader of the Peoples National Movement, 1970-86. Awards: The Order of Diplomatic Service Merit; Gwangha Medal by the Government of The Republic of Korea, 1986; The Gran Cordon of the Order of the Liberator by the Government of Venezuela, 1985. Address: PO box 42, San Fernando, Trinidad & Tobago.

**MAHADEVA SASTRI Korada,** b. 29 December 1921, Machilipatnam, Andhra Pradesh. Professor. m. Saraswathi, 3 sons, 1 daughter. Education: MA Economics, 1942, MA Telugu, 1957, Madras University; MA Comparative Philology, 1951, D Litt, 1961, Calcutta University. Appointments: Researcher in Indian History, Madras University, Research Department, Labour Investigation Committee, Simla, Research Department, Federation of Indian Chambers of Commerce and Industry, New Delhi, Anthropology Department, Indian Museum, Calcutta, 1944-51; Faculty Member, Department of Linguistics, Annamalai University, 1957-60; Faculty Member, Department of Telugu, S V University, Tirupati, 1960-68; Professor, Department of Telugu, S K University, Anantapur, 1968-81; Visiting Professor, Cologne University, Germany, 1976-78. Publications: Historical Grammar of Telugu, 1969; Descriptive Grammar and Handbook of Modern Telugu, 1985; Publications in Telugu on Telugu language and literature. Honours: President, Dravidian Culture Section of the All India Oriental Conference, Shantiniketan, 1976. Membership: Life Member of the Dravidian Linguistics Association, Trivandrum. Address: 1/92-C1-B2-A1, Dwarakanagar, Anantapur 515 004 (AP), India.

**MAHARAJA Suraksha,** b. 26 January 1935, Ahmedabad, India. Retired Government Officer. Education: BA, 1955-57; MEd, 1964; PhD, 1987. Appointments: Retired Government Officer, Department of Public Health, State Petrol. Honours: Distinguished Leadership Award, ABI, USA; Golden Poet ward, USA. Address: D3/Akashdeep Apartment, Ellisbridge, hmedabad 380006, Gujarat State, India.

**MAHBOOBANI Vinod,** b. 5 January 1966, Hong Kong. enior Attorney. m. Venita, 2 daughters. Education: LLB, 1988, ostgraduate Certificate in Laws, 1989, University of Hong ong; Masters in Applied Finance, Macquarie University, 1996. ppointments: Solicitor, Denton Hall, 1991-93; Solicitor, asons, 1993-96; Attorney, Pepsico Inc, 1996-97; Attorney, ricon Restaurants Intl, 1997-; all in Hong Kong. Honours: acquarie Prize in Management of Financial Institutions, 1996; reshfields Prize in Commercial Law, 1989. Memberships: Law ociety of Hong Kong, 1991-; Law Society of England and Vales, 1992-; Associate Member, Chartered Institute of rbitrators, 1991-; Rotary Club of Wanchai, Hong Kong, 1992-, oard Member, 1993-94, 1996-97. Address: Tsim Sha Tsui, O Box 97091, Kowloon, Hong Kong.

**MAHESH Virendra Bhusan,** b. 25 April 1932, India. ndocrinologist. m. Sushila Kumari Aggarwal, 1 son, 1 aughter. Education: BSc Hons, 1951, Patna University, India; Sc Chemistry, 1953, Delhi University; PhD, 1955; DPhil iological Science, 1958, Oxford University; James Hudson rown Memorial Fellow, Yale University, 1958-59. ppointments: Assistant Research Professor, Endocrinology, ledical College Georgia, Augusta, 1959-63; Associate esearch Professor, 1963-66; Professor, 1966-70; Regents rofessor, 1970-86; Robert B Greenblatt Professor, 1979-; hairman Endocrinology, 1972-86; Chairman, Regents rofessor Physiology and Endocrinology, 1986-; Chairman hysiology and Endocrinology, 1986-; Director, Centre for opulation Studies, 1971-; Editorial Board, Steroids, 1963, ournal of Steroid Biochemistry and Molecular Biology, 1991-, ndocrinology, 1999; Editor-in-Chief, Biology of Reproduction. ublications: Contributor articles to professional journals, hapters to books; Editor: The Pituitary, a Current Review; unctional Correlates of Hormone Receptors in Reproduction; Recent Advances in Fertility Research; Hirsuitism and Virilism; Regulation of Ovarian and Testicular Function; Excitatory mino Acids: Their Role in Neuroendocrine Function. Honours: Research Grantee NIH, 1960; Rubin Award, American Society tudy of Sterility, 1962; Billings Silver Medal, 1965; Best eacher Award, Freshman Class, 1969; Outstanding Faculty ward, 1981, 1994; Distinguished Teaching Award, 1988; Excellence in Research Award, 1987-91, 1993-95; Distinguished Scientist Award, Association of Scientist of Indian Origin in America, 1989; Carl G Hartman Award, Society fo the tudy of Reproduction, 1996; Lifetime Achievement Award, 997. Memberships include: Royal Society of Chemists Enland); Society of Biochemistry and Molecular Biology; American Physiological Society; Society Neuroscience; Endocrine Society; Society for Gynaecologic Investigation; nternational Society Reproductive Medicine. Address: Medical College of Georgia, Department Physiology & Endocrinology, Augusta, GA 30912-3000, USA.

**MAHESWARAN Kalaranji,** b. 5 December 1959, Sri Lanka. Researcher; Consultant. Education: MSc Hons Agronomy. Appointments: Research Scientist, 1984-86; Management Consultant, 1986-90; Free Lance Consultant, 1990-96; Partner, Consultant, MSK Consultancy and Research, 1996-. Membership: Life member, National Agricultural Association of Sri-Lanka. Address: 2B 10th Lane, Colombo-3, Sri Lanka.

**MAHMOUD Ben,** b. 6 October 1935, Charleston, West Virginia, USA. Artist; Professor. m. Wendy Ellen Kravit Mahmoud, 1 son, 2 daughters. Education: Prof Certificate, 1953, Columbus Art School, Ohio; BFA, 1958, MFA, 1960, Ohio University. Appointments: Instructor: Columbus College

of Art & Design, 1960-61, La Universidad Interamerican, Puerto Rico, 1961-63; Assistant Professor, 1965-68, Associate Professor, 1968-72, Professor, 1972-89, Presidential Research Professor, 1989-94, Distinguished Research Professor, 1994-98, Distinguished Professor Emeritus, 1998, Northern Illinois University; 300 solo exhibitions in USA, Holland and Germany; Represented in 10 public collections throughout the uSA. Honours: Appointed to the Board of Directors of Illinois Arts Council; Chair, Visual Arts Panel and Ethnic Arts Panel, 1974-78; Fellowship in Painting, National Endowment for the Arts, 1975. Address: 10/6 Market Street, De Kalb, IL 60115-3527, USA.

**MAI Yiu-Wing,** b. 5 January 1946, Hong Kong. Educator. m. Louisa Kit-Ling Mai. Education: BSc, Engineering, 1969; PhD, 1972. Appointments: Lecturer, 1976-78, Senior Lecturer, 1979-82, Associate Professor, 1983-87, Personal Chair, 1987-, Sydney University; Adjunct Professor, HKUST, 1995-. Publications: 3 books, over 350 papers in professional journals. Honour: Fellow, Australian Academy of Technological Sciences and Engineering, 1992. Memberships: FIEAust; FHKIE; MASME. Address: 20 Charles Street, Killara, NSW 2071, Australia.

**MAITLAND Geoffrey,b.** 27 August 1924. Physiotherapist. m. 1 son. Education: M in Applied Science, South Australian Institute of Technology, 1986. Appointments: Physiotherapy Department, Royal Adelaide Hospital, 1950-52; Adelaide Children's Hospital, 1951; Clinical Tutor, Physiotherapy University of Adelaide, 1952; Private Practice, 1952-98; Convenor, 2 physiotherapy congresses; RAF, 1942-45. Publications: Vertebral manipulations, 6 edits, 1964-97; Peripheral Manipulations, 3 edits, 1973-; Examination and Recording Guide, 6 edits; Co-author, Practical Orthapedic Medicine, 1983; Musculoskeletal and Sports Injuries, 1994; Vertebral Muskuloskeletal Disorders, 1998. Honour: Named to Most Excellent Order of the British Empire. Memberships: Anglican Church of Australia, Plympton, 1956; Server and counsellor, 1959; Server and sidesman, Lay Assistant, 1965; South Australian Registration Board, 1960-82; International Maitland Teachers Association, Switzerland, 1978-; Fellow, Australian Coll. Physiotherapists; Australian College Manipulative Physiotherapists; Chartered Society of Physiotherapy; Australian Physiotherapy Association; South African Society of Physiotherapists; Schwerischer Verband fur Manipulative Physiotherapie; Nederlandse Vereniging Manipulative Therapie; Deutscher Verband Manuelle Therapie; South Australian Cricket Association. Address: 7 Warburton Ct, Beaumont 5066, Australia.

**MAJASAN James Adeyemi,** b. 3 April 1917, Ipele, Nigeria. Teacher. m. Victoria Odole, 2 sons, 4 daughters. Education: BA, honours, 1956; Dip.Ed, 1957; PhD, 1967. Appointments: Primary School Teacher, 1933-45; Secondary School Teacher, 1945-60; University Teacher, University of Ibadan, 1960-79. Publications: Several articles in professional journals. Memberships: NUT; NGA; FRGS; ISRD; WCCL. Address: Department of Education, University of Ibadan, Ibadan Oyo State, Nigeria.

**MAJESKI James Anthony,** b. 29 January 1945, Newark, New Jersey, USA. Surgeon. m. Elizabeth D Majeski, 1 son, 2 daughters. Education: BS, The Citadel, 1966; MS, University of South Carolina, 1968; PhD, 1971, MD, 1974, Medical University of South Carolina. Appointments: Research Fellow, Pathology, Medical University of South Carolina, 1972-74; Surgical Residency and Transplantation Fellowship, University of Cincinnati, 1974-81; Instructor, Surgery, University of Cincinnati, 1979-81; Assistant Professor, Surgery, Medical

University of South Carolina, 1981-. Publications: Numerous articles in scientific journals and textbooks. Honours include: Eagle Scout Award, 1957; Roe Award, 1990; Jefferson Award, 1972; Mead Johnson Award, 1972; Mosby Award, 1973; Fellow, American College of Surgeons, 1994; Fellow, International College of Surgeons, 1995; George Meany Award, 1996; Spurgeon Award, 1997. Memberships: American Medical Association; Southern Medical Association; American Society of Transplant Surgeons; Sigma Xi. Address: 900 Bowman Road, Mount Pleasant, SC 29464, USA.

**MAJEWSKA Anna Cyryla,** b. 30 June 1953, Kepno, Poland. Parasitologist. Education: MSc, Adam Mickiewicz University, Poznan, 1977; PhD, Karol Marcinkowski University of Medical Science, Poznan, 1984; Postdoctoral Examination and Dissertation to qualify as Associate Professor, Witold Stefanski Institute of Parasitology, Polish Academy of Sciences, Warsaw, 1997. Appointments: Assistant Lecturer, 1977-80, Lecturer, 1980-84, Adjunct Professor, 1984-97, Associate Professor, 1997-, Department of Biology and Medical Parasitology, K Marcinkowski University of Medical Science. Publications: Contributor of over 100 articles to professional journals; Co-author of 18 handbooks. Honours: Science Awards, Rector of Karol Marcinkowski University of Medical Science, 1980, 1982, 1983, 1984, 1985, 1997, 1998; Science Awards, Polish Ministry of Health and Welfare, 1986, 1992, 1996. Memberships: Polish Parasitology Society; Polish Entomological Society; Protistology Club; National Geographic Society. Address: Department of Biology and Medical Parasitology, Karol Marcinkowski University of Medical Science, Fredry 10, 61-701 Poznan, Poland.

**MAJUMDAR Manas,** b. 28 November 1944, Mallarpur, Birbhum, West Bengal, India. Educator. m. Suprabha. Education: MA, 1966, PhD, 1980, Calcutta University. Appointments: Teacher: Jangipur College, 1967-68; Scottishchurch College, 1968-69; Chandernagore College, 1969-73; Goenka College of Commerce and Business Administration, 1973-74; Kalyni University, 1974; Calcutta University, 1974-. Publications: Natyakar Tarasankar, Tarasankar as a Dramatist, 1977; Akshoykumar Baral o Bangla Sahitya, 1983; Through the Mirror of Folk Tradition, 1993; Great Famine of 1350 BS as a Background of Bengali Short Stories, 1994; Ramalore and Rabindranath, 1995. Memberships: Folk & Tribal Cultural Centres, Calcutta; Bangla Akademy; Fellow, Royal Asiatic Society, London. Address: CA 187 Sector 1, Salt Lake City, Calcutta 700064 WB, India.

**MAKAI Frantisek,** b. 26 May 1933, Bratislava. Professor, Orthopaedic Surgeon. m. Izabella, 1 son, 1 daughter. Education: Doctor of Medicine, 1957; PhD, 1968; Associate Professor, 1983; DSc, 1989; Professor, 1990. Appointments: Head, Department of Orthopaedics, Bratislava; Head, Chair of Orthopaedics, Bratislava; Post Graduate, Medical Institute; President, Slovak Orthopaedic Trauma Society; Head, Scientific Committee, Slovak Ministry of Health; Chief, Orthopaedic Surgery, Ministry of Health. Publications: 80 Scientific Publications, 80 Over seas; 630 Scientific Papers. Honours: Gold Medal, Slovak Academy of Science; Gold Medal, Medical Faculty; Silver Medal, Medical Association. Memberships: Honorary Member, Polish, Hungaran, Czech Republic Orthpaedic Society; Hungarian, Slovak Rheumat Society. Address: Zrinskeno 7, Bratislava 81103, Slovak Republic.

**MAKAVICIUS Deividas,** b. 25 June 1972, Mazeikiai, Lithuania. Biologist. Education: Vilnius Pedagogical University, 1993-97. Appointments: Biologist in Kamanos State Nature Reserve, 1991-97; Assistant in Nemunas Delta Design, Ministry

of Environmental Protection, 1997; Director, Kamanos Stat Nature Reserve, 1997-. Memberships: Lithuania Ornithological Society of Biodiversity Protection Society Address: Naftininku 16-36, LT 5500 Mazeikiai, Lithuania.

**MAKI Andrea,** b. 10 September 1966, Seattle, Washingtor USA. Painter. Education: University of Washington, 1984-85 BS, Painting, New York University, New York City, 1988 Career: Solo Exhibitions: A Documentation, Union Settlemen New York City, 1988; Studio Exhibition, 711 John, Seattle USA, 1989; Jigging, 1988-91, Wilkey - Modern an Contemporary, Seattle, 1991; Jigging 2, 1988-92, J Rosentha Fine Arts Ltd, Chicago, USA, 1992; Dakota Zoo, Lannon-Cole Chicago, USA, 1992; Crazy River, Ratner Gallery, Chicago 1994; Maki/Maki, Butter's Gallery, Portland, OR, USA, 1994 Wild Rooster, Kantor Gallery, LA, 1995; Group Exhbitions 1990 Northwest International Art Competition, Whatcon Museum, Bellingham; Illiminance 90, Lubbock Fine Arts Center Lubbock, TX National Traveling Exhibition/Catalogue; 1991 The Artist in Art: Self Portraits, Bumbershoot 1991, Seattle Introductions 1991, William Traver Gallery, Seattle; 1991-92 Group Show, Wilkey - Modern and Contemporary, Seattle 1995: Pasted Papers - Collage and the Twentieth Century Louis Stern Fine Arts, Los Angeles, USA; Installations: Seattle Invitational - 20/20, Security Pacific Gallery, Seattle, 1992; The Single Guy, Attraction, NBC, Castle Rock Productions, 1995 Publications include: Photography: A Point of Departure, 1993 Father-daughter Exhibit Pushes as it Pulls, 1994; Form Follows Family, 1994; New American Paintings, 1996. Mentioned in "A Need for 'Accents' - Andrea Maki's Work Skillfully Balances Photography and Painting", by Alan G. Artner and "Andrea Maki at Wilkey - Modern & Contemporary", by Zoe Anglesey Address: 12239 10th Avenue, Seattle, WA 98168, USA.

**MAKOTA Cecilia Violet,** b. 30 May 1932, Butterworth South Africa. m. Jonathan D Makota, 1 son, 5 daughters Education: Upper Primary School Teachers' Certificate, 1952 Appointment: Executive Director. Honour: Women's Worlc Summit Foundation. Membership: Associated Country Womer of the World. Address: PO Box 50377, Lusaka, Zambia.

**MAKSTELE Jonas,** b. 27 April 1933, Ciuladai v Kupiskis D General Manager. m. Zita Vida, 1 son. Education: Kaunas Polytechnic Institute, 1953-58. Appointments: Senior Mechanic 1958-59; Senior Engineer, 1959-63; Director, Anyksciu Vynas 1963-86; Head, Beverages Department, Lithuanian Agro-industrial Centre, 1986-91; Chief Specialist, AIMA UAB 1991-95; General Manager, AB Zanyksciu, Vynas, 1995-. Honours: Merited Lithuanian Engineer, 1979; Honorary Inventor, 1975. Address: J Biliuno 10-2, LT 4930 Anyksciai, Lithuania.

**MALABA Griffiths,** b. 24 July 1924, Matobo, Zimbabwe. Josephine, 3 sons, 2 daughters. Education: BA, South Africa, 1949; UED, South Africa, 1950; Certificate in Advancec Religious Studies, 1958; Union Theological Seminary, New York, USA. Appointments: Headmaster, Thekwane Secondary School, 1951-66; Education Officer, 1966-68; Deputy Regional and later Regional Director of Education, 1972-78; Public Service Commissioner, 1979-83; Personnel Executive udc Ltd, 1983-89; Director, Air Zimbabwe and Affretair, 1990-; Trustee, Astra Pension Fund, 1997-; Trustee, Zimbabwe Mass Media Trust, 1994-; Director, Zimbabwe School Examinations Council 1995-; Vice Chairman, Presidential Education and Training Review Commission, 1998-. Methodist Minister; Chairman Zimbabwe Aids Prevention and Support Organisation, 1996- Publications: Ulunguza - A Ndebele Novel. Honours: Worlc Council of Churches Fellowship, 1957-58; Commonwealth Fellowship for Inspector Training, 1965. Address: udc Ltd, udc

Centre, Cnr First, Union Avenue, POB 1685, Harare, Zimbabwe.

**MALAKHOVSKII Alexander,** b. 6 January 1937, Kemezovo, USSR. Physicist. m. Ljubov Malakhovskaya, 1 son, 2 daughters. Education: Degree in electronic Engineering, 1960, V I Uliyanov Leningrad Institute; PhD Physics, 1974, USSR Academy, Krasnoyarsk; Postgrad 1983. Appointments: Senior Engineer, Machine Works, Krasnoyarsk, USSR, 1960-65; Senior Engineer, Institute Physics, Krasnoyarsk, 1965-69; Scientific Worker, 1969-80, Senior Scientific Worker, 1980-92; Senior Researcher, Bar-Ilan University, Ramat-Gan, Israel, 1994-. Publication: Monograph: Selected problems of optics and magneto-optics of transition elements compounds, 1992. Address: Bar-Ilan University, Department of Chemistry, 52900 Ramat-Gan, Israel.

**MALAYA Lubov,** b. 13 January 1919, Kopany Settlement, Zaporozhje, Ukraine. Professor of Medicine; Internist. Education: Diploma, Kharkov Medical Institute, 1938; Doctor of Medical Sciences, 1954; Professor, 1955. Appointments: Director, Ukranian Research Institute of Therapy; Chief, department of Internal Diseases, Kharkov State Medical University. Honours: Merited Figure of Science, 1968; Hero of the Socialist Labour, 1979; Laureat of the USSR State Prize, 1980; Awarded with 4 orders and 11 medals. Memberships: Academy of Medical Sciences of the USSR; National Academy of Sciences of Ukraine; Ukrainian Academy of Medical Sciences; International Association of Internists; International Society of Cardiovascular Pharmacotherapy; International Society of Hypertension. Address: Institute of Therapy, Prosp Postysheva 2A, Kharkov 310000, Ukraine.

**MALEKOPMATH Parvatidevi,** b. 29 June 1957, Belgaum. Musician, Industrialist. m. Vijaykumar, 2 sons, 1 daughter. Education: Vidwat Music Exam, 1990; Vishard Music Exam, 1992. Appointments: All India Radio Aroist, 1980-; Running Steel Furniture Manufacturing Unit, 1994-; Performing Artist, Performed in Noted Concerts. Honours: Gana Kogile, 1993; Pt Puttaraj Gawai, 1995. Memberships: Ganamadhuryam Nidhi, 1996; Swara-Shri, 1997; Mallikaye, Ghazal, 1998; Mallikaye, Tarannum, 1998. Address: Diamond Bldg Extension, Gadag 582 101, India.

**MALHAN Inder Vir,** b. 31 May 1954, India. Library and Information Scientist. m. Poonam Malhan, 2 sons. Education: BSc, 1975; BLib.Sc, 1976; MLib.Sc, 1977; PhD, 1986; Advanced Diploma, 1992. Appointments: Librarian, CAS Geology, PU, 1977-79; Lecturer, 1979-82; Research Fellow, 1982-83; Lecturer, 1983-87; Librarian, University of Jammu, 1987-. Honours: Leadership Development Grant, IASL, 1989; Fulbright Fellowship, Library and Information Science, 1996-97. Memberships: ILA; IATLIS; SIS; ISKO Germany; Association of Indian University Librarians. Address: Department of Library Science, University of Jammu, Canal Road, Jammu (Tawi), India.

**MALHOTRA Ashok,** b. 1 April 1940, India. Professor. Education: BA, 1961, MA, 1963, University of Rajasthan; PhD, University of Hawaii, USA, 1969. Appointment: Professor, Philosophy, State University of New York at Oneonta; Consultant, TV series, Kung Fu: The Legend Continues. Publications include: Books: Pathways to Philosophy: A Multidisciplinary Approach; Jean Paul Sartre's Existentialism in Nausea and Being and Nothingness; Sartre's Existentialism in Literature and Philosophy; Culture and Self; Transcreation of the Bhagavad Gita; Poetry: What is Love; What is Life; What is Death; Joyous Nothingness; Celebration of Life; Song of Love. Honours: Winner of Gold Medal in MA Examination; SUNY

Chancellor's Award for Excellence in Teaching; Certificate of Recognition for Bringing Cultural Understanding between East and West, University of Hawaii. Memberships: Association for Asian Studies; Society for Asian and Comparative Philosophy; Society for the Comparative Study of Civilizations; Jean-Paul Sartre Society; American Philosophical Association; International Phenomenological Society. Address: Department of Philosophy, University of New York, #513 Fitzelle Hall, Oneonta, NY 13820, USA.

**MALIK Raymond Howard,** b. 4 February 1933, Lebanon. Economist, Scientist, Corporate Executive, Inventor, Educator, Multilingual. 1 son, 1 daughter. Education: BA, 1950; BSBA, 1951; MSBA, 1956; PhD, ScD, 1959. Appointments: Arabian American Oil Company, Beirut, 1952-54; Faculty Advisor, Illinois State University, 1954-59; Professor, Head World Trade Programs, Central YMCA Community College, Chicago, 1966-74; President, Malik International Enterprises Ltd, Chicago, 1959-. Publications: The Guide to Youth, Health and Longevity, 1980; Do You Really Need Glasses, 1988. Honours: Fulbright Scholarship; Methodist Church Scholarship; Southern University Fellow. Memberships: Phi Beta Kappa; Alpha Phi Omega; Sigma Xi; Delta Rho; Beta Gamma Sigma; IREE. Address: P O Box 3194, Chicago, IL 60654-0194, USA.

**MALIK Vinay,** b. 23 September 1975, Haryana. Painter. Education: BFA in Painting, 1998, Government College of Art, Chandigarh, India. Appointments: Art Director, International Interior Designing, 1998-. Publications: The Tribune; Hindustan Times; Times of India; Danik Tribune; Punjab Kesri; Divya Himachal; Daily Sunshine; Chandigarh Newsline. Honours: Merit Certificate, Art Exhibition, 1989-90, Poster Competition, 1989; Participated in National Youth Meeting, Society for Promotion of Youth and Masses, New Delhi, 1992; Participated in National Workshop on Youth and AIDS, 1993; Regularly participated in art exhibitions, poster exhibitions, winning many honours & awards, Chandigarh Administration, India, 1994-96; Honourable Mention Awards in both Water Colour and Painting Exhibition organised by Avantika, 1997; Participated in exhibition, Yesterday - Today - Tomorrow to celebrate Golden Jubilee of Independent India, organised by Chandigarh Lalit Kala Academy, 1997; Scholarship Grant, Drawing Exhibition organised by All India Fine Arts and Crafts Society, 1997; Best Painting Award, Exhibition for Artists under 30 Years, Chd Lalit Kala Academy, 1998; Amrita Shergill Award for Best Painting of Year, 1998, Institute of Fine Arts, Chandigarh. Address: Chandigarh House No 74 L, Model Town, Rohtak 124001, India.

**MALINAUSKAS Albertas,** b. 24 November 1952, Vilnius, Lithuania. Chemist. m. Jule Vasiulyte, 1 son, 1 daughter. Education: MSc, University of Vilnius, 1975; PhD, University of Moscow, 1979; DrHabil, Institute of Chemistry, Vilnius, 1994. Appointments: From Engineer to Junior Scientist, Institute of Biochemistry, Vilnius, Lithuania, 1975-80; From Junior Scientist to Head of Department, Institute of Chemistry, Vilnius, 1980-. Publications: Over 100 scientific papers; 26 patents. Address: Institute of Chemistry, Gostauto Str 9, LT-2600 Vilnius, Lithuania.

**MALLIGA Vasantha,** b. 28 April 1944, Bangalore, India. Headmistress. m. B S Gopala Krishana, 16 February 1972, 2 sons. Education: BSc; BEd; FUWAI. Appointments: Monitor, Sree Saraswathi Vidaya Mandira; Teacher, Purna Prajana Education Society; Teacher, Parents Association High School; Headmistress, 1972-. Address: No CA-2, V Block, RPA High School, Rajajinagar, Bangalore 560010, India.

**MALLOUH Ahmad A,** b. 10 January 1945, Jaffa Palestine. m. Ayisha I, 2 sons, 3 daughters. Education: MB BCh, Cairo University, 1969; American Board of Pediatricians, 1975; American Board of Pediatrics Hematology, Oncology, 1980. Appointments: General Practitioner, 1970-72; Pediatric Resident, 1972-75; Locum Pediatrician, 1975; Pediatrician, 1976-77; Fellow Pediatric Hematology, Oncology, University of Alabama, 1977-79; Pediatric Hematologist, Oncologist, Dhahran Health Center, 1979-; Chief, General Pediatric Services Division, 1993-96; Chief, Speciality Pediatric Services Division, 1996-. Publications: 54 Publications; 35 Published abstracts in medical journals. Honours: Honour in MB MCH, Cairo University, 1969. Memberships: American Academy of Pediatric; American Society of Clinical Oncology; American Society of Pediatrics Hematology, Oncology; American Society of Hematology; Jordan Medical Association; Jordan Pediatrics Society; Jordan Society of Pediatric Hematology, Oncology. Address: P O Box 8250, Dhahran 31311, Saudi Arabia.

**MALMBORG Charles J,** b. 16 January 1955, Dunkirk, NY, USA. Professor. m. Candace. Education: BS IEOR, University of Massachusetts, 1976; MSIE, 1978, PhD, 1981, Georgia Tech. Appointments: Assistant Professor, 1985; Associate Professor, 1988; Full Professor RPI, 1995; Acting Chair, 1996-97; DSES Department, 1998-. Publications: 100 Technical Publications, International Journals. Memberships: IIE; IEEE; Alpha Pi Mu. Address: Rensselaer Polytechnic Inst, Dept of DSES-RPI, 110 8th St, Troy, NY 12180, USA.

**MALSCH Reinhard,** b. 5 September 1961, Bretten. Pharmacist. m. Doris Malsch, 1 son, 2 daughters. Education: Pharmacist, 1989; PhD, 1994. Appointments: Researcher, 1993-97; Pharmacist, 1997-99. Publication: German Patent, 1993. Honour: German Research Fund Grantee. Memberships: Society of Thrombosis and Haematosis (Germany); New York Academy of Science. Address: Markt Apotheke, Markstrasse 2, D-3155 Neustadt, Germany.

**MALTBY Per Eugen,** b. 3 November 1933, Oslo, Norway. Astrophysicist. m. Elisabet Ruud, 28 July 1956, 1 son, 1 daughter. Education: Candidate Degree, University of Oslo, 1957; Dr of Philosophiae, 1964. Appointments: Research Fellow, 1960-61, Senior Research Fellow, 1964-65, California Institute of Technology; Amanuensis, University of Bergen, 1961-63; Visiting Scientist, CSIRO, Sydney, Australia, 1974-75; Chairman, Astronomy Department, 1975-77; Chairman, Norwegian Council for Natural Science Research, 1978-80; Reader, 1963-67, Dosent, 1967-82, Professor, 1983-, University of Oslo. Memberships: International Astronomical Union; Norwegian Academy of Science and Letters; American Astronomical Society; European Physics Society; Norwegian Physics Society. Address: Postboks, 1029 Blindern, 0315 Oslo, Norway.

**MALYSHEV Anatoly,** b. 18 February 1937, Kirovsky, Russia. Surgeon. m. Vera. Education: Vladivostok Medical Institute, 1965; PhD, Professor, 1984. Career: Surgeon, 1965-; Assistant Professor, 1968; Associate Professor, 1974; Full Professor, 1984; Chairman, Marine, Medicine and Gepathology Chair, Vladivostok Medical University. Publications: 86 articles, 1 book. Honour: Ministry Certificate of the Best. Membership: Chairman, Primorsky Regional Association of Surgeons. Address: ostryakov av 2, 690600 Vladivostok, Russia.

**MAMMOLITI Anna Maria,** b. 28 August 1944, Melissano, Lecce, Italy. Editor; Journalist. m. Pierluigi Severi, 2 sons, 1 daughter. Education: Graduated Sociology summa cum laude, University of Rome. Appointments: Freelance Journalist, 1978-; National President, Club delle Donne, 1982; Founder, Premio Minerva, an award assigned yearly to women for personal merits and professional capabilities; Editor and Publisher, monthly magazine, Minerva; President, Minerva Publishing House; Editor and Publisher, Agenzia Minerva Informazione Donna, 1987; Town Councillor, Rome, 1989-91; Promoter of 2 year journalism course, Minerva Publishers, 1996-98. Publications: Essay, History of Feminism, 1975; 4 vols about Women's history in several fields of knowledge, 1992; Viaggio intorno alle donne, culture and worth in 80s, 1992; Vademecum del cittadino, 1996. Honours: Prize, Fregene for Peccato Capitale -la droga a Roma, 1982; Prize for Culture, Presidency of the Council of Ministers for Club delle Donne, 1985; Cavaliere Ufficiale della Repubblica, President of the Republic Francesco Cossiga, 1986; Recognition as one of the best Italian woman journalist by association Italia Nostra, 1987; Maggiore dei Corpi Sanitari Internazionali Garibaldini, 1988. Memberships include: President, Club Delle Donne. Address: Via Pierlugi, da Palestrina 48, 00193 Rome, Italy.

**MANDAL Gopal Prasad,** b. 15 May 1949, Tamluk, India. Teacher; Sculptor. m. Prabhati Mandal, 2 sons, 1 daughter. Education: BSc, 1970; Diploma, Modelling and Sculpture, 1975; Art Appreciation, 1976; Cultural Scholar, 1977-79; Teachership, 1978; MA, History of Art, 1981. Career: Assistant Professor, Modelling and Sculpture, 1990, Associate Professor, Department of Arts and Crafts, 1997, Government College of Education. Publications: Several articles in professional magazines. Memberships: Several. Address: College of Arts & Crafts, 28 J N Road, Calcutta 700016, India.

**MANDAL Jnanendra Nath,** b. 19 April 1951, Calcutta, India. Teacher, Researcher, Consultant. m. Mausumi, 1 son. Education: BE, Civil, 1974; M Tech, Geotechniques, 1977; PhD, Reinforced Soil, 1082. Appointments: Lecturer, 1980-82; Post Doctoral Fellow, 1982-84; Assistant Professor, 1984-90; Associate Professor, 1990-. Publications: More than 200 Papers, International Journals. Honours: 2 Indian Geotechnical Society Awards; Shamsher Prakash Research Award; Vijay Shree Award. Memberships: Institution of Engineers; Construction and Building Material; International Geosynthetic Society;Geotextiles and Geomembranes. Address: C-160 Hill Side IIT Powas, Block A-3rd Floor, Maharashtra, India.

**MANDEL H(arold) George,** b. 6 June 1924, Berlin. Pharmacologist. m. Marianne Klein, 2 daughters. Education: BS, 1944, Yale University; PhD, 1949. Appointments: Laboratory Instructor in Chemistry, Yale University, 1942-44, 1947-49; Research Associate, Department of Pharmacology, George Washington University, 1949-50, Assistant Research Professor, 1950-52, Associate Professor Pharmacology, 1952-58, Professor, 1958-, Chairman, Department of Pharmacology, 1960-96. Publications: Numerous publications on cancer chemotherapy, mechanism of growth inhibition, antimetabolites, drug disposition, chemical carcinogenesis. Honours: Advanced Commonwealth Fund Fellow, Molteno Institute, Cambridge (England) University, 1956; Commonwealth Fund Fellow, University Auckland, NZ, and University Medical Sciences, Bangkok, Thailand, 1964; American Cancer Society Eleanor Roosevelt International Fellow, Chester Beatty Research Institute, London, 1970-71; several other scholarships and research grants; Recipient, John J Abel Award in Pharmacology, Eli Lilly & Co, 1958; Distinguished Achievement Award, Washington Academy of Sciences, 1958; Golden Apple Teaching Award, AMA, 1969, 1985, 1997; George Washington Award, 1998. Memberships: Fellow, Medical Research Council Toxicology Unit, Carshalton, England, 1986; Cancer Chemotherapy Com International Union Against Cancer, 1966-73; Board of Advisors, Roswell Park Cancer Institute, Buffalo, NY, 1972-74; Fellow, Lyon, France,

1989; Honarary Fellow, University College, London, 1993-; Consultant, Bur Drugs, FDA, 1975-79, EPA, 1978-82; Member various NRC-NAS committees, 1965-86; AAAS; American Chemical Society; American Society Biochemistry and Molecular Biology; American Society Pharmacology and Experimental Therapeutics; Chairman, National Caucus of Basic Biomedical Science Chairs, 1991-; American Association for Cancer Research; and others. Address: 4956 Sentinel Drive, Bethesda, MD 20816 3562, USA.

**MANEVICH Michael,** b. 19 July 1946, Novosibirsk, Russia. Physicist; Researcher. m. Lyubov Belonosov, 1 son. Education: MS, Novosibirsk Inst of Electric Engineers, 1971; PhD, Novosibirsk, Russia, 1988. Appointments: Institute of Semiconductor Devices, 1971-75; Researcher, Novosibirsk Institute of Electrovacuum Devices, 1975-81; Head of Laboratory, Head of Department, Novosibirsk Institute of Applied Microelectronics, 1981-92; Lecturer, Associate Professor, Novosibirsk Institute of Electrotechnology Engineering, 1986-92; Senior Researcher, Jerusalem College of Technology, 1993-. Publications: Over 70 articles in professional journals. Address: Jerusalem College of Technology, 21 Havaad Haleumi Street #16031, Jerusalem 91160, Israel.

**MANFREDI Roberto,** b. 22 June 1964, Bologna, Italy. Physician; Researcher. Education: MD, University of Bologna, 1988; Infectious Disease Specialist, University of Bologna, 1992. Appointments: Researcher and Grantee, University of Bologna, 1986-91; Consultant for S Orsola-Malpighi Hospital, Rizzoli Hospital, Bellaria Hospital, Bologna, 1991-; Medical Assistant, Infectious Diseases, University of Bologna, 1991-93; Associate, Infectious Diseases, University of Bologna, 1993-; Contract Professor of Infectious Diseases, University of Bologna, 1996-. Publications: Nearly 600 in scientific journals, congress proceedings, books, monographs. Honours: L Concato Award, University of Bologna, 1988; F Schiassi Award, Medical-Surgical Society of Bologna, 1989; G Salvioli Award, University of Bologna, 1991. Memberships: International Society of Infectious Diseases; Italian Society of Infectious and Parasite Diseases, 1986-. Address: Instituto Malattie Infettive, Via Massarenti 11, 40138 Bologna, Italy.

**MANGA Vinod,** b. 29 December 1954, Jallandhar City. Researcher. m. Sudershan Manga, 1 son, 1 daughter. Education: BSc, 1974; MSc, Plant Breeding, 1977; PhD, 1995. Appointments: Senior Scientist, Plant Breeding, Cazri, Jodhpur, India, 1986-. Publications: 57. Honour: Fellow, Indian Society of Genetics and Plant Breeding. Memberships: Arid Zone Research Association of India; Crop Improvement Society of India; Indian Society of Genetics and Plant Breeding. Address: 1st Exit, B-31 Kamla Nehru Nagar, 1sr Ext, Jodhpur 342 009, India.

**MANGAL Lal Chand Gupta,** b. 15 March 1946, Lukhi, Kurukshetra, India. Professor. m. Usha Lal, 2 sons, 1 daughter. Education: BA, (Honours), 1965; MA, 1967; PhD, 1970. Appointments: Lecturer, 1970-78; Assistant Director, 1979-88; Lecturer, 1988-91; Associate Professor, 1992-94; Professor, 1994-. Publications: 12 books, over 100 articles in professional journals. Honour: Gold Medal. Address: Kurukshetra University, Kurukshetra, India.

**MANGERUD Jan,** b. 29 November 1937, Oslo, Norway. Professor of Geology. m. Bjorg Mangerud, 2 sons, 1 daughter. Education: Cand.mag, University of Oslo, 1961; Cand.real, University of Bergen, 1962; Dr.philos, University of Bergen, 1973. Appointments: Scientist, 1963-67, University Lecturer, 1967-77, Professor, 1977-, Head of Department, 1981-83,

Department of Geology, University of Bergen; Visiting Scientist, University of Stockholm, 1965, University of Minnesota, 1972; Visiting Professor, University of Colorado, 1982-83, 1990-91, 1997; Member, Natural Sciences Research Council, 1976-79; Chairman, National Radiocarbon Laboratory, 1994-97. Publications: Over 100 papers in international scientific journals on the dating, paleoclimate and development of the Ice Ages in NW Europe and the Arctic. Honours: Reusch Medal, Geological Society of Norway; Nansen Award for Polar Research, University of Oslo; Fellow, Royal Norwegian Society of Science, Norwegian Academy of Sciences, Academia Europea; Royal Physiographic Society, Lund, Sweden. Memberships: Geological Society of Norway; Norwegian Geographic Society; Geological Society of America; Quaternary Research Association, UK. Address: Department of Geology, University of Bergen, Allegt 41, 5007 Bergen, Norway.

**MANGUR Kader,** b. Jamtoil, Serajganj. m. Nilufa Yesmin, 2 daughters. Education: Hazi Korap Ali Memorial Degree College, Bangladesh; Library Science, Bangladesh. Publications: Prithibir Ajob Prani. Honours: Honoured, Culthara Accademy, Shaihtty Brova. Memberships: Joint Secretary, Bangladesh Cultural Association. Address: Bangladesh Shishu Academy, PO and Dist Pabna 6600, Bangladesh.

**MANICKATHAZHE Cherian Gudalur,** b. 18 October 1939, Kerala, India. Advocate. m. Mary Cherian, 1 son, 1 daughter. Education: BSc; MA; BL; PhD. Appointments: President, Gudalur Bar Association; UN Participant, 2nd World Conference, Human Rights, 1993; Trainee, NHRC, Delhi at Philippines, 1998. Publications: Gandhi's Concept of Truth and Justice. Honour: Best Social Worker Award. Memberships: Bar Association of India; Indian Society of Gandhian Studies. Address: Gudalur Bazor PO, Nilgiris Dt, TN India.

**MANKO Yuri I,** b. 25 November 1931, Russia. Head, Forestry Department. m. Nelli Manko, 1 son, 1 daughter. Education: Siberian Forestry Institute, 1954; Candidate of Science, Biology, 1962; DSc, Biology, 1985; Professor, Forestry, 1992. Appointments: Probationer, 1954, Junior Research Worker, 1954, Senior Research Worker, 1964, Head of Laboratory, 1968, Head of Department, 1981-. Publications: Over 180 in professional journals. Memberships: Russian Botanical Society; New York Academy of Sciences. Address: Institute of Biology & Soil Science, Forestry Department, 159 Prospect Stoletiya, 690022 Vladivostok, Russia.

**MANN Tejwant,** b. 1 January 1944, Mauran, Sangrur, Panjab, India. Senior Lecturer. m. Dhaminder Paulkaur, 1 son, 3 daughters. Education: BA, Hons, 1966; MA, 1972; MLitt, 1976; PhD, 1987. Appointment: Lecturer, Akal Degree College, Mastuana. Publications: Author, 24 books. Honours: Safdar Hashmi Award; Sant Singh Sehkon Award; Raslok Award; Panjab Raj Sahit Kala Prisad Award. Memberships: Vice President and General Secretary, Kendri Panjabi Lekhak Sabha. Address: Hargobindpura Basti, College Road, Sangrur Pbi, India.

**MANNAN Abdul,** b. 6 November 1948, Chittagong, Bangladesh. Vice Chancellor. m. Gulnahar Begum, 1 daughter. Education: B Com (Hons), 1970; M Com, 1971; MBA, 1978; Dip in Project Management, 1978. Appointments: Teaching, 1973-, University of Chittagong; Lecturer in Management, 1973-78; Assistant Professor of Management, 1978-87; Associate Professor of Management, 1987-89; Professor of Management, 1989-; Vice Chancellor, 1996. Publications: 4 books; Many research papers in Research Journals of National and International repute; 14 seminars and conferences; Regular column writer on socio-political and cultural issues.

Honours: 5 scholarships and fellowships awarded. Memberships: Association of Commonwealth Universities; Steering Committee of Bangladesh National Commission for UNESCO; Bangladesh Institute of Technology, Chittagong; Association of Universities in Bangladesh; Bangladesh Open University Steering Committee; Dhaka University Senate; Bangladesh Association for American Studies; Asiatic Society of Bangladesh, life member; Association of Management Development Institutions in South East Asia, Hyderabad; Chittagong University Teachers' Association; and others. Address: University of Chittagong, University Post Office, Chittagong, Bangladesh.

**MANOMAITIS Valdemaras,** b. 30 September 1912, Siauliai, Lithuania. Artist. m. Emilija Pranckeviciute, 2 sons, 1 daughter. Education: Diploma of the Art School of Kaunas, Lithuania, 1937. Appointment: Ceramics Art and Leather Decoration Art. Publications: 40 art works at Ceramics Museum of Kaunas, 1991; 400 art works, Applied Art Museum, Vilnius, 1975-97. Honour: Gold Medal, Art Exhibition, Paris, 1937. Membership: Lithuanian Artists Association, 1937-98. Address: Parodos 7-3, LT 3000 Kaunas, Lithuania.

**MANSELL Joyce,** b. 17 December 1934, Minot, North Dakota, USA. Retired Educator. m. Dudley J Mansell, 1 son, 1 daughter. Education: BS, University of Houston, 1968; MEd, Sam Houston State University, 1980; Cert Provisional Elementary Teacher 1-8; Provisional Mentally Retarded Teacher. Appointments: Provisional language and/or learning disabilities teacher; Professional elementary teacher 1-8; Professional reading specialist, 1st grade teacher, Johnson Elementary School, 1968-72; 2nd grade teacher, 1972-76, 3rd grade teacher, 1976-77; Special education teacher, mentally retarded, Memorial Parkway Junior High School, 1982-86; Waller Middle School, 1986-90; Royal Midddle School 1990-95; Royal High School, 1995-96. Membership: Holy Three-in-One, Lutheran Church of the Deaf. Address: 2155 Paso Rello Drive, Houston, TX 77077-5622, USA.

**MANSHARDT Thomas B,** b. 23 March 1927, Wai, India. Concert Pianist. Education: BMus, Oberlin College, 1953; Private Pupil, Alfred Cortot, Lausanne, Switzerland, 1957-62. Career: Debuts: Vienna, 1954; London, 1955; New York, 1965; Tours in Europe, Asia, USA, Canada; Professor Emeritus, University of Regina. Publications: Aspects of Cortot, 1994; CD: Thomas Manshardt: Alfred Cortot's Last Pupil. Address: 1830 College Ave Apt 1301, Regina, SK Canada S4P 1C2.

**MANSON Averill Faith,** b. 7 May 1953, Rochester, NY, USA. Special Education Musician. m. William Tinker, divorced 1989, 2 sons. Education: BME, Baldwin Wallace College, 1975; MM, Therapy, Southern Methodist University, 1978; Special Education Certificate, Texas Women's University, 1984. Appointments: Music Therapist, Terrell State Hospital, 1978-79, Fort Worth State School, 1979-84; Special Educator, Fort Worth State School, Fort Worth, TX, USA, 1985-86, SAU#43, Newport, NH, 1986-93; Dothan Brook School, Hartford, VT, USA, 1994-Present; Organist, Choir Director, St Paul's Episcopal Church, 1988-1999, Organist, W. Lebanon Congregational Church, 1999-Present. Honours: Mu Phi Epsilon, Honorary Music Sorority, 1973; Kappa Delta Pi, Honorary Education, 1975. Memberships: National Education Association; American Guild of Organists; American Guild of English Handbell Ringers. Address: 6 College Avenue, Lebanon, NH 03766-2504, USA.

**MANSOUR Alaa El-Din,** b. 5 February 1937, Zagazig, Egypt. Professor, Past Chair. m. Elizabeth, 2 sons. Education: BS, University of Cairo, Egypt, 1958; MS, University of

California, 1962; PhD, University of California, 1966 Appointments: Associate Professor, 1968-75; Professo Former Chair, Department of Naval Architecture and Offshor Engineering, University of California. Honours: Recipient Davidson Medal. Memberships: Society of Naval Architects an Haeinu Engineers. Address: University of California, 202 Nav Architecture Bldg, Berkeley, CA 94720-1781, USA.

**MANSOUR Awad Rasheed,** b. 13 March 1951, Jenir Chemical Engineer. m. Aishah Okur, 3 sons, 2 daughter Education: BSc, Chemical Engineering, University of Baghdad 1975; MSc, Chemical Engineering, University of Tulsa, 197 PhD, 1980. Appointments: Professor, Chemical Engineerinc Yarmouk University, 1980-. Publications: 72 Published Paper Refereed Journals; 57 Books Published. Honours: Man Scholarships; Candidate for UNESCO Prize for Science an Technology; International Man of the Year, 1998; 20th Centur Man of Achievements in Science and Technology; Internationa Man of 99. Memberships: American Society of Chemica Engineering; New York Academy of Sciences. Address Yarmouk University, P O Box 4455, Irbid, Jordan.

**MANSUROV Hamid,** b. 25 December 1925, Samarkanc Physician; Gastroenterologist. m. Daniyarova G, 4 sons, daughter. Education: First Degree, Medical University, 1947 Degree, Medical Sciences, 1951; Doctors Degree, Medica Sciences, 1958; Honoured Scientist, 1976; Academician, 1978 Appointments: Professor of the Chair, 1961; Director Gastroenterology Institute of the Academy of Sciences 1962-99; Deputy Chairman, Learned Society c Gastroenterologists, USSR, 1962; Chairman, Learned Societ of Gastroenterologists, Tajikistan, 1973; Vice President, Taji Academy of Sciences, 1990-95. Publications: Porta Hypertension, 1963; Biopsy of the Liver, 1964; Gallston Diseases, 1991; Problems of Dietology, Gastroenterology an Hepatology in Avicenna's Canon of Medicine, 1980. Honours Order of Lenin; Order of October Revolution; Tajik State Priz Laureate; Honourable Member, Gastroenterology Associatior of Hungary; Honourable Member, Gastroenterology Associatior of Bulgaria. Memberships: Corresponding, Medical Associatior of Internists, Poland. Address: Institute of Gastroenterology Parvina St 12, Dushanbe 734002, Tajikistan.

**MANTATOV Vyacheslav V,** b. 29 July 1941, Irkutsk, Russia Philosopher. m. Khakhalova Svetlana, 1 son, 1 daughter Education: MPhil, Moscow State University, 1965; PhD, Logic and Social Sciences, 1969; Grand DPhil, 1978. Appointments Head, Department of Philosophy, Eastern Siberian State University of Technology, Ulan-Ude, 1969-; President, Baika Fund, Ulan-Ude, 1991-; President, Peoples Academy o Buddhist Culture, Ulan-Ude, 1993-. Publications: Theory o Reflection and Heuristic Role of Signs, 1986; Dialectics o Social Cognition, 1988; Environmental Ethics: Buddhism anc Contemporaneity, 1997; Strategy of Mind: Sustainable Development, 1997. Honour: Honoured Scientist of Russia 1993. Memberships: Academician, International Informatior Academy; Russian Ecology Academy; Russian Academy o Humanities. Address; Solnetchnaya Street 24, Flat 2, 67003 Ulan-Ude Buryat, Russia.

**MANUILOV Boris,** b. 24 September 1956, Russia. Medica Doctor. m. 1 son, 1 daughter. Education: Graduate, Moscov Medical Academy, 1979; Postgraduate, 1980-85; Candidate o Biological Sciences, 1986. Career: Founder, Saluta-M Moscow, 1992. Publications: Over 51 scientific works i professional journals, 9 inventions and patents. Honours: The Best Young Inventor of Moscow, 1987; 2 Medals, 1994, 1995 RANS, 1997. Membership: Russian Academy of Natura Sciences. Address: Chikins Street 1, 123436 Moscow, Russia

**MANZER Alison Rosemary,** b. 1 July 1954, St John, New Brunswick, Canada. Lawyer. m. Glen De La Franier, 1 son, 1 daughter. Education: BSc, 1974, BSc, honours, 1977, LLB, 1977, Dalhousie University, Halifax, Nova Scotia; Barrister and Solicitor, Law Society of Upper Canada, 1979; MBA, University of Toronto, 1984; Securities Course, 1985; Canadian Investment Finance 1 and 2, 1986; LLM, Osgoode Hall Law School, York University, Toronto, 1997; PHDBA, California Coast University, in progress. Appointments: Associate Lawyer, Burt, Burt, Wolfe & Bowman, 1979-81; Partner, Robins, Appleby & Taub, 1981-90; Partner, Cassels Brock & Blackwell, 1990-. Publications: Several articles in professional journals; Several legal textbooks on banking, financial services and partnership. Memberships: Law Society of Upper Canada; Canadian Bar Association, Ontario, Finance Committee, Continuing Legal Education Committee, Governing Counsel, Financial Institution Legislation; Womens International Insolvency and Restructuring Association; Commercial Finance Attorneys Association. Address: Cassels Brock & Blackwell, Scotia Plaza, 40 King Street West, Ste 2100, Toronto, Ontario M5H 3C2, Canada.

**MAO Shengxian,** b. 28 November 1938, Hunan, China. Teacher. m. Wang Linying, 1 son, 1 daughter. Education: Beijing Normal University, 1957-62; University of Birmingham, England, 1981-83. Appointments: Assistant, Lecturer, Vice Professor, Beijing Normal University, 1962-93; Professor, Capital Normal University, 1994-. Publications include: Quantitative Genetics of Crops, 1984; Principles of Genetics, 1987; Population Genetics, 1993. Honour: Advancement Award, Science and Technology, Beijing Government, 1990. Memberships: Genetics Society of China; Beijing Genetics Society. Address: Department of Biology, Capital Normal University, 100037 Beijing, China.

**MAPLESDEN Carol Harper,** b. 27 August 1947, Philadelphia, Pennsylvania, USA. Family Therapist; Music Educator. m. James Paul Maplesden, 1 son, 1 daughter. Education: BA Psychology, 1979, Holy Family College; MA Marital and Family Therapy, 1984, LaSalle University. Appointments: Family Therapist: People Acting to Help, 1983-86, Benjamin Rush Mental Health, 1987-88; Clinical Supervisor, Interact Mental Health, 1989, Catholic Charities, 1989-90; Director, Seminar Lecturer, Carden Family Institute, 1984-; Northeast Treatment, 1988-89. Publications: Learning to Relax, audio tape exercise, 1984; Young Beginnings Piano Course I, 1993; Organist, Keyboard Instructor, Vocal Performer, carden Music, 1993-. Memberships: Licensed Counsellor of Mental Health; National Board of Certified Counsellors; American Counselling Association; National Board of Cognitive Therapists; National Association of Forensics Counsellors; National Board of Additions Counsellors. Address: PO Box 16096, Philadelphia, PA 19114-0096, USA.

**MARAI Ibrahim Fayez Mahmoud,** b. 10 January 1930, Giza, Egypt. Member of Academic Staff. m. Wafaa Mohamed Amin Salama, 2 sons, 1 daughter. Education: BSc, Agriculture, 1950, MSc, Animal Production, 1960, PhD, Animal Production, 1964, Cairo University. Appointments: Teacher in Agriculture, secondary schools; Demonstrator, Lecturer, Assistant Professor, 1960-76, Head of Department, 1972-82, Professor, 1976-, Department of Animal Production, Faculty of Agriculture, Zagazig University; Vice-Dean, Faculty of Agriculture, Zagazig University, 1982-85; Head, Zagazig University Buildings Construction Cooperative, 1985-92; Member, Board of Directors, Diarb-Negm Poultry Company, 1992-; Owner, Ben Abdel-Aziz Buildings Cooperative, 1995-. Publications: More than 200 scientific papers; Editor, author: New Techniques in Sheep Production, 1987, in Spanish as Nuevas Tecnicas de

Produccion Ovina, 1994; Pollution in Livestock Production System, 1994; Editor, 10 books in Arabic. Memberships: Head, City Council, Hesseneya, Sharkeya Governorate, 1968-72; Head, Egyptian Rabbit Science Association, 1998-. Address: Department of Animal Production, Faculty of Agriculture, Zagazig University, Zagazig, Egypt.

**MARCHANT Mary A,** b. California, USA. Associate Professor Agricultural Economics. m. James Marchant. Education: MA Economics, 1984, PhD Agricultural Economics, 1989, University California at Davis. Appointments: Assistant Professor, 1989-94, Associate Professor, 1995-, University of Kentucky. Publication: Hopes & Fears: The New Trade Agreement & Southern Agriculture, 1999. Honours: Fulbright Award, 1998; Distinguished Chair in Agricultural Economics, Italy. Membership: President, Southern Agricultural Economics Association, 1999. Address: 314 Agricultural Engineering Building, Department of Agricultural Economics, University of Kentucky, Lexington, KY 40546-0276, USA.

**MARCULESCU Alexandru-Sorin,** b. 15 September 1943, Iasi, Romania. 1 son, 1 daughter. Education: MS, University Bucharest, Romania, 1966; PhD, University Karlsruhe, Germany, 1973; Habilitation, University Siegen, Germany, 1987. Appointments: Assistant Professor, University Bucharest, 1966-71; 1973-81; Humboldt Fellow, 1971-73; Professor, Theoretical Physics, Siegen, 1995. Publications: Articles in various scientific journals, 1969-. Membership: German Physics Society. Address: University Siegen, Department Physics, Adolf Reichwein Str, D 57068 Siegen, Germany.

**MARCUS Solomon,** b. 1 March 1925, Bacau, Romania. Mathematician. m. Paula Diaconescu. Education: PhD in Mathematics, Faculty of Mathematics, 1956, DSc, 1966, University of Bucharest. Appointments: Assistant Professor, 1950-55, Associate Professor, 1955-66, Professor, 1966-91, Emeritus Professor, 1991-, Faculty of Mathematics, University of Bucharest; Permanent Invited Professor, Sai Paulo Catholic University, Brazil. Publications: 40 books and 350 research articles in mathematical analysis, computer science, linguistics, semiotics and poetics. Honours: Prize, Romanian Academy for Linguistics, 1974; Prize, Romanian Academy for Mathematics, 1967. Memberships: Vice-President, International Association for Semiotic Studies, 1989-99; Romanian Academy, 1993. Address: Str Sf Voievozi 41-45, Scara B, et V, Apart 32, SEctor I, 78109 Bucharest.

**MARDON Austin Albert,** b. 25 June 1962, Edmonton, Alberta, Canada. Writer; Researcher. m. Stephanie Ngar Ling Liu. Education: BA Geography, 1985, University of Lethbridge; MSc Geography, 1988, South Dakota State University; MEd Education, 1990, Texas A&M University. Publications: 14 books and 75 scholarly communications. Honours: Antarctic Service Medal, US Navy, 1987-88; Duke of Edinburgh Medal; Governor General's Caring Canadian Award, 1998; Texas State Proclaimation, presented to Canadian Senate. Memberships: Antarctic Institute of Canada; COSPAR; Clubhouse Society of Edmonton.

**MARDON Ernest George,** b. 21 December 1928, Harris County, Texas, USA. Professor; Author. m. May Knowler, 1 son, 2 daughters. Education: BEd, University of Alberta, 1961; MA, University of Ottawa, 1966; PhD, 1967. Appointments: Agricultural Worker, 1951; Purchaser, 1953-54; London Blitz Rubble Disposal Unit Leader; Staff Correspondent, Bureau Manager, 1954-58; Political Organiser, 1959; Teacher, 1961-63; Political Organiser, 1970; Professor, University of Lethbridge, 1967-89; Visiting Professor, University of Calgary; Visiting Professor, Laurentian University; Visiting Professor,

University of Saskatchewan; Visiting Professor, Nipissing University. Publications: The Narrative Unity of the Cursor Mundi; The Conflict Between the Individual and Society in the Plays of James Bridie; Southern Alberta Place Names; Community Names of Alberta; Alberta Mormón Politicians; Alberta Election Results, 1882-1992; Alberta Anglican Politicians. Address: 1007 7th Avenue South, Lethbridge AB, Canada, T1J 1K3.

**MARGATE Lorenzo Zamoras,** b. 10 August 1938, Maribojoc, Bohol, Philippines. Professor; Researcher. m. Epifania Matunog Exile, 3 sons, 1 daughter. Education: BSA, 1967, Central Mindanao University; MS Horticulture, 1975, PhD Horticulture, 1986, University of Philippines at Los Banos. Appointments: Coordinator, NOMCARRD, CMU, 1986-91; Professor VI, 1988-; Evaluator, TPAE, DECS, UPLB College, Laguna, 1990-95; Dean, College of Agriculture, CMU, 1991-94. Publications: As senior author, 17 articles in professional journals; As co-author or Junior Author, 15 abstracts and articles. Honours: 3rd Prize, Best Research Paper Award, 1990; Best Technology Award, Regional, 1990, 1994; Recognition for Significant Contribution to Research and Development, 1996. Memberships: Philippine Association of Research Managers; Society for Advancement of Vegetable Industry, Philippines; UP Alumni Association, Bukidnon Chapter; CMU Faculty Association; and others. Address: Central Mindanao University, MUSUAN, 8710 Bukidnon, The Philippines.

**MARGETA Jure,** b. 6 June 1950, Osijek, Croatia. University Professor. m. Silvana Kirhner, 1 son, 2 daughters. Education: BSc Civil Engineering, 1974, MSc Civil Engineering, 1980, PhD, 1983, University of Zagreb, Croatia; PhD study, Colorado State University, USA, 1981-82. Appointments: Assistant Professor, University of Zagreb and Split, 1985; Associate Professor, 1987, Full Professor, 1991, University of Split; Associate Dean of Faculty, 1996-98; UNEP-MAP/PAD Coordinator for Water Resources, 1985-. Publications: 5 books; Editor, 4 publications; 25 papers in domestic and international journals; 86 papers presented at conferences and published in procceddings of conferences. Memberships: American Water Works Association; American Water Resources Association; International Water Resources Association; Croatian Society of Civil Engineering; Croatian Society for Water Pollution Control. Address: Department Obalak Branimira 3, 21000 Split, Croatia.

**MARIK Ivo Antonin,** b. 6 February 1950, Prague, Czech Republic. Orthopaedic Surgeon; Paediatrician. m. Alena Marikova, 2 sons, 3 daughters. Education: Medical School Degree, 1975; Specialist in Paediatrics, 1979; Specialist in Orthopaedics, 1982; PhD, 1987; IIA Scientific Degree, Czech Academy of Sciences, 1991. Appointments: Senior Research Worker, Orthopaedic Clinic, 2nd Medical Faculty, Charles University, Prague, 1988-91; Assistant Professor, 1991-94; Head, Ambulant Centre for Defects of Locomotor Apparatus,Natural Historical Faculty, Charles University, Prague, 1994-. Publications: Over 50 papers in professional journals including: Osteitis caused by BCG Vaccination, J Pediatr Orthop, 8, 1988; Complications of intramedullary nailing and regeneration of long bones at some bone dysplasias, Locomotor System 4, 1997. Memberships: Founding Member. Czech Society for Surgery of the Hand and Rehabilitation, 1988; Founding Member, The Marik Foundation for Children with Disorders of Locomotor Apparatus, 1992-94; International Federation of Societies for Surgery of the Hand, 1992-; Czech Society for Connective Tissue Research and Biological Use, 1993-; Czech Society for Prosthetics and Orthotics, 1994-; Chief Editor of the Czech Journal, Locomotor System-Advances in Research, Diagnostics and Therapy,

1994-. Address: Olsanska 7, Prague 3, 130 00 Czech Republic

**MARINESCU Niculae Ion,** b. 19 January 1951, Bucharest, Romania. Engineer. m. Camelia-Elena, 2 daughters. Education: BSc, Polytechnical University of Bucharest, 1974; Specialization, Germany, 1977; DSc, 1979. Appointments: Manufacturing Technology Engineer, 1974-78, Assistant Lecturer, 1978-82, Lecturer, 1982-91, Senior Lecturer, 1991-95, Professor, Department of Manufacturing Technology, Faculty of Manufacturing Systems and Management, 1995-. Polytechnical University of Bucharest. Publications: 15 technical books, 16 handbooks, 144 papers in professional journals, 21 inventions and innovations, 3 training films, 48 research contracts with research institutes and plants. Honours: The Crystal Cup Award, Romania, 1984; International Training Film Festival Award, Brno, Czech Republic, 1985; President, Non-Conventional Technology Commission, Romanian Academy of Sciences, subsidiary of Bucharest, 1997-. Memberships: Association of Romanian Scientists; Romanian Association for Non-Convention Technologies; PHARE. Address: 68 Soseaua Iancului Sector 2, 73378 Bucharest, Romania.

**MARINKOVIC Dragan,** b. 31 August 1951, Belgrade, Yugoslavia. Psychiatrist. m. Olivera Ristic. Education: MD, 1976; Neuropsychiatry, 1983; Clinical Neurophysiology, 1994, Clincial Psychopharmacology, 1995; MSc, 1997. Appointments: Physician, Medical Centre, Gnjilane, Serbia; Psychiatrist, Institute of Psychiatry, University Clinical Centre, Serbia, Yugoslavia. Publications: Schizophrenia Beyond 2nd Millenium - Positive and Negative Syndrome Treatment (book); Over 70 articles in professional journals. Memberships: Serbian Medical Association; Association of European Psychiatrists. Address: Psychiatric Clinic of the Clincal Centre of Belgrade, 11000 Beograd, Yugoslavia.

**MARINOV Venelin Mladenov,** b. 16 September 1935, Sofia, Bulgaria. Radiochemist. m. Angelina Jekova Marinova, 1 son. Education: Magister of Chemistry, University of Sofia, 1957; 4 months, Max Plank Institute of Biophysics, Frankfurt, Germany, 1964; 12 months, Research Center, Seibersdorf, Austria, 1971; PhD, Chemistry, 1971; Training course, off-site emergency response to nuclear accident, Commission of the European Communities, Aghios Minas, Greece, 1993. Appointments: Chemist, Medical Division, Bulgarian Army, 1957; Scientific Fellow, Central Laboratory of Radiation Protection and Toxicology, Agricultural Academy, Sofia, 1966; Senior Scientist, 1975 Head, 1976, Radiation Protection Department, CLRPT; President, Dr of Science, 1985, Professor, 1986, Expert, Council on Radiation Protection, Scientific Co-ordination Council, Permanent Commission on Population Protection Against Emergencies and Disasters, Council of Ministers, Bulgaria, 1991; President, Consultative Council on Radiation Protection, Committee on the Use of Atomic Energy for Peaceful Purposes, Council of Ministers, Bulgaria, 1997. Publications: Over 200 as author or co-author in fields including: radio-chemistry analyses; microanalyses of trace elements; spectometry of $\rho$ emitters; methodology and metrology of radiation measurements; radiation control, radioecology and radiation protection; emergency response and emergency planning. Honours: include: Honorary Sign I Grade, Civil Protection of Bulgaria, 1987; Silver Medal, St Cyril and Metodi, State Snd of Bulgaria, 1985; Award, Ministry of Culture, Science and Education of a complex medical-biological system for radiation protection, 1988. Memberships: Scientific Council, CLRPT, 1968; Scientific and Educational Council, National Centre of Radiobiology and Radiation Protection, Ministry of Health, 1995. Address: Central Laboratory of adiation, Protection and Toxicology, Agricultural Academy, acaureno shosse str 1, 1360 Sofia, Bulgaria.

**MARINOVA Tsvetomira Angelova,** b. 7 May 1972, Trojan, Jlgaria. Singer. Education: Qualified Fitter of Industrial lectronics; Music School, Trojan, Bulgaria. Career: Singer. ddress: H Botev Str No 71 V, Town Trojan 5600, Bulgaria.

**MARISTANY Jaime,** b. 3 December 1935, Barcelona, pain. Management HHRR Consultant. m. Martha, 3 aughters. Education: LLM; Professor, HHRR Postgraduate. ppointments: Union Carbide Argentina; Eveready. ublications: 12 books on management, 15 papers, several ticles in professional journals and newspapers. Memberships: ersonnel Directors Association. Address: J Maristany SA, arrea 1367 P B 3, Buenos Aires 1117, Argentina.

**MARKATOS Nicholas-Chris G,** b. 1 March 1944, Athens, reece. Professor. m. Marina Verykiou, 1 son. Education: raduate, 1967, Department of Chemical Engineering, National echnical University of Athens; MA Business Administration, 970, Athens School of Economics; MSc Advanced Chemical ngineering and Technology, PhD, DIC, 1974, Department of hemical Engineering, Imperial College of Science and echnology, University of London. Appointments: Military ervice, 1967-69; Unit Operations Engineer and Cost and lethods Manager, VIOCHROM, Proctor & Gamble Hellas dustry, 1969-70; Post-Doctoral Research Assistant, Imperial ollege, Fluid Dynamics and Thermodynamics Section, lechanical Engineering Dept, 1974; Group Leader of erospace Group, 1976, Manager of Application Groups, 977-84, CHAM Ltd (Concentration Heat and Momentum Ltd), ondon; Extra-Mural Academic Advisor, Imperial College; rincipal Lecturer in Mathematical Modelling and Process nalysis, School of Math and Scientific Computing, University f Greenwich, London, 1982, Director of this Centre, 1983, leader, 1984; Visiting Lecturer, Computational Fluid Dynamics nit, Imperial College, 1983-; Technical Consultant for many esearch Centres, State Institutions and Industries in the UK, JSA, Germany, France, Japan etc, 1974-; Professor of hemical Engineering, National Technical University of Athens, 985, Head of Chemical Engineering Department, 1990-94, ector of the University, 1991-. Honours: Thomaidion Award, 966, 1967; Chrysovergion Award, 1967; Certificate of ecognition, Inventions Council of NASA, 1980; Embiricos nstitute Prize, 1994; Awarded Doctor Honoris Causa, echnical University of Sofia, Bulgaria, 1997; Elected City ouncillor, City of Athens, 1994; Chairman of the Acropolis ppeal for Peace and Civilization; Chairman of the Centre for ocial and Political Studies 'John Kapodistria'. Publications: )ver 100 original scientific papers in international journals; articipant and Organiser many international conferences, eminars and meetings; over 200 publications in proceedings; books; Many articles in popular press on Engineering Higher ducation. Memberships: FIChE; C Eng, Engineering Council f Gt Britain; MAIChE; MAIAA; UKSC; MISCME; and others. ddress: National Technical University of Athens, Zografou Jniversity Campus, 157 80 Athens, Greece.

**MARSH Harold Michael,** b. 7 March 1939, Sydney, ustralia. Physician; Anesthesiologist. m. Elizabeth Eleanor, 1 son, 2 daughters. Education: BSc, MB, BS, University of Sydney. Appointments: Professor, Chair of Anesthesiology, Wayne State University, Detroit. Honours: Gilbert Phillips Memorial Prize for Neuroanatomy; Gilbert Troup Anaesthesia Research Prize; Midwest Anesthesia Research Conference, Second Prize. Memberships: Numerous Including, Academy of Anesthesiology; American College of Chest Physicians; American Red Cross; American Society of Critical Care

Anesthesiologists; Association of University Anesthetists; Australian and New Zealand College of Anesthetists; Society of Critical Care Medicine. Address: Wayne State University, The Detroit Medical Center, Department of Anesthesiology, DRH/UHC Annex 2T, 4201 St Antoine, Detroit, Michigan 48201, USA.

**MARSHALL David,** b. 4 February 1914, Syracuse, New York, USA. Orthodontics Consultant. m. Margie Kaufman, 3 sons, 1 daughter. Education: BS, Syracuse University, 1936;DDS, School of Dentistry, University of Maryland, 1942; Orthodontics, Certificate of Proficiency, Columbia University, 1945; Graduate Work in Orthodontics, Tufts, 1951, Graduate Work in Orthodontics, University of Pennsylvania, 1959. Appointments: Staff Member, Crouse Irving Memorial Hospital; Founder, Cleft Palate, Syracuse University, School of Speach; State Consultant, Screening Center. Publications: Orthodontics of Adult, 1950; Changes in Dento-Facial Relationship, 1951; Rationale of Mandibular Prognathism, 1954; Dimensional Growth, 1958; Growth of Face, 1962; Growth, Heraldo Dental; X-ray Study of the Cranial and Facial Bones in Relation to the Profile, 1965; Skull Bones in Plastic, 1967; Interpretation of the Posterior Skull Radiograph, 1969; Interpretation of the Lateral Skull Radiograph, 1970. Honours: Men of Distinguished Achievement, 1972; Outstanding men of the 20th Century; Fellow Member, Royal Society of Medicines, 1992; Memberships: Syracuse Dental Society; New York State Society; American Dental Society; 5th District Dental Society; Northeastern Orthodontic Society; American Orthodontic Society; American Board of Orthodontics; Columbia Alumni of Orthodontics. Address: 5231 Brockway Lane, Fayetteville, NY 13066-1705, USA.

**MARTENSEN-LARSEN Britta Tanja,** b. 14 March 1944, Copenhagen. Art Historian. Education: MA History of Art, 1977, University Copenhagen. Appointments: Assistant Professor, Copenhagen University, Institute Art History, 1979, 1982; Curator, Ordrupgaard Collection, Copenhagen, 1982-83; Director, Gallery A Gruppen, Copenhagen, 1981-87; Secretary, Ministry of Culture, Copenhagen, 1988-89; Ministry Foreign Affairs, Copenhagen, 1991-92; Curator, The Danish Filmus, Copenhagen, 1996. Publications: Contributor articles to professional journals in Scandinavia, France, Germany; Catalogue: Carl Th Dreyer, Jehanne La Passion et la Morte d'Une Sainte (Joan of Arc), 1989-93, translated into French, Danish, Polish. Memberships: Danish Art History Society, University Copenhagen, 1980-; Danish Federation of University Women, 1996-; Fellow, International Biographical Association, Cambridge, 1998-. Address: Lundsgade 3, 2100 Copenhagen, Denmark.

**MARTIN Jeanette St Clair,** b. 25 September 1947, Jackson, Michigan, USA. Associate Professor. m. Stevens John Martin Jr, 1 daughter. Education: BA, 1970, Michigan State University; MBA, 1974, University Chicago; EdD, 1991, University Memphis. Appointments: Assistant Professor, 1991-98, Associate Professor, 1999-; Teaching Business Communication. Publications: Co-author, 20 articles in peer reviewed journals; 1 books in the field of business communications; 17 papers in national and regional proceedings; 8 proceedings; Associate editor, Journal of Business Communication. Memberships: Association of Business Communication; Delta Pi Epsilon, Beta Xi Chapter; Kappa Delta Pi; SIETAR; Academy International Business; Intercultural Communication Association. Address: University Miss School of Business, University, MS 38677, USA.

**MARTIN Kate,** b. 11 March 1952, Pasadena, California, USA. Lawyer. 1 daughter. Education: BA, cum laude,

Philosophy, Pomona College, 1973; JD, University of Virginia, 1977. Appointments include: Director, National Security Litigation Project, American Civil Liberties Union Foundation, 1988-92; Adjunct Professor, Georgetown University Law Center, 1993-; Director, Center for National Security Studies, 1992-. Publications: Safeguarding Liberty: National Security, Freedom of Expression, and Access to Information, 1999; Civil Liberties and National Security on the Internet, 1999. Address: Gelman Library, 2130 H St NW Ste 701, Washington, DC 20037-2521, USA.

**MARTIN Laurabelle,** b. 3 November 1915, Jackson County, Minnesota, USA. Educator. Education: Teacher training for rural schools, Renville Teachers Training Department, 1935; BS, 1968, Mankato State University. Appointments: Teacher, Rural Schools, 1936-41, 1945-50; Wabasso Public School, 1963-81; Real Estate Owner and Operator, 1952-86; President, Renville, Minnesota Farms and Feed Lot. Publications: Poetry: Think Success; What's Your Message; Treasures to Share; Lingering Memories; and more; Historical Biography of Joseph Renville, Early 1800s French Fur Trader, Interpreter and Guide in Minnesota, 1998. Memberships: WEA and NEA Teachers' Organisations; Secretary, Historical Preservation Commission, 1979-86; American Legion Auxiliary; Renville Town & Country Booster. Address: 334 NW 1201, Holden, MO 64040-9804, USA.

**MARTIN Laurel Lynn LeMay,** b. 20 April 1968, Loomis, New York, USA. Graduate Research Assistant. m. David Henry Martin. Education: BS, Cornell University, 1990; MS, 1996, PhD (in progress), Pennsylvania State University. Appointments: Research Technician, NCI-Frederick Cancer Research and Development Center, 1991-93; Graduate Research Assistant, Pennsylvania State University, 1994-; Statistical Consultant, Department of Womens Studies, 1996-; Educational Webpage Developer, 1998. Publications include: National Sheep Improvement Program: Heritability Estimates for 60-day Weaning Weight and Grease Fleece Weight in Columbia, Dorset, Hampshire and Rambouillet Breeds of Sheep, 1996. Honours: Gamma Sigma Delta, 1994; Phi Kappa Phi, 1995; John O Almquist Award, 1997. Memberships: American Society of Animal Science; Executive Secretary Pennsylvania State University Graduate Student Association; President, Graduate Women in Science; Founder, Chair, WEBMENTOR; National Association of Female Executives; National Wildlife Conservancy; Defenders of Wildlife; American Society for the Prevention of Cruelty to Animals; National Parks and Recreation; Pennsylvania State Alumni Association. Address: Pennsylvania State University, Department of Dairy and Animal Science, 324 Henning Building, University Park, PA 16802, USA.

**MARTIN Philip John Talbot,** b. 28 March 1931, Melbourne. Retired Academic; Poet. Education: BA, Melbourne, 1958. Appointments: Tutor, University of Melbourne, 1960-62; Lecturer, Australian National University, 1963; Lecturer, Senior Lecturer, English, Monash University, 1964-88. Address: 25/9 Nicholson St, Balmain 2041, Australia.

**MARTINAITYTE Sabina,** b. 29 August 1958, Kaunas, Lithuania. Singer. Education: Higher School of Music, 1976-80; Lithuanian Academy of Music, 1981-87. Appointments: Soloist, Kaunas State Musical Theater, 1987; Senior Assistant, Singing Department, Lithuanian Academy of Music, 1990-. Memberships: Lithuanian Misicians Society. Address: K Barsausko 71-17, LT 3031 Kaunas, Lithuania.

**MARTINEZ Jose Maria,** b. 8 September 1980, Madrid. Economist. m. Ana Maria, 1 son, 1 daughter. Education:

Graduate, Economics and Business, Universidad Autonom 1968-73; Master, Marketing, Instituto de Empresa, 1980; MB, Business, London Business School, 1981. Appointment Marketing Planning Manager, 1973-78; Marketing ar Business Development Director, 1978-84; Marketing Directc 1984-87; Business Development Director, 1987-90; Scienti Regulatory and External Affairs Director, 1994; Head of th Madrid Office, 1995; Head of Madrid Office, Head of the Duba Middle East Office, Head of the South Africa Office, Europe: Partnership and Special Projects Director, 1996. Publication Over 30 articles published in several local Profession Business and Research Magazines. Honours: Marketing Ma of the Year, 1982. Memberships: Multinational Ophthalmoloc Pharmaceutical Companies Group in Spain; PHARMA Grou FARMAINDUSTRIA; Founder, AIMFA; Scientific Board · Instituto de Empresa; Lierian Executive Committee; Europe: Management Institute; European Key Processes Analys Group; R and D European Board. Address: Avenida De Den 111, Alicante 03015, Spain.

**MARTINKUS Vytautas,** b. 28 May 1943, Lithuania. Write Novelist. m. Violeta, 2 daughters. Education; Graduat∈ Engineering, Kaunas Technology University, 1965; Doctor ⋅ Social Science, 1981; Associate Professor, 198⋅ Appointments: Assistant Professor, Lithuanian Literatur Department, Vilnius Pedagogical University; Presiden Lithuanian Association of Artists. Publications: 9 Books; 12 Essays. Honours: National, State, Award, 1985. Membership Member, Board of Lithuanian Writers Union; Member, Worl Association of Lithuanian Researchers; Members, UNESC( National Commission of Lithuania. Address: Dominikonu 15-⦰ LT 2001 Vilnius, Lithuania.

**MARTINOVA Elena Alexandrovna,** b. 13 June 195⦰ Armavir, Russia. Immunologist. Education: MD, Intern Medicine, N Semashko Moscow Medical Institute, 1980; MC Immunology and Allergology, Institute of Immunology, 198⦰ PhD, Biochemistry, 1992, Russian Academy of Medic⦰ Sciences, Moscow. Appointments: Postdoctoral Fellow Institute of Immunology, 1980-82; Researcher, All Union Cancer Research Center, Moscow, 1982-84; Scientist, Institut⦰ of Viral Products, Ministry of Public Health, Moscow, 1984-8⦰ Senior Scientist, Nutrition, Academy of Medical Science⦰ Moscow, 1987-95; Leader, Research Group, Cardiolog Scientific Center, Moscow, 1995-96; Leader, Research Grou⦰ Institute of Nutrition, 1996-. Publications: Several articles i professional journals. Honours: Grants, Russian Foundation fc Fundamental Investigations, 1995-99. Memberships: America Chemical Society; Federation of European Biochemic⦰ Societies; Euroscience; New York Academy of Science Address: Russian Academy of Medical Sciences, Institute c Nutrition, 2-14 Ustinsky Proezd, Moscow 109240, Russia.

**MARTINOVIC Dusan,** b. 1 March 1933, Cetinj⦰ Montenegro, Yugoslavia. Bibliographer. m. Marija V Kovgan, son, 1 daughter. Education: BSc, MSc, DSc, Natural Science⦰ Geography, University of Belgrade. Appointments: Teacher Grammar School, Cetinje, 1956-62; Headmaster, Cetinj Grammar School, 1963, 1973; Executive Board, Loc⦰ Assembly, Cetinje, 1973-76; Director, Central Library, Durdj⦰ Crnojevic, Cetinje, 1976-91; Editor-in-Chief, Montenegri⦰ Bibliography Project, 1990-; Board of Directors, Academy c Sciences and Arts, for Old Printing and Historical Sources fc Montenegrin History; Editorial, Montenegrin Encyclopedia Publications: 38 monographs; Numerous articles i professional journals. Honours: Liberation of Cetinje Priz⦰ Plaque, Assocition of Librarians of Yugoslavia; Order of Worl with Golden Wreath, 1970. Address: ul Bajova 133, Cetinj⦰ Montenegro 81250, Yugoslavia.

**MARTYNENKO Oleg G,** b. 12 March 1936, Kramatorsk, SSR. Mechanical Engineer. m. Zhanna Martynenko, 2 aughters. Education: PhD, 1964; Professor, 1974; cademician of Belarusian Academy of Sciences, 1979. ppointments: Head of Laboratory, 1963-65, Deputy Director, 966-87, Acting Director, 1987-88, Director, 1988-, Heat and ass Transfer Institute, Belarusian Academy of Sciences; esearcher, Stanford University, USA, 1965-66. Publications: 2 monographs; Over 200 scientific papers; Over 100 ertificates of authorship; Latest monographs: Free-Convective eat Transfer, handbook, 1982; Theory of Buoyancy Jets and 'akes, 1991. Honour: Fellowship Award, International Centre r Heat and Mass Transfer. Memberships: Academy of ciences of Belarus; Acting member, New York Academy of ciences; American Society Mechanical Engineers; Executive ommittee, International Centre of Heat and Mass Transfer; ational Committee for Heat and Mass Transfer, Academy of ciences of Russia; Editor, International Journal, Heat and lass Transfer; Editor-in-Chief, Engineering Physics; Member oard of Editors, International Journal, Experimental Heat ransfer, and Optical Sensors. Address: Skorina ave 13-72, 20050 Minsk, Belarus.

**MARUKOVICH Eugene I,** b. 22 August 1946, Smoliany, elarus. Engineer. m. Vera Petrovna, 2 sons. Education: MS, echanical Engineering, Belarussian Polytechnical Institute, 969; PhD, Foundry Production, 1975; DSc, Foundry roduction, 1992; Professor, 1994. Appointments: Senior ngineer, Institute of Technology of Metals, National Academy f Sciences, Belarus, 1971; Senior Scientist, 1978; Head of aboratory, 1979; Director, 1998. Publications: More than 180 apers; 3 Books; 260 Patents. Honours: Belarussian State rize, 1990; Honoured Inventor of Belarus, 1992. lemberships: Belarussian Association of Foundrymen. ddress: Mira Prospect 25/6 32, 212030 Mogilev, Rep Belarus.

**MARUYAMA Hiroshi,** b. 15 July 1924, Fukushima, Japan. rofessor. m. Tsuneko Fukuyama, 1 son. Education: BEng, 946, PhD, 1961, University of Tokyo. Appointments: esearcher, 1946, Director General, 1977, Railway Technical nstitute/Japanese National Railways; Professor, 1980, Dean, 984-88, Science University of Tokyo. Publication: Railway echnology, Safety of Machinery in the World. Honours: Medal, uper High Speed Vehicle Machine Tool, 1965; Recipient, MITI ward, 1983; Medal with Blue Ribbon, Emperor of Japan, 992. Memberships: Japan-British Society; America-Japan ociety Inc; American Society of Mechanical Engineering; lapan Society of Mechanical Engineering. Address: 11-18 ligashi-cho 1-chome, Koganei-shi, Tokyo-to, 184-0011, Japan.

**MARWAH Kanta,** b. India. University Professor of conomics. Education: BA First Class, Economics, 1955, MA irst Class with distinction, Economics, 1957, Panjab Jniversity; PhD Economics, 1964, University of Pennsylvania. ppointments: Research Assistant in Economics, University of ennsylvania, 1959-63; Assistant Professor, Economics epartment, Boston College, 1963-66; Associate Professor, 967-77, Professor, 1977-, Economics Department, Carleton Jniversity, Canada; Economist Consultant and Visiting rofessor, various establishments including World Bank, Vashington DC and UNCTAD, UN, New York. Publications: uthor or co-Author 3 books: An Econometric Model of Price ehaviour in India, 1964; A History of Macroeconometric Model-Building, 1991; Selected Papers of Lawrence R Klein: Theoretical Reflections and Econometric Applications, 1997; 53 efereed journal articles and book chapters; 41 monographs; 44 papers presented at learned societies; On Editorial and Executive Boards of 9 committees and journals. Memberships: Association of Indian Economic Studies; Canadian Society for Asian Studies; International Studies Association; Association for the Studies of Grants Economy; American Economic Association, Life member; AEA Committee on the Status of Women in the Economic Profession; Canadian Economics Association; Econometric Society, Life member; Eastern Economic Association, Founding Life Member; Indian Econometric Society, Life Member; Economists Alled for Arms Reduction; ECAAR Canada. Honours: 8 scholarly awards including fellowships; Book of the Year Award, 1991. Address: Department of Economics; Carleton University, Ottawa, Ontario, K1S 5B6, Canada.

**MARX Michael William,** b. 1 November 1951, Philadelphia, Pennsylvania, USA. Novelist. m. Betty Brown Marx, 2 daughters. Education: European Literature and Drama, Loyola University of Chicago; BA Political Science, Hobart and William Smith Colleges, 1973; MFA, 1976, New York University. Appointments: Wrote, published and sold own novels, door to door, 1976-; Owned and Managed restaurant business, Freelandville Novelist Cafe, 1990-95; Formed a publishing company, Marx & Marx Writers and Publishers, 1998-; Taught creative writing, English literature and composition at Vincennes University, Indiana Business College and Indiana State University at Terre Haute. Publications: A War Ends, war novel, 1977, 1985; Eric Greenfield-Middle American, novel, 1987; Cine-Marx, movie and video review, 1991-92; Commentaries by Eric Greenfield - Middle American op-editorial, 1991-92; Justus-A Utopia, novel, 1999. Honours: Artisan Award, 1978; Pharoah American History Trophy, 1968. Address: PO Box 190, Flat Rock, IL 62427, USA.

**MASCARENHAS Marcio Paulo B P,** b. 31 January 1944, Pirapora, MG, Brazil. Education Businessman. m. Cleosane C Mascarenhas, 2 sons. Education: BA, Education, 1971. Appointments: Founder, Number One English Schools; Author, Number One's method: Dynamic for teenagers and adults and Wave for children from 7 years old on. Publications: 32 titles published to 102 franchisees all over Brazil; Methods Dynamic and Wave. Address: Number One English Schools, Rua Maranhao 181 - Belo Horizonte, Minas Gerais 30150 330, Brazil.

**MASHAYEV Said-Magomed-Shahidovich,** b. 20 July 1950, Village Aksakovka, Urdjarsky District, Semipalatinsk region, Kazakhstan. Physicist; Teacher of Physics. m. Sura, 2 sons, 2 daughters. Education: Checheno-Ingush State University, Grosny, 1976. Appointments: Professor of Physics and Mathematics, 1992; Assistant Professor of Chair, Molecular Physics, State Chechen University, 1994; Chief of Laboratory of X-ray Structural Analysis and Messbauer Spectroscopy, SCU, 1994; University Senior Lecturer in the same, 1996. Publications: 37 articles in different scientific periodicals incl: Study of alloys by method of Messbauer Spectroscopy, 1993; Peculiarities of local distribution of atoms of Iron in alloys Mn-Sn-Fe, 1993. Address: Laboratory of X-ray Structural Analysis, Checheno-Ingush State University, 32 A Sheripova Str, Groznyi 364907, Russia.

**MASHIRINGWANI Edward,** b. 15 November 1954, Zimbabwe. Banker. m. Jane, 1 son, 3 daughters. Education: BSc, MSc, Economics. Appointments: Senior Ecomist, 1984; General Manager, 1984; Manager, PTA Clearing House, 1986; Section Manager, 1988; Senior Deputy General Manager; Director. Address: 80 Samora Machel Avenue, Harare, Zimbabwe.

**MASHONOV Nenko,** b. 29 September 1937, Bata, Bulgaria. Psychiatrist; Medical Educator. m. Todorka Trifonova, 1 son. Education: MSc, Dr, 1961, Higher Medical Institute, Plovdiv;

Postgrad specialisations in Psychiatry, 1967, Social Medicine, 1968; MD, 1989. Appointments: GP, 1962; Senior Health Expert, 1963-64; Intern of Psychiatry, 1964-68; Chief Health Expert, 1968-69; Head Physician, Dispensary for Mental Diseases, Haskovo, 1970-72; Assistant Professor of Psychiatry, Higher Medical Institute of Plovdiv, 1972-97, Associate Professor, 1997-. Publications: Many in scientific journals and newspapers. Memberships: Union of Scientists in Bulgaria; Bulgarian Psychiatric Association. Address: Higher Medicine Institute Plovdiv, 4000 Plovdiv, Bulgaria.

**MASLOG Crispin,** b. 5 December 1931, Maribojoc, Bohol. Professor. m. Florita, 1 son, 1 daughter. Education: Litt B, Journalism, University of Sto Tomas, 1955; PhB, Philosophy, 1960; Master of Arts, Journalism, University of Minnesota, 1962; PhD, Mass Communication, 1967. Appointments: News Editor, Agence France-Presse, Manila, 1956-60; Journalism Instructor, South Dakota State University, 1965-66; Professor, Director, 1967-82; Director, Information Office, Silliman University, 1973-82; Communication Director, Philippine Government Peace and Development Panel for Mindanao and the Cordilleras, 1987; Director, Publications Office, University of Philippines, 1984-91; Communication Consultant, International Rice Research Institute, 1992-93; Professor of Communication, UP Les Baños, 1982-98; Senior Vice President, Dean, Graduate School, Asian Institute of Journalism and Communication. Publications: 18 Books; At least 100 articles for scholary journals and magazines. Honours: Fulbright Scholarship; Philippine Communication for Education Distinguished Service Award; The Outstanding Filipino Award. Memberships: Asian Mass Communication Research and Information Centre; National Press Club; Philippine Association of Communication Educators; National Research Council of the Philipines; Leadership and Initiative for the Environment Foundation. Address: 21 Dao St, Forestry, Los Banos 4031, The Philippines.

**MASON Dean Towle,** b. 20 September 1932, Berkeley, California, USA. Physician; Cardiologist. m. Maureen O'Brien, 2 daughters. Education: BA, 1954, MD, 1958, Duke University; Resident, Johns Hopkins Hospital, Baltimore, 1958-61; Cardiology Fellow, National Heart Institute, National Institutes of Health, Bethesda, 1961-63. Appointments: Co-Director, Cardiac Catheterization Laboratory, National Institutes of Health, 1963-68; Professor of Medicine and Physiology, Chief of Cardiology Division, University of California at Davis, 1968-82; Editor-in-Chief, American Heart Journal, 1980-96; Physician-in-Chief, Western Heart Institute, Chairman, Department of Cardiovascular Medicine, St Mary's Medical Center, San Francisco, California, 1983-. Publications: Over 1000 scientific publications; 25 books on cardiovascular medicine. Honours: American Therapeutic Society Research Award, 1965; Outstanding Professor, 1972; Faculty Research Award, 1978; Wisdom Society Award Honor, 1997; Master, American College of Cardiology, 1998. Memberships: American Society for Clinical Investigation, 1965; American College of Cardiology, President, 1977-78. Address: 44725 Country Club Drive, Box 3051, El Macero, CA 95618, USA.

**MASSIER Paul F,** b. 22 July 1923, Pocatello, Idaho, USA. Engineer. Education: Mechanical Engineering Certificate, University of Idaho Southern Branch, Idaho State University, 1943; BS, Mechanical Engineering, Honors, University of Colorado, 1948; MS, Mechanical Engineering, Massachusetts Institute of Technology, 1949. Appointments: Engineer, Construction and Maintenance Department, Pan American Refining Corporation, Texas City, Texas, USA, 1948; Design Engineer, Maytag Company, Newton, Iowa, USA, 1949-50; Research Engineer, Boeing Company, Seattle Washington,

1950-55; Senior Research Engineer, Group Supervisc Member of the Technical Staff, Task Manager, Jet Propulsic Laboratory, California Institute of Technology, Pasadena California, USA, 1955-88; Retired, 1989; Continued a Member of the Technical Staff, JPL, on call until 199' Publications: Author, Co-author, 39 professional technic: articles in journals and book series. Honours: Military Un Citation Award, 1946; Apollo Achievement Award, NASA, 196⁹ Life Member Service Award, California Parent Teacher Association, 1970; Layman of the Year Award, Arcadi' Congregational Church, 1971; Basic Noise Research Teal Award, NASA, 1980; Sustained Service Award, AIAA, Lo Angeles Section, 1980-81; Engineering Profession: Achievement Award, Idaho State University, 199' Memberships: New York Academy of Sciences; Planeta Society; Associate Fellow, American Institute of Aeronautic and Astronautics; Member of the Order of the Enginee Academic Honor Fraternities: Tau Beta Pi; Sigma Tau; Pi Ta Sigma; Life Member, California Parent Teachers Association Fellow, International Biographical Association; Life Fellow American Biographical Institute Research Association International Board of Directors, Life Member, Bukovina Socie¹ of the Americas; Moderator, Arcadia Congregational Churcr 1996, 1997. Hobbies: Travelog and documentary motio picture production and presentations; Genealogy and famil history research; Travel; Old sheet music; Antique collectibles Address: 1000 North 1st Avenue, Arcadia, CA 91006-253⁹ USA.

**MASSOUD Mary May Farid. b. Cairo,** Egypt. Universit Professor. Appointments: Visiting Professor, Selly Oak Birmingham, UK, 1977-78; Visiting Professor, University c Utah, USA, 1980-81; Visiting Professor, University of Indiana Pennsylvania, USA, 1983-84; Head of Department of English Ain Shams University, 1984-1990; Professor of English Comparative Literature, Ain Shams University, Cairo, Egyp¹ Publications: Numerous articles in various periodicals o¹ English, American and Anglo Irish Literary Topics; Translate t Communicate; Our Father (play). Honours: Award for the Bes Literary Publication; Editor's Choice Poetry Award Memberships: International Biographical Association International Association for the Study of Irish Literatures Association of Literary Translators of America. Address: 2⁹ Emad El Drine Street, Cairo 11111, Egypt.

**MASSOULIER Chantal,** b. 1 September 1966, Brive Correze. Psycholinguist; Chartered Consultant (CC) Education: Psycholinguist Diploma, 1990; PhD, 1992 Appointments: Education; Psychology; Translations Communication. Honours: Distinguished Leadership Award USA, 1998; Testimonial of Merit, USA, 1998. Memberships Elected member, New York Academy of Sciences, 1994 American Consultants League. Address: 1 Avenue Winstor Churchill, Tulle 19000, France.

**MASTRANGELO Bobbi,** b. 16 May 1937, Youngstown Ohio, USA. Professional Artist; Teacher. m. Alfred Mastrangelo 20 Dec 1958, 2 sons, 1 daughter. Education: BS, Elementary Education, State Teacher's College, Buffalo, New York, USA 1959; Art Education: State University, Stony Brook, New York USA, 1969-79. Appointments: Elementary School Teacher, NY State, 1959-66; Writing Teacher, 1999; Title One Tutor Elementary Grades, Smithtown, NY, 1987-99; Professiona Artist. Publications: Manhole Covers Fascinate St James Artist TV Channel 12, 1987; The Manhole is the Message, Newsday 1990; Looking at the Grater Picture, 1994; Art Environmental 1995; Oxymoron, The Fringe, 1998; Rejection, poem, 1998 Grate Works, TV Channel 12, 1998. Memberships: Founder 1986, Director, 1986-88, Member, 1986-95, CLEAN ommittee for Litter Elimination and Neatness); Art ganisations National Association of Womens Artists; National iseum of Women in the Arts, Washington, DC; New York ists Equity Association; Friends of Dard Hunter. Address: 21 ncess Tree Court Port Jefferson, NY 11777-1741, USA.

**MATAITIS Povilas,** b. 26 June 1933, Drasutaiciai Village, niskis District. Conductor; Director. m. Dalia Mataitiene, 1 ughter. Education: Faculty of Economics, Vilnius University, 52-57; J Tallat-Kelpsa College of Music, 1952-53, 1954-58; ioral Conducting, Lithuania Conservatory, 1958-63; ofessional Advancement Training, Leningrad Conservatory, 66-68. Appointments: Choir Master, Vilnius College of ilture and Education, 1958-62; Choir Master, Mixed Choir of ip Teachers Centre, 1960-62; Instructor, 1962-66, 1973-74, nius J Tallat-Kelpsa College of Music; Chair, Department of erature on Music, VAGA Publishing House, 1968-73; isearch Adviser and Artistic Director, Lithuanian Folklore ieatre, Open Air Museum of Lithuania, 1974-90; Manager, P itaitis Lithuanian Folklore Theatre, 1992-96; Manager, huanian Folklore Theatre, Movement for Progressive ieative Initiative, 1996-; Instructor, Lithuanian Academy of isic, 1985-89, Vilnius University, 1990-93. Creative Works: ide the first step towards the revival and promotion of ithentic folklore in Lithuania, 1968; Linked folklore to modern ieatre art and founded the folklore theatre genre. Staged 12 irformances based on personal research work as well as ierent works on the folklore, ethnology, mythology, history d overall cultural heritage of Lithuania; Scene script and -author, Lithuanian Ethnography - That's Us, and Yesterdays d Always, films. Honours: Lithuanian Merited Artist, 1983; huanian State Award Laureate, 1988; Lithuanian Grand Duke idiminas First Medal Cavalier, 1998. Memberships include: huanian Musicians Society; Lithuanian Theatre Society. idress: Antakalnio 118-30, LT 2040 Vilnius, Lithuania.

**MATHER Ruth,** b. 14 February 1934, Waverly, Washington, iA. Writer; Editor. m. Fred J Morgan, 1 son, 1 daughter. iucation: BA, highest honors, Brigham Young University, 61, MA, 1965; Postgraduate work at University of issississippi, 1977-78; Certificate for secondary teacher in Idaho; irtificate for grades 7-14 in California schools and junior illeges. Appointments: Instructor at: Rama Roma, Iglesia de isu Cristo, Mexico City, Mexico, 1955-56; Lemhi County ihools, Leadore, Idaho, 1962-66; Yonsei University, Seoul, irea, 1973-75; Boise (Idaho) State University, 1978-79; illege of Redwoods, California, 1980-81; University of iryland, Far East Division, Seoul, Korea, 1975-77. iblications: 5 history books published by university presses: inging the Sheriff: Biography of Henry Plummer, 1987; John ivid Borthwick: Artist of Gold Rush, 1989; Gold Camp isperadoes, 1990; Vigilante Victims, 1991; Domestic ilence on the Frontier, 1998. Memberships: National Outlaw d Lawman Association; Western Outlaw and Lawman isociation; People for Ethical Treatment of Animals. Address: istory West Pub Company, PO Box 23133, Oklahoma City, K 73123, USA.

**MATHERS Daniel Eugene,** b. 22 September 1962, illahassee, Florida, USA. Musician. Education: BM, Music ieory, Florida State University, 1984; MM, Music Theory, irida State University, 1989; PhD, Music Theory, University Conconnati, 1989. Appointments: Music Director, Southern iademy of Ballet Arts and pas de Vie Dance Co, 1987-; isiting Instructor of Music Theory, University of Cincinnati, i95-96. Publications: Assistant Editor, Theory and Practice, i91-92; Closure in the Sextet and Short Symphony; iagments of Self: Aaron Coplands uses of Musical ilf-Borrowing. Honours: University Dean's Distinguished

Dissertation Fellowship, 1996-97. Memberships: American Musicological Society; Society for Music Theory; Copland Society; Sonneck Society for American Music. Address: 2105 Scenic Road, Tallahassee, FL 32303, USA.

**MATHIESON Donald Lindsay,** b. 7 May 1936, Wellington, New Zealand. m. Sally Barbara Gentry, 1 son, 2 daughters. Education: Nelson College; BA, LLB, 1959, Victoria University of Wellington; BCL, University College, Oxford, 1961; LLD, VUW, 1971. Appointments: Senior Lecturer, Reader and Associate Professor of Law, 1961-70; Crown Counsel, 1971-76; Professor of Law, VUW, 1977-81; Partner of Hogg Gillespie Carter and Oakley, 1981-85; Queen's Counsel, 1986-. Publications: Cross on Evidence, 1963-97; Industrial Law in NZ, 1971. Address: John Salmond Chambers 10th Floor, 86 Lambton Quay, Wellington, New Zealand.

**MATHUR Krishan D,** b. 22 April 1928, India. Educator. 1 son, 1 daughter. Education: MSc, Zoology, Osmania University, India; MA, Government, 1953, PhD, Political Science, 1958, George Washington University. Appointments: Member, National Advisory Board, International Education, US Department of Education, 1989-91; Visiting Professor, Political Science, Indian Institute of Technology, New Delhi, 1993-94; Member, Board of Health Professionals, Virginia, 1997-. Publications include: Conduct of India's Foreign Policy; Indian Astronomy in the Era of Copernicus; Tibet's Tears; Some Aspects of International Control and Peaceful Uses of Atomic Energy. Address: University of the District of Columbia, 4250 Connecticut Avenue North West, Washington, DC 20008-1174, USA.

**MATHUR Vishnu Dayal,** b. 28 August 1939, Ajmer, Rajasthan. Historian; Educator; Researcher. m. Saroj Mathur, 2 sons. Education: MA, History; PhD. Appointments: Teacher, History, M B College, Udaipur, Government College, Banswara, Agrawal College, Jaipur; Head, History Department, Agrawal College Jaipur; Taught history for 33 years. Publications include: States' People's conference, 1984; Research Papers: Afghanistan in 19th Century a Geopolitical Study, 1986; Rajastan mein rajnitik andolan ke prerak tatva, 1986; Freedom Struggle in Rajasthan, 1986; Book Reviews; Biographical Sketches. Membership: Indian History Congress, New Delhi. Address: Raghubar Bhawan, D-155 Bapu Nagar, Savitri Path, Jaipur 302 015, India.

**MATIC Tin,** b. 30 January 1961, Zagreb. Attorney at Law. m. Marina Matic, 1 son, 1 daughter. Education: Masters degree, Faculty of Law, Zagreb University. Appointments: Editor in Chief, Odujetnik, the Journal of Croatian Bar, 1996-. Publication: Legal Framework for Doing Business in Croatia, 1997, 1998. Memberships: Croatian Bar; IBA; Croatian Arbitration Association. Address: Matic Law Office, Marticeva 70, 10000 Zagreb, Croatia.

**MATISHOV Gennady,** b. 1 January 1945, Preobrazhenie, Primorsky Region, USSR. Geographer; Geologist. m. Ludmila Dumenko, 1966, 1 son. Education: MS, Geography, Geomorphology, 1967, Candidate of Geographical Science, 1973, Rostov State University, Rostov-on-Don; Doctor of Geographical Science, Moscow State University, 1981. Appointments: Junior Scientist, Senior Scientist, PINRO, 1968-91; Director, Murmansk Marine Biological Institute, Kola Scientific Centre, Russian Academy of Sciences, 1991-. Honours: Awarded status of Professor, 1990; Elected Member, 1990, elected Full Member, 1997, Russian Academy of Sciences. Memberships: Academician, Russian Academy of Sciences, 1997-; New York Academy of Sciences. Address: 19 Starostina Street, Flat 20, 183038 Murmansk, Russia.

**MATOUSEK Josef,** b. 12 March 1925, Ujezd u Chocne. Immunogeneticist. m. Vladimira Dvorakova, 1 son, 2 daughters. Education: Ing, University of Agriculture, 1951; Phd, Academy of Agriculture, Inst Animal Breeding, 1955; DSc, Academy of Science, 1964. Appointments: Doctoral Student, Institute of Animal Breeding, Prague, 1951-55; Research Worker, Libechov, Czech Republic, 1955-62; Laboratory Animal Genetics, 1962-72; Inst Animal Genetics, 1972-. Publications: Blood Groups of Animals, Editor, 1965; Contributor to Professional Journals, 1951-. Honours: Laureate Czechoslovak State Prize 1968; Honorary Member, International Society of Animal Genetics, 1996; Gregor Mendel Medal, Academy of Science, 1991. Memberships: European for Animal Production, 1966-86; Czech Gregor Medel Genetics Society, 1971-; Czech Academy Agricultural Science, 1990-; Slovak Academy Agricultural Science, 1995-. Address: Oddeleni Fysiologie a Gentiky Akademie Ved Cr, Libechov u Melnika, 27721 Melnik, Czech Republic.

**MATOUSEK Michael,** b. 3 June 1960, Plzen, Czechoslovakia. Medical Doctor. m. Louise Anna Maria Tottie, 1 daughter. Education: MD, Goteborg University, Sweden, 1984; PhD Medicine, 1995; Certificate specialist in somatic long-term care and Geriatric Medicine. Appointments: Physician, Sahlgren's and Vasa Hospital, Goteborg, 1984-91; Tutor, Department of Geriatric Medicine, 1991-96; Physician 1996-. Publication: Movement Performance in the Elderly, 1995. Honour: Honorary Citizen, Upper Dublin Twp, Montgomery County, Pennsylvania, 1978. Memberships: International Psychogeriatric Association; European Neuroscience Association; Swedish Medical Society. Address: Vasa Hospital, Department of Geriatric Medicine, 411 33 Goteburg, Sweden.

**MATROS Larisa,** b. Odessa, Ukraine. Writer; Researcher. m. Yurii Matros, 1 daughter. Education: LLM, 1963, State University Odessa; PhD, 1972, State University Novosibirsk, Russia. Appointments: Lawyer, Ruskultory Trading Co, Novosibirsk, 1962-64; Researcher, Institute of Clinical and Experimental Medicine, Novosibirsk, 1982-; Chief of Philosophy Department, Siberian Medical Academy. Publications: Over 100 publications including 2 books, articles, short stories, essays, poems. Honours: Honorary Diploma, Poetry Competitions, 1993, 1996, 1997, 1998; World Lifetime Achievement Award, 1996; Award of Excellence, 23rd International Congress of Art and Com, 1996. Memberships: PEN; International Platform Association. Address: 14963 Green Circle Drive, Chesterfield, MO 63017-7826, USA.

**MATROS Lillian Ennis Dotson,** b. 10 March 1940, Durham, North Carolina, USA. Social Security Examiner. m. Nathaniel H Matros (dec). Education: AB, 1960, Duke University; MEd Programme, Lynchburg College, current. Appointments: Completed Government career with Social Security Administration as Senior Disability Examiner; Undertaking training as Educator. Address: 232-A Warwick Lane, Lynchburg, VA 24503-2648, USA.

**MATSUHASHI Nobuyuki,** b. 7 November 1956, Tokyo, Japan. Physician. m. Mayumi Iwakiri, 3 daughters. Education: MB, 1982, MD, 1991, University of Tokyo. Appointments: Assistant Professor, Tokyo Women's Medical College, 1984; Resident, Jichi Medical College, 1985; Research Fellow, National Institute of Radiology Science, 1988; Assistant Professor, Department of Internal Medicine, University of Tokyo, 1989-. Publications: Articles in professional journals. Memberships: American Society for Gastrointestinal Endoscopy; Japanese Society for Gastroenterology; Society for Mucosal Immunology; Japanese Society for Immunology.

Address: University Tokyo, Dept Internal Medicine, 7-3 Hongo Bunkyo-ku, Tokyo 113, Japan.

**MATSUMOTO Seiichi,** b. 8 November 1916, Kamaku Japan. Chairman. m. Sadako Ohkochi, 1 son, 1 daughte Education: Graduate, Tokyo University School of Medicir 1941; Dr.Med.Sci, Tokyo University, 1947. Appointmen Assistant Professor, Showa Medical College, 1945-50; Chi Department of Maternal Health, Aiiku Institute, 1950-54; Chi Department of Obstetrics and Gynaecology, Kanto Teish Hospital, 1954-58; Professor, Obstetrics and Gynaecolog Gunma University School of Medicine, 1958-72; Professc Obstetrics and Gynaecology, Jichi Medical School, 1972-9 Director, Jichi Medical School Hospital, 1974-85; Preside Jichi Medical School, School of Nursing, 1987-91; Profess Emeritus, Gunma University, 1988-; Chairman, Japan Fam Planning Association 1991-; Professor Emeritus, Jichi Medic School, 1992-. Publications: Menstruation and its Disorde 1962; Physiology of Menstruation, 1964; Maternal Health Ca 1977; Adolescent Health, 1982; Studies on Women's Sens and Behaviours about Menstruation, 1990; Adolesce Gynaecology, 1995; Studies on PMS, 1995. Honours: Awa Japan Society of Obstetrics and Gynaecology, 1964; Awa Minister of Health and Welfare, 1977; The Public Health Awa 1989; Order of the Sacred Treasure, Gold and Silver St 1991; FIGO, 1994; Dobszay Award, Hungary, 199 Memberships: President, Japan Federation of Sexolog Chairman Emeritus, Japan Society of Adolescents; Jap Society of Maternal Health; Honorary Member, Japan Socie of Obstetrics and Gynaecology; Japan Association of Mater Welfare. Address: Yuigahama 1-11-17, Kamakura 248-001 Japan.

**MATSUMOTO Toshio,** b. 26 March 1932, Nagoya, Japa Professor of Art and Design. m. Yoko, 1 son. Educatic Bachelor of Arts, Tokyo University, 1955. Appointments: Ma Films; Professor, Kyushu Institute of Art and Design, 1980-8 Professor, Kyoto University of Art and Design, 198 Publications: Discovery of Films; Aesthetics of Vision; Study Image Arts. Honours: Grand Prize, 18th Venice Internatio Documentary Film Festival; Main Prize of 27th Internatio Westdentschen Kurzfilmtage Oberhausen. Membershir Japan Society of Image Arts and Sciences; Japan Society Aesthetics. Address: 3 2 12 Takaido Higashi, Suginami Ku, 16 0072, Japan.

**MATSUOKA Masato,** b. 9 May 1958, Kitakyushu, Japa Researcher, Physician. Education: MD, University Occupational and Environmental Health, 1984; PhD, 198 Appointments: Associate Professor, University of Occupatio and Environmental Health. Address: Department Environmental Toxicology, University of Occupational a Environmental Health, 1-1 Iseigaoka, Yahatanishi-k Kitakyushu 807-8555, Fukuoka, Japan.

**MATTESON Clarice Chris,** b. 9 February 1918, Winnipe Manitoba, Canada. Arts. m. Daniel Chester Matteson, 1 son, daughter. Education: BA, Metropolitan State University, 197 MA, Liberal Studies, Hamline University, 1986; Ph Humanities, LaSalle University, 1995. Career: Lyric Impressionist, Artist, Represented by James Gallery a Gallery 416; Art Lecturer, 3 School Districts; Producer, Acce on Art, Kid's Art and International Cafe Internet Ar (television). Publications: Several articles in profession journals. Honours: Television Award, Series Programs, 198 ASCAP Award, 1997-98, 1999; Honoured, One of Twenty Fi Outstanding Graduates in Past Twenty Five Years, Met State, 1997; Interviewed on WCCO TV, The Ralph Jon F Program, 1998; Award for Speech, Art Today, Internation

atform Association, Washington DC, 1998; Selected by
ourage Center Rehabilitation Center to design Christmas
ard, 1998. Memberships: Vice President, Minnesota Territorial
oneers; Minnesota Artists; American Pen Women; WAMSO;
innesota Artists Association; Minnesota Institute of Arts;
ternational Platform Association; Minnesota History Society;
nerican Composers Forum; Minnesota International Center;
oard Member, Highland Business Association. Address: 2119
argent Avenue, St Paul, MN 55105, USA.

**MATTHEWS Anthony,** b. 26 January 1949, Swansea, South
ales, UK. Author; Historian; Filmmaker. m. Lensie Joy.
ducation: BA Hons, 1988; PhD, 1995. Appointments:
ocumentary Producer, Writer, Director, 1982-84; Full time
uthor, 1984-; Lecturer, Hervey Bay Campus, University of
outhern Queensland, 1989, 1990-; Author and Filmmaker.
ublications: 12 books, historical, 2 in progress; 9 television
ocumentaries; 2 commissioned documentaries: Panorama of
rogress, 1998, The Last of the Bullockies, 1998; 17 radio
eries of programmes and documentaries; Total number of
ogrammes written, produced and presented for ABC Radio
xceed 400, 1986-90, all broadcast at least twice; Widely
ublished in many national Australian magazines and
ewspapers, also published in the USA, NZ and UK.
emberships: Australian Society of Authors; Fellowship of
ustralian Writers, Queensland and Victoria. Address: 32
arshall Street, Warwick Qld 4370, Australia.

**MATTHEWS Harry Bradshaw,** b. 16 May 1951, Denmark,
C, USA. Dean. m. Pamela Louise Davis. Education: BA,
UNY Oneonta, 1974; MA, North Michigan University, 1980;
ertified Developmental Education Specialist, Tri-State
stitute, Fairleigh Dickenson University, US Department of
ducation, 1982. Appointments: Asistant Dean in Residence,
UNY, 1974-78; Director, Black Student Services, Northern
ichigan Univ, 1978-81; Director, Minority Affairs, Higher
ducational Opportunities Programs, Hobart & William Smith
olleges, 1981-85; Dean, Intecultural Advancement,
ettysburg College, 1985-91; Diversity Consultant, Roosevelt
chool District, NY, 1992-93; Associate Dean, Director of U S,
luralism Programs, Hartwick College, Oneonta, NY, 1993-;
tern, Trainee, Research Division, NY State Assembly,
Lbany, NY, 1973; Member of Governor and State Board of
ducation Task Force, Lansing, MI, 1979-81; Member, Black
istory Advisory Committee, PA Historical and Museum
ommission, Harrisburg, 1989-91; Chairman, City Commission
n Community Relations and Human Rights, Oneonta, NY,
996-. Publications: African American Genealogy, 1988;
inority Admissions, 1989; New York's Black Civil War
oldiers, 1997, 1998. Honours: Campaigner for US Senator
arl Levin, Marquette, MI, 1978; Distinguished Visitor, US 8th
ir Force, Bossier City, LS, 1979; Martin Luther King, Jr.
oliday tech-in for Congressional Black Caucus, marquette, MI,
981. Memberships: Human Rights Commission, 1983-85;
fro-American Historical and Genealogical Society; Hudson
ohawk, Association of Colleges and Universities; American
ociety of Freedmen's Descendants; Founding President,
nited States Colored Troops Institute at Hartwick College;
lack Civil War Soliders Commemorative; Phi Kappa Phi.
ddress: 74 Dietz Street, Oneonta, NY 13820, USA.

**MATTOLI Sabrina,** b. 1 January 1957, Terni, Italy.
hysician; Researcher; Consultant; Owner. Education: MD,
niversity of Perugia, Italy, 1981; European Board in
espiratory Medicine, Catholic University, Rome, Italy, 1985.
ppointments: Researcher, Department of Medicine, Catholic
niversity, Rome, 1985-87; Researcher, Department of
edicine, McMaster University, Canada, 1987-89; Head,
enter of Respiratory Medicine, University of Milano, Italy,

1989-92; Head, Clinical Research and Medical Affairs, Ferring
Pharmaceuticals, Milan, 1992-94; Head, Diagnostic Center for
Respiratory and Allergic Diseases, Institute of Experimental
Medicine, Milan, 1989-94; Chair, Italian Foundation of
Experimental Medicine, 1997-98; Consultant, Pharmaceutical
Industries, 1995-; Owner, Managing Director, Avail Gmb, Basel,
Switzerland, 1998-. Publications: Over 120 articles in
professional journals. Honours: Several research awards.
Memberships: Italian College of Physicians; American Thoracic
Society; AAAS; European Respiratory Society. Address:
Spalentorweg 18, 4051 Basel, Switzerland.

**MATULIONIS Arvydas,** b. 1 April 1940, Kupiskis, Lithuania.
Professor of Physics. m. Ilona, 3 sons, 1 daughter. Education:
Diploma in Physics, 1961, Candidate of Science, Physics and
Mathematics, 1967, DrSc Physics and Mathematics, 1981,
Vilnius University; Doctor Habilitatus, Natural Science, 1993,
Lithuania. Appointments: Various lecture posts, Vilnius
University, 1961-72; Research Associate, Institute of Optics,
University Rochester, USA, 1969-70; Senior Research
Associate, 1972-74, Head of Laboratory, 1974-91, Professor of
Physics and Principal Research Associate, 1991-95, Professor
of Physics and Head of Laboratory, 1995-, Semiconductor
Physics Institute, Vilnius; Associate Professor, p-time, Vilnius
University, 1983-85; Professor of Physics, p-time, Vytautas
Magnus University, Kaunas, Lithuania, 1991-95. Publications:
Over 160 papers and conference presentations; Over 300 ISI
Citation Index. Honours: Lithuanian National Award in Science,
1983, 1995. Memberships: Lithuanian Physical Society;
International Advisory Committee of the International
Conference on Noise in Physical Systems and I/f Fluctuations;
Advisory Committee of European Workshop on Compound
Semiconductor Devices and Integrated Circuits. Address: A P
Kavoliuko 22-180, Vilnius, Lithuania.

**MATUSAK Piotr,** b. 7 September 1941, Sulislavice, Poland.
Historian. m. Krystyna Wisniewska, 1 son. Education: Degree
in History, Higher Pedagogical School, Cracow, 1966;
Doctorate, Jagiellonian University, 1973; Qualified as
Professor, 1989. Appointments: Member, Military Council of
Higher Education and Science, 1990-93; Dean, Historical
Department, Mazovian Higher School of Humanism and
Pedagogics, Lovicz, 1992-; Dean, Department of Humanism,
Academy of Podlasie, Siedlce; Currently: Director, Department
of History, Academy of Podlasie, Siedlce; Member, Council for
Higher Education in Poland. Publications: Resistance
Movement in Military Industry of the German Occupants in
1939-45, 1983; El Movimiento de Resistancia Polaco 1939-45,
1985; Peasants' Battalions 1939-45, 1987; Resistance
Movement in Poland 1939-45, 1988; Co-author: Military
Technique Policy and Strategy in History; The Policy and
Strategy of Poland in the Second World War; European
Integration, 1996; Education and Culture of Underground
Poland, 1939-45, 1997. Memberships: Sikorsky Institute and
Museum, London, 1986; Frankfurter Projekt Deutsch-Polnische
Geschichte Team; Cooperation with Polish Historical Society,
Stamford, England; Historical Committee of Polish Academy of
Science, 1999; Many historical associations, Poland and
abroad. Address: ul Dickensa 15 m 86, 02-372 Warsaw,
Poland.

**MATUZAS Vitas,** b. 10 July 1959, Radviliskio Region,
Lithuania. Radio Engineer. m. Danute, 1 son, 2 daughters.
Education: Graduated 1982, Kaunas Technological University.
Appointments: Production Director, UAB Distenas, 1982; Mayor
of Panevezys, 1997-. Membership: Board member, Lithuania
Association of Local Authorities. Address: Smelynes 40, LT
5300 Penevezys, Lithuania.

**MATVEYENKO Leonid**, b. 20 December 1929, Kirovograd, USSR. Radioastronomer. m. Pisareva Ludmila, 1 daughter. Education: Leningrad Politechnic Institute Physics Faculty, 1950-56; Candidate Degree, 1966; Doctor Degree, 1979; Professor, 1987. Appointments: Engineer, Scientist, Lebedev Physical Institute, 1956-69; Head, Very Long Baseline Interferometry Labaratory, Space Research Institute, 1969-. Publications: 290 articles and books. Honour: State Award of the USSR, 1986. Memberships: EVN; VLBI Consortium; International Astronomical Union; Russian Astronomical Society; Radio Astronomical Council; Soviet Astronomical Letters Journal; Zemlja i Vselennaja Journal. Address: Institute of Space Research, Russian Academy of Sciences, 84/32 Profsoyuznaya Str, GSP 7, Moscow 117810, Russia.

**MATVEYEV Alexey**, b. 23 May 1938, Minsk, Belarus. Geologist. m. Nelly Korizho, 1 son. Education: Graduate, Belarussian State University, 1960; Candidate of Sciences, 1966; DSc, 1977; Professor, 1990. Appointments: Junior Researcher, 1966, Senior Researcher, 1967, Head of Laboratory, 1975, Vice Director, 1989, Director, Institute of Geological Sciences, 1993. Publications: 196 including 14 monographs. Honour: Laureate of the State Prize, 1986. Memberships: National Academy of Sciences, Belarus; International Eurasian Academy of Sciences. Address: 4a/28 Chernyshevski Street, Minsk 220012, Belarus.

**MATYUSHKIN Alexey**, b. 20 December 1927, Saratovskaya, Grivki, Russia. Psychologist. m. Makarova Tamara, 2 daughters. Education: Graduate, Moscow State University, 1956; Dr of Psychological Science, 1974; Professor of General Psychology, 1982; Academician, Russian Academy of Education, 1990. Appointments: Scientific Investigator, field of psychology, 1957-74; Leader, Psychological Laboratory, Institute of Higher School, 1974-80; Leader, Laboratory Psychology of Thinking in Psychological Institute, 1980-83; Director, Institute of Psychology, USSR, 1983-82; Editor-in-Chief of journal, Voprosi Psichologii; Leader of laboratory, Creative Giftedness, 1992. Publications: Psychology of Thinking, 1965; Problem Solving Situations in Thinking and Education, 1972; Mysteries of Giftedness, 1993. Honours: Medal, Russian Government, 1988; Medal, Ministry of Education, 1997. Memberships: Moscow Psychological Society; Russian Psychological Society. Address: ul Kosinskaia dom 18 Kvartira 116, 1115138 Moscow, Russia.

**MAURYA Nand Lal**, b. 18 June 1946, Varanasi, India. Academic Administrator. m. Vimla Maurya, 2 sons, 1 daughter. Education: BSc Agricultural Engineering, 1965, Allahabad University; M Tech Agricultural Engineering, 1969, PhD Agricultural Engineering, 1982, IIT, Kharagour. Appointments: Lecturer in Agricultural Engineering, Agra University, 1965-67; Technical Teacher Trainee, Agricultural Engineering Dept, IIT Kharagpur, 1967-70; Assistant Professor of Farm Machinery, 1970-72, Associate Professor and Head of Department of Farm Machinery, 1972-76, Principal, 1976-87, Professor and Head Division of Agricultural Engineering, 1987-, Director of Instruction, Rural Home Science College, 1989-90, Dean, 1990-97, Acting Vice Chancellor, 1991, Director of Extension I/C, 1995, UAS, Bangalore/Dharwad; Assistant Director General, Academician, KAB, ICAR, Pusa, New Delhi, 1997-. Publications: 2 books; 50 scientific papers in national journals and conferences; 125 review papers, popular articles, practical manuals and extension bulletins. Honours: ISAE Distinguished Service Award, 1980, Commendation Medal for: contribution to Agricultural Engineering Education, 1982, outstanding research work on Animal Energy, 1984; IE(I)Award for Outstanding Professional Achievement, 1996. Memberships: Indian Society Agricultural Engineers, various positions; American Society Agricultural Engineers; Fellow, Institution of Engineers, variou positions; Life member, Indian Society Technical Education Indian Meteorology Society; International Disordered System Associates Society. Address: Indian Council of Agricultura Research, New Delhi 110012, India.

**MAVASHEV Boris Zalmanovich**, b. 9 May 1939, Tashken Physicist; Geochemist; Ecologist. m. Sarah Mushyahova, sons. Education: BS, MSc, University, 1962; Doctor, Institut Seismology, 1972; Diploma for Discovery, Moscow, 197 Consultant on Ecology, National University, 198 Appointments: Scientist Institute of Health, 1965-73; Scienti Leader Science Group, Mid Asian Meteorolgical Researc Institute, 1973-82, Automobile Institute, 1982-90; Scientis Jerusalem College of Technology, Centre for Technic Education, 1992-97. Memberships: New York Academ ECOST. Address: St Neve Yaqov 207/33, 97150 Jerusalem Israel.

**MAXWELL Richard Anthony**, b. 1 April 1933, New Yo City, New York, USA. International Trader. m. Jacqueline An Creamer. Education: New York University, 1956; Academy Advanced Traffic, New York, 1959. Appointments: Executiv Vice-President, ADG Marketing, New York, 1981-86 Presiden ADG Marketing Services srl, Florence, Italy, 1981-8 President, Associated Dry Goods (FE) Ltd, Hong Kong, 198 Executive Vice-President, Associated Dry Goods Corporatio New York, 1984; President, Inter Textile Corporation, 1987 Honours: Silver Medal and Citation, Republic of China, 198 Commander, Order of Merit, Italy, 1984. Memberships: Pa President, Director, Italy-America Chamber of Commerce In Past President, Director, American Association of Exporter and Importers; Past President, Shippers Conference of Greate New York; National Committee for International Trad Documentation, Past Vice-Chairman, General Busines Committee; Department of Transportation, Washington D Task Force 2 and 3, Past Member, Advisory Committee, Carg Security; New York Airport Security Council, Past Membe Advisory Committee; Transportation Association of America Past Member, Facilitation Committee; National Maritim Council, Past Member, Shipper Advisory Committee. Addres 2408 Stag Run Boulevard, Clearwater, FL 33765-1832, USA

**MAYANGLAMBAM Kishorkumar**, b. 1 March 1971, Khura Konsam, Leikai Imphal. Education: BA Arts. Honours Traditional Martial Arts Awards. Memberships: Meetei Ipa Ip Salai, Inat Khongul Leeba Lup (Musikholl); Imphal Manipu India. Address: Khurai Komsam Leikai, Heigrumak Lon Imphal, Manipur, India.

**MAYE Beatrice**, b. 23 April 1916, Wanneuco, NC. Educato BSLS Library Science. m. 1 son, 1 daughter. Education: BS North Carolina State University; MA, East Carolina University 1976; MA, Administration, 1977; MA, University of Minneapoli Spec Ed, MA, University ot Kansas City. Career: Principa Jasper County High School, Ridgeland, South Carolina Memberships: NEA; NCAE. Address: 1225 Davenport S Greenville, NC 27834, USA.

**MAYER G Roy**, b. 28 August 1940, National City, California USA. Educator; Psychologist. m. Jocelyn Finn Mayer, 1 son daughter. Education: BA, San Diego State University, 196 EdD, Indiana University, 1966; Nationally Certified Schoc Psychologist, 1993-; Certified Behaviour Analyst, 1998 Appointments: Assistant Professor, Southern Illinois University Carbondale, 1966-69; Professor, California State University Los Angeles, 1969-. Publications: Author, 10 books o Behaviour Analysis; Over 60 articles and book chapters Member, Editorial Board, 2 journals; Association Editor, journal. Honours: Outstanding Professor Award, 1987-88; Outstanding Contributor for Behaviour Analysis Award, 1998. Memberships: President, California Association for Behaviour Analysis; International Association for Behaviour Analysis; National Association for School Psychologists; Council for Exceptional Children; California Association for School Psychologists; Phi Kappa Phi Honor Society; Advisory Board, Cambridge Center for Behavioural Studies. Address: 10600 Pinyon Avenue, Tujunga, CA 91042, USA.

**MAYINGER Franz,** b. 2 September 1931, Augsburg, Germany. Full Professor. m. Franziska Lindermeir, 2 sons, 1 daughter. Education: Mechanical Engineering studies, 1951-55; Doctorate in Thermodynamics, 1961. Appointments: Manager, Divisions Director, MAN Nürnberg; Professor Technical University of Hanover; Professor, Chair of Thermodynamics, Technical University of Munich. Publications: 300 papers; 7 books; Editor and co-editor, several scientific journals. Honours: Max Jakob Award, American Society of Mechanical Engineers/American Institute of Chemical Engineers, 1991; Honorary Doctorate, University of Hanover, 1994; Bavarian Order of Merit, 1995. Memberships: Bavarian Academy of Sciences; European Academy of Science and Art. Address: Bolzmannstrasse 15, 85748 Garching, Germany.

**MBAH Samuel Ifeanyi,** b. 25 July 1963, Ugboka, Enugu, Nigeria. Solicitor, Attorney. m. Nkechi. Education: BSc, University of Nigeria, Nsukka, 1986; LLB, 1990, MSc, 1996, University of Lagos; BL, Nigerian Law School, 1991. Appointments: Journalist, 1987-91; Company Secretary, Cannon Pacific Inc, Link Group Ltd, 1992-94; Principal Partner, Veritas Law Firm, 1995-; Legal Adviser HBN Ltd. Publications: Author: Enugu Rangers, 1993; The Wawa Struggle, 1995; African Anarchism, 1997; A History of Ugboka, 1998; Fellow, Nkanu Cultural Forum. Memberships: Nigeran Bar Association; African Bar Association; Awareness League; Nigerian Institute of Advanced Legal Studies; Executive Director, Tropical Watch Environmental Society; Initiative for Democracy and Good Governance (IDGG). Address: Veritas Law Firm, 13 Inyi Street, Po box 1920, Enugu, Nigeria.

**MCCARTHY-TUCKER Sherri,** b. 6 February 1958, USA. College Professor, Educational Psychology. m. Scott Tucker, 1 son, 1 daughter. Education: AA, English Education, BEd, English, 1981; BA, Psychology, 1984; MA, Special Education, 1987; PhD, Educational Psychology, 1995. Appointments: Faculty, Psychology, English and ESL, Maricopa Comunity College, 1988-95; Assistant Profesor, Northern Arizona University, 1993-. Publications include: Improving Adolescent Region Skills by Teaching Logic. Memberships: American Psychological Association; American Psychological Society; American Educational Research Association; Western Psychological Association; Arizona Educational Research Association. Address: 698 South 10th Avenue, Yuma, AZ 85364, USA.

**MCCARTIN Brian James,** b. 26 August 1951, Providence, Rhode Island, USA. Professor of Applied Mathematics. 1 son. Education: BS, Applied Mathematics, 1976, MSc, Applied Mathematics, 1977, PhD, Courant Institute of Mathematical Sciences, New York University, 1981; BM, Music Theory summa cum laude), Hartt School of Music, 1994. Appointments include: Scientific Analyst, Pratt & Whitney Aircraft, 1977-81; Lecturer in Mathematics, Central Connecticut State University, 1982-84; Adjunct Associate Professor in Computer Science, Hartford Graduate Center, 1984-89; Senior Research Mathematician, 1981-89, Consultant to Computational Mathematics Group, 1989-93, United Technologies Research Center; Professor, 1989-92, Chairman,

1989-93, Computer Science, Hartford Graduate Center; Professor of Applied Mathematics, Kettering University, 1993-. Honours include: Phi Kappa Phi, URI Chapter, 1976; Elected to Electromagnetics Academy, Institute for Theory and Computation, 1990-95; Alpha Chi, 1993; Pi Kappa Lambda (Music), Hartt School of Music, 1994; Invited Lecturer at NASA Langley Research Center, 1995; Distinguished Visiting Professor, New Jersey Institute of Technology, 1997; Pi Mu Epsilon, URI Chapter, 1997; Kappa Mu Epsilon, 1998. Publications: 73 papers in professional publications; 54 presentations. Memberships: Mathematical Association of America (MAA); Society of Industrial and Applied Mathematics (SIAM). Address: 2310 Crestbrook Lane, Flint, MI 48507-2209, USA.

**MCCORMACK Michael Joseph,** b. 19 July 1952, St Ignatius, Montana. Actor. m. Eileen Turro McCormack. Education: BA, 1974, Harvard University. Appointments: Founder, Promoter, World Hello Day, 1973-, in 179 countries; Writing has appeared in 46 languages; Versatile character actor. Publications: Author of published fiction, non-fiction, children's books, commercial art, a technical book, poetry and song lyrics. Honours: Valley Forge Freedoms Foundation Award, 1969; Permanent Display International Museum of Peace and Solidarity, Samarkand, Uzbekistan. Memberships: Signet Society of Harvard; Nebraska Association of Film, Television and Video. Address: World Hello Day, PO Box 993, Omaha, NE 68101-0993, USA.

**MCCORMICK Michael Patrick,** b. 23 November 1940, Cononsburg, PA, USA. Physicist. m. Judy Moyer, 1 s, 1 d. Education: BA, Washington and Jefferson College, 1962; MA, William and Mary, 1964; PhD, William and Mary, 1967. Appointments: Nasa Langley Research Center, 1967-96; Professor, Physics Department, Hampton University, 1996-. Publications: Over 400 Publications. Honours: Arthur S Fleming Award; Jule G Charney Award; William T Pecora Award. Memberships: American Meteorology Society; International Radiation Commission; American Geophysical Union. Address: Center for Atmospheric Sciences, Hampton University, Hampton, VA 23668, USA.

**MCCOY Lee,** b. 27 July 1925, Ipswich, Massachusetts, USA. Public Relations; Public Speaker; Panelist; Judge. 2 daughters, 2 sons. Appointments: Corresponding Secretary, 1 year, President, 2 years, Board Member, 4 years, Quota Club of Mobile; Editor, Quota Care-Gram, weekly newsletter for nursing homes. World Traveller: travelled and studied in 51 countries, including a trip, Arts, Color and Design, in China. Publications: 10 books published including: Hurricane Frederic; Mobile on the Mend; Mobile, The Story of a Beautiful City Honours: Many awards include: Merit of Honour Award, Civic Roundtable; Service Award for District Eight, 1979; International Award for Serving Quota Objectives in Australia, 1980; Service Award, Women's Committee of the Spain Rehabilitation Centre, State of Alabama, 1980-81; Gayfer Outstanding Career Woman Award, 1988; J. C. Penny Golden Rule Award, 1991; Member of the Order of International Fellowship. Memberships: Chairman, President's Council, 1979; Chairman, 44th District Conference, 1980; Chairman, Community Service Committee of Quota International, 1980-82; International Service Committee South Areas, 1978-80; First Vice President, Civic Roundtable, 1980-81, President, 1981-82; Board Member, Friends of the City Museum of Mobile, 1978-84; Government's Committee for the Employment of the Handicapped, 1981-; Presidents; Committee Employment of Handicapped; World Committee International Decade Disabled Persons; Cultural Enrichment Task Force, Chamber of Commerce, Mobile; Board of Directors, Miss Wheelchair Alabama, 1980-84; Curator,

...rary, 1972-; Board Member, Old Dauphin ..., 1977-79; Vice President, Board Member, ...eaking Union, 1981-83, President, 1995-; Hobby: ...ue collecting; Public Speaking; World travel. Address: ...53 Monterey Place, Mobile, AL 36605-1227, USA.

**MCCULLOUGH Colleen,** b. 1 June 1937, Wellington, New South Wales, Australia. Author. m. Ric Robinson. Education: Holy Cross College, Woollahra; Sydney University; Institute of Child Health, London University. Appointments: Neurophysiologist, Sydney, London, Yale University Medical School, New Haven, Connecticut, USA, 1967-77. Publications: TIM, 1974; The Thorn Birds, 1977; An Indecent Obsession, 1981; Cooking With Colleen McCullough & Jean Easthope, 1982; A Creed For The Third Millennium, 1985; The Ladies of Missalonghi, 1987; The First Man In Rome, 1990; The Grass Crown, 1991; Fortune's Favorites, 1993; Caesar's Women, 1996; Caesar, 1997; The Song of Troy, 1998. Honour: Doctor of Letters, honoris causa, Macquarie University, 1993. Address: "Out Yenna", Norfolk Island, Oceania, Via Australia.

**MCCULLOUGH Edward Eugene,** b. 4 June 1923, Baldwin, North Dakota, USA. Patent Agent; Inventor. Education: BA, University of Minnesota, 1957; Miscellaneous Patent, law courses; Postgraduate work, Utah State University; Registered Patent Agent, 1965. Appointments: Machine Designer, Sperry Rand Corporation, 1952-58; Patent Administrator, Thiokol Corporation, 1958-86; Private practice, 1986-; Patent Consultant to Thiokol Corporation, 1986. Publications: 33 US patents and numerous foreign patents. Membership: Fellow, International Biographical Association. Address: PO Box 46 784 Highland Boulevard, Brigham City, UT 84302, USA.

**MCDONALD John W,** b. 18 February 1922. Peacebuilder. m. Christel Meyer, 1 son, 3 daughters. Education: AB, 1943, JD, 1947, University of Illinois; Graduated, National War College, 1967. Appointments: State Department assignments, Berlin, Frankfurt, Bonn, Paris, Washington DC, Ankara, Tehran, Karachi and Cairo, 1947-74; Deputy Director-General, International Labour Organisation, Geneva, Switzerland, 1974-78; Various State Department assignments in multilateral diplomacy including as Ambassador, 1978-83; Coordinator for Multilateral Affairs, Center for the Study of Foreign Affairs, State Department, 1983-87; Retired from US Foreign Service, 1987; Professor of Law, George Washington University Law School, Washington DC, 1987-88; Senior Adviser to Center for Conflict Analysis, George Mason University; Teaching and lecturing, Foreign Service Institute and Center for the Study of Foreign Affairs; President, Iowa Peace Institute, Grinnell, and Professor of Political Science, Grinnell College, 1988-92; Bryan Wedge Visiting Professor, Institute for Conflict Analysis and Resolution, Fairfax, Virginia, 1992; Currently Chairman, Co-Founder, Institute for Multi-Track Diplomacy, Washington DC. Publications: Author or editor, 8 books on negotiation and conflict resolution. Address: Institute for Multi-Track Diplomacy, 1819 H Street NW, Suite 1200, Washington, DC 20006-3603, USA.

**MCDONALD SMITH Paul,** b. 26 November 1956, Melbourne, Australia. Artist. Education: Scotch College, Melbourne, 1969-75; Private Study. 1974-79; Study tours, 1975, 1978-79, 1986, 1991; Fine Arts, RMIT, 1976-78. Appointments: Painter, Tutor, Judge, Curator, Professor, Painter, 1978-; Elected Fellow, 1998, President, 1999, Victorian Artists Society. Creative works 6 solo exhibitions, 1980, 1982, 1983, 1987, 1990, 1993; Many group exhibitions, Adelaide Festival, 1980. Publications: Oils - The Medium of The Masters, 1989; Alan Moore, biographical catalogue; Ludmilla Meilerts, biographical catalogue; Num contributions, VAS Newsletter,

1997-99; Various articles in professional journals. Honours: Camberwell Travel Scholarship, 1986; VAS Signatory Diploma, 1991; Norwich Union Award for Landscape, 1992; Ballarat Society of Artists Award, 1993; Preston Rotary Art Prize, 1994; Brighton City Council Art Award, 1994; Leongatha Rotary Art Prize, 1994; Warragul Rotary, 1994, 1995, 1996; Moreland City Council Art Award, 1994; Heidelberg Prize, 1994; Bendigo Rotary, 1995; National Australian Bank Award, 1995; Ringwood, The Maroondah City Council Award, 1995; Wimmera Art Prize, 1996; Korumburra Rotary, 1997; Mount View Award, 1997; Sorrento Art Competition Major Award, 1998; Outstanding Achievement Award, IBC, 1998; Drysdale Club, 1998; Camberwell Club Award, 1998; Peninsula Art Society Award, 1998; Mt Eliza Zonta, 1998; Brighton, 1998; Ballarat, 1998; Norman Kaye Memorial Medallion, 1998; Bright Art Award, 1999. Memberships: Fellow of the Royal Society of Arts, London; Councillor, Director, Editor, Victorian Artists Society; Invited Member, Twenty Melbourne Painters Society; Bottle Brush Club; Honorary Member, Cheltenham Art Group; Altona Artists Association; Box Hill City Art Group; Past Member, Australian Guild of Realist Artists; Malvern Artists Society; Doncaster Templestowe Artists Society; National Gallery Society; Member, Order of International Fellowship; FIBA; DDG, IBC; Fellow, VAS; Royal Art Society, New South Wales. Address: 3 Perry Court, Kew, Vic 3101, Australia. 152. 156. 190.

**MCGUIRE Matthew Judd,** b. 26 October 1964, Waterbury, Connecticut, USA. University Instructor. Education: BA, The Catholic University of America, 1987; MA, King's College London, 1990. Appointments: Adjunct Instructor, Middlesex Community College, 1991-92; Congressional Reference Division, Congressional Research Service; Staff, Library of Congress, 1994-1996; Adjunct-Instructor, Teikyo Post University, Waterbury, Connecticut, USA, 1997-98.

**MCGURN Barrett,** b. 6 August 1914, New York, USA. Author. m. Janice, 5 sons, 1 daughter. Education: AB Fordham, 1935; LittD, honorary, Fordham, 1958. Appointments Foreign Correspondent, New York and International Herald Tribune, 1946-60; US Foreign Service, 1966-73; Spokesman US Supreme Court, 1973-82. Publications include: Decade in Europe, 1958; A Reporter Looks at Vatican, 1960; A Reporter Looks at American Catholicism, 1967; America's Court, 1997 Pilgrim's Guide to Rome, 1998. Memberships: Overseas Press Club of America; Cosmos Club, Washington DC. Address 5229 Duvall Drive, Bethesda, MD 20816, USA.

**MCHEDLISHVILI George,** b. 16 June 1921, Tbilisi, Georgia Pathological Physiologist. m. Marina Adamia, 1 son, 1 daughter. Education: High Medical School, Tbilisi, 1944 Candidate of Medical Sciences, 1947; Doctor of Medical Sciences, 1957; Professor of Pathological Physiology, 1963 Appointments: Head, Microcirculation Research Centre Georgia; Professor, Pathological Physiology, High Medical Schools. Publications: 7 scientific monographs, Georgia, Russia and USA; Over 350 scientific papers in periodicals and books; Over 250 abstracts at scientific congresses and conferences worldwide. Memberships: President, Georgian Society for Microcirculation and Clinical Hemorheology Interrational Advisory Board, International Society for Clinical Hemorheology; and many others. Address: Microcirculation Research Centre, 34 Gotua Street, Thilisi 380060, Georgia.

**MCINTIRE William Allan,** b. 29 December 1946, Long Beach, California, USA. Communications Executive; Special Effects Supervisor. m. Kathryn Dugger, 2 sons, 1 daughter Education: Student, Valley Junior College, Long Beach City College. Appointments: General Manager, A & R For Music roup "Three Dog Night" at Reb Foster Associates and other usic groups; Roadie, Sound Engineer; Producers Assistant, erry La Croix and White Trash, Gayle Mc Cormick (Smith) and thers; Special Effects Supervisor, including special lighting fects for many motion pictures, television movies, theatrical nd others; Inventor, Magic Gadgets, Lighting and Effects quipment sold internationally by major resellers including lole-Richardson Company, Hollywood, WWW Magicgadgets om Website. Creative Works: Numerous music videos and ommercials. Memberships: Audio Engineering Society; Motion icture and Television Engineers; Society of Broadcast ngineers. Address: 12986 Mapleleaf Court, North East, urora, OR 97002, USA.

**MCKALE Michael J,** b. 14 November 1949, Piqua, Ohio, SA. Education. m. Margaret Morales, 1 son, 1 daughter. ducation: BA,University of Notre Dame, 1968-72; MA, Jesuit chool of Theology, 1973-75; PhD, Graduate Theological nion, 1983-86. Appointments: Professor. St Francis College, 986-. Honours: National Endowment for the Humanities Grant, 987; Excellence in Education Award, St Francis College, 988, 1990. Memberships: American Academy of Religion; ociety of Christian Ethics; Society for the Scientific Study of eligion. Address: St Francis College, Philosophy and eligious Studies Department, Loretto, PA 15940, USA.

**MCKEEVER Katherine Lorraine,** b. 16 October 1924, ineland, Ontario, Canada. President Owl Foundation. m. 1)Donald A MacFadyen, (2)James L McKeever, 1 son, 1 aughter. Education: Lisgar Collegiate, Ottawa. Appointments: Vomen's Division, Royal Canadian Air Force, 1942-45; Aerial urvey mapping division of Photo Survey Corporation, Toronto; lesigner, custom jewellery, 1952-56; Residential dwelling esign, 1956-, Canada; Rehabilitated injured raptorial birds, 965; Owl Rehabilitation Research Foundation made into haritable foundation in 1975, President. Publications: The are and Rehabilitation of Injured Owls, 1979; A Family for linerva, childrens book, 1983; Granny's Gang, 1984; Speaker n owls. Honour: Honorary LLD from Brock University for onservation work with birds of prey, 1977; Order of Canada, 986. Address: The Owl Foundation, 4117 21st Street RR1, ineland Stn, ON, Canada LOR 2EO.

**MCKENZIE David Charles Robb,** b. 25 August 1936, Voodville, New Zealand. Carpenter-Joiner; Teacher; Iraughtsman; Music Teacher. m. Marlene McKenzie, 2 sons. ducation: Higher Technical Teacher's Certificate, 1982. ppointments: Manual Training Teacher, Wairarapa South, 965-92; Carpenter, 1992-. Memberships: Salvation Army, 965-92; Carpenter, 1992-. Memberships: Salvation Army, 965-92; Pianist, 1973-; Gideon, 1980-; Vice-President, Cobblestones luseum, 1995-.

**MCKINNEY Monica Lorraine,** b. 22 June, San Diego, USA. Aedia/Communications Company Executive. Education: BBA Aanagement, 1984, University Miami; Certified Videographer, 988, University Georgia; Certified Television Producer and lirector, 1989, DCC. Appointments: Computer Instructor, lperator, ADIA, San Diego and Atlanta, 1985-90; International raining and Development Coordinator, The Coca-Cola lompany Headquarters, Atlanta, 1990-92; Film, Video, Print lroduction and Telecommunications Software Development lompany President, MLM Communications Inc, Atlanta and as Vegas, 1990-. Publication: Telecommunications Software, 998-99. Honours: Various awards 1990-92: Writer, Producer, lirector of multi cultural Public Service Announcements overing Child Abuse, Crack Cocaine, Drugs in the Work Place; lrack Down Trophy, 1995, Producer, Director for Crack Down ational radio special; The Communicator Award, 1997, Writer, lroducer, Director of Television Entertainment; The

Videographer Award, 1998, Writer, Producer, Director of Music Video Entertainment; The Silver Telly Award, 1998, Creator, Host, Writer, Producer of Television Entertainment CELEBS; Who's Who in the Media and Communications, 1998, 1999. Memberships: Executive Committee Chair, International Television Association, 1990-92; International Media Liaison for 25th Anniversary of the Martin Luther King Jr Centre, Atlanta, 1992; Executive Committee Chair, American Women in Radio & Television, 1992-93; National Association for Female Executives, 1996-; Small Business Administration, Nevada Self Employment Trust, 1995-; Woman Incorporated, 1997-. Address: MLM Communications Inc, 5445 W Reno Avenue, Suite 1811, Las Vegas, NV 89118-1571, USA.

**MCKINSTRY Ronald Eugene,** b. 11 August 1926, Bakersfield, California, USA. Lawyer. m. Shirley D McKinstry, 2 sons, 2 daughters. Education: BS, 1950, University WA; JD, 1951. Appointments: Associate, Evans, McLaren, Lane, Powell & Beeks, 1951-55; Associate, Bogle, Bogle & Gates, 1955-61; Partner, Bogle & Gates, 1961-75; Chairman Litigation Department, 1975-91; Sr Trial Partner, Ellis Li McKinstry, 1992-. Publications: WA Law Review; Appointed Special Master for discovery by US District Court (we dist) Wash, 1976-81; Author and Editor-in-Chief, Washington Civil Procedure Before Trial Deskbook, Supplement, 1986; Contributed numerous articles to professional journals. Honour: Service Award, Western Centre for Law and Religious Freedom, 1990. Memberships: Seattle Rotary, 1955-90; Fellow, American College of Trial Lawyers, 1971-, Regent 1978-82; International Association of Defense Counsel, 1971-, Executive Committee 1974-82; Mercer Island Covenant Church, 1972-96; Christ Memorial Church, Poulsbo, Washington, 1997-. Address: Ellis Li and McKinstry, 3700 First Interstate Center, 999 3rd Avenue, Seattle, WA 98104-4001, USA.

**MCNEILL John H,** b. 5 December 1938, Chicago, Illinois, USA. Professor; Pharmacologist. m. Sharon, 2 daughters. Education: BSc, 1960, MSc, 1962, University of Alberta; PhD, 1967, University of Michigan. Appointments: Laboratory Assistant, 1959-62, Lecturer in Pharmacy, 1963, University of Alberta; Lecturer in Pharmacy, Dalhousie University, 1962-63; Research Associate, 1963-65, Teaching Fellow, 1965-66, University of Michigan; Assistant Instructor, 1966-67, Assistant Professor, 1967-71, Associate Professor and Chairman, 1972-75, Professor and Chairman, 1975-81, Division of Pharmacology and Toxicology, Professor, 1975-, Director, Research and Graduate Studies, 1977-78, Assistant Dean, Research and Graduate Studies, 1978-81, Faculty of Pharmaceutical Sciences, Research Professor, Medical Research Council, 1981-82, Professor and Associate Dean, Research and Graduate Studies, 1982-84, Dean, Faculty of Pharmaceutical Sciences, 1985-96, Michigan State University. Publications: Author and co-author, 332 manuscripts in professional journals; 392 abstracts and presentations at meetings; 75 review articles and book chapters. Honours: Alberta Pharmaceutical Association: Scholarship, 1959, Gold Medal, 1960; Zeta Psi Educational Foundation Award, 1961. Memberships: Active member of 19 societies and associations including: American Society for Pharmacology and Therapeutics; New York Academy of Sciences; AAAS; International Society for Heart Research; American Diabetes Association. Address: Faculty Pharmaceutical Science, University BC, Vancouver BC, Canada V6T 1Z3.

**MCPHAIL JoAnn Winstead,** b. 17 February 1941, Trenton, Florida, USA. Writer; Publisher; Property Management. m. James M McPhail, 3 daughters. Education: Florida Southern College, 1959-60; St Johns River Junior College, 1960-61; Houston Community College, 1980s. Appointments: Legal

Secretary; Decorator; Fashion Display Artist; Writer-Publisher; Owner, Art Investments Marketing. Address: 2608 Stamford Street, Houston, TX 77006-2928, USA.

**MCRAE Roberta,** b. 6 September 1948, Italy. Public Servant. m. Ian Stewart, 3 sons. Education: BA; Graduate Diploma, English. Appointments: Teacher; Public Servant; Politician, Speaker, 1992-95; Shadow Minister, 1995-98. Honour: Order of Australia Medal, 1990. Memberships: Australian College Education Association; National Pen Club. Address: 38 Bindaga Street, Aranda, NSW 2614, Australia.

**MCWILLIAMS Charles Henry,** b. 11 September 1952, Coral Gables, Florida, USA. Physician; Educational Administrator; Researcher. m. Susan Robinson, 2 daughters. Education: D Acupuncture, 1980, Institute of Modern Sciences, Mexico City; D Homeopathic Medicine, 1981, International Institute of Homeopatia, Mexico City; Diploma in Herbal Medicine, 1982, National Institute Chinese Medicine, Hong Kong; MD, 1992, Open International University, Sri Lanka. Appointments: Director, American School Oriental and Homeopathic Medicine, Miami Beach, Florida, 1979-86, Jade Academy, Charlestown, St Kitts & Nevis, 1992-, Pan Am School of Bioenergetics, Charlestown, 1994-; President, Universal Technology Ltd, Charlestown, 1989-; MB BS, Univ of Medical Studies, Sri Lanka, 1998; Regional Consultant of Canada, 1998; One of world's experts on acupuncture, chromotherapy, electro-crystal therapy, thermotherapy, electrotherapy, and other methods of transdermal diagnosis and therapy. Publications: Author, Treatise of Acupuncture and Homeopathy, 19 vols, 1981-; Photobiotics, 1995; Your Cure for Cancer, Only Skin Deep, 1997. Address: Pan Am School of Bioenergetics, PO Box 553, Charlestown, St Kitts and Nevis.

**MCWILLIAMS Samuel Robert,** b. 4 May 1948, Wilkensburg, PA, USA. Teacher. m. Rita Mary Nock, 1 daughter. Education: BA, Elementary Education, West Virginia Wesleyan College, 1971; Masters, Equivalency Education, Pennsylvania State University, 1973; MA, Pennsylvania State University, 1974; MS, University of Pittsburgh, 1984. Appointments: Teacher, Pennsyvania Trafford School District, 27 Years. Honours: Life Member, National Education Association, 27 years; Life Member, National Dramatics, Honorary Alpha PSI Omega, 30 years; Life Member, Pennsylvania State Teachers Association, 27 years. Memberships: Bushy Run Lions Club; Pennsylvania Science Teachers Association, 23 Years. Address: 348 Meadowbrook Rd, Level Green, PA 15085-9712, USA.

**MEACHEM Margaret Ramsey,** b. Brooklyn, New York, USA. Composer; Flautist; Teacher. m. Sydney, 2 sons, 1 daughter. Education: BA, Music, Bennington College; MA, Music, University of Masschusetts at Amherst; DMA, Compostiion, University of Maryland, College Park. Appointments: Music School, 30 years; Private Teaching, Flute; Professor of Theory, University of Maryland. Memberships: NFA; IAWM; Composers Forum. Address: P O Boc 491, Dorset, VT 05251, USA.

**MEAD Frank W,** b. 11 June 1922, Columbus, Ohio, USA. Taxonomic Entomologist (ret). m. Eileen Cornwell Mead (dec), 2 sons. Education: BS, 1947, MS, 1949, Ohio State University; PhD, 1968, North Carolina State University. Appointments: Biological Aide, USDA Bureau of Entomology and Plant Quarantine, Columbus, Ohio, 1950-53; Taxonomic Entomologist, Florida Department of Agriculture, Division of Plant Industry, 1953-94, Emeritus, 1994-. Publications: 86. Honours: Sigma Xi Scientific Honorary; Gamma Sigma Delta Agricultural Honorary; Honorary Life member, Alachua County Historical Society. Memberships: Honorary member, Florida

Entomological Society; Entomological Society of America Emeritus Courtesy Association; Professor, University Florida Department of Entomology and Nematology. Address: 2035 N 6th Terrace, Gainesville, FL 32609-3758, USA.

**MEANS John Barkley,** b. 2 January 1939, Cincinnati, Ohio USA. University Professor. Education: BA Latin America Studies, 1960, MA Political Science, 1963, PhD Linguistics 1968, University of Illinois at Urbana. Appointments: Executive Director, National Association of Self-Instructional Language Programmes, 1977-98; Professor, Temple University, 1968- Publications: Editor, Essays on Brazilian Literature, 1971 Contributor to numerous professional and academic journals Memberships: National Council of Organisations of Les Commonly Taught Languages, Executive Secretary-Treasurer 1990-. Address: PO Box 565, Yardley, PA 19067-8565, USA

**MEFED Anatoly Egorovich,** b. 7 December 1938 Gorodishe, Bryansk, Russia. Physicist; Scientific Researcher m. Lyudmila I Putilova, 1 daughter. Education: Graduate Physical Department, Moscow State University, 1962 Postgraduate, Institute of Radioengineering and Electronics Russian Academy of Sciences, 1967-71; Doctor Degree, 1972 Professor, 1989. Publications: Over 70 research papers in scientific journals. Honours: Medal, USSR Inventor, 1982 USSR Diploma, 1987. Membership: New York Academy of Sciences. Address: Institute of Radioengineering and Electronics, 1 Vvedenskogo Square, Fryazino, Moscow 141120, Russia.

**MEHAFFEY John Allen,** b. 18 October 1936, Brainerd Minnesota, USA. Newspapers. m. Mary Jean, 3 sons Education: Business, Minnesota School, 1954. Appointments President, Mehaffey International; Entire career in print media including: Owner, Editor, Publisher of daily and weekly newspapers, sales, marketing and management service consultancy business. Memberships include: American Marketing Association; American Telemarketing Association Association of Free Community Papers; Central States Circulation Managers Association; American Entrepreneurs Association; Direct Marketing Association; Florida Press Association; Florida Advertising Publishers Association Florida's Southwest Direct Marketing Association; Illinois Press Association; Independent Free Papers of America; International Platform Association; National Press Club; Newspaper Association of America; National Newspaper Association of America; Naples Area Chamber of Commerce; Society of Professional Journalists; Sigma Delta Chi; Southeastern Advertising Publishers Association and Suburban Newspaper Association. Address: Mehaffey International, PO Box 2956 Naples, FL 34106-2956, USA.

**MEHAIA Mohamed Abd El-Fattah,** b. 10 March 1948 Shabas Omair, Kafer Elshikh, Egypt. Professor. m. Magda Mohamed Ali. Education: BSc Dairy Science, 1970, MSc Dairy Technology, 1974, Alexandria University, Egypt; PhD Food Science, 1983, University Illinois, USA. Appointments Demonstrator, 1970-74, Teaching Assistant, 1974-78 Department of Dairy Science, Alexandria University; Research Assistant, 1978-82, Research Associate, 1982-84, Department of Food Science, University Illinois; Assistant Professor 1984-89, Associate Professor, 1989-95, Dept Food Science Professor Food Technology, College Agriculture and Veterinary Medicine, 1995-, King Saud University, Saudi Arabia Publications: 56 papers published in international journals Honour: Assistantship from University of Illinois, 1978-82 Memberships: Institute of Food Technologists; American Dairy Science Association; Egyptian Dairy Science Association audi Biological Society. Address: King Saud University, ollege Agriculture Vet Medicine, Buraydah, Saudi Arabia.

**MEHANDJIEV Marin Roussev**, b. 8 March 1927, Sofia, ulgaria. Chemical Engineer, Ecologist. m. Krassimira, 1 son, daughter. Education: MSc Diploma, Engineer in Chemistry, lytechnic of Sofia, 1949; Associate Professor, Degree, Non errous Metallurgy, Polytechnic of Sofia, 1970; PhD, High hemistry Institute, Bourgas, 1971; Associate Professor, egree, Non Equilibrium Thermodynamics of Accumulation ocesses, 1989. Appointments: Manager, Chemical Factory, ofia; Manager, Hydrometallurgical Plant, 1959; Manager, esearch Centre; 1962; Senior Researcher, Institute of Non errous Metallurgy, 1964; Scientific Director of BIOTECH, cience and Engineering Company, 1987. Publications: More an 360 Scientific Publications; 16 Monographs. Memberships: nion of Bulgarian Scientists; International Committee of, The hievement of Science and Research for the Benefit of the orking People, General Foundation of Labour, Israel; ssociation of Bulgarian Environmentalists and Ecologists; alkan Union of Oncology; Corresponding Member, Ukrainian cological Academy of Sciences. Address: Ent A Ste 26, ompl Nadejda Bl 533, 1229 Sofia, Bulgaria.

**MEHDIZADEH Parviz**, b. 15 September 1934, Tehran, Iran. surance Executive. m. Manijeh Sadri, 2 sons, 1 daughter. ducation: BS, 1958; MS, 1961; PhD, 1965. Appointments: esident, Research Institute of Natural Resources, Tehran, 966; Professor, University of Tehran, 1973; President, ZMS nancial Network Corporation, 1995; Charter Member, US esidential Task Force, Washington DC, 1984; US Senatorial ub, Washington DC, 1984. Publications: Flowering Plants of emi-Arid Zones, 1976; Economizing of Water Use in griculture, 1977. Honour: Medal of Merit by US President eagan, 1984. Memberships: Association for the Advancement Science; Charter President, Rotary Club of Rancho Paris, os Angeles. Address: American Family Life Assurance Co, 301 Wilshire Boulevard, Ste 508, Beverly Hills, CA 90210, SA.

**MEHROTRA Ram Charan**, b. 16 February 1992, Kanpur, dia. Emeritus Professor of Chemistry; Coordinator, Special ssistance Programme. m. Dr Sumar Mehrotra, 1944, 1 son, daughters. Education: DPhil; PhD; DSc (Lond); FRIC; NASc; FASc; FNA; FFAACS. Appointments: Lecturer, lahabad University, 1944-54; Reader, Lucknow University, 954-58; Professor and Dean, Faculty of Science, 1958-62; rofessor, 1962-82, Dean Science, 1962-65, Vice Chancellor, 968-69, 1972, 1973, University of Rajasthan; Vice Chancellor, elhi University, 1974-79, Allahabad University, 1991-94. ublications: Several textbooks; About 700 research papers nd review articles in international journals; 4 treatises; Recent dvances and Future Potential of Sol-Gel Process, 1991; Van er Kirk Issue of the Recuil, 1988; Eaborn Issue of the Journal Organomegallic Chemistry, 1988. Honours include: Platinum ubilee Distinguished Service Award of ISCA, 1988; Atma Ram ward, 1988; N R Dhar Memorial Award, 1991; G P Chatterjee ward, 1991; Asutosh Mukherjee Award, 1993; Vidya achaspati, honoris causa, All India Sahitya Sammelan, 1995; K Bose Award, 1997; P C Ray Award, 1998. Memberships: ditorial Board, many international journals; Organosilicon hemistry, 1982-; Organometallic Chemistry, 1985-. Address: epartment of Chemistry, University of Rajasthan, Jaipur 302 04, India.

**MEHTA Naresh**, b. 6 March 1972, Saharanpur, Uttar radesh, India. Film Maker; Writer; Painter. Education: BFA Art istory and Aesthetics, 1996, MS University, Baroda, Gujarat, dia. Appointments: Film Direction and Screenplay, 1995-;

Kalant, 1996; Asti Kalash Shom; Shesh Chinhon Ki Upasna; Chequered Game of My Dices, 1997 Tadbhav; Mrig Bhig Kar Jal Jata Hay; Karmbhar Kaushiki; Black Mirror and Three Mannequins; 1998, Sambhavtah Kramahshah; Sarvam Sarveksh Sarvoksh; Founder, Kavya Bhumi. Honours: Awards for plays; Winner of award for play given by Northern India Culture Association, Baroda, India, 1993. Memberships: Shakespeare Society, Baroda; Indian People Theatre Association, Alwar; Poetry Society, MS University, Baroda. Address: Mehta Niwas, Janakpuri, Saharanpur Uttar Pradesh, 247001, India.

**MEIER Eric John**, b. 14 October 1946, Hindmarsh, South Australia. MHA. m. Ruth, 2 sons, 1 daughter. Education: Flinders University, Bedford Park Teachers College, 1966-69; Diploma of Teaching, 1970; Graduate Diploma, Education Administration, Adelaide College of Advanced Education, 1978; BA, Politics, Journalism, Deakin University, 1988. Appointments: Commissioned Officer, Adelaide University Regiment, 1971-74; Teacher, Gawler High School, 1970-73; Senior Master, Yorktown Area School, 1974-80; Deputy Principal, Immanuel College, 1981-82; Shadow Minister, Agriculture, Fisheries and Marine, 1990-91; Parliamentary Secretary to the Minister for Consumer Affairs, 1996; SA Government Whip, 1993-; Member of Parliament, 1982-. Honours: Robert McDonald Prize. Memberships: Lions Club of Yorktown and District; Hon Member, Maitland Rotary Club. Address: 25 Owen Terrace, Wallaroo, SA 5556, Australia.

**MEILAKHS Melikhov**, b. 29 July 1947, Rossosh, Russia. Writer. m. Nina Meilakhs, 2 sons. Education: Mathematics and Mechanics Faculty, Leningrad University, 1969; Dr, 1974. Publications: Several books. Address: Griboedov Chan 9 kv 79, 191186 St Petersburg, Russia.

**MEKHAIL Fikry Matta**, b. 10 April 1941, Cairo. Radiochemist. m. Salwa Labib, 1 s, 1 d. Education: BSc, Alexandria University, 1962; MSc, DIC Imperial College, London, 1968; PhD, Leicester University, 1972. Appointments: Professor of Radiochemistry, 1992; Head, Environmental Pollution Department, 1996; Head, Nuclear Fuel Processing, 1998. Publications: Fifty Papers in Professional Journals. Memberships: Royal Institute of Chemistry; Institution of Nuclear Engineers. Address: 22 Masaken El Taawinate, Cairo 11361, Egypt.

**MEKHTIEVA Salima I**, b. 21 May 1941, Nahchivan, Azerbaijan. Physicist. m. Talibov A M, 1 son, 1 daughter. Education: Candidate of Physico-Mathematical Sciences, 1967, Doctor of Physico-Mathematical Sciences, 1988, Azerbaijan State University. Appointments: Vice Director, Institute of Physics, Baku, Azerbaijan. Publications: 123. Membership: Active member, Physical Society of Russian Academy of Sciences. Address: Institute of Physics, Azerbaijan Academy of Sciences, G Javid Prospekt 33, Baku 370143, Azerbaijan.

**MELL Gertrud Maria**, b. 15 August 1947, Ed, Sweden. Composer; Sea Captain; Organist; Music Teacher. Education: Student Orchestra and Conducting, Organ, Music Conservatory, Lund, 1965-67, Graduate, 1967; Certified Ship's Mechanic, Ship's Telephone Operator, Ship's Engineer; Graduated, Sea Officer Mate, (Sea Officers High School) University of Sea Officers, Göteborg, 1979; Graduated, Sea Captain, 1981. Appointments: Organist; Music Teacher; Director Choirs and Orchestra; Music Teacher and Organist, Bengtsfors and Töftedal, 1967-76; Worker ships at sea, 1976-78; Organist, Göteborg, 1982-, conducting own Chamber Music, Göteborg. Publications: Composer and Pianist, long playing record Mell, including String Quartet with members of

Royal Court Orchestra, 1971; Composer and Singer, single record Mermaid, 1977; Composer 4 symphonies, 1 string quartet, chamber music, symphonic poems, organ-piano compositions. Honours: Älvsborgs Läns Landstings Kultur Scholar, 1975. Memberships: KMR; STIM. Address: Strömstadvägen 30, 66831 Ed, Sweden.

**MELNIK Roderick V N,** b. 1 June 1963, Sheptivka, Ukraine. Mathematician; University Lecturer. m. Katerina, 2 sons. Education: MSc, National University of Kiev, 1985; PhD, National University of Kiev, 1989; FIMA, Elected Fellow, Institute of Mathematics and its Applications, 1998. Appointments: Lecturer, National Technical University (KPI) Kiev, 1989-94; Lecturer, University of South Australia, 1994-97; Lecturer, University of Southern Queensland, Australia, 1997-99; Senior Research Scientist, CSIRO Mathematical and Information Sciences, Sydney, Australia, 1999-. Publications: Over 70 scientific papers, 1 book. Honours: Australian Research Council Grant; Associate Professor degree, National Technical University, Kiev, 1992. Memberships: Fellow, Institute of Mathematics and its applications (UK); American Mathematical Society; European Mathematical Society; London Mathematical Society; Australian Mathematical Society; ANZIAM. Address: CSIRO Mathematical and Information Sciences-Sydney, Macquarie University, North Ryde, NSW 2113, Australia.

**MELNIKAS Borisas,** b. 5 October 1950, Vilnius, Lithuania. Professor. m. Violeta Melnikiene, 1 daughter. Education: Dipl Engineer, 1973; Dipl Pedagogue, 1973; Dr Sc, 1979; Dr Habil, 1988; Professor, 1990. Appointments: Head of Department of Management, Vilnius Technical University, 1992; Professor, Lithuanian Law Academy, Lithuanian Military Academy, 1994-. Publications: 250 Publications, 30 Books and Booklets. Memberships: Lithuanian Europe Institute; Member of Lithuanian Management Association. Address: Ozo 30-10, LT 2010 Vilnius, Lithuania.

**MENDES Helen Althia,** b. 20 May 1935, New York City, USA. Social Worker, Management Consultant. m. Gregory R Love, 1 son, 1 daughter. Education: BA, Queens College, 1957; MSW, Columbia University, 1964; DSW, UCLA, 1975. Appointments: Director, 1970-72; Associate, 1972-75; Associate Professor, University of Southern California, 1975-86; President, Mendes Consultation Services, 1976-. Publications: African Heritage Cookbook and History; Professional Articles. Honours: Woman of the Year Award; Zeta Phi Beta; Women of Religious Achievement Award; Award of Merit. Memberships: Board of Directors, West Angeles Church of God in Christ; Hollgrove Childrens Home; Los Angeles House of Ruth. Address: Mendes Consultation Services, 3660 Wilshire Blvd Penthouse 1, Los Angeles, CA 900010, USA.

**MENGIS Christopher Ludwig III,** b. 6 July 1924, Monroe, Louisiana, USA. Medical Doctor. m. Marie Godspeed, 1 son, 3 daughters. Education: MD, Tulane University. Appointments: Research Assistant, JTF-1, 1946; Intern, Madigan Army Hospital, Tacoma, Washington, 1951-52; Surgeon, 370th Amphibious Brigade, Fort Sherman, Canal Zone, 1952-53; Resident in Internal Medicine, Brooke Army Hospital, Fort Sam Houston, Texas, 1953-55; Assistant Chief of Medicine, Post Hospital, Fort Jay, New York, 1955-59; Private practice, San Juan Clinic, Farmington, New Mexico, 1959-60; Past President of Medical Staff, St Vincent Hospital, Santa Fe, New Mexico; Assistant Chief of Internal Medicine, Walla Walla (Washington) Veterans Administration Hospital, 1980-93; Retired, 1993-. Publications: Articles in professional journals including: Eosinophilic Granuloma Confined to the Lung, 1959; Plague,

1962; Lactic acid acidemia and phenformin, 1964; Thos Infernal Medical Machines, 1972. Memberships: Board o Directors, New Mexico Tuberculosis Association, Santa Fe Active Santa Fe Volunteer, Fire Department; President, Sant Fe Community Council, 1964. Address: PO Box 149, Athena OR 97813-0149, USA.

**MENSAH Juliana,** b. 20 April 1970, Takoradi, Ghana Typist. Education: NACVET Certificates, Typist Grade, 199£ Stenographer Grade, 1996; WANG Computer Training in M' DOS, WINDOWS, MS WORLD, MS EXCEL, 1997 Appointments: Typist; Documentaries Officer. Address: Ghana National Chamber of Commerce, Box 45, Takoradi, Ghana.

**MENSHIKOV Anatolii Zoteevich,** b. 2 July 1934, Russia Physicist. m. Galina A Kravchenko, 2 sons. Educatior Diploma, 1956; DSc, 1979; Professor, 1988. Appointments Scientific Worker, 1958-65, Senior Scientific Worker, 1965-8£ Head of Laboratory, 1982-, Institute of Metals, Urals Divisior Russian Academy of Sciences. Publications: 220 scientific publications. Address: Laboratory of Magnetic Neutro Scattering, Institute of Metals, Urals Division of Russia Academy of Sciences, 18 S Kovalevskaya Street GSP-17C Ekaterinburg 620219, Russia.

**MERONI Rudolf,** b. 26 April 1953, Bellinzona. Attorney a Law. Education: Lic iur, University of Zurich, 1978; Master c Comparative Jurisprudence, New York University, 1981; Doctc of Laws, University of Zurich, 1982. Appointments: Associate International Legal Practice, Zurich, 1982-85; Partner, Lav Firm, International Practice, 1985; Partner, Meroni and Schmic Attorneys at Law. Publications: Bankers' Liability: Risk an Remedies; International Franchising Law; The Lawyers Guid to Transnational Corporate Acquisitions; The Internationa Franchising Option; Distributions Agency and Francising in a\ International Arena; Sub-Surface Ground Conditions; Civil Lav Projects; Legal and Contractual Approach in Switzerlanc Memberships: International Bar Association; Internationa Chamber of Commerce. Address: Meroni and Schmic Dufourstrasse 13, CH 8702, Zollikon-Zurich, Switzerland.

**MERRITT Danna Wray,** b. 23 July 1945, Pittsburg, Kansas USA. Social Worker. 2 daughters. Education: B£ Sociology/Psychology, 1967; MSW Social Work, 1984 Appointments: Clinical Caseworker, Psychiatric Social Worke Workshop/Day Program Supervisor, for the Disabled, 1967-7£ Adult Day Activity Program Supervisor, Field Placemer Supervisor, Madonna College, Adult Care Services fc Emotionally Impaired, Detroit, 1977-79; Director, Grie Counselling Program, Peer Training Program Developer an Coordinating Supervisor, Beginning Experience of Michigar 1979-82; Social Work Coordinator, Executive Director, Cysti Fibrosis Foundation of Detroit, 1984-86; Medical Social Worke Field Placement Supervisor, Wayne State University an University of Michigan, Regional Comprehensive Haemophili£ Clinic, Children's Hospital of Michigan, 1987-; AIDS/HIV Tes Counsellor, Michigan Department of Health, 1989-98; Cours Trainer, Partners in Haemophilia Care, 1994, Foundations i Haemophilia Care, 1995; Course Co-author, Developer an Trainer, Parents Empower Parents, 1996-. Publications: I books, chapters and articles in the field of haemophilia; abstracts. Honours: Outstanding Professional, 1989, 199C Appreciation Award, 1992, Haemophilia Foundation c Michigan; Social Worker of the Year, 1994, Nation£ Haemophilia Foundation, USA. Memberships Michigan/National Haemophilia Foundation; Michiga Inter-Professional Association, National/State Association c Social Workers; Michigan Rehabilitation Association; Michiga

Association of Professional AIDS Counsellors. Address: 5741 Houghten, Troy, MI 48098-2910, USA.

**MERVILLE Lawrence Joseph,** b. 7 April 1943, Nashville, Tennessee, USA. Professor. m. Sheryl W Merville, 1 daughter. Education: BA, Physics, Vanderbilt University, 1965; MBA, Finance, 1968, PhD, 1971, The University of Texas, Austin. Appointments: Financial Analyst, Texas Instruments, 1968; Assistant Professor of Finance, Indiana University, 1971; Professor of Finance, The University of Texas, Dallas, 1980-. Publications: Several articles in professional journals. Honours: Valedictorian, 1961-; NSF Fellow, 1965; Phi Beta Kappa, 1965. Memberships: American Finance Association; Dallas Economists Club. Address: The University of Texas, Dallas, 2601 North Floyd Road, Richardson, TX 75080, USA.

**MESA ORAMO Jesus de la Caridad,** b. 28 October 1952, Cuba. Researcher. m. Virginia. Education: BSc, Physics, 1979; Specialist, Digital Systems, 1982; Specialist, Microelectronics, 1985; MEcon, 1997. Appointments: Senior Researcher, 1987; Member, Science Council, Cuban Research Institute for Sugar Cane By-Products, 1992-98; Secretary, 4th International Congress of Sugar Cane and Sugar Cane By-Products. Publications: 40 papers in professional journals. Honours: 2 Gold Medals. Memberships: Several. Address: ICIDCA, PO Box 5134, Havana 10500, Cuba.

**MESHRAM Baliram Maharuji,** b. 1 July 1942, Rajoli. Awarded Teacher. m. 2 sons, 1 daughter. Education: 8th class pass, 1st Division first. Appointments: Awarded Teacher, 1964-. Honours: 7 Ideal Teachers Awards; 5 Social Awards; 3 Publications Awards. Memberships: 5 associations. Address: Rajoli, Taluka mula, Chandrapur, Maharastra, India 441212.

**MESKAUSKAS Kazimieras,** b. 19 October 1917, Lithuania. Economist. m. Rasciute Malvina, 1 son, 2 daughters. Education: Vilnius University, 1947; Academic, 1964, Lithuanian Academy of Sciences. Appointments: Hab Doctor, 1963; Professor of Social Sciences, 1966. Honour: Award of Lithuanian Republic, 1966. Membership: Russian Society of Economists. Address: D Poskos 31, 2004 Vilnius, Lithuania.

**MESSERSCHMIDT Albrecht Mattias Wilhelm,** b. 31 January 1945, Germany. Senior Scientist. m. Beate, 1 daughter. Education: Master in Crystallography, Humboldt University, Berlin, 1968; Dr rer nat, 1972; Dr rer nat habil, University of Konstanz, Germany, 1996. Appointments: Post Doctoral Fellow, Humboldt University, Berlin, 1971-75; Research Associate, Academy of Sciences, Berlin, 1975-81; Post Doctoral Fellow, Max Planck Institute for Biochemistry, Germany, 1983-90; Senior Scientist, 1990-. Publications: Editor, Multi Copper Oxidases, 1997; Handbook of Metaloproteins. Honours: Fichte Award of Humboldt University, 1972. Memberships: Society of Biological Inorganic Chemistry. Address: Max Planck Inst Biochem, Am Klopferspitz 18A, D-82152 Martinsried Bavaria, Germany.

**MESSINA Antoinette Josephine,** b. 30 October 1932, Newark, New Jersey, USA. Professor; Economist. m. Joseph A Pagano. Education: BA Economics, 1954, EdD, 1979, Rutgers State University; MBA Economics, Finance and Investments, 1958, NYU; MAE, 1969, Seton Hall University; PhD Equivalent, Finance, 1959, University of Rome; Certificate in Economics, 1963, Drew University; NJ Certificate, Social Studies Teacher, Student Personnel Services, Supervisor. Appointments: Assistant to traders and arbitragers in Foreign Dept, White, Weld & Company, New York, 1954-55; Assistant Trust Administrator, The Bank of New York, 1955-57; Assistant Economist and Assistant to Manager, Federal Reserve Bank of New York, 1957-61; Instructor, Union College, Cranford, 1961-62; Assistant Professor, Newark State College, Union, 1962-63; Instructor, Rutgers University, 1963-64; Assistant Professor of Economics and Finance, Assistant Graduate Dean and Registrar of Law School and Administration, Seton Hall University, 1964-72. Publications: Confidential publications for Federal Reserve System, 1957-61; 2 papers in Resources in Education, 1979, 1980. Memberships: Kappa Delta Pi; NJ Fulbright Association. Address: 26 Daugherty Avenue, Gillette, NJ 07933-1402, USA.

**MESSNER Reinhold,** b. 17 September 1944, Brixen, Italy. Writer, Speaker, Climber. 1 son, 2 daughters. Education: Surveying Studies, Bozen and Padova. Appointments: Climbed, Everest, 1978; 1st Solo Ascent, 1980; Climbed all 14 Eighthausenders; Crossing Antarctic by Foot, 2800km, 1989-90. Publications: 40 Books. Honours: Nepal, Pakistan, Italy, France. Address: Schloss Juval, 39020 Staben BZ, Italy.

**MESTARIHI Shaher Saleh,** b. Zarqa-Jordan. Petroleum Engineer; General Manager. m. Zainab Khan, 3 sons, 1 daughter. Education: BSc Hons Geology, 1981; MSc Petroleum Engineering, 1983. Appointments: General Manager, 1985-. Publication: Book, Diagnosis of Sind Area - Pakistan. Membership: Geological Association of Jordan. Address: Omar Bin Haroon, 3288 Doha, Qatar.

**MEŠTROVIĆ Julije,** b. 10 July 1959, Split, Croatia. Paediatrician. m. Marija Mestrovic. Education: MD, 1984, Zagreb (Croatia) University; MS, 1989; Certificate in Paediatrics, 1994; Certificate in Paediatric Intesivist, 1996, Universita Cattolica, Bambino Gesu, Rome, Italy. Appointments: General Physician Emergency, Split, 1984-89; Resident, Clinical Hospital, Split, 1989-94; Paediatrician, Intensive Care Unit, 1994-96, Director, 1996-; Consultant Paediatrician, Clin Hosp, Split. Publications: Clinical Experimental Metastasis, 1990; Undersea and Hyperbaric Medicine, 1996; Paediatric Dermatology, 1997; Periodicum Biologorum, 1990. Memberships: Croatian Society for Naval, Undersea and Hyperbaric Medicine; Croatian Society of Allergology; Croatian Cultural Literary Society. Address: Kneza Viseslava 1, 21000 Split, Croatia.

**METRAUX Jean-Claude,** b. 14 December 1955, Lausanne, Switzerland. Physician. m. Spomenka Alvir, 3 daughters. Education: Physician, 1980; MD, 1985; Privat Dozent, 1997, University of Lausanne. Appointments: Coordinator, Mental Health Programme for Child War Victims in Nicaragua, 1987-90; President, Association - Appartenances, Lausanne, Switzerland, 1991-98. Publications: Books: Los ninos victimas de la guerra, 1988, translated into English; Children War Victims, 1995; El nino, le familie y la comunidad, 1985. Honour: 1st Prize of Health Education in the Francophony. Memberships: Psychologists for Peace and Human Rights; International Society for Mental Health, 1996; University of Lausanne, Switzerland. Address: ch 1-de Montolieu 57, 1010 Lausanne, Switzerland.

**MEYBERG Bernhard Ulrich,** b. 29 August 1917, Norden. Owner; Manager. m. Lotte Essig, 1 son, 2 daughters. Education: Studium University, Greifswald, 1935-37. Appointments: Savings Bank Employee, 1937-38; First Lieutenant, Air Force, 1938-43; Wholesaler, 1948-70; Owner, Manager, Furniture Wholesale Company, 1970-. Publications: Contributor of essays to diverse newspapers. Memberships: Executive Committee, International Furniture and Carpentry Purchase Association; Committee, Chamber Industry and Trade; Italian Chamber of Trade for Germany; Union of Wholesalers, Cologne; International Trafic Association; Red

Cross Bayern. Address: Max Ostheimerstrasse 6, 87534 Oberstaufen, Germany.

**MEYER Russ,** b. 21 March 1922, Oakland, CA, USA. Film Maker. m. (1) Betty Valdarinos Meyer, (2) Eve Turner Meyer, (3) Edy Williams Meyer. Education: Junior College, Oakland, California; US Army WWII Combat Cameraman. Appointments: Former Photographer, Playboy Magazine; Partner, RM Films International Inc; Film Producer, Director, 1959-; Films include: Finders Keepers, Lovers, Weepers, 1967; Vixen, 1969; The Immoral Mr Teas, 1959; The Seven Minutes, 1971; Cherry, Harry and Racquel, 1970; Beyond the Valley of the Dolls, 1970; Blacksnake, 1973; Super Vixens, 1975; Up!, 1976; Beneath the Valley of the Ultravixens, 1979; Eve and the Handyman, Goodmorning and Goodbye Blacksnake. Address: c/o RM Films International, PO Box 3748 Los Angeles, CA 90078-3748, USA.

**MEYERS Carol,** b. 26 November 1942, Wilkes Barre, Penna. Professor; Archaeologist. m. Eric, 2 d. Education: AB, Hons, Wellesley College, 1964; MA, Brandeis University, 1966; PhD, 1975. Appointments: Editorial Assistant, 1964-65; Quadrangle Director, Brandeis University, 1965-67; Lecturer, University of North Carolina, Chapel Hill, 1971-79; Part-time Lecturer, 1976-77; Consultant, Various Media Productions, 1980-; Assistant Professor, Duke University, 1977-84; Co-Director, Duke University Summer Programme in Israel, 1980-; Research Faculty, Women's Studies, Duke University, 1983-; Associate Professor, Duke University, 1984-90; Member, Center of Theological Inquiry 1991-; Consultant, Lilith Publications Network, 1994-; Visiting Faculty, University of Connecticut, 1994-; Consultant, National Endowment for the Humanities, 1995; Consultant, Dream Works, 1997-98; Associate Director, 1986-90, 1992-98, Acting Director, 1992, Women's Studies Program, Duke University; Professor, Department of Religion, Duke University, 1990-. Publications: Many Publications. Honours: Wellesley College Scholar; Brandeis University Fellowship; Howard Foundation Fellowship; Wellesley College Alumni Achievement Award; Many other honours. Memberships: American Academy of Religion; American Schools of Oriental Research; Archaeological Institute of America; Archaelogical Society of Jordan; British School of Arcaeology in Jerusalem. Address: 3202 Waterbury Drive, Durham, NC 27707-2416, USA.

**MEZHIKOVSKII Semyon,** b. 18 November 1936, Odessa. Chemist. m. Tokar Marina J, 2 sons. Education: University, 1958; Candidate of Science, 1967; DSc, 1984; Professor, 1996. Appointment: Principal Researcher, N N Semenov Institute of Chemical Physics, Russian Academy of Science. Publications: Over 350 scientific papers; 5 monographs; About 100 patents. Honours: Named Hon Inventor USSR, 1985; Recipient Bronze, 1974, Silver, 1980, Medal Exhibition of National Economy Achievements; Award for Popularization of Science Academician, N N Semyonov, 1979. Memberships: D J Mendeleev Russian Chemistry Society; G V Vinogradov Rheol Society; Russian Academy of Sciences. Address: N N Semyonov Institute Chem Phys, Russian Academy S Kosygin Str 4, Russia.

**MIAN Nazir Azhar,** b. 1 March 1937, Rawalpindi. Advocate. Education: BA, honours, English Literature, 1958; Postgraduate, International Affairs, 1959; LLB, 1960; MA, Political Science, 1961. Career: Lecturer, Political Science, Gordon College, Rawalpindi; Customs Service, 1962; Trainee, Finance Services Academy, Lahore, 1964; Assistant Collector, Customs, Lahore, 1965-66; Karachi, 1966-69; Kohat, 1969-71; Deputy Collector, Customs, Lahore, 1971-73; Deputy Financial Advisor, Deputy Secretary, Administration, Ministry of Finance,

Government of Pakistan, Islamabad, 1973-76; Collector c Customs, Peshawar, 1976-81, Lahore, 1981-83; Directo Customs Intelligence and Investigation, Islamabad, 1983-8£ Chief, Survey and Rebate, Central Board of Revenue Islamabad, 1988-90; Director General, Customs Intelligenc and Investigation, Islamabad, 1990-95; Director Genera Administration, Pakistan Telecommunication Corporatio Islamabad, 1995-97; Advocate, High Courts of Pakistar Honours: 1st Prize, Philosophy, 1958; 1st Postion, Internation Affairs, 1959; Certificate of Merit, Political Science, 196 Memberships: Lahore Gym Khana; Islamabad Club; Pakista Cultural Society of Graduates; Society of Cultural Promotio Address: 2236 Archer Road, Shawsville, VA 24162, USA.

**MIAO Wuyi,** b. 1 May 1954, Tianjin, China. Banker. m. Xi Wang. Education: Graduate, Guangzhou Foreign Languag Institute, 1975. Appointments: Senior Vice President, Chie Representative. Address: Bayerische Landesbank Beijing, ( 302 B Beijing Lufthansa Center, 50 Llangmagiao Road, Beijin 100061, China.

**MICALLEF Doris,** b. 20 February 1938, Birkirkara. Maltes Artist; Business Executive. m. Max Micallef, 2 sons, ; daughters. Education: Augustinian Sisters; Malta Society c Arts, Manufactures and Commerce; School of Arts, Valletta Appointments: Co-Founder, Director, Man with husband Max of Dormax Press, 1970-. Creative Works: Exhibitions: Auberg De Provence, Valletta, 1985; Dormax Press, 1986; Medisl Village, 1987; Auberge De Provence, Valletta, 1990; Collective National Council of Women, Museum of Fine Arts, 1984 Permartex 1985, 1986, Royal British Legion, Valletta; Maltafes Auberge de Provence, Valletta, 1986-90; Malta 25 Sen Indipendenti Valletta, 1989; Malta International Trade Fai 1989; Cathedral Museum, Mdina, 1991; Woman Artists in Malt To-Day, 1994; Mediterranean Nights, 1994; The Sacred in An 1995; The Opposite Sex, 1996; Malta Society of Arts Manufacture and Commerce, 1996; Summer Exhibition Mediterranean Conference Centre, 1996; The Cathedra Museum - Mdina, 1996; Malta Society of Arts, Manufacture an Commerce, 1997; Exhibition by Female Artists, 1997 Maltafest, 1997; Mediterranean Nights, 1997; Bath, England 1997; Historical Maltese and Gozitan Arts - Europe Day, 1997 Sarasota Opera House, Florida, 1998. Address: Dormax, 5 Wignacourt Street, Birkirkara, BKR 08, Malta.

**MICHAELOWA Axel,** b. 8 April 1968, Heidelberg, German Economist. m. Katja Michaelowa, 1 son. Education: Diploma Mannheim University, 1993; PhD in Economics, Hambur University, 1996. Appointments: Research Fellow o International Climate Policy, Hamburg Institute for Economi Research, 1994-97; Consultant on Economic Instruments c Climate Policy, to UNCTAD, UNDP, Hamburg Institute, 1998 Publications: Over 20 including: Incentive Aspects of Joir Implementation of Greenhouse Gas Reduction, in Mitigatio and Adaptation Strategies for Global Change, 1996; Joir Implementation - The Baseline Issue, in Global Environmenta Change, 1998. Memberships: International Society fo Ecological Economics; Association of German-Speakin Economists; American Economic Association. Address: 17 Boulevard de la République, 92210 Saint-Cloud, France.

**MICHAELS Alan,** b. 29 November 1946, Stowe, USA Safety Manager. m. Glenda Becton, 2 daughters. Education Bachelor of Arts, Arizona State University, 1970; Master i Science, Industrial Safety Management, Colorado Stat University, 1979. Appointments: Public School Teache 1970-78; Safety Manager, Dunlop Tice Corp, Huntsville Alabama, 1979-; Director of Safety, Lafarge Corporatio Denver, Colorado. Publications: Articles in Professional Safet agazines. Honours: NIOSH Fellow; ASU Medallion of Merit; Ninninger Award. Memberships: American Society of Safety ngineers, various offices; Board of Certified Safety rofessionals. Address: 12340 Ivanhoe Street, Brighton, CO J601, USA

**MICHAELEWICZ Marek Tadeusz,** b. 1 March 1957, 'roclaw, Poland. Physicist; Computational Scientist. m. gnieszka, 1 son, 1 daughter. Education: University of 'rockaw, Poland, 1976-81; La Trobe University, 1982-84; ISc, 1984; The Australian University, 1984-87; PhD, heoretical Physics, 1987. Appointments: Computer onsultant, Scientific Software, Canberra, 1987-88; Research ssociate, University of Minnesota, Minneapolis, 1988-90; esearch Scientist, CSIRO, Australia, 1990-93; Senior esearch Scientist, CSIRO, 1993-97. Publications: Advances • Computational Life Sciences, 1997; Plants to Ecosystems, 997; Humans to Proteins, 1998; Over 35 contributions to iternational journals, book chapters and conference roceedings. Memberships: American Physical Society; ustralian Institute of Physics. Address: 112 Rankins Road, ensington, Vic 3031, Australia.

**MICHELUCCI Marco Américo,** b. 23 October 1967, Santos, razil. Physician. m. Silvana. Education: Bachelor of Medicine, 991; Specialist, Sports Medicine, Paulista Medical School ederal University, 1992; Specialist, Sports Sciences, ABC niversity, 1994; Residence, Community General Medicine, 994; Specialist, Sports Medicine, Sao Paulo University, 1998; laster in Experimental Physiopathology and Sports Medicine, ledical College, Sao Paulo University, 1999. Appointments: egional Coordinator, Agita Sao Paulo Program, 1998-; eacher, Human and Sports Physiology at Hogi University; eacher, Human and Sports Physiology, Physiotherapy ollege Nautico; Coordinator, Stage in Health Community and hysical Activity at Physical Education Nautical Sports. ublications: Paulista Medicine School's Journal of Sports ledicine. Memberships: American College of Sports Medicine CSM); International Federation of Sports Medicine (FIMS); anathlon International; Sao Paulo Sports Medicine Society; entre Français d'Informacion Permanente au Medicine, Paris. ddress: Maria Nascimento Boz, Vidal 415/34, 08810100 Mogi os Cruzes, Brazil.

**MIERTUS Stanislaw,** b. 26 April 1948, Slovakia. Research oordinator. m. Jana Miertusova, 1 son, 1 daughter. Education: ISc, Physical Chemistry, Slovak Technical University, 1971; hD, Physical and Macromolecular Chemistry, Slovak cademy of Sciences, Bratislava, 1975; DSc, Biophysical hemistry, 1988. Appointments include: Researcher, Institute f Polymers, Slovak Academy of Sciences, 1971-81; ostdoctoral Research, University of Pisa, 1977-78; esearcher, Institut de Chimie Biophysique, Paris, 1978; esearcher, University of Pisa, University of Milano, Italy, 979-86; Assistant Professor, 1981-83, Associate Professor, 983-89, Professor, 1989-, Vice Director, Department of nalytical Chemistry, 1985-91, Vice Dean 1988-1990, Slovak echnical University; Visiting Professor, Mount Sinai School of ledicine, University of New York, USA, 1988; Research director, PolyBios/PolyTech, 1992-1997; Area Coordinator, rogramme Officer, Pure and Applied Chemistry, ICS-UNIDO, 998-. Publications: Over 160 papers in professional journals. chievements: Inventor of Solid Binding Matrix Biosensors, 997; Co-author of PCM theory of solvent effect (called also liertus-Scrocco-Tomasi method) Honours: Named Best Junior esearcher in Czechoslovakia, 1977; DSc, University of ratislava, 1988; Gold Medal, Arab Society of Materials cience, Egypt, 1997. Memberships: American Academy for he Advancement of Science; New York Academy of Sciences;

Czech and Slovak Chemical Society. Address: UN Industrial Development Organization, International Center for Science Technology, UNIDO-ICS, Padriciano 99, Trieste 34012, Italy.

**MIHAESCU Grigore,** b. 8 October 1947, Celaru, Dolj, Romania. Professor, Microbiology, Virology, Immunology. m. Elena Mihaescu, 1 daughter. Education: Graduate, Faculty of Biology, 1970; PhD, 1975. Appointments: Assistant, 1975-79, Lecturer, 1979-89, Professor, Microbiology, Immunology, 1989-. Publications include: Biology of Nitrogen Fixing Microorganisms, 1989; Technics and Principles of Microbiology and Immunology, 1992, 1993, 1995, 1997. Address: Aleea Portocalelor 1-3 Sect 6, 77206 Bucharest, Romania.

**MIHAYLOVA Emilia,** b. 28 July 1959, Trud, Bulgaria. Lecturer. Education: Bachelor of Mathematics, 1981; master of Physics, 1982. Appointments: Teacher of Physics, 1982-84; Assistant Professor, University of Plovdiv, 1984-. Publications: Publications in Ferroelectrics, Physica State Solidi and Journal of Physics and Chemistry of Solids. Memberships: New York Academy of Sciences. Address: Agrl U, Mendeleev St 12, 4000 Plovdiv, Bulgaria.

**MIHEVC Marko,** b. 30 April 1957, Ljubljana, Slovenia. University Professor. m. Marija Jereb Mihevc, 1 daughter. Education: Diploma, Academy for music, University Ljubljana; Diploma, Masters degree, Hochschule fur Musik, Vienna, Austria. Creative Works: Children's opera, Aladdin and his wonder lamp; Concert for Violin & Orchestra, 1989; Symphonic poem, Equi, 1991; Initiator & Organiser, Night of Slovene Composers, annual concert, also called Father of the Night of Slovene Composers, 1991; Symphonic poem, In Signo tauri, 1992; Capriccios for Violin & Piano in Vienna, 1993; Professor for composition and Head of composition dept, 1994-; Symphonic poem, Miracula-miracles, 1994; Cantata, Proverbia, proverbs, 1995; Symphonic poem, Alibaba, 1995; Cantata Enigmata, riddles, 1998; Symphonic poem, The Planets, 1998. Memberships: President, Association of Slovene Composers; Vice President, Slovenian Society of Composers, Authors and Publishers. Address: Groharjeva 18, 1000 Ljubljana, Slovenia.

**MIHUT Lizica Marioara,** b. 9 October 1945, Cermei, Romania. Professor; Journalist; Critic. Divorced, 1 son. Education: University Timisoara, 1968; PhD, Philology, University Bucuresti, 1981. Publications: Over 500 studies and articles regarding the history of culture of Transylvania; 7 books; The History of Culture; Morphology and Syntax of Romanian Language. Memberships: League of University Professors of Romania; Association of Writers; Association of Journalists of Romania; Association of The Critics. Address: St Lucian Blaga nr 5, Arad 2900, Romania.

**MIKHAILOV Gennady Georgievich,** b. 26 September 1937, Chelyabinsk, Russia. Engineer; Metallurgist. m. Elvira Nikolaevna Mikhailova, 1 son, 2 daughters. Education: Diploma, Southern Ural State University, 1960; Candidate of Science, 1966; DSc, 1986. Appointments: Associate Professor, Physical Chemistry Department, 1966-85, Chair, Physical Chemistry Department, 1971-85, Professor, Metallurgical Faculty, 1986-, Dean, Metallurgical Faculty, 1986-, Vice President, Academic Affairs, 1988-, Southern Ural State University. Publications: 198 professional publictions. Honour: Honoured Figure of Science, 1987. Membership: Academy of Sciences of Institutes of Higher Education, 1985-. Address: Southern Ural State University, 76 Prospekt Lenina, Chelyabinsk 454080, Russia.

**MIKI Yoshitsugu,** b. 1 January 1954, Neyagawa, Osaka, Japan. Oncologist. m. Machiko Tsuchiya. Education: Doctor of

Medicine, Osaka University, 1984. Appointment: President, Miki Clinic, Neyagawa, 1985-. Publication: In Cancer Research no 57, 1997. Memberships: Japanese Society for Immunology; Japanese Cancer Association; Charles Darwin Associates of New York Academy of Sciences. Address: Miki Clinic, 2-2-1 Kuzuhara, Neyagawa, Osaka, 572-0075 Japan.

**MIKOV Metodi,** b. 10 July 1930, Strezimirovci, Yugoslavia. Medical Educator. m. Jovanka Jovanovic, 2 sons. Education: MD, Belgarde, 1955; Specialist in Health, Belgrade, 1962; DSc, Medical University, Novi Sad, 1970. Appointments: Head, Occupational Health Servies, Magnohrom Kraljevo, 1958-65; Chief, Department of Occupational Health, 1965-72; Director, Department of Occupational Health, 1972-77; Chief of Chair, Professor, Occupational Health, Medical Faculty, 1973-95. Publications: Author, Occupational Health; Practical Manuel in Occupational Health; Pesticides; Contributor, Articles to Professional Journals. Honours: Medallion VI Congress Occupational Health. Memberships: Serbian Medical Association; International Association of Agricultural Medicine and Rural Health. Address: Gagarinova 24, 21000 Novi Sad, Vojvodina, Yugoslavia.

**MIKUTENAS Algimantas,** b. 28 May 1949, Rokiskis, Lithuania. Director of Photography. m. Grazina Baikstyte, 2 sons. Education: Graduate, Institute of Cinematography in Moscow, 1975. Honours: Awards for films in Lobec (Germany), Strasbourg (France) and Bratislava (Slovakia), 1993, and Cork (Ireland), 1998. Membership: Cinematographyc Union of Lithuania. Address: Zemynos 19-45, LT 2022, Vilnius, Lithuania.

**MILENKOVIC Pavle,** b. 22 February 1944, Beograd, Serbia. Professor. m. Roksanda Stojanovic, 2 sons. Education: Medical Faculty, Beograd, 1967; Master degree, 1974; Doctor of Sciences, 1979; Medical Academy of Serbian Medical Association, 1996. Appointments: Institute for Medical Research, 1970-, Head of Haematology, 1991, President of Board of Directors, 1993-97, President Scientific Committee, 1989, Head of Pathophysiology, Faculty of Stomatology, 1985. Publications: Over 150 papers and meeting reports; 55 scientific papers in international journals. Memberships: International Society for Experimental Hematology; Cell Proliferation Society. Address: Dr Suboltica 4, POB 721, 11001 Beograd, Yugoslavia.

**MILLATMAL Tajuddin,** b. 1 May 1953, Chaparhar, Nangarhar, Afghanistan. MD; Public Administrator. m. Parveen Millatmal, 2 daughters. Education: BS, 1969, Nangarhar Lycee, Afghanistan; MD, 1976, University of Kabul, Nangarhar Medical College, Afghanistan; MPA, 1998; Certificate in Gerontology, 1999, University of Nebraska at Omaha. Appointments: Director of Health Committee, Samangan Province, Afghanistan, 1976-78; Medical Officer, Wazir Akbar Khan Hospital, Kabul, 1978-79; Executive Committee Member, Society of Afghan Doctors (SAD), Peshawar, Pakistan, 1980-85; Medical Officer, UN High Commissioner for Refugees, Pakistan, 1982-85; Co-Founder, Medical Director', Afghans' Health and Social Assistance Organisation, Pakistan, 1985-88; Instructor, American Red Cross, Omaha, USA, 1989-91; Clinical Research Specialist, University of Nebraska Medical Centre, Omaha, 1991-. Publications: 4 Inventions in field of calendars, 1987-88; Author 6 books; Co-author, 3 books; Published over 20 research articles in highly prestigious medical and social journals; Delivered over 30 speeches in national and international conventions; Many live interviews. Honours: 2 scholarship awards; National Leadership Honour Society, University of Nebraska at Omaha, 1997; Special Recognition Award in Research, American Lung Association

and American Thoracic Society, 1994; Personal Achieveme Award from Director of AHSAO, Pakistan, 1988; Inventic Award, Islamic Council of Afghanistan, Pakistan, 198 Recognition Award, Director of Public Power Departmer Afghanistan, 1977. Memberships: Afghan Millat Part Executive Board, Afghan Doctor Society, Pakistan; Founde and Vice President Afghans' Health and Social Assistanc Organisation, Pakistan, 1985; Founder and VP, Relie Organisation for Women in Afghanistan, USA; Islamic Medica Association of N America; Executive Board, USA Asia Newspaper Inc, Omaha; Afghan Medical Associatio California; Founder and Interim President, Alumni Associatio of Nangarhar Medical College, Omaha, Nebraska, 199 Address: Dept Internal Medicine, UNMC 600 S 42nd Stree Omaha, NE 68198-2465, USA.

**MILLER Eleanor,** b. San Francisco, California, USA. Colleg Professor. Education: BA, honours, 1966, PhD, 197C University of Nevada, Reno. Career: Crafton Hills College Redlands, California, 1984-86; College of the Desert, Palr Springs, California, 1986-90; College of Southern Nevada 1990-. Publications: Various articles in professional journals Honours: College Service Award, 1995; Excellence in Teachin Award, 1998. Memberships: Phi Kappa Phi; American Societ of University Women; University of Nevada Alumni Associatior National Council of Teachers of English; Nevada Humanitie Committee; Nevada State Teachers Council, Women i Communication; Mountain Plains Adult Education Associatior Address: Southern Nevada CC, 3200 East Cheyenne Avenue North Las Vegas, NV 89030, USA.

**MILLER Errol Constantine,** b. 1 March 1952, Gimmemebit Clarendon, Jamaica. Science Educator. Education: BA, Elysior College of Liberal Arts; DD, BD, 1976, National Society c Universalists; DP, 1976, Neofarian College of Philosophy; BS 1978, MA, 1980, Sussex College of Technology; Managemer Studies diploma, Institute of Management, England, 1982 Science Education qualifications, West Indies College, 1987 Hofstra University, 1995-97, San Francisco State University 1996, UNiversity of Nevada in Las Vegas, 1998; CPA, CPR CBC, CFLE, 1989, 1991-96, University of the West Indies; DSc 1996, Brandridge University; PhD in Public Administration 1998, La Salle University; PhD, California Coast University Century University, Pacific Western University; Currently doin PhD in Environmental Science, Curtin University c Technology, Perth, Australia; many other certificates an diplomas in field of agriculture, teaching, mathematics, biology hotel management, tourism and travel. Appointments: Teacher mainly science subjects, 20 high schools and colleges Jamaica. Publications: Author, co-author and writer c numerous science publications, conference proceedings an symposia. Honours: Award of National Science Teachers Association of USA, Association of Science Teachers o Jamaica, Caribbean Ministry of Education, and many others Memberships: Association of Science Teachers of Jamaica Jamaica Agricultural Science Teachers Association; Caribbear Science Teachers Association; 4-H Leaders Association Geological and Geographical Societies of Jamaica; Historica and Archaelogical Societies of Jamaica. Address: 10-1 Hanbury Heights, PO Box 9, Shooters Hill, Manchester Jamaica, West Indies.

**MILLER Judith Wolfe,** b. 19 August 1928, Boston, USA Consultant. m. Sanford A Miller, 2 daughters, Wallis and Debra Education: BS, Northeastern University, 1949. Appointments Research Technician, Massachussetts General Hospita Boston, 1949-51, New England Medical Center, Bostor 1951-52; Special Assistant, MIT, Cambridge, 1952-61 Chairman, MIT Matrons, 1972; New England Conservator

Prep School Parents Association, Boston, 1976; Vice Chairman: First Bicentennial '87 Symposium, "The Constitution", Washington, 1985; Montgomery County Chairman, National Symphony Orchestra Women's Committee, Washington, 1979-81; Boutique Chairman Decorators' Showhouse, National Symphony Orchestra, Washington 1981-86; Docent, 1979-, President 1983-84, National Arch. Vols., Washington; Co-chairman American Newspaper Publishers Association Foundation Colloquium, Washington, 1985; Vice Chairman Constitution Study Group at National Archives, Washington, 1982-87; Vice President, Treasurer, SA Miller & Associates Inc, San Antonio, Washington, 1987-; Consultant, 9th International Symposium on the US Constitution, Smithsonian Institute, Washington, 1987; Docent, Institute of Texan Culture, San Antonio, 1988-91; Programme Chairman Texas Health Science Centre Club, San Antonio 1988-89; White House Vol. Presidential Student Correspondence, 1996-. Address: SA Miller & Associates Inc, 5450 Whitley Park Terrace #704, Bethseda, MD 20814, USA.

**MILLER Phoebe,** b. 13 January 1948, Evanston, Illinois, USA. Computer Software Marketing Consultant. Education: BA, honours, Mathematics, University of Wisconsin, 1970; Graduate Work, Civil Engineering, Stanford University, 1973; MBA Work, Golden Gate University, 1978; ICP Sales Training, 1979. Appointments: Optics Analysis, Coherent Radiation, Palo Alto, California, 1970-72; Engineer, Bechtel Inc, 1972-77; Assistant Divisional Manager, Rand Information Systems, San Francisco, 1977-79; Senior Marketing Representative, Computer Sciences Corporation, San Francisco, 1979-81; Senior Marketing Consultant, 1981-84, Manager, Distributor Sales, 1984-86, Cognos Corporation, Walnut Creek, California; President, P A Miller & Associates Inc, San Francisco, 1986-. Publication: Computer Input Output Methods Useful for Engineers, 1976. Honours: Bechtel Award of Merit, 1977; Marketing Representative of the Year, New Account Leader, 1st & 3rd Quarters, Most New Accounts, Most Registered Accounts, Most Quality Accounts, Computer Sciences Corporation, Infonet Division, Northwest District, 1981; Vice President, Computer Sciences Corporation Achievement Club, 1981; Cognos Sales Honour Roll, 1982, 1983, 1984; Cognos Presidents Award, 1982, 1983; ICP Million Dollar Super Seller Award, 1983. Membership: International Platform Committee, 1993-98. Address: P A Miller & Associates Inc, 1750 Montgomery Street, San Francisco, CA 94111, USA.

**MILLER Richard Irwin,** b. 2 January 1924, Fairbury, Nebraska, USA. Educator. m. Peggy McLaren, 3 daughters. Address: College of Education, 314B McCracken, Ohio University, Athens, OH 45701, USA.

**MILLER Sandra Perry,** b. 8 March 1951, Nashville, TN, USA. Educator. m. William K Miller. Education: Portland High School, 1969; BS, Elementary Education and Music, 1973; MEd, Masters of Elementary Education, Curriculum Instruction, 1983; Fellowship, Princeton University, 1994. Appointments: Educator, 1973-; National Geographic Teacher Consultant; Teacher Reviewer, Houghton Mifflin Company, 1993; TN Curriculum Committee for the Social Studies. Honours: National Educator, 1992; Tennessee Teacher of the Year for the Middle School, 1992; Fellow, TN Humanities Council, 1994; Distinguished Teacher of the Year, 1992; TN Association of Middle School Teacher of the Year. Memberships: International Platform Association; National Council for the Social Studies; National Geographic Society; National Education Association; National Association for Middle Schools; National Educator Milken Foundation; TN Humanities Council. Address: Portland Middle School, 922 S Broadway, Portland, TN 37148-1624, USA.

**MILLS Frederick E,** b. 12 November 1928, Streator, Illinois, USA. Physicist. m. Joyanne B, 2 sons, 1 daughter. Education: BS, University of Illinois, 1949; MS, 1950; PhD, 1955. Appointments: Director, MURA, 1965-67; Director, Physical Sciences Laboratory, 1967-70; Chairman, Accelerator Department, Brookhaven National Laboratory, 1970-73; Scientist, National Accelerator Laboratory, 1973-92. Publications: about 150 non refereed and refereed publications. Honours: AEC Fellow; GE Fellow; University of Chicago Argonne Fellow. Memberships: American Physical Society; Phi Beta Kappa; Sigma Xi. Address: 40 W 665 Grand Monde Dr, Elburn, IL 60119, USA.

**MILONJIC Slobodan,** b. 10 June 1942, Spuz, Montenegro. Scientist. m. Branka Milonjic, 1 son, 1 daughter. Education: BSc, Chemical Engineering, 1968, MSc, Physical Chemistry, 1974, PhD, Physical Chemistry, 1982, Belgrade University. Appointments: Assistant, 1968-70, Researcher, 1970-74, Senior Researcher, 1974-82, Senior Scientist, 1982-, Vinca Institute of Nuclear Sciences, Belgrade University. Publications: 1 monograph, 2 textbooks, 100 scientific papers in international and national journals. Memberships: Editorial Board, 3 scientific journals; International Association of Colloid and Interface Scientists; European Materials Research Society; Serbian Chemical Society. Address: Lab 060, Vinca Institute, PO Box 522, 11001 Belgrade, Yugoslavia.

**MILOSAVLJEVIC Aleksije,** b. 22 October 1919, Rogaca, Serbia. Physician; Haematologist. m. Radica Milosavljevic, 12 Apr 1947, 1 son, 1 daughter. Education: Graduated, Belgrade School of Medicine, 1947; Specialisation in Haematology, 1953; PhD, 1976. Appointments: Joined, 1948, Assistant Professor, 1956-58, Clinic for Internal Diseases; Assistant Professor, 1958-76, Associate Professor, 1976-81, Professor, 1981-85, Institute of Oncology and Radiology; Retired, 1985. Publication: Anemias - Study of Erythropoiesis and its Disorders, 1983. Honour: Medal of Labour, Serbian Medical Society, 1970. Membership: International Society of Haematology, 1976. Address: Kumodraska Street 33A, 11000 Belgrade, Yugoslavia.

**MILUNIĆ Vlado,** b. 3 March 1941, Zagreb, Yugoslavia. Architect. m. Jirina Altner, 1 son, 2 daughters. Education: Faculty of Architecture ČVUT, -Prague CZ, 1960-66. Appointments: Architectural activities, 1966-; Leader of Studio VM, -1990. Honours: AIA LA Design Awards, -1993; TIME, the best design of 1996 with Frank Gehry for Dancing building-Prague. Membership: Czech chamber of architects. Address: Oldrichova 27, 12800 Prague 2, Czech Republic.

**MINDERMANN Thomas F G,** b. 10 Mar 1955, Schopfheim, Germany. Neurosurgeon. Education: MD, Medical School, 1983, Doctoral Thesis, Medical School, 1984, University of Basel; Board Certified Neurosurgeon, Swiss Board of Neurological Surgery, 1995. Appointments: Attending Neurosurgeon, University Hospitals, Basel, Switzerland, 1995-; Privatdozent, Medical School, University of Basel. Publications: Indications for Single-Dose Antibiotic Prophylaxis in Surgery and Gynaecology, 1985; Single-Dose Antiobiotikaprophylaxe, 1991; Chapters in: Neurosurgery '96, Cancer Medicine, 1997, Intracranial Pressure and Neuromonitoring in Brain Injury, 1998; Contributor to Journal of Neurosurgery, 1993, Neurosurgery, 1994, 1995, 1998, Lancet, 1998, other journals. Honours: Grantee: Lichtenstein-Stiftung, University of Basel; CIBA-Geigy Jubiläumsstiftung, Basel; Freiwillige Akademische Gesellschaft, Basel. Memberships include: American Association of Neurological Surgeons; Congress for Neurological Surgeons, USA; Pituitary Society, USA; Swiss

Medical Association. Address: Department of Neurosurgery, University Hospitals Basel, 4031 Basel, Switzerland.

**MINKO Bogomaz Tamara,** b. 16 October 1953, Kiev, Ukraine. Biologist. m. Vitaliy Pozharov, 1 son. Education: MS, Biochemistry, 1977; PhD, Physiology, 1984. Appointments: Institute of Physiology, Ukrainian Academy of Sciences, Kiev, Ukraine, 1977-93; University of Utah, Salt Lake City, Utah, USA, 1994-. Publications: 120 publications, 1977-98. Memberships: Ukrainian Physiological Society; Ukrainian Pathophysiological Society; American Assocation for Clinical Chemistry; Controlled Release Society. Address: University of Utah, 3662 Kaibabcr., Salt Lake City, UT 84109-2309, USA.

**MINTZ Kenneth Andrew,** b. 15 March 1951, Plattsburgh, New York, USA. Librarian. Education: BA, University of Redlands, 1973; MLS, Southern Connecticut State University, 1978; Appointments: Assistant Newsletter Editor, First Unitarian-Universalist Society of New Haven, Connecticut, 1979-80; Cataloger, Medford Public Library, 1980; Newsletter Editor, Unitarian Society of Rutherford, New Jersey, 1984-85; Book Reviewer, Library Journal, 1988-93; Director, Drama Group, Community Church of New York, 1993-; Librarian, Bayonne Public Library, 1980-88; Cataloger, Hoboken Public Library, 1991-99; Head of Technical Services, Newsletter Editor, Hoboken Public Library, 1999-. Publications: Cochran's Corner; Connecticut River Review; Bayonne Facts; Jersey City News; American Libraries; Quill Books; Many Reviews. Honours: Quill Poetry Award; Editors' Choice Award; New Jersey Essay Writer of the Year; Christmas Story Prize; Essay Prize; Writers Legion of Honour Award; Bayonne Writers Special Legion Award; Bayonne Writers Group Founders Competition Award; Many Other Awards. Memberships: Poetry Society of America; Academy of American Poets; The Modern Poetry Association; Hoboken Creative Alliance and Bayonne Writers' Group; New York Academy of Sciences; Poets House; Poets' Guild; The House of the Seven Gables Settlement Association; The Mark Twain House. Address: Hoboken Public Library, 500 Park Avenue, Hoboken, NJ 07030, USA.

**MIRAVALLES Lemuel M,** b. 16 July 1946, Philippines. Consultant; Educator. m. Myrna P Miravalles. Education: BS, Chemical Engineering, 1967, MEng, 1971, University of the Philippines; WWS, Princeton University, 1977-78; World Bank, EDI, Washington DC, 1981; HIID, Harvard University, 1989. Appointments: Faculty, College of Engineering, 1967-73; Graduate School of Engineering, 1971-73, 1987-88, University of the Philippines; Programme Director, Information Systems, Development Academy of the Philippines, 1973-75; Lecturer, MBA Programme, Ateneo de Manila University, 1974-80, 1988-96; Programme Director, Planning Support Services, Human Settlements Commission, 1975-77; Programme Director, Technobank, Technology Resource Center, 1977-80; Deputy Director General, Director General, National Manpower and Youth Council, 1980-86; Consultant, World Bank, 1988, 1993, USAID, 1989, 1990-92, Government of Kenya, 1992, Colombo Plan Staff College, 1992-95, Government of the Philippines, 1993-96, UNESCO, 1994-95; Asian Development Bank Team Leader, Bangladesh NFETA Project, 1996-2001. Honours: College Scholar, Phi Kappa Phi, University of the Philippines; Colombo Plan Fellow, 1974; Parvin Fellow, Princeton, 1977-78; RP-US Faculty Development Fellow, Harvard, 1989; Study visit fellowships. Memberships: Vice-President, Asian Regional Training and Development Organisation, Manila, 1980-84; Vice-President, Operations Research Society of the Philippines, 1990-92; President, Association of Management and Industrial Engineers of the Philippines, 1990-92; Association of Princeton Graduate Alumni; Society for International Development, Washington DC;

Project Management Institute, USA; University of the Philippines Alumni Engineers. Address: Asian Developmer Bank, NFETA Project, ADB BRM Office, Sheraton Annex Minto Road, Dhaka, Bangladesh.

**MIRIC Milutin,** b. 24 May 1957, Zagreb. Medical Doctor. m Mirjana, 3 sons. Education: MD, 1979; MDc, Medicine, 1983 DSc, Medicine, 1985; Specialist, Internal Medicine, 1985 Appointments: Resident, Internal Medicine, KBC "Zvezdara' Beograd, 1981; Chief CCU, KBC "Zvezdara", 1987; Director Cardiology Clinic, "Dedinje" CVI, Beograd, Professor c Medicine, University of Beograd Medical School, 1984 Memberships: Several articles in professional journals Memberships: International Society for Interferon and Cytokin Research; New York Academy of Sciences. Address Cardiovascular Institute Dedinje, Milana Tepica 1, 1100( Belgrade, Yugoslavia.

**MIRZA Abdur Rauf,** b. 7 February 1951, Pakistan Associate Professor. m. Samina Rauf, 3 sons, 1 daughter Education: BSc Mechanical Engineering, 1975, UET, Lahore Pakistan; MSc Mechanical Engineering, 1981, UPM, Dahrar KSA, Saudi Arabia. Appointments: Assistant Professor 1982-87, Associate Professor, 1987-, Mechanical Engineerin Department, UET Lahore. Publications: Proc 16th SE Semina on Thermal Sciences, 1982; Proc National Symposium o energy crises, 1986; 4 publications in UET Research Journa 1989-94; 1 paper in Institute of Engineers, Pakistan, 1996 Membership: Pakistan Engineering Council. Address University of Engineering & Technology, Lahore 54890 Pakistan.

**MISBAHUDDIN Mir,** b. 1 November 1955, Mymensingh Bangladesh. Associate Professor. m. Nazneen Sultana, 1 son 1 daughter. Education: MBBS, University of Dhaka, 1979; PhD University of Tokushima School of Medicine, Japan, 1988 Appointments: Lecturer, Department of Pharmacology Mymensingh Medical College, Bangladesh, 1981; Osak University of Foreign Studies, 1982-83; Department o Pharmacology, University of Tokushima School of Medicine Japan, 1983-88; Assistant Professor, Rajshahi Medica College, Bangladesh, 1988-93; Associate Professor Department of Pharmacology, Institute of Postgraduate Medicine and Research, Shahbag, Dhaka, Bangladesh, 1993-Publications: Books: General Principles of Pharmacology 1992, 4th edition, 1998; Introduction to Neuropharmacology 1994; Community Pharmacology; Numerous articles ir professional journals. Honour: Japanese Governmen Mombusho Scholarship, 1982. Address: Department o Pharmacology, IPGM & R, Shahbag, Dhaka 1000, Bangladesh

**MISCHENKO Alexei,** b. 27 January 1949, Kartaly, USSR Engineer. m. Nadezhda Mischenko, 1 son, 1 daughter Education: Degree in Electronics, Leningrad, USSR, 1973 PhD, Technics Science, Moscow, 1989; Certified Technics Engineer. Appointments: Deputy General Director, Dalnaya Sviaz, Leningrad, USSR, 1992; Sales Director, JV AT&T S Petersburg, 1995; Managing Director, JV AT&T St Petersburg 1996; Managing Director, Lucent Technologies, Russia, S Petersburg branch, 1996-; Deputy Managing Director, Lucen Technologies, Russia, 1997-. Publications: Over 20 articles tc professional journals. Honours: Recipient, Successful Labou Medal, USSR Government, Moscow, 1972; Friendship o People Order, USSR Government, Moscow, 1985 Memberships: International Telecommunications Academy Russia, 1998. Address: 63 Zhukovskogo Street, St Petersburg 193036, Russia.

**MISHEV Georgi**, b. 3 October 1947, Plovdiv, Bulgaria. Mechanical Engineer. m. Fanny Christeva, 1 son. Education: Mechanical Engineer, 1971; Assistant Professor, 1974; PhD, 1983; Professor, 1988. Appointments: Constructor in Industry, 1971-74; Assistant Professor, 1974-83; Professor, Technical University Sofia, 1986-; Dean, 1993. Publications: 71. Memberships: Union of the Scientists in Bulgaria; Union of Tribology in Bulgaria; Blakan Union of Tribology; Association of Machine Technological Faculties in Bulgaria. Address: Technical University Plovdiv, St Petersburg 61, Plovdiv, Bulgaria.

**MISHINA Mizuho**, b. 21 November 1942, Osaka, Japan. Artist. m. Masanori, 1s, 1d. Education: AD, Kawamura Womens College, Japan, 1963; BA, Art, Norhtern Illinois University, USA, 1986. Appointments: Secretary, Insitute for Nuclear Study, University of Tokyo, 1965-69; Gallery Assistant, Charles Bennett Gallery, Illinois, USA, 1984-85; Artist, 1986-. Honours: Golden Key Honour Society, 1986; Jewelry Award, 1996, 1997, 1998. Memberships: SNAG. Address: 322 Grant Ave, Geneva, IL 60134-1115, USA.

**MISHRA Ashok**, b. 8 January 1947, Jigini, India. Professor. m. Shanti Mishra, 1 son, 2 daughters. Education: BSc, Agriculture, 1966; MSc, honours, Agriculture, 1969; PhD, 1977. Appointments: Assistant Professor, Udaipur University, 1974-82; Associate Research Scientist, 1982-95, Professor, Plant Pathology, 1995-, Gujarat Agricultural University. Publications: Numerous papers in professional journals. Memberships: Indian Society of Mycology and Plant Pathology, Vice President, 1997; Indian Phytopathological Society; Indian Virological Society; Indian Society of Seed Science and Technology; Secretary (Plant Virology), International Working Group of Tropical Virology; Bean Crop Leader, International Seed Testing Association Working Gruop on Viruses. Address: Department of Plant Pathology, BA College of Agriculture, Gujarat Agricultural University, Anand 388 110, India.

**MISHRA Jayamanta**, b. 15 October 1925, V Haripur PO, Bihar. Retired University Professor. m. Sushila Devi, 1 son, 4 daughters. Education: BA Hons Sanskrit, First Class First, 1950, MA Sanskrit, First Class First, 1952, Patna University; PhD, 1961, Bihar University; Vyakarana Sastri, First Class, Varanasi, 1942; Sahitya Sastri, First Class, Bihar, 1944; Sahityacarya, First Class, Bihar, 1946; Vyakaranacarya, II, Varanasi, 1948. Appointments: Lecturer, Assistant Professor, Reader and Head, University Professor and Head, Senior University Professor and Head, Department of Sanskrit, Bihar University; Professor of Sanskrit, Ministry of External Affairs, Government of India, Tu, Nepal, 1963-1969, 1972-75; Vice Chancellor, KSDS University, Darbhanga, 1980-85. Publications: 10 books published; Over 100 research papers in different research journals; Edited 15 works and the 5th volume of the History of Sanskrit Literature. Honours: Sanskrit Ratnam, 1983; Kalidasa Puraskara, 1985; Certificate of Honour, President of India, 1986; Certificate of Honour of Mithila Vibhuti, 1987; Mithila Vibhuti Samman of Chetana Samiti, Patna, 1991; Sahitya Akademi Award, 1995; Presented a big Felicitation Volume, 1995. Memberships: Various posts including General President, All India Oriental Conference; and others. Address: Hanuman Ganj, Mishra tola, Darbhanga Bihar, India.

**MISHRA Kali Prasad**, b. 12 January 1956, Mawaiya Mirzapur. Doctor. m. Dr Kusum Mishra, 2 sons. Education: BSc; MBBS; MS General Surgery. Appointments: Surgeon, MCS Hospital Gyanpur, CCHC Gordair. Honours: Best Doctor and Leproscopic Surgeon of District Bhadohi. Memberships: Indian Medical Association; Association of Surgeons of India;

Indian Red Cross. Address: Mishra Clinic, Near Vijai Cinema, Gyanpur 221304 UP, India.

**MISIAK Zofia Anna**, b. 23 November 1950, Wroclaw, Poland. Artist. Education: Academy of Art, Warsaw, Poland; Private Lessons, Lecole Nationale Superieure des Beaux Arts, 1979. Appointments: Many Exhibitions, Individual, Group, 1975-. Honours: Silver Medal, Grand Concours International Academy; Diploma Di Benemerenca; Diploma Di Merito; Honorary Representative for Poland, International Academy of Leonardo De Vinci; Medal for Distinguished Achievement; Bronze Medal for Painting; Silver Medal, Jazz Festival; Silver Medal, Honours Diploma; Awards of Pictures, Fiera Del Libro Per Ra. Memberships: International Academy of Leonardo Da Vinci, Italy; International Academy of Lutece, Paris, France; Society Europeenne De Culture-Venise. Address: 31/37 rue Piekna Apt 16A, 00 677 Warsovie, Poland.

**MISKINIS Vytautas**, b. 20 July 1946, Panevezys Region, Lithuania. Electrical Engineer. m. Eleonora, 1 son, 3 daughters. Education: Master Technical Science, 1969, Kaunas Politechnical Institute; Doctor Technical Science, 1984, Minsk Politechnical Institute. Appointments: Technical Director, Vilnius Thermal Power Station, 1988-95; Head of State Energy Inspectorate, Ministry of Economy, Republic of Lithuania. Publications: Switchgears and Transformers; 40 brochures, articles and reports in ex-USSR and Lithuanian Press and Conferences; 3 inventions. Memberships: College member, Moe of The Republic of Lithuania; Long term member, Scientific Technical Society of the Lithuanian Power Specialists. Address: Kriviu 31-13, LT 2007 Vilnius, Lithuania.

**MISRA Alka**, b. 9 May 1968, Lucknow, Utter Pradesh, India. Research, Teaching. Education: BSc, Physics, Mathematics, Astronomy, 1987; MSc, Physics, Specilization in Mod Optics, 1989; Doctorate, Astrophysics, 1995; Post Doctorate, 1997. Appointments: Assistant Professor, University of Lucknow, 1991. Publications: 7 Research Publications, 1998-. Honours: Young Scientist Project Award, 1998; 1st Prize, Essay Competition; 1st Prize, Quitz Programme. Memberships: All India Lucknow University Physics Alumni Association. Address: Department of Mathematics and Astronomy, University of Lucknow, Lucknow, UP, India 226007.

**MISRA Dinesh Chandra**, b. 10 October 1940, Unnao, UP, India. Civil Servant. m. Meera Dube, 1 son, 1 daughter. Education: BA, 1960, MA,1962, Lucknow; PhD, 1991, JMI, New Delhi; Visiting Fellow, University of Oxford, Queen Elizabeth House, UK, 1993-94. Appointments: Joined Indian Administrative Service, 1965; Under Training, National Academy of Administration, 1965-66, Joint Magistrate and Assistant Collector, Dehra Dun (1966-67) and Delhi (1967-68). Sub-Divisional Magistrate, Delhi, 1968-69; Additional Deputy Commissioner, Seppa, NEFA, 1969-71; Deputy Secretary, Delhi Administration, 1971-72; Excise Commissioner, Delhi, 1972-74; Chief Secretary, Andaman and Nicobar Administration, Port Blair, 1974-77,Deputy Municipal Commissioner, Delhi, 1977-78; Deputy Secretary, Director and Joint Secretary, Department of Personnel and Administrative Reforms, Government of India, 1979-84; Development Commissioner, Delhi, 1984-88; Joint Secretary, Ministry of Agriculture, Government of India, 1988-93;Visiting Fellow, Queen Elizabeth House, University of Oxford, United Kingdom, 1993-94; Chief Secretary, Goa, 1994-95; Chief Secretary, Arunachal Pradesh, 1995-98; Chairman and Managing Director, Delhi Financial Corporation Ltd, and President, Confedation of State Industrial Development and Investment Corporation of India, 1998-. Publications: Ed, Drought of 1987, 2 vols; Ed, Training and Visit Extension in India in Action; New

Directions in Extension Training; Extension Monitoring and Evaluation (forthcoming). Memberships: Life: Indian Society of Extension Education; Indian Institute of Public Administration; Solar Energy Society of India; India Harbitat Centre; Oxford and Cambridge Society of India; and; Civil Services Officers Institute; others. Address: D-II/91 Kidwai Nagar East, New Delhi110 023,India.

**MISRA Ushakant,** b. 10 April 1952, India. Neurologist. m. Sunita Misra, 2 sons. Education: MD (Medical), 1978; MNAMS (Medical), 1979; DM Neurology, 1985. Appointments: Scientist Neurotoxicology, 1980-87; Lecturer Neurology, K G Medical College, Lucknow, 1987; Addl Professor Neurology, 1987-93, Professor and Head Neurology, 1993-, Sanjay Gandhi PG Institute Medical Sciences, Lucknow. Publications: 110 research papers; 1 book. Memberships: Corresponding Fellow, American Academy of Neurology, USA; Associate Member, American Association of Electrodiagnostic Medicine; World Federation of Neurology. Address: Sanjay Gandhi Postgrad Institute of Medical Sciences, 226014 Lucknow, India.

**MITCHELL Jacob B,** b. 19 June 1932, Boswell, Oklahoma, USA. Electrical Engineer; Project Leader. m. Erma Jean, 4 sons, 1 daughter. Education: AE, Armed Forces Inst, 1953; BSEE, UCLA, 1958; MSEE, 1963; PhD Program, City University of Los Angeles, 1979. Appointments: Senior Engineer, Librascope Inc, 1956-60; Systems Design Engineer, North American Aviation, 1960-62; Senior Electronic Engineer, Hughes Aircraft Co, 1962-64; Senior Research Engineer, NASA, 1964-68; Design Engineer, Beech Aircraft, 1968-73; Design Engineer, Cessna Aircraft, 1973-75; Engineering Consultant, Jacob B Mitchell Association, 1975-79; Systems Engineer, NCR, 1979-81; Research Engineer, Mitchell Enterprises, 1981-89; Research Engineer, Learjet Inc, 1989-. Publications: NASA Publications. Memberships: IEEE. Address: 1456 N Madison St, Wichita, KS, 67214, USA.

**MITOIU Corneliu Vasile,** b. 20 January 1940, Bucharest, Romania. Professor; Engineer. m. Romonita Mitoiu, 1 son. Education: PhD, Hydrotechnical Engineering and Land Reclamation, 1982; PhD, Faculty of Land Reclamation and Environmental Engineering, Bucharest, 1992. Appointments: Civil Technician, Forestry Plant, Suceava, Romania, 1959-63; Research Engineer, Research Institute for Waters Management, Bucharest, 1968-76; Associate Professor, 1972-91, Professor, 1992-, Faculty of Land Reclamation and Environmental Engineering, Bucharest; Design Engineer, Institute for Design and Waters Management, Bucharest, 1976-84; Manager, Special Hydrotechnics Corporation, Bucharest, 1984-90; Expert, Ministry of Environment, Bucharest, 1990, Romanian Waters, Bucharest, 1991-92; Technical Expert, Adviser, Ministry of Justice, Bucharest, 1992-; Consultant Adviser, SC Derol SA, Bucharest, 1993; Chief Inspector of State, Ministry of Waters, Forestry and Environmental Protection, Bucharest, 1994-98; Consultant Adviser, Ministry of Public Works, Bucharest, 1994-; Counsellor of Minister, Ministry of Waters, Forest & Environmental Protection, Bucharest, 1999. Publications: Over 60 articles and scientific communications. Memberships: Vice President, National Society of Scientific Writers, Bucharest, 1991-; President, National Eco-Foundation PROMERO, Bucharest, 1996-; International Geosyntetics Society; National Environmental Protection Society; PROTECAN Foundation of Navigable Channels; National Committee of Water Producers and Users in Romania; President, Environmental Scientific and Technic Council; Naval Lague Constantsa; General Association of Romanian Engineers. Address: Aleea Fetesi 6-12 Sector 3, Bucharest 74722, Romania.

**MITROVIC Dragisa,** b. 16 March 1922, Valjevo, Yugoslavia. Mathematician; Educator. m. Melita Klakocar, 1 son. Education: BSc, 1949, University Zagreb; DSc, 1958; Habilitation, 1959; Alexander von Humboldt Fellow, 1966-67, University Mainz, Germany. Appointments: Math Teacher, Zagreb, 1951-55; Teaching Assistant, 1955-60; Assistant Professor, 1960-63; Associate Professor, 1963-67; Professor, 1967-87; Research Counsellor, 1987-91. Publications: Numerous research papers in professional journals on Calculus of residues, Dirichlet series, Vectorvalued analytic functions, Distributions as boundary values of analytic functions; Co-author books: Distributions and analytic functions, 1989; Fundamentals of applied functional analysis, 1998. Memberships: Society of Mathematicians of Croatia; American Math Society; Reviewer, Mathematical Reviews, USA, and Zentralblatt für Mathematik, Berlin. Address: Kozarceva 19, Zagreb 10000, Croatia.

**MITROVIC M Predag,** b. 14 July 1966, Belgrade, Yugoslavia. Medical Doctor. m. Duska, 1 daughter. Education: Medical School, University of Belgrade, 1992; Specialisation in Internal Medicine, 1997; MSc in Cardiology, 1998. Publications: Over 350 published scientific materials. Honours: Acknowledgement as Outstanding Student at Medical School, Belgrade University, 1990; Professor Slobodan Krajinovic Annual Award of Belgrade University for best research paper in epidemiology, 1991; Second Prize of International Epidemiology Association for scientific researches, 1995. Memberships: Serbian Medical Society; European Society of Cardiology. Address: Cardiology Clinic, Clinical Centre, 29 novembra 102/30, 11000 Belgrade, Yugoslavia.

**MITRY Darryl Joseph,** b. 25 February 1943, Pittsburgh, Pennsylvania, USA. Professor. 1 daughter. Education: MA, 1968, PhD, 1971, University Southern California. Appointments: Served on faculty of eleven universities, including Associate Professor, University Kentucky; Professor, San Diego State University; Head of Faculty, School of Business and Technology, National University. Publications: Numerous. Honours: Numerous. Address: 10840 Queen Avenue, La Mesa, CA 91941-7124, USA.

**MITTAL Vibhu,** b. 2 December 1964, New Delhi, India. Scientist. Education: B Tech, 1986, MS, 1987, PhD, 1993, all Computer Science. Appointments: Faculty, University Pittsburgh, 1993-97; Scientist, Just Research, 1997-; Adjunct Professor, CMU, 1998-. Publications: 2 books; Over 50 scientific papers. Honour: IEEE Vincent Bendix Award, 1986. Memberships: AAAI; ACM. Address: Justsystem Pitts Research Centre, 4636 Henry Street, Pittsburgh, PA 15213-3715, USA.

**MITTELSTAEDT Elizabeth,** b. 18 April 1946, Subotoca, Yugoslavia. Editor. m. Ditmar Mittelstaedt. Education: Diploma, Darmstadt, Germany, 1971. Appointments: Editor, "Lydia", Christian Women's Magazine, Asslar, Germany, 1986; Editor, Publisher, "Lydia", in Rumanian and Hungarian languages; Director, Hope for Europe, Women's Leadership Conference. Publications: Publisher: Women's Devotional Bible and other books. Honour: Christian Woman of the Year Award, Germany. Memberships: Hope for Europe; ECPA, Evangelical Christian Publishers Association. Address: Lydia Verlag GMBH, Asslarer Weg, 35614 Asslar, Berghausen, Germany.

**MIURA Takaharu,** b. 19 March 1951, Toyama Prefecture, Japan. General Manager. m. Mutsuko Suenaga, 3 daughters. Education: BS Engineering, Tohoku University; MBA, Newport University. Appointments: General Manager, Stepper Design Division, Nikon Corporation. Honour: Development Award, Japanese Defense Agency, 1982. Membership: SPIE. Address: 2289-18 Shimotsuruma, Yamato City 242, Japan.

**MIYAMOTO Wayne Akira,** b. 6 September 1947, Honolulu, Hawaii. Artist, Teacher. 3 sons. Education: BA, University of Hawaii, 1970; BFA, University of Hawaii, 1970; MFA, University of Hawaii, 1974. Appointments: Lecturer in Art, 1974; Visiting Assistant Professor of Art, 1976; Assistant Professor of Art, 1976-78; Guest Artis, 1978; Guest Artist, 1978; Visiting Artist, 1980; Visiting Assistant Professor, 1980-81; Visiting Artist, 1981; Professor of Art, University of Hawaii, 1981-. Publications: Unique Art of Akaji, 1976; Lee Chesney, Twenty-Five years of Printmaking, 1978; Editor, Catalogue, Pacific States Regional Print Exhibition, 1982; Editor, Catalogue, Pacific States Regional Print and Drawing Exhibition, 1983, 1984, 1985, 1986; Editor, Catalogue, Pacific States Biennial National Print Exhibition, 1988, 1990, 1992, 1994, 1996, 1998; Editor, Catalogue, Pacific Rim International Print Exhibition, 1993, 1995, 1997; ; Prints, Hawaii and the Pacific Rim, 1996; Catalogue, 1991 Hilo National Drawing Exhibition; Catalogue, 1990 International Works on Paper Invitational Exhibition, 1992, 1993, 1994, 1995. 1996, 1997. Honours: Hawaiian Graphics Corporation Award; Juror's Award, Eugene Feldman Memorial Award; Regional Prize, National Society of Arts and Letters; Many Purchase Awards. Memberships: College Art Association; Boston Printmakers; Honolulu Printmakers Association; Florida Printmakers Association; Society of American Graphic Artists; The Print Club of Philadelphia; Northwest Print Council; The Print Consortium; Southern Graphics Council; Mid American Print Society. Address: Department of Art, University of Hawaii at Hilo, HI 96720, USA.

**MIYASAKA Kenji,** b. 14 July 1948, Osaka, Japan. Mechanical Engineering Educator; Researcher. m. Naoko Yamagata, 22 November 1986, 2 children. Education: BEng, 1971, MEng, 1973, University of Osaka Prefecture; PhD, University of Tokyo, 1982. Appointments: Research Associate, Osaka University, 1973-79; Postdoctoral Fellow, Northwestern University, Evanston, Illinois, USA, 1979-82; Assistant Professor, Southern Illinois University, Carbondale, 1982-85; Associate Professor of Mechanical Engineering, 1985-89, Professor of Mechanical Engineering, 1989-, Fukui University, Fukui, Japan; Research Scholar, Department of Mechanical Engineering, University of California at Berkeley, USA, 1994-. Address: 1-6-7 Machiya, Fukui 910, Japan.

**MIYASAKA Tsutomu,** b. 10 September 1953, Kamakura, Japan. Chemist. m. Yayoi, 2 sons. Education: BEng, 1973, Waseda University; MEng, 1978, PhD, 1981, University Tokyo. Appointments: Chemist, 1981-91, Manager & Research Associate, 1991-, Ashigara Research Laboratories Fuji Photo Film Co Ltd. Publications: 60 articles and 90 patents. Memberships: Chemical Society of Japan; Electrochemical Society Japan. Address: Ashigara Research Laboratories Fuji Photo Film Co Ltd, Nakanuma Minamiashigara, Kanagawa 250-0193, Japan.

**MIYAZAKI Koichi,** b. 7 December 1949, Yokohama, Japan. Professor in Economics. m. Mizuyo Muto. Education: BA, 1972, Yokohama National University; MA, 1974, University Tokyo. Appointments: Professor in Economics, Hosei University, 1986-. Memberships: American Economic Association; Japanese Economic Association; Tokyo Centre for Economic Research. Address: 565-10-202 Kitano-Machi, Hachioji-Shi, Tokyo 192-0906, Japan.

**MIYOSHI David Masao,** b. 2 January 1944, Overton, Nevada, USA. Attorney at Law. m. Teruko Ochiai, 2 sons. Education: BS, University of Southern California, 1966; JD, University of California, 1973; Certificate of Completion, Waseda University, 1976; MBA, Harvard University, 1978.

Appointments: USMC Captain, 1970; Attorney, Matsuo Law Office, 1974; Attorney, Morgan Lewis & Bockns, 1978. Honours include: International Man of the Year, 1995. Memberships: California Bar Association; Los Angeles Bar Association. Address: 4009 Via Largavista, Palos Verdes Estates, CA 90274, USA.

**MIYOSHI Shunkichi,** b. 16 March 1929. Engineer. Education: Graduate, First Faculty of Engineering, University of Tokyo, 1951. Appointments: Superintendent, Steel Making Shop, 1972-75, General Manager, Steel Making Department, 1975-79, General Manager, Iron and Steel Engineering Department, 1979-82, Board Director, 1982, General Manager, R&D Center, 1983, Managing Director, General Manager, Fukuyama Works, 1985-88, Senior Managing Director, Executive Director, Advanced Materials Division, 1988-90, Executive Vice President, Technical Issues, 1990-92, President, 1992-97, Chairman of the Board, 1997-, NKK Corporation. Memberships: The Coal Mining Council, Advisory panel for the Minister of International Trade and Industry, 1992-97; The Electric Power Development Co-ordination Council, 1996-, The Trade Council, 1997-, and the Central Environment Council, 1997-, Advisory Panels for the Prime Minister; President, The Iron and Steel Institute of Japan, 1992-94; Executive Member of the Board of Directors, The Japan Federation of Economic Organizations, 1992-97; Director, 1992-, Vice-Chairman, 1993-94, 1996-97, The Japan Iron and Steel Federation; Vice-Chairman, The Japan Federation of Employers' Associations, 1997-; Trustee, The Japan Association of Corporate Executives, 1996-. Address: NKK Corporation, 1-1-2 Marunouchi, Chiyoda-ku, Tokyo 100-8202, Japan.

**MIZUKAMI Yoshihiro,** b. 8 October 1961, Tokyo, Japan. Scientist. m. Yasumi Maekawa, 1 daughter. Education: Dr engineering, 1991, Kyoto University. Appointments: Associate Professor, Shiga University. Membership: American Chemical Society. Address: Kokubu 1-7-30-634, Otsu 520, Japan.

**MKHEIDZE Medeia,** b. 20 June 1945, Leningrad, USSR. Medical Geneticist. m. 4 March 1967 to 7 February 1980, 1 son. Education: LPM Institute Diploma Education, 1968; PhD, 1982; Secondary Education in Specialty Pianoforte Certificate, 1963; Music Therapist, Certificate of Completion, 1995. Appointments: Research Worker, 1974-87; Assistant, Department of Medical Genetics, MAPE, 1988-92; Assistant Professor, ibid, 1992-98; Academic Status of Assistant Professor, Testimonial, 1994; Medical Geneticist, Highest Category Certificate, 1996. Publications: 105 research publications. Honours: Diploma of Counsil of Student RSOC, 1978, 1979; Prize of AUSOE, G & S, 1978; M Pavlov's Prize of 1 L MInst, 1983; Diploma of Society Erudition, 1980. Memberships: Vavilov's Society Genetics and Sei. 1976; Research Society Medical Genetics, 1979; Chairman, Medical Genetics Section, Association Medical Labor Diagnostics, 1995; Kiwanis Club Certificate, 1996; Scientific Sec, Twins of St Petersburg, 1997; ESHG, 1997. Address: St Petersburg, Kamenoostrov Str Pz N 47, Kw 18, 197022, Russia.

**MKRTCHYAN Alpic,** b. 16 February 1937, Armenia. Physicist. m. Haikush Mkrtchyan. Education: Yerevan State University, 1959-64; Diploma of Doctorship in Solid State Physics and Acoustophysics, 1983; Diploma of Professorship, 1986; Diploma of Academician, 1996. Appointments: Head, Department of Applied Problems of Physics, 1980, Director, IAPP of NASRA. Publications: Over 205 professional publications. Honours: Kurchatov Premium of Double y-RCR, 1977; Gold and Silver Medals, Exhibition of National Economy of USSR, 1985, 1986, 1987; The Armenian Pope Katolicos

Medal for the Service to the Nation, 1989. Memberships: Editorial Board, Journal of NAS, RA, 1981-; Chairman, Scientific Council for Attribution of Scientific Degree of PhD and Mathematical Sciences, 1983-; Head of Chair, Scientific Instruments, Yerevan Engineering University, 1986-87; Chairman, Commission of Experts, Ministry of Science and Education RA for Awarding Grants in Physics, 1997. Address: Hrachia Kochar Str 20, Apt 3, Yerevan 375012, Armenia.

**MO Loar Ka-Keung,** b. Hong Kong. Physician. m. Yee-Man Chan, 1 son, 1 daughter. Education: MBCHB, CUHK, 1986; MRCP, UK, 1991; FHKCP, 1994; FHKAM, Med, 1995; MBA, CUHK, 1996. Appointments: Consultant Physician, Yan Chai Hospital; Adjunct Associate Professor, The Chinese University of Hong Kong; Part Time Lecturer, Hong Kong Baptist University; Part Time Instructor, Open University of Hong Kong; Honorary Clinical Supervisor, Hong Kong College of Family Medicine; Professional Advisor, Community Rehabilitation Network; Honorary Advisor, Hong Kong Stroke Association; Honorary Medical Advisor, Yan Chai Nursing Home; Honorary Medical Advisor, International Buddhist Progress Society. Publications: Dogma, A Guide or a Trap?, 1996; Road to Recovery, The Predischarge Programme, 1997; Ageing in Perspectives, 1997. Memberships: Council, Hong Kong Association of Gerontology, 1991-92; Council, Alzhimers Disease and Brain Failure Association, 1997; The Church of Mount Carmel, 1995-97. Address: Department of Medicine, Yan Chai Hospital, 7-11 Yan Chai Street Tsuen Wan, New Territories, Hong Kong.

**MO Wenyi,** b. 23 August 1936, Shanghai, China. Professor. m. Xingchu Zhang, 1 son, 1 daughter. Education: Mining Engineering Degree, Dnepropetrovsk Mining College, Ukraine, 1959. Appointments: Secretary General, Second World Congress on Nonmetallic Minerals, 1989; Secretary General, XVII International Congress on Glass, 1995; Chief Organizer, First Seven China International Glass Exhibitions, 1986-98. Honours: Proceedings of the XVII International Congress on Glass, 1995; 2000 Millennium Medal of Honour, 1998; 20th Century Award for Achievement, 1999. Memberships: Trustee, Director, Chinese Ceramic Society. Address: Chinese Ceramic Society, Baiwanzhuang, Beijing 100831, China.

**MOBERLY Elizabeth Rosamund,** b. 18 September 1949, Caterham, England. Health Educator. Education: BA, Hons, 1972, MA, 1975, DPhil, 1977, Oxford University. Appointments: Director, Psychosexual Education and Therapy, BCM International, 1989-95; Director, Cancer and Immune Deficiency Crisis Project, at present. Publications: Suffering, Innocent and Guilty, 1978; Psychogenesis, 1983; Homosexuality: A New Christian Ethic, 1983; The Psychology of Self and Other, 1985; Contributor to: A New Dictionary of Christian Ethics, 1986; Breaking Out, 1986; Lent for Busy People, 1987; New Dictionary of Christian Ethics and Pastoral Theology, 1995; Poetry Contributions in: Aspects of Faith, 1992; Fishers of Men, 1993; Sackcloth and Ashes, 1994; Faithful Poets, 1996; Articles and reviews in the London Times, The Times Literary Supplement, and numerous other journals. Honours: Distinguished Leadership Award; Most Admired Woman of the Decade; Twentieth Century Award for Achievement; Women's Inner Circle of Achievement; International Cultural Diploma of Honor; International Woman of the Year, 1994-95. Memberships: Association of Christian Therapists; American Association of Christian Counselors; Christian Society for the Healing of Dissociative Disorders; Christian Legal Society; International Society of Cryptozoology; Society for the Study of the Indigenous Languages of the Americas; Society for the Study of Christian Ethics; Society for the Study of Theology; Orthodox Theological Society of America. Address: 237 Fairfield Avenue, Upper Darby, PA 19082, USA.

**MOCKYEN Alma Hyacinth,** b. 15 November 1928, Kingston, Jamaica. Educator; Broadcaster; Radio Producer. m. John MockYen, div, 1 son. Education: Certificate, 1962, Sound Broadcasting BBC Overseas Training; Diploma Mass Communications, 1976, UWI, Mona; BA Hons Social Science with Language and Literature, 1980, UWI, Mona. Appointments: Staff Announcer, Traffic Manager, Radio Jamaica, 1954-58; Assistant to Staff Tutor in Radio Education, UWI, Radio Unit, 1958-77; Coordinator FM Talks Programmes, Jamaica Broadcasting Corporation, 1971-76; Supervisor of Broadcasting, Jamaica Literacy Board, 1973-74; Producer, Workers World (UWI/FES project), 1977-79; Production Assistant, CARIMAC/UWI, 1977-81; Director, Producer, Project Satellite, 1979; Editor, The Harbour Viewer, community newsletter, 1979-82; Lecturer, Caribbean Institute of Mass Communications, 1981-88; Consultant, UNESCO Caribbean, Radio Broadcasting Arts and Development Support Communication, 1982-; Staff Tutor in Radio Education, School of Continuing Studies, University of West Indies, 1987-97; Consultant in Media Education to the Vice-Chancellor UWI and Supervisor of the library of the Spoken Word UWI. Publications: Once Upon a Seaweed: Book and Lyrics for a Jamaican Musical, 1960; Re-Entry into Sound, parts 1-4, 1983; Potted Versions, collection of verse, 1992; Sound Advice, parts 1-4, 1995; Rewind with Footnotes: History of Radio Broadcasting in Jamaica, with publishers. Honours: Various trophies, medals and certificates for dance instruction and choreography, 1961-71; Various medals, cash awards, certificates for literature, mainly poetry, 1967-73; Centenary Medal (1879-1979) Institute of Jamaica for services to Arts, 1979; Many other awards and honours for work in radio broadcasting. Memberships: Commonwealth Association for Education in Journalism; and others. Address: 34 Harbour Drive, 17 Kingston, Jamaica.

**MODELL Stephen Mark,** b. 22 June 1958, Detroit, Michigan, USA. Researcher; Educator in Public Health Policy. m. 1 daughter. Education: AB, Philosophy, Stanford University, 1980; MD, Medical College of Ohio, 1984; MS, Clinical Research Design and Statistical Analysis, University of Michigan, 1991. Appointments: Assistant Coordinator, The Resource for Public Health Policy, University of Michigan School of Public Health, Ann Arbor, Michigan, 1987-89; Research Assistant, Department of Psychiatry, University of Michigan, 1989-90; Research Associate, Genome Ethics Committee, 1992-94; Research Associate, Council on Genetics and Society, Department of Health Management Policy, University of Michigan School of Public Health, 1995-98; Director of Research-Genetics Policy, 1999-. Publications: Several articles in professional journals. Honours: Honourable Mention, Nellie Westerman Prize Competition in Clinical Research Ethics, American Federation for Clinical Research, 1995. Memberships: Board of Directors, International Society for the Study of Human Ideas on Ultimate Reality and Meaning, 1994-, Treasurer, 1999-; President's Council, Medical College of Ohio; American Medical Association; American Federation for Medical Research; New York Academy of Sciences; Maimonides Society. Address: 3086 Deer Creek Court, Ann Arbor, MI 48105-9664, USA.

**MODI Anil,** b. 3 July 1975, Jamshedpur. Businessman. Education: Matriculation, 1991; I Com, 1993; Graduation, 1997; Studying, Chartered Accountancy. Honours: 1st Prize in Essay; 2nd Prize Essay and GK; Prizes for Debates and Speaches. Memberships: Marwari Yuva Manch; Giants International; Singhbhum Zila Marwari Sammelan; Seva Sadan Library;

Muslim Library. Address: Sonkar Katra, PO Jugsalai, Jamshedpur 831106, India.

**MOE Orville Leroy,** b. 26 November 1936, Spokane, Washington. President Auto Racing Facility. m. Deonne W Schultz, 3 daughters. Appointments: Co-Owner, Moe's Sudden Svc Fuel Co, Spokane, 1956-74; Sec, Gold Research Mining Corp, Spokane, 1973-89; Bonanza Gold Corporation, Spokane, 1973-85; President Founder, Spokane Raceway Park Inc, 1971-; Regional Vice President, American Hot Rod Association, Kansas, 1968-84, Marketing Director, 1978-84; Co-Producer, Spokane Auto Boat Speed Show, 1964-. Memberships: Nat Rep Senatorial Committee, 1984-; Trustee Rep Presidential Task Force, 1992, Presidential Trust Rep National Committee Member; ISCA; Eagles; American Hot Rod Association, Executive Vice President, Spokane, 1986-; International Footprint Association; American Auto Racing Association, regional vice president. Address: Spokane Raceway Park Inc, 101 N Hayford Road, Spokane, WA 99224 9510, USA.

**MOELJOPAWIRO Sugiono,** b. 25 November 1947, Yogyakarta, Indonesia. Plant Breeder. m. Ms Asseta, 1 son, 1 daughter. Education: Ir, Gadjah Mada University, 1973; MS, University of the Philippines, Los Baños, 1979; PhD, University of Arkansas, USA, 1986. Appointments: Leader, Lowland Rice Programme, 1986-90; Head, Biotechnology Division, 1990-95; Head, Molecular Biology Division, 1995-. Honours: Rockefeller Foundation Research Grantee, 1989, 1993, 1997. Memberships: CSSA; ASA; International Society for Plant Molecular Biology; Indonesian Society of Agriculture and Biotechnology. Address: Jl Cimanggu 74, Bogor 16114, West Java, Indonesia.

**MOHAMED Suhaila,** b. 12 September 1954, Malaysia. Professor. m. Dr Baharuddin Ali, 4 sons, 2 daughters. Education: BSc, 1977, PhD, 1981, Leeds University, England. Appointments: Member, Committee for the Certification of Herbal Products for Malaysia, 1982-; Director, Technology Commercialisation, University Business Center, 1996-97; Professor, Food Chemistry, University Putra Malaysia, 1996-. Publication: Food and Its Healing Power. Honours: Excellent Academic of Year; George Weston Award, Canada. Memberships: Institute of Food Technology; Malaysian Institute of Food Technology; New York Academy of Sciences; Malaysian Academy of Muslim Sciences. Address: Faculty of Food Science and Biotechnology, University Putra Malaysia, 43400 Serdang Upm, Selangor, Malaysia.

**MOHAMMADI FAR Ali Reza,** b. 11 February 1961, Tehran. Computer Engineer. 1 daughter. Education: BS, Shiraz University, 1986. Appointments: Researcher, Editor, Managing Director, Rizpardazande Magazine. Publications: Over 200 Articles, Computer Science. Address: Rizpardazande Mag, P O Box 16765-447, Tehran, Iran.

**MOHAMMED Jubril Bala,** b. 30 November 1960, Kaduna, Nigeria. Lecturer. m. Zainab Bala Suleiman, 1 son, 1 daughter. Education: BSc Hons Mass Communication, 1985, University of Lagos, Nigeria; MSc Mass Communications, 1989; PhD Political Science, 1998. Appointments: Teacher Grade 3, Government Secondary School, Yerwa, Maiduguri, 1981; Broadcaster, Federal Radio Corporation of Nigeria, 1982; Reporter, crime, police & court, Herald Newspaper, Ilorin, 1985-86; Lecturer, Dept of Mass Communication, University of Maiduguri, 1986-. Publications: Editor: Introduction to Human Rights Journalism, 1997; Introduction to Specialised Reporting, 1999. Memberships: Vice-Chairman, African Council on Communication Education, Nigerian Chapter, 1995-; Chairman, Borno Coalition for Democracy and Economic Prosperity,

1996-. Address: Dept of Mass Communication, University of Maiduguri, Nigeria.

**MOHAN Brij,** b. 9 August 1939, Mursan, India. Professor. m. Prem Sharma, 1 son, 1 daughter. Education: PhD, Social Work, Lucknow University, 1964; MSW, Agra University, India, 1960. Appointments: Researcher, Lecturer, Lucknow University, 1960-75; Academic Specialist, University of Wisconsin, 1975-76; Associate Professor, Louisiana State University, 1976-81; Dean, School of Social Work, 1981-86; Professor, 1981-. Publications: 11 Books; Over 150 articles and papers. Honours: Numerous Awards; Brij Mohan Distinguished Faculty Award. Memberships: National Association of Social Workers; Council on Social Work Education. Address: Louisiana State University, 1573 Leycester Dr, Baton Rouge, LA 70808, USA.

**MOHAN Jag,** b. 3 April 1945, Karnal, Haryana, India. Teacher and Researcher. m. Neelam Aggarwal, 1 daughter. Education: Passed Higher Secondary Examination, First Division, Punjab University, Chandigarh; BSc Hons, Chemistry, MSc, Organic Chemistry, First Division, Kurukshetra University, Kurukshetra, India, 1969; PhD Chemistry, 1974. Appointments: Postdoctoral Research Fellow, Kurushetra University, India, 1974-75; Postdoctoral Research Associate, University of Illinois, Chicago, USA, 1989-90; Taught MSc classes, Department of Chemistry, Kurukshetra University, India, 1973-75; Teaching Postgraduate classes, Department of Chemistry, Maharshi Dayanand University, Rohtak, India, 1975-. Publications: Advanced Practical Organic Chemistry, 2 volumes, book; Organic Spectroscopy (Principles and General Applications), under preparation. Honour: Nominated for Gold Record of Achievement Award, 1997. Memberships: Elected Fellow, Institution of Chemists, India, 1987; Elected Fellow, Indian Chemical Society, 1988; Life Member, Indian Science Congress Association, 1985-; Life Member, The National Academy of Sciences, India, 1987; American Chemical Society, USA. Address: Department of Chemistry, Maharshi Dayanand University, Rohtak 124 001, India.

**MOHAN Rakesh,** b. 14 January 1948, India. Education: BSc, Engineering, ACGI, 1969; Imperial College of Science and Technology, University of London, England, 1966-69; BA, Economics, 1971, Yale University, New Haven, Connecticut, 1969-71; MA, 1974, PhD, 1977, Department of Economics, Princeton University, Princeton, New Jersey, USA. Appointments include: Director, Small Industries Development Bank of India, Lucknow; member, Board of Trustees, Economic and Social Research Foundation, Tanzania; Director, Infrastructure Development Finance Corporation, Chennai; Honorary Visiting Professor, Indian Institute of Technology, New Delhi, India; member, Local Advisory Board, Dresdner Bank; member, Board of Governors, Institute of Economic Growth, Delhi; Economic Adviser, Government of India, Ministry of Industry, New Delhi, 1988-94; Director General, National Council of Applied Economic Research, New Delhi, 1996-. Publications: Urban Economic and Planning Models: Assessing the Potential for Cities in Developing Countries, 1979; Work, Wages and Welfare in a Developing Metropolis: Consequences of Growth in Bogota, Columbia, 1987; Understanding the Developing Metropolis: Lessons From the City Study of Bogota and California, Colombia, 1994. Address: Director General, National Council of Applied Economics Research, Parisila Bhawan 11 IP Estate, New Delhi 110091, India.

**MOHAN Sankaralingam,** b. 22 February 1959, Thanjavur. Professor in Civil Engineering. m. M Kala Mohan, 1 son, 1 daughter. Education: BE, 1981, Madurai Kamaraj University, India; ME, 1983, PhD, 1987, Indian Institute of Science,

Bangalore. Appointments: Lecturer, 1987-90, Assistant Professor, 1991-95, Associate Professor, 1995-, Department of Civil Engineering, Indian Institute of Technology, Madras; Visiting Scientist, School of Civil and Environmental Engineering, Cornell University, Ithaca, New York, USA, 1994. Publications: Author or co-Author, 29 articles in refereed national journals; 24 in refereed international journals; 20 papers presented at international conferences, 33 at national conferences; 3 research reports. Honours: Dorr Oliver Award, Indian Water Works Association, best paper, 1990; 3 other Best paper Awards, 1988, 1991, 1997; Certificate of Merit, Central Board of Irrigation and Power, for papers, 1991, 1993; DAAD Fellowship, 1993; Young Engineer Award for notable contributions in the field of water resources, Central Board of Irrigation and Power, Government of India, 1993; Indo-US Science and Technology Fellowship, USAID, 1994. Memberships: International Water Resources Association, Washington; Indian Water Resources Society; Institution of Engineers, India; Indian Association for Environmental Management; Indian Water Works Association; Institution of Public Health Engineers; Indian Association of Hydrologists; Indian Society for Technical Education. Address: IIT Campus, D-30/2 Adyar Avenue, Madras 600 036, India.

**MOHAN Srinivas,** b. 9 March 1945, Secunderabad, India. Professor. m. Saroja, 1 son. Education: BSc, 1965; MSc, 1968; PhD, 1975. Appointments: Research Associate, City University of New York, USA, 1976-77; Assistant Professor, Montana State University, USA, 1977-78; Research Associate, Texas A&M University, USA, 1979; Assistant Professor, 1980-84; Associate Professor, 1984-92; Professor, 1992-; Head, Department of Chemistry, Osmania University, Hyderabad, India 1996-. Publications: 35 Scientific Research Publications in International Chemistry Journals. Honours: Distinguished Leadership Award, American Biographical Institute, USA, 1998. Memberships: Royal Society of Chemistry; Indian Chemical Society; Catalysis Society of India. Address: H No 109 West Marredpally, Street No 4, Secunderabad 500 026, India.

**MOHAN Sriramulu,** b. 3 April 1947, Madras, India. Professor. m. Dr Selvarani, 1 daughter. Education: BSc, Madras University; MSc; PhD; DSc; Diploma in German. Appointments: Teaching Research Fellow, 1969-72; Assistant Professor, Presidency College, 1973-1980; Reader, Anna University, 1980-1987; Professor, Pondicherry University, 1988-. Publications: More than 370 papers, Various Journals. Honours: Doctor of Science, University of Madras; International Man of the Year, 1997; Five Hundred Leaders of Influence, American Biographical Institute, USA; International Man of the Year, International Biographical Centre, 1997; International Who's Who of Intellectuals, Thirteenth Edition, IBC; International Man of the Year, Global Laurates, India, 1998. Memberships: Spectroscopic Society; Indian Chemical Society; New York Academy of Sciences; Indian Society for Experimental Learning; Society for Chemists; Indian Physics Association; Society for the Progress of Science; International Consortium of Experimental Learning; Laser and Spectroscopy Society of India; Indian Council for Research in Educational Media. Address: Pondicherry Engring College, RMO Quarters, Pondicherry 605 014, India.

**MOHANAN P K,** b. 19 November 1948, Kerala, India. Stenographer. m. Sukla Devi, 1 son. Education: Pre-University, Arts, 1969. Appointments: Served in a number of private companies as Stenographer; Now serving in the Northeast Frontier Railway as a Stenographer, 1975-. Publication: Love Lyrics, 1993. Memberships: Life Member, Poetry Society, India; Honorary Secretary, Poets Guild, 1998. Address: 75/B Hathat

Colony, Rest Camp, Guwahati - 781 012, Dist Kamrup, Assam, India.

**MOHIUDDIN Akm,** b. 31 March 1954, Bangladesh. Educator. m. Rahima Afroz, 2 sons. Education: MSc First Class Hons, Mechanical Engineering, 1978, Peoples Friendship University, Moscow; MBA, Qualitative Business Analysis, 1988, Institute of Business Administration, University of Dhaka, Bangladesh; PhD, Mechanical Engineering, 1994, Indian Institute of Technology, Kanpur, India. Appointments: Mechanical Engineer, Executive Engineer, Bangladesh Diesel Plant, Gazipur, 1978-80; Engineer-in-Charge, Agri-Engg Ltd, Dhaka, 1980-83; Managing Partner, The Mechanical and Industrial Engineers, Dhaka, 1984-85; Project Manager, The Bengal Electric Ltd Dhaka, Sub-contractor of GEC Gas Turbine Services Ltd, England, 1985-86; Assistant Professor, 1986-94, Head, Dept of Mechanical Engineering, 1992-, Associate Professor, 1994-96, Professor, 1996-, Mechanical Engineering, Bangladesh Institute of Technology, Dhaka. Publications: Co-author, 14 papers in professional journals and proceedings; 3 technical reports. Honours: Fellow, Institution of Engineers, Bangladesh. Memberships: Bangladesh Computer Society; Bangladesh Environmental Society; IBA Alumni Association. Address: GP Chha 72, Mohakhali TB Gate, Dhaka 1212, Bangladesh.

**MOHR Lawrence Charles,** b. 8 July 1947, Staten Island, USA. Physician, Professor. m. Linda Johnson, 1 daughter. Education: AB with highest honours, 1975; MD, University of North Carolina, 1979; Resident, Chief Resident, Internal Medicine, Walter Reed Army Medical Center, 1986-87. Appointments: US Army Medical Corps, 1979-93; White House Physician, Washington DC, 1987-93; Associate Clinical Professor of Medicine, George Washington University, 1990-94; Professor of Medicine, Medical University of South Carolina, 1994-. Publications: International Case Studies in Risk Assessment and Management, 1997; Biomarkers, 1998; Numerous scientific articles and book chapters. Honours: Distinguished Service Medal; Silver Star Medal; Bronze Star Medal; Purple Heart; Erskine Award; Order of Military Medical Merit. Memberships: Fellow, American College of Physicians; Fellow, American College of Chest Physicians. Address: 673 Lake Frances Drive, Charleston, South Carolina 29412, USA.

**MOHSEN Zohair Husein,** b. 8 January 1948, Baghdad, Iraq. Technical Consultant. m. Sawsan M El Gamal, 2 sons, 1 daughter. Education: BSc Economic Entomology, 1970, Al-Azhar University, Cairo; MSc Entomology, 1973, University Baghdad, Iraq; PhD Entomology, 1981, University of California, Riverside, USA. Appointments: Instructor of Entomology, 1973-75, Head, Department of Plant Protection, 1974-75, Institute of Technical Agriculture (ITA), Foundation of Technical Institutes (FTI), Iraq; PhD Graduate Student, Penn State University and University California at Riverside, 1975-81; Research Scientist, 1981-87, Director General, Scientific Affairs Office, 1982-86, Head, Scientific Photography Unit, 1987-90, Senior Research Scientist, Biological Research Centre, 1987-90, Scientific Research Centre, Iraq; Senior Entomologist, Agricultural and Consultation Services Bureau, Iraq, 1990-91; Technical Consultant: Arab Pest Control Centre, Amman, 1991-, Zeneca Public Health (formerly ICI), 1991-, Jordan. Publications: Participated in 29 international meetings; 54 scientific publications in refereed journals; 6 full papers in conferences; 27 abstracts in conferences. Honours: Many letters of appreciation and thanks from the president of SRC for distinguished scientific achievements and performance, Iraq, 1981-90; Letter of Appreciation from Shuman Foundation for distinguished and intensive scientific publications, Jordan, 1988. Memberships: Arab Society for Plant Protection; Culex ɔipiens Society, Japan; Entomological Society of America; Iraqi Biological Society; Iraqi Photographers Society; Japan Society ɔf Sanitary Zoology; Jordan Environment Society; New York Academy of Sciences; Society for Invertebrate Pathology; Society for Vector Ecology; Royal Society for Conservation of Nature. Address: 1391 S Hidden Creek Dr, Salin, MI 48176-9021, USA.

**MOLNAR Gábor,** b. 17 July 1951, Debrecen, Hungary. Psychiatrist, Neurologist. m. Aseva Jelena, 2 sons, 1 daughter. Education: Medical Diploma, Sechenow Medical School, Moscow, 1975. Appointments: Senior Assistant Professor, Debrecen Medical School, 1975-90; Senior Registrar, City Hospital, Debrecen, 1990-94; Consultant activity, Debrecen, 1994- 1998; Psychiatrist-Neurologist, Budapest Social Center, Budapest, Hungary, 1998-. Publications: 75 papers, 5 expert reports. Honours: Hungarian Medical Association Awards, 1995; National Institute of Psychiatry and Neurology Award, 1996; 2000 Outstanding Achievement Diploma, 1998;International Man of the Millennium, 1999; Hungarian Psychiatric Association Award, 1999; 2000 Millennium Medal of Honor, 1999. Memberships: International Society of Psychoneuroendocrinology; Collegium Internationale Neuro-Psychopharmacologicum; New York Academy of Sciences; WPA Section of Mental Health; Hungarian Medical Association; Hungarian Psychiatric Association. Address: Solymárvölgyi út 78, Budapest, Hungary. .

**MOMBELLO Gianni,** b. 4 April 1933, Villanova, Monferrato. Professor. m. Laura Fontana, 2 sons, 1 daughter. Education: Arts Degree, 1959. Appointments: Assistant Professor, 1968, Professor, 1981.Honour: Commander in the Order of the Palmes Académiques. Memberships: Accademia Tiberina, 1970; Académie de Savoie, 1986; Académie Saint Anselme d'Aoste, 1989. Address: Lungo Po Antonelli 209, I 10153 Torino, Italy.

**MOMENI Ali-Zamen,** b. 23 September 1949, Bourujen. Dermatologist. m. Mali-Alsadat, 2 sons. Education: MD, School of Medicine, Isfahan University, Iran, 1978; Dermatology Residency, Shiraz University, Iran, 1979-83; Dermatology Board, Iranian Council of Medical Sciences, 1983; Fellow, Immunology and Allergy, 1985, Dermatopatology, 1986, University of Vienna; Special Training Course, Isfahan University, 1990. Appointments: Assistant Professor, Faculty of Medicine, Isfahan University, 1983; Head, Dermatology Clinic, Khorshid Hospital, Isfahan; Head, Leishmania Clinic, Amin Hospital, Isfahan. Publications: Several articles in professional medical journals. Honours: First Award and Special Diploma, Best Research, 1994, Special Award for Best Paper, 1995, First Award and Special Diploma, Best Paper, 1996, Isfahan University of Medical Sciences. Membership: Vice President, Isfahan Society of Dermatology. Address: Isfahan University of Medical Sciences, PO Box 81465-1191, Isfahan 81465, Iran.

**MONGE-NAJERA Julian,** b. 6 June 1960, San Jose, Costa Rica. Ecologist. m. Zaidett Barrientos, 1 son. Education: BSc Biology, 1985, Magister Scientiae Ecology, 1989, University Costa Rica. Appointments: Editor-in-Chief, University of Costa Rica, 1984; Researcher, Smithsonian Tropical Research Institute, 1986; Scientific Adviser, BBC, 1989; Adviser, Costa-Rican Oil Company, 1989; Adviser, National Geographic Society, Washington DC, 1992; Head, Research Div, Open University of Costa Rica, 1994; Director, International Neotropical Malacology Project, 1997; Project Evaluator, Inter-American Institute for Global Change Research, Sao Paulo, Brasil, 1998. Publications: 17 books and 40 scientific papers. Honours: Elected to Ombudsman Academic Board, Costa Rica, Organisation for Tropical Studies, Wilson Station

Board, 1996; Elected to Universidad FR de Rio de Janeiro Editorial Board. Memberships: Centre International de Mynapodologie, Paris; Societe de Biogeographie,Paris; Animal Behaviour Society, USA. Address: University Costa Rica, Biologia Tropical, 2050 San Jose, Costa Rica.

**MONREAL ACOSTA Antonio,** b. 16 July 1975, Murcia. Education: Degrees on piano and composition. Appointment: Pane Lucrando (concert). Publication: Pane Lucrando. Membership: Ego (et al?) Society for Music Theory. Address: C/Princesa #8-20 Dcha, 30 002 Murcia, Spain.

**MONTANA Rizalina A,** b. 15 August 1926, Bulan, Sorsogon, Philippines. Professor; Statistical Consultant. m. Peregrino C Montana, 3 sons, 1 daughter. Education: BS, Education, 1950; BS, Mathematics and Physics, 1955; MAT Physics, 1971; PhD, Mathematics Education, 1980. Appointments: Physics, Mathematics Teacher, Southern Luzon Institute, 1950-53; Physics Teacher, Mapa High School, 1953-63; Head, Natural School Department, RAHS, 1963-65; Physics, Mathematics, Statistics Professor, CEU, 1965-69; Mathematics, Statistics Professor, UST Commerce Graduate School, 1969-. Publications: Several professional publications. Honours: Presidents Award, Lions Club, Manila, 1978; St Antonino's Award, UST Graduate School, Manila, 1995. Memberships: AAAS, USA; PAUW; Mathematics Society of the Philippines; New York Academy of Sciences; National Geographic Society, USA. Address: Block 89, Lot 17, Novaliches, Quezon, The Philippines.

**MOON William Arthur Jr,** b. 20 October 1932, St Louis, Missouri, USA. Retired Petroleum Geologist. m. (1) Marlene Joan Johnson, 27 June 1959, dec, March 1976, 1 adopted son, (2) Erika Moon. Education: BSc, Geology, 1956, MSc, Geology, 1961, Virginia Polytechnic Institute. Appointments: Field Geologist, Norfolk and Western Railway, Pearisburg, Virginia, 1961-64; Petroleum Geologist, 1964-70, Staff Geologist, 1970, Assistant District Geologist, Howma District, 1970, Texaco Offshore Division, New Orleans; Senior Geologist, 1972-75, Manager, Exploration and Operations, 1985-90, Manager, Exploration, 1990-93, Consultant, Geoscience,, 1993-97, Texaco Ltd, London, England; Retired, 1997. Honour: Decorated Officer of the Most Excellent Order of the British Empire, 1998. Memberships: American Association of Petroleum Geologists; Geological Society of America; Petroleum Exploration Society of Great Britain; Sigma Xi; Sigma Gamma Epsilon. Address: 1602 Scott Drive, Farmville, VA 23901, USA.

**MOORE Emma Sims,** b. 27 October 1937, Mayo, Florida, USA. Educator. m. Dean Moore, 1 son. Education: BSc, Office Administration, Butler University, 1985; MSc, Management, Indiana Wesleyan University, 1989; MA, Human Development, The Fielding Institute, 1995; Doctorate of Education, The Fielding Institute, 1996. Appointments: General Motors Corporation, retired, 1956-92; Faculty, Adult and Professional Studies Program, Indiana Wesleyan University, 1993-94; Faculty, Adult and Graduate Studies Program, Southern Wesleyan University, 1996-. Publication: Utilization of the Group Process in Adult Learning in an Educational Setting, doctoral dissertation, 1996. Honours: State of Indiana Secretary of the Year, PSI, 1989-90; Resolutions by City/County Council, City of Indianapolis, Marion County, 1986, 1989; Valedictorian, Branford High School. Memberships: Association of University Women; Professional Secretaries International; National Association of Female Executives; Advisory Board, Littlejohn Community Center; Pickens County Accommodations Tax Advisory Committee; CPS Academy. Address: 107 Catawbah Road, Clemson, SC 29631-2826, USA.

**MOORE J Scott,** b. 27 September 1952, Detroit, Michigan, USA. Company President. m. Soon Ki Moore, 1 son. Education: BS, Physics, 1974; MS, Materials Engineer, 1977; PhD, 1981. Appointments: Staff Engineer, IBM East Fishkill Facility, 1981-85; Staff Engineer, IBM Research Division, Yorktown Heights, NY, 1985-88; Senior Administrator, IBM Research Division, 1989-92; Senior Administrator, IBM Research Division, 1992-95; President, Cybersea Inc, Mount Kisco, NY, 1995-. Publications: The Transit Response of Hot Electrons in Quasi Two Dimensional Semiconductors, 1979; Hot Carrier Transient Response in Bulk II-V Compounds, 1984; Two Dimensional Process Modeling, 1981; Monte Carlo Simulation of Ion Implantation in Crystalline Silicon Usine MARLOWE, 1985; Monte Carlo Simulation of Ion Implantation in Crystalline Silicon Usine MARLOWE, 1988; Channeling of Shallow Si Implants Into Ga As a Function of Tilt and Rotation Angles, 1988; Doping of III-V Compounds By Channeled Implants and its Applications, 1989; Several Other Publications. Memberships: IEEE; Sigma Xi, Societe de Chimie Industrielle. Address: 25-107 Barker St, Mount Kisco, NY 10549-1629, USA.

**MOORE Martin,** b. 16 June 1934, Wilson, Arkansas. Teacher. Education: BA, 1958, University of Mississippi. Appointments: Latin Teacher, Peekskill Military Academy, 1959-65; Latin Teacher, Browning School for Boys, 1965-66; Teacher of Latin and English, Hobbs High School, Hobbs, New Mexico, 1966-67; Teacher of Latin, Ancient History, French and English, 1967-98, Chair of Language Department, 1980-86, Brooklyn Friends School. Honour: Student at the American Academy at Rome, 1987. Membership: American Classical League; Classical Association of the Empire State; New York Classical Club; Classical Association of the Atlantic States. Address: c/o Brooklyn Friends School, 375 Pearl Street, Brooklyn, NY 11201, USA.

**MOORE MYERS John,** b. 24 January 1946, Urbana, Cuba. General Secretary. m. Nancy Lee, 2 sons. Education: BS, Education, Bowling Green State University, 1968; MS, Study Theatre, University of Kansas, 1971; Diploma, Professional Broadcasting, Columbia School of Broadcasting. Appointments: Announcer, Radio and TV, 1971-84; Director of Development, Kansas Masonic Home, 1984-86; General Secretary, Wichita Scottish Rite of Freemasonry, 1986-; Founding Partner, Planetalk Airshow Narration National, 1990-. Publications: Tom Destry in USO European Tour, Destry Rides Again. Honours: Member, Resident Acting Company, University of Kansas; Kansas Association of Broadcasters, Deejay Personality of the Year; 33 Highest Masonic Degree. Memberships: Rotary Club of Wichita; Scottish Rite Research Society; Kansas Aviation Museum Charter; Colonel, Confederate Air Force, Jayhawk Wing; Titanic Historical Museum; Sir John Falstaff Literary Society; The Royal Order of Scotland. Address: 2221 Bramblewood St #501, Wichita, KS 67226-1067, USA.

**MOOS Janusz Jan,** b. 10 July 1939, Rohatyn, Lwowa. Engineer; Pedagogue. Education: Diploma of Pedagogical Study, 1965; Qualification in Carry on Therapeutics Activities, 1969. Appointments: Director, Regional Centre of Vocational Education, Lodz, managing: Training Centre of Educational Systems for Vocational Training; Centre of Pre-Vocational Education; Centre of Shaping Vocational Skills; Programming Teams of National Education; Centre of Computer Education. Publications: 270 articles in various pedagogical magazines; 170 bulletins, scripts and other papers; 140 lectures made in national and international seminars, symposiums and conferences; Editor-in-Chief, Szkola Zawodawa, 1985-97. Honours: Many times awarded by Minister of National Education, and Head of Education, Lodz. Address: Regional Centre for Vocational Education, 29 Kopcinskiego St, 90 147 Lodz, Poland.

**MORALES Roberto Rodriguez,** b. 14 March 1953, Lawton, Ciudad Habana, Cuba. Scientist (Physics). 1 son, 1 daughter. Education: Diploma, Physics, Havana University, 1978; Titular Professor, PhD, Institute of Technology, José Antonio Echeveria, Havana, 1994. Appointments: Research Assistant, 1978-83, Digital Image Processing, Laboratory of Remote Sensing; Professor, Havana University, 1985-90; Morphometrical Analysis, "Dr Carlos J Finlay" Hospital, 1991; Associate Professor, Institute of Technology, José Antonio Echeveria, Titular Investigator, 1992-. Publications: Over 30 papers in professional journals and conference proceedings. Honours: 1st Award, Science Conference, Havana University, 1977; 3rd Award, Specialist Seminary, Cuba, 1988; Excellent Award, Science Conference, Cuba, 1996. Membership: Cuban Society of Bioengineering. Address: Group of Digital Sequel Processing, Institute of Cybernetics, Mathematics and Physics, Calle 15, No 551, ef CyD, CP 10 400, Havana, Cuba.

**MORELLO Celeste Anne,** b. 22 July 1958, Norristown, Pennsylvania, USA. Criminologist; Historian. Education: BA cum laude Classical Civilisations, BA magna cum laude Art History, Maria Rosa Award in Italian, Chestnut Hill College, Philadelphia, 1976-79; Courses in real estate and biology, Community College of Philadelphia, 1981-84; Paralegal Certificate, 1986, Villanova University; MS Sociology/Criminology, 1994, St Joseph's UNiversity Graduate School, Philadelphia; MA History Candidate, Villanova University Graduate School, 1997-. Appointments: Teacher History and Social Studies and Lecturer history and criminology, 1977-; Lecturer and Consultant in history and/or criminology to university and Law Enforcement; Pennsylvania Court Project, 1998; Historian, researched and wrote documentation for 22 individuals and places which were officially designated as historical by the Pennsylvania Historical and Museum Commission. Publications: Beyond History, 1992; The 9th Street 'Italian Market' in Philadelphia, 1993; History of South Philadelphia in Review, 1996; History of the Mafia and La Cosa Nostra in Philadelphia, c. 1880-1959, 1997; Survey of Illicit Narcotics Use in Philadelphia, 1900-1945, 1998; The Oral Histories of Three Men: All Mafiosi before 1930, 1998; Compact Disc on History of the Mafia and LCN in Philadelphia, 1997; Founder, Sicilian Culture Collection, Balch Institute for Ethnic Studies, Philadelphia, 1993; Co-wrote text on historical markers; 8 copyrighted and unpublished works; 6 published works. Address: 1234 S Sheridan Street, Philadelphia, PA 19147-4820, USA.

**MORII Hirotoshi,** b. 11 July 1933, Kobe, Japan. Professor. m. Kumi Shimizu, 2 sons, 4 daughters. Education: MD, University of Tokyo, Faculty of Medicine, 1958. Appointments: Professor, Medicine, 1984, Emeritus Professor, 1999, Osaka City University. Publications: Numerous articles in professional medical journals. Honour: International Distinguished Medal, US National Kidney Foundation, 1997. Memberships: Japanese Society of Internal Medicine; American Society of Bone & Mineral Research; US National Kidney Foundation. Address: 2-11-25 Mukoyama, Takarazuka City, 665 0005 Japan.

**MORRIS Una,** b. 17 January 1949, Kingston, Jamaica. Medical Doctor. m. Charles Chong, 1 daughter. Education: University of California at San Francisco, 1974; Residency Martin Luther King, 1979; Fellowship, 1980; BA, Science Honors, 1990. Appointment: Assistant Professor of Radiology, Los Angeles County, University of Southern California, 1980-93. Honours: 4th Placed Olympic 200 Metres, Tokyo, Japan, 1964; Olympian Bronze Medallist, 400 Metres, 1966

Commonwealth Games; Gold Medallist, 200 Metres and 4 x 00 Metres Relay Team, 1966; World Record Holder, 300 Metres, 1966. Memberships: LARS; ACR; CRS; Radiological Society of North America. Address: 817 Homewood Drive, Altadena, CA 91001-2638, USA.

**MORRISON Glenn Leslie,** b. 26 February 1929, Cortez, Colorado, USA. Minister. m. Beverly Joanne Buck, 3 sons, 2 daughters. Education: San Deigo University, 1948-49; Chabot College, 1968-69; Ordained to Ministry Evangelical Church Alliance, 1961. Appointments: Director, Counselling and Follow Up, Oakland (California Youth for Christ), 1954-56; President, Follow Up Ministries Inc, Castro Valley, California, 1956-; Associate Pastor, 1st Covenant Church, Oakland, 1956-58; Executive Director, East Bay Youth For Christ, Oakland, 1960-66; Supervising Chaplain, Alameda County Probation Department, California, 1971-90; Volunteer Chaplian, Alameda County Sheriffs Department, 1971-; Seminar Leader, California Department of Corrections, Sacramento, 1978-; Member, Chaplains Coordinating Committee, 1988-; Founder, Director, God Squad Volunteer Program for Prison Workers. Publications: Scripture Investigation Course, 1956. Memberships: American Correctional Association; American Correctional Chaplains Association. Address: PO Box 5226, Sun City West, AZ 85376-5226, USA.

**MORSE Joyce,** b. 20 July 1945, Brooklyn, New York, USA. Nurse Specialist. m. Mark B Schuman, 1 daughter. Education: BSN, Hunter College, 1966; MA, New York University, 1971; PNP, Seton Hall University, 1974; RN, New York. Appointments: Staff Nurse Emergency Room, Coney Island Hospital, Brooklyn, 1967-71; Pediatric Nursing Faculty, St Johns Episcopal Hospital School of Nursing, Brooklyn, 1967-71; Director, In-Service Education and Staff Development, Clove Lakes Nursing Home, Staten Island, 1974-76; Assistant to Medical Director, United Cerebral Palsy, New York State, 1976-84; Director, Nursing, Matheny School and Hospital, Peapack, New Jersey, 1984-93; Director, Childrens Service Division, Matheny School and Hospital, 1993-. Publications: Contributions to professional journals and magazines. Memberships: ANA; National Association of Pediatric Nurses and Practitioners; Nurses of the Developmentally Disabled; American Association of Mental Retardation; New Jersey State Nurses Association; Sigma Theta Tau. Address: Matheny School & Hospital, 244 Main Street, Peapack, NJ 07977, USA.

**MORSE-McNEELY Patricia,** b. 2 April 1998, Galveston, Texas, USA. Writer;Poet; Teacher. m. Chalmers Rankin McNeely (div), 1 son, 3 daughters. Education: BS Ed, 1972; MA Special Ed; LLD; MA Counselling & Special Education Counselling. Appointments: Clerk, Executive Secretary, 1941-43, 1945-49, 1960-74; Teacher, Counsellor, 1974-. Publications: Poetry: A Gift of Love; The Key; Various poems n anthologies, periodicals; Education: Citizenship Modules, 1979-80; Articles in educational newsletters. Honour: Bernice Milburn Moore Scholarship Award, 1972, 1st recipient. Memberships: Classroom Teachers of Dallas; Texas State Teachers Association; NEA; National Trust for Public Education; American Association of University Women; Academy of American Poets; International Society of Poets; Alumni Association, UNiversity of Texas; Alumni Association, University of Texas at San Antonio; Association for Supervision and Curriculum Development. Address: Dallas Ind School District, EB Comstock Middle School, 7044 Hodde Street, Dallas, TX 75217-4830, USA.

**MORTIMER Wendell Jr,** b. 7 April 1937, Alhambra, California, USA. Judge. m. Cecilia Vick Mortimer, 2 daughters.

Education: AB, Occidental College, 1958; JD, University of Southern California School of Law, 1964. Appointments: Attorney, 1965-95; Judge, Los Angeles Superior Court, 1995-. Memberships: Executive Committee, Los Angeles Superior Court; California Judges Association; American Judicature Society; American Bar Association; Los Angeles County Bar Association; American Judges Association; American Board of Trial Advocacy. Address: 1420 San Marino Avenue, San Marino, CA 91108-2042, USA.

**MORTON Richard Hugh,** b. 16 September 1946, Grahamstown, South Africa. Professor. m. Colleen Morton, 2 daughters. Education: BSc Honours, Rhodes University, 1968; MSc, University of Wales, 1970; MA, University of Cambridge, 1976; PhD, Massey University, 1985. Appointments: Lecturer in Statistics, University of Canberra, Australia, 1974-81; Senior Lecturer, Professor in Statistics, Massey University, Palmerston North, New Zealand. Publications: 61 academic research papers. Honours: Fulbright Fellow, 1996; Fellow, Institute of Statisticians. Memberships: New Zealand Statistical Association; Association of Track and Field Statisticians. Address: Institute of Food, Nutrition and Human Health, Massey University, Private Bag 11-222, Palmerston North, New Zealand.

**MOSELEY Mary Prudence,** b. 31 December 1922, Fort Worth, TX, USA. Educator. Education: BA, Southern Methodist University, 1943; MS, University of Iowa, 1945. Appointments: Supervisor, Penn Mutual Life Insurance Company, 1945-47; Computer Programmer, Southwestern Life Insurance Company, 1960-63; Substitute, Waco Indendent School District, 1986-. Memberships: American Association of Retired Persons; Associate, Sigma Xi, The Scientific Research Society. Address: 4018 Homan Avenue, Waco, TX 76707-1650, USA.

**MOSER Gabriel Andreas,** b. 24 March 1944, Berne, Switzerland. Researcher and University Professor. m. Dirce Takahashi, 3 sons, 1 daughter. Education: PhD, Social Psychology, 1977; Doctorat es Lettres et Sciences Humaines, 1991. Appointments: Laboratory of Applied Social Psychology, 1973; Head of the Laboratory of Environmental Psychology, Director of the Doctoral School in Social Psychology, Université René Descartes, Paris. Publications: L'aggression, 1987; Les stress urbains, 1992; Les relations interpersonelles, 1994. Memberships: New York Academy of Science; Board member, International Association of Applied Psychology; Board member, International Association of People, Environmental studies. Address: Laboratoire de Psychologie Environmentale, Université René Descartes - Paris V, France.

**MOSES Daniel,** b. 12 April 1954. Company President. m. Burlean Smith Moses, 1 son. Education: BS, Business Management, Coker College; Masters Degree, Human Resources, Kennedy Western. Publications: Poetic Living: The Mind of Young America, 1980; The History of the James Family: A Historical Perspective, 1989. Address: PO Box 2403, Jacksonville, FL 32203, USA.

**MOSESCU Nicolae,** b. 22 November 1942, Chipirceni-Orhei. Professor Physics. m. Viorica Simona, 1 daughter. Education: BSc Physics, 1966, University Iasi; PhD Physics, 1975, University Bucharest. Appointments: Scientific Researcher, Research Institute of well drilling and petroleum reservoir engineering, Ploiesti, 1966-78; Professor, University Petroleum and Gas, Ploiesti, Department of Physics, 1978-. Publications: 76 papers in journals in Romania and abroad; 2 patents; 8 scientific papers (books). Memberships: Romanian Physics Society; Men of Science Foundation, Prahova. Address: Str Dobrogeanu Gherea No 2, Bl A Ap 18, Ploiesti,

Romania.

**MOSKVIN Gennady Aleksejevich,** b. 14 August 1948, Valmiera, Latvia. Professor. m. Michailova Ludmila, 1 son, 1 daughter. Education: Diploma Ing, 1974; Dr Sc ing, 1987; Dr Dr Sc ing, 1988; Dr Dr Habil Sc ing, 1996. Appointments: Senior Researcher, Assistant, Lector, Doc, Assistant Professor, Professor, Department of Electroteknic, 1976-90, Department of Labour Environment, 1990-98, Latvian Academy of Agriculture, Latvia University of Agriculture. Publications: over 250; 75 PCT patents, 1989-96. Honours: 3 international gold medals: Moscow, SU, Russia, 1988; Nitra Slovac Republic, 1990; Geneva, Switzerland, 1993; 6 silver medals, Moscow, SU, Russia; 1 bronze medal, 1984-90. Memberships: International Federation of Automatic Control; IFAC, 1997; Latvian National Automatic Association, 1997. Address: Latvia University of Agriculture, Satixmes Stre 49-59, Jelgava LV 3007, Latvia.

**MOSLEY Glenn Richard,** b. 23 May 1935, Akron, Ohio, USA. Minister; Administrator. m. Martha Lorella Mosley, 2 sons, 2 daughters. Education: Ordained Unity Minister, 1961; DD, 1963, American Bible Institute; MA, 1976, Wayne State University; PhD, 1976, Walden University; MSc Ad, 1991, Central Michigan University. Appointments: Silent Unity Prayer Ministry and Minister of 6 churches in New York, Iowa, Ohio and Michigan, 1957-85; President, CEO, Association of Unity Churches International, 1985-. Publications: 3 book,authored; Co-authored 5 books; Over 300 monographs and articles. Address: c/o The Association of Unity Churches, PO Box 610, Lee's Summit MO 64063, USA.

**MOSLEY Martha Lorella,** b. 17 July 1952, Leesville, Louisiana, USA. Minister; Administrator. m. Glenn Richard Mosley, 2 sons, 2 daughters. Education: Associate Arts, 1988, Longview College, Lee's Summit; BA, 1990, Avila College; Ordained Unity Minister, Association of Unity Churches, 1993. Appointments: Management in Home Healthcare, 1970-85; Mid-Massaganon Management Association of Unity Churches, 1985-91; Vice President, Organisational Services, 1991-96, Vice President of Education, 1996-, Association of Unity Churches. Publications: Numerous articles and monographs. Honours: Graduated Summa Cum Laude in Public Administration and Management, 1990, Avila College, Kansas City; Masters in Family Therapy candidate; Friends University Mission, Kansas. Address: c/o The Association of Unity Churches, PO Box 610, Lee's Summit, MO 64063, USA.

**MOSZCZYNSKI Paulin,** b. 3 January 1936, Janów Lubelski, Poland. Hematologist. m. Maria Otto, 1 son, 1 daughter. Education: University Medical School, Cracow, Poland, 1960; MD, 1968; Postgraduate in Hematology, Medical Postgraduate Center, Warsaw, 1975; Full Professor of Medicine, Central Qualification Commission, Warsaw, Poland, 1991. Appointments: Registrar, Department of Medicine, 1960-75; Head of Department of Medicine, Rydygier Hospital, Brzesko, Poland, 1975-; Head, Province Immunology Laboratory, 1978-; President, International Institute of Universalistic Medicine, Tarnow, Poland, 1996-. Publications: Over 420 articles to professional journals. Honours: Prize, Ministry of Health and Social Welfare, Poland, 1989, 1995; Golden Medal Gloria Medicinae, 1994; A. Schweitzer Golden Medal, 1996, 1999. Memberships: Polish Academy of Medicine; New York Academy of Sciences; Albert Schweitzer World Academy of Medicine; Hon. degree, State Medical University, Odessa, Ukraine. Address: Wyzwolenia 7, 32-800 Brzesko, Poland.

**MOULDER T Earline,** b. 11 October, Buffalo, Missouri, USA. Organist; Composer; Author. m. R David Plank. Education:

BMus, BA Biology and French, 1973, Drury College; MMus Indiana University; D Musical Arts, 1991, University of Kansas Organ Study, Paris, with André Marcha, 1971; Piano with Soulima Stravinsky. Appointments: Concert Organist Professor, Drury College; Chair, Organ Department; College Organist 1991-; Executive Editor, Drury Mirror; Rank I Missour College Newspaper Association Journalist, US Navy Springfield, MO and Treasure Island, California, 1975-77 Publications: Organ Music of Elsa Barraine, 1995; Music o' Alice Jordan, 1998; Fugue, The Crucifixion, for organ, 1995 Memberships: American Guild of Organists; Mortar Board Sigma Alpha Iota; Alpha Lambda Delta; Pi Delta Phi; Beta Beta Beta; Pi Kappa Lambda. Address: 3563 E Linwood Drive Springfield, Missouri, MO 65809, USA.

**MOURA Romero Marinho de,** b. 3 September 1941, Recife Pernambuco, Brasil. University Professor; Researcher. m. div 3 sons, 2 daughters. Education: BS Agronomy, 1965, Federa Rural University of Pernambuco; MSc Plant Pathology, 1967 University Sao Paulo, Piracicaba, Sao Paulo, Brasil; PhD Plant Pathology, 1974, North Carolina State University; Post-Doctoral in Plant Pathology/Plant Nematology, 1992, University Georgia USA. Appointments: Researcher, Instituto de Pesquisas Agronomicas do Recife (IPA), State Research Institute of Pernambuco, 1966-93; Professor, 1968-, Vice President for Research and Graduate Studies, 1982-89, Universidade Federal Rural de Pernambuco; Research Fellow, Conselho Nacional de Pesquisa, CNPq, National Research Council, Brasil, 1976-; President: Brazilian Society of Phytopathology, 1976-77, Brazilian Society of Nematologists, 1992-94. Publications: 51 in scientific journals with board of referees. Honours: Gold Medal, The Honour Society of Agriculture, NCSU, Raleigh, USA, 1974; Medal of Scientific Merit, Brasilian Society of Nematologists, 1982, 1997, Brazilian Phytopathological Society, 1989. Memberships: Fellow: Agronomy Academy of Sciences of Pernambuco, Sciences Academy of Pernambuco, New York Academy of Sciences; Brazilian Society Nematologists; Brazilian Phytopathological Society; Society of Nematologists USA; Organisation of Nematologists of Tropical America, Address: Univ Fed Rural de Pe, Rua Manoel de Medeiros S/N, 52171-900 Recife PE. Dois, Irmaos, Brazil.

**MOURADOV Aidyn,** b. 15 June 1954, Mindzevan. Scientist. m. Ekaterina Vechikko, 1 son. Education: BA, honours, 1976; PhD, Plant Biochemistry, 1981. Appointment: Senior Principal Scientist, 1996-. Publications: Over 50 articles in professional journals. Memberships: AAAS; New York Academy of Sciences. Address: ForBio Research, 50 Meiers Road, Brisbane, Queensland 4069, Australia.

**MOUSTAFA Awad Moustafa,** b. 3 November 1944, Cairo, Egypt. Chief of Sector of Protocol Ministry of Agriculture and Democratic Party. m. 1 son, 1 daughter. Education: Licencee, Translation and Languages. Appointments: Undersecretary of State for Minister's Office for Land Reclamation; General Supervisor of Egyptian Zoos; Administration; Protocol management of foreign groups visit programs, VIP visitors for Agriculture ministry and Democratic party, political and scientific conventions; Zoos and Wildlife: Changed closed exhibition of animals to open yards; 7 Regional zoos belong to Giza Zoo. Honours include: 3 Awards from Armed Forces; Agriculture Production Heroes, 1995-96; Twentieth Century Achievement Award, American Biographical Institute. Address: Zoological Gardens, Giza, Egypt.

**MOYER Jack Thomson,** b. 7 March 1929, Topeka, Kansas, USA. Environmental Consultant; Author. m. Lorna Paragsa Moyer, 1 son, 1 daughter. Education: AB, Colgate University,

952; MA, University of Michigan, 1961; DSc, University of Tokyo, 1984. Appointments: Teacher, Administrator, American School in Japan, Tokyo, 1963-84; Director, Tatsuo Tanaka Memorial Biological Station, 1970-; Environmental Consultant, Government of Miyake-Mura, 1993-, Government of Bais City, Philippines, 1996-. Publications: Books include: Miyake-Jima Naturalist, 1993; The Joy of the Ocean, 1994; Discoveries of an Underwater Naturalist, 1994; A View of Japan from Southern Islands, 1995; The Mikura-jima Dolphins, 1997; Our Coral Seas, 1998; Numerous professional publications. Honours include: Conservation Award, Wild Bird Society, Japan, 1953, Japan Environment Agency, 1975, Worldwide Fund for Nature, Japan, 1994; Asahi News Service, Japan, 1996, Asahi Ocean Award; Selected by Government of Tokyo Prefecture for two years' service, Tokyo Prefectural Tourist Program Assessment Committee. Memberships include: Animal Behavoir Society; Coral Reef Society of Japan. Address: Miyake-Jima Nature Center, Tsubota, Miyake-Mura, Miyake-Jima, Tokyo 100-12, Japan.

**MOYOU Roger S,** b. 3 March 1949, Djesse, Cameroon. Researcher. m. Lucy Ako, 1 son, 2 daughters. Education: MD, 1976; High Diploma, Studies and Research in Human Biology, 1977; Docteur d'Etat ès Sciences (PhD), 1979. Appointments: Lecturer, Bordeaux University, France, 1974-79; Chief, Medical Research Station, Kumba, 1981-83; Senior Lecturer, 1985-96; Professor, 1996-, Yaounde University; Chief, Cameroon Medical Research Centre, Yaounde, 1993. Publications: 70 publications in various journals at home and abroad. Memberships: Cameroon Academy of Sciences; American Society of Tropical Medicine and Hygiene; French Society of Parasitologists; Cameroon National Epidemiology Board; New York Academy of Sciences; Pan African Malaria Team. Address: IMPM/Medical Research Centre, Yaounde, Cameroon.

**MRAZEK Jiri,** b. 22 April 1920, Praha, Czech Republic. Artist. m. Daisy Tronickova, 1 son, 1 daughter. Education: Prague College Applied Arts, graduated 1949. Appointments: Textile Designer, Institute of Apartment and Clothes Culture, 1950-67; Solo exhibitions of paintings: Praha, 1959, 64, 70, 82, 83, 86, 93, 94, 98, Karlovy Vary, 1988, Roudnice n L, 1988, Cheb, 1989, Olomouc, 1993, Zdar N.S, 1993, Louny, 1997. Membership: Umelecka beseda, Association of Artists, Musicians and Authors. Address: Sekaninova 54, 128 00 Praha 2, Czech Republic.

**MRAZKOVA Daisy,** b. 5 May 1923, Praha. Artist; Author of books for children. m. Jiri Mrazek, 1 son, 1 daughter. Education: Prague School of Applied Arts, 1943-44. Career: 25 solo exhibitions of paintings and drawings. Publications: 11 books for children including: What would happen if .... 1980; The Elephant and the Ant, 1982; Editor, Albatros. Honours: First Prize, Albatros, 1965, Don't Cry Little Toadstool; 3rd Review Prize 1970, The Boy and the Distance. Membership: Umelecka beseda, Association of Artists, Musicians and Authors. Address: Sekaninova 54, 128 00 Prague 2, Czech Republic.

**MUAMBE Kabasele,** Inventor. Appointments: Grand Officer Eurafrica; President, African Federation of Associations of Inventors; Captain of Industry; Senator, Parliament for Safety and Peace, Italy. Honours: Golden Medal of Angola; Awarded many times, Golden Medal of Salon; Diploma of Exposition and Seminary; Golden Medal, Fancy Fair of Pointe Noire; Decoration, Minister Ikunga Marchal; Certificate of Creativity; Certificate of Chemists; Golden Medal, WIPO; Golden Medal of Artists; Medal of Solidarity; Golden Medal 24 Jewels of 500 Premier, International Biographical Association; The First Five

Hundred, IBC; International Register of Profiles; Grand Officer of Merit; Golden Medal of International Quality of the Liquor; DG Deputy Governor; International Sash of Academia; Many other Honours. Memberships: Royal College of Tasmania; American Biographical Institute; African Federation of the Association of Inventors. Address: BP 852, Kinshsa 1, Democratic Republic of the Congo.

**MUCHIRI Stanley Charles,** b. 2 January 1946, Muranga, Kenya. Manager. m. Jerusha Muthoni, 4 sons, 1 daughter. Education: Diploma in Co-op Management, 1976, Turin, Italy. Appointments: Untrained Teacher, 1964-65; Society Secretary Manager, 1966-74; General Manager, 1974-96; Director and Vice Chairman, Co-op Bank of Kenya, 1982-98. Address: PO Box 14, Murang'a Central Province, Kenya.

**MUHAMMAD Sohail Ashraf,** b. 25 July 1964, Karachi. Travel Consultant. Education: Bachelor's, Sociology, Political Science, Civics, 1989; Masters, International Relations, 1992; Post Graduate Diploma, Public Administration, 1993. Appointmernts: Reservation Agent, Abudhabi, UAE; Reservation Officer, Gerry's International , Karachi; Travel Consultant, Matchless Travels, IATA, Karachi. Publications: Peace Loving Reader, Readers Digest, 1993; Passion for Love and belief, 1996. Honours: Peace Lover, University of Karachi, 1992; Peace Maker, University of Karachi, 1993. Memberships: Peace Society; Green Peace. Address: Adj Civic Ctr, Apt H-19, Karim Plaza, Karachi 75300, Pakistan.

**MUKHOPADHYAY Aditya,** b. 20 January 1958, Dharampur, PO-Barla, Birbhum, WB, India. Educator. m. Basanti Mukhopadhyay, 2 daughters. Education: BA, 1979; BEd, 1981; MA Bengali, 1982; PhD, 1991. Appointments: Assistant Teacher, Mayureswar High School, Birbhum. Publications: Arshinagar, 1988; Dharma-O-Sanaskritir Aloke Baul, 1988; Tarasankara: Samaya-O-Samaj, 1993; Nirbachita Kabita, 1996; and others. Honours: Tarasankara Award, 1993; Folk Culture Award, 1999; and others. Memberships: Brahmoni Magazine; Press Club; Baul Research Project, Calcutta & Delhi. Address: Mayureswar High School, Mayureswar, Birbhum 731218 WB, India.

**MUKHOPADHYAY Ashok Kumar,** b. 8 September 1948, Calcutta, India. Manager. m. Malabika Mukhopadhyay, 1 son, 1 daughter. Education: BSc, honours, Chemistry, 1970; MSc, Chemistry, 1972; PhD, Chemistry, 1989; FIC, 1990; MBA, Finance, 1993. Career: Research Chemist, Dien Chemical & Pharmaceutical Works, 1974-76; Cheif Chemist, Assistant Factory Manager, K.L.P Ltd, 1976-80; Assistant Works Manager, Radha Chemical Company Ltd, 2 years; Works Manager, Coalite Chemicals Ltd, 2 years; Project Manager, Rasoi Ltd, 1983-86; R&D cum Production Manager, West Bengal Chemical Industry Ltd, 1987-92; Manager, QC Development & Malt Plant, IFB Agro Industry Ltd, 1992-95; General Manager, Sangito Biochemicals Ltd. Publications: 12 papers. Memberships: Institute of Chemists, India; Indian Leather Technologists Association; Indian Science Congress Association; All India Bengali Literary Conference. Address: Sangita Biochemicals Ltd, 28 Strand Road, 2nd Floor, Calcutta 700 001, India.

**MUKHOPADHYAY Gautam,** b. 1 January 1946, Berhampore, West Bengal, India. Educator; Researcher. m. Pragati Chandravanshi, 1 son, 1 daughter. Education: BSc, Honours in Physics, Scottish Church College, Calcutta University, 1964; MSc, Physics, Indian Institutte of Technology, Kharagpur, West Bengal, 1966; BARC Training School, Bombay, 10th Batch, 1967; PhD, Physics, TIFR, under Bombay University, 1973. Appointments: Research Associate, TIFR,

Bombay, 1967-73; International Atomic Energy Agency Fellow, ICTP, 1972, Fellow, 1985-87, Trieste, Italy; Guest Scientist, Institute of Theoretical Physics, Chalmers University, Gothenburg, Sweden, 1973-78; Assistant Professor, 1978-87, Professor, 1987-, Physics Department, Indian Institute of Technology, Bombay. Publications: More than 80 in journals and proceedings. Honours: 1st Rank in MSc, 1966; 2nd Rank at BARC Training School, 1967; International Atomic Energy Agency Fellowship, 1972; Associate, ITCP, 1980-86; Senior Solid State Fellow, 1985-87. Memberships: Life Member, Indian Physics Association; Life Member, Materials Research Society of India; Minerals, Metals and Materials Society, USA. Address: Physics Department, Indian Institute of Technology, Powai, Mumbai 400076, India.

**MUKHTAR Ahmed,** b. 22 December 1959, Bahrain. Senior Lecturer; Associate Professor. m. Mahnaz Dashti, 1 son, 1 daughter. Education: BSc, BEd, 1979; MEd, 1980; MSc, 1982; MPhil, 1988; PhD, 1992. Appointments: Instructor, 1979; Development Trainee, 1979; Tutor, 1984; Research Pathologist, 1992; Senior Lecturer, 1992; Visiting Senior Lecturer, 1994. Publications: Several papers in professional journals. Honours: Amir of Bahrain Award, 1992; Research Grant, H H Amir, 1996. Memberships: MISHE; MIMLS; MCTPS. Address: College of Health Sciences, PO Box 12, Manama, Bahrain.

**MULEKAR Manohar Krishnaji,** b. 23 December, 1945. Scientist. m. 9 March 1973, 1 son. Education: BSc, Chemistry; MBA, Management. Appointments: Production and Analytical Chemist, Wadhus India Industries, Mumbai; Chemist, Film Processing, Ramnord Research Labs Ltd; Supervisor, manufacturing particles boards, Particles Boards Ltd; Supervisor, Swastik Oils Mills; Chemist, Nirlon Synthetic Fibers, Mumbai; Indofile Chemicals Ltd; Sonawala Industries Ltd; Hindustan Composite Ltd, Mumbai; Writer; Producer; Director. Publication: Divya Natya. Honours: AFJA Award, All India Freelance Journalists Association; Chess Champion 1st Prize, Hindustan Ferodo Chess Competition. Memberships include: Marathi Patra Lekhak Sangh Dadar, Bombay; Friends of Trees Association, Bombay; General Secretary, Mulund Bhandup Pawai Dyandeep Sangh; Life Member, Marathi Vidyan Parishad; Life Member, Anti Dowry Movement, Mumbai; Life Member, Deshast Rigkvedi Brahman Sangh Mulund; Life Member, Mulund Resident East Association. Address: Building No A-8, Block No 204, Veena Nagar, LBS Marg, Mulung (West), Mumbai 400080. Maharashtra State, India.

**MULL Jocelyn Bethe,** b. 21 October 1968, Nassau. School Administrator. 1 son. Education: BA, 1981, SUNY, Buffalo; MA, 1989. Appointments: Director of Education, Centre for Positive Thought, Museum of African American Arts and Antiquities, Buffalo, 1978-83; Teacher of English, Buffalo Board of Education, 1980-, Cons Teacher, Inclusion Project, 1991-93; Fed Magnet Curriculum Specialist, Futures Academy, 1993-; Case Manager, Special Education, Gifted and Comprehensive Programmes, Crenshaw High School, Los Angeles, 1995; Case Manager, Coordinator Special Education, GATE Coordinator, Peer Tutoring Coordinator, 1996-; Case Manager, Special Education and GATE Coordinator, Crenshaw High School; Compliance Facilitator, Case Manager for Special Education and Special Education Specialist, Dorsey High School, 1997; Founder, Publishing Company, 1998. Publications: The Knee, A Thigh and The Leg, poetry, 1980; Strength in the Water, 1995; Because of God, 1998. Honours: Educator of Excellence Award, PUSH Excel, Operation PUSH, 1981; NY State English Coun, 1994; Creative Arts Award, 1980; Citation Martin Luther King Jr, Arts and Sciences Award, 1986-; Outstanding Youth Award for Performing Arts; Educator of Excellence Award,

NYS, 1994; American Education Award, 1996-97. Memberships: Recording Coordinator, Publicist, Lighthouse Interdenominational Choir, 1988-94; Project Coordinator, Performing Artists Collective, Western NY United Against Drugs and Violence, 1995; ASCD; NEA; Buffalo Teachers Federation; AAUW. Address: Dorsey High School, 3637 Farmdale Avenue, Los Angeles, CA 90016, USA.

**MULLEN Rod.** Company Executive. m. Naya Arbiter, 1 son, 2 daughters. Education: AB Political Science, 1966, University California at Berkeley. Appointments: Director, Synanon Foundation, 1968-80; National Treatment Director, VisionQuest, Tucson, 1980-82; Executive Director, Amity Inc, 1982-95; President, CEO, Amity Foundation of California, 1995-98. Publications: Many presentations including: Prison-based Therapeutic Communities and Community-based Punishment Options, 1998; 12 book chapters, monographs and articles in professional journals including: Reducing Recidivism: Amity Foundation of California and the California Department of Corrections demonstrate how to do it, 1998. Memberships: Academy of Criminal Justice Sciences; American Correctional Association; California Therapeutic Community Association, Secretary 1997-; Therapeutic Communities of America, Executive Council 1988-94. Address: Amity Foundation of California, Post Office Box 713, Porterville, CA 93258, USA.

**MULLER-BUTTMANN Heinz E,** b. 11 September 1948, Karlsruhe, Germany. Managing Partner. m. Claudia Muller-Buttmann, 2 sons. Education: MLaw, 1977; Advocate, 1980; Admission to the Bar, 1980; MBA, 1987. Appointments: Legal Counsel, 1980; Division Manager, 1987, Regional Director, 1991, Roche; Managing Director, Givaudan Roure, 1995; Managing Partner, Lenser Prazisionstechnik, 1998-. Memberships: Rotary International; German Association of the Flavour Industry; Association of Vitamin Research; Association of Nutrition and Vitamin Information. Address: Lenser Prazisionstechnik, Kemptenev Str 48, D-89250 Sendeu, Germany.

**MUNASINGHE Mohan,** b. 25 July 1945, Colombo, Sri Lanka. Professor. m. Sria Munasinghe, 1 son, 1 daughter. Education: BA, honours, 1967, MA, 1968, Cambridge University; Michigan Institute of Technology; PhD, McGill University, 1973; MA, Economics, Concordia University, 1975. Appointments: Research Officer, Ceylon Institute of Science and Industrial Research, Colombo, 1968-70; Assistant Director, International Institute, Quantitative Economics, Montreal, 1973-75; Senior Energy Advisor to the President of Sri Lanka, 1982-87; Advisor, US Presidents Council on Environment Quality, 1990-92; Distinguished Visiting Professor, Colombo University, Sri Lanka, 1995-; Senior Advisor, World Bank, Washington, 1996-; Vice Chair, Intergovernmental Panel on Climate Change, 1997-; Special Advisor to President of Sri Lanka, 1998-. Publications: Author of 62 books and several hundred articles in professional journals. Honours include: Prize, Outstanding Achievement, Latin American and Caribbean Energy Conference, 1988; Exceptional Contributions Award, International Association of Energy Economics, 1987. Memberships: Fellow of the Third World Academy of Sciences; Sri Lanka Academy of Sciences; Sri Lanka Institute of Engineers; Royal Society of Arts; Institute of Electrical Engineers; Member of the American Economics Association; American Physical Society; Sri Lanka Association for the Advancement of Science. Address: 4201 East West Highway, Bethesda, MD 20815-5910, USA.

**MUNNINGS Gladys Rosina,** b. 27 January 1911, Belleville, Ontario, Canada. Secondary School Educator. Education: BA, Hons, Queen's University, Kingston, Ontario, Canada; Diploma,

932, College Education at Toronto, Ontario, Canada, 1932-39. Appointments: Teacher of English, Windsor, Ontario, 1933; Head of English Department, 1948; Academic Secondary School Inspector in English Teaching and Examinations for Ontario, 1957. Honours: Degree of Doctor of Laws, Honoris Causa, 1976; Queen's University, Kingston, Ontario, 1976. Membership: Chairman, Windsor, Library Board, 10 years. Address: 14 Hirondelle Place, Don Mills, North York, Ontario, M5A 1V8, Canada.

**MUNTEANU Ioan,** b. 23 June 1938, Igris, Romania. Physician. m. Gina Munteanu, 2 daughters. Education: Graduated, University of Medicine and Pharmacy, Timisoara, 1961; Doctor's degree as Physician, 1972. Appointment: Professor of Obstetrics and Gynaecology, Bega, University Clinic of Obstetrics and Gynaecology. Honours: Gh Marinescu Award, Romanian Academy, 1987; 1st in Romania to perform VF, 1995. Memberships: Chief, Romanian Society of Human Reproduction; President, Romanian Society of Human Assisted Reproduction; New York Academy of Sciences; UPIGO; European Association of Gynaecology and Obstetrics; ESHRE; Obstetrics and Gynaecology Gestosis; International Federation of Gynaecology and Obstetrics; SOFIGO. Address: Bega, University Clinic of Obstetrics and Gynaecology, Boulevard Victor Babes Nr 12, 1900 Timosoara, Romania.

**MUNTER Rein,** b. 23 December 1936, Tallinn. Professor. m. Helge-Liis, 1 son, 1 daughter. Education: Chem Eng, 1960; PhD, 1968; DSc, 1991. Appointments: Engineer, 1960; Assistant TTU, 1965-69; Senior Lecturer, 1969-74; Associate Professor, 1975-91; Professor of Environmental Technology, 1991-. Publications: 45 Papers in International Journals. Honours: TTU Award, Mente Et Manu, 1997. Memberships: New York Academy of Sciences, 1994-; International Ozone Association, 1996-; Director, Baltic University, 1997-. Address: Tallinn Technical University, 5 Ehitajate Tee, Tallinn, Estonia.

**MURATOV Gennady,** b. 21 March 1946, Sverdlowsk, Russia. Scientist. m. Liapina Tatiana, 1 son. Education: PhD, Physics and Maths, 1976. Appointments: Senior Research Worker, 1980-94; Scientific Sec of Institute, 1994-. Publications: Thermophysical Properties of Liquids in the Metastable States, New York, London, Paris, 1988. Address: Laboratory of Energetics and Cryogenics, Institute of Thermophysics, Urals Division of Russian Academy of Sciences, 91 Pervomaiskaya Str GSP-169, Ekaterinburg 620219, Russia.

**MURDARE Vasant,** b. 1 June 1957, Bhagur. m. 1 son, 2 daughters. Education: SSC, Poona Board, 1974; B Com, 1978; M Com, 1980. Publications: Bharat Mara Desh Ahe; Bobhata Poetry Seconm. Address: Shevago Khandoba Nagar, Dist Ahmed Nagar, India.

**MURIASOV Rakhim Zaki,** b. 14 January 1940, Sterlybash, Bashkortostan. Philologist. div, 1 son. Education: Diploma with Hons, 1963, Bashkirian University; Master Phil Sc, 1969, PhD, 1991, Prof Cert, 1992, Moscow. Appointments: Bashkirian State University, 1963-, Dean Faculty Foreign Languages, current. Publications: 5 monographs; Scientific articles in Russian Academy Sciences journal; 2 articles in Deutsche Sprache, 1994; 1 in Deutsch als Fremdsprache, 1976; and others. Membership: Editorial staff, Bashkirian State University Scientific Journal. Address: Faculty Foreign Languages, Bashkirian State University, Ul Frunze 32, 450074 Ufa, Russia.

**MURIN Boris Pavlovich,** b. 7 March 1926, Moscow, Russia. Radiophysicist. m. Lidia Murina, 1 daughter. Education: Radioengineer, 1952; Dr Techn of Sciences, 1967; Professor,

1974. Appointments: Engineer, Radiotechnical Institute, Russia, 1952; Chief, Linac Department, Radiotechnical Institute, 1963; Director, 1970-77, Chief, Linac Department, Moscow Radiotechnical Institute, 1977. Publications: Stabilization and Adjusting RF Accelerating Fields in Ions Linacs; Ion Linear Accelerators; Prospects for High Power Ion Linea Accelerator Construction for Energy Function. Honours: USSR State Prize Laureate, 1970; Great Revolution Order, 1971; Meritorious Science Worker, Russian Federation, 1996. Memberships: Science Council Charge Particles Accelerators of Nuclear Physics; Russian Academy of Sciences. Address: Laboratory of Linear Accelerators and Radioengineering Arrangements, Moscow Radiotechnical Institute, 132 Warsavskoe Shosse, Moscow 113519, Russia.

**MURPHEY Margaret Janice,** b. 24 July 1939, Taft, California, USA. Professional Counsellor; Psychologist. m. Russell W Murphey, 3 daughters. Education: BA, Social Science, California State University, Chicago, 1986; MA, Psychology, 1989; Postgraduate, La Salle University. Appointments: Secretary, Folson State Prison, California, USA, 1963-66; Teacher, Desert Sands Unified Schools, Indio, California, 1969-72; Claims Determiner, Employment Development Department, Redding, California, 1976-78; Secretary, Shasta County Pers, Redding, 1978-79; Welfare Worker, Shasta County Welfare Office, Redding, 1979-85; Therapy Intern Counseling Center, California State University, Chicago, 1989-90; Therapist, Family Service Association, Chicago, 1987-90; Butte County Drug and Alcohol Abuse Center, Chicago, 1989-90; Mental Health Counselor Cibecue, Indian Health Clinic, Arizona, 1990-; Kinisba Child Abuse Committee, 1994-; Volunteer, Pacheco School, Redding, 1972-76; Sunday School Teacher, Director, Vacation Bible School, Nazarene Church, Sacramento, Indio and Redding, 1958-85. Honour: School Bell Award, Pacheco School. Memberships: American Academy of Bereavement Facilitators; American Association Multi-Cultural Counselors; International Association Trauma Counselors. Address: PO Box 1114, Show Low, AZ 85902-1114, USA.

**MURPHY Kevin,** b. 29 February 1952, Albany, New York, USA. Author. m. Judith M Murphy, 1 son, 1 daughter. Education: Creative Writing, Empire State College, 1975. Career: Author. Publications: 27 books. Address: 125 Brittany C/Kingspoint, Delray Beach, FL 33446, USA.

**MURRAJ Xhelo,** b. 28 August 1932, Vlora. Biologist; Ecologist. m. Fato Murraj, 2 sons. Education: Graduate Dr of High School, 1957, St Petersburg (Leningrad). Appointments: University Lecturer, Scientific Worker of Institute of Agriculture and the Institute Fisica Nucleare, Tirana; Director of Laboratory for Biologica Struggle, Founder and Director of the Biomass Station; Projects in Biology-Ecology in Albania (Consultant). Publications: 8 teaching texts and scientific books; 12 articles in natural and agricultural sciences bulletins; 9 articles in professional magazines; Narration cycle for children about the biological riches and beauty of Albania; 25 problematic articles on agricultural and animal products; 7 main reports in national and regional conferences; Texts and stories of 18 documentary films. Address: Rr Muhamet Gjollesha Pall 5/2 Apt 6, Tirane, Albania.

**MURRAY David Robert,** b. 14 May 1960, Chicago, Illinois, USA. Cardiologist. m. Natalie Scott Callander, 2 sons, 1 daughter. Education: BA Biochemistry, Highest Distinction, Northwestern University, 1982; MD, Hons, University of Illinois, 1986. Appointments: Assistant Professor, Medicine, University of Texas, Health Science Center, San Antonio, 1992-. Publications: Original Publications in Circulation; Circulation

Research, American Journal of Physiology. Honours: Phi Beta Kappa; Alpha Omega Alpha. Memberships: American College of Cardiology; American College of Physicians. Address: 9223 St Ives, San Antonio, TX 78250, USA.

**MURRAY Pius Charles William**, b. 24 July 1957, Worcester, Massachusetts, USA. Priest; Librarian; Educator. Education: AB, College of the Holy Cross, 1979; MLS, Graduate Library School, University of Rhode Island, 1982; MA, 1990, M Div, 1991, Holy Apostles College and Seminary; SSL, Pontifical Biblical Institute, 1995. Appointments: Payroll Clerk, Worcester Public Library, 1980-82; Library Director, Greenfield Public Library, 1982-83; Library Supervisor, Dinand Library, College of the Holy Cross, 1980-86; Town Librarian, West Springfield Public Library, 1985-86; Student Assistant Librarian, Holy Apostles College and Seminary, 1988-90; Instructor, Sacred Scripture, Associate Director of Library Services, 1995-96; Adjunct Professor of Old Testament, Pope John XXIII National Seminary, 1995-96; Professor of Old Testament, Director of Library Services, 1996-. Publications: Many publications, books, abstracts, reviews. Honours: Invested as a Priest Knight; Order of International Fellowship, IBC; Deputy Director General; Phi Beta Kappa; Phi Sigma Iota; Alpha Sigma Nu; Beta Phi Mu. Memberships: American Academy of Religion; American Library Association; American Theological Library Association; Business Ethics Centre at Bentley College in Waltham; Catholic Biblical Association. Address: Stigmatine Fathers and Brothers, 54 Lexington Street, Waltham, MA 02452, USA.

**MURRELL Janice M**, b. 29 November 1937. Concert Opera Artiste; Writer. Education: Masters, Kroeger Institute of Music, 1971; Julliard School of Music, New York, 1979; Certificate, Washington University, 1972. Appointments: Member, Maestros Circle, St Louis Symphony Orchestra; Concert Presenter, Young Audience; Writer of Poetry. Publications: International Musicians Museum Londons, 1989; St Louis Symphony Chair of Honor, 1997; White House Committee, DNC, 1997; International Poetry Hall of Fame, 1997. Memberships: Metropolitan Opera Guild; World Concern; Platform Committee, St Louis Symphony Orchestra. Address: 5556 Riverview Boulevard, Saint Louis, MO 63120-2453, USA.

**MURTHY K N Balasubramanya**, b. 12 May 1957, Karnataka State, India. Teacher; Researcher. m. Jyothi Hebbur Thammaiah, 1 son, 1 daughter. Education: BE, Malnad College of Engineering, India, 1980; ME, Indian Institute of Science, India, 1986, PhD, 1996, Indian Institute of Technology, India, 1996. Appointments: Lecturer, Malnad College of Engineering, 1980-81, 1982-88; Lecturer, Siddaganga Institute of Technology, 1981-82; Lecturer, J M Institute of Technology, 1981; Assistant Professor, Malnad College of Engineering, 1988-; Visiting College Associate Professor, New Mexico State University, 1998-99. Publications: Several Papers in National and International Journals and Conferences; Coordinated: National Workshop on Energy Management Systems, 1997 and National Workshop on Energy Auditing and Demand Side Management, 1998. Honours: Best Student Award, 1980; Sathyanarayana Setty Superlative Award, 1991-92. Memberships: Indian Society for Technical Education; Institute of Electronics and Telecommunication Engineers. Address: Malnad College of Engineering, PB No. 21, Hassan 573-201, India.

**MURTI Kotikalapudi Venkata Suryananayana**, b. 9 May 1925, Parlakhemundi, Onissa, India. Educator; Researcher. Education: MA English Language and Literature, 1963, PhD English, 1972, Andhra University, Visakhapatnam; Intensive course Linguistics and Phonetics, 1969, Central Institute of English and Foreign Languages, Hyderabad. Appointments: Lecturer in English to 1984, Assistant Professor of English to 1985, Andhra University; Professor of English, MMA Law College, Madras, and Gangadran, Jr. College, Visakhapatman 1986-99. Publications: Several research papers on English and Telugu Linguistics and Literatures in international journals and anthologies; Several poems and book reviews; 2 books of criticism; Editor 2 anthologies, Andhra University Students Magazine, 1985, and Indian Editor of International Journal Poet; Author, 3 books of poetry in Telugu and 9 in English Several manuscripts awaiting publication, criticism, novels poetry in English and Teluga. Honours: Hon LLD conferred b Free University of Asia, Manila, 1976, and World University Tucson, USA, 1977; 5 Merit Certificates for Distinguished Achievement in poetry; 11 Awards for Literature in USA and India; Honoured as Chancellor, Congress of Poets, Baltimore USA and at other places and institutions. Memberships: Fellow International Academy of Poets, UK; Life member: World Poetry Society Intercontinental, Madras; World University Roundtable, Tucson; Indian PEN; Authors Guild of India; and many others. Address: 43-21-9A Venkatarajunagar Visakhapatnam 530016, India.

**MURTY S**, b. 7 February 1939, Poosad, India. Professor o Economics. m. A T Murty, 1 son, 1 daughter. Education: MA Economics, 1962; PhD, Economics, 1975. Appointments College Assistant Professor, 1962-75, College Professor 1975-82, Principal, 1982-86, Reader, 1986-90, Professor Head, 1990-; Dean, Faculty of Social Science, Vikram University; Academic Visitor, London School of Economics Publications: 12 books, 121 papers, 60 dissertations. Honours include: All India Sulekha Central Gold Medal; Gold Medal fo Excellence in Journalism, Seminar Research Centre Hyderabad; Fellowship, Young Scientist Exchange Scheme Best Youth Award, Ujjain JCCI. Memberships: Indian Economi Association; Indian Society of Labour Economics; President MP Economic Association; Computer Society of India Executive Member, Indian Economic Association; MF Economic Association; Centre for Management Studies Ghaziabad; Indian Institute of Economic Research, Allahabad Member, Indian Society of Agricultural Economics. Address Vikaram University, Ujjain MP, India.

**MURUGESAN Arunachalam Ganesan**, b. 10 April 1960 Ariyapuram, India. Researcher; Teacher; Consultant Education: MSc, 1982; PhD, 1988; DSc, 1998; Diploma i Gandhian Thought; Diploma in Health and Hygiene; Diploma ir World Religions. Appointments: Junior Research Fellow; Senio Research Fellow; Assistant Professor of Biology; Scientific Poo Officer; Lecturer in Environment. Publications: 165 Research Papers. Honours: Award for best Research Paper; Man of the Year, American Biographical Institute, 1998; Distinguished Leadership Award. Memberships: Academy of Environmenta Biology; Academy of Zoology; Society of Environmenta Sciences; Secretary Exnoa International; Director, Academy o Sustainable Agriculture and Environment; Ethological Society of India. Address: SPK Centre Env Sci, M S University, Alwark ichi 627412, Tamilnadu, India.

**MURUGESAN Sadasivam**, b. 15 June 1934, Erode. Editor m. S Radhamani, 1 son, 1 daughter. Education: BA Hons 1957; MA, 1958; Dip in Ling, 1972; M Litt, 1975; PhD, 1991 Appointments: Tutor, Tamil, 1957-58; Librarian, Government Oriental MSS Library, Madras, 1958-60; Editor, Saivasiddhanta Works Publishing Society, 1961-64; Professor, Tamil, Sr Vasavi College, Erode, 1967-93; Director, Saraswathi Maha Library, Thanjavur, 1989-91; Editor, Etymological Dictionary Project Government Museum, Madras, 1996-98. Publications 40 Books. 125 Articles in Magazines. Honours anmolippulavar Scholar; Sollàiyvuk Kalaiccelvar; 6 Research rizes. Memberships: All India Tamil Teachers Association; All outh Indian History Congress; Dravidian Linguistic ssociation. Address: 45 Valliammai II St, Erode 638004, India.

**MUSAAZI John C S,** b. 25 December 1947, Buteeka, ganda. Teacher. m. Sarah Kizza Namusoke, 2 sons, 2 aughters. Education: BEd Hons, University of East Africa, 967-1970; Diploma, Kansas University, 1972; MA, Duquesne niversity, 1972-73; PhD, University of Pittsburgh, 1973-76. ppointments: Teacher, 1970; Deputy Principal, 1971-72; esearch Assistant, 1972-73; Programme Assistant, 1974-75; enior Education Planning Officer, 1976-77; Senior Consultant, 977-78; Lecturer, 1978-79; Senior Lecturer, 1979-82; ssociate Professor, 1982-86; Professor, 1986-95; Professor, 995-96; Professor, Director, University of the West Indies, 996-. Publications: 42 Selected Papers; 10 Books. Honours: ganda Government Scholarship Award, 1967-70, 1972-76; ternational Institute of Education Scholarship Award, 972-76. Memberships: Institute of Management Consultants f Jamaica; Society for International Development; African tudies Association; Nigerian Institute of Management; ducational Studies Association of Nigeria; International and omparative Education Association; African Association for ublic Administration and Management; Uganda Education ssociation; American Association of School Administrators; merican Institute of Education Planners and American ducational Research Association; Nigerian Association for ducational Administration and Planning. Address: Education esearch Centre, University of the West Indies, Monai, West dies.

**MUSTAFA Hussein Darwish,** b. 25 March 1967, Cairo, gypt. Researcher. Education: BSc Chemistry, 1989; MSc hemistry, 1995; PhD Chemistry, 1998. Appointments: esearcher, Glass Research Department, National Research entre. Publications: Many publications in journals, 1990-. lemberships: Egyptian Chemistry Society; Science rofessionals Syndicate; Research Club in Egypt; Japan ternational Cooperation Agency (JICA). Address: National esearch Centre, Glass Research Department, Tahrir Street, airo, Dokki, Egypt.

**MUSTAFA Iqbal,** b. 11 April 1950, Amsterdam. Physician. 1. Titie Sayekti, 3 sons, 2 daughters. Education: MD, Faculty f Medicine, University of North Sumatra, 1976; nesthesiologist, Faculty of Medicine, University of Indonesia, 984. Appointments: Clinical Chief, Intensive Care Unit, ational Cardiac Center, Jakarta; President, Western Pacific ssociation of Critical Care Medicine (WPACCM). Honour: xecutive Award Grant, Indonesian-ASEAN Organization. Memberships: WPACCM; President, Indonesian Society of ritical Care Medicine; President, Indonesian Shock Society; hock Society of USA; European Shock Society; Society of ritical Care Medicine, USA; European Society of Intensive are Medicine; New York Academy of Science; American ssociation for Advancement of Science. Address: Cimahi treet No 19, Jakarta, Indonesia.

**MUSTAFAEVA Solmaz,** b. 1 January 1950, Dalny, China. hysicist. m. M M Asadov, 1 son. Education: Azerbaijan State Jniversity, 1972; Scientific degree of candidate of hysico-mathematical science, 1978; Degree of doctor of hysico-mathematical sciences, 1991. Appointment: Main cientific Worker, Institute of Physics, Baku, Azerbaijan. ublications: 150 publications, 25 patents. Honour: Soros rize, 1994. Memberships: Active Member, New York Academy f Sciences. Address: Institute of Physics, Azerbaijanian

Academy of Sciences, G Javid Prospekt 33, Baku 370143, Azerbaijan.

**MUSTAKIM Zihadi,** b. 13 April 1941, Munu Manzil, Bangladesh. Writer. m. Begum Jahanara Khatun, 2 sons, 1 daughter. Education: Matriculation, G C Institution, Pabna, Bangladesh. Appointments: Poems, Column, Novels and Cultural Articles, Writer. Publications: Namaz Porbo Na. Honours: Pabna District Cultural Accademy. Memberships: Deputy Secretary, Bangladesh Cultural Association. Address: c/o Me Jamat Ali Mian, Pabna Purashvava, PO and Dist Pabna 6600, Bangladesh.

**MUSTATA Gheorghe,** b. 6 March 1938, Adjud, Vrancea, Romania. Biologist. m. Maria Mitrofan, 1 son. Education: Graduate Natural Sciences and Geography, 1962, University Al I Cuza Iasi; Doctors degree in Biology, 1974. Appointments: Preparator, 1962-68; Teaching Assistant, 1968-71; Lecturer, 1971-91; Reader, 1991-93; Professor, 1993-; Director, Prof Ioan Borcea Marine Biology Station Amnea, 1990-. Publications: Over 100 scientific papers; 3 monographs; Author or co-author 5 books. Honour: Laureate of the Romanian Academy Emil Racovita Award, 199. Memberships: Moldavian National Academy of Ecology; International Society of Hymenopterology; Romanian Society of Biological Sciences; Romanian Society of Ecology. Address: Universitatea Al I Cuza Iasi, Romania, 6600 Iasi, Bd Copou 20 A.

**MUTHE Kunal,** b. 23 February 1964, Nashik. Physicist. m. Surekha Modak, 1 son. Education: BSc, 1984, MSc, 1986, University of Poona. Appointments: Scientific Officer, SC 1987-90, SD 1990-95, E 1995-. Publications: Around 20 articles in professional journals. Honours: Middle School Scholarship, 1973, High School Scholarship, 1976, Government of Maharashtra; Certificate of Merit, Ministry of Education and Culture, Government of India, 1979. Address: Akashganga, Anushaktinagar, Trombay, Mumbai 400 094, India.

**MUTHUKRISHNAN Ramasamy Kanagasamy Sennagasamy,** b. 22 March 1956, Bodinayakanur. Egyptologist; Anthro Biometric Researcher. m. Malleeswari, 3 sons, 3 daughters. Education: Diploma, Draftsman, 1974; MA, Sociology Discontinued, 1996. Appointments: Anthro Biometric Research, 1980-; Head of the Research Department, Anthro Biometric Research and Development Centre 1992-; Consultant, Ramses II Cosmetic Drawings and Interior Crafts and Textile Association, 1996-. Publications: Many Articles to Magazines and Journals. Memberships: Chairman, Sennaya Swamy Naickar Research Foundation, 1982; President, Global Cosmic Pyramidian Srichakra Spiritual Meditation Club, 1999. Address: 1 Sadaiyappan St, Madaiveli, Chennai 600 028, India.

**MWASAGA Belekebajobege,** b. 13 July 1948, Tukuyu, Tanzania. Chief Ecologist. m. Florida Mwambona, 2 sons, 3 daughters. Education: Diploma, Wildlife Management, 1975; BSc, Forestry, 1979; MSc, Forestry, 1984. Appointments: Chief Park Warden, 1979-87; Chief Ecologist, 1987-. Publications: Best Worker, 1987, 1988, 1990, 1991, 1992. Memberships: Wildlife Society of Tanzania; Task Force, World Commission on Protected Areas; Tourism and Protected Areas; Wildlife Sector Review, Tanzania; Italian Conservation Society. Address: Tanzania National Parks, POB 3134, Arusha, Tanzania.

**MYARTSEVA Svetlana Nikolaevna,** b. 29 January 1937, Turkmenistan. Scientist. m. Wjacheslav Myartsev, 2 daughters. Education: Turkmen State University, 1959; Candidate of Biological Sciences, 1965; Doctor of Biological Sciences, 1984; Professor of Entomology, 1995. Appointments: Assistant, Postgraduate, Scientific Worker, Head of Laboratory, Institute of Zoology, Academy of Sciences of Turkmenistan, 1959-. Publications: Over 270 articles and books on Entomology. Honours: 3 State Medals for Achievements, 1971, 1986, 1989. Memberships: Entomological Society; American Biographical Institute; New York Academy of Sciences; National Geographical Society. Address: Institute of Zoology, Academy of Sciences of Turkmenistan, 59 Azady Street, 744000 Ashgabat, Turkmenistan.

**MYASOEDOV Boris,** b. Fjodorovich, b. 2 September 1930, Ryazan, Russia. Radio and Analytical Chemist. m. Myasoedova Galina, 1 son. Education: Graduated from Mendeleyev Chemi-Technological College as M.Sci, 1953; PhD Degree, 1965; Full Doctor of Chemistry, 1975; Professor, 1976. Appointments: Vernadsky Institute of Geochemistry and Analytical Chemistry, Junior, 1953-60, Senior Scientist, 1960-70, Head of Radiochemical Lab, 1968-, Deputy Director, 1979-. Publications: More than 450 in professional field. Honours: State Prize of USSR, 1985; Prize of RAS, named Khlopin V G; Academician, Russian Academy of Sciences, 1994-. Memberships: IUPAC; Vice Chairman, Russian Committee of IUPAC; Editorial Boards of several international and Russian Scientific Journals. Address: V.I. Vernadsky Institute of Geochemistry and Analytical Chemistry, Russian Academy of Sciences, 19 A N Kosygina Str GSP1, Moscow 117975, Russia.

**MYBURGH Susan Elizabeth,** b. 29 June 1952, Cape Town, SA. Academic; Information Scientist. 1 son, 1 daughter. Education: Cert of Ind Design, 1973; BA (UCT), 1976; HDLIS (UCT), 1980; B Bibl (Hons)(UNISA), 1981; MSc (Simmons), 1983; PhD, 1995-, University of S Australia. Appointments: Lecturer, University Cape Town; Senior Lecturer, University South Australia. Publications: Published widely in the area of information management and Gender & Technology. Honour: Fulbright Fellow. Memberships: ALIA; RMAA; ASIS. Address: University South Australia, St Bernards Road, Magill, SA 5072 Adelaide, Australia.

**MYERS Dorothy Roatz,** b. 24 March 1921, Detroit, Michigan, USA. Artist; Writer. 2 sons, 1 daughter. Education: Antioch College, University of Iowa. Career: Fine Artist; Writer. Creative Works: Exhibits internationally. Honours: Numerous. Memberships: National Writers Union; Salmagundi Club; Art Students League; Academia Internationale Greci-Marino. Address: Box 518, Ocean Grove, NJ 07756, USA.

**MYERS Marilyn G,** b. 17 July 1930, Lyons, Nebraska, USA. Physician. m. Paul Frederick Motzkus, deceased. Education: BA, cum laude, University of Omaha, 1952-54; MD, University of Nebraska, College of Medicine, 1955-59; Rotating Internship, Orange County General Hospital, 1959-60; Pediatric Residency, Orange County General Hospital, 1960-62; Fellowship, Hematology, Oncology, Orange County General Hospital and Childrens Hospital of Los Angeles, 1962-64. Appointments: Coordinator, National Foundation of Birth Defects Clinic, 1964-72, Director, Outpatient Department, 1964-73, Chief, Department of Hematology, Oncology, 1964-80, Associate in Research, 1964-80, Associate Director, Leukapheresis Unit, 1971-80, Childrens Hospital, Orange County; Clinical Practice, Hematology, Oncology, Rheumatology, Orange, California, 1964-80; Assistant Clinical Professor, Pediatrics, University of California, Irvine, 1971-; Private Practice, Santa Ana, California, 1980-. Publications: Results of Combination Chemotherapy, Surgery and Radiotherapy in Children with Neuroblastoma, 1974; Emphysematous Gastritis in a Leukemic Child, 1976. Honours: Grant, American Leukemia Society, 1963; Grant, American Heart Association, 1964. Memberships include: American

Medical Association; Los Angeles County Medical Association Orange County Medical Association; California Medica Association; Orange County Pediatric Society; Southwestern Pediatric Society; American Heart Association Cardiopulmonary Council; Orange County Blood Bank Hemophiliac Foundation. Address: 2220 East Fruit Street Ste 217, Santa Ana, CA 92701, USA.

**MYFTARI Skender,** b. 10 July 1942, Fier. Albania.Micropaleontologist. m. Bukuroshe, 1 son, 3 daughters. Education: Engineer Geologist, Tirana University, 1968 Micropaleontologist, 1970; Doctor in Science, 1985; Professor Doctor, 1995. Honours: Albanian Medal, For Outstanding Mine and Geological Work. Memberships: Albanian Association of Engineering Geology and Geoenvironment; Albanian Geoscientists Association. Address: Instituti Naftos dhe Gazit Fier, Albania.

**MYO-KHIN,** b. 12 March 1953, Rangoon, Yangon. Physician. m. Khin-May-OO, 1 son, 2 daughters. Education: MBBS, 1976; MD, 1998, UNSW; DCH, 1986. Appointments: Research Officer, Department of Medical Research, 1981-92; Research Scientist, 1992-98; Deputy Director of Research, 1998-. Publications: Over 60 articles to professional journals. Honours: Grantee WHO 1989, 93, 97; Medal for Public Service, 1997. Memberships: Burma Medical Association; Executive member, Paediatric Section. Address: Department of Medical Research, Division of Experimental Medicine, 5 Ziwaka Road, Rangoon 11191, Myanmar.

# N

**NA Man Gyun**, b. 17 Feb 1963, Seocheon, Chungnam, )rea. Associate Professor of Nuclear Engineering. m. Byung Jn Lee, 1 son, 1 daughter. Education: BS, Nuclear ngineering, Seoul National University, 1986; MS, Nuclear ngineering, 1988, PhD, Nuclear Engineering, 1992, Korea dvanced Institute of Science and Technology. Appointments: ıll-time Instructor in Nuclear Engineering, 1992-94, Assistant 'ofessor of Nuclear Engineering, 1994-98, Associate 'ofessor of Nuclear Engineering, 1998-, Chosun University; siting Scholar, University of Tennessee, Knoxville, USA, ₩96-97. Publications: Articles in IEEE Transactions on Nuclear ;ience, 1998, Nuclear Science and Engineering, 1998, Jclear Technology, 1998, Journal of Korean Nuclear Society, )98. Memberships: New York Academy of Sciences; nerican Nuclear Society; Korean Nuclear Society; Institute of ectrical and Electronics Engineers; Korean Society of echanical Engineers. Address: Department of Nuclear ngineering, Chosun University, 375 Seosuk-dong, Dong-gu, wangju 501-759, Korea.

**NAAGAS Manolo**, b. 31 July 1953, Manila, Philippines. )rarian; Educator; Researcher. m. Amerlita P Alcantara, 3 )ns, 2 daughters. Education: BA Library Science, 1977, 'esleyan University of The Philippines; Master in anagement, Public Management, 1982, Central Luzon ılytechnic College. Appointments: Librarian, 1978-82, Faculty )unsellor, Office of Student Services, 1978-80, Central Luzon 'ate University; Librarian I, University of the Philippines, 1988; echnical Librarian, Saline Water Conversion Corporation, )89-. Publications: Focusing on Small Library Operations, )91; Path to the Truth, 1993; Between Fact and Fiction, 1995; tting the Librarian to the Latest Technologies, 1996. Honour: niversity of the Philippines - Central Luzon Polytechnic ıllege, Consortium Fellow, 1979. Memberships: American brary Association; Library Administration and Management ssociation; Association for Library Collections and Technical ervices; International Relations Round Table; Media Guild of Jeva Ecija. Address: Saline Water Conversion Corporation, ) Box 6, Shuqaiq Gizan, Saudi Arabia.

**NAAMAN Naji Mitri**, b. 19 May 1954, Harissa, Lebanon. ebanese Poet; Writer; Publisher. m. Fadia Tawfic Al-Hawa, 2 )ns, 1 daughter. Education: Auditing and Accounting Degree, )77, Centre Supérieur d'Etudes Commerciales, Beirut; LLB, )79, Lebanese University, Beirut; LLM (equivalent), 1979, niversity of Nantes, France; Licence en Sciences ommerciales, 1979, MBA (equivalent), BA History, 1979, Holy pirit University, USEK, Kaslik, Lebanon; Diplôme d'Etudes oprofondies en Histoire, 1980, University of Nantes. ppointments: Formerly Journalist; Joined Al-Jumhur agazine, 1970-74; Executive, Jordan National Bank, 1973-74; eacher, Ecole Professionnelle Pauliste, Lebanon, 1974-77; irector, Al-Manshuratul 'Arabiyya, Beirut-Lyon, 1978-79; 'ofessor of Economics and Management, Al-Markaziyya ıllege, 1978-79, and Centre International des Sciences echniques, Dora, 1980-85; Currently: Publisher, Founding ember, Dar Na'man lith Thaqafa (Maison Naaman pour la ulture-Publishing House), 1979; Sole Owner of the Said blishing house, 1983-; Founder, Markaz at-Tarbiya t-Tiqaniyya technical centre, 1987; Founder, Owner, Galerie Art Naaman art gallery, 1987-; Founder, Owner, NBC - aaman Biographical Centre, 1997-. Publications: Editor: olitics and Strategy, 1981-; The Arab World, 1985-, Press and nformation, 1987; Editor, Encyclopedia of Contemporary Arab Jorld, 1983-; Author 7 books, Principle Author 1 book; Articles

in media and poetry; Several courses in Economics and Management; Translator of 7 books from French to Arabic; Several manuscripts. Memberships: Founder, The Humanitarian Movement, 1971, and The Universal Unity of Man, 1976; Founding member, Al-Yunbu (Charity Association), 1991; Member, Lebanese Publishers Association. Address: PO Box 567, Jounieh, Lebanon.

**NACHANE Dilip Madhukar**, b. 5 February 1945, Mumbai, India. Academic. m. Sudaxina, 2 daughters. Education: BA Mathematics, 1965, BA Economics, 1966, MA Economics, 1968, PhD Economics, 1973, MA Mathematics, 1976, Bombay University. Appointments: Lecturer, 1971-73, Reader, 1976-78, Professor of Quantitative Economics, 1978-, Director, 1993-, Department Economics, University Bombay; Assistant Professor, National Institute Bank Management, India, 1973-76; Visited USSR under Indo-Soviet Academic Exchange Programme, 1982; Senior Fulbright Fellow, University Texas at Austin, 1983-84; Hallsworth Fellow, University Manchester, 1987-88; Visiting Professor, University British Columbia, 1988-89, University Manchester, 1990, University Ulster, 1991, University Avignon, France, 1997; Visited University Paris under Indo-French Cultural Exchange Programme, 1995; Visiting Scholar, European University Institute, Florence, Italy, 1998. Publications: Author and Co-author 57 articles & books including: Regional Trading Blocs and their implications for the Indian Economy, book chapter, 1997. Honours: Sir James Fergusson Scholarship, 1965, for securing 1st Rank at BA examination of Bombay University; Chancellor's Gold Medal and K T Telang Gold Medal, 1968, for securing 1st Rank at MA examination of Bombay University; Paper awarded D K Desai Prize by Indian Society Agricultural Economics, 1989; PaperReceived ANBAR Citation for Excellence; Chaired a session on Econometric Theory at 1992 India and South-East Asia Meeting of Econometric Society, Bombay. Memberships: Elected member: New York Academy Sciences; National Geographic Society; Member Board Directors: National Stock Exchange, India, 1997-; State Bank India (Gilts) Ltd, 1997-; Board Governers, Tata Institute Social Sciences, Mumbai. Address: University Bombay, Department Economics, CST Rd, Bombay 400 098, India.

**NADERI Ezatolah**, b. 19 July 1945, Arak, Iran. Full Professor. m. Mariam Seifnaraghi, 3 daughters. Education: BA, Teacher Education University, Tehran, Iran, 1967-71; MSc, 1973, MPA, 1975, University of Southern California, USA; Community College Instructor Credential, 1976; DPhil, University of Southern California, 1977. Appointments: Part time Teacher, private high schools, Tehran, Iran, 1968-71; School Counselor, Marjan High School, Tehran, Iran, 1971-72; Assistant Professor, 1977-84, Associate Professor, 1984-91, Full Professor, 1991-, School of Education and Psychology, Research Method, Statistics, Measurement and Evaluational Areas, Teacher Education University, Tehran, Iran. Publications include: Exeptional Pupils: Definition, Classification, Characteristics Causes and Diagnosis of Their Problems, 1994; Learning Disabilities: Historical Background, Definition, Classification, Stage of Diagnosis, Educational Methods and Clinical Cases, 1995; Sensation and Perception from the Psychological Point of View, 1990; Measurement and Evaluation and Analytical Foundations of It's Instruments in Education and Psychology, 1994; Address: University for Teacher Education, Dr Mofateh Avenue, Tehran 15614, Iran.

**NAESSENS Jan L G**, b. 7 February 1952, Kortrijk, Belgium. Scientist. m. Anne-Marie Vlieghe, 2 daughters. Education: Licentiate Chemistry, 1973, Doctorate Science, Immunology, 1981, Free University Brussels (VUB). Appointments: Postdoctoral Scientist, Ilrad, Nairobi; Scientist, International

Livestock Research Institute, Nairobi. Publications: Many in immunology journals; Organised several workshops and conferences; Editor-in-Chief, Veterinary Immunology and Immunopathology. Membership: New York Academy of Science. Address: International Livestock Research Institute, Nairobi, Kenya.

**NAGAHATA Yoshi,** b. 30 January 1955, Katsuta, Okayama, Japan. Surgeon. m. Masami Sakamoto, 2 sons. Education: MD, 1979, PhD, 1986, Kobe University School of Medicine. Appointments: Assistant Professor, Kobe University School of Medicine, 1989-98; Director of Surgery, Mitsubishi Kobe Hospital, 1998-. Publications: Actions of H2 Receptor Antagonist, 1992; Syndromes of Alimentary Tract, 1994; Helicobacter Pylori, 1996; Paradox of Helicobacter Pylori, 1998. Memberships: Councillor, Japanese Society Gastroenterology; Japan Society Coloproctology; Fellow, Japan Surgical Society; Japanese Society Gastroenterology; Asian-Pacific Congress Gastroenterology; and others. Address: Mitsubishi Kobe Hospital, 6-1-34 Wadamiya Dori, Hyogo-ku, Kobe 652-0863, Japan.

**NAGATSU Masayoshi,** b. 15 April 1957, Tokyo, Japan. MD; Cardiovascular Surgeon; Researcher. m. Yuko Komatsu, 3 sons. Education: Medical, 1983, National Tsukuba University. Appointments: Department of Surgery, Heart Institute of Japan, 1983-, Department of Pediatric Cardiovascular Surgery, 1989-, Tokyo Women's Medical College; Department of Cardiology, Gazes Cardiac Research Institute, Medical University of SC, USA, 1991-; Department Head of Pediatric Cardiac Surgery, Gifu Prefectural Hospital, 1997-. Publications: Articles and papers in professional journals. Memberships: Japan Surgical Society, 1983-, authorised surgeon, 1988-; Japan Association for Thoracic Surgery, 1983-, staff member 1990-, surgical instructor 1996-; American Heart Association; Asian Society for Cardiovascular Surgery. Address: Gifu Prefectural Hospital, 4-6-1 Noishiki, Gifu-shi, Gifu 500-8717, Japan.

**NAGATUCHI Yukihisa,** b. 10 June 1945, Saga, Japan. Medical Doctor; Surgeon. m. Etsuko Nagatuchi, 3 daughters. Education: MD, PhD, Kyushu University. Appointment: Associate Professor, University of Occupational and Environmental Health. Memberships: New York Academy of Sciences; Japan Surgical Society. Address: 20-21 3-Chome, Shiobaru, Minami-ku, Fukuoka 815, Japan.

**NAGRALE Mahadeo,** b. 1 July 1949, Palasgaon, India. Professor. m. Rama, 2 sons. Education: MCom, 1973; MA, Ecomics, 1973; MA, Political Science, 1979; LLB, 1978; PhD, 1983. Appointments: Lecturer, Commerce, 1973; Lawyer, 1980; Professor, 1985. Publictions: Several professional articles in journals. Honours: Dr Ambedkar Teachers Award, 1996. Memberships: Indian Society for Community Education; International Community Education Association; International Association of Educators for World Peace; Nagpur University Teachers Association. Address: Ashirwad, Kukde Layout, PO Bhagwan Nagar, Nagpur, India.

**NAIDU B Narasingaraja,** b. 13 October 1942, Tambaram. Teacher. m. Chandrika, 2 daughters. Education: MA, Madras Christian College, 1966; PhD, Wilson College, Bombay, 1988. Appointments: Tutor, 1966-67; Assistant Professor, 1968-72; Professor, HOD, Madras College, 1973; Lecturer, Bangalore University, 1974-94; Professor, 1994-. Publications: 4 research books; 8 research articles. Honours: Recipient, Best Cadet Cup, ACCTSG; Award, Awards Committee of the American Studies Research Centre; Twice Recipient, Thurso and Macphail Prizes for History. Memberships: Convener, Doctoral Committee, Madurai Kamaraj; Member, Board of Examiners;

Member, Board of Questions; Member, Board of Studie Member. Address: 18-379 B IInd Main, Vinayak Nagar, Koner Agrahara, HAL Post, Bangalore 560017, India.

**NAIK Suresh Ramnath,** b. 11 May 1945, Mirjan Karnatak India. Researcher; Educator. m. Ratnaprabha, 1 so Education: BSc, 1963; MSc Biochemistry, 1968; Ph Pharmacology, 1973; Postdoctoral Research, National Institu of Mental Health, Washington DC, USA, 1974-7 Appointments: Research Fellow, 1964-66; Research Associat 1966-68; Council Science and Industrial Research, Professo Federal University of Paraiba, Brazil, 1980-82; Current General Manager Research and Development, Quality Contro Quality Assurance, Hindustan Antibiotics Ltd, Pune, Indi Publications: 118 scientific publications and reviews in India and international journals; Chief Editor, Hindustan Antibio Bulletin, 1987-. Honours: National Research and Developme Corporation Award, Government of India, 1995; Awa Hexamar Agricultural Research and Development Foundatio Bombay, 1995; Fellow, Royal Society Chemistry, Englan 1996. Memberships: Indian Society Pharmacologists, 1975 New York Academy of Sciences, 1995. Address: F Hindustan, Antibiotics Colony, 411 018 Pune, India.

**NAIK Vihang,** b. 2 September 1969, Surat. Educato Education: BA English Literature and Philosophy, 1993, M English and Indian Literature, 1995, M S, University of Barod Appointments: Lecturer in English, Smt M C Desai Arts ar Commerce College, 1997, Ambaji Arts College, 1998 Publications: City Times, a book of poems, 1993; Poen published in various Indian leading journals and anthologie Critical essay, Manifesto from the Subaltern Stand, 199 Reviews and articles in publications in field. Honours: Micha Madhusudan Academy, Calcutta, for City Times, 199 Memberships: Poetry Society of India; Forum on Contempora Theory, Baroda; Gujarati Sahitya Parishad; The Poetry Circl Bombay; The PEN All-India Centre; Writers' Forum; Wor Poetry Society Intercontinental; United Writers Association; ar others. Address: 3 Kamdurga Society - 2, Naranpur Ahmedabad 380013, India.

**NAKAJIMA Kenji,** b. 29 June 1941, Kyoto, Japa Professor; Researcher. m. Junko Ohgushi, 2 sons. Educatio Graduated, 1966, completed postgraduate studies, 196 Doctorate, 1971, PhD, 1972, Kyoto University. Appointment Lecturer, Kyoto University, 1971-77; Lecturer, 1973-7 Associate Professor, 1979-87, Professor, 1987-, Koshie University; Co-Researcher, Biwa Lake Research Institut Shiga, 1988-. Publications: Methods in Enzymology, Vol 62, 6 1979, 1980; Vitaminology II, 1980; Chemical Stimulants f Feeding Behavior of Fish and Shellfish, 1994; Biology ar Environmental Chemistry of DMSP and Related Sulfoniu Compounds, 1995. Honour: Academic Award, The Vitam Society of Japan, 1971. Memberships: Japan Vitamin Socie Council Member, 1996; Japan Nutrition and Food, Coun Member, 1997-; Japanese Fish Science Socie Senescence-Accelerated Mouse Society, Council Memb 1997-. Address: Department of Nutrition, Koshien Universi 10-1 Momijigaoka, Takarazuka, Hyogo 665-0006, Japan.

**NAKAJIMA Osamu,** b. 1 August 1962, Shinmori, Asahi-k Osaka. Physician; Cardiologist. m. Chise Sagawa, 2 daughter Education: MD, 1989, Osaka Medical College, Takatsu Japan. Appointments: House Staff, Osaka Medical Colleg Takatsuki, 1989-90; Resident, Mishima Critical Care Centr Takatsuki, 1990-92; Chief, Nissay Hospital, Osaka, 199 Honour: Nissay Medical Award, 1997. Memberships: Japanes Society Internal Medicine; Japanese Circulation Socie Japanese Association for Acute Medicine; Japanes

Endocrinological Society; Japan Medical-Dental Association for Tobacco Control. Address: Nissay Hospital, 3-8 6-chome, Itachibori, Nishi-ku, Osaka 550-0012, Japan.

**NAKAMURA Keijiro,** b. 27 August 1935, Hita City, Japan. Consultant. m. Kinue Asakura, 2 sons, 1 daughter. Education: University of Fukuoka, 1957. Appointments: Consultant, Matsushita Electric Industrial Co Ltd, 1999-; Asahi Glass Co Ltd, 1999-; Municipal Disposal Plant, MITI: converting sea water into fresh water. Publications: Patent applications: Method for converting sea water into fresh water, Method for treating exhaust water using micro-organisms and enzymes hereof. Address: 4-18-1 Sakae-cho, Tachikawa 190-0003, Japan.

**NAKANISHI Shohachiro,** b. 13 February 1945, Kyoto, Japan. Professor Engineering. m. Michiko Saito, 1 son, 1 daughter. Education: B Eng, 1967, M Eng, 1969, PhD Eng, 1990, Tokai University. Appointments: Assistant Professor, 1972-85, Associate Professor, 1985-91, Professor, 1991-, Chair Electrical Engineering, Graduate School, 1996-98, Vice Dean, School of Engineering, 1998-, Tokai University. Publication: Electro-Magnetics, in Japanese. Membership: Director, Japan Society for Fuzzy Theory and Systems, 1991-95. Address: Department of Electrical Engineering, Tokai University, 1117 Kitakaname, Hiratsuka 259-1292, Japan.

**NAKANO Takeshi,** b. 7 December 1963, Japan. Derivatives Specialist. Education: BA, Law, University of Tokyo, 1986; MA, Economics, Hitotsubashi University, 1997. Appointments: Vice President, Dai-Ichi Kangyo Bank Ltd; Chartered Financial Analyst. Membership: Association for Investment Management and Research. Address: 49 Kanda-Kami, Houhoku-cho, Toyoura-gun, Yamaguchi Prefecture 759-6121.

**NAKASHIMA Toshio,** b. 6 September 1920, Japan. Professor. m. Sumiko Asakura, 1 son, 1 daughter. Education: DAgric, Hokkaido University, 1952; Exchange Programme, University of Massachusetts, USA, 1959-60. Appointments: Assistant, Faculty Agriculture, 1950, Lecturer, 1959, Assistant Professor, 1961, Professor, 1972-84, Member, University Senate, 1977-79, Hokkaido University; Professor, Hokkaido Musashi Women's Junior College, 1984-93. Publications: Over 50 scientific papers and books on ecology of Scarabaeidae and Ambrosia Beetles; New Applied Entomology, textbook. Honours: Emeritus Professor, Hokkaido University, 1984-; The Order of the Rising Sun, Third Class, The Emperor of Japan, 1995. Memberships: Japanese Society Applied Entomology and Zoology, Past Member Senate, Past Director Hokkaido Branch; Entomological Society Japan, Past Member Senate; Japanese Society Sericultural Science, Past Member Senate; Vice Chairman, Commission Drainage Canal of Chitose River; Past Vice Chairman, Commission Environmental Impact Assessment on Otarunai Dam; Past Vice Chairman, Development of Tokachi River. Address: 206 D Fureaino Machi, Noukendai 3-51-1, Kanazawa-ku, Yokohama 236-0057, Japan.

**NAKATA Toshihiko,** b. 12 October 1960, Hatano, Kanagawa, Japan. Mechanical Engineer; Researcher. m. Chiko Ando, 1990, 1 son, 2 daughters. Education: BEng, Mechanical Engineering, 1983, MEng, Mechanical Engineering, 1985, DEng, Mechanical Engineering, 1993, Tohoku University. Appointments: Researcher, Central Research Institute of Electric Power Industry, Tokyo, 1985-86; Researcher, 1986-92, Senior Researcher, 1992-93, Central Research Institute of Electric Power Industry, Yokosuka; Associate Professor, Graduate School of Engineering, Tohoku University, Sendai, 1993-; Fulbright Scholar, Lawrence Livermore National Laboratory, Livermore, California, USA, 1997-98. Publications: Author or co-author, numerous articles, papers, contributions to books, research reports, mostly on energy-economic modelling, fossil fuel combustion technology for power generation, industrial ecology; Patents: Gas Turbine Combustor, 1988; Low Calorific Gas Combustion and Combustor, 1988; Gas Turbine Combustion Equipment, 1990; Gas Turbine Combustor, 1993. Honours: President's Award, Central Research Institute of Electric Power Industry, 1991; Academic Award, Combustion Society of Japan, 1993; Fulbright Award, 1997-98. Memberships: International Association for Energy Economics; International Society for Ecological Economics; American Society of Mechanical Engineers; Japan Society of Energy and Resources; Japan Society of Mechanical Engineers; Gas Turbine Society of Japan; Combustion Society of Japan; Japan Institute of Energy; Several committees. Address: 4-14-13 Katsura, Izumi-ku, Sendai 981-3134, Japan.

**NAKATANI Kei,** b. 14 January 1952, Nara, Japan. Associate Professor. m. Yumiko Nakatani. Education: BS, 1976; MSc, 1978; PhD, 1982. Appointments: Postdoctoral Fellow, University of Texas Medical Branch, USA, 1982-86; Research Associate, Johns Hopkins University School of Medicine, 1986-92; Associate Professor, University of Tsukuba, Japan, 1992-. Publications: Scientific papers in Nature, Science, Journal of Physiology, Journal of General Physiology and others. Memberships: Society for Neuroscience, USA; Physiological Society of Japan; New York Academy of Sciences; Biophysical Society of Japan; and others. Address: University of Tsukuba Institute of Biological Sciences, Taukuba Ibaraki 305-8572, Japan.

**NAKAYAMA Takeo,** b. 19 July 1961, Tokyo, Japan. Epidemiologist. m. Erika, 1 son, 1 daughter. Education: MD, 1987, PhD, 1997, Tokyo Medical and Dental University. Appointments: Assistant Professor, Department of Epidemiology, Medical Research Institute, Tokyo Medical and Dental University, 1989-. Publications: Several articles in professional journals. Honour: Young Investigator Award, Japan Heart Foundation, 1993. Memberships: International Epidemiological Association; Fellow, International College of Angiology; American Association for the Advancement of Science. Address: 1-39-21-502 Hikari-cho, Kokubunji-shi, Tokyo 185-0034, Japan.

**NAMJIL Hurelsha,** b. 28 February 1950, Huria Banner, Inner Mongolia, China. Teacher. m. B Sechin, 2 sons, 1 daughter. Education: Masters Degree. Appointments: Dean, Mongolian Language and Literature, Inner Mongolia Teacher's College for Nationalities. Publications: Monographs; Studies of Mongols Mythology, 1996; Studies of Khorchin Shamnism, 1998; The Monastres of Jirim, 1993. Memberships: Institute of Khorchin Culture; Association of Mongolian Literature of China. Address: Department of Mongolian Language and Literature, Inner Mongolia Teacher's College for Nationalities, Tongliao, Inner Mongolia, China.

**NAMSRAI Khavtgain,** b. 15 September 1943, Taagaan Khairkhan Sun, Zavkhan Province, Mongolia. Education: MSc, Moscow State University, 1968; PhD, Theoretical and Maths Physics, Joint Institute Nuclear Research, Dubna, Russia, 1973, DSc, 1982. Appointments: Junior Scientific Worker, Institute of Chemistry and Physics, Ulaanbaatar, 1968-69; Scientific Worker, Joint Institute Nuclear Research, 1969-74; Dir, Institute Math Mongolian Academy Sciences, Ulaanbaatar, 1974-78; Lecturer, Mongolian State University, 1975-78, 1985-88; Senior Scientific Worker, Joint Institute Nuclear Research, 1978-83; Leading Scientific Worker, Institute of

Physics and Tech, Ulaanbaatar, 1983-; Head, Theoretical Physics Laboratory, Mongolian Academy of Sciences, 1985-; Visiting Scientist: University of Syracuse, New York, 1989, International Center for Theoretical Physics, Trieste, Italy, 1991, 1999, European Laboratory for Nuclear Research, Geneva, 1993, University of London, 1993; University of Heidelberg, 1995. Publications: Author: Nonlocal Quantum Field Theory and Stochastic Quantum Mechanics, 1986 (Mongolian Academy of Sciences Prize, 1988; Articles to professional journals. Honours: Vice President, Mongolian Scientific Worker Association, 1988-94; Diploma, World Cultural Committee, Cambridge, Massachusetts, 1989; Vice Chairman, State Awarding Committee, Mongolia, 1991-97; Order of Sukhbaatar President, Mongolia, 1996; Mongolian State Prize in Science, 1997. Memberships include: Fellow, Third World Academy of Sciences; Mongolian Physics Society, President, 1992-; Academician, Mongolian Academy of Sciences; Mongolian-USA Society, President, 1990-93. Address: Institute of Physics and Tech MAS, Zhukoff Ave 54A, Ulaanbaatar 51, Mongolia.

**NANDIBEWOOR Sharanappa**, b. 1 July 1953. Professor. m. Education: SSLC, 1968; BSc, 1972; MSc, 1974; PhD, 1979. Appointments: Lecturer, P G Department of Chemistry, Karnatak University, 1978-87; Reader, 1987-1996; Professor, Physical Chemistry, 1996-. Publications: 100 Publications. Memberships: Indian Chemical Society; Indian Council of Chemists; Association of Kineticists. Address: Department of Chemistry, Karnatak University, Dharwad 580 003, India.

**NARAGHI Ramin**, b. 16 July 1962, Vienna, Austria. Neurosurgeon. Education: Medical School, Hannover, Germany, 1982-88; Doctoral Thesis, 1990; Board Certificate Neurosurgeon, 1998. Appointments: Researcher; Scientific Assistant; Neurosurgeon, University of Erlangen. Publications: Neurovascular Compression and Hypertension in Journal of neurology; Neurosurgery; The Lancet. Address: University of Erlangen Dept Neurosurgery, Schwabachanlage 6, 91054 Erlangen, Germany.

**NARAYANAN Bernice Cynthia**, b. 22 July 1954, Malaysia. Publisher; Writer; Author. Education: Associate Diploma in Hotel and Catering Management, Australia; Diploma in Public Relations, Malaysia. Appointments: Travelwriter, Malaysia, 1973-75; Freelance Writer, Malaysia and Australia, 1976-80; Public Relations Manager, Orchard Hotel, Singapore, 1981-82; ASEAN Manager, Carl Byoir & Associates, Singapore, 1982-84; Mass Communications Consultant, 1985-87; Managing Director, Publisher, BN and Associates Sdn Bhd, Malaysia, 1987-; Managing Director, BN Communications Sdn Bhd, 1989-; Director, Mystical Renderings, Malaysia, 1990-. Publications: Tok Cerpen, Malaysian Short Stories; Tok Cerpen's, The Hero Within; The Fisherman's Daughter and Other Stories; Publisher: Travelogue - Mystical Malaysia 1988-92, 1998; Publicist for Selangor, Malaysia, 1994-96. Honours: Mystical Malaysia, Best Travel Publication, 1988, 1990; Best Travel Writers Award, 1989, 1992. Memberships: Royal Selangor Club; Royal Commonwealth Club; Malaysian Forum of Environmental Journalists. Address: BN & Associates Sdn Bhd, 17-1 Lorong Setiabistari Dua, Bukit Damansara, 50490 Kuala Lumpur, Malaysia.

**NARAYANAN P M**, b. 12 May 1945, Mudur, Malapuram. Bank Officer. m. K C Sumatuy, 1 son, 1 daughter. Education: B Com, 1964. Appointments: Bank Clerk, 1965-74; Bank Officer, State Bank of India, 1974-. Publications: Enthinu, 1974; Foot Ball, 1981; Thadakam, 1992; (all collections of poems); Swathanthryam Enna Sapam, 1981; Nhan Aaranu, 1996; (both collection of essays). Honour: Winner of Mudadi Damodaran

Award, 1993. Address: 14 Vidya State Bank Colony, Calicut 673016, India.

**NARAZANI Bardhyl**, b. 23 May 1936, Elbasan, Albania. Zootechnician. Education: Zootechnician Diploma, 1954, National School of Agriculture, Department of Zootechny, stock breeding. Appointments: Scientific Specialist, Department of Genetic Breed Improvement of Cows, National Institute of Zootechny (stock breeding) Studies, Shkoder, Albania, 1954-61; Specialist of Breed Improvement of Livestock, Agriculture Directorate, region of Elbasan, Albania, 1962-66; Chief Specialist of Livestock, Agricultural Livestock Cooperative, 1966-72, Chief Specialist of Livestock Sevice, Agriculture Directorate, region of Elbasan, 1972-77; Chief Specialist of Livestock, Agricultural-Livestock Cooperative, region of Elbasan, 1977-81; General Manager, Livestock Food Factory, Elbasan, 1981-87; Chief Specialist of Livestock, State Agricultural-Livestock Enterprise, region of Elbasan, 1987-92; Regional Chief of Livestock Service, Agricultural Directorate, Elbasan, 1992-98; Advisor of the Major of region of Elbasan for Agriculture and Lives, 19tock98-. Publications: Contributor to the Albania media with technical essays as well as essays on his fruitful experience in animal breeding. Memberships: Scientific Council, Institute of Livestock Research; Institute of Animal Feed; Deputy Chief, National Associations of Cow Breeders; Chief, Association of the Livestock Specialists of the region. Address: Pal 7, H 1 Ap 3, Bul Q Stafa, Elbasan, Albania.

**NARBUTAITE Ausra**, b. 19 May 1963, Moletai. Teacher. Education: Vilnius Pedagogical University, 1986. Appointments: Geography and PT Teacher, Vilnius Tuskulenu Secondary School, 1986-87; Geography Department, Vilnius Pedagogical University, 1987-91; Gymnasia, Moletai Secondary School, 1991-. Memberships: Association Geography Teachers, Lithuania; Association Gymnasia Head Teachers, Lithuania. Address: J Janonio 6-3, LT 4150 Moletai, Lithuania.

**NARBUTAS Motiejus**, b. 27 November 1934, Danevezys District. Artist; Sculptor. m. Janina Alejunaite, 3 sons, 1 daughter. Education: Executor of wooden artworks, 1955; Artist, Sculptor, 1965. Appointments: Teacher of Sculpture in Klaipeda Children's School of Arts. Honours: Membership acknowledgements in Art Symposia of Lithuanian Artists and Sculptors. Memberships: Lithuanian Folk Art Society; Klaipeda Department of Lithuanian National Union. Address: Kretingos 27-15, 5818 Klaipeda, Lithuania.

**NARVANE Deepak**, b. 2 January 1961, Parli-Vaijnath. Principal. m. Surekha. Education: Bachelor of Music, Vocal; Bachelor of Music, Tabla. Appointments: Principal, Naad-Brahma Music Institute, 11 Years. Honours: Honoured by Parli Rotary Club; Other Social Organisation. Memberships: Naad Brahma Music Institution. Address: Principal, Naad-Brahma Music Institute, Parli, Vaijnath, Dist-Beed, Maharashtra, India.

**NASH-ISAAC Eva M**, b. 24 July 1936, Natchitoches, Louisiana, USA. Educator; Counsellor. m. Will Isaac Jr, July 1971, deceased 1970. Education: City College of San Francisco; BA, Social Science, 1974, MA, Education, MA, Counselling, 1979, San Francisco State University; PhD Education, Walden University, Minneapolis, 1985. Appointments: Elementary School Teacher, Oakland Public Schools, Oakland, California, 1974-; Pupil Personnel Service Counsellor, Garfield School, Oakland, 1976-77, Roosevelt Junior High School, Oakland, 1977-78; Extended Opportunity Programme Service Counsellor, City College, San Francisco 1978-79; Lecturer to churches and schools, 1983-84, 1987-88 nours: Superteacher Award, Oakland Unified School District, 85, 1986; Community Service Award, California Association Counseling and Development, 1988; Citizen of the Day, dio Station KABL, 1988; Phi Delta Kappa Five-Year Award, 89, 1990; Certificate of Recognition, Beyond the Call of Duty, ard of Education, Oakland, 1990; Honorary Diploma, St bre Indian School, Ashland, Montana, 1991. Memberships: lifornia Association for Counseling and Development; sociation for Supervision and Curriculum Development; ernational Reading Association; Commonwealth Club of lifornia; California Teachers Association; National sociation for Female Executives; International Platform sociation; World Affairs Council; Leadership Circle, National mmittee to Preserve Social Security and Medicare; Black ucus; Phi Delta Kappa; National Alliance of Black Educators; tional Education Association. Address: 920 Felton Street, n Francisco, CA 94139-1471, USA.

**NASYROV Albert Makhmutovich,** b. 7 March 1940, Kazan, ssia. Radiophysicist. m. Valentina Semenovna, 10 cember 1965, 1 son, 1 daughter. Education: Radiophysics partment of Kazan State University, Diploma II, 1962, DPhil, 69, DSc, 1989, Certificate of Senior Research Worker, 1981, ofessor, 1997. Appointments: Student, Kazan State iversity, 1957-62; Research Worker, 1967-69, Senior search Worker, 1969-78; Head, Meteors Department of tronomical Observatory, Kazan State University; Head, dioelectronics Chair, Professor of Kazan State University, 91. Publications: 130 research papers and monographs. nours: Prize of Council of Minister USSR, 1983; Individual ant, International Fund Soros, 1993. Memberships: ademician, International Informatization Academy, 1997; sociate Member, Academy of Natural Sciences of Russia, 97; Member, Presidium and Chairman, section of Scientific uncil, Propagation of Radio Waves, Academy Science of ssia; Expert Advice of Physicist, Ministry Education of ssia; Member, Council on doctoral thesis protection of ofessional Theoretical basic of radio techniques, Kazan State iversity; Member, Presidium of Scientific Advisers, Kazan ate University; Scientific Leader, Main Scientific Direction, zan State University. Address: Physics Department, Kazan iversity, Kremlevskaya St, 18 Kazan 420008, Russia.

**NATH Abhijit,** b. 1 September 1964, Kankurgachi, Calcutta, dia. Physician. m. Pompiya, 1 daughter. Education: MBBS, lcutta; DMCW, Calcutta; MIPHA, India; FRJM, London; RSTM&H, London; FIAGP, India. Career: Practising ysician, working with various public health programmes. emberships: Fellow, Royal Society of Medicine; Fellow, Royal ciety of Tropical Medicine and Hygiene; Indian Public Health sociation; Fellow, Indian Academy of General Practice. ddress: P268 CIT Road Scheme WIM, Calcutta 700 054, est Bengal, India.

**NAUROSCHAT Juergen Thomas,** b. 10 September 1964, ologne, Germany. Biosystems Researcher; Mathematician; ucator. Education: BSc, 1988, MSc, 1993, Mathematics and ology, Cologne University. Appointments: Teacher, athematics, Adult Education Program, City of Cologne, 1989-; ientific Collaborator, Researcher, Biomathematics, University Witten/Herdecke, 1993-; Teacher, Mathematics, University Witten/Herdecke, 1994-. Publications: Several articles in ofessional journals and books. Honours: Fellowship, German ciety for the Advancement of Scientific Research, 1993, 96. Memberships: Society for Simulation in Engineering and atural Sciences; European Society for Mathematical and eoretical Biology; New York Academy of Sciences. Address: tring 75, 50259 Pulheim, Germany.

**NAVEH Zev,** b. 2 December 1919, Amsterdam. Landscape Ecologist. m. Ziona Blitzman, 1 son, 1 daughter. Education: MSc, Agriculture, 1950, PhD, 1960, Hebrew University, Jerusalem. Appointments: Research Scientist, Range Ecology, Israel Ministry of Agriculture, Research Station, Neve Yaar, 1950-65; Seconded by Israel Ministry of Foreign Affairs International Cooperation, to Tengeru, Northern Tanzania Agriculture Research Station for Pasture Research and Development, 1963-65; Faculty of Agriculture Engineering, Technion, Israel Institute of Technology, Haifa, Teaching and Research in Ecology, Ecological Engineering, Restoration and Landscape Ecology, 1965-88; Co-Founder, Scientific Director, First Environmental Highschool and Teacher Training Program in Israel at Sdeh Boker, 1975-78; Founder and Curator, Ecological Garden, Technion Campus, 1980-88; Professor Emeritus at Technion, 1988-; Chairman, Working Group on Landscape Conservation of IUCN-Commission for Environmental Strategies and Planning, 1989-94. Publications: Over 200 scientific publications; Author and Co-author of several Hebrew and Englishs books. Honours: Henrietta Szold Scholarship, Outstanding Students Award, Hebrew University, Jerusalem, 1946; British Council Bursery for Tour of British Hill Pasture Research, 1958; USA Academy of Sciences, Visiting Research Scientist Fellowship, School of Forestry, University of California, Berkeley, 1958-60; Henri Gutwwirth Fund Award for Outstanding Ecological Research at Technion, 1985; Distinguished Member, International Society for the Study of Mediterranean Ecosystems, 1987; Distinguished Member, Israel Society of Ecology and Environmental Quality Sciences. Memberships: Editorial Board of 4 International Scientific Journals. Address: The Lowdermilk Faculty of Agricultural Engineering, Technion City, Haifa 32000, Israel.

**NAVIKAS Audrius,** b. 5 August 1961, Vilnius, Lithuania. Diplomat. m. Aida Navikiene, 2 sons. Education: M Economics, 1984, Vilnius University; MBA, 1992, University of Illinois; PhD Economics and Management, 1990, Vilnius University. Appointments: Assistant Professor, Vilnius University, 1989-95; Director Economics Dept, Ministry of Foreign Affairs of Lithuania, 1994-96; Charge d'Affaires, Permanent Mission of Lithuania to the UN Office at Geneva, 1996-98. Address: Permanent Mission of the Republic of Lithuania to the UN Office at Geneva, 18 Ave du Bouchet, 1209 Geneva, Switzerland.

**NAVJIVAN Sankalp,** b. 23 February 1970, Lucknow. Operations Manager. m. Sona. Education: Bachelor of Engineerin, 1992; Master of Business Administration, Bowling Green State University, 1995. Appointments: Reengineering Coordinator, Century Marketing Corporation, 1995; Selected to Rubber Maids Prestigious Global Leaderships Development Program, 1995; ISO Coordinator, 1995-96; New Product Intro Project Leader, 1997; Planning and Materials Manager, 1998-. Honours: Certified Lead Assessor for ISO 9000; Passed Exam, Project Management Professional. Memberships: APICS. Address: Little Tikes Div of Rubbermaid, 2180 Barlow Road, Hudson, OH 44236, USA.

**NAVYS Evaldas Vylius,** b. 6 August 1937, Lithuania. Research Fellow Natural Science. m. Irena Rimkute, 1 son, 1 daughter. Education: Lithuanian Academy of Agriculture, Forestry Department, 1956-60; Doctor of Agricultural Science, 1981, Minsk Institute of Technology. Appointments: Director, Vilnius University Botanical Garden, Vice Dean Faculty of Natural Science of Vilnius University, Associate Professor, Department of Botany and Genetics, 1990-. Publications: 52 research works; 4 monographs; Over 175 popular articles contributed to encyclopaedias; Recently published books: Melliforms Trees and Shrubs, 1994; Horticulture Rare Plants,

1996. Memberships: Lithuanian Dendrology Society, Vice Chairman; Lithuanian Horticultural Society, Vice Chairman; Senior Editor, Dendrologia Lithuaniae; President, Association of Baltic States Botanical Gardens. Address: Saltiniu 11/15-42, 2600 Vilnius, Lithuania.

**NAWOJCZYK Maria,** b. 9 June 1958, Jelenia Gora, Poland. Sociologist. Education: MA Economics and Statistics, 1981, Wroclaw School of Economics; PhD Sociology, 1995, Jagiellonian University. Appointments: Research Assistant, Dept of Sociology, Academy of Mining and Metallurgy, 1982-90; Teaching Assistant, 1991-95, Assistant Professor, 1995-, Dept of Sociology, Nicolaus Copernicus University. Publications: One book; numerous Articles in Polish and 5 in English. Honour: Second degree Award of the President of NCU for Achievements in Academic Year 1996-97. Memberships: Polish Sociological Association, Chair Torun Branch 1995; European Sociology Association; European Association of Social Anthropologists. Address: Nicolaus Copernicus University, Dept of Sociology, Mickiewicza 121, 87 100 Torun, Poland.

**NAYDENKOV Mikhail N,** b. 5 January 1972, Dzerzhinsk, Russia. Research Engineer. m. Maria Naydenkova. Education: Department of Physical and Quantum Electronics, Moscow Institute of Physics and Technology, 1988-94, BSc, Applied Physics and Maths, 1992, MSc, Applied Physics, 1994, Graduate Student, 1994-95; Postgraduate Study, Department of Physical and Technological Problems of Microeletronics, 1995-97; PhD, Physics of semiconductor and dielectric materials, 1997. Appointments: Part-time Junior Scientific Researcher, Microstructuring and Submicron Devices Laboratory, Institute of Physics and Technology, 1994-97; Part-time Engineer, Optical Equipment and Passive Components, Telecomservice, Russia, 1997-98; Part-time Physics and Engineering Consultant in METHOD Company, 1998; Postdoctoral Scientific Researcher in Microstructuring and Submicron Devices Laboratory, Institute of Physics and Technology, 1997-98; Postdoctoral Research Engineer, Optoelectronic Circuits and Systems Laboratory, Department of Electrical Engineering, University of California at Los Angeles, 1998-. Publications: Numerous articles as co-author in scientific journals. Membership: American Physical Society. Address: 1711 Corinth Ave, Apt 301, Los Angeles, CA 90025, USA.

**NDOMA-EGBA Rowland,** b. 7 July 1951, Ikom. Consultant Surgeon. m. Dr Margaret Ndoma-Egba, 4 sons. Education: MBBS, Lagos, 1977; Royal College of Surgeons, 1986; International College of Surgeons, 1991; West African College of Surgeons, 1993. Appointments: House Officer, LUTH, 1977-78; NYSC, Gongola State, 1978-79; Senior House Officer, Registrar, UCTH, 1980-81; SHO General Surgery Westminister Hospital, 1982-83; SHO Accident Surgery, Bassetlaw District Hospital, Sheffield, 1983-84; SHO, Registrar, Orthapaedics & Trauma, Gloucester Royal Hospital, 1984-85; Honourable Research Registrar, UCH and Middlesex Hospitals, University of London, 1986-88; Consultant Surgeon, UCTH, 1988-. Honours: Best Corper Award, 1979; Merit Award, 1997, 1998; Certificate of Honour, 1997, 1998; Certificate of Excellence, 1998; Award of Excellence, 1998; Achievers Award, 1998; Best Employer of the Year Award, 1998. Memberships: World Association of Hepato-Pancreato Biliary Surgery; British Medical Association; Nigerian Medical Association; Nigerian Surgical Research Society; Nigerian Cancer Society; Association of Paediatric Surgeons of Nigeria; Disabled Sports Association.

**NDROQI Shefqet,** b. 21 March 1914, Tirana, Albania. Professor; Doctor of Medicine. m. Lumturi Petrela, 2 sons, daughter. Education: MD, 1962; Professor of Medicine, 1974. Appointments: Intern, Hospital Fontainbleau, 1939-40; Ci Hospital of Tirana, 1941; Qafshtama Battle, 1943; Docto Partisan Hospital of Peshkopia, 1944-45; Second Captai Head of Ward, Infective Disease and Tuberculosis, Gener Military Hospital of Tirana, 1945; Head, TBC Ward, Civ Hospital of Tirana, 1947; Consultant, Ministry of Health ar General Civil Hospital and Military Hospital, 1947; Fir Director, Sanatorium of Tirana, 1948; Staff, Faculty Medicine, University of Tirana, 1955; Chief, Clinic Tuberculosis, 1966-89; Head, KEMP, Superior Commission phtisiatry for invalidity at work, 1959-89. Publication Numerous articles in professional medical journals; 3 books c TBC. Honours: Order of Merit, 1950; Order Naim Frasheri, Fir Class, 1979; Order of Red Flag of Work, 1989; Teacher of th People Awards from the President, in Honour of contribution 1 humanism in the workplace and formation and qualification students and medical workers, 1994; Outstanding Personali of Albanian Medicine; Several Honorary titles. Membership include: Association of Teachers of Albania; Association of Wa Against Smoke; Association of Hygiene and Environment Work. Address: Rr Qemal Stafa 130, Tirana, Albania.

**NDUNDA James Musyoki,** b. 1950, Machakos. Hea Teacher. m. Margaret, 3 sons, 3 daughters. Educatio Bachelor of Education, University of Exeter, England, 198 Appointments: Headmaster, Kawgundo High School. Addres P O Box 1000, Kangudo, Machakos, Kenya.

**NEAD Morris James,** b. 10 May 1943, Lawrencevill Illinois, USA. University Professor. m. Dr Karen Lea Nead, sons, 1 daughter. Education: BA, 1980, Eastern Illino University; MS, 1981, Indiana State University; EdD, 199 Indiana University; PhD, 1996, DTS Cand, Bethany Theologic Seminary. Appointments: Professor of Management, Vincenne University, 1985-. Publications: in Business Education Forun 1995, 1997. Honour: NISOD Excellence Award, 199 University of Texas at Austin. Memberships: Alpha Be Gamma; Pi Lambda Theta. Address: 1209 Old Orchard Roa Vincennes, IN 47591, USA.

**NEAGOE Victor-Emil,** b. 31 May 1947, Pitesti, Romania Electronics and Informatics Diplomate. m. Iordana. Educatio Honour Diploma in Electronics and Telcommunications, 197( PhD Electronics, 1976, Applied Mathematics for Researc 1981, Polytechnic University of Bucharest. Appointment Assistant Professor, 1970, Lecturer, 1978, Professor teachin courses of Pattern Recognition and Artificial Intelligenc Information Theory, Computational Intelligence, Digital Sign Processing, 1991-, Polytechnic University of Buchares Publications: in periodicals and conference proceeding Patents; First Romanian monograph on pattern recognitio Memberships: IEEE; Senior member, IEEE; IAPR, New Yor EURASIP, Lausanne. Address: PO Box 16-37, 7750 Bucharest 16, Romania.

**NEAL Eric James,** b. 3 June 1924, London, Englan Engineer. m. Joan Bowden, 2 sons. Education: The Sou Australian School of Mines; C Eng; C P Eng; FIEAust; FIEGas (London). Appointments: Early training and experience with S Gas Company and Electricity Trust of South Australia, 1940-4 Gas Industry in Broken Hill and Ballarat, 1950-63; Assista General Manager, 1963-68, General Manager, 1968-71, Bor Gas Ltd; Chief General Manager, 1972-74, Chief Executive Managing Director, 1974-87, Boral Ltd Group; Director variou limited companies, 1970-96; Also government service 1981-9 including Chief Commissioner of the City of Sydney, 1987-8

Governor of South Australia, 1996. Honours include: Knight Bachelor, 1982; Companion of the Order of Australia, 1988; Commander of the Royal Victorian Order, USA Dept of Defence Medal for Distinguished Public Service, 1992; Knight of Grace, Most Venerable Order Hospital of St John of Jerusalem, 1997; Honorary Colonel, Royal South Australia Regiment, 1996; Emeritus Member, Australian Institute of Management, 1998. Memberships: Institution of Gas Engineers, London, 1965, Fellow, 1969; Fellow, Australian Institute Management, 1969; Fellow, Institution Engineers, Australia, 1982, Honorary Fellow, 1985; Fellow, Australian Academy Technological Sciences & Engineering, 1989; Foundation Fellow, Australian Institute Company Directors, 990. Address: Government House, Adelaide, SA 5000, Australia.

**NEDOSPASOV Arthur,** b. 13 June 1928, Miass, Cshelyabinsk Region, Russia. Physicist. m. Mudretskaya Evgeniya, 3 sons. Education: Physicist, Moscow State University, 1950; Doctor of Physics, 1958; Doctor of Science in Physics, 1965; Diploma of Professor, Plasma Physics, 1968. Appointments: Engineer, Moscow Electrical Lamp Factory, 950-58; Scientific Worker, Institute of Atomic Energy, 1958-62; Head of Division, 1962-1970; Head of Division, Institute for High Temperatures, Russian Academy of Sciences, 1970-; Professor, Moscow Physical Technical Institute, 1968-. Publications: 4 books, 1977, 1979, 1990, 1991; More than 200 articles; 2 inventions. Memberships: Fellow, Russian Academy of Natural Sciences, 1992; Vice Editor in Chief, Vestnik Akademii Nauk SSSR, 1973-89. Address: Institute High Temperatures, Izhorskaya 13/19, Moscow 127412, Russia.

**NEELEY Delmar George,** b. 4 June 1937, Charleston, Illinois, USA. Manager; Educator. m. Terry B Neeley, 2 sons. Education: BA, Philosophy, 1965, MA, Literature, 1969, Olivet Nazarene University; EdD, Counseling Psychology, University of Sarasota, 1996. Career: Manager, Management Development, Rauland Division, Zenith Corporation, Chicago, 1967-70; Senior Personnel Consultant, Mid West Services Company, Chicago, 1971-73; Human Resources, Nichols-Homeshield Inc, West Chicago, 1974-76, Gould Inc, Industry Battery Division, Langhorne, Pennsylvania, 1976-81; President, Owner, Barbour-Neeley Inc, Sarasota, Florida, 1982-91. Honours: Meritorious Service Award, Chicago Boys Club, 1970; Service Award, Chicago Jaycees, 1971. Memberships: ACA; American Association of Christian Counselors; American Association of Pastoral Counseling; American Association of Professional Chaplains; Florida Academy of Professional Mediators. Address: 3778 Bonaventure Court, Sarasota, FL 34243, USA.

**NEER SHABNAM Nirmala Shankarrao Chandekar,** b. 9 November 1939, Aheir, India. Professor. Education: BA, 1964; MA, English Literature, 1966. Appointments: Lecturer, English, 1966-; Principal, Janala College, 1999-. Publications: Gulmohari Sham; Band Lifafa; Badi Sab Kushal Hai; Guftagu. Honours: Jainendra Kumar Prize; Gyanbharti Prize; Mata Kusum Kumari Award; Mahadevi Berma Rashtriya Shikhar Samman Prize; International Woman of the Year, International Biographical Centre. Memberships: Community Education CEA, Asian Region. Address: Chitra-Withi, Samadkiward, Chandrapur 442402, India.

**NEGI Gorkhu Ram,** b. 1 April 1960, Suroo, India. Teacher; Lecturer in Indian and European History (College Cadre). Education: MA, History, 1982; MPhil History, 1984; Postgraduate Diploma in Adult Education, 1985; Doctoral Research Work, Christian Missionary Activities and Their Impact on Himachal Pradesh, 1840-1947 AD, in progress.

Appointments: Lecturer in History, Government College Rampur Bushhr, August 1985 to December 1986, Lecturer in History, (School Cadre), 10 + 2 or Secondary School, December 1986 to July 1987; Lecturer in History, (College Cadre), 1987-. Publications: Research papers including The Himalaya Mission with Special Reference to the Contribution of American Missionaries and Samuel Evanes Stokes in Indian Church History Review Vol XXXI, No 1. Memberships: Life Member, Himachal Pradesh History Congress; Life Member, American Studies Research Centre; Library Osmania University Campus, Hyderabad; Church History Association of India; Governing Body Member; Indian Confederation of Indigenous Tribal Peoples; Attended conference, Germany, 1995, Visits to Belgium, Netherlands, Luxembourg. Address: G B Pant Memorial Government, PG College, Rampur Bushahr 172001, DT Shimla HP, India.

**NEGOESCU Adrien N,** b. 2 March 1959, Bucharest, Romania. Biologist. Education: MD, Medical School, University of Bucharest, Romania, 1985. DEA (Diploma of Postgradute Studies), Medical & Biological Engineering, 1991, PhD, Cell Biology, 1995, MS, General Biology, 1998, Joseph Fourier University, Grenoble, France. Appointments: Researcher, Victor Babes Institute of Pathology and Medical Genetics, Electron Microscopy Department, Bucharest, 1987-90; DEA Research Program, 1990-91, PhD Research Program, 1991-95, National Institute of Health and Medical Resaerch (INSERM), Grenoble; Postdoctoral Fellow, Lung Cancer Research Group, Albert Bonniot Institute of Biotechnology, Grenoble, 1995-98. Publications: Reviews, book chapters, letters to journal editors and theses. Address: 1 rue Servan, 38000 Grenoble, France.

**NEISHTADT Naum,** b. 19 March 1929, Toropez town, Russia. Geophysicist. m. Div. 1 daughter. Education: MSc Geophysical Exploration, 1953, Leningrad Mining Institute, USSR; PhD Geophysical Exploration, 1967, DSc Geophysical Exploration, 1989, Mining Institute, USSR, Leningrad. Appointments: Professor, Dept Geophysics and Planning Science, Tel Aviv University; General Manager, Geoport Ltd. Publications: 85 in USSR, England, France, Israel. Honours: Bronze Medal, 1971; Silver Medal, 1982, for Exhibition of Achievements of National Economy, Moscow; Gold Medal, 1973, State Prize Laureate USSR; Badge of Honour, Ministry of Geology, USSR, 1975. Memberships: Geology Board of Leningrad Mining Institute; Scientific Referee, Ministry of Geology, USSR. Address: 11/20 Snapir Street, 67298 Tel Aviv, Israel.

**NEJOH Yasu-Nori,** b. 14 October 1947, Hachinohe, Japan. Professor. m. Yuko, 2 sons, 1 daughter. Education: PhD, Hokkaido University. Appointments: Professor, Hachinohe Institute of Technology, 1996-. Publications: 62 articles in society journals. Honour: Grantee, Ministry of Education Science Culture, 1989. Memberships: American Physical Society; IEEE; European Geophysics Society; Physical Society of Japan; Japanese Society Plasma Fusion Science; Japanese Society Fluid Mechanics. Address: 15-5 Kitsunekubo Uruichi, Hachinohe 031-0073, Japan.

**NEKHAMIKIN Yuri,** b. 1 March 1947, Leningrad, USSR. Mechanical Engineer. m. Ludmila, 1 son. Education: MSc, Mechanical Engineering, Faculty of Physics and Mechanics, Leningrad Polytechnic Institute, Leningrad, USSR, 1971. Publications: More than 60 articles, professional journals. Memberships: Israel Nuclear Society. Address: P O Box 1449, Ofakim St 7 Apt 32, 36770 Nesher, Israel.

**NEKRAŠAS Evaldas,** b. 29 May 1945, Ukmerge, Lithuania. Philosopher; Political Scientist. m. Vanda Nekrašiene, 1 daughter. Education: Mathematics major, 1962-67, Honours Diploma, 1967, Philosophy major, 1968-71, PhD, 1971, Vilnius University; Professor, Head, Department of Philosophy, 1988-, Professor, Institute of International Relations and Political Sciences, 1992-, Vilnius University; Senior Fulbright Scholar, Harvard University, USA, 1995-96; Visiting Professor, Salzburg University, Austria, 1998. Publications: 4 books including: Probable Knowledge, in Russian, 1987, in Polish, 1992; Legislature and the Executive in Foreign Policy Making, in English, 1994; About 100 other publications on philosophy and politics. Honours: Corresponding Member, Lithuanian Academy of Sciences, 1994-. Membership: President, Lithuanian Society of Philosophers. Address: V Druskio 10-32, LT-2050 Vilnius, Lithuania.

**NELSON Roger William,** b. 24 August 1947, Santa Cruz, California, USA. Conductor; Pianist; Educator. m. Karen Iglitzin, 1 daughter. Education: BA, Zoology, Pomona College, 1969; MMus, Choral Conducting, State University of New York at Stony Brook, 1974. Appointments: Professor, Cornish College of the Arts, 1979-; Pianist, New Performance Group, 1979-97; Conductor, Bainbridge Orchestra, 1987-, Seattle Creative Orchestra, 1996-. Publications: Fiddle Tunes with a Difference, contemporary gigs, reels, waltzes, 1993; Numerous recordings of music of Cage, Giteck, Dresher. Membership: ACDA. Address: 10734 38th Avenue NE, Seattle, WA 98125, USA.

**NEMECEK Eduard,** b. 2 July 1927, Hradec, Kralove, Czech Republic. Professor. m. Stychova Hana, 2 sons. Education: Juris Doctor, Charles University, Prague, 1950; CSc, Economics, Academy of Science, Prague, 1961. Appointments: Head, Public Finance and Banking Department, Law Faculty, Charles University, Prague. Publications include: Theory of Exchange Rates, 1967; Introduction in Financial Science and Czech Financial Law, 1994. Honours: Commemoration Medal, Charles University, Prague, 1975, 1998. Memberships: Network of Institutes and Schools of Public Administration in Central & Eastern Europe. Address: Charles University, Law Faculty, Nam Curieovych 7, 110 00 Prague 1, Czech Republic.

**NENKOV Milen,** b. 13 October 1963, Russe, Bulgaria. Senior Lecturer. m. 1 son, 2 daughters. Education: Physicist, Physics Department, Sofia University, 1986. Appointments: Lecturer, 1987-92, Senior Lecturer, 1992-, Department of Physics, University of Russe. Publications: Numerous publications in journals. Membership: Bulgarian Union of Scientists. Address: Department of Physics, University of Russe, Russe 7017, Bulgaria.

**NEOCLEUS Kyriakos,** b. 11 December 1922, Limassol, Cyprus. Educationist. m. Elsie Gaston, 5 sons. Education: Shorthand Teacher's Certificate, 1944, Pitman's College, London; Diploma in School Administration, 1964, Northwestern University, Illinois; Diploma in Education, 1969, Leeds University, England. Appointments: Founder and Teacher, Neocleus' Institute, 1943-47; Teacher, Samuel High School, 1947-50; Founder and Headmaster, Pancyprian Economic Lyceum, 1950-83; Founder and Principal, Neocleus' Evening Schools, 1953-60; Founder, Cyprus, 40th Scouts' Group; President, Cyprus Government Sport Organisation, 1983-88; Chief Examiner, Ministry of Education, in Typewriting, 1960-; Consultant to Ministry of Education, 1983-88. Publications: International Typewriting, 1947; The Headmaster in Cyprus, 1969; Golden Key to Classical Wisdom, 1971; School Pulses, 1972; Education in Yorkshire, 1973; Political Economy (with son Nelson), 1976; Chronicle of Sport in Cyprus (Centennial Edition), 1986; The Computer as a Word Processor, 1996.

Honours: Fulbright Scholarship, Northwestern University, 1964; Commonwealth Bursary, Leeds University, 1969; Unveiling by Education Minister and Alumni's Association of a built-in plaque for Substantial Contribution to Education, 1991; Award by Cyprus Sport Organisation for Contribution to Advancement of Sport; Author's Award by Ayios Dometios Co-op Society for Most Worthy Writing Work, 1995; Award by Greek Literary Society, Athens, for Substantial Contribution to the Cultivation and Advancement of Contemporary Greek Civilisation, 1995; Honorary Membership by City and Guilds of London Institute for Significant Involvement in, and Contribution to, the furtherance of the work of the institute in technical & vocational education and training, 1995. Address: 24 Smyrnis St, 2401 Engomi Nicosia, Cyprus.

**NEPERSHIN Rostislav Ivanovich,** b. 28 July 1938, Russia. Mechanical Engineer. 2 sons, 1 daughter. Education: Mechanical Engineering Degree, 1962; Candidate of Engineering Science, 1967; Doctor of Engineering Science, 1977. Appointments: Engineer, Automotive Technical Research Institute, Moscow, 1962-65; Research Scientist, Institute of Machine Research, 1965-91; Professor, Moscow State Academy of Instruments, Institute of Engineering and Informatics, Moscow, 1991-; Visiting Research Scientist, Alcoa Technical Centre, USA, 1996, 1998, 1999. Publications: Theory of Technological Plasticity, 1990; Problems of Technological Plasticity, 1994. Memberships: Science Council, Chuvash Pedagogical Institute, Russian Peoples Friendship University. Address: Moscow State Academy of Engineering, Stoenynka Street 20, Moscow 107846, Russia.

**NESIC Vojna,** b. 6 October 1947, Sarajevo. Composer. m. Milan Nesic, 1 son, 1 daughter. Education: Faculty of Musical Arts, Belgrade, Enriko Yosif; MA, Music Academy, Sarajevo, Vojin Komadina. Career: Professor of Harmony and Composition, Faculty of Arts Pristina and Sarajevo; Guest Lecturer, USA, 1991; School of Music, Kragujevac, 1977-1995. Publications: Several compositions. Acknowledgments: Mannheim, 1985; Miami, 1988, 1989; Corciano, 1989, 1990; Fairbanks, 1993; London 1994; Raleigh, 1996-98. Memberships: Frau und Musik, Kassel, Germany; International Alliance for Women in Music. Address: Kneza Mihaila 84 IV/44, 34000 Kragujevac, Yugoslavia.

**NESTEROV Alexander Ilyich,** b. 22 June 1950, Krasnogorsk, Russia. Physicist; Researcher. m. Elena Dmitrievna, 2 sons. Education: PhD, 1976; DSc, 1989; Professor, 1991. Appointments: Assistant Professor, 1977-80, Senior Lecturer, 1980-84, Associate Professor, 1984-86, 1988-90, Senior Researcher, 1986-88, Professor, 1990-97, Krasnoyarsk University, Russia; Visiting Professor, 1993-94, Professor, Researcher, 1994-, Guadalajara University, Mexico. Publications include: Dynamics of fields in general relativity, 1985. Honours: Gravity Research Foundation Honorable Mention, 1988, 1994, 1996; International Science Foundation Grant, 1993. Memberships: Mexican Academy of Science; Russian Gravitational Society; American Physical Society; American Mathematical Society; Mexican Physical Society. Address: Fray Antonio de Segovia 729, Guadalajara, Jalisco 44840, Mexico.

**NET Mariana,** b. 15 August 1956, Iasi, Romania. Senior Researcher in Linguistics. Education: MA, English and French, University of Bucharest, 1979; PhD, Linguistics, 1992. Appointments: Editor, Foreign Trade Publicity Agency Publicom, Bucharest, 1979-84; Researcher, Institute of Linguistics, Bucharest, 1984-91; Senior Researcher, Institute of Linguistics, 1991-. Publications: A Poetics of Atmosphere 1989; The Metalanguage of the Literary Text, 1989; Alexandre umas: Le Pays Où Il Fait Mort, 1997. Memberships: IASS; IS; OGS; DGS. Address: Str Obcina Mare 4 OS2 ScD, Et 1 ot 126 Of 66, 77368 Bucharest VI, Romania.

**NEUMANN Bernhard Hermann,** b. 15 October 1909, Berlin, ermany. Mathematician. m. (1) Hanna von Caemmerer, dec 971, 3 sons, 2 daughters, (2) Dorothea Frieda Auguste Zeim. ducation: University of Freiburg, 1928-29; DrPhil, University Berlin, 1929-32; PhD, University of Cambridge, England, 933-35; DSc, University of Manchester, 1954. Appointments: emporary Assistant Lecturer, University College, Cardiff, ales, 1937-40; Army Service, Pioneer Corps, Royal Artillery, telligence Corps, 1940-45; Lecturer, University College, Hull, ngland, 1946-48; Lecturer, Senior Lecturer, Reader, niversity of Manchester, 1948-61; Professor, Head of epartment of Mathematics, Institute of Advanced Studies, ustralian National University, Australia, 1962-74; Honorary ellow, Emeritus Professor, 1975-; Senior Research Fellow, SIRO Division of Mathematics and Statistics, 1975-77; onorary Research Fellow, 1978-, (now Mathematical and nformation Sciences). Publications: Contributor of over 120 apers in mathematical journals; Selected works of B H eumann and Hanna Neumann, 6 vols, 1988. Honours: Prize, Viskundig Genootschap to Amsterdam, 1949; Matthew linders Lecturer, Australian Academy of Science, 1984; dams Prize, University of Cambridge, 1952-53; Honorary Sc, Univesity of Newcastle, NSW, 1974, Monash University, 982; Honorary Dr Mathematics, University of Waterloo, 1986; onorary DSc, University of Western Australia, 1995; niversity of Hull, England, 1995; Dr rer nat hon causa, umboldt University, Berlin, 1992; Honorary Member, Canberra lathematical Association, 1975-, New Zealand Mathematical ociety, 1975-, Australian Association of Mathematics eachers, 1975-, Australian Mathematical Society, 1981-; AustMS, Fellow of the Australian Mathematical Society, 1994; ompanion of Order of Australia, 1994. Memberships: FRS; AA; FACE; FTICA (Hon); London Mathematical Society; Viskundig Genootschap; American, Canadian, Australian, New ealand and South East Asian Mathematical Societies; lathematical Asssociation; Mathematical Association of merica; Australian Association of Mathematics Teachers. ddress: The Australian National University, School of lathematical Sciences, ACT 0200, Australia.

**NEVES José Amarildo De Castro,** b. 14 November 1963, ortegaca, Portugal. Managing Director; Chartered Accountant. . Angela Frances, 1 son, 1 daughter. Education: BCom, 1985; ertificate in the Theory of Accountancy, 1986; Chartered ccountant (SA), 1990; ACMA, 1992. Appointments: Financial lanager, Formex Industries(Pty) Ltd, 1992-93; General lanager, 1993-97, Managing Director, 1997-, Coca-Cola abco (Mozambique) SARL. Honour: Manager Coca-Cola abco Plant of the Year, 1997. Memberships: South African nstitute of Chartered Accountants; Associate member, hartered Institute of Management Accountants; Management oard, South Africa/Mozambique Chamber of Commerce. ddress: PO Box 6783, Nelspuit 1200, South Africa.

**NEVO Eviatar,** b. 2 February 1929, Tel Aviv, Israel. volutionary Biologist. Divorced, 1 son, deceased, 1 daughter. ducation: MSc, special distinction, 1958, PhD, summa cum aude, Biology, 1964, Hebrew University, Jerusalem. ppointments include: Senior Lecturer in Genetics, Department f Genetics, Hebrew University, Jerusalem, 1970-71; Research ssociate, Museum of Vertebrate Zoology, University of alifornia, Berkeley, and Senior Postdoctoral Research, niversity of Chicago, 1972-73; Associate Professor of Biology, niversity of Haifa, 1973-75; Professor of Biology, 1975-, irector, Institute of Evolution, 1977-, University of Haifa;

Incumbent Chair of Evolutionary Biology, 1984-. Publications: 650 papers in various fields of evolutionary biology; Author and co-author of nine books including: Population Genetics and Ecology, 1976; The Evolutionary Significance of Genetic Diversity, 1984; Evolutionary Processes and Theory, 1986; Evolution of Subterranean Mammals at the Organismal and Molecular Levels, 1990; Evolutionary Theory and Processes of Active Speciation and Adaptive Radiation in Subterranean Mole Rats, 1991; The First Checklist of Lichen-Forming and Lichenicolous Fungi of Israel, 1996; Cyanophyta: Checklist of Continental Species from Israel, 1996; Medicinal Mushrooms Ganoderma Lucidum, 1997. Honours include: Foreign Member, The Linnean Society; Foreign Member, National Academy of Sciences of Ukraine; Fellow of the American Association of the Advancement of Science; Honoured Member, Ukrainian Botanical Society, 1995; Decree of Merit, International Biographical Centre, 1996; Presidential Seal of Honor, 1997; Life Fellow, International Biographical Association, 1997; Deputy Governor, American Biographical Institute, 1997. Memberships: Society for the Study of Evolution; International Society of Molecular Evolution; American Association for the Advancement of Science; American Society of Naturalists; Genetics Society of America; Genetical Society of Israel; Zoological Society of Israel; Geological Society of Israel. Address: Institute of Evolution, University of Haifa, Haifa, Israel.

**NEWKIRK Raymond,** b. 13 July 1944, Shreveport, Louisiana, USA. Management Consultant. m. Education: Dayton Comm Coll, 1973; BS in Behavioral Sciences, New York Institute Tech, 1976; MS in Philosophy, Columbia Pacific University, 1980; PhD, Behavioral Sci, 1982; PhD, Human Science, Saybrook Institute, 1992. Appointments: Clinical Intern Fielding Inst, 1995; Chief Executive Officer, cons, Newkirk & Assocs, Fort Lauderdale, Florida, 1980-84; Head Dept, ADP Royal Saudi Naval Forces, Jeddah, 1984-86; President, Cons Internal Association of Information Management, Santa Clara, California, 1984; Certified Quality Analyst, Quality Assurance Institute, Orlando, Florida, 1986-; Pris cons info Impact International, Nashville, 1988-; President, CEO Sys Mgmt Inst, Pleasant Hill, Calif, 1987; Pres, COO Pq Info Group, Egmont ann Haeff, The Netherlands, 1992-94; Pres, CEO Systems Mgmt Inst, 1994-; Prin, Forum 2000, 1996-; Deputy Governor, ABI, 1995. Publications: Chronicles of the Making of A Philosopher, 1983; contr, articles to professional journals. Honours: Phi Kappa, 1973; Confederation of Chivalry. Memberships: Speaker, Member, Union for Concerned Scientists, San Francisco, 1988; Fellow, British Institute of Management, IBA; Member, Association of Systems Management; Association of Professional Cons, Planetary Society, Columbia Pacific Alumni Association, 1985; Association of Computing Machinery, IEEE Computer Society, 1995. Address: 95 Greenock Lane, Pleasant Hill, CA 94523-2083, USA.

**NEWSOM James Thomas,** b. 6 October 1944, USA. Lawyer. m. Sherry Elaine, 1 stepson, 1 stepdaughter. Education: AB, 1966, JD, 1968, University of Missouri. Appointments: Lt Commander, Judge Advocate General's Corps, US Navy, 1968-72; Partner, Shook, Hardy & Bacon, Law Firm, 1972-. Publications: Several articles in professional journals. Honour: Order of the Coif, 1968. Memberships: University of Missouri Law Society; University of Missouri Jefferson Club; American Bar Association; Missouri Bar Association. Address: Shook, Hardy & Bacon, 1 Kansas City Place, 1200 Main Street Ste 3100, Kansas City, MO 64105-2139, USA.

**NEYMANN Monika Anna,** b. 22 September 1932, Warsaw, Poland. Academic Professor. m. 1 son. Education: MA, English

Philology, 1955; PhD, Humanistics, 1967; PhDhab, English Philology, 1976. Appointments: English Language Teacher, 1958-63; Lecturer, Reader, English, Warsaw School of Economics, 1962-67; Vice Director, Language Centre, Warsaw School of Economics, 1967-92; Professor, Head of the Chair of Business Communication, Warsaw School of Economics, 1992-; Professor, Business English Programme Consultant, Leon Kozminski Academy of Entrepreneurship and Management, 1995-. Publications: Over 100 in professional journals and books. Address: Warsaw School of Economics, Al Niepodleglosci 162, Warsaw 02554, Poland.

**NG Man-Lun,** b. 14 October 1946, Hong Kong. Psychiatry. m. Sui-May, 1 son, 1 daughter. Education: MBBS, Hong Kong; MD, Hong Kong; DPM, English; Diploma, American Board of Sexology; FRANZCP; FRCPsych, England; FHKAM, Psychiatry; FAACS. Career: Medical Officer, 1972, Lecturer, Psychiatry department, 1973-81, Senior Lecturer, 1981-92, Reader, 1992-96, Professor, 1996-, University of Hong Kong; Fellow, Hong Kong College of Psychiatrists. Publications include: Chinese: Sexual Medicine; A Modern Perspective; Sexual Behavior in Modern China - A Report of the Nationwide Sex-Civilization Survey on 20,000 Subjects in China; Chinese Dictionary of Sexology; Sexuality in Asia. Honourss: Sexologist of Asia, Asian Federation for Sexology, 1994. Memberships: Foundation President, Hong Kong Sex Education Association; Foundation President, Asian Federation for Sexology; President, 14th World Congress of Sexology. Address: Queen Mary Hospital, Department of Psychiatry, University of Hong Kong, Hong Kong.

**NG'OMBE Roger Mazauri Stephen (Reverend Canon),** b. 6 June 1932, Msoro, Chipata, Zambia. Journalist; Priest. m. Joyce Anne Chitalande Ng'ombe, 5 sons, 3 daughters. Education: Diploma in Journalism, 1965, University Nairobi, Kenya. Appointments: Newspaper Editor; Broadcasting Editor; Hansard Editor; Metric System Analyst; Director, Zambia Broadcasting Services (Radio and TV); Anglican Parish Priest; Diocesan Secretary; Chairman, Multimedia Zambia. Publications: Parliamentary Debates 1967-69; Zambia Goes Metric, film, 1970; Metrication in Zambia, 1973; Making Broadcasting Useful: The African Experience, Manchester, UK, 1986, co-author. Memberships: Zambia Agricultural and Commercial Society; Multimedia Zambia; Christian Council of Zambia; Bible Society of Zambia. Address: PO Box 37708, Lusaka, Zambia.

**NGANWA-BAGUMAH Alex Bernard,** b. 6 March 1946, Kabwohe, South Africa. Medicine. m. Margaret Jenny, 1 son, 3 daughters. Education: MBChB (Makerere), 1971; MMed (Surg)(Makerere), 1976; FRCS (Edinburgh), 1980; FRCS, RCPS (Glasgow), 1980; Dip Med Ed (Dundee), 1994. Appointments: Professor and Head of Department of Anatomy, Histology and Embryology. Honour: Hero of the Spear, University Hall, Makerere University. Memberships: ASSA; ASEA. Address: University of Transket, Alexandra Road, 5117 Unitra, South Africa.

**NGO Quang Xuan,** b. 1 January 1951, Vietnam. Diplomat. m. Mrs Le Thi Hoa, 2 daughters. Education: Diploma, Hanoi Institute of International Relations, 1974; Postgraduate studies, 1975-76, Postgraduate Degree, 1976, Institut des HEI, Geneva; Postgraduate studies, 1980-83, Postgraduate Degree, 1983-, Diplomatic Academy of Moscow. Appointment: Ambassador Extraordinary and Plenipotentiary and Permanent Representative of the Socialist Republic of Vietnam to the United Nations. Address: Permanent Mission of the Socialist Republic of Vietnam to the United Nations, 866 UN Plaza, Suite 435, New York, NY 10017, USA.

**NGUYEN Lai,** b. 4 March 1930. Professor; Linguist. m. sons. Education: Doctor Degree, 1976; DSc, 1984. Career Dean, Linguistics and Philosophy, College of Social Science and Humanities, Hanoi National University. Publications: Ove 30 articles on linguistics. Memberships: GAL, PALA; VN Linguistics Association. Address: College of Social Sciences Humanities, Hanoi National University, 90 Nguyen Trai Stree Hanoi, Vietnam.

**NGUYEN Lam Duc,** b. 20 July 1945, Vietnam. President. m Trang Thu Nghiem, 2 sons, 1 daughter. Education: BA Englisl and EFL/ESL Teaching, 1968, University of Saigon; Diploma i TEFL, 1973-74, Sydney University; ASCS, 1981, Condi College. Appointments: Deputy Executive Director, Director c Programmes, IRCC Inc, 1988-93; Special Refugee Consultan California State RIPB/DSS, 1993-94; President, Win-Visions 1994-. Publications: Co-author, Affirmative Action and Vie community, 1966; Author of hundreds of articles. Honour: Ma of the Year, ABI, USA, 1997. Memberships: America Individual Investors Association; American Managemer Association; National APA Educators Association. Address 4864 Miramar Avenue, San Jose, CA 95129, USA.

**NGUYEN Le Hieu,** b. 16 May 1965, Vietnam. Specialist. m Tram P T Truong. Education: Diploma, Electrical Engineering 1987; PhD, Electrical Engineering, 1996. Appointment Specialist, Federal Computing Center, Austria. Publications Several papers in professional journals. Memberships: IEEE Austrian Computer Association. Address: Eibengasse 59/32 A-1220 Vienna, Austria.

**NGUYEN Nhu Y,** b. 14 June 1942, Huong Son, Ha Tinh Vietnam. Science Researcher; Editor. m. Nguyen Thi Nhi, son. Education: BA, 1966, Hanoi University; PhD, 1983, USSF Academic Institute; Professor, 1996. Appointments: Deput Director, Linguistics Institute, 1985; Deputy Director, 1994 Deputy Director, Editor in Chief, current, Education Publishin House. Publications: Researching on Chinese and Frenc original term in Vietnamese, 1983; Language Policy, the polic for ethnic languages in Vietnam, 1986; Dictionary c Vietnamese Idioms, 1992; Vietnamese Great Dictionary, 1998 Memberships: Linguistics Association; Vietnamese Folklor Association; Chairman, Association of Teaching Vietnames Language; Deputy Director, Researching Centre for Se Education. Address: Education Publishing House, 81 Tran Hin Dao St, Hanoi, Vietnam.

**NGUYEN-CANH Toan,** b. 28 September 1926, Doluong Nghean, Vietnam. Professor. m. Nguyen-Thi-Ty, deceased, sons, 2 daughters. Education: Hanoi University, until 1946 Candidat's Masters Degree, 1958; Doctor's Degree, Moscoy University, 1963. Appointments: Teacher, secondary schoo 1947-51; Assistant Professor of university, 1951-; Dear Mathematical Faculty, 1958-66; President of university 1966-76; Vice Minister of Education, 1976-89; Professor, Hane National University, at present; Chairman of Math Methodology Founder and Editor in Chief, Toanhocvatuoitre (Math an Youth), journal, 1964-; Innovator of the ultra non-Euclidia geometry. Publications include: Books: Projective Geometr 1961, 1962; Bases of Geometry, 1962; Tensorial Algebra an Analyz, 1964; Vectorial Algebra, 1970; Higher Geometry, 1976 1979; Initiation of Good Pupils to Mathematical Researcl 1992, 1997; Some Problems in Teaching and Studying b Distance Education in Vietnam, 1993; Dissertation an Experiences in Self-Education, 1995; The Different Periods c the Development of the Pedagogical Training in Vietnam, 1996 1997; Materialists and Dialectical methodology in Service fc Learning, Teaching, Researching in the Domain Mathematics, 1997. Memberships: Vice President and Genera ecretary, 1964-80, Vietnamese Math Association; Chairman f Advisor Council, Vietnam Association Promoting and upporting Educational Development; Director, Research and Jevelopment Centre for Self Education, 1996-. Address: 55 Di 3iang Co, Ba Dinh, Hanoi, Vietnam.

**NI Wansun,** b. 14 May 1930, Anqing, Anhui, China. 'rofessor of Nanjing University. m. Yuhui Cheng, 3 daughters. :ducation: Graduate, Peking University, 1956. Appointments: 'rofessor, Department of Information Physics, Nanjing Jniversity, 1990. Publications: Solitary Wave in Water Trough, 1 Chinese, 1997; over 50 articles on physics. Honours: \wards: Second, 1986 and First, 1990 of progress of Science nd Technology of State Education Commission of China. Jembership: Council, Physical Acoustics of China. Address: nfo Physics Department, Nanjing University, Nanjing, Jiansu, China.

**NI Yixin,** b. 27 October 1946, Shanghai, China. Professor. 1. Wang Mi, 1 daughter. Education: Bachelor of Engineering, 968, Master of Engineering, 1981, Doctor of Engineering, 983, Electrical Engineering, Tsinghua University, Beijing, China. Appointments: Electrical Engineer, First Engineering Company, Northeastern Power Administration Bureau, China, 968-78; Instructor, 1983-86, Associate Professor, 1986-88, 'rofessor, 1988-96, Dept of EE, Tsinghua University, Beijing; 'ice-Chair for Teaching Affairs, 1988-89, Vice-Chair for 1esearch Affairs, 1989-91, Vice-Director of EERI, 1991-96, Jice-Director of National Power System Laboratory, 1993-95, Jirector of NPSL, 1995-96, Vice-Chair of Postgraduate Degree Committee, 1994-96, President Education Consultant, 1992-96, singhua University; Advisory Professor, He-hai University, China, Shanghai Electric Power Institute; Editor, Power System Technology, China; Editor, Modern Power System Series, Science Press, China; Associate Professor, Dept of EEE, Jniversity of Hong Kong, Hong Kong SAR, 1996-; Concurrent 'rofessor, Southeast University, China, North China Electric 'ower University; Visiting Scholar, Associate Professor, Scientist, 1985-87,, 1994-96. Publications: 5 books and book chapters; 33 papers published on refereed journals; 51 papers ublished on conferences. Honours: 14 awards including: Jutstanding Doctor Award for being the first woman doctor of engineering educated in China and the first doctor educated in singhua University, 1984. Memberships: Senior Member, EEE, 1994-; National Committee, Chinese Association for Science and Technology, 1990-95; Senior Member, Chinese Society of Electrical Engineers, 1998; Vice-Chair, All China Young Scientists and Engineers Association and All China Youth Federation, 1992-95. Address: Department of Electrical and Electronic Engineering, University of Hong Kong, Pokfulam 1oad, Hong Kong.

**NICHOLSON Benjamin,** b. 20 December 1927, Aberdeen, Scotland. Executive Director; Trade Unionist. m. Doris Elaine \ckermann, 5 August 1961, 1 daughter. Education: Diploma in Electronics, Cambridge, 1955. Appointments: Electrical Officer, 1oyal Navy, 1943-57; Research Officer, Computers, Elliot Brothers, 1957-58; Manager, After Sales, Instr Manufacturers CT, 1958-65; Trade Union Executive Director, 1965-97; Editor, 'ower Magazine, 1974-90. Publications: Contributor of numerous papers on industrial relations in South Africa, 1970-97. Memberships: National Industrial Council of Iron and Steel, Chair, 1978-80, 1985-87; Executive Director, South \frican Electrical Workers Association, 1965-; Executive Jirector, Confederation of Metal and Building Unions; Chair, Metal Industries Pension Fund; Chair, Electrical Industrial Council, Natal, 1974-, Transvaal, 1990; Chair, Mining Industry Training Board, 1980-90; Founder and President, South Africa Skills Foundation, Chair, 1988-92; Council of Mining Unions,

1984-96. Address: PO Box 45, Laezonia 0026, Republic of South Africa.

**NICKELL Joe Herman,** b. 1 December 1944, Lexington, Kentucky, USA, Paranormal Investigator. Education: BA, 1967, MA, 1982, PhD, 1987, University of Kentucky. Appointments: Stage Magician, 1968-73; Private Investigator, 1973-75; Teaching Assistant, Instructor, University of Kentucky, 1980-95; Senior Research Fellow, Committee for the Scientific Investigation of Claims of the Paranormal, 1995-. Publications: 16 books, including: Inquest on the Shroud of Turin, 1983, 1987; Looking for a Miracle, 1993; Camera Clues, 1994; Detecting Forgery, 1996. Address: 1992 Sheridan Drive, Buffalo, NY 14223-1249, USA.

**NICKERSON Richard Goram,** b. 20 November 1927, Harwich, USA. Organic Polymer Chemist. m. Eileen Florence Tressler, 3 daughters. Education: BS, cum laude, 1950; Phd, 1955; MBA, cum laude, 1983; Postdoctorate, Polytechnical Institute, Brooklyn. Publications: 8 US patents. Memberships: Sigma Xi; Phi Lambda Upsilon; Society of Plastics Engineers; Alpha Chi Sigma. Address: 9 Lyford Road, Hopkinton, MA 01748-1581, USA.

**NICOLAE Avram,** b. 15 Sept 1941, Casimcea-Tulcea, Romania. Engineer. m. Maria Nicolae. Education: Engineer, 1965; DSc, 1979; Qualified Professor, 1990. Appointment: Head, Department of Materials and Equipment for Metallurgical Instruments, Polytechnic University of Bucharest. Publications: Papers in specialist journals: Fonderie, France; Stahl und Eisen, Germany; Bulletin CEM, France; ISIJ International, Japan. Membership: Association of Senior Members International, Brussels. Address: Polytechnic University of Bucharest, Splaiul Independentei 313, 77206 Bucharest 6, Romania.

**NICOLODI Maria,** b. 2 June 1955, Florence, Italy. Physician; Researcher. Education: Laureate, Medicine, Florence University, 1984; Fellowship, Pathophysiology and Therapy of Pain, Rome, 1992; Specialization, Neurology, Pavia, 1994. Appointments: Adjoint Professor, Psychiatry, University of Catania, 1997; Referee Cephalalgia, Journal of International Headache Society; International Consultant, INMED, Santiago, Chile, 1997. Publications: Over 200 articles. Honours: International Greppi Junior Prize, Sydney, Australia, 1989; International Greppi Prize, Toronto, Canada, 1995. Memberships: Italian Society for the Study of Headache; International Headache Society; International Association for the Study of Pain; World Federation of Neurology; Founder, International Club, "Functional Organic and Non-Organic Nociceptive Diseases; General Secretary, Interuniversity Centre of Neurochemistry and Clinical Pharmacology of Idiopathic Headache. Address: Via G C Vanini 17, 50129 Florence, Italy.

**NICU Mihail,** b. 23 March 1937, Bucharest. Professor; Doctor. m. Silvia, 2 dughters. Education: Romanian Academy of Medical Sciences. Appointments: Head of Department, Bioengineering, Politechnical University of Bucharest. Publications: Over 500 papers; 20 books. Memberships: 7 International Associations. Address: Str Drumul Taberei Nr 82/BI, C16 Sc C Et I Apt 103 Sector G, Bucharest, Romania.

**NIETKABUL Sulaiyiman,** b. 15 March 1936, Uluchat County, China. Deputy Director. m. Alima Umet, 3 sons, 2 daughters. Education: National University of China, 1976; School of Central Committee of Communist Party of China, 1983. Appointments: Communist Party of China, 1956; Deputy Secretary, Communist Youth of Uluchat County, 1956; Deputy

Secretary, County Party Commission, 1976; Head of Uluchat County, 1979; Head of Kirghiz Prefecture, 1988; Vice Chair, XPPCC, 1993; Deputy Director, SCPC of Xinjimig, 1998. Memberships: Fourth Xinjiang Party Commission; Deputy to the Seventh National Peoples Congress of China; Delegate to the Party Congress of China; Study Society of Epic Manas of China. Address: The Standing Committee of Peoples Congress, Urmqi 83000, China.

**NIGAM Shyam Behari Lal,** b. 7 April 1924, District Etawah, India. United Nations Adviser. m. Prem Kumari, 2 s. Education: Ma, Economics; MCom, India; PhD, London School of Economics. Appointments: Lecturer, 1945-47; Head, Economics Department, 1951; Assistant Insurance Commissioner, 1952-54; Assistant, Deputy Economic and Statistical Adviser, 1954-57; Secretary, Government of India, Working Group on Unemployment Insurance; Member Secretary, Government of India Jute Enquiry Committee; Joint Director, Director, Indian Economic Service, 1958-63; ILO Manpower Planning Adviser, 1963-69; Regional Manpower Planning Adviser, 1969-72; First Member, 1973; Visiting Fellow, Institute of Development Studies, Sussex, England, 1974; Deputy Chief, ILO Jobs and Skills Programme, 1974-77; Chief, ILO Jobs and Skills Programme for Africa, 1978-84; ILO, UNDP, ADB Consultant, Guest Lecturer, Institute of Applied Manpower Research , Government of India, 1985-. Publications: State Regulation of Minimum Wages; The Utilisation of Manpower in the Public Services in Somalia; The Manpower Situation in Somalia; Employment and Income Distribution Approach in the Economic Development Plans of English Speaking Independent African Countries; Many others. Honours: Government of India Research Scholar, London School of Economics; Listed in many Who's Who Directories. Memberships: Member and Leader ILO/UNDP Employment Advisory Missions to Kenya, Tanzania, Somalia, Sudan, Lesotho, Nigeria, Togo, Sierra Leone, Zambia, Swaziland, Ethiopia; Leader, ILO Delegation to UNDP Conference on Human Resources Development; Leader, Core Group UNDP/ILO Human Resources Project, Malaysia; UNDP/ILO Employment Policy Mission to Papua New Guinea; Many others. Address: K-118 Hauz Khas Enclave, New Delhi 110016, India.

**NIJBAKKER Alexander Godfried Matthijs,** b. 7 June 1955, Naarden. Senior Information Analyst. m. A M J Meulman, 1 s, 2 d. Education: BSc, Electronics, HTS Zwolle; MSc, Knowledge Engineering, Middlesex, 1994; RISc, Registered Information Scientist, 1997; Senior Project Management, 1996; Diploma, Middle Management, 1998. Appointments: Test and Electronics Engineer, Siemens Gamma-Sonics, 1979-81; Design Engineer, Nieaf, 1981-83; Engineering Assistant, IBM Engineering, 1983; Associate Engineer, 1983; Senior Associate Engineer, 1986; Information Analyst, 1987; Senior Information Analyst, IBM Logics Engineering, 1993. Publications: Society for Judgement and Decision Making; Statistical Production Control 1984; Practical Application of Knowledge Management. Honours: Outstanding Technical Achievement Award; Administration Achievment Award; Customer Satisfaction Award. Memberships: AAAI; ACM; APICS; DSI; IEEE; Informs; J/DM; PMI/IPMA; SMA; VRI; Chartered Information Systems Practitioner; Lifetime Fellow, Royal Society of Arts, Manufacturing and Commerce; Lifetime Fellow International Biographical Association; Lifetime Deputy Director General, ABIRA; Lifetime Deputy Governor, IBC; Order of International Ambassadors, ABI. Address: AGM Nijbakker, Vlamoven 18, 3402 SE Ysselstein, Netherlands.

**NIKLUS Mart-Olav,** b. 22 September 1934, Tartu, Republic of Estonia. Pensioner; Freedom Fighter. Education: Graduate,

Biologist, Zoologist, Tartu University, 1957. Appointments: Teacher; Musician; Member of Parliament, 1992-95. Publications: About 12 papers on Ornithology and Nature Conservation; Trial in Vilnius Through the Eyes of an Estonian; Vilnius and the Vilniusites Through the Eyes of a Dissident; Account on Some Events in the National Movement of Estonia; Estonian Independence in Historical Perspective. Honours: Order of Merit, Republic of Estonia; Order of Merit, International Publicity; Prize Winner, Baltic American Freedom League. Memberships: Estonian Naturalists Society; Estonian Ornithological Society; Estonian Fund of Nature; Estonian Freedom Fighters Union; Estonian Union of Former Political Prisoners; Estonian Defence League; Ukrainian Helsinki Watch Group; International Society for Human Rights; International Association of Soviet Political Prisoners. Address: Vikerkaare 25, 51006 Tartu, Estonia.

**NIKOLOVA Svetlina,** b. 1 January 1942, Vratza, Bulgaria. Scientist. m. Ilia Todorov, 1 son. Education: PhD, State University, St Kliment of Ohrid, 1970. Appointments: Senior Research Associate, Cyrillo Methodian Research Centre, Bulgarian Academy of Sciences, 1971-; Director, 1993-. Publications: 150 Publications, Cyrillo methodian Studies, Slavonic Paleography, Old Bulgarian Literature, Medieval Slavic Studies. Memberships: FIBA; Early Slavic Studies Association. Address: Bozhuriste Street 131V/V Apt 53, 1309 Sofia, Bulgaria.

**NIMSOMBOON Nontaphon,** b. 22 February 1944, Bangkok, Thailand. Civil Servant. m. Salisa, 1 daughter. Education: BCom, honour, 1965, BAcct, 1968, Faculty of Commerce and Accountancy, Thammasart University; MBA, University of Iowa, 1972. Appointments: Lecturer, Faculty of Commerce & Accountancy, Thammasart University, 1967; Head of Section, Government Enterprises and Funds Audit Division, Office of the Auditor General of Thailand, 1980; Director of Performance Audit Division, 1985; Director, Regional Office, Chiang Mai, 1990; Assistant Auditor General, 1991; Deputy Auditor General, 1992; Auditor General, 1997-. Publications: Modern Internal Control; Administrative and Financial Accountability in Thailand. Honours: Thai Government Scholarship, 1969; Outstanding Alumni of Thammasart University, 1991. Memberships: President, Institute of Certified Accountants & Auditors of Thailand; Council, ASEAN Federation of Accountants; Executive Committee, Confederation of Asia & Pacific Accountants. Address: Office of the Auditor General of Thailand, Soi Areesampan, Rama 6 Road, Bangkok 10400, Thailand.

**NION Stevie Tsilih Sokou,** b. 26 October 1956, Pohowa Village, Manus Island, Papua New Guinea. Geologist. m. Julie Naba, 2 sons, 3 daughters. Education: BSc, 1978, UPNG; MSc, 1984, Sydney University. Appointments: Director, PNG Geological Survey; Chief Government Geologist. Publications: Geological Survey Reports. Memberships: PNG Association of Geoscientists; Australian Institute of Mining and Metallurgy. Address: Geological Survey Division, Dept of Mineral Resources, Private Mail Bag, Port Moresby NCD, Papua New Guinea.

**NIRANJAN Udipi Cholayya,** b. 11 April 1964, Sholapur, India. Professor. m. Vijayalaxmi. Education: BE, Electronics and Communication, 1985; MTech, Industrial Electronics, 1988; PhD, Electrical Science, 1993. Appointments: Professor, Manipal Institute of Technology, 1986-; Visiting Researcher, Parama Biomonitoring Institute, Japan, 1994, 1996. Publications: Several articles in professional journals. Honours: Winner, IEEE-EMBS Student Paper Competition, Paris, 1992; Young Investigator Award, ISCE, Arizona, USA, 1996.

emberships: IEEE; Biomedical Engineering Society of India. ddress: Jangam Mutt, 576 101 Udupi Karnataka, India.

**NISHIMURA Akitoshi,** b. 14 April 1950, Mie, Japan. esearcher (Physics and Electronics). m. Nori, 1 daughter. Jucation: BS, Kyoto University, 1972; MS, 1974, PhD, 1977, niversity of Tokyo. Appointments: Research Fellow, Glasgow niversity, Scotland, 1977-79; Researcher, High Energy hysics Laboratory, Japan, 1980-83; Technical Staff, Tex struments Japan, 1983-. Publications: 45 in science and chnology journals, 20 patents. Membership: IEEE. Address: ex Instruments Japan, 4-13-23 Shibaura, Minato-ku, Tokyo ●8, Japan.

**NISHIYAMA Misuzu,** b. 15 December 1951, Sapporo, ●pan. Anaesthesiologist. m. Hiroaki Nishiyama, 1 daughter. Jucation: Graduate, Hokkaido University, Sapporo, Japan, )76. Appointments: Resident, Hokkaido University, 1976-77; :aff Anaesthesiologist, St Luke's International Hospital, Tokyo, )86-95; Jikeikai University School of Medicine, 1996-. iblication: Anesthaesiology Resident Manual, 1994. Address: ●09, 2 18 1 Kachidoki, Tokyo, Japan.

**NIVENS Robert Glenn,** b. 15 March 1940, Chelsea, iabama, USA. Retired US Army Officer, Infantry. m. Linda ene Whitfield, 1 son, 2 daughters. Education: BA, 1974, MEd, )75, University of Montevallo. Appointments: US Army nlisted Man, 1957-64, Officer, Infantry, 1964-86, Retired eutenant Colonel, Infantry, 1986. Honours: Vietnam Service edal, Vietnam Campaigne Medal, 1967-70; Combat Infantry adge, Vietnam, 1969; Bronze Star Medal, 1970; Meritorious ervice Medal (3 awards), 1964-86; Army Achievement Medal, )80-86. Address: PO Box 307, Harpersville, AL 35078-0307, SA.

**NIVINSKAS Rimantas Steponas,** b. 5 May 1946, Joniškis, thuania. Scientist. m. Ona Diciũnaite, 1 son, 1 daughter. Jucation: BS Biochemistry, 1968, PhD Genetics, 1973, Habil octor, 1993, Vilnius University; Postgrad student, Institute of iochemistry, Lithuanian Academy of Sciences, 1968-71. ppointments: Junior Researcher, 1971-75, Senior esearcher, 1975-86, Head of Section of Gene Engineering, )86-90, Head of Lab of Gene Engineering, 1990-, Institute of iochemistry, Vilnius. Publications: Author and co-author of ver 100 scientific publications on gene structure, function, and ●e control of gene expression in bacteriophages. Honours: dividual Grant from International Science Foundation, 1993; thuanian State Scholarship of Supreme Level, 1994; ●ternational Research Scholars Grant from Howard Hughes ●edical Institute, 1995. Memberships: Lithuanian Biochemical ociety; Lithuanian Society of Genetics and Breeders. Address: ●stitute of Biochemistry, Mokslininku 12, LT 2600 Vilnius, thuania.

**NO Hee Cheon,** b. 1 April 1954, Pusam, Korea. Professor. ●. Jae Hee No, 3 daughters. Education: BS, 1976, Seoul ●ational University; PhD, 1983, MIT. Appointments: Professor, ept of Nuclear Engineering, KAIST, 1983-. Honours: Cum aude, 1976, Seoul National University; Academy Award, orean Nuclear Society, 1995. Memberships: ANS; ASME; ●NS; National Academy of Engineering of Korea. Address: ●ungdong Yusong-gu, Hanbit 122-1202, Taejon, Korea.

**NOAMESI Gottlieb Kofi,** b. 30 March 1917, Akpafu. cientist (Medicinal Plants Research and Development). m. ●elen Yawa Ikoide, 3 s. Education: MSc, 1956; PhD, Jisconsin, USA, 1958; Diploma, Applied Parasitology and ●ntomology, UK, 1959. Appointments: Research Officer, CSIR. ublications: Scientific Papers in the fields of Botany, Zoology,

Entemology; Transactions of Wisconsin Academy of Sciences; A Rivision of the Xylocarpeae; Bull, Wld, Hid, Org; Many others. Honours: Certificate of Honour, 1981; Africa Award, 1990; International Aurope Award, 1990. Address: Lab/OAU/STRCJP27, P O Box 383, Hohee Volta, Ghana.

**NOBLE Bruce Harvey,** b. 12 September 1937, Brisbane, Queensland, Australia. Catholic Priest. Education: BA, University of Queensland, Brisbane, 1961; ThL (Hons), St Francis Theological College, 1963; Ordained, St John's Anglican Cathedral, 1963; BA, Queen's College, Oxford, 1969; MA (Oxon), 1970; Ordained Catholic Priest, St Mary's Seminary, Houston, 1987. Appointments include: Curacies, Australia, 1963-67, several UK positions, Oxford, Preston, Coventry, 1967-83; International Spiritual Director, Anglican Engaged Encounter, 1983-86; Coordination of Catholic Chaplains, Methodist Hospital, Texas Medical Center, Houston, USA, 1987-; Priest-in-Charge, Our Lady of Walsingham Parish, 1994-96. Publications: Co-author: L J Harvey, the Gentle Humorist, The Australiuan Antique Collector, 46th edition, 1993; A Bed of Peace for Troubled Times: L J Harvey, the State of his Art and the Art of his State; Dynamic Integration from an Oxford Perspective: The Integral Harvey. Honours: Stained Glass Window Commemoration for 12 years of Worldwide Encounter Ministry, 1986; Silver Salver for 15 years service to widowed, divorced and their families, Texas BE, 1997; Plaque for 3 years Voluntary Service as Chaplain Member of St John Fellowship, to The Hospice, Texas Medical Center, 1998. Memberships include: Honorary Chaplain, Flying Angel Club, Port of Preston, 1970-72; Ministry to Commerce, Coventry Industrial Mission, 1975; Co-Curator, Braeswood House Houston, hospitality house and private museum for Australian artist, sculptor and wood carver L J Harvey, 1976-; Board, Houston Episcopal Team Beginning Experience, 1981-86; American Society for Training and Development, 1981-86; Catholic Chaplain Corps, Galveston-Houston Diocese, 1987-; Board, Institute of Worklife Ministry, Houston, 1993-94; President, Houston Oriental Rug Study Society, 1998-. Address: Braeswood House, 2330 Dorrington Boulevard, Houston, TX 77030, USA.

**NOAMESI Benjamin Kwame,** b. 12 February 1944, Ghana. University Lecturer. m. Susanna Noamesi, 1 son, 3 daughters. Education: B.Pharmacy, University of Science and Technology, 1973; M.Pharmacy, 1975; PhD, University Lagos, Nigeria, 1982; Registered Pharmacist, Ghana. Appointments: Demonstrator, University Science and Technology, Kumasi, 1973-75; Research Fellow, 1975-76; Senior Lecturer, 1988-; Lecturer, Illinois University, Lagos Medical College, 1976-78; Lecturer, 1979-82; Senior Lecturer, 1982-87. Publications: Articles to Professional Journals. Honours: Research Grantee. Memberships: New York Academy of Sciences; European Society for Medicinal Plant Research; American Society Pharmacognosy. Address: University of Science and Technology, Pvt Mail Bag, Kumasi Ashanta, Ghana.

**NOBLE David Harvey,** b. 12 September 1937, Brisbane, Queensland, Australia. Catholic Priest. Education: BA, University of Queensland, 1961; ThL Honours, St Francis Theological College, Brisbane, 1963; Ordained, St John's Anglican Cathedral, 1963; STB, General Theological Seminary, New York, 1970; STM, 1972, Ordained Catholic Priest, St Mary's Seminary, Houston, 1987. Appointments: Curate, New York Dioceses: Resurrection, Long Island, 1969-71, St Stephen, Manhattan, 1971-73; Assistant Chaplain, St Hilda and St Hugh's School, New York City, 1971-75; Associate Director, Trinity Institute, Corporation of Trinity Church, Wall Street, New York City, 1971-76; Resource Development Clergy, Marriage, Family and Youth Encounter, 1977-86; Civilian Clergy,

Episcopal Marriage Encounter to US German NATO Bases, 1982-86; Coordinator, Episcopal Team, Beginning Experience for Widowed and Divorced, Texas, 1984-86, Catholic Chaplain Corps, University of Texas M D Anderson Cancer Center, Texas Medical Center, Houston, 1987-; Civilian Catholic Chaplain, HHC 2nd Brigade, 75th Division E, Houston, 1995-; Diocesan Pastor, Deaf Community, 1998-. Publications: Co-author, L J Harvey, the Gentle Humorist, The Australian Antique Collector, 46th edition, 1993; A Bed of Peace for Troubled Times: L J Harvey, the State of his Art and the Art of his State; Dynamic Integration from an Oxford Perspective: the Integral Harvey (Bodleian Library Oxford). Honours: Stained-Glass Window Commemoration, Episcopal Marriage Encounter Community National Board, 1986; Silver Salver Service Award, Texas BE, 1997; Plaque, Service to Texas Medical Center Hospice, 1998. Memberships: Bush Brotherhood of St Paul, Outback, Queensland, 1964-68; American Society for Training and Development, 1984-85; Catholic Chaplain Corps, Galveston-Houston Diocese, 1987-; Librarian-Historian, Houston Oriental Rug Study Society, 1998; President, Textile Oriental Rug Club of Houston, 1998-. Address: Braeswood House, 2330 Dorrington Blvd, Old Braeswood, Houston, TX 77030, USA.

**NOBLE Weston H,** b. 30 November 1922, Riceville, Iowa. Professor of Music. Education: BA, 1943, Luther College; MM, 1953, University of Michigan; Hon Doctorate: Augustana College, Sioux Falls, South Dakota, 1971, St Olaf, Northfield, Minnesota, 1996. Appointments: Director of Band and Choir, Luverne High School, Iowa, 1946-48; Professor of Music, Music Dept, Luther College, Decorah, 1948-. Honours: First Recipient, Outstanding Music Educator of the United States, National Federation of High School Association; First Recipient, Weston H Noble Award for Lifetime Achievement in the Choral Art; Citation of Merit Award, University of Michigan; Presidential Award, Illinois Music Educators Association; St. Olaf Medallion from King of Norway; Robert Lawson Shaw Citation from American Choral Directors Association; Judge Henry and Helen Graven Award, given to an Outstanding Layperson whose life is nurtured by a strong sense of Christian Calling and who is making a significant contribution to community, church and society; Guest Director of over 800 music festivals in 48 states; Director over 50 All-State bands, choirs and orchestras; 8 concert tours of Europe; Conducted wide number of groups and Guest Adjudicator throughout Europe and Australia; Currently celebrating 51 years of teaching at Luther College; and others. Address: 602 Mound, Apt #4, Decorah, IA 52101, USA.

**NODA Nao-Aki,** b. 25 December 1956, Bisai City, Japan. Mechanical Engineering Researcher; Educator. m. Kaoru Noda, 1 son, 1 daughter. Education: B Engineering, 1979, M Engineering, 1981, Kyushu Institute of Technology, Kitakyusha, Japan; PhD Engineering, 1984, Kyushu University, Fukuoka, Japan. Appointments: Assistant Professor, 1984-87, Associate Professor, 1987-, Kyushu Institute of Technology; Visiting Professor, Lehigh University, Pennsylvania, USA, 1985-86. Honours: Fellow, Japanese Ministry of Education and Science, 1985-86; Honorary Professor, Shandong University of Technology, China, 1996. Memberships: Japan Society of Mechanical Engineers; Japan Society Material Sciences. Address: 1-2-37 Kawanaka-yutakamachi, Shimonoseki 751, Japan.

**NOGAMI Takashi,** b. 10 February 1943, Niigata Prefecture, Japan. Professor. m. Yumiko Kawamura, 1 daughter. Education: DSc, 1971, University of Tokyo. Appointments: Research Associate, Assistant Professor, Associate Professor, Osaka University; Professor, University Electro-Communications, Chofugaoka; Visiting Professor of

Institute for Molecular Science. Publications: About 14 research papers, 1969-. Memberships: Chemical Society of Japan; Polymer Science of Japan. Address: University of Electro-communications, Chofugaoka, Chofu, Tokyo 182-8585 Japan.

**NOLAN Patricia,** b. 15 January 1963, San Mateo, California Systems Engineer. m. Bryan Christopher Nolan, 2 sons Education: AAAS Music & Video Business, 1989; BAA Applied Technology Training and Development, 1995 Appointments: Airline Accounting Manager; Audio Marketing Producer; Instructional Media Producer; Systems Engineer and Distance Education Developer. Memberships: National Association of Female Executives; World Methodist Council Address: 504 N 3rd Street, Krum, TX 76249, USA.

**NOMURA Junji,** b. 10 April 1947, Kagawa, Japan. Engineer m. Mie, 3 sons, 1 daughter. Education: BS, Department of Electronics, 1971, DEng, 1988, Kyoto University Appointments: Research Engineer, 1971, Director, System Development Center, Research and Development, Matsushita Electric Works Ltd. Publication: Virtual Reality, 1997. Honour Excellent Application Award, Operations Research Society of Japan, 1986. Memberships: Virtual Reality Society of Japan Operations Research Society of Japan. Address: 1-16-15 Tamade-Nishi, Osaka 557, Japan.

**NOMURA Kaneo,** b. 9 June 1935, Tokyo, Japan. Guest Professor, Tokyo National University of Fine Arts and Music Diplomatic Architect, Japan. Appointments: Isoya Yoshida Architect and Associates, Tokyo, 1958-60; Diplomatic Architect Japan Ministry of Foreign Affairs, Rome, 1960-63; Principle Associate, 1963-73, Principle, 1974-77, Architect Kaneo Nomura, Architect & Associates, Tokyo, 1978-; Guest Professor, Tokyo National University of Fine Arts & Music 1993-. Honours: Recipient Gold Medal Kanagawa Architectura Contest, Japan, 1980, 1982, 1984; Architectural Designer Shigeru Yoshida Memorial Hall, 1987; Mitsukoshi Museum 1991; Gold Medal, Italian Marble Architectural Awards, 1992 Japanese Ambassador's Residence, Columbia, 1996; Public Residence Imperial Highnesses, Prince and Princess Akishinomiya, 1998-. Memberships: Japanese Institute of Architects (Corp); Architectural Institute Architects (Corp); The Japan-Italy Association; Kyoto Traditional Association of Architecture. Address: 15-13 Nishimagome 1 Chome, Ohta-ku Tokyo 143-0026, Japan.

**NOMURA Taisei,** b. 11 February 1942, Nagoya City, Japan Professor and Chairman. m. Ikuko Nomura, 4 sons. Education MD, Medicine, 1967, PhD, Medical Science, 1974, Osaka University. Appointments: Professor, Faculty of Medicine Osaka University, 1987-; Professor, Radiation Biology Center Kyoto University, 1988-92. Publications: Nature, 1975, 1976 1982, 1990, 1993. Honours: Prix Isabelle Decazes, 1978; Inoue Prize, 1991; Osaka Science Prize, 1992; Kihara Memoria Prize, 1993; Etoh Memorial Award, 1994. Memberships Japanese Association for Cancer Research; Genetics Society of America; American Association for Cancer Research; Japan Radiation Research Society; Japan Society of Environmental Science. Address: Department Radiation Biology, Osaka University Faculty of Medicine, B4, 2-2 Yamadaoka Suita-sh Osaka 565-0781, Japan.

**NORBECK Jack C.** Education: University of Connecticut Ratcliffe Hicks School of Agriculture, 1964; Opticians Institute Dale Carnegie. Appointment: President, Norbeck Research 1978-. Publication: Author, The Encyclopedia of American Steam Traction Engines; 44 magazine covers; over 6 magazine articles. Honours: International Man of the Year ternational Biographical Centre, Cambridge; Winner, umerous medals. Memberships: Historical Steam ssociations; American Society of Agricultural Engineers; The uthor's Guild; Union Historical Fire Society; YMCA; American egion; USA Gymnastics. Address: 117N Ruch Street, 8 oplay, PA 18037 1712, USA.

**NORCROSS John C,** b. 13 August 1957, New Jersey, USA. rofessor; Psychologist. m. Nancy A Caldwell, 1 son, 1 aughter. Education: BA, Rutgers University, 1990; MA, niversity of Rhode Island, 1981; PhD, University of Rhode sland, 1984; Internship, Brown University School of Medicine, 985. Appointments: Staff Clinician, University of Rhode Island, 980-84; Psychology Instructor, University of Rhode Island, 984; Clinical Psychologist, Private Practice, 1986-; hairperson, Department of Psychology, University of cranton, 1987-93; Assistant Professor, University of Scranton, 985-88; Associate Professor, University of Scranton, 1988-90; rofessor, University of Scranton, 1990-. Handbook of Eclectic sychotherapy, 1986; Casebook of Eclectic Psychotherapy, 987; Therapy Wars, 1990; A Dialogue with John Norcross, oward Integration, 1991; Handbook of Psychotherapy tegration, 1992; Changing for Good, 1995, Insider's Guide to iraduate Programs in Counseling and Clinical Psychology, 997; Systems of Psychotherapy, 1998; Psychologist's Desk eference, 1998 More than 150 other publications relating to sychotherapy. Honours: Jack D Krasner Memorial Award, 992; Professor of the Year, 1992; President, APA Division of sychotherapy, 2000. Memberships: American Psychological ssociation; Association for the Advancement of Psychology; merican Association of University Professors; Eastern sychological Association; Society for Psychotherapy esearch. Address: 300 Spangenberg Road, Lake Ariel, PA 8436, USA.

**NORLANDER Torsten Georg,** b. 8 August 1950, othenburg, Sweden. Leacturer; Researcher. m. Anne Sofie lorlander, 1 son. Education includes: PhD, 1997. Appointment: lead of Psychology Department, Karlstad University. Address: Jepartment of Pyschology, Karlstad University, S-651 88 arlstad, Sweden.

**NORMANTAS Valentinas,** b. 3 November 1941, 'anevezys, Lithuania. English and German Teacher; Chess oach. m. Zenona Jursyte, deceased, 1 daughter. Education: iraduated in foreign languages from Pedagogical Institute 'ilnius, 1965. Appointments: Worker, road building Dept, 1 silute, 1957-60; Military Service, 1966-70; Interpreter, omputer Design Office, Vilnius, 1970-71; Various ppointments, Chess sports school, Vilnius, 1971-. Honours: CF (correspondence chess) International grandmaster, 1996; nternational master, 1992; 34th European Champion, 1994; JSSR Champion, 1984, Vice Champion, 1987 with the team of .ithuania at the 7th and 8th USSR Team Championships; Top orrespondence Chess Player of Lithuania, 1992-; Ranked mong 40 best players on yearly ratings lists of ICCF, 1992-99. lembership: Deputy President, Lithuanian Correspondence hess Federation, 1995-. Address: Zerucio 20-37, LTU-2043 'ilnius, Lithuania.

**NORO Yoshio Hayashi,** b. 2 August 1925, Tokyo, Japan. heological Educator; Writer. m. Ruth Komatsu, 2 sons, 3 laughters. Education: Keio University Law School, 1942-45; okyo Union Theological Seminary, 1945-48; BD, 1952, Drew heological Seminary; ThD, 1955, Union Theological Seminary; loctor of Literature, 1970, Kyoto University. Appointments: ecturer, Aoyama Gakuin University, 1956-57; Associate rofessor, 1957-62, Professor, 1962-72, Dean of School of iterature, Aoyama Gakuin University, 1969-71; Professor,

Rikkyo University, Tokyo, Chairman of Dept Theology, Graduate School, 1984-91. Publications: John Wesley, 1963; AnExistentialist Theology, 1964; Life and Theology of John Wesley, 1975; Christianity and Japanese Popular Religions, 1991. Memberships: Society of Christian Studies in Japan; Trustee 1980-82, Minister of United Church of Christ. Address: 3 21 13 Midori-cho, Akishima-shi, Tokyo 196 0004, Japan.

**NORTON Eunice,** b. 30 June 1908, Minneapolis, Minnesota, USA. Pianist. m. Bernard Lewis, 4 1934, 1 son. Education: Music student, University of Minnesota, 1922-24; Tobias Matthay Pianoforte School, London, 1924-31; Schnabel Master Piano Classes, Germany, 1931-33; Artur Schnabel Master Piano Classes, Berlin, Italy, 1933. Career: Concert Pianist, USA, Europe, 1927-; Soloist, many symphony orchestras including New York Philharmonic, Boston, Philadelphia, Pittsburgh, Minneapolis, London and Berlin Symphony Orchestras, orchestras in Leipzig, Germany, Vienna, Austria, Birmingham and Manchester, England; Chamber Musician, Budapest, Juilliard and Griller String Quartets, American Chamber Orchestra; Performed all Beethoven piano sonatas, Carlow College, 1983, University of Pittsburgh, 1988; Visiting Professor of Piano, Lecturer, Carnegie Mellon University; Lecturer, University of Pittsburgh; Lecturer, Master Class Conductor, other universities; Conductor, private master classes, Pittsburgh, New York, Washington DC, Vermont; Director, Peacham Piano Festival, Vermont; Founder, Director, Pittsburgh New Friends of Music and Concert Artists of Pittsburgh; 4 video lectures on the teaching of Artu Schnabel; President, Norvald Records Inc, Classic CDs. Publications: Recordings: Well-tempered Clavier, Bach; 1988 performance of Beethoven Piano Sonatas; The Teaching of Tobias Matthey, 4 illustrated lectures, video, 1995; Complete piano repertoire on CDs include Bach's 48 Preludes and Fugues and 32 Beethoven Sonatas, 1995. Honours: Bach Prize, 1927; Chappell Gold Medal, Chappel Piano Co, London, 1928; Honorary Doctor of Music, Wooster College, 1997. Memberships: Founder Member, American Matthay Piano Association; Sigma Alpha Iota; Honorary Member, Tuesday Musical Club, Pittsburgh. Address: 5863 Marlborough Avenue, Pittsburgh, PA 15217-1415, USA.

**NORTON Jay,** b. 26 November 1968, Olathe, Kansas, USA. Attorney. m. Katherine. Education: Bachelor of Arts, English Literature, University of Kansas, 1991; Juris Doctorate, University of Kansas School of Law, 1994. Appointments: Partner, Erker and Moore, LLC. Memberships: National College for Dui Defence; Kansas Association of Criminal Defence Lawyers. Address: 4221 Oak St, Kansas City, MO 64111-1616, USA.

**NOSSAL Gustav Joseph Victor,** b. 4 June 1931, Bad Ischl, Austria. Professor Emeritus. m. Lyn Beatrix Dunnicliff, 2 sons, 2 daughters. Education: BSc, Medical, 1952, BMed and Surgery, 1954, University of Sydney; PhD, University of Melbourne, 1960. Appointments: Junior, Senior Resident Officer, Royal Prince Alfred Hospital, Sydney, 1955-56; Research Fellow, 1957-79, Deputy Director, Immunology, 1961-65, Director, 1965-96, The Walter and Eliza Hall Institute of Medical Research; Assistant Professor, Department of Genetics, Stanford University School of Medicine, California, 1959-61; Professor, Department of Medical Biology, University of Melbourne, 1965-96, Professor Emeritus, 1996-. Publications include: Antibodies and Immunity, 1968; Antigens, Lymphoid Cells and the Immune Response, 1971; Medical Science and Human Goals, 1975; Nature's Defences, 1978; Reshaping Life: Key Issues in Genetic Engineering, 1984. Honours include: Knight Bachelor, 1977; Companion of the Order of Australia in the General Division, 1989; OBE, 1970; Emil von Behring Prize,

Philipps University, Marburg, West Germany, 1971; Rabbi Shai Shacknai Memorial Prize, Israel, 1973; James Cook Medal, Royal Society of New South Wales, 1995. Honours include: Australian Academy of Science; US National Academy of Science; Indian National Science Academy; New York Academy of Medicine; American Association of Immunologists. Address: Department of Pathology, University of Melbourne, Parkville, Victoria 3052, Australia.

**NOVAK Joseph Anthony,** b. 8 February 1964, Detroit, USA. Librarian. Education: AA, Macomb Community College, 1984; BA, Oakland University, 1986; JD, Detroit College of Law, Michigan State University, 1991; MLIS, Wayne State University, 1998. Appointments: Intern, Wayne County Public Defender's Office, Detroit, 1986; Detroit Recorder's Court Office of Judicial Assistance, 1993; Law Clerk, Wayne County Circuit Court Judge Diane M Hathaway, 1996. Honours: Outstanding Volunteer Vita Tax Assistance Program, Detroit, Michigan, 1995,1996, 1998; Spirit of America is in the Hearts of its Volunteers, 1995, 1996, 1997. Memberships: American Association of Law Libraries; Special Libraries Association; Accounting Aid Society. Address: 36874 Myra Ct, Sterling Heights, MI 48312-3272, USA.

**NOVICKAS Julijus,** b. 26 July 1944, Panevezys. Engineer; Economist. m. Nadiezda Novickiene, 1 daughter. Education: Professor, habilit Dr Social Science, 1968, Kaunas Technological University. Appointments: Professor, Kaunas University of Technology, 1975-; Director, Lithuanian Information Institute, 1988-97; Secretary of Ministry governing Reforms and Local Government Affairs of Lithuania, 1994-97. Publications: Over 100 articles, several books, about technical innovation, information policy in Lithuania. Membership: Lithuanian Economists Association. Address: Rudens 4-26, LT 2055 Vilnius, Lithuania.

**NOVICKIENE Nadiezda,** b. 8 October 1951, Poltava, Ukraine. Banker. m. Julijus Novickas, 1 daughter. Education: Kharkov Politechnical Institute, 1969-75; Doctor Social Sciences, 1985, Kaunas Politechnical Institute. Appointments: Office worker different companies and organisations, 1975-82; Assistant, Kaunas Polytechnic Institute, 1982-85; Head Deputy Chairperson, Lithuanian Board of the USSR Bank of Construction, 1986-88; First Deputy Chairperson, Lithuanian Bank of the USSR Bank of Industry and Construction, 1988-90; Chairperson, Naujamiestis Division of Bank of Lithuania, 1990-91; Chairperson of Executive Committee, HERMIS Bank, 1991-. Publications: 4 books and brochures; 20 research studies and publications. Membership: Vilnius Club. Address: Rudens 4-26, LT 2000 Vilnius, Lithuania.

**NOVOA HECKEL German,** b. 1 March 1951, Mexico. Medical Director; Physician. m. Laura E Chavez, 1 daughter. Education: MD, 1976, National University Mexico City; Biostatistics, 1981, Clinical Pharmacology, 1993, with Medal and Recognition Award, UNAM; Diploma Business Administration, 1989, ICAM1; Diploma Marketing, 1997, ITAM. Appointments: Chief of Research, Boehringer Mannheim, Mexico City, 1980-81; Assistant to Medical Director, CIBA-GEIGY, Mexico City, 1982-87; Medical Director, Parke-Davis, Mexico City, 1987-. Publications: Editor and co-author 1 book chapter and book on Parmaceutical Medicine; Preparation and monitoring of trials and publications of 8 articles in specialised magazines; 8 other publications related to pharmaceutical medicine. Honours: President, Pharmaceutical Physicians Association, 1991-92; Fellow, Faculty of Pharmaceutical Medicine, FFPM, 1998. Memberships: AMEIFAC (Physicians in the Pharmaceutical Industry); New York Academy of Sciences; AMEFAR, Mexican

Association of Pharmacology; Faculty of Pharmaceutical Medicine, UK. Address: Arbol del Fuego 77-04, 04380 Mexico City, Mexico.

**NOVOPASHIN Mikhail,** b. 29 April, Sakha, Russia. Mechanical Engineer. m. Marianna Novopashina, 1 son, 1 daughter. Education: Diploma, Riga Flying University, 1968; Candidate of Technical Sciences, 1972; Doctor, Technical Sciences, 1989; Professor Degreem, 1991; Academician, Academy of Sciences, Sakha, 1995. Career: Principal, Mining Institute, North of the Siberian Branch, Russian Academy of Sciences. Publications: Raising of last Quality of Bearing Constructions of Career Dump Trucks; Eleastic Plastic Deformations and Maximum Conditions Element of Constructions with Concentration Tension. Membership: Academy of Sciences, Sakha. Address: United Institute for Physico-Technical Problems of Northern Territories, Siberian Division, Russian Academy of Sciences, 1 Oktyabrskaya Str, Yakutsk 7, 677077 Russia.

**NOVOSAD Jan,** b. 12 June 1930, Zlin, Czech Republic. Chemical Engineer. m. Alena Seifertova, 1 son, 1 daughter. Education: Prague Technical University, 1951; PhD, Czech Academy of Sciences, 1962. Appointments: Head, Research Group, Czech Academy of Sciences, 1961-91; Executive Secretary, Czech Society of Chemical Engineering, 1991-. Publications: Book, Mechanics of Particulate Solids, 1983; 39 original contributions in scientific journals. Membership: European Federation of Chemical Engineering, Chairman, Working Party on the Mechanics of Particulate Solids, 1971-, Member, Executive Board, 1996-. Address: Krohova 2212, 160 00 Praha, Czech Republic.

**NOWOK Jan W,** b. 15 June 1941, Poland. Research Scientist. m. Janina, 2 daughters. Education: MS, Silesian University, Katowice, Poland; PhD, Academy of Mining and Metallurgy, Cracow, Poland. Appointments: Dept of Solid State Physics, Polish Academy of Science, Zabrze, Poland, 1966-73; Senior Research Scientist, Silesian Polytechnical School, Katowice, Poland, 1973-82; Research Scientist, University of North Dakota, Grand Forks, USA, 1982-. Publications: Over 90 publications. Memberships: Materials Research Society; American Ceramic Society. Address: 815 Duke Drive #430, Grand Forks, ND 58201, USA.

**NUNEZ DE ARCO Jorge,** b. 23 April 1950, La Paz, Bolivia. Psychiatrist. m. Maria Dolores Valenzuela, 2 sons. Education: MS Biology, 1973; MD, 1979; Degree in Psychology, 1988; PhD, 1991; Professor Assistant Biology, 1973-75, Bolivia; Professor Psychobiology, 1985, Spain; Associate Professor Psychobiology, 1986-88; Professor Human Ecology, 1994-96, Spain. Appointments: Psychiatrist, 1981, Sevilla; Hospital America, 1982-84; Hospital Valme Sevilla, 1985-91; Chief of Area Psychiatric; Official Psychiatry Penitentiary Psychiatry, Ministry of Justice, 1991-94; Chief Psychiatry, Santa Isabel Clinic, Sevilla, 1995-98. Publications: Evaluation y Percepcion Paisases on Ninos en Situacion Quirurgica., 1993; Contributor of articles to professional journals. Honour: Honorary Consul of Bolivia. Memberships: APA; Royal Medical College, Sevilla; American Neurological Science Society; American Association of Study of Mental Retardation. Address: Avenue Republica Argentina 22A, Seville, Spain.

**NUSEIBEH Taj-Ul-Deen,** b. 15 September 1933, Jerusalem, Israel. Occupational Safety Adviser. m. Amal Hasan Nuseibeh, 2 sons, 2 daughters. Education: BSc, Mathematics and Physics, East Texas State College, 1958; BSc, Mechanical Engineering, Oklahoma State University, 1960. Appointments: Mechanical Engineer, Ministry of National Economy, 1961-62;

Safety Engineer, Ministry of Social Affairs and Labour, 1962-71; Consultant Engineer, Ministry of Health, 1971-72; Consultant Maintenance Engineer, Ministry of Public Work, 1972-73; Occupational Safety Advisor, Ministry of Labour, 1973-83; Mechanical Maintenance Engineer, Ministry of Water Authority and Irrigation, 1985-86. Publications: Several articles in professional journals on safety subjects. Memberships: Jordan Engineers Association; American Society of Mechanical Engineers; Institution of Occupational Safety and Health, England; American Conference of Governmental Industrial Hygienists; Jordan Society for the Prevention of Road Accidents; Jordan Environmental Society. Address: Dahayat El-Rabeya, PO Box 950 280, Amman 11195, Jordan.

**NWA Willia L,** b. 20 July, Chicago, Illinois, USA. Educator. m. Umoh Nwa, 2 sons, 3 daughters. Education: BS, Education/Psychology, 1971; MS, Educatgion, 1975; PhD, Education, 1992. Appointments: Educator, Northeastern Local Schools, Ohio, 1971-75; Canton City Schools, 1975-; Supervisor, University of Akron, Ohio, 1989-; Summer Lecturer, Sonoma State University, California, 1992-96; Adjunct Professor, Malone College, Ohio, 1997-. Publications: Extracurricular Activities with Exceptional Children, 1992; Article, Magazine Activities, 1996. Honours: Charles S Seelback and Alice A White Scholarships; Grant Recipient, Kurdziel Foundation, Impact 11, Edith and Helen Rank Charitable Trust, Pi Lambda Theta, Educational Enhancement Parternship; Outstanding Contribution in Education, Council for Exceptional Children, 1992; Outstanding Educator, Pi Lambda Theta, 1995; Inductee, YMCA Stark County Women's Hall of Fame, Education category, 1998; Nominee, Teacher of the Year, Canton Regional Chamber of Commerce, 1998. Memberships: Kappa Delta Phi; Pi Lambda Theta; Malone College Advisory Board; Association of Supervision and Curriculum Development; American Education Research Association; National Education Association; American Association of University Women; National Alliance of Black School Educators; Ohio Education Association State Superintendent's Task Force; Council for Exceptional Children. Address: Canton City Schools, 521 Tuscarawas-West Canton, OH 44702, USA.

# O

**O'BRIEN Peter L,** b. Australia. Company Executive. m. 3 children. Education: LLB, BCom, LLM, Queensland University; MBA, Australian Graduate School of Management, University of NSW, presently enrolled. Appointments: Business Development Manager, Defiance Mills Ltd, 1985-90; Corporate/Commercial Lawyer, Phillips Fox Lawyers, 1990-93; Executive Manager-Business Strategy, TNT Ltd, 1994-96; Director, Defiance Holdings Ltd, 1996-97; Executive Member, Nudgee College Management Committee, 1997-99; National Supply Chain Strategy Leader, Appointed by Federal Govt, 1998; Principal Consultant, PricewaterhouseCoopers Consultants, numerous Pricewaterhouse Coopers Management Committees including the National Supply Chain Committee and the National Strategy and Marketing Group, 1996-99; General Manager, Global Strategy and Costing, DHL Worldwide Express, Global Headquarters, Belgium, 1999-; Chairman, DHL Worldwide Express Global Costing Review Board, 1999-. Publications: 4 papers in professional journals. Honours: 3 academic awards including: The W Carlton-Smith Memorial Trophy for Conduct, Character, Leadership, Study and Sport, Nudgee College, Queensland. Memberships: Solicitor, High Court of Australia and Supreme Court of NSW, Queensland and Victoria; Barrister, Supreme Court of Victoria; American Management Association; Australia Institute of Management; Securities Institute of Australia; Logistics Management Association of Australia; Australian Institute of Management Consultants. Address: DHL Worldwide Express, Global Co-ordination Centre, Industriepark, Diegem-Zuid, De Kleet, De Kleetlaan 1, 1831 Diegem, Belgium.

**O'HARA Hiroshi,** b. 9 Sept 1952, Tokyo, Japan. Medical Doctor. m. Narumi Ishikawa. Education: Bachelor of Medicine, MD, Hiroshaki University, 1978; PhD, Diploma as Expert in Tropical Medicine, University of Tokyo, 1982. Appointments: Associate Professor, Saitama Medical School, 1985-92; Chief Medical Adviser, Japan Overseas Cooperation Volunteers, 1993-94; Team Leader, Medical Education Project, Nepal, 1995-96; Senior Medical Expert, International Medical Centre of Japan, 1996-. Publications: Infectious diseases and changing environment in Nepal, 1996; Prophylaxis of hepatitis in developing countries, 1997; Standard Textbook of Internal Medicine, 1999. Memberships: American Society of Tropical Medicine and Hygiene; International Society of Travel Medicine. Address: 1-41-11 Ishiharamachi, Kawagoe, Saitama 350, Japan.

**OAKES Ellen Ruth,** b. 19 August 1919, Bartlesville, USA. Clinical Psychology. 1 son, 2 daughters. Education: Scholarship in Human Relations, University of Concinnati, 1959; BA, Oklahoma City University, 1961; MS, University of Oklahoma, 1963; PhD, University of Oklahoma, 1967. Appointments: Psychotherapist, 1963-93; Assistant Professor, OU Medical School, 1967-70; Co Founder, Director, Timberridge Institute for Children, 1970-90; President, 1980-90; Private Practice, Edmond, 1990-92. Publications: Investigation of Male Pigeon Mate Choices as Influenced by Early Experiences; The Determinants of Social Status in a Colony of Female Macaca Speciosa; Tieing Between Stup Tailed Macaques During Mating; Understanding Parent Child Disturbances, Intensive Experience in Pastoral Counseling for Pastors; Critique of How to Raise a Human Being. Honours: Oklahoma State Honour Society and Letter D Award; Honorary Woodrow Wilson Scholar, 1960; Elected to OUC Advisory Council by Professors; Graduated Summa cum laude; Pioneering Psychologist, Certificate of Appreciation.

Memberships: American Psychological Association; Oklahoma Psychological Association; Oklahoma State Board of Examiners of Psychologists; Peer and Standards Review Committee; Southwestern Psychological Association. Address: 15821 Napa Ridge, Edmond, OK 73013-1420, USA.

**OBELIENIUS Vidmantas,** b. 28 September 1951, Kaunas, Lithuania. Doctor. m. Diana Kuzmickaite, 1 son, 1 daughter. Education: MD, Kaunas Medical University, 1974; PhD, Prague Institute for Clinical and Experimental Medicine, 1981; Doctor Habilis, Kaunas Medical Unviersity, 1991. Appointments: Surgeon, Kaunas Clinics, Lithuania, 1974-78; Postgraduate, Clinic of Experimental Medicine, Prague, 1978-81; Research Secretary, Kaunas Medical Institute, 1981-90; Director General, Kaunas Medical Centre, 1990-97; Director, Ilsanta Ltd, Vilnius, 1997-. Publications: Cardioendoscopic Laser Surgery for Cardiac Arrythmias Lasers Surgery Medicine, 1986. Memberships: Lithuanian Medical Association; Lithuanian Association for Social Adaptation. Address: P Dovydaicio 36, LT 3005 Kaunas, Lithuania.

**OBOT Patrick,** b. 5 May 1966, Anua. Manufacturing Engineer. m. Maria P Obot, 1 son, 1 daughter. Education: Master of Science, Advaced Manufacturing, 1998; Higher Technician Diploma, Mechanical Engineering, 1992. Appointments: Process Engineer. Memberships: The American Society of Mechanical Engineering. Address: 4 Seychell Bldg, Wilga St, Luqa, LQA 04, Malta.

**OBREGON Octavio,** b. 19 December 1945, Mexico City. Researcher in Theoretical Physics. m. 1 daughter. Education: BS Diploma, National Autonomous University, Mexico City, 1969; Dr Rer Nat, Konstanz University, Germany, 1973. Appointments: Research Professor, Department of Physics, Met U, Mexico City, 1974-92; Head, Department Physics, 1986-90; Researcher, Professor, Institute of Physics, Guanajuato, Leon, 1992-; Director, Institute of Physics, 1994-2000; Director, Latin American Center of Physics, Mexico, 1994. Memberships: Fellow, Mexican Academy of Sciences, member, International Society on General Relativity on Gravitations; American Physical Society. Address: Loma della Sauz No 203, 37150 Leon, Guanajuanto, Mexico.

**OBRETENOV Valentin,** b. 2 July 1950, Drianovo, Bulgaria. Educator. m. Diana Obretenova, 2 sons. Education: MSc, 1973, PhD, 1982, Technical University of Sofia; Specialization, Energy Institute, Moscow, 1979. Appointments: Designer, Institute for Building, 1973-75; Assistant, 1976-85, Associate Professor, 1985-, Technical University of Sofia; Visiting Professor, Nuclear Energy Institute, 1986-89; Consultant, National Electrical Company, 1984-, Electroimpex AS, 1990-. Publications: 87 papers, 6 books, 3 inventions in the field of hydraulic machines and hydropower. Membership: Association of Science & Technology, 1988-. Address: Technical University, 1756 Sofia, Bulgaria.

**OCAMPO Larry,** b. 23 May 1959, San Miguel, Bulacan. Philippines. Social Worker. m. Vilma Alberto, 2 sons, 1 daughter. Education: BA, 1983; BSc Social Work, 1992. Appointments: Social Worker, Dept Social Welfare and Development (DSWD). Honour: Commendation Award from DSWD Region III, 1998. Membership: Associate member, Philippine Association of Social Workers. Address: DSWD Mt Pinatubo Commission, No 1 Salangan San Miguel, Bulacan, Philippines.

**OCHIAI Shinya,** b. 6 June 1935, Kofu City, Japan. Process Control Engineer. m. Hisako Ochiai, 1 daughter. Education: BSME, Waseda University, Japan, 1960; MSME, Rice

University, Houston, Texas, 1962; PhD, Purdue University, West Lafayette, Indiana, 1966. Appointments: Instrumentation Development Engineer, 1965-68, Senior Process Systems Engineer, 1968-74, Engineering Associate, 1974-90, Senior Engineering Associate, 1990-, Celanese. Publications: 19 on automatic control. Honours: Schuck Best Paper Award, American Control Conference, 1974. Memberships: Fellow, Instrument Society of America; AIChE; Japanese Society of Instrument Control Engineers. Address: Celanese, Box 9077, Corpus Christi, TX 78469, USA.

**ODURO Daniel Boahne,** b. 12 July 1939, Mampong, Ghana. Minister of Religion. m. Margaret Oduro, 2 sons, 2 daughters. Education: Marine Engineer (Chartered), 1971; DipTheol, 1982. Appointments: Marine Engineer Officer, Ghana Navy, Afloat 1967-76, Ashore 1976-79, Headquarters 1979-80; District Pastor, 1982-. Publications: Several professional articles. Honours: 4 Military Medals. Membership: Institute of Marine Engineers, England. Address: Presbyterian Church, PO Box 129, Cape Coast, Ghana.

**OFOEFULE Sabinus Ifeanyi,** b. 22 September 1960, Orlu, Imostate, Nigeria. Pharmacist. m. Akuzuo Uwaoma, 1 son. Education: BPharm, 1988; MPharm, 1991; PhD, 1997. Appointments: Internee Pharmacist, Faculty of Pharmaceutical Sciences, University of Nigeria, Nsukka, 1988-89; National Youth Service Corps (NYSC) Superintendent Pharmacist, Christian Health Centre, Ilesa, Nigeria, 1989-90; Superintendent Pharmacist, Couple Pharmacy, Maiduguri, Nigeria, 1990-93; Lecturer II, 1993-97, Senior Lecturer, 1997-, Department of Pharmaceutical Technology and Industrial Pharmacy, University of Nigeria, Nsukka; Acting Head of Department, Department of Pharmaceutical Technology and Industrial Pharmacy, April to July 1998. Publications: Research articles in international journals in pharmacy, medicine and related fields. Honours: Best MPharm graduate, Faculty of Pharmaceutical Sciences, University of Nigeria, 1991; Bashir-Thomas Research Foundation Award, 1996; Biodata in Marquis Who's Who in the World. Memberships: Pharmaceutical Society of Nigeria (MPSN); National Association of Academic Pharmacists (MNAAP); New York Academy of Sciences; Associate Member, Bioencapsulation Research Group (AMBERG); Consultant, Biopharmaceutics and Pharmacokinetics Research Units, Nsukka and Nnewi. Address: University of Nigeria, Nsukka, Department Pharm Tech, Nsukka Enugu, Nigeria.

**OFOSU-MENSAH Samuel,** b. November 1935, Ghana. Reverend Minister. m. Janet, 5 sons, 2 daughters. Education: Presbyterian Seminary, 1960; Trinity College, Legon, 1967; Billy Graham School of Evangelism, Canada. Appointments: Evangelist, 1961-63; Full Time Ministry, 1967-. Honours: Presbyterial Youth Worker, 1967-78; 1st Presbytery Chairman, Asante Akyem, 1989-94. Memberships: Ghana Red Cross, 1950. Address: Presbyterian Church, Asankrangwa, Ghana.

**OGAH Gabriel Okhaisimhape,** b. 3 July 1954, Fugar, Nigeria. Medical Doctor. m. Celina Onotse Gbaghidi, 2 sons, 2 daughters. Education: MB BS, 1978, University of Ibadan; FWACS, 1987; Residency in Surgery, Ahmadu Bello University Hospital, 1980-87; Postgraduate Surgery Course, University of Edinburgh, 1987. Appointments: Senior Registrar Urology, Abu Hospital, 1985-87; Consultant Urologist, Nigerian National Petroleum Corporation, 1991-; Medical Director, Ogah Hospital, Lagos, 1991-. Publication: Book: For Everyman, 1995. Honours: Fellow, Association of General and Private Medical Practitioners of Nigeria, 1998; Chairman's Award, NYSC, Nigeria, 1979. Memberships: President, Association of General and Private Medical Practitioners of Nigeria, 1998; Nigerian

Association of Urological Surgeons, 1994; Fellow, West African College Surgeons. Address: Ogah Hospital Box 252, 18B Salvation Rd Opebi, Ikeja Lagos, Nigeria.

**OGAWARA Hiroshi,** b. 11 September 1935, Tokyo, Japan. Professor. m. Hiroko, 2 daughters. Education: Diploma, 1958, Faculty of Pharmaceutical Sciences; Dr of Pharmaceutical Sciences, 1968, University of Tokyo. Appointments: National Institute of Health of Japan, 1960-65; Meiji Pharmaceutical University, 1965-. Honour: The Society of Actinomycetes Japan Award, 1996. Memberships: American Society of Microbiology; New York Academy of Sciences; Biochemical Society of Japan; and others. Address: Meiji Pharmaceutical University, Noshio 2, Kiyose, Tokyo 204-8588, Japan.

**OGILVIE Kelvin Kenneth,** b. 6 November 1942, Summerville, Hants County, USA. University President. Education: BSc, Acadia University, 1963; BSc, Acadia University, 1964; PhD, Northwestern University, 1968. Appointments: Assistant Professor, University of Manatoba, 1968-72; Associate Professor, 1972-1974; Associate Professor, McGill University, 1974-1978; Professor, 1978-87; Canadian Pacific Professor, 1984-87; Director, 1984-87; Professor, Acadia University, 1987-; Vice President, 1987-1993; President, Vice Chancellor, 1993-. Publications: 150 Journal Publications; 104 Conference Papers; 117 Technology Presentations; 170 Invited Lectures; 14 Primary Patents; 31 Derivative Patents. Honours: Honorary Colonel, Canadian Air Force; Manning Principal Award; Order of Canada; Knight of Malta; Canadian Pacific Professor of Biotechnology; Buck-Whitney Medal of the Eastern New York Section of the Chemical Society; EWR Steacie Memorial Fellowship; Fellowship in the Chemical Institute of Canada; Upjohn Fellow. Memberships: New York Academy of Science; American Association for the Advancement of Science; Ordre des Chimistes du Quebec; Chemical Institute of Canada; American Chemical Society; Association Canadienne-Francaise pour l'Advancement des Sciences; Manitoba Environment Council; Voyageur Sled Dog Club; Manitoba Scientists to Combat Pollution. Address: Acadia University, Wolfville, Nova Scotia, Canada, B0P 1X0.

**OGISO Ken,** b. 9 September 1931, Tokyo. m. Kazuko Tazaki. Education: BEng, Tokyo University, 1957; MEng, 1959; Dr Eng, 1978. Appointments: Senior Researcher, NTT Lab; Professor, Tokyo University of Technology. Publications: Assessment of an Overall Cooling Performance of a Forced Convertion Cooling. Memberships: Japan Society of Mechanical Engineers; Society of University Graduates. Address: Tokyo University of Technology, 1404-1 Katakura, Hachiouji 192-8580, Japan.

**OGUN Oluremi,** b. 10 October 1957, Owo, Nigeria. Economist. m. Olubu Kunola Abetokunbo Ogun. Education: BSc (Hons) Economics, 1981; MSc Economics, 1983; PhD Economics (Ibadan), 1990; ACIB (London), 1991. Appointments: Assistant Lecturer, 1984-87; Lecturer II, 1987-91; Lecturer I, 1991-96; Senior Lecturer, 1996-. Publications: Several academic publications including one book on monetary and financial institutions. Honours: African Economic Research Consortium, Research Fellowship, 1994; Visiting Senior Economist, Financial Institutions Training Centre, 1994; Visiting Research Scholar, University California, Santa Barbara, 1994-96. Memberships: African Economic Research Consortium; African Technology Policy Studies; West African Economic Association; Nigerian Economic Society; Chartered Institute Bankers, London (Associate). Address: University Ibadan, Department Economics, Ibadan, Nigeria.

**OGWU David,** b. 22 June 1950, Abavo-Agbor, Nigeria. Veterinarian. m. Theresa N Ogwu, 1 son, 3 daughters. Education: DVM, 1975; MSc, 1978; PhD, 1983. Appointments: Lecturer, Ahmadu Bello University, Zaria, 1976; Professor of Theriogenology. Publications: Over 60 in renowned academic journals worldwide. Memberships: Nigerian Veterinary Medical Association. Address: Faculty of Veterinary Medicine, Ahmadu Bello University, Zaria, Nigeria.

**OGWUEGBU Martin,**b. 25 September 1956, Imo State, Nigeria. Chemist; Metallurgist. m. 1 son, 4 daughters. Education: BSc Chemistry, University of Calabar, 1980; Diploma Metallurgy, Univeristy of Sheffield, 1983; Master of Metallurgy, University of Sheffield, 1984; PhD Industrial Chemistry, University of Port Harcourt, 1991. Career: Assistant Lecturer, Imo State University, Nigeria, 1984-85; Lecturer II, Imo State University, Nigeria, 1985-91; Lecturer I, Abia State University, Nigeria, 1994; Senior Lecturer, Abia State Univeristy, Nigeria, 1994-96; Visiting Senior Lecturer on Sabbatical Leave, The Copperbelt University, Kitwe, Zambia, 1996-97; Senior Lecturer, The Copperbelt University, Kitwe, Zambia, 1998-; Unit Head, Chemistry Unit, Abia State University, Nigeria, 1994-96; Member, Technical Committee of Solid Minerals Producers and Marketers Association of Nigeria; Consultant for Shell-BP, University of Port Harcourt, 1988-91. Awards: Scholarship Award for first degree by the Imo State, Nigeria, University of Calabar; Scholarship Award for Masters Degree in Metallurgy, University of Sheffield, Federal Government of Nigeria; Fellowship grant for a PhD degree, University of Port Harcourt, Imo State University, Nigeria, 1988-91; Research grant, Abia State University for pollution control, 1992. Memberships: Nigeria Chemical Society; Metallurgy Society; Engineering Institute of Zambia; New York Academy of Sciences. Address: Copperbelt University, Riverside, PO Box 21692, Kitwe, Zambia.

**OHAEGBULAM Samuel C,** b. 3 May 1941, Nigeria. Neuro Surgeon. m. Marcelle Sadalla Saad, 3 sons. Education: Cairo University, 1962-67; MB, 1967; FRCS Ed, 1972; FRCS Eng, 1973; FWACS, 1975; FMCS, 1982; FICS, 1975. Appointments: Professor of Neurosurgery, University of Nigeria, 1980-93; Dean of Medicine, University of Nigeria, 1982-84; Deputy Vice Chancellor, University of Nigeria, 1987-89. Publications: About 95 Articles; Chapters to Books. Memberships: Royal College of Surgeons of Edinburgh; New York Academy of Science; Congress of Neuro Surgeons; Rotary Club; International College of Surgeons; Pan African Neuro Surgeons Association. Address: 11-15 Imoke Street, PO Box 2292, Gra-Rnugu, Enugu, Nigeria.

**OHASHI Tetsuya,** b. 21 August 1951, Sapporo. Scientist. m. Yoshie Yokouchi. Education: BS, 1974, MS, 1976, PhD, 1981, Hokkaido University. Appointments: Researcher, Hitachi Research Lab, Hitachi Ltd, 1982; Senior Researcher, 1990; Research Fellow, National Research Institute for Metals, 1997-. Publications: Numerical Modeling of Plastic Multiple Slip in Metal Crystals of FCC Type, 1994. Memberships: Japan Society for Mechanical Engineers; Japan Institute of Metals; Materials Research Society; and others. Address: 1-11-5 Mika-nohara, Hitachi 316-0026, Japan.

**OHKADO Masayuki,** b. 12 September 1963, Ise, Japan. Associate Professor. m. Kikuyo Suzuki, 2 daughters. Education: BA, Osaka University of Foreign Studies, 1986; MA, Nagoya University, 1988. Appointments: Lecturer, Osaka-Kyoiku University, 1989-96; Associate Professor, Chubu University, 1996-. Publication: On Nominative Case Assignment in Old English, 1998. Honour: IVY Award, 1996.

Membership: English Linguistic Society of Japan, National Conference Planning Committee Member.

**OHKURO Shigeru,** b. 29 November 1940, Sendai, Japan. Associate Professor. m. Noriko, 2 daughters. Education: MSc, 1965, Tohoku University, Sendai, Japan. Appointments: Research Assistant, Tohoku University, Sendai; Associate Professor, Hachinohe Institute of Technology, Hachinohe; Expert, Chamber of Commerce and Industry of Hachinohe. Publications: A substitute shig for latitude degree, 1979. Membership: International Federation of Non-linear Analysts. Address: Hachinohe Institute of Technology Myo, Hachinohe City 031-8501, Japan.

**OHNAKA Mitiyasu,** b. 11 September 1940, Yamaguchi Prefecture, Japan. University Professor. m. Yoshiko, 1 son, 1 daughter. Education: BS, Physics, 1966, MSc, Geophysics, 1968, DSc, Geophysics, 1975, University of Tokyo. Appointments: Research Associate, Earthquake Research Institute, 1970, Associate Professor, 1980, Professor, 1990, Director, Earthquake Prediction Research Center, Earthquake Research Institute, University of Tokyo. Publications: Earthquake Source Physics and Earthquake Precursors (editor and co-author); Theory of Earthquake Premonitory and Fracture Processes, 1995. Honour: Honorary Professor, University College, London, 1998. Memberships: American Geophysical Union; Seismological Society of Japan; New York Academy of Sciences. Address: Utsukushigaoka-nishi 3-40-19, Aoba-ku, Yokohama 225-0001, Japan.

**OHSAKI Katsuichiro,** b. 13 February 1935, Kyoto City, Japan. Otolaryngologist; Professor. m. Reiko Miyoshi, 2 sons, 1 daughter. Education: MD, 1959, PhD, 1965, Okayama University Medical School; Postgraduate Medical School, New York University, 1961-62. Appointments: Internship, 6022 USAF Hospital, 1959-60; Resident Otolaryngologist, New York Eye and Ear Infirmary, NYC, 1961-62; Otolaryngologist in Chief, Okayama Red Cross General Hospital, 1975-76; Otolaryngologist and Professor, School of Medicine, The University of Tokushima, 1976-81; Otolaryngologist and Professor, Division of Clinical Otology, University Hospital, University of Tokushima, 1981-. Publications: Author: Sudden Deafness, 1985; Co-author and Co-editor, Tinnitus, 1994; Patentee, Remedy for Sudden Deafness and Fluctuating Hearing Loss, 1982; Test Equipment of Tinnitus, 1992. Honours: Honorary Chair, Beijing International Symposium Otolaryngology, 1988; Most Admired Man of the Decade, 1995. Memberships: Otological Society of Japan, Councillor 1991-; New York Academy of Sciences, 1995-; Corresponding member, American Academy of Otolaryngology - Head and Neck Surgery, 1999-; Advisory Committee to be: 6th International Conference on Cholesteatoma and Ear Surgery; Sudden Deafness Research of Japan by Ministry of Health and Welfare of Japanese Government, 1973-76. Address: 3-5-36 Atake, Tokushima, Tokushima-ken 770-0863, Japan.

**OHTSUKA Toshiyuki,** b. 28 September 1967, Tokyo, Japan. Engineering Educator. Education: B Eng, 1990, M Eng, 1992, Dr Eng, 1995, Tokyo Metropolitan Institute of Technology, Hino, Japan. Appointments: Assistant Professor, University of Tsukuba, Japan, 1995-; Visiting Associate, California Institute of Technology, Pasadena, USA, 1996-97. Honour: Young Investigator Award, Japan Society for Aeronautical and Space Science, 1996. Memberships: Japan Society for Aeronautical and Space Sciences; American Institute of Aeronautics and Astronautics; Society for Instruments and Control Engineers; New York Academy of Sciences; Japan Society Mechanical Engineers; IEEE. Address: University Tsukuba Institute Engineering Mechanics,

-1-1 Tennodai, Tsukuba 305, Japan.

**OHWAKI Junichi,** b. 15 March 1953, Toyko, Japan. :lectrical Engineer. m. Nobuko, 1 son. Education: BA, Nihou ▮niversity, 1976; MA, 1978. Appointments: Engineer, Nippon ▮elegraph and Telephone Corporation, 1978-85; Senior ▮esearch Engineer, NTT, 1985-. Publications: Numerous ▮apers. Honours: Phosphor Prize, 1996. Memberships: Japan ▮ociety of Applied Physics; Institute of Electronics, Information ▮nd Communications Engineers; Phosphor Research Society; :lectrochemical Society of Japan. Address: 3-9-11 Midori-cho, ▮usashino-shi, Tokyo 180-8585, Japan.

**OI Walter Y,** b. 1 July 1929, Los Angeles, USA. Economist. ▮. Marjorie Robbins, 2 daughters. Education: BS, UCLA, 1952; ▮A, UCLA, 1954; PhD, University of Chicago, 1961. ▮ppointments: Associate Professor, Economics, University of ▮Vashington, 1962-67; Professor, University of Rochester, ▮967-77; Elmer B Milliman Professor, University of Rochester, ▮978-. Publications: Labor as a Quasi-Fixed Factor; The :conomic Cost of the Draft; On The Relationship of Different ▮embers of the K-Class; The Economics of Product Safety; On ▮he Economics of Industrial Safety; Safety at Any Price; ▮eterogeneous Firms and the Organization of Production; ▮Vork for Americans with Disabilities; On Working; Productivity ▮n the Distributive Trades; Firm Size and Wages. Honours: ▮ellow, Econometric Society; Fellow, American Academy of ▮rts and Sciences; Distinguished Fellow of the American :conomics Association. Memberships: Econometric Society; ▮merican Economics Association. Address: Department of :conomics, 211 Harkness Hall, University of Rochester, ▮ochester, NY 14627, USA.

**OJHA Mahendra,** b. 11 April 1968, Bombay, India. Health ▮ervices. m. Mitu, 1 daughter. Education: MBA; Master in ▮ealth Administration; Diploma in Hospital Management. ▮ppointments: Associate Manager, P D Hinduja Hospital, 1993; ▮irector, Hospital Consultancy Pvt Ltd, 1994-. Membership: ▮merican College of Healthcare Executives. Address: 105 ▮ehangir Mansion Office, Complex Metro Cinema Lane, ▮umbai 400 020, India.

**OKA Masahiro,** b. 15 February 1924, Hiroshima, Japan. ▮rofessor. 1 son, 2 daughters. Education: Postgraduate, ▮hilosophy, Kyoto Imperial University, 1948. Appointments: ▮hudo Junior College, 1953; Hiroshima Commercial College, ▮960; Hiroshima Shudo University, 1973. Publications: The ▮dea of Education; Contemprary Philosophy; German Ethics; Einladung zum Denken (in German); Conpleson's ▮onttemporary Philosophy (translated into Japanese); History ▮of Ethics; Moral Education; Philosophy of University Education; ▮usiness Ethics I and II; Philosophical Anthropology; Social ▮hilosophy; Philosophy of Literature, Art and Language; Many papers in professional journals. Honour: 3rd Cosmos Publishing Prize, 1994. Memberships: Japanese Society for Ethics; Aristotelian Society. Address: Fujidanchi 3-4, 2-chome, ▮Ohmachi-nishi, Asaminami-ku, Hiroshima 731-0125, Japan.

**OKAWA Antonia Camacho,** b. 13 March 1949, Saipan, USA. Classroom Teacher. m. Ryo Okawa, 1 son, 2 daughters. Education: AA, Education, Northern Marianas College, 1986; BA, Elementary Education, University of Guam, 1991. Appointments: Kindergarten Teacher, WSR School, Public School System, 1990-; Teacher of the Year, William S Reyes School, 1991-92; Tutorial Reading Teacher, K-6, WSR School and PTA Treasurer, 1998-. Honours: Presidential Awards for Excellence in Science and Mathematics Teaching, 1993, 1995; Author of Public School System Language Arts Standard and Benchmark CNMI, 1996, 1997, 1998; Biographee inclusion in

Who's Who in the West, 1998-99. Memberships: Association Supervision Curriculum Development; International Reading Association; National Council of Teachers in Mathematics; Restoration Advisory Board, CNMI Pacific Oceans Division; Parents Teachers Association. Address: Chalan Kanoa, PO Box 141, Saipan, MP 96950, USA.

**OKAZAKI Motoaki,** b. 17 July 1937, Tokyo, Japan. Engineer in Atomic Energy. m. Keiko Yamaguchi, 3 daughters. Education: BSc, Keio University, Tokyo, Japan, 1961. Appointments: Senior Engineer, Japan Atomic Energy Research Institute, Tokai-Mura, Japan, 1963-97. Publications include: Analysis of Density Wave Instability in a Boiling Flow Using a Characteristic Method, 1994. Memberships: Japan Society of Mechanical Engineers; Atomic Energy Society of Japan. Address: Sanai-cho 29 Ichigaya, Shinjuku-ku F162-0846, Tokyo, Japan.

**OKERE Chukwuma Onyeaghala (Chuma),** b. 20 March 1964, Enugu, Nigeria. Neuroscientist. m. Maria Anayo Iwuoha, 2 sons, 1 daughter. Education: BSc, Honours, 1987, MSc, 1990; PhD, 1997. Appointments: Lecturer in Physiology, University of Maiduguri, Nigeria, 1990-93; Postdoctoral Fellow, 1997-99, Research Associate, 1999-2000, Kochi Medical School, Japan. Honours: Anshin Tomonokai Research Award; Kochi Medical School. Memberships: International Behavioral Neuroscience Society; American Association for the Advancement of Science. Address: Department of Physiology, Kochi Medical School, Okoh-cho, Nanko-ku, Kochi 783-8505, Japan.

**OKEREKE-ONYIUKE Ndi,** b. 2 November 1950, Bonny, Rivers State, Nigeria. m. Charles Onyiuke. Address: Nigerian Stock Exchange, Custom Street, Lagos, Nigeria.

**OKOH Samuel E N,** b. 29 December 1942, Ekwuoma. Economist. m. Chief Florence, 4 sons, 1 daughter. Education: BA Economics, 1969, Bishop College, Dallas, Texas; MA Economics, 1970, North Texas State University, Denton; PhD coursework, 1973, Southern Methodist University, North Texas State University; AIB certificate in Banking, 1974, American Institute of Banking, Dallas, Texas. Appointments: Lecturer, Instructor, Dept Economics, Bishop College, Dallas, 1970-72; Lecturer Grade II, Dept Economics and Statistics, University of Benin, 1975-77, Lecturer Grade I, 1977-80, Senior Lecturer, 1980-88, Associate Professor, 1988-91, Head, 1990-96, Professor Economics, 1992, Acting Dean, 1992-96, Dean, 1996-, of Faculty of Social Sciences; President, Ekwuoma Development Union, Benin Branch, 1983-; Vice-President, Nigeria Economic Society, 1993-95. Publications: Editor-in-Chief: Economic and Financial Review, Benin Journal of Social Sciences, 1995-; Associate Editor, Nigerian Journal of Economics and Social Studies, 1991-93; Thesis, Education and Economic Growth in Nigeria, 1970; Co-author, book, Socio-Economic Development in Nigeria, 1981; 28 journal publications; 14 edited conference proceedings; Over 40 articles on various socio-economic issues in national newspapers. Memberships: Life member, Nigerian Economic Society; Nigerian Political Sciences Association; Population Association of Nigeria. Address: University of Benin, Department of Economics and Statistics, Benin City, Nigeria.

**OKREPILOV Vladimir Valentinovitch,** b. 23 February 1944, Leningrad. Economist. m. Irina Gennadievna, 1 son. Education: Engineer-Mechanic, 1970, Baltic State Technical University; Candidate of Science, Economics, 1986, State University of Economics and Finance; Doctor in Economics, 1992; Professor, 1993. Appointments: Engineer, Plant of Radio-Technical Equipment, 1965-70; Chief Engineer,

Research Institute of Metrology n.a. D.I. Mendeleev, 1979-86; Director, Leningrad Centre of Standardisation and Metrology, 1986-90; Director General, Centre for Testing and Certification, St Petersburg, 1990-. Publications: Over 150 scientific publications including books: Total Quality Management, 1996; Quality Management, 1998. Honours: Honoured Scientist and Technician of Russia, 1994; State Award of Russia in the field of Science and Techniques, 1997. Memberships: Head of sub-faculty, State University of Economics and Finance; Head of sub-faculty, Academy of Standardisation, Metrology and Certification; President St Petersburg's Branch, Russian Academy for Quality Problems. Address: Kurlyandskaya st 1, Centre for Testing and Certification, 198103 St Petersburg, Russia.

**OKUDA Yukichi,** b. 25 May 1954, Gunma, Japan. Associate Professor. m. Harumi Okuda, 2 daughters. Education: MD, Medical School, University of Tsukuba, 1980; PhD, University of Tsukuba, 1987. Appointments: Instructor, Department of Medicine, Baylor College of Medicine, USA, 1987-88; Assistant Professor, Institute of Clinical Medicine, University of Tsukuba, 1988-92. Honours: Excellent Investigator Award, Ibaraki Medical Association, 1996, Hypertension and Atherosclerosis Research Foundation for Community Medicine, 1998. Memberships: Endocrine Society, USA; American Diabetes Association; Japanese Society of Internal Medicine. Address: Institute of Clinical Medicine, University of Tsukuba, Tennodai 1-1-1, Tsukuba-shi, Ibaraki-ken 305-8575, Japan.

**OKWARE Ikwaras Samuel,** b. 16 August 1948, Tororo, Uganda. Medical Doctor. m. Daisy Okware, 3 sons, 2 daughters. Education: MB ChB, Makerere, Kampala, 1968-73; DPH, Public Health, Makerere University, Medical School, Kampala, 1975-76; MPH, Epidemiology and Public Health, 1978-79. Appointments: Medical Officer (Mulago Hospital), 1973, Medical Superintendent, 1974, Ministry of Health; Senior House Officer, Institute of Public Health, Kampala, 1975-76; Senior Medical Officer, Ministry of Health, 1976-77; WHO Fellow, University of Minnesota, USA, 1978-79; Assistant Director, Medical Services/Public Health, 1980-85; Director, National AIDS Control Programme, Ministry of Health, Entebbe, 1986-90; Chairman, National Committee for Prevention of AIDS, Uganda, 1986-90; Deputy Director, Medical Services In-charge of Public Health, 1990-94; Commissioner Health Services, Communicable Disease Control/AIDS, Ministry of Health, 1994; Commissioner, Health Services, Community Health, Ministry of Health, 1999. Publications: In national and international journals and conferences. Honour: 20th Century Award for Achievement for outstanding contribution to public health and AIDS work, International Biographical Centre, Cambridge, England, 1998. Memberships: American Public Health Association; Editorial Board, African Analysis Magazine, London; International AIDS in Africa; Society for AIDS in Africa. Address: Ministry of Health Headquarters, PO Box 8, Entebbe, Uganda.

**OLARU NENATI Lucia,** b. 20 February 1949, Romania. Writer; Journalist; Educator; Cultural Worker. m. Dumitru Olaru, 31 December 1969, 2 daughters. Education: Faculty of Philology, Cuza University, Jassy, 1967-72; Course in Journalism, California University; Doctorate in Literature, Cuza University. Appointments: Researcher, Museum Mihai Eminescu, Ipotesti, Botosani, 1972-77; Literary Secretary and Manager, Botosani Puppet Theatre, 1977-86; Manager, Mihai Eminescu Theatre, Botosani, 1986-90; Journalist, Manager, Vega S C, Editor, newspaper Gazeta de Botosani, 1990-97; Teacher, College of School Teachers, Botosani, 1997-. Publications: 12 books of essays, poems, prose and books and for children, including: Cea Mai Tinara Ecaterina; Cochilii

Cîntatoare; Drumuri; Serpentine; Numerous articles and studies. Honours: Medal of Cultural Merit, 1984; Award, National Literary Contests, Bucharest, 1975, Brasov, 1997, Calarasi, 1998, Cluj, 1999. Memberships: Writers Association of Romania; Association of Professional Journalists of Romania; Society for Romanian Culture and Literature in Bucovina; UNESCO; Women's National Association of Romania. Address: Str Cuza Voda Nr 25, Bloc L6, sc A, ap 1, 6800 Botosani, Romania.

**OLASZ Lajos,** b. 21 June 1948, Szegvar, Hungary. Oncology Researcher, Oral and Maxillofacial Surgeon. m. Aranka Fejes, 1 son, 1 daughter. Education: MD, Szent-Gyorgyi Albert Med U Szeged, 1973; DMD, Medical University Pecs, 1976; PhD, Hungarian Scientific Academy, Budapest, 1994. Appointments: Clinical Physician, Medical University, Pecs, Hungary, 1973-76; Assistant Lecturer, 1976-87; Lecturer, 1987-97; Associate Professor, 1997-. Publications: Contributor, articles for professional journals. Honours: Cons Orvosi Hetilap, Budapest, 1992-; Hungarian Dental Society Directory Member, 1978-; Oral and Maxillofacial Surgical Society secretary, 1990-96; Hungarian Oral and Maxillofacial Surgical Society, Directory Member, 1996-. Memberships: Hungarian Scientific Academy; Intern, Society of Chemotherapy; Intern, Society for Prev Onocology; Intern, Association of Oral and Maxillofacial Surgeons. Address: Dischka 5, 7621 Pecs, Hungary.

**OLATOREGUN Cecilia Mojisola,** b. 9 November 1954, Nigeria. Law. m. Frank Olatoregun, 1 son, 2 daughters. Education: LLB, honours, 1979; BL, 1981. Appointments: Chief Magistrate, Oyo State, Nigeria, 1986-96; Deputy Chief Registrar, Federal High Court, Nigeria, 1996-. Honour: Outstanding Achievement in Law, with Particular Emphasis on Public Administration. Memberships: Commonwealth Magistrates and Judges Association; Nigerian Bar Association. Address: Federal High Court, Oyinkan Abayomi Drive, Ikoyi Lagos, Nigeria.

**OLESEN Ole Frilev,** b. 30 June 1965, Denmark. Scientist. m. Elisabetta Vaudano, 1 daughter. Education: BSc, Biology, 1989; MSc, Molecular Biology, 1991; PhD, Neurobiology, 1996. Appointments: Research Fellow, MRC LMB, Cambridge, England, 1991-93; Research Fellow, Department of Molecular Biology, Aarhus University, 1993-94; Research Manager, H Lundbeck A/S, Denmark, 1994-98; International Project Manager, Ferring Pharmaceuticals, Denmark, 1998-. Publications: 20 scientific articles in professional journals; Mr Dupond (poetry collection), 1991. Memberships: American Society of Neuroscience; International Project Management Association; Danish Association for Foreign Trade. Address: Hyskenstraede 3, 1207-K Copenhagen, Denmark.

**OLESZEK Wieslaw Aleksander,** b. 27 February 1948, Belzyce, Phytochemist; Professor. m. Ewa Gozdzicka, 2 d. Education: MSc, 1975; PhD, 1985; Professor, 1997. Appointments: Visiting Fellow, Cornell University, 1980, 1987; Head of Biochemistry Department, Institute of Soil Science Plant Cultivation Pulawy, Poland, 1992-. Publications: 130 publications in international journals. Honour: Polish Academy of Science. Memberships: Phytochemical Society of Europe; New York Academy of Science; Polish Phytochemical Society. Address: Inst Soil Sci Plant Cultiv., Czartoryskich 8, Pulawy 24-100, Poland.

**OLIVER Dominick M,** b. 12 April 1962, Niagara Falls, New York. Educator. m. Vicki A. Education: AAS, 1982, Niagara County Community College; BS, 1984, MS Education, 1986, Niagara University. Appointments: Instructor, Kelley Business nstitute, Bryant & Stratton Business Institute; Academic Dean, Kelley Business Institute; Senior Mentor for New Instructors & Academic Committee Member, Bryant & Stratton Business Institute. Honours: Instructor of the Year, 1996, 1997, Bryant & Stratton Business Institute; Phi Delta Kappa. Memberships: National Business Education Association; New York State Association of Two Year Colleges; National Society of Public Accountants; New York State of Independent Accountants. Address: 119 Wendover Avenue, Buffalo, NY 14223-2731, USA.

**OLNESS Valerie Keeling,** b. 10 March 1944, Sheffield, England. Professor. m. Alan Earl, 3 sons, 1 daughter. Education: Research Assistant, University of Minn; Public School Teacher, Minnesota and Dares Salaam; Professor of Biology, Science, Augustana College, South Dakota, USA. Publications: Curriculum Development, FACETS; Hidden Curriculum Faculty made tests in Science. Memberships: National Science Teachers Association; Minnesota Academy of Science; Association for the Education of Teachers in Science; Association for Supervision and Curriculum Development. Address: Augustana Coll Dept Biology, 2001 S Summit Ave, Sioux Falls, SD 57197 0001, USA.

**OLSAUSKAS Algimantas Mecislovas,** b. 22 August 1942, Kaunas City, Lithuania. Lecturer. m. Viciute Elzbieta, 1 son, 1 daughter. Education: Botanist, Vilnius University, 1968-74; Post Grad, Institute of Botany, Lithuanian Academy of Science, 1978-82; Doctor of Physical Science. Appointments: Master, Klaipeda Greenery Planting Trust, 1972-76; Biology Teacher, Klaipeda Evening School, 1976-80; Research Fellow, Lithuanian Institute of Agriculture, 1980-86; Chief Research Fellow, Klaipeda Ecological Problems Center, Lithuanian Academy of Science, 1987-91; Associate Professor, Recreation Department, 1991-; Director, Botanical Garden, Klaipeda University, 1994-; President, Lithuanian Association for Coastal Conservation, 1998-. Publications: The Old Aurochs Field Park, 1993; Medical Properties of Plants, 1994; Author Monograph, Influence of Recreation on Plant Cover in West Lithuania, 1996; 200 Science and Popular Articles. Memberships: European Union for Coastal Conservation; Association of Baltic Botanical Gardens; Union of Lithuananian Dendrologists; Klaipeda Department, Lithuanian Nature Society; Lithuanian Scientists Union. Address: Liepojos 22-23, LT 5808 Klaipeda, Lithuania.

**OLSZEWSKI Stanislaw Marian,** b. 8 December 1932, Warsaw, Poland. Physicist. m. Widowed, 1 son. Education: MSc, Theoretical Physics, University Warsaw, 1954; Chemical Engineer, Polytechnical Institute, Warsaw, 1954; Doctor, Solid State Physics, University Paris at Orsay, 1962; Habilitation, Polish Academy of Sciences, 1964. Appointments: Research Worker, Institute Physical Chemistry, Polish Academy Sciences, 1955-, Professor, 1971, Head of Institute division, 1985. Publications: Original articles in scientific journals on quantum theory and its application to atoms, molecules and solids. Memberships: Polish Physical Society; Polish Chemical Society; European Academy of Sciences and Arts, elected 1991. Address: Platynowa 8/97, 00-808 Warsaw, Poland.

**OLSZOWSKA Marta,** b. 27 February 1950, Krakow, Poland. Fine Arts Artist. 1 daughter. Education: School of Fine Arts, Krakow, 1964-69; Studies: Academy of Fine Arts in Krakow, Print Faculty, Diploma in Lithography and Book Illustration, 1974. Appointments: Director Assistant, Krakow, Studio of Animated Film, 1976-; Work for Polish Music Publishers Exhibitions of Graphics (print), paintings, masks, religious paintings, copies and original works. Publications: Illustrations and Graphic Design of Books: Edward Pałtasz " Musical Journeys";" The Songs for Children";" Jazz Pieces for Various

Scoring";" Musical Games". Memberships: ZPAP-Zwiazek Poliskich Artystow Plastykow; Association of Polish Artists and Designers. Address: ul Zulawskiego 10/6, 31-145 Krakow, Poland.

**ONET Gheorghe Emil,** b. 24 July 1937, Romania. Doctor of Veterinary Medicine. m. Virginia, 2 daughters. Education: DVM, 1960, PhD, 1970, College of Veterinary Medicine, Bucharest, Romania. Appointments: Associate Professor, Head, Departments of Laboratory Diagnosis and Sanitary Veterinary Legislation, College of Veterinary Medicine, Cluj-Napoca, 1962; Research Group Leader, Director, Veterinary Diagnostic Laboratory, Larchwood, Iowa; Director, State Veterinary Diagnostic Laboratory, Richmond, Virginia, 1991; Animal Science Research Coordinator, National Institute for Discover Science, 1996-. Publications: 13 books, including: Viruses and Viral Diseases of Animals; Laboratory Diagnosis in Veterinary Medicine; 154 articles in professional journals. Memberships: World Association of Veterinary Pathologists; World Association of Avian Pathologists; International Union Against Tuberculosis; World Society of History of Veterinary Medicine; American Veterinary Medical Association; World Association of Microbiologists and Specialists in Infectious Diseases; World Association for Buiatrics; New York Academy of Sciences; American Association of Avian Pathologists. Address: National Institute for Discovery Science, 4640 South Eastern Avenue, Las Vegas, NV 89119, USA.

**ONGOCKA Dhimiter,** b. 21 October 1936, Korce. Actor, Producer. m. Theofani, 1 son, 1 daughter. Education: High Arts Institute, 1959. Appointments: Actor, Theatre A Z Cajuri Korce, 1955-1996; Producer, 1970-1996; Director, Cultural Center, 1996-. Honours: Merited Artist; Best Role. Memberships: Writers and Artists Link; New World Organizate. Address: Theatri A Z Gujupi, Kocca, Albania.

**ONOKPISE Oghenekome,**b. 10 May 1951, Lagos, Nigeria. University Teacher; Researcher. m. 4 sons. Education: PhD Forestry, Iowa State University, 1984; MSc Plant Breeding and Genetics, University of Guelph, 1980; BSc Agriculture, University of Ife, 1974; Post Doctorate Study in Biotechnology, Ohio State University, 1985-86. Appointments: Professor and Coordinator, Florida A&M University, 1994-; Associate Professor, Florida A&M University, 1991-94; Assistant Professor, Florida A&M University, 1986-91; Courtesy Professor, University of Florida, 1993-; Courtesy Professor, University of Cape Coast, 1998-; Post-Doctorate Researcher, Ohio State University, 1985-86; Research Assistant, Iowa State University, 1981-85; Research Officer, Rubber Research Institute of Nigeria, 1975-81; Instructor, School of Agriculture, Yandev, Nigeria, 1974-75; Over 7 International programs. Teaching responsibilities: Introduction to Agricultural Sciences; Principles of Field Crop Production; Pasture and Range Management; Plant Ecology; Special Problems in Agronomy; Plant Breeding and Genetics; Advanced Plant Sciences; Sees Science and Technology; Forestry in Rural and Urban Environments; Nature and Properties of Soils. Honours: University Service Award, Florida A&M University, 1996; Advanced Teacher of the Year, Florida A&M University, 1996; Dean's Award for Superior Accomplishment, CESTA, 1995; Nominated Outstanding Scienctist, Associate of Research Directors, 1994; Teacher Incentive Programme Award, FAMU and The Board of Regents, State of Florida, 1994; Teacher of the Year, FAMU, 1993; Agricultural Science Teacher of the Year, Students' Agricultural Science Club, 1993. Publications: Over 60 refereed symposia, workshop and conference papers; Natural Resources, Salem Press; Restoring wiregrass to longleaf pine stands, Restoration Ecology, 1999; Cogongrass Populations in North Florida and Southeast Alabama, 1999;

Germplast collection and evaluation of macabo cocoyam, 1998; Graduating blacks: Some joint programs show early sucess, 1997; Evaluation of European black alder provenances for short rotation forestry, 1994. Memberships: Society of American Foresters; International Society of Tropical Forestry; Agronomy Society of America; Commonwealth Forestry Association; Florida Academy of Sciences; Technical Advisory Committee, Southern Region Sustainable Agriculture; National Geographic Society; Association for the Advancement of Industrial Crops; Gamma Sigma Delta. Address: 2810 Kennesaw Pl, Tallahassee, FL 32301-1202, USA.

**ONUCHUKU Okechuku,** b. 4 April 1964, Emohua, Rivers State, Nigeria. Lecturer. m. Joy. Education: BSc, Economics, University of Port Harcourt, 1990; MSc, Economics, 1993; PhD, 1998. Appointments: Lecturer, Rivers State College of Arts and Science, 1992-94; Lecturer, University of Port Harcourt, 1995-. Publications: Econometrics: An Introduction to Ordinary Least Square Regression Analysis; Inflation and Stabilization Policy Measures in Nigeria; Applied Statistics for Economists; plus articles: An Econometric Study of Public Investment Behaviour in Nigeria (1970-1994); The Determinants of Investment Behaviour in Nigerian Manufacturing Sector; Exchange Rate Variation and Price Inflation in Nigeria. Honours: Best Graduating Student, Department of Economics; Uniport Award. Memberships: Nigerian Economic Society. Address: Department of Economics, University of Port Harcourt, Port Harcourt, Nigeria.

**ONYEMELUKWE Geoffrey C,** b. 7 April 1944, Onitsha, Nigeria. Medical. m. Ifeoma, 3 sons, 2 daughters. Education: BSc, University of Ibadan, 1964-67; MD, University of Ibadan, 1973; DTM and H, University of Liverpool, 1979; FMCP, Nigeria, 1981; FWACP, Nigeria, 1983, FICA, USA, 1983; FIAMN, Nigeria, 1988. Appointments: Consultant Physician, Lecturer, 1981; Professor of Medicine and Immunology, 1988; Medical Abu Zaria, 1988; President, Diabetics Association of Nigeria, 1992-98. Publications: More than 80 Scientific Publications, 1979-; Articles and Chapters in books, 1998. Honours: Best All Rounder, Kuti Hall, 1967; Robert White Fellowship in Immunology, 1988. Memberships: Pan African Study Group; International League Against Rheumatism; Diabetes Association of Nigeria; Pan African Mutagin City Society; New York Academy of Science. Address: Ahmadu Bello University Teaching Hospital, Dept Medicine, Zaria Kaduna, Nigeria.

**OOLUN Mukund Krishna,** b. 5 March 1968, Mauritius. Lecturer. m. Shailaja Seebaluck. Education: BTech, Electrical and Electronic Engineering, University of Mauritius, 1992; MSc, Instrumentation, distinction, England, 1996. Appointments: Electrical Engineer, CEB Mauritius, 1992-93; Lecturer, University of Mauritius, 1993-. Publications: Over 10 articles in professional journals. Memberships: IEEE; IEM. Address: University of Mauritius, Reduit, Mauritius.

**OOMMEN Thottathil,** b. 29 August 1934, Kerala, India. Executive Scientist. m. Annamma, 2 sons, 1 daughter. Education: BSc, 1954; MSc, 1965; PhD, 1970. Appointments: College Faculty, 1965-68; Research Faculty, 1971-76; Senior Scientist, Executive Consulting Research and Development Engineer, 1977-. Publications: 50 in scientific and engineering journals; Breakthrough research on elemental sulphur, static electrification, biodegradable insulating fluids - Outstanding papers, 1981, 1998. Memberships: IEEE, senior member; CIGRE; Fellow, American Institute of Chemists. Address: ABB Power T&D Co Inc, 1021 Main Campus Drive, Raleigh, NC 27606, USA.

**ORE Timothy,** b. 21 August 1955, Nigeria. Researcher; Bureaucrat. m. Radha Claridge, 1 s, 1 d. Education: BS, University of Lagos, Nigeria, 1975-78; MS, 1979-80; Japanese Language Student, Osaka University of Foreign Studies, 1980-81; Graduate Student, Hitotsubashi University, Tokyo, Japan, 1981-82; Doctor of Philosophy, University of New South Wales, 1982-86. Appointments: Lecturer, Faculty of Social Sciences, University of Lagos, 1986-89; Industrial Analyst, Victorian Department of Labour, Australia, 1990-91; Economic Adviser, National Occupational Health and Safety Commission, Sydney, 1991-92; Senior Policy Analyst, Federal Department of Industry, Science and Technology, Australia, 1992-95; Senior Research Associate, Division of Safety Research, National Institute of Occupational Safety and Health, West Virginia, USA, 1995-97; Senior Project Manager, Victorian Department of Human Services, Melbourne, Australia, 1998-. Publications: An Analysis of Fatal Occupational Injury Experience; Motor Vehicle Fatalities in the US Construction Industry Accident Analysis and Prevention; Many others. Honours: United States National Research Council Fellowship for Postdoctoral Research; Australian Government Fellowship for Doctoral Studies; Japanese Government Mombusho Fellowship; 3 University Awards for Best Graduating Student. Memberships: American Public Health Association. Address: 25 Kelson Street, Melbourne, VIC 3058, Australia.

**OREKONDY Siddalingeswara,** b. 1 May 1943, Gadag, India. Ophthalmologist. m. Nalini Basappa, 1 s, 2 d. Education: MBBS, Mysore, India, 1965; D.O RCP, RCS, Dublin, 1971; DO, London, 1972; FICS, 1993; FRACO, 1997. Publications: Non Traumatic Iris Retractor, British Journal of Optahlmology. Memberships: Kannada Balaga; Basava Samithi of Australasia; All India Institute of Opthalmology; American Academy of Opthalmology. Address: 30 Llandilo Ave, Strathfield, NSW 2135, Australia.

**ORENSTEIN Myra,** b. 18 February 1952, Malden, Massachusetts, USA. President, Advertising Agency. m. Louis J Orenstein, 1 son, 1 daughter. Education: BA, Case Western Reserve University. Appointments: President, CATV Inc; Consultant, Master Card International Fundraiser, Easter at The White House; Restaurant Reviewer, Northern Ohio Live Magazine. Membership: Cleveland Growth Association. Address: CATV Inc, 2533 Euclid Heights Blvd, Cleveland, OH 44106, USA.

**ORLU Levent,** b. 21 October 1953, Istanbul, Turkey. Divorced, 1 son. Education: Doctor, Faculty of Medicine, University of Istanbul. Certificate, University of Istanbul, Faculty of Economics, 1991; Les Laboratoires Servier, Paris; CEO, Orlu Ltd, 1991-; Certificate, Cambridge Academy of Transport, 1994. Appointments: Physician, Ministry of Health, Gumushane, Tirkey, 1984; Municipality of Besiktas, Istanbul, 1986; Project Manager, Servier, Paris, Istanbul, 1987; Servier ILAC, Istanbul, 1988-91; general Coordinator Research Studies in Field, 1989; CEO ORLU Ltd, Istanbul, 1991-; Consultant, SSM&A, Istanbul, 1993-98; SEO, SIGOR Ltd, Istanbul, 1995-; CEO GALEV Ltd, 1999-; CEO Ordent LTd, 1999-. Honours: Founder President, Fatih Leo Club, 1980; General Secretary Committee, 1982, Loyalty Plaque, 1981; Gratitude Plaque, 1982-83. Memberships: Beyazit Rotary Cercle d'Orient American Management Association International; Galatasaray Club; The Turkish Football Men Association; Alexander Hamilton Institute. Address: Address: SoyakSitesi1 BlokD:007, 81190, Istanbul, Turkey.

**ORNE Eadric,** b. 1938, London, England. Ex-Categorical Algebraist; Novelist; Poet; Playwright. Education: BA; MA; DPhil (Oxon). Publications: Supermate; Two Minus One;

harlacan; Clitorati; Zero on the Posmugraphy of Knowledge; ill Joy Limited. Membership: Oxford and Cambridge Club. ddress: 23 Rue des Martyrs, 75009 Paris, France.

**ORO John,** b. 26 October 1923, Lleida, Catalonia, Spain. iochemistry. m. Francisca Forteza, 3 sons, 1 daughter. :ducation: BS, Chemistry, University of Barcelona, 1947; PhD, iochemistry, Baylor University College of Medicine, Houston, 956. Appointments: Professor, Chemistry, 1955-67, Professor, iochemistry, 1967-94, Professor Emeritus, 1994-, University f Houston. Publications: 30 books, 250 research papers. lonour include: Cross of Saint George, Catalonia, Spain. Aembership: Member, Former President, International Society or the Study of the Origin of Life. Address: University of louston, 4800 Calhoun Road, Houston, TX 77204-5934, USA.

**ORSI Zsuzsanna,** b. 15 November 1940, Pecs, Hungary. iobelin Artist. m. Lorant Bencze, 1 son, 2 daughters. :ducation: Graphic Art, High School of Arts and Crafts, iudapest; Tapestry Designer, 1971, University of Arts and :rafts, Budapest. Appointments: Teacher at gobelin workshop, lungarian Academy of Applied Arts in Budapest, 1962-79; lead, Tapestry Workshop, University of Arts and Crafts, iudapest, 1971-79. Creative works: 3 solo exhibitions; 22 iroup exhibitions; Works in Education and Recreation Centre, IAV Hospital, Budapest, and Secondary School's Library, 'annonhalma; 13 works abroad in France, Belgium, iwitzerland, Germany and USA. Honour: Special Prize, Igriculture in Arts, Budapest, 1980. Membership: Association if Hungarian Artists. Address: H 2822 Szomor, Petofi S u 32, lungary.

**ORTMANN Bodo,** b. 25 November 1960, Hage. Scientist. :ducation: Diploma of Biology, 1988; PhD, 1991. Ippointments: Research Associate. Publications: J Immunol; Nature; PNAS; Science. Memberships: Society for mmunology; German Society of Cell Biology. Address: U :ologne Inst Genetics, Zuelpicher Str 47, D-50674, Cologne, iermany.

**ORZECHOWSKA-JUZWENKO Krystyna,** b. 18 April 1933, 'oland. Professor. m. Adolf Juzwenko, 1 son. Education: MD, Medical Faculty, Wroclaw University of Medicine, 1957; PhD, Medical Sciences, 1965; Assistant Professor, 1976; Professor, 1988. Appointments: Assistant, Tutor, Assistant Professor, Department of Pharmacology, Wroclaw University of Medicine, 1957-79, Head of Chair and Department of Clinical Pharmacology, 1979-. Publications: Author, co-author of 164 scientific publications in Polish and international medical ournals; Author, co-author or editor of 25 books; Author or :o-author of 109 scientific communications and 29 plenary lectures presented on Polish and international scientific medical congresses. Honours: Awards of Polish Minister of Health, Warsaw, 1958, 1972, 1986, 1998; Awards, 12 times Rector of Wroclaw University of Medicine, 1966, 1977, 1983, 1984, 1988, 1989, 1991, 1992, 1993, 1995, 1997, 1998; Golden Cross of Merit, Government of Poland, Warsaw, 1981; Order-Cross Polonia Restituta, President of Poland, Warsaw, 1990; Golden Award of Honour, Academia Medica Wratislaviensis, Rector of Wroclaw, University of Medicine, 1995. Memberships: Polish Academy of Sciences Committee of Clinical Pharmacology; Section of Clinical Pharmacology, Polish Pharmacological Society; Polish Society of Clinical Pharmacology and Therapeutics; Polish Society of Therapeutic Drug Monitoring; International Society of Therapeutic Drug Monitoring; New York Academy of Sciences; German Society of Clinical Pharmacology and Therapy. Address: ul Piotra Skargi 15/12, 50-082 Wroclaw, Poland.

**ORZESZEK Piotr Mark,** b. 30 August 1969, Cracow, Poland. Architect. m. Malgorzata Orzeszekova. Education: Diploma, High School, Cracow, 1993; Doctoral studies, 1995-98. Appointments: Taught Architecture course, Cracow Polytechnical School, 1993-94; Architect in architectural practice, 1994-98. Publications: 4 publications, Cracow University of Technology, 1994-98; Article in Polish monthly Architecture and Business, 1998. Membership: SARP, Polish Architects Society. Address: ul Batorego 24/8, Cracow, Poland.

**OSAKI Humio,** b. 4 June 1916, Hirosaki, Aomori Prefecture, Japan. Retired Doctor. m. Toyoko Omori, 2 daughters. Education: MD, 1942, Oakayama Medical College; D Med Sci, 1960, Osaka University. Appointments: Research Associate, Duke University, 1956-58; Instructor, Osaka University Dental School, 1959-61; Associate Professor, Okayama University Medical School, 1961-66; Professor, University of Tokushima School of Medicine, 1966-81; VP, Kochi Medical School, 1982-86; Honorary Director, Yagi Hospital, 1987-; Director, Special Nursing Home for Aged, Ojuen, 1987-. Honour: Koizumi-Syo Award, 1970. Memberships: Honorary member: Japanese Society of Parasitology; Japanese Society of Tropical Medicine; Japan Society of Protozoology; VP, Japanese-German Association on Protozoan Diseases; Emeritus, Society of Protozoologists; Royal Society of Tropical Medicine and Hygiene, London, Fellow; Mount Desert Island Biological Lab, USA, Life member; Friendship and Exchange, UK, Honorary Member; Life member, Society of Sigma Xi; Japan Medical Association. Address: 5-18 Mizugaoka, Tarumi-ku, Kobe, 655 0025 Japan.

**OSAWA Satoshi,** b. 5 June 1961, Tokyo, Japan. Associate Professor. m. Etsuko, 4 daughters. Education: BSc, 1986, PhD, 1991, University of Tokyo. Appointments: Departmental Assistant, University of Massachusetts, 1991-93; Research Associate of Science, University of Tokyo, 1993-96; Assistant Professor, 1996-98, Associate Professor, 1998-, Kanazawa Institute of Technology. Publication: Recent Research Developments in Macromoleculer Research, 1998. Honour: Award of Materials Technology, 1999. Memberships: American Chemical Society; Chemical Society of Japan; Society of Polymer Science. Address: Kanazawa Institute of Technology, Nonoichi, Ishikawa 921-8501, Japan.

**OSBORN Peter George,** b. 26 April 1914, Adelaide, South Australia, Australia. Education: BA, 1st Class Honours, University of Sydney; Frazer Postgraduate Research School, University of Glasgow; Diploma, Industrial Management, Cuddesdon Theological College. Appointments: Trained for Theatre, Embassy Theatre School, 15 roles in West End; Ordinary Seaman, RNVR, 5/4 Lieutenant; Instructor Officer, Commander, Royal Navy; Ordained, 1963; Curate, St John's, Gosport; Chaplain, Geelong Grammar School, Abingdon School; Archbishop's Chaplain for the Arts; Actor, Breaker Morant, Shine. Publications: MID, 1944; Exit Praying, 1995. Memberships: Naval Club, UK; NM and AF Club, Adelaide. Address: Unit 8, 33 Buxton Street, North Adelaide 5006, South Australia, Australia.

**OSINSKY Sergey Petrovich,** b. 5 November 1945, Mutishchy, Moscow, Russia. Scientist. m. Bubnovskaya Larissa N, 1 son. Education: Student, Medical University, Kiev, 1963-69; MD, 1969; Postgraduate, Institute of Oncology Problems, 1969-72; PhD, 1973. Appointments: Senior Scientist, Science Secretary, Chief Scientist, Head of Laboratory, Institute of Oncology Problems, Kiev, 1972-90; Doctor of Sciences (med.), 1987; Professor of Medicine, 1993, Head of Department, Institute of Experimental Pathology, Oncology and Radiobiology, Kiev, 1990-. Publications: 81 papers, 88 abstracts, 2 monographs, 7 patents. Memberships: Oncological Society of the Ukraine; International Society of Clinical Hyperthermia, USA; International Association for the Sensitization of Cancer Treatment, Japan. Address: 9 Ozernaya Street, Flat 18, Kiev 252110, Ukraine.

**OSMAN Mirghani Alielhag,** b. 20 April 1948, Kassala, Sudan. Medicine. m. Aida, 2 sons, 1 daughter. Education: MBBS, 1971; MSC, CAUB, 1976; Dip DERM, London, 1980; Dip VEN, London, 1981; PhD, London, 1981. Appointments: Associate Professor, Consultant Dermatologist. Honours: Salamabi Prize; W H O Fellowship. Memberships: Sudan Medical Association; British Association of Clinical Anatomists; European Academy of Dermatology and Ven; American Academy of Dermatology; American Association for Advancement of Science. Address: College of Medical Sciences, King Faisal University, P O Box 2114 Dammam 31451, Saudi Arabia.

**OSSOFSKY Helen,** b. 12 July 1923, Philadelphia, USA. Medical Doctor; Adolescent Psychiatrist. Education: BA, honours, Mt Holyoak College; MD, Johns Hopkins University School of Medicine, 1954. Appointments: Associate Professor, Georgetown University School of Medicine, 1959-79; Consultant, Program Development, NIH and NSDSP Division of PHS, 1962-64; Private Consultation Practice, Psychiatry, 1968-. Honours: Award, Outstanding Service, 1959. Memberships: American Psychiatrist Association; Washington Psychiatric Society. Address: 1333 Merie Ridge Road, McLean, VA 22101-1826, USA.

**OSTERKAMP Dalene Simmons,** b. 12 January 1932, Davenport, Iowa, USA. Professor; Psychologist; Artist. m. Donald Osterkamp, deceased. Education: PhD, 1989. Appointments: Professor, Counselor, Gallery Director. Publications: Several. Honours: Several in Psychology and Art. Memberships: American Psychological Association; California Printmakers Society. Address: PO Box 387, Glennville, CA 93226-0387, USA.

**OSTERN Hedvig Wright,** b. 5 February 1948, Modum, Norway. Illustration. m. Tore. Education: Diploma, National College of Art and Design, Norway, 1973. Appointments: Freelance Botanical Illustrator, 1980-. Publications: Many Exhibitions, collections and Commissions. Honours: Travel Grant, Book Illustrators Foundation; Travel Grant, GRAFILL. Memberships: GRAFILL; GNSI. Address: Torsrudstubben 25, 3430 Spikkestad, Norway.

**OSTRANDER Diane Lorraine,** b. 28 February 1952, Mason, Michigan, USA. Family Counsellor. m. Charles W Ostrander, 3 daughters. Education: BS, Colorado University; MA, Central Michigan University; PhD, Oklahoma State University. Career: University Assistant Professor, South Dakota University; Counselor, Family Life Consultant, Mental Health, North Carolina and Colorado; Self Employed Counselor and Family Life Consultant. Honours: New Professional of the Year, Oklahoma, 1991; Outstanding Teaching Award, 1994; Listed in biographical dictionaries. Memberships: National Council of Family Relations; American Association of Christian Counselors; Phi Kappa Phi. Address: PO Box 837, Arvada, CO 80001-0837, USA.

**OSTROWSKI-MEISSNER Henry,** b. 18 April 1940, Grochowce, Poland. Research Scientist in Biochemistry, Nutrition and Environment. m. Teresa, 1 son, 3 daughters. Education: BSc Agric Sciences, 1961; MSc Environmental Sciences, 1963; Diploma Chemistry of Radioisotopes, 1967; PhD Nutritional Biochemistry, 1968; Diploma in Computer

Techniques in Industrial Research, 1972. Appointments: OIC Nutritional Biochemistry Laboratory, Balice, Cracow, 1966-70 Department Head, Central Laboratory Feed Industry, Lubliu Poland, 1970-72; Leader, Extraction Project, Ruakura Research Centre, Hamilton, New Zealand, 1972-76; Lecturer Nutrition Biochemistry and Environmental Physics, University of Sydney, 1978-79; Programme Leader, Centre for Research and Development, Bogor, Indonesia, 1979-82; Senior Research Scientist, Commonwealth Scientific and Industrial Research Organisation, CSIRO, Australia, 1982-1993; Director AFIC-CSIRO, Australia, 1983-92; USDA Tropical Research Station, Mayorguez, Puerto Rico, 1984-85; Senior Consultant and Project Coordinator, UNIDO-IPS China, 1996-98 Executive Director, Research and Development, Technology Transfer and Development International Pty Ltd, Sydney 1993-; Director, Research and Development, Wild Herbs Australia Pty Ltd, 1998-. Publications: 279 research and technical publications in professional journals, 18 of them as books and 11 book chapters. Honours: Honorary Professor and Researcher, Chinese Academy of Science, Beijing, China 1996; Visiting Professor, Nagoya University, Japan, 1992-96. Memberships: Life member, President 1991-96, SGVR; Executive Committee member, Coordinator for Asia & Pacific Region 1984-, INFIC. Address: GPO Box 4792, Sydney 2001, Australia.

**OSTRY Sylvia,** b. Winnipeg, Canada. Economist. m. Bernard Ostry, 2 sons. Education: PhD Economics, McGill University and Cambridge University. Appointments: Educator and Researcher, number Canadian universities and University of Oxford Institute of Statistics; Joined Federal Government, 1964, Chief Statistician, Deputy Minister of Consumer and Corporate Affairs, Chairman of Economic Council of Canada, Deputy Minister of International Trade, Ambassador for Multilateral Trade Negotiations and Prime Minister's Personal Rep for the Economic Summit, and other posts; Head, Economics and Statistics Dept, OECD, Paris, 1979-83; Volvo Distinguished Visiting Fellow, Council on Foreign Relations, New York, 1989; Chairman, Centre for International Studies, University of Toronto, 1990-97; Distinguished Research Fellow, Centre for International Studies, University of Toronto. Publications: Governments and Corporations in a Shrinking World: The Search for Stability, 1990; Technonationalism and Technoglobalism: Conflict and Cooperation, 1995; Rethinking Federalism: Citizens, Markets and Governments in a Changing World, 1995; What's On First?: The Post-Cold War Trading System, 1997; Asia-Pacific Crossroads: Regime Creation and the Future of APEC, 1998; Reinforcing the WTO: Occasional Papers No 56, 1998. Honours: 18 honorary degrees from universities in Canada and abroad; Outstanding Achievement Award, Government of Canada, 1987; Companion of the Order of Canada, 1990; Fellow, Royal Society of Canada, 1991; 1992 the Sylvia Ostry Foundation annual lecture series was launched by Madam Sadako Ogata, UN High Commissioner for Refugees; and more. Memberships: Director, Power Financial Corporation; International Advisory Council, Power Financial Corporation; Power Corporation Inter-American Dialogue. Address: 44 Charles Street West, Apt 4111, Toronto, Ontario M4Y 1R8, Canada.

**OTAKE Yoshie,** b. 8 October 1960, Tokyo, Japan. Physicist. Education: BS, 1984, Waseda University, Tokyo; MS, 1986; DSc, 1989. Appointments: Research Associate, 1989-90, Assistant Professor Physics, 1990-96, National College Technology, Katsuta, Japan; Research Fellow, Kyoto University, Japan, 1993; Visiting Scientist, Institute Laue-Langevin, Grenoble, France, 1996; Researcher, Senior Researcher 1997-, RIKEN Institute Physics and Chemistry Research. Publications: Quantum Aspects of Optical

Communications, 1989; Contributor articles to professional journals. Honours: Recipient grant-in-aid for scientific research, Minister for Education in Science and Cl, 1992-97; Alexander von Humboldt Foundation Research Fellow Award. Memberships: Physical Society of Japan; Synchrotron Radiation Society of Japan. Address: Riken, Mihara Mikazuki, Sayo-gun, Hyogo-ken 678-5143, Japan.

**OTANI Yoshio,** b. 13 September 1939, Yokohama, Japan. Professor of Public International Law. m. Ishikawa Tamiko, 3 sons. Education: BA, Otaru University of Commerce, 1964; JSD, Hitotsubashi University, 1971. Appointments: Professor, Hitotsubashi University, 1989-; Invited Professor, University of Paris I, 1998; University of Paris II, 1999. Publications: European Community Law, Tokyo, 1982; Common Interests and International Law, 1992. Membership: French Society of International Law. Address: Hitotsubashi University, Faculty of Law, 2-1 Naka Kunitachi-shi, Tokyo 186, Japan.

**OTCHIROVA Alexandra,** b. 5 July 1949, Ryazan, Russia. Politician; Academic; Poet; Public Figure. m. Valeriy, 1 daughter. Education: Graduate, Moscow State University; Diplomatic Academy under the Russian Foreign Ministry. Appointments: Held a number of posts in government system; Former Deputy of Russian Parliament; Vice President, Committee on International Affairs of Duma. Publications: Author of many publications on problems of philosophy, promtoing women's rights. Honour: Laureate of State Prize. Memberships: Founder and President, Russian Woman's Future; VP, Russian Academy of Creative Arts; Various international forums. Address: 40/6-157 Dolgorukovskaya Str, Moscow, Russia.

**OTEWA John Odhiambo,** b. 27 August 1957, East Kochia, Kenya. Teacher. m. Florence Atieno, 2 sons, 2 daughters. Education: B Ed Science (Hons), 1981, Postgrad Diploma in Curriculum Development, 1983, Nairobi University, Kenya; Postgrad Diploma in Educational Studies, 1987, M Ed Environmental Education, 1988, Leeds University, UK. Appointments: Teacher of Biology & Chemistry, Rapogi High School, 1981-84; Lecturer in Environmental Education, Kisii Teachers College, 1984-89; Lecturer in Primary Science and Professional Studies, Kamagambo Adventist College, 1989-90, 1993-94, Deputy Principal, 1995-; Assistant Lecturer, 1990-91, Lecturer, 1991-93, in Environmental Education, Maseno University College, Kenya. Publications: Textbook, Primary Science and Environment, 1992; 2 Book Chapters entitled Environmental Education Programmes in Africa; Resources Management in Africa, 1992; 2 Papers: The SDA Church and the Worldwide Gender Crisis, 1997; The Man of the Environment?, 1997; The Hidden Curriculum and the Management of SDA Schools, 1998. Honours: 2 scholarships, 1982-83, 1986-88. Membership: Educational Research Network in Kenya. Address: Kamagambo University, PO Box 591, Kissii, Kenya.

**OTGON Munkdorjin,** b. 22 February 1939, Khujirt, Oudorhangai Somon, UVS Province, Mongolia. Medical Doctor. m. T Sarantsetseg, 2 sons. Education: MD Hons, 1962, Mongolia; Medical Biochemist diploma, 1964, Praha, Czechoslovakia; PhD in Medical Genetics, 1972, Moscow, USSR. Appointments: Medical Doctor, Second Hospital Ulaanbaatar, Mongolia, 1962; Assistant Professor and Professor, Medical University, Mongolia, 1972-84; Staff Member, WHO/SEARO, India, 1984-. Publications: 3 books; 80 scientific articles; Supervised 2 PhD students' dissertations, 1962-84. Memberships: Several National and International Scientific Associations and Working Groups. Address: D 383 Defence Colony, New Delhi 110024, India.

**OTOK S,** b. 1 September 1932, Poland. Professor. Education: MA, 1955; DSc, 1964; Dr.hab, 1972. Career: Professor, Geography, Warsaw University, 1984; Professor, Politics & Geopolitics, Catholic Theological Academy, Warsaw, 1998. Publications: 17 books and handbooks, 85 articles e.g. Social Geography, 1987; Environment in Social Policy of the State, 1990; Political Geography: Geopolitics-States-Ecopolitics, 1996, 1997, 1998. Memberships: Council, Center of Local Government, Warsaw; Studium Generale Europa, Warsaw. Home Address: Gen. Waltera 8, 04-991 Warsaw, Poland.

**OTSUKA Akio,** b. 28 January 1959, Tochigi, Japan. Attorney. Education: LLB, Hitotsubashi University, Tokyo, 1984; LLM, 1990, MBA, 1991, Southern Methodist University; Doctoral Program in Management Science and Policy Studies, Tsukuba University, 1998-. Appointments: Legal Trainee, Legal Training & Research Institute of the Supreme Court, Tokyo, 1984-86; Associate Lawyer, Shinmyo & Osanai Law Offices, Tokyo, 1986-89; Advisor, Tokyo Consulting International Inc, Dallas, Texas, USA, 1993-97; Lawyer, Hamayotsu & Hamayotsu Law Offices, Tokyo, 1991-. Publications: The Extraterritorial Applications of US Antitrust Law, 1992; Legal Problems on the Internet, 1997. Memberships: Japanese Bar Association; Daiichi Tokyo Bar Association. Address: 27-4 Yoyogi 4-chome #105, Shibuya-ku, Tokyo 151, Japan.

**OTT C(larence) H(enry),** b. 20 January 1918, Richmond, Michigan. Citizen Ambassador; Accounting Educator. m. Helen Louis McKay, deceased, 3 sons, 1 daughter. Education: BA, 1940, Valparaiso University; MBA, 1970, Northwestern University; PhD, 1980, Southeastern University; CPA, NY; Cert Management Accountant, NY. Appointments: Chief Accountant, G E X-Ray Corporation, Chicago, 1940-41; Public Auditor, Arthur Andersen & Co, Chicago, 1941-43; Renegotiator of Contracts, US Army Air Corps, Chicago, 1943-45; Internal Auditor, David Bradley Manufacturing Co. (Sears), Bradley, Illinois, 1945-48; Contr Treasurer, Manco Manufacturing Co, Bradley, 1948-59; Owner, Operator, Yellow-Checker Cab Co, Kankakee, Illinois, 1959=70; Chairman, Accounting Professor, Rochester (NY) Institute of Technology, 1970-73, Southwestern Michigan College, Dowagiac, Michigan, 1973-; Citizen Ambassador, People to People International, Kansas City, Missouri, 1992-, visiting Estonia, Finland, Spain, Portugal, Morocco, Mainland China, Hong Kong, Israel, Egypt, South Africa, Zambia, Zimbabwe, Botswana, Cape Town, British Isles, Fiji Islands, New Zealand, Australia, Singapore, India, Nepal, Oman, Japan and Paris; Curriculum Advisor, Southwestern Michigan College, 1992-; Delegate to Russia to facilitate their transition to Democratic form of government with Wharton School of Finance, University of Pennsylvania, acting as delegation leader, 1992. Memberships: National Association of Accountants; Institute of Certified Management Accountants; Planning Executives Institute; Alpha Kappa Psi; Pi Kappa Alpha; Pi Gamma Mu. Address: 30992 Middle Crossing Rd, Dowagiac, MI 49047-9268, USA.

**OURS Robert Maurice,** b. 15 September 1936, Parkersburg, West Virginia, USA. Professor; Writer. m. Ann Montague Ours, 2 daughters. Education: BS Journalism, 1958, West Virginia University; MA History, 1966, University Virginia; PhD History, 1974, College of William and Mary. Appointments: Newsman, The Associated Press, 1958-64; Professor of History, University of Virginia, 1966-68; Historian, Editor, Virginia State Library, 1971; Editor, Colonial Records Survey, Virginia Independence Bicentennial Commission, 1972; Professor Journalism, 1972-96, Professor Emeritus Journalism, 1997-, West Virginia University. Publications: Author, College Football Encyclopedia, 1997; College Football Almanac, 1984;

Contributor, Biographical Dictionary of American Journalism, 1989; American Writers Before 1800, 1983. Memberships: Kappa Tau Alpha, journalism honorary; Virginia Historical Society. Address: 209 Waitman Street, Morgantown, WV 26505 7531, USA.

**OURTSEV Vladimir,** b. 15 August 1962, Magnitogorsk, Russia. Researcher. m. Marina Laguza, 1 son, 1 daughter. Education: Magnitogorsk Metallurgical Academy, 1979-84. Appointments: Head, Physical Metallurgy Group, Research Center MMK, 1992-95; Research Manager, Research Center Ausferr, 1995. Publications: Evolution of Dislocations and Grain Structures During Hot Deformation, 1997; The Textures Analysis of Cube Polycrystals, 1997; Fundamentals of Strength and Plasticity, 1998. Address: Central Research Laboratory, Joint Stock Company V I Lenin, Magnitogorsk Metallurgic Production Association, 93 Kirova Str Magnitogorsk, 455002, Russia.

**OUYANG Quan,** b. 10 October 1929, Rucheng Town, Hunan, China. Forestry. m. Zhu Shu Rong, 1 son, 1 daughter. Education: BS, Hunan College of Agriculture, 1952. Appointments: Administrator, Operator, State-run Forest Farms, Guangxi Forestry Administration Department, 1952; Researcher, Guangxi Qinzhou Forestry Research Institute, 1978; Executive Chief Engineer, Guangxi Forestry Administration Department, 1982; Director, Guangxi Eucalyptus Research Group, 1991-93; Vice Technical Director, Sino-Wood Partners Ltd, Hong Kong, 1995-. Publications include: Studies on the development of embryoid from eucatyptus callus, 1980. Memberships: China Society of Eucatyptus; Guangxi Society of Eucatyptus Speciality; Guangxi Association for Forest Ecologic Balance and Environmental Protection. Address: Guangxi Guijia Forestry Co Ltd, No 30 Ren Ming Da Dao Zhong, Zhan Jian City, Guandong, China.

**OUZTS Eugene Thomas,** b. 7 June 1930, Thomasville, Georgia, USA. Minister; Educator. m. Mary Olive Vineyard. Education: BA, 1956, MA, 1957, Harding University; Postgraduate, Murray State University, University of Arkansas, University of Arizona, Arizona State University, Northern Arizona University. Appointments: Secondary Teacher, Arkansas, 1959-60; Secondary Teacher, Missouri, 1960-65; Secondary Teacher, Community College Teacher, Arizona, 1965-92; Ordained Minister, Church of Christ, Arizona, 1956; Minister, Arkansas, Texas, Missouri 1957-65; Minister, Arkansas, Clifton, Safford, Morenci, 1965-. Honours: Arizona Chaplain of the Year, 1984, Thomas C Casaday Unit Chaplain, 1985, Safety Officer, 1989, Senior Member, 1994, Meritorious Service, 1994, Southwest Region Senior Member, 1995, Exceptional Service Award, 1997, Civil Air Patrol. Memberships include: Military Chaplains Association; Disabled American Veterans; American Legion; Elks; Board, Arizona Church of Christ Bible Camp; Airport Advisory Board, Greenlee County; Civil Air Patrol, US Air Force Auxiliary. Address: HC 1 Box 557, Duncan, AZ 85534-9720, USA.

**OVINNIKOV Dmitrii A,** b. 8 November 1935, Chernava. Poet, Writer, Critic. Education: Graduate, Pedagigical University, 1965; PhD, VI Lenin Moscow State Pedagogical Institute. Appointments: Teacher of Literature, Alexin Chemical Technological School; Teacher of Literature, Leo Tolstoi Tula Sate Pedagogical University; Editor, Prioksk Publishing House, Fiction Department. Publications: Many poems published; Sergeui Esenin; I am With You Russia; Memory of My Childhood; The Singer of Russia; The Tzar; A Non Recognized Genious; A Point in the Universe Twilight; A Pearl in the Universe Crusification; Crusification. Memberships: Sain Petersburg Peter Academy of Science and Art; Academician

Petersburg Academy; International Association of the Land and Marine Battle Scenes Writers; USSR and the Russian Federation Writers Union. Address: Apt 4 Korpus 3, 9 Kaulja Str, Tula 300058, Russia.

**OWCZAREK Robert Michal,** b. 20 April 1962, Szczecin, Poland. Mathematical Physicist. m. Hanna E Makaruk. Education: MSc, Physics, Warsaw University, 1988; PhD summa cum laude, Technical Sciences, Institute of Fundamental Technological Research, Polish Academy of Sciences, 1993. Appointments: Research Associate, 1988-93, Associate Professor, 1993-, on leave, 1996-, Institute of Fundamental Technological Research, Polish Academy of Sciences; Postdoctoral Associate, Theoretical Divison, Los Alamos National Laboratory, Los Alamos, New Mexico, USA, 1997-; Referee, 4 journals. Publications: Author or co-author, papers in the field including: Topological Defects in Superfluid Helium, 1991; Quantum Vortex Waves in Superfluid Helium, 1992; Knotted Vortex Lines, Helicity and Superfluid Phase Transition, 1994; Interfacial Dymamics of Abelian Domains: Differential Geometric Methods, 1997; Spinor structures on coadjoint orbits of compact simple Lie groups, book chapter, 1997; Geometry of group and homogeneous manifolds in description of quantum fluids and low-dimensional organic conductors, report, 1998; On Group Theoretic Finite-Mode Approximation of 2D Ideal Hydrodynamics, submitted. Honours: Polish State Committee for Scientific Research Grants, 1993-94, 1995-97; Young Researcher's Fellowship, 1994, Young Doctor's International Fellowship, 1996, Foundation for Polish Science; Senior Fulbright Fellowship, 1997. Memberships: International Society for the Interaction Between Mechanics and Mathematics; American Mathematical Society; Polish Physical Society; Polish Society of Applied Electromagnetics. Address: T13 B213 Los Alamos National Laboratory, Los Alamos,, NM 87595, USA.

**OWENS Charles,** b. 11 August 1956, Champain, Illinois, USA. Medical Doctor. m. Susan, 2 sons, 1 daughter. Education: BS, Biology, University of Illinois, 1980; BS, Psychology, 1981; MD, 1985; Diplomate, National Board of Medical Examiners, 1986; Diplomate, American Board of Radiology, 1993-. Appointments: Residency Radiology, 1987-91; Assistant Professor, University of Illinois, 1992-97; Associate Professor, 1997-; Co Director, Cardiovascular and Intorventional Rediology, 1996-. Memberships: Society of Cardiovascular and Interventional Radiology; Radiological Society of North America; Cardiovascular and Interventional Society of Europe; American Gastro Enterological Association; International Hepatopancreato Biliary Association. Address: 331 Fuller Road, Hinsdale, IL 60521-3626, USA.

**OWENS Thomas,** b. 24 July 1938, Torrance, California, USA. Music Professor. m. Karen Ann, 2 sons, 1 daughter. Education: BA, 1961, MA, 1965, PhD, 1974, University of California at Los Angeles. Appointments: Music Professor, El Camino College, Torrance, 1966-; Visiting Professor of Ethnomusicology, UCLA, 1991-92. Publications: Articles in The New Grove Dictionary of Jazz, 1988; Author, Bebop, The Music and Its Players, 1995. Honours: Atwater-Kent Award in Musicology, 1964; National Endowment for the Humanities Stipend, 1980. Memberships: Society for Ethnomusicology; Music Association of California Community Colleges; American Federation of Musicians; American Federation of Teachers. Address: El Camino College, Dept of Music, 16007 Crenshaw Boulevard, Torrance, CA 90506-0001, USA.

**OWENS Wallace Junior,** b. 28 December 1932, Muskogee, Oklahoma, USA. College Professor (Retired). m. Carolyn Kornegay, 1 daughter. Education: BA, Art Education, Langston niversity, 1959; MA, Art Education, University Center, Klahoma, 1965; MFA, Instituto Allende, GTO, Mexico, 1966. ppointments: Professor, Art, Langston University, 1966; rofessor, Art History, University Central Oklahoma, 1980. onours: Fulbright Scholar, University Rome, Italy, 1969; ellow, African American Institute, 1974. Address: Rt 6 Box 12, Guthrie, OK 73044, USA.

**OYA Hiroshi,** b. 23 April 1936, Nagoya, Japan. University rofessor. m. Motoko Oya, 1 son, 1 daughter. Education: raduated, Department of Electronics, Kyoto University, 1959; Eng, 1961, PhD, 1967, Kyoto University. Appointments: esearch Associate, 1961-67, Assistant Professor, 1967-74, yoto University; Professor, Tohoku University, 1974-. Honour: atsunaga Prize for Outstanding Physicists in Japan, 1978. emberships: Society of Geomagnetism and Earth, Planetary nd Space Science; American Geophysical Union. Address: ohoku University, Department of Astronomy and Geophysics, ameki, Aoba, Sendei 980, Japan.

**OZOBIA Nnamdi Victor,** b. 21 April 1949, Onitsha, Nigeria. arine Engineer; Naval Architect. m. Sylvia Nkiru Ozobia, 1 on, 3 daughters. Education: University of Michigan, USA, 976-77; University of Michigan, Ann Arbor, USA, 1974-75; niversity of Hartford, 1972-74; Diploma in Mechanical ngineering, 1974; BSc, Naval Architecture, Marine ngineering, 1975, MSc, Engineering, 1977. Appointments: ngineer in charge of impact test, 1976; Senior Manager, lichelin overseas, France and Michelin Nigeria, 1978-80; Ag ead, Marine Maintenance, Nigerian Institute for ceanography and Marine Research, Victoria Island, Lagos, 980-81; The Engineer, Dockyard Projects/Head of ngineering Federal Ministry of Transport; Pioneering Project irector, Nigerdock Nigeria Limited, 1986. Publications include: ort Facilities in Trade and Shipping, 1989; Sourcing and ffective Management of Ship Acquisition and Building Fund, 990; Effective Strategic Management in the Maritime Industry The Case of Nigerdock Nigeria Limited, 1990; Development f Ship-building in Nigeria - A Case Study, 1991; Engineering conomy, 1993; Managing an Engineering Consultancy ractice in an Unstable Economy, 1994. Honours: IX ternational Trophy for Technology, 1988; Transport chievement Award, 1989; Recipient of the Maritime Reporters ssociation of Nigeria Merit Award, 1990; Contractor of the ear 1991 Award; Transport Expo 92 Golden Merit Award, 992; Abia State Government Award, 1992; Engineer of the ear Award, 1992; Illustrious Sons of Anambra State Awards, 992; Honorary Fellowship Award, 1993. Memberships: igerian Society of Engineers; Society of Naval Architects and arine Engineers; Institute of Marine Engineers; Council of legistered Engineers of Nigeria; Executive Council, Nigerian ociety of Engineers; Coordinator, Naval Architecture/Marine ivision, Nigerian Society of Engineers; Committee of Division hairman, Nigerian Society of Engineers. Address: 26 lakuwen, Ikoyi, Lagos, Nigeria.

**OZTURK Munir Ahmet,** b. 6 December 1943, Kashmir, urkey. Ecologist. m. Birsel, 2 sons, 1 daughter. Education: BSc, 1962; MSc, 1964; PhD, 1970; DSc, 1975. Appointments: Botany Department, Ege University. Publications include: Observations on the seed dormancy of three Ranunculus pecies; Studies on the autecology of Ranunculus arvensis; Some autecological studies on Ranunculus muricatus; Preliminary observations on the edaphic and biotic relations of Myrtus communis; Preliminary studies on the vegetation of neadows in Srinagar; Vegetation in Aegean region of Turkey; Studies on the germination of Asphodelus aestivus Brot. Address: Botany Department, E Block, Science Faculty, Ege University, 35100 Bornova-Izmir, Turkey.

# P

**PACE George Ernest,** b. 16 May 1961, Sliema, Malta. Hospital Engineer. Education: B Elec Eng Hons, University of Malta, 1987-1992; MBA, Henley Management College, 1998. Appointments: Trainee Engineer, Malta Development Corporation, 1987-92; Engineer, 1992-93; Hospital Engineer, Department of Health, 1993-. Address: 15/3 Sappers St, Valletia VLT 11, Malta.

**PADMANABH Jena,** b. 10 October 1930, Benjarapur Village. Social Worker; Teacher. m. Tulashi Dei, 2 sons, 1 daughter. Education: Graduate, Rural University, 1956; Diploma in Social Science; Trained in IDP, BT. Memberships: Afford, New Delhi. Address: Benjerapur, PO Mandari vai Bari Cuttack, Jajpur, Orissa, India.

**PAGE Linda Jewel,** b. 18 March 1941, Quanah, Texas, USA. Educator. m. Roger Hollander, divorced, 2 daughters. Education: PhD, Princeton University, 1973; MA, Counseling Psychology, Adler School of Professional Psychology, 1989. Appointments: Founder, Psychotherapy Institute of Toronto, 1987-92; Director, Adler Graduate School of Ontario, 1992-; Core Doctoral Faculty, Adler School of Professional Psychology, 1991-. Honours: Phi Beta Kappa, 1963; Woodrow Wilson Fellowship, 1963; National Science Foundation Fellowship, 1963-66. Memberships: North American Society of Adlerian Psychology; American Counseling Association; Society for the Exploration of Psychotherapy Integration; Society for Psychotherapy Research. Address: 134 Dovercliffe Road, Guelph, Ontario, Canada.

**PAK Mikhail Nikolaevich,** b. 21 June 1918, Yanchikhe, Hasan Region, Russia. Historian; Educator. m. Gorinstein Maria Yu, dec, 2 sons. Education: BA, 1941, Moscow University, Institute of History, Philosophy and Literature; PhD, History, 1947; Dr Sc, History, 1961; Professor, 1963. Appointments: Lecturer, Ukraine University, 1943-44; Lecturer and Assistant Professor, Ryazan Pedagogic Institute, 1945-49; Assistant Professor, 1949-61, Professor, 1961-71, Professor, Head of Dept, 1971-91, Director of International Centre for Korean Studies and Professor, 1992-, Moscow University. Publications: Over 250 works on Korean Studies; History of Korea, 1974; Outlines of Early History of Korea, 1979; Outlines of Korean Historiography, 1987; Kim Pu-sik's Samguk Sagi (History records of 3 kingdoms), translated into Russian, vol 1, 1959, vol 2, 1995. Honours: Certificate of Honour, Supreme Soviet of Russia, 1980; Fulbright Certificate, 1982; National Order Tongback-chang, Korea, 1992; Honorary Professor of MSU, 1993; Lomonosov Prize of MSU, 1997; National Prize for Overseas Koreans, 1999. Memberships: Head of Department, Eurasian Studies in Russian Academy for Natural Sciences; International Society for Korean Studies; and others. Address: Leningradsky Prospect 74-1-30, Moscow 125315, Russia.

**PALACIOS Ronald,** b. 11 January 1953, Camiri, Bolivia. Immunologist. 2 daughters, Catherine, Patricia. Education: Bachelor Degree, Humanities, Colegio Sagrado Corazon, Sucre, 1970; MD with distinction, 1976, Degree, Internal Medicine Speciality, 1979, University National Autonoma de Mexico; PhD, Karolinska Institute, Stockholm, 1982. Appointments: Instructor, Histology, 1973, Assistant Professor, Introduction to Medicine, University National Autonoma de Mexico; Fellow, Immunology, Institute National Nutrition, Mexico City, 1979-80; Member, Basel Institute of Immunology, Switzerland, 1982-92; Professor, Deputy Chairman, Department of Immunology, University of Texas, MD Anderson

Cancer Center, Houston, 1992-. Publications: Several article in peer-reviewed professional journals. Memberships: Fellow Mexican Board of Internal Medicine; AAAS; America Association of Hematology; Association Medicos Internista Mexico; Association Medicos Instituto National Nutritio American Association of Immunology; American Association Microbiology; Scandinavian Society of Immunology; Universi of Texas MD Anderson Associates; New York Academy Sciences. Address: PO Box 2795, Santa Cruz, Bolivia.

**PALAIMA Jurgis,** b. 18 October 1914, Jonava Distric Lithuania. Lecturer, Professor. m. Marina, 1 daughte Education: Lithuanian Institute of Physical Education, 1947-4 Graduate, Psychology Department, Leningrad Institute c Physical Education, 1954-58; Doctor of Social Sciences, 1979 Appointments: Chairman, Pedagogy and Psycholog Department, 1950-79; Director, 1954-61; Professor, Pedagogy Psychology and Sports Management Department, Lithuania Institute of Physical Education, 1979-94. Publications: autho and co-author of 8 books; Over 100 other Scientif Publications. Memberships: Lithuanian Association of Spo Psychologists. Address: Kovo II Osios 52-9, LT 3031 Kaunas Lithuania.

**PALICICA Radu Dimitrie,** b. 21 October 1945, Timisoara Romania. Professor, Veterinary Medicine. m. Maria Palicica, daughter. Education: Graduate, Veterinary Medicine Facult Timisoara, 1968; PhD, 1975. Appointments: Universi Assistant, Veterinary Medicine Faculty, Timisoara, 1968-7 University Professor, Constantine State University, Algeria 1979-80; Lecturer, Banat University of Agricultural Science and Veterinary Medicine, Timisoara, 1980-90; Universi Professor, Agricultural Institute, Moldavian Republic, 1990-9 Assistant Professor, 1992-96, Professor, 1996-, Bana University of Agricultural Sciences and Veterinary Medicine Timisoara. Publications: 126 scientific papers, 12 book Memberships: World Veterinary Anatomists Associatio Romanian Veterinary Surgeons Association; Veterinar Surgeons Association of Moldavian; Applied Biotechnologie Association, Romania. Address: Zborului Str Nr 18, Apt 1 Timisoara, Romania.

**PALLASCHKE Diethard Ernst,** b. 30 June 1940, Friedlanc Ostpr, Pravdinsk. Mathematician. m. Ingrid Marx, 1 daughte Education: Doctorate, University of Bonn, 1967; Habilitatior University of Bonn, 1970. Appointments: Assistant Professo Darmstadt, Germany, 1972-73, University of Münste Germany, 1973-77; Full Professor, University of Bonr Germany, 1977-81, University of Karlsruhe, Germany, 1981 Publications: Publication of research papers and textbooks i Functional Analysis, Mathematical Economics an Optimization. Memberships: American Mathematical Societ German Mathematical Society; Polish Mathematical Societ Intern Order of Merit, 1994-. Address: Institut fur Statisk an Mathematisch, Wirtshaftstheorie, Universitat Karlsruh Postfach 6980, D-76128 Karlsruhe 1, Germany.

**PALLONE Sharon Raney,** b. 8 August 1939, Little Rock Arkansas. Executive; Social Worker; Christian Counsellor. sons. Education: BS Psychology, 1961; BA Psychology, 197 Hon Doctorate Humanities, 1976. Appointments: Founder an Executive Director, SCAN Volunteer Services Inc; Nationa Child Abuse Treatment Centre - SCAN is Suspected Chil Abuse and Neglect. Publication: Book: Helping Parents wh Abuse their Children, 1984; 7 articles published. Honours Delegate to Governor's Conference on Early Childhoo Development, 1972; Award for Outstanding Services in th Field of Human Relations; Woman of the Year - Arkansa 1975; One Woman's War Against Child Abuse, Goo

Housekeeping, 1975; Notable Americans Award, 1977; They are to Care, Child Abuse Volunteers, 1978; Liberty Bell ward, Bar Association Award; Chosen one of Ten Outstanding Young Women of America. Memberships: Child Protection eam, University of Arkansas Medical Centre and Arkansas Children's Hospital; Arkansas Council for Child Protection; Pulaski County Task Force for Child Protection; SCAN Volunteer Service Inc; Woodlawn Day Care Centre for Abused Children; Arkansas Association for Children with Learning Disabilities; Ada Thompson Home; Deputy Investigator, Pulaski County Prosecuting Attorney's Office; Sudden Infant Death Syndrome; Arkansas Advocates for Families and Children; Rhodes Scholarship, Selection Committee, 1977-81; Access-Teenage Mothers; Coalition Against Family Violence; Kairos Prison Ministry; Governor's Crime Commission. Address: SCAN Volunteer Service Inc, 1400 West Markham Ste 300, Little Rock, AR 72201, USA.

**PALLOTTA Gail Cassady,** b. 7 January 1942, USA. Writer. m. Frederick V Pallotta, 1 daughter. Education: AB, Western Carolina University, 1964; Publications Certificate, Emory University, 1967; Long Ridge Writers Group, 1996; Institute of Childrens Literature, 1996. Appointments: Editorial Assistant, Life Insurance Company, Georgia, 1965-67; Editor, Employee Relations, Colonial Pipeline Company, 1967-68; Philip Denton Advertising, 1968-69; Assistant to Director of Nurses, Piedmont Hospital, 1970-72; Part Time, Cobb County After School Enrichment Program. Publications: Articles Including, Teachers Are Bridging the Gap, 1985; Austell Begins Second Century, 1986; Up By the Bootstraps, 1987; This Spring Health Is In, 1988; Woodruff Plantation, 1990; Tar Heel Towns - Saluda, 1993; The Outer Banks or Bust, 1995. Membership: First Presbyterian Church. Address: 251 Hunting Creek Drive, Marietta, GA 30068-3419, USA.

**PALOMÄKI Jari Juhani,** b. 24 May 1961, Turku, Finland. Philosopher; Librarian. Education: MS, University of Turku, 1989; Licentiate of Philosophy, 1994, PhD, 1994, Librarian degree, 1994, Docent (Theoretical Philosophy), 1996-, University of Tampere. Appointments: Library Assistant, 1981-, Turku City Library; Teacher, University of Turku, University of Tampere, Technical University of Tampere, Turku School of Economics, 1986; Researcher, 1990-, University of Tampere; Visiting Researcher, Academy of Sciences, Czech Republic, 1994-; Visiting Researcher, 1994, Assistant Research Professor, 1997, Technical University of Denmark. Publications: From Concepts to Concept Theory, 1994; Co-editor: On the Formal Representation of Knowledge (in Finnish), 1997; Several scientific articles. Honour: Grantee, Finnish Cultural Foundation, 1999. Memberships: Philosophical Society of Finland; Finnish Artificial Intelligence Society. Address: Vuorikatu 7aA4, FIN 20700, Turku, Finland.

**PÄLTÄNEA Radu,** b. 1 March 1953, Brasov, Romania. Professor of Mathematics. m. Cornelia, 2 sons. Education: University Brasov, 1976; PhD, University of Cluj-Napoca, 1992. Appointments: University Assistant, 1980, Lecturer, 1991, Associate Professor, 1996-, Transilvania University. Publications: 40 Papers. Memberships: Society for Mathematical Science of Romania; American Mathematical Society. Address: Transilvania University, Fac Sciences, Bd Eroilor Nr 29, Brasov 2200, Romania.

**PALTRIDGE Rosemary,** b. 2 August 1952, Adelaide, Australia. Social Welfare Administrator. m. Robert Wayne Paltridge (deceased 10 April 1995), 1 son, 1 daughter. Education: Psychology One - Human Behaviour, Adelaide Institute, 1996-97; BSA Business Services, Advanced Certificates in Computer Accounting and Computer Office

Software, 1998; Student, Tabor College Teachers, 1999. Appointments include: Teacher Aid, Trinity Christian School, Rosewater, South Australia, 1981-84; Assistant Administrator, Hebron Christian Centre, West Lakes, 1984-86; Missionary, Teacher, Accountant, Christian Revival Crusade International, Port Moresby, Papua New Guinea, 1989-91; Co-ordinator, Crusade Mercy Ministries, Ethelton, South Australia, 1995-; Advisor, Australian Cambodia Overseas Support Inc, Taperoo, South Australia, 1997-; Missions Co-ordinator, Pastoral Care Worker, Portside Community Church Inc, Ethelton, 1999-. Honour: Certificate, Who's Who in the World, 16th edition, 1999. Memberships: Community Member, St John's Ambulance, 1988; Pt Adelaide Division, SA; Life Member, Asian Action Love Australia; Portside Community Church Inc, Ethelton. Address: Crusade Mercy Ministries, 1 Causeway Road, Ethelton 5015, Australia.

**PALVA Ilmari Pellervo,** b. 5 May 1932, Finland. Physician. m. Seija Kaivola, 1 son, 3 daughters. Education: MD, University of Helsinki, 1956; PhD, 1962. Appointments: Registrar, 1959-63; Consultant, 1964-65, University Hospital of Helsinki; Associate Professor, University of Oulu, 1965-74; Professor of Medicine, University of Kuopio, 1974; Acting Professor of Medical Education, University of Tampere, 1975-76; Consultant, City Hospital, Tampere, 1976-92; Retired, 1992. Publications: Haematology Guide for Evaluation in Medical Education; Over 200 Scientific Papers on Haematology, Medical Education. Honours: Knight 1st Order, Finish White Rose. Memberships: Finnish Society Internal Medicine; Finnish Society of Haematology; International Society of Haematology; American Society of Haematology. Address: Oikotie 8, FIN-33950 Pirkkala, Finland.

**PAN Huo-Hsi,** b. 11 November 1918, Fuzhou China. Engineering Professor. m. Chao Pan, 2 daughters. Education: BS, ME, 1943; MS, ME, 1949; MS, Applied Mechanics, 1950; PhD, University of California at Berkeley, 1954. Appointments: Head of Inspection Department, 21st Arsenal, China, 1943-47; From Teaching Assistant to Associate in ME, University of California, 1950-53; Assistant Professor, University of Toledo, 1954-55; Univesity of Illinois, 1955-57; From Assistant Professor to Professor, Applied Mechanics, New York University, 1957-73; Proffers Applied Mechanics; Professor, Mechanical Engineering, Polytechnic University, 1973-90; Professor Emeritus, 1990-. Publications: Numerous Papers Published, Various Journals. Memberships: ASME; AIAA; American Academy of Mechanics; Society of Engineering Science; US and International Association for Computational Mechanics; Society for ndustrial and Applied Mathematics; Phi Kappa Phi; Sigma Xi; Tau Beta Pi; Pi Tau Sigma; Pi Mu Epsilon; Listed in Who's Who in Science and Engineering; Who's Who on America; Who's Who in the World. Address: 76 Edgars Ln, Hastings On Hudson, NY 10706, USA.

**PAN Xiaoyang,** b. 25 December 1953, Sichuan, China. Director; Professor. m. Huang Zhenghong, 1 son. Education: Bachelor Degree, Shanghai Drama Institute, 1984-88. Appointments: Director, Chongqing Television Station, 1980-84; Senior Director, Sichuan Television Station, 1988-96; Senior Director, China National Television Station, 1997-. Publictions include: Pason and His Brothers, 1988; South Traveling-History of Bordering Families, 1991; I Own The Blue Sky, 1992; Son of the Earth, 1994; Three Gorges of Long History, 1996. Honours: Gold Medal, 10th China National Flying Award, 1988; Golden Panda, International Television Festival, Sichuan, 1991; Gold Medal, Best Director, China National Television Show, 1992; Gold Medal, Best Director, Best Photographer, 12th China National Flying Award, 1992; Silver Medal, 12th China National Flying Award, 1992; Golden Fairy

Award, Monte Carlo International Television Festival, France, 1994; NHK Award, Japan, 1996. Address: No 15 Building, Hufang Road, Xuan Wu District, Beijing 100052, China.

**PANCHALE Bhimrao**, b. 30 March 1951, Amaravati, Maharashtra. Singer. Education: Bachelor of Commerce, 1972; Bachelor of Arts, Hindi Marathi Literature and Music, 1976-78; Study of Urdu Literature. Appointments: Dalit Sahitya Sammelan, Chandrapur, 1959; Classical Vocal Disciple, Guru Shri Bhaiyasaheb Deshpande, and Guru Shri Eknathpant Kulkarni of Akola; Singer, All India Radio; Performer, Various Programmes on Television; More than 450 public programmes of Gazal Singing; Some Major Concerts; Singer, 1972-; Akhil Bharitya Marathi Sahitya Sammeland, Akola, 1981; Radio Artists, Sammelan, Raipur, 1982; 21st Maharashtra State Music and Dance Conference, 1984; Maharashtra State Music Festivals, Beed, 1985; Publications: Gazalche Chhanda Shastra. Honours: Sur Singar Souvenir, Sur Singar Samsad; Dr Babasaheb Ambedkar Puraskar, 1998; Phule Shahu, Ambedkar Smruti Puraskar; Many other Awards. Address: 5th Floor HRD Section, State Bank of India, M Cama Road, Nariman Point, Mumbai 400021, India.

**PANDA Naresh Kumar**, b. 17 June 1959, Parlakhemundi, Orissa, India. Otolaryngologist. m. Nidhi Bidyut Panda, 2 sons. Education: MBBS, 1982; MS ENT, 1987; Dip NBE, 1987; Senior Resident, 1987-90. Appointments: Assistant Professor, 1990-97; Associate Professor, 1997-. Publications: 45. Honours: National Scholarship, 1975; Silver Medal, First Order, MS exam, 1987. Memberships: New York Academy of Sciences; Indian Society Head, Neck Oncology; Association of Otolaryngologists of India. Address: H-11/3 Chandra Sekharpur, Housing Board Colony, Bhubaneswar Orissa 751016, India.

**PANDA Subas Chandra**, b. 12 May 1960, Dalvanpur, India. Lecturer. m. Ratnamoni Panda, 3 sons. Education: MSc, 1981; MPhil, 1985; PhD, continuing under guidance of Dr B B Parida. Appointments: Biology Teacher, Sainik School, Utkal University, 1986; Lecturer, Nimapara College, at present. Publication: 1 paper in Nucleus Journal. Address: Nimapara College at Dalvanpur, PO Vanpur, District Puri 752 114, India.

**PANDE Deepa**, b. 6 July 1943, Haldwani, India. Teacher. m. Pande ID, 1 son, 1 daughter. Education: MA, Economics, Agra University, 1964; PhD, Agra University, 1970. Appointments: Lecturer, 1974-88; Reader, Kumaun University, India, 1988-. Publications: Articles Published in Encyclopaedia, Books and Journals. Memberships: All India Economic Association and Bhartiya Arthik Shodh Sansthan. Address: Sunny Bank, Ayarpata Tallital, Nainital UP, India.

**PANDE Ishwari Datt**, b. 18 January 1942, Almora, India. Forester. m. Deepa, 1 son, 1 daughter. Education: MSc, Chemistry, Agra University, 1963; AIFC, Indiana Forest College, Dehradun, 1966. Appointments: Various Assignments in Indian Forest Service, 1969-; Chief Conservator of Forests, 1996-. Publications: Articles Published in World Forestry Congress, Various Books, Journals. Honours: Agrawal Award in Soil Conservation, 1966. Memberships: Indian Forest Service Association. Address: Chief Conservator of Forest, Nainital UP, India.

**PANDE Piyush Chandra**, b. 9 December 1952, Haldwani, India. Scientist. m. Namita Pande, 1 son. Education: BSc, Agra University, 1972; MSc, Roorkee University, 1974; PhD, University of Durham, 1984. Appointments: Scientist, Physics, Agricultural Research Services of India, 1976, Head of Division, 1990-93, Senior Scientist. Publications: Over 104 research papers. Honours: Commonwealth Scholarship, 1981-84; Marie Curie Fellowship, 1995. Memberships: Solar Energy Society of India; Semiconductor Society of India; Indian Association of Physics Teachers. Address: Central Arid Zone Research Institute, Jodhpur 342003, India.

**PANDE Suresh Chandra**, b. 2 October 1955, Nainital, U.P. India. Lecturer. Education: MA, 1976, PhD, 1983, Kumaon University, Nainital, U.P., India. Appointment: Lecturer, English, UP Government, 1991-. Publications: Poems and research articles in professional journals, periodicals and magazines including: Indian Verse by Young Poets, 1980; Modern Trends in Indo-English Poetry, 1982; Bharat Protiva, 1982; Prevalent Aspects, 1983; Considerations, 1985; Poetry, 1985; Poetry Time, 1985; The Kalyana Kalptaru, English Monthly, 1995, 1996, 1997; A Am a Sea, 1995. Address: Government College, Maitakunda, PO Bansal District Garwal, India.

**PANDEY J N**, b. 15 August 1943, India. Teaching. m. R S Pandey, 2 sons, 1 daughter. Education: BA, 1963; BEd, 1964; MA, 1966; PhD, Geography, 1984. Appointments: Lecturer, Department of Geography, Banaras Hindu University, 1967-68; Lecturer, 1968-84, Reader, 1984-96, Professor, 1996-, Department of Geography, DDU Gorakhpur University. Publications: 3 books, 35 research papers. Honours: Gold Medal, 1965. Memberships: 12 associations and societies in India and abroad. Address: Department of Geography, DDU Gorakhpur University, Gorakhpur UP, India.

**PANDIT Ashok K**, b. 20 February 1952, Hawal, Pulwama, Kashmir, India. Postgraduate Teacher; Researcher. m. Anita, 23 June 1985, 2 sons. Education: BSc, Biology, 1971; MSc, Zoology, 1974; PhD, Aquatic Ecology, Kashmir University, 1980. Appointments: Junior Research Fellow, 1975-77, Senior Research Fellow, 1977-80, Scientist (Ecologist), 1980-97, Associate Professor, 1997-, Centre of Research for Development, University of Kashmir, Srinagar, India. Publications: 50 research papers and reviews in the area of limnology and wetland ecology, algology, fish and wildlife ecology, resource ecology, management of ecosystems in well known national and international journals and proceedings of international conferences; Ecology, Environment and Energy; Freshwater Ecosystems in the Himalaya; Natural Resources of Western Himalaya; Wetland Ecosystems in India. Honours: National Merit Scholarship, Higher Secondary Elective to MSc; UNESCO participant to Third International Wetlands Conference held in Rennes, France, 1988; International Environment Award, 1997. Memberships: International Society for Tropical Ecology; National Institute of Ecology; Indian Ecological Soicety; Indian Society of Naturalists; Indian Association of Pollution Chemists and Biologists; Founding Fellow, J & K Academy of Sciences; Founding Member, World Wetlands Partnership, Colorado, USA. Hobbies: Gardening; Photography; Hiking; Nature loving and making friends. Address: Centre of Research for Development, University of Kashmir, 190006, India.

**PANDYA Sumanchandra**, b. 16 August 1929, Davad, Gujarat, India. E D Physician. m. Subhadra, 1 son, 1 daughter. Education: MBBS, 1952, Gujarat University, India; ECFMG, 1971; FLEX, NY; ACLS; Fellow, American College of Emergency Medicine, Life; Diplomate, American Board Emergency Medicine, 1994. Appointments: Various posts including: Casualty Medical Officer, House Physician and Registrar in Internal Medicine, House Surgeon, Postgraduate Studentship in Obstetrics and Gynaecology, Chief Medical Officer, Surgical Resident in Trauma services and Cardiovascular Surgery, Chief Resident in Surgery, 1952-76; ED Physician, Good Samaritan Hospital, NY, 1976-77; ED ysician at Portsmouth, Ohio and at Westbranch, Michigan rking for Emergency Consultants, 1977-78; ED Physician at 1ens, Ohio, working for Spectrum, 197-79; ED Physician at oenix Medical Park Hospital, 1979-84; Director of 1ergency Medical Services, Phoenix Medical Park Hospital, 84-92; Medical Director, Emergency Dept, St Francis spital, Regional Heart Centre, Columbus, Georgia, 1992-94; ) Physician, Heart of Florida Hospital, 1994-95; ED ysician, Florida Hospital-Walker, 1995; ED Physician, St 1ud Hospital, 1995-. Memberships: Fellow, American College Emergency Physicians; Donor and Member, Trustee of veral educational institutions, hospitals and religious anisations in India. Address: 2223 Paprika Drive, Orlando, 32837, USA.

**PANERO Teresa,** b. 7 April 1929, Turin, Italy. urative-Symbolist Painter; Graphic Artist. m. Giovanni Bosio v), 2 daughters. Education: Autodidact. Appointments: Many lective exhibitions as well as personal exhibitions in Italy and road from 1981; Most relevant and recent participations: 12th ropean Biennial, Paris, 1998 (Gold Medal); 30th CEIC niversary, Moscow, 1998. Publications: Donne di Quadri, 81; Un Anno d'Arte, Mondadori, 1986; Il Quadrato, 1986; I 1estri Del Colore, 1987; Antologia Artisti Italiani, 1994; and 1ers. Honours: Golden Gondola, Milan, 1984; Trophy ly-China, Milan, 1984; 1st Prize, 8th European Biennial, me, 1988; Trophy, Tokyo 1992; International Prize, Silver 1ot Europe, London, 1994; and others. Memberships: cademia Santa Rita, Turin; European Union Artisti d'Europa, me; Italart, Lodi (Milan); Accademia Ferdinandea, Catania; cademia Internazionale dei Dioscuri, Taranto. Address: Via 1ntebello 1, 10098 Rivoli, Torino, Italy.

**PANG Tao,** b. 30 June 1935, Beijing, China. Professor. m. 1an Jialing, 1 son, 2 daughters. Education: Department of 1chanical Engineering, Harbin Institute Technology, 1955-60. 1pointments: Director Technical Section of Electrical 1gineering Factory, 1960-62, Teaching Assistant, 1962-74, 1cturer, 1974-85, Associate Professor, 1985-92, Professor, 92-, Harbin Institute Technology; Visiting Researcher, Osaka iversity of Japan, 1981-83. Publications: Books include: 1perprecise Processing Technique and Application; Over 20 1ademic papers. Honours: First Prize, Important Scientific 1search Achievement, National Defence Science and 1gineering Committee, 1980; 2nd and 3rd Prize, National 1ience and Technology Advancement, 1986, 1988. 1mberships: China Precision Engineering Speciality 1mmittee; Board Director, China Bao Yushi; Standing 1mmittee, Board Director, Shandong Bao Yushi; Senior 1mber, China Mechanical Engineering Institute. Address: 1partment of Mechanical Engineering, Weihai Campus, 1rbin Institute of Technology, 264209 Weihai Shangdong, 1ina.

**PANIN Victor Yevgenyevich,** b. 10 November 1930, 1azakhstan, Russia. Physicist. m. Panina Margarita, 2 sons. 1ucation: Graduate, Tomsk State University, 1952; PhD, 1stgraduate School, 1955; Professor, 1969. Appointments: 1ad of Division, Siberian Physics and Technology Institute, 169-79; Deputy Director, Institute of Atm Opt, Siberian 1anch, Academy of Sciences, Russia, 1979-84; Director, 1titute of Strength Physics and Materials Science, 1984. 1blications: The Theory of Phases in Alloys, 1984; Structural 1formation Levels of Solids, 1985; Physical Mesomechanics 1d Computer-Aided Design of Materials, 1995. Membership: 1ssian Academy of Sciences. Address: Institute for Physics 1 Strength and Materials Sciences, Siberian Division of 1ssian Academy of Sciences, 2/1 Prospekt Akademicheskii 1msk 55, 634021 Russia.

**PANKEY George Atkinson,** b. 11 August 1933, Shreveport, Louisiana, USA. Physician. Education: Student, La Poly Institute, 1950-51; BS, Tulane University, 1954, MD, 1957; MS, University Minnesota, 1961. Appointments: Diplomate, American Board of Internal Medicine, American Board Infectious Diseases; Intern, University Minnesota Medicine, 1958-60; Resident in Internal Medicine, 1958-60; Resident in Internal Medicine, Minneapolis VA Hospital, Minneapolis General Hospital, 1960-61; Practice Medicine, New Orleans, 1961-; Partner, Ochsner Clinic, New Orleans, 1968-; Assistant Visiting Physician, Charity Hospital, New Orleans, Lousiana, 1961-62; Senior Visiting Physician, 1975-95; Consultant, Infectious Diseases, Ochsner Clinic and Foundation Hospital, 1963-; Head, Section Infectious Diseases, 1972-94; Instructor, Department Medicine, Division Infectious Diseases, Tulane School Medicine, New Orleans, 1961-63; Clinical Instructor, Tulane University School Medicine, 1963-65; Clinical Assistant, Professor Medicine, 1965-68; Clinical Associate Professor, 1968-73; Clinical Professor, 1973-; Clinical Professor, Department Medicine, Louisiana State University School Medicine, 1979-; Clinical Professor, Oral Diagnosis, Medicine and Radiology, Louisiana State University School of Dentistry, 1983-; Consultant, World Health Information Services Information Services Inc, 1974-; Director, Founder, Century National Bank, New Orleans; Member, Medicine Test Committee, National Board Medical Examiners, 1979-83; Member, Infectious Diseases Advisory Board, Hoffman-LaRoche, 1982-; Consultant, Federal Air Surgeon, 1997-. Publications include: A Manual of Antimicrobial Therapy, 1969; Contemporary Diagnosis and Management of Sinusitis, with Charles W Gross and Michael G Mendelsohn, 1997; Editor: with Geoffrey A Kalish, Outpatient Antimicrobial Therapy - Recent Advances, 1989; Infectious Diseases Digest, 1983-95; Southern Medical Association Program for Infectious Diseases Dial-Access, 1983-92; Ochsner Clinic Reports on Serious Hospital Infections, 1985-; Ochsner Clinic Reports on Geriatric Infectious Diseases, 1990-93; Ochsner Clinic Reports on the Management of Sepsis, 1991-93; Infectious Disease Clinics of North America, 1994. Honours include: Fellow, ACP; Fellow Infectious Diseases Society of America; Clinician Award, 1996; Laureate Award, Louisiana Chapter, 1997. Memberships include: American Society Microbiology; American Thoracic Society; New Orleans Academy Internal Medicine, President, 1977-78, 1996-97; AMA; Aerospace Medical Association; American Society Tropical Medicine and Hygiene; American Venereal Disease Association; American Society Parasitologists. Address: 1514 Jefferson Highway, New Orleans, LA 70121-2429, USA.

**PANOSSIAN Alexander,** b. 31 January 1949, Yerevan, Armenia. Chemist. m. Susanna Panossian, 1 son, 1 daughter. Education: Diploma, Yerevan State University, 1971; Candidate of Science, Moscow Institute of Bioorganic Chemistry, 1975; DSc, Chemistry, Moscow Institute of Fine Chemical Technology, 1986; Professor, 1991. Appointments: Researcher, Institute of Fine Organic Chemistry, Yerevan, 1975-85, Karolinska Institute, Department of Physiological Chemistry, Stockholm, 1982-83, Institute of Pharmaceutical Biology, Munich University, 1993-94, 1995, Kings College, London, Department of Pharmacy, 1996; Head, Department of Medical Chemistry and Biochemical Pharmacology, Institute of Medical Radiology, Yerevan, 1985-94; Head of Research and Drug Quality Control Laboratories, Armenian Drug and Medical Technology Agency, Yerevan, 1994-. Publications: Over 100 papers in professional scientific journals; 14 patents. Honours: Diploma, Mendeleev All Union Chemical Society, 1976; Award, German Academy of Sciences, 1996. Memberships: Association of Pharmacologists of Armenia; New York Academy of Sciences. Address: Drug Agency, 15 Moscowian,

375002 Yerevan, Armenia.

**PAPADOPOULOS Constantinos,** b. 12 December 1962, Athens, Greece. Computer Scientist. Education: BSc Mathematics, 1984, Athens University, Greece; Postgraduate Diploma in Computer Studies, University of Essex, 1986; PhD, Computer Science, Lancaster University, forthcoming. Appointments: Programmer, Control Data Corporation, Athens, Greece, 1986-88; Systems Analyst, Greek Army's Computing Centre, 1988-90; Protocol Designer, Intracom SA, 1990-92; Instructor, American College of Greece, 1991-97; Project Leader, Computing Centre of the Greek Ministry of Finance, 1992-. Publications: 4 research papers in international computing journals; 9 research papers in international computer conferences. Memberships: IEEE; ACM; New York Academy of Sciences, 1996. Address: 77 Aristeidou Street, GR-17671 Kallithea Athens, Greece.

**PAPADOPOULOU Alexandra,** b. 3 January 1958, Patra, Achaia, Greece. Doctor. m. Mark Avrousin, 1 d. Education: MB BS, Medical Institute of Paediatrics, St Petersburg, 1983; Boards in Paediatrics, University of Athens, 1989; MD, University of Birmingham, UK, 1998. Appointments: Resident Doctor, 1983-84; House Officer, 1985-86; Senior House Officer, 1986-89; Junior Specialist, Childrens Hospital, Athens, 1989-91; Clinical Research Fellow, Paediatric Gastroenterology and Nutrition, University of Birmingham, 1991-94; Responsible for running the Paediatric Gastroenterology and Nutrition Department of Paediatrics, Faculty of Nursing, University of Athens, Paul A Kyriakou Children's Hospital, Athens, 1994-. Publications: 17 original papers reviewed; 4 reviews; 5 contributions to books; 17 published abstracts. Honours: Grant, Local Bone Marrow Transplantation Research Fund; First Award in Nutrition. Memberships: Greek Paediatric Society; Greek Gastroenterology Society; British Society of Paediatric Gastroenterology and Nutrition; European Society of Paediatric Gastroenterology and Nutrition. Address: Ag Anargyron 32B Marousi, 151 24 Athens, Greece.

**PAPAEVAGELOU George,** b. 19 December 1962, Thessaloniki, Greece. Professor. m. Maria Konsta. Education: Engineer, University of Thessaloniki, 1985; MSc, Hydrology, V U Brussels, Belgium, 1987; PhD, Mechanics, INP Grenoble, France, 1994. Appointment: Professor, Technical-Professional School of Kozani, Greece, 1995-. Publications: Several professional articles in international conferences and journals. Memberships: Society of Rheology; Technical Chamber of Greece. Address: Paraskevopoulou 19, 54640 Thessaloniki, Greece.

**PAPAVA Vladimer,** b. 25 March 1955, Tbilisi, Georgia. Economist. m. Elena Papava, 1 son, 1 daughter. Education: Diploma, 1977, Tbilisi State University; Candidate of Economic Sciences, 1982, Central Econimic-Mathematical Institute of Academy of Sciences of USSR; Doctor of Economic Sciences, 1990, Leningrad State University. Appointments: Researcher, 1982-91, Director, 1991-96, P Gugushvili Institute of Economics, Georgian Academy of Sciences; Professor of Macroeconomics, Tbilisi State University, 1990; Minister of Economy of Georgia, 1994-. Publications: 10 monographs and books; Over 100 papers. Honour: FIBA, 1998. Memberships: International Input-Output Association; International Informatization Academy; New York Academy of Sciences; Corresponding member, Georgian Academy of Sciences; International Academy of Sciences, Education, Industry and Arts; International Atlantic Economic Society. Address: 12 Chanturia Street, Tbilisi 380008, Georgia.

**PAPAVASILIOU Andreas,** b. 22 January 1939, Nicosia, Cyprus. Executive Director, Administration. m. Iro, 2 sons, daughters. Education: Certificate, English School, Nicosia 1957; ACIB, Chartered Institute of Bankers, England, 1976 Appointments: Assistant General Manager of Financia Services, 1990-91, General Manager of Banking, 1991-96 Memberships: Chairman, Nicosia School Committee, Ar Drugs Organization "Ayia Skepi". Address: Cyprus Popula Bank Limited, 154 Limassol Av, PO Box 2032, 1598 Nicosia Cyprus.

**PAPAZOGLOU Michael,** b. 2 December 1953, Cairo, Egyp Professor. m. Ingrid Heck. Education: BS, honours, 1978; MSc 1979; PhD, 1983. Appointments: Principal Researcher, GMC Germany, 1983-89; Reader, Computer Science, Australia National University, 1989-91; Professor, Information Systems Queensland University of Technology, 1991-96; Professo Computer Science, Director, Tilburg University, Netherlands 1996-. Publications: Over 100 scientific papers, 8 books Honour: Certificate of Appreciation, Distinguished Visitor, IEE Computer Society, 1998. Memberships: IEEE Compute Society; ACM; IFIP; American Association for the Advancemer of Science. Address: Tilburg University, Infola B, PO Bo 90153, Tilburg 5000LE, The Netherlands.

**PAPINEAU Patricia,** b. 9 July 1951, Rutland, Vermont, USA Business Owner; Former Ballerina; Professional Mode Education: Green Mountain College, Poultney, Vermon Indiana University, Bloomington, Indiana. Career: Owne Patrician Academy of Ballet, Rutland, 1966-74, Springfiel 1972-74; Owner, Patricia's Charm and Modeling Schoo Rutland, 1970-74, Pati Papineau Center for the Performin Arts, Clifton Park, New York, 1978-84; Hosts and produces ow TV Show, Conversations with Pati Papineau. Honours: Mis Green Mountain College, 1970; Miss Vermont, 1970; Mis Vermont-World, 1972. Memberships: Dance Masters c America; Professional Dance Teachers Association; Danc Educators of America; Soroptimist International; America Association of University Women; American Federation c Female Executives; Listed in numerous biographica dictionaries. Address: PO Box 367, Rutland, VT 05702, USA

**PAPOUTSOGLOU Sofronios,** b. 26 July 1943, Veria Greece. Applied Hydrobiology Educator; Researcher. m. El Papaparaskeva, 2 children. Education: BSc, Agriculture University of Thessalonika, Greece, 1967; MSc, Marine Biology, University of Southampton, England, 1972; PhD Icthylology, University of Patra, Greece, 1975. Appointments Researcher, 1972-74, Director, Laboratory of Fish Nutritior 1974-80, Hellenic Center of Marine Research, Athens, Greece Temporary Professor, 1977-80, Full Professor, 1980-, Dear Faculty of Animal Production, 1989-91, 1993-95, Vice Recto 1997, Agricultural University, Athens; President, Board c Directors, Hellenic Center of Marine Research, Athens 1991-93; National Representative, Intergovermenta Oceanographic Commission, UN Environmental Programme Paris, 1993-95. Publications include: The Aquatic Environmer and its Organisms, 1980; Introduction to Aquaculture, 1985 Agricultural Aquaculture, 1986; Aquaculture Engineering, 1989 Endocrinology of Fishes. Honours: Grant, Greek Governmer 1975; Fullbright Grant, 1982. Memberships: Marine Bioloc Association; European Aquaculture Association; New Yor Academy of Science; Aquacultural Engineering Associatior World Aquaculture Association. Address: Agricultura University, Iera Odos 75, 118 55 Athens, Greece.

**PAPULOV Yuri,** b. 4 June 1935, Troitsk, Russia. Chemis m. Chulkova Lucyh, 1 son, 1 daughter. Education: Diploma Moscow State University, 1958; Candidate Science, Leningra

State University, 1962; Dr Science, Moscow Institute of Education, 1969. Appointments: Research Worker, Institute of Synthetic Fibres, 1961-63; Assistant Professor, Kalinin Institute of Education, 1963-71; Professor, Tver State University, 1971-; Head of Chair, Tver State University, 1973-. Publications: Over 100 articles in professional journals, 16 books including Structure of Molecules, 1974, 1995; Molecular Symmetry, 1979; Physical Properties and Chemical Constitution, 1981. Honour: Meritorious Science Worker of Russia, 1995. Memberships: World Association Theoretical Organic Chemistry, 1990; Peter's Academy of Sciences and Arts, 1994; New York Academy of Sciences, 1995; Academy of Natural Sciences, 1996. Address: 43 Apt 26, Tver (Kalinin), Lenin Prosp 170023, Russia.

**PARDALA Antoni Jerzy,** b. 28 January 1949, Piolunka, Poland. University Lecturer. m. Teresa Stanek, 1 son, 1 daughter. Education: Master Mathematics, 1971, Rzeszow; PhD Mathematical Sciences, 1981, Cracow; PhD Mathematics Education, 1994, Moscow. Appointments: Institute of Mathematics, Head of Section of Mathematics, 1995-, Pedagogical University, 1971-75, Rzeszow; Professor, Department Mathematics, 1995-, Rzeszow University of Technology. Publications: 41 research works. Honours: Chancellor's Awards for Research Works, 1982, 1983, 1986, 1988, 1989, 1994, 1996, 1998. Membership: Polish Mathematical Association. Address: Rzeszow University of Technology, ul W Pola 2, PL 35959 Rzeszow, Poland.

**PARIKH Shirkant N,** b. 25 February 1956, Bombay, India. Computer Scientist. m. Dr Vandana, 1 daughter. Education: MS Computer Science, 1981, USA; PhD, 1988, USA; Certified Project Manager Professional, 1993. Publications: Filed for 19 patents, 10 granted so far. Honours: Awarded 9 Invention Achievement Awards from IBM. Membership: IEEE. Address: 54 Pirbhoy Mansion, 2d Fl A Block SVP Rd, Bombay 40004, India.

**PARK Chung,** b. 27 October 1941, Pusan, Korea. Art Educator, Businessman. m. Sue Bok, 1 son, 2 daughters. Education: Diploma, Pusan National Teachers College; BFA, University of Michigan; MFA, Pratt Institute Graduate School. Appointments: Trustee, Tenatly Board of Education, Advisory Committee of State Bilingual Education; College Teacher; Painter; Businessman. Honours: Citation, Jersey City; Citation, State of New Jersey. Memberships: College Art Association; Korean American Elected School Board Members Association. Address: 166 Hefferson Ave, Tenafly, NJ 07670-1628, USA.

**PARK Jong Kyun,** b. 16 April 1963, Jinryong, Kyungbuk Province, Korea. Professor. m. Kim So Young, 1 son, 1 daughter. Education: BS, 1986, MS, 1989, Kyungpook National University; Agricultural Doctor degree, 1995, Kyungpook National University. Appointments: Advisory Committee, Experimental Office, Sericulture and Entomology of Kyungbuk Province, 1997-; Chairman, Department of Sericulture and Entomology Resources, Sangju National University, 1998-. Publications: Books: 1999 Environmental Science, 1999 Natural Science; Over 30 articles or theses of Insect Taxonomy concerned with Coleoptera. Memberships: Korean Journal of Applied Entomology; The Entomological Society of Korea; Japan Society of Applied Entomology and Zoology; Editor, The Apicultural Society of Korea. Address: Department of Sericulture and Entomology, Sangju National University, Sangju Shi Kyonbuk 742 711, Korea.

**PARK Roy H Jr,** b. 23 July 1938, Raleigh, North Carolina, USA. Media Executive. m. Elizabeth Parham, 1 son, 1 daughter. Education: Journalism, University of North Carolina,

Chapel Hill, 1961; MBA, Cornell University Johnson Graduate School of Management, 1963. Appointments: Senior Account Executive, Review Board Executive, Advertising Planning Director, Awards Chairman, Personnel Group Head, J Walter Thompson Company, New York City and Miami, Florida, 1963-70; Vice President of Account Management, Kincaid Advertising Agency, 1970-71; Vice President, Park Outdoor Advertising, Ithaca, New York, 1971-75; Vice President, Advertising and Promotion, Park Broadcasting Inc, Ithaca, New York, 1976-81; Managing Editor, Park Communications, 1976-81; Managing Director, Ag Research Advertising Agency, Ithaca, New York, 1976-84; Vice President, General Manager, Park Outdoor Advertising, 1981-84; President, Chief Executive Officer, Director, Park Outdoor Advertising of New York Inc, 1984-; President, Roadside Business Association, New York Inc, 1985; Chairman, Outdoor Advertising Council of New York Inc, 1992-95; Director, Park Communications Inc, 1993-95; Director, Senior Vice President, RHP Inc and RHP Properties Inc, 1994-96; Board of Trustees, Park Foundation Inc, 1995-; Board of Visitors, University of North Carolina, School of Journalism and Mass Communications, 1994-; Advisory Council, Cornell University Johnson Graduate School of Management, 1996-. Memberships include: North Carolina Society of New York. Address: Park Outdoor Advertising of New York Inc, PO Box 6477, Ithaca, NY 14851-6477, USA.

**PARKER Andrew Richard,** b. 28 October 1967, Wolverhampton, England. Biologist. Education: BSc, honours, Biological Sciences, Liverpool John Moores University, 1988-90; PhD, Marine Biology and Evolution, Macquarie University, 1993-96. Appointments: Research Fellow, Australian Museum, Sydney, 1996-99; Lecturer, Marine Biology, University of Reading, England, 1999-. Publications: Numerous articles in professional journals. Honours: Smithsonian Institution and Australian Museum Awards; Several others. Memberships: Institute of Biology; European Optical Society. Address: School of Animal and Microbial Sciences, University of Reading, Whiteknights, Reading, RG6 6AJ, UK.

**PARMENTIER Claude Jean,** b. 23 April 1934, St Maur, France. Nuclear Medicine Physician. m. Nicole Le Moigne, 2 sons. Appointments: MD, University of Paris, 1965; Association Professor Medicine, University of Paris, 1971-91; Professor of Medicine, 1991-; Head Nuclear Medicine Department, Institute Gustave-Roussy, Villejuif, France, 1978-. Publications: Contributor to the discovery of calcitonin as a marker of Medullary Thyroid Carcinoma; Contributor to chapters in books; Over 300 articles to science publications. Memberships: ScienceAdv Board, Electricity of France; French Society Radioprotection; Interministerial Commn for Basic Nuclear Installations, France 1990-; French Biophysics and Nuclear Medicine Society. Address: 25 rue Georges Clemenceau, 91310 Leuville sur Orge, France.

**PARRAVANO Amelia Amy,** b. 5 April 1951, Providence, Rhode Island, USA. m. Grimaldo A Parravano, 1 son, 1 daughter. Education: AA, Liberal Arts, Roger Williams University, RI, USA, 1971. Appointments: Producer, President and Owner, Peridot Records Company; Owner and President, Parravano Music and Peridot Now Publishing Companies. Publications: Pre-Nominee Grammy Awards, Songwriter/Artist; Country Music Associations of America Award Plaques, Songwriter/Artist/Albums. Membership: IFCO Fan Clubs; ASCAP; BMI; Greater Southern Country Music Association. Address: 17 Woodbine Street, Cranston, RI 02910-1916, USA.

**PARSLOW Thomas,** b. 12 March 1920, Melbourne, Australia. Lawyer; Soldier, (Brigadier). m. Margaret Fraser dec'd, 2 daughters. Education: LLB, University of Queensland, 1950; Barrister at Law, 1950. Career: Commissioned, 1941, War Service, 1939-46, 47th Infantry, World War II, Co. Queensland University Regiment, Commander, 2 Support Group, Commander, 7 Task Force; Senior Crown Prosecutor, Deputy Parliamentary Counsel and Draftsman, Crown Solicitor, Solicitor General, Queensland, 1970-80. Honours: Reserve Forces Decoration; Efficiency Decoration and Two Bars; QC. Memberships: State Councillor, Returned Services League of Australia; President, Victoria Barracks Historical Society; Great Chancellor, Great Priory of Queensland; Past Assistant Grand Master, United Grand Lodge of Queensland. Address: 27 Southerden Street, Sandgate, Qld 4017, Australia.

**PARSONS Ivy,** b. 3 March 1955, Baltimore, Maryland, USA. Sculptor; Artist. Education: BFA cum laude, Sculpture, Maryland Institute College of Arts, 1977; MFA magna cum laude, Sculpture, Virginia Commonwealth University, 1980; Sculpture, Skowhegan School of Painting and Sculpture, 1980. Appointments: Faculty, Maryland Institute College of Art, 1998-99; Faculty, Director of The Gallery, Community College of Baltimore County at Catonsville, 1998-99. Honours: Fulbright-Hays Fellowship in Sculpture, Italy, 1982; Visual Arts Fellowship in Sculpture, National Endowment for the Arts, 1983; Pollock and Krasner Foundation Grant in Sculpture, 1987, 1999; Adolph and Esther Gottlieb Foundation Grant in Sculpture, 1994; Individual Artists Grant in New Genre, Maryland State Arts Council, 1996; Tyrone Guthrie Center Residency, County Monaghan, Ireland, 1997; Alfred and Trafford Klots Residency, Chateau Rochefort-en-Terre Museum, Brittany, France, 1999. Address: 503 South Patterson Park, Baltimore, MD 21232, USA.

**PARTINGTON John Edwin,** b. 13 November 1907, Union Springs, New York. Retired. m. Gwen L Gray. Education: AB, Earlham College, 1929; MA, Psychology, University of Kentucky, 1938; Postgrauate, University of Chicago, 1946; Purdue University, 1959-62. Appointments: Diplomate, Counseling American Board of Professional Psychology; Teacher, Kentucky Houses of Reform, Lexington, 1930-35; Assistant to Research Psychologist, USES Hospital, Lexington, 1935-40; Psychologist, USES, Washington, 1940-42; Counsellor, VA, Roanoke, 1946-50; Psychologist, US Naval Exam Centre, 1950-58; Chief Test Developer, 1958-70; Chief of Research, 1970-72. Publications: Leiter Partington Adult Performance Scale; Helpful Hints for Better Living, Vol 1, Vol 2. Honours: Outstanding Kentuckian Award; Certificate of Recognition, Distinguished Contribution to the Discipline of Clinical Psychology. Memberships: APA, Industry Psychology Association; International Society of Poets. Address: 3458 Flintridge Drive, Lexington, KY 40517, USA.

**PARVEZ Tariq,** b. 5 April 1952, Multan, Pakistan. Doctor. m. Kaniz Akhter, 2 sons, 1 daughter. Education: BSc, 1975; MBBS, 1976; MCPS, 1988; DMRT, 1988. Career: GDMO Pakistan Army, 1976-79; Demonstrator, AIMC Lahore, Pakistan, 1979-85; SMO, Radiotherapy, Mayo Hospital, Lahore, 1987-88; Incharge, Assistant Profesor, Radiotherapy, AIMC, Lahore, 1988-90; Incharge, Radiotherapy, Sir Ganga Ram Hospital, Lahore, 1990-97; Incharge, Radiotherapy Services Hospital, Lahore, 1997-. Publications: 12 research papers, 7 books on cancer, 150 articles for awareness to masses on chancer, 130 seminars, discussions and lecturers. Honour: President of Pakistan Gold Medal for Research and Publications on Cancer. Memberships: Chairman, Pakistan Society for Cancer Prevention; Fellow, Member, many national and international associations. Address: 231 T Phase 11 LCCHS, Lahore, Pakistan.

**PASCHKE Donald Vernon,** b. 22 October 1929 Menominee, MI, USA. Voice Teacher. m. Helen, 1 s, 1 d Education: BS, Music Education, University of Illinois, 1957 BM, Voice, 1957; MM, Voice, 1958; DMusA, Voca Performance and Pedagogy, University of Colorado, 1972 Appointments: US Army, 6th Armoured Division Band, 1951-53 Instructor of Music, Berea College, 1958-62; Assistan Professor of Music, Eastern New Mexico University, 1962-71 Associate Professor of Music, ENMU, 1971-76; Professor of Music, 1976-94; Professor Emeritus of Music, 1994- Publications: Translated Manuel Garcia's A Complete Treatise on the Art of Singing; Articles. Honours: Phi Kappa Phi University of Illinois, 1956; Pi Kappa Lambda, 1956; Graduate Fellow in Music, University of Illinois, 1957-58. Memberships National Association of Teachers of Singing. Address: 228 Kansas Dr, Portales, NM 88130-7121, USA.

**PASHIK Jury Aleksandrovich,** b. 26 January 1960, Minsk Radio Technician. m. Svetlana, 2 sons. Education: Minsk Radiotechnical Institute, 1976-83; Appointments: Engineer Head of Bureau, Deputy Workshop Manager, Deputy Production Manager, Head of Department, Director, JSC Bellis Publications: Valuation Methods of Radio Equipment; Means and Methods of Technological Process Improvement in Radio Equipment and Production; National System of Products Certification. Memberships: Belarussian Engineering Technological Academy. Address: Krasnaja Street 7, 220759 Minsk, Rep of Belarus.

**PASS Susan,** b. 30 September 1944. m. Ed Pass, 1 son, 2 daughters. Education: ABD in Education and American History University of Houston; MS, Education, Western Illinois University, 1986; BS, Georgetown University in Washington DC, USA, 1964. Appointments: Teacher, Inner City Public Schools, 1981-; Springfield, ISD, Illinois, 1981-86; Houstor ISD, Texas, 1986-. Honours: Outstanding Educator, ITISD 1991, 1992, 1993, 1994, for Texas, 1996; Lead Teacher, SHS 1997-98; Elected Secretary, SDMC, 1998-99. Memberships President, AERA; TEA; NCSS; Phi Beta Kappa. Address: 5031 Lymbar Street, Houston, TX 77096, USA.

**PATEL Bhikhubhai Narsinhbhai,** b. 17 August 1930 Gangpur, India. Agricultural Educator; Researcher and Educationist. m. Shantabeni, 2 sons. Education: BEd I, 1958 BSc I, 1954; MEd II, 1967; PhD, 1974. Appointments: Assistant Teacher; Principal; Director of the Diploma, Engineering College; Founder Headmaster in school; Researcher Publications: 2 books, 1976, 1981; and research papers 1971-99. Honours: In AAAS in USA; Local Award, 1958 Gujarat State Best Teacher, 1976; 2 medals; National awards from the Government and NCERT New Delhi, 1980, 1982 1993, 1997. Memberships: AAAS; UNESCO; NCERT, New Delhi. Address: AF Gangpur, Gangadhra Gujarat, India.

**PATEL Manan,** b. 15 July 1972, Baroda. Banking Consultant. Education: B Eng (Hons) Electronics with Computing and Business. Appointments: Supplementa Instruction Leader, Kingston University; Workshop Engineer Canon, UK; Trainee Aeronautical Engineer, Kenya Airways Financial Consultant, Head of Support and Development Fintech (K) Ltd. Publication: Fly by Light, thesis on avionics Honour: AMIEE Award by IEEE. Memberships: Environmenta Investigation Agency, UK; Associate Member, IEEE, UK Address: PO Box 44137, Nairobi, Kenya.

**PATEL Neeyati,** b. 22 January 1971, Nairobi, Kenya. United Nations Official. Education: Bachelor Degree, Managemen Information Systems, 1992; Master Degree, Internationa Business Administration, 1994. Appointments: Residen rector, Elderhoster, 1991-94; Editor, Board Director, Center International Studies, 1993-94; Remote Translation Officer, onference Services, 1995-96, Fund Programme Managment anch, 1996-97, Fund Management Officer, Biodiversity Unit, 97-98, United Nations Environment Programme; Iministrator, Fund Officer, Convention on Biological Diversity cretariat, UNEP, Montreal. Publications: Several articles in ofessional journals. Membership: National Geographic. Idress: PO Box 44137, Nairobi, Kenya.

**PATEL Ramnarayan,** b. 1 June 1956, Thakurdiya, Madhya adesh, India. Professor. m. Lata Chaudhary, 1 son, 1 ughter. Education: BSc, MA, PhD, DLitt, Sangit Visharad. iblications: Navgeet, haikus, stories, essays, criticisms, ners. Appointment: Professor, Department of Hindi, M G egree College, Bhukta, Bavgarih District. Honours: Awards luding: Sahitya Shiromani; Sahitya Vibhushan; Sahitya Shri; :harya. Memberships include: Akhil Bharatiya Sahityakar hinandan Samiti, Mathura, Uttar Pradesh; Akhil Bharatiya eetkar Parishad, Hyderabad, Andhra Pradesh. Address: epartment of Hindi, M G Degree College, Bhukta, Disst irgarh (Orissa) 768-045, India.

**PATEL Ramniklal V,** b. 1 September 1954, Supedi, Gujarat, lia. Paediatric Surgeon; Professor; Administrator; edicolegal Consultant. m. Dr R R Patel, 1 son. Education: BBS, 1979; LLBC, 1982-83; DTPL, 1982; DLLP, 1983; MS, 83; Mch, 1986; DNBS, 1986; TRAB, 1987; FRCS, 92;FFARCS, 1992; DNB, Paediatric Surgery, 1993; LLM, 95; DHE, 1997; DHAC, 1998; DHR, 1998. Appointments: egistrar, Sho and House Office; Senior Registrar; Associate cturer; Assistant Professor; Associate Professor; Professor; nief Medical Director. Publications: Numerous Publications. onours: Man of the Year, 1998, American Biographical stitute; 2000 Millennium Medal of Honour; International iltural Diploma of Honour; 5000 Personalities of the World, 31. Memberships: Indian Medical Association; IMA College of P; IMA Academy of Medicine; India Association of Surgery; lian Academy of Paediatrics; Indian Assocaition of Paediatric irgery; American Medical Society; New York Academy of :iences; International Medical Science Academy; American ollege of Surgeons. Address: Dhaval Clinic, Jyotinagar Main oad, Rajkot, Gujarat 360 005, India.

**PATEL Rasmika,** b. 29 November 1962, Contai. Teacher; esearcher. Education: BSc, 1984; MSc, 1986; PhD, 1990. ppointments: Senior Lecturer, Post Graduates Department of aterials Science, Sardar Patel Unversity, 1990-. Publications: out 12 Publications, National and International Journals. onours: Convention Award, Indian Chemical Society, 1988; iri Ohm Ashram Awards, 1989, 1991. Memberships: aterials Research Society of India; Society for Polymer :ience India. Address: G H Patel Institute of Materials :ience, Sardar Patel University, Vallabh Vidyanagar 388120, lia.

**PATEL Ray,** b. 16 November 1939, India. Architect. m. eena Patel, 1 son, 1 daughter. Education: BArch, 1963. areer: Planning Commissioner, City of Sugar Land; President, inicipal District 2, Fortbend County, Texas; Director, ecretary, Fortbend Appraisal District, Texas; Advisory Council, ivenile Probation Board, Fortbend County, Texas. Honours: itstanding Design Award in Architecture, 1994; Excellence in esign abd Outstanding Professional Service Award, ternational School of Vedant. Memberships: American stitute of Architects; National Council of Architectural egistration Board of USA. Address: DMP Architects Inc, 6776 outhwest Fwy #285, Houston, TX 77074, USA.

**PATEL Shailesh Chhaganlal,** b. 13 August 1965, Surat, Gujarat, India. Freelance Painter. m. Hema Patel. Education: BA, Fine Art, in Painting, 1986, Postgrad Diploma, Fine Art, in Murals, 1990, MA, Fine Art, in Creative Painting, 1993, Maharaja Sayajirao University of Baroda, India. Appointments: Freelance Painter, 1985-; Represented in many private and public collections; Murals commissioned at different hotels, offices, temples and private places; Participated in national and international group and solo exhibitions and competitions and artist workshops. Honours: Awards and prizes for outstanding paintings, drawings and photographs. Memberships: Life member, The Bombay Art Society, and Avantika, New Delhi. Address: C 21 Shreeji Dham Society, Opp Raneswar Mahadev, Saiyed Vasna Rd, Dist Baroda 3900015, Gujarath, India.

**PATERNÒ Lucio Gaetano,** b. 22 December 1939, Catania, Italy. Professor. m. Marcella Lanzetta, 1 son, 1 daughter. Education: Laurea, 1962, PhD, 1968, Catania University. Appointments: Assistant Professor, Catania University, 1969-71; Astronomer, Catania Astrophysical Observatory, 1971-83; Lecturer, 1973-83, Professor of Solar Physics, 1983-, Director, Institute of Astronomy, 1992-97, Catania University. Publications: Numerous articles in professional journals and international conferences. Memberships: French Academy of Sciences; Gioenia Academy of Natural Sciences, Catania; International Astronomical Union; European Astronomical Society; Italian Astronomical Society; Italian Physical Society. Address: Institute of Astronomia, Catania University, 95125 Catania, Sicily, Italy.

**PATHAK Bindeshwar,** b. 2 April 1943, Rampur, Bihar. Action Sociologist and Social Reformer. m. Amola Pathak, 2 July 1965, 1 son, 2 daughters. Education: Graduation in Sociology, 1964; Masters in Sociology, Patna University, 1980; PhD, 1985; Masters in English, Patna University, 1986; DLitt, Patna University, 1994. Appointments: Gandhi Centenary Celebration Commitee, 1968-70; Founder, Sulabh International Social Service Organisation, Founder Secretary, 197086, Founder Chairman, 1980-86, of the organisation; Member, Bhangi-Mukti Cell (Scavenging Liberation Cell) Bihar, India. Publications: Sulabh India, Sulabh Sansar, Sulabh Shauchalaya - A Study of Directed Change, Sulabh Shauchalaya _ a Simple Idea That Worked; Road to Freedom - a Sociological Study on the Abolition of Scavenging in India; Power generation from human excreta; An Innovative Approach to Provide Rural Sanitation; Violence in Rural Bihar. Honours include: K P Goenka Memorial Award, 1981; Prabandhak Mahan Muzzaffarpur, 1990; Builders Information Bureau Award, 1990; Civic Betterment Award, Bombay, 1990-91; National Citizens Award, 1991; Padma Bhushan, 1991; International St Francis award for the Environment, 1992; Shahid Bhup Singh Award for Social Work, New Delhi, 1992; Indira Gandhi Priyadarshini Award, 1994; NRI Golf Award, 1994; Manav Sewa Puraskar, 1995; Vitas Ratna Award, 1995; Limca Book of Records Man of the Year Award, 1995; Babu Jagjiwan Ram Award for Abolishing Scavenging, 1997; Madhusadan Dutt Award, 1997. Memberships include: Chairman, Indian Association of Action Sociologists; Life Member, Indian Science Congress. Address: Founder, Sulabh International Social Service Organisation, Sulabh Bhawan, Mahavir Enclave, New Delhi 110 045, India.

**PATHAK Chander Mohan,** b. 29 October 1948, Amritsar, India. Medical Scientist. m. Sudha, 1 son, 1 daughter. Education: BSc, (Hons), 1968, MSc, (Hons), 1970, PhD, 1980, Biophysics. Appointments: Tutor, 1971-82, Lecturer, 1982-85, Assistant Professor, 1986-87, Associate Professor, 1987-93, Additional Professor, 1993-, Pgimer, Chandigarh. Publictions: 32 in professional national and international journals. Honours:

University Merit Scholarship, 1968-70; Secretary, Society of Nuclear Medicine, India, 1985-86. Memberships: Society of Nuclear Medicine, India; Biophysical Society of India; Association of Medical Physicists, India; Society of Biophysicists, India. Address: Department of Biophysics, PG I Sector 12, Chandigarh 160012, India.

**PATHAK Kare Narain,** b. 30 July 1941, Bara, Gaon, Chaukhari. Professor. m. K Pathak, 2 sons, 3 daughters. Education: BSc, 1st Class, Agra University, 1960; MSc, 1st Class, Allahabad University, 1962; PhD, IIT, Kanpur, 1967. Appointments include: Senior Associate Member, International Centre for Theoretical Physics, Trieste, Italy, 1992-97; Senior Alexander Humboldt Fellow, Technical University, Munchen, Germany, 1992; Visiting Professor, Royal Military College of Canada, Kingston, Ontario, Canada, 1993, 1996, 1998; Visiting Professor, Lakehead University, Thunder Bay, Kingston, Ontario, Canada, 1984,1985, 1988, 1991. Publications: Over 120 research papers in International Journals of repute; Field of Specialization: Condensed Matter Physics. Honours: Government of India Merit Scholarship and UP Government Scholarship; UGC National Lecturer Awards, 1986-87; Founder Member, Society for Scientific Values, New Delhi; Fellow, National Academy of Sciences, 1983; UGC National Fellowship Award, 1991; Fellow, Indian Academy of Sciences, 1992. Address: Department of Physics, Panjab University, Chandigarh 160014, India.

**PATHAK Ved P,** b. 9 February 1958, New Delhi, India. Scientist. m. Urvashi Pathak, 2 sons. Education: MPhil, 1980, PhD, 1983, Delhi University. Appointments: Visiting Fellow, Pharmaceutical Sciences, Kyoto University, Japan, 1984-85; Alexander von Humboldt Fellow, Technical University of Berlin, Germany, 1985-86; Postdoctoral Research Associate, University of Hyderbad, India, 1986-87; NSERC Visiting Fellow, National Research Council of Canada, 1987-89; NIH Postdoctoral Research Fellow, University of South Alabama, Mobile, 1989-90; Research Chemist, Nutrimed Biotech Inc, Ithaca, New York, 1990-91; Research Scientist II, BioCryst Pharmaceuticals Inc, Birmingham, Alabama, 1991-95; Senior Chemist, GEM Pharmaceuticals, Birmingham, Alabama, 1996; Senior Scientist, Alanex Corporation, San Diego, 1996-. Publications: 45 research papers in professional journals. Honours: Presidents Award, NRC Canada, 1988. Membership: American Chemical Society. Address: Alanex Corporation, 3550 General Atomics Court, San Diego, CA 92121-1194, USA.

**PATHMANATHAN Sivasubramaniam,** b. 20 March 1940, Vaddukoddai, Jaffna. Professor. m.(1) Saradha Rajasundram, deceased, (2) Pathmaleela Navarajah, 3 sons, 2 daughters. Publications: Over 200 articles in professional journals. Honour: British Commonwealth Academic Staff Fellowship, 1978-79. Address: 20 Ward Place, Colombo 07, Sri Lanka.

**PATIL Ravindra,** b. 24 December 1940, Kelva Mahim. Scientist. m. Ashalata, 1 son, 1 daughter. Education: BSc Hons, 1962; MSc, 1968; PhD, 1980. Appointments: Chemist, National Rayon; Scientific Officer, Bhabha Atomic Research Centre, Mumbai, India; Visiting Scientist, Hahnmeitner Institute, Berlin. Publications: Over 30 research papers in international journals. Memberships: Life member, Nuclear Science Society; Vice Chairman, MMCBARD Education Trust. Address: 10A Kamet, Mumbai 400094, India.

**PATNAIK Simanchal,** b. 8 November 1928, Parlakhemundi. m. Sarala, 3 sons, 4 daughters. Education: BA; LLB. Appointments: Block Development Officer; Revenue Officer; Tahasildar Magistrate; Sub-divisional Magistrate; Judge.

Publications: Delightful World of Poems; Bedroom Poem Sonnets and other Poems; Poetry in Tranquility; Poetry Himalayan Wisdom; Malati Tolar Kavya. Honours: Micha Madhvsudan Award; Sahitya Akademi Award; Internatior Eminent Poet Award; DLitt; International Man of the Yea 1997-98. Membership: World Poetry Society. Address: Gano Nagar, Berhampore 760 001, India.

**PATRA Pradip Kumar,** b. 1 April 1966, Balasore. Teache m. Tanushree. Education: MA, Englishm 1988; M Phil, Englis 1990; PhD, English, 1992; D Litt, English, 1997. Appointmen Senior Lecturer, Head of English Department, B B Kisha College; Guest Lecturer, English Department, Gauha University. Publications: Panoramic Shillong; Summ Implications; The Winding Path; Denouement; Dewy Mornin Midnight Divinity. Memberships: American Studies Resear Centre; Writers Forum; Council of Courses of Studies. Addres AT PO Pathsala, Dt Barpeta 781 325, Assam, India.

**PATTON John A L.** Physician. m. Deborah Merley Paton son, 1 daughter. Education: BA, Chemistry, University Louisville, 1970; MD, University of Louisville, 1974; ABF 1977; FAAFP, 1978. Appointments: Physician, Ru Southeastern Kentucky, 1976-; University of Kentuc Voluntary Faculty, University of Louisville Voluntary Facult Honour: Citizen Family of Year, 1997. Memberships: AM KMA; Lions Club; AAFP; KAFP. Address: PO Box 189, Whitl City, McCreary, KY 42653, USA.

**PAUL Jose,** b. 17 August 1941, Narakkal, Kerala, Indi Government Worker. m. Rita Jose, 3 daughters. Educatio MA, Political Science, University of Mysore, India, 1980; Ph Port Management, University of Wales, England, 198 Appointments: Assistant Traffic Manager, 1968-70, Depu Traffic Manager, 1970-75, Additional Traffic Manager, 1982-8 Cochin Port Trust; Traffic Manager, New Mangalore Port Trus 1975-79; Traffic Manager, Tuticorin Port Trust, 1979-8 Deputy Chairman, New Mangalore Port Trust, 1989-94; Depu Chairman, Jawaharlal Nehru Port Trust, New Mumba 1994-95; Acting Chairman, 1995-96, Deputy Chairma 1996-97, Jawaharlal Nehru Port Trust; Chairman, Mormuga Port Trust, Goa, 1997-. Publications: Several articles newspapers and journals. Honours: 1st Prize, Akiyama Awar International Essay Competition, International Association Ports and Harbours, Tokyo, 1986; Silver Medal, Scroll, Cas Award, World Port Conference, Seoul, 1987; Speci Commendation Certificate, Secretary to the Government India, 1998. Memberships: Fellow, British Institute Management, Chartered Institute of Transport, Londo Address: Mormugao Port Trust, Headland Sada, Goa 40380 India.

**PAUL Peter,** b. 3 October 1964, Holland, Michigan, US, Educator. Education: MA Candidate, Politics in Educatio Teachers College, Columbia University; AB Summa Cu Laude, Hope College, 1989. Career: Founder, Principal ar President, NCA International Schools, 1990-; Progra Associate/NTPI Coordinator, The Teachers Network, 1999 Graduate Intern, The Teachers Network, 1998; Teacher, NY Public Schools, 1998-99. Honours: Honorary Fellow, Nation Teacher Policy Institute, 1999; Who's Who in the Worl 1997-99; Participant, UNESCO Regional Conferenc Hokkaido, 1995. Memberships: Member, Association f Supervision and Curriculum Development; Member, Unite Federation of Teachers; Member, American Federation Teachers. Address: 350 Richmond Terr 5H, Staten Island, N 10301-2673, USA.

**PAUL Vanaja,** b. 4 January 1942, Coimbatore District, India. Pharmacologist; Educator; Researcher. m. A Paul. Education: BSc Zoology, 1962; MSc Pharmacology, 1967; PhD Pharmacology, 1988. Appointments: Lecturer in Pharmacology, Christian Medical College, Vellore, 1967, J J M Medical College, Davangere, 1968, St John's Medical College, Bangalore, 1969, Christion Medical College, Ludhiana, 1976, Dr A L M Postgraduate Institute of Basic Medical Sciences, University of Madras, Taramani, Chennai, 1983; Reader in Pharmacology, 1990, Professor of Pharmacology, 1996-. Publications: in professional journals and bulletins, 1986-. Honours: Grants from Indian Council of Medical Research, New Delhi, 1989, 1993, R D Birla Smarak Kosh, Mumbai, 1995, 1998; Award, 1995, Indian Council of Medical Research, New Delhi, for Research in Pharmacology; Invited Member, New York Academy of Sciences, 1995. Address: Dr A L M Postgrad Institute of Basic Medical Science, Department of Pharmacology & Environmental Toxicology, Chennai 600 113, India.

**PAULOSE V D,** b. 22 March 1957, Kunnappillysery. Teacher. m. Fancy Varghese, 1 son, 1 daughter. Education: SSLC, 1974; PUC, 1977; BA, 1980; MA, 1982; PGDTE, 1994; MPhil Thesis, submitted October 1997. Appointments: Lecturer, Zunheboto College, 1982-86; Higher Secondary School Teacher, KHS School, 1988-90; Lecturer in Badarpur NC College, 1990-. Publications: The Brainwave, 1996; Poems in Poet, 1997; Metverse Muse, Canopy, Bridge-in Making, 1997; Kytherean Idea, 1997; Poets International and Poetcrit, 1997; The Quest, 1997; Samvedana, 1998; International Poetry Letter, 1998; World Poetry, 1998; The "O", 1998; Twilight Ending, 1998. Honour: Distinguished Leadership Award, ABI, USA. Memberships: United Writers Association of India; Madras World Congress of Poets, China. Address: St Joseph's Church, Badarpur 788806, Assam, India.

**PAULSEN Richard W,** b. 8 September 1945, Blue Island, Ilinios, USA. Administrator; Counsellor. m. Susan, 5 sons, 3 daughters. Education: BS, 1972; MBA, 1980; MEd, 1997. Appointments: State of Nevada, 1964-74; Continental Bank, 1974-81; WGUS Fargo Bank, 1981-85; First International Bank, 1985-90; Whimsy Wear, 1991-96; Garland Church, 1996-. Honour: Outstanding Gaduate Award, State of Nevada, 1969. Memberships: ACA; AACC; ISSD; CSHDD; GSAE. Address: Survivor Support Services, PO Box 10657, Spokane, WA 99209, USA.

**PAVEL Dumitru,** b. 1 September 1963, Vaslui, Romania. Research Scientist. Education: Bachelor of Polymer Engineering, 1988; Doctor of Philosophy, Polymer Science, 1999. Appointments: Research Engineer, Technical University of IASI, Romania, 1989; Research Scientist, RMIT University, Melborne, Australia, 1998-. Publications: More than 30 Scientific Papers; Liquid Crystalline Polymers, 1999; Cross Linkable Liquid Crystalline Polymers Containing Azobenzene Mesogenic Groups. Honours: RMIT University Award, 1996. Memberships: Insitution of Engineers, Australia. Address: RMIT University, Dept of Chemical Engineering, GPO Box 2476V, Melbourne, VIC 3001, Australia.

**PAVEL Nicolaie,** b. 5 December 1965, Stanesti-Arges, Romania. Researcher. m. Daniela Pavel. Education: MSc, Faculty of Physics, Bucharest University, 1990; PhD, Institute of Atomic Physics, Bucharest, 1997. Appointments: Junior Scientist, 1990-92, Researcher, 1992-, Institute of Atomic Physics, Bucharest; Visiting Researcher, Faculty of Engineering, Fukui University, Japan, 1996-98, Mitsubishi Electric Corporation Information Technology R&D Center, Kanagawa, Japan, 1998-99; Postdoctoral Scholarship, Institute

for Molecular Science, Lasers Research Center for Molecular Science, Okazaki, Japan, 1999-. Publications: Over 35 articles in professional journals and conferences. Memberships: Romanian Society of Physics; International Society for Optical Engineering. Address: Laser Research Center for Molecular Science, Institute for Molecular Science, 38 Nishigonaka, Myodaiji Okazaki 444-8585, Japan.

**PAVLICHENKOV Igor Mikhailovitch,** b. 4 December 1934, Reuton City, Moscow Region, Russia. Physicist; Theoretician. m. Olga Yavorskaya, 1 son. Education: Physicist, 1958, Moscow University; Candidate of Physics, 1964, JINR, Dubna; Doctor, 1982, Kurchatov Institute. Appointments: Junior Researcher, 1958-83, Senior Researcher, 1983-87, Leading Researcher, 1987-93, Principal Researcher, 1993-, Kurchatov Institute, Moscow. Publications: Contributor articles to scientific journals. Memberships: various scientific boards. Address: RRC Kurchatov Institute, Kurchatov Square 1, 123182 Moscow, Russia.

**PAVLIN Zdenko,** b. 16 February 1929, Sisak, Croatia. University Professor. m. Ana Stankovic, 1 daughter. Education: Engineer of Timber Industry, 1954, MSc, 1967, PhD, 1975, University of Zagreb. Appointments: Assistant Design Organisation; Investigator, Research Institute; Assistant on Faculty, Assistant Professor, Associate Professor, Full Professor, Associate Dean, Dean on Faculty, Faculty of Forestry, University of Zagreb. Publications: Wood Steaming, 1983; Wood Seasoning, 1984; Drying of Hardwood, 1986. Memberships: University Council, University of Zagreb; International Union of Forestry Research Organisation; IUFRO, working party for wood drying. Address: Panciceva 3, 10000 Zagreb, Croatia.

**PAVLOVIC Marius,** b. 8 August 1963, Martin, Slovakia. Engineer. m. Jarmila Pavlovicova, 2 sons. Education: Dipl.Ing, Slovak Technical University, 1986; PhD, 1994. Appointments: Slovak Technical University, 1986-96; CERN, Geneva, 1993-94; Slovak Institute of Metrology, 1996-99; Gesellschaft für Schwerionenforschung, Darmstadt, 1997-98; Austron Project, Vienna, 1999-. Publications: Scientific papers and proceedings. Honour: Award of Slovak Ministry of Education, 1986. Address: Bukovcana 28, 841 07 Bratislava, Slovak Republic.

**PAYNE Jiri Tomas,** b. 7 July 1956, Prague, Czech Republic. Member of Parliament. div., 2 sons, 1 daughter. Education: Graduated in Nuclear Physics, Charles University, Prague, 1981. Appointment: Member of Parliament, Czech Republic. Address: Mikovcova 5, 120 00 Prague, Czech Republic.

**PEACHES Daniel,** b. 9 February 1940, Kayenta,USA. Politician. m. Carlotta Boone, 1 son, 1 daughter. Education: BS, Political Science, Northern Arizona University, Flagstaff, 1967. Appointments: Arizona House of Representatives, Phoenix. Honour: Presidential Appointment to Commission on Education by President Richard Nixon, 1972. Membership: Governing Board, Northland Pioneer College, Holbrook. Address: PO Box 1801, Kayenta, AZ 86033, USA.

**PEAK Geoffrey Harold,** b. 1 March 1936, Auckland, New Zealand. Lawyer. m. Patricia Mary Briggs, 2 sons, 2 daughters. Education: LLB, Auckland University, 1961. Appointments: Lawyer in General Practice, 1960; Partner, Peak Rogers and Partners, 1960-90, Cairns Slane, 1990-; Legal Adviser to Methodist Church of New Zealand, 1977-; Director of several companies. Memberships: Formerly Auckland Grammar Schools Board of Governors, 6 years; Currently several charitable Boards, Methodist Church; Auckland District Law Society; Maungakiekie Golf Club. Address: 12 Wayne Place, Mt Roskill, Auckland 1004, New Zealand.

**PEARSON Helen Bruch,** b. 29 May 1937, Genoa, Colorado, USA. University Faculty Member; Seminary Administrator; Minister. 1 son, 1 daughter. Education: AA, distinction, Graceland College, 1958; BSc, distinction, Music Education, Kansas University, 1961; MDiv, magna cum laude, Emory University, 1982. Career: Public School Music Educator, Kansas, Missouri and Michigan; Arts Administrator, Dean of The Chapel, Cannon Chapel, Emory University; Dean for Community Life, Director of Womens Program, Candler School of Theology, Emory University. Publications: Bent Over Woman; Do What You Have the Power to Do; Numerous articles and religious curriculum pieces. Honour: Appointed World Council of Churches Worship Committee, 1996. Memberships: Omicron Delta Kappa; Sigma Alpha Iota; Phi Kappa Lambda; Delta Kappa Gamma; Theta Phi; National Association of Student Personnel Administrators. Address: Emory University, Candler School of Theology, 3290 Clairmont North, Atlanta, GA 30329, USA.

**PEARSON Paul David,** b. 22 January 1940, Boston, Massachusetts, USA. Attorney; Mediator. m. Carol A Munschauer, 1 son, 1 daughter. Education: BA Psychology and Sociology, 1961, Bucknell University, Lewisburg, Pennsylvania; LLB, 1964, University of Pennsylvania Law School, Philadelphia; Mediation training, 1985, 1995. Appointments: Laboratory of Community Psychiatry, Department of Psychiatry, Harvard Medical School, 1966-68; Partner, Snyder, Tepper & Berlin, Boston, 1968-79; Partner, Hill & Barlow, Boston, 1979-87; Partner, Hodgson, Russ, Andrews, Woods & Goodyear, Buffalo, 1987-96; Attorney & Mediator, Sullivan & Oliverio, Buffalo, 1996-; Instructor in Law and Mental Health, Boston Psychoanalytic Society and Institute, 1975-87; Frequent Lecturer at continuing legal education and interdisciplinary seminars; Chairman, Family Law Section, MA Bar Association, 1984-86; Chair, ADR Committee, Erie County (NY) Bar Association, 1992-96. Publications: Author, Family Law Quarterly, 1968, Trial Magazine, 1967. Membership: Fellow, American Academy of Matrimonial Lawyers, President, MA Chapter, 1986-87. Address: 605 Lebrun Rd, Buffalo, NY 14226-4232, USA.

**PECI Aleksander,** b. 11 July 1951, Tirana, Albania. Composer. m. Ana Koco, 2 sons. Education: Diploma, 1969, 1974; Specialist, 1993, 1994. Appointments: Director, Artistique Variete du Tirana, 1977; Director, Artistique de L'Ensemble des Chansoms et des Danses Poputaires, Tirana, 1979; Professor du Composition, L'Academie des Arts, 1979; Founder, President, L'Association de la Nouvella Musique, 1993-; Founder, Director, L'Ensemble, 1998. Publications: Numerous Articles in Professional Journals. Honours: Several. Memberships: SACEM; Eurn des Ptomoteurs de la Nouvelle Musique. Address: Rue Zhan D'Ark, Kulla Nr2 Kati 8/3 Midis Pall Laives, Tirane, Albania.

**PECSI Marton,** b. 29 December 1923, Budapest, Hungary. Research Professor. m. Eva Donath, 1 daughter. Education: PhD, P Pazmany University, Budapest, 1948; DrSc, Hungarian Academy of Sciences, 1962. Appointment: Titular Professor, University of L Eötvös, Budapest, 1966. Publications: 500 publications; Author of 25 books. Honours: Humbold Medal; State Prize; Lifetime Achievement Award. Memberships: Director of Earth Science Centre, Hungarian Academy of Sciences, 1963-90; Corresponding Member, 1965, Regular Member, 1976, Hungarian Academy of Sciences; 5 foreign Academies of Sciences; Honorary Member: Hungarian

Geographical Society; International Quaternary Research; 6 European Geographical Societies; Geographic Society of America. Address: Dozsa u 7, 2747 Tortel, Hungary.

**PEDAR Arul A,** b. 4 February 1943, Savariar Pattanam, India. Scientist. m. Sengole Pedar, 2 daughters. Education: BE Electrical Engineering, 1966, Madras University; PhD Computer Engineering, 1982, Indian Institute of Science. Appointments: Scientist at various levels, National Aerospace Labs, Bangalore, India. Honour: NASA Senior Research Associateship, 1991-93. Membership: Senior member, IEEE Address: National Aerospace Labs, PB No 1779, Bangalore 560017, India.

**PEI Xue-Tao,** b. 20 May 1962, Kunming, Yunnan, China. Professor. m. Ning Du. Education: Graduate, 3rd Medical College, Chongqing, 1983; MMedSc, PhD, 1987, MD, 1990, Beijing Institute of Radiation Medicine. Career: Professor, Director, Laboratory of Bioactive Substances Analysis, National Center of Biomedical Analysis; Deputy Director, Department of Experimental Hematology, Beijing Institute of Radiation Medicine; Deputy Secretary General, Standing Committee, Chinese Experimental Hematology Society. Publications: Over 80 research papers, books and monographs. Honours: 1st Class Prize, 3rd Class Prize, Scientific & Technological Progress, 1996. Memberships: Chinese Committee, International Association of Radiation Research; Committee, Chinese Radiological Medicine & Protection Association; International Association of Radiopathology; Editorial Board, Journal of Chinese Experimental Hematology, Journal of Clinical Molecular Biology. Address: Beijing Institute of Radiation Medicine, 27 Taiping Road, Beijing 100850, China.

**PEIKOV Tosho Kostadinov,** b. 17 January 1951, Slatina, Lovetch District. Economist. m. Maria Russeva, 2 daughters. Education: BA, 1980, MA, 1996, Varna University. Appointments: Department Chief, Lovetch Furniture Plant, 1981-90; CEO, Lovetch Furniture Plant, 1990-94; Member Bulgarian Parliament, 1991-94; Institute Sociology, Bulgarian Academy of Sciences, 1996-. Publications: Writings on Bulgarian Reforms, vol 1, Analysis of an Unsuccessful Period, 1996, vol 2, The Crash, 1998; Red Book of the Bulgarian People - An Endangered Species, 1995; Ferocious Arena of Circus, 1993; numerous articles. Memberships: Liberal Congress Party, Vice President, 1992-; Basic Institute for Research and Defense of Human Rights, member of the Board, 1995-. Address: 7 Pirotska Street, Sofia 1000, Bulgaria.

**PEIRIS Lakmal,** b. 17 December 1959, Colombo. Medical Doctor, Classical Guitarist, Producer. Education: MD, Superior Institute of Medical Sciences, 1987. Appointments: Medical Officer, European Medical Centre, 1988; Medical Director, Guadalmina Clinic General, 1989-. Publications: Vivencias, 1995; Nancy Casanova Dacosta, Federico Chopin, 1998; Homenaje, 1999. Honours: College Prizes, Botany, Zoology, 1976; Award in Scientific Exhibition for Invention, 1977; Most Outstanding Jaycee of the Year, 1979; Provinvincial Prize in Biochemistry, 1983; Provincial Prize in General Surgery, 1986; Provincial and National Prizes in Cardiology, 1986; Best Surgery Tutor, 1986; Provincial Vanguard, 1986; Title of Gold, 1987; The Most Outstanding Graduate of the Year, 1987; Most Excellent in Cultural Activities, 1987; Provincial Prize Instrumental Soloist, 1987. Memberships: Jaycees International; Young Zoologists Association; Field Ornithology Group. Address: Guadlamina Clinic Edif Barclays, Local 5 Alto Urb, Guadalmina Alta, 29678 San Pedro Alcantara, Malaga, Spain.

**PEIXOTO NETO José Ulysses,** b. 29 August 1930, Crato, Ceara, Brazil. Medical Doctor. m. Maria Isolda Cartaxo Peixoto, sons, 1 daughter. Education: MD, Medical School of Pernambuco, 1955. Career: Founder, Social Security, Crato, 958, St Michael Hospital, Crato, 1967, Crato School of Law, 978. Publication: Himathantus Articulata in Medicine, 1976. Honour: Award for Good Services, Lions Club of Crato, 1993. Memberships: New York Academy of Sciences; American Association for the Advancement of Science; American College of Physicians; Brazilian Medical Association; Brazilian Medical Clinic Society. Address: Rua Tristao Goncalves 568, Crato, Ceara, Brazil.

**PEKER Elya,** b. 15 June 1937, Moscow. Artist, Painter. m. Katrina Friedman, 1 son. Education: Diploma, Theater Decoration, Moscow Art Institute, 1956. Appointments: Artist, Painter. Creative Works: Large series of posters and reproductions of flowers and still life paintings published, 1991. Honours: Cross of the Order of International Ambassadors with the title of HE, American Biographical Institute, 1996. Memberships: Lima Licensing Industry Merchandisers Association; IPA. Address: 1673 East 16 Street, Suite 164, Brooklyn, NY 11229, USA.

**PELANT Ivan,** b. 12 December 1944, Uherske Hradiste. Physicist; Educator. m. Alena Beresova, 2 daughters. Education: MSc, 1967, PhD, 1976, DSc, 1990, Charles University, Prague. Appointments: Postdoctoral Fellow, Ecole Normale Superieure, Paris, 1976; Associate Professor, Charles University, 1983; Research Scientist, Academy of Sciences, Prague, 1994. Publications: Over 90 articles in professional journals. Memberships: SPIE; Society of Czech Mathematicians and Physicists. Address: Moravska 11, Prague 2000, Czech Republic.

**PELOQUIN Louis Omer,** b. 15 June 1957, Tracy, Canada. Executive; Lawyer. m. Carole Plante, 1 son, 1 daughter. Education: BBA, Laval University, 1980; LLB, University of Montreal, 1984; Graduate Studies, Economics, McGill University, 1984-85; LLM, New York University, 1987. Appointments: Solicitor, Martineau Walker, Montreal, Quebec, 1985-86; Solicitor, Paul, Weiss, Rifkind, Wharton & Garrison, New York City, 1987-89; Solicitor, Shearman & Sterling, New York City, 1989-91; Solicitor, McCarthy Tetrault, Montreal, 1991-93; Vice President, General Counsel, Secretary, Golden Star Resources Ltd, Denver, Colorado. Publications: La Nature Juridique de la responsabilile des architectes et entrepreneurs, 984; Negotiating Mineral Transactions in Latin America, International Oil Gas and Mining Development in Latin America, Paper No. 6 (Rocky Mountain Mineral Law Foundation), 1994. Memberships: American Bar Association; New York Bar; Bar of Province of Quebec, Canada; Association of American Corporate Counsel; Rocky Mountain Mineral Law Foundation; American Society of International Law. Address: 5300 East Nichols Drive, Littleton, CO 80122-3892, USA.

**PENA Lorenzo,** b. 29 August 1944, Alicante, Spain. University Professor. m. Teresa Alonso. Education: MA, Philosphy, Pontifical University, Quito, 1974; American Studies Certificate, 1978, PhD, 1979, University Liege, Belgium. Appointments: Instructor of Philosophy, 1974-75, Professor of Philosophy, 1979-82, Pontifical University, Quito, Ecuador; Untenured Associate Professor Philosophy, University Leon, Spain, 1983-87; Scientific Researcher, Institute of Philosophy, CSIC, 1987-; Visiting Professor, Australian National University, Research School of Social Sciences, Philosophy Programme, 1992-93. Publications: 6 books. Honours: Made eligible, on account of distinguished research achievements, for any vacant Full-Professorship at any Spanish University, 1985; Recipient Grant, Spanish Culture Ministry, 1987 for the publication of Spanish outstanding scientific contributions; Recipient, 1988 Literary Creation Prize, Spanish Culture Ministry for Research Essays in the Humanities. Memberships: Mind Association; Aristotelian Society; European Society for Analytical Philosophy. Address: Consejo Superior de Invest, Cientificas Inst of Philosophy, Pinar 25, E 28006 Madrid, Spain.

**PENBERTHY Stanley Josiah,** b. 3 September 1921, Des Moines, Iowa, USA. Broadcasting, Manufacturing, Publishing, Writer, Author. m. Dorothea Oehmke, 1 son. Appointments: Broadcasting, KSo and KRNT, Des Moines, Iowa, 1941-44; WjR Detroit, 1944-56; Vice President, Federal ID Corporation, 1952-62; Free Lance Broadcasting, 1956-96; President, Publishers Inc, 1976-97; Narator, Commercial and Industrial Films. Publications: These Were Our Presidents; Living Under Cover; Episodes of Life; Cottage Industry; Many Magazine Articles. Memberships: Screen Authors Guild; American Federation of Radio and Television Artists; Adcraft Club of Detroit; Detroit Executives Association; Detroit Producers Association; American Film Institute; Broadcasting Pioneers; Detroit Masonic Temple Association; Alpha Tau Omega Fraternity; Founders Society; Detroit Intitute of Arts; Michigan Historial Society; Heritage Village Condo Association. Address: 35560 Heritage Ln, Farmington, MI 48335-3136, USA.

**PENSOY Barbara,** b. 1 June 1961, Istanbul, Turkey. Interior Design. Education: Abitur 1980, German High School, Istanbul; Interior Design Diploma, 1981, Inchbald School of Design, London; BFA Honour Environmental Design, 1984, Parsons School of Design, New York. Appointments: Senior Designer, 1985-87, Partner, 1987-92, Sam Lopata Inc, New York; Own office in Soho, New York, 1992-95; Projects in Washington DC and Istanbul, 1996-98; Office in Istanbul, Atelye 5, 1998-. Publications: Featured in more than 40 newspaper and other professional publications. Address: Besi sokak 5, Yenikoy, Istanbul 80870, Turkey.

**PÉNZES Laszlo Geza,** b. 14 July 1930, Budapest, Hungary. Biological Scientist. m. Ilona Csáky, 1 son. Education: Degree in Agricultural Engineering, 1955, University Agricultural Sciences; PhD, 1960; UN Fellowship, IAEA, 1961-62; D Sc, 1982, Hungarian Academy Science; Dr Habil, 1996, Budapest University, ELTE. Appointments: Trainee, 1955-56; Postgraduate, 1956-59; Scientific Researcher, Institute for Animal Husbandry, Budapest, 1959-66; Scientific Adviser, Gerontology Centre, Semmelweis University of Medicine, Budapest, 1966-98, Vice Director, 1993-95; Guest Professor, Bologna University, Italy, 1993. Publications: Over 130 articles in field of experimental gerontology in scientific journals; Co-author, 3 books on gerontology, 1984, 1990, 1992. Honours: Berlin University of Medicine, 1985; Semmelweis Diploma of Merit, 1993; Ferd Med University L'Aquila, 1995. Memberships: Hungarian Association Gerontology; National Rep, Hungarian Association Gerontology, President 1985-89; Tempus Coordinator, Joint European Project, 1991-94; Public Body, Hungarian Academy of Sciences, 1994-. Address: Madách Imre u 2-6, 1075 Budapest, Hungary.

**PERELLO Jorge,** b. 5 May 1918, Barcelona, Spain. Physician. m. Nuria Scherdel, 2 sons, 1 daughter. Education: University of Barcelona, 1943. Appointments: Dr h C. Publications: 10 Volumes. Memberships: International Association of Logopedics. Address: Provenza 319, 08037 Barcelona, Spain.

**PERELLO Manuel,** b. 15 April 1935, Guadalcanal, Sevilla, Spain. Physician. m. Juani Miron, 5 sons, 3 daughters. Education: License of Physics Science, 1957, University

Madrid; Diploma in Nuclear Engineering, 1958, JEN Madrid; Diploma in Reactor Safety, 1972, Harwell (UK); Diploma in Regulatory Principles, 1973, Bethesda, Maryland, USA; Diploma in High Temperature Gas Reactor, 1974, General Atomic Company, California. Appointments: Investigator of Nuclear Safety Department (DSN); Inspector Nuclear Facilities, 1972; Chief of Nuclear Standards in DSN; Chief Nuclear Facilities in Operation, Nuclear Safety Council (CSN), 1982; Chief Relations with Comunidades Autonomas (CCAA); Coordinator to the International Nuclear Standards with IAEA. Publications: Various articles in professional reviews and journals in the field of nuclear safety. Memberships: Real Sociedad Espanola de Fisica; Colegio Oficial de Fisicos; Sociedad Nuclear Española (SNE); General Secretary, SNE, 1978-81; European Nuclear Society (ENS), member of Board, 1978-82, member Steering Committee, 1978-82, ENS. Address: Galileo 5, 28015 Madrid, Spain.

**PERENYI Andras,** b. 28 May 1949, Hungary. Psychiatrist. m. Kinga Paulheim, 1 daughter. Education: Medical Degree, Semmelweis Medical School, Budapest, 1973. Appointments: Trainee, Psychiatry, National Institute for Nervous and Mental Diseases, Budapest, 1973-77; Psychiatrist, Hungary, 1977; Research Fellow, Psychopharmacology, Harvard Medical School, 1980; Departmental Chief, National Institute for Nervous and Mental Diseases, Budapest, 1985-92; Consultant Psychiatrist, Monash Medical Center, Clayton, Australia, 1995-. Publications: Over 100 in professional medical journals. Memberships: Fellow, Royal Australian and New Zealand College of Psychiatrists; New York Academy of Sciences; American Association for the Advancement of Science. Address: Monash Medical Center of Adult Psychiatry, 246 Clayton Road, Clayton, Victoria 3168, Australia.

**PEREPELITSA Vitaly,** b. 4 August 1937, Ukraine. Mathematician. m. Nina A, 1 daughter. Education: Diploma of Mathematician, Novobirsk State University, 1960-65; Degree of Candidate of Sciences, 1971; Academic Title, Associate Professor, 1977; Degree, Doctor of Sciences, 1989; Academic Title, Professor, 1991. Appointments: Science Researcher, Institute of Mathematics, Siberian Branch, Academy of Sciences, 1965-81; Head of Department, Zaporozhye State University, -1994; Karachai, Cherkess Technological Institute, 1994-. Publications: Over 200 Scientific Papers. Memberships: American Mathematical Society; Academy of Social Sciences of Russia; Academy of Engineering Sciences, Ukraine. Address: Oktyabrskaya Str 309-18, Cherkessk-15 357100, Russia.

**PERETTI Lurdes Maria Bolognesi,** President, Society Educacional Provincia de Sao Pedro. m. Cicero de Quadros, 3 children. Education: Master Degree, Philosophy and History, Universidad de Caix do Sur, 1968. Appointments: Director, Founder, Castelinho Baby Bercario e Creche Ltda, 1979-; Headmaster, Owner, Founder, Colegio Provincia de Sao Pedro, 1985-; President, Society Educacional Provincia de Sao Pedro, 1992-. Memberships: Maria Montessori Brazillian Association; Association Montessori International; Committee, Santo Antonio Childrens Hospital. Address; Society Educacional Provincia de Sao Pedro, Rua Mal, Andrea 345, Porto Alegre, Brazil.

**PEREZ Reynolds,** b. 5 April 1961, La Vega. Surgeon; Theologian; Writer; Researcher. m. 1 son, 2 daughters. Education: Médico Cirujano General Vascular Y Laporoscopista; Teologo; Investigador en el Area de la Historia Y medicina; Universidad Católica Madre Y Maestra de Rep. Appointments: Entrenamientos en Hospitales en Cuba, Argentina, Puerto Rico; Y Estados Unidos; Los Estudios de

Teología en la Universidad Nacional Evangélica. Publication Más de cincuenta trabajos de investigacion científica médic. Historica y en el area del saber. Memberships: New Yo Academy of Sciences; Colegio Dominicano de Cirujano Sociedad de Hiperalimentación de los Estado Unido Sociedad de flebologia de Argentina y Republica Dominica; D grupo cooperativo latinamericano de estudios de trombosi Asesor musical del gran teatro clásico regional del cibao, E Santiago, Republica Dominicana; Societe Internationale c Chirurgie; Sociedad Shalom de Isareal; Who's Who in th World; Red International Sanofi de Trombosis; Nominado a Academia de Ciencias de la Rep. Dominicana. Address: Pad Fantino St 12, La Vega, Dominican Republic.

**PEREZ GOMEZ Augusto,** b. 15 May 1947, Bogota Columbia. Psychologist. m. Leonos Trujillo, 2 daughter. Education: Psychologist, National University of Columbia; Ph[ University of Louvain, Belgium. Appointments: Full Professc University of Los Andes; Visiting Professor, University London; Director, Presidential Program Against Drug Abuse Publications: 6 Books; 110 Articles and Papers. Honour National Award in Clinical Psychology; National Award Psychology. Memberships: APA; ICAA; SOS Drogu International. Address: Apt 302, Carrera 11 # 86-86, Bogot. Colombia.

**PÉREZ HERNANDEZ Ramón Esteban,** b. 3 August 195. Santa Clara. Professor. m. Adela Pairol Martínez, 2 sons, daughter. Education: English Professor, Agronomist ar Specialist on Information (Chief of a National Informatic Center). Publications: Brochures on tropical root and tube crops; Articles on scientific information. Memberships: INIVIᵀ AGROINFOR. Address: Marti Edif 2 Apto 14, Sauto Doming Villa Clara, Cuba.

**PERIC Veselin,** b. 20 January 1930, Podgorica Montenegro, Yugoslavia. m. Marianne Peric-Lehmann, 1 sol 1 daughter. Education: Podgorica, 1948; Graduate, studies maths, Zagreb, 1954; PhD, maths, University of Zagreb, 196E Appointments: Assistant, University of Sarajevo, 195! Assistant Professor, 1966, Associate Professor, 1972 Professor, 1977, University of Sarajevo; Professor, Universit of Montenegro in Podgorica, 1993. Publications: More than 3 scientific papers in different domains of Algebra; Sever. papers of popular and didactical character. Memberships President, Society of Mathematics and Physics of Bosnia an Herzegovina, 1968-72; Academy of Science and Arts c Republika Srpska, 1997; Editorial Boards of 3 journals in forme Yugoslavia; President, Yugoslav National Mathematic Committee, 1994-; President, Organizing Committee of Conference for Algebra and Logic, Sarajevo, 1987 and of th 9th Congress of Yugoslav Mathematics, Petrovac, Montenegr 1955. Address: PO Box 211, Cetinjski Put BB, Podgorica Yugoslavia.

**PERMADI Pudji,** b. 4 March 1953, Jakarta. m. 2 daughter: Education: Engineering degree, Petroleum Engineering, Institu Teknologi Bandung, 1979; Master of Science, Petroleur engineering, University of Southern California, 1985; Doctor c Philosophy, Petroleum Engineering, New Mexico Tech, 199C Appointment: Head of petroleum engineering departmen Institut Teknologi, Bandung. Publications: Author an Co-author of more than 30 technical papers, 1990-99 Contributing author of the standard handbook of petroleum an matural gas engineering, 1996; 10 year loyalty award fror Indonesian Government, 1997. Memberships: Society Petroleum Engineers; Indonesian Petroleum Association.

**PERNG Chin-Lin,** b. 15 October 1957, Hsinchu, Taiwan. Gastroenterologist. m. Hsiao-Feng Chung, 1 son, 2 daughters. Education: Bachelor Medicine, 1983, National Yang-Ming University, Taipei, Taiwan. Appointments: Attending Physician of Medicine, Veterans General Hospital, Taipei, Taiwan; Instructor of Medicine, National Yang-Ming University. Publications: Papers in professional journals in field of gastroenterology. Memberships: Gastroenterological Society of China; Digestive Endoscopy Society of China; American College of Gastroenterology. Address: Veterans General Hospital, Shih-Pai Road, Taipei, Taiwan 11217.

**PERRON Pierre,** b. 14 March 1959, Verdun, Canada. Professor. m. Regina Celia Cati, 2 daughters. Education: BA, 1981, McGill University, Montreal, Canada; MA, 1982, Queen's University, Kingston, Canada; PhD, 1986, Yale University. Appointments: Research Associate, 1986-, Director, 1995-97, Centre de Recherche et Developpement en Economique, Assistant Professor, 1986-88, Associate Professor, 1992-94, Professor, 1994-97, Universite de Montreal; Assistant Professor, Princeton University, 1988-92; Professor, Department of Economics, Boston University, USA, current; Visiting Professor: Pontifical Universidade Catelica de Rio de Janeiro, 1995, 1998; Universidade de Sao Paulo, Brasil, 1995, 1997; Universite de Lausanne, Switzerland, 1996; Editorial Board 10 professional journals in economics. Publications: Over 40 scientific articles published in econometric journals; Chapters in various books. Honours: Prix Triennal d'Excellence de la Societe Canadienne de Sciences Economiques, 1994; Econometric Theory Multa Scripsit Award, 1996; Fellow, Journal of Econometrics, 1999. Memberships: American Economic Association; Econometric Society; American Finance Association; American Statistical Association; Canadian Economic Association, executive council, 1995-97; Institute of Mathematical Statistics; Societe Canadienne de Sciences Economiques. Address: Boston University, Department of Economics, 270 Bay State Rd, Boston, MA 02215, USA.

**PERRY Robert Johnson,** b. 19 October 1949, Vicksburg, Mississippi. Plastic and Reconstructive Surgeon. m. Linda Baldi-Perry, 2 sons, 1 daughter. Education: BA, 1971, Vanderbilt University; MD, 1975, Southwestern Medical School; Surgery, Medical College of Virginia, 1976-77; Otolaryngology, SUNY at Buffalo, 1978-80; Board Certificate Otolaryngology, 1980; Plastic Surgery, University of Miami, 1980-81; Board Certificate Plastic Surgery, 1984; Fellow, American College of Surgeons, 1990. Appointments: Plastic Surgery practice, 1982-; Chief of Plastic Surgery, Children's Hospital of Buffalo and Craniofacial Centre of Western New York, 1986-; Clinical Associate Professor of Surgery (Plastic), 1990; Chairman, Division of Plastic Surgery, SUNY at Buffalo, 1990-91. Honour: Member, People to People Citizen Ambassador Programme to Soviet Union, Hungary, Czechoslovakia, 1986. Memberships: American College of Surgeons; American Society of Plastic and Reconstructive Surgery; American Society of Aesthetic Plastic Surgery; American Cleft Palate Association; American Academy of Otolaryngology, Head and Neck Surgery; American Medical Association; Medical Society of New York; Erie County Medical Society. Address: 191 North Street No 104, Buffalo, NY 14201, USA.

**PERRY Thomas Amherst,** b. 26 April 1912, Beaver City, Nebraska, USA. Retired University Professor. m. Lora Margaret Turner, 3 sons, 1 daughter. Education: BA, Honors, Park College, 1934; MA, 1936, PhD, 1943, University of Iowa, Iowa, USA; Oxford University International Summer School, 1964. Appointments: Assistant Professor, English, Park College, 1936-42; Instructor of English, University of Iowa, 1943; Professor of English, Department Head, Central Methodist

College, 1943-51, 1952-63; Visiting Professor of English, University of Missouri, 1951-52; Visiting Smith-Mundt Professor, University Aut Estado de Mexico, 1959; Fulbright Lecturer in American Language and Literature, University of Bucharest, Romania, 1963-64; Herman Brown Professor of English, Southwestern University, 1964-65; Visiting Professor of English NE Mo State University, summer 1965; Professor of English (Dept. Head, 1969-72), East Texas State University, now Texas A and M University-Commerce, 1965-1980; Professor Emeritus since 1980; Member, Committee on Doctorate in English, Federation North Texas State Universities, 1972-75; Member, Committee on Variorum Glossary, World Shakespeare Congress, Vancouver, BC, Canada, 1970-71; Member, Steering Committee, Romanian Studies Congress, Auckland, New Zealand, Summer 1973. Publications: Romanian Poetry in English Translation: An Annotated Bibliography, co-author, 1989, with supplement An Update with Over 60 Never Poets, 1997; A Bibliography of American Literature Translated into Romanian, 1984; From These Roots and Other Poems, author, 1996; From These Roots and Other Poems, author, 1996; Contributor, articles and criticism to professional journals, poems and poem translations to literary magazines. Honours: past member, Executive Committee, Hunt County Rep Party, Greenville, Texas, 1970-80; past member, Administrative Board, Methodist Church, Fayette; past member, Administrative Board, 1st Methodist Church, Commerce; Distinguished Alumnus Award, Park College, 1984; Smith-Mundt Grantee, Toluca, Mexico, 1959; Research Associate Travel Grantee, University Bucharest and University Cluj, 1968; American Council Learned Societies Research Grantee, Romania, 1978. Memberships: Modern Language Association of America, Senior Bibliographer, 1969-; Shakespeare Association of America; International Shakespeare Association; American Comparative Literature Association; International Comparative Literature Association; American Romanian Academy Arts and Sciences; Romanian Studies Association, Executive Board, 1946-48; Society Romanian Studies; Texas Association College Teachers; Texas Folklore Society; Omicron Delta Kappa. Hobbies: Numismatics; Photography; Travel. Address: 214 Brookhaven Terrace, Commerce, TX 75428, USA.

**PERSICO Joseph Edward,** b. 19 July 1930, Gloversville, New York, USA. Author. m. Sylvia LaVista, 2 daughters. Education: BA, State University of New York, 1952; Graduate Programme, Columbia University. Publications: Biographies: Edward R Murrow; William J Casey; Nelson Rockefeller; Histories: Piercing the Reich; Nuremberg: Infamy on Trial; My American Journey; Collaborator with General Colin Powell. Honour: Honorary PhD, State University of New York. Memberships: Authors Guild; PEN International. Address: 222 Heritage Road, Apt 215, Guilderland, NY 12084-9672, USA.

**PERSKII Nikolay Evgenevitch,** b. 23 May 1956, Novgorod, Russia. Physicist. m. Elena A Friendling, 2 sons. Education: Graduated, Doctor Degree of Physics, Petrozavodsk State University, 1979. Appointments: Lector in Petrozavodsk State University, 1991; Scientific Researcher, Northern Water Institute of Petrozavodsk, 1994. Publications: 40 publications including 10 in foreign. Address: Department of Electronic and Ionic Devices, O V Kuuskinen Petrozavodsk State University, 33 Prospekt Lenina, Petrozavodsk 185640, Russia.

**PERSLIDEN Jan R G,** b. 13 July 1950, Norrkoping. Medical Physicist. m. Lena, 1 son, 2 daughters. Education: PhD 1986; Associate Professor 1993. Appointments: Research Assistant, 1976-82, Medical Physicist, 1982-87, University Hospital Linkoping; Principal Medical Physicist, 1987-. Publications: Over 80 articles and conference reports. Membership: Sewdish

Society for Medical Radiation Physics, member board. Address: Department of Radiation Physics, University Hospital, 581 85 Linkoping, Sweden.

**PERSSON Roland S,** b. 7 October 1958, Sweden. Associate Professor; Reader. Education: Diploma, Church Music, 1979; MA, Music Education, 1983; PhD, Psychology, 1993. Appointments: Headteacher, Piano and Organ Performance, Uddevalla Pre-Conservatoire, Sweden, 1986-90; Researcher, Part-time Lecturer, Music Psychology, Huddersfield University, England, 1990-93; Assistant Professor, Senior Lecturer, Psychology, 1994-98, Associate Professor, Reader in Psychology, Center for Psychology, 1998-, School of Education and Communication, Jonkoping University, Sweden; Member, Board of Governors, Ingesund College of Music, Arvika, Sweden, 1994-98; Editor-in-Chief, High Ability Studies, Journal of European Council for High Ability, 1998-; Member, Jonkoping County Directorate Scientific Board for Health Care, Sweden, 1998-. Publications: Psyche, Stress and Artistic Freedom, 1996; Formal Structure and Personal Writing, 1997; In a Different Land: The Psychology of High Ability, 1997; Scientific Supervision, 1999. Honours: National Correspondent, European Council for High Ability, 1994-; National Representative, World Council for Gifted and Talented Children, 1997-. Memberships: British Psychological Society; American Psychological Association; Swedish Psychological Association; European Council for High Ability; World Council for Gifted and Talented Children; International Arts Medicine Association; Society for Research in the Psychology of Music and Music Education; European Society for the Cognitive Sciences of Music. Address: School of Education and Communication, Jonkoping University, PO Box 1026, SE-55111 Jonkoping, Sweden.

**PESTELL Richard,** b. 5 March 1958, Perth, Western Australia. Doctor. m. Nicola, 2 s. Education: MBBS, Australia, 1981; MRCP, London, 1983; FRACP, 1989; PhD, University of Melbourne, 1991; MD, 1997. Appointments: Tutor, Pathology, University of Western Australia, 1985; Tutor, Medicine, University of Melbourne, 1988-90; Tutor, Medicine, 1987-90; NHMRC Scholar, 1988-91; Consultant Endocrinologist, Northwest Hospital, 1990-91; Assistant Professor, Northwestern University Medical School, 1993-96; Assistant Professor, Albert Einstein College of Medicine, 1996-97; Associate Professor, 1997-; Visiting Attending, Weiler Hospital, Jacobi Hospital, New York, 1997-. Publications: 64 Publications; 10 Submited Manuscripts; 76 Abstracts. Honours: University Commonwealth Scholarship; Queens College Prize; The Royal Australian College of Physicians Clinical Examinations; PhD Thesis; Robert Wood Johnson Minority Medical Education Program Certificate for Contribution to Teaching; Pfieffer Award; Many others. Memberships: Robert H Lurie Cancer Center; Australian Medical Association; Endocrine Society of Australia; Australian Diabetes Association; International Diabetes Association; Australian Society of Medical Research; Endocrine Society of the USA; American Federation for Clinical Research; America Association for Cancer Research; Many others. Address: Albert Einstein College of Medicine, 1300 Morris Park Ave, Bronx, NY 10461-1926, USA.

**PETERS Connie Jane,** b. 21 October 1949, Decatur, Illinois, USA. Teacher. Education: BA, Millikin University, 1971; MA, Sangamon State University, 1972; MS, Library Science, Eastern Illinois University, 1973. Appointments: Librarian, St Teresa High School, 1982-92; Educational Specialist in Instructional Media, 1985-; Librarian, Stephen Decatur High School, 1995-. Memberships: Illinois School Libraries and Media Association; ALA; Association of Educational

Technology; Illinois Computing Educators. Address: 1 Educational Park, Decatur, IL 62526-2548, USA.

**PETERS Joseph Donald,** b. 7 March 1958, Montebello, California, USA. Film Maker. Education: BA, Communication, University of Southern California, Los Angeles, 1982. Career: Writer, Producer, Director, Films, Television. Creative Works: Films: Seniors and Alcohol Abuse, 1986; Eskimo Ice Cream Shoes, 1990; Rachel, 1994; Emotions, 1996; Sam and Kathy - Time Travelers, 1998. Honours: Finalist, 1987; Gold Award, 1991; Silver and Bronze Award, 1995. Memberships: American Film Institute; Independent Feature Project/West; Cinewomen. Address: Renaissance Productions Ltd, 301 North San Dimas Cyn Road #48, San Dimas, CA 91773, USA.

**PETERS Sally Ann,** b. 17 October 1938, New York, New York, USA. Writer; Professor; Consultant; Critic; Educator, Arts. 3 sons. Education: AB, magna cum laude, with Distinction in English, Salutarian; Temple University, 1960; MA, University of South Florida, 1970; PhD, Florida State University, 1973. Appointments: Assistant Professor of English, 1973-79, Supervisor, Teacher Preparation, Yale University. 1973-79; Director, Writing Workshop, Yale University, 1979; Lecturer, Graduate Liberal Studies Program, Wesleyan University, 1985-; Visiting Professor, Connecticut College, 1999. Publications: Bernard Shaw: The Ascent of Superman (book); Numerous publications in anthologies and journals. Honours: Alumni Prize, College of Liberal Arts; Kappa Delta Epsilon National Honour Society, English Honour Society, Women's Honour Society, Temple University; Four Year Competitive Scholarship, Florida State University; Elected to Phi Kappa Phi National Honour Society; Connecticut Humanities Scholar, 1987-88, 1988-89, 1998; Honoured by Bernard Shaw Society and American Irish History Society; Choice Outstanding Academic Book, 1996. Memberships: Vice President, Bernard Shaw Society of North America; Editorial Board, Annual of Shaw Studies, Author's Guild of America. Address: Wesleyan University Graduate Liberal Studies Program, Middletown, CT 06459, USA.

**PETERSON Barbara Bennett,** b. 6 September 1942, Oregon, USA. Professor. m. Frank Lynn. Education: BA, BS, Oregon State University, 1964; MA, Stanford University; PhD, University of Hawaii, 1978. Appointments: Emeritus Professor, University of Hawaii, 1967-95; World Campus Afloat, 1974; Associate Professor, SS Universe Campus, 1978. Publications: 60 Television Programs, Hawaiian Educational Channel; Numerous Book Chapters; Abstracts; Book Reviews; Papers for Conferences and Invited Lectures; News Paper, Magazine, Encyclopedia, Special Collection and Journal Articles. Honours: Honorary Doctorates, London Institute of Applied Research, Australian Institute for Coordinated Research; Drucilla Shepard Smith Award; Distinguished Alumni Award, University of Hawaii, 1997; Excellence in Teaching Award, Board of Regents University, Hawaii; Outstanding Teacher of the Year, Wuhan University. Memberships: World Literary Academy. Address: East West Center, 1633 East West Road, Honolulu, HI 96848-1633, USA.

**PETERSON Robert Scott,** b. 24 March 1930, McKeesport, Pennsylvania, USA. Electrical Systems Engineer. Widower. Education: BSEE, 1952, Pennsylvania State University; MSEE, 1961, University of Pittsburgh. Appointments: Fellow Design and Development Engineer, Westinghouse Electrical Corp, 1952-89; Fellow Design and Development Engineer, AEG Automation Corp, 1990-95; Consulting Engineer, 1996-. Publications: Granted 30th USA Patent pertaining to steel mill automation and drive system control, in 1995. Memberships:

EE; Association of Iron and Steel Engineers. Address: 719 eathergate Drive, Pittsburgh, PA 15238-1000, USA.

**PETKEVICIENE Laisvune,** b. 28 June 1940, Kretinga, ithuania. Physician; Dietologist; Poet. Widowed, 1 son, 1 aughter. Education: Graduated, Faculty of Medicine, Vilnius, 964; Postgraduate study, 1983-88, Candidate of Science, 988, Vilnius University; Highest Qualification as Dietologist, 989; DSc, 1993. Appointments: Siauliai Emergency Station, 966-66; Siauliai Maternity Home, 1966-75; Obstetrics and ynaecology Department, Vilnius Railway District Hospital, 975-78; Dietologist, Vilnius City Canteen Trust, 1978-87; ietologist, Vilnius City Trade Organisations Board, 1987-89; hief Specialist Dietologist, Lithuanian Ministry of Health, 989-; Chief Specialist Dietologist, Gastroenterology and ietetics Clinic, Vilnius University, 1989-; Instructor, Centre of ursing Specialists and Professional Advancement Training, 996-. Publications: Laumzirgiu sokis (Dragonflies Dance), petry book, 1993; Poems in medical poets' collection Skrenda aukste Baltaplunksne (The Bird of White Feathers Flies). onours: Winner, prizes for poetry, Poezijos Pavasaris medical riters' festival, 1983; Documents acknowledging rank of obility, 1996. Memberships: Founder, President, Lithuanian ietetics Society, 1990-; European Federation of Dietetics ssociations, 1995-; V Kudirka Society of Medical Writers; thuanian Samaritans Society; Commission for Certification of astroenterologists and Dietologists; Chair, Commission for ertification of Dietitians; Noblewoman, Lithuanian Royal Union Nobility. Address: Peteliskiu 46-19, LT-2007 Vilnius, ithuania.

**PETKOV Kiril Todorov,** b. 12 May 1943, Dolna Beshovitza, ulgaria. Physicist. m. Anelia Dilova, 2 sons. Education: raduate, University of Sofia, 1968; PhD, Bulgarian Academy Science, Sofia, 1988. Appointments: Physicist, Central aboratory of Photoprocesses, Sofia, 1968-73; Research ssociate, CLF, 1973-95; Associated Professor, 1995-. ublications: More than 65 Publications in Science Journals. lemberships: Union of Scientists, Bulgaria, New York cademy of Science. Address: Komplex Mladost Bl 87 Ent 9, 797 Sofia, Bulgaria.

**PETKOVA Marussya,** b. 20 September 1945, Sofia, ulgaria. Physician; Medical Journalist; Translator. Divorced, son, 1 daughter. Education: MD, Public Health, 1981; PhD, ledical Information, 1981; MD, Disaster Medicine, 1995. ppointments: Physician: National Institute of Public Health, 971-74; Medical Information Center, 1974-78; Government lospital, 1978-; Journalist: Freelance journalist, 1976-; Medical ditor, Ot.front daily, 1980-89; Editor-in-Chief, Med Magazin iweekly), 1997-. Publications: Over 100 science publications; lany translations - books, films, articles, from and into English, omanian, Polish, Moldavian, Russian; Author: Multilingual ictionary of Medical Prosthetics. Memberships: Bulgarian ociety of Public Health; Bulgarian Society History of Medicine; iternational Society Disaster Medicine (Geneva); New York cademy of Sciences; National Disaster Medical System, USA lon); Hon Member, IBC Advisory Council. Address: Mladost bl 224-14/34, 1799 Sofia, Bulgaria.

**PETRANOVIC Nadezda,** b. 6 December 1934, Beograd. rofessor. m. Branko, 2 daughters. Education: Graduate legree, 1959; MSc, 1967; PhD, 1972. Appointments: Head of epartment of Electrochemistry, Chemical Kinetics, Faculty of hysics, Chemistry, 1991; Full Professor, 1980; Associate rofessor, 1984; Docent, 1975; Assistant, 1960. Publications: hemical Thermodynamics; More than 100 articles in Journals; ongress Materials. Honours: Dictionary of International iography, 26th Edition, International Biographical Centre;

International Who's Who of Twentieth Century Achievement. Memberships: International Zeolite Association; American Chemical Society of Physical Chemistry of Serbia; Serbian Chemical Society; Yugoslav Material Research Association. Address: Beograd, Smiljaniceva 41, Serbia, Yugoslavia.

**PETRELLO George James,** b. 30 April 1938, New Jersey, USA. Economist, University Professor. m. Barbara A. Education: PhD, New York University; MBA, Seton Hall University; BA, Montclair State University; BCFE, American College of Forensic Examiners. Appointments: Professor of Economics and Business Administration, Eagner College and Montclair State University; Dean of the School of Business Administration, St Mary's University, 1978-83; Provost Dean of and Vice President for Academic Affairs, Bryant College, 1983-86; Andreas School of Business, 1986-1990; Professor, Long Island University, 1990-; Forensic Economist, Forensic Education Consultant, 1991-. Publications: Introduction to Business: An Integrated Approach, 1976; Personal Finance, 1978; Introduction to Business, 1979; Journal of Business Education, 1981-83; Delta PI Epsilon Journal, 1984-86; Journal of the Society of Educators and Scholars; AICS, In Service to America at 75, 1987; Various Articles, Abstracts, Monographs. Honours: Honorary Fellow in the Anglo American Academy, Cambridge; Delta Pi Epsilon National Honorary Graduate Society; Honorary Member, Delta Mu Delta National Honour Society; Founders Day Award, 1969; Honorary Member, Alpha Mu Alpha National Honour Society in Marketing Management. Memberships: National Association of Forensic Economics; National Business Education Association; American Assembly of Collegiate Schools of Business; Small Business Administration; American Assocaition of Collegiate Registrars and Admissions Officers. Address: LIU, University Plz, Brooklyn, NY 11201, USA.

**PETRIE Marie Rose,** b. 29 January 1937, Calvary, Wisconsin, USA. School Psychologist; Learning Specialist. Education: BA Education and Mathematics, 1969, Cardinal Stritch University, Milwaukee; MS School Psychology, 1974, University Wisconsin, Whitewater. Appointments: Have worked as School Psychologist in Jefferson, Milwaukee, and Sturgeon Bay, Wisconsin; Taught at elementary through college level; Currently, Learning Specialist, Sacred Heart School, Racine, Wisconsin. Honours: Theta Alpha Kappa, National Honour Society for Religious Studies; International Society of Poets, 1998. Memberships: Sisters of St Francis of Assisi; Spiritual Directors International; National Association School Psychologists; Wisconsin School Psychological Association. Address: Sacred Heart School, 2023 Northwestern Avenue, Racine, WI 53404-2514, USA.

**PETRO Nadia Shakir,** b. 26 July 1939, Cairo, Egypt. Research Chemist. m. Professor Nasr Z Misak, 1 son, 1 daughter. Education: BSc, Chemistry and Geology, 1960, MSc, Metallurgy, 1968, Cairo University; PhD, Physical Chemistry, Ain-Shams University, 1974. Appointments: Scholar, National Research Centre, 1961-63; Assistant Researcher, National Research Centre, 1963-74; Researcher, National Research Centre, 1974-83; Assistant Research Professor, National Research Centre, 1983-89; Professor, 1989-. Publications: 30 papers in international specialized journals; 2 papers in local journals. New Developments in Ion Exchange, paper, 1991. Honour: Visiting Scientist, Institute of Catalysis and Surface Chemistry Cracow, Poland; Participated in local and international scientific projects. Memberships: Syndicate, Scientific Professions; Egyptian Chemical Society; Egyptian Society for Surface Chemistry and Catalysis. Address: Surface Chemistry Laboratory, National Research Center, El Tahreer Street, Dokki, Cairo, Egypt.

**PETROFF Milan,** b. 27 March 1939, Bulgaria. Professor. m. Bogdana Petroff, 2 sons. Education: MD, 1965; PhD, 1977; MScD, 1990. Appointments: Chief Medical Doctor, 1965-60; Medical Corps, 1970-78; Chief of CACDS, 1978-92; Vice President, President of Military Academy for Education, 1993-93. Publications: Articles; Reports; Monographs. Honours: Ministry of Health Excellence Award, 1982; Under the Flags Order, 1996. Memberships: Committee of Medical Science; NYAS; Bulgarian Academy of Medical Science; Military Alliance Against Aids. Address: Military Medical Academy, 3 Georgi Sofijski Street, 1606 Sofia, Bulgaria.

**PETROIANU Andy,** b. 2 September 1952, Braila, Romania. Professor of Surgery. 1 daughter. Education: Graduate, Medicine, 1976; MSurg, 1981; PhD, Surgery, 1985; Specialized in Surgery, 1979; MS, Physiology, 1983; PhD, Physiology, 1998. Appointments: Professor of Surgery, Medical School, Federal University of Minas Gerais; Free Docent of Surgery, Medical School, Federal University of Sao Paulo; HSC-SUNY, 1986-87; Free Docent of Surgery, Medical School, University of Sao Paulo. Publictions: 154 publications in journals, 9 books. Honours: 28 awards. Memberships: Brazilian College of Surgeons; Brazilian Medical Association. Address: Apto 1901, Avenida Afonso Pena 1626, Belo Horizonte 30130005, Brazil.

**PETROLIAGI Zoe,** b. 26 October 1969, Athens, Greece. Doctor of Philosophy. Education: Degree in Classics, 1992, PhD, 1997, University of Athens. Appointments: Post-doctoral, UCL; Oral participation in VIIth Annual Conference of Euroclassica in Homer and European Literature, 1997. Publication: Dissertation, Zeus in Prometheia and Oresteia of Aeschylus, moral development. Honour: Scholarship from Sasakawa, Global Foundation Research and Scholarship, for dissertation. Memberships: Society of Greek Philologists, 1992; Secretary, VIIth Annual Conference of Euroclassica, 1997. Address: Dept of Philosophy and Classical Literature, Athens University, Zographou Athens, Greece.

**PETROSKEVICIUS Petras,** b. 29 June 1944, Pusalotas, Lithuania. Geodesist. m. Lina, 1 son, 1 daughter. Education: Dipl Eng, Moscow Engineering Institute of Geodesy, Aerophotography, 1970; Doctor of Technical Sciences, Moscow Engineering Institute of Geodesy, Aerophotography, 1978. Appointments: Lecturer, Department of Geodesy, Vilnius Technical University, 1970-71, 1973-78; Senior Lecturer, 1978; Professor, 1979; Director, 1992-. Publications: 38 Scientific Articles. Memberships: Estonian, Latvian and Lithuanian Geodetic Commission; International Association for EUREF Subcommission; FIG; Association of Surveyors of Lithuania; Geodesy and Cartography. Address: Rudninku 14-3, LT 2024 Vilnius, Lithuania.

**PETROV Valery Danilovich,** b. 13 February 1946, Moscow. Physicist; Educator. Education: Honoured Diploma Electronic Engineering, Moscow Institute of Energetics. Appointment: Consultant. Publications: Over 80 research papers and critical reviews in field of volumic imaging, human and robot vision, laser metrology, holography, optical data storage; More than 50 communications at International Conferences; Introduced a novel concept of human and animal volumic vision; Devised momental daylight holography, enabling the production of holograms rapidly in a brightly lit environment. Membership: European Optical Society. Address: Postfach 3350, D-89023, Ulm, Germany.

**PETROV Vladilen Vasilievich,** b. 13 March 1935, Ratislovo, Vladimir, Russia. Professor. m. Svetlana Vasilievna Petrova, 1 son. Education: Degree of Engineer, 1957; Degree of Candidate of Technical Science, 1962; Degree of Doctor of

Technical Science, 1971. Appointments: Assistant, Departme of Construction Mechanics and Theory of Elasticity, Sarato Polytechnic Institute, 1961; Associate Professor, Departme of Construction Mechanics and Theory of Elasticity, Saratc Polytechnic Institute, 1962; Head, Department of Constructio Mechanics and Theory of Elasticity, Saratov Polytechn Institute, 1970; Vice Rector in Research, Saratov Polytechn Institute, 1977; Rector, Saratov Polytechnic Institute, 198 Publications: 140 articles; 6 monographies. Honours: Medal f Excellent Labour, 1970; Award of a Sign of Honour, 198( Honourable Person of Science and Engineering of Russi 1985; Honourable Worker of Higher Education of Russi Memberships: Russian Academy of Architecture and Buildir Science; International Engineering Academy; Internation Academy of a Higher Education; Transport Academy of Russi Correspondent Member, Academy of Engineering Science Address: 778 Politeknicheskaya str, Saratov 410016, Russia

**PETROV Vladimir Ivanovich,** b. 30 June 1951, Orenburg Clinical Pharmacologist. m. Irina Alexandrovna Trishkova, son. Education: Physician, Medical Institute, Volgograd, 197 PhD, 1977; MD, 1988; Professor, 1989. Appointments: Hea Clinical Pharmacology Department, 1983-; Rector, 1990 Head, Pharmacology Research Institute, 1991-. Publication Clinical Toxicology in Pediatrics; Pharmacotherapy and Clinic Pharmacology; Excitatory Amino Acids; Hypertensive Diseas Emotional Stress; Bronecial Asthma in Children. Honou Honoured Physician of Russia, 1997; Lenin Comsomol Prize i Science. Memberships: Russian Pharmacology Society; Russi Academy of Medical Science; International Academy c Science; New York Academy of Science. Address: Mira S 6-46, 400 066 Volgograd, Russia.

**PETROV Yuriy V,** b. 8 May 1940, Tashkent, Uzbekistar Physicist, Ecologist. m. Lilia Avramova, 2 daughters. Educatior BS, Geophysics, Tashkent State University, 1962; Diploma Candidate Science, Physics and Mathematics, USSR Stat Committee of Education, Moscow, 1985; Diploma, Doctor c Science, USSR State Committee of Education, Moscow, 1991 Appointments: Assistant, Department of Physics, Tashker State University, 1957; Teacher, Physics, 1957-89; Heac Physics of Atmosphere Department, 1989-. Publications: Mor than 70 Articles, Physics of Atmosphere, Meteorolog Geophysics, Ecology, Various Scientific Journals. Honours: Certificates of Honour, Ministry of Public Education, Ministry c Higher Education; Many other awards. Memberships ECOSAN; Science Council of the Physics Faculty, Central Asi University of GydroMeteorological Research, and Educationa and Methodological Union; Educational and Scientific Cente Address: Dept of Physics of Atmosphere, Physical Faculty Tashkent State University, Vuzgorodok GSP Tashkent, 70009 Uzbekistan.

**PETROVA Palmira G,** b. 28 June 1944, Kougostach Ust-Yan Region, Sakha Republic (Yakutia), Russia. Physiciar Pathopathologist. m. Kim Petrov, 1 son, 1 daughter. Educatior Graduated, Medical Faculty, Yakutsk University, 196 Graduated, postgraduate study, Department c Pathophysiology, Moscow Mechnikov Medical Institute, 197( Candidate's degree, 1971; Title of Assistant Professor, 198 Doctor of Medical Sciences, 1995; Title of Professor, 199€ Appointments: Lecturer, Department of Physiology, 197 Senior Lecturer, Department of Physiology, 1978, Dean c Education, Medical Faculty, 1982-92, Head, Department c Human Physiology, Medical Institute, 1985-, Rector, Medic Institute, 1996-, Yakutsk State University. Publications: Mor than 100 scientific publications, including monographs: Ecolog of the River Vilui, 1993; Condition of human health in th Republic of Sakha (Yakutia), co-author, 1995; Man und conditions of the North, co-author, 1996; Ecology, adaptation and health, 1996; Human ecology under conditions of the North, co-author, 1996; The teaching about disease (Nosology), co-author, 1997; Integrative medicine and human ecology, 1998. Honour: Kapitza Memorial Medal, Russian Academy of Natural Sciences, 1995. Memberships: Academician, International Academy of Ecology and Life Protection Sciences, 1995; Academician, Academy of Sciences of the Republic of Sakha, 1996; Academician, International Academy of the North Forum, 1997; Academician, Russian Ecological Science, 1998. Address: Apt 20, 5 Chirajev Street, Yakutsk 677000, Russia.

**PETROVA Svetlana,** b. 21 July 1945, Yakutsk, Russia. Philologist. 1 daughter. Education: Yakut State University, 1967; Master of Pedagogical Sciences, 1982; Doctor of Pedagogical Sciences, 1996; Professor, 1997; Associate Member of Petrovsky Sciences and Art Academy, 1996. Appointments: Teacher, Russian Language and Literature, 1967; Lecturer, Yakutsk University, 1970-85; Assistant Professor, 1985-95; Doctor Professor, 1996. Publications: 70 publications, 3 monographs. Honours: Doctor, 1996; Professor, 1997; Honoured Peoples Education Worker of Republic of Sakha, 1995. Memberships: Associate Member, Petrovsky Sciences and Art Academy, 1996. Address: Apt 10, 21 Krupskaya st, Yakutsk 677002, Russia.

**PETURSSON Gisli Ragnar,** b. 8 December 1937, Reykjavik, Iceland. Accountant. div, 1 son, 1 daughter. Education: College of Iceland, 1956. Appointments: Clerk, USAF Keflavik, Iceland, 1955; Accountant, Co-Op, Reykjavik, 1956; Transport Manager, Iceland Product's Inc, New York City, 1957-58; Accountant, Co-Op, Reykjavik, 1959-60; General Manager, Co-Op, Thorsöfn, Iceland, 1961-69; Chief Accountant, Assistant Finance Manager, Veltir hf (Volvo) & Gunnar Asgeirsson hf, Reykjavik, 1970-75; Chief Accountant, Hafskip hf, Reykjavik, 1979-82; Construction Worker, Hagvirki hf, Sultartanga, Iceland, 1983; Dockworker, Co-Op, Samskip, Reykjavik, 1984-85; Financial Consultant, Iceland State Housing Institute, 1986; Chief Accountant, Office & Finance Manager, Co-Op, Kopasker, Iceland, 1987-88; Accountant Mcpl. Social Service, Reykjavik, 1989-; Founder, Owner, Petursson ehf, Accounting & Marketing Co, 1994-. Address: Kelduland 7, 108 Reykjavik, Iceland.

**PETVIASHVILI Rusudan,** b. 25 January 1968, Tbilisi, Georgia. Artist. m. Teimuraz Badriashvili. Education: Artist-Graphic, The Tbilisi State Art Academy, Diploma-the Artist-Graphic, 1990. Appointments: The Personal Exhibitions, Tbilisi, 1974, Moscow, 1977, 1978, 1981, Paris (Centre G Pompidou), 1983, Budapest, 1984, Moscow, 1985, Madrid, 1985, Vienna, 1988, London (Roy Miles Paintings, 27 Berkeley Square, USA, 1995-97). Honours: Golden Medal and I Rank Diploma, 1975, 1981, 1983 (The VIII, X, XI, Republic Olimpiad of Art Lover Youth). Membership: Georgian Artists' Association. Address: 209 Nutsubidze Str, 380086 Tbilisi, Georgia.

**PETZOLD Horst Willy,** b. 21 February 1923, Leipzig, Germany. Writer; Translator; Consultant. m. Margaret Reher, 20 January 1948, 1 son, 1 foster son. Education: Flight Training Certificate ABC; Pilot Licence; Industrial Engineering School; Flight Training in Gliders and Sailplanes. Appointments include: Luftwaffe; Flight testing new aeroplanes and equipment; General Manager, Public Relations Officer, Research Company Developing mainly Flying Wings, Seattle, 1962-. Publications: Numerous books and aviation stories; Correspondent for aviation magazines, Germany. Memberships: Aviation Space Writers Association; American Association for the Advancement of Science. Address: 710 Edward Avenue,

Everett, WA 98201-4644, USA.

**PFAFF Lucie,** b. 17 September 1929, Germany. Professor. Widow. 1 son. Education: PhD, 1972; MA, 1980; MBA, 1981; DBA, 1986. Appointments: Lecturer, 1973-77, Academic Recorder, 1977-80, Fairleigh Dickinson University; Professor, College of Mt St Vincent, 1982-. Publications: The Devil in Mann's Dr Faustus, 1976; The American and German Entrepreneur, 1986. Honours: Academic Excellence Award, 1968, Pace University; Founder's Day Award, 1973, NYU; Delta Mu Delta, 1993. Memberships: American Marketing Association; Association of Marketing Educators; International Studies Association; Midwest Business Administrators Association. Address: 300 Gorge Rd #25, Cliffside Park, NJ 07010, USA.

**PFANNER Helmut Franz,** b. 8 November 1933, Hohenweiler, Austria. Professor of German. m. Nasy I Pfanner, 1 son, 3 daughters. Education: Austrian Teaching Credentials, 1952; MA, 1961, PhD, 1965, Stanford University. Appointments: University of Washington, 1964-67; University of Virginia, 1967-69; University of New Hampshire, 1969-86; University of Nebraska, 1986-80; Vanderbilt University, 1990-. Publications: 10 books and numerous articles in professional journals. Memberships: Alexandria von Humboldt Association of America; American Association of Teachers of German; International A Döblin Society; International Association of Germanic Studies; International Pen Club. Address: Vanderbilt University, Department of Germanic and Slavic Languages, Box 1567, Sta B, Nashville, TN 37235, USA.

**PFANNSCHMIDT Heinz,** b. 7 June 1947, Salzgitter, Germany. Vice President. m. Gisela, 2 daughters. Education: Dipl.Ing, 1973; Dr.Ing, 1978. Appointments: Managing Director, Philips, Germany; Vice President, Philips Radio Communications; Board Member, PKI-AG; Executive Vice President, HELLA KG. Memberships: Lions Club; VDE; VDI. Address: TRW Automotive, Industriestr 20, 73551 Alfdorf, Germany.

**PFITZNER Roman Jerzy,** b. 19 December 1948, Katowice, Poland. Cardiac Surgeon. m. Irena Kasprzyk, 1 son, 1 daughter. Education: Graduate, Faculty of Medicine, Medical University, Cracow, 1972; Doctorate, 1979, Habilitation, 1996, Faculty of Medicine, Jagiellonian University, Cracow; Specialisation: General Surgery I degree, 1976, II degree, 1980, Cardiac Surgery (II degree), 1991. Appointments: Department of Experimental Physiology, 1968-85, II Department of Surgery, 1972-73, Medical University, Cracow; Department of Thoracic, Cardiac and General Surgery, Specialist Hospital, Cracow, 1974-79; Assistant Professor, 1980-96, Associate Professor, 1996-, Department of Cardiovascular Surgery, Institute of Cardiology, Collegium Medicum, Jagiellonian University, John Paul II Hospital, Cracow; Head, Consultative Cardiovascular Surgeon Outpatient Department, 1987-. Publications: Author and co-author of papers, chapters and books, scientific films in field of cardiac surgery, experimental cardiology and biomineralogy. Honours: Scholarship, Alexander von Humboldt Stiftung, Dusseldorf, Germany, 1985-86; Awards of Polish Cardiac Society for Education, 1995, 1996; Secretary General, Division for Cardiac, Thoracic and Vascular Surgery, Association of Polish Surgeons, 1986; Co-Chairman, Cardiosurgical congresses, 1993, 1997 on occasion of Papal visits. Memberships: Polish Medical Society, 1973-; Polish Cardiac Society, 1977-; Association of Polish Surgeons, 1978-; Club of Cardiac Surgeons, 1986- (charter member); Societas Humboldtiana Polonorum, 1989-; Polish Society of Angiology, 1993-; New York Academy of Sciences, 1997-; Polish Society of Transplantation, 1997-; Society of Thoracic Surgeons, 1996-; International Society of Cardio-Thoracic Surgeons, 1996-. Address: Inst of Cardiology Collegium Medicum, Jagiellonian Univ, Dept Cardiovascular Surgery, ul Pradnicka 80, 31 202 Cracow, Poland.

**PHALORA Onkar S,** b. 18 August 1938, India. Teacher. m. Satpal K, 2 sons. Education: DVM, Punjab Veterinary College, Punjab, India, 1961; PhD, Montana State University, 1966; Postdoctorate, University of Kansas, 1968. Appointment: Professor of Biology, Anderson University, 1968-. Publication: A Genetic Basis of Physiological Response to Stress. Honour: Gold Medallist, Punjab University, 1961. Memberships: Indiana Academy of Sciences; Indiana College Biology Teacher's Association. Address: Biology Department, Anderson University, 1100 East 5th Street, Anderson, IN 46012, USA.

**PHILLIPS Edward John,** b. 17 July 1937, Bristol, Pennsylvania, USA. Computer Scientist. Education: BA, Mathematics, Temple University, 1963; Stockbrokers Licence, Texas, USA, 1992. Appointments: Planetary Research Programmer, Jet Propulsion Laboratory, Pasadena, California, USA, 1969-78; Brain Research Programmer, University of California Medical School, Los Angeles, 1979-80; Scientific Systems Engineer, Electronic Data Systems, Riverside, California, Dallas, Texas, 1980-85; Senior Systems Analyst, US Navy, Corona, California, USA, 1986-89; Computer Scientist, Riverside, California, 1989-92, Dallas, Texas, 1992-93, Levittown, Pennsylvania, 1993-. Publications: The Computer and Statistics; The Prediction of Failure in Automobile Components and Systems. Membership: Broadcast Music Inc (BMI). Address: 80 Indian Red Road, Levittown, PA 19057, USA.

**PICCIONI Emanuele,** b. 25 July 1966, Assisi, Italy. University Technical Assistant. m. Fiorella Ascani, 2 daughters. Education: Degree in Agricultural Sciences, with honours, 1991; PhD, Seed Biotechnology, 1995. Appointments: Educational Educator, Science High School, 1995-; Assistant Researcher, 1997-98, University Assistant Technician, 1999-, University of Perugia. Publications: Articles in international science magazines, on research in synthetic seed production, 1995-99; Article in International Journal of Plant Science, on research in somaclonal variation in plant embryogenesis, 1998. Membership: Italian PhD Association. Address: Via S Pietro Campagna, Località Colderba, 06081 Assisi, Perugia, Italy.

**PICKER Eduard,** b. 3 November 1940, Koblenz, Germany. Law Educator. m. Elke Heinemeyer, 2 sons, 2 daughters. Eduction: Law, University of Cologne, 1967; Graduate, University of Bonn, 1971; Law, Dusseldorf, 1972; Habilitation, University of Bonn, 1978. Appointments: Scientific Assistant, 1972-73, Advisor, 1973-78, Lecturer, 1978-79, University of Bonn; Professor, Law, University Regensburg, Germany, 1979-86; Professor, University of Tubingen, Germany, 1986-. Publications: The Negating Claim for Removal, 1972; The Third Party Action to Prevent Execution in its Historical Development as an Example of the Interaction of Substantive and Procedural Law, 1981; The Token Strike and the Role of the Industrial Dispute Under the Private Law, 1983; Freedom of Industrial Dispute and its Limitations, 1986; The Regulation of "Conditions of Employment and Economy" - Principle of Contract or Principle of Dispute?, 1988; Judge-Made Law Instead of Systematric Doctrine?, 1988; Wrongful Life - Damages for Own Undesirable Life, 1995. Membership: Heidelberg Academy of Sciences. Address: Falkenweg 64, D-72076 Tubingen, Germany.

**PIEPENBRING Meike,** b. 26 December 1967, Wuppertal, Germany. Scientific Assistant. Education: Licence des sciences naturelles, 1990, Clermont-Ferrand, France; Diploma Biology, 1991, Cologne, Germany; PhD Biology, 1994, Tubingen, Germany. Appointments: At least one trip per year to Latin America for investigation and teaching, 1992-; Investigation grant for Central America, 1995; Course of plant anatomy in Honduras, 1997. Publications: Several in international journals. Memberships: Deutsche Botanische Gesellschaft; Society for Threatened People; Latin American Mycological Society. Address: Spezielle Botanik/Mykologie, Botanisches Institute, Auf der Morgenstelle 1, 72076 Tubingen, Germany.

**PIERSON Thomas Claude,** b. 13 May 1922, Houston, Texas, USA. Professor of Music. m. Beth Polhemus Pierson, 2 sons, 1 daughter. Education: BMusEd, 1943; MMus, Violin, 1947; PhD, Theory, Musicology and Composition, 1952. Appointments: Associate Professor, University of Houston, 1954-62; Associate Professor, Mt St Mary's College, California, 1962-66; Professor, Texas A&M University, Kingsville, 1966-91; Department Chairman, 1966-1978; Associate Concertmaster and Program Annot, Corpus Christi Symphony Orchestra, 1968-1995. Publications: Integrate Comprehension/Performance, Clavier Vol II, 1963. Honours: NEH Fellowship, 1981-82; 2 Faculty Grants; 2 Faculty Lectures. Memberships: American Association of University Professors; College Music Society. Address 5909 Fenway Drive, Corpus Christi, TX 78413-2715, USA.

**PIETSCHMANN Herbert Victor Richard,** b. 9 August 1936, Vienna, Austria. Professor of Physics. m. Edeltraud Sicka, 2 sons, 1 daughter. Appointments: Fellow, Centre Europ Res Nucleaire, 1960-61; Research Assistant, 1961-64, Associate Professor, 1968-71, Full Professor, 1971-, University Vienna; Research Associate, University Virginia, 1964-65; Docent, 1966, NORDITA Professor, 1975, Tech Univ Goteborg; Visiting Professor, University Bonn; Director, Institute High Energy Physics, Austrian Academy of Sciences, 1971-75. Publications: 10 books; Over 250 papers in journals and magazines in the fields of theoretical physics, general physics, didactics, philosophy, foundation of medicine and others. Honours: Promotion sub auspiciis praesidentis, 1961; Hon Member, Hungarian Physical Society, 1976; Eotvos Medal, 1976; City of Vienna Prize for Science & Technology, 1996; Gold Medal of Science Faculty, University Bratislava, 1996. Memberships: Member 16 association and institutes including: Faculty member, Hernstein International Management Institute; Vice Chairman, Academic Board, Vienna International Academy for Holistic Medicine; Austrian Academy of Science; New York Academy Sciences; Austrian/European Physical Society. Address: Institute for Theoretical Physics, Boltzmanng 5, A 1090 Vienna, Austria.

**PIIROLA Jouko,** b. 23 February 1935, Pukkila. Biologist; Geographer. m. Irma, 1 son, 1 daughter. Eduction: BSc, 1958, MSc, 1959, PhD, 1967, University of Helsinki. Appointments: Associate Professor, University of Joensuu, 1970-71; Docent, University of Helsinki, 1972-; Senior Lecturer, University of Lapland, 1979-98; Associate Professor, University of Zambia, 1991-93. Publications: Research report in Annals of Geomorphology; Articles in professional journals and magazines. Honour: Knight of the Order of White Rose of Finland. Memberships: Nonfiction Writers Union of Finland; Valamo. Address: Myllarinte 38 B9, 96400 Rovaniemi, Finland.

**PILECKIS Simonas,** b. 19 October 1927, Lithuania. Professor Biomedical Science and Biology. m. Valentina Pileckiene, 2 daughters. Education: Faculty of Forests, Agricultural Academy of Lithuania, 1949-54; PhD Biomedical

Science, Biology, 1969. Appointments: Assistant Professor, 1954-60, Docent, 1960-69, Professor and Chief, 1969-93, Professor of Biomedical Science, retired, 1993-, Institute for Prevention of Plants, Agricultural Academy of Lithuania. Publications: Over 25 monographs, textbooks and guidebooks in the field of classification of beetles, and prevention of plants against pests; Author and co-author, over 200 scientific articles. Honours: Cavalier of the Fifth Degree order of Lithuanian Duke Gediminas The Great, 1997; Honoured Man of Science of Lithuania, 1981; Laureate of the Award of the Republic of Lithuania, 1978; Silver Medal for achievements in entomology, 1974. Address: LZUA gyvenviete 7 9, 4324 Kauno raj, Lithuania.

**PILIPAUSKAS Albinas,** b. 1 March 1961, Raseiniai, Lithuania. Spokesman. m. Ina Vasauskaite, 1 son, 1 daughter. Education: Vilnius University. Appointments: Priminister's Spokesman, Dress of Government, Republic of Lithuania. Address: Lithuania.

**PIMENTAL Patricia Ann,** b. 2 February 1956, Warwick, Rhode Island, USA. Doctor; Clinical Neuropsychologist. m. Dr John V O'Hara, 2 sons. Education: BS, 1978, MA, 1980, Northwestern University; Psy D, 1987, Chicago School of Professional Psychology; Fellow, American College of Professional Neuropsychology; American Board of Professional Neuropsychology. Appointments: Director, Psychological Service Department, PM&R, University of Illinois College of Medicine; Director, Neurobehavioural Medicine Programme, GlenOaks Hospital, Illinois; President and Chief Executive Officer, Neurobehavioural Medicine Consultants Ltd. Publications: Numerous manuscripts in professional journals, book chapters, test battery Mini Inventory of Right Brain Injury, 1989; Book, Neuropsychological Aspects of Right Brain Injury, 1989. Memberships: Member many professional organisations; Past president, Illinois Psychological Association; American Psychological Association; National Academy of Neuropsychology; International Neuropsychological Society; International Society of Hypnosis. Address: Glen Oaks Hospital Medical Centre Neurobehavioural Medicine, 701 Winthrop Avenue, Glendale Heig, IL 60139, USA.

**PINKOWICZ Christine Ann,** b. 5 August 1961, York, Pennsylvania, USA. College English Professor. m. Brian Patrick Craig, 1 daughter. Education: BA, Shippensburg University, 1983; MFA, Columbia University, 1988; MPhil, ABD, CUNY Graduate Center, 1996; PhD, CUNY Graduate Center, in progress. Appointments: Instructor, English, The Mercersburg Academy, 1983-85; TA, English, Shippensburg University, 1984; Director of Development Circle In The Square Theatre, New York, New York, 1987-89; Director of Development Pieter Claesen Wyckoff House Museum, Blooklyn, New York, 1989-90; Director of Development Repertorio Español, New York, New York, 1990, 1993-; Instructor, Adult Education, Lehman College, 1990-91; Instructor, A B Program, The Wood School, 1990-93; Instructor, Theatre, Hunter College, 1991-93; Instructor, Workplace Education, CUNY Office of Academic Affairs, 1993-95; Instructor, Adult Education, Brooklyn College, 1991-96; Instructor, English, Kingsborough Community College, 1994-. Publications include: ART/NY Real Estate Project; The Real Estate Crisis in the New York City Not-for-Profit Theatre: Models for Solution; Theatre du Soleil: Merging the Artistic and Economic; The Bramhall Playhouse: New York's Oldest Off-Broadway Theatre; Havel's Vanek Plays at the Jean Cocteau Repertory. Honours include: Fellowship, 1989-92, Travel Grant, 1991, V.P. Doctoral Theatre Student's Association, 1989, CUNY; Fellowship, Columbia University, 1985-88; Jesse S Heiges English Award, Shippensburg

University, 1983; Alpha Psi Omega, Pi Nu Epsilon, Kappa Delta Pi. Memberships: Association for Theatre in Higher Education; Modern Language Association; National Council of Teachers of English. Address: 440 First Street, Dunellen, NJ 08812, USA.

**PINNEKER Eugene,** b. 22 June 1926, Saratov, Russia. Hydrogeologist. m. R F Ivanilova, 2 daughters. Education: Geological Engineer; Hydrogeologist. Appointment: Chief Scientific Researcher. Publications: Brines of the Angara-Lena Artesian Basin, 1966; Fundamentals of Hydrogeology, 6 vol, book, 1980-84. Memberships: Intern Associate, Hydrogeologists, 1968; USSR Academy of Sciences, 1990; New York Academy of Science, 1994. Address: Institute Earth Crust, 128 Lermontov St, 664033 Irkutsk, Russia.

**PINSON William Meredith,** b. 3 August 1934, Fort Worth, Texas, USA. Professor; Administrator. m. Bobbie Ruth Judd, 2 daughters. Education: BA, University of North Texas, 1955; M Div, Southwestern Baptist Seminary, 1959; ThD, 1963. Appointments: Professor, Christian Ethics, Southwestern Baptist Seminary, 1963-75; Pastor, First Baptist Church Wichita Falls, Texas, 1975-77; President, Golden Gate Seminary, 1977-82; Executive Director, Baptist General Convention of Texas, 1982-. Honours: Outstanding Alumnus, University of North Texas; Outstanding Alumnus, Southwestern Seminary. Memberships: Association of Convention Executive Directors; Association of Baptist Schools and Colleges. Address: 333 N Washington, Dallas, TX 75246, USA.

**PINTO Maxwell S C,** b. 10 March 1954, Goa, India. Management Analyst. 1 son, 1 daughter. Education: BA, honours, Economics, University of Leeds, England, 1978; PhD, Business Administration, Pacific Southern University, California, USA, 1988. Appointments: Management Analyst, New York, 1989-93; Business Associate, New York Life Insurance Company, 1993-97; Trust Accountant, CI Mutual Canada, 1998-. Honours: Student of the Year, Park Lane College, Leeds, England, 1975; Scholarships, Pacific Southern University, 1984. Membership: England and Wales Institute of Professional Managers. Address: 75 Pinto Drive, North York, Ontario M2J 3T9, Canada.

**PIRK Jan,** b. 20 April 1948, Prague, Czech Republic. Cardiac Surgeon. m. Blanka Pirková, 2 sons. Education: MUDr, Charles University, Prague, 1972; DSc, Czech Academy of Science, 1988; Assistant Professor, Surgery, Charles University, Prague. Appointment: Head of Department, Department of Cardiovascular and Transplant Surgery, Institute for Clinical and Experimental Medicine, Prague 4, Czech Republic. Publications: More than 100 publications in scientific journals. Memberships: STS, USA; EACTS, Europe; ISCTS, Japan; New York Academy of Science. Address: IKEM, Videnska 800, 140 00 Prague 4, Czech Republic.

**PIROGOV Yuri,** b. 20 December 1937, Vologda, Russia. Physics. m. Pirogova Ludmila, 1959, 1 daughter. Education: MS, Physics, 1961, PhD, Physics and Mathematics, 1966, DSc, Physics and Mathematicss, 1991, Full Professor of Physics, 1992, Moscow State University. Appointments: Engineer, 1961, Senior Engineer, 1963, Associate Professor, 1966, Leading Scientist, 1991, Director of Quantum Radiophysics Laboratory, 1992, Vice Dean of Faculty of Physics, Moscow State University, 1994-98; Director, Center of Magnetic Tomography. Publications: 250 papers and conference contributions, 8 books. Medals: 2 government medals, 1990, 1997; Silver Medal of Russian Science Technology Exhibition, 1987. Memberships: SPIE, 1994; Russian Physics Society, 1985; Director General, Microwave International Association, 1994;

Director, Radioastronomical Science Educational Center of Russia, 1997. Address: Physical Faculty, M V Lomonosov Moscow State University, Leninskie Gory, Moscow 119899, Russia.

**PIROZZO Ralph Steve,** b. 26 December 1946, 1 son. Consultant Education. m. Sandra Lynn, 1 son. Education: BSc, Toronto; BEd, Queen's; Respiratory Technologist, Canada; Graduate Diploma in Resource Teaching, QUT; Graduate Certificate in Management, QUT. Appointments: Science Teacher, Pimlico State High School, 1975-77; Science Teacher, Wavell State High School, 1977-78; Resource Teacher, Clontarf Beach High School, 1978-83; Head of Science, Morayfield State High School, 1983-88; Regional Consultant, Sunshine Coast Region, 1988-92; Head of Curriculum, Deception Bay High School, 1992-94; Director of Development, Nudgee College, 1994-97; Managing Director, Pirozzo Consultancy Services, 1997-. Publications: 63 articles in Australian and overseas journals, 1980-97. Honours: Founder/President, Peninsula Enrichment Program Inc, 1979-98; Jaycees Outstanding Young Australian, 1981; Honorary Visiting Teacher, QUT, 1987; CRA Fellow, 1988; Paul Harris Fellow, Rotary Club of Kippa Ring, 1992; Citizen Ambassador Delegate, People to People International, China, 1992; Australian Men and Women of Science, Engineering and Technology, 1995. Address: 3 Cathedral Street, Bridgeman Downs, Qld 4035, Australia.

**PISHARODI Madhavan,** b. 13 July 1945, India. Neurosurgeon. m. Veronica, 3 daughters. Education: MBBS, 1967; MS, 1972; MCh, 1974; MD, 1988. Appointments: Assistant Professor, Neurosurgery, Calcutta, India, 1974-77; Private Practice, USA, 1985-; Assistant Professor, UTMB, Galveston, 1993-. Publications: Several articles in professional medical journals. Memberships: AMA; American Association of Neurological Surgeons; North American Spine Society. Address: 942 Wild Rose Lane, Brownsville, TX 78520, USA.

**PITTS George,** b. 10 September 1951, Sewickly, PA, USA. Director of Photography, Painter, Photographer. m. Janis. Education: Howard University, Washington, DC, USA, 1969-70; Skowhegan School of Painting and Sculpture, Maine, USA, 1971; BA, Bennington College, Bennington, Vermont, 1970-73. Appointments: Art Instructor, Phillips Exeter Academy, 1972; Picture Researcher, Time Warner Inc, 1978-90; Assistant Photo Editor, Entertainment Weekly Magazine, 1990-93; Teacher, Parsons School of Design, 1998; Director of Photography, Vibe Magazine, 1993-. Publications: Many Published Writings. Honours: SPD, Citations in Photography; National Magazine Award, Nominations in General Excellence and Design; National Magazine Award, Nomination in Photography; The Visual Club, Publication Cover Award; National Magazine Award, Nomination in Photography; SPD, Gold Award for, Vibe October 1994, Wesley Snipes; Certificate of Excellence for Chaka Khan Series. Memberships: Society of Publication Design. Address: VIBE Magazine, 215 Lexington Ave, 6th Flr, New York, NY 10016, USA.

**PITTS Sidney Clark,** b. 1 November 1950, Lancaster, Pennsylvania, USA. Musician; Actor; Producer. Education: BA, Music Education, Lenoir-Rhyne College, 1972; MFA, Acting, Rutgers University, 1983. Appointments: Managing Director, Co-Founder, Actors' Inscape, 1984-86; Chair, Department of Theatre, Newberry College, 1988-94; Founder, Bay City Actor's Studio, 1994; Director of Music, First United Lutheran Church, 1995-; Director, San Francisco Small Choir Festival, 1997-. Honour: Fulbright-Hayes Grantee, 1990. Memberships: American Guild of Organists; Organ Historical Society; Boston Clavichord Society; San Francisco Gay Men's Chorus.

Address: 23 Baker Street, San Francisco, CA 94117-3019 USA.

**PLAISANT Paola,** b. 29 August 1956, Alghero. Biology Doctor. Education: Doctor in Biology, University of Sassari 1983; Specialist in Microbiology, Rome, 1987. Appointments Biologist, Catholic University, Rome, 1994; Professor Microbiology School, 1992. Memberships: New York Academy of Sciences. Address: 1st Microbiol U Cattolica, Largo F Vito 1 I-00168, Rome, Italy.

**PLEINER Radomir,** b. 26 April 1929, Prague. Archaeologist Archaeometallurgist. m. Ivana Hnizdova, 1 daughter Education: PhDr, 1952; CSc, 1956; Doctor, 1968; Professor 1993. Appointments: Research Fellow, Archaeologists Institute Academy of Sciences, Prague; Professor, University o Charles, Prague. Publications: About 250 Treatises, Science Literature; 10 Books. Memberships: Secretary, Comite pour la siderurgie anc de l'UISPP; Member, Archaeological Institute Berlin; History Metal Society, London. Address: Archeologicky Ustav, 1 Mala Strana, Letenska 4, 118 01 Praha, Czech Republic.

**PLENS Ole Emil,** b. 20 February 1948, Copenhagen. Doctor. Education: Medical Candidate, 1873. Appointments Flight Surgeon, 1979-80; Head Psychologist, Helsinborg Sweden, 1981-83, 1984-89; Denmark, 1983-84; Private Practice, Sweden, 1989-. Publications: The Elderly and Depression. Memberships: Swedish Medical Association Danish Medical Association.

**PLUMMER John Mitchell,** b. 18 November 1950, Waterbury, Connecticut, USA. Clerk, Historian. Education: MA, Columbian University, 1998. Appointments: Researcher, Historic and Architectural Surveys, Norwich, CT. Publications: Contributing Editor, The American Genealogist; Contributor, Fifty Great Migration Columnist to New England and their Origins, 1991. Memberships: Maine History Society; New York Genealogical and Biographical Society. Address: 148 Grand St Apt 34, Waterbury, CT, 06702-1922, USA.

**POCSI Istvan,** b. 5 May 1961, Debrecen, Hungary. Chemist; Biochemist. m. Edit Rizan, 1 son, 1 daughter. Education: MSc Hons in Chemistry, 1985; CSc Chemistry, 1993; PhD Chemistry, 1993. Appointments: Assistant Research Fellow, Department of Biochemistry, Kossuth Lajos University, 1985-87, 1991-92; Aspirant of the Hungarian Academy of Sciences, 1987-90; Research Fellow, Senior Research Fellow, Associate Professor, Department of Microbiology and Biotechnology, Kossuth Lajos University, Debrecen, 1992-. Publications: About 35 professional publications in fields of Chemistry, Biochemistry, Clinical Chemistry, Microbiology and Biotechnology. Memberships: Hungarian Society for Microbiology, 1993-; British Biochemical Society, 1989-92; Hungarian Biochemical Society, 1991-. Address: Department of Microbiology and Biotechnology, Kossuth Lajos University, PO Box 63, H-4010 Debrecen, Hungary.

**PODCHERNYAEVA Raisa,** b. 26 February 1933, Moscow Region. Virologist. m. V Podcheryaev, 1 son, 1 daughter. Education: MD, 1956; PhD, 1974; Professor, 1989. Appointments: Head of Genetics group of Influenza virus, 1976-85; Chief of Cell Culture Laboratory, 1986-. Publications: 260 articles; monographs; patents. Honours: Medals: Excellent Worker of Public Health, 1970; Achievement of National Economy, 1968. Memberships: All-Russian Society of Epidemiologists, Microbiologists, Parasitologists; Russian Association of Cell Cultures; Russian Virologist Society. Address: Rogova Str 7, 123470 Moscow, Russia.

**PODOBNIK Mario,** b. 13 August 1952, Rijeka. Consultant; Obstetrician; Gynecologist. m. Slava Podobnik. 1 daughter. Education: MD, University of Zagreb, Croatia, 1976; PhD, 1989. Appointments: Postdoctoral Student, University of London, 1990; Thomas Jefferson University, 1994; Head, Obstetric & Gynecology, University Hospital Merkur, Zagreb, 1994-97. Honour: First Prize, Academy of Science and Art, 1996. Memberships: Croatian Academy of Medical Science; International Society of Ultrasound in Obstetrics and Gynecology. Address: University Hospital Merkur, Department of Obstetricts and Gynecology, Zajceva 19, 10000 Zagreb, Croatia.

**POEHLMANN Gerhard M,** b. 28 November 1924, Gotha, Germany. Cartographer. m. Ilse I D Schmidt, 2 daughters. Education: Lieutenant, German Army Service, 1942-45; Education by Professor Dr Hermann Haack, Perthes, Gotha, 1945-47; Cartographer, 1947; Diploma Graduate Engineer, Academy of Architecture, Berlin, 1952; Postgraduate Studies, Geography and Cartography, ETH and University Zürich, 1956-59; Doctor's degree scl, FU Berlin, 1974. Appointments: Lumberjack, combine operator, fire-brigade command, bank manager, 1945-47; Map editor, production manager, Editor in Chief, Gotha, Darmstadt, Zürich, Stuttgart, 1947-62; Lecturer, Professor, TFH Berlin, 1962-88, retired, 1988. Publications: From copper engraved maps (Stieler 1948) to satellite based mapping of one million square kilometres (Geology Map of Egypt, 1982-88), 1945-88; Numerous literary publications in Germany, Austria, Switzerland, China, India, Egypt, Nigeria, the Netherlands. Memberships: Geogr-Ethnogr Ges Zürich, Switzerland; Schweiz Kartogr GEs Bern, Switzerland; Ges.f.Erdk zu Berlin, Germany; DtschGes.f.Kartographie, Germany; Deutsches Farbenzentrum, Germany. Address: Cimberstrasse 11/1, D-14129, Berlin, Germany.

**POETHIG Eunice Blanchard,** b. 16 January 1930, Hempstead, New York, USA. Clergy. m. Richard P Poethig, 1 son, 4 daughters. Education: BA, Depauw University, 1951; MA, McCormick Theological Seminary, 1952; M Div, 1975, PhD, 1985, Union Theological Seminary, NYC. Appointments: Missionary, Philippines, 1956-72; Associate Executive, Presbytery of Chicago, 1979-85; Executive Presbyter, Presbytery of Western New York, 1986-93; Director, Congregational Ministries Division, General Assembly Council, Presbyterian Church (USA), 1994-98. Publications: Good News Women, 1987; Sing, Shout & Clap for Joy, 1989; Social Themes of the Christian Year, 1983; Women of Faith, 1997. Honours: Walker Cup, 1951; Nettie F McCormick Award, 1975. Memberships: American Academy of Religion, Society of Biblical Literature; International Association Women Ministers. Address: 3606 Trail Ridge Rd, Louisville, KY 40241-6221, USA.

**POGGI Roberto,** b. 24 August 1950, Genova, Italy. Entomologist. Education: Laurea in Natural Sciences, 1973, Genoa University. Appointments: Curator, 1976, Assistant Director, 1989, Director, 1996-, Museo Civico di Storia Naturale G Doria, Genova. Publications: Over 100 scientific publications in Entomology, Museology etc. Memberships: Academician, Accademia Nazionale Italiana di Entomologie; Secretary, Società Entomologica Italiana; Societe Amici del Museo G Doria; and others. Address: Museo Civico di Storia Naturale G Doria, Via Brigata Liguria 9, 16121 Genova, Italy.

**POGOSIAN Sergey,** b. 3 June 1956, Astrakan, Russia. Vascular Surgeon. m. 1 son, 1 daughter. Education: Yerevan State Medical University, 1972-78; Residentship, 1986-87; Training Course, Moscow Postdoctoral Graduation Training Institute, 1983; Training Course, Moscow Surgical Institute, 1988; Candidate of Medical Science, 1992; MD, 1996.

Appointments: Professor of Surgery, Yerevan Sate Medical University, 1997-. Publications: Several articles in professional medical journals. Memberships: Surgical Association of Armenia; Russian Vascular Surgeons Association. Address: 36 app 6 Yerevan, 375037 Babayan Street, Armenia.

**POHRIBNYI Anatoliy,** b. 3 January 1942. Philologist, Literary Critic. 2 sons. Education: Kujiv State University, Ukraine, 1966; Cand Phil, 1969; Phd, Philology, 1982. Appointments: Journalist, Various Newspapers, 1966-69; Professor, Kujiv State University, 1970-92, 1994-; 1st Vice Minister Education, Ukraine 1992-94; Vice Head, Ukrainian Writers Union, 1994-. Publications: Artistic Conflict, 1981; Oles Honcha, 1987; The Wells Never to Become Shallow, 1994; If We Were Studying the Way We Should. Talks on Burning Issues, 1999; 10 Monographs; More than 700 articles. Honours: Honourable Worker of the Ukrainian Higher School, 1991. Memberships: High School Academy of Science, Ukraine; Ukrainian Academy Original Ideas; Shevchenko Scientific Society; Head of Ukrainian Pedagogical Society, 1995; Co-Leader, Ukrainian World Coord Council. Address: Budivelniky Str 32/2 Apt 4, Kijiv 100, Ukraine 252100.

**POINDEXTER Vernon Stephenson,** b. 28 November 1918, Roanoke, Virginia, USA. Artist; Illustrator. m. Ollie H Henry, 13 Sept 1947. Education: Art Student, Virginia State College, 1938; Art Students League of New York, 1945-48. Certificate, Cartography, US Army Map Service, 1951; Diploma, General Electric Sales College, 1958. Appointments: Freelance Illustrator, Combat Forces Magazine, Infantry Journal Magazine, 1950; Commercial Artist, 1956-78, retired as Advertising Specialist, 1978, General Electric Co; Courtroom Sketch Artist for Jet Magazine, 1978; Sketch Artist, TV Metromedia News Channel 5, Washington DC, 1981; Exhibited, groups shows including Library of Congress, 1946, Brookland Museum, ACA Gallery, New York City, Philadelphia Print Club, National Academy Galleries, 1947. Creative Works include: Lithograph on loan from Barnett Aden Galleries, Washington DC, to Metropolitan Museum, New York City, 1953; 3 works in Howard University Permanent Collection; Designed religious banners for church, 1974-84, Boy Scout uniform shoulder patches. Honours include: 5 Bronze Combat Stars, Silver Star, US Army, 1942-45; Meritorious Service Award, American Legion, 1954; 3 National Awards, General Electric Co; Outstanding Service Award, Lincoln Temple Congregational Church, 1981; Lincoln Douglas Gold Medal Award, North American Theatre Group, 1984; Nominated to Historical Preservations, American Hall of Fame, 1988. Memberships: Numerous professional organisations; Smithsonian Institution; American Legion; International Platform Association; Commander, Lifetime Membership, Confederation of Chivalry, Sydney, Australia, 1988. Address: 1826 Porter Avenue, Suitland, MD 20746, USA.

**POJE Mirko,** b. 22 June 1945, Zagreb, Croatia. Chemist. m. Nevenka Modric, 1 daughter. Education: BSc Chemical Engineering and Technology, 1970, MSc Organic Chemistry, 1974, PhD Chemistry, 1976, University Zagreb. Appointments: Research Assistant, Institute Organic Chemistry and Biochemistry, 1971-75, Member, Department Organic Chemistry, Faculty Natural Sciences and Mathematics, 1978-, Research Assistant Professor, 1978-82, Research Associate Professor, 1982-87, Research Professor of Chemistry, 1987-, University Zagreb. Publications: Numerous publications on chemistry of organic natural compounds, especially purines and biogenetically related heterocycles; Important contributions to understanding of mechanisms of uricolysis. Memberships: Croatian Chemical Society; American Chemical Society; New

York Academy of Sciences, 1996-. Address: Svacicev trg 10, 10000 Zagreb, Croatia.

**POKOEV Alexander Vladimirovich,** b. 3 July 1946, Kashalin, Poland. Physicist. m. Mashina Valentina Alekseyevna, 1 son, 1 daughter. Education: Candidate of Science Diploma, 1973, Scientific Degree of Candidate of Science in Physics and Mathematics; Assistant Professor Certificate, Solid State Physics Chair, 1978. Appointments: Finished Secondary School, Balashov, 1963; Graduated from Department of Physics, Voronezh State University, 1968; Service in Soviet Army, 1969-70; Completion of Postgraduate Course on Solid State Physics Chair, Voronezh State University, 1972; Assistant and Senior Teacher of General and Theoretical Physics Chair, 1973, Assistant Professor, 1978, Kuibyshev State University; Graduated the qualification improvement dept, Moscow State University specialisation Solid State Physics, 1982, 1987, in field of computer technique proficiency, 1986, Kuibyshev State University; Head of Solid State Chair of Samara State University, 1992-; Obtained Certificate of Specialist in Field of Technologies Commercialisation, International Technologies Incubator, Russian National Economy Academy, Russian Federation Government, 1998. Publications: 100 scientific publications, inventions and publications on teaching principles of Solid State Physics, Diffusion in Solids. Honour: Merited Worker of Russia's Higher Education badge, 1997. Memberships: Russian Metallurgists Association; Higher School and Scientific Institutions Trade Union; Vice President, Expert Commission of Samara State University. Address: Dept of Solid State Physics, Samara State University 1 Akademika, Pavlova Street, Samara 443011, Russia.

**POKULIS Janis,** b. 4 June 1938, Asune vol, Kraslava r. Educator; Associate Professor. m. Helga Pokule, 1 son. Education: Diploma of Teacher of Biology, Chemistry and Bases of Agriculture, 1962, Daugavpils Teacher Training College, Department Sciences; Candidate of Pedagogical Science, Branch of Natural Sciences Methodology, 1975, St Petersburg Teacher Training College; Certified by Latvian Scientific Board, 1991; Dr Paed habil, 1997. Appointments: Teacher of Biology, Chemistry and Bases of Agriculture, Vilyany Secondary School, 1962-63; Director, Daugavpils Teacher Training College Agrobiological Station, 1963-76; Lecturer, 1976-81; Head, 1984-93, Department of Botany and Biology Teaching Methodology, Daugavpils Teacher Training College; Head of Home Economics Dept, 1993, Rector and Associate Professor, 1998-, Daugavpils Pedagogical University. Publications: 70 including 3 monographs in field of pedagogy. Honour: Certificate of Honour awarded by Ministry of Education for fruitful and creative work in Higher School, 1996. Memberships: Participant, TEMPUS programme, 1993-; Expert, Promotion Board on Pedagogy, 1993-; Consulting Board, Home Economics Teaching of the Ministry of Education and Science of Latvia; Latgale Development Board, 1998-. Address: Jatnieku iela 76, 42 Daugavpils, LV-5410 Latvia.

**POLAND Anne Spellman,** b. 13 June 1922, Woodward, Iowa, USA. Educator. m. Philip H Poland, 6 sons, 6 daughters. Education: MSE, 1970, Drake University, Des Moines, Iowa; PhD Education, 1989, Iowa State University, Ames. Appointments: Home Economist, Carroll County Extension, 1944-47; Elementary School Teacher, 1967-74, Counsellor, 1974-, Carroll Community Schools. Honours: Global Peace Curriculum Presenter, World Children's Day, United Nations, High School Teacher, Social Studies, 1942-44. Membership: Association for Supervision and Curriculum Development. Address: 21507 180th Street, Carroll, IA 51401, USA.

**POLEMIKOS Nikitas E,** b. 10 February 1947, Karpathos, Greece. Psychologist. m. Stacey Psaros, 2 sons, 2 daughters. Education: BA, 1972, MA, 1973, University N Colorado; PhD, 1983, NYU. Appointments: Assistant Professor Psychology, 1986-. Publications: Co-editor, Persons with Special Needs, 2 vols, 1994; Co-author, School Phobia, 1994. Memberships: American Psychological Association; Founding member, European Institute in Psychological Therapies. Address: 27 Papachristodoulou, 85100 Rhodes, Greece.

**POLENZ Joanna Magda,** b. 20 October 1936, Cracow, Poland. Physician. m. Dary Louis Polenz, 1962, divorced 1991, 1 son, 2 daughters. Education: MD, University of Sydney, Australia, 1960; MPH, Columbia University, New York City, New York, USA, 1992. Appointments: President, Van Sant Healthcare Association, New York, USA; Surveyor, Joint Commission for Accreditation, Illinois, USA. Publications: In Defense of Marriage, 1981; Test Your Marriage IQ, with others, 1984; Test Your Success IQ, with others, 1985. Memberships: Fellow, American Psychiatric Association; AMA; Public Health Association; Royal Society of Health. Address: 360 E 88th St, Apt 37a, New York, NY 10128, USA.

**POLESHCHUK Oleg Khemovich,** b. 24 April 1947, Krasnojarsk, Russia. Chemist. m. Svetlana Poleshchuk, 2 daughters. Education: MSc, Tomsk University, 1970; PhD, Tomsk State University, 1975. Appointments: Institute of Oil Chemistry, Russian Academy of Sciences, 1970-82; Tomsk Pedagogical University, 1983-; Visiting Assistant Professor, Irkutsk Institute of Organic Chemistry, 1991; Visiting Professor, Institute of Physics, A Mickiweicz University, 1992, 1993, 1994, 1995, 1997, 1998. Publications: Over 130 in professional journals and books. Honours: Tomsk Party Organization Prize, 1975; Individual Grant, Soros Foundation, 1993; Several grants. Memberships: New York Academy of Sciences; Date Base Best Europe Carmell International Ltd Technology Centre, Scotland; Mössbauer Effect Data Center, USA. Address: Vavilova 4/52, Tomsk 634005, Siberia, Russia.

**POLK Benjamin Kauffman,** b. 18 May 1916, Des Moines, Iowa, USA. Architect; Planner. m. Emily Polk. Education: Amherst College, 1933-35; University Chicago, 1935-36; Iowa State College, 1936-38; Diploma for Research in Regional Development, 1951, School of Planning, London. Appointments: Self-employed Architect and Planner, in South Asia, 1952-64; Designer, Monumental, Industrial, Residential Work including: Tripitaka Library, Rangoon; US Library, Bharat Ram Residence, New Delhi; Palace for King of Nepal; Jalianwalla Bagh; Utkal University; Kala Mandir Theatres, Calcutta; Karachi Polytechnic Institute; Woodlands Calcutta; US Embassy House and Staff Apartment, Rangoon; Saharanpur Paper Mill; Lipton Tea Calcutta; Schools and Technical Institutes, Napal; Young Island Resort, St Vincent, WI. Publications: Books: Architecture and the Spirit of the Place, 1960; Building for South Asia, 1992; India Notebook, co-author with Emily Polk, 1986; Buddhist Monastic Architecture in Sri Lanka with Seneviratna, 1992; Christchurch Priory, Dorset, 1994; Orchestration of own compositions and Structure for Music, 1995. Honour: Gold Medal, Prime Minister of Burma; played own Piano compositions All India Radio, 1962; 50 pen and pencil Landscape Studies of California Series on display Devizes Museum, Wiltshire. Memberships: AIA; AICP; IIA; IICP; Vice-President, Service Civil International East India. Address: 2361 Claranita Avenue, Los Osos, CA 93402 4013, USA.

**POLLMANN Herbert Josef,** b. 30 June 1956. Mineralogist. m. Maria, 1 son. Education: Diploma, 1981; PhD, 1984; Habilitation, 1990. Appointments: Assistant Professor, 1984-90,

University Lecturer, 1990-94, Head of Department, Professor, 994-. Publications: Several articles in professional journals. Honours: Emmy-Nöther Award, 1990; Georg-Agricola Medal, 995. Memberships: GdCh; DMG; MSA; MSC; VFMG; ABG; New York Academy of Sciences; GUG; ICDD. Address: University Halle Mineralogy, Domstr 5, 06108 Halle/Saale, Germany.

**POLOSUKHIN Vasily V**, b. 22 April 1961, Tsvetnogorsk. Pathoanatomist. m. Polosukhina Dina, 2 sons. Education: MD, Omsk Mediacl Institute, Russia, 1984; PhD, 1991, DSc, 1998, Institute of Clinical and Experimental Lymphology, Novosibirsk, Russia. Appointments: Scientific Researcher, Laboratory of Ultrastructural Pathology, Institute of Clinical and Experimental Medicine, Novosibirsk, 1984-91; Scientific Researcher, Laboratory of Functional Morphology of the Lung, Institute of Physiology, Novosibirsk, 1991-95; Senior Scientific Researcher, Laboratory of Ultrastructural Researches, Institute of Clinical and Experimental Lymphology, 1995-99; Post-doctoral Research Visitor, Department of Internal Medicine, University of Nebraska Medical Center, Omaha, Nebraska, 1999-. Publications: 42 scientific publications including 4 monographs (as co-author) Morphogenetic effects of laser induced treatment in therapy of chronic inflammation of the bronchi, 1993; Diagnostic bronchoalveolar lavage, 1995; Anatomic pathology of inflammatory lung diseases, 1997; Chronic bronchitis: pathogenesis, diagnostics, clinical and anatomic description, 1998. Memebrships: Russian Association of Anatomic Pathologists; Siberian Association of Lymphologists. Address: Ekvatornaja 3-94 Box 15, 630060 Novosibirsk, 60 Russia.

**POLSTON Ronald Wayne**, b. 1 November 1931, USA. Law, Legal Educator. m. Mary Ann Campbell, 1 son, 1 daughter. Education: BS, Eastern Illinois University, 1953; JD, University of Illinois College of Law, 1958. Appointments: Associate, 1958-64, Partner, 1964-65, Craig & Craig, Illinois; Assistant Professor, 1965-68, Associate Professor, 1968-72, Assistant Dean, 1968-71, Professor, 1972-95, Professor Emeritus, 1995-, Indiana University School of Law, Idianapolis; Visiting Professor, Monash University, 1972-73; Lecturer, China University of Political Science and Law, 1993. Publications: Include, What Happens When Judges Make Law and Nobody Listens; Legislation Exisiting and Proposed Concerning Marketability of Mineral Titles; Mineral Ownership Theory; Doctrine inDisarray; The Fixtures Doctrine: Was It Ever Really the Law?; Current Issues in American Contracts Law. Address: 311 South McGown Street, PO Box 20, Raymond, Illinois 62560, USA.

**POMES Ramon**, b. 5 December 1947, Santiago de Cuba. Professor Physics. m. M Cobas, 1 daughter. Education: BSc Physics, 1970, University Oriente, Santiago de Cuba; PhD Physics and Mathematics, 1976, University St Petersburg; Dr Habil, 1982, University Humboldt, Berlin; Dr in Sciences, Crystallography, 1982, National Comm Academic Degrees, Cuba. Appointments: Initial School Teacher, 1961-64; Military School Teacher, 1964-66; Senior Professor and Professor, University Santiago de Cuba, 1970-82; Vice President, Academy of Sciences of Cuba, 1982-91, Full Professor and Head of Division, 1991-94, Head X Ray Laboratory, 1995-, National Centre for Scientific Research. Publications: around 220 publications and over 120 scientific reports in conferences and scientific meetings. Honours: Include: Order to the Scientific Merit from Minister of Higher Education of Cuba for research on structure of complex silicates; Medal, Rafael Maria Mendive for more than 25 consecutive years with satisfactory results in education granted by the National Union of Education Workers of Cuba; Commemorative Medal of XXV Anniversary

of Academy of Sciences of Cuba for contribution to development of research in Cuba; Medal as International Fighter granted by Council of State of Republic of Cuba for teaching and scientific work developed in Republic of Angola; Golden Medal from Intercosmos Commission of the Federal Czech and Slovak Republic for contribution to research and collaboration in space research. Memberships: Division Scientific Council in NCSR; Cuban Physics Society; Editorial Comm of 5 journals; Mexican Crystallographic Association; Royal Microscopical Society; Fellow, Royal Society of Chemistry. Address: Ave Camaguey 11238, Casino Deportivo, Havana, Cuba.

**PONNAMPALAM Andrew**, b. 17 February 1958, Petaling Jaya, Malaysia. Nature and Travel Writer; Ecotourism Consultant. Education: Diploma in Communications, Advertising & Marketing. Appointments: Consultant to tourism-related government departments, travel and airline industries, 1980-; Managing Director, Answers! Consultancy, 1988-; Consultant, Koh Design Consultants, 1988-, Falcon Press, 1991-, Buzzword Creative, 1998-. Publications: Waterfalls of Malaysia; Rivers of Malaysia; Marine Heritage of Malaysia; Evergreen Tropical Forests of Malaysia; Selangor, A Never-ending Discovery; Guide to Kuala Lumpur & The Klang Valley; Words & Wings, Jungle Journal, newspaper columns on wildlife, conservation and ecotourism; Invited speaker at local and international symposia on conservation and ecotourism, papers thereof published. Honours: Gold Awards: Tourism Malaysia, Best Book, 1990, Best Poster Series, 1991, Best Travel Article, 1994, 1995; Awards of Appreciation, Rotary Clubs, for lectures and talks. Memberships: Founder member, Bird Conservation Council of Malaysia; Birdlife International; Malaysian Nature Society; First Baptist Church, Petaling Jaya. Address: 2 Lorong 11/6B, 46200 Petaling Jaya, Selangor, Malaysia.

**PONOMAREVA Valentina**, b. 10 July 1939, Moscow, Russia. Vocalist. m. Konstantin Gogunsky, 1 son. Education: Classical Music Degree, Vocals and Piano, Khabarovsk Institute of Arts, 1960. Career: Soloist, Vocalist, Tula Jazz Big Band, 1967-70; Actress, Singer, Dancer, Moscow Gypsy Theatre "Romen", 1971-78; Soloist, Vocalist, Trio "Romen", 1973-84, State National Concert Tour Union of Russia "Roskonzert", 1979-90; Founder, Leader, Valentina Ponomareva Musical Theatre, 1991-. Creative Works: 35 recording albums; 25 film sound tracks. Honours: Participant in several music festivals worldwide. Memberships: Theatrical Artists Union, Moscow; Performing Right Society, London. Address: Valentina Ponomareva Musical Theatre, 14 Malaya Bronnaya Street, Apt 19, Moscow 103104, Russia.

**POON Chung Kowng**, b. 28 February 1940, Hong Kong. Education Administration, Chartered Chemist. m. Vivien, 1 son, 2 daughters. Education: BSc, General, 1963; BSc, Special, 1964; PhD, 1967. Appointments: Lecturer, University of Hong Kong, 1968-75; Senior Lecturer, 1975-77; Reader, 1977-82; Professor, 1982-90; Faculty Dean, 1983-90; Director, HK Polytechnic, 1991-94; President, HK Polytechnic University, 1994-. Honours: JP, 1989; CBE, 1991; Ten Outstanding Persons Award. Memberships: Fellow, University College, London; Fellow, Royal Society of Chemistry. Address: Hong KOng Polytechnic University, Yuk Choi Road, Hung Hom, Kowloon, Hong Kong.

**POONGOTHAI Ko**, b. 11 May 1955, Irumbulikhurichi. Magnetotherapist; Freelance Writer. m. Pon Kothanda-Raman, 1 son, 2 daughters. Education: Diploma in Magnetotherapy, Naturopathy. Appointments: Editor of Arivukkuurval. Publications: 5 Books. Honour: KRG Endowment Prize.

Memberships: Naturopathy Society. Address: 16/10 6th Cross Street, Sasthri Nagar, Adyar, Chennai 600 020, Tamil, Nadu, India.

**POP-JORDANOV Jordan,** b. 23 November 1925, Veliko Gradiste. University Professor. m. Nada, 1 son, 2 daughters. Education: BS, Philosophy, University of Skopje, 1956; BS, Electrical Engineering, 1960, DSc, Engineering Physics, 1964, University of Belgrade. Career: Research Associate, BK Institute of Nuclear Science, Vinca, Belgrade, 1960-71; Dean, Faculty of Electrical Engineering, University of Belgrade, 1977-79; President, Macedonian Academy of Sciences and Arts, 1984-91; Director, Research Center for Energy and Informatics, 1993-. Publications: 10 books, 200 science papers. Honours: 2 Annual Awards, 1960, 1964; 2 Jubilee Awards, 1967, 1968; 3 Gold Medals, 1965, 1980, 1988; WREN-UNESCO Award, 1996. Memberships: Macedonian Academy of Sciences and Arts; New York Academy of Sciences; European Academy of Sciences and Arts; American Physical Society; International Solar Energy Society; Club of Rome Council for the Future of Europe. Address: Macedonian Academy of Sciences and Arts, Bul Krste Misirkov 2, 91000 Skopje, Macedonia.

**POPA Constantin,** b. 26 April 1931, Panciu-Vrancea, Romania. Chemist; Chemical Engineer. m. Clemansa Popa, 1 son, 1 daughter. Education: MChemEng; PhD, Chemical Engineering. Career: Professor, Technical University Gheorghe Asachi. Publications: 76 theoretical publications and appliances in Chemistry, Descriptive Geometry and Technical Drawing. Address: Technical University Gheorghe Asachi, Faculty of Chemical Engineering, Iasi, Romania.

**POPA Vasile,** b. 16 April 1954, Constanta. Professor. m. Carmen Lucia, 1 son, 1 daughter. Education: Faculty of Law, Bucharest University, 1973-78; Postgraduate, Labour Law, University of Iasi, 1980; Postgraduate, Civil Law, University of Cluj-Napoca, 1982; Postgraduate studies in France, Universities of Lyon and Nice. Appointments: Legal Adivsor, Ministry of Industry, 1978-81; Lawyer, Timis Bar Association, 1981-90; Lecturer, Senior Lecturer, University of Timisoara, 1990-; Senior Lecturer, Faculty of Law, Banat, University of Timisoara, 1991; Vice Dean, Banat University, 1991; Dean, Faculty of Law, Banat University, 1992-; Professor, Vest University, 1993-; Rector of Banat University, Timisoara; Co-President, Balkan Association of Criminal Law; Co-Chairman of the Permanent Secretariat of the Balkan Association of Business Law; President, Central European Academy of Science & Art, 1994-. Publications: Over 200 articles and studies in law, in newspapers and magazines; Author of 42 monographs and student courses, six of which published abroad. Memberships: Balkan Association. Address: Colonel Enescu Street No 8, Timisoara 1900, Romania.

**POPE Robert,** b. 29 November 1948, Wayne County, Georgia, USA. 3 sons, 2 daughters. Education: BS, Magna Cum Laude, Valdosta State College, 1975; Juris Doctor, Law, John Marshall Law School, 1981. Appointments: Criminal Defense Attorney, 1981-; Member, Cobb County Indigent Defense Panel, 1987-. Honours: Has won many seemingly unwinable criminal trials. Membership: DA Association of Criminal Defense Attorneys; President, American Criminal Justice Organisation, Valdosta Chapter, 1975. Address: 74 Spruce Lane, Cartersville, GA 30120, USA.

**POPESCU Mihail,** b. 2 February 1946, Bucharest, Romania. Professor. m. Carmen, 1 son, 1 daughter. Education: MSc, Highway Engineering, University of Civil Engineering, 1968; PhD, Geotechnical Engineering, University of Civil Engineering,

1978. Appointments: University Assistant, 1968-80; Lecturer 1980-89; Reader, 1989-92; Professor, University of Civ Engineering, 1992-; Visiting Professor, University of Edinburgh UK, 1992, University of Tokushima, Japan, 1993-94, University of Natal, Durban, South Africa, 1995, Norwegian University of Science and Technology, Trondheim, Norway, 1997; Currentl Chairman of the Working Group on Landslide Causes and Co-Chairman of the Commission on Landslide Remediation United Nations International Decade for Natural Disaste Reduction, 1990-2000. Publications: More than 100 Research Papers, Romanian, English, French, Italian. Slope Stability Analysis and Control; Design Guide for Highway and Bridge Geotechincal Engieering; Soil Mechanics; Foundation Engineering. Memberships: International Society of So Mechanics and Foundation Engineering; International Union o Geological Sciences Working Group on Landslides Associazione Geotecnica Italiana; Comite Francais de Mecanique des Sols et des Travaux de Fondations; Association of Geoscientists for International Development; Association o Engineering Firms Practicing in the Geosciences. Address University of Civil Engineering, P O Box 2-45, 78172 Bucharest, Romania.

**POPESCU Mihail,** b. 22 January 1936, Romania. Engineer m. Rodica-Elena Popescu. Education: Engineer, 1958, PhD 1970, Institute of Civil Engineering, Bucharest, Romania Appointments: Engineer, Hydratechnics Company, Timisoara 1958-64; Senior Researcher, Hydraulic Engineering Research Institute, Bucharest, 1964-90; Senior Researcher, Research Institute for the Environment, Bucharest, 1990-97; Professor Department of Hydraulics, University of Constanta, 1992- Publications include: Applied Hydraulics, 1985; Hydroelectric Power Plants and Pumping Stations, 1987; Selected Problems of Mathematics, 1994; Selected Problems of Geometry, 1997 Honours: Romanian Academy Award, Traian Vuia in Technica Sciences, 1982; Gold Medal, 23rd International Exhibition of Inventions, Geneva, Switzerland, 1995. Memberships International Association for Hydraulic Research; New York Academy of Sciences; Romanian Academy of Sciences. Address: Bd Iuliu Maniu (Pacii), No 52-72 Bloc 3 ScB Ap 65 Bucharest 77536, Romania.

**POPOV Igor,** b. 12 December 1959, Krivoy Rog, Ukraine. Immunologist. m. Marina Sasikina, 1 son, 1 daughter. Education: MD, Crimean Medical University, 1983; PhD, Research Centre, Kiev, Ukraine, 1989; DM Sci, Medical University, Kiev, Ukraine, 1994. Appointments: Researcher, Crimean Medical University, USSR, 1984-89; Researcher, Cancer Research Centre, Moscow, 1990-93; Visiting Researcher, University of California, San Francisco, 1994-95; Professor, Crimean Medical University, Ukraine, 1995-96; Visiting Researcher, Australian National University, Canberra, 1996-. Publications: More than 100 Articles, Studies. Honours: Medal, 100 Years of Viedogy; Honorary Professor, The Crimean Medical University. Memberships: Russian Immunological Society; Ukrainian Microbiological Society; Crimean Branch of Sciences; Australian Society for Immunology. Address: The Australian National University JCSMR/WVH, Canberra, ACT 0200, Australia.

**POPOV Iliya Vassilev,** b. 13 November 1931, Belitza. Professor. m. Ljudmila Petkova Popova, 1 son, 1 daughter. Education: Dipl.Eng, Higher Mechanical and Electrical Institute, Technical University, Sofia, 1954; PhD, 1970, DSc, 1986, Technical University, Sofia. Appointments: Electroengineer, Cellulose Plant, Stambolijski, Bulgaria, 1954-59; Assistant Professor, Higher Institute of Food and Flavour Industries, Plovdiv, 1959-71; Associate Professor, Automation of Food Industry, Department of Atomation of Production, Plovdiv,

Bulgaria, 1971-88; Professor, Automation of Food Industry, 1988-, Head of Department of Atomation of Production, 1971-89, Dean of Postgraduate Studies, 1993-95, Vice Rector of R & D, 1994-95, Higher Institute of Food and Flavour Industries, Plovdiv, Bulgaria. Publications: More than 130 papers, 10 textbooks, 2 books, 5 patents, leader of 27 research and development projects, 32 popular articles. Memberships: Scientific Board of Automatics & Control Systems, Bulgaria, Scientific Board of Food Technologies, Bulgaria; Union of Automatics and Informatics in Bulgaria. Address: 26 Maritza Blvd, Higher Institute of Food and Flavour Industries, Plovdiv, Bulgaria.

**POPOV Nicolai,** b. 17 March 1934, Leningrad, USSR. Physicist. m. Lazerevich, 15 June 1962, 1 son. Education: BS, Leningrad Polytechnic Institute, 1958; PhD, Ioffe Physico-Technical Institute, Leningrad, 1966; DSc, Leningrad Nuclear Physics Institute, 1984. Appointments: Junior Scientist, Ioffe Physico-Technical Institute, 1958-71; Junior Scientist, 1971-92, Senior Scientist, 1972-87, Leading Scientist, 1987-90, Leningrad Nuclear Physics Institute; Professor, Ludwig-Maximilians University, Munich, 1992-. Publications: 150 in professional journals. Honours: Silver Medal, Secondary School, 1952; Grantee, Volkswagen-Stiftung, 1996-97. Memberships: AAAS, 1994-; Gesellschaft von Freunden und Förderen der Universität München, 1994-1998; New York Academy of Sciences, 1995-; International Society for Human Rights, 1995-. Address: Sektion Physik der Ludwig-Maximilians-Universität München, Schellingstr 4, 80799 Munich, Germany.

**PORADA Zbigniew Wladyslaw,** b. 5 July 1946, Rzeszow, Poland. Electronics Educator. m. Krystyna Kubel. Education: MSc 1970, PhD, 1978, Mining and Metallurgical Academy, Krakow; DSc, 1996, Institute Electron Technology, Warsaw. Appointments: Assistant, Mining and Metallurgical Academy, Krakow, 1970-75; Senior Assistant, 1975-78; Assistant Professor, Cracow University Technology, 1979-96; Associate Professor, 1996; Head Electronic Division, 1997-. Publications: About 120. Honours: Award of the Minister of Higher Education, 1981, 1989; Mark of Distinction, Cracow University of Technology, 1995. Memberships: Polish Physical Society; Electrical Engineers Association of Poland; International Microelectronics and Packaging Society, Poland Chapter; New York Academy of Sciences. Address: Witosa 21/75, PL-30612 Krakow, Poland.

**PORTEANU Mircea Julian,** b. 20 July 1938, Oradea, Romania. Electrical Engineering Educator, Consultant. Education: MSEE, Polytechnic Institute, Romania, 1960; PhD, Control Engineering, 1974; IPROMET, Institute of Metallurgy, Plants, Bucharest, 1960-62; IRME, Institute of Power Engineering, 1962-70; ICPET, 1970-77. Appointments: Assistant Professor, University of Oradea, 1977-82; Consultant, Expert, ICEM Institute of Metallurgy, 1982-; Associate Professor, Department of Engineering, Constantin Brancusi University, 1995-. Publications: TTL Integrated Cigruits; Trends in Power Systems and Equipment; Trends in Electric Machines and Power Electronics; Numerous Articles, Science Journals. Memberships: IEEE. Address: Calea Grivitei 139 Ap 91, 78102 Bucharest, Romania.

**PORTER Michael L,** b. 23 November 1947, Newport News, Virginia, USA. Poet; Philosopher; Writer; Advisor. Education: BA, Sociology, Virginia State University, Petersburg, USA, 1969; MA, History, Atlanta University, USA, 1972; PhD, History, Emory University, Atlanta, USA, 1974; Postdoctorate, Sorbonne University, Paris, 1979; Further study, Harvard University, 1982; Cambridge University, 1982. Appointments:

Assistant Professor, Hampton University, Virginia, 1977-80; Research Advisor, American Biographical Institute, 1980-. Publication: Black Atlanta; Read Between the Lines. Honours: Distinguished Poet; Outstanding Poet. Membership: Board of Governors, American Biographical Institute. Address: 3 Adrian Cir, Hampton, VA 23669 3814, USA.

**PRUDOMINSKY Vladimir,** b. 19 July 1928, Moscow, Russia. Writer. m. Nadejda Kolosova, 2 daughters. Education: Moscow High School for Poligraphy, 1950; Diploma of Literary Editor. Appointments: Journalist in Moscow magazines and newspapers to 1960; After 1960: Free Author in Biographic Literature; Member of the Journalists' Union of Russia, 1957-; Member, Writers' Union of Russia, 1969-. Publications: Author over 30 books and over 200 articles in magazines and various editions including: Biographical comment to the work of L Tolstoy, 1988; The Colours of Tolstoy, 1997. Memberships: Member of Scientific Councels of Pushkin Museum, Moscow and of Tolstoy Museum, Moscow. Address: Gleueler str 22, D 50931 Koln, Germany.

**POSPISIL Jaroslav,** b. 19 February 1935, Charvaty. University Professor. Education: MSc, 1957; MEng, 1964; PhD, 1968; RNDr, 1968; DSc, 1992. Appointments: Graduated in Physics and Mathematics, Palacky University Olomouc; Electrical Engineering, Technical University Brno; Finished research study of optics, University of Tokyo. Publications: Author of 200 research publications in periodicals, 1960-99. Honours: Gold Medal, Polacky University, 1995; Merit Member, Czech Mathematicians and Physicists, 1996. Memberships: International Society for Optical Engineering; Czech Committee of International Commission for Optics; Union of Czech Mathematicians and Physicists. Address: Ovesna 10, 77900 Olomouc, Czech Republic.

**POSTAN Mikhail Ya,** b. 3 February 1948, Odessa, Ukraine. Mathematician. m. Elena Fabian, 1 daughter. Education: MS, Economics and Organisation of Water Transport, 1972; Kandidat of Science Degree, Mathematical Methods and Models in Economics, 1984; Doctor of Science Degree, Mathematical Methods in Economics, 1991. Appointments: Science Associate, Junior and Senior, R and D Institute, 1972-87; Senior Science Associate, 1987-91; Associate Professor, Professor, Odessa State Maritime University, 1991-. Publications: Over 100 Scientific Articles; 2 Books. Honour: International Man of the Year, 1995-96. Memberships: American Mathematical Society; International Academy of Ecology; Trasport Academy of Ukraine; Man and Life Protection Sciences. Address: Odessa State Maritime University, 34 Mechnikov Str, Odessa 270029, Ukraine.

**POSTOLACHE Julian,** b. 7 November 1949, Romania. Environmental Specialist. m. Adriana, 2 sons, 1 daughter. Education: Engineer Licence, 1971. Appointments: Programmer; Environmental Specialist. Publications: Several papers concerning coastal engineering and environmental aspects. Memberships: Romanian Marine Research Institute; Impulse 2000. Address: Romanian Marine Research Institute, Bvd Mamaia No 300, RO 8700 Constant, Romania.

**POTUPA Alexander Sergeevich,** b. 21 March 1945, Sevastopol. Futurist, Sociologist, Author, Physicist. m. Lubov, 1 son, 1 daughter. Education: Dr Sci, Professor, International Academy of Information Processes and Technologies, 1995; PhD, Institute of Physics, Belarus Academy of Sciences, 1970; MS, Moscow State University, 1967. Appointments: President, Center for Future Studies, 1992-; Chairman, Belarussian Human Rights Convention, 1997-; Vice President, Belarussian Union of Entrepreneurs, 1994-. Publications: 11 Books;

Discovery of Universe: Past Present, Future; Something Unimaginable; 120 Articles. Honours: International Man of the Year. Memberships: International Institute of Sociology; World Future Society; International Academy of Information Processes and Technologies; New York Academy of Sciences; International Pen Club; Belarussian Association of Journalists; AAAS; International Academy for Leadership in Business and Administration; Belarussian Association of Think Tanks; Belarussian Human Rights Convention; Belarussian Euro Atlantic Association; Belarussian Union of Entrpreneurs.

**POTVIN Jean-Albert,** b. 8 March 1915, St Boniface, Manitoba, Canada. Priest; Educator. Education: Paris and Rome; Ordained Priest, 1937. Appointments: Teacher, St Joseph de Mont-Laurier High School; Royal Canadian Legion, 15 years; Curate of parishes including: Ste Anne du Lac, Nomininque, Lac des Seize Iles, Lac Marois; Almoner, Accueil Vert-Pre d'Huberdeau; Lectures to historical societies and scientific groups. Publications: Numerous articles in professional journals. Honours: Conseil de la Culture des Laurentides for Conservation of the Patrimony. Memberships: Past President, Montreal Mycological Society; Past Director, Quebec Young Naturalists Club; Founding member, Canadian Nature Federation; Founding member, Quebec 4H Clubs; Founding member, Les Amis du Jardin Botanique de Montreal; Honorary member, Montreal Mycological Society. Address: PO Box 149, Huberdeau, P Que, Canada J0T 1G0.

**POULSHOCK Normand Garber,** b. 7 February 1926, Philadelphia, USA. Educator; Musician. m. Barbara Baker, 2 sons, 1 daughter. Education: BA, 1954, MA, 1955, Long Beach State College. Appointments: 2nd French Horn, Honolulu Symphony, 1945-46; 4th Horn, Anaheim Symphony, California, 1954; 4th Horn, Long Beach Symphony, 1955; Alamitos School District, Garden Grove, California, 1955-59; Klamath Falls School, Districts 1 and 2, Oregon, 1959-64; Klamath County School District, 1966-68; Viola, Cascade Symphony, Edmonds, Washington, 1969-77; Shoreline Public Schools and Summer Music Camps, 1968-71; Sammamish High School, 1971-76; Pacific Lutheran University, 1974-94; Pianist at various nightclubs, dance bands, Honolulu, Long Beach, Los Angeles, Klamath Falls, Seattle; Pioneered Teaching Electronic Music, Washington Public Schools. Creative Works: Seattle Symphony commissioned and performed Encounter for Synthesizers and Orchestra, 1971; Cascade Symphony performed Viola Concerto, 1976. Honour: Washington State Composer of the Year 1990. Memberships: Society of Composers; Past member, Musicians Union, California, Oregon, Washington; Educator's Associations. Address: 29507 G Street, Ocean Park, WA 98640, USA.

**POUPKO Victor,** b. 18 March 1927, Charcov-City, Ukraine. Engineer; Physicist. m. 1 son, 1 daughter. Education: Diploma of Engineer-Physicist, Moscow Institute of Energy, 1950; Diploma of Physics and Mathematics, Scientific Council of IPPE, 1957; Diploma of Physics and Mathematics, Scientific Council of IPPE, 1964; Certificate of Nuclear Power Systems Professor, Scientific Council of IPPE, 1968. Appointments: Junior Research Worker, 1950-56; Research Worker, 1964-70; Head of Laboratory, 1970-80; Head of Sector, 1980-90; Director of Section, 1990-95; Consultant of Director, 1995-. Publications and Awards: Monographs Methods of Adjoint Functions in physics and engineering investigations, Moscow, 1986; Application of Perturbation Theory in Engineering problems of nuclear energy, Moscow, 1993. Awards: State award, 1972; Schreiber-Spence Award, 1995; Membership of IPPE Scientific Council, 1964-; Membership of IATE, 1991-95.

**POVILIUNAS Arturas,** b. 10 August 1951, Kaunas, Lithuania. Sport Specialist. m. Laimute Pilipauskaite, 1 son. Education: Qualified as Trainer-Teacher, 1973, Kaunas State Institute of Physical Education; Post-graduate course, 1979, Scientific Research Institute for Physical Education, Moscow. Appointments: Educationist, Institute of Physical Education, 1974-76; Vice-Chairman, State Committee for Physical Education and Sport, 1987-91; Advisor at the Supreme Council of Lithuania, 1991-93, to the Presidential Office of the Republic of Lithuania, 1993-98; President of the NOC of Lithuania elected in 1988, re-elected in 1992, 1996-. Publication: Olympic Flame Never Dies, 1995. Honours: Chevalier of the Cofraternity of Knights of Most Holy Trinity in Italy, 1998; Olympic Order Holder, 1998; Order of the Grand Duke of Gediminas, 1998. Membership: European Olympic Committees (EOC) Executive Committee member, elected 1995, re-elected 1997. Address: Svyturio 25-18, LT 2040, Vilnius, Lithuania.

**POWELL Eric,** b. 23 July 1958, Parkersburg, West Virginia, USA. Barrister. Education: BA, History, 1980, BS, Business Administration, 1981, West Virginia University; JD, Western State University, 1987. Appointments: Attorney, 1993-; Notary Public Commissioner, 1996-97. Honour: Honoured Eagle Scout. Memberships: American Bar Association; West Virginia State Bar; Georgia State Bar; Association of Trial Lawyers of America. Address: 2002 20th Street, Parkersburg, WV 26101-4125, USA.

**POWELL John Constantine,** b. 17 August 1960, Manchester, Jamaica. Artist. Education: Certificate, Edna Manley School for the Visual Arts, 1987-90; University of West Indies, 1993. Appointments: Teacher, St Andrew High School for Girls, 1990-91; Bridgeport Comprehensive High School, 1993-98. Honours: Recipient of Rotary Scholarships, 1986, 1987-90; JCDC Festial Merit, 1990, 1991. Memberships: Jamaican Artists and Craftsmen Guild. Address: Mandeville, P O Box 1229, Manchester, Jamaica.

**POWERS Alan William,** b. 15 November 1944, Springfield, MA, USA. Literature Educator. m. Susan Mohl, 2 d. Education: AB, Amherst College, 1966; MA, University of Minnesota, 1996; PhD, 1996; Post Doctoral Fellow, Brown University. Appointments: Bristol Community College; Berkshire Community College; University of Minnesota. Publications: Westport Soundiaps; Acting Funny in Shakespear; Others. Publications: NEMLA; MLA; ALSC; ASCAP; Others. Address: Bristol CC, 777 Elsbree St, Fall River, MA 02720-7307, USA.

**POWERS Martha Mary,** b. 8 January 1940, Medford, MA, USA. Nursing Consultant; Administrator; Educator. Education: Boston College School of Nursing, BS, 1962; MS, 1978; EdD, 1985. Appointments: Undergraduate Faculty Member, Boston College School of Nursing; Assistant Professor, Regis College Division of Nursing; Faculty Member, Curriculum Coordinator, Somerville Hospital School of Nursing; Health Care Consultant, NATO, Brussels; Curriculum Consultant, Education Specialist, National Institute of Health. Publications: Numerous including, Nursing Diagnosis: A Literature Review, 1992; Adult Learners in Non-Traditional Programs: The Teaching-Learning Process, 1996; Critical Thinking and Nursing Diagnoses, 1998. Honours: Pi Lambda Theta; Federal Traineeship Grant for Academic Pursuit. Memberships: American Association of University Professors; American Association for the Advancement of Science; American Nurses Association; American Association for Critical Care Nurses; American Red Cross; Massachusetts Association for the Blind; American Association of Nurse Researchers; New York Academy of Science; National League of Nurses. Address: 29 April Lane, Lexington, MA 02421-8116, USA.

POZDEEV Anatoly Dmitrievich, b. 12 March 1929, Russia. Iectrical Engineer. m. Pozdeeva Alla Grigorievna, 2 sons, 1 aughter. Education: Dipl.ing, Water Transport Institute, Nizhny ovgorod, 1952; Candidate of Science, Politechnical Institute, harkov, 1963; DSc, Power Institute, Moscow, 1977; Professor, 979; Academician, Electrotechnical Sciences Academy, ussia, 1993. Appointments: Chief, Automatics Laboratory, olga-Don Channel, 1952-55; Studentship, Polytechnical stitute, Kharkov, 1955-59; Chief, Electric Drives Department, eavy Machine Tools Bureau, Ulianovsk, 1959-65; Chief, lectric Drives Department, Deputy Director, Director of cientific Research, Institute of Electroengineering, heboksary, 1965-86; Professor, Chuvash State University, heboksary. Publications: Over 200 including 5 monographs. onours: Honoured Inventor of Russia, 1981; Honoured cientist of Russia, 1986. Membership: Editorial Board, lectroengineering magazine, Russia. Address: St Engels 4-35, heboksary 428003, Russia.

PRAAG Herman Meir Van, b. 17 October 1929, Schiedam. sychiatrist. m. C Eikens, 3 s, 1 d. Education: Md, State niversity, Leiden, 1948-56. Appointments: Chief of Staff, 963-66; Founder, First Head of Department of Biological sychiatry, University of Groningen, 1966-67; Associate rofessor, Psychiatry, 1968, Professor of Psychiatry, 1970, niversity of Groningen; Lady Davis Visiting Professor, 976-77; Professor, Head of Department, University of Utrecht, 977-82; Professor, Chairman, Albert Einstein College of 1edicine,1982-92; Psychiatrist in Chief, Montefiore Medical Center, 1982-92; Professor, Chairman, Maastricht University, 992-97; Emeritus Professor, Albert Einstein College of 1edicine, 1992-; Interim Head of Department of Psychiatry, europsychology, Academic Hospital, The Netherlands, 997-99; Scientific Adviser, Department of Psychiatry and leuropsychology, Maastricht University, 1999-. Publications: 31 Publications. Honours: Ramaer Medal; Anna-Monika Prize; aal van Zwanenberg Prize; Reynier de Graaf Medal; Bronze ledal; Duphar Award; Ezrath Nashim Medal; Knighted by Queen Beatrix of the Netherlands; Eli Lily CNS Award; New rontier Award; First Sylvia Best Hunter Distinguished Service ward; Open Mind Award; Albert Einstein Award; Erasmus ward; Others. Memberships: Royal Academy of Sciences, the letherlands; International Scientific Commission; Society of Biological Psychiatry; Collegium Internationale leuro-Psychopharmacologicum; Association for the dvancement of Psychotherapy; The European Brain and Behaviour Society; British Pharmacological Society; Israel ledical Association; Manu others. Address: Academic sychiatric Centre, Maastricht University, P O Box 616, laastricht, 6200 MS, The Netherlands.

PRABHAKAR Belavadi K, b. 17 November 1946, Hassan, Karnataka, India. Educator. m. Gayathri Devi, 2 sons. Education: BSc, 1966, MSc, 1968, PhD Chemistry, 1984, Karnatak University, Dharwar, Karnataka. Appointments: Lecturer, Reader and Professor in Chemistry, Garbarga University, Gulbarga, 1970-; Director of Physical Education, Student Welfare Officer; Director, Institute of Sugar Technology. Publications: 20 research papers. Honours: Talent ward, Indian Institute Tal SE; Coordinator, National Youth Festival; Best District Governor Award; Coordinator, SAARC outh Festival. Memberships: Life member, Servas nternational. Address: Institute for Sugar Technology, Udgir Road, Bidar 585401 Karnataka, India.

PRADHAN Ashoke Kumar, b. 15 July 1958, Midnapur, ndia. Homoeopathic Medical Practitioner; Oncological Consultant. Education: DMS, 1978; BHMS, 1983. Appointments: Founder of Hyd Therapy (Homoeopathy, yoga

and diet); Founder President, Institute of HYDT Research and Education in India, 1998; Founder, The American Institute of Hyd Therapy Clinic, 1998; Speaker, 2nd International Conference on Mathematical Population Dynamics, Rutger's University, USA; Speaker, 7th International Conference on Mathematical Computer Modelling, Chicago, USA. Publications: 5 papers published including: Cancer, its early detection and Homoeopathic Treatment, 1990. Memberships: Founder President, Institute of HYDT Research and Education, India; Honorary Founder President, American Institute of Hyd Therapy Clinic, USA; Founder President, American Institute of HYDT Research and Education, USA; Life Member, Forum for Advancement of Science of Human Development, Karikundi; Life Member Homeopathic Medical Asscociation of India. Address: 487 Rabindra Sarani, Calcutta 7000005, W.B.India.

PRAKASA RAO Bosukonda Surya, b. 1 July 1949, Dangeru, India. Teacher; Researcher; Associate Professor. m. Krishna Veni, 2 sons. Education: MSc Tech Geophysics, 1975; Senior Diploma in Russian, 1980; PhD Engineering, 1983. Appointments: Department Geophysical Engineering, 1990-93, Head of Department, 1996-98, Chairman, Board of Studies, 1998-2001, Andhra University. Honour: Best Researcher Award, 1995. Memberships: Association of Exploration Geophysicists; Indian Society for Technical Education; Indian Society for Remote Sensing. Address: Department of Geophysical Engineering, Andhra University, Visakhapatnam 530003, AP India.

PRAKASH Om, b. 18 August 1927, Lucknow, India. University Professor; Vice Chancellor. m. Sushil Kumari Mathur, 2 sons, 1 daughter. Education: BCom, 1st class, 1945, MCom, 1st class, 1947, PhD, 1951, D Litt, 1961, University of Allahabad. Appointments: Assistant Professor, University of Allahabad, 1947-62; Professor, Head, Panjab University, 1962-63; Professor, Director, Dean, Vice Chancellor, University of Rajasthan, 1963-87; Vice Chancellor, Bundelkhand University; Emeritus Fellow, Visiting Professor, 1988-98; Editor, Indian Journal of Economics. Publications include: Industrial Organization; State Corporations; Economic Sins of Nations; Guided Incomes Policy; Management Ratios; The Commercial Society. Honour: Winner of CED International Award on US Economy, New York. Memberships include: Indian Commerce Association; Indian Institute of Public Administration; Founder President, Agrawal Farm Mansarovar Mathur Society. Address: 1/245 SFS Mansarovar, Jaipur 302020, India.

PRAKHOVNIK Arthur, b. 21 December 1940, Gomel, USSR. Electrical Engineer; Educator. m. 2 daughters. Education: Degree in Engineering, Polytechnic Institute, Kiev, Ukraine, 1966; PhD, 1971; DSc, 1982. Appointments: Engineer and Professor, National Tech of Ukraine, Kiev Polytechnic Institute, 1966-84; Vice Rector, 1984-89; Director, SRI Energia, 1989-97; Head of Department, Electrical Power Engineering, 1989-97; Energy Saving and Management Institute, 1997-. Publications/Honours/Awards: President, Ukraine honoured title; Distinguished person in field of science and technology of Ukraine, 1988; 7 books; 26 inventions; more than 200 works incl in USA, Italy, Bulgaria, Netherlands, Brazil, Russia, Ukraine and Germany. Memberships: IEEE, International Inst Rsch and Edn, Power System Dynamics, Ukrainian Academy of Engineering Sciences. Address: 4 Pobedy Ave Bld 4 Apt 6, 252056 Kiev, Ukraine.

PRAMOD V, b. 8 July 1973, Bangalore, India. Senior Control Systems Engineer. Education: Pre University Diploma, 1991; Bachelor, Control Engineering, Mechanical, 1995. Appointments: Application Engineer, Motor Industries Co Ltd, 1995-97; Control Systems Engineer, Robert Bosch, Germany,

1997-98; Control Systems Engineer, Robert Bosch, India, 1998-; Built, programmed and operated a Robotic Actuator Arm for precise pick'n' place operation, 1994-95; Completed development and application of embedded control system for the Tata Safari, sports utility vehicle, 1998; Customising export version, 1999. Honours: All India First for Cryogenic Engine Controls; Fellow, College of Engineering, Technokrec; National Merit Scholarship Holder; All India Prize for paper on Automotive Control Applications of Memory Alloys. Memberships: International Rotary Club, 1992-95; President, Astronomy Club, Surathkal Chapter, 1994-95. Address: No 284/E 10th Main Road, 5th Block, Jayanagar, Bangalore 560041, India.

**PRASAD Suman Prabha,** b. Gaya. University Professor. m. Kameshwar, 1 son, 1 daughter. Education: BA Hons, English, MA, English, Patna University; MA, Leicester University, England, 1968; PhD, 1971. Appointments: Professor of English, Patna University, 1985-; Professor of English, Sanaa University, Yemen, 1993-95; Head, PG Department of English, Patna University, 1997-; Dean, Faculty of Humanities, Patna University, 1998-. Publications: Hardy and Lawrence; Kathghore Ka Vijeta; Hukum Ka Ekka; Mutthi Bhar Shabd. Honours: Prizes in Chess and table tennis. Memberships: International Society for Humor Studies; Indian Association of English Studies; American Studies Research Centre. Address: 61 Patliputra College, Patna 800013, Bihar, India.

**PRASAD SINGH Devendra,** b. 25 January 1958, Muzaffarpur, Bihar. Journalism. m. Renu Singh, 2 sons, 2 daughters. Education: Sahityacharya (euivalent to Master degree), Kameshwar Singh Sanskrit Vishwavidyalay Kameshwer Nagar Darbhanga, Bihar. Appointment: Sub-editor, Chamakta Aina Hindi Daily. Publications: Several research articles in Indian newspapers and magazines. Address: Chamakta Aina (Hindi Dainik), 26 New Development Area, Golmuri, Jamshedpur, Bihar.

**PRATT William Frederic,** b. 2 October 1929, New Zealand. Research Scientist. m. Margaret Bethea Ammundsen, 2 sons, 1 daughter. Education: BA (NZ) 1951. Appointments: Secondary School Teacher, General Subjects, 1952-62; Secondary School Teacher, Head of Language Department, Horowhenua College, Levin, New Zealand, 1962-75; Self Employed Research Scientist, radiomedical science and interdimensional physics, studying the ability of radio waves to boost immune responses, to inactivate some toxic substances in human and animal bodies and in the air, the water and the food chain, and to neutralise bacterial and viral infections, 1975-; for the purpose of neutralising infective organisms, eg HIV, it is necessary to use a radio wave that is capable of disrupting the chemical-electrical cycle of the target organism. The radio transmitter is the only invention capable of rapidly defeating biological wafare. Memberships: New York Academy of Sciences; American Association for the Advancement of Science; Royal Society of New Zealand; Royal Astronomical Society of New Zealand. Address: Waikupa Road, RD 12 Okoia, Wanganui 5021, New Zealand.

**PRECHT William F,** b. 26 December 1956, New York, USA. Coral Reef Scientist. m. Joni Lynn Ferden, 2 daughters. Education: BA, Geology, SUNY Oswego, 1978; MS, Earth Science Adelphi University, 1984; MA, Marine Geology, University Miami, 1994. Appointments: 18 years professional experience; Natural Resources Manager, Law Engineering and Environmental Services, at present. Publication: The Art and Science of Reef Restoration, 1988. Membership: AAPG; SEPM; AIPG; ISRS. Address: 7310 Ponciana Court, Miami Lakes, FL 33014, USA.

**PRESS Vello,** b. 13 October 1934, Tallinn, Estonia Scientific Worker. m. Lubomira Broniarz. Education: Graduat Engineer, Technical University, Tallinn, 1957; PhD, 197C Diploma of Senior Researcher, Academy of Sciences Estonia, 1974. Appointments: Heat Power Engineer, 1957-6C Junior Researcher, 1960-70; Senior Researcher, 1970-93 Senior Specialist, 1994-95; Senior Lecturer, 1995 Publications: 40 Papers, Reports, Field of the Combustion of Fuels and the Mass Transport in the Multicomponent Media Memberships: Research Board of Advisors, America Biographical Institute. Address: Brzoskwiniowa 4, Lubo Poznan, Poland.

**PRIDEAUX Bruce,** b. 6 October 1953, Townsville. Universit Lecturer. m. Linda Veronica, 3 sons, 2 daughters. Education BE, 1976. ME, 1986, James Cook University; BA, University c Queensland, 1979. Appointments: High School Teache Department of Education, Queensland, 1974-84; Transpo Analyst, Queensland Department of Transport, 1984-89 Regional Officer, 1989-92; Lecturer, University of Queenslanc 1992-; Principal, BRP Consulting, 1994-; Editor, Asia Pacifi Journal of Transport, 1996. Publications: Numerous includin The Role of the Transport System in Destination Developmen Is the Tourism Industry Prepared for the Bug's Bite Implications for Australia of the Asian Financial Crisis; A Stud of Opportunities for Rural Heritage Museums to Maximis Patronage; Effects of Crime on the Tourist Industry Memberships: Chartered Institute of Transport in Australia Australian Institute of Tourism and Travel; Asia Pacific Tourisr Association; Queensland Korean Chamber of Commerce.

**PRIEST Terrance Lee,** b. 20 January 1942, Shoshone Idaho, USA. Logistics Professional. m. (1) Pixie Ann Anderson 28 June 1965, deceased 28 Mar 1968, (2) Mary Coco Koep, 2. May 1971, 2 daughters. Education: BS, BA, BBA, Boise Stat University, 1972; Master of Transportation Law, College c Advanced Traffic, 1981; PhD, honoris causa, Gustavu Adolphus College and Delta Nu Alpha Transportatio Fraternity, 1986; Certified in Transportation and Logistics American Society of Transportation and Logistics, 1974 Reregistered Interstate Commerce Commission Practitioner 1975. Appointments include: Agent/Telegrapher, Union Pacifi Railroad, Pocatello, Idaho, 1961-69; US Army Combat Soldie and Personnel Specialist E-4, 1964-66; US Army, Idaho NC Personnel Specialist and Liaison Sergeant E-5, 1966-69 Corporate Traffic Manager, J R Simplot, Boise, Idaho, 1969-82 Corporate Commerce Manager - Logistics, Coors Brewing Golden, Colorado, 1982-. Publications: The Interstat Commerce Commission, 1973; Articles in trade journals Honours include: Professor of Transportation, Boise Stat University, 1974-79; Idaho Transportation Man of the Year 1981; Colorado Transportation Person of the Year, 1986 President Reagan Transportation Education Award, 1987; BC Society Transpportation Man of the Year, 1991; TC International Transportation Person of the Year, 1991 Outstanding Logician of North America, 1994; ANA International Transportation Logistician of the Year, 1997 Memberships include: WRVP, National AST, President 1991-92; Vice Chair, Legislative Committee, National Industria Transportation League, 1975-79; Association for Transportatio Law, Logistics and Policy, 1976-; National Association o Manufacturers, Chairman, 1982-, Transportation Task Force 1993-; Colorado Annual Operation Stimulu Transportation/Logistics Forum, 1984-, Chair, 1986-91 Co-Chair, 1984-85, 1992-; National Freight Transportatio Library Board of Governors, 1994-. Address: Coors Brewing Company, BC 41012th & Ford Streets, Golden, CO 80401 USA.

**PRILLINGER Hansjörg**, b. 3 October 1944, Vienna. Professor. m. Judith, 2 sons, 1 daughter. Education: PhD Thesis, Ruhr Universität, 1971-69; Habilitation, Universität Regensburg, 1975-83. Appointments: Assistant, 1969-1970; Assistant, 1971-75; Assistant, 1975-79; Assistant, 1979-80; Assistant, 1980-83; Habilitation, 1983; Head of Laboratory, Microbiology Raiffeisen Bioforschung, 1989-90; Visiting Professor, 1990-92; Visiting Professor, Institute of Applied Microbiology, Vienna, 1992-. Publications: 53 Publications. Address: U Bodenkultur, Muthgasse 18, A-1190 Wien, Austria.

**PRITCHARD Mary Elizabeth**, b. 14 December 1946, Kankakee, Illinois, USA. College Professor. m. Robert W Pritchard, 2 sons. Education: BS, University of Illinois, 1968; MS, Iowa State University, 1974; PhD, Purdue University, 1984. Appointments: Home Service Representative, Iowa-Illinois Gas & Electric Company, Cedar Rapids, Iowa, 1968-71; Teacher, Linn-mar High School, Marion, Iowa, 1971-72; Co-ordinator, Career Education, Iowa State University, Ames, 1972-74; Instructor, North Illinois University, DeKalb, 1975-81; Graduate Assistant, Purdue University, West Lafayette, Indiana, 1982-84; Assistant Professor, Northern Illinois University, 1984-90; Associate Professor, Coordinator family and child studies, 1990-92; Acting Chair, Department of Human and Family Resources, North Illinois University, 1992-93; Professor & Chair, School of Family, Consumer & Nutrition Sciences, 1993-. Publications: Contributor of articles to professional journals. Honours include: Phi Upsilon Omicron, 1966; Omicron Nu, 1967; Kappa Delta Pi, 1968; Phi Kappa Phi, 1974; Sigma Xi, 1988; Nominee, NIU Award for Excellence in Undergraduate Teaching, 1990; Kappa Omicron Nu National Honour Society, Adviser Award of Excellence, 1992-93 Academic Year; Gladys Bahr Award for Outstanding Service to Consumer Education, 1994; Various grants. Memberships include: Home Economics Association, State Board Directors, 1978-82; Kappa Omicron Mu honor Society, National President, 1993; National Board, 1992-93. Address: School of Family, Consumer & Nutrition Sciences, Northern Illinois University, Dekalb, IL 60115, USA.

**PROCHAZKA Ales**, b. 27 February 1948, Prague. Associate Professor, Lecturer. Education: MSc, Czech Technical University, 1971; PhD, 1983; Associate Professor, 1990. Appointments: Head of Department, 1997-; Vice-Dean, 1997-. Publications: 131 Papers, textbooks and reports; Signal Analysis and Prediction, 1998; Wavelet Use for Noise Rejection and Signal Modelling. Memberships: IEEE; Signal Processing Society; EURASIP. Address: Stareho 2168/11, 160 00 Prague, Czech Republic.

**PROCHAZKA Petr P**, b. 29 May 1945, Prague, Czech Republic. Structural Mechanic; Educator; Professor. 1 son, 3 daughters. Education: MS, CTU Prague, 1968; PhD, 1975; DS-CTU, Prague, 1990. Appointments: Assistant Professor, CTU Prague, 1968-72; Chief Analyst, 1972-79; Head of CAD Department, VHMP Prague, 1979-89; Principal Science Officer, ASCR Prague, 1989-92; Visiting Professor, RPI, Troy, New York, 1993-; Professor, CTU Prague. Publications: 7 Books, 1987, 1991, 1993, 1995; 200 Papers. Honours: Prizes for Best Publications in Applied Maths and Civil Engineering. Memberships: AMS; IACMAG; SMFE; Reviewer of Math Reviews. Address: Krkonosska 13, 120 00 Prague, Czech Republic.

**PROKHORENKO Victoria**, b. 12 August 1935, Zaporojie, Ukraine. Mathematician; Celestial Mechanics and Space Researcher. Divorced. Education: Mathematician, Moscow Lomonsov State University, Moscow, Russia, 1957; Candidate of Sciences (PhD), Space Research Institute, Russian

Academy of Sciences, Russia, 1989. Appointments: Engineer, Industry Institute, Moscow, 1957-60; Head of Mathematical Group, Central Institute of Mechanical Engineering, Moscow, 1960-68; Senior Scientist, Space Research Institute Russian Academy of Sciences, 1968-. Publications: Over 50 in professional journals. Honours: Medal: Veteran of Labour, Moscow Municipal Council, 1989; Medal: N Pilugin Space Science Federation of Russia, 1989. Membership: American Geophysical Union, 1996-. Address: Apt 193, Voronovskie Prudy Str 9, 117630 Moscow, Russia.

**PROKHOROV Evgeny Fedorovich**, b. 26 August 1948, Dnepropetrovsk, Ukraine. Physicist. m. Lyudmila A Fedotova, 1 son, 1 daughter. Education: MSc, Dnepropetrovsk State University, Dnepropetrovsk, Ukraine, 1971; PhD, Odessa State University, Odessa, Ukraine, 1979. Appointments: Engineer, 1971-73; Junior Researcher, 1973-82, Senior Researcher, 1982-89, Leading Researcher, 1989-91, Head of Department, 1991-, Institute of Technical Mechanics, Dnepropetrovsk, Ukraine. Publications: 82 publications. Honour: Badge, Inventor of the USSR, 1990. Membership: Ukrainian Physical Society, 1992-. Address: 6 Vokzalnaya st Apt 40, Dnepropetrovsk 320091, Ukraine.

**PROKOPOVICH Petr**, b. 3 November 1942, Brest, Belarus. Banker. m. Ludmila, 1 son, 1 daughter. Education: Dnepropetrovsk Construction Engineering Institute. Appointments: Director General, Brest Regional Planning and Construction Association, 1976-96; Member of Parliament, XII Supreme Soviet of the Republic of Belarus, 1990-95; Deputy Head, Belarussian President's Adminsitration, 1996; First Deputy Prime Minister, Republic of Belarus, 1996-; Chairman of the Board, National Bank of Belarus, 1998-. Publications: Various Belarussian and Foreign Editions. Memberships: Member of The Belarussian Engineering Academy; Address: Nat Bank of Belarus, 220008 Minsk Dr F, Skaryny 20, Belarus.

**PRONCKUS Mykolas**, b. 24 March 1936, Lithuania. Agronomist. 2s, 1d. Education. Agriculture Academy of Kaunas, 1965. Appointments: Agricultural Adviser; Head of Agricultural Department, Plunge; Member of Lithuanian Parliament, 1992-. Honours: Doctor Degree on Agricultural Science, 1982. Memberships: Lithuanian Labour Democratic Party. Address: Telsiu 1-12, LT 5640, Plunge, Lithuania.

**PRUSKUS Valdas**, b. 10 April 1950, Vilnius, Lithuania. Sociologist. m. Violeta, 2 sons. Education: Vilnius University, 1973; Dr of Humanities Philosophy, 1985; Dr Hab of Social Science in Sociology, 1997. Appointments: Professor, Social Science, Vilnius Gediminas Technical University, 1998-. Publications: Catholic Social Thought in Lithuania, late XIX - early XXC, 1997; Expression of Business Ideas in Lithuania, late XIX - 1940, 1997; Achievements of Public Education in Lithuania in the Context of OECD Countries, 1998. Memberships: Lithuanian Catholic Academy of Sciences; Lithuanian Sociology Society. Address: VGTU Sauletekio al 11, LT 2040, Vilnius, Lithuania.

**PSATHAS George**. Emeritus Professor. Education: BA (Honours), Sociology, Yale University, 1950; MA, University of Michigan, 1951; PhD, Yale University, 1956; Diploma, New England School of Photography, Boston, 1979. Appointments include: Research Associate, Social Science Institute, Washington University, 1963-68; Director, Center for Applied Social Science, Boston University, 1970-73; Co-Director, Sociology and Health Services Research Training Program, National Center for Health Services Research and Boston University, 1970-78; Co-Director, Post Doctoral Research Training Program in Sociology and Mental Health, NIMH and

Boston University, 1976-79; Visiting appointments in Greece, Turkey, Japan; Professor, 1968-, Acting Chairman, 1968-69, Associate Chairman, 1969-70, 1976-78, Chairman, 1984-85; Visiting Professor, Manchester, March 1996; Guest Professor, Institute for Human Sciences, Vienna, April, 1996. Publications: Over 60 articles in journals; Books and edited volumes include: Conservation Analysis: The Study of Talk-in-Interaction, 1995; Alfred Schutz Collected Papers Vol IV (co-editor), 1996. Address: Department of Sociology, Boston University, 100 Cummington Street, Boston, MA 02215, USA.

**PU Yongxiu,** b. 19 July 1937, Shanghai, China. Physical Oceanographer. m. Zhao Xiaomin, 1 son. Education: Graduate, Oceanographic Engineer, Leningrad Hydrometeological College, 1961. Appointments: Deputy Director, Second Institute of Oceanography, 1987-91; Director, National Marine Environmental Monitoring Centre, 1991-94. Honour: Certificate of the Outstanding Expert. Memberships: Chinese Society of Oceanography; Chinese Society of Oceanography and Limnology. Address: The Second Institute of Oceanography, Hangzhou 310012, China.

**PUCKETT Charles Lin,** b. 19 October 1940, Burlington, North Carolina, USA. Plastic Surgeon. m. Teresa Puckett, 2 sons, 2 daughters. Education: Elon College, 1959-62; MD, Bowman Gray School of Medicine, Wake Forest University, 1966; Internship, General and Plastic Surgery Residencies, Research Training, Duke University and Hospital, 1966-75; Diplomate, American Board of Surgery, 1972; Diplomate, American Board of Plastic Surgery, 1977; Certificate in Surgery of the Hand, American Board of Plastic Surgery, 1990. Appointments include: Attending Surgeon, Duke University Medical Center and Durham Veterans Administration Hospital, 1973; Chief of Plastic Surgery Service, 1976-78, Attending Plastic Surgeon, 1978-92, Harry S Truman Veterans Hospital; Associate Professor of Plastic Surgery, 1976-80, Chief of Plastic Surgery Service, 1976-, Professor of Plastic Surgery, 1980-, Vice-Chairman, Department of Surgery, 1986-98, University of Missouri Health Sciences Center, Columbia; Attending Plastic Surgeon, Boone Hospital Center, 1990-. Publications: Hand injuries, co-author, monograph, 1976; 17 contributions to books; More than 100 refereed publications in the field. Honours include: Hoffman La Roche Award, 1965; Alpha Omega Alpha, 1965; Numerous Visiting Professorships. Memberships: American Association of Hand Surgery, President 1988-89; Fellow, American College of Surgeons, Governor, 1991-97; American Association of Plastic Surgeons, Trustee, 1995-98; American Medical Association; American Society for Plastic and Reconstructive Surgeons Inc, Board of Directors, 1985-, Chairman, CAQ Task Force, 1996-, Vice-President, 1997-98, President-Elect, 1998-99, President, 1999-2000, other offices; American Society for Surgery of the Hand, Sigma Xi; Several others. Address: 14605 Wren School Road, Ashland, MO 65010, USA.

**PUDLOWSKI Zenon Jan,** b. 23 May 1943, Pruchnik, Poland. Professor; Director. Education: M Electrical Engineering, 1968, Academy of Mining and Metallurgy, Cracow, Poland; PhD, 1979, Jagiellonian University, Cracow. Appointments: Lecturer, Institute Technology, University Pedagogy, Cracow, 1969-76; Researcher, Institute Vocational Education, Warsaw, 1976-79; Adjunct Professor, Institute of Pedagogy, Jagiellonian University, 1979-81; Senior Lecturer, Department of Electrical Engineering, University of Sydney, 1981-93; Associate Professor, Associate Dean Engineering Education, 1994-98, Director of UNESCO International Centre for Engineering Education (UICEE), Faculty of Engineering, Monash University, Clayton, Australia, current; Established an International Faculty of Engineering, Technical University of Lodz, Poland, 1992, Foundation Dean and Professor (in absentia); Honorary Dean of English Engineering Faculty, Donetsk State Technical University, Ukraine, 1995. Publications: Books, manuals, over 200 scientific papers in refereed journals and conference proceedings. Honours: Fellow, Institution of Engineers, Australia; AAEE Medal for Distinguished Contributions to Engineering Education, Australasia, 1991; Order of the Egyptian Syndicate of Engineers for Contributions to the Development of Engineering Education on both National and International levels, 1994; Honorary doctorate, Donetsk State Technical University, 1996; Honorary Doctorate of Technology, Glasgow Caledonian University, Scotland, 1998. Memberships: Member editorial advisory boards many international journals; Founder, Australasian Association for Engineering Education; UNESCO International Committee on Engineering Education; Ukrainian Academy Engineering Sciences. Address: UICEE, Faculty of Engineering, Monash University, Clayton, Victoria 3168, Australia.

**PUGACHEVA Galina,** b. 25 April 1939, Moscow, Russia. Scientist, Space Physics. m. A Gusev. Education: Graduate, Moscow Engineering Physical Institute, 1962; MS, Institute of Physics, Russian Academy of Sciences, Moscow, 1962; PhD, Elementary Particle Physics, Institute of Nuclear Physics, Moscow University, 1973. Appointments: Engineer, Physics Institute and Institute of Nuclear Physics, Moscow University, 1962-74; Scientist, Institute of Nuclear Physics, Moscow University, 1974-92, Professor of UNICAMP, Brazil, 1993-. Publications: Numerous articles in professional journals. Memberships: American Geophysical Union; Sociedade Brasillia de Fisica. Address: UNICAMP IFGW DRCC, Cp 6165 Campinas SP, CEP 13083 970, Brazil.

**PUI Ching Hon,** b. 20 August 1951, Hong Kong. Pediatric Oncologist. Education: MD, National Taiwan University, 1976. Appointments: Fellow, Pediatric Hematology Oncology, St Judes Childrens Research Hospital, 1979-81; Research Associate, 1981-82; Assistant Member, 1982-86; Associate Member, 1986-89; Associate Professor, University of Tennessee, 1986-89; Professor, 1990-. Publications: 360 Articles, Reviews, Chapters. Honours: Book Coupon Award, 1971, 1974, 1975; Membership, Society for Pediatric Research, 1987; Honorary Professor, 1993; Membership, American Society for Clinical Investigation, 1996; Consultant Professorship, 1998; Fellow, American Association for the Advancement of Science, 1998; The Best Doctors in America, 1998; Membership, American Association of Physician, 1999. Memberships: NCI Ad Hoc Grant Reviewer; Pediatric Oncology Group; Project Hope; American Society of Clinical Oncology; ALL Guideline Committee; American Society of Hematology; American Society of Clinical Oncology. Address: St Jude Childrens Rsch Hosp, 332 N Lauderdale St, Memphis, TN 38105-2729, USA.

**PUIU Ligia,** b. 16 December 1955, Vasad, Jud, Bihor. Physician. Education: Physician, Medical School Cluj, Napoca, 1980. Appointments: Specialization Physician, Pneumophtysiology, Institute of Pneumophysiology, Bucharest, 1987-. Honours: High Physician, Institute of Pneumophysiology, Bucharest 1993; High Physician, Department Chief, Hospital of Pheumophtysiology, Baia Mare. Memberships: National Pneumophysiology Society, Romania; French Pneumology Society. Address: Str Victor Babes, 7/15, Baia Mare, Judet Maramures, Romania.

**PUKIENE-LAZAUSKAITE Alfreda,** b. 1 January 1961, Ignalia. Barrister. m. Milvydas Pukas. Education: Faculty of Law, Vilnius University, 1979-84. Appointments: Attorney,

Inius Attorneys Office No 1, 1985-. Publications: in Russia, stonia, Latvia, Belorussia 1981-89. Memberships: Lithuanian ollege of Attorneys; Lithuanian Attorney Court; International ar Association. Address: Vilnius 1-oji advokatu kontara, dminiu 3, 17 kab, LT 2000, Vilnius, Lithuania.

**PULIAEV Sergei**, b. 5 June 1954, St Petersburg, Russia. stronomer. m. Potemkina Galina, 1 s, 1 d. Education: ploma, St Petersburg University, 1976; PhD, Pulkovo bservatory, 1982. Appointments: Assistant astronomer, ulkovo Observatory, Russia, 1976; Associate Researcher, 981; Researcher, 1987; Professor, Visitant Observatory ational, Rio de Janeiro, Brazil, 1993-. Memberships: National cademy of Science; Russian Astronomical Society; Brazilian stonomy Society. Address: Rua Alm Tefe 632 AP 911 Niteroi, 1030080 Rio de Janeiro, Brazil.

**PULKIN Sergei Alexandrovich**, b. 5 December 1950, etrotovodsk, Russia. Physicist. m. Tatyana B Pulkina, 1 son, daughter. Education: Postgraduate, Leningrad State niversity, 1968-72; PhD, Optics and Spectroscopy, 1978. ppointments: Head, Department of Quantum Electronics, 979, Leading Scientific Researcher, 1987, DI Mendeleev I-Russia Research Institute for Metrology. Publications: Over J papers and 3 patents. Memberships: SPIE; Metrological cademy, Russia. Address: DI Mendellev All-Russia Institute r Metrology, 19 Moskovsky Prospekt, St Petersburg 198005, ussia.

**PUPLESIS Rimantas**, b. 26 August 1958, Klaipeda, thuania. University Professor. m. Jurate Puplesiene, 1 aughter. Education: Graduated, Vilnius Pedagogical niversity, 1982; PhD, 1985, Postdoctoral studies, 1989-92, Sc, 1992, Zoological Institute, Russian Academy of Sciences, t Petersburg; Professor, 1996. Appointments: Assistant, ecturer, Senior Lecturer, Associate Professor, Vilnius edagogical University, 1985-89; Postdoctoral Fellow, Russian cademy Sciences, 1989-92; Head of Scientific Biosystematic aboratory, Professor Zoology Department, Vilnius edagogical University, 1993-95, 1996-97, 1998-; Postdoctoral ellow, Copenhagen University, Denmark, 1995-96; NATO and oyal Society, London, Postdoctoral Fellow, Natural History useum, London, 1997-98. Publications: About 60 scientific apers and a few substantial monographs; About 180 new pecies have been discovered and described; Participated in 5 scientific expeditions to Eastern and Central Asia, India, lepal and Belize. Honours: Various stipends of the Lithuanian overnment and others; George Soros' Award for chievements in entomological studies, 1993; Prof M Hering lemorial Foundation Award, UK, 1993, 1995; George Soros' iploma and Award, 1994; National Foundation Award for cientific and pedagogical achievements, 1995; State Order of iediminas of the Fifth Class for the merits for Lithuanian ducation and Science, 1996; NATO Fellowship grant, 1997; odman Research Foundation Grant, UK, 1998. Memberships: ussian Entomological Society; European Lepidopterologists ociety; Tropical Lepidoptera Association, USA; Council lember, Vilnius Pedagogical University, Chairman Science ommittee; Council member, Lithuanian Entomological ociety. Address: VPU, Biosistematikos Lab, Zoologijos atedra, Studentu 39, LT 2034, Vilnius, Lithuania.

**PURAMKAR Khudram Govind**, b. 9 December 1945, lodra. Teacher, Administrator; Poet; Social Worker. m. Sarala, sons, 2 daughters. Education: BA, Nagpur University, 1968; Ed, Bombay University, 1973. Appointments: Teacher, amarth High School, Lakhani, 1968; Teacher, Adiwari Shiv idyalaya, Garada, 1968-69; Teacher, New English School, har, Bombay 1970-71; Probation Officer, Social Welfare

Department, Government of Maharashtra Yerwada Industrial School, 1971-72; Education Officer, Maharashtra Educational Service Class 1, 1973-77; Teacher, Adiwasi Shiv Vidyalaya Dawwa, 1987-. Publications: Vishwatmak Dharma. Memberships: Secretary, Bhandara District Development Front; Adviser, Adishakati Education Society; Adviser, Fishermen Co-operative Society Ekodi. Address: At Post Dawwa Palasgaon, Tah-Sadakarjuni, Dist-Bhandara MS, India.

**PURETIC Stefanija**, b. 2 July 1922, Prelog, Medjimurje, Croatia. Medical Doctor; Paediatrician; Dermatologist. m. Bozidar Puretic, 1 son, 1 daughter. Education: MD, 1946, Medical School, University Zagreb, Croatia; Paediatric Diplomate, 1951; Consultant, 1956-; MSc, 1980, Medical School, University Zagreb. Appointments: Assistant Physician, Anat Institute, University Zagreb, 1945-50; Research Assistant, 1951; Founder and Chief Paediatrics, Dermatology Ward Dermven Department, Medical School, Zagreb, 1953-81; Chief of Dermhist Labor, 1956-68, 1997. Publications: 95 professional papers and clinical reports and textbooks; Coauthor, Derm Paediatrics; Author, Puretic Syndrome, 1962; Birth Defects, 1973. Honours: Order of Labour (Gold); Hon causa for Dermatology, Croatia, 1993. Memberships: Academy Medical Sciences of Croatia, 1971- , Senate, 1993-; EAA; Secretary, Croat Medical Association (Derm Allerg lo y). Address: Petrova ulica 90, 10000 Zagreb, Croatia.

**PURETIC Zvonimir**, b. 25 May 1946, Zagreb, Croatia. Medical Doctor. 2 sons. Education: MD, Medical School, University Zagreb, Croatia, 1970; Pediatrician, 1977; Nephrologist, 1985; Master of Medical Science, 1989; Research Fellow, 1989; Abdominal Ultrasound Specialist, 1997. Appointments: Head of Pediatric Dialysis and Plasmaphe resis Unit, University Hospital Centre, Zagreb; Head of Dialysis Centre, Medical School, University of Zagreb. Publications: 198 scientific, professional and educational papers. Honours: Award for Human Approach, Ministry of Defence, Croatia. Memberships: CEE Advisory Board in Chronic Renal Failure; National Coordinator, European Dialysis Registry; Member, Croatia Medical Association; EDTA; ISAO; ESAO; ISN; ISPD; ISFA. Address: Dialysis Centre Urol Clin, University Medical Centre, KBC, Kispaticeva 12, 10000 Zagreb, Croatia.

**PURNATMANANDA Swami**, b. 26 October 1950. Editor, Orator, Essayist, Poet. Appointments: Associate Editor with Dr Suniti Kumar Chatterji and R C Majundar; Head of Publication Department, Ramakrishna Mission Instituteof Culture; Editor, Udbodhan, 1987-. Publications: Swami Vivekananda Ebong Bharater Swadhinata Sangram; Ebar Kendra Vivekananda; Vishwapathik Vivekananda; Chirantani Sarada; Sri Ramakrishner Astangik Marga; Yugapurush Sri Ramakrishna; Many other publications. Honors: Dictionary of International Biography, International Biographical Centre; International Who's Who of Intellectuals, IBC; 20th Century Award for Achievement, IBC; International Man of the Year, IBC; International Directory of Distinguished Leadership, American Biographical Institute; Five Thousand Personalities of the World, ABI; 2000 Millennium Medal of Honour, ABI. Memberships: Working Committee, Ramakrishna Math and Ramakrishna Mission, 1990-; Member, Research Faculty, Library Faculty, Managing Committee, Ramakrishna Mission Institute of Culture; Member, Research Board of Advisors, ABI; Lecture tours in different parts of India and abroad (Bangladesh, Sri Lanka, Malta, France, Holland, Switzerland, Italy and England). Address: Udbodhan Office, 1 Udbodhan Lane, Calcutta 700 003, India.

**PURSGLOVE Laurence**,b. 29 July 1924, Monogahela. Technical Writer; Computer Quality Tester. m. 5 daughters.

Education: BSChE, Carnegie Institute Tech, Pittsburg, 1944; MSChE, 1946; ScD Organic Chemistry, 1949; Cert US Patent agent. Appointments: Designer of pilot plant minn, 1944-46; Assistantt Professor of Chemistry, Morgantown, 1949-53; Chemist Dow Chem Co, Midland, Michigan, 1953-58; Assistant Professor, Department of Chemistry, Delta College, University Center, Michigan, 1958-63; Technical Writer, Dallas, 1964-74; Entelek Newburyport, Massachusetts, 1975-89; Michigan National Bank, Lansing, 1970-89; IBM, Santa Clara, Clalifornia, 1990-92; Software Quality Assurance Tester Aristacom International, California, 1993-96; Technical Writer, Oreg Department of Transport, Salem, 1996-97; Translator Chemical Abstracts, Ohio, 1950-63; Contributor of articles to professional journals; Patentee chemical products. Memberships: American Chemical Society; Sigma Xi; Phi Lambda Upsilon. Address: Box 3125, Applegate, OR 97530, USA.

**PURWONO Albertus Soegiarto,** b. 5 June 1945, Purwokerto. Head of R&D Department. m. Ruth Aryani, 1 son, 1 daughter. Education: Doctorandus in Biology, 1974. Appointments: Staff of Air Mancur, 1974; Purchasing Manager, 1979; Assistant Manager R&D Dept, 1984; Head of R&D Dept, PT Air Mancur, 1990-. Membership: Indonesian Traditional Herbal Society. Address: Melati 11 AA 80, 57171 Solo, Indonesia.

**PUZANOV Arii,** b. 7 February 1937, Sverdlovsk, USSR. Scientific Worker; High School Lecturer. m. Sofyina Lyubov, 1 son. Education: Student, Urals Polytechnical Institute, Physical-Technical Faculty, 1954-60; Postgraduate, 1963-66; Diploma of graduation, 1960; Diploma of candidate of Physico-Mathematical Sciences, 1969; Diploma of Associate Professor, Department of Experimental Physics, 1973. Appointments: Engineer, Senior Engineer, Electro-Physical Laboratory; Senior Lecturer, Associate Professor, Head of Electrophysical Laboratory. Publications: Over 100 publications on physics of atomic collisions in solids; State Prize Winner, Medal and Diploma of 4 November 1972; Medal for excellent successes in field of higher education, 1984. Memberships: Regional Council for Scientific and Technical Societies; Nuclear Physics Division of the Scientific and Technical Council, Ministry of Higher Education. Address: Department of Experimental Physics, Urals State Technical University, 19 Mira Street, Ekaterinburg 620002, Russia.

**PYATT Leo Anthony,** b. 20 October 1925, NJ, USA. Real Estate Broker. m. Geraldine Genevive Gibb, 1 s, 1 d. Education: Franklin University, 1947-49. Appointments: Sales Person, Standard Oil Co, Columbus, Ohio, 1947-49; Borden Dairy Co, Columbus, Ohio, 1950-57; Frito-Lay Inc, Columbus, 1958-74; Secretary Treasurer, Snack Time Inc, Columbus, 1974-75; Agent, N NE Realty Co, Columbus, 1976-86; Owner, Broker, Pyatt's Rose Realty Co, Columbus, 1986-; Presiding Judge, County Rep Party, Franklin County, 1991. Honours: Distinguished Flying Cross; Air Medal with Silver Star; Philippine Liberation Medal. Memberships: Citizens for an Alternative Tax System; US Naval Air, 1943-46. Address: 4400 Wanda Lane Road, Columbus, Ohio 43224, USA.

**PYLANT Faye Ables,** b. 17 March 1928, Fayetteville, Tennessee, USA. Teacher. m. Kenneth Dean Pylant, 1 son, 1 daughter. Education: BA, Elementary Education, Belhaven College; M Ed; GA State University; Education Specialist, Georgia State University. Appointments: Teacher, Sixth Grade, Two Years, Jackson, Miss; Teacher, Sixth Grade, Three Years, Orlando, Florida; Teacher, Sixth Grade, Thirteen Years, Columbus, Georgia; Teacher, Second Grade, Columbus, Georgia, Five Years. Honours: Named Outstanding Teacher of Musecogee County, 1978-79. Memberships: Delta Kappa

GAmma; Philonian Club; Musecogee County Retired Teachers Gracious Ladies of Georgia; Edgewood Church of Christ Address: 4114 Olympic Lane, Columbus, GA 31907, USA.

**PYNE Phul Chand,** b. 18 February 1933, Calcutta, Benga India. Sculptor. m. Aparna Pyne, 1 son, 2 daughters Education: Studied Fine Art, Painting, Indian College of Art and Draftsmanship, Calcutta, 1951-56; Graduated in Modelling and Sculpture, 1959, 1st Class, Government College of Art and Crafts, Madras. Appointments: Free Lance Artist 1959-61; Art Teacher, High School, Calcutta, 1962-63; Home Publicity Department, Government of West Bengal, 1963-64 Head Dept, Incharge Modelling Unit, Indian Museum, Calcutta 1964-91; Retired. Creative Works: Participated in Trends c Bengal Art, Commonwealth Institute, London and Crafts Council of India, London, 1986-87; Royal Society of British Sculptors, 1971; Special Exhibition on Dr B R Ambadakar National Academy of Art, New Delhi, 1991; Wood Sculpture exhibited in Expo-70, Osaka, Japan, Ministry of Foreign Trade Government of India; National and various All India Exhibition in India; 2 solo exhibitions, 1983, 1991, in Calcutta. Honours National Award on Sculpture, 1968, Academy of Fine Arts Calcutta, 1969; Other awards from different organisations institutions at different times; Several hundred sculptures in public and private collections. Membership: National Academy of Arts of India; Academy of Fine Arts, Calcutta. Address: 87E Sri Arabinda Sarani, Calcutta 700005, India.

# Q

**QADRI Sohan,** b. 2 November 1932, Chachoki, India. Artist; Poet. 1 son, 2 daughters. Education: MFA, India, 1960. Appointment: Assistant Professor, Art, 1965-; Freelance Artist. Publications include: The Dot and The Dot's, 1978; Mitti Mitti, 1987; Boond Samunder, 1990; Antar Joti, 1995. Honours: National Award, Painting, 1968. Address: Broholms Alle 21B, 2920 Charlottenlund, Denmark.

**QIAN Kun-Xi,** b. 10 August 1944, Wujing, China. Scientist. m. Li Su-hua, 3 sons. Education: BS, 1968, Fudan University, Shanghai; MS, 1980, Jiangsu University of Science and Technology. Appointments: Professor and Director, Institute of Biomedical Engineering, Jiangsu University of Science and Technology. Publications: 100s publications to professional journals. Honours: Recipient, Gold Prizes, Einstein Invention Expo Centre, 1997, Centre Edison Inv City, USA, 1998. Memberships: Chinese Society Mechanical Engineering, senior member; AAAS. Address: Institute of Biomedical Engineering, Jiangsu University of Science & Technology, 212013 Zhen iang, Jiangsu, China.

**QIN Anren,** b. 21 November 1950, Ruicheng County, Shanxi Province, China. Exploration Engineer. m. Xiangyue Yao, 1 son, 1 daughter. Appointments: Exploration Engineer, 1990-; Leader, Prospecting Team, Yuan Qu Manferrous Metal Company, 1991-. Publications: 11 Academic Essays, 1979-. Honours: Prize for National Workers; Medal, Worker of the Metal Department. Memberships: Geology Academy of China; Metal Academy of China. Address: Yuan Qu Monferrous Metal Company, Prospecting Team, Shanxi Prov, 043700, China.

**QIN Qing Hua,** b. 22 March 1958, Guangxi, China. Scientist. m. Yi Xiao, 1 daughter. Education: BSc, Xi'an Highway University, China, 1984-87; MSc, Huazhong University of Science and Technology (HUST), China, 1984; PhD, HUST, China, 1990. Appointments: Associate Lecturer, HUST, China, 1984-87; Lecturer, HUST, China, 1987-1994; DAAD-KC Wong Postdoctoral Fellow, University of Stuttgart, Germany, 1994; Postdoctoral Follow, Tsinghua University, China, 1995-96; Queen Elizabeth II Fellow, University of Sydney, 1997; Honours: DAAD-KC Wong Postdoctoral Fellowship, 1994; Postdoctoral Fellowship, 1995; Visiting Scholar, 1996; Queen Elizabeth II Fellow, 1997; J.G. Russell Award, 1998. Membership: Member, Chinese Mechanics Society, 1992. Address: Department of Mechanical Engineering, University of Sydney, Sydney, NSW 2006, Australia.

**QIN Yaokun,** b. 19 February 1936, Wuxi, Jiansu Province, China. Research Fellow. m. Yushu Chen, 1 daughter. Education: Nanking University, China, 1958. Appointments: Associate Engineer, Minerals Nuclear Technical, Sichuan, China, 1958-76; Engineer, Shanghai Transmission Lines Research Institute, China, 1976-81; Senior Engineer, 1981-85; Research Fellow, Professor, 1985-. Publications: Contributor to Articles, Professional Journals. Memberships: China Institute of Electronics; China Institute of Microwave. Address: Shanghai Transmission Lines, Research Institute, P O Box 437833, Shanghai 200437, China.

**QIN Zeng-Hao,** b. 14 August 1933, Ningbo, Zhejiang Province, China. Teacher; Researcher. m. Xue-Jun Feng, 2 sons. Education: Graduation Diploma, 1956, Department of Meteorology, Nanjing University. Appointments: Assistant, Nanjing University, 1956-57; Assistant, Shandong University, Qingdao, 1957-59; Lecturer, 1962, Associate Professor, 1978,

Professor, 1985, Deputy Director, Dept Physical Oceanography and Marine Meteorology, 1978-82, Deputy Director, Institute of Physical Oceanography, 1983-85, Shandong College of Oceanology; Supervisor of PhD Student, Shandong College of Oceanology and Ocean University of Qingdao, 1984-; Senior Research Scientist, Shanghai Typhoon Institute and concurrent Professor, Ocean University of Qingdao, Nanjing Institute of Meteorology and Air Force Institute of Meteorology, 1986-. Publications: 2 translated monographs; 109 papers published in international and domestic atmospheric, oceanic and geophysical journals and periodicals. Honours: Science and Technology Prize Winner, 3rd National Natural Science Prize of China, 1982; 2nd National Science and Technology Progress Prize of China, 1998; 1st and 2nd Science and Technology Progress Prizes awarded by the Chinese Meteorological Administration, 1997; 2nd Science and Technology Progress Prize awarded by State Educational Committee of China, 1986 and Shanghai Municipality, 1997, 1998; 3rd Science and Technology Progress Prizes awarded by Shandong Provincial Government, 1990, Shanghai Municipality, 1995, and State Oceanic Administration of China, 1997. Memberships: Editor in Chief 1 journal; Editorial Board 4 journals; Vice President, 2 commissions and 2 Societies; Chairperson, Commission on Marine Meteorology of Chinese Meteorological Society; Executive member: Commission for Natural Marine Hazards, International Association for Physical Science of Ocean; and many more. Address: Shanghai Typhoon Institute, 166 Puxi Road, Shanghai 200030, China.

**QIU Fengqiong,** b. 17 September 1925, Sichuan Province, China. Researcher in Soil Biochemistry. m. Xu Yingzhong, 4 sons. Education: Bachelor of Agrochemistry, 1950, National Sichuan University. Appointments: Professor, Institute of Applied Ecology Academia Sinica, 1983-. Publications: 6 journal articles, 1964-. Honours: Science Progress Award, 1963, Science Leader Office of Chenyang; 3 second and two third class awards of science progress, Academia Sinica, 1985, 1987. Membership: Institut of Pedology, China. Address: Institute of Applied Ecology, Chinese Academy of Science, 72 Wenhua Road, Shenyang Liaoning Prov 110015, China.

**QIU Shijie,** b. 13 January 1932, Guangzhou, China. Teacher; Researcher. m. Wu Yu-e, 1 daughter. Education: PhB, Wuhan University, 1956-61. Appointments: Professor, Sociology Department, Zhongshan University, 1987-92; Vice Chairman, Sociology Department, Zhongshan University, Guangzhou. Publications include: Introduction to Sociology. Memberships: Vice Chairman, Guangdong Sociology Society; Vice Chairman, Guangdong Civil Administration Society, Guangdong Zhu Xi's Thought Research Institute Society. Address: Sociology Department, Zhongshan University, Guangzhou, China.

**QIU Song Long,** b. May 1929, Meixian County, Guangdong, China. Professor. m. Xie Duan Fen, 2 sons, 1 daughter. Education: Completed graduate study of economics at China People's University, 1956. Appointments: Teacher, various universities, 1952-; Professor Economics, Jinan University, 1991; Director Economics Faculty, Vice Chairman Board of Guangzhou University of Applied Science and Technology; Principal, Training Centre of Vocational Skills; Honorary Director, Zhongshan College of Finance; Engaged in study of theories of economic construction in China, economic administration and economic administration in Hong Kong. Publications: Editor-in-Chief, Imperialism - the Highest Stage of Capitalism; Chief editor, Brief Introduction to Selected Works of Lenin; Co-author, Elementary of Politics; Political Economy (Socialism); Lectures on Developing Agfrarian Commodity Production; Hong Kong Economics; Chief Editor, Administration of Industrial Enterprises; Study Guide to Political Economy. Memberships: Standing Council member, Guangdong Cultural Association; Council member, Guangdong Association of Corporate Culture. Address: Economics Dept, Jinan University, Guangzhou 510632, China.

**QIU Zesheng,** b. 15 August 1936, Candong Province, China. Teacher; Professor. m. Zensheng Ma, 2 sons. Education: BSc, 1961, Department of Biology, Capital Normal University; Visiting Scholar, Department of Botany, University of Massachusetts, 1983-84; Senior Visiting Scholar, Plant Biochemistry Department, Lund University, Sweden, 1993. Appointments: Lecturer, 1978-86, Associate Professor, 1986-92, Professor, 1992-; Director of Plant Physiology and Molecular Biology Research and Teaching Section, 1988-; Vice Chairman, Department of Biology, Capital Normal University, 1991-94. Publications: 45 papers in professional journals; 2 book translations; 2 Textbooks: Plant Physiology, 1989; Gene Engineering, 1993. Honours: Prize of Advanced Individual by Higher Education Bureau of Beijing, 1986; Second Prize for Excellent Teaching by Government of Beijing, 1993. Memberships: Director, China Association for Plant Physiology; Director, Beijing Association for Plant Physiology; Member, Professional Commission for Plant Phyliology of Botanical Association of China. Address: Biology Department, Capital Normal University, West Thirdcircle Road, Beijing 100037, China.

**QU Lei,** b. 26 December 1922, Gaiping, Liaoning, China. Physician. m. Zheng Rujun, 2 sons, 1 daughter. Education: MD, Changchun Medical University, 1943. Appointments: Vice Director, Deputy Chief Physician, Zhangjiakou Medical College, 1975; Director, Professor, Rehabilitation Center, Hebei Provincial Peoples Hospital and Hebei Provincial Geriatric Institute, 1975-. Publications: 10 books, 60 academic papers. Honours: National Excellent Scientific and Technical Worker, National Scientific and Technical Association, 1997; 20 awards and prizes. Memberships: Vice President, Chinese Association of Rehabilitation Medicine; President, Geriatric Rehabilitation; Council Member, Chinese Society of Gerontology, Executive Member of Geriatric Medicine; Chinese Medical Association; International Rehabilitation Medicine Association; Advisory Committee, International Conference on Physical Activity, Aging and Sports. Address: Hebei Provincial Peoples Hospital, 348 Hepingxi Road, Shijiazhuang 050051, China.

**QUADRI Asghar Hussein,** b. 18 February 1943, Moshi, Tanzania. Insurance Consultant. m. Karin Klein, 1 son. Education: Cambridge School Certificate, 1960; Insurance Diploma. Appointments: Insurance Clerk, various consultancy firms, Tanzania, 1961-65; Manager, various consultancy firms, 1966-76; Managing Director, Meru Insurance Consultancy Ltd, 1976-; Sub-Broker, Insurance, Blackmore (Diplomat Services) Ltd, London, 1989-; Sub-Agent, Medicare International Health Plan, Birmingham, 1992-. Memberships: Tanzania Insurance Institute; IAPA, Croydon, Surrey; YMCA, Tanzania; The Flying Doctors Society of Africa. Address: Meru Insurance Consultancy Ltd, India Street, PO Box 7126, Arusha, Tanzania.

**QUAYE Samuel Wilkinson,** b. 19 January 1963, Tema, Ghana. Business Executive. Education: Diploma, Sotech, Somanya, Ghana, 1982; Diploma, Impex Consultants Ltd, London, 1989; Certificate, Accra Polytechnic, 1994. Appointments: Teacher, Anada Maga, Bankok, Thailand, 1975-77; Researcher, Tex International, 1977-88, Pertain Metal & Rubber International, Taipei, Taiwan, 1988-; Teacher, Redmen, Taipei, 1987-91, Pertain Logical, California, 1987-90, Polytex, Manchester, England, Representative, Taipei, Taiwan, 1989-93; Director of Operations, Jass Ltd, Sfiac-Ankobra

Mining Co, Ltd, Sfiac Mining Co Ltd, Ghana, 1996-97; Pertain Damsamik ENT, 1997-. Honours: Chinese Speech Contest in Mandarin, 1989. Membership: Oxford Club. Address: PO Box 632, Tema, Ghana.

**QUESENBERRY Jewel Delena,** b. 25 June 1928, Hellier, Kentucky, USA. Retired Carer; Poet. m. (1)Robert Lee Swick, div, (2)Thomas Francis Steffen, div, 3 sons, 1 daughter, (3)Aubrey Dale Green, 4 December 1998. Education: Self educated. Appointments: Telephone Operator, Pacific Bell Telephone, 1961-70; Jewelry Store Owner and Operator, 1975-77; Real Estate Broker, Owner and Manager, 1977-86; Trainer and Caretaker of mentally retarded adults, State of Arkansas, Department of Human Resources, 1987-93. Publications: Contributor poems to newspapers, magazines, journals, periodicals and hardcover books of collections of poems. Honours: 3rd Prize and honourable mention, California Federation of Chaparral Poets, 1943; The Golden Poet Award, National Library of Poetry, 1992-93. Address: 4665 Jack Creek Road, Booneville, AR 72927, USA.

**QUIJANO-RICO Marco Antonio,** b. 7 August 1933, Sogamoso. Wine Grower. 3 sons, 1 daughter. Education: Chemistry Diploma, University of Lausanne; PhD, University of Mainz. Appointments: Scientific Fellow, Max Planck Society; Scientific Assistant, Max Planck Institute for Chemistry; Scientific Director, National Federation of Coffee Growers, Colambia. Honours: President, Association Scientifique Internationale du Caffé, 1970-71, 1988-89; Pioneer, Tropical Highlands Viticulture, 1982. Memberships: Colambian Academy of Sciences, New York; Academy of Sciences; American Wine Society; Association Scientifique Internationale du Caffé. Address: P O Box AP 048, Sogamoso Boyaca, Columbia.

**QUILLIAM Derek Henry,** b. 17 April 1946, New Plymouth, New Zealand. Solicitor. m. Judith Wendy, 1 son, 1 daughter. Education: LLB, Victoria University of Wellington, New Zealand, 1972. Appointments: Member, Criminal Bar Association, Hawkes Bay, New Zealand; Member, Criminal Law Committee, Hawkes Bay District Law Society; Honorary Solicitor, German Shepherd Dog Association of Hawkes Bay. Publication: Represented in New Zealand Photography Year Book, 1992; The Complete Book of New Zealand Trout Lures - forthcoming. Memberships: Hawkes Bay District Law Society; New Zealand Law Society. Address: Quilliam & Co, RSA Building, Vautier Street, Napier, New Zealand.

# R

**RAAD Virginia,**b. 13 August 1925, Salem, WV. Musician; oncert pianist; Musicologist. BA, Art history, Wellesley ollege, 1947; New England Conservatory, 1948; Ecole ormale de Musique, Paris, 1950; Doctorate, University of aris, 1955; Other studies. Career: Salem College, 1957, ▪59-70; NC Community Colleges and Art Council Artist in esidence, 1971-72; Concerts; Lectures; Master Classes, ▪60-. Publications: Claude Debussy, Anglophile, Musical ourier, 1961; Debussy et l'evolution de la musique au XXe ecle, 1965; Claude Debussy, Gabriel Fauré, The New atholic Encyclopedia, 1967; The American Music Teacher, )68, 1971, 1976, 1977, 1986; Piano Guild Notes, 1973; lavier, 1979; The Piano Sonority of Claude Debussy, 1994; iano Guild Notes, 1995. Memberships: American usicological Society; International Musicological Society; ociete Francaise de Musicologie, College Music Society; merican Society for Aesthetics; American College of usicians; Music Teachers National Association. Address: 60 errace Avenue, Salem, WV 26426, USA.

**RAAFAT Aly,** b. 7 August 1928, Cairo, Egypt. Architectural onsultant. m. Zainab, 1 son, 3 daughters. Education: BArch, airo University, 1949; M.Arch, Michigan University, 1953; PhD olumbia University 1957. Appointments: Professor and Head, rchitectural Department, Cairo University, 1988; Architectural onsultant, Middle East. Publications: Several articles in rofessional journals; 4 volumes on Architectural Creativity. onour: National Merit of Appreciation, 1990. Memberships: ▪A; Trustees, I House, New York. Address: Interconsult, 32-C lourad Street, Giza, Cairo, Egypt.

**RABABAH Abedallah Mohamad,** b. 1 December 1963, Jeita, Irbid. Mathematician. m. Nisreen Al-Ibrahim, 1 son, 1 aughter. Education: BSc in Mathematics, 1986; MSc in lathematics, 1988; PhD in Mathematics, 1992. Appointments: ssistant, Department of Mathematics, Yarmouk University, ▪86-88; Assistant, Department of Mathematics, Stuttgart niversity, 1990-92; Assistant Professor, Stuttgart University, ▪92-94, Yarmouk University, 1994-95, Qatar University, ▪95-. Publications: in many professional journals worldwide. ▪emberships: American Mathematical Society; German athematical Society; IEEE Computer Society. Address: Qatar niversity, Department of Mathematics, PO Box 2713, Doha atar.

**RABINOVICH Boris,** b. 23 June 1924, Moscow, Russia. viation, Rocket Carriers and Spacecraft Enginering, Space esearcher. m. Natalia Sapozhnikova, 1 son. Education: ngineer of Military Air Forces, Joukowski Military Air Forces ngineerng Academy, Russia, 1948; Candidate Sciences ?hD), Artillery Sciences Academy, Moscow, 1952; DSc (Eng), entral Institute of Mechanical Engineering, Moscow, 1961. ppointments: Officer, Soviet Army Air Forces, USSR, ?42-60; Head, Dynamics Laboratory, Central Institute of lechanical Engineering, Moscow, 1960-74; Head, Dynamics epartment, Research-Production Association lydrotruprovod", Moscow, 1974-93; Professor, State cademy of Control Devices Design, Moscow, 1993-; Leading cientist, Space Research Institute, Russian Academy of ciences, Moscow, 1999. Publications: Over 100 in rofessional journals; 10 monographs (5 with co-authors). onours: Medals for Victory in the Great Patriot War, 1945, for e battle merits, 1957, Supreme Council, USSR; Medal Yuri ▪agarin, 1987, Medal S Korolev, 1990, Space Science ▪ederation of Russia. Memberships: Moscow House of

Scientists, Russian Academy of Sciences, 1987-; Planetary Society, USA, 1995-. Address: Dnepropetrovskaya 39-1 #248, 113570 Moscow, Russia.

**RABINOVITCH Aviva,** b. 23 March 1927, Israel. Ecologist. 2 sons, 1 daughter. Education: MSc, Ecology, Hebrew University, Jerusalem, 1970; PhD, Geology, Pedology, Botany, Hebrew University, Jerusalem, 1979. Appointments include: Ecologist, 1970-76; Management of professional team in Nature Reserves Authority Management, 1976-79; Chief Scientist, Nature Reserves Authority, Management of Professional Branch, Wildlife Protection Branch, Environment Branch, 1979-89; Guidance and assistance for research students of Nature Reserves Authority and Technion Landscape Architects, 1983-; Teaching at the Technion, Haifa, 1983-1999; Survey and research work at Guatemala and Cyprus, 1989-. Publications include: Articles: Nature Conservation in Israel - Researches and Surveys, 1977; Tree Upper-Storey Units in Israel's Mediterranean Zone, 1985; Books: Parent Rock, Soil and Vegetation in Galilee, 1986; Continuous Human Use as Tool for Species Richness in Protected Areas of Israel, 1991. Honour: Honour by UNEP for outstanding contributions toward a better planet, 1997. Memberships: Botanical Society of Israel, 1967; Geological Society of Israel, 1967. Address: Kabri, D N Oshrat, 25120, Israel.

**RACEK Jaroslav,** b. Plzen, Czechoslovakia. University Professor. m. 1 son, 2 daughters. Education: MD, 1975; PhD, 1985; Associate Professor, 1991; Professor, 1997; All degrees at Charles University, Prague; Specialisation in clinical biochemistry; 1st degree, 1978; 2nd degree, 1981. Career: Department of Clinical Biochemistry, University Hospital, Pilsen, 1991-97; Institute of Clinical Biochemistry Laboratory Diagnosis, Charles University Medical School, 1997-. Publications: 3 Czech Investigations; Cell-based Biosensors; Clinical Biochemistry. Memberships: Czech Society of Clinical Biochemistry; Czech Medical Chamber. Address: Brojova 19, 30704 Pilsen, Czech Republic.

**RACHKOVA M I,** b. 27 June 1955, Assenovgrad, Bulgaria. Medical Doctor. 2 daughters. Education: Medical Doctor Diploma, 1979; Diploma, Certified Clinical Biochemistry, Sofia, 1988. Appointments: Attendant Physician, General Hospital, Emergency, Stara Zagora, 1979-83; Chief Assistant Professor, Medical University, Stara Zagora, 1983-94; Scientist, Iriston Co and Asson - 93 Research Company, 1996-. Publications: Contributor, articles to professional journals. Honours: Grantee, European Society Pigment Cells Research, Milano, Italy, National Cancer Institute, 1991; Award, Brighton Melanoma Conference, 1991; Project Commission of the European Comtys, Belgium, 1993. Memberships: International Society Pigment Cells Research; American Association Cancer Research; European Association Cancer Research; New York Academy of Sciences. Address: Asson - 93 Research Company, 3115 West Leland Avenue Ste 2, Chicago, IL 60625, USA.

**RADHAMOHAN Charles K,** b. 13 May 1946, India. Engineering Designer m. Annie, 1 son, 1 daughter. Education: BEng, Mechanical; MSc, IE and Operations Research. Appointments: Xerox Corporation, 1973-90; Applied Materials Inc, 1990-. Honour: Xerox Engineering Team Excellence, 1987. Memberships: American Institute of Industrial Engineers; American Institute of Vacuum Science Engineers; American Society of Metals and Materials. Address: 1566 Taipei Drive, San Jose, CA 95131-2417, USA.

**RADIC Njegomir,** b. 17 September 1943, Vrgorac, Croatia. Professor of Chemistry. m. Ksenija, 1 son. Education: Graduate, Faculty of Chemical Technology, University of Split, 1969; MS, 1974, PhD, 1978, Chemical Sciences, University of Zagreb; Postdoctoral Fellow, University of Cincinnati, USA, 1981-82. Appointments: Teaching Assistant, Assistant Professor, Associate Professor, Professor, 1996-, Faculty of Chemical Technology, Split. Publications: Over 50 papers mostly in international journals; Main research interests include the preparation and application of potentiometric sensors. Memberships: American Chemical Society; Croatian Chemical Society. Address: Sizgoriceva 20, 21000 Split, Croatia.

**RADOMSKA Maria,** b. 19 August 1927, Nisko, Poland. Academic (Professor). 1 daughter. Education: MSc, 1951; PhD, 1961; Professor, 1985; Student, Agricultural Faculty's University of Wroclaw, Poland, 1947-51. Appointments: Assistant Professor, Agricultural University of Wroclaw, 1949-79; Head of Institute, Department of Agriculture, Production Technology, Agricultural University of Krakow, 1980; Dean of Faculty of Agriculture Production Economy, 1990-93. Publications: 140 scientific papers in area of soil tillage and plant cultivation; Co-author of 4 handbooks of general soil and plant cultivation. Honours: Warsaw Upraising Cross, 1982; National Education Commission, 1992. Memberships: Polish Soil Society; Scientific Society of Wroclaw; Polish Society of Agricultural Science; International Soil Tillage Research Organisation. Address: ul M Cwilinskiej 2, 35 959 Rzeszow, Poland.

**RADONJIC Svetozar Ras,** b. 23 February 1937, Podgorica, Montenegro. Writer. m. Dr Ljubica. Education: Graduated, Faculty of Law, Sarajevo, 1965. Appointments: Financial Department, Dalekovod, 1957-58; Free Artist, 1959-60; Personnel Department, Standard, Sarajevo, 1960-62; Organizer and Secretary, Association of Amateurs Theaters of Bosnia and Herzegovina, Sarajevo, 1962-65; Lecturer, Centre for Education of Personnel in Sarajevo, 1966-68; Counsellor for Theatre and Art, Ministry of Culture of Bosnia and Herzegovina in Sarajevo, 1968-92; Senior Adviser, Ministry of Culture of Serbia, Belgrade, 1992-95; Free Artist, 1996-. Publications: Poetry: Variants for Survival, 1965; Melancholy Report of Autumn, 1970; Curses 1972; From Sleeplessness to Reality, 1990; The Year of Shells, 1994; Floating Illusions, 1997; Stories: The Edelwiss of a Shill Velly, 1972; Whirlpools of Life, 1985; Abysness and Passions, 1994; When Happiness Comes, 1996; Novels: Dark Fragments of Summer, 1970; Uncovering, 1987; The South Day, 1990; Dramas: On the Horizon (1 play), 1997; The Play goes on (2 plays), 1979; Adam After (3 plays), 1982; My Way (1 play), 1987. Theatrology Studies: The Search in the Theatre, 1974; Theatre in Time, 1996; Sociology of Culture: Cultural Life in Communities of Bosnia and Herzegovina, 1974; Cretivity and Reality, 1990; Culture to Man, 1992. Honours: Awarded at Yugoslav competitions for poetry, story, drama, novel, essay, more than 20 times; First award for poetry at the competition, Youth League of Bosnia and Herzegovina, Sarajevo, 1959; Third Award, Drago Gairvais, Rijeka, 1966; Djuro Salaj, Belgrade, 1961; First Award, Theatre Communities in Rijeka, 1976; First Prize Award, Gradina, Nis, 1970; Two First Awards, Isak Samokovlija, Pljevlja, 1979, 1980; First Award, Ivo Andric, Sarajevo, 1987. Membership: Yugoslav Writers' Union and Bosnia and Herzegovina Writer's Union and Association of Theatre Critics and Theatrologists of Bosnia and Herzegovina, Sarajevo; Serbia's Writer's Union and Association of Theatre Critics and Theatrologists of Serbia in Belgrade. Address: Strugarska 2/27, 11000 Beograd, Yugoslavia.

**RADULESCU Elena,** b. 14 May 1927, Rosiorii de Vede, Teleorman. Haematologist. div. 1 son. Education: MD, 1953,

Faculty General Medicine, Cluj; PhD Medical Sciences, 197. University Medicine and Pharmacy, Cluj; Postgraduate, Roy Postgraduate Medical School, London, 1983-87, 199( Diploma, 1992, Honorary member Professorial Counc. University Medicine and Pharmacy, Cluj, 1983, 1987, 199( Accreditative Diploma, 1995, for Membership of Internation Society of Haematology. Appointments: Senior Researche Department Haematology, Oncology Institute, Cluj, 1966-9' 2nd Paediatric Clinic, Cluj, current; Chairman, Internation Congress of Histochemistry and Cytochemistry, Helsinki, 198. Washington, 1988, Paris, 1991, and others. Publications Cancer Malignant Haemopathies, 1982; Haematologica, 199. The Histochemical J and Tissue biochemistry, 199. Biotechnologya Stacastru 9, 1-2, 1993; and others Memberships: International Federation of Researchers fc Science and Technology; World Society Cellular and Molecula Biology; International Society Haematology, European an African Divisions. Address: Str Unirii Nr 1, Et III, Apt 16, 340 Cluj Napoca, Romania.

**RADZEVICH Stepan Pavlovich,** b. 19 February 1953, Bil. Tserkva, Ukraine. Mechanical Engineer. m. Natalie Radzevich, 1 son, 1 daughter. Education: MSc, 1976, PhC 1982, Kyiv Polytechnic Institute; DSc, Mechanical Engineerinç Tula Polytechnic Institute, 1991. Appointments: Enginee Senior Engineer, Junior Scholar, Department of Design an Production of Metal Cutting Tool, Kyiv Polytechnic Institute 1976-82; Assistant Professor, Department of Mechanica Engineering, Bila Tserkva Agricultural Institute, 1982-8£ Associate Professor, 1985-91, Professor, 1991-97, Dean Faculty of Mechanical Engineering, 1993-9€ Dnieprodzerzhinsk State Technical University; Professo Department of Cutting Tool Design and Production, Nationa Technical University of Ukraine, Kyiv Polytechnic Institute 1997-. Honours: Silver Medal and Diploma, 1985, Gold Meda & Diploma, 1986, Ukraine State Exhibition of the Achievement of National Economics, Kyiv; Silver Medal, 1986, Gold Meda 1986, USSR State Exhibition of the Achievements of Nationa Economics, Moscow; Honorary Inventor of Ukraine, 1989 Ukrainian State Prize, 1990; Honorary Docto Dnieprodzerzhinsk State Technical University, 1995 Memberships: New York Academy of Sciences; Internationa Academy of Science & Arts; Ukrainian Higher Educatio Academy of Sciences; National Ukrainian Committee in Theor of Mechanisms & Machines; American Society of Mechanica Engineers; All Ukrainian Independent Society; Doctora Dissertation Panel of National Mining Academy of Ukraine Address: Kalinovaya Ave, 8-209, Kiev, 252190, Ukraine.

**RADZIKOWSKI Wladyslaw,** b. 5 February 1929, Lodz Poland. Econometrician. m. Danuta Eleonora Kielkiewicz, : sons. Education: M Econ, 1955; PhD, Math Programming 1964; Degree in Econometrics, 1969. Appointments: Hea Department, 1955-66, Head Director, 1968-71, Institute Orga in Machine-Build Industry, Warsaw; Deputy Director, Researcl Institut Industry Economics and Organisation, Warsaw 1966-68; Deputy Director Research, Research an Development Centre of Informatics, Warsaw, 1971-73; Head c Chair, Warsaw University, 1974-. Publications: Over 20 book: and 260 other publications including Operations Research ii Organ and Management, 1985, 1997. Honours: Silver Cross c Merit, 1964; Gold Cross of Merit, 1969; Polonia Restituta Cros V Class, 1977, IV Class, 1985. Memberships: Polish Academ Sciences; Polish Society for Operations and System: Research; Member, Committee, Organisation an Management, Polish Economic Society; German Operation: Research; International Input-Output Association; Institute fo Operations Research and the Management Science: (INFORMS). Address: Marszalkowska 27/35/37, 00-63!

Warsaw, Poland.

**RAEUCHLE John,** b. 21 September 1955, Washington, DC, USA. Computer Engineer. Education: BS, Texas Christian University. Appointments: Senior Programmer, Analys Commodity News Services, Kansas City, USA; Project Manager, Logica PLC, 1986-89; Senior Computer Analyst, Credit Systems Inc, 1989-95; Software Engineer, MasterCard International, 1995-. Honours: Eagle Scout; Scouting District Award of Merit; Scouters Training Award; Commissioners Key; Commissioners Arrow Head Award; Wood Badge. Memberships: St Louis Junior Chamber of Commerce, 1986-95; St Louis Jaycee Foundation, 1988-; Missouri Jaycees, 1984-95; Missouri Junior Chamber International Senate, 1991-; United States Junior Chamber of Commerce Senate Foundation, 1998-; St Louis Ambassadors, 1989-98; Boy Scouts of America, 1964-. Address: 52 Country Creek Dr, Saint Peters, MO 63376-3041, USA.

**RAFIUL Islam,** b. 5 January 1951, Rajshahi, Bangladesh. Teacher; Researcher. m. Shamima Majid, 1 son, 1 daughter. Education: BS, honours, University of Rajshahi, 1972; MS, 1974; MPhil, 1978; PhD, University of Punjab, Pakistan, 1991. Appointments: Research Scholar, 1974-78, Senior Research Scholar, 1978-79, Assistant Professor, 1981-89, Associate Professor, 1989-94, Professor, 1994-, University of Rajshahi; Senior Research Officer cum Divisional Head, Bangladesh Sericult Research Institute, 1979-81; Research Scholar, University of Punjab, Pakistan, 1988-91; Visiting Scientist, International Crop Research Institute for Semi-Arid Tropics, India, 1992, International Maize & Wheat Improvement Centre, Mexico, 1996, Cornell University, USA, 1996, Southampton University, England, 1996, Federal Institute of Technology, Switzerland, 1996, Chulalongkorn University, Thailand, 1996. Publications: Numerous research articles and scientific papers. Memberships: Bangladesh Botanical Society; Bangladesh Association for Plant Tissue Culture; Bangladesh Genetical Society; Asiatic Society of Bangladesh; Indian Horticultural Society; International Association for Plant Tissue Culture; Asia-Pacific Association for Plant Micropropagators; Pakistan Plant Molecular Society. Address: H265 Bosepara, Rajshahi 6100, Bangladesh.

**RAGO Ann D'Amico,** b. 24 August 1957, Pittsburgh, PA, USA. Writer; Public Relations Professional. m. John T, 2 daughters. Education: BA, Duquesne University, 1979; MA, 1987. Appointments: Communications Associate, Director, Public Relations, Duquesne University, 1979-89; Coordinator, University Relations, 1989-93; Executive Director, Public Affairs, 1993-. Memberships: Public Relations Society of America; International Association of Business Communicators; Council for the Advancement and Support of Education. Address: Duquesne University, 600 Forbes Ave Pub Affairs Off, Pittsburgh, PA 15282, USA.

**RAGULSKIS Kazimieras,** b. 15 October 1926, Lithuania. Scientific Worker. m. V Kesgailaite, 2 sons. Education: Dr Degree, 1954; Dr.habil, 1963; Professor, 1967; Academician, 1987. Appointment: Research Chief, Scientific Group, Kaunas University of Technology. Publications: 23 monographs; Editor, 160 books; 700 scientific articles in professional journals; 1700 patents and inventions. Honours include: Honoured Inventor of the USSR; Honoured Laureate of the USSR; State Prizes in Science, Lithuania; Prize of the Council of Ministers of Lithuania; Honoured Laureate of Sciences, Lithuania; Five times Laureate of Academician Varilov Prize; Simonavichus Prize, Academy of Sciences; 5 Golden, 3 Memorial and several other medals of Exhibition Achievements, Russia; Golden Medal, World Invention Exhibition, 1981. Memberships:

Academy of Sciences, Lithuania; Corresponding Member, Academy of Sciences, Russia. Address: Geliu Ratas 15A, 3028 Kaunas, Lithuania.

**RAHIM Muhammed Zeaur,** b. 1 May 1955, Mukundapur. Microbiologist. m. Tania Rahman, 2 daughters. Education: MSc, University Dhaka, 1980; MPhil, University Dhaka, 1991; MS, University of Paris, 1993. Appointments: Research Trainee, ICDDR, 1981-84; Research Officer, ICDDR, 1984-86; Senior Research Officer, ICDDR, 1986-87; Assistant Scientist, ICDDR, 1987-92; Associate Scientist, 1992-. Publications: Articles in Scientific Journals. Honours: British Society General Microbiology Award; French Government Scholarship; British Society General Microbiology Award. Memberships: British Society General Microbiology; Bangladesh Society Microbiology; Bangladesh Society Botany; Bangladesh Society Zoology. Address: 109 Madha Basabo, Dhaka 1214, Bangladesh.

**RAHMAN Anis,** b. 6 December 1945, Azamgarh, India. Environmental Scientist. m. Qamar Shamim Rahman, 1 son, 2 daughters. Education: MSc Plant Ecology, 1968, University of Alberta, Canada; PhD Plant Science and Plant Physiology, 1971, University of Saskatchewan, Canada. Appointments: Graduate Research Assistant, University of Alberta and Saskatchewan, 1966-71; Postdoctoral Fellow, University of BC, 1971-72; Scientist, Weed Research, 1972-78, Section Leader, Weed Research, 1979-85, MAF, Ruakura; Group Leader, Plant Science, MAFTech North, 1985-92, Group Leader, Plant Protection, AgResearch, 1992-, Ruakura Agricultural Research Centre; National Programme Manager, Weed Research; Manager, Pesticides Research Unit, Ruakura Research Centre. Publications: 1 book; 6 book chapters; 67 science journals; 155 in refereed scientific conferences; 84 other conference and farming publications; all in field of Weed Management, Plant Protection, Pesticides. Honours: Best Research and Presentation Award, 1985; Co-operated in 5 international research projects; National Merit Scholarship, 1st class honours throughout academic career. Memberships: Past President, NZ Plant Protection Society, President Waikato Branch; Board of Directors, International Weed Science Society; Treasurer, Asian-Pacific Weed Science Society; Member 6 national and 5 international plant protection, horticultural, and soil societies; Associate Editor, 2 international journals, member 3 other editorial committees; Technical Adviser, NZ Pesticides Board and Noxious Plants Council. Address: AgResearch, Ruakura Research Centre, East St, PB 3123, Hamilton, New Zealand.

**RAHMAN Mohammad Habibur ,** b. 1 January 1942, Nabiganj, Habiganj, Bangladesh. Educator. m. Mamataz Sultana, 4 sons, 1 daughter. Education: MA Social Welfare 1st Class Hons, 1964, Dhaka University; Post-graduate Diploma in Community Development and Youth Studies, 1968, Edinburgh University, UK. Appointments: Lecturer in Social Work, 1964-65, Assistant Professor of Social Work, 1965-77, Associate Professor, Dept of Social Work, 1981-89, Professor of Social Work, 1989-92, Rajshahi University, Bangladesh; Deputy Director of Research, Social Science Research Council, Ministry of Planning, Govt of Bangladesh, 1977-81; Professor of Social Work, 1992-, Head, Department of Social Work, 1993-, Dean, School of Social Sciences, 1994-, Shahjalal University of Science and Technology, Sylhet, Bangladesh, Vice-Chancellor, Shahjalal University, Sylhet, Bangladesh, 1997-. Publications: 11 papers in foreign journals, 2 in domestic journals; 5 books in the field of social work and welfare, in Bengali and English; 11 publications in magazines and books; 7 research articles in conference proceedings, 9 as reports; 2 book reviews. Memberships: Correspondent, Community

Development Journal; District Governor, Apex Bangladesh; Editorial Board, Directory of Voluntary Social Welfare Agencies, Department of Social Services, Bangladesh; Book Review Editor, Sociological Perspectives; Secretary-General, Bangladesh Social Work Teachers' Association; Secretary, Rajshahi University Teachers' Association; Member, National Council of Social Welfare; Member, Executive Committee of National Council of Social Welfare, Ministry of Social Welfare, Government of the People's Republic of Bangladesh; Member of Presidium, Bangladesh Social Science Association; Life member, Bangla Academy, Dhaka; President, Shahjalal University Teachers' Association; Chairman, Editorial Board, SUST, Studies, Shahjalal University. Address: Shahjalal University of Science & Technology, Sylhet, Bangladesh.

**RAHMAN Muhammad Abdur,** b. 1 March 1930, Sylhet, Assam, India. Mechanical Engineer. Education: BSME, 1953, MSME, 1968, University of Toledo; PhD, Engineering, California Coast University, 1985. Appointments: Mechanical Design Engineer, various consultancy firms, Los Angeles, 1955-61; Aerospace Engineer, Douglas Aircraft Company, Santa Monica, California, 1962-63; North-American Aviation Inc, Los Angeles, 1963-64; NASA Manned Spacecraft Center, Gemini and Apollo Program Offices, Houston, 1964-70; Safety Engineer, US Department of Labor, OSHA, Washington, 1975-86; Invention Researcher, Arlington, Virginia, 1987-. Publications: Numerous articles in professional journals. Memberships: New York Academy of Sciences. Address: 1805 Crystal Drive, Apt 1013, Arlington, VA 22202-4407, USA.

**RAHMAN Syed Zillur,** b. 1 July 1940, Bhopal, India. Teacher. m. Ahmadi Begum, 1 son, 3 daughters. Education: BUMS, 1960. Appointments: Reader, 1973; Professor, 1983; Dean, 1988-90; Chairman, 1978-85, 1992-95. Publications: 22 books; 115 articles. Honours: President of India Award, 1995; Imtiaz-e Mir Award, 1997; Visiting Professor, Hamdard University, Pakistan, 1997. Memberships: Member, 44 learned association; WHO Consultant, Bangladesh, 1996. Address: Tijara House, Dodhpur, Aligarh 202002, India.

**RAI K B,** b. 20 June 1935, Sarai Sidhu, Pakistan. Retired. m. Smt Umesh Kanta Wig, 2 sons. Education: MA, English, Delhi University, 1968. Appointments: Retired as Administrative Officer, International Organization after 32 years of service. Publications: Men and Gods and Other Poems, 1985; Miscellany, 1994. Honour: Michael Madhusuddan Award for Miscellany. Memberships: Fellow Member of United Writers Association, Chennai; Member International Writers Association (IWA), USA. Address: BB 18C First Floor, Janakpuri, New Delhi 110058, India.

**RAI Markandey,** b. 1 February 1952, Ujiar, India. Statistician. m. Gayatri Rai, 1 son. Education: BA, honours, 1974, MA, 1976, Bhagalpur University; PhD, Patna University, 1983. Appointments: Reader, Patna University, 1987; Lecturer, University of Nairobi, 1987-92; Statistician, UNCHS (Habitat), Nairobi, 1992-. Publications include: Compendium of Human Settlements Statistics. Memberships: Indian Science Congress; Beroronlli Society. Address: UNCHS (Habitat), PO Box 67553, Nairobi, Kenya.

**RAINA J L,** b. 11 November 1943, Anantnag, India. Engineer. m. Nancy Raina, 1 son, 1 daughter. Education: Degree, Chemical Engineering. Appointment: Associate, Oil Refining Industry India. Publications: Various articles in professional leading journals. Membership: Northern Regional Committee, All India Council for Technical Education. Address: Executive Director, IOCL, Mathura Refinery, Mathura 281005 UP, India.

**RAINEY Derek Rexton,** b. 7 November 1949, Palo Alto, California, USA. Teacher; Sculptor. 1 son, 2 daughters. Education: Diploma, Phillips Academy, Andover, Massachusetts, 1967; BA, History, Philosophy, University of Michigan, 1971; Teacher Certificate, Art, History, Eastern Michigan University, 1975. Appointments: Educator, Portage, MI, USA, 1975-76; Educator, World History, Psychology, Art, Portland, MI, USA, 1977-. Creative Works: Michigan Vietnam Memorial Sculpture unveiled, 1994. Memberships: Honorary Member, Michigan Vietnam Veterans. Address: 8473 Riverest Drive, Portland, MI 48875-9692, USA.

**RAJ Janak,** b. 7 January 1939, India. University Librarian. Education: Postgraduate Diploma, Library Science, 1962; MA, Philosophy, 1967; MA, Linguistics, 1970; Certificate, French, 1971; PhD, Linguistics, 1979; MLibSc, 1980. Appointments: Librarian, GGD College, Baijnath, 1962-63; Librarian, Vaish College, Bhiwani, 1963-67; Assistant Librarian, 1967-68, Officiating Librarian, 1968, Librarian, 1968-81, Regional Engineering College, Kurukshetra; Deputy Librarian, 1981-88, Part-time Lecturer, Library and Information Science, 1984-86, 1987-88, University of Kurukshetra; University Librarian, Thapar Institute of Engineering and Technology, Deemed University, 1988-. Publications: Numerous articles in professional journals. Honours include: Most Disciplined Cadet Award of the Year, 1959-60; Decorated, Under-Officer, 1959-60. Memberships include: Indian Library Association; Indian Association of Special Libraries and Information Centres; Haryana Library Association; Indian Association of Academic Librarians; Punjab Library Association. Address: Thapar Institute of Engineering and Technology, Deemed University, Patiala 147 001, Punjab, India.

**RAJAMMA PREMACHAR G,** b. 8 February 1950, Bangalore. BEL Employee. m. A V Premachar, 1 son, 1 daughter. Education: Matriculation, 1968. Appointments: SKOP VIII; Bharal Electronics, Bangalore, 1975-. Honours: State Level, Industrial Level, India Radio, Bangalore; Organisation Level, India Radio, Bangalore; BEL Sponsorship for AIR, India Radio, Bangalore. Address: No 596 Ravi Arts, Near Government Middle School, Hesaraghatta, Bangalore 560 088, India.

**RAJAN P Bhupathi,** b. 5 September 1946, Madras State. Executive. m. Rajalakshmi, 2 sons, 1 daughter. Education: BE, Electrical, 1969; MSc, Engineering, 1973. Appointments: Power Engineer, 1970-78, Tamil Nadu Electricty Board; Executive, Bharat Heavy Elecls Ltd, 1978-. Publications: 2 Research Papers, Elecrical Engineering. Honours: Man of the Year, American Biographical Institute, 1998; Vice President, Rotaracy Club, 1968-69. Memberships: Fellow, Institution of Engineers, India; Fellow, Standards Engineers Institute, India; Founder Secretary, Volunteers Society of India. Address: C-376 BHEL Township, Ranipet 632406, Vellore Dist Tamil Nadu, India.

**RAJCANI Julius,** b. 9 February 1937, Bratislava. Virologist. m. Kamila Ballay, 2 sons. Education: MD, 1960, Faculty Medicine, Comenius University, Bratislava; PhD, 1970, Institute Virology, DrSc, 1985, Slovak Academy of Sciences, Bratislava. Appointments: Pathologist, Institute of Pathology, Faculty of Medicine, Comenius University, Bratislava, 1960-66; Specialisation in Pathology, lower degree, 1963; Research Fellow, 1966-70, Scientist, 1970-85, Senior Scientist, Head of Department of Pathogenesis and Medical Virology, 1985-, Institute of Virology, Slovak Academy of Sciences, Bratislava. Publications: Executive Editor, Acta virologica, 1982-91; 3 books; Over 140 genuine research papers in journals. Honours: Slovak Medical Society Award, 1979, for book; Golden esenius Medal of SAS for achievements in medical sciences, 997. Memberships: Slovak Medical Society; Czech and Slovak Society for Microbiology; Presidium member, Slovak Academy of Sciences, 1995-98. Address: Institute Virology, Dubravska cesta 9, 842 46 Bratislava, Slovakia.

**RAJECKAS Valentinas,** b. 9 May 1930, Siauliai, Lithuania. Professor. m. Laima Jekabsone, 2 daughters. Education: Kaunas Polytechnical Institute, Lithuania, 1953; Doctor Techn Scis, 1963, Doctor Scis Habilitus, 1972, Moscow Light Industry Institute, USSR. Appointments: Manager of Production and Chief Engineer, Leather and Shoe Factories in Lithuania, 953-59; Graduate Student, Moscow Light Industries Institute, 1959-62; Professor of Technology and Polymer Processing, Kaunas Polytechnical Institute (present Kaunas University of Technology), 1963-, Head of Department, 1975-91. Publications: Author or co-author over 300 scholarly publications including 6 books. Honours: Honoured Scientist of Lithuania, 1980; Lithuanian State Prize in Science, 1995; Editor-in-Chief, Journal Materials Science, Lithuania. Memberships: Adhesion Society, USA, 1982-90; Lithuanian Academy Sciences; Ukrainian Technological Academy. Address: S Lozoraicio 19-1, LT 3009, Kaunas, Lithuania.

**RAJENDRAN Narayanan,** b. 25 May 1956, Sri Kalhasti. Teacher. m. J Shanti, 1 son, 1 daughter. Education: MA, University of Madras, 1978; M Phil, University of Madras, 1981; PhD, University of Madras, 1988. Appointments: Assistant Professor of History, Pachaiyappas College, Chennai, 1982-89; Assistant Professor, Vivekananda College, Chennai, 1985; Assistant Professor, Vivekananda College, Chennai. Publications: National Movement in Tamid Nadu 1905-1914, 994. Memberships: Indian History Congress; South Indian History Congress; Tamil Nadu History Congress; Association of Third World Studies. Address: Bharattsidasan University, Tricy, Tamil Nadu, India.

**RAJPOOT Mubarik Ahmed,** b. 11 November 1937, Lahore, Pakistan. Teacher, Journalist. m. Robina S, 3 sons, 3 daughters. Education: BSc. Appointments: Teacher, AOF Evening School, Oslo, 1973-93; Teacher, Secondary School, Oslo, 1973-; Editor, Akhbar-E-Pakista, Weekly Newspaper, 973; Director, Islam Aymadiyyah, Radio/Television, 1981; Author: Urdu Compendium, 1973; Learn Urdu (written in Norwegian), 1988; Freelance Journalist, Photographer. Memberships: Norwegian Union of Journalists. Address: PB 233 Sentrum, 0103 Oslo, Norway.

**RAKIB-UZ-ZAMAN Md,** b. 26 November 1955, Jessore, Bangladesh. Educator. m. Rezina Aktar Banu, 1 son, 1 daughter. Education: BSc, 1975, Rajshahi University, Bangladesh; PhD, 1990, Banaras Hindu University, India. Appointments: Lecturer, 1981-85; Assistant Professor, 985-91; Associate Professor, 1991-96; Professor, 1996-, University Rajshahi, Bangladesh. Address: Rajshahi University, Dept Applied Chemistry, Rajshahi 6205, Bangladesh.

**RAKUS-ANDERSSON Elisabeth,** b. 10 September 1950, Lodz, Poland. Senior Lecturer. m. Seth Christer. Education: Master of Science Degree, 1974; Postgraduate Studies, 1978; Doctor's Degree, 1997; Swedish Teachers Competence, 1997. Appointments: Teacher, Mathematics, 1974-93; Mathematical Advisor, Medical Academy, Poland, 1980-93; Research Worker, University of Lodz, Poland, 1986-93; Senior Lecturer, Mathematics, University College, Halmstad and Karlskrona, Sweden, 1994-; Reviewer, Fuzzy Sets and Systems, 1993-. Publication: 18 Papers, 1988-98. Memberships: EUROFUSE; Polish Mathematical Society; EUSFLAT. Address: Hogskolan Karlskrona Ronneby, Inst for Hälsovård och Naturvetenskap

(Dept of Health and Natural Sciences), S 37179 Karlskrona, Sweden.

**RAKUSIC Neven,** b. 17 April 1949, Veliki Prolog. Physician. m. Spomenka Beker, 2 daughters. Education: MD, 1967; MSc, 1987; Consultant, 1988; Pulmonologist, 1979. Appointments: Head of Pulmonary Dept in Chest Clinic. Publications: Contributor in textbook on Internal Medicine, 1991, 1997; Articles in medical journals. Memberships: Croatian Medical Association; President, Croatian Respiratory Society, 1996-; European Respiratory Society, National Delegate. Address: Sermageova 4, 10000 Zagreb, Croatia.

**RALL Wilfrid,** b. 29 August 1922, Los Angeles, USA. Neuroscientist; Sculptor. m. Mary Ellen Condon-Rall, 2 daughters. Education: BS Highest Hons Physics, 1943, Yale University; MS Biophysics, 1948, University of Chicago; PhD Physiology, 1953, University of New Zealand. Appointments: Junior Physicist, Manhattan Project, 1943-46, Biophysics Fellow, 1946-48, University of Chicago; Lecturer, Senior Lecturer, Physiology & Biophysics, University Otago, Dunedin, New Zealand, 1949-56; Head Biophysics Division, Naval Research Institute, Bethesda, 1956-57; Biophysicist, Senior Research Physicist, National Institutes of Health, Bethesda, 1957-94; Scientist Emeritus, NIH, 1994-. Publications: in professional journals; Theoretical Foundation of Dendritic Function, selected papers, 1995. Memberships: Founding member, Society for Neuroscience, and of Biophysical Society; Physical Society, UK; American Physical Society; AAAS; Rockefeller Foundation Fellow, 1954-55; Central Committee, IBRO, USA National Committee 1972-76. Address: Math Resch Br NIDDK NIH, 9190 Wisconsin Avenue Ste 350, Bethesda, MD 20814-3897, USA.

**RAM Abha Devi,** b. 21 March 1956, Suya, Fiji. Doctor. m. Daya Singh, 2 sons. Education: Medical Degree; MBBS, Monash University, Victoria, AUstralia, 1979. Appointments: Private Medical Practitioner, Solo Practice, 1984-. Honours: Chairperson, Fiji Collegeof GP's. Memberships: Fiji College of GP's; Association Member, RACGP. Address: Rosawa St, P O Labasa, Fiji.

**RAMACHANDRAN K N,** b. 23 May 1969, Kerala, India. Scientist; Technologist. Education: BSc, Chemistry, 1985-88, MSc, 1988-90, PhD, 1990-93, Pt Ravishankar University, Raipur. Appointments: Scientist, Adviser, UN Environment Program, Asia-Pacific, Indian Revenue Service, 1992-94; Technology Manager Scientist, GE Silicones India, Shriram Institute for Industrial Research, 1994-96. Publications: 57 articles, 4 patents, 30 conference presentations, 9 project reports. Honours: National Talent Scholarship, 1979; MPCST Award, 1989; Indian Science Congress Young Scientist Award, 1993; Referee of American Chemical Society, 1993-; DAE Young Scientist Award, 1996. Memberships: Association of Official Analytical Chemists; Indian Science Congress Association; World Wild Life Forum; Society for Action Research and Appropriate Technology Innovations. Address: Shriram Institute for Industrial Research, 14 15 Sadararmangala Industrial Area, Whitefield Road, Bangalore 560 038, India.

**RAMAGE Jean.** Professor. Education: BA, University of Oregon; MA, PhD, University of California at Berkeley. Appointments: Assistant Professor, University of Oregon, 1971-73; Associate Professor, University of Massachusetts, 1973-75; Executive Manager, National Association of School Psychologists, 1976-85; Associate Professor, Assistant Dean, San Diego State University, 1975-89; Director, American Psychological Association, 1988-89; Dean, James Madison

University, 1989-91; Dean, California State University at San Bernardino, 1991-95; Dean, Professor, University of Nebraska, 1995-. Publications: Include, Regulation of Teacher Education; Handbook of Research on Teacher Education; The Dynamic Interaction of Higher Education, Teacher Education and School Reform; Teacher Education as an All Community Responsibility: A Proposal for Restructing California Teacher Education; Policy and Alternative Assessment Guideline Recommendations. Honours: Certificate of Recognition, Joe Baca, California State Assembly, Commonwealth Center for the Education of Teachers; Christa McAuliffe Award; Certificate of Appreciation, Association of Teacher Education; Sandra Goff Award; Outstanding Teacher Award. Memberships: Association of Teacher Educators; American Association of College of Teacher Education; American Psychological Association; National Association of School Psychologists. Address: University of Nebraska, College of Education, Kearney, NE 68849-4240, USA.

**RAMAIAH Chennupati Kodanda,** b. 12 November 1957, Katrapadu, India. Scientist. m. Lakshmi, twin daughters. Education: BSc Chemistry, Botany and Zoology, 1979, Silver Jubilee College, Kurnool; MSc Chemistry, 1982, Meerut University; BLISc Information Studies, 1983, Diploma in Hindi, 1983, MLISc Computer Applications in Libraries, 1984, University of Delhi; PhD Hypertext, 1993, Loughborough University of Technology, UK. Appointments: Trainee Librarian, Institute for Defence Studies and Analysis Library, New Delhi, 1983-84; Scientist B in Defence Scientific Information and Documentation Centre (DESIDOC), DR and DO, Ministry of Defence, Delhi, 1984-89; Conducted Research on Hypertext/Hypermedia at Loughborough University of Technology for PhD degree, 1989-93; Scientist C, Multimedia Division, DESIDOC, 1993-95; Scientist D and In-Charge Multimedia Laboratory, DESIDOC, 1995-. Publications: Author or co-Author 23 papers in professional journals and bulletins; 15 presented papers at national and international conferences and seminars; Guest Editor and Columnist, DESIDOC Bulletin on Information Technology. Honours: Commonwealth Scholarship in Information Science, 1989; Vergheeze Prize for best paper of year in ILA Bulletin, 1988. Memberships: Association of Computing Machinery, New York; American Society for Information Science; IEEE Computer Society; Institute of Information Scientists, London; Library Association, London; Life Member; Society for Information Science, New Delhi; Micrographics Congress of India; Association of Government Librarians and Information Specialists; Indian Association of Special Libraries and Information Centres; Indian Library Association; International Wild Waterfowl Association Inc; International Freelance Photographers Organisation, Washington. Address: DESIDOC, Metcalf House, Delhi 110054, India.

**RAMAKRISHNA Alappa,** b. 1 July 1958, Mysore, India. Scientist; Engineer. m. Savitha, 1 son, 1 daughter. Education: PUC, 1976, Sharadavila College, Mysore; ITI (Machinist), 1978, ITI, Mysore; DME Mechanical, 1982, CPC Polytechnic, Mysore; BE Mechanical Engineering, 1990, M Tech Maintenance Engineering, 1993, SJ College of Engineering, Mysore. Appointments: Designer, Electromobiles (I) Ltd, Mysore, 1981-82; Designer, Automotive Axles Ltd, Mysore, 1982-84; Scientist, Defence Food Research Laboratory, Defence Research and Development Organisation, Ministry of Defence, Siddarthanagar, Mysore, 1984-. Publications: Co-author 19 papers in field of design engineering, maintenance engineering, food process engineering, quality assurance and management and good manufacturing practice; Co-presenter of 8 presentations; Participated in 9 international and national seminars and symposia. Honours: Best Scientific Worker,

1988; Best Outstanding Engineer, 1990; Best Research Pape Awards, 1993, 1995; Defence R&D Award, 1993 Memberships: Indian Society for Technical Education Institution of Engineers, India; Indian Institute of Plan Engineers; Association of Food Scientists and Technologists India; Indian Plastic Institute. Address: 2256 Basaweswara Road, Mysore 570 004, India.

**RAMAKRISHNAMACHARYA Chintapatla,** b. 2 April 1957 Warangal, India. Ayurveda Medicine Specialist. m. Sree Padma, 1 son, 2 daughters. Education: Bachelor Ayurveda Medicine and Surgery, 1980; MD, 1985; PhD, 1997 Appointments: Lecturer, Venkataramana Ayurveda College 1986-87; Assistant Medical Officer, Government Tamil nadu 1987-. Publications: Articles in professional journals; Manual of Safe Motherhood, UNICEF, 1997. Honour: Appreciatior Awards, Lion's Club, 1994, 1996. Memberships: Indiar Practitioners Co-op Stores Ltd, 1987-; All India Ayurveda Congress, Executive member, 1998-99. Address: Governmen Anna Hospital Indian Medicine, Dept Ayurveda Arumbakkam Madras, Tamil nadu 600 106, India.

**RAMAMOORTHY Narayani,** b. 5 May 1966, Madras, India Educator. Education: BSc Biochemistry, 1987; MSc Biochemistry, 1989; PhD Biochemistry-Biomaterials, 1994 Postgraduate Diploma in Business Management, 1998 Appointments: Junior Research Fellow, 1989-91; Senior Research Fellow, 1991-94; Research Associate, 1995-96 Assistant Professor, 1996-97; Reader and Head of Department Biochemistry, 1997-98; Professor and Head, Biochemistry Department, SRM Dental College, Madras, India, 1998- Publications 12 in international and national journals. Honours Best Paper Award, IV National Conference of Society of Biomaterials and Artificial Organs. Memberships: Life Member Society Biomaterials and Artificial Organs; Association of Bharatnatyam Artists of India; Active member, New York Academy of Science. Address: 16 Thambia Reddy Street Mambalam, Madras 600 033, India.

**RAMAMURTHY Shanta,** b. 4 April 1945, Mysore, India Sports. m. Rao S, 1 son, 1 daughter. Education: Bachelor of Arts, Mysore University, 1963. Appointments: Captained Karnataka Womens Team to Victory 13 Times in National Ball Badminton Championships, -1980. Honours: Mysore Dasara State Award; Karnataka Sports Council Award. Memberships: Karnataka State Ball Badminton Association. Address: #134 Giriniwas II Cross III BlockJayanagar, Bangalore 560011, India

**RAMAMURTHY Temura,** b. 6 June 1936, Hyderabad, India Educator. m. Lakshmi Kamala, 2 sons. Education: BE Cibil 1958, Osmania University; ME from IISc, Bangalore with distinction, 1962; PhD, 1966, University of Birmingham, UK, as Commonwealth Scholar. Appointments: Consultant to abou 150 engineering works; Guided over 80 M Tech theses and 20 PhDs; Stated M Tech programme in Rock Mechanics, 1977 Established 3 laboratories: Rock Mechanics Laboratory Geomechanics Modelling Laboratory, and Foundatior Laboratory; Served Andhra Pradesh Engineering Research Labs, 1958-67; Lecturer, Assistant Professor, Professor, IIT Delhi, 1967-96. Publications: 140 technical papers; Editoria Board, International Journal of Geotechnical and Geologica Engineering, International Journal of Rock Mechanics and Mining Science and others; Editor, Indian Geotechnical Journal 2 years, Rock Mechanics in India; Contributor chapter Comprehensive Rock Engineering; Honours: 15 awards fo best papers published and for outstanding contributions made Nation's Inventions Award, Outstanding Contribution Awards to Soil Mechanics and Rock Mechanics. Memberships: President Indian Geotechnical Society; Founder President, Nationa

Committee of International Society of Rock Mechanics, former Vice President; Advisory Committee, International Congress on Rock Mechanics, Germany; Chairman Organising Committee of Asian Regional Symposium on Rock Slopes; Council Member, AICTE; PG Review Committee, AICTE; Board of Management, Tezpur University; and others; Fellow/member 7 professional societies at national and international level. Address: Civil Engineering Department, Indian Institute Technology Delhi, Hauz Khas, New Delhi 110016, India.

**RAMANA MURTY Tayya Venkata,** b. 25 August 1949, Calingapatnam. Joint Registrar; Controller of Examinations. m. Bhagya Lakshmi, 1 son, 2 daughters. Education: BSc, Andhra University; MA Sociology, Agra University; PG Diploma n Journalism and Mass Communication, IIMC, New Delhi. Appointments: Investigator, IIMC, New Delhi; News Reader and Translator, AIR, New Delhi; News Reporter, Samachar Bharati, New Delhi; PRO, DR, JR-FO, JR-CE, Andhra University. Publications: Yerra Jeera, 1995; East Wind, 1996; Andhra Fishermen, 1996. Memberships: Sarada Arts Theatre; Amnesty nternational; AU Officers Association; Andhra Fishermen Association; YMCA; Mutnuru Krishna Rao Sahitya Peetham; Junior Red Cross. Address: c/o Andhra University, 9 Sea Sands, Visakhaparnam AP, India.

**RAMESH BABU Nagalamadaka,** b. 5 May 1960, Y N Hosakote, India. Scientist. m. S R Shanthala Murthy, 1 daughter. Education: BVSc, 1983, MVSc, Microbiology, 1986, University of Agricultural Science, Bangalore; PhD, Biotechnology, Tamil Nadu Veterinary and Animal Sciences University, Madras, 1997. Appointments: Extension Officer, Animal Husbandry, 1985; Scientist 1, Institute of Animal Health and Veterinary Biologicals, Hebbal, Bangalore, 1986-89; Scientist, Institute of Animal Health and Veterinary Biologicals, Bangalore, 1989-. Publications: Co-author, articles in Veterinary Record, UK, Indian Journal of Comparative Microbiology, Immunology and Infectious Diseases, Indian Veterinary Journal, International Journal of Animal Sciences, Small Ruminant Research, USA, Indian Journal of Animal Sciences, Centaur, Indian Journal of Virology, Indian Journal of Experimental Biology, Journal of Clinical Microbiology, Avian Diseases; Conference and symposium papers. Honour: Recognition as Postgraduate Teacher, University of Agricultural Sciences, Bangalore. Memberships: New York Academy of Sciences; Association for the Promotion of DNA Finger-Printing and Other DNA Technologies; Indian Society of Veterinary Immunology and Biotechnology; Indian Association of Veterinary Microbiologists, Immunologists and Specialists in Infectious Diseases. Address: 1462, 14th Main, 17th Cross, Kumaraswamy Layout, 1st Stage, Bangalore 560-078, India.

**RAMESH BABU S,** b. 12 February 1957, Bangalore. Metallurgical Scientist. m. Usha Govind Tumkurkar, 2 daughters. Education: BSc, National College, Bangalore University, India, 1977; BE (Metallurgy), Indian Institute of Science, Bangalore, India, 1980; PhD (Metallurgy), Indian Institute of Science, Bangalore, India, 1985. Appointments: Visiting Scientist, NE Univ of Tech, Shenyang, People's Republic of China, 1986; Visiting Scientist, Tohoku Univ, Japan, 1986; Monbusho post doc Res Fellow, Tohoku University, Seudi, Japan, 1987; post doc Res Fellow, UBC, Vancouver, Canada, 1988-89; Research Engineer, Associate Head, Thapar Corporate Research and Development Centre, India, 1989-90; Assistant Director, National Metallurgical Laboratory, 1990-91; R & D Manager, Jindal Strips Ltd, India, 1991-94; Dy General Manager, NSL Ltd, India, 1994; General Manager, Isapt Profiles Ltd, India, 1994-95; Professor, M S Ramaiah Institute of Technology, 1995-97; Professor, P E S Institute of Technology, 1997-98; Senior Res. Scientist, Adv.

Forming Tech. Centre, Bangalore, 1999-. Publications: 7 Journal Publications; 4 Patents Filed; 29 Conference Papers; 23 Research Reports; Several Research Contributions. Honours: Golden Jubilee Eminent Person Honour, 1996; Outstanding Alumnus Felicitation, 1996; Outstanding Achiever Felicitation, 1996; Outstanding Young Person, 1997; Eminent Sports Person Felicitation, 1997; Outstanding Young Indian, 1997; Vivekananda Youth Day Honour, 1998; Outstanding Indian Achiever Award, 1998; Hundred Best Citizens of India Award, 1998; 16 International Awards/Honours; Holder of 16 World Records and 7 National Records in Table Tennis, Shuttle Badminton, Tennis, Kite Flying, Oratory, Cycling, Scooter Driving, Vegetable Cutting and many others. Memberships: Iron and Steel Society, 1992; Institute of Engineers, 1992; Indian Institute of Metals, 1992; Institute of Indian Foundrymen, 1992; Indian Society of Theoretical and Applied Mechanics, 1990; Indian Institute of Science Alumni Association, 1986; Hokkaido International Friendship Association, 1987; Uluchukamme Brahmana Maha Sabha, 1996. Address: No 27 Jaladarshini Layout, Nr old Punjab Ntl Bank, New BEL Road, Bangalore 560094, India.

**RAMIREZ Dolores A,** b. 20 September 1931, Calamba, Laguna, Philippines. Professor Emeritus of Genetics and Plant Breeding. Education: BS Agriculture Magna cum Laude, 1956, University of the Philippines; MSc Cytogenetics, 1958, University Minnesota; PhD Biochemical Genetics, 1963, Purdue University. Appointments: Research Fellow, 1956-57, Research Instructor, 1958-64, Research Assistant Professor, 1964-68, Associate Professor, 1969-73, University of Philippines College of Agriculture; Associate Professor, 1973-74, Professor, 1974-77, College of Science and Humanities, Researcher IV, 1977-79, Professor, 1979-95, University Professor, 1995-98, Professor Emeritus, 1998-, College of Agriculture, University Philippines Los Banos. Publications: Author or co-Author 98 journal or other technical publications; 18 books, lecture syllabus and laboratory manuals. Honours: 8 academic honours; Rockefeller Foundation Fellowship, Rockefeller Foundation, 1957-58, 1961-63; Riza Pro Patria Award for Outstanding Achievements in Science (Biochemical Genetics), President of the Republic of Philippines, 1981; First Maryang Maya Achievement Award in Science, 1983; D L Umali Professorial Chair in Genetics and Plant Breeding, UP, 1988-89; Recognition Award, Philippine Society for the Advancement of Genetics, 1996; National Scientist, President of the Republic of Philippines, 1998; and many others. Memberships: Society for the Advancement of Research, life member; Philippine Association for the Advancement of Science; Philippine Phytopathological Society; National Research Council of the Philippines; Society for the Advancement of Breeding Research in Asia and Oceania; Crop Science Society of the Philippines; Philippine Biochemical Society; Third World Organisation for Women in Science; Philippine Association of University Women; National Academy of Science and Technology, Philippines; and others. Address: Institute of Plant Breeding, UP Los Banos College, Laguna, Philippines 4031.

**RAMJEE Venkatraman,** b. 3 May 1942, Tiruchy, India. Researcher, Teacher. m. Vatsala, 1 son, 1 daughter. Education: BSc, 1962; MSc, 1964; PhD, 1969. Appointments: Lecturer, 1971; Assistant Professor, 1973; Associate Professor, 1985; Professor, Department of Applied Mechanics, 1987. Publications: Research Papers are published in journals; Many other publications. Memberships: Fellow, Aeronautical Society of India; FMFP India; Who's Whoo in the World. Address: 74 Kamaraj Ave II Street, Madras 6000 20, India.

**RAMOS-ALVAREZ Manuel,** b. 24 May 1926, Mexico City. Physician. m. Maria Eugenia Francia, 2 sons, 1 daughter. Education: MD, National University, Mexico City. Appointments: Research Fellow, 1952; Research Fellow, 1953; Research Fellow, 1953-54; Professor, Infectious Diseases, 1958-86; Founder, Director, General Biology Products, 1961-66; Head of Division, Infectious Diseases Childrens Hospital, 1965-86. Address: Blvd Virreyes 1135-PH, 11000 Mexico City, Mexico.

**RAMRAKHIANI Meera,** b. 5 June 1951, Mhow, India. Teacher; Researcher. Education: Higher Secondary School Certificate, M.P. Board of Secondary Education Bhopal, 1968; BSc, University of Jabalpur, 1971; MSc, University of Jabalpur, 1973; PhD, University of Jabalpur, 1979. Appointments: JRF, Physics Department, University of Jabalpur, 1974-77; Lecturer in Physics, Howabagh Women's College, Jabalpur, 1977-1989; Sr Lecturer in Physics, Physics Department, RD University, Jabalpur, 1989-90; Reader in Physics, R D University, 1990-. Publications: Co Author of a Text Book, 1991; 57 Resaerch Papers, Articles in International, National Journals. Honours: Vijau Shree Award, India International Friendship Society; Twentieth Century Award for Achievement, International Biographical Centre; 2000 Millennium Medal of Honour, American Biographical Institute. Memberships: Indian Science Congress Association; Indian Association of Physics Teachers; Biophysical Society of India; Luminescence Society of India; Third World Organization of Women in Science; Society for Biomaterials and Artificial Organs; Indian Physics Association. Address: Department of Post Graduate Studies and Res in Physics, Rani Durgavati, Vishwavidyalaya, Jabalpur, 482001, India.

**RAMSEY Sally Ann Seitz,** b. 15 February 1931, Columbus, Ohio, USA. Public Administrator. m. Edward Lewis Ramsey, div 1962, 1 son, 1 daughter. Education: BA, 1952, MA, 1955, Postgraduate, 1963-66, Ohio State University; Postgraduate, St Marys College, 1962, Florida State University, 1970-72. Appointments: Research Engineer, Senior Research Engineer, North American Aviation, 1962-67; Ohio Legislative Intern, 1964-65; Research and Information Officer, Ohio Department of Urban Affairs, 1967-68; Administrative Specialist, Ohio Department of Development, 1968; Planner, Senior Planner, Florida Department of Administration, 1968-76; Economic Analysis Supervisor, Florida Department of Commerce, 1976-93. Publications: Several articles in professional journals. Honour: US Economic Development Administration Fellow, 1978-79. Memberships: American Society for Public Administration; The Economic Club of Florida; DAR; Kappa Kappa Gamma; Pi Sigma Alpha. Address: 2429 Merrigan Place, Tallahassee, FL 32308-2346, USA.

**RAMU Tyamagondlu Sankarasastry,** b. 21 November 1950, Bangalore, India. Professor. m. Nalini, 2 sons. Education: BE, 1969; ME, 1971; PhD, 1974. Appointments: Research Fellow, University of Groningen, Netherlands, 1974-75; Assistant Professor, 1976-81, Associate Professor, 1981-87, Professor, 1988-, Department of High Voltage Engineering, Indian Institute of Science, India. Publications: Over 50 professional publications in scientific journals. Address: Department of High Voltage Engineering, Indian Institute of Science, Bangalore 560012, India.

**RAMUNAITE Aiste,** b. 14 March 1957, Kaunas, Lithuania. Graphic Artist. m. div. 1 son, 1 daughter. Education: J Naujalio Art School, 1973-75; Art Academy, Vilnius, 1975-82; Senege Art Camp Stipendium, Russia, 1986; Grant of Lippe District, Schwalenberg, Germany, 1991. Appointments: Graphic Art for Gertruda, the Contemporary Art Centre, Vilnius, 1992; Graphic about Birth, Kaunas Picture Gallery, 1995; Graphic on Paper,

Giedres Bartelt Gallery, Berlin, Germany, 1996; Stiffer Time Ornaments, Vartu Gallery, Vilnius, 1997. Honours: 1st Diploma, Biennalen Baltisk Grafik Nu Falu, 1993; State Grant of the Highest Degree, Lithuania, 1994-95, 1998-99. Memberships: Lithuanian Artist Union; Shareholder in Grafikenshus Mariefred Sweden, 1997-. Address: Aukstaiciu 44-2, LT 3005, Kaunas, Lithuania.

**RANDALL Elinor,** b. 3 July 1932, Connecticut, USA. Artist. m. James, 1 s, 1 d. Education: BFA, Wayne State University. Appointments: Instructor, Intaglio, Wayne State University 1969; Instructor, Drawings, Peacham, VT, 1970-73; Instructor Intaglio, San Francisco, 1982-86; Instructor, Art, National Institute of Art and Disabilities, 1990-92; Many Exhibitions. Publications: The Skipping Stone; Beyond Hadrian's Wall; Farewell Dundrennan; Going Down; New Politics. Memberships: Vermont Council of the Arts; Artisit's Conference Network; California Society of Printmakers; Artisit Enquiry; Graphi Art Workshop. Address: Maple Hill, P O Box 223, Plainfield, VT 05667-0223, USA.

**RANDMARK Henry,** b. 12 January 1937, Los Angeles, California, USA. Retired Colonel; Businessman. m. Silvia, 2 sons, 1 daughter from previous marriages. Education: MBA, University of California at Los Angeles; Journalist High School in Denmark; MBA, West Point Military Academy. Appointments: Chairman and Main Shareholder, IPA Randmark International AG. Hamburg. Honours: Highly decorated for Special Services in Vietnam. Memberships: Overseas Club of Hamburg; American Chamber of Commerce, Hamburg; Honorable Merchant of Hamburg; American German Business Club, vice-president, Hamburg Chapter; International Press Agency, president; Hearst Entertainment Group, L.A.; International Journalist Association; League of Preservation and Care of Landmarks in Germany. Address: IPA Randmark International AG, P.O. Box 60 53 61, D-22248 Hamburg, Germany.

**RANGASHREE,** b. 16 May 1967, Bangalore, India. Artistic Director; Performing Artist (Classical Dance). m. M K Srinivas, 2 sons. Education: BCom, 1989; Pre-Masters Inf Mass Communication and Journalism, 1998. Appointments: Artistic Director, KINKINI and Performing Artist-Classical Dance-Bharathanatyam, 1983-. Honours: Best Dancer Award, IFAS, Chennai, 1992; Selected to visit USA and Canada by Rotary International under GSE programme. Memberships: Life Member: Karnataka Nrithya Kala Parishad and Association of Bharathanatyam Dancers of India. Address: KINKINI, 308 10th Main 111 Block, Jayanagar, Bangalore 560011, India.

**RAO Akkinepalli B Narayan,** b. 7 October 1923, Hyderabad, India. Ear Nose and Throat Specialist. m. Norah Janet Gardner, 2 daughters. Education: MBBS (Osmania) 1947; DLO (Eng) 1951; FRCS (Eng) 1954; LRCP, MRCS (Eng) 1969; FRACS, 1978. Appointments: House Surgeon, Osmania General Hospital, Hyderabad, India, 1948-50; House Officer, Royal National Ear Nose and Throat Hospital, London, 1951-52; Registrar, Birmingham, UK, 1952-54; Professor of Ear Nose and Throat, Osmania Medical College, 1954-67; Consultant Ear Nose and Throat, Birmingham, 1967-69; Senior Specialist in Charge, Royal Darwin Hospital, Australia 1973-97; Part-time Ear Nose and Throat Consultant, Mackay Base Hospital, Australia, 1997-. Publications: 35 articles published in various journals in UK, Europe and India. Honours: Citizen of the Year, Darwin, 1996; Order of Australia (OAM) 1997 for Service to Medicine. Memberships: Fellow of the Royal Society of Medicine, London; Otolaryngological Society of Australia, UK and India; IMA; Australian Medical Association. Address: 57 Pamela Street, Mount Waverly, Victoria 3149, Australia.

**RAO Atul,** b. 28 May 1963, Budni (MP), India. Educator. m. ₁nagha, 1 son. Education: BSc, 1981; MSc, 1983; PhD, 1989, ₁aculty of Engineering. Appointments: Lecturer of Applied ₁hysics, 1983-92; Reader of Applied Physics, 1992-. ₁ublications: 8 articles in professional journals; 9 paper ₁resentations in research conferences. Memberships: Indian ₁ociety for Technical Education; Plasma Science Society of ₁dia; Indian Science Congress Association. Address: B N ₁ollege of Engineering, Dept of Applied Physics, 445215 ₁usad, India.

**RAO Dabeeru Chandrasekhara,** b. 6 April 1946, India. ₁cademic. m. Sarada, 1 son, 1 daughter. Education: B Stat, ₁967; M Stat, 1968; PhD, 1971. Appointments: Professor, ₁irector, Division of Biostatistics; Professor, Departments of ₁sychiatry and Genetics; Adjunct Professor, Department of ₁athematics, Washington University. Publications: 3 Books; ₁ver 300 Research Papers. Honours: Most Admired Man of the ₁ecade, American Biographical Institute, 1992; Outstanding ₁chievements in Science, Telugu Association of North ₁merica, 1993; IGES Leadership Award, International Genetic ₁pidemiology Soc, 1997. Memberships: Editorial Board, ₁besity Research, 1995-; Editorial Board, Annals of ₁pidemiology, 1995; Editorial Board, Human Heredity, 1997-. ₁ddress: Washington University School of Medicine, 660 S ₁uclid Avenue, Box 8067, Old Shriners Room 1100, St Louis, ₁O 6311-1010, USA.

**RAO Gopal Subba,** b. 12 August 1938, Mangalore, India. ₁xecutive. m. Harsha, 1 son. Education: BSc, 1958; MS, 1964; ₁hD, 1969. Appointments: Instructor, Pharmacognosy, Howard ₁niversity, 1962-64; Research Fellow, University of Michigan, ₁964-69, National Institutes of Health, 1969-74; Research ₁irector, American Dental Association Research Institute, ₁974-85; Professor, Loyola University Dental School, 1985-96; ₁resident, CEO, Multitek Circuitronics Incorporated, 1985-. ₁ublications: Over 100 original research papers. Honours: Eli ₁illy Award, University of Michigan, 1965-68; Horace H ₁ackham Award, University of Michigan, 1968-69; Numerous ₁esearch grants. Memberships: American Chemical Society; ₁merican Society of Pharmacology and Experimental Therapy; ₁merican Society of Experimental Biology; Chicago Printed ₁ircuit Association. Address: 1250 Crispin Drive, Elgin, IL ₁0123, USA.

**RAO Kotha Gangadhara,** b. 10 February 1926, Roddam ₁illage, Anantapur District, AP, India. Retired Administrative ₁xcise Officer. m. Manorama, 1 daughter. Education: LME ₁iploma, 1943, CNT Institute, Vepery, Madras. Appointments: ₁D Clerk; UD Clerk; Junior Deputy Office Superintendent; ₁enior Deputy Office Superintendent; Office Superintendent; ₁dministrative Officer, Central Excise Department, Government ₁f India; Presently, Eye Donation and Body Donation ₁ampaigner. Honours: 1st Prize by Chief Minister of Andhra ₁radesh for Telugu Essay; Appreciated by Government of India ₁hilst in service and during his Eye Donation Campaign, ₁ppreciated by press of India; His mission is - Support Eye ₁onation, Body Donation, Organ Transplantation and Organ ₁anks, Give Life after Death. Memberships: Central ₁overnment Pensioners Association, Mysore; Life member, ₁elugu Samskruthika Samithi, Mysore. Address: Shree # 40, ₁th Main, 7th Cross, Saraswathipuram, Mysore - 570 009, ₁dia.

**RAPP Lea,**b. 10 July 1946, Brooklyn, New York. Author. m. ₁son, 1 daughter. Education: BA, Journalism, Thomas Ediston ₁tate College, Trenton, NJ; College Alumni Award for ₁utstanding Professional Achievement; Additional coursework ₁nd seminars and research. Career: Magazine and Newspaper

Columnist; Freelance articles for 12 papers; Over 200 magazine articles; 20 books published; Freelance writing, newsletters; Co-author of book and lyrics, Smiling Faces, an educational audience participation musical for children; Teacher and Lecturer; TV and radio appearances. Awards: Unity Award in Media, 1999; 1st place, National Federation of Press Women, 1994, 1995; Society of Professional Journalists, 1994; Society of Professional Journalists Mark of Excellence Award, 1988; New Jersey Press Women Awards, 1998, 1997, 1995, 1994, 1993, 1992, 1991, 1989, 1988, 1987; North Jersey Press Club Award, Top Story of the Year, 1995, other awards in 1999, 1997, 1994, 1992, 1990; Capitol Award, 1991. Memberships: Authors Guild; Authors League of America; Society of Professional Journalists; National Federation of Press Women; New Jersey Press Women, 1990 Communications Coordinator; Investigative Reporters and Editors North Jersey Press club. Address: The Pub Eye, 82 Marsh Avenue, Sayreville, NJ 08872 1342, USA.

**RASAPUTRAM Warnasena,** b. 6 September 1927, Sri Lanka. Ambassador of Sri Lanka to USA. 1 son. Education: BA, 1950, Ceylon; MA Statistics, 1957, PhD Economics, 1959, Wisconsin. Appointments: Governor, Central Bank of Sri Lanka, 1979-89; Ambassador of Sri Lanka in Paris, Geneva and High Commissioner of Sri Lanka in Malaysia; Ambassador of Sri Lanka to USA; UN Advisor in Iraq, Bangkok, ILO, CRIAT, UNIDO; Alternate Executive Director, IMF. Publications: Over 50 articles in local and international journals. Honour: Kheimer Award for International Understanding, 1977, Kheimer Institute, Washington. Memberships: President, Sri Lanka Association of Economists; President, Disarmament Conference, Geneva, 1991; Fellow, Institute of Bankers; Honorary Member, Institute of Bankers in Sri Lanka; South Asia Development Fund. Address: 2503 30th Street, N.W., Washington, DC 20008, USA.

**RASHBA Emmanuel Iosif,** b. 30 October 1927, Kiev, Ukraine. Physics. m. Erna K Rashba, 1 daughter. Education: Diploma, honour, Kiev University, 1949; PhD, Kiev, 1956; DSc, Leningrad, 1964; Professor, Theoretical & Mathematical Physics, Moscow, 1967. Career: Junior, Senior Scientist, Institute of Physics, Kiev, 1954-60; Head, Theoretical Division, Institute of Semiconductors, Kiev, 1960-66; Head, Division for Theory of Semiconductors, Landau Institute for Theoretical Physics, Moscow, 1966-97; Professor, University of Utah, USA, 1992-. Publications: Several articles in professional journals. Honours: Lenin Prize, Sciences, 1966; A F Ioffe Prize, Academy of Sciences, Russia, 1987. Membership: Fellow, American Physical Society. Address: University of Utah, Department of Physics, 201 J Fletcher Building, Salt Lake City, UT 84112, USA.

**RASHED Youssef Fawzy,** b. 11 November 1970, Giza, Egypt. Structural Engineer; Educator. Education: BSc, Civil Engineering, 1990, MSc, 1993, Cairo University; PhD, Engineering, University of Wales, England, 1997. Appointments: Assistant Professor, Department of Structural Engineering, Cairo University; Visiting Scholar, Department of Mathematics & Science, University of Nevada; Structural Engineer, ORASCOM Company, Egypt. Publications: Several articles in professional journals. Memberships: Director, Computer Center, Giza; Coptic Metropolis; Saint George Cathedral. Address: 28 Rabie El Gizy Street, Giza, Egypt.

**RASTOGI Shekhar,** b. 10 March 1964, Kanpur. Doctor. m. Vibha, 1 son. Education: MBBS, 1988; MS, 1993. Appointments: Resident Ophthalmology, Gsum Medical College, Kanpur, 1989-92; Sr Fellow, Aravind Eye Hospital, Madurai, 1993-95; Consultant, Dr Jlrs Eye Hospital, 1995-96; Consultant, Regency Hospital. Publications: Research Papers,

Thesis. Memberships: All India Ophthalmic Society; International Iol and Refractive Society; Delhi Ophthalmic Society; Up State Ophlmic Society; Eye Bank Association, India. Address: 118 374A Kaushal Puri, Kanpur, India.

**RATEAVER Bargyla,** b. 3 August 1916, Madagascar. Writer; Publisher. 1 son. Education: Eminence Credential under the Einstein Clause (very rare), 1969; MS Botany, 1950, PhD Botany, 1951. Appointments: Introduced first in the world course in organic gardening & farming into the world's educational system, organising and introducing the first college & university level degree credit course in organic methods, entitled Conservation Gardening & Farming; Organised 2 symposia, 3 seminars, demonstrations and many lectures on the subject; Headed booths, debates, TV, Radio & Video programmes; Held the First International Conference on Organic Methods for Farm & Garden, San Francisco Hilton, 1973; Exhibitions of organic growing and other bestseller books; Other work includes plant collection in Madagascar, 1930-34; Organisation & preparation of herbarium in Palm Springs Desert Museum, 1944; Charting bestseller books of all time, 1958; Organised science libraries in California, 1959-64; Lectured and Wrote & Published books on organic gardening, 1965-; Taught organic method, 1965-77; Book Publishing, 1974-; and much more. Honours: Award for plant introduction of 1935 for USDA, and for Joel Springarn Clematis Collection; First Prize, Della Sizler Graphic Arts Collection, UC Berkeley, 1959, for collection entitled Preparation for botanical research in Madagascar; Grant, Longwood Gardens, 1955; Award: Chicago Museum of Natural History, 1955; American Academy of Arts & Sciences, 1955; Committee for Sustainable Agriculture (first), 1988; Acres USA, Lifetime Achievement (first), 1994; and others. Membership: International Federation of Organic Agriculture Movements. Address: 9049 Covina Street, San Diego, CA 92126-3717, USA.

**RATEAVER Bargyla,** b. 3 August 1916, Madagascar. Writer. 1 son. Education: AB Botany, 1938-43; MS, Botany, 1945-50; PhD, Botany, 1950-51; MSLS, Library Science, 1958-59. Eminence Credential, 1969. Appointments: Plant Collection, 1930-34; Plant Introduction, 1935; Plant Collection, 1936; Gardening, 1938-43; Organization and Preperation of Herbarium, 1944; Research Assistant, 1945-51; Specialist, 1951-52; Technical Work, 1953-54; Plant Propagation Experiments; 1954-55; Literature, 1956-58; Literature Search, 1958-59; Organized Science Libraries, 1959-64; Lecturing, 1965-; Teaching Organic Method, 1965-77; Reorganizing Science Collection, 1968-69; Promotion of International Liaison, 1972-; Organizational Full Member, IFOAM, 1978-; Editorial Board, IFOAM, 1988. Publications: Organic Method Primer; Many other publications. Honours: First Prize, Della Sizler Graphic Arts Collection; Chicago Museum of Natural History; American Academy of Arts and Sciences. Address: 9049 Covina Street, San Diego, CA 92126, USA.

**RATHBUN James Ronald,** b. 25 March 1934, Ozark, USA. Professor of Piano; Performer. m. Sharon Short Rathbun, 1 son, 1 daughter. Education: BSE, Diploma, Piano, Southwest Missouri State University, 1956; MME, Indiana University, 1957; DMA, Piano Performance and Pedagogy, University of Iowa, 1976. Career: Teacher, Public Schools, Missouri, 1957-63, Angelo State University, 1964-66, Concord College, Athens, West Virginia, 1968-70, University of Iowa, 1966-68, 1970-72, Abilene Christian University, 1972-. Creative Works: Concerto Performances in Korea, USA; Lecture Recital, Texas MTA State Meeting, 1996; Solo Appearances at Meyerson Symphony Center, Dallas, 1994, 1996, Wortham Center, Houston, Texas, 1997, Carnegie Hall and Kennedy Center, 1986; Music Director, Abilene Opera, Carmen, 1984, Madame

Butterfly, 1988. Memberships: MTNA; Texas MTA; Abilene MTA. Address: 1157 Highland Avenue, Abilene, TX 79605-4209, USA.

**RATHER Mehraj Ud Din,** b. 27 August 1960, Srinagar Kashmir, India. University Teacher; Researcher. Education: PhD in Botany, 1987; Passed Civil Services Examination, 1999. Appointments: Lecturer, Department of Botany, University of Kashmir, Srinagar, 1990; Assistant Director, Industries and Commerce Department, J & K Govt. Publications: 25 research publications in field of botany. Honours: Young Scientist Award and Fellowship, Department of Science and Technology, J & K Govt, 1995; Executive Member, research journal Nature and Biosphere. Memberships: Phycological Society of India; Editorial Board, research journal Vigyan Paridhi. Address: Department of Botany, University of Kashmir, Srinagar 190006, India.

**RATHIE Arjun Kumar,** b. 1 September 1954, Nasirabad, India. Educator; Researcher. m. Kavita, 2 sons. Education: BSc, 1974, MSc, 1976, PhD, 1981, University of Rajasthan; Postdoctoral Fellow, Visiting Professor: Canada, 1981, Brazil, 1988, 1996, South Korea, 1997, 1998. Appointments: Lecturer in Mathematics, Senior Lecturer, 1986-94, Lecturer in Selection Scale, 1994-, in Govt PG Colleges of Rajasthan State affiliated to University of Rajasthan and MDS University; Presently working at P G Dungar College, Bikaner. Publications: Over 70 research papers in various journals. Honours: Isheer Award 1995; Certificate of Appreciation from The Collector, Bikaner Rajasthan, 1993. Memberships: American Math Society; Isheer Society. Address: Colina Bloco F Apt 604, 709 10900 Brasilia Brazil.

**RATLIFF Robert Barns Jr,** b. 24 October 1950, Bluefield, West Virginia, USA. Executive Vice President. m. Marsha Meredith Ratliff, 1 son, 2 daughters. Education: BS, Mechanical Engineering, Virginia Tech, 1973. Appointments: Distribution Engineer, 1973-76, Staff Engineer, 1976-77, Superintendant 1977-79, Duke Power Company; Division Manager, 1979-89 Assistant Vice President, 1989, Vice President, 1990, Executive Vice President, 1991, Pike Electric. Memberships: National Society of Professional Engineers; Advisory Council John Locke Foundation; Board Director, NCFREE. Address: Pike Electric Inc, PO Box 868, Mount Airy, NC 27030-0868, USA.

**RATNAYAKE Paul,** b. 5 April 1946, Kandy. Healthcare Scientist. m. Chandani, 1 daughter. Education: PhD Naturopathic Medicine; Doctor Degree, Metaphysics; Doctor of the Universe. Appointments: Healthcare Assistant, Mental Retard Patients, Bexley Hospital, Kent, England, 1965-67; Tea Market Expansion Board, Ceylon Tea Centre, London Birmingham, Leeds and Glasgow Merchandising and Public Relations, 1965-67; Marketing Director, Zamag International Marketing Ltd, 1975-77; Human Sciences, Medicine and Healthcare Services, Developing and Manufacturing Pharmaceuticals, 1977-. Memberships include: Chairman Grounder, Association for Health and Human Sciences; Associate Member, British Holistic Health Sciences Association; American Metaphysical Doctors Association Chairman, Belgrave Management Ltd, The Bahamas; Pastoral Psychology Counsellors Association. Address: Parkstrasse 44, CH 4102, Binningen 2/BL, Switzerland.

**RAUH Hermann Rudolf (HE, The Honourable),** b. 8 March 1946, Metzingen, Germany. Physicist and Materials Scientist. m. Sigrid Ursula Löbker, 25 July 1980, 2 daughters. Education: Dipl Phys, University of Tübingen, Germany, 1971; Dr rer nat, University of Stuttgart, Germany, 1975; Dr rer nat habil and Priv

Doz, University of Osnabrück, Germany, 1985. Appointments: Research Associate, Max Planck Institute for Metals Research, Stuttgart, 1971-76; Assistant Professor, University of Osnabrück, 1976-86; Visiting Scientist, Harwell Lab, Oxfordshire, England, 1980-83; Visiting Scientist, Research Centre, Jülich, Germany, 1981; Visiting Fellow, University of Oxford, England, 1986-87; Visiting Scientist, Harwell Lab, Oxfordshire, 1987-88; Visiting Scientist, Interuniversity Microelectronics Centre, Leuven, Belgium, 1988; Research Fellow, Wolfson College, Oxford, 1988-94; Consultant, Harwell Lab, Oxfordshire, 1991-95; Professor, Theoretical Foundations of Materials Development, Darmstadt University of Technology, Germany, 1994-. Publications: Co-editor, book, Materials Modelling: From Theory to Technology, 1992; Contributor, numerous articles on electron optics, defect properties of the solid state, atomic diffusion and segregation in professional journals. Honours include: Scholar of the Commission of the European Communities, 1982; Chartered Physicist and Fellow of the Institute of Physics, 1985; Scholar of the Science and Engineering Research Council, 1986; MA of University of Oxford, 1990; 20th Century Achievement Award, American Biographical Institute, 1999; Medal of Honour, Order of International Ambassadors, 1999; Fellow of the Institute of Materials, 1999. Memberships: German Physical Society, 1970-; Wilhelm Busch Society, 1976-96; Institute of Physics, 1983-; St Edmund Hall, Oxford, 1986-87; Wolfson College, Oxford, 1988-; Congregation, University of Oxford, 1990-94; Ernst Ludwig Society, 1994-; European Physical Society, 1995-; Oxford Society, 1997-; Order of International Ambassadors, 1999-; Institute of Materials, 1999-. Address: Fachbereich Materialwissenschaft, Technische Universität Darmstadt, Petersenstrasse 23, D-64287 Darmstadt, Germany.

**RAUPP Manfred G von Staffort**, b. 13 November 1941, Staffort, Germany. Agrareconomist; Management Educator. m. Dorothee Gisela auf der Heide, 3 daughters. Education: Dipl Ing FH, 1962, Ed farming Augustenberg and farm-technic Nurtingen; Dipl Landwirt, 1968, Agricultural Science Stuttgart-Hohenheim; Dr oec, 1973, Scientific Assistant, Faculty of Economics, Hohenheim; Management, 1978, University Mannheim; Marketing, 1990, Insead Fontainebleau. Appointments: Management Consultant, agricultural related companies, 1971-73; Head of Seeds Division and Home and Garden Business, Ciba-Geigy Germany, 1974-86; Manager of Marketing and Sales for crop protection of Ciba/Novartis Switzerland in middle, eastern Europe and Central Asia, 1986-98; Lecturer of Marketing and Management, Czech Zemedelske University, Prague; President and Chief Exectutive Officer, Madora GmbH Germany. Publications: 6 articles in the field of Agrarmarketing, 1992-97. Address: Madora GmbH Dinkelbergstrasse 12, D 79540 Lorrach, Germany.

**RAVAL Vasantbhai Vitthaldas**, b. 10 May 1951, India. Educator. m. Ila, 1 son, 1 daughter. Education: BA, Sanskrit Gujarati, 1972; BEd, Sanskirt Gujarati, 1976; MA, Entive Sanskirt, 1978. Appointments: Headmaster, Dhraganvel Primary School, 1972-73; Teacher, Shri S S Dayapar High School, 1973-76; Teacher, Shri S S Ramaniya High School, 1976-87; Principal, Shri S S Bada High School, Bada, 1987-. Publications: 25 Compositions for Radio Broadcasting; Editor, Saraswatam; Editor, Mandvi Town national Language Souvenir; Compositions and Poems for various magazines. Honours: Best Principal Award; State Best Teacher Award. Memberships: Saraswatam Committee; District Principal Union; Treasurer, Kutch District Secondary School Examination Board; Treasurer, Mandvi Town National Language Committee; Education Improvement Committee; Converner Sanskrit Study Circle; Honorary Secretary, Shri Bada Vaishnav Society.

Address: High School, Bada TQ Mandvi, Kachchh Guj State, India.

**RAVETKAR Satish**, b. 14 July 1951, Pune, India. Scientist. m. Anjali, 2 daughters. Education: BSc, Chemistry, 1971; MSc, Microbiology, 1973; PhD, Microbiology, 1981; DBM, 1983; MDBA, 1984. Appointments: Director, Projects and materials, Serum Institute of India Ltd. Memberships: International Society of Ayurvedic Medicine; International Society for Pharmaceutical Engineering; Pharmaceutical Manufacturers Association; Indo-German Chamber of Commerce; Indian Academy of Vaccinology and Immunobiology; The All India Glass Manufacturers Federation; National Geographic Society. Address: 4 Sadashanti Apts Lm #9A, Prabhat Road, Pune 411 004, India.

**RAWAT Ajay Singh**, b. 13 July 1948, Naini Tal, India. History Professor. m. Sushma Rawat. Education: MA; PhD. Appointments: Head, History Department, Kumaon University, Naini Tal, 1976-92; Director of Research, Centre for Development Studies, UP Academy of Administration, Naini Tal, 1992-. Publications: Since 1998: Biodiversity Conservation in the UP Himalaya: A Peoples' View Point; Forestry in Central Himalaya; Corbett's Naini Tal; Forests on Fire: Ecology & Politics in the Himalayan Tarai; Nightmare Rides Through Gorakhpur: a Study on the Flood Situation of Gorakhpur Division. Honours: National Fellow, Nehru Memorial Museum & Library, Teen Murli House, New Delhi; Senior Fellow, Indian Council of Social Science Research, New Delhi. Memberships: Chairman, International Union of Forestry Research Organisations, Group 6.07.01, Vienna; Monitoring Committee for Naini Tal, Supreme Court of India, New Delhi; Forest History Society, USA; Indian History Congress; Institute of Historical Studies, Calcutta; Indian National Trust for Art and Cultural Heritage, New Delhi. Address: 2B Sleepy Hollow, Naini Tal 263001, India.

**RAWAT P Prasad**, b. 23 July 1947, Siddhartha Nagar, India. Chief Librarian. m. SMT Kamalesh Rawat, 2 sons, 2 daughters. Education: MA, Sociology, History; MLibSc and Information Science; PhD. Career: Chief Librarian, Government Ayurvedic Medical College, 1976-88; Chief Librarian, Sanjay Gandhi Postgraduate Institute of Medical Sciences, 1988-. Publications: Several articles in professional journals. Memberships: Indian Library Association; Medical Library Association; Association of Special Libraries and Information Centres; Association of Government Libraries and Information Centres; Indian Association of Teachers of Library and Information Science. Address: Sanjay Gandhi Postgraduate Institute of Medical Sciences, PB No 375, Lucknow 226001, India.

**RAWLINGS Robert**, b. 3 August 1924, Pueblo, Colorado, USA. Publisher; Editor. m. Sandy Graham, 1 son, 3 daughters. Education: Graduated, Colorado College, Colorado Springs, 1947; Navy ROTC Unit, University of Colorado. Appointments: Supply Officer, Executive Officer, Subchaser 648, US Navy; Reporter, Pueblo Chieftain; Pueblo Star Journal; Advertising Salesman, 1951; General Manager, 1962; Publisher, Editor, 1980-; President, Star Journal Publishing Corporation 1984-. Honours: Distinguished University Fellow, University of Southern Colorado; Outstanding Service to the University, USC Alumni Association; Citizen of the Year, Pueblo Chamber of Commerce; Colorado Newspaper Person of the Year; Man of the Year, Jaycees; Outstanding Professional for 1980, Southern Colorado Press Club; Named, Pueblo Chamber of Commerce, Citizen of the Year; Colorado Business Leader of the Year, 1989; Donor of the Year, Association of University Athletic Development Directors; Louis T Benezet Award,

Colorado College; Colorado Press Association's Golden Rule Makeup Award; Creative Spirit Award and Public Hall of Fame, 1999. Memberships: Colorado Press Association; Colorado Bar Press Committee; Rocky Mountain Ad Manager's Association; Colorado Associated Press; Colorado Mental Health Institute, Pueblo Community Planning Committee; University of Southern Colorado Foundation; Colorado Forum; Chairman, Southern Colorado Community Foundation; President, Medal of Honor Memorial Committee; President. Robert Hoad Rawlings Foundation. Address: 27 Calle del Sol, Pueblo, CO 81008, USA.

**RAY Kumar Sankar,** b. 24 June 1955, Burdwan, West Bengal. Professor; Researcher; Educator. m. Dhira Ray, 1 daughter. Education: B Engineering, 1977, PhD Engineering, 1987, Calcutta University, India; MSc Control Engineering, 1980, University Bradford, England; Postdoctoral Research, 1990, University of Texas at Austin, USA. Appointments: Instrumentation Engineer, Development Consultant Pvt Ltd, Calcutta, 1980-82; Computer Engineer, 1982-87, Associate Professor, 1987-93, Professor, 1993-, Electronics and Communications Sc Unit of Indian Statistical Institute, Calcutta. Publications: 50 research papers in different areas of computer science. Honours: Merit Scholar of Calcutta University, 1974-76; K S Krishnan Memorial Award for best paper on computer vision, 1991; UNDP Fellowship, 1990; Scholarship for study abroad, Rotary Club of India. Memberships: Founder member, Indian Society for Fuzzy Mathematics; Indian Unit for Pattern Recognition and Artificial Intelligence; President, Indian Statistical Institute's Workers Organisation, 1988-89, 1992-93; Founder member and Assistant Secretary of Faculty Association of ISI. Address: 28/7 College Road, Post Botanic Gardens, W Bengal Howrah 711 103, India.

**RAY Prasanta Kumar,** b. 29 September 1941, Narottampur, Barishal, India. Director, Bose Institute. m. Khana, 2 sons. Education: MSc, 1964; PhD, 1968; DSc, 1974. Appointments: Fellow, Senior Research, CSIR Junior Research, Department of Biochemistry, University of Calcutta, 1964-69; Senior Postdoctoral Fellow and Incharge of laboratory, 1969-70, Research Specialist, 1970-71, Instructor in Experimental Surgery, 1971-73, Department of Surgery, University of Minnesota, USA, 1969-73; Senior Scientific Officer, Head of Cancer Immunobiology Group, Medical Division, Biomedical Group, Bhabha Atomic Research Centre, 1973-76; Director, Chittaranjan National Cancer Research Centre, Calcutta, India, 1976-77; Research Head, Bengal Immunity Research Institute, Calcutta; Head of Department of Immunology and Biochemistry, Calcutta, India, 1977-78; Director, 1978-84, Assistant Professor, 1978-80, Associate Professor, 1980-84, Almea Dea Morani Laboratory of Surgical Immunobiology, Department of Surgery, The Medical College of Pennsylvania and Hospital, Philadelphia, Pennsylvania, USA; Director, Head, Department of Immunobiology and Preventive Toxicology, Industrial Toxicology Research Centre, 1984-92; Director, Bose Institute, Department of Science and Technology, Government of India, 1992-. Publications: 197 Research papers, 13 books, 5 patents. Honours: Ranbaxy National Research Award, 1985; Professor S C Roy Commemorative Medal, 1986; ICMR Cancer Research, 1977; VIII Dr N L Ramanathan Memorial Oration Medal, 1992; NII Senior Immunologist Award, 1995. Memberships: Fellow, Royal Institute of Biology, UK/Indian Academy of Sciences, Allahabad. Address: Bose Institute P-1/12, CIT Scheme VII-M, Calcutta 700 054, West Bengal, India.

**RAY Purnima,** b. 3 January 1959, Bajitpur, India. Teacher. m. Mohit Ray, 1 son, 1 daughter. Education: West Bengal Board of Secondary Education, 1975; English, honours,

Burdwan University, 1978; MA, English, Visva-Bharati, 1981; Advance Diploma, French, Burdwan University, 1991. Appointments: Teacher, Higher Secondary School, 1981; Lecturer, French, Burdwan University, 1993-. Publications: Kavita Utsab, 1990; Bikalpa Batayan, 1994; Chotder Samagra Shakespeare, 1997; Lalo Kalo, 1998. Memberships: Writers Forum; Ranchi India. Address: U5A Tarabag, Burdwan 713104, India.

**RAYEVSKY Kirill S,** b. 2 December 1931, Moscow, Russia. Researcher. m. Margarita Sazonova, 1 son. Education: Moscow Medical Academy, 1957; PhD, 1961; DSc, 1972; Professor of Pharmacology, 1983. Appointments: Researcher, 1959-62, Senior Researcher, 1962-75, Head of Department, 1975-, Institute of Pharmacology RAMS; Professor, Moscow State University, 1993-. Publications: Over 300 publications including 2 monographs. Honours: N P Krakkov Memorial Medal, 1975; A Humboldt Medal, 1983. Memberships: Corresponding member, Russian Academy of Medical Sciences; Society for Neuroscience, USA; European and International Society for Neurochemistry; Russian Society of Pharmacologists; and others. Address: Institute of Pharmacology, 8 Baltiyskaya, 125315 Moscow, Russia.

**RAYOME David Lee,** b. 13 August 1952, Dayton, Ohio, USA. Professor. m. Catherine A Rayome, 2 sons, 1 daughter. Education: PhD, Management, Kent State University, 1992. Appointment: Associate Professor, Finance, Northern Michigan University. Honours: Various Awards for International Financial Research, 1992-97. Memberships: International Trade & Finance Association; Financial Management Association. Address: 748 Baldwin Avenue, Negaunee, MI 49866-1406, USA.

**RAZENKOV Igor Alexandrovich,** b. 20 September 1957, Kamchatka, USSR. Physicist (Optics). m. Roubtsova Olga, 3 sons. Education: Tomsk State University, USSR, 1979; PhD, Tomsk State University, 1993. Appointments: Janitor, 1977-78; Plumber, 1978-80; Researcher, 1979-90; Builder, 1983-85; Senior Scientist, 1990-. Publications: Scientific papers, 1980-; Russian patents, 1982, 1985, 1987; Korean patents, 1997. Address: Laboratory of Optic Probe Analysis, Institute of Atmospheric Optics, Siberian Division of Russian Academy of Science, 1 Prospekt Akademicheskii Tomsk 55, 634055, Russia.

**RAZZAQ Zia,** b. 16 March 1945, Rawalpindi, Pakistan. Professor of Engineering; Businessman. m. Shahida Y Razzaq, 2 sons. Education: BEng, honours, University of Peshawar, Pakistan, 1966; MASc, University of Windsor, Canada, 1968; DSc, Washington Univerity, USA, 1974. Appointments: Assistant Professor, Arizona State University, 1974-77, South Illinois University, 1977-79, University of Notre Dame, 1979-82; Professor, Old Dominion University, 1982-; President, Neptune Engineering Corporation, PC, 1990-. Publications: Over 75 works published in structural engineering. Honours: Morgan Award for Excellence in Teaching & Research; Lincoln Award; NASA Fellowship. Memberships: Fellow, American Society of Civil Engineering; AISC; SSRC. Address: Neptune Engineering Corporation, PC, 4128 Cheswick Lane, Virginia Beach, VA 23455, USA.

**REBANE Karl K,** b. 11 April 1926, Parnu, Estonia. Physicist. m. Ljubov (Shagalova) Rebane (dec), 1 son, 1 daughter. Education: Tallinn Polytechnical Institute, Estonia, 1946-49; Diplomate Physicist, 1955, Leningrad State University, Russia. Appointments: Military Service, 1943-46; Student and Postgrad, Tallinn Polytechnical Institute, Leningrad State University, 1947-55; Senior Scientist, 1956-59, Deputy Director, 1959-64, istitute of Physics, Estonian Academy of Sciences, Tartu; cademician-Secretary of the Department of Physics, lathematics, Technology, 1964-68, Vice President, 1968-73, resident, 1973-90, Estonian Academy of Sciences, Tallinn; rofessor Emeritus, Senior Scientist, Institute of Physics of iartu University, 1990-; Head, Chair of Experimental Physics, 958-60, Head, Chair of Laser Optics, 1973-94, Tartu Iniversity; Chairman, Scientific Council for Optics, USSR cademy of Science, 1977-91. Publications: Author, Impurity pectra of Solids, Russian edition, 1968, 1970; Energy, ntropy, Environment, 1980, 1984; 5 other smaller books; uthor or co-author, 12 USSR Patents and 1 discovery; About 50 papers in various scientific journals on solid state physics, ptics, holography, neural networks modelling, spectral ole-burning, single molecule spectroscopy and applications. lonours: P N Lebedev Golden Medal for Physics, 1981; lexander von Humboldt Award, 1994; 2 Science Prizes of stonian Republic, Estonian Government, 1966, 1995; Various ʻar decorations; Hero of Socialist Labour for Physics Science nd Education, 1986; Presidium of Supreme Council of USSR. Memberships: Academician (Theoretical Physics), Estonian cademy of Sciences; Academician (Optics), Russian cademy of Science; European Academy (London), Section hysics; European Academy of Science and Arts, Saltzburg; lonorary Member, A F Ioffe Physico-Technical Institute, St etersburg; New York Academy of Sciences; Estonian Physical ociety; Italian Physical Society; Society for Simulation of nvironment. Address: Institute of Physics, Tartu University, 42 Riia Street, 51014 Tartu, Estonia.

**REBEIZ Karim,** b. 14 May 1962, Beirut, Lebanon. Scholar; rofessor. Education: BEng, 1984; MSE, Architectural :ngineering, 1986; PhD, Civil and Chemical Engineering, 1992; MBA, Graduate School of Business Administration, 1998. ppointments: Professor, Lafayette College, Department of :ngineering, Civil and Environmental Engineering; Scholar, Iarvard University, Graduate School of Business dministration. Publications: Numerous articles in profesional iurnals and magazines. Honours: Sherwin-Williams Finalist itudent Award, American Chemical Society, 1991; Award, iignificant Contribution to Research on Plastics Recycling, iociety of Plastic Engineers, 1990; Best of Session Paper iward, American Society of Civil Engineers, 1991, 1993, 1996. ddress: Harvard University, 348 Franklin Street #D, lambridge, MA 02139, USA.

**REBELLO Luiz-Francisco,** b. 10 September 1924, Lisboa, ʻortugal. Lawyer; Playwright. m. (dec), 1 daughter. Education: .aw Graduate, 1946, University of Lisbon. Appointments: lirector, Estudio do Salitre, 1946-48; Director, Municipal ʻheatre of Lisbon, 1971-72; President, Portuguese Society of ιuthors, 1973-; Vice President, International Confederacy of iocieties of Authors and Composers, 1976-78; Professor on lopyright, University of Coimbra. Publications: Over 30 books, ncluding plays staged in Portugal and abroad, drama, history, ιnd aesthetics. Honours: Twice winner of the Portuguese )rama Award, 1964, 1994. Memberships: Portuguese .cademy of Sciences; European Academy of Sciences and ιrts; Several Portuguese cultural organisations. Address: iociedade Portugesa Autores, Av Duque de Loule 31, 1069 .isbon, Portugal.

**REBOLJ Joan Marie Kaletta,** b. 17 September 1959, lleveland, Ohio, USA. Teacher, Technical Writer, Malcom ßaldrige Quality Specialist. m. John Adolph, 1 son, 1 daughter. :ducation: BA, Notre Dame College of Ohio, 1980; MA, John larroll University, 1983. Appointments: John Carroll College, 1983; Cuyahoga Community College, 1984-90; Ursuline lollege, 1990; Lakeland Community College, 1983-; Picker

International, 1997-. Address: Lakeland Community College, 7700 Clocktown Dr, Kirtland, OH 44094-5198, USA.

**RECUERO Alfonso,** b. 23 January 1944, Barcelona, Spain. Scientific Researcher. m. Esther, 3 daughters. Education: Civil Engineering, 1969; PhD, Civil Engineering, 1972; Degree in Informatics, 1972. Appointments: Eduardo Torroja Institute, 1969; Senior Researcher, 1973; Became blind in 1975; Head, Department of Civil Engineering, 1982-; Professor of Investigation, 1992. Publications: 56 Papers in Scientific Journals; 58 Communications to Congress; 20 Books and Monographs. Honours: H C Robert of Scholarship, 1971-72; National Award for Technical Resaerch, 1972. Memberships: ACHE; ONCE; Collegio de Caminos; Eurographics; SEMNI. Address: Eduardo Torroja Inst CSIC, Serrano Galvache s/n, 28033 Madrid, Spain.

**REDDY Junuthula N,** b. 12 August 1945, Warangal, AP, India. Professor. m. Aruna, 1 son, 1 daughter. Education: BE, Mechanical Engineering, 1968, Osmania University, Hyderabad, India; MS Mechanical Engineering, 1970, Oklahoma State University; PhD Engineering Mechanics, 1973, University of Alabama; Postdoctoral Fellow, University of Texas at Austin, 1973-74. Appointments: Research Scientist, Lockheed Missiles & Space Company, 1974-75; Assistant Professor, 1975-78, Associate Professor, 1978-80, University of Oklahoma; Professor, 1980-85, Clifton G Garvin Professor, 1986-92, Virginia Polytechnic Institute and State University; Oscar S Wyatt Jr Chair, 1992-, University Distinguished Professor, 1998-, Texas A&M University. Publications: Author over 200 journal papers and 10 text books on theoretical formulations and finite-element analysis of problems in solid and structural mechanics, computational fluid dynamics, numerical heat transfer and applied mathematics. Honours: 7 university awards; Ralph R Teetor Award, 1976; The Walter L Huber Civil Engineering Research Prize, 1983; The Worcester Reed Warner Medal of the American Society of Mechanical Engineers, 1992; Technical Achievement Award, NAE, 1995; Charles Russ Richards Memorial Award, ASME, 1995; Archie Higdon Distinguished Educator Award, American Society Engineering Education, 1997; Melvin R Lohmann Medal, Oklahoma State University, 1997. Memberships: Fellow: American Academy Mechanics; American Society Mechanical Engineers; Aeronautical Society of India; American Society Civil Engineers; US Association of Computational Mechanics, President, current; Associate Fellow, American Institute Aeronautics and Astronautics; Member, International Association Computational Mechanics, co-editor of bulletin; and others. Address: Texas A&M University, College Station, TX 778983 3123, USA.

**REECE Rodney Leon,** b. 9 January 1949, Bankstown, New South Wales, Australia. Veterinary Scientist. m. Janette Gladys Evelyn Mitchell, 11 May 1974, 1 son, 2 daughters. Education: BSc, Veterinary Science, Sydney University, 1971; MSc, James Cook University, 1975; Fellowship by examination in Avian Management and Diseases, Australian College of Veterinary Surgeons, London, 1987; DPhil, Bristol University, 1995; Diploma of Biblical Studies, Vision College, 1987. Appointments: Veterinary Practitioner, Wingham NSW, Australia, 1971-72; Australian Development Assistance Bureau, Honiara, Solomon Islands, 1974-77; Veterinary Pathologist, Victorian Department of Agriculture, Veterinary Research Institute, Victoria, Australia, 1977-87; Veterinary Pathologist, Institute for Animal Health, Houghton Laboratory, Houghton, Cambs. UK, 1987-92; Veterinary Pathologist, Taronga Zoo, Sydney, NSW, Australia, 1992-94; Registrar, National Registry of Domestic Animal Pathology, Camden, NSW, Australia, 1992-97; Veterinary Pathologist, NSW

Agriculture, Elizabeth Macarthur Agricultural Institute, Camden, NSW, 1995-. Publications: Color Atlas of Avian Histology, co-editor with C J Randall, 1996; Author of chapters in Diseases of Poultry, 1997, Poultry Diseases, 1996, Bone Biology and Skeletal Disorders of Poultry, 1992, Diseases and Threatened Birds, 1989; Companion Bird Medicine, 1987; Author, more than 50 original scientific articles; 8 refresher courses in veterinary science, 50 short communications and case reports to scientific journals, proceedings to learned societies and detailed reports; 2 theses. Honour: Registered with New South Wales Veterinary Surgeons Board as Specialist in Avian Medicine, 1997-. Memberships: Treasurer, Australian College of Veterinary Scientists, 1995-; Coordinator, Australian Society of Veterinary Pathologists slide of the month, 1994-; Secretary, British Veterinary Poultry Association, 1990-92; Australian Society of Veterinary Pathologists; Australian Veterinary Poultry Association; Wildlife Diseases Association, Australasian Division; World Poultry Science Association, NSW Division; Australian Christian Veterinary Fellowship. Address: 257 Camden Valley Way, Narellan, NSW 2567, Australia.

**REED Cheryl,** b. 8 Feb 1952, San Antonio, TX, USA. Assistant Professor. m. Anthony L Reed, 3 sons. Education: BA, Literature/Writing, 1991; MA, Literature, 1994; PhD, Literature, 1996. Appointments include: Writing Laboratory Tutor, San Diego Mesa College, 1994; Composition Instructor, San Diego Mesa College/Mira Mar College, 1995-97; Assistant Professor, Faculty Development Coordinator, Penn State Hazleton, 1997-. Publications include: Service Learning in the Writing Class, 1997; Working Without a Net: Making Connections in the Non-Electronic Classroom, 1998; Bibliographic Annotation of Journalism and Mass Communication Quarterly, 1998; The Enabling Face of the Dark: A Speculative Inquiry, 1998; Job Search in Academe: Strategic Rhetorics for Faculty Job Candidates, 1999. Honours: Service Award, Tarrant County Junior College, 1986; Academic Achievement Award, 1986; Soroptimist Charitable Foundation Scholarship, 1991; Outstanding Muir Scholar Award, 1991; Eleanor Roosevelt Summer Research Grant, 1993. Memberships: NCTE/CCCC - National Council of Teachers of English; Sisters in Crime (Women Mystery Writers). Address: PA State University Hazelton Division English, Hazelton, PA 18201, USA.

**REEVES III Ralph Bernard,** b. 2 April 1947, Raleigh, NC, USA. Publisher; Editor. m. Katherine Drewery Reid, 20 June 1998, 2 sons. Education: BA, University North Carolina, Chapel Hill, USA, 1970. Appointments: Editor, NC Architect, 1981-84; Founder, Editor, Publisher, 1978-98. Honours: Governor's Award for Arts, 1986; Benjamin Fine Award, 1991; City of Raleigh Gold Medal. Memberships: Chairman, Raleigh Downtown Advisory Committee, 1983-85. Address: 1707 McDonald Lane, Raleigh, NC 27608-2111, USA.

**REFSUM Helge,** b. 16 September 1947, Oslo. Professor; Research Leader. m. Nina Christensen, 1 son, 2 daughters. Education: MD, 1973, Dr Med, 1976, University of Oslo. Appointments: Research Fellow, Institute of Pharmacology, 1974-77, Professor, Institute for Experimental Medical Research, 1996-, University Oslo; Associate Professor, Departments of Physiology and Pharmacology, 1978-82, Chief, Department Clinical Pharmacology, 1983-84, Professor, Department of Medical Physiology, 1984-93, University Tromso, Norway; Visiting Research Associate, Cardiovascular Research Institute, University California, San Francisco, 1979-80; Visiting Professor, Department of Medicine, University Calgary, Canada, 1985-86; Manager, R&D, Nycomed Imaging AS, Oslo, 1993-. Publications: 7 books; Over 150 publications

in international medical journals. Honours: AC Houen Award 1978; Fogerty International Award, 1979; Alberta Heritage Foundations for Medical Research Award, 1985; Awards from Norwegian Council on Cardiovascular Diseases, and Norwegian Research Council for Science and Humanities. Memberships: International Union of Physiological Sciences, International Union of Pharmacologists; International Society for Heart Research; American Heart Association. Address: Risalleen 28B, N 0387 Oslo, Norway.

**REGNER Dubravka,** b. 18 December 1944, Zagreb, SFR Yugoslavia. Ecologist. m. Dr Slobodan Regner, 2 sons. Education: BSc Biology, 1967, University Belgrade; MSc Biology (Ecology), 1970, PhD Biology, 1980, University Zagreb. Appointments: Ecologist, Marine Biology (Plankton, Environmental Protection). Institute of Oceanography and Fisheries, Split, 1970-94; Institute of Marine Biology, Kotor 1994-; Deputy Director, Institute of Oceanography and Fisheries, 1983-88, Coordinator of the team for the Environmental protection, 1985-88, President of Scientific Council, 1989-91; Coordinator, FAO-UNEP project, Pollution induced ecosystem modification in the coastal area of the Central Adriatic, 1982-84; Coordinator various other projects. Publications: 78 scientific papers, mostly on the ecology of copepods (zooplankton), and on the protection of the coastal sea; 55 technical papers, studies and reviews. Memberships Committee for Marine Plankton of International Commission for the Scientific Exploration of Mediterranean Sea; Mediterranean Commission of Environmental protection, Serbian Ecologica Society; Yugoslav Association for the Protection of the Waters Address: Institute of Marine Biology, PO Box 69, 85330 Kotor Yugoslavia.

**REGNER Slobodan,** b. 4 November 1944, El-Shatt, Egypt Ecologist; Fisheries Biologist. m. Dubravka Regner, 2 sons Education: BSc, Biology, 1967, PhD, 1980, University of Belgrade; MSc, Biology, University of Zagreb, 1970 Appointments: Institute of Oceanography and Fisheries, Split 1970-91; Head, Laboratory for Ichthyoplankton, 1976-91 President, Scientific Council, 1985-87, Institute of Oceanography and Fisheries, Split; Head, Scientific Unit Natural History Museum, Belgrade, 1991-94; Institute of Marine Biology, Kotor, 1994-. Publications: 74 scientific papers Memberships: Committee, Marine Vertebrates and Cephalopodes of International Commission for the Scientific Exploration of Mediterranean Sea; Serbian Ecological Society Address: Institute of Marine Biology, PO Box 69, 85330 Kotor Yugoslavia.

**REIGELSBERGER Paul A,** b. 2 April 1973, Brookfield, MO USA. Artist, Designer, Financial Planner. Education: BA Independent Studies, Columbia College, 1997. Appointments Director, PAR Enterprises, 1994. Publications: Visions of Heaven. Honours: Delta Cgi Fraternity. Memberships: Human Rights Campaign. Address: 4341 Shaw Avenue, First Floor, St Louis, MO 63110, USA.

**REINGARDIENE Dagmara,** b. 12 January 1939, Siaulia, Lithuania. Physician. m. 1 son. Education: Kaunas Medical University, 1962; Thesis for a Candidates Degree of Cardiology, 1975; Thesis for a Doctors Degree of Cardiology 1989. Appointments: Professor, 1993; Chief of Intensive Care Medicine Clinic, 1994. Publications: Co-Author, 219 Articles 1975-98; Co-Author, Textbooks, 1984, 1985, 1987; Co-Author Monographs, 1984, 1988. Memberships: Lithuanian Intensive Care Society; Lithuanian Cardiology Society; European Society of Cardiology; World Cardiology Federation. Address: A Mickevicaus 9, LT 3000, Kaunas, Lithuania.

**REINOEHL Richard Louis,** b. 11 October 1944, Omaha, Nebraska, USA. Scholar; Artist; Martial Artist. m. Linda Dale Iroff, 1 daughter. Education: BS, Portland State University, 1962-69; MSW, University of Minnesota, 1975-77; PhD, Cornell University, 1984-88. Appointments: Acting Director, Vanguard Group Homes, Virginia, 1976-77; Director, Minnesota Chippewa Tribe Group Home, Duluth, 1977-78; Director, Human Development Consortium, 1978-; Editorial Board, Computers in Human Services, 1983-96; Affiliated Scholar, Oberlin College, 1991-; Artist in Residence, Studio Orpheus, Oberlin, 1992-; Director, Kung Fu Shu Studio, Oberlin, 1996-. Associate Editor, Computers in Human Services, 1996-. Publications: Books, Computer Literacy in Human Services, 1990; Numerous papers in professional journals. Memberships: Art Education Committee, FAVA; Fireland Association of the Visual Arts. Address: 46180 Butternut Ridge Road, Oberlin, OH 44074, USA.

**REMISON Samson Uduzel,** b. 17 February 1946, Afuze, Nigeria. Professor. m. Grace Remison, 3 sons, 1 daughter. Education: BSc, honours, Ibadam, 1969; PhD, 1973. Appointments: Research Officer, 1970-76, Senior Research Officer, 1977-78, Principal Research Officer, 1979-80, Chief Research Officer, 1981-86, Assistant Director, 1988-89, Reader, 1989-91, Professor, 1991-, Edo State University. Publications: Over 60 in professional journals. Memberships: Science Association of Nigeria; Agriculture Society of Nigeria. Address: Faculty of Agriculture, Edo State University, Eipoma, Nigeria.

**REMKO Milan,** b. 29 October 1948, Jasenova. Professor. m. Anna Okrucka, 2 daughters. Education: Graduate, Chemistry, Slovak Technical University, 1971; PhD, Physical Chemistry, 1977; Habilitation in Physical Chemistry, Comenius University, Bratislava, 1991; DSc, Physical Chemistry, Slovak Tehnical University, 1994. Appointments: Researcher, Institute of Polymers, 1972-74; Researcher, Pulp and Paper Research Institute, 1974-78; Scientific Worker, Faculty of Pharmacy, Comenius University, 1978-92; Associate Professor, 1992-98; Professor, 1998-. Publications: Theoretical Basis of Medicinal Chemistry; Molecular Basis of Drug Development; QSAR in Design of Bioactive Compounds; More than 120 papers in refereed chemical and pharmaceutical journals. Memberships: Royal Society of Chemistry; International Society for Theoretical Chemical Physics; World Association of Theoretically Oriented Chemists; International Biographical Association; Order of International Fellowship; Slovak Chemical Society; Slovak Pharmaceutical Society. Address: Department of Pharmaceutical Chemistry, Comenius University, Odbojarov 10, SK-832 32 Bratislava, Slovakia.

**RENCKEN-WENTZEL Anne Marie,** b. 29 October 1950, Vryburg, South Africa. Psychologist. 1 son, 2 daughters. Education: BA, 1971, BA, honours, 1978, University of Pretoria; MA, Psychology, Rand Afrikaans University, 1983; PhD, (3rd yr), University of Freestate; Teachers Diploma, Pretoria Teachers Training College. Appointments: Teacher, Ontdekkers High School, 1973-79; Therapist, Child and Adult Guidance Clinic, RAU, 1980-83; Private Practice, 1984-. Publications: Women's Bureau: Women of the Future; Is Your Child School Ready. Memberships: PASA; SAAM. Address: PO Box 5018, Horison, Gauteng 1730, South Africa.

**RENCZ Marta Kerecsen,** b. 24 July 1950, Szekszard, Hungary. Electrical Engineer. I Kerecsen, 1 son, 1 daughter. Education: MS Electrical Engineering, 1973, PhD Microelectronics, 1980, Technical University of Budapest, Hungary. Appointments: Associate Professor, Dept of Electron Devices, Technical University Budapest; CEO of MicRed Ltd,

Budapest. Publications: Over 120 international scientific publications; PC, OC member of over 20 international conferences. Memberships: IEEE; HTE. Address: Technical University of Budapest, Electrical Dept, Goldmann ter 3, 1521 Budapest, Hungary.

**REPSAS Konstantinas,** b. 31 August 1930, Kaunas, Lithuania. Scientist. m. Angele-Grazyte Repsiene, 3 sons. Education: Six High School Classes, 1948; Kaipeda Nautical School, 1948-52; Faculty of Physics, Vilnius University, 1955-60; MSc, 1960; PhD, 1967; Dr Sc, 1979; Professor, Semiconductor Physics Institute, Vilnius, 1980. Appointments: Junior Research Fellow, Institute of Physics and Mathematics, 1960-68; Senior Researcher Fellow, 1968-80; Laboratory Chief, 1980-92; Chief Research Fellow in Semiconduction, Physics Institute, Vilnius Lithuania, 1992-. Publications: Co Author of over 30 inventions. Honours: First Scientific Discovery in Lithuania Diploma N185 of the Discovery of Physics, USSR, 1977; 2 Lithuanian Awards in Physics, 1982; Over 150 Science Studies; Hon/Peter Kapica Medal, Russia Academy of Natural Science, 1995. Memberships: Physical Society of Lithuania; Chairman Department; Soviet and Secretariate of Scientists Union of Lithuania. Address: Kalvariju 134-1, LT 2042, Vilnius, Lithuania.

**RETOLA Jaidev Singh,** b. 1 April 1947, India. Health Worker. m. Renuka, 1 son, 1 daughter. Education: BSc; MBBS; CD. Appointments: MO, Civil Hospital, Rohru, 1976; MOI/c, PHC, Sarswatinagar, 1978; Block Medical Officer, PHC Tikkar, 1990; DYMS, Isolation Hospital, 1994; Chief Health Officer, Ripon Hospila Shimla, 1997; Chief Health Officer, Shimla, 1997-. Honours: 2 National Awards; Publically Honoured for standing 1st in University in BSc II Exam. Memberships: Medical Officers Association; Sages, Amateur Gardens and Environment; RSS Beas. Address: Senior Medical Officer, H P Vidhan Sabha C D, Shimla 171400, India.

**REVELL Dorothy Evangeline Tompkins,** b. 22 December 1911, Rugby, North Dakota, USA. Medical Dietician. m. Gene Allen Revell, 1 son (dec), 1 daughter. Education: BS Foods and Nutrition, 1933, University of North Dakota; Dietetic Internship, Harper Hospital, Detroit, Michigan, 1934. Appointments: Dietetic Department, Dakota Clinic, 18 1/2 years; Private Practice, -. Publications: Presented professional papers at International Congress of Dietetics, London, 1961, Hanover, Germany, 1973, Sydney, Australia, 1977; Authored 9 books on different phases of nutrition. Honours: Sioux Award for Distinguished Service and Outstanding Achievement, 1974, University of North Dakota. Memberships: American Dietetic Association, 1935-; Daughters of the American Colonists; United Empire Loyalists. Address: 2407 E Country Club Dr, Fargo, ND 58103-5730, USA.

**REVHIC Floarea,** b. 26 June 1950, Giurgiu, Romania. Assistant Professor; Senior Researcher. m. Dr Simion Revhic, 1 son. Education: BSc, Cell and Molecular Biology, King's College, University of London; PhD. Appointments: Assistant Professor, University of Agricultural Medicine, Faculty of Biotechnology. Publications: Publications in various journals. Honour: Honour Degree in Cell and Molecular Biology, King's College, London, England. Memberships: National Society of Gerontology; European Muscle Research; New York Academy of Science. Address: National Institute of Gerontology ANA, ASLAN, 9 Caldarusani Str 1, 78178 Bucharest, Romania.

**REY-BELLET Jean,** b. 15 January 1925, St Maurice, Valais, Switzerland. Physician (Neurology and Psychiatry). m. Monique Muller, 3 sons. Education: Medical Diploma, 1950, Medical Doctorate, 1952, Resident in Psychiatry, 1951, Geneva;

Resident in Pathology, Research Institute, Davos, 1952; Fellow in Neurology, Mayo Clinic, Rochester, 1953-54; Resident in Neurology, 1954-55, Chief Resident in Neurology, 1956-58, Bellevue Hospital, New York Uuniversity; Fellow in Neurology, Children's Hospital Harvard University, 1955-56; Resident in Medicine, Medical Policlinic University of Geneva, 1958-59; Chief Resident in Psychiatry and Child Psychiatry, Hopital Bel Air, Geneva University, 1958-64. Appointments: Medical Director, Psychiatric Hospital Malevoz, Monthey, Valais, 1965-90, Child Psychiatric Service of Valais, 1965-81; Retired 1990; Medicial Delegate, International Committee of the Red Cross, 1991-. Publications: Over 50 scientific publications in various neurologic and psychiatric journals. Memberships: President: Association Psychiatric Directors, 1979-82, Swiss Psychiatric Association, 1982-85; Member: Pro Infirmis Zurich; Association of Parents of Handicapped Children; Enfants du Monde, Geneva; Swiss Neurological Association; Swiss Psychiatric Association; Swiss Child Psychiatric Association; Swiss Neurophysiological Association; Swiss Association for Psychiatric Epidemiology; Swiss Psychoanalytical Association; American Academy of Neurology; New York Academy of Sciences; Societe Medicale du Valais; Federation des Medecins Suisses. Address: Ret de Martoret 29, 1870 Mothey, Switzerland.

**REYES Hernan M,** b. 5 April 1933, Alicia, Isabella, Philippines. Professor of Surgery. m. Dolores L Cruz, 1 son, 4 daughters. Education: Undergrad Studies, Pre-Med, University of Philippines, 1949-51; MD, 1957, University of Santo Tomas College of Medicine; Rotating Internship, University Santo Tomas Hospital, Manila, 1956-57, Cook County Hospital, Chicago, 1958-59; Residency, General Surgery and Paediatric Surgery, Cook County Hospital, 1959-65; Research Fellowship, Surgery, Cook County Hospital and Hektoen Institute of Medical Research, Chicago, 1964-65. Appointments: Clinical Assistant, Department of Surgery, Stritch School of Medicine, Loyola University, 1964-65, 1968-69; Instructor in Surgery and Chief, Section of Paediatric Surgery, Department of Surgery, University Santo Tomas College of Medicine, Manila, 1966-67; Lecturer, Cook County Graduate School of Medicine, Chicago, 1972-; Assistant Professor, 1969-73, Acting Chief of Section, Paediatric Surgery, 1973-76, Associate Professor, 1973-76, Department of Surgery, Pritzker School of Medicine, University Chicago; Professor of Surgery, Dept Surgery, 1976-94, Lecturer, Surgery, 1994-, Chief, Division Paediatric Surgery, 1976-90, Professor Clinical Paediatrics, 1982-, University Illinois College of Medicine at Chicago; Professor of Surgery, 1994-, Director, Surgical Academic Programmes, 1994-, Rush University/Rush Medical College at Cook County Hospital, Assistant Dean for Surgical Programmes, 1996, Member Academic Council, 1996; Attending Surgeon and Consultant, various hospitals and medical centres. Publications: 73 articles in journals; 21 book chapters; 41 bulletins and published abstracts; 74 presentations at national meetings. Honours: Very many awards and honours and certificates of appreciation. Address: Cook County Hospital Department Surgery M, 2201 1835 W Harrison Street, Chicago, IL 60612-3701, USA.

**REZNIK Leonid,** b. 18 October 1955, St Petersburg, Russia. Senior Lecturer. m. Olga Kuftova, 1 son. Education: Diploma Electrical Engineer, 1978, St Petersburg Aircraft Academy; PhD Engineering, 1983, St Petersburg University of Technology. Appointments: Programmer, Junior Scientist, Senior Scientist, Principal Scientist, Research Institute of Electromeasuring Instruments, St Petersburg; Principal Scientist, Research Institute of Shipbuilding Technology, St Petersburg; Principal Scientist, Interquadro, Moscow; Lecturer, Senior Lecturer, Victoria University of Technology, Melbourne, Australia. Publications: Fuzzy Controllers, 1997; Co-ed, Fuzzy Systems

Design: Social and Engineering Applications, 1998. Honour: Title of Senior Researcher, High Certifying Commission, Russia, 1986. Memberships: IEEE; New York Academy of Science. Address: Victoria University of Technology, MCMC, PO Box 14428, Melbourne, VIC 8001, Australia.

**RHEINSTEIN Peter Howard,** b. 7 September 1943, Cleveland, Ohio, USA. Physician; Attorney; Government Executive. m. Miriam Ruth Rheinstein, 1 son. Education: BA, honours, 1963, MS, 1964, Michigan University; MD, Johns Hopkins University, 1967; JD, University of Maryland, 1973. Appointments: Private Practice, Medicine, 1970-; Instructor, Medicine and Health Service Physician, University of Maryland School of Medicine, 1970-73; Medical Director, Extended Care Facilities, CHC Corp, Baltimore, 1972-74; President, Zimmerly, Rheinstein & Joson, 1975-76; Director, Division of Drug Advertising and Labeling, 1974-82, Acting Deputy Director, Office of Drugs, 1982-83, Acting Director, Office of Drugs, 1983-84, Director, Office of Drug Standards, 1984-90, Director, Medicine Staff, Office of Health Affairs, 1990-, US Food and Drug Administration. Publictions: Numerous articles in professional journals, several books. Honours include: American College of Legal Medicine Presidents Award, 1985, 1986, 1989, 1991, 1993; Federal Bar Association Distinguished Service Award, 1977; Drug Information Association Outstanding Service Award, 1990. Memberships include: Drug Information Association; American College of Legal Medicine; American Medical Association; Federal Bar Association; American Bar Association; Annapolis Yacht Club; Chartwell Golf and Country Club; John Hopkins Club. Address: 621 Holly Ridge Road, Severna Park, MD 21146-3520, USA.

**RIAZI Mohammad-Reza,** b. 27 July 1952, Rafsanjan, Iran. University Professor. m. Shiva Soleimani, 1 son. Education: BS (Hons) Chemical Engineering, 1974, Tehran University of Technology; MS Chemical Engineering, 1977, PhD Chemical Engineering, 1979, Pennsylvania State University, USA. Appointments: Research, Teaching Assistant, Tehran University Technology, 1974-75, Pennsylvania State University, 1976-79; Assistant Professor, Isfahan University of Technology, 1979-82, Wright State University, Dayton, Ohio, 1983-84, Pennsylvania State University, 1985-86; Visiting Professor, Norwegian Institute of Technology, University of Trondheim, 1988-89, University of Illinois, Chicago, 1992; Associate Professor, Sharif University of Technology, Tehran, 1987-93; Associate Professor, Kuwait University, 1994-. Publications: Author and co-author 40 publications, 14 significant reports and one book: Introduction to Petroleum Reservoir Engineering, 1994; 24 internal conferences; 31 invited seminars and lectures. Honours: Arya-Mehr University Outstanding Student Award, 1974; Sharif University of Technology Research Award, 1991; Diploma of Honour, American National Petroleum Association for Outstanding Services to Petroleum Industry, 1995. Memberships: AIChE Jornal, Journal Petroleum Science and Engineering, Ind Engineering Chem Res and Journal Fluid Phase Equil review boards; Scientific Research Society of N America; American Institute Chemical Engineers; Iranian Academy of Sciences; Editor, Scientia Iranica, 1992-95, Kuwait Journal of Science and Technology, 1998-. Address: Kuwait University Department of Chemical Engineering, PO Box 5969, Safar 13060, Kuwait.

**RICH Ray,** b. 10 December 1940, Oklahoma City, USA. College Professor. m. Julie Bennett Rich. Education: MS, BA, University of Nevada, Las Vegas. Career: Professional Musician, Hollywood, California, Las Vegas; Community College of Southern Nevada, 1981-. Creative Works: Recorded Three Record Albums, Two Movies Scores, Performed on Network Television, Toured Nationally and Internationally,

Honours: Outstanding Service to Humanity Award, Phi Theta Kappa, 1988; Burlington Award, Outstanding Teaching Faculty, 1988. Membership: Nevada Faculty Alliance. Address: 3332 Calle De Corrida, Las Vegas, NV 89102-1124, USA.

**RICHARDSON Robert Carleton,** b. 17 March 1925, Grand Junction, Colorado, USA. Engineering Consultant. m. Ruby Lucille Morrison, deceased, 1 son, 1 daughter. Education: Student, University of Colorado, Boulder, 1943-44, University of California, Berkeley, 1946-47, ICS, Scranton, 1947-50, California State University, Long Beach, 1983, John F Kennedy University. Appointments: Chief Engineer, General Manager, Gilmore Fabricators, Oakland, California, 1948-56; National Sales Manager, Gilmore Steel Contractors, Oakland, 1957-72; Vice President, Engineering, R&D Davis Walker Corporation, 1972-86; Member, Instructional Engineering Faculty of California State University, Long Beach, California, 1983-85; Technical Director, Ivy Steel Division, MMI, Houston, 1986-93; Engineering Consultant, R C Richardson & Associates, Sun Lakes, Arizona, 1993-. Honours: Outstanding Achievement Award, Wire Reinforcement Institute, 1993; Named Boss of the Year, Women in Construction, Oakland, 1964, 1965. Memberships: Fellow, American Concrete Institute; ASTM; ASCE/Federal Emergency Management Agency; Structural Engineers Association of California; Marines Memorial Assocaition; Earthquake Engineering Research Institute; Alliance for Concrete Codes & Standards; Building Seismic Safety Council. Address: 10930 East San Tan Boulevard, Sun Lakes, AZ 85248-7903, USA.

**RIDOUT Daniel III,** b. 13 June 1953, Salisbury, Maryland, USA. Physician. Education: BA Music, 1975, Dartmouth College; MD, 1979, College of Medicine, University Cincinnati. Appointments: General Internist via Chief Independent Contract, Methadone and Alcohol Rehabilitation Clinic, Thomas Jefferson University Hospital, Philadelphia, 1981-83; Attending, Emergency Service, Graduate Hospital, Part-time, 1982-83, 1984-86, Full-Time, 1983-84; Resident and Clinical Instructor of Internal Medicine, 1982-83, Clinical Instructor and Full-Time Attending, Emergency Medicine, Department of Emergency Medicine, 1983-84, Fellowship Appointment, Gatroenterology and Nutrition, 1984-86, Attending Physician and Teaching Staff, Gastroenterology/Internal Medicine, Department Medicine, 1986-94, Graduate Hospital, University of Pennsylvania; Chief, Gastroenterology Division, Veterans Administration Hospital, Coatesville, PA, 1987-89; Attending Physician, Gastroenterology Medicine, Crozer-Chester Medical Centre, Affiliated with Hahnemann University Medical School, 1988-; Attending and Teaching Staff, Gastroenterology, Community Hospital, Chester, PA, 1988-; Attending, Springfield Hospital, PA, 1991-; Attending, Riddle Memorial Hospital, PA, 1992-; Private Practice - Gastroenterology with Hospital Affiliation, Graduate Hospital, University Pennsylvania, 1986-; Group Specialty Practice, Crozer-Chester Medical Centre, Upland, PA, 1996-. Publications: in American Journal of Gastroenterology, 1988; Recent abstract acceptance in Abstracts International 1989. Honours: Paper Presentation, American College of Physicians, Eastern and Western Pennsylvania & West Virginia Scientific Meeting, 1986; Achievement and Service in Medicine Award from the Afro-American Historical Society of Delaware, 1989; Community Achievement Award, 1998. Memberships: in 14 professional associations and societies. Address: Crozer Chester Medical Centre, Suite 220 Bldg 2, Chester, PA 19013, USA.

**RIEHM Sarah Lawrence,** b. Iowa City, Iowa, USA. Writer; Lecturer. m. Charles C Riehm, 1 son, 2 daughters. Education: Bachelor General Studies, 1974, University of Iowa; Masters in International Management, 1980, University of Texas. Appointments: Founder and Executive Director, Playwrights' Project, 1991-95; Executive Director, Texas Composers Forum, 1996-97; Co-Founder and Partner, Azimuth, 1997-. Publications: 3 plays: Liberty, 1992; The King and Me, 1993; The Chute, 1994; 3 books: The Teenage Entrepreneur's Guide, 1987; Entrepreneurship: Building the American Dream, 1991; 50 Great Businesses for Teens, 1997. Honour: Winner, Southern Playwrights Competition, 1994. Memberships: Commissioner, Richardson Arts Commission; Elder, Presbyterian Church. Address: Azimuth, 819 Arapaho Village No 24B Ste 107, Richardson, TX 75080, USA.

**RIKE Susan,** b. 29 August 1952, New York, New York, USA. Publicist. Education: BA cum laude, Art History, 1975, Brooklyn College, New York. Appointments: Co-Owner, Say Cheese, Brooklyn, New York, 1977-82; Account Secretary, Robert Marston & Associates, New York, 1983-84; Assistant Account Executive, Marketshare, New York, 1984; Account Executive, Doremus Public Relations/BBO International, New York, 1984-86; President, Susan Rike Public Relations, Brooklyn, New York, 1986-. Memberships: Professional Member, The James Beard Foundation, 1993-; Professional Member, Women Chefs and Restauranteurs, 1997-; Professional Member, National Association for Female Executives, 1998-. Address: Susan Rike Public Relations, 335 State St Apt 3C, Brooklyn, NY 11217-1719, USA.

**RILEY Paul Richard,** b. 7 September 1968, Shipley, West Yorks, UK. Research Scientist. Education: BSc Hons Zoology, 1990, Leeds University; PhD Molecular Endocrinology, 1995, Institute of Zoology, University College London. Appointments: Senior Embryologist, London Fertility Clinic, 1990-92; Postdoctoral Research Fellow, SLRI Toronto, Canada, 1996-. Publications: Manuscript: Nature Genetics, 1998. Honours: BBSRC Scholarship 1992-95; Wellcome International Travelling Fellowship 1996-. Memberships: Fellow, Zoological Society of London; BSCB; BSDB. Address: 76 Grange Avenue, Toronto, ON, Canada M5T 3J5.

**RILEY Ronald Jim,** b. 10 June 1950, Flint, Michigan, USA. Inventor, Consultant. m. Laura Jean Gill, 2 daughters. Education: CS Mott CC, Flint, 1969-70. Appointments: Assistant Manager, Salesman Howat Electronics, 1968-70; Proprietor, Customtronics, 1970-74; Engineer, Medical Equipment Werby Labs, 1974-76; Plant Engineer, Cara Corp, 1976-78; Industrial Controls Engineer, Atlas Techs, 1978-84; Manager, JN Fauver Co Subs Sun Oil, Madison Heights, 1984-90; Inventor, Riley and Associates, 1990-. Publications: Contributor, Articles to Professional Journals. Memberships: ACLU; Union of Concerned Scientists; Action on Smoking and Health; Inventors Alliance; Alliance for American Innovation Inc; Intellectual Property Creators; Student Coalition for Handling Intellectual Property. Address: Riley and Associates, 1323 W Cook Rd, Grand Blanc, MI 48439-9364, USA.

**RIMAS Justinas,** b. 17 December 1955, Kaunas Region, Lithuania. Financier. m. Virginija Rimiene, 2 sons, 2 daughters. Education: Diploma, 1982, Kaunas Politech Institute; Master degree, 1994, Kaunas Vytautas Magnus University; Doctor of Management Sciences, Kaunas Technology University, 1998. Appointments: Vice Chairman, Planning Commission by Kaunas Executive Committee, 1983-90; Assistant Manager, Kaunas Centre Lithuanian Savings Bank, 1991-92; Director, Kaunas Branch by Vilnius Bank Public Stock Co, 1992-94; Head, Kaunas State Tax Inspection, 1995-97. Publications: Subauthor 4 books: Origin of Taxes and Social Economic Expression; Business and Taxes;Municipal Government Taxes and Fees; For Businessmen about Taxes.Memberships:

President, Lithuanian Boxing Federation; Financial Commission of European Boxing Association; Lithuanian National Olympic Committee; Member Economic & Finance Commission by Lithuanian Confederation ofIndustrialists; Kaunas Rotary Club. Address: Gailutes Str 8B, LT-3016, Kaunas, Lithuania.

**RIMDEIKA Jurgis Gediminas,** b. 23 April 1941, Vilnius, Lithuania. Director. m. Rimdeikiene Angele, 2 sons, 1 daughter. Education: Medical Faculty, Kaunas Medical Institute, 1959-65. Appointments: Physician, Chief Physician, Therapeutical Physical Training Park, Druskininkai, 1965-76; Deputy Chief Physician, Vilnius Outpatient Department, Town Clinics, Vilnius, 1976-82; Republican Clinics of Vilnius, 1984-93; Director, Sapeiga Hospital, 1993-. Honours: Bronze Medal, USSR National Economy Fair for the Creation and Usage of the New Medical Informative System in Lithuanian Institute, 1979; Memorial Honorable Sign, For Humanism, International Chernobyl Union, 1996. Memberships: Medical Issues of Lithuanian Social Movement; Union of Lithuanian Heads Physicians. Address: Birutes 40a-1, LT 2004 Vilnius, Lithuania.

**RIMMER Sheila Mary,** b. Scotland. m. Russell Rimmer. Education: DPhil, 1985; BEcons, First Class Hons, 1976; Certificate IV, Arts, Professional Writing and Editing, 1998. Appointments: Teacher, Deputy Principal, Victorian Education Department, 1963-76; Deputy Master, Ormond College, University of Melbourne, 1995-96; Academic Economist in numerous universities, 1978-85; Consultant Editor, National Council of Women of Australia; Research Economist, Melbourne Catholic Social Services; Literary Researcher, Searching Questions; Publications Assistant, the Australian Economic Review; Publications Assistant, the Australian Economic Review. Publications: More Brilliant Careers, 1994; Australian Labor Market and Microeconomic Reform, 1994; A Workbook to Introduce Macroeconomics, 1994; Opportunities Lost, 1997. Honours: D M Myers University Medal, La Trobe University, 1976; Awarded Annual Best Paper Prize, Economic Society of Australia, 1991. Address: 55 The Righi, Eaglemont, Victoria 3084, Australia.

**RIOS Elena Victoria,** b. 24 April 1955, Los Angeles, California, USA. Physician. Education: BA Human Biology and Public Administration, 1977, Stanford University; MSPH Health Planning and Policy Analysis, University of California, Los Angeles, School of Public Health, 1980; Pre-med Programme, Creighton University, 1981-82; MD, UCLA School of Medicine, 1987; Internal Medicine Residency, Santa Clara Valley Medical Centre, 1987-89, White Memorial Medical Centre, 1989-90; Primary Care Health Services Research Fellowship, NRSA, University of California, Los Angeles Division of General Internal Medicine, 1990-92. Appointments: Involvements in various medical associations, delegations and committees, task forces and Advisory Boards, 1989-97; Research Assistant, Intern, Health Planner, Counsellor, 1975-83; Director, Supernetwork Programme, Los Angeles, 1986-87; Medical Consultant, State of California Office of Statewide Health Planning and Development, Sacramento, 1992-94; Director, CMAC California Medical School Recruitment Programme; White House Healthcare Reform Taskforce, Coordinator of Outreach, 1993; Advisor for Regional and Minority Women's Health, US Department of Health and Human Services, Office of the Secretary, Office on Women's Health and Lecturer, UCLA School of Nursing, Division of Administration, 1994-98; Executive Director, Hispanic-Serving Health Professions Schools, 1998-. Publications: 9 reports, fact sheets and white papers. Honours: Include: Hispanic Woman of Promise Award, 1983; Outstanding Women of America Award, 1984; Lifetime Service Award, California Chicano/Latino Medical Student Association, 1991; American Association of Indian Physicians

Appreciation Award, 1995, AMA Leadership Program, 1998. Memberships: AMA; Society of General Internal Medicine; American Public Health Association; President, National Hispanic Medical Foundation and others. Address: 1700 17th Street NW, Suite 405, Washington DC 20009, USA.

**RÍOS José,** b. 18 December 1919, Rivera, Uruguay. m. Lira Santos. Address: Calle Clara 4558, Sayaga, 12.900, Montevideo, Uruguay.

**RISCH Victor Rene,** b. 9 August 1951, Vienna, Austria. Physician. m. Mary Jane Shelhamer, 2 sons, 1 daughter. Education: BS, 1972; MS, 1974; PhD, 1975; MD, 1980. Appointments: Instructor, 1975-80; Assistant, 1984-87; Assistant Professor, 1987-88; Clinical Assistant Professor, 1989-94; Associate Chair, Associate Professor, 1994-. Publications: 15 Published Abstracts; 18 Publications. Honours: Outstanding Young Men of America, 1989. Memberships: American Society for Therapeutic Radiology; American College of Radiology. Address: Lehigh Valley Hospital Morgan Cancer Ct, P O Box 689, Allentown, PA 18105-1556, USA.

**RITSILA Veiji Antti,** b. 27 April 1930, Sortavala, Finland. MD; Surgeon; Assistant Professor; Researcher. m. Irja Ritsila. Education: MD, 1956, Helsinki University; Medical Diploma, PhD, 1969, Helsinki University, Certificate in General Surgery, Plastic and Reconstructive Surgery, Orthopaedic Surgery, 1965-75; Appointments: Resident, General Surgery, University Central Hospital, Helsinki, 1956-66; Resident, Orthopaedic Surgery, Orthopaedic Hospital of Invalid Foundation, Helsinki, 1964-66; Resident, Plastic and Reconstructive Surgery, University Central Hospital, Helsinki, 1966-69; Senior Plastic Surgeon, University Central Hospital and Finnish Red Cross Hospital, Helsinki, 1969-78; Associate Chief Surgeon, Orthopaedic Hospital of Invalid Foundation, 1978-93; Head of Research Institute, Orton Orthopaedic Hospital, Invalid Foundation, 1988-93; Associate Professor, Plastic Surgery, Helsinki University, 1979-; Consultant Plastic Surgeon, Orton Orthopaedic Hospital, Invalid Foundation in Helsinki, 1993-97; Consultant Plastic Surgeon various clinics and surgeries; Lecturer in field, Helsinki University, 1978-; Council Member European Association of Plastic Surgeons, 1992-97; Editorial Board, European Journal Experimental Muscular-skeletal Rsck, and other professional journals. Publications: Over 150 publications in professional medical journals. Honours: Tord Skoog Society Grantee, 1973-74; Award: Paulo Foundation, 1969, Finnish Medical Society Duidecim, 1970, Sigrid Juselius Foundation, 1972-89, Finnish Orthopaedic and Traumatologic Research Foundation, 1974; Anders Langenskiold Medal, 1994. Memberships: AAAS; New York Academy of Sciences; International Confederation for Plastic and Reconstructive Surgery; International Society Orthopaedic Surgery and Traumatology; European Association of Plastic Surgeons; Nordic Surgical Association; Nordic Orthopaedic Federation; Scandinavian Association of Plastic Surgery; Nordic Scoliosis Research Association; Spinal Deformity Society; and others. Address: Lahnatie 4B, SF-02170 Rspoo, Finland.

**RITTNER Leona Phyllis,** b. 9 February 1948, Peekskill, New York, USA. Independent Scholar, Comparative Literature. Education: BA, 1973; MA Equivalent, CCNY, 1982; PhD, 1984. Appointments: Graduate Assistantship, Department of Romance Languages, CCNY, 1973; Executive Committee, Romance Literary Relations, 1987-91; Executive Committee, Women in French, 1988-90. Publications: Several abstracts, articles and reviews in professional journals; Presenter in field; Artist, Translator. Memberships: Modern Language Association of America; South Atlantic Modern Language Association; Women's Caucus for the Modern Languages; Women in

French; American Association of University Women; Rocky Mountain Modern Language Association; Society for Critical Exchange; CUNY Francophone Association; Society for Phenomenology and Existential Philosophy; Theatre Development Fund; Harvard English Institute; International Association for Philosophy and Literature; International Simone de Beauvoir Society; The Sartre Society of North America American Association of Teachers of French; National Coalition of Independent Schools; America-Italy Society Inc; Associates of the Rare Book and Manuscript Library of Columbia University; Association of French and Francophone Teachers of America; American Association of French-Language Philosophy; W B Yeats Society; G Bernard Shaw Society. Address: 120 Kenilworth Place, Apt 1J, Brooklyn, NY 11210, USA.

**ROATZ MYERS Dorothy,** b. 21 March 1921, Detroit, Michigan, USA. Artist. m. div. 2 sons, 1 daughter. Education: Corcoran Gallery Art School, Washington DC; Art Students League, NYC; Study with Yashuoa Kuniyoshi, William J Calfee, Ralph M Pearson; Fellowships and Residencies with Bay Street Studio, Maine, 1985, Cummington Community of the Arts, Massachusetts, 1993, Vermont Studio Centre, 1994, 1995. Career: Represented by Ward-Nasse Gallery, NYC, Exhibits regularly in Greece,France and Europe. Honours: International Awards including bronze medals and Certificates of Appreciation. Memberships: 14th Street Painters, NYC; C.O.G.A.P. (US Coast Guard Art Program); Hellenic Institute, Athens; Portrait Institute, NYC; Salmagundi Club, NYC; NY Artists Equity; Garrison Art Centre, NYC; Corresponding Academician (Dept Arts), Accademia Internazionale 'Greci - Marino', Accademia Del Verbano, Italia. Address: Box 518, Ocean Grove, NJ 07756, USA.

**ROBBINS Jeanette Lee Rassi,** b. 21 July 1956, Portland, Oregon, USA. Founder, Owner, Eye-Dea Development Sales and Manufacturing. m. Michael Keith Robbins, 22 May 1981. Education: AGenSci, Portland Community College, Oregon, 1982. Appointments: Correspondent Adviser, world government and national government, local government and business owners, 1978-; Salvation Army, Portland, Oregon, 1979; Detective Scientist, X, 1980-; Goodwill Industries, Denver, Colorado, 1983-87; Founder, Owner, Chief Executive Officer, Job Development Research Center, Portland, Oregon, USA, 1985-; St Vincent De Paul, Portland, 1987-88; Founder, Owner, Chief Executive Officer, Eye-Dea Development Sales and Manufacturing, Portland, 1988-; Certificate-Engineering Aide, Oregon, 1988. Publications: Artist, author: Artrithmetic, 1978, 1982; Author: Prime Factor Pattern, 1991; Prime Factor Pattern of Square Root Ends, 1994; Artist: Patricia Mae, 1996; Artist, Author: Artrithmetic - Reference, 1997. Honours include: Certificate of Merit Award for Distinguished Service, Certificate of Inclusion for Achievements and Contributions, Outstanding Achievement Diploma Outstanding Achievement Medal, Invitation for Fellowship with International Congress, International Biographical Centre, Cambridge, England; Key Award for Significant Accomplishments, American Biographical Institute. Address: Eye-Dea Development Sales and Manufacturing, PO Box 66221, Portland, OR 97290-6221, USA.

**ROBERTS Calvin W,** b. 7 September 1952, New York, USA. Medicine. m. Andrea Calvin Roberts, 1 son, 2 daughters. Education: AB, Princeton University, 1974; MD, Columbia University College of Physicians and Surgeons, 1978. Appointment: Professor of Ophthalmology, Cornell University Medical College, 1982-. Honour: Honor Award, American Academy of Ophthalmology, 1997. Memberships: Medical Director, The Fight for Sight; Medical Board, Eye Bank for Sight

Restoration; Board of Directors, The Louis Gibofsky Foundation; National Eye Care Project. Address: Cornell University Medical College, 520 E 70th Street, New York, NY 10021, USA.

**ROBINSON Arthur Napoleon Raymond,** b. 16 December 1926, Calder Hall, Tobago, Trinidad and Tobago. President of the Republic of Trinidad and Tobago; Lawyer. m. Patricia Rawlins, 1 son, 1 daughter. Education: LLB, London University, 1949; Bar Final Exam, Inner Temple, London, 1953; MA Philosophy, Politics, Economics, St John's College, Oxford, 1955. Appointments: Member of the Federal Parliament of the West Indies, 1958-60; Minister of Finance, 1961-67; Minister of External Affairs, 1967-70; First Chairman of the restored Tobago House of Assembly, 1980-86; Minister of Economy, 1986-88; Prime Minister, Republic of Trinidad and Tobago 1986-91; Minister Extraordinaire and of Tobago Affairs, 1995-97; President of the Republic of Trinidad and Tobago, 1997-. Honours: Senior Counsel, Trinidad and Tobago; Freeman of Los Angeles, and Thousand Oaks, 1987; Honorary Fellow St John's, Oxon, 1988; Gran Orden de El Libertador, 1990; Hon DCL, Obafemi Awolowo University, Nigeria, 1991; Chief of Ils Ife, 1991; Knight of St John; Defender of Democracy, Parliamentarians for Global Action, 1997; Trinity Cross, Highest National Award of Trindad and Tobago, 1997; Order of the Caribbean Community, 1998. Memberships: President, PGA, 1997; VC, International Council PGA, 1993; UN Expert Group on Crime & Abuse of Power, 1979; Director, Foundation for Establishment of International Criminal Court, 1972-87. Address: Office of the President of the Republic of Trinidad & Tobago, St Anns, Port of Spain, Trinidad & Tobago, West Indies.

**ROBINSON Barbara,** b. 7 March 1928, London, England. Painter. m. G W Robinson, 2 sons. Education: Lycée Francais du Royanne Uni, 1932-38; Slade and Ruskin Schools of Fine Art, 1943-47. Creative Works: Exhibitions 1959-74, 1983, New Art Centre, London, Geneva, New York; Bruton Street Gallery, London, 1999; Galerie Henri Bronne, Monaco, 1999. Honours: Medal, City of Monaco; Medal, City of Rodez; Lumières de Barbara Robinson, Geneviève Conte, 1985; Autres Lumières de Barbara Robinson, 1997. Address: Vic-le-Fesq, Gard, France.

**ROCHA-PEREIRA Maria Helena,** b. 3 September 1925, Oporto, Portugal. Professor. Education: Diploma, Hebrew, 1946, DLitt, 1956, University of Coimbra; Attended lectures, University of Oxford, 1950-51, 1954, 1959. Appointments: Lecturer, Greek, 1951-56, Reader, 1956-61, Associate Professor, 1961-64, Professor, 1964-95, Vice Chancellor, 1970-71, Emeritus, 1995, Coimbra University; President, Scientific Council, Faculty of Arts, Coimbra, 1977-89. Publications: Books and several professional articles in journals. Honours: Prize, Essay, 1966, 1988. Memberships: Societe Internationale d'Histoire de la Medecine; Lisbon Academy of Sciences; Hellenic Society, London; Foundation for Hellenic Culture, Athens. Address: Praceta Av Dias da Silva 1, 3000 Coimbra, Portugal.

**RODGERS Grace Anne,** b. 19 April 1936, South Bend, Indiana, USA. Associate Faculty. m. Eugene Merle, 1 son, 1 daughter. Education: Bachelor of Science, Indiana State University, 1981; Public Management Certificate, Indiana University, 1991; Master of Public Affairs, Indiana University, 1993. Appointments: Director of Special Programs, Ivy Tech State College, 1990-94; Marketing Consultant, Educational Institutions, 1994-96; Director of Internships and Student Services, Indiana University, 1994-98; Acting Director, Community Links, Indiana University, 1997-98; Associate

Faculty, Indiana University, 1994-. Publications: Resume and Beyond, 1990; Strategic Marketing Plan, 1994. Honours: Award for Outstanding Service to Students and Education, Ivy Tech State College, 1993; Phi Theta Kappa Award for Outstanding Contributions, 1993; Outstanding Associate Faculty Award, Indiana University, 1997; Lifetime Achievement Award for Outstanding Community and Student Service, Indiana University, 1998. Memberships: Indiana University Alumni Association, Pi Alpha Alpha, National Honour Society for Public Affairs, School of Public and Environmental Affairs Alumni Council, Associate Faculty Association, Phi Theta Kappa, Ivy Tech Foundation. Address: 17120 Killarney Ct, Granger, IN 46530-9771, USA.

**RODRIGUES Valerian,** b. 29 July 1949, Loreto, Mangalore, India. Professor. m. Betilda Rodrigues, 2 daughters. Education: MA, Poona University; MPhil, PhD, Jawaharlal Nehru University, New Delhi. Appointments: Lecturer, S D M College, 1976; Lecturer, Mangalore University, 1982; Reader, Mangalore University, 1989; Professor, Mangalore University, 1994; Dean, Faculty of Arts, Mangalore University. Publications: Over 25 research articles. Honours: UGC Junior Research Fellow, 1977-81; Agatha Harrison Fellow, St Antony's College, Oxford, 1989-91; Danti Award for Kannada. Memberships: University Bodies of Mangalore, Kuvempu, Goa, Gulbarga, Bangalore, Calcutta, Kerala; Subject Committee, University Grants Commission, India. Address: River View Ullas Nasgar, Kavoor, Mangalore 575015, Karnataka, India.

**ROGAN Richard A,** b. 6 September 1950, Los Angeles, California, USA. Attorney. 1 son, 1 daughter. Education: AB, honours, Hamilton College, 1972; JD, University of California, Hastings College of Law, 1975. Appointments: Carpenter & Fall, 1975-78; Managing Partner, Broad, Schulz, Larson & Wineberg, 1991-93; Jeffer Mangels, Butler Marmaro, 1994-. Publications: Several articles in professional journals. Memberships: American Bar Association; Business Bankruptcy Committee; State Bar of California; Bar Association of San Francisco; Commerical Law & Bankruptcy Section. Address: Jeffer Mangels Butler Marmaro, 12th Floor, One Sansome Street, San Francisco, CA 94104, USA.

**ROGERS Derry F M,** b. 6 January 1954, Derby, UK. Cosmetic Dentist. m. Trisha Chesney, 1 son. Education: BDS, 1977; Licentiate in Dental Surgery, 1977; Diploma CRE (Seattle), 1996; Fellowship American Academy of Cosmetic Dentistry, 1998. Appointments: International Editor: Journal Aesthetic Dental Research, USA; Cosmetic Dentistry for the GP, USA; Annals of Cosmetic Dentistry, USA; Co-Founder and Inaugural President, Australian Society of Dental Aesthetics; Director, Australian Centre for Facial Aesthetics; 36 Lecture Tours to Australia, Canada, New Zealand, USA and Far East. Address: 657 Chapel Street Suite G3, South Yarra, Victoria, Australia 3141.

**ROGERS Gary C,** b. 18 December 1936, Charleston, IL, USA. Educational Administrator. m. Phyllis J Reffeitt, 2 daughters. Education: BSc, Education, 1961; BSc, Business, 1962; MSc, Educational Administration, 1965. Appointments: Elementary Teacher and Assistant Principal, 7 years; Principal, Daniel and Douglas Elementary Schools, 11 years; Dean of Men, East Park Junior High School 3 years; Principal, East Park Middle School, 4 years. Honours: Illinois Those Who Excel in Education Governor's Award; American Heart Association Presidential Award. Memberships: Kiwanis of Danville, past President; YMCA Board Member, past President, District 118 School Board Member, 1995-; St James United Methodist Church Appalachian Service Project Leader. Address: 1314 N Gilbert Street, Danville, IL 61832, USA.

**ROGERS Kenneth A,** b. 17 July 1946, Hyannis, MA, USA. Professor. m. Donna L, 3 daughters. Education: USAF Russian Language School, Syracuse University, 1967; BS, Meterology, University of Oklahoma, 1970; MA, International Affairs, California State University, 1976; PhD, International Relations, American University, Washington DC, 1982. Appointments: Weather Forcaster, USAF, 1970-74; Soviet Affairs Analyst, Pentagon, Washington, 1977-81; International Political Affairs Officer, Washington DC, 1981-83; Research Fellow, University of Edinburgh, Scotland, 1983-84; Director of Comparative and Area Studies, USAF Academy, 1984-89; Professor of Political Science, Arkansas Tech University, 1989-. Publications: 9 Publications; Numerous Classified Articles, Assesments and Briefings. Honours: Post Doc Research Fellowship, University of Edinburgh; Fac of the Year, Arkansas Tech University. Memberships: American Political Science Association; International Studies Association; Arkansas Political Science Association. Address: Dept of Soc Sci and Philos, Arkansas Tech Univ, Russellville, AR 72801-2222, USA.

**ROGERS Mal David Jr,** b. 26 July 1922, Myrtle, Mississippi, USA. Chemical Engineer. m. Juanita Mills, 1 son, 3 daughters, 2 adopted daughters. Education: BS, Chemical Engineer, 1948; MChE Chemical Engineering, 1949; Nuclear Science/Engineering, 1957. Appointments: Shell Chemical Division at Shell Oil, 1951-56; General Dynamics (now McDonnell-Douglas), 1956-59; Texas Instruments, 1959-90. Publications: Internal Only. Honours: Awarded 9 Months Study of Nuclear Science/Engineering at Pennsylvania State University and Argonne National Laboratory. Membership: New York Academy of Sciences. Address: 1240 Derby Drive, Richardson, TX 75080, USA.

**ROHEKAR Joel Ezekiel,** b. 5 October 1942, Nadiad, Gujarat. Teacher. m. Sudha. Education: BA, Nagpur University; MA, Shivaji University; BEd, Shivaji University. Appointments: Teacher, English, 1971-; Lecturer, English, and Teacher in English, 1974-. Publication: Gomatesham Panamami, book, English. Honour: Distinguished Leadership Award, USA; Appointment to Research Board of Advisors, USA. Memberships: Life Member, International Writers and Artists Association, USA; Writers' Forum; Active Member: World Poetry Society; Intercontinental; American Biographical Centre, USA. Address: 164/65 South Sadar Bazaar, Solapur 413 003, India.

**ROHLENA Robert Charles,** b. 22 August 1932, Cedar Rapids, Iowa, USA. Retired Farmer. m. Sylvia Blaha, 2 sons, 1 daughter. Education: BSC, Commerce, 1959; MSS, Sociology, 1970. Appointments: Agriculture; Finance; Real Estate. Memberships: American Legion; Czech and Slovak Museum and Library. Address: 3105 76th Avenue Dr SW, Cedar Rapids, IA 52404-9004, USA.

**ROISMAN Isaac,** b. 9 February 1946, Landsberg, Germany. m. 5 children. Education: BA, Sociology and Anthropology, Tel-Aviv University, 1970; MD, Faculty of Medicine, Tel-Aviv University, 1974; Diploma in Surgery, Faculty of Medicine, School of Continuing Medical Education of Tel-Aviv University, 1986; Master of Surgery, Faculty of Medicine, School of Continuing Medical Education of Tel-Aviv University, 1991; DSc, Israel Institute of Technology, Bruce Rappaport Faculty of Medicine, Haifa, 1996. Appointments: Military Service: Infantry, compulsory service, 1964-66; Reserve forces, 1966-; Physician, 1974-; Rank of Major, 1991-97. Publications include: Surgical Considerations in the Treatment of Well-Differentiated Thyroid Cancer, 1996; Breast Cancer in a Nun, 1996; TNF and IL-1 in Cerebrospinal Fluid of Malignant Brain Tumors; Surgical Considerations in the Treatment of Gastric leiomyosarcoma,

996; Hodgkin's Disease of the Breast and the Anterior Chest Wall, 1996; Breast Cancer Detection by Mammography and CA 15-3; CSF Cytokine Levels of Deppressed Patients; TNF and IL-1 in Cerebrospinal Fluid of Malignant Brain Tumors. Honours include: Rotary Club Nazareth Cup, 1993; Special Prize, Presenting Unique Posters, New Delhi, India, 1994; Mark of Honor from Haifa Municipality to the President of The European Group for Breast Cancer Screening of 1997; Free Masons Mark of Appreciation, Haifa, 1997; Free Masons Mark of Appreciation, Haifa, 1997. Memberships: Israel Medical Association; Associate Member, European Group for Breast Cancer Research, USA; Active Member, The European Society of Mastology; European Association for Cancer Research; Executive Member, IATMO Conference in Jerusalem, 1997; Elected President, European Group for Breast Cancer Screening, 1997. Address: 27 Kabrim St PO Box 45470, 31453 Haifa, Israel.

**ROMANCE Ullod Joan,** b. 17 October 1951, Barcelona, Spain. Bank Executive; Marketing Consultant. m. Isabel Hernandez Esteban, 2 sons. Education: Licentiate in Psychology, 1975, Barcelona University; Licentiate of History, 1977; M of Marketing, 1980. Appointments: Junior Staff, Bank Auraly Mediterraneo, Barcelona, 1977-81; Director, Bank Exterior Espana, Barcelona, 1981-89, Argentaria's Bank, Barcelona, 1989-90; Business Manager, Director, Bank of Tokyo, Barcelona, 1990-96; with Bank of Tokyo-Mitsubishi, 1996-; Consultant, Ullod Associates, Barcelona, 1980-90; Marketing Consultant, Electronic Association of Barcelona, 1986-89, schools, Barcelona, 1984; Psychology Marketing Consultant, Marketing Club of Barcelona, 1990-. Publications: Psychology of Bank's Client, 1980; Introduction to Marketing, 5 vols, 1990; Bank's Marketing, 1992; Psychological Marketing, 1995. Honours: Gold Medal, Psychology Association, 1984; Silver Cup, Marketing Club, 1990. Memberships: Founder member, Key of City of Barcelona, 1980, member Board of Directors; Old Marist Students, Barcelona; Red Cross, Barcelona; Geographic Society; Master Annyssetiers; Psychology Professionals Association; International Association. Address: Bank of Tokyo-Mitsubishi Ltd, Diagonac 605 6 2, 08028 Barcelona, Spain.

**RONG Shi,** b. 10 October 1939, Dongtai, Jiangshu Province, China. Vice President. m. Wang Quai yun, 1 daughter. Education: Graduate, Shuzhou Medical College and Education School; Master of Philosophy, Huadong Teacher Training University. Appointment: Professor, Medical Ethics. Publications include: Country Medical Morality; Shi Rong, Professor's Collected Works. Memberships: Vice Chairman, Institutions of Higher Learnings; Director, Chinese Medical Committee; Deputy Director, National Medical Ethics for Young and Middle Aged Committee; Director, National Terminally Hospital Case Speciality Committee; East-Asia Life Ethics Committee and World Life Ethics Committee. Address: Shanghai Medical College, Fengxian Nao Qiao Town, Shanghai 201400, China.

**ROONGPISUTHIPONG Chulaporn,** b. 18 April 1952, Bangkok. Physician. m. Anuvat, 1 son, 2 daughters. Education: Bachelor of Sciences, Mahidol University, Bangkok, 1975; Doctor of Medicine, 1977; Graduate Diploma in Clinical Sciences, 1979; Diploma Thai Board of Internal Medicine, 1981; Diploma of Nutition, American Board Emory School of Medicine, Altanta, 1988. Appointments: Clinical Instructor, Mahidol University, 1982-83; Assistant Professor, 1983-88; Associate Professor, 1988-95; Professor of Medicine, 1995-. Publications: Author of 12 books. Honours: Commander of the Most Noble Order of the Crown of Thailand; Knight Commander, 1989; Knight Commander of the most Exalted

Order of the White Elephant, 1993; Knight Grand Cross of the most Noble Order of the Crown of Thailand, 1997. Memberships: American Institute of Nutrition; American Society of Clinical Nutrition; Federation Association of Societies Experimental Biology; Woman Medical Association of Thailand; The Royal College of Physicians; Nutrition Association of Thailand; Society of Parentoral and Enteral Nutrition; Medical Association of Thailand; National Research Institute. Address: 153/20 Roongpracha Road, Bangkok, Thailand 10700.

**ROOTS Ott,** b. 9 May 1946, Tallinn, Estonia. Chemist. m. Marika Voit, 1 son. Education: Chemist Technologist, Tallinn Technical University, 1969; Candidate of Chem Sci, Institute of Chemistry, Estonian Academy of Sciences, 1983. Appointments: Scientist, Institute of Zoology and Botany, 1971-74; Scientist, Institute of Thermo and Electrophysics, 1974-84; Chief Researcher, Institute of Applied Geophysics, 1984-90; Chief Researcher, Tallinn Technical University, 1990-92; Senior Scientist, Institute of Experimental and Clinical Medicine, 1992-94; Monitoring Councillor, Ministry of the Environment of Estonia, 1993-. Publications: Over 160 articles; Several reports, environmental issues; 4 Monographs. Honours: Bronze Medal, Environmental Protection Exhibition, Moscow, 1982; Honour Certificate, Ministry of the Environment of Estonia, 1996. Memberships: National Geographic Society, Washington, 1996; New York Academy of Sciences, USA, 1997. Address: Ministry of Environment, Environment Information Centre, Mustamae tee 33, 10616 Tallinn, Estonia.

**ROSCHER Nina Pauline Matheny,** b. 8 December 1938, Uniontown, Pennsylvania, USA. Professor of Chemistry. m. David Moore Roscher. Education: BS, University of Delaware, 1960; PhD, Purdue University, 1964. Appointments: Director of Academic Administration, 1974-76, Associate Professor, 1974-79, Associate Dean for Graduate Affairs and Research, College of Arts and Sciences, 1976-79, Professor of Chemistry, 1979-, Vice Provost for Academic Services, 1979-82, Dean for Faculty Affairs, 1981-85, Vice Provost for Academic Affairs, 1982-85, Department of Chemistry, Chair, 1991-, American University, Program Director, 1986-98, National Science Foundation. Honours include: Iota Sigma Pi; Sigma Xi; Phi Kappa Phi; Sigma Delta Epsilon; American Chemical Society Award, Dreyfus Foundation, 1996; Purdue University School of Science Distinguished Alumni Award, 1996; Charles Gordon Award, Chemical Society of Washington, 1996; American University Award for Outstanding Service by a Faculty Member, 1998; Senior Scholar Special Commendation of Honor, American Association for University Women, 1998; Presidential Award for Excellence in Science, Mathematics and Engineering Mentoring, Presented at White House, 1998; National Science Foundation Grant, 1998-2000. Memberships include: American Chemical Society; Fellow, American Institute of Chemists; Fellow, American Association for the Advancement of Science; New York Academy of Sciences; Fellow, Association of Women in Science; Fellow, Washington Academy of Sciences; Council of Chemical Research. Address: The American University, Washington DC 20016, USA.

**ROSENAU Pauline M Vaillancourt,** b. 14 June 1943, San Diego, California, USA. Professor. 1 daughter. Education:BA, Political Science, University of California, 1965; MA, Political Science, University of California, 1966; PhD, Political Science, University of California, Berkeley, 1972; Masters of Public Health, University of California, UCLA, 1992. Appointments: Assistant Professor, McGill University, 1969-73; Associate Professor, University of Quebec, 1973-1980; Full Professor, University of Quebec, 1980-93; Associate Professor, Management and Policy Sciences, School of Public Health, University of Texas, 1993-. Publications: Post-Modernism and the Social Sciences, Insights, Inroads and Intrusions; Health Case Reform in the Nineties: Public/Private Policy Patnerships; When Marxists Do Research; Section, Encyclopedia of Biomedical Policy; Several Book Chapters; Numerous Articles. Honours: International Authors and Writers Who's Who, Fifteenth Edition, International Biographical Centre; Dictionary of International Biography, Twenty-Sixth Edition, IBC; Appointment as Adjunct Associate Professor, School of Social Sciences, Rice University; Appointment as Adjunct Professor, University of Houston; Delta Omega; Phi Beta Kappa. Address: University of Texas, School of Public Health, 1200 Herman Pressler, P O Box 20186, Houston, TX 77225, USA.

**ROSENKNOP John,** b. 28 December 1929, Moscow. Mathematician. Education: MSc, 1952, Moscow University; DSc, 1962, Kazan University. Appointments: Scientific Associate, Zentralblatt fur Mathematik, Berlin; Independent Publisher. Publications: Over 30 in Mathematics. Honour: Special Grobner Bases Co-Inventor Award, Linz, Austria, 1998. Membership: American Mathematical Society. Address: Box 15 11 21, 10673 Berlin, Germany.

**ROSENSTREICH David,** b. 16 November 1942, New York City, USA. Physician, Scientist. m. Victoria Abokrek, 2 sons, 1 daughter. Education: BS, Cum Laude, City College of New York, 1959-63; MD Hons, New York University School of Medicine, 1963-67. Appointments: Senior Investigator, Cellular Immunology Section, National Institute of Dental Research, 1974-79; Visiting Associate Professor, Laboratory of Cellular Physiology and Immunology, Rockefella University, 1978-79; Associate Professor, Departments of Medicine and Microbiology and Immunology, Albert Einstein College of Medicine, 1980-84; Professor, Department of Medicine, 1984-; Professor, Department of Microbiology and Immunology, 1987-; Director, Division of Allergy and Immunology, 1982-. Publications: 107 Publications, Original Research Papers; 57 Invited Papers, Reviews. Honours: Tremaine Scholarship; Phi Beta Kappa, Honour Society; New York State Regents Scholarship; Alpha Omega Alpha; Founders Day Award for Excellence in Medical Studies; Publich Health Service Commendation Award; Danziger Distinguished Scholar in Microbiology and Immunology. Memberships: American Association of Physicians; American Society for Clinical Investigation; American Federation for Clinical Research; American Association of Immunologists; Fellow American Academy of Allergy and Immunology; Fellow American College of Allergy; NY Allergy Society. Address: 1300 Morris Park Avenue, Bronx, NY 10461 1926, USA.

**ROSENTHAL J William,** b. 30 October 1922, New Orleans, USA. Ophthalmologist. m. Harriet Stern Rosenthal, 1 son, 1 daughter. Education: BS, 1942, Tulane University; MD, 1945, Tulane Medical; MSc, 1951, DSc, 1956, University Pennsylvania; Diplomate, American Board of Ophthalmology. Appointments: Private Practice of Ophthalmology, 1951-; President, New Orleans Eye Specialists, 1950-98. Publications: 60 professional articles; 2 Book chapters; Editor, 3 ophthalmic Books; Spectacles & Other Vision Aids, 1996. Honours: Lion of the Year; Beta Mu, Biological; First Service Award, 1985, Honour Award, 1990, American Academy Ophthalmology. Memberships: Fellow: American College of Surgeons; International College of Surgeons; Royal Society Medicine, UK; French Ophthalmological Society; Member: American Academy Ophthalmology; History of Medicine Section, Philadelphia Medical Society; Louisiana-Mississippi O&O Society; Louisiana State Medical Society; Orleans Parish Medical Society; New Orleans Academy of Ophthalmology; Past President, Lions Club. Address: 1320 Valence Street, New Orleans, LA 70115 3934, USA.

**ROSENTHAL Mark J,** b. 15 December 1951, Los Angeles California. Professor. Education: Bachelor of Arts, Claremore Men's College, 1973; Doctor of Medicine, University o Pennsylvania, 1977. Appointments: Councilor, American Federation Clinical Research, 1983-86; Assistant Professor Gerontology Division, University of New Mexico School o Medicine, 1983-86; Assistant Professor, Geriatric Division University of California, 1986-89; Staff Physician, Sepulveda Veterans Affairs Medical Center; Associate Professor Department of Medicine, University of California, 1990- Publication: 6 Geriatrics Bibliographies; 82 Research Publications; 52 Published Abstracts; Honours: Outstanding People of the 20th Century, International Biographical Centre Dictionary of International Biography, IBC; Invitation to Presidential Inauguration, President Clinton, Washington Nationally Accepted Modality for Treatment of Decubitus Ulcers by VA Rehabilitation Engineering Service; Hall of Fame, US Grant High School; First Prize, Kaleidoscope Disability Fiction Award; First Award, National Institute of Health; New Investigator Award; Associate Investigator Award; Magna cum laude, Claremont Men's College; National Merit Review Committee. Memberships: Gerontological Society of America American Geriatrics Society; American Federation for Clinica Research; Endocrine Society; American Association fol Advancement of Science; American Diabetes Association. Address: 16161 Nordhoff St, Suite 293, North Hills, CA 91343. USA.

**ROSMUS Anna Elisabeth,** b. 29 March 1960, Passau, Germany. Author. 2 daughters. Education: Master's Degree in Sociology, German Literature and Fine Arts. Publications: Daten innerer und aeusserer Freiheit aus Geschichte und Politik Europas (Dates of Internal and External Freedoms Taken From the History and Politics of Europe), 1980; Widerstand und Verfolgung am Beispiel Passau 1933 - 1945 (Resistance and Persecution from 1933-1945 in Passau), 1983; Lieben Sie Deutschland - Leiden an Passau (Do You Love Germany - Sufferings in Passau), 1985; Abrahams Gold, 1987, published as a movie, 1991; Robert Klein - Ein Jude schaut zurueck (Robert Klein - A German Jew Looks Back), 1990; Wintergruen - Verdraengte Morde (Wintergreen - Suppressed Murders), 1993; Was ich denke (What I Think), 1995; Pocking - Ende und Anfang. Juedische Zeitzeugen ueber Befreier und Defreite (Pocking - End and Renewal. Jewish Witnesses about Liberators and Civilians), 1995; Out of Passau, 1999; Numerous publications as a Freelance Writer for different German magazines and international newspapers such as La Penseé et les Hommes, Holocaust and Genocide Studies, The New York Times, The European and Aufbau. Honours: Best German Writer, European Essay Competition, 1980; 3rd Place, The Prewar-years in My Hometown, Hamburg, Germany, 1981; The Death-Mask of Kurt Tucholsky for Civic Courage and Political Engagement, Hindas, Sweden, 1987; The Nasty Girl, movie, released and nominated for an Oscar, 1991; The Holocaust-Memorial-Award, Holocaust Survivors and Friends in Pursuit of Justice, Albany, New York, USA, 1992; Elected Member, International PEN Club, 1993-; Sarnat Award, 1994; Tree Dedication, Temple Israel, Albany, New York, 1994; Conscience-in-Media-Award, 1994; Myrtle Wreath Award, Washington DC, USA, 1995; Elected Honorary Member, 65th Infantry Division Association, 1995-; Heinz-Galinski-Award, 1996; Immigrant Achievement Award, Washington DC, 1998. Address: 11200 Lockwood Drive #805, Silver Spring, MD 20901, USA.

**ROSS E Wayne,** b. 26 April 1956, Greenville, SC, USA. Professor. m. Sandra Mathison. Education: MAT, AB, University North Carolina at Chapel Hill, USA; PhD, Ohio State University, USA. Appointments: Assistant Professor, State

University of New York at Albany, 1986-92; Associate Professor, State University of New York at Binghamton, 1992-. Publications: Teacher Personal Theorizing, 1992; Reflective Practice in Social Studies, 1994; The Social Studies Curriculum, 1997. Memberships: American Education Research Association; John Dewey Society; National Council for Social Studies; American Federation of Teachers. Address: SUNY School Education and Human Development, PO Box 6000, Binghamton, NY 13902-6000, USA.

**ROSSIKHIN Vladimir V,** b. 17 October 1938, Dnepropetrovsk, Ukraine. Physical Theorist. m. Galina A Vlasova, 1 daughter. Education: Diploma, Physics, 1960, Candidate of Science, 1968, Dnepropetrovsk University; DSc, Saratov University, 1986; Professor, 1987. Career: Docent, 1963-68, 1968-78, Dnepropetrovsk Institute of Railway Transport Engineering; Head, Physics Department, Dnepropetrovsk Technical University, 1979-. Publications: Several articles in professional journals. Honours: Medal, Veteran of Labour, USSR, 1988; Grant, ISF, Washington, 1993; Grant, DAAD, Bohn, 1996. Memberships: WATOC; New York Academy of Sciences. Address: 6 Acad Lazaryan Street, App 3, 320010 Dnepropetrovsk 10, Ukraine.

**ROTH Walter Emil von,** b. 10 August 1940, Lauchringen, Germany. Professor. m. Maria d I A Rechy, 3 sons. Education: Engineer, 1963; Diploma in Engineering, 1968; Diploma in Mechanics, 1970; Doctor of Engineering, 1978. Appointments: Senior Researcher, Federal Research Institute, Hamburg, 1970; Professor of Wood Technology, University of Monterrey, Mexico, 1989; Professor of Wood Construction, University of Applied Science, Neubrandenburg, Germany, 1994-. Publications: Various publications in international scientific journals. Honour: Gruen and Bilfinger Prize, 1968. Membership: German Foundation for Higher Education. Address: University of Applied Science, Brodaer Strasse 2, D-17033 Neubrandenburg, Germany.

**ROY P N,** b. 15 January 1940, Varanasi, UP, India. Doctor. m. S Roy (dec), 1 son, 1 daughter. Education: MS (Ophth), 1979; FICS, 1982; FICO, 1988. Appointments: Assistant Professor in Ophthalmology, 1974; Associate Professor in Ophthalmology, 1977; Professor of Ophthalmology, 1983; in A N M Medical College, Gaya Bihar, India. Publications: 8 papers including: Experimental penetrating injuries, 14th UPSO Conference at Jhansi, awarded Gold Medal for Best Paper; Uveilic and Filariasis, 11th UPSO conference at Mussorie, India, 2nd Best Prize Award for paper. Memberships: Life member: AIOS; UPOS; BOS. Address: 430 Anugrah Puri Colony, Gaya Bihar, India.

**ROY Santi,** b. 17 April 1945, India. State Government Servant. m. Purabi Roy, 1 son, 2 daughters. Education: Calcutta University. Appointment: Editor, Anami. Publications include: Poetry books: Mousumi, 1967; Smriti Santwana, Avista Sanlap, 1974. Memberships: Chairman, Swapnaneer Sahitya Basar, Kotulpur, Bankura District. Address: Villa & PO Kotalpur, District Bankura, West Bengal, India.

**ROZENBLAT Anatoly,** b. 25 August 1938, Russia. Scientist. 1 son, 1 daughter. Education: Bachelor of Science, Mechanical Engineering, 1967; Bachelor of Science, Computer Science, 1998. Appointments: Mechanical and Manufacturing Engineer; Independent Scientist, Inventor. Publications: 41 scientific papers; 24 innovations; 2 books. Memberships: ASME; SME; SNAME. Address: 1355 W Estes M1, Chicago, IL 60626, USA.

**ROZGONYI Ferenc,** b. 21 September 1938, Tarcal, Hungary. Medical Microbiologist. m. Katalin Szitha, 2

daughters. Education: Medical University of Debrecen, Hungary, 1957-63; Graduated Summa cum laude, 1963; Diploma, Specialist for Medical Laboratory Investigations, 1967; PhD, 1978; Diploma, Specialist for Medical Microbiology, 1979; Doctor of Medical Science, 1988. Appointments: Dr Med Habil, Debrecen, 1995; Professor, Debrecen, 1996; Director, Chairman, Institute of Microbiology, Semmelweis University Medicine, Budapest, 1996-. Publications: 106 Articles. Honours: 460 Citations; Doubly Awarded, Hungarian Academy of Sciences; Honoured by Ministry of Public Health, Minister of Welfare. Memberships: Active member in different bodies, committees, of numerous Hungarian and foreign or International scientific associations. Address: Inst Microbiology, Semmelweis Univ of Medicine, Nagyvarad ter 4, H-1089 Budapest, Hungary.

**ROZSIVAL Pavel,** b. 27 September 1950, Cheb. Physician, Ophthalmologist. m. Iva, 1 son, 1 daughter. Education: MD, Charles University, 1974; PhD, 1979; Fully Board Certificate, 1981; Associated Professor, 1991; Professor of Ophthalmology, 1996. Appointments: Postgraduate Student, 1974-79; Scientific Assistant, 1980-84; Head of District Department of Ophthalmology, 1984-86; Head of Regional Department of Ophthalmology, 1986-93; Head of Regional Department of Ophthalmology, School of Medicine, Charles University, 1993-. Publications: 185 Papers; 489 Lecturers. Honours: Medal on Occasion of 650 Anniversary, Charles University, 1998. Memberships: American Academy of Ophthalmology; American Society of Cataract and Refractive Surgery; Council of Cataract and Refractive Surgery; International Society of Refractive Surgery; European Society of Cataract and Refractive Surgery; European Glaucoma Society. Address: Kudrnova 756/34, 500 02 Hradec Kralove, Czech Republic.

**RUBACK Randall Scott,** b. 30 April 1958, Omaha, Nebraska, USA. Musician; Educator. Education: BM, Trombone Performance, Mannes College of Music, New York, 1981; Certificate of Performance, 1991, MM, Trombone Performance, 1992, Northwestern University. Career: Trombonist: Haifa Symphony Orchestra, Israel, 1984-86; Spoleto Orchestra, USA & Italy, 1987; Orchestra of Ancient Music, Rome, Italy, 1988; Municipal Opera Theatre "Giuseppe Verdi", Trieste, Italy, 1987-88; Symphonic Orchestra of the RAI of Rome, Italy, 1988-89; Milwaukee Ballet Orchestra, 1990-94; Skylight Opera, Milwaukee, 1990-. Assistant Music Director and Conductor: Milwaukee Repertory Theatre, 1994. Educator: Mannes College of Music, New York City, 1980-81; Haifa Youth Orchestra, Israel, 1984-86; National College of Education, Evanston, Illinois, 1987; Milwaukee Public Schools, 1990-91; Concordia University, Mequon, 1991-92; Milwaukee Institute of Art and Design, 1992; Alverno College, Milwaukee, 1993; University of Wisconsin, Parkside, 1990-94; Wisconsin Conservatory of Music, Milwaukee, 1990-95; Milwaukee Youth Symphony Orchestra, 1990-. Publications: Tips On Playing In An Orchestra, 1997; From Artisan to Artist, 1998. Honours: Finalist, Prize Winner, Israel Trombone Association and Band Federation Composition Contest, 1985. Address: 1609 North Prospect Avenue, Apt #904, Milwaukee, WI 53202, USA.

**RUBEL Marek J,** b.19 April 1953, Warsaw, Poland. m. Elzbieta Przyborowska, 2 sons 1 daughter. Education: Department of Chemistry, Warsaw, Poland, 1972-1977; MSc, Chemistry, 1977; Department of Materials, Science and Engineering, University of Warsaw, Poland, 1977-1981; PhD 1983; Docent in Plasma Physics, Royal Institute of Technology, Stockholm, Sweden, 1994. Appointments: Researcher, Warsaw, Poland, 1992-1994; Assistant Professor, 1985-1990; Associate Professor, Royal Institute of Technology, Stockholm,

Sweden, 1997. Publications: In the field of plasma-surface interactions in controlled fusion devices. Membership: European Microbeam Anelysis Society. Address: Royal Institute of Technology, Alfvén Laboratory, Teknikningen 31, SE-100 44 Stockholm, Sweden.

**RUBIN Robert E,** b. 29 August 1938, New York, USA. Secretary of the US Treasury. m. Judith Leah Oxenberg, 2 sons. Education: AB, Harvard University, 1960; Post Graduate Studies, London School of Economics, 1960-61; LLB, Yale University, 1964; DHL, Yeshiva University, 1996. Appointments: Attorney, Cleary, Gottlieb, Steen and Hamilton, New York City, 1964-66; Goldman, Sachs and Co, New York City, 26 Years; Assistant to the President for Economic Policy, White House, 1993-95; Secretary of the US Treasury, 1995-. Honours: Columbia Business Schools Distinguished Leadership in Government Award; Euromoney Magazine's Award of Finance Minister of the Year; Citizen's Budget Commission Award for High Civic Service; Foreign Policy Association Medal; Washington DC Greater Boys/Girls Clubs' Chairman's Award; Intrepid Sea Air Space Museum Award; American Institute for Public Service's Jefferson Award; Yale University's Award of Merit; Paul Tsongas Award; United Nations Association's Global Leadership Award; New York Legal Aid Society, Servant of Justice Award. Memberships: Phi Beta kappa; Harvard Club; Century Country Club. Address: Department of the Treasury Office of the Sec, 1500 Pennsylvania Avenue NW, Washington, DC 20220-0001, USA.

**RUCHIN Cecile,** b. 30 September 1936, Bay Shore, New York, USA. Communications Executive. m. John Quinn, 2 sons, 1 daughter. Education: Seton Hall Academy, 1954; New School, Social Research, 1960; New York University, 1963. Appointments: Production Assistant, ABC TV, Hollywood, California, 1959-60; Account Executive, Dirusso and Falborn Advertising, 1962-64; Assistant Producer, BBDO-TV, 1964-66; President, Complete News Paper Group, 1966-69; Founder, President, Holographic Design, Development Corporation, 1969-70; President, International Holographics Corporation, 1970-71; Holographic Communications Corporation, 1971-; Developed first commercial holographic products, produced all of Salvador Dali's art pieces, 1970-71. Publications: Holographic Special Effects for Theatre, 1988; Holography and Lasers for Human Energy Studies; Mental Energisms; Global Impact; Holography - Energy Field Physics and Metaphysics. Memberships: American Managment Association; Women in Film, Laser Institute; American International Society for Optical Engineering; US Psychotronics Association; International Platform Association; Union of Concerned Scientists; Film and VideoArts; Roman Catholic Avocations. Address: Holographic Communications Corp, 250 W 77th St, New York, NY 10024-4810, USA.

**RUDIK Stanislav Kostyantynovych,** b. 25 May 1940. Veterinary Anatomist. Education: Graduate, 1965, Faculty of Veterinary Medicine, National Agrarian University; Dr Sc Veterinary; PhD; DVM. Appointments: Professor, Chief of Dept of Anatomy, Ukraine National Agrarian University; Founder, Dept Anatomy, National School of Veterinary Medicine of Algeria University, 1972-75. Publications: 280 pub lications including 11 books and monographs in the field of investigation of the vertebrates head alimentary canal and the history of veterinary medicine; Includes: The Anatomy of Animals; The History of Veterinary Medicine in Ukraine. Honours: Gold Medal, Ankara University, Turkey, 1992; Honoured National Education Worker of Ukraine, 1993, President of Ukraine; Honourary Diploma of the Prime Minister of the Ukraine, 1998. Memberships: World Association of Veterinary Anatomists; European Association of Establishments for Veterinary Education, World Association for the History of Vetinary Medicine; Full member, Ukrainian Higher Education Academy of Sciences, Agrarian Sciences Section. Address: Faculty of Veterinary Medicine, National Agrarian University, Potehina 16, Kyev 252041, Ukraine.

**RUEDENBERG Klaus,** b. 25 August 1920, Bielefeld, Germany. Distinguished Professor Emeritus; Associate Senior Chemist. m. Veronika Kutter Ruedenberg, 1 son, 3 daughters. Education: Abitur, Gymnasium Bielefeld, 1938, English diploma of Cambridge University, 1939, MS Chemistry and Mathematics, 1944, University of Fribourg, Switzerland; PhD Theoretical Physics, 1950, University of Zurich; Graduate Fellow in Physics, University of Chicago, 1948-50. Appointments: Research Associate in Chemical Physics, University of Chicago, 1951-55; Assistant and Associate Professor of Chemistry and Physics, 1955-62, Professor of Chemistry and Physics, 1964-78, Distinguished Professor in Science and Humanities, 1978-91, Distinguished Professor Emeritus and Associate Senior Chemist, Ames Laboratory, US Dept of Energy, 1991-, Iowa State University; Professor of Chemistry, Johns Hopkins University, 1962-64. Publications: About 170 theoretical chemistry publications in professional journals; About 200 lectures at scientific conferences and departmental seminars; Associate or Advisory Editor to 5 prestigious journals; Editor-in-Chief, 1985-96, Honorary Editor, 1996-, Theoretical Chemistry Accounts. Honours: 5 fellowships, 1962-82; Elected to International Academy of Quantum Molecular Sciences, 1973; 3 Honorary PhDs in Switzerland and Germany; Midwest Award of American Chemical Society, 1982; Member of a committee of five to evaluate theoretical chemistry in Sweden for Swedish National Science Council, 1988. Address: Chemistry Dept, Iowa State University, Ames, IA 50011, USA.

**RUELAS-GOMEZ Roberto,** b. 2 January 1961, Guanajuato, Mexico. Electrical Engineer. m. Alicia Zermeno, 1 son, 2 daughters. Education: BSEE 1st in Class, 1983, Universidad A De San Cuis Potosi; MEng, 1986, McGill University. Appointments: Chief Maintenance Engineer, Polimenos y Derivados, 1986-87; Partner and Owner, Ruelsa & Electrinet, 1993, 1998. Publication: Grounding Systems, 1997. Memberships: New York Academy of Sciences; International Association of Electrical Inspectors; Counsellor, IEEE Student Branch Universidad del Bajio; Vice-Chairman, Board of Electrical Engineers, 1998-2000. Address: Av Americas 819, 37370 Leon, Mexico.

**RUHS Sven Hedin,** b. 4 March 1961, Sontheim, Germany. Executive Creative Officer; Partner. Education: Diploma, University of Stuttgart, 1987. Appointments: Copywriter, 1985-88; Creative Grouphead, 1988-90; Creative Director, 1990-94; Executive Creative Officer, Partner, Glanzer & Partner, Stuttgart, 1994-. Honours: Several creative awards. Address: Glanzer & Partner, Paracelsusstr 26, Stuttgart 70599, Germany.

**RAKSENAS Rimvydas,** b. 26 April 1941, Kaunas, Lithuania. Engineer. m. Nijole, 2 sons, 1 daughter. Education: Engineer-mechanic Diploma, 1965, Moscow Technical University. Appointments: Foreman, 1965, Senior Engineer, 1969, Deputy Shop Chief, 1969, Deputy Director, 1975, Director, 1983, Deputy Director General, 1994, Director General, 1996; President, National Electroenergetics Association, 1998. Honour: Honoured Engineer of Lithuania, 1986. Membership: National Electroenergetics Association. Address: Zuvedru 45B, LT 2016, Vilnius, Lithuania.

**RUMANE Abdul Razzak,** b. 8 June 1948, Chandve, India. Electrical Engineer. m. Noorjehan, 1 s, 1 d. Education: BE, Electrical Engineering, Marathwada University, 1972; Diploma n Modern Management, 1981; Diploma in International Trade, 982. Appointments: Trainee Production Engineer, 1972-73; Assistant Purchase Officer, 1973-76; Assistant Electrical Engineer, 1976-79; Staff Engineer, 1979-1980; Purchase Officer, 1980-81; Officer/Engineer, 1981-83; Electrical Engineer, 1983-84; Electrical Engineer, 1984-86; Electrical Engineer, Jassim Shaban and Sons Co, Kuwait, 1986-1990; Senior Electrical Engineer, Pan Arab Consulting Engineers, Kuwait, 1991-99; Senior Electrical Engineer, Dar Al Handasah, Kuwait, 1999-. Memberships: Kuwait Society of Engineers; Fellow of Institution of Engineers; Senior Member, IEEE; Affiliate Member of American Society of Civil Engineers; MEW Supervising Licence). Address: P O Box 5020, Salmiya 22061, Kuwait.

**RUNKLE James Reade,** b. 3 July 1951, Grove City, USA. Professor. m. Janet Kreps Runkle, 3 sons, 1 daughter. Education: BA, Ohio Wesleyan University, 1973; PhD, Cornell University, 1979. Appointment: Professor, Wright State University, Biological Sciences Faculty, 1979-. Publications: Many articles in professional journals, several book chapters. Memberships: AAAS; AIBS; ESA; BES; OAS; IAUS. Address: Wright State University, Department of Biological Sciences, Dayton, OH 45435, USA.

**RUPKUS Stasys,** b. 14 October 1949, Joniskis, Lithuania. Engineer. 1 daughter. Education: PhD, Kaunas University of Technology, 1979; DSc, 1990. Appointments: Assistant, 1973-80; Senior Assistant, 1980-81; Associate Professor, 1981-91; Professor, 1991-; Head of Department of Electronics, 1994-. Publications: 2 Monographs, 1991, 1996; 130 Articles. Honours: Lithuanian National Science Award, 1995. Memberships: IEEE; UFFC Soceity. Address: S Zukausko 16-16, LT 3043, Kaunas, Lithuania.

**RUSK Brian Dwight,** b. 2 May 1955, Buffalo, New York, USA. Public Relations Officer. m. Maureen M Rusk, 1 son, 1 daughter. Education: BA cum laude, State University of New York at Buffalo, 1974. Appointments: Public Relations Director, Daemen College, 1981-93; Erie County Legislator, 1993-95; Assistant Public Relations Officer, New York State Thruway, 1996-. Honours: Diploma, Polish Veterans of World War II, 1995; President's Award, Amherst Chamber of Commerce, 1979. Memberships: Executive Committee, Erie County Republican Committee, Board Member; International Institute, MDA, Kenmore Mercy Hospital, Polish American Congress. Address: 340 Wellingwood Drive, East Amherst, NY 14051-1751, USA.

**RUSSEV Vladimir,** b. 19 April 1959, Bulgarovo, Bulgaria. Executive President World Security Organisation. 2 sons, 1 daughter. Education: Pastor Superior, Orthodox Academy of Theology, Sofia, 1985; Paralegal, 1993, School of Paralegal Studies, Atlanta; Expert, 1994, International Management of Security, England. Appointments: Military Instructor, Ministry of Defense, Kurdjali, Bulgaria, 1977-81; Pastor Superior, St Pr Ilia Monastery, 1988-89; President, International Security Agency Valterkatany, Veliko Tarnovo, Bulgaria, 1990-93; Anglo-Bulgarian World Elite Security, World Security Trust, 1992-95; Executive President, World Security Organisation, Veliko Tarnovo, 1995-. Publications: Manual, Psychological Portrait of the Terrorist, 1985; Author of World Programmes. Honours: Order of Merit, Columbia, 1996, Spain, 1996; Honorary Sign, Ministry of Interior, Kazakhstan, 1994, Ministry of Interior, Russia, 1995. Memberships: Bundesverband Deutscher Detektive Association; Fachverband

Schweizerischer Privat-Detective Association; International Association Chiefs of Police, US. Address: World Security Organisation, Centre-2 Sq, Block 1 Fl 5, 5000 Veliko Tarnovo, Bulgaria.

**RUTBERG Philip Grigorievich,** b. 22 September 1931, Vinnitca. Scientist. m. Klara Leonidovna Emelianova, 1 son. Education: State University, St Petersburg, 1954; Polytechnical Institute, 1961; Doctor (Professor), 1981; Member Correspondent, Russian Academy of Sciences, 1990. Appointments: Teacher, college, 1954-60; Junior Researcher, Physical Technical Institute of Ioffe, 1961-63; Senior Researcher, Chief of Laboratory Vice Director, Institute of Electromechanics, RAS, 1963-91; Director, Institute of Problems of Electrophysics of RAS, 1992. Publications: 4 books; 243 papers. Honour: State Reward of USSR, 1982. Memberships: AIAA; IEEE; International Engineering Academy; Russian Academy of Sciences. Address: Institute for Problems of Electrophysics, Russian Academy of Sciences, 18 Dvortsvaaya Naberezhnaya, St Petersburg 191065, Russia.

**RUTKEVICH Igor,** b. 6 April 1944, Semipalatinsk. 1 daughter. Education: MS, Moscow University, 1966; PhD, Moscow University, 1971; DSc, USSR Academy of Sciences, 1988. Appointments: Deputy Head, Theoretical Physics Department, Institute for High Temperature, USSR Academy of Science, 1986-92; Research Professor, Department of Mechanical Engineering, Ben-Gurion University, Beer Sheva, Israel, 1993-. Publications: Books: Electric Breakdown Waves in a Bounded Plasma, 1989; Ionization Waves in Electrical Breakdown of Gases, 1994; Over 100 articles in scientific journals. Memberships: New York Academy of Sciences; American Physical Society. Address: Mechanical Engineering Department, Ben Gurion University, Beer Sheva 84105, Israel.

**RUVINSKII Mark,** b. 5 August 1938, Kiev, Ukraine. Physicist. m. Clara Pshenichniksova, 2 sons. Education: Honorary Diploma, Lviv, 1960; PhD, Odessa University, 1967; DSc, Institute Physics Academy Sciences, Ukraine, Kiev, 1994. Appointments: Assistant Lecturer, Drogobych Pedagogical Institute, Ukraine, 1967-71; Postgraduate, Lviv and Odessa Universities, Ukraine, 1964-67; Associate Professor, 1967-92; Professor, Precarpathian University, Jvano-Frankivsk, 1992-. Publications: 3 books; Course of Quantum Physics, 1992; 127 articles and studies in Russian, English and Ukrainian. Memberships: Ukrainian Physics Society, Coordinated Council, 1990-95, Co-Chairman, 1990-; American Physics Society, 1992-. Address: Precarpathian University, 57 Shevchenko Str, Ivano-Frankivsk 28400, Ukraine.

**RUZICKA Marek Captain,** b. 29 August 1960, Sobeslav, Czech Republic. Naturalist. m. Magdalena Zhofova, 2 sons. Education: MSc Environmental Engineering, 1984; Postgrad course, Applied Maths, 1987, Enzyme Engineering, 1988; PhD Chemical Engineering, 1990; Partial study, Physics, Charles University, Prague, 1990-94. Appointments: Scientist, Institute Chemical Process Fundamentals, Academy of Sciences of Czech Republic, 1990-; Hon Research Fellow, University Birmingham, England, 1994-95. Publications: Contributor to professional journals and to books Fractal Reviews in Natural and Applied Sciences, 1995, Fractals and Chaos in Chemical Engineering, 1997. Honour: Postdoct Fellowship, Royal Society London, 1994-95. Membership: Union Czech Mathematicians and Physicists, 1988-. Address: Institute of Chemical Process Fundamentals, Rozvojova 135, 16502 Prague, Czech Republic.

**RYAL Dick,** b. 21 June 1925, Corning, New York. Scriptwriter; Actor. Education: Student, Professional Children's School, NYC, 1942-43. Appointments: Host, Scriptwriter, The

Golden Key Station, KTTV-TV, Hollywood, late 1950's; Film, Radio, TV Actor NYC and Hollywood, California, 1960-83; Writer, Actor, Chevron Broadcast, San Francisco, 1969-72; Featured actor films, TV series Studiohouse, Hollywood, 1971-86; Voice over actor, Hanna-Barbera Animated Films, Hollywood, 1979. Creative Works: Scriptwriter, (documentary) Our Nation's Heritage, 1969-72; (drama) The Calumet, 1984; (comedy) Why Me?, 1985. Honours: Peabody Medal, 1975; Writers Guild America Award, 1984; Ohio State Award for network documentaries, 1972-74; Spl accolade award, 1979. Memberships: American Federation of Television and Radio Artists; Writers Guild of America, acad liaison com, tellers com; SAG; Pacific Pioneer Broadcasters. Address: PO Box 82, Beverly Hills, CA 90213-0082, USA.

**RYAN Frank James,** b. 12 March 1954, Bronxville, NY, USA. Executive. m. Jane Joan DeNunzio, 1 daughter. Education: Liberal Arts, Social Behaviour, Physical Education, Concordia, Bronxville, 1973-75. Appointments: Account Executive, Trans Western Regional Operations, 1981-98. Publications: Works Appearing in Many National, International Literary Anthologies; Over 60 Editorial Publishings, various topics; Author: The Verve of Passion and Peril. Honours: 1st Place, Int. Society Authors & Artists 'International Literary Competition', 1997; 2nd Place, 'North American Poetry Competition', 1998; Ten time Editors Choice Award Winner, International Library of Poetry, 1996-1999; International Poetry Hall of Fame; The Frank James Ryan Jr Internet Poetry Exhibit; International Poet of Merit. Memberships: International Society of Poets; Marquis Who's Who in the World, 17th Edition; Who's Who in the East, 1999-2000; National Library of Poetry; International Society of Authors and Artists; Poets Guild; Crative Arts and Science Enterprises; Poetry Guild. Address: 192 Midland Ave, Bronxville, NY 10707, USA.

**RYMSZA Janusz,** b. 4 January 1958, Bastuny, Belorussia. Bridge Research Engineer. m. Grazyna, 1 son, 2 daughters. Education: MSc, Warsaw Technical University; PhD, Poznan Technical University. Appointment: Chief, Bridge Division, Road and Bridge Research Institute, Warsaw, 1990-. Publications: Over 50, a few patents. Memberships: Secretary, Department of Polish Society of Bridge Engineers, 1992-; Secretary, Bridge Normalisation Sub-Committee, Polish Normalisation Committee, 1994-. Address: ul Krasnobrodzka 6/154, 03 216 Warsaw, Poland.

# S

**SAADY Marlow,** b. 8 August 1953, Quuens, NY, USA. Radio and TV Engineer. m. Ricki. Education: TV and Radio, Brooklyn College, 1971, uncompleted. Appointments: Engineering Aide, ABC-TV, 1978-79; UN Radio/TV, 1979-. Honour: SBE, Certified Broadcast Technologist. Membership: Senior member, Society of Broadcast Engineers. Address: 1305 75th Ave Apt 21, Bayside, NY 11364-3318, USA.

**SABININ Juri,** b. 25 November 1913, St Petersburg. Electric Engineer, Professor. m. Sabinina, 1 son, 1 daughter. Education: Doctor of Techincal Sciences, 1965; Professor, 966. Appointments: Professor, Faculty of Electrical Engineering, Precise Electromechanical Systems. Publications: 4 Books; Many other published works. Honours: Honoured Representative of Sciences and Technic of Russian Federation. Memberships: International Power Academy; Electromechanical Systems at the Technical Society of Power. Address: St Mochovaja 31-61, St Petersburg 191028, Russia.

**SABRI Osama,** b. 14 June 1963, Berlin. Physician, Researcher. Education: Freie Universitat Berlin, 1988; MD, 989; Assistant Medical Director, 1998; PhD, 1998. Appointments: Intern Fellowship, Berlin, 1987; Researcher, Institute Anatomy University Bonn, 1989-91; Resident University Aachen, 1991-96; Senior Physician Nuclear Medicine, 1997-98; Assistant Medical Director Nuclear Medicine, RWTH, 1998. Publications: Contributor to Professional Journals; Brain SPECT in Psychiatry, 1995; SPECT in Clinical and Psychiatry, 1998. Honours: Ludo Van Bogaert Award, 1995; Maliuckrodt Award, Brahms Award, German Association of Nuclear Medicine, 1999. Memberships: German Association of Nuclear Medicine, 1994; American Association for the Advancement of Science, 1997. Address: Hans-Boeckler Allee 155, App 126, D 52074 Aachen, Germany.

**SACHAR Rajindar,** b. 22 December 1923, Lahore. Retired High Court Chief Justice. m. Raj Nayar, 1 son, 1 daughter. Education: BA Hons, LLB. Appointments: Judge, Delhi High Court, 1970; Chief Justice, 1985; UN Sub Commission on Prevention of Discrimination and Protection of Minority, 1990; UN Special Reporter. Publications: Right to Adequate Housing, 1996, presented at Habitat II, Istanbul, Turkey. Membership: President, Peoples' Union for Civil Liberties, India. Address: A 19 New Friends Colony, New Delhi 110 065, India.

**SACHS Horst,** b. 27 March 1927, Magdeburg, Germany. Mathematician. m. Barbara. Education: Diploma, 1953; Dr rer nat, 1958; Dr rer nat habil, 1963. Appointments: Science Assistant, University Halle, 1953-63; Professor of Mathematics, Technical University of Ilmenau, Ilmenau, Germany, 1963-92; Retired, 1992-. Publications: Spectra of Graphs; Science Articles, Mainly Graph Theory. Memberships: Institute of Combinatorics and Its Applications. Address: Technical University of Ilmenau, Institute of Mathematics, PF 100 565, Ilmenau D 98684, Germany.

**SADCHIKOV Anatoly,** b. 25 November 1946, Vladivostok, Russia. Scientist. m. Galina V Kalinaeva, 1 son. Education: Oil College, 1967; MS, Moscow State University, 1975; PhD, Moscow State University, 1980; Doctor of Science, 1997. Appointments: Post Graduate Student, Biological Faculty, Moscow Lomonosov State University, 1975-78; Manager, Ministry of Higher Education, 1977-87; Assistant Professor, Associate Professor, Professor, Moscow Lomonosov State

University, 1987-. Publications: Over 120 Scientific Publications, 2 books. Address: Intern Biotechnol Centre, Moscow State University, 119899 Moscow Vorobjevy Gory, Russia.

**SADEK Hussein,** b. 15 January 1917, Cairo, Egypt. Professor. m. Soad Khaled, 2 sons, 1 daughter. Education: BSc, 1st class honours, Cairo University, 1938, MSc, 1941; PhD, Princeton University, USA, 1948. Appointments: Demonstrator, Cairo University, 1938; Lecturer, 1943, Assistant Professor, 1951, Professor of Physical Chemistry, 1956, Dean, Faculty of Science, 1970, Vice President, 1971, Alexandria University. Publications: 135 papers in professional journals. Honours: Alexandria University Award, 1959; National Prize, 1962; First National Prize, 1995. Memberships: American Chemical Society; Faraday Society; Indian Chemical Society; Pakistan Chemical Society. Address: Department of Chemistry, Faculty of Sciences, Alexandria University, Alexandria, Egypt.

**SADOWSKI Tomasz Stanislaw,** b. 6 April 1954, Lublin, Poland. Mechanical Engineering Educator. m. Jolanta Smok, 1 daughter. Education: MSc, Technical University, Lublin, 1978; Dr Eng, Institute of Fundamental Technological Research, Polish Academy of Sciences, 1985. Appointments: Assistant, Faculty of Mechanical Engineering, Technical University of Lublin, 1978-81; Lecturer Assistant, 1981-85; Assistant Professor, 1985-. Publications: Mechanics of Materials; Computational Mechanics; Archives of Applied Mechanics. Honours: Awards of the Rector of Technical University of Lublin. Memberships: Polish Society of Theoretical and Applied Mechanics; Polish Society for Composite Materials; Solid Mechanics Section of the Mechanics Committee, Polish Academy of Science; GAMM. Address: Technical University of Lublin, Faculty of Mechanical Engineering, Nadbystrzycka Str 36, 20-618 Lublin, Poland.

**SAENGHIRUNVATTANA Sawang,** b. 25 January 1955. Professor. m. Rungsima, 2 sons, 1 daughter. Education: Doctor of Medicine, 1978; Certificate in Internal Medicine, 1983; Fellow, Pulmonary Medicine, 1984; Fellow, Critical Care Medicine, 1986; Master of Management, SASIN, 1995. Appointments: Clinical Instructor, Ramathibodi Hospital, 1984-85; Assistant Professor, 1986-88; Associate Professor, 1989-94; Professor, 1994-. Honours: Best Instructor Award; Researcher Award; Knight Grand Cross; Commander; Knight Commander; The Royal Cypher Medal; 2000 Outstanding Scientists. Memberships: Student Council, School of Management; National Research Institute. Address: 1121 Praholyothin Road, 10400 Bangkok, Thailand.

**SAENZ Gilbert,** b. 17 October 1941, Detroit, Michigan, USA. Computer Specialist. Education: BA, English Literature, Wayne State University, Detroit, Michigan, 1968; Postdegree credits, Wayne State University, 2 years. Appointments: US Diplomatic Courier, Department of State, Washington DC, 1969-70; Computer Specialist, Detroit IRS Computing Center, Detroit, Michigan, 1974-. Honours: EEO Award, 1989; Detroit IRS Computing Center, Boy's Vocal Award, 1959. Memberships: Latino Poets Association, Detroit, Michigan; MDDA, Self-help support group, Detroit, Michigan; US Diplomatic Courier Association, 1970-. Address: 19211 Wall Street, Melvindale, MI 48122 1876, USA.

**SAFAR Zeinab Saleh,** b. 18 October 1948. 1 son, 1 daughter. Education: PhD, Mechanical Engineering, University of Pittsburgh, 1973. Appointment: Professor, Mechanical Engineering, Cairo University, 1984-; Member, Consultative Council, 1995-. Publications: Over 40 articles in professional journals. Membership: ASME. Address: Apt 51, 20 El Mansour Mohamed Street, Zamalek, Cairo, Egypt.

**SAFRONOV Michael Fedotovitch,** b. 16 March 1942, Yakutsk, Russia. Engineer; Metallurgist. m. Natalya Vishnya, 1 son, 3 daughters. Education: Diploma, 1966; Candidate of Technical Sciences, 1989. Appointments: Design Engineer, Foreman, Irkutsk Engineering Works, 1966; Agglomeration Supervisor, Magnitogorsk Iron and Steel Works, 1966-67; Design Engineer, Senior Design Engineer, Magitogorsk State Institute for Projects in Iron and Steel Industry, 1967-69; Senior Engineer, Head of Bureau, Deputy Head of Department, Magnitogorsk Iron and Steel Works, Capital Repairs Department, 1969-90; Head, Design Department, 1990-92, Chief Engineer Assistant, 1992-93, Magnitogorsk Iron and Steel Works; Director, Industrial Association, Metallurgreconstruktsyaremont, 1993-95; Associate Director, Trading House, Magnitogorsk Iron and Steel Works, 1995-96; Director, JSC, Complex of New Technologies, 1996-; Management Board Member, Magnitogorsk Iron and Steel Works, 1997. Publictions: 45 articles, 5 patents, 2 monographs. Honour: Prize Winner, Magnitogorsk Iron & Steel Works, 1982. Memberships: Quality Problems Academy. Address: Oktiabrskaiya str 17-12, Magnitogorsk 455023, Russia.

**SAGAR Ram,** b. 1 July 1952, Vill Baragaon, India. Scientist. m. Kiran Sagar, 4 daughters. Education: BSc, 1971, MSc, 1972, PhD, 1981, Gorakhpur University. Appointments: Research Fellow, 1973-74, Scientific Assistant, 1974-76, Scientific Officer, 1976-79, Director, 1996-, UP State Observatory, Naini Tal; Lecturer, Kumaon University, 1979-86; Reader, 1986-91, Associate Professor, 1991-96, IIA, Bangalore. Publications: 80 papers in refereed journals, 27 conference proceedings. Honours, Royal Society Commonwealth Bursary, Royal Society, London, 1983-84; Academic Consultant, Royal Observatory, England, 1984-85; Young Astronomers Award, Astronomical Society of India, 1984; Alexander von Humboldt Foundation Research Fellowship, 1989-90. Memberships include: Astronomical Society of India; International Astronomical Union. Address: UP State Observatory, Manora Peak, Naini Tal 263129, India.

**SAGGINO Aristide,** b. 3 September 1956, Napoli, Italy. Psychologist. m. Michelina Loré, 1 son. Education: Degree in Psychology, 1979, PhD Clinical Psychology, 1992, University of Rome La Sapienza. Appointments: Senior Clinical Psychologist, Italian National Health Service; Lecturer, Seconda Universita Di Napoli, Napoli, Italy; both current. Publications: Book: The Rorschach in the John E Exner's Comprehensive System, 1989; Book, The Myers-Briggs Type Indicator: Normative Data and Contribution to the Italian Standardisation of the Form F, 1993; 32 contributing articles to professional journals. Honour: NATO Senior Fellowship, 1994. Memberships: Society for the Exploration of Psychotherapy Integration, member board of directors, 1994-; New York Academy of Sciences; British Psychological Society; Italian Register of Professional Psychology. Address: Via Nazario Sauro 12, 80026 Casoria, Naples, Italy.

**SAHA Debashis,** b. 15 March 1965, India. Teacher. m. Sumita, 1 son. Education: BE, Jadavpur University, 1986; M Tech, IIT, Kharagpur, 1988; PhD, IIT, Kharagpur, 1996. Appointments: Lecturer, Computer Science and Engineering Department, Jadaupur University, 1990-96; Reader, Computer Science and Engineering Department, 1997-. Publications: More than 70 Papers, 2 Books, 1 Monograph. Honours: AICTE Career Award; Qualcomm Research Award; JIE Best Paper Award. Memberships: Senior Member, IEEE, USA; IEEE

Computer Society. Address: Jadavpur U, Dept Compute Sci/Engring, 700032 Calcutta, India.

**SAHANI Dharma Vir,** b. 15 March 1936, Kualalampore Malaysia. Educator. m. S D Sahani, 1 daughter. Education: MA Eco, 1962; M Com, 1964. Appointments: Director, Institute fo Economics and Social Sciences Research, Gondia, India Publications: 30 research papers in Indian and internationa journals; 8 prominent publications including: Fuelwood Famine in India, 1993; Lac Industry in India, 1994; Noise Pollution 1997; Air Pollution, 1998. Honours: Appointed PhD Guide or basis of research papers of high academic worth, Nagpur University; Appointed to Panel of Research Supervisors and Resource Persons, Centre for Advanced Research ir Commerce and Management, Nagpur; Invited to participate ir XV World Congress of Poets held in Almanty, Kazakhstan 1995; Participated in a number of poets' gatherings and also or All India Radio; Delivered a number of talks on All India Radio Recipient very many awards including: Award of Honour or research paper, Indian Shipping Industry: A Study, 1991 National Unity Award, 1994, for outstanding services achievements and contributions, All India National Unity Conference, New Delhi; Vikas Rattan Award, 1995; Indira Gandhi Solidarity Award, 1995; Bharat Vikas Award, 1996 Rashtriya Ekta Award, 1997; Winged Word Award, 1998 Michael Madhusudan Poet Award, 1998. Memberships: 27 including Life Fellow: Royal Geographical Society, London: United Writers' Association, Chennai; Frank Moraes Foundation, Chennai; Life Member: Indian Commerce Association; National Association of Geographers of India, New Delhi; Asian Environmental Council, Jaipur; Nagpur University Teachers' Association. Address: Nr Ramnagar School, Gondia 441601, India.

**SAHIN Sumer,** b. 9 June 1942, Kadirli, Turkey. Professor in Nuclear Energy. m. Ayse Oytun Hacieminoglu, 1 son, 1 daughter. Education: Dipl Ing Mech Eng, 1967; Dr Ing, 1970; Habilitation in Physics, 1973. Appointments: Professor, 1981-. Publications: 83 top journal articles; 65 international conference papers. Memberships: American Nuclear Society; Turkish Chamber of Mechanical Engineers. Address: Makina Bol, Teknik Egitim Fakultesi, Gazi University, Besevler, Ankara, Turkey.

**SAID Walid Abdulrahman,** b. 29 October 1947, Jenin, Jordan. Senior Financial Analyst. m. Fatima El-Qasem, 2 sons, 5 daughters. Education: Bachelor, Accounting, Arab University of Beirut, Lebanon, 1973; Bachelor, Business Administration, Arab University of Beirut, Lebanon, 1977; Certificate, Bookkeeping and Accounts, Stage I, 1984, Diploma, Bookkeeping and Accounts, 1985, Trans-World Tutorial College, England; Doctorate, Business and Management, Sussex College of Technology, England, 1988. Appointments: Accountant, The Public National Company for Mills and Fodders, Tripoli, Libya, 1977-80; Chief Accountant, Al Mimary Establishment, Amman, Jordan, 1981-82; Senior External Auditor, Saudi Accounting Bureau, Riyadh, Saudi Arabia, 1982-89; Senior Financial Analyst, Saudi Consolidated Electric Company, Central Region, Riyadh, Saudi Arabia, 1989-. Publication: Financial and Administrative Systems (By Laws and Procedures) for Companies, Establishments and Factories. Honours: Certificate, Association of Cost and Executive Accountants, 1986; Practicing Certificate, Association of Cost and Executive Accountants, England, 1989; Certificate, Institute of Internal Auditors, USA, 1990; Certificate, British Institute of Management, England, 1991. Memberships: Association of Cost and Executive Accountants, England; Association of Cost and Executive Accountants, England; Institute of Internal uditors, USA, 1990; British Institute of Management, England. Address: PO Box 42886, Riyadh 11551, Saudi Arabia.

**SAIFUL-ISLAM K M,** b. 29 July 1942, Jessore, Bangladesh. Educator. Information Scientist. Education: BA, Dacca College, 961; Diploma Library Science, University of Karachi, Pakistan, 963; MALS, University of Karachi, 1965; Certificate in French, University of Karachi, 1963; PhD, University of Dhaka, 1987. Appointments: Professor, LIS, DU, 1993-; Lecturer-Associate Professor, 1975-93; Lecturer, part time, DU, 1972-73; Librarian, CDDR, B, 1972-75; Lecturer, part time, University Karachi, 966-67; Incharge, Bengali Sec/Catal Librarian, Reference Librarian, University Karachi, 1965-71; Reference Librarian, Morning News, 1963-65. Publications: 3 books, 14 research works, over 50 research-oriented articles published in national nd international journals and periodicals. Memberships: Bangla Academy, Dhaka; Asiatic Society of Bangladesh. Address: Department of Library and Information Science, University of Dhaka, Dhaka 1000, Bangladesh.

**SAINT-JACQUES Bernard,** b. 26 Apr 1928, Montréal, Quebec, Canada. Professor. m. Education: BA, Classics, Philosophy, 1949, MA, Philosophy, 1954, Montreal University; MA, Japanese Culture and Religion, Sophia University, Tokyo, 962; MS, Linguistics, Georgetown University, Washington DC, 964; Doctorat de 3ème Cycle, Linguistics, Asian Studies, 966, Doctorat d'Etat-Doctorate ès Lettres et Sciences Humaines, 1975, University of Paris. Appointments: Instructor, Classics, Collège Jean de Brébeuf, Université de Montréal, 954-55; Instructor, French, Social Sciences, 1959-62, Assistant Professor, French, Linguistics, 1966-67, Sophia University, Tokyo, Japan; Assistant Professor, Linguistics, 967-69, Associate Professor, Linguistics, 1969-78, Acting Head of Department, 1969-72, 1978-80, Professor, Linguistics, 978-88, Graduate Adviser, Linguistics Department, 1984-88, Emeritus Professor, 1988-, University of British Columbia, Vancouver; Consultant, Inter Pacific Club, Vancouver, 1986-88; Professor, Linguistics, Intercultural Communication, 1988-, Director, Institute of Language and Culture, 1994-, Head, Intercultural Communication Graduate Programme, 1995-, Aichi Shukutoku University, Japan. Publications: Monographs and books including: Structural Analysis of Modern Japanese, 971; Aspects Sociolinguistiques du Bilinguisme Canadien, 976; Language and Ethnic Interaction, co-editor, 1979; Studies in Language and Culture, co-editor, 1995; Some 100 papers, articles, contributions to books and reviews. Memberships: Linguistic Society of America; Canadian Society for Asian Studies; Canadian Linguistic Association; Fellow, International Academy for Intercultural Research; Founding Member, British Columbia Society for Translators and Interpreters; Royal Society of Canada; SIETAR Japan and Chubu; New York Academy of Sciences; Others. Address: Aichi Shukutoku University, Katahira Nagakute, Aichi-gun, Aichi 480-1197, Japan.

**SAIYADAIN Mirza S,** b. 11 July 1942, Lucknow, India. Professor. m. Rosy Saiyadain, 1 son, 1 daughter. Education: BA, Aligarh Muslim University, India, 1959; MA, Psychology, University of Hawaii, 1965; PhD, Personnel Management and Social Psychology, University of Kansas, 1972. Appointments: Teaching Assistant, University of Kansas, Lawrence, 1969-72; Instructor, Training Program for Federal Employees, University of Kansas Extension Education; Assistant Professor, 1973-77, Associate Professor, 1977-80, Professor, 1980-93, Personnel and Industrial Relations Area, Indian Institute of Management, Ahmedabad, India; Visiting Faculty, Faculty of Business Administration, University of Lagos, Nigeria, 1977-79; Visiting Professor, Faculty of Management, McGill University, Canada, 1991-92; Professor, School of Management, Universiti Sains

Malaysia, 1992-. Publications include: Human Resources Management, 1988; Challenges in Adult Education, 1990; Managerial Training and Development in Malaysia, 1995; Human Resources Management in Forestry: Employees Concerns, 1997. Honour: Grantee, East-West Centre, Hawaii, 1963-65. Memberships include: Asian Academy of Management, Malaysia; Board, Macmillian India Ltd; Indian Society for Training and Development; Human Resources Development Network, India; Chairman, Programmes Committee, Ahmedabad Management Association, India; Advisor, National Institute of Personnel Management, India. Address: Universiti Sains Malaysia, School of Management, Penang 11800, Malaysia.

**SAJEDUR RAHMAN Sarker Mohammad,** b. 19 November 1943, Bangladesh. Journalist. m. Amina Khatun, 4 sons. Education: Diploma in Arts and Crafts, 1964; IA, 1972; Diploma in Secretarial Science, 1978. Appointments: Sub Editor, The Daily Awaz, Dhaka, Bangladesh, 1964-68; Literary Editor, Weekly Katha, Bangladesh, 1986-87; Literary Editor, Daily Icchamati, Bengali, 1997-; Photo Journalist; General Secretary, Bangladesh Sonskrity Parishad, Pabna, Bangladesh. Publications: About 300 Poems, sub editorials, articles, features, short stories. Honours: Poet Bonde Ali Literary Award; Pabna Bangladesh Honour with Kabbya Binod; Nandimi Literary Award, Ishwardi, Pabna, Bangaladesh. Memberships: Amnesty International; Bangladesh Society for the Enforcement of Human Rights; Bangladesh Journalist Association; Bangladesh Poet Club; Bangladesh Literary Association; Bangladesh Judge, Shishu Academy. Address: Dilalpur, Mohila College Lane, PO and Dist Pabna 6600, Bangladesh.

**SAJI Madathiparambil,** b. 2 October 1956. Orthopaedic Surgeon. m. Rosie Saji, 1 son, 1 daughter. Education: MBBS, 1979; MS Orthopaedic Surgery, 1983; Hodgson's Fellow, Hong Kong, 1992. Appointments: Clinical Tutor, 1983-84, Assistant Professor, 1984-91, Associate Professor, 1991-93, Professor, 1993-96, Orthopaedic Surgery, St John's Medical College; Senior Specialist and Head of Department of Orthopaedics, IBRI Regional Referral Hospital, 1994-. Publications: Co-author 16 publications in professional journals including: Increased Femoral Neck - Shaft Angles in Adolescent Idiopathic Scoliosis, 1995; An Analytic Study of Road Traffic Accidents 1996, Ibri Hospital Experience, 1997. Honours: Russell Hibb's Award, SRS Annual Meeting, Kansas City, USA, 1992; ENT Gold Medal, 1978, Association of ENT Surgeons of India. Memberships: Inspector, Indian Medical Council; Indian Orthopaedic Association; Spastic Society of India; National Institute of Public Co-operation and Child Development; NY Academy of Science, invited member; Paediatric Orthopaedic Society of India; Postgrad Examiner, Christian Medical College, Vellore; Accessing of Thesis, PGIMER, Chandigarh; Examiner, Bangalore University. Address: Virgonagar PO, Nirmala Farm, Bangalore 560049, India.

**SAKAC Dejan,** b. 11 November 1965, Novi Sad, Yugoslavia. Medical Doctor, Cardiologist. Education: Medical Doctor, 1991; Master of Science Pharmacology and Toxicology, 1993; Specialist in Internal Medicine, 1996; Subspecialist in Cardiology, 1998. Appointments: Research Assistant Professor, 1994; Assistant Professor, 1998. Publications: Associate Author, Textbook Cardiology. Memberships: Medical Society of Vojvodina; Serbian Medical Society; Mediterranean Association of Cardiology and Cardiac Surgery. Address: Institute for Cardiovascular Diseases, 21204 Sremska Kamenica, Yugoslavia.

**SAKAC Vladimir,** b. 18 October 1962, Novi Sad, Yugoslavia. Medical Doctor, Nephrologist, Immunologist. m.

Marijana, 1 son. Education: Medical Doctor, 1988; Master of Science, Pharmacology and Toxicology, 1994; Specialist, Internal Medicine, 1995; Subspecialist, Nephrology, 1998. Appointments: Research Assistant Professor, Medicine, University of Novi Sad, 1994; Assistant Professor, Medicine, University of Novi Sad, 1998; Clinical Doctor, Institute of Internal Diseases, Novi Sad. Publications: Treatment of Primary Dysmenorrhea, 1994; Neprotoxicity of Drugs, 1998. Honours: Young Investigator, University Award, 1986, 1987. Memberships: Medical Society of Vojvodina; Serbian Medical Society; EDTA. Address: Clinic for Internal Medicine, Hajduk Veljkova 3, 21000 Novi Sad, Yugoslavia.

**SAKALAS Aloyzas,** b. 6 July 1931, Lithuania. Member of Parliament. m. Rita, 1 son, 2 daughters. Education: Kaunas University, 1960; Dr.habil, 1977; Professor, 1993. Appointments: Assistant Professor, 1969; Associate Professor, 1971; Professor, 1978; Member of Parliament, Lithuanian Parliament. 1990-, Vice Speaker, 1992-96. Publications: 166 scientific articles in professional journals. Honours: State Award, 1981; Cabinet of Ministers Award, 1987. Memberships: President, Save the Children, 1986-; Chairman, Lithuanian Social Democratic Party, 1991-. Address: P Vileisio 12-55, 2055 Vilnius, Lithuania.

**SAKALAUSKAS Algimantas,** b. 22 September 1958, Vilkaviskis, Lithuania. Wood Sculpter. m. Raimonda, 2 sons. Education: Post Graduate, Kaunas Polytech, 1987. Appointments: Fitter, 1977-89; Joiner, 1989-91; Free Lance Artist, 1991-95; Wood Carver Artist, 1995-. Publications: Chronicle of Folk Art, 1998; Memberships: Lithuanian Folk Art Society, 1985. Address: Vytauto 27-60, LT 4340, Prienai, Lithuania.

**SAKSAGANSKII Georgii Leonidovich,** b. 13 July 1936, Sevastopol, Crimea, Russia. Physicist; Engineer. m. Olga Sergeevna Kononova, 1 son, 1 daughter. Education: Engineering Diploma, Polytechnic Institute, Leningrad, 1959; Northwestern Extramural Polytechnic Institute, Leningrad, 1964; Candidate of Science in Engineering, Engineering and Physics Institute, Moscow, 1972; DSc, Engineering, 1985. Appointments: Engineer, Researcher, 1959-61, Head of Group, 1961-67, Head of Laboratory, 1967-80, Head of Department, 1980-, DV Efremov Scientific Research Institute of Electrophysical Apparatus, Leningrad; Senior Lecturer, Northwestern Extramural Polytechnic Institute, Leningrad, 1963-76; Assistant Professor, 1982-84, Professor, 1989-92, Polytechnic Institute, Leningrad; Professor, Polytechnic University, St Petersburg, 1992-97. Publications include: Principles for Calculation and Design of Vacuum Apparatus, 1978; Molecular Flow in Complex Vacuum Systems, 1980; Electrophysical Vacuum Pumps, 1988; Getter and Getter-Ion Vacuum Pumps, 1994. Memberships: St Petersburg Engineering Academy; Russian Vacuum Society; American Vacuum Society. Address: DV Efremov Research Institute for Electrophysical Apparatus, Pos Metallostroi, St Petersburg 189631, Russia.

**SAKTHIVEL Marimuthu,** b. 8 July 1944, Paraipatty Village. Teacher, Researcher. m. Lalitha, 3 daughters. Education: BSc, Zoology, Alagappa College, 1966; MSc, Zoology, American College, 1969; M Phil, Zoology, Thiyagarajar College, 1986; PhD, Fish, Physiology, Madurai Kamaraj University, 1990. Appointments: Demonstrator, Zoology, 1971; Lecturer, Zoology, 1973; Assistant Professor, Zoology, 1974; Professor, Zoology, 1982; Principal, 1994. Publications: 21 Publications. Honours: Best national Service Scheme Officer Award, 1992-93. Memberships: Principal's Association. Address: Kamaraj College, Tufocorin, Tamilnadu, India.

**SALAEV Eldar Yunis,** b. 31 December 1933, Nakhichevan, Azerbaijan. Professor in Physics. m. Dilara Guseynova, 2 sons. Education: BSc, MSc, Azerbaijan State University, Faculty of Physics, 1956; PhD, Physics, 1963; DSc, Physics, 1975; Professor in Physics, 1976; Academician, 1983. Appointment: Director, Institute of Photoelectronics, Azerbaijan Academy of Sciences. Publications: More than 200 articles, 70 patents; 4 books. Honours: Azerbaijan State Prize, 1972; Academician S I Vavilov Award, 1976; Education S I Vavilov Award, 1985; Z Tagiev Premium, 1993; N Narimanov Premium, 1993; European Turkish Premium, 1994. Memberships: Azerbaijan Academy of Sciences, 1983; New York Academy of Sciences, 1997; International Islamic Academy, 1993; Intern Eastern Oil Academy, 1994. Address: Institute of Photoelectronics, Azerbaijanian Academy of Sciences, F. Agaeva 555, Baku 370141, Azerbaijan.

**SALAHUDDIN Ahmad,** b. 19 September 1941, Anbala, India. Professor. Education: BSc, Panjab University, Pakistan, 1961; MSc, Columbia University, USA, 1967; PhD, Concordia University, Canada, 1971. Appointments: Design Engineer, Pakistan, 1961-65; Research Associate, 1971-73, Assistant Professor, 1977-81, Concordia University, Canada; Consultant, Canadian Industry, 1973-76, 1981-83; Associate Professor, University of Bahrain, Arabian Gulf, 1983-85; Director, Canadian Institute of Technical Education, Canada, 1985-87; Senior Lecturer, University of Zimbabwe, 1987-. Publications: Book, Application of Science in the Analysis of Structural Components, ed, 1987, based on research in stuctural engineering; 13 book reviews in scientific journals; 20 technical reports to Canadian government and industry; 30 technical papers in engineering journals and conference proceedings. Honours: 3 scholarship and fellowships; Certificate of Achievement, University of Minnesota, USA, 1965; Certificate of Recognition, American Society of Mechanical Engineers, 1975. Memberships: American Society Civil Engineers; Canadian Society for Civil Engineering, and Engineering Institute of Canada; International Association for Bridge and Structural Engineering Switzerland, and International Association for Shell and Spatial Structures Spain; International Association for Structural Safety and Reliability, USA; Standards Association of Zimbabwe; Association for Computing Machinery, USA; Structural Engineering Institute - ASCE, USA; Computer Society IEEE, USA. Address: Civil Engineering Dept, University of Zimbabwe, PO Box MP 167, Harare, Zimbabwe.

**SALAJEGHEH Eysa,** b. 8 December 1951, Kerman, Iran. Professor. m. Souri Salajegheh, 2 sons, 1 daughter. Education: BSc Civil Engineering, 1975, Iran University of Science and Technology; MSc Structural Engineering, 1977, PhD Civil Engineering, 1981, Surrey University, Guildford, England. Appointments: Head of Civil Engineering Department, Assistant to Dean of College of Engineering, 1981-85, Academic and Research Assistant to Dean of College of Engineering, 1986-91, Dean of College of Engineering, 1992-94, Graduate Vice Chancellor, 1994-, University of Kerman, Iran; Sabbatical leave, University of California, Santa Barbara, 1985-86, 1991-92. Publications: 20 papers in professional journals; 44 conference presentations in proceedings; 6 lecture notes in Persian; 11 invited seminars. Honours: Distinguished Professor and Distinguished Researcher several times, 1990, 1995, 1996, 1997, 1998; Distinguished Professor, Universities of Iran, 1998, presented an award by the President of Iran. Memberships: Editorial Board: Journal of Engineering, Iran, Asian Journal of Structural Engineering; Member: International Society for Structural and Multidisciplinary Optimization; New York Academy of Science; Iranian Society Civil Engineers; Iranian Society of Earthquake Engineering; Member of the Founders of the Kerman Journal of Science and Engineering; Islamic

epublic of Iran Academy of Science. Address: No 12 1st St U
ousing, Amir-Kabir Boulevard, Kerman 76188, Iran

**SALAMA Mohamed Sayed,** b. 1 October 1955, Kena,
gypt. Professor. m. Sarnia M Negm, 1 son, 2 daughters.
ducation: MSc, Ain Shams University, 1985; Peace
ellowship, University of California Riverside, 1988-90; PhD,
SU, 1990; Post Doctor, UCR, 1991-93; BSc, ASU, 1997.
ppointments: Teaching Associate, Ain Shams University,
985-1990; Teaching Assistant, Ain Shams University,
985-97; Assistant Professor, Ain Shams University, 1990-95;
enior Scientist and Consultant, Agricultural Genetic
ngineering Research Istitute, 1994-; Associate Professor, Ain
hams University, 1995-; Teaching Assistant. Publications: 24
ublication, 1986-98. Honours: Best Scientific Conduct and
ttitude Award,Ain Shams University, 1993-94; State Award for
ncouragement of Science, Egypt, 1994; Third World Academy
f Science, Italy, 1994; Best Scientific Conduct and Attitude
ward, Ain Shams University, 1994-95; Best Scientific Conduct
nd Attitude Award, Ain Shams University, 1995-96; Man of the
ear, American Biographical Institute, 1998; Outstanding
eople of the 20th Century, International Biographical Centre,
998. Memberships: National Board of Specialists, 1994-;
gricultural Genetic Engineering Research Institute, 1993-;
oard of Directors of the Central Laboratory, 1995-; Egyptian
ociety of Gene Biotechnology and Genetic Engineering, 1998.
ddress: Department of Entomology, Faculty of Science, Ain
hams University, Abaasia, Cairo, Egypt.

**SALAMA Raphael,** b. 16 April 1929, Cairo. Orthopaedic
urgeon. m. Gisele, 1 daughter. Education: MB, BCH, Cairo,
953. Appointments: Assistant, Foch Hospital, France, 1957;
esearch Fellow, Visiting Lecturer, Royal National Orthopaedic
ospital, 1969-70; Head of Orthopaedic Department, Ichilov
ospital, Tel Aviv, 1977-94; Chairman of Orthopaedics, Sackler
chool of Medicine, Tel Aviv University, 1979-84; Full
rofessor, 1983; Research Fellow, Weizman Institute, Israel,
994-95; Professor Emeritus, 1997. Publications: 54 Major
ublications; More than 30 Short Reports and Abstracts.
lemberships: Israeli Orthopaedic Association, 1973-77; British
rthopaedic Research Society; Calcified Tissue Research
ociety; Nuclear Society of Israel European Tissue Bank
ssociation. Address: Rotschild Blvd 135, 65272 Tel Aviv,
srael.

**SALAMUN Elizabeth (Betty) A,** b. 13 June 1951,
lilwaukee, Wisonsin, USA. Performer; Choreographer. m.
avid H B Drake. Education: BFA, University of Wisconsin,
973; American University, Washington, DC; Colorado
omens College, Denver. Career: Artistic Director,
horeographer, Founder, Betty Salamun's DANCECIRCUS,
975-. Honours: National Endowment for the Arts Award, Art
pheres, 1980; Silver Plaque Award, Chicago International
ilm and Video Festival for Art Spheres, 1981; National
ndowment for the Arts and Joyce Foundation Awards, 1985;
st Place Performance, Emerald City Classic, 1985;
utstanding Contributions to Wisconsin Dance, Wisconsin
ance Council, 1987; Poetry Movement Award, New York
tate Council for the Arts, 1987; Choreographic Award,
Visconsin Arts Board, 1990; Non-Formal Educator of the Year
ward, Wisconsin Environmental Educators Association, 1993;
ollaborative and Community Production Awards, 1995-.
lemberships: Laban/Bartenieff Institute for Movement Studies;
hicago Dance Coalition; Minnesota Dance Allance; American
ance Guild; No Limits; Motus Humanus. Address: Betty
alamun's DANCECIRCUS, 810 South 37th Street, Milwaukee,
VI 53215-1023, USA.

**SALAS Henry,** b. 30 January 1947, New York City, USA.
Environmental Engineer. m. Mirna Bordalez, 1 son. Education:
BEng, Civil, 1969; MEng, Environmental, 1970. Appointments:
Registered Professional Engineer, New York State;
Hydroscience Incorporated, Westwood, New Jersey, 1970-79;
Environmental Quality Board, San Juan, Puerto Rico, 1979-82;
Pan American Health Organization, CEPIS, Lima, Peru, 1982-.
Publications: Manual for the Evaluation and Management of
Toxic Substances in Surface Water, 1988; Application of
Microbiological Water Quality Standards in the Marine
Environment, 1998. Memberships: ASCE; Water Environmental
Federation; Chi Episilon. Address: Malecon de la Reserva,
457/1102 Miraflores Lima 18, Peru.

**SALEH Hassan Abdul Kadir,** b. 25 May 1936, Al-Falujeh.
Professor of Geography; Dean, Faculty of Humanities and
Social Sciences. m. Laila Muteir, 5 sons, 3 daughters.
Education: BA, Geography, MA, Geography, 1964, Cairo
University; Diploma, Education, Ain Shams University, 1962;
PhD, Geography, Durham University, 1969. Appointments:
Assistant Professor, 1969, Currently, Professor fo Geography,
1979-, Head of the Geography Department, Head, Graduate
Department of the Biological and Agricultural Sciences and
Natural Resources, Faculty of Graduate Studies, Vice Dean,
Faculties of Graduate Studies and Arts, Dean, Faculty of
Humanities and Social Sciences, 1997-, University of Jordan,
Amman. Publications: Books in Arabic include: Food
Resources of Jordan, 1985; Khan Yunis City, 1988; The
Geographic Basis of the Desertification Problem, 1989;
Geography of Jordan; Geography of the Fertile Crescent
Region; The Geographical Encyclopedia of the Islamic World;
The Demographic State of Arab Palestine, in Palestine
Encyclopedia 2nd division, 1990; Geography of Palestine,
1995; Economic Geography, 1995; Geography of the Arab
World, 1996; Numerous papers. Honours: Man of the Year,
American Biographical Institute, 1988; Award, International
Biographical Centre, Cambridge, England, 1998. Memberships
include: Egyptian Geographical Association; International
Islamic Geographical Society; Arab Geographical Association;
Social Muslim Scientists of North America Association.
Address: Geography Department, Faculty of Humanities and
Social Sciences, University of Jordan, Amman, Jordan.

**SALEHI SHOKRAVAR Farhad,** b. 7 April 1965,
Masjed-E-Soleiman, Iran. Mechanical Engineer. m. Sonbol
Rooindej, 1 son. Education: BSc, Mechanical Engineering,
1995. Appointments: Piping Designer, Piping Design Engineer,
Head, CAD Department, Offshore Piping Specialist, 3D Plant
Design Specialist, Engineering Software Designer, Piping
Software Specialist, Trainer. Honour: 1st Place, Cadpipe Quest
for Excellence in the World, 1994; 2nd Place Cadworx/Pipe
Contest, Houston Texas Coade Inc, 1998. Memberships:
American Society of Mechanical Engineers, 1991-. Address: No
5 Mofateh Square, Nemati Avenue, Dowlat 8th Alley, Dowlat
19397, Tehran, Iran.

**SALEM Elsayed M,** b. 12 January 1932, Sharkia, Egypt.
Professor. m. Wafaa Salem, 2 sons, 1 daughter. Education: MB
Bch, Faculty of Medicine, Cairo University, 1953; Diploma,
1956, Doctorate, 1961. Appointments: Resident, Chest
Department, Cairo University Hospitals, 1954-56;
Demonstrator, 1956-61, Lecturer, 1961-66, Assistant Professor,
1966-72, Professor, 1972-, Faculty of Medicine, Chest
Department, Cairo University; Consultant, Chairman, Chest
Department, Italian Hospital, 1964-; President, Egyptian
Society of Chest Physicians, Cairo, 1988-93; President, Arab
Respiratory Society, 1997-; WHO Expert in Tuberculosis,
Geneva. Publications: Several articles in professional journals.
Memberships: American College of Chest Physicians;

American Thoracic Society. Address: 4 Roushody Street Abdin, Cairo, Egypt.

**SALIBA Holem Mansour,** b. 25 January 1967, Bteghrine, Lebanon. Teacher, Researcher. Education: PhD, 1997. Appointment: Assistant Professor, Notre Dame University, Lebanon. Publications: 1997-98. Address: Bteghrine Metn, Lebanon.

**SALIH Mustafa Abdalla Mohamed,** b. 5 January 1950, Kosti, Sudan. Paediatric Neurologist. m. Nadia Abdalla El Hassan, 1 son, 3 daughters. Education: MBBS, 1974, Master Paediatric and Child Health, 1980, MD, 1982, University Khartoum; ECFMG, 1985; Dr Med Sci, 1990, Uppsala University. Appointments: include: Appointed Lecturer, 1980, Associate Professor, 1985, Professor of Paediatrics, 1990, Department of Paediatrics, Faculty of Medicine, University of Khartoum; Professor of Paediatrics, College of Medicine, King Saud University, 1993-. Publications: Author and co-Author numerous articles and reports in field of paediatric neurology. Honours: Head of State Prize, 1964; 2 prizes, Faculty of Medicine, University Khartoum; Clinical Research Fellow, Newcastle General Hospital; Fellow to Department of Child Health, University of Newcastle Upon Tyne, 1980-82; Fellow, Department of Paediatrics, University Hospital, Uppsala, Sweden, 1984, 1985-90; Riyadh Neuroscis Club Award, 1996. Memberships: Editorial Board, Sudan Medical Journal, 1983-86; Editor, Sudanese Journal of Paediatrics, 1985-92; Sudan Association Paediatrics, 1983-; Council, Sudan Association of Paediatrics, 1983-91; World Federation Neurology, 1983-; International Society Tropical Paediatrics, 1986-; Saudi Paediatric Association, 1992-; NYAS, 1995-; International Child Neurology Association, 1996-; AAA, 1997-; National Geographic Society, 1997-. Address: Division of Paediatric Neurology, Department of Paediatrics, College of Medicine, King Saud University, PO Box 2925, Riyadh 11461, Saudi Arabia.

**SALOVA Nikolinka,** b. 27 November 1935, Ticha, Bulgaria. Professor. m. Stoyan Sulov, 1 son. Education: Dr Sc, Economics, University of Economics, 1968; MBA, University of Economics, 1958; PhD, University of National and World Economics, 1980. Appointments: Economist, 1958-61; Assistant, 1962-71; Assistant Professor, 1971-82; Chief of Department, 1973-93; Professor, 1982-; Deputy Rector, 1983-89. Publications: Over 150 Published Scientific Works. Memberships: Logman Association; Popular Bank; Union of Merchants; Union of Scientists. Address: U Econs, 77 Knyaz Boris 1 Blvd, 9002 Varna, Bulgaria.

**SALTINA Marina,** b. 9 August 1951, Kazan, Russia. Theatrical Director. Divorced. Education: Lenin Kazan State University, Historic and Philological Department, 1968-73; Lunacharsky State Institute of Theatrical Art in Moscow, Department of Producing, 1976-81; Trainee, Moscow Gogol Theatre and Moscow Art Theatre. Appointments: Theatrical Director, dramatic theatres in Kazan, Elista, Dzerzhinsk, Nizhny Novogorod, Moscow; Artistic Director, Dzerzhinsk Dramatic Theatre, 1988-90. Publications: About 50 performances; More than 500 publications. Honours: All-Russian Theatre Festival Diploma for performance The Little Boar, by V. Rozov, 1987; WTK Society International Diploma (Germany) for Organization of Educational Theatre in Russian State Humanitarian University, 1995. Memberships: Union of Theatrical Public Figures of Russia, 1983-; Union of Russian Literary Men, 1997-. Address: Miusskaja pl, 6, Korp 2, Moscow 125267, Russia.

**SALZMAN Eric,** b. 8 September 1933, New York, USA. Composer; Writer. m. Lorna Jackson, 2 daughters. Education: BA, Columbia College, Columbia University, 1954; MFA, Princeton University Graduate School, 1956; Fulbrigh Fellowship, Rome, 1956-58; Darmstadt Ferienkurse, Germany 1957. Appointments: Music Critic, New York Times, 1958-62; Music Director, WBAI FM, 1962-64; Music Correspondent and Critic, New York Herald Tribune, 1964-67; Assistant Professor of Music, Queens College, 1967-68; Music Director, WBAI FM, 1968-72; Founder, Director, The Electric Bar, 1967-68, New Image of Sound, 1968-71, Quog Music Theater, 1970-82, Free Music Store, 1970-72, American Music Theatre Festival 1982-93; Editor, The Musical Quarterly, 1984-91; Founder Director, Music Theatre, New York, 1994-. Publications Twentieth Century Music: An Introduction; Making Changes The Harmony of American Popular Music; The New Music Theatre; Contributing Editor and Critic. Honours: Armstrong Award; Prix Italia, Broadcast Award; Stereo Review Record o the Year Award; Seagram Production Award. Address: 29 Middagn Street, Brooklyn, New York 11201 1339, USA.

**SAMAHA Mohamed El-Said,** b. 24 October 1949, Cairo Egypt. Engineer. m. Nawal, 1 son, 3 daughters. Education BSc, Mechanical Engineering, Cairo University, Egypt, 1971 PhD, Mechanical Engineering, Concordia University, Canada 1978. Appointments: Pratt & Whitney, Aircraft, Canada 1978-80; Saudi Aramco, Dhahran, 1980-. Publications: Over 50 papers in professional journals in the fields of dynamic analysis equipment reliability and plant maintenance. Memberships ASME; CSME. Address: Saudi Aramco, Box 5689, Abqaic 31311, Saudi Arabia.

**SAMANTARAY Pramod C,** b. 29 November 1942, Cuttack Orissa, India. Medical Specialist. m. Ratna, 1 son, 1 daughter Education: MBBS (Utkal), 1966; DTM&H, 1971, DPH (Calcutta), 1972; MD (L N Mithila), 1974; DIH (Calcutta), 1975 DMM, Faculty of Management Studies (Delhi), 1987; DMPE (Punjabi), 1989. Appointments: Head, Medical and Health Services, MMC LTd, Calcutta, 1976-77; Executive Advisor Indian Medical Gazette, 1970-73; Manager, Medical Services 1978, Manager, Medical Services Training, 1982, Senior Manager, Medical Serices and Sales Promotion, 1988- Controller Medical Services, 1990, Senior Deputy Genera Manager (MS and T), 1993, General Manager (Acting), 1993 General Manager (Marketing and Medical Services), 1995 Indian Drugs and Pharmaceuticals Ltd (A Government of India Undertaking), Gurgaon, Haryana; Director, Orissa Drugs and Chemicals Ltd, Bhubanes war, Orissa, to 1997. Publications Papers in medical journals. Memberships: Fellow, Roya Society of Tropical Medicine and Hygiene, London; Fellow International College of Nutrition; Life Member: Indo-French Technical Association, Delhi Chapter, Indian Hospital Association; Indian Association of Occupational Health; Indian Medical Association; Association of Physicians of India Cardiological Society of India; Indian Public Health Association (Vice-president, 1978-79); Indian Society of Malaria and CD Indian Institute of Public Administration. Address: Genera Manager (MDHO), Corporate Office IDPL, Dundahera Industria Complex, Gurgaon 122016, Haryana State, India.

**SAMARASINGHE Colvin Ananda,** b. 11 December 1946 Colombo, Sri Lanka. Neurosurgeon. m. Charlotte Elizabeth, 1 daughter. Education: FRCS England, 1977; FRCS Edin, 1977 FACS, 1991; FCS (SL), 1992. Appointments: Senior Consultan Neurosurgeon, Department of Neurosurgery, National Hospita Colombo, Sri Lanka. Honours: Sir Nicholas Atygalle Oration 1989; Sir Arthur De Silva Oration, 1989; Travelling Fellow University of Minnesota, Mayo Clinic Rochester, University o Western Ontario, Canada, University of Chicago, University o olumbia New York, 1989; International Guest Scholar, merican College of Surgeons, 1989; British Council Scholar, 988; Travelling Fellow, Fujita Health University, Aichi, Japan, 998. Memberships: Executive Committee Member, Asian ongress of Neurosurgeons; International Associate Member, merican Association of Neurosurgeons; Congress of leurosurgeons. Address: 30/6 Longdon Place, Colombo 7, Sri anka.

**SAMES Martin,** b. 1 November 1963, Jabloncec nad Nisou, :zechoslovakia. Neurosurgeon. m. 1987, 2 daughters. ducation: MD, with Honours, Medical School, Charles lniversity, Prague, 1988; Anatomical Institute, 1 year; Scientific ellow, Neurosurgical Department. Appointments: leurosurgical Residency, Department of Neurosurgery, 1asaryk Hospital, Usti nad Labem, 1991-96; Lecturer, ostgraduate Course, Surgical Training, Postgraduate Institute f Medicine, 1992-98; Neuroscience Programme, 3rd Medical .chool, Charles University, Prague, 1995-98; Chairman, epartment of Neurosurgery, Masaryk Hospital, 1997; Lecturer, stitute of Postgraduate Education of Physicians, Prague, 999; Professional residencies in many Neurosurgical epartments in the USA and Europe. Publications: Numerous ticles in professional medical journals; Abstracts and posters. onours: Grants, IGA MZ. 1992-94. Memberships: Czech ledical Society; Czech Society J E Purkyne; Czech leuroscience Society; Czech Neurosurgical Society; Czech ociety of Traumatology; EANS. Address: Jezkova 20, 400 11 lsti nad Labem, Czech Republic.

**SAMOYLENKO Mykola,** b. 4 Septmeber 1947, Riga. lystem Analyst. m.Samoylenko, Nina. 2 sons. Education: MSc, 970, Candidate of Sciences, 1979, DSc, 1996, Kharkov State echnical University of Radioelectronics (KhTURE). ppointments: Docent DAMC, 1980-96, Head of Department, :AM/CAD, Kharkov State Academy of Municipal Economy <hSAME); Professor, Department of Applied Mathematics and :omputers (DAMC), KhSAME, 1996-99. Publications: 4 andbooks; 3 books; 30 scientific articles, 1975-99. Honour: )iploma, Ministry of Education, 1988. Memberships: Post PhD :ouncil, KhTURE; PhD Council, KhSAME; Scientific Council at hSAME; Regional Ecology Commission of Experts. Address: ./2 Mykola Samoylenko, 2/2 Moskovsky Ave #130, 310003 <harkov, Ukraine.

**SAMSONOVA Tatiana,** b. 28 March 1953, Orel, Russia. °olitical Scientist. Education: MA, Department of Philosophy, Moscow State University, 1975; PhD, Department of °hilosophy, Moscow State University, 1979. Appointments: Assistant Professor, Department of Philosophy, Moscow State Jniversity, 1979-89; Associate Professor, Department of °hilosophy, Moscow State University, 1989-91; Associate °rofessor, Department of Sociology, 1991-. Publications: The lustice of Equality and the Equality of Justice, monograph, 996; About 50 articles, chapters, translations, etc. Memberships: Russian Philosophical Society, 1974-; Russian °olitical Science Association, 1992-; The Transnational /ladimir Solovyov Society, 1994-; International Political 3cience Association, 1997-. Address: Department of Sociology, Moscow State University, Moscow 119899, Russia.

**SAMUELS Shirley C,** b. 12 December 1930, The Bronx, New York, USA. Mental Health Administrator; Psychotherapist. n. Stanley Samuels, 2 sons, 1 daughter. Education: BS, 1952, MS, 1957, Syracuse University; EdD Marriage and Family Therapy Education Degree, Columbia University, 1969; °ostgraduate Degree, Center for Preventive Psychiatry in Child °sychotherapy, White Plains, New York, 1977. Appointments: Teacher, Cleveland, Hartsdale, New York Pre-School, 1957-63;

School Director, Mt Vernon, New York, New York City, 1963-68; Associate Professor, Manhattanville College, Purchase, New York, 1969-80; Assistant Clinic Director, Center for Preventive Psychiatry, White Plains, New York, 1977-. Publications: Self-Concept in Early Childhood, 1977; Disturbed Exceptional Children, 1981, 1986; Ideal Adoption, 1990. Memberships: National Association Marriage and Family Therapy; American Psychological Association; Association for Child Psychoanalisis; Fellow, American Orthopsychiatric Association. Address: 10 Crest Drive, White Plains, NY 10607-2702, USA.

**SAN JUAN Enrico,** b. 29 April 1952, Manila. Journalist; Political Analyst; Author. div. 2 sons, 1 daughter. Education: BSc Commerce, San Sebastian College, Manila, 1975; MBA, Units, Ateno Graduate School of Business, The Philippines, 1977. Appointments: Radio Commentator DWAN, Quezon City, The Philippines; DWBL, Pasig; Columnist Northern Times, The Philippines; Director, News Asia; Analyst San Juan & Assoc, The Philippines. Publications: Author, Marcos Legacy Revisited, Conspiracies and Controversies. Honours: Most outstanding Jaycee Senator of The World, Cartagena, Columbia, 1975; Who's Who in the World, 1999. Address: San Juan & Associates, Rm 1402 PDCP Bank Ctr Pas de Roxas, Makati City, The Philippines.

**SANCHES Aderito,** b. 27 November 1945, Porto Alexandre, Angola. Psychology Educator; Researcher; Consultant. div 2 sons. Education: Psychology (licence), University of Paris, 1968; Biology, (licence), University of Nice, 1970; Psychology (maitrise) University of Nice, 1971; Doctorate in Social Sciences (doctorate d'Etat), University of Nice, 1981; Capacity to Direct Doctoral Research, University of Nice, 1981. Appointments: Assistant Professor, Faculty of Science, 1968-70, Assistant Professor, Faculty of Arts and Human Sciences, 1970-83, Senior Lecturer, Faculty of Arts and Human Sciences, 1985-; Joint Director, Laboratory of General, Differential and Applied Psychology, 1983-89; Head, Department of Psychology, 1983-85, University of Nice; Research Director, European Institute for Advanced International Studies, 1984-85; Guest Lecturer, University of Coimbra, Portugal, 1983-84; (Doctorat HEC: Hautes Etudes Commerciales, Jouy-en Josas) 16 month programme for the Training of Trainers for Trainers of Enterprise Managers, 1990-91; Head, Department of International Relations for Southern Europe Universities, 1990-91; Head, Continuing Education Programme, 1990-91; Professor, Member of the Pedagogical Committee, 1989-91; Over 120 consultancy and training field missions in 25 countries for governments and international organisations. Publications: Over 13 books; Over 100 papers and other publications, 1989-99. Memberships: American Association of Science, 1976; The New York Academy of Sciences (life), 1981; Societe Europeenne de Culture, 1983; National Council of Teachers of Mathematics, 1976; The Mathematical Association, 1976; Association of Teachers of Mathematics, 1976; Association des Enseignants de Psychologie des Universites, 1976; World Association for Educational Research, 1983. Address: 18 Ave des Mimosas, 06800 Cagnes-Sur-|Mer, France.

**SANDER Louis Wilson,** b. 31 July 1918, San Francisco, California, USA. Professor of Psychiatry. m. Betty E Thorpe, 2 sons, 1 daughter. Education: AB, University California, 1939; MD, University California Medical School, 1942; Intern, University of California Hospital SF, 1942-43; Resident in Psychiatry to Professor of Psychiatry, Boston University School of Medicine, 1947-68; Diplomate, American Board Psychiatry and Neurology, 1951; Phi Beta Kappa, Alpha Omega Alpha. Appointments: Served to Major, USAAF, 1943-46;

Inventor/Developer, Infant Bassinet Sleep-State Monitor, 1958-87; Senior Scholar, University of Colorado Medical School, 1977-87; Professor of Psychiatry, Boston University School of Medicine, 1968-78, University of Colorado School of Medicine, 1978-87; Professor of Psychiatry, Principal Investigator, 254 longit Study, Boston University, 1963-87. Publications: Contributor over 50 articles, book chapters, reviews to professional publications. Honours: Recipient, Research Career Development Awards, USPHS, 1963-78; Research grantee, USPHS March of Dimes, W Grant Foundation, MacArthur Foundation, Spencer Foundation, National Council on Alcoholism, Development Psychobiology Research Group, and others. Memberships: American Medical Association; American Psychiatric Association; American College of Psychoanalysts; Boston Psychoanalytic Society and Institute; AAAS; Society for Research on Child Development; American Academy on Child Psychology; Denver Psychoanalyst Society; World Association for Infant Mental Health; Boston Change Process Study Group, 1995-. Address: 2525 Madrona Avenue, St Helena, CA 94574, USA.

**SANDERS Marion Yvonne,** b. 4 December 1936, Saint Petersburg, Florida, USA. Nurse. 1 son, 1 daughter. Education: BS Nursing Education, 1959, Florida A&M University; 20 credits, 1962, 1963, Indiana University; Masters in Health Service Administration, 1992, Nova University. Appointments: Staff Nurse, General Duty, Private Duty Nursing, 1959-94; Home Nursing, Geriatric, Volunteer, 1994-, Urban Jacksonville Inc. Memberships: American Nurses Association; Florida Nurses Association; Brewsters Community Nurses; Ideals for America's Future. Address: 4832 North Main Street=14, Jacksonville, FL 32206, USA.

**SANDHAWALIA Sarbjeet Kaur,** b. 1 August 1955. Professor and Head. m. Sandhawalia H S, 3 daughter. Education: MSc, Botany, Pbi University, Patiala, 1974; MA, Education, HP University, Shimla, 1976; MA, Music, Pracheen Kala Kendra, Chandigarh, 1978; MA, Punjabi, Punjabi University, Patiala, 1980; MA, Sociology, Panjab University, Chandigarh, 1982; MA, Psychology, Panjab University, Chandigarh, 1984; MA, English, HP University, Shimla, 1986; PhD, 1993; Captain, NCC, 1994. Appointments: Research Officer, Language Department, Punjab, 1976-77; Lecturer, Botany, at present. Publications: 7 books written in Prose and Poetry; 1 manuscript; 100 reseach articles published and presented in national and international seminars and conferences; Regular features and articles published in newspapers, magazines and journals both in India and abroad. Honours: Awaj-e-Wattan Award; Honoured by Overseas Congress abroad; Best Director Award; Best Seminar in Punjabi University; Best presentation in India's Silver Jubilee celebrations; Best comparer in Apna Utsav, New Delhi; many other honours received by various literary societies. Address: 20C Baradari Garden, Patiala, Punjab 147001, India.

**SANDHU Shingara S,** b. 10 October 1932, Amristar, India. Director of Research; College Teacher. m. Jatinder K, 3 sons, 1 daughter. Education: BS, Chemistry, 1952, MS, Chemistry, 1954, Punjab University; PhD, Environmental Cemistry, Utah State University, 1970. Appointments: Assistant Professor, Chemistry, Punjab Agricultural University, 1955-65; Graduate Research Assistant, Utah State University, 1965-69; Professor of Chemistry, P.I and Director of Special Projects, 1969-80, Chair, Department of Chemistry and Chair, Division of Science and Mathematics, 1980-87, Distinguished Professor of Chemistry, Chairman, Division of Science and Mathematics, Director of Special Projects, 1987-93-, Claflin College; Director of Research and Grants, Director, Center for Excellence in Science and Maths, 1994-. Publications include: Degradation

Mechanisms of Tetraphenylboron (TPB) on Minerals, 1993 Leachability of Ni, Cd, Cr, and As form Coal Ash Impoundments of Different Ages on the Savannah River Site in Trace Medals, 1994; FTIR Analysis of Gaseous Products From Hazardous Waste Combustion, 1996; Detection of Transien Species From Laser Ablated polymer via FTIR, 1998. Honours include: South Carolina Governor's Professor of the Year 1996; Award of Honour, Alumnus of the Year, Punjab Agricultural University, 1997; Recognition Award, Savannah River Ecology Laboratory, University of Georgia, 1998 Memberships include: American Chemical Society; American Association for the Advancement of Science; Smithsonian Association. Address: Claflin College, College Avenue JST 125, Orangeburg, SC 29115, USA.

**SANDORSKI Jan Tadeusz,** b. 28 January 1940, Poznan Poland. Lawyer; Scientist. m. Urszula Rozanska, 2 sons, 2 daughters. Education: DSc Law, 1967; Doctor Habilitatus 1977; Professor, 1992. Appointments: Professor, Public International Law Chair, Law Faculty, UAM, Poznan, 1992- Rector of School of Advanced Studies on Humanistic Science and Journalism, Poznan, 1997-. Publications: Invalidity of International Treaties, 1978; June 1956 in Poznan, 1981 Memberships: President, Board of Directors, All Polands Eugeniusz Kwiatkowski Association; American Society of International Law; International Law Association; Poznan Bar Association. Address: Ul Wiedenska 44, 60-683 Poznan Poland.

**SANLI N Oya,** b. 15 July 1948, Aksehir, Konya, Turkey Chemistry Professor; Academician. 1 son, 1 daughter Education: BS, 1971, MS, 1973, Middle East Technical University, Chemical Engineering Department; PhD, Ankara University, Chemistry Department, 1978. Appointments Assistant, 1971-78, Assistant Professor, 1978-82, Chemistry Department, Academy of Architecture and Engineering Associated Professor, Chemistry Department, Professor 1989-, Vice Dean, 1997-, Faculty of Art and Sciences, Gaz University. Publications: Various papers in professional journals Honours: Awards from Turkish Science and Research Association and Gazi University. Memberships: Turkish Chemistry Association; Polymer Association; Soroptimis Organization; New York Academy of Sciences; American Association for the Advancement of Science. Address: Gaz Universitesi Fen-Edebiyat Fakultesi Dekan Yardimcisi Teknikokullar, 06500 Ankara, Turkey.

**SANO Hirotoshi,** b. 11 March 1945, Tokyo, Japan Neurosurgery. m. Tomoko, 2 daughters. Education: Medical Doctor, Shool of Medicine, Keio University, 1970. Appointment Associate Professor of Neurosurgery. Honour: President, 9th Annual Conference on Neurosurgical Techniques and Tools Memberships: AANS; CNS; Japan Neurosurgical Society IWCVS; Japanese Congress of Neurological Surgeons Address: Fujita Health University, 1-98 Dengakugakubo, Aich 470 1192, Japan.

**SANTANA-GARCIA Mario Arturo,** b. 16 November 1956 Pabellon, Aguascalientes, Mexico. Agronomic Engineer. m Maria Irene Santana-García, 3 sons, 1 daughter. Education BS, Agronomic Engineering, Chapingo National Agriculture School, 1978; Horticulture Specialty, Centre for International Technical Cooperation, Istituto Sperimentale per lorticolture de Salerno, Italy, 1985; MS, Horticulture, 1987, PhD Agronomy-Plant Physiology, 1996, New Mexico State University, USA; Diploma, Public Policies of Agriculture Livestock and Forestry, National Institute of Public Administration and Postgraduate College in Agricultural Sciences, 1995; Diploma, English Language Teaching

Aguascalientes Technological University and Angloamerican Superior Institute, 1999. Appointments: Several research, professorial and administrative posts, 1978-95; Professor-Researcher, Technological Agriculture and Livestock Institute No 20, General Director of Agriculture and Livestock Education, Secretariat of Public Education, 1995-. Publications include: Effects of cultural practices and natural acclimation on cold hardiness of overwintered short-day onions, PhD dissertation, 1996; Soil temperature monitoring in different depths and water content at the freezing time, 1997; Guava (Psidium guajava L) micrograft surviving under preconditioning before acclimation, 1997; Methodology to obtain Opuntia spp flour to be used as forage, 1998. Honours include: Honour Frame, National Agriculture School, 1974; Academic Excellence Recognition, New Mexico State University, 1988. Memberships: American Society for Horticultural Science; Crop Science Society of Agronomy, USA; American Society of Agronomy; Soil Science Society of America; Sociedad Mexicana de Fitogenética; Sociedad Mexicana de Fruticultura; Sociedad Mexicana de Ciencias Horticolas; Pi Alpha Xi, USA; Golden Key National Honor Society, USA. Address: Secretariat of Public Education, Paseo de la Cruz 803, 20250 Aguascalientes, Mexico.

**SANTOS Gonzalo Jr,** b. 25 January 1936, Cabanatuan, Philippines. Lawyer. m. Virginia Cabaccang, 2 sons, 1 daughter. Education: AA, 1953, BA, Economics, 1957, LLB, 1957, University of the Philippines; LLM, Yale Law School, 1958; Certificta d'Application, Academie De Droit International De La Haye, 1971; MA, summa cum laude, University of Manila, 1973; Master in National Security Administration, National Defense College of the Philippines, 1975; PhD, Meritissimus, Real y Pontificia Universidad de Santo Tomas, 1977. Appointments include: Arbitrator, ICC International Court of Arbitration, Paris and Geneva; Arbitrator, American Arbitration Association, New York; Arbitrator, Conciliator, International Centre for Settlement of Investment Disputes, Washington, DC; Arbitrator, International Centers for Arbitration, Houston, Texas; Philippine Representative, UN Commission on Transnational Corporations, New York; Philippine Representative, UN Conference on Trade and Development, Intergovernmental Group of Experts on Restrictive Business Practices, Geneva; Negotiator, Philippine Panel for Negotiation of Investment Treaties. Publications: Numerous articles in professional journals. Honours include: Cultural Doctorate in Philosophy of Economics, honoris causa, World University Roundtable, Arizona, USA, 1984; Special Citation, University of the Philippines Alumni Association, 1996. Memberships: American Society of International Law; World Association of Law Professors; Internationales Fachinstitut fur Steuer-Und Wirth Schaft Srecht; Phi Kappa Phi; Pi Gamma Mu; Phi Delta Kappa. Address: Unit 606 Royal View Mansion, 242 Artiaga Street, San Juan, Metro Manila, The Philippines.

**SANTOS-TAVERAS Jose,** b. 26 July 1946, Villa Gonzalez, Dominican Republic. Economist. m. 1 son, 2 daughters. Education: MA, Economics; PhD, Political Science. Appointments: Minister of Finance; Ambassador to UN; Governor, Central Bank; Superintendent of Banks. Publication: US Sugar Consumption and its Incidence into the Dominican Economy, 1973. Memberships: American Economic Association; Colegio Dominicano de Economistas. Address: Planeta Azul, Av Central Esq Av Primera, Reparto Gala, Santo Domingo, Dominican Republic.

**SANTURJIAN Ohanes,** b. 21 February 1938, Sofia. Hydraulic Engineer. m. Evelina, 1 son. Education: MSc, 1962; PhD, 1974; DSc, 1991.Appointments: Designer, 1962-66; Researcher, 1966-84; Senior Resident, 1984-1993; Prfessor,

Director of Institute of Water, 1993-. Publications: 60 Papers; 2 Monographs. Honours: Civil Order; Method Order. Memberships: Bulgarian Committees of Large Dams of Irrigation and Drainage. Address: Graf Ignatiev Str #23, 1000 Sofia, Bulgaria.

**SARACAYDIN Aytac,** b. 4 April 1966, Izmir. Medical Doctor. m. Ozleni, 1 son. Education: Medical School of Istanbul, 1984-90, Graduated with high degree, 1990. Appointments: Specialisation Ear-Nose-Throat Surgery, Istanbul University School of Medicine, 1990-94; Dept Otorhinolaryngology, Mayo Clinic, Rochester, USA, 1994-95; University of Michigan, Michigan Ear Institute, Michigan, USA, 1992. Publications: Handbook of Antimicrobial Therapy, 1994; Chondroma of the Larynx, Azathioprine in the Treatment of Autoimmune Inner Ear Disease; Primary Malignant Uelanoma of Ethmoid and Sphenoid Sinuses. Honour: Most Successful Young Person of the Year. Memberships: New York Academy of Sciences; American Association for the Advancement of Science. Address: Kececizade Sok Poyraz, Apt 28 Pink House, 80880 Tarabaya, Istanbul, Turkey.

**SARANGI Alekha Chandra,** b. 26 March 1949, Birgovind Pur, Puri, Orissa, India. Professor of Sanskrit. m. Smt Pramila Mishra, 2 sons, 1 daughter. Education: MA 1972; Diploma in German, 1976; Certificate in French, 1978; PhD 1978; Vyakarana carya, 1979; M Phil, 1991. Appointments: Lecturer in Sanskrit, 1977; Reader in Sanskrit, 1990; Professor of Sanskrit, 1996; Mombusho Fellow, Japan, 1984-85 Visiting Professor, Udayana University, Bali, Indonesia, 1990-91. Publications: 4 books on development of Sanskrit; 30 papers. Memberships include: International Association of Sanskrit Studies, Paris; All India Oriental Conference, Puni; Bhandarkar Oriental Research Institute, Pune. Address: c 16 Utkal University Campus, Vani Vihar, Bhubaneswar 751004, India.

**SARASWATHI M,** b. 30 August 1969, Chickballapur. Social Worker. m. M Subramanyam. Education: Bachelor of Arts; Nursery Teacher Training; Typewriting Course. Appointments: Programme Officer, Vice Chairman, Farmers Development Agency; K V English School; Pavan English School. Honours: Momentues, Youth and Sports Department, Government of Karnataka; Institute of Public Corperation and Child Development. Address: 240 1st Cross, Nagarthpet, Chickballapur 562101, Karnataka State, India.

**SARCHET Bernard Reginald,** b. 13 June 1917, Byesville, Ohio, USA. Engineering Management Educator. m. Lena Virginia Fisher, 3 daughters. Education: BS, Chemical Engineering, Ohio State University, 1939; MS, Chemical Engineering, University of Delaware, 1941; Advanced Management Program, Harvard Business School, 1955. Appointments: Engineer, Plant Manager, Department Manager, Director, Commercial Development, 1941-67; Professor, Founding Chairman, Department of Engineering Management, University of Missouri, Rolla, 1967-88. Publications: Numerous articles in professional journals. Honours include: Certificate of Achievement, University of Delaware, 1952; Four George Washington Awards, Freedoms Foundation, Valley Forge; Award of Merit, University of Missouri, Rolla. Memberships include: Founding President, American Society for Engineering Management; American Chemical Society. Address: PO Box 68, Rolla, MO 65402-0068, USA.

**SARKAR Gerlinde,** b. 5 November 1942, Germany. EducationAdministrator. m. Dr Kit Sarkar, 3 sons. Education: BEd; BA; MBA. Appointments: Teacher, Edmonton School Board, 1963-67; Lecturer, University of Saskatchewan College of Commerce, 1986-89; President, TARA Management

Consulting, 1987-90; Research Officer, 1990-93, Director, Planning and Research, 1993-, Saskatchewan Institute of Applied Science and Technology. Publications: Agriculture Business Certificate Course, modules 1-4, 1988; Various articles in professional journals. Memberships: President, Saskatchewan and Saskatoon Business and Professional Women's Clubs; President of the Board, Saskatoon YWCA; Canadian Institutional Researchers and Planners Association; American Institutional Researchers Association; Women Studies Research Group, University of Saskatchewan; Canadian Labour Force Development Board - Education Reference Group. Address: Saskatchewan Institute of Applied Science and Technology, SIAST Administrative Offices, 119-4th Avenue S Ste 401, Saskatoon SK, Canada S7K 5X2.

**SARKAR Subir,** b. 3 January 1970, Cooch Behar, India. Writer (Poet). Education: BA, 1994; BEd, 1997; MA, studying at present. Publications: Japanchitra, a collection of self composed poems, 1996; Sada Karataler, 1998. Memberships: Fortnight Journal, Kabitapakshik; Cooch Behar Journalist Club. Address: Department Bari Nutan Para, Coochbehar, India.

**SARKAR Sunil Kumar,** b. 1 February 1948, Mymensingh, Bangladesh. Doctor. m. Doli Sarkar, 2 sons, 1 daughter. Education: MBBS, 1972; MD, 1993; PhD, 1995; DSc, 1998. Appointments: Private Practice, 1973-; Emeritus Professor, 1990; Honorary Senior Medical Consultant, Professor of Medicine, 1993. Publications: Several articles in professional medical journals. Honours: Gold Record of Achievement Award, 1997; Visisht Chikitsa Medal, 1997; Gold Medal, 1997. Memberships: Fellow, Association of College of Chest Physicians, India, Society for Advanced Studies in Medical Sciences, New Delhi. Address: "Anupal", House No 119, Road No 9, Nirala Residential Area, Khulna 9100, Bangladesh.

**SARMA K V,** b. 22 December 1919, Kerala, India. Professor of Sanskrit. m. Sarada L, 1 son, 1 daughter. Education: BSc, 1940; MA, 1942; Diploma in French, 1953; Diploma in German, 1954; DLitt, 1979. Appointments: Lecturer, Madras University; Curator, 1962, Reader, 1972, Ag Director, Director-Professor, 1975, Vishveshvarnand Institute, Hoshiarpur; Professor, Adyar Library Research Centre; Director, SSES Research Centre, 1997. Publications: 85 books; 600 articles. Honours: Maharani Sethu Parvathi Bayi Prize, All India, 1976; Certificate of Honour in Sanskrit from the President of India, 1991; International Man of the Year 1997-98; 20th Century Award for Achievers 1998, IBC, Cambridge, England; Life Time Excellence Award, United Writers' Association 1998, Madras, India. Memberships: Bhandarkar Or Research Institute, Poona; Vishveshvaranand Vedic Research Institute, Hoshiarpur; World Theosophical Society, Madras. Address: 63-B III Main Road, Gandhi Nagar, Adyar, Madras 600-020, India.

**SARRAFZADEGAN Nizal,** b. 1959, Iraq. Medical Doctor. m. Homayoon Ranjbar, 2 daughters. Education: General Physician, 1984; Board in Internal Medicine, 1987; Subspeciality in Cardiology, 1992; Associate Professor, Isfahan University of Medical Sciences. Appointments: Director, Isfahan Cardiovascular Research Center; Consultant, Member, Several Local and International Research Committees. Publications: 22 Full Articles in International and Local Journals. 10 Articles in Press. Memberships: International Fellowship of American Heart Association; Member, Several Scientific Councils of AMH; International Society and Federation of Cardiology; European Society of Rehabilitation of Cardial Patients; Heart Friends Around the World; Local Societies of Cardiology and Internal Medicine. Address: Charbagbala, Hedayat-Shahrokh 47, Isfahan, Iran.

**SARVESWARA RAO Bhavaraju,** b. 4 November 1915, Peddapuram, East Godavari District, Andhra Pradesh, India. Emeritus Professor; EconomistResearcher; Educator. m. Mrs Venkata Ratnam, 6 sons, 2 daughters. Education: BA Hons, MA Economics, Andhra University, 1935-39; PhD, 1953, University of Cambridge, UK. Appointments: Professor and Head, Department of Economics, 1958-75, Emeritus Professor, 1975-85, Principal, University College of Arts and Commerce, 1966-68, Founder Director, Agro-Economic Research Centre (Government of India), 1968-76, Andhra University; Senior Economist, UN Institute for Economic and Social Development, Bangkok, 1964; Economic Adviser, Government of East Nigeria, 1964-66; Research Fellow, Indian Council for Social Science Research, Madras Institute of Development Studies, Madras, 1976-78; Vice Chancellor, Nagarjuna University, Guntur, Andhra Pradesh, 1979-81; Founder Director, Institute of Development and Planning Studies, Visakhapatnam, 1983-93, Honorary Professor and Chairman, 1993-96; Honorary Professor and Chairman, Indian Institute of Advanced Management, Visakhapatnam, 1985-95; President, Gayatri Vidya Parishad and Chairman, Management Committees of G V P Junior College, G V P College for Degree and Post-Graduate Courses, and G V P College of Engineering, 1990-. Honours: Honorary D Litt, Andhra University, 1979, Nagarjuna University, 1981; President, Indian Economic Association, 1982, A P Economic Association, 1983; Indian Economic Association's honour with a citation at its 80th Jubilee Conference in 1997. Publications: 5 books; 20 papers; 25 project study reports. Address: 8-59-5, 2nd Lane, Vidyanagar, Visakhapatnam 530 003, Andhra Pradesh, India.

**SASTRI Suri Rama Subbaraya,** b. 16 November 1942, Nuzvid, India. Research Engineer. m. Veluri Sumathi, 1 son, 1 daughter. Education: BTech Chemical Engineering, Andhra University, Waltair, India. Senior Scientific Assistant, National Chemical Laboratory, Council of Scientific & Industrial Research, Pune, 1963-68; Scientist B, 1968-73, Scientist C, 1973-83, Scientist EI, Assistant Director 1, 1981-87, Scientist EII, Assistant Director 2, 1987-93, Scientist F, Deputy Director, 1993-, Regional Research Laboratory, Council of Scientific and Industrial Research, Bhubaneswar; Guest Scientist, Niproruda, Sofia, Bulgaria, 1975-76; Consultant, institutional Tata Iron and Steel Co Ltd, National Mineral Development Corporation Ltd, Birla Periclase Ltd, Mecon (India) Ltd, Uranium Corporation of India Ltd, and Hindustan Zinc Ltd, 1987-. Publications: Co-patentee 3 patents; Associate Editor, International Series on Chemical Engineering: Utilisation of Natural Resources: Chemical Engineering Approach, 1994; Co-Editor, Indian Mineral Industry: Energy Environment and Resources Development, 1995; co-editor, Benefication, Agglomeration and Environment, 1999; Principal author, 18 research papers on Chemical Engineering in journals; Author or Co-author, 25 research papers on Mineral Processing; 24 papers published in proceedings of seminar symposia; 26 technical reports. Memberships: Life member: Indian Institute of Chemical Engineers; Indian Institute of Metals; Indian Institute of Mineral Engineers. Address: 503 RRL Colony, Bhubaneswar, Orissa 751013, India.

**SATA Toshikatsu,** b. 16 May 1933, Fukuoka City, Japan. Educator; Engineering Consultant. m. Takako Sata, 1 son, 2 daughters. Education: BS, 1963, Kyushu University, Fukuoka City; Dr Sc, 1975. Appointments: Head Staff of Research, Tokuyama Soda Co Ltd, Tokuyama City, Japan, 1963-92; Professor, Faculty of Engineering, Yamaguchi University, Ube City, 1992-97; Japanese Government Authorized Engineering Consultant, 1992-. Publications: Contributor of many papers to various journals. Honours: Hatsumei Sho (Invention Prize) Award, Nippon Hatsumei Kyoukai, 1974; Person of Science nd Technology Merits Award, Science and Technical Agency of Japanese Government, 1979; Tanahashi Sho (Technical Prize) Award, The Electrochemical Society of Japan, 1979; Gijitsu Sho (Technical Prize) Award, Nippon Kagaku Kyokai, 980, Gijitsu Sho (Technical Prize) award Nippon Soda Kogyokai, 1982; Gakujutsu Sho (Science Prize) Award, The Society of Sea Water Science of Japan, 1997. Memberships: Chemical Society of Japan; Electrochemical Society of Japan; Electrochemical Society Inc (USA); Society of Polymer Science of Japan; Society of Sea Water Science of Japan; AAAS; and others. Address: Ohoshima Ohara 89-57, Takuyama City, Yamagudi Pref, 745-0803, Japan.

**SATHYANARAYANA Kestur,** b. 8 October 1942, India. Scientist. m. T S Bhavani, 2 sons. Appointments: Demonstrator, Government Arts and Science College, Bangalore, 1965-68; Research Fellow, Department of Metallurgy, BHU, Varanasi, 1968-74; Pool Officer, National Aeronautical Laboratory, Bangalore, 1974; Visiting Scientist, Tohoku University, Sendai, Japan, 1975-76; Pool Officer, Hindustan Aeronautics Ltd, Bangalore, 1976-78; Scientist C, 978-81, Scientist EI, 1981-86, Scientist EII, 1986-90, Scientist F, Deputy Director 1990-, Regional Research Laboratory, Trivandrum. Publications: Over 180 articles in professional journals. Honours include: Joint Winner, Binani Gold Medal, Indian Institute of Metals, 1993; Cash Prize, Certificate, 2nd Best Presentation; Certificate and Shawl, All India Kannada Cultural and Literary Conference, 1993; Recognised Supervisor, Kerala University; Editorial Board Member, Bulletin of Materials Science of India; Listed in many biographical publications. Memberships: American Society of Materials; Fellow, Institution of Engineers, India; Life Member, Indian Institute of Metals; Materials Research Society of India; Indian Society for Nondestructive Testing; Indian Society of Composite Materials; Electron Microscope Society of India; Society for Research Managers of India; Kerala Academy of Sciences; Indian Society for Materials & Process Engineering. Address: Regional Research Laboratory, Industrial Estate PO, Thiruvananthapuram 695 019, Kerala, India.

**SATIJA M P,** b. 6 June 1949, Sangrur, India. Library Science Teacher. m. Amrita, 1 daughter, 1 son. Education: PhD, 1990; MA, English Literature, 1981. Appointment: Associate Professor, 1991-. Membership: International Society for Knowledge Organisation. Address: Guru Nanak Dev University, Amritsar-143005, India.

**SATO Kazuo,** b. 15 March 1932, Doshimura, Japan. Professor; Inventor and Designer. m. 5 May 1961, 2 sons. Education: BEng, 1957, MEng, 1959, DEng, 1983, Meiji University. Appointments: Engineering Educator, 1955-63; Lecturer, 1963-71, Assistant Professor to Professor, 1971-, Shibaura Institute of Technology, Monato, Tokyo. Publications: Some 500 papers, books: Mechanical Engineering, 1975; Engine Engineering, 1991; Contributor to professional association journals. Honour: Prize for invention of the two-stroke SL engine, Kanagawa, 1991; Swedish Award for Research, 1992; Award for High Technology in Mechanical Devices, the Fire Association. Memberships: Society of Automotive Engineers; Japan Society for Design Engineering; Japan Society for Agricultural Machinery. Address: 3-11-21 Vabe, Sagamihara-shi, Kanagawa-ken 229, Japan.

**SATOMURA Kisaku,** b. 8 July 1928, Wakayama, Japan. President Japanese Red Cross. m. Kimiko Satomura, 1 son, 1 daughter. Education: MD, 1953, School of Medicine, PhD, 1959, Postgrad School, Kyoto University. Appointments: Associate Professor, Kyoto University School of Medicine, 1976-86; Vice President, Wakayama Red Cross Hospital,

1986-92; President, Japanese Red Cross, Wakayama Medical Centre, 1992-. Honours: Pediatric Surgery, 1980; Wakayama Prefectual Prize for Health Care, 1998. Memberships: International College of Surgeons, Chicago; Pacific Association Pediatric Surgeons, Seattle. Address: Japanese Red Cross Society, Wakayama Medical Centre, Wakayama-shi 640-8558, Japan.

**SATTAR Abdus,** b. 3 January 1944, Dist Pabna, Bangladesh. Teacher. m. Nasima, 1 daughter. Education: BA Hons, 1972; MA, Bengali, 1972. Appointment: Professor, Department of Bengali, Bhangura College, Bangladesh. Publications: Poems and Articles in Different Dailies, Weeklies and Journals. Honours: Shahitya Shekwar Title; Championship in Literary and Cultural Competition of Students Union; First Prize, All Bangladesh Essay Competition. Memberships: Director General, Bangladesh Coltural Parishad Central Office; General Secretary, Bangladesh College Teachers Association; Bangladesh Poet Club; Students Union Cabinet. Address: Bhangura College, P O Box Bhangura, Dist Pabna, Bangladesh.

**SATTAR Abdus,** b. 31 December 1954, Bogra, Bangladesh. Scientific Officer. m. Nazma Akhter, 1 son, 1 daughter. Education: BSc.Ag, honours, BAU, Mymensingh, 1976; MSc.Ag, 1978, PhD, IARI, New Delhi, 1983; Postdoctoral, Dundee University, 1992. Appointments: Officer, NPS V, Sonali Bank, 1977-79; Scientific Officer, 1979-85, Senior Scientific Officer, 1979-85, Principal Scientific Officer, 1985-90, BINA; CSO, 1998-. Honours include: BAAS Award, 1990; Certificate of Achievement, BINA, 1993; NST Expert Fellowship, 1998-99; Indian Government PhD Scholarship; EEC Postdoctoral Fellowship. Memberships: Several. Address: Bangladesh Institute of Nuclear Agr, BAU Campus, 2200 Mymensingh, Bangladesh.

**SAUCIER Guylaine,** b. Noranda, Quebec. Chairwoman, CBC Board of Directors. Education: Graduate, College Marguerite-Bourgeois, Ecole des Hautes etudes commerciales, Montreal; Fellow, Institute of Chartered Accountants. Appointments: President and Chief Executive Officer, Groupe Gerard Saucier Ltee, major company specialising in forest products, 1975-89; Sits on board several major Canadian businesses including Northern Telecom, Petro-Canada and Bank of Montreal; Board of Directors, Bank of Canada, 1987-91; Member of Commission of Inquiry on Unemployment Insurance, 1986; Member Ministerial Taskforce on Social Security Reforms, 1994; First Woman President, Quebec Chamber of Commerce; Chairwoman, Canadian . HoBraodcasting Corporation Board of Directors. Honour: Member, Order of Canada, 1989 for displaying exeptional civic-mindedness and for making a significant contribution to the business world. Memberships: Member of board of various bodies including the University of Montreal, Montreal Symphony Orchestra, Hotel-Dieu de Montreal. Address: Canadian Broadcasting Corporation, 250 Leonark Avenue, Ottawa, Ontario, Canada K12 6R5.

**SAUER Timothy Duwayne,** b. 21 May 1956, Valley City, ND, USA. Mathematician. m. Kathleen T Alligood, 1 daughter. Education: BA, Mathematics, Michigan State University, 1977; PhD, Mathematics, University of California, 1982. Appointments: Lecturer, Michigan State University, 1982-85; Assistant Professor, George Mason University, 1985-90; Associate Professor, George Mason University, 1990-96; Professor, GMU, 1996-. Publications: Co-Author, Coping with Chaos; Co-Author, An Introduction to Dynamical Systems. Memberships: American Mathematical Society; SIAM; American Physical Society. Address: Math Sci Dept George

Mason Univ, Fairfax, VA 22030, USA.

**SAUTER Friedrich,** b. 23 May 1930, Vienna, Austria. University Professor. m. Susanne. Education: PhD, University Vienna, 1954. Appointments: Assistant Professor, University Professor, Full Professor, Head of the Chemistry Section, Vienna University of Technology. Honours: Honorary Member, Slovak Chemistry Society; Egyptian Heterocyclic Society. Memberships: Many scientific societies. Address: Vienna University of Technology, Institute of Organic Chemistry, A1060 Vienna, Getreidemarkt 9, Austria.

**SAVONA-VENTURA Charles,** b. 18 February 1955, Malta. Lecturer. m. Marylene Simler, 2 children. Education: MD, University of Malta, 1979; ACOG, Catholic University of Leuven, Belgium, 1985; MRCOG, Royal College of Obstetricians and Gynaecologists, England, 1986; PhD, Research Institute for Mother and Child Care, Poland, 1997. Appointments: Chemistry Research Technician, University of Malta, 1973-74; Trainee Specialist, Obstetrics and Gynaecology, 1979-85, Specialist, 1985-98, Consultant Specialist, 1998-, Department of Health, Malta; Lecturer, Obstetrics and Gynaecology, Faculty of Medicine and Surgery, University of Malta, 1980-87, Institute of Health Care, University of Malta, 1998-. Publications: Numerous articles in professional medical journals. Honours: Craig Memorial Research Scholarship, University of Malta, 1988; Medical Research Grant, BMA (Malta Branch), BUPA Foundation, 1991; Essay Prize, Medical Association of Malta, 1991. Memberships include: New York Academy of Sciences. Address: Northwyndo 40, Triq Antonio Zammit, Ix-Xwieki, L/O Gharghur, NXR 08 Malta.

**SAVU George,** b. 26 February 1949, Paulis, Romania. Aerodynamics. m. Popescu Daniela, 1 son, 1 daughter. Education: Aerospace Engineer, 1973, PhD, 1990, Politechnica University, Bucharest. Appointments: Research Scientist, Programs Engineer, 1973-84, Senior Scientist, 1984-96, Aviation Institute, Bucharest; Space Programs Director, Comoti, Bucharest, 1996-. Publications: Over 50 professional papers. Honours: Over 50 Citations; Nominated, FXB Aerospace Prize, USA, 1993, 1997. Membership: AIAA. Address: Comoti Institute, Bd Iuliu Maniu 220, Bucharest Sector 6, Romania.

**SAWAHEL Wagdy A,** b. 25 September 1964, El-Mahalla El-Kobra, Egypt. m. Education: BSc, Botany, Tanta University, Faculty of Science, 1983-87; PhD, Transgenic Plant Technology, 1991-94. Appointments: Research Assistant, 1988-91; Teaching Assistant, 1996-93; Post Doctoral Research Fellow, 1996-98; Researcher, Genetic Engineering and Biotechnology Division, National Research Centre, Egypt, 1995-. Publications: 21 Research and Review Papers, Plant Biotechnology Research; 2 Academic Books, Plant Biotechnology and Research; 10 Abstracts, Plant Biotechnology Research; 1 Article, Biotechnology Education and Training Programmes; 2 Books, Biotechnology Education and Training Programmes; 4 Articles, Biotechnology Related Issues; 2 Books, Biotechnology Related Issues; 19 Articles, Public Understanding of Biotechnology. Honours: ICG Grant, 1993; British Council Grant, 1993; SEB Society Grant, 1993; Genetical Society Grant, 1993; CBT Fellowship, 1991; Edward Boyle Research Scholarship, 1991-94; Foreign and Commonwealth Scholarship, 1991-94. Memberships: Egyptian Society of Genetic Engineering; Genetical Society of Great Britian; The Society of Experimental Biology; Institute of Biology; New York Academy of Sciences; Many other memberships. Address: National Res Center Genetic Engrg and Biotech Division, Tahrir St, Dokki Cairo, Egypt.

**SAWANT Bhausaheb,** b. 28 June 1964, Chilekhanwadi. m. Padma. Education: BSc, 1990; BPed, 1994; MA, 1996; BA, 1998. Appointments: 1992-. Publications: Padzad, story, 1995. B G Rohamare State Award; Parabhav, novel, unpublished, D E Ambedkar Fellowship Award; Matimol, story. Membership: Maharastea Sanskrutik Kala Abhiyan; President, Shyog Prrtisttan; President, Janata Library. Address: Jijamata College, Bhenda Tal Newasa, Dist Ahmednagar, India.

**SAWAYA Michael George,** b. 26 September 1949, Trinidad, Colorado, USA. Lawyer. m. Louise Ortiz, 2 sons, 1 daughter. Education: BA, Sociology, Colorado College, 1971; BA, Economics, University of Colorado, 1972; JD, Texas Technical University School of Law, 1975. Career: Founder, Law Firm, Sawaya & Rose PC, 1977; President, Cranmer Park Hilltop Civic Association, 1985-87. Honours: Order of the Coif, 1975; Master, Neurolinguistic Programming, 1998. Memberships: American Trial Lawyers Association; Denver Bar Association; Colorado Trial Lawyers Association; Colorado Bar Asscciation. Address: Sawaya & Rose PC, 1650 Emerson Street, Denver, CO 80218-1412, USA.

**SAXENA D C,** b. 12 August 1938, Delhi, India. University Professor. m. Prabha, 1 son, 2 daughters. Education: BA, honours; MA; PhD; LLB. Appointments: Professor, Director University P G Centre; Chairman, Haryana State Board of Education; Convener, All India Committee on Teaching of English in Schools; Professor, Chairman, Department of English, Punjab University. Publications: New College Essays, 1963; Youth Speaks, 1965; Merchant of Venice, 1975; 2 articles. Membership: Charles Lamb Society, England. Address: Department of English, Punjab University, Chandigarh 160014, USA.

**SAYEED M F,** b. 3 February 1933, Hyderabad, Andhra Pradesh, India. m. Munira D/O K Hyder Hussain, 1 son, 3 daughters. Education: BA, 1950; MA, 1957; PhD, International Economics and International Finance. Appointments: former Economic, Banking and Finance Advisor, Government of Kuwait; Notary. Publications: Guidelines: Offset and Counter Trade Program Government of Kuwait and planned Reconstruction of Kuwait After Iraq Invasion. Honours: Awards, Government of Kuwait; Award and Medal, Republican Senatorial Inner Circle; Advisory Board Member Chairman, National Republican Party. Address: The Sayeed International Corporation, 8161 Middle Fork Way, Jacksonville, FL 32256, USA.

**SAZDOV Tome Simon,** b. 8 February 1934, Skopje, Macedonia. University Professor. m. Danica Krsto Ilievska, 2 sons. Education: Faculty of Philosophy, University of Skopje, 1957; PhD, Faculty of Philosophy, University of Skopje, 1969. Appointments: University of Skopje, 1961-70, Assistant Professor, 1970-75, Associate Professor, 1975-79, Professor, 1979; Journalist at Nova Makedonija, newspaper, Skopje, 1956-60, Assistant Lecturer. Publications: Macedonian Folk Literature, 1987, Best Book of Folklore, 1991; Macedonian Folk Works and Their Collectors, 1995. Honours: Oktomvri Award; Kliment Ohridski Award. Memberships: Science Association Bitola; Writers Association of Macedonia; Matica Srpska. Address: Filoloski Fakultet Krste Misirkov, CC 9100 Skopje, Macedonia.

**SCALES John Thomas,** b. 5 July 1935, Cambridge, Massachusetts, USA. State Official. Education: Graduate, Cambridge, MA, High and Latin School, 1953. Appointments: Assistant Law Librarian, Essex County New Jersey Law Library, 1972-80; Technical Assistant Legal Activities, State of New Jersey, 1981-. Honour: Certified Law Librarian, American

Association of Law Libraries, 1962. Address: 628 Arnold Ave, Point Pleasant Beach, NJ 08742-2531, USA.

**SCALISE Randall J,** b. 2 November 1965, Scranton, Pennsylvania, USA. Professor of Physics. Education: BA, magna cum laude, Physics, Cornell University, Ithaca, New York, 1987; PhD, Theoretical Elementary Particle Physics, Pennsylvania State University, 1991. Appointments: Teaching Assistant, 1987-90, Computer System Administrator, Lab for Elementary Particle Science (PSULEPS) Vaxcluster, 1990-92; Computer System Administrator, Department of Physics SUN network, 1990-91, Graduate Research Assistant, Professor John C Collins, 1992-94, Postdoctoral Teaching Assistant, Fall, 1994; Postdoctoral Research Assistant to Professor Collins, 1994-96; Lecturer, Introductory Mechanics, Spring & Summer, 1995; Visting Assistant Professor of Physics, 1995-. Publications: (co-author) 6 refereed in professional journals, 11 others. Honours: Braddock Graduate Fellowship, Pennsylvania State University, 1987-90; Phi Beta Kappa; Teacher of the Year Award, Southern Methodist University Physics Department, 1996-97; Sigma Pi Sigma, Southern Methodist University Chapter Faculty Advisor, 1996-. Memberships: American Physical Society; American Association of Physics Teachers; Mathematical Association of America. Address: Department of Physics, Fondren Science Building, Southern Methodist University, Dallas, TX 75275-0175, USA.

**SCATENA Lorraine Borba,** b. 18 February 1924, San Rafael, California, USA. Teacher; Rancher; Women's Rights Advocate. m. Louis G Scatena, 1 son, 1 daughter. Education: BA, Dominican College, San Rafael, 1945; Postgraduate, California School of Fine Arts, 1948. Appointments: Teacher, Dominican College, 1946, San Anselmo School District, 1946-53, Fairfax Public Elementary School System; Assistant to the Mayor of Fairfax; Teacher, Librarian, US Dependent School Mainz-am-Rhine, Germany, 1953-56; Translator, Portugal Travel Tours, Lisbon, 1954; Bonding Secretary, American Fore Insurance Group, San Francisco. Honour: Travel Award, American Association of University Women, President Yerington Branch, 1975; AAUW Nevada State President, 1981-83; National Future Fund Award, 1983; Nevada Humanities Award; Nevada Named Endowment Gift Awarded for Significant Contributions to the AAUW Educational Foundation, 1997. Memberships: American Association of University Women; Unit President Nevada Retired Teachers; President, Yerington, Nevada Italian Catholic Federation, 1986-88. Address: PO Box 247, Yerington, NV 894470247, USA.

**SCHACH Barbara Jean,** b. 3 December 1945, Bakersfield, California, USA. Educator. m. Henry, 1 son, 1 daughter. Education: BS, 1967; MS, 1994. Appointments: Teacher, 1967-96; Administrator, 1996-. Honours: Educator of the Year, 1994-96; Phi Kappa Phi, 1994. Memberships: Phi Delta Kappa; Association of University Women; Association of Supervision & Curriculum; Delta Delta Delta. Address: 6917 Hartcrest Drive, Rancho Palos Verdes, CA 90275, USA.

**SCHAUBERGER Amanda (Louise),** b. 11 February 1925, Iowa, USA. Author. Education: Hamilton School of Commerce, Mason City, Iowa, 1943-44; 3rd Class Operator's License, Federal Communications Commission, 1929. Appointments: Assembly Worker, General Dry Batteries Inc, 1945-46; Self employed sales worker, Dubuque, Iowa, 1946-49; David Lionel Press of Chicago, Illinois, Knitcraft Hosiery of Brooklyn, New York; Freelance author, 1958-; Disabled American Veterans Thrift Store Phone Solicitor, 1972-1991. Publications: Contributor feature articles and articles on toy making weekly press; Fillers in weekly newspapers; Weekly column in the

Arlington Citizen, 1961-67; Column Writer, Recollections with Mandy, 1984-; Volunteer disc jockey, KFAi-6m, 1978-87. Memberships: Indiana Recording Club of Indianapolis, 1990-; One Man's Family, 1996-; Iowa Antique Radio, 1996-. Address: 555 Fifth Avenue, Apt 1011, Des Moines, IA 50309 2300, USA.

**SCHEIBER Ernest,** b. 3 February 1950, Brasov, Romania. Professor. m. Puscas Floare, 2 sons. Education: Graduate, Faculty of Mathematics, Babes Bolyai, University of Cluj, Romania, 1974; Degree in Mathematics, 1987. Appointments: Transilvanian University of Brasov, 1978; Associate Professor, Computer Science Department, Faculty of Science. Publications: Co-Author, Mathematics for Engineers, Computer Aided Problem Solving Using Derive, MathCAD, Maple and Mathematica; Co-author, Math CAD Presentation and Applications; About 20 Scientific Papers. Memberships: Member, Institutes, Associations; American Mathematical Society. Address: Transilvania University, Faculty of Science, Bd Froilor Nr 29, Brasov 2200, Romania.

**SCHERBAKOV Alexey,** b. 24 February 1954, Leningrad, Russia. Physicist. m. L Zaremba, 2 sons, 1 daughter. Education: High Education, Moscow Physical and Technical Institute, 1978; Dr Sc, 1981; Assistant Professor, 1988. Appointments: Chief Engineer, 1981; Scientific Worker, 1983; Head of Scientific Department, 1988; Head of Scientific Laboratory, 1988; Assistant Professor, 1988. Publications: Advanced Technology of Plasticity, 1990. Honour: Komsomol Prize Winner in Science, 1984, for Numerical Modelling of High Technology Processes. Memberships: Assistant Professor at Moscow Aviation and Technology Institute, Department of Metal-working Treatment, 1988-. Address: Komsomolskaya str Bldg 9 96, Odintsovo, 143000 Moscow Region, Russia.

**SCHIFFNER Charles Robert,** b. 2 September 1948, Reno, USA. Architect. m. Adrienne Andrews. Education: The Frank Lloyd Wright School of Architecture, 1968-73. Appointments: Designer, Project Manager, Taliesin Associated Architects, 1973-78; Staff Architect, Taliesin Associated Architects, Scottsdale, 1978-83; President, Charles Robert Schiffner Architect Ltd, Phoenix, 1983-; Visiting Lecturer, The Frank Lloyd Wright School of Architecture, 1993-. Honours include: Award of Merit, Phoenix Home and Garden, Arizona Homes of the Year Award, 1990; Merit Award, Central Arizona Chapter for the Restoration of the Raymond Carlson House, 1993; Award of Excellence, AIA Arizona, 1993; Federal Design Achievement Award, 1995; ACEA Engineering Excellence Award, 1996. Memberships include: Public Art Committee, Scottsdale; Board Director, Scottsdale Cultural Council. Address: 5202 East Osborn Road, Phoenix, AZ 85018-6137, USA.

**SCHILLER Sophie,** b. 2 October 1940, Moscow. Artist. m. Mikhail, 1 daughter. Education: MA, Moscow Polygraphic Institute, 1958; Certificate, Massachusets College of Art, 1977. Appointments: Free Lance, Moscow Publishing Houses, USA Publishing Houses. Memberships: National Museum Women in Arts. Address: 63 University Road, Brookline, MA 02146-4532, USA.

**SCHLARB Bernhard,** b. 31 March 1958, Koblenz, Germany. Chemist. Education: Abitur, 1977; Chemistry Diploma, 1983; PhD, 1988. Appointments: Scientific Assistant, University of Mainz, Germany, 1983-84; Technical Trainee, Eastman Kodak Company, Rochester, USA, 1986; Scientific Employee, University of Mainz, 1987-88; Scientist, BASF AG, Ludwigshafen, Germany, 1988-. Publications: 14 Publications, 1984-. Memberships: German Chemical Society, 1985-. Address: Dhauner Str 15A, 67067 Ludwigshafen, Germany.

**SCHLEMAN Margo M,** b. 20 March 1945. Physician. m. Samuel, 1 son, 2 daughters. Education: BA, New York University, 1966; MD, New York School of Medicine, 1970. Appointments: Pediatric Residency, Long Island Jewish Hillside Medical Center, New York, USA, 1970-72; Executive Director, Clinical Research, Astra Merck Inc, Wayne, PA, USA, 1994-98. Honour: Pediatric Cardiology Fellowship, 1972-75. Memberships: Fellow, American Academy Pediatric; Fellow, American College of Cardiology. Address: Astra Merck Inc, 725 Chesterbrook Boulevard, Wayne, PA 19087, USA.

**SCHLESINGER John Richard,** b. 16 February 1926, London. Film Director. Education: BA, English Literature, Balliol College, 1950. Appointments: Professional Actor, 1950-58; Director, Documentary Films for TV, 1958-60; Associate Director, National Theatre, 1973; Many Films Directed. Honours: Golden Lion, Venice Film Festival; Golden Bear, Berlin Film Festival; New York Critics Award; Academy Award, Best Director; David de Donatello Special Award for Best Director, Best Film; New Evening Standard Award, Best Film; Society of West End Theatre Award; British Academy Award; Broadcasting Press Guild Award; Barcelona Film Festival, Best Fiction Film for an Englishman Abroad; British Academy Award, Best Single Drama; Lifetime Achievment Award. Address: United Talent Agy, Attn Jeremy Zimmer, 9560 Wilshire Blvd, Beverly Hills, CA 90212, USA.

**SCHMIDLI Keith William,** b. 11 October 1952, Niagara Falls, New York. Educational Administrator. Education: AA, Liberal Arts and Sciences, Niagara County Community College, 1972; Journeyman Certificate, Auto Diesel Mechanics, Trott Vocational School, 1982; BS, Vocational-Technical Education, Summa Cum Laude, SUNY College at Buffalo, 1992; MS, Education, Summa Cum Laude, SUNY College at Buffalo, 1993; PhD, Magna Cum Laude, University of Buffalo, 1999; MBA, DBA, Cambridge State University, 1999. Appointments: Certified Teacher, New York; Maintenance Mechanic, Operating Engineer, Machinist, Great Lakes Carbon Corp, 1973-82; Owner, Manager, Apartment Rental Units, 1975-86; Industrial Tuck Mechanic, New York State Dept of Labour, 1982; Mechanic, Tracy Luckey Co, 1984-85; Mechanic, Operating Engineer, Niagra Falls Country Club, 1985-86; Millwright Custom Maintenance, 1986-87; Pipefitter, John Martin Plumbing, 1987; Engineering Technician, Precious Plate, Niagra Falls, 1987-90; Graduate Administrative Assistant, SUNY College at Buffalo, 1993-94; Administrator, Niagra County Community College, 1995-96; Member, Faculty Selection Committee, Department of Technology, SUNY College at Buffalo, 1992-94; Teaching, Curriculum Cons, LaSalle Senior High School, 1992-. Publications: Increasing Enrollment in Secondary Vocational Education Programs Through Teacher Based Promotion, 1993; Career Education: Exploring the Unfinished Agenda of Providing Applied Practical Knowledge and Skills Needed in a Changing Economy, 1999; Contributor, Articles to Professional Journals. Memberships: ASCD; SME; Association for the Study of Higher Education; Council for Exceptional Children, American Society of Quality; Alpha Sigma Lambda; Kappa Delta Pi. Address: 209 Sabre Park, Niagara Falls, NY 14304-1754, USA.

**SCHMIDT Axel,** b. 29 May 1962, Krefeld, Germany. Physician; Philosopher; Scientist. m. Doris Bade, 1 daughter. Education: Candidate Philosophy, 1987, University Duesseldorf, Germany; MD, 1988; Cert MD, Clinical Microbiologist, 1993, University Hospital Duesseldorf. Appointments: Director, Bayer Pharmaceutical Research, Wuppertal, Germany, 1993-; Associate Professor, University Witten, Herdecke, Witten, 1997-. Publications: Editor: (book series) Contributions to Microbiology, 1996-; Editorial Board,

Chemotherapy, 1996-, Drug Research, 1996-, Haut, 1996-, Alternatives to Laboratory Animals, 1997-, Mikrobiologe, 1998-; Member Scientific Board, Fortschritte de Meditin, 1996-; Mycoses, 1998-; Reviewer, New England Journal of Medicine, 1997-; Contributor, numerous scientific papers; Patentee in field. Honours: Dorothy Hegarty Award, 1997-; Twentieth Century Achievement Award, 1998. Memberships: President, North-Rhine Westfalia, Union of German Clinical Microbiologists, 1995-; Member Board Curators, Manfred Plempel Stipendium for Medical Mycology, 1997-; Union German Clinical Microbiologists; German Society for Mycology; German Hygiene and Microbiology Association; German Association for Natural Sciences and Medicine; Virology Association; Paul Ehrlich Association; French Society for Medical Mycology; International Society of Human/Animal Mycoses; Robert Koch Foundation. Address: Bahnstrasse 118, D-42327 Wuppertal, Germany.

**SCHMIDT Gunter,** b. 22 August 1913, Germany. Dentist. m. Corrine Mitchell, 2 daughters. Education: University of Munich, 1932-33; University of Wurzburg, 1933; Washington University, 1933-37. Appointments: Practice of General Dentistry, 1937-59; Parkway Tower Building, Clayton, 1959-85. Publications: Penicillin Mouthwash for Treatment of Vincent's Stomatitis; Penicillin Reaction in Endodontic Treatment; Neuropsychiatrist and Dentist, A Need for Cooperation; The American Society for Geriatric Dentistry. Honours: 3 Battle Stars; Diamond Pin Award American Academy of Oral Medicine; Honorary Fellow American Academy of Oral Medicine; Academic Fellow American Academy of Oral Medicine; Fellow American College of Dentist; Gold Medal, Greater St Louis Dental Society; Distinguished Service Award; Herschfus Memorial Award. Memberships: Staff Dentist, Shriners Hospital for Crippled Children; Senior Dentist, Jewish Hospital; Anaesthetist, Jewish Hospital; Council on Dental Education; Council on Legislation; AARP; American Dental Association; American Academy of Oral Medicine; American Society for Geriatric Dentistry; Pierre Fauchard Academy; Academy of General Dentistry; Chicago Dental Society; Federation Dentaire International. Address: 7777 Bonhomme, Suite 1400, Clayton, Missouri 63105, USA.

**SCHNEIDER David Paul,** b. 18 December 1954, Kansas City, Missouri, USA. CFO. m. Christine, 1 son. Appointments: OCA Diocese of New York, New Jersey; Secretary, Treasurer, Personal Secretary to Archbishop Peter, 1990-. Address: Diocese of NJ and NJ, 53 Hewitt Avenue, Bronxville, NY 10708-2333, USA.

**SCHNEIDER Dennis Ray,** b. 10 June 1952, Sinton, Texas. Micro Biologist. 1 son, 1 Daughter. Education: BA, University of Texas, Austin, 1974; PhD, University of Texas, Austin, 1978; Appointments: Director for Research and Development, Austin, 1982-88; ADJ Associate Professor, University of Texas, Austin, 1988-. Publications: Numerous Scientific Publications. Memberships: AAAS; ASM; PAOI; SPE. Address: MicroBac Internat, 3200 N H 35, Round Rock, TX 78681-2410, USA.

**SCHOELLER Wolfgang Wilhelm,** b. 3 July 1941, Illertissen, Bavaria. Engineer; Chemist. m. Johanna Stäbler, 1 son, 1 daughter. Education: Diploma of Engineering, 1963, Chemistry, 1966; Doctorate, 1969. Appointment: Professor of Chemistry, University of Bielefeld. Address: University of Bielefeld, Faculty of Chemistry, Postfach 100131, Bielefeld 33501, Germany.

**SCHOENEMANN Ernst A K,** b. 11 May 1940, Ballenstedt, Germany. Professor of Chemical Engineering. m. Hildegard Oellermann, 3 daughters. Education: DIPL-ING Chemist, Technical University, Darmstadt, 1965; DR-ING Chemist, Technical University, Darmstadt, 1967. Appointments:

esearch, Hoechst Ag, Frankfurt Main, 1968; Patents, CIBA ieigy Ag, Basel Switzerland, 1968; Professor of Chemical ngineering, Fachhoch Schule Darmstadt, University for pplied Sciences, 1971. Memberships: AIChE; IUPAC; EFCE; ECHEMA; GDNA. Address: Balkhauser Tal 44, 64342 eeheim-Jugeheim, Germany.

**SCHOONOVER Amy Jo,** b. 25 April 1937, Glen Ellyn, inois, USA. College Instructor; Writer. m. Samuel J Zook Jr, sons, 1 daughter. Education: BA, 1969, Wittenberg niversity; MA, 1982, PhD, 1993, West Virginia University. ppointments: Part-time and fulltime teaching in junior and enior high schools in Champaign, Logan, Madison and Clark ounties, 1961-80; Instructed professional writing course for hio Peace Officers Training Academy, 1979; Taught college evel poetry course for Free University Network in Columbus, hio, 1980; Graduate Teaching Assistant in English at West irginia University, 1981-82, 1984-85; Adjunct English istructor, Urbana University, 1986-88, 1991-, Clark State ommunity College, 1989-90; Taught creative writing course, rbana Senior Citizens Centre, 1991-, Elderly United in pringfield, 1995. Publications: Many papers and articles; egular columnist on arts and general insterest subjects; Over 000 poems published in journals, anthologies and textbooks; ook reviewer; Texts for 5 ensembles; 5 books of poetry; much ore. Honours: Ohio Poet of the Year in 1988 for New & Used oems; Listed in Poets and Writers. Memberships: Society for ie Study of Midwestern Literature; Verse Writers' Guild of hio, several posts; Illinois State Poetry Society; West Virginia oetry Society; National Federation of State Poetry Societies, everal posts; Executive Board, Ohio Poetry Day Association; lational League of American Pen Women in Letters. Address: 520 State Route 56, Mechanicsburg, OH 43044, USA.

**SCHORER Suki,** b. 3 November 1939, Boston, lassachusetts, USA. Ballet Teacher. 1 daughter. ppointments: Member, 1959-72, Principal Dancer, 1968, New ork City Ballet; Teacher, Ballet, 1960, Permanent Member of aculty, 1972, Balanchine Company and School of American allet. Creative Works: Several roles and many ballets. ublications: Blanchine Technique. Honour: Dance Magazine ward, 1998. Address: School of American Ballet, 70 Lincoln enter Plz, New York, NY 10023-6548, USA.

**SCHRIFT Alan Douglas,** b. 2 March 1955, Brooklyn, New ork, USA. Philosophy Professor. m. Jill Lynn Davis. ducation: BA, Brown University, Rhode Island, 1977; MA, 980, PhD, 1983, Purdue University. Appointments: Visiting ssistant Professor, Purdue University, 1983-85; Visiting ssistant Professor, Center for Liberal Studies, Clarkson Jniversity, 1985-87; Visiting Professor, Institute of Philosophy, atholieke University; Assistant Professor, Department of hilosophy, Grinnell College, 1987-91; Associate Professor, 991-97; Department Chair, 1993-; Professor, 1998-. ublications: Nietzsche's French Legacy; Nietzsche and the Question of Interpretation; Why Nietzsche Still?; The Logic of he Gift; The Hermeneutic Tradition; Transforming the lermeneutic Context; Editor, International Studies in hilosophy. Honours: National Endowment for the Humanities; Vestern European Studies Travel Grant; External Fellow, )regon Humanities Centre; American Council of Learned ocieties; Purdue University Fellowship; Baccalaureate lonours Degree. Memberships: American Philosophical ssociation; Society for Phenomenology and Existential hilosophy; North American Nietzsche Society; Nietzsche ociety; Friedrich Nietzsche Society; International Association or Philosophy and Literature. Address: 1032 Chatterton St, irinnell, IA 50012-1734, USA.

**SCHROEDER Jorg Ulrich,** b. 31 October 1953, Sigmaringen. Teacher. Education: Abitur, 1972; State Examination, 1979; MA, 1980; 2 State Exam, 1982. Appointments: Teacher, 1980-82; Music Teacher, 1982-83; Organist, Choirmaster, 1982-83; Teacher, 1983-. Honours: Key Award; Decree of Merit, 1994; Man of the Year, 1994; International Cultural Diploma of Honour,1994; 500 Leaders of Influence; 5000 Personalities of the World; Leaders in Achievement; International Biographical Association Directory. Memberships: Foreign Affairs Association, Munich; Order of International Fellowship; International Biographical Centre, Advisory Council; American Biographical Institute, Research Associate; ABI, Research Board; Life Fellow, International Biographical Association. Address: Gabelsbergstrasse 60B, D-80333 Munich, Germany.

**SCHUELER Karl,** b. 28 December 1956. Operator of a Communications Service. Education: Electronics degree in Communication and Computer Systems, Northwestern, 1978; General education, North Iowa Community College, Mason City, 1981-83; Avionics, Spartan School of Aeronautics, 1986; Computer Science, College of St Teresa, Winona, Minnesota, 1987; Harris Broadcasting: AM/FM/TV Transmitters, 1988; Fiber Optics Splicing & Maintenance, Kris Kellen Fiber Optics Services with Crowder College, Missouri, 1994; Internet, protocols, software, systems, Deing Management, supervisory techniques and workforce utilization in modern business; Warren Hardy, San Miguel de Allende Gto, Mexico: Spanish Intensive. Appointments: various employment, Rush Arbor Ranch, Rushford, Minnesota, 1964-76, 1986-88, 1992-94; Cashier/waiter, Land O'Lakes, Minneapolis, Minnesota, 1976-78; Final Test Technician, Speery Corporation, Clear Lake, Iowa, 1978-84; Technician, Minneapolis Public Schools, Minneapolis, Minnesota, 1985; Salesman, Radio Shack, City Center, Minneapolis, 1985-86; Communications Engineer, IBM, Rochester, Minneapolis, 1989; Chief Engineer, Brookdale College, New Jersey, 1990-91; Contractor, KS Services, offering, independent engineering, facility and equipment maintenance, training others in PC usage, 1987-; Currently in Mexico, operating a communications service: email, phone, fax, publishing, graphics, information, legal and other services, 1996-. Address: Portal de Allende, San Miguel de Allende, CP 37700, Gto, Mexico.

**SCHULZ John Joseph,** b. 28 September 1940, Gt Falls, Montana, USA. Journalist; Educator. m. Linda Seligman Schulz, 2 daughters. Education: BA Journalism, 1962, University Montana; USAF Flight School, 1964; M Phil International Relations, 1979, D Phil International Relations, 1981, Oxford University; National War College, 1986. Appointments: Reporter, UPI San Francisco Bureau, 1962; Fighter, Instructor Pilot, Staff Officer, USAF, 1963-71; Newswriter-Reporter, VOA News, Washington, 1971-72; Regional Correspondent, VOA Hong Kong, 1972-74; Bureau Chief, VOA Tokyo, 1974-77; BBC Commentator and Think Tank Consultant, 1977-79; Deputy Director, VOA News Division, 1982-84; Coverage Editor, 1979-82; South Asia Correspondent, Voice of America News, Islamabad, 1987-89; Oxford Analytica Analyst, 1984-88; Professor, National War College, Washington DC, 1989-91; Senior Correspondent, VOA News, 1984-87, 1991-92; Associate Director for Publications, the Arms Control Association, and Editor, Arms Control Today magazine, 1992-95; Director, London Summer Graduate Programme, 1995-, Professor of International Communications, 1995-, Chair, Dept Mass Communications, Advertising & Public Relations, 1998-, Acting Chair, 1997-98, Boston University. Publications: Scholarly articles and papers presented; Testimony on China's Military Plans and Capabilities, presented to the Senate Foreign Relations Subcommittee on

East Asia/Pacific Affairs, 1995; Featured University Guest Lecturer; Arms Control & National Security Issues: A Guide for VOA Editors and Writers, 1986; VOA Style Guide, book chapters, 1979, 1984; Writing for Your Commander, guidebook, 1968; Author & Publisher 2 periodic newsletters: The St Catherine Wheel; Eagle's Views and News; Final Draft Editor, 3 publications. Address: College of Communications, 640 Commonwealth Avenue, Boston, MA 02215-2422, USA.

**SCHULZE Mark Levon,** b. 30 October 1958, Joliet, Illinois, USA. Video Producer; Business Owner. m. Patricia K Mooney. Education: BA, Communications, Sociology, University of California, San Diego, 1977-82. Appointments include: Producer, Director, DP, Cameraman, Steppin' Out, video, 1994; Producer, Director, DP, Cameraman, Full Cycle: A World Odyssey, 1995; Producer, Director, DP, Cameraman, Location Scout, 1996-. Honours include: Classic Telly Award, 1999; Gold Aurora Award, 1997; Top 100 Producers of the Year, 1997; Aegis Award, 1998 (twice); Communicator Award, 1998; Communicator Jade Crystal Award, 1998; International Sports Video and Film Festival 98 Spirit Award, 1998. Memberships: Special Interest Video Association, 1987-; Video Producers Association of America, 1983-; Alumni Association, 1982-; National Association of TV Arts and Sciences, 1991-. Address: Crystal Pyramid Productions, 7323 Rondel Ct, San Diego, CA 92105, USA.

**SCHUSELKA Elfi,** b. Vienna, Austria. Education: Graphic and Experimental Institute Vienna; University of Vienna; Academy of Applied Arts, Vienna; School of Vision; Academy of Fine Arts, Naples; Art Students League, Pratt Graphics, New York City. Appointments: School of Visual Arts, New York City, 1970-72; Pratt Institute, Phoenix, New York City, 1974; Rutgers University, New Jersey; Visiting Artist, 1976; Pratt Graphics Center, New York City, 1978, 1979, 1980; Baruch College, CUNY, 1989, 1990, 1991. Creative Works: Solo Exhibits include: Condeso/Lawler Gallery, New York City, 1987; Neue Galerie, Vienna, Austria, 1988; Henry Chauncey Conference Center, Princeton, NJ, 1990; Verita Gallery, Tokyo, Japan, 1990; Al Galerie Gerlinde Walz, Stuttgart, Germany, 1993; Glaskasten, Leonberg (Stuttgart), Germany, 1996; Selected Group Shows include: Invited Intern Biennale Bharat Bhavan, Roopankar (Bhopal), India, 1989, 1991, 1995; Intern, Print Triennale Miniature, Frederikstad, Norway, 1988, 1991, 1994, 1996; Intern, Triennial of Graphic Art, Bitola, Macedonia, 1994, 1997. Honours: Awards: International Exhibition of Graphic Art, Frechen, Germany, 1978; Ibizagraphic, Spain, 1982; International Exhibition of Graphic Art, Ljubljana, Jug, 1985, 1987; Invited Intern, Biennale Frederikstad, Norway, 1986; New York Foundation for the Arts, Painting, 1986; Artist Space, New York City, 1988. Address: 133 Eldridge Street, New York, NY 10002, USA.

**SCHWAB Adrijano,** b. 21 February 1965, Postojna, Slovenia. Professor. Education: MD, Medical Faculty, Ljubljanam Slovenia, 1991. Appointments: Professor, Rep of Eli Lilly; Mark Coordinator, 1995-96; Medical Coordinator, 1996-. Memberships: New York Academy of Sciences; National Geographic Society. Address: Na Grivi 61, 1351 Dragomer, Slovenia.

**SCHWARTZ Charles Robert,** b. 3 January 1951, West Virgina, USA. Photographer. 1 daughter. Education: Rochester Institute of Technology, 1968-69; University of Hawaii, 1980-81; University of Maryland, 1984-85; La Verne University, 1985-86. Appointments: Owner, Bob Schwartz Photography, Honolulu, 1974-82; Naples, 1982-85, Milan, 1985-. Membership: TAU Visual, Milan. Address: Via Franza 3, 10010 Lessolo (to), Italy.

**SCHWARTZ Lillian,** b. 13 July 1927, Cincinnati, Ohio, USA. Artist; Author. m. Jack J Schwartz, 2 sons. Education: RN University of Cincinnati, College of Nursing and Health, 194?. Honorary Degree, Seton Hal University; Doctor, Humanities. Appointments: Nurse, Cincinnati General Hospital, 1947; Head Supreme Premature Nursery, St Louis Maternity Hospital 1947-48; Consultant, Bell Laboratories, 1968-; Consultant AT&T Bell Laboratories, Murray Hill, New Jersey, 1968-9? Consultant, Lucent Technologies 1996-; President, Compute Creations Corp, Watchung, New Jersey, 1989-; Consultant Bell Communications Research, Morristown, New Jersey 1984-92; Artist-in-Residence, Sta WNET, New York City 1972-74; Consultant, T J Watson Research Laboratory, IBM Corp, Yorktown, New York, 1975, 1982-84; Visiting Member Computer Science Department, University Maryland, College Park, 1974-80; Adjunct Professor, Fine Arts, Kean College Union, New Jersey, 1980-82; Rutgers University, New Brunswick, New Jersey, 1982-83; Adjunct Professor Department Psychology, New York University, New York City 1985-86; Associate Professor, Computer Science; Guest Lecturer, Princeton University, Columbia University, Yale University, Rockefeller University; Member, Graduate Faculty School Visual Arts, New York City, 1990-. Publications: The Computer Artist's Handbook, co-author; Contributed articles to professional journals; Contributor, chapters to books Membership: World Academy Arts and Sciences.

**SCHWARTZ Sergiu,** b. 1957, Romania (Israeli/US Citizen). Concert Violinist; Conductor; Pedagogue. Education: Studies with Stefan Gheorghiu, Romania; Rami Shevelov, Rubin Academy, Tel Aviv; Yfrah Neaman, Guildhall School, London Dorothy DeLay, Juilliard School, New York; Additional studies with Sandor Vegh, Felix Galimir, Leon Fleisher, Isaac Stern and Sergiu Celibidache. Debut: New York debut at Carnegie Recital Hall; London debut at Wigmore Hall in the Outstanding Israel Artists series; North American debut at the Museum of Fine Arts, Montreal. Career: Soloist with leading orchestras in Europe and throughout the USA, including the Dresden Staatskapelle under Giuseppe Sinopoli, the Jerusalem Symphony under Sergiu Comissiona, the Slovak Philharmonic, the Dresden Philharmonic, the London Symphony at Barbican Hall, London Soloists at Queen Elizabeth Hall, the Bern Symphony under Peter Maag, the Polish National Radio and TV Orchestra under Antoni Wit, the Florida Philharmonic under James Judd, the Orchestra of St Luke's at New York's Lincoln Centre, the Chicago Grant Park Symphony; Soloist and Conductor with the Sarajevo Philharmonic, the Concentus Hungaricus, the European Community Chamber Orchestra, the New York Master Players; Music Advisor and Principal Guest Conductor of the Ashdod Chamber Orchestra of Israel; Recitals at major music centres throughout the US, including Carnegie's Weill Recital Hall, 92nd Street Y, Town Hall, Merkin Hall in New York; Kennedy Centre and the Library of Congress in Washington; Royce Hall (UCLA) and Ambassador Auditorium in Los Angeles; Recital and chamber music appearances at music festivals, including Newport, Rhode Island, Interlochen Michigan, Interlaken, Switzerland, Music at La Gesse, France Kuhmo, Finland; Broadcast recitals in Jerusalem, New York Los Angeles, Washington, Boston, Chicago and London (BBC) including premiere of the Concerto by Samuel Coleridge-Taylor; Teaching position, artist faculty, The Harid Conservatory School of Music, Lynn University, Florida, USA Master classes at music schools, colleges, universities throughout the USA including Interlochen Arts Academy, UCLA, Oberlin Conservatory and Idyllwild School of Music Rubin Academy in Jerusalem, Franz Liszt Academy in Budapest, Rejna Sofia Academy in Madrid; Master courses in Romania, Bulgaria, Switzerland, Holland and Germany; Judge international violin competitions in France, Italy and the USA

Recordings: Works by Sibelius with the London Symphony, Svendsen and Grieg; Works by Spohr; Debussy, Schumann, R Strauss, Bloch, Enescu and Smetana. Honours: America-Isreal Cultural Foundation Award; National Endowment for the Arts Solo Recitalist Fellowship; Prizewinner, international violin competitions in the US, England, Switzerland and Chile. Address: c/o Joanne Rile Artists Management, 801 Old York Road, Noble Plaza, Suite 212, Jenkintown, PA 19046, USA.

**SCHWARZ Louis J**, b. 15 May 1946, Illinois, USA. Financial Advisor. m. Doris, 3 daughters. Education: BA, Chemistry, Gallaudet University, Washington, D.C., USA, 1968; Postgraduate Studies, Illinois Institute of Technology, Chicago, Illinois, USA, 1968-69; Postgraduate Studies, University of Maryland, College Park, Maryland, USA, 1970-72; Certified Financial Planner Designation, College for Financial Planning, Denver, Colorado, USA, 1986. Appointments: High School Science Instructor, Illinois School for the Deaf, Jacksonville, Illinois, USA, 1969-70; Chemist, US Geological Survey, Reston, Virginia, USA, 1970-85; Registered Representative, Integrated Resources Equity Corporation, Silver Spring, Maryland, USA, 1984-89; President, Giuntoli & Schwarz Inc d/a Mail Boxes, USA, Gaithersburg and Germantown, Maryland, USA, 1987-91; Adjunct Professor, School of Management, Gallaudet University, Washington, D.C., USA, 1993, 1994, 1997; President, Metro, Washington Telecommunication Directory for the Deaf Inc, Silver Spring, Maryland, USA, 1988-; Tax Preparer, Income Tax Service for the Deaf, Silver Spring, Maryland, USA, 1971-; Registered Representative, Royal Alliance Associates Inc, Silver Spring, Maryland, USA, 1989-; Financial Planning Advisor, Schwarz Financial Concepts, Silver Spring, Maryland, USA, 1983-. Publications include: Editor, Publisher, Schwarz Signs, newsletter, 1986-87, 1993-; Columnist for various financial periodicals; Contributing Author, About Your Future, 1988. Honours: Top Producer, National Fraternal Society of the Deaf, 1979, 1983; Named Outstanding Handicapped Federal Employee of US Department of Interior, 1974, 1977; Recipient of International Year of Disabled Persons' Honor Award, US Department of Interior, 1981; Recipient of Montgomery County Council's Business Services Award, 1988, 1989; Recipient of National Association of the Deaf's Knight of Flying Fingers, 1990; Recipient of Dee Cee Eye's Appreciation, 1991; Recipient of Maryland Association of the Deaf Distinguished Service Award, 1993; Recipient of Silent News's Certificate of Appreciation, 1993; Recipient of Montgomery County Association of the Deaf's 1997 Business of the Year. Memberships: Institute of Certified Financial Planner; International Association of Registered Financial Consultants Inc; International Association for Financial Planning; Deaf and Hard of Hearing Entrepreneurs Council, Past President and Founder. Address: Schwarz Financial Concepts, 814 Thayer Ave Ste 301, Silver Spring, MD 20910-4500, USA.

**SCIANNAMEO Franco**, b. 5 August 1942, Maglie, Italy. Professor. m. Louise G Cavanaugh. Education: Diploma, Professor of Music; Conservatorio Santa Cecilia, Rome, 1963; Certificate, Professor of Violin, Accademia Nazionale Santa Cecilia, Rome, 1967; MA, Musicology, University of Pittsburgh, 1996; MA, Cultural Studies, University of Pittsburgh, 1996. Appointments: Professor, Hartford Conservatory, Hartford, USA, 1968-80; Director, LSF Publications, 1981-89; Professor, Carnegie Mellon University, Pittsburgh, 1990-. Publications: Scoring Fellini; Giacinto Scelsi; Filippo Traetta; Roman Soundtrack. Recordings: Felix Draeseke, Sonatas for Viola and Piano. Memberships: ASTA; AAIS; AISLLI. Address: Carnegie Mellon University Sch Music, 5000 Forbes Ave, Pittsburgh, PA 15213-3890, USA.

**SCOTT Georgia Dyke**, b. 25 Feburary 1946, Bedford, Virginia, USA. Educator. m. Waldron Scott, 1 son, 2 daughters. Education: BA, Rutgers University, 1976; MA, William Paterson University, 1989. Appointments: Mayor's Aide, Program Analyst, Office of the Mayor, East Orange, New Jersey and Newark, New Jersey, 1976-77; Benefits Coordinator, Ford Motor Company, Metuchen, New Jersey, 1978-83; Director, Administrative Services, American Leprosy Missions, Elmwood Park, New Jersey, 1982-84; Founder, Director, Loving Care Early Learning Center, Paterson, New Jersey, 1985-; President, Holistic Ministries International, Paterson, New Jersey, 1995-; Passaic County (NJ) Freeholder, 1997-. Publication: Bring Forth Justice. Memberships: Board of Chosen Freeholders, Passaic County, New Jersey; Chair, Planning and Economic Development Committee, Board of Chosen Freeholders; Trustee, Passaic County Juvenile Justice Commission & Passaic County Workforce Development Center, Clifton, New Jersey; Chair, CEO, Holistic Ministries International, Paterson, New Jersey; Madison Avenue Christian Reformed Church, Paterson, New Jersey; Pi Lambda Theta; Life Member, National Council of Negro Women; Democratic Party, Passaic County, New Jersey; President, Citizens' Alliance for Drug-Free Paterson; Program Coordinator, Youth Leadership, Leadership Paterson Alumni Association; Board Director, Passaic County Child Care Coordinating Agency; Child Care Committee, Passaic County REACH Project; Consultant, Advance Program, Patterson, New Jersey. Address: 401 East 40th Street, Paterson, NJ 07504, USA.

**SCOTT Pamela Moyers**, b. 1 May 1961, Clarksburg, West Virginia, USA. Physician Assistant. m. Troy Allen Scott. Education: BS, 1983, summa cum laude, Alderson-Broaddus College. Appointments: Physician Assistant, Weston State Hospital, Weston, West Virginia, 1983; Physician Assistant, Rainelle Medical Centre, Rainelle, West Virginia, 1984-. Publications: 26 articles in professional journals including: Setraline for otitis media, 1998; Evaluating a breast mass with fine needle aspiration, 1998. Honours: Business and Professional Woman's Club Young Career Woman of the Year for the Rainelle Club and District V of WV Citation of Honour at state level of competition, 1985-86; West Virginia Women's Commission Celebrate Woman Awards, recognised nominee, 1996, 1997; American Academy of Physician Assistants' Outstanding Physician Assistant of the Year, 1991; West Virginia Governor's Award for Outstanding Rural Health Practitioner, 1997; 6 collegiate awards. Memberships: American Academy Physician Assistant, various posts; Editorial Board member, Journal American Academy of Physician Assistants; West Virginia Association Physician Assistants, various posts; West Virginia State Task Force on Adolescent Pregnancy & Parenting; West Virginia Governor's Rural Health Awards Programme, Judge; West Virginia Coalition for Managed Care Options' Provider Sponsored Network Committee; Mississippi Academy of Physician Assistants; and others. Address: PO Box 43, Williamsburg, WV 24991, USA.

**SCZAKIEL Georg Alois**, b. 7 July 1956, Kaiserslautern, Germany. Scientist; Biochemist. m. Jutta Sczakiel, 1 son, 1 daughter. Education: Diploma in Chemistry, University of Freiburg; PhD, Max Planck Institute, Heidelberg; Venia Legendi, University of Heidelberg. Appointments: Researcher, German Cancer Research Centre, Heidelberg; Lecturer, University of Heidelberg; Project Leader, Steinbeis-Transferzentrum for Genome Informatics, Heidelberg; Co-Founder, Chief Executive Officer, A3D GmbH Antisense Design and Drug Development. Publications: Author of over 75 books and scientific articles; Patentee in the field. Memberships: Editorial Board, Antisense and Nucleic Acid Drug Development; Gesellschaft Deutscher Chemiker;

Gesellschaft für Biochemie und Molekularbiologie. Address: German Cancer Research Centre, Im Neuenheimer Feld 242, D-69120 Heidelberg, Germany.

**SEABOURN Connie,** b. 20 September 1951, Purcell, Oklahoma, USA. Visual Artist. 1 daughter. Education: BA, University of Oklahoma, 1980. Career: Numerous exhibitions worldwide, including The Kennedy Center for Performing Arts, Washington, DC; The Museum of Man, San Diego; Represented in private collections; Several workshops. Address: PO Box 23795, Oklahoma City, OK 73123, USA.

**SEBEOK Thomas A,** b. 1920, Budapest. Professor, Linguistics. Education: BA, University of Chicago, 1941; MA, 1943, PhD, 1945, Princeton University; Doctor hon causa, University of Budapest, 1990; Dr.Sci, hon causa, University of Southern Illinois, 1991, New Bulgarian University, 1996; PhD, hon causa, University of Helsinki, 1997. Appointments include: Member, Indiana University Faculty, 1943-; Numerous visiting appointments. Publications: Numerous in professional journals. Honours include: Distinguished Service Award, American Anthropological Association, 1984; Presidents Medal of Excellence, 1991; Professional Achievement Citation, University of Chicago, 1992; Honorary Member, Hungarian Academy of Sciences, 1993-; Honorary Fellow, Victoria College, University of Toronto, Canada, 1995-; Distinguished Senior Fellow Emeritus, Institute for Advanced Study, Budapest, 1996-. Memberships include: Linguistic Society of America; Semiotic Society of America; American Anthropological Association; American Folklore Society; American Association for the Advancement of Science; New York Academy of Sciences. Address: Indiana University, PO Box 10, Bloomington, IN 47402-0010, USA.

**SEDACCA Angelo,** b. 14 March 1971, Bronx, New York, USA. Police Officer. m. Diane Bockino, 2 sons. Education: BA French and Italian Studies, 1993, Fordham University, Bronx; MA French Language and Civilisation, 1995, NYU; MA cand Religious Studies, St Joseph's Seminary, Institute of Religious Studies, Yonkers, New York. Appointments: Assistant Martial Arts Instructor, USA Martial Arts Fitness Centre, Bronx, 1991-94; RCIA Catechist, Our Lady of Solace Church, Bronx, 1993-; Translator, Legal Language Services, 1994-97, Franciscans International, 1995-; Educator, Salesian High School, 1995-96, Our Lady of Solace School, 1996, Riverdale Community Centre, 1996-97; Production Assistant, AI Credit Corporation, 1996-97; Bartender, Pelham Country Club, 1997-98; Police Officer, NY City Police Dept, 1998-. Memberships: Fraternal Order of Police, 1998-; International Police Association; Anchor Club; Holy Name Society; Hispanic Society; Columbia Association; New York City Police Department, 1998-; Eucharistic Minister, 1997-; Parish Council member, 1997-98, St Theresa Church; Treasurer, Secular Franciscan Order, St Barnabus Fraternity, Professed Member, 1996-; National Notary Association, 1997-; American Society of Notaries; and many others. Honours: La Medaille du Grand Maitre aux Pelerins de l'ordre, Sovereign Military Order of Malta, 1996; Presidential Sports Award, Amateur Athletic Union, 1994; Tae Kwon Do Times Magazine Recognition Award, 1994; Heydt French Gold Medal, 1993; Michael Marinaro Award, 1993. Address: 1650 Hutchinson River Parkway East, Apt 5B, Bronx, NY 10461-4313, USA.

**SEDLAK Shirley A,** b. 6 September, Chicago, Illinois. Freelance Writer. m. Harold Otto, 1 daughter. Education: Morton College, Cicero, Illinois. Appointments: Editor of children books, Benefic Press, Westchester, Illinois, 1973-75; Publicity/Public Relations, National League of American Pen Women Inc, Chicago Branch, 1987-89; Novelist. Honours:

Listed in various Marquis Who's Who. Membership: Toastmaster International, West Suburban 939, 1989-90. Address: 2226 S 9th Avenue, North Riverside, IL 60546, USA.

**SEFR Roman,** b. 8 February 1963, Brno, Czech Republic. Surgeon. m. Dana Klempusova, 1 son. Education: MD, 1988, Masaryk University, Brno. Appointment: Chief of Surgical Endoscopy, Bakes Hospital, Brno. Publications: Surgical Endoscopy; International Surgery. Memberships: EAES; Czech Surgical Society; IGSC. Address: Bakes Surgical Hospital, Zluty Kopec 5, 60200 Brno, Czech Republic.

**SEGAL Heshie,** b. 8 October 1944, Atlantic City, New Jersey, USA. Entrepreneur; Teacher; Author; Speaker; Trainer; Designer. 1 son, 1 daughter. Education: BA, 1966, Douglass College, New Jersey; Graduate Studies, Trenton State College, 1967-70. Appointments: International Mail Order Company Owner, Operator, 1989-; International, National, Local Educator, Lecturer, 1966-; National Speakers Association/Liberty Bell; Embroiderers' Guild of America; National Needlework Association; American Needlepoint Guild; International and National Design Company Owner, Operator, Fleur de Paris, Rainbow Gallery, Harriet Segal Designs, 1991-; Consultant, Advisor to start-up needlework businesses nationally, 1986-; Small Business Owner, Sr Executive for Motivational TV Network, 1994-, The Embroidery Stop, Retail Embroidery, 1975-; Consultant for future business owners, Founder and Director of the What If Organisation producing results from possibilities, 1990-; Author, 1981-; Needlework Judge, Nationally and locally, 1981-; Led 6 week educational teen tour to Israel, 1991; Developed and taught language, history and culture for grades 5-10, 1964-; Developed and taught needlework programmes for children nursery through grade 12, nationally and locally, 1978-; National Chairman, Children's Programming for Embroiderer's Guild of America, 1982-89; Founder/Creator, Leadership educational programmmes in lay, civic, and religious organisations for adults and children, 1974-; Student Advisor and mentor in schools and non-profit organisations, 1988-. Publications: Phoenix, Instruction Book, 1996; Many articles and instruction booklets and 3 magazine covers in the field of needlework; Writings also included in Needlejoy and Jewish Yellow Pages. Honours: Many awards from National Council of Jewish Federation and Welfare Funds, Jewish Federation, Women's Division, Embroiderers' Guild of America, Jewish Community Centre, National Frame Factory, Elsa Williams School of Needle Art. Memberships: business/education community, Chamber of Commerce, 1996-. Address: 1042 Victory Drive, Yardley, PA 19067, USA.

**SEGALA Carlo,** b. 26 November 1924, Golasecca, Varese, Italy. Inventor. Education: High School Diploma. Appointments: President, International Association Inventors. Honours: 104 Gold Medals; 32 Silver Medals; 18 Bronze Medals. Memberships: Counsellor and Deputy of the World Parliament for Security and Peace. Address: Via Cesare Battisti 47, 21010 Golasecca, Varese, Italy.

**SEGETH Karel,** b. 10 May 1943, Prague, Czech Republic. Mathematician. m. Jitka, 2 daughters. Education: MS, Charles University, Prague, 1964; PhD, Mathematics Institute, Academy of Sciences, Prague, 1972. Appointments: Research Assistant, 1966-72, Researcher, 1972-77, Senior Researcher, 1977-93, Department Head, 1993-96, Director, 1996-, Mathematics Institute, Academy of Sciences, Prague. Publications: Mathematics Modeling in Electromagnetic Prospecting Methods, 1982; Survey of Applicable Mathematics, 1994. Membership: Union of Czech Mathematicians and Physicists.

Address: Mathematics Institute, Academy of Sciences, Zitna 5, CZ 11567 Praha 1, Czech Republic.

**SEIFRITZ Walter, b.** 14 June 1939, Tuttlingen, Germany. Professor. m. Birgit. Education: Diploma in Physics, University of Karlsruhe, 1994; PhD, Reactor Engineering, 1969; Habilitation, University of Hannover, 1972; Professor, 1978. Appointments: Research Center Karlsruhe, 1964-69; University of Hannover, 1969-73; OECD Halde Reactor Project, 1971-72; Head, Physics Department, Swiss Federal Institute, Reactor Research, 1982-92; Retired, 1992. Publications: More than 300 publications; Many books; Articles in Scientific Journals. Memberships: International Association for Hydrogen Energy. Address: Mulacherstr 44, CH 5212 Hausen, Switzerland.

**SEILER Ernst Friedrich, b.** 6 September 1934, arrived in Japan, 1961. Pianist. m. (1) Mie Ogiso, 16 September 1959 (divorced March 1976), 4 children; (2) Kazuko Masada, 3 March 1976, 2 children. Appointments: Professor, Kobe (Japan) College, 1961-67; Head Professor, City Music College, Kyoto, Japan, 1961-67; Lehrauftrag Mozarteum, Salzburg, Austria, 1968-72; Professor Bunri University, Tokushima, Japan, 1974-96; Senzoku University, Tokyo, 1983-85; Advisor, Yamaha Music Foundation, Tokyo, 1961-68; Chairman, The first Kayabuki Ongaku-do Competition for Piano Duet, Japan, 1998. Publications: Co-auth: Seiko-Uso, 1992; CDs include Encores from Kayabuki, 1994; The Seasons of Japan, 1995. Honours: Recipient, 1st Prize, Colony Club, 1959; Distinguished Services Award, Hiyoshi County, Japan, 1995; Kyoto Prefecture, 1995; Distinguished Services Award, Japan, 1997. Memberships: Piano Instructors Association; Founding Member, Japan Piano Teachers Association; Member of the Board, Kyoto Prefecture International Center. Address: Awagakaki Uchi-cho 30, 603 Kyoto-Kitaku, Japan.

**SEK Danuta, b.** 8 December 1935, Katowice, Poland. Chemist; Scientist. m. Mieczyslaw Sek, 1 son. Education: MS, 958; PhD, 1967; DSc, 1983. Appointments: Head of Laboratory, Cefarm, Katowice, 1959-64; Assistant, Technical University, Gliwice, 1964-67; Head of Laboratory, Institute of Polymere Chemistry, Zabrze, 1967-74; Deputy Director, 1974, Director, 1998-, Institute of Polymere Chemistry, Zabrze. Publications: Over 50 articles in professional scientific journals. Honours: Award of Scientific and Technical Committee, Warsaw, 1967; Award, Scientific Secretary of Polish Academy of Sciences, 1973. Membership: New York Academy of Sciences. Address: 40-713 Katowice ul, Slupska 19 m 16, Poland.

**SEKAJUGO James, b.** 18 February 1954, Kampala, Uganda. Medical Doctor. Education: Bachelor of Medicine, Bachelor of Surgery, Makerere University, 1978; Postgraduate Diploma in Sports Medicine, LHMC London, 1983. Appointments: Medical Officer, Special Grade, Ministry of Education and Sports; Member, Supreme Council for Sports in Africa, Medical Commission. Membership: International Federation of Sports Medicine. Address: Plot 5, William Street, PO Box 9194, Kampala, Uganda.

**SEKINE Hideki, b.** 22 March 1943, Tokyo. Professor. m. Yukimi Sekine. Education: Doctor of Engineering, 1977. Appointments: Associate Professor, Tohoku University, Japan, 1980-87; Professor, 1987-. Publications: Theory of Elasticity, 1983. Honours: MMIJ Prize, 1985; Yamazaki Prize, 1992. Memberships: Japan Society of Mechanical Engineers; Japan Society for COmposite Materials. Address: 7-9-904 Itsutsu Bashi 2 chome, Aoba Ku Sendai 980 0022, Japan.

**SELANDIA Elizabeth, b.** 3 April 1945, Santa Barbara, California, USA. Doctor of Oriental Medicine; Acupuncturist; Freelance Author. Divorced, 1 daughter. Education: AA, Behavioral Sciences, French, Humanities, College of Marian, Kentfield, 1992; BA, honours, Native American Studies and Linguistics, University of California, Berkeley, 1994; MA, Museum Studies, San Francisco State University, in progress. Career: Freelance Author, 1981-; Editorial Assistant, UNIX World Magazine, 1985-91; Doctor of Oriental Medicine, Licenced Acupuncturist, 1987-. Publications include: Dead Heat - A Pictorial: the Importation of Arabian Horses From the Middle East to San Simeon Stables, 1998. Address: PO Box 827, Larkspur, CA 94977, USA.

**SELVIN Nancy, b.** 19 August 1943, Los Angeles, USA. Artist. m. Steve Selvin, 1 daughter. Education: MA Ceramics, 1970, University California at Berkeley. Career: 15 solo exhibitions including: Sybaris Gallery, Royal Oak, Missouri, City of Las Vegas, Charleston Heights Art Centre, Nevada, 1999; Represented in 24 public and private collections throughout USA and Japan; On several art advisory committees; Since 1970 taken part in exhibitions all over the USA, Czech Republic, Japan and England; 40 lectures and workshops, 1980-; Featured in many publications in the field of ceramics and women artists; Owner, Founder, After School Arts, Cragmont, Prospect Schools, 1983-89; Co-Owner, Brushstrokes Studio, Berkeley, 1996-98. Publications: 4 articles: Tepcoware, 1982; Bulmer Brick and Tile, 1985; How I Got Here, 1989; Decorating Tile, 1993. Honours: California Craftsman Award, 1978; Westwood Ceramic National, Purchase Award, 1980; NEA Individual Artist Fellowship, 1980, 1988; Skaggs Foundation, Programme Development Grant, 1986; Outstanding Educator, Studio Potter Foundation, 1988; Oakland Business Arts Award, Individual Artist, 1990; Guest Artist, Watershed Centre for Ceramic Arts, 1998. Address: 745 Page Street, Berkeley, CA 94710, USA.

**SEMBULINGAM K, b.** 27 July 1947, Thirunelveli, India. Teaching. m. Prema Sembulingam, 1 son. Education: BSc, Zoology, 1967, MSc, Physiology, 1970, PhD, Physiology, 1994, University of Madras. Career: Lecturer, JJM Medical College, Davanagere, Karnataka, 1970-71; Lecturer, 1971-84, Assistant Professor, 1984-86, MR Medical College, Gulbarga, Karnataka; Assistant Professor, 1986-95, Reader, 1995-96, Associate Professor, 1997-, Sri Ramachandra Medical College & Research Institute Madras. Publications include: Effect of acute noise stress on some selected stress indices, 1996; Effect of Ocimum Sanctum Linn on noise induced changes in Plasma Corticosterone level, 1997; Effect of chronic noise stress on some selected stress indices in albino rats, 1997. Memberships: Indian Association of Biomedical Scientists; Association of Physiologists & Pharmacologists of India. Address: Sri Ramachandra Medical College & Research Institute, Madras 600 116, India.

**SEMBULINGAM Prema, b.** 10 November 1944, Chittoor, India. Teacher. m. K Sembulingam, 1 son. Education: BSc, Zoology, 1966, MSc, Physiology, 1969, University of Madras; PhD, Physiology, The Dr. M.G.R. Medical University, Chennai. Appointments: Lecturer, 1970-84, Assistant Professor, 1984-86, MR Medical College, Gulbarga, Karnataka; Assistant Professor, Sri Ramachandra Medical College and Research Institute, Chennai, 1986-. Publications include: Finger pulse volume in patients with panic attacks, 1992; Finger pulse volume during $CO_2$ induced panic states, 1992; R-R variance in patients with panic disorder and generalized anxiety disorder, 1994; R-R variance during CO2 induced panic attacks; Effect of acute noise stress on cholinergic neurotransmitter in corpus striatum of albino rats, 1996; Effect of Ocimum Sanctum Linn on noise induced changes in Plasma Corticosterone level, 1997; Effect of chronic noise stress on some selected stress indices in albino rats; 20 papers presented in conferences. Memberships: Fellow, Indian Association of Biomedical Scientists; Association of Physiologists and Pharmacologists, India. Address: Sri Ramachandra Medical College & Research Institute, Porur, Chennai 600 116, India.

**SEME Phillipine J Nomathemba**, b. 15 May 1957, Durban, South Africa. Assistant Professor. m. Joseph M Kargbo, 1 daughter. Education: MS, Curriculum and Instruction, Oklahoma State University, Stillwater, Oklahoma, USA, 1987; MEd, Reading and Language, Harvard Graduate School of Education, Massachusetts, USA, 1991; EdD, Harvard Graduate School of Education, Cambridge, Massachusetts, USA, 1993. Appointments: Assistant Professor, Old Dominion University, Norfolk, Virginia, USA; Teaching Fellow and Research Assistant, Harvard Graduate School of Education, Massachusetts, USA. Awards: Research Grant, Harvard Institute of International Development; Research Grant, Old Dominion University Summer Faculty Research. Memberships: National Council of Teachers of English; Teachers of English to Speakers of Other Languages; ASCD. Address: 901E Armfield Circle #104, Norfolk, VA 23505, USA.

**SEMON Mark David**, b. 27 March 1950, Milwaukee, Wisconsin, USA. Physicist. Education: AB, Colgate University, 1971; PhD, University of Colorado, 1976. Appointments: Demonstrator, Imperial College, 1973-74; Summer Research Student, Kitt Peak Obs, 1970; Summer Research Student, Los Alamos Scientific lab, 1975; Professor, Bates College, 1976-. Honours: Magna Cum Laude, With High Honours in Physics. Memberships: Phi Beta Kappa; Woodrow Wilson Fellows; Kappa Mu Epsilon; American Physical Society; American Association of Forensic Scientists; American College of Forensic Examiners. Address: Bates College Department of Physics, 44 Campus Avenue, Lewiston, ME 04240-6018, USA.

**SENCENBAUGH Joseph Buz**, b. 17 June 1951, New London, USA. Consulting Musician. Education: BA, Mathematics, University of Colorado, 1983. Appointments: Teacher, Substitute Teacher, Professional Musician, Photographer. Creative Works: Album: Take The Time, 1985; Tape: Reach For The Top, 1988. Honours: National Photographic Award, Canadian Figure Skating Club, 1975; 1st Class Hiking Counsellor, Ski Hi Camp, Cheley, Colorado Camps; Most Philosophical Sub Coronado High School, 1996; Special Sub Award, Palmer High School, 1997. Address: 7413 Tudor Road, Colorado Springs, CO 80919-2614, USA.

**SENDA Kei**, b. 17 August 1963, Toyama, Japan. Associate Professor. m. Yoko, 1 son. Education: BS, 1986, MS, 1988, in Aerospace Engineering, PhD Engineering, 1993, Osaka Prefecture University. Appointments: Research Associate, 1988-94, Lecturer, 1994, Associate Professor, 1994-, Department of Aerospace Engineering, College of Engineering, Osaka Prefecture University; Visiting Professor, Michigan State University, 1996-97. Publications: Over 30 journal papers; Co-author, in Japanese, book, Introduction to Aerospace Engineering, 1998. Memberships: Senior member, AIAA; Member: Japan Society Mechanical Engineers; Robotics Society of Japan; Institute of System, Control and Information Engineers; Society of Instrument and Control Engineers; Japan Society for Aeronautical and Space Sciences. Address: Osaka Prefecture University, College of Engineering, 1-1 Gakuen-cho, Sakai Osaka 599-8531, Japan.

**SENEVIRATNA Peter**, b. 30 December 1927, Colombo, Sri Lanaka. Retired Veterinarian. m. Kamanee, 2 sons, 2 daughters. Education: BVSc, Madras, 1951; PhD, London 1957; MRCVS, England, 1958; FRCVS, England, 1964 MACVS, Australia, 1981; DSc (honoris causa), 1998 Appointments: Dean, Faculty of Agriculture and Veterinar Science, University of Ceylon; Post Doctoral, Fulbrigh Research Scholar, University of California, 1963-64; Visiting Professor, Wayne State University, Michigan; Veterinar Officer, Department of Primary Industries, Canberra; Senic Lecturer, Murdoch University, Perth. Publications: Diseases c Poultry; Manual of Meat Inspection for Developing Countrie with Four Others; Over 60 Research Papers. Memberships Australian Veterinary Association; Australian College c Veterinary Scientists; Royal Society for Prevention of Cruelty t Animals. Address: 25 Broadbent Loop, Leeming, WA 6149 Australia.

**SENGUPTA Subodh C**, b. 20 April 1935, Maymyo, Burma Retired Civil Servant. m. Krishna Sengupta, 1 son, 1 daughter Education: BA, 1957, MA, 1960, Calcutta University Intermediate Arts, Dacca University, 1995. Appointments School Teacher, 1957-64; Librarian, The Army Ordnance Club Calcutta, 1958-60; Deputy Commissioner, Law, West Benga Excise Service, 1995. Publictions: 12 anthologies of poems, 2 collections of short stories, 6 novels, 2 collections of poems or English, several articles in professional journals. Honour: include: Michael Madhu Sudan Award, 1992; Bishnudey Award 1995. Memberships: Social Welfare Organization; Literar Forum. Address: Judges Bagan, West Putiary, Calcutta 700082, India.

**SENVALTIENE-JASINEVICIUTE Jurate**, b. 29 February 1956, Vilnius, Lithuania. Restoration Scientist. m. Senvaiti Vidmantas, 1 daughter. Education: Diploma, Vilnius University 1979. Appointments: Chemist, Restoration Centre of Lithuania Art Museum, 1979-83; Head of Department, Scientific Research, Restoration Centre of Lithuanian Art Museum 1983-97; Head of Restoration Centre, Lithuanian Art Museum 1997-. Publications: Prano Gudyno Restaurauimo Centras 1997. Memberships: Lithuanian Council of Museums. Address Taikos 43-16, LT 2017, Vilnius, Lithuania.

**SENZIA Musa Saidi**, b. 4 October 1937, Mwanga District Laboratory Technician. m. Rukia, 8 sons. Appointments: IC, S Elizabeth Laboratory. Membership: American Association fo Clinical Chemistry. Address: RC Mission Bagamoyo, Dept c Lab, Begamoyo, Tanzania, Africa.

**SERDANS Rebecca**, b. 26 November 1965, Munster Germany. Registered Nurse, Writer. Education: BSN University of Rochester, NY, 1990; Registered Nurse, 1987 Pre Med Studies, 1992; Certified Diabetes Educator Appointments: Staff RN, Charge RN, Highland Hospital Rochester, 1987-; Staff Nurse, New York Presbyterian Hospital 1998-; Staff RN, Lenox Hill Hospital, 1998-; Research Assistant, St Mary's Hospital, 1996-. Publications: Clues tc Managing Endocrine Disorders in the ICU; Re Discovering Diabetes; UN Masking Parkinsons Disease; Dystonia is, / Personal Poem; De Mystifying Dystonia. Memberships American Latvian Relief Organization; Bachmann Strauss Dystonia and Parkinson Foundation; National Spasmodic Torhcollis Association; American Association of Neuroscience Nursing; American Association Diabetes Educators; Dystonia Medical Research Foundation. Address: 440 East 78th St, Nev York, NY 10021, USA.

**SEREDA Yuri Stepanovitch**, b. 23 November 1937 Ordzhonikidze, North Osetian ASSR, USSR. Physicist. m Evelina Alexeevna Sereda, 1 son, 1 daughter. Education Diploma, Gorky State University, 1961; Doctorate i

Radiophysics, 1980. Appointments: Engineer, Special Bureau ofAutomatics, 1968; Head of Research Group, V A Kargin Polymer Research Institute, 1968-78; Senior Scientific Associate, Institute of Mechanics, Gorky State University, 1978-89; Scientific Secretary, Blagonravov Mechanical Research Institute, Gorky branch, 1989-98. Publications: Statistical Models of Synergetics, 1997; Problems ofInformational-Statistical Theory, 1998; 50 articles. Address: 85 Belinskogo Str, Nizhny Novgorod 603024, Russia.

**SERES Laszlo,** b. 10 January 1939, Mindszent, Hungary. Professor of Chemistry. m. Edit Magocsi, 1 son, 1 daughter. Education: Graduate, University of Szeged, Faculty of Sciences, 1962; PhD, University of Szeged, Faculty of Sciences, 1973; DSc, Hungarian Academy of Sciences, 1994. Appointments: Professor's Assistant, Institute of General and Physical Chemistry, University of Szeged, Hungary, 1962-67; First Assistant to Professor, Institute of General and Physical Chemistry, University of Szeged, Hungary, 1967-74; Lecturer, Institute of General and Physical Chemistry, University of Szeged, 1974-91; College Professor, Chief of Chemistry Department, Teachers' Training College, Szeged, 1991-96; Professor of Chemistry, Department of Chemistry, Teachers' Training College, Szeged, 1996-; Vice General Director, Teachers' Training College, Szeged, 1995-; Member, Senate of Szeged University, 1998-. Publications: Over 50 research papers in different journals of chemistry; Co-author, Fortran Programs for Solution of Physical Chemistry Problems, 1978. Honours: Excellent Worker of Education, Ministry of Education, 1975; Decoration of Work, silver grade, Ministry of Education, 1983; Szent-Gyorgyi Albert Award, Ministry of Education, 1998. Memberships: Working Committee, Reaction Kinetics and Photochemistry, Hungarian Academy of Sciences, 1987-; Correlation Analysis in Organic Chemistry, 1985-. Address: Gy Juhasz Teachers College, 6720 Szeged Boldogasszony sgt 6, Hungary.

**SERYS Vytautas,** b. 24 January 1931, Naujasodziai village, Anyksciai district. Sculptor; Painter. m. Judita Zaveckyte-Seriene, 1 daughter. Education: Diploma Professional Sculptor, 1956, Lithuanian SSR State Art Institute. Career: Participator in group and one-man exhibitions, 1957-. Honour: National Prize, 1995. Memberships: Lithuanian Artists Union, 1964-; Artists Organisation Group "24", 1991-. Address: Vilneles 7, 2014, Vilnius, Lithuania.

**SETH Prahlad Kishore,** b. 15 June 1943, Lakhimpur, Kheri, India. Scientist. m. Manju, 1 son, 2 daughters. Education: BSc, 1960; MSc, 1962; PhD, 1967. Appointments: Assistant Professor, The Chicago Medical School, Chicago, USA, 1970-71; Scientist, Industrial Toxicology Research Center, 1971-97; Director, Industrial Toxicology Research Center, 1997-. Honours: Board of Trustees Research Award of the Chicago Medical School; Schewppe Foundation Award; C R Krishnamurti Lecture Award; Bharat Joyti Award. Memberships: Fellow, Indian National Science Academy; The National Science Academy, India; Society of Toxicology, India; Indian Academy of Neurosciences. Address: Director, Industrial Toxicology Research Center, Lucknow 226001, India.

**SETHY Andreas von,** b. 27 August 1932, Budapest. Researcher. m. Christiane Countesse Schall-Raucour, 2 sons, 2 daughters. Eduction: Dipl.Eng, Budapest, 1954; Tu-Wien, 1958; Dr, University of Wien, 1964. Appointments: Electronics Industry, 1954-67; Head of Department, Electronics Institute, Vienna, 1967-95; Division of Technology, College Mödling, Austria, 1973-96. Publications: Books for research policy, 1969, 1983; Memoirs, 1997, 1998; Over 100 articles in professional

journals. Memberships include: IEEE. Address: Liechtensteinstrasse 32/6, A 1090 Vienna, Austria.

**SETOGUCHI Toshiaki,** b. 19 June 1951, Fukuoka, Japan. Professor. m. Kyoko Setoguchi, 1 son, 1 daughter. Education: DrEng, Kyushu University, 1981. Appointment: Professor, Saga University, 1993-. Publications: Paper Awards, Journal, Society of Turbomachinery, 1993; 2 books in Japanese. Memberships: MJSME; International Society of Offshore and Polar Engineers. Address: Department of Mechanical Engineering, Saga University, Saga 840 8502, Japan.

**SETTY Anantha Padmanbha,** b. 19 September 1926, Huliyar, Karnataka, India. Scientist. m. Vimala, 1 son, 1 daughter. Education: BSc Hons, University of Mysore, 1949; MSc, University of Mysore, 1950; PhD University of Utah, 1963. Appointments: Professor, Head of Department, BMS College of Engineering, 1954-55; Lecturer in Geology, University of Mysore, 1955-59; Research Assistant, University of Utah, 1959-63; Research Geologist, International Indian Ocean Expedition, UNESCO, 1964-66; Scientist in Charge, National Institute of Oceanography, Goa, 1967-70; Project Leader, Senior Research Scientist, Assistant Director, National Institute of Oceanography; Disaster Control Management, Oil Spills, Karnataka Coast, 1970-86; Visiting Professor, PhD Examiner, Book Reviewer, Invited Scientist, International Geological Congress, Washington, 1970-85; Many international Conferences. Publications: Many Indian and international journals; Papers on fossils and sediments. Honours: University Merit Scholarship, 1946; Tuition Waiver Fellowship, 1946-50; Award of Teaching and Research Fellowship and Tuition Waiver Fellowship, 1959-63. Memberships: Sigma Gamma Epsilon; Society of Economic Paleontologists and Minerologists; Geological Society of India; Indian Society of Earth Scientists; Paleontological Society of India; Sigma XI, The Scientific Research Soceity of North America; American Association for the Advancement of Science; New York Academy of Sciences; Association of Micropaleontologists; Rotary International; Many other Memberships. Address: Shangri la 130 V Main IV, Blk II Banashankari III STG, Bangalore 560085, India.

**SEVASTAKIEV Venelin,** b. 7 February 1934, Montana, Bulgaria. Professor. m. Margarita Sevastakieva, 1 son, 2 daughters. Education: Graduate diploma, 1956, Ship Mechanic Engineer, Varna, Bulgaria; Graduate diploma, 1963, Internal Combustion Engines Engineer, Sofia, Bulgaria; PhD, 1970, Moscow, Russia. Appointments: Assistant, 1964, Senior Assistant, 1970, Lecturer, Chief Assistant, 1972, Assistant Professor, 1973; Professor, 1989-, Technical University, Varna. Publications: Over 115 articles, research reports, books for Dynamics and authorship certificates, 1968-97; Created and published own formulas in the books and reference manuals all over the world. Honour: National Order, Kiril and Methody, for scientific research, 1989. Memberships: Bulgarian Union of Scientists; Scientific Boards: Energetic Technologies, Shipbuilding and Navigation; Supreme Attestation Commission of Ministry of Sciences and Higher Education for academic ranking in Bulgaria, 1988-97. Address: Technical University, Studentsko Str No 1, G010 Varna, Bulgaria.

**SEVASTIANOV Viktor,** b. 28 August 1945, Russia. Biophysicist. m. Irina A Sevastianova, 2 daughters. Education: MSc, Biophysics, 1969; Candidate of Science, 1973; DSc, Biophysics, 1973; Professor of Biophysics, 1985. Appointments: Head, Professor, State Center for Research of Blood Compatible Biomaterials, Institute of Transplantology and Artificial Organs, Moscow; Professor, Chair of Physics of Living Systems, Moscow Institute of Physics and Technology.

Publications: Several articles in professional journals. Honours: Outstanding Achievement Diploma; Awards for Basic Research. Memberships: International Society for Artificial Organs; American Society for Artificial Organs; Moscow Society for Transplant and Artificial Organs; New York Academy of Science. Address: Institute of Transplant & Artificial Organs, 1 Schukinskaya Street, Moscow 123182, Russia.

**SEYRANIAN Alexander P,** b. 15 February 1947, Moscow, Russia. Scientist. m. Eleonora A Saakian, 1 son, 1 daughter. Education: MSc, Moscow Physical Technical Institute, 1971; PhD, USSR Academy of Sciences, Moscow, 1977; DSc, USSR Academy of Sciences, 1988. Appointments: Engineer, Central Aero-Hydrodynamic Institute, Moscow, 1971-73; Researcher, Institute of Mechanics, USSR Academy of Sciences, 1973-91; Guest Professor, Technical University of Denmark, Copenhagen, 1991-92; Leading Researcher, Moscow State Lomonosov University, 1993-. Publications: Strutural Optimization under Stability and Vibration Constraints, 1989; Optimization of Aviation Structures (co-author), 1989; Over 100 papers on mechanics and applied mathematics in scientific journals. Memberships: New York Academy of Sciences, 1994-96; International Society of Structural and Multidisciplinary Optimization, 1994; Honorary Advisor, National Laboratory, Dalian University of Technology, China, 1994; Editorial Board, International Journal of Theoretical and Applied Mechanics, Yugoslavia. Address: Moscow State Lomonosov University, Institute of Mechanics, Michurynski pr 1, 117192 Moscow, Russia.

**SHABNAM Nirmala Shankarrao Chandekar,** b. 9 November 1939, Aheri, India. Professor. Education: BA, 1964; MA, 1966. Appointments: Lecturer, English, 1966-; Editor, Woman's Column, Hindi Magazine Mahan Asia of Mumbai, 1987-88; Principal, 1999-. Publications: Gulmohar Antar Ka; Nayak; Kasturi Gandh; Gulmohari Sham; Band Lifafa; Baki Sab Kushal Hai; Guftagu; Ek Tha Balak Dhrav; Guldasta; Seven Stars of Galaxy; Wanderlust. Honours: Jainendra Kumar Prize; Gyanbharti Prize; Mata Kusum Kumari Award; Mahadevi Verma Rashtriya Shikhar Samman Prize; International Woman of the Year, International Biographical Centre. Memberships: Community Education ICEA. Address: Chitravithi, Samadhivad, Chandrapur 442 402, India.

**SHAGHIROV Amin Kabtsuyevich,** b. 8 January 1930, Village 2nd Lesken, Urwan district, Kabardino-Balkaria. Linguist. 1 son, 1 daughter. Education: Graduated 1952, Tbilisi University, Georgia; BSc, 1955, DSc, 1971, Institute of Linguistics, Russian Academy of Sciences. Appointments: Senior Scientist, 1965-; Professor in Caucasian Languages, 1991-; Honoured Scientist of Kabardino-Balkarian ASSR; Chief Scientist, Russian Academy of Sciences, 1991-. Publications: Around 80 works including: An Essay of Comparative Lexicology of Adygh Languages, 1962; Etymological Dictionary of Circassian Languages, 2 vols, 1977; Material and Structural Communities in Vocabulary of Abchazian-adygh Languages, 1982; Lexical Borrowings in Abchazian-adygh Languages, 1989. Address: Profsoyuznaya str 99 193, 117279 Moscow, Russia.

**SHAH Ajendra Chhotalal,** b. 2 November 1941, Bombay, India. Medical Doctor. m. Usha, 1 son, 1 daughter. Education: MBBS, 1965, MD General Medicine, 1969, Mumbai University; FCCP, 1982, USA; Mini Fellowship in Pulmonary Medicine, 1982, USA. Appointments: Practising Pulmonary Medicine last 27 years; Visiting Honorary Assistant Physician and Honorary Assistant Professor of Medicine, 1976-86; Honorary Associate Physician and Honorary Associate Professor of Medicine, 1989-93; Honorary Associate Physician and Honorary

Associate Professor of TB and Chest Medicine, 1993-95; Honorary Professor of TB and Chest, Lokmanya Tilak Municipal General Hospital and Medical College, Mumbai, GTB Group of Hospitals, Sewree, Mumbai, 1995; Founder Member, Department of Respiratory Diseases, 1997-. Publications: 90 papers; 1 book: Mara Videshna Sansmarono, 1989; 1 booklet: Common Poisoning, 1972; 1 Book Chapter; 40 papers presented at national and international conferences; 9 original research data presented at congresses and conferences. Honours: 5 awards received during undergraduate and postgraduate examinations; 5 research grants and fellowships. Memberships: Jaycees International, Ghatkopar Branch; Life member, Association of Physicians of India, 1996-; Fellow American College Association, 1982-; Life member, Indian Occupational Health, 1976-. Address: 4 Golwala House, Hingwala Lane PB No 7294, Ghatkopar E, Bombay 400 077, India.

**SHAH Amritlai,** b. 6 November 1941, Mombasa, Kenya. Industrialist. m. 1 son, 1 daughter. Education: BCom, 1963. Appointments: Chairman and Managing Director, Garments Manufacturers Ltd. Memberships: Institute of Directors; Institute of Management. Address: POB 2358, Off Halle Sellasie Road, Dar En Salaam, Tanzania.

**SHAH Jatin P,** b. 31 December 1940, India. Head and Neck Surgeon. m. Bharti J, 1 daughter. Education: MD, 1964; MS Surg, 1967; FACS, 1977; FRCS Hon, 1998; FDSRC Hon, 1998. Appointments: Chief, Head and Neck Surgery; Professor of Surgery, Memorial-Sloan Kettering Cancer Center, New York. Publications: 181 Peer Reviewed Publications. Honours: 1st Prize from British Medical Association. Memberships: President, Society of the Head and Neck Surgeons; President, New York Cancer Society; President, New York Head and Neck Society; International Federation of Head and Neck Societies; Secretary General, American Surgical Association. Address: Meml. Sloan Kettering Cancer Center, 1275 York Ave, NY 10021-6094, USA.

**SHAH Sayid Ghulam Mustafa,** b. 18 October 1918, Sujawal, Thatta, Sindh. Retired Teacher. m. Aziza Mustafa, 1 son, 4 daughters. Education: BA, MA, LLB, Muslim University Aligarh, 1943; MEd, Kings College University of Darham, Exeter College Oxford University, 1949. Appointments: Principal, Sindh Muslim College, Karachi, 14 years; Director of Education, Pakistan provinces, 10 years; Vice Chancellor, University of Sindh, 5 years. Publications: Bhutto - The Man and the Martyr; General Zia - His Winged Death and the Aftermath; Jam and His Politics; English Literary Essays of Pakistan; British in the Sub-Continent; Legacy of Britain; A Principal's Papers; Towards Understanding the Muslims of Sindh; Indus Seals and Inscriptions - Pakistan, volume II, Co-Editor with Dr Asko Parpola; Aboriginal Tribes of India. Memberships: Life Member, President, 10 years, Sindh Madressah Board, Pakistan; Trusteee, Estate of Quaid-e-Azam; Founder of Pakistan; National Commissioner, Pakistan Scouts Association, 10 years; Secretary, Board of Trustees, Shaheed Zulfikar Ali Bhutto Institute of Science and Technology; Chairman, Shah Abdul Latif Cultural Society, 1972; President, Servants of Sindh Society, 1982-. Address: Sindh Quarterly, 36D Karachi Admin Coop Housing Society off Shaheed e Millat Road, Karachi 75350, Pakistan.

**SHAHIM Sima,** b. 1953, Shiraz, Iran. School Psychologist; University Teacher. m. Parviz Hajivandi, 1 daughter. Education: BA, Pahlavi University, Shiraz, 1975; MS, University of Dayton, Ohio, 1977. Appointments: School Principal, 1987-80, University Teacher, 1980-, Shiraz University; Associate Dean for Research, Shiraz University School of Education, 1991-95;

Chair, Department of Special Education, 1998-. Publication: Adaptation and standardization of Wechsler Intelligence Scale for Iranian children, 1994. Honours: Best Iranian Lady Researcher, 1992; Recipient, 1st and 3rd Awards of Iranian Congress of Research in Psychology, 1992, 1998. Memberships: Council for Exceptional Children; Iranian Psychological Association. Address: 314 69th Street, Ghasrodasht Ave, Shiraz, Iran.

**SHAIKH Amir Ahmed,** b. 14 February 1954, Bombay. Group Financial Controller. m. Shaista M I Shaikh, 4 daughters. Education: B Com (Hons); ACA; MBA, USA; CPA, USA; FCPA, UK; Fellow, Association of Certified Public Accountants-International, UK; PhD by Research, UK. Appointments: Served in various positions as Chief Executive Officer, VP, Executive Director, Group Financial Controller and Manager Finance & Administration 1979-, currently Clovergem AG, Basle, Switzerland, Clovergem BV, Barendrecht, Holland, Clovergem Fish & Foods Ltd, Entebbe, Uganda, 1998-. Address: 203 Moti Villa Fatima Nagar, Poona 411013, India.

**SHAIMIEV Mintimer,** b. 20 January 1937, Anyakovo, Tatarstan, Russia. Government Officer. m. Sakina Shakirovna Shaimieva, 2 sons. Education: Mechanical Engineer, Kazan Institute of Agriculture, 1959; Academician, Academy of Technological Sciences of Russian Federation; Honorary Academician, International Academy of Informatization. Appointments: President, Republic of Tatarstan. Honours: Koul-Gali International Prize of Tatar People; Order of Lenin, 1966; Order of the October Revolution, 1976; Order of the Red Banner of Labour; Order of the Peoples Friendship; Order of the Service for the Fatherland, II Degree, 1997; 2 Medals. Memberships: Federation Council, Federal Assembly of the Russian Federation; Honorary Member, Presidum of International Parliment of the World Knight Confederation Under the Auspices of UN. Address:

**SHALI Peniel Trophimo,** b. 9 December 1952, Machame, Kilimanjaro. Engineer. m. Esther P Shali, 2 sons, 2 daughters. Education: BSc Engineering, 1977, University Daressalaam, Tanzania. Appointments: Assistant Chief Engineer (Civil), Williamson Diamonds Ltd, 1986; Principal, Mwadui Training Centre, 1988; Engineer, Estate Care (T) Ltd, 1998. Memberships: Institute Engineers, Tanzania; Registered, Engineers Registration Board, Tanzania. Address: PO Box 3485, Moshi, Tanzania, Africa.

**SHALINI Khosla,** b. 24 December 1976, Kalka. Student. Education: BA, Psychology, Government College of Kalka; MA, English; 6 months diploma in computers. Appointments: Owner, Shop Selling Handloom Items. Publications: Articles Published in College Magazine. Honours: Awarded with Books and Certificates, 1st in college. Memberships: Rotaract Club Kalka; Pahal an Association of Jalandhar; Ponds and Milkmaid Institute; Britania Institute. Address: M/S Handloom Home, Gandhi Chowk, Kalka 133302, Haryana, India.

**SHAMANNA K N,** b. 6 June 1948, India. Engineer, Director. m. Vani, 1 son, 1 daughter. Education: BE, Electronics, Bangalore University, 1970; M Tech, Microwaves, IIT, Kharagpur, India, 1972. Appointments: Head, Engineer-SF, Special Test Section, ISRO Satellite Centre, 1972-89; Group Director, Scientist-G, ADA, 1989-. Publications: More than 35 publications, National and International Journals. Memberships: Aeronautical Society of India, Society of EMC Engineers, India. Address: ADA, P B No 1718, Vimanapura Post, Bangalore 560017, India.

**SHAMLIAN Tatiana,** b. 21 April 1961, Stavropol, Russia. Education: MD, Stravropol Medical School, 1984; PhD, Rostov Medical University, 1994. Appointments: Physician, City Hospital, Stavropol, 1984-85; Anaesthesiologist, Regional Clinical Hospital, Stavropol, 1985-86; Cardiologist, Stavropol District Cardiology Centre, 1986-. Publications: Contributor of articles to scientific journals. Memberships: New York Academy of Sciences; Armenian Catholic Church. Address: Stavropol District Cardiology, St Prigorodraya 244, Stavropol, Russia.

**SHAN Ying Gui,** b. 13 September 1933, Gaomi City, Shandong, China. Educator; Painter. m. Qin Sheng Zhou, 1 son, 1 daughter. Education: studied in Chinese Painting Department, Central Art Academy, 1956-61. Appointments: Professor, Shandong Arts College; Director, Folk Arts Research Office. Publication: Selected Paintings of Shan Ying Gui, 1975. Honours: Winner, 2 2nd Prizes, 6th National Exhibition of Works of Art, for paintings Wedding on the Lake, and Making Shoes for the Army; Special Prize, International Exhibition of Works of Art for 50th Anniversary of the Anti-Fascist Victory, for Chinese painting Fleeing From Home. Memberships: Director, Spring Festival Pictures Committee Member, China Artists' Society; Consultant, Shandong Artists Society; President, Shandong Women Calligraphers and Painters Society; Humane and Societal Studies Comment Committee, National Education Department. Address: Art Department, Shandong Art Gallery, Jinan, China.

**SHANG Longan,** b. 27 January 1964, Xian, China. Researcher. m. Hong Ren, 1 son. Education: BS, 1986, MS, 1989, Northwest University, Xian, China. Appointments: Researcher, Institute of Chemical Engineering, Xian, 1989-92; Teacher, Northwest University, Xian, 1992-97; Researcher, KAIST, Korea, 1998-. Publications: Several articles in professional journals. Honours: Certificate for Science Research, Shaanxi Science Commission, 1997. Membership: Shaanxi Chemical Engineering Commission, Xian, 1995-. Address: Chemical Engineering Department, Northwest University, Xian Shanxi 710069, China.

**SHANKANGA Anderson Bunham,** b. 15 April 1939, Mumbwa, Zambia. m. Joy Theresa, 2 sons, 2 daughters. Education: BA, University of Zambia, 1970; MEd, University of Alberta, 1972; EdD University of Southern California, 1985. Appointments: Teacher, Principal, Director of Curriculum Research and Development, 1962-74; International Adviser on Education, Programme Development, Director UNESCO Office, South Africa. Publications: Research and Reports on Education Development in Africa, 1973-90; Research on Curriculum Reform Practices Around the World, 1985. Memberships: Association for Supervision and Curriculum Development; African Curriculum Organisation. Address: Education Sector - UNESCO, 7 Place de Fonenoy, 75700 Paris, France.

**SHAO Wei Wen,** b. 1 October 1934, Huangyan, Zhejiang. Senior Engineer. m. Zhang Xiuwen, 2 daughters. Education: Bachelor, Fudan University. Appointments: Senior Engineer, CSSRC; Chief Editor, Journal of Hydrodynamics; Professor, Yunnan University. Publication: Chief Editor, English-Chinese Dictionary of New and Developing Science and Technology, 1992. Membership: Shanghai Maritime Exchange Association. Address: Editorial Board of the Journal of Research and Advance of Hydrodynamics, 185 Gaoxiong Rd, Shanghai 200011, China.

**SHAPIRO Harvey Allan,** b. 21 April 1941, Toledo, Ohio, USA. University Professor. m. Fukiko N Shapiro, 2 daughters. Education: BArch, University of Detroit, 1965; Master of Regional Planning, Pennsylvania University, 1970; DAgricl,

Kyoto National University of Japan, 1997. Appointments: Professor, Department of Environmental Planning, Osaka Geijutsu University, 1971-; Associate, Regional Planning Team Association Inc, 1974-. Publications include: Introduction of the McHargian Method to Japan, 1979; Coastal Area Management in Japan, 1984. Memberships: Pacific Science Association; World Conservation Union; Sierra Club; Coastal Society of America; Japan Geography Society; Japan Environment Society. Address: Osaka Geijutsu University, Minami Kawachi-Gun, Kannan-cho, Higashiyama, Osaka 585-8555, Japan.

**SHAPIRO Yury Eugen,** b. 28 February 1947, Zhitomir, Ukraine. Biochemist. m. Tatyana Klyukina, 1 daughter. Education: MS, Polytechnic Institute, Yaroslavl, Russia, 1970; PhD, Shemyakin Institute of Bioorganic Chemistry, Moscow, 1974; DSc, Institute of Macromolecular Chemistry, National Academy of Sciences, Kiev, Ukraine, 1990. Appointments: Lecturer, Laboratory Head, Polytechnic Institute, Yaroslavl, 1974-88; Senior Researcher, Chief Researcher, Laboratory Head, Bogatsky Physico-Chemical Institute, National Academy of Sciences, Odessa, Ukraine, 1988-97; Professor of Chemistry, Mechnikov State University, Odessa, 1992-; Visiting Professor, Royal Institute of Technology, Stockholm, Sweden, 1997; Visiting Professor, Bar-Ilan University, Ramat-Gan, Israel, 1998. Publications: Author of 200 papers in field of NMR spectroscopy and conformational analysis. Honours: INTAS Grantee, Belgium, 1992; Svenska Institutet Grantee, Sweden, 1997; Royal Academy of Sciences Grantee, Sweden, 1998. Memberships: New York Academy of Sciences; Pharmacological Committee of Ukraine; International Liquid Crystal Society; World Association of the Theoretically Oriented Chemists; Association of the NMR Spectroscopists, Russia; Mendeleyev Chemical Society, Russia. Address: Bar Ilan University, Department of Life Sciences, 52900 Ramat Gan, Israel.

**SHARAN Vishwa Mohan,** b. 2 January 1942, Gaya, India. Radiologist. m. Bimal Sharan, 1 son, 2 daughters. Education: MBBS, University of Patna; DMRT, London University; ABR, Therapy. Appointments: Assistant Professor in Radiology, Case Western Reserve University, Cleveland, Ohio, USA; Director, Marion Regional Cancer Center, Marion, Ohio. Memberships: ASTRO; AAPI. Address: Marion Regional Cancer Center, 1150 Crescent Heights Road, Marion, OH 43302-6406, USA.

**SHARIPOV Kongratbay,** b. 24 March 1963, Kungrad Town, Karakalpak Republic, Uzbekistan. Scientist, Teacher. m. Lidia, 1 son, 2 daughters. Education: Mechanical Engineer, Tashkent Institute of Engineers of Irrigationa and Agricultural Mechanization, 1986; PhD, Moscow Agro Engineering University, 1992. Appointments: Mechanical Engineer, 1986; Senior Engineer, 1987; Postgraduate, Moscow Agro-Engineering University, 1988-92; Assistant TIEIAM, 1992; Assistant of Professor, TIEIAM, 1993-94; Associate Professor, Department of Tractors and Automobiles, TIEIAM, 1995-98; Senior Scientific Worker, TIEIAM, 1996-98. Publications: 2 Monographs; 77 Articles; 12 Patents; 9 Methodological Instructions. Honours: International Certificate at the International Exhibition on Minitechnology, 1998. Memberships: Scientific Director, Agricultural Mechanization Faculty; Member, Institute Education Reform Committee, TIEIAM. Address: 39 Kari Niyazov Str, Tashkent Inst of Engineers of Irrigation and Agricultural Mechanization, Tashkent, Republic of Uzbekistan, 700000.

**SHARMA Bhuvnesh K,** b. 2 June 1955. Assistant Director (Immunology). m. Education: BS, 1972, Msc, 1974, Agra University; PhD, Meerut University, 1981. Appointments: Senior Research Fellow, National Institute of Communicable Diseases Government of India, Delhi, 1975-81; Research Assistant Immunology, Cytology Research Cenre, New Delhi, 1981-82; Visiting Scientist, Department of Cytopathology, St Mary's Hospital Medical School, University of London, 1983-84; Research Officer, Immunology, Cytology Research Centre, New Delhi, 1983-87; Senior Research Officer, Institute of Cytology and Preventive Oncology, New Delhi, 1987-93; Visiting Faculty (Scholar), Johns Hopkins University, School of Hygiene and Public Health, Department of Immunology and Infectious Diseases, Baltimore, Maryland, USA, 1989-91; Visiting Research Scientist, University of Baltimore, 1991-92; Assistant Director (Immunology), Institute of Cytology and Prev Oncology, Maulana Azad Medical College Campus, New Delhi 1993-. Publications: Molecular oncology research, 33 papers in professional journals. Honours; Government of India Biotechnology Overseas Associateship (long term), at Johns Hopkins University, Baltimore, 1989-92; Fellowship in Medical Sciences, National Environmental Science Academy, 1997. Memberships: Life Member, Indian Association of Cancer Research; Indian Association of Blood Banks; Fellow International Research into Science and Technology, UK; Fellow, National Environmental Science Academy. Address: B-105 A, Sec 27, Noida-201301, India.

**SHARMA Gita,** b. 21 April 1948, Madras, India. Scientist; Educator. m. B T Sharma. Education: PhD, 1976. Appointments: Lecturer, 1974-86; Reader, 1986-, Department of Microbiology, Chairperson, Board of Studies, 1992-95, Head, Department of Microbiology, 1995-97, Co-Ordinator, DRS-UGC, 1995-95, Osmania University; Scientific Advisor, Shantha Biotechnics Ltd, Hyderabad, 1990-95; Vice President, Head, Department of Biotechnology, Cadila Healthcare Ltd, Ahmedabad, 1997-; Main person involved in the first DNA derived HBs vaccine in India. Publications: Several articles in professional journals. Memberships: Society of Biological Chemistry, India; Association of Microbiologists; Yeast Group of India; Society of Virologists, India. Address: Department of Biotechnology, Cadila Healthcare Ltd, 244 Ghodasar Maninagar, Ahmedabad 380008, India.

**SHARMA Kamla Nath,** b. 3 March 1946, Jaipur, India. Water Management Specialist. m. Chandrika Sharma, 1 son, 1 daughter. Education: BEng, University of Jodhpur, 1967; MEng, BITS, Pilani, 1970. Appointments: Lecturer, Department of Civil Engineering, MR Engineering College, Jaipur, 1969-81; Assistant Specialist, Water Management, University of California, Davis, USA, 1976-77; Manager, Head, Hydrology Wing, National Hydro-Electric Power Corporation, Ltd, 1981-89; ICID Central Secretariat, 1989-. Publications: Several articles in professional journals, conferences; Book on Water Power Engineering. Honours: Fellowship, University Grants Commission, 1972-75; Ford Foundation Fellowship, University of California, Davis, USA, 1976-77. Address: ICID, 48 Nyaya Marg, Chanakyapuri, New Delhi 110021, India.

**SHARMA Ravindra Nath,** b. 22 October 1944, Panjab, India. Director. m. Mithlesh Kumari Joshi, 2 daughters. Education: BA Hons, University of Delhi, India; MA, University of Delhi, 1966; MLS, North Texas State University, USA, 1970; PhD, State University of New York, 1982. Appointments: Editor, Library Times International, 1984-; Assistant Director, University of Wisconsin, Oshkosh, 1985-89; Director of Libraries, University of Evansville, 1989-95; Director of Libraries, West Virginia State College, 1996-. Publications: 9 Books; 300 Articles, Interviews, Editorials, Reports, Books Reviews. Honours: Forest Press Award, ALA for International Librarianship, 1997; Memberships: American Library Association; Association of College and Research

Libraries.Address: West Virginia State College, P O Box 1002, Institute, WV 25112, USA.

**SHARMAN Diane Lee,** b. 5 December 1948, Harvey, Illinois, USA. Educator. m. Richard Sharman, 2 daughters. Education: BS, Purdue University, 1970; MBA, University of Chicago, 1973. Appointments: Computer Sales, General Electric Company, 1970-73; Financial Operations Management, Xerox Corporation, 1973-84. Honour: University of Chicago Alumni Association. Memberships: DAR; National Council of Teachers of Mathematics; Purdue Alumni Association; Texas Professional Educators Association. Address: 26 Fernglen Drive, Woodlands, TX 77380, USA.

**SHASHIDHARA PRASAD J,** b. 18 November 1947, Thimmasandra, India. Researcher; Teacher. m. Ms Revathi, 1 son. Education: MSc Physics, Solid State Physics, 1968, PhD Physics, Liquid Crystals, Crystallography, 1972, University of Mysore. Appointments: Research Scholar, University of Mysore, University Grants Commission, 1968-71; Lecturer, 1971-75, Reader, 1975-84, Professor, 1984-, Department of Physics, Chairman, Department of Studies in Physics, 1989-91, Dean, Faculty of Science and Technology, 1989-91, Acting Vice-Chancellor, 1990, University of Mysore; Commonwealth Academic Staff Fellow, Oxford University, England, 1976-77; UGC career Awardee in Science, 1980-83. Publications: Various articles in encyclopedia and other professional publications in the field of cryogenics, x-ray crystallography, molecular structure and physical properties of liquid crystals, biological and drug molecules and superionics etc. Honours: Post-matric National Merit Scholar, Government of India; Mysore University Golden Jubilee Science Award. Memberships: Indian Association of Physics Teachers; Indian Physics Association; Fellow, Institute of Physics, London; American Institute of Physics, USA, ex-officio; Optical Society of America; Australian Institute of Physics; American Physical Society; International Liquid Crystal Society; Indian Liquid Crystal Society. Address: 49/2 5th Main 3rd Block, Jayalakshmipuram, Mysore 570012, India.

**SHASTRI H H Accharya Vagish,** b. 24 July 1934, Madhya Pradesh, India. Spiritual Teacher. m. Sanskrit Bharati, 3 sons. Education: PhD, 1964; DLitt, 1969. Appointments: Lecturer, Bharatiya Sahitya Vidyalay, 1956; Principal, Laleshvar Pathashala, 1954-56; Teacher, Philosophy and Sanskrit Literature, Teekamani Sanskrit College, 1959-64; Senior Research Fellow, Assistant Researcher, Director, Research Institute, S Sanskrit University, 1964-96; Kundalin Yoga and Sanskrit Teacher, 1996-. Publications: Over 200 papers in professional journals; 16 books on Yoga Tantra. Honours: 10 awards. Memberships: Executive and Academic Councils of S Sanskrit University. Address: Vagyogachetanapitham, B 3/131A Shivala, Varanasi 221 001, Uttar Pradesh, India.

**SHASTRI Padam Nath,** b. 2 October 1929, Jagron, India. Retired Sanskrit Research Scholar. m. Shanti Devi, 3 sons. Education: PhD, Sanskrit Language. Appointments: Chairman, Punjab Sanskrit Academy, 1985-98; President, Brahmin Sabha Punyas. Honours: Gold Medal, President of India; Government Medal and Citation, State Government, Punjab; Chief Minister Award. Memberships: Chairman, Punjab Sanskrit Academy; Secretary General, Sanskrit Vishar Parshad. Address: Bhogian Muhalla, Jagron, India.

**SHATILOV Ivan Semeonovich,** b. 19 January 1917, Makhrovka Village, Russia. Agronomist. m. Lavrova, 1 son, 1 daugther. Education: Moscow Academy of Agricultural Sciences; Diplomas of Candidate; Doctor of Sciences; Certificate of Sciences Professor; Degree of Full Member, Russian Academy of Sciences. Appointments: Pro Rector, Moscow Academy of Sciences; 1961-63; President, 1963-71; Academician Secretary, Russian Academy of Sciences, 1971-75; First Vice President, 1975-79; President, All Russian Department, 1979-89; Deputy Minister of Agriculture, 1979-89; Professor, Plant Growing Department, 1991-. Publications: 380 Publications. Honors: Title, Hero of Socialistic Labour; Three Orders Lenin; Order of Russian Revolution; Two Orders of Red Labour Banner; Order of Great Patriotic War; Order for Services to Motherland; Gold, Silver Medals, All Russian Exhibition; Medals, Participation in Great Patriotic War. Memberships: International Academy of Scientific Works; National Academy Knowledge; Bashkir Academy of Sciences; Poland Acadmey of Sciences; Honorary Doctor of University; Orlov Academy; Academician, Russian Academy of Agricultural Science. Address: Timiryazevskays St 29, Department of Plant Growing, 125550 Moscow, Russia.

**SHAUKAT QADIR Soomro,** b. 12 March 1947, Shikarpur, Sindh. Government Official. m. Mufeeda Shaukat, 2 sons, 1 daughter. Education: Bachelor degree, 1967, Masters in Economics, 1971, University of Sindh; Central Superior Service of Pakistan, 1976. Appointments: Additional Commissioner, Income Tax and Wealth Tax, Karachi, Pakistan. Honours: Numerous awards for Meritorious Service. Membership: Pakistan Taxation Club, Karachi. Address: C6/B3 Street No 2, Bath Island, Clifton Karachi, Pakistan.

**SHAYEGANI Mehdi,** b. 2 April 1926, Rasht, Iran. Medical Microbiologist. m. Asieh, 1 son, Bobeck, 2 daughters, Aryan and Susan. Education: Pharm D, 1953, University Tehran; MS, 1958, PhD Medical Microbiology, 1961, University Pennsylvania. Appointments: Instructor to Assistant Professor, University of Pennsylvania, 1958-72; Associate Professor, 1984-95, Professor, 1995-, State University of New York, School of Public Health; Chief, Bacterial Disease, NY State Dept Health, Albany, 1973-. Publications: Over 70 publications in scientific journals, 1959-. Memberships: American Society for Microbiology; Sigma Xi. Address: New York State Department of Health, PO Box 22002, Albany, NY 12201-2002, USA.

**SHCHOKIN George Vasilievich,** b. 27 May 1954, Zaporozhye, Ukraine. Human Resources Management. m. Rimma, 1 son. Education: Master Degree, Pedagogical Sciences, Kyiv, 1981; PhD, Psychological Sciences, Kyiv, 1989; Doctor in Sociological Sciences, Moscow, 1996; PhD, Business Administration, Vienna, 1997. Appointments: President, Inter-Regional Academy of Personnel Management, 1989-, International Personnel Academy, 1992-; Head Editor, The Personnel, magazine, 1991-. Publications: Over 150 articles including 30 books. Honours: Honoured Worker of National Education in Ukraine; Knight of International Order of Winged Lion. Memberships: International Personnel Academy; Baltic Pedagogical Academy; Russian Pedagogical Society; Romanian Academic Society "Hyperion". Address: Academy of Personnel Management, 2 Frometivska Street, Kyiv 2520329, Ukraine.

**SHEA Brent Mack,** b. 3 June 1946, Oneida, New York. Professor. Education: BA, Harpur College, 1964-68; MA, 1970-72; PhD, 1972-77. Appointments: Visiting Instructor of Sociology, 1975-76; Resident Director, 1976-78; Research Associate, 1977-78; Assistant Professor of Sociology, 1978-84; Acting Chairman, 1980-81; Associate Professor, 1984-92; Visiting Fellow, 1984-85; Postdoctoral Fellow, 1985-86; Scientific Collaborator, 1990-; Visiting Scholar, 1991; Secretary of the Faculty, 1991-92; Professor of Sociology, 1992-; Chairman, 1986-90, 1996-. Publications: 14 publications; Co-Author, 39 Papers, Nantional and International. Honours:

New York State Regents Scholarship, 1964-68; State University of New York Graduate Research Fellowships, 1971, 1974; State University of New York at Binghamton Faculty Research Grant, 1976; National Institute of Mental Health Postdoctoral Research Fellowship, 1985-86; Sweet Briar College Faculty Fellowship, 1984-85, 1992-93. Memberships: Eastern Educational Research Association, 1983-87; Virginia Sociological Association, 1981-82; International Sociological Association Mental Health and Illness Research Committee, 1993; Ilus Primi Viri International Association, 1994-; American Assocaition of University Professors, 1996-. Address: P O Box 1, Sweet Briar, VA 24595-0001, USA.

**SHEHU Avni,** b. 2 June 1957, Burrel. President of the Court of Cassation. m. 1 son, 1 daughter. Education: Faculty of Law, University of Tirana, 1977-81. Career: Lawyer, 1981-83, Judge, 1983-87, District Court, Mirdita; Justice, Civil Cases, Supreme Court, Tirana, 1987-92; Professor, Faculty of Law, University of Tirana, 1990-; Vice President, Court of Cassation, Tirana, 1992-95; President, Court of Cassation, 1995-; Chairman, Board of Directors, School of Magistrates, 1996-; Professor, School of Magistrates, Tirana, 1997-. Publications: Some issues which come out in the judicial practice related to the contract of house leasing; The property under the new Civil Code; The constitutional guarantees for a just judicial process; The Ownership, textbook. Membership: Deputy Chairman, Jurists Association; Board Director, The Justice, Jurisprudence, magazines; Commission, Drafting of the Constitution of the Republic of Albania. Address: Sami Frasheri, Str Pa 20/3, Shk 3, App 5, Tirana, Albania.

**SHEHU Hazbi,** b. 14 February 1933, Berat. Geologist. m. Sheriban, 2 daughters. Education: First Scientific Degree, 1982; Old Scientific Collaborator, 1985; Scientific Doctor, 1993; Professor, 1995. Appointments: Prime Geologist, Enterprise of Marinez, 1957-63; Chief of Cabinet of Prospect, 1969-89; Specialist, Cabinet of Generalising and Projecting Oil Wells; Professor, Faculty of Geology in Tirana. Honours: Honourable Prize of Labour, 1978; Price of Republic of the Second Grade, 1979. Memberships: Scientific Council of Gas and Oil Scientific Labroatory; Scientific Council of Gas and Oil Geological Institute. Address: Lagia Glirim, Pallati 63, Berat, Albania.

**SHEHU Namik,** b. 28 August 1935, Berat, Albania. Doctor. m. Engjellushe, 1 son, 2 daughters. Education: Diploma, 1957; Docent, 1988; Doctor, 1993. Appointments: Conference in Pavia, Italy, 1993, Liege, Belgium, 1994; Upheld scientific articles in 17 conferences and 7 symposia 1971-94. Publications: 30 scientific articles 1966-94; 4 books on Blood Pressure Pathologies and Treatment. Memberships: Cardiology European Society; Scientific Secretary, Albanian-American Academy of Sciences, New York. Address: 21035 21 Ave #3R, Astoria, NY 11105, USA.

**SHEIRR Olga,** b. 6 July 1931, New York City, USA. Artist. m. Maurice Krolik. Education: BA, Brooklyn College, New York; Graduate Studies, New York Institute of Fine Arts, New York. Career: Solo exhibitions, New Jersey, Connecticut, New York, include: Gallery Juno, New York, 1996, 1998; The Jewish Center of the Hamptons, East Hampton, New York, 1996; Group Exhibitions, in USA, Argentina, Italy, China, France, include: Ashwagh Hall, Springs, New York, 1998; The Watermille Museum, Watermill, New York, 1998; The Carriage Barn Art Center, New Canaaan, Connecticut, USA, 1998; Public Collections: Springfield Art Museum, Missouri; Bank of Tokyo, New York; National Museum of Women in the Arts, Washington DC; Museum of the City of New York; St Vincent's Hospital, New York; Greenville County Museum, Greenville, South Carolina. Publications: Art Resources and Treasures Ltd,

2 limited editions. Honours: Heckscher Museum, Nora Mirmont Hambuechen Award, 1990; National Academy of Design, Adolph and Clara Obrig Award, 1990; New York Artists Equity Annual Award, 1991; Paterson Museum, Honorable Mention, 1993; Maryland Federation of Art, 1st Prize, Drawing, 1993; Springfield Museum of Art, Patron's Purchase Award, 1997. Memberships include: Women in the Arts, 1977-; New York Artists Equity, 1978-; Womens Caucus for Art, 1981-; The New York Society of Women Artists, 1984-. Address: 360 First Avenue Apt 11G, New York, NY 10010, USA.

**SHEKH Arvindbhai,** b. 1 May 1949, Vaso, India. Professor Agrometeorology. m. Mukundben, 2 sons, 1 daughter. Education: BSc Agri, 1970; MSc Agri, 1976; PhD, 1985; Postdoct, 1989. Appointments: Associate Professor and Agrometeorologist, 1984-93; Professor and Head, Department of Agrcultural Meteorology, 1993-. Publications: 106 scientific publications in national and international journals. Honours: Merit Award, Central Board of Irrigation and Power. Memberships: Life member, 8 scientific societies; Ordinary member, 6 scientific societies; Appointed member, different committees at central & state level. Address: 10 New B Quarter Guj Agri University, 388110 Anand Kheda, India.

**SHELDON David,** b. New York, USA. Producer; Director; Writer. m. Joan McCall. Education: MFA, Yale University School of Drama; BA, Principia College. Career: Producer, Director, Writer, Ten Motion Pictures; Television Producer; Writer; Founder, Director, Gateway Playhouse, New York; Television Producer. Memberships: Actors Studio; Writers Guild of America. Address: Joda Productions Inc, 1437 Rising Glen Road, Los Angeles, CA 90069-1243, USA.

**SHELDRICK Katherine Elizabeth,** b. 31 March 1948, Boston, USA. Musician; Writer. m. G M Sheldrick, 2 sons, 2 daughters. Education: LLB, 1966-68; MA, Knightsbridge University, 1993-95. Career: Legal Secretary, Pye of Cambridge, 1970-73; Solo Clarinet, Cambridge Philharmonic, 1974-76. Publictions: Blackbird Has Spoken; Hymn of the Universe; Echoes of Yesterday. Memberships: MUSA; International Society of Poets; Little Pen. Address: Heinrich Deppe Ring 51, 37120 Bovenden, Germany.

**SHEN Ya Ching,** b. 30 May 1953, Taipei, Republic of China. Professor. m. Show-Ching Dai, 1 son, 1 daughter. Education: PhD, 1987. Appointment: Professor, Institute of Marine Resources, Taiwan. Publications: 50 papers in journals. Membership: American Society of Pharmacognosy. Address: Institute of Marine Resources, National Sun Yat-Sen University, Kaohsiung, Taiwan, ROC.

**SHENG Zhuping,** b. 2 October 1962, Jiangsu, China. Geological Engineer, Hydrogeologist. m. Min Yao, 1 son, 1 daughter. Education: B Eng, Tongji University, China, 1983; MS, Chinese Academy of Sciences, 1987; PhD, University of Nevada, USA, 1996. Appointments: Research Assistant, Chinese Academy of Sciences, 1983-89; Assistant Professor, Chinese Academy of Sciences, 1989-91; Research Assistant, Nevada Bureau of Mines and Geology, 1991-96; Assistant Professor, Morgan State University, 1997-98; Hydrogeologist, El Paso Water Utilities, Texas, USA, 1998-. Publications: Investigation on Stability of High Dip Bankslopes for Yongtze Gorges Key Water Control Project, 1993. Honours: Certificate of Achievement; State Scientific and Technologic Commission; Hon Certificate of Achievement; Scientific and Technical Award, Chinese Academy of Sciences. Memberships: Association of Engineering Geologists; National Ground Water Association; Geological Society of America. Address: 1481 Desierto Rico, El Paso, TX 79912, USA.

**SHENGELIA Ramaz,** b. 28 September 1952, Tbilisi, Georgia. Surgeon. m. Nan Misidze, 1 son. Education: Tbilisi State Medical University, 1975; Art Faculty, State University, 976. Appointments: Senior Surgeon, 1975-91; Head, Chair, History of Medicine, Museum of History of Medicine, 1991-. Publications: 102 Publications, Georgia, Russia, USA, UK, Italy, Germany, Croatia. Honours: Various Medals. Memberships: Administrative Council of International Society of History of medicine; NYAS; Russian Academy. Address: 7 Asatiani Str, 380077 Tbilissi, Georgia.

**SHER Emmanuil Moiseyevich,** b. 29 March 1929, Port Khorly, Ukraine. Physicist Researcher. m. Elena Stepanovna Sher, 1 son. Education: BS, Moscow State University, 1951; Physicist, St Petersburg State University, 1952; PhD, Physical Electronics, 1967; DSc, Physics of Semiconductors and Dielectrics, 1983. Appointments: Senior Engineer, Vacuum Technology, 1952-59; A F Ioffe Physico-Technical Institute, Russian Academy of Sciences, 1959-; Researcher, Senior Researcher, Leading Researcher, Physics of Thermoelectricity, Electron Emission, High Temperature Superconductors and Thin Solid Films, 1959-99. Publications: 80 publications in field; 21 patents. Honours: Bronze, 1963, Silver, 1983, Medals for Thermoelectric Devices; Honorary Academician, International Academy of Refrigeration, 1999. Memberships: International Thermoelectric Society, 1991; New York Academy of Sciences, 996. Address: 20 Orbely Str, Apt 73, 194223 St Petersburg, Russia.

**SHERESHEVSKY August Moiseyevich,** b. 16 August 925, Leningrad, USSR. Psychiatrist. m. Alla Brilliant, 2 daughters. Education: Medical Diplomate, Military Medical Academy, Leningrad, USSR, 1951; Candidate Medical Science, 1966; MD, 1983; Professor, 1992; FNYAS, 1994. Appointments: Student, military school, Sergeant, Student, Scientist, Head of Department, Chief Scientist, Bekhterev Institute, St Petersburg, Russia, 1970-98; Academician, Russian Academy of Humanities, 1998. Publications: Author, 5 books, 1998; 176 articles in Russian and foreign scientific journals. Honours: 16 military and civic medals, USSR; Excellent Work Public Health, badge. Memberships: Executive Scientific Sec, SPb Society of Psychiatrists; Associate Chairman, SPb Society Medical Historians; Officer, Russian Association of Historians of Medicine. Address: VM Bekhterev Psychoneurology Research Institute, 3 Bekhterev St., 193019 St Petersburg, Russia.

**SHERIDAN Sonia,** b. 10 April 1925, Newark, Ohio, USA. Professor Emerita; Artist. m. James Edward Sheridan. Education: BA, Hunter College New York City, 1945; MFA, California College of Arts and Crafts, 1961. Appointments: Professor Emerita, School of the Art Institute of Chicago, 1961-80; Founder, Generative Systems Program, Art Institute of Chicago, 1970; Co-Editor, Leonardo, International Journal of Art Science Technology, at present. Honours: Guggenheim Fellow, 1973; National Endowment for the Arts, 1974, 1976, 1981. Memberships: College Art Association; International Symmetry Society. Address: 80 Lyme Road Apartment 438, Hanover, NH 03755-1236, USA.

**SHETTY A Chandra,** b. 20 July 1958, Akkunje. Consultant. m. Sadhana C, 1 son, 1 daughter. Education: B Tech Degree, Mechanical Engineering, University of Calicut; Diploma, Export Marketing Management, LIEx, Baroda; Diploma, Small Industries Management, ILM, CBE; Diploma, Refridgeration and Air Conditioning; Diploma, Business Administration. Appointments: Chief Executive, M/S Kohinoor Computers Service; Director, MS Freight Links Put Ltd; Director, MS Goodwill SOftware and Technology International Ltd. Honours:

GMP Award in Production Management; Vijaya Shree Award; Super Intellectual Award; Best Citizen of India Award. Memberships: IFE; IIPE; FPSI; ISHRAE; AIMC; MSPI. Address: Kohinoor Computer Services, 53 S C Road Opp Royal Lodge, Bangalore 560009, India.

**SHEU Wayne Huey-Herng,** b. 17 November 1957, Taiwan. Medical Doctor. m. Terry Chen, 2 daughters. Education: MD 1983; PhD 1989. Appointments: Director, Endocrinology and Metabolism, Taichung Veterans General Hospital, Taichung, Taiwan. Publications: Over 60 medical articles published. Membership: American Diabetes Association. Address: Taichung Veterans General Hospital, No 160 Sect 3 Chung Kang Road, 407 Taichung, Taiwan.

**SHEVCHENKO Vladimir,** b. 18 August 1958, Krasnoyarsk, Russia. Physicist. m. Marina Shevchenko, 1 son, 1 daughter. Education: MSc, 1981; PhD, 1996; DSc, 1998. Appointments: Leading Researcher, TRINITI, Moscow; Temporary Research Associate, UKAEA Culham Science Centre, Abingdon, UK. Publications: Over 40 at conferences and in journals on Plasma Physics. Address: Microraion B 38 ap 119, 142092 Troitsk, Moscow, Russia.

**SHI Bingxia,** b. 9 April 1939, Shandong, Qingdao, China. Professor. m. 1961, 1 daughter. Education: Bachelor Degree, Shandong Medical College, 1961. Career: Director, Cerebrovascular Disease Institute, Qingdao Medical College; Vice President, Blood Therapy Branch, Chinese Biomedical and Engineering Academy; Vice President, National Low Energy Laser Therapy Co-operative Committee; President, Shandong Low Energy Laser Therapy Co-operative Committee; President, Shandong Blood Therapy Society, Chinese Medical Association; Committee, Chinese Ultrasound Medical Engineering Association, Cerebral Ultrasound Diagnosis Committee; Board, Chinese Journal of Cerebrovascular Rehabilitation Committee; Board, Journal of Rehabilitation & Recuperation. Publications: Over 20 articles in professional journals. Honours: Golden Cup Prize, 1st International Meeting of Human Body, USA; Outstanding Worker, Qingdao Medical College. Address: Institute of Cerebrovascular Diseases, Qingdao Medical College, Qingdao 266003, China.

**SHI Feng,** b. 1949, Tianjin. Professor. m. Tian Meihua, 1 son. Education: MA, Chinese People University, Beijing, 1982; PhD, Nankai University, 1990. Appointments: Faculty, Tianjin Foreign Languages College, 1982-85; Teacher, Nankai University, 1985; Professor, Nankai University, 1993; Professor, Nagoya Gakain University, 1998; Professor, Beijing Langauge and Culture University. Publications: About 50 Articles, China, Overseas; Studies in Tone and Stops; Papers on Phonetics; Overseas China Linguistics; Chinese Linguistics Abroad. Memeberships: Society of Chinese Phonology; Society of Chinese Dialectology. Address: Graduate School of Foreign Langauges Studie, Nagoya Gakuin University, Seto, Aichi, Japan.

**SHI Feng Sheng,** b. 28 September 1935, Shanghai, China. Mathematician. m. Dorothy. Career: Author. Honours: Son of the Year, Hall of Fame; many more. Address: 1000 8th Street, St Petersburg, FL 33701, USA.

**SHI Hong Hui,** b. 11 November 1962, Fuzhou, China. Lecturer. m. Bin Xu, 1 daughter. Education: BSc, 1983, MSc, 1986, PhD, 1989, Xian Jiaotong University; DSc, Tohoku University, 1995. Appointments: Visiting Scientist, University of Cambridge, England, 1990-91; Assistant Professor, 1995-97; Lecturer, 1997-, Nagoya Institute of Technology. Honours:

Tang Zhao-Qian Scholarship, Xian Jiaotong University for Overseas Study, 1990-91; Japanese Government Scholarship for Foreign Students, 1992-95. Memberships: JSME; JSASS; Japan Explosives Society; Gas Turbine Society of Japan; Turbomachinery Society of Japan; AIAA; New York Academy of Sciences; American Association for the Advancement of Science. Address: Nagoya Institute of Technology, Department of Mechanical Engineering, Gokiso-cho, Showa-ku, Nagoya 466-8555, Aichi, Japan.

**SHI Jiuyong,** b. 9 October 1926, Zhejiang, China. Judge. m. Zhang Guoying, 1 son. Education: BA Government and Public Law, 1948, St John's University, Shanghai; MA International Law, 1951, Research in International Law, 1951-54, Columbia University, New York. Appointments: Professor of International Law, Foreign Affairs College, Beijing, 1984-93; Legal Adviser, Ministry of Foreign Affairs, China, 1980-93; Member, International Law Commission, United Nations, 1987-93; Judge, International Court of Justice, The Hague, The Netherlands, 1994-. Publications: Author of numerous publications on international law. Memberships: American Society of International Law; Member and Adviser, Chinese Society of International Law. Address: International Court of Justice, Peace Palace, 2517 KJ, The Hague, The Netherlands.

**SHIBAMOTO Yuta,** b. 13 December 1955, Kakogawa, Japan. Educator; Radiation Oncologist. m. Hiromi Yanagawa, 1 son, 2 daughters. Education: MD, 1980, Dr.Med.Sc, 1987, Kyoto University. Apointments: Assistant Professor, Lecturer, Associate Professor, Kyoto University. Honour: Hanns Langendorff Prize, 1992. Membership: Councilor, Japan Society for Therapeutic Radiology and Oncology. Address: Department of Oncology, Institute for Fronier Medical Sciences, Kyoto University, Kyoto 606-8397, Japan.

**SHIBAYAMA Hiroshi,** b. 15 December 1919, Kyoto, Japan. Professor Emeritus. m. Chieko Kubo dec'd. Education: BE, Electrical Engineering, 1942, DEng, 1962, Kyoto University. Appointments: Research Engineer, Mitsubishi Electric Corporation, 1942-46; Teacher, Rakuyo High School, Kyoto, 1946-50; Lecturer, Electrical Engineering, 1950-56, Assistant Professor, 1956-62, Professor, 1962-90, Visiting Professor, 1990-92, Professor Emeritus, 1992-, Osaka Institute of Technology. Publications: Numerous papers in professional journals. Honours include: 4th Order of Sacred Treasure, Emperor of Japan, 1993. Memberships: Institute of Electrical Engineers, Japan; Institute of Electronics, Information & Communication Engineers. Address: KouriMinamino-cho 28-24-806, Neyagawa, Osaka 572-0084, Japan.

**SHIBUE Yasuhiro,** b. 9 September 1955, Osaka, Japan. Professor. m. Yumiko Yanai, 1 son, 1 daughter. Education: BSc, 1979, PhD, 1986, University of Tokyo. Appointments: Research Assistant, 1987-88, Assistant Professor, 1988-90, Associate Professor, 1990-99, Professor, 1999-, Hyogo University of Teacher Education. Publications: Paper in Proceedings of the IAGOD 8th IAGOD Symposium, 1993; Separation Science and Technology, 1998. Memberships: The Geochemical Society; American Geophysical Union. Address: Suehiro Mansion A 3, Oomura 426, Miki City 673-0404, Hyogo, Japan.

**SHIELDS Allan Oakley,** b. 23 May 1943, Bakersfield, California, USA. Entomology. Education: BS, 1966, MS, 1968, Biology, San Diego State University; PhD, Entomology, University of California at Davis, 1977. Appointments: Caretaker, Carnegie Experimental Garden, 1964-66; Senior Graduate Research Associate for Professor S Warren Carey, 1975-78; Field Collections of Camel Crickets for Dr Theodore

J Cohn, 1978-88; Entomological Consulting Services Ltd, 1989-. Publications: 108 scientific publications in 30 journals in entomology and geology. Honour: Phi Kappa Phi, 1971. Memberships: Lepidopterists' Society; Association of the Lepidoptera Research Foundation. Address: 555 Matmor Road, Apt 108, Woodland, California 95776, USA.

**SHIEU Fuh-Sheng,** b. 22 August 1959, Taiwan. Professor of Materials Engineering. m. Mei-Lih Chi Shieu, 1 son, 3 daughters. Education: BS, National Tsing-Hua University, 1981; MS, 1988, PhD, 1990, Cornell University, USA. Appointments: Product Engineer, China Steel Company, Taiwan, 1983-85; Senior Research Engineer, The Dow Chemical Company, USA, Associate Professor, 1993-98, Professor, 1998, National Chung-Hsing University, Taiwan. Publications: Author: Relaxation of Thermal Stress at Metal-Ceramic Interfaces by a Dislocation Mechanism, 1994; Production of the Critical Particle Size for Toughening a Glassy Polymer, 1997; Co-author, some 26 other articles, 1990-. Address: Institute of Materials Engineering, National Chung-Hsing University, 250 Kuo Kuang Road, Taichung 40227, Taiwan, USA.

**SHIH Ting-Fang Tiffany,** b. 2 January 1959, Taipei, Taiwan. Medical Doctor. m. Walter T W Liu, 1 son. Education: MD, 1984. Appointments: Rotating Intern, 1983-84, Resident, Department of Internal Medicine, 1984-85, Resident, Department of Radiology, 1985-87, Chief Resident, Department of Radiology, 1987-88, Visiting Staff, Department of Radiology, 1988-, Assistant Professor, School of Medicine, 1989-96, Associate Professor, School of Medicine, 1996-, National Taiwan University Hospital; Clinical Instructor, Department of Radiological Science, UCLA Medical Center, 1989-90; Organizer, Consultant, An-Drukon Buddhist Hospital, Taipei, 1994-; Organizer, Consultant, Breast Cancer Screening Center, National Institute of Health, Taiwan, 1994-; Head, Section of Musculoskeletal Radiology, National Taiwan University Hospital, 1995-. Publications include: Magnetic Resonance Imaging of Vertebral Compression Fracture, 1996; Magnetic Resonance Imaging in Patients with Hemodialysis-Related Arthropathy, 1997; Bone Marrow Perfusion of the Hip After Core Decompression: Evaluated with Dynamic Contrast-Enhanced MR Imaging, 1997. Honours include: Several Best Article Awards; Best Scientific Presentation, International Symposium on Radiology, Beijing, 1993. Memberships: Formosan Medical Association; Radiological Society of China; Radiological Society of North America; American Roentgen Ray Society; Orthopaedic Research Society; Western Pacific Orthopedic Association; International Congress of Spinal Surgery; International Congress of Radiology. Address: National Taiwan University Hospital, Department of Radiology, 7 Chung-Shan South Road, Taipei, Taiwan.

**SHILAKADZE Tamaz A,** b. 19 February 1932, Georgia, Tbilisi. Engineer. m. Ketevan Natsvlishvili, 1 son, 1 daughter. Education: Degree of Engineer, Georgian Technical University, Tbilisi, 1955; Postgraduate, 1961, Degree of Candidate of Science, 1980, Moscow Institute of Highways, Technical University; Degree of Inventor's Adviser, Moscow Institute of Patent Systems, 1967; Degree of Inventor's Adviser, Georgian Institute of Patent Systems and Technical Work, 1978. Appointments: Director, Road Scientific-Research Institute; Director General, Road Amalgamation; First Deputy Minister, Ministry of Georgian Highways; Deputy Chairman, State Concern "Sakavtogza"; At present, Director General, Georgian State Road Scientific-Research and Industrial-Technological Institute "Sakgzametsniereba"; Chairman, Association of Inventors of Georgia; Rector, Institute of Patent Systems and Technical Work; State Patent Attorney. Publications: Books, articles, brochures and inventions, with over 50 patents. Honours: Honoured Engineer of Georgia; Honoured Inventor of Georgia; State Prize Winner, Science and Technology; Honoured Professor of Moscow Institute of Highways, Technical University; Honorary Degree of Community Association of European Order of Merit, 1994. Exhibitions of inventions at International Fairs: Moscow, USSR, 1967-88; Spokane, USA, 1974; Izmir, Turkey, 1978; London, UK, 1979; Barcelona, Spain, 1986, Brussels, Belgium, 1994; Budapest, Hungary, 1996. Awarded Gold Silver and Bronze medals. Memberships: Active Member, Academician, Georgian National Academy; Active Member, Academician, Georgian Academy of Ecological Science; Corresponding Member, Georgian Academy of Engineering; Academician, Academy of Transport, Russian Federation; Active Member, International Academy of Sciences, Industry, Education and Arts, California, USA; Active Member, New York Academy of Sciences, USA; Senatore Accademico di Accademia Universale Gugliemo Marconi, Art-Letter-Scienze. Address: 29a Gagarin Street, 380060 Tbilisi, Georgia.

**SHIM Sang-Tai,** b. 29 July 1940, Seoul. Professor. Education: BA, 1968, Catholic University of Korea; ThD, 1975, Tubingen University, Germany. Appointments: Ordination as Catholic Priest, 1971; Professor. 1976-93, Dean of the Theological Faculty, 1985-88, Catholic University of Korea; Director, Korean Christian Thought Institute, Hwasong, Seoul, 1992-; Professor, Suwon Catholic University, Hwasong, 1993-; Guest Professor, Graduate School of Sogang University, Seoul, 1995-. Publications: Author 8 books; Co-author 6 books; Editor, New Selection of Theological Works Vol I - XV, 1979-; Editor periodical, Korean Christian Thought, 1993-; Numerous articles. Memberships: International Study Group 'Inculturation', Aachen, Germany, 1994-; Member and Supervisor, Research Institute for Life and Culture, Seoul, 1992-; Honorary Director, A Catholic Charity Work, House of Hope, Yongmun, Korea, 1980-. Address: Korean Christian Thought Institute, 168 Wangnim-ri, Pongdam-myon, Hwasong-gun, Kyounggi-do, 445-890 South Korea.

**SHIMADA Akihiko,** b. 8 November 1953, Nishinomiya, Japan. Assistant Professor of University of Tsukuba. m. Yoshie Shimada, 2 sons, 2 daughters. Education: Faculty of Science, Osaka University, 1977; Masters program of Graduate School of Osaka University, 1980; Doctoral Program of Graduate School of Osaka University, 1986; Doctor of Agriculture, University of Tsukuba, 1989. Appointments: Research Associate, University of Tsukuba, 1987-90; Assistant Professor, 1991-. Publications: The role of radiation in the origin and evolution of life. Honour: Who's Who in the World, 1999. Membership: International Society for the Study of the Origin of Life; Society for the Study of the Origin and Evolution of Life of Japan. Address: Kaname 710, 300-2622 Tsukuba-shi, Ibaraki, Japan.

**SHIMOYAMA Ryushi,** b. 15 October 1952, Sapporo, Japan. Physician; Medical Scientist. m. Midori Saito, 1 son, 1 daughter. Education: MD, Hokkaido University School of Medicine, 1977; PhD, 1985. Appointments: Vising Research Fellow, Temple University, 1982-84; Vice-Director, Medical Section, Hokkaido Red Cross Blood Center, 1993-. Publications: Current Transfusion; What is a Virus Carrier?; Transfusion Handbook; How to Interpret Laboratory Data. Honour: Sol Shelly Award, Temple University, 1983. Membership: Fellow, Japan Society of Int Medicine; MACP. Address: Hokkaido Red Cross Blood Center, Yamanote 2-2, Sapporo 063, Japan.

**SHIN Dong-Keun,** b. 13 June 1959, Incheon, Korea. Independent Researcher in Computer Science. m. Helen

Chang, MD, 2 sons. Education: BA Computer Science, 1983, UC Berkeley, USA; MS Computer Science, 1985, DSc Computer Science, 1991, George Washington University, USA. Appointments: Engineer, Analyst, Programmer, BT-Dialcom, Xerox, CBSI, SRA, Samsung Electronics. Publications: Co-author, A New Join Algorithm, 1994; Author, The Theory of Massive Cross-Referencing, 1996. Memberships: Association for Computing Machinery; IEEE Computer Society. Address: Hwa Shin Building, Suite 701, 705-22 Yuksam-dong, Kangnam-gu, Seoul 135 080, Korea.

**SHINOHARA Kunio,** b. 9 February 1943, Fukuoka-shi, Japan. Professor. m. Sachiko, 3 sons. Education: B Eng Applied Physics, 1966, MSc Physics, 1968, Waseda University; PhD Radiation Biophysics, 1975, University of Tokyo. Appointments: Research Official, National Institute of Radiological Sciences, 1972-77; Associate Professor, School of Medicine, Kobe University, 1977-83; Head, Department of Radiation Research, Tokyo Metropolitan Institute of Medical Science, 1983-96; Professor and Director, Radiation Research Institute, Faculty of Medicine, University of Tokyo, 1996-. Publications: Ed, X-Ray Miscroscopy in Biology & Medicine, 1990; Co-author, Fine Structure of unstained human chromosome fibres dried with mofixative as observed by X-ray contact microscopy, 1990; Apoptosis induction resulting from proteasome inhibition, 1996; and others. Memberships: Royal Microscopical Society; American Association for the Advancement of Science; Japanese Society for Synchrotron Radiation Research; Japan Radiation Research Society; Biophysical Society of Japan; Japan Radiological Society; and others. Address: Radiation Research Institute, Faculty of Medicine, University of Tokyo, 7-3-1 Hongo Bunkyo ku, Tokyo 113 0033, Japan.

**SHIRINOV Timur,** b. 10 March 1950, Farish City. Archaeologist. m. Mavludakhon Sh Rasulovna, 1 son, 1 daughter. Education: Diploma, Termiz State University, 1972; Postgraduate, 1976-79; Candidate of Historical Sciences, 1980; Candidate for Doctors Degree, 1989-92; Doctor of Historical Sciences, 1993. Appointments: Technician, 1972-76, Junior, Senior Researcher, 1979-89, Uzbnek Academy of Sciences, Institute of Archaeology; Director, Institute of Archaeology, Samarkand, 1993-. Publications: Tools of Production and Weapons of Bronze Age of Central Asia; Early Urban Culture in Bronze Age of South of Central Asia; 60 articles in Uzbnek, Russian, English and French languages. Memberships: German Institute of Archaeology; French Society of Culture and History Studies of Timurids Epoch; French-Uzbnek Friendship in Paris. Address: Institute of Archeology, Uzbnek Academy of Sciences, Abdulaeva str 3, Samarakand 703051, Uzbekistan.

**SHIROKOV Aleksandr Mikhailovich,** b. 14 September 1924, Zaovrak, Russian. Physicist. m. Galina Petrovna Ivanchenko, 1 daughter. Education: Artillery Radio Engineering Academy, 1953; Doctor of Engineering, 1960; Assistant Professor, 1965; Master of Engineering, 1972; Professor, 1973; Correspondent Member, Belarus National Academy of Sciences, 1977. Appointments: Artillery Academy, Lecturer, 1959-63; Higher Missile Engineering College, Head of Chair, 1963-70; Vice Rector, 1970-80; Dean, Belarus University, 1980-87; Head of Chair, 1987-90; Rector, Institute of Modern Knowledge, 1990-. Publications: Over 200 Publications in Physics. Honours: 4 orders; 20 medals. Memberships: Academician of International Academy of Informatisation; Academician of the International Academy of Information Processes and Technologies. Address: Chornog Str 13a 22, 220012 Minsk, Belarus.

**SHIVADAS Kakkadan N,** b. 28 October 1936, Madras, India. Pharmaceutical Consultant. m. Pushpa Sukumaran, 1 son. Education: BSc Chemistry, 1956; BSPharm, 1961, Philadelphia College of Pharmacology and Science; MS Industrial Pharmacology, 1963, Purdue University, USA. Appointments: Analyst Control Department, Boots, 1956-58; Head Sterile Bulk Manufacturing, Sarabhai Squibb, 1963-64; Assistant Superintendent, Process Control, Indian Drugs and Pharmaceuticals, 1964-69; Executive Production, Glaxo Laboratories, 1969-76; Product Supply Manager, Procter & Gamble India Ltd, 1976-96, retired; Consultant to Pharmaceutical Industry, 1997-. Honours: Rho Chi Society, 1962; Sigma Xi Society, 1962. Memberships: Exec Committee, Indian Pharmaceutical Association; Rotary Board of Directors, Jinnaram Club; Procter & Gamble Europe Technical Services Task Force; Procter & Gamble Global Improving Production Quality Team. Address: Pooja 8-2-674/2/B/2, Road No 13, Banjara Hills, Hyderabad-500 034 , India.

**SHKATOVA Ludmila Alexandrovna,** b. 7 August 1939, Belinskii, Penza Oblast. Linguist. m. Vladimir Shkatov, 1 son, 1 daughter. Education: Graduate, Faculty of History and Philology, Chelyabinsk Pedagogical State Institute, 1961; Postgraduate Student, Moscow Institute of Russian Language of USSR Academy of Sciences, 1967. Appointments: Assistant Lecturer, Chelyabinsk Pedagogical State Institute, 1957-64; Postgraduate Student, Moscow Institute of Russian Language, 1964-67; Senior Lecturer, Chelyabinsk Pedagogical State Institute, 1968-76; Dean, Pro-Rector, Chelyabinsk State University, 1976-89; Professor, Department of the Russian Language, Chelyabinsk State University, 1989-. Publications: 150 publications including 4 monographs and 7 books. Honours: Received a Badge for Outstanding Worker of Education; Received a Badge for Outstanding Worker of Higher School; Veteran of Labour Medal. Memberships: Scientific Council of Terminology Society of Russia; Association of Researchers, Lecturers and Teachers of Russia in Rhetoric; Association in Support of International Academy of Sciences, Scientific Council of Regional Branch; Council on the Russian Language and the Russian Philology, Deputy Chair; Scientific Council to award the degree of Doctor (Philology), Ural State University, Yekaterinburg; Council Degree of Candidate of Science (Philology), Chelyabinsk University; Council to the degree of Doctor (Pedagogic), Chelyabinsk State University; Vice President, Znaniye Society, Chelyabinsk Branch. Address: Chelyabinsk State University, Ul Br, Kashirinykh 129, Chelyabinsk 454021, Russia.

**SHKODRA Zija,** b. 14 August 1925, Shkoder, Albania. Historian. m. Nahide, 1 son, 2 daughters. Education: Classical Lyceum, 1945; Diploma Marketing Economy, 1950; Diploma Political Economy, 1953; Universities in Bucharest, Romania. Appointments: In Beograd, 1988, Seminar Aisse, the theme of the reference, Balkans Corporations, in 17-18 centuries; Jordan Malfrag, The fifth International Seminar on Islamic Arts, Architecture, the Islamic Architecture in Albania, 1996. Publications: Destruction of the Albanian Feudalism, 1957; Albania in the Period of Tanzimat, 1959; The Albanian Craftsman, 1973; The Albanian City during National Renaissance, 1984; La ville .... national, 1988; The Albanian cities during Renaissance, 1990; Documents about Albania of the 18th century, vol 1 (1696-1707), 1975; The History of Albania, vol 1, (co-author), 1959; Le marche Albanais au 18 siècles Tirana, 1966; The Albanian encyclopaedic dictionary (co-author); 2500 total pages of scientific articles. Honours: 2nd Class Prize, Naim Frasheri, 1982; First Class Prize of Naim Frasheri, Presidium of the People's Assembly, 1989; 2nd Prize of Republic, 1989; Granted title Professor, 1995, Council of Ministers, Commission of scientific qualifications; Distinguished

Worker of Science and Technics, Republic of Albania, President of Republic, 1995. Memberships: Institute of History, Academy of Sciences, Tirana; Academy of Albanian Intellectuals of the Academy of Arts Prishtina, Istanbul, Tirana, 1993. Address: Rr Ali Demi, Pall 67/1 Shk 11 ap 14, Tirana, Albania.

**SHKROB O S,** b. 27 January 1920, Russia. Surgeon. m. L A Chernyavskay, 2 daughters. Education: 1st Medical Institute, 1941; Dr.Ph, 1953; MD, 1967; MMD N, 1967. Appointment: Professor of Surgery, MPR, 1968. Publications: Over 250 in thoracic and abdominal, endocrinology surgery. Memberships: Several. Address: Moscow Medical Academy, Great Pirogov St 2-6, 119435 Moscow, Russia.

**SHLAYEN Pinkhus,b.** 6 June 1923, Poltava, Ukraine. Ergomist. m. 1 son, 1 daughter. Education: Dr. of Technical Sciences, 1988. Appointments: President, Inter-Regional Ergonomic Association; Chief Research Worker, Ergocentre. Publications: Editor, Scientific Bulletin Theory and Practice, 1996; Editor, Problems of Psychology and Ergonomics, 1999. Honours: Awards: State Prize of Soviet Government, 1975; Three Orders for service in battle; State Committee of Defence Industry Prize Winner, 1995; Honoured Scientist, Russian Federation, 1996; Chizhevsky Prize Winner, 1997; Diploma of Brussels Eureka, 1997, 46th World Exhibition, 1997; Silver Medal, Outstanding merits in decision info problems in world cmty. Internal. Processes and Techs., 1998; Order for profl. merits in psychology Internat. Acad. Psychology, 1998. Memberships: President, Inter-Regional Ergonomic Association of the Russian Federation, 1996; Active Member, New York Academy of Scientices, 1996; Academician, Academy of Transport, 1992; Academician, International informatization Academy, 1992; Academician, International Academy for Information Processes and Technologies, 1993; Academician, Academy of Medical Technical Sciences, 1995; Academician, Military Sciences Academy, 1997; Academician, Russian Academy for Cosmonautics, 1998; Academician, Russian Ecological Academy, 1998; Academician, International Academy for Psychology, 1998. Address: Ergocentre,PO Box 0533, 17000 Tver, Russia.

**SHOL Kim Durand,** b. 19 October 1955, Fergus Falls, Minnesota, USA. Accountant; Computer Programmer. m. Cheryl Renee Casmey Shol, 2 daughters. Education: Associate of Applied Science in Business Computer Systems, University of Minnesota at Crookston, 1988. Appointments: Programme Assistant, Northwestern Apartments, Crookston, 1982-86; Junior Programmer, University of Minnesota at Crookston, 1988-90; Accounting Technician, Northwestern Mental Health Centre, Crookston, 1991-. Honour: Scholarship, Minneapolis Tribune, Minneapolis, Minnesota, 1970. Memberships: Computer Advisory Committee, University of Minnesota; New York Academy of Sciences, 1998-. Address: 917 Memorial Drive, Crookston, MN 56716, USA.

**SHRESTHA Bharat,** b. 2 February 1956, Nepal. Development Economist. m. Sheemela Shrestha, 1 son, 1 daughter. Education: MBA, 1980; MA, Economics, 1983; Post Graduate, Ecology and Environment, 1996. Appointments: Lecturer, Tribhuvan University, Consultancy Work, 1981-82; Development Economist, Agriculture Projects Services Centre, 1983-. Publications: Social Synamics of Deforestation in Nepal; Operational Stratergies of Sustainable Management of Forest; Community Bayed Forest Conservation. Memberships: Society for International Development; The World Conservation Union; IUCN; The Mountain Forum. Address: Gpo Box 1440, APROSC, Kathmandu, Nepal.

**SHRESTHA Bijaya,** b. 8 July 1955, Kathmandu, Nepal. Professor. m. Puja, 1 son, 3 daughters. Education: MS, Nuclear Physics, Louisiana St University, 1988; PhD, Nuclear Engineering, University Ma-Rolla, 1995. Appointments: Faculty, Department of Electrical Engineering, 1996-; Postdoctoral Fellow, Department of Nuclear Engineering, 1996. Honours: Fulbright Scholar, 1985; Outstanding Research Paper Award, 1994. Memberships: American Physical Society; American Mathematical Society; Nepal Physics Society; American Nuclear Society; American Engineering Society. Address: 1602 W Cedar, Rolla, MO 65401, USA.

**SHRIVASTAVA Harihar Charan,** b. 15 May 1927, Akaltara, MP. Social Worker. m. Kumudini Shrivastava, 1 son, 3 daughters. Education: Diploma in Agriculture, 1946, Raipur; Diploma in Journalism, 1948, Delhi; Stock Supervisor cum Health Assistant, 1951, Wardha; Extension Training, 1956, Betul; Several short and long term training in information and communication systems, commercial poultry enterprise, egg industry and poultry diseases, Production of low cost high protein food and beverage from soybean, USA, and Administrative Training. Appointments: Agricultural Overseer, 1946; Agricultural Assistant, 1958; Block Development Officer, Maheshwar in West Nimar District of MP; Agricultural Assistant, 1958, 1971, Class II service, 1981; Radio Officer, Jawahar Lal Nehru Agricultural University, Jabalpur; Mass Media Communication Officer, Dairy Development Corp, earning Golden Laurels; Publicity Officer Class I, FAO/UK/FCI; Information and Public Relations Officer, Tilhan Sangh; Administration and Accounts, Directorate, Indore; Social Worker, current; Contested election for Parliament, 1996. Publications: Several articles in USA agricultural journals and local Hindi and English journals. Memberships: Life member, Indian Institute of Public Administration; Chairman, People's Action for Development, MP. Address: Retired Assistant Director of Agriculture, 113 Usha Nagar (Main), Indore (MP) 452009, India.

**SHU Hao Wu,** b. 31 March 1931, Wuhan, Hubei, China. Senior Engineer; Professor. m. Qiu Zeyin, 1 son, 1 daughter. Education: Bachelor degree, 1952, Department Chemical Engineering, Qinhua University, Beijing. Appointments: Teaching work of a military academy, Beijing, 1952-64; Design Engineer, Technical Process Division, 1964-85, Deputy Chief Engineer of Institute and Director of Dept of Total Quality Control, 1985-94, Consulting Engineer, 1994-, Sichuan Chemical Engineering Design Institute, Chengdu. Publications: Took part in compiling text books in the military academy in the 1950s; Over 20 scientific papers in different periodicals in field of Sulfric acid, phosphorus fertiliser and compound fertiliser, and fine chemicals. Honours: Provincial Excellent Design Prize and 2nd Prize in National Excellent Design Prize, 1979 for a project; National 6th Five-year Plan Scientific and Technologic Key Project Prize, 1986; 1st Prize in Sichuan Provincial Excellent Design Prize for a project, 1998. Memberships: Society of Chemical Engineers of China; Vice Chairman, Chengdu Society of Chemical Engineering, 1980s; 6th Sichuan Committee member of CPPCC; Editorial Board, Sichuan Chemical Industry, Special Auditor of Sichuan Province, 1980s. Address: Sichuan Chemical Engineering Design Institute, No 35 Jinhe Road, Chengdu, Sichuan 610015, China.

**SHU Sing-Rong,** b. 28 January 1952, Maouli, Taiwan, China. m. Siau-Yui Lin, 2 sons, 1 daughter. Education: Graduate, Majored in Accounting, National Taichung Commercial College; Business Management, Japan Tokyo National University. Appointments: Assistant of President, Marketing Manager; Association Secretary; Director; Project Leader; Department Manager; Administration Department Manager; Chief of Trading Department, Kun Nan Enterprise Co; Supervisor of Import and Export Department, Kou Hwa Ceramic Co; Trading Specialist, Taichung Funai Electrics Co. Publications: Handbook of Sintered Part's Design and Production; How to Launch International Marketing at Low Expense; Factory Management Handbook of 5S with Checking List; The Management and Control Skill of Small Lot Multi Model Production Style; Just in Time Management Skill; How to Create the Idea and Wake up the Smart Brain; The Promoting Practice of 5S; The Children Growing Record Photo Collection. Address: 2F No 7 Ln 270 Chun-Hsin Rd, Sec 1 Hsin Tien, Taipei, Taiwan.

**SHU Wei-Der,** b. 2 November 1965, Taipei, Taiwan. Sociologist. m. Pei-Chi Chung. Education: BA, 1991, Department of Sociology, National Taiwan University; PhD candidate, 1998, Department of Sociology, Syracuse University, New York. Publications: 6 articles and conference proceedings. Honours: Book Coupon Award, National Taiwan University, 1989, 1990; Distinguished Graduate Student Paper Award, Political Sociology Section, American Sociological Association, 1995; Taiwanese Import and Export Association Scholarship, New York City, 1996. Memberships: American Sociological Association; American Political Science Association; Association for Asian Studies; North America Taiwan Studies Conference; Taiwanese Collegian; Syracuse Taiwanese Association. Address: 6210 The Hamlet, Jamesville, NY 13078, USA.

**SHUBIN Gregory,** b. 28 December 1925, Minsk, Belorussia. Engineering Educator and Researcher in Heat and Mass Transfer. m. Iliana Shubina, 1 son. Education: Honoured Diploma of Higher Education, Moscow State Forest University, Russia, 1951; PhD, 1964; Doctor of Technical Sciences, 1986. Appointments: Assistant Professor, 1955-61, Senior Lecturer, 1961-65, Associate Professor, 1965-86, Professor, 1986-, Moscow State University, Russia. Publications: Author, many books including: Physical Principles and Calculations of Wood Drying Processes, 1973; Drying and Heat Treatment of Wood, 1990; Over 250 articles. Honours: Honoured Worker of Science and Technic by Government of Russia, 1995; Decorated various medals for WWII by Government of Soviet Union. Memberships: Russian Academy of Natural Sciences (honorary); International Academy of Energy-Informative Sciences; New York Academy Sciences; International Union of Forest Research Organizations. Address: 2d Schelcovsky 9 2 48, 141 007 Moscow, Russia.

**SHUGALEI Irina,** b. 13 December 1950, Leningrad, Russia. Chemist. m. Mr Ilyushin M, 1 daughter. Education: Engineer of Chemical Technology, 1974; PhD, Chemical Sciences, 1978; Doctor of Chemical Sciences, 1996. Appointments: Researcher, 1974-75, 1978-83; Postgraduate, 1975-78; Assistant Professor, 1983-91, 1994-97; Doctorant, 1991-94; Professor, 1997-. Publications: In professional journals. Membership: New York Academy of Sciences. Address: Institute of Technology, Moskovsky pr 26, St Petersburg 198013, Russia.

**SHUGUROV Victor,** b. 15 January 1928, Samara, Russia. Physicist. m. Catherine Marchenko, 1 son, 1 daughter. Education: Physics Department, 1950, PhD, 1953, Hab dr, 1966, Vilnius University. Appointments: Lecturer, 1953, Associate Professor, 1957, Professor, 1967-, Physics Department, Vilnius University. Publications: Textbook; 2 books on microwave ferrite electrodynamics; About 150 papers. Honours: Honoured Scientist of Lithuania, 1978; National Prize, 1979; Some decorations. Memberships: IEEE; Lithuanian

Physicists' Society. Address: Svyturio 25-6, LT 2040, Vilnius, Lithuania.

**SHUKLA Priyendra,** b. 25 October 1975, Delhi, India. Artist (Creative Painting). Education: BFA, 1997. Honours: 2nd Prize in BFA Final Year, 1997; Participated in Nifals 1998 All India Fine Arts and Crafts Society; Particpated in South Asian Fraternity Youth Camp Nagaland 1996, won Good Work Certificate. Address: G 30 52 Sector 3, Rohini Delhi, 110085 India.

**SHUKSO Oodru Dorje,** b. 1 July 1944, Shigatse. Conductor. m. Dawa Drolgar, 1 daughter. Education: Degree in music composition and conducting, 1978, Shanghai Music Conservatory. Appointments: 1st Conductor, Tibetan Music Ensemble, 1979-84; Deputy Director, 1985-94, Director, 1994-, Tibetan Song and Dance Ensemble. Honour: HBS Broadcasting Award, Great Prayer Festival of Snowland. Memberships: Chinese Musicians Association; Director and life member, Tibetan Musicians Association. Address: Tibetan Song and Dance Ensemble, Lasa, Tibet 850000, China.

**SHUM Choi Sang,** b. 24 January 1922, Hong Kong. Merchant. m. Lee Sau Ling, 3 sons, 2 daughters. Education: MA, Economics, New York University. Career: Merchant. Memberships include: Barristers Disciplinary Tribunal Panel; Council of the Chinese University, Hong Kong; Selection Committee, Hong Kong Special Administrative Region; Hong Kong Country Club; Hong Kong Jockey Club; Hong Kong Red Cross; Hong Kong Society for Protection of Children; Hong Kong Tuberculosis, Chest and Heart Diseases Association. Address: c/o Overseas Chinese Enterprises Group Ltd, 21st Floor, Thyrse House, 16 Pottinger Street, Hong Kong.

**SHUMEIKO Nikolai M,** b. 22 September 1942, Belarus. Physicist. m. Zoya A Shumeiko, 2 sons. Education: Belarussian State University, 1960; Moscow State University, 1966; PhD, 1971; Assistant Professor Diploma, 1976; DSc, 1984; Professor Diploma, 1987. Appointments: Assistant, 1970, Senior Assistant, 1973, Assistant Professor, 1974, Senior Scientist, 1977, Associate Professor, 1985, Belarussian State University; Deputy Director, Research Institute for Nuclear Problems, 1986; Director, National Centre of Particle and High Energy Physics. Publications: Over 100 scientific papers. Honour: Distinguished Feature of Ministry of Education, Belarus, 1997. Membership: Corresponding Member, Belarussian Engineering Technological Academy, 1991. Address: National Centre of Particle and High Energy Physics, 153 Bogdanovich Str, Minsk 220 040, Belarus.

**SHUNDI Andrea,** b. 15 November 1934, Tirana, Albania. Agronomist. m. Vangelica, 2 sons. Education: Faculty of Agronomy, Tirana, 1952-56; Masters Degree, Candidate of Agricultural Sciences, 1981; Professor Assistant, Docent, 1985; PhD, Doctor of Agricultural Sciences, 1990; Professor, 1994. Appointments: Researcher, 1956-60; Agronomist in Chief, 1960-62; Agronomist in Chief, 1962-64; Head of Division of Livestock, Agronomist in Chief, Head of Division of Scientific Research, 1964-75; Head of Agriculture Department, 1975-76; Head of Seed's Enterprise of Tirana, 1976-80; Chair of Phytotechny, Lecturer on the subject, Dean, Faculty of Agronomy, 1980-92; Academy of Sciences, Tirana Scientific Secretary and Technical Sciences Section, 1994-. Publications: Many Papers and Posters in Scientific and Didactic Activities; 11 Monographs; 6 Textbooks; Several Booklets, Scientific Articles, Articles in Magazines and Newspapers. Memberships: Bulletin of Agricultural Sciences; Society of Albanian Agronomists; National Committee of Science and Technique; Scientific Council of Agricultural University; Scientific Council of

Faculty of Agronomy; National Commission of Post University Qualification; Scientific Council of Politechnical University Scientific Council of Institute for Forages Researches; Scientific Council of Institute for Agricultural Researches; Project Tempus of CEE in Albania; European Society for Grasslands; Albanian Journal of Natural and Technical Sciences. Address: Academy of Sciences, Tirana, Albania.

**SHURRAB Deya'a M,** b. 7 April 1970, Dubai, UAE. Electronics Engineer. m. Rasha Na'em, 1 daughter. Education: BSc Electronics Engineering, 1994, Ajman University Science and Technology, UAE. Appointments: Electronics Engineer, Fujairah Cement Industries, 1994-96; Communication Engineer, Fujairah International Airport, 1996-98; Computer Engineer, General Postal Authority, 1998-. Membership: IEEE. Address: PO Box 310, Fujairah, United Arab Emirates.

**SIBALSZKY Zoltan Georg,** b. 29 July 1926, Budapest. Professor Education: Diploma Electronic Engineering, Budapest, 1949; Dr Eng, Gödöllo, Hungary, 1972. Appointments: Assistant Professor, Technical University, Budapest, 1949; Chief Researcher, Central Physical Research Institute, Budapest, 1951-55; Professor, Agrarian Sciences University, Gödöllo, Hungary, 1955. Publications: 235 publications. Honours: French Ordre du Mérite Agricole, 1977; Bláthy Prize, 1982; Grand Prize of Electrotechnics, 1990; Recognition of Mérit of CIGR, 1998. Memberships: Commission Internationale du Genie Rural; Hungarian Electronic Association; Hungarian Agrarian Society. Address: Villanyi ut 9, HG 1114 Budapest, Hungary.

**SICUTERI Federigo,** b. 13 April 1920, Borgo, San Lorenzo, Florence, Italy. Physician; Researcher. divorced, 2 daughters. Appointments: Ordinary Professor and Chairman, Clinical Pharmacology, Florence, 1978-83; Chairman, Headache Centre, Florence, 1980-97; Ordinary Professor and Chairman, Medical Pathology, Florence, 1983-87; Ordinary Professor and Chairman, Internal Medicine and Therapeutics, Florence, 1987-90; Chairman, Interuniversity Centre of Neurochemistry and Clinical Pharmacology of Primary Headache, 1990-96; General Coordinator, Interuniversity Centre of Neurochemistry and Clinical Pharmacology of Primary Headache, 1997-; Emeritus Professor of Internal Medicine, 1997. Publications: Author, over 1700 articles; Editor, 5 volumes on kinins, 7 volumes on primary headache. Honours: First Prize of Italian Internal Medicine, 1961; Marzotto Prize for Medicine, 1965; Harold G Wolff Prize, 1966; Bormio 2000 Prize, 1978; International Greppi Prize, 1981; The Golden Guiness - International Prize for Medicine, 1985; Honorary President, Italian Society for the Study of Headache, 1992; Honorary Life Member, International Headache Society, 1998. Memberships: Italian Society for the Study of Headache, President, 1972-76; International Headache Society, Vice President, 1989-91; International Headache Society, President, 1991-93; Founder, International Club, Functional Organic and Non-Organic Nociceptive Diseases, FOND, President, 1991-. Address: Via Costa Dei Magnoli 28, 50125 Firenze, Italy.

**SIDAROSS Mona,** b. Egypt. Engineer. m. Joseph Tawfik. Education: BSc, Civil Engineering, 1977, Postgraduate Diploma, Structural Engineering, 1982, University of Alexandria, Egypt; Master Degree, Civil/Structural Engineering, University of Southern California, Los Angeles, 1997. Appointments: Project Engineer, County of Alexandria, Egypt, 1978-86; Bridge Engineer, Office of Structural Maintenance and Investigation, Caltrans, California, 1998-. Publications: Several reports. Honours: Silver Medal, Religieuse Franciscaine High School, Paris, 1967; Cash Scholarship, University of Alexandria, Egypt, 1973; Gold Medal, 20th Century Award for

Achievement, Cambridge, England, 1996; Member, Los Angeles World Affairs Council, 1997; US Citizen, 1998. Address: PO Box 6705, Rosemead, CA 91770, USA.

**SIDDIKY Sayeed A,** b. 21 February 1956, Narayanganj, Bangladesh. General and Plastic Surgeon. m. Fahmida Siddiky, 1 son, 1 daughter. Education: MBBS, 1982; FCPS (Surg), 1989; FICS, 1993; FRCS (Glasg), 1995; FACS, 1996. Appointments: Assistant Professor of Surgery, Z H Sikder Medical College and Hospital, Dhaka, Bangladesh. Publications: 9 articles in professional journals; 4 papers presented in international scientific conferences. Memberships: Society of Surgeons of Bangladesh; Life member, Bangladesh Medical Association; Life member, American Medical Society of Vienna, Austria; New York Academy of Sciences. Address: c/o 2/1 Naya Paltan, Amena Manjil (2nd Floor), Dhaka 1000, Bangladesh.

**SIDDIQUI Dilnawaz Ahmed,** b. 4 July 1937, Amroha, UP, India. Professor; International HRDEP Advisor. m. Narjis B Naqvi, 1 son, 1 daughter. Education: MA, BEd, Aligarh Muslim University, India; Postgrad Dip Ed, University of London, UK; PhD, Syracuse University, Syracuse, New York, USA. Appointments: US Chief Advisory Team to Yemen, 1980-83; Advisory Team Leader (Evaluation) to Jordan, 1992; HRD Advisor to Gov. of Sudan, 1994-95; Professor, Communication, Clarion University of Pennsylvania, current. Publications: CAE: State of the Art, 1989; The Gulf War, 1992. Honours: AFMI Professional Excellence Award, 1997; Saifi Burhanuddin Gold Medal, Aligarh Muslim University, India, 1958; Russian Academy for Humanities, Honoris causa, 1996; USA/NGO Delegate to UNESCO, 1997. Memberships: American Society for Training and Development, Editorial Board; Association of Muslim Social Scientists, President 1994-96; International Communication Association, Editorial Board; Islamic Horizons, Editorial Board. Address: 510 Ridgewood Road, Marianne Est, Shippenville, PA 16254, USA.

**SIDDIQUI Majeed,** b. 5 August 1956, Hyderabad, India. Doctor of Medicine. m. Salima, 1 son, 1 daughter. Education: MBBS, 1983; Doctorate in Clinical Neurology, 1987. Appointments: Senior Medical Officer; Visiting Medical Officer; Family Practitioner. Publications: Research in Parkinsons Disease, Pathophysiology, Journal of Neurology. Memberships: President, Australian Doctors Trained Overseas Association Inc; Member, British Postgraduate Medical Federation. Address: 1/56 Belford Rd, East Kew, Vic 3102, Australia.

**SIDERIDOU Niki Stella,** b. 1915, Smyrna. Writer; Honorary General Inspectress. m. John Thomopoulos, 2 d. Appointments: Secondary Education, Greece, 35 Years. Publications: 25 Books include: A. Kackavitsas and his Era, study; Impressions from Ethiopia; Zacharias Papantoniou, study; Uncertain Wall, poems; The Song of Loneliness, short stories; Poems, Short Stories, Travelogues, Pedagogical Works; A Fairy Tale for Peace. Honours: Literary Prizes of the Accademia Ferdinandea, La Sicula Athenae; Attestato Di Merito; Primavera Catanese; Catania Duomo; Certificate of Distinguished Achievements; Lady of Olympoetry; Woman of the Year, 1997; Director Generals Honours List; Prize, Athens Academy; Prize Supreme Council of National Education; Many other honours and awards for educational, social, humanitarian contributions in a career of 35 years. Memberships: Greek Litterteurs International Society; International Writers and Artists Academy; International Writers and Artists Association; Olympoetry Movement Committee; International Biographical Association; Order of International Fellowship; Many other memberships. Address: 17 Galaxidiou, Athens, Greece 104 43.

**SIEBERT Traute,** b. 1943, Neumünster, Germany. Registered Nurse; Businesswoman; Entrepreneur. m. Dietrich E Siebert, 1 child. Education: RN, 1963, Nursing Academy in Germany. Appointments: Registered Nurse, Germany; High Fashion Model, Canada, 1965; Modelling Teacher; VP, Eurocommerce Canada Inc; School Director, Eleanor Fulcher Ltd, VP 1990, Owner and President 1991-; Director: Eleanor Fulcher International Ltd, Can-Am International Properties Inc, Euro-commerce Canada Inc; President, Blast Models Inc. Honours: Award of Educational Excellence, International Model and Talent Association, since 1990. Memberships: AFFH; International Model and Talent Association; Women Entrepreneurs of Canada; Speakers Forum. Address: Eleanor Fulcher Intl Ltd, 615 Yonge Street Ste 200, Toronto ON, Canada M4Y 1Z5.

**SIEGEL Stuart Elliott,** b. 16 July 1943, New Jersey, USA. Physician. m. Linda, 1 son. Education: BA, Summa Cum Laude, Boston University, 1967; Doctor of Medicine, Magna Cum Laude, 1967. Appointments: Intern, Department of Pediatrics, University of Minnesota Hospitals, 1967-68; Resident, Department of Pediatrics, 1968-69; Associate Hematologist, Attending Physician, 1972-76; Assistant Professor, 1972-76; Head of Division of Hematology, Oncology, Childrens Hospital of Los Angeles, 1976-; Coordinator for Pediatric Oncology, US School of Medicine, 1976-; Associate Professor of Pediatrics, 1976-81; Professor of Pediatrics, USC School of Medicine, 1981-; Head of Division of Oncology, 1986-; Acting Physician in Chief, 1987; Deputy Physician in Chief, 1987-91; Associate Director, Kenneth Norris Jr Comprehensive Cancer Center, 1989-; Associate Chair, Childrens Hospital of Los Angeles, 1994-96; Vice Chairman, Department of Pediatrics, USC, 1994-. Publications: Many Publications. Honours: Phi Beta Kappa; Medical Staff of Childrens Hospital of Los Angeles Distinguished Service Award; The Best Doctors in America; Many other honours and awards. Memberships: Los Angeles County Medical Association; Los Angeles Pediatric Society; Western Society for Pediatric Research; American Academy of Pediatrics; Many other memberships. Address: Childrens Hospital of Los Angeles, 4650 Sunset Boulevard, Los Angeles, CA 90027, USA.

**SIGLER Lois Olivier,** b. 8 September 1923, Piney Flats, Tennessee, USA. Educator. m. William Vigil Sigler Junior, 1 son, William Oliver. Education: BS, East Tennessee State University, 1944; MS, plus 45 hours, University of Tennessee, 1952; MS, University of Tennessee and Memphis State University. Appointments: Home Economics Teacher, Buchanan, Virginia, 1944-46; Area Supervisor, Home Economics Education and School Lunch Program, State Department of Education, Commonwealth of Virginia, 1946-54; Assistant National Adviser, 1954-56, National Adviser, 1956-63, New Homemakers of America, Department of Health, Education and Welfare, Washington, DC; Coordinator, Family Living Pilot Program, Columbus, Ohio, 1963; Home Economics Teacher, Millington, Tennessee, 1966-92. Honours: Honorary Member, Future Homemakers of America, 1956; Tennessee Home Economics Teacher of the Year, 1975; Outstanding Service Award, Tennessee Association Vocational Home Economics Teachers, 1986; Master Adviser, Futuree Homemakers of America, 1988; Honorary Member, Tennessee Assocation, Future Homemakers of America, 1988; Adviser Mentor, Tennessee Association of Vocational Home Economics Teachers, 1992; Woman of the Year, 1991; Twentieth Century Award for Achievements. Memberships: American and Tennessee Home Economics Associations; American and Tennessee Vocational Associations; National and Tennessee Vocational Home Economics Teachers Association,

Secretary-Treasurer of TAVHET, 1974-75, Served on NAVHET Awards Committee, 1975-76; West Tennessee Home Economics Education Association Secretary, 1972-73; National, Tennessee, West Tennessee and Shelby County Education Associations, SCEA School Representative, 1975-77, Executive Committee SC-PAGE, 1976, TEA Board of Directors, 1977-80; Delta District Chairman, Home Economics Teachers, 1981-83. President Eisenhower's Advisory Committee on Youth Fitness; President Kennedy's Food for Peace Council. Address: 4785 Rolling Meadows Drive, Memphis, Tennessee 38128, USA.

**SIIVOLA Jouko Reino,** b. 13 January 1944, Hameenlinna. Clinical Neurophysiologist. m. Seija Jarvi, 1 son, 1 daughter. Education: MD, 1973; Doctor of Philosophy, 1982. Appointments: Clinical Neurophysiologist, 1979; Chief, Clinic of Neurophysiology, Kainuu Central Hospital, 1990-. Publication: Clinical applications of evoked potentials and elctrically active polymers. Memberships: Finnish Brain Research Association, 1981-; New York Academy of Sciences, 1996-. Address: Kainuu Central Hospital, 87140 Kajaani, Finland.

**SIKKA Desh Bandhu,** b. 1 November 1927, India. Consulting Geologist. m. Mira, 2 sons, 1 daughter. Education: BSc, Punjab, 1945; MS, New York, 1954; PhD, McGill, 1960. Appointments: Mineral Exploration, Brazil, Canada, Egypt, Greece, India, Mexico, Sierra Leone, Sudan, USA, Over 44 years; Honourary Advisor, Hindustan Copper Ltd, 1981-85; Advisor, Uranium Corporation of India, 1981-; Chief Geologist, National Mining Development Corporation, 1966-68; Chief Geologist, Acting Chief Executive Planning, Hindustan Copper Ltd, 1968-71. Publications: 26 Papers Published. Honour: President's Gold Medal for Doctoral Thesis, 1960. Memberships: Canadian Institute of Mining and Metallurgy; Geological Society of India; Mining Geological Metallurgical Institute of India; Association of Professional Geologists and Geophysicists of Quebec; Professional Geoscientist, Association of Professional Engineers and Geoscientists of Saskatchewan; Life Member, Association of Exploration Geophysicists, India. Address: 2108 3463 Rue Ste Famile, Montreal, Quebec, Canada, H2X 2K7.

**SIKULA Josef,** b. 14 January 1933, Bystrice nad Pernstejnem. Professor of Physics. m. Marie Sikulova, 4 daughters. Education: MSc, Electronics, 1957, Czech Technical University, Prague; MSc, Experimental Physics, Comenius University, Bratislava, 1960; PhD, Semiconductor Physics, TU Leningrad, USSR, 1965; RNDr Solid State Physics, Masaryk University of Brno, 1965; DSc, Phys Math Sciences, Czech TU, Prague, 1980. Appointments: Head of Physics Department, Technical College Cairo, Egypt, 1967-72; Associated Professor of Applied Physics, Technical University Brno, 1969; Professor of Applied Physics, Czech TU Prague, 1980; Vice Dean for Research, 1975-85, Head of Physics Department, 1975-94, TU Brno; Head of the Board for PhD, 1985-98, Member of the Board for DSc, 1985-92, Theses in Physics of Condensed Matter and Acoustics; Director, Czech Noise Research Laboratory, TU Brno, 1997-. Publications: 92 scientific works related to problems in physics of fluctuation processes in solid states. Honours: Project Leader and Co-ordinator of grants supported by Commission of European Communities and by Czech Grant Agency, 1994-98; Silver Medal, TU Brno, 1983; Gold Medal, TU Gdansk, 1997. Memberships: Union of Czechoslovak Mathematicians and Physicists; Permanent International Committee for Conferences on Noise in Physical Systems and I/f Fluctuations; Programme Committee, CARTS-EUROPE conferences; Technical Committee, European Symposium Quality and Reliability of Electron Devices. Address: TU Brno, Zizkova 17, 6000 Brno, Czech Republic.

**SILERIO ESPARZA Maximiliano,** b. 14 March 1939, Yerbabuena, Dgo, Mexico. Attorney-at-Law. m. Elvira Diaz Quinones, 4 sons, 2 daughters. Education: Attorney at Law, Juarez University, State of Durango, 1964. Appointments: District Attorney of Durango, 1963-64; State Congressman in Durango, 1968-71; Mayor, City of Durango, 1971-74; Secretary of State, State of Durango, 1974-75; Federal Congressman, House of Representatives, Mexico, 1976-79; Leader of the House, 1977; Speaker of the House, 1978; Federal Congressman, 1982-85; Senator, Republic, representing Durango, 1988-92; Governor, State of Durango, 1992-98. Memberships: Secretary General, Durango Student Federation, 1962; Univesity Council, 1962; Youth State Director, 1965, President of Municipal Committee, 1966, President, 1969-71, Revolutionary Institutional Party of Durango; Secretary of Administration of National Commitee, 1985-86, Deputy Secretary General of National Commitee, 1987, Revolutionary Institutional Party; Secretary General, National Peasants Confederation, 1989-92. Address: Valle del Guadiana 212, CP 84000 Deranges, Mexico.

**SILVA Joao,** b. 5 Feb 1949, Sao Paulo, Brazil. Geophysicist. m. Hiroko Sido, 1 son. Education: BSc, Geology, 1972; MSc, Geophysics, 1976; PhD, Geophysics, 1982. Appointment: Professor, Geophysics, Federal University of Para, Brazil. Publications: 28 papers in specialised periodicals, 1981-99. Membership: Society of Exploration Geophysicists. Address: CG-UFPA, Calxa Postal 1611, 66017-900 Belem, Brazil.

**SILVA Lawrence K,** b. 27 June 1948, Lagos, Nigeria. m. Mojisola A Silva, 3 sons, 1 daughter. Education: NCE, Institute of Education, ABU, Nigeria, 1971; BS, Benedict College Columbia, South Carolina, 1976; MAT, University of South Carolina, Columbia, South Carolina, USA, 1978; PhD, Ahmadu Bello University, Zaria, Nigeria, 1987. Appointments: Education Officer, Kaduna, Nigeria, 1971-78; Senior Lecturer, Ahmadu Bello University, Zaria, Nigeria, 1979-90; Associate Professor, Bowie State University, 1990-. Publications: Motivational Dimensions of Nigerian Elite Athletes in Selected Sports, in the Journal of the International Council of Health, Physical, Education and Recreation, 1991; Reviewer, Sports and Recreational Activities. Honours: Certificate of Recognition in Coaching Athletics, Ahmadu Bello University , 1986; World Fitness Ambassador, 1990; Outstanding Professor, 1993; Who's Who of Professionals, 1996-; Certificate of Appreciation, Maryland Charity Campaign, 1996, 1997. Memberships: International Council for Health, Physical Education, Recreation and Dance; AAHPERD; Maryland Association for Health, Physical Education, Recreation and Dance; Sport Science Exchange. Address: Bowie State University, 9104 6th Street, Lanham, MD 20706, USA.

**SILVA Luis Antonio Rebello Da,** b. 20 September 1931, Albergaria A Velha. Mechanical Engineer. m. Maria Teresa, 1 son, 3 daughters. Education: Degree, Mechanical Engineering, Higher Institute of Technology, Technical University of Lisbon, 1949-55; Post Graduate Studies, Department of Glass Technology, Faculty of Engineering, University of Sheffield, England, 1958-59. Appointments: Assistant, Lecturer of Mathematics, Higher Institute of Technology, 1954-55, 1956-57; Factory Manager, Vigola, 1957-58; Factory Manager, Produtora Garrafas, SA, Marinha Grande, 1964-66; Senior Executive, CIVE, SA, 1967-70; Managing Director, Barbosa and Almeida, 1971-77; General Manager, Fonseca Internacional Vinhos, 1978-80; Chairman, Board of Covina, 1980-88; Chairman, Board of ACTA, 1988-91; Chairman, Board f UTIC, 1991-95; Chairman, Complexo do Cachao, 1992-93; :hairman, Board of CIVE, 1992-93; Chairman, Board of MECI, 993-95; Chairman, Board of INTERFORMA, 1993-95; .hairman, Board of Sodia, 1996-; Director, SANEST, 1995-. ublications: Vidros e Seus Componentes, 1961; A qualidade uma Fabrica de Vidros, 1966. Memberships: Forum dos dministradores de Empresas; APM; Gremio Literario; Society f Glass Technology; American Club of Lisbon; Sporting Clube e Portugal. Address: Cascais, Ave de Sintra, 267-r/c Esq, 750 Lisbon, Portugal.

**SILVA Rene Charles,** b. 2 January 1930, Lobito. Inspector ieneral of Education. m. Matilde, 1 son, 2 daughters. ducation: Bachelor, Overseas Administration, 1953; Doctor in 'olitical and Social Science, 1968. Appointments: Portuguese iuinea, 1955; Inspector General of Education, High Office. ionours: Councillor of the Lisbon Technical University, Lifetime iignity. Memberships: Pluridimensional Education and Cultural ichool Association. Address: Rua Curry Cabral 2 Esq, 2780 'aco De Arcos, Portugal.

**SILVERSON Rex Allen,** b. 31 May 1940, Waterloo, Iowa. .ducation. m. Karen, 1 son. Education: BA, 1972; Teachers :redentials, 1973; Master of Arts, Education Degree, 1988. ppointments: Teaher,College Administration, High School, lementary School; Home Builder; Restoration Auto Builder; .rt Designer. Honours: Numerous Artisitc and Design Awards. 1emberships: ISEA; NEA; IPERS. Address: 2301 Sunset Blvd, :edar Falls, IA 50613-5653, USA.

**SILYANOV Valentin V,** b. 19 June 1937, Moscow, Russia. ransport Engineer. m. Nellya, 1 son. Education: Eng, 1960; hD, 1968; DSc, 1979; Professor, 1982. Career: Road Forman, 1oscow Road Building Company, 1960-62; Faculty Lecturer, 964-; Dean, Highway Engineering Department, Head, icientific Laboratory on Road Traffic Safety of MADI-TU, 978-; Vice Rector, Moscow State Automobile and Road echnical University,(MADI TU) 1987-. Publications: 7 books, ver 200 scientific papers on theory of traffic flow, road traffic afety, highway capacity, road design and road rehabilitation. Jonour: Honorary Scientist of the Russian Federation; lonorary Road Engineer of Mongolia. Memberships: Vice 'resident, International Association for Automotive and Road ngineering Education; Russian Academy of Transport; nternational Higher Education Academy of Sciences; Ukranian .cademy of Transport; International Academy of Creative :ndeavors; New York Academy of Sciences. Address: eningradskoe Shosse, Building 35, App 85, Moscow 125212, {ussia.

**SIM Terence Chet Hong,** b. 21 April 1948, Singapore. Trade ipecialist. m. Grace P G Chng, 1 daughter. Education: 3achelor of Commerce, 1972, Saint Olav's Academy, Paris, rance. Appointments: Representative, Vavasseur Levetus :xport Ltd, UK, 1968-72; Representative, American Minerals & 'etroleum Corp (US), 1973; Representative, Dominion ihippers Ltd (UK), 1974-78; Representative, Gordon & Gotch :xport Services Ltd, UK, 1979-80; Representative, Dalgety :xport Services Div, UK, 1981-83; Founder/President, 3eneficial Offshore Trading House, 1984-98; Company )irector, Global Exports Network, 1986-92. Honours: In ecognition of Merit for a World Trade Certificate by The 1ellinger Company, Los Angeles, USA as a member of nternational Traders, 1970; Certificate of Excellence and 3arons Fellowship Award, 1996. Address: Blk 108 Simei St *04-740, Singapore 520108, Singapore.

**SIMAL-GANDARA Jesus,** b. 5 April 1966, Santiago de Compostela, Spain. Associate Professor of Nutrition and Food Science. Education: Graduate, 1989, Licentiate, 1989, Doctorate, 1991, University of Santiago. Appointments: Provisional Associate Professor, 1991-93, Associate Professor, 1993-, University of Vigo; Trainee Researcher's Fellowship, CSIC, 1988-89; Researcher's Fellowship, Ministry of Education & Science, 1989-91. Publications: Research Articles Referee, Journal of Agriculture and Food Chemistry, Water Research, Journal of AOAC International, Vibrational Spectroscopy, Food Science and Technology (Spanish); Editor, Social Anthropology Journal of Ourense; Author many books and publications in journals. Honours: Eloy Diez Prize for Best Doctoral Thesis; Prize for Distinction, Pharmacy Doctorate; Galician Section, Royal Society of Medicine and Surgery; National Prize for Students Completing Licentiate in Pharmacy; Prize for Distinction, Licentiate in Pharmacy. Memberships: Programme D'Echanges Avec Les Anciens Chercheurs, Stagiaires et Etudiants Etrangers en France; Spanish Section, European Association for Food Legislation; Association of Food Scientists & Technologists of Madrid. Spanish Nutrition Association; Spanish Food Science Association. Address: Rua Paris 7B, (Area Central 14) 2A, 15703 Santiago de Compostela, Spain.

**SIMANANAVICIUS Leonas,** b. 28 June 1929, Panevezys, Lithuania. Chemist. m. 1 daughter. Education: Graduate, Vilnius University, 1954; PhD, Leningrad University, 1958; DSc, Institute of Chemistry, Vilnius, 1988. Appointments: Lecturer, 1957-60, Docent, 1960-65, Dean, Chemistry Faculty, 1961-64, Vilnius University; Senior Research Fellow, 1965-75, Head of Department, 1975-, Assistant Director, 1990-92, Institute of Chemistry, Vilnius. Publications: Over 100 articles in professional chemical journals. Memberships: Lithuanian Academy of Sciences; American Chemical Society; International Society of Electrochemistry. Address: Rintines 21-156, 2051 Vilnius, Lithuania.

**SIMANCAS ROBLES Antonio,** b. 22 November 1945, Tepic, Nayarit, Mexico. CPA. 1 son, 1 daughter. Education: CPA degree, Universidad Nacional Autonoma of Mexico, 1969; MBA, 1971-72, not concluded; Specialist in Finance and Taxes. Appointments: Senior Partner, Antonio Simancas Robles & Associates, Public Accountants and Business Consultants; Professor, University of Mexico; Partner, Moores Rowland International, International Latin American Controller for ICI Ltd. Publications: Several essays and articles on taxes, economics and politics in local newspapers 1989-. Memberships: Instituto Mexicao de Contadores Publicos and Colegio de Contadores Publicos de Estado de Nayarit. Address: Priv Cipres No 7, Col Versalles, 63128 Tepic Nayarit, Mexico.

**SIMASCHEVICI Alexei,** b. 27 June 1929, Kishinau, Moldova. Physicist. m. Inna Kromida-Rekken, 1 s, 1 d. Education: Kishinau State University, 1952; PhD, 1963; Dr Sc, 1979. Appointments: Professor, Head of Semiconductor Physics Department, Moldavian State University, 1955-95; Head of Physics, Mathematics Section, Academy of Sciences, Moldova, 1995-. Publications: 450 Publications, 5 Books, 162 Papers, 231 Communications to Scientific Meetings; 21 Patents. Honours: State Prize of Republic of Mildva. Memberships: Solar Energy Society of Moldova; Renewable Energy Sociaty of Romania. Address: Str Academiei 5, MD2028 Chisinau, Rep of Moldova.

**SIMICEVIC Velimir Nicholas,** b. 12 October 1968, New York, USA. MD. Education: MD, 1995, Postgrad Programme in Biomedicine, 1998, University of Zagreb. Appointments: Research Associate, Department of Biomedicine, 1995-97, Clinical Research Physician, Medical Department, 1997-, Pliva Research Institute. Publications: Over 20 articles, 1992-. Honours: University Chancellor's Award for Best Student

Paper, 1994. Memberships: AAPP; IUPHAR; NYAS; ACRPI; European Society of Clinical Pharmacology. Address: Pliva Pharmaceutical Co Research Institute, Prilaz B Filipovica 25, HR 1000 Zagreb, Croatia.

**SIMMS Albert,** b. 21 January 1931, Claremont, WV, USA. Pastor, Evangelist. Appointments: Past Historian, Baptist Convention, 1973; Chairman, State Baptist Advisory Board; Chairman, State Order Nation Committee, 1973; Field Representative, Hill Top Baptist Seminary, 1975. Honours: Award of Merit; Outstanding Achievement Diplomas; Certificate in Religious Education; Diploma in Education; Diploma in Pastoral Ministries; Advance Diploma in Pastoral Ministeries; Honorary Doctorate, Community College, Opelika, Alabama, 1978. Memberships: Member, Cripple Children Division Association; Moderation of New River Baptist Association; Treasurer, New Rivers Baptist Association. Address: 216 Broadway Ave, Oak Hill, WV 25901, USA.

**SIMON Rita James,** b. New York. Sociologist, Professor. 2 sons, 1 daughter. Appointments: Research Fellowship, Law and Behavioral Sciences, University of Chicago, 1957-58; Research Associate, 1958-59; Assistant Professor, 1959-61; Research Associate, Columbia University, 1961-62; Annie W Goodrich Visiting Professor, 1962-63; Associate Professor, Professor, University of Illinois, 1963-67; Visiting Lecturer, Hebrew University, Jerusalem, 1967-68; Professor, Head of Sociology Department, 1968-70; Visiting Professor, Hebrew University, 1970-71; Professor of Sociology, University of Illinois, 1971-74; Visiting Professor, Hebrew University, 1974-75; Director, University of Illinois, 1975-80; Professor of Sociology, University of Illinois, 1968-83; Dean, School of Justice, The American University, 1983-87; Acting Dean, School of Public Affairs, 1987-88; Professor, Justice, Law and Society, American University, 1988-; University Professor, 1989-. Publications: Authored many books and monographs. Memberships: American Sociological Association; American Society of Criminology; Law and Society Association; Advisory Screening Committee in Sociology for Fulbright Hays Application; NIMH Crime and Delinquency Review Council. Address: 110 Primrose Street, Chevy Chase, MD 20815, USA.

**SIMPSON John Berchman Jr,** b. 18 July 1938, Hartford, Connecticut, USA. Retired Chaplain; Retired military law enforcement officer. m. (1) Yvonne Elaine McGruder, 4 sons, 1 daughter, (2) Donna Jean Hadra, 1 son, 2 daughters. Education: BA Journalism, 1963, Brooklyn College; BS Divinity, 1984, DD, 1989, Houston Divinity College; Certified Protection Professional, Arizona. Appointments: Editor, USAF, 1956-65; Managing Editor, Enfield (Conn) Press, 1967; Director, Public Affairs, US Coast Guard Res, New London, Connecticut, 1970-89; President, Loss Prevention Institute, Houston, 1980-84; Assistant Pastor, Chapel of Prayer, Houston, 1982-84; Officer, Chaplain, Maricopa County Sheriff's Office, Phoenix, 1985-96; Pastor, Chapel of Divine Faith, Scottsdale, Arizona, 1996-. Publications: Author, Retail Loss Prevention, 1983; Editor, Aetna-izer, 1969, The Deputy, 1986; Board of Directors, Maricopa County Deputy Sheriff's Association, Phoenix, 1986-93; Council of Churches, Houston, 1984, Phoenix, 1996; Chaplain, VA Hospital, Houston, 1980-84; Commander, US Coast Guard, 1989. Honours: Named Editor of the Year, Sigma Delta Chi, Hartford, 1966; Recipient, Medal of Valor, New Haven (Conn) Police Department, 1972; Distinguished Service Award, VA Hospital, Houston, 1984. Memberships: DAV (life); Res Officers Association, life, Chaplain, 1993-94; US Naval Institute, life; Society Professional Journalists, Presidents Club; American Legion, Chaplain, 1993-98; Retired Officers Association. Address: 6226 East Anaheim Street, Mesa, AZ 85205, USA.

**SIMSON Daniel,** b. 18 January 1942, Zajaczkowo, Poland Mathematician; University Professor. m. Sabina Mielcarek Education: MS, 1966, PhD Mathematics, 1974, Doctorate Habilitation in Mathematics, 1974, Nicholas Copernicus University. Appointments: Assistant, 1966, Adjunct, 1974 Docent, 1975, Professor in Mathematics, 1987, Nichola Copernicus University; Head of Institute of Maths, 1975-87 Head of Algebra and Topology Department, 1976-95, Dean Faculty of Mathematics and Informatics, 1993-, Nicholas Copernicus University; Visiting Professor to 18 universities Attended 28 international conferences on Algebra. Publications Linear Representations of Partially Ordered Sets and Vector Space Categories, book, 1992; Over 100 research articles on algebra and related topics. Honours: For Mathematical results and research awarded Prize from Polish Ministry of Science and Higher Education, 1975, Zaremba Prize from the Polish Mathematics Society, 1978, Prize from Ministry of National Education of Poland, 1993, 1996. Memberships: Mathematics Committee, Polish Academy Sciences; Mathematics Section of State Committee KBN for Scientific Research in Poland Committee of Experts in Mathematics of Ministry of National Education in Poland. Address: Faculty of Mathematics and Informatics, N Copernicus University, ul Chopina 12/18, 87 100 Torun, Poland.

**SINANI Shaban,** b. 16 April 1958, Diber, Albania Ethno-Sociologist. m. Alma Hasani, 2 daughters. Education Graduate, University of Tirana, 1982; Master Degree, 1993 DSc, Ethnology, 1998. Appointments: Pedagogue of Albanian Language, University of Tirana, 1983; Journalist, 1983, Specia Correspondent, 1985, "Voice of People"; Editor-in-Chief Presidium of Peoples Council, 1985; Consultant, President of Republic R Alia, 1991; Specialist, Epic of Bravemen, Institute of Folk Culture, Academy of Sciences, 1992; Chief, Department of Folklore, 1998. Publications include: Albanian Folk Songs (southern regions), compiler and editor with glossary, 1988 northern regions, 1998; The Pawn of Misunderstanding, 1997 Mythology in Epic of Bravemen, 1998; Superlative, 1998 Kosovo in Geopolitic, 1998; Honours: Medal, Naim Frashëri. 1984; Order, Naim Frashëri, 1987. Memberships: Chief, Department of Literary Folklore, Institute of Folk Culture, Academy of Sciences; General Secretary, Cultural Foundation D&D; Board of Editors, "Popular Culture" and "Perla". Address Instituti i Kulturës Popullore, Kont Urani 3, Tirana, Albania.

**SINGAL Savita,** b. 30 June 1956, Pilani, Rajasthan, India Teacher; Researcher. m. Shiv K Singal, 2 sons. Education: BSc Home Science, 1974, BSc Hons Home Management, 1975 MSc Home Management, 1977, Punjab Agricultural University, Ladhiana; PhD Home Management, 1989, MS University of Baroda, Gujarat. Appointments: Lecturer in Home Science, Bhiwani, 1977-78; Lecturer in Home Science, Kaithal, 1978-80 Assistant Professor, 1980-89, Scientist, 1989-96, Professor and Head, Department of Family Resource Management, 1996- CCS Haryana Agricultural University, Hisar. Publications: 50 research papers; 34 Research abstracts; 47 extension articles; 15 booklets and leaflets; 5 research reports; 2 textbooks; Participated in 50 seminars and conferences, 5 at international level. Memberships: Life Member: Home Science Association of India; Society for Home Scientists of State Agricultural Universities and Rural Development Institutes; Network Member, Women Household Development Studies Information Centre; Associate Member, Third World Organisation of Women Scientists; Member: International Organisation for Science & Technology; Managing Committee for Jindal Modern School. Address: 403 Defence Colony, Hisar 125001, Haryana, India.

**SINGANAYAGAM Indrapalan,** b. 26 December 1961, Trincomalee, Sri Lanka. Engineering Manager. m. Thilagadevi, son, 1 daughter. Education: BSc Eng (Civil), 1984; Diploma n Computer Programming, 1986; Chartered Engineer; Internal Quality Auditing; Quality Management. Appointments: Civil Engineer, Coomsco Pvt Ltd, Sri Lanka, 1985; Chief Engineer, Site Agent, Balfour Beatty Intl Construction Ltd of UK, 1985-89; Bridge Engineer, Highway Engineer, Randel Palmer and Tritton of UK, Transport and Road Research Lab of UK (Overseas Unit), Consulting Engineers and Architects Associated, 1989-91; Engineering Manager, Head of Health, Safety and Environment, Haji Adinin and Sons Pte Ltd, Brunei, 1992-98; Director, Business Powercom Link (NZ) Ltd, New Zealand, 1998-; Managing Director, Antsteck Engineering Consultants Ltd, New Zealand, 1998-. Honours: Safety Awards, 1996, 1997, 1998. Memberships: Corporate Member: American Society of Civil Engineers, Institution of Engineers, Sri Lanka; Institution of Highways and Transportation, London, Institution of Professional Engineers, New Zealand. Address: PO Box 27-465, Mt Roskill, Auckland, New Zealand.

**SINGH Amarjit,** b. 10 August 1952, New Delhi, India. Civil Engineer. m. Harkiran Singh, 2 sons, 1 daughter. Education: BTech, Civil Engineering, Indian Institute of Technology, 1976; Postgraduate Diploma in Construction Management, Delhi Productivity Council, 1985-86; MEng, Civil Engineering, Texas A&M University, 1987; PhD, Civil Engineering, Purdue University, 1990; Licensed Professional Engineer, Ontario; Chartered Engineer, UK; Certified Project Management Professional, USA. Appointments: Engineering Assistant, Hindustan Prefab Ltd, 1975-76; Construction Manager, Gammon India Ltd, 1976-79; Resident Engineer, Sami Badr Consulting Architect Ltd, Brian Colquhoun & Partners Ltd, Estimating Engineer, Al-Hamra Kuwait Co, Project Planning Engineer, M A Kharafi Construction Co, Kuwait, 1980-86; Research Assistant, Texas Transportation Institute, Bechtel National Inc and Indiana Mining and Minerals Resources Research Institute, USA, 1987-90; Construction Consultant, Foundation Company of Canada Ltd, Scarborough, Ontario, 1990-91; Assistant Professor, Construction Management Engineering, North Dakota State University, Fargo, 1991-93; Assistant Professor, Civil Engineering, 1993-97, Associate Professor, Civil Engineering, 1997-, University of Hawaii at Manoa. Publications: Refereed articles in international and national journals and conference proceedings; Technical reports. Honours: 7 Research Awards; Eminent Scholar, invited to present Eminent Scholar Lecture, University of Florida, Gainesville. Memberships: Institution of Civil Engineers, UK; American Society of Civil Engineers; American Association of Cost Engineers; Performance Management Association; Society of Cost Estimating and Analysis. Address: University of Hawaii at Manoa, 2540 Dole Street, Holmes Hall, Honolulu, HI 96822, USA.

**SINGH Bajrang,** b. 1 December 1952, Barabanki, India. Scientist. m. Manju Singh, 1 son, 1 daughter. Education: PhD, Botany, 1979. Appointments: Scientist, 1983-; Scientist-in-Charge, ULRU Project, Aligarh, 1983-89. Specialization: Ecology, Silviculture, Soil Reclamation. Publications: 25 articles in professional journals. Memberships: International Society of Environmental Botanists; NBRI, Lucknow, India. Address: National Botanical Research Institute, Rana Pratap Marg, Lucknow 226001 UP, India.

**SINGH Baljit Paul,** b. 14 March 1956, Jhanda Kalan, India. Teacher. m. Narinder Kaur, 1 son, 1 daughter. Education: BEd; MA Political Science. Appointments: Teacher, 1980-. Publications: One poetry book; Over a dozen research publications in reputed newspapers. Membership: Sahitya Sabha Gardulgarh. Address: V & PO Jhanda Kalan, Teh Sardulgarh, Distt Mansa Punjab, India.

**SINGH Bhisham Prasad,** b. 18 August 1937, India. Director. Education: BSc, 1st class with distinction, Patna University, 1955; MSc, 1st class, Bihar University, 1957; MSc, Queen's University, Kingston, Canada, 1969, PhD, 1972. Appointments: Lecturer, Physics, R.D.S. College, Muzaffarpur, 1957-58; Lecturer, Physics, Ranchi College, 1958-65; Graduate Student, Queens University, Canada, 1956-72; CSIR Pool Officer, Physical Research Laboratory, Ahmedabad, 1972-73; Reader, 1973-78, Associate Professor, 1978-83, Professor, 1983-91, Director, 1991-, Indian Institute of Geomagnetism; Research study of the earth's interior through geoelectromagnetism, 1998-. Publications include: Calculation of energy levels and transition rates for oddes muclei, 1972; Coreparticle approach to nuclear structure; Electromagnetic studies of the Zinc isotopes; Odd zinc isotopes in unified vibrational model; Structure of some odd-A cuclei in f-p shell and unified vibrational model. Honours include: Fellow, National Academy of Sciences, India, Indian Geophysical Union, Hyderabad, Association of Exploration Geophysicists, Hyderabad, Geological Society of India, Bangalore; Medal, Soviet Geophysical Commission; Commendation Certificate, NASA. Memberships include: Mining Geological & Metallurgical Institute of India. Address: Indian Institute of Geomagnetism, Colaba, Mumbai 400 005, India.

**SINGH Brij Narayan,** b. 12 August 1949, Pratapgarh, UP, India. Veterinarian. m. Smt Bimla Singh, 4 daughters. Education: Bachelor of Veterinary Science and Animal Husbandry, 1970, Master of Veterinary Science and AH, Honours, 1974 J N Agriculture University, Jabalpur; Diploma Animal Management and Reproductive Biology, 1976, Dr Med Vet (Phd), 1977, Veterinary University, Vienna, Austria. Appointments: Research Assistant, 1971, Senior Researcch Assistant, 1971-75, Assistant Professor, 1975-81, Associate Professor, Animal Production and Management, 1981-83, Vice Chancellor J N Agriculture University, Jabalpur; Executive Director, 1983-88, Managing Director, 1988-, MP Livestock and Poultry Development Corporation and MP State Poultry Cooperative Federation. Publications: 40 research papers published in different Indian and foreign journals. Honours: Awarded Major G C Juneja and Dr R L Kaushal Trophy, 1969-70; Rajiv Gandhi Excellance Award, 1996; Awarded University Merit Scholarship; Gold Medale, J N Agriculture University, 1997; Awarded Austrian-Unesco Scholarship. Memberships: Poultry Federation of India; World Poultry Science Association; Animal Production and Management Association of India; World Cattle Blood Group Association. Address: A 46 Padmansh, Nager, Bhopal, India.

**SINGH Dina Nath,** b. 31 December 1937, Monghyr, Bihar, India. Professor. m. Shakunfala Devi, 4 sons, 1 daughter. Education: BA, Hons, Hindi, 1959; MA, Hindi, 1961; PhD, 1973; DLitt, 1990. Appointments: Lecturer in Hindi, 1961; Reader, 1981; Professor, 1985. Publications: 4 books; 100 articles published in different journals. Memberships: Head of Department in PG Hindi, VKSU Ara; Dean of Humanities; President of Teachers Association. Address: HOD PG Department of Hindi, VKS University, Ara Bihar 802301, India.

**SINGH G K K,** b. 20 July 1951, New Delhi, India. Businessman; Educator. m. Ms Kawaljit, 1 son. Education: BTech, IIT Bombay; MBA, IIM Calcutta. Appointments: Regional Manager, Johnson & Johnson; Marketing Manager, Horstmann India; Director, Enertech Electronics; Director, Galaxy Institute of Interaction Training. Publication: Relationship Management in 21st Century Organizations.

Honours: Silver Medalist, IIT Bombay; Bharat Ratna Award, Outstanding Growth in Business. Memberships: IIT Alumni Association; IIM Alumni Association; YMCA; World Trade Centre; Mahratta Chamber of Commerce and Industry. Address: Galaxy Electronics, 64 Lullanagar, Pune 40, (411040), India.

**SINGH Harpal,** b. 16 August 1947, Pakistan, India. Professor. m. Jan, 2 sons, 1 daughter. Education: BS, Punjab University, India, 1962; MS, 1964; PhD, University of Tennessee, 1970; MPH, 1974. Appointments: Associate Director, Research and Sponsore Programs, 1995- Acting Head, Biology and Life Sciences, SSU, 1998. Honours: 20 Years of Grants. Memberships: Society of Toxicology; Society of Research Administration. Address: Savannah State University, P O Box 20425, Drew Giffith Building, Savannah, GA 31404, USA.

**SINGH Jagdamba,** b. 1 January 1944, Azamgarh, UP, India. Senior Research Officer. m. Smt Usha Singh, 1 son, 2 daughters. Education: BSc Agricultural Engineering and Technology, 1969; PG Diploma in Business Management, 1971; Current, PhD on Energy and Sustainable Development. Appointments: Engineer, Consultant, Adviser and presently Senior Executive in Research. Publications: Over 60 publications in national and international journals and books. Memberships: 9 associations and institutions. Address: Senior Research Officer (Energy & Environment Division), Sah Industrial Research Institute, Sa 15/171 Gautam Buddha Rajpath, Samath, Varanasi 221007, India.

**SINGH Lala Aswini Kumar,** b. 19 June 1953, Puri, Orissa, India. Wildlife Researcher. m. Puspalata, 1 son, 1 daughter. Education: BSc (Hons) 1972; MSc, 1974; PhD, 1980; Animal Management Course, Cambridge, 1990. Appointments: Research Scholar, 1975-79; Research Officer, Government of Orissa, Forest and Environment Department, 1979-; Government of India, Ministry of Environment, and for Wildlife Institute of India, 1981-87. Publications: Over 180 scientific articles on Crocodile, Turtle, Dolphin, Birds, Tiger, Elephant, Wildlife-Conservation/Techniques. Honours: FAO Fellow, 1982; Conservation Treaty Support Fund Fellowship, 1990; Chaturvedi Prize, 1983-84, 1990; International Man of the Year, 1997-98. Memberships include: IUCN/SSC Specialist Groups; Science Academies; Wildlife Societies; Environmental Societies. Address: Research Officer, Similipal Tiger Reserve, Baripada, Orissa 757 002, India.

**SINGH Nityanand,** b. 14 August 1953, Varanasi, Uttar Pradesh, India. Civil Servant; Scientist. m. Urmila Singh, 2 sons, 1 daughter. Education: BSc; MSc, Geophysics with Meteorology; PhD, Geophysics. Appointments: Research Scholar, 1976-79; Junior Hydrometeorologist, 1979-82, Senior Scientific Officer, 1982-94, Assistant Director, 1994-, Indian Institute of Tropical Meteorology, Government of India. Publications: 3 books; 45 scientific publications. Honours: Fellowship, World Meteorological Organization; 13th SAARC Young Scientist Award in Meteorology and Environment, 1993-94. Memberships: Indian Meteorological Society; Indian Agrometeorological Society; Indian Hydrologists Society. Address: Indian Institute of Tropical Meteorology, Dr Homi Bhabha Road, Pashan, Pune 411-008, India.

**SINGH Paula Kaur.** International Peace and Technological Advancement Worker. Education: BS, University of California at Davis, 1988; Executive Education Programs, Stanford University, 1996; Senior Executive Education Programs, Harvard University and Massachusetts Institute of Technology, 1997; Stanford Leadership Academy, Stanford University,

1998; The Oxford Strategic Leadership Programme, Oxford University, 1998; Numerous national and international forums, symposiums, and conferences. Appointments: Founder, President and CEO Medical Information Management, Research and Development, 1984-; Director of Seminars and Information Services, Mind Matter Seminars, Stanford, CA, 1993; Founder, President and CEO, The International Academy of Information Sciences, Systems and Technologies, 1994-. Memberships: Board of Advisors, International Who's Who of Professionals; Board of Advisors, International Who's Who of Professional Management; Board of Advisors, International Who's Who of Information Technology; Board of Advisors, International Who's Who of Entrepreneurs; International Association of Women in Technology; American Association for the Advancement of Science; Scientist/Mentor, Boston Museum of Science; Member, Smithsonian Institute; Founding Member, the Library of Congress; Association of Women in Science; American Public Health Association - Forum on Bioethics, Health Education, and Legislative Action Committee National Association of Female Executives; American Association of University Women; International Federation of University Women; Citizen Ambassador, People to People International; World Affairs Council. Address: International Academy Information Science Systems and Technology, 160 West Portola Avenue, Los Altos, CA 94022-1251, USA.

**SINGH Pramod Kumar,** b. 11 March 1967, Bihar, India. Artist; Muralist. Education: BFA Painting, 1991, Viswa Bharat Santiniketan; MFA Mural-Painting, 1993, Faculty Fine Arts, MS University, Baroda, India. Appointments: Ceramic Colour Designer, Siddhartha Ceramics, GIDC, Makarpura, Baroda 1995-96; Lecturer in Painting, Dayanand College, Ajmer, Rajasthan, India, 1998-. Publications: Poems in Indian journals; Poetry published in The Nearness of Day, 1998, USA. Honours: French Government Scholarship in Painting, Ecole Regionale des Beaux-Arts de Rouen, France, 1994-95; Charles Wallace Fellowship, Edinburgh College of Art, UK, Glass & Architectural Stained Glass, 1998-. Address: c/o K P Singh Wz 1, Gali No 3, Chhatri Wala Marg, Raj Nagar I, Palam Colony, New Delhi 110045, India.

**SINGH Prem,** b. 15 April 1943, Patiala, India. Painter. m. Navpreet Kaur, 2 sons. Education: 5 year Diploma in Applied Art, 1967; MA in Fine Arts, Gold Medallist, 1975. Appointments: Faculty, Government College of Art, Chandigarh, Head Applied Art Department, current; Art Critic for a newspaper in Chandigarh. Creative Works: Indiviual Shows throughout India including: Vadhera Art Gallery, New Delhi, 1990; LTG Art Gallery, New Delhi, 1992, 1995; Participated 11 exhibitions including: Hundred Years: from the NGMA Collection, 1994; Work shown in 17 public galleries and several private collectors in India, Hong Kong, Japan, Netherlands, Antilles, Denmark, Egypt, USA, UK, South Africa, Italy and elsewhere. Honours: Punjab Lalit Kala Akademi, Chandigarh; Indian Academy of Fine Arts, Amritsar; Academy of Fine Arts, Calcutta; Government Museum and Art Gallery, Chandigarh; Triennale India International Award, 1994, Lalit Kala Akademi New Delhi; Parasmani Award, 1988; The Living Glory - a memento presented by Mohindra College, Patiala, 1988; Artist of the Year Award, Art Society of India, 1989; Om Parkesh Memorial Award, Prakash Kala Sangam, Chandigarh, 1993; Honoured by Chandigarh Administration on Republic Day 1994 in recognition of contribution to art and culture. Memberships: General Council, Lalit Kala Akademi, New Delhi, 1983-96; Executive Board, North Zone Cultural Centre, Patiala; Secretary, Chandigarh Lalit Kala Akademi, 1989-97; Founder-Secretary, The SOLIDS, Chandigarh; Steering Committee, Shilpgram, North Zone Cultural Centre, Patiala; Core Committee, Chandigarh 2020, Chandigarh Administration; Art Adviser, The nvironment Society of India, Chandigarh. Address: 374/1 ector 44A, Chandigarh 160047, India.

**SINGH Rana P B,** b. 15 December 1950, Majhanpura, Bihar, ndia. Educator; Researcher; Eco-tourism Guide. m. Manju ingh, 2 sons, 2 daughters. Education: MA Geography, 1971; ʰD, 1974; Dipl Computer Appl, 1976. Appointments: Lecturer ɪ Geography, BHU, 1977-80; Japan Foundation Scholar, )kayama University, 1980; Visiting Professor, Environmental ystems and Geography, Virginia Tech, USA, 1981; CSIR Sct, Ieerut University, 1981-83; Lecturer, Associate Professor ɟeography, BHU, 1983-; Visiting Professor, University ̇arlstad, Sweden, 1989, 1993, 1995, 1999; Ron Lister ecturer, Otago University, New Zealand, 1995; As Visiting and ʌvited Fellow gave lectures in many countries including, ̇apan, USA, USSR, Australia, New Zealand. Publications: 125 ̇esearch papers and articles in professional journals; 10 ̇esearch monographs; 17 edited anthologies; 3 textbooks. Ǝemberships: Founding President, Indian Society of ̇nvironment and Culture; Society of Pilgrimage Students; ̇ociety of Heritage Ecology and Environmental Health; Life ɴember, Environmental Monitoring Society; NAGI; NGSI; Ron ̇ister Lecturer, Otago University, New Zealand, 1995. Address: ̇anaras Hindu University, Department Geography, Varnasi, UP ̇21005, India.

**SINGH Ravi Prakash,** b. 24 June 1957, Varanasi, India. ̇cientist. m. Alka Rani Sachan, 2 sons, 1 daughter. Education: ̇S, 1977, MS, 1979, Banaras Hindu University, India; PhD, ̇niversity of Sydney, Australia, 1984. Appointments: ̇ostdoctoral Fellow, 1983-85, Senior Scientist, 1985-98, ̇rincipal Scientist, Coordinator of Global Project on Wheat ̇iotic Stresses, 1998-, International Maize & Wheat ̇nprovement Center, Mexico. Publications: 51 research articles ̇ɪ professional scientific journals, 6 book chapters, 65 ̇dditional scientific articles and bulletins in conference ̇roceedings; Co-author of book, Rust Diseases of Wheat. ̇onours: University Medals; University of Sydney Fellowship. Ǝemberships: American Phytopathological Society; Crop ̇cience Society of America; American Society of Agronomy; ̇nternational Society of Plant Pathology. Address: International Ǝaize & Wheat Improvement Center, Lisboa 27 Col Juarez, Ǝexico City 06600, Mexico.

**SINGH Satya Prakash,** b. 12 August 1939, Paina, Deoria, ̇P, India. Educator. m. Bisen Shashi, 2 sons. 2 daughters. ̇ducation: MSc, Botany, 1959, MEd, 1963, BHU; Certificate in ̇cience, Institute of Education, Hull University, England, 1968; ̇ʰD, Education, Gorakhpur University, 1975. Appointments: ̇ecturer in Biology, S K Intermediate College, Barhaj, Deoria, ̇959-61; Reader in Education, SMM Town College, Ballia and ̇ N Institute of Science and Technology, Sultanpur, 1963-; ̇ean, Faculty of Education, Avadh University, Faizabad. ̇ublications: Books: Bhartiya Shiksha Ke Ayam (Aspects of ̇ndian Education); Elementary Educational Statistics; Founder ̇ditor-in-Chief, Journal of Educo-Ecology; The concept ̇ropounder of ecology of Education - Educo-ecology. Address: ̇48 Gola Ghat, Sultanpur 228001, UP, India.

**SINGH Shiva D,** b. 1 January 1954, Motiyari, Banda, India. ̇rofessor; Principal Scientist. m. Rita, 2 sons. Education: BSc, ̇972; MSc, 1974; Proficiency Certificate, German, 1976; ̇roficiency Certificate, French, 1978; PhD, Biochemistry, 1982. ̇ppointments: Research Assistant, Allahabad University, ̇974-77; Scientist, Biochemistry Division, Indian Veterinary ̇esearch Institute, Izatnagar, 1978-84; National Associate, ̇ndian Institute of Science, Bangalore, 1985; National ̇ssociate, Jawaharlal Nehru University, New Delhi, 1986; ̇enior Scientist, National Biotechnology Centre, Indian

Veterinary Research Institute, Izatnagar, 1986-96; Professor, 1996-98; Professor and Principal Scientist, Central Institute of Fisheries Education, Mumbai, 1998-. Publications: 16 Research Papers; 49 Abstracts. Honours: FAO Fellowship for Advanced Research in Australia, 1993-94; Best Poster Award, 1991; Nature Scholarship Award, 1985, 1987; Award by British National Committee for Microbiology, 1986; National Associate (DBT) Award, 1985-86. Memberships: Indian Science Congress; Society of Biological Chemists, India; Association of Microbiologists of India; National Academy of Science, India; Association for DNA Fingerprinting and other related Technologies; Member od Society of General Microbiology, UK, 1987. Address: Head Division of Biochemistry, Nutrition and Post Harvest Technology, Central Institute of Fisheries Education, Mumbai 400061, India.

**SINGH Shyam,** b. 2 July 1946, Rajender Nagar, UP, India. Research Management. m. Nirmala Singh, 1 son, 1 daughter. Appointments: Agricultural and Laboratory Assistant, Department of Horticulture, Udaipur University, Rajasthan, 1971-75; Scientist S-1, Horticulture, ICAR Research Complex, for NEH Region, Shillong, 1975-80; Scientist S-2 (Hort), TTC for NEH Region, Medziphema, 1980-83; Scientist S-3 (Hort), Central Agricultural Research Institute, Portblair Andaman and Nicobar Islands, 1983-85; Principal Scientist, Horticulture, Central Agricultural Research Institute, Portblair, Andaman and Nicobar Islands, 1986-89; Director of Agriculture, Andaman and Nicobar Administration, Portblair, Andaman and Nicobar Islands, 1989-91; Principal Scientist, Horticulture, National Research Centre for Citrus, Nagpur, India, 1992-97; Director, National Research Centre for Citrus, ICAR, Nagpur, India, 1997-. Publications: 178 research papers and articles; 29 folders; 27 extension bulletins; 6 technical bulletins; 7 technical reports. Honours: Fakhruddin Ali Ahmed Biennial Award, 1986-1987, ICAR, for Research contributions in the field of Horticulture in Andaman and Nicobar Islands; Pioneer Scientist of Horticulture working under Hill conditions in Tribal areas of Mizoram, Meghalaya, Nagaland and Andaman and Nicobar Islands for 17 years, 1975-92. Memberships: International Society of Citriculture, California; Life Member, Horticultural Society of India, New Delhi, India; Life Member, and Secretary, Indian Society of Citriculture, Nagpur, India; Punjab State Co-operative Fruit Development Federation Ltd, Chandigarh, India. Address: National Research Centre for Citrus, ICAR, Amravati Rd, Nagpur-440 010, Maharashtra, India.

**SINGH V R,** b. 24 February 1946, India. m. Chitra Singh, 2 daughters. Education: BE, Electrical Engineering, 1968; PhD, ITT, Delhi, 1973. Appointments: Postdoc Fellow, University of Toronto, Canada, 1974-77; Scientist, NPL, New Delhi, 1968-; Visiting Scientist, TU - Delhi, Netherlands, 1991-92. Publications: 300 papers; 13 patents; 24 consultancies. Honours: INSA, 1974; ICMR, 1985; AFSUMB, Australia, 1991; NPL, 1993. Memberships: Fellow, IEEE, USA; Fellow, IE, India; Fellow, IETE; Fellow, IFUMB. Address: National Physical Laboratory, DRKS Krishnan Road, New Delhi 110012, India.

**SINGLETON Robert Culton,** b. 17 October 1950, Amarillo, Texas, USA. Bible Educator. m. Stephanie Diane, 1 son, 1 daughter. Education: BS, Electrical Engineering, University of Texas, 1973; ThM, Bible Exposition, Dallas Theological Seminary, 1977; PhD, Higher Education, University of Texas, 1993. Appointments: Campus Staff, Campus Crusade for Christ, 1974-77; Dean, Director, Founder, Nairobi International School of Theology, 1978-83; Graduate Studies Staff, Campus Crusdae for Christ, 1984-92; Dean of Faculty, East Asia School of Theology, 1993-96; Faculty, The Orlando Institute, 1997-. Publications: Our Lord's Use of Questions in Matthew, 1977; The I/O Port, 1980; The I/O Port, 1993; Mentorship and

Professional Socialization in a Theological Seminary Setting, 1993.Honours: 15 Year Award, Campus Crusade for Christ, 1989; 25 year Award, 1999. Memberships: Kappa Delta Pi An Honor Society in Education; Honours Society of Phi Kappa Phi. Address: 100 Support Lane 3000, Orlando, FL 32809, USA.

**SINGOUNAS Evangelos G,** b. 1938, Arta, Greece. Neurosurgeon. m. P Neou, 1 daughter. Education: MD, 1955, Thesis submitted, 1972, PhD, 1989, Assistant Professor, University Athens; Training in Neurosurgery, Glasgow (Killearn Hospital-Western infirmary), 1966-69. Appointments: Newcastle General Hospital; Pinderfilds General Hospital, Leeds; Middlesex Hospital, London; Central University Hospital, Helsinki; Deputy Director, Evagelismos Medical Centre, 1978-82; Consultant, Children's Hospital, Athens; Consultant in Neurosurgery, Evagelismos Medical Centre, 1982-; Visiting Professor, Umea Sweden, 1977. Publications: 6 books concerning Neurosurgery in Greek; 43 publications in English in various journals; 70 in Greek journals; 20 presentations in international meetings; 15 lectures. Honour: Awarded membership of Greek literature association, 1977. Memberships: New York Academy of Sciences; Associate member, British and Scandinavian Neurosurgical societies; Founding member, Psychiatric Neurosurgery; Fellow, American College of Surgeons. Address: Tositsa 26, 106 83 Athens, Greece.

**SINHA Asit Kumar,** b. 19 September 1941, Pipra, Bihar. Service. m. Gita, 2 sons, 1 daughter. Education: HS, 1960; D Man, 1962. Appointments: Tracer, 1963. Honours: Story Competition, 1st Prize. Address: Vill and PO, Kenduadihi St, Bankuna, WB, India.

**SINHA Daisy,** b. 26 July 1963, Muzzaipui. Social Worker. m. L P Sinha, 1 d. Education: MA; BA; Intermediate of Arts. Honours: Kustuska Gandhi, Bepol Award. Memberships: USO; AIWC; AIR, Iamshedpul. Address: Sushiula Bhawan, Dimna Road, Mango, Jamshedpur 831012, India.

**SINHA Ishita,** b. 19 March 1973, Bihar, India. Artist. Education: Graduate, Arts, Delhi University, 1994; Art Appreciation Course, National Gallery of Modern Art, New Delhi, Indian Art and Culture Course, National Museum, New Delhi, 1996. Creative Works: Several exhibitions at national and international level, including National Exhibition of Contemporary Art, Lalitkala Academy, 1994, 1996, 1997; National Exhibition of All India Fine Arts and Craft Society, 1994, 1997; Golden Jubilee of India's Independence Through Indian Art, 1997; Major Solo Exhibition: Ialit Kala Gallery, 1996. Address: 266 Vinay Marg, Chanakyapuri, New Delhi 110021, India.

**SINHA Sunil Kumar,** b. 3 January 1953, Braipura, Birpur, Bihar, India. Professor of Mathematics. m. Manjula Prasad, 1 son. Education: MSc, 1973; PhD, 1979; DSc, 1988. Appointments: Lecturer in Mathematics, 1978-86, Reader in Mathematics, 1986-94, University of Mathematics, 1994-, Tata College, Chaibasa. Publications: 2 books; 35 research papers. Memberships: Member of 10 mathematical societies; Editorial Board of Mathematics Education. Address: Department of Maths, Tata College, Chaibasa 833202, Bihar, India.

**SINKARIUKAS Viktoras,** b. 17 October 1947, Lithuania. Actor, Director. 1 son. Education: Kaunas Drama Theatre, Acting Higher School, 1968; Giti, S, Institute of Theatre Arts in Moscow, 1975. Appointments: Actor. Honours: Honoured Artist of Lithuania, 1987; Best Actor of Lithuania, 1990; Best Actor of Baltic States, 1992; Lithuanian Government Grant for Artist of Merit, 1998-2000. Memberships: Lithuanian Theatre Union.

Address: J Basanaviciaus al 51-19, LT 3000, Kaunas Lithuania.

**SINKEVICH Oleg,** b. 24 November 1934, Pskov, Russia. Physicist. m. Ludmila Butchkova, 1 daughter. Education: BSc Engineering, 1955; MSc, Heat Physics and Engineering, 1966. PhD, Physics and Mathematics, 1970; Diplomas of Dr of Physics and Mathematics, 1981; Diploma of Professor of Mechanical Engineering, 1985. Appointments: Assistant Professor, 1968-74, Associate Professor, 1974-83, Full Professor, 1984, Moscow Power Institute; Research Scientist 1966-81, Chief Scientist, 1981-; Head, Plasma Laboratory 1968-; Consulting, 1968-. Publications: Plasma Physics co-author, book, 1994; Instabilities and Turbulence in Low Temperature Plasmas, co-author, 1994. Memberships Low-temp Plasma Science Council, Russian Academy Science Editorial Board, High Temperature Journal; Executive Board Moscow Physics Society; Editorial Board, MPEI Publishing House. Address: 15-75 Korchagina St, Moscow 129278 Russia.

**SINNATHURAI Sothirachae,** b. 12 August 1946, Batugajah Malaysia. Professor, Dean. m. S Jaya Ranee, 2 daughters Education: BA, University of Malaya, 1968; Post Graduate Diploma of Arts, University of Otago, 1971; MA, 1972; PhD SOAS University of London, 1978; Diploma in Law, 1978 Barrister at Law, Lincolns Inn, 1984; LLM, University of Bristol 1990. Appointments: Teacher, 1968-69; Teaching Assistant University of Otago, 1971-72; Lecturer, 1972-81; Associate Professor, 1982-92; Associate Professor, 1992-94; Professor Dean, Faculty of Law, University of Malaya, 1994- Publications: Law and the Electoral Process in Malaysia, 1993 Honours: Tokoh Pengguna; Darjah Dato Paduka Mahkota Perak. Memberships: Ministry of Trade and Consumer Affairs Ministry of Science; Ministry of Energy; Bar Council of Malaya Insurance Meditation Bureau; Federation of Consumers Associations; Health Action International; Consumers International; IUCN; International Association for Consume Laws; LAWASIA; ASEAN. Address: University of Malaya Pantai Valley 50603, Kuala Lumpur, Malaysia.

**SINOHARA Hyogo,** b. 16 January 1931, Kitaibaraki, Japan Professor. m. Makiko Susuki, 1 son, 1 daughter. Education BMed, 1955, DMed, 1960, Tohoku University, Sendai, Japan Appointments: Research Associate, Preston-St Lukes Hospital Chicago, 1960-65; Assistant Professor, Iwate Medical School Morioka, 1965-74; Professor, Kinki University, 1974- Publications: Life Science in the Living Room, 1983 Forerunners of Life Science, 1983. Memberships: New York Academy of Sciences; Japanese Biochemical Society Address: 3-16-7 Onodai, Osaka Sayama, Osaka 589-0023 Japan.

**SIRIWARDHANA Sita Eileen,** b. 1 April 1928, Matara School Principal. m. Dbips Siriwardhana, 2 sons, 1 daughter Education: Visakha Vidyalaya, Colombo, 1946-47; BA, 1950 Sinhalese, English, Pali, University Ceylon. Appointments Assistant Teacher, 1950-61; Deputy Principal, 1973, Principal 1978, Samudra Devi Balika Vidyalaya, Nugegoda; Officer Class 1, Sri Lanka Educational Administrative Service, 1983 Principal, Visakha Vidyalaya, Colombo, 1983-88; Director Sahanaya, Colombo Community Mental Health Centre 1989-90; Principal, Shinyo-En-Lanka, Kohuwela, Colombo Free Nursery School, 1991-92; Principal, Buddhist Ladies' College Colombo, 1995-. Publications: Translator and Author 23 novels short stories or books of verse; 2 novels made into films Contributions in English and Sinhala to magazines, journals and local press. Honours: Poems included in internationa anthologies of poems; Many awards for poems and other literary works including First recipient of the D R Wijewardena Award, 1985, organised on lines of British Booker Award. Memberships: PEN; Friends of Sumithrayo; Committee, All Ceylon Women's Buddhist Congress; Advisory Committee, Ministry of Women's Affairs; Working Committee, Seva Vanitha Movement; Trustee and Board member, Individual Development Education School for Special Children; Consultant on Youth Problems in Lawyers for Human Rights Development Organisation; Governing Council of Sahanaya, organisation for mental health; and many others. Address: 57 Railway Avenue, Nugegoda, Sri Lanka.

**SIRIWEERA Wathuge Indrakeerti,** b. 26 April 1942, Sri Lanka. Professor. m. Lalitha, 1 son, 1 daughter. Education: BA Hons, 1964, University Ceylon; PhD, 1969, London School of Oriental and African Studies. Appointments: Professor, University of Peradeniya, Sri Lanka, 1991-; Chairman, University Grants Commission, Sri Lanka, 1994-95; Vice Chancellor, Rajarata University, 1995-. Publications: 6 books on history; Over 50 articles on Asian History, Economy and Politics; 2 collections short stories; 2 novels. Memberships: Editor, Sri Lanka Historical Association, 1991-92; Member, Governing Board of the Kotelawala Defense Academy, National Education Commission, Human Resources Development Council, Sri Lanka, 1994-95; President, Rajarata Professional's Association, 1996-97. Address: University of Sri Lanka, Mihintale, Sri Lanka.

**SITNIKOV Aleksandr,** b. 1945, Iva, Russia. Painter. Education: Graduate, Surikov Art Academy, 1972. Appointments: Member, Union of Soviet Painters, 1975; Paintings exhibited in many countries, Russia, Bulgaria, Germany, USA, Italy, France, India, Czechoslovakia, Autria, Sweden, Latvia, Estonia, Portugal. Honours: First International Drawing Competition for Young Artists, 1979; Grand Prize of the 5th Triennial of Fine Arts in New Delhi, 1982; First Prize of the International Painting Exhibition in Kosice, 1984. Address: Staropimenovsky 8-11, Moscow 103006, Russia.

**SITSKY Larry,** b. 10 September 1934, Tianjing, China. Musician. m. Magda Wlczek, 1 son, 1 daughter. Education: Cambridge University, 1950; Tiensin Jewish School, 1950; Matriculation Status, University of Sydney, 1951; Graduate, NSW State Conservatorium of Music; Post Graduate Studies, NSW State Conservatorium, 1956-58; Post Graduate Studies, San Francisco Conservatory of Music, 1959-61. Appointments: Chief Study Piano Teacher, 1961-65; Head of Keyboard Studies, 1966-78; Head of Department, Composition and Electronic Music, 1978-81; Head of Department, Composition and Musicology, 1981-83; Head of Department, Composition, 1983-. Publications: Many Article about Music. Honours: Myer Research Foundation Grants; Vaccari Foundation Grant; Music Board, Australia Council; Composition Fellowship; Australian Research Grants Scheme; Travelling Research Fellowship; Fulbright Australian, American Fellowship; Advance Australia Award; Anu Publishing Grant; Anu Research Grant; Critics Circle Award. Address: 29 Threlfall Street, Chifley, ACT 2606, Australia.

**SIUMBEREVICIUS Mindaugas,** b. 29 August 1973, Siauliai, Lithuania. Security Officer. Education: Graduated, Dainu Higher School, Siauliai, 1991. Career: Security Officer, 1991-. Honours: Selected as Best Rugby Player of Lithuania, 1996, 1997. Address: K Korsako 117-16, LT-5400 Siauliai, Lithuania.

**SKACEL Alexander,** b. 2 November 1955, Ostrava, Czech Republic. Biologist. 2 sons, 1 daughter. Education: Graduate, Brno University; PhD, Charles University, Prague, 1986; Postgraduate, EIPOS Institute, Dresden, Germany.

Appointments: Institute of Industrial Landscape Ecology, Czech Academy of Sciences, 1980-93; University of Ostrava, 1993-. Honour: Award, Czech Literary Fund, 1988. Memberships: Czech Limnological Society; SETAC; SECOTOX. Address: University of Ostrava, Bralova 7, 700 00 Ostrava, Czech Republic.

**SKANDA PRASAD Vaidya,** b. 6 September 1949, Mysore City, India. Bank Executive. m. 1 son. Education: MSc; DLitt; PBA; IM. Appointments: Research Scholar; Lecturer; Bank Executive. Publications: 5 collections of poems, 5 international anthologies of poems, edited over 20 books of poems. Honours: Several international awards. Address: Corporation Bank, Mangalore, India.

**SKOBELIN Eugene Alekseevich,** b. 3 June 1936. Geologist. m. Voloshina, 2 sons, 1 daughter. Education: Diploma, Mining Geologist Engineer. Appointments: Senior Geologist, 1958-61; Senior Geologist of the Party; Geologist, 1962-64; Chief of a party, 1964-66; Senior Geologist, 1966-68; Chief of the Geological Department, 1968-72; Senior Geologist; 1972-73; Chief Geologist, 1973-75; Geologist, 1975-76; Senior Geologist, 1976-; Chief of a Detachment; 1976-79; Senior Geologist, 1979-80; Chief of Thematic Trap Party, 1980-86. Publications: Many Publications in Russian, English, Japanese. Address: P O Box 12640, Krasnoyarsk 660021, Russia.

**SKOLYSZEWSKI Jan,** b. 27 January 1935, Krakow, Poland. Radiation Oncologist. m. Romana Machowska, 1 daughter. Education: Diploma in Medicine, School of Medicine, Krakow, 1958; MD, 1964; PhD, 1975; Diploma in Radiation Oncology, 1966. Appointments: Clinical Assistant, Centre of Oncology in Krakow, 1959-74; Head of Radiation Oncology Department, 1974-; Director of Centre of Oncology, Krakow, 1981-. Publications: About 160 articles in scientific journals; 3 manuals on radiation oncology. Honours: Prizes of Polish Ministry of Health, 1965, Mayor of Krakow City, 1980; M Sklodowska-Curie Medal, Polish Society of Radiation Research, 1995. Memberships: Polish Oncology Society; Polish Society Radiation Oncology; Polish Society Radiation Research; European Society Therapeutic Radiology Oncology; Radiotherapy Club, UK. Address: Centre of Oncology M Sklodowska-Curie Memorial Institute, Branch Krakow, 11 Garncarska St, 31-115 Krakow, Poland.

**SKRABKA-BLOTNICKA Teresa,** b. 4 January 1933, Przemysl. Academical Teacher. m. Henryk Skrabka, 1 son, 1 daughter. Education: MSc Chemistry, 1956, Technical College in Gliwice; DrPh, 1965, University of Medicine Wroclaw Faculty of Pharmacy; DrSci, 1987, University Agriculture Poznan Faculty of Food Technology; Various professional experiences in Hungary, Germany and Moscow. Appointments: Assistant, 1956, Assistant Lecturer, 1958, Tutor, 1965, Senior Lecturer, 1973, Assistant Professor, 1974, Associate Professor, 1990, Full Professor, 1995, Head of Dept of Animal Food Technology, 1989, Head of Department of Food Technology, 1988-89, Vice Dean of Faculty of Industrial Engineering and Economics, 1973-81, University of Economics, Wroclaw. Publications: Author 2, Co-author 1 monograph; Author book, Bioengineering, materials to lectures, 1981; Co-author and Editor, General Food Technology, 1976, 1984; Co-author, Food Technology, 1978, 1985; Author or co-author: 70 original experimental papers, 17 review papers, 31 abstracts published in conference proceedings, 1 patent. Honours: Medal of 30th Anniversary of Polish People's Republic, 1974; Gold Cross of Merit, 1975; Order of National Education Committee, 1980; Cavalier's Cross of Polonia Restitute, 1987; Awards of The Ministry of Science, Higher Education and Technics, 1977, 1982. Memberships: Polish Chemistry Society; Polish

Commodity Society; World's Poultry Science Association; Polish Food Technologist's Society, Organiser and Chairperson, Wroclaw Branch, member of Chief Board; Science and Technology Association of Food Industry Engineers, Central Technical Organisation. Address: ul Komandorska 118/120, 53 345 Wroclaw, Poland.

**SKROMME Arnold Burton,** b. Zearing, Iowa, USA. Agricultural Engineering. m. Lois L Fausch, 3 sons, 1 daughter. Education: BS, Agricultural Engineering, Iowa State University, Ames, 1941. Appointments: Agricultural Engineer, Firestone, Auto Speciality Company, Pineapple Research Institute; Assistant Chief Engineer, John Deere Ottumwa Works; Chief Engineer, Deere Spreader Works; Research Engineer, Deere Harvester Works; Retired 1984. Publications: Several papers in agricultural engineering journals and magazines; Books: The 7-Ability Plan, 1989; The Cause and Cure of Dropouts, 1998. Honour: Honoured by Alpha Zeta Fraternity, 1997. Memberships: American Society of Agricultural Engineers, 1941-; Society of Automotive Engineers, 1957-. Address: 2605 31st Street, Moline, IL 61265-5309, USA.

**SKWARA Erich Wolfgang,** b. 4 November 1948, Salzburg, Austria. Novelist; Poet; Educator. m. Gloria E Skwara, 2 daughters. Education: PhD, 1986. Appointments: Instructor, University of Maryland, Baltimore, 1975-77; Freelance Author, Baltimore and Paris, 1977-82; Visiting Lecturer, Georgetown University, 1982-84; Freelance Author, Salzburg, 1984-86; Professor, Humanities, Comparative Literature and German, San Diego University, 1986-; Deputy Editor-in-Chief, Cultural Affairs, Die Welt, Berlin, 1993; Cultural and Literature Correspondent, several German and Austrian newspapers and media. Publications include: Black Sails, 1979, 1998; The Cool Million, 1990; Tristan Island, 1992; Die Heimlichen Könige, 1995; Plague in Siena, 1995; Ice on the Bridge, 1997; Versuch einer Heimkehr, 1998; Nach deu Nordeu, 1998. Memberships: International PEN; PEN Center of German Speaking Authors Abroad; PEN Center of Austria; PEN Center of France. Address: San Diego University, Department of Classics/Humanities, San Diego, CA 92182, USA.

**SLAMET Yohan,** b. 9 January 1950, Bogor, Indonesia. Vice Director. m. Maria Magdalena Budiman. Education: Bachelor, University of Jayabaya, 1976; Master, School of Ministry, 1980; Master, Institute of Development Management, 1983; Master, Institute of Prasetia Mulia, 1985. Appointments: Store Manager, CV Toko Buku Tropen; Manager, Tropen Groups; General Manager, PT Panca Sakti Jaya; Managing Distributor, Asian Productivity Organisation; Vice Director, Persatuan Abadi. Publications: What is Youth Speak About?, 1975; Organisation, What is About, 1976; Who is the Real Leader, 1976; What is the Truth, 1977; What is Love, 1978; Management the Nations, 1980. Honours: Best Student Community Coordinator, 1975; Best National Young Generation Movement, 1976; Distributor of Asian Productivity Organisation, 1985. Address: Persatuan Abadi, Jalan Pasar Baru 113, Jakarta Punat 10710, Indonesia.

**SLEKAITIS Vidas,** b. 1 May 1952, Silale, Lithuania. Economist. m. Irena Slekaitiene. Education: Economist, Vilnius University, Economic of Industry, 1970-75. Appointments: Chief Specialist of Standard, Vilnius factory of furs, 1975-77; Chief Economist of Department, Ministry of Light Industry, 1977-84; Economical Adviser, Havana factory of textile, 1984-87; Deputy Director, Knitted factory, Sparta, 1987-90; Deputy Head of Department, Ministry of Social Security, 1990-92; Director General of Lithuanian Labour Exchange, 1992-. Address: Respublikine darbo birza, Saltoniskiu 19, LT 26600, Vilnius, Lithuania.

**SLEPUKHINA Tatyana,** b. 27 February 1937, Ukraine. Hydrobiology; Limnology. 1 daughter. Education: Leningrad State University, 1959; PhD, 1967; DSc, 1991. Appointments: Research Assistant, 1959-68, Scientific Secretary, 1968-76, Senior Research Scientist, 1976-81, Leading Research Scientist, 1981-, Institute of Limnology, Russian Academy of Sciences. Publications: Over 100 articles in professional journals. Memberships: Scientific Council, Institute of Limnology, Fishery Institute of St Petersburg. Address: Institute of Limnology, Russian Academy of Sciences, Sevastyanova Street 9, St Petersburg 196105, Russia.

**SLOBOZHANIN Lev,** b. 1 September 1941, Nylga, Russia. Fluid Mechanics Researcher. 1 son, 1 daughter. Education: Degree in Mechanical Engineering (Honours), Kharkov, Ukraine, Aviation Institute, 1963; PhD, Physics and Mathematics, Institute for Low Temperature Physics and Engineering, Kharkov, 1968; Cert Senior Research Scientist, Academy of Sciences of Ukraine, 1975; DSc, Physics and Maths, Lavrentyev Institute Hydrodynamics, Novosibirisk, Russia, 1989. Appointments: Engineer, 1963-66, Senior Engineer, 1966-69, Junior Scientist, 1969-71, Senior Scientist, 1971-89, Leading Scientist, 1989-98, B Verkin Institute of Low Temperature Physics and Engineering, National Academy of Sciences of Ukraine, Kharkov; Professor, Kharkov Aviation Institute, 1989-90; Visiting Professor, Madrid Polytechnic University, 1993-94; Visiting Scholar, University of Alabama, Huntsville, 1995-. Publications: Co-author, books: Fluid Mechanics of Weightlessness, 1976; Low Gravity Fluid Mechanics, 1987; Solution Methods for Fluid Mechanics Problems Under Weightlessness Conditions, 1992. Memberships: American Physics Society; American Institute of Aeronautics and Astronautics (AIAA). Address: University of Alabama, Huntsville, Research Institute D 29 CMMR, AL 35899, USA.

**SMAGIN ALexander Garasim,** b. 30 May 1930, Staro-Juryevo, Russia. Physicist; Researcher. Education: Moscow State Lomonosov University, 1949-54; PhD, Moscow State Bauman University, 1965; DSc, Physics, Maths, Institute of Electronics and Mathematics, Moscow, 1988; Professor, Physics, State Com, USSR of Peoples Education, 1990. Appointments: Scientist, Research Institute Mendeleevo, Moscow, 1955; Senior Scientist, 1955-60; Chief of Laboratory, 1960-63; Chief of Laboratory, Fonon Co, Moscow, 1963-67; Chief of Laboratory, Research Institute of Mashinbilding, Moscow, 1968-71; Professor, Physics, Engineering Institute, Moscow, 1972-93; Chief, Crystal Co, Moscow, 1994-98; Professor, Physicis, Engineering Institute, Moscow, 1999. Publications: Higher High Q Quality and Highstability Resonators for State Frequency and Time Standards, 1962; Methods of Elimination Dissipation Energy in Subsurface Layers of Crystals, 1959; Precision Quartz Resonators, Physical Grounds, 1964; Piezoelectric Resonators and Their Application, 1967; co-author, Atomic Energy, 1968; Piezoelectricity of Quartz and Quartz Resonators, 1969; Creation, Industry and Application of Quartz Resonators, 1971; Low Temperature Oscillator Instability 4.10-14, 1975; Fundamental Energetic Losses in Crystals, 1988; Fundamentals of Crystalochemical Physics, 1991; General Methods and Principals of Designing Higher Q Quality Crystals Vibrational Systems, 1994; Contributor to over 250 articles in professional journals. Honours: Diploma of Cambridge, 2 Diplomas of Presidium Academy of Sciences; Diploma of Statstandard. Memberships: New York Academy of Sciences; IEEE; UFFC; Internal Information Academy. Address: 9 Park Street 47-1-29, 105425 Moscow, Russia.

**SMATRAKALEV Gueorgui,** b. 9 March 1958, Bulgaria. conomist. m. Violeta, 2 daughters. Education: English anguage School, Plovdiv, 1972-77; UNWE Sofia, 1977-82; 'hD, Institute of Economics, BAS, 1983-88. Appointments: lesearch Fellow, Institute of Economics, BAS, 1988-98; ssociate Professor, New Bulgarian University, 1993-; hairman, Rehabilitation and Social Integration Fund, 1998-. ublications: 12 Books; 10 Studies; Over 100 Articles. lemberships: Zalburg Seminar; ISA; ISINI; IRMI. Address: 64 juben Karavelov Street, 1000 Sofia, Bulgaria.

**SMELOV Sergey,** b. 1964, Saratov, Russia. Psychologist. ı. 1 son, 1 daughter. Education: Moscow Medical College. areer: Director General, Psychosuggestive Programming 'enter, Serso. Publications: Several articles in professional edical journals. Honour: Winner, International Congress of raditional Medicine Award, Moscow, 1995. Membership: lussian Academy of Medical and Technical Science. Address: olskay Street 2, Poliklinik N 6, 00 Serso Moscow, Russia.

**SMETANA Karel,** b. 28 October 1930, Prague. Physician; cientist. m. Vlasta Smetanova, 1 son. Education: MUDr(MD), 955; CSc(PhD), 1962; DrSc(DSc), 1967, Charles University, 'rague; Certificate for Internal Medicine I, 1986, Institute for ostgraduate Medical Studies, Prague. Appointments: ecturer, Department of Histology, Charles University, Prague, 955-62; Scientific Officer, Senior Scientific Officer, Head of epartment of Blood Cytology, Laboratory of Ultrastruct esearch, Czechoslovak Academy of Sciences, Prague, 962-84; Director, Institute of Haematology and Blood ransfusion, Prague, 1984-90, Senior Scientific Officer, Head f Laboratory of Cytology and Electron Microscopy, 1990-; ;hair of Haematology and Transfusion Service, Institute of ostgrad Medical Studies, Prague, 1985-93, Lecturer, 1993; lesearch Fellow, Department of Pharmacology, Baylor College f Medicine, Houston, Texas, 1962, Visiting Associate 'rofessor, 1963,Professor, 1970; Chairman, Board of Postgrad ;cientific Studies in Cell Biology and Pathology, Charles Iniversity, Prague, 1994-. Publications: 245 articles on cell ucleus, nucleolus, malignant cells, including leukemic cells nd blood cells in scientific journals; 1 monograph; 6 ıonographic chapters in various scientific monographies; ;hapters in 6 textbooks in biology and medicine. Honours: 11 rizes and medals in field; Honorarydiplomas of various cientific institutions including Purkynje Medal for chievements in Medicine; State Prize; Gold Medal of the ;lovak Medical Society; Gold Medal for Achievements in 'eterinary Medicine. Memberships: Czech Histochemical ociety; Czech Hematological Society; American Association ır Cancer Research; W Bernhard Workshop on the Cell lucleus; Austrian Hematological Society; Society Clinical ;ytology; and others. Address: Puchovska 2, Prague 4, Czech lepublic 141 00.

**SMIRNOV Yuri A,** b. 30 April 1935, Petrozavodsk, Russia. :cologist. m. Zoya N Smirnova, 1 daughter. Education: )iploma, Petrozavodsk University, 1958; Diploma, dr. Biology, 967; Diploma, Senior Researcher, 1974. Appointments: ;enior Ichthyologist, Fishery Inspection, 1959; Senior lesearcher, Laboratory of Water Ecology, Institute of Biology, cademy of Sciences, Karelia, 1967; Head of Laboratory, Vater Ecology, 1978; Leading Researcher, Academy of ciences, Karelia, 1986; Ecology Engineer, Energetics :ompany, 1992. Publications include: Books: Salmon of Lake )nego, 1971, translated in Canada, 1972; Freshwater Salmon, 979; Salmon Spawning Rivers, 1978, with others; Over 100 ırticles. Honours: Silver Medal, 1975, Bronze Medal, 1981, JSSR Exhibition of Economical Achievements; 2 Medals, 1981, 987, Government of Russia. Memberships: Russian

Hydrobiological Society; Salmon Committee, Ichthyological Commission of Russia. Address: Moscovskaya str 13, app 20, Petrozavodsk 185031, Russia.

**SMITH Charles F Jr,** b. 5 January 1933, Cleveland, Ohio, USA. Professor Emeritus of Education. m. Lois Thompson Smith, 1 son, 1 daughter. Education: BS Ed, Bowling Green State University, 1960; EdM, Kent State University, 1963; CAS, Harvard University Graduate School of Education, 1965; EdD, Michigan State University, 1969. Appointments: Military Service, Staff Sergeant, Medical Corps, 1954-56; 5th Grade Teacher, Lorain, Ohio, 1960-62; Academic Director, Peace Corp Training Camp, Puerto Rico, 1962-63; Teaching Fellow, Harvard University School of Education, 1963-65; Assistant Director, Elementary Education, Flint, Michigan, 1965-66; Instructor, Michigan State University, 1966-68; Professor Emeritus, Boston College, 1968-. Honours: Danforth Associate, 1974; Visiting Scholar, University of Michigan, 1990, Atlanta University, 1993, Yale University, 1995; Phi Delta Kappa Emeritus, 1998; Numerous Travel Fellowships. Memberships: Board of Directors, National Council for the Social Studies, 1990-97; American Association of Colleges for Teacher Education; American Association of University Professors; American Association of School Administrators; Association for Supervision and Curriculum Development; Department of Elementary School Principals; National Council for the Social Studies; Phi Delta Kappa. Address: 194 Parker Street, Newton Centre, MA 02459, USA.

**SMITH Doris Corinne,** b. 22 November, Bogalusa, USA. Registered Nurse. m. Joseph William Smith. Education: BS, Nursing, 1957, MS, Nursing Administration, 1958, University of Colorado, Boulder; Registered Nurse Diploma, City Hospital, Mobile, 1940. Appointments: Head Nurse, Chicago Bridge and Iron Company, Morgan City, 1941-45; Head Nurse, Shannon Hospital, San Angelo, Texas, 1945-50; Director, Nursing, Yoacum City Hospital, 1951-52; Supervisor, Medical Centre Hospital, Odessa, Texas, 1952-55; Director, In-Service Editor, St Anthony Hospital, Denver; Coordinator, School of Nursing, Kiamichi Area, 1969-97. Publications include: Survey Nurses Functions, 1958; Nursing Practice Guides. Honours: ABWA Woman of the Year, 1995. Memberships: Steering Committee, WICHE, 1963-65. Address: 2103 55th Street, Lubbock, TX 79412-2612, USA.

**SMITH Irving,** b. 4 June 1948, Washington, DC, USA. Gerontologist. 5 sons. Education: PhD Candidate, Walden University; Master of Human Services, Lincoln University, 1995; Graduate Certificate Advanced Gerontology, 1995; Fellow, Washington, DC Area Geriatric Education Center Consortium. Appointments: Director, Leisure and Aging Programs, 32 years; Forum Speaker, International, National on Leisure and Aging Issues; Licensed Professional Counsellor; Senior Center Director; Sports Science Instructor, American Sports Education Program; CPR, First Aid Instructor, American Red Cross; Defensive Driving Instructor, National Safety Council. Publications: Off Your Rocker, 1995; Still Off Your Rocker. Memberships: National Recreational and Park Association; Pi Gamma Mu International Honour Society; Charter Chapter, Lincoln University. Address: 503 Pacer Dr, Hyattsville, MD 20785-4639, USA.

**SMITH John Wilson,** b. 2 June 1935, Pottsville, Pennsylvania, USA. Journalist. m. Jean A Longenecker, 1 son, 2 daughters. Education: BA History magna cum laude, Franklin & Marshall College, 1957; MA Journalism, Syracuse University, 1959. Appointments: Sports Writer, 1958-82, Sports Editor, 1981-82, Reading Eagle; News Editor, 1982-87, Copy Chief, Columnist, Religious Editor, 1987-, Reading Eagle Times;

OUTSTANDING PEOPLE OF THE 20TH CENTURY

Statistician, Eastern Football Conference, 1981-, District 11, 1984-. Honours: Pa, American Legion Baseball Hall of Fame, 1971; Moderator, Reading Baptist Association, 1965-67. Memberships: Phi Beta Kappa; Sigma Delta Chi. Address: 1121 Whitfield Boulevard, West Lawn, PA 19609-1137, USA.

**SMITH Kenneth George,** b. 16 November 1929, Auckland, New Zealand. Musician. m. Lois Nola Smith, 3 sons, 1 daughter. Appointments: Co-Principal Cornet, The Fairey Aviation Band, England, 1950-55; Senior Brass Specialist, Victorian Education Department, Australia; Professor, Trumpet, Head, Brass, Sydney Conservatorium of Music, 1974-89; Conductor, New Zealand National Band, 1985 Honours: Winner, International World Championship, The Netherlands, 1985; Awarded, MNZM; Order of Merit, Queens Birthday Honours, 1997. Address: 2/28 Francesca Street, North Box Hill, Melbourne, Australia.

**SMITH Lincoln Cain,** b. 8 October 1971, Taree. Banker. m. Helen Grace Smith. Appointments: Banking Executive, Relationship Management, Commonwealth Bank of Australia. Membership: Australian Institute of Bankers. Address: PO Box 917, Maroubra, NSW 2035, Australia.

**SMITH Philip Gene,** b. 3 March 1928, Chicago, Illinois. m. Elaine Keherer Smith, 2 sons. Education: BA, Kentucky State College, 1949; BE, Chicago Teachers College, 1953; MA, Antioch College School of Law, 1982. Appointments: Political Science Adjucant Professor, Georgia Perometer College, Wayne County Michigan Community College, Highland Park, Michigan Community College. Publications: One Step Forward, Two Steps Backwards. Address: 955 Hargett Court, Stone Mountain, GA 30083 2401, USA.

**SMITH Roger Leroy,** b. 15 May 1946, New York, USA. Aviation Electronics. m. Maneewan Smith, 2 sons, 4 daughters. Education: AA, Criminal Justice, Nassau Community College, 1975. Appointments: USN Petty Officer 2nd Class, 1965-69; Federal Law Enforcement US Customs, 1971-74; FAA Air Traffic Controller, 1974-76, Flight Inspection, 1976-. Honour: Vietnam Service Medal, 1966-69. Address: 1444 Crystal Springs Drive, Woodland, CA 95776, USA.

**SMITH Shirley,** b. Wichita, Kansas. Actress; Artist. Education: BFA, Kansas State University; Wichita State University; Provincetown Workshop, Massachusetts; Arts Students League, New York City. Career: Actress 1952-63, appeared on Broadway in Picnic, Eugenia and the Highest Tree, on tour, on television and in commercials; In Feature Film, Pretty Boy Floyd and 3 industrial films, Suburban Housewife, To Live Again, College Life. Artist, 1963-: Represented in 7 museum and 6 public collections in USA; 7 solo exhibitions and 36 group exhibitions. Publications: Featured in various publications and reviews. Honours: 2 art grants, 1998, 1999; Grumbacher Cash Award for Mixed Media, New England Exhibition, Connecticut, 1967; Academy-Institute Painting Award, American Academy and Instutute of Arts and Letters, New York City, 1991. Address: 141 Wooster Street, New York, NY 10012, USA.

**SMITH Stafford,** b. 11 January 1956, Wilkes-Barre, PA, USA. Cardiologist. m. Mary Rose A Smith, 2 sons, 1 daughter. Education: Clinical Chemistry, University of South Florida, USA, 1981; MD, St George's University School of Medicine, 1985. Appointments: Intern, Veterans Administration Medical Center, Hahnemann University, Northeastern Pennsylvania Affiliated Hospitals, Scranton, PA, USA, 1986-87; Residency, Internal Medicine, University of Pennsylvania, Presbyterian/University of Pennsylvania Medical Center, Philadelphia, PA, USA,

1987-89; Fellowships: Cardiovascular Disease, Presbyterian Medical Center of Philadelphia, University of Pennsylvania, PA 1989-91; Invasive/Interventional Adult Cardiology, Medical College of Virginia Hospital, Virginia Commonwealth University, Medical College of Virginia, 1991-92; Invasive and Interventional Adult Cardiovascular Diseases, Blair Medical Associates, Altoona, PA, 1992-93; Invasive and Interventional Adult Cardiovascular Diseases, Giamber, Dale and Smith Bethlehem, PA, USA, 1993-. Publications: Essentials for the Diagnosis and Therapy of Glaucoma, 1986; Spontaneou Coronary Artery Dissection, 1994; Results of the Splinting for Acute Closure Trial, 1994; Long Term Results of the Multicenter Splinting for Acute Closure, 1995; Current Management of Acute Myocardial Infarction, 1995; Vasospasm Relieved by Intracoronary Nicardipine Administration, 1997 Transthoracic Echocardiography is Inadequate to Diagnose Acute Mitral Insufficiency in Papillary Rupture, 1997. Honour Physicians Recognition Award. Memberships: American College of Physicians; Fellow, American College of Cardiology Fellow, American College of Chest Physicians; Fellow International Society of Cardiovascular Interventionists; Fellow Society for Cardiac Angiography and Interventions; Fellow American Heart Association Scientific Council on Clinica Cardiology. Address: 504 Eagle Drive, Emmaus, PA 18049-1929, USA.

**SMITH Verna Green,** b. 23 August 1919, Oklee, Minnesota USA. Journalist; Educator. m. Alfred N Smith Jr, dec, 3 sons Education: BA, Journalism, University of Montana; MA Education, Washington University, St Louis; PhD, Education St Louis University. Appointments include: Public Relation Director, English Teacher, Ritenour School District, St Loui County, 1956-66; Communication Services Director, Editor CEMREL Reports, CEMREL Inc, St Louis, 1966-82 Publications Director, Editor, R&D Notes, Regional Educational Laboratory, St Louis, 1983-85; Volunteer Editorial Director 1986-, Editor, UPDATE, 1986-89, Volunteer Coordinator, Oral History Project, 1992-94, Contributor, OASIS OUTLOOK 1993-, Peer Counsellor, Person to Person Program, 1996 Older Adult Service and Information System, St Louis Volunteer Coordinator, Media Archives, St Louis Public Library 1986-. Publications: Arts Education, co-author, 1982; Editor OASIS Arts and Humanities Training Manual, 1986; OASIS Activate Your Health Training Manual, 1987; Positive Attitudes Positive Aging Training Manual, 1992; Movers and Shakers Men Who Shaped St Louis, co-editor, 1992; Articles on educational topics. Honours include: Charter Member, F Lambda Theta, 1969; 2 1st Prizes, 1969, 2nd Prize, 1970, 3r Prize, 1982, National Federation of Press Women Writing Contests; Member, Catfish Club, Press Club of Metropolitan S Louis, 1991; Quest Award, Missouri Press Women, 1992 Woman of Worth, Older Women's League, 1995; Olympi Torchbearer, St Louis, 1996. Memberships include: Nationa School Public Relations Association; Charter Member Conference on Education, St Louis; Press Club of Metropolita St Louis, Board of Directors, Treasurer, Vice-President; Societ of Professional Journalists; National Federation of Pres Women; Women in Communications; Many more. Address 10311 Pineview Court, St Louis, MO 63114-1436, USA.

**SMITH Walter Delos,** b. 7 June 1936, Rensselaer, Indiana Accountant; Professional Speaker. m. Yvonne Marie Dietz, sons, 2 daughters. Education: BS in Accounting, 1960, Walto School of Commerce, Chicago. Appointments: CPA Wisconsin, Illinois Accountants, Frazer & Torbet CPAs Chicago, 1960-66; Assistant Contr, Rath-Packing Company Waterloo, Iowa, 1966-68; Contr, Treasurer, DeLeuw, Cather Co, Chicago, 1968-72; Corporate Contr, Mohawk Dat Sciences, Utica, New York, 1972-75; Management Consultan

Walter D Smith and Associates, New Hartford, New York, 1975-76; VP, General Manager, Flambeau-Plastics, Baraboo, Wisconsin, 1976-83; Principal, Walter D Smith, CPA, Baraboo, 1983-; Ad hoc faculty, University of Wisconsin Management Institute, 1988-; Director, Trachte Building Systems, Sun Prairie, Wisconsin, Baraboo Mutual Fire Insurance Company, Baraboo, Skyward Inc, Stevens Point, Wi. Memberships: Board of Directors, New Hartford School District, 1974-76, Baraboo School District, 1980-83; AUS, 1955-56; National Society Public Accountants; National Conference CPA Practitioners; National Speakers Association; Wisconsin Professional Speakers Association; Institute Management Accountants; Alliance Practicing CPA's; Baraboo Toastmasters; American Legion; VFW; Kiwanis; Elks. Address: 809 Iroquois Cir, Baraboo, WI 53913-1248, USA.

**SMITH-LUNDBECK Penny,** b. 28 September 1940, Dayton, Ohio, USA. Middle School Educator. m. (1) Mark Richard Smith, deceased, (2) Gordon E Lundbeck, 1 son, 1 daughter. Education: BS, Education, Taylor University, 1963; MEd, Bowling Green State University, 1966; Teaching Certificate. Appointments: 3rd Grade Teacher, East Auburn (Ind) Elementary School, 1963-66, Skycrest Elementary School, Clearwater, Florida, 1972-73; 1st Grade Teacher, John Wilson Elementary School, Honolulu, 1966-67; 4th Grade Teacher, Harrison-McKinney Elementary School, Auburn, 1967-71; 4th-6th Grade Teacher, Prospect Elementary School, Monroe, North Carolina, 1973-75; 6th Grade Teacher, Parkwood Middle School, Monroe, 1975-96. Honours: Terry Sanford Organization Award, 1980; Outstanding Young Educator Award, Auburn Jaycees, 1964; Named Union County Teacher of the Year, 1976, Parkwood Middle School Teacher of the Year, 1992; Fulbright Scholar, India, 1992. Memberships: NEA; North Carolina County Social Studies Association; English Teachers Association; Classroom Teachers Association; Association of North Carolina Educators; Friendship Force. Address: 493 Haven Point Drive, Treasure Island, FL 33706, USA.

**SMOOT Nelson Christian,** b. 13 August 1942, Richmond, VA, USA. Marine Geomorphologist. m. Jane Berrong Smoot, 1 son. Education: BS, Clemson University, 1966; MS, University South Miss, 1986. Appointments: Making Classified Surveys and Maps for the Submarine Community by Evolving Technology, 1966-75, 1977-98. Publications: 150 assorted Newsletters; Abstracts; Presentations; Papers; Books. Honours: OSP Award, 1971; Realm of Artic Circle, 1970; Royal Order of Atlantic Voyageurs, 1972; Domin of the Golden Dragon, 1979; Vigil Honour, Boy Scouts, 1983; Solemn Mysteries of the Ancient Order of the Deep, 1985; Tung Belt District Order of the Arrow Service Award, 1986; EEO Certificate of Award, 1989; Tung Belt District Pine Burr Award, 1991; SCV Camp Historian Award, 1997; Contributor of the Year, 1998. Memberships: Sigma Xi; Geological Society of America; Marine Technology Society; Kiwanis Club; Boy Scouts of America; Sons of Confederate Veterans; Sons of the American Revolution; Bonnie Blue Society. Address: 104 Williamsburg Road, Picayune, MS 39446-8415, USA.

**SMUTS Malie,** b. 27 February 1933. Retired Professor of Veterinary Anatomy. Eduction: BVSc, 1954, DVSc, 1976, University of Pretoria. Appointments: Private Veterinary Practice, 1955; Volunteer Worker, WI Moral Re-Armament, 1956-69; Lecturer, Professor, Anatomy, 1970-93. Publication: Anatomy of the Dromedary, 1987. Honour: Best Student, 1954. Membership: World Association of Veterinary Anatomists. Address: 26 Lynnwood Mews, Kings Highway, Lynnwood, Pretoria 0081, South Africa.

**SNAITANG Overland,** b. 13 April 1952, Mawkyrwat. Professor. m. Diana Hadem, 3 sons, 1 daughter. Education: BA, 1974; BD, 1978; MTh, 1981; DTh, 1990. Appointments: Lecturer, Cherra Theological College, Meghalaya, 1978-94; Visiting Professor, Sacred Heart College, Shillong, 1993-; Professor, Serampore College, Serampore and Eastern Theological College, Jorhat, 1994-, Official Historian for the Asia-Pacific Church of God Conference. Publications: Christianity and Social Change in Northeast India, 1993; Memoirs of Life and Political Writings of the Honourable Reverend J J M Nichols-Roy, 1997. Memberships: Northeast India History Association; Board, MTh Studies and D Min Programme; Senate of Serampore College. Address: Kench's Trace, Shillong 793004, Meghalaya, India.

**SNIEZAK Gary,** b. 20 May 1957, Mineola, New York, USA. Engineer. 1 son. Education: BSME, 1985, MSME, 1992, Western New England College, Springfield. Appointments: Machinist, Falls Machine Screw Inc, Chicopee, Massachusetts, 1976-77; Tool and Dye Designer, HBA Cast Products Inc, Springfield, Massachusetts, 1977-79; Checker, Draftsman, 1979-81, Design Engineer, 1981-84, Product Engineer, 1984-87, Senior Product Engineer, 1987-89, Engineering Product Manager, 1989-94, Smith & Wesson Inc, Springfield, Massachusetts; Director of Engineering, FN Manufacturing Inc, Columbia, South Carolina, 1994-. Publications: Several papers at various professional conferences, 9 patents. Membership: American Society of Mechanical Engineers. Address: FN Manufacturing Inc, PO Box 24257, Columbia, SC 29224-4257, USA.

**SNIPAS Pranas,** b. 13 March 1930, Deguciai, Lithuania. Physician. 3 daughters. Education: Graduate, Liburio College in Sakiai, Lithuania, 1950; Graduate, Kaunas Medical Institute (now Kaunas Medical Academy), 1956. Appointments: Head, Department of Internal Diseases, K Naumiesti's Hospital, 1956-57; Dr, Kaunas Academical Clinic, 1957; Medical Dr and Assistant Professor, Kaunas Medical Institute, Chair of Internal Diseases, 1958-68; Doctor Habilitated of Medecine, Professor, Kaunas Medical Institute, Chair of Internal Diseases, 1968-69; Director, Central Laboratory of Medical Research, 1969-72; Head, Clinic of Internal Diseases, Kaunas Medical Academy, 1972-94; Professor, Kaunas Medical Academy, 1994-. Publications: Author of 7 investigations; 2 monographs, 30 studying materials for students; Author of 475 articles. Memberships: Association of Lithuanian Internists; European Respiratory Society. Address: Perkuno al 46-3, 3000 Kaunas, Lithuania.

**SNOW Peter John,** b. 25 February 1948, Jubbulpore, India. Professor Neurobiology. 1 son, 2 daughters. Education: BSc 1st Hons, 1970, University Tasmania; PhD, 1974, University Alberta; Canadian Medical Research Fellowship, University Edinburgh, 1974-76; Queen's Fellowship, Australian National University, 1976-78; Travelling Fellowship, 1982. Appointments: Lecturer, 1978-83, Senior Lecturer, Department of Anatomy, Associate Professor, Department of Anatomical Sciences, 1989-, Director, Cerebral and Sensory Function Unit, current, University Queensland; Visiting Research Fellow and Professor, University College, London, 1981-82, University of California at San Francisco, 1985-86, Bristol University, UK, 1988, University of Pisa, Italy, 1988. Publications: Over 65 major papers; Book, Brain Plasticity, 1991; 13 papers in preparation/submitted. Memberships: International Association for the Study of Pain; US Society for Neuroscience; International Brain Research Organisation; Primate Society of America; Australian Neuroscience Society; Australian Physiological and Pharmacological Society. Address: Cerebral

& Sensory Function Unit, Anatomy Department, University of Queensland, St Lucia, QLD 4072, Australia.

**SNOWDEN-WILSON Bertha Jeanne,** b. 26 August 1948, Lowell, Massachusetts, USA. Musician and Educator. m. Alan Lee Wilson, div 1992, 1 son. Education: BMus, Berklee College of Music, 1973. Career: Music Teacher, Choral Director, Narragansett Regional School District, Otter River, Massachusetts, 1994-95; Music Teacher, Choral Director, Boston Public Schools, 1995-. Publications: Life in the US and Canada, 1990. Memberships: Broadcast Music Inc; American Federation of Teachers; American Federation of Musicians. Address: Gingercake Publishers, PO Box 285, Billerica, MA 01821-0285, USA.

**SNYDER Francis Gregory,** b. 26 June 1942, Madison, Wisconsin, USA. Professor. Appointments: Research Fellow, Yale Law School, 1970-71; Asstistant Professor, Associate Professor, York University, Canada, 1971-78; Senior Lecturer, Reader, Warwick University, 1978-87; Reader, European Professor of Law, Univrsity College London, 1987-92; Professor of European Community Law, European University Institute, 1992-; Visiting Professor of Law, College of Europe, 1989-; Honorary Visiting Professor of Law, University College London, 1992-. Publications: 20 Books; Over 100 Articles. Honours: Wrexham Prize, Yale University, 1967; Clark Prize, Yale University, 1967; Phi Beta Kappa, Yale University, 1967; Research Associate Award, International Development Research Centre, 1974; Officier De L'Ordre des Palmes Academiques, 1988; Medal of the Town of Segowzac, 1993. Memberships: International Bar Association; Massachusetts Bar Association; United Kingdom Association for European Law; International Biographical Association; Law and Society Association; The Athenaeum; Yale Club, New York; Yale Club, London; Harvard Club, London. Address: European University Institute Department of Law, via Boccaccio 121, I-50133 Firenze, Italy.

**SOAI Kenso,** b. 3 May 1950, Hiroshima, Japan. Professor of Chemistry; Educator. m. Hiroko Ogino, 1 daughter. Education: BSc, 1974, MSc, 1976, PhD, 1979, University of Tokyo; Postdoctoral Fellow, University of North Carolina at Chapel Hill, 1979-81. Appointments: Lecturer at Science University of Tokyo, 1981-86, Associate Professor, 1986-91, Full Professor, 1991-. Publications: in professional journals. Honours: Recipient Progress Award in Synthetic Organic Chemistry, 1988; Chisso Award in Synthetic Organic Chemistry, 1990. Memberships: American Chemical Society; Chemical Society of Japan; American Association for the Advancement of Science; Society of Synthetic Organic Chemistry Japan. Address: Science University of Tokyo, Department of Applied Chemistry, Kagurazaka Shinjuku-ku, Tokyo 162-8601, Japan.

**SODOMKA Lubomir,** b. 29 July 1930, Hlinsko, Czech Republic. Professor. m. Vladimira Grygarkova, 1 son, 3 daughters. Education: Mathematical Physical Faculty, Charles University, Prague; Postgraduate, Institute of Solid State Physics, Academy of Sciences, Prague, 1965; Technical University, Liberec, 1981; Technical University, Brno. Appointment: Professor of Physics and Textile Science. Publications: Several in professional journals. Memberships: FABI; MDFABI; Czech Mathematical Physical Society. Address: Horska 16, 46014 Liberec, Czech Republic.

**SOETANTO Melinda,** b. 10 October 1964, Indonesia. Education: BS, Computer Applications and Systems, California State University, Fresno, 1987; MBA, International Business, National University, Los Angeles, 1989. Appointments:

Accountant, T and J Products, Los Angeles, California, USA, 1987-88; Financial Analyst, Angeles Corporation, Los Angeles, 1988-90; Assistant Manager, Nomura Securities, Jakarta, Indonesia, 1991-93; Director, Pacific Place Holdings, Singapore, 1994-98, Director, P T MacLand Mulia Sentosa, Jakarta, 1996-. Address: Orchard PO Box 224, Singapore 912308.

**SOFOWORA Abayomi,** b. 16 May 1941, Lagos, Nigeria. Pharmacist. m. Florence, Oluwajemite, 2 sons, 2 daughters. Education: BPharm, Hons, 1964; PhD, Pharmacognosy, Nottingham, 1967; MPS, 1968; FPC, Pharm. Appointments: Lecturer, 1967, Senior Lecturer, 1970, Reader, 1975, Professor, 1979, Obafemi Awolowo University, Ile-Ife, Nigeria. Publications: Medicinal Plants and Traditional Medicine in Africa, Spectrum, Ibadan, 1993; Fellowship of the Sickle Cell Association of Nigeria, 1997. Memberships: Institute of Public Analysts, Nigeria; Pharmaceutical Society of Nigeria. Address: Faculty of Pharmacy, Obafemi Awolowo University, Ile-Ife, Oshun State, Nigeria.

**SOKOLOV Vladimir V,** b. 24 November 1932, Rostov-on-Don, 24 November 1932. Clinical Anatomist. m. Sokolova M T, 2 daughters. Education: MD, Rostov State Medical Institute, 1956; PhD, Medicine, 1960; DSc, Medicine, 1971. Appointments: Professor, Normal Anatomy Department, 1973; Head, Normal Anatomy Department, 1975; Deputy Rector, Rostov State Medical University, 1994. Publications: 300 scientific publications including monographs: Cardiac Vessels. Honours: Excellent Physician, 1967; For Excellent Work, 1970; Veteran of Labour, 1985; Scientist Emeritus of Russia, 1991; Order of Esteem, 1996. Memberships: Russian Society of Anatomists Gystologists; IAM, Advisory Board; Euro-Asian Medical Academy; Russian Teriological Society; Advisory Board on Anatomy, Ministry of Public Health. Address: Krasnoarmeiskaya Str 63/90 - 43, 344010 Rostov on Don, Russia.

**SOLBRIG Ingeborg Hildegard,** b. 31 July 1923, Weissenfels, Germany; US Citizen. Education: BA summa cum laude, 1964, San Francisco State University; MA German Studies, 1966, PhD Humanities, German, 1969, Stanford University. Appointments: Assistant Professor, Universities of Rhode Island, Kingston, Chattanooga, Tennessee and Lexington, Kentucky; Associate Professor, University Iowa, 1975-81, Professor, 1981-93; Professor Emeritus, 1993-. Address: 1126 Pine Street, Iowa City, IA 52240, USA.

**SOLJIC Zvonimir,** b. 6 April 1935, Herzegovina. University Professor; Researcher. m. Ina Vidovic, 2 daughters. Education: BS Chemistry, 1961, MSc, 1968, PhD Chemistry, 1973, University Zagreb. Appointments: Assistant, Faculty Technology, 1961-71, Lecturer Chemistry, 1971-75, Docent, 1975-79, Associate Professor, 1979-85, Professor, Faculty Chemical Engineering and Technology, 1985-, University Zagreb. Publications: Qualitative Inorganic Chemistry Analysis, 1984, 1992; Analytical Chemistry, 1985, 1992; Calculations in Analytical Chemistry, 1987, 1998; Scientific articles in analytical chemistry in many scientific journals. Memberships: Croatian Chemical Society; Croatian Society of Chemical Engineers and Technologists; New York Academy of Sciences. Address: University Zagreb, Faculty Chemical Engineering-Technology, Marulicev trg 20, 10000 Zagreb, Croatia.

**SOLOGOUB Elena Borisovna,** b. 11 September 1929, St Petersburg, Russia. Physiology Educator, Researcher, Consultant. m. Sologoub Mikhail Ivanovich, 1 son, 1 daughter. Education: MSc, Biology, Physiology Summa cum laud, State University of St Petersburg, 1952; PhD, Human and Animal

Physiogy, 1955; DSc, Biology, Lesgaft, St Academy of Physics, St Petersburg, 1967. Appointments: Tutor, Physiol, State University, 1955-56; Tutor, Physiology, Legstaft State Academy, 1956-62; Researcher, 1962-64; Assistant Professor, 1964-74; Professor, 1974-; Acting Head Department of Physiology, 1983-86. Publications: Electrical Activity of Human Brain in Course of Movement, 1973; Elektroenzephalografie in Sport; Cortical Regulation of Human Movement; Over 250 Articles. Honours: Honorary Award of State Sport Com, Moscow. Memberships: Editorial Council Journal Human Physiol; Baltic Academy Education; Russian Academy of Med-Technical Sciences; Physiology Society of Russia; Honorary Educator of Russian Highest Education. Address: O Forsh St 13 Apt 211, 195269 Saint Petersburg, Russia.

**SOLOGOUB Mikhail Ivanovich,** b. 17 November 1928, Kursk Region, Russia. Physiology Educator, Researcher, Consultant. m. Shturmer Elena Borisovna, 2 sons, 1 daughter. Education: Graduate Engineer, Mechanic Poly Institute, Ukraine; MSc, Biology, Physiology, State University, Russia, 1953; PhD, Biology, Physics, 1958; Dr Scs, Biology, 1970; Professor, Physiology, 1979. Appointments: Laboratory Technician, Researcher, Lecturer, State University, 1956-77; Director of Research Laboratory, 1971-77; Professor, Head of Department, Anatomy and Physiology State Pedag University, St Petersburg, 1977-94; Professor, State Technical University, 1995-96; Professor, Lesgaft, St Academy of Physic al Culture, 1996-. Publications: Motor Activity Control in Crayfish; Neurophysiol Mechanics of Motor Activity in Crayfish; Over 100 Articles to Scientific Journals. Memberships: Academy Boards in Physiology and Biophysics; Physiology Society of Russia. Address: O Forsh St 13 Apt 211, 195269 Saint Petersburg, Russia.

**SOLOMON Jerry,** b. 11 June 1954, New York, New York, USA. Sports Marketing. m. Nancy Kerrigan, 2 sons. Education: Bachelors, 1976, UCLA; Masters, 1978, Columbia University. Appointments: Chairman, Kidsports Foundation, 1989-95; President, Prosen, 1991-95; President, PS/StarGames, 1995-; Founder Kidsports Magazine; Chief Executive Officer, Association of Volleyball Professionals, 1995-97. Honours: Top 100 Most Powerful People in Sport, 1992; Top 25 Most Influential in Figure Skating, 1995. Memberships: Young Presidents Organisation; Committee of Sports for Israel. Address: PS/StarGames, 40 Salem St. Bldg 1, Lynnfield, MA 01940, USA.

**SOLOMON Phyllis,** b. 6 December 1945, Hartford, Ronn, USA. Professor. Education: BA, Sociology, Russell Sage College, 1968; MA, Case Western Reserve University, 1970; PhD, 1978. Appointments: Teaching Assistant, 1976, Lecturer, 1985-86, Adjunct Instructor, 1986, Lecturer, 1986, Adjunct Professor, 1987-88, Case Weston University; Professor, Hahnemann University, 1988-94; Professor, School of Social Work, 1994-; Professor, Social Work of Psychiatry, 1995-. Publications: Psychiatric Rehabilitation in Practice; New Developments in Psychiatric Rehabilitation; Community Services to Discharged Psychiatric Patients; Many Book Chapters; Numerous other publications. Honours: Dictionary of International Biography, International Biographical Centre; Honorary Master of Arts; Evaluator of the Year; Kellas Scholar; Many others. Memberships: Society for Social Work and Research; International Association of Psychosocial Rehabilitation Services. Address: 104 Woodside Rd, Apt 108-A, Haverford, PA 19041, USA.

**SOLOMON Robert Douglas,** b. 28 August 1917, Delavan, Wisconsin, USA. Medical Researcher. m. Helen Fisher, 2 sons, 2 daughters. Education: BS, Biochemistry, University Chicago,

1938; MD, Johns Hopkins University, 1942. Appointments: Associate Professor, Pathology, USC, 1962; Professor, Pathology, State University of New York, 1978-86; Professor, Pathology, University Missouri, 1976-78; Adjunct Professor, Biology, University North Carolina, Wilmington. Publications: 45 publications in pathogenesis of cancer and atherosclerosis. Memberships: FACS; FCAP; FASCP; RSM; ACS; Sigma Xi; Phi Beta Kappa; International Academy Pathologists; Association Clinical Scientists. Address: 113 S Belvedere Drive, Hampstead, NC 28443-2904, USA.

**SOLOMONOW Moshe,** b. 24 October 1944, Tel-Aviv, Israel. Professor, Scientist. m. Susanne, 2 daughters. Education: BSc, University of California, Los Angeles, 1970; MSc, 1972; PhD, 1976. Appointments: Assistant Professor, University of California, 1976-80; Associate Professor, Tulane University, 1980-83; Professor, Louisianna State University, 1983-. Publications: 105 Scientific Papers. Honours: Volvo Award, 1999; Doctor Medicine Honouris Causa; Cahen Professorship; Editor in Chief, Journal of Electronography and Kinesology. Memberships: ISEK; ISB; IEEE; ORS. Address: Dept Orthopedic Surgery, 2025 Gravier St Ste 400, New Orleans, LA 70112-2289, USA.

**SOLOVIEVA Vera,** b. 30 September 1921, Satka, Cheliabinskaya, Russia. Doctor; Pharmacologist. 1 son. Education: BM, Tomsk Medical Institute, 1941. Appointments: Commander, Surgical Department, Red Army, 1942-45; Assistant, Ufa Medical Institute Chair of Pharmacology, 1946-53; Head, 1946-53, Professor, 1991-, Laboratory of Tissue Therapy. Publications: 4 monographs. Honours: Honoured Scientist of Ukraine; 16 military orders and medals. Membership: International Peat Society, Representative of Ukraine in VIth Commission, 1976-. Address: Boulevard Le France 43 Apt 11, 270061 Odessa, Ukraine.

**SOMKUAN Kaviya,** b. 14 January 1935, Suratthani, Thailand. Associate Professor. m. Duangjai Naewbanij, 1 son, 1 daughter. Education: BA Journalism, 1963, Thammasat University; Diploma in Public Information, 1966, CIESJ, Strasbourg; Docteur en Journalisme, 1969, Universite de Strasbourg; MPA Economics and Finance, 1973, IIAP, Paris. Appointments: Associate Professor in Communication, Dhurakijpundit University; Committee Member, National Broadcasting Board. Publications: Mass Communication: Functions, Freedom and Responsibility, 1996; Media transorms my life, 1997; Eco-Communication, 1998. Membership: Asian Media, Information and Communication Centre, Singapore. Address: 3/170 Muangthong 1, Laksi, Bangkok 10210, Thailand.

**SOMMERLATTE Werner Hermann Albert Tom,** b. 24 March 1938, Dessau, Germany. Management Consultant. m. Christine, 4 sons, 7 daughters. Education: Master of Science, University of Berlin, 1964; PhD, University of Paris, 1968; MBA, INSEAD, France, 1970. Appointments: European Director, Arthur D Little Inc, 1976; Managing Director, Arthur D Little Inc, 1983; Senior Vice-President, Arthur D Little Inc, 1990-. Publications: 15 Books and many Articles on current management issues, 1983-. Memberships: Rotary; Board of Deutsche Bank AG; Board of Alchemy. Address: Falkenweg 6, D 65537 Engenhaln Wildpark, Hessen, Germany.

**SONDEL Paul M,** b. 14 August 1950, Milwaukee, Wisconsin, USA. Professor. Education: BS Hons, University of Wisconsin, 1968-71; PhD, University of Wisconsin, 1974-75; Medical School, Harvard Medical School, 1972-74; MD, Magna cum laude, 1975-77. Appointments: Various Teaching, Research, Posts, 1970-80; Sub Fellowship, Pediatric Oncology, Midwest

Children's Cancer Center, 1980; Assistant Professor, Department of Pediatrics, Human Onocology and Genetics, University of Wisconsin, 1980-84; Associate Professor, 1984-86; Visiting Scientist, Weizmann Institute of Science, 1987; Professor, University of Wisconsin, 1987-; Head, Division of Pediatric Hematology, Oncology, 1990-; Program Leader, 1990-; Associate Director, UWCCC Laboratory Research, 1996-; Harold P Rusch Professorship, 1996-. Publications: 277 Publication. Honours: Rensselaer Award for Achievement in Mathematics and Science; Harvard Medical School HA Christian Award; Madison Jewish Community Council YoungLeadership Award; University of Wisconsin Romnes Faculty Research Award; State of Wisconsin Combined Health Appeal Advancement Award; Dean's Award for Excellence in Health Communication; The Best Doctors in the USA. Memberships: American Society of Bone Marrow Transplantation; Editorial Board, Journal of Clinical Immunology; Senior Editor, Clinical Cancer Research; International Cytokine Society; National Cancer Institute; Many other Memberships. Address: 1114 Winston Drive, Madison, Wisconsin, WI 53711, USA.

**SONG Chunshan,** b. 11 February 1961, Shijiazhuang, Hebei, China. Chemist and Chemical Engineer; University Professor. m. Lu Sun, 1 son, 1 daughter. Education: BS, Chemical Engineering, Dalian University of Technology, Dalian, China, 1982; Diploma in Japanese, Northeast Shifan University, China, 1983; MS Applied Chemistry, Osaka University, Japan, 1986; PhD, Applied Chemistry, Osaka University, Japan, 1989. Appointments: Osaka Gas R&D Center, Japan, 1989; Research Associate, 1989-1994; Assistant Professor, 1994-97, Associate Professor, 1997-, Pennsylvania State University. Publications: Over 60 peer-reviewed papers in many journals. Honours: Won several awards. Memberships: American Chemical Society; American Institute of Chemical Engineers; American Association for Advancement of Science; International Zeolite Association. Address: Pennsylvania State University, Fuel Science Program/209 Academic Project Building, University Park, PA 16802, USA.

**SONG Guo Dong,** b. 1 June 1933, Sun, Lin AI, Zhejiang Province, China. Professor of History and Literature. m. Lu Jing, 1 son. Education: BA History, 1961, Fudan University, Shanghai. Appointments: Land Reform, 1951-56; Lecturer, History Department, Fudan University, 1961-66; Cultural Revolution, 1966-77; Member Shanghai Academic Society, Adviser in Chinese Presentation and Speach Society, Founder and Head of Administration Department at Shanghai Administration Institute, Head of History and Literature Department at Shanghai Administration Institute, 1978-97. Publications: 20 papers published in professional journals; Books: Knowledge Based on Administration; Modern Chinese Social Structures and the Conflict between the Eastern and the Western Culture; History and Literature Encyclopedia for Leaders; Presentation and Speach Skills; Chinese Temple, Tower and Caves; The Development of Modern Chinese Culture and the Construction of a Civilised Society. Membership: Shanghai Academic Society. Address: Shanghai Administration Institute, Nozoo Hong Cao Nan Rd, Shanghai 200233, China.

**SONG Hong Zhao,** b. 13 August 1915, Sazhou, Jiansu, China. Professor. 3 sons, 1 daughter. Education: BS, Soochow University, 1934-38; MD, Beijing Union Medical College, 1938-43. Appointments: Intern, 1943-45; Resident, 1945-49; Chief Resident, 1949-51; Assistant Instructor, 1951-66; Assistant Professor, Associate Professor, 1966-78; Professor of Obs and Gyn, 1978-. Publications: 20 papers; 3 Books,

Tropical Diseases. Honours: First Grande Prize, Achievemer on the Diagnosis and Treatement of Tropho Blastic Disease Honour, Advanced Scientist; First Medical Prize; Ho Leung, Hc Lee Prize for Promotion of Medical Sciences. Memberships Society of Obs, Gyne Chinese medical Association International Society on the Study of Trophoblastic Diseases International Society of Gynaecology and Onocology; Chinese Adademy of Engineering. Address: Deparment of Obs Gyn Beijing Union Medical College, Beijing 1000730, China.

**SONG Iickho,** b. 20 February 1960, Seoul, Korea Professor. m. Taeyoung Seong, 2 daughters. Education: BS Electronics Engineering magna cum laude, 1982, MSE Electronics Engineering, 1984, Seoul National University; MSE Electrical Engineering, 1985, PhD Electrical Engineering, 1987 University Pennsylvania, USA. Appointments: Teachinç Assistant, Department of Electronics Engineering, Seou National University, 1982-83; Research Assistant, Departmen of Systems Engineering, 1984, Department of Electrica Engineering, 1984-87, University Pennsylvania; Membe Technical Staff, Digital Communications Research Group, Bel Communications Research, Morristown, NJ, 1987-88 Associate Editor, Communications Technology, Acoustica Society of Korea, 1990-91; Assistant Professor, KAIST, Seoul 1988-91; Teaching Fellow, Department of Electrica Engineering, National University of Singapore, 1992; Associate Professor, 1991-98, Professor, 1998-, Department of Electrica Engineering, KAIST, Daejeon, Korea; Associate Editor Modulation, Demodulation and Communications Network 1995-96, English Edition of Journal of Acoustical Society o' Korea, 1996-, Editor, Journal of Communications anc Networks, 1998-; Visiting Associate Professor, Communications Research Laboratory, Department oi Electrical and Computer Engineering, McMaster University, Hamilton, Ontario, 1996-97. Publications: Over 250 papers ir international and Korean journals and conferences. Honours 7 academic awards including LG Academic Award, Korear Institute of Communication Sciences, 1998; 3 scholarships including Korean Honour Scholarship, Korean Embassy in USA, 1985, 1986; Young Scientists Award, 1989, 1990, Union Radio-Scientifique Internationale; Best Research Award, 1993, Acoustical Society of Korea. Memberships: 6 professional societies. Address: KAIST Department of Electrica Engineering, 373-1 Guseong Dong, 305-701 Daejeon, Korea

**SONG Yi Ying,** b. 17 March 1930, Tianjin City, China. Professor. Education: Graduate, Northeast Commercial Institute, China, 1955. Graduate, Harbin Military Engineering Graduate Academy, 1961. Appointments: Assistan' Researcher, 1980; Professor, Researcher, 1990; Chairman, Valiant Shiping Trading Co Ltd, Hua Ding Engineering Equipment Co Ltd, Marinequip China Co Ltd, Hong Kong Huo Bin Holdings Ltd, Hong Kong Hua Da Development Co Ltd; Arbitrator, China International Economy and Trade Arbitration Commission; President, Technology Economic and Modern Management Institution; Chief Editor, Journal of Technology Introduction; Investment Consultant, Japan, 1991; Founder, Jilin Coyo Engineering Equipment Rental Co Ltd, Hong Kong. Publications: A Handbook on the Procedures of International Trade; Practical Contracts for International Trade; Modes of Payment for International Trade - Letter of Credit; Guide tc Checking Documents Drawn Under Documentary Credits; Over 30 research papers. Address: Changchun Coyo Co Ltd, No 188 Renmin Street, Changchun 130000, China.

**SONI Jagdish Chand,** b. 20 November 1951, Hamirpur, India. Teacher. m. Santosh Soni, 2 sons, 1 daughter. Education: MSc, Mathematics, 1974; MEd, 1976; MPhil, Education, 1978; PhD, Education, 1985; MA, Sociology, 1987.

Diplomas, German and Russian; BA, German. Appointments: Lecturer, Department of Education, North-Eastern Hill University, 1980-88; Reader, Department of Education, 1988-95, Professor, Head, Dean, Faculty of Education, 1995-, Arunachal University. Publications: Several articles in professional journals. Honours: UGC Fellowship, 1977-80; Faculty Research Fellowship, Shastri Indo-Canadian Institute, 1994. Memberships: 10 national level associations. Address: Aruachal University, Rono Hills, Itanagar 791 111, India.

**SONNENFELD Elio Moti,** b. 15 May 1956, Sao Paulo, Brazil. Industrial Engineer; International Consultant. m. Rachel, 1 son, 2 daughters. Education: BSc, Industrial Engineering, 1978, MSc, Industrial Engineering, 1980, Polytechnic Institute; Courses in Engineering, Management and History, Harvard University, 1980, Columbia University, 1977-79. Appointment: President and Chief Executive Officer, Logistica Group, 1978-. Publications: Computerized Traffic Control in the Island of Manhattan, 1979; Transfer of Technology to Developing Countries, 1980. Memberships: Officer of the Aeronautical Order of Brazil, Presidential Decree, 1988; American Institute of Industrial Engineers; New York Society of Professional Engineers; American Society for Engineering Education; American Institute of Aeronautics and Astronautics. Address: Logistica, Praia de Botafogo 228/1102, Rio de Janeiro 22359 900, Brazil.

**SONNINO Giorgio,** b. 6 November 1960, Genova, Italy. Scientist, Scientific Officer. m. Carla Di Nicola, 2 sons, 1 daughter. Education: Graduate in Physics, 1985; PhD, Physics, 1992. Appointments: Professor, University of Genova. Publications: Many Publications on various topics. Honours: NATO Award, 1992. Memberships: New York Academy of Science; Darwin Academy; AAAS Association. Address: Free U Brussels Ser Chim Ph, Blvd du Triomphe CP 231, 1050 Brussels, Belgium.

**SONTAKKE Neelima,** b. 4 April 1949, Pune India. Climatologist; Researcher. m. Ashwinikumar Sontakke, 3 daughters. Education: BSc, 1969, MSc, 1990, PhD, 1997, University of Pune. Appointments: Senior Scientific Officer Grade I, Indian Institute of Tropical Meteorology, Pune, 1985-98. Publications: 35 research publications: 16 in journals, 11 books and proceedings, 8 research reports, lecture notes and thesis. Honours: UNDP Fellowship awarded by World Meteorological Organisation at National Centre for Atmospheric Research, Colorado, USA, 1993-94. Membership: Life member, Indian Meteorological Society, Delhi, 1985-. Address: Shahu Coll Rd, 12-B Saurabha Soc, Pune 411009, India.

**SORIANO Debbie,** b. 10 December 1963, Montebello, California, USA. Teacher. m. Marcos Soriano, 1 son. Education: BA, 1982; MA, 1983; MBA, 1998; Doctorate, 1998. Appointments: Teacher, 1983-98; US Naval Reserves, 1996-. Honour: National Endowment of the Humanities Scholarship, 1994, 1995. Memberships: American Association of University Women; Pi Lambda Theta; United Nations Development for Women. Address: PO Box 2095, Arcadia, CA 91077-2095, USA.

**SOROKIN Garald K,** b. 30 January 1939, Nizhny Novgorod, Russia. Founder. m. Margarita Saianova, 18 March 1961, 2 daughters. Education: Diploma, Metallurgy Engineer, 1961; Diploma, Dr Tech, 1971; Diploma, Dr Phi, 1989. Appointments: Test Engineer, 1961-65; Superior of Friction Laboratory, 1965-80; Secretary of Party Committee, 1980-86; Branch Director, A A Blagonravov Institute of Machine Science, 1986-98. Publications: Business Mystery, 1997; Publicity Mystery, 1998; Memory Mystery, 1998. Honour: Medal, 300

Years Russian Navy, 1996. Memberships: Active Member, New York Academy of Sciences; USSR Chess Master, 1971; International Correspondence Chess Master. Address: A A Blagonravov Institute of Machine Science, Russian Academy of Sciences, 85 Belinskogo Str, Nizhny Novogorod 603024, Russia.

**SOTAMAA Yrjo Kalervo,** b. 25 September 1942, Helsinki, Finland. Professor; University President. m. Pirko Sotamaa, 1 son, 1 daughter. Education: MA, 1969, University of Art and Design Helsinki. Appointments: Visiting Assistant Professor, Purdue University, USA, 1969-70; Head of Department, 1975-85, Professor, 1987-, President, 1986-, University of Art and Design Helsinki. Honours: Honorary Fellow, Finnish Association of Graphic Designers, 1991, Finnish Association of Designers Ornamo, 1992, Royal College of Art, London, 1994; Kommander, Orde Van Oranje, Netherlands, 1995. Memberships: Finnish Association of Interior Architects; Society of Finnish Cultural Foundation; Finnish Council of University Rectors, Vice Chairman, 1996-. Address: University of Art & Design Helsinki, Hameentie 135 C, 00560 Helsinki, Finland.

**SOTONYI Jozsef,** b. 27 Oct 1949, Hungary. General Director. m. Mary Guablocwe, 2 daughters. Education: University of Science, Eötvös Lorand, Tech University. Appointment: General Director, Alfa Television. Publications: Television Practice, book, 1988; Several publications in professional journals. Memberships: numerous foundations. Address: Fahej Utca 22, 1162 Budapest, Hungary.

**SOUDAN Jean Pol (Lord John's),** b. 2 July 1953, Louise-Marie, Belgium. Artist; Painter. Div. 1 son. Education: Academy of Tournai, 1968-70; Academy of London, 1972-73; Academy of Lille, 1973-74; Academie of Brussel, 1974-76. Career: Painter, originally inspired by the Ardennes countryside and the North Sea, then a more fantastic and symbolic style; Represented in many different museums in Belgium and other countries. Publications: Featured in such noted reference publications as Artists and Galleries, Brussels; Lexion Spectraal, Gent; International Art Guide Sermardiras, Paris; and others. Memberships: Royal Association and Royal Foundation of the Professional Belgian Artists Painters; Royal Association and Royal Foundation 'Sabam' of Belgium Authors Rights Copyright and Preservations for the Belgian Artists; Accademia Del Verbano, Vinzaglio, Italia. Address: 95 Rue de la Lorette, Le Vieux Memphis, Renaix 9600, Flandre Orientale, Belgium.

**SOUETOV Nicolay Micaylovich,** b. 6 August 1926, Saratov, Russia. Professor of Electronics. m. Victoriya, 2 sons. Education: Moscow Aviation Institute, 1949; Postgrad Student, Physical Faculty, Saratov State University, 1952; Dr Physics and Mathematics, 1952; Dr Industrial Arts, 1980; Professor of Electronics, 1981. Appointments: Student: Aviation College, Saratov, 1941-44, Moscow Aviation Institute, 1944-49; Postgrad Student, 1949-52; Assistant Professor, Saratov State University, 1952-56; Director of Professorship, Taganrog Radioinstitute, 1956-61; Director of Professorship then Professor of Electronical Device School, Saratov State Technical University, 1961-. Publications: Over 150 including: 5 scientific monographs; 6 belles-lettres. Memberships: Master of Sport USSR, yachtsmen; Member, Alliance Writers of Russia. Address: 2 Poperechnaya 205, Saratov 410053, Russia.

**SOULE Lucile Snyder,** b. 21 September 1922, Fargo, North Dakota, USA. Musician; Pianist Teacher. m. Leon C Soule dec, 1 son, 1 daughter. Education: BMus, BMusEd, MacPhail College of Music, 1943; MA, Smith College, Northampton,

1945; Postgraduate Diploma, Juilliard School of Music, 1948. Appointments: Organist, various churches in Montana, Louisiana and Ohio, 1935-68; Instructor, Smith College, Northampton, 1945-46; Freelance Pianist, Juilliard School of Music and Private Groups and Individuals, New York City, 1946-49; Instructor, Assistant, Associate Professor, Newcomb College, Tulane University, 1949-51, 1952-61; Staff Pianist, Soloist, New Orleans Symphony, 1954-61; Guest Artist, Contemporary Music Festival, LSU, Baton Rouge, 1953-61; Lecturer, Lakewood Branch, Ohio University, 1964-66; Music Teacher, East Cleveland Ohio Public Schools, 1969-85; Music Director, East Cleveland Theatre, 1985-; Pianist, Zhao Rongchun, Cleveland, 1995-. Publication: Master of the Erhu (cassette and CD), 1996. Honours: Scholarship, MacPhail College of Music, 1938-40, 1941-43; Teaching Fellowship, Smith College, 1943-45; Scholarship, Juilliard, 1946-48; Woolley Foundation Fellowship, 1950-51; Teaching Fellowship, CWRU, Cleveland, 1967-68. Memberships include: Darias Milhaud Society; New Orleans Music Teachers Association; Rocky River Chamber Music Society. Address: 15617 Hazel Road, East Cleveland, OH 44112, USA.

**SOUTHARD James B,** b. 31 March, Brooklyn, New York, USA. Lecturer; Painter. m. Katherine Folbert, 1 daughter. Education: National Academy of Design, 1939-41; Beaux Arts Institute of Design, 1941; Art Students League, 1946-49; Escuela de Pintura y Escultura, Mexico. Career: Palace Legion Honor, San Francisco, Stockton Museum of Art, Health Center No 3, Department of Health, San Francisco, San Francisco General Hospital, Carnegie Art Museum. Creative Works: Numerous exhibitions and one man shows. Honours: Home Savings Purchase Award; Awards of Merit. Memberships: Artists Equity Association; International Society of Artists; Society of Western Artists; East Bay Watercolor Society; Duchess County Art Association. Address: 100 Font Boulevard 4G, San Francisco, CA 94132, USA.

**SPAAR Friedrich-Wilhelm,** b. 19 March 1921, Dresden, Germany. Professor. m. Ursula Karheiding. Education: Medical Studies, Marburg, Lahn; State Examination and Graduation, Marburg, 1951; habilitation, 1975; Professor of Neuropathology, University of Göttingen, 1978; Specialist in Neurology, Psychiatry and Neuropathology-Histology. Appointments: Assistant Physician, 1951-52, Volunteer Assistant Physician, 1953-55; Assistant Research Physician, Max Planck Institute for Brain Research, 1956-62; Neurology Clinic, University of Göttingen, 1962-; Emeritus, 1986-. Publications include: Impfstoffprüfg Gegen Poliomyelitis; Akute nekrotis Encephalitis; Encephalitis Pette-Döhring; Polyneuritis mit Adrenalitis kindl Hirntrauma; Amyloidoma cerebri; CSF-Zytologie von Tumoren; FCM-DNA Messungen am Gewebe von Glioblastomen, Meningeomen; monographs: Die Menschl Herpes Simplex Encephalitis und Meningitis, 1976; Handbuch Clinische Neurologie (Vol 39); Paraproteinaemias and Multiple Myeloma, 1980. Honours: Iron Cross, 1st and 2nd Class, World War II; Gold Bar (for work at the front); Military Service Order of Savoy, Italy. Memberships: Naval Officers Association; Deutsche Gesellschaft für Neurologie; Deutsche Gesellschaft für Neuropathologie und Neuroanat; Pforter Bund und Verein d. ehem Schuler des Eberh-Ludwigs-Gymnasiums, Stuutgart. Address: Department of Neuropathology, Robert Kochstr 40, D-37075 Gottingen, Germany.

**SPAHIU Xhevahir,** b. 1 March 1945, Malind, Skrapar, Albania. Writer. m. Marjeta Qejvani, 2 sons. Education: University of Tirana, Faculty of History and Philology, Dept of Albanian Language and Literature; Department of Journalism, 1967. Appointments: Journalist, 1968-77; Editorial Board, 1978-86; Teacher, 1986-89; Libretto Ed, 1989-92; General

Secretary, 1993-98; Chairman, Writers' and Artists' League of Albania, 1998-. Publications: Books of poems, selected essays, translations etc. Honours: National Literature Award Migjeni, 1987, 1991; Literature National Award, 1989, 1994; Velia National Literature Award, 1996; and others. Memberships: Writers' and Artists' League of Albania; Albanian Helsinki Committee; Journalist Association of Albania. Address: Rruga Qemal Stafa, pall.217/1, shk.1, ap.6, Tirané, Albania.

**SPARR Marie-Brigitte,** b. 2 February 1958, Colmar, France. General and Vascular Surgeon. Education: Doctorate of Medicine, 1984; Residency, 1983-87; Fellowship, 1987-91; Qualification in Surgery, 1991; Senior Registrar, Cardio-thoracic Surgery, 1991, General and Digestive Surgery, 1994. Appointments: Hospitals of Paris, London, Montreal, Washington DC, Cleveland Clinic, Mayo Clinic. Honour: Member, New York Academy of Sciences. Memberships: European Digestive Surgery; Fellow, Royal College of Surgeons. Address: Ave de Brunerie, 77330 Ozoir-la-Ferrière, France.

**SPASIC Aleksandar Miodrag,** b. 28 December 1945, Belgrade, Serbia, Yugoslavia. Chemical Engineer. m. Dusica Popovic Jovan, 1 son. Education: BSc, 1977, MSc, 1989, PhD, 1992, University Belgrade, Yugoslavia; IAEA Fellow, 1983, OUN/CNRS, Odeillo, France. Appointments: R&D Engineer, 1978-81, Research Attached, 1984-86, Research Assistant, 1987-89, Research Associate, 1990-92, Research Fellow, 1993-, Institute Technology Nuclear Materials, Belgrade; IAEA Fellow, 1982-83. Publications: Author or co-author, 1 review paper, 10 original scientific papers, 3 patents, 50 congress presentations, 18 R&D Projects; Editor, Contributor, Reviewer, JCIS and Chemical Industry. Memberships: Serbian Chemical Society, Belgrade; Society Physical Chemists of Serbia, Belgrade; ElectroChemical Society, Penington, New Jersey; Radio Amateur Society of Yugoslavia; American Radio Relay League, Newington, USA. Address: ITNMS/86 F d'Esperey Street, PO Box 390, 11000 Belgrade, Serbia, Yugoslavia.

**SPENCER David Anthony,** b. 7 November 1963, Stepney, London, UK. Geologist. m. Cinzia, 1 daughter. Education: Bachelor of Science with Honours, Geology, University of Exeter, 1983-86; Diploma of Imperial College, Structural Geology and Rock Mechanics, University of London, 1987-88; Master of Science, Structural Geology and Rock Mechanics, University of London, 1987-88; Doctor of Natural Science, Tectonics of the NW Himalaya, Swiss Federal Institute of Technology, 1989-93. Appointments: Insurance Claims Broker Department, 1982-83; Platinum Exploration Geologist, Gencor, 1986-87; Visiting Scientist, University of Beijing, 1986; Pre-Doctoral Research Fellow, 1988-89, Research and Teaching Assistant, 1989-1992, Visiting Post Doctoral Research Fellow 1993-94, ETH-Zürich; Visiting Lecturer, University of Punjab, 1995; Visiting Scientist, TIT 1996; Post Doctoral Research Fellow, ETH-Zürich, 1994-97; Visiting Professor, University of the Punjab, Pakistan. 1997-; Senior Post Doctoral Research Fellow, various universities, 1997-; Research Assistant Professor, Lecturer, Structural Geology, University of Maine, 1997-98; Staff Geologist/Project Manager, Saga Petroleum ASA, 1998-. Publications: Over 200 Scientific Publications, articles, abstracts and reports. Many Postions of Responsibility; Many Scholarships and Awards. Memberships: Member of Many Societies. Address: P O Box 23, N-1312 Slependen, Norway.

**SPENTZAS Constantin,** b. 24 May 1944, Athens, Greece. Professor; Consulting Engineer. 1 daughter. Education: Certificate MPC, Mathematics, Physics, Chemistry, University of Paris, France, 1963; Diploma, Mechanical Engineering,

1968, Certificate, Postgraduate Studies, Physical Metallurgy, 1972, University of Lausanne Engineering School, Switzerland; )TechSc, Federal Technical University of Lausanne, 1972. Appointments: Assistant II, 1970-71, Assistant I, 1971-72, University of Lausanne Engineering School; Professor, Group of Technical Schools, Hellenic Army, 1973-78; Professor, Higher School of Engineers, Athens, 1974-75; Engineer, Public Petroleum Corporation, Athens, 1976-77; Engineer, Bureau of Military Works, Hellenic Army, Athens, 1977-78; Consulting Engineer, Independent, Athens, 1978-; Research Assistant, 1982, Lecturer, 1982-88, Professor, 1988-98, 1998-, National Technical University of Athens. Publications include: JOMINY Hardenability Tests, 1970; Mechanical Tests of Metals, 1970; On a Variational Method of Computation of Axisymetric Shells, 1976; Introduction to Vehicle Design, 1993; Vehicle Design, 1994. Honours: Diploma of Honour, Union of Hellenic Writers, 1996, Athens College. Memberships: Switzerland Society of Engineers and Architects; Hellenic Technical Chamber; USA Society of Automotive Engineers; AVERE-Greece; New York Academy of Sciences; Hellenic Leica Club of Photography. Address: Deliyanni 52, 14562 Kifissia, Athens Greece.

**SPERELAKIS Nicholas,** b. 3 March 1930, Joliet, Illinois, USA. University Professor. m. Dolores Martinis, 2 sons, 2 daughters. Education: PhD Physiology, 1957, University Illinois. Appointments: Associate Professor, Case Western Reserve University, 1957-66; Professor, University Virginia, 1966-83; Professor and Chairman, University Cincinnati, 1983-96; Eichberg Professor Emeritus, 1996-. Publications: Over 500 published papers; Several books. Honours: Distinguished Research Awards from American Heart Association, Ohio and SW Ohio. Memberships: American Physiological Society; Biophysical Society; International Society for Heart Research. Address: 12114 Paulmeadows Drive, Cincinnati, OH 45249, USA.

**SPINOSA Gary Paul,** b. 26 December 1947, Memphis, TN, USA. Visual Artist. Education: Yale Summer School for Art and Music, 1970; BFA, Cleveland Institute of Art, 1972; MFA, Edinboro University of Pennsylvania, 1988. Career: Independent Visual Artist. Honours: Ohio Arts Council Grant, 1978; Ohio Arts Council Fellowship, 1979; Cleveland Museum of Art Sculpture Award, 1981; Pennsylvania Council on the Arts Fellowship, 1988; Works in collector: Southern Alleghenies Museum of Art; The Butler Institute of American Art; Lock Haven University. Address: 22778 Blystone Road, Venango, PA 16440, USA.

**SPIRIDONOVA Irina,** b. 12 September 1938, Dniepropetrovsk, Ukraine. Researcher; Teacher of Physics. m. 1 son. Education: Master Degree, Metallurgical Institute, 1961; Doctor Degree, Solid State Physics, 1973; Professor, University, Dniepropetrovsk, 1987; Academician of Academy of Engineering Science of Ukraine, 1992. Appointments: Research Engineer of Dniepropetrovsk State University, 1961-72; Head, Research Laboratory of Applied Physics DSU, 1972-81; Professor of Chair of Physics of Metals, Supervisor of Research Department of Dynamic Metal-Physics of DSU. Publications: 250 papers, 48 patents. Honours: Honour of Labour; Bronze Medal of VDNKH of USSR; Bronze and Silver Medals of VDNKH of UkSSR. Memberships: ASM International; Editorial Boards of 2 scientific journals; National Welding Committee of Ukraine. Address: Department of Physics of Metals, Physical Faculty, Dniepropetrovsk State University, 13 Nauchny Lane, Dniepropetrovsk 10, 320625, Ukraine.

**SPIRNAK John,** b. 17 March 1951, Cleveland, Ohio, USA. Urologist. m. Diane, 2 sons, 1 daughter. Education: BS, Zoology, Ohio University, 1969-73; MD, Emory University,

Atlanta, 1973-77. Appointments: Senior Instructor, Case Western Reserve University, 1983-85; Consultant, Veterans Administration Hospital, 1984-; Assistant Professor, Case Western Reserve University, 1985-91; Associate Professor, 1991-; Director of Urology, Metro Health Medical Center, Cleveland, 1991-. Publications: 53 Publications; 80 Book Chapters; Many other publications. Honours: First Prize, Residents Essay Contest. Memberships: American Medical Association; North Central Section; American Urological Association; American College of Surgeons; The Cleveland Urological Society; Ohio Urological Society; Ohio State Medical Association; Endourological Society; American Association for Surgical Trauma; Lorain County Medical Center. Address: 2178 Silveridge Trl, Westlake, OH 44145-1797, USA.

**SPIVAK Maurice Sidney,** b. 1 January 1926, Milford, USA. Biochemist; Engineer. m. Annette, 1 son, 2 daughters. Education: BS, 1950; MS, 1955; Certificate, MIT, 1960; Certificate, Infrared Analysis, 1961-68; PhD, 1993. Appointments: Biochemist, Massachusetts General Hospital, 1950-52; Biochemist, Worcester Foundation, 1952-57; Chemical Engineer, Springfield Armory, 1957-66; Chemical Engineer, Edgewood Arsenal, 1967-73; Chief, Industrial Section, Supervisory Civil Engineer; Chief, Management Corps Engineering, 1980; USNR Engineering Officer, by Direct Commission. Honours include: Numerous Fellowships; Army Roll Economy Champion, 1956; US Army Bronze Star Medal; Worcester Foundation Fellowship, 1956; Who's Who. Memberships: American Society of Civil Engineers; American Electroplaters Society; Military Army Society; Professional Engineers Society. Address: US Army Corps of Engineers, 821 Jennings Street, Virginia Beach, VA 23464, USA.

**SPJELDVIK Walther Nordmann,** b. 4 May 1945, Bergen, Norway. Space Physicist; Professor; President. 2 daughters. Education: CMag, Mathematics and Physics, Faculty of Mathematics and Natural Sciences, University of Bergen, Norway, 1969; MS, Physics, Department of Physics, 1971, CPhil, Department of Meteorology, 1974, PhD, Department of Atmospheric Sciences, 1974, University of California, Los Angeles. Appointments: Adjunct Assistant Professor, Meteorology, University of California, Los Angeles, 1975; NAS Resident Research Associate, National Academy of Sciences, Washington,DC, 1976-77; Research Associate, Space Physics, University of Colorado, 1978-83; Senior Research Physicist, Department of Physics, Boston College, Massachusetts, 1983-85; Chief Scientist, Hughes STX Corporation, Maryland, 1990-91; President, Nordmann Research and Development Inc; Discipline Scientist, NASA Headquarters, 1992-94; Professor of Physics, Department of Physics, Weber State University, Utah, 1985-. Publications: Numerous articles in professional journals. Memberships: American Geophysical Union; European Geophysical Society; Sigma Xi; Phi Kappa Phi. Address: Department of Physics, Weber State University, Ogden, UT 84408-2508, USA.

**SPRAGUE Raymond,** b. 28 November 1947, Yonkers, New York, USA. Professor of Music; Choral Conductor. m. Kathleen Jane Turner. Education: BA, Williams College, Massachusetts, 1969; MMus, Theory and Composition, University of New Mexico, Albuquerque, 1973; DMA, Choral Performance and Literature, University of Colorado, Boulder, 1979. Appointments: Director of Choral Activities, St Mary's Church, 1977-84; Director, Choral Activities, Professor of Music, University of New Orleans, 1985-; Director of Music, St Charles Avenue Baptist Church, 1985-91; Founder, Artistic Director Louisiana Vocal Arts Choral, 1992-. Publications include: Literature of Quality for the Treble Choir, 1984; Music and Letters: 1920-1980. Honours: 1st Virginia Koch Endowed

Professor of Music, UNO, 1997-99. Memberships: American Choral Directors Association; Music Educators National Conference; College Music Society. Address: University of New Orleans, Department of Music, New Orleans, LA 70148, USA.

**SPROSTY Joseph,b.** 25 August 1947, Cleveland, Ohio, USA. Entertainment Industry Writer; Producer; Director; Actor. m. Education: Student, San Diego City College, 1972-73; Class 2 firearms license; Property Builder, the Gouliardi Show, Cleveland, 1962-65; Sub-Agent International Artists Agency, San Diego and LA, 1982-83; Casting Director, Cinemode Films, 1982; Operator, Owner Actors Artists Agency, LA, 1983-87; Founder, Producer, Director Magnum Prodns, 1985; Founder, Sprosty Productions, 1990; Demonstrator weapons and handling of weapons Beth Holmes, Propmaster TV Co, Van Nuys, California, 1992; Expect witness Laser WeaponsScam, 1984; Visiting lecturer, firearms safety, handling, rules and regulations governing use of firearms in motion picture, TV Productions U, SO, California, 1996-; Animal wrangler specialising in opossums; Scriptwriter, Vanishing Points II, The Apartment Manager, The Big House, Rambo III, Rambo IV, Boneyard, Mister Ed - Talking Again, Mister Ed, - Radio Talk, Brick, Life Plus One, Gun Slave, Fixation, Last Chance (renamed Terminal Virus), numerous others; Producer, Director Break Disc, 1985; Location Manager, Armourer, Weapons Specialist, Heat From Another Sun (retitled Maladiction), 1988; Armourer, 2nd Assistant Director, Associate Producer, Weapons Specialist, Provoked, 1989; Weapons Specialist, Armourer, Big City, 1990; Co-producer, Animal Wrangler, Weapons specialist, Opossum de Oro, 1996; Weapons specialist, Jake and the Fat Man, Black's Magic, Hill Street Blues, Murder She Wrote, On The Edge of Death, Emerald Point NAS, America's Most Wanted, FBI: The Untold Story, numerous others, Revolt, Rocky IV, Streets of Fire, Walk in the Sun, Cloak & Dagger, One Man's Poison, Killing Zoe, Desert Storm, The Movie, Live Shot, Outer Heat, Zipperhead, Four Minute Warning, The Robbery, Spirit, Texas Payback, High Adventure, The Waterfront, The Philadelphia Experiment II,Oppossum de Oro, Harlem Nights, Tango & Cash, Die Hard, Provoked, Beverly Hills Cop II, Big City, numerous others; Speaker Veterans Day California State University, Dominguez Hills, 1993; Served with USN, 1965-67; Memberships: ASTRA, SAG. Address: 305 South Lincoln Street, Burbank, CA 91506-2612, USA.

**SRAJER Val,** b. 4 September 1941, Klobuky, Czechoslovakia. Engineering Manager. m. Jarka, 1 son, 1 daughter. Education: Engineering Technologist, Industrial High School, Czechoslovakia, 1955-59; MEng, Industrial Engineering, Technical University, Faculty of Industrial Engineering, Czechoslovakia, 1959-64; PhD, University of Nottingham, England, 1983-87. Appointments : Assistant Professor, Department of Surveying, Technical University, Czechoslovakia, 1963; Military Training, 1965; Independent Engineer, 1967; Chief Engineer, Kam-Kotia Mines, Fort Nelson, British Columbia, Canada, 1969-71; Planning Engineer, Cominco Limited, Kimberley, British Columbia, 1971-75; Senior Field Engineer, Syncrude Canada Limited, Fort McMurray, Alberta, 1975-76; Head, Operations Research, Federal Government of Canada, Department of Energy and Mines, CANMET Mining Research Laboratory, Calgary and Devon, Alberta, 1976-90; Regional Manager, Federal Government of Canada, Department of Solicitor General, Saskatoon, 1990-. Publications: Several in journals and magazines. Memberships: Association of Professional Engineers, Canada; Chartered Engineer in UK; Canadian Engineering Institute; American Institute of Engineers; Industrial Engineering Society, Canada; Fellow, Institute of Engineers, England; EUR ING, European Federation of National Engineer, Associate Member;

International Who's Who of Professionals. Address: CSC-RHC Prairies, PO Box 9223, Saskatoon, SASK S7K 3X5, Canada.

**SREY Chanthy,** b. 9 November 1964, Cambodia Consultant; Agro-Economist. m. Kao Sokuntheavy, 1 daughter Education: BSc Agronomy, 1992; MSc Agricultural Systems 1995. Appointments: Agro-Economist, Consultant, Mekong River Commission and Asian Development Bank, Royal University of Agriculture. Publications: Farming Systems Practices in Tasa-any, 1991; Potentials and Constraints or Agricultural Production in Bati, Takeo, 1995; Development Potentials of Wasteland in the Tonle Sap Area, 1998 Memberships: Asian Institute of Technology Alumn Association; LIDEE Khmer; Royal University of Agriculture Address: 25E2 Road 199, Tuol Svay Prey 2, Chamcar Morn Phnom Penh, Cambodia.

**SRINIVASAN Indira,** b. 30 May 1938, Visakhapatnam Musician, Poet, Publisher. m. P K Srinivasan, 3 sons Education: Graduate, Music, Kalakshetra, Adyar and Centra College of Music, 1957; MA, Sociology, Mysore University Diploma, Officer Management, IIMS; MBA, Doctorate in Music California University; D Litt, International University Appointments: Temporary Teacher, Calcutta; Conducter Organiser of Councerts; Tutor, South Indian Classical Music Given Many Concerts; Musician, Self Employed. Publications Many Poems Published, International and National Monthlies and Annuals; Booklet, Indian Festivals and Culture. Honours Several Certificates, Testimonials and Gifts; Severa Certificates, Annual Hortocultural Exhibitions. Memberships World Centre of Tamil Studies; DDLA; World Tamil Writers Group; Writers Forum, Bihar. Address: 22 K South Ave Thiruvanmiyur, Chennai-41/TN 600041, India.

**SRISA-AN Wichit,** b. 22 December 1934, Chachoengsao Thailand. Rector. m. Sukon, 2 sons. Education: BA, Faculty of Arts, Chulalongkorn University, Thailand, 1959; BEd, Faculty of Education, 1961; MA,Educational Administration, University of Minnesota, USA, 1964; PhD, Educational Administration, 1967. National Defence College, Thailand, 1997. Appointments: Chief, Administrative Department, Chulalongkorn University, 1961-62; Principal, 1969-70; Administrative Secretary General. 1970-71; Acting Secretary General, 1971-72; Secretary General, 1972-73; Vice Rector, Planning and Development 1973-75; Secretary to the Ministry of University Affairs. 1973-74; Acting Secretary General, 1974; Director, University Development Commission, 1974-78; Deputy Permanent Secretary, Ministry of University Affairs, 1974-87; Acting Rector, Thammasart University, 1977; Acting Rector, Khon Kean University, 1978; Founding Rector, Sukhothai Thammathirat Open University, 1978-87; Permanent Secretary, Ministry of University Affairs, 1987-94; Director, Management Center, WORLDTECH 95, Thailand, 1995-. Publications: 3 Research Works; 10 Text Books; Approximately 60 Articles, Education, Domestic and International Journals. Honours: Distinguished Fellow, International Council on Education for Teaching, 1984; Doctor of the University, The Open University, 1986; Outstanding Civil Servant of the Year; Silver Conch Award; Honorary Degree of Doctor of Letters; Many other Honours. Memberships: International Council on Education for Teaching; Council of the United Nations; Many other memberships. Address: Suranaree Uni, 111 Univ, Muang Nakhon R, Thailand.

**SRIVASTAVA Radhey Shyam,** b. 7 June 1931, Bahadurganj, UP, India. Scientist. m. Vijay Laxmi, 1 son, 2 daughters. Education: BSc, 1951, MSc, 1953, PhD, 1963 Certificate in Proficiency in French, 1957, Lucknow University. Appointments: Research Fellow, Lecturer, Lucknow University

1954-58; Junior Scientific Officer, 1958-61, Senior Scientific Officer, 1961-71, Principal Scientific Officer, 1971-80, Defence Science Laboratory, New Delhi; Deputy Chief Scientific Officer, Defence Science Centre, New Delhi, 1980-91; Private Researcher, 1991-. Publications: 2 books: Turbulence (Pipe Flow), 1979; Interaction of Shockwaves, 1994; Several internationally recognised research papers. Honours: Five distinguished assignments abroad. Memberships: Life Fellow, National Academy of Sciences, India; Life member, Bharat Ganita Parishad, Lucknow University; Indian Science Congress, 1972-74. Address: A-3/260 Janakpuri, New Delhi 110058, India.

**SRIVASTAVA Suresh Chandra,** b. 16 December 1940, Saharanpur, India. Teacher. m. Padma Srivastava, 1 son, 1 daughter. Education: BSc, 1958; MSc, Physics, 1961; DPhil, 1964; German Diploma, 1964. Appointments: Lecturer, Physics, 1967-84, Reader, Physics, 1984-95, Professor, Physics, 1995-, Allahabad University. Publications: 30 research papers in national and international journals. Honour: Postdoctoral Fellow, Canada, 1976. Memberships: National Academy of Sciences, India; Institution of Electronics and Telecommunication Engineers, India. Address: Physics Department, Allahabad University, Allahabad 211002, India.

**STACHNIAK Donald Edward,** b. 1 August 1938, Chicago, Illinois, USA. Engineering Manager. m. Rita M Radous, 1 son, 2 daughters. Education: Physics, University of Chicago, 1969. Appointments: Founder, South Grove Water Utility; Founder Security Computer Systems. Publications: Several Articles in Power Engineering, Nuclear News. Memberships: American Nuclear Society. Address: Security Computer Systems, 164 W Sequoia Ct, Claremont, CA 91711-1763, USA.

**STACK Frank H,** b. 31 October 1937, Houston, Texas, USA. Artist. m. Mildred Roberta Powell, 1 son, 1 daughter. Education: BFA, University of Texas, Austin, 1959; School of the Art Institute of Chicago, 1960-61; MA, University of Wyoming, Laramie, 1963. Appointments: Associate, Fine Arts, The Houston Chronicle, 1959; Instructor, Through Ranks to Professor of Art, 1963-; Holder, Catherine Paine Middle Bush Chair of Fine and Performing Arts, University of Missouri, Columbia, Missouri, 1995-. Publications: Etchings and Lithography by Frank Stack, 1976; Dorman's Doggie, 1990; Our Cancer Year, 1993; Naked Glory: The Erotic Art of Frank Stack, 1997. Memberships: Kansas Watercolor Society; The Print Consortium. Address: 409 Thilly Avenue, Columbia, MO 65203-3458, USA.

**STAFF Sue-Ann Elizabeth,** b. 3 January 1971, St Catharines, Canada. Winemaster. Education: BSc Agriculture, Hons Horticulture, 1994, University Guelph, Canada; Graduate degree Oenology, 1996, University of Adelaide, Australia. Appointments: Trainee Winemaker, Simon Gilbert Wine Services, Upper Hunter, NSW, Australia; Winemaster, Pillitteri Estates Winery, Niagara-on-the-Lake, Canada. Publications: in Canadian Journal of Plant Science; Fruit Zone leaf removal influences vegetative, yield, disease, fruit composition and wine sensory attributes of Vitis vinifera L "Optima" and "Cabernet franc". Honours include: Canadian Figure Skating Association Triple Gold Medallist, 1990; Top Undergraduate Research Paper, American Society for Horticultural Science, 1993; Ontario Grape Growers Marketing Board Scholarship, 1995; Gold, Drinks China, 1998; Gold, International Wine Challenge, 1998; Silver, Pacific Rim Wine Competition, 1998; Gold, Air Ontario Wine Awards, 1998; Superlative, Beverage Tasting Institute, top scoring wine competition, 1999. Memberships: Winetasters Society of Toronto; Australian Wine Society; Ontario Institute of Agrologists. Address: Pillitteri Estates

Winery, 1696 Niagara Stone Road, Niagara on the Lake ON, Canada LO5 1JO.

**STAFFORD Preston Clay,** b. 23 December 1961, Chattonoga, Tennessee, USA. Writer; Film Director; Producer; Actor. m. Jacqueline Ellis. Education: BA, Film and Television, The Union Institute, 1989; MFA, Motion Pictures, University of Miami, 1992. Appointments: Studio Support Services Employee, Universal Studios, MCA Records, 1985-86; Assistant to the Director of Program Development, Producer, Writer, Director, WLRN TV, PBS, 1987-90; Writer, Director, Producer, Actor, The Clay Stafford Company, 1986-.Publications: Patterns of Power; Mazatlan Mangle; Lost Amulet of Abalone Cove; Proud to be Me; New Horizons in Bonsai; We Are Family; New Horizons in Bonsai II; For Lee's Sake; Bad Loch; Sewing Without Pins TV; How to Win Auditions, An Actors Guide to Success; Marine Inboard Diesel Engine Maintenance; Marine Inboard Gasoline Engine Maintenance; Many others. Honours: Southeastern Theatre Conference; Valediction Scholar; Chancellor's Scholar; Vocal Performance Scholar; Tennessee Theater Conference; Graduate Teaching Assistant; Many others. Memberships: American Federation of Television and Radio Artists; Authors Guild; Authors League Fund; Mortar Board Society; Screen Actors Guild; Toastmaster'sInternational; Williamson County Literary Council. Address: The Clay Stafford Co, P O Box 680686, Franklin, TN 37068-0680, USA.

**STALILIUNAITE Regina Ruta,** b. 21 January 1938, Siauliai, Lietuva, Lithuania. Actress. m. div. Education: Gruodis Conservatory, 1956-59; Diploma of Actress, 1963, Academy of Music. Career: Actress, Kaunas Drama Theatre. Honours: 1998 Lithuanian Government Award for Achievement in Arts and Culture; Knight of Lithuanian Grand Duke Gediminas Order; Cristophor Prize, Annual Theatre Award. Memberships: Association of Lithuanian Theatre; M K Ciurlionis Society. Address: Kestucio 87-1, LT 3000, Kaunas, Lithuania.

**STALLINGS Viola,** b. 6 November 1946, Norfolk, Virginia, USA. Certified Project Manager. 1 daughter. Education: Diploma, BT Washington High School, 1964; BS, Virginia State University, 1968; MBA, Wharton Graduate School, University of Pennsylvania, 1976; EdD, Nova Southeastern University, 1996. Appointments:Teacher/Supervisor, Peace Corps Volunteer, Liberia, 1968-71; Teacher and Substitute Teacher, Philadelphia School District, 1972-76; IBM Professional, 1976-. Memberships: ASCD; AAUW; AECT; World Affair Council of Philadelphia; PMI; International Platform Association; Women of the Arts; Beta Gamma Sigma Honor Society. Address: 105 Burnamwood Court, Mount Laurel, NJ 08054 3106, USA.

**STALLMAN Robert,** b. 12 June 1946, Boston, USA. Flautist. m. Hannah Woods. Education: BMus, 1968, MMus, 1971, New England Conservatory of Music; Paris Conservatoire, France, 1968-69. Career: Major solo performances include Carnegie Hall, Alice Tully Hall, Avery Fisher Hall (New York), Symphony Hall (Boston), Library of Congress (DC), Salle Pleyel (Paris), Suntory Hall (Tokyo), Wigmore Hall (London); Guest Artist appearances include American Symphony, Mostly Mozart Festival Orchestra, Netherlands Chamber Orchestra, Northern Sinfonia, Royal Philharmonic, Virtuosi di Praga, Lincoln Center Chamber Music Society, Speculum Musicae, Muir, Mendelssohn and Orion String Quartets; Festivals: Canada, Finland, France, Netherlands, Japan, Spain, USA; Founder, Artistic Director, Cambridge Chamber Players and Marblehead Music Festival, 1976-96; Radio and Television appearances: Nationwide USA, Canada, England, France, Spain; Recordings: works by JS Bach, Blavet, Dodgson, Handel, Leclair, McKinley, Mozart, Schubert, Telemann, Vivaldi, albums of American, French and 20th Century collections. Teaching: New England Conservatory, 1978-82, Académie Internationale d'Eté, France, 1985, Boston Conservatory, 1986-89, Queens College, New York, 1980-95, Masterclasses, Canada, England, France, Japan, Mexico. Publications: 30 performance editions, transcriptions, and technique books with International Music Co., G. Schirmer and Schott. Honours: Fulbright Grant, 1968-69; Chadwick Medal, 1968; Koussevitsky Fellowship, 1970; CD Jackson Prize, Tanglewood, 1970; 1st Prize, USA National Collegiate Artists Competition, 1970; Solo Recitalist Award, National Endowment for the Arts, 1983; Arcadia Foundation Grant, 1994. Membership: National Flute Association, USA. Address: 1530 Locust Street, Philadelphia, PA 19102-4415, USA.

**STAMATI Aleksi,** b. 29 July 1951, Saranda, Albania. Explorationist. m. Lindita, 1 son, 1 daughter. Education: Diploma, Physicist, 1974; Degree, Geophysics, 1976; Dr, 1990. Appointments: Director, Geology and Geophysics Company, Anglo Albanian Petroleum; Member of Board of Directors, Consultant Institution, National Petroleum Agency. Memberships: Geophysics Society, Albania; Physic Society, Albania. Address: Anglo Albanian Petroleum, Vila Lagia 29 Nentori, Fier, Albania.

**STAMBERG Susan Levitt,** b. 7 September 1938, Newark, New Jersey, USA. Broadcast Journalist. m. Louis C Stamberg, 1 son. Education: BA, 1959, Barnard College. Appointments: Producer, Programme Director, General Manager, NPR member station, WAMU-FM/Washington DC; Co-Host, NPR's newsmagazine, All Things Considered, 1972; Host, Weekend Edition/Sunday, NPR's morning newsmagazine, 1987-89; Guest Host, NPR's Morning Edition, Weekend Edition/Saturday, and Weekly Edition, current; Special Correspondent, National Public Radio; Anchor, National Nightly News Programme; Commentator, Guest or co-Host various commercial TV programmes; Narrator, St Louis and National Symphony Orchestras; Voice appeared on Broadway in Wendy Wasserstein's play, An American Daughter. Publications: 2 books; Co-editor, 1 book. Honours: Winner of every major award in broadcasting; Inducted into Broadcasting Hall of Fame, 1994, Radio Hall of Fame, 1996; Armstrong & Dupont Awards; Edward R Murrow Award, Corporation for Public Broadcasting; Distinguished Broadcaster Award, American Women in Radio and Television; Jefferson Fellowship for Journalism, East-West Centre in Hawaii. Memberships: Fellow, Silliman College, Yale University; Serves on boards of PEN/Faulkner Fiction Award Foundation and Columbia University's National Arts Journalism Programme. Address: National Public Radio, 635 Massachusetts Avenue NW, Washington DC 20001-3752, USA.

**STANASILA Octavian Nicolae,** b. 19 May 1939, Stoenesti-Olt, Romania. Mathematician. m. Tatiana, 1 son. Education: Graduate, Mathematics Faculty, 1960; PhD, 1969. Appointments: Researcher, 1960-73, Assistant Professor, 1973-77, Professor, 1977-, Head, Department of Mathematics, 1982-, University Polytechnica Bucharest. Deputy Minister, Ministry of Education, 1990. Publications: 75 scientific papers, 10 textbooks, 15 patents. Honours: Prize of Academy, 1974. Memberships: American Mathematical Society. Address: University Polytechnica Bucharest, Department of Mathematics, Splaiul Independentei 313, Bucharest, Romania.

**STANCEVICIUS Antanas,** b. 8 January 1920, Lomiai Village, Taurage Region. Diplomaed Agronomist. 1 son, 2 daughters. Education: Master of Science, 1943; Doctor of Biomedical Sciences, 1958; Associated Professor, 1961; Professor, 1991. Appointments: Professor, Agricultural Department, Lithuanian University of Agriculture, 1990-; Chairman, Lithuanian Chamber of Agriculture,1991-. Publications: Weed Control, 1948; Lithuanian Flora, II, III, IV, V, VI, 1962-82; Reference of Grain Crops and Leguminous Forage Plants, 1968; Field and Pasture Forage Plants, 1977. Honours: Honorary Doctor; Lithuanian Grand Duke; Gediminas Order; State Award Lecurate; Merited Agronomist. Memberships: Lithuanian Agronomists Union; European Weed Research Society. Address: Kestucio 27a-5, LT 3000, Kaunas, Lithuania.

**STANFORD Linda Oliphant,** b. 11 February 1946, Hollis, New York, USA. Art Historian; Art Administrator. m. Richard M Stanford, 1 son. Education: PhD, University of North Carolina, Chapel Hill, 1976. Appointments: Associate Dean, College of Arts and Letters, 1989-92; Assistant to Full Professor, Michigan State University, 1975-; Chair, Department of Art, 1993-. Honours: American Council on Education Fellow, 1989-90; Outstanding Faculty Woman, Faculty and Professional Women's Association, Michigan State University, 1991; Elected Member, Hall of Fame, Alumni Association of Hunter college, City University of New York, 1994. Memberships: College Art Association; Society of Architectural Historians. Address: Department of Art, 113 Kresge Art Centre, Michigan State University, East Lansing, MI 48824-1119, USA.

**STANIKUNAS Rimantas,** b. 17 August 1952, Lithuania. m. Irena, 1 son. Education: PhD, Economics. Appointments: Chairman of Competition Council. Address: Virsuliskiu 75-25, LT 2000, Vilnius, Lithuania.

**STANKEVICIENE-MARCINKEVICIUTE Virginia,** b. 30 December 1954, Vilnius, Lithuania. Sports Shooting Coach; Economist. m. Gediminas Stankevicius, 2 daughters. Education: Faculty of Economics, Vilnius University, 1973-78. Appointments: Coach, 1972-82, Chief Coach, 1982-92, Lithuanian Republic Council, Dinamo Sports Society; Coach, USSR Teens Team, 1985-87, USSR Women Team, 1987; Senior Economist, Vilnius University Red Cross Hospital, 1997-. Honours: Medal, Uz aukstus sportinius pasiekimus, for High Merits in Sports, 1972; Honour Certificate, Vilnius City Council for high Merits in European Championship, 1975, and LSSR Ministry of Interior for Merits in physical education and sports development, 1980; Mentioned in Soviet Lithuania encyclopedia in 2 vols; Gold Medal winner, European Championship, Skeet, Lachti, Finland, 1987; 2 Gold Medals for team training; Many times winner in Skeet and double trap championships. Address: Zalgirio 66, LT 2005, Vilnius, Lithuania.

**STANKEVICIUS Henrikas,** b. 29 October 1933, Kaunas, Lithuania. Veterinary Surgeon. m. Marija, 2 sons. Education: PhD, Biology, 1972; Senior Research Fellow, 1984; Dr Habil, Zootechnics, Biomedical Science, 1992; Professor, 1995. Appointments: Director, Siauliai District Veterinary Laboratory, 1964-74; Director, Swine Breeders Union, Jonava District, 1974-78; Laboratory Head, 1978-92; Senior Research Fellow, Lithuanian Food Institute, 1992-. Publications: 157 Publications, 1969-89; 15 Authorships. Honours: 15 Authorship Certificates; 16 Normative Technicion Documents; 4 Gold, 2 Bronze, Medals; 2 Honorary Diplomas. Memberships: Lithuanian Veterinary Academy; Lithuanian Academy of Sciences. Address: V Landsbergio-Zemkalnio 16-36, LT 3042, Kaunas, Lithuania.

**STANKOVIC Milorad Dragutin of Yugoslavia (Sir),** b. 1928, Leskovac, Srbija, Yugoslavia. Education: Medical Degree, University of Belgrade, 1955; Specialist, Pneumophthisiology, University of Belgrade, 1960, Graduate

Studies, Cardiorespiratory Pathology, 1970; Chief Physician, Primarius, 1971. Appointments: Military Physician, Dubrovnik, Yugoslavia, 1955-56; Pneumophthisiologist, Central Scholar Polyclinic, Belgrade; Director, Anti-Tuberculosis Dispensary, Stara Pazova, Indjiija and Pecinci, Yugoslavia, 1962; Chief, Anti-Tuberculosis Dispensary, T B Hospital, Apatin, Yugoslavia, 1964-73; Chief, Anti-Tuberculosis Dispensary Medical Center, Paracin, 1973-. Publications: Numerous books including: The Real View and the Prior Problems in the Fight Against Tuberculosis, 1972; Archives in the History of Medicine, 1982; Many articles in professional medical journals. Honours: Special Award, Albert Einstein Academy; Bronze Medal with Collar Ribbon; PhD honoris causa, Albert Einstein International Academy Foundation, 1984; Noble by Grant of Arms, Royal College of Heraldry, UK; World Decoration of Excellence, Historical Preservation of America, 1990. Memberships include: Commission for Medical Science, Serbia; Serbian Medical Association; Balkan Medical Union, Bucharest; Serbian Medical Intercommunity Organization. Address: Soliter 2, Lole Ribara, Paracin, SR Srbija, Yugoslavia.

**STANKUNAS Jonas,** b. 11 April 1949, Rokiskis, Lithuania. Professor of Electronics. m. Vladislava Stankuniene, 1 son, 1 daughter. Education: Diploma, College of Aviation, 1970; Diploma, Electronics Engineer, 1976; PhD, 1981; Associate Professor, 1990; Doctor Habilitus, 1995; Professor, 1996. Appointments: Technician on Avionics, Vilnius Airport, 1970-72; Engineer, 1972-75, Leader, Science Laboratory, 1973-87, Senior Engineer, 1975-78, Associate Professor, 1987-93, Vilnius Gediminas Technical University; Director, Antanas Gustaitis Aviation Institute, 1993, Professor, 1995-. Publications include: Super-Wide Band Tracts of the Travelling-Wave Catode-Ray Tubes. Honours: Lithuanian State Scientific Prize, 1997. Address: Taikos 24-4, 2029 Vilnius, Lithuania.

**STANTON Harry Edward,** b. 18 April 1932, Melbourne, Australia. Clinical Psychologist. m. Valerie Joy Hands, 1 son, 1 daughter. Eduction: BA, 1955; BEd, 1963; MA, 1969; PhD, 1972. Appointments: Lecturer, Senior Lecturer, Flinders University, South Australia; Director, Higher Education Research and Advisory, University of Tasmania; Private Practice, Clinical Psychologist. Publications: 9 books, numerous articles in professional journals. Memberships: Australian Psychological Society; International Society of Hypnosis; Australian Society of Hypnosis; American Society of Clinical Hypnosis. Address: 12 Sonning Crescent, Sandy Bay, Tas 7005, Australia.

**STAREVA Lilia Petrova,** b. 29 August 1954, Sofia, Bulgaria. Publisher. m. Plamen Starev, 1 son, 2 daughters. Education: Graduate, University of Sofia, 1977; PhD, 1991. Appointments: Expert, Research Institute of Culture, 1978-92; Owner and Director, Publishing House, Lista, 1992-. Publications: Author, Annunciation, 1989; Compiler, Editor:Bulgarian Folk Tales, 1993; Krali Marko, Bulgarian Folk Tales, Songs & Legends, 1995; Bulgarian Folk Proverbs, Sayings & Riddles, 1996; Children's Folklore Encyclopedia, 1996. Address: Publishing House Lista, Lulin Planina #4, 1606 Sofia, Bulgaria.

**STASHANS Arvids,** b. 29 December 1965, Kraslava, Latvia. Physicist. Education: BSc, University of Latvia, 1991; MSc, University of Latvia, 1991; PhD, Daugavpils Pedagogical University, 1993. Appointments: Assistant to Senior Scientist, Institute of Solid State Physics, 1989-95; Postdoctoral Position, Department of Quantum Chemistry, 1995-97; Professor, Department of Fisica, 1998-. Publications: More than 30 International Publications. Honours: Fellowship of Svenska Institute, 1993; Matsumae International Foundation, 1995. Memberships: New York Academy of Sciences, 1995-.

Address: Dept of Fisica, Escuela Politechnica Nacional, Apto 17-01-2759, Quito, Ecuador.

**STAUB August William,** b. 9 October 1931, New Orleans, USA. Retired University Professor. m. Patricia Gebhart, 1 daughter. Education: BA, English, MA, Theatre, 1958, PhD, Theatre, 1960, Lousiana State University. Appointments: Instructor, Theatre, Lousiana State University, 1957; Instructor, English, Eastern Michigan University, 1958-60; Assistant Professor, Speech and Theatre, University of Florida, 1960-64; Associate Professor, English and Drama, University of New Orleans, 1964-66; Professor of Drama, Head, Department of Drama and Communication, University of New Orleans, 1966-76; Professor, Head, Department of Drama, 1976-95, Professor Emeritus, 1996-, University of Georgia. Publications: Books: Creating Theatre; Introduction to Theatrical Arts; Varities of Theatrical Art; Several professional articles in journals, 4 chapters in books, 2 monographs, 4 produced plays. Honours include: Lifetime Achievement Award, Southwest Theatre Conference, 1986; Fellow, Southwest Theatre Association, 1996. Memberships: College of Fellows of the American Theatre; National Theatre Conference; National Association of Schools of Theatre; American Society for Theatre Research; International Federation for Theatre Research; Congress of European Theatres; Southwest Theatre Association; Society for Science & Literature. Address: 400 Ponderosa Drive, Athens, GA 30605-3324, USA.

**STEELE-EYTLE C Michael,** b. 28 May 1951, Port of Spain, Trinidad. Teacher; Conductor. Education: BMus, 1975, MMus, 1991, Temple University. Career: Baritone; Educator; Musical Director; Composer; Arranger. Creative Works: Numerous educational and professional performances in Eastern and Western Europe, USA, England, South America and West Indies. Memberships: Conductors Guild; Music Educators National Conference; American Choral Directors Association. Address: 4503 Chester Avenue, Philadelphia, PA 19143-3706, USA.

**STEFANOV Stefan Minev,** b. 8 August 1964, Sevlievo, Bulgaria. Professor of Mathematics. Education: BA, 1986; BSc, 1988; MS, 1989; MEd, 1989; PhD, 1991; DSc, 1996. Appointments: Assistant Professor, 1991-96, Associate Professor, 1996-97, Professor, 1997-, Neofit Rilski South-West University, Blagoevgrad. Publications: 4 textbooks and monographs; 36 papers in professional journals. Honours: Medal of the Ministry of Education, Republic of Bulgaria, 1982; Awards for contribution to mathematics/science, 1996, 1998 Memberships: Union of Bulgarian Mathematicians; Union of Bulgarian Scientists; AMS; Mathematical Programming Society, USA; Society for Industrial and Applied Mathematics (SIAM), USA; SIAM Activity Group on Optimization; London/European/Canadian Mathematical Societies; Canadian Applied and Industrial Mathematics Society; IEEE Computer Society. Address: 4 Ilio Vlaev Str, 5400 Sevlievo, Bulgaria.

**STEIN Robert A,** b. 5 August 1933, Duluth, Minnesota, USA. Writer; Educator; The Black Samaritan. m. Betty L Pavlik, 3 sons. Education: BSc Industrial Management, 1956, MA Counselling/Education, 1968, MA Writing, 1986, University of Iowa; Permanent Professional Counselling/Teaching Certificate, 1968; Various Air Force Schools and Colleges. Appointments: Officer and Pilot, USAF, 1956-77; Director, Safety and Security Department, University of Iowa Hospitals, Clinics in Iowa City, 1977-85; Writer, Educator, 1985-; Faculty Writing Division, Kirkwood Community College, Iowa City, 1985-89; Instructor, Creative Writing Program, Iowa City, Johnson County Senior Centre, 1994-. Publications: Books: The Chase, 1988; Apollyon: A Novel, 1985; The Black

Samaritan, 1997; Also short stories, articles and his flying story, Death Defied. Honours: Inducted into Minnesota Authors' Collection, 1987; His books are in a special collection in the Duluth Public Library, and in the Iowa Authors' Collection, 1985; International Literary Award for Excellence, for Death Defied, 1988; Selected to be in first edition of Directory of Iowa Artists, 1996; 9 Air Force Service Awards and Medals for Merit; 5 Combat Medals including the Bronze Star; One of only 10 honoured 1967-68 Outstanding Faculty at the University of Iowa. Memberships: include: The Authors' League of America; The Authors' Guild; Iowa Authors' Collection; Minnesota Authors' Collection; Rotary International, Paul Harris Fellow; AFA, Lifetime member; Military Affairs Association, Charter member. Address: 2020 Ridgeway Drive, Iowa City, IA 52245, USA.

**STEINBERG Mark David,** b. 8 June 1953, San Francisco, CA, USA. Historian; Teacher; Administrator. m. Jane T Hedges, 1 s. Education: BA, University of California, 1978; MA, 1982; PhD, 1987. Appointments: Acting Instructor, University of California, 1986; Visiting Instructor, University of Oregon, 1987; Assistant Professor, Harvard University, 1987-89; Assistant Professor, Associate Professor, Yale University, 1989-96; Professor of History, University of Illinois, 1996-98; Helen Corley Petit Professor, 1998-99; Associate Professor, 1998-; Director, Russian and East European Center, 1998-. Publications: The Fall of the Romanovs: Political Dreams and Personal Struggles in a Time of Revolution; Moral Communities: The Culture of Class Relations in the Russian Priniting Industry; Untimely Thoughts: Essays on Revolution, Culture and the Bolsheviks; Many others. Honours: National Endowment for the Humanities; William and Flora Hewlett Summer International Research Grant; A Whitney Griswold Faculty Research Award; George and Gladys Queen Excelence in Teaching Award; Sarai Ribicoff Prize for Teaching, 1993; Many others. Memberships: American Association for the Advancement of Slavic Studies; American Historial Association; At Petersburg Academy for the Humanities. Address: University of Illinois Urbana Champaign, Department of History; 309 Gregory Hall, 810 S Wright St, Urbana, IL 61801, USA.

**STEJSKALOVA Marina Anatolievna,** b. 13 November 1957, Astrachan, Russia. Music Scientist. m. Jirí Stejskal, 2 daughters. Education: Diploma, Music Scientist, Novosibirsk Music Academy, 1981; Doctorate in Music Science, Masaryk University, Brno, 1988. Appointments: Novosibirsk Music Academy, Russia, 1981-83; Masaryk University, Brno, Czech Republic, 1983-88; Music Therapist, Motol Children;s Hospital Psychiatric Clinic, Prague, 1998-. Publications: Janácek's Russian Operatic Fragments, 1988; Janácek's Conception for Russian Town, 1994; Janácek's Collection of Russian Speaking Motives, 1997. Membership: Janácek Music Association. Address: Ciolkovskeho 849, 16101 Prague 6, Czech Republic.

**STELIAN Stojanov,** b. 16 August 1955. Artist. m. Dona Stelianova, 1 son. Membership: Union of Bulgarian Artists. Address: Debritch 9300, Drigba 3 41 7, Bulgaria.

**STENFLO Lennart,** b. 27 November 1939, Eksjo, Sweden. Professor. m. Karin Elmhed, 2 sons, 1 daughter. Education: PhD, 1968, Uppsala University, Sweden. Appointments: Professor of Physics, Umea University, Sweden, 1971-. Publications: Papers in scientific journals in field of plasma physics and space physics. Membership: Royal Swedish Academy of Sciences. Address: Department of Plasma Physics, Umea University, S 90187 Umea, Sweden.

**STEPANIAN Arnold,** b. 15 May 1931, C Baku, Azerbaijan Astrophysicist. m. Nataly Stepanian, 2 sons. Education: Physical Department (Faculty), Moscow University, Physicist Appointments: Scientist, Crimean Astrophysical Observatory, 1955; PhD, Moscow Institute of Nuclear Physicst, 1963; Senior Scientist, 1968; Head of Laboratory, 1979; Dr of Science, 1982. Honour: Badge of Honour, 1976. Memberships: International Astronomical Union, 1965-; Council on Cosmic Ray Problem of the USSR's Academy, 1970-. Address: Crimean Astrophysical Laboratory, p/o Nauchny, Crimea 334413, Ukraine.

**STEPANOV Nikolay,** b. 30 April 1936, Bayaulovo, Russia. University Professor. m. Eleonora Krikunova, 3 daughters. Education: MSc, 1958, PhD, 1964, DSc, 1979, University of Nizhny Novgorod. Appointments: Assistant Professor, General Physics Department, University of Nizhny Novgorod, 1961-65, Associated Professor, 1965. Publications: More than 150 articles; Merited Worker of Science of Russia, 1987; Fulbright Grantee, 1993; Soros Professor, 1997. Membership: Vice President, Nizhny Novgorod Region Physical Society. Address: 23 Gagerin Avenue, 603600 Nizhny Novogord, Russia.

**STEPHEN Rajan Samson,** b. 2 June 1951, Mayyanad. Freelance Writer. m. Annaamma, 1 son, 1 daughter. Education: BA Hons, Economics, University of Bombay, 1974. Appointments: Gandhi Peace Foundation, New Delhi; Technical Aluminium Industries, Ajman, UAE, USSR Book Centre, New Delhi. Publications: Fettered Verse; My Mango Tree; Situation Vacant; On a Rainy Night; One Word; Deep and Dark; Father; Love; How Green is Kerala. Membership: Writers Forum, Ranchi. Address: Pavel purayidom House, Kackottumoola, Mayyanand PO, Kollam, 691 303 India.

**STEPHENS Wanda Brewer,** b. 6 November 1932, Bolckow, Missouri, USA. Social Services Administrator. m. Lloyd W Stephens, 1 son, 3 daughters. Education: BS, Home Economics, 1954, MS, Home Economics, 1958, University of Arkansas. Appointments: Home Economics Teacher, West Fork, Arkansas, 1954-58; Developmental Child Care Association President, 1971-74; Infant Development Center President, 1972-75, Treasurer, 1975-81; American Association of University Women, Fayetteville, President, 1976-79; League of Women Voters, Washington County, Arkansas, President, 1979-83; National Organization for Women Fayetteville, Arkansas, President, 1983-89, State President, 1991-93, State Vice President, 1993-. Honours: International 4-H Youth Exchange, 1953-54; Infant Development Center Founder Plaque, 1987; Lay Person of the Year, Central United Methodist Church, 1977; Mental Health Association Community Service Award, 1972; American Civil Liberties Union Susan B Anthony Award, 1985; Arkansas Women's Political Caucus Uppity Women Award, 1987, 1992. Address: 1177 E Ridgeway Drive, Fayetteville, AR 72701-2612, USA.

**STEPHENSON Frank Alex,** b. 4 May 1940, Helena, Montana, USA. Professional Engineer. m. Brenda Vitales, 1 son, 2 daughters. Education: BS, Civil Engineering, 1967; MS, Civil Engineering, 1973; PhD, Environmental Engineering, 1975. Appointments: Registered Professional Engineer, South Dakota, 1971-; Consulting Engineer, 1975-. Honours: World Health Organization Scholarship, 1972; Ernest Coor Research Fellowship, 1973. Memberships: American Society of Civil Engineers; American College of Forensic Examiners. Address: 1702 East Aurelius Avenue, Phoenix, AZ 85020, USA.

**STEPHENSON Maureen,** b. 29 March 1932, New York. Author. m. Robert Evarts, 1 son, 1 daughter. Education: Associate Science degree, 1951, New York State University; Journalism, 1976, University of California at Los Angeles; PhD,

Biblical Studies, American College, Minnesota; Theology, 1982, PWM Ministry, Los Angeles; Ministerial Ordination, Non-Denominational, 1983, Unlimited Faith Ministry, Fontana, California. Appointments: Journalist and Editor of Special Sections, Burbank Daily Review Newspaper, 1977-78; Free-lance Journalist, TV Guide, American Newspaper Chain, 1979-80; Secretary-Treasurer, 1982-85, Prison Chaplain, 1983-85, Unlimited Faith Ministry, California; Chaplain/Counsellor, Olive View Medical Centre, California, 1985-86; Chaplain, St Jude's Home for Women, Santa Clarita, 1986-90; Executive Administrator, International Technical Services, Sherman Oaks, California, 1986; Owner, MWS Business Services, Sherman Oaks, 1987-88; Executive Assistant to VP, CIGNA HealthCare of California, Glendale, 1988-96; Owner-Publisher and Advertising Consultant, REMS, Valencia, California, 1996-. Publications: 6 books on Home-Based Businesses and Entrepreneurial Success, 1998; 2 children's books, 1996, 1997; Poem, Robin, 1998. Honours: Mass Media Award, Burbank Exchange Club, 1978; Recognition Award, Burbank Women's Chamber of Commerce, 1978; Guest Speaker, Women's Career Conference, College of the Canyons, Santa Clarita, 1998. Memberships: Board of Directors, Home Visitation Centre, Pacoima, California; American Association University Women, Washington DC; Highlanders Club, Baltimore; Past President and Charter member, Naomi's Hope of St Jude's Home, Santa Clarita; World Jewish Congress, Washington DC; National Association for Female Executives, Escondido, California. Address: 21310 Seep Willow Way, Canyon Country, CA 91351, USA.

**STERE Constantine Aurel,** b. 21 May 1944, Cocisc Snagov, Romania. International Consultant. m. Georgeta, 2 sons. Education: MSc, Civil and Hydraulic Engineering, Bucharest, Romania, 1967; Diploma, Hydrolic Engineering, Netherlands, 1969-70; PhD, Hydraulic Engineering, 1977. Appointments: Researcher, Institute of Hydraulic Research, Bucharest, 1967-75; Assistant Professor, 1977-80; Professor, Port and Coastal Engineering, 1981-91; Researcher, CNB, Lyon, France, 1991-92; International Consultant, Haskoning, Nehterlands, 1991-. Publications: 4 Books; More than 90 Scientific Papers. Honours: Honorary Member, US PIANC; Distinguished Leadership Award. Memberships: PIANC, International; ICOLD. Address: Mozartstraat, Elst Gelderlan, Netherlands.

**STERZL Ivan,** b. 10 January 1954, Prague, Czech Republic. Physician. 1 son. Education: MD, 1979, PhD, 1985, Research Assistant, 1982, Assistant Professor, 1991, Associate Professor Clinical Immunology, 1997, Charles University. Appointments: Postdoctoral Fellow, Research Institute Endocrinology, 1982; Chief of Laboratory, 1986; Head of Department, 1993-; Visiting Scientist, UT, SWMC, 1989-91; Consultant, University Alabama, Birmingham, 1997. Publications: 105 publications; 7 monographs. Honour: Grantee in field. Memberships: International Union of Immunological Societies; International Brain Research Organisation, Purkynje Society. Address: Praha 4, Kvetnoveho vitezstvi, 1629 Czech Republic.

**STEVENS Kenneth John,** b. 29 June 1946, Tekuiti, New Zealand. Professor. m. Susan Mary Tatham Stevens, 2 daughters. Education: BA, University of Waikato, Hamilton, New Zealand, 1969; DipEdSt, University of Waikato, Hamilton, New Zealand, 1972; MSocSc, University of Waikato, Hamilton, 1975; PhD, James Cook University of North Queensland, Townville, Australia, Faculty of Education, 1989. Appointments: Temporary High School Teacher, 1967, 1968, English and French, Te Kuiti High School, Te Kuiti, New Zealand; High School Teacher, English and Social Studies, Fairfield College,

Hamilton, New Zealand, 1971-72; Tutor in Sociology, Department of Sociology, School of Social Sciences, University of Waikato, 1973; Junior Lecturer, Faculty of Education, Victoria University of Wellington, 1974-75; Lecturer, Faculty of Education, James Cook University of North Queensland, Townville, Queensland, Australia, 1976-80; Lecturer in Education, Department of Education, Victoria University of Wellington, Wellington, New Zealand, 1980-83; Senior Lecturer in Education, 1983-90, Senior Lecturer in Education, 1984-91, Senior Lecturer in Education (extended scale), 1992-96; Department of Education, Victoria University of Wellington, New Zealand; Professor of Education, 1997, Chair of Telelearning, 1997, Faculty of Education, Memorial University of Newfoundland, St Johns, Newfoundland, Canada. Publications include: Management, Technology and Future Directions in Distance Education in New Zealand, Wellington, 1991; Contemporary Developments in Learning and Instruction by Distance Education In New Zealand, 1991; The Learner - Proceedings of the Seventh Annual Conference of the Distance Education Association of New Zealand, 1992. Chair of Telelearning, Faculty of Education. Honours: Post Primary Teachers' Studentship, 1966-68; Lincoln University College Foundation Travel Award, 1988; Honorary Fellow of Hughes Hall, 1990; New Zealand Vice Chancellor's Committee Claude McCarthy Fellow, 1992-93; Bicentennial Fellow, Northern College, Aberdeen, Scotland, 1997. Memberships: Canadian Association of Distance Education; Commonwealth Council for Educational Administration; Distance Education Association of New Zealand; National Rural and Small Schools Consortium; New Zealand Association for Research in Education; New Zealand Institute of Management, Associate Fellow; Rural Education Reference Group New Zealand; Wellington Institute for Educational Research. Address: Chair of Telelearning, Faculty of Education, Memorial University of Newfoundland, St John's N7, Canada A1Q 557.

**STEWARD Harold (Hal) David,** b. 2 December 1918, East St Louis, Illinois, USA. Author; Journalist. Education: LLB, 1949, LaSalle Extension University, Chicago; BS, 1961, Boston University; PhD Economics, 1979, Columbia Pacific University, San Rafael. Appointments: High Official under Ronald Reagan in California State Government; Staff Reporter, Los Angeles Examiner and San Diego Union; Executive Editor, The Daily Chronicle; Centralia Washington; National Correspondent, North American Newspaper Alliance; Foreign Correspondent, Copley News Service; Instrument rated commercial pilot; Certified flight instructor; Retire US Army Lieutenant Colonel. Publications: 6 books including 2 fiction and Money Making Secrets of the Millionaires, 1970; The Successful Writer's Guide. Memberships: The Author's Guild; The National Press Club; The San Diego Press Club; Society of Professional Journalists; Rancho Bernardo Press Club; San Diego Press Club. Address: 5240 Fiore Ter #J-306, San Diego, CA 92122-5636, USA.

**STEWART Bobby G,** b. 18 April 1940, Jesse, West Virginia, USA. Medical Technologist. m. Linda M Smith, 2 daughters. Education: Medical Laboratory Technology Course, Brooke Army Medical Centre, Fort Sam, Houston, Texas, 1959-60; Advance Blood Banking Course, 10th Medical Research Lab, Landstuhl, Germany, 1961; Continuing Educations courses at various universities and numerous workshops, scientific seminars and lectures. Appointments: US Army Hospitals and Medical Facilities, US and Europe, 1959-62; Chief Medical and X-Ray Technologist, Oceana Medical Centre, West Virginia, 1962-68; Clinic Manager and Medical Technologist, Sigourney Medical Clinic, Iowa, 1968-70; Staff Medical and X-Ray Technologist, Van Buren County Memorial Hospital, Keosauqua, Iowa, 1970; Laboratory Director and Chief Medical and X-Ray Technologist, Scotland County Memorial Hospital, Memphis, 1970-71; Director of Medical Laboratory Services, Keller Memorial Hospital, Fayette, Missouri, 1971-95; Director of Laboratory Services, Keller Medical Laboratory, 1995-97; Staff Medical Technologist, Regional Medical Plaza, Woodrail Lab, Columbia, Missouri, 1997-; Acting Mayor, 1982, Mayor Pro-Tem, 1979-83, City of Fayette, Missouri. Honours: Various Achievement Awards and Exceptional Merit Awards as Medical Technologist; Albert M Keller Memorial Hospital Nominee for Employee of the Year Award, 1977-80, 1985, 1990; National Silver Service Award, American Medical Technologists, 1997. Memberships: American Society for Medical Technology; Clinical Lab Management Association; Missouri League of Nursing Home Administrators; Missouri State Society of American Medical Technologists; American Medical Technologists. Address: 410 Cooper Street, Fayette, MO 65248-9630, USA.

**STEWART Patricia Ann,** b. 23 September 1940, Australia. Sociologist. m. Terry, 1 son, 2 daughters. Education: BA, University of New South Wales, 1986. Appointments: Research Officer, Australian Multiple Birth Association; Manager, Stock Broking; Senior Lecturer, Securities Institute of Australia. Publications: Parenting Triplets. Memberships: Australian Multiple Birth Association; Australian Twin Register; International Society for Twin Studies. Address: 7/44 Waratah Avenue, Randwick, Sydney, NSW 2031, Australia.

**STEWART Tonea,** b. Greenwood, Mississippi, USA. Tenured Professor; Director of Theatre Arts; Actress. m. Dr Allen Stewart, 3 children. Education: BS Speech and Theatre, Jackson State University; MA Theatre Arts, University California at Santa Barbara; Doctoral studies, Florida State University, 1989; PhD Theatre Arts, FSU School of Theatre; McKnight Doctoral Fellow in Theatre Arts; Fellowship, National Endowment for the Humanities. Appointments: Teacher, role model, Mentor, Director of Theatre Arts, tenured Professor, Alabama State University; Professional Actress, 1969-; Theatre Artists Performance School and Camp 3T (Teaching Through Theatre) summer performance and enrichment camps; Performed on stage throughout the United States, including Carnegie Hall and the Kennedy Center, and internationally in Canada, Mexico, South Korea; Appeared on screen and television; Notable titles include: A Time to Kill; Mississippi Burning, Invasion of the Body Snatcher III, Living Large, My Stepson/My Lover, Walker, Texas Ranger, Matlock, Leave of Absence, I know Why the Caged Bird Sings. Honours: Inducted into the National Black College Alumni Hall of Fame, 1995; NAACP Image Award nomination for A Time to Kill, 1997; World Gold Medal Winner, Best Narrator Internationally, New York World Festival, 1999; First African American female to receive a doctorate from FSU School of Theatre; First African American to direct and appear on stage at New Stage Theatre; Honorary doctorates from Buenos Vista University, Iowa; Jarvis Christian College, Hawkins, Texas; Numerous keys to cities throughout the USA. Memberships: Order of the Golden Circle; Life Member, NAACP; Zeta Phi Beta Sorority Inc; Hutchinson Baptist Church. Address: Alabama State University, Dept Theatre, Montgomery, AL 36101, USA.

**STICKLER John Cobb,** b. 18 July 1937, Washington, USA. Journalist; Author. m. Lucy Han, 1964, 2 sons. Education: BA, Honors, Yale University, 1959; Certificate, Peace Corps, Pennsylvania State University, 1961; CBS Radio News, Seoul, Korea, 1967-76; Owner, Manager, S/K International Advertising, Seoul, 1966-76; Publisher, Owner Journal Applied Management, Walnut Creek, California, 1978-81; Account Executive, Cunningham & Walsh, San Francisco, 1981; Director, Marketing Neighbourhood Housing Services, Tucson,

1982; Director, Public Relations Sheraton Tucson El Conquistador Resort, 1983-92; Editor, Aging Well Newsletter. Publications: Books: Editor, Advertising in Korea, 1973, 2nd revised edition, 1975; Growing Up Afraid, 1985; Contributor, Exporting to Mexico, 1992; Berlitz American Southwest, 1993; Fodor's B&B Guide, Southwest, 1994; Fodor's Southwest's Best Bed and Breakfasts, 1996; Author: Exporting to the USA, 1992; Contributor, numerous articles to magazines. Honours: Served with US Army, 1962-64; Recipient, advert prize Hotel Sales and Marketing Association, 1974; CLIO Award, 1975; Poetry Award, National Writers Club, 1978. Memberships: Public Relations Society America, President So Arizona Chapter, 1991; America Society Journalists and Authors; International Association Business Communicators, President, Tucson Chapter, 1985-86; Society Southwestern Authors, President, 1988-90; UNESCO Association USA, Board Directors, 1981-90; International Advert Association, Founder Korea Chapter, 1967; Society American Travel Writers; Royal Asiatic Society, Korea Branch; Tucson Press Club; UN Association Southern Arizona; Yale Club Tucson, Vice President, 1988. Address: PO Box 358, Aromas, CA 95004, USA.

**STIGEBRANDT Anders Gosta,** b. 10 November 1942, Uddevalla, Sweden. Oceanography Educator; Researcher. m. Siv Lilian Emanuelsson, 3 sons. Education: PhD, 1978, Goteborg University, Sweden. Appointments: Educational and Research Assistant, Goteborg University, 1968-73; Scholar, Nordic University Group for Phys Oceanography, 1973-74; Researcher, SINTEF, Trondheim, Norway, 1974-76; Assistant Professor, Goteborg University, 1977-83; Professor Oceanography, 1986-; Senior Researcher, Swedish Natural Science Research Council, 1983-86; Chairman, Nomination Committee, Stockholm Water Prize, 1998-; Consultant to Institute Marine Research Bergen, Norwegian Institute Water Research Oslo. Publications: Contributor articles to professional journals, chapters to books; Author computer programmes for computation of ocean circulation and environmental effects of fish farming, sewage etc. Honours: Recipient, Fridtjof Nansen Medal, European Geophysics Society, 1996; Fellow, Royal Swedish Academy Sciences. Address: Goteborg University, Department Oceanography, Earth Sciences Centre, PO Box 460, 40530 Goteborg, Sweden.

**STIGLITZ Beatrice,** b. 24 April 1945, Russia. Professor. Education: MS, Romania, 1963; BA, Hunter College, 1970; MA, Sorbonne, Paris, France, 1971; MPh, 1978; Graduate, School of CUNY, French Literature, 1981; Appointments: Lecturer, ORT School, NY, 1977-78; Instructor, University of Vermont, 1978-79; Professor, French and Italian, University of Charleston, 1979-. Publications: Research Publications; Newspaper Reviews. Honours: Phi Kappa Phi; Pi Delta Phi; Distinguished Teaching Award; Golden Key Award. Memberships: Modern Language Association; American Organisation of Teachers of French. Address: 186 Queen St, Charleston, SC 29402, USA.

**STOKES Alexia,** b. 1 December 1968, Dublin, Eire. Researcher; Lecturer. Education: BSc Hons Botany, University Newcastle Upon Tyne, UK, 1990; DPhil Biology, University York, UK, 1994. Appointments: Guest Scientist, Forschungszentrum Karlsruhe, Germany, 1994-95; Researcher, INRA, Bordeaux, France, 1995-97; Researcher, Lecturer, University Bordeaux I, France, 1997-. Publications: Articles in international scientific journals. Address: LRBB BP 10, Domaine de L'Hermitage, 33610 Cestas-Gazinet, France.

**STOLBOV Vladimir I,** b. 26 February 1932, Kirov, Russia. Mechanical Engineer. m. Eleonora A Stolbova, 1 son, 1

aughter. Education: Ural Polytechnic Institute, 1954; Candidate of Technical Science, 1965; Doctor of Technical Science, 1984. Appointment: Rector, Togliatti Polytechnic Institute. Publications: Over 200 scientific works. Honour: Medal, 100 years since Lenin's Birthday, 1970. Memberships: International Institute of Welding, 1996. Address: 14 Byelorusskaya Street, Togliatti, Samara 445002, Russia.

**STONE Dulcie May,** b. 29 May 1924, Melbourne, Australia. Teacher, Author. m. David, 1 son, 3 daughters. Education: Victoria Education Department, 1940-42. Appointments: Student Teacher, Victorian Education Department, 1940-42; Metrology Laboratory Assistant, Department of Aircraft Production, 1942-44; Kindergarten Teacher, Sunraysia Non Profit Kindergarten, 1948-51; Principal, W J Christie Centre, Mildura, 1959-83; Foundation Principal, Handfield Park, 1983-85; Foundation Co-ordinator, Tutor, Upper Yarra Community House, 1987-88; Tutor, Springdale Community Cottage, 1992-; Tutor, Geelong, 1996-. Publications: 8 non-fiction publications; 5 fiction publications; various articles and papers. Honours: Honorary Life Governor, Royal Childrens Hospital, 1962; Life Member, W J Christie Centre, 1979; MBE, 1981; Community Service Award, 1983; Finalist, Upper Yarra Citizen of the Century Award, 1988-98; Apostolic Blessing, 1989; Community Service Award, 1990; Life Member, Upper Yarra Community House Inc, 1990; International Woman of the Year, International Biographical Center, 1996-97. Memberships: W J Christie Centre, 1959-82; Mildura Residentials for People with Intellectual Disability; Mildura and District Educational Council; OPTIONS; Melba Day Centre; Outer East Regional Planning Committee; Council of Women; Warburton Annual Book Fest; Karingal; SpringDale Community Cottage Inc; Geelong Adult Education and Training; Springdale Writers; VALID. Address: 15 Central Rd, Clifton Springs, Australia 3222.

**STONE John Owen,** b. 31 January 1929, Perth, Western Australia. Columnist. m. Nancy Enid, 4 sons, 1 daughter. Education: BSc, Hons, University of Western Australia, 1950; BA, Hons, University of Oxford, 1954. Appointments: Assistant to the Australian Treasury Representative in London, 1954-56; Senior Research Officer, 1956-57; Australian Treasury Representative in London, 1958-61; Chief Finance Officer, 1961-62; Assistant Secretary, 1963-66; First Assistant Secretary, 1971; Deputy Secretary (Economic), 1971; Member, Committee of Review, 1973; Deputy Secretary, 1976; Secretary to the Treasury, 1979-84; Professor, Monash University, 1984; Consultant, Potter Partners, 1985-87; Director, Peko Wallsend Ltd, 1986-87; Elected Senator for Queensland, 1987; Opposition Finance Spokesman, 1987-88, 1989-90; Member, Opposition Leadership Group, 1989-90; Senior Fellow, Institute of Public Affairs, 1985-87, 1990-95; Chairman, J T Campbell and Co Ltd, 1994-96; Member, Defence Efficiency Review Committee, 1996-97; Weekly Columnist, The Australian Financial Review, 1990-. Publications: Upholding the Australian Constitution, Vol 1-10. Memberships: Council of the National Interest; Board of Management; HR Nicholls Society; The Samuel Griffith Society, Editor and Publisher, Society's Proceedings. Address: 70 Gipps St, East Melbourne, Vic 3002, Australia.

**STOPLER Traian,** b. 30 March 1924, Bacau, Moldavia, Romania. Physician; Microbiologist. m. dec, 1 daughter. Education: Diploma of Physician, 1953, Institute of Medicine and Pharmacology, Bucharest; Head Physician in Urban Hygiene, 1960, Bucharest; Head Physician in Microbiology, 1967, Bucharest. Appointments: Scientific Researcher, Institute of Hygiene, Bucharest, 1953-62; Laboratory Chief, Infectious Diseases, Hospital Colentina, Bucharest, 1962-72; Government

Central Laboratories, Ministry of Health, Israel, 1972-94. Publications: 18 in Journal of Antimicrobial Chemo, 1986; 16 in Israel Journal of Medical Science, 1980; 24 in FEMS Microbiology Letter, 1984; 5 in Microb Parazitologia-Epidemiologia, 1964. Membership: International Organisation for Mycoplasmology. Address: Etzel 2/12, 32427 Jerusalem 91323, Israel.

**STORM-MATHISEN Jon,** b. 16 January 1941, Oslo, Norway. Neuroscientist. m. Ingebsorg, 2 sons, 1 daughter. Education: MD, 1965; PhD, 1976. Appointments: Research Physician, Norwegian Defense Research Establishment, 1967-77; Associate Professor, 1977-85, Professor, 1985-, University of Oslo. Publications: Over 200 scientific papers. Honours: Voss' Award, 1981; Monrad Krohn's Prize, 1989; Fellow of the Norwegian Academy of Science and Letters, 1993. Memberships: Society of Neuroscience; International Society Neurochemistry. Address: University of Oslo, Anatomical Institute, PO Box 1105, N-0317 Oslo, Norway.

**STORMER Chris,** b. 22 May 1950, Nairobi, Kenya. Nurse. Education: SRN; Midwifery. Appointments: Staff Nurse, Assistant Head Nurse, John Peter Smith Hospital, Tarrant County, Texas, 1974-75; Consultancy, Trumps Nursing Agency, Kingston-upon-Thames, Surrey, 1975; Territorial Army, Queen Alexandra Royal Nursing Corps, London General Hospital; Sister, Occupational Health, New Charing Cross Hospital, London, 1975-77; Health Visitor, Croydon Area Health Authority, 1977-78; Drake Personnel, 1980-87; Self Employed, Sunphysique Health Studio, 1988-90; President, Founder, Reflexology Academy of Southern Africa, 1989-. Publications: Author of 5 books; Numerous articles in professional journals. Address: PO Box 1280, Rivonia 2128, Gauteng, South Africa.

**STRAKHOV Alexander,** b. 10 December 1948, Moscow, Russia. Scholar. m. Strakhov Olga, 1 son, 1 daughter. Education: BA, Moscow Lomonosov University, 1974; PhD, Institute of Slavic and Balkan Studies, Russian Academy of Sciences, Moscow. Appointments: Assistant Professor, Department of Russian Language, Moscow Lomonosov University, 1976-88; Guest Lecturer, Department of Belorussian Linguistics, Belorussian State University, 1989; Guest Lecturer, Instituto di Linguistica, Salerno University, Italy, 1989; Guest Lecturer, Slavic Department, Yale University, 1989; Visiting Scholar, Davis Center for Russian Studies, Harvard University, 1990-92; Fellow, Davis Center for Russian Studies, Harvard University, 1992-. Publications include: Collecting Russian Ritual Calendar Folklore: Methodological Guide, 1982; The Terminology and Semiotics of Slavic Everyday and Ritual Bread, 1986; The Cult of Bread Among the East Slavs: Attempt at an Ethnolinguistic Study, 1991. Address: 820 Mt Auburn Str Apt 5, Watertown, MA 02172, USA.

**STRAKOVSKY Igor,** b. 28 September 1945, Cheljabinsk, Russia. Physicist. m. Natalia Urieva, 1 son. Education: BA, Physics, St Petersburg State Technical University, 1965; MS, Physics, 1969; PhD, Physics, 1984. Appointments: Assistant Research Scientist, Russia, 1969-71; Research Scientist, Nuclear Physics Institute, 1971-98; Visiting Research Scientist, Canada, 1989-94; Research Assistant, Visiting Research Scientist, Physics Department, 1992-97; Visiting Professor, Physics Department, 1997-98; Senior Research Scientist, Physics Department, 1998-. Publications: 50 Papers, Reference Journals, 1976-. Honours: 250th Anniversary Commendation for Excellence in Research, Academy of Sciences of Russia, 1974. Memberships: APS. Address: Department of Physics, George Washington University, 725 21st Street NW, Washington DC 20052, USA.

**STREET Jennifer Louise,** b. 18 November 1965, Carlinville, Illinois, USA. Broadcaster. m. Gary L Street. Education: AAS Radio Broadcasting, 1985, Lewis & Clark Community Centre, Godfrey, Illinois. Appointments: Programme/Promotion Coordinator, WRSP-TV/WCCU-TV Springfield, 1989-93; Programme Director, In-House Producer, WFHL-TV Decatur, Illinois, 1993-98; Continuity Director, WPXU-TV Decatur, Illinois, 1998-. Membership: National Religious Broadcasters, via Corporate Membership, 1993-. Address: WPXU-TV, 2510 N Parkway Ct, Decatur, IL 62526-5227, USA.

**STRINGER Samuel,** b. 28 July 1928, Edlington, Nr Doncaster, UK. Metallurgist. m. Enid Ogilvie, 4 sons, 1 daughter. Education: Graduate Diploma Plastics Fundamentals, 1969; B App Sc Secondary Metallurgy, 1972. Appointments: Assistant Chief Engineering Inspector, International Harvester, Doncaster, England, 1950-54; Office in Charge materials testing, Electricity Trust of South Australia, Adelaide, 1958-70; Materials Technologist, AMDEL, Adelaide, 1970-72; Supervising Scientist, South Australian Public Service, Highways Department, Adelaide, 1972-88; Consultant, Adelaide, 1989-; Materials Signatory and Assessor, National Association Testing Authorities, Melbourne, 1968-89; Computing and Materials Consultant, Adelaide, 1975-. Publications: Contributor around 30 articles to various professional publications. Honours: Named Fellow Australian Welding Institute, Adelaide, 1974. Memberships: Member various coms Standards Associations, Australia, Sydney, Melbourne, 1976-89; S Australia representative, Australian Road Research Board, Melbourne, 1979-85; Member Technical Committee, National Association State Road Authorities, Sydney, 1980-89. Address: The Palms, Supple Rd, Virginia SA 5120, Australia.

**STROGANOV Anatolii Iljitch,** b. 16 November 1927, Orlov Gai, Novousensky, Saratov, Russia. Engineer-Metallurgist. m. Nina Markelova, 1 son. Education: Diploma of Engineer-Metallurgist, 1949; Diploma Master of Science, 1952; Certificate of Reader Chair of Metallurgy of Steel, 1955; Diploma Doctor of Technology, 1970; Certificate of Professor, 1970. Appointments: Graduate, Moscow Institute of Steel, 1949; Senior Laboratory of Department of the Metallurgy Steel, 1949; Junior Researcher of that Institute, 1952; Senior Teacher, Chelyabinsk Politechnical Institute, 1952; Reader, Department Metallurgy Steel of ChPI, 1955; Dean of metallurgical Faculty ChPI, 1968; Director, Department of Analytical Chemistry, 1970; Conferring the title of Professor, 1970; Director of Department of corrosion and protection of metal, 1974. Publications: Deoxide of Opean-Hearth Steel, 1955; Application of Oxygen to Convert of Production Steel, 1958; Arc Furnace, 1972; Production of Steel and Ferro-alloy, 1974; Quality Surface Metals, 1985; Perspective Production of Chromiste Alloys on Chelyabinske Electrometallurgical Plant, 1997. Honours: Graduate with Honour, Moscow Institute of Steel, 1949; Order Friendship of Peoples, 1981. Address: South Ural State University, 76 Prospekt Lenina, Chelyabinsk 454080, Russia.

**STROME Marshall,** b. 27 April 1940, Lynn, Massachusetts. Physician. m. Deena (Lazarov) Strome, 2 sons. Education: LS&A, 1960, MD, 1964, MS, Otorhinolarygology, 1970, University of Michigan. Appointments include: Assistant Surgeon, Otolaryngology, Beth Israel Hospital, Boston, 1971-77, Associate Staff in Otolaryngology: New England Deaconess Hospital, 1972-93, Mt Auburn Hospital, Cambridge (Massachusetts), 1972-93, Senior Associate in Otolaryngology, Children's Hospital Medical Center, Boston, 1974-93; Surgeon and Chief, Otolaryngology, Beth Israel Hospital, 1977-93; Associate Surgeon in Otolaryngology, Massachusetts Eye and Ear Infirmary, Boston, 1978-93; Chief, Otolaryngology 1978-93, Associate Surgeon, 1979-82, Senior Surgeon 1982-93, Brigham and Women's Hospital, Boston; Associate Professor of Otolaryngology, Harvard Medical School, Boston 1979-93; Otolaryngology Consultant, Sidney Farber Cance Institute, Boston, 1980-93; Longwood Otolaryngology Coordinator, Harvard Medical School, Boston, 1980-86 Chairman, 1993-, Professor of Otolaryngology, 1994 Department of Otolaryngology and Communicative Disorders Cleveland Clinic Foundation, Ohio. Publications: 107 origina papers; 44 reviews, chapters, editorials; 20 books and monographs. Memberships include: Cartesian Society Triological Society; American Academy of Otolarygology - Head & Neck Surgery; Society of University Otolaryngologists American College of Surgeons; American Medical Association Address: Department of Otolaryngology and Communicative Disorders, The Cleveland Clinic Foundation, 9500 Euclid Avenue, Cleveland, OH 44195, USA.

**STROUD-HARVEY Gloria,** b. 16 April, Washington, DC USA. Physicians Assistant. m. Jimmy Harvey, 3 sons, 1 daughter. Education: BS, University of Maryland, 1968 Physicians Assistant Certificate, Howard University, 1978 Appointments: Physicians Assistant, Weaver Clinic, 1977-80 Western State Hospital, John Hemstead Hospital, University of North Carolina, Chapel Hill, Maria Parham Hospital Memberships: American Business Womens Association; North Carolina State Employees Association; North Carolina Association for Physician Assistants; Triangle Association for Physician Assistants. Address: 3582 GG Tar River Road, Oxford, NC 27565, USA.

**STROUKEN Ineke,** b. 10 November 1951, Tegelen, Netherlands. Education: History, University of Utrecht, Netherlands. Appointments: Manager, Goirles Nieuwsblad Goirle, 1974-80; Teacher, various schemes, 1980-85; Director, Nederlands Centrum voor Volkscultuur. Publications: Editor, Alledaagse Dingen, 1992-; Editor, Traditie, 1995-; Editor, Volkscultuur; Author, Marriage Customs, 1993; Birth Customs, 1991; Joepie Joepi, 1994. Memberships include: Chairman, Brieven aan de Toekomst; Vlaams-Nederlandse werkgroep volkscultuur; Vrienden van het Maliebaanfestival; Stichting Cultuur Projecten; Board Member: Foundation for Dutch National Costumes; Chair, Brabant Folklore; Farmyards studygroup; Tourism Prize, 1998; Staring Institute; Foundation for historical wallpapers and wall decorations. Address: Lucasbolwerk 11, NL 3512, EH Utrecht, Netherlands.

**STRUKCINSKAS Mindaugas,** b. 25 June 1925, Kaunas, Lithuania. Phytopathologist. m. Aldona Aleknaviciute, 1 daughter. Education: Graduate, 1950, DAgricSci, 1955, Docent, 1959, Lithuanian Academy of Agriculture; Habilitated Doctor, Natural Sciences, Vilnius University, 1974; Professor, Lithuanian Academy of Sciences, Institute of Botany, 1977. Appointments: Laboratory Head, Lithuanian State Selection Station, 1951-56; Senior Lecturer, Lithuanian Academy of Agriculture, 1957-60; Senior Research Fellow, 1960-61, Phytopathogenic Microorganism Laboratory Head, 1961-93, Lithuanian Academy of Sciences, Institute of Botany; Member, Lithuanian Academy of Sciences, Agriculture and Forestry Section, 1985-; Research Fellow, Institute of Botany, 1993-. Publictions: Several articles in professional journals. Honours: Lithuanian Distinguished Scientist. Memberships: Lithuanian Botanist Association; Lithuanian Horticulturalists Association; Lithuanian Scientists Union; Lithuanian Phytopathologists Association. Address: J Basanaviciaus 16/5-125, 2009 Vilnius, Lithuania.

**STRUNECKA Anna**, b. 24 January 1944, Prague, Czech Republic. Professor of Physiology. m. Otakar Strunecky, 1 son, 1 daughter. Education: Faculty of Sciences, Charles University, Prague, 1966. Appointments: Head, Department of Physiology, 1981-90, Professor, 1988-, Faculty of Sciences, Charles University, Prague. Publications: Over 150 publications in scientific journals, 4 textbooks. Honours: Silver Medal, Charles University, 1988; Woman of the Year, American Biographical Institute, USA, 1995. Memberships: IUPS; IUBS; New York Academy of Sciences; Czech Cosmetic Union; Red Cross. Address: Vinicna 7, Prague 2 12800, Czech Republic.

**STRUNK Betsy Ann Whitenight**, b. 28 May 1942, Bloomsburg, Pennsylvania. Educator. 2 sons. Education: BS Education, 1964, Bloomsburg University; MEd, 1969, West Chester University; Certificate, Mentally/Physically Handicapped, 1981, Pennsylvania State University; Certified in Elementary Education, Special Education; Post-Graduate Study, Wilkes University, Joseph's University, Drexel University, Western Maryland College. Appointments: Teacher, Faust School, Bensalem Township, 1964, Eddystone (Pennsylvania) Elementary School, 1964-66, Lima Elementary School, Rose Tree Media School District, 1966-69, Rose Tree Media School District, 1977-; Owner, Designer, Betsy's Belts, 1970-74; Instructor, Introduction to Flying and Pilot Companion Course; Curriculum Designer, Private Pilot Ground School; Special Education Resource Room Specialist, Teacher Consultant, Media Elementary School, Rose Tree Media School District; Instructor, Performance Learning Systems Inc, 1981-; AdjunctProfessor, Wilkes College, 1981-86; Instructor, Delaware Community College, 1986; FAA Representative, Philadelphia, 1986-88; Director, Ground School Education, Brandywine Airport, West Chester, 1986-88;Instructor, Drexel University, 1989-; Learning Support Teacher, Glenwood Elementary School, Media, 1994-; Academically Gifted Programme teacher, Glenwood Elementary School and Indian Lane Elementary School, 1998-. Publications: Contributor of articles to professional journals. Honours: Exeptional School Service Award, Rose Tree Media School District; Various fine artsand photography awards. Memberships: National Education Association; Association for Supervision and Curriculum Development; Pennsylvania Association for Supervision and Curriculum Development; Rose Tree Media Education Association, various positions; Pennsylvania State Education Association; National Staff Development Council; Aircraft Owners and Pilots Association; Media Society of Performing Arts; Independent School Teachers Association; and others. Address: 203 Cohasset Lane, WestChester PA 19380-6507, USA.

**STRUZHANOV Valerii Vladimirovich**, b. 14 December 1946, Tallin, Russia. Scientist. m. Valentina Bryuhova, 1 daughter. Education: Dr 1977, Professor, 1994, Urals State University, 1970. Appointments: Associate Professor, 1978; Scientific Researcher, 1979; Head of Laboratory, 1982. Publications: Monograph: Material Deformation Softening in Structural Elements, 1985; Textbook: Methods of Strength of Materials in Mechanics of Solids, 1996. Address: Institute of Machine Sciences, Urals Division of Russian Academy of Sciences, 91 Pervomaiskaya Str, GSP-207 Ekaterinburg 620219, Russia.

**STUBER William Charles**, b. 25 September 1951, Rochester, New York, USA. Engineer; Producer. m. Irene, 1 son. Education: Stonybrook University; Cleveland Institute of Electronics; Recording Institute of America; Peninsula College. Appointments: Owner, Operator, Road Runner Recordings, The Recording Studio, Western Audio Recording, Triangle Recording, Visioneering, Shabda Publishing. Publications:

Gems of the Seven Colour Rays; Ultimate Love; Devotion; Love's Heavenly Dream. Memberships: Seattle Writers Association; AES. Address: Triangle Recording, PO Box 21, Carlsborg, WA 98324 0021, USA.

**STULGIENE Liucija**, b. 27 Jaunary 1941, Parrvojis, Lithuania. Professor. m. Vaclovas Juddpusis, 1 daughter. Education: University of Bianhai, Lithuania, 1958-63. Appointments: Professor of University, 1963-69; Vice Chief, Bianhai City Council, 1969-76; Counselor, Culture of Premier Ministry of Lithuania, 1976-91; Director, Support for Musicians Foundation, 1991-. Honours: Honours for the Culture, Parliament of Lithuania, 1970, 1985; Prize for Culture, Parliament of Lithuania, 1997; Honours for the Help of Musicians, President of Lithuania, 1997; Expert Consultant of Ministry of Education. Memberships: Ministry of Culture; Community of Samaritans. Address: Lietuvos Muziku Remimo Fondas, Bernardinu 8/8, LT 2001, Vilnius, Lithuania.

**STULGINSKAS Kestutis**, b. 9 October 1955, Raseiniai, Lithuania. Lawyer. div. Education: State Manager, Vilnius Conservatoire, 1980; Lawyer, Moscow Juridical Academy, 1988. Memberships: Rotary Club; President, Lithuanian Trade Union of State Workers. Address: Urvikiu 18, LT-5500 Mazeikiai, Lithuania.

**STULPINIENE Sniraite Genovaite**, b. 9 June 1932, Ukmerge, Lithuania. Teacher; Doctor of Humanities; Academician. m. 1 son. Education: Vilnius Tallat-Kelpsa College of Music, 1956-59; Siauliai Pedagogical Institute, 1964-66; Postgrad, Vilnius University, 1978-82. Appointments: Teacher, Ukmerge and Siauliai district schools, 1951-66; Director, Sakyna 8 year school, Siauliai district, 1966-68; Instructor, Kaunas Polytechnical Institute, 1969-86; Instructor, Kaunas Technical College, 1975-80; Private vocational and higher education organiser, 1987; President of Management College, 1993; President of Institute of Management and Law, 1995. Publications: Academician; Writer; Author complete works, A way to Recognition, in 10 parts; History dissertation, Cultural contacts with other countries. Honours: Founder, non-state educational institutions and initiator of first private studies in Lithuania. Memberships: Founder, Owner and President, Kaliningrad (Russia) International Academy of Ecotechnology and Management; Section for International Relations, Dante Alighieri Committee; Real Member of Academy of Natural Sciences; International Society of Scientifical Organizations of Education. Address: Trumpoji 4, LT 3000, Kaunas, Lithuania.

**STUMP M Pamela**, b. 8 July 1928, Detroit, Michigan, USA. Sculptor. m. Richard T White, 1 son, 2 daughters. Education: Bachalor, Master, University of Michigan, 1950-51. Appointments: Professional Sculptor, 1950-; Teacher, Ann Arbor Michigan Adult Education, 1950-51; Saginaw Museum School, Michigan, 1963-68; Birmingham Bloomfield Art Association, Washtenaw Community College, 1968; Cranbrook Educational Community, 1969-90. Honours include: Award, Excellence in Teaching, 1990; Distinguished Alumna Medal, Cranbrook Educational Community. Memberships: National Museum of Women in the Arts; Detroit Institute of Art Founders Society; National Association of Women Artists, New York City. Address: 19629 Parke Lane, Grosse Ile, MI 48138-1024, USA.

**STUPPERICH Hans Reinhard**, b. 26 July 1951, Münster, Germany. Archaeologist. m. Sylvia Sosna, 4 daughters. Education: Abitur, 1970; Studies, Münster and Oxford; State Exam, History, Latin and Archaeology, 1975; DPhil, Archaeology in Münster, 1977; Habilitation in Archaeology, Münster, 1989. Appointments: University Assistant, Münster,

1977; Professor, Classical Archaeology, Mannheim University, 1990. Publications: Books: Staatsbegrabnis und Privat Grabmal im Klassischen Athen, 1977; Romische Funde in Westtalen, 1980; Antiken Investfälischen Museen, 1984; Vasen Dersammlung Peek, 1990; Untersuchungen Zuden Figurlichen Römischen Metallarbeiten, 1988. Memberships: German Archaeological Institute; Curatorium, Historical Museum of Palatinate at Spever; Several scholarly societies. Address: Markgrafen Str 1, D 69412 Eberbach, Germany.

**STÜTZ Anton,** b. 11 June 1947, Schärding, Austria. Chemist. m. Edelfriede, 1 son, 1 daughter. Education: PhD, University of Vienna, 1972; Post Doctor, Max Planck Institute, 1972-74; Habilitation, University of Vienna, 1987; University Professor, Pharmaceutical Chemistry, 1994. Appointments: Head of Laborototy, 1974; Senior Scientist, 1982; Head of Dermatology. 1992; Head of Chemistry, Pharmacology, 1997-. Publications: 60 Scientific Articles; 60 Abstracts, 25 Patents in Fields of Synthetic and Medicinal Chemistry, Biochemistry, Pharmacology, Antifungal Chemotherapy, Inflammation, Immunosuppression, Oncology, Dermatology; 50 Invited Lectures, Congresses and Universities. Honours: Sandoz Golden Triangle, 1993. Memberships: Verein Osterreichischer Chemiker; Gesellschaft Deutscher Chemiker; Society for Investigative Dermatology; Skin Pharmacology Society; New York Academy of Sciences; European Dermatology Forum. Address: Lindauergasse 35, A-1238 Vienna, Austria.

**STYLES Richard Wayne,** b. 22 June 1939, Waterbury, Connecticut. Pastor. m. Helen Horton Styles, 2 sons, 1 daughter. Education: BA, 1965, Shaw University; MDiv, Southeastern Baptist Theological Seminary; DDiv, 1987, Union Christian Bible Institute. Appointments: Tupper Memorial Baptist Church, Raleigh, NC, 1965-68; Star of Bethel Baptist Church, Hendersonville, NC, 1968-73; First Baptist Church, Burlington, NC, 1973-. Memberships: General Board, Trustee, of General Baptist State Conventions of NC; Hampton Ministers Institute; Progressive National Baptist Convention. Address: 612 Crestview Drive, Burlington, NC 27215, USA.

**SU Der-Ruenn,** b. 1937, Chekiang, China. Professor. m. Cheng-Chuang Ch'ang, 1 son, 1 daughter. Education: BSc, Physics, National Taiwan University, Taipei; MSc, University of Pennsylvania; PhD, University of New York. Appointments: Assistant Instructor, University of Pennsylvania; Researcher, State University of New York; Visiting Professor, Fu-Jen University, Taiwan, National Taiwan University, National Central University; Professor, National Taiwan Normal University. Publications: Numerous papers in professional journals. Honours include: Bravery Prize, 1975; Charity Prize, 1978; Six-Art Medal, China Ministry of Education; DSc (Hon.), Marquis Scicluna International University; DPhil (Hon.), Albert Einstein International Academy. Address: Physics Department, National Taiwan University, Taipei, Taiwan 10617, China.

**SU Fong-Chin,** b. 1 September 1958, Taiwan. Professor. m. Rey-Chuan Chang, 1 s, 1 d. Education: BS, National Cheng Kung University, 1980; MS, National Taiwan University, 1982; PhD, University of Rochester, USA, 1989. Appointments: Co-Director, Motion Analysis Laboratory, National Cheng Kung University, Taiwan, 1989-; Associate Professor, Institute of Biomedical Engineering, 1989-96; Professor, 1997-. Honours: National Science Council Fellowship; Li Foundation Fellowship. Memberships: Formosan Society of Biomechanics; Orthopaedic Research Society. Address: National Cheng Kung University, Inst Biomed Eng, 1 Univ Road Tainan 701, Taiwan.

**SU Xing.** Address: Party School of CC of CPC, Mailbox 1070, Beijing 100091, China.

**SU Yi,** b. 12 December 1963, Jiangsu, China. IC Engineer. m. Weihua Song. Education: BSc Semiconductor Physics, 1986, Nanjing University, China; MSc Semiconductor Physics and Device Physics, 1991, Shanghai Institute of Metallurgy, Chinese Academy of Sciences; PhD, 1997, Southampton University, UK. Appointments: Technician, CMOS Lab, Institute of Semiconductors, Chinese Academy of Sciences, 1986-88; Lecturer, Semiconductor Research Group, Department Physics, Fudan University, Shanghai, 1991-94; Research Engineer, Microelectronic Process Technology Group, Institute of Microelectronics, Singapore, 1997-. Publications: 14 papers in international journals, 11 in Chinese journals; 9 papers presented in international conferences, 10 in Chinese conferences. Honours: Joint holder of 2 patents on optical instruments in China; Grant supported from the Human Capital and Mobility Programme, Micromechanics Europe of the European Union in ESSDERC'96 in Italy, 1996. Membership: IEEE, student member. Address: Institute of Microelectronics, 11 Science Park Road, Singapore Science Park II, 117685 Singapore.

**SUAREZ Louis,** b. 30 December 1947, Hauana, Cuba. Cardio Thoracic Surgeon. m. Denise Boland, 2 sons, 1 daughter. Education: MD, University of Illinois, College of Medicine, 1974; University of Wisconsin Hospital, Surgery, Cardio Thoracic Surgery, 1974-83. Appointments: Appleton Heart Surgery, 1984; Staff Physician, Appleton Medical Centre; Theda Clock Medical Center, 1991. Honours: Best Doctor, America. Memberships: AMA; FACS; FACCP; FACC; STS. Address: 2011 N Nicholas St, Appleton, WI 54914-2211, USA.

**SUBBARAO Barry Venkata,** b. 10 January 1936, Visakhapatnam. Teacher. Education: BSc Hons; MSc; DSc Andhra; DSc HC; MBA; MD AM; DEMM; DPRM; DUNIU; DBP; DcFM; D ACU; D MAG; D ACU MAG; D MAG ACU; CHART MIE; FMSPI; FISE; FIIPE; FIC; FIE; FIMS; MIICh E; MISTE; MCSI; MIMS; MCAM; MIT; MSASMS: MWTA; MISAM; MIRS; MYMCA. Appointments: Class 1, Ex Officio Member of Academic Senate; Chairman; Faculty of Chemical Engineering; Board of Studies, Chemical Engineering; Professor, Reader, Lecturer, Chemical Engineering, Andhra University; Post Doctoral Research Fellow, National Research Council, California University. Publications: 40 Publications, Chemical Engineering; 15 Publications, Management; 12 Publications, Drugless Therapies; 12 Publications, Freemasonry; 4 Publications, Rotary; 8 Articles, Chemical Engineering; Presentation of Papers in Chemical Engineering at National and International Conferences. Honours: Eminent Citizen of India, 1994; Doctor of Science, Honoris Causa, Sri Lanka, 1995; Outstanding Acheivement Award, 1996; Gems Award, 1997; 25 Years Service, Jewel in Freemasonry, 1997. Memberships: Institution of Engineers; Indian Chemical Society; Indian Institute of Plant Engineers; Management Studies Promotion Institute; International Magnetotherapist Service; Indian Society of Engineers and Chartered Member of Institution of Engineers; Research Society for the Study of Diabetes; Institute of Teaching; Indian Membrane Society; Centre of Applied Medicine; Society for Advanced Medicine, Many other Memberships. Address: 4-45-14 Vani Nilayam, Vijayanagaram Colony, Peda Waltair, Visakhapatnam 530 017, Andhra Pradesh, S India.

**SUBHA Kezhakumkara,** b. 19 March 1960, Kumaraneloor, Kerala, India. Social Scientist. m. Suresh, 1 daughter. Education: BA, 1st class, 1980, MA, 1st class, 1982, Bangalore University; PhD, Political Science, Institute for Social and Economic Change, Bangalore, 1993. Appointments: Senior Researcher, Project UMA, Institute of Social Studies Trust, 1993-94; Regional Co-ordinator, Southern Region of Institute f Social Sciences, 1994-. Publications include: Books: Develpment Planning and Administration, 1992; Women in Local Governance, 1994; Karnataka Panchayat Elections, 1995; Numerous articles in professional journals. Memberships: Vice President, Karnataka Panchayat Parishat; General Secretary, Womens Wing, Karnataka Panchayat Parishat. Address: B-203 Kasturi Dhama Apts, 8th Main Road, 9th Cross Road, Mallewswaram, Bangalore 560003, India.

**SUBRAMANIAN Muthurangam,** b. 25 May 1946, Coimbatore, India. General Manager. m. Vijayalakshmi S, 2 sons. Education: Degree/Diploma, Computers, German, French, Business Administration, Industrial Management, Electronics and Communication Engineering; BSc, Physics, 1967; B.Tech, 1970; MBA, 1976. Appointments: Technical Manager, Toshiba Anand Batteries Limited, 1970-80; Projects/Operations Manager, Comcraft Services Limited/Booth Manufacturing Company, 1980-85; General Manager, Saudi Polystyrene Plant, 1985-. Publications: Progress in Batteries and Solar Cells; Productivity Improvement; Simple Approach to Dry Batteries. Memberships: Fellow, Institution of Engineers; British Institute of Management. Address: PO Box 40147, Riyadh 11499, Saudi Arabia.

**SUBRT Oldrich,** b. 4 January 1957, Prague. Physician. m. Ludmila, 3 sons, 1 daughter. Education: MD, 1982, PhD, 1988, Assistant Professor, 1989, Charles University, 1st School of Medicine. Appointments: CEO, Na Homolce Hospital, Prague; Assistant Professor, Department of Neurosurgery, Charles University, Prague; Physician, Regional Hospital, Ostrava. Publications: 64 papers in the field of functional neurosurgery. Memberships: International Stereotactic Surgery; Vice Chairman, Czech Neurosurgical Society; Association of the Czech Hospitals, member of the board. Address: Roentgenova 2, 5 Prague 15119, Czech Republic.

**SUBULWA Leonard Simukwela,** b. 5 May 1928, Mongu-Lealui, Zambia. Politician. m. Florence Sepiso, 1 son, 7 daughters. Education: Diploma in Educational Administration, Leeds University, England, 1967. Appointments: Member of Parliament for Mulobezi, 1978-96; Deputy Minister of Commerce and Industry, 1978-83; Minister of Commerce and Industry, 1983-86; Minister of Mines, 1986; Minister of Tourism, 1986-88; Minister for Western Province, 1992-96. Publication: The Developing Role of a Manager of School as a School Administrator, 1967. Address: Namatanda Ltd, PO Box 910125, Mongu, Zambia.

**SUGIMOTO Tadao,** b. 11 January 1941, Chiba City, Japan. University Professor. m. Taeko, 3 sons. Education: BSc, 1964, ME, 1966, DrE, 1977, Department of Industrial Chemistry, Tokyo University and Graduate School of Tokyo University. Appointments: Research Associate, 1966, Senior Research Associate, 1980, Fuji Photo Film Co; Professor, Tohoku University, 1991-. Publications: Colloid Science, 1995; Handbook of Crystal Growth, 1995; Fine Particles Science and Technology, 1995. Honours: Photographic Technology Award, 1983; Metallic Materials Award, 1993; Moet Hennessy Lous Viniton Vinci d'Excellence Award, 1997. Memberships: Chemical Society of Japan; Japan Institute of Metals; Japanese Association for Crystal Growth; American Chemical Society. Address: Kawauchi Jutaku 4-204, Kawauchi Motohasekura 35, Aobaku, Sendai 980-0861, Japan.

**SUKAJ Syrja,** b. 22 January 1942, Tirana, Albania. Director. m., 2 sons, 1 daughter. Education: Graduate, Mechanic Engineering, 1964. Appointments: Chairman, Department of Technological and Constructive Studies and Projections, Institute of the Study and Projection of Geology and Mining,

1964-78; Chairman, State Group Technological and Constructive Studies, Institute of Mineral Studies and Projection, 1978-82; Chairman, Department of Technological and Constructive Studies and Projections, Institute of Chemical Studies and Projections, 1982-93; Director, Economic Development Department in Tirana Municipality, 1996-; Publications: The Enrichment of Minerals, 1981; The Baking of Calcereous Phosphated with Poor Coal in Rotative Furnice; Design Difficulties and the Way Out for the Plants of the Enrichment of Phosphated Calcerous; Design in Chemical Industry and Problems of the Future. Memberships: Association of the Mechanic Engineers; Association of the Chemist Engineers. Address: Rruga Gemal Stafa MR417, Tirane, Albania.

**SUKER Davor,** b. 1 January 1968, Osijek. Football Player. Honours: World Champion Junior, 1987; Golden Boot, 1988-89; League Champion, 1996-97; Silver Boot, 1997; Europe Champion, 1997-98; World Intercontinental Champion, 1998; Bronze Medal, France World Cup, 1998; Golden Boot, 1998; Third Fifa Player in the World, 1998; Silver Ball, 1998. Address: Real Madrid Estadio Santiago Bernab'ev, Concha Espira 1, 208036 Madrid, Spain.

**SUKHERA Rehana,** b. 7 May 1946, Rawalpindi, Pakistan. Professor of Medicine. m. Muzaffar Sukhera. Education: MBBS, 1969; FCPS, 1975; Training in Cardiology, England, 1980. Appointments: Professor of Medicine, 1997-; Associate Professor, 1985-97; Assistant Professor, 1977-85; Senior Registrar, 1976-77; Registrar, 1971-76. Publications: Several publications in Pakistani journals (Medicine). Honours: Merit Certificate, premedical, 1964; Merit Scholarship, 1964, 1969; First Position, PPSC, 1984. Memberships: Pakistan Medical Association; Punjab Teachers Association; Pakistan College of Physicians and Surgeons; Academic Council Rawalpadi Medical College, Pakistan; Associate Member, British Medical Association. Address: House No 4, Street 25, F6/2, Islamabad, Pakistan.

**SULEIMAN Ahmed,** b. 1 April 1950, Dagauda, Africa. Civil Servant. Education: BA, Administration, Ahmadu Bello University, Zaria, 1970-73; National Institute of Policy and Strategic Studies, Kuru, 1992. Appointments: Assistant Secretary II, Lagos State Ministry of Information, 1973; Assistant Secretary II, Federal Ministry of Agriculture, 1974-75; Acting Assistant Secretary I, Federal Ministry of Water Resources, 1975-77; Senior Assistant Secretary, 1977-78, Principal Assistant Secretary, 1978-80, Upper Benue River Basin Development Authority, Yola; Principal Private Secretary to Executive Governor of Bauchi State, 1981-83; Deputy Secretary, Ministry of Works, Bauchi, 1984; Permanent Secretary, Ministry of Health, Bauchi, 1984-85; Permanent Secretary, Establishment and Service Matters, Bauchi, 1985-86; Permanent Secretary, Ministry of Commerce, Industry and Tourism, Bauchi, 1986-87; Permanent Secretary, 1987-88, Director-General, 1988-89, General Administration, Bauchi; Director-General, Hospitals Management Board, Bauchi, 1989-90, 1993; Director-General, Deputy Governor's Office, Bauchi, 1990-92; General Manager, Yankari Express, Bauchi, 1994-96; Secretary, Bauchi State Government, 1996-. Address: Secretary to State Government, Government House, Bauchi, Nigeria, Africa.

**SULEIMAN Michael Wadie,** b. 26 February 1934, Palestine. Professor. m. Penelope A Suleiman, 1 son, 1 daughter. Education: BA, Bradley University, 1960; MS, 1962, PhD, 1965, University of Wisconsin. Appointments: Teacher, Amman, Jordan, 1953-55; Teacher, England, 1955-56; Assistant Professor, KSU, 1965-68; Inter University Consortium, Politcal

Research, University of Michigan, 1967; Visiting Scholar, University of London, 1969-70; Associate Professor, KSU, 1968-72; Professor, KSU, 1972-90; Visiting Scholar, University of California, 1979; Head, Department of Political Science, KSU, 1975-82; University Distinguished Professor, KSU, 1990-. Publications: Numerous Journal Articles, Essays and Books. Honours: Phi Kappa Phi Scholar Award; Distinguished Graduate Faculty Member Award. Memberships: American Political Science Association; Middle East Studies Association; International Association for Mass Communication Research; American Institute of Maghribi Studies; Arab Sociological Association; Arab International Studies Association. Address: Department of Political Science, Kansas State University, Manhattan, Kansas 66506, USA.

**SULEIMAN Yahia Mustafa**, b. 22 October 1941, Coast Banias. Vice Dean. m. Ghazwah Kamal Aabdeen, 2 sons, 3 daughters. Address: P O BOx 163, Coast Banias, Syria.

**SULIAUSKAITE Elena-Gerarda**, b. 30 December 1932, Prienai, Lithuania. Specialist in Lithuanian Philology; Sister of Congregation of Eucharistic Jesus. Education: Studies at Vilnius (Lithuania) Pedagogical Institute, 1953-56, Excluded because of participation at anti-Soviet demonstration, 1956; Studies at Vilnius University, Bachelor on Lithuanian Philology, 1961-68. Appointments: Soviet Government only permitted unqualified labour: Conductor, Telegraph Operator; Secretary, 1956-61; Secretary, Vilnius University, 1968-73; Removed by Soviet Power, 1973; Librarian, later Head Editor, Kate Library, 1973-75; Underground activity, publishing of Chronicle of the Lithuanian Catholic Church; Technical Editor, Stylist, Proof-Reader, Author of many articles; Chairwoman of the Caritas of Vilnius diocese, 1989-92; Redactor, magazine, Caritas, 1989-90. Publications: Articles in the republic newspapers and magazines. Honours: Medal of Saurio 13-osios atminimui, 1993; Granted state pension. Address: Didzioji 36A, LT 2001 Vilnius, Lithuania.

**SULLIVAN Carol**, b. 18 March 1961, New York, USA. Architect. Education: BS, Architecture, Kent State University, Ohio, 1985. Appointments: Project Architect, Ferguson Murray Shamamian Architects, PC, New York, 1988-90; Television, Theatre Set Designer, Production Design Group, New York, 1993-94; Project Architect, The Office of Thierry Despont, New York, 1994; Project Manager, Architect, Mark Hampton Inc, New York, 1995-96; Manager, Naomi Leff & Associates Inc, New York, 1996-. Honour: National Deans List. Membership: Tau Sigma Delta. Address: 154 Saint Johns Place, Brooklyn, NY 11217-3402, USA.

**SULLIVAN Edwin Percy Albert**, b. 16 February 1924, Randwick, Sydney, Australia. Retired. m. Eva Weiszberger, 1 son, 1 daughter. Education: BSc Hons, University of Sydney, 1950; MSc, University of Sydney, 1951; PhD, University of Sydney, 1954. Appointments: Lecturer, Chemistry, University of Malaya, Singapore, 1954-1956; Teaching Fellow, Physico-Chemical Laboratories, University of Sydney, 1956-57; Lecturer, Chemistry, Newcastle University College and University of New South Wales, 1958-61; Lecturer, Chemistry, University of Sydney, 1961-65; Senior Lecturer, 1965-67; Reader, Chemistry Department, Victoria University of Wellington, 1967-69; Lecturer, Physics, 1969-70; Senior Lecturer in Physics, New South Wales Institute of Technology, Sydney, 1970-84. Publications: 41 Publications. Honours: Several Honourary Positions. Memberships: Life Member, University of Sydney Union; Union Life Member, University of Technology, Sydney; Australian Institute of Physics; New York Academy of Science; Returned Sericemens League of Australia; 52nd Australian Composite A A Regiment; AIF

Association. Address: 29 Howard St, Randwick, 2031 Sydney, NSW, Australia.

**SULOV Vladimir**, b. 27 March 1972, Varna, Bulgaria. University Professor. Education: Bachelor of Art, 1995. Graduate (MBA) Degree, University of Economics, Varna, Burgaria 1996. Appointments: Founder, Reality Software, 1984; Lieutenant, Chief of Information Squad, Bulgarian Navy General Staff Headquarters, 1996-1997; Assistant Professor, University of Economics, Varna, 1997. Publications: One book and two studies in journals about the Internet. Honours: Scientific Sessions Awards, 1995-96; Award, National Academic Foundation of Bulgaria, 1994. Memberships: Scientific Centre for Business Information Technologies Chairman, Division of the Scientific and Technical Union of Bulgaria. Address: 19 Bratya Miladinovi Street, Varna 9002, Bulgaria.

**SUMMERS Patsy**, b. 26 September 1942, Springfield, USA. Educator. m. Gail Eugene Summers, 1 son, 1 daughter. Education: Drury College, 1964. Appointments: Teacher, Springfield Public School, 1965-; Suprvising Teacher, Drury, 1980-; Summer Quest Instructor, Drury College, 1987-. Honours: Jif Teacher of the Year, 1990; Kids Choice Teacher of the Year, 1994; Teacher of the Year Finalist, 1995. Memberships: President, ACEI Drug Alumni Assistant Committee; Area Arts Council; PALS Board of Directors; NFL Judge; Board of Christian Education, St Johns Church; IRA; Twin Oaks Tennis Board; PTA/VP; GAAM; WINGS Board; SEA; MSTA; LAD Fair Dance A Poem Chair; DIG Founder; Park View Partners Founder, SITE Council; LAD; LIFE. Address: 1340 South Delaware, Springfield, MO 65804, USA.

**SUN Haiyin**, b. 17 July 1958, China. Optical Engineer. m. Nah Yang, 1 son, 1 daughter. Education: BS, Shanghai Teachers University 1982; MS, Shanghai Institute of Optics, 1985; PhD, University of Arkansas, 1994. Appointments: Product Manager, Coherent Inc, 1998; Senior Engineer, Coherent Inc, 1997. Publications: 30 in International Journals. Honours: Outstanding Researcher. Address: 8328 Northvale Way, Citrus Heights, CA 95610, USA.

**SUN Hugo Sui-Hwan**, b. 19 October 1940, Hong Kong. Mathematician. m. Ixin Wen, 1 son, 3 daughters. Education: BA, 1963, University of California at Berkeley; MA, 1966, University of Maryland; PhD, 1969, University of New Brunswick. Appointments: Assistant Professor, University of New Brunswick, 1969-70; Assistant Professor, 1970-; Professor, 1978-, California State University, Fresno; Visiting Research Professor, Academia Sinica, 1980, Peking University, 1987. Honour: First Award in Anthology, 5th World Congress of Poets, San Francisco, 1981. Membership: Hongkong Mathematics Association. Address: Mathematics Department, California State University, Fresno, CA 93740-0108, USA.

**SUN Qian-Zhang**, b. 5 June 1938, Zibo City, Shandong, China. Educator. m. 2 sons. Education: BA, Political Economics, Department of Politics, Shandong University, 1960-64. Appointments: Teacher, Central Academy of CCP and Beijing University, 1964-77; Vice Director, Administrative Bureau, Vice Director, Central Office, Vice Chairman, Training Department, Director, Academy Library, Central Academy of CCP, 1977-93; Vice President, President, Correspondence College, Central Academy of CCP, 1993-96; Member, School Affair Committee, President, Correspondence College, Central Academy of CCP, 1997-. Publications include: Management Studies of the National Economics; Policy-Making of Socialist Economy; Introduction to the Science of Leadership; Science of Industrial Management; A History of Management Ideologies;

f China and of Foreign Countries. Honours: 1st Class Award, China Education Commission; Publication Award, Japan; Award of Excellent, China Association of Leadership Sciences. Memberships: China Association of the National Economic Management; China Academy of Management Sciences; China Institute of the National Economic Management. Address: Department of Economics, Party University of C C of CPC, Beijing, China.

**SUN Shiying,** b. 11 March 1933, Shanghai. Microwave and Communications Expert. m. Zhang Han-Yang, 1 daughter. Education: Graduate, Department, Electronic Engineering, Shanghai Jiaotong University, 1953; Graduate, Department of Russian, Harbin Foreign Language Institute, 1955; Graduate Student, University of Electronic Science and Technology of China, UESTC, in Chengdu, Sichuan Province. Appointments: Lecturer, University of Electronic Science and Technology of China in Chengdu, 1961-; Associate Professor, 1982-, Full Professor, 1988-, Shanghai Jiaotong University; Co-Chair, AMIC Session of APMC'88, 1988. Publications: Over 50 scientific papers including 11 of the International Microwave Symposium; Book, Measurement of Microwave Devices; Co-author, several other books including: Microwave Techniques, Microwave Electronic Devices, Vol I and II. Honours: 5 certificates of National Science and Technological Achievements, State Science and Technology Committee of China, 1992; Third Prize and Diploma for Microwave Achievements, Pei-Yuan Zhou Foundation, 1998; First Prize, Excellent Advisor to graduate students by Shanghai Jiao-Tong University, 1986; and others. Memberships: IEEE, Senior member; Chinese Institute of Electronics, Senior member; Member Microwave Committee of Shanghai Institute of Electronics. Address: Department of Electronic Engineering, Shanghai Jiao Tong University, No 535 Fahuazhen Rd, Shanghai 200052, China.

**SUN Wen Shan,** b. 16 October 1942, Xia Men City, China. Senior Enginer. m. Gui Lan Ma, 1 son, 1 daughter. Education: Three year high school course, No Five Middle School, Xia Men, 1960; Graduate, Beijing Iron and Steel University, Metallurgic Department, 1965. Appointments: Worked on metallic materials research in Nei Meng Gu Metallic Materials Research Institute, 1965-98; Senior Engineer. Publications: Published 21 papers in journals, magazines; Behaviour of Ce in Duplex Stainless Steel, 1996. Honours: Awarded three prizes and third prize, National Science Committee and North Corporation, 1967-91; Won Invention Patent, 1995. Memberships: Director; Chinese Society for Special Steel and Bao Tou Society for Rare Earth, 1994-98. Address: No 4 Hu Dei Mu Lin Street, Qing Shan Section, Baotou City, Nei Meng Gu Province, China.

**SUN Yun Song,** b. 11 July 1934, Dalian, China. Professor. m. Xue Yu Xia, 1 son, 2 daughters. Eduction: BS, Jilin University, 1961. Appointment: Research Fellow, Dalian Institute of Chemical Physics. Publications include: The Development of Anti-Smell Fabric, 1988; Composition of Water-Soluble Protein of Tussah Silk, 1990; Thermal Analysis of The Wild Cocoon, 1990; The Study on Yellowing and Yellowing-Resistant of Tussah Silk, 1991; Vegetation and Dyestuff, 1997. Membership: China Chemical Association. Address: Dalian Institute of Chemical Physics, Chinese Academy of Sciences, PO Box 110, Dalian 116 023, China.

**SUN Zhen Pei,** b. 11 October 1937, Wuhang, Hubai, China. Professor. m. Jinxiao Zhong, 2 sons. Education: Graduate, Chongqing Jiangzhu University, 1960. Appointments: Teacher, Chongqing Jianzhu University, 1960-. Publications: Basic Theory of Hydraulic Technology; Hydraulic and Pneumatical

Seal Technology. Honours: 8 First, Second or Third Prizes of the Province, Ministry or City Rank. Memberships: Secretary-General, Hydraulic and Pneumatic Technology Communicated Centre of China Mechanics Associations Fluid Control Experts Committee; Advisor, Sichuan Giving Water Association; Director, Sichuan Town-Heads Association. Address: Mechanical & Electrical School, Chongqing Jianzhu University, Chongqing, China.

**SUN Zhongcai,** b. 21 March 1950, Liaoning, China. Professor. m. Lanfen Liu, 1 daughter. Education: Master of Economics, 1987; Doctor of Economics, 1994. Appointments: Associate Professor, Department of Agricultural Economics, Remin University of China, 1993-97; Professor, Department of Agricultural Economics, Renmin University of China, 1997-. Publications: Agriculture and Economic Growth, 1995; Introduction to Agricultural Information Systems, 1996; Agricultural Economics: A Theoretical Inquiry, 1998. Honours: Folkswagen Award, 1992. Memberships: New York Academy of Sciences. Address: Renmin U China Rural Devel, Haidaian Rd 175, Beijing 100872, China.

**SUNDARESHAN Tambarahalli,** b. 30 June 1955, Mysore, Karnataka, India. Scientist; Researcher. m. Suma Sundareshan, 2 daughters. Education: MSc, 1976; PhD Oncology, 1995. Appointments: Research Assistant, Department of Microbiology and Cell Biology, Indian Institute of Science, Bangalore, 1977-81; Senior Cytogeneticist, Medical Genetics Centre, Kuwait, 1981-89; Lecturer in Cytogenetics, Department of Pathology, Kidwai Memorial Institute of Oncology, Bangalore, 1990-. Publications: Author or co-Author, over 40 articles in professional journals in field of cancer cytogenetics and clinical cytogenetics. Membership: Kidwai Memorial Institute of Oncology, Bangalore. Address: 599 SWATI 10th B Cross, 4th Main WCR II Stage, Bangalore 560 086, India.

**SUPANICH Barbara,** b. 24 September 1952, Detroit, Michigan, USA. Associate Professor, Family Practice and Medical Ethics. Education: BS, Chemistry, Mercy College of Detroit, 1974; MD, Michigan State University, 1980; Residency in FP, Creighton University, 1980-83; Fellowship in Clinical Medical Ethics, Michigan State University, 1992-. Appointments: FP Residency, Creighton University, Omaha, NB, 1980-83; Family Physician, Rural Practice, 1983-92; Faculty MSU, CHM, 1993-. Publications include: Management of the Perimoenopause, 1996; Pallative Care and Physician-assisted Death, 1997; Approach to the Patient, in Taylor's Family Medicine, 1997; Ethical Issues in Physician-assisted Suicide, 1997; Menstrual Disorders, in Essentials of Family Medicine, 1997. Honours: Sigma Phi Sigma, 1972; Physician's Recognition Award, AMA, 1983-; Fellow, American Academy of Family Physicians, 1985; Member, American College of Physician Executives, 1996; CHM Teacher Scholar Award, 1997. Memberships: American College of Physician Executives, 1995-; Society of Teachers of Family Medicine, 1993-; Society for Health and Human Values, 1992-; Association of Sister, Brother, and Priest Physicians, 1983-; Michigan State Medical Society, 1983-; Michigan Academy of Family Physicians, 1983-; American Academy of Family Physicians, 1980-; American Medical Women's Association, 1980-; North Central Medical Society, 1986-92. Michigan State University, Department Family Practice, B100 Clinical Center, East Lansing, MI 48824, USA.

**SUPHIOGLU Cenk,** b. 28 February 1966, Cyprus. Senior Research Officer. m. Dianna Hocking. Education: BSc Hons, 1989; PhD, 1994. Appointments: Post-doctoral Fellow, Research Officer, University of Melbourne, 1994-97; Senior

Research Officer, Monash Medical School, 1998-. Publications: Over 40 publications in refereed journals; 3 patents. Honours: PhD Scholarship, 1990-93; Young Achiever of the Year Award, 1991; Lilian Roxon Travel Award, 1992; AAAAI Travel Award, 1994. Memberships: Australasian Society of Clinical Immunology and Allergy; American Association for the Advancement of Science. Address: Department of Allergy & Clinical Immunology, Monash Medical School, Alfred Hospital, Prahran 3181, Victoria, Australia.

**SURABHI Gopinath,** b. 6 September 1941, Tirupati. Teacher. m. Sasirekha, 2 s. Education: BVSc, 1964; MSc, Veterinary, 1974; PhD, 1985. Appointments: Assistant Professor, 1966; Associate Professor, 1989; Professor, 1999. Memberships: Indian Association of Veterinary Anatomists; Andhra Pradesh Veterinary Association. Address: Department of Anatomy, College of Veterinary Science, Gannavaram, Krishna District 521 102, Inida.

**SURESH Lekha,** b. 17 May 1955, Ernakulam, India. Legal Advocate. m. Ashok Suresh, 1 son. Education: BSc, 1975; LLB, 1979. Appointment: Lawyer, High Court of Kerala, 1979-. Publications: Articles in periodicals to spread legal literacy. Memberships: Indian Federation of Women Lawyers; Kerala High Court Advocates Association; Sangamithra. Address: High Court, Vayanappillil, PO Poothotta, Ernakulam District, Kerala 682307, India.

**SURIYAMOORTHY Marimuthu,** b. 16 August 1944, Neidavasal, India. International Artist; Writer. 1 son, 3 daughters. Education: 1st Class, 1st Rank, G D Arts at Government College of Arts and Crafts, Madras, 1963. Career: Solo exhibitions in India include: 750 works at Pondicherry, sponsored by Alliance Française and Raoul Follereau Foundation, 1987; Lilit Kian Akademi, Madras, 1987; Government Museum, Madras, 1988; Airport, Madras, 1990; 1200 works at Lilit Kala Akademi, Madras, 1994; Foreign exhibitions in countries including, London, Spain, Bulgaria, New Zealand, Mexico, include: Mini Graphic International Exhibition, Spain, 1984, 1985, 1991, 1993, 1994, 1997; International Biennial Art Exhibition, Bulgaria, 1987, 1991, 1993, 1994, 1995, 1997; 3rd Biennale International Pastel Exhibition, France, 1992; International Poster Exhibition, Mexico, 1994; Collections include: 14 works, Tamil Cultural Centre, Madras; 19 works, Easel Art Gallery Madras; 11 works, National Gallery of Modern Art, New Delhi; 2 works, Government Museum, Punjab; Many works in private collections and 685 throughout five continents worldwide. Honours: Numerous include: Five Prizes, Directorate of Health, Government of India, New Delhi, 1963-65; UP Governor Award, 1965; Gujarat State Award, Ahmedabad, 1967; Silver Medal, Hyderabad Art Society, 1967; All India Exhibition, Ambain Cantt (Gold Medal) and Memento Award, 1990-91. Address: Kadaiku Neidaysala PO, Poompuhar Via Sirkali 609105, Tamil Nadu, India.

**SURJANA Vinsensius,** b. 9 September 1939, Bandung, West Java, Indonesia. Pharmacist. m. Augustina Remita Kakisina, 2 sons, 3 daughters. Education: Registered Pharmacist, 1967. Appointments: Plant Manager, Sanbe Farma. Membership: PDA, USA. Address: Gq Adi Sahid No 11, RT 09/03, Bantar Pete, Tajur, Bogor 16720, Indonesia.

**SURKOVA Tatyana Petrovna,** b. 3 July 1948, Russia. Physicist. Education: Graduate, Ural University, 1971; PhD, 1977. Appointments: Postgraduate, Junior Scientist, Researcher, Senior Researcher, Institute of Metal Physics, Russian Academy of Sciences, 1973-. Publications: Over 70 on optical properties of semiconductors. Membership: Rozhdestrensky Optical Society. Address: Institute of Metal

Physics, Russian Academy of Sciences, 18 S Kovalevskaya St, GSP 170, Ekaterinburg 620219, Russia.

**SUROWIEC Andrew Julius,** b. 13 April 1940, Poland. Biophysicist. m. Irene Baranowski, 1 daughter. Education: BS 1962, MSc, 1964, Technical University; PhD, Silesian University, 1972. Appointments: Postdoctoral Fellow, Centre de L'Energie Nucleaire, Mol, Belgium, 1973-74; Assistan Professor, Silesian School of Medicine, Katowice, Poland, 1970-81; Distinguished Visiting Scientist, University of Ottawa, Ontario, Canada, 1983-88; Assistant Professor, Bowman Grey School of Medicine, Winstom-Salem, North Carolina, USA, 1988-89; Assistant Professor, University of Southern California, Los Angeles, USA, 1989-94; Senior Medical Physicist, Centennial Medical Center, Nashville, Tennesssee, 1994-. Publications: 43 peer reviewed publications; 51 paper presentations on international and national scientific meetings, symposia and congresses. Honours: Award, Natural Science and Engineering Research Council, Canada; Peer reviewer, Cancer Journal. Memberships: New York Academy of Sciences; Radiation Research Society; International Clinical Hyperthermia Society. Address: 8209 Londomberry Road, Nashville, TN 37221-4640, USA.

**SURUSHE Ashok Rangnathrao,** b. 8 January 1950, Hingoli. Wooden Sculptor. m. Sow Chandrakala, 3 sons. Education: BA, Traditional Sculptor. Appointments: Traditional Sculptor, All over India. Publications: Articles Published in Prominent and Eminent News Papers in India. Memberships: Maharashtra Kala Sanshodhan Mandal Hingoli Dist; Indian Working President; Vishvakarmamaya Vikas Mandal Maharashtra. Address: Vishwaharma Chowk, Hingoli, Dist Parbhani, India.

**SUSANTO Harta,** b. 6 August 1931, Medan, Indonesia. Publisher; Journalist. m. Widijawanti Susanto, 1 son, 3 daughters. Appointments: Chairman, Founder, Harian Analisa, 1972-; Executive Director, Harian Garuda, 1976-. Honours: Best Publisher in Indonesia, 1994, 1995. Memberships: Indonesian Journalists Association; Indonesian Publishers Association; Board Chairman, General Sudirman School of Business and Academy Foundation. Address: Harian Analisa, JL Jend A Yani 35-43 Medan, 20111 North Sumatra, Indonesia.

**SUSLA Jeffrey,** b. 30 October 1958, Bridgeport, Connecticut, USA. English Teacher. Education: BA, 1982, Wesleyan University, Middletown; MALS, 1991, Dartmouth College, Hanover. Appointments: English Teacher, Woodstock Academy, Connecticut, 1993-. Honours: 21st Century Educator of Year, 1996; National Endowment for the Humanities Fellow, 1996; Fulbright Memorial Fund Fellow, 1997; Teaching Excellence Award Fellow, 1998. Memberships: National Council of Teachers of English; Connecticut Council of Teachers of English; National Peace Corps Association. Address: PO Box 27, Woodstock Ct, CT 06281-0027, USA.

**SUSLOV Valentin Vasilievich,** b. 5 June 1931, Voznesensk, Ukraine. Anesthesiologist. m. Tamara Starostenko, 1 son, 1 daughter. Education: Physican Diploma, Medical Institute Odessa, Ukraine, 1957; Candidate Medical Sciences, Donetsk, Ukraine, 1967; Doctor of Medical Sciences, Kiev, 1973; Professor of Anesthesiology, Kiev, 1980. Appointments: Surgeon Medical Institute, Donetsk, Ukraine, 1957-61; Anesthesiologist, Medical Institute, Donetsk, 1961-65; Head, Anesthesiology Department, 1965-72; Chief, Anesthesiology Service Institute of Urology, Kiev, 1972-. Publications: Author, monograph: Intensive Care and Anesthesia in Urology, 1981; Co-author: Functional Diagnostics in Urology and Nephrology, 1977; Manual on Anesthesiology,

994. Memberships: Ukrainain Sciety of Anesthesiologists; olish Society Anesthesiologists (hon); German Society nesthesiologists (association); European Academy nesthesiology (academician). Address: Gogolevskaya Str 23, pt 11, 252054 Kiev, Ukraine.

**SUTCLIFFE James Helme,** b. 26 November 1929, Suzhou, hina. Music Critic; Teacher; Composer. Education: University Melbourne Conservatory, 1948; BSc, Piano, Juilliard School f Music, 1949-53; MA, Composition and Theory, Eastman chool of Music, 1955-58. Appointments: Assistant Professor f Music, Duquesne University, Pittsburgh, Pennsylvania, 957-61; Music Critic, Opera News, New York Times, Opera anada, Musical America, Int Herald Tribune, 1964-99; pernwelt; Opera (London; Retired as Critic for Opera, 1999; uthor for Salzburg Festival, and Opera Houses, Vienna, erlin, Hamburg, Munich. Compositions: Numerous for full and ring orchestra, chorus, harp, organ, piano, song cycles, namber music. Memberships: American Society of omposers, Authors and Publishers (ASCAP); German Society f Composers, Authors and Publishers (GEMA). Address: /ilmersdorger Str 94, D-10629 Berlin, Germany.

**SUTKUS Antanas,** b. 27 June 1939, Kaunas Region. hotographer. m. Rima Kiubaraite, 1 s, 2 d. Education: Vilnius niversity, 1958-66; Appointments: President, Union of hotoartists of Lithuania. Honours: 4 Grand Prix; 3 FIAM Gold ledals; 3 Gold Medals; More than 70 awards; Decorated with ne Dukes Gediminas Order of the 4th Rawr. Memberships: :HAP, 1994; Rotary International. Address: Mindaugo 19-34, 006 Vilnius, Lithuania.

**SUTTON Kerry Peter,** b. 22 September 1944, Matamata, lew Zealand. Industrial Designer. Education: Diploma in ndustrial Design, Wellington Polytechnic, 1964; Art Center, :ollege of Design, Los Angeles, California, 1966-68. Iembership: Royal Overseas League. Address: Apt 2, 10 lutton Street, Otahuhu, Auckland, New Zealand.

**SUVALOVA Elena,** b. 13 August 1946, Kiev, Ukraine. Irganic Chemist; Researcher. widow, 1 daughter. Education: iiploma of Engineer, Technology Institute of Food Industry, iiev, 1969; Candidate of Chemical Sciences, Kiev, 1977. ppointments: Engineer, 1971-77, Researcher, 1977-, Institute f Organic Chemistry, National Academy of Sciences, Ukraine. ublications: Several articles and patent. Honour: Diploma, Ilendeleev Chemical Society, 1977. Memberships: Ukrainian :hemical Association; Green Peace. Address: Pobeda Street 3-B 77, Kiev 252057, Ukraine.

**SUZUKI Akira,** b. 28 June 1948, Nagasaki, Japan. Irthodontist; Teacher. m. Hiromi Suzuki, 1 son, 2 daughters. :ducation: DDSurg, Faculty of Dentistry, Kyushu University, apan, 1973, PhD, 1991. Appointments: Instructor, 1973-98, ecturer, 1998-, Kyushu University. Publications include: *arental data used to predict growth of craniofacial form, 1991; A longitudinal study of changes of the primary dental arch limensions in the cleft lip and/or palate subjects, 1992; Tooth rown affinities among South Korean, Central Taiwanese and ertain Japanese Populations, 1994; Cephalometrical omparison of craniofacial morphology between primary bone rafted and non-grafted complete unilateral cleft lip and palate dults, 1996. Memberships: Japanese Orthodontic Society; Imerican Association of Orthodontists; Japanese Cleft Palate Issociation; American Cleft Palate-Crainofacial Association; Korean Cleft Lip and Palate Association; Anthropological Society of Nippon; International Association for Dental Research; Japanese Society of Pediatric Dentistry; Japanese Society of Oral & Maxillofacial Surgeons; Japanese Society of

Pediatric Oral and Maxillofacial Surgery. Address: Kyushu University School of Dentistry, 61/Department of Ortho Maedashi 3-1-1, Higashi-ku, Fukuoka 812-8582, Japan.

**SUZUKI Osamu,** b. 30 January 1930, Gero, Gifu, Japan. Business Executive. m. Shoko Suzuki, 2 sons, 1 daughter. Education: Chuo University, 1953. Appointments: Joined Suzuki Motor Corporation Ltd, 1958, Various Management Positions, 1958-63, Director, 1963-66, Junior Managing Director, 1967-72, Senior Managing Director, 1973-77, President, CEO, 1978-. Honours: Sitara-I-Pakistan Award, Government of Pakistan, 1985; Honour with Blue Ribbon Medal, 1987; Mid Cross of Order, Hungary, 1993. Address: Suzuki Motor Corporation, 300 Takatsuka-cho, Hamamatsu-shi, Shizuoka-ken 432-8611, Japan.

**SVIKLAS Alfredas Martynas,** b. 16 May 1972, Rokishkis, Lithuania. Engineer. m. Regina, 1 son, 1 daughter. Education: Diploma of Technologist Engineer, 1965; Doctor of Chemistry, 1978; Habilitat doctor, 1993; Professor, 1996. Appointments: Engineer, Head Laboratory, Jonava, Azotas, 1966-92; Docent, Kaunas University of Technology, 1991-96; Professor, 1966-. Publications: 102 publications; 29 invention certificates and patents. Honour: Award, Lithuanian Technical Science Society, 1988. Memberships: Lithuanian Chemist Association; Expert of Standard Department of Lithuania. Address: Veterinarijos 9, LT 5000, Jonava, Lithuania.

**SVINKIN R Mark,** b. 29 April 1935, Kharkov, Russia. Civil Engineer. m. Margarita, 1 son. Education: MS, Civil Engineering, 1958; MS, Mathematics, 1968; PhD, Civil Engineering, 1978. Appointments: Senior Research Associate, 1963-87; Consulting Engineer, GRL & Associates, 1991-96; Independent Consulting Engineer, 1996-. Publications: Over 100 papers published. Honour: Medal, Exhibition of Achievements of National Economy, USSR. Memberships: ASCE; ISSMFE; DFI; PDCA. Address: 13821 Cedar Road, Apt 205, Cleveland, OH 44118, USA.

**SVIRNOVSKI Arcadi,** b. 14 February 1938, Minsk, Belarus. Physician. m. Esfir Geller, 1 son. Education: Physician, State Medical Institute, Minsk, 1955-61; Educator, Pedagogical Institute of Foreign Languages,Minsk, 1955-60; Certificated Specialist, Cytology and Hematology, State Institute of Medical Training, Moscow, 1963; PhD, Med, National Centre of Hematology, Moscow, 1968; MD 1979; Professor, Higher Qualification Committee for Academic Degrees and Scientific Titles, Moscow, 1990. Appointments: Research Fellow, Hematology and Blood Transfusion Research Institute, 1961-66; Head of Laboratory, Leukemia Pathophysiology, 1967-; Part Time Teacher, High Medical School, 1964-79; State Medical Institute, Minsk, 1988-89; Consultant, Hospital N 9, 1977-; Consultant, Bone Marrow Transplantation Centre, Minsk, 1994-; Consultant, Children's Oncohematological Centre, Minsk 1996-; Scientific Secretary of the Expert Council, National Higher Qualification Committee for Academic Degrees and Scientific Titles, 1994-. Publications: More than 270 Publications, National and International Proceedings, Collections of Scientific Works and Scientific Journals. Memberships: Belarus Association of Hematologists and Transfusiologists; European Hematology Association; International Society for Hemotherapy and Graft Engineering; Board of International Journal Hematology; Belarussian Academy of Ecological Anthropology. Address: 34a K MArx St Apt 12, Minsk 220030, Belarus.

**SVYAZHIN Anatoly,** b. 11 October 1934, Verkhnaya Tura, Russia. Metallurgy Educator; Researcher. m. 1 son. Education: Diploma, Engineering, 1962, PhD, 1966, DSc, 1987, Professor,

1989, Moscow Steel and Alloys Institute. Appointments: Senior Research Scientist, 1967-71, Head, Steelmaking Division Research Laboratory, 1972-76, Head, Research Laboratory of Metals and Alloys, 1977-, Moscow Steel and Alloys Institute; Visiting Professor, Technical University of Czestochowa, Poland, 1994-99. Publications: Over 200 articles in professional scientific journals. Honours: Awards, Ministers of Education and Ferrous Metallurgy, 1980-95; Prize, Board of Ministers, USSR, 1987. Memberships include: Association of Steelmakers and International Metallurgist Union of Commonwealth Independent States. Address: Steel and Alloys Institute, Leninsky Prospect 4, Moscow 117936, Russia.

**SWAIM Mark Wendell,** b. 4 December 1960. Hepatologist. Education: BA, summa cum laude, University of North Carolina, Greensboro, 1979-83; PhD, honours, 1989, MD, 1990, Duke University Medical Center. Appointments: Attending Physician, Duke University Medical Center, Durham Medical Center, 1998. Publications include: Rethinking the Art of Medicine, 1996; The DCC Protein and Colon Cancer, 1997; Dr Stead on Doctoring: Advice to Emerging Physicians, 1998; Teaching the Context of Doctoring, 1998; Therapeutic Considerations for Geriatric Gastrointestinal Emergencies, 1998. Honours include: CRC Freshman Chemistry Award, 1980; Phi Beta Omega Alpha; First Walter A Puterbaugh Memorial Award, 1983; Conoco Chemistry Research Fellowship; Several scholarships. Memberships: American College of Physicians; American Society of Internal Medicine; Sigma Xi; Reticuloendothelial Society; American Board of Forensic Examiners; American Board of Forensic Medicine; American Society for Gastrointestinal Endoscopy; American College of Forensic Examiners; American College of Gastroenterology; North Carolina Medical History Society; North Carolina Medical Society. Address: 4208 Five Oaks, Durham, NC 27707, USA.

**SWAMIJI Swami Chidanand Saraswatiji (Muniji),** b. 3 June 1955, Rishikesh, India. Spiritual Leader. Education: Master Degrees in Sanskrit and Philosophy. Appointments: President, Parmarth Niketan Ashram; Founder/Chairman, India Heritage Research Foundation. Honours: Hindu of the Year Award; Mahatma Gandhi Humanitarian Award; Guest Delegate, United Nations Golden Jubilee. Address: India Heritage Research Foundation, Parmarth Niketan, Rishikesh 249304, India.

**SWAMY M R Kumara,** b. 23 January 1938, Mysore, India. Financial Management Researcher. m. Shaila, 1 son, 1 daughter. Education: BA Hons 1958 and MA Economics, Delhi, India, 1960; PhD Economics, Central Christian College, Huntington, USA, 1965. Appointments: Social Worker, Bharat Sevak Samaj, Delhi, 1956-57; Research Fellow Delhi School of Economics, 1960-61; Economic Investigator, National Council of Applied Economic Research, Delhi, 1961-62; Consultant, Cassa Per Il Mezzogiorno, Rome, 1965-66; Advising Oil Economist, Government of Qatar, Doha, 1967-69; Senior Research Officer, Commerce Research Bureau, Bombay, 1969-77; Professor of Economics and Finance and Head of Finance Department, Institute of Management and Technology, and Anambra State University of Technology, Nigeria, 1977-87; Director and Managing Editor, Journal of Financial Management and Analysis, Om Sai Ram Centre for Financial Management Research, India, 1987-; Chairman Public Lectures Committee, Institute of Management and Technology, Enugu, 1979-87; Expert Member, Appointments and Promotions Committee, Professorial Appointments, University of Ibadan, Nigeria; Member Editorial Board International Journal of Business, USA, 1999-. Publications: Over 175 papers in professional journals of international repute; Founder and Editorial Adviser, Nigerian Journal of Financial

Management, 1982-87. Honours: Delivered Distinguishe Economist Guest Lectures at University of Rome, 1965-6( Memberships: Financial Management Association Internationa Life Member, Lisle Fellowship. Address: Om Sai Ram Cent for Financial Management Research, 15 Prakash Coo Housing Society, Relief Road, Santacruz West, Mumb. 400054, India.

**SWANEK Susan,** b. 21 October 1955, Pihstor Pennsylvania, USA. Medical Technology, Quality Improvemen Education: Certified Laboratory Assistant, 1974; Laborator Technologist, 1977; AS Medical Laboratory Technology, 1992 BS, Health Administration, 1993; Graduate, Adificato in Quali Management, 1994; MBA, 1995. Appointments: Medic. Technologist, 1974-79; Microbiologist, 1979-93; Quali Improvement Coordinator, 1993-96; Technical Specialist, Poin of Case Testing, 1996-. Honours: Scientific Award, 1985, 198! 1987; PA Technologist of the Year Award, 1988; Informatio Laboratory Technical Writing Award, 1988, 1989, 1994; AM" Scholarships Award, 1991; Exceptional Award, 1994 Memberships: American Society of Quality; American Medic. Technologists. Address: PA State Geisinger Wyo Valley Me Ctr, 1000 E Mountian Dr, Wilkes Barre, PA 18711-0027, USA

**SWANSON William F, III,** b. 3 June 1960, Pittsburgh, PA USA. Manufacturing Manager. m. Jane Crosby, 1 son, daughter. Education: BS, Mechanical Engineering, Universit of Virginia, 1982; Master of Management, J L Kellogg Graduat School of Management, Northwestern University, 1985 Appointments: Assistant to UP, Manufacturin Bridgestone/Firestone Inc, 1985-87; Project Manager Bridgestone/Firestone Inc, 1987-89; Operating Manage 1989-92; Plant Manager, American Roller Company, 1992-95 Manufacturing Manager, 1995-. Address: 304 Sterbenz C Antioch, IL 60002-2601, USA.

**SWEETING Charles Harvard,** b. 14 July. Author. Education MA, Trinity College, Dublin, 1959. Appointments: Writer Associated British Studios, Elstree, Herts, England, 1954-55 Film Coordinator, Pennsylvania State University, 1968-69 Publications: A Film Course Manual, author, 1971; Columnist Union Jack monthly. Memberships: London Press Club Overseas Press Club of America; Savage Club. Address: c/ Savage Club, 1 Whitehall Place, London SW1A 2HD, England

**SWETCHARNIK Sara Morris,** b. 21 May 1955, Shelby North Carolina, USA. Artist; Sculptor; Painter; Writer. m William Norton Swetcharnik. Education: Art Students League New York, 1979-81; Postgraduate, Schuler School of Fine Arts Baltimore, 1973-78; Private Study, Melvin Gerhold Studio Frederick. Appointments: Exhibitions include: Reptile House National Zoological Park, Washington, DC; Weinberg Cente for the Arts, Frederick, Maryland; US State Department of Art Embassies Exhibition, Tegucigalpa, Honduras. Solo Exhibition include: Showcase of Terra-cotta Animal Sculpture, Weinberg Center for the Arts, Frederick, Maryland; Frederick Community College Art Gallery; Landon School Gallery, Washington, DC Holly Hills Country Club, Frederick. Numerous Group Exhibitions. Publications include: White Faced Capuchin Romeo's Offering; The General; Pancha and the Burro Honours include: IIE Fulbright Fellowship, 1987-88, 1988-89 Archibald King Memorial Award, Best Sculpture, 43rd Annua Exhibition of the Miniature Painters, Sculptors, Gravers Society Washington, DC. Memberships: Delaplaine Visual Art Center Frederick; Fulbright Association. Address: 7044 Woodville Road, Mount Airy, MD 21771, USA.

**SWIEZEWSKA Ewa,** b. 7 January 1953, Lodz. Chemist. m Marek Swiezewski, 2 sons, 2 daughters. Education: MSi, 1977

PhD, 1990; Dr Habilitatus, 1996. Appointments: Assistant, Assistant Professor, Associate Professor, Institute of Biochemistry & Biophysics, 1983-. Publications: Co-author, 25 publications. Membership: AOCS. Address: Institute of Biochemistry and Biophysics, ul Pawinskiego 5a, PL 02 106 Warsaw, Poland.

**SWITZER Les,** b. 4 September 1935. Professor. m. Hazel, 5 children. Education: PhD, African History, University of Natal, South Africa, 1972. Appointments include: Professor, School of Communication, 1983-; Professor, African American Studies Program, 1983-86; Adjunct Professor, Department of History, 1986-. Publications include: 7 books and monographs, edited conference proceedings, 25 book chapters, articles and essays in scholarly journals; The Black Press in South Africa and Lesotho: A Descriptive Bibliographic Guide 1836-1976, 1979; Media and Dependency in South Africa, 1985, 1987; Power and Resistance in an African Society: The Ciskei Xhosa and the Making of South Africa, 1993; South Africa's Alternative Press: Voices of Protest and Resistance, 1880-1960, 1997; South Africa's Resistance Press: Dissident Voices in the Last Generation Under Apartheid, 2000. Honours: 30 individual grants from Britain, South Africa and USA; Fulbright Senior Scholar Award; Distinguished Faculty Recognition Award. Address: University Houston, School of Communication, Houston, TX 77204-3786, USA.

**SWOGER James Wesley,** b. 26 January 1918, Wilkinsburg, Pennsylvania, USA. Magician. m. (1) Willie Williams, 8 January 1944, divorced 1967, 1 son, 2 daughters, (2) Violet Elizabeth Pettit, 29 October 1968. Appointments: Magician, more than 75 years; Owner, House of Enchantment, Oceanside, California, 1937-; Owner, Magician, Museum of Magic, 1937, Magic Follies of Tomorrow, 1938-41; Magician, Pittsburgh Children's Theatre, 1941-43, Bascom Productions, 1941-43, Austin Productions, 1941-43; Numerous war bond drive shows, camp shows, ship entertainment and concert tours, Australia, New Guinea and Philippines, 1943-46; Starred in Magic on Showboat Rhododendron Season, 1965-; Lecturer, Magic Castle, 1995; Inventor, stage effects and model illusions. Honours: Named Magician of the Year, 1960; 50 Years of Service to Magic, International Magicians Ring 13 IBM, 1973; Faithful Year of Service to Magic, 42nd Annual Magicfest, 1973; 60 Years of Service to Magic, 1983. Memberships: Society of American Magicians, President; International Brotherhood of Magicians, President of Order of Merlin Excalibur, 1996; Mystic 52, President; Academy of Magical Arts and Sciences; Fellowship of Christian Magicians; San Diego Ring 76 IBM. Address: House of Enchantment, 3542 Mira Pacific Drive, Oceanville, CA 92056-3932, USA.

**SYCHUGOV Nikolay Pavlovich,** b. 25 November 1936, Kirov, Russia. Engineer. m. 1 son. Education: Engineering Diploma, 1959; TSC Diploma, 1966; Senior Lecturer Certificate, 1969; Dr.techn, 1979; Professor Certificate, 1990. Appointments: Chief Engineer, Collective Farm, Kirov Region, 1959; Assistant, Kirov Agriculture Insütute, 1961; Postgraduate, Leningrad Agricultural Academy, 1963-66, Vyatka State Agricultural Academy, 1966-97. Publications: Author or co-author of 8 books, 250 science articles and 90 inventions. Memberships: St Petersburg State Agricultural University Thesis Council; Science Research Agricultural North-East Institute; Kazan State Agricultural Academy Thesis Council; Agroindustry Group of Kirov Region Administration. Address: ul Moskovskaya 15-51, Kirov 610000, Russia.

**SYED Anisuddin,** b. 22 October 1962, Warangal, AP, India. Professor Civil Engineering. m. Dr Sofia Tahseen, 2 daughters. Education: BTech Civil Engineering, First with Distinction, 1983,

MTech Transportation Engineering, First Class, 1986, PhD, 1998, REC, Warangal, Kakatiya University. Appointments: Consultant, Civil Engineering. Publications: 3 in journals; 2 communicated to J of Advanced Transportation and IRC; 14 in conferences. Memberships: Institution of Engineers, India; Indian Roads Congress; Indian Society for Technical Education; Indian Society for Rock Mechanics and Tunnel Technology; Association for Transport Development in India. Address: Department of Civil Engineering, Kakatiya Institute of Technology and Science, Kakatiya University, Warangal 506 015 AP, India.

**SYED Ibrahim Bijli,** b. 16 March 1939, Bellary, India. Nuclear Physicist; Professor. m. Sajida, 1 son, 1 daughter. Education: DSc, Johns Hopkins University, 1972. Appointments: Director of Medical Physics, Professor of Medicine and Nuclear Cardiology, University of Louisville, Louisville, Kentucky, USA. Publications: 200 papers, 2 books. Honours: PhD, Hon Causa, 1985; Hind Rattan, Jewel of India, 1994. Memberships: FRSH; FACR; F INST P, UK; FAIC; DABR; DABHP. Address: 7102 Shefford Lane, West Louisville, KY 40242-6462, USA.

**SYED Sarfaraz Ali,** b. 1 September 1943, Ajmir, Pakistan. Engineer. m. Rafat Syed, 1 son, 3 daughters. Education: BE, Electrical Engineering, University of Sindh, 1967; MBA, USA, 1993. Appointments: Junior Engineer, 1967-74, Senior Engineer, 1975-87, Director of Engineering, 1987-90, Pakistan Water and Power Development Authority; Project Engineer, seconded to Tabouk, Saudi Arabia, 1990-99. Publications: Articles including: Village Electrification in Pakistan, 1993; Energy Conservation, 1995; 15 conference, symposium and seminar papers including: Electricity and Pollution in Gulf Countries, 1995; Testing and Commissioning of Power Transformers, 1995; Global Technology Management, 1996; Quality Engineering - A New Potential, 1997; Managing Technology Dynamics, 1998; Electric Industry and 21st Century Issues and Challenges, 1999; Comprehensive Power System Maintenance, 1999. Memberships: Institute of Electrical and Electronics Engineers; Institution of Electrical Engineers; Institute of Quality Assurance; New York Academy of Sciences; Conférence Internationale des Grands Réseaux Electriques; American Management Association. Address: Tabouk Electricity Co, PO Box 34, Tabouk, Saudi Arabia.

**SYED Younus M,** b. 13 March 1948, Karachi, Pakistan. Consultant. m. Zubeda Begum, 2 sons, 4 daughters. Education: BSc, 1970; MBA, 1986; DSc, 1989. Appointments: Unilever, 1975-85; Almutlaq, 1989-93; Gen Y A Mouam, 1993-96; Namma Scvs Co, 1998. Publications: Books, 1978; Desert Shield, 1991. Memberships: Fellow, ISMM; Fellow, BRSH; Fellow, BTM. Address: c/o 2 Begum #075990, Dhahran Mail Centre, Saudi Arabia.

**SYED Zahid Feroze Sarfaraz,** b. 12 Nov 1951, Karachi, Pakistan. Senior Business IT Consultant; Expert on World Economics and Chemical/Mineral Industry; Marketing Specialist. m. Yasmin Bibi Zahid, 2 sons, 1 daughter. Education: Fellowship, Institute of Sales and Marketing Management; Certified ISO Internal Assessor. Appointments: 27 years experience with multinational trading, manufacturing, industrial and chemical groups, London, Riyadh and Jeddah, including previously Group Commercial Manager, currently Senior Business Consultant, chemical industry, and Marketing Specialist. Honours: Chess Championship Trophies, Inter-College and Inter-Company Tournaments. Memberships include: Institute of Export; American Management Institute; Institute of Management Services; Institute of Purchasing and Supply Management; Institute of Sales Technology

Management; Institute of Professional Managers. Address: PO Box 13586, Jeddah 21414, Saudi Arabia.

**SYRISTIVA Eva,** b. 7 November 1928, Prague. Professor Emeritus of Psychopathology and Psychotherapy. m. Syriste Jaroslav MD, 1 son. Education: PhD, 1951, C Scientiarum in psychopatology and psychotherapy, Charles University, 1962. Appointments: Editor, SPN Publications, Prague, 1951-53; Clinical Psychologist, Institute of Psychiatry, Prague, 1953-57; Lecturer, 1957-67, Professor 1967-94, Prodean for Scientific Research, 1992-94, Professor Emeritus, 1994-, Psychopathology, Psychotherapy, Charles University, Prague. Publications: The Possibilities and Limitations of Schizophrenic Diseases, 1965; The Imaginary World, 1973; Normality of the Personality, 1973; The Cracked Time, 1988; The Group Psychotherapy of Psychoses, 1989; Man in Crisis, 1994; The Poem as a Home in the Homelessness of Paul Cealan, 1994. Honours: Honorary Appreciation CZ Medical Society for contribution to CZ Sciences, 1978; Honorary Prize for Translation of Celan's Poetry, 1983. Memberships: IAAP; IBRO; International Association of Phenomenology and Sciences of Life; New York Academy of Sciences; Czech Medical, Psychiatric & Artistic Association; Director, White Rawen for Non-professional Art in Prague. Address: Sluknovska 316, 190 00 Prague 9, Czech Republic.

**SYTENKO Alex (Oleksiy),** b. 12 February 1927, Baturyn, Ukraine. Scientist (Physicist). m. Joanna, 2 sons, 1 daughter (deceased). Education: MA, Kharkiv University, 1949; PhD, 1952; DSc, 1959; Full Professor, Kharkiv University, 1961. Appointments: Director, 1988-, Head, Nuclear Theory Department, 1968-, Bogolyubov Institute for Theoretical Physics, Kiev; Professor, Kiev University, 1963-; Head, Institute of Physics, Kiev, 1961-68; Lecturer, Kharkiv University, 1949-63. Publications: Author, numerous books. Honours: Sinelnikov Prize, 1978; State Prize, Government of Ukraine, 1992; Bogolyubov Prize, 1993; Soros Professor, 1994; Honoured Scientist of Ukraine, 1996. Memberships: Academician, National Academy of Sciences of Ukraine; Foreign Member, Royal Swedish Academy of Sciences; Honorary Member, Ukrainian Mohylo-Mazepian Academy, Canada; Member, Ukrainian Higher Education Academy of Sciences; New York Academy of Sciences; American Physics Society; Editor-in-Chief, Ukrainian Journal of Physics. Address: Institute of Theoretical Physics, Ukrainian National Academy of Sciences, 14 B Metrologichna Str, Kiev 252130, Ukraine.

**SZABADOS Tamas,** b. 14 May 1948, Budapest, Hungary. Mathematician; Educator. m. Eva Kosa, 1 son, 1 daughter. Education: Diploma in Electrical Engineering, 1972; Diploma in Mathematics, 1978; PhD Mathematics, 1982, ELTE, Budapest. Appointments: Research Fellow, Technical University of Budapest, 1972-74; Assistant Professor, 1974-96, Associate Professor, 1996-; Adjunct Professor, Budapest Semester in Mathematics, 1996-, and Western Maryland College, Budapest, 1998-. Publications: 1 textbook; 20 research papers. Memberships: Janos Bolyai Mathematical Society; American Mathematical Society; Bernoulli Society. Address: Dept Math, Technical University EGRY U 20-22, Budapest 1521, Hungary.

**SZABO Karalin,** b. 5 November 1944, Godollo, Hungary. Professor. m. Balazs Hamori, 2 sons. Education: MBA, Karl Marx University of Economic Sciences, 1966; PhD, Hungarian Academy of Sciences, 1975; Doctor of Economic Sciences, Hungarian Academy of Sciences, 1988. Appointments: Editor in Chief, Kozgazdasagi Szemle, 1986-; Head of Department of Economics, 1988-92. Honours: International Academic Award, 1983; Szechenyi Scholarship of Professors, 1996. Memberships: Economic Committee of Hungarian Academy of

Science. Address: Fovah ter 8, Budapest 1093, Hungary.

**SZALACSI Joseph S,** b. 11 December 1946, USA. Educator. m. Kathleen Jo Szalacsi, 2 daughters. Education: BS, Music, Mannes College of Music, 1969; MMus, Education, Manhattan School of Music, 1972; Professional Diploma, 1975; Certified School Administrator. Appointments: Teacher, Brass Instruments, Public Schools, 1971; Coordinator, Music and Art Department, John Bowne High School, 1990-; Performed with Bronx Symphonic Orchestra, 1995-. Memberships: United Federation of Teachers; United Federation of Musicians; International Trumpet Guild. Address: 13018 16th Avenue, Flushing, NY 11355-5115, USA.

**SZALACSI Joseph S,** b. 11 December 1946, Flushing, New York, USA. Pedagogue of Music, Professional Musician. m. Kathleen, 1 daughter. Education: Master of Music, Music Education, Mannes Colllege of Music, 1972; Professional Diploma, Administration and Supevision, Manhattan School of Music, 1975; BS, Music and Performance, 1969. Appointments: Music Teacher, Band Director, Newtown High School, 1979-83; Band Director, Morris High School, 1983-96; Coordinator of Music and Art, JOhn Bowne High School, 1996-. Publiactions: Teaching Brass Instruments in the Public Schools. Honours: Teacher of the Year Award. Memberships: United Federation of Techers. Address: 13018 60th Ave, Flushing, NY 11355 5115, USA.

**SZEGEDI Ladislau,** b. 12 July 1939, Oradea, Romania. Anesthesiologist. m. Erzsebet Francisca, 1 son. Education: University of Medicine, Cluj, 1965; Anesthesiologist, Hospital Fundeni, Bucharest, 1965-68; Specialist Anesthesiologist, 1968-71; Chief Physician, Anesthesiology, 1971-79; PhD, Pharmacology, 1979. Appointments: Professor of Anesthesiology, University of Medicine, Oradea, 1991-. Publications: Author of 11 books; Several articles in professional journals. Memberships: Romanian Society of Emergency Medicine and Disasters; Romanian Society of Regional Anesthesiology; Council, Romanian Society of Anaesthesiologists and Intensive Care; European Society of Anaesthesiologists (ESA); Vice-President, Romanian Society of Cardiopulminary and Cerebral Resuscitation; College of Publication of 2 Anaesthesiology and Intensive Care Romanian Journals. Address: 88 Ady Endre, Oradea 3700, Romania.

**SZEGHY Iris,** b. 5 March 1956, Presov, Slovakia. Composer. Education: Degree of Art, Composition, 1981, Doctoral Degree, Composition, 1989, Academy of Music, Bratislava. Career: Freelance Composer. Honours: Several Scholarships; Domestic & International Awards; Composition Prizes. Memberships: Slovak Composers Union; Hungarian Composers Union; ISCM Slovak Section. Address: Tematinska 4, 85105 Bratislava, Slovakia.

**SZYMANSKI George,** b. 12 August 1947, Pittsburgh, Pennsylvania, USA. Education. m. Sharon Linn, 1 son, 1 daughter. Education: BSc, 1969; MEd, 1972; PhD, 1980. Appointments: Mathematics Teacher, 1969-79, Assistant Principal, 1979-81, Acting Superintendent, 1983, Assistant Superintendent, Staff, Personel Services, 1981-87, North Allegheny School District; Superintendent of Schools, South Dise Area School District, 1987-93, Pine-Richland School District, 1993-. Publications include: Redefining Organization to Accomplish Your Strategic Plan; Site-Based Planning in Food Services; Communicating Strategic Planning; Education: Pressures and Concerns; Labor Peace in Public Schools. Honours include: Outstanding Young Educator Award, North Hills Jaycees, 1981; Project of the Year Award, North Hills Jaycees, 1983; Leadership for America Award, 3rd Place, US

aycees, 1983; US Department of Education, District
ecognition Committee, 1996. Address: Superintendent, Pine
ichland Schools, Ewalt Road, Gibsonia, PA 15044, USA.

# T

**TABLER Shirley,** b. 18 March 1936, Washington, USA. Retired Librarian. m. Carlton Byard, 2 sons, 1 daughter, 1 stepson, 1 stepdaughter. Education: BS, Art, University of Maryland, 1977; BA, Library Science, 1978; MA, Art , 1981; MLS, 1990. Appointments: Secretary, National Capital Housing Authority, Washington, 1954-55; Clerk, Vitro Corp, Silver Springs, 1956-57; Hostess, Cashier Hot Shoppes, Wheaton, 1960-63; New Accounts Secreatry, State National Bank, Bethesda, 1966-68; Art Teacher, Montgomery County Public Schools, Rockville, 1968-86; Librarian, Cataloguer, Computer Technology, 1986-93. Memberships: ALA; Society Librarians International; American Art League; Maryland Printmakers, Washington Printmakers Gallery; Miniature Painters, Sculptors and Gravers Society; Rockville Art League; Olwey Art Association; Miniature Art Society of Florida. Address: 123 Charles St, Rockville, MD 20850-1510, USA.

**TABUTIN Jacques,** b. 22 August 1948, Moulins, France. Orthopaedic Surgeon. m. Chantal Gounot, 1 son, 3 daughters. Education: BA, 1966, Moulins, France; MD, 1977, MA Human Biology, 1980, University Lyon, France. Appointments: Intern, Lyon, 1972-77; Attache Anatomie, Lyon, 1974-77; Chef de Clinique, Lyon, 1977-81; Head of Orthopaedic Surgery, Cannes, 1981. Honour: Expert les Tribunaux Aix, 1990. Memberships: SOFCOT; SICOT; ESSKA; ESSES; European Hip Society; Gerhardt Küntscher Kreis; EBJIS; AOLF. Address: 8 Rue de Madrid, 06110 Le Cannet, France.

**TADA Tomio,** b. 31 March 1934, Yuki City, Ibaraki, Japan. Scientist. m. 1 son, 2 daughters. Education: MD, 1959, DMS, 1964, Chiba University School of Medicine. Appointments: Professor, Laboratories for Immunology, Chiba University, School of Medicine; Professor and Chairman, Dept of Immunology, Faculty of Medicine, University of Tokyo; Director, Research Institute for Biological Science, Science University of Tokyo. Publication: The Immune System as a Supersystem, 1997. Honours: Hideyo Noguchi Memorial Award, 1976; Emil Von Behring Prize, 1980; Distinguished Service Award, International Congress of Allergy & Clinical Immunology, 1988. Memberships: International Union of Immunological Societies; American Association of Immunologists; Japanese Society of Immunology. Address: Research Institute for Biological Sciences, Science University of Tokyo, 2669 Yamakazi, Noda City Chiba, Japan 278.

**TAGILAEV Azmudin,** b. 29 May 1959, Village of Khardik. Radio Engineer. m. Dinara Tagilaeva, 1 son, 1 daughter. Education: Doctor of Technical Science. Appointment: Professor, Daghestan State Technical University. Publications: Broadband Microstrip Controlling Devices of a Microwave; Projection of Phase Automation Direction. Honour: Honourable Radioman Russia. Memberships: Editorial Staff, Journal Electrodynamics. Address: Marksa Str 94 A Apt 27, Mahhachkala 367014, Russia.

**TAI Xue Cheng,** b. 15 July 1965, Henan, China. Professor. m. Xin Feng Xia, 1 son. Education: Bachelor Degree, Zhengzhou University, 1985; Institute of Systems Science, 1985-88; Licentiate Degree, University of Jyvaskyla, Finland, 1989; PhD Degree, 1991. Appointments: Doctoral Researcher, University of Jyvaskyla, 1988-91; Researcher, 1991-92; Visiting Researcher, University of Graz, Austria, 1992; Researcher, University of Jyvaskyla, 1992-93; Visiting Researcher, University of Heidelberg, Germany, 1994; Associate Professor, University of Bergen, Norway, 1994-97; Professor, Department of Mathematics, University of Bergen, Norway, 1997-. Publications: 35 journal articles. Honours: Men of Achievement 1996; Dictionary of International Biography, 1997 Memberships: Society for Applied and Industrial Mathematics. Address: University of Bergen, Dept Math, Alleg 55, Berger 5007, Norway.

**TAIWO Ladi,** b. 17 September 1948, Benin City, Nigeria. Business Law Practitioner. m. Ibitola Shonibare, 2 sons, 1 daughter. Education: LLB Hons, 1972, University Lagos. Certificate of the Council of Legal Education, 1973; Notary Public, 1988; Fellow, Centre for International Legal Studies, Salzburg, Austria, 1994. Appointments: Called to Bar & Admitted as Solicitor and Advocate of Supreme Court of Nigeria, 1973; Associate Counsel, David Garrick & Co, 1973-74; State Counsel, Ministry of Justice, Lagos State, 1974-75; Co-Founder and Senior Partner, Abdulai, Taiwo & Co, Solicitors, 1975-; Visiting Lecturer, Nigerian Law School, 1994; Consultant to Nigerian Investment Promotion Commission, 1998; Editorial Consultant, Modus International, 1996-. Publications: Author, co-author or contributing author, 9 books including: Registration of Trademarks, Patent and Technology Transfer Licences, 1998; Registration and Regulation of Foreign Investments and Enterprises, 1998. Honours: Junior Chambers International Medallion award for recognition as Outstanding National President of the Year, 1983; Lions International Award of Meritorious Service to Mankind, 1984; Conferred with the traditional Chieftaincy title of Olotu (Ilamuren) of Ijebu-Oru (ie Prime Minister of the Council of Chiefs) in his native town of Ijebu-Oru, 1989. Memberships: Nigerian Bar Association; Nigerian Institute of Management; Chartered Institute of Arbitrators, London; International Trade Mark Association; International Association of Practising Lawyers; Industrial Property Law Interest Group; Life-Patron, Nigerian-Belgian Chamber of Commerce; International Business Network; and others. Address: Abdulai Taiwo & Co, Goodwill House, 278 Ikorodu Rd PO Box 536, Yaba Lagos, Nigeria.

**TAJIRI Masayoshi,** b. 30 November 1937, Himeji Hyogo, Japan. Physicist. m. Yoshiko, 1 son, 2 daughter. Education: BS, Kobe University, 1960; DSc, Nagoya University, 1967. Appointments: Research Associate, Osaka Prefecture University, 1961-66; Assistant Professor at Osaka Prefecture University, 1966-74; Associate Professor at Osaka Prefecture University, 1974-94; Professor of Mathematical Sciences at Osaka Prefecture University, 1994-. Publications: Contributor of articles to professional journals. Memberships: Japanese Physical Society, 1960-; Japan Society of Fluid Mechanics, 1982; Japan Society of Plasma and Nuclear Fusion Research, 1983-. Address: 7-17-7 Ohno-dai, Osaka-Syama, 5890023, Japan.

**TAKADA Goro,** b. 27 September 1941, Pyong Yang. Professor. m. Hiroko, 1 son, 1 daughter. Education: MD, Tohoku University School of Medicine, 1967. Appointments: Professor, Chairman, Akita University, School of Medicine, 1982-. Honours: Osaka City Mayors Award, 1975; Osaka Medical Award, 1975; Arakawa Memorial Award, 1981. Memberships: Japan Paediatric Society; Society for the Study of Inborn Errors of Metabolism. Address: 3-12-20 Sakuraga-oka, 010 Akita Shi, Japan.

**TAKAGI Ryosuke,** b. 10 February 1947, Kobe, Japan. Professor. m. Akiko, 1 son. Education: BSc, Kwansei Gakuin University, 1970; MSc, 1972; Dr Pharm Sci, Kyoto University, 1986. Appointments: Researcher, 1972-77; Researcher, Kyoto University, 1977-87; Lecturer, Shukugawa Gakuin College, 1977-83; Associate Professor, 1983-96; Post Doctor, LMPM

ENSCM, France, 1994; Associate Director of Research, CNRS, Montpellier, 1995; Professor, 1996-. Publications: Membranes and Membrane Processes; Setai Korido; Contributor, Articles to professional journals. Memberships: Membrane Society, Japan; Chemical Society of Japan; Physics Society of Japan; Pharmaceutical Society of Japan. Address: Shukugawa Gakuin Coll, 6-58 Koshikiiwa-cho, Nishinomiya 662-8555, Japan.

**TAKAHASHI Kazuo,** b. 11 May 1945, Oita, Japan. Professor. m. Hiroko, 1 son, 2 daughters. Education: Bachelor of Engineering, Kyushu University, 1968; Master of Engineering, Kyushu University,1970; Doctor of Engineering, Kyushu University, 1984. Appointments: Research Associate, Nagasaki University, 1970; Lecture, Nagasaki University, 1971; Associate Professor, Nagasaki University, 1975; Professor, Nagasaki University, 1992. Publications: Car Life and Flood Disaster, 1989; Unzen Volcano the 1990-92 Eruption, 1992. Honours: Academic Prize, Japan Society for Natural Disaster Science, 1997. Memberships: International Association of Computational Mechanics, 1988; Japan Society of Civil Engineering, 1995; Council Japan Society for Natural Disaster Science, 1996; City Planning Institute, Japan, 1997. Address: Department of Civil Engineering, Nagasaki University, 1-14 Bunkyo-machi, Nagasaki City, Nagasaki 852, Japan.

**TAKAISHI Noboru,** b. Japan. Psychiatrist. Education: MD, Nippon Medical School, 1954; Diplomate, Japanese National Board of Medical Examiners, 1955; DMedSci, Osaka University, 1959; Senior Visiting Fellow in Psychiatry, University of Oregon Medical School, USA, 1964-65; Research Fellow in Psychiatry, Albert Einstein College of Medicine, 1983. Appointments: Assistant Professor of Psychiatry, Osaka University Medical School, 1966-69; Chief, Department of Psychiatry, Osaka University Branch Hospital, 1966-69; Private Practice in Psychiatry, Takaishi Clinic, Osaka, 1969-; Lecturer in Psychiatry, 1969-; Clinical Professor of Psychiatry, Nippon Medical School, 1999-. Publications: Contributor, articles to professional journals and chapters to books; Translator, various articles. Memberships: Fellow, Representative, International Society of Hypnosis; Approved Consultant, American Society for Clinical Hypnosis; Association for Advancement of Behavior Therapy; Scientific Associate, American Academy of Psychoanalysis; Japan Psychiatry Association, Board Member, 1979-81; Board Member, Japan Society for Hypnosis; Board Member, Japan Society of Behavior Therapy. Address: Takaishi Clinic, 1-2-2-200 Umeda Kita-ku, Osaka 530-0001, Japan.

**TAKAMATSU Takejiro,** b. 9 February 1946, Kyoto, Japan. Soil Chemist. m. Yoshie Ishikawa, 2 daughters. Education: Bachelor's degree, 1968, Master's degree, 1970, DSc, 1974, Kyoto University. Appointments: Chief, Soil Science Section, National Institute for Environmental Studies; Visiting Professor, Chiba University. Publications: Contributor to Soil Science, 1992, European Journal of Soil Science, 1994, Plant and Soil, 1997, Canadian Journal of Forest Research, 1998, other journals. Memberships include: Japanese Society of Soil Science and Plant Nutrition; Japan Society of Analytical Chemistry; Geochemical Society, Japan; Japanese Society of Limnology. Address: 3-12-11 Matsushiro, Tsukuba, Ibaraki 305-0035, Japan.

**TAKANAKA Kimio,** b. 14 August 1961, Tokyo, Japan. Professor; Economist. m. Miki Takanaka, 1 son, 1 daughter. Education: BA, Economics, St Paul's University, 1984; MS, Yale University, 1986; MSc, Pacific Western University, 1990; PhD in Economics, Yale University/Pacific University, 1991; Doctor of Engineering, Tokyo Institute of Technology, 1999-2000. Appointments: Senior Fellow, Stanford University,

California, USA; Senior Fellow, World Economic Information Services, 1989-91; Chief Economist, Japan External Trade Organization, 1986-97. Publication: Foreign Direct Investment in the United States, 1993. Honour: Inazo Nitobe Memorial Award, 1984. Memberships include: American Economic Association; American Political Science Association; Econometric Society; International Economic and Finance Society. Address: 14-5, Kami-kitazawa 1-chome, Suite 205, Setagaya-ku, Tokyo 156-0057, Japan.

**TAKAYAMA Shigemi,** b. 24 January 1933, Tokyo, Japan. Professor. m. Machiko Hosoda, 2 sons. Education: MSci, 1957, DSci, 1963, Tokyo University of Education. Appointments: Professor, University of Tsukuba; Professor, Keiai University. Publication: River Morphology, 1974. Memberships: American Geophysical Union; Association of Japanese Geographers. Address: 2-20-14 Aoyamadai, Abiko, Chiba 270-1175, Japan.

**TAKEDA Yasuhiko,** b. 16 March 1927, Japan. Physician; Professor; Researcher; Educator. m. Tamako Kawai, 2 sons, 2 daughters. Education: MD, Chiba School of Medicine, 1952; Sacred Heart Hospital, 1954-56; University of Colorado School of Medicine, 1956-60; Diplomate, American Board of Pathology, 1970. Appointments: Director, Immunoassay Laboratory, 1972-86, Director, Pathophysiology Course, 1970-85, Professor of Medicine, 1979-88, UCHSC. Publications: Over 60 original publications in the area of coagulation. Honours include: Career Development Award. Memberships include: College of American Pathologists; American Society of Clinical Pathology; American Physiological Society; International Society on Thrombosis and Hemostasis; Central Society for Clinical Investigation; Western Society for Clinical Investigation. Addresss: 635 Dexter, Denver, CO 80220, USA.

**TAKEOKA Norio,** b. 23 July 1914, Shizuoka, Japan. Poet; Writer. 1 son, 2 daughters. Education: Department Pedagogy, Waseda University and College of Buddhism; Doctrine of St Shinran in Hongangji Temple. Appointment: Chief Priest, Hofukuji Temple. Publications: Contributed to numerous anthologies, books and I (International) W (Writers) A (Association), USA. Honours: From Kyoto Newspapers Co, Mayor of Kyoto, Marseille; Golden Prize from Japanese Red Cross, International Academy Prize from Japan Culture Society, 1975; MM Award. Address: 1 18 36 Shimo da shi, Shizuoka ken, 415 Japan.

**TAKEOKA Yukiharu,** b. 23 January 1932, Kyoto, Japan. Professor of Economic History. m. Kazuko Yamamoto, 2 sons. Education: BA, 1954, MA, 1957, Kyoto University; MA, 1962, DEcon, 1974, Osaka University. Appointments: Lecturer, 1963-68, Assistant Professor, 1968-75, Professor, 1975-95, Emeritus Professor, 1995-, Osaka Univesity; Professor, Osaka Gakuin University, 1995. Publications: Author: Study of Price Revolution in France, 1974; Des entreprises françaises et japonaises face à la mécantronique, 1988; Annales School and Social History, 1990; Editor: Economic History of Europe and America, 1980; Adoption of New Technology in Modern Machine Industry, 1993; Introduction to Social History, 1995. Memberships: Socio-Economic History Society, Director, 1987-97, Advisor, 1997-; French-Japanese History Society, Director, 1982-. Address: 3-2-70 Seiwadai-Higashi, Kawanishi, Hyogo-ken 666-0142, Japan.

**TAKESHITA Toru,** b. 16 December 1931, Nishinomiya, Japan. University Professor. m. Yumiko Taniguchi, 1 son, 1 daughter. Education: BS Mathematics, Kyoto University, 1957; PhD Computer Science, 1983. Appointments: Applied Science Representative, IBM Japan, 1957; Senior Programmer, IBM

Data Systems Applied Programming, 1960-62; Manager, IBM Tokyo Olympic Information Systems, 1962-64; Consultant, Software Technology, IBM CHQ, 1983-87; Manager, CSI, IBM Tokyo Research Laboratory, 1989-91; Professor, Chuba University, 1991-. Honour: Outstanding Achievement Award, IPSJ, 1984. Memberships: ACM; IEEE Computer Society; IPSJ; JAIS; JSST. Address: 3-11-1-410 Soshigaya, Setagaya-ku, Tokyo 157-0072, Japan.

**TAKROURI Mohamad Said,** b. 16 May 1946, Damascus, Syria. Doctor; Professor of Anaesthesia. m. Tharwat Hilwani, 2 sons, 2 daughters. Education: MB ChB, Alexandria University; FFARCS, Faculty of Anaesthesia, Royal College of Surgeons, Ireland. Appointments: Consultant and Professor of Anaesthesia, College of Medicine, King Saud University. Publications: Principles of First Aid; Obstetric Anaesthesia. Memberships: Saudi Anaesthesia Association; Pan Arab Anaesthesia Society. Address: College of Medicine, King Saud University, PO Box 2925, Riyadh 11461, Saudi Arabia.

**TALAIE Afshad,** b. 2 September 1961, Tehran. Scientist. Education: BE Chemical Engineering, 1985; ME Polymer Engineering, 1988; MSc Information Technology, 1991; PhD Chemistry, 1994; MER in Artificial Intelligence. Appointments: Postdoctoral at Sydney University, Australia, 1994-97; Selected Scientist Fellow, Osaka National Research Institute, Japan, 1997-99. Publications: Over 80 publications and an average of 10 plenary/invited lectures at international conferences every year. Honours: 4 scholarships for degrees; 2 Fellowships by Australian Academy of Science, 1996, 1998; OPRA Award by Australian Government, 1992. Memberships: International member: Material Research Society; Japan Polymer Society; Solid State Ionics; New York Academy of Science by Special Invitation; American Association of Advancement of Science by Special Invitation; Society for Advancement of Material and Process Engineering. Address: 20 Murranar Road, Towradgi, Wollongong, NSW 2518, Australia.

**TALBOT Norman Clare,** b. 14 September 1936, Gislingham, England. Poet; Writer; Editor. m. Jean Margaret, 1 son, 2 daughters. Education: BA, English, Durham University, 1956-59; PhD, American Literature, Leeds University, 1959-62. Appointments: Lecturer in English, University of New South Wales, 1962; Lecturer in English, American and Australian Literature University of Newcastle, New South Wales, 1965; Senior Lecturer, 1968; Associate Professor, 1972; Retired, 1993. Publications: Poems for a Female Universe, 1968; Son of a Female Universe, 1972; The Fishing Boy, 1973; Find the Lady, 1978; Where Two Rivers Meet, 1980; The Kelly Haiku, 1985; Four Zoas of Australia, 1992; Australian Quaker Christmases, 1993; A Moment for Morris, 1996; Australian Skin, Suffolk Bones, 1997; Song Cycle of the Birds, Lake Macquarie, 1998. Honours: E C Gregory Award for Poetry, 1965; American Council of Learned Societies Fellowship, 1967-68; City of Lake Macquarie Award for Services to Poetry, 1994; Various Local Prizes for Poetry. Memberships: Society of Friends; Mythopoeic Society; Mythopoeic Literature Association of Australia; Newcastle Poetry at the Pub; Newcastle Writers' Centre; Nimrod Publications and Literary Consultancy. Address: P O Box 170, New Lambton, NSW 2305, Australia.

**TALMY Leonard,** b. 17 June 1942, Chicago, Illinois, USA. Professor. Education: BA, Linguistics, 1963, PhD in Linguistics, 1972, University of California at Berkeley. Appointments: Director, Center for Cognitive Science and Professor, Department of Linguistics, State University of New York at Buffalo. Publications: Toward a Cognitive Semantics, volumes 1 and 2; Force Dynamics in Language and Cognition; How

Language Structures Space. Memberships: Founding Member, Cognitive Science Society; International Cognitive Linguistics Association, Governing Board, 1990-97; Editorial Board, Cognitive Linguistics Journal. Address: Linguistics Department, State University of New York at Buffalo, 685 Baldy Hall, Buffalo, NY 14260, USA.

**TALOCKIENE-GASPARIUNAITE Emilija,** b. 12 July 1946, Lithuania. Artist. m. Ricardas Talocka, 1 son. Education: Art Academy of Lithuania, 1975. Appointments: Artist; Painter. Memberships: President, Sculptor J Zikaras' Foundation; Association of Artists, Lithuania. Address: Shuletekio 56-6, Vilnius, Lithuania.

**TAM Paul Wing Ming,** b. 27 July 1956, Hong Kong. Civil Engineer. Education: BSc Honours, Civil Engineering, University of Edinburgh, Scotland, 1980; PhD, Construction Management, Civil Engineering, University of Waterloo, Canada, 1992. Appointments include: Executive Engineer, Meinhardt (C&S) Ltd, 1992-93; Engineer, Agriculture and Fisheries Department, Hong Kong, 1993-95; Lecturer, Department of Civil Engineering, University of Hong Kong, 1995-98; Assistant Vice-President, Parsons Brinckerhoff (Asia) Ltd, 1999-. Publications: Book chapters: State Space Representation of Linear Project, co-author, 1996; Optimization of Linear Construction Projects Using Optional Control, co-author, 1996; Procurement of Specialised Civil Engineering Facility by Design and Build Contract, author, to appear; Papers and reports. Honours: Faculty of Engineering Scholarship, 1989, 1990, 1991, University Graduate Scholarship, 1991, University of Waterloo. Memberships: Institution of Civil Engineers, 1985; Chartered Engineer, 1985; Fellow, Geological Society, 1985; New York Academy of Sciences, 1997. Address: Parsons Brinckerhoff (Asia) Ltd, 23rd Floor, AIA Tower, 183 Electric Road, North Point, Hong Kong.

**TAMAOKI Bun-Ichi,** b. 24 July 1925, Tokyo, Japan. Biochemist. m. Shoko Sasaki, 2 sons. Education: School of Pharmaceutical Sciences, Tokyo Imperial University, 1947; Diploma, Pharmacist, 1947; PhD, University of Tokyo, 1959. Appointments: Research Associate, University of Tokyo, 1947-61; Section Chief, 1961-74; Division Director, National Institute of Radiological Sciences, 1974-86; Professor, School of Pharmaceutical Sciences, Nagasaki University, 1986-91. Publications: More than 200. Honours: Research Award, Minister of Science and Technology Agency; Medal of Achievement, Emperor of Japan, 1995. Memberships: Japan Society of Comparative Endocrinology; Japan Society of Andrology, New York Academy of Sciences. Address: 238 21 Sonnocho, Inageku, Chibashi 263-0051, Japan.

**TAMAS Christian,** b. 13 November 1964, Letca, Salaj, Romania. Writer. m. Brandusa Bardas. Education: Foreign Languages, University of Bucharest. Appointments: Lecturer, University of Kishinev; Editor, Junimea Publishing House; Editor in Chief, Graphix Publishing House; President, Ars Longa Publishing House; Translator of Seven Languages, English, French, Italian, Spanish, Portuguese, Irish and Arabic. Publications: The Black Knight; The Curse of the Cathars; Labyrinth; Awakening to Immortality. Memberships: Aspro; Litter Art XXI. Address: Str Elena Doamna 2, 6600 Iasi, Romania.

**TAMBA Nobuo,** b. 3 January 1958, Hamamatsu, Shizuoka, Japan. Electrical Engineer. m. Yuko Nakadai. Education: BS, 1980, Waseda University, Tokyo; MS, 1982, Tsukuba University, Ibaraki, Japan; PhD, 1998, Kyushu University, Fukuoka, Japan. Appointments: Engineer 1982-88, Assistant Senior Engineer 1989-94, Senior Engineer 1994-, Hitachi Ltd, okyo; Visiting Scholar, Stanford University, California, USA, 988-89. Publications: Contributor of articles to professional ournals. Memberships: IEEE; Physical Society of Japan. address: Hitachi Ltd Device Development, 2326 Imai, Ome, okyo 198, Japan.

**TAMINSKAS Algirdas,** b. 9 February 1962, Birzai. Lawyer. n. Nerija, 1 son, 1 daughter. Education: Faculty of Law, Vilnius University, 1981-86, Doctoral Studies, 1989-93. Appointments: nstitute, 1986-96, Associate Professor, 1996-, Faculty of Law, Vilnius University; Advisor State and Law Comm, Lithuania Rep Seimas, 1993-94; Ombudsmen and Head, Ombudsmen's Office of the Lithuania Republic Seimas, 1994-. Publications: Reorganisation of Legal Ownership Relations in Lithuania, dissertation, 1993; Co-author, Human Rights and Liberties, 995; Civil Law, 1997. Address: Zirgo 3a-21, LT 2040, Vilnius, Lithuania.

**TAMOSIUNAS Vytas Antanas,** b. 1942, Pasvalys, Lithuania. Scientist. m. Laima, 1 son, 1 daughter. Education: DSc, Natural Science, 1970; DHabil, Allergology and Immunology, 1986; Professor, Immunology, 1988. Career: Junior Researcher, Institute of Biochemistry, Lithuanian Academy of Sciences, 1969-71; Senior Researcher, 1971-74, Head of Laboratory, 1974-90, Professor, Chair, 1988-, Head of Laboratory, Institute of Immunology, 1990-, Vilnius University. Publications: 240 and 3 monographs. Membership: Corresponding Member, Lithuanian Academy of Sciences. Address: Kestucio 12-1, 2004 Vilnius, Lithuania.

**TAN Masaki,** b. 13 February 1946, Akita, Japan. Surgeon. n. Keiko Takahashi, 1 son, 1 daughter. Education: MD, Tohoku University, 1978; LLB, Kinki University, 1985. Appointments: Associate Professor, Tohoku University, 1973-85; Head of Department, Ohfunato Prefectural Hospital, 1985-88; Kitakami Prefetural Hospital, 1988-94; Isawa Prefectural Hospital, 994-98; Vice Director, Wakayanagi NHI Hospital, 1998-. Publications: Recent Advances in Chemotherapy New Applications of OK-432. Memberships: AAAS; ISPO; New York Academy of Science. Address: 112 Kawakitafurukawa Wakayanagi, Kurihara, Miyagi 989 5501, Japan.

**TANAKA Hiroshi,** b. 6 October 1939, Fukuoka, Japan. Professor of Meteorology. m. Noriko Katayama, 2 sons. Education: BSc Geophysics, 1964, MSc Geophysics, 1966, PhD Geophysics, 1973, University of Tokyo. Appointments: Research Officer, 1969, Principal Research Officer, 1975, Radio Research Laboratories of Ministry of Post and Telecommunications; Associate Professor of Meteorology, 1978, Professor of Meteorology, 1988, Water Research Institute, Nagoya University; Professor of Meteorology, 1993, Director, 1995-, Institute for Hydrospheric-Atmospheric Sciences, Nagoya University; Visiting Scientist: LAR of University of Illinois at Champaign-Urbana, 1973; Mesoscale Research Section of National Centre for Atmospheric Research, 1981; Lab of Atmosphere of NASA Goddard Space Flight Centre, 1987. Publications: 56 refereed papers of atmospheric sciences; Books written in Japanese. Honour: Award of the Meteorological Society of Japan, Waves and Wavebreaking in the Middle Atmosphere, 1989. Memberships: Member, Meteorological Society of Japan; Management Board of the Meteorological Society of Japan; SCOSTEP Science Discipline Representative. Address: Institute for Hydrospheric-Atmospheric Sciences, Nagoya University, Furo-cho, Chikusa-ku, Nagoya 464-8601, Japan.

**TANAKA Masayuki,** b. 15 April 1935, Yamanashi Prefecture, Japan. Professor. m. Mayumi, 4 sons. Education: Bachelor of Science; Tohoku University, 1959; Master of

Science, Tohoku University, 1961; Doctor of Science, Tohoku University, 1971. Appointments: Research Associate, 1961-71; Associate Professor, 1971-73; Professor, 1973-1985; Director, Upper Atmospheric Research Labs, 1990-; Oceanic Studies, 1993-96. Publication: Global Warming, Japanese; More than 200 Treatises. Honours: Meritorious Environment Preservation Award, 1997; Purple Ribbon Medal, 1998. Memberships: Science Council of Japan; Council of Geology and Geophysics of Japan. Address: Graduate School of Science, Tohoku University, Aoba Ku, Sendai, Japan.

**TANAKA Shigeki,** b. 23 August 1953, Asahikawa, Japan. Neurologist. m. Kumiko Sakai, 3 sons. Education: MD, 1979, PhD, 1988, Juntendo University. Appointments: Neurologist, Japanese Society of Neurology, 1983; Lecturer, 1988, Associate Professor, 1998-, Juntendo University. Publications: Several articles in professional journals. Honours: Badges: Council of Japanese Society of Neurology, 1999; Grantee, Ministry of Education, Japanese Government, 1988. Memberships: Japanese Society of Neurology; Royal Society of Medicine, England; American Academy of Neurology. Address: 1-19-12 Himonya Meguroku, Tokyo 152-0003, Japan.

**TANAKA Yoshihiro,** b. 21 February 1960, Kobe, Japan. Associate Professor. Education: BE, 1982, ME, 1984, DEng, 1988, Kyoto University. Appointments: Senior Researcher, CRIEPI, 1989-91; Associate Professor, Hokkaido University, 1991-; Research Fellow, University of California, Berkeley, USA, 1994-95. Publications: Several articles in professional journals. Honour: Visiting Scholar Fellowship, Ministry of Education, 1994. Memberships: SIAM, Philadelphia, USA; Mathematics Program Society, The Netherlands. Address: Hokkaido University, Kita 9 Nishi 7 Kita-ku, Sapporo 060-0809, Japan.

**TANDON Parshotam Lal,** b. 7 May 1945, India. Agricultural Scientist. m. Rekha, 1 son, 1 daughter. Education: BSc, Punjab Agricultural University, 1967; MSc, Himachal Agriculture College, 1970; PhD, University of Agricultural Sciences, 1985. Appointments: Research Assistant, 1967-71; Senior Research Assistant, 1971-74; Scientist, 1974-76; Senior Scientist, Indian Institute of Horticultural Research, 1976-82; Head, Division of Entomology, 1988-91; Principal Scientist, 1982-96; Principal Scientist, Project Directorate of Biological, Bangalore, 1996-. Honours: University Medal; Mr N M Mohan Memorial Gold Medal; British Council Scholarship; Hexamar Award; Medal and Citation. Memberships: Vice President, Association for Advancement of Pest Management in Horticultural Ecosystems; Chief Editor, Society for Biocontrol Advancement; Agriculture Scientists Research Forum; Indian Journal of Plant Protection; International Working Group on Mango. Address: PB No 2491, H A Farm Post, Bellary Road, Bangalore 560 024, India.

**TANG Alice Xiao-Jing,** b. 3 July 1962, Chengdu, Sichuan, China. Senior Researcher. 1 son. Education: BSc Chemistry and Chemical Engineering, 1983, University of Hunan, China; PhD Analytical Chemistry, 1997, Lund University, Sweden. Appointments: Undergrad student, University Hunan, 1979-83; Assistant Lecturer, University Wuhan Technology, China, 1983-89; Researcher, 1990-91, 1992-93, PhD Student, 1993-97, Senior Researcher, 1998-, Lund University, Sweden. Publications: In Analytical Letters, 1995, 1997, Biotechnology Techniques, 1997, Analytica Chimica Acta, 1998. Membership: Swedish Centre for Bioseparation, Lund, Sweden. Address: Uardavagen 14E, 22471 Lund, Sweden.

**TANG George,** b. 8 November 1964, Hong Kong. Money Manager. Education: BSc, Electrical Engineering, Case

Western Reserve University, 1987; MSc, Northwestern University, 1989. Appointment: Second Vice President, Investments, Financial Consultant, Smith Barney. Memberships: Association for Investment Management and Research; Institute for Investment Management Consultants. Address: Smith Barney, 1 Tower Lane, Villa Park, IL 60181-4671, USA.

**TANG Jian Zheng,** b. 5 December 1938, Nantong, China. Physicist. m. Zhi Min Wang, 1 son, 1 daughter. Education: BS, MS, Peking University. Appointments: Lecturer, Associate Professor, Peking University, 1963-90; Senior Research Engineer, University of Sydney, 1990-99. Honour: Löf/Duffie Best Paper Award, International Solar Energy Society, 1997. Address: University of Sydney, Department of Applied Physics, Sydney, NSW 2006, Australia.

**TANG Ling-Yu,** b. 4 December 1938, Jiangsu, China. Professor. m. Hui-Lan Gao, 1 son, 1 daughter. Education: Bachelor's degree, Nanjing University, 1963; Doctorate, Australian National University, 1988. Appointments: Research Assistant, Lanzhou Institute of Glaciology and Cryopedology, 1963-75; Assistant Professor, 1975-83, Professor, Head of Palynology Department, 1988-, Nanjing Institute of Geology and Palaeontology. Publications: More than 70. Membership: Director, Palynological Society of China. Address: Nanjing Institute of Geology and Palaeontology, Academia Sinica, 39 East Beijing Road, Nanjing 210008, China.

**TANIGAKI Masataka,** b. 2 October 1942, Kobe, Japan. Professor. m. Tomoyo Ohmura, 2 daughters. Education: BS, Kyoto University, 1965; PhD, University of Wisconsin, USA, 1972. Appointments: Research Associate, Institute of Atomic Energy, 1972-83, Associate Professor, 1983-94, Professor, 1994-, Department of Chemical Engineering, Kyoto University. Publications include: Separation Engineering, 1992. Memberships: SCEJ; AIChE; Japan Membrane Society; Japan Society of Polymer Processing. Address: Department of Chemical Engineering, Kyoto University, Honmachi, Yoshida, Sakyo-ku, Kyoto 606, Japan.

**TAO Cheng,** b. December 1924, Beijing, China. Professor. m. Shu Xin Chen, 1 d. Education: Graduate, Department of Aeronautical Engineering, Shanghai Jiao Tong University, 1950. Appointments: Teacher, Revolution School, Yucai School, 1942-43; Teacher, Lecturer, Associate Professor, Professor, Harbin Institute of Technology, 1958; Professor, Department of Astronautical Engineering and Mechanics, School of Astronautics, HIT. Publications: Using Heng Chih Tao's Educational Thought with the Help of Music to Save the Juvenile Delinquents Holding Highly the Great Banner of the Combination of Patriotism and Internationalism Advocated by My Father Mr Heng Chih Tao; The Review of the Forty Years of Harbin Society of Theoretical and Applied Mechanics; More than 20 papers on gas dynamics, mechanics of the viscous flow, turbulent flow and aeroelasticity at international conferences and symposiums and in international journals. Honours: Awarded Title of Oustanding Secretary General, Harbin Association of Science and Technology; Second Prize of the National Progression of National Science and Technology, 1985; Memberships: Honorary Chairman, Harbin Society of Theoretics and Applied Mechanics; Honorary Chairman, Shanghai Maritime Exchange Association; Heilongjiang Provincial Committee of the Chinese People's Political Consultative Conference; China Heng Chih Tao Foundation; China Society for Study of Heng Chih Tao. Address: Apt III, Gate 1, 138-1 Fanrong Street, Nangang District, Harbin 150001, China.

**TAO Long-Xiang,** b. 14 September 1933, Peking. Professor; Senior Researcher. m. Zou Duo-Xiu, 1 son, 1 daughter. Education: Tsinghua University, 1952-53; Peking Institute of Petroleum, 1954-56; Zelinsky Institute of Organic Chemistry, Russian Academy of Sciences, Moscow, 1962-66; DSc, 1966. Appointments: Head, Scientific Research Group, 1966-92, President, 3 Projects, National Natural Science Foundation of China, 1985-87, 1990-92, 1992-94; 2 Projects, Foundation of SINOPEC, 1986-89, 1987-89. Publications: Over 100 papers in professional journals. Honours: Certificate of Merit, Science Research, 1977; Achievement Award, Science and Technology, 1980; Government Special Subsidy, Council of China, 1992-. Memberships: Chinese Chemical Society; Chinese Petroleum Society. Address: Dalian Institute of Chemical Physics, Chinese Academy of Sciences, PO Box 110, Dalian 116023, China.

**TAO Zhiguang,** b. 23 February 1937, Guangxi, China. Teacher. m. Sha Xiaoci, 2 sons. Education: Graduate, Department of Mathematics, Fudan University, Shanghai, China, 1964. Appointment: Professor of Mathematics, 1992. Honour: Given title of Specialist with Outstanding Contributions, State Council of China, 1994. Membership: Mathematical Society of China. Address: Department of Mathematics, Guangxi University, Guangxi 530004, China.

**TAORMINA Charles Anthony,** b. 2 April 1948, Johnstown, Pennsylvania, USA. Author; Playwright. m. Brenda Gilbert, divorced, 1 daughter. Education: 1 January, Indiana University of Pennsylvania. Appointments: Author and Playwright; Editor, Times of Charlottesville, 1976-78, Blue Ridge Review, 1978-79, Virtù, 1993-94; Author, Playwright, The Renaissance Workshop, 1990-98; Playwright, Actor, Theatrix Unlimited, 1993, Gemini Theatre, 1998; Speaker, World Future Society, 1979, 1993; Artist and Consultant, Downsizing and Sketches Performed, 1998. Publications: Novels include: Abbas and Merdan; Endgames; Karma Bums; Gratuity; Legacy; Drama: Freedom One; The Catalyst; Nonfiction: Along the Journalistic Path, Infinity; Vision; Ardour; Keystone; Poetry: Rain Folio; also independent monographs and audio cassette; story collection, Moments published on-line, 1998; Contributor fiction and nonfiction to other collections. Honours: Nominated Pushcart Prize, 1979; Honourable Mention for essay, Society of American Cuisine, 1987; Interviewed WPFW Radio, 1978. Memberships: Authors League; Dramatists Guild; American Christian Writers Association; World Vision; Amnesty International; Union of Concerned Scientists. Address: 860 Chalkei St, ist Fl Apt, Akron, OH 44310, USA.

**TARASENKO Yuri P,** b. 29 May 1946, Poltava Region, Ukraine. Researcher in Physics. m. Natalia A Muraviova, 1 son. Education: Diploma, Physicist, 1969; DPhys, 1986. Appointments: Engineer Researcher, Scientific Researcher, Senior Researcher, Institute of Chemistry, N Lobatchesky University, 1973-86; Head of Laboratory, A Blagonravov Institute of Machine Science, 1986-; General Director, Scientific and Production Enterprise, Tribonika, with important research and development works in the field of ion-plasma vacuum coatings for aviation, gas and automobile industries, 1994-; Founder, developer, high plasma technologies in Russia. Publications: Over 80 scientific articles in Russia and foreign professional journals; Holder of 10 Russian patents. Membership: Technical Academy of Russia. Address: A Blagonravov Institute of Machine Science, Russian Academy of Sciences, 85 Belinsky Str, 603024 Nizhny Novgorod, Russia.

**TAREEN J A,** b. 26 April 1947, Mysore, India. Professor. m. Syeda Gulnaz Tareen, 1 daughter. Education: MSc, Geology, 1967; PhD, Experimental Mineralogy, 1978, Mysore University;

DSc, Solid State Chemistry, Bordeaux University, 1983. Appointments: Research Assistant, 1967-74, Research Officer, 1974-83, Assistant Director, 1983-87, Mineralogical Institute; Professor, Mineralogy, University of Mysore, 1987-97; Visiting Professor, Mekelle University, 1997-. Publications: Over 60 research papers in international journals. Honours: Golden Jubilee Science and Technology Award, Mysore University, 1982; National Mineral Award, Government of India, 1997. Memberships: Geological Society of India; Mineralogical Society of India; Muslim Education Society, Mysore. Address: Department of Geology, Mysore University, Mysore 570006, Karnatak, India.

**TARGOS Julie Diana,** b. 21 July 1944, Rib Lake, Wisconsin, USA. Marketing and Advertising Executive. Education: BA Communications and Journalism, University of Detroit; AA General Business and Accounting, Macomb County Community College; Certificate, IBM Data Processing School; Middleton Real Estate School. Appointments: Assistant to the Director of Antibiotic Research and Biological Development, Data Processing, Computer Operator, Parke-Davis & Co Division of Warner-Lambert), 1962-79; Editor, Office Manager, Brooks & Perkins (Division of AAR Corp.), 1979-81; Art Director, Account Executive, Project Coordinator, Copywriter, G&D Communications Inc, 1979-85; Account Executive, Marketing Associates Inc, 1985-89; President and Sole Owner, JDT Associates Inc, 1989-94; President and Sole Owner, Nonpareil Communications Inc, 1993-; Creative Services Manager, Sun Technicom Inc, 1997; Executive Producer, Kelly Technical Services, 1997; Proposal Manager, Graphic Artist, Technical Representative, Adecco Technical Services, 1994-98; Certified Rehabilitation Skills Technician, Special Tree Rehabilitation Institute, 1998. Honour: University of Detroit Jesuit Founders' Scholarship, 1981. Memberships: Adcraft Club of Detroit; Adobe Technology Exchange; American Marketing Association; Marketing Research Association; Greater Detroit Chamber of Commerce; American Advertising Federation; World Trade Club; Women in Communications Inc. Address: Nonpareil Communications Inc, 427 Jeffrey Avenue, Royal oak, MI 48073-2521, USA.

**TARNOPOLSKII Yuri,** b. 16 December 1929, Sevastopol, Russia. Scientific Worker. m. Rita Kalnberinga, 2 daughters. Education: Graduated with Honours Degree, Latvian State University, 1952; Candidate of Technical Sciences, 1957; PhD, Latvian State University, 1968. Appointments: Professor, Riga Technical University, 1969; Latvian Academy of Sciences, 1954-. Publications: Static Test Methods for Composites, 1985; Handbook og Composites, 1989; Structural Composites, 1990; Spatially Reinforced Composites, 1993; Composites Engineering Handbook, 1997; Lubin's Handbook of Composites II, 1998. Honours: Latvian State Prize Winner, 1965; USSR State Prize Winner, 1985. Memberships: Latvian Academy of Sciences; National Committee on Theoretical and Applied Mechanics of the former USSR; International Committee for Composite Materials, ICCM. Address: 79-81 Flat 41, Kr Valdemara St, LV-1013, Riga, Latvia.

**TARNOPOLSKY Oleg Borisovich,** b. 21 December 1950, Dnepropetrovsk, Ukraine. English Educator; Professor of English; Researcher in Teaching English as a Foreign Language. m. Natalia Tolstikh, 20 September 1969, 1 daughter. Education: Diploma as Teacher of English, Dnepropetrovsk State University, 1972; Candidate of Pedagogy, Moscow State Pedagogical Institute of Foreign Languages, 1979; Doctor of Pedagogy (DSc equivalent), Moscow State University, 1992. Appointments: Senior Librarian, 1972-73, Instructor in English, 1973-75, Dnepropetrovsk Medical Institute; Instructor in English, 1975-81, Chairperson, Foreign Language Department,

1980-, Associate Professor, 1981-92, Full Professor, 1992-, Dnepropetrovsk State Technical University of Railway Transport. Publications: 81 research publications including: Methods of teaching English to 1st year Technical Students, book; Methods of teaching English to 2nd year Technical Students, book; Articles and abstracts of papers in professional publications, Ukraine, Russia, USA, UK, France, Spain. Honours include: Fulbright Award, 1994. Memberships: International Association for Teachers of English as a Foreign Language, UK; Teachers of English to Speakers of Other Languages, USA; AEDEAN, Spain; European Society for Studies of English. Address: ul Chkalova 4, apt 8, Dnepropetrovsk 49029, Ukraine.

**TASHA Lawrence Loweh,** b. 25 August 1947, Kumbo, NSO, Cameroun. Banking. m. Mary Electa Barkisu, 3 sons, 2 daughters. Education: BA, Distinction, Maths, De Pauw University, Greencastle, USA; MSc, 1969-71; PhD Program in Mathematics, 1973-75; MBA, University of British Columbia, Vancouver, Canada, 1975-77. Appointments: Principal Promoter, Creation of Amity Bank, 1988-91; Founder, Chairman and Managing Director, Amity Bank Cameroon SA, Douala, Cameroon, 1992-. Publication: Capital of Banks. Honour: Banker of the Year, Comite D'Excellence Africaine, 1995. Memberships: APECCAM; GICAM; General President, Kumbo Strikers. Address: Amity Bank Cameroon SA, BP 2705, Douala, Cameroun.

**TATEIBA Mitsuo,** b. 24 May 1944, Beppu, Japan. Professor. m. Junko, 2 sons, 1 daughter. Education: BEng, Kyushu University, 1967; MEng, Kyushu University, 1969; DEng, Kyushu University, 1977. Appointments: Research Associate, Kyushu University, 1969-77; Associate Professor, Nagasaki University, 1977-83; Associate Professor, Kyushu University, 1983-90; Full Professor, Kyushu University, 1990-. Honours: Yonezawa Prize, IEICE, 1975; The 7th Institute Comm Res Prize, 1986. Memberships: IEICE; IEEJ; ITEJ; JSIAM; AGU; Electromagnetics Academy; AAAS. Address: 3-14-3 Miwadai Higashi-ku, Fukuoka 811-02, Japan.

**TATIC Darko,** b. 22 December 1932, Belgrade. University Professor, Senior Drama Director. m. Ljubica Milenkovic, 1 son. Education: Degree in Acting, Academy of Theatrical Arts, 1961; Degree in Directing, Academy of Theatrical Arts, 1963. Appointments: Radio Drama Director, Radio Belgrade, 1961-; Lecturer, 1973-87; Professor, 1987-. Publications: The Essence of the Contemporary Radio Drama; History of Serbian Radio; Poetics of Radiophony; Centaurs; Hydrocialectica alias Aquae Rondo; Campo Santo; Dragoslav Jelic-a Man of Planetary Culture; Plato in Serbia; Photo Boo-hoo; Fe male Strom; Das Fraulein; Rabies; Secondary Heaven. Honours: Prix Italia Capri, 1983; Premio Ondas Internacional Barcelona, 1977, 1980, 1990; Prix Monte Carlo, 1991; OIRT Varna, 1990; 11 awards, The Festivals of Yugoslav Radio Television, 1968-91; FEDOR Belgrade, 1990; International Man of the Year, International Biographical Centre, 1998. Memberships: Association for the Protection of Architectural and Environmental Heritage; Serbia Nostra; Association for German Serbian Cooperation; Yugoslav French Allicance. Address: Radio Belgrad, Hilendarska 2a, 11000 Beograd, Yugoslavia.

**TAUB Edward,** b. 22 October 1931, Brooklyn, USA. Psychology Researcher. m. Mildred Allen Taub, 13 August 1959. Education: BA, Brooklyn College, 1953; MA, Columbia University, 1959; PhD, New York University, 1969. Appointments: Research Assistant, Columbia University, New York City, 1956; Department Experimental Neurology, Jewish Chronic Disease Hospital, New York City, 1957-60; Research Associate, Department Experimental Neurology, Jewish

Chronic Disease Hospital, 1960-68; Director, Behavioral Biology Center, Institute for Behavioral Research, 1968-83; Associate Director, Institute for Behavioral Research, 1978-83; Director, Feedback Research Center, Birmingham, Alabama, USA, 1984-91; Professor, Psychology, University Alabama, Birmingham, 1986-; Senior Scientist, Center for Aging; Guest Professor, University Konstanz, Germany, 1995-96; University Jena, Germany, 1996-97; Assistant Professor, Department Psychiatry, Johns Hopkins University, Balt, 1972-82; Visiting Professor, Graduate Program, Department Psychology, CUNY, 1984-85; Visiting Professor, University Tuebingen, University Trier, University Muenster, Humboldt University, Germany, 1993-. Publications: Contributor, articles to professional journals; Co-inventor, Technique of Thermal Biofeedback, 1970-71. Honours: Award Association Applied Psychophysiol and Biofeedback, 1989; Distinguished Scientist of 1998 Award; Ireland Prize for Scholarly Distinction, University of Alabama, Birmingham, 1997; Guggenheim Foundation Fellow, 1983-84; Fellow, 1997, AAAS; APA, Executive Com Div 6; Society for Behavioral Medicine; American Psychological Society, Charter, William James Fellow Award 1997); Society for Neuroscience; Biofeedback Society America, President 1978-79, Outstanding Research Contribution Award, 1988; American Physiological Society, Executive Com Neuroscience Section, 1988-91. Address: 1428 Shades Crest Road, Birmingham, AL 35226-3120, USA.

**TAVARTKILADZE George A,** b. 23 August 1948, Tbilisi, Georgia. Otorhinolaryngologist. m. Natalia Baltiyskaya. Education: Graduated, Russian State Medical University, 1973; MD, 1975, PhD, 1977, Moscow Ear, Nose and Throat Research Institute; Academician, International Academy of Sciences, 1994. Appointments: Senior Researcher, 1978-83, Laboratory Head, 1983-88, Moscow Ear, Nose and Throat Research Institute; Director, Research Centre for Audiology and Hearing Rehabilitation, Moscow, 1988-; WHO Expert. Publications: 210 publications in professional journals and chapters in books. Honour: Named to Russian Order of Friendship by President of the Russian Federation, 1996. Memberships: American Academy of Audiology; New York Academy of Sciences; Association for Research in Otorhinolaryngology; International Evoked Respiratory Audiometry Study Group. Address: 3 Romanov Per, Apt 69, Moscow 103009, Russia.

**TAWIL George,** b. 14 April 1947, Lattakia, Syria. Psychiatrist. m. Eleftheria Tsakalou. Education: MD, 1981, PhD Psychosomatics, 1986, University of Athens, Medical School. Appointments: Scientific worker (unpaid), Electro-Engephalic Lab, Psychiatric Clinic, State Mental Hospital of Athens, 1981-86; Specialist, Neurological Clinic, Psychiatric Hospital of Attica, 1986-87; Specialist, 14th Psychiatric Hospital of Attica, 1988-91; Specialist in Psychiatry, 1991; Researcher on new methods of confronting psychosomatic diseases and the problems of drug abuse in youth, team psychotherapy and Psychosomatic Study, various medical colleges and hospitals in the United States, 1991-; Academic Advisor, La Salle University, 1996-. Publications: 5 major published works including: Influence of Family Relations on the Chronic Asthmatics, 1987; Family Structure and the Third Age, 1991; Co-author, Hostile Personality Characteristics, Dysthymic States and Neurotic Symptoms in Urticaris, Psoriasis and Alopecia, 1985; various unpublished works; 28 conferences. Honours: Fulbright Grant, 1991. Memberships: American Psychiatric Association; American Association for the History of Medicine Inc; Illinois Psychological Association; American Association for the Advancement of Science; American Psychosomatic Society; Academy Psychosomatic Society; American Society for Psychosomatic, Obstetrics and Gynaecology; International Psychogeriatric Association; and others. Address: 54 Michalakopoulou Street, 115-28 Athens, Greece.

**TAYADE Ganesh,** b. 13 March 1954, Telhara, India. District Librarian. m. Padmatai, 1 son, 2 daughters. Education: BA, 1977; BLib and Information Science, 1978; Diploma, Public Relations, 1988. Appointments: Editor, Maharashtra Granthalaya Patrika, Dhamma Saurabh, Buldhana Sarswat, Jaibhim - Dindarshika; Co-Editor, Gram Darshan; Sub Editor, Republican Sandesh. Memberships include: Satyashodhak Mitra Mandal; Sarwajanik Maitrey Wachanalaya, Talhara; Samrat Ashoka Bahuddheshiya Sikshan Prasarak Mandal, Telhara; The Buddhist Co-operative Credit Society, Bombay; Bhartiya Dalit Sahitya Academy, New Delhi. Address: Government Librarian, Buldara MS, 443001 Maharashtra, India.

**TAYLOE Marjorie Zaerr,** b. 15 February, Los Angeles, California, USA. Musician. m. Ralph Tayloe, 2 sons, 3 daughters. Education: Teachers Diploma, Samoiloff Opera Academy, Los Angeles, 1952; Student, Whittier College, Los Angeles Valley College, Occidental College. Appointments: Harpist, Phil Kerr's Harmony Chorus, 1949-53; Founder, Director, Music Arts Academy, North Hollywood, 1950-; Soloist, Harpist, Beverly Hills Symphony, California, 1962-; Director, Harps of Hollywood, 1984-; Director, Tayloe Family Ringers and Singers, Royal Harpist of Hollywood, 1986-. Creative Works: Appeared Seattle World's Fair Concert, 1963; 16 European Concert Tours; Played Before Queen of England; Numerous Private Concerts; 1800 Weddings; Concerts in 20 Countries; 8 Solo Tapes. Honours include: Pen Woman of the Year, 1994. Memberships include: DAR Minstrel Harpers Society; American Pen Women. Address: 340 3rd Street, Solvang, CA 93463-2724, USA.

**TAYLOR Anthony B,** b. 25 November 1971, Nassau, Bahamas. Civil Engineer. m. Kaaryn Taylor, 1 son. Education: BS, Civil Engineering, 1994; MBA, 1995; PhD, 1997. Appointments: Construction engineering and management, Parsons Constructors Inc; Resident Engineer, Federal Medical Center Project. Publication: The Taylor Research Model, article, 1998. Memberships: Institution of Civil Engineering; AACE International. Address: Parsons Constructors Inc, 5404 Wine Court, Raleigh, NC 27610, USA.

**TAYLOR Ellis Clarence,** b. 4 Feb 1931, New Hebron, Missouri, USA. Retired, Electronic Engineer. Education: Universal TV Electronics Diploma, 1953; Cleveland Institute of Electronics, 1956; Diploma, 1988; 2nd CIRE Diploma, Engineering Technology, 1959-63; University of Kansas City, 1978-81; University of Missourie. Appointments: Mayor of Kansas City, Missouri; Kansas City Board of Radio and TV Examiners, 1961-84; Executive Council, International Brotherhood Electronic Workers, 1976-79. Honours: Medal of Freedom; veteran of Foreign Wars, US Navy, 7th Fleet Flagship, Carrier-gunnery. Memberships: Audio Engineering Society; Alumni Association. Address: P O Box 320541, Kansas City. MO 64132, USA.

**TAYLOR Mary Jane,** b. 30 May 1953, Schenectady, New York, USA. Professor; Studio Art; Art Education; Clay Artist. m. George Richter Taylor, 1 son, 1 daughter. Education: Clay Artist, Art Education; BFA, Art Education, Valdosta State University, 1975; MEd, Art Education, University of Georgia, 1980; EdD, Art Education, University of Georgia, 1995. Appointments: Certified Teacher, Art, K-12; Art Teacher, 9-12, Colquitt Co Schools, Moultrie, Georgia, 1975-76; 9-12 Valdosta City Schools, Valdosta, Georgia, 1976-78; K-6 Art Teacher,

Clarke Co Schools, Athens, Georgia, 1978-79; Faculty Brenau University, Gainesville, Georgia, 1979-; Full Professor, Director, Visual Arts Department, 1979-97; Acting Chair, Fine Arts, 1990-92; Chair Fine Arts, 1993-94; Director, Galleries, Brenau, 1974-90; Faculty Elderhostel, Brenau University. Honours: Art and Museum Program Grantee, The Coca Cola Foundation, 1993-96, 1997-2000; One Woman Show Brenau University, 1988; 1st Place, Philadelphia Rug and Carpets Des Competition, 1975; 1st Place, Clay National Invitational Art Exhibition, 1992-. Memberships: National Art Education Association; Higher Education Division State Representative, 1995-97; Georgia Art Education Association; Omicron Delta Kappa; Sigma Alpha Iota; AAUP. Address: 3581 Meadow Lane, Gainesville, GA 30506, USA.

**TAYLOR Paul David,** b. 1 May 1937, Lexington, Tennessee, USA. Health Services Administrator; Educator. Divorced, 2 sons. Education: AS, 1957, Garden City Community College; University of Kansas, 1958. Appointments: Biology Lab Technician, University of Colorado Health Science Centre, 1962-65; Coordinator of Organ Transplant Programme, 1962-92; Research Associate, 196587, Senior Instructor, 1969-92, Professor Emeritus, 1992; Transplant Administrator, Presbyterian University Hospital of the University of Pittsburgh, 1989-98; Health Technician, Veterans Administration Hospital, Pittsburgh, 1990-97. Honours: Citizenship Award, Prince Hall Masons CO & Jurisdiction, 1982, Hattie Anthony Resource Centre, 1986; Guest Lecturer, Denver Public Schools, 1983-89; Inaugural inductee, High School Hall of Fame, Garden City, 1985; Man of Distinction, Lane Contemporaries of Lane College Alumni Association, 1989; Colorado's Own African-American History Maker Honoree, 1993; BTAC, Denver, Black Transplantation Committee, 1993; Inaugural Member of The National Minority Transplant Hall of Fame sponsored by MOTTEP, The National Minority Organ/Tissue Transplant Program, 1996; Special Achievement, member of world's first human liver transplant team, Denver, 1963. Memberships: Task Force on Minority Organ Donation of Western Pennsylvania; National Kidney Foundation of Western Pennsylvania, Minority Affairs Committee; Editorial Board, Journal of Transplant Coordination; American Society of Minority Health and Transplant Professionals; Knights of Pythsgorus; Prince Hall Masons; North American Transplant Coordinators Organisation; CO Society to Prevent Blindness. Address: PO Box 200026, Denver, CO 80220 0026, USA.

**TAZEWELL Calvert Walke,** b. 13 April 1917, Wilmington, Delaware, USA. Air Force Officer; Publisher; Author; Historian; Webmaster. m. Therese Hoey, 1 s, 5 d. Education: USAF Air University, 1952; Indiana University, 1956; New York University, 1962-63; Fisk University, 1964; Old Dominion University, 1964-65; Sophia University, Tokyo, 1952. Appointments: U S Army, U S Airforce, 1937-59; Retired at Lt Colonel, Regular Air Force; Founder, Metro Dade County Public Library System, 1963-64; Norfolk Historical Society, 1965; Virginia History Federation, 1967. Publications: Over 36 Books. Honours: Writers Digest; National Writers Club; Bronze Star Medal; Member of the Year, 1998, National Weather Association. Memberships: The Retired Officers Association; National Writers Association; Air Weather Association; Norfolk Historical Society. Address: 704 Green Tree Circle, Apt #103, Chesapeake, VA 23320, USA.

**TCHENG James Enlou,** b. 15 September 1956, Covington, Kentucky, USA. m. Mary Ann Powers. Education: BS, 1978; MD, 1982. Appointments include: Department of Critical Care, Bridgeton, Missouri, 1985-86; Fellow, Division of Cardiology, 1986-88, Associate in Medicine, 1988-89, Director of Interventional Cardiovascular Databank, 1988-, Assistant

Professor of Medicine, 1990-97, Director, Quality Assurance, Division of Cardiology, 1994-, Associate Professor of Medicine, 1997-, Department of Medicine, Duke University Medical Center, Durham, North Carolina, USA. Publications: Peer reviewed manuscripts, abstracts, invited manuscripts. Memberships: American College of Physicans; American College of Cardiology; American Heart Association, Council on Clinical Cardiology; Fellow, Society for Cardiac Angiography and Interventions; Fellow, American Colleg of Cardiology; Associate Editor, American Heart Journal. Address: Duke University Medical Center, Box 3275, Durham, NC 27710, USA.

**TCHIZHIK Andrey Aleksandrovich, Jr,** b. 15 March 1937, St Petersburg, Russia. Physical Mechanical Metallurgist; Metal Scientist. m. Karina Markovna Poliatskina, 1 daughter. Education: Diploma, Metal Science, St Petersburg Technical University, 1961; PhD, 1966, DSc, 1977, Prof (hon), 1986, Metal Sciences, Polzunov Central Boiler and Turbine Institute, St Petersburg. Appointments: Scientist, Research Laboratory of Boiler and Piping Systems Materials, Department of New Materials, 1961-66, Head, Research Laboratory, Steam Turbine Materials, Department of New Materials, 1966-85, Head of Research Department of the Fatigue Life of Materials for Power Plant Equipments, 1985-, Polzunov Central Boiler and Turbine Institute; Assistant Visiting Professor, Institute of Fine Mechanics and Optics, St Petersburg, 1961-68; Visiting Professor, Institute of Machine Building, St Petersburg, 1975-88, St Petersburg Technical University, 1992-95. Publications: Numerous articles in professional journals. Honours: Government Science Laureate, 1983; Russian State Science Laureate, 1985; Medal of Work, Government of Russia, 1989; Prize, WWII Civic Government, 1989; Medal, 50 years of Victory of WWII, Government of Russia, 1995. Memberships: New York Academy of Sciences; ASME; ESIS. Address:51 2nd Murinsky Avenue, app 70, 194021 St Petersburg, Russia.

**TCHORZ Tadeusz Stefan,** b. 8 July 1946, Babimost. Artist. m. Danuta, 1 daughter. Education: MA, Fine Arts Education, 1986. Appointments: Exhibitions Held, Theme, Horse, Poland, 1981-; Hunfeld, Germany, 1987; Kuopio, Finland, 1988; Panama, 1993. Honours: Diploma from Minister of Culture. Memberships: Association of the Fine Arts Education. Address: ul, Daleka 27-10, 25319 Bielce, Poland.

**TEDER Priit,** b. 14 April 1964, Tartu, Estonia. Physician; Scientist. m. Divorced, 2 daughters. Education: MD, 1988; Specialist in Lung Medicine and Allergology, 1990; PhD Lung Medicine, 1996. Appointments: Physician-intern Internal Medicine, Lung Hospital, 1988, Pulmonary Fellow, 1988-90, Postgraduate Student, 1990-91, Department of Lung Medicine, Head, 2nd Ward of Lung Medicine, Head, Endoscopy Unit at ICU, 1991-92, 1997, Lung Hospital, Tartu University, Estonia; Visiting Scientist, 1992-93, Postgrad student, 1993-96, Postdoctoral fellow, 1996-97, Dept Lung Medicine, Pulmonary fellow, Dept Anaesthesiology, 1995, Junior Physician, Lung Hospital, 1997-98, Uppsala University, Sweden; Postdoctoral associate, Section of Pulmonary and Critical Care, Yale University, USA, 1998-. Publications: 9 original papers; 2 reviews; 15 abstracts. Honour: Swedish Heart Lung Foundation Grant, 1995-98. Memberships: Estonian Association for Lung Medicine; Swedish Association for Lung Medicine; Swedish Medical Association; European Respiratory Society. Address: Uppsala University, Dept Lung Medicine, Akademiska Sjukhuset, S-75185, Uppsala, Sweden.

**TELLENNE Eric François,** b. 22 Nov 1953, Paris, France. Writer; Poet. Education: BA, University of Paris IV, Sorbonne,

1973. Appointments: Literary Reviewer, Valeurs Actuelles, 1980-84; Radio Host, Radio-Nova, 1985-87; Television Writer, Canal-Plus, 1988-98. Publications: Books: Les Oeufs Frits, short stories, 1988; La Clé des Chants, poems, 1998. Honours: Poetry Prize, Académie Française, 1998; Poetry Prize, Société des Gens de Lettres, 1998. Address: 4 Square de Robiac, 75007 Paris, France.

**TEO Huat,** b. 15 December 1939, Muar, Malaysia. Educator; Author. m. Koh Gek Hua, 2 sons. Education: DTC, 1960. Appointments: Teacher, Principal Lecturer, Government Textbook Writer, Contract Teacher of Chinese, Ministry of Education, Malaysia; Professional Author; Adviser, Unified Chinese School Teachers' Association, Malaysia. Publications: 79 books including short stories, poetry, prose, children's literature and primary school textbooks. Honours: Malaysian Prime Minister Tun Abdul Razak Literature Award, 1971; Children's Literature Award, Malaysia Chinese Cultural Association, 1978, 1982; National Chinese Literature Award, 1991, Chinese Language Medal, 1995, Taiwan; Name listed in World VIP Center, China, 1993. Memberships: Former Vice President, National Translation and Creative Society of Malaysia; Vice President, Chinese Writers Association; President, Literature and Art Society of South Malaya. Address: 66-9 Jalan Hj Jaib, 84000 Muar, Johor, Malaysia.

**TEODORESCU Nicolae,** b. 14 November 1947, Lipova. University Professor. m. 24 April 1970. Education: Graduate, Academy of Economic Studies, Bucharest, 1970; Doctor of Economics, Academy of Economic Studies, Bucharest, 1980. Appointments: Professor, Academy of Economic Studies, Bucharest, 1992-; Research, Marketing Research, 1970-. Publications: Consumer Behaviour Investigation Patterns, 1984; Consumer Behaviour, 1997. Memberships: ESOMAR (European Society for Opinion and Marketing Resaerch); AMA (American Marketing Association). Address: 10 Fibrei Street, 72304 Bucharest, Romania.

**TEPOOL Harold E,** b. 13 June 1952, Evansville, Indiana, USA. Professor. 1 daughter. Education: BA, University of Southern Indiana, 1980; MPA, Indiana State University, 1987. Appointments: Assistant Professor, 1987-93; Associate Professor, 1993-97; Professor of Business, 1997-. Honour: Award for Exemplary Service, 1991. Memberships: Phi Delta Kappa; Alpha Beta Gamma; Alpha Psi Omega. Address: 1410 Sandalwood Court, Evansville, IN 47720, USA.

**TEPPER Howard,** b. 31 January 1963, New York, New York, USA. Healthcare Executive. m. Bash B Tepper, 2 sons. Education: MBA, Healthcare Administration, Barvah College, Mt Sinai School of Medicine of the City University of New York, 1988; BA, Accounting and Information Systems, Queens College of the City of University of New York. Appointments: Administrator, Beth Israel Medical Center, 1989-91; Administrative Director, St Vincent's Hospital and Medical Center, 1991-93; Director of Administration, University of Medicine and Dentistry of New Jersey, 1993-. Publications: Clinical Computer Systems, in One Revolution Managing the Academic Practice in an Era of Rapid Change; New Informational Technologies Influence Practice Management, in The Patient Account Managers Handbook. Memberships: Fellow, Healthcare Financial Management Association; Certified Managed Care Professional; Editorial Review Board, American College of Healthcare Executives, Diplomate; Fellow, American College of Medical Practice Executives. Address: University of Medicine and Dentistry of New Jersey, 185 South Orange Avenue, MSB1-506, Newark, NJ 07103, USA.

**TEPTIN Guerman Mikhaylovich,** b. 19 June 1937, Kazan, Russia. Physicist. m. Teptina Natalia Vladimirovna, 1 daughter. Education: Red Diploma, Kazan State University, 1954; Degree of Kandidate Physical and Mathematical Sciences, 1966; Senior Scientist, 1969; Degree Doctor of Physical and Mathematical Sciences, 1986; Professor, 1989. Appointments: Head, Radioastronomy Department, Chief of Scientific Applied Radiophysics Research Section, Physics Faculty, Kazan St University; Editor-in-Chief, International Journal Environmental Radioecology and Applied Ecology. Publications: 3 scientific books, 1976, 1986, 1989; 113 articles. Honour: Honoured Scientist of Tatarstan, 1996. Memberships: International Association of Meteorology and Atmospheric Physics; International Association of Geomagnetism and Aeronomy, 1978-85; Member Correspondent, St Petersburg Peter's Academy of Science and Arts, 1997. Address: Physics Department, Kazan University, 420008 Kazan, Russia.

**TERAMOTO Tetsu,** b. 19 January 1954, Kumamoto City, Japan. Architect. Education: Master of Architecture, graduate school, Kumamoto University, 1980. Appointments: Staff Architect, Azusa Sekkai Co Ltd, Tokyo, 1980-82; Sub-Chief Architect, Osaka branch, Azusa Sekkai Co Ltd, Osaka, 1983-85; Principal, Tetsu Teramoto Architect Office, Kumamoto, 1986-. Membership: Architectural Institute of Japan. Address: Tetsu S Teramoto, 2-17-3 Hirata, 860-0826 Kumamoto City, Japan.

**TERAMURA Shoji,** b. 25 February 1949, Osaka, Japan. Linguist; Educator. Education: BA, 1971, MA, 1973, Osaka University, Toyonaka. Appointments: Teaching English and English Linguistics, Wakayama University, 1973-. Publication: A Functional Approach to (Epistemic) Modality, paper, 1981-83, 1991. Membership: English Linguistic Society of Japan. Address: Sakaigodoshukusha 124, Nagasone-cho 1180, Sakai, Osaka 591-8025, Japan.

**TERAUCHI Hajime,** b. 7 January 1960, Gunma, Japan. Associate Professor. m. Mayumi Terauchi. Education: Bachelor of Law, Faculty of Law, Keio University, 1984; Certificate in Language Improvement and Methodologies for Overseas Teachers of English, Centre for English Language Teaching, 1991, MA, English Language Teaching, Centre for English Language Teaching, 1992, PhD, English Language Teaching, Centre for English Language Teacher Education, 1997, University of Warwick, England. Appointments: Assistant Professor, 1998-99, Associate Professor, 1999-, Faculty of Commerce, Takachiho University, Suginami, Tokyo. Publications: Issues in English Language Teaching in Universities in Japan, 1995; English for Academic Purposes in Japan: An Investigation of Language Attitudes and Language Needs in a Department of Law, PhD thesis, 1997; Several others on legal language and English language teaching. Membership: President, Warwick Graduate Association of Japan. Address: 2-5-49-529, Minami-Koshigaya, Koshigaya City, Saitama 343-0845, Japan.

**TERCERO SIERRA Domingo,** b. 14 May 1962, Barcelona, Spain. Transportation Executive. 1 son, Domenic. Education: BBA, University of Barcelona, 1990; MA, Economics, 1994; Postgraduate, University of Central Florida, 1994; London School of Economics, 1994; Harvard-MIT, 1995; PhD, Business Administration, California Coast University, forthcoming. Appointments: Area Manager, Tudor SA, Barcelona, 1990-92; International Purchasing Manager, American Medical Dental, Miami, Florida, 1992-94; International Sales Manager, Decoy Safe Company, Orlando, Florida, 1994-97; Executive Vice President, Partner, Truck and Wheel SL, Navarra, Spain, 1997-; Presenter in field. Honours: Spanish State Department,

Madrid, Spain; MIT, Cambridge, MA, USA; London School of Economics, England; Spanish Army, Sebta, Morocco; In-Mark AB, Stockholm, Sweden. Memberships: UNICEF; Catalonia Economy Association; United Hands Association; Oxford Club; '5 Points' Investment Club. Address: Trav Corts, 371 2 4a 08029, Barcelona, Spain.

**TERPUGOVA Anna Fuodorovna,** b. 19 February 1934, Tomsk, Russia. Physicist. 1 son. Education: PhD, Tomsk State University, 1964. Appointment: Assistant Professor, Tomsk State University. Publications: 170 Articles in Scientific Journals. Address: Physical Faculty, VV Kuibyshev Tonsk State University, 36 prospekt Lenina, Tomsk 10, 634010 Russia.

**TERRY Russell,** b. 12 August 1943, Michigan, USA. Home Health Aide. Education: Ministry Degree, Great Lakes Christian College, Lansing, Michigan, USA, 1979. Appointments: Home Health Aide, Sparrow HELPS, Lansing; Home Health Aide, Visiting Nurse Service, Lansing. Honours: Certificate of Recognition, USA; Certificate of Appreciation, APCOA. Memberships: Golden Rollers of America, Florida; National Museum of Roller Skating, Nebraska, USA. Address: 121 E Mount Hope Ave, Lansing, MI 48910-9132, USA.

**TERTAK Adam,** b. 22 January 1953, Budapest, Hungary. Economist. m. 2 daughters. Education: BA, University Degree in Economics, Harvard Business School. Appointments: SZKI Computer Software Company, 1971-75; Head of Main Frame Computer Centre, EGSZI, 1975-82; Director, SZAMREND, 1982-87; General Venture and Trust Co, Advisor, 1988; Bonitas, Director, 1988; Director, Ernst and Young, 1989; Managing Partner, 1990-. Memberships: American Chamber of Commerce, Hungary; Transparency International; Rotary Club; Joint Venture Association; Hungarian Management Institute. Address: Ernst and Young, 17 Hermina Str, 1146 Budapest, Hungary.

**TERZIEV Fedor Semenovich,** b. 23 February 1923, Marinovka, Ukraine, USSR. Oceanologist. m. Lidya Ivanovna Terzieva, 1 son. Education: Oceanologist Diploma, 1941, Feodosya Hydrometeorological Technical School; Physicist-Mathematician Diploma, 1955, Azerbaijan State Pedagogical Institute; Oceanologist Certificate, 1970, PhD of Natural Science, Geography, Oceanology, Post-grad School in State Oceanographic Institute; Senior Scientific Researcher Diploma, 1982, State Oceanographic Institute. Appointments: Senior Engineer, Chief of Hydrometeorological Station, Chief of Dept of Marine Researches, Deputy Chief of Azerbaijan Dept of Hydrometeorological Service, Hydrometeorological Service of Caspian Sea, 1941-58; Chief of Murmansk Administration of Hydrometeorological Service, 1958-77, Director Murmansk Branch Office of Arctic and Antarctic Institute, 1972-77; Director, State Oceanographic Institute, Hydrometeorological Service, 1977-88; Chief of Lab of Marine Researches in State Oceanographic Institute, 1988-. Publications: Nearly 140 publications on oceanology, marine meteorology and climatology, hydrochemistry, protection of environment, complex hydrometeorological and hydrochemical monitoring, scientific operative maintenance of human activity etc. Honours: 15 governmental awards of USSR and Russia including Order of Labour Red Banner, 1976; Order of Friendship of Peoples, 1986; Order Sign of Honour, 1967; Medal for Labour Valour, 1963; Honorary Meteorologist of Russian Federation, 1998. Memberships: Participator of many international organisations, scientific commissions, scholar councils and associations in USSR and Russia. Address: Kropotkinsky per d 6, Moscow 119838, Russia.

**TETELBAUM David Isaakovich,** b. 23 June 1932, Arzamas, Gorki, Region, Russia. Physicist. m. Nina Ezhova, 1 daughter. Education: Graduate, Nizhnii Novgorod University, 1955; Candidate of Phys-Math Science, 1969; Senior Research Worker, 1970; Doctor of Phys-Math Science, 1988; Professor, 1997. Appointments: Junior Research Worker, 1956-70; Senior Research Worker, 1970-88; Leading Research Worker, 1988-. Publications: Near 200 articles; Monographie, with E I Zorin and P V Pavlov, Ion Doping of Semiconductors, 1975. Memberships: Russian Physical Society; Russian Vacuum Society; Ion Implantation Section of Semiconductor Physics Council of Russian Academy Science. Address: Physico Technology Research Institute, 23/3 Gagarin Prospekt, 603600 Nizhnii Novgorod, Russia.

**TEWOLDE Assefaw,** b. 21 August 1949, Addi-Ugri, Eritrea. Animal Scientist. m. MA Socorro Serrano, 2 sons, 1 daughter. Education: BSc, Animal Science, University Ethiopia, 1973; MSc, Animal Breeding, University of Florida, Gainesville, Florida, USA. Appointments: Professor, University of Chapingo, Mexico; International Staff, Catie, Costa Rica; Program Director, Education, Catie, Costa Rica; International Program Director, University Autonoma de Tamaulipas, Mexico. Memberships: Advisory Council to Ministry of Agriculture; Board of Directors, Latin American Association of Animal Production; ASASS. Address: Facultad de Argonomia, Universidad Autonoma de Tamaulipas, Ciudad Victoria, Tamaulipas, Mexico.

**THADANI Udho,** b. 1 April 1941, Hyderabad Sind, India. Physician. m. Dorothy Ann, 1 daughter. Education: MBBS; MRCP; FRCPC; FACC. Appointments: Intern, 1964-65, House Physician and Surgeon, 1965-66, All India Institute of Medical Sciences, New Delhi; House Physician in Medicine, Joyce Green Hospital, England, 1966-67; Senior House Physician in Medicine, Kingston General Hospital, England, 1967-69; Registrar and Research Fellow in Medicine and Cardiology, Kingston General Hospital and Royal Infirmary, Hull, 1969-71, University of Leeds, General Infirmary, 1971-75; Senior Research Fellow and Clinical Assistant in Medicine, 1975-78, Assistant Professor of Medicine, 1978-80, Queen's University, Kingston General Hospital, Canada; Associate Professor of Medicine, 1980-83, Professor of Medicine, Vice Chief Cardiovascular Section, 1983-, Oklahoma University Health Sciences Centre. Publications: 3 books; 42 book chapters; 150 articles in peer reviewed journals; 41 symposia and invited articles; 197 abstracts. Honours: Roll of Honour, Premedical, Delhi University, 1959; Merit Scholarship, 1960-63; Provost's Research Award for Senior Faculty, University of Oklahoma, Health Sciences Centre, 1995. Memberships: Fellow, 5 professional societies; Member: Royal College Physicians, London; Canadian Cardiovascular Society; American Federation for Clinical Research; American Association for Advancement of Sciences; and others. Address: Oklahoma University Health Science Centre Cardiology Section, 920 SL Young WP-3120, Oklahoma City, OK 73104, USA.

**THAN Swe,** b. 30 March 1938, Myanmar. Doctor. m. Daw Khin San Myint, 3 sons, 2 daughters. Education: MBBS, 1962; D Bact, 1972; DS, 1977; FRCP, Edin, 1995. Appointments: Consultant Virologist; Director (Research); Deputy Director-General; Director-General. Publications: 36 in national and international journals. Honours: Public Service Medal, 1990; Good Public Service Medal, 1990; Medal on Excellent Performance in Administrative Field, 1st Class, 1997. Memberships: Myanmar Medical Association; Royal College of Physicians, Edinburgh, 1995. Address: Dept of Medical Research, 5 Ziwaka Road, Dagon PO, Yangon, Myanmar.

**THANASI Ana,** b. 8 February 1941, Albania. Chemist. m. Vasil Thanasi, 1 son, 1 daughter. Education: Higher Chemical Technological Institute, Czech Republic, 1958-61; Diploma, Tirana University, 1961-63. Career: Technical Scientific Co-Worker, Faculty of Geology-Mining, 1963-67; Technical Scientific Co-Worker, Geological Enterprise, Tirana, 1967-73; Scientific Co-Worker, 1973-78, Chief of Analytic Sector, 1978-88, Geological Institute, Tirana; Doctor, Department of Chemical-Physical Analysis, 1988-93; Part-time Professor, Faculty of Natural Sciences, Analytic Chair, 1984-89. Publications include: Methods of chemical analysis of rocks and ores; Study on methods of complex analysis of Titanium mineral and chemical evaluation of totanomagnetits of Kashnjet and other forms; Chemical analysis of minerals: Sulfide ore, polimetals, phosphorites, bauxite, carbonic rocks, silicate. Honours: Medal, Remarkable Work in Mining Geology, 1983; Candidate of Science, 1983; Assistant Professor Doctor, 1995. Memberships: Association of Geologists of Albania. Address: Laboratory Oendro Geologice, Biiku Sossil, Tirana, Albania.

**THEVOZ Jacqueline,** b. 29 April 1926, Estavayer le Lac. Teacher. 2 daughters. Education: Diploma, Catholic Institute, Switzerland; Diploma, Conservatory of Music University; Diploma, Stenographic Swiss Institute; Diploma, Dance, Conservatory of Music, Lausanne-Paris. Appointments: Teacher, Ballet, Pensionnat La Chassotte; Director, Studio of Zaehringen; Director, Studio du Theatre of Fribourg (Ballet). Publications: 23 Books, Poetry, Novels, Treatises of Dance. Honours: Knight of the Internationale des Arts; Numerous Gold and Silver Medals Prize Folloppe of the Faculte des Lettres, University of Lausanne; Dr ad honorem, Centro Cultural; Literario e Artistico de Felgueiras. Address: Verossier Haut, F 74500 Larringes sur Evian, France.

**THIBAULT Paul John,** b. 1 July 1953, Newcastle, Australia. University Professor in Linguistics. m. Divorced, 1 daughter. Education: BA Hons Class 1, 1976, Newcastle, NSW; PhD, 1985, University Sydney. Appointments: Tutor, Murdoch University, Perth, Australia, 1982-83; Postdoc Research, University Bologna, 1984; Lecturer, University Sydney, 1986-88; Visiting Professor, University Verona, 1989-90; Associate Professor, University Padua, 1992-95, University Venice, 1995-. Publications: Social Semiotics as Praxis, 1991; Re-reading Saussure, 1997; Plus articles, chapters etc. Honours: Northrop Frye Fellow, University Toronto, 1996; Foundation Faculty, Cyber Semiotics Institute; Advisory board, TEXT. Address: Via Oblach 8, 40141 Bologna, Italy.

**THIELE Colin Milton,** b. 16 November 1920, Eudunda, South Australia. Author; Educator. m. Rhonda Gill, 2 daughters. Education: BA, 1942; Dip Ed, 1947; DipT, 1963, University of Adelaide. Appointments: Senior Master, High Schools; Lecturer, Wattle Park Teachers' College; Principal, 1965-72, Director, 1973, Murray Park College of Advanced Education; Director, Wattle Park Teachers' Centre, 1973-81. Publications: 65 children's books; 6 books of verse; 10 environmental books; 7 books of history and biography; 3 one-act plays for secondary schools; 9 other educational books; 2 books of fiction. Honours: Many awards for his books including: The Book of the Year Award of the Children's Book Council of Australia; The Austrian State Prize for Children's Books, twice; Award of the Silver Pencil in the Netherlands; Certificate of Honour from the International Board on Books for Young People; 2 Commonwealth Jubilee Literary Awards; and many other commendations, medals and awards. Memberships: Australian Society of Authors; Australian College of Education. Address: Endeavour Lane, King Scrib, via Dayboro Qld 4521, Australia.

**THISTEL James Norman,** b. 24 December 1950, Baltimore, Maryland,USA. Clinical Psychologist; Management. m. Cynthia Lee Thistel, 1daughter. Education: BS Psychology, Townson State University; MA ClinicalPsychology, Loyola College at Baltimore. Appointments: Practicum inClinical Psychology, Spring Grove Hospital Centre, 1974-75; Mental HealthAssistant IV, Southeastern Community Mental Health Centre, BaltimoreCounty, 1973-75; Social Worker, Salvation Army, Baltimore, Maryland,1975-76; Coordinator of Counselling & Diagnostic Services, Baltimore PREPProgramme, Mayor's Office of Manpower Resources, Baltimore, 1976-78; DeptHead, Director of Youth and Family Services, City of College Park,Maryland, 1978-90; Manager, Oasis in the Flats-Employee AssistanceProgramme, Dept Energy,EG&G/Kaiser-Hill/Dyncorp of Colorado Inc, RockyFlats Environmental Technology Site, Golden, Colorado, 1990-; President,Oasis in the Workplace Inc, Private Intergrated Health Care Services,Evergreen, Colorado, 1996-. Publications: 19 papers in professionaljournals and Chairman of National Conference on Employee AssistancePrograms (EAP) and Statewide Conference in Maryland on Juvenile Justice; Pimary author for a Worldwide website on Mental Health, oganisational management, stress, addiction & recovery, family therapy and specific physical health areas. Honours: National Lead for Employee Assistance Programs (EAP) in the US Dept of Energy Complex; Poclamation 89-R-14, Mayor and Council of the City of College Park,Maryland for Outstanding Professional, Administrative and CommunityContributions to the City; Global Five Hundred Outstanding Leaders of the20th Century; Lifetime member, Who's Who Worldwide; member, Who's Who ofProfessionals.Memberships: American Psychological Association; SocietyofPsychologists in Management; American Counselling Association; NorthAmerican Association for Masters in Psychology; Licensed ProfessionalCounselor in the State of Colorado and certified as a NationalPsychologist. Address: 4633 Bannock Lane, Evergreen, CO 80439, USA.

**THOMAS I D E,** b. 30 April 1921, Wales. Minister; Author. m. Mildred Thomas, 1 son. Education: BA, 1943, BD, 1946, University of Wales, Bangor; PhD, California Graduate School of Theology, 1971. Appointments: Minister of Religion; Author; BBC Correspondent; Chancellor, Seminary, California Pacific School of Theology, Glendale. Publications: Author, 15 books. Honours: Winner, Drama Award, Royal National Eisteddfod, Wales, 1949; Honors Certificate for Outstanding Achievement, Freedoms Foundation, Valley Forge, USA, 1973. Address: United Community Church, 333 E Colorado Street, Glendale, CA 91205, USA.

**THOMAS James Edward,** b. 18 October 1944, Darlington, USA. Accountant. m. Joan Yvette Grant, 1 son. Education: BS, Accounting, Johnson C Smith College, Charlotte, North Carolina, 1966; MA, Finance, C W Post College, Greenvale, New York, 1980; PhD, Education, Fordham University, New York, 1996. Appointments: Assistant Manager, Manufacturers, Hanover Trust, New York City, 1970-78; Met, Sava Bank, New York City, 1978-81; Auditor, New York State Department, Social Services, 1981-83; Accountant, New York City Board of Education, 1983-86; Accountant, Agent, IRS, New York City, 1987-; Instructor, Katherine L Gibbs Inc, New York City, 1987-89; Instructor, Queen's College, Flushing, New York, 1998-99. Memberships: MBA Executives Association Management; Association of International Platform Association; Sigma Rho Sigma. Address: 37-06 104th St Apt 4C, Flushing, NY 11368-1901, USA.

**THOMAS Jerome (Jerry) Lefede,** b. 11 May 1927, Fort Worth, Texas, USA. Public Relations Specialist; Teacher. m.

essyl A Mitchell, 2 sons, 1 daughter. Education: BA, Drama, minor Social Psychology, 1953; Graduate courses, Texas Wesleyan University. Appointments: Programme Director, Disc Jockey, KNOK Radio Station, Fort Worth, 1955-69; Reporter, Newscaster, KTVT Television, Minority Affairs Director, Fort Worth, 1970-81; Producer, Host, What About People talk show, Fort Worth, 1981-87; Account Executive, KDLZ/KHVN Radio Station, Fort Worth, 1987-89; Managing Sales Director, KSGB Radio Station, Fort Worth, 1989-90; Managing Editor, Columnist, La Vida News, 1990-; Substitute Teacher, Fort Worth Independent School District, 1990-. Honours: Outstanding Citizen Award, National Association of Radio Announcers, 1966; Outstanding Citizen Award, National Association of Television and Radio Announcers, 1967; Man of the Year, Florence B Brooks Culture Club, 1972; Man of the Year, Mayor's Council on Youth Opportunities, 1973; Media Black Achiever, 1977; Man of the Year, Omega Psi Phi, 1978; Appreciation Award, Historic Allen Chapel AMEC, 1982; Various citations. Memberships include: Board of Directors, Sickle Cell Anemia Association of Texas Inc; Lifetime Member, United Negro College Fund; Lifetime Member, National Association for the Advancement of Colored People; Omega Psi Phi; Board of Directors, Bethlehem Community Center, 1955-62; National Association of Television and Radio Announcers, 1967-69; National Association of Radio Announcers, 1967-89; President, Forth Worth Catholic Board of Education, 1977; President, Texas Catholic Conference, 1978; President, Ambassadors Club, 1989-92. Address: 5677 Comer Drive, Fort Worth, TX 76134, USA.

**THOMAS Marianna,** b. 9 December 1927, Darke County, Ohio, USA. Executive Director; Fundraiser; Farmer; Writer. m. Lowell Thomas, deceased, 3 sons, 2 daughters. Education: Student, Dayton Art Institute; MA, Hons, Union College, Kentucky, 1978. Appointments: Advertising, Broadcasting, Greenville, 1965-67; Executive Director, Help for Children in the Holy Land, 1969-76. Publication: Catitudes. Honours: Honorary Member, Dayton Engineer's Club; Honorary Degree, Union College. Memberships: Board Member, National Platform Association; Founder, US Civil Responsibilities; Citizens for Moral War; Former National Board Member, American Judicature Society, Family Service America; Former National Council, Freedoms Foundation at Valley Forge. Address: P O Box 626, Dayton, OH 45405-0626, USA.

**THOMAS Zdenek,** b. 11 May 1929, Opava. Civil Engineer. m. Jitka Kadlecova, 1 son. Education: Civil Engineer, 1954; PhD, 1967; DrSc, 1992. Appointments: Water Research Institute, Prague, 1954; Water-Loopkundig Lab, Delft, The Netherlands, 1968; Institut fur Wasserbau, University of Stuttgart, Germany, 1989; Instituto de Ingenieria, Universidad Autonoma de Mexico, Mexico, 1996. Publications: 34 including 4 monographs; 8 patents. Honour: 1989 Deutsche Forschungsgemeinschaft Grantee. Memberships: Scientific-Technical Society, Prague; Czech Society for Chemical Technology, Prague; Union of Czech Mathematicians and Physicists, Prague. Address: Instttuto Mexicano del Petroleo, Eje Central Lazaro Cárdenas 152, 2 do piso Torre Administrativa, Col San Bartolo Atepehuacan, 07730 Mexico.

**THOMASCHEWSKI Dieter,** b. 24 March 1944, Weissenburg. m. Barbara Birk-Thomaschewski, 1 son. Education: Diploma in Business Administration, University of Saarbrucken. Appointments: Various positions in marketing, sales oeganisation, as Senior Executive with BASF Corporation, 1969-86; President, BASF Venezolana, 1987-90, Group VP, BASF Information Systems, USA, 1990-91; Executive VP, President Fertilisers Div, BASF Mg, 1992-98; Executive VP, President Reg Div Central Europe, 1999-.

Membership: Schmalenbach Gesellschaft; Lions Club. Address: BASF Anbiengeschaft, Ludwigshafen am Rhein, Germany.

**THOMPSON Eric Thomas,** b. 19 July 1962, Trumbull County, Ohio, USA. Business Owner. m. Susan, 1 son, 2 daughter. Education: Kent State University; Youngstown State University. Appointment: Partner, Owner, NLS Inc Satolli Carpet. Publications: Articles. Memberships: Newton Falls Youth Baseball Association; Newton Falls United Methodist Church Youth Advisor; Friends of Newton Falls Library; Newton Falls Chamber of Commerce; Church Pastor Parish Relations Board; Ohio High School Athletic Association; Shoes for Kids; Many other memberships. Address: 315 Marshall St, Newton Falls, OH 4444-1426, USA.

**THOMPSON Lynn Renee,** b. 19 September 1955, Rockford, Illinois, USA. Chiropractor. m. (1) John Michael Thompson, 27 August 1975, divorced February 1985, 1 daughter, (2) Leonard Alan Conant, 29 May 1993, divorced March 1996. Education: AD, Medical Laboratory Technologist, Chippewa Valley Technical College, 1979; BAAS, Midwestern State University, 1985; D of Chiropractic, Palmer College of Chiropractic, Davenport, Iowa, USA, 1993; Licenced Chiropractor, Iowa, Illinois, Wisconsin, USA; Medical Laboratory Technician, Laughlin Osteo Hospital, Kirksville, Missouri, USA, 1979-82; Medical Technologist, Hamilton Hospital, Olney, Texas, 1982-83; Bethania Regional Hospital, Wichita Falls, Texas, USA, 1983-87; St Clare Hospital, Baraboo, Wisconsin, USA, 1987-88; Samaritan Health Care, Clinton, Iowa, 1993-95; Chiropractor, Yours For Health, Chiropractic, Chippewa Falls, Wisconsin, USA, 1995-97; Chiropractor, Owner, Thompson Chiropractic Clinic, Eau Claire, Wiconsin, USA, 1996-; Foster Chiropractic, Osseo, Wisconsin, USA, 1996-; Owner, Conant Chiropractic Clinic, LeClaire, Iowa, 1993-96; Board Advisors Iowa Commission on Persons with Disabilities, Davenport, 1993-94; Board Directors, Quint Cities Handicap Group, Davenport, 1989-94; Sigma Phi Chi, Sorority National Board, 1993-; President, 1997-. Memberships: International Chiropractors Association; American Society Clinical Pathologists; American Medical Technologists; Eau Claire Women's Network; Newcomers Club of Eau Claire. Lutheran. Address: E10834 Park Avenue, Osseo, WI, 54758-8826, USA.

**THOMPSON Lynn Helen,** b. 22 July 1922, Plainfield, USA. m. David Duvell Thompson, 3 sons. Education: BS, Douglas College, 1940-43; Student, Jackson Laboratory, 1942; Cornell Medical College, 1943-46; Music, Hunter College, 1947; National Academy of Design, 1970. Publications: Several articles in professional journals. Memberships: Rockefeller Institute of Medical Research; AWS; Salamundi Club. Address: Box 54, Hulls Cove, ME 04644, USA.

**THOMPSON Paul Alastair,** b. 16 November 1942, Orpington, England. Business Improvement Consultant. m. Sarah Jean, 1 son. Education: BA, honours, Economics, 1965, MA, Economics, 1969, Cambridge University, England. Appointments: Horse Breaker, Rodeo Rider, California, 1965-69; Senior Analyst, Shell Mex & BP, 1966-70; Senior Business Analyst, Westinghouse Electric Corporation, 1970-76; Site Manager, Westinghouse, Richmond, Virginia, 1976-79; RSCDS Teacher, Socttish Dance Workshops, 1976-; Program Chairman, Pittsburgh Folk Festival, 1977-95; Founder, Senior Consultant, Westinghouse Productivity and Quality Center, 1979; Leading Innovator, TQM Tools, 1979-94; Advisor to US Congress, 1980-84; Visiting Lecturer, US and Overseas Universities, 1990-; Chairman, Strategic Planning for Westmoreland County Presbytery, 1990-92; President, Childrens Festival Chorus, 1990-95; Founder, Chairman,

Reengineering Users Group, 1992-95; International Consultant, 1994-; Editorial Board, Focus on Change Management, magazine, 1994-; Founder, Director, Productivity & Leadership Consortium in Arabian Gulf, 1995-; Founding Member, UAE Technology Park, 1996-; Founder, Chairman, Productivity and Leadership Forum, 1996-; Founder, Editor, Forum, TQM magazine, 1997-; Cambridge Society UAE Representative, 1997-99. Publications: Several articles in professional journals. Address: 127 Surrey Drive, Belmont, PA 15626-1539, USA.

**THOMPSON Theodis,** b. 10 August 1944, Arkansas, USA. Health Care Executive. m. Patricia Holley, 2 son, 1 daughter. Education: BS, Tuskegee Institute, 1968; MPA, 1969; PhD, University of Michigan, 1972; Certificate, Health Systems Management, Harvard University, 1977. Appointments: Assistant Professor, Howard University, 1973-78; Associate Professor, University of Southern California, Los Angeles, 1978-79; Acting CEO, Director, Planning, Memphis Health Centre Inc, 1979-88; CEO, Brooklyn Plaza Medical Center Inc, 1988-. Honours: USDHHS, HRSA Administrators Award; Distinguished Service Award. Memberships: American Public Health Association; Alpha Phi Alpha Fraternity. Address: Brooklyn Plaza Medical Center Inc, 650 Fulton St, Brooklyn, NY 11217, USA.

**THOMPSON-COUCH Nancy,** b. 30 December 1939, North Carolina, USA. Business; Psychology. 2 sons, 1 daughter. Education: BA, Accounting, MBA, Business, University of La Verne; DCH, American Institute Hypnotherapy, Irvine, California; PhD, Doctor of Psychology, American Pacific University, Honolulu, Hawaii, USA. Appointments: President, NTC Business Services Inc; President, Center Dynamic Change. Memberships: Toastmasters CTM; ATM; NAEA; CSEA. Address: NTC Services Inc, 5196 Benito Street '1, Montclair, CA 91763, USA.

**THROWER Muzetta,** b. 25 May 1938, Yazoo City, Michigan, USA. Educator. m. Robert L Sr, 2 sons, 2 daughters. Education: MS, Jackson State University; Master of Arts, Ball State University; Adult Education Certificate, University of California; Administration Certification Courses, California State University; Labor Management Relations Certificate, University of California. Appointments: Administrative Intern, California Medical Facility, 1979-81; Summer School Vice Principal, Vacaville United School District, 1982; Summer School Principal, Vacaville United School District, 1983; Summer School Principal, Vacaville United School District, 1984; Vice Principal, Fairmont Elementary School, 1989-90; Vice Principal, Callison Elementary School, 1990-91; Principal, Country High School, 1991-96; Director of Student Services, Vacaville Unified, 1996-. Honours: Teacher of the Year, Country High School; Woman of Distinction, Soroptomist; Tri City Educator of the Year, Martin Luther King Committee; Outstanding Elementary Assistant Principal, ACSA; Insperational Mother of the Year, Travis AFB Chapel; Mother of the Year, Travis AFB Chapel. Address: 751 School Street Vacaville, CA 95688-3945, USA.

**THUEME William Harold,** b. 4 September 1945, St Clair, Michigan, USA. Teacher. 2 sons, 2 daughters. Education: BA, Michigan State University, 1967; MA, 1969; PULC, PhD, 1997. Appointments: Teacher, Charlotte, Michgan, 1967-69; Teacher, Ann Arbor Public School, 1969-. Memberships: National Education Association; International Reading Association. Address: 5187 Palms Road, Casco, MI 48064, USA.

**TIAN Enrui,** b. 3 December 1937, Yutian County, Hebei Province, China. Teacher. m. Xu Xiulan, 1 son, 1 daughter. Education: Graduate, Harbin Institute of Technology.

Appointments: Vice Chairman, Applied Physics, Harbin Institute of technology, 1985; President, Harbin University, 1985-1988; President, Harbin Teachers College, 1988-. Publications: Educational Reform and Development of Teachers Colleges in the 21st Century, 1998; Quality of Efficiency of Teachers, 1997; Collegiate Physical Experiments, 1989. Honours: National Ministerial Level Scientific Achievement Award, 1983; The State Council Special Subsidy Award, 1992. Memberships: National Teachers Colleges Association, 1994, 1998; National Teachers Colleges and Universities Education Research Association. Address: Harbin Teachers Training College, 3 Xue Fu Road, Nangang District, Harbin 150086, China.

**TIAN Lian-Tao,** b. 23 January 1930, Tianjin City. Ethnomusicologist; Composer. m. Song, 1 daughter. Education: Graduate, Central Conservatory of Music, Beijing, China, 1955-60. Appointments: Ethnomusicologist, Composer; Professor, Research Fellow, Central Conservatory of Music, Beijing, China; Deputy Director, Institute in Central Conservatory. Publications: The Essence of Tibetan Traditional Music; The Traditional Music of Chinese Ethnic Minorities. Memberships: Chinese Minority Music Society; Chinese Traditional Musical Society. Address: Institute of Music Research, Central Music Conservatory, #43 Baojin Street, Xi Cheng District, Beijing 100031, China.

**TIBBS Thomas Stansbury,** b. 30 August 1917, Indianapolis, Indiana, USA. Art Museum Director; Educator. m. Ruth M Northup. Education: BA, Fine Arts, 1946, MA, Fine Arts, 1948, University of Rochester, New York, USA; Postgraduate Courses, Columbia University, 1948. Appointments: Associate Director of Education, Memorial Art Gallery, University of Rochester, 1948-52; Director, Huntington Museum of Art, West Virginia, USA, 1952-56; Director, American Crafts Museum, New York, USA, 1956-60; Director, Des Moines Art Center, Iowa, 1960-68; Founding Director, San Diego Museum of Contemporary Art, 1968-72; Graduate Seminars, San Diego State University, 1970-90. Honours: Elected Fellow, Royal Society of Arts, London, England, 1962; Many exhibitions and catalogues including L C Tiffany, 1958, Josse de Rivera, 1972. Memberships: American Association Museums, 1948-72; Association Art Museum Directors, 1962-72. Address: 12202 A Rancho Bernardo Road, San Diego, CA 92128, USA.

**TIUECO Ruben,** b. 8 November 1958. Salesman. Education: Bachelor of Science and Business Administration. Appointment: UNEP San Rouque, Iriga City, Philippines. Membership: AMA International, USA. Address: Highway #69 San Isidro, Iriga City, 4431 The Philippines.

**TILININ Igor Stanislavovich,** b. 2 December 1952, Vladivostock, Russia. Educator; Physicist; Software Engineer. m. Nadezhda Yaroshuk. Education: Engineer diploma with Distinction (MS), 1976, Candidate of Sciences Physics and Maths, 1981, DSc Theoretical Physics, 1994, Moscow Institute for Physics and Engineering. Appointments: Docent, Institute of Physical Chemistry, Warsaw, Poland, 1994-; Research Scientist, Lawrence Berkeley National Labor, CA, USA, 1996-; Software Engineer, D W Smith & Associates, CA, USA, 1998-. Publications: About 80 and two monographs. Memberships: American Association for Advancement in Science; American Physical Society; New York Academy of Sciences; European Microlearn Analysis Society. Address: 1555 West Hillsdale Br #307, San Mateo, CA 94402-3784, USA.

**TIMEN Grigory,** b. 19 February 1937, Kharkiv. Otorhinolaringologist. m. Kopaygorodskaya Asya, 1 son, 1 daughter. Education: Diploma, Kiev Medical Institute, 1960; MD, Kiev Research Institute of Otolaryngology, 1983;

Professor, 1990. Appointments: Doctor (Surgeon), 1960; Junior Scientist, Kiev Research Institute of Otolaryngology, 1967-68; Senior Scientist, 1968-85; Chief, Pediatrical Department of Otorhinolaryngology, 1985-; Head, Ukrainian Hearing Centre, 1986-; Chief, Surdologist f Ukraine; Vice General Secretary, Ukrainian Otolarygology Society. Publications: The Use of Laser in Medicine and Biology, 1974; Ear, Nose and Throat Disorders, 1986; Laser Medical Appliances, 1984; Laser Endoscopic Surgery of the Upper Airways, 1990; Over 200 articles. Honour: Emeritus Promoter Science, Ukraine Award. Memberships: International Academy of Oto-Rhino-Laryngology; New York Academy of Science; Ukrainian Oto-Rhino-Larygology Society, 1995-; Ukranian Academy of Science; European Oto-Rhino-Larygological Society Council Member; Medical Trade Union. Address: Kiev Resaerch Institute of Otolaryngology, 3 Zoologichna Street, 252057 Kiev, Ukraine.

**TIMI Jorge,** b. 11 Nov 1957, Curitiba, Brazil. Vascular Surgeon. m. Melania Timi, 1 son, 1 daughter. Education: MD, University of Parana, 1980; MS, 1992, PhD, 1998, Surgery, University of Parana. Appointments: Certificate Vascular Surgeon, Brazilian Council of Medicine; Vascular Surgeon, Hospital N S Gracas, 1983-; Hops Cajuru, 1986-; University of Parana, 1997-. Publications: Brazilian Index of Vascular Surgery, editor, 1995; Revista Cirurgia Vascular, associate editor, 1993-95; Revista Cirurgia Vascular, editorial board, 1996-. Honour: L E Puech Leao Award, Panamerican Congress of Phebology, 1998. Memberships: International Society for Cardiovascular Surgery; Brazilian Society for Vascular Surgery, Director, 1993-95; Society for Vascular Surgery of Parana, President, 1991-93; Brazilian College of Surgeons. Address: 369 Bruno Filgueria Street, 80240000 Curitiba, Brazil.

**TIMMONS Gerald Dean,** b. 1 June 1931, USA. Child Neurologist; Physician. m. Lynne R Timmons, 4 daughters. Education: AB, 1953, MD, 1954, Indiana University. Appointments: Clinical Professor of Pediatrics; Chairman, Division of Neurology, Northeastern Ohio Universities College of Medicine. Publications: 2 Books. Memberships: American Academy of Neurology; American Medical Association; Child Neurology Society. Address: Akron Pediatric Neurology, 300 Locust St, Ste 460, Akron, OH 44302-1804, USA.

**TIMOSHENKO Jaroslava,** b. 14 December 1944, Belokurakino, Lugansk, Ukraine. Doctor; Mathematician; Pharmacologist; Scientist. m. Anton P Gusty, 1 son, 1 daughter. Education: BM, Department of Pediatrics, Kyiv Medical Institute, 1967; BS, Kyiv Pedagogical Institute, Mathematics, 1977. Appointments: Lecturer, 1987-94, MD, 1990, Professor, 1993, Kuban Medical Institute; Academy of Sciences of Ukraine, 1967-87. Publications: 150 scientific works; 4 patents. Membership: Ukrainian Assocation of Computer Medicine. Address: Admiralsky Ave 1 B Apt 133, 270009 Odessa, Ukraine.

**TINITIGAN Joel,** b. 5 November 1967, San Mateo, Rizal. CPA; Lawyer; Educator. m. Graciela Ely S Tan-Tinitigan. Education: BBA Accounting, San Sebastian College, Recoletos, Cavite City, 1989; JD, Ateneo de Manila University, School of Law, 1994. Appointments: Administrative Officer, 1985-91, President, 1991-, Rosario Institute; Proprietor, JT Lending, 1993-; Chairman, RI Multi-Purpose Cooperative, 1993-; Partner, Ignacio & Tinitigan Law Firm, 1995-; Chairman, Bukas Palad Lending Corporation, 1996-; Chairman, Limbas Security Services Inc, 1998-. Publications: A Feasibility Study on the Offering of 2-Year Automotive Course, 1989; Thesis, The Taxing Powers of Local Government Units over the Export Processing Zones, 1994. Honours: 8 academic awards; Plaque

of Recognition given by the Integrated Bar of Philippines for being BAR Topnotcher No 8, 1995; 3 awards from the Rotary Club of Rosario, 1995, 1997, 1997; Plaque of Recognition for Support to Mat Caparas Scholarship Fund, 1998; Most Outstanding Club President, District 3810, RY, 1997-98. Memberships: Education Committee, Rosario Anti-Drug Council, 1993-; Rotary Club of Rosario, various posts; Assistant Governor, Rotary International, District 3810; Cavite Association of Private Schools; Philippine Institute of Certified Public Accountants; Integrated Bar of Philippines; and others. Address: 10 C Abueg St, Rosario Cavite 4106, The Philippines.

**TISCHENDORF Frank Walter,** b. 12 October 1936, Gera, Thuringia, Germany. Physician; Scientist. 2 sons. Education: MD, University of Goettingen, Germany, 1963; Research Fellow, Columbia University, New York, 1965-67; Scientific Assistant, Dept of Medicine, University of Tuebingen, 1967-77; Diploma, Internal Medicine, 1972; Habilitation (Experimental Medicine), 1976; Senior Physician, Municipal Hospital Esslingen, University of Tuebingen, 1977-80; Diploma, Laboratory Medicine, 1979. Appointments: Docent, Technical Academy of Esslingen, Germany, 1975-80; Head, Physician in Chief, Department of Clinical Chemistry, Bernhard-Nocht-Institute for Tropical Medicine, Hamburg, 1980-; Consultant, Harbour Hopsital, Hamburg, 1980-97; Docent, University of Tuebingen, 1976-85; Docent, University of Hamburg, Germany, 1986-; Director, Tropical Medicine Course, Bernhard-Nocht-Institute, 1988-89; Associated Editor, Member, editorial boards of 5 scientific journals. Publications: Author: Editor: External Manifestations of Disease, 1973, 6th edition, 1998; Prima Vista Diagnosis, 1995; Co-editor: The Eye in Systemic Disease (with C Meyer), 1999; Over 100 contributions to books and scientific journals. Memberships: New York Academy of Sciences; German Society of Tropical Medicine. Address: Tropical Institute, Bernhard Nocht-Strasse 74, 20359 Hamburg, Germany.

**TISDALE James Edward,** b. 23 April 1960, Winnipeg, Canada. Associate Professor. Education: BSc, Pharm, University of Manitoba, 1983; Pharmacy Residency, Health Sciences Center, Winnipeg, 1983-84; Doctor of Pharmacy, State University of New York, 1988; Fellowship, Cardiovascular Pahrmacotherapy, Hartford Hospital and University of Connecticut, 1988-90. Appointments: Assistant Clinical Professor, School of Pharmacy, University of Connecticut, 1988-90; Adjunct Clinical Instructor, Massachusetts College of Pharmacy and Allied Health Sciences, 1988-90; Assistant Professor, College of Pharmacy, 1990-96; Associate Professor, Wayne State University, 1996-. Publications: Over 30 Publications, Peer reviewed journals. Honours: Teaching Awards; Fellow, American College of Clinical Pharmacy. Memberships: American Heart Association; American College of Clinical Pharmacy; American Pharmaceutical Association; American Society of Health System Pharmacists. Address: Wayne State University, Coll Pharmacy 230 Shapero Hall, Detroit, MI 48202, USA.

**TISSUE Mike,** b. 24 August 1941, Garfield, Washington, USA. Respiratory Therapy Educator. 1 son, 3 daughters. Education: 4 AAS Degrees; Honors, Spokane CC, Washington, USA, 1985; BS, Respiratory Therapy cum laude, Loma Linda University, California, 1987; MS, Respiratory Care, Georgia State University, 1998; Registered Cardiovascular Technologist; Registered Respiratory Therapist, Registered Pulmonary Function Technologist, Perinatal/Pediatric Specialist, NBRC; Registered Respiratory Care Practitioner, California, Georgia; Respiratory Intern, Level III, NICU Therapist Loma Linda University Medical Center, California, 1985-87; Educator, Therapist, Riyadh Armed Forces Hospital,

Saudi Arabia, 1987-91; Department Head Respiratory Care Security Forces Hospital, Riyadh, 1991-93; Assistant Professor, Director, Clinical Education Respiratory Therapy Program Morehead State University, Kentucky, USA, 1993-94; Program Director, Associate Degree Respiratory Therapy, Chattahoochee Technology Institute, Marietta, Georgia, 1994-; President, Founder, Riyadh Cardiorespiratory Society, 1988-93; Researcher, Loma Linda University, 1987, Riyadh Armed Forces Hospital, 1988; Instructor and Affiliate Faculty, ACLS, Washington State Heart Association, 1983-85, California Heart Association, 1985-87, Saudi Heart Association, 1987-93, Kentucky Heart Association, 1993-94, Georgia Affiliate, 1994-; Instructor and Affiliate Faculty Pediatric Advanced Life Support Saudi Heart Association, 1987-93; Instructor and Affiliate, Faculty Basic Life Support/CPR Washington State, 1974-85, California, 1985-87, Saudi Heart Association, 1987-93; Kentucky Heart Association, 1993-94, Georgia Affiliate, 1994-; Consultant, ARC, Tacoma, Washington, 1984; Instructor, Advanced 1st Aid, Standard 1st Aid, CPR, 1975-; Inland Empire Chapter, Spokane, Washington, 1975-94; San Bernardino/Redlands Service Center, Loma Linda, 1985-87; American Community Services US Embassy, Riyadh, 1991-93; US Military Operation Desert Storm, Riyadh, 1991-93, Georgia Affiliate Cobb County Chapter, Marietta, 1994-; Instructor, Freedom From Smoking Clinic Program American Lung Association, California, 1985-87, Saudi Arabia, 1987-93, Smyrna, Georgia, 1994-; Member, Institutional Effectiveness Committee, Campus Computer Chattahoochee Technology Institute, 1994-. Publications: Contributor, articles to professional journals. Honours: Commissioners Key, 1977; Scouters Key, 1979; Named Citizen of Day KGA Radio, Spokane, 1983. Memberships: AAUP 1993-; Legislature Committee, Atlanta, 1995-; American Association Respiratory Care, 1984-; Georgia Society Respiratory Care, 1994-; Georgia Society Respiratory Care, Chair Cardiopulmonary Committee 1995,1996; Phi Delta Kappa 1994-; Lifetime Certification/Membership American Board of Disability Analysts; Alliance of Cardiovascular Professionals, 1996-present. Address: 1881 Arnold Drive SW, Austell, GA 30106-2907, USA.

**TITANI-KOSTALLARI Gjergji P,** b. 23 January 1937, Korce, Albania. Pensioner; Poet; Historian; Translator. m. Jlda Deli, 2 sons. Education: Military Academy, Skenderbej, 1954; Naval Military Academy, Shore Artillery, 1959; Defence Academy, Albania, 1969. Appointments: Platoon Commander, Shore Artillery; Vice Commander, Mine Sweeper; Executive Vice Head, Military Corpus; Chief of Headquarters, Shore Defence Brigade; Head of Department, Ministry of Defence; Chief, Corpus Headquarters. Publications: Literature and historical translations from the Russian language; 2500 pages of scientific publications, Albania and Overseas; Poetry: Italian, Greek War of 1940-41; Study on Military History; Albanian Military Personalities of 1912-97. Memberships: Secretary General, Albanian Commission of Military History; Administrative Director, Dhora LEKA Foundation; Amnesty International; Secretary General, Greece Albania Friendship Association; Secretary General Puchkins Friends Association. Address: Rr Komunae Parisit, Pallati 1 Shk 3 Ap 19, Tirana, Albania.

**TITOV Alexander,** b. 16 February 1943, Barnaul, Russia. Physicist. m. Madlen Erin, 2 sons, 1 daughter. Education: PhD, Physics, Moscow Physical-Technical Institute, 1972. Appointments: Senior Research Fellow, Institute for Physical-Technical Mcas, 1972-93. Publications: Over 120 scientific publications. Honour: Senior Research Fellow certificate, 1978. Membership: United Nations (UNIDO) expert in Metrology, 1991-.

**TIUECO Ruben,** b. 8 November 1958, Iriga City, Philippines. Salesman. Education: BSc, Commerce. Career: Salesman. Membership: AMA International. Address: The Way Passed Away, Highway #60, San Isidro, Iriga City, Philippines.

**TIWARI Ram Kalp,** b. 12 January 1942, Rae Bareli. Educator; Principal. m. Smt Raj Pati, 2 sons, 2 daughters. Education: MA Economics, 1969; MA Political Science, 1974; MA Hindi, 1976; L T Diploma of Tecahing, 1972; PhD, 1988, Kanpur University; Higher Training of Scouting. Appointments: Teacher, higher secondary school, 1969; Principal, Inter College Shukul Bagar, 1978; Worked honorary as District Scout Commissioner, Sultanpur, 1981-87. Honours: State Award of Teachers, UP State Government, 1994, for best ideal services as teacher/principal. Memberships: VP, UP Bharat Scout and Guide of UP State; Games Secretary, Sultanpur District; Talker of All India Radio Station, Lucknow, 1991-; Life member, Bharat Scout and Guide; VP, UP Principal's Association; Many other social and educational institutions. Address: K C RCI C Shukul Bazar, Shultanpur, UP India.

**TIWARI Ravi Prakash,** b. 12 December 1959, Hastinapur, India. Molecular Biologist. m. Laxmi, 1 son, 1 daughter. Education: BSc, Gold Medal, 1978; MSc, Biochemistry, 1981; PhD, Biochemistry, 1986. Appointments: Research Fellow. Publications: 15 Research Papers. Memberships: Indian Association of WA; Hindi Academy. Address: 30 parkway Road Bibra Lake, Perth, Western Australia, Australia.

**TLASKALOVA-HOGENOVA Helena,** b. 29 December 1938, Prague, Czech Republic. Researcher. m. Vlastimil Tlaskal, 1 son, 1 daughter. Education: MD, 1962, Associate Professor, 1995, First Medical Faculty, Charles University, Prague; PhD, 1968, Institute of Microbiology, Czech Academy of Science, Prague. Appointments: Clinician, Deptartment of Haematology, Hospital Usti n Labem, Czech Republic, 1962-64; PhD Student, 1964-68; Scientific Worker, 1968-91; Head, Dept Immunological Gnotobiology, Institute of Microbiology, Prague, 1991-. Publications: 145 papers in international journals and proceedings; 55 chapters in books; Editor, Advanced Mucosal Immunology, 1995. Honours: J E Purkyne Medal, 1987; Awards of the Czech Academy of Science and Society of Clinical Immunology and Allergology. Memberships: President, Czech Immunological Society; International Endotoxin Society; International Society for Mucosal Immunology; International Society of Development and Comp Immunology. Address: Konevoa 59, 130 00 Prague 3, Czech Republic.

**TO Luen Bik,** b. 14 July 1949, Hong Kong. Haematologist. m. 3 children. Education: Bachelor Medicine, Bachelor Surgery, 1973, University Hong Kong; MD, 1985, University Adelaide; MRCP, UK, 1979; FRCPath Australasia, 1986; FRACP, 1995. Appointments: Royal Adelaide Hospital Research Fellow, 1981-83, Registrar, 1980-81, 1983-87, Senior Registrar, 1987, Haematologist-in-Charge, Leukaemia Research Unit, 1987-91, Division of Haematology, Institute of Medical and Veterinary Science, Adelaide; Visiting Haematologist, Royal Adelaide Hospital, 1987-91; Member, 1992-, Director, 1992-94, Acting Clinical Director, 1995-96, Acting Head of Haematology, 1995-97, Clinical Director, 1997-, Hanson Centre for Cancer Research, Institute of Medical and Veterinary Science; Director, Clinical Haematology, Bone Marrow Transplant Unit, Royal Adelaide Hospital, Director, Clinical Science and Research, Division of Haematology, Institute of Medical and Veterinary Science, 1994-95, Head of Haematology, 1997-; Clinical Senior Lecturer, Department of Medicine, University Adelaide, 1989-. Publications: Author or co-Author, 77 papers in refereed journals including 18 of significance; 14 book chapters; 18 proceedings; 9 letters. Honours: Mun's Gold Medal in

Psychiatry, University of Hong Kong, 1972; A J Baikie Memorial Medal, Haematology Society of Australia, 1983; 25 research grants awarded. Memberships: Haematology Society of Australia; International Society Experimental Haematology; International Society Haematotherapy and Graft Engineering; American Society of Haematology; Australian Leukaemia Study Group; Apheresis Association of Australia; Health Informatic Society of South Australia. Address: Hanson Centre for Cancer Research, PO Box 14 Rundle Mall, Adelaide SA 5000, Australia.

**TOBIAS Philip W,** b. 8 November 1949, Evanston, Illinois. Business and Communications Specialist. 1 daughter. Education: Miami-Dade Community College, Florida; HOM Seminary, San Francisco; Continuing Professional Education, throughout the USA, 1970-. Appointments: Founder, Director, Tobias Photo/Graphics, Business Management and Marketing, DTP, Photographer, Writer, 1973-95; Copy Editor, Quark Inc, 1996-98; Technical Writer, Eclipse Inc, 1998-; Extensive Media and Publishing Experience; Graphic Artist; Photographer. Publications: Nationally Published Writer, 1975-; Editor, Guide to Colour Management and Prepress, A Guide to QuarkXPress, A Preview to QuarkXPress, Global Communications: A Guide to International Publishing, QuarkEd, books 1 and 2, What's New in 4.0? Honour: Eastman Kodak Book, Feature Subject: Marketing Professional Photography. Memberships: Internet, DTP, PR & Marketing Forums; Boulder Writers Alliance. Address: 1750 30th Street #603, Boulder, CO 80301, USA.

**TOBIN Thomas Vincent,** b. 8 April 1926, Plymouth, USA. Associate Professor of Biology; Chief Health Professions Advisor; Director, Clinical Laboratory Science Program. m. Dolores Mary Chewey, 1 daughter. Education: BS, cum laude, Biology, King's College, Willes-Barre, 1951; MS, Biology, Boston College, 1953; Graduate Student, LeHigh University, Bethlehem, 1960. Career: Graduate Assistant, Boston College, 1951-52; Instructor, Biology, 1952-54, Assistant Professor, Biology, 1955-61, Chairman, Natural Science Division, 1971-77, King's College; Associate Professor, Biology, 1962-, Chief Health Professions Advisor, 1989-, Director, Clinical Laboratory Science, 1990-, King's College; Lecturer, Biology, Pennsylvania State University, University Park, 1972-77; Lecturer, Biology, College Misericordia, Dallas, 1977-78; Chairman, Department of Biology, King's College, 1985-91. Honours: NSF Science Faculty Fellow, 1960, 1961; O'Hara Distinguished Service Professor of Science, King's College, 1984; Thomas V Tobin Faculty Development & Research Fund in Science, King's, 1991; Charter Member, Alpha Epsilon Delta, 1989. Memberships: National Association of Advisors for the Health Professions; Pennsylvania Register of Biologists; Pennsylvania Society of Medical Technology. Address: 124 Forest Road, Mountain Top, PA 18707-1320, USA.

**TOCAN Dumitru,** b. 11 February 1926, Ocnita-Dambovita, Romania. Professor, Poet. m. Valeria. Education: BS, Petroleum Engineering, Petroleum and Gas Institute, 1951; MS, Petroleum Engineering, 1952; PhD, Petroleum Engineering, Petroleum, Gas and Geology Institute, 1962. Appointments: Tutor, 1950-51; Petroleum Engineer, 1951-54; Scientific Adviser for MS Degree, Petroleum Engineering, 1954-; Instructor, 1954-56; Assistant Professor, 1954-56; Scientific Adviser for PhD Degree, Petroleum Engineering, 1968-; Associate Professor, 1956-64, 1964-75, 1975-78; Professor, Petrolem, Gas and Geology Institute, 1978-; EducationalDirector, 1959-63; Principal Inspector for Mining and Petroleum Higher Education, 1963-67; Chief of Drilling, Engineering Department, 1966-72; Scientific Secretary, 1968-72; Professor, Ecological University, 1990-; Scientific Counsellor, Future Telecom Romania, 1997-. Publications:

More than 30 techincal and scientific works; Books; Manuals; Textbooks for Students; Technical Dictionary. Honours: Jubilee Plate, 1968, 1978; Medalia a 50-a Aniversare, 1971; Distinction Award, 1971, 1998; Ordinul Muncii, 1972. Memberships: Trade Union of Professors and Students; University House; Scientific Association of Engineers and Technicians; National Council for Science and Technology; Industrial Group for Drilling and Producation; The General Association of Engineers. Address: Str Barbu Delavrance No 27, Sector 1, Bucharest, Romania.

**TODA Susumu,** b. 1 December 1940, Yamagata, Japan. Aerospace Researcher. m. Sahoko Miwa, 2 sons. Education: BEng, Waseda University, 1964; MEng, 1966; DEng, 1980. Appointments: Senior Researcher, National Aerospace Laboratory (NAL); Senior Engineer, NASDA; Head, Structural Dynamics Lab, NAL; Director, Structural Mechanics Division; Director, Space Technology Research Group; Director Director-General. Honour: Distinguished Research Award, Ministry of Science and Technology, 1996. Memberships: Committee Member, Space Debris NRC, Washington, 1993; Associate Fellow, AIAA; SEM; Planetary Society; JSAS; JSME. Address: 1-4-6 Sekimae, Musashino-shi, Tokyo 180-0014, Japan.

**TODD Charles O,** b. 12 November 1915. Art Education. m. Geraldine, 2 daughters. Education: BS, Education, Emporia State University, 1936-40; MS, Art Education, Kansas University, 1948; MFA, University of Southern California, 1957. Appointment: Educator, Tucson; Retired. Membership: Phi Delta Kappa. Address: 848 E Grant Road, Tucson, AZ 85719, USA.

**TODOROV Vasil,** b. 15 October 1953, Sofia. Physician. m. Maia Todorova, 1 son, 1 daughter. Education: MD, 1979, Medical Academy of Sofia; Dipl internal medicine, 1984; Diploma nephrology, 1986; PhD, 1990, National Attest Com, Sofia. Appointments: Physician, Emergency Centre, Pleven, 1979-80; Teaching Assistant, Medical University, Pleven, 1980-88; Senior Teaching Assistant, 1988-95; Associate Professor, 1995-; Head of Clinic of Nephrology & Haemodialysis, Medical University, Pleven, 1995-. Memberships: European Dialysis and Transplant Association; New York Academy of Sciences; Balkan Association Nephrology Dialysis Transplant and Artificial Organs. Address: St Karadja 23 B Apt 13, 5800 Pleven, Bulgaria.

**TOIDA Makota,** b. 20 February 1958, Ogaki, Japan. Dentist. m. Kyoko Toida, 3 daughters. Education: DDS, 1982, Aichi-Gakuin University; DMSc, PhD, 1986, Nagoya University. Appointments: Head, Dept Oral Surgery and Oral Medicine, Ibi General Hospital, 1989-. Publication: Tumor Matrix Biology. Honours: Kancho Award, 1982; Decree of Merit in the Field of Dentistry and Oral Surgery, 1996; 20th Century Achievement Award, 1997. Memberships: International Association of Oral and Maxillofacial Surgeons; Asian Association of Oral and Maxillofacial Surgeons; Japanese Society of Pathology, councilor; and others. Address: 7 902 Hayashi Machi, Ogakai 503-0015, Japan.

**TOKARCZYK Roman Andrzej,** b. 16 March 1942, Grudki, Poland. University Full Professor. m. Czeslawa Malec, 1 daughter. Education: LLM, 1966, PhD Law, 1970, PhD Law and Philosophy, 1976, Marie Curie-Sktodowska University in Lublin; Research Associate Professor, Notre Dame University, USA; Visiting Associate Professor, Harvard University, Wayne University, Berkeley University, UCLA and several others in USA, France, Italy, Germany, Denmark, Israel; Visiting Professor in Madrid, Haifa and Harvard University. Appointments: From Assistant, 1966, to Full Professor, Marie

Curie Sktodowska University, Lublin; Dean of Faculty of Law and Economics, Studium Generale Sandomiriense. Publications: Author over 400 publications including books in Polish, articles in English, French, German and Russian, and conference papers; Creator of Biojun's Prudence. Honours: Awards given by Ministry of Education and Rector many times; Received grants from USA, NATO, Italy, Germany, France, Israel, Denmark, Finland, Spain and others. Memberships: Member of national and international professional organisations; Member of Tribunale of State. Address: Dudzinskiego 16, 20 815 Lublin, Poland.

**TOKARSKAYA Zoya Borisovna,** b. 16 June 1924, Borovichi Novgorod, Russia. Radiobiologist; Researcher. m. Gartsev Vitalii Petr, 1 son. Education: MD, Medical Institute, St Petersburg, 1951; Postgraduate, Radiobiology, Roentgen Radiological Institute, St Petersburg, 1957; MD, (hon), Biophysics Institute, Moscow, 1979. Appointments: Medical Radiology Lecturer, Institute of Continuing Education, Kharkov, Ukraine, 1957-59; Scientist, Branch N1 Biophysics Institute, Ozyorsk, 1959-63; Senior Scientist, Branch N1, 1963-. Publications: Health Physics, 1995, 1997; Voprosy Oncologii, 1994, 1995. Honour: Excellent Worker of Public Health, Health Ministry, 1968. Memberships: Russian Radiology Society; Russian Biochemical Society; Nuclear Society International. Address: Sverdlova Street 16-21, Ozyorsk 456780, Russia.

**TOKARSKI Juliusz Jan,** b. 7 October 1931, Krzemieniec, Poland. Physiologist. m. Magorzata Tokarska Schlattner, PhD. Education: Medical Diploma, 1959; PhD, 1965. Appointments: Associate Professor, Gdansk University, 1972-92; Head, Department Animal Physiology, Gdansk University, 1972-; Dean, Gdansk University, 1987-90; Professor, 1992-. Publications: Articles in professional journals. Honours: Award Minister Science and Education, 1978; Award Science Polish Academy Science, 1987. Memberships: Polish Physiological Society; Chairman, Gdansk Section, 1972-87, 1990-93; American Society Animal Science; European Neuroscience Association. Address: Gdansk University, Animal Physiology, Kladki 24, 80 822 Gdansk, Poland.

**TOKUMARU Hiroshi,** b. 5 February 1953, Tokyo, Japan. Aerospace Engineering Management. Education: BS, Mechanical Engineering, St Sophia University, 1976; MS, Aeronautics and Astronautics, Stanford University, 1982. Appointments: Assistant Manager, Mitsubishi Heavy Industries Aircraft Works, 1982-89; Deputy Director, Technology, Black & Decker Nippon Pop Rivets and Fasteners Co Ltd, 1989-91; Engineering Manager, Teijin Skiki Co Ltd, 1991-93; Engineering Sales Manager, Feintool Japan, 1995-96; President, Global Co Ltd, 1993-. Publications include: 100 Year History of Aerospace Technology; Air Flight 2000: Free Flight; Air Safety Beyaond 2000, presented at Total Flight Operation Study Group Conference, Tokyo, 1998. Honour: Excellence Award, Boeing Commercial Airplane Group, 1986. Memberships: AIAA; SAE; New York Academy of Sciences; AAAS; TFOS. Address: 2-6-18 Takamoridai, Kangawa Isehaba 259-11, Japan.

**TOLDSEPP Aarne,** b. 6 February 1942, Tartu, Estonia. Professor. m. Vilja Toots, 2 sons, 1 daughter. Education: Bachelor of Chemistry, 1965; PhD, 1970; Dr habil, 1985. Appointments: Postgraduate Student, 1966-69; Lecturer, Assistant Professor, 1970-84; Professor, 1985-. Publications: 350 publications including 45 textbooks, workbooks etc on chemistry and didactics of chemistry. Memberships: Estonian Association of Chemistry Teachers; IOSTE; ICASE. Address: Department of Chemistry, Tartun University, Yakobi 2, EE 2400 Tartu, Estonia.

**TOLER Michael Morgan (Lieutenant-Colonel),** b. 12 March 1950, Oklahoma City, Oklahoma, USA. Soldier; Educator; Industrial Manager. m. Mary Elizabeth Creagh, 3 sons. Education: Graduated with Honours, Peacock Military Academy, 1968; BS, General Engineering, US Military Academy, West Point, New York, 1972; MS, Systems Management, University of Southern California, 1986; MA, Strategic Studies, USA War College, 1997. Appointments: Commissioned 2nd Lieutenant, Infantry, US Army, 1972; Company Commander and Staff Officer, 1973-81; Contracting Officer, 1981-84; Inspector General, 1984-86; Chief of Operations and Training, 1986-88; Programme Manager, GE Aerospace, 1988-89; Adjunct Professor, Middlesex College, 1989; Director of Programme and Technical Support, Defense Logistics Agency, 1989-92; Director, Acquisition and International Support Operation Restore Hope, Somalia, 1992-93; Director, Contracting, and Associate Professor, US Military Academy, 1993-99. Publications: Contributions to Army Magazine, 1990, Army Times, 1993, Contract Manager, 1995, Acquisition Review Quarterly, 1998. Honours: Ancient Order of St Barbara Medal, 1981; Army Procurement Savings Award, 1985; Defense Meritorious Service Medal, 1993; Legion of Merit, 1999. Memberships: Army Acquisition Corps; Association of US Army; National Contract Management Association; Academy of Political Science; National Geographic Society; Association of Graduates of US Military Academy; TROA; Army Athletic Association. Address: 15B Wilson Road, West Point, NY 10996, USA.

**TOLLAN Arne,** b. 19 June 1938, Kristiansund, Norway. Hydrologist. m. Elin Kirsti Tollan, 2 sons, 1 daughter. Education: Cand Real, 1962, University of Oslo; National Academy of Defence, Oslo, 1991. Appointments: since 1980: Research Manager, Deputy Director, Norwegian Institute for Water Research, Oslo, 1980-86; Chief, Air Pollution Unit, UNECE, Geneva, 1983-85; Director, Hydrology Department, Norwegian Water Resources and Energy Administration, Oslo, 1986-98; National Expert, European Environment Agency, Brussels, 1992-93. Publications: Book: Water, A Natural Resource; Editor and contributor to several textbooks and conference proceedings. Over 50 papers in scientific journals in field of Hydrology, Water Management, Environment. Memberships: Norwegian Geophysical Society, President 1991-92; Norwegian Hydrological Council, Chairman 1995-; European Geophysical Society; Nordic Hydrological Association; and others. Address: Norwegian Water Resources and Energy Administration, Box 5091, 0301 Oslo, Norway.

**TOLSTOGOZOV Vladimir,** b. 22 April 1937, Moscow, Russia. Physical Chemistry. m. Davidova Ophelia. Education: BS, Chemistry, 1959, PhD, 1962, Mendeleev Institute of Chemical Technology, Moscow; DSc, Institute of Organoelement Compounds, USSR Academy of Sciences, Moscow, 1975; Professor, Food Science and Technology, USSR Academy of Sciences, Moscow, 1980. Appointments: Head, Laboratory of Novel Food Forms, 1975-91; The USSR Academy of Science, 1975-94; Head of the Laboratory of Functional Properties of Biopolymers, 1991-94; Senior Scientists in Food Science and Technology, Nestec. Publications: 5 books; 390 papers; 140 patents; 150 invited lectures. Address: Nestec Ltd Research Center, Vers-chez-les Blanc Box 44, CH-1000 Lausanne 26, Switzerland.

**TOMAS Ivan,** b. 12 May 1943, Praha, Czechoslovakia. Physicist. m. Vera Tomasova, 1 son, 2 daughters. Education: MSc, Charles University, 1967; PhD, Czechoslovakia Academy of Science, 1974. Appointments: Deputy Director, Institute of Physics, 1990-93; Head of Department, Institute of Physics, 1997-. Publications: 100 publications. Memberships:

Union of Czech Mathematics and Physics; IOPAP. Address: Slavikova 11, 12000 Prague, Czech Republic.

**TOMAS Srecko**, b. 23 January 1954, Drinovci, Croatia. Professor of Chemical Engineering. m. Ruzica, 1 son. Education: BSc, Chemical Faculty, Split, Croatia, 1977; MSc, 1989, DSc, 1993, Faculty of Chemical Engineering and Technology, Zagreb. Application: Technologist, Zagorka, Bedekovcina, Croatia, 1977-79; Designer, Borovo-Engineering, Vukovar, Croatia, 1979-80; Main Technologist, Opaka, Oijek, Croatia, 1980-87; Assistant Lecturer, 1987-95, Assistant Professor, 1995-, Associate Professor, 1998-, Food Technology Faculty, Osijek, Croatia. Publications: Numerous articles in professional journals. Memberships: Fellow, Croatian Society of Chemical Engineers, Almae Matris Alumni Chemicae Ingeniarie Zagrabiensis, Croatian Systems Society, Technical Information Services, Bangkok, New York Academy of Sciences, Biotechnology TIS, Ratburana, Bangkok; Committee, Napredak; HDZ. Address: Food Technology Faculty, University of JJ Strossmayer, F Kuhaca 18, 31000 Osijek, Croatia.

**TOMASEVICIUS Janas Vitoldas**, b. 25 June 1937, Vilnius, Lithuania. Cameraman; Director. m. Grazina Peciulyte, 2 sons. Education: Camermans Faculty, All Union Institute, Russia, 1960-65; Appointments: Assistant Camerman, 2nd Cameraman, Lithuania Cinema Studio, 1955-66; Director of Photography, 1966-. Membership: Lithuanian Cinematography Society. Address: Architektu 76-11, LT 2043, Vilnius, Lithuania.

**TOMASOV Pavol**, b. 26 March 1939, Richnava. University Professor. m. Marta Gecziova, 1 son, 1 daughter. Education: Electrical Engineering, 1963; PhD, 1971; Associate Professor, 1984; Professor, 1997. Appointments: Dean of Faculty, Zilinska Universita, 1992. Publications: 3 Monographs; 18 articles in foreign languages, 53 in Slovak language; 21 university textbooks including: Telecommunication and Safety Systems, co-author, 1990; Transmission Engineering, 1994. Membership: Scientific Council of University, 1992. Address: Zilinska Universita, Velky Diel, 01088 Zilina, Slovakia.

**TOMESCU Carmen Viorica Bela Cotofana**, b. 12 January 1961, Tulcea, Romania. Engineer. m. Sorin Cotofana. Education: MSc Mechanical Engineering, 1984, Polytechnic University of Bucharest; Chartered Design Engineer in Microelectronics, 1996, Delft University of Technology, Netherlands. Appointments: Maintenance Mechanical Engineer, Technical Rubber Artifacts Enterprise, Jilava, Romania, 1984-85; Scientific Researcher, Research and Development Institute for Electronic Components and Technological Equipment, Bucharest, 1985-93; Manager, Cartel Alfa Trade Union, International Relations Dept, Bucharest, 1993-94; Chartered Design Engineer, 1994-96, PhD Student, 1996-98, Delft University, Faculty of Information Technology and Systems, Electronic Instrumentation Lab, Delft. Publications: co-Author 10 papers in professional publications. Memberships: IEEE Components, Packaging and Manufacturing Technology Society. Address: Delft University of Technology, Information Technology and Systems, Mekelweg 4, Delft, CD 2628, The Netherlands.

**TOMIKAWA Soji**, b. 13 July 1918, Nagoya, Japan. International Civil Service and Education. Education: Law degree (Hogakushi), Tohoku University, Japan, 1942; MA, Public Administration, Syracuse University, Syracuse, New York, USA, 1955; PhD, Political Science, Syracuse University, 1966. Appointments: Member, Facilities Sub-Committee, Administrative Agreement, US-Japan Security Treaty, Prime Minister's Office, Japan, 1950; Senior Procurement Officer, United Nations Headquarters, New York, 1960; Office-in-Charge, UN Peace Keeping Emergency Forces, Middle East, Jerusalem, Israel, 1973; Executive Secretary, Japanese Educational Institute of New York, USA, 1982; Special Advisor, Council for Founding the Greenwich Japanese School, Greenwich, Connecticut, USA, 1990. Publications: Impact of Public Opinion on the Post-War Administration of Japan, Tokyo, 1965; Five Surprises Happened in Connection With the Relocation of the Japanese School in New York to Greenwich, 1997. Honours: Fulbright Exchange Program Scholarship to Syracuse University, New York, 1953; Order of Rising Sun, Gold and Silver Rays, His Majesty, the Emperor of Japan, 1994; Yomiuri Press (Tokyo) Education Award of Excellence in category of Community Relations Activities, 1997. Memberships: The Nippon Club, New York, 1982; The Japanese American Association of New York (Board of Directors), 1989; US-Japan Society of Fairfield County, Connecticut, 1990; US-Japan Fulbright Alumni Association, New York, 1990. Address: 68-28A 136th Street, Flushing, NY 11367, USA.

**TOMITA Akihiko**, b. 7 November 1967, Osaka, Japan. Astronomer. m. Yuko T Hanba. Education: Bachelor of Science, 1991, Dr of Science, Astronomy, 1996, Kyoto University. Appointments: Research Fellow, Department of Astronomy, Kyoto University, 1995-96; Research Fellow, Institute of Astronomy, University of Tokyo, 1996-97; Assistant Professor, 1997-99, Associate Professor, 1999-, Faculty of Education, Wakayama University. Publications: Many astronomical articles to journals including the Astronomical Journal and publications of the Astronomical Society of Japan. Memberships: Astronomical Society of Japan; Astronomical Society of the Pacific. Address: Wakayama University, 930 Sakae-Dani, Wakayama 640-8510, Japan.

**TOMIZ UDDIN**, b. 21 May 1958, Dist Pabna, Bangladesh. Physician. m. Shamima Begum, 2 sons. Education: DHMS Diploma, 1980; HSC, 1988. Appointments: Professor, Homoeopathic Medical College, Dist Pabna, Bangladesh, 1981-. Publications: Columnist and Feature Writer, different journals and dailies of Bangladesh. Memberships: Life Member, Bangladesh Probin Hitaishi Sangha, Pabna Dist Branch. Address: Tanti Market, PO & District, Pabna 6600, Bangladesh.

**TOMOV Botu Nicolov**, b. 19 December 1934, Dervischka Moguila, Bulgaria. m. Stoyanka, 2 sons. Education: Diploma Engineer, Technological Institute for Refrigeration Industry, Leningrad, 1957. Appointments: Designer, Technologist and Chief Engineer, Factory for Refrigeration, Sofia, Bulgaria; Director of Direction for Industrial Air-conditioning and Ventilation, Committee for Basic Machine Industry, Sofia, Bulgaria; Expert in Industrial and Commercial Refrigeration and Chief Technical Adviser, Project UNESCO/SIDA-2, Santa Clara, Cuba; Expert in Industrial and Commercial Refrigeration of the ILO Project in Luanda, Angola; Director, Intervodootchistka, Sofia, Bulgaria. Publications: Refrigeration Installations -Exploitation, Mounting and Reparation, textbook; Instalaciones Frigorificas, 2 vols, textbook; more than 20 manuals and brochures mainly written in Spanish. Address: Bl 335 B Zaichar Str, 1309 Sofia, Bulgaria.

**TOMOVA-STANKEVA Galina**, b. 31 January 1960, Sofia, Bulgaria. Publisher; Translator; Journalist. m. Emilian Stankev. Education: BA, English Philology, St Kliment Ohridski, Sofia University, 1979-84; Specialization, Leeds University, 1984-85; MA, English Literature, Sofia University, 1985; Hubert H Humphrey Program, School of Communications, School of Managemnt, Boston University, 1996-97. Publications: Translations of 27 plays including the works of Harold Pinter; 65 feature films, 4 novels; Author: Bulgarian-English

Phrasebook; Concise English-Bulgarian Dictionary; Articles, essays, editorials; Selector, editor: Bulgarian Love Poetry, Bulgarian Women's Poetry, Haiku, P B Shelley, Paul Cezanne. Honours: Certificate, Edinburgh University, 1990; Certificate, Boston University, 1997; Certificate, Government of the USA, 1997. Memberships: Bulgarian Translator's Union; Union of Bulgarian Journalists; United Nations of Greater Boston; Modern Language Association (New York); American Association for the Advancement of Slavic Studies, Cambridge, Massachussetts; Bulgarian Studies Association; Women of the World Initiative, Boston. Address: Compl Ovcha Kupel 2, BC 15, Entr G, Apt 102, Sofia 1632, Bulgaria.

**TOMS Kathleen M,** b. 31 December 1943, San Francisco, California, USA. Nurse. m. Benjamin Peskoff, 2 daughters. Education: AA, RN Diploma, City College, 1963; BS, Elizabethtown College, 1973; MS Ed, Temple University, 1977; MSN, Gwynedd Mercy College, 1988. Appointments: COL AN USAR, 2nd Medical Brigade, CA, USA; Nurse Manager, VA Northern CA Health Care System. Memberships: Alumni; US Army War College; American Nurses Association. Address: 2098 Sea Mist Dr, Vallejo, CA 9591 7748, USA.

**TONFONI Graziella,** b. 23 July 1957, Bologna, Italy. Research Professor. Education: Bachelor Degree, Humanities, 1976; Doctorate in Linguistics, magna cum laude, University of Bologna, 1980. Appointments: Researcher, University of Bologna, 1983-90; Visiting Scholar, Massachusetts Institute of Technology, Harvard University, Bolt Beranek & Newman, NASA, Lyndon Johnson Space Center, 1981-96; Research Professor, University of Bologna, 1991-96; Visiting Professor, College of Library and Information Services, University of Maryland, College Park, 1997-98; Visiting Research Professor, George Washington University, School of Engineering and Applied Science, 1998-99; Research Professor, Computational Linguistics, University of Bologna, 1998-. Publications: 17 books and over 100 scientific papers. Honours: Lega Navale Italiana Award, 1974; Ettore Majorana Award, 1975; Minerva Award, 1984. Memberships: American Association for Artificial Intelligence; Italian Association for Artificial Intelligence; Information Design Society, England; Sign Design Society, England. Address: University of Bologna, Via Zamboni 16, 40126 Bologna, Italy.

**TONG Zhe,** b. 16 June 1940, Beijing, China. Plant Physiologist. m. Yi-Lin Chen, 2 sons, 1 daughter. Education: Grad 1964, Department Biology, Beijing University. Appointments: Professor, 1991-, Director of Department of Developmental Botany, 1995-, Member Academic Committee, Institute of Botany, CAS. Publications: Over 70 research papers and reviews including: Coaction of light and cytokinin in photomorphogenesis, Planta, 1983; Evidence for involvement of phytochrome regulation in male-sterility of a mutant of Oryza Sativa, Photochem Photobiol, 1990; Studies on photoperiod-sensitive genetic male sterile rice in terms of developmental biology, Acta Bot Sin, 1998. Honours: Awards, National Science and Technical Committee, and CAS, 1991. Memberships: Board member, Chinese Society Plant Physiology; Standing Editorial Board, Acta Botanica Sinica. Address: No 20 Nanxin Village, Xiangshan, Beijing 100093, China.

**TOOMING Heino Ulo,** b. 22 October 1930, Mustvee, Estonia. Agrometeorologist. m. 1 son, 1 daughter. Education: Diploma, Geophysics, Tartu University, 1954; Candidate of Physics and Mathematics, 1961; DSc, Biology, 1972; Senior Research Scientist in Geophysics Diploma, 1967; Professor of Meteorology, Agrometeorology, Climatology Diploma, 1990. Appointments include: Fellow, Institute of Physics and Astronomy, Estonian Academy of Sciences, Tartu, 1954-74; Fellow, Estonian Agrometeorological Laboratory, 1974-91; Estonian Meteorological and Hydrological Institute, 1991-; Professor of Applied Meteorology, Estonian National Defence and Public Service Academy, 1995-. Publications: Several booka and over 300 pepers in professional journals; Essays. Memberships: European and African Region International Association of Wind Engineering; Estonian Ecological Council; Estonian Geographical Society; Honorary Member, Estonian Naturalists' Society; Honorary Corresponding Member, Russian Society of Plant Physiology. Address: Estonian Meteorological and Hydrological Institute, Teaduse 2, 75501 Saku Harjumaa, Estonia.

**TOPA Dan-Ion,** b. 2 August 1958, Targoviste, Romania. Theatre Director. m. Gabriela Oprea, 1 son, 1 daughter. Education: Stage Management, 1982, Scene Painting, 1986, Art School; Theatre Academy, 1988; Alternative Theatre Courses, 1991. Career includes: Personal Exposition Decorative Art, Buzau, Romania, 1975, Bucharest, Saloon Comentar, Romania, 1976, Targoviste, Culture Palace, Romania, 1977; Binala Scenografie, Bucharest, Dallas Hall, 1977; Scene Painting of The Head, 1979; Direction and Scence Painting of Flight or Freedom, 1979 & Mos Naca, 1978. Publications: Dambovita Sheet, Cultural Editor; Resocialization Course by Theatre, Uniter Year Book; Monthly Review, Neghinita; Theatre's Influence in Rural Environment, in progress. Honours: Interpretation Prize, Postdzam, Germany, 1985; National Prize, 1986, 1987, 1988. Memberships: President, Dambovita's School; Founder President, Theatrical Company, Thalia; Founder President, Arts Academy, Targoviste; Manager, Neghinita Theatre; Paradoxist Literary Association; Union of Theatre People, Romania; Contemporary Theatre Teachers at Art School; Cultural Foundation, Ileana Sararoiu. Address: PO Box 1-6, 0200 Targoviste, Romania.

**TOPPOZADA Mokhtar K,** b. 11 March 1939, Giza, Egypt. Prof of Obstetrics and Gynaecology. m. Jane Toppozada, 1 son, 1 daughter. Education: MBBch, 1962; Diploma Obs and Gyn, 1964; Diploma Surgery, 1966; MD, 1969. Appointments: Post-doctoral Training, Stockholm, Sweden, 1971-73; Lecturer Obstetrics and Gynaecology, 1969-74; Assistant Professor, 1974-79; Professor, 1979-. Publications: 248 scientific papers; 16 books and book chapters. Honours: Temporary Adviser for WHO Geneva 21 years; Member 3 Steering WHO Committees and WHO Advisory Board; Consultant, US Congress special hearing; International Health Foundations Geneva Award, 1972; National Medical Science Award, 1975. Memberships: 15 local and international associations and boards. Address: Shatby University Hospital, Alexandria, Egypt.

**TOPTSIS Anestis A,** b, 7 July 1959, Alexandroupolis, Greece. Educator. m. Urania, 1 son. Education: BA Mathematics, 1982; MA Mathematics, 1985; PhD Computer Science, 1992. Appointments: Assistant Professor, 1990-94, Associate Professor, 1994-, York University; Founder and Director, Heuritek and Heuritek Inc (an educational and software consulting corporation), Ontario, Canada, 1995-. Publications: 33 scientific publications 1985-. Honours: Honorary member, International Association of Knowledge Engineers (IAKE) 1992-93; Research funding from the Natural Sciences and Engineering Research Council of Canada, 1993-. Memberships: ACM; IEEE Computer Society, 1986-96. Address: Department of Computer Science and Mathematics, Atkinson College, 4700 Keele Street, North York, Ontario, Canada M3J 1P3.

**TOROSYAN Gagik.** Professor; Rector Advisor; Senior Scientific Assistant. Education: Yerevan Polytechnic Institute,

Chemistry, 1965-70; Institute of Organic Chemistry of National Academy of Sciences, RA, 1970-74, PhD Chemistry; Institute of Organic Chemistry of the NAS, Dr Chem Scis, 1975-85. Appointments: Aspirant, 1970-74, Scientific Assistant, 1974-80, Senior Scientific Assistant, 1980-85, Leading Scientific Assistant, 1985-89, Head of the Laboratory, 1989-90, to the Institute of Organic Chemistry, of the NAS RA; Head of Higher Education Dept, Ministry of Higher Education and Science RA, 1991-94; Professor of Yerevan Institute of Architecture and Construction/YerIAC, Rector Advisor, Vice-Rector, Yerevan University Hrachya Acharian, Senior Scientific Assistant, Yerevan State University, 1994-. Publications: 15 papers in professional journals; 2 academic courses taught; 14 presentations at professional conferences. Honours: 3 research grants in France, Italy and Germany, 1982, 1988, 1989; The Higher Award for Academic Excellence, 1967-70. Memberships: Ararat International Academy of Sciences; Scientific Council, Ministry of Agriculture & Food Industry RA; Scientific Council, Hrachia Acharian University; New York Academy Sciences. Address: Yerevan State University, Yerevan Hrachya Acharian University, 3 Moscovian, 375011, Yerevan RA.

**TOROSYAN Toros Sh,** b. 23 July 1950, Yerevan, Armenia. University Professor. m. 2 children. Education: Undergrad Student, Faculty Economics, 1968-73; Postgraduate Student, 1973-76, Research Assistant, 1976-79, PhD, 1978, Economics Institute of Armenian NAS; Dr Econ Scis, 1986. Appointments: Scientific Secretary of Economics, Institute of Armenia NAS, 1979-92, Head of Department of Foreign Economic Relations, 1989-92; Professor, YSU, 1989; Head Dept International Economics, YSU, 1992-, ErHAU, 1997-. Publications: 100 including: Perspectives of foreign economic relations of Armenia, Collection of Articles, 1989; State and perspectives of the external economic relations - Information Reference Book, 1992. Address: Yerevan State University, Faculty of Economics, Yerevan Hrachya Acharian University, 3 Moscovian 375001, Yerevan, Armenia.

**TORRENS Michael John,** b. 25 June 1942, Taunton, Somerset, England. Neurosurgeon. m. Maria Papageorgiou, 1 son, 2 daughters. Education: BSc (1st Class Honours), London, 1963; MB BS, MPhil, London, 1967; FRCS, England, 1972; ChM Bristol, 1975; Appointments: MRC Fellow, 1963, 1973; Duke University Scholar, 1967; Consultant Neurosurgeon and Clinical Lecturer, University of Bristol, 1976-90; Consulting Neurosurgeon and Chairman of Neurosurgery, Hygeia Hospital, Athens, Greece, 1991-99. Publications: Author: Urodynamics, 1983; The Physiology of the Lower Urinary Tract, 1987; Operative Spinal Surgery, 1991, reprinted 1992; Operative Skull Base Surgery, 1997. Memberships: Past President, ICS; SBNS; EANS; HNS; BCSS; BGS; New York Academy of Sciences; Fellow, Royal College of Surgeons. Address: Dionysou 10, Halandri, Athens 15234, Greece.

**TORRES Rafael,** b. 29 December 1950, Frank Pais, Cuba. Academic Administrator; Pediatrics Specialist; Magister in Bioethic. 4 children. Education: MD, University Oriente, 1975. Appointments: Director, Childrens Hospital, Holquin, Cuba, 1979-80, Banes (Cuba) General Hospital, 1982-83; Vice Director, Pediatric Services, Holquin, 1987-89; 1st Vice Director, Childrens Hospital, 1989-94; Teaching Vice Dean, Nursing School, Holquin, 1994-95; Head, Center for the Study of Bioethics, Holquin, 1995-; Associate Professor, Medical School, Holquin, 1996-; Head, Department of Post-Graduate Medical School, 1999-. Publications: Nutrition and Health in Children, 2nd edition, 1992; Bioetica: Desda UUA Perspectiva Cubana, 1997; Elementor Dara la Ensenanza de la Bioetica, 1998. Memberships: Cuban Society of Pediatrics; Cuban

Society of Neurosciences; Cuban Society of Pedagogy; Caribean Society of Physicians. Address: Apt Building 15-B, Apt 3, 31 St, R Lenin, PC 80100 Holquin, Cuba.

**TOSSETT Gloria Vay,** b. 31 January 1926, Hamar, North Dakota, USA. Educator. m. Arthur A Borstad, 1 son, 1 daughter. Education: BS, Concordia College, Moorhead, 1968; MS, North Dakota University, Fargo, 1972. Appointments: School Superintendent, Balfour, Flaxton and Buchanan Public Schools, North Dakota. Honour: Centennial Commission Recognition, State of North Dakota, 1989. Memberships: North Dakota Daughters of the Pioneers; Eastern Star Masonic Lodge. Address: Box 115, Sheyonne, ND 58374, USA.

**TOUGHLAJIAN Parsegh,** b. 1 April 1933, Istanbul. Historian; Author; Linguist; Lexicographer; Translator; Researcher; Writer. m. Irma, 2 sons. Education: Melkonian Educational Institute, Cyprus, 1951; Doctors degree, 1955, Michigan University, Ann Arbour, USA. Appointments: Linguist; Lexicographer; Encyclopedist; Historian; Translator; Researcher; Writer; Teacher of English, Gulhane Military Medical Academy, Ankara, and secondary schools, Istanbul. Publications include: English-Turkish Dictionary of Idioms, 1961, 16th edition, 1993; Comprehensive Turkish-English Dictionary, 1966; Comprehensive Turkish-French Dictionary, 1968; Okyanus Encyclopedic Turkish Dictionary, 1974, 10th ed, 1995; Bulgaria and Turkish-Bulgarian Relations, 1984; Contemporary Turkey, 3 volumes, 1987-90; Selections from Armenian Literature, 1992; Numerous articles on linguistics and history in various periodicals; Cagdas Turkiye, six vols; 28 published and 40 non-published works. Honours include: 32 international honours and 15 awards; Knighthood and Medal, Lofsensus Ursinus Committee, Germany, 1991; Most Admired Man of the Decade, American Biographical Institue, 1992; Order of Universal Knighthood, Supreme Council of International Knights Union of Spain, 1992; Order of the Holy Cross of Jerusalem, 1992; Deputy, Assembly of the International Parliament for Safety and Peace; Invitee, 21st International Congress on Arts and Communications, Edinburgh, 1994; Décoration au Grade de Commandeur de l'Ordre du Mérite Natioal du Caricom, 1995; Participated in 22nd Congress, Sidney, 1995, 23rd Congress, San Francisco, 1996, 24th Congress, Oxford, England, 1997; Military Order of Aigle de Mer, 1992; Albert Einstein Medal for Science, 1993; Many Honorary Doctorates and Professorships. Memberships: Numerous international and world scientific and social institutions including: Turkish Press Union, 1964; Writers Syndicate of Turkey, 1974; Supreme Council of the Turkish Press Union, 1983; Australian Institute for Coordinated Research; Deputy, Assembly of International Parliament for Safety and Peace, Parliament's Envoy-at-Large to Turkey, 1991; International Intellectuals Academy, Paris, 1991; Institut Des Affaires Internationales, Paris, 1994; Official Representative, World Institute of Achievement, USA; Life Fellow, International Biographical Association; Order of International Fellowship, Deputy Director General, Advisory Council, International Biographical Centre; Life Patron, Deputy Governor, American Biographical Institute Research Association. Address: PO Box 193, Levent, Istanbul, Turkey.

**TOURTELLOTTE Mills C,** b. 16 December 1922, Great Falls, Montana, USA. Engineer. m. Linda M Tourtellotte, 1 son, 2 daughters. Education: BSc, 1947, MSc, 1952, Mechanical Engineering. Appointment: Senior Project Engineer, Gulf States Tube Division, 1956-. Publications: Several articles and 3 patents. Honour: Junior Prize Paper, American Society of Mechanical Engineers. Memberships: American Society of Mechanical Engineers; Association of Iron and Steel Engineers;

Veterans of Foreign Wars. Address: Gulf States Tube Division, PO Box 952, Rosenberg, TX 77471-0952, USA.

**TOWNSEND Marilyn Moran,** b. 9 December 1954, Seminolo, Oklahoma. Chief Executive Officer; Owner, Communications Company. m. Bill, 2 daughters. Education: BA Radio, TV, Film and Journalism, Political Science minor, 1976, Purdue University. Appointments: News Reporter, WBBH TV, 1976-77; News Anchor, Reporter, WKJG TV, 1977-81; CEO/Owner, CVC Communications, 1981-. Honours: Indiana Small Business Person of 1988; Indiana Woman Entrepreneur of 1988; Fort Wayne Business Woman of Year 1991; Indiana United Way Volunteer of Year, 1997; 100 Most Influential Business Leaders, 1997, Issues in Business Magazine. Memberships: Chairman, Indiana Chamber of Commerce, 1995-96 (first woman); Chairman, Allen County United Way, 1994-95; Vice Chair, Indiana Economic Development Council, 1996. Address: 5131 Binford Lane, Fort Wayne, IN 46804-6503, USA.

**TOZER William Evans,** b. 7 July 1947, Binghamton, New York, USA. Entomologist; Educator. Education: BS, Natural Sciences, Niagara University, 1969; MS, Biology, Ball State University, 1979; PhD, Entomology, University of California, Berkeley, 1986; Certified Instructor, Biology, Zoology, California Community College. Career: Junior High School Teacher, 1969-71; Teaching Assistant, Biology, Ball State University, 1974-76; Private Practice, Biological Environmental Consultant, Berkeley, California, 1974-79, 1986-88; Research Assistant, University of California, Berkeley, 1979-86; Department Head, Education and Training, USN Disease Vector Ecology and Control Center, 1988-. Publications: Several articles in professional journals. Memberships: Chairman, Committee Member, Armed Forces Pest Management Board, Washington, DC, 1994-; American Entomology Society; Sigma Xi. Address: 1407 Northwest Santa Fe Lane, Apt 304, Silverdale, WA 98383, USA.

**TRAN Manh Tri,** b. 29 November 1937, Phu Yen, Vietnam. Scientist. m. Phan Kim Anh, 1 son, 1 daughter. Education: Engineer, Chemical Technology, 1961; PhD, Chemistry, Moscow Oil and Gas Institute, Russia, 1972; DSc, Chemistry, Institute of Catalyse, Villeurbanne, CNRS, France, 1982. Appointments: Director, Institute of Chemical Technology, National Centre for Natural Science and Technology of Vietnam. Honours: Professor, Superior Researcher. Memberships: Editorial Board Member, Journal of Chemistry, Vietnam; Editor in Chief, Journal of Chemical Society, Hochiminh City. Address: Institute of Chemical Technology, 1 Mac Dinh Chi, District 1, Hochi Minh City, Vietnam.

**TRAUBE Charles,** b. 18 October 1950, USA. Medical Doctor; Cardiologist. m. Shoshana, 1 son, 2 daughters. Education: BS, Brooklyn College, 1968-72; MD, Albert Einstein Medical College, 1972-1975. Appointments: Assistant Clinical Professor, Downsmre Medical School. Memberships: AMA; American College of Cardiology. Address: Traube Marush and Plawes, 2270 Kimball Street Suite 101, Brooklyn, NY 11234, USA.

**TRAYKOVA Maria Lozanova Valcheva,** b. 16 August 1952, Sofia, Bulgaria. Researcher. m. Trayko Traykov, 1 son. Education: MSc in Chemistry, 1978, University of Sofia; PhD in Catalysis, 1993. Appointments: Research Fellow, Bulgarian Academy of Sciences, 1978-98; Senior Research Associate, NASA-CAMMP, Northeastern University, Boston, USA. Publications: 27 papers in scientific journals. Memberships: IZA; FIZA; European Catalytic Society. Address: CAMMP, Dept Chemical Engineering, Northeastern University, 342 Snell

Engineering Centre, 360 Huntington Avenue, Boston, MA 02115, USA.

**TREJOS Charlotte,** b. 5 July 1920, Michigan, USA. Teacher. m. J M Trejos, deceased, 1 son. Education: MA Education, 1975, Hawthorne Christian College. Appointments: Retired Teacher since 1985; Lectures at high school, current; Registered Artist, Museum of Latin American Art; Artist, Huntington Botanical Gardens Art Guild. Publications: Books: My Carson, Your Carson, 1987; Yesterday Was Sunday, 1990; Magazine and newspaper articles. Memberships: National Museum of Women in Art; American Legion Post 287, Past Commander; Charter member, WIMSA (Women in Military Service for America). Address: 22325 So Vermont #13, Torrance, CA 90502, USA.

**TRESKOVA Svetlana Harnisch,** b. 21 July 1944, Kherson, USSR. Researcher. m. Jorg-Henner Harnisch, 1 son. Education: German Philology, Moscow State University, 1968; PhD, Institute of Linguistics, USSR Academy of Sciences, 1976. Appointments: Chairman, Research Committee, Sociolinguisitics, Soviet Sociological Association, 1986-90; 2nd Director, Institute of Cultural and Economic Analysis, USA, Great Britain, 1990-99. Publications: Russian in Ten Days, 1st and 2nd edition, in over 4 languages, 1988, 1992, 1993; Sociolinguistic Foundation of Mass Media, 1996; Editor, several books in Russian, German, 1970-99. Address: Rhoenstrassse 13, 36 0 37 Fulda, Germany.

**TRIFONOV Nikolai,** b. 27 June 1948, Voronezh, USSR. Real Estate Executive. m. Evgeniia, 2 sons. Education: Physics Faculty, Belarusian State Unversity, 1971; Special Faculty of Applied Maths, Belarusian State University, 1975; Cand Sci, Physics and Maths, 1987. Appointments: Reader, Belarusian Polytech Inst, 1988-91; Co-Chair of Council, Minsk Exchange, 1991; Vice President, Western Real Estate Exchange, 1991-94; President, Belarusian Real Estate Guild, 1994-; Expert, WP5 of Economic Commission for Europe of UNO, 1995-; President, Belarusian Society of Valuers, 1996-; Editor, Accounting and Analysing Journal, 1996-; Co-Chair, Coordination Council of Valuation for CIS, 1998-; Editor, Valuation Questions Journal, 1998-; Director, European Real Estate Society, 1998-. Publications: More than 150 Publications, Maths, Physics, Chemistry, Economics including Valuation, Law. Honours: Honourary Member of OSV; Honourary Member of AAPOR. Memberships: BREG; ERES; BSV. Address: Belarusian Society of Valuers, 17A Kalvaryiskaya Str, Minsk 22004, Belarus.

**TRIFONOVA Todorka,** b. 25 August 1955, Davidkovo, Bulgaria. Psychiatrist; Medical Educator; Writer. m. Nenko Mashonov, 1 son. Education: English Language School, Plovdiv, 1974; MSc, Dr, 1981, Higher Medical Institute, Plovdiv; Post-grad Specialisation in Psychiatry, 1990. Appointments: Intern, District Hospital of Mental Diseases, Patalenitsa, 1981; Intern, Dept Psychiatry, District Hospital, Pazardzhik, 1981-86; Assistant Professor of Psychiatry, 1986-90, Senior Assistant Professor of Psychiatry, 1990-93, Chief Assistant Professor of Psychiatry, 1993-99, Higher Medical Institute, Plovdiv. Publications: Monograph, Eastern Martial Arts - a Way to Health and Self-control, 1997; 51 scientific publications in Bulgarian scientific journals and collections of research works; 42 scientific papers presented at scientific congresses and symposia; Over 200 popular scientific and publicistic articles, short stories and feuilletons in Bulgarian newspapers and journals. Honours: 3 Certificates of Innovations in the fields of psychometrics, statistics and pharmacology. Memberships: Union of Scientists in Bulgaria; New York Academy of Sciences; Bulgarian Psychiatric Association. Address: Dept of

Psychiatry, Higher Medical Institute, 4000 Plovdiv, Bulgaria.

**TRIMONIS Algis Egidijus,** b. 10 June 1939, Utena, Lithuania. Geologist. m. Rimute Gagyte, 1 son, 1 daughter. Education: Geologist Diploma, Vilnius University, Lithuania, 1962; Candidate of Geology and Mineralogy Sciences, Moscow State University, Russia, 1972; Doctor of Geology and Mineralogy Sciences Diploma, Institue of Oceanology, Moscow, Russia, 1990. Appointments: Senior Technician, Geological Research and Survey Expedition, Vilnius, 1962-64; Junior Research Fellow, Southern Department of the Institute of Oceanology, Russia, 1964-73; Senior Scientist, Atlantic Department of the Institute of Oceanology, Russia, 1973-1999; Chief Scientist, Head of Division, Institute of Geography, Lithuania, 1992-; Professor, Vilnius University, Lithuania, 1996-. Publications: Author, Co Author of more than 190 Scientific publications. Honours: Senior Scientist Academic Rank, Academy of Sciences of Russia, 1982. Memberships: Geological Union of Lithuania; Geographical Society of Lithuania; Geographical Society of Russia. Address: Zirmunu 56A-14, Vilnius, LT 2012, Lithuania.

**TRIOLO Lelio,** b. 10 July 1948, Genova, Italy. Physician. m. F M. Education: MD, 1973. Appointment: Chief, 1st Medical Department, Trieste, Italy. Publications: 50 medical papers; 2 textbooks. Honours: 5 Medical Prizes won. Memberships: Augusto Murri's Club; Richard Feynman's Club; Paul Ehrlich's Club; Italian Hematological Society. Address: Via Picciola 1, 34123 Trieste, Italy.

**TRIPATHI Satya Narain,** b. 10 January 1950, Jaunpur. Educator. m. Smt Shail Kumati Tripathi, 2 sons, 2 daughters. Education: BSc I Div, 1970; MSc Phy II Div, 1972; BEd, II, II, 1975; MEd II, 1976; PhD, 1994. Appointments: Reader, Dept of Education, Co-ordinator Exam Reform Unit, DDU Gorakhpur University. Publications: 2 papers, 1992, 1997; One paper on Whistalers Research in India, 1971; One book, 1996. Memberships: Indian Association of Teacher Education, Life member; Indian Association of Educational Technology, Life member. Address: Dept of Education, DDU Gorakhpur University, Gorakhpur 273009, India.

**TRIPATHY Iswar,** b. 31 May 1941, Saitora, Bankura, West Bengal, India. Teacher. m. Parbati, 1 son, 1 daughter. Education: MA, Economics, 1963, English, 1965, Calcutta University, India. Appointments: Lecturer, Commerce, Burdwan University, India, 1974-75; Head, Department of Economics, Bankura Christian College, West Bengal, India, at present. Publications include: Poems: Hymns From the Womb, in English, 1982; Jeev Ebong Chaldal, 1984; Nirbachita Kobita, 1986; Aarshi Tower, 1989; Rupsayar, 1993; Short Story: Ghare Fera, 1978; Ashok Phool O Anyanya Galpa, 1994; Essays: Gram Banglar Arthaniti, 1983; Bankura Zillar Arthaniti, vol 1, 1989; Bankura Zilar Arthaniti, vol 2, 1993; Sahitya O Arthaniti, 1996; Drama: Kaagaj, 1983; Rangamancher Baire, 1997; Scenario: Rataner Prithiby, 1984; Anthology: Iswarer Biruddhe, 1987. Honours: Felicitation conferred by Durgapur Sahitya Sabha, 1996; Tarak Sen Prize, awarded by Jodhan Sahitya Sangstha, Hindusthan Cables, Burdwan, 1995. Address: PO and District Bankura, 722101 West Bengal, India.

**TRISCHIN Valerij Alexejewitsch,** b. 13 June 1947, Nischni Nowgorod. Conductor. m. Pentina Elvina Michailna, 2 sons, 1 daughter. Education: Studies in the Glinka, Conservatory in Nischni Nowgorod, 1970-75; Conductor, 1975; Conductor, children's choir school, Cokoleta, Rybinsk, 1972-87; Conductor, Glass, choir, 1987-90, and Ssallowuschki. Honours: Prize Winner, Sobinow, 1995; Prize Winner, Silver, International Choir Competition, Dautphetal, 1996; Prize Winner,

International Choir Competition, Athen, 1996. Address: Zhukova 29-32, 150043 Yaroslavl, Russia.

**TROFIMOV Anatoly,** b. 22 July 1937, Kazan, Tatarstan, Russia. Professor. m. Tatjana Pigour, 1 daughter. Education: Diploma, Kazan University, 1961. Appointments: Professor, Kazan State University. Publictions: Over 750 works including 22 monographs. Honours include: Several honorary diplomas; Honary Science Worker, Republic of Tatarstan, 1987, 1998. Memberships include: Informational International Academy; Russian Ecology Academy; International Academy of Humanitary Sciences; International Academy of Euroasian Sciences;. Address: Galeeva 8-99, 420061 Kazan, Tatarstan, Russia.

**TROMPF Garry Winston,** b. 27 November 1940, Melbourne, Australia. Academic. m. Robyn Trompf, 1 son, 4 daughters. Education: BA, Hons, Melbourne, 1962; MA, Monash, 1967; MA, Oxon, 1974; PhD, 1975; Dip Ed Hons, Melbourne, 1963. Appointments: Professor of History, University of Papua New Guinea, 1983-85; Associate Professor of Religious Studies, 1986-94, Professor in the History of Ideas, 1995, University of Sydney. Publications: 11 books including monographs and edited volumes. Memberships: Research Institute for Asia and the Pacific; International Association of the History of Religions; Association of the Journal of Religious History, Chairman, 1997-; and others. Address: School of Studies in Religion, University of Sydney, Sydney, NSW 2006, Australia.

**TRUEB Beat,** b. 21 Oct 1954, Zurich, Switzerland. Biochemist. m. Judith Köppel, 1 son, 1 daughter. Education: MSc, 1978, PhD, 1981, Habilitation, 1991, ETH, Zurich; Postdoctoral research, University of Washington, Seattle, 1983, Fred Hutchinson Cancer Research Center, Seattle, 1984. Appointments: Assistant Professor, ETH, Zurich, 1985-94; Associate Head, M E Müller Institute for Biomechanics, Bern, 1995-. Publications: Articles in scientific journals; Editor, J Biochim Biophys Acta. Honours: START Career Development Award, 1987; Jucker Cancer Award, 1992; Töndury Award, 1993. Memberships: Vice-President, Swiss Society for Biochemistry; Chairman, Swiss Connective Tissue Society. Address: Sunnhaldeweg 14, CH-3097 Liebefeld, Switzerland.

**TRUSOV Peter,** b. 7 May 1948, Lvov, Ukraine. Physicist (Mechanics); Researcher. m. Trusova Valentina, 1 son, 1 daughter. Education: PhD, Moscow Institute of Electronic Machinebuilding, 1978; DSc, Moscow State University, 1987. Appointments: Research Worker, 1971-78, Teacher, 1978-88, Decan of the Faculty, 1988-93, Head of Department, 1992-, Perm State Technical University. Publications: 2 monographs; over 60 articles. Memberships: Professor, Perm State Technical University; Euromech (European Mechanics Society); Corresponding Member of Russian Academy of Natural Sciences; Fellow for conferment of PhD and DSc degrees, Institute of Continuous Media Mechanics, Ural Department of Russian Academy of Science. Address: 29A Komsomolskiy av, 614000 Perm, Russia.

**TRUTER Patricia-Ann,** b. 10 January 1964, Pretoria, South Africa. Scientist. m. Hugo Johannes. Education: PhD Science, 1993. Appointments: Scientist 1986-89; Project Manager 1989-93; Programme Manager Polymers, 1993-. Publications: Patents, Artificial Skin, 1995; Controlled Release Products for Pharmaceutical Activities, 1996. Honours: Presidents Medal for Outstanding Performance, 1994, 1998. Memberships: American Association of Pharmaceutical Sciences; International Controlled Release Society; South African Chemical Society; Plastics Institute of South Africa; Society of

Plastics Engineering, USA. Address: Box 553, Irene 0062, South Africa.

**TSAI Ching-Piao,** b. 4 Sept 1957, Kaohsiung County, Taiwan. Professor of Civil Engineering. m. Lisa Tsai, 2 sons. Education: BS, 1979, PhD, 1988, National Cheng-Kung University; MS, National Taiwan University, 1981. Appointments: Lecturer, 1984-88, Associate Professor, 1988-95, Professor, 1995-, Department of Civil Engineering, National Chung-Hsing University, Taichung. Publications: Contributor of articles to professional journals including American Society of Civil Engineers Journals, Ocean Engineering, International Journal of Offshore and Polar Engineering, Applied Ocean Research, International Journal for Numerical and Analytical Methods in Geomechanics. Honour: Best Paper Award, Journal of Chinese Institute of Civil and Hydraulic Engineers, 1993. Memberships: American Society of Civil Engineers; International Society of Offshore and Polar Engineers; Soka Gakki International. Address: Department of Civil Engineering, National Chung-Hsing University, 402 Taichung, Taiwan.

**TSAI Chong-Shien,** b. 23 December 1953, Taiwan, China. Professor and Manager. m. Min-Whei Tsai, 1 daughter. Education: BS, National Cheng-kung University, Taiwan, China, 1977; MS, National Taiwan University, Taiwan, 1979; PhD, State University of New York at Buffalo, USA, 1987. Appointments: Associate Professor, Department of Civil Engineering of Feng Chia University, Taichung, Taiwan, China; Manager, Earthquake Hazard Prevention Inc, New York, USA. Publications: Recipient, First Prize for paper competition, International Bridge Conference, 1986; Excellent Award 1990, United University Professions. Memberships: American Society of Civil Engineering; American Society for Computational Mechanics; International Society for Computational Mechanics; Mentioned in biographical dictionaries. Address: Earthquake Hazard Prevention Inc, 76 Summerview Road, Buffalo, NY 14221, USA.

**TSAI Chung Jyi,** b. 18 October 1958, Taiwan. Medical Doctor. m. Hsian Chuan Huang, 3 sons. Education: Medical Degree, Taipei Medical College, Department of Medicine, 1984. Appointments: Intern Physician, 1983-84; Army Medical Officer, 1984-86; Resident Physician in Internal Medicine, 1986-89; Fellow Physician, Gastroenterology, Hepatology, 1989-91; Instructor Physician in Clinical Medicine, 1994-95; Assistant Professor, Medicine, China College of Medical Technology, 1995-; Attending Physician in Internal Medical, Gastroenterology, Hepatology, Chi Mei Foundation Hospital, 1992-. Publications: Many Refered Papers in Scientific Journals. Honours: Young Investigator Award, 1998. Memberships: New York Academy of Sciences; American Gastroenterologic Association; The Formosan Medical Association; The Society of Internal Medicine of Taiwan; Society of Gatroenterology of Taiwan; Society of Digestive Endoscopy of Taiwan; Society of Ultrasound in Medicine of Taiwan. Address: Chi Mei Found Hosp, 901 Chung Hwa Rd, Tainan 710, Taiwan.

**TSAI John,** b. 9 September 1942, Taiwan. Ocean Physicist. m. Lois, 1 son, 1 daughter. Education: PhD Physics, 1977, University Miami, Coral Gables; MBA Business, 1987, Florida International University. Appointments: Research Physicist, Ocean Acoustics Division, Atlantic Oceanographic and Meteorological Laboratory, NOAA, 1977-; Publisher & Editor, Overseas Chinese News, 1991-. Honours: Distinguished Authorship Award, NOAA/ERL/Department of Commerce, 1986; Annual Award for Outstanding Paper, Applied Physics Lab, Johns Hopkins University, 1986. Memberships: American

Geophysical Union, 1978-; Acoustical Society of America, 1978-. Address: 8100 SW 92 Ct, Miami, FL 33173, USA.

**TSAI Wu-Fu,** b. 28 September 1939, Taipei, Taiwan. Ophthalmologist. m. Diana Tsai, 1 son, 3 daughters. Education: MD, National Taiwan University, 1958-65. Appointments: Clinical Professor of National Taiwan University, 1985-; Chief, Chi-Mei Foundation Hospital, 1990-. Publications: 123 articles to professional journals; 5 books on Ophthalmology, 1983-98. Honour: Excellence Achievement Medal of Ministry of Education, 1984. Memberships: Fellow, International College of Surgeons; International Schepens Society; American Academy of Ophthalmology. Address: Chi-Mei Foundation Hospital, 901 Chung Hwa Road, Yung Kang, Tainan, Taiwan.

**TSAO Shyh-Lin,** b. 3 October 1965, Taipei, Taiwan. Associate Professor. m. Mei-Ling Kuo, 1 son, 1 daughter. Education: BS, Physics, 1987; MS, Opto Electronics Eng, 1989; PhD, Electrical Engineering, 1995. Appointments: Lecturer, Tairkang University, 1994; Lecturer, Fu Jen University, 1995; Associate Professor, St Johns and St Mary's Institute of Technology, 1995-97; Associate Professor, Yuan Ze University, 1997-. Publications: 12 Referred Paper; 43 Conference Papers; 1 Book Chapter, A High Speed Self Routing WDM ATM Network for Wireless Personal Communication Services; 1 Patent, An Optical Frequency and Temperature Sensor by Applying two Fiber Rin Resonators. Memberships: IEEE; SPIE; OSA. Address: Hsing Chuang, P O Box 1-236, Taipei, Taiwan.

**TSAPENKO Nikolai Evgenievich,** b. 22 May 1953, Nizhniy Novgorod, Russia. Mathematician. 1 son. Education: Diploma in Radio Physics, Moscow Power Engineering Institute, 1976; Postgraduate studies at the Department of Mathematics of Moscow Mining Institute, 1979-82; PhD, Mathematical Physics, Belarusian Academy of Sciences, Minsk, 1992. Appointments: Research Associate, Radio Engineering and Electronics Institute, Academy of Sciences, Moscow, 1977-79; Assistant Professor, Academy of Water-Transport, Moscow, 1985-91; Associate Professor, Moscow Power Engineering Institute, 1992-95; Lecturer, Moscow State Technical University, 1995-. Publications: Professional book and articles to professional journals. Honour: Medal, Defender of Free Russia. Memberships: New York Academy of Sciences; Party of Democratic Choice of Russia. Address: Malysheva St 26 Bldg 1, Apt 25, 109263 Moscow, Russia.

**TSARENKOV Boris Vasil'Yevich,** b. 19 June 1930, Bykhov, Belarus, USSR. Education: Master in Electrical Engineering, Leningrad Electrotechnical Institute, USSR, 1954; PhD, Physics and Mathematics, 1967; Doctor of Science, Physics and Mathematics, Ioffe Physico Technical Institute, Leningrad, USSR Academy of Sciences, 1986; Certificate of Professor, Physics of Semiconductors and Dielectrics, Highest Certifying Commission, USSR Government, 1991. Appointments: Junior Research Scientist, Physico Technical Institute, 1954-68; Senior Research Scientist, 1968-86; Principal Research Scientist, 1986-96; Head of Laboratory, Physical Problems, Semiconductor Electronics, 1993-96; Associate Research Scientist, 1997-. Publications: Over 250 Articles in Russian and International Scientific Journals, Physics of Semiconductors and Semiconductor Optoelectronics. Honors: Laureate of the Lenin Prize, For Participation in Fundamental Research Led to the Creation of Semiconductor Lasers, USSR Government, 1964; Recipient of Gold, 1977; Silver, Bronze; Medals of the USSR National Economic Achievement Exhibition. Memberships: General Meeting, Russian Academy of Sciences. Address: 805 Ditmas Ave #3J, Brooklyn, NY 11218, USA.

**TSARENKOV Gennadiy Vasil'yevich,** b. 29 July 1939, Bykhov, Belarus, USSR. Physicist. m. Nina Pugach, 1 son. Education: MS, Physics, Leningrad Polytechnical Institute, 1962; PhD, Physics and Mathematics, 1968, DSc, Physics and Mathematics, 1990, Ioffe Physico-Technical Institute, Russian Academy of Sciences. Appointments: Junior Research Scientist, 1966-86, Senior Research Scientist, 1986-91, Leading Research Scientist, 1991-94, Ioffe Physico-Technical Institute, Russian Academy of Sciences; Freelance Consultant, Brooklyn, New York, 1994-. Publications: 60 articles in Russian and international scientific journals, 19 invention certifications; Discovery of Phenomenon of Recombination Waves in Semiconductors, 1980. Honours: Co-recipient, Discovery Diploma # 226, USSR Inventions and Discoveries State Committee, 1980; Petr Kapitza Medal, Russian Academy of Natural Sciences, 1997. Address: 1086 Ocean Ave Apt B6, Brooklyn, NY 11230, USA.

**TSENG Chin-Hsiao,** b. 4 August 1958, Cambodia. Doctor. m. Choon-Khim Chong, 2 daughters. Education: MD, College of Medicine, National Taiwan University, Tapei, 1979-86; PhD, Graduate Institue of Public Health, College of Public Health, National Taiwan University, Taipei, 1993-96. Appointments: Resident, Department of Internal Medicine, 1986-91, Attending Physician, 1991-, National Taiwan University Hospital, Taipei. Publications include: Peripheral vascular disease and microcirculating defects among residents in the endemic areas of blackfoot disease (PhD dissertation); Atherosclerotic vascular diseases and associated risk factors among diabetic patients in Taiwan; Cardiovascular mortality in diabetic patients; Calcium antagonists in treating diabetic patients with hypertension implications from ABCD and FACET. Honours: Professor Chen Fang-Wu Award, 1991; Harvester Trading Company Ltd Award for Diabetic Research, Taipei, 1991, 1992, 1993; Merck-Sharp-Dohme Award, Diabetic Research, Taipei, 1995, 1997, 1998; Taiwan Medical Promotion Award, 1995; National Taiwan University Hospital Award for Research, 1996; Novo Nordisk Award, 1996; National Science Council Research Award, Taipei, 1996, 1997; Laser Medicine Society Award, Taipei, 1997; Fellow of American College of Angiology, 1999-. Memberships: American Diabetes Association; Formosan Medical Association; International Medical Association, Taiwan; Diabetes Association, Taiwan; European Society for Microcirculation; Laser Medicine Society, Taiwan; Gerontological Society, Taiwan; Taiwan Society of Atherosclerosis and Vascular Disease. Address: National Taiwan University Hospital, 7 Chung-Shan South Road, Taipei, Taiwan.

**TSENOGLOU Christos,** b. 26 July 1954, Athens, Greece. Chemical Engineer, Polymer Scientist, Educator. Education: Diploma Chemical Engineering, National Tech, University of Athens, 1978; MSc, Northwestern University Evanston, Illinois, USA, 1981; PhD, Northwestern University Evanston, Illinois, USA, 1985. Appointments: Assistant Professor, Stevens Inst of Technology, Hoboken, New Jersey, USA, 1985-91; Associate Professor, Stevens Institute of Technology, Hoboken, 1991-95; Visiting Research Professor, Dept of Chemistry, University of Athens, 1996-97; Visiting Professor, Dept of Chemistry, NTUA Greece, 1998-. Publications: Viscoelasticity of Polymer Blends, Macromolecules, 1989 and 1991; Journal of Polymer Science, Physics editor, 1988; Rheologica Acta, 1989; Fractal Suspension Rheology, Journal of Rheology, 1990. Memberships: AIChE; ACS; Soc Rheology; British Society of Rheology; AAAS; NYASc; Hellenic Society of Rheology. Address: 49 Fokionos Negri St, 113-61 Athens, Greece.

**TSHERNYSHEV Wladimir,** b. 16 May 1936, Moscow, Russia. Biologist. m. Afonina Valentina, 1 son. Education: MSc,

1958, PhD, 1963, DSc, 1978, Professor, 1989, Moscow State University. Appointments: Professor, Moscow State University; Chairman, Moscow Branch, The Russian Entomological Society. Publications: More than 200 scientific publications including monograph, Diurnal Rhythms of Activity in Insects; Insect Ecology, textbook. Honours: Honorary Member, Russian Entomological Society; Soros Professor. Memberships: Russian Entomological Society; Moscow Society of Natural History. Address: Department of Entomology, Faculty of Biology, Moscow State University, Moscow 119899, Russia.

**TSINTSADZE Nodar,** b. 22 February 1930, Tbilisi, Georgia. Physicist. m. Nelly Tsintsadze, 1 son, 1 daughter. Education: MS, Physics and Mathematics, Tbilisi State University, 1955; PhD, Physics and Maths, Kharkov State University, 1958; DSc, Physics and Maths, Tbilisi State University, 1966; Professor, Tbilisi State University, 1967. Appointments: Head, Plasma Physics Department, Institute of Physics, Georgian Academy of Sciences; Head, Physics Department, Tbilisi State University. Publications: More than 200 publications: Relativistic Nonlinear Effects in Plasma, 1989. Honours: Award, Georgian Government for Excellence in Science; Award, Ministry of Education for Outstanding Contribution to Education; Award for Contribution to Foundation of Tbilisi State University. Memberships: Georgian Academy of Sciences; Honorary Member, Hiroshima University; Problem Council, Plasma Physics, Russia; Problem Council of Plasma Electronics, Russia. Address: Institute of Physics, Georgian Academy of Sciences, Tamarashvili 6, Tbilisi 380077, Georgia.

**TSIRLIN Mark S,** b. 4 March 1939, Moscow, USSR. Chemist. m. Granik Marina G, 1 son, 1 daughter. Education: MSc Chemical Technology, 1962, Institute of Fine Chemical Technology, Moscow; PhD Inorganic Chemistry, 1968, Moscow State University; DrSc Physical Chemistry, 1984, Institute of Physical Chemistry of Academy of Science, Moscow. Appointments: Pulsar Research Engineer, Moscow, 1962-65; Junior Researcher, 1968-73, Senior Researcher, 1973-87, Leading Researcher, 1987-89, Head of Lab, 1989-92, Institute of Physical Chemistry of Academy of Science, Moscow; Head Mater Group, Solmecs (Israel) Ltd, Beer-Sheva, Israel, 1992-. Publications: Author, Editor: High Temp Corrosion and Protection Methods, 1973; Author: High Temp Corrosion and Protection of Ref2 Metals, 1977, 2 editions; Contributor articles to professional journals. Honour: Honour Order, USSR, 1990. Memberships: American Chemical Society; Scientific Council, Institute of Physical Chemistry, Academy of Sciences, Moscow; Scientific Council of USSR Academy Science, New Materials. Address: Omer Industrial Park, POB 3026, Omer 84965, Israel.

**TSOCHAS Constantinos,** b. 18 September 1933, Thessaloniki, Greece. Professor of Clinical Pharmacology. m. Elisabeth Mavridou, 1 daughter. Education: MD, Aristotelian University, Thessaloniki, 1959; Specialist in Internal Medicine, 1963; Specialist in Pneumonology-Phthysiology, 1964; PhD, 1968. Appointments: Licenced Physician Intern, internal medicine, Ahepa Hospital, Thessaloniki, 1959-60; Resident, Hospital Chest Diseases of North Greece, Thessaloniki, 1961-63; Assistant Director, Clinics Internal Medicine Hospital Mental Diseases, Thessaloniki, 1964-65; Assistant Director, General Central Hospital, Thessaloniki, 1966-69; Director, St Georges Clinic, Athens, Greece, 1972-79; Professor, Higher Technical Education Centre, Athens, 1973-83; Head, School of Paramedical Professions, 1973-76, 1982-83; President, Technological Educational Institution (TEI), Athens, 1983-87; Professor, Faculty Health and Caring Professions of Technological Educational Institution (TEI), Athens, 1983-; Medical Director, Faran SA Pharmaceutical, Athens, 1971-72, Eaton Pharmaceutical SA (subsidiary of Morton-Norwich

International, USA), Athens, 1972-74. Publications: Numerous scientific publications in many periodicals; Books include: Clinical Pharmacology (editor), 1996; Optical Pharmacology (editor), 1997; First Aids (author, editor), 1998. Honours include: Silver Medal, International Red Cross, 1968; Award, Greek Writers Association, 1998. Memberships include: Fellow, Royal Society of Health (London); Athens Medical Association. Address: Tech Education Institute Athens, Ag Spirdonos St, GR 12210 Athens, Egaleo, Greece.

**TSUBOMURA Hiroshi,** b. 12 August 1927, Nara, Japan. Professor. m. Michi, 3 sons. Education: BSc, University of Tokyo, 1950; DSc, University of Tokyo, 1957. Appointments: Research Associate, University of Tokyo, 1955-60; Assistant Professor, University of Tokyo, 1960-62; Professor of Chemistry, Osaka University, 1962-91; Professor, Kobe-Gakuin University, 1993-98. Publications: Chemistry of Excited States; Structural Physical Chemistry; New Physical Chemistry. Honour: Purple Ribbon Medal. Memberships include: Chemical Society of Japan. Address: 8-19-38 Mino, Mino 562-0001, Japan.

**TSUI Chih Ya,** b. June 1921, Wuhan, China. Education: Graduate, Mechanical Engineering Department, Central University, China; PhD, London University, 1950. Appointments: Professor, Yunnan University and then in Beijing Institute of Engineering, 1951-52; Joined new Beijing Institute of Aeronautics until present. Publications: More than 40 originals, major in Engineering Thermodynamics, Heat Transfer and Turbomachinery; Translated English, Russian, German, Japanese and French Literature. Honours: Awarded Honor Certificates for Outstanding Service from State Education Commission and Ministry of Aero and Astronautical Industries. Memberships: President, BUAA Federation of Returned Oversea Chinese, 1986-. Address: Department of Jet Propulsion, Beijing University of Aero and Astronautics (BUAA), Beijing, China.

**TSUJI Toshizo,** b. 2 January 1932, Kyoto, Japan. Hospital Administrator; Educator; Physician. m. Yoshiko Taniguchi, 1 son, 1 daughter. Education: MD, 1957, DSc, 1964, Kyoto Prefectural University of Medicine; Medical Diploma, Japanese Ministry of Health and Welfare. Appointments: Clinical Fellow, 1959-60, Assistant Professor, 1971-74, Associate Professor, 1974-97, Kyoto Prefecture University of Medicine; Clinical Fellow, 1964-67, Instructor Medicine, 1967-68, University Alabama Medical Centre, Birmingham, USA; Postdoctoral Fellow in Molecular Biology, University of Edinburgh, Scotland, 1968-70; President, The Medical Juridical Person, Ohta Foundation, Ohta Hospital, 1997-. Publication: Marine Hepatitis Virus, Effect on Live RNA, 1968. Honours: Fellow, NIH, 1965; Senior Fellow, EMBO, 1968. Memberships: New York Academy of Sciences; Internal Medicine, Gastroenterology, Hepatology, Clinical Oncology, Gastroenterological Endoscopy of Japanese Society; AAAS; WHO, Kyoto, Japan; OMGE. Address: 988 Uoya, Miyazu Kyoto, Japan.

**TSUJII Kaoru,** b. 22 March 1945, Sakai, Osaka, Japan. Scientist. m. Yukiko Tsujii, 2 sons. Education: Graduate, Department of Chemistry, Faculty of Science, 1968, MSc, 1970, PhD, 1983, Osaka University. Appointments: Joined Kao Corporation, 1970; Director, Tokyo 1st Research Laboratories, 1988, Director, Institute for Fundamental Research, 1990; Principal Researcher, Tsujii Research Laboratory, Institute for Fundamental Research, 1994, Research Fellow, Tokyo Research Center, 1996, Kao Corporation; Team Leader, DEEPSTAR Group, Japan Marine Science & Technology Center, 1998-. Publications include: Surface Activity - Principles, Phenomena and Applications; Chemistry and Applications of Surface Activity. Honours: Progress Award, Japan Oil Chemists Society, 1982; Outstanding Paper Presentation Award, American Oil Chemists Society, 1993; Most Valuable Paper Award, Association of Oil and Fat Industry, Japan, 1998; Divisional Award, Chemical Society of Japan, 1999. Memberships: Chemical Society of Japan; Japan Oil Chemists Society; Polymer Society of Japan; The Surface Science Society of Japan; Kinki Chemical Society; The Japan Society of High Pressure Science and Technology. Address: 3-9-26 Shodo, Sakae-ku, Yokohama 247-0022, Japan.

**TSUNO Katsushige,** b. 23 July 1945, Japan. Researcher. m. Shoko, 2 sons, 1 daughter. Education: Graduate, 1968, Master Degree, 1970, Engineering Department, Tohoku University. Appointments: Doctor of Engineering, Tohoku University, 1981. Honours: Seto Award, Japan Electronic Microscopic Society, 1998. Memberships: Electronic Microscopic Society, Japan; Royap Microscopical Society; Microscopical Society of America. Address: 2-10-11 Mihori, Akishima 196, Japan.

**TSUNOGAE Hiroshi,** b. 19 April 1935, Shimizu City, Japan. Emeritus Professor. m. Yoshiko Tsunogae, 1 son, 1 daughter. Education: BEd, 1958; MEd, 1960. Appointments: Professor, 1977-99, Dean, Department of Education, 1996-99, Emeritus Professor, 1999-, Shizuoka University; Professor, Tokoha Gakuen University, 1999-. Publication: An Introduction to the Study of Lifelong Learning, 1999. Honour: Minister of Education Award, Ministry of Education, 1993. Membership: Director, Japanese Society of Lifelong Education. Address: Tokoha Gakuen University, 1-22-1 Sena, Shizouka 420-0811, Japan.

**TSYFANSKY Semyon,** b. 16 August 1932, Ukraine, Kiev region. Mechanical Engineer. m. Tsyfanskaya Nadezhda, 1 son, 1 daughter. Education: Mechanical Engineer, 1955, Aviation Eng School, Kharkov, Ukraine; DrSc Eng, 1965, Air Force Academy, Leningrad, Russia; Dr Habil Sc Eng, 1992, Latvian Council of Sciences, Riga. Appointments: Assistant Professor, Chief of Dept, Military Engineering School, Perm, Russia, 1965-75; Professor in Strength of Materials, 1975-86, Chief of Laboratory, 1986-, Riga Technical University, Latvia. Publications: 250 scientific works, 1955-98, books, papers, patents and others. Honours: Laureate of Latvian State Prize in Science, 1990; Silver Medal, USSR State Exhibition, Moscow, 1984. Memberships: New York Academy of Sciences; National Committee in Mechanics, Latvia. Address: Riga Technical University, Material Strength Department, Ikalvu Street, Riga, LV 1658, Latvia.

**TSYKALO Alfred Leonidovich,** b. 20 Feb 1939, Odessa, Ukraine. Professor of Chemistry and Ecology. m. Tetyana Chorna, 2 sons. Education: Magister, Odessa Institute of Marine Engineers, 1961; PhD, Lomonosov Technological Institute, Odessa, 1967; DrSci, Institute of Non-Water Solutions, USSR Academy of Sciences, 1984. Appointments: Lecturer; Docent, 1967; Professor, Chair of Chemistry and Ecology Department, Odessa State Academy of Refrigeration. Publications: Thermophysical Properties of Liquid Crystals, monograph, 1991; 20 other books: 250 articles and reports. Honours: Ist Prize, International Association of Theoretical Chemistry, 1993; Soros Professor, 1994-95, 1997. Memberships include: Ukrainian Ecological Academy of Sciences, 1992; Academician, International Academy of Ecology and Life Protection Sciences, 1995; New York Academy of Sciences, 1996; Head, Odessa Ecological Association. Address: Malaia Arnautskaia Str 73, Apt 21-A, Odessa 270023, Ukraine.

**TU Ching-I,** b. 13 May 1935, Nanking, China. Educator. m. Sabrina S Tu, 1 son, 1 daughter. Education: BA, National Taiwan University; PhD, University of Washington, Seattle. Appointments: Assistant Professor, 1966-71, Associate Professor, 1971-75, Professor, 1975-, Chair, Department of Chinese, Comparative Literature and Slavic Languages, 1981-, Chair, Department of East Asian Languages and Cultures, 1990-, Rutgers University. Publications: Poetic Remarks in the Human World, 1970; Anthology of Chinese Literature, 1972; Readings in Classical Chinese Literature, 1981; Tradition and Creativity: Essays on East Asian Civilisation, 1988; Classics and Interpretations, 1999, (forthcoming). Memberships: Association for Asian Studies; MLA; Chinese American Academic and Professional Society; American Association for Chinese Studies; and others. Address: Dept of East Asian Languages and Cultures, Rutgers University, College Avenue, Scott Hall, Room 330, New Brunswick, NJ 08903, USA.

**TU Guoquan,** b. August 1947, Jiangxi, China. Professor; Teacher. m. Shuiyin Xiong, 1 son, 1 daughter. Education: Agronomic Department, Jiangxi Agricultural University, 1970-72, 1983-86; Glasgow University, 1994. Appointments: Assistant, 1972-83, Lecturer, 1986-91, Department of Agronomy, Jiangxi Agricultural University; Deputy Director, Assistant Professor, 1991-92, Director, Professor, 1993-, Biotechnique Research Centre, Jiangxi Agricultural University. Publications include: Physiological Studies on the Growth and Production of Steptomyces nanchangensis, 1990; Studies on the Biochemical Mechanism of Keratin Decomposed by Streptomyces II. Primary Study on the Transferring Laws of Thio-Compounds During Keratin Decomposition, 1998; Studies on the Biochemical Mechanism of Keratin Decomposed by Streptomyces III. Primary Studies on the Thio-Compounds Effects on the Mechanism of Keratinase and Biochemical Mechanism of Keratinase in the Course of Keratinolysis, 1998. Honours: State Council Special Allowance, 1993; Jiangxi Province Prominent Contribution Expert, 1994; Winner, Certificate of Finisher of State Grade Science and Technique Achievement Award, State Science and Technique Committee, 1995. Memberships: Chinese Society for Microorganism; Society for Invertebrate Pathology. Address: Biotechnique Research Centre, Jiangxi Agricultural University, Jiangxi Province, China.

**TU Jenn-hwa,** b. 26 December 1954, Taiwan. Professor; Politician. Education. m. Ma Yin-chuan, 1 son, 1 daughter. Education: BS, Agricultural Economics, National Taiwan University, 1977; MS, Economics, Thammasat University, 1981; PhD, Economics, Johns Hopkins University, 1991. Appointments: Assistant Research Fellow, 1987-90, Associate Research Fellow, 1990-92, Institute of Economics, Academia Sinica; Associate Professor, National Taiwan University, 1992-; National Assembly Member, 1996-. Publications include: Asia-Pacific Regional Operations Center: Theory and Practice, 1995; International Trade, Investment and Economic Growth, 1996. Membership: Taiwan Economic Association. Address: Graduate Institute of the 3 Peoples Principles, National Taiwan University, 1 Roosevelt Road, Sect 4, Taipei, Taiwan.

**TU Shan-Tung,** b. 4 November 1961, Fujian, China. Professor. m. F N Liang. Education: MSc, 1985, PhD, 1988, Nanjing University of Chemical Technology. Career: Vice President, Nanjing University of Chemical Technology; Chief Engineer, Sinopec Equipment Failure Analysis and Prevention Center, Nanjing. Publications: 70 papers on creep, fatigue and heat pipe technology. Honours: Excellent Young Scientist Award, China, 1990; Top Ten Best Young Teachers of Jiangsu, 1995; 1st Prize, Science and Technology Progress, Jiangsu, 1995. Memberships: Director, Chinese Chemical Engineering Society; First Vice Chairman, High Temperature Strength Committee. Address: Nanjing University of Chemical Technology, Nanjing 210009, China.

**TU Shiu-Tien,** b. 28 July 1944, Taiwan. Dentist. m. Tzeng Chiou-Jyu, 2 sons, 1 daughter. Education: DDS, Kaohsiung Medical College, 1969; Postgraduate, Tokyo University, 1974-76; Diplomate, International Congress of Oral Implantologists. Appointments: Chief Director, Kaohsiung Childrens Literature Association, 1992-98; Director, Chinese Poetry Association, 1995-98; Director, Association of Oral Implantology, China, 1997-99. Publications: The Running Sound of the Sun; The Spiritual Sea, Hollow Shells; The Singing River. Honours: DLitt, World Academy of Arts and Culture, 1990; International Poet of Merit Award, International Society of Poets, 1995. Memberships: World Academy of Arts and Culture; International Society of Poets; Fellow, World Literary Academy; Trustee, The Olympoetry Movement Fund Committee. Address: 228 Jen Ai 1st Street, 80027 Kaohsiung, Taiwan, China.

**TUBBS Charles A,** b. 21 October, 1953, Beloit, USA. Law Enforcement Officer. m. Cindy Olstead, 3 sons, 1 daughter. Education: Sociology, University of Wisconsin, 1972-1974; Graduate, Police Academy, Blackhawk Technical College, 1974; Graduate, Special Studies, Wisconsin State Patrol Academy, 1978; Graduate, Senior Police Executive Institute, University of Wisconsin, 1987; Graduate, Northwestern University School of Police Staff and Command, 1995; BS, Criminal Justice Administration, Mount Senario College, 1997. Appointments: Jr Police Officer, 1969-70; Field Patrol Officer, 1974-79; Police School Liaison Officer, 1979-80; Patrol Sergeant, 1980-83; Administrative Captain, 1983-87; Captain of the Records Bureau, 1987; Captain of Professional Standards and Training, 1987-88; Captain of Patrol, 1988-90; Interim Chief of Police, 1990-91; Captain of People and Public Issues, 1991-96; East Side Patrol Captain District Commander, 1996-98; Deputy Police Chief, 1998-. Honours: Numerous Awards and Honours include: Distinguished Officer of the Year in USA, National United Law officers Association (Top Blacks in Law Enforcement), 1993; Wisconsin Professional Police Association Certificate of Merit, 1996; Thrasher Award, National Gang Crime Research center, 1996, 1998; Distinguished Service Award for Appreciation, Brother Dutton Parochial School, 1998; Leadership Appreciation Certificate, Louis Porter Club, 1998. Memberships include: National Black Police Officer Association; National Organization of Black Law Enforcement Executives; Wisconsin Law Enforcement Officers Association; Wisconsin Police Women Association; National Association of School Safety and Law Enforcement Officers; Central Christian Church; New Zion Baptist Church; Black Professional Role Models. Address: 2690 Chatsworth Dr, Beloit, WI 53511-2306, USA.

**TUGBIYELE Emmanuel Akande,** b. 22 April 1923, Igbajo, Nigeria. Management and Training Consultant. m. C F W Tugbiyele, 2 sons, 3 daughters. Education: BA, magna cum laude, 1954; MA, Harvard, 1955. Appointments: Professor, Director, Continuing Education Center, University of Lagos, 1969-76; Depty Vice Chancellor, 1973-75. Publications include: The Education System - Philosophy, Form and Content, 1976. Memberships: Fellow, Nigerian Institute of Management, Institute of Personnel Management of Nigeria, Nigerian Institute for Training & Development. Address: PO Box 89, Unilag, Akoka Yaba, Lagos, Nigeria.

**TUKSAR Stanislav,** b. 27 July 1945, Gornji Kraljevec. University Professor. m. Vjera Katalinic, 2 sons, 2 daughters. Education: Faculty of Philosophy, 1970; Academy of Music,

1972; MA, 1978; PhD Philosophy, 1990. Appointments: Secretary, Croat Musicological Society, 1992-97; Vice Dean, Academy of Music, 1997-2000; Full Professor, University of Zagreb, 1998. Publications: Croatian Renaissance Music Theorists, 1980; Croatian Baroque Music Terminology, 1992. Memberships: Croatian Academy of Sciences and Arts; Croatian Musicological Society. Address: University Zagreb Academy of Music, Gunduliceva 6, 10000 Zagreb, Croatia.

**TUMAKOV Vladimir L,** b. 16 February 1957, Rustavi City, Georgia, Russia. Physicist. m. Tatiana P Gordeeva, 1 son, 1 daughter. Education: Graduate, Moscow Physical Engineering Institute, 1980; PhD, Physics and Mathematics, Institute for Energy Physics, Protvino, 1996. Appointments: Institute for High Energy Physics, Protvino, 1980-97; KEK (High Energy Accelerator Research Organization), Tsukuba, Japan, 1997-98; University of California, Irvine, USA, 1999-. Honour: International Science Foundation Grantee, 1994. Address: Institute of High Energy Physics, Protvino 142284, Moscow, Russia.

**TUNG Yeou-Koung,** b. 4 March 1954, Taiwan. Professor. m. Be-Ling Lee, 4 daughters. Education: BS, 1976; MS, 1978; PhD, 1980. Appointments: Assistant Professor of Civil Engineering, University of Nevada-Reno, 1981-84; Statistical Hydrologist, Wyoming Water Resources Center, University of Wyoming, 1985-1995; Professor, Civil Engineering Dept, Hong Kong University of Science and Technology, 1996-. Honours: Collingwood Prize of American Society of Civil Engineers, 1987; Arthur Thomas Ippen Award of International Association of Hydraulic Research, 1993; Walter L Huber Civil Engineering Research Prize of American Society of Civil Engineers, 1995. Memberships: American Society Civil Engineers; International Association Hydraulic Research; International Water Resource Association. Address: Hong Kong University of Science and Technology, Civil Engineering Dept, Clear Water Bay, Kowloon, Hong Kong.

**TUORI Timo Kustaa,** b. 24 November 1955, Pori. Detached National Expert. m. Taru Kirsti Sinikka (Orre), 3 sons, 1 daughter. Education: MSc, 1987; PhD, 1998. Appointments: Research Scientist, 1987-95; Product Manager, 1995-; Coord European Commission, 1996-; Invited Detached National Expert European Commission, 1998. Publications: Publications, lectures and patents in fields. Memberships: IEEE; ASA; ASS. Address: European Commission, DG XII, Rue de la Loi 200, B-1049 Bruxelles, Belgium.

**TURBALI Yadi,** b. 13 March 1931, Baghdad. BBA. m. Zainab, 2 sons, 3 daughters. Education: BBA, Guam, USA, 1954. Appointments: Business Manager, Financial Consultant, Private Sector, 1960-98. Honour: MBA. Memberships: Financial and Industrial. Address: MITCO Ltd Iran, PO Box 13145-964, Tehran, Iran.

**TURNER Marjorie Shepherd,** b. 12 December 1921, Beaumont, Texas, USA. Economics Professor. m. Merle Brandt Turner, 1 son. Education: BA, 1943; MA, 1945; PhD, University of Texas, Austin, 1954. Appointments: Professor, Department of Economics, San Diego State University, 1954-76. Publications: Books: Joan Robinson and the Americans, 1989; Nicholas Kaldor and the Real World, 1993. Honour: Phi Beta Kappa. Address: Box 8005 Black Butte Ranch, Sisters, OR 97759, USA.

**TURNER Ralph James,** b. 24 October 1935, Ashland, OR, USA. Artist. m. Phyllis I Wilson, 1 son, 3 daughters. Education: Diploma, Portland Art Museum School, 1958; BA, Reed College, 1958; MFA, University of Oregon, 1962.

Appointments: Director, Rock Creek Experimental Station, 1973-; Research Associate, Lunar and Planetary Laboratory, University of Arizona, 1965-75; Assistant Professor, Syracuse University, New York School of Architecture, 1966-70; Instructor, University of Arizona Art Department, 1962-65. Publications: Extraterrestrial Landscapes, 1972; Modeling and Mapping Photos, 1978; NE Rim of Tycho, 1970. Membership: Fellow, National Endowment for the Arts and Humanities, 1972-73. Address: 14320 SW Rock Creek Road, Sheridan, OR 97378, USA.

**TURNER Robert Comrie,** b. 6 June 1920, Montreal, Canada. Composer. m. Sara Scott Turner, 2 sons, 1 daughter. Education: BMus, 1943; MMus, 1950; DMus, 1953, (McGill). Appointments: Senior Music Producer, Canadian Broadcasting Corporation, Vancouver, 1952-68; Professor of Composition, University of Manitoba, 1969-85; Composer in Residence, the McDowell Colony, Peterborough, New Hampshire, 1987. Creative Works: Over 70 compositions including: Orchestral, A Children's Overture, 1958, Shades of Autumn, 1987, Diverti-Memento, 1997; Opera, Vile Shadows, 1983-86; Instrumental and Vocal, String Quartets No 1 and 2, 1949, 1954, Ten Canadian Folksongs, 1973. Honours include: Several major arts grants, from Canada Council, Manitoba Arts Council; Commemorative Medal, 125th Anniversary of Confederation of Canada, 1993; Listings in several Who's Who Biographical Dictionaries. Memberships: SOCAN; Canadian League of Composers; Canadian Music Centre; MacDonald Colony. Address: 126 Handsart Boulevard, Winnipeg, MB R3P 0C5, Canada.

**TYKOT Robert Howard,** b. 30 June 1961, New York, USA. Archaeologist. m. Cynthia Grant Tykot, 2 sons. Education: BS, 1983, MA, 1984, Tufts University; MA, 1993, PhD, 1995, Harvard University. Appointments: Manager, Archaeometry Laboratories, Harvard University, 1990-96; Lecturer, Department of Anthropology, University of Massachusetts, Boston, 1995-96; Assistant Professor, Department of Anthropology, University of South Florida, 1996-. Publications: Over 50 articles and professional reports. Honour: USF Presidential Young Faculty Award, 1998. Memberships: American Anthropological Association; Archaeological Institute of America; Association for the Study of Marble and Other Stones in Antiquity; Harvard Archaeological Society; International Association for Obsidian Studies; Society for American Archaeology; Society for Archaeological Sciences. Address: Department of Anthropology, University of South Florida, Tampa, FL 33620, USA.

**TYLEVICH Alexander,** b. 12 September 1947, Minsk, Belarus. Sculptor, Architect, Educator. m. Poline, 1 son, 1 daughter. Education: BA, Architecture, Minsk Architectural Institute, 1965; MA, Architecture, Byelorussian Poly Inst, Minsk, 1971. Appointments: Senior Architect, Minsk Project, 1971-84; Artist, Architect, Fine Arts Foundation, Minsk, 1984-89; Sculptor, Architect, Tylevich Arts, 1989-. Honours: Elected Fellow, Architectural Association of the USSR, 1976; Member, Project Team Awarded Gold Medals, First Prizes, Byelorussian and National USSR Competitions; Contributor to Art Exhibitions. Memberships: Architecture Association. Address: 1937 Highland Parkway, Saint Paul, MN 55116-1350, USA.

**TYURKYAN Raffi Armenakovich,** b. 3 April 1929, Poti, Georgia, arrived in Ukraine, 1951. Mining Executive. m. Liana G Aristesyan, September 1954, 1 daughter. Education: Diploma in Engineering, Institute of Technology, Tbilisi, Georgia, 1951; Candidate of Science, Mining Institute, Moscow, 1965, DSc, 1989. Appointments: Executive Director, Mine Building, Donetsk, 1953-55; Director, Vertical Mine Tunnel

Building, Ukrainian Mining Architecture Trust Donetskshakhtoprokhodka, 1955-76; General Director, Ukranian Ministry Mining Blgd, 1976-87; Orthekhshakhtostroy Project Institute, Donetsk, 1987-; Technical Supervisor, Building of underground section of hull Chernobyl (Ukraine) Atomic Station, 1986; Ukrainian Professor, Donetsk University Technology, 1991-. Publications: Author: Technic and Technology of Building of Vertical Mines Tunnels, 1970; Building and Digging of Vertical Mines Tunnels, 1982; Work of Miners in Chernobyl for Liquidation of Accident in Chernobyl Atomic Station, 1996; Contributor of chapters to books, numerous articles to scientific journals; 45 patents in field. Honours: Lenin Premium Award, Cabinet of Ministries, Moscow, 1957; Order for Participation in Liquidation of Accident in Chernobyl Atomic Station, Supreme Council, USSR, 1986; 2 Order of Lenin Medals; 15 others, 1955-85. Memberships: Ukrainian Aacdemy of Mining Science; Ukrainian Academy of Mining Architecture; New York Academy of Sciences. Address: Str Kobozeva 68/11, 340000 Dobetsk, Ukraine.

**TYUTYUNNIK V M,** b. 4 October 1949, Kupyansk, Ukraine. Information Scientist. m. Elvira A Tyutyunnik, 1 son. Education: Mechanical Engineer, Tambov, Russia, 1972; Dr.Chem, Mendeleev Institute of Chemical Technology, Moscow, 1977; Associate Professor, Institute of Culture, Tambov, 1981; Professor, State University of Tambov, 1992. Appointments: Head Chair of Information Systems, 1981-; President, Intern Information Nobel Centre, Tambov, 1992-; Chief, Tambov Department, Russian Academy of Natural Sciences, 1997-; Holder, Tambov Center of Moscow State University of Culture, 1997-. Publications include: Atom's Biography, 1984. Honours include: Best Book Award, 1986, 1989, 1992; Nobel Prizes, 1988, 1991; Nobel Prize Winner, Literature, 1991; Nobel Prize Winner, Chemistry, 1991; Honour Prize, Russian Ministry of Culture, 1992; J Soros Prize, 1993; Silver Medal & Diploma, 1997. Address: 6 Soviet Street, Tambov 2 392002, Russia.

**TZVETKOV Dimiter,** b. 14 November 1937, Sofia, Bulgaria. Physician; Professor. m. Kristina Tzvetkova, 2 daughters. Education: MD, 1961, Higher Medical School. Appointments: Assistant, 1963; PhD, 1973; Associate Professor, 1977; DSc, 1990; Professor, 1992; Head of Dept of Hygiene, Ecology and Occupational Health, 1990-; Vice Dean, Medical Faculty, Sofia, 1990-91; Vice Rector, Medical University, Sofia, 1991-92; President, National Centre of Hygiene, 1995. Publications: Over 150 articles; 9 textbooks and manuals; 1 monograph; on Hygiene and Ecology. Honours: Medal, Cyril and Methodius, 1987, for scientific, teaching, popularizing and prophylactic activity. Memberships: Bulgarian National Academy of Medicine; Management Board, Bulgarian Scientific Society of Hygiene; New York Academy of Sciences; Polish Society of Hygiene; Atlantic Euro-Mediterranean Academy of Medical Sciences; National Geographic Society, USA; VP, Bulgarian Lipid Association; Editorial Board several medical journals; International contributing editors, Central European Journal of Public Health; Responsible for the EC Programme, Tempus - Education and Ecology; and others. Address: 73 Boulevard Evl Georgiev, 1000 Sofia, Bulgaria.

# U

**UBUKATA Makoto,** b. 16 July 1951, Katashina. Professor; Chemist. m. Satomi Kawakatsu, 1 son, 2 daughters. Education: BS, 1977, PhD, 1980, Hokkaido University. Appointments: Research Associate, Indiana University, Bloomington, 1980-81; Research Associate, Inst Phys Chem Research, Wako, Japan, 1982-83; Research Scientist, Research Institute of Life Science, Snow Brand Co Ltd, Ishibashi, Japan, 1983-84; Research Scientist, 1984-92; Senior Research Scientist, 1992-95; Professor, Toyama Prefect University, Japan, 1995-. Honours: Research Promotion Award, Agricultural Chemical Society, Japan, 1988; Sumiki-Umezawa Memorial Award, 1995. Memberships: Ameican Chemistry Society; AAAS; Japanese Society for Biosci Biotech Agrochem. Address: Toyama Prefect University, Biotech Research Center, Kosugi, Toyama 939-0398, Japan.

**UCEL Gulgun,** b. 8 January 1943, Kadiköy, Istanbul. Historian; Soprano. m. Cahid Aybet, 1 daughter. Education: Operatic Singing, 1985, Mozarteum, Salzburg; PhD History, 1981, University of Istanbul. Appointments: History Teacher, American Robert College, Istanbul, 1974-75; Scholar, B L Eng, 1981-91; History Teacher, American College, Izmir, 1975-77; Assistant Professor, Aegean University, 1977-81; Lecturer, MSU, Istanbul, 1992-99. Publications: Social Policy of the Ottoman State, 1987; Social and Economic Life in 16th Century Bosnia, 1995; Contributions to: Urban Administration and Housing in Istanbul in the 17th Century, 1993; Festivities in Istanbul in 16th and 17th Centuries, 1996; Evaluation and Interpretation of Re-Discovered Sources of Ottoman Social History, Archivum Ottomanicum, Hungary, 1999. Honours: BA Hons in History; Award winner, Glasgow Music Festival, 1972. Memberships: CIEPO; Association of International Congress of Social and Economic History; BRISMES; MESA. Address: Caddebostan, Iskele Caddesi No 32/17, Erenkoy 81060, Istanbul, Turkey.

**UCHAEVA Inna Mikhailovna,** b. 28 August 1970, Saratov, Russia. Chemistry Educator; Scientist in Chemistry. Education: MSc, Department of Chemistry, 1992, Postgraduate Student, 1992, PhD, 1997, N G Chernyshevskii Saratov State University, Saratov, Russia. Appointments: Laboratory Assistant, 1989-95, Senior Laboratory Assistant, 1995-96, Engineer, 1996-, N G Chernyshevskii Saratov State University. Publications: Over 40 publications including 5 articles; Chemical and Electrochemical Oxidation of Phenothiazine, 1993; Spectrophotometric, Voltammetric and Quantum Chemical Investigation of Phenothiazine Oxidation Reaction, in Russian, 1994; Data for Teaching-and-Controlling Software on Sections of Analytical Chemistry Course for Universities, in Russian, 1995; Concentration of Hydronium Ions in the Solutions of Biprotic Acids Completely Dissociated on the First Step: Substantiation of Limiting Cases, 1996; Participation in state program, Russia Universities, 1992-94. Memberships: International Society for Theoretical Chemical Physics, 1993-; D I Mendeleev Russian Chemical Society, 1996-. Address: Department of Chemistry, N G Chernyshevskii Saratov State University, 83 Astrakhanskaya Street, Saratov, 410026, Russia.

**UDEH Kenneth Ogbonna,** b. 26 May 1959, Naze-Owerri, Nigeria. Biotechnologist. m. Zofia Skrzydlewska Udeh, 2 daughters. Education: Diploma in Cold Storage Technology; MSc, Agricultural Science; PhD, Food Biotechnology. Appointments: Doctoral Student, 1991-96; Research Fellow, 1996-. Publications: Articles in professional journals. Honours: Polish Patent, 1998; World Patent pending. Memberships: New York Academy of Sciences, 1995; Polish Food Technologists Society, 1991. Address: Przy Stawie Street 4/3, 20-067 Lublin, Poland.

**UDLER Rubin Y,** b. 27 September 1925, Braila, Romania. Linguist. m. Malka I Alexenberg, 1 son, 1 daughter. Education: Bachelor of Philological Science, University of Chernovtsy, Ukrainian SSR, 1951; Master of Philological Science, Institute of Linguistics, USSR Academy of Sciences, Moscow, 1961; Doctor of Philological Science, Institute of Linguistics, USSR Academy of Sciences, Leningrad, 1974. Appointments: Translator, Soviet Bucovina, newspaper, Chernovtsy, 1951-52; Professor and Deputy Chairman, Foreign Languages Department, Chernovtsy State Pedagogical Institute, Chernovtsy, Ukrainian SSR, 1951-56; Junior Scientific Researcher of the Dialectology Section of the Moldavian Branch of the USSR Academy of Sciences, Kishinev, Moldavian SSR, 1956-61; Chief of Dialectology and Experimental Phonetics Section of the Language and Literature Institute 1961-85; Chief of Dialectology and History of Language Section of the Language and Literature Institute, 1980-86; Chief of Dialectology and Linguistic Geography Department of the Language and Literature Institute, Academy of Sciences of Moldova, 1986-92; Deputy of Academician-Secretary, Social Studies Department, Academy of Sciences, Moldova Kishinev, Moldovian SSR, 1989-92; Centre Associate, University Centre for International Studies, University of Pittsburgh, 1994-. Publications include: Moldavian Dialects of the Chernovtsy Area Consonantism, author, 1964; The Moldavian Linguistic Atlas, 4 parts, co-author, 1968-73; Dialectological Dictionary: Words, Meanings, Forms, 5 volumes, co-author, 1985-86; The Historical Grammar of the Moldavian Language, co-author, 1964; The Carpathian Dialectological Atlas, 5 volumes, co-author, 1987-93; More than 230 published works with total volume of more than 420 editorial sheets; Managing Editor and Co-Editor, about 60 monographs, dictionaries, atlases, collection of dialectological texts, collections of articles, theses. Honours: Corresponding Member, Academy of Sciences of Moldova; Appointed by Presidium of Academy of Sciences of Moldova, Kishinev, Moldavian SSR, 1989; Laureate of the Award of the Presidium of Academy of Sciences of Moldova, Kishinev, Moldavian SSR, 1980; Senior Scientific Researcher, appointed by the All-Union Certification Committee, Moscow, USSR, 1963. Memberships include: American Society of Romanian Studies, 1992-; Modern Language Association 1993-; American Association of Teachers of Slavic and East European Languages, 1995-; Holocaust Center of United Jewish Federation of Greater Pittsburgh, 1993-; Editorial Board, Philological Journals, Moldavian Language and Literature, Kishinev, 1961-91, and Journal of Linguistics and Study of Literature, Kishinev, 1991-92. Address: 1535 Shady Avenue, Pittsburgh, PA 15217, USA.

**UDOMON Henry,** b. 11 November 1953, Mbioto II, Akwa Ibom, Nigeria. Metallurgical Engineer; University Lecturer. m. Aniefiok Udomon, 3 sons, 1 daughter. Education: BS, Metallurgical Engineering, 1979, MS, Metallurgical Engineering, 1980, Michigan Technological University; PhD, Metallurgical Engineering, University of Wisconsin at Madison, 1986. Appointments: Metallurgist, Madison-Kipp Corporation, Madison, Wisconsin, USA, 1986-87; Senior Lecturer, 1992-, Head of Department, 1992-96, Deputy Director, 1996-, Federal University of Technology, Owerri, Nigeria. Publication: Effects of Bismuth on the Structure and Mechanical Properties of Grey Cast Iron and Its Neutralisation with Rare Earth Metals, PhD dissertation, 1986. Memberships: The Minerals, Metals and Materials Society, USA; American Association for the Advancement of Science. Address: Federal University of

Technology, PMB 1526, Owerri, Imo, Nigeria.

**UEDA Kosuke,** b. 10 May 1945, China. Professor. m. 2 sons. Education: Nagoya City University Medical School. Appointment: Professor, Department of Urology, Nagoya City University Medical School. Publications: Numerous articles in professional journals. Membership: International Society of Urology. Address: Department of Urology, Nagoya City University Medical School, 1 Kawasumi Mizuho-cho, Mizuho-ku, Nagoya 467, Japan.

**UEDA Yuichi,** b. 14 November 1951, Nara, Japan. Cardiac Surgeon. m. Keiko Kumaki, 2 sons. Education: MD, 1976, Kobe University School of Medicine; PhD, 1994, Kyoto University. Appointments: General Surgery Residency, 1976-79, Cardiovascular Surgery Residency, 1979-83, Staff Surgeon, 1983-84, 1986-93, Vice Director, 1994-95, Director, 1996, Dept CV Surgery, Tenri Hospital; Registrar, National Heart Hospital, London, 1985-86; Clinical Professor of CV Surgery, Kyoto University, 1998. Memberships: European Association for Cardio-thoracic Surgery; Society of Thoracic Surgeons. Address: Tenri Hospital, 200 Mishima, 632-8552, Tenri Nara, Japan.

**UEMICHI Isao S,** b. 13 January 1934, Tokyo, Japan. University Professor. m. Keiko N Suga, 7 January 1962, 1 son, 1 daughter. Education: BA, 1956, MA, Graduate School, 1959, Kansai University; PhD, World University, Arizona, 1986. Appointments: Lecturer, 1961-66, Associate Professor, 1966-68, Ryukoku University, Kyoto; Associate Professor, Mukogawa Women's College, Nishinomiya, 1968-70; Professor, Himeji Women's Junior College, 1988-90; Professor of English, Aichi University, Toyohashi, 1991-. Publications: Articles in professional journals. Honours: Bronze Medal for Peace, Third Class with Ribbon, 1988; Alfred Nobel Medal with Collar Ribbon; Special Award, Albert Einstein Academy Foundation, 1991. Memberships: Fellow, United Writers Association; English Association; Modern Language Association. Address: 13 Douzaka, Toyohashi 441-8038, Japan.

**UGAJIN Ryuichi,** b. 17 June 1963, Tokyo, Japan. Physicist. Education: PhB, 1988, MSc, 1990, PhD, 1997, University of Tokyo. Appointments: Research Scientist, Sony Corporation Research Centre, 1990-. Publications: Physical Review Letters; Applied Physics Letters; and others. Membership: Physical Society of Japan. Address: Sony Corporation Research Centre, 134 Goudo-cho, Hodogaya-ku, Yokohama 240-0005, Japan.

**UGGERHOJ Lars,** b. 2 November 1952, Frederikshavn, Denmark. Researcher. m. Vinnie Thomsen, 1 son, 1 step-daughter. Education: MSW, 1978; Advanced course in social work, 1986; PhD, Social Work, 1995. Appointments: Social Worker, Centerprise, London, England, 1973-74; Social Worker, Project Developer and Community Worker, Department of Social Services, Aarhus, Denmark, 1978-91; Research Fellow, Aalborg University, Denmark, 1991-95; Visiting Professor, Boston University, USA, 1993; Researcher, Danish Research Centre for Social Work, 1995-; External Associate Professor, Aalborg University, 1995-; Main external examiner, KaosPilot University, Aarhus, 1993-; Lecturer and Consultant to universities, schools of social work, local and governmental departments, conferences, primarily in Denmark, Norway and Sweden, 1980-; Member of boards in different private, city and governmental committees, 1986-. Publications: Author or Co-author, 19 articles, books or book chapters. Honour: The social encouraging Prize, Danish Association of Social Workers, 1994. Membership: Danish Governmental

Prevention Committee, 1997-. Address: Piganavej 9, 8320 Marslet, Denmark.

**ULIERU Mihaela,** b. 1 February 1962, Bucuresti, Romania. Professor. 2 sons. Education: PhD, Control Engineering, 1995, Darmstadt Institute of Technology, Germany. Appointments: Assistant Professor, Brunel University, London, England, 1995-97; Postdoctoral Fellow, Simon Fraser University, Vancouver, Canada, 1997-98; Associate Professor, University of Calgary, Canada, 1998-. Publications: 40 publications in professional journals; 1 book. Honour: Best Plenary Presentation Award, ISRPC, 1995. Memberships: New York Academy of Science; IEEE Systems, Inau of Cybernetics Society; IFAC Technical Committee on Diagnosis. Address: School of Engineering Designs, Simon Fraser University, Burnaby, BC W5A 1A6, Canada.

**ULLAH M Tobarak,** b. 20 August 1954, Comilla, Bangladesh. Environmental Engineer. m. Yasmin Akhter, 2 daughters. Education: Registered Professional Engineer, State of California and Nevada, USA; Registered Environmental Assessor, California State Environmental Protection Agency; Graduate Studies in Structural Engineering, Northrop University, Los Angeles, California; BS, Civil Engineering, Bangladesh University of Engineering and Technology, 1977. Appointments: Assistant Design Engineer, EAH Consultants Ltd, Bangladesh, 1977-79; Project/Material Engineer, BDC and Anderson Associates, Abu Dhabi, UAE, 1979-87; Project Manager, RAD Construction Co, California, 1987-90; Project/Resident Engineer, Kern County Waste Management Department, California, 1990-96; Construction Engineer, Harris and Associates Consulting Engineers, California, 1996-97; Staff Engineer, State of Nevada, Department of Conservation and Natural Resources, Division of Environmental Protection, 1997-. Honour: Certificate of Appreciation from Kern County Waste Management Department, California. Memberships: American Society of Civil Engineers; National Society of Professional Engineers; Associate Member, Institute of Engineers, Bangladesh. Address: 1350 Grand Summit Drive Apt. No.129, Reno, NV 89523, USA.

**ULLMAN Susanne,** b. 15 May 1938, Copenhagen, Denmark. Physician; Professor of Dermatology. Education: MD, 1965, University of Copenhagen; Postgrad training in Dermatology, Rigshospital, University of Copenhagen; 1988 Doctoral thesis: Immunofluorescence and diseases of the skin. Appointments: Visiting Professor, University of Minnesota, USA, 1974-76; Professor of Dermatology, Rigshospital, University of Copenhagen, 1979-; Visiting Professor, King Faisal University, Saudi Arabia, 1981, Hunan Medical University, Changsa, China, 1989; Professor of Dermatology, Bispebjerg Hospital and Rigshospital, University of Copenhagen, 1996-; Member of the National Board of Health's Advisory Group on AIDS, 1984-89; Member National Board of Health's Advisory group on STD, 1987-. Publications: Author and Co-Author, 85 publications in international and Danish journals on connective tissue diseases, bullous diseases, immunofluorescence microscopy and sexually transmitted diseases including AIDS. Address: Bispebjerg Hospital, Department of Dermatology, DK 2400 Copenhagen NV, Denmark.

**ULREY Prescott,** b. 1 April 1966, Atlanta, Georgia, USA. Attorney. Education: AB, University of California, Berkeley, 1988; MALD, The Fletcher School of Law and Diplomacy, 1991; JD, Columbia Law School, 1994. Appointments: Associate, Brown & Wood, 1994-97; Deputy Counsel, New York City Office of Management and Budget, 1997-. Memberships: New York City Bar Association; National

Association of Bond Lawyers. Address: NYC Office of Management and Budget, 75 Park Place, New York, NY 10007-2146, USA.

**ULYANENKOV Alexander,** b. 7 May 1963, Poltava, Ukraine. Physicist. m. Svetlana, 1 son, 1 daughter. Education: MS, Theoretical Physics, 1985; PhD, Theoretical Physics, 1990. Appointments: Institute of Nuclear Problems, 1990-98; Rigaku Corp, Tokyo, Japan, 1998-. Publications: Annals of Physics, 1995; Applied Physics, 1997; Physica B, 1998; Journal of Applied Physics, 1999. Memberships: New York Academy of Sciences. Address: Rigaku Corp, 3-9-12 Matsubara Cho. Akishima, Tokyo 196, Japan.

**UMALI Filemon,** b. 8 August 1925, Manila, Philippines. Physician. m. Nancy Lynn Fuller, 1 son, 3 daughters. Education: BS, Cosmopolitan College, Manila, 1948; MD, Manila Central University, 1956. Appointments: Obstetrician Gynaecologist, Wytheville, Virginia, 1967-85; Obstetrician Gynaecologist, Huntington East Valley Hospital, Glendora, California, 1985-. Memberships: Fellow, American Society of Abdominal Surgeons, Society of Philippine Surgeons of America. Address: 1347 Candish Avenue, Glendora, CA 91740, USA.

**UNGARO Maria Regina Goncalves,** b. 15 November 1951, Sao Paulo, Brazil. Agronomist. m. Fernando Ungaro, 2 sons, 1 daughter. Education: BSc, 1973, MSc, 1981, Dr, 1994, University of Sao Paulo. Appointments: Scientific Researcher, 1974-, Head, Oilseed Department, 1985-89, 1993-97, Agronomic Institute-IAC, Campinas, Brazil; National Research Council, Brazil, 1995-; Scientific Adviser, Research Support Foundation of Sao Paulo, 1997-. Publications: Several scientific papers in professional journals. Honour: Sao Paulo State Government Award, 1981. Memberships: Foundation Member, International Sunflower Association; Lions Club International. Address: Rua Dr Socrates de Oliveira, 99 Chacara Urbana, Jundiai 13201838, Sao Paulo, Brazil.

**UNGARO Susan Kelliher,** b. 7 June 1953, New York City, Magazine Editor. m. Colin, 2 sons, 1 daughter. Education: Bachelor of Arts, William Paterson University, 1975; Master of Arts, Wiliam Paterson University, 1976. Appointments: Editor in Chief, Family Circle Magazine, 1994-. Publications: H & R Block Family Financial Planning Workbook, 1980. Honours: President's Award, New Jersey Press Women's Association, 1995; William Paterson University Legacy Award, 1998; Irish America Top 100, 1999. Memberships: American Society of Magazine Editors; Women's Media Group; Women in Communications; New York Women in Communications; Brazelton Foundation; National Marrow Foundation; HELP. Address: Gruner and Jahr, 375 Lexington Ave, New York, NY 10017, USA.

**UNGUREANU Octavian,** b. 13 September 1922, Cornesti, Gorj, Romania. Journalist. m. Denise, 1 son. Education: Graduate, History Writing, Book Publishing. Appointments: Journalist. Publications: The Book of Heroes; Review of Military History; Nation Voice. Honours: 3 Jubilee Medals. Memberships: Professional Journalsits Union; Organisation of International Journalists; Society of Romanian Science and Culture. Address: Str Livezilor bl 11 Sc C, et II ap 12, Municipiul Pitesti, Jud Arges, Romania.

**UNNIKRISHNAN Seema,** b. 3 May 1967, India. Assistant Professor; Teacher. m. 1 daughter. Education: BSc, 1987; MSc, 1989. Doctorate, 1997, Hazardous Waste. Appointments: Trainee Scientist, Central Pollution Control Board, 1989-92; Faculty of Environmental Management, NITIE, 1993-. Honours:

University Gold Medalist; Jawahailal Nehru Award for Proficiency. Memberships: National Safety Council; Indian Environmental Association; National Solid Waste Association. Address: NITIE, Vihar Lake, Mumbai 400087, India.

**UNVER Ismail Hakki Olcay,** b. 2 February 1957, Erzurum, Turkey. Water Resources Engineer. m. Sumru Unver, 1 son, 1 daughter. Education: BS Hons, 1979, MS, 1981, Civil Engineering, Middle East Technical University; PhD Civil Engineering, 1987, University of Texas at Austin, USA. Appointments: Project Engineer, Municipality of Ankara, 1979-80; Private Consultant, Ankara, 1980; Lecturer, Research Assistant and Associate, various universities, 1978-91; Consultant, Co-Founder, Water Resources and Irrigation Cnsulting/Software Company, IRRISCO, Texas and New Mexico, 1987-88; Water Resources Engineer, Lower Colorado River Authority, an Agency of State of Texas, 1986-88; Water Resources Specialist and Deputy Director, Republic of Turkey Prime Ministry, State Planning Organisation, Southeastern Anatolia Project management Unit, Turkey, 1988-89; Regional Director, Republic of Turkey Prime Ministry, GAP Regional Development Administration, 1989-91; President, Republic of Turkey Prime Ministry, Southeastern Anatolia Project (GAP) Regional Development Administration, Ankara, 1991-. Publications: 38 publications and presentations. Honours: Science Fellow, NATO, 1981-84; Honour Fellow, Turkish Scientific and Technical Research Council, 1981-87; Honorary Governor, Agricultural Energy and Mechanisation Foundation of Turkey, 1996-; Agricultural Sector Award, Agriculturalists Association of Turkey, 1998; Nominee, Entering Graduate Student Award, 1981; Work referred to in 3 hydrology books. Memberships: World Water Council, various offices; International Hydropower Association, Council member; Consultative Group, Global Water Partnership, Sweden; Editorial Board, International Journal of Water Resources Development, and Hydro Review Worldwide; Black Sea Economic Cooperation Foundation of US; National Olympics Committee of Turkey; and others. Address: Birlik Mah Balta Sitesi #30, Cankaya Ankara, Turkey.

**UOGINTAS Arunas,** b. 26 March 1960, Siauliai, Lithuania. Art Teacher; Artist. m. Reda Uogintiene, 2 sons. Education: Art Dept, Siauliai University, 1983; Member, Lithuanian Artists' Association, 1992-. Appointments: Teacher of Art, various educational establishments; Director, Siauliai Art School, 1990-94, Teacher, currently; Works in fields of painting, fashion and wood miniatures. Creative works: Works exhibited in 13 joint Lithuanian Painting Exhibitions, 1983-89; Participated in group exhibitions in Vilnius, Lithuania, 1985, Siauliai, Lithuania, 1987, Klaipeda, Lithuania, 1988, Jelgava, Latvia, 1990; Personal exhibits at Siauliai Art Gallery entitled RA, 1989, and PARADAS, 1992; Creator, with wife, multi-part exhibition about the Gilia region near Kaliningrad, 1992, 1994, 1997, and theme based shows and performances entitled Archaeologists, 1993, 1994; Joined by other artists and musicians in 1995 taking part in 9 shows 1995-98; Works exhibited in several exhibitions, 1990-94. Address: P Cvirkos 106, LT 5400, Siauliai, Lithuania.

**UOSUKAINEN Riitta Maria,** b. 18 June 1942, Jääski, Finland. MP; Speaker. m. Toivo Uosukainen. Education: Matriculated, 1961; BA, 1964; MA, 1969; Lic Phil, 1970. Appointments: Teacher, Imatrankoski Upper Secondary School, 1969-; Provincial Instructor, Finnish Language, Kymi Province, 1976-83; Member, Imatra Town Council, 1977-92; Vice Chair, 1980-86; Member of Parliament, 1983-; Minister of Education, 1991-94; Speaker of Parliament, 1994-. Publications: 3 publications concerning Finnish language and mother tongue speaking; Liehuva Liekinvarsi, 1996 (Speeches and Letters). Honours: Commander of Order of the White Rose f Finland, 1992; Commander of the Italian Republic, 1993; Order of 1st Class of White Star of Republic of Estonia, 1995; Grand Cross, 1st Class of Order of Merit of Federal Republic of Germany, 1996; Grand Cross, Order of the Crown, Belgium, 1996; Commander, Grand Cross, Swedish Royal Order of Polar Star, 1996; Grand Cross of Order of Honour, Greece, 1996; Commanders Cross, The Icelandic Order of the Falcon, 1997; Doctor of Humane Letters, Suomi College, USA, 1997. Address: Parliament of Finland, Eduskunta, Fin 00102 Helsinki, Finland.

**UOTINEN Jorma.** Ballet Director. Appointments: Dancing career, Finnish National Opera, 1970's, First choreography, ASPECTS to Aulis Sallinen's music, Finnish National Opera, 1974; Choreographed the Forgotton Horizon, commissioned by the Helsinki Festival to Matti Bergström's music, 1980; Choreographed a solo piece, B12, for the dancer Tero Saarinen, 1988; Guest Choreographer, A Bird is a Bird is a Bird to Serge Aubry's music, 1991; Choreographed Rendering to the music of Luciano Berio and Franz Schubert for the Zürich Opera Ballet, 1993; Choreographer, La Neige Noire, 1997. Creative Works: White on White, performed 1991; Sketches, performed 1993; Swirls, 1997. Honours: Pro Finlandia, 1985; Helsinki City Cultural Award and major Finnish Award; Third Prize Winner, Groupe International des 8; French Medal, Chevalier des Arts et des Lettres. Address: The Finnish National Opera, Box 176, 00251 Helsinki, Finland.

**UPADHYE Milind,** b. 23 May 1961, Pune, India. Engineer. m. Neeta M Pangarkar, 1 son. Education: BSc Physics, 1981, MSc Electronics Instrumentation, 1983, PhD currently submitted, University Bombay. Appointments: Technician, Neharu Planetarium, 1982-83; Lecturer, Elphinstone College, 1983-85; Manager R&D, MIRC Electronics Ltd, ONIDA group, 1985-91; Digital Circuit Designer, Victor Company of Japan (JVC) in Japan, 1991-93; CEO, Kaihatsu Techno Centre Pvt Ltd, 1993-95; Managing Director, Asian Compusoft Ltd, 1995-. Publications: Problems faced by Indian Software Companies, forthcoming; 6 papers in professional journals. Address: Flat 05, Madhuban Bldg Raheja Twp, Malad Mumbai 400 097, India.

**UPHOFF Joseph Anthony Jr,** b. 15 March 1950, Colorado Springs, USA. Surrealist. Education: AA, 1975, EPCC; BA, 1977, UCCS; Shodan (Black Belt), 1989, IMA; Nidan, 1994, JJI; Hon LLD, 1992; D Div, Hon PhD, 1993, ULC; Honorary Professor, Fine Arts, Documentation and Mathematics, 1993, IDP. Appointments: Examiner, NJI, 1995-2001; Sovereign Military Order of the Knights Templar of Jerusalem, Corps Diplomatique, 1994-1999. Honours: Grand Council, World Parliament, 1993; Knight of the Year, International Writers and Artists Association, 1995, Lord Senator, Council of States, Count, San Ciriaco, 1996; International Poetry Hall of Fame, National Library of Poetry, 1997; Outstanding Poets of 1998, ILP. Address: 1025 Garner St Ste D Space 18, Colorado Springs, CO 80905 1774, USA.

**URABE Akio,** b. 1 April 1946, Japan. Haematologist. m. Hiroko Kato, 1 son, 1 daughter. Education: MD, 1973, PhD, 1980, University of Tokyo. Appointments: Assistant Professor of Medicine, University of Tokyo, 1979-89; Associate Professor of Medicine, Teikyo University, 1989-91; Director, Division of Haematology, Kanto Teishin Hospital, 1991-. Honours: Physician to Crown Prince, 1987-91; Physician to Emperor, 1989-91. Memberships: New York Academy of Sciences; International Society for Experimental Haematology. Address: 4-9-20 Den-en-chofu, Ota-ku, Tokyo 145-0071, Japan.

**URATA Kenji,** b. 25 February 1935, Kumamoto, Japan. Law Professor. m. Atsuko, 1 son, 2 daughters. Edcation: LLB, 1959, LLM, 1961, Doctorate, 1961-64, Waseda University. Appointments: Research Assistant, 1962-65, Lecturer, 1965-67, Assistant Professor, 1967-72, Professor, Constitutional Law, 1972-, Waseda University Law School; Academic Visitor, London University Institute for Advanced Legal Studies, 1978-80; Fellow, Science Council of Japan, 1985-94; Acting Vice President, Association of Asian Social Science Research Councils, 1989-91; Board Director, Japan Association of Lawyers Against Nuclear Arms, 1994-, International Association of Lawyers Against Nuclear Arms, 1995-; Representative, Japanese Association for Studies of Constitutional Law, 1995-97. Publications include: Nelson Mandela, Black Lawyers, and the IADL: Impression of the Cape Town Congress, 1996; Judging the Illegality of the Threat or Use of Nuclear Weapons: An Examination of the ICJ's Advisory Opinion, 1996; Peace Constitution's Ideal Still Worth Upholding, 1997. Membership: Vice President, IALANA. Address: Waseda University School of Law, 1-6-1 Nishi-waseda, Shinjuku, Tokyo 169-8050, Japan.

**URBAITIS Mindaugas,** b. 1 June 1952, Kaunas, Lithuania. Composer. m. Zivile Karkauskaite Urbaitiene, 1 son. Education: Graduate cum laude, 1970, Kaunas Juozas Gruodis Music School; Studied Composition with Prof Dr Julius Juzeliunas, Lithuanian Academy of Music, Diploma cum laude of Composer, Lecturer of Musical-Theoretical Disciplines, 1970-75, Postgrad course, 1975-77. Appointments: Lecturer, Musical-theoretical disciplines, Lithuanian Academy of Music, 1975-78; Freelance Composer, 1978-89; Delivered series of lectures, Klaipeda Faculties, Lithuanian Academy of Music, 1980-88, Lecturer, 1989-, Associate Professor, 1992-; Contemporary Music Producer, Radio Station Vilniaus varpas, Vilnius, 1991-94; Artistic Director, Baltic Music Festival, Gaida, Vilnius, 1991-95; Chairman of the Lithuanian Composers Union, 1991-96; Elected as a Member of the Senate of the Lithuanian Academy of Music, 1999-; Guest Composer, various music festivals; Commissioned to write a work for 50th anniversary of UNESCO, Paris, 1995, for the Vale of Glamorgan Festival, Wales, Great Britain, 1996, for Jauna Muzika Festival, Vilnius, 1998, to write a work for Wien Modern Festival, Vienna, 1998. Honours: Recipient several travel scholarships; Stasys Simkus 2nd Award for Parein jauteliai, 1980, 3rd Award for Kas?, 1987; Diploma for Music to G Buchner's Woyzeck, Moscow, 1981; Laureate Diploma, Ministry of Culture for Music, Vilnius, 1985; Jonas Svedas 1st Award for Dilio melnycia, and Rotas roto nepoveja, 1986; Balys Dvarionas 1989 Year Award; 1991 Year Award of monthly journal of culture and art, Kulturos barai, for Lithuanian Folk Music, 1991; Fellow, Salzburg Seminar Session 352 for Music for a New Millenium, 1997. Memberships: Lithuanian Composers Union, 1977-; International Society of Contemporary Music (ISCM), Lithuanian section; VP, 1991-94, President, 1994-96, Lithuanian Copyright Protection Association. Address: Fabijoniskiu 10-8, LT-2029 Vilnius, Lithuania.

**URBAN Joseph-Jaroslav,** b. 11 March 1922, Chocen, Czechoslovakia. P.Eng.; Consultant Engineer. 1 son, 1 daughter. Education: Diploma Engineering, Mechanical Engineering, University in Prague; Associate Professor of Engineers, University of Toronto, Canada. Appointments: Designer, Inventor, War High Speed Auto Machines; Patentee in fields: Pinsetters, Computers, Print Presses, Book Binders and Glass Class Machines; Vice President, Huck Co Montvale, New Jersey, USA, 1958-72; Board of Directors, Executive Consultant, Crown Cork & Seal, USA, 1972-92; Private Consultant Engineer, 1993-. Honour: Recipient, World War I,

Decoration from Brit Field Marshall Alexander. Memberships: Association Professional Engineers; Society of Art and Science; Professor Emeritus University Nurnberg, Germany; Sir Knight of Columbus, USA. Address: 71 Bacon Hill Road, Pleasantville, NY 10570-3501, USA.

**URMANIENE Liia,** b. 12 September 1945, Tallinn, Estonia. Diplomatic Engineer. m. Raimundas, 2 daughters. Education: Diplomatic Engineer, 1970. Appointments: Head of International Relations, Vilnius CCI, 1980-95; Deutsch Messe Ag Representative in Baltic Countries. Address: Lietuvos estu draugjia, Raugyklos 25, LT 2600 Vilnius, Lithuania.

**USMAN Rudolf G,** b. 1953, Padang, West Sumatra, Indonesia. Artist. Creative Works: Institute of Fine Art, Jakarta, Indonesia, 1974; Solo exhibitions in Indonesia, Kuala Lumpur, Australia; Group exhibitions in Singapore, Malaysia, Thailand, Taiwan, Korea, Japan, China, Australia and The Netherland; Co-founder, Indonesian Watercolour Society, 1992; Watercolour Album, 1993; Watercolour book, Tropical Tranquility, 1997; Art book, Rudolf's Journey, 1969-99, 1999. Honours: First Prize in painting competition, Padang, 1972; Certificate of Recognition, Jiangsu Province Watercolour Research Society, China, 1996. Address: Taman Kedoya Permai, Jl Limas VII, Blok C3 No 8, Jakarta-11530, Indonesia.

# V

**VADASDI Karoly Gabor,** b. 30 October 1942, Hungary. Chemist. m. Divorced, 1 son. Education: MS, Chemistry, 1965; PhD, Chemistry, 1969; CSc Techn Science, 1992. Appointments: Head Dept Chemistry, 1972-86, Head, Division Metal Research, 1987-97, Research Institute Technical Physics, Hungary Academy of Sciences. Publications: 60 scientific publications; 1 monograph; 19 patents on Tungsten and Molybdenum. Honours: Award and Medal of Research Institute of Technical Physics, Hungarian Academy of Science, 1997. Membership: Chemical Metallurgy Committee, Hungarian Academy of Science, 1993-. Address: Korong u 31/B, H 1145 Budapest, Hungary.

**VAFAI Abolhassan,** b. 25 October 1949. Professor. m. Mahshid, 1 son, 1 daughter. Education: MS, Civil Engineering, University of Southwestern Louisiana, USA, 1968; BS, 1968; PhD, Structures, University of Houston, 1972; Registered Professional Engineer, State of Texas, 1972. Appointments: Chief Structural Engineer, 1965-68; Assistant Professor, 1972-74; Associate Professor, 1974-78; Associate Professor, 1978-80; Chairman, 1980-84; Chairman, 1983-89; Professor, Civil Engineering, 1980-90; Chairman, Regional Coordinating and Scientific Cooperation, Sharif University of Technology, 1990-; Professor of Civil Engineering, Sharif University of Technology, 1990-. Publications: Approximately 200 Articles publishied in National and International Journals; Several Books. Honours: World Who's Who Hall of Fame, International Biographical Centre; Man of the Year, American Biographical Institute; 20th Century Achievement Award; ABI; Many other honours. Memberships: Organization of Professional managers; Iranian Society of Civil Engineers; American Society of Civil Engineers; American Society of Engineering Education; Americal Society of Experimental Stress Analysis. Address: Office of International and Scientific Cooperation, Sharif University of Technology, Azadi Aveue, P O Box 11365-8639, Tehran, Iran.

**VALK Harold Wessel de,** b. 25 October 1959, Bilthoven, The Netherlands. Physician, Internal Medicine, Endocrinology and Metabolism. Education: Propedeuse Pharmacy, 1977-78, Pharmaceutics University of Amsterdam; MD, 1985, Erasmus University, Rotterdam; Specialist training in internal medicine: Department of Internal Medicine, St Elisabeth Ziekenhuis, Amersfoort, 1985-87; Department of Internal Medicine, Utrecht University Hospital, 1988-90; Internist, Utrecht University Hospital, 1991-; Registration as Endocrinologist, 1994; PhD, Utrecht University, 1997. Appointments: Managing Director and diabetes expert, Utrecht Diabetes Project; Out-Patient Clinic of Diabetology, Utrecht University Hospital; Combined Clinic for Obstetrics and Metabolic diseases; Out-Patient of General Internal Medicine; Lipid Clinic; Consultant for Internal Medecine: Department of Neurology, Department of Psychiatry, Department of Rehabilitation Medicine, Bartimeushage (Doorn) Centre. Membership: Educational Board, Utrecht University Hospital, 1998-. Address: Utrecht U Hospital, G02-228 Heidelberglaan 100, 3584 CZ Utrecht, The Netherlands.

**VALNERE Rita,** b. 21 September 1929, Latvia. Painter. m. Kalnins Eduards, 1 daughter. Education: Gold Medal, 1949, J Rozentals Art School of Riga; Diploma with Honours, 1956, Latvian Academy of Arts, Painting Department; Masters in Art, 1992. Career: Began to participate in Exhibitions in Latvia and abroad, 1955; Creative trip to France, 1965; Teacher, 1967, Assistant Professor, 1978, Professor, 1985-, Chair of Painting, Latvian Academy of Arts; Creative trip to Italy, 1970; Creative trip to Japan, 1977; Member, International Art Association B-13, 1993. Exhibitions: 7 one-man shows including, Nepartrauktiba, Latvian Art Museum, 1996-97; 15 major group expositions including participating in jubilee exhibition of the Latvian Academy of Arts in Cologne and Dusseldorf, 1990; Works in collections in State Art Museum of Latvia and Latvian Artists' Union; Gekosso Gallery in Japan; Tretiakov Gallery in Moscow; Ministry of Culture of Russia; Tukums Art Museum, Latvia; many private collections in Latvia, India, Germany, USA. Publications: 4 monographic character publications; 3 catalogues; 7 books, including: Latvian Academy of Arts 1921-1996, 1996; 5 albums; 1 publication in Soviet Literature; 400 paintings. Honours: Laureate, Baltics Second Painting triennal, Vilnius, diploma and prize of the Lithuanian Artists' Union, 1972; Honorary Title of Latvian SSR, 1977; Diploma, Artists' Union of Latvia, medal and prize for best creative work, 1978; Order, Goda Zime, 1986; Honorary title of Peoples' Artist of Latvian SSR, 1987. Memberships: Artists' Union of Latvia, 1957; International Art Association B-13, 1993. Address: A Caka Iela 67/69, 14a Riga, Latvia, LV 1001.

**VALSALA Kizhakkae Valappil,** b. 6 June 1944, Edappil. University Professor. m. Dr A Rajan, 3 sons. Education: BSc, 1965; MSc, 1968; PhD, 1986. Appointments: Veterinary Surgeon, 1965-72; Assistant Professor, 1976; Associate Professor, 1981; Professor, Center of Excellence in Pathology, 1986. Publications: 62 Research Publications. Honours; DST Award for Outstanding Research; Best Research Article Award; Mycotoxin Research Award. Memberships: Indian Association of Veterinary Pathologists; Kerala Veterinary Association; Indian Veterinary Association. Address: College of Veterinary and Animal Science, Mannuthy Thrissur Kerala, 680651 India.

**VALSAN E H,** b. 30 August 1933, Trichur, India. Education. m. Srilakshmi, 1 son, 1 daughter. Education: BA, Madras, 1953; MA, Nagpur, 1956; PhD, Indiana, 1967. Appointments: Lecturer, Nagpur University, India, 1956-62; International Development Fellow, East-West Center, Hawaii, 1964-66; Professor, Public Administration, American University, Cairo, 1967-. Publications: Community Development Programs and Rural Local Government, 1970. Honours: Trustees Award, Meritorious Faculty, American University, Cairo, 1996. Memberships: Indian Institute of Public Administration; Chairperson, Local Government Working Group, International Association of Schools and Institutes of Administration; American Society for Public Administration. Address: American University, Cairo, Egypt.

**VAN ALLEN-HELSBY Veronica Elaine,** b. 6 May 1936, New York, USA. Marketing Executive. m. Ian Helsby, 2 daughters. Education: BEd, 1963, University of Miami. Appointments: Teacher of English and Physical Education, 1963-67; Executive Director, Royal Palm Festival, 1978-83; Executive Vice President, Northern Palm Beaches Chamber of Commerce, 1983-88; Marketing Director and in charge of Operation Explore, 1993-98. Honours: Graduated Dean's Commendation, University of Miami; International Festivals Association Award; Advertising Club of Palm Beaches and Florida Awards. Memberships: Leadership Palm Beach County; Rotary Club of West Palm Beach. Address: 192 Hampton Cir, Jupiter, FL 334458, USA.

**VAN BOXTEL Randall Anthony,** b. 27 February 1949, Appleton, Wisconsin, USA. Teacher; Theatre Director. Education: Bachelor of Arts Degree, Magna Cum Laude, St Norbert College, 1971. Appointments: English Teacher, Green Bay Public Schools, 1971-72; English Teacher, Kimberly Public Schools, 1972-. Honours: District Teacher of the Year, 1978, 1981; Presenter, Arts World Teacher Camp, 1990, 1991; Care

Community Award, 1997. Memberships: National Education Association, 1971-; National Council of Teachers of English, 1992-. Address: 714 E Lincoln Ave, Little Chute, WI 54140-2215, USA.

**VAN DE BOVENKAMP Hans, b.** 6 January 1938, Holland. Sculptor; Designer. 2 sons. Education: School of Architecture, Amsterdam, Holland, 1958; University of Michigan, Ann Arbor, Michigan, 1958-61. Career: Selected exhibitions include: Lowe Gallery, one man show, Atlanta, Georgia, 1989-96; Alcan-Lavelin, Montreal, Canada, 1989; Cameno Real, Boca Raton, Florida, 1990-96; Benkert Gallerie, Zurich, Switzerland, 1991, 1993, 1994; Omega Institute, Rhinebeck, New York, USA, 1992; Couturier Gallery, Los Angeles, California, 1993-94; Cast Iron Gallery, New York, New York, USA, 1993; Quietude Gallery, one man show, East Brunswick, New Jersey, USA, 1994, 1995, 1996; Dietrich Contemporary Arts, one man show, New York, New York, 1994; Cavalier Gallery, Stamford, Connecticut, 1994; Cavalier Gallery, Stamford, Connecticut, USA, 1994, 1995, 1996; PPG, Pittsburgh, Pennsylvania, 1995; Sculpture Showcase, New Hope, Pennsylvania, USA, 1995-96; Lumina Gallery, Taos, New Mexico, USA, 1995-96; 110 Greene St, New York, New York, 1995, 1996; Michener Museum, Doyles Town, Pennsylvania, 1996; Stamford Museum, Connecticut, USA, 1996; Elena Zang, Woodstock, New York, USA, 1996. Honours: Emily Lowe Award, 1964; American Institute Arts and Letters, 1976; Nebraska Bicentennial Competition; Sanctuary for Omega Holistic Health Institute, 1996. Address: 661 Springtown Road, Tillson, NY 12486, USA.

**VAN DE PAS Leonardus Franciscus Maria.** b. 28 October 1942, The Netherlands. Genealogist. Education: St Bonifacius Lyceum, The Netherlands. Appointments: Boekhandel Van Rossum, Utrecht, 1958-59; OPG, Pharmaceutical Wholesalers, 1959-60; Amsterdamse Balvast Mij, Jutphaas, 1960-64; Netherlands Department of Customs, 1964-48; Assistant, Author G M Glaskin, 1968-73; Genealegy, 1995-. Publications: Genealogical Compilations; HRH Charles Prince of Wales; Lord Frederick Windsor; Sarah Ferguson; Clifton Ancestry; Father of Europe; Giscard; Cupid and the King by HRH Princess Michael of Kent; Diana, Princess of Wales; Crommelin. Memberships: Dutch Genealogical Society; Friends of the Central Bureau for Genealogy; Australian Genealogical Society; WA Genealogical Society, Perth. Address: P.O. Box 79, Mosman Park, WA 6012, Australia.

**VAN DEN AKKER Johannes Archibald, b.** 5 December 1904, Los Angeles, California, USA. Physicist. m. Margaret W Koller, 1 daughter. Education: BS, California Inst of Technology, 1926; PhD, Californian Institute of Technology, 1931. Publications: More than 100 published papers in science journals. Memberships: American Physical Society; Optical Society of America; Technical Associate of the Pulp and Paper Association. Address: 1101 E Glendale Ave, Appleton, WI 54911-3144, USA.

**VAN DER WAL Eelco, b.** 2 November 1958, Baarn, The Netherlands. Managing Director. Education: Technical Science, University Groningen. Appointments: Product Manager, Business Manager, Motion Control, Chief Executive Officer, Forum Foundation. Memberships: NNI; IEEE. Address: Forum Foundation, PO Box 2015, NL 5300CA Zaltbommei, The Netherlands.

**VAN DER WESTHUIZEN Jacob, b.** 15 September 1929, Heidelberg, Gauteng, South Africa. Criminological Researcher. m. Debora Magrietha, 1 son, 2 daughters. Education: BA, Honours, University of South Africa, 1968; MA, cum laude, 1970; PhD, 1977; Teachers Diploma, 1954. Appointments:

Clerk, Farmers Cooperative, Nylstroom, South Africa, 1948-50; Laboratory Assistant, Researcher, Industrial Firm, Germiston, South Africa, 1951-53; Teacher, Division Head, Education Department, Gauteng, South Africa, 1954-70; Lecturer, Senior Lecturer, University of South Africa, Pretoria, 1970-75; Senior Research Officer, Institute Criminology, 1976-79; Professor, Criminal Justice and Director Research, Institute Criminology, 1980-89; Research Consultant, University and South African Police, 1990-. Publications: Descriptive Analysis of Housebreaking in the Area of the Norwood Police Station, 1979; Prediction of Parole Failure and Maladjustment, editor, co-author, 1983; Measurement of Crime, handbook, author, 1983; Wheels of Misfortune, editor, co-author, 1988; Security Management, handbook, author, 1990; Forensic Criminalistics, editor, co-author, handbook, 1993; Videotapes: Security - A Way of Life; The Quest for Balance, 1988. Memberships: Founder Member, Institute for Criminology; Board Member, Institute of Security; Associate Member, International Association of Chiefs of Police; Africa Representative, International Narcotic Enforcement Officer Association, USA; Chancellors Club of the University of South Africa; Planetary Society; International Police Association. Address: 37 Buffels Road, Rietondale, Pretoria 0084, South Africa.

**VAN DER WERSTHUIZEN Jacob, b.** 8 February 1960, South Africa. Orthopaedic Spinal Surgeon. m. Karin Verschave, 2 sons. Education: MBChB, University of Pretoria, 1983; Microsurgery Diploma, 1988; MMed, Prthopaedic Surgery, 1992; Spine Fellowship, 1992. Appointments: Orthopaedic Spinal Surgeon; Consultant, Spinal Unit, Pretoria Academic Hospital; Consultant Spinal Surgeon, Kalafong Hospital, Pretoria; Lecturer, Department of Orthopaedic Surgery, University of Pretoria; Private Practice, Pretoria East Hospital. Publications: Several articles in professional journals. Honours: Lecturer, International Spine Congresses, South Africa, 1996, 1997, 1998, Spain, 1998. Memberships: Orthopaedic and Neurosurgery Institute, Pretoria; South African Orthopaedic Association; South African Spine Association; European Spine Association; Founder, Eugene Marais Hospital Spinal Unit. Address: Pta-East Orthopaedic & Neuro Institute, Suite 4, PO Box 27098, Sunnyside 0132, South Africa.

**VAN DETH Jan Willem, b.** 27 May 1950, Utrecht. Professor of Political Science and International Comparative Research. m. Education: Mechanical Engineering, Polytechnic, Utrecht, 1969-74; Political Science, University of Amsterdam, 1974-79; PhD Political Science, 1984, University of Twente. Appointments: Assistant Professor, 1979-84, Associate Professor, in field of Political Behaviour, 1984-89, University Twente; Full Professor of Political Science and Chair of Department of Political Science, University Nijmegen, 1989-94; Visiting Professor, University Iowa, 1992; Full Professor of Political Science and International Comparative Research, University of Mannheim, Germany, 1995-; Head of Research Dept II, Problems of Governance in Industrial Societies, and Deputy Director, Mannheimer Centre for European Research, 1996-. Publications: 2 research notes; co-author, 12 book chapters and 10 books; Editor, several book chapters; over 40 articles; Number of book reviews in professional journals and articles in journals and newspapers; 21 papers. Honours: Winner of yearly award of Dutch Political Science Association for best book in Dutch Political Science; Co-winner 3rd Prize of Foundation for Research and Marketing for article; Various research grants. Memberships: Corresponding Member, Royal Danish Academy of Science and Arts. Address: University Mannheim, Lehrstuhl Polit Wissensch, D-68131 Mannheim, Germany.

**VAN DOOREN Rene,** b. 17 May 1943, Willebroek, Belgium. Professor. m. Roelants Denise. Education: Doctor Degree in Sciences, Free University of Brussels, Belgium, 1972. Appointments: Assistant, 1965-72; 1st Assistant, 1972-78; Assistant Professor, 1978-86; Professor, 1986-. Publications: Around 80 Scientific Papers in International Journals. Honours: About 40 Prizes and Honours; Spec Prize, Het Belgisch Schaakbord L'échiquier Belge, 1979; 2nd Prize, Schach-Echo, 1983; 2nd Prize, The Problemist, 1984; 2nd Prize, Szachy, 1985; 2nd Prize, Buletin Problemistic, 1987; 1st Prize, The Problemist, 1987; 2nd prize, Hlas L'udu, 1991; 1st Prize, Hlas L'udu, 1993. Memberships: Belgian Association of Problemists. Address: Free U Brussels, Dept Mech E, Pleinlaan 2, 1050 Brussels, Belgium.

**VAN LOON Antonius J,** b. 6 May 1944, Delft, Netherlands. Geologist; Author. m. Marion C A Kooreman, 2 sons. Education: MSc, State University Leyden, 1970; PhD, State University, Leyden, 1972. Appointments: Director of Geocom, Scientific Editor, Publisher, Anvers, (Belgium), Associate Professor Geology, Amsterdam. Publications: Numerous professional articles in English, French, German, Spanish, Finnish, Polish, Chinese and Dutch. Honours: Recognition of Outstanding Achievements in the German Language, 1963; Engineer of Honour, Belchatow Browncoal Mine, Poland. Memberships: International Association Sedimentologists; Society for Sedimentary Geology; Royal Geological and Mining Society Netherlands; Netherlands Geological Society; Working Group for Tertiary and Quaternary Geology; Leiden Geological Society; European Association Scientific Editors, Netherlands Association Scientific Editors; Lions Club, Renkum-Ostrabeke. Address: Benedendorpsweg 61, 6862 WC Oosterbeek, The Netherlands.

**VAN NORDEN Bryan William,** b. 9 December 1962, Latrobe, Pennsylvania, USA. Educator. m. Sarah Rebecca Thomas, 1 son, 1 daughter. Education: BA magna cum laude, Philosophy, University of Pennsylvania, 1985; PhD, Philosophy, Stanford University, 1991. Appointments: Lecturer, Stanford University, 1990-91; Visiting Assistant Professor, Philosophy Department, University of Vermont, 1991-93, Department of Philosophy and Religion, University of Northern Iowa, 1994-95; Assistant Professor, Philosophy Department and Asian Studies Program, Vassar College, 1995-. Publications include: Kwong-loi Shun on Moral Reasons in Mencius, 1991; Mengzi and Xunzi: Two Views of Human Agency, 1992; Hansen on Hsün-tzu, 1993; Yearley on Mencius, 1993; What Should Western Philosophy Learn from Chinese Philosophy?, 1996; Competing Interpretations of the Inner Chapters, 1996; The Ways of Confucianism: Investigations in Chinese Philosophy, editor and author of Introduction, 1996; Mencius on Courage, 1997; Method in the Madness of the Laozi, 1999; Essays on Confucius and the Analects, editor, contributor, forthcoming; Readings in Classical Chinese Philosophy, co-editor, contributor, forthcoming; Entries in reference books; Reviews. Honours: Mellon Fellowship in the Humanities, 1985; Stanford Center for East Asian Studies Foreign Language and Area Studies Fellowship, 1989; Chiang Ching-kuo Fellowship, 1993; Vassar College Research Grant, 1998. Address: Vassar College, 124 Raymond Avenue, Poughkeepsie, NY 12604-0310, USA.

**VAN PRAAG Herman M,** b. 17 October 1929, Schiedam, Netherlands. Professor of Psychiatry. m. Nelleke Eikens, 3 sons, 1 daughter. Education: MD, State University, Leiden, 1948-56. Appointments: Chief of Staff, Department of Psychiatry, Dijkzigt Hospital, Rotterdam, 1963-66; Founder, Head, Department of Biological Psychiatry, 1966-77, Associate Professor, 1968, Professor, 1970, State University, Groningen;

Lady Davis Visiting Professor, Hebrew University, Hadassah University Hospital, Jerusalem, Israel, 1976-77; Professor, Head, Department of Psychiatry, Academic Hospital, State University, Utrecht, 1977-82; Professor, Chairman, Department of Psychiatry, Albert Einstein College of Medicine, Bronx, New York, 1982-92; Psychiatrist-in-Chief, Montefiore Medical Center, Bronx, New York, 1982-92; Professor, Chairman, Department of Psychiatry, State University of Limburg, Netherlands, 1992-97; Emeritus Professor of Psychiatry, Albert Einstein College of Medicine, Bronx, New York, 1992-; Interim Head, Department of Psychiatry and Neuropsychology, Academic Hospital, Maastricht, Netherlands, 1997-. Publications: Numerous articles in professional journals. Honours include: Duphar Award, 1986; Knighted by Queen Beatrix of the Netherlands, 1989; New Frontier Award, Jerusalem Mental Health Center, 1991; Albert Einstein Award, 1993. Memberships include: Royal Netherlands Academy of Arts and Sciences. Address: Academic Hospital, Department of Psychiatry, Derylaan 25, 6202 AZ Maastricht, Netherlands.

**VANAHALLI Shivaram Mahadevappa,** b. 6 October 1937, Doddwad. Rural Developer. m. Smt Shakuntala, 2 sons, 1 daughter. Appointments: Self Practice, 15 years; Founder-President, Kalaposaka Sangha. Honours: Many awards in Karnataka States, 1965-. Memberships: Yes, Award DDU Marga New Delhi; ICURD; Gole Market, New Delhi. Address: Dodwad 591104, Bailahonghal Talu, Belgaum District, Karnataka State India.

**VANDERHEYDEN Mirna-Mar,** b. 8 October 1932, Freeport, Illinois, USA. Corporate President, Resort Management. 2 sons, 3 daughters. Education: Certificate, Browns Business College, 1949; BA, Milliken University, 1953. Appointments: Paralegal; Legal Administrator; Resort Managment Corporation President. Honours: Platinum Record, Exceptional Performance, 1997; Order of International Fellowship, 1997; Certificate of Merit, Distinguished Service, 1997; Citation of Meritorious Achievement in Finance and Industry, 1997. Membership: American Water Works Association. Address: 609 West Apple Drive, Delta, CO 81416, USA.

**VANICEK Jiri,** b. 3 February 1937, Prague, Czechoslovakia. University Professor in Computer Science; Government Council-in-Chief. m. 3 sons. Education: MSc Mathematics, Charles University, Prague, 1960; PhD Mathematics, Charles University, Prague, 1964; PhD Computer Science, Czech Technical University, Prague, 1986; Professor in Computer Science, Czech Techical University, Prague, 1996. Appointments: Professor in Computer Science, Czech Univeristy of Agriculture in Prague, Department Head, Inforamation Engineering, 1997-; Governor Councillor-in-Chief, Government Office for the State Information System, Czech Republic, 1995-; Professor in Computer Science, Czech Technical University, Prague, 1995-97; General Director, Gov Inst for Inforatics in Education, Prague, 1990-94; Head of Software Research, Research Institute for Computers, Prague, 1965-90; Assistant Professor in Mathematics, Charles University, Prague, 1960-65. Publications: 100 scientific papers and momographs from the areas of topology, functional analysis, numerical methods, optimal control theory, operation systems for computers, software development methodology, theory of information and data, software engineering, software quality and electronics association, 1960-. Honours: 1st award for the scientific work in the category of univeristy teachers in the area of electronics equipment, control, information and communication systems - AFCEA, 1996; Achievement Award from the Software Engineering Standards Committee, 1999. Memberships: President, Czech National Committee for Standardisation in Information Technology, 1990; Scientific Advisor, Czech

Republic Government, 1995. Address: Czech University for Agr PEF K1, Kamycka 129, CZ 16521 Prague 6, Czech Republic.

**VANISTENDAEL Marilyn,** b. 4 December 1933, Greensburg, Pennsylvania, USA. Janitor. m. David Marcel Vanistendael, 8 December 1958, divorced 19 May 1971, 3 sons, 3 daughters. Education: BA, Art, Seton Hill College, Greensburg, Pennsylvania, USA, 1955; Greensburg Business School, 1955; Medical School, Washington, Pennsylvania, 1990. Appointments: Camp Counsellor, Girl Scouts,, 1948-49, 1951, 1955; Artist, TV Station, WQED, Pittsburgh, Pennsylvania, 1955; Elementary Teacher, Texas, 1955, 1956, 1957. Publications: Falling For You, cassette, 1986; Golden Poetry, 1960; Sparrowgrass Poetry, 1986. Honours: Golden Poet Award, World of Poetry, Orlando, Florida, USA, 1986. Memberships: Honorary Crew Member, USSWVA, 1990; Historical Society Bedford, Pennsylvania, 1973-85; Library of Congress, Ancient Astronaut Society, 1998; American Museum of Women in Arts, Washington, D.C., 1978-90. Address: 304 Valley View Terrace, Canonsburg, PA 15317-1224, USA.

**VANITHAKUMARI Gopal,** b. 21 October 1946, Coimbatore. Professor. m. K Sunderraj. Education: BSc, Madras University, 1967; MSc, Madras University, 1969; Diploma, German, Madras University, 1972; PhD, Madras University, 1978. Appointments: Lecturer, Endocrinology, Madras University, 1973; Reader, Endocrinology, Madras University, 1982; Reader, Zoology, Bharathiar University, 1998; Professor of Zoology, 1994. Publications: 48 international research papers; 28 national research papers. Honours: Fellow, New York Academy of Sciences; Member, Advisory Board, American Biographical Institute. Memberships: Endocrine Society of India; Asian Society of Andrology; Medicina Alternativa International; Indian Society for Study of Reproduction and Fertility. Address: Bharathiar University, Marudamalai Rd, Tamil Nd, Coimbatore 641 046, India.

**VARCUS Flore,** b. 25 April 1958, Urvis de Beliu, Romania. Surgeon. Education: MD; General Surgeon; Master in Surgical Sciences, Paris, 1996; Doctorate in Surgical Sciences, Lyon, 1966. Appointment: Lecturer, University of Medicine, Timisoara. Publications: Co-author, 3 surgical books; 40 articles in surgical field; Thyroid Nodule: Diagnosis and Treatment, doctoral thesis, 1996. Memberships: French Society of Laparoscopic Surgery; Romanian Society of Surgery; Balkanic Medical Society. Address: Uvis Nr 75, 2856 Arad, Romania.

**VARGA Stefan,** b. 21 July 1942, Timisoara, Romania. Mechanical Engineer. m. Margareta Varga, 2 sons. Education: Diploma of Graduation, 1960; Diploma of Technician, 1962; Diploma of Engineer, 1971; Doctorate, Robotics, 1997. Career: Researcher Technician, 1962-71, Designer Engineer, 1971-78, University Assistant, 1978-85, Working Head, 1985-97, Lecturer, 1998-, Politechnical University of Timisoara. Publications: 1 book, 6 handbooks for students, 70 articles. Honours: Golden Medal, International Market of Bucharest, 1988. Memberships: Romanian Robotics Association; IFTOM. Address: Bv Mihai Viteazul Nr 1, 1900 Timisoara, Romania.

**VARKONYI Anna,** b. 18 Dec 1946, Budapest, Hungary. Environmental Consultant. m. Tamas Revesz, 1 son, 1 daughter. Education: Bachelor's and Master's degrees in Chemical Engineering, 1970; PhD, Environmental Sciences, 1996. Appointments: President Herald Agency, Hungary, 1991; Environmental Consultant for Tetra Pak, 1994-; President, Ecovision LLC, 1996-. Publications: Numerous articles in Hungarian dailies and magazines; People and the Planet, 1988, 1994. Memberships: Hungarian Committee of Sustainable Development; Society of Environmental

Journalism; Environmental Management and Law Association Danube Circle. Address: 300 Winston Drive, Cliffside Park, N 07010, USA.

**VARMA Avnish Kumar,** b. 8 August 1936, Lahore Physician. m. Usha Varma, 1 son, 1 daughter. Education: BDS 1958; MDS, 1972; DMFS, 1981; DMFD, 1982; DOS, 1983 Appointments: ADC, AFCDE, Bangalore, 1991; Director Denta Service, Army, 1994; Honorary Surgeon to President of India 1995-. Publications: Oral Oncology, vol I & II, 1992, vol III 1994, vol IV, 1995, vol V, 1997. Honour: Ati Vashisht Seva Medal, 1985. Memberships: EACMFS, Europe; IAOMFS, USA AAOMFS, USA; ICOMFS, Germany. Address: Internationa Congress on Oral Cancer, 509 B Sarita Vihar, New Delh 110044, India.

**VARMA Baidya Nath,** b. 10 March 1921, India. Professor o Sociology. m. Savitri D Varma, 2 sons, 2 daughters. Education BA, distinction, Patna University, 1941; MA, University c Missouri School of Journalism, 1949; PhD, Sociology Columbia University, 1958. Appointments: Radio Broadcaste to India, from United Nations, New York; Interviewer, Voice c America; Asian News Moderator, National Educationa Network, Station WNDT, New York; Professor of Sociology currently Emeritus Professor, City College, City University c New York; Guest Fellow, Indian Institute of Advanced Study Simla, Jawaharlal Nehru University, New Delhi, Oxfor University, Sorbonne, Paris; Lecturer, universities, India, USA Canada, UK; Consultant to National Endowment for the Humanities, Wenner-Gren Foundation for Anthropologica Research, Center for Migration Studies, Population Council, US Department of Energy, Canada Council. Publications: Book including: The New Social Sciences; Contemporary India; New Directions in Theory and Methodology; Social Science and Indian Society: A Civilizational Perspective; The Sociology and Politics of Development: A Theoretical Study; Threads of Love Kama Sutra - the Vision of Romance, commentary; Conference papers; Many documentary filmscripts; Poems. Honours Distinguished Poet of the Year 1996, International Society o Poets; International Poetry Hall of Fame, USA, 1996; Founding Member, US Library of Congress, 1997. Memberships Chairman, International Committee on Sociological History 1978; Fellow, Royal Anthropological Institute of Great Britain and Ireland, 1985; New York Academy of Sciences, 1986 Trustee, The Wordsworth Trust, UK, 1988; President, Sout Asian Sociologists; India Council, Asia Society of New York Patron, Academy of American Poets; Numerous editoria boards. Address: 62 Belvedere Drive, Yonkers, NY 10705-2814, USA.

**VARVARA Mircea,** b. 13 August 1932, Dealul Morii, Bacau County, Romania. Professor. m. Elena Vidvischi, 2 sons Education: Diploma, Pedagogical School, Bârlad, 1952 Diploma, Faculty of Natural Sciences and Chemistry, Alex Cuza University of Iasi, 1957; DBiol, Alexandru Ioan Cuza University, 1972. Appointments: Head of Laboratory, 1958 Assistant Professor, 1960, Lecturer, 1966, Reader, Genera Ecology, 1990, Professor, General Ecology, Faculty of Biology 1994-, Alexandru Ioan Cuza University. Publications: 85 scientific papers, 7 books. Memberships: Society of Ecology Romania; Academy of Scientists, Romania; Society o Entomology, Romania. Address: Alexandru Ioan Cuza University, Faculty of Biology, Str Bulevardul Copou 20A, 6600 Iasi, Romania.

**VASEK Stefan,** b. 25 December 1936, Lucenec. Specia Pedagogue. m. Emilia Vasekova, 1 daughter. Education Vyssia Skola Pedagogicka, Bratislava, 1959; Vysoka Skola Pedagogicka, Bratislava, 1962; PhDr, 1975; PhD, 1979

Associate Professor, 1982; Professor, 1997. Appointments: Vice Dean, Faculty of Education, Comenius University, Bratislava. Publications: Aktualne Problemy deti s Poruchami reci a Citania, 1979; Specialno Pedagogicka Diagnostika, 1990; Speciano Pedagogicky Terminologicky a vykladovy slovnik, 1994; Pedagogika Mentalne Postihnutych, 1995; Specialna Pedagogika, 1996; Pedagogika Viacnasobne Postihnutych, 1998; Various Articles in Magazines. Honours: Association of Hungarian Special Padagogues, Comenius University, Bratislava. Memberships: Vice Chairman, Association of Special Education of the Slovak Republic. Address: Pedagogicka Fakulta UK, Racianska 59, 813 34 Bratislava, Slovak Republic.

**VASIC Smiljka,** b. 20 October 1919, Belgrade, Yugoslavia. Psycholinguist. m. Zivorad Vasic, 1 son. Education: BA Serbian Language and Literature, 1941, University of Belgrade; PhD Philosophy, 1965. Appointments: Teacher of Serbian Language and History, Secondary Economic School, 1946-58; Advisor, Institute for Experimental Phonetics and Speech Pathology, Belgrade, 1958-65, Scientific Advisor, 1965-84; Consultant and Researcher, Pedagogical Institute, 1958-; Reader, Dept of Pedagogy, Faculty of Philosophy, University of Belgrade, 1970-73; Visiting Professor of Psycholinguistics, Nis University, 1985; Visiting Professor, Centre for Multidisciplinary Studies, 1985; Visiting Professor, Faculty of Drama, University of Belgrade, post-graduate studies, 1982-85; Retired. Publications: 32 Monographs in psychology, linguistics, psycholinguistics, including: Your Child's Speech, 1967; Development of Child Articulation, 1970; Definitions and Defining, 1988; Culture of Speech Communication, 1990; Psycholinguistics, 1994; Frequency Dictionary of Pavic's Dictionary of the Khazars, 1997; Over 260 articles in journals,magazines and proceedings. Honours: Radio-Television Award for Speech Culture, 1978, 1983. Memberships: Society of Psychologists, Belgrade, 1965-; Yugoslav Society of Applied Linguistics, 1977-90; Serbian Society of Applied Linguistics, 1972-90; International Society of Applied Psycholinguistics, committee member 1989-; ISAPL; AILA; Scientific Commission for Language Methodology, 1990; Serbian-Canadian Society, 1993-. Address: Cara Urosa 19/11, Belgrade, Yugoslavia 11000.

**VASIC Voislav,** b. 9 March 1945, Belgrade, Yugoslavia. Biologist. m. Olga Vasic, 1 son, 1 daughter. Education: PhD, Faculty of Biology, University of Belgrade, 1984. Appointment: Director, Natural History Museum of Belgrade. Publications: Catalogue of Birds of Yugoslavia, 1973; Biodiversity of Yugoslavia, 1995. Memberships: President, Yugoslav Union of Ornithological Associations; President, Serbian Ecological Society; Committee of Faunistica; Montenegrian Academy; President of Yugoslav Ramsar Committee.

**VASILESCU Alexandru A,** b. 10 March 1926, Romania. University Professor. m. Motrea Rohovski, 1 son. Education: Diploma in Engineering, Polytechnic Institute of Timisoara, 1951; PhD, Polytechnic Institute of Iassy, 1973. Appointments: Assistant Professor, Engineering, University Galati, Romania, 1951-53, Lecturer, 1953-65, Senior Lecturer, 1965-74; Professor Fluid Mechanics, 1975-; Professor, Chairman, Department of Applied Mechanics, 1975-90; Appointed Supervisor of doctoral degree course, 1975. Publications: Many papers and books concerning fluid mechanics, the theory of the similitude, gravity theory and relativity theory; In a new outlook, together with his son, has published the correlation between the thinking of Newton and Descartes in the gravity domain, with extensions in the relativity theory. Membership: National Geographic Society, Washington DC, USA. Address: University

Dunarea de Jos din Galati, Faculty of Naval and Electrical Engineering, 6200 Galati, Romania.

**VASILIEV Aleksey,** b. 25 April 1960, Kiev, Ukraine. Chemist. m. Larisa Vasilieva, 1 daughter. Education: MS, Organic Chemistry, Kiev State University, 1982; Postgraduate studies, 1986-89, PhD, 1991, Institute of Physical Organic Chemistry and Coal Chemistry, Academy of Sciences of Ukraine, 1986-89. Appointments: Engineer, Institute of Molecular Biology and Genetics, Kiev, 1982-83, Institute of Organic Chemistry, Kiev, 1983-86; Research Assistant, Institute of Physical Organic Chemistry and Coal Chemistry, Kiev, 1987-89; Researcher, Institute of Bioorganic Chemistry and Petrochemistry, Kiev, 1989-96; Representative for MV Technologies Inc (Akron, Ohio, USA) in Ukraine and Russia, 1995-; Invited Professor, National Technological University, Cordoba Faculty, Argentina, 1997-; Associate Professor, Faculty of Engineering, University of Buenos Aires, 1997-, Consultant, Tecnomyl srl, Villete, Paraguay, 1998-. Publications: Co-author, more than 40 research and review papers; Author or co-author, papers in conference and symposia proceedings or on internet, including: Prevention of water and soil pollution from mining and minerals, 1996; On the problem of deactivation of land areas contaminated with radionuclides, 1996; Transgenic plants capable of accumulating copper and cadmium, 1998; Catalytic properties of polycationic forms of zeolites in the conversion of hydrocarbons, 1998; 4 patents. Honour: Individual Grant, International Science Foundation, New York, 1994. Memberships: New York Academy of Sciences, 1995-; International Society of Heterocyclic Chemistry, 1999-. Address: National Technological University, CC17, 5016 Cordoba, Argentina.

**VASILIUNAS Kestutis,** b. 17 July 1964, Vilnius, Lithuania. Artist. m. Roberta, 1 son, 1 daughter. Education: Vilnius Art Institute (now Art Academy), 1982-88; Diploma, Vilnius Art Institute. Appointments: Professor, Vilnius Art Academy, Graphic Department, 1994-; Director, Public Institute, Bookart, Exhibitions and Edition, 1998-. Honours: Scholarship of Brandenburg Ministry of Culture, Germany, 1993; The Premium, Republican Exhibition of Visual Arts, Vilnius, 1993; The Jury Honorable Mention, Falubiennelen, Swerige, 1993. Memberships: Lithuanian Artists Association, 1990-; Baltic Scandinavian Artists Group, 1997-. Address: Filaretu 9-5, Vilnius, Lithuania.

**VASILKO Karol,** b. 17 February 1942, Vaniskovce. Professor; Dean. m. Darina Vasilkova, 2 sons. Education: Ing, 1964; CSc, 1972; Doctor, 1977; Professor, 1983; DSc, 1984. Appointments: Vural Zilina, 1965-69; Vukov Presov, 1970-72; ZVL Presov, 1973-78; VSDS Zilina, 1979-92; TU Kosice, 1993. Publications include: New approach to design of geometry of cutting tools, 1995; Historie of Technic and Technologies, 1998. Memberships: Academy of Science, Bratislava. Address: Technical University of Kosice, Faculty of Production Technologies, 080 01 Presov, Slovakia.

**VASSILEVA-ALEXANDROVA Petrana,** b. 21 March 1933, Preslav, Bulgaria. Associate Professor. m. Alexander Alexandrov, 1 daughter. Education: Magister of Chemistry, 1957. Appointments: Assistant, 1959, Associate Professor, 1971. Publications: Over 90 articles in professional scientific journals. Membership: Union of Scientists, Bulgaria. Address: 104 Vasil Aprilov Boulevard, Plovdiv 4002, Bulgaria.

**VASUDEORAO Patil,** b. 24 February 1917, Akoli Jahagir. Social Work. Education: Ayurvedacharya, 1961. Appointments: Honorary Principal, Bhagavat Dharma Education Society, Nagzari District, 1945-53. Publications: Gajanam Bhaskar;

Daily Worship of Gajanam Maharaj; Changdeo Pasasti; Biography of Lord Shrikrishna; Biography of Sant Dnyaneshwar Maharaj; Biography of Sant Namdeo Maharaj; Biography of Sant Eknath Maharaj; Biography of Jagadguru Sant Tukaram Maharaj; Biography of Niloba; Biography of Gajanam Maharaj; Biography of Bhaskar Maharaj; Biography of Narsinha Maharaj; Biography of Sakharam Maharaj; Biography of Pitambar Maharaj; Biography if Ekviva Devi; Biography of Gadge Baba; Biography of Ramnath Swami; Shrimadbhagavadgita Abhangas; Shrimadbhagvat Mahapuran; Amrutanubhao; Jai Jai Ram Krishna Hari; Dnyanoba Tukaram; Gajanan Bhaskar; Simple Household Medical Treatment; Gajanam Vitthal Charitra. Memberships: Shri Bhaskar Mahoraj Sanstham Adgaon Dist, Akola, MS, India. Address: Gawalipura, Akot, Dist Akola MS, India.

**VASYLYEV Konstantin Konstantinovitch,** b. 25 February 1951, Riga, Latvia. Medical Researcher. m. Lyudmila Gordeeva, 1 son. Education: Graduate, Odessa State Medical Institute, 1974; MSc, 1981; DSc, 1994. Appointments: Intern, Hospital of Odessa, 1974-75; Doctor, Hospital of Odessa, 1975-84; Teacher, Ternopol Medical Institute, 1984-94; Head, Social Medicine Department, Sumy State University, 1994-. Publications: Over 150 published works. Address: Sumy Ukraine, 244035 P Box 36, Ukraine.

**VAZQEZ Ernesto V,** b. 25 August 1969, Cienfuegos, Cuba. Painter. m. Janet Rodriguez, 1 son. Education: Independent Creator, 1993. Creative Works: Gallery Wavana, Expo Prural Track, La Rama Dorada Gallery Panama. Memberships: ACAA. Address: Bellavista #55 la y Zda, Rpt Apolo CP 10900 C Habana, Cuba.

**VEDANAND Swaroop,** b. 4 May 1962, Jammalamadugu, India. Scientist. Education: BSc, 1982; MSc, 1985; MPhil, 1989; PhD, 1993. Appointments: Junior Research Fellow, 1988-92, Project Assistant, 1992-93, Department of Physics, SV University; Scientific Assistant, Forensic Science Laboratory, Hyderabad, 1993-96; Lecturer, Department of Advanced Mathematical Science and Engineering, Yamaguchi University, Japan, 1996-97. Publications include: Electronic and Vibrational Absorption Spectra in Nickelblodite, 1996; Spectral Studies on Ni(II) in Sepiolite Mineral, 1996; EPMA, EPR, Electronic and Vibrational Studies on Natural Aurichalcite, 1996. Honour: Junior Research Fellowship, Council of Scientific and Industrial Research (CSIR) New Delhi, India, 1988. Memberships: South Asia Pacific Physics Association; Union of Evangilical Students of India. Address: Silas Compound, Jammalamadugu Andhra Pradesh, 516 434 India.

**VEERAKYATHIAH V D,** b. 25 June 1926, Vaddagere. Retired Public Administrator. m. V Rajamma, 2 sons. Education: BScAgr, 1951; Indian Administrative Service, 1980. Appointments: Village Level Worker; Block Development Officer; Deputy Development Commissioner; Director; Head of Department. Publications: 3 papers in Indian Science Congressions sessions. Honour: Outstanding Achievement in Rural Development and Welfare Services. Memberships: Advisor, Charitable Trust Devoted for Rural Development. Address: 596 IInd Stage 1 E Block; Rajajinagar, Bangalore 560010, India.

**VEKSLER Vladimir Isaakovich,** b. 11 January 1927, Kiev. Scientist m. Elena Lyubovskaya, 1 daughter. Education: Diploma, honours, 1949; Candidate of Science Degree, 1953; DSc, 1968. Appointments: Assistant, 1953, Docent, 1957, Professor, 1969, Department of Physical Electronics, Tashkent State University. Publications: Over 200 in professional leading journals. Honours: Honoured Figure in Science, 1980.

Memberships: New York Academy of Sciences, 1995-. Address: Department of Physical Electronics, Tashkent State University, Tashkent 700095, Uzbekistan.

**VEKTARIENE Ausra,** b. 6 June 1959, Lithuania. Chemist; Researcher. m. Gytis Vektaris, 1 daughter. Education: Faculty of Chemistry, Vilnius University, 1977-82; PhD, 1989. Appointments: Research Associate, 1984, Chemical Engineer, 1989, Head, Patent Analysis Department, 1993-98, Institute of Biochemistry; Coordinator of Innovation Centre, 1996. Publications: Contributor of articles to professional journals, 1985-; Co-editor, Scientific Reports, 1995; Co-author, inventions. Address: Sevcenkos 10-2, 2009 Vilnius, Lithuania.

**VELANISKYTE Egle,** b. 28 May 1958, Kaunas, Lithuania. Artist-Painter. m. Gediminas Borisevicius, 1 son, 2 daughters. Education: Student, 1976-82, Artist-Painter, 1982, Vilnius Art Institute. Appointment: Teacher, Art and Art History, Salakas Secondary School, 1991-. Membership: Lithuanian Artists Association, 1992-. Address: Sabalunku k, LT-4795 Salakas, Zarasu raj, Lithuania.

**VELARDO Joseph Thomas,** b. 27 January 1923, Essex County, N.J. Biomedical Scientist; Professor; Lecturer-speaker; Writer. m. Forresta M.M. Power (dec). Education: Certificate, US Army, Air Force, 1944; AB Biology, Physical Sciences and Humanities, 1948, University Northern Colorado; SM, Zoology, Physiology, 1949, Miami University, Oxford, Ohio; PhD, Biology and Physiology, 1952, Harvard University. Appointments: Research and Teaching Fellow, Organic Chemistry, Colorado State College of Education, University of Northern Colorado, 1946-47; Research & Teaching Fellow, Heredity and Zoology, Miami University, 1948-49; Research and Teaching Fellow, Endocrinology, Research Fellow, Endocrinology, Harvard Univ, 1949-1954; Research Associate in Pathology, Obstetrics and Gynecology, Surgery, Endocrinology, Harvard University, School of Medicine, 1954-55; Asst Prof Anatomy and Endocrinology, 1955-62; Professor and Director, Institute for the Study of Human Reproduction, 1962-68; Professor, Biology and Endocrinology, John Carroll University, Hts and Cleveland, Ohio, 1962-68; Professor and Chairman, Department of Anatomy, Loyola University of Chicago-Stritch School of Medicine, 1968-74; Professor, Anatomy and Endocrinology, 1974-1988;.Emeritus 1988, Loyola University ofChicago-Stritch School of Medicine. Professor, Chairman, Dept of Anatomy, New York Medical College, New York, 1991-1999. Publications: Editor, Endocrinology of Reproduction; Essentials of Human Reproduction; The Uterus; Co-Editor, Biology of Reproduction. Honours: Lederle Medical Faculty Award, 1955-58, Yale University School of Medicine; Vatican Consultant to the World Congress on Reproduction, 1954; William R Ross Distinguished Alumni Award in Science at the University of Northern Colorado, 1999; Certificate of Achievements, Republican Task Force, 1999. Memberships: Fellow, American Association for the Advancement of Science; Fellow, New York Academy of Sciences; Fellow, Gerontological Society; American Physiological Society; Endocrine Society, UK; Endocrine Society, USA; American Society of Zoologists; Histochemical Society; Society of Experimental Biology and Medicines; American Society for Study of Sterility (Rubin Award); and others. Address: Wilson House, 607 E Wilson Avenue, Lombard, IL 60148-4062, USA.

**VENKATARATNAM Lukka,** b. 26 March 1944, Guntur Dt, AP, India. Scientist. m. Ms Padmavathi, 1 daughter. Education: BSc Agri, 1964; MSc Agri, 1966; PhD, 1970; PG Certificate in Soil Science, 1971; Certificate in Photogrammetry and Photointerpretation, 1976. Appointments: Assistant Soil Chemist, 1973-75; Scientist SC, 1975-81; Scientist SD,

1978-81; Scientist SE, 1981-83; Scientist SF, Head Soils Division, 1983-87; Scientist SF, Head Agri and Soils Division, 1987-92; Scientist SG, Group Head, Agri and Soils, 1992-. Publications: 102 research papers. Honours: Elected as Fellow, Andhra Pradesh Akademy of Sciences, Hyderabad, 1995; Leadership Award, Soil Conservation Society of India, 1996. Memberships: Life Member: Indian Society of Remote Sensing, Dehra Dun, India; Indian Society of Soil Survey and Landuse Planning, Nagpur; Soil Conservation Society of India; Indian Society of Coastal Agricultural Research, Canning, WB, India. Address: National Remote Sensing Agency, Balangar, Hyderabad 500037 AP, India.

**VENKOV Pencho,** b. 5 December 1934, Sofia, Bulgaria. Research Professor. m. Liliana Waltshewa, 1 son. Education: Sofia School of Medicine, 1960; MD, 1961; PhD, 1980; DSci, 1985. Appointments: Associate Professor, Professor, 1985, Head Dept, Institute of Molecular Biology, Bulgarian Academy of Sciences. Publications: 94 research communications; 1 textbook. Memberships: International Society for Yeast; International Conference on Yeast Genetics and Molecular Biology; Molecular Cell Biology Network of UNESCO; Bulgarian Union of Scientists. Address: St Naum St 49, 1126 Sofia, Bulgaria.

**VERCELLI, Alessandro,** b. 17 April 1945, Torino, Italy. University Professor. m. Sinischalchi Maria Carmen, 1 son. Education: Graduate, Political Science, University of Torino, 1979. Appointments: Lecturer, University of Torino, 1973-76; Professor, Economics, University of Siena, Italy, 1976-; Board of Directors of the Banks, MPS, Siena, INCA, Florence, MP Belgio, Brussels, 1997-. Publications: Methodological Foundations of Macroeconomics, 1991; Macroeconomics - A Survey of Research Strategies, 1992; Substainability, Dynamics and Uncertainty, 1998. Honours: Fulbright Social Science Research Council Award, 1982; St Vincent Prize, 1988; Senior Research Fellow, St Antony's College, Oxford, 1996; Life Visitor Member, Clare Hall, Cambridge, MA. Memberships: NY Academy of Sciences; Academia La Colombaria, Florence. Address: Pian dei Mantellini 24/A, 53100 Siena Toscana, Italy.

**VERGILIS Joseph,** b. 14 August 1934, Odessa, Ukraine. Educator, Mechanical Engineering. m. Zhanna Vergilis, 2 daughters. Education: MS, Polytechnic Institute, Odessa, 1958; PhD, Mechanical Engineering, Research and Development Institute of Machine Tools, Moscow, 1973. Appointments: Senior Scientist, Research and Development, Institute, ENIM, Moscow, 1966-87; Professor, Mechanical Engineering, Murray, Kansas State University, 1990-92, University Turabo, 1993-94, CUNY, 1994-. Publictions: Several articles in professional journals. Memberships: ASME; SME; ASEE. Address: PO Box 100104, Brooklyn, NY 11210, USA.

**VERHESE Cherian,** b. 14 June 1962. Professor. m. Suja, 1 daughter. Education: MBBS, Medical College, University of Kerala, 1979-85; DMRT, Christian Medical College, University of Madras, 1986-88; MD, 1988-90; Dip NB, National Board of Examinations, New Delhi, 1990; M Phil, Institute of Public Health, University of Cambridge, UK, 1992-93; PhD, Institute of Cancer Research, University of London, 1998. Appointments: Registrar, Department of Radiotherapy, CMC Hospital, 1986-90; Lecturer, Division of Medical Oncology, Regional Cancer Centre, 1990-91; Research Fellow, Yorkshire Cancer Organisation, University of Leeds, UK, 1995-96; Associate Professor, Division of Epidemiology, Regional Cancer Centre, 1996-. Publications: 36 Publications. Honours: Travel Scholarship; UICC - ICRETT Fellowship; IARC, Research Training Fellowship; Khandelwal Junior Oncology

Award for Scientific Excellence; Parvathy Sethi Best Paper Award. Address: Division of Cancer Epidemiology and Clinical Research, Regional Cancer Centre, Trivandrum, India 695 011.

**VERLI Merushe,** b. 8 February 1962, Albania. Audit Manager. m. Kliton Verli, 1 son, 1 daughter. Education: Bachelor of Geological Engineering, 1979-94; Diploma in Economy, 1985-90, University of Tirana; ESS Masters, Institue National Olitechnique De Lorraine, 1992-93. Appointments: Assistant Lecturer, 1985-91, Lecturer, University of Tirana, 1991-; Director of Industrial Policies Department, Ministry of Mineral Resources, 1994-94; Consultant, Albanian Copper Corporation, 1994; Chief Administrator, Supervising Accountant, Corexland Company, Tirana, 1996; Senior Audit, Audit Manager, KPMG Audit, Tirana, 1998-. Publications: Include, International Mining Investment and Regulation Seminar; Management of the Small Business; Economical Analysis of Mining Fields in Albania; Qualitative Analyses of the Coal Fields Around Tirana. Address: Rr Ndre Mjeda, Pall 3 Sh 2 Ap 19, Tirana, Albania.

**VERLOREN VAN THEMAAT Pieter,** b. 16 March 1916, Rotterdam, Netherlands. Emeritus Professor. m. Maria, 3 sons, 1 daughter. Education: ML, University of Leiden, 1939; DL, 1946. Appointments: Ministry of Economic Affairs, Netherlands, 1945-58; Director General, Commission of European Economic Community, Brussels, 1958-67; Professor of European and International Economic Law, Utrecht University, 1967-81; Advocate General, Court of Justice, European Communities, 1981-86. Publications include: International Fiscal Law, 1946; The Changing Structure of International Economic Law, 1981; Introduction to the Law of the European Community, Third Edition, 1998. Honours: 5 Dutch Awards, 1970-90. Memberships: Royal Dutch Academy of Sciences; Address: Mozartlaan 4, 3723 JM Bilthoven, Netherlands.

**VERMA Pratibha,** b. 25 December 1947, Patna, India. Service. m. Vijayendra Kishore Verma, India. 2 sons, 1 daughter. Education: MA, English, Patna University, 1971; BA, Lucknow University, 1968; PhD, English, Patna University, 1984. Appointments: Magadh University, Bihar, India, 1975-; Reader, English, A.N. College, Patna, Bihar, India, at present. Publications: Sri Sunil Prasad, 1986; The Peon, in Canopy, 1988; Happiness, in Hesperus Review, 1988; A Boy and a Dog, in Canopy, 1991; Examination, in Canopy, 1989; Cultural Variation of Speech in Anita Desai's Novel Bye Bye Blackbird, in Quest, 1989; Growing Up, in Canopy, 1997; A Sociolinguistic Study of The Novel Adam Bede, in Explorer, 1997; many others. Address: c/o V K Verma, I F S, East Patel Nagor, Patna 23, Bihar, 800 023, India.

**VERMA Ram Sagar,** b. 3 March 1946, India. Professor; Director. m. Shakuntala D Verma, 2 sons. Education: BSc Agriculture, 1965, MSc Quantitative Genetics, 1967, Agra University, India; PhD Cytogenetics, 1972, University of Western Ontario, Canada; Postdoctoral-Research Associate Cytogenetics, Department Paediatrics, Colorado Medical Centre, Denver, 1973-76; DipRCPath Clinical Cytogenetics, 1984, FRCPath Clinical Cytogenetics and Genetics, 1995, Royal College of Pathologists, London, UK. Appointments: Research and Teaching Assistant, Department Plant Sciences, University of Western Ontario, 1967-73; Postdoctoral Research Associate, Dept Paediatrics, University Colorado, 1973-76; Instructor, 1976-79, Assistant Professor, 1976-79, Associate Professor, 1979-85, Professor, 1985-, Dept Medicine, Professor, School of Graduate Studies, 1990-, Professor, Dept Anatomy and Cell Biology, 1988-, State University of New York Health Science Centre, Brooklyn; Associate Director of Cytogenetics, Division of Haematology and Cytogenetics,

1976-78, Chief, Division of Cytogenetics, 1978-88, Jewish Hospital and Medical Centre of Brooklyn; Chief, Division of Genetics, Long Island College Hospital, Brooklyn, 1986-97; Director, Institute of Molecular Biology and Genetics, Brooklyn, 1997-. Publications: Editor-in-Chief, Advances in Genome Biology; Author and Co-author of 12 books and monographs and 322 publications in professional journals and meetings. Honours: Mario Toppo Distinguished Scientist Award, ASIOA, 1995; Pride of India Award, 1994; Global Distinction Award, 1994-95; and many others. Memberships: American Association for: Advancement of Science, Clinical Research; American College of Medical Genetics; 19 others. Address: Institute of Molecular Biology and Genetics, 6910-12 Fort Hamilton Parkway, Brooklyn, NY 11228, USA.

**VERMA Ramesh Chand,** b. 18 October 1953, Kalka, Haryana, India. Teacher; Researcher. m. Saroj Bala Verma, 2 sons. Education: BSc, Honours, 1973, MSc, Honours, 1974, PhD, 1978, Panjab University, Chandigarh, India. Appointments: Visiting Scientist, University Alberta, Canada, 1979-81, 1986, 1990, 1991, 1995; Lecturer, Kumaun Univerity, 1981-84, Panjab University, 1984-94; Reader, Himachal P University, 1990-92; Panjab University, 1994-95; Professor, Punjabi University, Patiala, 1995-. Publications: 93 research papers in journals of international repute; 14 general articles in physics; 2 books on computational physics. Honour: Award, Hari Ohm Ashram National Research Award, S Patel University, 1994. Memberships: Life Member, Indian Physical Society, Indian Association of Physics Teachers; Indian National Science Congress Association; Punjab Academy of Sciences. Address: Department of Physics, Punjabi University, Patiala, Punjab, India.

**VERMA Veena Rashmi.** Teacher. m. Harbansh Prasad, 4 children. Education: MSc Research Scholar; Bachelor in Law. Appointment: Teaching in Jamshedpur Women's College. Publications: Poems, published in magazines and journals. Honours: Received Award for Best Cadets in National Cadet Corps; Awarded with various medals in classical and vocal music. Address: Flat No N142/1, Telco Colony, Jamshedpur 831 004, India.

**VERMA Vimal Kumar,** b. 15 August 1967, Sarwan Bhadsara, Patna, India. Lecturer. m. Raj Kumari. Education: BA, honours, English, St Columba's College; MA, English, Patna College. Appointment: Lecturer, English, Bailey Baptist College, Workha, Nagaland. Publications: Several poems; One Poem translated and published in Kannada; Two novels and one poetry book ready for publication. Address: PO Box 99, Workha 797111, Nagaland, India.

**VERMAAT John Arthur Emerson,** b. 22 October 1947, Arnhem, the Netherlands. Television Reporter; Writer. Divorced. Education: Law Degree, State University, Leyden, The Netherlands. Appointments: Government Official, 1969-73; Senior Television Reporter, 1973-. Publications: Co-author: The New Image Makers, 1987; Author: The World Council of Churches and Politics, 1989; Reporting in Situations of War and Crisis (in Dutch), 1995; In the Name of Allah... Islamic Fundamentalism and Terrorism (in Dutch) 1997; Islamic Fundamentalism and European Security, 1998; The Turn of the Millenium (in Dutch), 1998, new edition 1999. Honours: Finalist Award, International Film and Television Festival, New York, for documentary: Return to Auschwitz (director, Franz Arnold). Memberships: Dutch Association of Journalists; Netherlands International Law Association; Royal Association "Our Army"; Netherlands Association of International Affairs. Address: PO Box 1944, 1200 BX Hilversum, The Netherlands.

**VERTES Arpad,** b. 20 July 1940, Turje, Hungary Contractor; City Mayor. m. Margit Kiss, 1 son, 1 daughter Education: Degree, Commerce, 1960-64. Career: Hotel Owner Contractor; Mayor, City of Heviz, 1994-. Honours: Gold Cross Hungarian Republic; 1st Class Award, National Defense Address: City Hall, Heviz, Kossuth ul, 8380 Hungary.

**VEST Steven Lee,** b. 30 July 1948, Minneapolis, USA Physician. m. Gayle S Vest, 1 son. Education: BA Premec Psychology, 1970, Medical School, 1970-74, University o' Minnesota, Twin Cities; Rotating Medicine Internship Milwaukee County General Hospital, 1974-75; Internship Medicine Residency, Southern Illinois University School o' Medicine, Springfield, 1975-77; Gastroenterology Fellowship Duke University Medical Centre, Durham, 1978-80; ABIM Board Certifications in Internal Medicine, 1981, Gatroenterology and Hepatology, 1987. Appointments: Various positions in Wise County and Virginia Medical Societies and several committees 1982-; Board of Directors, Dickenson-Wise Medical Group 1982-88, Norton Community Hospital, 1993-; Gastroenterology and Hepatology Consultant, Lonesome Pine Hospital, Big Stone Gap, Virginia, 1980-, St Mary's Hospital, Norton, 1983-Norton Community Hospital, 1985-. Memberships: Fellow American College of Physicians; American College o' Gastroenterology; Member: American Gastroenterologica Association; American Society of Internal Medicine; Virginia Medical Society; American Association of Christian Counsellors; Wise County Chamber of Commerce. Address 1800 Egan Road, Powell Valley, Big Stone Gap, VA 24219-4224, USA.

**VETTER Ralf-Achim Horst,** b. 3 August 1962, Duisburg Physiologist. m. Susanne Glang-Vetter, 1 daughter. Education Abitur, 1981; Prediploma Biology, 1985; Diploma Biology, 1989 PhD Biology, 1992. Appointments: Sales Manager Tobaccoland, Mulheim, 1982-83; Scientist, Institute for Marine Sciences, Kiel, 1989-92; Scientist, University Bochum, Bochum, 1992-93; Vice Head, Ecophysiology Laboratory, Bio Anstalt, Helgoland, 1993-. Publications: Biochemical Adaptions in Crustacea, 1992; Crustaceologen, 1997; Several articles in profiled journals. Memberships: Studienstiftung Des Deutschen Volkes; New York Academy of Sciences; Deutsche Zoologische Gesellschaft. Address: Bop Stak 681, D-27498 Helgoland, Germany.

**VIDAL GH Pedro,** b. 7 April 1959, Santiago, Chile. Plastic Surgeon, Entomologist. m. Dawn Lesley, 3 children. Education BSc, Zoology, Catholic University, Chile, 1980; MD, 1986; CM British National Health Services, 1990; MS, Plastic and Reconstructive Surgery, British Association of Plastic Surgeons, 1993. Appointments: Plastic Surgeon, Yorkshire England, Plastic Surgery University, Wakefield, 1988-91; Welsh Regional Plastic Surgery Services, Wales, England, 1991-94 Professor, Chairman, Department of Plastic Surgery; Professor Human Anatomy, in charge of Plastic Surgery Post Graduate Training, Catholic University, Santiago, 1994-; Associate Entomologist, National Museum of Natural History Publications: Co-author, Cancer, 1996; Contributor to many Artices, Professional Journals. Memberships: Fellow, Roya College of Surgeons, England; Member, British Association o' Plastic Surgeons; Chilean Society of Plastic Surgeons; Chilean Society of Surgery. Address: Av Apoquindo 3990, OF 1003 Los Condes Santiago, Chile.

**VIDAVER Anne Marie,** b. 29 March 1930, Vienna, Austria Plant Pathologist. m. George A, 1 son, 1 daughter. Education BA, Biology, 1960; MA, Bacteriology, 1962; PhD, Bacteriology 1963. Appointments: Research Assistant, 1958-59; Graduate Student in Bacteriology, 1960-65; Lecturer in Bacteriology

1965-66; Research Associate, 1966-72; Assistant Professor, 1972-74; Associate Professor, 1974-79; Professor of Plant Pathology, University of Nebraska, 1979-; Head, Department of Plant Pathology, University of Nebraska, 1984-; Director, Center for Biotechnology, 1997-. Publications: Author, Co-Author of 75 Refereed Journals. Honours: New York State Regents Scholarship; Rose Simon Memorial Award in Biology; Graduation with High Honours in Biology; Floyd Fund Fellowship; National Institute of Health; Public Service Award; Election to Fellow Status, American Association for the Advancement of Sciences; Election to Fellow Status, American Phytopathological Society; Science Award for Agricultural Excellence; Science Award for Agricultural Excellence, National Award Winner, Award of Merit for Distinguished Service to Agriculture; Election to Fellow Status, American Academy of Microbiology; Award of Distinction. Memberships: American Phytopathological Society; American Society for Microbiology. Address: Department of Plant Pathology, University of Nebraska, Lincoln 406 Plant Science Hall, East Campus Lincoln, NE 68583, USA.

**VIDYAKAR S,** b. 16 April 1953, India. Social Worker. Education: MA, Social Work, 1974-76; MA, Sociology, 1981-83. Appointment: Social Worker. Publications: Several articles in professional journals. Honours: Outstanding Young Person State Award, Jaycees; Award of Excellence, Loud Thinking Forum; L R Swamy Award of the Year, 1991; Exemplary Citizenship Award, Rishi Sumskruiti Vidya Kendra; Best Social Worker Award, National Youth Federation; Lakshya Vasakar Award, Vikatan Group, Ananda Vikatan; For the Sake of Honour Award, Rotary Club of Madras; Lions Club International Award of Excellence; Indian Health Mission Award; Tamil Nadu Brahmin's Association Award; Kannada Rajothjsava Award; International Award for Best Voluntary Service in India, Matsustuta, Japan; MaschioHumanitarian Award, Bombay. 1996. Address: Udavum Karangal, 460 N S K Nagar, Chennai 600 106, India.

**VIEIRA David Gueiros,** b. 9 December 1929, Garanhuns, Brazil. Historian; Educator. m. (1) Anne Taylor Pettit, divorced 1965, (2) Heloisa Domingues, 3 sons, 1 daughter. Education: Diploma, Arts and Sciences, Colégio 15 de Novembro, Garanhuns, Brazil, 1947; BA, History, King College, Bristol, USA, 1952; MA, History, University of Richmond, USA, 1961; PhD, History, American University of Washington, USA, 1973; Diploma, Strategic Planning, National War College, Rio de Janeiro, 1979. Appointments: Professor of History, Longwood College, Farmville, Virginia, USA, 1960-65; Editor, SOILS magazine, Joseph Ward & Associates, Caldwell, New Jersey, USA, 1968-73; Assistant to the President, Total Environment Group, New York, USA, 1970-73; Professor of History, 1973-93, Chairperson, History Department, 1974-78, President, University Press, 1976-79, University of Brasilia; Aide to Brazil's National Constituent Assembly, 1987-88; Federal Intervenor, Serra Pelada Gold Mine, 1988; Consultant, Brazilian Foundation of Education, 1997-98, Federal University of Amapa Macapa, 1997-98; Pro-tempore Vice Rector, UNIFAP, 1998-99; Dean of Research and Graduate Studies, UNIFAP, 1999. Publications: Books: Protestantism, Massonry and the Religious Question in Brazil, 1980, A Light on the Mountain: Protestant Education in Brazil, 1999; Numerous articles in professional journals. Memberships: Phi Alpha Theta; Pi Sigma Alpha. Address: UNB Colina Block A Apt 14, 70910-900 Brasilia DF, Brazil.

**VILENCHIK Michael,** b. 30 May 1938, Bransk, Russia. Research Scientist. Education: MD, First Leningrad Institute of Medicine, 1961; PhD, Moscow Institute of Virology, 1966. Appointments: Researcher, Institute of Virology, Moscow,

1963-66; Research Scientist, 1966-81; Research Fellow, Institute of Biophysics, Pushino, 1981-90; Researcher, Institute for Environmentl Research, Tel-Aviv University, 1991; Research Scientist, State University of New York, 1991; Research Scientist, Longevity Achievement Foundation, 1994-. Publications: Many including, Realization of the Mechanisms of the Spontaneous DNA Instability in Vivo and its Quantification: Discovery of the Spontaneous DNA Repair synthesis Connected with this Instability; Evidence for the Age-Dependent Decline of DNA Repair and Accumulation of the DNA Damage Similar to Spontaneous and Rediation-Induced Damage; Radiobiological Effects and Environment; Late Health Consequences of the Accident at Chernobyl; Oxidative Damage. Address: PO Box 1407, Media, PA 19063, USA.

**VILKAS Algirdas.** b. 11 February 1960, Mazeikiai District, Lithuania. Biologist, Teacher. Education: Diploma, Biologist, Vilnius University, 1986. Appointments: Director, Station of Young Naturalists Mazeikiai City, 1998-; Teacher, Methodist Biology, 1995-. Publication: Lithuanian Spider Names, 1996; A Brief Guide of Bryopsids, 1997; The Checklist of Spiders of Lithuania, 1992. Memberships: European Arachnological Society; Lithuanian Teriological; Ornitological; Entomological Societes. Address: Station of Young Naturalists, Laisves g 30a, 5500 Mazeikiai, Lithuania.

**VILKOV Gennady,** b. 10 March 1937, Vladikavkaz. Psychoneurology; Pathophisiologist. Education: BS, 1960, DSc, 1974, Rostov on Don Medical Institute. Appointments: Psychoneurologist; Junior & Senior Researcher; Head of CR Laboratory. Publications: Nearly 300 in Central Home and Foreign Editions. Membership: Rostov Medical Institute and University. Address: Central Research Laboratory, Thalman Str 41, 344010 Rostov on Don, Russia.

**VILKOVISKIJ Emmanuil,** b. 21 November 1936, Novosibirsk, Russia. Astrophysicist. m. Pavlova Larisa, 2 sons. Education: BA, Physics, Almaty, Kazakhstan, 1960; PhD, Izmiran, Moscow, 1972; Doctor of Physics and Mathematical Science, Gaish, Moscow, 1992. Appointments: Nuclear Physics Institute, Almaty, kazakhstan, 1960; Postgraduate, Ioffe Physics and Technology Institute, Leningrad, 1964; Professor, Fesenkov Astrophysical Institute, Almaty, Kazakhstan, 1967. Publications: Over 100 scientific papers, 2 monographs. Memberships: IAU; International (Euro-Asian) Astrophysics Society; Almaty Astrophysics Society. Address: Laboratory of Spectrophotometry of Stars, VF Fesenkov Astrophysical Institute, Kazakhstan Academy of Sciences, Observatory Alma-Ata 68, 480068 Kazakhstan.

**VILLARETE Horacio A,** b. 23 July 1954, Panganiban, Catanduanes, Philippines. Journalist; Economist; Political Activist; Developer. Education: BSc Business Administration, 1975, University of Santo Thomas, Manila. Appointments: Journalist and Economist, Political Activist, 1975-, Philippine Islands. Publications: Contributor and News Correspondent, local tabloids in territory; Columnist. Honour: Outstanding Stud Leader of the Year, UST, Manila, 1975. Memberships: Society for International Development, 1997; National Geographic Society, 1997; American Society of International Law, 1997; AMA, 1996; New York Academy of Sciences, 1996; AAAS, 1997. Address: 25 Sto Santiago Street, Panganiban, Catanduanes 4806, The Philippines.

**VINEETH V Francis,** b. 15 May 1935, Kandassankadavu, India. Professor. Education: PhD, Philosophy, Gregorian University, Rome, 1965; PhD, Theology, Oxford University, 1975. Appointments: Fordham University, Bronx, New York,

1974-75; Dharmaram Vidya-kshetram, Bangalore, 1965-70, 1976-; University of Tuebingen, Germany, 1992. Publications include: Discovery of Being, 1970; Call to Integration: New Perspectives in the Theology of Religious Life, 1981; Justice and Reconciliation, 1983; Manunaniswanam (Voice of Silence), 1984; Foundations of World Vision, 1985; Song of Solitude, 1992; Yoga of Spirituality, 1995; Self and Salvation in Hinduism and Christianity, 1997; Founded Vidyavanam Ashram, Bangalore, 1996. Memberships include: American Academy of Religion, 1974-76; All Kerala Philosophical Association, 1968-70; Indian Theological Association, 1975-96. Address: Dharmaram Vidya Kshetram, Hosur Road, Bangalore 560029, India.

**VINOGRADOVA Marina,** b. 14 November 1969, Vyshnij Volochek, Russia. Chemist. Education: Diploma, Tver State University, 1993; Candidate Science, Tver State University, 1996. Appointments: Research Worker, Tver State University, 1996-. Publications: Over 30 articles in prose journals, 2 books. Membership: Mendeleev's Chemical Society, Tver, 1992-. Address: Department of Chemistry, Tver State University, Sadovy per 35, Tver 170002, Russia.

**VIRZI MARIOTTI Gabriele,** b. 21 April 1949, Palermo, Italy. Professor. m. Bruno Sigismunda. Education: Graduate, Engineering, 1974. Appointments: Researcher, 1980-93, Associate Professor, 1993-, Palermo University; Professor, Arcavacata Di Rende University, 1978-88. Membership: Editorial Board, Mobility Vehicle Mechanics Journal, 1995-. Address: Mechanics & Aeronautics, University Viale Delle Scienze, Palermo 90128, Italy.

**VISSARION Torop,** b. 14 January 1961, Krasnodar, Russia. Artist. m. Ljubov Torop, 4 sons, 1 daughter. Appointments: Founder, The Last Testament Church. Publications: The Last Testament, 2 volumes. Address: 21 Beregovja str, Village Petropavlovka, Kuraginskij raion Krasnojarskij, Kraj 662 925, Russia.

**VITALETTI Giuseppe,** b. 13 March 1950, Sassoferrato. University Professor. m. Pietrunti Anna. Education: BA, University of Rome, 1974; MSc, University of York, England, 1978. Appointments: Researcher, University of Rome, 1976-88; Professor, Public Finance, University of Macerata, 1989-. Publications include: The Italian Pensions, 1988; The Tax Fair, 1991; Hypotheses for a Fiscal System Based Upon the Benefit Principle, 1996. Honours: Stringher Grantee, Bank of Italy, 1975; Canova Prize, 1994. Memberships: Italian Society of Public Economics; Italian Society of Economists. Address: Via Nazionale N 243, 00184 Rome, Italy.

**VITALI Julius,** b. 1 July 1952, Queens, New York, USA. Author; Artist. Education: BA, State University of New York at Fredonia, New York, USA. Appointment: Gallery Director, Open Space Gallery, Allentown, Pennsylnania, USA, 1996-98. Publication: Fine Artists Guide to Marketing and Self-Promotion, Author. Honours: Pennsylvania Council on the Arts Special Projects Award, 1987, 1991, 1997. Address: 308 N 2nd Street, Allentown, PA 18102, USA.

**VITCU Dumitru,** b. 2 March 1940, Ibanesti, Romania. Historian. m. Reveca Vitcu, 1 son. Education: BA, History and Romanian Language and Literature, Al I Cuza University of Iasi, Romania, 1962; PhD, History, Al I Cuza University of Iasi, 1974. Appointments: Senior Scientific Researcher, A D Xenopol Institute of Romanian Academy; Professor on Modern History, Stefan Cel Mare, University of SUCEAVA, Romania, 1994-. Publications: Diplomats of the Union, 1979; History of the Moldavian Salt Mines during Modern Times, 1987; George

Enesco in the American Musical World, 1994; Intre Revolutie si Unire: Pagini de istorie socialä, 1997; Editor, "Studia et Acto Historiae Iudaeorum Romaniae", I,II,III-, 1996, 1997, 1998-; Fulbright Fellow, Boston College, 1983-84. Memberships: Romanian National Committee of Historians, Member of the Board, 1996-; American Society for Romanian Studies, 1983-. Address: Institute of History, Str Lascar Catargi 15, 6600 Iasi, Romania.

**VITENSON Anatoly S,** b. 28 June 1924, Moscow, Russia. Doctor. m. R A Vitenson, 2 daughters. Education: Medical Institute, 1948; Medical Science Candidate, 1955; MD, 1983; Professor, 1989. Appointments: Head, Biomechanics Department, Central Research Institute for Prosthetics and Prosthesis Design. Honours: Honoured Scientist of Russia, 1993. Academician of Academy of Medico-Technical Sciences of Russia, 1996. Membership: Biomechanics Society of Russia. Address: Central Research Institute for Prosthetics & Prosthesis Design, 127486 Moscow, Russia.

**VITT Walter,** b. 2 October 1936, Gera, Germany. Art Writer. m. Luiza Aschenbrenner, 1 son, 2 daughters. Education: Germanistics, Journalism, Historical Research, University of Müenster, 1957-63; Appointments: Editorship, 1961-98; Vice Head, Department for News Service, 1989-98; Westdeütscher Ründfünk, Koeln. Publications: Lienhard von Monkiewitsch, 1994; Kûenstler Traeûme, 1994; Enzo Maiolino, 1996; Walter Dexel Werkverzeichuis der Drûckgrafik, 1998; Schriften zur Kûnstkrifik (editor), 8 Volumes, 1993-1999. Membership: Association International de Critiques d'Art, President, German Section, 1989-. Address: Maternusstr 29, D-50678, Koeln, Germany.

**VLAD Melu,** b. 5 March 1955, Braila, Romania. Engineer. m. Florica, 2 daughters. Education: Graduated ENG, Politechnical University, BUH, Computers and Automation, 1980; Postgraduate Course, Microprocessors, 1990. Appointments: Research Engineer, Factory for Electronics and Automation (FEA), 1980-89; Head of Laboratory Research and Development (FEA), 1990-92; Senior Project Manager Research and Development (FEA), 1992-98; Head of Automation Department, 1999. Publications: Technical contributions and many scientific contributions on industrial measurement. Honour: Second Prize, yearly session, University. Membership: Instrument Association of Romania. Address: Odobesti 5 Bl Zl Sc 4 Apt 57, 74576 Bucharest, Romania.

**VLADIMIROV Alexander Petrovich,** b. 10 August 1952, Narophominsk, Moscow, Russia. Scientist. m. Valentina Korshunkova, 3 sons. Education: Chuvash State University, 1975, Dr, 1989. Appointments: Engineer, 1975; Scientific Researcher, 1979. Publication: Dissertation, 1989. Memberships: Russian Physical Society, 1989; Holographic Working Group of SPIE, 1993; Society for Experimental Mechanics, 1994. Address: Institute of Engineering Science, Urals Division of Russian Academy of Sciences, 91 Pervomaiskaya Str, GSP-207 Ekaterinburg 620219, Russia.

**VLADIMIROV Serguel V,** b. 1 October 1961, St Petersburg, Russia. Physicist. m. Galina Vladimirova, 1 son, 1 daughter. Education: MSc, 1984, PhD, 1988, Moscow Institute of Physics and Technology, DSc, 1999, General Physics Institute. Appointments: Junior Research Fellow, Research Fellow, General Physics Institute, Moscow; Research Fellow, Ruhr University, Germany; Research Fellow, Kyushu University, Japan; Research Fellow, University of Sydney, Australia. Publications include: Modulational Interactions in Plasmas, 1995. Honours include: Alexander von Humboldt Fellowship,

1992; JSPS Fellowship, Japan, 1994; ARC Fellowship, Australia, 1995. Address: University of Sydney, School of Physics, Sydney, NSW 2006, Australia.

**VLASE Ioan-Orest,** b. 4 January 1955, Brasov, Romania. Electrical Engineer. m. Stanca-Mihaela Jurescu, 1 daughter. Education: Degree, Electrical Engineer, 1980, PhD, 1991, Polytechnic Institute, Bucharest; MS, Mathematics, Univerity of Bucharest, 1989. Appointments: Developer Engineer, National Institute for Automation, Bucharest, 1980-82; Research Engineer, Scientific Assistant, Lecturer, Polytechnic Institute, Bucharest, 1982-91; Researcher, Darmstadt University of Technology, 1982. Publications include: Electromagnetic Shielding in the Technical of Heavy Currents, 1990; Archiv für Elektrotechnik, 1992. Memberships: International Computer Society; IEEE; ACM; New York Academy of Sciences. Address: Grafenstrasse 33, D-64283 Darmstadt, Germany.

**VLASOV Gennadii,**b. 3 April 1939, Karaganda, Russia. Physicist. m. 1 daughter. Education: Kiev State University, 1961-66; PhD, Theoretical Physics, Kiev Institute of Physics, 1970. Appointments: Senior Science Worker, Institute of Physics, Kiev, 1973-84; Space Research Institute, Moscow, 1989-92; Leading Science Worker, Center for Program Studies, 1992-. Publications: Spherical Excitons in many electron atoms, International Journal of Infrared and Millimeter Waves, 1991; Sun as many-particled spherical exciton, 1997; Superphotons and Natural Holograms, 1998. Membership: Member of New York Academy of Sciences. Address: Center for Program Studies, Ul Profsoyuznaya 84/32, 117810 Moscow, Russia.

**VLASOV Kirill Borisovitch,** b. 4 April 1920, Novocherkassk, Russia. Scientist; Physicist. m. Vera N Vlasova, 2 daughters. Education: Graduate, Ural Polytechnical Institute, Sverdlovsk, 1942; PhD, 1949; Doctor of Physical and Mathematical Sciences Degree, 1966; Professor, 1984. Appointments: Electrical Engineer, 1942-45; Postgraduate Student, Science Researcher, Head, Laboratory of Electric Phenomena, Leading Scientific Researcher, Institute of Physics of Metals, Ural Branch, Academy of Sciences, Russia. Publications: Several articles in professional scientific journals. Honour: Laureate of the National Prize, Ukraine, 1986. Memberships: Council, Russian Academy of Sciences. Address: Laboratory of Electric Phenomena, Institute of Metal Physics, Urals Division, Russian Academy of Sciences, 18 s Kovalevskaya Str GSP-170, Ekaterinburg 620219, Russia.

**VLECK Donald,** b. 30 October 1949, Chicago, Illinois, USA. Personal Coach; Consultant; Keynote Speaker. m. Valeria, 1 son, 2 daughters. Education: Bachelor of Business Administration, University of Michigan. Appointments: General Manger, Popps INC Hamtramck, 1971-76; Vice President, Domino's Pizza, 1978-94; President, Don Vlcek Associates Ltd, 1994-. Publications: The Domino Effect, 1992; Business One Irwin. Honours: Best of Business, American Library Association, 1992; Top 30 Business Books, Soundview. Memberships: Professional Member, National Speakers Association; Professional Certified Coach; International Coaching Federation. Address: POB 701353, Plymouth, MI 48170-0963, USA.

**VOLPE Andrew Arnold,** b. 17 February 1952, Moscow, Russia. Financial Company Executive; Mathematician; Computer Science Engineering Educator. m. Natalia Volpe, 1 son, 1 daughter. Education: Master Degree, Computer-Aided Control Systems, 1969-75, MS, Technique, 1975, Riga Red Banner Civil Aviation Engineering Institute; Postgraduate, Engineering Cybernetics, 1979-83; PhD, 1985; DSc, 1993. Appointments: Mathematician, Programmer, Senior Engineer,

Laboratory of Control Information Systems, 1975-78, Lecturer, Senior Teacher, Chair of Mathematical Method and Programming, 1978-88, Assistant Professor, Chair of Software and Computer Science, 1988-92, Riga Red Banner Civil Aviation Engineering Institute; Vince Chairman of the Board, Joint Stock Company Slavu Bank, Riga, 1992-93; Director, Computer Technology and Information Systems Department, Joint Stock Company Bonus Inc, Riga, 1993; Senior Manager, Commercial Firm Bonus Trust Ltd, Riga, 1993-94; Director, Moscow's Representative Office, 1994-95, Director, Inter-Regional Relationships Department, Riga, 1995, Joint Stock Company Kredo Bank, Riga, Latvia/Moscow, Russia; General Manager, Commercial Firm Remora Ltd, Riga, 1995-96; President, Brokerage Joint Stock Company Fincross Securities, Riga, Latvia/San Francsico, California, USA, 1996-. Publications: Over 36 scientific papers in professional journals. Honours: Several. Memberships: Latvian Association for Professional Participants of Securities Market, Riga; Research Board of Advisors, American Biographical Institute. Address: 11 Cesu Street, Apt #23, LV-1012 Riga, Latvia.

**VOLPE Eugene Arnold,** b. 31 October 1947, Moscow, Russia. Researcher. Education: MS, Medicine, Riga Medical Institute, 1972; PhD, Medicine, Academy of Medical Sciences, Moscow, 1976; Diploma, Political University, Riga, 1985; Postdoctoral Research Training, Natural Anti-Tumour Resistance Effector Cells, N.N. Blokhin Centre for Cancer Research, Moscow, 1989-95; Visiting Scientist, Mario Negri Institute for Pharmacological Research, Milan, Italy, 1996; Diploma Dr Med, Institute for Experimental and Clinical Medicine, Riga, 1992; Dr Habil Med, 1997. Appointments: Junior Research Scientist, 1975-80; Senior Research Scientist, Group Leader, 1981-94; Leading Research Scientist, 1994-, Lab of Host Biostimulators, Dept of Oncology, Inst for Exp. & Cein. Med., Riga. Publications: More than 75 Scientific Publications, Tumour Immunology, Professional Journals. Honours: Many HOnours and Prizes. Memberships: CPSU; Baltic Immunological Society; European Association for Cancer Research; European Macrophage Study Group; International Society for Preventive Oncology; Society for Experimental Biology and Medicine; Society for Leukocyte Biology; New York Academy of Sciences; Research Board of Advisors, ABI Inc.; Habilitation and Promotion Council. Address: 4 Gailezera Street, Apt 89, Riga LV 1079, Latvia.

**VOLYNCHIK Eugeny Pavlovich,** b. 8 March 1939, Ukraine. Surgeon. m. Galina L Minkova, 1 son. Education: Medical Institute in Odessa, 1968; Diploma of Candidate of Medical Sciences, 1981; Senior Research Fellow degree, 1985; Docent, State Medical Academy n.a. I.M.Sechenov, 1990. Appointments: Leading Research Fellow, Department of Kidney Transplantation, 1990-; Docent, Chair of Hospital Surgery, Moscow Medical Academy; Consultant Surgeon in Transplantology; Consultant, Medical Air Force Service of Russia. Publications: 80 scientific publications, articles and books, 1968-97. Honour: Diploma Winner of Highest Category, Cambridge University. Memberships: Society of Surgeons of Russia n.a. Pirogov; Society Transplantologists of Russia; New York Academy of Science. Address: Malaya Pirogovskaia St 27 Bldg 1, Flat 16, 119435 Moscow, Russia.

**VON FEILITZEN (Maria) Cecilia,** b. 26 September 1945, Stockholm, Sweden. Researcher. Education: BA, 1969, PhD Sociology, 1971, Stockholm University. Appointments: Media Researcher, Swedish Broadcasting Corporation, 1964-96; Senior Researcher, Dept Journalism, Media & Communication, Stockholm University, 1981-, Board of Directors, Head of Centre for Mass Communication Research, 1990-93, Stockholm University; Film Examiner, Board of Films for

Children and Young People, Swedish Film Institute, 1983-88; Expert Council on Media Violence, Ministry of Culture, Sweden, 1991-; Scientific Coordinator, UNESCO International Clearinghouse on Children and Violence on the Screen, 1997-; Co-Editor, several scientific journals on Media and Communication, 1974-. Publications: About 150 reports, articles and books in the field of Media and Communication research. Memberships: Amnesty International; Association of Swedish Media and Communication Science, President 1979-81, VP 1981-83, Board of Directors 1996-; International Association for Media and Communication Research. Address: Stockholm University, PO Box 27861, Journalism, S-11593 Stockholm, Sweden.

**VON KROGH Geo,** b. 25 January 1943, Bergen, Norway. Medical Doctor. Education: Medical School, University of Bergen, Norway, 1967; Specialist of Dermatology, 1976; PhD, 1981, Karolinska Institute. Appointment: Associate Professor, Department of Dermatology, Karolinska Hospital, 1988. Publications include: Current treatment of genital warts; External genital wart treatment; Clinical management of penile HPV-associated lesions. Memberships: Swedish Academy of Dermatology; Scandinavian Society of Genito-Urinary Medicine; International Society for the Study of Vulvar Disease; International Papillomavirus Workshop Group; Swedish Physicians Against AIDS; European Academy of Dermatology and Venereology; International AIDS Society; International Society for STD Research, European Course HPV-associated Pathology. Address: Bondegatan 1C, Stockholm 11623, Sweden.

**VONK Gerrit Rokus,** b. 1 August 1962, Utrecht. Radio Station Owner. Education: BBA, 1984, MBA, 1988, Erasmus University, Rotterdam, Netherlands. Appointments: Senior Consultant, Europe Transfer Consultants, 1988-90; Owner, General Manager, HOLLAND FM Radio Chain, 1991-95; Project Coordinator, MSF, Doctors Without Borders, 1996-97; Owner, General Manager, City FM Radio Chain, 1997-. Publications: Author, Venture Capital Beyond Boundaries, 1988; Co-author, A natural link: Building European Ventures, 1990. Address: Veldlaan 13, 3737 AM Groenekan, The Netherlands.

**VONKA Vladimir,** b. 31 July 1930, Prague, Czech Republic. Physician; Virologist. m. Jarmila Vonkova, 1 son. Education: MD, CSc (PhD), Professor Microbiology, Charles University, Prague; DSc, 1981, Czechoslovak Academy Science, Prague; Visiting Professor Virology, Baylor College Medicine, Houston, Texas, 1968-69. Appointments: Postdoctoral Fellow, Research Institute Immunology, Prague, 1956-60, Head Department Virus Biology, 1961-70; Head, Department Experimental Virology, Institute Sera and Vaccines, 1971-91; Head Department Experimental Virology, Institute Haematol Blood Transfusion, 1991-. Publications: Over 230 scientific publications; 7 monographs or chapters in monographs. Honours: 1991 G Mendel Medal; 1973 Reiman Medal; J E Purkynje Medal, 1988-; Trapl Medal, 1995-; Award of Minister of Health for Research, 1984, 1994, 1997; Fellow, American Academy Microbiology, 1992-; Academia Scientiarum et Artium Europea, 1997-. Memberships: Czech Medical Society; European Association CanResearch; Founding member, Learned Society of Czech Republic. Address: Virology Department, UHKT U nemocnice 1, Prague 2 120 00, Czech Republic.

**VORA Laxmikant N,** b. 12 March 1931, Bhavnagar, India. Orthopaedic Surgeon. m. Bindu, 1 son, 1 daughter. Education: MBBS, 1954, MS, 1957, FCPS, 1957, Bombay; FRCS, 1958, England; M Ch Orth, 1959, Liverpool. Appointments: Honorary

Professor Orthopaedics, Seth G S Medical College, Honorary Orthopaedic Surgeon, KEM Hospital, Bombay, 1962-89 Honorary Orthopaedic Surgeon, Dr B Manaiati Hospital 1961-73; Sizhn Hospital, 1973-. Memberships: Formerly VP SICOT, Indian Orthopaedic Association; Indian Arthroscop Society; Indian Rheumatism Association, Treasurer; British Orthopaedic Association. Address: 7 Adarsh, 94 Walkeshwa Road, Mumbai 400 006, India.

**VOROB'EV Adolf,** b. 23 October 1931, Russia. Chemist. m Moisseeva Nelya, 1 daughter. Education: Diploma, Chemistry Moscow State University, 1954; PhD, 1958; DSc, 1971 Appointments: Scientific Worker, Moscow State University 1954-77; Professor, Chief of the Chair, Moscow Chemica Technological Institute, 1977-. Publications: Several articles in professional journals. Honours: Medal, 25 years of the Cosmi Era, 1982; Title, Meritorious Science Worker of Russia, 1996 Memberships: Academician, International Higher Educatio Academy of Sciences, Academy of Creative Endeavors Address: D I Mendeleev Moscow Chemical Technologica University, 9 Miusskaya Ploschad, A-47 GSP Moscow 125820 Russia.

**VORONOV Gennadii Stepanovich,** b. 14 June 1937 Moscow, Russia. Physics. m. Anna Voronova, 1 daughter Education: Moscow Physical and Technical Institute, 1960 PhD, 1960; Magistr of Physics and Mathematical Science 1966. Appointments: Assistant, Tractor Research Institute 1951-54; Engineer, PN Lebedev Physics Institute, 1960-65 Research Scientist, PN Lebedev Physics Institute, 1965-79 Senior Scientist, PN Lebedev Physics Institute, 1979-82; Senio Scientist, General Physics Institute, Moscow, 1982-98 Publications: Around 100 in professional journals. Address Russian Academy of Sciences, 38 Vavivlova Str GSP, Moscov 1179442, Russia.

**VOROS Imre,** b. 20 October 1944, Budapest, Hungary Lawyer. m. Krisztina Veress, 2 sons. Education: Lawyers Diploma, 1968. Appointments: Legal Counsel, 1967-69 Researcher, Academy of Sciences, 1969-90; Professor of Law University of Uiskolc, 1983-98; Györ, 1998-; Donau Universita Krems, Austria; Central European University Budapest, 1992- Judge, Constitutional Court, 1990-. Publications include: Marke Behaviour - Competition Law, 1981; Public Tenders, 1984 International Co-Operation Contracts, 1995; Handbook o European Competition Laws, 1996. Memberships: Associatior Internationale de Droit Economique; Hungarian Association o Competition Law; Hungarian Association for the Protection o Industrial Property. Address: Constitutional Court, Donati 31-35, 1015 Budapest, Hungary.

**VORSTER Len,** b. 17 November 1954, Johannesburg South Africa. Musician. Education: BMus Degree, Cape Tow University, South Africa, 1976; Postgraduate Performers Diploma in Chamber Music and Accompanying, Cape Towr University, 1982. Appointments: Piano Lecturer, Cape Tow University, 1981, 1982; Proof-Reader, Editor, Allans Publishing in Melbourne, Australia, 1985-89; Piano Lecturer, University o Melbourne, 1992-. Publications: Edition of Mozart Flute Sonatas; Several CD's released. Memberships: Artistic Director, Port Fairy Spring Music Festival; Artistic Director o Schirmer Ensemble; Vice-President, Camberwell Music Society. Address: 70 Merton Street, Albert Park, Vic 3206 Australia.

**VOSEVICH Kathi Ann,** b. 12 October 1957, St Louis, USA Writer; Scholar. m. James H Meredith. Education: AB, honours English, 1980, MA, English, 1983, St Louis University; PhD Rhetoric & Shakespeare, University of Denver, 1988

Appointments: English Professor, BNM, NL. 1988-91; Education Officer, Volkel, NL, 1988-91; English Instructor, University of Georgia, 1991-94; Visiting Assistant Professor of English, Colorado College, 1994; Head of Documentation, Senior Technical Writer, Editor, Titan, 1994-97; Documentation Manager, Beechwood, 1997-. Publications: CTAS User's Guide; The Education of a Prince(ss): Tutoring the Tudors; Conversations with Joseph Heller; Interview with Joseph Heller. Honours: NCTE National Writing Award, 1975; National Merit Scholarship, St Louis University, 1976-80; Phi Beta Kappa, 1978; Teaching Fellowship, St Louis University, 1980-83; Alpha Sigma Nu, 1983; Academic Advising Fellowship, St Louis University, 1983-84; University Scholarship, University of Denver, 1985; Colorado Scholar, University of Denver, 1985-86; Teaching Fellowship, University of Denver, 1985-87; Graduate Dean Scholarship, University of Denver, 1988; National Endowment for the Humanities Fellowship, 1994. Membership: Modern Language Association. Address: 6535 Hawkeye Circle, Colorado Springs, CO 80919, USA.

**VOUDOURIS Konstantinos,** b. 4 January 1938, Thessaloniki, Greece. Rheumatologist; Medical Doctor. m. Ekaterini, 1 son, 1 daughter. Education: Medical Diploma, 1962, MD, 1972, University Thessaloniki. Appointments: Post-grad training as Assistant, SHO, Registrar etc, 4 years in GB, 5 years in Greece; Consultant in Medicine, 1976-85; Consultant in Rheumatology, 1986-. Publications: Diagnostic Rheumatology, 1987; Rheumatological Dictionary, 1998. Honour: Honorary Professor, Open University of Thessaloniki. Memberships: President, Hellenic Society Rheumatology, 1989-90; Foundation Member, Hellenic Foundation of Rheumatology Research, 1992-. Address: 20 Chrisostomou Smirnis Street, 54622 Thessaloniki, Greece.

**VOYKOVA Rositsa,** b. 16 September 1973, Troyan, Bulgaria. Economist. Education: Business Academy, D A Tsenov, Svishtov, Bulgaria. Appointment: Owner, IRMA, 1992-. Address: IRMA, V Levski #264 Str, 5600 Troyan, Bulgaria.

**VRANES Jasmina,** b. 20 February 1961, Gospic, Croatia. Assistant Professor. Education: MD, Zagreb University Medical School, 1984; MSc, 1989, PhD, Zagreb University. Appointments: Intern, University Hospital, Osijek, 1984-86; Staff Associate, Medical School, Zagreb University, 1986-89; Research Assistant, 1989-97, Assistant Professor, 1997-. Publications: Several articles in professional medical journals. Memberships include: Croatian Society of Medical Microbiology; International Society for Infectious Diseases; New York Academy of Sciences. Address: Zagreb University Medical School, Rockefeller Street 4, Zagreb 1000, Croatia.

**VRONSKY Petr,** b. 4 March 1946, Prague. Conductor. 1 daughter. Education: Violin Conservatoire Pilsen, 1967; Conducting, Academy of Music Arts, Prague, 1972; Senior Lecturer, Prague, 1990. Career: Opera Pilsen, 1971; Opera Aussig, 1974; State Philharmonic Orchestra, Brno, 1979-91; Guest Conductor, Czech Philharmonic Orchestra, Prague, National Theatre, Prague, Metropolitan Orchestra, Tokyo, Radio Symphony Orchestra, Munich, Kammeroper Vienna Dance Theatre, Haag; Several recordings. Membership: Association of Music Scientists and Musicians, Prague. Address: Majerskeho 2049, PO Box 29, 14901 Praha, Czech Republic.

**VUKASINOVIC Zoran,** b. 12 July 1959, Valjevo. Medical Doctor. m. Zorica, 1 son, 1 daughter. Education: MD, 1982; Specialist in Orthopaedics, 1990; MSc, 1991; PhD, 1993. Appointments: Assistant Professor, 1989; Head of US Department, 1990; Head of Pediatric Orthopaedics

Department, 1995; Professor, 1996. Honours: Pediatric Hip Diseases, 1994; Pediatric Orthopaedics. Memberships: SICOT; EFORT; EPOS; Balkan Orthopaedic Association; Yugoslavia Orthopaedic Association. Address: Special Orthopaedic Hospital Banjica, 28 Mihajla Avramovica, P O Box 803, 11041 Belgrade, Yugoslavia.

**VUKIC Zoran,** b. 3 April 1962, Croatia. Attorney at Law. m. Gina Vukic, 1 son, 2 daughters. Education: LLB, University of Rijeka, 1985. Appointments: Associate, Sprajc Law Office, Rijeka, 1985-88; Partner, Sprajc & Vukic, Rijeka, 1989-95; Senior Partner, Vukic Jelusic & Sulina, Rijeka, 1996-. Publications: Several articles in professional journals. Memberships: International Bar Association; Croatian Bar Assocaition. Address: N Tesle 9/V1, Rijeka 51000, Croatia.

**VULCHANOV Nikolai L,** b. 3 September 1948, Sofia, Bulgaria. Heat Transfer Applied Mathematics. m. (1) 2 daughters, (2) Iliana Vulchanova. Education: Graduate, 114 English Language School, Sofia, 1962-67; High, Heat Transfer Engineering, 1967-72, Master Applied Mathematics, 1972-73, PhD, Applied Mathematics, 1973-76, School for Mechanical and Electrical Engineering, Sofia. Appointments: Assistant Professor, Department Mathematics, School for Mechanical and Electrical Engineering, Gabrovo, 1978-80; Research Fellow, Central Laboratory of Chemical Engineering, Bulgarian Academy of Sciences, 1980-86; Senior Research Fellow, Secctretary for Research, ICL, 1986-87; Associate Professor, Department of Mathematics, School for Mechanical and Electrical Engineering, Gabrovo, 1988-91; Senior Research Fellow, Department Head, ICL, Sofia, 1991-92, 1995-. Publications: Co-author 2 monographs in Computational Mathematics; Author, co-author, over 50 scientific/research papers in international and local periodicals; Translations from English of 3 monographs; Over 100 newspaper articles; Reviewer: Zentralblatt fur Mathematik, 1978-, Mathematical Reviews, 1988-. Memberships: Union of Bulgarian Mathematicians, 1976; American Mathematical Society, 1988; National Geographic Society, 1996. Address: 159 Nikola Popov Str, BG-1444 Sofia, Bistrica, Bulgaria.

**VUZA Dan Tudor,** b. 26 January 1955, Bucharest, Romania. Mathematician. Education: Graduate in Mathematics, 1978, Doctor degree in Mathematics, 1984, University Bucharest. Appointments: Senior Researcher Degree I, Institute of Mathematics, Romanian Academy. Publications: 65 in functional analysis, signal processing and mathematical theory of music. Honour: Simion Stoilow Prize, Romanian Academy, 1987. Membership: Member of Committee for Functional Analysis, Romanian Academy. Address: Calea Victoriei 12A Bloc B, 70412 Bucharest, Romania.

**VYAS Girish,** b. 11 June 1933, Aglod, India. Professor. m. Devi R Trivedi, 2 daughters. Education: BSc Hons, 1954, MSc, 1956, PhD, 1964, University Bombay, India; Postdoctoral fellowships, Case Western Reserve University, Cleveland, Ohio, University of California. Appointments: Professor of Laboratory Medicine, 1977-, Director of Blood Bank, 1969-89, Director, current, Transfusion Medicine Programme, UCSF, California. Publications: Edited 9 books and monographs; Published over 210 original scientific papers in peer-reviewed journals of medical science. Honours: Numerous awards. Memberships: American Society of Haematology; American Association of Blood Banks; American Association for the Study of Liver Diseases; American Association for Advancement of Science; International Association of Biological Standards. Address: University of California School of Medicine, 513 Parnassus Avenue, Medical Sciences Room S-555, San Francisco, CA 94143-0134, USA.

# W

**WABREK Alan John,** b. 12 October 1937, Philadelphia, Pennsylvania, USA. Physician; Public Health Specialist; Professor. m. Lynn Wabrek, 1 son, 1 daughter. Education: MD, 1963; Master of Public Health, 1994; Doctor of Public Health, 1997. Appointments: Professor of Obstetrics and Gynaecology, University of Connecticut, 1985-96; Professor of Population Medicine, Syracuse University Health Sciences Center, 1999-; Medical Director, Broome County Health Department. Publications: 86 publications. Memberships: President, World Association for Sexology; President, Society for Sex Therapy and Research; President, American Society for Psychosomatic Obstetrics and Gynaecology; President, Hartford Medical Society. Address: Clinical Campus, 425 Robinson Street, Binghamton, NY 13901, USA.

**WAGNER Edyth E,** b. 15 October 1916, Brooklyn, New York, USA. Music Professor; Pianist; Writer. m. Frederick C Roop. Education: Diploma, Piano, Institute Medical Art, New York, 1941; BS, Piano, Juilliard School of Music, New York, 1947; M M Piano, University of Southern California, Los Angeles, 1951; Dr of Music Arts, CA, 1968. Appointments: Juilliard School, 1945-47; Hockaday Jn College; University of Houston; San Bernardino Valley College; Long Beach City College; Lecturer, University Southern California; Chicago State University; Private Studio, Retired, 1985. Piano Technique for the First Years; Raymond Burroughs and his Contributions to Music Education; Brazilian Folksongs. Honours: Honorary Plaque, National Federation of Music Clubs, 1990; Pi Kappa Lambda, 1953. Memberships: National Guild of Piano Teachers; Music Teachers National Association; California Association Professional Music Teachers; International Society of Music Education; American Musicological Society; Music Educators National Conference; Mu Phi Epsilon Fraternity. Address: 506 Oak Creek Lane, Ojai, CA 93023 3208, USA.

**WAHBA Ayman,** b. 1 August 1965, El-Guiza, Egypt. Assistant Professor. Education: BSc Electrical Engineering, 1988; MSc Electrical Engineering, 1991; DEA, 1993; PhD Computer Engineering, 1997. Appointments: Assistant Professor, Ain Shams University, Cairo, teaching and research projects. Publications: in scientific journals and conferences. Memberships: IEEE Computer Society; ACM. Address: Ain Shams University Faculty Engineering, 1 El Sarayay Street, Cairo, Egypt.

**WÅHLIN Vagn,** b. 16 January 1935, Copenhagen, Denmark. History Educator. m. (1) Birgitte, 1964, divorced 1981, 1 son, 1 daughter, (2) Barbara E Dunn, 1984, divorced 1991, (3) Kaisu K Salmia, 1995. Education: Mag art, Copenhagen University, 1968; Senior Professor exam, Aalborg University, 1981. Appointments: Amanuensis, History Department, Aarhus University, 1968-73; Visiting Research Fellow, University College, London, 1973-74; Lecturer, 1974-89, Docent, 1989-Aarhus University; Director, Centre for North Atlantic Studies, 1991-94; Vice-Chairman, Research Board, Centre for Maritime and Regional History, Esbjerg. Publications: Several in the fields of Nordic cultural history, the Faroe Islands, American History; Over 50 articles in Danish and international journals; Editor for several journals. Memberships: Several historical research associations; Board of History Studies, Aarhus University. Address: Emmasvej 18, 1, DK 8220 Brabrand, Denmark.

**WAITZMAN Daniel Robert,** b. 15 July 1943, Rochester, New York, USA. Musician. m. Mona Good. Education: BA, 1965, MA, Musicology, 1968, Columbia College; ABD, Columbia University Teachers College, 1970. Appointments: Flutist, Queens Chamber Band, Trio Bell Arte, New Baroque Soloists, Long Island Baroque Ensemble; Professor, Flute and Recorder, The Aaron Copland School of Music; Professor of Flute, Hofstra University. Publications: The Art of Playing the Recorder, 1978; String Quartet in D Minor, 1996; Quintet in E Flat Major, 1996; Sonata in A Major for Flute and Harpsichord, 1998; Trio in E Major for Flute Oboe d'Amore and Harpsichord, 1998. Honours: Concert Artists Award Winner, 1971; International Bach Society Award Winner, 1973; National Endowment for the Arts Solo Recitalist Fellowship Grant, 1986; ASCAP Awards, 1997, 1998. Address: 28-02 Parsons Boulevard, Flushing, NY 11354-1346, USA.

**WALD Lucia,** b. 1 October 1923, Iasi, Romania. University Professor. Education: Master Degree in Arts, 1948; Doctor's Degree in Philology, 1968. Appointments: University Degree in Classical Philology and General Linguistics: Assistant Lecturer, 1949, Lecturer, 1951, Reader, 1963, Professor, 1970, University of Bucharest. Publications: 7 books on General Linguistics, History of Linguistics, Indo European Linguistics; 130 articles and reviews. Honour: Prize of Romanian Academy, 1996. Membership: Romanian Society of Classical Studies. Address: Str Garii de Nord Nr 2 BL C, SC 3 ap 31, R078123 Bucharest, Romania.

**WALKER Claudia T,** b. 2 September 1943, St Croix, Virgin Islands. Business Manager. m. 2 sons, 1 daughter. Education: BA, Management, 1990, Personnel Management, 1990; AA Accounting, 1990, Marketing and Sales, 1980. Appointment: Founder and President of Gospel Tent Ministries. Memberships: Ordained and Licensed Pastor; International Third World Leaders Association, 1996; Morris Cerullo World Evangelism, 1994. Address: Government of Virgin Islands, Department Licensing and Consumer Affairs, Golden Rock Shopping Center, Christiansted, St Croix, VI 00820, USA.

**WALKER Clive Thomas,** b. 22 November 1947, Coalville, England. Nuclear Fuel Technologist; Microbeam Analyst. m. Janet Patricia Vernon. Education: Metallurgy Diploma, 1971, PhD, 1974, University of Surrey, Guildford. Appointments: Head of EPMA Laboratory, European Institute for Transuranium Elements, Karlsruhe, Germany, 1978-; Deputy Head, Tech Physics, 1998-; Advisor ISO, Geneva, Switzerland, 1997-; ICXOM, 1998-. Publications: Articles in professional journals. Honour: Freedom of the City of London, 1998. Memberships: Executive Board, European Microbeam Analysis Society, 94th Livery Company of the City of London; Fellow: Institute of Physics; Institute of Materials; Royal Microscopical Society. Address: Hegenbergstr 8, D 76327 Woeschbach, Germany.

**WALL Judith Lindley,** b. 18 October 1943, Burley, Idaho, USA. Data Entry. Education: BA, German University of California, Berkeley, USA, 1964; MA, Social Science, California State University at Chico, USA, 1976. Appointments: Researcher and Creator and Owner, Basic Patent on a Structural Object and Process; Writer. Publications: 4 articles with the Christian Science Publishing Society. Honour: Fellowship in Writing at Chico, California State University. Memberships: Library of Congress; Smithsonian and US Naval Institute; Charter Member, Women in the Arts Museum, Washington, DC, USA; First Church of Christ, Scientist, Boston, Massachusetts, USA. Address: 2209 Brumback Street, Boise, ID 83702, USA.

**WALL Matthew Jr,** b. 22 June 1958, USA. Surgeon; Scientist. m. Barbara M, 2 sons. Education: BS, Rice University, 1980; MD, Baylor College of Medicine. Appointments: Assistant Professor, Associate Professor, Baylor College of Medicine, 1991-. Publications: Numerous Articles in Scientific Journals and Textbooks. Memberships: America College of Surgeons; America Association for the Surport of Trauma. Address: Baylor College of Medicine, 1 Baylor Plaza, Houston, TX 77030, USA.

**WALLACE Roger James,** b. 29 August 1950, Swan Hill, Victoria, Australia. Educator; Researcher. m. Cheryl Lynn Evans, 1 son. Education: B App Sc, RMIT, 1973; BSc Hons, 1975, Monash University; Dip Ed, 1981, Melbourne University; PhD, 1988, La Trobe University. Appointments: Tutor in Mathematics, La Trobe University, 1983-85; Lecturer in Management Information Systems, Deakin University, 1985-; Exchange Professor, Winthrop University, Rock Hill, SC, USA, 1992; Statistical Consultant, Pacific Plants, Vancouver, Canada, 1992, 1993, 1996; Speaker in the field, Europe, Australia. Publications: Co-author 3 books on Statistics, 1988, and International Student Exchange, 1994, 1995; Numerous papers in professional journals and proceedings. Honours: Siddons Industries Travelling Scholarship, West Germany, 1983; Bowater Industries Travel Grants, Poland, England, 1987, Poland, 1991; Co-Designer, FECRT field test, 1992-. Address: Deakin University School Management Information Systems, Burwood Highway, Burwood, Victoria 3125, Australia.

**WALLAERT Benoit,** b. 17 March 1952. Professor. m. Tillie Wallaert, 3 sons, 2 daughters. Education: MD, 1982. Appointments: Professor of Medicine, 1989-. Publications: Author or co-Author, 233 original articles; 91 abstracts; 6 invited conferences; 9 book chapters and congress reports; 37 other papers; in fields of pneumology, allergology, and oncology. Honours: Prix de Medecine de l'Association des Internes et Anciens Internes de Lille, 1980; Prix de la Societe de Medecine du Nord, 1982; Prix Louis Christiaens, 1984; Prix Fred Siguier de la Societe Nationale Francaise de Medecine Interne, 1986; Prix Arsac, 1987; Bourse de Recherche GLAXO, 1988; Cournand Lecture, European Respiratory Society, 1996. Memberships: Societe de Pneumologie de Langue Francaise; Societe Francaise d'Allergologie; Societe de Pathologie Thoracique du Nord; American Thoracic Society; European Society of Pneumology. Address: BLD Leclerq-Hosp Calmette, Dept Pneumology, 59037 Lille, France.

**WALLER Robert Rex,** b. 19 February 1937, New York, New York, USA. Consultant in Ophthalmology. m. Sarah Elizabeth Pickens, 1 son, 2 daughters. Education: BA, 1958, Duke University, Durham, North Carolina; MD, University of Tennessee College of Medicine, 1963; Internship, City of Memphis Hospitals, Memphis, 1963-64; Residency, Internal Medicine, 1966-67, Ophthalmology, 1967-70, Mayo Graduate School of Medicine, Rochester; Heed Foundation Fellow, Oculoplastic Surgery, University California at San Francisco, 1973. Appointments: Surgeon, US Public Health Service, National Institute of Arthritis and Metabolic Disease, National Institutes of Health, 1964-66; Consultant in Ophthalmology, Mayo Clinic, Rochester, 1970-; Professor of Ophthalmology, Mayo Medical School. Publications: 65 articles, abstracts and book chapters in professional publications. Honours: Marvin H Quickert Award, 1977; Teacher of Year Award for Ophthalmology, Mayo Graduate School, 1977; Heed Award in recognition of contributions to American Ophthalmology, 1985; Distinguished Alumnus Award, 1987; Hon Doctorate of Humane Letters, 1991, Jacksonville University; Medical Executive Award, 1992; Guest of Honour, American Academy of Ophthalmology Annual Meeting, 1993; Yater Award, 1996;

Honorary Fellowship, Royal College of Surgeons in Ireland, 1998. Memberships: Olmsted County Medical Society; Minnesota Medical Association; AMA; American Society of Ophthalmic Plastic and Reconstructive Surgery; Orbital Society; International Orbital Society; American Ophthalmological Society; American Board of Ophthalmology, Director, 1982-89, Vice Chair, 1988, Chair, 1989; Society of Heed Fellows, Board of Trustees; Society of Medical Administrators; Member, Board of Trustees, 1978-99, President and CEO, 1988-98, President Emeritus, 1999-, Mayo Foundation. Address: 199 Greenbriar Drive, Memphis, TN 38117, USA.

**WALLEY W W,** b. 2 August 1916, Richton, Mississippi, USA. Medical Practitioner; Church Lay Worker. m. Eletha Green, 7 June 1943, 2 sons, 2 daughters. Education: BS, University of Mississippi, 1946; MD, University of Pennsylvania, 1950. Appointments: Served to Captain, US Army Medical Corps, 1941-45; Intern, Jefferson Hillman Hospital, Birmingham, Alabama; Private Practice of Medicine, Mississippi, many years; Member, Medical Staff, Wayne General Hospital; Sunday School Teacher, Deacon, Chairman, First Baptist Church; Director, Agricultural Missions Foundation; Director, Universal Concern Incorporated; Participant, Layman's Crusades to Montana and California; Participant, Baptist Medical Missions to Korea, Bangladesh, Thailand, other Far Eastern countries. Publications include: Amniotic Fluid as a Cause of Death; How a Preacher Should Behave in Regard to His Health; The Diary of a Country Doctor. Memberships: Men's Department, Baptist World Alliance; Chairman, Christian Acting Commission, Mississippi State Baptists Association; Chairman, Committee on Boards, Southern Baptist Convention; Chairman, South and Southeast Asia Committee, Chairman, Retirement Committee, Foreign Mission Board; Executive Committee, Mississippi Baptist Convention; Vice-Chairman, Salry Study Committee; Founder, Board Member, Owen Cooper Foundation; Former Vice-President, Gideon, Laurel Camp. Address: 606 South Street, Waynesboro, MS 39367, USA.

**WALSH Thomas,** b. 15 August 1956, New York, USA. Co-Chairman; Chief Executive Officer. m. Adriana Stastny. Education: BFA, New York University, 1977. Appointments: Director, Producer, The Whole Truth, documentary, 1977; Chairman, Chief Executive Officer, Tom Walsh Productions Inc, 1977-89; Executive Producer, Creator, Mismatch, 1979, House to House, 1982, We Dare You, 1992; Chairman, Chief Executive Officer, Woderland Dream Factory Inc, 1989-91; Producer, Denial, 1991, The Arrival CD-ROM, 1996; Co-Chairman, Chief Executive Officer, Enteraktion Inc, 1993-98. Honours: 1st Prize, Best Television Show, Connecticut Association of Professional Communicators, 1974; Bronze and Silver Awards, National Forensic League, 1974; Helena Rubenstein Scholar, Helena Rubenstein Company, 1976-77; Kate Garland Award, 1977. Memberships: Psi Upsilon; Alpha Epsilon Rho. Address: Enteraktion Inc, 15200 Sunset Boulevard, Pacific Palisades, CA 90272, USA.

**WALTER Hugo,** b. 12 March 1959, Philadelphia, Pennsylvania, USA. College Professor of Humanities and Literature. Education: BA, Princeton University, 1981; PhD, Literature, Yale University, 1985. Appointments: Teaching Fellow, Yale College, 1982-85; Assistant Professor, Rhodes College, 1986-87; Assistant Professor, University of Missouri, 1987-88; Adjunct Assistant Professor, Old Dominion University, 1988-89; Assistant Professor, Washington and Jefferson College, 1989-92; Assistant Professor, Fairleigh Dickinson University, 1992-96; Assistant Professor, Kettering University, 1996-. Publications: Books of Poetry: The Fragile Edge, 1988;

Velvet Rhythms, 1989; Amber Blossoms, 1990; Golden Thorns of Light and Sterling Silhouettes, 1991; Amaranth-Sage Epiphanies of Dusk-Weaving Paradise, 1995. Address: 157 Loomis Court, Princeton, NJ 08540, USA.

**WAMSTEKER Kees,** b. 29 May 1946, Haarlem, The Netherlands. Gynaecologist. m. Yvonne M L Bylsma, 3 daughters. Education: MD, 1971, State University, Leiden; PhD, 1977; Board Cert Ob/Gyn, 1976; Ob/Gyn Resident, State University, Leiden, 1971-76. Appointments: Senior Consultant, Dept Ob/Gyn: Maria Stichting, Haarlem, 1977-89, Spaarne Hospital, Haarlem, 1989-. Publications: 43 papers in professional journals including: Hysteroscopie, 1977, thesis; Imaging and Visual Documentation in Medicine, 1987, Diagnostic Imaging and Endoscopy in Gynaecology: a practical guide, 1997. Memberships: International Society for Gynaecologic Endoscopy; European Society of Gynaecologic Endoscopy; Uropean Society for Human Reproduction and Embryology; Dutch Ob/Gyn Society. Address: Spaarne Hospital, Van Heythujzenweg 1, 2012 CE Haarlem, The Netherlands.

**WAN Danny T F,** b. 24 April 1964, Hong Kong. Executive Director. m. Ingrid Ying Kei Leung. Education: Diploma; BSc; MBA. Appointments: Jun Gao Real Estate Development Company Ltd; Jun Gao Holdings Company Ltd; Jun Gao Trading Development Ltd; Jun Gao Agency and Consultants Ltd; Jun Gao Property Management Ltd. Memberships: Chairman, Property Owners Incorporation; The Highlander Club. Address: Jun Gao Holdings Company Ltd, PO Box 166, Tsuen Wan Post Office, Hong Kong, China.

**WANG Allan Xuhui,** b. 14 May 1955, Zhejiang, China. Doctor. m. Huang Hui, 1 daughter. Education: MD, 1977, Postdoctoral, 1984, Shanghai University of Chinese Medicine. Appointments: Professor, Doctor, shanghai College of Traditional Chinese Medicine, 1977-85; Vice President, Institute of Traumatology and Orthopedics, Shanghai Academy of Traditional Chinese Medicine, 1985-92; Vice President, International Medical Research Inc, 1993-. Honours: 2nd Class Prize, Scientific Advancement, Shanghai Science & Technology Committee, 1990; 2nd Class Prize, Scientific Advancement, All China Traditional Chinese Medicine, 1990; Special Subsidy, State Council, 1992. Memberships: Committee, International Association for the Study of Pain and The Task Force on Cancer Pain of IASP; Vice Chairman, All China T-W Society of Rheumatism & The Task Force on Rheumatism. Address: 800 West Zhong Shan 57, Zihong Building 21A, Shanghai 200051, China.

**WANG Bing-Hong,** b. 4 October 1944, Wuyuan, Jiangxi, China. Professor. m. Liu Ru Zhen, 2 sons. Education: PhD, USTC, 1982; Post Doctor Research, Stevens Institute of Technology, 1982-85. Appointments: Associate Professor, USTC, 1989; Professor, USTC, 1996; PhD Doctors Advisor, USTC, 1997-. Research Projects in Charge: Stochastic Heating and Acceloration of Particles in Plasma by Electromagnetic Wave, 1989-91; Chaos in Conservative System, 1991-95; Interpretation of Earthquake Time Series and Research on Prediction Alorithums, 1993-95; Nonlinear Analysis of Time Series and Application to Earth Science, 1995-97; Research on Complex System and Chaos Theory, 1997-2002; Research on Instabilities of Basic Fire Combustion System, 1999-2001. Honours: Transition from Conservative Chaos to Dissipative Chaos, Science and Technology Research Advance Award, Education Council of Anhui Province, 1995; Universal Behaviours for Bifurcation, Chaos and Intermittancy, Sience and Technology Research Advance Award, National Education Council, 1996; Education Award, Wang Kuan-Cheng

Foundation, 1996; New Dynamical Behaviour of the Relaxation Oscillation System, 1996; Sience and Technology Research Advance Award, Education Council of Shanxi Province, 1997. Memberships: MPHY, USTC; NSC, USTC; Director of Anhui Society of Nonlinear Science; Research Professor, College of Systems Science, Shanghai Science and Technology University. Address: University Sci and Tech of China, Dept Modern Physics, Anhui Hefei 230026, China.

**WANG Da Peng,** b. 28 August 1946, Nanjing, China. Medicine. m. Xu Mezi, 2 daughters. Education: MD, 1981. Appointment: Professor, Tianjin Traditional Medicine University. Publications: Thinking Mode and Basic Viewpoints of Traditional Medicine; 14 books, 170 articles, 130 compositions. Memberships: Countrywide Committee; Traditional Medicine Learned Society. Address: Chinese Medicine Institute of Wang Da Peng, Room 3, 4 Building, Linxiang Li Lane, Qijin Lu Road, Hedongqu, Tianjing 300171, China.

**WANG Dehua,** b. 27 September 1937, Shaoxing, China. Physical Chemistry. m. Xiaolong Xu, 2 daughters. Education: PhD, Syracuse University, USA, 1985. Appointments: Research Scienctist, Kimberley clark Corp, 1985-. Publications: Over 50 Publications including, Magnetic Resonance in Chemistry, 1995. Address: Kimberly Clark Corp, 1400 Holcomb Br Road, Roswell, GA 30076, USA.

**WANG Erich Jiansheng,** b. 29 September 1941, Linyi, China. Computer Scientist; Sinologist; Economist. m. Marianne Grundtner, 3 sons. Education: Diploma, Foreign Languages, Pedagogical Institute, Jiangsu Province, 1963; Postgraduate Diploma, Economics, Institute for Advanced Studies, Vienna, 1970; PhD, Sinology, Vienna University, 1986. Appointments: Assistant, Institute for Advanced Studies, Vienna, Austria; Research Member, Austrian Institute of Economic Research; Head, Information Department, Computing Centre for Economics and Social Sciences; Project Manager for Computer Science, Vienna University; Project Manager for Computer Science, Austrian Computer Society; Guest Professor, University of Science and Technology, Jiangsu Province, China; External Lecturer, University of Economics and Business Administration, Vienna. Publications: Science and Technology in China, 1975; Using databases for Economic Decision-Making, 1990; Using National and International Databases for Information and Decision-Making, forthcoming; Internet for Economists, forthcoming. Membership: Austrian Computer Society. Address: Laudongasse 22/2, A-1080 Vienna, Austria.

**WANG Fengyun,** b. 17 October 1960, Jianhu, Jiangsu, China. Professor. m. Zhanzhi Yang, 1 son. Education: BSc, University of Science and Technology, China, 1981; MS, Nanjing University of Science and Technology, 1984. Career: Lecturer, Chemistry Department, 1985-90, Associate Professor, Chemistry Department, 1990-93, Professor, Dean, 1993-97, Professor, Head, Water Treatment Institute, 1997-, Nanjing University of Science and Technology. Honours: Model Citizen of Jiangsu Province, 1991; Special Allowance, Chinese Government, 1992-; Outstanding Professor of Jiangsu Province, 1996. Membership: Chinese Chemical Society. Address: Chemical Engineering School, Nanjing University of Science and Technology, 200 Xiao Ling Wei, Nanjing, Jiangsu 210014, China.

**WANG Han Gong,** b. 16 October 1940, Jiyuan, Henan Province, China. Professor. m. Zhang Hui Qing, 1 son, 1 daughter, Education: Graduate, Xi'an Shaangxi Province, China. Appointments: Vice Director, Faculty Office; Director, Faculty Office; Vice Director, Secons Artillery Logistics Science and Technology Institute. Publications: Maintenance Management of Equipment; Operation and Maintenance Engineering of Missiles; Optics Apparatus Basics. Honours: National Science and Technology Progress Award; Army Science and Technology Progress Award. Memberships: Technology Committee of the Chinese Equipment Association; Surface Engineering Branch; Chinese Mechanism Engineering Association. Address: 203 Office Secondary Artillery Engrg Inst, Xian 710025, China.

**WANG Jianjiang,** b. 26 August 1995, Hei Longjiang Province. Professor. m. Mrs Zhang, 1 s. Education: Graduate, North West Teachers College, 1982; Graduate, Normal University, 1988. Appointments: North West Techers College, 1982-85; Assistant Lecturer, Vice Professor, Professor, North West Normal Unviersity, 1988-. Publications: The Aesthetics of Self Adjustment; Zhuangzi And Zens Aesthetics. Honours: The Leading Expert of Gansu Province; The Highest Social Science Science Prize, Gansu; First Class Prize of Teaching Study. Memberships: Association of All China Aesthetics; Gansu Aesthetics Association; Lanzhou Lif Sciences. Address: Chinese Department, North West Normal University, Lanzhou Gansu, China.

**WANG Jiuling,** b. 26 April 1932, Gao Yang County, Hebei Province, China. Teacher. m. Li Yingxiu, 1 son, 1 daughter. Education: BA, College of Beijing Forestry, 1955; PhD, Leningrad Forestry University, 1960. Appointments: Leader, Silvicuture Laboratory, 1980-87. Publications: Collectors of Forestry Technology in North China; Forestry Division Chinese Agricultural Encyclopedia. Memberships: Chinese Forestry Society; National Natural Science Committee. Address: Beijing Forestry University, Beijing 100083, China.

**WANG Jizhi,** b. 20 March 1932, Jiangxi, China. Professor of Soil Science. m. Rengai Zhou, 1 son, 1 daughter. Education: Graduate, 1954, Huazhong Agriculture College. Appointments: President, Ningxia Institute of Agriculture Survey and Design. Publications: Soils in Yinchen Plain, 1963; Soils in Ningxia, 1990; Irrigating Warped Soils in China, 1996. Memberships: Chairman, Soil Science Society of Ningxia; Council member, Soil Society of China. Address: Ningxia Institute of Agricultural Survey and Design, Yingchuan 750000, Ningxia, China.

**WANG Keping,** b. 19 May 1955, China. Professor. m. Li Zhongze, 1 daughter. Education: MA, Canberra University, 1983. Appointments: Professor, English Department, Beijing 2nd Foreign Languages Institute (University); Deputy Director, Institute of Inter-cultural Studies (BSFLU). Publications: Sightseeing as an Aesthetic Activity, 1991; Applied Aesthetics in Tourism, 1997; The Classic of the Dao: An New Investigation, 1998; Essays on Sino-Occidental Aesthetic Cultures, 1998. Honours: Book Prize, 1992; Leading Scholar of Youth, 1993; All China Outstanding Scholar Studied Overseas, 1997. Membership: China Aesthetic Society. Address: Department of English, Beijing 2nd Foreign Languages Institute (University), Beijing 100024, China.

**WANG Lefu,** b. 15 August 1941, Hainan, China. Professor. m. Yunyu Mu, 2 daughters. Education: Bachelor Degree, Philosophy Department, Zhongshan University, 1965. Appointments: Professor, Chairman, Faculty of Law & Politics, Zhongshan University, 1993-. Publications include: Administration Management; Public Relations. Honours: 1st Prize, National Administration Best Sellers, 1985; National Excellent Education Material Prize, 1995. Memberships: Director, Administration Management Committee of China; Director, Politics Institute of China. Address: Department of Politics & Administration, Zhongshan University, Guangzhou, China.

**WANG Lei,** b. 12 February 1970, Nanjing, China. Communications Engineer. m. Xin Zhao. Education: BE, 1991; ME, 1993; PhD, 1996. Appointments: Senior Communications Engineer and Network Consultant; Chief Network Planner and Designer of China Telecom. Honours: Minister Prize, 1989, 1991; Nortel Scholarship, 1990; AT&T Scholarship, 1994. Membership: IEEE. Address: Data Comm Bur MPT China, A12 Xin-Jie-kou-wai St, Beijing 100088, China.

**WANG Liqian,** b. 23 January 1933, Nanjing, China. Chairman. m. Zhang Bentao, 1 s. Education: BS, 1952; Professor, 1988. Appointments: Chairman, Chinese Society of Electrostatic Precipitation. Publications: Fluidization Engineering. Honours: Scientific and Technology Award. Memberships: International Society of Electrstatic Precipitation. Address: Nanjing Electric Power Environmental Protection Science Research Institute, 10 Pudong Road 210031, Nanjing, China.

**WANG Mingqi,** b. 1 October 1963, Shanghai, China. Physicist. Education: Bachelor in Engineering, 1985; Licentiate of Philosophy, 1995; PhD, 1997. Membership: New York Academy of Sciences. Address: Department of Physics, Uppsala University, Box 530, S-751 21 Uppsala, Sweden.

**WANG Mintong,** b. 23 November 1925, Baodi, Hebei, China. History of South East Asia. m. Ge Jifang, 1 son, 1 daughter. Education: Master of History, Dongbei Normal College, 1949-54; Bachelor of Law, Dongbei University, 1946-48. Appointments: Professor, History Department, Yunnan Normal University, Tutor of Postgraduates majored in SE Asian Studies, 1954-97. Publications: The Industrial Revolution of Britain; A Brief History of Modern World Political Thinking; A Brief Introduction of SE Asian History. Honours: Often awarded by Yunnan Provincial Government for excellent works. Memberships: Board Member, Association of China SE Asian Studies; Deputy Director, Association of Yunnan SE Asian Studies. Address: History Department, Yunnan Normal University, Kunming, Yunnan, 650092, China.

**WANG Qinglan,** b. 30 November 1936, Henan, China. Professor. Education: Graduate, Veterinary Department, Beijing Agricultural University, 1963. Appointments: Beijing Agricultural University, Vice Dean and Active Dean Veterinary College; Professor of Chinese Traditional Veterinary Medicine, 1994-; First PhD Student Supervisor, 1995-; Organiser of the International Veterinary Acupuncture Training Course, 1989-. Publications include: Veterinary Acupuncture Treatment; Advances on Veterinary Research Methods; 80 professional papers. Honours include: 2nd Class Prize, Science and Technology; Two 3rd Class Prizes, Science and Technology; Special Government Award, State Council. Memberships: Animal Husbandry and Veterinary Association of China; National Association of Veterinary Surgery; Vice-Secretary General of the Chinese Traditional Medicine and Instruments Association Address: Veterinary College, China Agricultural University, Beijing 100094, China.

**WANG Richard Hsu-shien,** b. 2 January 1932, Anqing, China. Research Chemist. m. Josephine Sun Wang, 1 son, 2 daughters. Education: BS, National Taiwan University, Taipei, 1956; PhD, University of Kansas, Lawrence, 1968. Appointments: Research Associate, Eastman Chemical Company, 1968-97; Retired 1997. Publications: 56 US patents. Honour: Eastman Chemical Company Inventor Appreciation Award, 1993. Memberships: American Chemical Society; Phi

Lambda Upsilon, Chemistry Honour Society. Address: 182 Crown Point Road, Pasippany, NJ 07054, USA.

**WANG Rubin,** b. 23 February 1951, Zhe Jiang, China. Research Scientist. m. 18 November 1992, 1 son. Education: Diploma, China Shaanxi TV Telecom Univeristy, 1982; MSc, Kyushu Sangyo University, Japan, 1996; PhD, Nagoya University, 1998. Appointments: Mechanical Designer, Ligh Industry Mechanics Co, Shanghai, 1982-92; Postdoctoral Fellow, Nagoya University, 1998-; Fellow, Japan Society for the Promotion of Science. Publications: Over 20 research papers in various international journals and conferences. Memberships: Japan Society of Mechanical Engineers; Chinese Academy of Sciences and Engineering. Address: Nagoya University Department of Electrical and Mechanical Engineering, Faculty of Engineering, Furocho, Chikusa-ku 464-8603, Japan.

**WANG Shizhen,** b. 4 September 1933, Llellong, Jiang Province, China. Senior Engineer; Professor. m. Feng Huiming, 1 son, 3 daughters. Education: BSc, 1956, North-East University of China. Appointments: Technician, Beijing Architectural Design Institute of Cities Building Ministry, China, 1956-57; Technician, Engineer, 4th Design Institute of Chemical Industry Ministry, China, 1958-93; Senior Engineer to Senior Engineer at Professor Rank, 1988. Publications: Prilling Tower and Prilling Spray Head; and others. Honours: Title of Advanced Worker in Chemical Industry System of China, 1991; Model Worker of Hubei Province, China, 1990; Winner of First Ten Inventions-Creations Golden Prize of China Patents, WIPO of UH and PO China, 1989 for one of his inventions. Memberships: Director, Chinese Fluid Engineering Society; Jet Technical Council. Address: China Five-Ring Chemical Engineering Corp, No 31 Zhuo-dao-quan Rd, Wuchang Hubei Province 430079, China.

**WANG Shou Chun,** b. 26 December 1930, Jiangyin, Jiangsu, China. Education. m. Guo Juan Fen, 1 son, 1 daughter. Education: Master Degree, University of International Business and Economics, Beijing, 1955. Appointments: Assistant Professor, 1956, Lecturer, 1960, Associate Professor, 1981, Professor, 1987-. Publictions include: Theory and Policy of China's Foreign Trade; China's Foreign Trade Economics. Honours: University Textbook Awqard, 1992, 1995. Memberships: Council, China Association of International Trade, Beijing. Address: University of International Business and Economics, Hepingjie Beikou, Beijing 100029, China.

**WANG Susheng,** b. 13 July 1957, Suzhou, China. Professor of Economics. m. Wei Yang, 2 sons. Education: BS Mathematics, 1982, MS Mathematics, 1985, Nankai University; PhD Economics, 1991, University Toronto. Appointments: Lecturer, Dept Mathematics, Nankai University, 1985; Assistant Professor of Economics, Concordia University, 1991-93; Assistant Professor of Economics, HKUST, 1993-. Publications: 3 articles in Journal of Economic Theory; 1 article in American Economic Review; 1 in Economic Theory. Memberships: Reviewer, American Mathematical Society, 1985-; Econometric Society. Address: Econ Dept, Hkust, Clear Water Bay, Hong Kong, China.

**WANG Tao,** b. 1 June 1936, Shandong, China. Researcher. m. Fan Ying-han, 1 son. Education: Bachelor Degree, Department of Forestry, Beijing Forestry University, 1955-59. Appointments: Professor, Researcher, Institute of Forestry, Chinese Academy of Forestry. Publications include: How to select the technology suitable for rural area extension through technical market and how to play the part of women scientists in extension, 1990; ABT Rooting Powder Principle and Application, 1991; Summary of the Project Extension, 1993; ABT Rooting Powder Introduction, 1994; Selected Papers of ABT, 1994; Papers of ABT Application Techniques Part 4, 1995; Polarization of ABT Rooting Powder Series, 1995. Honours include: National Outstanding Worker, State Council, 1989; 1st Prize, Outstanding Inventor, Society of Inventors, Romania, 1993; Officer Medal, King of Belgium, 1993; Title of National Outstanding Women Staff, One of National Key Cited Outstanding Science and Technology Workers, All-China Federation Trade Unions, 1996; Prize of Yilida Science and Technology, Appraisal Office, Yilida Science & Technology; Special Class, Prize of National Science & Technology Advancement, 1997. Address: ABT Research & Development Centre, Chinese Academy of Forestry, Wan Shou Shan, Beijing 100091, China.

**WANG Tao,** b. 2 December 1942, Wuhan, China. Metal Plastic Forming Technologist. m. Zhao Lizhen, 1 son, 1 daughter. Education: Bachelor Degree, 1966, Master of Science, 1982, Harbin Institute of Technology. Appointments: President, Heads Specialty Committee, CFIA, 1990-99; Professor, Harbin Institute of Technology, 1991-99. Publications: Numerous papers and several books; Technical Performance and Structural Specifications of WT6500-32 Spinning Equipment for Large Heads, Proceedings of the 4th ICTP, 1993. Membership: Council Member, China Forging Industry Association. Address: Harbin Institute of Technology, 92 West Dazhi Street, Harbin 150001, China.

**WANG Tiandong,** b. 2 September 1939, Zotou Town, Wendeng, China. Director of the Board. m. Jihua Lin, 2 sons, 1 daughter. Education: Graduate, High School, 1960. Appointments: Director, Nowoven Clothing Factory, Wendeng City, 1980-; Director of the Board, Decorative Clothing Company, Ltd. Honour: Title, National Model Worker, 1995. Membership: Representative, Peoples Congress. Address: The Decorative Clothing Company Ltd, Wendeng, Shandong 264400, China.

**WANG Weiqiang,** b. 22 August 1959, Qingdao, Tsingtao, China. Professor. m. Aiju Li, 1 son. Education: BS, 1982, Qingdao Institute of Chemical Technology; MSc, 1984, PhD, 1990, East China University of Science and Technology. Appointments: Professor, Dept Chemical Engineering, Shandong University of Technology. Honour: Award of Shandong Youth Scientists, 1996. Memberships: Chinese Society of Mechanics; Mechanical Engineering Society of China. Address: Shandong University of Technology, Dept of Chemical Engineering, 73 JingShi Road, 250061 Jinan, China.

**WANG Weiti,** b. 25 May 1938, China. Professor. m. Chengyuan Xue, 1 son, 1 daughter. Education: ScB, Shandong University of Technology, 1958-63. Appointment: Dean of College of Materials Science, Shandong University of Technology. Publication: Foundry Machine Theory, 1990. Membership: Vice President, Shandong Foundry Association. Address: College of Materials Science, Shandong University of Technology, Jinan 250061, China.

**WANG Xiaoming,** b. 20 April 1965, Sichuan, China. Professor, Academic Researcher. Education: BA, English, Southwest China Teachers University, 1991; MA, English Literary Translation, World Literature, Shanghai Normal University, 1996; PhD, Aesthetics, Shandong University, 1999. Appointments: Agronomist of Silkworm and Mulberry, Fruit and Tea, Kaijiang Agricultural Bureau, Sichuan, 1982-85; English Teacher, Daxian, Sichuan 1985-87, 1991-93. Publications: Translation, Aesthetic Life in the Anti-Urban Culture of Japan; Aesthetics as Mass Culture in Indian Antiquity; Modern Beauty

Seeking Opposition; Where to Go for the World Aesthetics Study; Introduction to Contemporary Chinese Aesthetics; A Summary of the XIVth International Congress of Aesthetics. Memberships: International Association for Aesthetics; The Chinese Society for Aesthetics. Address: Institute of Aesthetics, New Campus, Shandong University, Jinan 250100, China.

**WANG Yong Tai,** b. 1 September 1955, Hengyang, China. Associate Professor. m. Wei Shi, 2 sons. Education: MS, Wuhan Institute of Physical Education, Wuhan, 1985; MA, Ball State University, Muncie, Indiana, USA, 1988; PhD, University of Illinois at Urbana-Champaign, 1991. Appointments: Formerly Auburn University, Auburn, Alabama, USA; Currently Associate Professor, Department of Physical Therapy, Georgia State University, Atlanta. Honours: Outstanding Teaching Professor Award, Auburn University and State of Alabama, 1994. Memberships: American College of Sports Medicine; American Alliance of Health, Physical Education, Recreation and Dance; Chair of International Relations Council, American Association of Active Lifestyle and Fitness, 1996. Address: Department of Physical Therapy, Georgia State University, 700 Kell Hall, University Plaza, Atlanta, GA 30303, USA.

**WANYANGA John Nathan,** b. 4 April 1947, Kakamega. Controller. 2 sons. Education: Advanced Cambridge School Certificate, 1967. Appointments: Aviation Controller, 1968-78; Aviation Manager, 1978-96; Principal, Aviation School, 1996-. Address: PO Box 53362, Nairobi, Kenya.

**WARAKAULLE Herath Mudiyanselage Nissanka,** b. 13 July 1937, Peradeniya. Director. m. Rachel Mallika, 2 sons. Education: BA, 1962; Diploma in Tertiary, New England, Australia, 1981. Appointments: Teacher, 1962-1966; Assistant Manager, CTB, 1966-1972; Senior Assistant Registrar, University of Sri Lanka, 1972-1979; Senior Assistant Registrar, Colombo, 1979-1982; Registrar, Open University, 1982-1984; Registrar, Colombo, 1984-1997; Secretary, Committee of Vice-Chancellors and Directors, Sri Lanka, 1992, 1997-; Director, Institutee of Workers' Education, 1997-. Publications: Priorities and Control of Science, 1980; The Amalgamation and Decentralisation of Universities in Sri Lanka, 1985. Honours:Association of Commonwealth Universities Administrative Travelling Fellowship, 1977; Australian Government Award, 1980; Outstanding People of the 20th Century, 1998. Memberships: Colombo Hockey Association; State Services Cricket Association. Address: Committee of Vice Chancellors and Directors, Institute of Workers Education, 275 Bauddhaloka Mawatha, Colombo 7, Sri Lanka.

**WARD Donald E,** b. 30 November 1946. Professor. m. Susan Jane Gordon Ward, 27 November 1971, 1 son, 1 daughter. Education: BA, Psychology, DePauw University, Greencastle, Indiana, 1969; MS, Counseling, 1970, PhD, Counselor Education, 1973, Purdue University; Licensed Professional Counselor, Kansas; National Certified Counselor; Approved Clinical Supervisor; NBCC; Clinical Member, Approved Supervisor, American Association for Marriage and Family Therapy. Appointments: Graduate Teaching Assistant, Purdue University, 1972-73; Assistant Professor, Department of Counseling Psychology and Guidance Services, Counseling Psychologist, University Counseling and Psychological Services Center, Ball State University, 1973-76; Assistant, 1976-81, Chair of Counseling Committee, 1980-, Associate, 1981-87, Acting Department Chairperson, 1985, Professor, 1987-, Pittsburg State University. Publications: Numerous papers in professional journals; 1 book. Honours include: Psi Chi National Psychology Honorary; Chi Sigma Iota National Counseling Honorary (Charter Member); Phi Kappa Phi; NDEA Title IV Fellow, Purdue University; US Department of Education

Title III Faculty Collegial Research Mentoring Grant, 1987-89; ASGW Fellow. Memberships include: American Counseling Association; American Association for Marriage and Family Therapy; American Mental Health Counselors Association; American Psychological Association; Association for Counselor Education and Supervision; Council for the Accreditation of Counselling and Related Educational Programmes, Board, 1995-, Vice Chair, 1997-2000; Associate Editor, Journal for Specialists in Group Work, 1999-. Address: 2002 Countryside Drive, Pittsburg, KS 66762, USA.

**WARD Jon,** b. 30 Nove,ber 1944, Marshalltown, Iowa, USA. Internal Auditor. m. Judy Ann Ward, deceased, 1 son, 2 daughters. Education: BS, Accounting, University of Northern Iowa, 1969; MBA, Illinois State University, 1973. Appointments: Various internal audit positions, currently Audit Manager, State Farm Insurance Companies, Bloomington, Illinois, USA, 1969-. Publication: Internal Control, article, co-author. Honour: Award for Outstanding Article, Internal Auditor Journal, 1990. Memberships: Institute of Internal Auditors, Board of Directors, 1984-97; Children's Protection Network and Advocacy Center, Bloomington, Illinois, USA. Address: Rr 1 Box 359, Bloomington, IL 61704-9758, USA.

**WARE Barbara A Scott,** b. 17 February 1955, Brooklyn, New York, USA. Construction Consultant; Radio Broadcaster. m. Morris, 1 son, 1 daughter. Appointments: Costruction, 1974-90; Business Consultant, 1990-95; Citizens Advocate, 1995-99; Radio Broadcasting, 1995-. Publications: Essence Magazine; Savvy Magazine. Honours: Outstanding Women in Business. Memberships: Women in Broadcasting; Governors Taskforce on Womens Issues. Address: Jow Construction, 316 Nassau Road Ste 426, Roosevelt, NY 11575, USA.

**WARRIER Sankara,**b. 7 December 1946, Poothrikka. Teacher. m. 1 son, 1 daughter. Education: BA History, First class and first rank; MA History, First class and first rank. Appointments: Lecturer, Maharata's College, Ernakulam; Professor, Govi College, Thrissur. Publications: KP Gopalamean prize for history; Gurvuayurtemple, Mphil thesis. Membership: Indian History Congress. Address: Govt College, Kuttanallur PO, Trissur-14, Kerala, S India.

**WASHBURN Robert Brooks,** b. 7 November 1928, USA. Composer; Conductor; Author; College Professor. m. Beverly Darnell, 1 son, 1 daughter. Education: PhD, Eastman School of Music, 1960. Appointment: Professor of Music, Crane School of Music, Potsdam, 1954-. Publications: Numerous. Honours: Danforth Foundation Grant, 1959; Ford Foundation Grant, 1960; ASCAP Awards, annually, 1960-; Fulbright Fellowship, 1986. Memberships: ASCAP; MENC. Address: 87 State Highway 72, Potsdam, NY 13676-3478, USA.

**WASHINGTON Anthony Nathaniel,** b. 19 January 1969, Los Angeles, California, USA. Engineer. Education: Prairie View A and M University. Appointments: Forecasting Engineer, Planner, Detroit Edison Co, 1992-95; Advanced Manufacturing Engineer, General Motors Corp, 1995-96; Consultant, Optimum Gain Engineering Inc, 1996-97; Production Supervisor, Daimler Chrysler, 1997-. Memberships: Pitau Sigma; National Honorary Mechanical Engineering Fraternity. Address: 28678 E Carriage Park Dr, Southfield, MI 48034-6151, USA.

**WASHINGTON Johnnie Marian,** b. 23 September 1936, Paris. Minister. m. Naamon, 2 daughters. Education: Faith Bible Institute, Chicago, 1952-54; Religious Education, University of Maryland, Frankfort, Germany, 1963-65; Ministers Certificate of Ordination, 1972; Bachelor of Theology, International Seminary, Orlando, Florida, 1986; Certified Learing

Coordinator, Behavioral Modification, Performax System International, Minneoplis, 1985-86. Appointments: Supervisor in Charge, Hotel Dieu Hospital, -1987; Pastor, Full Gospel Evangelistic Temple Inc; Superintendent, El Paso District of Christ Holy Sanctified Churches of America, 1988-; Chairwoman, El Paso Black Chamber of Commerce, 1996; President, Interdenominational Ministerial Alliance. Honours: Many Awards from National State and Local NAACP; Honorary Doctor of Divinity; Outstanding Mother of the Year Award; Outstanding Black Personality Award; Outstanding Woman of the Year; Martin Luther King Award; Public Service Award; many other awards. Memberships: Attourney Generals Child Support Board; Mayor's Ethic Community; Aids Review Board; Fair HousingBoard; Texas Coalition of Black Democrats; Many other memberships. Address: 4631 Atlas, El Paso, TX 79904, USA.

**WATABE Tomiji,** b. 26 October 1927, Tokyo, Japan. Research and Engineering Consultant. m. Akiko, 1 son, 1 daughter. Education: Mechanical Engineering Dept, Tokyo Technical College, 1950; Dr Eng, 1970, Tokyo University. Appointments: Machine Designer, Kameari Works Hitachi Co Ltd, 1950-71; Researcher, Mechanical Engineering Lab Hitachi Co Ltd, 1972-77; Part-time Lecturer, Electric Technical University of Tokyo, 1971-77; Professor, Muroran Institute of Technology, 1978-93; Volunteer, Research & Engineering Consultant of T-Wave, 1974-; Consulting: Muroran Institute of Technology, Narasaki Machine Manufacturing Co Ltd, Hitachi Co Ltd, Hokkaido Development Bureau, Ocean Engineering Institute of Teanjin, China, Haiyou Machine Mnaufacturing Co, China. Publications: 11 books; 15 journal papers; 14 proceedings; 150 patents. Honours: Honorable Mention Prize, Hyd and Pneu Prize paper contest, 1977, 1978; Invention Prize, Japan Society of Invention, 1978; Award for Superior Paper, Foundation for Promotion of Hyd and Pneu Tech, 1990. Address: 5-23-3 Misono, Noboribetsu 059-0036, Japan.

**WATERS Jack,** b. 14 October 1954, Philadelphia, Pennsylvania, USA. Artist; Writer; Film Maker; Performer. Education: BFA, Dance, Juilliard, New York City, USA. Appointments: Founder, Allied Productions Inc; Former Co-Director, ABC No Rio; Co-Director, Naked Eye Cinema. Publications: Outweek, 1989; Village Voice, 1989; Das Tanz Archives, 1980; New York Times, 1989; Art in America, 1983. Membership: New York State Council on the Arts, 1985-90. Address: PO Box 20260, New York, NY 10009, USA.

**WATIE Hadiah,** b. 7 April 1948, Indonesia. Director. m. Ferrydear Ronald Rumampuk, 2 daughters. Education: BSc, Banking. Appointments: Secretary, Staff, Marine and Aviation Department, Superintendent, Marine Hull and Aviation Department, Manager, Reinsurance Department, Deputy Branch Head and Marine Underwriter, General Manager, General Underwriting Division, Asuransi Indrapura, 1975-85; Technical Director, Asuransi Dharma Bangsa, 1985-89; Technical Director, Asuransi Summa, 1989-93; Technical Director, Asuransi Tugo Indo, 1993-; Lecturer. Publications: Several articles and reports. Address: Duri Intan Raya T 402, Duri Kepa, Kebon Jeruk, Jakarta 11510, Indonesia.

**WATSON Alan Gordon,** b. 19 December 1964, Bulawayo, Zimbabwe. Software Engineering Consultant. Education: Transvaal Senior Certificate with Matriculation Exemption, St Benedict's College, South Africa, 1981; BSc, Computer Science, University of the Witwatersrand, South Africs, 1985; BSc, Hons, 1986; MSc, Computer Science, 1988; PhD, Geo Engineering, University of Minnesota, USA, 1990. Appointments: Systems Programmer, Mathematical Analyst, 1985-86; Software Consultant, 1986; Director, 1986-91; Software

Engineer, 1988; Research Assistant, 1988-90; Project Leader 1991-97; Proprietor, Manager, Corporate Technologies, 1997-. Publications: 3 refereed publications; 6 Conferences; 3 Interna Reports. Honours: Colin James Young Prize; Freda Lawensk Scholarship; AECI Research Fellowship; CSIR Studentship; National Postgraduate Scholarship; CSIR Information Services Star Performer Award; Outstanding Services Award; ICL Service Excellence Award. Memberships: International Association for mathematical Geology; International Statistics Institute; Geostatistics Association of South Africa. Address: 16 2nd Ave, Edenvale 1609, South Africa.

**WATSON Clarissa Alden,** b. 8 April 1928, Ashland, Wisconsin, USA. Author; Art Director; Curator. m. Edward L Watson, 1 son, 1 daughter. Education: BA, Milwaukee-Downe College; Layton Art School, University of Wisconsin. Career Director, Co-Founder, Country Art Gallery, Locust Valley, New York, 1953-90; Trustee, Nassau County Museum of Art, Roslyn, New York, 1980-84; Trustee, Heckscher Museum, Huntington, New York, 1984-88; Producer, International Chairman, Normandy Remembered, 1994. Publications: The Sensuous Carrot, 1975; The Fourth Stage of Gainsborough Brown, 1976; The Bishop in the Back Seat, 1980; Runaway, 1985; Last Plane From Nice, 1987; Somebody Killed the Messenger, 1990. Address: 1011 Wolver Hollow Road, Oyster Bay, NY 11771, USA.

**WATSON Duane Frederick,** b. 15 May 1956, Watertown, New York, USA. Professor; Author. m. Joann Ford, 1 daughter. Education: Bachelor of Arts, Houghton College, 1974-78; Master of Divinity, Princeton Theological Seminary, 1978-81; Doctor of Philosophy, Duke University, 1981-86. Appointments: Assistant Professor, Biblical Studies, 1984-86; Post Doctoral Study, Emory University, 1986-87; Pastor, Tri Church Parish United Methodist Churches of North Western, 1987-1989; Professor, Malone College, 1989-. Publications: Rhetorical Criticism of the Bible; Persuasive Artistry, Studies in New Testament Rhetoric in Honor of George A; Invention, Arrangement and Style, Rhetorical Criticism of Jude and 2 Peter; Several Articles. Honours: Dictionary of International Biography, Twenty Fifth Edition, International Biographical Centre; First Distinguished Faculty Award for Scholarship, Malone College; Forum Showcase of Research Award, Malone College; American Bible Society Scholarly Achievement Award for Excellence in Biblical Studies; Summa Cum Laude Graduate, Houghton College; Comprehensive Examination Honours, Houghton College. Memberships: Studiorum Novi Testamenti Societas; Society of Biblical Literature; Catholic Biblical Associations of America; Eastern Great Lakes Biblical Society; Institute for Biblical Research; International Society for the History of Rhetoric; Rhetoric Society of America; John Wesley Fellowship. Address: Malone College, 515 25th St NW, Canton, OH 44709, USA.

**WATSON Roberta Casper,** b. 7 November 1949, Boise, Idaho, USA. Attorney. m. Robert G Watson, 1 daughter. Education: JD, Harvard, Cambridge, MA, USA, 1974; BA, University of Idaho, Moscow, ID, USA, 1971. Appointments: Peabody and Brown, Boston, Massachusetts, 1974-78; Mintz, Levin, Cohn, Glovsky and Popeo, PA, Boston, Massachusetts, 1978-84; Trenam, Kemker, Scharf, Barkin, Frye, O'Neill & Mullis, Tampa, Florida, 1985-. Publications include: Employees Leased by Doctors Get Tax Scrutiny, 1986; 401(K) Plans Today... And Tomorrow, 1986; An ESOP Can Be AN Anti-Takeover Device, 1986; Spouse Wins Rights Under Pension Law, 1986; In Divorce, Who Gets Pensions?, 1986; COBRA As It Applies to Flexible Benefit Plans, 1993; What Is Gross Misconduct Under COBRA?, 1994; Special Fiduciary Responsibility Issues in Managed Health Care Plans, 1994.

Honour: Florida Council for Community Mental Health, Member of the Year, 1994. Memberships: American Bar Association; The Florida Bar; American Law Institute; Harvard Club-West Coast Florida; The Ivy League Club of Tampa Bay; Tampa Bay Pension Council; Florida West Coast Employee Benefits Council; The ESOP Association. Address: 124 Adalia Avenue, Tampa, FL 33606 3304, USA.

**WATSON Thomas Carl,** b. 26 February 1945, USA. Lawyer. m. Sharlene Dee, 5 sons. Education: BS, University of Memphis, 1967; MEd, University of Memphis, 1968; JD,Washington University, 1972. Appointments: Chair, Senior Partner, Crowell & Maring; Senior Partner, Watson & Renner. Publications: 20 Publications. Memberships: American Trial Lawyers Association. Address: Watson & Renner, 2000 M St, Washington, DC 20036, USA.

**WAYITI Lucas,** b. 19 August 1961, Nyangana. Education. m. Anna Wayiti, 4 sons. Education: Proposed BEd course. Appointments: 1984. Honour: HPEC Teaching Certificate. Memberships: NANTU; SWAPO. Address: PO Box 753, Rundu, Namibia.

**WEBER Richard Anthony,** b. 23 December 1929, Indianapolis, Indiana, USA. Professional Bowler. m. Juanita Delk, 3 sons, 1 daughter. Appointment: Charter Member, Professional Bowlers Association. Honours: American Bowling Congress Hall of Fame; Professional Bowlers Association Hall of Fame; Missouri State Sports Hall of Fame. Memberships: PBA; ABC. Address: 1305 Arlington Drive, Florissant, MO 63033-2201, USA.

**WEBSTER Alan Charles,** b. 22 May 1929, Cheviot, New Zealand. Social Researcher; Psychologist; Minister; Educator; Futurist. m. Janice M Fogg, 3 daughters. Education: L Th, 1955, Melbourne; BA, 1962, William Jewell College, Missouri; MDiv, 1963, Colgate Rochester Divinity School, New York; MA, 1965, Syracuse University; EdD, 1966, Syracuse University; PhD, 1972, Massey University, New Zealand. Appointments: Minister, New Zealand & USA, 1954-66; Assistant Professor Psychology, SUNY, 1965-66; Lecturer, Associate Professor, Education & Human Development, Massey University, New Zealand, 1966-95; Research Director, NZ Study of Values, from 1985; Executive Director, NZ Study of Values Trust, from 1997. Publications: Education with a Human Face; The Religious Factor in NZ Society; NZ Values Today. Honours: Bishop Ledden Fellow, Syracuse University, 1963-66; Yates Distinguished Alumnus Medal, William Jewell College, 1987; Visiting Scholar, Hughes Hall, Cambridge University, 1981-82. Memberships: Registered Psychologist; International Learning Styles Network; Steering Committee, World Values Survey; Board of Studies, NZ College of Early Childhood Education; Research Director, NZ Learning Styles Centre; NZ Association of Psychological Type; World Future Society. Address: 1 Awatea Terrace, Palmerston North, New Zealand.

**WEI Wei,** b. 4 April 1947, Tianjin, China. Entrepreneur. m. Liu Baozhen, 1 son. Education: Economic Management, Beijing Economy Correspondence University, 1989. Appointments: Section Chief, Shop Head, 1970-83, Director, 1984-, Tianjin Art Printing Factory; Member, Production and Technology Division, Tianjin Publishing Administration, 1983-84. Publication: Practical Color Standard, 1993. Honours: Advanced Worker of National Book Printing, 1980; Tianjin "Seven Five" Meritorious Medal, 1985, 1987; Tianjin Model Worker, 1986-95; First Session Printing Enterprise Management Prize, 1993; Tianjin Excellent Manager, 1994; National Model Worker, and Tianjin Special Class Model Worker, 1995; Morisawa Nobuo Printing 1st Award, 1995. Memberships: Enterprise Management

Committee, Printing Technology Association, China; Director, Standing Director, Tianjin Printing Technology Association; Director, Tianjin Enterprise Management Association & Enterprisers Association. Address: No 12 Binxi Road, Hexi District, Tianjin 300061, China.

**WEI Xiyun,** b. 3 October 1940, Nanjing, China. Professor of Anatomy. m. Zhang Jinkun, 1 son. Education: BS, Nanjing Railway Medical College, 1964. Appointments: Lecturer, Department of Anatomy, Nanjing Railway Medical College, 1964-87; Vice Professor, Department of Anatomy, China Pharmaceutical University, 1987-92; Professor, Head of Department of Anatomy, Shantou University Medical College, 1992-. Publications: 40 Articles; Observations of the Dorsal Scapular Nerve ans its Clinical Application; Anatomical Study on Compression Syndrome of Common Peroneal Nerve; Morphological Observation of Thymic Changes of Aged Mice After Excising Sex Glands; Morphological Quantitative Study of Protective Effect of Tonic Traditional Chinese Medicines on Thymus in Mice. Honours: 2nd Grade Prize, Science and Technology Progression of the Department of Railways. Memberships: Chinese Society of Anatomical Science; Chinese Society for Stereology. Address: Department of Anatomy, Shantou University Medical College, Xingling Road, Shantou 515031, Shantou Guangdong Province, China.

**WEIL Marlyn E,** b. 8 January 1949, Johnstown, Pennsylvania, USA. Early Childhood Educator. m. Charles Weil, 2 sons. Education: BSEd, 1970, Otterbein College; MEd, 1996, Benedictine University. Appointments: Child Care Licensing, Illinois Dept Children and Family Services, Glen Ellyn, 1986-; Instructor, Early Childhood Education, Elgin Community College, 1989-95, Benedictine University, 1996. Publication: Positive Social Interactions of Four-Year-Old Children with and without Disabilities, 1996. Memberships: NAEYC, Life member; Association of Child Care Consultants, Life Member; Fox Valley Association for the Education of Young Children, Founding Member. Address: Illinois Departmentt Children and Family Services, 800 Roosevelt Rd Bldg D Ste 10, Glen Ellyn, IL 60137, USA.

**WEINBAUM William,** b. 12 September 1960, New York City, USA. Television Producer. m. Joy Caslowitz. Education: International Baccalaureate, United Nations International School, 1978; BS, 1982, MS, 1983, Northwestern University, Medill School of Journalism. : Feature Producer, This Week in Baseball, Sports Newsatellite, 1984-95, ESPN, Sportscenter, Outside the Lines, 1995-. Honours: Deadline Club Television Feature Reporting Award, 1994; Emmy Awards, 1995, 1996; Ace Award, 1997; Northeastern University Sport in Society Journalism Award, 1997. Memberships: Society of Professional Journalists; National Academy of Television Arts and Sciences; International Radio and Television Society; Radio and Television News Directors Association; Deadline Club. Address: 81 Bangall Road, Stamford, CT 06903-4318, USA.

**WEINKAUF David.** Education: BS, Television, Radio, Ithaca College, 1963; MS in Film, Boston University, 1965. Appointments: Director, Announcer, Director of Traffic, WHCU-AM-FM, Cornell University, 1960-63; Graduate Assistant, Teacher, Boston University, 1963-65; Engineer, WBZ-TV, Boston, Massachusetts, 1964-65; Instructor of Speech, University of South Dakota, 1965-66; Engineer, WOR-TV, New York, USA, 1966-68; Designer, Builder; Frequent Contributor; Negotiator; Supervisor; Initiator; Advisor; Co-Advisor; Co-Founder; Founder; Initiator; Guest Lecturer; Creator; Co-Author; Teacher; Assistant Professor, Edinboro University of Pennsylvania, 1966-. Publications: High Tech Radio Days; Chuck Jones A Life of Animation; Radio Days at

Edinboro; Animation Is It Headed For Extinction?; Pioneering Life Styles in Nearby Pennsylvania in the Age of the Atom; Teaching Politics With Film At Edinboro; Weinkauf Surowiecki, Roberts. Honours: Pennsylvania Council on the Arts; Case Professor of the Year Nomination; Senate Faculty Research Grant; Many others. Memberships: Society for Animation Studies; American Federation of Film Societies; American Federation of Teachers; Association of Pennsylvania State College and University Faculties; National Association of Educational Broadcasters; Many others. Address: P O Box 145, Edinboro, PA 6412 0145, USA.

**WEINTRAUB Stanley,** b. 17 April 1929, Philadelphia, Pennsylvania, USA. Biographer; Historian; Professor. m. Rodelle S Weintraub, 2 sons, 1 daughter. Education: BS, 1949, West Chester University; MA, 1951, Temple University; PhD, 1956, Pennsylvania State University. Appointments: Evan Pugh Professor of Arts and Humanities, Pennsylvania State University; Visiting Professor, UCLA, University Hawaii, University Malaya, National University of Singapore. Publications: Author or Editor, 50 books, including biographies of Victoria, Albert, Disraeli, Whistler, Shaw, Beardsley, Rossetti, and histories of World War I and World War II. Honours: Bronze Star Medal, Korean War; Guggenheim Fellowship, 1968-69. Membership: National Book Critics Circle, USA. Address: 840 Outer Drive, State College, PA 16801-8233, USA.

**WEIR Sonja Ann,** b. 10 December 1934, Hazleton, Pennsylvania, USA. Artist. m. Richard C Weir, 2 sons, 3 daughters. Education: Student, Mary Ellen Silkotch, 1963-83; Art Students League, New York City, 1985-87. Career: President, Raritan Valley Art Association, 1982-84; President, American Artist Professional League, New Jersey Chapter, 1992-95, Editor of Newsletter, 1992-98; Artist, National Board AAPL, New York City, 1998. Honours: Grumbacher Art Award, 1981-83; Soho International Art Competition winner, 1992. Memberships: American Artists Pro League, New Jersey Chapter; Association of National Miniature Art; Raritan Valley Arts Association; New Jersey Watercolor Society. Address: 25 Madison Street, South Bound Brook, NJ 08880, USA.

**WEISS Susette Marie,** b. 14 June 1957, New Orleans, Louisiana, USA. Imaging (Photographic); Consultant and Technical Specialist. Education: AA, Photojournalism, Northern Louisiana University, Monroe, 1977; PhD, Religion, Universal Life College, Modesto, California, 1990; Certified Retinal Angiographer; Certified Ophthalmic Assistant; Certified CPR. Appointments: Production Supervisor, Laboratory Manager, Colorpix Custom Photographics Inc, New Orleans, 1978-84; Ophthalmic Photographer, Ochsner Clinic, New Orleans, 1984-85; Director, Ophthalmic Photography Omni/Medivision, Metairie, Louisiana, 1986-87; Audiovisual Meeting Planner, Technician and Consultant, New Orleans, 1988-89; Technical Supervisor, Retina and Vitreous Associates of Alabama, Mobile, 1989; Director, Photography, Dauphin West Eye, Ear, Nose and Throat Specialists, Mobile, 1989-91; Technical Sales Representative, Technical Specialist, Nikon Inc, Melville, New York, 1992-95; Contractual Consultant, Simply Susette Inc, New Orleans, 1995-; Inventor, Stereo-imaging Calibrator and Quantitiative Stereopsis Technique. Publication: Redefining the Wheel: Stereo-Photomicroscopy and Ophthalmology, author. Honours: Recipient, Best of Show Photography Award, Biological Photographers' Association, 1991; 1st Place General Photography Award, Biological Photographers' Association, 1991. Memberships: Ophthalmic Photographers' Society, Audio-visual Chair, 1991, Audio-visual Co-chair, 1992. Address: 5905 Colbert St, New Orleans, LA 70124, USA.

**WELCH J Kathleen,** b. 28 January 1950, Pensacola, Florida. Entrepreneur. Education: Kofutu Touch Healer, 1994; Reiki Practitioner, 1995; Kineseology, 1995; Regenesis Practitioner, 1996; Advanced Clinical Hypnotist, 1997; Massage Therapist, 1998. Appointments: Salesperson and Senior Salesperson, Arthur Murray International, Denver, 1970-72, Hollywood, Florida, 1972-73, Philadelphia, 1973-75, Chatham, 1975-81; Sales Rep, Warner-Lambert International Inc, 1981-83; Manager and Supervisor, TC Dance Club International, 1983-90; District Rep, NFIB - National Federation Independent Business, 1990-95; Radio Buyer, Frees Media, Springfield, 1995-96; Sales Rep, Atlantic Lucent Technologies, 1997; Computer Operator, Mailcraft Inc, Elizabeth, New Jersey, 1997-98. Honours: 6 Awards, Arthur Murray International, 1971, 1972, 1976, 1978, 1981; First Place Counsellor, Arthur-Murray All Star Tournament, 1977; 5 Awards, Dance Club International, Tournament of Champions, 1984-87; First Place New York Division, Professional Corner, National Federation of Independent Business, 1991, 1992. Memberships: Associate, Ballroom and Latin American, Imperial Society of Teachers of Dancing; Adjudicator, Ballroom and Latin American, National Dance Council of America; Ballroom and Latin American, American Dance Teachers Association. Address: 2000 W 92nd Ave No 443, Denver, CO 80221, USA.

**WELCH Richard LeRoy,** b. 15 October 1939, Lincoln, USA. Chief Executive Officer. m. Donna Lee Welch, 1 stepson, 2 daughters. Education: University of Nebraska, 1959. Appointmetns: CEO, Educom Inc, Subliminal Dynamics, International Speed Reading Institute and American Speed Reading Academy; Known as the Father of Mental Photography. Membership: Masons. Address: Educom Inc dba Subliminal Dynamics, 19744 East Union Drivce, Aurora, CO 80015, USA.

**WELLER Walter,** b. 30 November 1939, Vienna, Austria. Conductor. m. Elisabeth, 1 son. Education: Violin and Conducting Studies, Vienna Music High School. Appointments: Chief Conductor Emeritus, Royal Scottish National Orchestra, 1997-; Chief Guest Conductor, Orquesta Nacionel de España; Music Director, Basle Theatre; Leader, Allgemeinen Musikgesellschaft Basle; Conductor Laureate, Royal Liverpool Philharmonic; Conductor, major orchestras of Europe, Japan, USA and Israel; Many recordings for major record companies. Honours: Mozart Interpretations Prize; Beethoven Medal; The Grand Silver Medal for Services to the Austrian Republic, 1998. Membership: State Opera, Vienna. Address: Doblinger Hauptstrasse 40, 1190 Vienna, Austria.

**WELLS Clyde K,** b. 9 November 1937, Buchans Junction, Newfoundland. Chief Justice of Newfoundland. m. Eleanor Bishop, 2 sons, 1 daughter. Education: BA, 1959, Memorial University Newfoundland; LLB, 1962, Dalhousie University Newfoundland; Called to Bar Nova Scotia, 1963, Newfoundland, 1964. Appointments: Queen's Counsel, 1977; Captain, Judge, Advocate General's Office, Canadian Army, 1962-64; Senior Partner, Wells and Company, General Practice, 1964-87; MHA, 1966-71; Minister of Labour, 1966-68; Elected Leader, Liberal Party of Newfoundland and Labrador, 1987; Elected to House of Assembly, 1987, Premier of Newfoundland and Labrador, 1989-92, 1993-96; MHA Bay of Islands, 1989, 1993; Practiced law, O'Reilly, Noseworthy, St John's, Newfoundland, 1996-98; Justice, Court of Appeal, Supreme Court of Newfoundland, 1998; Chief Justice of Newfoundland, 1999-; Former Director, Board Chairman: Newfoundland Light and Power Company Ltd. Honour: Honorary LLD, Memorial University Newfoundland, 1996.

Address: Court of Appeal, 287 Duckworth Street, PO Box 937, St John's Newfoundland, Canada A1C 5M3.

**WELLS Lois Florence Campbell,** b. 25 December 1935, Christchurch, New Zealand. Retired Teacher. m. Peter Alan Vells, deceased. Education: English graduate; Christchurch Teacher's College, 1959; 2 year course Theory and Practice of Social Work; SPELD-Trained teacher, 1983; Naturopathic Diploma, Queensland Institute of Natural Science, 1986; studies on Mauri Psychology. Appointments: Teacher, Papanui High School; Lincoln High, Girl's Career Adviser, 1968. Child Welfare Officer; Medical Social Worker; Teacher, Allan Gardiner's Modern School of Music; Established own studio, 1984; Producer, series, Reading and Spelling Programmes based on accelerated learning techniques and SPELD teaching methods. Publications: 9 booklets on Reading and Spelling Programmes; Loving Fingers; Don't Be a Victim: Plug Up Your Boundaries, 1998; Stop the Game of Passing Round the Guilt: Walk the Path of Truth, 1999. Address: 85A Roberta Drive, Christchurch 2, New Zealand.

**WELLS Merle William,** b. 1 December 1918, Lethbridge, Alberta, Canada. Historian. Education: AB, College of Idaho, 1941; MA, 1947, PhD, 1950, University of California. Appointments: Instructor in History, College of Idaho, 1942-46; Associate Professor of History, Dean of Students, Alliance College, 1950-56; Consulting Historian, 1956-58, Historian, Archivist, 1959-86, Idaho State Historical Society; Idaho State Historic Preservation Officer, 1968-86. Publications include: Anti-Mormonism in Idaho, 1978; Boise: An Illustrated History, 1982; Gold Camps and Silver Cities, 1984; Idaho: Gem of the Mountains, 1985. Honours: LHD, College of Idaho, 1981; LHD, University of Idaho, 1990. Memberships: Treasurer, Graduate Students Association; University of California; Chairman, Southern Idaho Migrant Ministry; Department of History, United Presbyterian Church, USA; US State Historic Preservation Officers Council; Director, Idaho Zoological Society; Idaho Commission of Arts and Humanities; Many others. Address: Idaho State Historical Society, 210 Main Street, Boise, ID 83702-7264, USA.

**WENGER Ronald David,** b. 1 May 1944, Philadelphia. Physician, Surgeon. m. Judy Anderson, 1 son, 1 daughter. Education: BA, Ohio Wesleyan University, 1966; MD, Case Western Reserve University School of Medicine, 1970; Mano Clinic, Graduate School of Medicine, 1973-77; Intern, University of Oregon, School of Medicine, 1970-71. Appointments: Associate Clinical Professor, Surgery, University of Wisconsin School of Medicine. Honours: Diplomat American Board of Surgery. Memberships: American College of Surgeons; Past President Madison Surgical Society; AMA; WI Medical Society; WI Surgical Society; Society for Surgery of Alimentary Tract; Society of American Gastro Intestinal Surgeons. Address: 726 Farwell Dr, Madison, WI 53704 6052, USA.

**WENGLER Marguerite,** b. 18 November 1943, Kokomo, Indiana, USA. Author; Director; College Instructor. m. James Burton, 2 sons, 1 daughter. Education: BS, Education, Hofstra University, 1964; St John's University; MA, Moderate Special Needs, Assumption College, 1991. Appointments: Teacher, Public School, Elementary, High School, 1965-85; Special Needs Director, Montessori School, Lexington; Senior Lecturer, Curry College, 1993-. Publications: 60 Minutes in Much Higher Grades, A Closer Look. Honours: US Delegate, China. Memberships: Director, Learning Success Helpline; Learning Disabilities Network; Director, A Friend in Need. Address: Program Advancement Learning, Curry Coll Blue Hill Ave, Milton, MA 02186 2302, USA.

**WENINGER Mark Alexander,** b. 20 August 1962, Cleveland, Ohio, USA. Advertising and Marketing Executive. m. Julie Ann Jungels. Education: BA, summa cum laude, Borromeo College, Ohio, 1984. Career: Copywriter, Suarez Direct Incorporated, Canton, Ohio, 1984-86; Creative Group Head, Wyse Advertising Incorporated, Cleveland, Ohio, 1986-90; Group Creative Director, Cooperative Marketing Concepts Incorporated, Memphis, Tennessee, 1990-92; Vice President, Creative Director, Valentine Radford Advertising Incorporated, Kansas City, Missouri, 1992-94; Senior Vice President, Executive Creative Director Worldwide, Carlson Marketing Group Incorporated, Minneapolis, Minnesota, 1994-. Publication: More Facing Pages, Poems and More by Chris Holt and Friends, 1998. Honours: Spokesman for Freedom Award, Veterans of Foreign Awards, Washington, DC, 1980; Omni Award, Bronze (3), Kansas City Advertising Club, 1994; ARC Award, 1st Place Gold, Midwest Direct Marketing Association, 1996; Best of Category Award, Printing Industries of America, 1994; Pathfinder of the Year, Carlson Marketing Group, 1996; Presidents Award, Association of Graphic Communications, 1996; Echo Award, Silver, 1987, Bronze, 1994, 1996, 1997, Direct Marketing Association; Corporate Advertising of the Year, American Corporate Identity, 1998; 1st Place Trophies (6), Best of Category Trophies (4), Best of Show Trophy, The Astrid Awards, 1998; 1st Place Gold Statues (7), The Mobius International Advertising Awards, 1998; Gold Finalist, (2), New York Festivals, 1998. Memberships: American Institute of Graphic Arts; Direct Marketing Association; British Airways plc. Address: Carlson Marketing Group, 12755 Highway 55, Dept 8272, Minneapolis, MN 55441, USA.

**WERNER Yehudah Leopold,** b. 16 June 1931, Munich, Germany. Zoologist. m. Nurit Meyerstein, 1 son, 2 daughters. Education: MSc, 1956, PhD, 1961, Hebrew University of Jerusalem. Appointments: Assistant, 1953, to Professor, 1978-, Dept Zoology, Hebrew University of Jerusalem. Publications: Guide to the Reptiles and Amphibians of Israel, 1995; 280 assorted articles and papers mostly on reptiles 1948-98. Membership: Executive Committee, International Society of Morphologists. Address: Hebrew University of Jerusalem, 91904 Jerusalem, Israel.

**WERT Ned Oliver,** b. 26 May 1936, Sunbury, Pennsylvania, USA. Artist; Museum Director; Retired Professor. Education: BSEd Art, Indiana University of Pennsylvania, 1958; MEd Art, Pennsylvania University, 1964; Postgraduate, Kent University, 1970. Career: Artist, 1968-; Professor of Painting, 1970-88; Director, University Museum, Indiana, 1988-96. Honours: Outstanding Art Educator, National Art Education Association; Distinguished Service to the Arts, Indiana Arts Council; Carnegie Museum of Art Jurors Awards, twice. Memberships: Associated Artists of Pittsburgh; Pennsylvania Art Educators Fellow; Millersburg Historical Society; Friends of the University Museum, Indiana. Address: PO Box 1, Brush Valley, PA 15720, USA.

**WESOLOWSKI Andy,** b. 19 November 1953, Glogow, Poland. Computer Scientist. m. Margaret, 1 son, 1 daughter. Education: Technical Mechanics, Byogoszcz, Poland, 1968-73; Master Degree, 1973-79; National College of Education, 1983-85. Appointments: Wood Federation, Gdynia, Poland; Andres Fotolab, Chicago; Prismatec, USA. Address: 315-B Hawthorn, Glencoe, IL 60022, USA.

**WESSON Alphonzo,** b. 14 July 1960, Canton. Motion Picture Director. 1 son, 2 daughters. Education: PhD, University of Public Library. Appointments: Drama Instructor; Director, Film and Video Division; Senior Manager; Director, Proctor and Gamble Worldwide. Honours: 2 Emmys; 3 Tellys; 6 Angels.

Memberships: SMPTE; NATAS. Address: 637 Redna Ter, Cincinnati, OH 45215-1108, USA.

**WEST Roberta Bertha,** b. 7 September 1904, Farm, Saline Co, Missouri, USA. Educator; Writer. m. Harold C West, 3 daughters. Education: Graduate, Slater, Missouri. Appointment: Library Service. Publications: 3 publications 1972-75; North Montana Methodist History, 1971; Contributor to Upper Room, Methodist Encyclopaedia. Honour: Wedgewood Jasper Plate awarded at 70th anniversary of Class of 1927 by Wm Journalist College. Memberships: Missouri and Montana Educational Associations. Address: PO Box 583, Viburnum, MO 65566-0583, USA.

**WESTERBERG Siv,** b. 11 June 1932, Boraos, Sweden. Lawyer. m. Per Westerberg, 2 sons, 1 daughter. Education: Medicine Kandidat, 1954, Medicine Licentiat, 1960, University Uppsala; Juris kandidat, 1982, University of Lund. Appointments: Hospital Doctor, University Clinics in Gothenburg, Sweden, 1960-63; GP, Gothenburg, 1964-79; Lawyer, Gothenburg, 1982-; Specialised in medical and sociomedical cases; Tried and won several cases in the European Court of Human Rights. Publication: Book, To be a Physician, 1977. Memberships: Board of Nordisk Kommitte for Menneske-re forttigheder, Commission for critical investigation of unnecessary taking of children into public care in the Nordic Countries. Address: Skarsgatan 45, S-412 69, Goteborg, Sweden.

**WESTIN Steinar,** b. 21 June 1944, Oslo. Physician; Professor. m. (1) Rigmor Austgulen, 28 December 1970, divorced 1985, 1 son, 2 daughters, (2) Lise Skjaak Braek, 25 May 1991. Education: Medical School, University of Bergen, 1963-70; Wien/Fulbright Scholar, Brandeis University, Massachusetts, USA, 1966-67; MD, PhD, 1990, University Trondheim; Specialist of General Practice, 1986. Appointments: Junior Registrar, 1970-71, Research Fellow, 1972, Neevengaarden Psychiatric Hospital, Bergen; Intern, Haraldsplass Hospital, Bergen and Asköy district, 1973; General Practitioner, District Physician, Asköy district, 1973-78; Senior Lecturer, 1979-83, Associate Professor, 1983-90, Professor and Dept Chairman, 1990-, Dept of Community Medicine and General Practice, University Trondheim. Publications: Research in General Practice, 1983; The Educational Handbook for General Practitioners, 1985, 1996; Problem Solving in General Practice, 1987; Unemployment and Health, 1990; Becoming Disabled, 1990; Over 150 articles. Honours: Visiting Professor, Royal Australian College of General Practitioners, 1995. Memberships: Royal Norwegian Society of Sciences and Letters; Chairman Editorial Board, Journal of the Norwegian Medical Association; Editorial Board, British Medical Journal and European Journal of General Practice. Address: Deptartment of Community Medicine and General Practice, Norwegian University of Science & Technology, Medisinsk Teknisk Senter, N-7005, Trondheim, Norway.

**WESTLUND Hans Gustav,** b. 22 June 1957, Sweden. Researcher. m. Loulou Hasselquist, 1 daughter. Education: BA, Umea University, 1986; PhD, Economic History, Umea University, 1992. Appointments: Lecturer, Umea University, 1987-92, Mid-Sweden University, 1992-93; Communication Official, Jamtland County Administration, 1993-94; Researcher, Institute for Regional Research, 1993-; Researcher, 1994-95, Associate Professor, 1999-, Royal Institute of Technology, Stockholm; Researcher, Norwegian Institute for Regional and Urban Research, Oslo, 1997-98. Publication: Regional Development in Russia, 1999. Memberships: Swedish Historical Association; European Regional Science Association;

Western Regional Science Association. Address: Vallsjo 4552, SE 84064 Kalarne, Sweden.

**WEYHENMEYER Gesa Antonie,** b. 4 November 1969 Bonn, Germany. University Researcher. Education: Preliminary Diploma, Freiburg, Germany, 1991; Bachelor of Science Peterborough, Canada, 1992; Filosofie Liantiatsexamen, 1995 PhD, 1996, Uppsala, Sweden. Appointments: Aquatic Ecologist, European Union Project Response of Freshwater Lakes to Environmental and Climatic Change. Publications: In Limnology and Oceanography; Many publications reviewed in international journals. Honours: Several major research grants Memberships: ASLO; AGU; SIL. Address: Erken Laboratory Uppsala University, Norr Malma 4200, 76173 Norrtälje Sweden.

**WHALEY Lucille,** b. 17 May 1923, Garfield. Nursing Consultant; Educator. m. 2 daughters. Education: Diploma, S Marks Hospital School Nursing, Salt Lake City, 1944; BS, Sar Jose State College, 1962; MSu California, San Francisco 1963; EdD University of South, California, 1986; Professo Emeritus Nursing, San Jose State University, 1963-83 Appointments: Consultant, private practice, Sunnyvale California, 1974-. Publications: Author of 11 major nursing textbooks; Contributor of articles to professional journals books. Memberships: ANA, California Nurses Association Sigma Theta Tau. Address: 1652 Lachine Dr, Sunnyvale, CA 940876-4207, USA.

**WHELAN James R,** b. 27 July 1933, Buffalo, New York USA. Author; Business Executive. m. Guadalupe Aguirre Whelan, 1 son, 1 daughter. Education: BA, Florida Internationa University, 1972; Nieman Fellow, Harvard University, 1966-67 Appointments: United Press (International), 1953-67; ITT 1968-70; Managing Editor, Miami News, 1970-73; Editor Sacramento Union, 1980-82; Founding Editor, Publisher, CEO Washington Times, 1982-85; Silver Standard Resources President, Latin America, 1994, President (inter alia) Publications: Books: Through the American Looking Glass Central America's Crisis, 1980; Allende: Death of a Marxist Dream, 1981; Catastrophe in the Caribbean: The Failure of America's Human Rights Policy in Central America, 1984; The Soviet Assault on America's Southern Flank, 1988; Out of the Ashes: Life, Death and Transfiguration of Democracy in Chile 1833-1988, 1988; Hunters in the Sky, 1991; Hundreds of articles in newspapers, magazines and academic journals in dozens of countries in North and South America and Europe. Memberships: Harvard Club, New York City; Cosmos Club Washington; Board, Latin American Journalism Center; Institute O'Higginiano (Chile), Council on National Policy. Address: Orquideas 163 Bugambilias, Saltillo, Coahuila 25296, Mexico.

**WHINERY Linda,** b. 12 February 1949, Phoenix, Arizona, USA. Psychotherapist. m. Marvin R Whinery, 1 son, 2 daughters. Education: BS, University of Arizona; MS, Counselling, California University, Long Beach. Appointments: Rehabilitation Counsellor, Easter Seals; Director, Juvenile Division, Police Department, 1976-80; Private Therapist, Tucson, 1988-. Honour: Guest Lecturer, Chapman College, Arizona State University. Membership: Juvenile Officers Association. Address: 7321 East Wikieup Circle, Tucson, AZ 85750, USA.

**WHITE Ian,** b. 5 August 1943, Woonona, Australia. Professor. m. Elaine Lesley Le Meuri, 1 son, 3 daughters. Education: BSc, University of Sydney, 1964; MSc, University of Sydney, 1966; PhD, University of Sydney, 1971. Appointments: Research Chemist, Rochester Institute of Technology, 1970-72; Research Associate, University of Pennsylvania, 1972-74;

Research Scientist, CSIRO Australia, 1974-96; Professor, ANU, 1996-. Honours: Burton Medal, ACT Hydrol Society, 1994, 1998. Memberships: American Geophysics Union; Soil Society of America; Australian Soil Science Society; Australian Water Waste Water Association. Address: Australian National University, Canberra, ACT 0200, Australia.

**WHITE John Kenneth,** b. 10 October 1952, Providence, Rhode Island, USA. Professor; Author. m. Yvonne, 1 daughter. Education: BA, University Rhode Island, 1975; MA, University of Connecticut, 1976; PhD, 1980. Appointments: Professor, SUNY Potsdam, New York, 1980-88; Professor, Catholic University of America, Washington, DC, 1988-. Publications: Still Seeing Red; The New Politics of Old Values. Honours: Carnegie Association, Washington, DC; Professor of the Year, 1997. Memberships: American Political Science Association; Center for Party Development. Address: Dept Politics, Catholic University of America, Washington, DC 20036, USA.

**WHITE Judith Mary,** b. 7 January 1933, Sydney, Australia. Author; Publisher. m. Michael F White, 5 sons, 2 daughters. Education: BEc. 1956; MLitt, 1984; MA, Honoris Causa, 1988. Appointments: Boards, Australian Elizabethan Theatre Trust; Hunter Economic Development Corp; Hunter Institute of Technology; Hunter Valley Research Foundation; Upper Hunter Development Team, Business Enterprise Centre. Publications: 8 books; Belltrees; Memories Sydney, 1920-60; Memories Country NSW, 1920-60; Memories Sydney, 1920-60; S W Jackson; Family Album. Memberships: Royal Sydney Golf Club; Royal Australian Historical Society; Royal Agricultural Society. Address: Belltrees, Scone, NSW 2337, Australia.

**WHITE Ralph Ernest Jr,** b. 1 March 1921, Minneapolis, Minnesota, USA. Artist; Professor. m. Ruby Irene Bergherr, 2 sons, 1 daughter. Education: Minneapolis School of Art, 1942; Van Der Lip Fellow, 1942; Pratt Institute, New York City, USA, 1946. Appointments: Professor, University of Texas, Austin, USA, 1946-82; Professor Emeritus, 1983-. Publications: Over 100 exhibitions; Solo shows; Major collections, US, UK. Address: 4701 Agarita Road, Austin, TX 78734, USA.

**WHITE Sallie Vine,** b. 22 June 1959, Birmingham, Alabama, USA. Professional Educator; Musician. m. Noah White, 1 son, 2 daughters. Education: BA, Anderson College, Anderson, Indiana, 1982; Masters of Music Education, Indiana University, Bloomington, Indiana, 1985. Appointments: Assistant Band Director, Jess Lanier High School, Bessemer Alabama, 1982-84; Band Director Davis Middle School, Bessemer, Alabama, 1982-84; Associate Instructor, Music Education, Indiana University, 1984-85; Jazz Band Instructor, University of Montevallo, Alabama, 1987-88, University of Alabama at Birmingham, 1988-94, Jess Lanier High School, 1987-89; Assistant Band Director, 1987-89, Band Director, 1989-90, Jess Lanier High School; Choir Director, Riverchase South Church, Hoover, Alabama, 1990-; Saxophone Instructor, Samford University, Birmingham, Alabama, 1990-; Jazz and Concert Band Director, Hoover High School, Hoover, Alabama, 1990-; Band Director, Simmons Middle School, Hoover, Alabama, 1990-; Many professional engagements including: Anderson, Indiana Symphony; Bill Gaither Trio; Superjazz Ensemble; Summerfest Orchestra; Engagements with Bob Hope, Stevie Wonder, Glen Campbell; Andy Williams and many others. Honours: Magna Cum Laude; Undergraduate Honours in Psychology; National Dean's List; Pi Kappa Lambda; Fiesta Marching Band, 3rd Place, Phoenix, Arizona; First Place, Orange Bowl Marching Band Award, Miami, Florida. Memberships: Alabama Band Masters Association; International Association of Jazz Education; American Federation of Musicians, Music Educators National Conference; National League of American Women. Address: 411 Valley Lake Drive, Birmingham, Alabama, AL 35206, USA

**WHITE Sally Ann,** b. 20 January 1961, England. University Professor. Education: BEd, 1983; MS, 1985; PhD, 1988. Appointments: Assistant Professor, University New Hampshire and Illinois State University, 1988-93; Assistant Dean, College of Applied Science and Technology, 1993-98; Associate Dean, Graduate School Towson University, 1998-. Publications: 24 refereed publications; 65 international and national refereed presentations. Memberships: Fellow, AAHPERD; AAASP; Member, NCURA; CGS; NASPSPA. Address: Illinois State University, 227 F Horton Fieldhouse, Normal, IL 61790-5120, USA.

**WHITEHORN-RANDAZZO Willa Elizabeth,** b. 15 May 1954, New Orleans, Louisiana, USA. Public Accountant. Education: Bachelor of Arts, University of New Orleans, 1976; Bachelor of Science, University of New Orleans; Certified Public Accountant, State of Louisianna, 1981. Appointments: Book Keeper, Office Manager, French Quarter hotel, 1975-78; Parson-Gilbane, 1978-79; Accounting, Tax Pratice, 1979-83; Public Accountant, 1983-. Memberships: Daughters of American Revolution Francois Delery Chapter; Louisiana Society of Certified Public Accountants. Address: 3108 Cleary Ave Ste 108, Metairie, LA 70002-5755, USA.

**WICKER Franklin Michael,** b. 6 March 1924, St Paul, USA. Financial Advisor; Analyst; Consultant; Builder. m. Alice M Wicker. Education: BA, Macalester College, 1948; Financial Planner, 1948. Appointments: Fuel Coordinator, Central Pacific, US Navy Air Corps, 1943-46; Investment Trustee, St James Luth Church, St Paul, 1974-86; Small Business Counsellor, US Government, 1979-. Honours: Several in Financial Planning. Memberships: International Association for Financial Planning; SBA. Address: 9991 Oak Shore Drive, Lakeville, MN 55044-7655, USA.

**WIEDEMANN Ramona Diane Fay,** b. 1 October 1962, Topeka, Kansas. Occupational Therapist; Registered OTR. m. Bill Wiedemann, 3 sons, 2 daughters. Education: BSc Occupational Therapy, 1988. Appointments: Healthcare Staff Resources, 1988-91; OTR in psychiatric setting, Associated Rehabilitation Services, 1991-; OTR in nursing homes, Out-Patient rehab, in house rehab, paediatric OT in schools, homehealth. Memberships: American Occupational Therapy Association; International Platform Association. Address: 210 Winding Creek Drive, Highland Village, TX 75077, USA.

**WIEDMER Terry Lynn Boyer,** b. 15 February 1951, Missoula, Montana, USA. Education: Education: BA, Elementary Education, University of Montana, 1972; ME, Educational Administration, 1975; EdD, 1983. Appointments: 1st Grade Teacher, 1972; 2nd Grade Teacher, 1972-76; 4th Grade Teacher, 1976-77; Graduate Teaching Assistant, 4th Grade Teacher, 1977-82; Grades 7 and 8, Mathematics, Computer Teacher, 1983-84; Administrative Assistant, 1984-85; Post Doctoral Study, Research, 1984-85; Adjunct Assistant Professor, 1984-85; Principal, Computer Education Coordinator, 1985-87; Administrative Assistant, 1987-92; IASCW Executive Secretary, 1992-94; Director, Resource Center for Educational Services, 1992-95; Executive Director, National State Teachers of the Year, 1993-95; Director, INSPRA Public Relations, 1995-96; Vice President, Indianna School Public Relations Association, 1996-97; Director of NSTOY Membership, 1996-97; Executive Secretary, Upper Wabash Valley School Study Council, 1995-; Assistant Professor, Educational Leaderships Department, 1992-98; Associate Professor, Ball State University, 1998-. Publications:

Book Chapter; Many Articles, Professional Journals; Book Reviews; 2 Books. Honours: Phi Delta Kappa International; Outstanding People of the 20th Century, International Biographical Centre; Service to Education Award; Service to Society Award; Many other honours. Memberships: American Association of Colleges for Teacher Education; American Association of University Women; Many other memberships. Address: 1923 E Robinwood Dr, Muncie, IN 47304-2854, USA.

**WIENER Stan,** b. 24 March 1950, Ceska, Lipa. m. Vladimira, 3 sons, 2 daughters. Education: University of Economy. Appointments: General Manager, Consultant, Compass CPC Knorr, Grand Metropolitan, P and O Transeuropean. Honours: Best Services, Madrid, 1996. Memberships: Chamber of Commerce, UK in Prague. Address: SW Consulting, Hrebenka 490, 473 01 Novy BOR, Czech Republic.

**WIERCINSKI Andrzej Kazimierz,** b. 22 April 1930, Chorzow, Poland. Anthropologist. m. Alina Morat, 2 sons, 1 daughter. Education: MSc, University of Warsaw, 1951; PhD, University of Lodz, 1957; Doc Habil, University of Wroclaw, 1968. Appointments: Assistant, Department of Anthropology, 1950-68, Assistant Professor, 1968-78, Full Professor, Head of Department of Historical Anthropology, 1978-, Warsaw University; Head, Department of General Anthropology, Pedagogical University of Kielce. Publications: 170 publications. Honours: Gold Cross of Merit, 1973; Polonia Restituta Cross, 1980; Medal of National Education. 1980; Honorary Member, Ligurian Academy of Sciences and Letters, Genoa, Italy, 1991; Fellow, Explorers Club of New York, 1993. Memberships: Polish Anthropological Society; European Anthropological Association; Polish Society for Jewish Studies. Address: Department of Historical Anthropology, University of Warsaw, ul Krakowskie Przediniescie 26/28, 00-325 Warsaw, Poland.

**WIJESINGHE Bandupala,** b. 18 January 1948, Sri Lanka. Process Engineer. m. Marthupitiya Epage, 3 daughters. Education: MSc, Mendeleev Institute, Moscow, 1973; PhD, 1976; MBA, 1997. Appointments: Lecturer, Senior Lecturer, University of Moratuwa, Sri Lanka, 1977-88; Research Fellow, University of Karlsruhe, Germany, 1981-82; Research Engineer, University of New South Wales, Sydney, 1989-93; Executive Engineer, DPI, Queensland, Australia, 1992-. Publications: Over 20 Publications. Honours: Fellowship Awards from USSR, Germany and Canada. Memberships: Institution of Engineers; Association of Professional Engineers, Scientists and Managers. Address: Centre for Food Technology, 19 Hercules Str, Hamilton, Queensland, Brisbane 4007, Australia.

**WILAIRAT Prapon,** b. 30 June 1944, Bangkok, Thailand. University Faculty. m. Mullika Wilairat, 1 son. Education: BSc, Honours, Chemistry, Australian National University, 1966; PhD, Biochemistry, University of Oregon, USA, 1974. Appointments: Chairman, Department of Biochemistry, Faculty of Science, Mahidol University, 1988-91; Chairman, Biochemistry Section, Science Society of Thailand, 1988-89; Editor, Journal of the Science Society of Thailand, 1990-91; Editorial Board, Journal of the Science Society of Thailand, 1975-; Editorial Board, Asia Pacific Journal of Molecular Biology and Biotechnology, 1992-. Publications: Over 80 publications. Honours: Australian Government Colombo Plan Undergraduate Scholarship, 1963-66; Rockefeller Foundation Pre-doctoral Fellowship, 1967-73; Mahidol University Prize in Research, shared, 1987; Mahidol University Prize in Teaching, 1993; National Research Council of Thailand First Prize for Invention, shared, 1996; National Research Council of Thailand Outstanding

Researcher, 1996; Thailand Research Fund Senior Research Scholar Award, 1996; Thailand Outstanding Scientist, 1997. Address: Department of Biochemistry, Faculty of Science, Mahidol University, Rama 6 Road, Bangkok 10400, Thailand.

**WILCZYNSKI Krzysztof,** b. 5 September 1953, Bydgoszcz, Poland. Researcher. m. Gertruda Barbara Wilczynska, 2 sons. Education: MSc, Bydgoszcz University of Technology, 1978; PhD, 1982, DSc, 1990, Warsaw University of Technology. Appointments: Adjunct Professor, 1983-89, Associate Professor, 1990-94, Professor, 1994-, Head, Polymer Processing Institute, 1994-, Warsaw University of Technology; Visiting Professor, Kyushu Institute of Technology, Kitakyushu, Japan, 1990-91; Visiting Professor, Stevens Institute of Technology, Hoboken, New Jersey, USA, 1993. Publications: Books: Theory of Polymer Single-Screw Extrusion; Handbook of Polymer Science, co-author; Contributions to journals on polymer science. Memberships: The Society of Rheology; Polymer Processing Society; Society of Plastics Engineers. Address: Zamoyskiego 13/6, 85-063 Bydgoszcz, Poland.

**WILDE Alan Conrad,** b. 30 March 1946, Baltimore, Maryland, USA. Mathematician. Education: BS honours, Mathematics, College of Literature, Science and the Arts, 1970, MA, Mathematics, Rackham School of Graduate Studies, 1973, University of Michigan, Ann Arbor. Appointments: Independent Study Teacher, Department of Mathematics and Extension Service, University of Michigan, 1966-; Private Practice, Ann Arbor, 1992-. Publications: Articles in American Mathematical Monthly, Journal of Undergraduate Mathematics, Notre Dame Journal of Formal Logic, Rocky Mountain Journal of Mathematics, Pi Mu Epsilon Journal, Proceedings of the American Mathematical Society, Journal of the University of Kuwait, Atti del Seminario Matematico e Fisico dell'Università di Modena, Rivista di Matematica della Università di Parma, Linear Algebra and Its Applications, Journal of the Technical University of Plovdiv, including: Solutions of equations containing primitive roots of unity, 1971; Generalizations of the distributive and associative laws, 1974; Complex matrices and polynomials, 1984; Algebras of operators isomorphic to the circulant algebra, 1989; Generalized trigonometric functions, circulant matrices, and Fermat's Last Theorem, 1992; Nearly commuting projections, 1993. Honours: Silver Medal, Michigan Mathematics Prize Competition Examination, 1963; 1st Prize in Mathematics, 4th Prize overall and Navy Science Cruise, Southeastern Michigan Science Fair, 1964; Regional Award, Future Scientists of America, 1964. Memberships: Co-Chair, Committee to Aid Disabled Students, University of Michigan, 1972-73, Chair, Disabled Student Services Programme Policy Board, 1973; Homeless Action Committee, Ann Arbor, 1990-97; American Association for the Advancement of Science, 1996; New York Academy of Sciences, 1997. Address: 601 Pearl, Ypsilanti, MI 48197-2616, USA.

**WILKIN Karen,** b. New York, New York, USA. Independent Curator; Critic. m. Donald Clinton. Education: BA, cum laude, Barnard College; MFA, Columbia University. Appointments: Chief Curator, The Edmonton Art Gallery, Edmonton, Canada, 1971-78; Independent Curator, Critic, 1978-. Publications: Books: Modern Painting in Canada, co-author Terry Fenton, 1978; Jack Bush, editor, contributor, 1984; David Smith, 1984; Frankenthaler on Paper, 1985; Stuart Davis, 1987; Kenneth Noland, 1990; Anthony Caro, 1991; Georges Braque, 1992; Paul Cézanne, 1996; Giorgio Morandi, 1998; Isaac Witkin, 1998; Contributor: Abstract Painting and Sculpture in America: 1927-44, 1983; The Canadian Encyclopaedia, 1985; Contemporary Artists; The Dictionary of Art, 1996; Stuart Davis: American Painter, 1991; Stuart Davis: A Retrospective, 1997. Memberships: International Association of Art Critics; PEN;

College Art Association. Address: 28 W 38th Street, New York, NY 10018, USA.

**WILKINS Daniel Chaim,** b. 28 April 1947, New York, New York, USA. Physicist. Education: BA, Amherst College, 1967; MS, Stanford University, 1968; PhD, Stanford University, 1972. Appointments: Postdoctoral Fellow, USA, India, Europe, 1972-81; Assistant Professor, University of Nebraska and Oakland University, 1981-89; Associate Professor, University of Nebraska, 1989-. Publications: About 2 dozen articles published in professional journals, mostly on gravity or astronomy/astrophysics. Memberships: NSF Traineeship, Stanford University, 1967-68; Sigma Xi 1982; Graduate Faculty Fellow, UNO, 1984; NASA-ASEE Summer Faculty Fellow, 1985-86; NASA Jove Fellow, 1991-94. Address: Department Physics, University Nebraska, 60th and Dodge, Omaha, NE 68182, USA.

**WILLIAMS Lawrence A D,** b. 5 October 1962, Siloah, St Elizabeth, Jamaica. Researcher. m. Lisa Simone Caleb. Education: BSc Hons, University of the West Indies, Kingston, Jamaica, 1987; PhD, 1992. Appointments: Scientific Officer, Scientific Research Council, Jamaica, 1987-92; Post Doctoral, University of the West Indies, Jamaica, 1993-94; Assistant Lecturer, 1994-95; Lecturer, 1995-. Publications: Phyto Chemistry; Pesticide Science. Honours: Caribbean and Third World Academy Award. Memberships: Jamaica Society of Scientists and Technologists; Jamaica Natural History Society; New York Academy of Sciences. Address: Department of Chemistry, University of the West Indies, Mona Campus, Kingston 7, Jamaica.

**WILLIAMS Mark Leon,** b. 25 July 1953, Portsmouth, Virginia, USA. Behavioral Scientist. Education: BGS, University of Iowa; MA, University of Nebraska, Lincoln, NE, USA; PhD, University of Iowa. Appointments: Assistant Professor, University of St Thomas; Vice President, Behavioral Research, Nova Research Company; Adjunct Assistant Professor, University of Miami; Adjunct Assistant Professor, University of Texas. Publications: over 50 articles and book chapters. Membership: American Public Health Association. Address: NOVA Research Company, 1214 Alabama Street, Houston, TX 77006, USA.

**WILLIAMS-PFISTER Gail,** b. 6 May 1936, Seattle, Washington, USA. Economist; Educator; Author. m. Cloyd H Pfister, 1 son, 1 daughter. Education: BA Economics, 1957, Oberlin College; MAT History magna cum laude, 1968, Fairleigh Dickinson University; Graduate Studies Economics, 1972, McGill University; MA Economics, 1976, New York University. Appointments: Teacher & Instructor Economics, 1957-79; Assistant Professor Economics, George Mason University, 1979-82; Lecturer in Economics and History, University of Maryland, European Division, 1982-84; Lecturer in Economics: University of Arizona, 1984-86, University So Florida, 1986-88, Marymount University and USDA Graduate School, 1989-96; Review Boards Health and Human Services, 1992-96. Publications include: Multinational Corporations: Problems and Prospects, 1975, 1976, 1982; Economists in the Job Market, 1984; The Multinational Dragons, 1976; Multinationals: Friends or Foes, 1975; The US Trade Deficit - Long Term, 1990. Honours: Certificate of Merit, NJ Institute of Technology, 1976; President, US Award for Outstanding Contributions to the White House Conference on Small Business, 1980; Outstanding Civilian Service Medal, US Dept of the Army, 1994. Memberships: Middle East Institute; World Affairs Council; AAUW; AEA. Address: 4653 Kirkpatrick Lane, Alexandria, VA 22311, USA.

**WILLIS Barbara,** b. 17 December 1932, Bronx, New York, USA. Artist. m. Sidney F Willis, 2 sons. Education: Vesper George School of Art, Boston. Career: Artist. Honours: Over 15 awards, including Master Pastelist Designation from PSA, 1995. Memberships: American Artists Professional League, Inc, New York, New York; Pastel Society of America; Academic Artists Association, Springfield; Copley Society, Boston; New Hampshire Art Association; Allied Artists of America; Audubon Artists, New York; Connecticut Pastel Society. Address; 64 State Route 202, Bennington, NH 03442, USA.

**WILLIS Sidney.** Education: Graduate, Vesper George School of Art, Boston, Massachusetts, USA; Further study under Robert Douglas Hunter. Appointments: Teaching positions: Franklin Pierce College; Sharon Art Center; Vesper George Art School; Artist, Boston School. Honours: Four Gold Medals, Jordan Show, Boston, Massachusetts; Still Life Prize, Pastel Society of America Show, 1990; The Vayana Memorial Grand Prize, Ogunquit Art Center, Maine; Still Life Prize, Pastel Society of America Show, 1990; Still Life Prize, Ellsworth Gallery, Simsbury, Connecticut; Acrylic Prize, Cape Cod Art Association, Barnstable, Massachusetts; Gold Medal, Heritage Salon Invitational, Alexandria, Virginia, 1988. Memberships: Guild of Boston Artists; Pastel Society of America; The Southern Vermont Art Association; The American Artists Professional League; The New Hampshire Art Association; The Copley Society. Address: 64 Rte 202, Bennington, NH 03442, USA.

**WILSON Ben,** b. 23 June 1913, Philadelphia, USA. Lecturer. m. Evelyn, 1 daughter. Education: National Academy of Design, 1931-34; BS, City University, New York, 1935; Academy Julien, 1953-54. Appointments: Art Instructor, Franklin School of Design, New York; Lecturer, Art, New York University. Honours: Ford Foundation Grant, 1965; Artist in Residence, Everhart Museum; Milhouse Bundy Foundation. Memberships: Modern Artists Guild; Association of Artists of New Jersey. Address: 2720 Herwald Street, Sarasota, FL 34231-5116, USA.

**WILSON Elizabeth Hornabrook (Lady),** b. 25 January 1907, Adelaide, South Australia, Australia. Former Member of Voluntary Organisations. m. Keith Cameron Wilson, dec, 2 sons, 1 daughter. Appointments: Chairman, 1951-54, Chairman, National Committee, 1952-59, 1967-70, Victoria League for Commonwealth Friendship, South Australia. Honours: MBE, 1946; CBE, 1959. Memberships: Royal Commonwealth Society; Chairman, SA Division, Red Cross, 1968-71; Chairman, Joint Commonwealth Societies Council in South Australia, 1970-73; Executive Member, Australia Red Cross Society; Commandant, Red Cross Aids, South Australia Division; President, Tusmore Red Cross Branch; Central Committee, Mothers and Babies Health Association; Volunteer Association of the Child and Family Health Services; Burnside War Memorial Hospital Board; Founding President, Milpara Nursing Home Auxiliary; Patron, Civilian Widows Association. Address: 79 Tusmore Avenue, Tusmore, South Australia 5065, Australia.

**WILSON Geraldine,** b. 18 October 1933, Hartford, Connecticut, USA. Psychologist. m. Richard T, 4 daughters. Education: BA, Mary Mount College, 6th Year; Diploma of Advanced Studies, 1976, Southern Connecticut State University; MS, 1971. Appointments: Social Worker, 1956-58; School Psychologist, 1971-95; Private Practice, 1995-. Honours: Practitioner of the Year, 1995; Nationally Certified School Psychologist, 1989. Memberships: NASP; CASP. Address: 51 Stillson Rd, Southbury, CT 06488-1116, USA.

**WINDHAGER Reinhard,** b. 13 September 1957, Linz. Physician. m. Silvia Windhager, 1 son, 1 daughter. Education: MD, 1981, University Innsbruck. Appointments: Resident, General Hospital, Linz, 1982-84; Resident, 1982-84, Consultant, 1988-91, Dept of Orthopaedics, University of Vienna; Assistant Professor, 1991-95, Associate Professor, 1995-97, Professor and Chairman of Orthopaedic Surgery, 1997-, Dept of Orthopaedics, University of Graz. Honours: Recipient, M Jaegar Award, Society of Orthopaedic Sport Medicine, 1986; Austrian Society of Radiology Award, 1994; Lorenz-Bohler Foundation Grantee, 1990; Patent Automatic growing prosthesis, 1992. Memberships: European Musculo-Skeletal Oncology Society; New York Academy of Science. Address: Budinskygasse 9/19, A-1190 Vienna, Austria.

**WINDHAUSER John W,** b. 30 January 1943, College Teacher. 1 son. Education: PhD, Ohio University, 1975. Appointments: Professor, Louisana State University. Publications: 100 plus research papers and articles. Address: 2826 Dakin Avenue, Baton Rouge, LA 70820, USA.

**WININGS Kathy,** Education: BA, Media Communications; Professional Degree, Elementary Education, Forham University, Summa Cum Laude; Fordham's Elementary Education Program; MRE M Divinity; Doctor of Education. Appointments: Assistant Professor, Religious Education and Ministry Unification Theological Seminary, 1990-; Instructor, College of New Rochelle, 1990-92; National Co-Director, Unification Campus Ministry Association, New York, 1990-94; Director, Ecumenical Affairs for HSA UWC, 1992-98; Executive Director, International Relief Friendship Foundation, New York, 1994-; National Educational Consultant, World CARP, New York, 1994-97; Director, National Youth Ministry Program Family Federation for World Peace, 1995-; Senior Developer, Designer, Curriculum Unification, Church of America, 1995-; Founder, President, Educare, Tarrytown, New York, 1998-; Director, Doctor of Ministry Program, Unification Theological Seminary, 1997-. Publications: Building Character Through Service Learning; Christian Traditions in America; Many Articles and Book Chapters. Honours: Kappa Delta Pi. Memberships: American Academy of Religion; Association for Doctor of Ministry Education; Association of Professors and Researchers of Religious Education; Association for Theological Field Education; Religious Education Association; National Association of Ecumenical Staff; Association of University Women. Address: 177 White Plains Road, Tarrytown, NY 10591, USA.

**WININGS Kathy,** b. 4 April 1953, Indianapolis, Indiana, USA. Educator; Humanitarian Aid. Education: BA (summa cum laude), Elementary Education, Media Communications, Fordham University; MRE/MDivinity; Doctor of Education, Religion and Education Teachers College, GPA, 3.199. Appointments include: Assistant Professor, Religious Education and Ministry Unification Theological Seminary, Barrytown, New York, 1990-; Director, Ecumenical Affairs for HSA-UWC, 1992-; Executive Director, International Relief Friendship Foundation, New York, 1994-; National Educational Consultant, World CARP, 1994-; Director, National Youth Ministry Program, Family Federation for World Peace, 1995-; Senior Developer and Designer, Curriculum HSA - UWC, 1995-; Director, Doctor of Ministry program Unification Seminary, Barrytown, New York, 1997-; Founder, President, Edcare, Tarrytown, New York, 1998-. Publications: Mind and Body: The Role of Service Learning in the Curriculum, 1999; articles, conference papers, curriculum materials. Honour: Kappa Delta Pi. Memberships: Association of Professors and Researchers of Religious Education; Religous Education Association; National

Association of Ecumenical Staff; Aassociation of University Women; American Academy of Education; Association c Doctors of Ministry Education; Association of Theological Fiel Education. Address: 177 White Plains Road, 50F, Tarrytown NY 10591, USA.

**WINKELMANN John Paul,** b. 14 September 1933, St Louis Missouri, USA. Pharmacist. m. Margaret Ann Grandy, 5 sons Education: BSc, 1955; BSc Pharmacy, 1960; Doctor c Pharmacy, 1972; DSc, 1972. Appointments: Captain, US Ai Force Reserve, (Retired); President and Chief Pharmacist Winkelmann Apothecary Ltd, professional prescriptior pharmacy, Founding Member, 1962, President, 1968-70 1979-83, 1985-, Executive Director, 1970-; Editor, Nationa Catholic Pharmacists Guild of the US, 1968-. Publications History of the St Louis College of Pharmacy, 1964; Catholic Pharmacy, 1966; Founding Editor, The Catholic Pharmacis Quarterly Journal, 1968-; Over 500 professional articles Memberships: Board of Trustees, St Louis College o Pharmacy, 1961-83; Appointed by Governor as Charte Member, Missouri Statewide Professional Services Rewview Organisation Commission, 1976-. Address: 1012 Surrey Hills Drive, St Louis, MO 63117-1438, USA.

**WINSTIN Robert Ian,** b. 6 June 1959, Chicao, Illinois, USA Composer; Conductor. m. Judy Ann Poklenkowski. Education Roosevelt University, Chicago Musical College, 1977-81 University of Colorado at Boulder, 1981-83; Advanced Studies at the Foundation for New Music, 1984-85, and the Centre for Contemporary Music, 1990-91. Appointments: Composer in Residence, Classical Symphony, 1995-98; Music Director and Principal Conductor, The Derriere Guard Festival Orchestra 1998; Music Director and Principal Conductor, Millenium Orchestra, 1998; Metropolis Youth Symphony, 1999. Publications: Numerous works published and recorded on CD's; Works in magazines, books, records, CD's etc. Honour Barrettson Prize for American Music, 1990; First American Composer/Pianist to perform in China, 1995. Memberships Executive Director, Foundation for New Music; ASCAP Conductor's Guild. Address: Editions de la Rue Margot, 3712 Broadway St #264, Chicago, IL 60613-4105, USA.

**WINTER Susan Hettel,** b. USA. Health Care Professional. Education: Michigan University, East Lansing; Summers National Music Camp, Interlochen, Michigan. Appointments: Researcher, Washington University Medical School, 10 years; Open Heart Surgery Team, Saint Louis University Medical Hospital, 1 year; Health Care Professional, Jewish Hospital, Saint Louis, Missouri. Publications: Poetry in books, journals and magazines. Memberships: International Society of Poets. Address: PO Box 16021, Saint Louis, MO 63105, USA.

**WISE Stephen,** b. 26 November 1939, Seattle, Washington, USA. Teacher. m. Jeanne Marie Wise, 2 daughters. Education: BA, Education, Indiana University, 1963; MA, Art, San Jose State University, 1966. Appointments: College Art Teacher, 1964-67; Secondary Art Teacher, 1968-. Creative Works: Many one person art shows in the Bay Area and nationwide; Group Shows include: 85th Annual National Exhibition, Museum of Art, San Francisco; Owens Corning Fiberglas Corporation, Santa Clara, California; Pavilion Gallery, Los Gatos, California; Discovery Gallery, San Jose; Ages Gallery, San Jose; Greenleaf Gallery, Saratoga; The San Jose Art Museum. Memberships: Society of Western Artists; National Education Association; California Teachers Association; Los Gatos Art Association. Address: 4383 Glenmont Drive, San Jose, CA 95136-1747, USA.

**WISEMAN Gloria,** b. Manhattan, New York, USA. Physician. Education: BS, CUNY, 1977; MD, Columbia University, 1981. Career: Intern, Resident, Pediatrics, New York University Medical Center, 1981-84, Teaching Assistant, 1983-84; Neonatal-Perinatal Medicine Fellow, Babies Hospital, Columbia University, 1984-86, Assistant Pediatrician, 1984-86, Staff Associate, 1984-86, Babies Hospital; Instructor, University of Medicine & Dentistry of New Jersey, New Jersey Medical School, 1986-87, Assistant Professor, Clinical Pediatrics, 1987-88; Neonatology, Pediatric Attending Physician, University Hospital of New Jersey, 1986-88; Research Fellow, Allergy & Immunology, Albert Einstein College of Medicine, Bronx, New York, 1988-91; Fellow, Weiler Hospital, Albert Einstein College of Medicine, Bronx, 1988-91; Director, Neonatal-Perinatal Medicine, Englewood (NJ) Hospital, 1991-96, Holy Name Hospital, New Jersey, 1996-; Assistant, Newborn Medicine, Mount Sinai Babies and Childrens Hospital of New York, New York City, 1991-; Attending Physician, Columbia-Presbyterian Medical Center, New York City, 1996-; Assistant Professor, Columbia University, New York City, 1996-. Honours include: Diploma of Honor; Order of Merit, Womens Inner Circle of Achievement. Memberships include: New York Perinatal Society; Babies Hospital Alumni Association; New York University Pediatric Alumni Association; Phi Beta Kappa. Address: 570 Fort Washington Avenue, New York, NY 10033, USA.

**WITHERSPOON John Thomas,** b. 25 June 1947, Springfield, Missouri, USA. Water Resources Manager. m. C Frances. Education: BS, Southwest Missouri State University, 1969; MA, 1971; PhD, University of Montana, 1975. Appointments: Water Pollution Control Inspector, City of Springfield, 1976-78; City Utilities of Springfield, Maryland, Laboratory Director, 1978-91; Manager, Water Treatment and Supply, 1991-. Honours: Chair, Missouri Safe Drinking Water Commision, 1995-; Boyd Utility Manager Award, American Water Works Association, 1996; Chair, Missouri Section, American Waterworks Association, 1997. Memberships: Watershed Committee of the Ozarks, 1983-; University Club President, 1989. Address: 1927 E Lark St, Springfield, MO 65804-4345, USA.

**WLODARSKI Ziemowit Franciszek,** b. 5 January 1925, Poznan, Poland. Psychologist; Researcher; Educator. Education: Master in Psychology, Warsaw University, 1949; Dr in Psychology, Warsaw University, 1958; Associate Professor, Psychology, 1959; Professor, 1964; Full Professor, 1980. Appointments: Teacher, Elementary and Secondary Schools, 1945-57; Psychologist Guiding Centers, 1948-57; Assistant Associate Professor, Psychology, Nencki Institute, Biology, 1956-61; Associate Professor, Full Professor, Psychology, Warsaw University, 1959-; Full Professor, Psychology, Emeritus, Warsaw University, 1997-; Full Professor, Psychology, Higher School Education, Warsaw, 1997-. Publications: The Reception of Information in the Learning Process, 1978, 1983; Psychology of Learning, 1989, 1998; Secrets of Human Memory, 1985, 1990; Educational Psychology, co-author, 1978, 1998; Editor, bimonthly journal, Psychologia Wychowawcza, Educational Psychology, 1978-. Address: ul Hoza 5/7 m 36, 00-528 Warsaw, Poland.

**WNENDT Stephan,** b. 2 October 1962, Detrold. Biochemist. m. Petra, 2 daughters. Education: Diploma, Biochemistry, Free University Berlin, 1987; Doctorate, University of Technology, Berlin, 1991. Appointments: Head of Research Lab, Aachen, 1991-95; Head of Department of Molecular Pharmacology, 1995-. Publications: About 20 Papers, Peer reviewed journals. Memberships: New York Academy of Sciences; Society for Neuroscience. Address: Adenauer Allee 203, 52066 Aachen, Germany.

**WOELFEL Joseph Donald,** b. 3 June 1940, Buffalo, New York, USA. Professor, 4 sons, 3 daughters. Eduction: BA, Cansisus College, Buffalo, 1962; MA, 1963, PhD, 1968, University of Wisconsin, Madison. Career: Instructor, Canisius College, 1965-66; Research Associate, University of Wisconsin, 1966-68; Assistant Professor, University of Illinois, 1968-72; Associate Professor, Michigan University, 1972-79; Visiting Professor, 1978-79, Associate Professor, 1979-81, Professor, Acting Chair, Communiction, 1982, SUNY, Albany; Director of Research, SUNY Institute for the Study of Information Science, 1988-89; Professor, Chair, 1989-95, Professor, 1995-, SUNY, Buffalo. Publications: Numerous articles in professional journals. Honours include: Senior Fellow, East-West Communication Institute, Honolulu, 1977-83; Presidents Award for Excellence in Research, SUNY, 1983; Fullbright Award, Conference at Dubrovnik, 1983; Richard W D Nicholas Agricultural Science Scholarship, University of Melbourne, 1986. Memberships: American Association for the Advancement of Science; Inernational Society for Network Analysis; Neural Network Society; New York Academy of Sciences; North American Classification Society; Psychometric Society. Address: University of Buffalo, Department of Communication, 332 MFAC-Fillmore, NY 14261, USA.

**WOLFE Burton H,** b. 2 September 1932, Washington, District of Columbia, USA. Free Lance Writer, Director of Non Profit Organization. 2 sons, 1 daughter. Education: BA, George Washington University, 1954. Memberships: Phi Beta Kappa; American Legion; Smithsonian Association. Address: 1095 Market Street, #814 San Francisco, CA 94103-1631, USA.

**WOLFE-COOTE Sonia,** b. 8 November 1936, London, England. Medical Researcher. m. Gerald Wolfe-Coote, 2 sons, 1 daughter. Education: BSc, Edinburgh, 1961; PhD, RSA, 1985. Appointments: Research Assistant, Royal College of Surgeons, London; Technician, Senior Professional Officer, Department of Virology, US Medical School; Medical Researcher, Chief Specialist Scientist, Director, MRC Experimental Biology Programme. Publications: 2 books, 5 invited chapters, 120 peer reviewed manuscripts. Honours: 1st Women President of South African Scientific Society, 1987. Memberships: Microscopy Society of South Africa; American Society of Histochemistry; International Society for Stereology; Royal Microscopy Society, England; European Association for Study of Diabetes; African Society for Cell and Developmental Biology; South African Physiology Society; Association of Medical Scientists. Address: Experimental Biology, MRC PO Box 19070, Tygerberg 7505, South Africa.

**WOLK Howard,** b. 20 April 1920, USA. Poet. Education: Wright Junior College. Appointments: 40 years in office retiring as Vice President of small corporation. Publications: Contributor of poems to many poetry magazines and books of poetry including, Poetic Voices of America; A Prism of Thoughts; Great American Poetry Anthology; Today's Best Poems; Our World's Most Treasured Poems; American Poetry Showcase. Honours: Awards of Merit, silver and gold; Poet Laureate; Award of Appreciation; Editor's Choice Award. Memberships: ROTC; Variety Club; American Philatelic Society; Academy of American Poets; International Society of Poets; Advisory Council, IBC. Address: 6007 N Sheridan Road, Chicago, IL 606660, USA.

**WOLKENBERG Andrzej,** b. 30 November 1931, Poland. Professor. Widower, 2 daughters. Education: MSc, 1956; PhD, 1964; DSc, 1982. Career: Professor, Materials Engineering,

Technical University and Institute of Electronic Technology, Warsaw. Publications: Various scientific papers in professional journals. Membership: American Electrochemical Society. Address: ul Woloska 51, 02-583 Warsaw, Poland.

**WOLLINA Uwe,** b. 31 January 1956, Jena, Germany. Dermatologist. m. Karin Wollina, 2 sons. Education: Medicine, Friedrich Schiller University, Jena, 1976-82. Appointments: Acting Head of Department, 1992-97, Senior Adviser, Department Dermatology, University Jena, 1997-. Publications: Author or co-author 85 publications in field of wound healing, keratinocyte biology, neuropeptides and oncology; Contributor to 37 books. Memberships: 14 professional societies including: American Association for the Advancement of Science; New York Academy of Science; European Tissue Repair Society; European Photopheresis Society. Address: Friedrich-Schiller University, Erfurter St 35, 07740 Jena, Germany.

**WON Sangchul,** b. 19 January 1951, Korea. Professor. m. Haeryung Ha Won, 2 sons. Education includes: PhD, Electrical Engineering, University of Iowa, USA, 1985. Appointments: Professor, Electrical Engineering Department; Director, SPARC, POSTECH. Honour: Korean Presidential Commendation, 1994. Membership: Control System Society, Institute of Electrical and Electronics Engineers. Address: Faculty Apt 5-1104, 756 Jikockdong, Namku, Pohang 790-390, Korea.

**WON Youkyung,** b. 12 July 1957, Injae, Kangwon-do, Korea. Professor. m. Soonoak Kim, 1 s. Education: BBA, Sung Kyun Kwan University, 1981; MBA, Seoul National University, 1983; PhD, Korea Advanced Institute of Science and Technology, 1994. Appointments: Assistant Professor, Jeonju University, 1995-. Publications: Engineering Optimization; Computers and Industrial Engineering; International J Production Research. Address: Jeonju University 1200, 3 Ga Hyoja dong, Wansan gu Chonju Chonbuk, 560-759 South Korea.

**WONG Kit Pong,** b. 15 September 1963, Hong Kong. Assistant Professor of Finance. m. Floriana Ng, 1 son, 1 daughter. Education: MA, Economics, 1989; PhD, Finance, 1993. Appointments: Assistant Professor of Finance, University of Hong Kong. Publications: Articles in Journal of Banking and Finance, 1995, 1997, Economica, 1999. Memberships: American Finance Association; Canadian Economics Association. Address: School of Economics and Finance, University of Hong Kong, Pokfulam Road, Hong Kong, China.

**WONG Kok Cheong,** b. 11 September 1965, Singapore. Director, Computer Graphics. m. Lee Hock Mui, 1 daughter. Education: B Eng First Class Honours Electronics and Electricals, 1989, PhD Engineering, 1993, University of Surrey, UK. Appointments: Lecturer, 1993, Deputy Director, 1993-96, Research Director, 1996-98, Director, 1998-, Centre for Graphics & Imaging Technology, Nanyang Technological University, Singapore. Publications: 1 short computer animated film entitled Litter Bug, International Symposium on Computer Graphics, Image Processing & Vision, 1998; 4 journal papers; 18 conference papers; 1 book chapter. Honours: Oversea Research Student Award, UK, 1989-92; IEE Prize, UK, Blumlein-Browne-Willans Premium Award for a journal paper, 1993. Membership: Association for Computing Machinery. Address: Apt Blk 553, Choa Chu Kang N 6 #07-02, Singapore 680553, Singapore.

**WONG Kon Max,** b. 11 June 1945, Macau. Mitel Professor of Signal Processing, McMaster University. m. Margaret E Rumsey, 2 sons. Education: BS (Eng), 1969; DIC, 1972; PhD,

1974; DSc(Eng), 1995; CEng, FIEE, FInstP, FSS. Appointments: Prinicipal Research Engineer, Plessey Telecom Research Ltd, UK; Assistant Professor, Technical University of Nova Scotia; Associate Professor, Professor, Chairman, McMaster University; Visiting Professor of Electronic Engineering, Chinese University of Hong Kong; Honorary Professor, Southeast University; Mitel Professor of Signal Processing, McMaster University. Publications: 130 in journals and international conferences; Chapters in four textbooks. Honour: IEE Overseas Premium, 1989. Memberships: Chartered Engineer, UK; Professional Engineer, APEO, Canada; Senior Member, IEEE; Fellow, IEE; Fellow, Institute of Physics; Fellow, Royal Statistical Society. Address: Department of Electrical and Computer Engineering, McMaster University, Hamilton, Ontario, Canada L8S 4K1.

**WONG Lucille,** b. 20 October 1949, Mexico City, Mexico. Painter. Education: BA, Universidad Nacional Autonoma de Mexico, 1974; MA, University of Kent, 1976; Eastern Arts, Colegio de Mexico, 1976. Appointments: Museo Ateneo de Yucatan, 1996; Museo Contemporaneo de Arte, Universidad Nacional, 1997. Memberships: Association International d'Artistes; UNESCO; Consejo Mundial de Artistas Visuales. Address: Calle da la Otra Banda, 80-14 San Angel DP, CP 01090 Mexico DF, Mexico.

**WONG Tommy Sai Wai,** b. 14 December 1952, Hong Kong. Civil Engineering Educator. m. Christina Sum, 3 sons. Education: BSc, honours, Leeds University, 1974; Certificate in Engineering, Cambridge University, 1975; MSc, Birmingham University, 1976; PhD, National University of Singapore. Appointments: Assistant Engineer, Wessex Water Authority, England, 1976-80; Manager, Tung Sun Investment Company, Hong Kong, 1980-81; Engineer/Resident Engineer, Charles Haswell & Partners (FE), Hong Kong, 1981-85; Senior Engineer, China Overseas Building Development Company Ltd, Hong Kong, 1985; Senior Lecturer, Associate Professor Nanyang Technological University, Singapore, 1985-. Publication: An Introduction to Kinematic Wave Method for Storm Drainage Design, 1992; Numerous articles in international professional journals and conference proceedings. Honours: John Illingworth Prize, Leeds University, 1974. Memberships: American Society of Civil Engineers; Hong Kong Management Association; Institution of Engineers, Singapore; International Association for Hydraulic Research; Singapore Institute of Management; Institution of Civil Engineers, England; International Association of Hydrological Sciences. Address: 135 Sunset Way #06-13, Singapore 597158, Singapore.

**WONG Wendell P,** b. 16 May 1953, Chicago, Illinois, USA. Surgeon; Specialist in Laser Vision Correction. m. Terry, 1 daughter. Education: BA, 1973, Northwestern University; MD, 1977, University of Illinois. Appointments: Chief of Laser Eye Surgery, Natural Sight Laser Vision Centre. Memberships: Fellow, American Academy of Ophthalmology; Diplomate, Natural Board of Medical Examiners. Address: Natural Sight Laser Vision Centre, 3445 Pacific Coast Highway, Ste 200, Torrance, CA 90505, USA.

**WONGCHAROEN Tiparatana.** Lecturer. m. Surapong Pinitglang. Education: BSc, Physics, Silpakorn University, Thailand, 1983; MSc, Applied Mathematics, Mahidol University, Bangkok, 1986; PhD, Electronics Engineering, City University, London, England, 1995. Appointments: Visiting Lecturer, Bumrongvithaya School, Thailand, 1980-82, Satreepatheongvithaya School, Bangkok, 1983-85; Satit of Kasetsart University, Bangkok, 1986-87; Department of Physics, Civil Aviation Training Institute, Bangkok, 1991; Lecturer, School of Science, Bangkok University, 1987-92,

School of Engineering, Bangkok University, 1992-; Researcher, King Mongkut's Institute of Technology Thonburi, Thailand, 1988-92; Postdoctoral Research Fellow, Department of Electrical, Electronic and Information Engineering, City University, London, 1995-96, 1998; Visiting Fellow, Politechnic of Torino, Italy, 1996; Head, Department of Electrical Engineering, School of Engineering, Bangkok University, 1997-. Publications include: Spot size transformations for laser-fiber integration; Rigorous Characterization of MMI-based Photonic Devices. Honours: Scholarships, John F Kennedy Foundation, 1979-83, Dr Tab Foundation, Bangkok, 1984-85, Bangkok University, 1992-96, Royal Society, UK Academy of Sciences, 1998; Gold Medal, Buddhism Society, Thailand, 1982, Dr Tab Foundation, Bangkok, 1983; Honour Certificate, Dr Tab Foundation, Bangkok, 1983. Memberships: IEEE; IEEE Computer Society; Optical Society of America; Science Society of Thailand; Mathematics Society of Thailand; Physics Society of Thailand. Address: School of Engineering, Bangkok University, 9/1 Klong-one Sub District, Klonglaung District, Pathumthani 12120, Thailand.

**WOOD Robert Warren**, b. 5 July 1955, Des Moines, Iowa, USA. Attorney. m. Beatrice Wood, 1 daughter. Education: AB summa cum laude, English, Humboldt State University, 1976; University of Sheffield, England, 1975-76; University of the Witwatersrand, South Africa, 1977; JD, University of Chicago, 1979; Admitted, Bars of California, New York, Washington DC, Montana, Arizona; US Tax Court, Northern and Central Districts of California; Solicitor, Supreme Court of England and Wales; Certified Tax Specialist, California Board of Legal Specialization. Appointments: Attorney with several large law firms, 1979-93; Instructor, Hastings College of the Law, University of California, 1981-82; Director, Harvey L and Maud C Sorensen Foundation, 1992-93; Founder, Attorney, Robert W Wood Professional Corporation, San Francisco, California, 1993-; Past Director, Nutriceutical Products Corporation; Director, Tax Institute; Director, Doverwood Corporation. Publications: Author or editor, some 2 dozen books related to business and corporate taxation, including tax guides; Numerous articles on taxation in legal, accounting and business publications. Honours: President's Scholar, Humboldt State University; Scholarship, University of Chicago; Florence James Adams Prize, University of Chicago Law School. Memberships include: Fellow, American College of Tax Counsel; Law Society of England and Wales; Associate, Canadian Bar Association; Past Trustee and Secretary, Mzuri Wildlife Foundation; Commonwealth Club; International Order of St Hubert. Address: 477 Pacific Avenue #300, San Francisco, CA 94133-4614, USA.

**WOODBURY Arthur**, b. 20 June 1930, Kimball, Nebraska, USA. Musician; Composer; Professor of Music. m. Sharon, 2 daughters. Education: BSc, Music, 1951; MMus, 1955. Appointments: Lecturer, Music, University of California, Davis, 1963-72; Professor, University of South Florida, Tampa, 1972-. Publications include: Music In The United States, 1998. Honours: Performance Award, Faculty Jazz Trio, University of South Florida, 1981; Sabbatical Awards, University of South Florida, 184, 1993; Pi Kappa Lambda, 1993; TIP Award, 1994. Memberships: American Federation of Musicians; Broadcast Music International; National Association of Jazz Educators; North American Saxophone Alliance. Address: 7407 19th Street South East, Snohomish, WA 98296, USA.

**WOODSON Gayle Ellen**, b. 6 September 1950, Galveston, Texas, USA. Surgeon. m. Kevin Thomas Robbins, 2 sons, 1 daughter. Education: BA, Rice University, 1972; MD, Baylor College, 1975. Appointments: Assistant Professor, Baylor College of Medicine, 1982-87; Assistant Professor, 1987,

Associate Professor, 1991, UC San Diego; Professor, UT, Memphis, 1992-. Memberships include: Harris County Medical Society, 1982-87; Society of Head and Neck Oncologists of Great Britain, 1982-; Royal College of Surgeons, Canada, 1983-; Society of University Otolaryngologists, 1984, Council, 1992-95, President Elect, 1996; American College of Surgeons, 1985-, Board of Governors, 1995-, Advisory Council for Otolaryngology, 1995-; American Physiological Society, 1988-; Association of Women Surgeons, 1989-; American Laryngological Association, 1994-. University of Tennessee, College of Medicine, Department of Otolaryngology, Head and Neck Surgery, 956 Court Avenue, Suite B226, Memphis, TN 38163, USA.

**WOODWARD Vern Harvey**, b. 18 October 1899, Hawkeye, Iowa, USA. Engineering Sales Executive. m. Florence Thompson, 11 July 1927, deceased January 1989. Education: University of Pittsburg, 1923; Carnegie Tech, 1929; Westinghouse Technical School, 1924-28. Appointments: Engineer, Westinghouse Electricity, East Pittsburgh, 1922-31; Engineering Sales Representative, Equitable Gas Co (now Equitable Resources), Pittsburgh, 1935-40; Supervisor, Architects, 1940-45; Supervisor, Architects and Engineering Services, 1945-64; Member, Operating Committee, 1960-64; Auditor, Churchill Boro, 1957-69. Honours: Recipient, 3 Outstanding Achievement Awards, National Library of Poetry. Memberships: Scottish Rite, 33 deg Supreme Council, 1968-97; Distinguished Member, KT International Society of Poets; Masons; Red Cross of Constantine, US Premier Conclave, 1965-97; Golden Triangle York Rite College No 32; Joshua Association of Western Pennsylvania; Association of Masonic Veterans of Western Pennsylvania. Address: 1 Masonic Drive, Elizabethtown, PA 17022, USA.

**WORK Mitchell R**, b. 17 March 1947, Vienna, Autria. Health Care Information Consulting, Market Intelligence. m. Susan, 2 daughters. Education: BA, Political Sceince, Pennsylvanian State University, 1969; MPA, Public Administration, American University, 1971. Appointments: Professor of Sociology, 1970-71; Senior Trainer, 1971-73; Executive Director, 1973-78; Director, IMS America Ltd, 1982-86; Director, 1986-91; Senior Vice President, Sheldon I Dosenfort And Associates, 1991-. Memberships: CHIM Centre for Healthcare Information Management. Address: 2936 Grant St, Evanston, IL 60201-2059, USA.

**WORKMAN George Henry**, b. 18 September 1939, Muskegon, Michigan, USA. Structural Engineer. m. Vicki Sue Hanish, 2 sons. Education: Associate of Science, Muskegon Community College, 1960; BSE, 1966, MSE, 1966, PhD, 1969, University of Michigan. Appointments: Served US Navy, 1961-64; Principal Engineer, Battelle Memorial Institute, Columbus, Ohio, 1969-76; Instructor, Department of Civil Engineering, Ohio State University, 1973, 1982; President, Applied Mechanics Inc, Longboat Key, Florida, 1976-. Publications: Contributor of 27 technical papers to national and international conferences. Honours: Named Outstanding Undergraduate Student, EM Department, 1966, named Outstanding Graduate Student, Civil Engineering Department, 1969, University of Michigan. Memberships: Professional Engineer, Ohio; American Society of Mechanical Engineers; American Academy of Mechanics; Sigma Xi; Chi Epsilon; Phi Kappa Phi; Phi Theta Kappa. Address: 3431 Bayou Court, Longboat Key, FL 34228-3028, USA.

**WORKMAN Jerome James Jr**, b. 6 August 1952, Northfield, Minnesota, USA. Chemist. m. Rebecca Marie, 2 sons, 3 daughters. Education: BA Natural Sciences, St Mary's University, 1975-76; MA, Biological Sciences, Genetics, St

Mary's University, 1976-80; PhD, Biological Chemistry, Columbia Pacific University, 1982-84; EPM, Columbia University, 1990-91, 1999. Appointments: Supervising Scientist and Chemist, Technicon Instruments, New York, 1984-87; Senior Scientist, Hitachi Instruments, California, 1987-89; Director of Technical Support and Marketing, Perstorp Analytical, Maryland, 1989-93; Principal Scientist, Perkin-Elmer Corporation, Connecticut, 1993-96; Research Fellow, Kimberley-Clark Corporation, Wisconsin, 1996-. Publications: 225 Scientific Papers, abstracts and book chapters on Spectroscopy, Statistics, Process Analysis and Chemometrics; Over 100 Proprietary Corporate Research Technical Reports, and four inventions disclosures and patents; Books include: Statistics in Spectroscopy, 1991; UV-VIS Spectroscopy, 1993; Applied Spectroscopy, 1998. Honours: Outstanding Student Achievement Award, St Mary's University, 1978; Heart of Gold Award, 1983; Technicon Instruments Performance Award, 1987; Award of Excellence, Perstorp Analytical, 1992. Memberships: National Honor Society, 1970; New York Academy of Sciences, 1982; Fellow, American Institute of Chemists, 1989-; Fellow and Chartered Chemist, Royal Society of Chemistry, 1996; ASTM Committee, 1999-. Address: Analytical Science and Technology, Kimberley-Clark Corp, 2100 Winchester Rd, Neenah, WI 54956, USA.

**WORTHAM Christopher John,** b. 11 November 1940, South Africa. Academic. m. Maryanne Courtenay Wortham, 1 son, 1 daughter. Education: BA, Law, 1962, BA, hons, 1964, MA, 1967, Rhodes University; PhD, University of London, 1974. Appointments: Lecturer, University of Rhodesia, 1967-76; Lecturer, 1977-86, Senior Lecturer, 1987-91, Assoicate Professor, 1992-, University of Western Australia. Publications include: Shakespeare, James I and the Matter of Britain, 1996; Shakespeare: Readers, Audiences, Players, 1998; Australasian Drama Studies: Renaissance in the South, 1998; Andrew Marvell: Lyric and Pastoral Poetry, 1999. Memberships: Australian and New Zealand Association for Medieval and Early Modern Studies; Australian and New Zealand Shakespeare Association. Address: 12 Boreham Street West, Austr Perth, Western Australia 6011, Australia.

**WORTHING Carol Marie,** b. 27 December 1934, Duluth, Minnesota, USA. Ecumenical Minister. Widow, 2 sons. Education: BS, 1965; MDiv, 1982; DMin, 1988; MBA, 1993; Candidate for PhD. Appointments: Teaching, 1965-78; Pastoral Ministry, 1982-90; Executive Director, IL Conference of Churches, 1990-96; Texas Conference, 1996-. Publications: Contributing Editor, Lutheran Partners Magazine, 1984-; many articles. Memberships: National Association of Ecumenical Staff; National Association of Female Executives. Address: 40N IH35, Ste 2B4, Austin, TX 78701, USA.

**WOSSNER Mark,** b. 14 October 1938, Berlin, Germany. Executive. Education: Mechanical Engineering, Technical University, karlsruhe; Dr.Ing. Career: Management Assistant, Bertelsemann, 1968; Production Manager, 1970, Technical Director, 1972, Managing Director, 1974, Mohndruck; Executive Board, 1976, Deputy Chairman of Executive Board, 1981, Chairman, Chief Executive Officer, Bertelsmann AG; Executive Board, Bertelsmann Foundation, 1996. Address: Bertelsmann AG, Carl Bertelsmann Str 270, D-33311 Gütersloh, Germany.

**WOUDE Ad van der,** b. 11 July 1932, Utrecht, Netherlands. Historian. m. Francine Peppelenbosch, 1 son, 1 daughter. Education: University Degree in History, 1958; Doctorate in History, cum laude, 1972. Appointments: Military Intelligence Service, 1958-60; Assistant Professor, 1966-74, Full Professor, 1975-, Agricultural University, Wageningen. Publications: Het Noorderkwartier, 3 vols, 1972; The First Modern Economy,

1997. Honour: Knight in the Order of the Dutch Lion, 1994-. Membership: Chairman, Dutch Union of University Professors and Lecturers. Address: Agricultural University Department of Rural History, Hollandse weg 1, 6706 KN Wageningen, The Netherlands.

**WRIGHT Anne,** b. 10 June 1929, Liss, Hampshire. Conservationist; Stud Farmer. m. Robert, 1 son, 1 daughter. Appointments: Founder, Trustee, WWF India, 1972-95; Equestrian Judge, Asiads, 1992; Honours: MBE, Golden Ark of Holland. Memberships: Rhino Foundation; Wildlife Protection Society of India; International Centre; IUCN Cat Specialist Group. Address: c/o Tollygunge Club Ltd, 120 Deshapran Sasmal Road, Calcutta 700033, India.

**WRIGHT John Cardwell II,** b. 16 June 1927, Sodus, New York, USA. Medicine. 1 son, 3 daughters. Education: BM, University of Buffalo, 1950; MD, New York Medical College, Lower Fifth Avenue Hospital, New York, New York 1955; Internship, 1955-56; Residency, IM, 1956-57; Waterbury Hospital, Connecticut, 1956-57. BA, University of Buffalo, Buffalo, New York, USA, 1950; Rotating Internship, Waterbury Hospital, Waterbury, Connecticut, USA, 1955-56; Residency in Medicine, Waterbury Hospital, Connecticut, USA, 1956-57; Appointments include: Chairman Department of Family Practice, 1978-81; Director, Geriatric Programs, 1981-91, Director and Co-Founder, Geriatric Evaluation and Treatment Unit, 1981-91, Acting Director, Founder - Urban Center on Aging, 1985-89, Research Associate, Telecommunications Research Center, 1991-92, Director, Division of Geriatric Medicine, 1991-93, Director, Memory Disorders Clinic, 1991-95, Professor, Department of Family and Community Medicine, 1992-95, Professor Emeritus, 1995-, University of Louisville, Louisville, Kentucky, USA. Publications include: Family Medicine Principles and Practice, book chapter, 1983; Prevalence of Pseudohypertension in 3436 Persons Screened for the Systolic Hypertension in the Elderly Program, abstract, 1991; Clues to Depression in Primary Care Practice, 1996; Prevelance of Positive Osler's Maneuver in 3387 Persons Screened for the Systolic Hypertension in the Elderly Program, 1997. Honours include: Fellow, World Health Organization, 1986; Certificate of Appreciation, 1988; Certificate of Recognition, 1993; Award for Exemplary and Distinguished contribution to the field of gerontology and practice of geriatrics, 1993. Memberships include: International Committee, 1981-85, Constitution and Bylaws Committee, 1982-84, Society of Teachers of Family Medicine; Alternate Delegate, House of Delegates, 1970-75, American Academy of Family Physicians; Section of Medical Schools, 1979-86, Section on Hospital Staffs, 1984-86, American Medical Association; Certification Planning Committee, 1989-91, Certification Council, 1991-94, American Medical Directors Association; Board of Directors, 1994-97, Certification Council of the American Medical Directors Association Inc. Address: 3696 Webb Road, Simpsonville, KY 40067 6435, USA.

**WRIGHT John MacNair Jr,** b. 14 April 1916, Los Angeles, California, USA. Retired. m. Helene Tribit, 2 sons. Education: Bachelor of Science, United States Military Academy, West Point, NY, 1940; Master of Business Administration, University of Southern California, Los Angeles, 1956; Master of Science, International Affairs, George Washington University, DC, 1973. Appointments: Battery Commander, 1940-41; Prisoner of War, 1942-45; War Department General Staff, 1946-48; Military Attache, 1948-50; Executive Officer, 1950; Commander, 1951-52; Assistant Chief of Staff, 1953-54; Office of Deputy Chief, Officer of Chief, 1956-60; Chief of Staff, 1961-63; Assistant Chief of Staff, 1962-63; Assistant Division Commander, 1963-66; Office of Assistant Chief, 1966-67;

Commanding General, 101st Airborne Division, Vietnam, 1967-70; Comptroller of the Army, 1970-72; Retired from Army, 1972; National Director, Exploring, Boy Scouts of America, 1973-81; Retired from Boy Scouts, 1981. Publications: Captured on Corregidor. Honours: George Washington Honour Medal; Silver Beaver; Silver Antelope; Distinguished Eagle Scout Award; Exploring Leadership Award; Army Aviation Hall of Fame; Distinguished Service Medal, Two Oak Leaf Clusters; Silver Star, Oak Leaf Cluster; Many Other Awards. Memberships: Evergreen Masonic Lodge; National Sojourners Shrine; Phi Kappa Phi; National Congress of Patriotic Organizations; Many other memberships: Address: 21227 George Brown Avenue, Riverside, CA 92518-2881, USA.

**WRIGHT Stephanie,** b. 4 September 1948, Boulder, Colorado, USA. Director. 2 sons. Education: Bachelor of Arts, University of Delaware, 1970; Master of Education, 1976; Doctor of Education, Temple University, 1987. Appointments: Music Educator, 1970-89; Director of Aerospace Education, Delaware, 1989-. Honours: She Knows Where She's Going Award; Oustanding Education Alumna; Education Achievement Award; Distinguished Citizen Award. Memberships: Air Force Association; Civil Air Patrol; Defence Orientation Conference; Challenger Center; Association of American University Women; Phi Delta Kappa; International Tech Association; Women in Aerospace. Address: 5 Essex Drive, Bear, DE 19701-1602, USA.

**WRIGHT Thomas Parker,** b. 3 July 1924, Springfield, Missouri, USA. Educator. m. Elizabeth, 2 sons, 3 daughters. Education: BA, Mathematics, Henderson University, Arkansas, 1948; MA, Mathematics, Louisiana University, Baton Rouge, 1962. Appointments: Secondary Mathematics and Science Teacher, 1949-63; College Computer Science Teacher, 1963-71; College Administrative Dean, 1971-79; Art Gallery Owner, 1979-83; College Teacher, 1983-94; Director, 1994-98. Memberships: University of Hawaii Professional Assembly; National Education Association. Address: 811 South Kihei Road, Apt 3L, Kihei, HI 96753-90896, USA.

**WU Aicheng,** b. 19 April 1942, Shaoyang, Hunan, China. Professor. 2 sons, 1 daughter. Education: Majored in English, College of Foreign Languages, Hunan Normal University, 1963-68; Studied further, Beijing University, Beijing University of Foreign Languages and Beijing Medical University. Appointments: Interpreter and Translator, Asia, Europe and Africa, 1972-80; Professor, Hunan University; Expert, China Association of Translation and Interpretation on Science and Technology, current. Publications: Monographs: A Guide to Learning English Words, 1987; Successful Strategy and Skill in Taking English Examinations, 1990; Chief Editor, Lexicology and Methods of Memorizing English Words, 1993; Chemistry & Chemical Engineering, 1996; Editor, national text books of Specialised Intensive Reading English, 14 books, 1994-97; Five papers in national journals and magazines. Memberships: Vice Academic Dean and Professor, Changsha Foreign Languages College for Foreign Trade and International Development; Research Fellow, West Asia and Africa Study Association; Consultant in Behaviour Science Research Society of Hunan Province; Secretary General and Managing Director, Hunan Provincial Association for Studies in Theory and Teaching of Translation; Managing Vice Chairman, Training Centre of Overseas Persons of Hunan Provincial Commission for Foreign Trade and Economic Relations with Foreign Countries. Address: Room 203, Building One, Feng Huang Cun, Hunan University, Changsha, Hunan 410082, China.

**WU Cheng-Wen,** b. 19 June 1938, Taipei, Taiwan, China. m. Felicia Y-H Chen, 2 sons, 1 daughter. Education: MD, National Taiwan University, 1964; PhD, Biochemistry, Care Western Reserve University, 1969. Appointment: Founding President, Distinguished Investigator, National Health Research Institute, China, 1996-. Publications: 168 papers published in refereed international journals. Honours: Fellow, NIH Special Fellowship, USA, 1972; Academia Sinica, China, 1984; Fellow, American Institute of Chemists, USA, 1986. Memberships: Trustee, The Chinese Oncology Society, 1991-; President, The Chinese Society of Cell and Molecular Biology, 1992-. Address: President, National Health Research Institute, 128 Sec 2, Yenchiouyuan Road, Nanking, Taipei, 115 Taiwan.

**WU Ching-mu,** b. 16 May 1929, Tainan, Taiwan, China. Professor. m. Nuan Shy, 2 sons, 2 daughters. Education: BS, 1953, National Taiwan University; DS (PhD), 1971, Osaka City University, Japan. Appointments: Assistant and Instructor to Associate Professor, Cheng-Kung University, Taiwan, 1953-65; Associate Professor, Professor, Tunghai University, Taiwan, 1965-72; Research Fellow, Research Institute for Mathematical Sciences, National Kyoto University, Japan, 1969-71; Professor and Director, Graduate School of Mathematics, Tamkang University, 1972-78; Chair Professor (retired), Tamkang University, Taiwan, 1980-95; Visiting Professor: University of West Florida, USA, 1978-80, Private Teikyo University, Japan, 1993-94. Honours: Honorary Citizen, City of Pensacola, Florida, USA, 1979; Chair, Professor, (Professorship of authority), Tamkang University, 1980-95; Recipient, Decoration for Distinguished Educator, Ministry of Education, 1983, 1993. Address: 2F, No 6, Alley 18, Lane 250, Sec 5, Nanking East Road, Taipei, Taiwan 105.

**WU Delong,** b. 5 November 1935, Anhui, China. Professor. m. Zhenni Liu, 2 sons. Education: Graduate, Shanghai Jiaotong University, 1960; Scholarship, Athens National Technical University, Greece, 1982-83; PhD, World Open University, New York, USA, 1997. Appointments: Senior Research Scientist, Beijing Institute of Astronomical Systems Engineering, 1986-; Vice Secretary, General of Degree Committee, China National Space Administration, 1994-. Honours: Scientist and Returned Student of Distinguished Achievement of Aero-Astronautical Ministry; The National Special Allowance for Outstanding Contribution. Memberships: Specialized Committee of Chinese Society of Mechanics; Chinese Society of Composites. Address: P O Box 9208, Beijing 100076, China.

**WU Dong Tung,** b. 31 October 1936, Shanghai, China. Doctor. m. Jin Yun Li, 2 sons. Education: Graduate, Japanese Language, Beijing University, 1955-57; Masters Degree, Surgery, Beijing Medical University, 1962; National Tokyo University, Japan Medical and Dental University, 1978-81. Appointments: Chairman of Students' Union, Beijing Medical University, 1960-61; Lecturer for Cardiac Surgery, Physician in Charge, 1961-1998; Physician of Cardiac Surgery, Lecturer, Kameda General Hospital, Japan, 1989-91. Publications: Surgery of Carcinoma of Esophagus, 1980; Diagnosis and Surgical Treatment of Membranous Septal Aneurysms, 1988; Coronary Artery Bypass Surgery with Bilateral Internal Mammary Artery, 1992. Honours: Award for Contribution, Professor Asano Kenichi, 1981; First Qualified Physician from China that is Permitted to Exercise Surgery in Japan, Department of Health, Japan, 1989. Memberships: International Exchange Center, Beijing; Magazine of Cardiac Surgery, China; Department of Health, China; Special Expert of Health, Newspaper; Complier of the Magazine of Circulation, China. Address: First Teaching Hospital, Beijing Medical University, Beijing 100034, China.

**WU Felicia Ying-Hsiueh**, b. 27 February 1939, Taipei, Taiwan. Research Fellow. m. Cheng-Wen Wu, 2 sons, 1 daughter. Education: BS Chemistry summa cum laude, 1961, National Taiwan University; MS Organic Chemistry & Biochemistry, 1963, University of Minnesota at Minneapolis; PhD Organic Chemistry, 1969, Case Western Reserve University, Cleveland, Ohio. Appointments: Various research posts in USA and Taiwan, 1961-72, 1988-92; Instructor, Associate, Dept Biophysics, 1972-78, Assistant Professor, Dept Biochemistry, 1978-79, Albert Einstein College of Medicine, Bronx, USA; Visiting Professor, Department of Molecular Biology, Institut Pasteur, Paris, and Unite de Physiochimie Macromoleculaire, Institut Gustave-Roussy, France, 1979-80; Professor, Associate Professor, Catacosinos Professorship, Department of Pharmacological Sciences, SUNY at Stony Brook, 1980-90; Adjunct Professor, Dept Pharmaceutical Chemistry, University California at San Francisco, 1991-96; Adjunct Professor, Institute of Life Sciences, Academia Sinica/National Defense Medical Centre Joint PhD Programme, Taipei, 1992-; Adjunct Professor, Department of Pharmaclogy, 1988-90, Institute of Toxicology, 1990-97, Joint Professor, Institute of Toxicology, 1998-, National Taiwan University; Coordinator, Cancer & Virus, Gene Regulation and Cancer, and Genetic Toxicology Groups, Institute of Biomedical Sciences (IBMS), Academia Sinica, 1988-89; Special Medical Research Chair, 1989-, Research Fellow, 1988-, Coordinator, 1989-97, Division of Cancer Research, IBMS. Publications: 85 peer-reviewed papers; 165 conference papers; Edited book, Structure and Function of Nucleic Acids and Proteins, 1990. Honours: Vary many honours and awards including Model Youth Award from China Government, 1957; Catacominos Professorship, 1980-88; Grant Awards from US and ROC organisations, 1972-; Outstanding Basic Cancer Research Award from the Chinese Oncology Society, 1998. Memberships: American, International and Chinese Oncology, Genetic and Biochemical societies and associations. Address: Inst Biomed Sciences, Academia Sinica, 128 Yen Chiu Yuan Rd, Sect II, Taipei 11529, Taiwan, R.O.C.

**WU Huiding**, b. 13 May 1937, Anhui, China. Professor. m. Sili Xie, 1 son, 1 daughter. Education: Graduate, 1960, Geophysics Dept, Peking University, Beijing. Appointments: Assistant, Lecturer and Associate Professor, Peking University, 1960-85; Professor, National Research Centre for Marine Environment Forecasts (NRCMEF), Beijing, 1986-98; Heads of Numerical Marine Environmental Forecast Division, NRCMEF, 1986-93, Sea Ice Division, 1993-95, Second Oceanography Division, 1995-98; Part-time Professor and PhD Supervisor at Qingdao Ocean University, Qingdao, 1986-98, and at Peking University, 1996-98. Publications: 2 books: Numerical Weather Prediction, 1986; Sea Ice: Observation & Modelling, 1994; Over 70 papers on sea ice, storm surges, typhoon, planetary boundary layer, numerical weather prediction and rotting dishpan experiment for the general atmospheric circulation. Honours: Young and Middle Aged Expert with Outstanding Contributions, 1990, Ministry of Personnel; Special allowance for an Outstanding Contribution from Chinese Government, 1991; First and Third National Prizes of Advance in Science and Technology for research on numerical weather prediction in 1986 and on sea ice modelling and forecasting, 1992; 1st, 2nd & 3rd SOA Prizes of Advance in Science and Technology for storm surges study in 1989, sea ice study in 1991 and atmospheric boundary layer modelling and its application in 1986; The Prize for the Achievements of National Scientific and Technolegical Key Projects for the 8th 5 year Plan of China, 1996. Memberships: Sea Ice Working Group of WMO Commission for Marine Meteorology; Numerical Weather Prediction Committee, Chinese Society of Meteorology; and others. Address: National Research Centre for Marine Environment Forecasts, 8 Dahuisi Road, Beijing 100081, China.

**WU Jianguo**, b. 17 January 1929, Chongqing, China. Professor of Computer Control Automation. m. Xie Lianzhou, 4 sons. Education: Graduated, Machinery and Electricity Department, Chongqing University, 1950. Appointments: Professor; Senior Engineer, Centre Experiment and Research Institute of Chongqing Electric Power Bureau. Publications: Over 60 research papers, books and monographs, 1954-. Honours: Technical Golden Award by China Scientific and Technical Committee for Step by Step Revolution Type Pulse Width Modulation with Constant Flux Variable Frequency Electric Source. Membership: China Power Electronic Academy. Address: No 55-5-6, Pibashan Main Street, Yuzhong District, Chonqing 400013, China.

**WU Penyen**, b. 23 August 1938, Shanghai. Aero-Scientist. Education: BE, BSc, University of Aeronautics & Astronautics, 1961. Appointments: Supervisor of Postgraduate, University; Rsch Fell; Chartered Scientist; Certified Science Author. Publications: 7 awarded science books and numerous professional articles. Awards: 10 worldwide, Natl, State Awds and Medal; Creating New Design Method; Creating New Science Theory; Creative New Science Idea. Address: PO Box A2511, Sydney South, NSW 1235, Australia.

**WU Qing-Yu**, b. 27 January 1952, Heilongjiang Province, China. Cardiovascular Surgeon. m. 1 daughter. Education: MD, 1976. Appointments: Consultant Cardiovascular Surgeon, 1985; Chief, 1989; Director and Professor of Cardiovascular Surgery, 1993. Memberships: International Eurasian Academy of Sciences. Address: Department of Cardiovascular Surgery, Fuwai Hospital, North Li Shi Road, Beijing, China.

**WU Qun**, b. 30 September 1955, China. Physician. m. You Li Na, 1 son. Education: BMed, 1982; MMed, 1988; PhD, 1995-. Appointments: PhD Candidate, Department of Biological Sciences, Illinois University, USA. Publications: Several articles in professional journals. Memberships: Society of Neuroscience; China Association of Acupuncture and Moxibustion. Address: J116 Cardinal Court, Normal, IL 61761, USA.

**WU Ru Shan**, b. 9 December 1938, Henan, China. Geophysicist. 1 son, 1 daughter. Education: BSc, Physics, 1962; PhD, Geophysics; MIT. Appointments: Research Geophysicist, Director, Modeling and Imaging Lab, Institute of Tectonics, University of California, Santa Cruz, USA. Publications: Scattering and Attenuation of Seismic Waves, 1988-90. Honours: Certificate of Merit, National Conference of Science and Technology, China. Memberships: Geophysics Association; SEG; AGU; SSA. Address: Institute of Tectonics University of California, Santa Cruz, 1156 High Street, Santa Cruz, CA 95064, USA.

**WU San Giang**, b. 21 July 1954, Tainan, Taiwan. Physician. m. Shu-Ling, 2 sons, 1 daughter. Education: Nat Def, Med Ctr, Taipei, 1979. Appointments: Resident, Cheif, Army General Hospital, Taiwan, 1981-90; Chief, Kaohsiung Municipal Womens and Childrens Hospital, 1990-. Honours: Nephron, 1993; Nephron, 1998. Memberships: Cons in Field, Society of Nephrology, 1993-96. Address: Kaohsiung Mcpl W & C Hospital, #976 Chung Hwa 1st Rd, Kaosiung, Taiwan.

**WU Tiee-Jian**, b. 16 September 1949, Kaohsiung, Taiwan. Professor. m. Chung-Li Yuan, 1 daughter. Education: BS, National Cheng-Kung University, 1972; MA, Wake Forest University, 1976; PhD, Indiana University, 1982; MA, Indiana

University, 1983. Appointments: Visiting Scholar, Institute of Statistical Science, Academia Sinica, 1991-92; Professor, National Dong-hwa University, 1995-97; Assocaite Professor, University of Houston, 1989-. Publications: Adaptive root n Estitimates of Integrated Squared Density Derivatives, Anm Statist, 1995; Root n Bandwidth Selectors for Estimation of Density Derivatives, J Amen Statist Association, 1997. Honours: Elected Member, International Statistical Institute, 1996. Memberships: International Statistical Institute; Institute of mathematical Statistics; American Statistical Association; International Chinese Statistical Assocaition. Address: Department of Mathematics, University of Houston, 4800 Calhoun, Houston, TX 77204-3476, USA.

**WU Tony,** b. 5 January 1956, Koashiung, Taiwan. Neurologist. m. Ming-Yu Bai, 1 son, 1 daughter. Education: MD, 1983, Taipei Medical College; DMS, 1995, Chang Gung University. Appointments: Associate Professor, Chang Gung University; Head evoked potential section, Neurology Dept, Chang Gung Memorial Hospital; Secretary-General, Taiwanese Society of Clinical Neurophysiology. Publications: Editor, Atlas of Histology, 1983; Author, Clinical Application of Magnetic Transcranial Stimulation. Memberships: Taiwan Neurology Society; Basic Neuroscience Society; Taiwanese Society of Clinical Neurphysiology. Address: Chang Gung Memorial Hospital, Department of Neurology, No 199 Tung-Hwa North Road, Taipei, Taiwan.

**WU Xing Hui,** b. October 1940, Yunnan, China. Teacher. m. Zhan Ui Fen, 2 sons. Education: Graduate, Physics Department, Yunnan University, 1963. Career: Professor, Director, SABA Transduction Technology Research Center, Head, Semiconductor Section, Department of Physics Yunnan University. Publications: Over 70 research papers and monographs in professional journals, 2 books. Honours: 10 National and Provincial Awards; Model Worker, Government of Yunnan, 1992; Excellent Worker Prize, Government of Chinese Center, 1995. Memberships: Board, China Society of Reliability and Quality Control of Electronic Products; Director, Sensor Technology Society; Director, Yunnan Society of Physics and Solar Energy Research; Chairman, Semiconductor Special Committee, Society of Physics; Committee, Yunnan Society of Invention. Address: Department of Physics, Yunnan University, Kunming, Yunnan 650091, China.

**WU Xing Yong,** b. 28 November 1938, Hunan, China. Research Fellow. m. Liu Guoying, 2 sons. Education: BA, History Department, Sun Yat-Sen University, 1956-60. Appointments: Assistant Research Fellow, 1980-86, Associate Fellow, 1985-96, Research Fellow, 1997-, Hunan Academy of Social Sciences. Publications: Biography of Nightingale, 1998; Biography of Helen Keller, 1998; Biography of Andrew Carnegie, 1998; Caption of Origin of the Yan-ti and Hwang Ti; The Three Loves of Dostoyevsky; Living and Death: An Inside Story of an Upstart. Membership: Chinese Association for Soviet-East European Philosophy. Address: Academy of Social Sciences, Changsha Hunan, China.

**WU Yang-Chang,** b. 24 January 1951, Taiwan. Professor of Pharmacognosy. m. 2 sons. Education: BS, Pharmacy, 1975, Master of Science, 1982, PhD, 1986, Kaohsiung Medical College, Taiwan; Postdoctoral fellow, School of Pharmacy, University of North Carolina at Chapel Hill, USA, 1986-87. Appointments: Teaching Assistant, 1977-82, Instructor, 1982-86, Associate Professor, 1986-1990, Professor, 1990-, School of Pharmacy, Professor and Director, Graduate Institute of Natural Products, 1992-, Kaohsiung Medical College. Publications: Over 100 papers; Over 100 invited and conference lectures. Honours: Excellent Research Award,

National Science Council, Taiwan, 1992; Excellent Teaching Prize, Ministry of Education, Taiwan, 1992; Examination Committee of Ministry of Examination, Taiwan, 1994; Consultant of Committee on Chinese Medicine and Pharmacy, Department of Health, Executive Yuan, Taiwan, 1995. Memberships: Pharmaceutical Society of Taiwan; Chinese Chemical Society of Taiwan; Natural Medicinal Products Society of Taiwan; Society of Chinese Biochemists in America. Address: Graduate Institute of Natural Products, Kaohsiung Medical College, Kaohsiung 807, Taiwan.

**WU Zuojun,** b. 21 June 1939, Shanghai, China. Professor; Chief Physician. m. 1 daughter. Education: Graduated from Medical University. Appointments: Phsyician, Shanghai Ren-ji Hospital, 1963-66; Engaged in prevention and treatment of schistosomiasis and training of rural doctors in Jiading County, 1967-69; Director and Chief Physician, An-ting Hospital, Jiading County, 1970-89; Director, WHO Collaborating Centre for PHC, Jiading, VP Red Cross, Jiading District, Director, Jiading District Public Health Bureau, 1990. Publications: 5 academic thesis; Professional writing: Cough; Participated in editing, Handbook of Appropriate Technology and Essential Drugs for Rural Areas in China. Address: WHO Collaborating Centre for PHC, Jiading District, 255 Jinsha Shanghai 201800, China.

**WULFF Donald H,** b. 5 August 1944, Billings, Montana, USA. University Professor; Administrator. 1 son, 1 daughter. Education: BS, General Studies, Montana State University, 1966; MA, Interpersonal Communication, University of Montana, 1975; PhD, Instructional Communication, University of Washington, 1985. Appointments: Secondary Instructor, 1965-80; Assistant/Associate Director, 1988-. Publications: Numerous Research Publications. Honours: Distinguished Teaching Awards. Memberships: University of Washington Teaching Academy; National Communication Association; Professional and Organizational Development Network in Higher Education. Address: University of Washington, Center for Instructional Develompent and Research, 396 Bagley Hall, Box 351725, Seattle, WA 98195-1725, USA.

**WUORINEN Charles,** b. 9 June 1938, New York City, USA. Composer. Education: BA, 1961, MA, 1963, Columbia University. Appointments: Academic Appointments: New England Conservatory, 1968-71, Manhattan School of Music, 1971-79, Rutgers University, 1984-; Composer, over 200 works. Honours include: Pulitzer Prize, 1970; MacArthur Foundation Fellowship, 1986-91. Memberships: American Academy of Arts and Letters; American Academy of Arts and Sciences. Address: c/o Howard Stokar Management, 870 West End Avenue, New York, NY 10025-4948, USA.

**WURZBURGER Judith,** b. 20 January 1935, Frankfurt, Germany. Senior Lecturer. m. Simon, 2 sons, 1 daughters. Education: Degree in Sport Education, Wingate College, 1953; MSc, Life Sciences, Hebrew University, 1959; PhD, Bar Ilan University, 1974. Appointments: Senior Assistant, Bar Ilan University, 1960-75; Postdoctoral Fellow, Hebrew University, 1975-76; Lecturer, Open University, Tel Aviv, Israel, 1976-77; Senior Lecturer, Levinsky College for Education, Tel Aviv, Israel, 1978-; Head of Biology Department, 1985-. Publications: Germination behaviour of Aegilops Kotschyi Boiss; Gibberellin and hull controled inhibition of germination in Aegilops Kotschyi Boiss; Many other articles on the germination of Aegilops Kotschyi seeds. Memberships: Israel Society of Plant Science, and FESPP. Address: P O Box 11282, 61112 Tel Aviv, Israel.

**WYNESS Steven C,** b. 25 September 1967, Carmel, New York, USA. Artist; Designer. m. Lorraine E Disanza-Wyness, 2 sons, 1 daughter. Education: AAS, Dutchess Community

College, 1987; BA, Western Connecticut State University, 1990. Appointments: Photographer; Illustrator; Designer; Sculpter; Art Director. Honours: Dutchess United Educators Award, Academic Excellence in Visual Arts, 1987; Best in Show Fourth Annual Photographic Eye, 1990. Address: 77 Joes Hill Road, Brewster, NY 10509-5322, USA.

**WYNN Valree Fletcher,** b. 9 May 1922, Mineral Wells, Texas, USA. Educator. m. Phail, 2 sons, 1 daughter. Education: MA, Oklahoma State University, 1951; PhD, 1976. Appointments: Gubernatorial Appointment, Board of Regents of Oklahoma Colleges, 1986; Full Professor, Cameron University, Lawton Oklahoma; Retired, 1985. Honours: Appointed 2 International Committees in Alpha Kappa Alpha; Numerous Awards and Certificates, For Excellence in the field of Education; Numerous Positions on Boards of Directors; Inducted in Oklahoma Women's Hall of Fame, 1996; Graduate Excellence Award, Oklahoma State University. Memberships: Phi Kappa Phi; AAUW. Address: 6901 Sprucewood Dr, Lawton, OK 73505, USA.

**WYRSCH James Robert,** b. 23 February 1942, Springfield, Missouri, USA. Lawyer. m. B Darlene, 4 sons, 1 daughter. Education: BA, University of Notre Dame, 1963; JD, Georgetown University, 1966; LLM, University of Missouri, Kansas City, 1972. Appointments: Lawyer; Adjunct Professor; Lecturer; Captain, United States Army. Publications: Co-Author, Criminal Intent and Due Process, 1991; Co-Author, Missouri Criminal Trial Practice, 1994. Memberships: American Bar Association; Association of Trial Lawyers of America; Fellow, American College of Trial Lawyers; Missouri Supreme Court Committee. Address: 1501 NE Sunny Creek Lane, Blue Springs, MO 64014-2044, USA.

**WYSINSKA Elzbieta,** b. 18 November 1934, Warsaw, Poland. Theatrologist. m. Kazimierz A Wysinski. Education: MS, University of Warsaw, 1956. Appointments: Editor, Dialog, magazine, 1956-; Editorial General Secreatary, 1961-84; Deputy Editor, 1985-90; Literary Manager, Theatre Na Woli, Warsaw, 1990-91; Editor-in-Chief, Theatre in Poland, 1992-. Publications: First Nights and Other Theatre Events, 1977; Dictionary of Contemporary Theatre, 1980, 1990 (with co-author); Several articles. Honours: Awards, 1973, 1980. Memberships: Polish Writers Society; Polish Centre of International Theatre Institute. Address: Theatre in Poland, Pilsudskiego 9, 00-078 Warsaw, Poland.

# X

**XANTHEAS Sotiris,** b. 20 June 1961, Athens, Greece. Chemist. m. Maria Annmari Hadjos, 2 daughters. Education: Diploma, Chemical Engineering, National Technical University of Athens, Greece, 1984; PhD, Physical Chemistry, Iowa University, Ames, USA, 1991. Appointments: Postdoctoral Fellow, Molecular Science Research Center, Richland, 1990-92; Research Scientist, 1992-93, Senior Research Scientist, 1992-97, Chief Scientist, 1998-, Environmental Molecular Sciences Laboratory, Richland. Publications: Several in professional journals. Honours: Alpha Chi Sigma; Outstanding Teaching Award, 1990. Memberships: American Chemical Society; American Physical Society; Adjunct Member, Institute of Electronic Structure and Laser, Foundation for Research and Technology-Hellas, Heraklion, Crete, Greece. Address: Environmental Molecular Sciences Laboratory, Pacific Northwest National Laboratory, PO Box 999, MS K1-96, Richland, WA 99352. USA.

**XIA Jisong,** b. 15 May 1925, Hangzhou, China. Professor of Philosophy. m. Feifeng Shen, 1 son, 1 daughter. Education: BA, National Central University of China, 1948; MA, Peoples University of China, 1954. Appointments: Associate Professor and Deputy Chairman, Department of Philosophy, Nanjing, 1975-82; Professor and Chairman, Department of Philosophy, Nanjing University, 1982-90; Professor, Department of Philosophy, Hangzhou University, 1990-98; Professor, Department of Philosophy, Zhejiang University, 1998-. Publications: Over 10 books, Course of the Modern Philosophy in the West, 1986; Mathematics Philosophy in the West, 1986; Philosophy of Science in the West, 1986. Memberships; Vice-Chairman, Society of Modern Foreign Philosophy Study in China; Chairman, Society of Foreign Philosophy Study in East China. Address: Department of Philosophy, Hangzou University, Hangzou 310007, China.

**XIA Yun,** b. 27 December 1927, Jiangxi, China. Teacher. m. Zhang Yiren, 1 son, 1 daughter. Education: Student, Beijing University, 1950-52; Architecture Diploma, 1954, Tsinghua University. Appointments: Assistant in Architecture in Tsinghua University, 1954-57; Assistant, Lecturer, Associate Professor and Professor, 1957-97, Professor and Educational Inspector, College of Architecture, 1997-, Xian University of Architecture and Technology. Publications: Books: Foundations of Energy and Land Saving Buildings; Energy and Land Saving Buildings; 2 translations English to Chinese: Earth Sheltered Habitat; Foundations of Architectural Science; 4 collections of teaching slides. Honours: Excellent Science Researcher, Shaanxi Province, 1989; Special Subsidy of the State Council of China for Outstanding Teaching and Research, 1992-; With 3 other teachers won the 3rd Professional Prize of UIA and UNESCO, 1993 International Design Compt; 2nd Prize of Advanced Science and Technology of Ministry level. Membership: International Energy Foundation. Address: Xian University of Architecture and Technology, College of Architecture, Xian City 710055, China.

**XIAO Da Zhun,** b. 25 December 1938, Pingxiang City, Jiangxi, China. Professor of Mechanical Engineering. m. Shu Yuan Chen, 2 daughters. Education: Graduate, Power Engineering Department, Huazhong University of Science and Technology, Wuhan, 1955-60. Appointments: Teaching Assistant, Lecturer, Associate Professor, Professor, Dalian University of Technology, 1960-80, 1983-; Visiting Assistant Professor, University of California, Davis, USA, 1981-82. Publications include: Computer aided design software package for conjugate helical surfaces, 1996; Features of the negative torque on female rotor in twin screw compressors, 1996; Kinematic differential geometry of a rigid body in spatial motion, 1997; Geometrical analysis for inter-groove passage of the conjugate helical surfaces, 1997. Honours: Graduate Award, HUST, 1960; Advanced Faculty Member Award, DUT, 1978, 1987; Science and Technology Progress Award, Liaoning Education Commission, 1996; Excellent Teacher Award, Bao Steel Education Fund, 1997; Model Worker, Dalian Municipal Government, 1998. Memberships: Senior Member, Chinese Mechanical Engineering Society, 1986-; Teaching Directing Committee on Theory of Machines and Mechanisms, 1990-; Deputy Chief of Council, Chinese Education Society for Theory of Machines and Mechanisms, 1992-; Committee, International Federation for Theory of Machines and Mechanisms, 1998. Address: Department of Mechanical Engineering, Dalian Unviersity of Technology, Dalian 116024, China.

**XIE Guozhang,** b. 18 June 1929, Jiangxi, China. Researcher; Professor. m. Wu Hezheng, 2 daughters. Education: BSc, 1951, Physics Departmentt, Tsing Hua University, Beijing. Appointments: Researcher, Institute of Applied Physics, The Academy of Science of China, Beijing, 1951-60; Researcher, Institute of Electro-Mechanics, 1960-66; Senior Engineer, Changzhou Semi-Conductor Factory, 1966-85; Professor, Hehai University, 1985-95; Director, Institute of Micromechanism, 1995-. Publications: 2 books; Over 100 papers; Discovered a metastable phase in AB alloy; Invented a new technology for fabricating high-temp CMOS. Honours: 1st Prizes, Ministry and City Government, 1987-88. Memberships: China Physics Association; China Electronics Association; Tsing Hua Alumni Association; China Translation Association. Address: 85-2-301 South LaoDon XinCun, Changzhou, Jiangsu, 213001, China.

**XIE Yi-Min,** b. 23 December 1963, Jiangsu, China. Engineering Educator. m. Grace, 1 son, 1 daughter. Education: BSc, Jiao Tong University, China, 1984; PhD, University of Wales, UK, 1991. Appointments: Research Fellow, University of Sydney, Australia, 1992-93; Lecturer, 1993-95; Senior Lecturer, 1995-97; Associate Professor, Victoria University of Technology, Melbourne, 1998-. Publications: Evolutionary Structural Optimisation, 1997. Honours: Best Student Award, K C Wong Education Foundation, Hong Kong, 1985. Address: Victoria U Tech Civil Engr, P O Box 14428 MCMC, Victoria 8001, Australia.

**XING Qiwu,** b. 29 December 1953, Shanghai. Chemist. m. Hong Zhu, 1 son. Education: Anhui Normal University, Wuhu, China, 1975-78; MSc, 1983, Hangzhou University, Zhejiang; Julius-Maximilians-Universitaet Wuerzburg, Bayern, Germany, 1989-90; Dr rer nat, 1993, Universitaet Bayreuth, Bayern. Appointments: Agricultural Labourer, Mechanic, Skilled Worker of Chemical plant, Product Manager in Anhui, China, 1970-75; University Assistant, Anhui Normal University, 1978-80; Hangzhou University, 1984-86; Lecturer, Hangzhou University, 1986-89; Teaching Assistant, Universitaet Bayreuth, 1990-93; Researcher, Forschunginstitut fur Chemie und Erdoel, Technische Universitaet Wien, Austria, 1993, Institut fur Neue Materialien gem GmbH, Saarbruecken, Germany, 1993-98; Chairman of Board of Directors, 1997-98, Member of Board of Directors, 1998-, Society of Chinese Chemists and Chemical Engineers in Germany; Head of Development, Graf Papiere GmbH, Grimma, Germany, 1998-. Publications: 12 articles in scientific publications. Membership: Society of Chinese Chemists and Chemical Engineers. Address: Graf Papiere GmbH, Sudstrasse 80, D-04668 Grimma, Germany.

**XIONG Yeping,** b. 26 May 1959, Zhengzhou, Henan, China. Researcher; Educator of Solid Mechanics, Vibration and Noise Control. m. Han Yuchang, 1 daughter. Education: BS, 1982, Petroleum University; MSc, 1988, PhD, 1996, Shandong University of Technology. Appointments: Assistant Lecturer, Lanzhou Petroleum School, 1982-85; Chief Lecturer, 1991-93, Associate Professor, 1993-96, Professor, 1996-, Shandong University of Technology. Publications: Over 35 journal papers both at home and abroad. Honours: Three Advanced Science and Technology Achievements Awards of Provincial level, 1992, 1992, 1994; Distinguished Teacher Award, Shandong University of Technology, 1993; 1st Prizewinner for Excellent Teaching, SDUT, 1995; National Award for Excellence in attending the UN World Conference on Women, 1995; Honoured as Provincial Top Level Professional Technical Personnel, 1998; Honoured as Representative of People's Congress of capital city Jinan, Shandong, 1998. Memberships: Chief Councillor of Shandong Society of Vibration Engineering; Councillor of the Chinese Society of Vibration Engineering for Structure Control; Chinese Society of Mechanics; Chinese Society of Vibration Engineering; Chinese Society Mechanical Engineering. Address: Institute of Engineering Mechanics, College of Materials Science & Engineering, Shandong University of Technology, 250061 Jinan, Shandong, China.

**XIU-LI Zheng.** b. 28 November 1933, Shanghai, China. Oncologist. Education: MD, Shanghai Second Medical University. Appointments: Clinical Oncologist; Chief, Department of Internal Medicine, Pioneering Research in Cancer Diagnosis and Therapy, 35 years. Memberships: Jiansu Provincial Cancer Association; China Medical Association. Address: Jiangsu Provincial Cancer Hospital, No. 42 Bai Zi Ting, Nanjing City 210009, Jiangsu Province, China.

**XU Bo-Qing,** b. 24 June 1961, Jiangxi, China. University Professor. m. Lily Song, 2 daughters. Education: BSc Chemistry, 1982, Jiangxi University; MSc, 1985, PhD, 1988, Dalian Institute Chem Phys, Academia Sinica; Research Fellow, Hokkaido University, Japan, 1986-88. Appointments: Research Associate, Dalian Inst Chem Phys, 1988-91; Professor, Dalian University of Technology, 1992-98; Professor, Tsinghua University, 1998-; Visiting Scholar, Northwestern University, USA, 1995-96; Research Associate, Georgia Tech, USA, 1996-97; Research Associate, Northwestern University, USA, 1997-98. Publications: Over 60 publications in field of Catalysis, Physical Chemistry. Honours: Monbusho Scholarship, Japanese Government; Young Investigator Award, NSFC, China Young Scientist Awards, Liaoning Province, Dalian City, China. Memberships: International Zeolite Association; Chinese Chemical Society. Address: State Key Lab of C1 Chemistry and Chemical Technology, Dept of Chemistry, Tsinghua University, Beijing 100084, China.

**XU Gang,** b. 26 August 1955, Hefei, China. Associate Professor. 1 son. Education: MS, Psychology, Ohio University, 1984; PhD, Psychology, Ohio University, 1989. Appointments: Assistant Professor, Jefferson Medical College, 1992-97; Associate Professor, Jefferson Medical College, 1997-. Publications: 50 Publications in USA, England, Canada; 72 Publications in China; 2 Books, China. Memberships: American Psychological Association. Address: 139 Ashley Ct, Cherry Hill, NJ 08003 3743, USA.

**XU Hongqi,** b. 20 August 1956, Liaoning, China. Scientist. m. Min Lu, 1 son. Education: BSc, 1982; PhD, 1991; Docent, 1995. Appointment: Assistant Professor, Lund University, Sweden. Publications: Numerous, in Physical Review, Journal of Applied Physics, other journals. Honour: Adjunct Professor, Institute of Semiconductors, Chinese Academy of Sciences, 1998. Memberships: American Physical Society; American Association for the Advancement of Science; New York Academy of Sciences. Address: Solid State Physics, Lund University, Box 118, SE-22100 Lund, Sweden.

**XU Jianping,** b. 29 October 1936, Shanghai. Professor; Chief Doctor. m. Chiu Yin Ping, 1 son, 1 daughter. Education: An Hui Medical University; Moscow Neurosurgical Researching Institute. Appointments: Assistant Professor, Doctor, Hospital of An Hui Medical University, 1956-83; Professor, President, Anhui Medical University, 1983-. Publications: 4 Books, Stereotactio, Functional Nuerosurgery; More than 150 Articles. Honours: The Whole Nation Outstanding Model; The Whole Nation Labour Model; Outstanding Expert Enjoying Special Subsidy from the State Department; State Scientific and Technological Advanced Prize. Address: 12E Biyunge Zhonglu Plaza, Huaqiao Cheng, Shenzhou, 518053, China.

**XU Jingze,** University Professor. Education: BA Sociology, 1949, East China University; MA, 1953, Graduate School of China People's University. Appointments: Lifelong Professor of Shandong University, 1960-91; Director of Political Science Department, Director of Sociology Department, President of the Library, Shandong University; President of Folklore Study magazine. Publications: The Introduction of Sociology; The Theories and Methods of Social Investigation; The Introduction of Social Security; Sociology in China; Towards the Society; The Modernisation of Dongying Village; Modernisation, the Choice of Countryside. Memberships: Executive Council of Chinese Sociology Association; President, Shandong Sociology Institute.

**XU Jun Quan,** b. 24 December 1941, Jiangyin City, China. Scientist. m. Sheng Yin Jun, 2 sons. Education: Bachelor, Department of Engineering Physics, Tsing Hua University, China, 1965. Appointments: Scientific Research, Shanghai Institute of Nuclear Research, Chinese Academy of Sciences, 1965-; Senior Researcher, 1978- 1988; Associate Professor, 1988-1995; Professor, 1995-. Publications: Radioisotope X-ray Fluorescence Analysis; Interpretation of Diagram and Satellite L X-ray Transition Around Z=50; L-Subshell Flourescence Yields for Elements with $73{\le}Z{\le}83$; Au L X-ray Relative Intensities Induced by Proton Impact, etc. Honours: 3rd Award of Important Scientific Achievements (Shanghai); 2nd Award of Scientific and Technological Advances (Chinese Academy of Sciences); 3rd Award of Natural Sciences (Chinese Academy of Sciences). Memberships: Chinese Nuclear Society; Chinese Nuclear Physics Society; International Radiation Physics Society; Shanghai Eighth and Ninth Committee, Chinese Peoples Political Consultative Conference. Address: Shanghai Inst of Nuclear Research, Chinese Academy of Sciences, P O Box 800-204, Jiading, Shanghai 201800, China.

**XU Kelin,** b. 28 July 1945, Chengdu, Sichuan, China. Professor. m. Qin Hua Bai, 1 daughter. Education: Graduate, Tianjin University, 1968. Appointments: Chongqing Making-Ball Factory; Chongqing Leather Corporation; Teacher, Chongqing Jiangzhu University, 1974-. Publications include: Pneamatical Technology Basement; Research of Technology of Hydraulic System's Fuzzy Control; Research of Continuous Casting Machine's Hydraulic System Experiments. Honours: Over ten awards and honours in scientific research and teaching. Memberships: Sichuan Hydraulic and Pneumatic Chapter, China Mechanics Association; Secretary, Chapter of Tianjin University Alumni Association; Sichuan Writers Union. Address: Mechanical and Electrical School, Chongqing Jiangzhu University, Chongqing, China.

**XU Lisheng,** b. 3 May 1940, Guiping, Guangxi. Educator; Researcher. m. Hongmao Jiang, 1 son. Education: Department of Geophysics, Peking University, 1958-64. Appointments: Visiting Scholar, Space Science and Engineering Centre, University Wisconsin-Madison, 1982-85; Associate Professor, 1987-93, Professor, 1993-, Chengdu Meteorological College, Chengdu, China; Guest Professor, National Satellite Meteorological Centre of China, Beijing, 1997-; Guest Professor, Centre for Environmental Remote Sensing, Chiba University, Japan, 1997-98; Research Fellow, Department Physics and Material Science, City University of Hong Kong, 1999-. Publications: Author or co-Author, more than 60 papers in fields of environmental remote sensing and light scattering by nonspherical particles. Honours: 3rd Award of meteorological sciences, 1990, 2nd Award, 1996, 1998, Meteorological Administration of China; Specialist with special contribution award, the State Council of China, 1991-. Memberships: New York Academy of Sciences; American Association for the Advancement of Sciences; Optical Society of America; American Institute of Physics; European Optical Society; Planetary Society. Address: Chengdu Meteor Coll ARSRSL, Renmin South Road, Chengdu Sichuan 610041, China.

**XU Man,** b. 23 April 1948, Beijing, China. Pharmacologist. Education: PhD, Tokyo Institute of Technology, 1990. Appointments: Senior Scientist, Nippon Roche Research Centre, 1992-98; International Project Manager, Applied Analytical Industries Japan, 1998-. Membership: Japanese Contract Research Organization Association. Address: 7-10 Nihnbashi-Honcho, 4-chome, Chuo-ku, Tokyo 103-0023, Japan.

**XU Qinghua,** b. 28 September 1952, Beijing, China. Engineer; Manager. m. J Y Zhou, 1 daughter. Education: Master Degree, Science. Appointments: Deputy Director, Planning Department, 1985, Director, Standards Department, 1988, NEPA; Vice President, Chinese Research Academy of Environment Sciences, 1991; Deputy Permanent Representative of China to UNEP, 1993; Secretary General, CEPE, 1996. Memberships: Secretary General, Chinese Water Quality Committee. Address: CEPF, Yuhninan Road, Beijing 100029, China.

**XU Ruiwei,** b. 4 May 1933, Shanghai, China. Environmental Chemistry. m. Yongxin Ji, 1 son, 1 daughter. Education: Undergraduate, Zhejiang University, 1951-55; Postgraduate, Chinese Academy of Sciences, 1959-63. Appointments: Research Assistant, 1955-59, Postgraduate Student, 1959-63, Research Associate, 1964-82, Associate Professor, 1983-89, Professor, 1990-97, Group Leader, 1984-97, Institute of Soil Science. Publications: 63 papers in professional journals. Honours: Development Prize, Science and Technology, Academia Sinica, 1981, 1985, 1987, 1988; Nature Science Prize, Academia Sinica, 1995. Memberships: Environmental Chemistry Committee, Chinese Society of Environmental Science; Soil Science Society of China; Chemistry Society of China. Address: Institute of Soil Science, Academia Sinica, PO Box 821, Nanjing, China.

**XU Yingpei,** b. 31 January, Ningbo, China. Artist. m. Jun Bi, 1 son, 1 daughter. Education: BA, China Academy of Art, 1965; MA, China Academy of Art, 1980; Exchange Scholar, Hochschule Fur Bildende Kunste, Hamburg, Germany, 1992. Appointments: Editor, Jiangxi Province Federation of Literacy and Art Workers, China, 1965-68; Artist, Jiangxi Province Museum, Nan Chang, China, 1968-78; Professor, Academy of Fine Arts, Hangzhou, 1980-92; Artist, Two World Arts Inc, USA, 1993-94; Artist, Julia Gray Ltd, USA, 1994. Publications: Canadian Eskimos Art, 1987; The World of Printmaking, 1988.

Honours: Third Prize, 4th International Graphic Art Exhibition, Sweden, 1997; Certificate of Merit, WC the Slmagundi Club 21st Annual Non Member Art Exhibition, 1998; C & S Studio Award, Community Arts Association 5th National Open Exhibition, USA, 1999. Memberships: Art League of Long Island; American Artists Professional League; China Artists Association. Address: 89-10 Whitney Ave Apt 5P, Elmhurst, NY 11373, USA.

**XUE Qunying,** b. 21 December 1950, Hebei, China. Lawyer, Doctor. m. Zhao Zhenxue, 1 son, 1 daughter. Education: Masters Degree, Institution of Law, 1989. Appointments: President, Qiushi School of Law, 197-; Lawyer, Fatongs Lawyer's Office, 1997. Publications: Discussions in Chinese Criminal Law; A New Theory of Jural Psychology; Over 50 Thesis, Value Engineering, Lawyers. Honours: Present Day Famous Persons of China, 1994; Self Study Talent of China, 1991; Who's Who of Intellectuals, Thirteenth Edition, International Biographical Centre. Address: Qiushi School of Law, Hengshui 05300, Hebei, China.

# Y

**YACOUT Maged Mahmoud,** b. 7 May 1946, Cairo, Egypt. Physiologist. Education: MB, BCh, Ain Shams University, Cairo, 1969; DMSc, Al Azhar University, Cairo, 1973; MD, Physiology, 1976. Appointments: Senior Professor, Physiology, Faculty of Medicine, Zagazig University, 1984-; Member, Scientific Permanent Committee for Evaluation and Promotion of Physiologist in the Supreme Council of Egyptian Universities, 1985-. Publications: Principals of Human Physiology, 5 Volumes, 6 Editions; Editor in Chief, Zagazig Journal of Medical Physiology. Memberships: Egyptian Medical Association; Egyptian Society for Physiological Sciences; Egyptian Society for Basic Medical Sciences; Zagazig Clinical Medical Society. Address: Department of Physiology, Zagazig University Faculty of Medicine, Zagazig, Egypt.

**YADAV Mahendra Pal,** b. 2 June 1945, Surkhuroo Village, Bulandshahar (UP), India. Government Service. m. Kanti Yadav, 1 son, 1 daughter. Education: BVSc and AH, 1966, MVSC, 1968, PhD, 1973, University of Agra. Appointments: Demonstrator, Bacteriology, Veterinary College, Mathura, 1968-69; ICAR Senior Research Fellow, 1969-72, Postdoctoral Fellow, 1973-74, Graduate Assistant, 1972-73, Professor Virology, 1981-82, Head, Division Virology, 1982-87, IVRI, Mukteswar; Assistant Professor Virology, 1974-76, Associate Professor Virology, SRO, 1976-81, Agricultural University Pantnagar; Scientist In Charge of Animal Health Unit and Infectious Disease Unit, 1987-93, Director, 1993-, National Research Centre on Equines, Hisar. Publications: 107 Research papers; 12 review papers and book chapters; 137 seminar, symposia and workshop proceedings; 29 scientific bulletins, reports and proceedings; 26 popular articles; 54 newspaper articles. Honours: Chancellor's Medal, 1966; 3 Silver and 1 Bronze Medal for merits, 1963-66; Junior, 1967-68, Senior, 1969-72, and Postdoctoral, 1973-74, Research Fellowships, Indian Council of Agricultural Research; Lance Award of 61 Cavalry, 1996 for promotion of equine sports; Best Research Paper Award, 1996; ICAR Special Award for developing a low cost equine influenza vaccine, 1998; Fellow, National Academy of Veterinary Sciences, New Delhi, 1996. Memberships: President, Indian Virological Society, 1996-98, Joint Secretary, 1988-91, Councillor, 1983-88; VP, Indian Association of Veterinary Microbiologists, Immunologists and Specialists in Infectious Diseases, 1993-96, Executive Committee, 1985-91, 1997-; Founder member, Transport Animal Welfare Studies; Indian Science Congress; 5 other societies. Address: National Research Centre on Equines, Sirsa Road, Hisar 125001, India.

**YAKES Barbara Lee,** b. Detroit, Michigan, USA. Physician. m. Richard Jankowics, 1 son. Education: BA, 1973, BSN, 1978, Wayne State University; DO, 1986, Michigan State University; MOccHealth, 1989, Harvard. Appointments: Medical Director, General Motors Corporation, 1989-. Publications: 5. Honours: Phi Beta Kappa, 1972; Bubeck OB-Gyn Award, 1984; Michigan Cancer Society Award, 1990; Mead Johnson Research Award, 1986. Memberships: Fellow, American College of Preventive Medicine; ACOEM; American College of Occupational and Environmental Medicine. Address: General Motors Corporation, Powertrain Group, Medical Department, 12200 Middlebelt Road, Livonia, MI 48150, USA.

**YAKIMENKO Stanislav A,** b. 3 September 1938, Rijevka, Umanskogo, Cherkasskiy, Ukraine. Ophthalmologist. m. V A Yakimenko, 1 daughter. Education: Medical Institute, Ternopol Ukraine, 1955-61; Postgraduate Course, Filatov Institute of Eye

Diseases and Tissue Therapy. Appointments: Candidate of Medical Science, 1973; Dr of Medical Science, 1986; Professor, 1993; Ophthalmosurgery of high qualification, 1991; Performed 10000 opthalmological operations, 750 keratoprosthetics; Chief of Eye Burns Department, Filatov Institute, 1988-. Publications: Monographs: Optical Keratoprosthesis, 1986; Eye Burns, 1998; Diploma of Medical Academy of USSR, 1987; Scientific works on ophthalmosurgery, 1969-97; 3 patents. Memberships: Government of Ukrainian Association of Ophthalmologists; Scientific Counsil of Filatov Institute of Eye Diseases and Tissue Therapy. Address: The Filatov Eye Institute, Boulevard Le France 49/51, Odessa 61, 270061 Ukraine.

**YAKOVER Yosef,** b. 21 December 1950, Moscow, USSR. Physicist. m. Diana, 2 sons. Education: MSc, University of Vilnius, USSR, 1973; PhD, University of Minsk, USSR, 1984. Appointments: Engineer, Senior Engineer, Researcher, Scientific Research Institute of Radio Meas Instr, Vilnius, 1973-89; Senior Researcher, Zondas Co, Vilnius, 1990; Senior Researcher, Department Physical El, University Tel-Aviv, 1991-. Publications: About 60 papers in scientific journals. Honours: 4 USSR patents; USSR Inventor Medal, 1989. Address: Tel Aviv University, Department Electrical Engineering and Physical Electrics, PO Box 39040, 69978 Ramat Aviv, Israel.

**YAKOVLEV Anatoly Ivanovych,** b. 1 November 1937, Kharkov, Ukraine. Economist; Academic. m. Nina Khitushchenko, 18 May 1986. Education: MEng, 1961; DS (Kandidat Nauk), 1969; DSc, Industrial Economics and Management, 1982. Appointment: Head and Full Professor of the Chair, Department of Economics and Marketing, Economics Faculty, Kharkov State Politech University. Publications: 230 scientific publications including 23 books (monographs and textbooks): Economic Estimation of Automation Instruments, 1982; Socio-Economic Effectiveness of Innovations, 1994; Creating New Technogical Systems: Efficiency Planning, Optimization Under Conditions of Market Relations, Kiev, 1998; Marketing of Innovation Processes, Kiev, 1998; Management of Investment and Innovation Activity on the basis of the Project Analysis; Choice of System Alternatives of Management of Investment of Project Risk, 14th World Congress on Project Management, Intl Project Mngmt Assn Proceedings, Vol 1, Lithuania, co-author, 1998. Honours: Winner, Ukrainian Professors' Competition, 1990; Electing Academician, Academy of Engineering Sciences of the Ukraine, 1991; Honoured Professor, Ukraine, 1991. Memberships: International Project Management Association, 1993-; Journalists Association of the Ukraine, 1965; Ukrainian Supreme (Verchovnaya) Rada Councillor-Consultant on Innovation Policy and New Technology. Address: 22 Krasnoshkolnaya naberezhnaya Str, Apt 53, Kharkiv 310125, Ukraine.

**YAKOVLEV Genrikh Vasilievich,** b. 30 May 1932, Cheboksary, Russia. PhD. m. Ludmila Vasilievna, 1 son. Education: Diploma, Moscow Engineering and Physics Institute, magna cum laude, 1956; PhD, 1985. Appointments: Engineer, Senior Engineer, Head of Group, Head of Laboratory, Head of Division, Director of Department of Electronics, Russian Research Center, Kurchatov Institute, 1956-. Publications: Over 120 publications, 2 Russian patents. Honours: Prize, USSR Ministry Council, 1985; State Order of Friendship of the People. Memberships: Bureau of Applied Physics; Council of the Russian Academy of Sciences; Nuclear Society of Russia. Address: RRC Kurchatov Institute, 1 Kurchatov Square, 123182 Moscow, Russia.

**YALKOVSKY Rafael,** b. 11 October 1917, Chicago, Illinois, USA. Professor. Education: SB, 1946; MS, 1955; PhD, University of Chicago, 1956. Appointments: US Air Corps, England, 1943-45; Western Geophysical Company, 1950-54; Research Laboratory, Crane Co, 1954-56; Assistant Professor, University of Montana, 1956-61; Professor, Buffalo State University, 1962-84. Publications: Over 30 Publications, Papers, Abstracts, Poems, Short Stories. Memberships: Fellow, American Association for the Advancement of Science; Fellow, New York Academy of Sciences. Address: P O Box 544, Grand Island, NY 14072 0544, USA.

**YAMAGUCHI Akira,** b. 15 October 1940, Kyoto, Japan. Professor. m. Toshimi, 2 sons, 1 daughter. Education: BS, Nagoya Institute of Technology, 1964; PhD, Nagoya University, 1977. Appointments: Associate Professor, 1972-78, Professor, 1989-, Nagoya Institute of Technology. Publications: Numerous professionl articles in journals. Honours: New Technology Development Foundation Award, 1981; Technical Association Refractories of Japan Award, 1993; Excellent Writings Award, Japanese Society for Engineering Education, 1994; Ceramic Society of Japan Award, 1995. Memberships: Ceramic Society of Japan; Technical Association of Refractories, Japan; American Ceramic Society; Iron and Steel Institute, Japan. Address: 5-5-3 Iwanaridai, Kasugai 487-0033, Japan.

**YAMAGUCHI Jun,** b. 6 September 1957, Osaka, Japan. Medical Doctor. Education: MD, 1984, PhD, Postgrad Course of Physiology, 1990, Osaka Medical College. Appointments: Assistant Professor of Rehabilitation Medicine, Osaka Medical College, 1996-. Memberships: Japan Medical Association; Japanese Association of Rehab Medicine; Japanese Orthopaedic Association; Physiological Society of Japan; Japanese Society for Bone and Mineral Research. Address: Dept of Rehabilitation Medicine, Osaka Medical College, 2-7 Daigaku-machi, Takatsuki 569-8686, Japan.

**YAMAGUCHI Shigehiro,** b. 22 July 1961, Nagasaki, Japan. Chemist; Educator. Education: B Eng, 1984, M Eng, 1988, Yokohama National University. Appointments: Research Associate, Teikyo Heisei University, 1989-. Publications: Articles in professional journals. Memberships: AAAS; Chemical Society of Japan; Japan Oil Chemists' Society. Address: 5-6-9-201 Oyumino, Midori-ku, Chiba 266-0016, Japan.

**YAMATOYA Kazuhiko,** b. 11 July 1961, Osaka, Japan. Company Executive. m. Michiyo Shigi. Education: BS, 1984, MS, 1986, Osaka University. Appointments: Development Section, 1986-, Deputy Manager, 1995-, Dainippon Pharmaceutical Co Ltd. Publications: Advances in Food Science and Technology, 1997; The Science of Dietary Fiber, 1997; Maruzen Food Encyclopedia, 1998. Memberships: Fellow, Japan Association for Dietary Fiber Research; Super Glycomolecules Society. Address: Food, Food Additives and Chemicals Division, 25-6 Yanaka 3-chome, Taito-ku, Tokyo 110, Japan.

**YAMAZAKI Yoshio,** b. 7 September 1953, Saitama, Japan. Railman. Appointments: Railman, Seibu Railway, 1969; Railman, Eidan Subway, 1970; Various, 1970-74; Japan National Railway, 1974; East Japan Railway Company, 1987-. Memberships: International Passengers Association, Hong Kong. Address: 7 18 Iwasawa, Hannoshi Saitama-Ken 357, Japan.

**YAMPOLSKY Phyllis,** b. 23 August 1932, Philadelphia, USA. Conceptual Artist; Painter. Education: Philadelphia College of Art, 1950-52; Institute Allende, 1952-53; Hans Hoffman School, New York, 1955-58; Ecole de Beaux Arts, Fontainbleau, France, 1957. Career: Collections of Dallas Museum of Fine Arts, Texas; Museum Erotic Art, Stockholm, Sweden; National Archives, Washington; Several Private Collections. Creative Works: Exhibitions include: Philadelphia Museum of Art, 1957; McNay Institute, San Antonio, Texas, 1977-78; Teilhard and Metamorphosis, Arcosanti, Arizona, 1981; America's Reunion on the Mall, Clinton Inaugural Committee, Washington, 1993. Honours: Walter Damrosch Award, Ecole de Beaux Arts, Fontainbleau, France, 1957; New York State Council Arts Award, 1967; Ann Valentine Awards, of Cue Magazine, 1967. Memberships: Founding Member, The Brooklyn Accent, Greenpoint Council of Arts; Co-Founder, McCarren Park Conservancy; Independent Friends of McCarren Park; Northeast Windham Council on the Arts, Vermont; New Vermont School of the Arts. Address: 888 Manhattan Avenue, Brooklyn, NY 11222, USA.

**YAN Weixing,** b. 26 July 1957, China. Medical Scientist. m. Changsong Cai, 1 son. Education: Bachelor Degree, Medicine, 1983; Master Degree, Physiology, 1990. Appointments: Teaching Assistant, 1983-86, Lecturer, 1990-95, Department of Physiology, Nantong Medical College, China; Researcher, Neurology Department, Faculty of Medicine, University of Sydney, Australia, 1995-. Publications: Several articles in professional journals. Honours: 2nd Prize, National Medicine Examination, China, 1983; 1st Prize, Public Speech Competition, China, 1991. Memberships: Chinese Medical Association; Neurosciences Association; Immunology Association of China. Address: Medicine Department D06, University of Sydney, Sydney, NSW 2006, Australia.

**YAN Zhenghua,** b. 14 January 1968, Lin Chuan, Jiangxi, China. Researcher. m. Yan Liu. Education: BSc, 1990; MSc, 1992; PhD, 1999. Appointment: Researcher, Lund University. Publications: Articles in professional scientific journals. Honours: Chinese National Academy President Prize, 1992; 2nd Class Prize, Chinese National Academy, 1993. Address: Lund University, Fire Safety Engineering Department, 221 00 Lund, Sweden.

**YANG BaoZhi,** b. 29 October 1935, Foshan, Guangdong Province. Professor of Violin. m. Sun Huijin, 1 son. Education: Studied violin with Ma Sicong, Central Conservatory of Music, 1952, graduated with distinguished achievements, 1957. Appointments: Violinist, Conductor, Composer, Chongqing Opera House, 1957-84; Professor, Central Conservatory of Music, researcher on sophisticated combination of Chinese and western music, 1984-91; Guest Professor, Shanghai Conservatory and Tianjing Conservatory same time; Professor of violin and chamber music, 1991-; Special concert of works, 1997. Publications: Works and debut: About 50 violin pieces based on Chinese traditional tunes; About 30 pieces of chamber music. Honours: The Joyful Greetings violin piece awarded Prize in 1st Instrumental Music Competition, Central Conservatory of Music, 1956; Torch Festival, an opera, Second Prize, 1984, All-China Theatrical Opera Performance. Memberships: Chinese Musicians Association; Founder, Chinese Children's Federation of Violin Education. Address: Sichuan Music College, Chengdu, China 610021.

**YANG Bo-Suk,** b. 8 February 1956, Kangwon, South Korea. Professor. m. Jung-Mi Um, 2 sons. Education: BS, 1978, MS, 1980, PhD, 1985, Engineering. Appointments: Assistant Professor, 1985-90, Associate Professor, 1990-95, Professor, 1995-; Visiting Professor, University of Virginia, 1989-90; Visiting Scientist, Kobe University, 1990-91. Publications: Several articles in professional journals. Honours: H H Jeffcott Award, 1987; Distinguished Research Award, 1988;

Outstanding Paper Award, 1994. Memberships: American Society of Mechanical Engineers; Korean Society of Mechanical Engineers; Vibration Institute; Korean Society for Noise and Vibration Engineering. Address: Pukyong National University, School of Mechanical and Automotive Engineering, San 100 Yongdang-dong, Nam-ku, Pusan 608-739, South Korea.

**YANG Chih-Ping,** b. 5 July 1959, Taipei, Taiwan. Pharmaceutical Researcher. m. Professor Shir-ly Huang, 1 daughter. Education: BS, Chemistry, 1982; PhD, Organic Chemistry, 1990; EMBA, General Management, 1998. Appointments: Research Scientist, Upjohn, USA, 1990-92; Research Fellow, Development Center for Biotechnology, Taiwan, 1992-96; Medical Department Manager, Bayer Taiwan, 1996-99; Medical Director, Schering-Plough, Taiwan. Publications: 23 in journals; 7 patents. Memberships: AAAS; NYAS; DIA; IUPAB; IRPMA. Address: 7F #8-2, Lane 280, Section 6, Min-Chuan East Road, Nei-Hu, Taipei, Taiwan 114.

**YANG Chunxia,** b. 15 February 1943, Shanghai, China. Actress. m. Lin Xintao, 1 son. Education: Shanghai School of Chinese Opera, 1954-60. Career: Actress, Shanghai Youth Theatre of Chinese Opera, 1960-71; Actress, Beijing Theatre of Peking Opera, 1971-79; Actress, China Theatre of Peking Opera, 1979-. Honour: Plum Blossom Medal, Performing Art, 1989. Memberships: Chinese Dramatists Association; Chinese People's Political Consultative Conference. Address: Hong Tudian, 6th Building 1-303, Beijing 100054, China.

**YANG Ji Wu,** b. 22 June 1941, Shenyang, Liaoning, China. Agrometeorology. n. Yong Sheng, 1 son, 1 daughter. Education: Bachelor of Science, 1964. Appointments: Vice Dean, Agronomy Department, 1980-84. Publications: Agrometeorology Predicition and Information; Agrometeorology; Introduction to Agrometeorological Prediction; CLimate Change and Crop Yield; The Impact of Climate Variations on Agriculture and Its Stratergic Countermeasure. Honours: Excellent Scientific Acheivement of Central Meteorology Bureau; Scientific Progress Award; Scientific Progress Award of Agricultural Ministry of China. Memberships: Director, Agrometeorology Division, Agronomy of Chino; Vice President, Agrometeorology Association of Northeast China; Membership, Agrometeorology Council of the Meterology Association of China. Address: Agrometeorology Department, Agricultural College, Shanyang Agricultural University, 120 Dongling Road, Shenyang, Liaoning 110161, China.

**YANG Jiben,** b. 25 September 1918, Zengzhou, Henan Province, China. Professor. m. Mrs Meihua Song, 1 son, 2 daughters. Education: BEd, 1942, National South-Western United University; MA of Educational Psychology, 1945, National Central University; Graduate of the class for advanced studies for teachers in-service at universities, 1953, Peijing Normal University. Appointments: Professor, Honorary President, (former) Research Institute of Education and Psychology, Hunan Normal University, Honorary President, Hunan Province Social Psychology Society; Adviser, Hunan Psychology Society; Adviser on Scientific Affairs to China Information Company; Head of Hunan Provincial Editorial Branch under the leadership of magazine Chinese Information Processing; Specially invited editors committee member, China International Education Press O/B HK CIIP Ltd. Publications: 9 important papers in professional journals and proceedings; Translator 4 psychological and educational books from English and Russian, 1948-83; 2 inventions; Present research fields: Application of Psychology on Cognitive Aspect of Chinese Characters. Honours: Government Special Subsidy for Scientists with outstanding achievements, State Council of China, 1993; Excellent Achievement Certificate in research of humanistic and social science, 2nd Class Prize, Sate Education Commission of PR China, 1995; Excellent Natural Science Essay Certificate, 1st Class Prize, Government of Hunan Province, 1994; Honorary Social Science Specialist working in Hunan Province, Government of Hunan Province, 1998. Memberships: Standing member in Council, China Social Psychology Society, 1982-95; Editorial Committee member, Journal of Social Psychology Research; President, 1983-95, Honorary President, 1996-, Hunan Province Social Psychology Society; Advisor, Hunan Province Psychology Society, 1985-; Committee member, Hunan Province Union of Social Science Scientists, 1991-95; and others. Address: College of Educational Science, Hunan Normal University, Changsha, Hunan 410081, China.

**YANG Li Qing,** b. 30 April 1942, Sichuan, China. Composer. 1 daughter. Education: BA, Shenyang Conservatory, 1970; MA, Composition, Shanghai Conservatory, 1980; Diplomas of Solistenklasse and Ausbildungsklasse, Musikhochschule, Hannover, Germany, 1983. Appointments: Assistant, Shenyang Conservatory, 1970-78; Lecturer, Composition, 1983-86, Assistant Professor, 1986-89, Professor, Dean, Department of Composition, 1991-96, Vice President, 1996-, Shanghai Conservatory; Guest Professor, Music College Mozarteum, Salzburg, Austria, 1990; Visiting Professor, Cornell University, USA, 1995. Publications include: The Compositional Techniques of Olivier Messiaen, 1989. Honours: Chinese Record Prize, 1986; DAAD Scholarship, Germany, 1990; Literary and Arts Prize of Shanghai, 1991; Distinguished Achievement Awards, Classic Arts, 1994; ACC Grant, USA, 1995; CSCC Grant, USA, 1995. Memberships: Chinese Musicians Association; Shanghai Musicians Association; Modern Music Society, Shanghai. Address: Shanghai Conservatory of Music, 20 Fen Yang Road, Shanghai 200031, China.

**YANG Liguo.** Address: College of Animal Science and Technology, Nanjing Agricultural University, Nanjing 210095, China.

**YANG Pengji,** b. 19 July 1913, Shanghai. Professor. m. Chen Qinying, 3 sons, 3 daughters. Education: Tsinghua University, China,1931-1933; Ecole des Mines de Mons, Belgium, 1934-36; Universite de Liege, Belgium, 1936-39. Appointments: Engineer, Renard des Constr. Aero., Bruxelles, 1939-40; Engineer, Central Aircraft Manufacturing, 1940-42; Director, Chengdu Gilder Manufacturing, 1943. Professor, Southwest United University, Jiao-tong Univ, 1944-; Director of CAD/CAM Research Centre, 1981-. Publications: 8 books; 72 theses. Honours: Prominent Contribution Expert, 1992; Award for Devotion to Science and Tech of National Defence, 1988; Governmental Special Allowance, 1991. Memberships: FABI; VRS. Address: CAD CAM Research Center, Northwestern Polytechnical University, Xian 710072, China.

**YANG Renjing,** b. 6 December 1937, Jinjiang, China. College Professor. m. Baurui Xu, 1 son, 1 daughter. Education: BA, 1958, Xiamen University; MA, 1966, Nanjing University; Postdoctoral, Harvard University, 1980-81. Appointments: Assistant, 1958-63, Professor and Doctoral Tutor, 1986-, Xiamen University; Lecturer, Associate Professor, Nanjing University, 1966-85; Fulbright Scholar, Harvard and Duke Universities, 1993-94. Publications: Hemingway in China, 1990; Hemingway: the self made giant, 1996; Over 70 articles published; Translated 8 books from English to Chinese. Honours: Various Fellowships and Grants; First Class Award, Xiamen Social Sciences, 1994; Excellent Books for Teenagers

Award, Beijing, 1992, for translations; Nanqian Award, the top award for Outstanding Faculty of Xiamen University in Teaching and Research Work, 1991. Memberships: Director, Institute of Foreign Literature and Languages, Xiamen University; Council member, China Foreign Literature Society; Standing Committee, China Association for the Study of American Literature; Standing Committee, China English Literature Society; President, Fujian Foreign Languages Society; International Committee, the Hemingway Review, the Hemingway Society; Modern Language Association. Address: Jingxian 7-602, Xiamen University, Xiamen 361005, China.

**YANG XinHui,** b. 11 July 1935, Pingxiang, Jiangxi, China. Professor. m. Li Zhiping, 1 son. Education: BA Education Dept, 1958, Central China Normal University. Appointments: Professor, Master Mentor, Dean of the Department, Jiangxi Normal University, 1978-94; Professor, Doctor Mentor, Nanjing Normal University, 1995-. Publications: 26 academic books; Over 120 papers in academic journals and university journals; Editor-in-Chief, Exploration of Psychology, 1994-. Honours: National-level Expert with Special Contributions, 1988; Nation's Excellent Teacher, 1989; Governmental subsidy offered by State Council, 1991-; 10 provincial awards of 1st and 2nd prizes for academic publications. Memberships: China Psychology Society, Director 1984-; Permanent Director, 1997-; Chair of Specialty Committee of Theoretical Psychology and Psychological History; Editorial Board, Acta Psychologia Sinica, 1997-; Specialty Committee, Human, Machine and Environment of China Human Efficiency Society and China Systematic Engineering Society; Director, China Socio-psychology Society. Address: Nanjing Normal University, Nanjing, China.

**YANG Xiyao,** b. 25 January 1937, Java, Indonesia. Professor. m. Huang Xiuzhen, 1 son. Education: Graduate, Peking University, 1960. Appointments: Professor, College of Chemistry, Peking University. Publication: Physicochemical Research by Gas Chromatography, 1989. Membership: Chinese Chemical Society. Address: College of Chemistry, Peking University, Beijing 100871, China.

**YANG Yu-Qi,** b. 5 August 1946, Jiangsu, China. Director Professor. m. Wang Li-Jun, 1 son. Education: Postgraduate, Nanjing Teachers' University, 1984-86. Appointments: Director Professor, Yang Yu-Qi College of Art. Publications: Design of Fine Arts; The Collected Works of Yang Yu-Qi Vol 1 and 2; The Collected Works of Professor Yang Yu-Qi and Students. Honours: Prize for National Popular Science Works, China, 1983; Prize for Fine Works at Nationwide Chinese Calligraphy; Certificate of Award in Recognition of Outstanding Contribution in Support of Canada Day, 1991; International Chinese Water Colour Art Award, 1990. Memberships: Vice Chairman, Taizhou Artists Association, 1979-; Chairman, International Chinese Artists Association, 1991. Address: Canada Y & J International Chinese Artists Association, 206 Wintermute Boulevard, Scarborough Ont, M1W 3L5, Canada.

**YANG Zhu-Liang,** b. 30 June 1963, Qujing, Yunnan, China. Associate Professor. m. Hai-Yan He. Education: Bachelor, Biology, Xiamen University, 1983; Master degree, Mycology, Kunming Institute of Botany, 1990; Doctor, Mycology, Institute of Botany, Eberhard-Karls University, Tuebingen, 1997. Appointment: Scientific Probationer, Yunnan Institute of Tropical Botany, 1983-87; Scientific Probationer, 1990-92; Scientific Assistant, Kunming Institute of Botany, 1992-98; Associate Professor, Kunming Institute of Botany, Academia Sinica, 1998-. Publications: Over 20 papers and 2 monographs. Honour: Dissertation, awarded as one of best of 1997 by University of Tuebingen, Germany, 1997. Membership:

Mycological Association of China. Address: Kunming Institute of Botany, Aacdemia Sinica, Heilongtan, Kunming 650204 Yunnan Privince, China.

**YANKOV Rossen Angelov,** b. 11 August 1949, Archar, Montana, Bulgaria. Physicist. m. Lena Karagyaurova, 1 daughter. Education: BSc Physics, 1973; MSc Solid State Physics, 1974; PhD Applied Physics, 1981. Appointments: Researcher, Bulgarian Academy Sciences, 1977-93; Executive Joint Com, Royal Society London and Bulgarian Academy Sciences, 1985-88; Researcher and Executive, Research Centre Rossendorf and Deutsche Forschungsgemeinschaft, Germany, 1993-98; Senior Principal Scientist, R&D Dept, CCR GmbH, Germany, 1998-. Publications: Over 120 articles; Co-patentee 9 patents. Honour: Recipient Fellowship International Atomic Energy Agency, Vienna, 1983-85. Memberships: New York Academy of Sciences; National Geographic Society; Materials Research Society; European Materials Research Society; Bulgarian Physics Society. Address: CCR GmbH, Maarveg 30, D-53619, Rheinbreitbach, Germany.

**YANOFF Arthur,** b. 9 May 1939, Boston, Massachusetts, USA. Artist; Painter. divorced, 1 son, 2 daughters. Education: Boston Museum School of Fine Arts, 1958-61; Studied painting privately with Jason Berger, 1962-65. Career: Studio instruction of private students, 1967-; Art Therapist, private clinic, Concord, New Hampshire, USA, 1975-; Instructor, Manchester Institute of Art, Manchester, New Hampshire, 1973-74; Art Design Consultant, Lillabulero Press, Northwood Narrows, New Hampshire, 1967-74; Art Instructor, Adult Education Program, Coe-Brown Academy, Northwood, New Hampshire, 1972; Art Therapist, New Hampshire Hospital, 1970-71; Instructor, Children's Summer Art Program, Temple Beth Jacob, Concord, New Hampshire, 1969. Honours: Purchase Prize, Laconia Citizen, New Hampshire Bicentennial, Laconia, New Hampshire, USA, 1975; Memorial Foundation for Jewish Culture, New York, New York Fellowship, 1989-90; International Man of the Year, 1993; Grant: The Max and Anna Levinson Foundation, Santa Fe, New Mexico, USA. Publications include: The Paste-up Autobiography, article, 1973; The Direct Vision, lecture, 1975; Painting From a Painter's Point of View, lecture, 1975; The Emergence of the Visual Memory in My Painting, lecture, 1983; Creative Works: Exhibitions include: Museum of Fine Arts, Boston, Massachusetts, USA 1983; Mast Cove Galleries, Kennebunkport, Maine, USA, 1983-; Harcus Gallery, Boston, Massachusetts, USA, 1983-; Sound Shore Gallery, Cross River, New York,USA, 1986-; The Currier Gallery of Art, New Directions, Contemporary Art from the Currier Collection, Manchester, New Hampshire, 1994; New England College Gallery, The Artist's Champion, 1994; Cline Fine Art Gallery, The Luria Series, 1995; NUAR Contemporary Art, Quartet, Santa Fe, New Mexico, USA, 1995; Yeshiva University Museum, "The Teaching of Isaac Luria", New York, New York, USA, 1997; Warehouse Gallery, Lee, Massachusetts, USA, 1998. Public Collections: Museum of Fine Arts, Boston, Massachusetts, USA; Detroit Institute of Arts, Detroit, Michigam, USA; Rose Art Museum, Brandois University, Waltham, Massachusetts, USA; Museum of Art, Fort Lauderdale, Florida, USA. Memberships include: Boston Painters and Sculptors; New Hampshire Art Association; American Art Therapy Association; Centre for Jewish Culture and Creativity, Los Angeles, California, USA; New Hampshire Sheep and Wool Growers Association. Address: 50 Lenox Road, PO Box 233, West Stockbridge, MA 01266, USA.

**YAPOUJIAN Nerses,** b. 19 June 1950, Yerevan, Armeuia. Senior Executive. Education: MS, Electrical Engineering; MS,

Physics, 1973. Appointments: Senior Executive. Publications: Over 50 Publications, Electronic Design, Americas Network. Address: Gen Protective Corp, P O Box 597631, Chicago, IL 60659-7631, USA.

**YARROW Andrew Louis,** b. 11 June 1957, Washington, DC, USA. Writer. m. Shari Targom, 1 son. Education: BA, University of California, 1979; MA, Princeton University, 1981; MPA, Harvard University, 1994. Appointments: The New York Times, 1981-92; International Relations Consultant, The World Bank, The United Nations, Carnegie Commission, on Preventing Deadly Conflict, 1994-95; Speech Writer, Department of Labor, 1995-. Publications: Latecomers: Children of Parents Over 35, 1991; Articles published in professional journals. Honours: European Union Visitors Program, 1993; French Government Fellowship, 1992-93. Address: 4122 Jenifer Street Northwest, Washington, DC 20015, USA.

**YASHROY Rakesh Chander,** b. 13 January 1947, Lahore. Researcher. m. Sudesh, 1 son, 1 daughter. Education: BSc Hons, Gold Medalist, 1968; MSc Hons, Gold Medalist, Panjab University, India, 1970; PhD, Carleton University, Canada, 1980. Appointments: Lecturer, Biophysics Department, Panjab University, India, 1971-81; Principal Scientist, Professor, 1981-; Chief, Biophysics Section, 1987-. Honours: Discoverer, Liquid Bilayer Organization of Chloroplast Thylakois Memb; Discoverer, Exocytosis in Prokaryotes; Discoverer, Mechanism of Salmonella Invasion. Honours: Comminwealth Awardee. Memberships: New York Academy of Sciences; Electron Microscope Society of India; Indian Poultry Science Association. Address: Indian Vet Rsch Inst, Biophysics EM and I Sect, Bareilly UP 243122, India.

**YASUDA Keigo,** b. 10 November 1939, Furukawa, Miyagi, Japan. Researcher, Professor, Physician. m. Kieko Marumori, 1 daughter. Education: MD, Tohoku University, 1965; PhD, Tohoku University, Graduate School, 1970. Appointments: Assistant Professor, Gifu University, 1976; Research Fellow, University Tenn, Memphis, 1979; Associate Professor, Gifu University, 1986; Professor, Chief, Department of Int Med III, 1993; Director, Health Management Centre, 1994. Publications: New England J Med; Secondary Diabetes; Prevention and Treatment of NIDDM; Diabetes. Memberships: American Diabetes Association; American Endocrine Society; Japanese Diabetes Association; Japanese Endrine Society; Japanese Geriatric Medical Association. Address: Dept of Intl Med III, School of Medicine, Gifu University, 40 Tsukasa Machi Gifu 500 8705, Japan.

**YASUHARA Michiru,** b. 22 March 1928, Taiwan. Educator (Aerospace and Mechanical). m. Yumiko Shinohara, 1 son. Education: Bachelor Degree, Engineering, 1951, Dr Engrg, 1962, Department of Applied Mathematics, University Tokyo. Appointments: Research Associate, University of Tokyo, 1954-58; Associate Professor, 1958-67, Professor, 1967-91, Nagoya University; Professor, Aichi Institute of Technology, 1991-; Research Associate: Cornell University, 1963-65; Associate Professor, University Southern California, 1965; Managing Committee Member, Institute of Space and Astronomical Science, 1987-91. Publications: The Day Japanese Space Shuttle Flies, 1984; Computational Fluid Dynamics, co-ed, 1992. Honours: Professor Emeritus, Nagoya University, 1991; Paper Awards, 1993; Honorary member, Japan Society for Aeronautical and Space Science, 1997-. Memberships: JSASS; Japan Society for Mechanical Engineers. Address: 34-18 Neura Iwasaki, 470-01 Nissin Aichi, Japan.

**YATES Marvin,** b. 22 September 1943, Jackson, USA. Art Director; Painter. m. Margaret Lea Yates, 1 son, 1 daughter. Education: BA, Memphis College of Art. Career: Co-Founder, Tennessee Watercolor Society, Memphis Watercolor Society. Honours: American Watercolor Society Washington School of Art Award, 1975. Membership: American Watercolor Society. Address: 1457 Highway 304, Hernando, MS 38632, USA.

**YATES Steven Audus,** b. 14 November 1949, Chicago, Illinois, USA. Curator of Photography; Associate Adjunct Professor. m. Lynne Ann Smith, 1 daughter. Education: BFA, University of Nebraska, 1972; MA, University of New Mexico, 1975; MFA (doctorate), University of New Mexico, 1978. Appointments: Teaching, photography and history of photography, University of New Mexico and Pomona College, California, 1975-78; Instructor, History of Photography, Santa Fe Community College, 1998-; Photographers Fellowship, National Endowment for the Arts, 1979; Curatorial Assistant, Art Museum, University of New Mexico and Sheldon Memorial Art Gallery, University of Nebraska, 1972-75; Curator, Photography, Museum of New Mexico, Santa Fe, 1980-. Publications: The Essential Landscape, with John Brinkerhoff Jackson, 1982; The Poetics of Space, A Critical Photographic Anthology, 1996; Betty Hahn, 1996. Honours: Senior Fulbright Scholars Award, USSR, 1991; Senior Fulbright Scholar Award, Russia, 1995. Address: c/o Museum of Fine Arts, PO Box 2087, Santa Fe, NM 87504-2087, USA.

**YATSENKO Nikolai,** b. 1 January 1948, Russia. Physics Researcher; Educator. m. Lyudmila Fedyanina, 1 daughter. Education: MS, Physics, 1973, PhD, Physics, Mathematics, 1978, Moscow Institute of Physics and Technology; DSc, Physics, Mathematics, Russian Academy of Sciences, Moscow, 1992. Appointments: Full Professor of Physics, 1993-; Head Researcher, Gas Discharge and Laser Group, Institute for Problems in Mechanics, Russian Academy of Sciences, Moscow, 1995-; Project Scientist, Optical Engineering Inc, Santa Rosa, California, USA, 1996-. Publications: Co-author, books: Thermal Plasma Diagnostics, 1994; Radio-Frequency Capacitive Discharges, 1995; Gas Lasers: Recent Developments and Future Prospects, 1996; Articles in journals on plasma physics and gas lasers, 1978-; 10 patents. Honours: Awards for Best Research Works, Institute for Problems in Mechanics, Russian Academy of Sciences, 1984-90; Grantee: Ministry of Education, Moscow, 1992-97; International Science Foundation, 1993, 1994; Joint Russian and International Science Foundation, 1995; Medal in Honour of 850th Anniversary of Moscow, 1997. Memberships: Fellow, Institute of Physics, London; Senior Member, Institute of Electrical and Electronics Engineers; American Physical Society; American Vacuum Society; Sigma Xi; European Physics Society; American Association of Physics Teachers. Address: 2389 McBride Lane #60, Santa Rosa, CA 95403, USA.

**YE Dequan,** b. 10 May 1942, Rong Xian City, Sichuan, China. Professor. m. Gong Fu Zhen, 3 sons. Education: Graduate, Chemistry Department, Lu Zhou Chemical Academy of Si Chuan an Prov, 1964. Appointments: Southwestern Physics Institute, Chinese Academy of Science, 1964-76; Scientific and Technological Committee, Gong Jing District of Zigong City, currently. Publication: Rapid Pig-Raising Method, 1989. Honours: Excellent Prize, 1988; Called 'The Man Who Solved an International Problem', by the China's Technical Market Newspaper, 1994; Gold Medal, International Honour Judgement Committee of Aomen Inventional City Center, 1996. Memberships: Sichuan Patent Association of China. Address: Gong Jing District Committee of Scientific and Technological Zigong City, Sichuan, China.

**YE Gao-xiang**, b. 25 July 1958, Zhejiang, China. Professor in Physics. m. Hui-li Wang, 1 daughter. Education: PhD, 1994, Zhejiang University. Appointments: Professor, Director of Physics Department, Hangzhou University; President Assistant of Hangzhou University. Publications: Co-author papers in Physical Review Letters and Physical Review B. Membership: Member of Council, Zhejiang Provincial Physics Association. Address: Department of Physics, Hangzhou University, Hangzhou 310028, Zhejiang, China.

**YE Yun-Hua**, b. 15 August 1936, Nanjing, Jiangsu. Professor. m. Xuan-Wen Li, 1 son, 2 daughters. Education: Graduate, Peking University, Beijing, 1960. Appointments: Associate Professor, 1985-92; Professor, 1993-. Publications: More than 90 Papers. Honours: Co-recipient Research Prize; 1st Prize, State National Science, 1982; 2nd Prize, 1988; 1st Prize 1995; Cathay Award, 1998; Recipient Reserch Prize, State Education Commission. Memberships: American Paptide Society; Chinese Chemical Society; Chinese Biochemical Society. Address: Department of Chemistry, Peking University, Beijing 100871, China.

**YEADON-MCGINNIS Pearl**, b. 2 March 1948, Missoula, Montana, USA. Musician; Opera and Concert Soloist; Educator; Artist; Author; Composer. m. Douglas E Erny, div 1982, 1 daughter. Education: BMusEd, 1969, MMus, Opera, 1970, University of Montana; Doctorate, Musical Arts in Vocal Performance, Literature and German, University of Illinois, Champaign-Urbana, 1995. Career: Performer, Opera, Concert, Broadway, Recital Soloist, 1972-; Opera Tours, Opera Soloist; Opera Stage Director; Assistant Professor of Music, Millikin University, Decatur, Illinois, 1989-91; Director of Opera Workshop, Director, Collectors Series; Director, School Outreach Program; Associate Professor of Voice, Southwest Missouri University, 1993-; Producer-Director, World Premier, Many Thousand Gone, opera by Brian Cain, April 6, 1998. Publications include: From Bed to Breakfast; Shadows from the Moon; Wings; Goodby John. Honours: Faculty Development Grant, Metropolitan Opera in New York City; University Award for Teaching, 1997. Memberships: Actors Equity; American Guild of Musical Artists; Gewerkshaft fur Musik; Missouri Music Teachers Association; Pi Kappa Lamda. Address: Southwest Missouri State University, 901 South National Avenue, Springfield, MO 65804-0027, USA.

**YEE Herbert Sun Jun**, b. 16 September 1946, China. Professor. m. Jenny Fan Hong Po, 2 sons, 2 daughters. Education: BA, 1970; MA, 1973; PhD, 1976. Appointment: Course Leader, China Studies Program. Publications: China in Transition: Issues and Policies, 1998; The Political Culture of Chinese Univesity Students, 1998; Macau in Transition, 1999. Address: Department of Government & International Studies, Hong Kong Baptist University, Hong Kong.

**YEH An-I**, b. 16 November 1953, Hsin-Ying, Taiwan. Food Engineer; Educator. m. Yueh-Ing Chang, 1 s, 1 d. Education: BS, Chung-Hsing University, 1977; MS, Montana State University, 1983; PhD, 1986. Appointments: Sales Engineer, Shei-Tai Co, Taiwan, 1979-80; Professor, National Taiwan University, Taiwan, 1992-. Honours: Graduate Research Achievement Award; Outstanding Researcher. Memberships: Institute for food technologists. Address: 59 Lane 144, Keelung Rd, Sec 4, Taipei, Taiwan, China.

**YEH Ming-Neng**, b. 13 October 1938, Taiwan. Obstetrician; Gynecologist. m. Lisa Lie-Yu Lin, 3 daughters. Education: MD, National Taiwan University, 1964. Appointments: Diplomate, American Board Obstetrician, Gynecologists; Intern, Johnston-Willis Hospital, 1966-67; Resident, Brooklyn,

Cumberland Hospital, 1967-68; St Lukes Hospital Centre, 1968-71; Fellow, Fetal Medicine, Columbia-Presbyn Medical Centre, 1971-73; Attending Obstetrician, 1987-; Clinical Professor, Columbia University, 1987-; Fellow, New York Academy of Medicine; New York Academy of Science. Memberships: American Fertility Society; American Institute of Ultrasound Medicine; American College of Obstetricians, Gynecologists; New York Obstetricians Society; New York Gynecologists Society. Address: 161 Fort Washington Avenue, New York, NY 10032, USA.

**YEISER Charles William**, b. 20 November 1925, USA. Painter; Art Dealer. m. Adele A Simola Yeiser, 1 son, 1 daughter. Education: Certificate, Pratt Institute Art School, 1949; Art History, New York University, 1949-51. Appointments: Commission, The Good Shepherd, 4 x 7 foot oil on canvas, Dutch Reformed Church, West Nyack, New York, 1960; Board of Directors, Exhibition, Hopper House, Nyack, New York, 1976; The American still Life Tradition, Montgomery Gallery, San Francisco, 1985. Honour: 1st Prize, watercolor, Railway Public Library, New Jersey, 1948. Membership: Board of Directors, Rockland Center for the Arts, West Nyack, New York. Address: 11 Wheller Place, West Nyack, NY 10994, USA.

**YELOVICHEVA Yadviga**, b. 5 June 1946, Alexandrovo, Minsk. Palynologyst. Divorced, 1 daughter. Education: Diploma, 1969, Belarus University; Diploma of Candidate of Sciences, 1977; Diploma of DrSc, 1992. Appointments: Aspirant, 1969-72, Junior Researcher, 1972-81, Senior Researcher, 1981-93, Chief Researcher, 1993-94, Leading Researcher, 1994-98, Institute of Geology, Academy of Sciences Belarus. Publications: 197: 7 monographs, 105 articles, including 10 in foreign publications, 2 brochures, 6 reports, 2 dissertations, 75 abstracts, 11 at international conferences. Address: Institute of Geology, Belarus Academy of Sciences, Zkodinskaya 7, 220141 Minsk, Belarus.

**YEN Ben Chie**, b. 14 April 1935, China. Engineer; Professor. m. Ruth H Chao. Education: BS, 1956, National Taiwan University; MS, 1959, PhD, 1965, University of Iowa. Appointments: Assistant Professor, 1966-70, Associate Professor, 1970-76, Professor, 1976-, University of Illinois at Urbana-Champaign; Professor of Civil Engineering and Centre for Advanced Studies, University of Virginia, 1988-91. Publications: 9 books; 220 articles. Honours: Fulbright Distinguished Lecture Award, 1988; International Water Resources Association V T Chow memorial Award, 1996. Memberships: American Society of Civil Engineers, Fellow; International Water Resources Association, Fellow; International Association Hydraulic Research; American Geophysical Union; Chinese American Water Resources Association, Founding President, 1993-95. Address: Department of Civil Engineering, University of Illinois, 205 N Mathews Avenue, Urbana, IL 61801, USA.

**YEN Gili**, b. 8 March 1953, Taipei, Taiwan. Economist. m. Eva Chung-chiung Lin, 1 son. Education: BA, Economics, 1975, MA, Economics, 1978, National Taiwan University, Taipei; PhD, Economics, Washington University, St Louis, USA, 1983. Appointments: Associate Research Fellow, Chung-Hua Institute for Economic Research, 1983-86; Associate Professor, Professor, Director, Graduate Institute of Industrial Economics, 1985-89; Professor and Founding Director, Graduate Institute of Financial Management, 1989-92, National Central University, Chung-li; Senior Research Fellow and Division Director, Taiwan Institute of Economic Research, Taipei, 1992-93; First Vice-President, China Development Industrial Bank, Taipei, 1994-97; Senior Research Fellow, Taiwan Research Institute, Taipei, 1994-; Dean, School of

Management, Chaoyang University of Technology, Taichung, 1998-. Publications: New Directions in Regional Trade Liberalization and Investment Cooperation, editor, 1994; Empirical Studies on Business Finance and Government Policy in Taiwan (a collection of academic articles), author, 1996; Author, co-author, more than 30 academic articles in international journals. Honours: Dissertation Fellowship, Washington University, 1981; Outstanding Professorship Award, National Central University, 1989; Research Awards, National Science Council, various years; Outstanding Research Award, Chaoyang University of Technology, 1999. Memberships: Chinese Economic Association, Governor, 1991-94; Chinese Finance Association, Secretary-General, Executive Director, 1992-96; The International Society for New Institutional Economics, Country Representative, 1997. Address: School of Management, Chaoyang University of Technology, 168 Gifeng E Road, Wufeng Township, Taichung County, Taiwan.

**YEN Kang K,** b. 15 June 1952, Taiwan, China. Educator. m. Siulan M Yen, 2 sons. Education: BS Physics, 1974, National Central University; MEE, 1979, University of Virginia; PhD Electrical Engineering, 1985, Vanderbilt University. Appointments: Professor, Department of Electrical and Computer Engineering, Florida International University. Publications: Over 70 research papers. Membership: IEEE. Address: Department of Electrical and Computer Engineering, Florida International University, University Park, Miami, FL 33199, USA.

**YEUNG Chap-yung,** b. 29 December 1936. Professor. m. Helen K S Chiu, 2 daughters. Education: MBBS, Hong Kong, 1961; DCH, London, 1967; MRCP, Edinburgh, 1967; FRCP, 1973; Dip.Am.Ped, 1974; FRCP, Edinburgh, 1975; FRCP, Glasgow, 1981; FRCP, London, 1993; FRACP, 1993; FRCP, Ireland, 1993. Career: Paediatric Consultant, Hong Kong, 1970-72; Neonatal Research Associate, 1972, Assistant Professor, 1972-76, Associate Director, Neonatal Unit, 1974-76, McMaster University; Consultant Paediatrician, Toronto, Canada, 1977-80; Professor, Head, Paediatrics, University of Hong Kong, 1980-. Publications: 200 papers, 180 abstracts, 22 chapters, 2 books. Visiting Professorships: Beijing University of Medical Science; Capital University PUMC; Sun Yet Sen University of Medical Science; Chongqing University of Medical Science; Shanghai First Medical University; Jinan University. Address: University of Hong Kong, Pediatric Department, Queen Mary Hospital, Hong Kong.

**YI Peter,** b. 18 July 1956, Seoul, Korea. MD. m. Alice Kim, 2 sons. Education: BS, 1980, SUNY at Stony Brook; MD, 1984, Cornell Medical College. Appointments: Medical Internship, 1984-85, Junior Assistant Resident in Medicine, 1985-86, Senior Assistant Resident, 1986-87, Brigham and Women's Hospital, Harvard Medical School, Boston; Chief Medical Resident in Medicine, Brocton Veteran Administration Medical Centre, 1986, Medical Residency at Dana-Farber Cancer Institute, 1984-87, Harvard Medical School; Clinical Fellow, 1987-88, Research Fellow, 1988-89, Chief Fellow, 1989-90, Haematology-Oncology, New York Hospital-Cornell Medical Centre, New York; Internal Medicine, Haematology, Medical Oncology, The Princeton Medical Group, PA, 1990-; Attending Physician, The Medical Centre at Princeton, 1990-; Clinical Assistant Professor in Dept of Medicine, UMDNJ-Robert Wood Johnson Medical School, 1992-; President, Board of Managers Mercer County Unit, NJ Division, American Cancer Society, 1996-98; Consultant, Dept Medicine, Memorial Sloan-Kettering Cancer Centre. Publications: Co-author: 3 research publications; 2 reviews; 4 abstracts and letters. Honours: Physician Recognition Award for Continuing Medical Education,

American Medical Association, 1993-96, 1996-99; Good Guys Award for Compassionate Care of Women with Cancer, 1993; Good Physicians Award, Cornell University Medical College, 1984; Weiss Prize for Excellence in Clinical Medicine, 1984. Memberships: American Society Oncology, of Haematology; Harvey Society; Society for Study of Blood; AMA; Academy of Medicine of NJ; NJ Medical Society; Mercer County Medical Society; Oncology Society NJ; American Cancer Society. Address: 419 North Harrison Street, Princeton, NJ 08540, USA.

**YIN Yizhi,** b. 1925, Honghu, Hubei, China. Writer; Professor. m. Wang Xuan Hiu, 2 sons, 1 daughter. Education: Graduate, Literature Lecture Institute, Chinese Writers Union; Bachelor Degree, Luxun Literature College, 1956. Appointments: Rector, Personnel of Army; Rector, Opus of Shikan; Teacher, Professor, Chinese Literature Department, Beijing Film Academy. Publications include: 21st Century's Dawn; Shengchang's Scientific Technique of Human Body; Open the Door to Wisdom and Health; Secret History of Yongzheng. Memberships: Chinese Writers Union; Chinese Film Artists Association; Council, Chinese Popular Literature and Art Research Institute. Address: Beijing Film College, Beijing, China.

**YODER Luella May Nafzinger,** b. 17 May 1913, Belleville, Pennsylvania, USA. English Teacher. m. Urie P Yoder. Education: BS, Shippensburg State Teachers College; MEd, Pennsylvania State University; University of Dublin; Cambridge University; Oxford University; University of North Wales. Appointments: English Teacher, Derry Township High School, Yeagertown, Pennsylvania, 1938-45; Instructor, Special Training Unit, 3rd Service Command, US Army, Indian Town Gap Military Reservation, Pennsylvania, 1946; Post and Technical Librarian, Aberdeen Proving Ground, Maryland, 1947-48; English and Latin Teacher, Bratton-McVeytown-Oliver Joint High School, McVeytown, Pennsylvania, 1948-52; English and Social Studies Teacher, Menno-Union Joint High School, Belleville, 1953-55; Chairman, English Department, Kishacoquillas Senior High School, Reedsville, 1955-76; Peace Corps English Instructor, Sana'a University, Yemen Arab Republic, 1989-90. Publications: Numerous articles in newspapers. Honours: Silver Medal of Congress, 1985; Silver Bar, 1987; Bronze Medal, 1996; International Order of Merit, 1990. Memberships: Delta Kappa Gamma; National Council of Teachers of English; Pennsylvania Council of Teachers of English; Mifflin County Association of School Retirees. Address: 2701 Regenfcy Oats Boulevard, Clearwater, FL 33759, USA.

**YOKOSAWA Kazuhiko,** b. 6 September 1956, Chiba, Japan. Psychologist. m. Sakura, 2 sons. Education: PhD, 1990. Appointments: Researcher, NTT Basic Research Laboratories, 1981-98; Associate Professor, University of Tokyo, 1998-. Honours: Best Paper Award, 1995. Memberships: IEEE; ARVO. Address: Univ of Tokyo, 7-3-1 Hongo, Bunkyo-ku, Tokyo 113-0033, Japan.

**YOKOYAMA Hirokazu,** b. 22 April 1959, Tokyo Japan. Physician. Education: Graduate, School of Medicine, Keio University, 1985; MD, 1985; PhD, 1994. Appointments: Assistant Professor, School of Medicine, Keio University; Assistant Professor, Keio University. Publications: Demmstation of Hepatotoxicity Via Immune Veaction Against Acetaldehyde Adduct, 1993, 1995; Cloning of Human Class IV Alcohol Dehydrogenase CDNA, 1994. Memberships: New York Academy of Science. Address: Keio U Sch Medicine, 35 Shinanomachi Shinjukuku, Tokyo 160, Japan.

**YOKOYAMA Shoichi,** b. 9 November 1945, Japan. Managing Director. m. Emi Yokoyama, 1 son, 1 daughter. Education: BA, 1969; Diploma, 1972. Appointments: Assistant Manager, Tokyo, 1977-86; Manager, Middle East, 1986; Managing Director, IHI UAE Co, 1986-. Publication: Asagiri. Memberships: International House of Japan; Mitakai AbuDhabi; Royal Automobile Club. Address: IHI UAE Company Limited, PO Box 2374, Abu Dhabi, United Arab Emirates.

**YONDEMLI Fuat,** b. 24 March 1951, Nevsehir, Turkey. Dr. m. Lilya Kurtayeva, 1 son, 1 daughter. Education: Medical Doctor, Ankara University Medical School, 1974; Specialization, Ear, Nose and Throat, Hacettepe University Medical School, 1979. Appointments: Associate Professor, Selcuk University Medical School, Konya, Turkey, 1982; Professor, 1992-. Publications: KBB El Kitabi, 1987; KBB Ders Kitation, 1989. Memberships: Chamber of Turkish Medical Doctors. Address: Askan Cad Muge Sitesi 120/3, 42090 Konya, Turkey.

**YONEDA Masashi,** b. 24 April 1957, Tokyo, Japan. Associate Professor. m. Eriko, 1 daughter. Education: MD, Hirosaki University, School of Medicine, 1983; PhD, 1987. Appointments: Medical Staff, Hirosaki University; Visiting Researcher, University of California, 1989-92; Medical Staff, Hirosaki University, 1992-94; Assistant Professor, Asalikawa Medical College, 1994-98; Associate Professor, IUHW, 1998-. Publications: Gastroenterology, Hepatology, American J Physiology. Honours: Young Investigator Award. Memeberships: American Gastroenterological Association; Japanese Society of Gastroenterology. Address: Murasakizuka Maison 308, Murasakizuka 1-3-10, Otawara 324-0058, Japan.

**YONEI Yoshikazu,** b. 18 January 1958, Tokyo, Japan. m. Keiko Nakatani, 1 son, 1 daughter. Education: MD, Keio University, Tokyo, 1982; PhD, 1986. Appointments: Visiting Researcher, Center for Ulcer Research and Education, 1986-89; Attending Physician, Nippon Kokan Hospital, 1989-; Chairman, Board of Directors, Keio Kai Medical Foundation, Tokyo, 1998-. Memberships: Keio Sakura Reunion, President, 1992-; Keio Medical School Yacht Club, Board of Directors, 1993-98; Medical Consultant, Asakusa Police Station, Tokyo, 1997-. Address: Nippon Kokan Hospital, 1-2-1 Kokan-dori, Kawasaki-ku, Kawasaki, Kanagawa 210-0852, Japan.

**YONEZAWA Katsuei,** b. 28 February 1942, Hirosaki City, Japan. Educator; Researcher. m. Masako Yonezawa, 1 son, 2 daughters. Education includes: PhD, Plant Genetics and Breeding, 1971. Appointment: Professor of Plant Genetics and Breeding, Department of Biotechnology, Kyoto Sangyo University. Publications: Biostatistics; Plant Genetics and Breeding. Honour: Award, Japanese Society of Breeding, 1997. Memberships include: Japanese Society of Breeding; SABRAO; Eucarpia; Japanese Society of Genetics. Address: Hiyoshidai 4-10-7, Ohtsu, Shiga 520-0112, Japan.

**YOON Ill-Hee,** b. 22 September 1954, Miryang Kyungsang-namdo, Korea. Professor. m. Young-Hee Lee, 2 daughters. Education: BS, Earth Science, Kyungpook National University, Taegu, Korea, 1978; MS, Meteorology, 1983, PhD, Atmospheric Sciences, 1991, Seoul National University. Appointments: Research Assistant, 1982-90, Assistant, 1986-88, Seoul National University; Lecturer, 1990-92, Assistant Professor, 1992-96, Associate Professor, 1996-, Kyungpook National University; Postdoctoral, CSIRO DAR, Aspendale, Australia, 1995. Publications include: Air Pollution Meteorology, 1998; Introductory of Atmospheric Sciences and Manual, 1998; Introduction to Earth Sciences, 1998. Memberships: AAAS; Royal Meteorological Society; American Meteorological Society; American Geophysical Union; Australian Meteorological and Oceanographic Society; Clean Air Society of Australia and New Zealand; Korean Atmospheric Environment Society; Korean Environmental Science Society; Korean Earth Science Society; Korean Meteorological Society. Address: 103-805 Nokwon Apt, Jisandong, 706-091 Taegu, Korea.

**YOSELOFF Thomas,** b. 8 September 1913, Sioux City, Iowa, USA. Publisher. m. (1) Sara Rothfuss, 2 sons, (2) Lauretta Sellitti, 1 daughter. Education: AB, University of Iowa, 1934; LittD, Bucknell University, 1982; LHD, Fairleigh Dickinson University, 1982. Appointments: Chairman, Rosemont Publishing & Printing Corporation, 1969-, Associated University Presses, 1969-, Golden Cockerel Press, London, 1979-. Publications: A Fellow of Infinite Jest, 1946; Merry Adventures of Till Eulenspiegel, 1944; Further Adventures of Till Eulenspiegel, 1957; The Time of My Life, 1979; Editor of several publications. Honours: Award of Merit, Bucknell University, 1975, University of Delaware, 1987. Memberships: Phi Beta Kappa; Sigma Delta Chi; Delta Sigma Rho. Address: 68 Cedar Drive, Colts Neck, NJ 07722-1672, USA.

**YOSHIDA Junichi,** b. 26 June 1955, Nagoya, Japan. Surgeon. m. Yukimi Yoshida, 2 sons. Education: MD, Kyushu University, 1981; MS, University Illinios Graduate College, 1986. Appointments: Assistant Professor, Kyushu University, 1993-96; Division Chief, Chest Surgery, Shimonoseki City Hospital, 1996-. Publications: Number of articles in professional medical journals. Memberships: FACS; Warren H Cole Society. Address: Shimonoseki City Hospital, 1-13-1 Koyo-cho, 750-8520 Shimonoseki, Japan.

**YOSHIHARA Ken-ichi,** b. 20 February 1932, Zushi, Kanagawa, Japan. Professor. m. Yasuko Terasaki, 2 sons, 1 daughter. Education: Bachelor and Master degrees; Doctoral studies, DSc, 1964, Tokyo University of Education. Appointments: Researcher and Educator, Lecturer, 1963, Assistant professor, 1965, Full Professor, 1973, Professor Emeritus, 1997, Yokohama National University. Publications: Author of many publications including a survey of statistics, and a work on mathematical education by CAI, a series of 9 volumes. Honours: Life Fellow, Honorary Professor of Statistics, Australian Institute for Coordinated Research; Honorary Professor in Asymptotic Statistics, Institut de Documentation et d'Etudes Europennes; Several other honorary doctorates; Lord of Knights and Knight of Humanity of the Order of the White Cross International; Presidential decree of Nomination of the World Parliament Confederation of Chivalry; Chevalier Grand Croix de l'Ordre Souverain et Militaire de la Milice du Saint Sepulcre; Member of Merit for Life of the Confederation of Chivalry; Knight Commander of the Lofsensischen Ursinius Order. Memberships: New York Academy of Sciences; Bernoulli Society for Mathematical Statistics and Probabilities; American Mathematical Society, Institute of Mathematical Statistics, USA; Mathematical Society of Japan. Address: 2-9-26 Yamanone, Zushi, Kanagawa, Japan.

**YOSHIMOTO Watson T,** b. 21 November 1909, Punaluu, Oahu, Hawaii, USA. Contractor. m. Katherine K Endo, 1 son, deceased, 2 daughters. Appointments: President, Oahu Construction Company Ltd, 1940-91; President, General Contractors Association of Hawaii, 1954; President, 1958-60, Secretary, Treasurer, 1960-65, Associated Field Trial Club, Hawaii; President, W T Yoshimoto Corporation, 1963-; President, Classic Bowling Center, 1965-92; President, Mak Bowl Incorporated, 1967-; President, Safari Club International Hawaii Chapter, 1978-81, President Emeritus, 1982-. Honours: Weatherby Big Game Trophy Award, 1980; Safari Club

International Hunting Hall of Fame, 1982; Field Trial Hall of Fame, 1991. Memberships include: Adventurers Club of Honolulu; American Automobile Association; American Air Museum; Montana Wildlife Federation; World War II Veterans Committee; Japanese American National Museum; National Rifle Association; Society for Conservation of Bighorn Sheep. Address: PO Box 4234, Honolulu, HI 96812-4234, USA.

**YOSHIMURA Masataka,** b. 15 May 1945, Japan. University Professor. m. Machiko, 2 sons. Education: Bachelor of Engineering, 1968, Master of Engineering, 1970, Doctor of Engineering, 1976, Kyoto University. Appointments: Lecturer, 1988, Associate Professor, 1994, Professor, 1998-, Kyoto University. Publications: Principles of CIM, 1993; Design for X: Concurrent Engineering, 1996; Numerous articles to professional journals. Memberships: AIAA; ASME; JSME; JSPE. Address: Department of Precision Engineering, Graduate School of Engineering, Kyoto 606-8501, Japan.

**YOSHINO Jajime,** b. 23 February 1939, Matsuyama, Japan. Professor of Law. m. Kazuko Shigenobu, 2 sons, 3 daughters. Education: LLB, Keio University, Tokyo, 1962; LLM, 1965. Appointments: Assistant Professor of Law, Meiji Gakuin University, Tokyo, 1973-76; Associate Professor of Law, Meiji Gakuin University, Tokyo, 1976-83; Professor of Law, Meiji Gakuin University, Tokyo, 1983-; Leader of Legal Expert System Project, 1983-84, 1986-87, 1993-94; 1994-. Publications: Foundation of Legal Expert System. Honours: Recipient, Yomiuri Prize, Yomiuri Shinbun, Tokyo. Memberships: Japanese Association of Legal Philosophy; Law and Computers Association; IVR; Japanese Society for Artificial Intelligence; Representative of Legal Expert Project. Address: Meiji Gakuin University of Law, 1-2-37 Shirokanedai, Minato, Tokyo 108-8636, Japan.

**YOSHIURA Kazunori,** b. 11 February 1959, Fukuoka, Japan. Oral Radiologist. m. Junko, 1 son, 2 daughters. Education: DDS, 1983, PhD, 1989, Kyushu University; Diplomate, JBOMR, 1996. Appointments: Resident, 1987-88, Instructor, 1990-91, Assistant Professor, 1991-99, Associate Professor, 1999-, Kyushu University; Instructor, Nagasaki University, 1988-90. Publication: Analysis of the diagnostic process in sialography, 1989. Memberships: Department of Oral and Maxillofacial Radiology, Faculty of Dentistry, Kyushu University; International Association of Dentomaxillofacial Radiology. Address: Miwadai 1-18-5, Fukuoka 811-0212, Japan.

**YOUNG Ming-an,** b. 7 January 1937, Chongzhou, Si-Chuan, China. Professor. m. Yu Su-Fang, January 1963, 2 daughters. Education: Graduated in Physical Chemistry, Si-Chun University, China, 1961. Appointments: Engineer, Senior Engineer, Professor, Manager, Information Centre of Surface Engineering, Wuhan Research Institute of Materials Protection, Ministry of Machinery Industry, 1961-. Publications: Various publications, 1961-. Honours: Second Grade Award of national and department science-technic advance, 1989-90. Memberships: General Secretary, Consulting Committee, National Standardigation Technic Committee of Metallic and Non-Metallic Coating; Vice General Director, National Technic and Standardic Information Centre of Surface Engineering for Machinery Industry. Address: Wuhan Research Institute of Materials Protection, Ministry Of Machinery and Electronics Industry, Wuhan 430030, China.

**YOUNG Tsen Men,** b. 1 April 1928, Shandong, China. Professor. m. Pei Lan Liu, 2 sons, 2 daughters. Education: Electrical Engineer, 1950, Chinese Air Force Technology Institute, Taiwan; MS Electronics, 1962, University of Paraiba,

Brasil. Appointments: Professor Electronics, University Brasilia, 1972-; Visiting Professor, Rockefeller University, New York, 1981, 1984-97, Harvard University, Massachusetts Institute Technology, Cambridge, 1982-83. Publications: Articles in professional journals. Address: Colina Bloco A Apt 23, University of Brasilia, Brasilia DF 70919-970, Brasil.

**YOUNG Walter,** b. 24 September 1934, Honolulu, Hawaii. Physician. m. John Audrey Nichols, 2 s, 1 d. Education:BA, Gettysburg College, PA, 1956; MD, Jefferson Medical College, Philadelphia, 1960; Intern, St Lukes Hospital, 1960-61; Residency, St Lukes Hospital, 1961-62; Residency, Graduate Hospital, 1962-63; Residency, Upstate Medical Center, 1963-65. Appointments: Assistant Instructor in Otolatyngology, University of Penna, 1962-63; Assistant Instructor in Otolaryngology, Upstate Med Center, 1963-65; Chief of Otolaryngology, Chanute AF Base, IL, 1965-67; 154th Air National Guard Disp, HI, 1968-69; Private Practice, 1968-; USAF Academy Liaison Officer, 1972-91; Clinical Assistant Professor in Surgery, University of Hawaii, 1973-; Deputy Liason Officer, 1974-80; LiaisonOfficer Commander, 1980-91. Honours: Outstanding DLOC in the Nation; Commendation Medal; Meritorious Service Medal; The Best Doctors in America; Best Doctors in America, 1997, 1998. Memberships: American Academy of Otolaryngology; American Audiology Society; American College of Surgeons; American Medical Association; Hawaii Ears, Nose and Throat, Nead and Neck Surgery Society; Hawaii Medical Association; Honolulu County Medical Society; Pacific Coast Ophthalmology and Otolaryngology Society; Society for Ears, Nose and Throat Advances in Children. Address: 1380 Lusitant Street Suite 615, Honolulu, HI 96813, USA.

**YOUSRIYA Loza,** b. 1 March 1936, Assuit, Egypt. Financial Advisor. m. Eng Onsi Sawiris, 3 sons. Education: Bachelor of Commerce, 1969, Cairo University; Diploma, Management, 1979, American University of Cairo; Master of Arts (MBA), 1982, American University of Cairo. Appointments: Financial Advisor, Qualified Accountant, Private Office. Publications: Solid Waste Management in Cairo. Memberships: Association for Protection of Environment; Ecumenical Development Cooperative Society. Address: 3 El Nessim St, Zamalek, Cairo 11211, Egypt.

**YOUSSEF Mohmed Kamal E,** b. 28 February 1938, Tahta, Egypt. Professor. m. Khadiga A Hassan, 1 son, 2 daughters. Education: BSc Food Science, 1958, Alexandra; Diploma, 1960, PhD, 1962, Meat Science and Technology, Moscow. Appointments: Demonstrator, 1958; Lecturer, 1963; Associate Professor, 1968; Professor, 1973-; Head, Food Science and Technology, Faculty of Agriculture, Assiut University, 1968-98. Publications: 210 scientific papers; Author 3 books, co-Author 2 books in Food Science and Technology and Nutrition; Author or co-Author 20 booklets on Human Nutrition. Honours: Holder of Golden Medal of Association of Agricultural Faculties in Egypt, 1958; Holder of King Faisal Medal of SASO Saudi Arabia, 1977. Memberships: AAAS; American Academy of Science; Egyptian Association of Food Science and Technology; Scientific Association of Food Industries; Egyptian Agricultural Engineers Syndicate; Assiut University Staff Members Club; Assiut University Club. Address: Assiut University Faculty Agriculture, University Street, Assiut 71516, Egypt.

**Yu Ai-Bing,** b. 18 January 1963, China. University Lecturer. m. Rui-Ping Zou, 1 son, 1 daughter. Education: B Eng, 1978-82, M Eng, 1982-85, Northeastern University, Shenyang; PhD, University of Wollongong, 1986-89. Appointments: Research Associate, University of Wollongong, 1989;

Postdoctoral Fellow, CSIRO Division of Mineral & Process Engineering, 1990-91; Research Fellow, University of Wollongong, 1992; Lectruer, 1992-95, QE II Fellow, 1993-98, Senior Lecturer, 1995-98, Associate Professor, 1998-, University of New South Wales. Publications: Over 140 Journal and Conference Publications. Honours: CSIRO Postdocoral Fellowship Award, 1990; ARC Queen Elizabeth II Fellowship Award, 1993. Memberships: TMS; AIChE; American Ceramic Society. Address: University New South Wales, School of Materials & Scientific Engineering, 2052 Sydney, New South Wales, Australia.

**YU Chien-Chih,** b. 4 February 1953, Keelung, Taiwan. Educator. m. Hsiu-Yuan Hsu, 1 son, 2 daughters. Education: BA, National Chengchi University, Taipei, 1975; MS, University of Toledo, Ohio, 1980; MA, 1983, PhD, 1985, University of Texas, Austin. Appointments: Teaching Assistant, Chengchi University, 1979-80, University of Toledo, 1980-83; Assistant Instructor, University of Texas, Austin, 1983-85; Associate Professor, 1985-91, Chairperson, 1986-90, Professor, 1991-, Department of Management Information Systems, National Chengchi University. Publictions: Integrated Expert Decision Support Systems: Architecture, Development and Applications; Electronic Commerce: Technology, Management and Applications. Honours include: Excellent Research Award, National Chengchi University, 1995. Memberships: ACM; IEEE; CS. Address: Department of Management Information Systems, National Chengchi University, 64 Sec 2 Chinan Road, Taipei, Taiwan.

**YU De-Quan,** b. 22 October 1932, Shan Dong, China. Scientific Researcher. m. Hui-Lan Zhang, 1 son, 1 daughter. Education: Beijing Medical University, 1956. Appointments: Professor of Chemistry, Institute of Materia Medica, Chinese Academy of Medical Sciences and Peking Union Medical College. Publications: 180 research papers; 6 books. Honours: 5 national and ministerial awards, 1980-98. Memberships: Consultative Committee, Specialist in Pharmacy, Ministry of Public Health, 1987-; Scientific Council of Chinese Academy of Medical Sciences and Peking Union Medical College, 1992-; Academic Chairman of Key Subject of Pharmaceutical Chemistry, State Commission of Education; Councillor of Chinese Chemical Society; Chinese Pharmaceutical Association; American Society of Pharmacognosy; New York Academy of Sciences; American Association for Advancement of Science; Examiner and Appraiser Member for Organic Chemistry Section, National Natural Science Foundation of China; Editorial Board: Acta Pharmaceutica Sinica, 1984-; Chemical Newsletter, 1996-; Analytical Chemistry Handbook, 1996-; Vice Editor in Chief, Journal of Asian Natural Products Research, 1998-. Address: Institute of Materia Medica, Chinese Academy of Medical Sciences, Beijing 100050, China.

**YU Guanghai,** b. September 1934, Long Chang, China. Professor. Education: Graduate, Sichuan University, 1956. Career: Professor, Deputy, Sichuan Livestock & Veterinary University; Director, Veterinary Microbiology Research Institute; Committee, China Committee of Microbiology Term Examination; Member, World Association of Rabbit Science; Managing Director, Sichuan Microbiology Institute; Editor, China Magazine of Rabbit Feeding; Deputy President, Chong Qing Tao Xing Zhi Research Institute; General Technical Inspector, Zhu Hai Wanhe Animal Medicine Factory; Deputy County Head, Sichuan Advanced Science. Publications: 25 books, numerous articles in professional journals. Honours include: Certificate of Glory, Russian Agriculture University & Kirghis Agricultural University. Address: Sichuan Institute of Animal Husbandry & Veterinary Medicine, No 5 Xueyuan Road, Rongchang, Chongqing 402460, China.

**YU He,** b. 19 May 1903, Beijing, China. Microbiologist; Immunologist. m. Liu Shuwei, 2 sons. Education: Bachelor Degree, Peking Medical College, 1929; PhD, Medicine, Harvard University, 1923. Appointments: Professor of Microbiology, Shanghai Second Medical University; Director, Shanghai Institute of Immunology; Director, Immuno-Genetics Research and Collaboration Center of World Hygiene Organization. Publications: Aetiology, 1933; Auto Immunization and Autoimmune Diseases, 1965; Medical Microbiology (textbook), 1958-1990); China Medical Encyclopedia, Microbiology, 1984. Honours: Gold Medal, American Society of Hygiene, Award, Advancing the New Theory of the Difference Between Antitoxin Immunity and Antibiotic Immunity, 1929; Diploma for brilliant contribution to Microbiology and Immunology, National Science Conference of China, 1978. Memberships: Founder, Director, International Society of Immuno-Pharmacology; President, Chinese Society of Microbiology, 1959-88. Address: Kang Ping Road, Lane 172, No 32, Shanghai 200030, China.

**YU Huey-Jen,** b. 14 April 1953, Hwa-Lien. Associated Professor. m. Ben-ray Jai, 1 son, 1 daughter. Education: PhD, 1992, TungHai University, Taiwan. Appointments: Associated Professor, Dept Chinese Literature, National Chung Cheng University, 1993-96; Associated Professor, Graduate Institute of Philosophy, Nan-hwa Management College, 1996-. Publication: The Study of the Shing-Chu Perfective Teaching in the Tien-Tai School, 1993. Memberships: Chinese Philosophical Research Centre; Foundation of the Oriental Humanity. Address: 32 Chung Keng Li, Dalin Chiayi 622, Taiwan, China.

**YU Ming-guang,** b. 6 September 1935, Wuhan, Hubei, China. Historian. m. Youming Zhou, 1 son, 2 daughters. Education: BA, History Department, Zhongshan University, 1956-60. Appointments: Professor, Head, History Department, Xiangtan University; Director, Institute of Chinese Culture; China Democratic League Xiangtan Committee; Deputy Chairman, Stading Committee, Xiangtan Peoples Congress. Publications: 5 books, over 40 papers in professional journals. Honours: Provincial Prize, 1992; National Prize, 1994. Memberships: Vice Chair, Hunan History Association, 1986-; Director, Chinese Philosophy Association, 1990-; Standing Director, Chuanshan Association, 1990-. Address: Research Office of Chinese Culture, Xiangtan University, Xiangtan, Hunan 411105, China.

**YU Richard Shue-Tak,** b. 27 June 1943, Quangzhou, Qangdong. Biochemist. m. Miu-Ling Yu, 3 daughters. Education: BS, Monash University, 1966; MSc, Monash, 1968; PhD, ANU, 1972; DEd, Melbourne, 1998. Appointments: Alexander Von Humboldt Fellow, 1972; CSIRO Postdoctoral Fellow, 1973; Research Fellow and Senior Research Fellow, ANU, 1974-80; Section Leader, Food Research Institute, Melbourne, 1980-89; Chief Scientist, Drug Implant Technology, Daratech Pty Ltd, Melbourne, 1990-94. Honours: Visiting Professor, Northeast Agricultural College, Harbin, China, 1988; Nanking Agricultural University, Nanking, China, 1993; Managing Director, Bonaphyte Products P/L, Melbourne, 1995-. Memberships: Alexander Von Humboldt Foundation; New York Academy of Sciences; AAAS: Controlled Release Society Inc. Address: Bonaphyte Products Pty Ltd, 33 Slattery Street, Werribee, VIC 3030, Australia.

**YU Sen-Hai,** b. 18 November 1938, Zhejiang, China. Medical Parasitologist. m. Liu Rui-Jun, 1 son, 1 daughter. Education: MD, 1962, Shanghai Second Medical College; MPH and Tropical Medicine, 1984, Tulane School of Public Health, USA. Appointments: Research Associate, Division Chief,

Professor, Director of the Institute of Parasitic Diseases, Chinese Academy of Preventive Medicine, 1962-92; Part-time Professor, Beijing Medical University, 1996-; Medical Officer, Health Education Specialist WHO, Geneva, 1992-. Publications: 70 papers; 5 books. Honours: Nati onalScience Congress Award, 1978; Scientific Achievement Award, Health Ministry, 1994; National Science Award, 1995; Special Allowance as Scientist with Outstanding Achievement, State Council, 1991-. Memberships: American Hon Public Health Society; Chinese Medical Association; Chinese Preventive Medical Association; Editorial Board, Acta Tropica, South East Asian Journal of Tropical Medicine and Public Health, Chinese Journal of Preventative Medicine. Address: 6 rue Zurlinden, 1207 Geneva, Switzerland.

**YU Shen,** b. 3 April 1933, Shanghai, China. Scientist. m. Erying Chen, 1 son, 1 daughter. Education: Graduate, Jiaotong University, 1953; Postgraduate, Institute of Mechanics, Chinese Academy of Sciences, Beijing, 1967. Appointments: Professor, Aerodynamics, Institute of Engineering Thermophysics, Chinese Academy of Sciences, 1987-; Guest Scientist, DFVLR, 1984-85, University of Karlsruhe, 1989-93. Publications: Passive Control of Shock-Boundary Layer Interaction in Transonic Axial Compressor Cascade Flow, 1994; Aerothermodynamics of Internal Flows III, 1996. Honour: Diploma for Outstanding Achievement in Science and Technology, State Council of china, 1992. Memberships: International Editorial Board, International Journal of Turbo and Jet Engines, 1996-. Address: PO Box 2706, Beijing 100080, China.

**YU Xiaoyang,** b. 27 August 1962, Beijing, China. Director, Photography. m. Wang Shumin, 1 son. Education: Graduate, Film Department, Zhong Hua Social University, Beijing, 1985; Graduate, Beijing Film Academy, 1996-97. Career: 3rd Photography Art Exhibition, Photography Association in Chinese Art Gallery, 1983; Joint Exhbition of Four People, 1986; Director, Television Series, "Warp & Weft", 1987; Personal Photography Exhibition, 1989; Yierfu Cup, National Photography Competition, 1992; Photographer, Film "Hanging Love", 1993; Director, Television Documentary Film "The Poet of the Lunati Hospital", 1994; Director, Feature Film "The Misty Land", 1995-96. Honours include: Modern Awareness Expression Award, 1988; Gold Medal, Yierfu Cup National Photography Competition, 1992; Best Critics Award, 1993. Address: Room 4741, No 16 Chenglzhuang lu, Fengtaiqu, Beijing 100071, China.

**YU Xingbo,** b. 9 January 1943, Changchun, China. Teacher. m. Zhao, 2 daughters. Education: Harbin University of Technology, 1962-67; MSc, 1993; Certificate, Intermediate English, Beijing Language and Culture University, 1994. Appointments: Chairman, Department of Mechanical Engineering, 1983-90, Senior Visiting Scholar, 1991-92, Jilin University of Technology; Vice President, College of Package Correspondence of China, 1985-87; Senior Visiting Scholar, Loughborough University of Technology, England, 1994-95. Publications: Over 34 papers in professional journals. Honours: Certificate of Excellent Teacher, Money Award, 1996; 3rd Class Award, Science and Technology, State Educational Committee of China. Memberships: China Translating Newspaper for Science and Technology; Jilin Mechanical Engineering Society; Vice Director, Educational Committee, Jilin Packaging Technology Society. Address: Jilin Institute of Technology, 17 Yanan Avenue, Changchun 130012, China.

**YU Xixian,** b. 19 July 1940, Kunming, Yunnan, China. Teacher. m. Sha Luyin, 2 daughters. Education: MA, Department of Geography, Peking University, 1981.

Appointments: Teacher, 1964-; Professor, Department of Geography, Peking University, 1986-. Publications: 10 books, 120 papers in professional journals. Honours: 1st Prize, Scientific Progress, China, 1992; 1st Prize, Educational Ministry of China, 1993; 1st Prize, Chinese Academy of Science, 1996. Memberships: Vice Chairman, Speciality Committee of Historical Geography, Geographical Society of China; Vice Chairman, Association for the Research on Xu Xiake of China. Address: Department of Geography, Peking University, Beijing 100871, China.

**YUAN Huang,** b. 2 March 1961, Hangzhou, China. Scientist. m. Jieping Chen, 2 daughters. Education: BEng, Polytech University, Hefei, 1981; MSc, Zhejiang University, China, 1984; Dr Ing, Technical University, Berlin, 1990. Appointments: Habilitation, Ruhr Uni, Bochum, Germany; Senior Research Scientist, Paul Scherrer Inst, Switzerland. Publications: Over 60 Scientific and Technical Papers; 2 Books. Memberships: DVM, ESIS. Address: Paul Scherrer Inst, 5232 Villigen PSI, Switzerland.

**YUAN Jinxiang,** b. 1 January 1929, Zhongshan, Guangdong, China. English Professor. m. Chen Changling, 1 son, 1 daughter. Education: BA, Central University, 1945-49; BA, Peking Foreign Languages Institute, 1950; Visiting Scholar, English Department, University of Illinois, Urbana-Champaign, USA, 1981-82. Appointments: Professor of English, Wuhan University, 1985-; Translator, General Red Cross Society of China, Peking, 1954-58; Translator, Chinese People's Volunteers, DPRK, 1950-53. Honours: Works: Studies in Famous Translators and Their Works, 1990, awarded a national 1st prize; Co-editor, A Dictionary of Chinese Translators, 1988; Vice Editor-in-Chief, A Companion for Chinese Translators, 1997; nearly 40 theses, 1978-88. Memberships: Modern Language Association of America, 1982-83; Councillor, China Translators Association, 1992-. Address: College of Foreign Languages, Wuhan University, Wuhan 430072, China.

**YUAN Shao Wen,** b. 16 April 1914, Shanghai, China. Professor. m. Hui Chih Hu. Education: BS Aeronautical Engineering, 1936, University Michigan; Engineer degree, 1939, Stanford University; MS Mechanical Engineering, 1937, PhD Aeronautics, 1942, California Institute of Technology. Appointments: Professor, Polytechnic University, 1946-57; Professor, University of Texas at Austin, 1958-65; Professor and Chairman, George Washington University, 1968-84. Publications: 3 books and over 100 papers and reports; Over 20 US and foreign patents. Honour: Canadian Chair Professor, 1957-58. Memberships: Fellow, American Association for the Advancement of Science; American Institute for Aeronautics and Astronautics. Address: 1400 Geary Blvd Apt 1595, San Francisco, CA 94109-6570, USA.

**YUDAKIN Anatoliy Petrovich,** b. 5 March 1941, Donetsk, Ukraine. Linguist. 1 daughter. Education: Diploma, Moscow State University, 1974; Candidate of Humanities, 1978. Appointments: Junior Scientist, Institute of Linguistics, Russian Academy of Sciences, 1978, Senior Scientist, 1987-. Publications: Several books and numerous articles in professional journals. Address: Istrinskaya 10-1-29, 121467 Moscow, Russia.

**YUEN Lung Cheong,** b. 14 April 1944, Fuchow, China. Doctor of Oriental Medicine. m. Lily Chang. Education: Bachelor of Medicine, 1957, Shan Dong Medical School. Appointments: Practised medicine with the Integration of Chinese and Western Medicine for 40 years; Internal Medicine Physician, Zhee Nang Municipal Medical Centre, Shang Dong

Province, 1957-61; ENT Specialist, Chief Physician, Fuching People's Hospital, Fukien Province, 1961- 78; Traditional Chinese medicine Practitioner, self owned Chinese Medicine Clinic, Hong Kong. Publications: Academic theses with combination of Chinese and Western Medicine in treatment of Internal Medicine and ENT problems. Honour: Outstanding Paper, 1997, World Chinese Medicine Conference; Hwong Di Prize, 7th International Chinese Medicine Conference. Address: 1326 Bay Ridge Avenue, 2nd Floor, Brooklyn, NY 11719, USA.

**YUN Chang Hee,** b. 6 February 1967, Chung Song County, Korea. Researcher. Education: Graduate, Hankuk University of Foreign Studies, 1993. Appointments: Volunteer English Interpreter, Seoul Olympics International Weightlifting Federation, Seoul, 1988, Boy Scouts 17th World Jamboree, Korea, 1991; Served Korean Army, 1989-90; Guaranteeing personal real estate, Samsung Fire and Marine Insurance Corporation Ltd, Seoul, 1993-94; Assistant Manager, Korea Management Association, 1995-, with International Cooperation Team, then Research and Publishing Team, currently at KMA Training Centre; Chief of Management, Asian Boy Scout Jamboree, Mt Sorak, 1996. Publication: Cook Grammar with 7 Elements, Cooked is Complicated English, 1999. Address: Korea Management Association, 3rd Floor, Koryo Building, 544, Dohwa-Dong, Mapo-ku, Seoul 121-041, Korea.

**YUNG Hsiwen,** b. 10 June 1961, Taipei, Taiwan. Ceramic Educator. m. Chang Yin-Lin, 2 sons, 1 daughter. Education: MSc, 1985, PhD, 1993, National Cheng Kung University, China. Appointments: Teaching Assistant, National Cheng Kung University, China, 1989-92; Visiting Scholar, University of Nebraska at Lincoln, USA, 1992-93; Associate Professor, Ceramics, Lienho College of Technology, 1993-. Publications: Articles in professional journals. Honours: Research Scholarship, 1996-97; Government Scholarship for studying abroad, Ministry of Education, 1992-93. Memberships: New York Academy of Science; American Ceramic Society; Chinese Association for Magnetic Technology; Chinese Ceramic Society; Chinese Society for Materials Science. Address: Lienhe College of Technology, Dept of Ceramic Engineering, Miaoli 36012, Taiwan.

**YURTSEVEN Omer,** b. Bursa, Turkey. Marketing, Business Educator. Education: BA, Ankara Academy, 1974; MBA, University of New Haven, 1981; MA, University of Texas, 1984; PhD, University of Texas, 1988. Appointments: Business Analyst, Pusan, Ankara, 1976-77; Manager, Ramada Conn, 1979-81; Research Assistant, University of Texas, 1983-88; Managing Director, Chelsea International, 1989-93; Vice Chairman, Hacettepe University, 1993-. Publications: Co-Author, Population Issues in Turkey; A Case Study Prepared for UNICEF; Texas Public Education Grant. Memberships: Executive Board Member, Turkish Scientific Research Council's; Turkish Industry Management Association. Address: Hacettepe University, 11BF Department of Business Administration, 06532 Beytepe Ankara, Turkey.

**YUSHINA Ludmila Dmitrievna,** b. 14 October 1929, Kazan Tatarstan, USSR. Physico-Chemist. m. Brajnin Semion Abramovich, 1 son. Education: Diploma with Distinction, Ural State University, 1947-52; Diploma of the Candidate of Chemical Sciences, 1958; Diploma of Doctor of Chemical Sciences, 1984. Appointments: Master of Shop, Optical plant, 1952-53; Scientific Worker, Institute of Electrochemistry, Russian Academy of Sciences, Ural Division, 1953-; Scientific Counsellor of the Institute of High Temperature Electrochemistry, Russian Academy of Sciences, 1986-. Publications: Over 150 and 14 inventions. Honours: Over 30 different Diplomas, 1960-; Medal, Inventor of the USSR, 1979;

Medal, Veteran of Labour, 1984. Memberships: International Society for Solid State Ionics, 1989-; Active member, New York Academy of Sciences, 1997. Address: Institute of High Temperature Electrochemistry, Russian Academy of Science, 620219 Ekaterinburg, Russia.

# Z

**ZACCAGNI James Louis,** b. 12 October 1945, Springfield, Illinois, USA. Public Accountant. m. Jennifer G, 2 sons, 2 daughters. Education: BS, Accounting, Southern Illinois University, 1969. Appointments: Personnel Manager, Senior Partner, Illinois CPA Firm, 1976; Partner, Shareholder, Lowrey Zaccagni & Powell, 1985-. Publications: Several articles in professional journals. Memberships: International Association of Financial Planners; American Institute of Certified Public Accountants; Texas Society of Certified Public Accountants; Texas Society of Public Accountants, San Antonio Chapter. Address: Lowrey Zaccagni & Powell, 14100 San Pedro Avenue, Ste 300, San Antonio, TX 78232-2361, USA.

**ZAGOROV Konstantin,** b. 7 November 1932, Bourgas, Bulgaria. Producer; Researcher-Creator. m. (2)Lily, 2 daughters. Education: Diploma, 1954, Staging at National Academy of Theatrical and Film Art Krustju Sarafov. Appointments: Producer of over 90 theatrical productions; Chief, specially founded Loichron Laboratory, Plovdiv University Paissii Hilendarsky, 1982-91; Chief, Liochronic notation author's school, 1992-98. Publications: Monograph, Liochron Notation and study Liochron, 1984; Ready for publication: Liochronic Orthography; Textbooks: Symbols system; Formalised grammar; Method of teaching; 4 vols of lectures; 4 vols of laboratory exercises. Honours: From Ministry of Education, Plovdiv Technology University, KTPU, and others; Avangard's National Award, 1989; International Award; Interface 87 International Award. Address: 5 Kiev Street, Plovdiv 4000, Bulgaria.

**ZAGOROVA Lilyana,** b. 11 September 1945, Lorn, Bulgaria. Expert, Liochron Notation. m. Konstantin, 1 daughter. Education: Violin, Secondary School of Music; Bulgarian Philology. Appointments: Director, Liochron Informantiks, Liochron Notation, Plovdiv University; Lecturer, Kiochron Notation and Experimenter. Publications: An Attempt for a Scientific Theoretical. Honours: Avangard, National Award and International Award, Interface 87. Address: Plovidv 5, Kiev St, 40000 Bulgaria.

**ZAHARESCU Maria Magdalena,** b. 20 January 1938, Cluj, Romania. Chemist. m. Bogdan Zaharescu, 1 daughter. Education: Master of Science, 1959; PhD, 1971; Post Graduate Scholarship, Denmark, 1974. Appointments: Scientific Researcher, Romania; Scientific Researcher; Senior Researcher; Research Professor; Head of Department, Institute of Physical Chemistry, Bucharest. Publications: Over 130 Scientific Papers. Honours: Third Class Award for research activity, Romanian Ministry of Education, 1967; Gheorghe Spacu, Romanian Academy's Award, 1971; Scientific Merit Medal, 1983; Third Class Order, 1984. Memberships: Romanian Chemical Society; Romanian Ceramic Society; Romanian Society of Glass. Address: Institutul Chimie Fizica, Academia Romana, Spl Indepentei 202, Bucharest, Romania.

**ZAHRADNIK Rudolf,** b. 20 October 1928, Bratislava, former Czechoslovakia. Chemist. m. Milena Bílková, 1 daughter. Education: Diploma Engineer, 1952; CSc, PhD, 1956, DSc, 1968, Professor of Charles University, Prague, 1967-. Appointments: Director, The J Heyrovsky Ins Phys Chem AS CR, 1990-93; President, Academy Science CR, 1992-; President, Czech Learned Society, 1994-97. Publications: 350 papers and 9 books on applied quantum chemistry. Honours: Gold Heyrovsky Medal, Votocek Medal; Gold Medal of Charles University. Memberships: Honorary Member, Swiss and German Chemical Societies; International Academy of Quantum Molecular Sciences, 1982; European Academy of Arts, Science and Literature; Member, European Academy of Sciences and Arts (Salsburg); Dr hc, University of Fribourg, Georgetown University, Charles University, Clarkson University, New York; TU Dresden, TU Pardubice. Address: Czech Academy Science, Narodni 3, 111 42 Prague 2, Czech Republic.

**ZAHRAN Mohsen,** b. 8 August, Cairo, Egypt. Professor. m. Gayle Zahran, 1 son, 1 daughter. Education: BArch, Ain-Shams University, March, MIT, Cambridge, Massachusetts, USA; MFA Arch, Princeton University; PhD, Princeton University, New Jersey. Appointments: Professor of Urban Design and Architecture, Former Dean, Faculty of Architecture, BAU, Beirut; Chairman, Department of Architecture, Alexandrian University; Executive Director, Alexandria Library. Honour: Medal of Distinction. Publications: Philosophy of Oration; Challenges of the Urban Environment; College Housing; Validity and Illusions in Architecture. Memberships: ESA; EES; Associate of AIA; Fellow of the Salzburg Seminar. Address: 23 Roushdy Street, Roushdy, Alexandria, Egypt.

**ZAINEA Liviu-Nicolae,** b. 11 April 1953, Ploiesti, Romania. Acoustics Consultant. m. Lyra Maria, 1 son, 3 daughters. Education: University Brasou, Romania, 1972-76; Mechanical Engineering, Auto Design. Appointments: Mechanical Engineering in Romania, until 1983; Acoustics Consultant and RPG Diffusor System Representative, 1990-. Publications: 6 articles. Memberships: Hellenic Acoustics Society; Audio European Society; Acoust Society of America. Address: 14 Peresiadou, 11141 Athens, Greece.

**ZAKHARCHENKO Mikhail Petrovich,** b. 24 January 1950, Gomel, Russia. Instructor. m. Galina Vladimirovna Zakharchenko, 2 sons. Education: Graduate, Kuibyshev Military Medical Faculty, 1973; Postgraduate, Military Medical Academy; Candidate of Medical Sciences, 1979; Doctor of Medical Sciences, 1987; Professor, 1990. Appointments: Postgraduate Instructor, Head of Studies, Military Medical Academy, 1976-90; Colonel, Medical Services of Reserves, 1990; Head of Department, St Petersburg Medical Academy, 1990-. Publications include: Ecologic and Hygienic Problems of Investigation of Man's and Population Immune Status, 1992; Modern Problems of Ecohygiene, 1993; Problems of Hygienic Diagnostics Today, 1994; Hygienic Diagnostics Under Extreme Conditions, 1995; Hygienic diagnostics of the water environment, 1996; Diagnostics in preventive medcine, 1997; Harmful habits, 1997; Electromagnetic radiation and health, 1998. Honours: 8 governmental awards; Order of Courage, 1997. Memberships include: St Petersburg Union of Scientific and Engineering Societies; Geographical Society of Russia. Address: PO Box 148, 194356 St Petersburg, Russia.

**ZAKI Fayez Nazir,** b. 16 August 1939, Cairo, Egypt. Professor. m. Nadia Kamil, 1 son, 1 daughter. Education: BSc, Agriculture, 1960; MSc, Entomology, 1966; PhD, Entomology, 1975. Career: Research Assistant, 1961-75, Researcher, 1975-82, Associate Professor, 1982-87, Research Professor, 1987-, National Research Centre, Egypt. Publications: Over 62 papers in national and international professional journals and conferences. Honours: Bronze Medal, National Research Centre Silver Jubilee, 1982; National Research Centre Prize, Scientific Contribution, 1985; State Prize, Biology, 1986; Prize, Distinguished Scientists in Agriculture, 1997. Address: National Research Centre, Tahrir Street, Dokki 12311, Giza, Egypt.

**ZALIKHANOV Mikhail,** b. 22 June 1939, Russia. Geophysicist. m. Akaeva Lidiya, 2 sons, 1 daughter. Education:

Mathematics Faculty, 1962, Agriculture Faculty, 1965, Engineering Faculty, 1971, Honours Diploma, Kabardino Balkarian State University. Appointments: Junior, Senior Scientific Researcher, Director, High-Mountain Geophysical Institute, 1962-; Head of Faculty, University; General Director, Aircraft Research Center; Member, UN Supreme Consultative Committee on Disasters. Publications: Over 350 professional works. Honours: Hero of Social Labour; State Prize of USSR and Russian Federation; Fedorov Prize; Glushkov-Uryvaev Prize; Multanovski Prize. Memberships: Academy of Sciences of USSR; Fellow, 15 other academies. Address: High-Mountain Geophysical Institute, Russian Hydrometerological Service, 6 Tarchokova Street, Nalchik 360030, Russia.

**ZAMAN CHISHTI Sher Muhammad,** b. 11 September 1933, Pak Pattan, Punjab-Pakistan. Educator. m. Kishwar Zaman, 1 son, 3 daughters. Education: BA, 1954, MA, 1956, MA, 1959, Punjab University; PhD, Harvard, 1968. Appointments: Vice Chancellor, Allama Iqbal Open University, Islamabad, 1976-80; Joint Secretary, Government of Pakistan and Director, National Documentation Centre, 1981-83; Director General, Islamic Research Institute, International Islamic University, Islamabad, 1983-88; Chairman, Literacy and Mass Education Commission, 1989-91; Director, National Institute of Historical and Cultural Research, Islamabad, 1991-93; Chairman, Council of Islamic Ideology, 1997. Memberships include: Pakistan Education Review, Islamic Studies, 1983-88; Al-Dirasat al-Islamiyyah, 1983-88; Fikr-o-Azam Academy, 1985; Oriental College Committee, University of Punjab, 1989; Advisory Committee National Documentation Centre, Islamabad, 1991-; Academic Council, Allama Iqbal Open University, International Islamic University, Islamabad. Address: House No 142, Street No 14, Sector E/7, Islamabad, Pakistan.

**ZAMMIT Charles Elia,** b. 8 December 1933, Hamrun, Malta. Director; Lecturer; Conductor. m. Michelina, 1 son. Education: PhD, 1989; DMus, 1990; 10 Fellowship Diplomas. Appointments: Musician; Manager; Lecturer; Conductor; Director, National Academy of Music, Malta; Radio and Television Personality. Publications: Sound Methods in Piano Pedagogy, 1989; Touch and Tone in Piano, 1991. Honours: Gold Medal, Artistic Achievements, Malta; Gold Medal, Composition, London; Silver Medal, International Biographical Centre; International Man of the Year, 1992-93; International Cultural Diploma of Honor; 5-Star Leader Award; 2 Knighthoods. Memberships: MIDI Academy, Germany; Music Education Council, London; National Association of Music Educators; International Society of Musicians; American Musicological Society; Senator, Music Consultant, International Parliament for Safety and Peace, Palermo. Address: Excelsior House, Valletta Road, Luqa LQA03, Malta.

**ZAMRAZIL Václav,** b. Prague, Czechoslovakia. Physician. m. Elvíra Zamrazilová, 1 son, 1 daughter. Education: Faculty Medicine, Charles University, Prague, 1960; Doctor of Medical Science, 1989; Associate Professor, Internal Medicine, 1993; Professor, Internal Medicine, Charles University, Prague, 1997. Appointments: Physician-Internist, 1960, Research Fellow, Research Institute Endocrinology, 1965; Resident, 1972, Chief of Clinical Department, 1983, Institute Endocrinology, Prague; Teacher, Medical Faculty II, Charles University, 1979. Publications: 11 monographs. Memberships: Czech Endocrinology Society; Czech Diabetology Society; International Council for Control of Iodine Deficiency Disorders. Address: Institute Endocrinology Národní 8, CZ 11694, Praha 1, Czech Republic.

**ZAPALSKA Alina M,** b. 25 November 1958, Krakow, Poland. Associate Professor of Economics. Education: BA,

Krakow College, 1977; MSc, 1982; MSc, University of Kentucky, 1987; MA, 1990; PhD, 1991. Appointments: Assistant Professor, Krakow Agricultural University, 1983-85; Research Assistant, University of Kentucky, 1985-87; Research Assistant, University of Kentucky, 1987-88; Teaching Assistant, University of Kentucky, 1988-91; Tenured, Associate Professor, Marshall University, 1991-; Assistant Professor, University of Kentucky, 1991-97; Tenured, Associate Professor, 1997-; Visiting Professor, Auckland Institute of Technology, New Zealand, 1998. Publications: Many, Publications, Refereed Journals, Papers. Honours: Teaching Honours Course; Multicultural, Social Justice Research Award; West Virginia University Research Award; 20th Annual Leavey Awards for Excellence; Outstanding Faculty; Research Summer Grant Award; Many others. Memberships: The Midwest Business Economics Association; American Society of Business and Behavioral Sciences Program; Polich Economic Advising Committee; Summer Institute for the West Virginia High School Teachers. Address: Department of Economics, Marshall University, Huntington, WV 25755, USA.

**ZAPOROZHAN Valery Nicolaevich,** b. 2 March 1947, Ismail, Odessa region. Medical Doctor. m. Natalia Zaporozhan, 1 son. Education: Distinguished Diploma, 1971, Odessa Pirogov's Medical Institute. Appointments: Chief Laboratorian, Research Worker, Assistant Professor, Professor, Dept Obstetrics and Gynaecology, Odessa State Medical University, 1971-86, Head of Department, 1986-; Rector, Odessa State Medical University, 1994-; Head, first Cryosurgery Centre in Ukraine for treatment of pre-oncology conditions in Gynaecology, 1978-; Created first in Ukraine Department of Immunodiagnosis and Immunocorrection in Gynaecology, 1983; Created the Family Health Centre in Odessa, 1989; Created, Endoscopy Laser Surgery Centre, Odessa. Publication: 37 inventions; 230 research papers; 8 monographs; 37 scientific articles; Book, Obstetrics and Gynaecology, in Ukrainian language. Honours: Honored Inventor of Ukraine; Ukrainian Order of Merit, International Gold Medal of Albert Shveytcher, 1997. Memberships: Corresponding member, Ukrainian Academy of Medical Sciences; Head, Republican Problem's Commission, Obstetrics and Gynaecology of Ukrainian Academy of Medical Sciences; President, Republican Association of Endoscopy and Laser Surgery; Honorary Academician, Polish Academy of Sciences; Professor, Johns Hopkins University, USA; European Society of Gynaecologists-Oncologists; American Association Gynaecologists-Laparoscopists; Editorial Commissions several medical journals. Address: Odessa State Medical University, N Narimanova Str 2, Odessa 270 100, Ukraine.

**ZARIC Katarina,** b. 15 June 1966, Belgrade, Yugoslavia. Professor. m. Dejan, 1 s. Education: Masters Degree, Academy of Fine Arts, 1993; Studies of Printmaking, 1999. Appointments: Professor Assistant, Fine Arts Academy, Belgrade, 1993-. Honours: Awards for Best Printmaking, 1990, 1991, 1993, 1995, 1997. Memberships: ULUS, Association of Fine Artists of Serbia. Address: 11080 Novi Beookad, Klare Cetkin 7, Serbia, Yugoslavia.

**ZAZOE Laila Saleh,** b. 6 March 1954, Mecca, Saudi Arabia. Assistant Professor. m. Jawad Koheil. Education: BA with highest honours, 1977, MA with highest honours, 1988, King Abdulaziz University, Jeddah; PhD with highest honours, Imam Mohamed University, Riyadh, 1996. Appointments: Teaching Assistant, 1977-88, Lecturer, 1988-96, Assistant Professor, 1996-, King Abdulaziz University. Publications: Columnist, weekly newspaper, 1997; Some articles in geographical publications. Memberships: American Association of Geographers; Royal Geographical Society; Saudi Geographical

Society; Saudi Disabled Children; Honorary Member, Saudi Ear, Nose and Throat. Address: PO Box 6080, 21442 Jeddah, Saudi Arabia.

**ZEBALLOS HURTADO Hernán,** b. 3 Sept 1934, Bolivia. Agricultural Economist. m. Brunilda Vargas, 2 sons, 1 daughter. Education: MSc, Agricultural Economics, University of Visosa, Minas Gerais, Brazil, 1966; MSc, PhD, Agricultural Economics, University of Wisconsin, Madison, USA, 1975. Appointments: Vice-Minister of Agriculture, Ministry of Agriculture, 1989-91; National Director of Governmental Coordination, Ministry of Presidency, 1997-99. Publications: Agriculture and Economic Development, 1-II, 1988, 1995; Economic Aspects of Potato Production in Bolivia, International Potato Center, 1997. Membership: President, National Consulting Companies Association, 1987-88. Address: PO Box 3499, La Paz, Bolivia.

**ZEHEB Ezra,** b. 2 March 1937, Haifa, Israel. Professor. m. Ruth, 3 sons. Education: BSc, Electrical Engineering, 1958; MSc, 1962; DSc, 1966. Appointments: Director of Electronics Department, 1970-72; Professor, Electrical Engineering, 1985-87; Professor, Electrical Engineering; Visiting Professor, University of California, USA, 1976. Publications: Over 75 Research Papers; 4 Chapters in Books. Memberships: IEEE; American Maths Society; Israel Maths Union; Sigma Xi; New York Academy of Science. Address: Technion, Israel Institute of Technology, Haifa 32000, Israel.

**ZEL Jana,** b. 7 February 1958, Ljubljana, Slovenia. Plant Biotechnologist. m. Zdravko Podlesek, 1 son. Education: Diploma, 1981; MSc, 1985; DSc, 1990. Appointments: Researcher on Plant Physiology and Biotechnology; Head of Plant Physiology Lab, National Institute of Biology, 1995-. Publications: in different research journals and books. Honour: Award of Boris Kidric Foundation, 1989. Memberships: IAPTC; FESPP; Slovene Society of Plant Physiology. Address: National Institute of Biology, Vecna Pot 111, 1000 Ljubljana, Slovenia.

**ZELASCHI Norberto Mario,** b. 26 December 1945, Buenos Aires, Argentina. Psychiatrist; Researcher. Education: Medical degree, 1974, Doctor of Medicine, 1978, Qualified as University Professor, 1984, National University of La Plata; Certification as Psychiatrist. Appointments: Medical Staff, 1974-77, Medical Head of Ward, 1978-79, Director, 1988-92, Department Head of Psychiatry, Mental Health Department, Public Health Administration, 1992-, Dr Alejandro Korn Neuropsychiatric Hospital; Medical Assistant, Institute of Psychiatry, Brugmann Hospital, Free University of Brussels, Belgium, 1979-; Head Coordinator of Clinical Psychiatry, 1987-, Assistant Professor of Psychiatry, 1992-, College of Medicine, Universidad Nacional de La Plata. Publications include: Ethical, Legal and Medical Consequences of the Intake of Amphetamines, doctoral thesis, 1978; Efectos Colaterales Neurológicos y Neuroendócrinos de los Antipsicóticos, 1997; Co-author, several papers, articles and abstracts in the field. Honours: Fellowship, Ministère de l'Education et de la Culture Française, Belgium, 1979-82; Grant, Fondation J Renson, Brussels, 1983-84; Fellowship, National Council of Scientific and Technological Research, Buenos Aires, 1987-89; Fellowship, Consultant to Scientific Investigative Committee, Province of Buenos Aires, 1992-. Membership: La Plata Psychiatric Association, President, 1991-92; Argentinian Society of Clinical Research, 1991-; American Association for the Advancement of Science, 1997-; New York Academy of Sciences, 1997-. Address: Calle 44, No 325, Dept 16-4B, La Plata 1900, Buenos Aires, Argentina.

**ZELECHOWER Michal,** b. 20 October 1947, Mieroszow, Poland. Physicist. Education: MSc, 1970; PhD, 1976.

Appointments: Polish Academy of Sciences, 1970-72; Silesian University of Technology, 1972-; Member of University Senate. Publications: 48. Honour: Ministry of Science Award, 1977. Membership: European Microbeam Analysis Society. Address: Silesian University of Technology, ul Krasinskiego 8, 40 019 Katowice PO Box 221, Poland.

**ZEMVA Boris,** b. 8 June 1940, Ljubljana. University Professor. m. Majda-Marija Brus, 2 daughters. Education: PhD Chemistry, 1971, University Ljubljana; BA Economics, 1983, University Maribor. Appointments: Head of Department, 1983, Deputy Director, 1996, Jozef Stefan Institute Ljubljana, Slovenia; Full Professor, University Ljubljana, 1985; Senior Researcher, Lawrence Berkeley Laboratory, California, USA, 1992. Honours: Boris Kidric Award, Prime Slovenian Award for Achievements in Science, 1989; Visiting Miller Research Professor, University California at Berkeley, USA, 1993; Visiting Professor, Universite de Bordeaux, France, 1997. Memberships: Engineering Academy of Slovenia; Chemical Society, Slovenia; Fluorine Division, ACS, USA; Josef Stefan Institute, Slovenia. Address: Pod Konstanji 42, 1000 Ljubljana, Slovenia.

**ZENG Hualin,** b. 30 May 1939, Xindu, Sichuan, China. Geophysicist. m. Xiangying Li, 1 son, 1 daughter. Education: Graduate 1960, Beijing College of Geology. Appointments: Assistant, 1960-77, Lecturer, 1977-86, Associate Professor, 1986-92, Professor, 1992-, China University of Geosciences, Beijing. Publications: 5 books; 10 Papers published and presented in English professional journals and at UK and USA Geophysical Conferences; Over 30 papers published and presented in Chinese professional journals and meetings; Translations from English and Russian into Chinese. Honours: Science and Technology Awards by the former Ministry of Geology and Mineral Resources, 1985, 1987, 1992, 1994, 1995. Memberships: Chinese Geophysical Society; Chinese Geological Society; Society of Exploration Geophysicists of USA; New York Academy of Science. Address: China University of Geosciences, Beijing, 29 Xueyuan Rd, 100083 Beijing, China.

**ZENG Kejun,** b. 12 December 1956, Hunan, China. Scientist. m. Weiqun Peng, 1 son. Education: BSc, 1981; MSc, 1986; PhD, 1992; Dr Technology, 1996. Appointments: Teaching Assistant, Hebei University of Mining, 1982; Researcher, Central South University of Technology (CSUT), 1986-90; Teaching Assistant, CSUT, 1988-89; Lecturer, CSUT, 1990; Research Fellow, Helsinki University of Technology (HUT), 1991-94; Advisor for PhD Thesis, HUT, 1994; Post Doctoral Researcher, Clausthal University of Technology (CUT), 1994-97; Teaching Assistant, CUT, 1996; Doctoral Thesis Opponent, HUT, 1997; Senior Researcher, GKSS Research Center, 1997-98; Associate Professor, Hunan University, 1998; Senior Scientist, Helsinki University of Technology, 1998. Publications: 35 Papers. Honours: Post Graduate Scholarship; Natural Science Award; Excellent Young Teacher; Scientific and Technological Achievement Award; Excellent Postgarduate Student; Excellent Undergraduate Student; Excellent Teacher. Address: Laboratory of Electrical Production Technology, Department of Electrical and Communications Engineering, Helsinki University of Technology, P O Box 3000, Otakaari 5A, FIN-02015 TKK, Finland.

**ZENG Yueping,** b. 23 April 1958, China. Reconstruction Software Specialist. m. Jenny, 1 daughter. Education: BS, Physics, Wuhan University, 1982; MS, Physics, Beijing University, 1987; MS, Computer Science, Wake Forest University, 1996; PhD, Physics, Wake Forest University, 1997.

Appointments: Teaching Assistant, Wuhan University, 1982-85; Research Engineer, Central Iron and Steel Research Institute, 1987-91; Research and Teaching Assistant, 1991-96; Software Design Engineer, Schlumberger Industries Inc, 1996-98; Reconstruction Software Specialist, Imaging Diagnostic Systems Inc, 1998-. Publications: 8 Publications. Honours: Sigma Xi, Xi Gsa Research Awards, 1995; Assistantship Award. Memberships: Sigma Xi; American Physical Society. Address: Imaging Diagnostic Systems Inc, 6531 NW 18th Court, Plantation, FL 33313, USA.

**ZERILLI Andrea,** b. 28 July 1952, Fiorenzuola, Italy. Geophysicist. Education: DSc, Earth Sciences, 1979. Appointments: Senior Researcher, Eni/Agip Division. Honour: ENI, Technological Award, 1998. Memberships: IEEE; SEG; EAGE; ASEG; EEGS. Address: Via Liberazione 36, 29017 Fiorenzuola d'Arada, Italy.

**ZEVNIK-SANATZKY Donna D,** b. 15 December 1946, Tulsa, Oklahoma, USA. Litigation Coordinator. m. Kenneth Sawatzky, 1 son, 1 daughter. Education: Student, University of Central Oklahoma, 1977; Oklahoma State University, 1984. Appointments: Secretary, Farmers Insurance Company, Oklahoma City, 1974-80; Office Manager, SAFE Incorporated, Oklahoma City, 1980-83; Junior Accountant, Southeast Exploration Corporation, Oklahoma City, 1983-84; Accountant, Young Brothers Incorporated, Oklahoma City, 1984-88, The Denman Company Incorporated, Oklahoma City, 1988-89; Litigation Coordinator, ACLU Oklahoma, Oklahoma City, 1994-; Founder, Executive Director, ASIA/COFWA Arachnoiditis Sufferer Worldwide Support Group, 1996-. Publications: Childrens Book: That Place - Otherwhere, 1994; Something for Otherwhere, 1995. Honours include: Outstanding DHS Volunteer Legislation Commendation, State of Oklahoma, 1987; Outstanding Volunteer, Child Advocacy, Oklahoma State Department of Human Services, 1987. Memberships: Amnesty International; Interfaith Alliance; ACLU. Address: 3012 North Lee Ste A, Oklahoma, OK 73103, USA.

**ZHA Yi-Min,** b. 25 April 1941, Shanghai, China. Professor; Chief Editor. m. Ding Bao-fen, 1 daughter. Education: Graduate in Water Resources, 1963, East China Technical University; M Eng, 1982, Hohai University. Appointments: Director and Chief Editor, Hohai University Press, 1986-; Associate Professor, 1987-92; Professor, Hohai University, 1993-. Publications: China Coastal Engineering; The Photographic Atlas of Geological Landscapes of Qinghai-Xizang (TIBET) Plateau; Handbook on Water Resources Protection; and others. Honour: National Excellent Book Prize. Memberships: VP, China Water Resources History Academy; Director, China Water Resources History Institute, Hohai University. Address: #1 Xikang Road, Hohai University Press, Nanjing 210024, China.

**ZHA Zizhong,** b. 28 October 1936, An Hui, China. Teacher andresearcher. m. Rui Liu, 1 son, 1 daughter. Education: Diploma, AtomicNucleus, Harbin Institute of Technology, China, 1964. Appointments:Assistant, Harbin Institute of Technology, China, 1964-75; Lecturer, Laser Physics and Nonlinear Optics, Harbin Institute of Technology,1976-86; Professor, Head of Research Group, Optical Bistable and Optical Computing as well as Laser Protection, Department of Applied Physics and Institute of Opto Electronics, Harbin Institute of Technology, 1987-95. Professor, Head of Research Group, Laser Protection, Institute of Opto-Electronics, Harbin Institute of Technology, 1996-99. Publications: 25 Papers in all kinds of Journals and Meetings at Home and Abroad. Honours: Third Class Award, Nature and Science, Academy of Sciences, China, 1992. Memberships: Association of Physics and Optics, Heilongjiang Province, China. Address: Institute of Opto-Electronics Harbin Institute of technology, P O Box 309 92 W Da Zhi, Harbin 150001, China.

**ZHANG Chunting,** b. 30 August 1934, Shandong Province, China. Senior Editor; Reporter. m. Zhang Yuee, 2 daughters. Education: Bachelor degree, 1960, Shandong Teacher's University. Appointments: Senior Editor, Xinhua News Agency. Honours: Excellent Reporter, 1990; Excellent Worker, 1994; Prize for Excellent Newsworkers. Memberships: China Reporters Association; China Old Professor Association. Address: Huayanli 33-808, Deshengmenwai, Chaoyang District, Beijing 100029, China.

**ZHANG Dazhi,** b. 3 April 1933, Penglai, China. Teacher; Professor. m. Shizhen Lieng, 1 son, 1 daughter. Education: Fudan University, 1955-60. Career: Cadre, Yantai City Office, Zhejiang Province Office, 1948-55; Director, Dean, Journalism Department, 1987-94, Vice Professor, 1986, Professor, 1990, Hangzhou University. Publications include: Fundamental Theory of Journalism, 1990; Anthology of Maokun, 1993; Developmental History of Literature on Chinese Ancient, 1996. Honours: Advanced Worker Award, 1990; 1st Degree Taofen Teacher Award, 1996. Memberships: Zhejiang Province Journalism Workers Association; Chinese Journalism Education Association. Address: No 33 Wensan New Village, Wensan Road, Hangzhou, China.

**ZHANG Fuqi,** b. 22 February 1937, Jinzhou, Liaoning, China. Senior Teacher of Mathematics. m. Yuezhe Sun, 1 son, 2 daughters. Education: Bachelor's degree, Department of Mathematics, Capital Normal University. Appointment: Currently Principal, Beijing 21st Experimental School. Publications: Analysis of Senior High School Mathematics Subjects, 1995; Series of Lectures on Middle School Mathematics, 1996; Behaviour, 1997. Honour: Outstanding Teacher Award, 1992. Memberships: Director, China Senior Professors Association; Executive Director, National Association of Scientific Research of Key Middle Schools; Deputy Director, Management Institute of China; Deputy Director, Educational Management Committee. Address: No 46 Enjihuang, Haidian District, Beijing 100036, China.

**ZHANG Huiming,** b. 11 October 1962, China. Civil Engineer. m. Hong Zhu, 1 son, 2 daughters. Education: BS, Changsha Railway University; MS, China Academy of Railway Sciences; PhD, University of Ottawa. Appointment: Senior Engineer. Publications include: Quasi-steady state: A real behaviour, 1997; Volume changes in undrained triaxial tests on sands; Steady state strength in quasi-steady state behaviour, 1998; Accuracy and uniqueness of steady state strength in triaxial tests, 1998. Membership: MCSCE. Address: Unit F, 12/f, Everwin Building, 406 King's Road, North Point, Hong Kong.

**ZHANG Huisen,** b. 21 February 1933, Hebei, China. Professor; Educator. m. 2 daughters. Education: Graduate, Harbin Foreign Languages Institute, 1953; Leningrad University. Career: Teacher, Harbin Foreign Languages Institute, 1953; Teacher, PhD Candidates; Professor, Russian Department, Heilongjiang University; Head, Graduate Teaching & Research Office; head, Russian Language Institute; Professor, Russian, Jilin University; Visiting Professor, Russian Far Eastern University. Publications include: New Modern Russian Grammar, 1979; Changes and Development in Modern Russian, 1984; Functional Russian Grammar, 1992; Selected Papers by Zhang Huisen, 1992; On Contrastive Linguistics, 1992. Memberships: Standing Board of Directors, China's Rhetoric and Stylistics Institute, China's Institute of Comparative Studies of Sino-Foreign Languages and Culture;

Head, China's Northeast Rhetoric and Stylistics Institute; Acaemic Consultant, Northeast Document Materials Center of China. Address: Russian Department, Heilongjiang University, Xuefu Street 74, Harbin 150080, China.

**ZHANG Jian,** b. 29 July 1955, Chengdu, China. Teacher. m. Fan Jin, 1 daughter. Education: Bachelor Degree, 1982, Master Degree, 1985, Historical Department, Sichuang University. Appointments: Lecturer, 1987, Assistant Professor, 1984, Sichuan University. Publications: The Jewish Giants Who Are Affecting the World; Researches of the Great Geographical Discovery. Memberships: Director, Chinese Society of Ancient and Medieval History of the World. Address: Department of History, Sichuan Union University, Chengdu 610064, China.

**ZHANG Jian,** b. 15 January 1963, Hunan, China. Thermal Engineering. m. Liu Hui, 1 son. Education: BA, Thermal Engineering, Dynamics Department, Harbin Industry University, 1985. Career: President, Broad Air Conditioning, Changsha. Honours: Special Guest, China Business Summit, 1998. Membership: Congressman, Hunan Province. Address: Broad Air Conditioning, Broad Town, Changsha, Hunan 410001, China.

**ZHANG Jian-Guo,** b. 27 January 1964, Chongqing, Sichuan, China. Researcher; Optical Communications Educator. Education: BSc Electronic Engineering, 1985, Shenyang Institute of Aeronautical Technology, Shenyang, China; MSc Electronic Engineering, 1988, Beijing University of Aeronautics and Astronautics, Beijing, China; PhD Information Technology, 1994, University of Parma, Italy. Appointments: Research Engineer in Development Division, Chengdu Aircraft Company, China, 1988-90; Visiting Associate and Research Associate, Department of Information Engineering, Chinese University of Hong Kong, 1994-95; Assistant Professor, 1995-98, Associate Professor, 1998-, Telecommunications Programme, Asian Institute of Technology, Thailand. Publications: 51 international journal papers including 17 IEEE journal and magazine papers, 13 IEE journal papers, 6 SPIE journal papers, 3 ISA journal papers, 3 OSA journal papers, 2 IEICE journal papers, 3 EOS journal papers; 2 EUREL journal papers. Honours: URSI Young Scientist Award, International Union of Radio Science, 1996; Twentieth Century Achievement Award, American Biographical Institute, 1998; Young Scientist Award, International Symposium on Signals, Systems and Electronics, 1995; Outstanding Achievement medal, International Biographical Centre, 1999; Special 1993 EMCSC Scholarship granted by World Federation of Scientists; Ing Migliorini Scholarship, Faculty of Engineering of Parma University. Memberships: New York Academy of Sciences; IEEE; OSA; SPIE; ISA; SAE. Address: Asian Institute of Technology, Telecommunications Programme, PO Box 4, Klong Luang Pathumthani 12120, Thailand.

**ZHANG Jianyi,** b. 3 August 1959, Zhejiang Province, China. Opera singer. m. Weiping Yang, 1 daughter. Education: BAm MA, The Shanghai Conservatory of Music, 1981-85; Young Artist Diploma, 1989, Juilliard School. Appointments: Leading tenor roles with Metropolitan Opera, Opera National de Paris, Bastille, Hamburg Staatsoper, Teatro Comunale di Firenze, Opera de Lyon and others. Honours: First Prize Winner of the Third Belvedere International Opera Singer Competition 84 in Vienna; Grand Prizewinner of Luciano Pavarotti Competition 88 in US. Memberships: Opera America; Council of China Musician Association. Address: 62-54 97th Pl #PH-I, Rego Park, NY 11374, USA.

**ZHANG Jinkun,** b. 7 March 1943, Shanghai, China. Professor of Histology and Embryology. m. Wei Xiyun, 1 son.

Education: BS, Nanjing Railway Medical College, 1965. Appointments: Lecturer, Department of Histology and Embryology, Nanjing Railway Medical College, 1965-87; Vice Professor, Graduate Advisor, Head of the Department of Histology and Embryology, Nanjing Railway Medical College, 1987-92; Professor, Graduate Advisor, Head of Department, Histology and Embryology, Head of Cancer and Cell Biology Laboratory, Shantou University Medical College, 1992-. Publications: More than 40 Publications. Honours: 3rd Grade Prize of Science and Technology Progression of the Department of Railways. Memberships: Chinese Society of Anatomical Science; Councilor of Guangdong Society of Anatomical Sciences; Chinese Society of Cell Biology; Chinese Society for Stereology. Address: Department of Histology and Embryology, Shantou University Medical College, Xingling Road, Shantou 515031, Shantou Guangdong Province, China.

**ZHANG Li,** b. 5 May 1963, Jilin, China. Teacher. m. Hongyu Chen, 1 son. Education: BA, 1985, Postgrad Study, 1987, Peking University. Appointments: Lecturer, Beijing Language Institute, 1987-94; Associate Professor, Moscow State Institute International Relations, 1994-97; Associate Professor, Beijing Language and Culture University, 1997-. Publications: A Dictionary of Semantic Variation in Current Chinese, 1998; Qingxilan Xi, poem collection, 1994; Foreign Trade Chinese : 30 lessons, 1991. Membership: Association of Teaching Chinese Language for Foreigner of China. Address: Dept of Chinese Language & Culture, Beijing Language and Culture University, Beijing 100083, China.

**ZHANG Ming,** b. 29 July 1949, Shanghai, China. Computer Scientist. m. Zhao Qing, 1 daughter. Education: MS, 1982; PhD, 1989. Appointments: PhD Supervisor, University of Western Sydney. Publications: Visual Cognition, 1991; IEEE Transactions on Neural Networks, Paper, 1996; International Journal of Nurocomputing, Paper, 1997. Memberships: Senior Member, IEEE. Address: University of Western Sydney, Department of Computing Information Systems, Campbelltown 2560, New South Wales, Australia.

**ZHANG Ming,** b. 29 May 1964, Nantong, China. Researcher. m. Yiming Weng, 1 son. Education: BS, 1986, MS, 1989, China University of Mining and Technology; PhD, Kyushu University, Japan, 1996. Appointments: Teaching Assistant, China University of Mining and Technology, 1989; Visiting Scholar, 1992, Visiting Researcher, 1996, Kyushu University; Researcher, Geological Survey of Japan/Research Fellow, Japan Science and Technology Corporation, 1996; Senior Researcher, Geological Survey of Japan, 1999. Publications: Underground Construction, 1995; Articles in ASTM Geotechnical Testing Journal, Scientific Basis for Nuclear Waste Management. Address: Environmental Geology Department, Geological Survey of Japan; Higashi 1-1-3, Tsukuba, Ibaraki 305-8567, Japan.

**ZHANG Minglong,** b. 28 March 1953, Haiyou, Sanmen, Zhejiang, China. Professor of Economics. m. 20 January 1981. Education: BA, Zhejiang Normal University, 1981; MEcons, Fudan University, 1984; DEcons, People's University, 1992. Appointments: Assistant, 1981-87, Lecturer, 1987-91, Associate Professor, 1991-95, Deputy Lecturer, 1992-95, Institute of Economics; Director of the Liaison Office, 1993-; Lecturer, Professor, Institute of Economics, Zhejiang Normal University, 1995-; Member, Zhejiang Provincial People's Political Consultative Conference, 1995-. Publications: Economy Movement and Adjustment, 1993; The Dictionary of Chinese and Western Thinking Comparison, co-author, 1993; There Is No Negative Effect in Socialist Competitions, 1986; Competition and Production Anarchy Aren't an Identical Law,

1988; Observations Crosswise the Socialist Mechanism of Competition, 1989; To Form and to Apply the Funds to Be Responsible for Loss in the Contractsystem Enterprises, 1990; Comparison Between Two Regulative Mechanisms in Socialist Market Economy, 1992; On the Signal Mechanism of Market, 1993; The Cause and Counteragent of a Few Productive Main Factor Income Overdid, 1994; The Connotations, Quantification and Protection of the Intangible Assets of State-Owned Enterprises, 1996; Establishing Central Mechanisms of Macroscopic Control, 1997; Accelerating the Reform of State-Owned Enterprises According to the Normative Requirements of the Corporation System, 1998. Honour: Outstanding Professor of Social Sciences of Zhejiang Province, 1997. Address: PO Box No 17 Normal University of Zhejiang, Jinhua, Zhejiang, 321004, China.

**ZHANG Niancun,** b. 25 February 1924, Zhuzhou City, China. Professor. m. He Wei, 2 sons, 1 daughter. Education: BEE, 1949, Jiaotong University, Shanghai. Appointments: Assistant Researcher, Changchun Electro-Mech Institute, 1949-56; Assistant Researcher, Institute of Automation, Chinese Academy of Sciences, 1957-63; Lecturer, Associate Professor, Professor, University Science and Technology of China, 1964-86; Professor, Beijing University Aeronautics and Astronautics, 1987-. Honour: Diploma of Merit, State Education Commission of China, 1990. Membership: Director, Chinese Federation of Automation, 1978-86. Address: Room 313 Bldg 23, Beijing University of Aeronautics and Astronautics, 37 Xueyuan Rd, Beijing 100083, China.

**ZHANG Peisheng,** b. 10 October 1941, Faku Town, Liaoning, China. Petroleum-Refining Engineer. m. Yang Ling Yun, 2 sons. Education: Student, 1961-66, Bachelor's degree, 1966, North-East Petroleum Institute of Technology. Appointments: General Manager, Shijiazhuang Chemical Fibre Co Ltd; Vice-President, Shijiazhuang Refinery, Sinopec International. Publications: 23 papers in national professional journals, 1983-98. Honours: 7 National Technical Prizes in field of Petroleum, 1983-98; One of 100 Famous Scientists in Hebei Province, 1992; State Special Contribution Prize, 1995-. Memberships: Vice-Director, Hebei Petroleum Institute; Committeeman, China Petroleum Institute. Address: Shijiazhuang Refinery, Shijiazhuang 050032, Hebei, China.

**ZHANG Qingchun,** b. 21 March 1964, Henan Province, China. Petroleum Geologist. m. Qizhi Wang, 1 daughter. Education: BSc, Northwest University, 1986; MEng, Graduate School, Research Institute of Petroleum Exploration and Development, China National Petroleum Corporation, 1989. Appointments: Assistant Engineer, Oil Production Plant, Jidong Petroleum Exploration and Development Company, 1989-90; Geologist, 1990-93, Senior Geologist, 1993-, Computer Application Technology Dept of RIPED. Publications: 19 publications including: Petroliferous Sedimantary Basins in China and basin Analysis, 1997; Principles and Methods of Basin Modelling, 1998. Honours: Gold Medal (First Prize), Popularization of New Technology, China National Petroleum Corporation, 1991; First Prize, Progresses of Science and Technology, China National Petroleum Corporation, 1992, Third Prize, 1993. Membership: Chinese Petroleum Society, 1993-. Address: Computer Centre, PO Box 910, Beijing 100083, China.

**ZHANG Tongzhu,** b. 10 October 1915. Education: Graduate, Department of History and Geography, National Central University, 1943; Graduate, Board of History Research, National Central University, 1947; Graduate, Postgraduate in Economic Geography in China People's University, 1955; Professor, Department of Geography and African Institute, Nanjing University, 1978. Appointments: Deputy Head, Department of Geography, 1961-80; Director, African Economic Geography Section, 1972-84; Advisor, Overall Territory Plan of Jiangsu Province; Associate Editor, Editorial Committee of Encyclopedia of China, World Geography. Honours: 5 Honor Citations from Nanjing University; National Educational Committee of China; Information Publication Bureau of China; China Geography Society and China Figure Dictionary. Memberships: Main Founder, China Society for African Studies and President of the Society for 20 years, 1979-99; Vice President, Advisor, China Society for Middle East, 1985-93; Vice Director, World Geography Specialized Committee, China Geography Society, 1987-94; Member of the Council, World Economic Society of China, 1980-93. Address: Rm 101 Jia Lou, 52-1 Hankou Road, Nanjing 210008, China.

**ZHANG Wei,** b. 22 May 1913, Beijing, China. Professor. m. Lu Shi-Jia, 1 son, 1 daughter. Education: BSc, 1933; DIC, 1938; Dr.Ing, 1944. Appointments: Research Engineer, 1945-46; Professor, Tungjie University, 1946, Beiyang University, 1946-47, Tsinghua University, 1947-. Publications: 1 book, numerous articles in professional journals. Honours include: Grossverdienstkreuz by the Bundespraesident of FRG, 1988; Science and Technology Award, Chinese Academy of Engineering, 1996. Memberships: Chinese Society of Mechanics; IABSE; GAMM; AIAA; VDI. Address: Tsinghua University, Beijing 100084, China.

**ZHANG Wenqi,** b. 29 June 1963, Hebei, China. Researcher; Educator. m. Chunyan Wang, 1 s, 1 d. Education: BSc, Northeastern University, Shenyang, China, 1985; MSc, 1988; PhD, Technical University of Denmark, 1994. Appointments: Senior Researcher, Technical University of Denmark, 1994-97; Associate Professor, 1997-; President, SWANTEC Software and Engineering ApS, 1999-. Publications: Articles to Professional Journals. Honours: Excellent Graduate, Northeastern University; F W Taylor Medal. Memberships: American Welding Society. Address: Technical University of Denmark, Bldg 425, 2800 Lyngby, Denmark.

**ZHANG Xian Min,** b. 25 November 1964, Hebei, China. Mechanical Engineer. m. Ren Shao Jing, 1 daughter. Education: MSc, 1991, Xian University of Technology; PhD, 1993, Beijing University of Aeronautics and Astronautics. Appointments: Postdoctoral Research work, Northwest Polytechnical University, 1995; Associate Professor, Shantou University, Head Dept Mechatronic Engineering, 1996-. Publications: 54 publications in journals. Honours: 10 Outstanding People of Science and Technology of Shantou Awards; Outstanding Teacher of Guangdong Province; 1994, 1996, 1997 Award of Science and Technology, Ministry of National Mechanical Engineering, State Education Commission of China; Many other awards. Memberships: Senior member, CMES; IFTTOMM China Committee; Director, Mechanical Engineering Society of Guangdong Province; and others. Address: Department of Mechatronic Engineering, Shantou University, Shantou 515063, Guangdong, China.

**ZHANG Yusheng,** b. 15 January 1939, Xiong County, Hebei Province, China. Teacher. m. Zhou Jianmin, 1 son, 1 daughter. Education: Diplomas of undergraduate course, Department of Chinese Language and Literature, Northwest China University, 1963. Appointments: Teacher, No 1 College of Xinjiang, 1963; Secretary of Revolution Committee of Urumchi, 1975; Teacher, Xinjiang Normal University, 1979. Honours: Silver Medal, Outstanding Behaviour in Teaching, 1991; Award for Excellent Works, 1994. Memberships: Council Member, China Society for the Study of the Book of Song; Society for the Study of Si Magian; Chinese Sanegu Association; Chinese Literature

Association of Tourism. Address: Xinjiang Normal University, Xinjiang, China.

**ZHANG Zhan Lin,** b. 29 January 1936, Daxing County, China. Director. m. Hao Kun Qin, 3 sons, 2 daughters. Education: Graduate, Middle School. Appointments: Director, Liu Min Ying Ecological Farm, Daxing County; Honorary Professor, Adult College of Beijing. Honours: Deputy to the 6th, 7th, 8th and 9th National Peoples Congress of China; National Model Worker, 1986; One of the Best 500 Global Environmental Protectors Awarded by the Office of the Environmental Plan of the UN, 1987. Address: Director of Ecological Forestry Farm, Liumingyin Daxing County, Beijing 102611, China.

**ZHANG Zhenxiang,** b. 30 August 1947, Jiangsu, China. Professor. m. Chen Xiuzhen, 2 sons. Education: Bachelor, Automation Department, Tsing Hua University, 1970; Master, Math Department, Anhui Normal University, 1981; PhD, Mathematics Department, University of Limoges, France, 1993. Appointments: Professor, Mathematicss Department, Anhui Normal University. Publications: On a Conjection of Edos on the sum, 1991; Upper Bound of 1, 1993; On a Problem of Erdos Concerning Primitive Sequences, Math Comp, 1993; A B2 Sequence with larger reciprocal sum, 1993; Upper Bound of 1, 1993; Finding Finite B2 Sequence with larger m-a, 1994. Honours: Anhui Province Learning Institutions Science and Technique Progress Awards, First Proze, 1997; Anhui Province Natural Science Awards, Second Prize, 1998. Memberships: Amer Math Society. Address: Anhui Normal University, Mathematics Department, 241000 Wuhu Anhui, China.

**ZHANG Zhiqiang,** b. 23 December 1967, Zhong Yang country, Shanxi, China. Orthopaedic Doctor. m. 1 son. Education: Medical Department, The Capital Medical College. Appointments: Doctor in Charge. Publications: Papers in professional journals. Honour: The Science-Technology Progress Award of Shanxi Provinces. Membership: Orthopaedic Association of Shanxi. Address: Orthopaedics, 2nd Teaching Hospital, Shanxi Medical College, Taiyuan 030001, China.

**ZHANG Zhiyuan,** b. 26 December 1941, Changsha, China. Painter. m. Yuping Li, 1 son, 1 daughter. Education: Harbin Art School, 1966-69; MA, Jiangsu Art College, 1980-83. Appointments: Artist-in-Residence, Jiangsu International Cultural Exchange Center, 1988-; Professor, Oriental Painting Institute, 1995-. Honours: Gold Medal, The Exhibition of All China Young Painters, 1979; Silver Medal, 3rd World Calligraphy-Painting Art Works Exhibition in Japan, 1995. Memberships: China Folk Artists' Association, 1995; Vice Director, Modern Painter's and Calligrapher's Association, 1995. Address: Apt 301, Building 14, Gate 43, Yu Tang Village, Nanhu Nanjing 210017, China.

**ZHAO Ming Jiu,** b. 6 November 1923, Shandong, China. Professor. m. Zhang Qing Lan, 1 son, 2 daughters. Education: Graduate, Department of Education, Northwest Normal College, 1953. Career: Director, Institute of Educational Science, Northwest Normal University, 1983-91; Member, Scholastic Delegation to USA, Northwest University, 1987. Publications inciude: Selection Reference Resources Materials of Psychology, 1989; Educational Psychology Branch of Hughe Educational Dictionary, 1990; Psychology for College Teachers, 1995; Folk Psychology, 1996. Honours: Teaching and Nurturing Prize, Gansu Provincial Higher School, 1987; Excellent Teacher and Prize of Gardener, Gansu Provincial Peoples Government, 1988; 1st Class Prize, State Education Committee, China. Memberships: Gansu Provincial

Psychological Association; Council, Psychological Association of China; Council, China Social Psychological Association. Address: Institute of Educational Science, Northwest Normal University, Lanzhou, Gansu 730070, China.

**ZHAO ShuJiang,** b. 21 November 1936, Tsinan, Shandong, China. Teacher; Professor. m. Miss Liu, 2 sons. Education: Physics graduate, 1958, Wuhen University, China. Appointments: Lecturer, Associate Professor, Professor, Wuhan Yejih University of Science and Technology, 1978, 1987, 1994. Honour: Title, 07 Project Technical Specialist, 1980. Membership: CIE Circuits and Systems Society. Address: Automation Department, WuHan Institute of Steel and Iron, Wu Han Hubei, China.

**ZHAO Song,** b. 19 January 1953, Beijing, China. Computer. m. Jianguo Shang, 1 daughter. Education: Business School of University of Maryland, 1988; BS, Computer Science, East-China Technology University. Appointments: System Administrator, College of Behavioral and Social Sciences, University of Maryland; System Administrator, Ministry of Water Resources, China. Honours: Outstanding Employee of College at University of MD, 1994; Outstanding Computer Expert, Department of Psychology of UM, 1993. Address: University Maryland - Academic Computing, 221 Lefrak Hall, College Park, MD 20742, USA.

**ZHAO You Bin,** b. 25 July 1945, Shaanxi, China. Director; Senior Engineer. m. Li Weiping, 2 daughters. Education: Graduate, 1978, Mechanical and Electrical Engineering College. Appointments: Director, Extrahigh Voltage Dept, Xi'an High Voltage Apparatus Research Institute. Publications: 35 papers in magazines; Patent for rod-rod gap awarded by Patent Bureau of China, 1991. Memberships: Vice Director, Technical Committee, High Voltage Testing and Measuring of China Electric and Mechanical Engineering Association, 1997. Address: 29 Daqing Rd, Xian High Pressure Electric Institute, Xian 710077, China.

**ZHAO Zong Fu,** b. 25 October 1995, Qinghai Province. Teacher. m. Yixiang Meng, 1 son, 1 daughter. Education: BA Chinese, 1981. Appointments: Dean of Chinese Department, 1993-95, Dean of Studies, 1995-98, Director of Dept for Chinese Literature, Qinghai Normal University, Xining Qinghai, China. Publications: Poems Collection of Qinghai Province, 1986; Collection of Tibetan Poems, 1987; North-West Literature of China, 1991; Folk Custom and Touring of Qinghai Province, 1995. Honours: Excellent Undergraduate Award, 1990; Excellent Works of Literature, 1994; Professional Talent, 1995; Model Workers, 1995; First Prize, Northern Folk Literature of China, 1995. Memberships: Chinese Folk Custom Institute, Director; Vice President: Folk Artist Association of Qinghai Province; Literature Institute of Qinghai Province; Literary and Art Critic Institute of Qinghai Province. Address: Department for Chinese Literature, Qinghai Normal University, Xining Qinghai 810008, China.

**ZHARIKOV Alexander Nicolaevich,** b. 2 January 1945, Russia. Engineer. m. Sukhova Olga, 1 son. Education: Shipbuilding Institute, Leningrad, 1969. Appointments: Secretary, Leningrad Youth Organization, 1971-74; Vice Chairman, Committee of Youth Organization, 1974-76; President, Student Council of Russia, 1976-78; Vice President, International Union of Students, 1978-84; CPSU, International Department, Central Committee, 1984-88; Director, International Department, All Union Central Council of Trade Unions, 1988-90; General Secretary, World Federation of Trade Unions, 1990-. Address: Branicka 112, 14000 Prague 4, Czech Republic.

**ZHENG Bin,** b. 1 January 1959, Shanghai, China. Assistant Professor. m. Jing Xu, 1 son. Education: BS, East China University of Technology, 1978-82; MS, East China University of Technology, 1982-84; PhD, University of Delaware, 1988-93. Appointments: Instructor, East China University of Technology, 1984-88; Research Assistant, University of Delaware, 1988-92; Teaching Assistant, University of Delaware, 1992-93; Research Associate, University of Pittsburgh, 1993-94; Assistant Professor, University of Pittsburgh, 1994-1997; Assistant Professor, Allegheny University of the Health Sciences Imaging Technology Division, 1997-1998; Assistant Professor, University of Pittsburgh, 1998-. Publications: 20 Refereed Articles; 8 Published Abstracts. Honours: Laser Doppler Spectrometer for the Statistical Study of the Behavior of Microscopic Organisms, 1993; Identification of Suspicious Mass Region in Mammograms, 1997; Computerized Detection of Masses and Microcalcifications in Digital Mammograms, 1997. Memberships: International Society for Optical Engineering, 1990. Address: 6581 Rosemoor Street, Pittsburgh, PA 15217-3025, USA.

**ZHENG Huai-mei,** b. 18 July 1918, Shanghai, China. MD; Professor. m. X G Zhou, 3 sons, 1 daughter. Education: Premedical Education, University Shanghai, 1935-38; MD, 1943, Women's Medical College of Shanghai and St Johns University School of Medicine, Shanghai; Postgraduate Medical Training and courses, USA, 1946-48. Appointments: Residency, Margaret Williamson Hospital, 1943-46; Visiting MD, full time, Gynaecological and Obstetrics Hospital, 1949-54; Deputy Chief, Gynaecological Service, 1954-58, Vice Director, 1979-89, Gynaecological and Obstetrics Hospital, Shanghai; Associate Professor, 1958, Vice Chairman, 1959, Professor, 1980, Department of Gynaecology and Obstetrics, First Shanghai Medical College, Shanghai; Cultural Revolution, 1966-76; Retirement, University Post, 1989-. Publications: 15 papers in Gynaecological and Obstetrical field. Honours: 4 National Awards in Science and Technology (Clinical Research), National Family Planning Commission, 1986-94; Personal Certificate of Honour, 1990; Citation of Honour, 1991; Certificate of Honour, Ministry of Public Health, 1987; Award, 1990, Certificate of Honour, 1991, Chinese Medical Association, ; Certificate of Honour, Ministry of Education, 1990; Special Cognitive Award, The State Dept, 1992; Quality Award for Textbook of Obstetrics and Gynaecology, II Ed, 1992, III Ed, 1996; Citation, The Chinese Organisational Committee of the UN 4th International Women's Congress for Outstanding Achievements, 1995. Memberships: Member 7 editorial boards; Ad hoc Editor, Journal of International Gynaecologic Laparoscopic Association, USA; Various positions, 6 other professional associations. Address: 7 Fl No 34 Fushing Xi Road, Shanghai 200031, China.

**ZHENG Peiyu,** b. 26 March 1937, Guangzhou, China. Educator. m. Zhaolian Tang, 1 daughter. Education: Bachelor of Economics Degree, Jilin University, 1960. Appointments: Lecturer, 1980-85, Associate Professor, 1985-92, Economics Department, Zhongshan University; Director, 1991-, Professor, 1992-, Hong Kong and Macau Research Institute, Zhongshan University; Deputy Chief, Center for Hong kong and Macao Research, Zhongshan University, 1991-. Publications include: Survey of Hong Kong Economy, 1985; A Precise Course on Modern Capitalist Economy, 1987; The Mabamen are on the Way of Growth, 1989; Contemporary Capitalist Economy, 1993; Strategic Research on Cooperation Between Mainland China and Hong Kong in Biological Medicine (joint project), 1997; Research on Hong Kong's Development in Science, Technology and High-tech Sectors, 1997; Development and Prospects of Hong Kong Foreign Economic Relations, 1998. Honours: 2nd Prize, Outstanding Works, Guangdong Higher Education Commission, 1988; 3rd Prize, Outstanding Textbooks, 1989; 2nd Prize, Outstanding Textbooks, Higher Education Commission of Central-South China 1995; State Special Subsidy for Outstanding Contributions to the Development of China's Higher Education, 1995; Honour for Scientific and Technological Advance of Guangdong Province, 1998. Memberships: Vice-President, Guangdong Hong Kong and Macau Economic Research Association; Council, Centre for Taiwan-Hong Kong-Macau Economic Studies, Foreign Economics and Trade University; Academic Committee, Zhongshan University; Administrative Affairs Committee, Zhongshan University; State Education Department Advisory Committee of Research Experts in Humanity and Social Science; Appointed Researcher of Hong Kong and Macao Research Centre of Guangdong Provincial Academy of Social Science; Appointed Researcher, Research Centre of Social and Economic Development of Guangdong Government. Address: Hong Kong-Macau Research Institute, Zhongshan University, Guangzhou 510275, China.

**ZHENG Qiguang,** b. 4 December 1944, Heng Yang, Hunan, China. Professor, Optic Educator. m. Zhongying Tao, 2 daughters. Education: Hua Zhong University of Science and Technology, 1964-69. Appointments: Assistant, Hua Zhong University, China, 1971-79; Lecturer, Hua Zhong University, China, 1980-88; Associant Professor, Hua Zhong University, China, 1989-92; Professor, Hua Zhong University, China, 1993-. Publications: Laser Machining; Interaction of Laser and Matter; 140 papers, Journals of Science and Technology, Inner and Abroad. Honours: 1st Award State Education Committee; 2nd Award, Hubei Province. Memberships: Optic Associations; National Laboratory of Laser Technology of Hua Zhong University of Science and Technology. Address: National Laboratory of Laser, Hua Zhong University of Science and Technology, Wuhan, Hubei, China.

**ZHENG Wenxin,** b. 13 November 1953, Beijing, China. Optical Communication Engineer. m. Sun Baihua, 1 son. Education: PhD, Electrical Engineering, Royal Institute of Technology, Sweden, 1989. Appointment: Senior Specialist. Publications: Over 30 articles to professional journals; 25 patents. Memberships: IEEE; SPIE. Address: Ericsson Cables AB, Landsvagen 66, 17287 Sundbyberg, Sweden.

**ZHENG Xinsheng,** b. 8 February 1951, Jiangsu, China. Executive. m. Xiang Guanghong, 1 son. Education: Master Degree, Development Administration, Birmingham University, England. Appointments: Deputy Director, Department of Cultural and Educational Experts; State Administration of Foreign Experts Affairs. Publications: Editor, Selected Articles, Foreign Experts Work. Honours: Awards for Distinguished work of Foreign Experts Affairs. Memberships: China Association for International Experts Exchange and Development; China Center for International Legal Study. Address: 61634 Freindship Hotel, Beijing 100873, China.

**ZHIGAL'SKII Gennadii Pavlovich,** b. 15 April 1939, Bryanskaya, Russia. Professor of Radiophysics. m. Zhigal'skaya Albina, 1 son. Education: Graduate, Moscow State University; Physical Faculty, 1962; Candidate of Science Degree and PhD Degree, MSU, 1967, 1993. Appointments: Professor in Chair of Physics and Technology of Integrated Circuits, Moscow Institute of Electronics Technology, Technical University. Publications: Author, more than 120 publications; Vacancy Model of 1/f Noise in Metal Films, 1991; Nonequilibrium Flicker Fluctuation in Conducting Films, 1995; Current Research Interests are in Excess Noise and Nonlinearity of Microwave Devices. Address: Moscow Institute of Electronics Technology Zelenograd, Moscow 103489, Russia.

**ZHIMIN Gu,** b. 1 July 1927, Beijing, China. Doctor of Medicine. m. Wong Wenjing, 1 son, 1 daughter. Education: Graduate, Department of Medical Science, Anhui Medical University, 1952; Graduate, 2 Year Chinese Medical Course, Shanghai, 1957; ICCI Honorary Doctor of Medicine. Appointments: Advisor, First Shanghai Hospital, PLA Air Force, 1987; Medical Director, International Old Folk Association of UN, 1987; Advisor, Daqing Forth Hospital. Publications: Equilibrium Detector and Equilibrator for Channels and Network; The Theory On the Equilibration Of Bioelectricity and its Medical Effects. Honours: Prize, International Exhibition of Inventions. Memberships: Association de Accupuncture China en Argentina; Chinese Society of Somatic Science. Address: No 22 Xijiaminxiang St, 100031 Beijing, China.

**ZHONG Kehuang,** b. 1 April 1936, Taoyuan, Hunan, China. Researcher. m. Li Zhongyi, 1 son, 1 daughter. Education: Graduate, Chemical Engineering Department, Changsha Polytechnic College, 1953. Appointments: Technician, Chief Technician, Engineer and Senior Engineer; Professor, Director, research lab, Xiangfan Institute of Adhesive Bonding Technology. Publications: More than 60 articles and books. Honours: China National Award for Progress in Science and Technology, 1989; China Chemical Industry Ministry Award for Progress in Science and Technology, 1988. Memberships: China Invention and Innovation Committee; Invention Association of Hubei Province; Editorial Board Member, Adhesive, magazine. Address: No 8 Chunyuan Road, Xiangfan City, Hubei 441003, China.

**ZHONG Yixin,** b. 14 February 1940, Jiangxi Province, China. Teacher; Researcher. m. Zhang Maolin, 1 son, 1 daughter. Education: BSc Communication Engineering, 1962; MSc Information Theory, 1965. Appointments: Lecturer of Radio Engineering, 1965; Associate Professor, 1983; Full Professor, 1989; Dean of Department of Information Engineering, 1987; Vice President, University of Posts and Telecommunications, Beijing, 1992. Publications: 16 books including: Intelligence Theory and Technology - Artificial Intelligence and Neural Networks, 1992; General Introduction to Information Technology, 1994; Principles of Information Science, 1996. Honours: Distinguished Mid-aged Scientist, awarded by Ministry of Human Resources, State Council, China, 1989; Outstanding Professor, awarded by State Commission of Education, State Council, China, 1989; Distinguished Scholar returned from abroad, 1991; First Expert of China Telecommunications High Technology Group, 1992; Outstanding Leadership of Neural Networks, awarded by International Society of Neural Networks, 1994. Memberships: Vice President, China Association of Artificial Intelligence; Vice Chairman, China Council of Neural Networks; Vice President, China Society of Information Economics; Director, Communication Theory Committee, China Institute of Communication; Vice Chairman, Chinese Committee for World Federation of Engineering Organisations; Associate Editor, IEEE Transactions on Neural Networks; Fellow, IEE, UK; Senior member, IEEE; New York Academy of Sciences. Address: Department of Information Engineering, University of Posts and Telecommunication, Beijing 1000876, China.

**ZHONG Zilin,** b. 1 January 1933, Hangzhou, Zhejiang, China. Musicologist. m. He Qiansan, 1 son. Education: Department of Musicology, Central Conservatory of Music, Beijing, 1956-62. Appointments: Visiting Professor, New England Conservatory, Boston, Michigan University, 1985; Professor, Central Conservatory of Music, 1992; Chairman,

Department of Musicology, 1990-93. Publications: An Introduction to Contemporary Western Music, 1991; The History and Style of Rock'n'Roll, 1998. Memberships: Chinese Musicians Association; Director, American Music Research Society, China. Address: Central Music Institute, Baojia Street, Beijing 100031, China.

**ZHOU Bosheng,** b. 23 February 1935, Jiangsu, China. Professor. m. Zirang Zhang, 1 son, 1 daughter. Education: Diploma in Automatic Control, 1958, Beijing University of Aeronautics and Astronautics; Senior Visiting Scholar, University of Maryland, 1981-84. Appointments: Director of Engineering, International Software Systems Inc, 1991-; Director, 1986-94, Honorary Director, 1995-, Software Engineering Institute, Beijing University of Aeronautics and Astronautics; PhD Students Supervisor, Education Committee of China, 1990-. Publications: Software Engineering Standard, 1988; Process Engineering and Process Engineering Environments, 1999; Over 30 papers in professional magazines. Memberships: IEEE Computer Society; Association of Computing; Computer Society of China; Automatic Control Association of China; Aeronautics and Astronautics Association of China. Address: 13509 Albania Way, Austin, TX 78729, USA.

**ZHOU Juan,** b. 18 July 1963, Xi'an, Shaanxin, China. Research Associate. m. Lei Jiang, 1 son, 1 daughter. Education: MD, 1986, Dept Medicine, Xi'an Medical University, China; MSc Biology, 1993, PhD Microbiology & Immunology, 2000, Dalhousie University, Halifax, Canada. Appointments: Ophthalmologist, Shaanxi Provincial Hospital, China, 1986-88; Teaching Assistant, Dept Biology, 1991-92, Research Technician, Dept Anatomy & Neurobiology, 1993-94, Research Associate & Microsurgeon, Dept Surgery, 1994-, Dalhousie University; Research Assistant, Institute for Marine Biosciences, National Research Council of Canada, 1991-93. Publications: Co-author 8 refereed journal papers, 13 refereed conference publications. Honours: 5 scholarships and travel awards. Memberships: Canadian Society for Immunology; Microscopical Society of Canada; Halifax Chapter of Neuroscience Society. Address: 44 Plateau Crescent, Halifax NS, Canada B3M 2V8.

**ZHOU Liaxiang,** b. 12 September 1929, Gaoqing County, Shandong, China. Professor. m. Dai Lei, 1 son, 2 daughters. Education: Graduate, Shandong University, 1953. Appointments: Lecturer, 1961, Associate Professor, 1978, Professor, 1983, Tutor of PhD Students, 1986, Director of Aesthetics Institute, 1987, Shandong University. Publications: 13 monographs, 200 papers. Honour: Special Subsidy for Elite Experts of China. Memberships: Executive Committee, International Association for Aesthetics; President, Shandong Aesthetics Society. Address: Institute of Aesthetics, Shandong University, Jinan 250100, China.

**ZHOU Nan-Zhao,** b. 20 October 1942, Jiangsu, China. Professor. m. Liu You-Yi, 2 sons. Education: BA, English Literature, Beijing Normal University, 1960-64; MA, Education, 1983-85, PhD, Education, 1985-89, State University of New York at Buffalo, USA. Appointments: Vice President, Professor, China National Institute of Education Research, 1991-. Publications: Over 100 articles in professional journals, including: Interactions of Education and Culture, 1996. Honours: 2nd Place award, Scholarship Essay Competition, International Underwriters, Washington, DC, 1985. Memberships: UNESCO International Commission on Education for the Twenty First Century; Comparative Education Society of Asia; Chinese Association of Education; Asia-Pacific Network of International Education & Values Education.

Address: Bei-San-Huan-Zhong-Lu, BeiTaiping Zhuang,Beijing 100088, China.

**ZHOU Shuxia**, b. 23 June 1923, Zhejiang, China. Professor; Chief Physician of maxillofacial surgery. m. Gao Yuan, 2 daughters. Education: DDS, Dental College of National Centre University, Nanjing. Appointments: Resident, Assistant, 1947; Physician-in-Charge, Lecturer, 1953; Vice Chief Physician, Associate Professor, 1963; Chief Physician, Professor, 1981; Professor, Chief Physician of Oral and Maxillofacial Surgery, 4th Military Medical University, Xi'an, Shaanxi; Director of PhD. Publications: Therapeutics of Trauma of Oral and Maxillofacial Region, Chief Editor, 1988; Operative for Oral and Maxillofacial Surgery, Chief Editor, 1994; Oral and Maxillofacial Surgery, Chief Editor, 1991, 1987. Honours: 2nd Prize, Medical Science Achievement in the Army, 1986, 1990, 1991, 1992, 1995, 1997; 3rd Prize, National Medical Science Achievement, 1996. Memberships: Chinese Medical Association; Standing Committee, Society of Traumatology; Society of Oncological Surgery of Head and Neck; cp, National Science and Technology Awards Committee, Branch of Military Medicine, PLA; International Association of Dental Research; Consultant of Chinese Stomatological Association. Address: Department of Oral and Maxillofacial Surgery, Stomatological College, 4th Military Medical University, 1 Kangfu Rd, Xi'an, Shaanxi, 710032, China.

**ZHOU Wei**, b. 7 February 1934, Anhui, China. Senior Researcher. m. Shunhua Li, 1 son, 1 daughter. Education: Undergraduate, Moscow University, 1953; Phd, Academy of Sciences, Russia, 1958-61. Appointments: Associate Professor, Chinese Academyof Agricultural Sciences, 1961-79; Visiting Scholar, Novi Sad University, Yugoslavia, 1980-83, Glessen University, Germany, 1983-84; Professor, Chinese Academy of Agricultural Sciences, 1985-95; Senior Economic Affairs Officer, United Nations World Food Council, 1995-97; Visiting Professor, Iowa University, 1997-; Professor, Chinese Academy of Agricultural Sciences, 1997-. Publications: Several articles in professional journals. Honours: 1st State Premium of Science Progress, 1984; 2nd Premium of Science Progress, Ministry of Agriculture, 1985. Membership: All Chinas Association of Agricultural Economists. Address: Institute of Agricultural Economics, Chinese Academy of Agricultural Sciences, 30 Baishiqiao Road, Xijiao 100081, Beijing, China.

**ZHOU Yaoqi**, b. 24 October 1963, Yueyang, Hunan, China. Geoscientist. m. Xia Changlan, 1 son. Education: BA, China University of Geosciences, 1983; MA, 1989; PhD, 1993. Appointments: Assistant Engineer, Geological Survey of Heilongjiang, 198-85; Visited Researcher, Institute of High Energy Physics, 1985-87; Postdoctoral Researcher, China University of Geosciences, 1993-95; Professor, Director of Institute of Petroleum Resources and Environmental Geology Research Institute, University of Petroleum, 1995. Publications: about 63 scientific publications. Honours: International Meteoritics Congress Praise Award; First Class Award of Natural Science in Academia Sinica; Excellent Award of Fellowship; Golden Hammer; Many other awards. Memberships: International Meteoritics Academy; Geological Society of China; Science Society of China; Nature Dialectics Academy of China. Address: Institute of Petroleum Resources and Environment Geology, University of Petroleum, Dongying 257062 Shandong, China.

**ZHOU Zhi-Gang**, b. 22 August 1931, Shanghai, China. Professor. m. Cui Wen-Jun, 1 son, 1 daughter. Education: BE, Tongji University, Shanghai, 1953; ME, Tsinghua University, Beijing, 1956. Appointments: Professor, Department of Materials Science and Engineering, University of Tsinghua;

Expert/Consultant, United Nations Industrial Development Organization, 1988-91; Director, Department of Engineering and Materials, National Natural Science Foundation of China, 1991-95; President, Dielectrics Physics Committee, Chinese Physics Society, Vice President, SensorTech, CIE, 1989-99. Publications: 3 books: Ferrite, Elemental Theory of Piezoelectric Physics; Physics of Ferroelectrics; More than 150 papers; 4 patents, US, Europe and China. Honours: Awards, Chinese Institute of Electronics and Chinese Physical Society, 1981, 1983, 1985, 1987, 1989, 1992; Second Prize, CMEIST, 1985. Memberships: Fellow, Institute of Electrical and Electronics Engineers; Senior Member, Institution of Electrical Engineers; Fellow, Chinese Institute of Electronics; Senior Member, CSS; New York Academy of Sciences. Address: Department of Materials Science and Engineering, Tsinghua University, Hai-Dian District, Beijing 100084, China.

**ZHOU Zonglu**, b. 5 May 1935, Nanxi, Sichuan, China. Telecommunications Interference. m. X G Huang, 1 daughter. Education: Bachelor Degree, Chengging University, 1955. Appointments: Project Chief Engineer of TL Design, 1958-; Chief Editor, Code for Design of Telecommunications Lines Against Danger Effects from Electric Power Lines. Publications: Code for Design of Telecommunications Lines Against Danger Effects from Electric Power Lines; Design Handbook for Protection of Telecommunication Lines Against Overhead Telecommunication Lines. Honours: 2nd Grade Award, Science and Technology Progress; First Grade Award, Science and Technology Progress Award. Memberships: Electric Magnetic Interference Committee; China Project Construction Standardization Association. Address: The Southwest Electric Power Designing Institute, Chengdu 610061, China.

**ZHU Jinrong**, b. 10 Dec 1963, Taicang, Jiangsu, China. m. Guping Lu, 1 son. Education: PhD, Southeast University, 1990. Appointment: Associate Professor. Publications: Journal of Chinese Electrical Engineering, 1991; Power Engineering, Chinese, 1990. Honour: Named Young Electrical Profession Lead Candidate for Next Century, Chinese Ministry of Electric Power Industry, 1996. Memberships: Chinese Society of Electric Engineering; Chinese Society of Energy. Address: Nanjing Institute of Technology, 74 West Beijing Road, Jiangsu Nanjing 210013, China.

**ZHU Jizhong**, b. 17 January 1965, Sichuan, China. Educator; Professor. m. Yuan Yao, 1 son. Education: BS, Electrical Engineering, 1985, MS, Electrical Engineering, 1987, PhD, Electrical Engineering, 1990, Chongqing University. Appointments: Research Assistant, 1987-90, Lecturer, 1990-92, Associate Professor, 1992-96, Full Professor, 1996-, Electrical Engineering Department, Chongqing University; Royal Society Fellow, Visiting Fellow, Brunel University, England, 1995-96; Postdoctoral Fellow, National University of Singapore, 1996-97; Visiting Scholar, Senior Research Fellow, Center for Energy Systems and Control, Electrical Engineering Department, Howard University, USA, 1997-. Publications: Power system section in Comprehensive Dictionary of Electrical Engineering, 1999; 70 publications in national journals, refereed international journals and proceedings of international conferences, in field of power systems. Honours: Excellent Youth Teacher Award, 1992, Excellent Doctor Award, 1992, Chongqing University; Science and Technology New Idea Prize, 1992, Outstanding Youth Scientist Award, 1993, Sichuan Province Science and Technology Association; Science and Technology Progress Prize, Sichuan Provincial Government, 1992, 1993, 1994; Science and Technology Progress Prize, State Education Commission, 1992, 1994; Excellent Youth Teacher Award, Chongqing City Government, 1992; Outstanding Youth Scientist Working in China, Chinese

Science and Technology Association and Royal Society, UK, 1994; 12-month Royal Fellowship, Royal Society, 1994; Huo Ying-Dong Excellent Youth Teacher Prize, State Education Commission and Huo Ying-Dong Education Foundation, 1996; Invited Assessor, Australia Research Council, 1997. Membership: Senior Member, Institute of Electrical and Electronic Engineers. Address: 501 Domer Avenue, Apt 102, Takoma Park, MD 20912-7139, USA.

**ZHU Min,** b. 4 April 1956, Beijing, China. Pharmaceutical Scientist. m. Li Rong, 1 daughter. Education: BSc, 1982, Department of Chemistry, Peking University, Beijing; M Phil, 1988, Department of Pharmacognosy, Peking Union Medical College, Beijing; PhD, 1994, School of Pharmacy, University of London, England. Appointments: Research Assistant, Institute of Materia Medica, Chinese Academy of Medical Sciences, 1982-85; Research Associate, Institute of Medicinal Plant Development, Beijing, 1988-91; Assistant Professor, Department of Pharmacy, Chinese University of Hong Kong, 1994-. Publications: Over 50 scientific research papers in international journals. Honour: Pfizer Studentship for PhD study in London, 1991-94. Memberships: American Society of Pharmaceutical Scientists; American Society of Pharmacognosy; European Society of Phytochemistry; Hong Kong Pharmacology Society; Hong Kong Society for Traditional Medicine and Natural Product Research; China Pharmaceutical Society. Address: Department of Pharmacy, Faculty of Medicine, Chinese University of Hong Kong, Shatin, Hong Kong.

**ZHU Ning,** b. 18 August 1935, Hangzhou, China. Professor. m. Xiaofang Zhang, 2 daughters. Education: BA, Northeast Forestry University, 1957. Appointments: Professor, Northeast Forestry University. Publications include: Advance and Present Situation in Plant Population Ecology; Introduction to Plant Population Ecology. Membership: Chinese Society of Ecology. Address: Northeast Forestry University, Harbin 150040, China.

**ZHU Qi Chang,** b. 17 November 1922, Zhejiang, China. Petroleum Engineer. m. Li Desheng, 1 son, 3 daughters. Education: BA, 1946, National Central University of China; BS, 1966, Beijing Petroleum Institute. Appointments: Senior Engineer, China Research Institute of Petroleum E&D; Professorships of Nanjing University, Zhejiang University and Southwest Petroleum Institute. Honour: National Science and Technology Progress Award, 3rd Class, 1991. Membership: Society of Petroleum Engineers. Address: PO Box 910 of Beijing, Beijing 100083, China.

**ZHU Qingsheng,** b. 27 December 1956, Chongqing, China. Professor. m. Yong Wang, 1 son. Education: BSc Computer Engineering, 1982, MSc Computer Science, 1986, Chongqing University, China. Appointments: Lecturer, 1986-90, Associate Professor, 1990-95, Professor, 1996-, Chairman of Department, 1994-97, Dean of College, 1998-, College of Computer, Chongqing University; Visiting Scholar, Department of Computer, Birbeck College, University of London, UK, 1993-94; Visiting Research Scholar, Computer Studies Department, Hong Kong Baptist University, 1998. Publications: Over 30 publications including 3 books. Honours: 7 Awards of Achievement in Science and Technology, Chongqing Government, 1988-98; Outstanding Young Teacher Award, National Education Committee, China, 1995. Memberships: General Secretary, Computer Education Committee of Chinese Universities, and Chongqing Computer Federation; Senior member, Chinese Electronic Federation; Director, Computer Committee of Chongqing Electronic Federation; Education Committee of Chinese Computer Federation; Editorial Board,

Journal of Chongqing University. Address: College of Computers, Chongqing University, Chongqing 440044, China.

**ZHU Shanli,** b. 26 September 1953, Jiangsu, China. Professor of Economics. m. Suping Fang, 1 daughter. Education: BA, Economics, 1982; MA, Economics, 1984; PhD, Economics, 1992. Appointments: Assistant Professor, 1984-86, Assistant Dean, Economics Management Department, 1985-87, Lecturer, 1986-91, Associate Professor, 1992-94, Dean, Economics Management Department, 1992-97, Professor, 1994-, Deputy Director, Center for Management Science, 1995-, Dean, Applied Economics Department, 1997-, Peking University. Publications include: The Road towards Prosperity of Economy - Efficient Allocation of Resources and Property Right, 1994. Honours: 1st Class Prize, Youth Teachers of Colleges and Universities, Fok Ying Tong Education Foundation, 1994. Memberships: Director, Special Committee of Overseas Market Economy, Research Institute of Market Economy, China. Address: Guanghua School of Management, Peking University, Beijing 100871, China.

**ZHU Xian,** b. 21 October 1957, Xiamen, Fujian, China. Medical Researcher. m. Weng Shong Lian, 1 daughter. Education: MS, Fujian Medical University, 1982. Appointments: Physician, Su Ming People Hospital, Xiamen City, China, 1982-87; Director, Medical Research Department, Xiamen Institute of Medicine and Pharmacy, 1987-. Honours: First Prize, Scientific Research Award, Fujian Government, Sanitary Department, 1993; Third Prize, Scientific Research Award, Fujian Government, 1994. Membership: China Medical Association. Address: 2 Tongan Road, Xiamen City, Fujian, China.

**ZHU Yi,** b. 7 July 1937, Jiangsu, China. Professor. m. Gu Qi Xiu, 2 daughters. Education: Graduate, Beijing Tsinghua University, 1959. Appointments: Director, Computer Center, 1983-93; Director; Network and Information Center, 1994-. Honours: Shanghai Government Research Award, 1988; Central Government Award, 1994. Memberships: Director, CDC and UNISYS Computer User Group, China. Address: Network and Information Center, Shanghai Jiao-Tong University, 1954 Hua Shan Road, Shanghai 200030, China.

**ZHU Yuanwu,** b. 5 May 1943, Jilin Province. Professor. m. Junying Zhou, 1 son, 1 daughter. Education: Undergraduate Diploma, 1966. Appointments: Professor, International Business School, Nanjing University, Nanjing, China. Publication: Financial Accounting - Theories & Practices in Reform, 1993. Honour: Excellent Achievement Award, Jiangsu People's Government, 1997. Memberships: Standing Director, Chinese Accounting Association; Chinese Accounting Professor Association. Address: International Commerce Department, Nanjing University, Nanjing 210093, China.

**ZHU Zhaoda,** b. 9 March 1939, Qingdao, China. Electronic Engineering Educator. m. Fengin Shu, 1 son. Education: Diploma, 1960, Nanjing Aeronautical Institute, China. Appointments: From Assistant to Professor of Electronic Engineering, Nanjing Aeronautical Institute, 1960-86; Professor of Electronic Engineering, Nanjing University of Aeronautics and Astronautics, 1986-; Director of Electronic Engineering Research Institute, Nanjing University of Aeronautics and Astronautics, 1993-. Publication: Contributor, Radar Array Processing, 1993. Honours: First Award, The Ministry of Aeronautical and Astronautical Industry, China, 1992; National Outstanding Expert, China, 1994. Memberships: Fellow, Chinese Institute of Electronics; Senior member, IEEE. Address: Nanjing University of Aeronautics and Astronautics,

Department of Electronic Engineering, 29 Yudao Street, 210016 Nanjing, China.

**ZHUO Baoxi,** b. 16 February 1934, Fuzhou, Fujian Province, China. Specialist in Remote Sensing in Geology. m. Zhenmin Lu, 2 sons. Education: Graduated from Tongji University, 1954. Appointments: Director, Science and Technology Information Center of Railway Ministry for Aerial Survey and Remote Sensing, 1995-; Professor Senior Engineer, 1995-; Guest Professor, Northern Jiaotong University and Southwestern Jiaotong University, 1995-; Vice-Chief Engineer, Professional Design Institute of Ministry of Railways, 1996-. Publications: Remote Sensing Principle and Engineering Geology Interpretation (Second Prize, Highly Rated Science and Technology Books of China, 1982; Technical Code for Remote Sensing of Railway Engineering Geology, 1982; Typical Photos of Remote Sensing Image for Engineering Geology, 1999. Honours: Scientific and Technical Star, 1992; National Government Subsidy, 1992; National Master in Engineering Survey, 1994. Memberships: Adviser, National Remote Sensing Association of Locality; Vice-Chief Editor, The Chinese Journal of Geological Hazard and Control; Photogrammetry and Remote Sensing Committee, China Survey and Mapping Institution; Vice Director, Remote Sensing Committee, China Geology Calamity Resaerch Institution; Compiler Member, Remote Sensing Information (publication). Address: 227 Chaowai Street, Beijing 100020, China.

**ZHVAKOLIUK Yury,** b. 18 August 1970, Armiansk, Ukraine. Business. m. Elena V Lobachyova, 1 son. Education: Odessa Financial College, Odessa, Ukraine, 1997; The Consultants Institute, American Consultants League, 1998. Appointments: Odd jobs, Form-Express, Simferopol, 1991-92; Financial Director, Printing House, Simferopol, 1992-93; President, Printing House, 1993-99. Publications: Businessman's Help, 1993; About Georde Soros' Reflection Theory, 1997; 'TVT' School Book I Five Rarities, 1999. Honour: Honorary Academician Award, Energy Academy. Membership: Representative of Netherlands Management and Cooperation Programme (NMCP). Address: Form Express, 3 Bakhchisarayskaya Str, Crimea 333015, Ukraine.

**ZIARATI Mohammad Reza,** b. 30 January 1952, Sary, Iran. Academic Director; Dean; Professor. 1 son. Education: BSc Honours; MSc; PhD, Bath University; Certificate of Education. Appointments: Researcher, Lecturer, Head of Department, Associate Dean, Dean and Academic Director; Educational Advisor to European Union, British Government, Governments of Oman and Gibraltar, EDEXCEL, and various universities. Publications: Over 100 technical and educational papers, books and articles. Honours: National Diploma, Best Lecture and Paper, Institute of Transport Engineers; European Enterprise Award. Memberships: Chartered Engineer; Fellow, Institution of Mechanical Engineers; Fellow, Institution of Electrical Engineers; Accreditation Committee, Institution of Electrical Engineers. Address: 4 Highgrove, Westwood Heath, Coventry CV4 8JJ, England.

**ZIFFRIN Marilyn Jane,** b. 7 August 1926, Moline, Illinois, USA. Classical Composer. Education: BM, 1948, University of Wisconsin; Private study in Conducting, Dr Sigfrid Prager, 1947-48; MA, 1949, Columbia University, New York; Graduate Work in Musicology, University of Chicago, 1950s; Private Composition Study with: Karl Ahrendt, 1950, Alexander Tcherepnin, 1952-56. Appointments: Head, Music Department, Northwest Miss Agriculture High School and Junior College, Senatobia, 1949-50; Assistant Head, Transcription Department, WGN Radio and TV Station, Chicago, 1950-52; Office Manager, W M Simeral & Co, Commodity Brokers, Chicago,

1952-56; Teacher, Second Grade, Chicago Public Schools, 1956-61; Assistant Professor of Music, Northeastern Illinois University, Chicago, 1961-67; Associate Professor of Music, New England College, Henniker, 1967-82; Composition Teacher, St Paul's School, Concord, 1972-84. Publications: Trio for Clarinet, Bassoon and Piano; Four Pieces for Tuba; Rhapsody for Guitar; Book, Carl Ruggles: Composer, Painter, Storyteller, 1994; Co-contributor, Grove's Dictionary of Music and Musicians, New Grove Dictionary of American Music; 5 articles about Carl Ruggles; 7 recordings; 13 solo compositions; 26 compositions of chamber music; 9 choral; 9 for orchestra; 2 for band. Honours: 6 grants; Honorable Mention, MTNA-Shepherd Competition, 1998; Prizes awarded for compositions in six competitions; Residence, Virginia Centre for the Creative Arts, 1987; Fellow, MacDowell Colony, 1961, 1963, 1971, 1977, 1980, 1989; New Hampshire MTA Composer of the Year, 1997. Memberships: ASCAP; Sigma Alpha Iota, life member; Society of Composers Inc; International League of Women Composers; American Women Composers Inc; Composers Forum Inc; American Music Centre; National Association of Composers; and others. Address: PO Box 179, Bradford, NH 03221, USA.

**ZIKA Sheryl C,** b. 8 July 1952, Los Angeles, USA. Psychologist, Researcher. m. Bill, 2 sons, 2 daughters. Education: BA, California State University, 1974; MA, Massey University, New Zealand, 1983; PhD, Massey University, New Zealand, 1996. Appointments: Research Associate, Massey University, New Zealand, 1985-88; Psychologist, Private Practice, New Zealand, 1996-97; Director, Senior Peer Counseling Program, Alliance on Aging, USA, 1998-. Publications: 7 Journal Publications; 1 Chapter in book, from 1987-1992. Honours: Vice Chancelors PhD Study Award, 1989-1992. Memberships: New Zealand Registered Psychologist, 1987-; New Zealand Health Psychology Society. Address: 280 Dickman Avenue, Monterey, CA 93940, USA.

**ZIMERING Mark Bernard,** b. 7 February 1955, St Paul, Minnesota, USA. Physician; Scientist. m. Laurie Friedlander, 1 son, 1 daughter. Education: Valedictorian, Blake School, 1973; AB, Harvard College, Cambridge, Massachusetts, USA, 1977; PhD, 1983, MD, 1984, Albert Einstein College of Medicine, Bronx, New York. Appointments: Diplomate, American Board Internal Medicine; Internal Medicine Intern, Resident, Hennepin County Medical Center, Minn, Minnesota, 1984-86; Medical Staff Fellow, NIH Bethesda, Maryland, 1986-90; Staff Physician, Veterans Affairs Medical Center, Lyons, New Jersey, USA, 1990-; Associate Professor of Medicine, UMDNJ, Robert Wood Johnson Medical School, 1997-. Publications: Contributed articles to professional journals; Reviewer, journals, 1994, 1998. Honours: Awarded grants. Memberships: American Association for the Advancement of Science; The Endocrine Society; The American Diabetes Association. Address: Vets Affairs Medical Center, Medical Service, Lyons, NJ 07939, USA.

**ZOLOTUKHIN Anatoly Boris,** b. 11 March 1946, Moscow, Russia. Professor; Petroleum Engineer. m. Gladkova Alla, 1 son. Education: MS, Petroleum Engineering, 1969; PhD, Mechanics of Fluids and Gases, 1973; MS, Applied Mathematics, 1976; DSc, Petroleum Engineering, 1991. Appointments: Researcher, Senior Researcher, Gubkin Institute of Oil and Gas, Moscow, 1973-82; Docent, Gubkin Institute, 1982-87; Department Head, Oil and Gas Research Institute, Moscow, 1988-91; Professor, Gubkin Institute and Stavanger College, 1991-; Project Manager, Statol Stavanger, 1999-. Publications: 4 books, over 100 papers in professional journals. Memberships: Society of Petroleum Engineers; European Association of Petroleum Geoscientists; Norwegian

Petroleum Society. Address: Stavanger College, Ullandhaug, PO Box 2557, N-4004 Stavanger Rogaland, Norway.

**ZORBOSKI Mitko,** b. 21 July 1924, Macedonia. Professor. m. Ivanka Polh-Zorboska, 1 son, 1 daughter. Education: Forestry Engineer, 1950, Doctor of Forestry, 1959, Faculty of Agriculture and Forestry, Skopje. Appointments: Director, Forest Economic Property, 1950-52; Assistant Professor 1952-59, Docent, Department of Forestry, 1959-66, Visiting Professor, 1966-71, Professor, 1971-88, Forestry Department, Faculty of Agriculture and Forestry, Skopje; Lecturer, Organization and Economics of Wood Processing Industry. Publications: Over 140 scientific and professional works, studies, analyses, reviews, elaborate studies and projects. Honours: Medal of Merit, City of Skopje, 1967; Commemorative Certificate of Merit, 1968; Order of Labour with Golden Wreath, Presidency of SFRYu, 1986; Medal of Merit, Faculty of Forestry, Skopje, 1987; Plauqe, Faculty of Forestry, Skopje, 1997. Memberships: Macedonian Association of Forestry and Wood Processing Industry Engineers and Technicians; Macedonian University Professors Society. Address: kej 13 Noemvri, kula Iv st 17, 91000 Skopje, Macedonia.

**ZOU Zhen,** b. 12 September 1954, Jiangxi, China. Education. m. Ling Wang, 1 s. Education: BA, Jiangxi Normal University, 1982; MA, Peking University, 1989; PhD, 1999. Appointments: Lecturer, Jiangxi Normal University, 1982-86; Teaching Assistant, Peking University, 1986-89; Assistant Professor, 1989-95; Director of Graudate English Teaching Division, 1989-91; Visiting Scholar, SUNY New Paltz, 1991-92; Teaching Assistant, Purdue University, 1995-97; Associate Professor, 1997-;Instructor, Purdue University, 1998-. Publications: An English Listening and Speaking Course for Graduate Students, 1996; Contributor of Ten Essays and Articles in Literary Critisism to Professional Journals. Honors: Winner, Translation Contest; Guanghua Award. Memberships: Peking University Literature and Translation Research Society; Modern Language Assocaition of America. Address: Department of Foreign Languages, Stanley Coulter Hall, Purdue University, IN 47907, USA.

**ZUCHMAN Philip Abrim,** b. 3 March 1942, New York City, USA. Artist. m. Deborah, 2 sons. Education: BA, Philosophy, Queens College, City University; MA, Fine Art, Goddard College. Appointments: Teacher, The Art Institute of Philadelphia, 1984-; Teacher, Brandeis Collegiate Institute, 1997; Honours: Villanova University Award for Oil Painting; US State Department, Art in Embassies Program; Salmagundi Club Young Artists Scholarship; Peter Pauper Press Award. Memberships: American Artist Gallery; Artists Equity; The College Art Association of America; Americans for the Arts. Address: 4724 Springfield Avenue, Philadelphia, PA 19143-3515, USA.

**ZULBERTI C,** b. 22 January 1944, Argentina. Economist. m. Ester, 1 son 1 daughter. Education: Engeniero Agronomo University de Mar del Plata, 1960; MS, Agricultural Economics, Cornell University, 1974; PhD, Agricultral Economics, Cornell University, 1974. Appointments: Chief, Corporate Planning and Accountability Service. Publications: Several. Membership: Several. Address: 304 E 45th Street, New York, NY 10017, USA.

**ZUREK Witold Stanislaw,** b. 18 March 1918, Poland. Scientific Worker. Education: MSc, 1948; Dr.Techn.Sc, Lodz Polytechnic, 1956. Appointments: Assistant, Assistant Professor, 1945-64; Professor, 1964-. Publications: 7 books, over 200 papers. Honour: Doctor Degree, Hon Causa, Lodz Polytechnic, 1995. Memberships: Real Academia de Ciencias

y Artes de Barcelona, 1990. Address: Wierzbowa 38-55, 90 245 Lodz, Poland.

**ZURINI Cristian,** b. 22 January 1954, Bucharest. Engineer. m. Carmen Elisabeth, 1 son, 1 daughter. Education: Diploma, Chemical Engineering, Polytechnical Academy, Bucharest, 1977. Appointments: Danubiana, Curing Division Manager, 1980-85; Quality Department Manager, 1985-88; Technical, Production Manager, 1988-91; President, General Manager, 1991-97; Tofan Grup, Senior Vice President, 1996-; Chemical Engineering and Management Consulting, Chairman, 1997-; SCHCC, Chairman, 1999-. Memberships: Romanian Society for Chemical Engineering; Society of Automotive Engineers of Romania; Employers Federation Chemistry; Trade Leaders Club; Golden World Club. Address: 28 Fluierului Street, Sector 2, Bucharest, Romania.

**ZUROWSKI Andrzej,** b. 24 September 1944, Poland. Theatre Critic; Writer; Essayist. m. Magda Oller, 1 son, 3 daughters. Education: MA, Polish Philology University, Gdansk, 1967; PhD, Arts in Theatre Studies, Gdansk University, 1973. Appointments: Editorial Staff, 1967-73, Editor in Chief, Theatre Section, 1973-80, Artistic Manager, 1980-83, Commentator, 1983-87, 1990-, Editor in Chief, Artistic Programs, 1987-90, Polish Television, Gdansk. Publications: 16 books and several articles in professional journals. Membership: Vice President, International Association of Theatre Critics. Address: Glogowa 21, 81-589 Gdynia, Poland.

**ZVIRGZDAS Stanislovas,** b. 13 September 1941. Photographer. Education: History, University of Vilnius, 1960-61; Photography, Institute of Peoples Art, Moscow, 1972. Appointments: Photographic Artist, Photoartists Union, 1972-92; Chairman, Photoartists Union, 1992-96; Secretary of the Board, Photoartists Union, 1996-. Publications: Photographs. Honours: 2 Grande Prix; 6 FIAP Gold Medals; 6 Silver FIAP Medals; 3 FIAP Diplomas; 8 Gold Medals; 4 Silver Medals; 3 Bronze Medals; More than 170 other awards. Memberships: Photoartists Union. Address: Gerove's St 9-2, 2041 Vilnius, Lithuania.

# Honours List

**NAME:**      Dr Abdel-Kader Abbadi

**ADDRESS:**      431 East 20, Apt 4-G
New York
NY 10010
USA

**OCCUPATION:**      UN Official

**YEAR OF ENTRY:**      1986

**CITATION:**      For your Outstanding Contribution to
the United Nations

---

**NAME:**      His Excellency Salim R Absy, FIBA

**ADDRESS:**      PO Box 1040
Manama
Bahrain

**OCCUPATION:**      Diplomat

**YEAR OF ENTRY:**      1986

**CITATION:**      For your Outstanding Contribution to
International Relations

---

**NAME:**      Dr Farid A Akasheh, LFIBA

**ADDRESS:**      PO Box 2173
Amman
Jordan

**OCCUPATION:**      Doctor (Consultant Obstetrician and
Gynaecologist)

**YEAR OF ENTRY:**      1986

**CITATION:**      For your Outstanding Contribution to
Medicine

**NAME:** Dr Farouk M Akhdar

**ADDRESS:** The Economic Bureau
PO Box 86619
Riyadh 11632
Kingdom of Saudi Arabia

**OCCUPATION:** President of the Economic Bureau

**YEAR OF ENTRY:** 1989

**CITATION:** For your Outstanding Contribution to
Economics and to the development of
Saudi Arabia

---

**NAME:** Mr Abdullatif A R Al-Bahar

**ADDRESS:** PO Box 89
Safat
13001 Kuwait City
Kuwait

**OCCUPATION:** Director General, Office of H H The Crown
Prince & Prime Minister - Kuwait

**YEAR OF ENTRY:** 1989

**CITATION:** For you Outstanding Contribution to
his present position within the field of
Political & Economics Institutions

---

**NAME:** Mr Said Jawdat Al-Dajani

**ADDRESS:** PO Box 927260
Amman
Jordan

**OCCUPATION:** Attorney At-Law and Legal Consultant

**YEAR OF ENTRY:** 1986

**CITATION:** For you Outstanding Contribution to
The Law and your Country

| | |
|---|---|
| **NAME:** | Mr Ahmad Mohamad Ali |
| **ADDRESS:** | Islamic Development Bank<br>PO Box 5925<br>Jeddah 21432<br>Saudi Arabia |
| **OCCUPATION:** | President, Islamic Development Bank |
| **YEAR OF ENTRY:** | 1990 |
| **CITATION:** | For your Outstanding Contribution to the Banking Business |

| | |
|---|---|
| **NAME:** | Mr Jacob Oladele Amao |
| **ADDRESS:** | PO Box 51722<br>Ikoyi<br>Lagos<br>Nigeria |
| **OCCUPATION:** | Company President - Executive |
| **YEAR OF ENTRY:** | 1990 |
| **CITATION:** | For your Outstanding Contribution to the Banking Business |

| | |
|---|---|
| **NAME:** | Professor Basile Angelopoulos, MD, PhD, LFIBA, DDG |
| **ADDRESS:** | Ipsilantou Str 37<br>Athens 106-76<br>Greece |
| **OCCUPATION:** | Professor in Pathologic Physiology |
| **YEAR OF ENTRY:** | 1986 |
| **CITATION:** | For your Outstanding Contribution to Medicine |

**NAME:**          Ms Liliane Atlan

**ADDRESS:**       70 Rue du Javelot
                   Cedex 13
                   75645 Paris
                   France

**OCCUPATION:**    Author, Writer, Playwright

**YEAR OF ENTRY:** 1991

**CITATION:**      For your Outstanding Contribution to
                   Literature

---

**NAME:**          Mrs Kathlyn Ballard, FIBA

**ADDRESS:**       40 Mont Victor Road
                   Kew
                   Victoria 3101
                   Australia

**OCCUPATION:**    Artist

**YEAR OF ENTRY:** 1986

**CITATION:**      For your Outstanding Contribution to Art

---

**NAME:**          Ms Elisabeth Barker

**ADDRESS:**       433 Simi Place
                   Santa Rosa
                   CA 95409-3621
                   USA

**OCCUPATION:**    Business Owner/Entrepeneur

**YEAR OF ENTRY:** 1991

**CITATION:**      For your Outstanding Contribution to
                   Business

| **NAME:** | Mr Abdul Rahman Batal, LFIBA, LFWLA |
|---|---|
| **ADDRESS:** | Chairman, Hannibal Tourism & Transport Co<br>PO Box 4088<br>Damascus<br>Syria |
| **OCCUPATION:** | Company Chairman |
| **YEAR OF ENTRY:** | 1986 |
| **CITATION:** | For your Outstanding Contribution to<br>Tourism and Transport |

| **NAME:** | Ms Winogene L Bergman, FIBA |
|---|---|
| **ADDRESS:** | 709 E Juneau Avenue<br>Milwaukee<br>WI 53202<br>USA |
| **OCCUPATION:** | Retired School Library Coordinator |
| **YEAR OF ENTRY:** | 1986 |
| **CITATION:** | For your Outstanding Contribution to<br>Education |

| **NAME:** | Ms Henriette Hannah Bodenheimer |
|---|---|
| **ADDRESS:** | Sadja Gaon Street 8<br>Jerusalem<br>Israel |
| **OCCUPATION:** | Educator, Writer, Historian of Political<br>Zionismus |
| **YEAR OF ENTRY:** | 1988 |
| **CITATION:** | For your Outstanding Contribution to<br>Education and to the State of Israel |

| | |
|---|---|
| **NAME:** | Mr Adrian R Boller |
| **ADDRESS:** | Belvedere 5<br>5400 Baden<br>Switzerland |
| **OCCUPATION:** | Trading Executive |
| **YEAR OF ENTRY:** | 1986 |
| **CITATION:** | For your Outstanding Contribution to Commerce |

---

| | |
|---|---|
| **NAME:** | Ms Shauna D Boulton, LFIBA, DDG |
| **ADDRESS:** | 1516 Glen Arbor<br>Salt Lake City<br>UT 84105<br>USA |
| **OCCUPATION:** | Educator |
| **YEAR OF ENTRY:** | 1986 |
| **CITATION:** | For your Outstanding Contribution to Education |

---

| | |
|---|---|
| **NAME:** | Dr Alexander Noble Burns, FIBA |
| **ADDRESS:** | No 9 Short Street<br>Burleigh Heads<br>Queensland 4220<br>Australia |
| **OCCUPATION:** | Biologist |
| **YEAR OF ENTRY:** | 1986 |
| **CITATION:** | For your Outstanding Contribution to Science |

**NAME:**            Mr Georg Brutian

**ADDRESS:**         Pushkin Street 40, Apt 90
                     Yerevan 375010
                     Armenia
                     USSR

**OCCUPATION:**      Teacher

**YEAR OF ENTRY:**   1990

**CITATION:**        For your Outstanding Contribution to
                     Education & Teaching

---

**NAME:**            Mr Hubert A Buchanan, LFIBA

**ADDRESS:**         209 West 19th Street
                     Pueblo
                     CO 81003
                     USA

**OCCUPATION:**      Retired Life Insurance Agent

**YEAR OF ENTRY:**   1990

**CITATION:**        For your Outstanding Contribution to the
                     Life Insurance Industry

---

**NAME:**            Mr Richard E Butler

**ADDRESS:**         40 Barrington Avenue
                     Kew 3101
                     Victoria
                     Australia

**OCCUPATION:**      International Official

**YEAR OF ENTRY:**   1990

**CITATION:**        For your Outstanding Contribution to
                     International Cooperation and to World-
                     wide Telecommunication Development

**NAME:** Mr Manfredo L Castro, LFIBA

**ADDRESS:** 1613 Cypress
Dasmarinas Village
Makati
Metro Manila
Philippines

**OCCUPATION:** Businessman

**YEAR OF ENTRY:** 1986

**CITATION:** For your Outstanding Contribution to
Business and Finance

---

**NAME:** Professor Chen Jian Hong

**ADDRESS:** Gansu University of Tech
Lanzhou
Gansu
China

**OCCUPATION:** President, Professor

**YEAR OF ENTRY:** 1989

**CITATION:** For your Outstanding Contribution to the
Science and Education of China

---

**NAME:** Mr Thomas J Cleary

**ADDRESS:** 933 Kiowa
Burkburnett
TX 76354
USA

**OCCUPATION:** Clinical Social Worker, Teaching Assistant,
Graduate Student US History MSU

**YEAR OF ENTRY:** 1989

**CITATION:** For your Outstanding Contribution to
Social Work Service

**NAME:**              Ms Irene Coates, LFIBA

**ADDRESS:**           Kaldadoon, 140 Station Street
                       Blackheath
                       NSW 2785
                       Australia

**OCCUPATION:**        Artist, Writer

**YEAR OF ENTRY:**     1987

**CITATION:**          For your Outstanding Contribution to Art

---

**NAME:**              Mr Colin Cecil Coleman, OAM, FIBA,
                       MSAE, TTC

**ADDRESS:**           43 Woolston Drive
                       Frankston
                       Victoria 3199
                       Australia

**OCCUPATION:**        Technical Senior Teacher

**YEAR OF ENTRY:**     1986

**CITATION:**          For your Outstanding Contribution to
                       Education

---

**NAME:**              Dr George Edward Corder, LFIBA, FWLA,
                       DDG

**ADDRESS:**           PO Box 1723
                       Hollywood
                       CA 90078
                       USA

**OCCUPATION:**        Scientist of Human Behaviour

**YEAR OF ENTRY:**     1986

**CITATION:**          For your Outstanding Contribution to
                       Science and Education

**NAME:** Professor Dr Erika Cremer

**ADDRESS:** Reitmannstrasse 20
A-6020
Innsbruck
Austria

**OCCUPATION:** Research and Education

**YEAR OF ENTRY:** 1991

**CITATION:** For your Outstanding Contribution to
Reaction Kinetics (branching of chain
reactions) and pioneer work in Gas
Chromatography

---

**NAME:** The Hon Dame Dr Joy Beaudette Cripps,
DCMSS, MCC, LFIAP, LFWLA, LittD

**ADDRESS:** 3 Mill Street
Aspendale
Victoria 3195
Australia

**OCCUPATION:** Publisher, Poet, Photographer

**YEAR OF ENTRY:** 1988

**CITATION:** For your Outstanding Contribution to Literature

---

**NAME:** Mr Glen Laban Cross, LFIBA

**ADDRESS:** 2841 Cottingham Street
Oceanside
CA 92054
USA

**OCCUPATION:** International Development Planner

**YEAR OF ENTRY:** 1986

**CITATION:** For your Outstanding Contribution to
International Development

| | |
|---|---|
| **NAME:** | Basil V Damalas |
| **ADDRESS:** | Patission 171<br>Athens 112 52<br>Greece |
| **OCCUPATION:** | Publicist and Economist |
| **YEAR OF ENTRY:** | 1986 |
| **CITATION:** | For your Outstanding Contribution to Economics |

---

| | |
|---|---|
| **NAME:** | Mr J Edward Dealy, MS, PhD |
| **ADDRESS:** | 800 F Street, No P-3<br>Juneau<br>AK 99801<br>USA |
| **OCCUPATION:** | Forestry |
| **YEAR OF ENTRY:** | 1986 |
| **CITATION:** | For your Outstanding Contribution to Forestry |

---

| | |
|---|---|
| **NAME:** | Mr Ronald Joseph Godfrey De Mel, MP |
| **ADDRESS:** | Ministry of Finance and Planning<br>Old Secretariat<br>Colombo 1<br>Sri Lanka |
| **OCCUPATION:** | Minister of Finance and Planning |
| **YEAR OF ENTRY:** | 1986 |
| **CITATION:** | For your Outstanding Contribution for 9 years as Minister |

**NAME:**    Sir Bayard Dill, CBE, JP, DDG

**ADDRESS:**    Newbold Place
Devonshire
Bermuda 1, 41

**OCCUPATION:**    Barrister-at-Law

**YEAR OF ENTRY:**    1986

**CITATION:**    For your Outstanding Contribution to
over 60 years law work and 34 years
Bermuda Government Political Life

---

**NAME:**    O Leonard Doellner, FIBA

**ADDRESS:**    PO Box 43392
Tucson
AZ 85733
USA

**OCCUPATION:**    Independent Consultant

**YEAR OF ENTRY:**    1986

**CITATION:**    For your Outstanding Contribution to
Science and Engineering

---

**NAME:**    Dr Luis Dolcet-Buxeres, LPIBA

**ADDRESS:**    Muntaner 350
08021 Barcelona
Spain

**OCCUPATION:**    Surgeon

**YEAR OF ENTRY:**    1987

**CITATION:**    For your Outstanding Contribution to
Medicine

| | |
|---|---|
| **NAME:** | Mr Alfons F Donko, DIPL-ING, HE, DG, FIBA, ABIRA |
| **ADDRESS:** | c/o Oesterr Normungsintitut Postf 130 Heinstr 38 A-1021 Vienna Austria |
| **OCCUPATION:** | Deputy Managing Director |
| **YEAR OF ENTRY:** | 1988 |
| **CITATION:** | For your Outstanding Contribution to Business |

| | |
|---|---|
| **NAME:** | Mrs Estelle Cecilia D Dunlap, LPIBA |
| **ADDRESS:** | 719 Shepherd Street, NW Washington DC 20011 USA |
| **OCCUPATION:** | Educator and Mathematician |
| **YEAR OF ENTRY:** | 1986 |
| **CITATION:** | For your Outstanding Contribution to Education |

| | |
|---|---|
| **NAME:** | Mr Howard M Dupuy Jr, BA, LLP |
| **ADDRESS:** | 16116 NE Stanton Street Portland OR 97230 USA |
| **OCCUPATION:** | Lawyer |
| **YEAR OF ENTRY:** | 1986 |
| **CITATION:** | For your Outstanding Contribution to The Law |

**NAME:**           Mr Dewey Bert Durrett

**ADDRESS:**        377 Main Street
                    Salem
                    NH 03079
                    USA

**OCCUPATION:**     Real Estate Agent

**YEAR OF ENTRY:**  1990

**CITATION:**       For your Outstanding Contribution to
                    Real Estate and Housing

---

**NAME:**           Dr Judith Marilyn Ebner

**ADDRESS:**        3601 Balfour Court
                    Flint
                    MI 48507
                    USA

**OCCUPATION:**     Educational Administrator

**YEAR OF ENTRY:**  1986

**CITATION:**       For your Outstanding Contribution to
                    Education

---

**NAME:**           Mr Chris Economides

**ADDRESS:**        PO Box 1632
                    Nicosia
                    Cyprus

**OCCUPATION:**     Director

**YEAR OF ENTRY:**  1988

**CITATION:**       For your Outstanding Contribution to
                    Economics

**NAME:**                Mr Earl Otto Ellison

**ADDRESS:**          6324 Telegraph Road
Alexandria
VA 22310
USA

**OCCUPATION:**    Computer Systems Contracting Officer

**YEAR OF ENTRY:**  1992

**CITATION:**       For your Outstanding Contribution to
Management and Finance

---

**NAME:**                Mr Wilhelm Flöttmann, LPIBA, DDG, IOM

**ADDRESS:**          Schülterstraße 11
33330 Güersloh
Germany

**OCCUPATION:**    Medicine

**YEAR OF ENTRY:**  1990

**CITATION:**       For your Outstanding Contribution to
Medicine

---

**NAME:**                Dr Gordon Buell Ford Jr, AB, AM, PhD,
LPIBA, LFWLA

**ADDRESS:**          3619 Brownsboro Road
Louisville
KY 40207
USA

**OCCUPATION:**    Educator, Univ Prof, Author, Hospital Industry
Executive, and Financial Management
Corporation Director

**YEAR OF ENTRY:**  1988

**CITATION:**       For your Outstanding Contribution to University Education and to Financial Management

| NAME: | Mr Joseph Edward Garrett, FIBA |
|---|---|
| ADDRESS: | 2291 Goodrum Lane<br>Marietta<br>GA 30066<br>USA |
| OCCUPATION: | Aeronautical Engineer |
| YEAR OF ENTRY: | 1986 |
| CITATION: | For your Outstanding Contribution to Engineering |

| NAME: | Professor M Gembicki, MD |
|---|---|
| ADDRESS: | Department of Endocrinology<br>University School of Medicine in Poznan<br>Al Przybyszewskiego 49<br>PL-60 355, Poland |
| OCCUPATION: | Doctor |
| YEAR OF ENTRY: | 1986 |
| CITATION: | For your Outstanding Contribution to Medicine |

| NAME: | Dr Ashraf Ghani |
|---|---|
| ADDRESS: | PO Box 16176<br>Riyadh<br>Saudi Arabia 11464 |
| OCCUPATION: | Engineering and Management Executive |
| YEAR OF ENTRY: | 1986 |
| CITATION: | For your Outstanding Contribution to Project Engineering and Management |

**NAME:**           Dr Richard Sherwin Gothard

**ADDRESS:**        Gothard House
Henley-on-Thames
Oxon RE9 1AJ
England

**OCCUPATION:**    Information Scientist

**YEAR OF ENTRY:**   1986

**CITATION:**        For your Outstanding Contribution to
Information Science

---

**NAME:**           Dr Francis W Graham

**ADDRESS:**        28 Pasley Street
South Yarra
Victoria 3141
Australia

**OCCUPATION:**    Physician, Psychiatrist & Psycho-analyst

**YEAR OF ENTRY:**   1988

**CITATION:**        For your Outstanding Contribution to Psychiatry,
Psycho-analysis and Group Psycho-therapy

---

**NAME:**           Professor Dr G Griesser

**ADDRESS:**        Universitätspräsident a D
Barstenkamp 51 - Rammsee
2300 Molfsee
Germany

**OCCUPATION:**    Professor of Medical Informatics and
Statistics Manager of ITK Information
Technology Giel Ltd

**YEAR OF ENTRY:**   1989

**CITATION:**        For your Outstanding Contribution to Medicine, Psychology, Hospitals and Dentists

**NAME:**               Professor Ghassan Haddad, PhD, DSc,
                        LPIBA, DDG

**ADDRESS:**            PO Box 6025
                        Mansour
                        Baghdad
                        Iraq

**OCCUPATION:**         Professor of Economics

**YEAR OF ENTRY:**      1986

**CITATION:**           For your Outstanding Contribution to
                        Science

---

**NAME:**               Ms Violet Edna Hobbs Hain

**ADDRESS:**            3530 Raymoor Road
                        Kensington
                        MD 20895
                        USA

**OCCUPATION:**         Artist

**YEAR OF ENTRY:**      1986

**CITATION:**           For your Outstanding Contribution to
                        Art

---

**NAME:**               Dr Paul L C Hao

**ADDRESS:**            10Fl No 116
                        Nanking East Road, Sec 2
                        Taipei
                        Taiwan

**OCCUPATION:**         Biochemist

**YEAR OF ENTRY:**      1986

**CITATION:**           For your Outstanding Contribution to
                        Science

**NAME:** Mr Christopher Philip Harding, FIBA

**ADDRESS:** PO Box 5271
Rockhampton Mail Centre
Queensland 4702
Australia

**OCCUPATION:** Market Analyst

**YEAR OF ENTRY:** 1986

**CITATION:** For your Outstanding Contribution to
Psychometrics

---

**NAME:** Louise Harris, FIBC, LPIBA, LFWLA,
LPWIA, LPABI, DG, DDG

**ADDRESS:** Steere House, #205th
100 Border Street
Providence, RI 02983
USA

**OCCUPATION:** Researcher and Writer

**YEAR OF ENTRY:** 1986

**CITATION:** For your Outstanding Contribution to
Research and Writing

---

**NAME:** Dr Kazuyuki Hatada, DDG, LFIBA, IOM

**ADDRESS:** Department of Mathematics
Faculty of Education, Gifu University
1-1 Yanagido, Gifu City
Gifu Prefecture 501-11, Japan

**OCCUPATION:** Mathematician

**YEAR OF ENTRY:** 1990

**CITATION:** For your Outstanding Contribution to
Pure Mathematics, especially to the
Theory of Modular Forms

**NAME:** Mr Diego C J F Hidalgo, LFIBA

**ADDRESS:** Felipe Cuarto 9
28014 Madrid
Spain

**OCCUPATION:** Lawyer

**YEAR OF ENTRY:** 1989

**CITATION:** For your Outstanding Contribution to Law

---

**NAME:** Reverend Reuben Arthur Houseal, ThD, PhD, LLD, LFIBA

**ADDRESS:** 132 South Erie Street, PO Box 132
Mercer
PA 16137
USA

**OCCUPATION:** Clergyman, Educator, Writer

**YEAR OF ENTRY:** 1986

**CITATION:** For your Outstanding Contribution for Distinguished Service to the Cause of Christ

---

**NAME:** Mrs Ruth Arnold Houseal, DRE, LHD, LFIBA

**ADDRESS:** 132 South Erie Street, PO Box 132
Mercer
PA 16137
USA

**OCCUPATION:** Educator

**YEAR OF ENTRY:** 1986

**CITATION:** For your Outstanding Contribution to Education

**NAME:**              Professor Zuey-Shin Hsu, MD, LFIBA, DDG, IOM

**ADDRESS:**           Department of Physiology
                       Kaohsiung Medical College No 100
                       Shih-Chuan 1st Road, Kaohsiung
                       Taiwan

**OCCUPATION:**        Professor of Physiology

**YEAR OF ENTRY:**     1989

**CITATION:**          For your Outstanding Contribution to
                       Medical Science and the Teaching
                       Profession

---

**NAME:**              Mr John Chih-An Hu, FIBA

**ADDRESS:**           16212 122 Se
                       Renton
                       WA 98058
                       USA

**OCCUPATION:**        Chemist and Chemical Engineer

**YEAR OF ENTRY:**     1986

**CITATION:**          For your Outstanding Contribution to
                       Chemistry

---

**NAME:**              Professor Qi Shu Hua, LFIBA

**ADDRESS:**           Tianjin Vocational Technical Teachers' College
                       Tianjin
                       China

**OCCUPATION:**        Professor, Vice-President

**YEAR OF ENTRY:**     1989

**CITATION:**          For your Outstanding Contribution to
                       researches on welding and the admini-
                       stration of vocational education

| | |
|---|---|
| **NAME:** | Dr Bettina S Hurni |
| **ADDRESS:** | Rue Saint - Jean 98<br>1211 Geneva 11<br>Switzerland |
| **OCCUPATION:** | Professor of Economics |
| **YEAR OF ENTRY:** | 1991 |
| **CITATION:** | For your Outstanding Contribution to<br>Economics |

---

| | |
|---|---|
| **NAME:** | Professor Dr Kazuyosi Ikeda, LPIBA, LFIBA,<br>DDG, IOM, LFWLA |
| **ADDRESS:** | Nisi - 7 - 7 - 11 Aomadani<br>Minoo-Si<br>Osaka 562<br>Japan |
| **OCCUPATION:** | Professor of Theoretical Physics and Poet |
| **YEAR OF ENTRY:** | 1989 |
| **CITATION:** | For your Outstanding Contribution to<br>Theoretical Physics and Poetry |

---

| | |
|---|---|
| **NAME:** | Dr Drago Ikic, LFIBA |
| **ADDRESS:** | Yugoslav Academy of Science and Arts<br>Inst for Research and Standardization of<br>Immunologic Substances<br>Demetrova 18, 41000 Zagreb<br>Yugoslavia |
| **OCCUPATION:** | Doctor |
| **YEAR OF ENTRY:** | 1986 |
| **CITATION:** | For your Outstanding Contribution to<br>Medicine |

| | |
|---|---|
| **NAME:** | Sir James Irwin |
| **ADDRESS:** | 124 Brougham Place<br>North Adelaide<br>SA 5006<br>Australia |
| **OCCUPATION:** | Retired Architect |
| **YEAR OF ENTRY:** | 1988 |
| **CITATION:** | For your Outstanding Contribution to<br>Architecture, the Arts and the Community |

| | |
|---|---|
| **NAME:** | Geo E Johnston, FIBA |
| **ADDRESS:** | PO Box 806<br>Marco Island<br>FL 33969<br>USA |
| **OCCUPATION:** | Multi-Faceted Entrepreneur |
| **YEAR OF ENTRY:** | 1988 |
| **CITATION:** | For your Outstanding Contribution to<br>Business and Commerce |

| | |
|---|---|
| **NAME:** | Ms Clare L Jones |
| **ADDRESS:** | 40 C Petherto Road<br>London<br>N5 2RE<br>England |
| **OCCUPATION:** | Pianist and Accompanist |
| **YEAR OF ENTRY:** | 1986 |
| **CITATION:** | For your Outstanding Contribution to<br>Music |

**NAME:** Mrs Hazel Emma Jones, FIBA

**ADDRESS:** 35 Greer Street
Bardon
Queensland 4065
Australia

**OCCUPATION:** Librarian

**YEAR OF ENTRY:** 1986

**CITATION:** For your Outstanding Contribution to
Librarianship

---

**NAME:** Mr Halldor H Jonsson, LFIBA

**ADDRESS:** Hyerfisgata 4-6
Reykjavik
Iceland

**OCCUPATION:** Architect and Company Director

**YEAR OF ENTRY:** 1986

**CITATION:** For your Outstanding Contribution to
Architecture

---

**NAME:** Denise M (Koppenhagen) Kalker-Harris,
FIL, LPIBA

**ADDRESS:** c/o M Harris & Sons
Gayfere House
22/23 Gayfere Street
London SW1P 3HP
England

**OCCUPATION:** Social Worker

**YEAR OF ENTRY:** 1986

**CITATION:** For your Outstanding Contribution to the
Community

| | |
|---|---|
| **NAME:** | Ms Catherine Earl Bailey Kerr, LPIBA |
| **ADDRESS:** | 1412 West Hendricks<br>Roswell<br>NM 88201<br>USA |
| **OCCUPATION:** | Artist, Art and Music Teacher, Architect, Designer |
| **YEAR OF ENTRY:** | 1986 |
| **CITATION:** | For your Outstanding Contrbution to Art and the Handicapped |

| | |
|---|---|
| **NAME:** | Dr Mohammed Vahid Husain Khan, FIBA |
| **ADDRESS:** | 9939 Affton Place<br>St Louis<br>MO 63123<br>USA |
| **OCCUPATION:** | Physician |
| **YEAR OF ENTRY:** | 1986 |
| **CITATION:** | For your Outstanding Contribution to Medicine |

| | |
|---|---|
| **NAME:** | Dr Rachel Hadley King |
| **ADDRESS:** | 60 Broadway, Apt 905<br>Providence<br>RI 02903<br>USA |
| **OCCUPATION:** | Teacher |
| **YEAR OF ENTRY:** | 1986 |
| **CITATION:** | For your Outstanding Contribution to Education |

**NAME:** Ms Isabella J Kirstein née Grobbelaar
(known as Lulu)

**ADDRESS:** PO Box 11260
Johannesburg 2000
Republic of South Africa

**OCCUPATION:** Executive Chairman - Marketing & Socio-
Political Research Co

**YEAR OF ENTRY:** 1989

**CITATION:** For your Outstanding Contribution to
Marketing & Socio-Political Research as
a profession and specifically for women

---

**NAME:** Mrs Nagiko Sato Kiser, LFIBA

**ADDRESS:** 1101 Mission Verde Drive
Camarillo
CA 93012
USA

**OCCUPATION:** Senior Librarian

**YEAR OF ENTRY:** 1991

**CITATION:** For your Outstanding Contribution to the
Community

---

**NAME:** Kristjan G Kjartansson

**ADDRESS:** Einimelur 7
107 Reykjavik
Iceland

**OCCUPATION:** Company Vice President

**YEAR OF ENTRY:** 1986

**CITATION:** For your Outstanding Contribution to
Commerce

**NAME:**                    Mr Tsuneo Koike, LFIBA

**ADDRESS:**                 39 Mauna Loa Street
                             Hilo
                             HI 96720
                             USA

**OCCUPATION:**              Engineering and Surveying Consultant

**YEAR OF ENTRY:**           1989

**CITATION:**                For your Outstanding Contribution to
                             Engineering

---

**NAME:**                    Professor Lidia Agnes Kozubek

**ADDRESS:**                 Al Waszyngtona 116/98
                             04-074 Warsaw
                             Poland

**OCCUPATION:**              Pianist, Educator and Musicologist

**YEAR OF ENTRY:**           1986

**CITATION:**                For your Outstanding Contribution to
                             Music

---

**NAME:**                    Mrs Pansy Daegling Kraus, LFIBA

**ADDRESS:**                 PO Box 600908
                             San Diego
                             CA 92120
                             USA

**OCCUPATION:**              Editor, Gemologist

**YEAR OF ENTRY:**           1991

**CITATION:**                For your Outstanding Contribution to
                             Writing

**NAME:**            Dr Rolf Kraus-Ruppert, LFIBA

**ADDRESS:**         Zelgli 41 C
                    CH-3179 Kriechenwil
                    Switzerland

**OCCUPATION:**      Neuropathologist and Physician

**YEAR OF ENTRY:**  1986

**CITATION:**        For your Outstanding Contribution to
                    Science

---

**NAME:**            Professor Raphael Hoegh Krohn, LPIBA, DDG

**ADDRESS:**         Mathematic Institution
                    Oslo University
                    PO Box 1053
                    Blindern
                    0316 Oslo 6
                    Norway

**OCCUPATION:**      Professor of Mathematics

**YEAR OF ENTRY:**  1986

**CITATION:**        For your Outstanding Contribution to
                    Education and Research

---

**NAME:**            Ms Mary Krueger-Ortlip

**ADDRESS:**         2917 So Ocean Blvd 703
                    Highland Beach
                    FL 33487
                    USA

**OCCUPATION:**      Artist

**YEAR OF ENTRY:**  1991

**CITATION:**        For your Outstanding Contribution to Art

**NAME:**              Mr Prem Chand Kulleen, LFIBA

**ADDRESS:**           PO Box 35173
                       Lusaka
                       Zambia

**OCCUPATION:**        Librarian

**YEAR OF ENTRY:**     1986

**CITATION:**          For your Outstanding Contribution to
                       Librarianship

---

**NAME:**              Professor Jean-Paul Labelle, SS, LFIBA

**ADDRESS:**           St Sulpice Seminary
                       Matsuyama 1-1-1
                       Jonan-ku, Fukuoka 814-01
                       Japan

**OCCUPATION:**        University Professor

**YEAR OF ENTRY:**     1986

**CITATION:**          For your Outstanding Contribution to
                       The Canon Law

---

**NAME:**              Dr Joyce M Laborde, PhD, RN, LFIBA

**ADDRESS:**           College of Nursing, Univ of ND
                       PO Box 8195, Univ Station
                       Grand Forks
                       ND 58202
                       USA

**OCCUPATION:**        Professor

**YEAR OF ENTRY:**     1986

**CITATION:**          For your Outstanding Contribution to
                       Nursing

| | |
|---|---|
| **NAME:** | Dr Vernette Landers, LFIBA, LFWLA, DDG |
| **ADDRESS:** | PO Box 3839<br>Landers<br>CA 92284<br>USA |
| **OCCUPATION:** | Educator |
| **YEAR OF ENTRY:** | 1986 |
| **CITATION:** | For your Outstanding Contribution to Education and Community |

---

| | |
|---|---|
| **NAME:** | Professor Chang Bin Lee, PhD |
| **ADDRESS:** | 18 Donui-dong<br>Chongro-ku<br>Seoul<br>Korea |
| **OCCUPATION:** | Professor of Medicine |
| **YEAR OF ENTRY:** | 1986 |
| **CITATION:** | For your Outstanding Contribution to Medicine |

---

| | |
|---|---|
| **NAME:** | Dr Joseph Le Jeune |
| **ADDRESS:** | 6 Square Castiglione<br>78150 Le Chesney<br>France |
| **OCCUPATION:** | International Industrial Development Projects Consultant |
| **YEAR OF ENTRY:** | 1986 |
| **CITATION:** | For your Outstanding Contribution to Industrial Development |

| | |
|---|---|
| **NAME:** | Dato Dr Sip Hon Lew |
| **ADDRESS:** | 25 Jalan 14/3<br>Taman Tun Abdul Razak<br>Ampany Jaya<br>Selangor, Malaysia |
| **OCCUPATION:** | Company Director, Retired Ambassador |
| **YEAR OF ENTRY:** | 1988 |
| **CITATION:** | For your Outstanding Contribution to the economic, political and cultural life of Malaysia and to your role in the larger world community |

| | |
|---|---|
| **NAME:** | Professor Jong-Teh Lin, FWLA, FIBA, DDG |
| **ADDRESS:** | No 185-6 Nan Men Road<br>700 Tainan<br>Taiwan<br>Formosa |
| **OCCUPATION:** | Teacher |
| **YEAR OF ENTRY:** | 1988 |
| **CITATION:** | For your Outstanding Contribution to Education |

| | |
|---|---|
| **NAME:** | Mrs Anneliese List, FWLA, FIBA<br>(Pseudonym Alice Pervin) |
| **ADDRESS:** | Fuenfbronn 26<br>8545 Spalt<br>Germany |
| **OCCUPATION:** | Soubrette |
| **YEAR OF ENTRY:** | 1986 |
| **CITATION:** | For your Outstanding Contribution to Literature |

**NAME:**              Ms Sonia Lynch

**ADDRESS:**           13705 Beret Place
                       Silver Spring
                       MD 20906
                       USA

**OCCUPATION:**        Consultant

**YEAR OF ENTRY:**     1991

**CITATION:**          For your Outstanding Contribution as a
                       Consultant in the Data Processing Field

---

**NAME:**              Mr Konstantin Mandic

**ADDRESS:**           Gaborone
                       Private Bag - BR38
                       Botswana
                       Africa

**OCCUPATION:**        Architect

**YEAR OF ENTRY:**     1989

**CITATION:**          For your Outstanding Contribution to
                       Architecture

---

**NAME:**              Professor Dr Mitsuo Masai, FIBA

**ADDRESS:**           Faculty of Engineering
                       Kobe University
                       Rokkadai
                       Nada
                       Kobe 657
                       Japan

**OCCUPATION:**        University Professor

**YEAR OF ENTRY:**     1986

**CITATION:**          For your Outstanding Contribution to
                       Catalysis

**NAME:**              Emeritus Professor Junji Matsumoto, FIBA

**ADDRESS:**           2-3-14 Asukano Minami
                       Ikoma City
                       630-01 Japan

**OCCUPATION:**        Neuroscientist

**YEAR OF ENTRY:**     1988

**CITATION:**          For your Outstanding Contribution to
                       Science

---

**NAME:**              Mr Seiichi Matsumoto, FIBA

**ADDRESS:**           Yuigahama 1-11-17
                       Kamakura 248
                       Japan

**OCCUPATION:**        Director and Professor

**YEAR OF ENTRY:**     1986

**CITATION:**          For your Outstanding Contribution to
                       Medicine

---

**NAME:**              Very Reverend Stanley Matuszewski

**ADDRESS:**           Box 777
                       Twin Lakes
                       WI 53181
                       USA

**OCCUPATION:**        Priest

**YEAR OF ENTRY:**     1986

**CITATION:**          For your Outstanding Contribution to
                       Architecture

**NAME:** Mrs Madella Rigby Maurer

**ADDRESS:** The Pennsfield, Apt C10
802 Broad Street
Selinsgrove
PA 17870
USA

**OCCUPATION:** Psychologist

**YEAR OF ENTRY:** 1986

**CITATION:** For your Outstanding Contribution to
Psychology

---

**NAME:** Ms Barbara Johnston McCrary

**ADDRESS:** PO Box 1017
Merced
CA 95341
USA

**OCCUPATION:** Business Women - Prudential Insurance, Financial Service Rep Dist Agent

**YEAR OF ENTRY:** 1991

**CITATION:** For your Outstanding Contribution to the
Business Profession

---

**NAME:** Helen McGinty

**ADDRESS:** 3755 Peachtree Road, Apt 410
Atlanta
GA 30319
USA

**OCCUPATION:** Retired Teacher

**YEAR OF ENTRY:** 1989

**CITATION:** For your Outstanding Contribution to
Teaching

**NAME:**              Dr John H McGovern

**ADDRESS:**           53 East 70th Street
                       New York
                       NY 10021
                       USA

**OCCUPATION:**        Professor of Clinical Surgery (Urology)

**YEAR OF ENTRY:**     1986

**CITATION:**          For your Outstanding Contribution to
                       Clinical Surgery

---

**NAME:**              Mrs Carmon Ramona McHugh

**ADDRESS:**           Casa de Rosas 11
                       1220 Avenida Caballeros
                       Palm Springs
                       CA 92262
                       USA

**OCCUPATION:**        Artist

**YEAR OF ENTRY:**     1986

**CITATION:**          For your Outstanding Contribution to Art

---

**NAME:**              Mr John Joseph Mehalchin

**ADDRESS:**           c/o Highline Financial Serv Inc
                       1881 9th Street, No 320
                       Boulder
                       CO 80302
                       USA

**OCCUPATION:**        Entrepreneur, Financial Executive

**YEAR OF ENTRY:**     1991

**CITATION:**          For your Outstanding Contribution to
                       Business

**NAME:** Mrs Josephine Mellichamp, FIBA

**ADDRESS:** 1124 Reeder Circle NE
Atlanta
GA 30306
USA

**OCCUPATION:** Former Librarian, Writer, Historian
and Teacher

**YEAR OF ENTRY:** 1986

**CITATION:** For your Outstanding Contribution to
Librarianship, Writing and Education

---

**NAME:** Dr Kathleen Louise Mendrey

**ADDRESS:** 791 Tremont Street West 403
Boston
MA 02118
USA

**OCCUPATION:** Management Consultant

**YEAR OF ENTRY:** 1991

**CITATION:** For your Outstanding Contribution to
Business

---

**NAME:** Mr Ralph E Montijo, DDG, IOM

**ADDRESS:** c/o Omniplan Corporation
5839 Green Valley Cir - 203
Culver City
CA 90230
USA

**OCCUPATION:** Company President, Executive

**YEAR OF ENTRY:** 1987

**CITATION:** For your Outstanding Contribution to
Business

**NAME:** Professor James Crutchfield Morelock, FIBA

**ADDRESS:** 2917 Garth Road, SE
Huntsville
AL 35801
USA

**OCCUPATION:** Mathematician

**YEAR OF ENTRY:** 1986

**CITATION:** For your Outstanding Contribution to
Mathematics

---

**NAME:** Ms Peggy Jean Mueller

**ADDRESS:** 1506 Hardouin Avenue
Austin
TX 78703
USA

**OCCUPATION:** Dance Teacher/Choreographer

**YEAR OF ENTRY:** 1990

**CITATION:** For your Outstanding Contribution to
Dancing, Ranching and Trail Riding

---

**NAME:** Mr Hassenally Nanuck, LFIBA

**ADDRESS:** PO Box 40346
Gaborone
Botswana
Southern Africa

**OCCUPATION:** Auto Body Mechanic and Panel Beater

**YEAR OF ENTRY:** 1992

**CITATION:** For your Outstanding Contribution to Auto
Body Mechanics and Panel Beating

| | |
|---|---|
| **NAME:** | Col Leon D Nobes, HOSJ, FIBA |
| **ADDRESS:** | 2033 Crozier Avenue<br>Muskegin<br>MI 49441<br>USA |
| **OCCUPATION:** | Retired University Professor |
| **YEAR OF ENTRY:** | 1986 |
| **CITATION:** | For your Outstanding Contribution to Education |

| | |
|---|---|
| **NAME:** | Professor Henry Ian A Nowik |
| **ADDRESS:** | 1250 Merchant Lane<br>McLean<br>VA 22101<br>USA |
| **OCCUPATION:** | Education |
| **YEAR OF ENTRY:** | 1990 |
| **CITATION:** | For your Outstanding Contribution to Education |

| | |
|---|---|
| **NAME:** | Dr Wilson Reid Ogg, LPIBA, LFWLA, DDG |
| **ADDRESS:** | Pinebrook<br>1104 Keith Avenue<br>Berkeley<br>CA 94708<br>USA |
| **OCCUPATION:** | Poet, Graphic Illustrator, Publisher, Retired Lawyer and Educator |
| **YEAR OF ENTRY:** | 1991 |
| **CITATION:** | For your Outstanding Contribution to the Legal Profession |

**NAME:**             Mr Masa Aki Oka

**ADDRESS:**          3-24-15-401
                     Tsurumaki
                     Setagaya-ku
                     Tokyo 154
                     Japan

**OCCUPATION:**       Businessman

**YEAR OF ENTRY:**    1991

**CITATION:**         For your Outstaniding Contribution to
                     Finance and Banking

---

**NAME:**             Mr Greensill Selby Old, FIBA

**ADDRESS:**          2/74 Milray Avenue
                     Wellstonecraft
                     NSW 2065
                     Australia

**OCCUPATION:**       Librarian

**YEAR OF ENTRY:**    1986

**CITATION:**         For your Outstanding Contribution to
                     Librarianship

---

**NAME:**             Mr Pedro T Orata

**ADDRESS:**          Urdaneta Community College
                     Urdaneta
                     Pargsinan
                     Philippines

**OCCUPATION:**       Teacher

**YEAR OF ENTRY:**    1986

**CITATION:**         For your Outstanding Contribution to
                     Education

| | |
|---|---|
| **NAME:** | Dr Pola Ortiz |
| **ADDRESS:** | Urbanizacion La Paz<br>El Paraiso<br>Calle 6<br>Quinta 'Pola'<br>Caracas 102<br>Venezuela |
| **OCCUPATION:** | Economist |
| **YEAR OF ENTRY:** | 1986 |
| **CITATION:** | For your Outstanding Contribution to Economy |

---

| | |
|---|---|
| **NAME:** | Dr Irene M K Ovenstone, FIBA |
| **ADDRESS:** | 10 Moor Road<br>Calverton<br>Nottingham<br>NG14 6FW<br>England |
| **OCCUPATION:** | Consultant Psychiatrist |
| **YEAR OF ENTRY:** | 1986 |
| **CITATION:** | For your Outstanding Contribution to Psychiatry |

---

| | |
|---|---|
| **NAME:** | Mr Pritam Singh Panesar, LFIBA, DDG |
| **ADDRESS:** | PO Box 46235<br>Nairobi<br>Kenya |
| **OCCUPATION:** | Engineer and Pilot |
| **YEAR OF ENTRY:** | 1986 |
| **CITATION:** | For your Outstanding Contribution to Engineering |

**NAME:**              Dr Lucy T Parker, LPIBA, DDG

**ADDRESS:**           The Parker Academy
                       248 Concord Road
                       Sudbury
                       MA 01776
                       USA

**OCCUPATION:**        Director, The Parker Academy

**YEAR OF ENTRY:**     1986

**CITATION:**          For your Outstanding Contribution to
                       Education

---

**NAME:**              Ms Marion L Patterson Beard, FIBA

**ADDRESS:**           Route 1
                       Vincennes
                       IN 47591
                       USA

**OCCUPATION:**        Artist

**YEAR OF ENTRY:**     1986

**CITATION:**          For your Outstanding Contribution to Art

---

**NAME:**              Ms Coralynn Pence

**ADDRESS:**           5009-48th NE
                       Seattle
                       WA 98105
                       USA

**OCCUPATION:**        Artist, Goldsmith

**YEAR OF ENTRY:**     1991

**CITATION:**          For your Outstanding Contribution for
                       Privately Commissioned Jewellery

**NAME:** Mr E Allen Propst, LFIBA

**ADDRESS:** 253 S E Scravel Hill Road
Houston
Albany
OR 97321
USA

**OCCUPATION:** Retired

**YEAR OF ENTRY:** 1991

**CITATION:** For your Outstandig Cotribution to
Public Affairs of All Countries

---

**NAME:** Mr George Earl Pyper

**ADDRESS:** 320-3120 North Island Hwy
Campbell River
British Columbia
Canada
V9W 2H7

**OCCUPATION:** Violinist and Columnist

**YEAR OF ENTRY:** 1991

**CITATION:** For your Outstanding Contribution to
Arts and Communities

---

**NAME:** Ms Sherry Swett Raatz, LPIBA, DDG

**ADDRESS:** 7500-27th NE
Seattle
WA 98115
USA

**OCCUPATION:** Community Leader

**YEAR OF ENTRY:** 1986

**CITATION:** For your Outstanding Contribution to the
Community

**NAME:**      Mr Charles R J Rapin

**ADDRESS:**      Laboratoire de Complilation
Department d'Informatique EPFL
Ecublens (MA)
CH-1015 Lausanne, Switzerland

**OCCUPATION:**      Professor of Computer Science

**YEAR OF ENTRY:**      1989

**CITATION:**      For your Outstanding Contribution to
Computer Science

---

**NAME:**      Mr John D Regan, CLU, Ch FC

**ADDRESS:**      Gen Services Life Insurance Co
201 Glameda Del Prado
Novato, CA 94949
USA

**OCCUPATION:**      President and Chief Executive Officer
GSLIC, GSL Holding, Federation for
Financial Independent

**YEAR OF ENTRY:**      1989

**CITATION:**      For your Outstanding Contribution to the
Insurance Industry in the USA

---

**NAME:**      Dr Ralph R Robinson, IOM, DDG

**ADDRESS:**      PO Box 668
Middlesboro
KS 40965, USA

**OCCUPATION:**      Medical Doctor

**YEAR OF ENTRY:**      1986

**CITATION:**      For your Outstanding Contribution to
Medicine

| | |
|---|---|
| **NAME:** | Captain Suleiman Sa'idu, FSS, PSC, MSC, LPIBA |
| **ADDRESS:** | PO Box 54119<br>Ikoyi<br>Lagos<br>Nigeria |
| **OCCUPATION:** | Naval Officer |
| **YEAR OF ENTRY:** | 1986 |
| **CITATION:** | For your Outstanding Contribution to the Armed Forces |

| | |
|---|---|
| **NAME:** | Dr Frank Samlot, FIBA |
| **ADDRESS:** | 2669 Gerda Bella Avenue<br>St Augustine<br>FL 32086<br>USA |
| **OCCUPATION:** | Forensic Technologist |
| **YEAR OF ENTRY:** | 1989 |
| **CITATION:** | For your Outstanding Contribution to Forensic Technology |

| | |
|---|---|
| **NAME:** | Dr Aiko Satow |
| **ADDRESS:** | c/o Department of Psychology<br>Hamamatsu University School of Medicine<br>Handa-cho<br>Hamamatsu 431-31<br>Japan |
| **OCCUPATION:** | Professor of Behavioural Science |
| **YEAR OF ENTRY:** | 1991 |
| **CITATION:** | For your Outstanding Contribution to Behavioural Study in Technology and Medicine |

**NAME:**          Mr J W Scheja, ScD, FIBA

**ADDRESS:**       Institute of Thrombosis & Transfusion Medicine
Universitat Dusseldorf
5 Morrensraße
D-4000 Dusseldorf 1
Germany

**OCCUPATION:**   Medical Doctor

**YEAR OF ENTRY:**   1986

**CITATION:**     For your Outstanding Contribution to
Engineering

---

**NAME:**          Mr Dennis Screpatis, PE, LFIBA, DDG

**ADDRESS:**       2200 North Central Road
Fort Lee
NJ 07024
USA

**OCCUPATION:**   Consulting Engineer

**YEAR OF ENTRY:**   1986

**CITATION:**     For your Outstanding Contribution to
Engineering

---

**NAME:**          Professor Maurice K Seguin, FIBA

**ADDRESS:**       Suite 7584 Pavillion Lemieux
Univerisite Laval
Quebec
Canada 6IK 7P4

**OCCUPATION:**   Professor of Geophysics

**YEAR OF ENTRY:**   1986

**CITATION:**     For your Outstanding Contribution to
Science

**NAME:**    Mr Philip Selby, LPIBA

**ADDRESS:**    Hill Cottage
Via Primo Maggio 93
00068 Rignano Flaminio
Rome
Italy

**OCCUPATION:**    Composer

**YEAR OF ENTRY:**    1991

**CITATION:**    For your Outstanding Contribution to
Music

---

**NAME:**    Mr Robert Al Serlippens

**ADDRESS:**    PO Box 2639
Kinshasa
Zaire

**OCCUPATION:**    Attorney at Law

**YEAR OF ENTRY:**    1986

**CITATION:**    For your Outstanding Contribution to
The Law

---

**NAME:**    Dr Isadore Shapiro, BChE, PhD, DDG, IOM

**ADDRESS:**    5624 West 62nd Street
Los Angeles
CA 90056
USA

**OCCUPATION:**    Material Scientist

**YEAR OF ENTRY:**    1990

**CITATION:**    For your Outstanding Contribution to
Science

| | |
|---|---|
| **NAME:** | Ms Carolyn Juanita Shearer |
| **ADDRESS:** | 205 South Tucson Circle<br>Aurora<br>CO 80012<br>USA |
| **OCCUPATION:** | Educator |
| **YEAR OF ENTRY:** | 1990 |
| **CITATION:** | For your Outstanding Contribution to<br>Education |

---

| | |
|---|---|
| **NAME:** | Dr Muhammad M Mukram Sheikh, PhD,<br>HLFIBA, DDG |
| **ADDRESS:** | PO Box 1974<br>Gaborone<br>Botswana<br>Southern Africa |
| **OCCUPATION:** | Government Official, Marketing Executive,<br>Public Relations Specialist |
| **YEAR OF ENTRY:** | 1992 |
| **CITATION:** | For your Outstanding Contribution to<br>Trade Journalism |

---

| | |
|---|---|
| **NAME:** | Ms Daphne Marjorie Sheldrick |
| **ADDRESS:** | David Sheldrick Wildlife Trust<br>Box 15555<br>Nairobi<br>Kenya |
| **OCCUPATION:** | Authoress and Wildlife Specialist |
| **YEAR OF ENTRY:** | 1989 |
| **CITATION:** | For your Outstanding Contribution to<br>Wildlife Conservation |

**NAME:**    Professor Koki Shimoji, MD, DDG

**ADDRESS:**    Department of Anesthesiology
Niigata University School of Medicine
1-757 Asahi-Machi
Niigata 951
Japan

**OCCUPATION:**    Professor and Chairman

**YEAR OF ENTRY:**    1986

**CITATION:**    For your Outstanding Contribution to Medicine

---

**NAME:**    Thaneswari De Silva, LFIBA

**ADDRESS:**    148/2A Kynsey Road
Colombo 8
Sri Lanka

**OCCUPATION:**    Estate Proprietoress and Directress
'Leighton Park' Montessori and Junior School

**YEAR OF ENTRY:**    1986

**CITATION:**    For your Outstanding Contribution as Montessori and Junior School Directress

---

**NAME:**    Professor Dr Adelbert Agustin Sitompul

**ADDRESS:**    Jalan Sang Nawaluh 6
P Siantar 21132
Sumatra Utara
Indonesia

**OCCUPATION:**    Teaching/Education

**YEAR OF ENTRY:**    1990

**CITATION:**    For your Outstanding Contribution to Education

| | |
|---|---|
| **NAME:** | Mr Demetre B Sochos, FIBA |
| **ADDRESS:** | Vattugatan 9 3 TR<br>Sundbyberg 1<br>S-17234<br>Sweden |
| **OCCUPATION:** | Retired Workshop Employee |
| **YEAR OF ENTRY** | 1991 |
| **CITATION:** | For your Outstanding Contribution to Architecture |

---

| | |
|---|---|
| **NAME:** | Mr Amadou Sow, FIBA |
| **ADDRESS:** | 4 Rue Carnot BP 192<br>Dakar<br>Senegal |
| **OCCUPATION:** | Company Chairman |
| **YEAR OF ENTRY:** | 1986 |
| **CITATION:** | For your Outstanding Contribution to Commerce |

---

| | |
|---|---|
| **NAME:** | Dr Elizabeth V Stewart, LFIBA, DDG |
| **ADDRESS:** | 77 Watkins Park Drive<br>Upper Marlboro<br>MD 20772<br>USA |
| **OCCUPATION:** | Nurse |
| **YEAR OF ENTRY:** | 1991 |
| **CITATION:** | For your Outstanding Contribution to the Nursing Profession |

**NAME:**               Eugene Lawrence Stewart, Esq

**ADDRESS:**            Stewart & Stewart
                        808 Seventeenth St NW Suite 300
                        Washington
                        DC 20006
                        USA

**OCCUPATION:**         Attorney at Law

**YEAR OF ENTRY:**      1989

**CITATION:**           For your Outstanding Contribution to
                        International Trade Law

---

**NAME:**               Mrs Kathleen Stuart Strehlow, LFIBA

**ADDRESS:**            30 Da Costa Avenue
                        Prospect 5082
                        South Australia

**OCCUPATION:**         Research Director

**YEAR OF ENTRY:**      1986

**CITATION:**           For your Outstanding Contribution to
                        Education

---

**NAME:**               Ms June Conran Sutherland, LFIBA

**ADDRESS:**            29 Swinburne Avenue
                        Hawthorn
                        Vic 3122
                        Australia

**OCCUPATION:**         Midwife

**YEAR OF ENTRY:**      1989

**CITATION:**           For your Outstanding Contribution to
                        Midwifery

**NAME:** Dr Srikanta M N Swamy, LFIBA, DDG

**ADDRESS:** 275 Des Landes
St Lambert
Quebec
Canada J4S 1V9

**OCCUPATION:** Electrical Engineer

**YEAR OF ENTRY:** 1986

**CITATION:** For your Outstanding Contribution of Engineering

---

**NAME:** Dr Clement D Tessa, LFIBA

**ADDRESS:** PO Box 9175
North Hollywood
CA 91609
USA

**OCCUPATION:** Doctor

**YEAR OF ENTRY:** 1991

**CITATION:** For your Outstanding Contribution to Medicine

---

**NAME:** Dr Grace Fern Thomas, FIBA, FWLA

**ADDRESS:** 2001 La Jolla Court
Madesto
CA 95305
USA

**OCCUPATION:** Physician, Specialist in Psychiatry

**YEAR OF ENTRY:** 1986

**CITATION:** For your Outstanding Contribution to Medicine

**NAME:** Ms Joyce Trickett, FIBA

**ADDRESS:** 23 Lavender Crescent
Lavender Bay
North Sydney
NSW 2060
Australia

**OCCUPATION:** Writer, Entertainment, Artist

**YEAR OF ENTRY:** 1986

**CITATION:** For your Outstanding Contribution to
Poetry, Literature and Entertainment

---

**NAME:** Vern William Urry, PhD, LPABI, LFIBA,
LFWLA

**ADDRESS:** 3301 Accolade Drive
Clinton
MD 20735
USA

**OCCUPATION:** Personnel Research Psychologist

**YEAR OF ENTRY:** 1986

**CITATION:** For your Outstanding Contribution to
Research Psychology

---

**NAME:** Mrs Marion Griffin Vedder

**ADDRESS:** 108 Ketewamoke Avenue
Babylon
NY 11702
USA

**OCCUPATION:** School Principal

**YEAR OF ENTRY:** 1992

**CITATION:** For your Outstanding Contribution to
Education

**NAME:**     Mr Jan Vegelius

**ADDRESS:**     Department of Statistics
PO Box 513
751 20 Uppsala
Sweden

**OCCUPATION:**     University Teacher of Statistics

**YEAR OF ENTRY:**     1986

**CITATION:**     For your Outstanding Contribution to
Scientific Research

---

**NAME:**     Dr Constantin Kimon Vereketi, LPIBA, DDG

**ADDRESS:**     Semitelou St No 7
Athens 115-28
Greece

**OCCUPATION:**     Company Director

**YEAR OF ENTRY:**     1986

**CITATION:**     For your Outstanding Contribution to
Commerce and Sport

---

**NAME:**     H E Hon Steven A Vladem, PhD, FUWAI,
LFABIRA, DG, LFIBA, DDG, IOM

**ADDRESS:**     6237 N Hamlin Avenue
Chicago
IL 60659
USA

**OCCUPATION:**     Mathematician, Educator, Computer Specialist

**YEAR OF ENTRY:**     1991

**CITATION:**     For your Outstanding Contribution in the
Field of Computer-Assisted Instruction

**NAME:**          Professor R F Vliegen, LFIBA, DDG, IOM

**ADDRESS:**       Honorary Consul of Belgium
Belgium Flanders Exchange Center
2-6 Uehonmachi 8
Tennojiku, 543 Osaka
Japan

**OCCUPATION:**    Honorary Consul of Belgium

**YEAR OF ENTRY:** 1991

**CITATION:**      For your Outstanding Contribution to
Musicology Related Education and
International Exchange

---

**NAME:**          Professor Dr Mohamed F Wazna, LFIBA, MD,
FRCSE, FRCS, FISS

**ADDRESS:**       8929 Wilshire Blvd, Suite 120
Beverly Hills
CA 90211
USA

**OCCUPATION:**    Professor of Surgery

**YEAR OF ENTRY:** 1986

**CITATION:**      For your Outstanding Contribution to
Medicine

---

**NAME:**          Franz Joseph Bernard Weiling

**ADDRESS:**       Zur Marterkapelle 65
D-5300 Bonn
Lengsdorf, Germany

**OCCUPATION:**    University Professor

**YEAR OF ENTRY:** 1986

**CITATION:**      For your Outstanding Contribution to
Education

| | |
|---|---|
| **NAME:** | Mr M R Wiemann, LPIBA, LFWLA, DDG, IOM |
| **ADDRESS:** | 418 South 9th Street<br>PO Box 532<br>Chesterton<br>IN 46304<br>USA |
| **OCCUPATION:** | Biologist, Microscopist |
| **YEAR OF ENTRY:** | 1991 |
| **CITATION:** | For your Outstanding Contribution to Theoretical and Applied Biology |

| | |
|---|---|
| **NAME:** | Dr Winifred Margaret Wilcox |
| **ADDRESS:** | 'Auld Reekie'<br>1 Sloss Road<br>Healesville<br>Victoria 3777<br>Australia |
| **OCCUPATION:** | University Lecturer |
| **YEAR OF ENTRY:** | 1986 |
| **CITATION:** | For your Outstanding Contribution to Education |

| | |
|---|---|
| **NAME:** | Dr Azi Wolfenson U, PhD, LFIBA, DDG |
| **ADDRESS:** | Haldenstraße 24<br>6006 Luzern<br>Switzerland |
| **OCCUPATION:** | Engineer |
| **YEAR OF ENTRY:** | 1986 |
| **CITATION:** | For your Outstanding Contribution to Engineering and Development |

**NAME:** Mr Vincent W S Wong, LPIBA, DDG, IOM

**ADDRESS:** 41A Jalan SS 21/1A
Damansara Utara
47400 Petaling Jaya
Selangor
West Malaysia

**OCCUPATION:** Company President, Financial Economist

**YEAR OF ENTRY:** 1991

**CITATION:** For your Outstanding Contribution to
Banking and Finance

---

**NAME:** Dr William L S Wu, MD, IPA, LPIBA,
ABIRA, DR YOU MING WU (HON)

**ADDRESS:** Corinthian House 219
250 Budd Avenue
Campbell
CA 95008, USA

**OCCUPATION:** Practising Physician and Flight Surgeon

**YEAR OF ENTRY:** 1986

**CITATION:** For your Outstanding Contribution to
Space Medicine and Bioastronautics

---

**NAME:** Dr Kemp Plummer Yarborough

**ADDRESS:** Department of History and Government
Texas Woman's University
Denton
TX 76204, USA

**OCCUPATION:** University Professor

**YEAR OF ENTRY:** 1986

**CITATION:** For your Outstanding Contribution to
Education

**NAME:**              Professor Chap-Yung Yeung

**ADDRESS:**           Dept of Paediatrics
                       Queen Mary Hospital
                       University of Hong Kong
                       Hong Kong

**OCCUPATION:**        Professor of Paediatrics

**YEAR OF ENTRY:**     1989

**CITATION:**          For your Outstanding Contribution to
                       Paediatrics

---

**NAME:**              Ken-ichi Yoshihara, LPIBA, DDG, IOM

**ADDRESS:**           2-9-26 Yamanone
                       Zushi
                       Kanagawa
                       Japan

**OCCUPATION:**        Professor of Engineering

**YEAR OF ENTRY:**     1988

**CITATION:**          For your Outstanding Contribution to
                       Mathematical Statistics

---

**NAME:**              Professor Zhang Shi-ding

**ADDRESS:**           Dorm 30, Room 401
                       Shanghai Teacher's University
                       No 10 Guilin Road
                       Shanghai 200 234
                       China

**OCCUPATION:**        Teacher

**YEAR OF ENTRY:**     1991

**CITATION:**          For your Outstanding Contribution to
                       Education

**NAME:** Mr Kees Zwikker

**ADDRESS:** 3674 Nautilus Trail
Aurora
OH 44202
USA

**OCCUPATION:** International Business Consultant

**YEAR OF ENTRY:** 1989

**CITATION:** For your Outstanding Contribution to
Business